3 Enoch

Eupolemus

Pseudo-Eupolemus

Apocryphon of Ezekiel

Ezekiel the Tragedian

Fourth Book of Ezra

Greek Apocalypse of Ezra

Questions of Ezra

Revelation of Ezra

Vision of Ezra

Fragments of Pseudo-Greek Poets

Pseudo-Hecataeus

Hellenistic Synagogal Prayers

Martyrdom and Ascension of Isaiah

Ladder of Jacob

Prayer of Jacob

Jannes and Jambres

Testament of Job

Joseph and Aseneth

History of Joseph

Prayer of Joseph

Jubilees

3 Maccabees

4 Maccabees

Prayer of Manasseh

Syriac Menander

Testament of Moses

Orphica

Philo the Epic Poet

Pseudo-Philo

Pseudo-Phocylides

The Lives of the Prophets

History of the Rechabites

Apocalypse of Sedrach

Treatise of Shem

Sibylline Oracles

Odes of Solomon

Psalms of Solomon

Testament of Solomon

Theodotus

Testaments of the Three Patriarchs

Testaments of the Twelve Patriarchs

Apocalypse of Zephaniah

THE OLD TESTAMENT PSEUDEPIGRAPHA

YALE

AYBRL

THE ANCHOR YALE BIBLE REFERENCE LIBRARY

THE OLD TESTAMENT
Pseudepigrapha

VOLUME 2

Expansions of the "Old Testament" and Legends,
Wisdom and Philosophical Literature,
Prayers, Psalms, and Odes,
Fragments of Lost Judeo-Hellenistic Works

EDITED BY
JAMES H. CHARLESWORTH

YALE
AYBRL

Yale University Press New Haven and London

First published in 1985 by Doubleday, a division of Random House, Inc.
First Yale University Press impression 2010.

Copyright © 1985 by James H. Charlesworth.

The Anchor Yale logo is a trademark of Yale University.

Printed in the United States of America.

Library of Congress Cataloging-in-Publication Data
Main entry under title:
Old testament pseudepigrapha.
Includes indexes.
1. Apocryphal books (Old Testament) — Criticism, interpretation, etc.
I. Charlesworth, James H.
BS1830.A3   1985   229   80–2443
ISBN 978-0-300-14020-0 (hardcover : alk. paper)

A catalogue record for this book is available from the British Library.

This paper meets the requirements of ANSI/NISO Z39.48-1992
(Permanence of Paper).

Dedicated to my family
—Jerrie, Michelle, Eve, and James—
to other families supporting our
common labors,
and to families who read these
documents.

CONTENTS

DOCUMENTS

EXPANSIONS OF THE "OLD TESTAMENT" AND LEGENDS

WISDOM AND PHILOSOPHICAL LITERATURE

FOREWORD

GEORGE W. MACRAE, S.J.

The ancient Jewish and Jewish-Christian documents that are here called Pseudepigrapha have in their long history been both problematic and promising in both
Jewish and Christian communities. It is heartening to observe that the very
publication of this new collection testifies more to their promise than to their
problems. An ancient witness to both problem and promise can be found within
two late books of the New Testament itself. The Epistle of Jude, in its strong
antiheretical polemic, refers at least twice to the language of the book we call
1 Enoch and in a third instance quotes it in an authoritative manner as prophetic.
It also refers to a legend about the body of Moses known to us in the book called
the Assumption of Moses. The Second Epistle of Peter, generally regarded as the
latest of the New Testament books, incorporates much of Jude into its second
chapter, but it is very careful to excise all of the allusions to the Pseudepigrapha.

The problem to which this situation points is that of the canonical status of the
Pseudepigrapha in early Christianity—and the consequent propriety or impropriety
of citing them in public documents. Clearly the authors of Jude and 2 Peter reflect
different views. This problem persisted for centuries in the Church and can further
be seen in the reluctance of some churches to accept Jude into the New Testament
because of its controversial sources. In the synagogue the problem did not persist
so long, and the decision was clearly against the Pseudepigrapha.

The promise to which the episode of Jude and 2 Peter points is the value of
studying the Pseudepigrapha for a better understanding of prerabbinic Judaism and
of the religious matrix of Christianity. Whatever canonical decisions were taken
by the official leadership, it is clear that in popular religious circles, especially
Christian ones, this literature continued to be prominent and to influence thought
and piety.

The most recent decades have seen an astonishing rebirth of scholarly interest
in the Pseudepigrapha, and these volumes are an excellent guide to much of it.
The renewed interest has been and continues to be stimulated in part by new
manuscript discoveries. One thinks of the Dead Sea Scrolls among others. These
have provided access to much more extensive knowledge of Judaism in the period
immediately following the Old Testament. But perhaps even more important than
such a largely accidental factor as manuscript discoveries has been the ever
increasing acceptance of historical-critical method on the part of students of the
Bible at all levels. To study the Bible by this method involves knowing as much
as one can about the biblical world in all of its facets. And this of course includes
knowing the Jewish and Christian religious literature that ultimately did not become

part of the Bible. What we find, as these volumes show, is a bewildering variety of ideas, styles, and literary genres that is as diversified as the Bible itself yet often quite different from it. One of the merits of this edition, especially when compared to the few earlier ones in modern languages, is that it is inclusive rather than exclusive. It includes much more of the surviving literature than others have. Thus it affords a rich insight into the creative religious imagination from a singularly important formative period in Western religious culture.

Readers of these volumes and those who consult them for reference should include scholars and teachers, students, and any others who have an interest in the biblical world. All will be grateful to the many scholars who have contributed to the work. But more especially, they will have an enormous debt of gratitude to Professor Charlesworth and his immediate associates who boldly undertook and so competently executed the formidable task of editing this major work.

FOREWORD FOR CHRISTIANS

JAMES T. CLELAND

As one brought up in the home of a Church of Scotland minister, my father, and as one prepared for the Christian ministry in the Divinity Hall of Glasgow University, I have been trying to recall any unique impact made upon me by these related experiences, apart from family worship; the daily reading of the Word of God: Genesis to Revelation, one chapter per night, before falling asleep. The unexpected outcome is that I still find it somewhat difficult to decide if a Scots Presbyterian is an Old Testament Christian, with a stress on the Law and the Psalms, or a New Testament Jew, who attends his synagogue—as Jesus' custom was—on the sabbath day (Luke 4:16). There he hears a sermon which may be based on the Old Testament, or on the New Testament, or on both, as equally valid, equally authoritative. Why not? Is it not the same God in both testaments?

Many years later, in a Duke Divinity School morning chapel service, instead of a meditation, I just read the Prayer of Manasseh, now recognized, in its own right, as one of the Pseudepigrapha. After the service, a colleague asked me, "Where did you find that?" I told him. His surprised, almost awed, comment was: "That is the gospel outside of the Gospels." Why such a reaction? Manasseh was acknowledged to be the wickedest king of Judah, one who both majored and minored in iniquity, and yet maintained his throne in Jerusalem for fifty-five years, which was something of a record. Dr. James Moffatt sums up Manasseh, that royal rake, in a few simple words: "He did ample evil in the sight of the eternal to vex him" (2Chr 33:6). That is the emphasis of underemphasis. However, Manasseh repented; he prayed; God forgave (2Chr 33:13). The God who forgave is the same, yesterday, today, and forever, the God of Jew and Christian alike.

What I, a pulpiteer, hope from this volume, supervised by Professor Charlesworth, aided and abetted by scholars throughout the world, is that, as never before, Judaism and Christianity will be recognized as heirs of the same God, with what Jew and Christian have in common uniting us, rather than continuing a separation which may be emotionally understandable but is spiritually devitalizing. The very text of parts of the Pseudepigrapha may have been edited by later Jews *or* Christians. It would be good if one of the scholars discovered in his research that a section was prepared by Jew *and* Christian working together, not always in agreement in minor matters, but one in scholarship and editing because each had faith, academic and spiritual, in the same Father, who is at the heart of both testaments, and to be found in the Pseudepigrapha.

So, may it come to pass that what unites us as brethren will far surpass what seems to separate us, too often, even too willingly. We need each other. We are both children of the Kingdom, and the Pseudepigrapha may become a bridge between the Old and New testaments, helping us cross to and fro, back and forth, until we are equally at home in both, to our mental satisfaction, and our spiritual growth in grace.

So read the Prayer of Manasseh in the Pseudepigrapha. It is a model for a prayer, public or private: the invocation of God: "O Lord, God of our fathers, . . . unending and immeasurable are your promised mercies" (vss. 1–6); the confession of sin, verses 9–10: "O Lord, I am justly afflicted . . . because I did evil things before you"; the entreaty for forgiveness, verses 11–15, including the wonderful metaphor of complete surrender to God: "And now behold I am bending the knees of my heart" (v. 11); "Forgive me, O Lord, forgive me" (v. 13); "I shall praise you continually all the days of my life" (v. 15). It is a bonny prayer; my gratitude to the Jew who wrote it. I shall use it.

This prayer is to more than a few people the most famous instance of "the infinite compassion of God." If a Manasseh can be absolved, there is hope for anyone—including me. No wonder that I bend "the knees of my heart." It is the gospel outside the Gospels.

FOREWORD FOR JEWS

SAMUEL SANDMEL

By the strangest quirk of fate respecting literature that I know of, large numbers of writings by Jews were completely lost from the transmitted Jewish heritage. These documents stem roughly from 200 B.C. to A.D. 200. Not only the so-called Pseudepigrapha, but even such important and extensive writings as those by Philo and Josephus have not been part of the Jewish inheritance from its past; these were preserved and transmitted by Christians. It was rather only in the backwash of the Renaissance that Jews began to encounter Philo and Josephus. A sixteenth-century Italian rabbi, Azariah de Rossi, in a book called *Me-or Enayim* ("Light for the

Eyes''), inaugurated this Jewish rediscovery of the "lost" literature. He wrote with great praise of Philo, but with only reserved admiration for Josephus, whose Jewish loyalty he doubted. After de Rossi, Jews began slowly to deepen their study of Josephus and Philo, and thereafter the other literature, as legitimate parts of the Jewish heritage.

The ancient literary legacy which Jews did preserve and transmit was primarily the rabbinic literature. This huge body of writings might be divided into three categories: one, the Midrashim; two, Mishna and Gemara; and three, the Targumim. The Midrashim are commentaries on Scripture arranged according to the sequence of the biblical verses. The Mishna is a laconic statement of the secondary laws (Halacha) derived from Scripture. The Targumim allude to the Aramaic translation of Scripture; these translations have come down to us in differing styles and in somewhat differing ages. While within the rabbinic literature, especially in passages called haggadic ("narrative"), there are allusions to some of the documents found in the Apocrypha and occasionally to those in the Pseudepigrapha, it is only Ecclesiasticus (Jesus, the son of Sirach) who figures in any prominence at all in the talmudic literature. The Pseudepigrapha as such might be said with very little exaggeration to be without reflection in rabbinic literature.

As is known, the Pseudepigrapha were first gathered by Johannes Fabricius in the early part of the eighteenth century. Subsequent collectors of this material were able to·add certain books that were unknown to Fabricius and certain editors, such as R. H. Charles, included in editions of the Pseudepigrapha materials the presence of which might be questioned. Charles, for example, included the talmudic tractate the Ethics of the Fathers. The point is that there is no such thing as a "canon" of the Pseudepigrapha. Rather, there is an abundance of this scattered literature, some of it preserved in entirety and some preserved in part, usually in translation rather than in the original Hebrew or Aramaic. It is in reality only in the eighteenth century that the earnest and ever increasing study of the Pseudepigrapha began. Because most of the Pseudepigrapha were not preserved in Hebrew or Aramaic, it has been only the rare Jewish scholar who has made this study a major concern. By and large it has been Christians who have done the painstaking work of gathering this material, comparing the various manuscripts, producing critical editions, and providing translations into modern languages.

I do not think it is wrong to say that much of the Christian interest in the Pseudepigrapha in the early nineteenth century was based on the light this literature was deemed to throw on early Christianity. Since the documents in the Pseudepigrapha were not being studied for their own sake, often that roundedness which one should expect from the best of scientific scholarship was absent. Even more to be deplored was the circumstance that there were Christian scholars who seemed to feel the need to choose, as it were, between the Pseudepigrapha on the one hand and the rabbinic literature on the other hand, and who, on the basis of only part of the total Jewish literary productivity, came to some occasionally quixotic or reckless or even partisan conclusions about the nature of Judaism at the time of the birth of Christianity. Such an allegation would not be unjust respecting R. H. Charles.

A complete turnaround in the approach to the Pseudepigrapha in the last decades has been most gratifying. These writings have become the object of study for their own sake, part of the wish to illuminate the totality of the Jewish creativity of that bygone age. The recent scholarship has not tried to make the literature fit into a procrustean bed for some parochial purpose. It should be said that the relevancy of the Pseudepigrapha to early Christianity is not in any way diminished by the recent admirable mode of the study of Pseudepigrapha.

The result of the work of fine scholars, such as are represented herein, has been a significant broadening and deepening of the appreciation of the Jewish literary creativity. The cooperative study enlisting the gifted minds of Christians of various denominations and Jews of varying backgrounds is surely as moving and exciting a development as any cooperative academic venture could be. Perhaps it was the abundance of this ancient literature which the author of Ecclesiastes had in mind when he spoke rather cynically in these words: "of making many books there is no end and most of them are a weariness of the flesh." Obviously the author of Ecclesiastes did not admire every bit of writing that was in his ken. I do not think that the modern student needs to admire every example of the Pseudepigrapha, any more than we today need to regard every novel as a masterpiece. But he can still be astonished, amazed, enlightened, and overwhelmed by the abundance and variety and recurrent high quality of the Jewish literary activity of that period.

Old as this literature is for most modern people, it is also in a sense something brand-new, for most American laypeople have never heard the word Pseudepigrapha, or, if they have heard it, are not sure what it means. Now through the work of Professor Charlesworth and his associates a door is being opened anew to treasures that are very old. How gratifying it is that scholars devote themselves to the recovery of that which was lost or strayed or hidden. How gratifying that cooperative study is reviving this literature. How much such study contributes to understanding the richness of the Jewish legacy, now the heritage of both Jews and Christians.

EDITOR'S PREFACE

The present work is designed for the scholar and for the interested non-specialist. The general introduction, the introductions to each subdivision and to each document, and the translations with accompanying notes are shaped to help the reader understand these ancient writings. At the outset it is wise to stress three caveats for the general reader: 1) The following collection of writings, many of which claim to preserve a message from God for his people, are not gathered here in order to replace or add to those scriptures considered canonical by Jews or the larger collections claimed to be canonical by various groups of Christians. 2) In order to understand the Bible better the Pseudepigrapha should not be read in isolation, but along with the writings collected in the Old and New testaments (terms used for convenience and without confessional bias), and in ten other collections of ancient Jewish or early Christian writings (see Introduction). 3) The expanded definition of the Pseudepigrapha, now universally recognized as necessary by scholars, represents a more extended historical period than Charles's selection of writings; hence it must not be used *prima facie* as a group of writings representative of Early Judaism. The late documents, and Christian expansions of early Jewish writings, as the contributors themselves clarify, must not be read as if they were composed by contemporaries of the early ones. Conversely, late writings must not be ignored in a search for ideas possibly characteristic of Early Judaism; these documents frequently preserve edited portions of early Jewish writings.

In the fall of 1972, an editor at Doubleday, John J. Delaney, on the advice of his consultants, invited me to prepare a new edition of the Pseudepigrapha. The present work, completed ten years later, is the product of an international team of collaborators. Because it is a widely used term today, we have decided to retain the technical term "Pseudepigrapha"; it is explained in the following Introduction.

Each contributor was asked to discuss all issues requisite for a meaningful reading of the document translated, and given some freedom in utilizing the following format:

> The contributor begins the presentation either with a synopsis of the narrative or with a discussion of the key characteristics and central ideas in a non-narrative writing.
>
> *Texts.* The scholar discusses only the most important extant texts, and clarifies the textual base or the critical edition behind the translation.
>
> *Original Language.* The translator briefly discusses the original language of the document, reviews published scholarly conclusions, and usually advocates one possibility.
>
> *Date.* The contributor assesses the debates (if any) over the date of the original composition, explains, if appropriate, the dates of any subsequent expansions or interpolations, and then presents his or her own scholarly opinion.

Provenance. The expert briefly evaluates the hypotheses regarding the place or places in which the work may have been composed, and subsequently voices his or her own judgment.

Historical Importance. The contributor discusses the importance of the document for an appreciation of the historical period in which it was composed.

Theological Importance. The specialist explains the motifs, symbols, and major theological ideas contained in the pseudepigraphon.

Relation to Canonical Books. The expert assesses the possible relationships between the pseudepigraphon and writings now customarily judged canonical.

Relation to Apocryphal Books. The scholar succinctly discusses the apocryphal books to which the document is especially close.

Cultural Importance. If appropriate, the contributor discusses the importance of the pseudepigraphon for a better understanding of the origin of our culture. Briefly mentioned are possible parallels between it and the great classics, such as Plato's *Dialogues,* Dante's *Divina Commedia,* and Milton's *Paradise Lost.*

At the end of each introduction to a document the contributor lists the most important publications on the document.

The organization of these documents follows considerable discussion with the Board of Advisors and the contributors themselves. Any system for ordering these documents has weaknesses. A listing of the documents in chronological order is impractical at the present time. We are still uncertain about the date or dates of composition for many of these writings; moreover, some are composite and represent more than one century. Merely placing them in alphabetical order is attractive in the sense that one knows where a particular document is in such a recognized sequence; hence, an alphabetical listing on the endpapers of this volume. An alphabetical listing is confusing, however, because some of the documents collected below are known by more than one title, some may be listed alphabetically according to more than one word in the title, and—most importantly— an alphabetical order is artificial and does not signal the relationships between documents that are related. We have decided to organize the documents according to broadly conceived literary types. Within these groups they are listed chronologically in terms of the earliest probable date with the exception that cycles of traditions, like the Enoch and Ezra books, are grouped together.

In the past scholars often felt free to emend a text and to aim at a loose idiomatic translation (although Charles himself was a literalist). Modern scholarship has demanded more rigorous devotion to extant readings, more thorough attempts to understand the grammar and syntax of ancient languages, and, in general, more loyalty to the manuscripts. While we have aimed whenever possible at an idiomatic rendering, we have avoided the temptation to paraphrase the meaning of a complicated passage or to conceal sometimes confusing readings behind elegant English prose. Besides trustworthiness to the transmitted text, there are other advantages in these literal renderings: The reader is introduced to the flavor of ancient expressions, phrases, and images. We have also presented literal translations of texts written in a language two or three times removed from that of the lost original. For example, Pseudo-Philo is extant in Latin but the original was composed in another language, probably Hebrew. The same situation lies behind 1 Enoch and Jubilees; both seem to derive ultimately from a Semitic language, which may be immediately behind the Ethiopic or be separated from it by an intermediary Greek version.

The preparation of this volume has been financed by generous grants and gifts from the Phillips Investment Corporation, the Phillips family, the Mary Duke Biddle Foundation, Brigham Young University's Religious Studies Center, Raymond and Hazel Mueller, Frances DeMott, the Welch family, and the Duke University Research Council. I am deeply grateful to each of them.

Finally after years of sacrificial work by so many it is difficult to articulate my deep appreciation and indebtedness to all those who have helped in the completion of the present edition of the Pseudepigrapha. I am indebted to the editors and staff at Doubleday, to my Board of Advisors, to the external readers, notably H. D. Betz, I. Gruenwald, J. Neusner, J. F. Oates, B. Schaller, J. L. Sharpe III, J. F. Strange, N. Turner, J. C. VanderKam, and F. W. Young, who have labored over many of these contributions, and to the contributors, who had to live for a long time with a frequently stern and demanding editor. I am grateful to my colleagues here at Duke, who had to live with unexpected responsibilities due to the tasks that fell my way, to the administrators, especially President Sanford, Chairman Bill Poteat, Chairman Bob Osborn, and Dean Langford, who provided space for editing and preparing the work. W. D. Davies, Moody Smith, Ray Brown, and John Strugnell helped me improve the Introduction. Many of my assistants worked long and hard hours, often during the trying summer months in Durham, and I wish to express my appreciation to all of them, notably Gary Martin, Jim Dumke, Dave Fiensy, Steve Robinson, George Zervos, and most especially to James Mueller, who served the longest, saw the task through to completion, and has proved to be a gifted and dedicated assistant. Marie Smith, my secretary, has without complaint typed and retyped much of the manuscript, and all of the voluminous correspondence. To all of these mentioned and many others I wish to express my sincere appreciation and hope that the final product is worthy of their sacrifices and support.

J. H. Charlesworth

Duke University
December 1982

BOARD OF ADVISORS

CONTRIBUTORS TO VOLUME TWO

Doran, R., Department of Religion, Amherst College, Amherst, Massachusetts
Aristeas the Exegete, Pseudo-Eupolemus, Cleodemus Malchus, Pseudo-Hecataeus

Fallon, F., Visiting Assistant Professor, Boston College, Chestnut Hill, Massachusetts
Theodotus, Eupolemus

Fiensy, D. A., Assistant Professor of Religion, Kentucky Christian College, Grayson, Kentucky
Hellenistic Synagogal Prayers

Hanson, J., Department of Religious Studies, University of Kansas, Lawrence, Kansas
Demetrius the Chronographer

Hare, D. R. A., William F. Orr Professor of New Testament, Pittsburgh Theological Seminary, Pittsburgh, Pennsylvania
The Lives of the Prophets

Harrington, D. J., S.J., Associate Professor of New Testament, Weston School of Theology, Cambridge, Massachusetts
Pseudo-Philo

Johnson, M. D., Academic Editor, Augsburg Publishing House, Minneapolis, Minnesota
Life of Adam and Eve

Knibb, M. A., Lecturer in Old Testament Studies, University of London, King's College, London, England
Martyrdom and Ascension of Isaiah

Lafargue, M., Lecturer, Religion Department, University of Massachusetts at Boston
Orphica

Lindenberger, J. M., Associate Professor of Old Testament, Director of Graduate Studies, Vancouver School of Theology, Vancouver, British Columbia, Canada
Ahiqar

Lunt, H. G., Samuel Hazzard Cross Professor of Slavic Languages and Literatures, Harvard University, Cambridge, Massachusetts
Ladder of Jacob

Lutz, R. T., Department of Near Eastern Studies, University of Toronto, Toronto, Ontario, Canada
Jannes and Jambres

Martin, E. G., Perkins Library, Duke University, Durham, North Carolina
Eldad and Modad

Pietersma, A., Department of Near Eastern Studies, University of Toronto, Toronto, Ontario, Canada
Jannes and Jambres

Robinson, S. E., Assistant Professor of Religion, Lycoming College, Williamsport, Pennsylvania
4 Baruch

Robertson, R. G., Federated Church of Ashland, Ashland, Massachusetts
Ezekiel the Tragedian

Sanders, J. A., President, Ancient Manuscript Center for Preservation and Research, School of Theology at Claremont and Claremont Graduate School, Claremont, California
More Psalms of David

Shutt, R. J. H., Professor Emeritus, Department of Religious Studies, Worcester College of Education, Worcester, England
Letter of Aristeas

Smith, J. Z., William Benton Professor of Religion and Human Sciences, The Divinity School, University of Chicago, Chicago, Illinois
Prayer of Joseph

Strugnell, J., Professor of Christian Origins, Harvard Divinity School, Cambridge, Massachusetts
Introduction to Fragments of Lost Judeo-Hellenistic Works

Van der Horst, P. W., Lecturer of New Testament Exegesis and New Testament Background, Faculty of Theology, University of Utrecht, Utrecht, The Netherlands
Pseudo-Phocylides

Wintermute, O. S., Professor of Religion, Duke University, Durham, North Carolina
Jubilees

Wright, R. B., Director of Graduate Religion Studies, Temple University, Philadelphia, Pennsylvania
Psalms of Solomon

Zervos, G. T., Research Assistant, Duke University, Durham, North Carolina
History of Joseph

INTRODUCTION FOR THE GENERAL READER

BY J. H. CHARLESWORTH

Western culture has been largely shaped by a unique collection of ancient books: the Bible. Not only our culture's language, but also its theology, philosophy, art, and law have been affected profoundly by the ideas, symbols, morality, commitments, perceptions, and dreams preserved in the biblical books. In the attempt to understand these books, scholars, especially since the time of the European Enlightenment, in the seventeenth and eighteenth centuries, have coupled an intensive study of them with a search for other ancient writings related to them.

The search for lost writings

Mere perusal of the biblical books discloses that their authors depended upon sources that are no longer extant. We know so little about these sources that we cannot be certain of the extent to which they were actual documents. A list of these lost sources would be extensive; it would include at least the following: the Book of the Wars of Yahweh (Num 21:14), the Book of the Just (Josh 10:13, 2Sam 1:18), the Book of the Acts of Solomon (1Kgs 11:41), the Book of the Annals of the Kings of Israel (1Kgs 14:19, 2Chr 33:18; cf. 2Chr 20:34), the Book of the Annals of the Kings of Judah (1Kgs 14:29, 15:7), the Annals of Samuel the seer (1Chr 29:29), the History of Nathan the prophet (2Chr 9:29), the Annals of Shemaiah the prophet and of Iddo the seer (2Chr 12:15), the Annals of Jehu son of Hanani (2Chr 20:34), an unknown and untitled writing of Isaiah (2Chr 26:22), the Annals of Hozai (2Chr 33:18), and an unknown lament for Josiah by Jeremiah (2Chr 35:25). In the Apocrypha (defined below) lost books also are mentioned; in particular, 1 Maccabees 16:24 refers to the Annals of John Hyrcanus. Within the Pseudepigrapha themselves there are references to "documents" now lost (cf. e.g. TJob 40:14, 41:6, 49:3, 50:3).

Christianity and rabbinic Judaism evolved within a milieu that was distinguished by considerable and significant literary activity. Some of the documents composed during the early centuries have been transmitted by copyists; many remain lost; and others have been recovered during the last two centuries. The search for lost writings is aided by ancient lists of "extracanonical" books. One of these lists is a catalogue, perhaps from the sixth century, falsely attributed to Athanasius of Alexandria (c. 296–373). The author includes among the disputed parts of the Old Testament (*ta antilegomena tēs palaias diathēkēs*), the four Books of the Maccabees (1–4 Mac), the Psalms and Ode (*sic*) of Solomon. He defines the Apocrypha of the Old Testament (*ta de apokrupha palin tēs palaias diathēkēs tauta*) as follows:

Enoch	Elijah the Prophet
Patriarchs	Zephaniah the Prophet
Prayer of Joseph	Zechariah the Father of John
Testament of Moses	Baruch
Assumption of Moses	Habakkuk
(And the) pseudepigrapha	Ezekiel
(*pseudepigrapha*) of Abraham	Daniel
Eldad and Modad	

All of the documents judged to be disputed parts of the Old Testament or the Apocrypha (if we understand their titles correctly) are included, if only fragmentarily, in the present collection, except for 1 and 2 Maccabees (which belong in the Apocrypha), and except for the lost pseudepigrapha attributed to Habakkuk and Zechariah (which is to be placed among the New Testament Pseudepigrapha because it is related to Zechariah the father of John the Baptist).

Numerous writings not mentioned by Pseudo-Athanasius are included in this volume. Many of these are named in other canonical lists, notably the List of Sixty Books (c. sixth to seventh century?) and the list of Mechitar of Ayrivank' (c. 1290). Others do not appear in any early list. Some pseudepigrapha mentioned in medieval lists are not included; they are judged to be characteristically different from and too late for the present collection (see below). The search continues for documents not yet found but cited in the classical lists: an Apocryphon of Lamech (Sixty Books), the Interdiction of Solomon (Gelasian Decree), and the Book of the Daughters of Adam (Gelasian Decree; perhaps this document is another name for Jubilees). Likewise scholars are seeking to understand the origin of ancient quotations from or allusions to unnamed Jewish apocryphal documents. Many of these citations or traditions are preserved by the Church Fathers, especially Clement of Rome, Clement of Alexandria, Hippolytus, Tertullian, Origen, and the compiler of the Apostolic Constitutions, as well as by the Byzantine chroniclers (especially George Syncellus [c. 800] and George Cedrenus [c. 1057]).

The present edition of the Pseudepigrapha reflects the search for lost writings. We have included many apocryphal documents, fragmentary or complete, which may be related to those named in the canonical lists or cited by the Church Fathers; note, for example, the following: Apocalypse of Adam, Apocalypse of Abraham, Testament of Abraham, Prayer of Joseph, Eldad and Modad (still preserved in only one brief quotation), Apocalypse of Elijah, Apocryphon of Ezekiel, Apocalypse of Zephaniah, and Apocalypse of Ezra.

Many documents, recently discovered in the Near East or recognized in distinguished libraries, are translated here into English for the first time. Not including the documents placed in the Supplement, the writings now available for the first time in English are the Testament of Adam, the Testaments of Isaac and Jacob (from the Arabic), the Apocalypse of Daniel, the Revelation of Ezra, the Vision of Ezra, the History of Joseph, Syriac Menander, and the History of the Rechabites (from the Syriac). Additional writings translated for the first time in a full English translation are the Questions of Ezra, the Ladder of Jacob, Jannes and Jambres, and the Apocalypse of Sedrach.

In addition to these documents, four writings presented only in a truncated version in Charles's edition are presented here in their full extant form. From the

Martyrdom of Isaiah Charles himself included only chapters 1, 2, 3, and 5; the present edition presents all of that document along with the other traditions now preserved in the Martyrdom and Ascension of Isaiah. From 2 Enoch Forbes and Charles omitted the conclusion to the document; the present edition includes chapters 68 through 73, which contain the fascinating account of Melchisedek's miraculous birth. From the Sibylline Oracles Lanchester collected only the fragments and Books 3, 4, and 5; the present edition includes all of the Sibylline Oracles now extant. Finally, from 4 Ezra Box selected chapters 3–14; the present edition also includes the Christian additions (chapters 1 and 2, and 15 and 16).

Canon

The preceding discussion brings forward the question of the origin of the closed canons of the Old and New Testaments. Impressive research is presently focused upon these issues, and it is possible to summarize only briefly my own opinions regarding this complex issue. For a long time scholars postulated that two canons of the Old Testament developed, one in Palestine and another in Egypt, and that Alexandrian Jews added the Apocrypha (see below) to the Hebrew canon. It now seems clear that there never was a rival Alexandrian canon. Philo and other Jews in Alexandria did not cite the Apocrypha, and the Alexandrian Church Fathers witness to the fact that Alexandrian Jews did not have an expanded canon.

When R. H. Charles published his edition of the Pseudepigrapha there was widespread agreement that the Hebrew canon, the Old Testament, was fixed finally at Jamnia around A.D. 90. Today there is considerable debate regarding the importance of the rabbinic school at Jamnia in the history of the codification of the Hebrew canon. On the one hand, it is becoming obvious that the process of canonization began long before the first century A.D., and that perhaps the earliest part of the Bible, the Law, had been closed and defined as authoritative well before the second century B.C., and the Prophets surely by that time. On the other hand, it is clear that after A.D. 90 there were still debates regarding the canonicity of such writings as the Song of Songs, Ecclesiastes, and Esther, but it is not clear what were the full ramifications of these debates. It seems to follow, therefore, both that the early pseudepigrapha were composed during a period in which the limits of the canon apparently remained fluid at least to some Jews, and that some Jews and Christians inherited and passed on these documents as inspired. They did not necessarily regard them as apocryphal, or outside a canon.

The writings collected into the New Testament were written during the end of this same period since they are dated from about A.D. 50 to 150. The New Testament canon was not closed in the Latin Church until much later; certainly not before the late fourth century and long after Constantine the Great established Christianity as the official religion of the Roman Empire. All the twenty-seven books of the New Testament, for example, are listed for the first time as the *only* canonical New Testament scriptures by Athanasius, bishop of Alexandria, in his Easter letter of A.D. 367. If the Latin Church finally accepted twenty-seven books as the canonical New Testament by the fifth century, the Greek Church apparently was not thoroughly convinced about the canonicity of one book, Revelation, until about the tenth century. The Syrian Church witnessed to an even more complicated debate over the canon of the New Testament; for many east Syrians today the

Peshitta is the canon and it contains only twenty-two documents, excluding 2 Peter, 2 and 3 John, Jude, and Revelation. Moreover, the assumption that all Christians have the same canon is further shattered by the recognition that the Copts and Ethiopians have added other documents to the canon.

Even in America today there are different canons among the various Christian communions: for example, Protestants exclude from the canon the Apocrypha, the additional books in the Greek Old Testament; the Roman Catholics, following the edicts of the Council of Trent in 1546, include them as deuterocanonical. The Mormons, moreover, argue that more books belong in the canon, and that it should remain open.

Most Jews throughout the world acknowledge only the Old Testament as canonical (cf. e.g. 4Ezra 14:37–48). The Falashas, Ethiopian Jews probably dependent on Ethiopian Christianity, however, have an expanded canon, including various apocrypha and pseudepigrapha, especially the Prayer of Manasseh, Jubilees, 1 Enoch, 3 and 4 Ezra.

For our present purposes it is wise to add to the above insights the recognition that many authors of pseudepigrapha believed they were recording God's infallible words. Early communities, both Jewish and Christian, apparently took some pseudepigrapha very seriously. The author of Jude, in verses 14 and 15, quoted as prophecy a portion of 1 Enoch, and this passage, 1 Enoch 1:9, has now been recovered in Aramaic from one of the caves that contained the Dead Sea Scrolls. Jude probably also was dependent, in verses 9 and 10, upon a lost Jewish apocryphon about Moses.

This brief overview of the historical development of the canons reveals that to call the Pseudepigrapha "non-canonical," or the biblical books "canonical," can be historically inaccurate prior to A.D. 100 and the period in which most of these documents were written. These terms should be used as an expression of some later "orthodoxy" with regard to a collection that is well defined regarding what belongs within and what is to be excluded from it. It is potentially misleading to use the terms "non-canonical," "canonical," "heresy," and "orthodoxy" when describing either Early Judaism or Early Christianity.

Definition of pseudepigrapha

The technical term "pseudepigrapha" has a long and distinguished history. It was used in the late second century by Serapion when he referred to the New Testament Pseudepigrapha (*ta pseudepigrapha*, "with false superscription"; cf. Eusebius, *HE* 6.12). It was given prominence in the early years of the eighteenth century by J. A. Fabricius, who called the first volume of his massive work *Codex pseudepigraphus veteris testamenti*. The nineteenth-century collection of "pseudepigrapha" was by the Roman Catholic M. L'Abbé J.-P. Migne and titled *Dictionnaire des apocryphes, ou collection de tous les livres apocryphes relatifs à l'ancien et au nouveau testament*; this work did not use the term "pseudepigrapha" because Roman Catholics consider the Apocrypha to be deuterocanonical writings and refer to the Pseudepigrapha as "the Apocrypha." In the year 1900, E. Kautzsch edited the first German collection of the Pseudepigrapha, titled *Die Apokryphen und Pseudepigraphen des Alten Testaments*. The first, and until the present the only, English collection of the Pseudepigrapha was published in 1913 by the Clarendon Press of Oxford, England, and edited by R. H. Charles; he included in his large two-volume work both *The Apocrypha and Pseudepigrapha of the Old Testament*. The importance of the Pseudepigrapha in the international community at the present time is evidenced by the preparation of translations into Danish, Italian, French, German, modern Greek, Japanese, Dutch, and Spanish.

It is appropriate at this point to clarify the meaning of the term "pseudepigrapha." Several definitions are current. Webster's Third New International Dictionary (p. 1830) defines the term as denoting "spurious works purporting to emanate from biblical characters." That definition is misleading; ancient writings are dismissed subjectively as illegitimate. The Random House Dictionary of the English Language (the Unabridged Edition, p. 1159) offers the following: "Certain writings (other than the canonical books and the Apocrypha) professing to be Biblical in character, but not considered canonical or inspired." Three reactions appear to this definition: First, it would have been informative to clarify for whom the writings are "not considered canonical or inspired." Second, it is good to see a recognition of the claim to be "Biblical in character," which I believe is implied by some pseudepigrapha of the Old Testament. Third, it is unfortunate that neither of the two definitions presented by these authoritative volumes recognizes that this term is also employed for documents not related to the Bible. Scholars have used the term, for example, to denote some rabbinic writings, referring to the *Othijoth de Rabbi 'Akiba* and the *Pirķê de Rabbi Eliezer* as rabbinic pseudepigrapha; moreover, "pseudepigrapha" is a technical term for some writings by the post-Platonic Pythagoreans.

Strictly speaking, the term "pseudepigrapha" has evolved from *pseudepigrapha*, a transliteration of a Greek plural noun that denotes writings "with false super-scription." *The Old Testament Pseudepigrapha*, the title of this collection, etymologically denotes writings falsely attributed to ideal figures featured in the Old Testament. Contemporary scholars employ the term "pseudepigrapha" not because it denotes something spurious about the documents collected under that title, but because the term has been inherited and is now used internationally.

In entitling the volume *The Old Testament Pseudepigrapha*, I have had to take a stance on the definition of "pseudepigrapha" as illustrated by the selection of works other than those included by Charles. Only two works from Charles's volume of seventeen documents are not included: Pirke Aboth and "The Fragments of a Zadokite Work," the former because it is rabbinic and the latter because it is now recognized to belong among the Dead Sea Scrolls. The following collection of fifty-two writings together with a long Supplement has evolved from the consensus that the Pseudepigrapha must be defined broadly so as to include all documents that conceivably belong to the Old Testament Pseudepigrapha. The present description of the Pseudepigrapha is as follows: Those writings 1) that, with the exception of Ahiqar, are Jewish or Christian; 2) that are often attributed to ideal figures in Israel's past; 3) that customarily claim to contain God's word or message; 4) that frequently build upon ideas and narratives present in the Old Testament; 5) and that almost always were composed either during the period 200 B.C. to A.D. 200 or, though late, apparently preserve, albeit in an edited form, Jewish traditions that date from that period. Obviously, the numerous qualifications (e.g. "with the exception of," "often," "customarily," "frequently," "almost always") warn that the above comments do not define the term "pseudepigrapha"; they merely describe the features of this collection.

Writings cognate to the Pseudepigrapha

Including fifty-two documents plus a Supplement in the present collection of the Pseudepigrapha meant excluding other writings, although they may have some characteristics of the Pseudepigrapha. These writings were usually omitted because they were far removed from the Old Testament in date and character. Most notable among them are the following: The Vision of Daniel, The Death of Abraham (both ed. by A. Vassiliev in *Anecdota Graeco-Byzantina*, vol. 1. Moscow, 1893), the Hebrew Apocalypse of Elijah (ed. and trans. M. Buttenwieser, *Die hebräische Elias-Apokalypse*. Leipzig, 1897), the Book of Jasher (ed. J. Ilive, *The Book of Jasher*. Bristol, 1829), the Conflict of Adam and Eve with Satan (ed. A. Dillmann, *Das christliche Adambuch des Orients*. Göttingen, 1853; ET: S. C. Malan, *The Book of Adam and Eve*. London, 1882), the Cave of Treasures (ed. C. Bezold, *Die Schatzhöhle: Syrisch und Deutsch*, 2 vols. Leipzig, 1883, 1888; ET: E. A. W. Budge, *The Book of the Cave of Treasures*. London, 1927), the Book of the Rolls (cf. M. D. Gibson, *Apocrypha Arabica*. Studia Sinaitica 8. London, 1901), the Sin of Solomon (unpublished, probably a homily, cf. Cod. Par. Gr. 1021, fols. 184v–185v in the Bibliothèque Nationale), *Pirķê de Rabbi Eliezer* (trans. G. Friedlander, *Pirķê de Rabbi Eliezer*. New York, 1981⁴), the Syriac Apocalypse of Ezra (ed. and trans. J.-B. Chabot, "L'Apocalypse d'Esdras," *Revue sémitique* 2 [1894] 242–50, 333–46), the Book of the Bee (ed. and trans. E. A. W. Budge, *The Book of the Bee*. Anecdota Oxoniensia, Sem. Ser. 1.2. Oxford, 1886), and the Questions Addressed by the Queen (of Sheba), and Answers Given by Solomon (trans. J. Issaverdens, *The Uncanonical Writings of the Old Testament*. Venice, 1901).

Later documents related to the Pseudepigrapha have been edited in important collections; most important are those from Armenian by Jacques Issaverdens, from Ethiopic by Wolf Leslau, and from rabbinic Hebrew by Adolph Jellinek (cf. the German translation by A. Wünsche). Recently Father Martin McNamara in *The Apocrypha in the Irish Church* (Dublin, 1975) drew attention to "probably the richest crop of apocrypha in any of the European vernaculars, possibly in any vernacular language" (p. 2).

While some of the documents mentioned above may prove to be ancient or preserve portions of early Jewish pseudepigrapha, the following ten collections of ancient Jewish or early Christian writings are recognized as important for understanding the period in which the Pseudepigrapha were composed. First and second are the works of the Jewish philosopher and exegete Philo of Alexandria (c. 20 B.C.–A.D. 50) and the Jewish historian Josephus (c. A.D. 37–c. 100); these are essential reading for an understanding of first-century Jewish life and thought. Third are the Dead Sea Scrolls, which are Jewish sectarian documents first found in 1947 in caves to the west of the Dead Sea; these inform us of the apocalyptic and eschatological ideas and of the surprising interpretations of the Old Testament by one sect of Jews, which flourished from the second century B.C. (c. 150 B.C.) to the first century A.D. (viz. A.D. 68). These scrolls are extremely important for an understanding of many pseudepigrapha, especially Jubilees, the Testaments of the Twelve Patriarchs, 1 Enoch, and the Odes of Solomon. Fourth are the rabbinic writings, and there can be no doubt that some of the traditions recorded in these documents predate the destruction of the Temple in A.D. 70; these early traditions are helpful in understanding the daily life of the religious Jew before the destruction of the nation and the Temple. Fifth are the targums, which are Aramaic translations and expansive interpretations of the Hebrew scriptures; these sometimes seem to preserve important evidence of an ancient understanding of the Old Testament. Since a Targum of Job, dating from the first half of the first century A.D., was found at Qumran, it is now clear that the earliest traditions in the other, but much later, targums must be included in an assessment of early Judaism. Sixth are the "Jewish" magical papyri, especially those edited by K. L. Preisendanz; these should not be ignored, as should become evident from a careful reading of some pseudepigrapha, especially the Prayer of Jacob, the Prayer of Joseph, and the History of Joseph. Seventh are the Hermetica, which are writings of the first few centuries A.D. attributed to Hermes that describe the means to personal salvation; these may contain (although I personally am not convinced) some early Jewish traditions that are important for an understanding of Early Judaism and earliest Christianity. Eighth are the Nag Hammadi codices; these Coptic codices were composed from perhaps the first to the fourth centuries A.D., but were not found until 1945 in Upper Egypt. These writings, most of which are gnostic, are intermittently influenced by early Jewish traditions. Of special importance among these codices is the Apocalypse of Adam included below. Ninth are the New Testament Apocrypha and Pseudepigrapha, which contain many early Christian writings that are usually legendary expansions of the New Testament itself; these only infrequently were shaped by early Jewish traditions.

Tenth are the Apocrypha, which are writings that like many pseudepigrapha are usually related to the Hebrew scriptures; as indicated earlier, the Apocrypha are documents preserved in the Greek, but not in the Hebrew, Old Testament. These documents are often designated by Roman Catholics as "deuterocanonical," but most scholars have now accepted the Protestant terminology and call them "Apocrypha."

Different collections of the Apocrypha are available today. In order to harmonize with the contemporary, enlarged concept of Pseudepigrapha the Apocrypha should include only the additional writings preserved in almost all Septuagint manuscripts, and not the additional documents in the Vulgate (see *PMR*, p. 19). The Apocrypha, therefore, includes thirteen documents: 2 Ezra (= 1 Esdras),* Tobit, Judith, Additions to Esther, Wisdom of Solomon, Sirach, 1 Baruch, Letter of Jeremiah, Prayer of Azariah with the Song of the Three Young Men, Susanna, Bel and the Dragon, 1 Maccabees, and 2 Maccabees. Often two pseudepigrapha, 4 Ezra (= 2 Esdras)* and the Prayer of Manasseh,* are considered part of the Apocrypha. The thirteen documents in the Apocrypha, with the exception of Tobit, which may be much earlier, date from the last two centuries before the common era. These documents may be found in Protestant ecumenical Bibles that contain the Apocrypha in a center section between the testaments, or at the end of the two testaments. All except the three marked with asterisks will be found in Roman Catholic Bibles interspersed among the Old Testament writings or even as part of them (esp. Esth and Dan).

It is important to draw attention to these other significant collections of early Jewish and Christian documents. Along with them, the Pseudepigrapha preserve ideas essential for an understanding of Early Judaism and Early Christianity.

Importance of the Pseudepigrapha

We may now assess briefly the importance of the Pseudepigrapha for a better understanding of the history and thought of Jews during the centuries that preceded and followed the beginning of the common era. Four aspects of that period are impressive. First, there is the very abundance of the literature, although we possess only part of the writings produced by Jews during the period 200 B.C. to A.D. 200. We know many works are lost since early Christians quoted from and referred to documents now lost, since some writings are available only in truncated manuscripts or in fragments, since there are references to lost volumes produced, for example, by Jason of Cyrene, Justus of Tiberias, and Nicolaus of Damascus, and since each new discovery of a manuscript reminds us that there are still more works to be recovered.

It is obvious that post-exilic Judaism was distinguished by voluminous and varied literature: from the production of epics or tragedies in hexameters or iambic trimeters (viz. PhEPoet, EzekTrag) to philosophical tractates (viz. Aristob, Philo, 4Mac), from perhaps reliable histories (viz. 1Mac, some of Josephus' publications) to imaginative recreations of the past (viz. the Chronicler, 3Mac, JosAsen), from apocalyptic dreams and visions of another world (viz. 1En, 2Bar; cf. HistRech) to humanistic wisdom (viz. Sir, Ps-Phoc), and even from charges against God in seemingly Promethean arrogance (viz. Eccl; cf. ApSedr) to hymnic and introspective submissions to God as the sole means of righteousness and salvation (viz. 1QH, PrMan; cf. OdesSol). During the post-exilic period, the Jewish genius exploded into creative new writings.

Second, the Pseudepigrapha illustrate the pervasive influence of the Old Testament books upon Early Judaism. That is seen not only in the following group of works designated "Expansions of the Old Testament," but also in many similar ones, especially in the selection of "apocalypses" and "testaments." Judaism became for all time a religion of the Book, God's eternal message.

Third, we learn from the Pseudepigrapha that the consecutive conquests of Palestinian Jews by Persians, Greeks, and Romans, and the intermittent invasions by Syrian, Egyptian, and Parthian armies did not dampen the enthusiasm of religious Jews for their ancestral traditions. The ancient Davidic Psalter was constantly expanded until some collections included 155 psalms. Other psalmbooks appeared, especially the Psalms of Solomon, the Hodayoth, the Odes of Solomon, and perhaps the Hellenistic Synagogal Hymns. Apocalypses that stressed the grandeur and transcendence of God were customarily interspersed with hymns that celebrated God's nearness, and by prayers that were perceived as heard and answered. Post-exilic Judaism was a living and devout religion. New hymns, psalms, and odes witness to the fact that persecution could not choke the blessings by the faithful.

Fourth, the Pseudepigrapha attest that post-exilic Jews often were torn within by divisions and sects, and intermittently conquered from without by foreign nations who insulted, abused, and frequently employed fatal torture. Persecutions inflamed the desire to revolt and some pseudepigrapha mirror the tensions among the Jews. Especially noteworthy are the Psalms of Solomon and the Testament of Moses, which record the idea that God alone is the source of power; it is he who will initiate action against the gentiles and purge Jerusalem of the foreigners. The apocalypses usually are pessimistic about the present: God had withdrawn from the arena of history and from the earth; he would return only to consummate the end and to inaugurate the new. Thereby the apocalyptists affirm the loyalty of God to covenant, invite the reader to live in terms of, indeed within, another world, and envisage an optimistic conclusion for Israel in God's completed story.

The Pseudepigrapha, therefore, are an important source for understanding the social dimensions of Early Judaism. The simplistic picture of Early Judaism should be recast; it certainly was neither a religion which had fallen into arduous legalism due to the crippling demands of the Law, nor was it characterized by four dominant sects. A new picture has been emerging because of ideas preserved in the documents collected below. Three examples suffice to demonstrate this insight: First, none of the present translators strives to identify a document with a particular Jewish sect. We cannot identify with certainty any author of a pseudepigraphon as being a Pharisee or an Essene or a member of another sect. Second, Palestinian Jews were influenced by Egyptian, Persian, and Greek ideas. Hence, the old distinction between "Palestinian Judaism" and "Hellenistic Judaism" must be either redefined or discarded. Third, because of the variegated, even contradictory, nature of the ideas popular in many sectors of post-exilic Judaism, it is obvious that Judaism was not monolithically structured or shaped by a central and all-powerful "orthodoxy."

When Charles published his edition of the Pseudepigrapha, it was widely held that Early Judaism was shaped and characterized by "normative Judaism" or a ruling orthodoxy centered in Jerusalem. This idea is no longer defended by most biblical scholars. Since 1947, when the first of the Dead Sea Scrolls were discovered, there has even been a tendency to emphasize unduly the diversity in Early Judaism. While it is now recognized that foreign ideas penetrated deep into many aspects of Jewish thought, and that sometimes it is difficult to decide whether an early document is essentially Jewish or Christian, it is, nevertheless, unwise to exaggerate the diversity in Early Judaism. In the first century Judaism was neither uniformly normative nor chaotically diverse.

The above discussion leads to the following observations that should be emphasized. The documents contained herein certainly demonstrate the rich vitality and diversity of Judaism during the early centuries. This is not the place to attempt to articulate further what, if anything, seems to unify them. Certainly confirmed is Charles's own statement that was controversial in his time: Without the Apocrypha and Pseudepigrapha (and we would add other documents recovered since his time, notably the Dead Sea Scrolls) "it is absolutely impossible to explain the course of religious development between 200 B.C. and A.D. 100" (*APOT*, vol. 1, p. x).

Significant theological conceptions

The general reader will find it helpful, when reading the documents collected below, to learn that at least four significant theological concerns are frequently found in the Pseudepigrapha: preoccupations with the meaning of sin, the origins of evil, and the problem of theodicy; stresses upon God's transcendence; concerns with the coming of the Messiah; and beliefs in a resurrection that are often accompanied with descriptions of Paradise. Each of these interests was developed—

at least partly—from ideas and beliefs found in the Old Testament. At the beginning it is prudent to emphasize that scholars' understanding of early Jewish theology has evolved from decades of research not only upon the Pseudepigrapha, but also upon the Old Testament, the Apocrypha, early rabbinics, Philo, Josephus, and the Dead Sea Scrolls.

Sin, Evil, and the Problem of Theodicy. The Jews who returned to Palestine following the sixth-century B.C. exile in Babylon attempted to be faithful to the covenant; they rebuilt the Temple and emphasized the study of the Torah. Dedication to purity involved not only heightened rules for worship and daily life but also racial purity and separation from the heathen. Despite renewed dedication and faithfulness, the righteous did not prosper and live in a holy land free from domination. It was the sinners and the unfaithful who seemed to be rewarded, and the land—indeed the land promised to Abraham as an inheritance—was ruled by foreign oppressors. Sin and injustice were rewarded; evil appeared to be the ruling power in a world created by God. Raised repeatedly was the question: "How could the God of Israel be holy, just, and all-powerful, and at the same time permit evil forces to oppress the righteous?" Many pseudepigrapha are shaped by this question and the problem of theodicy (see especially 4Ezra, 2Bar, ApAbr, 3Bar).

This problem evoked mutually exclusive reactions in Judaism. Qoheleth concluded, "Vanity of vanities. All is vanity!" (Eccl 1:2). Authors of some pseudepigrapha, basing their insight upon the story of Adam and Eve's first sin, described in Genesis 3, took the position that evil was dominant in the world because of Eve's sin. The author of the Life of Adam and Eve 18:1, as the author of Sirach 25:24 (in the Apocrypha), put the blame squarely upon Eve. The source of the guilt shifts completely from Eve to Adam in 4 Ezra. Evil reigns in the world certainly not because of God's actions, but because of Adam, who "transgressed" and was overcome, and not only he himself but all who descend from him (4Ezra 3:20f.; cf. 7:118). About the same time as 4 Ezra, the author of 2 Baruch argued that sin is in the world and continues to be a power because each individual chooses to sin (2Bar 54:15, 19; cf. 1En 98:4f.).

An appreciably different explanation for the origin of sin is found emphasized in numerous pseudepigrapha. Taking as their starting point the story in Genesis 6 about "the sons of God" who married "the daughters of men," the authors of some pseudepigrapha—especially the authors of 1 and 2 Enoch—claim that evil is in the world and is a powerful force because of evil angels. Four possible explanations for the fall of these angels may be discerned: 1) The angels had lusted for earth's beautiful women (1En 6:1–16:4, 40:7, 54:6; 2En 18). 2) The angels perhaps had desired to reproduce themselves (1En 6:2b, 7:1–3). 3) The Devil and his followers refused to worship Adam (*Vita* 14:3). 4) An angel and his legions desired to exalt themselves (2En 29:4f.). All these explanations, despite their significant differences, reflect the seriousness with which evil was perceived by post-exilic Jews, and all attempt to absolve God of the responsibility for evil. This balanced perspective is upset in a much later document, the Apocalypse of Sedrach (ch. 5).

Evil is a dominant force in the world, despite God's will and actions. The righteous suffer primarily because of the power evil has obtained on the earth. The land of Israel has been engulfed by nations either sent by God to punish his sinful people or by foreigners ruled by evil forces or angels; hence God can both send evil and allow it to continue. God's people suffer, and he tends to remove himself from a special portion of his creation.

Transcendence of God. The emphasis in many pseudepigrapha that God is far from Israel contrasts markedly with earlier traditions, especially two accounts: According to Genesis 18 God encountered Abraham on the earth and by the oaks of Mamre, just north of Hebron; according to Exodus 3 the Lord God calls Moses from a burning bush on Mount Horeb, and the presence of God defines the place as "holy ground." After the exile God is usually perceived as one who is above. The apocalyptists place him in the highest heaven, far removed from the earth (1En 1:4, 71:5–11; 2En 20:5), but the prayers interspersed through the apocalypses reveal that he is not inaccessible. He has withdrawn from the world and no longer acts in its history; he will, however, act again, probably through intermediaries (PssSol 17, TLevi 18, TJud 24, 4Ezra 7, 2Bar 72f.). Most pseudepigrapha, in contrast to earlier Jewish writings, are characterized by an increasing claim that God is thoroughly majestic and transcendent (2Mac 3:39; 3Mac 2:15; SibOr 3.1, 11, 81, 807; 5.298, 352; MartIs 1:6b; 1En 71:5–11; 2En 20:5). Knowledge of him is obtained almost always only through the sacred books, the descent of angels (TAb 2:15), the gift of vision (1En 1:2), or the journey of a seer through the various heavens (2En, AscenIs). The contrast of these ideas with earlier ones is demonstrated by the way the author of the Testament of Abraham rewrites Genesis 18: God does not descend to visit Abraham; he sends his angel Michael to speak with the patriarch (TAb 1; cf. 16).

The contrast between ideas or tendencies in early documents, such as Genesis, and those in the Pseudepigrapha should not be exaggerated; and the rewriting of God's encounter with Abraham should not be interpreted to mean that religious Jews came to believe that God was absolutely extramundane, remote, and exiled. As the hymns, odes, and prayers in the apocalypses themselves demonstrate, the Jew continued to affirm efficacious and personal communion with God. With these caveats it is possible to point out that early Jews tended to *emphasize* God's holiness, majesty, gloriousness, and sovereignty; he was transcendent.

Messianism. The belief in a Messiah—a term which here means an ideal person, probably a king or priest, who will bring in perfect peace—is not found in the Old Testament, in the Apocrypha, or in Philo and Josephus (except for allusions). The belief in a future messianic Davidic king, however, is recorded in the prophets (viz. Isa 9:2–7, 11:1–9; Jer 33:14–22; Ezek 37:24–28); and the belief in a future Messiah (or Anointed One) of Aaron and Israel (CD Text B 19.10f.; cf. 1QS 9.11) is recorded in the Dead Sea Scrolls. The term "Messiah" also appears in the later Targums (especially Pseudo-Jonathan [Jerusalem Targum] at Gen 49:1 and Num 24:17–24). Numerous titles were given to the expected messianic figure; but since it is difficult to be certain in which passages these are indeed titles for the Messiah, it is wise to limit this overview only to the places in the Pseudepigrapha which mention the terms "the Messiah" (the Heb. noun) or "the Christ" (the Gk. translation) or "the Anointed One" (which is the meaning of both the Heb. and the Gk.).

Significantly, most pseudepigrapha do *not* contain a reference to the coming of a Messiah; and it is impossible to derive a systematic description of the functions of the Messiah from the extant references to him. Only five pseudepigrapha contain clearly Jewish traditions about the Messiah. Late in the first century B.C. the author of the Psalms of Solomon yearned for the coming of the Messiah, who will "purge Jerusalem from gentiles." Notably he shall perform this task "with the word of his mouth," and do this not from his own initiative, but because he is God's agent and belongs to God (PssSol 17f.).

Apparently late in the first century A.D.—when many of the New Testament writings were being written, especially Matthew, Luke, and John—three authors of pseudepigrapha elaborated on traditions concerning the Messiah. The author of 2 Baruch focused upon the role of the Messiah in three separate sections (chs. 29f., 39–42, 72–74). When "all is accomplished" the Messiah will be revealed and the righteous resurrected (2Bar 29f.). In contrast to this apparently passive role, the Messiah, according to the second section (2Bar 39–42), will act decisively, convicting and putting to death the last evil leader, and protecting God's people. The Messiah is also active in the third section (2Bar 72–74): He shall summon all the nations, sparing those who have not mistreated Israel, and slaying those who have ruled over her. In both the second and third messianic sections the Messiah appears to be described as a militant warrior who slays the gentiles by the sword (72:6).

At about the same time as the author of 2 Baruch the author of 4 Ezra, in three passages (chs. 7, 11:37–12:34, 13:3–14:9), discusses the functions of the Messiah. According to the first of these (4Ezra 7), in the future age, the world to come (7:50, 8:1), the Messiah shall be revealed, bringing rejoicing for four hundred years, and eventually die (7:28f.). According to the second passage (4Ezra 11:37–12:34), the Messiah, who is depicted as "the lion," will denounce, judge, and destroy the ungodly; but he shall deliver the faithful and make them joyful. According to the third section (4Ezra 13:3–14:9), the Messiah, who is "my son" (13:32, 37, 52; 14:9; cf. 7:28f.) and "a man" (13:26, 32), withstands a warring multitude and consumes them with "a stream of fire" that proceeds from his mouth.

Perhaps roughly contemporaneously with 2 Baruch and 4 Ezra (see the introduction to 1En), the author of 1 Enoch 37–71 recorded his ideas about the Messiah. In contrast to his vivid depictions of "the Son of Man," "the Righteous One," and "the Elect One," the author's two meager references to the Messiah (or "the Anointed One") are surprisingly brief (48:10, 52:4). No functions are attributed to the Messiah.

The fifth document in the Pseudepigrapha that contains a clearly Jewish perspective on the Messiah is the late document titled 3 Enoch. Noteworthy is the portrayal of a Messiah who is son of Joseph, and a Messiah who is son of David (45:5). It is possible that one Messiah is meant; but if two Messiahs are denoted, then the Messiahs of Israel will wage war against Gog and Magog at the end of time. This war appears to end in a draw; God himself eventually enters the war and wins the last battle. Subsequently the author of 3 Enoch describes the celebration of Israel's salvation (48:10A). The possibly early date of these traditions has been raised by the discovery of similar ones in the Dead Sea Scrolls (especially 1QS, CD, 1QM).

Obviously different from the above are the references to "the Messiah" (and derived terms) in the pseudepigrapha that appear to be Christian compositions. Observe especially the use of the term in the Odes of Solomon (9:3, 17:17, 24:1, 29:6, 39:11, 41:3, 41:15), the Apocalypse of Zephaniah (10:24–12:32), the

Apocalypse of Elijah (13:15–15:14, 25:8–19), and the Apocalypse of Sedrach (ch. 12). Lengthy Christian additions in the Vision of Isaiah (9:12–13, 30:7–15) and the Testament of Adam (Rec. 2) also contain significant references to "the Anointed One" or "the Christ."

Resurrection and Paradise. Scholars generally agree that the Old Testament writings, with the possible exception of Isaiah 26 and Daniel 12, do not contain explicit references to the resurrection of the dead. At death the individual simply is gathered to his final (or father's) place, the tomb. Sheol and the netherworld (*'ereṣ*) is described as the abode of the dead, not of people who continue to live after death (cf. Isa 38:18, Sir 17:28, 14:12–19). Only through his reputation or a son does his life continue on the earth. In contrast to this perception are the ideas developed in post-exilic Judaism. Some books in the Apocrypha contain numerous explicit references to the resurrection of the dead (see especially 2Mac 7, 14), or possibly even to the immortality of the soul (WisSol), and the Dead Sea Scrolls preserve ambiguous sections possibly referring to an afterlife (see especially 1QH 5.34, 6.29f., 11.10–14). Some pseudepigrapha, even more than these other documents, contain many passages that with pellucid clarity express the belief in a resurrection after death (viz. TJob, PssSol, 4Mac, Ps-Phoc, 2En, HistRech). The author of 2 Baruch, moreover, devotes a section, 49–52, to the description of the resurrected body.

Logically subsequent to the development of this idea is the attempt to describe the future place of rest for the righteous. Hence, picturesque images of Paradise appear in many pseudepigrapha. The various pictoral descriptions are characterized by mutually exclusive ideas. Paradise is placed sometimes in the third heaven (2En 8A, ApMos 37:5, 40:1), and sometimes on the earth (1En 32; 2En 8:1–6A, 30:1A; ApMos 38:5). It is depicted as either without inhabitants (1En 32, 2En 8f., 4Ezra 8:52) or with inhabitants (PssSol 14, 2En 42:3B, ApAb 21, OdesSol 11:16–24; cf. HistRech). It is portrayed as both an eternal inheritance (PssSol 14:3f.; 2En 65:10A; OdesSol 11:16d, 16f.; 4Ezra 8:52) and a state preceding the end (ApMos 37:5, 40:1–41:3; *Vita* 48:6f.; AscenIs 9; cf. HistRech 13–15). There are some common beliefs, notably that Paradise is full of fruitful trees (see 2En 8A, OdesSol 11:11–16, 23) and distinguished by a sweet-smelling odor (viz. see 1En 32:3, 2En 8A, OdesSol 11:15, 2En 23:18).

The contradicting ideas should not be explained away or forced into an artificial system. Such ideas in the Pseudepigrapha witness to the fact that Early Judaism was not a speculative philosophical movement or theological system, even though the Jews demonstrated impressive speculative fecundity. The Pseudepigrapha mirror a living religion in which the attempt was made to come to terms with the dynamic phenomena of history and experience.

These are only four of the theological characteristics of the Pseudepigrapha, namely the problems of sin and theodicy, emphasis upon God's transcendence, speculations about the Messiah, and the ideas concerning the afterlife. Many other theological features could also be highlighted. The choice between a lunar and a solar calendar (see Jub and 1En) produced major upheavals in Judaism in the second century B.C. Calendrical issues contained cosmic and profound theological dimensions. How exasperating to discover you were not observing the Sabbath on the correct day and with the angels and the rest of the universe. How astounding to learn that Passover was celebrated at the wrong time. Similarly, the search for authority and reliable insight into God's will is reflected in the search for the quintessence of Torah and its text. The search for God himself and the tendency toward belief in a transcendent and apparently aloof Creator spawned complex angelologies. The impossibility of obtaining satisfactory meaning in present history helped produce the theological perspectives behind apocalypticism.

Conclusion

These introductory comments are far too brief to constitute an introduction to the Pseudepigrapha, and they should not be taken to indicate that scholars have arrived at anything like a consensus on the major issues. These few comments should, however, enable the general reader to understand better the documents collected below; at least they reflect how the editor perceives them. Each of the Pseudepigrapha is preceded by an introduction (see Editor's Preface) and organized under categories which also have brief introductions. These collectively serve to help the reader appreciate the documents themselves.

EXPLANATION OF TYPOGRAPHICAL
AND REFERENCE SYSTEMS

Chapter and verse numbers

We have endeavored to present the documents below in a format similar to that of the Jerusalem Bible. Hence, chapters and verses are supplied. A new chapter is indicated by a large bold numeral. Verse numbers are placed in the margin in ordinary roman type; in the text itself, the beginning of each verse is marked by a • which precedes the first word of the verse except when the verse begins a new line or a new chapter. Because of their linguistic nature, some documents—such as the Sibylline Oracles, Letter of Aristeas, and Syriac Menander—are not divided into chapters and verses. These are presented so that the beginning of each line or section of text is noted in the margin with numbers in ordinary roman type as with verse numbers.

Italics in the text

Italic type in the text denotes full or partial quotations of the Bible. The biblical passage from which the quotation is derived is noted in the margin.

Brackets and other sigla in the translation

[ ]   Square brackets denote restorations.

⟨ ⟩   Pointed brackets signify corrections to a text.

( )   Parentheses circumscribe words added by the translator. Ancient languages are cryptic; verbs, nouns, and pronouns are often omitted. These are, of course, necessary for idiomatic English and are presented within parentheses.

| | This siglum indicates a letter incorrectly omitted by an ancient scribe.

{ }   Braces denote unnecessary words or letters in an ancient text.

Footnotes

In each chapter, footnotes are lettered alphabetically. The footnotes are not intended to be a mini-commentary, but to supply significant information, such as important related thoughts contained in ancient writings not considered either canonical or extracanonical. Only significant variants in the manuscripts are cited. These notes assume that the reader has read the general introduction and the introduction to each document being footnoted.

Punctuation of biblical references

Chapter and verse are separated by a colon, e.g. Ex 20:7. A subsequent verse in the same chapter is separated from the preceding by a comma. Subsequent citations in other biblical or apocryphal writings are separated by semicolons: e.g. Ex 20:17, 20; Lev 9:15. Citations which are not preceded by an abbreviation refer to the respective passage in a document being footnoted.

Marginal references

Marginal references are kept to a minimum and except in rare occasions are limited to significant parallels in biblical and apocryphal writings. These marginal references should help the reader better understand the relevant passage by drawing attention to the source of a biblical quotation, and to other uses of special terms, phrases, or images. The references in the margin often occur in groups all relating to one text line; in such cases, the position of the first reference indicates the line to which the whole group applies. Marginal references not preceded by the abbreviation of a book indicate a passage elsewhere in the document before the reader.

Care has been taken to assure that each marginal reference begins on the line to which it refers. However, in some cases this is not possible because of the length of necessary marginal references. In these cases, the marginal reference is preceded by a verse reference (i.e. the letter *v* plus the number of the verse) so the reader can attach the marginal references to the correct verses.

Secondary divisions within the document

The manuscripts from which the translators have worked usually do not separate the text so that each new thought or development in the narrative is indicated. The translators have supplied the subdivisions to help the reader follow the flow of the document.

LIST OF ABBREVIATIONS

I. MODERN PUBLICATIONS

AAR	American Academy of Religion
AcOr	*Acta orientalia*
AGAJU	Arbeiten zur Geschichte des antiken Judentums und des Urchristentums
Agrapha	Resch, A., ed. *Agrapha: Aussercanonische Schriftfragmente.* TU 30.3–4; Leipzig, 1906.
ALBO	Analecta lovaniensia biblica et orientalia
ALGHJ	Arbeiten zur Literatur und Geschichte des hellenistischen Judentums
ALUOS	*Annual of the Leeds University Oriental Society*
ANET	Pritchard, J. B., ed. *Ancient Near Eastern Texts*. Princeton, 1969³.
ANF	Roberts, A., and J. Donaldson, eds. *The Ante-Nicene Fathers: Translations of the Writings of the Fathers down to A.D. 325.* 10 vols. Edinburgh, 1868–72; rev. and repr. Grand Rapids, Mich., 1950–52.
ANRW	Haase, W., and H. Temporini, eds. *Aufstieg und Niedergang der römischen Welt*. Berlin, New York, 1979– .
ANT	James, M. R. *The Apocryphal New Testament*. Oxford, 1924; corrected ed., 1955.
APAT	Kautzsch, E., ed. *Die Apokryphen und Pseudepigraphen des Alten Testaments*. 2 vols. Tübingen, 1900.
Apoc. Lit.	Torrey, C. C. *The Apocryphal Literature: A Brief Introduction.* New Haven, Conn., 1945; repr. Hamden, Conn., 1963.
Apocrifi del NT	Erbetta, M. *Gli Apocrifi del Nuovo Testamento*. 3 vols. Turin, 1966–69.
APOT	Charles, R. H., ed. *The Apocrypha and Pseudepigrapha of the Old Testament in English.* 2 vols. Oxford, 1913.
ArOr	*Archiv orientální*
ASOR	American Schools of Oriental Research
ASTI	*Annual of the Swedish Theological Institute*
ATANT	Abhandlungen zur Theologie des Alten und Neuen Testaments
ATR	*Anglican Theological Review*
AusBR	*Australian Biblical Review*
BA	*The Biblical Archeologist*
BASOR	*Bulletin of the American Schools of Oriental Research*
BDT	Harrison, E. F., et al., eds. *Baker's Dictionary of Theology.* Grand Rapids, Mich., 1960.
BEvT	Beiträge zur evangelischen Theologie
BHH	Reicke, B., and L. Rost, eds. *Biblisch-historisches Handwörterbuch*. 3 vols. Göttingen, 1962–66.

BHM	Jellinek, A. *Bet ha-Midrasch*. 2 vols. Jerusalem, 1967³.
Bib	*Biblica*
Biblia Sacra	Weber, R., *et al.*, eds. *Biblia Sacra: Iuxta Vulgatam Versionem*. 2 vols. Stuttgart, 1969.
Bibliographie	Delling, G. *Bibliographie zur jüdisch-hellenistischen und intertestamentarischen Literatur 1900–1970*. TU 106²; Berlin, 1975².
BibSt	Biblische Studien
BIFAO	*Bulletin de l'institut français d'archéologie orientale*
BiKi	*Bibel und Kirche*
BIOSCS	*Bulletin of the International Organization for Septuagint and Cognate Studies*
BJRL, BJRULM	*Bulletin of the John Rylands Library, Bulletin of the John Rylands University Library of Manchester*
B-L²	Haag, H., ed. *Bibel-Lexikon*. Zurich, 1968².
BLE	*Bulletin de littérature ecclésiastique*
BO	*Bibliotheca orientalis*
BSOAS	*Bulletin of the School of Oriental and African Studies*
BZ	*Biblische Zeitschrift*
BZAW	Beihefte zur Zeitschrift für die alttestamentliche Wissenschaft
BZNW	Beihefte zur Zeitschrift für die neutestamentliche Wissenschaft und die Kunde der älteren Kirche
CB	*Cultura bíblica*
CBQ	*Catholic Biblical Quarterly*
CCSL	Corpus Christianorum. Series Latina.
CETEDOC	Centre de traitement électronique des documents
CG	Cairensis Gnosticus
Crucible	Toynbee, A., ed. *The Crucible of Christianity: Judaism, Hellenism and the Historical Background to the Christian Faith*. New York, 1969.
CSCO	Corpus scriptorum christianorum orientalium
CTM	*Concordia Theological Monthly*
DB	Vigouroux, F., ed. *Dictionnaire de la Bible*. 5 vols. Paris, 1895–1912.
DBSup	Pirot, L., *et al.*, eds. *Dictionnaire de la Bible, Suppléments*. Paris, 1928– .
DJD	Discoveries in the Judaean Desert
Dogmengeschichte⁴	Harnack, A. *Lehrbuch der Dogmengeschichte*. 3 vols. Tübingen, 1909–10⁴.
DTT	*Dansk teologisk Tidsskrift*
Enciclopedia de la Biblia	Gutiérrez-Larraya, J. A., ed. *Enciclopedia de la Biblia*. 6 vols. Barcelona, 1963.
Encyclopedia of Christianity	Palmer, E. H., *et al.*, eds. *The Encyclopedia of Christianity*. Wilmington, Del., 1964–
EncyJud	Roth, C., *et al.*, eds. *Encyclopedia Judaica*. 16 vols. New York, 1971–72.
EOS	*Eos. Commentarii Societatis Philologae Polonorum*
ETL	*Ephemerides theologicae lovanienses*
EvT	*Evangelische Theologie*
Exégèse biblique et judaïsme	Ménard, J.-E., ed. *Exégèse biblique et judaïsme*. Strasbourg, 1973.
ExpT	*Expository Times*

Falasha Anthology	Leslau, W. *Falasha Anthology*. Yale Judaica Series 6; New Haven, 1951.
FBBS	Facet Books, Biblical Series
FGH	Jacoby, F., ed. *Fragmente der griechischen Historiker*. 3 vols. Leiden, 1923–
FRLANT	Forschungen zur Religion und Literatur des Alten und Neuen Testaments
GamPseud	Hammershaimb, E., *et al.*, eds. *De Gammeltestamentlige Pseudepigrapher*. 2 vols. Copenhagen, 1953–76.
GCS	Die griechischen christlichen Schriftsteller der ersten drei Jahrhunderte
GDBL	Nielsen, E., and B. Noack, eds. *Gads Danske Bibel Leksikon*. 2 vols. Copenhagen, 1965–66.
Geschichte [Baumstark]	Baumstark, A. *Geschichte der syrischen Literatur mit Ausschluss der christlichpalästinensischen Texte*. Bonn, 1922.
Geschichte [Graf]	Graf, G. "Apokryphen und Pseudepigraphen," *Geschichte der christlichen arabischen Literatur*. Studi e Testi 118; Vatican, 1944; vol. 1, pp. 196–297.
GLAJJ	Stern, M., ed. *Greek and Latin Authors on Jews and Judaism*. Vol. 1: *From Herodotus to Plutarch*. Jerusalem, 1974.
GNT	Grundrisse zum Neuen Testament
Goodenough Festschrift	Neusner, J., ed. *Religions in Antiquity: Essays in Memory of Erwin Ramsdell Goodenough*. Sup *Numen* 14; Leiden, 1968.
Gottesvolk	Janssen, E. *Das Gottesvolk und seine Geschichte: Geschichtsbild und Selbstverständnis im palästinensischen Schrifttum von Jesus Sirach bis Jehuda ha-Nasi*. Neukirchen-Vluyn, 1971.
Gunkel Festschrift	Schmidt, H., ed. *Eucharistērion: Studien zur Religion des Alten und Neuen Testaments*. H. Gunkel Festschrift. Part 2: *Zur Religion und Literatur des Neuen Testaments*. Göttingen, 1923.
Hastings' *DB*	Hastings, J., ed. *Dictionary of the Bible*, rev. ed. by F. C. Grant and H. H. Rowley. New York, 1963.
HAW	Handbuch der Altertumswissenschaft
HeyJ	*Heythrop Journal*
History [Pfeiffer]	Pfeiffer, R. H. *History of the New Testament Times with an Introduction to the Apocrypha*. New York, 1949.
History [Schürer]	Schürer, E. *A History of the Jewish People in the Time of Jesus Christ*. 5 vols., plus index, trans. J. MacPherson et al. Edinburgh, 1897–98.
History . . . The Time of the Apostles	Hausrath, A. *A History of New Testament Times: The Time of the Apostles*. 4 vols., trans. L. Huxley. London, 1895.
HNT	Handbuch zum Neuen Testament
HSW	Hennecke, E., W. Schneemelcher, and R. McL. Wilson, eds. *New Testament Apocrypha*. 2 vols. London, 1963–65.
HTKNT	Herders theologischer Kommentar zum Neuen Testament
HTR	*Harvard Theological Review*
HTS	Harvard Theological Studies

HUCA	*Hebrew Union College Annual*
IB	Buttrick, G. A., *et al.*, eds. *The Interpreter's Bible.* 12 vols. New York, 1952–57.
ICC	International Critical Commentary
IDB	Buttrick, G. A., *et al.*, eds. *The Interpreter's Dictionary of the Bible.* 4 vols. New York, 1962.
IDBS	Crim, K., *et al.*, eds. *The Interpreter's Dictionary of the Bible, Supplementary Volume.* Nashville, Tenn., 1976.
IEJ	*Israel Exploration Journal*
Int	*Interpretation*
Intr. to the Apoc.	Metzger, B. M. *An Introduction to the Apocrypha.* New York, 1957.
Introduction	Denis, A.-M. *Introduction aux pseudépigraphes grecs d'Ancien Testament.* SVTP 1; Leiden, 1970.
IOCB	Laymon, C. M., ed. *The Interpreter's One-Volume Commentary on the Bible.* New York, 1971.
ITQ	*Irish Theological Quarterly*
JA	*Journal asiatique*
JAAR	*Journal of the American Academy of Religion*
JAC	*Jahrbuch für Antike und Christentum*
JAL	Jewish Apocryphal Literature
JAOS	*Journal of the American Oriental Society*
JBC	Brown, R. E., J. A. Fitzmyer, and R. E. Murphy, eds. *The Jerome Biblical Commentary.* Englewood Cliffs, N.J., 1968.
JBL	*Journal of Biblical Literature*
JBLMS	Journal of Biblical Literature Monograph Series
JE	Singer, I., *et al.*, eds. *The Jewish Encyclopedia.* 12 vols. New York, London, 1901–6.
Jewish Symbols	Goodenough, E. R. *Jewish Symbols in the Greco-Roman Period.* 13 vols. New York, 1953–68.
JJS	*Journal of Jewish Studies*
JNES	*Journal of Near Eastern Studies*
JPOS	*Journal of the Palestine Oriental Society*
JQR	*Jewish Quarterly Review*
JRAS	*Journal of the Royal Asiatic Society*
JSHRZ	Kümmel, W. G., *et al. Jüdische Schriften aus hellenistisch-römischer Zeit.* Gütersloh, 1973–
JSJ	*Journal for the Study of Judaism*
JSS	*Journal of Semitic Studies*
JThC	*Journal for Theology and the Church*
JTS	*Journal of Theological Studies*
Judaic Tradition	Glatzer, N. N. *The Judaic Tradition: Texts Edited and Introduced.* Boston, 1969.
Kommentar	Strack, H. L., and P. Billerbeck. *Kommentar zum Neuen Testament aus Talmud und Midrasch.* 5 vols. Munich, 1922–56.
KS	*Kirjath Sepher*
Kuhn Festschrift	Jeremias, G., H.-W. Kuhn, and H. Stegemann, eds. *Tradition und Glaube: Das frühe Christentum in seiner Umwelt. Festgabe für Karl Georg Kuhn zum 65. Geburtstag.* Göttingen, 1971.

Lampe	Lampe, G. W. H., ed. *A Patristic Greek Lexicon.* Oxford, 1961–68.
LAOT	James, M. R. *The Lost Apocrypha of the Old Testament.* TED; London, New York, 1920.
LCL	Loeb Classical Library
Legends	Ginzberg, L. *The Legends of the Jews.* 7 vols., trans. H. Szold. Philadelphia, 1909–38; repr. 1937–66.
Literatur und Religion des Frühjudentums	Maier, J., and J. Schreiner, eds. *Literatur und Religion des Frühjudentums.* Gütersloh, 1973.
LSJM	Liddell, H. G., and R. Scott. *A Greek-English Lexicon,* rev. by H. S. Jones and R. McKenzie. Oxford, 1940.
*LTK*²	Buchberger, M., J. Höfer, and K. Rahner, eds. *Lexikon für Theologie und Kirche.* 11 vols. Freiburg, 1957–67².
LUOS MS	Leeds University Oriental Society Monograph Series
MBPAR	Münchener Beiträge zur Papyrusforschung und Antiken Rechtsgeschichte
McCQ	*McCormick Quarterly*
MGWJ	*Monatsschrift für Geschichte und Wissenschaft des Judentums*
Missionsliteratur	Dalbert, P. *Die Theologie der hellenistisch-jüdischen Missionsliteratur unter Ausschluss von Philo und Josephus.* Hamburg-Volksdorf, 1954.
M. Smith Festschrift	Neusner, J., ed. *Christianity, Judaism and Other Greco-Roman Cults: Studies for Morton Smith at Sixty.* SJLA 12; Leiden, 1975.
NCCHS	Fuller, R. C., *et al.,* eds. *A New Catholic Commentary on Holy Scripture.* London, 1969.
NCE	McDonald, W. J., *et al.,* eds. *New Catholic Encyclopedia.* 15 vols. New York, 1967–
NEB	New English Bible
NHC	Nag Hammadi Codex
NHL	Nag Hammadi Library
NHS	Nag Hammadi Studies
NovT	*Novum Testamentum*
*NovT*Sup	*Novum Testamentum,* Supplements
NTS	*New Testament Studies*
NTTS	New Testament Tools and Studies
OCA	*Orientalia Christiana Analeta*
Or	*Orientalia*
OrChr	*Orientalia Christiana*
OrSyr	*L'Orient syrien*
OTS	Oudtestamentische Studiën
Pauly-Wissowa	Wissowa, G., *et al.,* eds. *Paulys Real-Encyclopädie der classischen Altertumswissenschaft,* neue Bearbeitung. Stuttgart, Munich, 1893–1972.
PCB	Peake, A. S., M. Black, and H. H. Rowley, eds. *Peake's Commentary on the Bible.* London, New York, 1962.
PEQ	*Palestine Exploration Quarterly*
PETSE	Papers of the Estonian Theological Society in Exile
Peshitta	*The Old Testament in Syriac According to the Peshitta Version.* Leiden, 1966–
PG	Patrologiae graecae, ed. J. Migne
PIOL	Publications de l'institut orientaliste de Louvain

PL	Patrologiae latinae, ed. J. Migne
PMR	Charlesworth, J. H. *The Pseudepigrapha and Modern Research*. SCS 7; Missoula, Mont., 1976.
Pseud I	Fritz, K. von, ed. *Pseudepigrapha I: Pseudopythagorica, lettres de Platon, littérature pseudépigraphe juive*. Entretiens sur l'antiquité classique 18; Geneva, 1972.
Pseudépigraphes	Philonenko, M., *et al. Pseudépigraphes de l'Ancien Testament et manuscrits de la mer morte*. Cahiers de la *RHPR* 41; Paris, 1967.
PVTG	Pseudepigrapha Veteris Testamenti Graece
RAC	Klauser, T., *et al.*, eds. *Reallexikon für Antike und Christentum: Sachwörterbuch zur Auseinandersetzung des Christentums mit der antiken Welt*. Stuttgart, 1950– .
RB	*Revue biblique*
RBen	*Revue bénédictine*
RechBib	Recherches bibliques
REJ	*Revue des études juives*
RESl	*Revue des études slaves*
RevistB	*Revista bíblica*
RevSem	*Revue sémitique*
RGG³	Galling, K., *et al.*, eds. *Die Religion in Geschichte und Gegenwart*. 6 vols. plus index. Tübingen, 1957–65³.
RHPR	*Revue d'histoire et de philosophie religieuse*
RHR	*Revue de l'histoire des religions*
Riessler	Riessler, P. *Altjüdisches Schrifttum ausserhalb der Bibel*. Heidelberg, 1927; repr. 1966.
RivB	*Rivista biblica*
ROC	*Revue de l'orient chrétien*
RQ	*Revue de Qumran*
RSR	*Recherches de science religieuse*
RSV	Revised Standard Version
RTP	*Revue de théologie et de philosophie*
Sacramentum Mundi	Rahner, K., *et al.*, eds. *Sacramentum Mundi: An Encyclopedia of Theology*. 6 vols. New York, 1968–70.
SBFLA	*Studii biblici franciscani liber annuus*
SBLDS	Society of Biblical Literature Dissertation Series
SBLMS	Society of Biblical Literature Monograph Series
SBL 1971 Seminar Papers	*The Society of Biblical Literature One Hundred Seventh Annual Meeting Seminar Papers—28–31 October 1971, Regency Hyatt House—Atlanta, Ga*. 2 vols. Missoula, Mont., 1971.
SBL 1972 Seminar Papers	McGaughy, L. C., ed. *The Society of Biblical Literature One Hundred Eighth Annual Meeting Book of Seminar Papers: Friday–Tuesday, 1–5 September 1972, Century Plaza Hotel—Los Angeles, Ca*. 2 vols. Missoula, Mont., 1972.
SBL 1974 Seminar Papers	MacRae, G., ed. *Society of Biblical Literature 1974 Seminar Papers: One Hundred Tenth Annual Meeting, 24–27 October 1974, Washington Hilton, Washington, D.C*. 2 vols. Cambridge, Mass., 1974.
SBT	Studies in Biblical Theology

SC	Sources chrétiennes
ScEs	*Science et esprit*
SCS	Septuagint and Cognate Studies
SCS 2	Kraft, R. A., ed. *1972 Proceedings: International Organization for Septuagint and Cognate Studies and the Society of Biblical Literature Pseudepigrapha Seminar.* SCS 2; Missoula, Mont., 1972.
SCS 4	Nickelsburg, G. W. E. Jr., ed. *Studies on the Testament of Moses: Seminar Papers.* SCS 4; Cambridge, Mass., 1973.
SCS 5	Nickelsburg, G. W. E. Jr., ed. *Studies on the Testament of Joseph.* SCS 5; Missoula, Mont., 1975.
SCS 6	Nickelsburg, G. W. E. Jr., ed. *Studies on the Testament of Abraham.* SCS 6; Missoula, Mont., 1976.
SEA	*Svensk exegetisk Årsbok*
Sem	*Semitica*
Septuaginta	Rahlfs, A., ed. *Septuaginta: Id est Vetus Testamentum graece iuxta LXX interpretes.* 2 vols. Stuttgart, 1935; repr. 1965.
SJLA	Studies in Judaism in Late Antiquity
SJT	*Scottish Journal of Theology*
SNTS MS	*Studiorum Novi Testamenti Societas* Monograph Series
SPB	Studia postbiblica
ST	*Studia Theologica*
StANT	Studien zum Alten und Neuen Testament.
Studien	Eltester, W., ed. *Studien zu den Testamenten der zwölf Patriarchen.* BZNW 36; Berlin, 1969.
Studies on T12P	Jonge, M. de. *Studies on the Testaments of the Twelve Patriarchs: Text and Interpretation.* SVTP 3; Leiden, 1975.
Sup *Numen*	Supplements to *Numen*
SVTP	Studia in Veteris Testamenti Pseudepigrapha
T&S	Texts and Studies
T&T	Texts and Translations
TBT	*The Bible Today*
TDNT	Kittel, G., ed. *Theological Dictionary of the New Testament.* 10 vols., trans. G. W. Bromiley. Grand Rapids, Mich., London, 1964–76.
TED	Translations of Early Documents
ThĒE	Martinos, A., ed. *Thrēskeutikē kai Ēthikē Enkuklopaideia.* 12 vols. Athens, 1962–68.
ThRu	*Theologische Rundschau*
TLZ	*Theologische Literaturzeitung*
TQ	*Theologische Quartalschrift*
TU	Texte und Untersuchungen
TWAT	Botterweck, G. J., and H. Ringgren, eds. *Theologisches Wörterbuch zum Alten Testament.* Stuttgart, 1970–
TZ	*Theologische Zeitschrift*
USQR	*Union Seminar Quarterly Review*
VC	*Vigiliae christianae*
VT	*Vetus Testamentum*

*VT*Sup 22	Boer, P. A. H. de, ed. *Congress Volume: Uppsala 1971.* Supplements to *VT* 22; Leiden, 1972.
Widengren Festschrift	Bergman, J., *et al.*, eds. *Ex Orbe Religionum: Studia Geo Widengren.* 2 vols. Studies in the History of Religions 21, 22; Leiden, 1972.
WUNT	Wissenschaftliche Untersuchungen zum Neuen Testament
WZHalle	*Wissenschaftliche Zeitschrift der Martin-Luther-Universität, Halle-Wittenberg. Gesellschafts- und Sprachwissenschaftliche Reihe*
WZJena	*Wissenschaftliche Zeitschrift der Friedrich-Schiller-Universität, Jena. Gesellschafts- und Sprachwissenschaftliche Reihe*
WZKM	*Wiener Zeitschrift für die Kunde des Morgenlandes*
ZAW	*Zeitschrift für die alttestamentliche Wissenschaft*
ZDMG	*Zeitschrift der deutschen morgenländischen Gesellschaft*
ZKG	*Zeitschrift für Kirchengeschichte*
ZNW	*Zeitschrift für die neutestamentliche Wissenschaft und die Kunde der älteren Kirche*
ZPEB	Tenney, M. C., ed. *The Zondervan Pictorial Encyclopedia of the Bible.* 5 vols. Grand Rapids, Mich., 1975.
ZRGG	*Zeitschrift für Religions- und Geistesgeschichte*
ZTK	*Zeitschrift für Theologie und Kirche*
ZWT	*Zeitschrift für wissenschaftliche Theologie*

Additional Abbreviations

Ar.	Arabic	lit.	literally
Aram.	Aramaic	LXX	Septuagint
Arm.	Armenian	MS(S)	Manuscript(s)
BM	British Museum	MT	Masoretic Text
c.	circa	n. nn.	note(s)
cf.	compare	NAB	New American Bible
ch(s).	chapter(s)	NEB	New English Bible
col(s).	column(s)	NT	New Testament
Cop.	Coptic	OT	Old Testament
ET	English translation	pt(s).	part(s)
Eth.	Ethiopic	rec(s).	recension(s)
fol(s).	folio(s)	RSV	Revised Standard Version
Gk.	Greek	Russ.	Russian
GNMM	Good News for Modern Man	SBL	Society of Biblical Literature
Heb.	Hebrew	Slav.	Slavic
JB	Jerusalem Bible	SV	Standard Version
Kar.	Karshuni	Syr.	Syriac
KJV	King James Version	Vat.	Vatican
l. ll.	line(s)	vs(s).	verse(s)
Lat.	Latin		

II. ANCIENT DOCUMENTS

Bible and Apocrypha

Gen	Genesis	Tob	Tobit
Ex	Exodus	Jdt	Judith
Lev	Leviticus	AddEsth	Additions to Esther
Num	Numbers	WisSol	Wisdom of Solomon
Deut	Deuteronomy	Sir	Sirach
Josh	Joshua	1Bar	1 Baruch
Judg	Judges	LetJer	Letter of Jeremiah
Ruth	Ruth	PrAzar	Prayer of Azariah
1Sam	1 Samuel	Sus	Susanna
2Sam	2 Samuel	Bel	Bel and the Dragon
1Kgs	1 Kings	1Mac	1 Maccabees
2Kgs	2 Kings	2Mac	2 Maccabees
1Chr	1 Chronicles	Mt	Matthew
2Chr	2 Chronicles	Mk	Mark
Ezra	Ezra	Lk	Luke
Neh	Nehemiah	Jn	John
Esth	Esther	Acts	Acts
Job	Job	Rom	Romans
Ps(s)	Psalms	1Cor	1 Corinthians
Prov	Proverbs	2Cor	2 Corinthians
Eccl (Qoh)	Ecclesiastes	Gal	Galatians
Song	Song of Songs	Eph	Ephesians
Isa	Isaiah	Phil	Philippians
Jer	Jeremiah	Col	Colossians
Lam	Lamentations	1Thes	1 Thessalonians
Ezek	Ezekiel	2Thes	2 Thessalonians
Dan	Daniel	1Tim	1 Timothy
Hos	Hosea	2Tim	2 Timothy
Joel	Joel	Tit	Titus
Amos	Amos	Phlm	Philemon
Obad	Obadiah	Heb	Hebrews
Jonah	Jonah	Jas	James
Micah	Micah	1Pet	1 Peter
Nah	Nahum	2Pet	2 Peter
Hab	Habakkuk	1Jn	1 John
Zeph	Zephaniah	2Jn	2 John
Hag	Haggai	3Jn	3 John
Zech	Zechariah	Jude	Jude
Mal	Malachi	Rev	Revelation
2Ezra	2 Ezra		

Pseudepigrapha

ApAb	Apocalypse of Abraham
TAb	Testament of Abraham
ApAdam	Apocalypse of Adam
TAdam	Testament of Adam
LAE	Life of Adam and Eve
Ah	Ahiqar
AnonSam	An Anonymous Samaritan Text

LetAris	Letter of Aristeas
ArisEx	Aristeas the Exegete
Aristob	Aristobulus
Art	Artapanus
2Bar	2 (Syriac Apocalypse of) Baruch
3Bar	3 (Greek Apocalypse of) Baruch
4Bar	4 Baruch
CavTr	Cave of Treasures
ClMal	Cleodemus Malchus
ApDan	Apocalypse of Daniel
Dem	Demetrius
ElMod	Eldad and Modad
ApEl	Apocalypse of Elijah
HebApEl	Hebrew Apocalypse of Elijah
1En	1 (Ethiopic Apocalypse of) Enoch
2En	2 (Slavonic Apocalypse of) Enoch
3En	3 (Hebrew Apocalypse of) Enoch
Eup	Eupolemus
Ps-Eup	Pseudo-Eupolemus
ApocEzek	Apocryphon of Ezekiel
ApEzek	Apocalypse of Ezekiel
EzekTrag	Ezekiel the Tragedian
4Ezra	4 Ezra
GkApEzra	Greek Apocalypse of Ezra
QuesEzra	Questions of Ezra
RevEzra	Revelation of Ezra
VisEzra	Vision of Ezra
HecAb	Hecataeus of Abdera
Ps-Hec	Pseudo-Hecataeus
HelSynPr	Hellenistic Synagogal Prayers
THez	Testament of Hezekiah
FrgsHistWrks	Fragments of Historical Works
TIsaac	Testament of Isaac
AscenIs	Ascension of Isaiah
MartIs	Martyrdom of Isaiah
VisIs	Vision of Isaiah
LadJac	Ladder of Jacob
PrJac	Prayer of Jacob
TJac	Testament of Jacob
JanJam	Jannes and Jambres
TJob	Testament of Job
JosAsen	Joseph and Aseneth
HistJos	History of Joseph
PrJos	Prayer of Joseph
Jub	Jubilees
LAB	*Liber Antiquitatum Biblicarum*
LosTr	The Lost Tribes
3Mac	3 Maccabees
4Mac	4 Maccabees
5Mac	5 Maccabees
PrMan	Prayer of Manasseh
SyrMen	Syriac Menander

ApMos	Apocalypse of Moses
AsMos	Assumption of Moses
PrMos	Prayer of Moses
TMos	Testament of Moses
BkNoah	Book of Noah
Ps-Orph	Pseudo-Orpheus
PJ	*Paraleipomena Jeremiou*
PhEPoet	Philo the Epic Poet
Ps-Philo	Pseudo-Philo
Ps-Phoc	Pseudo-Phocylides
FrgsPoetWrks	Fragments of Poetical Works
LivPro	Lives of the Prophets
HistRech	History of the Rechabites
ApSedr	Apocalypse of Sedrach
TrShem	Treatise of Shem
SibOr	Sibylline Oracles
OdesSol	Odes of Solomon
PssSol	Psalms of Solomon
TSol	Testament of Solomon
5ApocSyrPss	Five Apocryphal Syriac Psalms
Thal	Thallus
Theod	Theodotus
T12P	Testaments of the Twelve Patriarchs
TReu	Testament of Reuben
TSim	Testament of Simeon
TLevi	Testament of Levi
TJud	Testament of Judah
TIss	Testament of Issachar
TZeb	Testament of Zebulun
TDan	Testament of Dan
TNaph	Testament of Naphtali
TGad	Testament of Gad
TAsh	Testament of Asher
TJos	Testament of Joseph
TBenj	Testament of Benjamin
Vita	*Vita Adae et Evae*
ApZeph	Apocalypse of Zephaniah
ApZos	Apocalypse of Zosimus

Other Writings

Dead Sea Scrolls

All abbreviations are according to J. A. Fitzmyer, S.J. *The Dead Sea Scrolls: Major Publications and Tools for Study.* SBL Sources for Biblical Study 8; Missoula, Mont., 1975; expanded ed., 1977.

Philo

All abbreviations are according to *Studia Philonica* with the exception that titles of Philonic treatises are italicized.

Josephus

Ant	Jewish Antiquities
Apion	Against Apion
Life	Life of Josephus
War	Jewish Wars

New Testament Apocrypha and Pseudepigrapha

EBar	Epistle of Barnabas
GBart	Gospel of Bartholomew
QuesBart	Questions of Bartholomew
1Clem	1 Clement
2Clem	2 Clement
PseudClemRec	Pseudo-Clementine Recognitions
Did	Didache
GEbion	Gospel of the Ebionites
GEgyp	Gospel of the Egyptians
GHeb	Gospel of the Hebrews
ShepHerm	Shepherd of Hermes
ApIoan	*Apokalypsis tou hagiou Iōannou*
ProtJames	Protoevangelium of James
ActsJn	Acts of John
GMatthias	Gospel of Matthias
GNic	Gospel of Nicodemus
ActsPaul	Acts of Paul
ApPaul	Apocalypse of Paul
ApPet	Apocalypse of Peter
GPet	Gospel of Peter
PrPet	Preaching of Peter
ActsPhil	Acts of Philip
GPhil	Gospel of Philip
RevSteph	Revelation of Stephen
ActsThom	Acts of Thomas
ApThom	Apocalypse of Thomas
GThom	Gospel of Thomas
GTr	Gospel of Truth
ApVirg	Apocalypse of the Virgin

Early Fathers

AdvHaer	Epiphanius, *Adversus haereses*
AposCon	Apostolic Constitutions

CommGen	Procopius of Gaza, *Commentary on Genesis*, part I
CommIsa	Basil Caesar, *Commentary on Isaiah*
CommJn	Origen, *Commentary on the Gospel of St. John*
DialTrypho	Justin, *Dialogue with Trypho*
DivInst	Lactantius, *Divine Institutes*
ExcerPss	Origen, *Excerpta in Psalmos*
HE	Eusebius, *Historia ecclesiastica*
HebQuaestinLibGen	Jerome, *Hebrew Questions on the Book of Genesis*
Hom	Macarius, *Spiritual Homilies*
Paid	Clement of Alexandria, *The Tutor* (*Paidagōgos*)
Philoc	Origen, *Philocalia*
PrEv	Eusebius, *Praeparatio evangelica*
Princ	Origen, *De principiis*
Ref	Hippolytus, *Refutation of All Heresies*
Strom	Clement of Alexandria, *Stromata*

Rabbinics

Ab	Abot
ARN	Abot de-Rabbi Nathan
AZ	'Abodah Zarah
b. (before a rabbinic text)	Babylonian Talmud
BB	Baba Batra
Bek	Bekorot
Ber	Berakot
BHM	Bet ha-Midrasch
Bikk	Bikkurim
BM	Batei Midrashot
BMeṣ	Baba Meṣi'a (Talmudic tractate)
DeutR	Debarim Rabbah
EcclR	Qohelet Rabbah
'Eduy	'Eduyyot
'Erub	'Erubin
ExR	Šemot Rabbah
GedMos	Gedulah Moshe
GenR	Bere'šit Rabbah
Giṭṭ	Giṭṭin
Ḥag	Ḥagigah
Ḥall	Ḥallah
Ḥull	Ḥullin
Ker	Keritot
Ket	Ketubot
Kid	Kiddushin
LamR	Ekah Rabbah
LevR	Wayyiqra Rabbah
m. (before a rabbinic text)	Mishnah
Makk	Makkot
Meg	Megillah
Men	Menaḥot
Mik	Mikwa'ot
MK	Mo'ed Katan
Naz	Nazir
Ned	Nedarim

LIST OF ABBREVIATIONS

Nidd	Niddah
NumR	Bemidbar Rabbah
OM	Ozar Midrashim
Pes	Pesaḥim
PetMos	Petiroth Moshe
PR	Pesikta Rabbati
PRE	Pirke de-Rabbi Eliezer
RH	Rosh Hashanah
RuthR	Ruth Rabbah
Sanh	Sanhedrin
SER	Seder Eliyahu Rabbah
Shab	Shabbat
SifDeut	Sifre Deuteronomy
SongR	Šir Hašširim Rabbah
Soṭ	Soṭah
Sukk	Sukkah
t. (before a rabbinic text)	Tosephta
Ta'an	Ta'anit
TargOnk	Targum Onkelos
TargYer	Targum Yerushalmi
TarJon	Targum Jonathan
Ter	Terumot
y. (before a rabbinic text)	Jerusalem Talmud
Yad	Yadayim
Yeb	Yebamot
Zeb	Zebahim

THE OLD TESTAMENT PSEUDEPIGRAPHA

DOCUMENTS

EXPANSIONS OF THE ''OLD TESTAMENT'' AND LEGENDS

INTRODUCTION

BY J. H. CHARLESWORTH

Early Judaism was a religion bound to and defined by the Book, the Torah. Because God had chosen to reveal himself in history, a sacred aura surrounded the events in Israel's past. These stories preserved in the books in the Old Testament were told and retold not only in the synagogues but also around the evening fires or wherever Jews would congregate. The biblical narratives were clarified, enriched, expanded, and sometimes retold from a different perspective. Often circulating first as oral legends, some stories eventually evolved into the documents collected here. Distinguishable from the others is the Letter of Aristeas; it does not center upon a biblical narrative, but glorifies the translation of the Hebrew scriptures into Greek.

Frequently the expansions explain the superiority of Judaism over other religions and may have an apologetic or missionary purpose; almost always they celebrate God's covenant with and guidance of the faithful. The primary focus is upon God's story in history, an ongoing drama in which the author claims to be a participant.

The early Jewish strata of the Martyrdom and Ascension of Isaiah belong to the present category; in its final and present form, however, it is clearly an apocalyptic work (especially chs. 6–11). Also related to the apocalyptic writings are Jubilees and 4 Baruch.

The expansions to sacred stories in the Old Testament should be studied in light of similar writings, such as some of the documents in the Apocrypha, the rabbinic Targumim and Midrashim, the Qumran Pesharim, and other exegetical documents (especially 1QapGen), a few of Philo of Alexandria's writings, Josephus' histories, and the Christian historians and chronographers. The Testament of Job, translated above, is an expansion of the biblical narrative in a testament form.

CONTENTS

LETTER OF ARISTEAS

(Third Century B.C.–First Century A.D.)

A NEW TRANSLATION AND INTRODUCTION

BY R. J. H. SHUTT

The so-called Letter of Aristeas is a primary source for understanding the Septuagint, the version of the Jewish Scriptures in Greek. It purports to describe how the Jewish Law was translated from Hebrew into Greek by seventy-two Jews sent to Alexandria for this purpose. The author, Aristeas, writes to his brother Philocrates about this mission. Presumably, Aristeas, who was a Jew from Alexandria, participated in the mission.

The contents are briefly as follows: The Egyptian king Ptolemy II (285–247 B.C.) wants Demetrius of Phalerum, his librarian, to collect all the books in the world for the library at Alexandria. Demetrius thinks that such a collection should include a copy of the Jewish Law in a Greek translation, and so he orders a letter to be written to the high priest at Jerusalem.

In a digression (vss. 12–27), Aristeas successfully petitions the king for the release of those Jews forcibly deported to Egypt by his father, King Ptolemy, son of Lagos. The relevant royal decree is quoted.

Returning to the main theme, Aristeas quotes the letter which Demetrius, the librarian, is instructed to send to the high priest (vss. 28–34). It suggests that the translation be made by six suitable members from each of the twelve tribes (vss. 35–40). The suggestion is accepted, and the names of the translators are given (vss. 47–50). Gifts are sent from the king to the high priest (vss. 51–82). Aristeas himself is mentioned as one of the ambassadors (vs. 43).

A description of Palestine follows, including the Temple and the high priest's vestments (vss. 83–120), but the account of the journey, though promised, is not given. The qualifications and virtues of the translators are given and extolled (vss. 121–27).

Then there is a further digression on the Law in Judaism (vss. 128–72). The arrival of the translators in Alexandria and their welcome are described; a royal banquet is prepared (vss. 173–86).

Even the author apologizes for the length of the next section, which is about a third of Aristeas (vss. 187–294). He describes the questions put by the king during the seven days of the banquet to each of the translators in turn, and their replies.

Finally the translators are conducted to their well-furnished quarters by Demetrius, and the work begins. Drafts of the translation are made, and the final version is completed in exactly seventy-two days (vss. 301–7).

The version is read to the Jewish community; Demetrius is asked to complete the project by arranging for the translation of the rest of the Law, and steps are taken, by pronouncing a curse on any who should change it in any way, to ensure that this is established as the authorized and official Greek translation (vss. 308–11).

The king shares in the rejoicing at the completion of the initial task, the sacred character of the Law is emphasized, and Demetrius receives instructions to guard the books with special care (vss. 312–17).

Further compliments and gifts are given, and the translators depart for home with a guard of honor, a letter, and further gifts to Eleazar (vss. 318–21).

A brief epilogue addressed to Philocrates, recalling his interest in such projects, brings Aristeas to a close.

Texts[1]

"There are more than twenty mss. containing the text or significant extracts from the Letter of Aristeas."[2] They range from the eleventh to the sixteenth centuries.

Thackeray describes these manuscripts in detail; Pelletier gives them in chronological groups according to the century to which they belong, adding six to Thackeray's list, and paying special attention to two of them: U, Seragliensis 8 of Istanbul, belonging to the twelfth or thirteenth centuries, and O, Monacensis 9 Munich of the eleventh century.

Thackeray and Pelletier agree that what Thackeray calls group A manuscripts are of special importance and antiquity. The group is subdivided as follows:

H Vaticanus 747. Rome (11th cent.)
K Vaticanus 383. Rome (12th–13th cent.)
A Regius 128. Paris, Bibliothèque Nationale (12th–13th cent.)

and (very similar to the above-mentioned):

G Venetus 534. Venice Marcianus (11th cent.)
I Palatinus 203. Rome, Bibl. Vatic. Pal. (11th cent.)
M Ottobonianus 32. Bibl. Vatic. Ottobon (15th cent.)

The earliest printed edition was a Latin translation by M. Palmerius of Pisa in 1471. A Greek text, the work of S. Schard, was published by Oporinus in 1561 at Basel, based mainly on O, Codex Monacensis 9 Munich.

The genuineness of Aristeas as a contemporary account of the proceedings by an eyewitness was seriously doubted by Hody (1659–1707). His position was rejected in 1870 by Schmidt, who was followed by Mendelssohn in 1897 and Wendland in 1900. The first edition of Thackeray's work also appeared in 1902 as an appendix to Swete's *An Introduction to the Old Testament in Greek*. Thackeray's text has been adopted in the works of Meecham (1935) and Hadas (1951). It is used as the basis of this translation; divergences from his text are indicated in the notes.

English translations have been published by H. St. J. Thackeray (1903), H. T. Andrews (in R. H. Charles, *APOT*, vol. 1, 1913), H. G. Meecham (1935), and M. Hadas (1951).

Original language

The original language of Aristeas is Greek, but not a particularly distinguished or elegant type of Greek. Some of its sentences are cumbersome, some of its words unusual, and some of its phrases striking because of their awkwardness. It hardly reaches the heights needed for a work to be classed as literature.

Date

It is impossible to be certain about the date of this work. The king referred to is Ptolemy II (Philadelphus, 285–247 B.C.). There is a reference in Aristeas to this king's father, Ptolemy I (Lagos), who abdicated in 285 and died in 283. Josephus (A.D. 37–?110) paraphrases the work in his *Jewish Antiquities* 12.12–118. From this we must conclude that it was written between approximately 250 B.C. and A.D. 100. To venture further with the dating demands some conjecture.

Jellicoe[3] summarizes the main categories of conjectured dates as follows:

1. early (i.e. 250–200 B.C.)
2. about 150–100 B.C.
3. first century A.D.

The majority of the views is in favor of c. 150–100 B.C. In deciding which conjecture is

---

[1] For further reference to the MSS see H. St. J. Thackeray, *Introduction to the Old Testament in Greek* (Cambridge, 1902) pp. 501–18, and A. Pelletier, *Lettre d'Aristée à Philocrate*, pp. 8–41.
[2] Pelletier, *Lettre d'Aristée*, p. 8.
[3] S. Jellicoe, *The Septuagint and Modern Study*. p. 48, n. 1.

preferable, we first have to decide on the occasion (and purpose) of the work. It has a decidedly Jewish background and provides an exposition and defense of the Law, seeking to indicate its relation in thought and political philosophy to Hellenism. This would be consistent with the view that the work emanated from Alexandria, a hellenistic center where there was a significant Jewish element in the population. There was consequently a need to promote integration and to avoid friction between Jew and non-Jew. There was presumably an immediate occasion for the composition of the work: Such an occasion would probably have been one during which an anti-Jewish policy was being carried out. A serious occasion of this sort occurred when Antiochus Epiphanes sought to carry out his pro-hellenistic or anti-Jewish policy, which caused such a strong reaction in Judea among, for example, the Maccabees. There would have been repercussions and unease in Alexandria about that time, i.e. about 170 B.C. Any attempt to consolidate the links between the two communities and to prevent a deterioration of the situation would have been worthwhile. Such an attempt, we may conjecture, underlies Aristeas. On these grounds we may with Jellicoe[4] and Orlinsky date the work about 170 B.C., thus putting it approximately in the second of the categories mentioned above.

Assuming some such occasion and date, what is the purpose of the work? It can hardly be regarded as a document written at the same time as the translation of the Law into Greek, known as the Septuagint. From this point of view, therefore, if that is the expectation, the work may be a disappointment. What is more important, it concerns Judaism and is a defense of Judaism in the light of its Law as available in a Greek version. The story of the making of that version underlines the toleration and respect which the Jews of Alexandria enjoyed and the integration of Jew and non-Jew in that city. Events in Jerusalem about 170 B.C. threatened such a community. Aristeas is an attempt by the author, himself presumably a Jew,[5] to show the links between Jew and Greek and to underline them by narrating the particular story of the translation of the Jewish Scriptures. Such we may conjecture is the occasion, date, and purpose of this work.

Provenance

A gentile, even a proselyte to Judaism, would hardly have attained such a knowledge of Jewish practices, and of the Temple worship, as the Letter of Aristeas exhibits (e.g. vss. 83–120). It is highly probable therefore that the author was a Jew. His knowledge of Alexandria needs also to be taken into account (e.g. vs. 301). The most attractive conjecture is that he lived in Alexandria.[6]

Historical and theological importance

It is difficult, as shown above, to date this document, and therefore difficult also to assess its importance for the time when it was composed.

However, its importance goes further and deeper than its historical setting because it raises a question implicit in Judaism that emerges in times of special crisis: If the Jews are God's special people, a chosen race, how are they to regard non-Jews? Can they live with them, or must they simply remove themselves and live exclusive lives? Is there any temporary arrangement of mutual recognition and respect that can be evolved? The case for the Jewish Law and attitude to life is set out in this work, and in confirmation of this, an appeal is made to the history of the Jews in Egypt and Alexandria, with special reference to the Law and its translation into Greek. It is also meant to show that there is some affinity between Jew and Greek, but not necessarily an identity, so that it is possible for them to live together. The difficulties are recognized, however: It is the merit of Aristeas that the author is alive to this recurring problem in the history of Judaism. For example, he describes how special arrangements were made for the banquet when the king and the Jews ate together (vs. 181). The implied warning is twofold: The danger with some of the Jews was that they might become excessively exclusive in their attitude to others, and the danger with

---

[4] Ibid., p. 49.

[5] In spite of LetAris, vs. 16.

[6] For details on the exact status of the Jews in Alexandria, see Josephus, *Ant* 19.279 (LCL ed., vol. 9, n. *ad loc.*, and App. Q. 583–85).

the Greeks, or the Hellenists, was that their attitude might be too syncretistic.[7] The moral was the need for mutual recognition of different customs and cultures.

Relation to canonical books

There is no evidence in Aristeas either to indicate which books in the Old Testament have exercised most influence upon it or to indicate which books in the New Testament it has influenced. Aristeas holds the Law in the highest esteem and is concerned with narrating the story of the translation of the Jewish Scriptures into Greek.

Relation to apocryphal books

Similarly, there is no evidence that any of the apocryphal books directly influenced Aristeas. There are no apocryphal books with which Aristeas is especially close; with some there is only the general link shown by hellenistic influence.

Cultural importance

Aristeas provides no specific detail either on the methods and aims of the translators or on the text used. Indeed, a look at the contents shows that the space devoted to the translators and their work is only a small proportion of the total length of Aristeas. The project and the names of the translators appear in verses 1–50; their actual work is described in verses 301–21. A digression on the questions put to the translators during the seven-day banquet occupies about a third of the whole work; other digressions include details of gifts from the king (vss. 51–82) and a description of Palestine, the Temple, and the high priest's vestments (vss. 83–120).

Nevertheless, the work is important, for it is the only ancient document on the subject that has survived. How is it then to be regarded? Opinions differ.[8] It has been regarded as a work of Jewish apologetics, aimed at the Greeks. Tcherikover suggested that it was "not written with the aim of self-defence or propaganda, and was addressed not to Greek, but to Jewish readers."[9] In either case, perhaps such a precise dichotomy obscures rather than illuminates: It may well be that we are nearer to the truth if we say that its underlying motive and purpose are mixed.

The background of the work is Alexandria, where a Jewish community lived among a predominantly gentile population. There were obvious differences in culture and religion, but Judaism and Hellenism largely succeeded in living side by side there in comparative harmony. Was any mutual assimilation possible? If so, would it take place? These questions were bound to arise, and indeed had arisen ever since some of the Jews had been forced to live in captivity in Babylon. To some extent, the result was the Judaism of the Dispersion, which was liberal as compared with the Judaism of Palestine, with the Temple at Jerusalem as the focus of its religion. This was inevitable and is associated with the rise and development of the synagogues, but even so, the Judaism of the Diaspora maintained its identity. On the other hand, the gentile population among whom the Dispersion lived was not always satisfied with such a situation, although there was little general hostile expression of such dissatisfaction. The ideals of Hellenism, however, aspired to a universalism in culture and religion, which could be intolerant of what might be regarded as Jewish separatism and exclusiveness.

The clash under Antiochus Epiphanes, which resulted in the persecution of the Jews in Palestine and an attempt to eradicate them, may have taken place shortly before Aristeas was written.[10] There may well have been repercussions and anxiety among the Jews in Alexandria and in the Dispersion. In any case, the situation existed either actually or potentially and was unavoidable as long as Jews lived among gentiles and, characteristically, exercised a noticeable presence and influence to a greater or lesser extent at different times.

---

[7] (Exclusiveness is found in Jub, syncretism in 4 Mac.—J.H.C.)

[8] See article by V. Tcherikover in *Studies in the Septuagint: Origins, Recensions, and Interpretations*, ed. S. Jellicoe.

[9] Ibid., p. 182.

[10] 175–64 B.C. See also "Date."

The author of Aristeas was aware of this situation—and its danger, and he saw in the translation of the Jewish Scriptures a phenomenal event important in itself for Judaism and its understanding by Jews and non-Jews. He recognized that in process of time, through lack of use in ordinary communication with gentiles, the native language of the Jews might become less familiar. He also saw in the translation a sort of parable of the relationship between the Judaism of the Dispersion and the Hellenism of the gentiles among whom these Jews lived. Hence he acclaimed in this work the actual project and those responsible for its execution, showing the attitudes of both groups to each other. Perhaps it is to be regarded as an attempt at a compromise, which well may be criticized for its emphasis on and even bias toward Judaism, but which, nevertheless, deserves credit for its basic concept and vision. In this sense, Aristeas is not to be regarded as aimed only at Greeks or at Jews; it was probably aimed at both.

SELECT BIBLIOGRAPHY

Charlesworth, *PMR*, pp. 78–80.
Delling, *Bibliographie*, pp. 97f.
Denis, *Introduction*, pp. 105–10.

Hadas, M. *Aristeas to Philocrates*. New York and London, 1951. (This translation follows Thackeray's text.)
Jellicoe, S. *The Septuagint and Modern Study*. Oxford, 1968. (A most important work, including chs. on Aristeas and its relation to LXX studies to date.)
Jellicoe, S., ed. *Studies in the Septuagint: Origins, Recensions, and Interpretations*. New York, 1974. (This vol. contains articles on Aristeas by D. W. Gooding, V. Tcherikover, and G. Zuntz which appeared in learned journals between 1958 and 1963, assembled in convenient form for reference and prefaced with a masterly introduction by Jellicoe.)
Marcus, R. *Josephus: Jewish Antiquities XII–XIV*. LCL edition, vol. VII; London and Cambridge, Mass., 1943. (Josephus used Aristeas as a source in *Ant* 12.11–118. See the appendix for a consideration of the method which Josephus adopted with this source.)
Meecham, H. G. *The Letter of Aristeas*. Manchester, 1935. (The text of Thackeray is given here, without translation. There are appendices in which philological studies are paramount.)
Nestle, E. "Septuagint" in J. Hastings, *Dictionary of the Bible*. Edinburgh, 1902. (This article contains much useful information, but now needs supplementing with the work of S. Jellicoe.)
Pelletier, A. *Lettre d'Aristée à Philocrate*. SC 89; Paris, 1962. (This vol. contains an introduction, text, and translation, with critical nn. and appendices. The introduction includes important sections on MSS, author and date, the Library of Alexandria, and the Jewish community there.)
Shutt, R. J. H. "Notes on the Letter of Aristeas." *BIOSCS* 10 (1977) 22–30.
Swete, H. B. *An Introduction to the Old Testament in Greek*. Cambridge, 1902; text: 519–74, introduction: 501–18. (The introduction is valuable for detailed descriptions of the MSS of LetAris.)
Thackeray, H. St. J., ed. "The Letter of Aristeas," in *An Introduction to the Old Testament in Greek*, by H. B. Swete. Cambridge, 1902. (This edition of LetAris is the basis for the present translation.)

ARISTEAS TO PHILOCRATES

1   A trustworthy narrative has been compiled, Philocrates, of the meeting which we had
with Eleazar, high priest of the Jews, arising out of your attaching great importance to
hearing a personal account of our mission, its content and purpose. By detailing[a] each
aspect I have tried to give you a clear exposition of it, realizing your scholarly disposition,
2 which is a supreme quality in any man who has tried continually to increase his learning
and understanding, whether from the accounts (of others) or by actual experience. This is
the way in which a pure disposition of mind is acquired, by the attainment of the noblest
ends, and which, turning to piety, the highest of all ends, lives by adopting a rule which
3 does not err. •We have a set purpose devoted to the special study of the things of God, and
offered ourselves as a deputation to the aforesaid gentleman, whose integrity and reputation
have won him preeminent honor in the eyes of citizens and others alike, and who has gained
a very great benefit for his own circle and for (fellow) citizens in other places. Our deputation
(waited upon him) with a view to the translation of the divine Law, due to its being written
4 by them on parchments in Hebrew characters. •We undertook this task with enthusiasm,
seizing an opportunity with the king in connection with those who were transported to Egypt
from Judea by the king his father, who was the original founder of the city and took over
5 the government of Egypt. It is worthwhile telling you this as well, •for I am convinced that
because you are more favorably inclined toward the piety and disposition of those who live
by the sacred Law, concerning whom we propose to write, you will gladly listen,[b] since
you have paid a special visit to us from your island, and wish to hear with us of matters
6 pertaining to the edification of the soul. •I had previously sent you the account of what I
regarded as the most memorable matters. We received this account of the people of the
7 Jews from the most renowned high priests in renowned Egypt. •You are studiously disposed
toward what can help the mind and it is my duty to share this with all like-minded persons,
and all the more so with you, for you have a kindred spirit, being not only a blood brother
8 in character but also in the pursuit of beauty the same as we are. •The value of gold or any
other treasure among those highly prized by the empty-headed does not possess the same
value, as compared with the pursuit of culture and caring for these things. But lest we
prolong the introduction and indulge in idle chatter, we will proceed to the main part of the
narrative.

9   On his appointment as keeper of the king's library, Demetrius of Phalerum undertook
many different negotiations aimed at collecting, if possible, all the books in the world. By
purchase and translation he brought to a successful conclusion, as far as lay in his power,
10 the king's plan. •We were present when the question was put to him, "How many thousand[c]
books are there (in the royal library)?" His reply was, "Over two hundred thousand, O
King. I shall take urgent steps to increase in a short time the total to five hundred thousand.
Information has reached me that the lawbooks of the Jews are worth translation and inclusion
in your royal library."
11   "What is there to prevent you from doing this?" he said. "Everything for your needs
has been put at your disposal."
    Demetrius replied, "Translation is needed. They use letters characteristic of the language
of the Jews, just as Egyptians use the formation of their letters in accordance with their
own language. The Jews are supposed to use Syrian language, but this is not so, for it is
another form (of language)."
    The king, in answer to each point, gave orders that a letter be written to the high priest
12 of the Jews that the aforementioned project might be carried out. •I considered that it was
an opportunity in connection with the matters on which I had often asked Sosibius of

---

a. The text is corrupt here, but the general sense is
clear.
b. Thackeray adopts the emendation of Schmidt.

c. Lit. "How many ten thousands of books are there?"
His reply was, "Over twenty, O King. I shall take urgent
steps to increase in a short time the total to fifty."

Tarentum and Andreas, the chief bodyguards, concerning the release of those deported from
Judaea by the father of the king. He invaded the whole of Coele-Syria and Phoenicia, and
by a combination of success and bravery deported some and took others prisoners, bringing
everything into subjection by fear. In the course of this he removed from the land of the
13 Jews into Egypt up to one hundred thousand people, •from whom he armed about thirty
thousand chosen men and settled them throughout the land in the forts. (Already in earlier
times as well a fair number had entered the country with the Persian, and before them other
confederate troops had been dispatched to fight with Psammitichus against the king of the
Ethiopians, but they were not so many in number as those brought over by Ptolemy the son
14 of Lagos.) •As we said previously, he selected the best, outstanding in youth and strength,
and armed them. The remaining number, old men, children, and women also, he let go
into slavery, not so much out of any personal predilection for such a course, but because
he was prevailed upon by his troops on account of the services which they had given in the
trials of war. When therefore we came upon some opportunity for their release, as we have
15 shown before, we spoke the following words to the king. •"Let it never be unreasonable
to be refuted by events themselves, O King. The laws have been established for all the
Jews, and it is our plan not only to translate but also to interpret them, but what justification
shall we have for our mission, as long as large numbers are in subjection in your kingdom?
But out of your unsullied and magnanimous soul release those who are subject to misery;
the (same) God who appointed them their Law prospers your kingdom, as I have been at
16 pains to show. •These people worship God the overseer and creator of all, whom all men
worship including ourselves, O King, except that we have a different name. Their name
for him is Zeus and Jove. The primitive men, consistently with this, demonstrated that the
one by whom all live and are created is the master and Lord of all. In your excelling all
17 men by your nobility of soul, I beg you to release those held in slavery." •He wasted no
time, while we offered hearty prayer to God to dispose his mind to the release of them all.
(Mankind is God's creation and is changed and converted by him. Wherefore with many
diverse prayers I besought the Lord with all my heart that he might be prevailed upon to
18 accomplish my request. •For I had great hope, as I presented the case for the saving of
men, that God would execute the fulfillment of my requests, inasmuch as whatsoever men
think to do in piety in the way of righteousness and attention to good works, God the Lord
19 of all directs their acts and intentions.) •(The king) looked up and, looking on me with
gracious countenance, said, "How many thousand[d] do you consider there will be?" Andreas,
standing by, answered, "A little more than one hundred thousand." He said, "It is a small
request that Aristeas makes of us." Sosibius and some of those present thus said, "It is
worthy of your magnanimity to offer the release of these men as a thank offering to the
Most High God. You are highly honored by the Lord of all, and have been glorified beyond
20 your ancestors, so if you make even the greatest thank offerings, it befits you." •The king
was absolutely confounded, and ordered an increase in army pay, and the payment of twenty
drachmas for each slave, together with the publication of an edict on these matters, and the
compilation of a register accordingly. He exercised his zeal on a grand scale, God having
fulfilled all our purpose, and compelled him to release not only those who came into his
kingdom with his father's army but also any others who were there previously or were
subsequently taken there. They revealed that the gift amounted to more than four hundred
21 talents. •As regards the copy of the decree, I consider its recording to be of no small value,
because the generosity of the king will be more clearly manifested thereby, as God gives
22 him strength to bring salvation to large multitudes. •It was as follows. "By order of the
king—as many as joined our father's campaigns in the regions of Syria and Phoenicia and
in their advance into the territory of the Jews became masters of Jewish personnel which
they transported into the city or the country or sold to others, and likewise any such who
were there before the advance or were subsequently brought in—those who hold such
persons shall forthwith release them, receiving as the price for each individual twenty
drachmas, such money to be paid in the case of soldiers with the issue of their pay, and in
23 the case of the remainder from the royal treasury. •It is our opinion that these prisoners
were taken contrary to the wishes of our father in a manner quite improper, and that

d. Lit. "How many ten thousands do you consider
there will be?" Andreas, standing by, answered, "A
little more than ten ten thousands."

excessively drastic military action caused the destruction of their land and the transportation of the Jews into Egypt. The assistance from the soldiers given along the plain was quite
24 enough, and the enslavement of these men is accordingly entirely inequitable. •We have a reputation of dispensing justice to all men, and all the more to those who are enslaved without good reason; our overall aim is that which promotes justice and piety in all things. We have accordingly decreed that all Jewish personnel in slavery (everywhere) in the kingdom for whatever reason shall be released, their owners to receive the payment laid down above, and that no one shall deal in a slow manner in these matters. Three days from the day of publication of this decree, the owners shall furnish registers to those appointed
25 over these matters, giving immediate details of these persons. •We have concluded that it is in the interest of ourselves and our royal affairs that this matter shall be accomplished. Anyone who so wishes may give information concerning those who have disobeyed (this edict) on the understanding that he will assume the office of the accused if found guilty;
26 the possessions of such men shall be appropriated into the royal treasury." •This decree was submitted to the king for his perusal. It was identical in all other respects except for the clause "and likewise any such who were there before the advance or were subsequently brought in," which the king added with his own hand, showing his magnificent magnanimity. He gave orders also that a generous gift of expenses should be divided among the servants
27 of the troops and the royal bankers. •Once so decided, it was implemented in seven days. The gift amounted to more than six hundred and sixty talents. A large number of children at the breast were also set free, with their mothers. There was an additional proposal to the effect that twenty drachmas should be given for these, and the king commanded that this also should be done, thus completely accomplishing every detail of his policy.
28 When this had been completed, he commanded Demetrius to report on the copying of the Jewish books. All measures were taken by these kings by means of edicts and in complete safety, with no trace of negligence or carelessness. For this reason I have set down the copies of the report and of the letters, as well as the number of those returned and the state of each, because each of them was outstanding in magnificence and skill.
29 The copy of the memorandum is as follows: "To the great king from Demetrius. Your command, O King, concerned the collection of missing volumes needed to complete the library, and of items which accidentally fell short of the requisite condition. I gave highest
30 priority and attention to these matters, and now make the following further report: •Scrolls of the Law of the Jews, together with a few others, are missing (from the library), for these (works) are written in Hebrew characters and language. But they have been transcribed[e] somewhat carelessly and not as they should be,[f] according to the report of the experts,

e. Lit. "have been indicated." The major problem in understanding vs. 30 is this verb, *sesēmantai* (perfect passive 3rd plural), which comes from *sēmainō* and can mean "to show by a sign, indicate, appear, be manifest, give a signal, signify" (LSJM and similarly Preisigke); "to indicate, signify, to mean (of words)" (Sophocles); or "to make known, report, communicate" (Bauer-Arndt-Gingrich). As translated above the vs. refers to copies of Heb. scrolls (cf. the judicious comments by Shutt in "Notes on the Letter of Aristeas," *BIOSCS* 10 [1977] 22–30. —J.H.C.). Andrews (*APOT*, vol. 2, p. 98) took *sesēmantai* to mean "interpreted" and noted that the "exact force" of this verb "is uncertain. If we translate 'interpreted' it involves the supposition that an earlier, though imperfect, translation of the law into Greek was in existence." Andrews translated the passage as follows: "They are written in the Hebrew characters and language and have been carelessly interpreted, and do not represent the original text as I am informed by those who know . . ." Andrews' rendering supports P. Kahle's hypothesis; Kahle claimed that the LetAris refers not to "the *first* Greek translation of the Law" but to "a revision of already existing translations." (*The Cairo Geniza* [Oxford, 1959²] p. 212; italics his). Kahle demands that *sesēmantai* be translated "interpreted" or "written" and claims it refers to earlier translations of the Law into Gk.;

yet he admits the expressions in LetAris 30 "are not clear" and "not good Greek" (p. 213). He is wrong in demanding that *amelesteron*, which he translated "rather carelessly," "can only be taken as referring to earlier *translations* . . ." (italics his).

The translation given above supports the position presented in 1863 by P. de Lagarde and defended more recently by H. M. Orlinsky, D. Barthélemy, F. M. Cross, H. H. Rowley, and S. Jellicoe (for details and bibliographical data see Jellicoe's *The Septuagint and Modern Study*, pp. 59–63). LetAris 30 is not referring to other Gk. translations of the Law; it appears to refer to unreliable Heb. MSS. There does appear to be an *Urtext* of the LXX; but the author of LetAris is, among other concerns, apparently defending the LXX against one or more rival Gk. translations [perhaps emanating from Leontopolis, as Jellicoe, p. 50, suggested. —J.H.C.].

f. Lit. "as is the case." Everyone recognizes the phrase *kai ouch·hōs huparchei* as "difficult Greek" (Hadas); it is translated variously: "and not acccording to their true meaning" (Thackeray); "and not adequately" (Hadas). Since the author of LetAris has the Heb. text of the Torah brought from Jerusalem, he may well have meant to indicate here that the copies available in Alexandria were inadequate. [I am indebted here to conversations with H. Orlinsky. —J.H.C.]

31 because they have not received royal patronage. •These (books) also must be in your library[g] in an accurate version, because this legislation, as could be expected from its divine nature, is very philosophical and genuine. Writers therefore and poets and the whole army of historians have been reluctant to refer to the aforementioned books, and to the men past (and present) who featured largely in them, because the consideration of them is sacred and 32 hallowed, as Hecataeus of Abdera says. •If you approve, O King, a letter shall be written to the high priest at Jerusalem, asking him to dispatch men of the most exemplary lives and mature experience, skilled in matters pertaining to their Law, six in number from each tribe, in order that after the examination of the text agreed by the majority, and the achievement of accuracy in the translation, we may produce an outstanding version in a manner worthy 33 both of the contents and of your purpose. Farewell always." •On receiving this report, the king ordered a letter to be written to Eleazar regarding these matters, announcing also the actual release of the prisoners. He made them a gift also for the provision of cups and goblets and a table and libation vessels weighing fifty talents of gold, seventy talents of silver, and a goodly number of (precious) stones—he commanded the treasurers to allow the craftsmen to select whatever they might prefer—and of currency for sacrifices and other 34 requirements one hundred talents. •We will show you details of the provisions after we have given the copies of the letters. The letter of the king was of the following pattern. 35 "King Ptolemy to Eleazar the high priest, hearty greetings. It is a fact that a large number of the Jews settled in our country after being uprooted from Jerusalem by the Persians during the time of their ascendancy, and also came with our father into Egypt as prisoners. 36 He put many of them into the military forces on generous pay, and in the same way, having judged the veterans to be trustworthy, he set up establishments which he handed over to them, to prevent the Egyptian people feeling any apprehension on their account. Having now inherited the throne, we adopt a more liberal attitude to all our subjects, and 37 more especially to your citizens. •We have freed more than a hundred thousand prisoners,[h] paying to their captors the price in silver proportionate to their rank. We also make amends for any damage caused by mob violence. We decided to do this as a religious obligation, making of it a thank offering to the Most High God, who has preserved the kingdom for us in peace and highest renown throughout the whole world. Those at the peak of their youth we have appointed to the army, and those who are able to be at our court, being 38 worthy of confidence in our household, we have put in charge of (some) ministries. •It is our wish to grant favors to them and to all the Jews throughout the world, including future generations. We have accordingly decided that your Law shall be translated into Greek letters from what you call the Hebrew letters, in order that they too should take their place 39 with us in our library with the other royal books. •You will therefore act well, and in a manner worthy of our zeal, by selecting elders of exemplary lives, with experience of the Law and ability to translate it, six from each tribe, so that an agreed version may be found from the large majority, in view of the great importance of the matters under consideration. 40 We believe that the completion of this project will win (us) high reputation. •We have dispatched on this business Andreas of the chief bodyguards and Aristeas, men held in high esteem by you, to confer with you; they bring with them first fruits of offerings for the Temple and one hundred talents of silver for sacrifices and the other requirements. Write to us on any matters you wish, and your requests will be gratified; you will be performing also an act worthy of friendship for what you choose will be carried out with all dispatch. 41 Farewell." •In reply to this letter Eleazar wrote in acceptance as follows: "Eleazar the high priest to King Ptolemy, dear friend, greeting. Good health to you and to Queen Arsinoe, your sister, and to your children; if that is so, it would be well, and as we wish. We too 42 are in good health. •On receipt of your letter we rejoiced greatly because of your purpose and noble plan; we therefore collected together the whole multitude and read it to them, that they might know your piety toward our God. We also showed them the vessels which you sent, twenty of silver and thirty of gold, five cups, and a table for offering, and for the performance of the sacrifices and the furnishing of the Temple requirements one hundred 43 talents of silver, •brought by two men highly esteemed by you, Andreas and Aristeas,

g. Lit. "with you," i.e. in your library, presumably, though not all commentators would wish to be so specific.
h. Lit. "ten ten thousands."

gentlemen of integrity,[i] outstanding in education, worthy in every respect of your conduct and justice. They also communicated to us your messages, in reply to which they have
44 heard from us also sentiments consistent with what you wrote. •Everything which is to your advantage, even if it is unnatural, we will carry out; this is a sign of friendship and love.
45 You have also bestowed great unexpected benefits upon our citizens in many ways. •We therefore offered sacrifices without delay for you, your sister, your children, and your friends. The whole multitude made supplication that it should come to pass for you entirely as you desire, and that God the ruler of all should preserve your kingdom in peace and glory, and that the translation of the sacred Law should come to pass in a manner expedient
46 to you and in safety. •In the presence of the whole assembly we selected elders, honorable men and true, six from each tribe, whom we have sent with the Law in their possession. It will be a noble deed, O righteous King, if you command that once the translation of the
47 books is complete these men be restored to us again in safety. Farewell.'' •The names of the men are as follows: First tribe:[j] Joseph, Ezekiah, Zachariah, John, Ezekiah, and Elissaeus; second tribe: Judas, Simon, Somoel, Adaeus, Mattathias, and Esclemias; third tribe:
48 Neemiah, Joseph, Theodosius, Baseas, Ornias, and Dakis; •fourth tribe: Jonathan, Abraeus, Elissaeus, Ananias, Chabrias;[k] fifth tribe: Isaac, Jacob, Jesus, Sabbataeus, Simon, Levi;
49 sixth tribe: Judas, Joseph, Simon, Zachariah, Somoel, and Selemiah; •seventh tribe: Sabbataeus, Sedekiah, Jacob, Isaac, Jesias, Natthaeus; eighth tribe: Theodosius, Jason, Jesus, Theodotus, John, and Jonathan; ninth tribe: Theophilus, Abram, Arsam, Jason,
50 Endemias, and Daniel; •tenth tribe: Jeremiah, Eleazar, Zachariah, Baneas, Elissaeus, and Dathaeus; eleventh tribe: Samuel, Joseph, Judas, Jonathan, Chabeu,[l] and Dositheus; twelfth
51 tribe: Isael, John, Theodosius, Arsamus, Abietes, and Ezekiel. Seventy-two in all. •The matters relating to the king's letter received the aforementioned reply from Eleazar and his advisers.

Since I promised to give full details of the furnishings, I will now do so. The finished objects were conspicuous for their variety of craftsmanship; the king made a generous contribution and oversaw the craftsman in each case, so that they could not neglect anything
52 or finish it off thoughtlessly. First I will describe the details of the table. •The king's main plan was to make the furnishing an object outstanding in its measurements, and commanded inquiries to be made of the local people concerning the size of the previous one set up in
53 the Temple at Jerusalem. •When they gave him the measurements he asked a further question, whether he should make it larger. Some of the priests and the others said that there was nothing to prevent this. The king replied that though he was quite willing to make it even five times as large in size, he hesitated in case it proved to be useless for the services;
54 he not only chose, he said, that his gifts should be placed in that building, but would be much more pleased if the appointed ministers duly performed the appropriate rites upon the
55 furnishings which he had provided. •Lack of money was not the reason he had made the measurements of the previously completed offerings short, but it is plain, he said, for what reason they were so constituted in their measurements. Had there been any (precise) order (to that effect) there would be nothing lacking now. Accordingly, we must not transgress
56 nor overstep what is right and proper. •He commanded that the fullest use should be made of the variety of the arts, his intentions being pious in every respect, and having naturally a good eye for appreciating how things will look. In cases of unspecified items he commanded that they should make them with an eye to their beauty (not expense); in cases of specified items, measurements should tally with them.
57   Their finished work was two cubits in length, one and a half[m] in height; they made it solid all over with highly precious gold, by which I mean not just an outer covering of
58 gold, but the plate itself superimposed. •They made the crown a palm's radius in size; the moldings twined, with coiled work in low relief, the relief-work marvelously executed on
59 the three sides. (It formed a triangle.) •On each side the shape of the workmanship was identical in arrangement, so that whichever side it was turned, the appearance was identical,

---

i. See also vs. 46. This phrase, *kaloi kai agathoi* (lit. "beautiful and good"), expresses the Gk. ideal of manhood and is almost untranslatable.
  j. Lit. "There are of the first tribe."
  k. The name of the sixth member from the fourth tribe

is missing. "Chelkias" has been suggested.
  l. "Chabeu" seems wrong. "Caleb" has been suggested.
  m. The addition "and a half" comes from Josephus, *Ant* 12.64.

and when one side of the crown was placed downward the slope downward to the surface of the table kept its beautiful shape, and the outer slope was facing the view of anyone

60 approaching it. •So the prominence of the two sloping sides stood out sharply, being raised high as we have said, and of triangular construction, whichever side it was turned. There were arrangements of precious stones upon it between the patterns of lines: Each overlapped

61 the other, unsurpassed in craftsmanship. •They were all fastened through the holes with

62 golden pins for safety. At the corners the clasps closed to keep them together. •On the sides on the crown all around as one looked at the top an ovate border had been fashioned set with precious stones, [in prominent relief][n] with uninterrupted striped reliefs, closely

63 connected with each other around the whole of the table. •Beneath the relief of the precious stones which made the (aforesaid) ovate border the craftsmen made a crown adorned with all sorts of fruit, preeminently conspicuous with grapes and ears of corn, also dates, apples, olives, pomegranates, and the like. Thus they fashioned the stones in the shape of the aforesaid fruits, in the color appropriate to each type, and then attached them with the

64 golden band around the whole design of the table in profile. •After the disposition of the crown a similar arrangement had been designed to match the scheme of the border, and likewise the rest of the fluting and engraving, because the table had been made for use on both sides whichever side they began, so that the position of the moldings and of the crown

65 matched the side where the feet were. •They made a solid metal plate over the whole breadth of the table, four fingers[o] deep, so that into it the feet fitted which had fasteners with holes for attaching under the crown to ensure its use whichever side they began. This

66 is seen plainly on the outside, the construction being visible on both sides. •On the actual table they made an intricate pattern in relief with very costly stones in profusion in the middle, consisting of rubies of many types and emeralds, onyx also, and the other kinds

67 conspicuous for their beauty. •After the arrangement of the (aforesaid) pattern there was superimposed a web with interstices, marvelously contrived, which made the central view rhomboid in shape; on it was put in relief a stone of crystal and what is called amber,

68 providing the viewers with a sight beyond compare. •They made the feet with the capitals adorned with lilies, the lilies opening out underneath the table; the inside parts which could

69 be seen they made with a real covering of gold leaf. •The support of the foot on the ground

70 was adorned liberally with rubies, having an arrangement of a foot at the front, eight fingers wide. On it was placed all the stress of the foot. •They made a sprouting ivy cluster of stone entwined in acanthus, and surrounded all around the foot with a vine together with the grape clusters, all fashioned out of stone, as far as the head. The same pattern was applied to the four feet; everything was artistically contrived and introduced, uniformly showing preeminence of experience and art with an emphasis on realism, so that the arrangement of the leaves seemed actually to receive a movement of breath in the air fanning

71 them. •Everything was modeled for realistic representation. They made the mouth of the table threefold, of three layers as it were, each layer fitted to each other with dovetailing joints through the thickness of the piece (of furniture): they made the joints so closely fitting as to be invisible and incapable of detection. The thickness of the whole table was not less

72 than half a cubit, so that the whole piece weighed many talents. •For since the king had decided to add nothing to the measurements insofar as greater expenditure was required for making them bigger, he increased the number of talents' weight, and so in accordance with his purpose every detail was completed in an extraordinary and remarkable way, unparalleled

73 in craftsmanship and outstanding in beauty. •Two of the drinking bowls were made of solid gold of overlapping design in relief from the base to the center, with very artistic joining

74 together of the stones in the middle of the layers. •There was superimposed an intricate pattern a cubit high, incorporated into the design by intricate work in precious stones, exhibiting meticulous art combined with beauty. On this was fluting intermingled with

75 circular patterns, giving a meshlike appearance as far as the mouth. •On the central part small bosses of stones, one group close to another, and of varied types, not less than four fingers in size, complemented the conspicuous beauty (of the whole). On the brim of the

---

n. The text here is corrupt. The general meaning is given, following Schmidt's conjecture *prooch*ē*s*, ''a prominent point,'' for *prosoch*ē*s*, ''attention.''

o. A ''finger'' is reckoned as equivalent to seven tenths of an inch, so that four fingers would be approximately three inches.

mouth shapes of lilies with flowers and interwoven clusters of grapes were fashioned all
76 around. •Such was the pattern of the golden (drinking bowls), holding above two[p] large
measures. The silver ones had a smooth appearance, being a reflector marvelously adapted
for this very effect, so that everything brought near it flashed more clearly than in mirrors.
77 It is not, however, possible to relate the additional details added to give the impression of
realism. When it was finished and the pieces put one upon another, that is to say a silver
drinking bowl first, then a gold, then one in silver and one in gold, the overall effect of the
sight was entirely beyond description, and even those who approached to view it were
78 unable to tear themselves away from the brilliance and delight in what they saw. •The living
craftsmanship of the work now made visible was subtly diverse. As people looked at the
actual furnishing in gold, a certain fascination ensued, coupled with awed amazement, as
the attention concentrated on each artistic device in turn. And again, when anyone wanted
to gaze at the arrangement of the silver, everything reflected all around, however one stood,
and caused even greater amazement among the spectators. So that the manifold artistry of
79 the masterpieces was absolutely indescribable. •They engraved the golden goblets with
crowns of grapes in the middle, and around the edges they plaited in relief a crown of ivy,
myrtle, and olive, into which they inserted precious stones; the remaining carvings the
craftsmen finished individually, competing with one another to do everything to the
80 preeminent glory of the king. •There was absolutely no work of art comparable in
magnificence and craftsmanship, either in the royal treasuries or in any other. The king
81 took no small interest in the work, because of his dedication to works of art. •Many a time
he laid aside public business and sat attentively among the craftsmen, in order that they
might complete the work in a manner consistent with the place for which the entire enterprise
was destined. So everything was done in solemnity and in a manner worthy of the king,
82 who sent (the gifts), and of the high priest, who presided over the place. •The number of
the stones was without limit, and they were great in size, not less than five thousand in
number. Everything was excellent in craftsmanship so that the gift of the stones and the
actual artistic work was worth five times more than the gold.
83 I assumed that the description of these details was indispensable, so I have narrated it to
you. What follows embraces the road to Eleazar that we took. First I will describe the
layout of the whole countryside. When we approached near the site, we saw the city built
in the midst of the whole land of the Jews, upon a hill which extended to a great height.
84 On the top of the hill the Temple had been constructed, towering above all. There were
three enclosing walls, over seventy cubits in size, the width being proportionate and the
length of the equipment of the house likewise; everything was built with a magnificence
85 and expense which excelled in every respect. •It was obvious that the expenditure of money
had been unrestricted upon the door, the fastenings upon it by the doorposts, and the
86 strength of the lintels. •The configuration of the veil was in respects very similar to the
door furnishing, and most of all in view of continuous movement caused to the material by
the undercurrent of the air. It was continuous because the undercurrent started from the
bottom and the billowing extended[q] to the rippling at the top—the phenomenon making a
pleasant and unforgettable spectacle.
87 The furnishing of the altar was constructed in a manner commensurate with the place and
the sacrifices consumed in the fire, and that of the ascent to it likewise—the site had the
ladder designed in a manner consistent with seemliness for the ministering priests swathed
88 up to the loins in "leather garments." •The house faces east, and the rear of it faces west.
The whole foundation was decked with (precious) stones and had slopes leading to the
appropriate places for carrying the water which is (needed) for the cleansing of the blood
from the sacrifices. (Many thousands[r] of animals are brought there in the festival days.)
89 There is an uninterrupted supply not only of water, just as if there were a plentiful spring
rising naturally from within, but also of indescribably wonderful underground reservoirs,
which within a radius of five stades[s] from the foundation of the Temple revealed innumerable
90 channels for each of them, the streams joining together on each side. •All these were

---

p. Perhaps about fifteen gallons. The Athenian measure
held nine gallons; others five or six.

q. Adopting Schmidt's conjecture *katateinein*, "extend."

r. Lit. "Many ten thousands."

s. A stade is one eighth of a Roman mile, i.e. one
eighth of 1,618 yards or approximately 200 yards.

covered with lead down to the foundation of the wall; on top of them a thick layer of pitch, all done very effectively. There were many mouths at the base, which were completely invisible except for those responsible for the ministry, so that the large amounts of blood which collected from the sacrifices were all cleansed by the downward pressure and

91 momentum. •Being personally convinced, I will describe the building plan of the reservoirs just as I understood it. They conducted me more than four stades outside the city, and told me to bend down at a certain spot and listen to the noise at the meeting of the waters. The result was that the size of the conduits became clear to me, as has been demonstrated.

92 The ministering of the priests was absolutely unsurpassable in its vigor and the arrangement of its well-ordered silence: All work hard of their own accord, with much exertion, and each one looks after his appointed task. Their service is unremitting, sharing the sacrifices, some undertaking the carrying of wood, others oil, others wheaten flour, others the sweet spices, others offering burnt offerings of the parts of the flesh—all of them exerting their

93 strength in different ways. •They divide the legs of the bullocks with both hands, though they are more than two talents[t] in weight in almost every case, and then with an upward movement rip off with each hand in an amazing way a sufficiently large portion[u] with unerring accuracy.[v] The sheep and the goats are similarly treated in a remarkable way, weight and fat notwithstanding. Those whose concern it is choose in every case spotless

94 specimens outstanding for fatness: Thus the aforesaid procedure is carried out. •They have a rest room set aside, where those who are resting sit down. When this happens, some of those who are rested stand up with alacrity, but no one orders the arrangements of their

95 ministry. •A general silence reigns, so that one might think that there was not a single man in the place although the number of ministers in attendance is more than seven hundred, in addition to a large number of the assistants bringing forward the animals for sacrifice:

96 Everything is carried out with reverence and in a manner befitting supreme divinity. •It was an occasion of great amazement to us when we saw Eleazar engaged on his ministry, and all the glorious vestments, including the wearing of the "garment"[w] with precious stones upon it in which he is vested; golden bells surround the hem (at his feet) and make a very special sound. Alongside each of them are "tassels" adorned with "flowers," and of

97 marvelous colors. •He was clad in an outstandingly magnificent "girdle," woven in the most beautiful colors. On his breast he wears what is called the "oracle," to which are attached "twelve stones" of different kinds, set in gold, giving the names of the patriarchs in what was the original order, each stone flashing its own natural distinctive color—quite

98 indescribable. •Upon his head he has what is called the "tiara," and upon this the inimitable "mitre," the hallowed diadem having in relief on the front in the middle in holy letters on a golden leaf the name of God, ineffable in glory. The wearer is considered worthy of such

99 vestments at the services. •Their appearance makes one awe-struck and dumbfounded: A man would think he had come out of this world into another one. I emphatically assert that every man who comes near the spectacle of what I have described will experience astonishment and amazement beyond words, his very being transformed by the hallowed

100 arrangement on every single detail. •For the inspection of the entire scene we climbed the neighboring citadel, and viewed it from there. It is situated on a lofty site, fortified with a number of towers, which in their turn are built of sizable stones right up to the top, according

101 to our information, for the protection of the area around the Temple, •so that, in case of any assault or revolt or enemy attack, no one could force his way into the precincts surrounding the house. There were catapults in position upon the towers of the citadel and

102 a variety of engines; the place dominated the aforementioned precincts. •The towers were, so to speak, guarded by most trustworthy sentries who had given distinguished service to their country. They had no permit to leave the citadel, except at festivals, and then not as

103 a body: They did not allow a soul to enter. •In the case of any order from their commander to admit any visitors to watch, as for example in our case, they observed the order very strictly, very reluctantly admitting us, though only two in number and unarmed, to observe

104 the proceedings at the sacrifices. •Such a procedure was, they said, confirmed by oath, for every man had sworn that, in the necessary and solemn discharge of the matter according

---

t. The actual weight of a talent varied between fifty and eighty lbs.

u. Lit. "height."

v. Lit. "and they do not fail in the attempt."

w. Cf. Ex 28:4, 27–31.

to the oath,[x] they would not admit more than five persons at the same time, although they themselves were five hundred in number. The citadel, they said, provided the whole protection for the Temple, and its founder had in this way secured the advanced protection
105 for the places which we have described. •The size of the city is well proportioned, about forty stades in circumference, as far as one can estimate. The setting of its towers looks like a theater, and that of thoroughfares, too, which stand out, some set lower down, some higher up, all in the accustomed manner;[y] the same applies to the roads which cross them.
106 Since the city is built on a hill, the layout of the terrain is sloping. •There are steps leading to the thoroughfares. Some people make their way above them, others go underneath them, their principal aim being to keep away from the main road for the sake of those who are
107 involved in purification rites, so as not to touch any forbidden object. •There was good reason for the building of the city by its pioneers in appropriate harmony, and their plan was a wise one. The terrain was ample and beautiful; parts were flat, such as the area around Samaria and the neighborhood of Idumaea; other parts were hilly, such as the neighborhood of Judea.[z] Continuous attention to husbandry and the care of the land is necessary, to ensure good yield as a result for the inhabitants. When this attention is paid,
108 all farming is accompanied by abundant yield on all the aforesaid land. •In such of the cities as achieve large size and its accompanying prosperity, the result is abundance of population and neglect of the land, because everyone is bent on cultural delights, and the
109 whole population in its philosophy is inclined to pleasure. •This is what happened with Alexandria, which excelled all cities in size and prosperity: Dwellers from the country
110 migrated to that city and remained there, thus bringing agriculture into decline. •So the king, to prevent their settling, gave orders that their stay should not be longer than twenty days. To those also in charge of business matters he gave written instructions that, should it be necessary to summon anyone to attend, the matter should be dealt with in five days.
111 As an indication of the importance he attached to this, he appointed officials[a2] and their staff by districts, to prevent the farmers and chief men of the city engaging in business,
112 thus diminishing the treasury, that is to say the profits of farming. •We have made this digression because Eleazar has traced out the aforementioned facts for us so well. The zeal of the farmers is indeed remarkable. In fact their land is thickly covered with large numbers of olive trees and corn crops and pulse, and moreover with vines and abundant honey. As for the fruit trees and date palms which they have, no number can be given. They have
113 many flocks and herds of various kinds, with ample pasture for them. •So they perceived clearly that the areas needed to be well populated, and designed the city and the villages
114 accordingly. •A large quantity of spices and precious stones and gold is brought to the area by means of the Arabs. The land is agricultural and well fitted also for commerce; the city
115 is the home of many crafts, and there is no lack of goods imported from overseas, •because of its convenient harbors which supply them, such as Ascelon, Joppa, and Gaza, and also Ptolemais,[b2] which the king founded in a central situation in regard to the aforementioned places, not far away from them. The district is well watered everywhere, has everything in
116 abundance, and is very secure. •The river Jordan flows around it and never dries up. The land originally measured not less than sixty million acres;[c2] subsequently, neighboring peoples overran it. Six hundred thousand[d2] settlers were established upon it, each having one hundred acres. As the river rises, like the Nile, in the days approaching harvest, it
117 waters much of the land, •discharging its waters into another river in the region of Ptolemais, which in turn flows into the sea. Other torrents, as they are called, also flow down, covering
118 the parts toward Gaza and the district of Azotus. •The countryside is surrounded with natural defenses, being difficult to invade and not negotiable for large numbers because of the narrow approaches, with overhanging precipices and deep ravines, and the whole mountainous

---

x. Translating with Mendelssohn, *horkismon,* "oath"; the Gk. MSS read *horismon,* "a fixed course."

y. The conjecture of Redpath, accepted by Thackeray.

z. The text is incomplete here. This is Thackeray's emendation.

a2. A technical term; these officials may be compared loosely with the judges of an assembly.

b2. These are extravagant claims, if they imply that

these harbors were permanent Jewish possessions. The abundance of water (116f.) is also exaggerated.

c2. Lit. "six thousand ten thousands *aroura.*" The *aroura* was approximately the size of the Roman *jugerum* (two thirds of an acre). Contrast Josephus, *Apion* 1.195 (quoting Hecataeus), according to which the area of Palestine is "about three million *arourae.*"

d2. Lit. "sixty ten thousands."

119 surroundings of the entire area being very rugged. •It used to be said that copper and iron mines were formerly sunk in the neighboring hills of Arabia, but in the time of the Persian supremacy they were abandoned because of the false allegation by the responsible authorities
120 of the time that their working was unprofitable and very expensive. •The purpose of closure was also to prevent the resulting ruination of the countryside by the working of the aforesaid mines, and even perhaps its alienation through their tyranny, because they had seized the pretext of moving into the mining areas on account of this allegation which had been made.

     I have explained to you in summary form, brother Philocrates, as much as was needful
121 concerning these matters, and we will next expound details of the translation. •Eleazar selected men of the highest merit and of excellent education due to the distinction of their parentage; they had not only mastered the Jewish literature, but had made a serious study
122 of that of the Greeks as well. •They were therefore well qualified for the embassy, and brought it to fruition as occasion demanded; they had a tremendous natural facility for the negotiations and questions arising from the Law, with the middle way as their commendable ideal; they forsook any uncouth and uncultured attitude of mind; in the same way they rose above conceit and contempt of other people, and instead engaged in discourse and listening to and answering each and every one, as is meet and right. They all observed these aims, and went further in wishing to excel each other in them; they were, one and all, worthy of
123 their leader and his outstanding qualities. •It was possible to perceive how inseparable was their attachment to Eleazar, and his to them. In addition to writing to the king concerning their reestablishment, he urged Andreas to take many[e2] active steps to this end, asking him
124 to collaborate to the utmost extent of our ability. •We affirmed that we would pay good heed to these matters, to which he replied that he was very apprehensive, because he knew that the king, out of his love of culture, considered it of supreme importance to bring to his court any man, wherever he might be found,[f2] of outstanding culture and prudence
125 which excelled his contemporaries. •I understand too that he made the noble statement that by having at his court men of integrity and wisdom he would provide the greatest protection for his kingdom; this was the frank advice given him by his friends for his benefit. The
126 point is amply confirmed in the delegates whom he sent. •(Eleazar) also affirmed on oath that he would not permit the men to leave if any other consideration militated against his own personal advantage; he was only dispatching them for the common improvement of all
127 the citizens. •The good life, he said, consisted in observing the laws, and this aim was achieved by hearing much more than by reading. By these pronouncements and others similar to them he clearly showed his attitude toward them.
128   It is worthwhile mentioning briefly his intimations in reply to the questions raised through us. It is my opinion that mankind as a whole shows a certain amount of concern for the parts of their legislation concerning meats and drink and beasts considered to be unclean.
129 For example, we inquired why, since there is one creation only, some things are considered unclean for eating, others for touching—legislation being scrupulous in most matters, but
130 in these especially so. In reply, he began as follows: •"You observe," he said, "the important matter raised by modes of life and relationships, inasmuch as through bad relationships men become perverted, and are miserable their whole life long; if, however, they mix with wise and prudent companions, they rise above ignorance and achieve progress
131 in life. •First, our lawgiver gave express commands relating to religious observance and justice, and issued precise sets of instructions about them, not only negatively but positively, together with the manifest damages and the visitations sent by God upon the guilty."
132 (Eleazar) began first of all by demonstrating that God is one, that his power is shown in everything, every place being filled with his sovereignty, and that none of the things on earth which men do secretly are hidden from him, but rather that all the deeds of any man
133 are manifest to him, as well as that which is to come to pass. •So by establishing these matters accurately and setting them out plainly, he demonstrated that even if a man thinks of doing evil he would not escape, let alone after the deed is done—thus indicating the
134 power of God through the entire legislation. •This was his introduction: He proceeded to show that all the rest of mankind ("except ourselves," as he said) believe that there are

e2. Translating *polla*, "many things," with *poiēsai*,   "he made many representations to . . ."
"to do." With *parekalese*, "he exhorted," it would read,   f2. Lit. "named."

135 many gods, because men themselves are much more powerful than the gods whom they vainly worship; •they make images of stone and wood, and declare that they are likenesses of those who have made some beneficial discovery for their living, and whom they worship,

136 even though the insensibility (of the images) is close at hand to appreciate. •For if the existence of any god[g2] depended on the criterion of invention, it would be absolutely foolish, because in that case the inventors would have taken some of the created things and given an added demonstration of their usefulness without themselves being their creators. Therefore

137 it is profitless and useless to deify equals. •And yet, even today, there are many of greater inventiveness and learning than the men of old, who nevertheless would be the first to worship them. Those who have invented these fabrications and myths are usually ranked to

138 be the wisest of the Greeks. •There is surely no need to mention the rest of the very foolish people, Egyptians and those like them, who have put their confidence in beasts and most of the serpents and monsters, worship them, and sacrifice to them both while alive and

139 dead. •In his wisdom the legislator, in a comprehensive survey of each particular part, and being endowed by God for the knowledge of universal truths, surrounded us with unbroken[h2] palisades and iron walls to prevent our mixing with any of the other peoples in any matter, being thus kept pure in body and soul, preserved from false beliefs, and worshiping the

140 only God omnipotent over all creation. •Hence the leading priests among the Egyptians, conducting many close investigations and with practical experience of affairs, gave us the title "men of God," which is ascribed exclusively to those who worship the true God, and not to those who are concerned with meat and drink and clothes, their whole attitude (to

141 life) being concentrated on these concerns. •Such concerns are of no account among the people of our race, but throughout the whole of their lives their main objective is concerned

142 with the sovereignty of God. •So, to prevent our being perverted by contact with others or by mixing with bad influences, he hedged us in on all sides with strict observances[i2] connected with meat and drink and touch and hearing and sight, after the manner of the

143 Law. •In general everything is similarly constituted in regard to natural reasoning, being governed by one supreme power, and in each particular everything has a profound reason for it, both the things from which we abstain in use and those of which we partake. For

144 illustration I will briefly give you one or two examples. •Do not take the contemptible view that Moses enacted this legislation because of an excessive preoccupation with mice and weasels or suchlike creatures. The fact is that everything has been solemnly set in order for

145 unblemished investigation and amendment of life for the sake of righteousness. •The birds which we use are all domesticated and of exceptional cleanliness, their food consisting of wheat and pulse—such birds as pigeons, turtledoves, locusts, partridges, and, in addition,

146 geese and others of the same kind. •As to the birds which are forbidden, you will find wild and carnivorous kinds, and the rest which dominate by their own strength, and who find their food at the expense of the aforementioned domesticated birds—which is an injustice; and not only that, they also seize lambs and kids and outrage human beings dead or alive.

147 By calling them impure, he has thereby indicated that it is the solemn binding duty of those for whom the legislation has been established to practice righteousness and not to lord it over anyone in reliance upon their own strength, nor to deprive him of anything, but to govern their lives righteously, in the manner of the gentle creatures among the aforementioned birds which feed on those plants which grow on the ground and do not exercise a domination

148 leading to the destruction of their fellow creatures. •By means of creatures like this the legislator has handed down (the lesson) to be noted by men of wisdom, that they should be righteous, and not achieve anything by brute force, nor lord it over others in reliance upon

149 their own strength. •In cases where it is not meet even to touch any of the aforesaid creatures because of their natural habits with other creatures, surely all possible precautions must be

150 taken to prevent (human) morals degenerating to their level? •Everything pertaining to conduct permitted us toward these creatures and toward beasts has been set out symbolically. Thus the cloven hoof, that is the separation of the claws of the hoof, is a sign of setting

151 apart each of our actions for good, •because the strength of the whole body with its action

g2. Thackeray's emendation *Theos eiē*, "a god may be"; the Gk. MSS have *theiē*.

h2. Or "unbreakable."

i2. Lit. "purities" or "purifications."

rests upon the shoulders and the legs.[j2] The symbolism[k2] conveyed by these things compels us to make a distinction in the performance of all our acts, with righteousness as our aim.

152 This moreover explains why we are distinct from all other men. •The majority of other men defile themselves in their relationships, thereby committing a serious offense, and lands and whole cities take pride in it: they not only procure[l2] the males, they also defile mothers and

153 daughters. We are quite separated from these practices. •The man with whom the aforesaid manner of disposition is concerned is the man on whom the legislator has also stamped that of memory. For example, all cloven-footed creatures and ruminants quite clearly express,

154 to those who perceive it, the phenomenon of memory. •Rumination is nothing but the recalling of (the creature's) life and constitution, life being usually constituted by nourishment.

155 So we are exhorted through scripture[m2] also by the one who says thus, "Thou shalt remember the Lord, who did great and wonderful deeds in thee." When they are (really) understood they are manifestly "great and glorious"; first, there is the construction of the

156 body, the digestion of the food, and the specific function connected with each limb. •Much more, the orderly arrangement of the senses, the operation and unseen activity of the mind, and the speed of its reaction to each stimulus and its invention of arts and crafts involves

157 an infinite variety of methods. •So he exhorts us to remember how the aforesaid blessings are maintained and preserved by divine power under his providence, for he has ordained every time and place for a continual reminder of the supreme God and upholder (of all).

158 Accordingly in the matter of meats and drinks he commands men to offer first fruits and to consume[n2] them there and then straightaway. Furthermore in our clothes he has given us a distinguishing mark as a reminder, and similarly on our gates and doors he has commanded

159 us to set up the "Words,"[o2] so as to be a reminder of God. •He also strictly commands that the sign shall be worn on our hands,[p2] clearly indicating that it is our duty to fulfill every activity with justice, having in mind our own condition, and above all the fear of God.

160 He also commands that "on going to bed and rising" men should meditate on the ordinances of God, observing not only in word but in understanding the movement and impression which they have when they go to sleep, and waking too, what a divine change there is

161 between them—quite beyond understanding. •I have already demonstrated to you the extraordinary nature of the sound reason behind our distinctive characteristic of memory when we expounded the cloven hoof and chewing the cud. It is no chance accident that it has been ordained as part of our very soul; but it is bound up with truth and the expression

162 of the right reason. •After prescribing each set of regulations concerning meats and drinks and matters relating to touch, he commands that no act be done nor word be heard to no purpose and that no use should be made of the power of the (spoken) word to incline toward

163 injustice. •The same principle can be found in the case of beasts, because the character of "weasels," and "mice," and all creatures like them which have been described is

164 mischievous. •Mice pollute and defile everything not only for their own nourishment, but also to the extent of rendering absolutely useless for human beings everything which comes

165 their way to defile. •The species of weasel is unique: Apart from the aforementioned characteristic, it has another polluting feature, that of conceiving through its ears and

166 producing its young through its mouth. •So for this reason any similar feature in men is unclean; men who hear anything and give physical expression to it by word of mouth, thus embroiling other people in evil, commit no ordinary act of uncleanliness, and are themselves completely defiled with the taint of impiety. Your king's action in removing such people—

167 for so we are informed—is amply justified. •I said, "You refer to informers, I suppose, for he systematically imposes upon them punishment and painful death." "Indeed I do refer

168 to them," he replied. "Being on the lookout to murder men is unholy. •Our Law forbids harming anyone in thought or in deed. I have therefore given a brief résumé of these matters, indicating further to you that all the regulations have been made with righteousness in mind,

---

j2. The underlying thought here is that the cloven, separate hoof is symbolic of the Jews and of their being separate and distinct from other people.

k2. The text is corrupt: Thackeray's suggestion *ho semeioutai*, "he signifies by symbols," is adopted here.

l2. Thackeray adopts Schmidt's emendation *proagousi*, "they procure."

m2. I.e. the OT.

n2. The text is corrupt, but the meaning is clear.

o2. Namely "of the Law." This is perhaps the earliest use of "Words" in this manner. Cf. Pelletier, *Lettre d'Aristée, ad loc.*

p2. Perhaps a reference of "phylacteries."

and that no ordinances have been made in scripture without purpose or fancifully, but to the intent that through the whole of our lives we may also practice justice to all mankind 169 in our acts, remembering the all-sovereign God. •In the matter of meats, the unclean reptiles, the beasts, the whole underlying rationale is directed toward righteousness and righteous 170 human relationships." •In my view, he habitually made out a good case for each separate category. For example, in the case of victims offered, calves, rams, and goats, he stated that it was our duty to take them from our herds and flocks, thus sacrificing domestic animals, but not a wild one, to prevent those who offer sacrifices being conscious in themselves of any excess, seeing that they follow the symbol of their legislator. Thus the 171 man who offers the sacrifice makes an offering of every facet of his being.[q2] •Indeed, I consider that, on these matters, details of our way of life are worth narrating. Wherefore, in view of your love of learning, I have been induced, Philocrates, to expound to you the solemnity and characteristic outlook of the Law.

172   Eleazar offered sacrifice, selected the men, and made ready an abundance of gifts for the 173 king. He then sent us forth on our journey with a large escort. •When we reached Alexandria, news of our arrival was given to the king. Andreas and I were introduced[r2] to the court, 174 we paid our warm respects to the king, and presented the letters from Eleazar. •The king was anxious to meet the members of the deputation, so he gave orders to dismiss all the 175 other court officials, and to summon these delegates. •The unprecedented nature of this step was very clear to all, because it was an established procedure that important bona fide visitors should be granted an audience with the king only four days after arrival,[s2] while representatives of kings or important cities are rarely admitted to the court within thirty days. However, he deemed the present arrivals to be deserving of greater honor, having regard to the preeminence of him who had sent them. So he dismissed all the officials whom he considered superfluous and remained walking among the delegates until he had 176 greeted the whole delegation. •So they arrived with the gifts which had been sent at their hands and with the fine skins on which the Law had been written in letters of gold in Jewish characters; the parchment had been excellently worked, and the joining together of the letters was imperceptible. When the king saw the delegates, he proceeded to ask questions 177 about the books, •and when they had shown what had been covered and unrolled the parchments, he paused for a long time, did obeisance about seven times, and said, "I offer to you my thanks, gentlemen, and to him who sent you even more, and most of all to the 178 God whose oracles these are." •They all, visitors and the court present alike, said together and with one voice, "It is well, O King." At this the king was moved to tears, so deeply was he filled with joy. Intensity of feeling coupled with the greatness of the honor received 179 do force men to tears in the moment of success. •The king commanded the parcels to be returned in order, and then immediately greeted the delegates with these words: "It is (meet and) right, O men of God, first to render homage to the documents for the sake of which I have sent for you, and after that to extend to you the right hand of greeting. This explains 180 my first action. •I regard this day of your arrival as of great importance, and it shall be specially marked year by year throughout the time of our life, for by a happy chance it coincides with our victory at sea against Antigonus.[t2] It will therefore be my wish to dine 181 with you this day. •Everything of which you partake," he said, "will be served in compliance with your habits; it will be served to me as well as to you." They expressed their pleasure and the king ordered the finest apartments to be given them near the citadel, and the preparations for the banquet to be made.

182   The chief steward[u2] Nicanor summoned Dorotheus, who was appointed in charge of these matters,[v2] and bade him complete preparations for each guest. "These," he said, "are the king's orders; some of them you still see now." The number of prominent delegates

q2. Lit. "soul."

r2. Thackeray accepts Schmidt's conjecture *pareimen-oi*, "being introduced," for the corrupt *pareimen*, "we may be present," or *parēmen*, "we were present," of the Gk. MSS.

s2. Lit. "on the fifth day."

t2. There are two battles to which reference may be

made, one c. 260 B.C. and one c. 245 B.C. However, according to LetAris, vs. 41, Eleazar wrote to Queen Arsinoe, who died in 269 B.C.

u2. A conjecture of Letronne adopted by Thackeray and Pelletier.

v2. Or "these men," but less probable in view of vs. 183 below.

corresponds to the number of cities, all having the same customs in matters of drink and food and bedding. All preparations were made in accordance with these customs, so that when they came in the presence of the kings they would have a happy visit, with no cause 183 for complaint. •This was their experience. Dorotheus, who had the charge of such matters, was a most punctilious man. He arranged all the furniture of which he had charge, all reserved for this type of reception. He set out the couches in two lines, in accordance with the royal command, because the king had ordered that half should sit at his right hand, and the rest behind his royal couch, leaving no stone unturned in his desire to do these delegates 184 honor. •When they had taken their places, he ordered Dorotheus to carry everything out in accordance with the customs practiced by all his visitors from Judea. So Dorotheus passed over the sacred heralds, the sacrificial ministers and the rest, whose habitual role was to offer the prayers. Instead, he invited Eleazar, "the oldest of the priests, our guests," to 185 offer a prayer. He stood and spoke these memorable words: •"May the almighty God fill you, O King, with all the blessings which he has created—and may he grant you, your wife, and children, and those of the same mind to enjoy all blessings without end all the 186 days of your life." •At these words from this man thunderous applause broke out with cries and rapturous joy, lasting a long time. Then they straightway turned to the enjoyment provided by the foods which had been made ready, all the service being carried out through the organization of Dorotheus, including the royal pages and the king's honored guests.

187   When after an interval he found an opportunity, (the king) asked the occupant of the first couch (they were seated according to age), "How can one keep his kingdom without offense 188 to the end?" •After a short pause he replied, "You would administer it best by imitating the eternal goodness of God. By using longsuffering and treatment[w2] of those who merit[x2] (punishment) more leniently than they deserve, you will convert them from evil and bring 189 them to repentance." •The king commended the answer and asked the next guest, "How should one act in each case?" The reply was, "If he practiced just dealing toward all, he will perform each task well for himself, believing that every thought is manifest to God. 190 Take the fear of God as your guiding principle, and you will not fail in anything." •He received him warmly and asked another guest, "How can one make his friends like himself?" He replied, "If your friends saw that you showed intense concern for the people whom you rule. This you will do by observing how God blesses the human race, giving 191 them health and food and all other gifts in their season." •He commended him, and asked the next guest, "How in his dealings and judgments can one gain the approbation even of those who lose their cases?" The reply was, "If you are fair to all in what you say, and if 192 you take no action arrogantly or in your own strength against wrongdoers. •This you will achieve if you have regard to the method of God. For the prayers of the deserving are fulfilled, but to those who fail, either through visions or acts, that which is harmful to them is demonstrated, for God does not smite them in proportion to their offenses nor by the 193 greatness of his strength, but exercises clemency." •(The king) highly approved this guest also, and asked the next guest, "How then can one be undefeated in the necessities of war?" To which he replied, "If he did not place his confidence in his numbers and his forces, but continually invoked God to direct his enterprises aright as he dealt justly in 194 everything." •He commended this guest also, and asked the next one, "How can one be respected by his enemies?" The reply was, "If in spite of deploying his great array of arms and forces, he knew that these things are useless in bringing anything to a lasting conclusion. For God by granting a truce and thus demonstrating the fear of his power implants it in 195 every breast." •He commended this guest also, and said to the next, "What would be for you (lit. him) the supreme blessing for living?" The reply was, "To know that God is Lord over all, and that we do not ourselves direct our plans in the finest of actions, but God brings to completion the affairs of all men and guides (them) with (his) sovereign power." 196 He acknowledged to this guest also that he spoke well, and asked the next guest, "Supposing one observed all (these principles) in their entirety, how can one transmit the same attitude to his descendants in the end?" His reply was, "By continual prayer to God that he may

w2. A rare word, *blimadzōn,* "inflicting punishment." Zuntz, followed by Pelletier, conjectured *koladzōn,* "punishing," but the Gk. MSS are unanimous.

x2. Lit. "worthy," i.e. of punishment. The Gk. MSS are virtually unanimous here. Zuntz conjectures *aitious,* "guilty," which clarifies the text but is hardly necessary.

receive good designs for what is to be done, and by exhorting his descendants not to be dazzled by fame or riches—the bestower of these things is God himself, and men do not

197 have excess of anything through their own merits." •(The king) commended these sentiments and inquired of the next guest, "How can one endure with equanimity what happens?" His reply was, "Only if you adopted as a basic principle that all men have been created by God to share the greatest ills as well as the greatest blessings, and that it is impossible, being a man, to be without some of both. But God, to whom we must pray, gives good

198 courage." •He was pleased with this guest too, and said that everyone gave good answers. "I will question yet one more," (he said), "after which I will cease for the time being, so that we can turn our attention to enjoying (the banquet) and pass the time pleasantly. In the

199 next six days following I will learn a little more from the others in turn." •Then he asked the (next) man, "What is the boundary of courage?" The reply was, "If the intent were rightly accomplished as planned in acts involving risks. If your intentions are honorable, O

200 King, everything is brought to pass advantageously for you by God." •All the assembled company acclaimed and applauded loudly, and the king said to the philosophers, of whom there were many among them, "I think that these men excel in virtue and have a fuller understanding, because when asked questions of this sort unexpectedly they give appropriate

201 answers, all making God the basis of their argument." •The philosopher Menedemus of Eritrea said, "Yes, indeed, O King, for since the whole universe is governed by providence, and on the correct assumption that man is a creature of God, it follows that all power and

202 beauty of argument has its origin in God." •The king agreed, and this questioning ceased. They then turned to the enjoyment of the feast, and the banquet came to an end when the evening had come.

203 On the day afterward the seating and banqueting arrangements were again carried out in the same order. When the king considered it opportune to put some questions to the men,

204 he proceeded to ask the neighbors of those who had answered on the previous day. •He began a dialogue with the eleventh. (On the previous day ten had been questioned.) When

205 silence reigned he inquired, "How can (one) remain rich?" •After a short pause the guest who received the question said, "If he did nothing outrageous or unworthy of his sovereignty, and did not by his spending contribute to vain and pointless objectives, while at the same time by well-doing attracting the goodwill of his subjects toward him. For the source of

206 blessings to everyone is God himself, who must be followed." •The king commended this man and asked the next guest, "How can one maintain the truth?" The answer to this was, "By realizing that the lie brings terrible disgrace upon every man, and much more so upon kings. For if they have the power to do what they wish, what reason would they have for telling lies? It is your duty, O King, to accept this further principle that God loves the

207 truth." •He warmly approved this man also, and looking closely at the next guest said, "What does wisdom teach?" This next guest replied, "Insofar as you do not wish evils to come upon you, but to partake of every blessing, (it would be wisdom) if you put this into practice with your subjects, including the wrongdoers, and if you admonished the good and

208 upright also mercifully. For God guides all men in mercy." •The king commended him (for his answer) and said to the guest after him, "How might one be a friend of man?" He replied, "By observing that the human race increases and is created over many years and in painful suffering, so that it is your duty neither to inflict punishments easily nor to submit men to torments, knowing that the life of mankind is constituted in pain and punishment. If you bear in mind each set of facts, you will be inclined to mercy, even as God is

209 merciful." •(The king) welcomed this man's answer and inquired of the next guest, "What is the most needful characteristic of kingship?" The reply was, "That (the king) should keep himself incorruptible, practice moderation throughout all his life, respect justice beyond

210 all else, and cultivate such men as friends, because God himself loves justice." •He commended this guest also, and said to his neighbor, "What is the essence of godliness?" He replied, "The realization that God is continually at work in everything and is omniscient, and that man cannot hide from him an unjust deed or an evil action. For, as God does good

211 to the whole world, so you by imitating him would be without offense." •(The king) agreed with him and said to the next guest, "What is the definition of kingship?" The reply was, "Real self-mastery, not being carried away by wealth and glamour, nor having, as a result, overweening or unworthy ambitions—(that would be kingship) if you reasoned well. You

have everything you need[y2] at hand. God likewise does not want anything and yet is merciful. You too must think in human terms, do not desire overmuch, but only what is
212 sufficient for reigning." •He complimented him, and asked the next guest, "How would one think the finest thoughts?" He replied, "By setting justice before him continually in everything, and thinking that injustice is negation of life. For God always provides for the
213 just the greatest blessings." •He commended this guest and said to the next, "How can one sleep undisturbed?" He replied, "You have asked a question on a matter which is difficult to answer, because self-consciousness is impossible in this realm of sleep, and we
214 are confined in this sphere to a sensation which goes beyond the rational. •Deep down in us, our experience of the things that happen (in sleep) is just as if they were actually seen; nevertheless we are irrational insofar as we imagine that we are on the sea and in boats, or that we are carried aloft on wings and fly to other places, and other suchlike things, and
215 we think this is really happening.[z2] •I have stated this as clearly as I can. In every respect, O King, I beg you to lift up your words and actions to reverence for God, so that your conscience may be quite clear that you are following the path of virtue. Do not deliberately
216 show favors unreasonably, nor destroy justice in your exercise of power. •For the most part, indeed, the matters which occupy each man in his waking hours are those on which the mind dwells in sleep as well, and God[a3] directs a man's every thought and action, awake or asleep, when aimed at the highest (goals). Hence the stability which continually
217 surrounds you." •(The king) complimented this guest also, and said to the next one, "Since you are the tenth one to answer we will turn our attention to dinner (after this question)."
218 So he asked him, "How can we avoid doing anything unworthy of ourselves?" •The reply was, "Always have an eye to your glory and prominence, so that you may say and think what is consistent with it, knowing that all your subjects have you in mind and speak of
219 you. •You must really be not the least among the actors! They observe the character which they have to portray and do all their actions consistently with it. Yours however is no acting role, you are really a king, God having granted you authority as your manner deserves."
220 The king responded with prolonged hearty and genial applause, after which they invited the guests to sleep. When he had finished entertaining them, they turned (their) attention to the next day's arrangements for the banquet.
221   On the next day, the same arrangement was made, and when the king deemed it an appropriate time to ask the guests questions, he asked the first of those left over for
222 subsequent questioning, "What is the highest form of sovereignty?" •He replied, "Control of oneself, and not being carried away by one's impulses." He said that it was quite natural
223 for all men to incline their thoughts in one direction (or another). •"The majority are likely to incline toward things to eat and drink and pleasure, but kings toward territorial conquest, depending on the greatness of their standing. And yet, in everyone moderation is a good
224 thing. What therefore God gives you, take and keep; do not covet the unattainable." •(The king) was pleased with this reply and said to the next guest, "How could one be free from envy?" After a pause he replied, "First of all, by realizing that God assigns glory and greatness of wealth to kings, each and every one, and that no king is independent. All of
225 them wish to share this glory, but they cannot—it is a gift of God." •(The king) gave a long commendation to this guest, and asked the next, "How can one despise his enemies?" He replied, "By practicing goodwill to all men and by forming friendships, you would owe no obligation to anyone. To practice goodwill to all men, and to receive a handsome gift
226 from God—this is the highest good." •He approved these words, and bade the next guest answer, asking him, "How can one maintain the honor he received?" The reply was, "If by earnestness and favors he showed munificence and liberality toward others, he would never lack honor. Pray God continually that these qualities which I have mentioned may
227 abide with you." •He complimented him, and asked the next guest, "To whom must a man be generous?" "It is a man's duty," he replied, "(to be generous) toward those who are amicably disposed to us. That is the general opinion. My belief is that we must (also) show liberal charity to our opponents so that in this manner we may convert them to what

---

y2. I adopt Wendland's conjecture *hosa deon*, "as much as is needed.".

z2. The text is here manifestly corrupt. Thackeray's conjecture is translated to provide the sense of the passage.

a3. Thackeray's conjecture *theos*, "God," is here translated; so also "awake," i.e. *egrēgorotos*, for the adverbial form, *egrēgorōs*, in the Gk. MSS.

is proper and fitting to them. You must pray God that these things be brought to pass, for
228 he rules the minds of all." •(The king) consented to these words, and asked the sixth guest
to answer. His question was, "To whom must one show favor?" The answer was, "To his
parents, always, for God's very great commandment concerns the honor due to parents.
Next (and closely connected) he reckons the honor due to friends, calling the friend an
equal of one's own self. You do well if you bring all men into friendship with yourself."
229 (The king) commended this guest too, and inquired of the next one, "What deserves to be
regarded as beauty?" He replied, "Piety, for this is a preeminent form of beauty. Its
dynamic is love, a divine gift which you too have acquired, including in it all blessings."
230 (The king) applauded him very warmly and said to his neighbor, "How can one after a false
step recover once more the same glory?" The reply was, "For you, a fall is impossible,
because you have bestowed on everyone favors which produce goodwill, and this, because
231 it is stronger than the greatest of weapons, produces the greatest security. •If, however,
some do slip, they must avoid in future the course of action which caused their fall, win
friends, and act justly. It is a gift of God to be a doer of good works and not of the
232 opposite." •He was pleased with these words, and said to the next guest, "How can (one)
be free from sorrow?" The reply was, "By pursuing righteousness, doing no harm to
anyone, and helping everyone. The fruits of righteousness make for freedom from sorrow.
233 You must," he said, "pray God that harm may not come to you from occurrences
inconsistent with our conduct—I mean, death, disease, pain, and suchlike. As for you, God
234 fearing as you are, none of these evils would befall you." •(The king) praised him generously
and asked the tenth guest, "What is the highest form of glory?" The reply was, "Honoring
God. This is not done with gifts or sacrifices, but with purity of heart and of devout
disposition, as everything is ordained by God and ordered according to his will. This is
also your attitude, evidence of which can be seen by all from your past and present
235 accomplishments." •With a loud voice the king complimented and encouraged them all;
the audience raised their voices in approval, and especially the philosophers, for these men
far surpassed them in attitudes and eloquence, their starting point being God himself. After
this the king led the way in showing goodwill to them in the toasts.
236 On the following day the arrangements for the banquet were the same as before, and
when it seemed suitable to the king he began to question the guests next to those who had
already replied, and said to the first, "Can (practical) wisdom be taught?" The reply was,
"It is a disposition of the soul, mediated by the power of God, to accept everything of
237 beauty, and to reject its opposite." •He concurred, and proceeded to ask the next guest,
"What makes the greatest contribution to health?" He replied, "Self-control, which it is
238 impossible to achieve unless God disposes the heart and mind[b3] toward it." •(The king)
congratulated this guest, and said to the next, "How can one show toward his parents the
gratitude which they deserve?" The reply was, "By causing them no pain—which is
239 impossible unless God guides the mind[c3] toward the noblest ends." •He nodded approval
of this man, and asked the next guest, "How can one be an attentive listener?" He replied,
"By perceiving that all knowledge is of value, so that in the face of events a man can select
one of the lessons he has heard, counteract the immediate situation and so remedy it[d3] with
the guidance of God—this means that the fulfillment of our deeds comes through him."
240 (The king) commended this man, and said to the next, "How can one avoid doing anything
contrary to the Law?" To this he replied, "By realizing that God has given to legislators
241 the purpose of saving men's lives, you would follow them." •(The king) approved this
guest, and said to the next, "What is the value of the family?" He replied, "If we think
that we are afflicted by adverse circumstances, and suffer as they do, the great strength of
242 the family bond is manifest, •and when that trouble is over, glory and success will be ours
in the eyes of such folk, for cooperation when given with goodwill is of itself indestructible
in the face of everything; with prosperity, there is no further need of their help, except that
243 you must pray God to bestow every blessing." •(The king) gave him the same welcome as
the others, and then asked another guest, "How does fearlessness come about?" He replied,
"When the mind is conscious that it has done no evil, for God directs men toward good

---

b3. "Heart and mind" is an attempt to bring out the meaning of one Gk. word, *dianoian*.

c3. See previous n.

d3. The text is uncertain but the meaning is clear.

244 deliberations on everything." •(The king) approved this man and said to the next, "How
can one have the right reasoning at hand?" He replied, "By always having an eye to the
misfortunes of mankind, knowing that God takes away prosperity (from some) while
245 magnifying others and promoting them to receive honor." •(The king) warmly approved
this man also, and asked the next guest to answer, "How can one avoid having recourse to
idleness and pleasures?" "By having in the forefront of his mind," he said, "that he rules
a large kingdom and leads many people, and it is his duty not to have his mind centered
on anything else but thinking of their care. He should ask God that no part of his duties be
246 lacking." •(The king) commended this man also and asked the tenth guest, "How can one
recognize those who are acting falsely toward him?" The reply to this question was, "By
observing whether their conduct was generous, and whether their orderly behavior persisted
in the greetings and consultations and the rest of the social life of his companions; and
(seeing that) they do not go beyond the proper limit in their entertainments and the other
247 features of their conduct. •God will direct your mind, O King, to the noblest ends." He
applauded them all and congratulated them by name; the company present followed suit,
and so they turned to celebrations.
248   On the following day (the king) seized the opportunity and asked the next guest, "What
is the worst (type of) neglect?" To this he replied, "If a man were neglectful of children,
and did not use every endeavor to bring them up. For we continually pray to God for
ourselves as also for our children, that all blessings may rest upon them. The petition that
children may have some discretion is something which comes to pass only by the power of
249 God." •(The king) said that he spoke well, and asked another guest, "How can one be a
patriot?" He replied, "By adopting the view that it is a noble thing to live and to die in
one's own country. A foreign country produces for the poor contempt, and for the rich
disgrace, as for men exiled for crimes. By doing good to all, while you continually carry
out this policy, you will undoubtedly be a patriot, God giving you favor in the sight of
250 all." •He heard this man, and then asked the next guest in order, "How can one reach
agreement with a woman?" "By recognizing," he replied, "that the female sex is bold,
positively active for something which it desires, easily liable to change its mind because of
poor reasoning powers, and of naturally weak constitution. It is necessary to have dealings
251 with them in a sound way, avoiding provocation which may lead to a quarrel. •Life prospers
when the helmsman knows the goal to which he must make the passage. Life is completely
252 steered by invocation of God." •(The king) gave assent to this man, and asked the next
guest, "How can one be without fault?" The reply was, "By doing everything with
considered judgment, not influenced by misrepresentations, but being your own judge of
what is said, and in your judgment directing aright matters concerned with petitions made
to you, and through your judgment bringing them to pass—that is how you would be without
fault, O King. To have these intentions and to conduct oneself in the light of them is a task
253 involving God's power." •He was cheered by what was said, and asked the next guest,
"How can one avoid anger?" To this the reply was, "By realizing that he has absolute
power, and that any recourse to anger brings death, which is indeed a useless and painful
254 thing to do if many are deprived of life simply because he is lord. •But if all are obedient
and there is no opposition, what will be the point of getting angry? You must know that
God governs the whole universe with kindliness and without any anger, and you, O King,"
255 he said, "must follow him." •He said that he had given a good answer, and inquired of
the next guest, "What is sound judgment?" "Doing everything well," was the reply, "with
due consultation, in your deliberation taking into account as well the harmful features of
the opposite side of the argument, in order that after paying attention to each detail our
deliberations may be good and our object achieved. What is most important, by the power
256 of God your every purpose will be accomplished if you practice piety." •(The king) said
that this man also had done well, and asked another guest, "What is philosophy?" "To
have a well-reasoned assessment of each occurrence," was the reply, "and not to be carried
away by impulses but to study carefully the harmful consequences of the passions, and by
exercising proper and necessary restraint in carrying out what the occasion demands. But
257 in order to have due care for these things, it is necessary to serve God." •(The king)
applauded this man, and asked another guest, "How can one find welcome abroad among
strangers?" "By equal treatment to everyone," he replied, "and by appearing inferior

rather than superior to those among whom he is a stranger. For, in general, God by his very nature welcomes that which is humbled, and the human race deals kindly with those
258 in subjection.'' •(The king) bore witness to these sentiments and asked another, "How will the structure which one builds survive in the future as well?'' To this the reply was, "If his accomplishments by his actions are great and glorious, so that those who see them show forbearance because of their beauty; and if he does not neglect a single one of those who carry out such works, and does not compel the rest to complete their part of the business
259 without any payment. •By considering how God cares for the human race in providing them with health and discernment and suchlike, he will himself do something accordingly by paying some compensation for sufferings endured. For the deeds which are of permanent
260 value are those performed out of righteousness.'' •(The king) said that this man had spoken well, and asked the tenth guest, "What is the fruit of wisdom?'' His reply was, "A clear
261 conscience of no evil done, and of living one's life in truth. •From these result for you the greatest joy and steadfast self-possession, O mighty King, and good hopes in God as you rule your realm with due reverence.'' When they heard this, all voiced their approval with loud applause. After this the king, filled with joy, proceeded to drink their health.
262 On the next day the arrangement was the same as before for the details of the banquet, and when an opportunity presented itself the king began to question the remainder (of the
263 guests). To the first he said, "How can a man avoid giving way to arrogance?'' •The reply was, "By maintaining impartiality, and by reminding himself in the case of each individual that he is a ruler of men and still a man himself. Moreover, God destroys the proud, and
264 exalts the gentle and humble.'' •(The king) commended him, and asked the next guest, "Of whom must one avail himself as counselors?'' "Those who have won experience in many affairs of state,'' he said, "and still maintain untarnished their loyalty to him and to all who share his ways. God manifests himself to such qualities in those who deserve it.''
265 He congratulated him and asked another guest, "What is the possession most essential for a king?'' "The love and affection of his subjects,'' he replied. "By these means the bond of goodwill is unbreakable. As for the realization of these aims, God fulfills them according
266 to his will.'' •(The king) commended him and inquired of another guest, "What is the purpose of speaking?'' "To persuade your opponent in debate,'' was his reply, "by pointing out his errors in an orderly list. In this way you will win over your listener, not being antagonistic but using some commendation to persuade him. And persuasion succeeds
267 through the activity of God.'' •(The king) said that he spoke well, and asked the next guest, "In view of the heterogeneous multitudes in the kingdom, how can one be in harmony with them?'' "By adopting the role appropriate to each one, with justice as your guiding
268 principle—as indeed is now your practice, God granting you sound reasoning.'' •(The king) was pleased with this man, and said to the next guest, "At what things ought one to feel pain?'' To which he replied, "At the misfortunes of our friends, when we see them long-drawn-out and incurable. When they are dead and released from evils, reason does not indicate for them any pain. But when human beings attribute to themselves even what is to their advantage, everyone suffers. The escape from every evil takes place only through the
269 power of God.'' •(The king) declared that this man replied as he ought to have done, and said to the next guest, "How does unpopularity arise?'' He replied, "When arrogance and boundless self-confidence are predominant, dishonor ensues and destruction of good
270 reputation. God controls all reputation, directing it where he wishes.'' •He confirmed this man's answer and asked the next guest, "To whom must one entrust himself?'' "To those who are drawn to you by loyalty,'' he replied, "and not through fear or flattery, with (personal) gain as their only objective. The former is a sign of affection, the latter of disaffection and expediency. The man whose aim is mere success is a natural traitor. As
271 for you, you have the goodwill of all, as God bestows upon you sound counsels.'' •He declared that this man's answer was wise, and said to another guest, "What preserves a kingdom?'' To this the reply was, "Concern and care that no harm shall come upon the multitudes through the officials appointed to serve their needs—which indeed is your policy,
272 God bestowing upon you such noble intent.'' •(The king) gave this man a word of encouragement, and asked another guest, "What maintains favor and respect?'' He said, "Virtue, for it accomplishes good works and renounces evil; just as you keep your noble
273 integrity toward all, having this gift from God.'' •(The king) gave this man a favorable

reception, and asked the eleventh guest (there being two over the seventy), "How can one be peacefully disposed at heart even in war?" The answer was, "By the knowledge that no evil has been committed upon any of your subjects, and that all are fighting for blessings received, knowing that even if they give their lives, you will take care of their property.

274 You do not cease helping everyone, for God has given you the gift of kindliness." (The king) applauded them all heartily and greeted them with acclamation, drank the health of each one, and turned his attention to enjoying (the feast), mingling among the guests with geniality and great delight.

275 On the seventh day, after much preparation, and amid the additional company of many others from the cities—for there was a large number of delegates—the king, at a suitable opportunity, asked the first of those who had not yet been questioned, "How can one avoid

276 being deceived?" •The reply was, "By investigating the speaker, his speech and the subject of it, and by making the same inquiries over a longer period by other means. The possession of an acute mind and the ability to discern everything, that is an excellent gift from God—

277 which indeed you possess, O King." •The king heartily applauded, and asked the next guest, "Why do not the majority of human beings recognize virtue?" "Because all men," he said, "have become naturally intemperate, and inclined to pleasures, as a result of which

278 injustice came about and the mass of greed. •The virtuous disposition, on the other hand, restrains those who are attracted to the rule of pleasure, and commands them to respect

279 self-control and justice more highly. God directs all these matters." •The king affirmed that this man had given a good answer, and asked (the next guest),[e3] "Whose guidance must kings follow?" The answer was, "The laws, so that by practicing justice they may improve the lives of men. In the same way that you by doing this have established an everlasting

280 memory of yourself, following the commandment of God." •He said that this man also gave a good answer, and asked the next guest, "Whom ought one appoint as chief ministers?" He replied, "Men who hate wickedness, and in imitation of his way of life do justice, so as to earn themselves good repute continually—just as you, O mighty King,"

281 he said, "achieve this aim, God having granted you a crown of righteousness." •He loudly approved him, looked toward the next guest, and said, "Whom must one appoint as commanders of his forces?" He replied, "Men of outstanding bravery and justice, who prefer saving men's lives to victory at the reckless risk[f3] of lives. As God showers blessings

282 upon all, you too in imitation of him are a benefactor to your subjects." •(The king) said that he had given a good answer, and asked another guest, "What man deserves admiration?" The reply was, "The man endowed with glory and wealth and power, who deep at heart is the equal of everyone. Just as you by your conduct deserve admiration, God giving you the

283 gift of caring for these things." •(The king) commended this man also, and said to the next guest, "On what matters ought kings to spend most of their time?" He said, "Time should be spent on reading and on the accounts of travels, which have been written and dedicated to thrones for the permanent betterment of mankind. This indeed you do, thereby winning

284 glory beyond the reach of others, with God fulfilling your plans." •(The king) warmly commended this man also, and asked another guest, "What must be one's conduct in relaxation and leisure?" The reply was, "Be a spectator of entertainments which exercise restraint and keep before your eyes things in life done with decency and moderation—that

285 is suitable and appropriate to life. •There is indeed a therapeutic value in these things, for often even from the smallest items something worthwhile stands out. You are well versed in all restraint, and show love of wisdom in your activities, receiving your reward from

286 God because of your moral goodness." •(The king) was well pleased with what had just been said, and addressed the ninth guest, "How ought one to conduct himself at banquets?" The reply was, "By inviting men of learning, with the ability to remind him of matters

287 advantageous to the kingdom and to the lives of the subjects. •Better harmony or music than these you would never find, because these men are beloved of God, having trained their minds for the noblest ends. This is your practice also, all your plans being directed

288 aright by God." •He was delighted at these words, and inquired of the next guest, "What is thought finer by the multitude, to have a king set over them who was once a commoner,

---

e3. Not in the text but required by the sense.
f3. Schmidt's emendation, adopted by Thackeray.

289 or a king of royal blood?'' He replied, ''The alternative which is by nature best. •Some kings of royal birth show themselves hard and cruel to their subjects; much worse—some kings of common origin with their experience of misfortune and their share of poverty, when given rule over people, have turned out to be more harsh than the foulest tyrants.

290 But, as I said before, a noble character which has had its share of (suitable) education is capable of ruling. Just as you rule, O mighty King, and are distinguished not so much by the outstanding glory and wealth of your kingdom but because you excel all men in your

291 moderation and humanity—God having endowed you with these gifts.'' •(The king) congratulated this man also with long applause, and asked the last guest of all, ''What is the most important feature in a kingdom?'' To this he replied, ''To establish the subjects

292 continually at peace, and guarantee that they obtain justice quickly in verdicts. •The sovereign brings about these aims when he hates evil and loves good and holds in high esteem the saving of a human life. In the same way that you consider injustice the greatest evil, and by your just government in all things have won glory for yourself which is

293 imperishable—God granting you to have a pure mind untainted by any evil.'' •When he had finished speaking there was a long burst of applause accompanied by delighted cheers. When it subsided, the king took a cup and drank a toast to all the assembled company and to the speeches which they had made. He addressed them all thus: ''The greatest benefits

294 have fallen on me through your visit. •I have been assisted a great deal by your giving me essential teaching on kingship.'' He commanded that three talents of silver should be given to each one, together with the slave who would hand it over to him. All joined in the acclamation, the guests were filled with rejoicing, and the king turned his attention to festivities unreservedly.

295 If I have dwelt at length[g3] on these matters, Philocrates, I beg your pardon. I admired these men tremendously, the way in which they gave immediate answers which needed a

296 long time (to ponder), •and while the questioner had thought out details in each case, those answering gave their replies immediately one after another—they were manifestly deserving of admiration to me and to the audience, but especially to the philosophers. All who will

297 inherit this narrative will, I think, find it incredible. •To tell lies concerning matters which are being chronicled is inappropriate: If I were to make a single error, it would be impious in these matters. On the contrary, we narrate things as they happened, eschewing any error. I therefore, heartily accepting the force of their argument, have tried to present from the

298 records the details of events at the audiences with the king and at the banquets. •It is, as you know, the custom that, from the beginning of the king's audiences until he retires to

299 bed, a record be made of everything said and done. •This is an excellent and worthwhile procedure, because on the next day, before the (day's) business begins, all that was done

300 and spoken is read out, and if any action needs it, it is corrected. •So this whole account we have produced by accurate reference to the records, as I have said, knowing your keen desire to learn what is of value.

301 Three days afterward, Demetrius took the men with him, traversed the mile-long jetty into the sea toward the island, crossed the bridge, and went in the direction of the north. There he assembled them in a house which had been duly furnished near the shore—a magnificent building in a very quiet situation—and invited the men to carry out the work

302 of translation, all that they would require being handsomely provided. •They set to completing their several tasks, reaching agreement among themselves on each by comparing versions.[h3]

---

g3. Mendelssohn's emendation, adopted by Thackeray.

h3. This passage alone (vss. 302–7) deals with the process of translation and forms a very insignificant part of the whole of LetAris. This section includes the description of the place where the work was done (vs. 302), the translators' manner of relaxing after each day's work (vss. 303f.), their practice of washing hands (vs. 305), with an exposition of the meaning of this symbolic rite of purification (vs. 303), and concludes with the statement that the task of the seventy-two was completed in seventy-two days. The actual work of translation is

discussed in one single sentence (part of vs. 302), which identifies in three stages the whole process:

1. The elders . . . ''completed their several tasks.'' If we hoped for details concerning the method of assignment of these tasks, we are disappointed. If there was anything like a collation of MSS, we are not told, and it is not implied. (See Pelletier, Lettre d'Aristée, ad loc., and Zuntz's article in Jellicoe, Studies in the Septuagint.)

2. They reached harmony in their completed tasks by comparing them. The word used, antibolais, ''comparison,'' sometimes has a technical connotation, but Aristeas does not say or imply that such is the case here. Neither

303 The result of their agreement thus was made into a fair copy by Demetrius. •The business of their meeting occupied them until the ninth hour,[i3] after which they were free for bodily
304 rest and relaxation, everything which they desired being furnished on a lavish scale. •Apart from all this, Dorotheus also provided for them all that was prepared for the king—this was the order which he had received from the king. At the first hour of the day they attended the court daily, and after offering salutations to the king, retired to their own quarters.
305 Following the custom of all the Jews, they washed their hands in the sea in the course of
306 their prayers to God, and then proceeded to the reading and explication[j3] of each point. •I asked this question: "What is their purpose in washing their hands while saying their prayers?" They explained that it is evidence that they have done no evil, for all activity takes place by means of the hands. Thus they nobly and piously refer everything to
307 righteousness and truth. •In this way, as we said previously, each day they assembled in their quarters, which were pleasantly situated for quiet and light, and proceeded to fulfill their prescribed task. The outcome was such that in seventy-two days the business of translation was completed, just as if such a result was achieved by some deliberate design.
308 When it was completed, Demetrius assembled the company of the Jews in the place where the task of the translation had been finished, and read it to all, in the presence of the translators, who received a great ovation from the crowded audience for being responsible
309 for great blessings. •Likewise also they gave an ovation to Demetrius and asked him, now
310 that he had transcribed[k3] the whole Law, to give a copy to their leaders. •As the books were read, the priests stood up, with the elders from among the translators and from the representatives of the "Community,"[l3] and with the leaders of the people, and said, "Since this version has been made rightly and reverently, and in every respect accurately, it is
311 good that this should remain exactly so, and that there should be no revision." •There was general approval of what they said, and they commanded that a curse should be laid, as was their custom, on anyone who should alter the version by any addition or change to any part of the written text, or any deletion either. This was a good step taken, to ensure that the words were preserved completely and permanently in perpetuity.
312 When the king received messages about these events, he rejoiced greatly, because it seemed that the purpose which he shared had been safely accomplished. All of the version was read by him, and he marveled profoundly at the genius of the lawgiver.[m3] He said to Demetrius, "How is it that after such great works were (originally) completed, none of the
313 historians or poets took it upon himself to refer to them?" •He said, "Because the legislation was holy and had come from God, and indeed, some of those who made the attempt were
314 smitten by God, and refrained from their design." •Moreover, he said that he had heard Theopompus declare that, just when he was about to quote in a misleading way some of the previously translated passages from the Law, he had a mental upset for more than thirty days; at its abatement, he besought God to make clear to him the cause of this occurrence.
315 It was revealed to him in a dream that it was due to his meddlesome desire to disclose the
316 things of God to common man, and then—he said—he ceased and so recovered. •I have

is there any reference to the criteria used for obtaining agreement or for resolving disagreement.

3. Demetrius made a fair copy of what was agreed. (There is no mention of any check or method of checking.)

The presentation of the completed work to the Jews is described in vss. 308–11, and to the king in vss. 312–16.

i3. I.e. 3 P.M. The Roman method of calculating is used, beginning at 6 A.M.

j3. The exact meaning of this word here is not clear; an attempt has been made to reflect this ambiguity by the rendering "explication." (See Zuntz in Jellicoe, *Studies in the Septuagint*, pp. 210f.) The word used is *diasaphēsin*, "explication." Its root meaning is that of clarifying, or making clear, without indicating whether the clarification is a translation or a commentary or both.

k3. "Transcribed the whole Law." This is a vague statement; if it had been precise, giving more details of the task undertaken and the exact books dealt with, many of the chief critical problems connected with LetAris

would have been solved. This section (vss. 308–11) describes the steps taken to secure the integrity of the text as translated and to avoid any revision. The attitude to the words themselves, not to mention the inspiration of the version, is noteworthy.

l3. See Pelletier, *Lettre d'Aristée, ad loc.* The term translated "community" was applied to the Jews of Alexandria, among others, and refers to the special status which they enjoyed.

m3. This section describes the presentation of the work to the king. Concern for its preservation is underlined here by the cautionary talk of the experience of Theopompus, with its warning against misquotation, or even quotation, of the Jewish Scriptures. See Zuntz's article in Jellicoe, *Studies in the Septuagint*, p. 223, and Pelletier, *Lettre d'Aristée, ad loc.* It is impossible to decide, with the evidence available to us, whether this warning was prompted by any particular experience of misquotation or misuse.

also received from Theodectus the tragic poet (the report) that when he was about to include in a play a passage from what is written in the Bible,[n3] he was afflicted with cataract of the eyes. He suspected that this was why the affliction had befallen him, so he besought God
317 for many days[o3] and recovered. •When the king had received, as I previously mentioned, Demetrius' account on these matters, he bowed and gave orders for great care to be taken
318 of the books and for their hallowed preservation. •He invited the translators to visit him often after their return to Judea. It was, he said, only fair for their departure to take place, but when they returned he would, as was right, treat them as friends, and they would receive
319 the most liberal hospitality[p3] at his hands. •He ordered preparations to be made for their departure, and treated the men magnificently, presenting to each one three robes of the finest materials, two talents of gold, a cup worth a talent, and complete furnishing for a
320 dining room.[q3] •He also sent to Eleazar, along with their luggage, ten silver-footed couches, with all accessories to go with them, a cup worth thirty talents,[r3] ten robes, purple cloth, a magnificent crown, one hundred lengths of finest linen, vessels, bowls, and two golden
321 goblets for a dedication. •He also wrote with an invitation that if any of the men desired to return to him, there would be no impediment, because he attached great importance to the company of men of culture, and invested his wealth liberally in such men, and not in useless expenditure.

322 There you have, Philocrates, as I promised, my narrative. These matters I think delight you more than the books of the mythologists, for your inclination lies in the direction of concern for things that benefit the mind, and to them you devote the greater time. I will also attempt to write down the remainder of what is worthwhile, in order that in going through it you may achieve the very noble reward of your purpose.

n3. Apparently the first time the term "Bible" was used to mean the OT.

o3. Taken with "recovered," it could be translated "recovered after many days."

p3. Thackeray adopts Mahaffy's emendation *polyōrias*, "hospitality," for *polydōrias*, "presents," in the Gk. MSS. Cf. vs. 270.

q3. Cf. the Roman *Triclinium*, which seems to be what Aristeas has in mind.

r3. "Thirty talents" presumably refers to its value in money, rather than to its weight. (Thirty talents is roughly equivalent to $1,200.) It would make more sense if we read *talantou*, "talent," instead of *talantōn*, "talents," i.e. "thirty cups [each] worth [or weighing] a talent."

JUBILEES

(Second Century B.C.)

A NEW TRANSLATION AND INTRODUCTION

BY O. S. WINTERMUTE

The Book of Jubilees is an account of matters revealed to Moses during the forty days that he spent on Mount Sinai (Ex 24:18). In the first chapter God describes to Moses the apostasy and ultimate restoration of his people, which will take place in the future. The remaining chapters (2–50) contain an extended revelation to Moses by an angel of the presence. The angel recounts for Moses the primeval history of mankind and the subsequent history of God's chosen people until the time of Moses. The author followed the outline of Israel's history that is given in Genesis and the early chapters of Exodus. In retelling the biblical narratives, the author has freely condensed (e.g. the story of plagues on Pharaoh, Ex 7–10 = Jub 48:4–11), omitted (e.g. the blessing of Ephraim and Manasseh, Gen 48:1–20), expurgated (e.g. the notice of Abraham's presenting his wife to foreign rulers as his sister, Gen 12:10–20; 20:2–7), explained (e.g. Reuben's apparent incest, Gen 35:22 = Jub 33:2–20), supplemented (e.g. tales of Abraham's youth, Jub 12:1–9, 12f., 16–21, 25–27), and sometimes radically recast the biblical episodes (e.g. Isaac's covenant with Abimelech, Gen 26:23–33 = Jub 24:21–33).

Jubilees may be outlined in the following manner:

Chapter
1	Introduction
2–4	Creation and Adam stories
5–10	Noah stories
11–23:8	Abraham stories
23:9–32	Digression on Abraham's death
24–45	Jacob and his family
46–50	Moses stories

The introduction and the digression at 23:9–32 are marked off in the preceding outline because they are the two sections in which the author looks beyond the time of Moses to describe what will happen in the distant future. The Abraham and Jacob stories are separated in the outline at the death of Abraham; the author of Jubilees, however, causes them to overlap by having Abraham express a special concern and blessing for Jacob.

The author's treatment of Adam in chapter 3:1–31 is characteristic of much of his writing. In verses 1–7 he gives Jubilees' version of Genesis 2:18–24 with some rearrangement of verses, slight expansion, and minor variations in the text. Verses 8–14 contain halakah for the purification of women after childbirth, which the author relates to the example of Adam and Eve in the garden of Eden. Verses 15–26 contain Jubilees' modified version of the Fall (Gen 3). Verses 27–29 contain extrabiblical traditions about events on the day of Adam's expulsion, i.e. a sacrifice was offered and the animals became mute. Verses 30f. interpret the biblical account of God's clothing Adam (cf. Jub 3:26) as the basis for an eternal decree prohibiting nudity, thereby distinguishing man from the animals.

In the Noah stories, the author has sharply abbreviated the account of the Flood. He has, moreover, inserted a considerable amount of extrabiblical material, including accounts and discussions of the following: the judgment of the Watchers (5:6–16), the feast of weeks (6:17–22), the calendar (6:23–28), the testament of Noah (7:20–39), the division of the world (8:10–9:15), Noah's effective intercession against Mastema (10:1–14), and Canaan's occupation of land belonging to Israel (10:28–34).

The account of Abraham begins in chapters 11f. with a series of haggadic tales about the youthful piety and wisdom of that hero. The end of his account is dominated by a series of speeches, testaments, and blessings in chapters 19:10–22:30. Chapters 13–19 follow the biblical account of the wanderings of Abraham, God's promises to him, and the birth of Isaac. The biblical account is frequently abbreviated to eliminate details such as Sarah's cruel treatment of Hagar in Genesis 16:4–14. The biblical account is also supplemented at points. The author, for example, has inserted an account of the trials of Abraham (17:15–18) and a theophany (16:15–19); his interest in ritual law leads him to report that Abraham celebrated both the Feast of Firstfruits (15:1f.; cf. 22:1) and the Feast of Tabernacles (16:20–31). He also supplies a lengthy discussion of circumcision (15:25–34).

In Jubilees, Jacob is the central figure. He is frequently praised or blessed by Abraham (19:17–25, 27–29; 22:10–24, 26–30), Rebecca (25:11–13, 14–23; 27:11; 35:6, 9–12), Isaac (26:22–24; 27:14–17; 35:13–17; 36:15f.), and God (27:22–24; 44:5f.). In poetic passages (e.g. 23:23; 31:15) Jacob is identified as Israel, the eponymous ancestor of all of the children of Israel. The stories of Jacob and his sons therefore both represent and explain his nation's justified hostility toward Philistines (24:25–33), Canaanites (25:1–10), Amorites (34:1–9), and Edomites (chs. 37f.). Only four sons of Jacob are singled out for special attention. The Joseph stories (chs. 39f., 42–45) are simply a condensed version of the biblical account. Reuben's incest with Bilhah (ch. 33) is given elaborate treatment as a warning against incest. In the case of Judah and Tamar, however, the story is retold in order to permit the confession, forgiveness, and defense of Judah's righteous intent in the matter (41:23–28). Judah is singled out again in chapter 31, where he shares a blessing with Levi, who is prominently treated in chapters 30–32. Judah and Levi, of course, were the two most prominent tribes at the time of the writing of Jubilees.

In chapters 24–29 the author of Jubilees supplements the biblical account of Jacob's early life and sojourn in Mesopotamia. He takes every opportunity to justify Rebecca's favoritism for Jacob over Esau. Jacob represents the highest degree of filial piety whereas Esau was disloyal to his parents.

Chapters 30–32 supplement biblical material with traditions about the priestly role of Levi. In chapter 31 Judah shares a blessing with Levi, but elsewhere Levi tends to be prominent.

Chapter 33 is a Midrash on Reuben's sin in Genesis 35:22.

Chapters 34–38 supplement the biblical account by describing in detail the wars of Jacob. Chapter 34 describes an Amorite war, while chapters 35–38 show how the relationship between Jacob and Esau ended in hostility and the defeat of Edom.

Chapters 39–45 are the writer's condensation of the Joseph stories.

The Moses story begins with a mention of his father in chapter 46, a chapter which explains the transition from an idyllic life under Joseph's rule, when there was no Satan in the land (vss. 1f.), to a scene of harsh slavery at the end of the chapter (vss. 14–16). The death of Joseph and war between the Canaanites and Egypt account for the deteriorating conditions.

The Moses story ends in chapters 49f. with a collection of laws concerning Passover (49), Jubilees (50:1–5), and the sabbath (50:6–13). The events of Moses' own life are quickly sketched in chapters 47f. Although the account is ultimately based on the Old Testament, the Exodus story in chapter 48 has been rewritten to explain how Mastema sought to help the Egyptians.

It is easier to describe the literary character of Jubilees than it is to name its genre. M. Testuz sought to identify its genre in terms of its relationship to five different types of literature: history, testament, apocalyptic, ritual law, and chronology. He concluded that Jubilees was a work of composite genre sharing features of each of the types mentioned. Although "composite" is too vague a term to be entirely satisfying, Testuz's method of describing the genres to which Jubilees is related enables one to provide a fair accounting of the distinctive combination which characterizes the genre of Jubilees.[1]

To the casual reader, Jubilees presents itself as a historical account of past events. R. H. Charles classified it as "Primitive History Rewritten from the Standpoint of Law."[2] The setting, the actors, and the episodes are all depicted in the past time. The most important source which the author used in writing his account was the biblical text, but he supplemented it with a considerable amount of traditional material which came to him in either written or oral form. The final result was a relatively well-integrated account.

Like most writers of history, the author of Jubilees was concerned to review critical events of the past in order to expose their significance for understanding his own contemporary political, social, or cultural situation. In Jubilees 10:29–34, for example, he has preserved an account of how the Canaanites came to inhabit the promised land in order to prove that any contemporary claim to it was illegitimate. His method of explaining contemporary realities is generally in line with methods used in the Old Testament. In Genesis 48, the Old Testament writers explain the division and priority of the Joseph tribes in later Israel by reporting that their eponymous ancestors had been singled out for a blessing by Jacob. In a similar manner, Jubilees accounts for the new political reality of its own time by preserving a report that Isaac had given a special blessing to Judah and Levi (Jub 31:1–22). In both content and method, the Book of Jubilees shares features of a historical genre.

The Catena of Nicephorus (1.175) cites the "Testament" (diathēkē) as the source of a quotation which matches Jubilees 10:21. There is some reason to believe that either Jubilees or some portion of that work circulated in antiquity as "The Testament of Moses." A number of the speeches of the ancestors appear in Jubilees as testaments (e.g. Noah, 7:20–39; Abraham, 20:2–11; Isaac, 36:1–17). Since everything contained in Jubilees was to be delivered to the children of Israel by Moses, one might possibly conceive of it as his testament. In its present form, however, it appears as a revelation to Moses rather than a testament from him.

A book which presents itself as an account of matters revealed by God and his angel to Moses might be identified as an apocalypse, but R. H. Charles did not list it among the apocalypses in his edition of the Pseudepigrapha.[3] Charles's position seems justified. Despite the fact that it shares many features of apocalyptic writings, Jubilees lacks certain characteristics of that genre. In agreement with apocalyptic writings: (1) Jubilees is a pseudonymous work which presents itself as (2) a book of revelations given privately (3) to a heroic figure from Israel's past (4) by an angel (5) in the form of a world history divided into balanced periods of time measured by weeks of years and jubilees (6) in an attempt to instruct the author's contemporaries about matters of vital importance for their own time.

The characteristics of apocalyptic writings which Jubilees does not share are: (1) bizarre imagery, (2) limited esoteric appeal, and (3) preoccupation with the type of eschatology characteristic of apocalyptic writings. The beasts, the horns, the heavenly scenes, the thrones, the rivers of fire, the otherworldly figures with brightly shining bodies, and the many other terrifying objects that populate the visionary world of Daniel, Enoch, and other apocalyptic writings are not found in Jubilees. Granted the presence of angels, demons, and an occasional prodigy (23:25), the world described in the revelation to Moses is very much like the historical world in which the author of Jubilees lived.

The bizarre visions contribute to the esoteric atmosphere of most apocalyptic writings. Behind such documents there is a small community of "the elect"; the writing is directed to them and often contains hostile words for members of the larger religious community from which they have separated. Apocalyptic writings are frequently described as being hidden until a determined time when they will be understood only by those who are pure (Dan 12:9f.). Jubilees is not written from that perspective. Although the revelation is given privately to Moses, and there are suggestions that there was a body of secret lore passed down in the family of Levi (Jub 32:22–26; 45:16), the content of Jubilees' revelation is

---

[1] M. Testuz, Les Idées religieuses du livre des Jubilés, pp. 11f. I am grateful to the editors and J. C. VanderKam for helpful suggestions and improvements.
[2] R. H. Charles, APOT, vol. 2, p. v.
[3] Cf. his table of contents at the beginning of APOT, vol. 2.

directed toward all of Israel and not to just a small group of embattled faithful. The author of the book may have been a member of a relatively small band of Hasidim, but there is no reason to believe that his group had yet broken sharply away from the larger Jewish community.

The matter of vital importance about which the author of Jubilees wishes to instruct his contemporaries is the necessity of strictly obeying the Law in the critical age in which they are living. The writer anticipates an age of increasing blessings in his own time which will result from renewed loyalty to the Law. The author of Jubilees is only slightly concerned with eschatological themes that preoccupy the writers of apocalyptic literature generally, notably, the abrupt end of the age together with wars and natural disasters which accompany it, the appearance of the Messiah, and the inauguration of the messianic age, or the revelation of heavenly realms prepared for the punishment of the wicked and reward of the righteous. Davenport has examined *The Eschatology of the Book of Jubilees* and sharply limited the number of "Passages Intended to Teach Eschatology" (i.e. 1:4–29; 23:14–31). Although there are other passages in which eschatological elements or terminology are present, Davenport has argued that they are not "eschatological in function," i.e. the writer was not primarily concerned to write eschatology.[4]

To the extent that the Torah could be designated a legal genre, one could argue that Jubilees deserves a similar title. In supporting the validity of certain laws, the writer appealed to the fact that they were given in "the book of the first law" (6:22), i.e. the biblical Torah. By doing that, he wished to present his own work as a second book of law given to Moses on Mount Sinai.

The author of Jubilees deals with law in a number of different ways. Sometimes he gathers together a group of laws pertaining to a particular subject, for example, the list of sabbath laws in chapter 50:6–13. Sometimes he is more concerned to elaborate the theological rationale for supporting a particular observance. In chapter 2:17–33, for example, he describes the sabbath as a sign of the election of Israel. The children of Israel are to keep it as a sign of their unique relationship to God and his highest angels—angels of the presence and angels of sanctification—who have kept the sabbath since the first week of creation. He further proves that the family of Jacob alone has been singled out for this honor because God created twenty-two works before the first sabbath and there are twenty-two heads of mankind from Adam to Jacob.

The writer was concerned to demonstrate the authoritative status of his laws. One method was to stress their antiquity. He is careful to note the first observance of particular rites. Thus the feast of Shevuoth was celebrated in heaven from the day of creation and subsequently first celebrated on earth by Noah (6:17f.). Even the practices that were initiated by the patriarchs have eternal validity because they were according to the testimony of the heavenly tablets, and they are to be observed forever (16:21–30). In a more pragmatic manner, he proves the validity of the Law by providing examples of the punishment of those who disobeyed (7:20–25; 16:5–9) and the blessing of those who obeyed (17:17f.; 18:14–16; 39:6f.; 40:8–10). He urged his own generation to follow the laws of God by means of the testimonies of the patriarchs, who regularly exhorted their offspring to avoid fornication, uncleanness, idolatry, drinking or shedding of blood; and to observe justice, righteousness, brotherly love, circumcision, and proper ritual practice (e.g. 7:20–39; 20:2–11; 21:1–25; 36:1–17).

The author's concern for chronological matters is illustrated by the earliest Hebrew description of the book "The book of the divisions of the times according to their jubilees and their weeks."[5] If that title leads one to expect a work seriously concerned with chronological matters, the reader will not be disappointed. The writer has a theological concern for time which is reflected in the structure of the book.

The author believed that there was a theological value inherent in certain special times. Unlike modern man, he did not limit himself to the *quantitative* measuring or counting of days from an arbitrary starting point. For him, the days were also to be divided on a

---

[4] G. L. Davenport, *The Eschatology of the Book of Jubilees*, pp. 47–71, 81–87.

[5] The Heb. description is found in CD, a sectarian document from Qumran. The most complete text was discovered in 1896 in Cairo, but subsequent discoveries of portions of the work at Qumran have led to its identification with that community. The mention of Jub is found at plate 16, ll. 2–4.

qualitative scale with respect to their sanctity. Some days were sacred and others profane. In 6:33–37, the writer describes a situation in which confusion prevails and sacred feasts are observed on unclean days. Although he does not explicitly say why he finds such a situation to be scandalous, he undoubtedly believed that sacred rituals for forgiveness, atonement, and communal well-being could not be valid unless observed at a sacred time.

For the author of Jubilees, the sabbath, which fell regularly on the seventh day of every week, was particularly sacred. A. Jaubert in her study of the calendar has demonstrated that Sunday and Wednesday were also frequently designated as festival days by the author of Jubilees.[6] It was important for the author of Jubilees to be assured that the festivals of Israel would fall on the same day of the week year after year. That was possible only if the readers would make use of the special calendar of 364 days (divisible by seven) that was adopted by the particular Jewish community to which the author belonged. Each year in that calendar began on Wednesday and lasted precisely fifty-two weeks so that the following year would also begin on Wednesday and all of the dates in that year would fall on the same day of the week as they had in any previous year.

The author of Jubilees is an outspoken opponent of the lunar month, which alternated in length between months of twenty-nine and thirty days, because it resulted in a year of 354 days, ten days too few. Nevertheless, his calendar was constructed within a society where the concept of "month" was too important in dating to be disregarded. Therefore the calendar was divided into twelve non-lunar months of thirty days each for a total of 360 days. In order to bring the final yearly total to 364 days, the year was divided into four seasons of three months each with an extra day inserted between each of the four seasons but not counted within any month.

Although months and seasons are accounted for in the calendar of Jubilees, it was the recurring cycle of seven-day weeks that was used as the basic model for structuring larger periods of time. Each period of seven years is referred to as a "week of years" or simply as a "week." Each period of seven weeks of years, i.e. forty-nine years, is designated a jubilee. And it is also possible that the period of forty-nine jubilees is significant for the structure of the book. According to the Book of Jubilees, the Exodus took place 2,410 years after the creation of the world. Adam remained in Eden until the eighth year. Between year eight and year 2410 there are 2,401 full years, i.e. forty-nine jubilees. Testuz has suggested that the period of forty-nine jubilees represents a complete era in world history. If that is true, then the reference to the passing of that period of time at the end of Jubilees (50:4) was written to call attention to the fact that a new era in world history had begun with the giving of the Law on Mount Sinai.[7]

In addition to the literary genres listed by Testuz, it is helpful to see Jubilees in relation to the genre Midrash. The compatibility of subject matter is obvious if simply because a number of episodes in Jubilees are also preserved in later Midrashim. One striking example is found in Midrash *Wayyissau*, which has preserved a detailed account of the war between Jacob and Esau that is similar to Jubilees 37f.[8]

Unfortunately, the nature of Midrash and even its existence as a separate genre is still being debated. R. Bloch's description of its characteristics, however, may serve as a starting point.[9] The first characteristic is that Midrash has its point of departure in the Scripture. Midrash is the form taken by rabbinic interpretation of Scripture. Although not produced in rabbinic circles, Jubilees shows evidence of a very similar type of scriptural interpretation. It may be regarded as a continuous interpretation of Genesis 1 through Exodus 12. It may also be understood as a Midrashic reflection on Exodus 24:18. Pious curiosity wished to know everything that Moses learned during his forty days on Mount Sinai.

A second characteristic of Midrash is its "homiletical" character. In contrast to a precise scholarly exegesis, it is a popular genre. The term "homiletical" reflects a presumed *Sitz im Leben* of rabbinic Midrashim, i.e. the reading and explanation of Scripture within the

---

[6] A. Jaubert, "The Calendar of *Jubilees*," *The Date of the Last Supper*, pp. 15–30.

[7] Testuz, *Les Idées religieuses*, pp. 138–40. Cf. also E. Wiesenberg, "The Jubilee of Jubilees," *RQ* 3 (1961/1962) 3–40.

[8] The text of Midrash *Wayyissau* has been published by A. Jellinek in *BHM*, pt. 3, pp. 1–5.

[9] R. Bloch, "Midrash," *DBS*, vol. 6, pp. 1263–81. ET by M. H. Callaway in *Approaches to Ancient Judaism: Theory and Practice*, ed. W. S. Green (Brown Judaic Studies 1; Missoula, Mont., 1978) pp. 29–50.

synagogue by means of a sermon designed to instruct the hearers. Jubilees was probably produced by someone within priestly circles who drew freely upon analogous instructive materials from an earlier generation. Notice how the reader is instructed by means of explanation, illustrative stories, and morals drawn from the biblical text designed to warn against nudity (3:26, 30f.) and incest (ch. 33) or to encourage the observance of the sabbath (2:16–21), circumcision (15:24–34), laws of purification (3:8–14), and tithes (32:1–15).

A third characteristic is careful attention to the text. Midrashic interpretation, which sometimes wanders far from what we might consider the original meaning of the text, is also capable of pausing to explain the significance of a single word or name. The author of Jubilees is also fond of this method, as, for example, in his treatment of Jared (4:15) and Rew (10:18). The author of Jubilees also has an extensive knowledge of Scripture which enables him to bring to bear widely scattered biblical texts in his discussion of a problem. Compare, for example, his discussion of Passover and the sabbath in chapters 49f.

The fourth characteristic is an adaptation to the present. The method of Midrashic interpretation has two foci: the text of Scripture and the writer's contemporary situation. The writer seeks the word of God within the text for the practical purpose of instructing the life of his contemporaries. That is clearly the intent of Jubilees. His contemporaries are faced with arguments that Jewish ritual law and piety are no longer relevant, that it was a law and piety freely adopted in the past and subject to arbitrary change in the present. Jubilees denies that. For Jubilees, the rites of Judaism are not recent. They were observed by the patriarchs. They are ordained by God and written on heavenly tablets. Gentiles who lived among the author's people did not observe the sabbath. They were uncircumcised. They appeared nude in athletic exercise. Many Jews were undoubtedly tempted to intermarry with them, adopt their customs, and abandon a pattern of Jewish piety. Jubilees preaches against all those evils through the words and examples of angels and patriarchs. Obedience to the Law is the central message of Jubilees.

The fifth characteristic of Midrash is the presence of halakah and haggada. The halakah consists of exegetical conclusions in the form of rules for a pious way of life such as we find collected in Jubilees 50:6–13. The exegetical conclusions of haggada are non-legal. Thus Jubilees is able to answer the question of where Cain found a wife by mentioning the birth of Adam's daughter Awan (4:1). The problem of a talking serpent is set in a new perspective by assuming that all of the animals spoke (3:28) Hebrew (12:26) in the garden of Eden. Haggadic commentary sometimes resolves minor problems, but at times it seems to serve a broader creative impulse. In Genesis 15:11 we are told that Abram once had to drive some birds away. Who sent the birds? Obviously, it was Mastema. In Jubilees 11:11–24 his reputation for combating the birds sent by Mastema has developed into one of the most charming tales in Jubilees. In Genesis 15:5, God orders Abram to look (Heb. *habbet*) toward the sky and count the stars if he is able. Such a passage can easily account for his reputation as a frustrated astrologer, which is reflected in Jubilees 12:16–20.

With regard to the literary structure of Midrashim, A. G. Wright has written "there are several rather diverse forms of literature that are designated as midrash. There are the exegetical, homiletic, and narrative midrashim."[10] The exegetical Midrash sets forth the biblical text and discusses it phrase by phrase. Homiletical Midrashim, on the other hand, begin with a portion of text which forms the basis for a thematic treatment of a specific subject which the Scripture evokes. The theme is frequently repeated and supported by texts drawn from various parts of the Old Testament. Finally, the narrative Midrash scarcely distinguishes between text and comment, but interweaves them to form a continuous narrative. In terms of overall structure, Jubilees is similar to the narrative Midrashim.

Two of the texts most closely related to Jubilees in terms of literary characteristics are Chronicles and the Genesis Apocryphon. Both of these works share certain characteristics of Midrash. Chronicles is similar to Jubilees in its intent to interpret Scripture in light of contemporary concerns. A central concern of the Chronicler was the Temple cultus. In his restatement of traditions recorded in 1–2 Samuel–1 Kings, King David provided the prototype for a proper attitude toward the cultus. Jubilees' dominant concern was for ritual law and Jewish piety. Consequently the patriarchs became the embodiment of piety and of the proper

---

[10] A. G. Wright, "The Literary Genre Midrash," *CBQ* 28 (1966) 133.

concern for sacred festivals. The Genesis Apocryphon is too fragmentary to permit one to discern its overall tendency, but P. Weimar has used it to illustrate the genre of narrative Midrash. In doing so he compared a portion of the text with the text of Genesis and showed how the author expanded upon it, occasionally making use of data found in Jubilees.[11]

Title

The earliest mention of Jubilees is found in the Qumran texts (CD 16.2–4), where the writer reports that an accurate account of Israel's periods of blindness may be found in "The book of the divisions of the times according to their jubilees and their weeks." The Ethiopic version of the text was expanded on that title to describe the work in the following manner: "This is the account of the division of days of the Law and the testimony for annual observance according to their weeks (and) their jubilees throughout all the years of the world."

In Greek, Syriac, Latin, and later Hebrew witnesses, however, the work was generally designated more briefly as either "The (Book) of Jubilees" or "The Little Genesis." The first of these titles probably represents a simple abbreviation of the longer description attested at Qumran. The second title serves as an appropriate description of the content of the work. Just as the Chronicler recapitulated and supplemented many of the episodes reported in the books of Samuel and Kings with a special concern to emphasize the Davidic foundation of many cultic details, the author of Jubilees likewise recapitulated and supplemented many of the episodes found in Genesis with the intention of stressing the eternal validity of the Law and explaining additional cultic details. Since the work is actually longer than the biblical book of Genesis, Charles has suggested that the adjective "Little" (Gk., *ta lepta*) was used to characterize the document's concern to provide fuller treatment of minor details not available in the canonical work.[12]

The significance of other titles attested by ancient authorities is less clear. Syncellus (*Chronographia* 1.5) reported that some people spoke of "The Little Genesis" as "an apocalypse of Moses," but elsewhere (*Chronographia* 1.48) Syncellus uses the title "The Apocalypse of Moses" to refer to a work which is quite distinct from "The Little Genesis."

In the Catena of Nicephorus 1.175 a quotation from Jubilees 10:21 is prefaced by the phrase *hē diathēkē*, which H. Rönsch explained as referring to "The Testament of Moses," a work known from four of the ancient catalogs which were prepared to define canonical boundaries. Although Rönsch may have been justified in interpreting the cryptic *hē diathēkē* as representing "The Testament of Moses,"[13] a simple identification of Jubilees with the work listed by that name in the catalogs has been rejected because the number of stichoi assigned in the catalog of Nicephorus (1,100) is scarcely one fourth the length of Jubilees.

"The Book of Adam's Daughters" was identified with Jubilees in the Decree of Gelasius; and Syncellus (1.7) reported that "The Little Genesis" was also called "The Life of Adam." It is generally assumed that the titles which relate the book to Adam are justified only when referring to certain limited portions of Jubilees. These titles may have originated to designate earlier works incorporated in Jubilees or portions later excerpted from the work.

Texts

In reviewing the textual history of Jubilees, it is difficult to be more succinct than J. C. VanderKam, who outlined its history thus:

1. Jubilees was written in Hebrew.
2. Jubilees was translated from Hebrew into Greek.
3. Jubilees was translated from Hebrew into Syriac.
4. Jubilees was translated from Greek into Latin.
5. Jubilees was translated from Greek into Ethiopic.[14]

---

[11] P. Weimar, "Formen frühjüdischer Literatur. Eine Skizze," *Literatur und Religion des Frühjudentums*, eds. J. Maier and J. Schreiner (Würzburg, 1973) pp. 123–62.

[12] R. H. Charles, *The Book of Jubilees or the Little Genesis*, p. xv. A similar opinion was expressed earlier by H. Rönsch in *Das Buch der Jubiläen oder die kleine Genesis*, pp. 467f.

[13] Rönsch, *Das Buch der Jubiläen*, pp. 479–82.

[14] J. C. VanderKam, *Textual and Historical Studies in the Book of Jubilees*, p. vi. The description of the texts is actually quoted from the table of contents.

Only fragments of the Greek text survive, in the form of quotations and summaries in Greek sources. The Greek fragments have recently been collected by A.-M. Denis and conveniently presented in his *Fragmenta Pseudepigraphorum Graeca*.[15] It is unfortunate that the Greek text has not survived in its entirety because both the Latin and Ethiopic versions were translated from it. The primary basis for assuming that both of the later versions are based upon a Greek text is the internal evidence of Greek loanwords, idioms, and obvious mistranslations. H. Rönsch presented data supporting a Greek base for the Latin version,[16] and R. H. Charles provided a smaller but no less convincing group of examples to demonstrate that the Ethiopic version was translated from Greek.[17]

The existence of a Syriac version of Jubilees was still open to question when R. H. Charles wrote his introduction to Jubilees in volume 2 of *The Apocrypha and Pseudepigrapha of the Old Testament*.[18] The evidence available in 1913 was slight. It consisted of a list of names of the wives of the patriarchs originally published by Ceriani[19] and reprinted by Charles as appendix III to his text of Jubilees. In 1921, however, E. Tisserant published "Fragments syriaques du Livre des Jubilés."[20] The fragments were discovered in an anonymous Syriac chronicle. Since the author of the chronicle used only Syriac and Arabic sources, these fragments bear witness to the existence of a Syriac text of Jubilees. Tisserant found no internal evidence to suggest a Greek antecedent and concluded that the Syriac Jubilees must have been translated directly from the Hebrew.

Approximately one fourth of the Latin text has survived. It was first published by Ceriani in 1861 and re-edited by both Rönsch and Charles.[21] The Latin text, which Rönsch dated in the mid-fifth century, is important because of its date, the length of the surviving manuscript, and the relative care with which it was originally translated. Its editors have noted lacunae and a number of corruptions. Charles, in particular, called attention to the fact that its biblical quotations had been corrected to agree with the standard Septuagint or Vulgate texts. Nevertheless, the Latin text is generally regarded as being almost as reliable a witness as the Ethiopic text. Although Charles was cautious he occasionally relied upon the Latin reading to emend his Ethiopic text. The Latin also provides help in interpreting ambiguous Ethiopic phrases.

The Ethiopic text is the only text that has survived in a form that is virtually complete. Therefore all complete translations of Jubilees are based on some form of the Ethiopic text. The present translation was made from the Ethiopic text edited by R. H. Charles in 1895.[22] That text was based on four manuscripts which he designated A–D. The best manuscript available to him was B, a sixteenth-century text preserved in the British Museum (B.M. Orient. 485), which he used as the basis of his edition.

A number of shortcomings in Charles's edition, particularly his failure to list all of the variant readings in his apparatus, have been noted by W. Baars and R. Zuurmond, who were preparing a new critical edition.[23] Nevertheless, Charles's text has several obvious virtues. His decision to follow manuscript B seems wise. He skillfully treated the biblical quotations in a systematic manner in an attempt to eliminate readings that contain scribal corrections intended to make the text agree with that of the Ethiopic Old Testament. Charles also exercised good judgment in sorting out and evaluating the particular tendencies of the Greek, Latin, and Ethiopic witnesses. Consequently his text is generally superior to any single manuscript, and corrections to his text made without an intimate knowledge of all of the witnesses are apt to be mistaken.

The preparation of a new text will probably require years to complete, because the task is very difficult. Nevertheless, the rationale and need for it are obvious. There is a group

---

[15] A.-M. Denis, ed., *Fragmenta pseudepigraphorum quae supersunt graeca*, pp. 70–102. Cf. also J. T. Milik, "Recherches sur la version grecque du livre des Jubilés," *RB* 78 (1971) 545–57.

[16] Rönsch, *Das Buch der Jubiläen*, pp. 439–60.

[17] Charles, *The Book of Jubilees*, pp. xxxf.

[18] Charles, *APOT*, vol. 2, p. 3.

[19] A. M. Ceriani, *Monumenta Sacra et Profana* (Milan, 1861) vol. 2, pp. 9f.

[20] E. Tisserant, *RB* 30 (1921) 55–86, 206–32.

[21] Rönsch, *Das Buch der Jubiläen*; R. H. Charles, *The Ethiopic Version of the Hebrew Book of Jubilees*.

[22] Charles, *Ethiopic Version*.

[23] W. Baars and R. Zuurmond, "The Project for a New Edition of the Ethiopic Book of Jubilees," *JSS* 9 (1964) 67–74. [Baars and Zuurmond have ceased work on this project. —J.H.C.]

of Ethiopic manuscripts now available which were unknown to Charles. Baars and Zuurmond describe five manuscripts which they examined; all are from European collections. VanderKam has assigned them the letters E–I.[24] More recently, three additional manuscripts have been copied by the Ethiopian Manuscript Microfilm Library Project. They are available on microfilm at the Monastic Manuscript Microfilm Library, St. John's Abbey and University in Collegeville, Minnesota. It is quite likely that additional Ethiopic manuscripts will be discovered.

A new critical text will have to include variant readings from the Syriac text published by E. Tisserant, which were also unknown to Charles. It will have to include all of the Qumran texts, some of which have not yet been published. In the present translation, both the Syriac text and the group of Qumran texts studied by VanderKam have been carefully examined and used to improve Charles's text. No other major change has been made.

Original language

There is no longer any reason to doubt that Jubilees was originally written in Hebrew. That was a view most forcefully argued by R. H. Charles over seventy years ago vis-à-vis the possibility of a Greek or Aramaic original. Nevertheless, there was still considerable latitude for debate until the discovery of fragments of the Hebrew text at both Qumran and Masada. The fragments from Qumran are especially significant. They include the earliest known manuscript, datable on paleographic grounds to the late Hasmonaean period (c. 75–50 B.C.), and their presence at Qumran called immediate attention to the many close parallels between the views of the author of Jubilees and the teaching within that community. The manuscripts from Qumran are near enough to the date of the text's composition and close enough to its original social matrix virtually to exclude the possibility that they are translations from some other language. Consequently, it is generally maintained that the text was written in Hebrew.

Date

The discoveries at Qumran have also helped narrow the limits for dating Jubilees. They provide new data for determining the latest possible date. Jubliees must have been written before: (1) the date of the earliest fragment of the text discovered at Qumran; (2) the date of Qumran documents which depend on Jubilees; (3) the date of the split between the Maccabean establishment and the sect which settled at Qumran.

The earliest published fragment of Jubilees from Qumran is dated in the late Hasmonaean period (c. 75–50 B.C.), but VanderKam has reported that two unpublished fragments (4Qm16Jub[a] and 4Qm17Jub[b]) have been dated by F. M. Cross to 125–75 B.C., with circa 100 as the preferred date. VanderKam justly observes that it is unlikely that the two unpublished fragments, which are written in a semicursive script, belong to the original manuscript of Jubilees. Therefore, paleographic dating of the earliest fragments points to a date prior to 100 B.C.[25]

There are two texts from Qumran which may have used Jubilees. In the case of the Damascus Rule (CD), most scholars are convinced that there is an explicit reference to Jubilees (CD 16.2–4). The earliest Hebrew fragment of the Damascus Document is dated to 75–50 B.C., but its composition is certainly earlier than that; perhaps it was composed at the end of the second or beginning of the first century B.C. That simply confirms a date prior to 100 B.C. for Jubilees. The Genesis Apocryphon (1QapGen) clearly shares common traditions and a common biblical text with Jubilees. Scholars are still debating the precise nature of the relationship between the two documents. It is unlikely that the Genesis Apocryphon served as a source for Jubilees; J. Fitzmyer, for example, claims that the Genesis Apocryphon "depends on . . . Jubilees."[26] By assuming that priority, P. Weimar

[24] VanderKam, *Textual and Historical Studies*, pp. 14f.

[25] Ibid., pp. 215f. [My latest information is that there are now nineteen Eth. MSS of Jub. —J. C. VanderKam.]

[26] J. A. Fitzmyer, *The Genesis Apocryphon of Qumran Cave 1: A Commentary*. (Biblica et Orientalia 18A; Rome, 1966) p. 14.

was able to provide an impressive illustration of the manner in which the writer of the Genesis Aprocryphon made use of Jubilees.[27] The date of the Genesis Aprocryphon is uncertain, but it was probably composed in the first century B.C. By itself, the evidence provided by the Genesis Apocryphon is less helpful for dating Jubilees than the witness of the Damascus Document, but taken together, the fact that two separate first-century writers treat Jubilees as an authoritative source indicates that Jubilees was already sufficiently established to warrant that status.

A still earlier date can be supported, but it depends on a different, somewhat less objective type of evidence. The majority of scholars who have studied the relationship between Jubilees and the doctrines of the sect at Qumran have noted a strong kinship. The parallels are overwhelming. They include numerous similarities in theology, ritual, law, and piety, as well as outright literary dependence and a common official calendar. Differences between Jubilees and Qumran in matters of eschatology (viz. messiah), ritual practice (viz. baptism and communal meals), details of theology, and attitudes toward the Temple and war were pointed out by B. Noack in an attempt to correct the assumption that Jubilees was written at Qumran.[28] It is more accurate to think of Jubilees as a work that was produced within a community of Hasidim or Essenes prior to the withdrawal of some of the members of the sect to Qumran.

The most significant difference between Jubilees and the writings from Qumran for the purpose of dating is the fact that Jubilees does not reflect any significant break with the larger national body whereas the Qumran sect has broken with the establishment and its priesthood, which it judges apostate. Although the author of Jubilees was one of the spiritual parents of the Qumran sect, he accepted the establishment and was filled with the joy of Maccabean triumphs and hopes for the future. Years ago R. H. Charles noted the proestablishment stance in Jubilees. He thought that Jubilees was written by a Pharisee, so he concluded that "it was written before the public breach between Hyrcanus and the Pharisees."[29] In the light of Qumran, the author is no longer considered to be a Pharisee. He belongs within the Hasidic or Essene tradition. It is therefore necessary to conclude that Jubilees was written before the breach between the Maccabeans and the Essenes. Unfortunately, that breach was not public. Our evidence for it comes from cryptic references to the "wicked priest" in the Qumran documents. The split probably occurred in the time of Jonathan or Simon (160–134 B.C.). Since the issue was a dispute over the high priesthood, two dates compete for attention: 152 B.C., the year that Jonathan was appointed high priest by Balas, and 140 B.C., the year that Simon was recognized as high priest by the people (1Mac 14:34–49). Since Jubilees was written before the split, the latest possible date should be set at either 140 B.C. or 152 B.C., depending on the identification of the "wicked priest."

A certain amount of subjective judgment is also involved in determining the earliest possible date for the writing of Jubilees. The work can be no earlier than the latest historical event to which it alludes. The majority of scholars assume that the writer composed his account of Jacob's wars against the Amorites and Edomites (chs. 34, 38) under the influence of certain Maccabean triumphs to which he alludes. In the war against the Amorites, for example, Jubilees describes the participation of the king of Bethhoron and confederates from the immediate area (34:4–7), recalling Judas Maccabeus' smashing victory over Nicanor at Bethhoron (1Mac 7:39–50). Both Judas and John Hyrcanus defeated the Edomites. Charles, who would set the earliest possible date for Jubilees as late as the breach between the Pharisees and Hyrcanus, assumed that Jubilees contained allusions to the subjugation of Edom by that ruler.[30] That was not a necessary conclusion, however, since the account in Jubilees could equally have been influenced by historical campaigns of Judas, which are noted in 1 Maccabees 5:3, 65. Recently, VanderKam carefully studied all the apparent allusions to Maccabean history and concluded that "the latest events to which I can find reference in Jubilees are Judas Maccabeus' wars in 161 B.C."[31] If that is correct, the date of Jubilees must be set between 161–140 B.C.

---

[27] Weimar, *Literatur und Religion des Frühjudentums*, pp. 144–55.
[28] B. Noack, "Qumran and the Book of Jubilees," *SEA* 22–23 (1957–58) 191–207.
[29] Charles, *APOT*, vol. 2, p. 6.
[30] Charles, *The Book of Jubilees*, p. lxii.
[31] VanderKam, *Textual and Historical Studies*, p. 283.

Provenance

The author of Jubilees was a Jew who lived in Palestine. That view may be supported by a number of observations. The fact that he wrote in Hebrew would favor a Palestinian background. His writing may reflect an awareness that not all of his contemporaries were thoroughly familiar with the language because he reports that even father Abraham had to learn Hebrew. Nevertheless, he understood that a knowledge of Hebrew was absolutely necessary for the study of sacred books (12:25–27). He made use of a Palestinian biblical text. The earliest external witness to his work is found in a writing from Qumran (CD). He has special praise for the land of Lebanon from the Jordan to the sea (10:29). Jerusalem was holy (1:28), and Zion was the navel of the earth (8:19). Although his knowledge of world geography in chapters 8–10 is seriously deficient at many points, it is clear that he is more familiar with the area assigned to Shem than that assigned to Ham or Japheth. Within the area assigned to Shem, his knowledge of Canaan from the Jordan to the sea (10:29) is the greatest. Despite the fact that many place names have been corrupted in the transmission of the Ethiopic text, scholars have been able to reconstruct most of them, indicating that the author of Jubilees had a detailed knowledge of many cities and towns within ancient Canaan.

The author probably belonged to a priestly family. That may account for his special interest in the origin of festivals, the determination of sacred times, and his incessant concern for ritual details (21:7–18). In the supplemental material which he brings to the Genesis account, Levi is given priority over the sons of Jacob (chs. 30–32), even being set before Judah (31:12f.). Levi is also the one who is entrusted with a library of books (45:16) containing heavenly lore revealed to Jacob (32:21–26) and sacred traditions passed down from earlier patriarchs. One of the duties of Levi was to preserve and renew the books. If our author defines his own vocation at any point, it must be here. He undoubtedly saw himself as part of a continuous chain of priestly writers going back to Levi. The idea of renewing ancestral books probably implied a license to do more than just make new copies. He was commissioned to bring ancient traditions up to date.

The author's strict interpretation of the Law, his appeal to a distinct set of traditions which reported the cultic life and piety of the patriarchs, his hostility to surrounding nations, his abhorrence of gentile practices, his insistent demand for obedience to God's commands in a time of apostasy, his belief that God was about to create a new spirit within his people which would make possible a proper relationship between God and Israel, and his preoccupation with adherence to a calendar of 364 days are some of the characteristics which identify him as part of a zealous, conservative, pious segment of Judaism which was bound together by its own set of traditions, expectations, and practices. It is well known that such groups played a significant role in the struggles of the Maccabean age. First Maccabees 2:29–42 reports about one group that withdrew to the wilderness in their search for justice. When they were attacked on the sabbath by troops of the Seleucid king, they refused to defend themselves because war on the sabbath was forbidden. A similar prohibition is found in Jubilees 50:12. The group described in 1 Maccabees was slaughtered, but when Mattathias, the leader of the Maccabean revolt, made a public display of mourning for them, other pious groups of Hasidim joined forces with him. The spiritual genealogy of both the Pharisees and Essenes should probably be traced back to those groups of pious Hasidim. The author of Jubilees belonged to the Hasidic or Essene branch of Judaism.

Historical importance

Although Jubilees presumes to give an account of the history of the world prior to the time of Moses, it does not add any trustworthy information beyond that which may incidentally be contained in the biblical writings. That does not mean that all of the supplemental information presented in Jubilees was composed on the basis of the author's imagination or his own contemporary history. It is obvious that he used a number of earlier sources. Unfortunately, all of the traditions were transposed into a patriarchal setting whether they belonged there or not. Thus accounts of wars against the Amorites and Edomites, which the author reinterpreted in light of the Maccabean battles, undoubtedly had a long prehistory in extrabiblical traditions. In Jubilees, however, they were radically recast and set within the patriarchal period, thus obscuring them and depriving them of their value as a witness to any original historical event that they may have once had.

As a witness to the author's own time, Jubilees is extremely important. Once the approximate date of Jubilees has been determined, it provides an excellent original source for the study of the social, political, and religious views of one group of Hasidim who lived near the middle of the second century B.C. It can, for example, provide evidence of Jewish reaction to some of the policies of Antiochus IV. According to 1 Maccabees, he was tolerant of apostate Jews who joined his cause, permitting them to build a gymnasium where they could imitate gentile ways, exercising in the nude, and disguising "their circumcision" (1Mac 1:14f.). Both of those evils are sharply criticized in Jubilees (3:31; 15:33f.). Antiochus is also credited with directing other actions that certainly must have outraged the community to which the author of Jubilees belonged. The king's orders led to the shedding of innocent blood (1Mac 1:37; cf. Jub 7:23–29), the banning of sacrifices (1Mac 1:45; cf. Jub 32:4–22), the profaning of the sabbath and festival days (1Mac 1:46; cf. Jub 23:19; 6:37), the prohibiting of circumcision (1Mac 1:47; cf. Jub 15:24–29), and a burning of books (1Mac 1:56; cf. Jub 45:16).

If Jubilees is dated between 161–140 B.C., it becomes an important primary source for studying the evolution of the various religious parties which became prominent in Judea just before the birth of Christ. Its kinship with the sect at Qumran and its relationship to certain other writings has been described by F. M. Cross in the following terms:

> The concrete contacts in theology, terminology, calendrical peculiarities, and priestly interests, between the editions of Enoch, Jubilees, and the Testaments of Levi and Naphtali found at Qumran on the one hand, and the demonstrably sectarian works of Qumran on the other, are so systematic and detailed that we must place the composition of these works within a single line of tradition.[32]

As an early witness to that "line of tradition," Jubilees may be understood to be a product of one of the "proto-Essene (presumably Hasidic) communities" mentioned elsewhere by Cross.[33] There are also parallels between Jubilees and later rabbinic attitudes. We can no longer agree with Charles's judgment that the author was "a pharisee of the straitest sect,"[34] but his view was not absurd. Before the discovery of the library at Qumran, it was quite reasonable to read Jubilees in light of the more abundant literature from Pharisaic circles. That a kinship exists between Jubilees and later works by the Pharisees is due to the fact that the Pharisees also had roots in the Hasidic movement of the Maccabean age. To the degree that Jubilees accurately reflects a proto-Essene position, it also provides evidence that at the time of its writing the boundaries between Pharisees and Essenes were not as sharply drawn as they were a hundred years later. Finally, if Milik is correct in tracing the early Enoch books to Samaritan circles, the obvious relationships between Jubilees and Enoch raise interesting questions about the openness of the Hasidim to Samaritan influences during the Maccabean period.[35]

Theological importance

There are a number of excellent discussions of the theology of Jubilees. One of the finest is that of M. Testuz.[36] He was able to go beyond most earlier studies because he saw clearly the nature of the theological parallels between Jubilees and Qumran. G. Davenport has also made an important contribution to the study of Jubilees by carefully examining its eschatology.[37] As a result of his study it would appear that the writer of Jubilees was scarcely interested in events which might occur beyond his own historical lifetime. He is

[32] F. M. Cross, *The Ancient Library of Qumran and Modern Biblical Studies* (rev. ed.; Garden City, N.Y., 1961) p. 199.

[33] Ibid., p. 200.

[34] Charles, *The Book of Jubilees*, p. lxxiii.

[35] J. T. Milik, *The Books of Enoch: Aramaic Fragments of Qumrân Cave 4* (Oxford, 1976) pp. 9f., 13.

[36] Testuz, *Les Idées religieuses.*

[37] Davenport, *The Eschatology of the Book of Jubilees.*

not concerned to describe a future Messiah, to give a detailed account of a coming messianic age, or to discuss at length an afterlife. The first concern of the eschatological passages in Jubilees is to teach that God is now about to restore a proper relationship with his people and to call the readers to obedience. If one is aware of the new information to be gleaned from the Qumran texts and adopts a cautious view regarding the interpretation of the eschatological passages, most of the earlier discussions of the theology of Jubilees may be read with profit. Only the briefest outline is possible in the present work.

In general, the writer of Jubilees expected his readers to share a common view of God derived from the Old Testament, together with all which that implied about the power, glory, majesty, wisdom, justice, creativity, compassion, or wrath of an ethical deity who had called forth a unique people to serve him in righteousness. His view of God's intent for Israel vis-à-vis the other nations, however, falls short of Second Isaiah's "light of the nations" (Isa 42:6) or Jonah's mission to Nineveh, siding instead with the Chronicler in calling for a rejection of all things gentile. In describing God's control of history, he has introduced certain nuances which lead in the direction of a rather strict determinism. It is clear that the author assumed that men were both free and culpable for their sins. Nevertheless, when he makes God the speaker of the prophetic words in chapter 1, they are no longer prophetic words. They become facts present in the foreknowledge of God. Prophetic words are not necessarily inevitable; but there is no avoiding what God knows to be the future. The fact that certain predictions are inscribed on heavenly tablets (5:13) implies the same fixed order of events. Even the evil forces of the world are fixed by God. Mastema, who has been allotted exactly one tenth of the demons born in the days of Noah (10:9), may be bound by God at will (48:15).

Between God and man, Jubilees introduces us to a host of angels and demons. The author stands at the beginning of a long history of speculation regarding that realm. In his account, only the prince of evil spirits, Mastema (= Satan), is named (10:8). The angels are described only by rank. There are two high ranks of angels: the angels of the presence and the angels of sanctification. They are born circumcised (15:27) and are therefore able to participate with Israel in all of her rites and feasts, including the sabbath rest (2:18). Lest the world go uncared for on the seventh day, however, God also created lesser angelic powers such as the spirits of wind, darkness, snow, and heat (2:2). There is also a class of angels known as Watchers, who were sent to instruct men and to do righteousness (4:15), but they corrupted themselves by having intercourse with the daughters of men who bore them giants (7:21f.). The Watchers also fathered a host of evil demons who plagued the sons of Noah (10:1–6).

Both angels and demons have their proper work to do within the world. Angelic spirits control the forces of nature within the world (2:2f.). Good angels teach men skills (3:15; 12:26f.), inform them of God's will (12:22), test them (19:3), report their sins to God (4:6), announce future events (16:1–4, 16), reveal secret cosmic lore (4:21), bind up evil spirits (10:9f.), and actively assist those who are attacked by the forces of evil (48:4, 13). Good angels may be assigned to guard men (35:17), but those assigned to direct the gentile nations lead them astray (15:31). The Watchers were originally good angels (4:15) who fell into sin with the daughters of men and were bound in the midst of the earth (5:6–11). Their children, the giants, were destroyed, but the spirits of their children (1En 15:8f.) wander the earth as demons, causing diseases (10:11f.), leading men astray (10:1f.), seeking human sacrifice, and encouraging idolatry (1:11).

The author's interest in demonic powers provided a practical way of dealing with the problem of evil: How can one affirm both the omnipotence and goodness of God in the presence of manifest evil? In other words, where does evil come from? The author of Jubilees would teach us three things about evil: (1) It is superhuman; (2) but it is not caused by God; (3) therefore it comes from the angelic world, which has suffered a breach from God's good order. The author of Jubilees does not blame Adam for the continuing diseases and sins of mankind. The cause of evil is clearly superhuman, and Jubilees continually stresses the helplessness of men (10:1f., 8) and nations (15:31) before its power. Nevertheless God cannot be held responsible. The author of Jubilees is so certain of that point that he can recast the biblical traditions with confidence. It was Mastema and not God who tempted Abraham to kill Isaac (17:15–18:13; cf. Gen 22:1–19), who provoked the Egyptians to pursue Israel (48:12; cf. Ex 14:8f.), and who sought to kill Moses on the way to Egypt (48:2f.; cf. Ex 4:24). The origin of Mastema is not separately discussed in Jubilees, but the spirits which serve him are all traced to a cosmic breach which occurred when the Watchers violated their natural order to mate with the daughters of men. The story of the fall of Adam is repeated in Jubilees, but it is the fall in the superhuman or semidivine realm that most readily explains the presence of evil in the world since the time of the Flood.

The dualism of the angelic world was reflected in the world of men. The good kingdom was identified with the children of Israel. God, their Father (1:28), selected them as a special people above all peoples (2:21) to be marked by circumcision (15:11) and to participate with him and his highest angels in the sabbath and all of the other festivals of Israel. The other nations are separated from God because he has placed spirits in authority over them to lead them astray. God alone rules Israel (15:32f.). Israel is qualitatively different from all other nations. In the context of such an understanding, the hostility between Israel and surrounding nations may be seen as a conflict between good and evil. The Lord destroyed the Rephaim because of their evil (29:11). The Egyptians were motivated to pursue Israel by the prince of evil, Mastema (48:12). The Philistines were cursed by Isaac (24:28–33), and the Canaanites were described as being more cursed than all the sons of Noah for illegitimately seizing the land that Israel was to occupy (10:32). The Shechemites (30:4–6), the Amorites (34:1–9), and the Edomites (38:1–10) were all destroyed by the righteous sons of Israel. On a theological level, we are to understand that those who do not belong to the children of the convenant belong to the children of destruction (15:26). It is possible, of course, for even the children of Israel to be subject to attack by the spiritual powers of evil (48:2f.). In such a case, the good angels of God will save them (48:4), and God himself will call to account both his angels and spirits in order to preserve and bless the children of Israel (15:32). When the children of Israel sin, however, God provides a day in which they may repent and be forgiven (5:17f.).

The priestly author of Jubilees presents his theological work with the authority of one who understands himself to be representing "the normative, orthodox" position. He knows of periods of apostasy when the children of Israel will go astray (1:8–11). In some cases sinners will act so outrageously that they will have to be cut off from the covenant and left without pardon or forgiveness (15:34). Nevertheless, he is writing at a time when he expects a general return to the "normative" position which he represents (23:26). Undoubtedly, his hope was frustrated. It would not be too long before his views would be ignored or contested, particularly his view of the calendar. Chapter 6:34–38 bears witness to the fact that there were many who did not observe it in his own time. He accuses them of sharing the ignorance and errors of the gentiles (6:35), but there is no evidence that they were in any position to threaten or prevent his own proper observance of festival times. He does not give us any reason to believe that he belonged to a small sectarian minority. It was only at a later time when intense party strife broke out in the struggles for the office of high priest and the rival lunar calendar was fixed in such a way as to exclude competition that those who followed the calendar of Jubilees would have to acknowledge their minority position. The theology of Jubilees has a uniqueness over against the views put forth by other groups, but it was not directed toward a small embattled minority. It was a theology appealing to all of the pious sons of Israel to return to strict obedience to the law and a proper observance of sacred times in accordance with God's covenant.

Relation to canonical books

The author of Jubilees had before him most of the books of the Old Testament. His use of the Pentateuch is extensive. Genesis 1 through Exodus 24:18 provided the major source used by the author, but he also used legal and cultic data found elsewhere in the first five books. In several passages the author refers or alludes to the book of the "first law" (6:22; 30:12, 21; 50:6). The most obvious identification for that book of law is the Pentateuch.

The author was also familiar with the books contained in that portion of the Hebrew Bible known as the Prophets. He makes use of expressions and data familiar from Kings, Isaiah, Jeremiah, Ezekiel, and several of the twelve minor prophets. Examples are cited in the margin of the translation of Jubilees which follows.

The author's familiarity with books contained in the portion of the Hebrew Bible known as the Writings is less clear. Granted the date of Jubilees and its provenance, he was probably not familiar with the Book of Esther. The marginal citations indicate a familiarity with Psalms and the work of the Chronicler (1Chr, 2Chr, Ezra, Neh). The temptations of Abraham in Jubilees 17f. clearly reflect the motif found in Job. Evidence for his familiarity with other books in the collection of Writings is not clearly present.

Evidence for the use of data appearing in Jubilees by writers of the New Testament is conveniently summarized by Charles. On the basis of the evidence which he provided,[38] it is clear that Paul and the authors of Luke-Acts, James, Hebrews, and 2 Peter were familiar with expressions and ideas that appear in Jubilees.

Relation to apocryphal books

The relationship of Jubilees to other apocryphal writings remains an open and perplexing question. The recovery of fragments of both previously known and newly discovered apocryphal works from Qumran has led to a general reappraisal of many of the documents. In the case of Jubilees, the discoveries led to a new understanding of its proto-Essene provenance and support for dating the work prior to the Essene split with the Maccabean rulers. In the case of Enoch and the Testaments of the Twelve Patriarchs, the finds at Qumran have opened up a new discussion of the evolution of those documents. Inasmuch as they are composite works, the question of dating the separate parts of each text has generated considerable debate.[39] In the case of the so-called Hymn to the Creator from the Qumran Psalms Scroll and the better-known Genesis Apocryphon (1QapGen), we are confronted with two entirely new texts which are very closely related to Jubilees. A clear understanding of their relationship to Jubilees would require a firm dating for both texts.

Inasmuch as Jubilees was part of a rather vast library of texts of uncertain date which were either used or written by the sect at Qumran, it will require much more research before the relative relationships between interdependent texts can be clearly demonstrated. In the process of publishing additional fragments from Qumran many new parallels to Jubilees will undoubtedly be uncovered. It will also require time to fix their relationship precisely. In the meantime, the best that can be done is to offer reasonable suggestions in the light of our present knowledge.

It is generally agreed that Jubilees is dependent on parts of the book of Enoch (1En). At the same time, it seems likely that the later portions of Enoch may be based on Jubilees. The question has been dealt with most recently by J. T. Milik, who argues that only four books of the later Enochic Pentateuch were known at Qumran. The four were: (1) a larger version of the Astronomical Book (1En 72–82); (2) the Book of Watchers (1En 1–36); (3) the Book of Dreams (1En 83–90); and (4) the Epistle of Enoch (1En 91–108). From that list, he dated the first three prior to Jubilees, following Charles in the assumption that Jubilees made use of them. With regard to the epistle, Milik assumed that it depended on Jubilees.[40]

The relationship which exists between the Aramaic apocryphal text of Levi, the Testament of Levi, and the Book of Jubilees has been most recently studied by A. Hultgård. It is his opinion that the apocryphal text and Jubilees depend on a common source. He claims, however, that the author of the Testament of Levi made use of the Aramaic apocryphal text of Levi in writing his testament. Thus the parallels which are noted between Jubilees and the Testament of Levi are less immediate.[41] That interpretation appears justified in light of our present understanding of the texts.

---

[38] Charles, *The Book of Jubilees*, pp. lxxxiii–lxxxv.

[39] The problem of the evolution of Jub has also been raised anew. G. L. Davenport began the investigation in his study of *The Eschatology of the Book of Jubilees*. Davenport's analysis of the structure of those chs. of Jub with which he dealt was very carefully done, but he treated only a limited amount of text.

[40] Milik, *The Books of Enoch*. Milik mentioned the dependence of Jub on the Astronomical Book (p. 11), the Watchers (p. 24), and the Book of Dreams (p. 45). On p. 255 he suggested that the epistle was dependent on Jubilees. More recently VanderKam has argued that the reverse is true ("Enoch Traditions in Jubilees and Other Second-Century Sources," *Seminar Papers of the Society of Biblical Literature* [Missoula, Mont., 1978] vol. 1, pp. 229–51).

[41] A. Hultgård, *L'Eschatologie des Testaments des Douze Patriarches* (Uppsala, Sweden, 1977) vol. 1, pp. 24, 45.

P. W. Skehan was the first to point out the close relationship between Jubilees and the Hymn to the Creator from the Psalms Scroll. He accepted Milik's judgment that Jubilees was to be dated from the end of the second century and assumed that it was dependent on the hymn.[42] When Avigad and Yadin published the Genesis Apocryphon in 1956, they assumed that it was also earlier than the Book of Jubilees and served as a source for it.[43] It is our opinion that in the case of both documents that judgment must now be reversed. Jubilees was written earlier and served as a source for both the Hymn to the Creator and the Genesis Apocryphon.

Other texts from Qumran that use expressions or ideas which are also found in Jubilees include the Damascus Document, which cites Jubilees by name (CD 16.2–4), the Manual of Discipline, the Hymns, and the Florilegium from Cave 4.

Note on the translation

The translation which follows is quite literal. The majority of students who make use of the translation will probably not be familiar with Ge'ez, the ancient dialect of Ethiopic used in writing the text. Therefore we have tried to remain as close to the simple wording of the text as possible. Significant words or phrases inserted to aid in the translation are put in parentheses. When square brackets are used, an accompanying footnote will explain their significance.

In the notes which accompany the translation an attempt has been made to indicate those passages for which there exists a parallel text in Hebrew, Latin, or Syriac.

The Ethiopic and Latin texts which have been used are those published by R. H. Charles in *The Ethiopic Version of the Hebrew Book of Jubilees* (Oxford, 1895). A number of significant textual comments were subsequently made by Charles in *The Book of Jubilees or the Little Genesis* (London, 1902). References in the notes to Charles's English translation are citations of this work.

The Hebrew text which was used was taken from J. VanderKam's convenient summary in *Textual and Historical Studies in the Book of Jubilees*. References to VanderKam's discussion of the Hebrew text are to be found in that volume unless otherwise noted.

The Syriac text which was used was published by E. Tisserant in "Fragments syriaques du Livre des Jubilés," *RB* 30 (1921), 55–86; 206–32. References to Tisserant's discussion of the Syriac text are to be found in that volume.

No attempt was made to cite all parallels in Greek texts. A large group is contained in A.-M. Denis's *Fragmenta pseudepigraphorum quae supersunt graeca* (Leiden, 1970; pp. 70–102). A number of them are also found in Charles's *The Ethiopic Version of the Hebrew Book of Jubilees* and his English translation, cited above.

[42] P. W. Skehan, "Jubilees and the Qumran Psalter," *CBQ* 37 (1975) 343–47.

[43] N. Avigad and Y. Yadin, *A Genesis Apocryphon: A Scroll from the Wilderness of Judea* (Jerusalem, 1956) p. 38.

BIBLIOGRAPHY

Charlesworth, *PMR*, pp. 143–47.
Delling, *Bibliographie*, pp. 172–74.
Denis, *Introduction*, pp. 150–62.

Charles, R. H. *The Ethiopic Version of the Hebrew Book of Jubilees*. Oxford, 1895. (This edition contains an Eth. text edited from four MSS. In separate appendices Charles has provided parallel portions from (1) the Heb. Book of Noah, (2) the Midrash *Wayyissau*, and (3) a Syr. text naming the wives of the Patriarchs.)
———. *The Book of Jubilees or the Little Genesis*. London, 1902. (This vol. contains an ET, introduction, and commentary on the text. It includes an annotated bibliography on previous editions, translations, and critical studies of the text.)
Davenport, G. L. *The Eschatology of the Book of Jubilees*. SPB 20; Leiden, 1971. (An attempt to deal with Jubilees in terms of redaction criticism.)
Denis, A.-M. "Liber Jubilaeorum," *Fragmenta pseudepigraphorum quae supersunt graeca*. PVTG 3; Leiden, 1970; pp. 70–102. (A collection of Gk. parallels and citations.)
Hölscher, G. "Die Karte des Jubiläenbuches," *Drei Erdkarten*. Heidelberg, 1949; pp. 57–73.
Jaubert, A. "The Calendar of *Jubilees*," *The Date of the Last Supper*, trans. I. Rafferty. Staten Island, N.Y., 1965; pp. 15–30. (A good summation of Jaubert's important discoveries regarding the calendar.)
Martin, F. "Le Livre des Jubilés. But ét procédés de l'auteur. Ses doctrines," *RB* 8 (1911) 321–44; 502–33. (A relatively brief, well-written introduction. Although written prior to the Qumran discoveries, it reflects sensitive theological insight.)
Rönsch, H. *Das Buch der Jubiläen oder die kleine Genesis*, Leipzig, 1874; repr. Amsterdam, 1970. (This edition contains a Lat. text, which Charles sought to improve upon. It also contains a mine of interesting material dealing with parallel literature, including handy German translations of parallel texts that are sometimes hard to find.)
Testuz, M. *Les Idées religieuses du livre des Jubilés*. Geneva, 1960. (Although Testuz ties the author too closely to the Essenes of Qumran, he provides an outstanding introduction to the religious issues in Jub.)
VanderKam, J. C. *Textual and Historical Studies in the Book of Jubilees*. Harvard Semitic Museum, Harvard Semitic Monograph 14; Missoula, Mont., 1977. (Provides a summary of the Heb. texts from Qumran which have been published thus far. Includes an important discussion of the dating of Jub and a study of textual affinities of biblical citations in Jub.)

THE BOOK OF DIVISION

Title[a]

This is *The Account of the Division of Days of the Law and the Testimony for Annual Observance according to their Weeks* (of years) *and their Jubilees[b] throughout all the Years of the World* just as the LORD told it to Moses on Mount Sinai when he went up to receive the tablets of the Law and the commandment[c] by the word of the LORD, as he said to him, "Come up to the top of the mountain." Ex 24:12

Moses is summoned to the mountain

1 **1** In the first year of the Exodus of the children of Israel from Egypt, in the third month on the sixteenth day of that month, the LORD spoke to Moses, saying, "Come up to me on the mountain, and I shall give you two stone tablets of the Ex 31:18 Law and the commandment, which I have written, so that you may teach them." Deut 9:11 Ex 32:15
2 And Moses went up to the mountain of the LORD. And the glory of the LORD
3 dwelt upon Mount Sinai, and a cloud overshadowed it for six days. •And he called to Moses on the seventh day from[d] the midst of the cloud. And the appearance of the glory of the LORD was like fire burning on top of the mountain.
4 And Moses was on the mountain forty days and forty nights.

Moses instructed to write a book

And the LORD revealed to him both what (was) in the beginning and what will occur (in the future), the account of the division of all of the days of the Law and
5 the testimony. •And he said, "Set your mind on every thing which I shall tell you on this mountain, and write it in a book so that their descendants might see Ex 34:27 that I have not abandoned them on account of all of the evil which they have done to instigate transgression[e] of the convenant which I am establishing between
6 me and you today on Mount Sinai for their descendants. •And thus it will be, when all of these things happen to them, that they will know that I have been Deut 30:1 more righteous than they in all their judgments and deeds. And they will know that I have truly been with them.

Moses is told how the people will forsake the LORD in the land of promise

7 "And you, write for yourself all of these words which I shall cause you to Deut 31:27 know today, for I know their rebelliousness and their stubbornness before I cause Deut 30:20 them to enter the land which I swore to their fathers, Abraham, Isaac, and Jacob, Ex 33:1 Deut 31:20
8 saying, 'I will give to your seed a land flowing with milk and honey.' •And they will eat and be satisfied, and they will turn to strange gods, to those who

---

1 a. MS B begins with a trinitarian formula and the blessing "May the LORD God of all spirit and all flesh be blessed."

b. In order to provide a chronological framework for dealing with events covering a long period of time, the author has used a system based on multiples of seven, the number of days in the week. Seven years are treated as a week of years, and seven weeks of years equal a jubilee.

c. "The Law and the Commandment" are mentioned in Ex 24:12. The Heb. is *hattôrâ* and *hammiṣwâ*.

d. The preposition "from" is supplied from the reading in Ex 24:16. The Eth. text reads "in." The corruption may have occurred in reading the Heb. text in a scriptorium. The labial "m" in *mittok* may have been heard as the labial "b" in *bětok*.

e. The translation "to instigate transgression" is an attempt to render the causative form of the verb which appears in the Eth. MSS. In his English translation, Charles emended the form to read as a basic tense he rendered "in transgressing."

cannot save them from any of their affliction. And this testimony will be heard
9 as testimony against them, •for they will forget all of my commandments, 2Kgs 17:15
everything which I shall command them, and they will walk after the gentiles and Ezra 9:10f.
after their defilement and shame. And they will serve their gods, and they will 2Kgs 17:2
10 become a scandal for them and an affliction and a torment and a snare. •And Ex 23:33
many will be destroyed and seized and will fall into the hand of the enemy because Josh 23:13
they have forsaken my ordinances and my commandments and the feasts of my
covenant and my sabbaths and my sacred place, which I sanctified for myself
among them, and my tabernacle and my sanctuary, which I sanctified for myself
in the midst of the land so that I might set my name upon it and might dwell Ezek 20:28
11 (there). •And they will make for themselves high places and groves and carved
idols. And each of them will worship his own (idol) so as to go astray. And they 2Chr 28:3
will sacrifice their children to the demons and to every work of the error of their Ezek 20:31
heart. 1En 99:7

The murder of prophets, the captivity, and the loss of the cult

12 "And I shall send to them witnesses so that I might witness to them, but they 2Chr 24:19
will not hear. And they will even kill the witnesses. And they will persecute those Jer 25:4
who search out the Law, and they will neglect everything and begin^f to do evil Neh 9:26
13 in my sight. •And I shall hide my face from them, and I shall give them over to Isa 1:15
the power of the nations to be captive, and for plunder, and to be devoured. And 2Kgs 21:14
I shall remove them from the midst of the land, and I shall scatter them among CD 1.2-8
14 the nations. •And they will forget all of my laws and all of my commandments Deut 4:28;
and all of my judgments, and they will err concerning new moons, sabbaths, 28:36,64
festivals, jubilees, and ordinances. CD 3.13-15

Repentance and restoration

15 "And afterward they will turn to me from among the nations with all their heart Deut 4:29f.
and with all their soul and with all their might. And I shall gather them from the
midst of all the nations. And they will seek me so that I might be found by them. Jer 29:14
When they seek me with all their heart and with all their soul, I shall reveal to Jer 29:13
16 them an abundance of peace in righteousness. •And with all my heart and with Jer 32:41
all my soul I shall transplant^g them as a righteous plant. And they will be a Zech 8:13
17 blessing and not a curse. And they will be the head and not the tail. •And I shall CD 1.7
build my sanctuary in their midst, and I shall dwell with them. And I shall be Ex 25:8; 29:45
18 their God and they will be my people truly and rightly. •And I shall not forsake Lev 26:12
them, and I shall not be alienated from them because I am the LORD their God." Jer 24:7
Deut 31:6

Moses' prayer of intercession

19 And Moses fell upon his face, and he prayed and said, "O Lord, my God, do
not abandon your people and your inheritance to walk in the error of their heart. 2Kgs 21:14
And do not deliver them into the hand of their enemy, the gentiles, lest they rule Ps 106:41
over them and cause them to sin against you. Deut 9:26
20 "O Lord, let your mercy be lifted up upon your people, and create for them Ps 51:10
an upright spirit. And do not let the spirit of Beliar^h rule over them to accuse 1QS 1.24
them before you and ensnare them from every path of righteousness so that they
21 might be destroyed from before your face. •But they are your people and your Deut 9:26,29
inheritance, whom you saved by your great might from the hand of the Egyptians.

f. The reading "begin" is found in MSS B C D. Charles preferred to follow MS A in his text, which reads "change."

g. The Eth. word means "remove." It has the sense of moving away from one's home and is hardly suitable in this context. The passage appears to be corrupt, and "transplant" is, at best, a weak attempt to make sense of a difficult text.

h. In 1Sam 2:12 the Heb. expression "sons of Beliar" is translated "worthless men." Later the term "Beliar" came to designate a demonic power; here it refers to Satan.

Create a pure heart and a holy spirit for them. And do not let them be ensnared
by their sin henceforth and forever."

The LORD predicts a restoration of the people

22   And the LORD said to Moses, "I know their contrariness and their thoughts   Deut 31:27
and their stubbornness. And they will not obey until they acknowledge their sin   Lev 26:40
23   and the sins of their fathers. •But after this they will return to me in all   Neh 9:2
uprighteousness and with all of (their) heart and soul. And I shall cut off the   2Chr 6:38
foreskin of their heart and the foreskin of the heart of their descendants. And I   Deut 10:16; 30:6
shall create for them a holy spirit, and I shall purify them so that they will not
24   turn away from following me from that day and forever. •And their souls will
cleave to me and to all my commandments. And they will do my commandments.   Jer 31:9
25   And I shall be a father to them, and they will be sons to me. •And they will all   Deut 14:1
be called 'sons of the living God.' And every angel and spirit will know and   Hos 1:10
acknowledge that they are my sons and I am their father in uprightness and
righteousness. And I shall love them.

Moses told again to write

26   "And you write down for yourself[i] all of the matters which I shall make known   Ex 34:27
to you on this mountain: what (was) in the beginning and what (will be) at the
end, what will happen in all of the divisions of the days which are in the Law   4Ezra 14:4f.
and testimony and throughout their weeks (of years) according to the jubilees
forever,[j] until I shall descend and dwell with them in all the ages of eternity."

The Angel of the presence is instructed to write the history for Moses

27   And he said to the angel of the presence, "Write for Moses from the first   1QH 6.13
28   creation until my sanctuary is built in their midst forever and ever. •And the   Deut 33:2
LORD will appear in the sight of all. And everyone will know that I am the God   Acts 7:53
of Israel and the father of all the children of Jacob and king upon Mount Zion   Gal 3:19
forever and ever. And Zion and Jerusalem will be holy."   Ex 24:10
                                                                                        Isa 24:23

The Angel of the presence receives the tablets containing the history

29   And the angel of the presence, who went before the camp of Israel, took the   Ex 14:19
tablets of the division of years from the time of the creation of the law and   Isa 63:9
testimony according to their weeks (of years), according to the jubilees, year by   TJud 25
year throughout the full number of jubilees, from[k] [the day of creation until][l] the   2Pet 3:13
day of the new creation when the heaven and earth and all of their creatures shall   Isa 65:17; 66:22
be renewed according to the powers of heaven and according to the whole nature   1En 91:16
of earth, until the sanctuary of the LORD is created in Jerusalem upon Mount
Zion. And all of the lights will be renewed for healing and peace and blessing for

---

i. The four MSS consulted by Charles differ on
the text at this point. MSS A D read "And I shall
write down for you." Charles used that reading in
his Eth. text, but turned to the reading of B C in
his English translation. We have also followed B
C.
    j. This sentence contains phrases similar to those
which appear in the title and in vs. 1:4. The book
that Moses is asked to write is a "second law."
The Pentateuch was apparently the book of the first
law, which was written by God himself, according
to Jub 6:22. In Ex 34:27 Moses was directed to
write certain laws, but in Ex 34:1 God wrote the
famous tablets of stone.
    k. Charles's Eth. text contains a fuller reading,

i.e. "year by year from." The repetition of "year
by year" appears to be a gloss resulting from
dittography. MS B does not repeat "year by year"
at this point.
    l. The portion of text between brackets has been
restored following a suggestion by M. Stone,
"Apocryphal Notes and Readings," *Israel Oriental
Studies* 1 (1971) 125f. It is assumed that a scribe
had to copy the phrase "from [the day of creation
until] the day of the new creation." By homoeoteleuton, in which his eye skipped from the first
"the day" to the second, he omitted the phrase
between brackets. The suggestion by Stone makes
sense of a passage that has long puzzled commentators.

all of the elect of Israel and in order that it might be thus from that day and unto all the days of the earth.

Description of six days of creation

1 **2** And the angel of the presence spoke to Moses by the word of the LORD, saying, "Write the whole account of creation, that in six days the LORD God completed all his work and all that he created. And he observed a sabbath the seventh day, and he sanctified it for all ages. And he set it (as) a sign for all his works."

2 For[a] on the first day he created the heavens, which are above, and the earth, Job 38:7 and the waters and all of the spirits which minister before him:

> the angels of the presence,
> and the angels of sanctification,   Ps 104:4
> and the angels of the spirit of fire,[b]   1En 60:12-21
> and the angels of the spirit of the winds,   1En 75
> and the angels of the spirit of the clouds and darkness and snow[c] and hail   1En 80
> and frost,   2En 19:1-4
> and the angels of resoundings[d] and thunder and lightning,   Ps 77:18; 104:7
> and the angels of the spirits of cold and heat and winter and springtime Job 37:4
> and harvest and summer,
> and all of the spirits of his creatures which are in heaven and on earth.

And (he created) the abysses[e] and darkness—both evening and night[f]—and light—both dawn and daylight[g]—which he prepared in the knowledge of his heart.
3 Then we saw his works and we blessed him[h] and offered praise before him on account of all his works because he made seven[i] great works on the first day.

---

2 a. There is a Gk. text contained in a work by Epiphanius entitled *De mensuris et ponderibus,* which is parallel to Jub 2:2–21. Charles published the relevant portions of that text in parallel columns opposite his Eth. text. Although the Gk. text is frequently abbreviated, it is, however, quite close to the Eth. in the passages which remain.

A portion of the Syr. text published by E. Tisserant also begins at this point and continues through vs. 16. The Syr. parallel is not as precise as the Gk., but it is helpful in confirming a few readings.

b. The "angels of the spirit of fire" are mentioned in MSS B C D, but are lacking in MS A and the Gk. text of Epiphanius. Charles did not include the phrase in his Eth. text, but he had it printed between brackets in his English translation. The phrase is also lacking in Syr., but that text is drastically abbreviated.

c. The word "snow" is supplied from the Gk. text of Epiphanius. Eth. MSS C D omit the word and MSS A B read "and everything," which is difficult.

d. The Eth. word which appears in the MSS means "depths," but Charles emended it to read "voices" in agreement with the reading in Epiphanius. If translated literally, the Eth. word for "voices" would not appear to be as suitable to read beside "thunder and lightning" as "depths," but the Heb. word *qōl,* which was probably used in this passage, means both "voice" and "thunder." It is in the latter sense that it is used here.

e. The Eth. MS reads "what is in the abysses," but Charles emended his text to agree with the Gk. The Syr. text also agrees with the Gk. The abyss is one of the seven works created by God on the

first day. It is the abyss itself and not just its content that needed to be created the first day.

f. The word "night" is restored from the Gk. text of Epiphanius. It also seems justified to balance the structure of the sentence.

g. Only one Eth. MS (A) has the word "daylight," but its presence in the Gk. text supports the reading. The word order of the sentence from "darkness" to "daylight" follows the order in the Gk. text of Epiphanius. The word order in Eth. differs.

h. There is an interesting parallel in a text from a Qumran collection of Psalms (11QPs[a]). P. W. Skehan referred to it as the "Hymn to the Creator" ("*Jubilees* and the Qumran Psalter" *CBQ* 37 [1975] 343–47). He demonstrated that vss. 4–6 of that hymn, in which the author describes God's creative acts and the hymnic response of the angels, are closely related to Jub 2:2f. The number of literal parallels is striking.

This theme of angelic praise to the Creator on the day when the angels were created has more recently appeared in the famous collection of Coptic gnostic tractates from Nag Hammadi. In the Apocryphon of John, for example, as each pair of invisible eons is created they glorify the Invisible One and his perfect power, Barbelo (5:18–9:25; cf. *NHL,* pp. 98–116).

This theme already appears in Job 38:7 where "the morning stars sang together and all the sons of God shouted for joy," but both the Qumran and later Nag Hammadi texts reflect an elaboration of the motif suggested by Jub.

i. The seven created works were: heaven, earth, waters, all the ministering spirits, the abyss, darkness, and light.

4   And on the second day he made the firmament in the midst of the water. And Gen 1:7
2En 26f. the waters were divided on that day. One half of them went up above, and one half of them went down beneath the firmament (which is) in the middle over the surface of all of the earth. And he made only this (one) work on the second day.

5   On the third day he did as he said[j] to the waters, "Let them pass from the 2En 30:1
6 surface of the whole earth into one place, and let the dry land appear." • And the waters did as he said. And they turned aside from upon the surface of the earth
7 into one place outside of this firmament.[k] And dry land appeared. • And on that day he created for it all of the seas in each of their gathering places, and all of the rivers, and the gathering places of the waters on the mountains and in all the earth, and all of the ponds, and all of the dew of the earth, and the seed which is 4Ezra 3:6 sown, and everything which is eaten,[l] and trees which bear fruit and (other) trees, and the garden of Eden in Eden—in (the place of) luxury[m]—and everything.[n] These four great species the LORD made on the third day.[o]

8   And on the fourth day he made the sun and the moon and the stars. And he set Gen 1:14-19
2En 30:2-6 them in the firmament of heaven so that they might give light upon the whole
9 earth and rule over the day and the night and separate light and darkness. • And the LORD set the sun[p] as a great sign upon the earth for days, sabbaths, months, feast (days), years, sabbaths of years, jubilees, and for all of the (appointed) times
10 of the years—• and it separates the light from the darkness—and so that everything which sprouts and grows upon the earth might surely prosper. These three kinds he made on the fourth day.[q]

11   And on the fifth day he created the great sea monsters in the midst of the depths Gen 1:20-23
2En 30:7 of the waters—for these were made by his hands as the first corporeal beings— and all the fish which move in the waters,[r] and all the birds which fly, and all of
12 their kind. • And the sun rose above them to make them prosper and above

---

j. In translating this vs. it was assumed that the phrase "as he said" was a citation formula of the type which is now well known from Qumran. It is also assumed that the quotation is an attempt to approximate Gen 1:9. The text of Jub, however, differs from both Heb. and Gk. texts of Gen 1:9, directing the waters to "pass over from" rather than being "gathered together into." This text may, however, provide the basis for an unusual statement which appears in the Nag Hammadi tractate On the Origin of the World (CG2, 100:10–14). In that text the unintentional creative force is Pistis Sophia, and the primordial, chaotic waters of Gen 1 are the wellspring of evil within the world, which is controlled by Yaldabaoth. The text is filled with a number of verbal allusions to Gen 1. The biblical background of CG2, 100:10–14 has not been explained, but it could quite easily be based on the wording of the present text of Jub. The passage reads as follows: "Then when Pistis Sophia saw him moving in the depth of the waters, she said to him, 'O youth, pass over here,' which is interpreted Yaldabaoth." NHL, p. 163.

The phrase "from the surface of the whole earth" could also be translated "from the presence of the whole earth." In vs. 6 the waters are actually removed to a place "outside this firmament." Both readings would have pleased the gnostics, who understood what happened to Yaldabaoth in a similar manner, as he exalted himself and moved above this firmament.

k. The Syr. text describes the place to which the waters are removed as "the midst of the firmament." In his commentary, Tisserant suggested that the variant texts were due to a confusion between the Heb. forms mittôk and bêtôk (cf. ch. 1, n. d).

l. The Gk. text of Epiphanius reads "the sprouts." Charles emended his Eth. text to read "everything which sprouts," in agreement with the Gk.

m. Read batadlâ for latadlâ. The Gk. phrase would have been en truphê, which is an attempt to translate the Heb. phrase "in Eden" into Gk. That emendation was suggested by Charles in the notes to his English translation. It is now possible to provide an additional support for this reading. The Nag Hammadi tractate On the Origin of the World, which reflects a number of contacts with the wording of Jub, has preserved a description of Paradise. According to that text, Paradise is located "outside the circuit of the moon and the circuit of the sun in the luxuriant [truphê] earth" (CG2, 110:3–5). The reason for creating it outside the circuit of the moon and the sun is probably related to the fact that neither sun nor moon had yet been created. In the book of Jub, which is the most likely source of this detail, the sun and moon are mentioned in the following vs., which describes the creative acts of the fourth day.

n. The Gk. text of Epiphanius reads "and all the plants according to (their) kind."

o. The four works are the creation of dry land, bodies of water, flora, and Eden.

p. The writer mentions only the sun, and not the moon, as the determinant for holy days. This is in keeping with his quasi-solar year of 364 days and his strident opposition to lunar calculations.

q. The three are the sun, moon, and stars.

r. The Gk. text of Epiphanius reads "the fish and the other crawling things in the water." Charles rearranged the Eth. word order to agree with the reading of the Gk.

s. The three are sea monsters, fish, and birds.

everything which was on the earth, everything which sprouts from the earth, and every tree which bears fruit, and all flesh. These three kinds he made on the fifth day.[s]

13 And on the sixth day he made all of the beasts of the earth and all of the cattle
14 and everything which moves upon the earth. •And after all of this, he made man—male and female he made them—and he gave him dominion over everything which was upon the earth and which was in the seas and over everything which flies, and over beasts and cattle and everything which moves upon the earth or above the whole earth. And over all this he gave him dominion. And these four
15,16 kinds he made on the sixth day.[t] •And the total was twenty-two kinds. •And he completed all of his work on the sixth day, everything which is in the heavens and the earth and the seas and the depths and in the light and in the darkness and in every place.

Gen 1:24-28
2En 30:8

Ex 20:11

The significance of the sabbath

17 And he gave us a great sign, the sabbath day, so that we might work six days
18 and observe a sabbath from all work on the seventh day. •And he told us—all of the angels of the presence and all of the angels of sanctification, these two great
19 kinds—that we might keep the sabbath with him in heaven and on earth. •And he said to us, "Behold I shall separate for myself a people from among all the nations. And they will also keep the sabbath. And I will sanctify them for myself,[u] and I will bless them. Just as I have sanctified and shall sanctify the sabbath day for myself thus shall I bless them. And they will be my people and I will be their
20 God. •And I have chosen the seed of Jacob from among all that I have seen. And I have recorded him as my firstborn son, and have sanctified him for myself forever and ever. And I will make known to them the sabbath day so that they might observe therein a sabbath from all work."
21 And thus he created therein a sign by which they might keep the sabbath with us on the seventh day, to eat and drink and bless the one who created all things just as he blessed and sanctified for himself a people who appeared[v] from all the
22 nations so that they might keep the sabbath together with us.[w] •And he caused their desires[x] to go up as pleasing fragrance, which is acceptable before him always.
23 There were twenty-two chief men from Adam until Jacob,[y] and twenty-two kinds of works were made before the seventh day. The former is blessed and sanctified, and the latter is also blessed and sanctified. One was like the other
24 with respect to sanctification and blessing. •And it was granted to the former that they[z] should always be the blessed and sanctified ones of the testimony and the first law just as he[a2] had sanctified and blessed sabbath day on the seventh day.

Ex 31:13

1Kgs 8:53

Ex 31:13,17
Ezek 20:12

Isa 41:8; 44:1
Ex 4:22
Jer 31:9

Ex 31:13,17
Ezek 20:12

---

t. The four are wild beasts, domestic animals, reptiles, and man.

u. A adds "(as) my (own) people."

v. Charles emended his Eth. text to read "whom he would possess" in agreement with Deut 7:6.

w. Charles has suggested that the phrase "so that they might keep the sabbath together with us" might be a dittography from the second clause in this vs.

x. The text reads "his desires," but the pronoun probably refers to "the people," which can be regarded as masculine singular in Heb. "Their desires" would then be the prayers of the people, which are like good incense.

y. Eth. "from Adam until him." Charles was able to restore "Jacob" on the basis of the parallel which is found in Epiphanius' *De mensuris et ponderibus*, ch. 22. That text goes on to point out

that there are twenty-two letters in the Heb. alphabet and twenty-two sacred books. In his English translation of 1902, Charles assembled an impressive group of ancient witnesses which shared the expanded tradition of Epiphanius. He was also persuaded that there was a lacuna at the beginning of vs. 23 and proposed to restore it as follows: "As there were two and twenty letters and two and twenty (sacred) books and two and twenty heads of mankind from Adam . . ."

z. Apparently Jacob and his seed since Jacob is being likened to the sabbath. A reads "he" at this point, but the other MSS have "they," agreeing with the plural forms used for "blessed" and "sanctified."

a2. A fragment of the Syr. text begins at this point and continues through vs. 2:25a.

The laws for keeping the sabbath

25　He created heaven and earth and everything which he created in six days. And
the LORD made the seventh day holy for all of his works. Therefore he commanded
concerning it, "Let everyone who will do any work therein die. And also whoever Ex 31:14f.; 35:2
Num 15:32-36
defiles it let him surely die."

26　And you, command the children of Israel, and let them guard this day so that Ex 20:8; 31:13
they might sanctify it and not do any work therein, and not defile it because it is
27 more holy than any day. •And everyone who pollutes it let him surely die. And
anyone who will do any work therein, let him surely die forever so that the
children of Israel might guard this day throughout their generations and not be Deut 29:28
28 uprooted from the land because it is a holy day and a blessed day. •And every
man who guards it and keeps therein a sabbath from all his work will be holy and
blessed always like us.

29　Make known and recount to the children of Israel the judgment of the day that CD 10.22
they should keep the sabbath thereon and not forsake it in the error of their hearts.
And (make known) that it is not permitted to do work thereon which is unlawful,
(it being) unseemly to do their pleasure thereon. And (make known) that they Isa 58:13
Ex 35:3
should not prepare thereon anything which will be eaten or drunk, which they
have not prepared for themselves on the sixth day.[b2] And (make known that it is
not lawful) to draw water or to bring in or to take out any work within their Jer 17:21
30 dwellings which is carried in their gates.[c2] •And they shall not bring in or take Neh 13:19
Jer 17:27
out from house to house on that day because it is more holy and it is more blessed
than any day of the jubilee of jubilees. On this day we kept the sabbath in heaven
before it was made known to any human to keep the sabbath thereon upon the
earth.

31　The Creator of all blessed it, but he did not sanctify any people or nations to
keep the sabbath thereon with the sole exception of Israel. He granted to them
alone that they might eat and drink and keep the sabbath thereon upon the earth.
32 And the Creator of all, who created this day for a blessing and sanctification and
33 glory, blessed it more than all days. •This law and testimony was given to the Ex 27:21
Lev 7:36; 23:14
children of Israel as an eternal law for their generations.

The naming of animals Gen 2:19f.

1 **3** And in six days of the second week, by the word of the LORD, we brought to
Adam all of the beasts, and all of the cattle, and all of the birds, and everything
which moves on the earth, and everything which moves in the water, each one
according to its kind, and each one according to its likeness: the[a] beasts on the
first day, and cattle on the second day, and the birds on the third day, and
everything which moves upon the earth on the fourth day, and whatever moves
2 in the water on the fifth day. •And Adam named all of them, each one according
3 to its name, and whatever he called them became their names. •And during these
five days Adam was observing all of these, male and female according to every
kind which was on the earth, but he was alone and there was none whom he
found for himself, who was like himself, who would help him.

---

b2. In the Eth. text, the relative clause "which
they have not prepared for themselves on the sixth
day" follows the phrase "to bring in or to take
out." The obvious misplacement of the relative
was noted by Charles in his English translation.

c2. The whole of vs. 29 is a single sentence in
Eth. Its length and complexity make it difficult to
reproduce in English. Therefore it is necessary to
restructure the clauses in translating.

3 a. There is a Gk. parallel from the *Chronographia* of Georgius Syncellus, which is based on the
present ch. His description of the order in which
Adam named the animals is very close to the
description which appears in Jub. Elsewhere in the
ch., the parallels are limited to a few phrases. The
relevant portions of the Gk. text are available in
A.-M. Denis' *Fragmenta Pseudepigraphorum
Graeca* (PVTG 3; Leiden, 1970) pp. 76–78.

The creation of Eve

4   And the LORD said to us, "It is not good that the man should be alone. Let
5 us make for him a helper who is like him." •And the LORD our God cast a deep
sleep upon him, and he slept. And he took one bone from the midst of his bones
for the woman. And that rib was the origin of the woman from the midst of his
bones. And he built up the flesh in place of it, and he constructed a woman.
6   And he awakened Adam from his sleep, and when he awoke, he stood up on
the sixth day. And he brought her to him and he knew her and said to her, "This
is now bone of my bone and flesh from my flesh. This one will be called my wife
because she was taken from her husband."
7   Therefore a man and woman shall be one. And therefore it shall be that a man
will leave his father and his mother and he will join with his wife and they will
become one flesh.

The laws of purification after childbirth

8   In the first week Adam was created and also the rib, his wife. And in the
second week he showed her to him. And therefore the commandment was given   Lev 12:2-5
to observe seven days for a male, but for a female twice seven days in their
impurity.
9   And after forty days were completed for Adam in the land where he was created,
we brought him into the garden of Eden so that he might work it and guard it.
And on the eighth day his wife was also brought in. And after this she entered
10 the garden of Eden. •And therefore the command was written in the heavenly
tablets for one who bears, "If she bears a male, she shall remain seven days in   1En 81:1
her impurity like the first seven days. And thirty-three days she shall remain in   TLevi 5
the blood of her purity. And she shall not touch anything holy. And she shall not
enter the sanctuary until she has completed these days which are in accord with
11 (the rule for) a male (child). •And that which is in accord with (the rule for) a
female is two weeks—like the two first weeks—in her impurity. And sixty-six
days she shall remain in the blood of her purity. And their total will be eighty
days."
12   And when she finished those eighty days, we brought her into the garden of
Eden because it is more holy than any land. And every tree which is planted in
13 it is holy. •Therefore the ordinances of these days were ordained for anyone who
bears a male or female that she might not touch anything holy and she might not
14 enter the sanctuary until these days are completed for a male or female. •This is
the law and testimony which is written for Israel so that they might keep it always.

The first seven years in Eden

15   And during the first week of the first jubilee Adam and his wife had been in
the garden of Eden for seven years tilling and guarding it. And we gave him
work and we were teaching him to do everything which was appropriate[b] for
16 tilling. •And he was tilling. And he was naked, but he neither knew it nor was   Gen 2:25
he ashamed. And he was guarding the garden from the birds and beasts and cattle
and gathering its fruit and eating. And he used to set aside the rest for himself
and his wife. And what was being guarded he set aside.

The Fall
                                                        Gen 3:1-19

17   At the end of seven years which he completed there, seven years exactly, in
the second month on the seventeenth day, the serpent came and drew near to the

---

b. Lit. "which appeared," or "which was obvious."

woman. And the serpent said to the woman, "The LORD commanded you,
18 saying, 'You shall not eat from any tree[c] which is in the garden.'" •And she
said to him, "The LORD said, 'Eat from all of the fruit of the trees which are in
the garden.' But the LORD said to us, 'You shall not eat from the fruit of the tree
which is in the midst of the garden, and you shall not touch it lest you die.'"
19 And the serpent said to the woman, "It is not (true) that you shall surely die because
the LORD knows that on the day you eat of it your eyes will become opened and
you will become like gods, and you will know good and evil."
20   And the woman saw the tree that it was pleasant and it was pleasing to the eye
21 and its fruit was good to eat and she took some of it and she ate. •And she first
covered her shame with a fig leaf, and then she gave it to Adam and he ate and
22 his eyes were opened and he saw that he was naked. •And he took a fig leaf and
sewed it and made an apron for himself. And he covered his shame.
23   And the LORD cursed the serpent and he was angry with it forever.[d] And he
was angry with the woman also because she had listened to the voice of the
24 serpent and had eaten. And he said to her, •"I will surely multiply your grief and
your birth pangs. Bear children in grief. And to your husband is your return and
25 he will rule over you." •And to Adam he said, "Because you listened to the
voice of your wife and you ate from that tree from which I commanded you that
you should not eat, the land shall be cursed because of you. Thorns and thistles
shall sprout up for you. And eat your bread in the sweat of your face until you
return to the earth from which you were taken because you are earth and to the
earth you will return."

Expulsion-day sacrifice and the law of covering shame

Gen 3:21,23

26   And he made for them garments of skin and he dressed them and sent them
27 from the garden of Eden. •And on that day when Adam went out from the garden
of Eden, he offered a sweet-smelling sacrifice—frankincense, galbanum, stacte,   Ex 30:34
and spices—in the morning with the rising of the sun from the day he covered
28 his shame. •On[e] that day the mouth of all the beasts and cattle and birds and   Ex 20:26; 28:42
whatever walked or moved was stopped from speaking because all of them used
29 to speak with one another with one speech and one language.[f] •And he sent from
the garden of Eden all of the flesh which was in the garden of Eden and all of
the flesh was scattered, each one according to its kind and each one according to
30 its family, into the place which was created for them. •But from all the beasts
and all the cattle he granted to Adam alone that he might cover his shame.
31 Therefore it is commanded in the heavenly tablets to all who will know the
judgment of the Law that they should cover their shame and they should not be
uncovered as the gentiles are uncovered.

The end of the first jubilee in 'Elda

32   And on the first[g] of the fourth month Adam and his wife went out from the
garden of Eden and dwelt in the land of 'Elda, in the land of their creation.[h]   Gen 3:23
33,34 And Adam named his wife Eve. •They had no son until the first jubilee but after

---

c. B C read "from any fruit of the tree."
d. At this point in his English translation Charles
indicated a lacuna because an impressive number
of ancient witnesses who are dependent on Jub
claim that the serpent originally had four legs. It
therefore seemed appropriate that the text should
contain some reference to cutting them off.
e. There is a small portion of the Syr. text which
is parallel to the first half of this vs.
f. On the basis of Jub 12:26, it is reasonable to
assume that all the animals spoke Heb.
g. Lit. "new moon," but the calendar used in
Jub speaks against that usage. The calendar was

made up of twelve months of thirty days plus four
days added at the end of each of the seasons. There
is no way that a new moon would be able to
coincide on a regular basis with the first of every
month in that system. Both the Lat. (28:24) and
the Syr. (6:1) texts use words for "first," which
cannot be translated "new moon."
h. Gen 3:23b says that Adam is to till the earth
"from which he was taken." Apparently that phrase
led to speculation that Adam did not originate in
Eden but was taken from another place to which
the author of Jub would return him.

35 this he knew her. •And he tilled the land as he had been taught in the garden of Eden.

The first murder and the law of manslaughter

Gen 4:1-14

1 **4** And in the third week in the second jubilee, she bore Cain. And in the fourth
2 she bore Abel. And in the fifth she bore 'Awan, his daughter. •And at the
beginning of the third jubilee, Cain killed Abel because the sacrifice of Abel was
3 accepted, but the offering of Cain was not accepted. •And he killed him in the
field, and his blood cried out from the earth to heaven, making accusation because
4 he killed him. •And the LORD rebuked Cain on account of Abel because he killed
him. And he made him a fugitive[a] on the earth because of the blood of his brother.
5 And he cursed him upon the earth. •And therefore it is written in the heavenly
tablets, "Cursed is one who strikes his fellow with malice. And all who have Deut 27:24
seen and heard shall say 'so be it.' And the man who saw and did not report (it)
6 shall be cursed like him." •Therefore when we come before the LORD our God
we will make known all of the sins which occur in heaven and earth and which
are in the light or in the darkness or in any (place).

The descendants of Adam

Gen 4:17,25f.;
5:6-15

7 And Adam and his wife were mourning four weeks of years on account of
Abel. And in[b] the fourth year of the fifth week they rejoiced. And Adam again
knew his wife and she bore a son for him. And he named him Seth because he
said, "The LORD has raised up another seed[c] for us upon the earth in place of
8 Abel because Cain killed him." •And in the sixth week he begat 'Azūra, his
daughter.
9 And Cain took his sister, 'Awan,[d] as a wife, and she bore for him Enoch at
the end of the fourth jubilee. And in the first year of the first week of the fifth
jubilee, buildings were constructed in the land. And Cain built a city and he
10 named it with the name of his son, Enoch. •And Adam knew Eve, his wife, and
she bore nine more children.
11 And in the fifth week of the fifth jubilee, Seth took 'Azūra, his sister, as a
12 wife. And in the fourth year of that week, she bore for him Enos. •He was first
to call the name of the LORD upon the earth.
13 And in the seventh jubilee in the third week, Enos took Noam, his sister, as a
wife. And she bore a son[e] for him in the third year of the fifth week. And he
named him Kenān.
14 And at the end of the eighth jubilee, Kenān took for himself a wife, Mu'aleleth,
his sister, (as) a wife.[f] And she bore a son for him in the ninth jubilee in the first
week in the third year of that (week). And he called him Mahalalel.
15 And in the second week of the tenth jubilee, Mahalalel took for himself a wife, CD 2.18
1QapGen 2.1
Dinah, the daughter of Baraki'el, the daughter of his father's brother,[g] as a wife.

---

4 a. In his edition of the Eth. text, Charles suggested that the Ethiopic word *nūḥa* was a corrupt transliteration of the word *nāʿ*, "fugitive," which appears in Gen 4:14.

b. A fragment of the Heb. text from Qumran (11QJub 1) begins at this point and continues to the beginning of vs. 11.

c. The Eth. word order is a bit unusual at this point. It reads lit. "raised up for us seed in the earth, another one," but the same word order is found in the Heb. fragment from Qumran.

d. The word order for "his sister, 'Awan" is provided by the Heb. fragment from Qumran. The Eth. text reads "'Awan, his sister."

e. A fragment of the Heb. text from Qumran begins at this point and continues into vs. 14.

f. B and D read "Kenan took for himself a wife, Mu'aleleth, his sister (as) a wife." The repetition of "wife" would appear to be redundant, but the Heb. text from Qumran clearly includes the second mention of wife and apparently provides sufficient space in the lacuna for its first mention. A C omit the final phrase "(as) a wife."

g. Eth. reads "father's sister." Where this reading occurred, Charles systematically changed it to read "father's brother." In his English translation he assembled a number of ancient texts which bear witness to the marriage of the patriarchs to the daughter of their "father's brother." The witnesses include the Syr. "Names of the Wives of the Patriarchs" which he published as Appendix III to his Eth. text. One might also note in support of

And she bore a son for him in the third week in the sixth year. And he called him
Jared because in his days the angels of the LORD, who were called Watchers,   Dan 4:13
came down to the earth in order to teach the sons of man, and perform judgment   1En 1:5
and uprightness upon the earth.

The birth and work of Enoch   Gen 5:18-24

16   And in the eleventh jubilee Jared took for himself a wife and her name was
Bāraka, the daughter of Rasuyal, the daughter of his father's brother, as a wife,
in the fourth week of that jubilee. And she bore a son for him in the fifth[h] week,
in the fourth year of the jubilee. And he called him Enoch.

17   This one[i] was the first who learned writing and knowledge and wisdom, from   1En 12:3f.
(among) the sons of men, from (among) those who were born upon earth. And
who wrote in a book the signs of the heaven according to the order of their
months, so that the sons of man might know the (appointed) times of the years   1En 72-82

18 according to their order, with respect to each of their months. •This one was the
first (who) wrote a testimony and testified to the children of men throughout the
generations of the earth. And their weeks according to jubilees he recounted; and
the days of the years he made known. And the months he set in order, and the

19 sabbaths of the years he recounted, just as we made it known to him.[j] •And he
saw what was and what will be in a vision of his sleep as it will happen among
the children of men in their generations until the day of judgment. He saw and
knew everything and wrote his testimony and deposited the testimony upon the   1En 37:2-4
earth against all the children of men and their generations.

20   And in the twelfth jubilee in its seventh week, he took for himself a wife and   1En 85:3
her name was 'Edni, the daughter of Dan'el, his father's brother, as a wife, and
in the sixth year of this week she bore a son for him. And he called him
Methuselah.

21   And he was therefore with the angels of God six jubilees of years. And they   1QapGen 2.21
showed him everything which is on earth and in the heavens, the dominion of the

22 sun. And he wrote everything, •and bore witness to the Watchers, the ones who
sinned with the daughters of men because they began to mingle themselves with
the daughters of men so that they might be polluted. And Enoch bore witness

23 against all of them. •And he was taken from among the children of men, and we   1En 70:1-3
led him to the garden of Eden for greatness and honor. And behold, he is there

---

the change that the names Baraki'el (vs. 15) and
Rasuyal (vs. 16) are masculine forms. Wintermute
attempts to follow the inconsistencies in the spelling
of the proper names in the Ethiopic text. —J.H.C.

h. A fragment of the Heb. text from Qumran
begins at this point and continues into vs. 17.

i. A portion of the Syr. text begins at this point
and continues into vs. 21.

The fragment from Qumran has a blank space
before the first word, which indicates that it marked
a new section of narrative. The reading "This one"
is clearly found in the Qumran text, from which it
has been restored. Charles's Eth. text began "He
was therefore the first." The "therefore" was
attested only in MS A, however, so it should now
be eliminated.

j. The suggestion that vss. 17f. were poetic
came from J. VanderKam, "Enoch Traditions in
Jubilees and Other Second-Century Sources," *SBL
1978 Seminar Papers* (Missoula, Mont., 1978) vol.
1, pp. 228–51.

Although there are some phrases in vss. 17f.
which are a bit difficult to put in poetic lines, the
case for an original poetic structure is strong. The

parallelism in ll. 3f. of vs. 17 and ll. 4f. and 6f.
of vs. 18 is convincing. There may, however, be
some expansion in the Eth. version. The Syr. text
contains a much shorter reading which preserves
the same poetic pattern with its obvious parallelism.
Inasmuch as the Syr. text is generally abbreviated,
there is no reason to believe that it preserves the
original text at this point. Nevertheless, it provides
an interesting variant in support of the original
poetic structure. It reads as follows:

17. This Enoch was the first (who) learned
       writing and knowledge and wisdom,
       and (who) wrote the signs of heaven in a book,
       to teach to the sons of men,
       the changes of the times and the years,
       according to their orders and their months.
       And he made known the days of the years
       and the number of the months he established.

The discussion of Enoch in Jub is closely related
to the account which appears in the book of 1En.
VanderKam's paper refers to the most important
current studies and introduces a number of significant new observations.

writing condemnation and judgment of the world, and all of the evils of the
24 children of men. •And because of him none of the water of the Flood came[k] upon
the whole land of Eden, for he was put there for a sign and so that he might bear   2En 34:3
witness against all of the children of men so that he might relate all of the deeds
25 of the generations until the day of judgment. •And[l] he offered the incense which
is acceptable before the LORD in the evening (at) the holy place[m] on Mount
26 Qater.[n] •For the LORD has four (sacred) places upon the earth: the garden of
Eden and the mountain of the East and this mountain which you are upon today,
Mount Sinai, and Mount Zion, which will be sanctified in the new creation for
the sanctification of the earth. On account of this the earth will be sanctified from
all sin and from pollution throughout eternal generations.

The generations from Enoch to Noah   Gen 5:25-29

27   And in the fourteenth jubilee Methuselah took as his wife 'Edna, daughter of
'Azri'al, his father's brother, as a wife, in the third week in the first year of that
week. And he begot a son. And he called him Lamech.
28   And in the fifteenth jubilee in the third week, Lamech took for himself a wife,   1QapGen 2.3
and her name was Betenos, the daughter of Baraki'il, the daughter of his father's
brother, (as) a wife. And in that week she bore a son for him and he called him
Noah, saying, "This one will console me from my grief and from all of my labor
and from the land which the LORD cursed."

The death of Adam

29   And[o] at the end of the nineteenth jubilee in the seventh week, in the sixth year,
Adam died. And all of his children buried him in the land of his creation. And
30 he was the first who was buried[p] in the earth. •And he lacked seventy years from
one thousand years, for a thousand years are like one day in the testimony of   2Pet 3:8

k. The reading is based on MS EMML3, the oldest known MS of Jub and one that was not known by Charles. The reading has already been noted by VanderKam, *SBL 1978 Seminar Papers*, vol. 1, pp. 228–51.

l. A portion of the Syr. text begins at this point and continues through the list of four mountains in vs. 26.

m. The reading "in the evening" is found in MSS C D. The reading was rejected by Charles, but has subsequently been confirmed by the presence of the word for "evening" in the Syr. text. The reading of "holy place" which follows in the Eth. text has no counterpart in the Syr. In commenting on the Syr. text, E. Tisserant suggested that *maqdas*, "holy place," was a corruption of *qaddmi*, "first," which agrees with the Syr. text. Thus one could read "and he offered incense which is acceptable to the LORD in the evening first on Mount Qater." The suggestion is attractive. In any case, Enoch is here being designated as the instigator of the ritual of evening incense, which was part of normal daily service in the Temple in Jerusalem.

n. "Qater" may be translated in Eth. as "noon." It seems likely, however, that it was originally the proper name of a mountain which was simply transcribed into Gk. and then Eth. just as Eden, Sinai, and Zion were. The Heb. root *qtr* is used to describe the burning of incense, and it is likely that some formation from that root was used to designate the place where Enoch burned incense.

Mount Qater is undoubtedly to be identified with the mountain of the East in vs. 26. The Syr. text uses the same word in both places, and its presence in both places proves that some designation of the mountain should be retained in vs. 25. The Syr. name for the mountain could be read as "South" or as "Taiman." If it is read as "South," then one would assume a corruption or confusion of a word for "East." If it is read as "Taiman," one might guess that it had reference to Taima in Arabia, about halfway between Damascus and Mecca, where Nabonidus spent about eight years of his reign. As a center for caravans (Job 6:19), Taima was undoubtedly identified with the incense trade, and might be an appropriate place to locate Enoch's mountain. Although Taima lies south of Jerusalem, it is also suitably eastward. In all probability the Syr. Taiman is simply a later attempt to identify the mountain with a known location. As it appeared in the earliest text it was simply an eastern mountain identified with incense; its actual location remains a subject of speculation. Compare Charles's discussion in his English translation and the discussion by Tisserant which accompanies his Syr. text for additional suggestions.

o. A portion of the Syr. text begins at this point. It contains the first part of vs. 1 and part of vs. 2. The second part of vs. 1 is contained in a separate fragment of the Syr. text noted below.

p. A fragment of the Heb. text from Qumran (11QJub 2) begins at this point and continues through most of vs. 30.

heaven and therefore it was written concerning the tree of knowledge, "In the day you eat from it you will die." Therefore he did not complete the years of this day because he died in it.

Abel avenged—law of retaliation

31 At the end of that jubilee Cain was killed one year after him. And his house fell upon him, and he died in the midst of his house. And he was killed by its Ex 21:24 stones because he killed Abel with a stone, and with a stone he was killed by 32 righteous judgment. •Therefore it is ordained in the heavenly tablets:

> "With the weapons with which a man kills his fellow
> he shall be killed
> just as he wounded him,
> thus shall they do to him."

The birth of Noah's sons

Gen 5:32

33 And in the twenty-fifth jubilee Noah took a wife for himself and her name was 'Emzara, daughter of Rake'el, daughter of his father's brother, as a wife, in the first year, in the fifth week. And in its third year she bore for him Shem. And in its fifth year she bore for him Ham. And in the first year of the sixth week she bore for him Japheth.

Corruption of all flesh when angels mate with humans

Gen 6:1-5

1 **5** And when[a] the children of men began to multiply on the surface of the earth 1QapGen 2.1 and daughters were born to them, that the angels of the LORD saw in a certain 1En 6:1f. year of that jubilee that they were good to look at. And they took wives for 1En 7:1,2 themselves from all of those whom they chose. And they bore children for them; 2 and they were the giants. •And injustice increased upon the earth, and all flesh corrupted its way; man and cattle and beasts and birds and everything which walks on the earth. And they all corrupted their way and their ordinances, and they 1En 7:5 began to eat one another. And injustice grew upon the earth and every imagination of the thoughts of all mankind was thus continually evil.

The punishment of angels and annihilation of their offspring

Gen 6:7-13

3 And the LORD saw the earth, and behold it was corrupted and all flesh had corrupted its order and all who were on the earth had done every sort of evil in 4 his sight. •And he said, "I will wipe out man and all flesh which I have created 5 from upon the surface of the earth." •But Noah alone found favor in the sight of the LORD.
6 And against his angels whom he had sent to the earth he was very angry. He 1QH 10.34f. commanded that they be uprooted from all their dominion. And he told us to bind them in the depths of the earth, and behold, they are bound in the midst of them, 7 and they are isolated. •And against their children a word went forth from before his presence so that he might smite them[b] with the sword and remove them from 8 under heaven. •And he said, "My spirit will not dwell upon man forever; for 9 they are flesh, and their days will be one hundred and ten years." •And he sent his sword among them so that each one might kill his fellow and they began to kill one[c] another until they all fell on the sword and they were wiped out from 1QH 10.34f. 10 the earth. •And their parents also watched. And subsequently they were bound in

---

5 a. A portion of the Syr. text begins at this point and continues to the end of the vs.

b. The phrase could be impersonal, "(one) might smite them," i.e. "they might be smitten."

c. There is a portion of the Syr. text which begins at this point and contains the sense of the present vs. although the wording is quite different.

the depths of the earth forever, until the day of great judgment in order for judgment to be executed upon all of those who corrupted their ways and their
11 deeds before the LORD. •And he wiped out every one from their places and not one of them remained whom he did not judge according to all his wickedness.

A new righteousness. The impartial judge will forgive

12 And he made for all his works a new and righteous nature so that they might not sin in all their nature forever, and so that they might all be righteous, each in IQS 3.16
13 his kind, always. •And the judgment of all of them has been ordained and written in the heavenly tablets without injustice. And (if)[d] any of them transgress from their way with respect to what was ordained for them to walk in, or if they do not walk in it, the judgment for every (sort of) nature and every kind has been
14 written. •And there is nothing excluded[e] which is in heaven or on earth or in the light or in the darkness or in Sheol or in the depths or in the place of darkness.
15 And all their judgments are ordained, written, and engraved. •He will judge concerning every one: the great one according to his greatness and the small one
16 according to his smallness, and each one according to his way. •And he is not IQH 15.24 one who accepts persons,[f] and he is not one who accepts gifts when he says that he will execute judgment upon each one. If one gave everything which is in the Deut 10:17 earth, he would not accept gifts or persons. And he would not accept (anything) 2Chr 19:7 from his hand because he is a righteous judge.
17 And for the children of Israel it has been written and ordained, "If they return Jer 36:3 to him in righteousness, he will forgive all of their sins and he will pardon all of Jer 18:8
18 their transgressions." •It is written and it is ordained, "He will have mercy on
19 all who return from all their error, once each year." •But to any who corrupted their way and their counsel before the Flood, he did not show partiality, except Noah alone, for he showed partiality to him for the sake of his sons whom he saved from the waters of the Flood (and) for his sake because his heart was righteous in all of his ways just as it was commanded concerning him. And he did not transgress anything which was ordained for him.

The Flood

Gen 6:14-8:19

20 And the LORD said, "Let everything which is upon dry land be blotted out: men and cattle and beasts and birds of the heaven and whatever moves on the
21 earth." •And he commanded Noah to make an ark for himself so that he might
22 save himself from the water of the Flood. •And Noah made an ark in all respects just as he commanded him in the twenty-second jubilee of years in the fifth week
23 in the fifth year. •And he entered it in the sixth year in the second month on the first of the second month until the sixteenth day. And he and everything which we brought to him entered into the ark. And the LORD shut it up from outside on the evening of the seventeenth.

24 And the LORD opened the seven floodgates of heaven,
and the mouths of the springs of the great deep were seven mouths in 1En 89:2-7 number;
25 and these floodgates sent down water from heaven forty days and forty nights,
and the springs of the deep sent up water until the whole world was full of water.

---

d. There is no external marker to indicate that this first clause is conditional, and Charles did not translate it as such. The sentence is admittedly difficult. Charles's Eth. text reads "all who," but we have followed the reading of MS A, which does not use a relative.

e. Nothing is excluded from liability before the judgment mentioned in vs. 13.

f. Lit. "accepts a face." What it means, of course, is that "he does not show partiality," but the parallelism involved in describing one who accepts both persons and gifts (i.e. bribes) seemed worth preserving in this vs.

26   And the water increased upon the earth,
        fifteen cubits the water rose over every tall mountain;
        and the ark rose from upon the earth,
        and it moved upon the surface of the water.

27 And all of the water stayed upon the surface of the earth five months, one
28 hundred and fifty days. •And the ark went and rested on the top of Lubar, one of
29 the mountains of Ararat. •And in the fourth month the springs of the great deep
    were closed and the floodgates of heaven were held shut. And on the new moon
    of the seventh month, all of the mouths of the deeps of the earth were opened.
30 And the water began to go down into the depths below. •And on the first of the
    tenth month, the heads of the mountains appeared, and on the first of the first
31 month, the land appeared. •And the water dried up from upon the earth in the
    fifth week, in its seventh year. And on the seventeenth day in the second month,
32 the land was dry. •And on its twenty-seventh day, he opened the ark and he sent
    out of it the beasts, and cattle and birds and whatever moved.

Debarkation and sacrifice   Gen 8:20

1   **6** And[a] on the first of the third month, he went out of the ark, and he built an   1QapGen 10.13
2   altar on that mountain. •And he made atonement for the land. And he took the
    kid of a goat, and he made atonement with its blood for all the sins of the land   Lev 18:26-28
    because everything which was on it had been blotted out except those who were   Num 35:33f.
3   in the ark with Noah. •And he offered up the fat upon the altar. And he took a   1QapGen 10.15
    calf,[b] a goat, a lamb, [kids[c]], salt, a turtledove, and a young dove,[d] and he offered
    up a burnt offering on the altar. And he placed upon them an offering kneaded
    with oil. And he sprinkled wine, and placed frankincense upon everything. And   Ex 29:40
    he offered up a sweet aroma which was pleasing before the LORD.   Lev 2:2-5

The covenant with Noah and laws prohibiting the eating of blood   Gen 8:21-9:17

4   And the LORD smelled the sweet aroma, and he made a covenant with him so
    that there might not be floodwaters which would destroy the earth. All the days
    of the earth, seed (time) and harvest will not cease. Cold and heat and summer
    and winter and day and night will not change their ordinances or cease forever.
5   "But as for you, increase and be multiplied on the earth and become many upon
    it, and become a blessing upon it. Fear and terror of you I will set upon everything
6   which is on the land or in the sea. •And behold, I have given you all of the beasts
    and everything which flies and everything which moves upon the earth and in the
    water, the fish and everything, for food like the green herbs. And I have given
7   you everything so that you might eat. •But flesh which is (filled) with life, (that
    is) with blood, you shall not eat—because the life of all flesh is in the blood—
    lest your blood be sought for your lives.

        From the hand of every man,
        from the hand of every (creature),
        I will seek the blood of a man.
8   Whoever pours out the blood of a man,
        by man his blood shall be poured out,
        because in the image of the LORD he made Adam.

6 a. A portion of the Syr. text begins at this point
and continues through vs. 3.
    b. The Eth. word which is translated "calf" is
ambiguous. It could also mean "bull" or "cow,"
but the Syr. text clearly reads "calf."
    c. The sudden appearance of "kids" in the
plural is unusual. It is not the same word for "kid"
that was used in vs. 2, but it is the word which

was translated "goat" in vs. 2. The word is lacking
in the Syr. and is therefore best understood as an
Eth. gloss.
    d. The words for "turtledove" and "young
dove" are plural in Syr. In editing the Syr. text,
Tisserant suggested that the plural forms were
preferable because those birds were regularly offered in pairs.

9 And as for you, increase and become many in the land."
10   And Noah and his sons swore that they would not eat any blood which was in
any flesh. And he made a covenant before the LORD God forever in all of the
generations of the earth in that month.
11   Therefore, he spoke to you so that you also might make a covenant with the
children of Israel with an oath in this month upon the mountain. And you will   Ex 19:1
sprinkle blood upon them on account of all of the words of the covenant which   Lev 17:10,12
12 the LORD made with them for all time. •This testimony is written concerning
you so that you might keep it always lest you ever eat any blood of the beasts or   Deut 12:23
birds or cattle throughout all of the days of the earth. And the man who eats the
blood of the beasts or cattle or birds throughout all of the days of the earth shall
13 be uprooted, he and his seed from the earth. •And you, command the children of   1QapGen 11.17
Israel not to eat any blood so that their names and seed might be before the LORD
14 God always. •And there is no limit of days for this law because it is forever.
They shall keep it for their generations so that they might make supplication on
your behalf with blood before the altar on every day. And at the hour of daybreak   Lev 17:11
and evening they will seek atonement on their own[e] behalf continually before the
LORD so that they might guard it and not be rooted out.   Num 28:3-8
15   And he gave a sign to Noah and his children that there should not again be a
16 flood upon the earth. •He set his bow in the clouds for a sign of the covenant
which is forever, that the water of the Flood should therefore not be upon the
earth to destroy it all of the days of the earth.

The feast of Shebuot

17   Therefore, it is ordained and written in the heavenly tablets that they should
observe the feast of Shebuot[f] in this month, once per year, in order to renew the   Ex 34:22
18 covenant in all (respects), year by year. •And all of this feast was celebrated in
heaven from the day of creation until the days of Noah, twenty-six jubilees and
five weeks of years. And Noah and his children kept it for seven jubilees and one
week of years until the day of the death of Noah. And from the day of the death
of Noah, his sons corrupted it until the days of Abraham, and they ate blood.   CD 3.6
19 But Abraham alone kept it. And Isaac and Jacob and his sons kept it until your
days, but in your days the children of Israel forgot it until you renewed it for
them on this mountain.
20   And you, command the children of Israel so that they might keep this feast in
all of their generations as a commandment to them. One day per year in this
21 month they shall celebrate the feast, •for it is the feast of Shebuot and it is the   Ex 23:16
feast of the first fruits. This feast is twofold and of two natures.[g] Just as it is   Num 28:26

e. The Eth. MSS provide three different readings
here: "on behalf of them," "it," or "you" (masculine plural).
   f. Although the Eth. word means "weeks,"
"Shebuot" was used in an attempt to maintain a
degree of openness to the double meaning of the
Heb. word which undoubtedly appeared in the
original text of Jub. In an unpointed Heb. text the
consonants *šb'wt* could be translated either "weeks"
or "oaths." The MT vocalizes the absolute form
of the word for "weeks" as *šābu'ot* and the word
for "oaths" as *šĕbu'ōt*, but "weeks" also appears
as *šĕbu'ōt* in the construct. We have chosen the
less precise spelling Shebuot to reflect the ambiguity
of an unpointed text, and do not intend to favor
one meaning over the other.
   The feast referred to by the Eth. word is, of
course, better known by the name of Pentecost or
weeks, but both of these names are supposedly
derived from the number of days (or weeks) which
separate that feast from the offering of the Omer
(Lev 23:9–17). Since the book of Jub, which is

particularly sensitive to chronology, does not identify this feast in relation to the passing of seven
weeks, S. Zeitlin (*The Book of Jubilees: Its Character and Its Significance* [Philadelphia, 1939])
made the following observation: "I venture to say
that even the name Shabuot in the Book of Jubilees
has not the connotation of 'weeks,' but means
'oaths' " (p. 6). Zeitlin supported his statement by
noting that the covenant between God and Noah
provided the context for establishing the feast and
that the covenant with Abraham in ch. 15 also
occurred on this festival. The significance of this
double meaning of weeks and oaths was probably
not lost on the author of Jub. The spelling Shebuot
is an attempt to maintain that double meaning.
   g. The "double nature" may be due to the
double sense of Shebuot discussed in the preceding
n. Although not mentioned in Jub, the feast may
have marked the passing of "weeks" in the agricultural year and also celebrated the "oaths" made
to Noah and Abraham.

22 written and engraved concerning it, observe it. •This is because I have written it
in the book of the first law, which I wrote for you, so that you might observe it
in each of its appointed times, one day per year. And I have told you its sacrificial
offering so that the children of Israel might remember them and observe them in
their generations in this month one day each year.

23 And on the first of the first month and on the first of the fourth month and on   1QS 10.5
the first of the seventh month and on the first of the tenth month are the days of   Lev 23:24
remembrance and they are the days of appointed times in the four parts of the
24 year. They are written and inscribed for an eternal witness. •And Noah ordained
them for himself as feasts for eternal generations because they were a memorial
25 for him. •And on the first of the first month, he was told to make an ark. And on
26 it the land dried up, and he opened up and saw the land. •And on the first of the   1En 89:7f.
fourth month, the mouths of the deeps of the abysses which were beneath were
shut. And on the first of the seventh month, all of the mouths of the depths of
27 the earth were opened, and the water began to go down into them. •On the first
28 of the tenth month the heads of the mountains appeared, and Noah rejoiced. •And
therefore he ordained them for himself as feasts of remembrance forever, and thus
29 they are ordained. •And they set them upon the heavenly tablets. Each one of
them is thirteen weeks from one to another of the remembrances, from the first
to the second, and from the second to the third, and from the third to the fourth.
30 And all of the days which will be commanded will be fifty-two weeks of days,
31 and all of them are a complete year. •Thus it is engraved and ordained on the
heavenly tablets, and there is no transgressing in a single year, from year to year.

The danger in failing to observe a 364-day calendar

32 And you, command the children of Israel so that they shall guard the years in   1QS 1.14f.
this number, three hundred and sixty-four days, and it will be a complete year.   1QH 12.8f.
                                                                                   1En 74:10,12;
And no one shall corrupt its (appointed) time from its days or from its feasts   75:2
because all (of the appointed times) will arrive in them according to their testimony,   2En 48:1
33 and they will not pass over a day, and they will not corrupt a feast. •But if they   1En 82:4-6
are transgressed, and they do not observe them according to his commandment,
then they will corrupt all of their (fixed) times, and the years will be moved from
34 within this (order), and they will transgress their ordinances. •And all of the sons   CD 3.14
of Israel will forget, and they will not find the way of the years. And they will
forget the new moons and (appointed) times and sabbaths. And they will set awry
35 all of the ordinances of the years. •For I know and henceforth I shall make you
know—but not from my own heart, because the book is written before me and is
ordained in the heavenly tablets of the division of days—lest they forget the feasts
of the covenant and walk in the feasts of the gentiles, after their errors and after
their ignorance.
36 And there will be those who will examine the moon diligently because it will
corrupt the (appointed) times and it will advance from year to year ten days.
37 Therefore, the years will come to them as they corrupt and make a day of testimony
a reproach and a profane day a festival, and they will mix up everything, a holy
day (as) profaned and a profane (one) for a holy day, because they will set awry
38 the months and sabbaths and feasts and jubilees. •Therefore, I shall command you
and I shall bear witness to you so that you may bear witness to them because
after you have died your sons will be corrupted so that they will not make a year
only three hundred and sixty-four days. And therefore, they will set awry the
months and the (appointed) times and the sabbaths and the feasts, and they will
eat all of the blood with all flesh.

Noah's sacrifice   Gen 9:20

1 **7** And in the seventh week in the first year in that jubilee, Noah planted a vine   1QapGen 12.13
on the mountain on which the ark rested, whose name is Lubar, (one) of the

mountains of Ararat. And it produced fruit in the fourth year, and he guarded its
2 fruit; and he picked it in that year in the seventh month, •and he made wine from 1QapGen 12.15
it, and he put it in a vessel, and he guarded it until the fifth year, until the first
3 day on the first of the first month. •And on that day he made a feast with rejoicing.
And he made a burnt offering to the LORD, one calf from the bulls, one ram, a Num 29:2-5
lamb of seven years, and one kid of the goats in order that he might thereby seek
4 atonement for himself and for his sons. •And he prepared the kid first. And he
placed some of its blood on the flesh which was on the altar which he had made.
And all of the fat and the bull and the ram and the lamb he offered up upon the
altar, where he made the burnt offering. And he offered up all of their flesh upon
5 the altar. •And he placed all of their sacrifice upon it, kneaded with oil. And after
that, he sprinkled wine in the fire which he had placed upon the altar. And he
presented frankincense upon the altar, and offered up a sweet odor which is
6 pleasing before the LORD his God, •and rejoiced. And he drank some of that
wine, he and his sons, with rejoicing.

The curse of Canaan and the blessing of Shem   Gen 9:21-27

7   And when evening came, he entered into his tent, and lay down drunk. And
8 he slept, and was uncovered in his tent as he was sleeping. •And Ham saw Noah,
9 his father, naked. And he went out, and told his two brothers outside. •And Shem
took his garment, and he stood up, he and Japheth, and they placed the garment
on their shoulders and, turning backward, they covered the shame of their father,
and their faces were backward.
10   And Noah woke up from his wine, and knew everything which his youngest
son had done to him. And he cursed his son and said, "Cursed is Canaan, let
11 him be an enslaved servant of his brothers." •And he blessed Shem, and said:

> "May the LORD, the God of Shem, be blessed.
> And may Canaan be his servant.
12   May the LORD enlarge Japheth,
> and may the LORD dwell in the dwelling place of Shem,
> and may Canaan be his servant."

13 And Ham knew that his father cursed his youngest son, and it was disgusting to
him that he cursed his son. And he separated from his father, he and his sons
with him: Cush and Mizraim and Put and Canaan.

The cities of Noah's three sons

14   And he (Ham) built a city for himself and he named it after his wife,
15 Na'eltama'uk. •And Japheth saw it and was jealous of his brother. And he also
16 built a city for himself and named it after his wife, 'Adataneses. •And Shem dwelt
with his father, Noah, and built a city near his father on the mountain. And he
17 also named it after his wife, Sedeqetelebab. •And behold, these three cities were
near Mount Lubar, Sedeqetelebab was in front of the mountain on its east, and
Na'eltama'uk was facing south, and 'Adataneses was toward the west.

The sons of Shem and Japheth

18   And these are the sons of Shem: Elam and Ashur and Arpachshad, who was 1QapGen 12.10
19 born two years after the Flood, and Lud and Aram. •The sons of Japheth are:
Gomer and Magog and Madai and Javon, Tubal and Meshech and Tiras. These
are sons of Noah.

The testament of Noah: avoid fornication, blood pollution, injustice

20   And in the twenty-eighth jubilee Noaḥ began to command his grandsons with
ordinances and commandments and all of the judgments which he knew. And he 2Pet 2:5

bore witness to his sons so that they might do justice and cover the shame of their
flesh and bless the one who created them and honor father and mother, and each
one love his neighbor and preserve themselves from fornication and pollution and   CD 4.14f.
21 from all injustice. •For on account of these three the Flood came upon the earth.
For (it was) because of the fornication which the Watchers, apart from the mandate   Lev 17:7
of their authority, fornicated with the daughters of men and took for themselves   1En 7:1
22 wives from all whom they chose and made a beginning of impurity. •And they
begot sons, the Naphidim, and all of them were dissimilar. And each one ate his   1En 86:4; 88:2
fellow. The giants killed the Naphil, and the Naphil killed the Elyo, and the Elyo   1En 15:11
23 mankind, and man his neighbor. •And everyone sold himself in order that he
might do injustice and pour out much blood, and the earth was full of injustice.   1Kgs 21:20
24 And afterward, they sinned against beasts, and birds and everything which moves   1En 9:1,9
or walks upon the earth. And they poured out much blood upon the earth. And   1En 7:5
all the thoughts and desires of men were always contemplating vanity and evil.
25 And the LORD blotted out everything from the face of the earth on account of
the evil of their deeds. And on account of the blood which they poured out in the
midst of the land, he blotted out everything.
26   "And[a] we were left, I and you, my children, and everything which entered
with us into the ark. And behold, I see your deeds before me that you have not
been ones who walked in righteousness because you have begun to walk in the
paths of corruption. And each one of you will be separated from his neighbor.
And this one will be jealous of that one, and (I see) that you will not be together,
27 O my sons, each one with his brother. •For I see, and behold, the demons have
begun to mislead you and your children. And now I fear for your sakes that after
I die, you will pour out the blood of men upon the earth. And you will be blotted
28 out from the surface of the earth. •For all who eat the blood of man and all who
eat the blood of any flesh will be blotted out, all of them, from the earth.   Lev 7:27

29   And no man who eats blood or sheds the blood of man will remain upon
     the earth;
     and neither seed nor posterity will remain alive for him under heaven.
     For they will go down into Sheol,   1En 103:7f.
     and into the place of judgment they will descend.
     And into the darkness of the depths they will all be removed with a cruel
     death.

30   "And let no blood from any of the blood which is in anything be seen upon   Ezek 24:7
you on the day when you sacrifice any beast or cattle or what flies upon the earth.   Lev 17:13
But do a good deed for yourselves by covering that which will be poured out
31 upon the surface of the earth. •And you shall not be like one who eats with blood,   Lev 19:26
but beware lest they should eat blood before you. Cover the blood, because thus
I was commanded to testify to you and to your children together with all flesh.
32 And you shall not eat living flesh lest it be that your blood which is your life be   Lev 17:10,11,14
33 sought by the hand of all flesh which eats upon the earth. •For the land will not
be cleansed of the blood which is poured out upon it, because by the blood of   Num 35:33
one who poured it out will the land be cleansed in all of its generations.

The testament of Noah and the law of reserving first fruits

34   "And now, my children, hear (and) do justice and righteousness so that you   Jer 11:17
might be planted in righteousness on the surface of the whole earth, and your   Amos 9:15
                                                                                     1En 10:16; 93:5,
                                                                                     10

7 a. The point at which direct discourse begins is
not certain. It might have begun with vs. 21.
  b. B C read "be consecrated."
  c. Against the unanimous witness of all of the
Eth. MSS known to me, I have emended the "fifth
year" to read "seventh year." The year of release
mentioned in Deut 15:1, 9 is the seventh year.

Charles dealt with the problem by assuming a
lacuna. The missing section would have described
the events of the fifth year and then introduced the
seventh year as the year of release. Compare Lev
19:25 and the practice of Noah in Jub 7:2 in support
of a lacuna dealing with the fifth year.

honor may be lifted up before my God who saved me from the water of the Flood.
35 And behold, you will go and build for yourselves cities, and you will plant in 1En 84:6
2Pet 2:5
them every plant which is upon the earth and every tree, moreover, which bears
36 fruit. •For three years its fruit will not be gathered from everything which may Lev 19:23f.
be eaten, but in the fourth year its fruit will be gathered.[b] And let one offer up
the first fruits which are acceptable before the LORD Most High, who made
heaven and earth and everything, so that they might offer up in the juice the first
of the wine and the oil as first fruits upon the altar of the LORD, who will accept
it. And that which is left the servants of the house of the LORD will eat before
37 the altar which receives (it). •And in the seventh year[c] make its release so that Deut 15:1,9
Lev 25:2-7
you might release it in righteousness and uprightness. And you will be righteous
38 and all your plants will be upright, •because, thus, Enoch, the father of your
father, commanded Methuselah, his son, and Methuselah (commanded) Lamech,
his son. And Lamech commanded me everything which his fathers commanded
39 him. •And I am commanding you, my sons, just as Enoch commanded his son in
the first jubilees. While he was alive in his seventh generation, he commanded 1En 60:8; 93:3
Jude 14
and bore witness to his son and his grandsons until the day of his death."

Cainan's discovery of astrological lore

1 **8** And on the twenty-ninth jubilee in the first week, at its beginning Arpachshad
took a wife and her name was Rasu'eya, daughter of Susan, daughter of Elam,
as a wife. And she bore a son for him in the third year of that week, and he called
2 him Cainan,[a] •and the child grew. And his father taught him writing. And he Lk 3:36
3 went forth in order that he might seek a place where he could build[b] a city. •And
he found a writing which the ancestors engraved on stone. And he read what was
in it. And he transcribed it. And he sinned because of what was in it, since there
was in it the teaching of the Watchers by which they used to observe the omens
4 of the sun and moon and stars within all the signs of heaven. •And he copied it
down, but he did not tell about it because he feared to tell Noah about it lest he
be angry with him because of it.

The descendants of Cainan

Gen 10:24f.

5 And in the thirtieth jubilee in the second week in its first year, he took a wife
and her name was Melka, daughter of Madai,[c] son of Japheth. And in its fourth
year he begot a son and he called him Shelah because, he said, "I have certainly
been sent out."[d]
6 And in the fourth year Shelah was born and he grew up. And he took a wife
and her name was Mu'ak, daughter of Kesed, his father's brother, as a wife in
the thirty-first[e] jubilee in the fifth week in the first year. And she bore a son for
him in its fifth year, and he called him 'Eber.
7 And he took a wife, and her name was 'Azurad, daughter of Nebrod, in the
8 thirty-second jubilee in the seventh week in its third year. •And in its sixth year
she bore a son for him. And he called him Peleg because in the days when he
was born the sons of Noah began dividing up the earth for themselves. Therefore
9 he called him Peleg.[f] •And they divided it in an evil (manner) among themselves,
and they told it to Noah.

---

8 a. A portion of the Syr. text begins at this point
and continues through vs. 4. The proper spelling
of Cainan appears in the Syr. The Eth. text spells
it with a final "m."

b. The reading "build" is supplied by the Syr.
The Eth. reads "acquire" or "possess." As Tisserant pointed out in his discussion of the Syr., the
confusion is probably due to a misreading of Heb.
bn' as *qn'*.

c. The spelling of the name has been altered to
agree with the reading which is given in *codex*

Basil. gr. 1 edited by de Lagarde. The relevant
portion of text has been reproduced by Denis,
Fragmenta, p. 86. The Eth. reads *'Abadāy*.

d. The Heb. root for the verb "to send" contains
the same consonants (*Šlḥ*) as the name Shelah.

e. The Eth. has the word for "year," but the
emendation to "first" is obvious.

f. The Heb. root for the verb "to divide"
contains the same consonants (*plg*) as the name
Peleg.

The division of the earth

10 And it came to pass at the beginning of the thirty-third jubilee, that they divided the land (in) three parts, for Shem, Ham, and Japheth, according to the inheritance of each, in the first year in the first week, while one of us who were sent was
11 dwelling with them. •And he called his children, and they came to him, they and their children. And heᵍ divided by lot the land which his three sons would possess. And they stretched out their hands and took the document from the bosom of Noah, their father.

Shem's portion

Gen 10:26-31

12 And the lot of Shem was assigned in the document as the middle of the earth, which he would take for his possession and for his sons for eternal generations from the midst of the Rafa Mountains,ʰ from the mouth of the water of the river Tina.ⁱ And his portion goes on toward the west through the midst of this river, and it goes on until it draws near to the water of the abysses from which this river goes forth. And its waters pour forth into the Me'atʲ Sea. And this river goes on into the Great Sea. And everything which is toward the north belongs to Japheth,
13 and everything which is toward the south belongs to Shem. •And (his portion) goes on until it draws near Karaso,ᵏ which is in the bosom of the tongue which
14 looks toward the south. •And his portion goes on toward the Great Sea. And it goes straight until it draws near to the west of the tongue which looks toward the
15 south because the name of this sea is the tongue of the Sea of Egypt. •And it is turned from there toward the south, toward the mouth of the Great Seaˡ on the shore of the waters. And it goes on toward the west of 'Afra.ᵐ And it goes on until it draws near the water of the river Gihon,ⁿ and toward the south of the
16 water of Gihon, toward the shore of that river. •And it goes on toward the east until it draws near to the garden of Eden toward its south, to the south and east of all the land of Eden, and to all of the east. And it turns in the east, and it comes forth until it draws near toward the last of the mountain whose name is
17 Rafa. And it goes down toward the shore of the mouth of the Tina River. •This portion was assigned by lot to Shem and to his sons to possess it forever for his generations forever.
18 And Noah rejoiced because this portion was assigned to Shem and for his sons. And he remembered everything which he spoke with his mouth concerning him because he said:

Ezek 38:12
1En 26:1

Gen 2:13

---

g. A portion of the Syr. text begins at this point and summarizes the remainder of the ch.

h. Rafa is probably the vague Rhipaean Mountains of early Gk. geographers whence the major rivers flowed.

i. The Tina is the river Don, which set the boundary between the land of Shem and Japheth. At this point the author of Jub is following hellenistic views of geography. Some geographers took the Don and the Nile (Gihon in Jub) as the boundaries of the three continents. It has been suggested that such a view may have been held by Hecataeus of Miletus (c. 500 B.C.) with whom Herodotus disputed in his Histories 2.16 regarding the use of the Nile to divide the continents.

j. Me'at is Lake Maeotis.

k. Karaso is probably Chersonese, an ancient name for the Gallipoli Peninsula, which extends into the Aegean Sea west of the Hellespont. In order to make this identification, which Charles rejected, it is necessary to assume that the author of Jub divided the Great Sea, i.e. the Mediterranean,

into at least four regions. In the north there were three "tongues," the Aegean, the Adriatic, and the Tyrrhenian seas. In the south there was a region known as the Sea of Egypt. From that perspective, the Aegean was the tongue which looked toward Egypt. Likewise from that perspective, Chersonese lies in the bosom of the tongue which looks south. For further discussion consult G. Hölscher, *Drei Erdkarten* (Heidelberg, 1949) pp. 57–73.

l. The Great Sea is the Mediterranean.

m. Africa, at least the portion through which the Nile flows. See also nn. w and x.

n. The Nile. The early geographers were uninformed about the sources of the Nile. For them, it apparently flowed south beyond the borders of Egypt and then flowed sharply eastward. Inasmuch as our writer identifies it with Gihon, one of the four rivers flowing out of the garden of Eden, it was obvious to him that it must have flowed eastward so that one could reach Eden by following it.

May the LORD God of Shem be blessed,
and may the LORD dwell in the dwelling place of Shem.

19 And he knew that the garden of Eden was the holy of holies and the dwelling of
the LORD. And Mount Sinai (was) in the midst of the desert and Mount Zion
(was) in the midst of the navel of the earth. The three of these were created as
20 holy places, one facing the other. •And he blessed the God of gods, who placed
21 in his mouth the word of the LORD, and also the Eternal God.° •And he knew
that a blessed portion and blessing had reached Shem and his sons for eternal
generations: all the land of Eden, all of the land of the Red Sea, all of the land
of the East, India, along the Red Sea, and its mountains, all of the land of Basa,
all of the land of Lebanon, the islands of Caphtor, all of Mount Senir, Amanus,
Mount Asshur, which is north, all of the land of Elam, Asshur, Babel, Susa,
Media, all of the mountains of Ararat, and all of the region beyond the sea,ᵖ
which is beyond Mount Asshur, which is toward the north, the blessed and wide
land. And everything which is in it is very good.

1QapGen 19.8
Ezek 38:12
1En 26:1

1QapGen
21.15f.

Jer 47:4
Amos 9:7
Song 4:8

Ham's portion

Gen 10:6-20

22 And to Ham was assigned the second portion toward the other side of the
Gihon, toward the south on the right of the garden. And it goes on toward the
south, and it goes along all of the mountains of fire.�q And (his portion) goes on
toward the west, toward the Atelʳ Sea. And it goes on westward until it draws
23 near the Ma'ukˢ Sea, to which nothing descends without perishing.ᵗ •And it goes
forth in the north to the end of Gadir.ᵘ And it goes forth along the edge of the
water of the sea into the waters of the Great Sea until it approaches the river
Gihon. And it goes on along the Gihon River until it approaches the right side of
24 the garden of Eden. •And this is the land that went forth to Ham as̬ a portion
which he will possess forever for himself and for his children for their generations
forever.

1QapGen 19.13
1En 18:6-9;
24:1-3

Japheth's portion

Gen 10:2-5

25 And for Japheth the third portion was assigned beyond the Tina River toward
the north of the mouth of its waters. And it goes on toward the northeast of all
26 of the region of Gog and everything east of it. •And it goes on toward the north
to the north. And it goes toward the mountains of Qeltᵛ toward the north, toward

---

o. The Eth. text reads "the LORD forever," but
that is probably a slight corruption of the Heb. 'ēl
'ōlām. Cf. Gen 21:33 and Isa 40:28.

p. Probably the Caspian.

q. Apparently a long range of mountains ringing
the southern boundary of the world just as the Rafa
Mountains marked a northern border. See G.
Hölscher, *Drei Erdkarten*, p. 58, for a map.

r. The Atlantic.

s. The word Ma'uk is spelled *ma'kaka* in EMML
101. In the Syr. text the spelling suggested by
Tisserant was *Maḥouq*. The Ma'uk Sea is the world
ocean, known to the Greeks as *ōkeanos*. Charles
sought to derive Ma'uk from Gk. word, but
that now seems impossible in light of the Syr.
spelling. I would suggest that it is a *mem* prefor-
mative noun from the Heb. root *ḥqq* with the
meaning "place of the boundary (of waters)." The
same root is used in Prov 8:29: "when he assigned
the sea its *limit*." The consonantal spelling of the
name would be *mḥqq*. The precise phonetic value
of each of the consonants has been preserved in
Syr., a fact which both depends on and reinforces

the view that the Syr. text was translated directly
from the Heb. The final double consonant is
reflected by the reading of EMML 101, which
preserves a form that could easily represent a Gk.
transcription of the Heb. original. The Syr. form
may also reflect a final double consonant if we
assume a simple misreading of *mḥqq* as *mḥwq*.
The confusion of "w" and "q" is relatively simple,
depending on the Syr. script that is used.

t. The reading of the final phrase is based on an
interpretation of the Syr. text. The Eth. text is
seriously confused at this point. At best we can
offer an awkward literal rendering of MS C and
EMML 101: "Ma'uk, which is that one into which
that which will be destroyed descends." All other
MSS read "that which will not be destroyed."

u. Cadiz, located on the southern Atlantic coast
of Spain. The name Gadir is Semitic, meaning a
"walled" or "fortified" place. It was founded as
a distant colony of Tyre.

v. This refers to the Celts who live in the far
northwest toward the Ma'uk Sea.

the Ma'uk Sea, and it comes toward the east of Gadir up toward the edge of the
27 water of the sea. •And it goes on until it draws near toward the west of Fereg^w
and it returns toward 'Afreg.^x And it goes on toward the east, toward the water
28 of the Me'at Sea. •And it goes on toward the side of the Tina River, toward the
northeast until it approaches the end of its waters, toward Mount Rafa. And it
29 goes around to the north. •This is the land which came to Japheth and to his sons
as the portion of his inheritance which he will possess for himself and for his sons
for their generations forever: the five great islands and a great land in the north.
30 But it is cold, and the land of Ham is hot, but the land of Shem is not hot or cold
because it is mixed with cold and heat.

The portions of the sons of Ham, Shem, and Japheth

Gen 10

1 **9** And Ham divided (his land) among his sons. And the first portion was assigned
to Cush^a toward the east, and west of him for Mizraim.^b And west of him for
2 Put.^c And west of him for Canaan. And toward his west was the sea. •And Shem
also divided among his sons. And the first portion was assigned to Elam and his
sons toward the east of the Tigris River until it approaches toward the east of all
of the land of India, along the Red Sea^d on its shore, the waters of Dedan,^e and
all of the mountains of Mebri^f and Elam^g all of the land of Susa, and everything
3 which is beside Pharnak^h as far as the Red Sea and up to the Tina River. •And
also to Asshur was assigned the second portion, all of the land of Asshur and
Nineveh and Shinar^i and as far as the vicinity of India. And then it goes up and
4 skirts the river.^j •And to Arpachshad was assigned the third portion, all of the
land of the region of Chaldea^k toward the east of the Euphrates, which is near the
Red Sea, and all of the waters of the desert as far as the vicinity of the tongue of
the sea which faces toward Egypt, all of the land of Lebanon and Senir^l and
5 Amana as far as the vicinity of the Euphrates. •And to Aram the fourth portion

w. *Fērēg* is the reading found in MS A, and is
probably closest to the original text. The spelling
of this name, which apparently represents Africa,
differs from MS to MS and from place to place in
the text. The Syr. form which occurs at this point
is *'afgerā*, with an initial *aleph* and metathesis of
the "g" and "r." The name also appears in vs.
15 and possibly a second time in the present vs.
The significance of drawing toward the west of
Africa may simply indicate the southward movement around the boot of Italy or it may imply that
the boundary between Japheth and Ham is in the
southern Mediterranean in order to claim the islands
for Japheth.

x. *'Afrēg* is the spelling in MS B. It is closest to
the Heb. and Aram. spelling for Africa (*'aphrīqī*)
of the forms given thus far. Hölscher assumes
that it represents a second mention of Africa (*Drei
Erdkarten*, p. 71). Charles, however, suggested in
his English translation that it referred to Phrygia.
Phrygia could easily be a stopping point in the
direction of the Me'at Sea. According to Josephus
(*Ant* 1.6.1), Phrygia belonged to Japheth. A further
bit of evidence may also be added to Charles's
argument; GenR refers to Phrygia (at the beginning
of ch. 37) by the name *'aphrīqī*, a homograph for
Africa. Inasmuch as that fact shows that it was
possible to use the same spelling when referring to
Africa or to Phrygia, we may not be able to
determine which one is intended here. Nevertheless,
it may be noted that in vs. 15 and in the first
mention of Africa in the present vs., the phrase
"west of" is used to define the location more
specifically. It is possible that such a phrase was

used to distinguish Africa from Phrygia inasmuch
as they were spelled alike.

9 a. The Eth. text has *kwes* for Cush, but the
intent of the author is clear. In this vs. he is dealing
with the four sons of Ham mentioned in Gen 10:6.
Cush is the land located directly south of Egypt.

b. Egypt.

c. Libya, or some part of it.

d. In the mind of the geographer, the Red Sea
was a huge eastern sea. Balancing the Mediterranean in the west, it included the Indian Ocean,
thus reaching to India.

e. The biblical Dedan is a prosperous caravan
city in northeast Arabia somewhere near Taima
(Isa 21:13; Ezek 25:13).

f. Mebrī is also spelled Mazbār. The site is
unknown.

g. Only MS A reads *'Ēlām*. The other MSS read
'Ēlā. One might not ordinarily expect Elam to be
part of a list mentioning the holdings of Elam, but
in vs. 3 the land of Asshur is given to Asshur.

h. Hölscher (*Drei Erdkarten*, p. 69f.) has identified Pharnak with a site along the Farah River
near the border of Iran and Afghanistan, and has
cited a passage in which Assarhadon represented
himself as subduer of the land of Parnaki.

i. Babylon.

j. The reading follows an emendation suggested
by Charles.

k. Chaldea is the homeland of the Neo-Babylonian Empire.

l. In the neighborhood of Mount Hermon (Song
4:8).

was assigned, all of the land of Mesopotamia, between the Tigris and the Euphrates, toward the north of the Chaldeans up to the vicinity of Mount Asshur and the
6 land of Arara.[m] • And to Lud[n] the fifth portion was assigned, Mount Asshur and everything pertaining to it until it approaches the Great Sea. And it draws near toward the east of Asshur, his brother.

7,8   And Japheth also divided the land of his inheritance between his sons. • And the first portion was assigned to Gomer[o] toward the east from the north side up to the river Tina. And in the north to Magog[p] was assigned all of the inner parts
9 of the north until it approaches toward the Sea of Me'at. • And to Madai[q] his portion was assigned that he should take from the west of his two brothers as far
10 as the islands and up to the coasts of the islands. • And to Javan[r] the fourth portion was assigned, every island and the islands which are toward the side of Lud.
11 And to Tubal[s] the fifth portion was assigned in the midst of the tongue which draws near toward the side of Lud's portion as far as the second tongue into the
12 region beyond the second tongue into the third tongue. • And to Meshech[t] the sixth portion was assigned, everything on the other side of the third tongue until it
13 approaches the east of Gadir. • And to Tiras[u] the seventh portion was assigned, four great islands in the midst of the sea which approaches the portion of Ham. And the islands of Kamaturi[v] were assigned by lot to the sons of Arpachshad as an inheritance for him.

The curse against violating boundaries

14   And thus the sons of Noah divided for their children before Noah, their father. And he made them all swear an oath to curse each and every one who desired to
15 seize a portion which did not come in his lot. • And they all said, "So be it and so let it be to them and to their sons forever in their generations until the day of judgment in which the LORD God will judge them with a sword and with fire on account of all the evil of the pollution of their errors which have filled the earth with sin and pollution and fornication and transgression."

Noah's prayer against the demons

1 **10** In the third week of that jubilee the polluted demons began to lead astray the
2 children of Noah's sons and to lead them to folly and to destroy them. • And the sons of Noah came to Noah, their father, and they told him about the demons
3 who were leading astray and blinding and killing his grandchildren. • And he prayed before the LORD his God and he said, "God of the spirits which are in all flesh, who has acted mercifully with me and saved me and my sons from the water of the Flood and did not let me perish as you did the children of perdition, because

Margin references: 1QapGen 17.16; Ezek 27:13; 1En 15f.; Num 16:22; 27:16; 2Thes 2:3

m. Ararat.

n. Ancient Lydia in Asia Minor.

o. Associated with the Cimmerians, who invaded Asia Minor in the eighth century B.C.

p. Associated with the Sythiör hordes whom Herodotus locates in this area (Histories, 4). The identification of Magog with the Scythians is found in Josephus, Ant 1.6.1.

q. The Medes.

r. Designates Ionians living in Asia Minor.

s. Identified with the Tabal, which is known from Akkadian texts of the ninth century B.C. and later. It was located somewhere in Asia Minor near the area of Cappadocia.

t. Equated with the Muski mentioned in Akkadian texts. It is located west of Tubal in Asia Minor.

u. Identified by Charles in his English translation as "the Tyrseni, a branch of the Pelasgians who lived by piracy on the coasts and islands of the Aegean."

v. From Jub 8:29 we learn that there are five great islands that were assigned to Japheth. 1En 77:8 mentions that there are five great islands in the Mediterranean. Enoch's islands would be Corsica, Sardinia, Sicily, Cyprus, and Crete. In the present vs. the writer may be modifying the view of 8:29 because he assigns only four to Japheth. The fifth belongs to Arpachshad, a son of Shem. If we are to select one of Enoch's five islands for Shem, it would obviously be Crete (Caphtor), in accord with 8:21. Therefore, it seems likely that Kamaturi may be a corruption of Caphtor. It involves the substitution of a labial "m" for a labial "p." There could, of course, be five Mediterranean islands reserved for Japheth, as Jub 8:29 maintains, if we were to count Malta.

> Great was your grace upon me,
> and great was your mercy upon my soul.
> Let your grace be lifted up upon my sons,
> and do not let the evil spirits rule over them,
> lest they destroy them from the earth.

4,5 But bless me and my sons. And let us grow and increase and fill the earth. •And you know that which your Watchers, the fathers of these spirits, did in my days and also these spirits who are alive. Shut them up and take them to the place of judgment. And do not let them cause corruption among the sons of your servant,
6 O my God, because they are cruel and were created to destroy. •And let them not rule over the spirits of the living because you alone know their judgment, and do not let them have power over the children of the righteous henceforth and forever.''

The binding of nine tenths of the demons

7,8 And the LORD our God spoke to us so that we might bind all of them. •And the chief of the spirits, Mastema, came and he said, "O Lord, Creator, leave some of them before me, and let them obey my voice. And let them do everything which I tell them, because if some of them are not left for me, I will not be able to exercise the authority of my will among the children of men because they are (intended) to corrupt and lead astray before my judgment because the evil of the
9 sons of men is great.'' •And he said, "Let a tenth of them remain before him, but let nine parts go down into the place of judgment.''
10 And he told one of us to teach Noah all of their healing because he knew that
11 they would not walk uprightly and would not strive righteously. •And we acted in accord with all of his words. All of the evil ones, who were cruel, we bound in the place of judgment, but a tenth of them we let remain so that they might be
12 subject to Satan upon the earth. •And the healing of all their illnesses together with their seductions we told Noah so that he might heal by means of herbs of
13 the earth. •And Noah wrote everything in a book just as we taught him according to every kind of healing. And the evil spirits were restrained from following the
14 sons of Noah. •And he gave everything which he wrote to Shem, his oldest son, because he loved him much more than all of his sons.

1En 10:4,12
Mk 3:22
1En 69:4,6
1En 15:11f.

1En 10:11-13;
15f.

The death of Noah

15 And Noah slept with his fathers and was buried on Mount Lubar in the land of
16 Ararat. •Nine hundred and fifty years he completed in his life, nineteen jubilees
17 and two weeks and five years. •On account of his righteousness in which he was perfected, his life on earth was more excellent than (any of) the sons of men except Enoch, for the work of Enoch had been created as a witness to the generations of the world so that he might report every deed of each generation in the day of judgment.

Gen 9:28

The Tower of Babel

Gen 11:18;
11:1-9

18 And in the thirty-third jubilee, in the first year of this second week, Peleg took a wife whose name was Lomna, daughter of Sina'ar. And she bore a son for him in the fourth year of that week. And he called him Reu because, he said, "Behold, the sons of man have become evil with perverse counsel so that they are building
19 a city and a tower for themselves in the land of Shinar.'' •For they departed from the land of Ararat toward the east into Shinar, because in his days they built a city and a tower, saying, "Come let us go up in it into heaven.''
20 And they began building. And in the fourth week they baked bricks in fire, and bricks were for them like stones. And the mud with which they plastered was bitumen, which came out of the sea, and the springs of water in the land of

21 Shinar. •And they built it; forty-three years they were building it. Its width was two hundred and three bricks. And the height of a brick was one third its length. Five thousand, four hundred and thirty-three cubits and two palms its height rose
22 up. And thirteen stades (was its wall).ᵃ •And the LORD our God said to us, "Behold, the people are one and they have begun working. Now nothing will escape them. Behold, let us go down and let us mix up their tongues so each one will not hear another's word, and they will be scattered into cities and nations, and, therefore, one counsel will not reside with them until the day of judgment."
23 And the LORD went down and we went down with him. And we saw the city
24 and the tower which the sons of men had built. •And he mixed up their tongues, and, therefore, one did not hear another's word. And so they ceased to build the
25 city and the tower. •Therefore, all of the land of Shinar is called Babel because there the LORD mixed up all the languages of the sons of men. And from there they were scattered into their cities according to each of their languages and
26 nations. •And the LORD sent a great wind upon the tower and overthrew it on   SibOr 3.98-103 the earth. And behold, it is between Asshur and Babylon in the land of Shinar and he called it "the Overthrow."

Canaan's seizure of land in Shem's portion

27 And in the fourth week in the first year in the beginning of it, in the thirty-
28 fourth jubilee, they were scattered from the land of Shinar. •And Ham and his sons went into the land which was his possession, which he found in his portion
29 in the land of the south. •But Canaanᵇ saw that the land of Lebanon as far as the river of Egypt was very good. And he did not go into the land of his inheritance toward the west, that is the sea, but he dwelt in the land of Lebanon, eastward
30 and westward, from the bank of the Jordan and from the shore of the sea. •And Ham, his father, and Cush and Mizraim, his brothers, said to him, "You have dwelt in a land which is not yours nor did it come forth for us by lot. Do not do this, because if you do this, you and your children will fall in the land and be cursed with sedition because by sedition you have dwelt and by sedition your
31 children will fall and you will be uprooted forever. •Do not dwell in the dwelling
32 of Shem because it came to Shem and his sons by lot. •You are cursed and you will be cursed more than all of the sons of Noah by the curse which we swore
33 with an oath before the holy judge and before Noah, our father." •But he would   2Chr 7:8 not listen to them and he dwelt in the land of Lebanon from Hamath to the
34 entrance of Egypt, he and his sons, until this day. •And, therefore, that land is called Canaan.

The settlement of Japheth's sons

35 And Japheth and his sons went toward the sea, and they dwelt in the land of their portion, but Madai saw the land of the sea and it did not please him. And he begged it from Elam and Asshur and Arpachshad, from the brother of his wife. And he dwelt in the land of Media near his wife's brother until this day. And he called his dwelling place and the dwelling place of his sons Media after their father, Madai.

---

10 a. This sentence requires considerable adjust-
ment in translating. There is a parallel Gk. text
preserved in the Catena of Nicephorus. Charles
published the relevant portion with his Eth. text.
The second sentence in this vs. is translated from
that Gk. text. The Eth. is more difficult to fit in
the context. It reads "thirteen solid bricks (were)
in it."

The third sentence is a free translation. The
literal translation reads "And one third of one (was)
its height."
In the last sentence, which mentions "thirteen
stades," the Eth. word translated "stades" is a
measure of an unknown distance.
b. There is a portion of the Syr. text which is
parallel to the first part of this vs.

The birth of Serug marks the rise of war and other evils Gen 11:20

1 **11** And in the thirty-fifth jubilee, in the third week, in the first year thereof, Reu took a wife and her name was 'Ora,[a] daughter of 'Ur, son of Kesed.[b] And she bore a son for him and he called him Seroh in the seventh year of that week in 2 that jubilee. •And the sons of Noah began fighting in order to take captive and to kill each other, to pour the blood of man upon the earth, to eat blood, to build fortified cities and walls and towers, so that (one) man will be raised up over the people, to set up the first kingdoms to go to war, people against people and nation against nation and city against city, and everyone (will act) to do evil and to acquire weapons of battle and to teach their sons war. And they began to take 3 captive a city and to sell male and female slaves. •And 'Ur, the son of Kesed, built the city of 'Ur of the Chaldees[c] and he named it after his name and his 4 father's name. •And they made for themselves molten images, and everyone worshiped the icon which they made for themselves as a molten image. And they began making graven images and polluted likenesses. And cruel spirits assisted 5 them and led them astray so that they might commit sin and pollution. •And the prince, Mastema, acted forcefully to do all of this. And he sent other spirits to 1En 10:8 those who were set under his hand to practice all error and sin and all transgression, 6 to destroy, to cause to perish and to pour out blood upon the earth. •Therefore he called the name of Seroh, "Serug," because everyone had turned back to commit all sin and transgression.[d]

The birth of Nahor Gen 11:22

7 And he grew up and dwelt in 'Ur of the Chaldees near the father of his wife's mother. And he used to worship idols. And he took a wife in the thirty-sixth jubilee, in the fifth week, in the first year thereof. And her name was Melka,[e] 8 daughter of Kaber, daughter of his father's brother. •And she bore for him Nahor in the first year of that week. And he grew up and he dwelt in 'Ur among the Chaldeans, and his father taught him the researches of the Chaldeans in order to practice divination and astrology according to the signs of heaven.

The birth of Terah marks a devastation by crows Gen 11:24

9 And in the thirty-seventh jubilee, in the sixth week, in the first year thereof, he took a wife. And her name was 'Iyaska,[f] daughter of Nestag of the Chaldees. 10,11 And she bore for him Terah in the seventh year of that week. •And Prince Mastema sent crows and birds so that they might eat the seed which was being sown in the earth in order to spoil the earth so that they might rob mankind of their labors. Before they plowed in the seed, the crows picked it off the surface 12 of the earth. •And therefore he called him Terah because the crows and birds 13 were impoverishing them.[g] And they ate their seed. •And the years began being

---

11 a. A feminine name meaning "light." It is a feminine form made with the same consonants as 'Ur, the name of her father.

b. The Heb. phrase *'ur kasdim*, "Ur of the Chaldeans," was apparently taken as a starting point for this genealogical note. In the singular, *'ur kesed* could easily be read "Ur, son of Kesed."

c. In this sentence the pun is complete; *'ur kesed* built the city of *'ur kasdim*. The Eth. text has corrupted the name of the city to *'ara*, but the correction is obvious.

d. The name Serug is provided with a rather feeble interpretation which is probably based on alliteration between the first syllable of the name (*ser*) and the Heb. roots *sur*, "turn," and *sara*, "turning away, apostasy, sin." Although the sib-

ilant in Serug is a *šin* and the sibilants in the words for "turn" and "sin" are *sameks*, the sounds were probably pronounced alike in the Heb. circles where this interpretation of Serug was proposed.

e. A feminine name which appears in Gen 11:29 as the name of Nahor's wife. Here she is the mother of a Nahor. The Nahor of Gen 11:29 is the son of Terah. The Nahor mentioned here is his grandfather.

f. There is a Iascah in Gen 11:29, but there she is the daughter of Haran.

g. There is an Ar. root *trh*, which means "to grieve, be sad." A Heb. or Aram. cognate may have existed to explain the meaning of Terah's name.

barren because of the birds. And they ate all of the fruit of the trees from the groves. If ever they were able to save a little from all of the fruit of the earth in their days, it was with great effort.

The birth of Abram and his piety

Gen 11:26

14 And in this thirty-ninth jubilee, in the second week, in the first year, Terah took a wife and her name was 'Edna, daughter of 'Abram, daughter of his father's
15 sister. •And in the seventh year of that week, she bore a son for him, and he called him Abram, after the name of his mother's father because he died before
16 his daughter conceived a son. •And the lad began understanding[h] the straying of the land, that everyone went astray after graven images and after pollution. And his father taught him writing. And he was two weeks of years old. And he
17 separated from his father so that he might not worship the idols with him. •And he began to pray to the Creator of all so that he might save him from the straying of the sons of men, and so that his portion might not fall into straying after the pollution and scorn.

Abram's successful efforts against the crows[i]

18 And the seed time arrived for sowing in the land. And they all went out together so that they might guard their seed from before the crows. And Abram went out
19 with those who went out. And the lad was fourteen years old. •And a cloud of crows came so that they might eat the seed, and Abram used to run up to them before they settled upon the earth. And he would call out to them before they settled upon the earth to eat seed, and he said, "Don't come down. Return to the
20 place whence you came." And they turned back. •And he caused the cloud of crows to turn back[j] seventy times in that day. And none of the crows settled on
21 any of the fields where Abram was, not one. •And all who were with him in all of the fields saw him as he was calling out. And all of the crows turned away.
22 And his reputation was great in all the land of Chaldea. •And all who would sow came to him during that year. And he used to go with them until the seed time passed. And they sowed their land and harvested in that year enough food, and they ate and were satisfied.
23 And in the first year of the fifth week, Abram taught those who were making the implements for oxen, the skilled carpenters. And they made implements above the ground facing the handle of the plow so that they might place seed upon it. And the seed would go down from within it onto the point of the plow, and it would be hidden in the earth. And therefore they were not afraid of the crows.
24 And they did likewise upon all of the plow handles above the ground. And they sowed and tilled all of the earth just as Abram commanded them. And therefore they were not afraid of the birds.

Abram's plea to avoid idolatry

1 **12** And it came to pass in the sixth week, in its seventh year, that Abram spoke to Terah, his father, saying, "O father." And he said, "Behold, here I am, my
2 son." •And he said:

---

h. A portion of the Syr. text is parallel to this vs. It excerpts portions of vss. from 11:16 to 12:29.

i. In his English translation, p. 88, Charles cited subsequent accounts of this episode by Jerome, St. Ephraem, and Bar. Hebraeus, but he concluded that all of the later accounts were derived from Jub. More recently, S. P. Brock has brought together Syr. evidence from the *Catena Serevi* on Gen and a letter written by Jacob of Edessa to John of Litarba and has sought to demonstrate that it reflects an independent tradition about Abraham.

In that account it is God rather than Mastema who sends the ravens. Abraham is unable to drive the ravens away until he calls out to God for help ("Abraham and the Ravens: A Syriac Counterpart to Jubilees 11–12 and Its Implications," *JSJ* 9 [1979] 135–52).

j. Various Eth. MSS read "he did," "they did," or "he returned." The emendation required for the present reading is slight and it is now supported by the Syr.

"What help or advantage do we have from these idols before which you
worship and bow down?

3 Because there is not any spirit in them,
for they are mute,
and they are the misleading of the heart.
Do not worship them.[a]

4 Worship the God of heaven,
who sends down rain and dew upon the earth,
and who makes everything upon the earth,
and created everything by his word,
and all life is in his presence.

5 Why do you worship those who have no spirit in them?
Because they are works of the hands,
and you are carrying them upon your shoulders,
and there is no help from them for you,
except great shame for those who made them
and the misleading of the heart for those who worship them.
Do not worship them."

6 And his father said to him, "I also know (that), my son, but what shall I do to
7 the people who have made me minister before them?[b] •And if I speak to them in
righteousness, they will kill me because their souls cleave to them[c] so that they
might worship them and praise them. Be silent, my son, lest they kill you."
8 And he told this matter to two of his brothers, and they were angry with him, and
he kept quiet.

The marriages of Abram and his brothers

9 And in the fortieth jubilee, in the second week, in its seventh year, Abram took
a wife and her name was Sarai,[d] daughter of his father, and she became a wife
for him.
10 And Haran, his brother, took a wife in the third year of the third week, and
she bore a son for him in the seventh year of that week. And he called him Lot.
11 And Nahor, his brother, took a wife.

Abram burns the house of idols

12 In the sixtieth year of the life of Abram, i.e. the fourth week, in its fourth year,
Abram arose in the night and burned the house of idols. And he burned everything
13 in the house. And there was no man who knew. •And they rose up in the night,
14 and they wanted to save their gods from the midst of the fire. •And Haran rushed
to save them, and the fire flared up over him. And he was burned in the fire and
died in Ur of the Chaldees before Terah, his father. And they buried him in Ur
of the Chaldees.

Ps 135:17

Jer 10:3,9
Amos 5:26
Isa 46:7

Gen 11:29

Gen 20:12

---

12 a. The imperatives and the second person pronouns ("you") are all plural in vss. 3–5. The
author of the text has apparently made use of a
liturgical unit written for a communal setting.
Certain poetic features appear if the unit is divided
into three stanzas in the following manner: (1) vs.
3; (2) vss. 4–5a; (3) the remainder of 5. Stanzas 1
and 3 begin with "because" and end with the
refrain "Do not worship them"; they describe the
worthlessness of idols. Stanza 2 provides an internal
contrast by describing the creative and providential

power of God. It seems reasonable to put vs. 2
outside the poetic unit because the second person
pronoun (you) is singular and refers only to Abram's
father. The Syr. has drastically abbreviated and
rearranged the statements which appear in these
vss.
  b. The pronoun refers to the idols which were
described in vss. 3–5.
  c. See previous n.
  d. The Eth. has "Sarah," but spellings have
been standardized to agree with the biblical text.

Departure to Haran Gen 11:31

15   And Terah went out of Ur of the Chaldees, he[e] and his sons, so that they might come into the land of Lebanon and into the land of Canaan. And he dwelt in Haran.[f] And Abram dwelt with Terah, his father, in Haran two weeks of years.

Abram's night vigil

16   And in the sixth week, in its fifth year, Abram sat up during the night on the first of the seventh month, so that he might observe the stars from evening until daybreak so that he might see what the nature of the year would be with respect
17 to rain. And he was sitting alone and making observations; •and a word came into his heart, saying, "All of the signs of the stars and the signs of the sun and the moon are all in the hand of the LORD. Why am I seeking?

18   If he desires, he will make it rain morning and evening,
       and if he desires he will not send (it) down;
       and everything is in his hand."

19 And he prayed on that night, saying:

       "My God, the Most High God, you alone are God to me.
       And you created everything,
       and everything which is was the work of your hands,
       and you and your kingdom I have chosen.
20   Save me from the hands of evil spirits
       which rule over the thought of the heart of man,
       and do not let them lead me astray from following you, O my God;
       but establish me and my seed forever,
       and let us not go astray henceforth and forever."

21 And he said, "Shall I return unto Ur of the Chaldees who seek my face so that I should return to them? Or shall I dwell here in this place? Make the straight path prosper before you in the hand of your servant that he might serve. And do not let me walk in the error of my heart, O my God."

Abram is called to the land of promise Gen 12:1-3

22   And he finished talking and praying and behold, the word of the LORD was sent to him by my hand, saying, "Come forth from your land and from your kin and from your father's house into the land which I shall show you, and I shall establish you as a great and numerous people.

23   And I shall bless you
       and I shall make your name great,
       and you will be blessed in the land
       and all the nations of the earth will bless themselves by you.
       And whoever blesses you I shall bless
       and whoever curses you I shall curse.

24 And I shall be God for you and your son and for the son of your son and for all of your seed. Do not fear henceforth and for all the generations of the earth. I am your God."

---

e. There is a small fragment of a Heb. text from Qumran which is parallel to vss. 15–17.

f. The printed Eth. text would give a reading "the land of Haran," but the Syr. and one Eth.

MS (D) omit the phrase "the land of." VanderKam has argued that the Qumran fragment scarcely has room for it either.

The revival of Hebrew

25 And the LORD God said to me, "Open his mouth and his ears so that he might
hear and speak with his mouth in the language which is revealed because it ceased
26 from the mouth of all of the sons of men from the day of the Fall." •And I opened
his mouth and his ears and his lips and I began to speak with him in Hebrew, in
27 the tongue of creation. •And he took his father's books—and they were written   1QapGen 19.25
in Hebrew—and he copied them. And he began studying them thereafter. And I
caused him to know everything which he was unable (to understand). And he
studied them (in) the six months of rain.

The blessing of Terah

28 And it came to pass[g] in the seventh year of the sixth week that he spoke with
his father and let him know that he was going from Haran to walk (in) the land
29 of Canaan so that he might see it and return to him. •And Terah, his father, said
to him:

> "Go in peace.
> May God eternal make straight your path
> and the LORD be with you
> and protect you from all evil
> [and grant favor upon you and mercy and grace before those who see
>   you.][h]
> May none of the sons of men rule over you to do evil to you.
> Go in peace.

30 And when you have seen a land pleasant to your eyes to dwell in, come and take
me to you. And take Lot, the son of Haran your brother with you (as) a son for
31 yourself. The LORD be with you. •But Nahor, your brother, leave with me until
you return in peace. And we will all go together with you."

Abram's sojourn at Bethel   Gen 12:4-8

1 **13** And Abram went from Haran. And he took Sarai, his wife, and Lot, his
brother Haran's son, into the land of Canaan. And he came to Asshur. And he
2 walked to Shechem. And he dwelt by a tall oak. •And he saw, and behold the
3 land was very pleasant from the entrance of Hamath to the tall oak. •And the
4 LORD said to him, "To you and to your seed I will give this land." •And he
built there an altar and he offered up upon it a burnt offering to the LORD, who
appeared to him.
5 And he removed from there into the mountain, with Bethel toward the west
6 and Ai toward the east, and he pitched his tent there. •And he saw and behold,
the land was wide and very good and everything was growing upon it: vines and
figs and pomegranate trees, oaks and ilexes and terebinths and olive trees and
cedars and cypresses and date trees[a] and every tree of the field, and water was

g. A fragment of a Heb. MS from Qumran has
provided a parallel for vss. 28f.

h. The words within the brackets, which have
strong support in the Eth. MSS, are not attested in
the fragment from Qumran. They are also missing
from the Syr. text, which omits the phrase "and
the LORD be with you and protect you from all
evil." Since the Syr. text is frequently abbreviated,
its witness alone would scarcely be significant. The
fact that there is not room for it in an early Heb.
text, however, raises serious questions about its
authenticity.

13 a. There is a degree of uncertainty about the

Eth. names for some of the trees in this list. The
more familiar words for "vines," "figs," "pomegranate," and "olive" are quite clear. The words
for cypress and cedar and terebinth are Eth. transcriptions of the Gk. terms. The word for oak
represents a transcription of the Gk. *balanos*. The
word which Charles rendered "ilex" is a transcription of the Gk. *drus*. Thus he used the Lat. name
to distinguish it in translation from *balanos*. The
"date trees" are the result of Charles's emendation
of the Eth. text. Most of the Eth. MSS transcribed
the Gk. *libanos*, "frankincense," but that would
be out of place in Canaan.

7 upon the mountains. •And he blessed the LORD who brought him out of Ur of
8 Chaldees and brought him into this land. •And it came to pass in the first year,
   in the seventh week, on the first of the first month, (that) he built an altar on that
   mountain and he called on the name of the LORD: "You (are) my God, the
9 eternal God." •And he offered up a burnt offering to the LORD upon the altar
   so that he might be with him and not forsake him all the days of his life.

Abram travels south to Hebron and Egypt

Gen 12:9-13:2
1QapGen 19f.

10 And he arose from there and he went toward the South and he reached Hebron—
    and Hebron was built then. And^b he dwelt there two years. And he went to the
11 land of the South as far as Bealoth. And there was a famine in the land. •And
    Abram went into Egypt in the third year of the week and he stayed in Egypt five
12 years before his wife was taken from him. •And Tanis of Egypt was built then, Num 13:22
    seven years after Hebron.
13 And it came to pass when Pharaoh took Sarai, the wife of Abram, that the
    LORD plagued Pharaoh and his house with great plagues on account of Sarai, the
14 wife of Abram. •And Abram was honored with many possessions: sheep and oxen
    and asses and horses and camels and male and female servants and silver and
15 much gold. And Lot, his brother's son, also had possessions. •And Pharaoh
    returned Sarai, the wife of Abram. And he sent him out from the land of Egypt.

Abram returns to Bethel and is promised the land

Gen 13:3-17

    And he went to the place where he had pitched his tent first, to the place of
    the altar. Ai was east and Bethel west. And he blessed the LORD his God who 1QapGen 21.2f
16 brought him back in peace. •And it came to pass in that forty-first jubilee, in the
    third year of the first week, (that) he returned to this place. And he offered up
    upon it a burnt offering and he called upon the name of the LORD. And he said:

> "You, O God, Most High, (are) my God
> forever and ever."

17 And in the fourth year of that week Lot separated from him. And Lot^c dwelt in 1QapGen 21.4f.
18 Sodom. And the men of Sodom were great sinners. •And his heart was sad because
    his brother's son had separated from him because he had no sons.
19 (It was) in that year, when Lot was taken captive, that the LORD spoke to 1QapGen 21.8-
10
    Abram after Lot had separated from him, in the fourth year of that week: "Lift
    up your eyes from the place where you are dwelling toward the North and South
20 and West and East •because all of the land which you see I will give to you and
    your seed forever. And I will make your seed like the sands of the sea. (Even) if
    a man were able to number the sands of the earth,^d he would not (be able) to
21 number your seed. •Arise and walk in the land in its length and its breadth and 1QapGen 21.11
    see all (of it) because I will give it to your seed."

Abram at Hebron reacts to Lot's capture

Gen 14:1-14

22 And Abram went to Hebron and he dwelt there. •And in that year Chedorlaomer, 1QapGen 21.23-
22.17
    king of Elam; and Amraphel, king of Shinar; and Arioch, king of Sellasar; and
    Tergal,^e king of the nations, came and killed the king of Gomorrah, but the king
    of Sodom fled. And many fell with wounds in the valley of Siddim, by the sea
23 of salt. •And they took captive Sodom and Adam and Zeboim. And they took

b. A portion of the Lat. text begins at this point
and continues through vs. 21.

c. A portion of the Syr. text begins at this point
and continues through vs. 29.

d. The first half of this sentence is omitted from
the Lat. text.

e. These names differ from the spelling in Gen
14. The Eth. spelling reflects that of an intermediate
Gk. text.

Lot, the son of Abram's brother, captive and all of his possessions. And he went
24 to Dan. •And one who escaped came and told Abram that his brother's son had
25 been taken captive. •And he armed the servants of his house.[f]

The law of the tithe

Gen 14:20

. . . upon Abram and his seed a tenth of the firstfruits to the LORD. And the
LORD ordained it (as) an ordinance forever that they should give it to the priests,
26 to those who minister before him so that they might possess it forever. •And there
is no limit of days for this law because he ordained it for eternal generations so
that they might give one tenth of everything to the LORD: grain and wine and oil
27 and oxen and sheep. •And he gave (it) to his priests to eat and drink with rejoicing
before him.

Abram restores booty to the king of Sodom

Gen 14:21-24

28 And the king of Sodom approached him and bowed down before him. And he [1QapGen 22.18-
said, "Our lord Abram, give us the people whom you saved, but let the booty 26]
29 belong to you." •And Abraham said to him, "I lift up my hand[g] to the God Most
High (that) I will (not) take anything of yours, (even) a thread or shoelace lest
you say 'I have made Abram rich,' but only what the young men have eaten and
the portion of the men who went with me, 'Aner and 'Eschol and Mamre. Let
them take their portion."

Abram's dream and sacrifice at Mamre

Gen 15:1-17

1 **14** And after these things, in the fourth year of this week, on the first of the [1QapGen 22.26-
third month, the word of the LORD came to Abram in a dream, saying, "Don't 34]
2 fear, Abram. I am your defender and your reward (will be) very great." •And he
said, "O Lord, O Lord what will you give me? I am going on without children.
And the son of Maseq,[a] the son of my handmaid, is Eliezer of Damascus. He will
3 be my heir, but you have not given seed to me." •And he said to him, "This one
will not be your heir, but one who will come from your loins will be your heir."
4 And he took him outside and he said to him, "Look into heaven and count the
stars if you are able to count them."
5 And he looked at the heaven and he saw the stars. And he said to him, "Thus
shall your seed be."
6,7 And he believed the LORD and it was counted for him as righteousness. •And
he said to him, "I am the LORD who brought you from Ur of the Chaldees so
that I might give you the land of the Canaanites to possess forever and (so that I
8 might) be God for you and for your seed after you." •And he said, "O Lord, O
9 Lord, how shall I know that I shall inherit?" •And he said, "Take for me a young
animal of three years and a goat of three years and a sheep of three years and a
turtledove and a pigeon."

---

f. There is an obvious lacuna in the text at this point. The biblical account of Abraham's pursuit of the invading army, his recapture of Lot, and an encounter with Melchizedek are all missing from the Eth. text. The Syr. text also omits the Melchizedek episode, but it contains a phrase not found in our text, i.e. "and he pursued the kings and he returned everything which they had taken captive from Sodom."

There is no way to determine whether the text originally follows the biblical account of Abraham giving a tithe to Melchizedek or not. Nevertheless, some incident involving a tithe must have been part of the text because vs. 24 continues the account as though a precedent for the tithe had just been described.

The loss of the Melchizedek passage leads one to wonder how the author of Jub dealt with the fact that the Bible describes him as "priest of God Most High," a title used elsewhere of Levi (cf. 32:1).

g. The lifting up of the hand signifies the swearing of an oath. It is a Semitic idiom taken from Gen 14:22.

14 a. The Heb. text of Gen 15:2 is difficult. The term *ben-mešeq* does not occur elsewhere in the OT, and its translation remains uncertain. The translators of the LXX were also confused by the phrase, which they mistook as a personal name. The Eth. reading "son of Maseq" follows that tradition.

10 And he took all of these in the middle of the month. And he was dwelling by
11 the oak of Mamre, which is near Hebron. •And he built an altar there. And he
slaughtered all of these, and he poured out their blood upon the altar. And he
divided them in the middle. And he placed them facing one another, but the birds
12 he did not cut up. •And the birds came down upon the pieces[b] and Abram kept
turning them away and he did not let the birds touch them.
13 And it came to pass when the sun set that a terror fell upon Abram. And behold
a great dark horror fell upon him. And it was said to Abram, "Surely know that
your seed will be strangers in an alien land. And they will serve them. And they
14 will make them suffer four hundred years. •But I will judge the people whom
they will serve. And afterward they will come forth from there with many
15 possessions. •And you will go to your fathers in peace and be buried in a good
16 old age. •And in the fourth generation they will return here because the sins of
the Amorites have not yet been completed."

The covenant with Abram
Gen 15:17-21

17 And he woke up from his sleep and stood up. And the sun had set and there
was a flame. And behold an oven was smoking and flames of fire passed between
18 the pieces. •And on that day the LORD made a covenant with Abram, saying,
"To your seed I will give this land from the river of Egypt to the great river, the
Euphrates River: the Kenites, the Kenizzites, the Kadmonites, the Perizzites, and
the Rephaim, the Phakorites, and the Hivites, and the Amorites, and the Canaanites,
and the Girgashites, and the Jebusites."[c]
19 And that day passed and Abram offered up the pieces and the birds and their
20 (fruit) offering and their libation. And the fire consumed them. •And on that day
we made a covenant with Abram just as we had made a covenant in that month
with Noah. And Abram renewed the feast and the ordinance for himself forever.

Sarai offers her handmaid, Hagar, to Abram
Gen 16:1-4,15

21 And Abram rejoiced and he told all of these things to Sarai, his wife. And he
22 believed that he would have seed, but she did not give birth. •And Sarai advised
Abram, her husband, and she said to him, "Go into Hagar, my Egyptian maid.
23 It may be that I will build seed for you from her." •And Abram heard his wife
Sarai's word and he said, "Do (it)!" And Sarai took Hagar, her Egyptian maid,
24 and she gave her to Abram, her husband, so that she might be a wife. •And he
went into her. And she conceived and bore a son and he called him Ishmael, in
the fifth year of that week. And that year was the eighty-sixth year in the life of
Abram.

The offering of firstfruits and the covenant changing Abram's name
Gen 17:1-16

1 **15** In the fifth year of the fourth week of that jubilee in the third month, in the
middle of the month, Abram made a feast of the firstfruits of the harvest of grain.
2 And he offered up a new sacrifice upon the altar, the firstfruits of the food for Lev 23:15-20
the LORD, a bull and a goat and a sheep upon the altar (as) burnt offering to the
LORD. And their (fruit) offering and their libation he offered up upon the altar
3 with frankincense. •And the LORD appeared to Abram and he said to him, "I
4 am God Shaddai. Be pleasing before me and be perfect. •And I will make my
covenant between me and you and I will make you increase very much."
5,6 And Abram fell on his face and the LORD spoke to him, saying, •"Behold, my

---

b. Charles corrected the Eth. text at this point
to agree with the biblical Heb. The Eth. MSS
contain a word meaning "wide," probably having
in mind that which is spread out.

c. This list differs from the list in Gen 15:19–
21. The present list lacks Hittites, but includes
Phakorites and Hivites, who are not in the Heb.
text. The Hivites, however, appear in the LXX.

7 ordinance is with you and you will be the father of many nations. •And your
name therefore will not be called Abram, but your name will henceforth and
forever be Abraham because I have established you (as) the father of many nations.
8 And I shall make you very great and I shall make you into nations. And kings
9 will come from you. •And I shall establish my covenant between me and you and
your seed after you in their generations for an eternal ordinance so that I might
10 be God for you and your seed after you. •And I shall give to you and your seed
after you[a] the land where you sojourn, the land of Canaan, which you will possess
forever. And I shall be God for them.''
11 And the LORD said to Abraham, ''And you also keep my covenant, you and
your seed after you. And you[b] will circumcise all of your[b] males. And you[b] shall
circumcise your foreskins and it will be a sign of the eternal ordinance between
12 me and you.[b] •And a son on the eighth day you will circumcise, every male in
your generations, the servant of the house and whomever you purchase with
money from all of the sons of the foreigner, whom you have acquired, who was
13 not from your seed. •The (servant) born in your house will certainly be circumcised
and the one whom you have purchased with money will be circumcised. And my
14 covenant will be in your flesh for an eternal ordinance. •And whatever male is
not circumcised, the flesh of whose foreskin was not circumcised on the eighth
day, that soul shall be uprooted from its family because he has broken my
15 covenant.'' •And the LORD said to Abraham, ''Sarai, your wife, will therefore not
16 be called Sarai because Sarah is her name. •And I will bless her and I will give
you a son from her. And I will bless him. And he will become a people. And
kings of nations will come from him.''

Abraham's concern for Ishmael
Gen 17:17-22

17 And Abraham fell on his face and he rejoiced and pondered in his heart whether
a son would be born to one who was one hundred years old or (whether) Sarah,
18 who was ninety years, would give birth. •And Abraham said to the LORD,
19 ''Would that Ishmael might live before you.'' •And the LORD said, ''Yes, but
Sarah will bear a son for you and you will call him Isaac. And I shall raise up
20 my covenant (as) an eternal covenant with him and with his seed after him. •And
concerning Ishmael I have heard you. And behold I shall bless him,[c] and make
him grow and increase him very much. And twelve princes he will beget. And I
21 shall make him into a great people. •But my covenant I shall establish with Isaac,
22 whom Sarah will bear for you in another year during these days.''[d] •And he
finished talking with him and the LORD ascended from Abraham.

The circumcision of Abraham's household
Gen 17:23-27

23 And Abraham did as the LORD said to him and he took Ishmael, his son, and
all of the male servants of his house and also whomever he bought with money,
every male who was in his house, and he circumcised the flesh of their foreskins.
24 And that very same[e] day Abraham was circumcised and every man of his house
and the servant of his house.[f] And all of those who were purchased for money
from the sons of aliens were also circumcised with him.

---

15 a. The first phrase in the sentence is missing
in the MSS, but restored in the printed text on the
basis of Gen 17:8.

b. The pronouns are in the second masculine
plural. The construction is dependent on the Heb.
text of the OT, which reflects a liturgical usage.
The force of the statements in this sentence is
imperative.

c. A portion of the Lat. text begins at this point
and continues through vs. 31a.

d. Isaac is to be born during the period of sacred

days associated with the celebration of the feast of
the firstfruits of the grain harvest, i.e. the middle
of the third month. Cf. the account of his birth in
16:13.

e. The Eth. phrase reads ''in the time of that
day,'' which is also found in the LXX as an attempt
to translate a somewhat unusual Heb. idiom which
means ''that very same day.''

f. The phrase ''and the servant of his house,''
is found in the Lat. text, but is missing from the
Eth. MSS used by Charles.

The laws of circumcision

25   This law is for all the eternal generations and there is no circumcising[g] of days
and there is no passing a single day beyond eight days because it is an eternal
26   ordinance ordained and written in the heavenly tablets. •And anyone who is born
whose own flesh is not circumcised on the eighth day is not from the sons of the
covenant which the LORD made for Abraham since (he is) from the children of
destruction. And there is therefore no sign upon him so that he might belong to
the LORD because (he is destined) to be destroyed and annihilated from the earth
and to be uprooted from the earth because he has broken the covenant of the
27   LORD our God. •Because the nature of all of the angels of the presence and all
of the angels of sanctification was thus from the day of their creation. And in the
presence of the angels of the presence and the angels of sanctification he sanctified
Israel so that they might be with him and with his holy angels.
28   And you command the sons of Israel and let them keep this sign of the covenant
for their generations for an eternal ordinance. And they will not be uprooted from
29   the land •because the commandment was ordained for the covenant so that they
30   might keep it forever for all of the children of Israel. •For the LORD did not
draw Ishmael and his sons and his brothers and Esau near to himself, and he did
not elect them because they are the sons of Abraham, for he knew them. But he
31   chose Israel that they might be a people for himself. •And he sanctified them and   Deut 32:8f.
gathered them from all of the sons of man because (there are) many nations and   Sir 17:17
many people, and they all belong to him, but over all of them he caused spirits
32   to rule so that they might lead them astray[h] from following him. •But over Israel   Dan 10:13
he did not cause any angel or spirit to rule because he alone is their ruler and he   1En 90:22f.
will protect them and he will seek for them at the hand of his angels and at the   Isa 24:21f.
hand of his spirits and at the hand of all of his authorities so that he might guard
them and bless them and they might be his and he might be theirs henceforth and
forever.

A prediction of future faithlessness regarding circumcision

33   And now I shall announce to you that the sons of Israel will deny this ordinance
and they will not circumcise their sons according to all of this law because some
of the flesh of their circumcision they will leave in the circumcision of their sons.
And all of the sons of Beliar will leave their sons without circumcising just as   TDan 5
34   they were born. •And great wrath from the LORD will be upon the sons of Israel
because they have left his covenant and have turned aside from his words. And
they have provoked and blasphemed inasmuch as they have not done the ordinance
of this law because they have made themselves like the gentiles to be removed
and be uprooted from the land. And there is therefore for them no forgiveness or
pardon so that they might be pardoned and forgiven[i] from all of the sins of this
eternal error.

Account of Sarah's laughter   Gen 18:1-15

1   **16** And on the new moon of the fourth month, we appeared to Abraham at the
oak of Mamre and we talked with him and we also caused him to know that a
2   son would be given to him by Sarah, his wife. •And Sarah laughed because she
heard that we discussed this matter with Abraham. And we reproached her. And
3   she was afraid and denied that she laughed about the matter. •And we told her

---

g. This is the writer's way of suggesting that no
day should be cut off to shorten the total number
of days.

h. The spirits are the descendants of the Watch-

ers discussed in ch. 10:2–9.

i. This phrase is found in MS B. Charles thought
the phrase was a corruption due to dittography.

the name of her son Isaac—just as his name was ordained and written in the
4 heavenly tablets—•and (that) when we returned to her at a specific time she would
have conceived a son.

The destruction of Sodom
Gen 18:16-19:20

5   And in that month the LORD executed the judgment of Sodom and Gomorrah
and Zeboim and all of the district of the Jordan. And he burned them with fire Gen 19:24
and sulphur and he annihilated them till this day just as (he said), "Behold, I
have made known to you all[a] of their deeds that (they were) cruel and great sinners
and they were polluting themselves and they were fornicating in their flesh and
6 they were causing pollution upon the earth." •And thus the LORD will execute
judgment like the judgment of Sodom on places where they act according to the
pollution of Sodom.

The sin of Lot's daughters
Gen 19:30-38

7   And we saved Lot because the LORD remembered Abraham and he brought
8 him out from the midst of the overthrow. •And he and his daughters also committed
sins upon the earth which were not (committed) on the earth from the days of
9 Adam until his time because the man lay with his daughters. •And behold it is
commanded and it is engraved concerning all of his seed in the heavenly tablets
so that he will remove them and uproot them and execute their judgment just like
the judgment of Sodom and so that he will not leave seed of man for him on the
earth in the day of judgment.

Events surrounding the birth of Isaac at Beer-sheba
Gen 20:1-21:7

10   And in this month Abraham moved from Hebron and went and dwelt between
11 Qadesh and Shur in the mountains of Gerar. •And in the middle of the fifth month
12 he moved from there and he dwelt by the Well of the Oath. •And in the middle
13 of the sixth month the LORD visited Sarah and did for her as he had said. •And
she conceived and she bore a son in the third month, in the middle of the month,
in the time when the LORD told Abraham. Isaac was born on the feast of the
14 firstfruits of the harvest. •And Abraham circumcised his son on the eighth day.
He was the first one circumcised according to the covenant which was ordained
forever.
15   And in the sixth year of the fourth week we went forth to Abraham at the Well
of the Oath. And we appeared to him [just as we said to Sarah that we would
16 return to her. And she had conceived a son. •And we returned in the seventh
month and we found Sarah pregnant before us.][b] And we blessed him and we
announced to him everything which was commanded for him that he would not
die until he begot six more sons and he would see (them) before he died. And Gen 25:2
17 through Isaac a name and seed would be named for him. •And all of the seed of Gen 21:12
his sons would become nations. And they would be counted with the nations. But
from the sons of Isaac one would become a holy seed and he would not be counted
18 among the nations •because he would become the portion of the Most High and
all his seed would fall (by lot) into that which God will rule so that he might
become a people (belonging) to the LORD, a (special) possession from all people, Deut 4:20
19 and so that he might become a kingdom of priests and a holy people. •And we Ex 19:6
went our way and we announced to Sarah everything which we had told him. 1Pet 2:9
And both of them rejoiced very greatly. Rev 5:10

---

16 a. A portion of the Lat. text resumes at this
point and continues through 17:6a.
  b. The section marked off by brackets is found

in both Lat. and Eth. MSS, but it appears out of
place here as a gloss which interrupts the text.

Abraham observes the feast of Booths at Beer-sheba

Gen 21:8
Num 29:12-40

20 And he built an altar there to the LORD who delivered him and who made him rejoice in the land of his sojourn. And he celebrated a feast of rejoicing in this

21 month, seven days, near the altar which he built by the Well of the Oath. •And he built booths for himself and for his servants on that festival. And he first

22 observed the feast of the booths on the earth. •And in these seven days he was making offering every day, day by day, on the altar a burnt offering to the LORD: two bulls, and two rams, and seven lambs, one kid on behalf of sins so that he

23 might atone thereby on behalf of himself and his seed. •And for a thank offering: seven rams and seven sheep and seven lambs and seven he-goats and their (fruit) offerings and their libations and all their fat he offered upon the altar as chosen burnt offering to the LORD for a sweet-smelling odor.

24 And in the morning and evening he offered the fragrance of frankincense, and galbanum, and stacte, and nard, and myrrh, and spices, and costum.[c] All seven

Ex 30:34
Sir 24:15

25 of these he offered, crushed, mixed in equal parts (and) pure. •And he observed this feast seven days, rejoicing with all his heart and with all his soul, he and all of those who were in his house. And there was no alien with him or any who

26 were not circumcised. •And he blessed his Creator who created him in his generation because by his will he created him for he knew and he perceived that from him there would be a righteous planting for eternal generations and a holy

1En 10:16;
93:5,10

27 seed from him so that he might be like the one who made everything. •And he blessed and rejoiced and called the name of this festival "the festival of the LORD," a joy acceptable to God Most High.

28 And we eternally blessed him and his seed who are after him in every generation of the earth because he observed this feast in its (appointed) time according to the

29 testimony of the heavenly tablets. •Therefore it is ordained in the heavenly tablets concerning Israel that they will be observers of the feast of booths seven days with joy in the seventh month which is acceptable before the LORD (as) an eternal

Lev 23:40-42

30 law in their generations throughout all (time), year by year. •And there is no limit of days for this because it is ordained forever concerning Israel so that they should observe it and they should dwell in tents and that they should place crowns on their heads and so that they should take branches of leaves and willow from the

31 stream. •And Abraham took branches[d] of palm trees and fruit of good trees and each day of the days he used to go around the altar with branches. Seven times per day, in the morning, he was praising and giving thanks to his God for all things.

The feast for the weaning of Isaac

Gen 21:8

1 **17** In the first of the fifth week in that jubilee Isaac was weaned. And Abraham celebrated a great feast in the third month on the day that his son, Isaac, was

2 weaned. •And Ishmael, the son of Hagar, the Egyptian woman, was in the presence of Abraham, his father, in his place. And Abraham rejoiced and he blessed the

3 LORD because he had seen his sons and had not died without sons. •And he remembered the word which was told to him on the day that Lot separated from him. And he rejoiced because the LORD had given him seed upon the earth so

---

c. The list of incense contains some uncertain elements. The Eth. words for "frankincense," "myrrh," and "spices" are fairly well known. The Eth. word for "nard" is *nārdōs*, a simple transcription of the Gk., and the word for "costum" is *kwast*, which probably reflects the Gk. *kostos*. The word that is translated "galbanum" is used in Eth. to represent either the Gk. *staktē* or *chalbanē*, but at Ex 30:34, which probably provided the

inspiration for the present text, the Eth. text uses it to translate "galbanum." The word that is translated "stacte" also appears in Ex 30:34 with that meaning.

d. The word which appears in both Lat. and Eth. MSS translates into English as "heart" (of palm trees). That is apparently due to a confusion between the Heb. words *lūlab*, "branches," and *leb*, "heart." The correction is obvious.

that they might inherit the land. And he blessed the Creator of all with all his
eloquence.[a]

The banishment of Hagar

Gen 21:9-21

4   And Sarah saw Ishmael playing and dancing and Abraham rejoicing very
greatly. And she was jealous of Ishmael and she said to Abraham, "Drive out
this girl and her son because the son of this girl will not inherit with my son,
5   Isaac." •And the matter was grievous in the sight of Abraham because of his
maidservant and because of his son that he should drive them away from him.
6   And the LORD said to Abraham, "Let it not be grievous in your sight on account
of the lad and the girl. (As for) everything which Sarah said to you, obey her
words and do (it) because it is through Isaac that a name and seed will be named
7   for you. •But regarding the son of this girl, I will make him into a great people
because he is from your seed."
8   And Abraham rose at the crack of dawn and he took bread and a water skin
9   and set it on the shoulder of Hagar and the lad and he sent her away. •And she
went and wandered in the desert of Beer-sheba and the water was used up from
10 the skin and the lad thirsted and was unable to walk and he fell. •And his mother
took him and cast him under one of the olive trees and she went and sat opposite
him a distance of one (arrow) shot because, she said, "Let me not see the death
of my child." And sitting down, she wept.
11   And an angel of the LORD, one of the holy ones, said to her, "What are you
weeping for, Hagar? Having arisen, pick up the child and take him in your arms
12 because the LORD has heard your voice and he has seen the child." •And she
opened her eyes and she saw a well of water. And she went and filled the water
skin. And she gave the child a drink and arose and went toward the desert of
13 Paran. •And the child grew and was a hunter. And the LORD was with him. And
14 his mother took a wife for him from the maids of Egypt. •And she bore a son for
him and he called him Nebaioth because, she said, "The LORD was near to me
when I called to him."

Mastema's plot to test Abraham

Gen 22:1

15   And it came to pass in the seventh week, in its first year, in the first month, in
that jubilee, on the twelfth of that month, that words came in heaven concerning
Abraham that he was faithful in everything which was told him and he loved the
16 LORD and was faithful in all affliction. •And Prince Mastema came and he said
before God, "Behold, Abraham loves Isaac, his son. And he is more pleased
with him than everything. Tell him to offer him (as) a burnt offering upon the
altar. And you will see whether he will do this thing. And you will know whether
he is faithful in everything in which you test him."
17   And the LORD was aware that Abraham was faithful in all of his afflictions
because he tested him with his land, and with famine. And he tested him with the
wealth of kings. And he tested him again with his wife, when she was taken
(from him), and with circumcision. And he tested him with Ishmael and with
18 Hagar, his maidservant, when he sent them away. •And in everything in which
he tested him, he was found faithful. And his soul was not impatient. And he was
not slow to act because he was faithful and a lover of the LORD.

The sacrifice of Isaac

Gen 22:1-19

1   **18** And the LORD said to him, "Abraham, Abraham." And he said, "Here I
2   am." •And he said, "Take your beloved son, whom you love, Isaac, and go into

---

17 a. Lit. "with all his mouth."

the high land and offer him up on one of the mountains that I will make known to you.''

3   And he arose while it was still dark at daybreak and he loaded his ass and took two of his young men servants with him and Isaac, his son. And he split the wood of the sacrifice and he went to the place on the third day. And he saw the place
4 from afar. •And he arrived at a well of water and he said to the young men, ''Stay here with the ass and I and the child shall go. And when we have worshiped we shall return to you.''
5   And he took the wood of the sacrifice and put it on the shoulder of Isaac, his son, and he took the fire and the knife in his hand. And the two of them went
6 together to that place. •And Isaac said to his father, ''Father.'' And he said, ''Here I am, my son.'' And he said to him, ''Behold, the fire and the knife and
7 the wood, but where is the lamb for the burnt offering, father?'' •And he said, ''The LORD will see about the lamb for the burnt offering, my son.''
8   And they drew near to the (holy) place of the mountain of the LORD. •And he built an altar and he placed the wood on the altar. And he bound Isaac, his son, and he placed him on the wood which was on top of the altar, and he stretched forth his hand, and took the knife in order to slaughter Isaac, his son.
9   And I stood before him and before Prince Mastema. And the LORD said, ''Speak to him. Do not let his hand descend upon the child. And do not let him
10 do anything to him because I know that he is one who fears the LORD.'' •And I called out to him from heaven and I said to him, ''Abraham, Abraham.'' And he
11 was terrified[a] and said, ''Here I am.'' •And I said to him, ''Do not put forth your hand against the child and do not do anything to him because now I know that you are one who fears the LORD and you did not deny your firstborn son to me.''
12   And Prince Mastema was shamed. And Abraham lifted up his eyes and saw a ram was caught in the thicket[b] by his horns. And Abraham went and took the ram
13 and offered it up for a burnt offering instead of his son. •And Abraham called that place ''The LORD has seen,'' so that it is said ''in the mountain[c] the LORD has seen.'' It is Mount Zion.
14   And the LORD called Abraham by his name again from heaven just as he caused us to appear so that we might speak to him in the name of the LORD.
15 And he said, ''I swear by myself, says the LORD, because you have done this thing and you have not denied your firstborn[d] son, whom you love, to me that I shall surely bless you and I shall surely multiply your seed like the stars of heaven and like the sand of the seashore and your seed will inherit the cities of their
16 enemies. •And all of the nations of the earth will bless themselves by your seed because you obeyed my word. And I have made known to all that you are faithful to me in everything which I say to you. Go in peace.''   ISam 1:17
17   And Abraham went to his young men and they got up and went (to) Beer-sheba
18 together. And Abraham dwelt by the Well of the Oath. •And he observed this festival every year (for) seven days with rejoicing. And he named it ''the feast of the LORD'' according to the seven days during which he went and returned in
19 peace. •And thus it is ordained and written in the heavenly tablets concerning Israel and his seed to observe this festival seven days with festal joy.

The death and burial of Sarah   Gen 23:1-20

1 **19** In the first year of the first week in this forty-second jubilee Abraham returned
2 and dwelt two weeks of years opposite Hebron, i.e. Kiryath Arba. •And in the

---

18 a. A portion of the Lat. text begins at this point and continues through 19:26a.

b. The Eth. words for ''in the thicket'' are based on a reasonable emendation by Charles. The Eth. MSS have a meaningless ''and he came.'' The Lat. MS reads ''caught by his horns,'' with no added

phrase at this point.

c. The phrase ''in the mountain'' is found only in the Lat. MS.

d. The reading is found in two of the Eth. MSS. Lat.: ''only begotten.''

first year of the third week of this jubilee, the days of Sarah's life were completed
3 and she died in Hebron. •And Abraham went to weep for her and bury her.

And we were testing him whether he would exercise self-control. And he was
not impatient with the words of his mouth and he was found self-controlled in
4 this also and he was not filled with anxiety •because with the self-control of his
spirit he spoke with the sons of Heth so that they might give him a place in which
5 to bury his dead. •And the LORD gave him favor in the presence of all who saw
him. And he begged politely from the sons of Heth and they sold him the land of
the cave of Machpelah,[a] which is opposite Mamre, i.e. Hebron, for four hundred[b]
6 silver (pieces). •And they begged him, saying, "Let us give (it) to you free."

But he did not take (it) from their control free because he gave the price for
the place (in) full silver. And he bowed down to them twice and afterward he
7 buried his dead in the cave of Machpelah. •And all the days of the life of Sarah
were one hundred and twenty-seven. These (are) two jubilees and four weeks and
8 one year. These (are) the days of the life of Sarah. •This (is) the tenth trial with
9 which Abraham was tried. And he was found faithful, controlled of spirit. •And CD 3.2
he did not say a word concerning the rumor which was in the land that the LORD
said he would give it to him and to his seed after him, but he begged a place Jas 2:23
there so that he might bury his dead because he was found faithful and he was 2Chr 20:7
Isa 41:8
recorded as a friend of the LORD in the heavenly tablets.

The marriage of Isaac and the birth of his children   Gen 24:1-
25:3,24-28

10   And in the fourth year thereof he took a wife for his son, Isaac, and her name
was Rebecca, daughter of Bethuel, the son of Nahor, Abraham's brother, the
sister of Laban and daughter of Bethuel. And Bethuel[c] was the son of Melca, who
11 was the wife of Nahor, Abraham's brother. •And Abraham took a third wife and
her name was Keturah from the daughters of his household servants because Hagar
12 died before Sarah. •And she bore six sons for him: Zimram, and Jokshan, and
Medan, and Midian, and Ishbak, and Shuah,[d] in two weeks of years.
13   And in the sixth week in the second year Rebecca bore two children for Isaac,
Jacob and Esau. And Jacob was smooth and upright, but Esau was a fierce man
14 and rustic and hairy. And Jacob used to dwell in the tents. •And the youths grew
up and Jacob learned writing, but Esau did not learn because he was a rustic man
and a hunter. And he learned war, and all of his deeds were fierce.

Abraham's blessings for Jacob   Gen 25:28

15,16   And Abraham loved Jacob, but Isaac loved Esau. •And Abraham saw the deeds
of Esau and he knew that in Jacob a name and seed would be named for him.
And he called Rebecca and he commanded concerning Jacob because he knew
17 that she loved Jacob more than Esau. •And he said to her, "My daughter, guard
my son Jacob because he will be in place of me upon the earth and for a blessing
18 in the midst of the sons of men and a glory to all of the seed of Shem •because I
know that the LORD will choose him for himself as a people who will rise up[e]

---

19 a. The Eth. text has translated this phrase to
read "double cave." There was never any doubt
that the familiar biblical phrase "cave of Machpelah" was the ultimate source of the Eth. "double
cave," but now two fragments of the Heb. text
from Qumran (3Q5, F.3 and 2Q19) contain the
word *mkplh*. Therefore there is scarcely any reason
to avoid using it.
  b. Charles emended the Eth. text to read "four
hundred," which agrees with the Lat. The Eth.
MSS read "forty."
  c. The reading "daughter of Bethuel. And Bethuel" follows the Lat. text. The Eth. MSS have

a corrupt reading which does not fit the context.
The vs. as a whole has clearly suffered in transmission. Both the Lat. and Eth. mention a daughter
of Bethuel twice in vs. 10. That would suggest
that the dittography was also present in the earlier
Gk. text.
  d. The names of the six sons are spelled in
agreement with Gen 25:2. The Eth. spellings are
slightly different. The Lat. spellings are even more
remote.
  e. The vs. is based on Deut 7:6, where the
chosen people are described as God's "own possession." The Lat. text describes them as a "holy

19 from all the nations[f] which are upon the earth. •And behold, Isaac, my son, loves
20 Esau more than Jacob, but I see you as one who loves Jacob rightly. •Be even
better to him and let your eyes be lovingly upon him because he will be for us a
21 blessing upon the earth henceforth and for all generations of the earth. •Let your
hands be strong and let your heart rejoice in your son, Jacob. Because I love him
more than all of my sons. He will be blessed forever and his seed will be one
22 which fills all of the earth. •If a man is able to count the sand of the earth, then   Gen 13:16
23 his seed will be counted. •And all of the blessings with which the LORD blessed
24 me and my seed will be for Jacob and his seed always. •And in his seed my name
will be blessed and the names of my fathers Shem and Noah, and Enoch, and
25 Mahalalel, and Enos, and Seth, and Adam.[g] •And they will serve to establish
heaven and to strengthen the earth and to renew all of the lights which are above
the firmament."
26   And he called to Jacob in the sight of Rebecca, his mother, and he kissed him
27 and blessed him, and said, •"'Jacob, my beloved son, whom my soul loves, may
God from above the firmament bless and may he give you all of the blessings
with which he blessed Adam and Enoch and Noah and Shem. And everything
which he told me and everything which he said that he would give me may he
cause to cleave to you and your seed forever according to the days of heaven
28 above the earth. •And may the spirit of Mastema not rule over you or over your   CD 12.2f.
seed in order to remove you from following the LORD who is your God henceforth
29 and forever •and may the LORD God be for you and for the people a father
always and may you be a firstborn son. Go, my son, in peace."
30,31   And the two of them went out together from Abraham. •And Rebecca loved
Jacob with all of her heart and all of her soul much more than Esau, but Isaac
loved Esau more than Jacob.

Abraham's farewell testimony for his children   Gen 25:5f.

1 **20** And in the forty-second jubilee, in the first year on the seventh week, Abraham
called Ishmael and his twelve children and Isaac and his two children and Keturah's   Gen 25:13-15
2 six children and their sons. •And he commanded them (a) that they should guard   CD 6.20-7.4
the way of the LORD so that they might do righteousness and each
one might love his neighbor, and (b) that it should be thus among all men so that
each one might proceed to act justly and rightly toward them upon the earth,
3 and (c) that they should circumcise their sons in the covenant which he made with
them, and (d) that they should not cross over either to the right or left from all of
the ways which the LORD commanded us and (e) that we should keep ourselves
from all fornication and pollution, and (f) that we should set aside from among
4 us all fornication and pollution.[a] •And when any woman or girl fornicates among   Deut 22:23
you you will burn her[b] with fire, and let them not fornicate with her after their   Ezek 16:40
                                                                                   Lev 20:10; 21:9
                                                                                   Gen 38:24

people," and the Eth. describes them as "a people
who will rise up." Charles assumed that it was
due to a misunderstanding of the Gk. word *periou-
sios*, which is also mistranslated in the Eth. version
of the Bible.
    f. The word "nations" is restored from the Lat.
text. It is missing in the Eth. MSS.
    g. In the genealogy of Enoch in Gen 5, the
seven generations are listed as Adam, Seth, Enosh,
Kenan, Mahalalel, Jared, and Enoch. Jared may
be left out of the present list because of the evil
associations derived from the meaning of his name
when the Watchers "descended" in his lifetime
(cf. Jub 4:15). The omission of Kenan may be due
to the fact that it is similar to Cain. Within the
remaining group Mahalalel is the least famous, but
his name means "God shines forth," an appropriate
name for a patriarch in this context where there is

mention of renewing "all the lights which are
above the firmament."

20 a. Vss. 2f. are written with a rambling syntax.
The designation of separate commands with letters
(a) through (f) was introduced by the translator to
break up the long sentence. In his translation,
Charles bracketed the last injunction in this series
as an example of dittography. Vs. 4, however,
describes in greater detail the manner in which
fornication is to be set aside. The shifting of
pronouns from "they" to "us" is similar to the
pattern found in the ancient liturgical fragment
preserved in Deut 26:5–11.
    b. Death by fire is the punishment which is
appropriate for the daughter of a priest according
to Lev 21:9; in other cases the OT required stoning,
e.g. Deut 22:23f. Jub's order for burning, which

eyes and hearts and let them not take wives from the girls of Canaan because the
seed of Canaan will be rooted out of the land.

5   And he told them the judgment of the giants and the judgments of the Sodomites
just as[c] they had been judged on account of their evil. And on account of their
fornication and impurity and the corruption among themselves with fornication
they died.

6   And you guard yourself from all fornication and impurity,
            and from all corruption of sin,
            so that you might not make our name a curse,   Isa 65:15
            and all your life a hissing,   Jer 29:18
                                                                            1En 5:6
            and all your sons a destruction by the sword.
            And you will be cursed like Sodom,
            and all your remnant like the sons of Gomorrah.
7   I exhort you, my sons, love the God of heaven,
            and be joined to all of his commands.
            And do not go after their idols and after their defilement.
8   And do not make gods of molten or carved images for yourselves, Deut 27:15
            because it is vain and they have no spirit.
            Because they are the work of hands,
            and all those who trust in them trust in nothing.
            Do not worship them and do not bow down to them.   Ex 20:5
9   But worship the Most High God,
            and bow down to him continually,
            and hope for his countenance always,
            and do what is upright and righteous before him,
            so that he might be pleased with you,[d]
            and grant you his mercy,
            and bring down rain for you morning and evening,
            and bless all your works   Deut 28:8
            which you have made on the earth
            and bless your food and your water,
            and bless the fruit of your womb and the fruit of your land,   Deut 7:13
            and the herds of your cattle and the flocks of your sheep.
10   And you will become a blessing upon the earth,   Gen 12:2
            and all of the nations of the earth will desire you,
            and they will bless your sons in my name,
            so that they might be blessed just as I am.

11   And he gave gifts to Ishmael and to his sons and to the sons of Keturah and he
sent them away from Isaac, his son, and he gave everything to Isaac, his son.
12 And Ishmael and his sons and the sons of Keturah and their sons went together
and they dwelt from Paran to the entrance to Babylon in all of the land which
13 faces the east opposite the desert. •And these mixed with each other, and they
are called[e] Arabs or Ishmaelites.

Abraham's farewell testimony for Isaac   Gen 25:5,7

1 **21** And in the sixth year of the seventh week of this jubilee Abraham called TLevi 9
Isaac, his son, and he commanded him, saying, "I am old and I do not know the Gen 27:2

---

appears to be a harsher form of death, may be
attributed to either the strictness of the community
to which the author belonged or to its priestly
orientation. It might also be influenced by Judah's
example in Gen 38:24.

c. A portion of the Lat. text begins at this point
and continues through 21:10a.

d. The reading "be pleased with you" is found
in the Eth. MSS. Charles had emended the printed

text to agree with the Lat., which reads "direct
you aright," but in his subsequent translations he
chose to follow the Eth. MSS.

e. The reading "are called" is found in the Eth.
MSS. Charles had emended the printed text to read
"were joined" to agree with the Lat., but changed
his mind in subsequent translations and followed
the Eth. MSS.

2 day of my death and I am filled with my days. •Behold I am one hundred and
seventy-five years old, and throughout all of the days of my life I have been
remembering the LORD and sought with all my heart to do his will and walk
3 uprightly in all his ways. •I hated idols, and those who serve them I have rejected.
And I have offered my heart and spirit[a] so that I might be careful to do the will
4 of the one who created me •because he is the living God. And he is holy, and
faithful, and he is more righteous than all (others) and there is no accepting of Deut 10:17
persons with him or accepting of gifts because he is a righteous God and he is
the one who executes judgment with all who transgress his commandments and
5 despise his covenant. •And you, my son, keep his commandments and ordinances
and judgments, and do not follow pollutions or graven images or molten images. Lev 7:26
6 And do not eat any blood[b] of beasts or cattle or any bird which flies in heaven.
7 And if you slaughter a sacrifice as an acceptable burnt offering of peace, slaughter Lev 3:7-10
it, but pour out its blood on the altar. And offer up all the fat of the burnt offering
on the altar with fine flour kneaded with oil, together with its libation. You will
offer it all together on the altar (as) a burnt offering, (as) a sweet aroma before
8 the LORD, •and the fat of the thanksgiving offering you will place upon the fire
which is on the altar. You shall remove the fat which is on the belly, all of the
fat of the internal organs and the two kidneys, all of the fat which is on them and
9 on the thighs and the liver together with the kidneys. •And you will offer all of
this up as a sweet aroma which is acceptable before the LORD together with its Lev 3:11
(fruit) offering and its libation for a sweet odor, the bread of a burnt offering to
10 the LORD. •And eat its flesh on that day and in the second (day), but do not let
the sun of the second (day) set upon it until it is consumed. And do not let it
remain until the third day because it will not be acceptable since it was not chosen.
Therefore, it will not be eaten. And all of those who eat it will raise up sin against
themselves. Because thus I have found written in the books of my forefathers and
11 in the words of Enoch and in the words of Noah.[c] •And you shall put salt in all TLevi 9
of your offerings, and you shall not omit the salt of the covenant from any of
12 your offerings before the LORD. •And take caution with the wood of the offering TLevi 2:13
that you do not bring wood for the offering except of such as these: cypress, bay,
almond, fir, pine, cedar, juniper, fig, olive, myrtle, laurel, and asphalathos.[d]

---

21 a. The statement "and those who serve . . .
heart and spirit" is not found in Eth., but appears
in the Lat. text. The additional text provides a
smoother reading.

b. The instructions which follow through vs. 20
concern the proper regulations for offering bloody
sacrifices. This portion of the text shares a number
of parallel passages with two other texts: TLevi 9
and fragments of an apocryphal work about Levi
which has survived in Gk., Syr., and Aram.
fragments. Charles has published the latter as
Appendix III in his volume entitled *The Greek
Versions of the Testaments of the Twelve Patriarchs*
(Oxford, 1908).

In both TLevi and the apocryphal fragments,
the instructions for performing sacrifice are given to
Levi by Isaac. In Jub, the instructions are given to
Isaac by Abraham. Since Levi is the central priestly
figure in Jub just as he is in the other two texts,
there is no reason to suspect that liturgical instructions given to him at some earlier stage in the
development of these interrelated traditions would
subsequently be applied to Isaac. The converse is
much more likely. In other words, these instructions
were probably intended for Isaac, as Jub reports,
but were subsequently reinterpreted to apply to
Levi.

The fact that Jub preserves an earlier order of
speakers does not necessarily prove that Jub is
earlier or that the other two accounts are dependent

on Jub. A. Hultgård has worked on the relationship
of these three documents most recently in his
*L'Eschatologie des Testaments des Douze Patri-
arches* (Uppsala, Sweden, 1977) vol. 1, pp. 15–
44. He is probably correct in his opinion that Jub
is related to the other two documents through a
common source (pp. 24, 45).

c. In both TLevi (9:12) and the apocryphal
fragments (vs. 22), Isaac describes Abraham as the
authority for the proper knowledge which he gives
to Levi. In the case of Jub, however, Abraham is
speaking. He claims that the authority is to be
found in the books of Enoch and Noah. Cf. 7:38.

d. Charles read the names of fourteen different
trees in his printed Eth. text and called attention
to the fact that Enoch speaks of fourteen evergreen
trees in ch. 3. He also noted that there are fourteen
trees listed in *Geoponica* XI. Subsequently, however, he discovered the list of twelve trees in the
fragmentary apocryphal work about Levi which he
published as Appendix III in *The Greek Versions
of the Testaments of the Twelve Patriarchs*. The
list contained in the fragmentary apocryphal work
has been preserved in both Aram. and Gk. Charles
compared the Aram. and Gk. lists with the Eth.
list in Jub and concluded that Jub also contained
just twelve trees. It goes without saying that there
is a considerable amount of uncertainty in the final
list. The word translated as "olive" is clear. It is
written with the familiar Eth. word for "olive."

13 But place some of these trees under the burnt offering on the altar (with) their appearance tested. And you will not place any split or dark wood, (but) wood strong and pure which has no spots, perfect, and new growth. And you will not place old wood (there) because its aroma has gone out because there is not,
14 therefore, an aroma upon it as before. •Except for these trees, there is none other that you will put on (the altar) because its aroma has separated and the smell of
15 its aroma will go up to heaven. •Keep this commandment and do it, my son, so
16 that you might act uprightly in all of your deeds. •And at all of the (appointed) times be pure in your body and wash yourself with water before you go to make an offering upon the altar. And wash your hands and your feet before you approach the altar. And when you have completed making the offering, wash your hands
17 and feet again. •And let there not be seen any blood upon you or your garments.
18 Be careful, my son, be extremely careful of blood. Cover it in the earth. •And, therefore, do not eat blood because it is life, and you shall not eat any blood.
19 And do not accept gifts for any human blood lest it be poured out in vain, without judgment, because it is blood which is poured out to cause sin for the earth. And the earth is not able to be purified of human blood except by blood of one who
20 shed it. •And you shall not accept gifts or tribute for human blood—blood through blood—so that you may be accepted before the LORD God Most High, and he will be the protector of the good, and so that you might guard yourself from all evil, and so that he might save you from all death,

21   I see, my son,
          every deed of mankind, that (they are) sins and evils;
          and all of their deeds are defilement and corruption and contamination;
          and there is no righteousness with them.
22   Be careful not to walk in their ways,
          and to tread in their^e path,
          or to commit a mortal sin before God Most High
          so that he will hide his face from you,
          and deliver you into the power of your sin,
          and uproot you from the earth,
          and your seed from beneath the sky,
          and your name and seed^f will perish from all the earth.
23   Turn yourself aside from all their deeds and from all their defilement;
          and keep the commands of God Most High,
          and perform his will, and act uprightly in all things.^g
24   And he will bless you in all your deeds,

Lev 17:13f.
Deut 12:23
1QapGen 11.17

Num 35:33

1Jn 5:16

All of the other Eth. words in the list are transliterations of Gk. spellings, some of which are themselves transliterations of Semitic names. The word for "fig" is ultimately derived from Aram. *tī'nā'*. The word that is translated "juniper" represents the same tree which appears in the OT as *bĕrôsh/bĕrôth*. It is frequently translated as "fir," but our list also includes the Gk. *strobilos* and *pitus*, which have been rendered "fir" and "pine" respectively. The word for "almond" is ultimately related to the Heb. word *shôqēd*. The most severe corruption is found at the end of the Eth. list, which reads "cedar which is named *'arbāt* and balsam." The word *asphalathos* is clearly written at the end of the list of twelve trees in the Gk. MS of the fragmentary apocryphal text. Since the list is derived from a source which it shares with Jub and since the Eth. word *'arbit* makes little sense, it is possible that the phrase " *'arbāt* and balsam" reflects a corrupted spelling of *asphalathos*, which was not understood. Subsequently it was broken up and reinterpreted to yield at least one intelligible word, "balsam." The phrase "cedar which is

named" was probably inserted to explain the strange word *'arbāt*, which survived in the text.
   e. Fragments of the Heb. text found at Qumran begin at this point and are parallel to phrases found in vss. 22–24.
   f. The Eth. clearly reads "seed" at this point. There is less certainty about the reading of the Heb. parallel from Qumran. In "Fragment d'une source du Psautier (4QPs 89) et fragments des Jubilés, du Document de Damas, d'un phylactère dans la grotte 4 de Qumran," *RB* 73 (1966) 104, Milik reads the Heb. as *zkrk*, "your memory," instead of a parallel *zr'k*, "your seed." The picture which appears on plate 9 in that article is not clear enough to confirm either reading. If Milik's reading proves to be correct, then the text should be altered to read "your memory."
   g. The parallel fragment from Qumran shows signs of a dittography at this point. The writer apparently began with the phrase "and from all their defilements" and repeated the text to this point.

and he will raise up from you a righteous plant in all[h] the earth throughout
  all the generations of the earth;
and my name and your name shall not cease from beneath heaven forever.

25 Go, my son, in peace. May God Most High, my God, and your God strengthen
you to do his will, and may he bless all of your seed and the remnant of your
seed for eternal generations with all righteous blessing so that you might be a
26 blessing in all of the earth." •And he went out from him rejoicing.

Abraham's celebration of the feast of firstfruits

1 **22** And it came to pass in the first week of this forty-fourth jubilee in the second
year, that year in which Abraham died, that Isaac and Ishmael came from the
Well of the Oath to Abraham, their father, to observe the feast of Shebuot,[a] which
is the feast of the firstfruits of the harvest. And Abraham rejoiced because both
2 of his children came,[b] •for Isaac had many possessions in Beer-sheba. And Isaac
used to go and inspect his possessions and return to his father.
3   And in those days Ishmael came to see his father. And both of them came
together, and Isaac slaughtered a sacrifice as a burnt offering and offered (it) up
4 upon the altar of his father which he built in Hebron. •And he sacrificed a thank
offering and made a feast of joy before Ishmael, his brother. And Rebecca made
new round cakes of new grain. And she gave them to Jacob, her son, to take to
Abraham, his father, from the firstfruits of the land so that he might eat and bless
5 the Creator of all before he died. •And Isaac also sent by the hand of Jacob a   Sir 24:8
6 good thank offering to Abraham so that he might eat and drink. •And he ate and   2Mac 1:24
drank and blessed God Most High who created heaven and earth and who made
all the fat of the earth and gave it to the sons of man so that they might eat and
7 drink and bless their Creator: •"And now I thank you, my God, because you have
let me see this day. Behold, I am one hundred and seventy-five years old, and
8 fulfilled in days. And all of my days were peaceful for me. •The sword of the   Jer 6:25
enemy did not triumph over me in anything which you gave to me or my sons all
9 of the days of my life until this day. •O my God, may your mercy and your peace
be upon your servant and upon the seed of his sons so that they might become an
elect people for you and an inheritance from all of the nations of the earth from   Deut 4:20
henceforth and for all the days of the generations of the earth forever."

Abraham's blessing for Jacob

10   And he called Jacob and said, "My son, Jacob, may the God of all bless you
and strengthen you to do righteousness and his will before him. And may he elect
you and your seed so that you become a people for him who always belong to
his inheritance according to his will. And you, my son, Jacob, draw near and kiss
11 me." •And he drew near and kissed him. And he said:

> "Blessed is my son, Jacob, and all his sons,
> unto the LORD, Most High, forever.   Gen 14:19
> May the LORD give you righteous seed,
> and may he sanctify some of your sons in the midst of all the earth.
> May the nations serve you,   Gen 27:29
> and all the nations bow down before your seed.
12 Be strong before men;
> and rule[c] over all the seed of Seth,   Num 24:17

---

h. The word "all" may be lacking in the Qumran
parallel. It is a matter of judgment regarding the
number of Heb. letters needed to fill up a lacuna.

22 a. Shabuot for this feast; see ch. 6, n. f.

b. A portion of the surviving Lat. text begins at
this point and continues to the last word of 22:19.
c. The Eth. text reads "while you rule." The
Lat. text has *potestatem exerce.* An imperative
form of the Eth. verb seems preferable.

then may your ways be righteous, and the ways of your sons,
in order to be a holy people.

13 May the Most High God give you all the blessings
(with) which he blessed me,
and (with) which he blessed Noah and Adam;
may they rest upon the holy head of your seed throughout each generation
and forever.

14 May he cleanse you from all sin and defilement,
so that he might forgive all your transgressions, and your erring through
ignorance.
May he strengthen you and bless you,
and may you inherit all of the earth.

15 And may he renew his covenant with you,
so that you might be a people for him, belonging to his inheritance forever.
And he will be God for you and for your seed in truth and righteousness
throughout all the days of the earth.

16 And you also, my son, Jacob, remember my words,
and keep the commandments of Abraham, your father.
Separate yourself from the gentiles,   Isa 52:11
and do not eat with them,[d]
and do not perform deeds like theirs.
And do not become associates of theirs.
Because their deeds are defiled,
and all of their ways are contaminated, and despicable, and abominable.

17 They slaughter their sacrifices to the dead,   Deut 26:14
and to the demons they bow down.   Ps 106:28
And they eat in tombs.[e]
And all their deeds are worthless and vain.

18 And they have no heart to perceive,
and they have no eyes to see what their deeds are,
and where they wander astray,
saying to the tree 'you are my god,'
and to a stone 'you are my lord, and you are my savior';
and they have no heart.[f]

19 But (as for) you, my son, Jacob,
may God Most High help you,
and the God of heaven bless you.
And may he turn you from their defilement,
and from all their errors.

20 Be careful, my son, Jacob, that you do not take a wife from any of the   Gen 28:1
seed of the daughters of Canaan,
because all of his seed is (destined) for uprooting from the earth;

21 because through the sin of Ham, Canaan sinned,
and all of his seed will be blotted out from the earth,
and all his remnant,
and there is none of his who will be saved.

22 And for all of those who worship idols and for the hated ones,
there is no hope in the land of the living;
because they will go down into Sheol.   1En 103:7f.
And in the place of judgment they will walk,

d. The implication is that the food prepared by
the gentiles would not be prepared in accord with
Jewish laws of purity. The issue became particularly
acute in the writer's own time in light of the fact
that servants of Antiochus IV tried to force Jews
to eat impure food such as pork. Cf. 1Mac 1:47f.;
62f.; 2Mac 6:18–21; 7:1.

e. Sacrificial offerings to or for the dead would

be consumed in the tombs. For a wide-ranging
recent discussion see M. Pope, *Song of Songs*
(Garden City, N.Y., 1977) pp. 210–29.

f. The phrase "and they have no heart" was
considered by Charles to be a dittography based
on the opening phrase in vs. 18, but it is found in
both Lat. and Eth. texts.

and they will have no memory upon the earth.[g]
Just as the sons of Sodom were taken from the earth,
so (too) all of those who worship idols shall be taken away.

23 Do not fear, my son, Jacob,
and do not be in terror, O son of Abraham.
The Most High God shall protect you from destruction,
and from all the ways of error he will deliver you.

24 This house I have built for myself so that I might cause my name to dwell upon it in the land. It has been given to you and to your seed forever.[h] And it will be called the house of Abraham and will be given to you and to your seed forever because you will build my house, and you will raise up my name before God forever. Your seed and your name will remain in all the earth's generations."

A second blessing for Jacob

25,26 And he ceased commanding him and blessing him. • And both of them lay down together on one bed. And Jacob slept on the bosom of Abraham, his father's father. And he[i] kissed him seven (times), and his compassionate heart[j] rejoiced

27 over him, • and he blessed him with all his heart and he said, "God Most High (is) the God of all, and Creator of all who brought me out from Ur of the Chaldees so that he might give me this land to inherit it forever and to raise up a holy seed

28 so that the Most High may be blessed forever." • And he blessed Jacob, saying, "My son (is) one in whom I rejoice with all my heart and all my emotion. And

29 may your favor and your mercy rest upon him and upon his seed always. • And do not forsake him and neglect him henceforth and for the eternal days. And may your eyes be open upon him and upon his seed so that you might protect him and

30 bless him and sanctify him for a people who belong to your heritage. • And bless him with all of your blessings henceforth and for all of the eternal days. And renew your covenant and your mercy with him and with his seed with all your will in all of the earth's generations."

Neh 9:6f.
Gen 15:7

1Kgs 8:29,52
Neh 1:6
Dan 9:18

The death and burial of Abraham

Gen 25:8f.

1 **23** And he placed the two fingers of Jacob on his eyes and he blessed the God of gods. And he covered his face, and stretched out his feet and slept the eternal

2 sleep, and he was gathered to his fathers. • During all of this (time) Jacob was lying on his bosom and did not know that Abraham, his grandfather, was dead.

3 And Jacob awoke from his sleep and, behold, Abraham was cold as ice, and he said, "O father, father!" And none spoke. And he knew that he was dead.

4 And he rose up from his bosom and ran and told Rebecca, his mother. And Rebecca went to Isaac in the night and told him. And they went together and Jacob was also with them, and a lamp was in his hand. And when they went,

5 they found Abraham lying dead. • And Isaac fell upon his father's face and wept

6 and kissed him. • And the sound was[a] heard in Abraham's house and Ishmael, his son, arose and went to Abraham, his father. And he wept for Abraham, his father,

7 he and all[b] of Abraham's house, and they wept greatly. • And his sons, Isaac and

Gen 46:4
Gen 49:33
Judg 2:10

g. In his English translation, Charles rearranged ll. 2–5 of this vs. so that l. 5 followed immediately after l. 2, with which it forms an exact parallel. The present translation simply follows the order of the Eth. text.

h. The phrase "It has been given . . . seed forever" is repeated with a slight variation again in the same vs. The repetition is cumbersome and probably due to dittography.

i. Abraham kissed Jacob.

j. Lit. "his mercy and his heart."

23 a. One of the fragments of the Heb. text found at Qumran (3Q5 F.3) begins at this point and continues through vs. 7a.

b. It is possible that the Qumran fragment differs at this point, but the script is difficult to read. VanderKam has restored '*n*)*śy*, "(me)n," in the Heb. text (*Textual and Historical Studies*, p. 62). That would mean that the earliest text read "all of the men of Abraham's house." Since the text is difficult to read at that point, VanderKam does not seriously press the case for his reading.

Ishmael, buried him in the cave of Macnpelah[c] near Sarah, his wife.[d] And all of
the men of his house and Isaac and Ishmael and all of their sons and all of the
sons of Keturah wept for him forty days in their places. And the days[e] of
Abraham's weeping were completed.

A discussion of the general decline in longevity   Gen 25:8

8   And he lived three jubilees and four weeks of years,[f] one hundred and seventy-
9 five years. And he completed the days of his life, being old and full of days. •For[g]
the days of the lives of the ancients were nineteen jubilees. And after the Flood
they began to be less than nineteen jubilees and to grow old quickly and to shorten
the days of their lives due to much suffering and through the evil of their ways—
10 except Abraham. •For Abraham was perfect in all of his actions with the
LORD and was pleasing through righteousness all of the days of his life. And
behold, he[h] did not complete four jubilees in his life until he grew old in the
presence of evil (and) his days were full.
11   And all of the generations which will arise henceforth and until the day of the   CD 10.8f.
great judgment will grow old quickly before they complete two jubilees, and their
knowledge will forsake them because of their old age.[i] And all of their knowledge
12 will be removed.[j] •And in those days if a man will live a jubilee and a half, they[k]
will say about him, "He prolonged his life, but the majority of his days were
13 suffering and anxiety and affliction. And there was no peace, •because plague   Ps 90:10
(came) upon plague, and wound upon wound, and affliction upon affliction, and
evil report upon evil report, and sickness upon sickness, and every evil judgment
of this sort one with another: sickness, and downfall, and sleet, and hail, and
frost, and fever, and chills, and stupor, and famine, and death, and sword, and
captivity, and all plagues, and suffering."
14   And all of this will come in the evil generation which sins in the land. Pollution
15 and fornication and contamination and abomination are their deeds. •Then they
will say, "The days of the ancients were as many as one thousand years and
good. But behold, (as for) the days of our lives, if a man should extend his life
seventy years or if he is strong (for) eighty years, then these are evil. And there   Ps 90:10
is not any peace in the days of this evil generation."

c. Another fragment of Heb. text (2Q19) begins
at this point. It overlaps the preceding fragment
(3Q5 F.3) on one word, i.e. *mkplh*, "Machpelah."
The Eth. text contains a word meaning "double,"
which is simply a translation of "Machpelah," but
since the Heb. original clearly contained the form
which is most familiar to readers of the Bible, we
have restored it.
   The two Heb. fragments also provide evidence
for changing the order of words in the Eth. text in
this vs., but that change of word order in Eth.
would not be reflected in the English translation.
   d. VanderKam has argued rather convincingly
that the lacuna in the Heb. MS (2Q19) at this point
indicates that the Heb. text had a fuller reading
than the one preserved in Eth. (*Textual and Historical Studies*, p. 66). Nevertheless, what might
have been in the additional text (approximately
twenty-two letters) is anyone's guess.
   e. Charles restored the word "days" on the
basis of Gen 50:4. His MSS B D read "the grief
of Abraham's weeping."
   f. The parallel Lat. text begins again at this
point and continues through 23:23a.
   g. An important digression from the continuing
account of the patriarchs begins here and runs to
the end of the ch. This is one of the main passages
to be investigated by anyone wishing to discover

the writer's view of his own age. G. L. Davenport
has made a careful study of this passage in his
volume *The Eschatology of the Book of Jubilees*
(Leiden, 1971). See especially pp. 32–40 and the
extensive footnotes on pp. 32f., where he attempts
to discern the structure of the passage in relation
to surrounding material.
   h. M. Baillet suggested that the Qumran fragment (3Q5 F.4) was to be identified with this
portion of the text of Jub. In his "Remarques sur
le manuscrit du Livre des Jubilés de la grotte 3
de Qumran," *RQ* 5 (1964–66) 323–33, he reconstructed a phrase which reads "(behol)d he did not
complete." VanderKam has challenged the reading
of the line and its appropriateness at this point in
Jub (*Textual and Historical Studies*, pp. 100f.); his
judgment seems justified.
   i. This is the reading of the Eth. MSS. Charles
followed the MSS in preparing his own translation,
but he had earlier emended the Eth. text to read
"because of their spirits" to agree with the Lat.
text.
   j. The last sentence in vs. 11 does not appear
in the Lat. text. Charles judged that the Eth. reading
was due to dittography.
   k. There is a Heb. fragment from Qumran (3Q5
F.1) which begins at this point.

The description of the future evil generation

16 And in this generation children will reproach their parents and their elders on 1En 90:6f.
account of sin, and on account of injustice, and on account of the words of their
mouth, and on account of great evil which they will do, and on account of their
forsaking the covenant which the LORD made between them and himself so that Dan 11:30
they might be careful and observe all of his commandments and his ordinances 1Mac 1:15
                                                                                 Deut 5:31f.
17 and all of his law without turning aside to the right or left. •For they all did evil
and every mouth speaks of sin and all of their deeds (are) polluted and abominable. 1Mac 1:52f.
And all of their ways (are) contamination and pollution and corruption.
18 Behold, the land will be corrupted on account of all their deeds, and there will
be no seed of the vine, and there will be no oil because their works are entirely
faithless. And all of them will be destroyed together: beast, cattle, birds, and all Hos 4:3
                                                                                 Ezek 38:20
19 of the fish of the sea on account of the sons of man. •Some of these will strive Zeph 1:3
with others, youths with old men and old men with youths, the poor with the
rich, the lowly with the great, and the beggar with the judge concerning the Law
and the Covenant because they have forgotten the commandments and covenant
and festivals and months and sabbaths and jubilees and all of the judgments.
20 And they will stand up with bow and[l] swords and war in order to return them to
"the way," but they will not be returned until much blood is shed upon the earth
21 by each (group). •And those who escape will not be turned back from their evils
to the way of righteousness because they will lift themselves up for deceit and
wealth so that one shall take everything of his neighbor; and they will pronounce
the great name but not in truth or righteousness. And they will pollute the holy
of holies with their pollution and with the corruption of their contamination.

Punishment on that generation followed by repentance and God's blessings

22 And there will be a great plague upon the deeds of that generation from the
LORD and he will give them to the sword and to judgment and to captivity and
23 pillage and destruction. •And he will rouse up against them the sinners of the Ezek 9:6
nations who have no mercy[m] or grace for them and who have no regard for any
persons old or young or anyone. For (they will be) cruel and powerful so that
they will act more evilly than any of the sons of men.

> And they will cause turmoil in Israel and sin against Jacob;
> and much blood will be shed upon the earth;[n]
> and there will be no one who will gather and no one who will bury. Jer 8:2

24 In those days, they will cry out and call and pray
to be saved from the hand of the sinners, the gentiles, Gal 2:15
but there will be none who will be saved,

25 and the heads of children will be white with gray hairs,
and an infant three weeks old will look aged
like one whose years (are) one hundred,
and their stature will be destroyed by affliction and torment.

26 And in those days, children will begin to search the law,
and to search the commandments
and to return to the way of righteousness.

27 And the days will begin to increase and grow longer

---

l. The phrase "with bow and" is found only in
the Lat. MS.
m. There is a Heb. fragment from Qumran (3Q5
F.3) which contains the Heb. word for "mercy."
A. Rofe (*Tarbiz*, 34 [1965] 333–36) proposed that
the passage matched the text of Jub at this point.
VanderKam (*Textual and Historical Studies*, pp.
60–65) has argued convincingly that the Heb. text

did not match the text of Jub at this point.
n. In his work on *The Eschatology of the Book
of Jubilees*, Davenport gathered together a selected
list of authors who describe the "messianic woes"
similar to those depicted in the following lines. He
rightly objects to the adjective "messianic," but
the type of literature is widely known (cf. especially
p. 37).

among those sons of men, generation by generation,
and year by year, until
their days approach a thousand years,
and to a greater number of years than days.

28 And there (will be) no old men and none who is full of days.[o]   Isa 65:20
Because all of them will be infants and children.

29 And all of their days they will be complete
and live in peace and rejoicing
and there will be no Satan and no evil (one) who will destroy,   AsMos 10:1
because all of their days will be days of blessing and healing.

30 And then the LORD will heal his servants,
and they will rise up and see great peace.
And they will drive out their enemies,
and the righteous ones will see and give praise,
and rejoice forever and ever with joy;
and they will see all of their judgments and all of their curses among their
enemies.

31 And their bones will rest in the earth,   1En 91:10; 92:3
and their spirits will increase joy,[p]
and they will know that the LORD is an executor of judgment;
but he will show mercy to hundreds and thousands,
to all who love him.

32 And you, Moses, write these words because thus it is written and set upon the
heavenly tablets as a testimony for eternal generations.

Jacob buys the right of firstborn from Esau   Gen 25:11,27-34

1 **24** And it happened after the death of Abraham that the LORD blessed Isaac,
his son. And he arose from Hebron and went to the Well of the Vision[a] in the   Gen 16:14
first year of the third week of this jubilee, and he lived there seven years.

2 And in the first year of the fourth week a famine began in the land other than   Gen 26:1
3 the first famine which occurred in the days of Abraham. •And Jacob was cooking
lentil soup, and Esau came in from the field hungry, and he said to Jacob, his
brother, "Give me some of this reddish-colored[b] soup." And Jacob said to him,
"Hand over your primogeniture (i.e.) this right of firstborn, and I will give you
4 bread and also some of this lentil soup." •And Esau thought, "I will die. Of what
use is this right of firstborn to me?" And he said to Jacob, "I give it (to) you."
5,6 And Jacob said, "Swear to me today." And he swore for him. •And Jacob gave
his brother, Esau, bread and soup. And he ate until he was satisfied. And Esau
despised his right of firstborn. Therefore, Esau's name was called Edom,[c] on
account of the reddish-colored soup which Jacob gave him for his right of firstborn.
7 And Jacob became the older one but Esau was lowered from his seniority.

---

o. Reading with the MSS, Charles inserted a
negative in his text to suggest there were none
"whose days would not be full." As VanderKam
has pointed out, the negative is not needed (*Textual
and Historical Studies*, p. 269).

p. This vs. is subject to two quite different
interpretations. It could be understood as a description of spirits which remain conscious and aware
of postmortem events while their bones rest in
peace. It could also be understood as an example
of poetic hyperbole, describing those who die with
assurance that justice has been done. They are
portrayed as joyous dead who lie in the earth

contented with God's certain vindication of the
righteous.

24 a. The Well of the Vision is the biblical *Beer
Lahai-roi*. See Gen 16:13f.

b. The Eth. text has "wheat soup," but Charles
has pointed out that the word for wheat arose in
the Gk. MS tradition where *puros*, "wheat,"
resulted from a misspelling of *purros*, "red, red-
dish."

c. A name formed from the Heb. root meaning
red.

Isaac's sojourn at Gerar

Gen 26:1-5

8 And there was a famine upon the earth, and Isaac started to go down to Egypt in the second year of this week and he went to the Philistine king at Gerar, to
9 Abimelek. •And the LORD appeared to him and he said to him, "Do not go down to Egypt. Dwell in the land where I shall tell you. And sojourn in that land.
10 And I shall be with you and bless you •because I will give all of this land to you and to your seed. And I will carry out my oath which I swore to Abraham, your father. And I will multiply your seed as the stars of the sky. And I will give to
11 your seed all of this land. • And all of the nations of the earth will bless themselves by your seed because your father obeyed me and observed my restrictions and my commandments and my laws and my ordinances and my covenant. And now,
12 obey my voice, and dwell in this land." •And he dwelt at Gerar three weeks of
13 years.d •And Abimelek gave orders concerning him and everything which was his, saying, "Any man who touches him or anything which is his let him surely Gen 26:11 die."

An account of the wells dug by Jacob from Gerar to Beer-sheba

Gen 26:12-33

14 And Jacob grew prosperous among the Philistines and had many possessions:
15 oxen, and sheep, and camels, and asses, and much property.e •And he sowed in the land of the Philistines, and he raised grain one hundredfold. And Isaac became
16 very wealthy, and the Philistines became jealous of him. •And all of the wells which the servants of Abraham dug during Abraham's lifetime the Philistines
17 stopped up and filled them with dirt after Abraham's death. •And Abimelek said to Isaac, "Go away from us because you are much greater than we."

And Isaac went away from there in the first year of the seventh week. And he
18 sojourned in the valleys of Gerar, •and they dug again the wells of water which the servants of Abraham, his father, had dug—and the Philistines stopped them up after the death of Abraham, his father. And he named them just as his father,
19 Abraham, had named them. •And the servants of Isaac dug wells in the valley, and they found running water. And the shepherds of Gerar became angry with the shepherds of Jacob, saying, "The water is ours." And Isaac named that well "Harshness," because they had been harsh with us.
20 And they dug another well and they also contended about it. And he named it "Hostility." And he rose from there, and they dug another well, but they were not angered about that, and he called it "Breadth," and Isaac said, "Now the LORD has made wide (a place) for us. And we have increased in the land."
21 And he went up from there to the Well of the Oath in the first year of the first
22 week in the forty-fourth jubilee. •And the LORD appeared to him during that night, on the new moon of the first month, and he said to him, "I am the God of Abraham, your father. Do not fear, because I am with you and I shall bless you and I shall surely multiply your seed like the sand of the earth because of Abraham,
23 my servant." •And he built an altar there where Abraham, his father, had built at first and called upon the name of the LORD and he offered a sacrifice to the God of Abraham, his father.
24,25 And they dug a well and found running water. •But the servants of Isaac dug another well and did not find water. And they went and told Isaac that they did not find water. And Isaac said, "I have sworn (an oath) on this day to the
26 Philistines. And this thing has happened to us." •And he named that place "the Well of the Oath," because he swore an oath there to Abimelek and to 'Ahuzzat, his friend, and to Phicol, the commander of his army.

---

d. The Lat. text resumes at this point and continues through 25:1a.

e. The Lat. text has *ministerium magnum,* "a

great (household) staff," which agrees with the Heb. of Gen 26:14.

Isaac curses the Philistines

27 And Isaac knew on that day that under pressure he swore an oath to them to
28 make peace with them. •And Isaac cursed the Philistines on that day, and he said,
"Cursed be the Philistines[f] for the day of wrath and anger from among all the
nations. May the LORD make them as scorn and a curse and (the object of) wrath
and anger at the hands of the sinners, the nations, and in the hands of the Kittim.
29 And whoever escapes from the sword of the enemy and from the Kittim, may   Dan 11:30
the righteous people uproot them from beneath the sky with judgment, because   Gen 10:4
they will be enemies and foes to my sons in their generations upon the earth.   1Mac 1:1; 8:5

30   And no remnant will be left to them,
             nor one who escapes on the day of the wrath of judgment;
         because all of the Philistine seed is (destined) for destruction and uprooting
                 and removal from the earth.
         And, therefore, there will not be any name or seed which remains upon   Amos 9:7
                 the earth for any of[g] the Caphtorim.   Deut 2:23
31   Because if they go up to heaven, from there they will fall;
         and if they are set firm in[h] the earth, from there they will be torn out;
         and if they are hidden among the nations, from there they will be uprooted; Amos 9:2-4
         and if they go down to Sheol, even there their judgment will multiply, Ps 139:8f.
         and also there will be no peace for them there.
32   And if they go into captivity by the hand of those who seek their life, they
                 will kill them along the way.
         And neither name nor seed will be left for them in all the earth,
         because they shall walk in an eternal curse."

33   And thus it is written and engraved concerning him in the heavenly tablets to
be done to him in the day of judgment so that they might be uprooted from the
earth.

Rebecca gives instruction to Jacob regarding marriage

1 **25** In the second year of this week, in this jubilee, Rebecca called Jacob, her
son, and spoke to him, saying, "My son, do not take for yourself a wife from   Gen 28:1
the daughters of Canaan as (did) Esau your brother, who took for himself two
wives from the daughters of Canaan. And they have embittered my soul with all   Gen 27:46
their impure deeds, because all of their deeds (are) fornication and lust. And there Gen 26:35
2 is not any righteousness with them because (their deeds are) evil. •And I love you
very much, my son. And my heart and affection bless you at every hour of the
3 day and (every) watch of the night. •And now, my son, heed my voice, and do   Gen 28:1f.
the will of your mother. And do not take for yourself a wife from the daughters
of this land, but from my father's house and my father's kin. You will take for
yourself a wife from my father's house. And the Most High God will bless you,
and your children will be a righteous generation and a holy seed."

---

f. This cursing of the Philistines is not part of
the biblical tradition. It reflects the writer's attitude
with respect to the contemporary inhabitants of the
area regarded as Philistia. The Philistines are not
to be defeated by the Jews in the first instance, but
by the Kittim. The identity of the Kittim is still a
subject of debate. See J. C. Greenfield, "Kittim,"
in *IDB*, vol. 3, p. 40f., and Davenport's discussion
in *The Eschatology of the Book of Jubilees* (p. 56).

g. Charles emended the text to read "for these
Caphtorium" with the Lat. text, but the Eth. MSS
read "all Caphtorim."

h. The Lat. text reads "and where he flees."
The text in vs. 31 is obviously dependent on Amos
9:2–4. The writer may have been attracted to that
passage because of the somewhat confusing reference to the "way of Beer-sheba" in 8:14. In the
present text, Jacob is portrayed as cursing the
Philistines in Beer-sheba after having made his way
there through Philistine territory. Although there is
no description of the patriarch Jacob cursing the
Philistines, Amos 8:14 does provide a biblical basis
of sorts for cursing those who live in that area.

Jacob's response

4   And then Jacob spoke with Rebecca, his mother, and said to her, "Behold, O mother, I am nine weeks of years old. And I have not known or touched or been betrothed to any woman. Nor have I been thinking about taking for myself a wife
5 from the daughters of Canaan, •because I recall, O mother, the words of Abraham, our father. For he commanded me that I should not take a wife from the daughters of Canaan because I should take for myself a wife from the seed of my father's
6 house and from my (own) kin. •I heard some time ago that daughters had been born to your brother, Laban. And I have set my heart upon them that I might take
7 a wife from among them. •And, therefore, I have guarded myself in my soul lest I sin or be corrupted in any of my ways all the days of my life because my father,
8 Abraham, gave me many commands regarding lust and fornication. •In spite of everything which he commanded me, for these twenty-two years my brother has contended with me and he frequently spoke with me and said, 'My brother, take as a wife one of the sisters of my two wives.' But I did not desire to do as he
9 had done. •I swear, O mother, before you all the days of my life, that I will not take for myself a wife from the daughters of the seed of Canaan and I will not
10 act wickedly as my brother has done. •Do not fear, O mother. Trust that I will do your will. And I will walk uprightly and will never corrupt my ways."

Rebecca's blessing for Jacob

11   And then she lifted her face toward heaven and spread out the fingers of her hands[a] and opened her mouth and blessed the Most High God who created heaven
12 and earth. And she gave to him glory and praise. •And she said, "May the LORD God be blessed, and may his holy name be blessed forever and ever, he who gave to me Jacob, a pure son and a holy seed; because he is yours and his seed will
13 (belong) to you for all times and in all generations forever. •O LORD, bless him
14 and place in my mouth a righteous blessing so that I might bless him." •And at   Jn 14:17
that time, when a spirit of truth[b] descended upon her mouth, she placed her two hands upon the head of Jacob and said:

15   "Blessed are you, O LORD of righteousness and God of Ages;
            and may he bless you more than all the generations of man.
            May he grant to you the way of righteousness, my son;
            and to your seed, may he reveal righteousness.
16   May he multiply your sons in your life(time);
            may they rise up according to the number of the months of the year.
            And may their sons be more numerous and greater than the stars of heaven;
            and more than the sand of the sea, may their number increase.
17   And may he give to them this pleasant land,
            just as he said that he would give it to Abraham and his seed after him
                  always;
            and may they hold it (as a) possession forever.
18   And may I see, O my son, that you shall have blessed sons in my lifetime;
            and a blessed and holy seed, may all your seed be.
19   And just as you have given rest to your mother's soul in her lifetime;
            the womb of the one who bore you likewise blesses you.
            My affection and my breasts are blessing you;
            and my mouth and tongue are praising you greatly.
20   Increase and overflow in the land,
            and may your seed be perfected in every age in the joy of heaven and
                  earth.

25 a. She held her hands in a traditional attitude   majority of MSS read "spirit of truth." Either
of prayer.   reading would be appropriate in this context.
   b. Eth. MS C reads "a holy spirit," but the

And may your seed be glad;
and on the great day of peace, may it have peace.

21 May your name and your seed stand for all the ages;
and may God Most High be their God.
And may the God of Righteousness dwell with them;
and with them may his sanctuary be built in all ages.

22 The one who blesses you will be blessed,   Gen 27:29
and all flesh which curses you falsely will be cursed.''

23 And she kissed him and said to him:

"May the LORD of the world^c love you;
just as the heart and affection of your mother rejoices in you and blesses
you.''

And she stopped blessing him.

The account of how Jacob received a blessing intended for Esau   Gen 27:1-40

1 **26** And in the seventh year of this week Isaac called Esau, his elder son, and
said to him, "My son, I am old, and behold my eyes are too dim to see. And I
2 do not know the day of my death. •And now take your hunting gear, your quiver
and your bow. And go out to the field and hunt for me and catch something for
me, my son. And prepare for me food, such as my soul desires. And fetch it to
3 me so that I might eat and my soul might bless you before I die.'' •Now Rebecca
4 was listening as Isaac spoke to Esau. •And Esau went out early to the field so
5 that he might snare and take something and bring it to his father. •And Rebecca
called Jacob, her son, and said to him, "Behold, I heard Isaac, your father,
speaking with Esau, your brother, saying, 'Snare something for me and prepare
food for me. And bring it to me. And I will eat, and bless you before the LORD
6 before I die.' •And now listen, my son, to my words which I command you. Go
to your flock and take for me two good goat kids. And I will prepare them as
food for your father just as he desires. And you shall take it in to your father and
he will eat and bless you before the LORD before he dies. And you shall be
7 blessed.'' •And Jacob said to Rebecca, his mother, "O mother, I will not refuse
anything which my father would eat and which would please him, but I am afraid,
8 my mother, lest he recognize my voice and wish to touch me. •And you know
that I am smooth and Esau, my brother, is hairy. And I shall become in his sight
like one who acts wickedly and I shall be doing a deed which he did not command^a
me to do. And he will be angry with me and I shall bring upon myself a curse
9 and not a blessing.'' •And Rebecca, his mother, said to him, "Upon me let your
10 curse be, my son, but obey me.'' •And Jacob obeyed Rebecca, his mother. And
he went and took two good and fat goat kids. And he brought them to his mother.
11 And his mother prepared them just as he liked. •And Rebecca took the favorite
clothing of her elder son, Esau, which was with her in the house. And she put it
on Jacob, her youngest son, and hides of the goat kids she placed on his hands
12 and on the bare parts of his neck. •And she gave the stew and bread which she
13 had prepared into the hand of Jacob, her son. •And Jacob entered to his father
and said, "I am your son. I have done as you said to me. Come, and sit down
and eat from what I have snared, O father, so that your soul might bless me.''
14,15 And Isaac said to his son, "How have you found (it) so quickly, my son?'' •And
16 Jacob said, "It is because your God directed me.'' •And Isaac said to him, "Draw
near, and let me touch you, my son, to know whether you are my son Esau or
17 not.'' •And Jacob drew near to Isaac, his father. And he touched him and said,
18 "The voice is the voice of Jacob, but the hands are the hands of Esau.''

---

c. The Eth. word which is translated "world"
is '*ôlam;* just as its Aram. counterpart, it may also
refer to a period of time, a world age, or eon.

26 a. A portion of the Lat. text begins at this
point and continues through the first three words
of vs. 23.

And he did not know him because the change was from heaven in order to 1Kgs 12:15
distract his mind, and Isaac was unaware because his hands were hairy like the
19 hands of Esau[b] so that he blessed him. •And he said, "Are you my son Esau?"
And he said, "I am your son." And he said, "Bring it near to me and I will eat
20 some of what you snared, my son, so that my soul might bless you." •And he
brought it near to him, and he ate. And he brought him wine, and he drank.
21 And Isaac, his father, said, "Come to me and kiss me, my son." And he drew
22 near and he kissed him. •And he smelled the fragrance of the odor of his garments,
and he blessed him and he said:

> "Behold, the odor of my son is like the odor of a field[c] which the LORD
> has blessed.
23　May the LORD give and multiply to you from the dew of heaven and from
> the dew of earth,
> and an abundance of wheat and oil may he multiply for you.
> May nations serve you,
> and the people bow down to you.
24　Become a lord to your brothers,
> and may your mother's sons bow down to you.
> And may all of the blessings with which the LORD blessed me and blessed
> Abraham, my father,
> belong to you and to your seed forever.
> May the one who curses you be cursed,
> and the one who blesses you be blessed."

25 And it came to pass after Isaac ceased blessing his son Jacob, and after Jacob
went out from Isaac, his father, that he hid himself. And Esau, his brother, arrived
26 from his hunting. •And he also prepared food and brought (it) to his father and
said to his father, "Let my father arise and eat from what I have snared so that
27 your soul may bless me." •And Isaac, his father, said to him, "Who are you?"
And he said to him, "I am your firstborn, Esau, your son. I have done as you
28 commanded me." •And Isaac was very greatly astonished, and he said, "Who is
this who hunted and snared (game) and brought (it) to me, and I ate from all (of
it) before you came, and I blessed him. And he and all his seed will be blessed
29 forever." •And it came to pass when Esau heard the words of his father, Isaac,
that he cried out with a very loud and bitter voice and said to his father, "Bless
30 me also, O father!" •And he said to him, "Your brother came fraudulently and
took your blessings." And he said, "Now I know why his name was called Jacob.
Behold he has defrauded[d] me twice. He has taken my right of firstborn and now
31 he has taken my blessing." •And he said, "Have you not retained a blessing for
me, father?" And Isaac answered and said to Esau, "Behold, I have set him up
as lord over you, and all his brothers I have given to him that they might be
servants to him. And with abundance of wheat, and wine, and oil I have
32 strengthened him. But for you, what shall I now establish, my son?" •And Esau
said to Isaac, his father, "Is there only one blessing of yours, father? Bless me
33 also, father." And Esau raised his voice and wept. •And Isaac answered and said
to him:

> "Behold, apart from the dew of the land shall be your dwelling,
> and apart from the dew of heaven from above.
34　And by your sword you shall live,
> and you will serve your brother.
> And it will happen when you become great,
> and you will remove his yoke from your neck,
> that then you will surely sin completely unto death,
> and your seed will be rooted out from under heaven."

b. The Lat. text adds "his brother."
c. The Lat. text reads "full field."

d. In Heb. the word meaning "defraud" contains the same consonants as the name "Jacob."

Esau's resolve to kill Jacob

Gen 27:41

35 And Esau kept threatening Jacob on account of the blessing with which his father blessed him. And he said in his heart, "Now let the days of mourning for my father draw near. And I will kill Jacob, my brother."

Rebecca and Isaac counsel Jacob to go to Haran

Gen 27:42-28:5

1 **27** And the words of Esau, her elder son, were told to Rebecca in a dream, and 2 Rebecca sent and called Jacob, her younger son, and she said to him, •"Behold, 3 Esau, your brother, will take vengeance in order to kill you. •So now, my son, obey me and arise and flee to Laban, my brother, to Haran. And dwell with him a few days until your brother's anger is turned away and he abandons his anger with you and forgets the full extent of what you did to him. And I will send and 4 bring you from there." •And Jacob said, "I am not afraid. If he desires to kill 5 me, I shall kill him." •And she said to him, "(No),[a] lest I be bereaved of both 6 of my sons in one day." •And Jacob said to Rebecca, his mother, "Behold, you know that my father is old. And he does not see because his eyes are dim. And if I leave him it will be grievous in his sight because I am leaving and going from you. And my father will be angry and curse me. I will not go. But when he sends 7 me, only then will I go." •And Rebecca said to Jacob, "I will go in and I will 8 speak to him. And he will send you." •And Rebecca entered and she said to Isaac, "I despise my life because of the two daughters of Heth whom Esau took as wives for himself. And if Jacob takes a wife from among the daughters of the land who are like these, why then shall I live, because the daughters of Canaan 9 are evil." •And Isaac called Jacob and he blessed him and admonished him and 10 said to him, •"Do not take for yourself a wife from any of the daughters of Canaan. Arise and go into Mesopotamia to the house of Bethuel, your mother's father, and take a wife for yourself from there, from the daughters of Laban, your 11 mother's brother. •And may God Almighty[b] bless and increase and multiply you. And become a company of nations. And may he grant the blessings of my father, Abraham, to you and[c] to your seed after you so that you will inherit the land of your sojournings and all of the land which the LORD gave to Abraham. Go, my 12 son, in peace." •And Isaac sent Jacob. And he went to Mesopotamia, to Laban, the son of Bethuel, the Syrian, the brother of Rebecca, the mother of Jacob.

Isaac consoles Rebecca regarding Jacob's future

13 And it came to pass after Jacob arose to travel to Mesopotamia that the spirit 14 of Rebecca grieved after her son. And she wept. •And Isaac said to Rebecca, "My sister, do not weep on account of Jacob, my son, because in peace he will Song 4:9,10,12 15 journey and in peace he will return. •God Most High will protect him from all 16 evil and he will be with him because he will not forsake him all of his days, •for I know that he will make his ways prosper everywhere he goes until he returns to 17 us in peace and we see him in peace. •Do not fear on his account, my sister, because he is upright in his way and he is a perfect man. And he is faithful. And 18 he will not perish. Do not weep." •And Isaac comforted Rebecca on account of Jacob, her son, and he blessed him.

Jacob's dream and vow at Bethel

Gen 28:10-22

19 And Jacob went forth from the Well of the Oath in order to travel[d] to Haran in

---

27 a. The word "no" is lacking in the Eth. text, but the syntax is awkward without it.

b. "God Almighty" from Heb. *El Shadday*. Two Eth. MSS have written *šamáy*, "heaven," instead of *šadáy* = *Shadday*.

c. A portion of the Lat. text begins at this point and continues through the first two words of vs. 24.

d. Another fragment of the Heb. text from Qumran (1Q17) begins at this point.

the first year of the second week of the forty-fourth jubilee. And he arrived at Luz, which is in the mountains, i.e. Bethel, on the first of the first month of this week. And he reached the place when it was evening. And he turned aside from the way toward the west of the public road on that night. And he slept there 20 because the sun had set. •And he took one of the stones of that place and he placed it at his head[e] beneath that tree and he was traveling alone, and he slept.

21 And he dreamed on that night and behold a staircase was set up upon the earth and its head touched heaven. And behold, angels of the LORD were going up 22 and down upon it. And behold, the LORD was standing upon it. •And he spoke with Jacob and he said, "I am the LORD, the God of Abraham, your father and the God of Isaac. The land upon which you are sleeping I will give to you and to 23 your seed after you. •And your seed shall be like the sand of the earth. And you shall increase in the West and the East and North and South. And all the peoples 24 of the nations will be blessed in you and in your seed. •And behold, I shall be with you and I shall protect you everywhere you go. And I shall bring you back into this land in peace because I shall not forsake you until I do everything which 25 I have said to you." •And Jacob awoke from his sleep and he said, "Truly this place is the house of the LORD, and I did not know it." And he was afraid and said, "Dreadful is this place which is none other than the house of God.[f] And this is the gate of heaven."

26 And rising early in the morning, Jacob took the stone which he had placed at his head and he set it up as a pillar for a sign. And he poured out oil on top of it and he named that place "Bethel." But formerly the name of that area was Luz.

27 And Jacob vowed a vow to the LORD, saying, "If the LORD will be with me and protect me in this way in which I am traveling, and if he will give me bread to eat and clothing to put on, and I return to the house of my father in peace, then the LORD will be my God and this stone which I have set up as a pillar for a sign in this place shall be the house of the LORD and everything which you have given me I will tithe to you, my God."

Jacob is given Leah as a wife
Gen 29:1-25

1 **28** And he traveled[a] to the land of the East, to Laban, Rebecca's brother. And 2 he was with him and served him for Rachel, his daughter, one week. •And in the first year of the third week, he said to him, "Give me my wife for whom I have served you seven years." And Laban said to Jacob, "I will give you your wife." 3 And Laban prepared a banquet and he took Leah, his elder daughter, and he gave her to Jacob as a wife. And he gave to her Zilpah, his handmaid, as an attendant. But Jacob did not know it because Jacob assumed that she was Rachel. 4 And he entered into her and behold, she was Leah. And Jacob was angry with Laban and he said to him, "Why have you treated me thus? Was it not for Rachel that I served you, and not for Leah? Why have you offended me? Take your 5 daughter, and I will go because you have done evil against me." •For Jacob loved Rachel more than Leah because the eyes of Leah were weak, but her appearance was very beautiful, and Rachel (had) good eyes and good appearance and she was very beautiful.

The rule regarding the marriage of the elder daughter first
Gen 29:26f.

6 And Laban said to Jacob, "It does not happen thus in our land, to give the younger woman before the elder." And it is not right to do this because thus it

---

e. The phrase "at his head" is lacking in the Eth. text, but is present in the Lat. text and its presence in the Heb. text may be implied by the length of the lacuna at the point where it should appear.

f. The Eth. word for God which is used here is ʾegzīʾabḥēr. Elsewhere it has consistently been translated LORD because it most frequently corresponds to the Heb. name *YHWH*. In this passage, however, the writer is presenting an explanation of the name "Bethel," "house of God."

28 a. The Eth. text reads lit. "he picked up his feet and traveled," thus preserving the quaint idiom which appears in the Heb. of Gen 29:1.

is ordained and written in the heavenly tablets that no one should give his younger   Lev 18:18
daughter before the elder because he should first give the elder and after her the
younger. And they will write it down as sin in heaven concerning the man who
acts thus. And no one who does this thing will be righteous because this deed is
7 evil before the LORD. •And you command the children of Israel so that they will
not do this thing: "Let not the younger woman be taken or given without the
8 elder one being first (given) because that is very evil." •And Laban said to Jacob,
"Let the seven days of banquet for this woman continue and then I will give you
Rachel so that you might serve me another seven years (and) pasture my sheep
just as you did in the previous week."

The marriage to Rachel and the birth of children   Gen 29:28-30:24

9   And on the day when the seven days of Leah's banquet passed, Laban gave
Rachel to Jacob so that he might serve him another seven years. And he gave to
10 Rachel, Bilhah, the sister of Zilpah, as an attendant. •And he served seven years
11 more on account of Rachel because Leah had been given to him gratis. •And the
LORD opened the womb of Leah and she conceived and she bore a son to Jacob,
and he called him Reuben, on the fourteenth of the ninth month, in the first year
12 of the third week. •But the womb of Rachel was closed because the LORD saw
13 that Leah was hated, but Rachel was loved. •And Jacob again went into Leah,
and she conceived and she bore another son to Jacob, and he called him Simeon,
14 on the twenty-first of the tenth month and in the third year of this week. •And
Jacob again went into Leah and she conceived and she bore the third son to him
and he called him Levi, on the first day of the first month, in the sixth year of
15 this week. •And again Jacob went into her and she conceived and she bore the
fourth son to him and he called him Judah, on the fifteenth of the third month, in
16 the first year of the fourth week. •And in all of this Rachel was jealous of Leah
since she was not giving birth, and she said to Jacob, "Give me sons." And
Jacob said, "Have I withheld from you the fruit of your[b] womb? Have I forsaken
you?"
17   And when Rachel saw that Leah had borne four sons to Jacob, Reuben and
Simeon and Levi and Judah, she said to him, "Go into Bilhah, my maid, and she
18 will conceive and bear a son for me." •And she gave Bilhah, her maid, to him
so that she might be his wife.[c] And he went into her and she conceived and she
bore a son to him, and he called him Dan, on the ninth day of the sixth month in
19 the sixth year of the third week. •And Jacob went into Bilhah again a second
time, and she conceived and bore another son to Jacob, and Rachel called him
Naphtali, on the fifth of the seventh month, in the second year of the fourth week.
20 And when Leah saw that she was sterile[d] and was not bearing children, she took
and she also gave Zilpah, her attendant, to Jacob as a wife. And she conceived
and bore a son to him and Leah called him Gad, on the twelfth of the eighth
21 month in the third year of the fourth week. •And he went into her again and she
conceived and bore another son to him, and Leah called him Asher, on the second
22 of the eleventh month in the fifth year of the fourth week. •And Jacob went into
Leah and she conceived and she bore a son and she called him Issachar, on the
fourth day of the fifth month in the fourth year of the fourth week. And she gave
23 him to a nurse. •And Jacob went into her again and she conceived and she bore
twins, a boy and a girl, and she called the boy Zebulun and the girl's name was
Dinah, in the seventh day of the seventh month in the sixth year of the fourth
24 week. •And the LORD had mercy upon Rachel and opened her womb. And she

b. A portion of the Lat. text begins at this point
and continues through vs. 27a.
c. The first sentence in this vs. is lacking in
Eth., but it is found in Gen 30:4, and is also
attested in the Lat. text of Jub.
d. This is the reading of the Eth. MSS. Charles

in his edition of the Eth. text emended the text to
read "stopped" (bearing children) to agree with
the Lat. text and the Heb. of Gen 30:9, but
subsequently he followed the MS reading in his
English translation.

conceived and bore a son and called him Joseph, on the first of the fourth month
in the sixth year of that fourth week.

Laban persuades Jacob to continue working for wages

Gen 30:25-31:1

25   And at the time when Joseph was born, Jacob said to Laban, "Give me my
wives and my children. And let me go to my father, Isaac. And let me make a
house for myself because I have completed the years which I served you for your
26 two daughters. And I will travel to my father's house." •And Laban said to Jacob,
"Remain with me for your wages and pasture my flock for me again and accept
27 your wages." •And they agreed with one another that he would give to him as
his wages each of the lambs and kids which were born (and) on which there were
28 black or spots or white. It would be his wages. •And all of the sheep bore spotted
(lambs) and ones which had variegated markings and ones which had various
shades of black. And the sheep bore again lambs which looked like themselves
and all which had markings belonged to Jacob and those which had no marking
29 belonged to Laban. •And the possessions of Jacob multiplied greatly. And he
acquired oxen and sheep and asses and camels and male and female servants.
30 And Laban and his sons were jealous of Jacob. And Laban collected his sheep
from him, and kept watch on him with evil intent.

Jacob flees secretly to Gilead

Gen 31:2-21

1 **29** And it came to pass after Rachel bore Joseph that Laban went to shear his
sheep because they were the distance of a three days' journey away from him.
2 And Jacob saw that Laban was going to shear his sheep and Jacob called Leah
and Rachel and spoke intimately with them so that they might go with him to the
3 land of Canaan. •For he told them everything, as he had seen it in the dream, and
everything which he[a] told him, that he would return to the house of his father.
4 And they said, "We will go with you anywhere you go." •And Jacob blessed
the God of Isaac, his father, and the God of Abraham, his father's father. And
he arose and loaded up his wives and children and took all of his possessions and
crossed over the river and arrived at the land of Gilead. But Jacob concealed his
intention from Laban and did not tell him.

The oath between Jacob and Laban and their separation

Gen 31:21-55

5   And in the seventh year of the fourth week, Jacob returned to Gilead, in the
first month on the twenty-first day of the month. And Laban pursued him. And
he found Jacob in the mountain of Gilead in the third month on the thirteenth
6 day. •But the LORD did not permit him to deal cruelly with Jacob because he
7 appeared to him in a dream at night. And Laban spoke to Jacob. •And on the
fifteenth of those days Jacob prepared a banquet for Laban and for all who came
with him. And Jacob swore to Laban on that day. And Laban also swore to Jacob
that one would not cross over on the mountain of Gilead against the other with
8 evil intent. •And they made there a heap for a witness. Therefore[b] that place is
called "the Heap of Witness" after this heap.[c]
9   But formerly the land of Gilead was called "the land of Raphaim" because it
was the land of the Raphaim. And the Raphaim were born as giants whose height
10 was ten cubits, nine cubits, eight cubits, or down to seven cubits. •And their
dwelling was from the land of the Ammonites to Mount Hermon and their royal
11 palaces were in Qarnaim, and Ashtaroth, and Edrei, and Misur, and Beon. •But
the LORD destroyed them because of the evil of their deeds since they were very
cruel. And the Amorites dwelt there instead of them, evil and sinful, and there is

---

29 a. The pronoun refers to God.
  b. A portion of the Lat. text begins at this point
and continues through 31:1a.

c. "Heap of witnesses" was the presumed meaning of Gilead.

no people today who have fully equalled all of their sins. And therefore they had no length of life in the land.

12 And Jacob dismissed Laban, and he traveled to Mesopotamia, the land of the
13 East. And Jacob returned to the land of Gilead. •And he crossed over the Jabbok   Gen 32:22 in the ninth month on the eleventh day of the month. And on that day Esau, his brother, came to him and was reconciled to him. And he went away from him to the land of Seir; but Jacob dwelled in tents.

Jacob's respect for his parents contrasted with Esau's disrespect

14 And in the first year of the fifth week in that jubilee, he crossed over the Jordan and he dwelt on the other side of the Jordan. And he was pasturing his sheep from the Sea of the Heap as far as Bethshan and Dothan and the forest of
15 Akrabbim. •And he sent to his father, Isaac, some of all his possessions: clothing, and food, and meat, and drink, and milk, and butter, and cheese, and some dates
16 of the valley. •And (he also sent) to his mother, Rebecca, four times per year— between the appointed times[d] of the months and between plowing and reaping, and between fall and the rainy season and between winter and spring—to the
17 tower of Abraham. •For Isaac had returned from the Well of the Oath and had gone up to the tower of his father, Abraham. And he dwelt there away from his
18 son Esau •because in the days when Jacob journeyed to Mesopotamia, Esau took   Gen 28:9 for himself as a wife Mahalath, daughter of Ishmael, and gathered together all of   Gen 36:6,8 his father's flocks and his own wives and went up and dwelt in Mount Seir. And
19 he left his father, Isaac, alone at the Well of the Oath. •And Isaac went up from the Well of the Oath and dwelt in the tower of Abraham, his father, in the
20 mountain of Hebron. •And Jacob sent there everything which he sent to his father and mother from time to time, all of their needs. And they blessed Jacob with all their heart and all their soul.

Levi and Simeon avenge the shame of Dinah

   Gen 33:17-34:31

1 **30** And in the first year of the sixth week he went up to Salem, which is east of
2 Shechem, in peace in the fourth month. •And there Dinah, the daughter of Jacob, was snatched away to the house of Shechem, son of Hamor, the Hivite, the ruler of the land. And he lay with her and defiled her, but she was little, only twelve
3 years old. •And he begged his father and her brothers that she be given to him as a wife, but Jacob and his sons were angry at the men of Shechem because they defiled Dinah, their sister. And so they spoke treacherously with them and
4 defrauded them and seduced them. •And Simeon and Levi entered Shechem   TLevi 6 suddenly. And they executed judgment upon all of the men of Shechem and killed every man they found therein and did not leave in it even one. They killed
5 everyone painfully because they had polluted Dinah, their sister. •And therefore let nothing like this be done henceforth to defile a daughter of Israel because the judgment was ordered in heaven against them that they might annihilate with a
6 sword all of the men of Shechem because they caused a shame in Israel. •And the LORD handed them over into the hand of the sons of Jacob so that they might destroy them with the sword and execute judgment against them, and so that nothing like this might therefore happen in Israel to defile an Israelite virgin.

The law prohibiting marriage with foreigners

7 And if there is any man in Israel who wishes to give his daughter or his sister to any man who is from the seed of the gentiles, let him surely die, and let him be stoned because he has caused shame in Israel. And also the woman will be   Gen 34:7 burned with fire because she has defiled the name of her father's house and so

---

d. These are probably the four feast days estab- lished by Noah in Jub 6:23–32. There are twelve months of thirty days plus four intercalary days, which provide a year of 364 days.

8 she will be uprooted from Israel. •And do not let an adultress or defilement be
found in Israel all of the days of the generations of the earth because Israel is
holy to the LORD. And let any man who causes defilement surely die, let him be

9 stoned •because thus it is decreed and written in the heavenly tablets concerning
all of the seed of Israel: "Let anyone who causes defilement surely die. And let
him be stoned."

10 And there is no limit of days for this law. And there is no remission or
forgiveness except that the man who caused defilement of his daughter will be
rooted out from the midst of all Israel because he has given some of his seed to

11 Moloch and sinned so as to defile it. •And you, Moses, command the children of
Israel and exhort them not to give any of their daughters to the gentiles and not
to take for their sons any of the daughters of the gentiles because that is contemptible

12 before the LORD. •Therefore I have written for you in the words of the law all
of the deeds of the Shechemites which they did against Dinah and how the sons
of Jacob spoke, saying, "We will not give our daughter to a man who is   Gen 34:14
uncircumcised because that is a reproach to us."

13 And it is a reproach to Israel, to those who give and those who take any of the
daughters of the gentile nations because it is a defilement and it is contemptible

14 to Israel. •And Israel will not be cleansed from this defilement if there is in it a
woman from the daughters of gentiles or one who has given any of his daughters

15 to a man who is from any of the gentiles. •For there will be plague upon plague
and curse upon curse, and every judgment, and plague, and curse will come. And
if he does this thing, or if he blinds his eyes from those who cause defilement
and from those who defile the sanctuary of the LORD and from those who profane
his holy name, (then) all of the people will be judged together on account of all

16 of the defilement and the profaning of this one. •And there is no accepting of
person or regarding appearance[a] or taking from his hand either fruit or sacrifice
or holocaust or fat or the aroma of sweet-smelling sacrifice so that he[b] might
accept it. And let any man or woman in Israel who defiled his sanctuary be (dealt

17 with likewise). •Therefore I command you, saying, "Proclaim this testimony to
Israel: 'See how it was for the Shechemites and their sons, how they were given
into the hand of the two children of Jacob and they killed them painfully. And it
was a righteousness for them and it was written down for them for righteousness.' "

Levi is chosen for priesthood in recognition of his zeal

18 And the seed of Levi was chosen for the priesthood and levitical (orders) to   TLevi 4
minister before the LORD always just as we[c] do. And Levi and his sons will be
blessed forever because he was zealous to do righteousness and judgment and

19 vengeance against all who rose up against Israel. •And thus a blessing and
righteousness will be written (on high) as a testimony for him in the heavenly

20 tablets before the God of all. •And we will remember for a thousand generations
the righteousness which a man did during his life in all of the (appointed) times
of the year. And (it) will be written (on high) and it will come to him and his
descendants after him. And he will be written down as a friend and a righteous
one in the heavenly tablets.

A warning against breach of covenant

21 All of these words I have written for you, and I have commanded you to speak
to the children of Israel that they might not commit sin or transgress the ordinances
or break the covenant which was ordained for them so that they might do it and

---

30 a. The expressions "accepting of person" (lit.
accepting of face) and "regarding appearance" (lit.
regarding of face) are idioms which mean essentially the same thing, i.e. "showing partiality."
The use of them together is somewhat redundant.
The Lat. text omits the phrase "or regarding

appearance."
    b. The pronoun refers to God.
    c. The "we" refers to the host of angels who
minister before the LORD continually. The Levites
are to minister on earth as the angels do in heaven.

22 be written down as friends. •But if they transgress and act in all the ways of defilement, they will be recorded in the heavenly tablets as enemies. And they will be blotted out of the book of life and written in the book of those who will
23 be destroyed and with those who will be rooted out from the land. •And on the day that the children of Jacob killed Shechem he wrote (on high)[d] for them a book in heaven that they did righteousness and uprightness and vengeance against the sinners and it was written down for a blessing.

The conclusion of the Shechem incident

Gen 34:26-31;
35:5

24 And they brought forth Dinah, their sister, from the house of Shechem and they took captive everything which was in Shechem: their sheep and their oxen and their asses and all their herds and all their goods. And they brought forth everything
25 to Jacob, their father. •And he spoke with them because they slaughtered the citizens,[e] for he was afraid of those who inhabited the land: the Canaanites and the Perizzites. But the terror of the LORD was in all of the cities which surrounded Shechem and they did not rise up to pursue the sons of Jacob because a dread had fallen upon them.

The preparation for pilgrimage to Bethel

Gen 35:1-4

1 **31** And on the first of the month, Jacob spoke to all of the men of his house, saying, "Purify and change your clothes, and having arisen, let us go up to Bethel, where on the day when I fled from the face of Esau, my brother, I made a vow to him who has been with me and has returned me unto this land in peace.
2 Remove the strange gods that are among you." •And they handed over[a] the strange gods and what was on their ears and what was on their necks and the idols which Rachel stole from Laban, her father,[b] and she gave everything to Jacob, and he burned it and crushed it and destroyed it and hid it under an oak which was in the Land of Shechem.

Jacob invites his father to come to Bethel

Gen 35:7
TLevi 9

3 And he went up on the first of the seventh month into Bethel. And he built an altar in the place where he had slept and had erected a pillar. And he invited his father, Isaac, and his mother, Rebecca, to come to him in the (time of) sacrifice.
4 And Isaac said, "Let my son Jacob come and let me see him before I die."

Jacob's visit to his father, Isaac

5 And Jacob went to his father, Isaac, and to his mother, Rebecca, at the house of his father, Abraham, and he took with him two of his sons, Levi and Judah.
6 And he came to his father, Isaac, and his mother, Rebecca. •And Rebecca went out from the tower at the gates of the tower to kiss Jacob and embrace him because it revived her soul when she heard, "Behold, Jacob, your son, has arrived."
7 And she kissed him, and she saw his two sons and she recognized them and she

---

d. The use of the word *'arega* in Jub needs further study. Normally the word means "to ascend." In a few passages, the word involves writing on heavenly tablets. In the present translation such passages are rendered "to write (on high)," i.e. "to go up (in writing)." In the process of reviewing the work for publication, J. VanderKam has suggested the possibility of reading this vs. as "a book/writing went up to heaven." He may be on the right track. The Lat. would appear to support such a reading. I have retained an earlier translation, however, pending a study of all of the relevant passages.

e. The text reads lit. "they killed the city," but the "city" is used by the writer to refer to all citizens.

31 a. The reading "handed over" is an emendation based on Gen 35:4. The Eth. MSS read either "melt" or "seize" at this point.

b. Charles emended his Eth. text to read "her brother," but he subsequently read "her father" in English translation published in his *APOT*, vol. 2.

said to him, "Are these your sons, my son?" And she embraced them and kissed them and blessed them, saying, "In you may he bless the seed of Abraham, and may you become a blessing upon the earth."

8 And Jacob went in to Isaac, his father, in the chamber where he was lying down, and his two children were with him. And he took the hand of his father, and, bowing down, he kissed him. And Isaac hung on the neck of Jacob, his son, 9 and he wept on his neck. •And the darkness passed from the eyes of Isaac and he saw Jacob's two sons, Levi and Judah, and he said, "Are these your sons, my 10 son, because[c] they resemble you?" •And he told him that they were truly his sons: "And certainly you have seen that they are truly my sons."

The blessing of Levi

11 And they drew near to him and he turned and kissed them and embraced the 12 both of them together. •And a spirit of prophecy came down upon his mouth. 13 And he took Levi in his right hand and Judah in his left hand. •And he turned to | 1QapGen 2.4
Levi first and he began to bless him first, and he said to him, "May the God of | TLevi 9
14 all, i.e. the LORD of all ages, bless you and your sons in all ages. •May the LORD give you and your seed very great honor.[d] May he draw you and your seed near to him from all flesh to serve in his sanctuary as the angels of the presence and the holy ones. May your sons' seed be like them with respect to honor and 15 greatness and sanctification. And may he make them great in every age. •And | TLevi 8
they will become judges and rulers and leaders[e] for all of the seed of the sons of Jacob.

> The word of the LORD they will speak righteously,
> and all of his judgments they will execute righteously.
> And they will tell my ways to Jacob,
> and my paths to Israel.
> The blessing of the LORD shall be placed in their mouth,
> so that they might bless all of the seed of the beloved.
16   (As for) you, your mother has named you 'Levi,'
> and truly she has named you.
> You will be joined[f] to the LORD
> and be the companion of all the sons of Jacob. | Lev 18:2,4
> His table will belong to you, | TLevi 8
> and you and your sons will eat (from) it, | TJud 21
> and in all generations your table will be full,
> and your food will not be lacking in any age.
17   And all who hate you will fall before you,
> and all your enemies will be uprooted and perish,
> and whoever blesses you will be blessed,
> and any nation which curses you will be cursed."

The blessing of Judah

18 And to Judah he said:

> "May the LORD give you might and strength
> to tread upon all who hate you.
> Be a prince, you and one of your sons for the sons of Jacob;
> may your name and the name of your son be one which travels and goes
>   about in all the lands and cities.

c. A portion of the Lat. text begins at this point and continues through 31:18.

d. The phrase "very great honor" is based on MS B, which reads "great greatness of honor"; the Lat. reads "to understand his glory." Charles emended his Eth. text to agree with the Lat., but returned to the Eth. MSS in preparing his own translation as "greatness and great glory."

e. The Lat. text omits "leaders."

f. In Heb. the name Levi and the verbal root meaning "to cleave, be joined to" share similar consonants and were presumed to be related.

Then may the nations fear before your face,
and all of the nations tremble,
[and every nation trembles].[g]

19   And with you will be the help of Jacob
and with you will be found the salvation of Israel.

20   And on the day when you sit on your righteous throne of honor,
there will be great peace for all the seed of the beloved's sons.
Whoever blesses you will be blessed,
and all who hate you and afflict you and curse you
will be uprooted and destroyed from the earth and they shall be cursed."

Jacob's visit with Isaac

21   And turning, he kissed him again and embraced him and rejoiced greatly because
22   he had seen the sons of Jacob, his own true son. •And he withdrew from his
embrace and fell down and bowed down to him. And he blessed them. And he
rested there near Isaac, his father, during that night. And they ate and drank
23   joyfully. •And he made the two sons of Jacob sleep, one on his right and one on
24   his left, and it was counted to him (as) righteousness. •And Jacob told his father
everything during the night, how the LORD had shown him great mercy, and how
25   he had made all of his affairs prosper and protected him from all evil. •And Isaac
blessed the God of his father, Abraham, who did not withhold his mercy and his
righteousness from the son of his servant Isaac.

Isaac's farewell to Jacob

26   And in the morning, Jacob told his father, Isaac, (about) the vow which he had
made to the LORD and the vision which he had seen and that he had built an altar
and everything was prepared to make a sacrifice before the LORD just as he had
27   vowed and that he had come to set him upon an ass. •And Isaac said to Jacob,
his son, "I am not able to come with you because I have grown old and I am not
able to endure on the way. Go, my son, in peace, because I am one hundred and
sixty-five years old today. Therefore I am not able to travel. Set your mother (on
28   the ass) and let her go with you. •I know, my son, that you came for my sake.
And let this day be blessed on which you have seen me alive and I have also seen
29   you, my son. •Prosper and perform the vow which you made and do not delay
your vow because the vow will be sought. And now hasten to do it, and may the
30   one who created[h] everything, to whom you vowed the vow, be pleased." •And
he said to Rebecca, "Go with Jacob, your son." And Rebecca went with Jacob,
her son. And Deborah (was) with her. And they reached Bethel.

Jacob reflects on the blessing of his sons

31   And Jacob remembered the prayer (with) which his father blessed him and his
two sons, Levi and Judah, and he rejoiced and he blessed the God of his fathers,
32   Abraham and Isaac. •And he said, "Now I know that I and my sons have an
eternal hope before the God of all." And thus it is ordained concerning the two
of them, and it has been written (on high) for them as an eternal testimony in the
heavenly tablets, just as Isaac blessed them.

Jacob's tithe and sacrifice at Bethel

1   **32** And he stayed that night in Bethel. And Levi dreamed that he had been TLevi 8
appointed and ordained priest of the Most High God, he and his sons forever.

---

g. The phrase that is written between brackets   h. A portion of the Lat. text begins at this point
is a rather obvious dittography.   and continues through the first three words of 32:8.

2 And he woke from his sleep and blessed the LORD. •And Jacob rose early in the TLevi 9
morning on the fourteenth of that month and he gave a tenth of everything which
came with him: man, (and) beast, gold, (and) all (sorts of) vessels and clothes.
And he gave a tenth of everything.
3 And in those days Rachel conceived Benjamin, her son. And Jacob counted his
sons from him and upward, and (the lot of) Levi fell with the portion of the
LORD. And his father put garments of the priesthood upon him and he filled his
4 hands. •And on the fifteenth of this month he brought to the altar fourteen bulls Num 29:12-40
from the herd and twenty-eight rams and forty-nine sheep and seven lambs and Lev 23:34-44
twenty-one[a] kids of the goats (as) a burnt offering upon the altar of sacrifices,
5 well pleasing for a sweet-smelling aroma before God. •This was his offering from Gen 28:22
the vow which he made to tithe together with their (fruit) offerings and their
6 libations. •And when the fire consumed it he burned incense upon the fire above
it. And for a thank offering: two bulls and four rams and four sheep and four he-
goats and two lambs, each a year old, and two kids of the goats. Thus he did at
7 dawn for seven days. •And it happened as he and all his sons and his men ate
there joyfully for seven days that he blessed and praised the LORD, the one who
8 delivered him from all his affliction and who granted him his prayers. •And he
gave a tithe of every clean animal and he made a burnt offering, but the unclean
animals he did (not)[b] give to Levi, his son, but every human soul he gave to him.
9 And Levi served as priest in Bethel before Jacob, his father, (apart) from his ten
brothers. And he was a priest there. And Jacob gave his vow. Thus he tithed a
second tithe to the LORD and he sanctified it and it was sanctified to him.

The law of the tithe

10 And therefore it is decreed in the heavenly tablets as a law to tithe the tithe Deut 14:22f.
again in order to eat it before the LORD from year to year in the place where it is
determined that his name shall dwell. And there is no limit of days to this law
11 forever. •This ordinance is written to observe it year after year to eat the second
tithe before the LORD in the place where it is determined. And there is not to be
12 (anything) left over from it from this year to the year which is to come. •For in
its year the grain will be eaten until the days of the harvest of the grain of the
year, and the wine (will be drunk) until the days of the wine, and the olive (will
13 be used) until the day of its season. •And everything which is left over from it
and which grows old will be unclean. Let it be burned in the fire because it has
14 become impure. •And thus they shall eat it together in the sanctuary and they
15 shall not let it become old. •And the whole tithe of oxen and sheep is holy to the Lev 27:32
LORD and it will belong to the priests who will eat it before him year after year 2Chr 31:6
because it is so ordered and engraved on the heavenly tablets concerning the tithe.

Jacob's vision which prevented him from sanctifying the court at Bethel

16 And in the second night, on the twenty-second day of this month, Jacob planned
to build up that place and to build a wall around the court and to sanctify it and
17 to make it eternally holy for himself and his sons after him. •And the LORD
appeared to him in the night and blessed him and said to him, "Your name will
18 not be called Jacob, but you will be named Israel." •And he said to him again,
"I am the LORD who created heaven and earth, and I shall increase you and
multiply you very much. And there will be kings from you; they will rule
19 everywhere[c] that the tracks of mankind have been trod. •And I shall give to your CD 1.7f.
seed all of the land under heaven and they will rule in all nations as they have

---

32 a. The numbers "seven" and "twenty-one"
are found correctly in the Lat. text. The Eth. text
has "sixty" and "twenty-nine" respectively, but
the series of animals offered were most likely
presented in multiples of seven.

b. The MSS lack the negative, but the sense
requires it.

c. A portion of the Lat. text begins at this point
and continues through the first three words of 33:9.

desired. And after this all of the earth will be gathered together[d] and they will
inherit it forever.''

20 And he finished speaking with him, and he went up from him. And Jacob
21 watched until he went up into heaven. •And he saw in a vision of the night, and
behold an angel was descending from heaven, and there were seven tablets in his
hands. And he gave (them) to Jacob, and he read them, and he knew everything
which was written in them, which would happen to him and to his sons during
22 all the ages. •And he showed him everything which was written on the tablets.
23 And he said to him, "Do not build this place, and do not make an eternal
sanctuary, and do not dwell here because this is not the place. Go to the house
of Abraham, your father, and dwell with Isaac, your father, until the day of your
24 father's death •because you will die peacefully in Egypt and you will be buried
honorably in this land in the tomb of your fathers with Abraham and Isaac. Do
not fear, because just as you have seen and read, thus will everything come to
25 pass. But you write down everything just as you have seen and read (it)." •And
Jacob said, "O LORD, how will I remember everything that I read and saw?"
26 And he said to him, "I will cause you to remember everything." •And he went
up from him and he woke up from his sleep and he recalled everything that he
had read and seen and he wrote down all of the matters which he had read and
seen.

The institution of the day of "Addition" to the feast

27 And he observed there yet one (more) day and he sacrificed in it according to 2Chr 7:9
everything which he had been sacrificing on the previous days. And he called it
"Addition" because that day was added, but the previous (days) he called "the
28 feast." •And thus it was revealed that it should be. And it is written in the
heavenly tablets. Therefore it was revealed to him so that he might observe it and
29 add it to the seven days of the feast. •And it was called "Addition" because it is
written (on high) in the attestation[e] of feast days according to the number of days
of the year.

The death of Deborah   Gen 35:8

30 And on the night of the twenty-third of that month Deborah, the nurse of
Rebecca, died. And she was buried south of the city under the oak at the river.
And that place was called "Deborah's River" and the oak (was called) "the Oak
of Sorrow for Deborah."

Rebecca's departure

31 And Rebecca went and returned to her house, to his father, Isaac, and Jacob
sent in her hands rams and sheep and he-goats so that she might make for his
32 father a meal such as he desired. •And he traveled after his mother until he
approached the land of Kabrâtân. And he dwelt there.

The birth of Benjamin and death of Rachel   Gen 35:16-20

33 And Rachel bore a son in the night and called him "son of my sorrow,"
because she suffered when she bore him, but his father called him Benjamin, on
the eleventh of the eighth month in the first year of the sixth week of that jubilee.
34 And Rachel died there and she was buried in the land of Ephrata, i.e. Bethlehem.
And Jacob built a pillar on the tomb of Rachel, on the road above her tomb.

d. This phrase could be translated lit. "they will
gather together all of the earth." The third person
plural may, however, be regarded as an impersonal
subject and rendered equally well as a passive.

e. This is the reading of the MSS. In his Eth.
text and English translation, Charles followed the
Lat. text, which reads "among the days of the
feast days."

The account of Reuben's sin with Bilhah

Gen 35:21f.

1 **33** And Jacob went and dwelt toward the south of Magdaladra'ef.[a] And he and Leah, his wife, went to his father, Isaac, on the new moon of the tenth month.
2 And Reuben[b] saw Bilhah, the attendant of Rachel (and) his father's concubine, TReu 3
3 washing in the water privately, and he desired her. •And hiding at night, he entered Bilhah's house at night[c] and found her sleeping in her bed, alone in her
4 house. •And he lay with her. And she woke up and looked, and behold, Reuben was lying with her on the bed. And she uncovered the hem of her (skirt) and
5 seized him and screamed and recognized that it was Reuben. •And she was
6 ashamed because of him and released her hand from upon him. And he fled. •And she lamented greatly concerning this matter. And she did not tell anyone at all.
7 And when Jacob came and sought her, she said to him, "I am not clean for you since I have become polluted for you because Reuben has defiled me and lay with me at night, but I was sleeping and I was unaware until he had uncovered my Deut 22:30
8 skirt and lain with me." •And Jacob was very angry with Reuben because he had
9 lain with Bilhah, for he had uncovered his father's robe. •And therefore Jacob did not draw near her since Reuben had defiled her. And the deed of any man who uncovers his father's robe is very evil because he is despicable before the LORD.

The laws of incest

10 Therefore it is written and ordered in the heavenly tablets that a man should not lie with his father's wife, and he should not uncover his father's robe because Lev 20:11 that is defilement. They shall certainly die together, the man who lies with his father's wife and also the wife because they have made a defilement upon the
11 earth. •And there shall be no defilement before our God among the people whom
12 he has chosen for himself as a possession. •And again it is written a second time: "Let anyone who lies with his father's wife be cursed because he has uncovered Deut 22:30 his father's shame." And all the holy ones of the LORD said, "So be it, so be it."
13 And you, Moses, command the children of Israel and let them keep this word because it is a judgment worthy of death. And it is a defilement. And there is no forgiveness in order to atone for a man who has done this, forever, but only to execute him and kill him and stone him and to uproot him from the midst of the
14 people of our God. •For any man who does this in Israel should not have life for a single day upon the earth because he is despicable and polluted.

The example of Reuben does not permit exception to law of incest

15 And let them not say, "Reuben had life and forgiveness after he lay with his father's concubine and while she had a husband and while her husband, Jacob,
16 his father, was alive." •For the ordinance and judgment and law had not been Rom 4:15 revealed till then (as) completed for everyone, but in your days (it is) like the law of (appointed) times and days and an eternal law for everlasting generations. •And
17 this law has no consummation of days. And also there is no forgiveness for it but only that both of them should be uprooted from the midst of the people. On the day when they have done this they shall be killed.

---

33 a. In Gen 35:21 it is reported that Jacob dwelt near the "tower of Eder" (Heb., *migdal-ēder*). That tower was in the region of "Ephrath." The Eth. spelling is therefore a corruption of the phrase "the tower of Eder at Ephrath" or "the Ephrathite tower of Eder."

b. A portion of the Syr. text begins at this point and continues through vs. 16a. The Syr. text is considerably abbreviated.

c. The repetition of "at night" seems unnecessary. The Lat. text mentions "night" only once in this vs.

Moses is directed to warn people of laws of sexual defilement

18   And you, Moses, write for Israel, and let them keep this. And let them do
according to these words. And let them not commit a sin worthy of death because
19 the LORD our God is a judge who does not accept[d] persons or gifts. •And say to
them these words of the ordinance that they might hear and guard and watch
themselves concerning them and they will not be destroyed or uprooted from the
earth. For defiled, and an abomination, and blemished, and polluted are all who
20 do them upon the earth before our God. •And there is no sin greater than the
fornication which they commit upon the earth because Israel is a holy nation to
the LORD his God, and a nation of inheritance, and a nation of priests, and a royal
nation, and a (special) possession. And there is nothing which appears which is
as defiled as this among the holy people.

The children of Jacob appear before Isaac

Gen 35:22-27

21   And in the third year of this sixth week it came to pass as Jacob and all his
sons were traveling that they dwelt (at) the house of Abraham near Isaac, his
22 father, and Rebecca, his mother. •And these are the names of the children of
Jacob: his firstborn, Reuben, and Simeon and Levi and Judah, and Issachar, and
Zebulun, the sons of Leah. And the sons of Rachel (are) Joseph and Benjamin.
And the sons of Bilhah (are) Dan and Naphtali. And the sons of Zilpah (are) Gad
and Asher. And Dinah (is) the daughter of Leah, the only daughter of Jacob.
23 And when they came, they bowed down to Isaac and Rebecca. And when they
saw them, they blessed Jacob and all of his sons. And Isaac rejoiced greatly
because he saw the sons of Jacob, his younger son. And he blessed them.

The sons of Jacob successfully defeat an Amorite coalition

Gen 37:12

1 **34** And in the sixth year of this week from this forty-fourth jubilee, Jacob sent
2 his sons with their servants to pasture their sheep in the field of Shechem. •And
while hiding themselves under the trees, seven kings of the Amorites assembled
3 themselves to fight against them and to plunder their animals. •And Jacob and
Levi and Judah and Joseph were at home with Isaac, their father, because his soul
grieved him, and they were unable to leave him. And Benjamin was the youngest
and therefore he dwelt with his father.
4   And the kings of Tafu, and the kings of 'Aresa, and the kings of Seragān, and
the kings of Sèlo, and the kings of Gā'as, and the kings of Bethoron, and the
king of Ma'anisakir,[a] and all of those who dwelt in that mountain, who dwelt in
5 the woods of the land of Canaan, came. •And they reported it to Jacob, saying
that, "Behold, the kings of the Amorites have surrounded your sons and they
6 have plundered their herds." •And he and his three sons and all of his father's
servants and his servants arose from his house and went against them with six
7 thousand men who carried swords. •And he killed them in the field of Shechem Gen 48:22
TJud 4
and he pursued those who fled and killed them with the edge of the sword. And
he killed 'Aresa and Tafu and Seragān and Sèlo and Ma'anisakir and Gā'as, and
8 he collected his herds. •And he prevailed over them and decreed a tribute against TJud 4

---

d. A portion of the Lat. text begins at this point
and continues through 35:5a.

34 a. For a recent discussion of the place-names
mentioned in this vs. see VanderKam, *Textual and
Historical Studies*, pp. 220–29.
    This account of the Amorite war against the sons
of Jacob is not biblical, but it is found in two
Jewish texts in a form which provides witness to
a version of the story which was independent of

Jub. See TJud 3–7 and Midrash *Wayyissau* in A.
Jellinek's *Bet ha-Midrasch* (Jerusalem, 1938²) part
3, pp. 1–5. In the Midrash *Wayyissau* it is explained
that the Amorites were provoked by the action of
two of Jacob's sons against Shechem, but waited
seven years to mount an attack against the family
of Jacob. In both the account of *Wayyissau* and
TJud, Judah plays a leading role in the war against
the Amorites.

them so that they might give a tribute of five of the fruits of their land. And he
9 built Robel and Tamnatares. •And he returned peacefully and he made peace with
them and they became servants to him until the day he and his sons went down
into Egypt.

The brothers sell Joseph and deceive their father   Gen 37:13-35

10 And in the seventh year of this week he sent Joseph from his house to the land
of Shechem in order that he might know about the welfare of his brothers, and
11 he found them in the land of Dothan. •And they acted fraudulently and made a
plot against him to kill him, but they repented and sold him to a band of
Ishmaelites. And they took him down to Egypt and sold him to Potiphar, a eunuch
12 of Pharaoh, the chief guard,[b] the priest of the city of Heliopolis.[c] •And the sons
of Jacob slaughtered a kid and dipped Joseph's garment into the blood and sent
13 (it) to Jacob, their father, on the tenth of the seventh month. •And he lamented
all of that night, because they had brought it to him in the evening. And he
became feverish in lamenting his death, and said that, "A cruel beast has eaten
Joseph." And all of the men of his house lamented with him on that day. And it
14 happened as they were mourning and lamenting with him all that day •that his
sons and his daughter rose up to comfort him but he was not comforted concerning
his son.

The death and burial of Bilhah and Dinah

15 And on that day Bilhah heard that Joseph had perished and she died while
mourning for him. And she was dwelling in Qafratef. And Dinah, his daughter,
also died after Joseph perished. And these three lamentations came upon Israel in
16 a single month. •And they buried Bilhah opposite the tomb of Rachel, and they
17 also buried Dinah, his daughter, there. •And it happened, as they lamented for
Joseph one year, that he was not consoled, because he said, "I will go down to
the grave lamenting for my son."

A day of memorial established for the crime against Joseph

18 Therefore it is decreed for the children of Israel that they mourn on the tenth   Lev 16:29,34
(day) of the seventh month—on the day when that which caused him to weep for
Joseph came to Jacob, his father—so that they might atone for them(selves) with
a young kid on the tenth (day) of the seventh month, once a year, on account of
their sin because they caused the affection of their father to grieve for Joseph, his
19 son. •And this day is decreed so that they might mourn on it on account of their
sins and on account of all their transgressions and on account of all their errors
in order to purify themselves on this day, once a year.

The wives of the sons of Jacob   Gen 38:2

20 And after Joseph perished, the sons of Jacob took wives for themselves. The
name of the wife of Reuben (was) 'Ada.[d] And the name of the wife of Simeon
(was) 'Adiba'a, a Canaanite. And the name of the wife of Levi (was) Melka,   Gen 46:10
from the daughters of Aram, from the seed of the sons of Terah. And the name

---

b. The Eth. MSS read "chief cook," but that
is due to a confusion about the meaning of the
Heb. word *ṭabbaḥ*, which lit. means "one who
slaughters." It was apparently applied to one who
slaughtered animals, i.e. a butcher, but in the
passing of time it became the title for a high official,
in this case the keeper of prison in Gen 39:1.
c. The Eth. spelling *'Elēw* is a transcription of

the Gk. *'ēliou*, "sun" (genitive).
d. In his edition of the Eth. text, Charles included
a Syr. fragment as Appendix III. The Syr. fragment
contained a list of the wives of the patriarchs which
generally agrees with the names found in Jub.
Charles provided a detailed comparison of the forms
in the notes to his 1902 English translation.

of the wife of Judah (was) Betasu'el, a Canaanite. And the name of the wife of Issachar (was) Hezaqa. And the name of the wife of Zebulun (was) Ni'iman. And the name of the wife of Dan (was) 'Egla. And the name of the wife of Naphtali (was) Rasu'u, who (was) Mesopotamian. And the name of the wife of Gad (was) Maka. And the name of the wife of Asher (was) 'Iyona. And the name of the wife of Joseph (was) Asenath, an Egyptian. And the name of the wife of Benjamin (was) 'Iyasaka. •And Simeon repented and took another wife from Mesopotamia as his brothers had.

Rebecca's conversation with Jacob predicting her death

1 **35** And in the first year of the first week in this forty-fifth jubilee, Rebecca called to Jacob, her son. And she commanded him with regard to his father and brother 2 that he should honor them all the days of Jacob's life. •And Jacob said, "I will do everything just as you have commanded me because this thing is an honor and a greatness for me and a righteousness for me before the LORD, that I should 3 honor them. •And you, mother, know from the day I was born until[a] this day all of my deeds and everything which is in my heart, that I always think of good for 4 everyone. •And why would I not do this thing which you have commanded me, 5 that I should honor my father and my brother. •Tell me, mother, what perversity you have seen against me and I will withdraw from it and mercy[b] will be upon 6 me." •And she said, "My son, all my days I have never seen against you anything perverse but only uprightness. But I will rightly tell you, my son, (that) I shall die within this year, and I shall not pass through this year alive because I have seen in a dream the day of my death, that I shall not live more than one hundred and fifty-five years. And behold, I have completed all of the days of my life which I will live."

7 And Jacob laughed about his mother's words, because his mother said that she would die, but she was sitting opposite him, and her strength was in her. And she was not suffering loss of strength, because she was coming and going and seeing (clearly), and her teeth were sound, and no disease had touched her all the 8 days of her life. •And Jacob said, "I (would be) happy, mother, if my days approached the days of your life and my powers were thus in me as your powers. And you will not die because you have spoken to me[c] (in) idle jest concerning your death."

Rebecca's conversation with Isaac concerning Jacob and Esau

9 And she went in to Isaac and she said to him, "One request I beg of you. Make Esau swear that he will not harm Jacob and will not pursue him hostilely because you know Esau's inclination,[d] that it has been evil since his youth. [And there is 10 no goodness in him because he wants to kill him after your death.][e] •And you know everything that he has done from the day that Jacob, his brother, traveled to Haran until this day, that he abandoned us with all his heart and did evil with us. He gathered your flocks and robbed all of your possessions before your face. 11 And while we were begging and asking for what was ours he acted like a man

---

35 a. A portion of the Lat. text begins at this point and continues through 35:12a.

    b. The Lat. text reads "mercy of the Lord."

    c. A Heb. fragment from Qumran begins at this point and is parallel through vs. 10a.

    d. The Heb. word in the Qumran text is *yēṣer*. The *yēṣer* of Esau is "evil."

    e. The sentence enclosed in brackets is lacking from the Heb. text. There is, of course, no way of knowing whether the Heb. text originally lacked the sentence, which appears in both Eth. and Lat., or whether the sentence was simply lost from a single Heb. manuscript. VanderKam, in his *Textual and Historical Studies*, pp. 85–87, concluded that

the sentence was probably in the original text. I am almost persuaded that he is right. I am, however, struck by the fact that vs. 13 contains a phrase which is quite similar to the sentiment expressed here, but the phrase in vs. 13 was identified as an addition to the text by Charles in his translation. If the two sentences 9 and 13 are read together with the bracketed phrases treated as glosses, one could imagine that some scribe was impressed with the total depravity of Esau which was discussed in this ch. and wrote in two marginal comments, perhaps to remind himself of a choice sermon illustration.

12 who was taking pity on us. •And he is bitter against you because you blessed Jacob, your perfect and upright son, because he has no evil but only goodness. And since he came from Haran until this day he has not been depriving us of anything, for he has always been bringing us everything in its season. And he rejoices with his whole heart whenever we accept (anything) from his hand. And he has been blessing us and has not separated from us since he came from Haran until this day. But he has been dwelling with us continually at home honoring

13 us." •And Isaac said to her, "I know and see the deeds of Jacob, who is with us, that with all his heart he is honoring us. And I first loved Esau more than Jacob because he was born first, but now I love Jacob more than Esau because he has increasingly made his deeds evil. And he has no righteousness because all of his ways are injustice and violence. [And he has no righteousness around him.]f

14 And now my heart is vexed on account of all his deeds. And neither he nor his seed is to be saved for they will be destroyed from the earth, and they will be uprooted from under the heaven since he has forsaken the God of Abraham and he has gone after his wives and after their defilement and after their errors, (both)

15 he and his sons. •And you say to me that I should make him swear that he will not kill his brother, Jacob. If he swears he will not abide by his oath, and he will

16 not do goodness, but only evil. •But if he wishes to kill Jacob, his brother, he will be given into the hand of Jacob. And he will not escape from his hand

17 because he will fall into his hand. •And you should not fear on account of Jacob because the protector of Jacob is greater and mightier and more honored and praised than the protector of Esau."

Rebecca seeks assurances of fraternal love between Jacob and Esau

18   And Rebecca sent and called Esau. And he came to her and she said to him, "I have a request, my son, which I will ask of you. Say that you will do it, my

19 son." •And he said, "I will do everything which you say to me. And I will not

20 refuse your request." •And she said to him, "I ask of you on the day when I die that you bring me and bury me near Sarah, your father's mother, and that you and Jacob love one another, and that one will not seek evil for his brother, but only love him. And you will prosper, my sons, and be honored in the midst of the earth and the enemy will not rejoice over you. And you will become a blessing

21 and a mercy in the sight of all who love you." •And he said, "I shall do everything which you have been saying to me. And I shall bury you on the day when you die near Sarah, my father's mother, just as you have desired so that your bones

22 will be near her bones. •And Jacob, my brother, I shall love more than all flesh. And I have no brother in all the earth except him alone. And this is not a great (thing) for me if I love him because he is my brother and together we were sown in your belly and together we came forth from your womb. And if I do not love

23 my brother, whom shall I love? •But I beg of you only that you admonish Jacob concerning my sons because I know that he will certainly rule over me and my sons because on the day my father blessed him he set him above and me beneath.

24 And I swear to you that I will love him and that I will not seek evil for him all the days of my life, but only good." And he swore to her concerning all of these matters.

25   And she called Jacob in the sight of Esau, and she commanded him according

26 to what she had spoken with Esau. •And he said, "I will do your pleasure. Trust me, that evil will not proceed from me or my sons against Esau and I will not act

27 first in anything except to love (him) only." •And they ate and they drank, she and her sons, that night. And she died (at the age of) three jubilees and one week and one year on that night. And her two sons, Esau and Jacob, buried her in the cave of Machpelah near Sarah, their father's mother.

---

f. The sentence within the brackets was identified by Charles as "either a corruption or, as I take
it, a dittography," p. 209 in his 1902 English
translation.

Isaac's farewell advice and blessings for Jacob and Esau

1 **36** And in the sixth year of this week, Isaac called his two sons, Esau and Jacob.
And they came to him and he said to them, "My sons, I am going in the way of Eccl 12:5
2 my fathers to the eternal home where my fathers are. •Bury me near Abraham,
my father, in the cave of Machpelah in the field of Ephron the Hittite which
Abraham acquired for a burial place there. In the tomb which I dug for myself
3 there, bury me. •And I am commanding this, my sons, that you might perform
righteousness and uprightness upon the earth so that the LORD will bring upon
you everything which the LORD said that he would do for Abraham and for his
4 seed. •And among yourselves, my sons, be loving of your brothers as a man loves
himself, with each man seeking for his brother what is good for him, and acting
5 together on the earth, and loving each other as themselves. •And regarding the
matter of idols, I command you and admonish you to scorn them and hate them
and not to love them because they are full of error for those who worship and
6 bow down to them. •Remember, my sons, the LORD, the God of Abraham, your
father, and (that) I subsequently worshiped and served him in righteousness and
joy so that he might multiply you and increase your seed like the stars of heaven
with regard to number and (so that) he will plant you on the earth as a righteous
7 planting which will not be uprooted for all the eternal generations. •And now I
will make you swear by the great oath—because there is not an oath which is
greater than it, by the glorious and honored and great and splendid and amazing
and mighty name which created heaven and earth and everything together—that
8 you will fear him and worship him. •And (that) each one will love his brother
with compassion and righteousness and no one will desire evil for his brother
from now and forever all the days of your lives so that you will prosper in all
9 your deeds and not be destroyed. •And if either of you seeks evil against his
brother, know that hereafter each one who seeks evil against his brother will fall
into his hands and be uprooted from the land of the living and his seed will be
10 destroyed from under heaven. •And on the day of turmoil and execration and
indignation and wrath, (then) with devouring burning fire just as he burned Sodom
so too he will burn up his land and his city and everything which will be his.
And he will be wiped out from the book of the discipline of mankind, and he will
not be written (on high) in The Book of Life for (he is written) in the one which
will be destroyed and pass on to eternal execration so that their judgment will
always be renewed with eternal reproach and execration and wrath and torment
11 and indignation and plagues and sickness. •I have been speaking and exhorting
you, my sons, according to the judgment which will come upon the man who
desires to harm his brother."
12 And he divided[a] all his possessions which he had with the two of them on that
day, and he gave a larger (portion) to the one whose birth was first: both the
tower and everything which surrounded it and everything which Abraham acquired
13 at the Well of the Oath. •And he said, "I will surely increase this (portion) for
14 the one whose birth was first." •And Esau said, "I have sold to Jacob and I have
delivered my right of seniority to Jacob and so let it be given to him, and there
15 is not anything which I can say concerning it because it is his." •And Isaac said,
"May a blessing rest upon you and upon your seed on this day, my sons, because
you have given rest to me, and my heart has not been grieved concerning the
16 right of seniority lest you act perversely concerning it. •May the LORD Most High
bless the man who does righteousness, him and his seed forever."
17 And he finished commanding them and blessing them. And they ate and drank
together before him. And he rejoiced because they were in mutual agreement.

---

36 a. There is a Heb. fragment from Qumran (1Q
18) which contains the Heb. letters *plg*, "divide."
In the official publication of DJD (Oxford, 1955),
vol. 1, p. 84, Milik suggested that it might possibly
be placed at Jub 36:12, but a remnant of the
preceding word in the Heb. text matches nothing
in this vs. of Jub so the identification is unlikely.

18 And they went out from him and they rested that day and they slept. •And Isaac
slept on his bed on that day rejoicing. And he slept the eternal sleep. And he died Gen 35:29
at the age of one hundred and eighty years. He completed twenty-five weeks and
19 five years. And his two sons, Esau and Jacob, buried him. •And Esau traveled to
the land of Edom, to the mountain of Seir, and he dwelt there.
20 And Jacob dwelt in Mount Hebron in the tower of the land of the sojourning
of his father, Abraham. And[b] he worshiped the LORD with all of his heart and
according to the commands which were revealed (and) according to the division
of the days of his generations.

The death of Leah

21 And Leah, his wife, died in the fourth year of the second week of the forty-
fifth jubilee. And he buried her in the cave of Machpelah near Rebecca, his
22 mother, and north[c] of the tomb of Sarah, his father's mother. •And all of her
children and his children went out to weep with him for Leah, his wife, and to
23 comfort him concerning her because he was lamenting her. •For he loved her very
much after Rachel, her sister, died since she was perfect and upright in all of her
ways, and she honored Jacob. And in all of the days which she lived with him
he never heard a harsh word from her mouth because she possessed gentleness,
24 peace, uprightness, and honor. •And he remembered all of her deeds which she
had done in her life, and he lamented greatly for her because he loved her with
all his heart and all his soul.

Esau's sons reprove him for yielding to Jacob

1 **37** And on the day that Isaac,[a] the father of Jacob and Esau, died, the sons of
Esau heard that Isaac had given the right of seniority to Jacob, his younger son,
2 and they were very angry. •And they argued with their father, saying,[b] "Why,
since you are the elder and Jacob the younger, did your father give the right of
3 seniority to Jacob and abandon you?" •And he[c] said to them, "Because I sold
my right of firstborn to Jacob for a little dish of lentils. And on the day that my
father sent me to hunt and snare [and bring to him][d] so that he might eat and bless
me, he went with guile and brought food and drink to my father and my father
4 blessed him and placed me under his hand. •And now our father has made us
swear, (both) me and him, that we will not seek after evil, either one against his
brother, but that we will continue with an affection and a peace, each one with
5 his brother, so that we will not corrupt our ways."[e] •And they said, "We will
not listen to you in order to make peace with him because our might is stronger
than his might and we are stronger than he. We will go against him and we will
kill and destroy him and his sons. And if you do not go with us we will do harm
6 to you. •And now listen to us, and we will send to Aram and to Philistia and to
Moab and to Ammon and we will choose for ourselves chosen men who are ardent
in battle and we will go against him and we will fight with him and we will uproot
7 him from the land before he seizes power." •And their father said to them, "Do
8 not go and make war with him lest you fall before him." •And they said to him,

b. A portion of the Lat. text begins at this point
and continues through 37:5a.

c. The word for "north" is literally "left." In
ancient Israel directions were given while facing
the east so that "left" is "north" and "right" is
"south."

37 a. A portion of the Syr. text begins at this
point and continues through 38:9.

b. The Lat. and Syr. versions of this quotation
are worded differently. The Lat. reads "why is
Jacob set before you inasmuch as he is younger,

and your father has given him the larger portion
and made you lower?" The Syr. reads "why, since
you are older than Jacob your brother, did your
father then give to him the right of first born and
the primacy, since he is younger than you."

c. Both the Syr. and Lat. read "Esau."

d. The phrase in brackets is lacking in both Syr.
and Lat.

e. The last phrase has a different Lat. text,
which reads "so that we will not mutually engage
in malice." The Syr. text lacks this phrase.

"This very (thing) is your (type of) act from your youth until this day, and you put your neck under his yoke. But we will not listen to these words."

Esau's sons hire mercenaries for war against Jacob

9   And they sent to Aram and to Aduram, to their father's friend, and they hired from them one thousand fighting men, chosen warriors. And they came to them:
10   from Moab and from the Ammonites, those who were hired, one thousand chosen men, and from Philistia one thousand chosen fighting men, and from Edom and from the Hurrians one thousand chosen fighting men, and from the Kittim strong men, warriors.

Esau's approach to battle against Jacob

11   And they said to their father, "Go forth with them and lead them. And if not,
12   we will kill you." •And he was filled with wrath and indignation when he saw that his sons were forcing him to go before (them) in order to lead them to Jacob,
13   his brother. •But afterward he remembered all of the evil which was hidden in his heart against Jacob, his brother, and he did not remember the oath which he swore to his father and his mother that he would not seek any evil against Jacob, his brother, all of his days.
14   And with all of this, Jacob did not know that they were coming against him for battle. But he was lamenting Leah, his wife, until they drew very near the
15   tower with four thousand men, warriors and chosen fighting men. •And the men of Hebron sent to him, saying, "Behold, your brother has come up against you in order to fight with you with four thousand men (who are) girded (with) swords and bear shields and military weapons"; because they loved Jacob more than Esau. And they spoke to him because Jacob was a more generous and merciful man than Esau.
16,17 But Jacob did not believe (them) until they drew very close to the tower. •And he closed the gates of the tower and he stood on the battlement and spoke with his brother, Esau, and he said, "Is the consolation (with) which you have come in order to console me concerning my wife who died good?[f] Is this the oath which you swore to your father and again to your mother before they died? You have sinned against the oath. And on the day when you swore to your father, you were
18   condemned."[g] •And (at) that time, Esau answered and said to him:

"Mankind and beasts of the field have no righteous oath which they have
    surely sworn forever.
But daily they seek evil, one against the other, and each one (seeks) to
    kill his enemy and adversary.
19 And you will hate me and my sons forever.
And so there is no observing of fraternity with you.

[And Jacob said, "Do not act (thus), my brother. As for me, there is no evil in my heart against you. Do not plan evil against me. Know that there is a God and he sees what is hidden and requites to everyone according to his deeds. Calm down the heat of your anger and do not do anything rashly so that evil will come upon you." Then Esau turned and said harshly:][h]

20 Hear these words of mine which I will speak to you.
If a boar changes his hide and his bristles (and) makes (them) soft as wool,

---

f. This question has no grammatical marker in Charles's printed text, but MS C provides one, and the context is appropriate for a question. The Syr. text inserts the interrogative word *mā*, "what?" or "how?" at the beginning of this sentence.

g. The Syr. text lacks the last sentence of this vs.

h. The portion of text which is set between brackets is lacking in Eth. It is found only in Syr. The sentiments expressed in the Syr. text are appropriate to the present context.

and if he brings forth horns upon his head like the horns of a stag or
    sheep;[i]
then I will observe fraternity with you.
[And if sucklings separate themselves from their mother, you would not
    be a brother to me.][j]

21 And if the wolves make peace with lambs so as not to eat them or assault
    them,[k]
and if their hearts are (set) upon them to do good,
then peace will be in my heart for you.

22 And if the lion becomes a friend of the ox,
and if he is bound with him in a single yoke,
and he plows with him and makes peace with him,
then I will make peace with you.

23 And if the raven becomes white like the Raza[l] bird,
then know that I will love you and I will make peace with you.
You will be uprooted,
and your sons will be uprooted,
but you will have no peace."

24 And when Jacob saw that he had planned evil against him from his heart and
from his whole being so that he might kill him, and (that) he had come leaping
like a wandering boar who had come upon a spear which was piercing him and
killing him, and he would not withdraw from it, then he spoke to his own
(followers) and to his servants so that they might attack him and all his friends.

The defeat of Esau and his forces

1 **38** And afterward Judah spoke to Jacob, his father, and he said to him, "O
father, stretch your bow and shoot your arrows and strike down the enemy and
kill the adversary. And may you have might because we will not kill your brother
(inasmuch as) he is near to you and with us he is like you with respect to honor."[a]
2 And then when Jacob drew his bow and shot an arrow and struck Esau, his   TJud 9
3 brother, on his right breast,[b] he killed him. •And again, he shot an arrow and
struck Adoran, the Aramean, in his left breast and drove him back and killed him.
4 And afterward, the sons of Jacob and their servants went forth to divide
5 themselves on the four (sides) of the tower. •And Judah went out in front and
Naphtali and Gad and fifty servants with him on the south side of the tower. And

---

i. The phrase "or sheep" is lacking in the Syr.
The text reads more easily without it, but that could
also explain why someone would drop it.

j. There is obviously something wrong with the
phrase between brackets. The word which is translated "sucklings" is lit. "breasts." The root from
which the word is derived means "to suck milk."
Charles emended his Eth. text to read "since the
males have been separated from . . ." but he
returned to follow a MS reading in his English
translation. The Syr. text lacks this sentence. In
this case, however, the Syr. omission does not
provide clear evidence of the original text because
the Syr. text has apparently shortened its reading
of all of vss. 20–23 quite drastically.

k. Instead of "to eat them or assault them," the
Syr. reads "they will not harm them."

l. The Syr. has "pelican," which might be
found in Palestine. Its white color is also appropriate
for the present context. The Raza bird has been
identified as *ciconia ephippiorhynca*, a type of
stork. See Tisserant, *RB* 30 (1921) p. 223, for a
discussion of the word.

38 a. A portion of the Lat. text begins at this

point and continues through 38:16, lacking only
the last two words in that vs.
    Charles had emended his Eth. text and translation
to agree with the Lat. text and reads the end of vs.
1 as "let us give him (this) honor." We have
followed the MS reading instead.
    Charles's emendation is attractive, but the Syr.
text also differs from the Eth. and it would appear
that this vs. suffered in transmission. Nevertheless,
the Syr. text does give some support for reading
with the Eth. MSS. The Syr. text reads as follows:
"Judah said to Jacob, his father, 'We are not able
to unsheath the sword before your brother because
he is like you in our sight. Bend your bow and
destroy your enemy and kill your adversary because
he is your brother, and leave to us the rest of the
warriors.' "

b. The phrase "his right breast" is lacking in
Eth., but it is restored from the Lat. text. The Lat.
version is supported by a parallel account of the
war between Jacob and Esau which is reported in
Midrash *Wayyissau*. Charles printed the relevant
portion of the text as Appendix II in his edition of
the Eth. text. There is a brief parallel to this battle
and the death of Esau in TJud 9.

they killed everyone they found before them. And not a single one escaped from
6 them. •And Levi and Dan and Asher went forth on the east side of the tower and
fifty (men were) with them. And they killed the warriors of Moab and Ammon.
7 And Reuben and Issachar and Zebulun (went) forth on the north side of the tower
and fifty (men were) with them. And they killed the fighting men of the Philistines.
8 And Simeon and Benjamin and Enoch,[c] the son of Reuben, went forth on the
west side of the tower, and fifty (men were) with them. And they killed four
hundred strong men, warriors, of the Edomites and Hurrians. And six hundred TJud 9
fled. And the four sons of Esau fled with them and they left their slain father just
9 as he had fallen on the hill which is in Aduram. •And the sons of Jacob pursued
them as far as the mountain of Seir. But Jacob buried his brother in the hill which
is in Aduram and he returned to his house.
10 And Jacob's sons besieged[d] the children of Esau on the mountain of Seir. And
11 they bowed down their necks to become servants of the children of Jacob. •And
they sent to their father (to ask) whether they should make peace with them or
12 whether they should kill them. •And Jacob sent notice to his sons to make peace.
And they made peace with them and placed a yoke of servitude upon them so
13 that they might pay tribute to Jacob and his sons always. •And they continued
14 paying tribute to Jacob until the day that he went down to Egypt. •And the
children of Edom have not ceased from the yoke of servitude which the twelve
sons of Jacob ordered upon them until today.

The kings of Edom   Gen 36:31-39

15 And these are the kings who ruled in Edom before a king ruled the children of
16 Israel until today in the land of Edom. •And Balaq, son of Be'or, ruled in Edom.
17 And the name of his city was Danaba. •And Balaq died, and Yobab, son of Zara,
18 who was from Boser, ruled instead of him. •And Yobab died. And Asam, who
19 was from the land[e] of Teman, ruled instead of him. •And Asam died. And 'Adath,
son of Barad, who killed Median in the field of Moab, ruled instead of him. And
20 the name of his city was 'Avith. •And 'Adath died. And Salman, who was from
21 'Amaseqa, ruled instead of him. •And Salman died. And Saul, who was from
22 Ra'aboth, (by the) river, ruled instead of him. •And Saul died. And Ba'elunan,
23 son of 'Achbor, ruled instead of him. •And Ba'elunan, son of 'Achbor, died. And
'Adath ruled instead of him. And the name of his wife was Maitabith, daughter
24 of Matarat, daughter of Metabedza'ab. •These are the kings who ruled in the land
of Edom.

Joseph in the house of Potiphar   Gen 37:1f.;
                                                                            39:1-40:23
1 **39** And Jacob dwelt in the land of his father's sojourning, (in) the land of Canaan.
2 These are the generations of Jacob. And Joseph was seventeen years old (when)
they brought him down into Egypt, and Potiphar, Pharaoh's eunuch, the chief of
3 the guard, bought him. •And he set Joseph over all of his house and the blessing
of the LORD was upon the house of the Egyptian because of Joseph and the LORD
4 caused everything which he did to prosper. •And the Egyptian left everything in
the hands of[a] Joseph because he saw that the LORD was with him and the LORD
caused everything which he did to prosper.
5 And Joseph was good-looking and very handsome. And the wife of his master
lifted up her eyes and saw Joseph and desired him. And she begged him to lie

---

c. As if to explain why Enoch had to fight, the
Midrash *Wayyissau* notes that Joseph had already
been sold at this time.

d. Charles emended his Eth. text to read "encircled" in agreement with the Lat., but then
returned to the MS reading in his English translation.

e. The translation "land" is given in agreement

with Gen 36:34. The Eth. word which is being
translated more frequently means "mountain" or
"mountain region."

39 a. The phrase "in the hands of" was suggested
by Charles as an emendation. The Eth. MSS read
"before."

6 with her. •And he did not surrender himself but he remembered the LORD and the words which Jacob, his father, used to read, which were from the words of Abraham, that there is no man who (may) fornicate with a woman who has a husband (and) that there is a judgment of death which is decreed for him in heaven before the LORD Most High. And the sin is written (on high) concerning him in
7 the eternal books always before the LORD. •And Joseph remembered these words
8 and he did not want to lie with her. •And she begged him (for) one year. And he turned away and refused to listen to her.

9 And[b] she embraced him and seized him in the house so that she might force him to lie with her. And she shut the door of the house and seized him. And he left his garment in her hand and he broke the door and fled outside (away) from
10 her presence. •And that woman saw that he would not lie with her and she falsely accused him before his master, saying, "Your Hebrew servant, whom you love, desired to seduce me so that he might lie with me. And it came to pass when I raised my voice that he fled and he left his garment in my hand when I seized him. And he broke the door."

Joseph in prison

11 And the Egyptian saw Joseph's garments and the broken door and he heard his wife's story and he put Joseph in prison, in the place where the prisoners whom
12 the king imprisoned stayed. •And he was there in the prison and the LORD gave Joseph favor and mercy before the chief guard of the prison because he saw that the LORD was with him and the LORD caused everything which he did to prosper.
13 And he left everything in his hands,[c] and the chief guard of the prison knew nothing which was with him •because Joseph did everything, and the LORD
14 perfected (it). •And he dwelt there two years.

And in those days, Pharaoh, the king of Egypt, was angry with two of his eunuchs, with the chief of the butlers and with the chief of the bakers. And he put them in prison, in the house of the chief of the guard, in the prison where
15 Joseph was held. •And the chief of the guard of the prison ordered Joseph to
16 serve them. And he served before them. •And both of them had a dream, the
17 chief of the butlers and the chief of the bakers, and they told it to Joseph. •And just as he interpreted to them so it happened to them. And Pharaoh returned the chief of the butlers to his task, but he killed the baker[d] just as Joseph interpreted
18 for them. •But the chief of the butlers forgot Joseph in the prison when he made known to him what would happen to him, and he did not remember to tell the Pharaoh what Joseph told him because he forgot.

Joseph as an interpreter of Pharaoh's dreams

Gen 41:1-38

1 **40** And in those days, Pharaoh dreamed two dreams in a single night concerning the matter of the famine which would come upon all of the land. And he awoke from his sleep and called all of the interpreters of dreams and magicians who were in Egypt. And he told them of both of his dreams but they were unable to
2 explain (them). •Then the chief of the butlers remembered Joseph and he told the king about him. And he brought him out of the prison and told both of the dreams
3 in his presence. •And he said in the presence of the Pharaoh that both of his dreams were one. And he said to him, "Seven years will come. Abundance will be in all the land of Egypt, but afterward seven years of famine, which (is) unlike
4 any (previous) famine, (will be) in all the land. •And now let Pharaoh appoint overseers[a] in all the land and let them store up food for a city within the city

---

b. A portion of the Lat. text begins at this point and continues through 40:8a.

c. The phrase "in his hands" was emended to agree with the Lat. text and Gen 39:22. The Eth. MSS read "before him."

d. The Lat. text reads "chief baker."

40 a. The word "overseers" is supplied from Lat. The Eth. reading makes no sense at this point.

during the days of the plentiful years. And there will be food for the seven years
of famine. And the land will not perish in the presence of the famine because it
5 will be very severe." •And the LORD gave Joseph favor and mercy in the sight
of the Pharaoh. And the Pharaoh said to his servants, "We will not find a man
wise and knowledgeable as this man because the spirit of the LORD is with him."

Joseph becomes a ruler in Egypt

Gen 41:39-49

6 And he set him second in all his kingdom and he made him rule in all of Egypt
7 and he made him ride upon the second chariot of the Pharaoh. •And he invested
him with a garment of byssus and hung a golden chain on his neck and they
proclaimed before him *"El, El wa Abirer"* and he gave him the signet ring on Gen 41:43
his hand and he made him rule over all his house and he made him great and he
said to him, "I will not be greater than you except (regarding) the throne alone."
8 And Joseph ruled in all the land of Egypt and all of the judges and all of the
servants of the Pharaoh and all of those who did the king's work loved him
because he walked uprightly and he had no pompousness or arrogance or partiality,
and there was no bribery because he ruled all the people of the land uprightly.
9 And the land of Egypt was at peace before the Pharaoh on account of Joseph
because the LORD was with him and gave him favor and mercy for all his family
before all who knew him and those who heard witness of him. And the kingdom
10 of the Pharaoh was upright. And there was no Satan and there was no evil. •And
the king called Joseph "Sephantiphans." And he gave the daughter of Potiphar,
the daughter of the priest of Heliopolis, the chief of the guard, to Joseph (as) a
11 wife. •And on the day that Joseph stood with the Pharaoh he was thirty years old,
[when he stood with the Pharaoh.][b]
12 And in that year Isaac died. And it came (about) just as Joseph related concerning
the interpretation of the two dreams, and there were seven abundant years in all
of the land of Egypt. And the land of Egypt was very fruitful, one measure
13 (yielding) eighteen hundred measures. •And Joseph gathered the food of a city
into the city until it was full of grain, until they were unable to count or measure
it because of its magnitude.

The story of Judah and Tamar

Gen 38:1-30

1 **41** And in the forty-fifth jubilee, in the second week, in the second year, Judah Gen 38:6f.
took a wife for Er, his firstborn, from the daughters of Aram, and her name was TJud 12
2 Tamar. •But he hated (her) and would not lie with her because his mother was
from the daughters of Canaan. And he wanted to take a wife from his mother's
3 people, but Judah, his father, did not permit him. •And Er, the firstborn of Judah,
4 was evil and the LORD killed him. •And[a] Judah said to 'Onan, his brother, "Go
to your brother's wife and act as levirate and raise up seed for your brother."
5 And 'Onan knew that the seed would not be his (but) only his brother's and he
entered the house of his brother's wife and poured out (his) seed on the ground
6 and he was evil in the sight of the LORD and he killed him. •And Judah said to
Tamar,[b] his daughter-in-law, "Remain at the house of your father as a widow
7 until Selah, my son, grows up. And I will give you to him (as) a wife." •And he
grew up, but Bedsuel, Judah's wife, did not permit Selah, her son, to marry. And
Bedsuel, Judah's wife, died in the fifth year of that week.
8 And in the sixth year, Judah went up in order to shear his sheep at Timnah.
And they told Tamar, "Behold, your father-in-law is going up to shear his sheep
9 at Timnah." •And she put off the clothes of her widowhood. And she put on a
veil. And she made herself beautiful and sat by the gates which are toward the

---

b. The words in brackets appear to be an obvious
gloss caused by dittography.

41 a. A portion of the Syr. text begins at this

point and continues through 41:24.
    b. A portion of the Lat. text begins at this point
and continues through the first word of 41:19.

10 Timnah road. •And when Judah walked along he found her and presumed that
    she was a prostitute. And he said to her, "Let me enter into you." And she said
11 to him, "Come on." And he entered. •And she said to him, "Give me my fee."
    And he said to her, "I have nothing in my hand except my signet ring of my
12 finger and my necklace and my staff which is in my hand." •And she said to
    him, "Give them to me until you send my fee to me." And he said to her, "I
    will send to you a young goat." And he gave them to her, and he was with her,[c]
    and she became pregnant by him.
13,14   And Judah went to his sheep and she went to her father's house. •And Judah
    sent a young goat in the hand of his shepherd, an Adulamite, but he did not find
    her. And he asked the men of the district, saying, "Where is the prostitute who
15 was here?" And they said to him, "There is no prostitute here with us." •And
    he returned and told him that he did not find (her).[d] And he said, "I inquired of
    the men of the district. And they said to me, 'There is no prostitute here.' " And
16 he said, "Let her take (it) lest we become an object of scorn." •And when she
    completed three months it was obvious that she was pregnant. And they told
    Judah, saying, "Behold, Tamar, your daughter-in-law is pregnant through pros-
17 titution." •And Judah went to her father's house and said to her father and her
    brothers, "Bring her out and let them burn her because she has caused a defilement
    in Israel."
18   And it came to pass when they brought her out to burn her that she sent to her
    father-in-law the signet ring and the necklace and the staff. And she said,
19 "Recognize whose these are because I am pregnant by him." •And Judah
    recognized (them) and said, "Tamar was more righteous than I. And therefore let
20 them not burn her." •And on account of that she was not given to Selah. And
21 therefore he did not approach her again. •And after this she bore two children,
22 Perez and Zerah, in the seventh year of this second week. •And after this the   Gen 41:53
    seven years of full harvest which Joseph told Pharaoh (about) were completed.

Judah's repentance

23   And Judah knew that the deed which he did was evil because he lay with his   TJud 14
    daughter-in-law. And he condemned himself in his own sight. And he knew that
    he had sinned and gone astray because he uncovered the robe of his son. And he
    began to mourn and make supplication before the LORD on account of his sin.
24 And we told him in a dream that it was forgiven him because he made great
    supplication and because he mourned and did not do it again.

Judah's forgiveness contrasted with subsequent
strict enforcement of the law

25   And there was forgiveness for him because he turned from his sin and from his   TJud 19
    ignorance because the sin was great before our God. And anyone who does
    anything like this, who lies with his mother-in-law, they shall burn with fire so
    that he might burn in it because defilement and impurity have come upon them.
    In the fire they shall burn them.
26   And you command the children of Israel and there will be no defilement in
    their midst because everyone who lies with his daughter-in-law or with his mother-   Lev 20:14
    in-law causes defilement. In the fire they shall burn the man who has lain with   Lev 18:15
    her and also the woman. And the wrath and punishment he will cause to cease   Lev 20:12
    from Israel.

c. Both Syr. and Lat. MSS read "he was with
her." Charles emended Lat. from *fuit* to *coiit* and
then restored an Eth. phrase meaning "he entered
into her" to agree with his emended Lat. text.
Charles, of course, did not know the Syr. text, and
without its witness his reconstruction was reasonable.

d. This follows the reading of the MSS. Charles
emended the Eth. text to read "made known to
him. And he said, 'I did not find her. And I
inquired.' " The altered word order agrees with
the word order in the Lat. text.

27 And we told Judah that his two sons had not lain with her and therefore his
28 seed stood for a second generation and it would not be uprooted •because in the
integrity of his eyes he went and sought judgment because by the judgment of
Abraham, which he commanded his sons, Judah wanted to burn her with fire.

The arrival of the years of famine

Gen 41:53-56

1 **42** In the first year of the third week of the forty-fifth jubilee the famine began
to come upon the land and rain refused to be given to the land because there was
2 nothing which would come down. •And the earth suffered famine but in[a] the land
of Egypt there was food because Joseph gathered the grain of the land during the
3 seven years of full harvest and he guarded it. •And Egypt came to Joseph so that
he might give them food. And he opened up the storehouses where the wheat of
the first year was and he sold it to the people of the land for gold.

The sons of Jacob travel to Egypt for grain

Gen 42:1-28

4 [And the famine was very severe in the land of Canaan.][b] And Jacob heard that
there was food in Egypt and he sent ten of his sons to get food for him in Egypt,
but he did not send Benjamin. [And the ten sons of Jacob][b] arrived [in Egypt][b]
5 with those who were traveling (there). •And Joseph knew them, but they did not
know him. And he spoke with them and interrogated them[c] and said to them,
"Are you men not spies? And you have come to examine the paths of the land."
6 And he locked them up. •But afterward he released them again, and he made only
7 Simeon stay.[d] And he sent his nine brothers away. •And he filled their grain sacks
with grain and he also put their gold in their grain sacks, but they did not know
8 (it). •And he commanded them that they should bring their little brother because
they told him that their father was alive and also their little brother.

The sons of Jacob recount their adventures in Egypt

9 And they went up from the land of Egypt. And they arrived in the land of Gen 42:29-38
Canaan, and told their father everything just as they experienced (it) and how the
overseer of the district had spoken harshly with them and held Simeon until they
10 would bring Benjamin. •And Jacob said, "You have therefore bereaved me.
Joseph is not (here) and Simeon is not (here) either and you will take Benjamin.
11 Your evil has therefore come upon me." •And he said, "My son will not go
down with you—perhaps he might become ill—because their mother bore two,
and one has perished, and you will take this one from me. If perhaps he became
feverish on the way then you would send down my old age to death in grief."
12 For he saw that the money of each one had been returned in his sack, and he
feared to send him on account of that.

The famine causes the sons of Jacob to return to Egypt

Gen 43:1-44:2

13 But the famine increased and became severe in the land of Canaan and in all
the earth except in the land of Egypt. For many of the Egyptians stored up their
grain for food after they saw that Joseph was gathering grain and placing it in
14 storehouses and guarding it for the year of famine. •And the men of Egypt ate it
15 in the first year of their famine. •And when Israel saw that the famine was very
severe in the land and there was no escaping, he said to his sons, "Go, return,

---

42 a. A portion of the Lat. text begins at this
point and continues through 42:14a.

b. The portions of text found between brackets
was restored from the Lat. text.

c. The Lat. text has "harshly" instead of "and

interrogated them." The Lat. agrees with Gen 43:7.
Cf. vs. 9 below.

d. The Lat. text reads "and sending he summoned them. And taking Simeon alone, he bound
him."

16 and get food for us lest we die." •And they said, "We shall not go. If our little
17 brother does not come with us, we shall not go." •And Israel saw (that) if he did
18 not send him with them they would all be destroyed due to the famine. •And
Reuben said, "Place him in my hands, and if I do not return him to you, kill
both of my sons for his life." And he said to him, "He will not go with you."
19 And Judah drew near and said, "Send him with me. And if I do not return him
to you, I will be guilty before you all the days of my life."
20   And he sent him with them in the second year of that week on the first of the
month and they arrived at the district of Egypt with all of those who were traveling
(there). And their presents (were) in their hands: stacte, almonds, terebinth nuts,
21 and pure honey. •And they arrived and stood before Joseph. And he saw Benjamin,
his brother, and he knew him. And he said to them, "Is this your little brother?"
And they said to him, "He is." And he said, "May the LORD be merciful to you,
22 my son." •And he sent him into his house. And he brought Simeon to them, and
made a banquet for them. And they presented him with his gift, which they
23 brought in their hands. •And they ate before him. And he gave a portion to all of
them. And he increased Benjamin's portion seven times more than any of their
24 portions. •And they ate and drank, and got up and stayed with their asses.
25   And Joseph thought of an idea by means of which he might learn their thoughts,
whether they had thoughts of peace for one another. And he said to the man who
was over his house, "Fill all of their bags with food for them. And also return
their money to them in the midst of their containers. And place my cup from
which I drink, the silver cup, in the bag of the youngest one and send them off."

Joseph's stratagem to test his brothers

Gen 44:2-34

1 **43** And he did as Joseph told him. And he filled all their bags for them (with)
food. And he also put their money in their bags. And the cup he put in Benjamin's
2 bag. •And (at) daybreak in the morning, they went. And it came to pass when
they departed from there, that Joseph said to the man of his house, "Pursue them.
Run and reproach them,[a] saying, 'You have repaid me evil in place of good. You
have robbed me of the silver cup from which my lord drinks.' And return to me
their little brother. And hurry, bring (him) before I go to my judgment seat."
3,4   And he ran after them and he spoke to them according to these words. •And
they said to him, "May God forbid that your servants would do this thing or steal
any vessel from your lord's house. But rather our money which we found at first
5 in our bags your servants have brought back from the land of Canaan. •Therefore,
why would we steal any vessel? Behold, search both us and our animals and
wherever you find the cup, in the bag of any one of our men, let him be killed,
6 and both we and our asses will become slaves to your lord." •And he said to
them, "It will not be so, (but) with the man with whom I find it, he alone, I will
take as a servant, but you will return in peace to your house."
7   And when he searched in their baggage, he started from the eldest and ended
8 with the youngest. And it was found in the bag of Benjamin. •And they tore their
clothes and loaded up their donkeys and returned to the city. And they reached
9 Joseph's house, and they all bowed to him with their face on the ground. •And
Joseph said to them, "You have done evil." And they said, "What can we say?
(With) what can we defend ourselves? Our lord has found the guilt of his servants.
10 Behold, we (are) servants of our lord and also our donkeys." •And Joseph said
to them, "I fear the LORD. You, go to your houses, but let your brother alone be
my servant because you have done evil. Did you not know that a man would be
11 pleased with[b] his cup as I am with this cup? And you stole it from me." •And
Judah said, "I pray,[c] O lord, let me, your servant, speak a word in my lord's

---

43 a. The reading is based on the MSS. Charles
emended his Eth. text to read "seize them" in
agreement with Gen 44:4.

b. The phrase "be pleased with" is found in
the MSS. Charles emended his text to read "divine"

in agreement with Gen 44:15, but returned to the
MS reading in his translation.

c. The Eth. text reads "upon me," which Charles
has identified as a simple mistranslation of Heb.
bî, which is found in Gen 44:18.

ear. His mother bore two brothers to our father, your servant. One went forth and
12 was lost, and was not found. •And he alone was left from his mother, and your
servant, our father, loves him. And his life is bound with the life of this (one).
And it will come to pass that if we go to your servant, our father, and if the lad
is not with us, he will die. And we will bring down our father to death with
13 sorrow. •And let me, your servant, remain alone instead of the child as a servant
to my lord, and let the lad go with his brothers because I was put as a pledge for
him at the hand of your servant, our father. And if I should not return him your
servant will always be guilty to our father."

Joseph reveals himself to his brothers   Gen 45:1-13

14   And Joseph saw that the heart of all of them was in accord one with another
for good. And he was unable to control his emotion and he told them that he was
15 Joseph. •And he conversed with them in the Hebrew language and embraced their
16 necks and wept. But they did not recognize him. And they began to weep. •And
he said to them, "Do not weep for me, but hasten and bring my father to me.
And I shall see him before I die even as the eyes of my brother Benjamin see.[d]
17 For behold this is the second year of famine, and there will still be five years.
18 And there will be no harvest or fruit of the tree or plowing. •Hasten, come down,
you and your households, lest you be destroyed in the famine. And you shall not
grieve for your possessions. For the LORD has sent me first to prepare before you
19 so that many people might live. •And tell my father that I am still alive and
behold, you were seeing that the LORD ordained me as a father to the Pharaoh
20 and so that I might rule in his house and over all the land of Egypt. •And tell my
father about all my honor and all the wealth and honor which the LORD has given
to me."

The brothers return to Canaan to get their father   Gen 45:17-28

21   And by the word of the mouth of the Pharaoh he gave them chariots and
provisions for the way. And he gave them all clothing of many colors and money.
22 And he also sent to their father clothing and money and ten asses which were
23 carrying wheat. And he sent them off. •And they went up and they told their
father that Joseph was alive and that he was distributing grain to all of the people
24 of the land. And he ruled over all the land of Egypt. •And their father did not
believe because there was a confusion in his mind. And after this he saw the
chariots which Joseph sent and the life of his soul was renewed. And he said, "It
is enough for me if Joseph is alive. I will go down and I will see him before I
die."

Jacob observes a feast of firstfruits at Beer-sheba   Gen 46:1

1 **44** And Israel rose up from Haran,[a] from his house on the first of the third month
and he went by the way of the Well of the Oath. And he offered up a sacrifice to
2 the God of his father, Isaac, on the seventh day of that month. •And Jacob recalled
the dream which he dreamed in Bethel, and he was afraid to go down into Egypt.
3 And as he was planning to send to Joseph so that he might come to him, and he
would not go down, he remained there seven days (to learn) if he would see a
4 vision (concerning) whether he should remain or go down. •And he observed the
feast of the harvest of the firstfruits from old wheat for there was not in the whole
land of Canaan a handful of any seed in the land because there was a famine for
all the wild animals and the cattle and the birds and also man.

---

d. This sentence is translated in agreement with
the Eth. MS. Charles emended the sentence to read
"and you see that it is my mouth that speaks and
the eyes of my brother Benjamin see." The emendation was based on Gen 45:12.

44 a. According to the biblical account, the location of Jacob is near Hebron. Cf. Gen 37:14.
Haran is apparently a corruption.

Jacob's theophany at Beer-sheba

Gen 46:2-4

5　And on the sixteenth day the LORD appeared to him and he said to him, "Jacob, Jacob." And he said to him, "Here I am." And he again said to him, "I am the God of your fathers, the God of Abraham and Isaac. Do not fear to go down to
6 Egypt because I will make you into a great people there. •I shall go down with you and I shall bring you (back) and you will be buried in this land. And Joseph will place his hand upon your eyes. Do not fear. Go down into Egypt."

The preparation for the journey to Egypt

Gen 46:5-7,28-34

7　And his children and grandchildren rose up and they loaded their father and
8 their possessions on the chariots. •And Israel rose up from the Well of the Oath
9 on the sixteenth day of this third month and he went to the land of Egypt. •And Israel sent Judah before him to Joseph, his son, so that he might examine the land of Goshen, for Joseph told his brothers that they should come to dwell there so
10 they might be his neighbor. •And it was the best in the land of Egypt. And it was near him for all (of them) and for the cattle.

A list of the children of Jacob

Gen 46:8-27

11　And these are the names of the sons of Jacob who went into Egypt with their
12 father, Jacob. •Reuben was the firstborn of Israel. And these (are) the names of his sons: Enoch, and Pallu, and Hezron, and Carmi—five.
13　Simeon and his sons; and these (are) the names of his sons: Jemuel, and Jamin, and Ohad, and Jachin, and Zohar, and Shaul, the son of a Zephathite woman[b]—seven.
14　Levi and his sons; and these (are) the names of his sons: Gershon, and Kohath, and Merari—four.
15　Judah and his sons; and these are the names of his sons: Shela, and Perez, and Zerah—four.
16　Issachar and his sons; and these are the names of his sons: Tola, and Phua, and Jasub, and Shimron—five.
17　Zebulun and his sons; and these are the names of his sons: Sered, and Elon,
18 and Jahleel—four. •And these are the sons of Jacob and their sons whom Leah bore to Jacob in Mesopotamia, six, plus one girl, Dinah, their sister. And all of the persons who (were) sons of Leah and their sons, who entered Egypt with Jacob, their father, were twenty-nine. And Jacob, their father, was with them. And they totaled thirty.
19　And the sons of Zilpah, the attendant of Leah, the wife of Jacob, which she
20 bore to Jacob, were Gad and Asher. •And these are the names of their sons who entered into Egypt with him.
　　The sons of Gad (are) Ziphion, and Gaggi, and Shuni, and Ezbon, and Eri,[c] and Areli, and Arodi—eight.
21　And the sons of Asher (are) Imnah, and Ishvah, [and Ishvi],[c] and Beriah, and
22 Serah, their one sister—six. •And all of the persons (were) fourteen. And the total of Leah was forty-four.
23　And the sons of Rachel, who (was) the wife of Jacob, (were) Joseph and Benjamin.
24　And (sons) were born to Joseph in Egypt before his father entered Egypt whom Asenath, the daughter of Potiphar, the priest of Heliopolis, bore to him, (namely) Manasseh and Ephraim—three.
25　And the sons of Benjamin (are) Bela, and Becher, and Ashbel, and Gera, and

---

b. A woman from the Canaanite city of *Zephath.* Cf. Judg 1:17. The reading is found in MS B.

c. The names in brackets were restored from Gen. They are lacking in the Eth. text. The spelling of names has also been standardized to agree with Gen.

26 Naaman, and Ehi, and Rosh, and Muppim, and Huppim, and Ard—eleven. •And all of the persons of Rachel were fourteen.

27 And the sons of Bilhah, the attendant of Rachel, the wife of Jacob, which she bore to Jacob, (are) Dan and Naphthali, and these are the names of their sons who entered Egypt with them.

28 And the sons of Dan (are) Hushim, and Samon, and Asudi, and 'Ijaka, and
29 Solomon—six. •And they died during the year they entered Egypt and there was left to Dan only Hushim.

30 And these are the names of the sons of Naphthali: Jaziel, and Guni, and Jezer, 1Chr 7:13
31 and Shallum, and 'Iv. •And 'Iv, who was born after the years of the famine, died
32 in Egypt. •And all of the persons of Rachel were twenty-six.

33 And all of the persons of Jacob who entered Egypt were seventy persons. Therefore all these sons and grandsons of his were seventy, but five died in Egypt
34 before Joseph, and they had no children. •And two sons of Judah, Er and Onan, died in the land of Canaan. And they had no children. And the children of Israel buried those who perished. And they were set among the seventy nations.

The family of Jacob is settled in Goshen

Gen 46:29-47:12

1 **45** And Israel entered into the land of Egypt into the land of Goshen on the first of the fourth month in the second year of the third week of the forty-fifth jubilee.
2 And Joseph came to greet his father, Jacob, in the land of Goshen. And he
3 embraced the neck of his father and wept. •And Israel said to Joseph, "Let me die now after I have seen you. And now let the LORD, the God of Israel, be blessed, the God of Abraham and the God of Isaac, who did not withhold his
4 mercy and his kindness from his servant Jacob. •It is enough for me that I have seen your face while I was alive, for the vision which I saw in Bethel was certainly true. May the LORD my God be blessed forever and ever and blessed (be) his name."

5 And Joseph and his brothers ate bread before their father, and they drank wine. And Jacob rejoiced very greatly because he saw Joseph eating and drinking with his brothers before him. And he blessed the Creator of all who kept him and kept
6 for him his twelve sons. •And Joseph gave to his father and his brothers (as) a gift that they might dwell in the land of Goshen and Ramses and all of the districts (belonging) to them which he ruled over before the Pharaoh. And Israel and his sons dwelt in the land of Goshen, the best of the land of Egypt. And Israel was
7 one hundred and thirty years old when he entered Egypt. •And Joseph provided bread for his father and his brothers and their possessions, as much as was sufficient for them for the seven years of famine.

Joseph's skill as an administrator

Gen 47:13-26

8 And[a] the land of Egypt suffered in view of the famine. And Joseph gathered all of the land of Egypt for the Pharaoh by means of the food. And men and their
9 cattle and everything he acquired for Pharaoh. •And the years of the famine were completed. And Joseph gave seed and food to the people who were in the land so that they might sow the land[b] in the eighth year because the river was full in
10 all the land of Egypt. •For during the seven years of famine it was not[c] full. And it did not irrigate except a few places by the shore of the river. But now it was full and the Egyptians sowed the land and it bore[d] much wheat[e] in that year.
11,12 And that was the first year of the fourth week of the forty-fifth jubilee. •And

---

45 a. A portion of the Lat. text begins at this point and continues through 46:1a.

b. "The land" is restored from the Lat. text.

c. The "not" is restored from the Lat. text.

d. The Lat. text reads "they harvested" instead of "it bore." Charles emended his text to follow the Lat.

e. The Lat. text reads "good fruit" for "much wheat."

Joseph took for the king one fifth of everything which bore fruit,[f] and he left four parts for them for food and seed. And Joseph set it up as an ordinance for the land of Egypt until this day.

The death of Jacob

Gen 47:28-31;
49:1-50:41

13   And Israel lived in the land of Egypt seventeen years, and all of the days which he lived were three jubilees, one hundred and forty-seven years. And he died in
14 the fourth year of the fifth week of the forty-fifth jubilee. •And Israel blessed his sons before he died. And he told them everything which was going to happen to them in the land of Egypt and in the latter days; he made them know how it would come upon them. And he blessed them and he gave to Joseph a double portion
15 upon the land. •And he slept with his fathers. And he was buried in the cave of Machpelah in the land of Canaan near Abraham, his father, in the tomb which he excavated for himself in the cave of Machpelah in the land of Hebron. And he gave all of his books and his fathers' books to Levi, his son, so that he might preserve them and renew them for his sons until this day.

The death of Joseph and his generation

Gen 50:15-26

1 **46** And it came to pass after Jacob died that the children of Israel increased in the land of Egypt. And they became a numerous people, and they were all in Ex 1:7 accord in their hearts so that each one loved his brother and each man helped his brother, and they increased exceedingly and increased very much for ten weeks[a]
2 of years, all the days of the life of Joseph.[b] •And there was no Satan or anything evil all the days of the life of Joseph which he lived after his father, Jacob, because all of the Egyptians were honoring the children of Israel all the days of
3 the life of Joseph. •And Joseph died at one hundred and ten years of age. And seventeen years he dwelt in the land of Canaan and ten years he remained as a slave and three years in the prison and eighty years under the king ruling all of Ex 1:6
4 the land of Egypt. •And he died and all of his brothers and all of that generation.

The removal of Jacob's bones and a comment on Joseph's burial

5   And he commanded the children of Israel before he died to carry his bones at
6 the time when they would go out of the land of Egypt. •And he made them swear TSim 8
TBenj 12 an oath concerning his bones because he knew that Egypt would not again bring them forth and bury them in the land of Canaan because when Makamaron, the king of Canaan, was dwelling in the land of Asshur, he fought in the valley with the king of Egypt. And he killed him there. And he pursued after the Egyptians
7 as far as the gates of Ermon. •And he was unable to enter because another new king ruled Egypt and he was stronger than he. And he returned to the land of Canaan and the gates of Egypt were shut up and there was none who could leave
8 or enter Egypt. •And Joseph died in this forty-sixth jubilee in the sixth week in the second year. And they buried him in the land of Egypt. And all of his brothers died after him.

---

f. The reading "everything which bore fruit" is a correction based on the Lat. text. The Eth. MSS read "grain which they sowed," which is not strictly logical.

46 a. A fragment of Heb. text from Qumran (2Q 20) begins at this point and continues through vs. 3a. It confirms the Eth. text.
  b. The spelling of this name was misprinted in

the Eth. text edited by Charles. That was pointed out by W. Baars and R. Zuurmond in their article "The Project for a New Edition of the Ethiopic Book of Jubilees," *JSS* 9 (1964) 71. In that article they recollated ch. 46 of Charles's Eth. text against MS B, calling attention to a number of interesting variations. None of the variations which they noted, however, require any change in the translation.

The removal of the bones of the children of Jacob

9 And the king of Egypt went forth to fight with the king of Canaan in this forty-seventh jubilee in the second week in the second year. And the children of Israel brought forth the bones of the children of Jacob, all except the bones of Joseph. And they buried them in the field in the cave of Machpelah in the mountain. 10 And many returned into Egypt but a few of them were left in Mount Hebron. Acts 7:15f. And Amram, your father, was left with them.

The children of Israel are reduced to slavery   Ex 1:1-14

11 And the king of Canaan was victorious over the king of Egypt and he closed 12 the gates of Egypt. •And[c] he conceived an evil thought against the children of Israel so that he might cause them to suffer. And he said to the men of Egypt, 13 "Behold, the people of the sons of Israel have grown and increased more than we. Come let us act wisely concerning them before they increase. And let us cause them to suffer in slavery before war comes to us, or before they battle with us, or if not (that, then) they will mix with our[d] enemy. And they will depart from our land because their hearts and their faces are upon the land of Canaan." 14 And they appointed over them taskmasters to make them suffer in slavery. And they built strengthened cities for Pharaoh, Pithom, and Ramses.[e] And they built all of the walls and all of the ramparts[f] which had fallen in the cities of Egypt. 15 And they made them slaves by force. And to the extent that they acted cruelly 16 against them, they likewise increased and multiplied. •And the men of Egypt regarded the sons of Israel as defiled.

The birth and early life of Moses   Ex 2:1-15

1 **47** And in the seventh week, in the seventh year in this forty-seventh jubilee, your father came from the land of Canaan. And you were born in the fourth week, in the sixth year, in this forty-eighth jubilee, which were days of affliction upon 2 the children of Israel. •And the king of Egypt, Pharaoh, issued an order concerning Ex 1:22 them that they should throw all of their male children who were born into the 3 river. •And they continued throwing (them into the river) seven months, until the day when you were born. And your mother hid you three months, and they 4 reported concerning her. •And she made an ark for you. And she covered it with pitch and asphalt. And she placed it among the reeds by the shore of the river and she placed you in it seven days. And your mother came in the night and suckled you and (in) the day Miriam, your sister, guarded you from the birds. 5 And in those days Tharmuth, the daughter of Pharaoh, came in order to bathe in the river and she heard your voice as you were crying and she told her maids[a] 6 to fetch you. And they brought you to her. •And she took you from the ark and 7 had pity on you. •And your sister said to her, "Shall I go and call for you one of the Hebrew women who will nurse and suckle the infant for you?" And she 8 said to her, "Go!" •And she went and called your mother, Jochebed. And she Ex 6:20 gave a wage to her. And she nursed you.   Num 26:59 9 And after this when you had grown they brought you to the daughter[b] of Pharaoh and you became her son. And Amram, your father, taught you writing. And after

---

c. A portion of the Lat. text begins at this point and continues through 48:5, except for the last six words.

d. "Our" is supplied from the Lat. text.

e. The Lat. text also includes the city of On.

f. The phrase "and all of the ramparts" is lacking in Lat.

47 a. The Eth. text has "her Hebrew women,"

but that is probably based on a mistranslation of the Gk. dative plural *abrais,* "maids." The Lat. text is correct. The Eth. text may also have been influenced by the appearance of "Hebrew women" in vs. 7.

b. The Eth. and Lat. MSS read "house" for "daughter." Apparently the Gk. texts on which the later versions were based misread the Heb. consonants *bt* as "house" instead of "daughter."

10 you completed three weeks (of years) they brought you into the royal court. •And
you were in the court three weeks of years until the day when you went out of
the royal court. And you saw an Egyptian beating your friend who was from the Acts 7:23
11 children of Israel. And you killed him and hid him in the sand. •And on the
second day you found two of the children of Israel striving together. And you
said to that one who was acting falsely, "Why are you striking your brother?"
12 And he was angry and indignant and said, "Who set you as a ruler and judge
over us? Do you also desire to kill me as you killed the Egyptian yesterday?"
And you were afraid and you fled because of those words.

Moses' experience in Midian and encounter with Mastema Ex 2:15-4:26

1 **48** And on the sixth year of the third week of the forty-ninth jubilee you went
and dwelt in the land of Midian[a] five weeks and one year and you returned to
2 Egypt on the second week in the second year in the fiftieth jubilee. •And you Acts 7:30
know what was related to you on Mount Sinai, and what Prince Mastema desired
to do with you when you returned to Egypt, on the way when you met him[b] at
3 the shelter. •Did he not desire to kill you with all of his might and save the
Egyptians from your hand because he saw that you were sent to execute judgment
4 and vengeance upon the Egyptians? •And I delivered you from his hand and you
did the signs and wonders which you were sent to perform in Egypt against
Pharaoh, and all his house, and his servants, and his people.

The plagues on Egypt Ex 7:1-12:39

5 And the LORD executed great vengeance upon them on account of Israel. And
he smote them with blood, and frogs, and lice, and dog flies; and evil boils which
break out (as) blisters; and their cattle with death; and hailstones with which he
destroyed everything which sprouted up for them; and with locust who ate the
remainder which was left from the hail; and with darkness, and (with death of)
the firstborn of men, and cattle; and upon all of their gods the LORD took vengeance
6 and he burned them[c] with fire. •And everything was sent in your hand to announce[d]
before it was done. And you related it to the king of Egypt before all of his
7 servants and before his people. •And everything happened according to your word,
ten great and cruel judgments came on the land of Egypt so that you might execute
8 vengeance upon it for Israel. •And the LORD did everything on account of Israel
and according to his covenant which he made with Abraham that he would take
vengeance upon them just as they had made them serve by force. Gen 15:13f.

The escape from Egypt and a discussion of Mastema's deeds Ex 7-14

9 And Prince Mastema stood up before you and desired to make you fall into the
hand of Pharaoh. And he aided the magicians of the Egyptians, and they stood
10 up and acted before you. •Thus we let them do evil, but we did not empower
11 them with healing so that it might be done by their hands. •And the LORD smote
them with evil wounds and they were unable to stand because we destroyed (their Ex 9:11
12 ability) to do any single sign. •And despite all the signs and wonders, Prince Ex 14:8f.
Mastema was not[e] shamed until he had become strong and called to the Egyptians
so that they might pursue after you with all the army of Egyptians, with their

---

48 a. The phrase "in the land of Midian" was
restored from the Lat. text. The Eth. MSS simply
read "there."

b. The reading "on the way where you met
him" is supplied by the Lat. text. The Eth. text is
corrupt at this point.

c. The writer is thinking of the icons of the
gods.

d. In his translation Charles suggested this emen-

dation. The Eth. MSS have "to do," which makes
a difficult reading. Perhaps one could retain the
Eth. text by assuming a command to work sympathetic magic: "Everything was sent in your hand
so that you might act (it out) before it was done."

e. The "not" appears in all MSS; Charles
omitted "not" from his text because he thought
that "it conflicts with the sense."

chariots, and with their horses, and with all the multitude of the peoples of Egypt.
13 And I stood between the Egyptians and Israel,[f] and we delivered Israel from
his hand and from the hand of his people. And the LORD brought them out through
14 the midst of the sea as through dry land. •And all of the people whom he brought
out to pursue after Israel the LORD our God threw into the middle of the sea into
the depths of the abyss beneath the children of Israel. Just as the men of Egypt
cast their sons into the river he avenged one million. And one thousand strong WisSol 18:5
and ardent men perished on account of one infant whom they threw into the midst
of the river from the sons of your people.
15 And on the fourteenth day, and on the fifteenth, and on the sixteenth, and on
the seventeenth, and on the eighteenth Prince Mastema was bound and shut up
16 from (coming) after the children of Israel so that he might not accuse them. •And
on the nineteenth day we released them so that they might help the Egyptians and
17 pursue after the children of Israel. •And he hardened their hearts and strengthened Ex 14:8
them. And it was conceived of by the LORD our God that he might smite the
18 Egyptians and throw them into the midst of the sea. •And on the fourteenth[g] day
we bound him so that he might not accuse the children of Israel on the day when
they were requesting vessels and clothing from the men of Egypt—vessels of
silver, and vessels of gold, and vessels of bronze—so that they might plunder the
Egyptians in exchange for the servitude which they subjected them to by force.
19 And we did not bring the children of Israel from Egypt in their nakedness.

The feast of Passover, its institution and observance   Ex 12f.

1 **49** Remember the commandment which the LORD commanded you concerning
Passover, that you observe it in its time, on the fourteenth of the first month, so
that you might sacrifice it before it becomes evening and so that you might eat it
2 during the night on the evening of the fifteenth from the time of sunset. •For on
this night there was the beginning of the feast and there was the beginning of joy.
You continued eating the Passover in Egypt and all of the powers of Mastema
were sent to kill all of the firstborn in the land of Egypt, from the firstborn of
Pharaoh to the firstborn of the captive maidservant who was at the millstone and
3 to the cattle. •And this is the sign which the LORD gave to them in every house
where they saw the blood of a year-old lamb upon its doors so that they would
not enter into the house to kill, they would pass over so that all who were in the
house might be saved because the sign of the blood was on its doors.
4 And the host of the LORD did everything which the LORD commanded them.
And they passed over all the children of Israel. And the plague did not come upon
5 them to destroy any life from them whether cattle or men or dogs. •And there
was a very great plague in Egypt. And there was no house in Egypt in which
6 there was no corpse and weeping and lamenting. •And all of Israel remained
eating the flesh of the Passover and drinking wine and praising and blessing and
glorifying the LORD the God of their fathers. And they were prepared to depart
from the yoke of Egypt and from evil slavery.
7 And you, remember this day all of the days[a] of your life and observe it from
year to year all the days of your life, once per year on its day according to all of
its law and you will not delay (one) day from (its) day or from (one) month to
8 (another) month. •For it is an eternal decree and engraved upon the heavenly
tablets for all of the children of Israel that they might observe it in each and every
year in its day once per year in all of their generations. And there is no limit of
days because it is ordained forever.

---

f. The Eth. MSS also insert "between you" to
this series. The "you" refers to Moses. A B read
"I stood between you, the Egyptians, and Israel."
C D read "I stood between the Egyptians, and
you, and Israel."
    g. "Fourteenth" is the reading of MS B. Charles

used that reading in his translation, but his Eth.
text had "seventeenth" in agreement with MSS A
D. MS C has "fifteenth."

49 a. A portion of the Lat. text begins at this
point and continues through 49:22a.

9 And (as for) the man who is purified and does not come so that he might
observe it on its appointed day to bring a gift which is acceptable before the LORD
and to eat and to drink before the LORD on the day of his feast, that man who is Num 9:13
purified and nearby shall be uprooted because he did not bring a gift of the LORD
10 in its (appointed) time. That man shall lift up sin upon himself. •So that the
children of Israel will be ones who come and observe Passover on its appointed
day on the fourteenth of the first month between the evenings from the third (part)
of the day until the third (part) of the night because two parts of the day are given
11 for light and one third for evening. •This is what the LORD commanded you so
that you might observe it between the evenings.
12 And it is not fitting to sacrifice it during any time of light except during the
time of the border of evening. And they shall eat it during the time of evening
until a third of the night. And what is left of all its flesh from the third of the
13 night and beyond, they shall burn with fire. •And it is not fitting that they should
boil it in water. And they shall not eat it raw but roasted in the fire, cooked[b] with
care, its head with its inner organs and with its feet. They shall roast it in fire
without breaking any of its bones within it because no bone of the children of
14 Israel will be broken. •Therefore the LORD commanded the children of Israel to
observe the Passover on its appointed day. And it is not fitting to break any bone
from it because it is the day of the feast and it is the day of the command. And
there is no passing over in it (one) day from (its) day or from month (to) month
because it shall be observed on the day of the feast.
15 And you command the children of Israel to observe the Passover in their days
in every year, once per year, on its appointed day. And it will come as an
acceptable memorial from before the LORD. And the plague will not come to kill
or to smite during that year when they have observed the Passover in its (appointed)
time in all (respects) according to his command.
16 And it is not fitting to eat it outside of the sanctuary of the LORD, but facing
the sanctuary of the LORD. And all the people of the congregation of Israel will
17 observe it in its (appointed) time. •And all the men who come on its day will eat
it in the sanctuary of your God before the LORD, whoever is twenty years or older, Ex 30:14
because thus it is written and decreed that they shall eat it in the sanctuary of the
LORD.
18 And whenever the children of Israel enter into the land which they will possess,
into the land of Canaan, they will set up the tabernacle of the LORD in the midst
of the land, in one of their tribes, until the sanctuary of the LORD is built upon
the land. And it will come to pass when[c] they come and observe the Passover in
the midst of the tabernacle of the LORD that they will sacrifice it before the LORD[d]
19 from year to year. •And in the days when a house is built in the name of the
LORD in the land of their inheritance, they shall go there and they shall sacrifice
the Passover at evening when the sun is setting on the third (part) of the day.
20 And they shall offer up its blood on the threshold of the altar. And its fat they Deut 16:5-7
shall place on the fire which is above the altar. And they shall eat its flesh cooked
in fire within the court of the house which is sanctified in the name of the LORD.
21 And they shall not be able to observe the Passover in their cities or in any district
except before the tabernacle of the LORD or before his house in which his name
dwells. And let them not stray from after the LORD.
22 And you, Moses, command the children of Israel so that they shall keep the
ordinance of the Passover just as it was commanded to you so that you might
relate to them its annual (occurrence) each year, both its period of days and the
feast of unleavened bread so that they might eat unleavened bread for seven days
so that they might observe its feast, and so that they might bring its gift, day by

---

b. "Cooked" is the MS reading. Charles emended
his text on the basis of the Lat. text to read "they
shall eat it."

c. The phrase "it will come to pass when" is
not found in the Lat. text or in Eth. MS A. Charles

put the phrase in his text, but removed it from his
translation.

d. The Lat. text also omits the phrase "that they
will sacrifice it before the LORD."

day, during those seven days to rejoice before the LORD upon the altar of your
23 God. •For this feast you observed with nervousness when you went out from
Egypt until you entered into the wilderness of Sur because you completed it on   Ex 15:22
the shore of the sea.

The laws pertaining to the sabbath   Ex 16:1

1 **50** And after this law I made you know the days of the sabbaths in the wilderness   CD 10.14-11.18
2 of Sin^a which is between Elim and Sinai. •And I also related to you the sabbaths
of the land on Mount Sinai. And the years of jubilee in the sabbaths of years I   Lev 25:8
related to you. But its year I have not related to you until you enter into the land
3 which you will possess. •And the land will keep its sabbaths when they dwell   Lev 26:34
upon it. And they will know the year of jubilee.
4   On account of this I ordained for you the weeks of years, and the years, and
the jubilees (as) forty-nine jubilees from the days of Adam until this day and one
week and two years. And they are still forty further years to learn the commands
of the LORD until they cross over the shore of the land of Canaan, crossing over
5 the Jordan to its western side. •And jubilees will pass until Israel is purified from
all the sin of fornication, and defilement, and uncleanness, and sin and error. And
they will dwell in confidence in all the land. And then it will not have any Satan
or any evil (one). And the land will be purified from that time and forever.
6   And behold the commandment of the sabbaths I have written for you and all
7 of the judgments of its law. •Six days you will work, but the seventh day is the   Ex 20:9f.
sabbath of the LORD your God. You shall not do any work in it, you, or your
children, or your manservant or your maidservant, or any of your cattle or the
8 stranger who is with you. •And let the man who does anything on it die. Every   CD 11.1f.
man who will profane this day, who will lie with his wife, and whoever will   CD 10.22f.
discuss a matter that he will do on it so that he might make on it a journey for
any buying or selling, and whoever draws water on it, which was not prepared   Neh 10:31;
for him on the sixth day, and whoever lifts up anything that he will carry to take   13:16f.
9 out of his tent or from his house, let him die. •You shall not do any work upon
the day of the sabbath except what you prepared for yourself on the sixth day to
eat and to drink and to rest and to observe a sabbath from all work of that day
and to bless the LORD your God who gave to you the day of festival and the holy
day. And a day of the holy kingdom for all Israel is this day among their days
10 always. •For great is the honor which the LORD gave to Israel to eat and to drink
and to be satisfied on this day of festival and to rest in it from all work of the
occupations of the children of men except to offer incense and to bring gifts and
11 sacrifices before the LORD for the days and the sabbaths. •This work alone shall
be done on the day of the sabbath in the sanctuary of the LORD your God so that
they might atone for Israel (with) continual gift day by day for an acceptable
memorial before the LORD. And so that he might accept them forever, day by
day, just as he commanded you.
12   And (as for) any man who does work on it, or who goes on a journey, or who   CD 12.5f.
plows a field either at home or any (other) place, or who kindles a fire, or who
rides on any animal, or who travels the sea in a boat, and any man who slaughters   1Mac 2:31-38
or kills anything, or who slashes the throat of cattle or bird, or who snares any   2Mac 6:11
13 beast or bird or fish, or who fasts or makes war on the day of the sabbath, •let
the man who does any of these on the day of the sabbath die so that the children
of Israel might keep the sabbath according to the commands of the sabbaths of
the land just as it was written in the tablets which he placed in my hands so that
I might write for you the law of each time and according to each division of its
days.
     The account of the division of days is finished here.

50 a. The Eth. text has written "sina" instead of
"sin."

MARTYRDOM AND ASCENSION
OF ISAIAH

(Second Century B.C.–Fourth Century A.D.)

A NEW TRANSLATION AND INTRODUCTION

BY M. A. KNIBB

The Ascension of Isaiah is a composite work which falls very obviously into two parts, chapters 1–5 and chapters 6–11; the first part is now known as the Martyrdom of Isaiah, the second bears the title the Vision of Isaiah. However, the Martyrdom of Isaiah is itself composite; included within these chapters is an independent section, 3:13–4:22, which is sometimes called the Testament of Hezekiah. Apart from these three main sections there are a number of additions and insertions which are to be attributed to the final editor of the whole book.

The Martyrdom of Isaiah (the basic material in 1:1–3:12 and 5:1–16) is the oldest element in the Ascension. It is a Jewish work which tells, in legendary form, of the martyr's death which Isaiah suffered at the hands of Manasseh. The narrative begins by describing how, in the twenty-sixth year of his reign, Hezekiah summoned his son Manasseh in order to instruct him, and how, on that occasion, Isaiah prophesied that Manasseh would ignore his father's words and, inspired by Beliar, bring about the death of the prophet (ch. 1). The remainder of the narrative describes the fulfillment of this prophecy. The wickedness of Manasseh's reign (2:1–6) leads Isaiah, in company with other prophets and faithful men, to flee from Jerusalem, first to Bethlehem, and then to a mountain in the desert (2:7–11). However, Isaiah's hiding place is discovered by a Samaritan who accuses Isaiah of treason and blasphemy (2:12a; 3:1–10). Manasseh has Isaiah arrested (3:11f.) and put to death (5:1–16). Included within this narrative is a digression (2:12b–16) which deals with the story of Micaiah son of Imlah (cf. 1Kgs 22:5–28).

A Christian addition to the Martyrdom of Isaiah, sometimes given the title the Testament of Hezekiah (3:13–4:22), is in reality presented as the account of a vision which Isaiah himself had experienced before his arrest by Manasseh. The account describes the life and death of the Beloved (3:13–20), the corruption of the Church (3:21–31), the reign of Beliar (4:1–13), and the second coming of the Lord (4:14–22).

The Vision of Isaiah (chs. 6–11) is likewise a Christian work. The introduction to the narrative tells how Isaiah, while present at the court of Hezekiah in the twentieth year of Hezekiah's reign, was carried up in his mind into heaven and had a vision (ch. 6). In the report of the vision itself (chs. 7–11) Isaiah describes his journey up through the seven heavens (7:1–9:26); it is this ascension which gives the title to the whole book. In the seventh heaven he sees the Lord and the Holy Spirit, and is given a glimpse of the glory of God; he himself joins in the worship which is offered to them (9:27–10:6). He then hears the Lord being commissioned by God to descend into the world (10:7–16); he sees the descent of the Lord through the seven heavens (10:17–31), his miraculous birth (11:1–16), his life, death, and resurrection (11:17–21), and his ascension once more into heaven (11:22–33). Verses 34–43 of chapter 11 form the conclusion to the vision and the book.

Texts[1]

The different elements within the Ascension of Isaiah were composed either in Greek or, in the case of the Martyrdom, in Hebrew, and at an early stage translated into Greek. The Greek text was translated into a number of different languages: Ethiopic, Latin, Slavonic, Coptic. Of these translations the Ethiopic is the most important, because it is only in Ethiopic that an entire version of the Ascension has survived.

The translation into Ethiopic of the Ascension of Isaiah, which was regarded in Abyssinia as a genuine work of the prophet, was probably undertaken as part of the translation into Ethiopic of the books of the Bible and Apocrypha. As such it is to be dated at some time after the introduction of Christianity into Abyssinia in the fourth century, but before the end of the sixth century.[2] A comparison of the Ethiopic translation with the fragment of the Greek text that has survived (see below) shows that on the whole the Ethiopic has faithfully rendered the original.[3] Many of the corruptions in the Ethiopic are to be attributed to faults in the underlying Greek, but there are also, of course, corruptions that are peculiar to the Ethiopic version. The following manuscripts of the Ethiopic version were used.

A   Bodleian Library, MS Aeth.d.13 (Dillmann's Catalogue, No. 7), 15th century, fols. 95–115.
B   British Library, Or. 501 (Wright's Catalogue, No. 25), 15th century, fols. 62–69.
C   British Library, Or. 503 (Wright's Catalogue, No. 27), 18th century, fols. 57–62.
D   Vatican Library, Eth. 263, 14th–15th century, fols. 85–104.
E   A fragment of the Ascension in an Abba Garima codex (a microfilm of the codex is deposited at the Hill Monastic Manuscript Library). The fragment covers 1:4–2:2, and its text is closely similar to that of D.

The Ethiopic text of the Ascension was first published in 1819 by R. Laurence; his edition consisted of a transcript of A, the only manuscript known at the time. Subsequently, critical editions of the text were published by A. Dillmann (1877) and by R. H. Charles (1900), in both cases based on the three manuscripts A, B, and C. Dillmann and Charles regarded A as the best manuscript and used it as their base text; Charles's edition contains a fair number of somewhat uncertain conjectural emendations.[4] D (unknown to Dillmann and Charles) is as important as A; and it often agrees with A. However, D sometimes supports the readings of B and C. The present translation of the Ascension is based on a fresh collation of these five Ethiopic manuscripts; in practice the translation often, but by no means always, follows Dillmann's edition of the text.

As has already been indicated, only a fragment of the Greek text of the Ascension has survived. The fragment, containing 2:4–4:4, was discovered in a papyrus of the Amherst collection dating from the fifth or sixth century. As will be recognized, the fragment covers both part of the original Martyrdom of Isaiah (the basic material in 1:1–3:12 and 5:1–16) and part of the inserted Christian section (3:13–4:22). Despite its limited extent the fragment is important because of the light it casts on the Ethiopic and Latin translations.[5]

Two quite different Latin translations of the Ascension are in existence. The first of these (Lat1) is represented by two fragments in a palimpsest belonging to the Vatican Library (Vatic. Lat. 5750) which were published by A. Mai in 1828.[6] The fragments, which cover

---

[1] For a survey of the textual evidence see A.-M. Denis, *Introduction*, pp. 170–76.

[2] On Ethiopic Bible translations see E. Ullendorff, *Ethiopia and the Bible* (The Schweich Lectures of the British Academy, 1967; London, 1968) pp. 31–59, especially pp. 55–59.

[3] Cf. B. P. Grenfell and A. S. Hunt, *The Amherst Papyri . . . Part 1. The Ascension of Isaiah and Other Theological Fragments* (London, 1900) p. 3.

[4] R. Laurence, *Ascensio Isaiae Vatis*; A. Dillmann, *Ascensio Isaiae, aethiopice et latine*; R. H. Charles, *The Ascension of Isaiah*.

[5] For further details see the excellent edition by Grenfell and Hunt (see n. 3). The text is also given by Charles (*Ascension*, pp. 84–95) and by A.-M. Denis (*Fragmenta Pseudepigraphorum Graeca* [PVTG 3; Leiden, 1970] pp. 108–13; Denis gives only the part which covers the Martyrdom, i.e. 2:4–3:12).

[6] A. Mai, *Scriptorum veterum nova collectio* 3.2 (1828) 238f. (not seen). The fragments were identified by B. G. Niebuhr and republished by I. Nitzsch ("Nachweisung zweier Bruchstücke einer alten lateinischen Übersetzung vom

2:14–3:13 and 7:1–19, form part of the original writing in the manuscript and date from the fifth or sixth century; the translation itself may have been made in the fifth century.

The Ethiopic, Greek, and Latin texts which have been mentioned so far, despite many differences of detail, all represent essentially the same textual tradition. This is not the case with the second Latin translation and the Slavonic, which both belong to a quite different textual tradition. These translations cover only chapters 6–11, the Vision of Isaiah, and thus provide evidence for the independent existence of this part of the Ascension.

The second Latin translation (Lat2) was first published by A. de Fantis in 1522 from a manuscript whose whereabouts is now unknown.[7] At the time when Laurence published the Ethiopic text of the Ascension in 1819 the edition by De Fantis of the Latin version appeared to have been lost, although Laurence knew of the edition because of a reference to it by Sixtus of Siena, who, in the sixteenth century, had condemned the Vision of Isaiah as a heretical work.[8] However, copies of the edition of De Fantis were discovered by J. C. L. Gieseler, who republished the text in 1832.[9]

The Slavonic translation[10] exists in two forms, of which the second is an abridgment of the first. The complete version (with which we are here concerned) is represented by a Russian manuscript of the twelfth century and by several later manuscripts of diverse origin. An edition of the Russian manuscript, with variants from a fourteenth-century Serbian manuscript, was published by A. Popov in 1879, and it was from this edition that N. Bonwetsch made the Latin translation of the Slavonic version which is given in Charles's edition of the Ascension.[11] The variants of the Slavonic version which are given in the notes in the present work have been taken from Bonwetsch, but it must be pointed out that his translation is now seen to be insufficiently precise.[12] An edition of the Russian manuscript, with the principal variants of the other manuscripts, was published by A. A. Šachmatov and P. A. Lavrov in 1899.[13]

The second Latin translation and the Slavonic clearly belong closely together and form a distinct recension of the Vision of Isaiah, but the relationship of the two translations to one another has been the subject of debate in recent years. Earlier this century it was argued that the character of the mistakes in Lat2 showed that this Latin version had been translated from a Slavonic text, and that the Slavonic version had been not merely adopted by the Bogomils (S. J. Ivanov), but also subjected to Bogomil editing (such was the view of E. Turdeanu); it was held that the translation into Latin was made by the Cathari.[14] In contrast, it has been argued by A. Vaillant[15] that those features in Lat2 which were held to show the dependence of Lat2 on the Slavonic are better explained in terms of the independent use by Lat2 and the Slavonic of a common Greek original, and that the differences between Lat2 and the Slavonic confirm this. Furthermore, the Vision of Isaiah, in the form known to us

---

Anabatikon Esaiou,'' *Theologische Studien und Kritiken* 3 [1830] 209–46). The text of the fragments is also given by Dillmann (*Ascensio,* pp. 83–85); J.-P. Migne (PL 13, cols. 629–32); Charles (*Ascension,* pp. 87–92, 102–8), and E. Tisserant (*Ascension d'Isaïe,* pp. 100–9, 142–54). The text of the first fragment (2:14–3:13, but with the exception of 3:13, since it is not part of the Martyrdom) is likewise reproduced in Denis (*Fragmenta,* pp. 111–13).

[7] A. de Fantis, *Opera nuper in lucem prodeuntia* (Venice, 1522). The Vision is included among several other religious writings.

[8] Cf. Laurence, *Ascensio,* p. 151.

[9] *Programma quo Academiae Georgiae Augustae prorector et senatus sacra pentecostalia anni MDCCCXXXII pie concelebranda indixerunt* (not seen). The text was reproduced by Dillmann (*Ascensio,* pp. 76–83), Charles (*Ascension,* pp. 98–139), and Tisserant (*Ascension,* pp. 133–214).

[10] The information given about the Slav. version is taken from the following sources: E. Kozak, "Bibliographische Übersicht der biblisch-apokryphen Literatur bei den Slaven," *Jahrbücher für Protestantische Theologie* 18 (1892) 138f.; N. Bonwetsch in A. Harnack, *Geschichte der altchristlichen Literatur* (Leipzig, 1893) vol. 1.2, p. 916; W. Lüdtke, "Beiträge zu slavischen Apokryphen," *ZAW* 31 (1911) 222f.; E. Turdeanu, "Apocryphes bogomiles et apocryphes pseudo-bogomiles," *RHR* 138 (1950) 214; A. Vaillant, *RESl* 42 (1963) 110; Turdeanu, *Apocryphes slaves et roumains,* pp. 70, 145–72.

[11] Cf. Charles, *Ascension,* pp. 98–139, and the statement on pp. xxivf.

[12] Cf. Vaillant, *RESl* 42 (1963) 110.

[13] A. A. Šachmatov and P. A. Lavrov, *Sbornik XII vĕka Moskovskago Uspenskago Sobora, I* (Moscow, 1899) (not seen).

[14] Cf. Turdeanu, *RHR* 138 (1950) 214–18; information about the views of J. Ivanov (given in his book *Bogomilski knigi i legendi* [Sofia, 1925]) has been taken from Turdeanu's article. The theory that Lat2 was translated from the Slav., which was put forward by Ivanov and accepted by Turdeanu, had earlier been presented by Lüdtke (*ZAW* 31 (1911) 223f.). See also Turdeanu, *Apocryphes slaves et roumains,* pp. 70–74, 150–72.

[15] Cf. Vaillant, *RESl* 42 (1963) 109–21.

from Lat2 and the Slavonic, contains no Bogomil doctrines, or even traces of Bogomil editing, even though the Vision was taken over by the Bogomils because they found in it similarities with their own doctrines. Rather, Lat2 and the Slavonic are independent translations of a Greek version of the Vision of Isaiah which had been revised to make it more orthodox (thus e.g. the account of the birth and life of the Lord in the Ethiopic version of 11:2–22 has been replaced in Lat2 and the Slavonic by a short statement which lacks the legendary features of the Ethiopic). The translation into Slavonic was made in the tenth or eleventh century. In a more recent article Turdeanu, while reaffirming the idea of Bogomil editing, apparently accepts the view that Lat2 is dependent on a Greek text.

Fragments of the Ascension of Isaiah in two Coptic dialects (Sahidic and Akhmimic) are also in existence. The fragments in Sahidic were published by L. T. Lefort;[16] some of the Akhmimic fragments were likewise published by Lefort, but a more complete version was later issued by P. Lacau.[17]

Finally, reference should be made to the Legend about Isaiah which was discovered by O. von Gebhardt in a twelfth-century Greek manuscript (Paris, Cod. Gr. 1534) and published by him in 1878.[18] The Legend is largely based on a Greek text of the Ascension of the type which is represented by the Ethiopic version, the Greek fragment, and Lat1, but the material has been completely recast. One very obvious feature is that the various incidents in the Ascension have been rearranged in a more coherent order, with the equivalent of the Vision (Eth. chs. 6–11) coming before the account of the martyrdom. The importance of the Greek Legend lies in the fact that it sometimes gives us the Greek wording underlying the Ethiopic and Lat1. A second manuscript of this Greek Legend is now known.[19]

Laurence, Dillmann, and Charles all included translations of the Ascension of Isaiah in their editions of the Ethiopic text (see n. 4); other translations have also been published in several languages.[20]

The translation given in the present volume has been made from the Ethiopic version on the basis of a fresh collation of the five Ethiopic manuscripts mentioned above. In the notes to the translation the more important variants of the Greek fragment and the first Latin translation, on the one hand, and of the second Latin translation and the Slavonic, on the other, have been given. Where appropriate, the evidence of the Greek Legend has also been cited.

Original language

In considering the question of the original language of the Ascension, it is necessary to distinguish between the Martyrdom and the remaining sections of the book. So far as the Martyrdom is concerned, there is good evidence for the view that is was composed in Hebrew. First, the form of the sentences in 1:1, 2:1, and 3:2 is typically Hebraic and points to the use of a construction with *way‘hî*. Second, in 2:1 there is a play on words linking the name Manasseh with the Hebrew verb "to forget" (*nāšāh*, cf. Gen 41:31) which is most naturally explained on the assumption that the Martyrdom was composed in Hebrew. Finally, in 5:1, 11 the Ethiopic states that Isaiah was sawed in half with "a wood saw" (i.e. a saw to cut wood). But the Ethiopic expression is ambiguous and could be translated "a wooden saw" (a saw made out of wood), and the corresponding passage in the Greek Legend (3:16) actually has this. The context and sense obviously require the meaning "a

[16] L. T. Lefort, "Coptica Lovaniensia (suite)," *Le Muséon* 51 (1938) 24–30, plate IVa.

[17] L. T. Lefort, "Fragments d'apocryphes en copte-akhmîmique," *Le Muséon* 52 (1939) 7–10, plate II; P. Lacau, "Fragments de l'Ascension d'Isaïe en copte," *Le Muséon* 59 (1946) 453–67.

[18] O. von Gebhardt, "Die Ascensio Isaiae als Heiligenlegende," *ZWT* 21 (1878) 330–53. The text was subsequently republished by Charles (*Ascension*, pp. 141–48); for a French translation see Tisserant (*Ascension*, pp. 217–26).

[19] Vatic. Palat. 27 of the 11th cent. (cf. Denis, *Introduction*, p. 172).

[20] English: Charles's translation was reproduced in *APOT*, vol. 2, pp. 155–62 (the Martyrdom only), and in TED; London, 1917 (Introduction by G. H. Box). Danish: E. Hammershaimb in *De Gammeltestamentlige Pseudepigrafer*, vol. 3 (1958) pp. 303–15 (not seen). French: R. Basset, *Les apocryphes Éthiopiens traduit en Français. III. L'Ascension d'Isaïe* (Paris, 1894); Tisserant, *Ascension* (see n. 6). German: G. Beer, *APAT*, vol. 2, pp. 119–27 (Martyrdom only); P. Riessler, *Altjüdisches Schrifttum ausserhalb der Bibel* (Augsburg, 1928) pp. 481–84, 1300f. (Martyrdom only); J. Flemming and H. Duensing in E. Hennecke and W. Schneemelcher, *Neutestamentliche Apokryphen* (Tübingen, 1964³) vol. 2, pp. 454–68 (ET, HSW, vol. 2, pp. 642–63); E. Hammershaimb, *JSHRZ* 2 (1973) 15–34 (Martyrdom only).

wood saw," but the evidence of the Greek Legend suggests that in the original a Hebrew construct-relationship was used, for which the translations "a wood saw" and "a wooden saw" would both be possible, and that the Hebrew was incorrectly translated into Greek as the latter.

The Hebrew Martyrdom of Isaiah was translated into Greek, and, as we have seen, a fragment of this Greek translation has survived. It is generally assumed that the remaining sections of the Ascension were composed in Greek, and there seems no reason to doubt this.

Composite character of the Ascension

It was stated at the outset that the Ascension of Isaiah is a composite work, and this view has been presupposed in the discussion so far. It is necessary here to say a little more about the evidence on which this view is based.[21]

The first point to be noticed is that a clear distinction has to be drawn between chapters 1–5 and chapters 6–11. On even a superficial reading it is obvious that chapters 6–11 are Christian in origin, and that chapters 1–5 at the very least include a good deal of Jewish material. But beyond this the evidence of the second Latin translation and the Slavonic translation shows that chapters 6–11 circulated independently of chapters 1–5 under the title "the Vision of Isaiah."[22] The awkwardness inherent in the fact that the events described in chapters 6–11 are set at an earlier stage in Isaiah's life than those described in chapters 1–5 suggests that chapters 6–11 not only circulated independently of chapters 1–5, but also had a quite independent origin. The combination of chapters 1–5 and 6–11 is the result of subsequent editorial activity.

In modern times chapters 1–5 have been given the title "the Martyrdom of Isaiah." So far as these chapters are concerned, 3:13–4:22 stands out as being an addition to the text. The basic narrative of chapters 1–5 is Jewish, but 3:13–4:22 is manifestly Christian. Apart from this, 3:13–4:22 forms a very harsh break in the narrative between 3:12 and 5:1. So much is clear; what is not clear is whether 3:13–4:22 originally formed part of an independent work, or whether it was composed specifically for the context which it now occupies as an addition to the narrative of the Martyrdom of Isaiah.

R. H. Charles took the view that 3:13–4:22 did at one time have an independent existence, and his view has been accepted by a number of scholars. Charles drew attention, on the one hand, to the fact that 1:2b–5a alludes, apparently with reference to 3:13–4:22, to a vision which Hezekiah saw in the fifteenth year of his reign; and, on the other hand, to the fact that the eleventh-century chronicler George Cedrenus quotes 4:12, but attributes the passage to "the Testament of Hezekiah." Charles concluded that 3:13–4:22 belonged originally to an independent work called the Testament of Hezekiah, although he thought the beginning and end of the work had been removed.[23]

There are, however, a number of difficulties with Charles's views about the Testament of Hezekiah. In the first place, the revelation given in 3:13–4:22 is attributed to Isaiah, not the king. This difficulty might be avoided by assuming that the revelation was transferred from Hezekiah to Isaiah when 3:13–4:22 was inserted in the Ascension; against this it must be pointed out that Cedrenus likewise places his quotation of 4:12 in the mouth of Isaiah ("In the Testament of Hezekiah, king of Judah, Isaiah the prophet says . . ."). Unless it is to be assumed that Cedrenus made a mistake, it is difficult to take his quotation of 4:12 as providing evidence for the existence of an independent work attached to the name of Hezekiah. It seems more likely that by "the Testament of Hezekiah" Cedrenus was referring to chapters 1–5 as a whole,[24] the first chapter of which does have the character of a testament

---

[21] For earlier discussions of this problem see Charles (*Ascension*, pp. xxxiv–xliii) and Tisserant (*Ascension*, pp. 42–61).

[22] In full "The Vision which Isaiah the prophet [Slav "the holy Isaiah, the prophet"], the son of Amoz, saw." Eth gives virtually the same heading at 6:1.

[23] Cf. Charles, *Ascension*, pp. xiiif., xlii, 2, 29. For the text of Cedrenus (quoted by Charles, p. 29) see I. Becker, *Georgius Cedrenus*, Corpus Scriptorum Historiae Byzantinae (Bonn, 1838) vol. 1, pp. 120f.

[24] Hammershaimb, *JSHRZ* 2 (1973) 17. Cf. also the critical comments of A. Caquot ("Bref commentaire du 'Martyre d'Isaïe,' " *Semitica* 23 [1973] 69) on the likelihood of the existence of an independent work called "the Testament of Hezekiah."

given by Hezekiah (see particularly n. g on 1:2). In the second place, it is not at all obvious that 1:2b–5a really does refer to 3:13–4:22; here the contrast with 1:5b–6a, which clearly was written with reference to chapters 6–11, is significant. Thus 1:2b–6a comes from the hand of the final editor of the Ascension and replaces an earlier narrative in which Hezekiah summoned Manasseh in order to instruct him about the fear of God and about how he should rule (see n. g on 1:2). In the present narrative we are told that Hezekiah summoned Manasseh in order to give him an account of a vision which he had seen about the judgment of the prince of this world and about faith in the Beloved (vss. 2b–5a), and an account of a vision which Isaiah had seen (vss. 5b–6a, referring to chs. 6–11). The combination of chapters 1–5 with chapters 6–11 gave the complete book predominantly the character of an apocalypse, and it was because of this that the final editor was led to describe Hezekiah as if he were an apocalyptic seer giving a revelation, rather than as a king giving practical advice to his son. It is unnecessary, therefore, to assume that 1:2b–5a refers to a particular section of the Ascension.

Even if the evidence for the view that 3:13–4:22 originally belonged to a work called the Testament of Hezekiah is unconvincing, it is nonetheless possible that this section of the Ascension has been taken from another, now unknown work. This question cannot be answered with any degree of certainty. All that can be said is that in its present form 3:13–4:22 presupposes the joining of chapters 1–5 (the Martyrdom) with chapters 6–11 (the Vision); 3:13 clearly alludes to chapters 6–11, and there are also a number of other links between 3:13–4:22 and the Vision.

The material that is left to the Martyrdom after the removal of 3:13–4:22 consists of 1:1–3:12 and 5:1–16 (minus a number of obvious editorial additions). At an earlier stage some scholars argued that chapter 1 did not form part of the original Martyrdom, but Charles[25] has convincingly shown that this chapter is presupposed by 2:1, even though it now contains a number of passages which stem from the final editor of the book (cf. vss. 2b–6a, 7, 13). The final editor was also responsible for a number of other passages in the Ascension (cf. 2:9; 4:19–5:1a; 5:15f.; 11:41–43).

The view that the Ascension is a composite work has been accepted by virtually every scholar who has studied this book, and the debate has really been concerned with the questions of the extent of the different elements within the Ascension, and the way in which they were put together. Since the time of Laurence, only two scholars, F. C. Burkitt and V. Burch, have maintained that the Ascension is a unity.[26] Burkitt (whose discussion is the more important) argued that it was impossible to remove the narrative portions of the Ascension (i.e. the Martyrdom) from the remainder of the work; rather he regarded the Martyrdom "as an integral part of the Ascension, constructed from the writer's knowledge of the early imperfect Greek translation of the Books of Kings, supplemented here and there by stray fragments of Jewish lore."[27] Burkitt believed that the unsatisfactory impression which the Ascension gives is due to the fact that the writer tried to deal in an apocalypse both with the last judgment and with the incarnation; the latter does not, in his view, really belong in the literary genre of an apocalypse. However, Burkitt's views do not really do justice to the very different character of 1:1–3:12, plus 5:1–16, 3:13–4:22, and chapters 6–11. Furthermore, even if it were to be accepted that it is not entirely possible to remove the Martyrdom from the Ascension, it would still be necessary to assume for the narrative portions of chapters 1–5 the use of a much more substantial Jewish substratum than Burkitt's "stray fragments of Jewish lore"; but in this case we are effectively dealing once more with sources. Burkitt's discussion does, nonetheless, have some importance inasmuch as it serves as a warning of the difficulties of recovering the text of the original Martyrdom. It cannot simply be assumed that what we are left with after the removal of the Christian elements in the Ascension and the obvious editorial additions is the Jewish Martyrdom of Isaiah; the possibility of Christian reworking of what appears to be Jewish material needs to be kept in mind.

---

[25] *Ascension*, pp. xl–xlii.
[26] F. C. Burkitt, *Jewish and Christian Apocalypses* (The Schweich Lectures of the British Academy, 1913; London, 1914) pp. 45–48, 72–74. V. Burch, "The Literary Unity of the Ascension of Isaiah," *JTS* 20 (1918–19) 17–23.
[27] *Jewish and Christian Apocalypses*, pp. 45f.

In the course of this discussion reference has been made to a number of titles which have been given to different parts of the Ascension, namely the Martyrdom (a modern title given to the basic material in 1:1–3:12 and 5:1–16), the Testament of Hezekiah (a title attached by George Cedrenus to a quotation of 4:12; it was thought by Charles to refer to 3:13–4:22, but has been taken here as a title of chs. 1–5), and the Vision of Isaiah (the title given to chs. 6–11 in the Eth. translation, the second Lat. translation, and the Slav.). It is convenient at this point to mention briefly the other titles that have been given to this book.[28]

The title conventionally given to the whole book—the Ascension of Isaiah—is the title which is found in the Ethiopic version at the beginning of the book. The same title is found twice in Epiphanius, on one occasion attached to a quotation of 9:35f.,[29] and, with reference to 11:34, in Jerome.[30] Since Jerome alludes elsewhere to the charges brought against Isaiah in 3:6–10,[31] it seems likely that he knew the Ascension in its complete form; but it is not clear from Epiphanius' use of the title whether he meant by it the whole book or only chapters 6–11. A similar uncertainty surrounds the use by Origen of the title "the Apocryphon of Isaiah";[32] Origen indicates that the story of the sawing of Isaiah in half was to be found in this "Apocryphon," but it is not clear what else it contained.

Date

It is difficult to date the different sections of the Ascension with any precision, but it is possible to give a general indication of when they were composed.[33]

Both Justin Martyr and Tertullian[34] refer to the tradition that Isaiah met his death by being sawed in half, and this same tradition about Isaiah was probably in the mind of the author of Hebrews 11:37. If this last point is correct, it suggests that the Martyrdom was composed not later than the first century A.D. But the narrative, like the stories of the martyrdom of Eleazar and the martyrdom of the seven brothers and their mother (2Mac 6:18–7:42), is probably much older than this and goes back ultimately to the period of the persecution of the Jews by Antiochus Epiphanes in 167–164 B.C.[35]

There are a number of indications which point to the view that 3:13–4:22 was composed at about the end of the first century A.D. This section of the Ascension is clearly later than the death of Nero in A.D. 68 because it refers to the expectation that Nero would come again as the "Antichrist" (see 4:2b–4a); presumably a little time would have been needed for this belief to develop, and this suggests a date at the earliest toward the end of the first century. On the other hand, the picture of the corruption of the Church which is given in 3:21–31 invites comparison with the descriptions of the Church given in 1 and 2 Timothy, 2 Peter, and 1 Clement 3; the similarities with these writings likewise suggest that 3:13–4:22 dates from about the end of the first century. Two other pieces of evidence also point toward this date. First, the author of 4 Baruch 9:18, 20, a work attributed to the early second century, betrays a knowledge of chapters 1–5 of the Ascension in their Christian form and may even have known the complete book; he gives in 9:18 what appears to be a loose quotation of 3:17 of the Ascension. Second, this same passage of the Ascension (3:17) provides a description of the emergence of the Beloved (Jesus) from the tomb which is similar to the description given in the Gospel of Peter 39f., a work which dates from the middle of the second century. Taken together, these indications suggest a date for the composition of 3:13–4:22 at about the end of the first century.

The date of the Vision of Isaiah is rather more difficult to determine. The fact that Jerome refers to 11:34, and that Epiphanius gives a quotation of 9:35f., suggests that this part of

[28] Cf. Charles, *Ascension*, pp. xii–xiv; Denis, *Introduction*, pp. 170f.

[29] The quotation of 9:35f. occurs in *AdvHaer* 67:3 (GCS 37 [1933] pp. 135f.); cf. *AdvHaer* 40:2 (GCS 31 [1922] p. 82).

[30] Cf. Jerome, *CommIsa* 64:4 (PL, vol. 24, col. 622).

[31] Jerome, *CommIsa* 1:10 (PL, vol. 24, col. 33).

[32] Origen, *CommMt* 13:57 (GCS 40, p. 24); cf. *EpAfr* 9 (PL, vol. 11, col. 65).

[33] For earlier discussions see Charles (*Ascension*, pp. xlivf.); Tisserant (*Ascension*, pp. 59f.).

[34] *DialTrypho* 120:5; Tertullian, *De patientia* 14 (Corpus scriptorum ecclesiasticorum latinorum 47 [1906] p. 21); *Scorpicae* 8 (Corpus scriptorum ecclesiasticorum latinorum 20 [1890] p. 161).

[35] Cf. O. Eissfeldt, *The Old Testament. An Introduction*, trans. P. R. Ackroyd (Oxford, 1966) p. 609.

the Ascension was in existence, at the latest, by the end of the third century A.D. But it is probably much older than the third century. The Acts of Peter 24, which dates from the second half of the second century, appears to quote 11:14, while the narrative of the miraculous birth of the Lord in 11:2–16[36] shows some similarities with the Protoevangelium of James, a work attributed to about A.D. 150. It thus seems likely that the Vision comes from the second century A.D. The date of composition was carried back even earlier (to the close of the first century) by Charles,[37] because he believed that 11:16 was quoted in Ignatius, Epistle to the Ephesians 19, "And hidden from the prince of this world were the virginity of Mary and her child-bearing and likewise also the death of the Lord." But it is not at all clear that Ignatius really is quoting from the Ascension.

It is not known when exactly the three sections of the Ascension were combined. The Greek fragment[38] (from the 5th–6th cent.), the palimpsest giving the text of the fragments of the first Latin translation (likewise from the 5th–6th cent.), and the Ethiopic translation (which was made some time during the 4th–6th cent.) all presuppose the existence of the complete work. But the character of the mistakes in the Greek fragment and the Latin palimpsest suggests that the complete work had already been in existence for some time when these manuscripts were copied. It thus seems likely that the three sections of the Ascension were brought together in the third or fourth century A.D., and this is confirmed by the fact that Jerome seems to have known the complete book. It is possible that there were two stages in this process, first the combination of 3:13–4:22 with the Martyrdom, and second the combination of the enlarged Martyrdom with the Vision.[39]

Provenance

It is generally assumed that the Martyrdom was composed in Palestine, and this seems to be correct given that the language of composition was almost certainly Hebrew, and given the hostility that is shown toward the Samaritans (cf. 2:12, 14; 3:1, 3). The fact that the legend is referred to in the rabbinic writings tends to support the view of Palestinian composition. There is no evidence to suggest where either 3:13–4:22 or the Vision was composed. It is also not known where the three parts of the Ascension were put together.

Historical and theological importance

The Martyrdom of Isaiah belongs with the martyr stories of the Old Testament (cf. Dan 3 and 6) and the Apocrypha (cf. 2Mac 6:18–7:42), but it is the latter which provides the closest parallel. The legend about the martyr's death which Isaiah suffered, like the stories about Eleazar and about the mother and her seven sons, goes back ultimately to the time of the persecution of Antiochus Epiphanes. Stories such as this were written to encourage the Jews to remain faithful to their religion, but unlike the somewhat older stories in Daniel 3 and 6 there is no happy ending; rather it is accepted that the cost of remaining faithful to God will indeed be death.

The narrative of the Martyrdom, as will be apparent from the references and notes appended to the translation, draws its inspiration to a very great extent from the Old Testament, and particularly from 1 and 2 Kings. The author takes over the contrast that is drawn in 2 Kings between the good Hezekiah and the wicked Manasseh, and there is no trace of the more sympathetic picture of Manasseh which is given in 2 Chronicles 33 and is presupposed in the Prayer of Manasseh. There is nothing in the Old Testament, of course, about the death of Isaiah, but the impetus for the development of the story of the martyrdom was perhaps provided by the note in 2 Kings 21:16 that "Manasseh shed innocent blood . . . in such great quantity that he flooded Jerusalem from end to end."

---

[36] The section 11:2–22 is attested only by the Eth. version and is omitted by the second Lat. translation and the Slav. But the primitive character of the narrative of the birth of Jesus suggests very strongly that the Eth. has preserved the original form of the text.

[37] *Ascension*, p. xlv.

[38] Although the Gk. fragment only covers 2:4–4:4, its text of 3:13 alludes to the content of chs. 6–11; the Gk. fragment thus presupposes the combination of the three elements in the Ascension to form the complete book we know.

[39] Cf. Eissfeldt, *Introduction*, p. 610.

The particular detail that Isaiah met his death by being sawed in half is at first sight somewhat surprising and has been the source of a good deal of speculation. But it is probably to be explained by the fact that the author here presupposes a tradition which is given in more complete form in the Talmuds. According to the tradition preserved in the Babylonian Talmud (Yeb 49b) Isaiah was put on trial by Manasseh on a variety of charges; included among these is the charge made in the Ascension (3:8f.) that Isaiah claimed to have seen God, despite the fact that Moses said that no one can see God and live. Isaiah, in order to escape, pronounced the name of God and, in consequence, was swallowed up by a cedar. The cedar was brought and sawed in half, and this caused the death of Isaiah. In this tradition Isaiah's death is interpreted as a punishment for saying, "and I live among a people of unclean lips" (Isa 6:5). Elsewhere the Babylonian Talmud only mentions the fact that Manasseh slew Isaiah (cf. b.Sanh 103b), but the Jerusalem Talmud (y.Sanh 10.2 [ed. M. Schwab, vol. 11, p. 49]) preserves a variant of the tradition linking Isaiah with a cedar. According to the Jerusalem Talmud Isaiah hid in a cedar to escape from Manasseh, but the fringes of his garment stuck out and betrayed his presence. Manasseh ordered the tree to be cut, and Isaiah was discovered.[40] It would appear that the Martyrdom presupposes a tradition, comparable to those in the Talmuds, according to which Isaiah took refuge in a tree trunk, and that it was for this reason that he is said to have met his death by being sawed in half. This view seems more likely than the view that the motif has been borrowed from non-Israelite sources. Thus a number of scholars believed that the motif of the sawing in half was Iranian in origin,[41] but it seems rather unlikely that the Iranian traditions which were held to provide the evidence for this view are sufficiently old for them to have influenced the author of the Martyrdom.[42] K. Galling linked the traditions about Isaiah in the Martyrdom with those about Isaiah and the cedar in the Talmuds and attempted to explain them as a reinterpretation of the mythology connected with Adonis,[43] but again this seems improbable.[44]

The demonology of the Martyrdom of Isaiah is a matter of some interest. The leader of the forces of evil, who has at his disposal a host of subordinate angels (2:2; cf. 5:9), is called variously Sammael (1:8, 11; 2:1; 5:15f.), Beliar (1:8f.; 2:4; 3:11; 5:1, [4], 15), and Satan (2:2, 7; 5:16). These three names, which are, of course, well known from other sources, appear to be used synonymously, and there is no real evidence to support the view of Charles that Sammael is subordinate to Beliar.[45] Two other names are also applied to this figure. The first, Malkira, is given in 1:8 as an additional name of Sammael and means in Hebrew "king of evil." The second, Matanbukus (2:4; there is a corrupt variant in 5:3, Mekembekus), apparently derives from a Hebrew expression meaning "gift of desolation."[46]

In different places both Beliar (1:9; 3:11; 5:1) and Sammael (2:1) are said to dwell in the heart of Manasseh, and it is under the inspiration of Beliar (or Sammael) that Manasseh, at the instigation of a Samaritan, has Isaiah put to death. This Samaritan is presented in the narrative as the agent of Beliar. The exact form of his name poses a particular problem. In the Greek fragment the name occurs as Belicheiar, Becheira, Melcheira, and Belchira; in the Latin palimpsest as Bechira; in the Ethiopic in a variety of forms, of which the most important are Belkira or Balkira, and Melkira or Malkira; in the Coptic as Belch[ira]; and finally in the Greek Legend as Melchias or Becheiras[47] (see the notes on 2:5, 12, 16; 3:1, 6, 11; 5:2, 3, 4, 5, 8, 12, 15, where the full evidence is given). Despite the wide range of the evidence for this name, it seems clear that we have to do essentially with only two

---

[40] For other Jewish traditions about Manasseh and Isaiah see L. Ginzberg, *The Legends of the Jews* (Philadelphia, 1946) vol. 6, pp. 370–76.

[41] The evidence for this view is summarized in Charles, *Ascension*. pp. xlviif. Cf. recently M. Philonenko, "Le Martyre d'Ésaïe et l'histoire de la secte de Qoumrân," *Pseudépigraphes*, vol. 1, p. 10.

[42] Cf. Caquot, *Semitica* 23 (1973) 87–89. V. Nikiprowetzky ("Pseudépigraphes de l'Ancien Testament et manuscrits de la Mer Mort: Réflexions sur une publication récente," *REJ* 128 [1969] 12f.) thinks that although the traditions about Isaiah in the Martyrdom were not based on Iranian sources, those in the Talmuds were.

[43] K. Galling, "Jesaia-Adonis," *Orientalistische Literaturzeitung* 33 (1930) cols. 98–102.

[44] Cf. Caquot, *Semitica* 23 (1973) 86f.

[45] *Ascension*, p. 7.

[46] Caquot (*Semitica* 23 [1973] 75) thinks the variant given in 5:3, Mekembekus, is preferable and argues that the name derives from a Hebrew expression meaning "He who creates tears." But this seems less likely.

[47] The story of the Martyrdom is given in ch. 3 of the Greek Legend, and "Melchias the false prophet" is mentioned in vss. 5, 7, 17, 18. But in vs. 10 there is a reference to "Melchias and Becheiras the false prophets."

alternatives, a name such as Belch(e)ira or Becheira, and a name such as Melcheira, and that one is an ancient variant or corruption of the other. The task is to discern the original form of the name and how the range of evidence for this name is to be explained.

A number of scholars have argued that the name of the Samaritan is derived from the Hebrew *bᵉḥîr-raᶜ*, "the elect of evil,"[48] and this would appear to be correct despite an apparent difficulty. The Greek variant Becheira (2:16; 3:1; cf. Becheiras in Greek Legend 3:10) and the Latin Bechira can readily be explained in terms of such a Hebrew name, but there is strong evidence in the Greek, Ethiopic, and Coptic versions, as well as in the Greek Legend (Melchias), for the occurrence of an *l* at the end of the first syllable of the name, and it is not so obvious that a form such as Belchira (Gk. 3:11) derives from the Hebrew *bᵉḥîr-raᶜ*. However, Caquot has pointed out that a superfluous *l* is also found in the name Melchol, the Septuagint form of the Hebrew *mîcāl*,[49] and in any case it would be easy in the Ascension for an *l* to be introduced in view of the occurrence in the same context of a name with a similar beginning, i.e. Beliar.

The greater part of the evidence from the various translations points to the view that the name of the Samaritan was in Hebrew *bᵉḥîr-raᶜ*, and that this passed into Greek as Becheira, and then as Belch(e)ira, but there is some evidence for an alternative name (cf. Gk. 3:6, Melcheira; similarly the Eth., MS D in 5:2, 3, 8, 12, 15 and MS A in 5:8, 12; Greek Legend, Melchias) and it remains to be asked how this is to be explained. The variants of this type point back to a Hebrew *malkira'*, "the king of evil," and this name also occurs as an additional name of Sammael in 1:8. There are two factors which could have contributed to the appearance of Melcheira as an alternative to Belcheira. The first is that it would not be difficult for the labials *B* and *M* to be confused; a comparable instance is found in 1 Enoch 6:7, where the Aramaic name *mᵉṭarʾēl* occurs in one Greek version and in the Ethiopic as Batriel. The second is that there is a tendency in the narrative for Beliar (or Sammael) and his human agent to be confused; in 5:4–9 the Samaritan is actually presented as the devil in human form; and in view of this it is perhaps hardly surprising that he should in some instances be given a name (*malkiraᶜ*) which also occurs as an additional name of Sammael.

In the present translation the name has been consistently given as Belkira, a transliteration of the Ethiopic form which appears to come closest to the original Hebrew, but all the variant spellings which the different translations attest have been supplied in the notes.

A study of the demonology of the Martyrdom led D. Flusser to the view that it reflected the dualistic theology of the Dead Sea community. He further argued that the author projected the religious disputes of his own day into the period of Isaiah, and that there are a number of parallels between the persons and events mentioned in the Martyrdom and those mentioned in the documents of the Qumran sect. In his view Isaiah represents the Teacher of Righteousness, Manasseh the Wicked Priest, and Belkira (interpreted as *bᵉḥîr-raᶜ*, "the elect of evil") the Teacher of the Lie. The withdrawal of Isaiah and his fellow prophets from Jerusalem to a mountain in a desert place corresponds to the withdrawal of the community to the wilderness; the arrest of Isaiah corresponds to the persecution of the community; and the command to Isaiah's followers to go to the district of Tyre and Sidon (5:13) corresponds to the flight of the community to the land of Damascus.[50] Flusser's views were accepted by J. van der Ploeg[51] and by M. Philonenko; but the latter, although accepting the main thrust of Flusser's arguments, offered a distinctive interpretation of his own. According to Philonenko, who accepts the views of A. Dupont-Sommer as to the origins of the Qumran community, the story of the Teacher of Righteousness, at least in its final stages, was a drama of three persons: the Teacher of Righteousness himself, and his opponents, Aristobulus II and Hyrcanus II. But the Martyrdom of Isaiah is also a drama of

[48] Cf. G. H. Box in TED, p. xvii. This explanation is accepted by D. Flusser, *IEJ* 3 (1953) 35 (see n. 50); Philonenko, *Pseudépigraphes*, vol. 1, p. 7; Caquot, *Semitica* 23 (1973) 75. The explanation suggested by W. Gesenius, *Theologische Studien und Kritiken* 3 [1830] 244; cf. Charles, *Ascension*. p. 14), that the name is derived from *belqiryâh = bᵉᶜal qiryâh* = "lord of the world," is impossible.

[49] *Semitica* 23 (1973) 75.

[50] Flusser, *IEJ* 3 (1953) 34–47. See also H. Burgmann, "Gerichtsherr und Generalankläger: Jonathan und Simon," *RB* 9 (1977) 28–33, 70–72.

[51] J. van der Ploeg, "Les manuscrits du Désert de Juda: Études et découvertes récentes," *BO* 11 (1954) 154f.

three persons: Isaiah, Manasseh, and the false prophet Belkira. Philonenko identifies Isaiah with the Teacher of Righteousness, Manasseh with Aristobulus II, and Belkira with Hyrcanus II, the person he, following Dupont-Sommer, believes to be the Wicked Priest. Furthermore, although Flusser specifically rejected the suggestion that we should conclude from the fact that Isaiah was martyred that the Teacher of Righteousness was executed by his opponents, Philonenko believes that the Martyrdom of Isaiah only makes sense if the Teacher of Righteousness was himself martyred.[52] Other scholars have accepted that there is a connection between the Martyrdom of Isaiah and the Qumran community, but without going into details.[53]

In comment on these views it must be said that although the idea that the Martyrdom of Isaiah offers a veiled history of the Qumran community is not impossible, it does seem rather unlikely. The Martyrdom is quite different in form from those Qumran writings, i.e. the biblical commentaries, which quite deliberately set out to reapply the Old Testament text to the events of the time in which the Qumran community existed, and in itself the Martyrdom offers no clue that it is to be interpreted in the way suggested by Flusser and Philonenko. The particular theory offered by Philonenko is also open to question on the grounds that an increasing number of scholars, if not the majority, are of the opinion that the Wicked Priest is to be identified, not with Hyrcanus II, but with either Jonathan or Simon.

Even if the Martyrdom does not provide a veiled history of the Qumran community, it might still be argued that this is a Qumran work. But although the dualistic theology of the Martyrdom is not out of accord with that contained in the Qumran writings, the distinctive language and theological emphasis of these writings are lacking. It thus seems unlikely that the Martyrdom is a sectarian document, and the most that could be said is that it was a writing used by the Qumran community. But, in fact, no traces of the Martyrdom have been found among the Qumran writings.[54]

The Martyrdom has the style of a narrative, but 3:13–4:22 is cast in the form of a prophecy given by Isaiah. The prophecy is linked rather awkwardly to the narrative (cf. 3:13) under the pretense that the giving of the prophecy was the reason for Beliar's anger with Isaiah. However, although presented as a revelation of the future, half of this material (3:13–31) is pseudo-prophecy and refers to events that at the time this passage was written had either already taken place (the life and death of the Beloved, 3:13–20) or were still in existence (the corruption of the Church, 3:21–31); it is only when the author refers to the reign of Beliar (4:1–13) and the second coming of the Lord (4:13–18) that we have genuine prophecy.

The description of the corruption of the Church (3:21–31) casts an interesting light on conditions in the area in which this section of the Ascension was written and provides a clue as to the purpose of its composition. The author, like the authors of 1 and 2 Timothy and 2 Peter, was concerned to warn his readers in no uncertain terms of the dangers which faced the Christian community. At the same time he wished to encourage them by insisting that the end of this age was near; the Church will be affected by false teaching and will suffer at the hands of wicked elders who seek office for the sake of money, but this will occur at the "approach" of the Beloved (3:21f.), i.e. when his second coming is near, and will be a sign of "the completion of the world" (4:1). The reign of Beliar, the length of which has been predetermined (4:12), will shortly begin, and then the Lord will come again both to punish Beliar and his hosts (4:14), and impious men (4:18), and to reward those Christians who have remained faithful to him (4:15–17). It may be observed that what is said here in a Christian context about Beliar provides a theological link with the surrounding narrative of the Martyrdom, where, as we have seen, a good deal of attention is paid to the role of this figure.

The Vision of Isaiah belongs, from a literary point of view, among the apocalyptic writings, and more precisely among those which take the form of an account of a heavenly

---

[52] Philonenko, *Pseudépigraphes*, vol. 1, pp. 1–10 (see n. 41).

[53] Cf. R. Meyer, "Himmelfahrt und Martyrium des Jesaja," *RGG*³, vol. 3, col. 336; L. Rost, *Judaism outside the Hebrew Canon. An Introduction to the Documents*, trans. D. E. Green (Nashville, 1976) p. 151.

[54] Cf. the comments of Hammershaimb, *JSHRZ* 2 (1973) 19; Nikiprowetzky, *REJ* 128 (1969) 5–13.

journey. Perhaps the best-known example of this type is to be found in the Similitudes of Enoch (1En 37–71), but the closest parallels to the Vision of Isaiah are the accounts of journeys through several heavens in the Testament of Levi 2:6–3:10, 3 Baruch, and 2 Enoch. However, the Vision of Isaiah is unlike many earlier apocalypses: There is little emphasis on the end of this age; and the author is more concerned to describe the heavens and to give an account of past events, especially the life and death of the Lord.

The author's purpose in writing the Vision seems to have been twofold. On the one hand he wished to encourage and reassure his readers by describing the blessings which awaited them in heaven. A good deal of attention is paid to the heavenly robes which the righteous will put on (a symbol of the transformation they will undergo in heaven), and to the crowns which they will wear and the thrones on which they will sit; the thrones are symbols of the fact that the righteous dead in heaven will share in the reign of Jesus, and the crowns are symbols of the reward which faithful Christians, particularly martyrs, will enjoy (see esp. 9:9–18, 24–26, and nn. i–k on 9:9f.). As further encouragement, the author hints that the righteous dead will enjoy a higher status in heaven than the angels (cf. 9:28, 33, 38, 41, and n. x[2] on 9:38).

On the other hand the author wished to present, as well as defend, certain views about the Trinity and the incarnation. What he has to say about the Trinity is of particular interest. In 9:27–42 Isaiah describes how, in the seventh heaven, he saw "the Lord" (9:27–32) and the Holy Spirit (9:33–36), and was given a glimpse of the glory of God (9:37–42). The Holy Spirit is described as an angel (9:36), as he is, in fact, frequently throughout the Ascension (see the list of references at n. s on 3:15). What is perhaps of greater interest is that a superior status is attributed to the Father in that "the Lord" and the angel of the Holy Spirit are presented as worshiping him (9:40).

In the last part of the Vision the author describes how Isaiah saw the descent of "the Lord" through the seven heavens, his birth, life, death, resurrection, and ascension (10:7–11:33), and what is said here is of interest from the point of view of his beliefs about the incarnation. Two emphases stand out. The author is concerned to explain how it was that the Lord's true nature remained concealed from the angels in the lower heavens (10:20–27), from the prince of this world and his hosts (10:29–31), and from men (11:14, 19). It is only when "the Lord" begins his ascent through the heavens that at last his true nature is recognized (11:23f.). The author's explanation for the fact that the identity of "the Lord" remained concealed (11:16) is that at the command of the Father (10:7–15) he progressively transformed himself. The author is also concerned to defend the reality of the Virgin Birth (11:2–16). This passage forms part of that section (11:2–22) which is attested only by the Ethiopic version, and is lacking in the second Latin translation and the Slavonic. But the primitive character of the narrative makes it difficult to believe that it did not form part of the original text. The concern to defend the reality of the Virgin Birth suggests that in this respect the Vision is to be compared with such writings as the Protoevangelium of James (which has often been seen to possess similarities with the Vision) and, in general, with the Infancy Gospels.[55]

It has been argued recently, on the basis of a number of parallels between the Vision of Isaiah and certain gnostic sources, that the Vision comes from "semi-Christian circles" or "Christian-gnostic circles."[56] However, although parallels do exist, it is not clear how far it is right to regard the Vision as a gnostic work.

[55] Cf. the comments of O. Cullmann on the purposes of the Infancy Gospels in HSW, vol. 1, p. 367. (Also cf. OdesSol, introduced and translated in the present collection. —J.H.C.)

[56] Cf. A. K. Helmbold, NTS 18 (1972) 222–27.

SELECT BIBLIOGRAPHY

Charlesworth, *PMR*, pp. 125–30.
Delling, *Bibliographie*, p. 166.
Denis, *Introduction*, pp. 170–76.

Caquot, A. "Bref commentaire du 'Martyre d'Isaïe,' " *Sem* 23 (1973) 65–93.
Charles, R. H. *The Ascension of Isaiah*. London, 1900.
Dillmann, A. *Ascensio Isaiae, aethiopice et latine*. Leipzig, 1877.
Flusser, D. "The Apocryphal Book of *Ascensio Isaiae* and the Dead Sea Sect," *IEJ* 3 (1953) 34–47.
Hammershaimb, E. "Das Martyrium Jesajas," *JSHRZ* 2 (1973) 15–34.
Helmbold, A. K. "Gnostic Elements in the 'Ascension of Isaiah,' " *NTS* 18 (1972) 222–27.
Laurence, R. *Ascensio Isaiae Vatis*. Oxford, 1819.
Philonenko, M. "Le *Martyre d'Ésaïe* et l'histoire de la secte de Qoumrân," *Pseudépigraphes*, pp. 1–10.
Tisserant, E. *Ascension d'Isaïe*. Documents pour l'étude de la Bible; Paris, 1909. Pp. 100–9, 142–54.
Vaillant, A. "Un Apocryphe pseudo-bogomile: La Vision d'Isaïe," *RESl* 42 (1963) 109–21.

(After the preparation of this contribution, the following volume of collected essays appeared: Turdeanu, E. *Apocryphes slaves et roumains de l'Ancien Testament* [SVTP 5; Leiden, 1981]. In this book see the following: "Apocryphes bogomiles et apocryphes pseudo-bogomiles" [pp. 1–74], "La Vision d'Isaïe: Tradition orthodoxe et tradition hérétique" [pp. 145–72]; and the additional notes on pp. 436f., 438f. [with reference to an edition and translation of the Slav. version of the Vision of Isaiah by A. Vaillant].)

ABBREVIATIONS USED IN FOOTNOTES ON PAGES 156–176:

The following abbreviations have been used; for more details see Texts.

Eth	=	the Eth. version of the Ascen Is on which the following translation is based.
A, B, C, D, E	=	manuscripts of the Eth. version.
Cop	=	the Cop. version of the Ascen Is.
Gk	=	the Gk. fragment.
Lat1	=	a Lat. version of the Ascen Is.
Lat2	=	a second Lat. version of the Vis Is.
Slav	=	tthe Slav. version of the Vis Is.

THE ASCENSION OF ISAIAH THE PROPHET

1. THE MARTYRDOM OF ISAIAH[a]

Hezekiah summons Manasseh

1 **1** In the twenty-sixth year[a] of his reign Hezekiah king of Judah summoned[b]
2 Manasseh his son,[c] for he was his only son.[d] •He summoned him in the presence
   of Isaiah, the son of Amoz, the prophet,[e] and in the presence of Josab[f] the son of
   Isaiah, in order to hand over to him the words of righteousness which the king
3 himself had seen,[g] •and (the words concerning) the eternal judgments,[h] and the
   torments of Gehenna,[i] and the prince of this world,[j] and his angels, and his
4 authorities, and his powers, •and the words concerning faith in the Beloved[k] which
5 he himself had seen in the fifteenth year of his reign during his sickness.[l] •And
   he handed to him the written words which Samnas[m] the secretary had written out,[n]
   and also those which Isaiah the son of Amoz had given to him, and to the prophets

1Pet 3:22
Eph 6:12
Mk 1:11; 9:7
Mt 12:18
Eph 1:6

a. The title "The Ascension of Isaiah the Prophet" is given in the Eth. MSS; the heading "1. The Martyrdom of Isaiah" has been supplied by the editor. Contrast the heading at ch. 6.

1 a. Greek Legend 1:1 "twenty-fifth"; Cop "sixteenth." "Sixteenth" would link more appropriately with the date given for Hezekiah's vision in vs. 4, but does not fit with the mention of Hezekiah's twentieth year in vs. 6.

b. Lit. "of the reign of Hezekiah king of Judah he summoned."

c. Greek Legend 1:1 adds "who was eleven years old," but this is inconsistent with its dating of the events in the twenty-fifth year of Hezekiah's reign. According to 2Kgs 18:2 and 21:1 Hezekiah reigned for twenty-nine years, and Manasseh was twelve years old when he began to reign; this would mean that Manasseh was only eight in Hezekiah's twenty-fifth year.

d. Lit. "for he alone (was) to him."

e. The translation assumes that "the prophet" refers to Isaiah, but it could refer to Amoz; this latter view would imply that Amoz, the father of Isaiah (Isa 1:1), was identified with the prophet Amos, an identification that is explicitly made in 4:22. B reads "Isaiah the prophet, the son of Amoz the prophet." In late Jewish tradition Amoz was regarded as a prophet, while in Christian tradition Amoz and Amos were frequently confused with one another; in the LXX and the Eth. OT the names Amoz and Amos are spelled the same way.

f. I.e. Shear-jashub, cf. Isa 7:3. The Eth. Josab (the variant Joseb occurs throughout) is the form used in the Eth. version of Isa 7:3.

g. Vss. 2b–6a are a Christian interpolation in the original Martyrdom whose purpose is in part to link together the different elements in the Ascension; vss. 5b–6a, which describe a vision of Isaiah, allude clearly to chs. 6–11; vss. 2b–5a, which describe a vision seen by the king, have sometimes been thought to allude to 3:13–4:22, but in fact 3:13–4:22 is presented as a revelation given through Isaiah, not the king. What appears to be a more original version of the scene described in ch. 1 is preserved in the *Opus Imperfectum*, an

incomplete work on Mt attributed to the sixth century. According to this work it was when Hezekiah fell ill that he summoned Manasseh; his purpose was to give him commands (for which cf. vss. 6b, 7) about the fear of God, and about how he should rule. The account in the *Opus Imperfectum* has, to a greater extent than the account in the Ascension, the character of a testament scene, i.e. a scene in which a great figure gives his last commands to his children or followers on his deathbed. For the text (quoted in Charles, *Ascension*, pp. 8f.) see PG, vol. 56, col. 626.

h. B C D "the judgments of this world."

i. Gehenna is mentioned elsewhere in AscenIs only in 4:14.

j. "and the prince of this world": translation based on a minor correction of the text, cf. 10:29; B C D "and [D "which is"] the place of punishment of this world"; A "which is the eternal place of punishment."

k. The title "the Beloved" occurs frequently in AscenIs as a Christian designation of Jesus. Thus it is used in the section 3:13–4:22 (cf. 3:13, 17, 18; 4:3, 6, 9, 18, 21) and in chs. 6–11 (cf. 7:17, 23; 8:18, 25; 9:12); the remaining occurrences (1:4, 5, 7, 13; 5:15) are all to be attributed to the Christian editor of AscenIs.

l. Cf. 2Kgs 20:1–11; Isa 38; 2Chr 32:24. The date "in the fifteenth year" has been deduced from the OT; Hezekiah reigned for twenty-nine years (2Kgs 18:2), but at the time of his sickness was promised a further fifteen years of life (2Kgs 20:6). There is no OT tradition that Hezekiah saw a vision when he was ill, but the author was perhaps building on the tradition that he was given a "sign" (cf. 2Kgs 20:8; 2Chr 32:24).

m. I.e. Shebnah, cf. 6:17 and 2Kgs 18:18. The Eth. Samnas (var. Samenas) reflects the spelling of the name in the Eth. OT and the LXX.

n. These words appear to imply that Hezekiah dictated the content of his vision to Samnas; they are perhaps based on the tradition in Isa 38:9 that Hezekiah composed a "writing" (so the Heb.; JB "canticle") at the time of his sickness. The remainder of vs. 5 and vs. 6a refer to VisIs, chs. 6–11.

also, that they might write out and store up with him what he himself had seen in the house of the king° concerning the judgment of the angels, and concerning the destruction of this world, and concerning the robes of the saints^p and their going out,^q and concerning their transformation and the persecution and ascension 6 of the Beloved. •In the twentieth year of the reign of Hezekiah Isaiah had seen the words of this prophecy and had handed them to Josab his son. And^r while (Hezekiah) was giving his commands, with Josab the son of Isaiah standing by, 7 Isaiah said to Hezekiah the king, and not only in the presence of Manasseh did he say (it) to him, "As the LORD lives^s whose name has not been transmitted to this world, and as the Beloved of my LORD lives, and as the Spirit which speaks in me lives,^t all these commands and these words will have no effect on Manasseh your son, and through the deeds of his hands, tormented in body I will depart. 8 And Sammael Malkira^u will serve Manasseh and will do everything he wishes, 9 and he will be a follower of Beliar^v rather than of me. •He will cause many in Jerusalem and Judah to desert the true faith, and Beliar^w will dwell in Manasseh, 10 and by his hands I will be sawed in half." •And when Hezekiah heard these words, he wept very bitterly, and tore his robes, and threw earth on his head, and 11 fell on his face.^x •And Isaiah said to him, "Sammael's^y plan against Manasseh is 12 complete; there will be no benefit to you from this day."^z •And Hezekiah thought 13 in his heart that he would kill Manasseh his son, •but Isaiah said to Hezekiah, "The Beloved^a2 has made your plan ineffective, and the thought of your heart will not come about; for with this calling have I been called, and the inheritance of the Beloved will I inherit."^b2

Margin references:
10:12
11:19f., 22-32
3:13, 18
6:1
7:37; 8:7
9:36; Mt 10:20
1:6; 2:1
2Kgs 21:9;
2Chr 33:9
2:1; 3:11; 5:1

Manasseh's wicked reign

1 **2** And it came about that after Hezekiah had died, and Manasseh had become king, (Manasseh) did not remember the commands of Hezekiah his father, but 2 forgot^a them; and Sammael dwelt in Manasseh and clung closely to him. •And

Margin references:
1:6f.
1:9; 3:11; 5:1

o. A D E "what the king alone had seen."

p. D E "the righteous." The heavenly robes which the saints put on after death are a symbol of their transformed state; they are mentioned frequently in the Christian portions of AscenIs; cf. 3:25; 4:16f.; 7:22; 8:14, 26; 9:2, 9–11, 17f., 24–26; 11:40. Cf. also 2Cor 5:1–4; Rev 3:4f.; 6:11; 7:9, 13f.; 4Ezra 2:39, 44f.

q. I.e. their departure from this life. But Greek Legend 1:2 more plausibly refers both the "going out" and the "transformation" to the Beloved; hence perhaps read "and concerning the going out, and the transformation, and the persecution and ascension of the Beloved." In this case the "going out" will be the descent of the Beloved through the seven heavens, cf. 3:13; 10:7–31.

r. The narrative of the Martyrdom is resumed here from vs. 2a.

s. "As the LORD lives": the common OT oath formula, cf. e.g. 1Sam 14:39, 45. I have rendered Eth. Ɜgzi²ᵃbāḥer by "LORD"; Ɜgzi²ᵃ by "Lord"; and Āmlak by "God." The first of these commonly translates Heb. "Yahweh" (LXX: kurios), the last the Heb. "Elohim" (LXX: theos).

t. "and as the Beloved . . . in me lives": Christian editorial addition, see n. k on vs. 4.

u. According to Jewish tradition Sammael was originally one of the chief archangels, but after inciting the serpent to tempt Eve he became the leader of the Satans. It is in such a role that he appears in AscenIs, where Sammael seems to be merely another name for Beliar (see n. v). Sammael is mentioned also in 1:11; 2:1; 3:13; 5:15f.; 7:9; 11:41 (in the last passage called Sammael Satan). Malkira, used here as an additional name for

Sammael, means in Heb. "king of evil"; elsewhere this name occurs as a variant of Belkira, the name of the Samaritan opponent of Isaiah (see 2:12); cf. Intro.

v. Beliar: a variant form of Belial, a common name for the devil in the period, cf. 2Cor 6:15; Jub 1:20; 15:33; TLevi 3:3; 18:12; 19:1; TDan 5:1, 10f. (and pass. in T12P); 1QS 1.17, 23f.; CD 4.13, 15; 5.8. In AscenIs Beliar is mentioned elsewhere in 1:9; 2:4; 3:11, 13; 4:2, 4, 14, 16, 18; 5:1, (4), 15.

w. Greek Legend 1:9 "Satan."

x. Conventional signs of distress, cf. 2Sam 13:19, 31; Job 2:12.

y. Greek Legend 1:11 has "Satan" for "Sammael."

z. "from this day": so B C; D E "from that day" (Greek Legend 1:11f. takes the phrase with the following vs., "And at that time Hezekiah thought . . ."); A "from those words," an allusion to the commands mentioned in vss. 6b, 7.

a2. "The Beloved": the use of the title betrays Christian influence, see n. k on vs. 4.

b2. "and the inheritance . . . inherit": Christian editorial addition, as the use of the title "the Beloved" indicates; as an heir of Jesus, Isaiah's fate is to be one of suffering, cf. 8:12; Rom 8:17.

2 a. A play on words linking the name Manasseh with the Heb. verb "to forget" (nāšāh), cf. Gen 41:31; the existence of this wordplay points to the fact that MartIs was composed in Heb. The description of the reign of Manasseh (vss. 1–6) reflects that of 2Kgs 21:1–18; 2Chr 33:1–10.

Manasseh abandoned the service of the LORD of his father, and he served Satan,[b]
3 and his angels, and his powers. •And he turned his father's house, which had
been in the presence of Hezekiah, away [from][c] the words of wisdom and the
4 service of the LORD. •Manasseh turned them away so that they served[d] Beliar; for
the angel of iniquity who rules this world is Beliar, whose name is Matanbukus.[e]
And he rejoiced over Jerusalem because of Manasseh, [and he strengthened him][f]
in causing apostasy, and in the iniquity which was disseminated in Jerusalem.
5 And sorcery and magic, augury and divination, fornication and adultery,[g] and the
persecution of the righteous increased through Manasseh, and through Belkira,[h]
and through Tobiah the Canaanite, and through John of Anathoth, and through
6 Zaliq Neway.[i] •And the rest of the acts, behold they are written in the book of
the kings of Judah and Israel.

1:8
1:3; 4:2; 10:29
Jn 12:31; 14:30;
16:11; 2Cor 4:4
Eph 2:2
2Kgs 21:9;
2Chr 33:9
2Kgs 21:6;
2Chr 33:6
2Kgs 21:16

2Kgs 21:17
2Chr 33:18

Isaiah withdraws from Jerusalem

7 And when Isaiah the son of Amoz saw the great[j] iniquity which was being
committed in Jerusalem, and the service of Satan, and his wantonness,[k] he withdrew
8 from Jerusalem and dwelt in Bethlehem of Judah. •And there also there was great
iniquity; and he withdrew from Bethlehem and dwelt on a mountain[l] in a desert
9 place. •And Micah the prophet, and the aged Ananias, and Joel, and Habakkuk,
and Josab his son,[m] and many of the faithful who believed in the ascension into
10 heaven,[n] withdrew and dwelt on the mountain. •All of them were clothed in
sackcloth, and all of them were prophets; they had nothing with them, but were
11 destitute, and they all lamented bitterly over the going astray of Israel. •And they
had nothing to eat except wild herbs (which) they gathered from the mountains,
and when they had cooked (them), they ate (them) with Isaiah the prophet. And
they dwelt on the mountains and on the hills for two years of days.

2:2

1:2

2Kgs 1:8
Zech 13:4
Mt 3:4; Mk 1:6
2Kgs 4:38f.
4Ezra 9:26;
12:51

The story of Zedekiah and Micaiah

12 And after this, while they were in the desert, there was a certain man in Samaria
named Belkira,[o] of the family of Zedekiah[p] the son of Chenaanah, the false
prophet, whose dwelling (was) in Bethlehem.[q] And Zedekiah[r] the son of Chenaanah,

1Kgs 22:11

---

b. The very common name for the devil; in the
Ascension used synonymously with Beliar and
Sammael and mentioned elsewhere in 2:7; 5:16;
7:9; 11:23, 41, 43.

c. Correction based on Greek Legend 3:3.

d. So D; A B C "Manasseh turned his heart
away to serve."

e. Another name for Beliar which possibly derives from a Heb. expression meaning "gift of
desolation" (contrast the OT name Mattaniah [cf.
e.g. 2Kgs 24:17], which means "gift of Yahweh");
see also 5:3.

f. Correction (apparently supported by Gk); Eth
"and he held him firmly."

g. "and adultery": so Eth; Gk omits.

h. So D; A "Belakira"; B C "Balkira"; Gk
omits. Since Belkira is apparently introduced for
the first time in vs. 12, the name is probably an
addition in Eth. here. The origin of the following
list of names is uncertain; they are not mentioned
in 2Kgs 21 or 2Chr 33.

i. So A; B C D "Zaliqa"; Gk "Zadok, the
overseer of the works." The Eth. names are
probably corruptions of an expression meaning
"the overseer of the works."

j. "great": so A; B C D omit.

k. Gk "and his triumph."

l. The narrative has possibly been influenced by
the story of Elijah, 1Kgs 19:1–8.

m. Micah, Joel, and Habakkuk are presented as

contemporaries of Isaiah, but this was, in fact, true
only of Micah. It is not known who is meant by
"the aged Ananias." Micah, Ananias, Joel, and
Josab are mentioned together in 6:7, and it is
possible that the names have been taken from there.
In Gk. and Eth. the names Micah (cf. 4:22) and
Micaiah (cf. 2:12, 13, 16) are identical, and it
could be the latter who is meant here (and in 6:7,
17; 7:1; 8:24).

n. So Eth; Gk "who believed that (he) had
ascended into heaven." Gk refers to the ascension
of Isaiah and makes no sense; Eth is much more
vague, but apparently refers to the ascension of
Jesus; neither version seems to preserve the original
(Jewish) text of MartIs.

o. So A; B C D "Balkira"; Gk "Belicheiar."
It is this individual—in fact the agent of the devil
who in 5:4–9 is presented as the devil himself in
human form—who brings about the death of Isaiah;
he is mentioned further in 3:1, 6, 11; 5:2, 3, 4, 5,
8, 12, 15; cf. 1:8; 2:5, 16.

p. D "Hezekiah," cf. n. r.

q. Gk "Bethany."

r. So Gk; Eth by mistake "Hezekiah," cf. n.
p. The account of the martyrdom is interrupted at
this point by a digression about Zedekiah and
Micaiah (vss. 12b–16). The narrative of the martyrdom is resumed in 3:1. The text of vss. 12b–16
is corrupt and difficult in a number of places.

who was the brother of his father,[s] was the teacher in the days of Ahab, king of Israel, of the four hundred prophets of Baal.[t] And he struck and abused Micaiah,
13 the son of Amida,[u] the prophet. •And he[v] was abused by Ahab, and Micaiah[w] was thrown into prison with Zedekiah the prophet;[x] they were with Ahaziah the son
14 of Alamerem Balalaaw.[y] •And Elijah the prophet from Tishbe in Gilead reproved Ahaziah and Samaria, and he prophesied concerning Ahaziah that he would die on his bed of sickness, [and] Samaria[z] would be given into the hand of
15 Shalmaneser,[a2] because he had killed the prophets of the LORD. •And when the false[b2] prophets who (were) with Ahaziah the son of Ahab[c2] and their teacher
16 Jalerias[d2] from mount Joel[e2] heard— •now he[f2] was a brother of Zedekiah—when they heard, they persuaded Ahaziah the king of Aguaron[g2] and [killed][h2] Micaiah.

1Kgs 22:6
1Kgs 22:24

1Kgs 22:24-28
1Kgs 22:52
1Kgs 17:1

2Kgs 1:1-8

3:2; 2Kgs 17:1-6

Isaiah is accused[a]

1 **3** And Belkira[b] discovered and saw the place of Isaiah and of the prophets who were with him, for he himself dwelt[c] in the district of Bethlehem, and he was a follower of Manasseh. And he prophesied lies in Jerusalem, and there were many
2 from Jerusalem who joined with him, but he himself was from Samaria. •And it came about, when Shalmaneser[d] the king of Assyria came and captured Samaria, and took the nine[e] tribes into captivity, and led them to the provinces[f] of the
3 Medes and the rivers of Gozan,[g] •this youth escaped and came to Jerusalem in the days of Hezekiah king of Judah, but he did not walk in the ways of his
4 Samaritan father because he feared Hezekiah. •And he was found in the days of
5 Hezekiah speaking words of iniquity in Jerusalem. •And the servants of Hezekiah

2Kgs 17:1-6;
18:9-11
4Ezra 13:40
2Bar 62:5;
77:19; 78:1

---

s. I.e. Zedekiah was the uncle of Belkira.

t. "of Baal": so A, Gk; B C D omit. The writer has confused the 400 prophets of Yahweh of 1Kgs 22:6 with the prophets of Baal mentioned in 1Kgs 18:19, 22.

u. Eth "Amida" or "Amada"; Gk "Iemmada." All the forms are corrupt for an original "Imlah" (1Kgs 22:8).

v. The reference is apparently to Micaiah, although this is not made clear in either Eth or Gk.

w. "Micaiah": so A C D, Gk; B omits (which makes better sense).

x. "with Zedekiah the prophet": so Eth; Gk "and he was with Zedekiah the false prophet." But in either case it is nonsense to say that Zedekiah was "with" Micaiah in prison. Possibly the original Heb. text read "The people of Zedekiah the false prophet were with Ahaziah . . ." but the word for "people" ('am) was wrongly taken by the Gk. translator as the word for "with" ('im). Underlying vss. 13b–16 is an otherwise unknown tradition about the fate of Micaiah in the reign of Ahaziah, but many details are obscure.

y. "Alamerem Balalaaw" (B "Balaaw"; D "Balew"): so Eth; Gk "Ala[m] in Semmôma." The text is obscure. "Alam" and "Alamerem" are corruptions of "Ahab," cf. Gk in vs. 15; the remainder of the expression (in Gk and Eth) is perhaps a corruption of "in Samaria."

z. So Gk; Eth by mistake "in Samaria." There is nothing in 2Kgs 1 to provide a basis for what is said about Samaria in this verse.

a2. Correction; Eth "Leba Naser" (or similar); Gk "Alnasar."

b2. "false": Gk omits.

c2. Gk "Alam," cf. n. y on vs. 13.

d2. So B, C; Gk "Iallarias"; Latl "Gamarias." The OT contains no reference to a person with such a name. A D omit "and their teacher Jalerias."

e2. So Eth; Gk "Islal," assumed to be corrupt

for "Israel"; Latl "Efrem." "Mount Ephraim" (JB: "the highlands of Ephraim") is mentioned frequently in the OT (e.g. Josh 17:15) and is probably the reading to be preferred; it is possible that "Israel" was substituted for "Ephraim," and that "Islal" and "Joel" are corruptions of this.

f2. "now he": so Latl, the reference correctly being to Jalerias. Eth and Gk add a gloss: Gk "now he, Becheir(a)"; Eth "now that Ibkira [so A; B "Abkira"; C "Ibakira"; D "Barakira"—the Eth. forms are all corruptions of the Gk.]." But a reference to this enemy of Isaiah, who in any case is said to be the nephew of Zedekiah (2:12), is out of place here.

g2. "Aguaron": so Eth; Gk, Latl "Gomorrah" (used here as a contemptuous name for Samaria, cf. 3:10; Isa 1:10; Jer 23:14). Eth. "Aguaron" is either a corruption of "Gomorrah" or, more naturally in Eth., of "Ekron." Ahaziah is king of Ekron because he consults the god of Ekron (2Kgs 1:1–16).

h2. Supplied from Gk, Latl; Eth omits by mistake.

3 a. The narrative of the martyrdom is resumed from 2:12a.

b. A B C "Balkira"; D "Borakira"; Gk "Becheira"; Latl "Bechira." See 2:12. Eth by mistake links the name with the previous vs. ("[killed] Micaiah and Belkira. And he discovered . . .").

c. "dwelt": so D, Gk, Latl; A B C corrupt.

d. So Latl; Eth "Alagar Zagar" (or similar); Gk "Algasar"; for these corruptions of "Shalmaneser" cf. 2:14.

e. Gk, Latl "nine and a half."

f. "provinces": so Eth, cf. MT of 2Kgs 17:6; 18:11; Gk "mountains" (Latl "mountain") = LXX of 2Kgs 17:6; 18:11. (Eth. OT follows former in 18:11, latter in 17:6).

g. So Gk, Latl; Eth "Tazon."

accused him, and he escaped to the district of Bethlehem and persuaded[h] . . .
6 And Belkira[i] accused Isaiah and the prophets who (were) with him, saying, "Isaiah and the prophets[j] who (are) with him prophesy against Jerusalem and against the cities of Judah that they will be laid waste, and also (against) Benjamin that it will go into captivity, and also against you, O lord king, that you will go (bound)
7 with hooks and chains of iron. •But they prophesy lies against Israel and Judah.[k]   2Chr 33:11
8,9 And Isaiah himself has said, 'I see more than Moses the prophet.' •Moses said, 'There is no man who can see the LORD and live.' But Isaiah has said, 'I have   Ex 33:20
10 seen the LORD, and behold I am alive.' •Know, therefore, O king, that they (are)   Isa 6:1
false prophets.[l] And he has called Jerusalem Sodom, and the princes of Judah and Jerusalem he has declared (to be) the people of Gomorrah." And he brought many   Isa 1:10
11 accusations against Isaiah and the prophets before Manasseh. •But Beliar dwelt   1:8
in the heart of Manasseh and in the heart of the princes of Judah and Benjamin,   1:9; 2:1; 5:1
and of the eunuchs, and of the king's counselors. And the words of Belkira[m]
12 pleased him very much, •and he sent and seized Isaiah.[n]

A prophecy about the Beloved and the Church[o]

13 For Beliar was very angry with Isaiah because of the vision, and because of the   5:15
exposure with which he had exposed Sammael, and that through him there had   1:8
been revealed the coming of the Beloved from the seventh heaven, and his   1:4
transformation, and his descent, and the form into which he must be transformed,   4:14, 16; 6:13;
(namely) the form of a man, and the persecution with which he would be   9:6
persecuted, and the torments with which the children of Israel must torment him,
and the coming of the twelve disciples, and the teaching,[p] and that before the
sabbath he must be crucified on a tree, and be crucified with wicked men[q] and   Jn 19:31
14 that he would be buried in a grave, •and the twelve who (were) with him would   Mt 26:31
15 be offended at him; and the guards who would guard the grave;[r] •and the descent   Mt 27:62-66;
of the angel of the church which is in the heavens, whom he will summon in the   28:4
Rev 2:1, 8
16 last days; and that the angel of the Holy Spirit[s] •and Michael, the chief of the   Heb 12:22;
Rev 3:12; 21:2
17 holy angels, will open his grave on the third day, •and that[t] Beloved, sitting on   Lk 24:4;
18 their shoulders,[u] will come forth and send out his twelve[v] disciples, •and they will   Jn 20:12
teach all nations and every tongue the resurrection of the Beloved, and those who   11:22
Mt 28:19
believe in his cross will be saved, and in[w] his ascension[x] to the seventh heaven   9:26
19 from where he came; •and that many who believe in him will speak through the
20 Holy Spirit, •and there will be many signs and miracles in those days.   11:18

---

h. So Eth; Gk "and they persuaded"; Latl omits; Cop "he persuaded Belch[ira]." The text is defective in Eth and Gk, but the fragmentary evidence of Cop confirms the old suggestion that the missing object of the verb was Belkira; for the construction cf. 2:16. The subject of the verb remains uncertain; it has been thought to be either the false prophets (cf. the plural verb in Gk) or Beliar (cf. the singular verb in Eth and Cop); but we expect a human subject as in 2:16.
i. A B C "Balkira"; D "Barakira"; Gk "Melcheira"; Latl "Bechira." Cf. 2:12.
j. "the prophets": so C D, Gk, Latl; A B "those."
k. "against Israel and Judah": so Eth, Latl (Latl adds "and Jerusalem"); Gk "and they hate Israel and Judah and Benjamin, and their word (is) evil against Judah and Israel."
l. Gk, Latl "that he is a liar."
m. So A D; B C "Balkira"; Gk "Belchira"; Latl "Bechire." See 2:12.
n. The narrative of the martyrdom is resumed in 5:1.
o. Section 3:13–4:22 is a Christian interpolation within the Jewish MartIs; cf. Intro. This section is presented as an account of a vision which Isaiah

had experienced earlier in his life; the account of the vision describes the life and death of the Beloved, the early history of the Church, the reign of Beliar, and the second coming of the Lord. The beginning of vs. 13 provides a summary of chs. 6–11.
p. "and the coming . . . teaching": so Eth; Gk "and the teaching of the twelve."
q. "and that before . . . men": so Eth; Gk "and that he must be crucified with wicked men."
r. Gk "and the guarding of the guards of the tomb."
s. "the angel of the Holy Spirit": for this expression (instead of "the Holy Spirit" or "the Spirit") cf. 4:21; 7:23; 8:14; 9:36, 39, 40; 10:4; 11:4, 33. In Gk there is a lacuna before "the angel of the Holy Spirit," and it has been suggested that the name "Gabriel" stood there.
t. Gk "the."
u. Cf. GPet 39f., where Jesus emerges from the tomb supported by two angelic figures.
v. "twelve": Gk omits.
w. "and in": so Gk; A omits "in"; B C D omit "and."
x. "ascension": so Gk; in Eth the word is normally translated "resurrection."

The corruption of the Church

21 And afterwards,[y] at his approach, his disciples will abandon the teaching[z] of the
22 twelve apostles, and their faith, and their love, and their purity. •And there will   1Tim 4:12
23 be much contention[a2] at his coming and[b2] at his approach. •And in those days
24 (there will be) many who will love office, although lacking wisdom. •And there
    will be many wicked elders and shepherds who wrong their sheep, [and they will
25 be rapacious because they do not have holy shepherds].[c2] •And many will exchange
    the glory of the robes of the saints[d2] for the robes of those who love money; and
    there will be much respect of persons in those days, and lovers of the glory of
26 this world. •And there will be many slanderers[e2] and [much][f2] vainglory at the
27 approach of the LORD, and the Holy Spirit will withdraw from many. •And in
    those days there will not be many prophets, nor those who speak reliable words,
28 except one here and there in different places, •because of the spirit of error[g2] and
    of fornication, and of vainglory, and of the love of money, which there will be
    among those who are said to be servants of that One, and among those who   4:9
29 receive that One. •And among the shepherds and the elders there will be great
30 hatred towards one another. •For there will be great jealousy in the last days, for
31 everyone will speak whatever pleases him in his own eyes. •And they will make
    ineffective[h2] the prophecy of the prophets who were before me, and my visions
    also[i2] . . . they will make ineffective, in order that they may speak what bursts
    out of their heart.

The reign of Beliar[a]

1 **4** Now, therefore, Hezekiah and Josab my son, [these are the days of the
2 completion of the world].[b] •And after it has been brought to completion, Beliar   1:8
    will descend, the great angel,[c] the king of this world, which he has ruled ever   1:3; 2:4; 10:29
    since it existed. He will descend from his firmament in the form of a man, a king   7:12
3 of iniquity, a murderer of his mother[d]—this is the king of this world— •and[e] will   6:13; 7:9–12;
    persecute the plant which the twelve apostles of the Beloved will have planted;   10:29; 11:23
4 some of the twelve will be given into his hand.[f] •This angel,[g] Beliar, will come   1En 93:2, 5, 7;
    in the form of that king, and with him will come all the powers of this world,   CD 1:7
5 and they will obey him in every wish. •By his word he will cause the sun to rise[h]   1:4
6 by night, and the moon also he will make to appear at the sixth hour. •And he   1:3
    will do everything he wishes in the world; he will act and speak like the Beloved,
7 and will say, "I am the LORD, and before me there was no one." •And all men   4:8; 10:13;
                                                                                      2Thes 2:4;

---

y. "afterwards": Gk omits. For the thought of
vss. 21–31 cf. Acts 20:29f.; 1Tim 1:3–7; 4:1; 2Tim
3:1–9; 4:3f.; 2Pet 2:1.
z. Gk "prophecy."
a2. Gk "many heresies."
b2. "at his coming and": so Eth; Gk omits.
c2. "and they . . . shepherds": correction of A
C D based on Gk, which apparently read "[which
will be ravag]ed because they do not have pure
shepherds"; B "and they will ravage the holy
flock."
d2. Perhaps an indication that Christians adopted
a special form of dress.
e2. Gk "slanders"; Eth by mistake repeats the
word for "slanderers," but in a different form.
f2. Supplied from the Gk.
g2. "error": so B C, Gk; A D "lying."
h2. Gk "will neglect."
i2. Eth adds "which," possibly a corruption of
the word for "these"; Gk "and these visions of
mine."
4 a. Vss. 1–13 describe the coming of Beliar as
the "Antichrist," the demonic ruler of the last
days, cf. 1Jn 2:18, 22; 4:3; 2Jn 7; 2Thes 2:3–10;

SibOr 3:63–76. In vss. 2b–4a this belief is linked
with the expectation, which was current for some
time after his death, that Nero would return, cf.
SibOr 4:119–39; 5:28–34, 99–110, 137–54, 361–
85; Suetonius, *Nero* 57; Tacitus, *Histories* 2:8f.
b. "these . . . world": correction based on Gk;
Eth corrupt.
c. Or "ruler," cf. vs. 4.
d. Nero had his mother, Agrippina, murdered
in A.D. 59; cf. SibOr 4:121; 5:29f., 142, 363.
e. "this is . . . world—and": so Eth (B "who
is . . ."; C omits "world"), a corruption of Gk
"who himself, even this king."
f. Gk is apparently more precise, "[one] of the
twelve"—an allusion to the martyrdom of Peter or
Paul. In vs. 3 the author refers to events of history,
Nero's persecution of the Church ("the plant"),
rather than to the future activities of Beliar, the
"Antichrist." The description reverts to the future
in vs. 4.
g. Or "ruler" (Gk actually has "ruler"), cf.
vs. 2. C D, Gk omit "Beliar."
h. "he will cause . . . to rise": so D; A B C
"the sun will rise." Cf. SibOr 3:63–65; 4Ezra 5:4.

8 in the world will believe in him. •They will sacrifice to him and will serve him,
9 saying, "This is the LORD, and besides him there is no other." •And the majority
of those who have associated together to receive the Beloved he will turn aside
10,11 after him. •And the power of his miracles will be in every city and district, •and
12 he will set up his image before him in every city.ⁱ •And he will rule for three
13 years and seven months and twenty-seven days.ʲ •And many faithful and saints,
when they saw him for whom they were hoping, who was crucified, Jesus the
LORD Christ—after I, Isaiah, had seen him who was crucified and ascendedᵏ—
and who believed in him, of these few will be leftˡ in those days as his servants,
fleeing from desert to desertᵐ as they await his coming.ⁿ

SibOr 5:34
Rev 13:4, 8, 12

3:28
2Thes 2:9; Rev
13:14; 19:20;
Mt 24:24; Mk
13:22
Rev 13:14f.;
14:11

Cor 1:7; Phil
3:20; 1Thes
1:10; Heb 9:28

The second coming of the Lord

14 And after [one thousand] three hundred and thirty-two daysᵒ the LORD will come
with his angels and with the hosts of the saints from the seventh heaven, with the
glory of the seventh heaven, and will drag Beliar, and his hosts also, into Gehenna.
15 And he will give rest to the pious whom he finds in the body in this world, but
16 *the sun will be ashamed,*ᵖ •and (to) all who because of their faith in him have
cursed Beliar and his kings. But the saints will come with the LORD with their
robes�q which are stored up in the seventh heaven above; with the LORD will come
those whose spirits are clothed, they will descend and be present in the world,
and the LORD will strengthen those who are found in the body, together with the
saints in the robes of the saints, and will serve those who have kept watch in this
17 world. •And after this they will be turned in their robes upwards, and their body
18 will be left in the world. •Then the voice of the Beloved will reprove in anger
this heaven, and this earth, and the mountains, and the hills, and the cities, and
the desert, and the trees, and the angel of the sun,ʳ and that of the moon, and
everywhere that Beliar has appeared and acted openly in this world. There will
be a resurrection and a judgment in their midst in those days, and the Beloved
will cause fire to rise from him, and it will consume all the impious, and they
19 will become as if they had not been created.ˢ •And the rest of the words of the
20 vision are written in the vision of Babylon.ᵗ •And the rest of the vision about the
LORD, behold it is written in parables in the words of mine that are written in the
21 book which I prophesied openly. •And the descent of the Beloved into Sheol,
behold it is written in the section where the LORD says, *"Behold, my son shall*

1Thes 3:13;
2Thes 1:7; 1En
1:4, 9; Jude 14
3:13; 4:16; 6:13;
9:6
1:3; Rev 19:20
2Thes 1:7
Isa 24:23
1Thes 3:13; 4:14

Rev 20:4

Lk 12:37

1Cor 15:50-53;
2Cor 5:1-4;
Phil 3:21

Rev 20:11-15

2Thes 1:8; 2:8;
Isa 11:4

9:16; 10:8

Isa 52:13 LXX

---

i. An allusion to the cult of the Roman emperors and the practice of erecting statues of them.

j. I.e. 1,335 days according to the Julian calendar; the author is drawing on Dan 12:12, itself an elaboration of the tradition in Dan 7:25; 12:7 that the persecution of Antiochus Epiphanes would last three and a half years ("a time, two times, and half a time"; cf. Rev 11:2f.; 12:6, 14; 13:5 and Lk 4:25; Jas 5:17). Ascenls 4:12, 14 are cited by the 11th-cent. chronicler George Cedrenus, who attributes the passage to THez. According to Cedrenus the reign of the Antichrist would last 1,290 days; for this variant cf. Dan 12:11.

k. "after I . . . ascended": an editorial insertion linking 3:13–4:22 to its context.

l. "And many faithful . . . few will be left": the translation reflects the somewhat awkward Eth.; the sense seems to be that of the many faithful and saints who saw and believed in Jesus, few will be left.

m. The desert was the traditional place of safety in times of persecution, cf. 1Kgs 17:2f.; 19:3f.; 1Mac 2:28–30; Rev 12:6, 14.

n. B C D "the coming of the Beloved."

o. "one thousand" was omitted by mistake, and similarly "two" written by mistake for "five,"

see vs. 12. Translation follows A; B C "thirty hundred and thirty-two"; D "thirty hundred and two."

p. "but the sun will be ashamed": a gloss which interrupts the sequence of thought in vss. 15f. and was probably occasioned by the reference to the sun in vs. 18. The words are quoted from Isa 24:23.

q. I.e. with the robes for the living righteous, those who are found "in the body." Alternatively it could mean "with [i.e. "in"] their own robes." On the robes see n. p on 1:5.

r. Angels or spirits were thought to have been placed in charge of the various created elements; for the sun cf. Rev 7:2; 19:17; cf. also Rev 7:11; 9:11; 14:18; 1En 60:12–21; Jub 2:2.

s. "and they will become . . . created": the language reflects the Eth. version of Job 10:19.

t. "the vision of Babylon": reflects the LXX text of Isa 13:1. Vss. 19–22 are an editorial conclusion to 3:13–4:22 which serves to link this section of Ascenls with the canonical Book of Isaiah (vss. 19f.) and makes the claim that what is said here was already (implicitly) contained in the OT (vss. 21f.).

understand."ᵘ And all these things, behold they are written in the Psalms,ᵛ in the parablesʷ of David the son of Jesse, and in the Proverbs of Solomon his son, and in the words of Korahˣ and of Ethan the Israelite,ʸ and in the words of Asaph,ᶻ
22 and in the rest of the psalms which the angel of the spirit has inspired, •(namely)   3:15 in those which have no name written, and in the words of Amos my fatherᵃ² and of Hosea the prophet, and of Micah, and of Joel, and of Nahum, and of Jonah, and of Obadiah, and of Habakkuk, and of Haggai, and of Zephaniah, and of Zechariah, and of Malachi,ᵇ² and in the words of the righteous Joseph,ᶜ² and in the words of Daniel.

The execution of Isaiah

1 **5** Because of these visions, therefore, Beliar was angry with Isaiah, and he dwelt   1:8
2 in the heart of Manasseh, and he sawed Isaiah in half with a wood saw.ᵃ •And   1:9; 2:1; 3:11 while Isaiah was being sawed in half, his accuser, Belkira,ᵇ stood by, and all the false prophets stood by, laughing and (maliciously) joyful because of Isaiah.
3 And Belkira,ᶜ through Mekembekus,ᵈ stood before Isaiah, laughingᵉ and deriding.
4 And Belkiraᶠ said to Isaiah, "Say, 'I have lied in everything I have spoken; the
5 ways of Manasseh are good and right, •and also the ways of Belkiraᵍ and those
6 who are with him are good.' " •And he said this to him when he began to be
7 sawed in half. •And Isaiah was in a vision of the LORD, but his eyes were open,
8 and he saw them.ʰ •And Belkiraⁱ spoke thus to Isaiah, "Say what I say to you,

---

u. "Behold, my son shall understand": a quotation of Isa 52:13, but reflecting the LXX form of the text. The quotation points to the messianic interpretation of Isa 52:13–53:12. In referring to the descent of the Beloved into Sheol the author perhaps had in mind Isa 53:8 in its LXX form (so JB "struck down in death").

v. "the Psalms": either a general heading for the various psalms and proverbs described in more detail in the remainder of the vs. and at the beginning of vs. 22, or a gloss on the word "parables," which is used here with a not very common meaning.

w. "the parables": the Eth. reflects Gk. *parabolē* and Heb. *māšāl*, a word with a wide range of meanings. It is used in Pss 49:4 (JB: "proverb") and 78:2 with the sense "a didactic poem"; here the plural form has the rather general sense "poems" or "psalms."

x. "Korah": cf. e.g. the headings of Pss 42, 44.

y. "Ethan the Israelite": text follows the LXX form of the heading of Ps 89 (LXX 88), where the MT reads "Ethan the Ezrahite" (= JB: "Ethan the native-born"); cf. the LXX and MT of 1Kgs 5:11.

z. "Asaph": cf. the headings of Pss 50; 73–83.

a2. Cf. n. e on 1:2.

b2. The twelve minor prophets; the order in which they are listed follows neither the MT, nor the LXX, but is nearer to the latter than the former. It might have been expected that there would be a reference to Jeremiah and Ezekiel, but cf. the similar list in 4Ezra 1:39f., in which neither they nor Isaiah himself is mentioned.

c2. Apparently a reference to PrJos; this work is mentioned in lists of pseudepigraphic books, but has been lost apart from some short excerpts in early Christian writings. It is a little surprising that this pseudepigraphon should alone be mentioned in the context of the books of the OT. [See the contribution on PrJos by J. Z. Smith elsewhere in the present collection. —J.H.C.]

5 a. "and he sawed . . . saw": the narrative of the martyrdom is resumed here from 3:12. The first half of the vs. is a redactional link. For the expression "a wood saw" see "Original Language."

b. So A: B C "Balkira"; D "Malkira"; see 2:12.

c. A B C "Balkira"; D "Malkira."

d. "through Mekembekus": so A C D; B "and Mekembekus." The reading of B is grammatically easier because the following verbs are in the plural in all MSS with the exception that C has "stood" in the singular. But the plural forms could have been introduced under the influence of the plurals at the end of the previous vs., and it is easier to make sense of the reading "through." "Mekembekus" is a corruption of "Matanbukus" (2:4), another name for Beliar; inspired by, and with the help of Beliar, Belkira now mocks Isaiah. In Eth. MSS "and" (*wa-*) and "through" (*ba-*) are frequently confused.

e. "laughing": possibly a marginal variant of "deriding" which has now come into the text. The following "and" is omitted by A, but is present in B C D.

f. B "Balkira"; A C D "Beliar." Since Belkira is presented in vss. 4–9 as the devil himself in human form (cf. particularly vs. 9), it is perhaps hardly surprising that there should be a confusion between Belkira and Beliar at this point. In vs. 8 it is Belkira, not Beliar, who addresses Isaiah, and correspondingly Greek Legend 3:17 (which summarizes 5:4–8 of AscenIs) refers to "Melchias, the false prophet." On the other hand 5:4 and 8 are cited by Ambrose (*Expositio in psalmum 118* 12.32), and there it is the devil (Lat. *diabolus*) who addresses Isaiah; for the text (quoted in Charles, *Ascension*, p. 40) see Corpus scriptorum ecclesiasticorum latinorum vol. 62 (1913) p. 270.

g. So D; A B C "Balkira."

h. Possibly to be emended, "and (although) his eyes were open, he did [not] see them," cf. 6:10.

i. B C "Balkira"; A "Milkiras"; D "Malkira."

and I will turn their heart and make Manasseh, and the princes of Judah, and the
9 people, and all Jerusalem worship you."[j] •And Isaiah answered and said,[k] "If it
is within my power to say, 'Condemned and cursed be you,[l] and all your hosts,
10 and all your house!'[m] •For there is nothing further that you can take except the
11 skin of my body." •And they seized Isaiah the son of Amoz and sawed him in
12 half with a wood saw. •And Manasseh, and Belkira,[n] and the false prophets, and
13 the princes, and the people, and all stood by looking on. •And to the prophets
who (were) with him he said before he was sawed in half, "Go to the district of
14 Tyre and Sidon,[o] because for me alone the LORD has mixed the cup."[p] •And
while Isaiah was being sawed in half, he did not cry out, or weep, but his mouth
15 spoke with the Holy Spirit until he was sawed in two. •Beliar did this to Isaiah
through Belkira[q] and through Manasseh, for Sammael was very angry with Isaiah   1:8; 3:13; 5:1
from the days of Hezekiah, king of Judah, because of the things which he had
16 seen concerning the Beloved, •and because of the destruction of Sammael which   1:4
he had seen through the LORD, while Hezekiah his father was king. And he[r] did
as Satan wished.[s]   2:2

2. THE VISION WHICH ISAIAH THE SON OF AMOZ SAW[a]

Isaiah visits Hezekiah and has a vision[a]

1 **6** In the twentieth year of the reign of Hezekiah, king of Judah, Isaiah the son
of Amoz and Josab the son of Isaiah came to Hezekiah in Jerusalem from Gilgal.[b]
2 And he sat on the couch of the king, and they brought a seat for him, but he
3 would not sit (on it). •And when Isaiah began to speak with Hezekiah the king
the words of faith and righteousness, all the princes of Israel were sitting (there),
and the eunuchs and the king's counselors. And there were there forty[c] prophets
and sons of the prophets; they had come from the neighboring districts, and from
the mountains, and from the country, when they had heard that Isaiah was coming
4 from Gilgal[d] to Hezekiah. •They came that they might greet him, and that they
5 might hear his words, •and that he might lay his hand on them, and that they
might prophesy, and that he might hear their prophecy; and they were all in the
6 presence of Isaiah.[e] •And when Isaiah[f] spoke with Hezekiah the words of
righteousness and faith, they all heard a door being opened[g] and the voice of the
7 Spirit.[h] •And the king summoned all the prophets and all the people who were to

j. There are some similarities with the temptation of Jesus, cf. Mt 4:8–10; Lk 4:5–8.

k. C D add "to him."

l. A C D "If (it is) within my power, 'Cursed, that is to say, you.' "

m. In vs. 9 Belkira is presented as the devil in human form, with his "hosts" of spirits at his disposal (cf. 2:2). What is implicit in AscenIs is made explicit in the parallel passage in the Greek Legend (3:18), "Accursed be you, O Melchias the false prophet, O devil."

n. B C "Balkira"; A "Melakira"; D "Melkira."

o. It is not clear why this particular region should be mentioned; it has been suggested that the tradition of Elijah's association with Sidon (1Kgs 17:7–24) may have inspired the author at this point.

p. "cup": a symbolic term for the vocation to which Isaiah was called, cf. Mk 10:38f.; 14:36.

q. A B C "Balkira"; D "Malkira."

r. I.e. Manasseh.

s. Vss. 15 and 16 are an editorial addition which serves to link 3:13–4:22 with the narrative of the martyrdom.

a. The heading (apart from "2") is given in Eth, Lat2, Slav, but Lat2 has "Isaiah the prophet, the son of Amoz" and Slav "the holy Isaiah, the prophet, the son of Amoz."

6 a. The VisIs (chs. 6–11) is a Christian work which was originally quite independent of the Jewish MartIs (the basic narrative of chs. 1–5); cf. Intro.

b. A B D "from Galilee," cf. vs. 3; Lat2, Slav omit. It is not clear why Gilgal should be mentioned.

c. It is not clear why there should be *forty* prophets; the figure is given in Eth and Greek Legend 1:3, but is absent from Lat2, Slav.

d. A "from Galilee," cf. vs. 1; Lat2 "from Galgatha."

e. Lat2, Slav are much shorter than Eth in vss. 3–5.

f. C D, Lat2, Slav "he."

g. Lit. "a door which (someone) opened."

h. "they all . . . the Spirit [C "the Holy Spirit"]": so Eth; Lat2, Slav "the Holy Spirit came upon him, and they all saw and heard the words of the Holy Spirit." Eth seems to be dependent on the corrupt Eth. text of vs. 9 and is probably secondary.

be found there, and they came. And Micah, and the aged Ananias, and Joel, and
8 Josab were sitting on his right.[i] •And when they all heard the voice of the Holy　2:9
Spirit, they all worshiped on their knees, and they praised the God of righteousness,
the Most High, the One who (dwells) in the upper world and who sits on high,
9 the Holy One, the One who rests among the holy ones,[j] •and they ascribed glory
to the One who had thus graciously given a door in an alien world, had graciously
10 given it to a man.[k] •And while he was speaking with the Holy Spirit in the hearing
of them all, he became silent, and his mind was taken up from him,[l] and he did
11 not see the men who were standing before him. •His eyes indeed were open, but
12 his mouth was silent, and the mind in his body was taken up from him.[m] •But his
13 breath was (still) in him,[n] for he was seeing a vision. •And the angel who was
sent to show him (the vision) was not of this firmament, nor was he from the　4:2; 7:9–12;
14 angels of glory of this world, but he came from the seventh heaven. •And　10:29; 11:23
3:13; 4:14, 16;
the people who were standing by, apart from the circle of prophets, did [not][o]　9:6
15 think that the holy Isaiah had been taken up. •And the vision which he saw was
16 not from this world, but from the world which is hidden from the flesh.[p] •And
after Isaiah had seen this vision he recounted it to Hezekiah, and to Josab his
17 son,[q] and to the other prophets who had come. •But the officials, and the eunuchs,
and the people did not hear, apart from Samnas the secretary, and Jehoiakim,[r]　1:5
and Asaph the recorder,[s] for they (were) doers of righteousness, and the fragrance
of the Spirit was in them; but the people did not hear, for Micah and Josab his
son had sent them out when the wisdom of this world was taken from him as if
he were dead.

Isaiah's journey through the seven heavens

1 **7** The vision which Isaiah saw he told to Hezekiah, and to Josab his son, and to
2 Micah, and to the other prophets; •it was as follows. When I prophesied in
accordance with the message which you have heard, I saw a glorious angel; his
glory[a] was not like the glory of the angels which I always used to see, but he had
great glory, and an office,[b] such that I cannot describe the glory of this angel.
3 And I saw when he took hold of me by my hand,[c] and I said to him, "Who are
you? And what is your name? And where are you taking me up?" For strength
4 had been given to me that I might speak with him. •And he said to me, "When
I have taken you up through (all) the stages and have shown you the vision on
account of which I was sent, then you will understand who I am; but my name
5 you will not know, •for you have to return into this body. But where[d] I take you　8:11, 23; 9:5
6 up, you will see, because for this purpose I was sent."[e] •And I rejoiced because

<hr />

i. Lat2, Slav add "and on his left."

j. The description of God, and particularly the
phrase "the One who rests among the holy ones,"
reflects the LXX text of Isa 57:15, cf. n. h on
10:6. Lat2, Slav have a shorter text in vs. 8.

k. "who . . . a man": so Eth, but probably
corrupt; Lat2 (and similarly Slav) "who had given
such a power of words in the world."

l. "and his mind . . . from him": so Eth,
supported by Greek Legend 2:1; Lat2, Slav omit.

m. "and the mind . . . from him": so Eth; Lat2,
Slav omit.

n. "But his breath . . . him": so Eth, supported
by Greek Legend 2:2; Lat2, Slav "But the inspiration of the Spirit [Lat2 "Holy Spirit"] was with
him." Lat2, Slav omit the rest of vs. 12 and vs.
13.

o. Restoration based on Lat2, Slav.

p. So D; Lat2, Slav "from all flesh"; A C
"which was hidden from his flesh," and similarly
B.

q. Lat2, Slav omit the remainder of vs. 16, vs.
17, and the beginning of 7:1 by homoeoteleuton.

r. No person with this name is mentioned in the
OT as living during the reign of Hezekiah. We
might have expected the name "Eliakim" (cf.
2Kgs 18:18; Isa 36:3), but it is also possible (cf.
Charles, *Ascension*, p. 46) that the text is corrupt
for "and Joah son of Asaph, the recorder." In the
OT Asaph is not the recorder himself, but the father
of the person who is.

s. "the recorder": in Eth the same expression
that is used in the Eth. version of Isa 36:3, 22; it
corresponds to what JB translates as "the herald."

7 a. So B; A C D "he."

b. "and an office": so Eth, cf. 3:23: Lat1, Slav
"but he had a great and holy glory"; Lat2 corrupt.

c. So Eth, but the text seems corrupt; Lat1 "And
he approached and held my hand"; Lat2, Slav
"And he took me by (my) hand and led me on
high."

d. Lat1, Lat2, Slav "when."

e. "because for this . . . was sent": Lat2, Slav
omit.

7 he spoke to me with kindness. •And he said to me, "Do you rejoice because I
have spoken kindly to you?" And he said, "You will see one greater than me,
8 how he will speak kindly and gently with you; •and the Father of the one who is
greater[f] you will also see, because for this purpose I was sent from the seventh
heaven, that I might make all this clear to you."

The firmament

10:29–31

9 And we went up into the firmament,[g] I and he, and there I saw Sammael[h] and his   1:8
hosts; and there was a great struggle in it, and the words of Satan, and they were   2:2
10 envying one another.[i] •And as above, so also on earth, for the likeness of what
11 (is) in the firmament is here on earth. •And I said to the angel, "What is this
12 envying?"[j] •And he said to me, "So it has been ever since this world existed   4:2
until now,[k] and this struggle (will last) until the one comes whom you are to see,
and he will destroy him."   10:12

The first heaven

10:27

13 And after this he took me up above the firmament; this is the [first][l] heaven.
14 There I saw a throne in the middle,[m] and on the right and on the left of it there
15 were angels. •And [the angels on the left][n] were not like the angels who stood on
the right, but those who stood on the right had more glory, and they all sang
praises with one voice. And the throne was in the middle,[o] and it they praised,
and those on the left after them;[p] but their voice was not like the voice of those
16 on the right, nor their praise like the praise of those (on the right). •And I asked
17 the angel who led me and said to him, "To whom is this praise directed?"[q] •And
he said to me, "To the praise of [the One who sits in][r] the seventh heaven, the
One who rests in the holy world,[s] and to his Beloved, from where I was sent to
you. To there it is directed."

The second heaven

10:25f.

18 And again, he took me up into the second heaven, and the height of that heaven   7:28
19 is like that from heaven to earth and to the firmament.[t] •And [I saw there, as][u] in
the first heaven, angels on the right and on the left,[v] and a throne in the middle,
and the praise of the angels who (were) in the second heaven; and the one who
20 sat on the throne in the second heaven had more glory than all (the rest). •And

---

f. Lat1 "and One more eminent than the greater
one himself"; Lat2, Slav differ.

g. "the firmament": the vault of the sky (cf.
Gen 1:6–8), here thought of as separating the earth
from the seven heavens.

h. Lat2, Slav, and Greek Legend 2:9 "Satan."

i. So Eth, but corrupt; read with Lat1 "and the
angels of Satan were envying one another"; Lat2,
Slav differ.

j. Lat1 "What is this war, and what is this
envying?"; Lat2, Slav "What is this war and
envying and struggle?" Cf. 10:29.

k. "So . . . now": so Eth, Lat1; Lat2, Slav
"That war is of the devil."

l. Supplied from Lat2, Slav. In AscenIs heaven
is thought of as being divided into seven layers,
each one more glorious than the one below. For
the idea of gradations within heaven, and particularly for the idea of seven heavens, cf. TLevi 2:7–
3:10; cf. also 3Bar; 2Cor 12:2; Eph 4:10; Heb
4:14; 7:26.

m. Lat2, Slav. add "and on it there sat an angel
in great glory." A comparable statement occurs in
the Eth. version of vss. 19, 24, 27, 29, 31 (also

in Lat2, Slav), 33, 35, 37. In Col 1:16; TLevi 3:8
the word "thrones" is used absolutely as the name
of a class of angels, and a similar usage is to be
found in AscenIs in 7:21, and in the Eth. version
of 7:15, 27; 8:8; 11:25 (cf. Greek Legend 2:40).

n. Supplied from Lat1.

o. "And the throne was in the middle": so Eth,
Lat1; Lat2, Slav omit, cf. n. m on vs. 14.

p. "and it they praised, and those on the left
after them": so Eth; Lat1 "and (those) on the left
blessed afterwards"; Lat2 (partially corrupt), Slav
"and those who were on the left sang praises after
them."

q. Lit. "sent."

r. Supplied from Lat1; Lat2, Slav "of God who
is above the seventh heaven."

s. "the One who rests in the holy world [B
"among the holy ones of the world"]": so Eth
(cf. 6:8), but the text appears corrupt; Lat1 "who
belongs to the everlasting age"; Lat2, Slav omit.

t. A "from earth to heaven and to the firmament"; Lat2, Slav "from the first heaven to earth."

u. Supplied from Lat1, Lat2, Slav.

v. Lat2, Slav omit the rest of the vs.

there was great glory in the second heaven, and their praise was not like the praise
21 of those who (were) in the first heaven. •And I fell on my face to worship him,[w]
and the angel who led me would not let me, but said to me, "Worship neither
throne,[x] nor angel from the six heavens,[y] from where[z] I was sent to lead you,
22 before I tell you in the seventh heaven.[a2] •For above all the heavens and their
angels is placed your throne, and also your robes and your crown[b2] which you are
23 to see." •And I rejoiced very much that those who love the Most High and his
Beloved will at their end go up there through the angel of the Holy Spirit.

Rev 19:10;
22:8f.;
Col 2:18

8:14; 9:2;
Rev 4:4

3:15

The third heaven

10:23f.

24 And he took me up into the third heaven, and in the same way I saw those who
(were) on the right and on the left, and there also (there was) a throne in the
middle and one who sat (on it),[c2] but no mention of this world was made[d2] there.
25 And I said to the angel who (was) with me, for the glory of my face[e2] was being
transformed as I went up from heaven to heaven, "Nothing of the vanity of that
26 world is named here." •And he answered me, saying, "Nothing is named because
27 of its weakness, but nothing is hidden which is done there."[f2] •And I wished to
find out how it is known; and he answered me, saying, "When I have taken you
up into the seventh heaven, from where I was sent, to the One which (is) above
these, then you will know that nothing is hidden from the thrones[g2] and those who
dwell in the heavens, nor from the angels." And the praises which they sang and
the glory of the one who sat on the throne were great, and the angels who (were)
on the right and on the left had more glory than (those in) the heaven which (was)
below them.[h2]

9:19-23

The fourth heaven

10:21f.

28 And again he took me up into the fourth heaven, and the height from the third to
29 the fourth heaven was greater than (from) earth to the firmament.[i2] •And there I
again saw those who (were) on the right and those who (were) on the left, and
the one who sat on the throne was in the middle,[j2] and there also they were singing
30 praises. •And the praise and glory of the angels on the right was greater than that
31 of those on the left. •And again the glory of the one who sat on the throne was
greater than that of the angels who (were) on the right, but their glory (was)
greater than that of those below.

7:18

The fifth heaven

10:20

32,33 And he took me up into the fifth heaven. •And again I saw those who (were) on
the right and the left, and the one who sat on the throne had more glory than
34 those of the fourth heaven. •And the glory of those who (were) on the right was
35 greater than that of those who (were) on the left . . .[k2] •The glory of the one on
36 the throne was greater than that of the angels who (were) on the right, •but their

w. I.e. the one sitting on the throne, vs. 19.

x. See n. m on vs. 14.

y. Lat2 "of that heaven"; Slav "from heaven."

z. "from where": so Eth. but elsewhere the
angel is specifically said to come from the seventh
heaven (cf. 6:13; 7:8); Lat2 "for this purpose";
Slav "because this purpose." Lat2, Slav do not
make any better sense, but may go back to the
same Gk. original as Eth. Possibly the whole clause
was misplaced from the end of the vs. at an early
stage in the transmission of the text.

a2. Lat2 (similarly Slav) "but only the one
whom I shall tell you."

b2. Traditional Christian symbols of the glorious
and transformed state of the righteous in heaven,
see n. p on 1:5 and notes i–k on 9:9f.

c2. "and one who sat (on it)": so Eth (B

defective); Lat2, Slav omit.

d2. Lit. "named."

e2. Lat2, Slav "spirit."

f2. So (C) D and similarly Slav; B (and similarly
Lat2) "there which is done"; A "which is done
here."

g2. Cf. n. m on vs. 14.

h2. Lat2, Slav have a much shorter text in vs.
27.

i2. "than (from) earth . . . firmament": Lat2,
Slav omit.

j2. "and the one . . . middle": Lat2, Slav omit.
Lat2 also omits the rest of vs. 29 and vs. 30.

k2. All Eth. MSS add "from the third to the
fourth." These words make no sense in their
context, but are perhaps a fragment of a sentence
comparable to vs. 28.

37 praise was more glorious than that of the fourth heaven.[12] •And I praised the One
who is not named[m2] and is unique, who dwells in the heavens, whose name is   8:7; 1:7
unknown to all flesh, the One who has given such glory to the different heavens,[n2]
who makes the glory of the angels great and the glory of the one who sits on the
throne (even) greater.[o2]

The air of the sixth heaven

1 **8** And again, he took me up into the air of the sixth heaven, and I saw a splendor
2 such as I had not seen in the five heavens as I went up; •the angels possessed
3,4 great glory, •and the praise there was holy and wonderful.[a] •And I said to the
5 angel who led me, "What (is) this which I see, my lord?" •And he said to me,[b]
6 "I am not your lord, but your companion." •And again I asked him, and I said   Rev 19:10;
7 to him, "Why (are there) not corresponding groups of angels?"[c] •And he said to   22:8f.
me,[d] "From the sixth heaven and upwards there are no longer those on the left,[e]
nor is there a throne placed in the middle, but [they are directed][f] by the power of
the seventh heaven, where the One who is not named dwells, and his Chosen   7:37
8 One,[g] whose name is unknown, and no heaven can learn his name;[h] •for he is   Isa 42:1;
alone, (he) whose voice all the heavens and thrones answer.[i] I, therefore, have   Lk 9:35; 23:35; 1En 45:3f.
9 been empowered and sent to bring you up here that you may see this glory, •and
10 (that) you may see the LORD of all these[j] heavens and of these thrones[k] •being   10:8–10
11 transformed until he resembles your appearance and your likeness.[l] •But I say to   7:5; 8:23; 9:5
you, Isaiah, that no man who has to return into a body of that world [has come
12 up, or seen],[m] or understood what you have seen[n] •and what you are to see, for   11:34
you are destined in the lot of the LORD, the lot of the tree,[o] to come here, and
13 from there is the power of the sixth heaven and of the air."[p] •And I proclaimed
the greatness of my LORD with praise, that through his lot I should come here.
14 And he said to me,[q] "Hear then this also from your companion: [when from the
body by the will of God you have come up here],[r] then you will receive the robe[s]   7:22; 9:2
which you will see, and also other numbered robes placed (there) you will see,   9:24f.
15 and then you will be equal to the angels who (are) in the seventh heaven."

12. Vss. 33–36 are considerably abbreviated in
Lat2, Slav.

m2. The thought is that the name of God is too
sacred to be uttered by men.

n2. Lit. "from heaven to heaven."

o2. Lat2, Slav differ considerably in vs. 37; in
particular, Isaiah does not himself praise God, but
marvels at the sight of the angels praising him.

8 a. "wonderful": so D, Lat2, Slav; A B C
corrupt.

b. "to me": so B D, Lat2, Slav; A C omit.

c. Lit. "companions of angels." The meaning
of the question is clarified by the following vs.:
why is there no longer one group of angels on the
left and one on the right? Lat2, Slav omit vs. 6.

d. "to me": so C (corrected reading) D, Lat2,
Slav; A B C (original reading) omit.

e. D adds "or right."

f. Supplied from Lat2, Slav.

g. "where the One . . . and his [B C D "the"]
Chosen One": so Eth; Lat2, Slav corrupt; Lat2
"where the bounteous [?] son of God is"; Slav
"where that famous one is and his only begotten
son."

h. "whose name . . . his name": Lat2, Slav
omit, cf. 7:37. If genuine, these clauses perhaps
refer to a secret name of the Chosen One, cf. 9:5;

Rev 19:12. [Also see PrJac, introduced and translated elsewhere in this collection. —J.H.C.]

i. Lat2, Slav "And all the heavens and
angels hear him."

j. A "those"; B "the."

k. Lat2, Slav "of all the heavens, and his [Slav
"the"] angels and powers."

l. Lat2, Slav omit vs. 10.

m. Correction based on Greek Legend 2:29; Eth
"has seen this, or come up."

n. B "see"; A "have understood."

o. "the lot of the tree [i.e. the cross]": lacking
in Lat2, Slav, and probably a gloss making explicit
the link between the martyrdom of Isaiah and the
crucifixion of Jesus which is indicated in the phrase
"the lot of the Lord," cf. 1:13.

p. "and from there . . . the air": a gloss based
on a misunderstanding of vs. 7, lacking in Lat2,
Slav.

q. "to me": so D, Lat2, Slav; A B C omit.

r. "when . . . here": correction based on Lat2,
Slav; A (and virtually C) "when from (your) alien
body by the angel of the spirit you have come up
here" (cf. 7:23); B "when in an alien body the
God of the spirit has brought you up here"; D
"when from (your) alien body the God of the spirit
you have come up here."

s. Lat2, Slav omit the rest of vs. 14.

The sixth heaven

10:17–19

16 And he took me up into the sixth heaven, and there were none on the left,ᵗ nor a
   throne in the middle, but all (were) of one appearance, and their praise (was)
17 equal. • And (strength) was given to me, and I also sang praises with them, and
18 that angel also, and our praise was like theirs. • And there they all named the
   primalᵘ Father and hisᵛ Beloved, Christ, and the Holy Spirit,ʷ all with one voice,
19,20 but it was not like the voice of the angels who (were) in the five heavens, •nor
   (was it) like their speech, but there was a different voice there, and there was
21 much light there. • And then, when I was in the sixth heaven, I thought that light
22 which I had seen in the five heavens darkness. • And I rejoiced and praised the
23 One who has graciously given such light to those who await his promise.ˣ • And Acts 1:4
   I entreated the angel who led me that from then on I should not return to the
24 world of flesh. • Indeed I say to you, Hezekiah and Josab, my son, and Micah,ʸ 7:5; 8:11; 9:5
25 that there is much darkness here. • And the angel who led me knew what I thought
   and said to me,ᶻ "If you rejoice over this light, how much more (will you rejoice)
   in the seventh heaven when you see the light where the LORD is and his Belovedᵃ²—
26 from where I was sent—who is to be called in the world the Son! • He who is to
   be in the corruptible world has not (yet) been revealed,ᵇ² nor the robes, nor the
   thrones, nor the crowns which are placed (there) for the righteous, for those who 7:22; 9:9f.
   believe in that LORD who will descend in your form. For the light which (is) there
27 (is) great and wonderful.ᶜ² • But as regards your not returning into the body, your
28 days are not yet complete for coming here." • And when I heard (this), I was sad; 11:35
   and he said to me,ᵈ² "Do not be sad."

The air of the seventh heaven

1 **9** And he led me into the air of the seventh heaven, and moreover I heard a voice
   saying, "How far is he who dwells among aliensᵃ to go up?" And I was afraid
2 and was trembling. • And he said to me when I was trembling, "Behold! From
   there another voice which was sent out has come, and it says,ᵇ 'The holy Isaiah
3 is permitted to come up here, for his robe is here.' " • And I asked the angel who 7:22; 8:14
   (was) with me and said, "Who is the one who prevented me, and who is this one
4 who turned to me that I might go up?"ᶜ • And he said to me, "The one who
   prevented you, this is the one [who (is) in charge of]ᵈ the praise of the sixth
5 heaven. • And the one who turned to you,ᵉ this is your LORD, the LORD, the LORD

---

t. D adds "or the right"; Lat2, Slav "no angels
on the right or left."
   u. "primal": C omits.
   v. B C D "the."
   w. Lat2, Slav "they praised the Father of all
and his [Slav "the"] Beloved Son and the Holy
Spirit." Lat2, Slav do not mention the name
"Christ" (cf. 9:5, 13, 17; 10:7) or "Jesus" (cf.
9:5; 10:7). But Greek Legend 2:37 supports Eth in
10:7.
   x. Lat2, Slav "such joy [Slav "such things"]
to those who receive his mercy."
   y. "Hezekiah . . . Micah": Lat2, Slav omit.
   z. "to me": so D, Lat2, Slav; A B C omit.
   a2. Lat2, Slav "the heavenly Father sits and his
only begotten Son."
   b2. "from where I was sent . . . been revealed":
Lat2, Slav omit, and the whole (or at least the
beginning of vs. 26) is probably an interpolation;
if it has all been interpolated, the passage would
have originally read, "where the Lord is and his
Beloved, and also the robes and the thrones and
the crowns which . . ." For "who is to be called
. . . the Son" cf. 9:5, 13; 10:7; in all these passages

Lat2, Slav do not have the clause, cf. n. w on vs.
18.
   c2. "for those . . . wonderful": Lat2, Slav omit.
   d2. "to me": so C D, Slav; A B omit; Lat2
defective.

9 a. Lat2, Slav, and Greek Legend 2:23 "in the
flesh."
   b. Lat2, Slav (and similarly Greek Legend 2:23)
"And again I heard another voice saying." In Eth
"he said to me" is awkward and probably an
addition; this suggests that Eth originally read "And
when I was trembling, behold from there another
voice . . . came, and it said." D adds "to me"
after "has come/came," which points to such a
text.
   c. So Eth, but a misunderstanding of the underlying Gk., which ought to have been rendered
"who permitted me to go up" (cf. Greek Legend
2:24).
   d. Correction based on Lat2, Slav, and Greek
Legend 2:25; Eth "on whom (is)."
   e. See n. c on vs. 3.

Christ, who is to be called in the world Jesus,[f] but you cannot hear his name[g]
until you have come up from this body."   7:5; 8:11, 23

The seventh heaven

6 And he took me up into the seventh heaven, and there I saw a wonderful light,
7 and also angels without number. •And there I saw all the righteous from the time
8,9 of Adam onwards. •And there I saw the holy Abel and all the righteous. •And
there I saw Enoch and all who (were) with him,[h] stripped of (their) robes of the
flesh; and I saw them in their robes of above,[i] and they were like the angels who
10 stand there in great glory. •But they were not sitting on their thrones,[j] nor were
11 their crowns of glory[k] on them. •And I asked the angel who (was) with me,[l]   7:22; 8:26; 9:18,
"How is it that they have received these robes, but are not on (their) thrones nor   24f.; 11:40
12 in (their) crowns?" •And he said to me, "They do not receive the crowns and
thrones of glory—nevertheless, they do see and know whose (will be) the thrones
and whose the crowns—until the Beloved descends in the form in which you will
13 see him descend. •The LORD will indeed descend into the world[m] in the last days,
(he) who is to be called Christ after he has descended and become like you in
14 form,[n] and they will think that he is flesh and a man.[o] •And the god of that world
will stretch out [his hand against the Son],[p] and they will lay their hands upon
15 him and hang him upon a tree,[q] not knowing who he is. •And thus his descent,
as you will see, will be concealed even from the heavens so that it will not be
16 known who he is.[r] •And when he has plundered the angel[s] of death, he will rise[t]   10:8, 10, 14;
on the third day[u] and will remain in that world for five hundred and forty-five   11:19;
17 days.[v] •And then many of the righteous will ascend with him, whose spirits do   1Pet 3:18–20;
not receive (their) robes until the LORD Christ ascends and they ascend with him.[w]   Mt 27:52f.
18 Then indeed they will receive their robes and[x] their thrones and their crowns,
when he has ascended into the seventh heaven."

f. "this is your Lord . . . Jesus": Lat2, Slav
"this is the Son of God," cf. n. w on 8:18 and n.
b2 on 8:25f.

g. Apparently a reference to a secret name of
Jesus, cf. 8:7; Rev 19:12. If not, it is necessary to
assume that all the references to "Jesus" and
"Christ" in chs. 6–11 are secondary.

h. For vss. 7–9a Lat2, Slav have only "And I
saw certain righteous men," but Greek Legend
2:27 supports Eth.

i. The heavenly robes of the righteous symbolize
their transformed state; they are mentioned elsewhere in 1:5; 3:25; 4:16f.; 7:22; 8:14, 26; 9:2,
17f., 24–26; 11:40. Cf. Rev 3:4f.; 6:11; 7:9, 13f.;
4Ezra 2:39, 44f.; 2Cor 5:1–4.

j. The thrones symbolize that the righteous dead
in heaven share in the reign of the Lord, cf. Rev
3:21; 4:4; Mt 19:28; Lk 22:30.

k. In the ancient world victorious athletes were
crowned. In a Christian context crowns are symbols
of the reward which Christians who are faithful are
to enjoy in heaven, cf. Rev 2:10; 3:11; 4:4; 1Cor
9:25; 2Tim 4:7f.; Jas 1:12; 1Pet 5:4; 4Ezra 2:43–
45; ShepHerm Similitudes 8:2, 1 and 3, 6.

l. "who (was) with me": so Eth, but D adds
"and I said to him"; Lat2, Slav "and I said."

m. "into the world": B C D omit.

n. Lit. "like your form."

o. For vss. 12f. Slav (and similarly the corrupt
Lat2) reads "And he said to me, 'They do not
receive these until this Son of God first descends;
nevertheless, they know whose (will be) [lit. "are"]
the thrones and whose the crowns when he descends
and is like you in form [lit. "like your form"].' "
For "who is to be called Christ" cf. n. b2 on

8:25f.

p. Correction based on Lat2 (which adds "of
God"); Eth "by the hand of his son"; Slav corrupt.

q. "and they will lay . . . a tree": Lat2, Slav
"and he will hang him upon a tree and kill him"
(Slav "and they will hang . . . and he will kill
him").

r. Lat2 (and similarly Slav) "And he will descend into hell and make it and all the phantoms
of hell desolate." Lat2, Slav differ considerably
from Eth in vss. 15–17.

s. Or "prince."

t. Lit. "ascend."

u. Lat2 (and similarly Slav) "And he will seize
the prince of death, and will plunder him, and will
crush all his powers, and will rise on the third
day."

v. "and will remain . . . days": Lat2, Slav omit
and the words may be an addition to the text. The
belief that Jesus remained on the earth after the
resurrection for 545 days is apparently taken from
gnostic sources; Irenaeus (*Adversus haereses* 1.3:2;
30:14 [PG, vol. 7, cols. 469f., 703]) states that
both the Valentinians and the Ophites believed that
Jesus remained with the disciples after the resurrection for eighteen months (i.e. approximately 545
days).

w. Lat2 (and similarly Slav) "having certain
righteous men with him, and will send his preachers
into the whole world [cf. 3:17f.; 11:22], and will
ascend into heaven." For the reference in Eth to
Christ cf. n. w on 8:18.

x. "their robes and": Lat2, Slav omit. Mention
of the robes is unexpected in what is intended as
an answer to the question of vs. 11; it was included

The record of men's deeds

19,20 And I said to him what I had asked him in the third heaven, •["Show me how   7:27
21 everything]ʸ which is done in that world is known here." •And while I was still
speaking to him, behold one of the angels who were standing by, more glorious
22 than that angelᶻ who had brought me up from the world, •showed me (some)
books,ᵃ² but not like the books of this world;ᵇ² and he opened them, and the books   Dan 7:10;
had writing in them, but not like the books of this world. And they were given   Rev 20:12;
to me, and I read them, and behold the deeds of the children of Israelᶜ² were   4Ezra 6:20;
                                                                                       1En 89:61-64;
23 written there, their deeds which you know, my son Josab.ᵈ² •And I said, "Truly,   98:6-8
nothing which is done in this world is hidden in the seventh heaven."ᵉ²

The robes and thrones and crowns

24,25 And I saw many robes placed there, and many thrones and many crowns, •and I   7:22; 9:9f.
said to the angel who led me, "Whose (are) these robes and thrones and crowns?"
26 And he said to me, "As for these robes, there are many from that world who
will receive (them)ᶠ² through believing in the words of that one who will be named
as I have told you,ᵍ² and they will keep them, and believe in them,ʰ² and believe
in his cross; [for them (are) these]ⁱ² placed (here)."   3:18

The worship of the Lord

27 And I saw one standing (there) whose glory surpassed that of all,ʲ² and his glory
28 was great and wonderful. •And when theyᵏ² saw him, all the righteous whom I
had seen and the angelsˡ² came to him. And Adam and Abel and Seth and all the
righteous approached first and worshiped him, and they all praised him with one
voice, and I also was singing praises with them, and my praise was like theirs.ᵐ²
29,30 And then all the angels approached, andⁿ² worshiped, and sang praises. •And he
31 was transformed and became like an angel.ᵒ² •And then the angel who led me
32 said to me, "Worship this one," and I worshiped and sang praises. •And the
angel said to me, "This is the LORD of all the praise which you have seen."

because both the righteous who are already in
heaven (vss. 7-12) and the righteous who ascend
with Christ (vs. 17) are in mind in Eth.

y. Correction based on Lat2, Slav; Eth "and he
said to me, 'Everything.'"

z. Lit. "more glorious than the glory of that
angel."

a2. Lat2, Slav "a book" (and consequently
singular for plural in the rest of the vs).

b2. "but not . . . this world": lacking in Lat2,
Slav, and probably a doublet.

c2. "of the children of Israel": Lat2, Slav "of
Jerusalem."

d2. "and their deeds . . . Josab": so Eth; Slav
"and I saw the deeds of men whom I did not
know"; Lat2 corrupt, but refers to "the deeds of
all men."

e2. Lat2, Slav add "And I asked the angel,
'Who is that person who is pre-eminent over all
[Slav omits "all"] the angels in his glory?' And
he answered and said to me, 'That [Slav "That
pre-eminent angel"] is the great angel [Slav "archangel"] Michael, ever praying on behalf of
humanity.'" Cf. Lat2, Slav in vss. 29, 42.

f2. Lat2 (and similarly Slav) "These robes many
from that world will lose." On this text the one in
whose words they believe is presumably meant to
be the Antichrist, but there is then nothing in chs.

6-11 to which this statement might refer, and vs.
26 is no longer an answer to vs. 25.

g2. "who will . . . told you": so Eth, cf. vs.
5; Lat2, Slav "about whom I told you." Lat2,
Slav omit the rest of vs. 26.

h2. B C D "him."

i2. Correction; A C "but for them (they are)";
B D "for whom (they are)."

j2. "one standing . . . of all": Lat2, Slav "the
Lord in great glory."

k2. A "I."

l2. A adds "whom I had seen"; D "all the
righteous and the angels whom [I] had seen."

m2. Lat2, Slav are much shorter than Eth in
vss. 27f. and omit mention of Adam, Abel, and
Seth; cf. n. h on vs. 9.

n2. Lat2, Slav "And then [Lat2 omits "then"]
Michael approached and worshiped, and with him
all the angels"; cf. n. e2 on vs. 23.

o2. The meaning seems to be that the appearance
of Jesus was transformed for the sake of Isaiah (cf.
vss. 33, 37). Lat2, Slav (preferred by some commentators) read "And again I was transformed and
became like an angel [Lat2 "the angels"]." But
the transformation of Isaiah took place progressively as he ascended from heaven to heaven (7:25),
and mention of it here comes too late; in any case,
the easier reading "I" is unlikely to be original.

The worship of the angel of the Holy Spirit

33 And while I was still speaking,[p2] I saw another glorious (person) who was like him, and the righteous approached him, and worshiped, and sang praises, and I also sang praises with them; but his glory[q2] was not transformed to accord with[r2]
34,35 their form. •And then the angels approached and worshiped him.[s2] •And I saw
36 the LORD and the second angel, and they were standing, •and the second one whom I saw (was) on the left of my LORD. And I asked the angel who led me and I said to him,[t2] "Who is this one?" And he said to me, "Worship him, for this is the angel of the Holy Spirit who has spoken[u2] in you and also in the other   1:7 righteous."[v2]

The worship of God

37 And I saw the Great Glory while the eyes of my spirit were open, but I could not   10:16; 11:32; thereafter see,[w2] nor the angel who (was) with me, nor any of the angels whom I   1En 14:20
38 had seen worship my LORD. •But I saw the righteous as they beheld with great   1En 14:21
39 power[x2] the glory of that one. •And my[y2] LORD approached me, and the angel of the Spirit, and said,[z2] "See how it has been given to you to see the LORD,[a3] and (how) because of you power has been given to the angel who (is) with you."   8:8
40 And I saw how my LORD and the angel of the Holy Spirit worshiped and [b3] both
41 together praised the LORD.[c3] •And then all the righteous approached and worshiped,[d3]
42 and the angels[e3] approached and worshiped, and all the angels sang praises.

The worship of the Father by the six lower heavens

1 **10** And then I heard the voices and the hymns of praise which I had heard in
2 each of the six heavens—which I had heard as I ascended[a] there;[b] •and all (the voices and hymns of praise) were directed to that Glorious One[c] whose glory I   7:16f.
3 could not see.[d] •And I also heard and saw the praise (which was directed to) him,
4 and the LORD and the angel of the Spirit heard everything and saw everything.[e]   9:37
5 And all the praise which was sent (up) from the six heavens was not only heard,

---

p2. Slav "while he was still speaking"; Lat2 omits.

q2. "his glory": so Eth; Lat2, Slav "he." The glory of the Holy Spirit was not such that it needed transformation for the sake of Isaiah; contrast vs. 30. However, some commentators would emend the text to read "my glory."

r2. Lit. "according to."

s2. "him": so B, Lat2, Slav; A C D omit. Slav adds "And the angel said to me, 'Worship him and sing praises.' And I worshiped him and sang praises." Lat2 adds the second sentence.

t2. "the angel . . . to him": so D; A B omit; C "him." For vss. 35, 36a Lat2, Slav read "And again I saw the other one in great glory. And I asked the angel who was walking [Lat2 "And walking, I asked the angel"]."

u2. Lat2, Slav "speaks."

v2. Vss. 35f. were used by the heretic Hieracas according to Epiphanius (*AdvHaer* 67:3), who quotes them. The text of Epiphanius is fuller than that of Eth and of Lat2, Slav, and contains elements which only occur separately in the two textual traditions. See "Composite Character of the Ascension," and n. 29.

w2. Lat2, Slav "And after these things another indescribable glory was revealed which, although the eyes of my spirit were open, I could not see."

x2. Lat2, Slav "in great glory." The righteous

dead, but not the angels, can look at the glory of God, cf. Rev. 22:4; for the privileged position of the righteous cf. also vss. 28, 33, 41.

y2. B C D "the."

z2. C D add "to me."

a3. Apparently an allusion to the momentary vision of God which, according to Eth in vs. 37, Isaiah was granted.

b3. B C D "how he worshiped my Lord and the angel of the Spirit, and they."

c3. For vss. 39f. Lat2 (similarly Slav) has only "And first my Lord approached, and the spiritual angel, and they worshiped him and [both] together sang praises."

d3. A C D add by mistake "and all the righteous" (C without "and"); B omits these words by homoeoteleuton together with the preceding "approached and worshiped."

e3. Lat2, Slav include a reference to Michael, cf. n. e2 on vs. 23.

10 a. "as I ascended": B "ascending."

b. Lat2, Slav corrupt, but Lat2 points to a text "which I had heard in the six heavens, ascending and being heard in the seventh heaven."

c. Lat2, Slav "And all praised that One"; D "and all praised that Glorious One."

d. D adds "to him (the praise) was directed."

e. Lat2, Slav omit vss. 3f.

6 but seen. •And I heard the angel who led me, and he said to me,[f] "This is the Most High of the high ones, who dwells in the holy world,[g] who rests among the holy ones,[h] who will be called[i] by the Holy Spirit in the mouth of the righteous the Father of the LORD."

The Lord Christ is commissioned by the Father

7 And I heard the voice of the Most High, the Father of my LORD, as he said to
8 my LORD Christ, who will be called Jesus,[j] •"Go out and descend through all the heavens. You shall descend through the firmament and through that world as far
9 as the angel who (is) in Sheol,[k] but you shall not go as far as Perdition.[l] •And
10 you shall make your likeness like that of all who (are) in the five heavens,[m] •and you shall take care to make your form like that of the angels of the firmament
11 and also (like that) of the angels who (are) in Sheol.[n] •And none of the angels[o] of that world shall know that you (are) LORD with me of the seven heavens and
12 of their angels. And they shall not know that you (are) with me •when[p] with the voice of the heavens[q] I summon you,[r] and their angels and their lights,[s] and when I lift up (my voice)[t] to the sixth heaven, that you may judge and destroy the princes and the angels and the gods of that world, and the world which is ruled
13 by them,[u] •for they have denied me and said, 'We alone are, and there is no one
14 besides us.' •And afterwards you shall ascend from the gods of death to your place,[v] and you shall not be transformed in each of the heavens, but in glory you
15 shall ascend and sit at my right hand, •and then the princes and the powers of
16 that world[w] will worship you." •This command I heard the Great Glory giving to my LORD.

(margin references: 9:16; 10:10, 14; 11:19 · 1Cor 2:8 · Ps 50:4 · 7:12 · 4:6 10:8 · 11:32 Phil 2:10 9:37)

The descent of the Lord through the seven heavens

17 And thus[x] I saw when my LORD went out from the seventh heaven into the sixth
18 heaven. •And the angel who had led me from this[y] world was with me, and he said to me, "Understand, Isaiah, and look, that you may see the transformation

---

f. "to me": A B omit.

g. Lat2, Slav "This is the one eternal (being), who dwells in the high world."

h. The description of God is based on the LXX text of Isa 57:15, cf. n. j on 6:8. Lat2, Slav add "whose name and appearance we cannot endure."

i. Lat2, Slav "who is praised" and omit "the Father of the Lord."

j. Lat2, Slav "the voice of the Eternal One saying to the Lord, the Son," but Greek Legend 2:37 supports Eth; cf. n. w on 8:18 and n. b2 on 8:25f.

k. B C D add "you shall descend."

l. The Eth. word *haguel*, which means "perdition," "destruction" is probably intended here as the name of the final place of punishment for the wicked; cf. Job 26:6; 28:22; Ps 88:11; Prov 15:11, where the word rendered in JB as "Perdition" is the Heb. *ᵓbaddôn*, i.e. "(place of) destruction." "Abaddon" occurs as the name of the angel of the Abyss in Rev 9:11. "You shall descend . . . Perdition": Lat2, Slav "You shall be in the world, and go as far as the angel who is in hell."

m. I.e. in the five lower heavens; in the sixth heaven he retains his divine form, cf. vs. 19.

n. Lat2, Slav abbreviate vs. 9 and omit vs. 10.

o. Or "rulers."

p. "And they shall . . . when": so A B D. Jesus will only be recognized by the angels of this world when he has actually ascended to heaven to sit at the right hand of God, cf. vss. 14f. It is thus possible to make sense of the text. However, some commentators have thought the text unintelligible and have emended it to read "And they shall not know that you (are) with me until"; a simpler alternative would be to omit the negative: "But they shall know that you (are) with me when." For Lat2, Slav see n. u. C has "then" for "when" in both places in vs. 12.

q. I.e. with thunder.

r. "you": A omits (hence "summon both their angels and . . .").

s. The angels and lights of heaven are meant.

t. "and when I lift up (my voice)": probable interpretation, text obscure. The sixth heaven is singled out for mention because, in association with the seventh, it enjoys a special status; thus e.g. the Lord does not change his appearance in the sixth heaven, cf. vs. 19.

u. For vss. 11f. Lat2, Slav have only "And they will not recognize you, nor will the angels and the princes of that world; and you will judge the prince of that world [Slav omits "of that world"] and his angels, and the world ruled by them [Lat2 "and the rulers of the world"]."

v. B "And after you have died and risen, you shall ascend to your place"; Lat2 omits; Slav "And when you have been raised from the earth, afterwards."

w. Lat2 (similarly Slav) "the princes and the powers and all the angels and all the rulers of heaven and earth and hell."

x. Lat2, Slav "then."

y. B "that."

19 and descent of the LORD." •And I looked, and when the angels who (were) in
the sixth heaven saw him, they praised him and glorified him, for he had not been
transformed into the form of the angels there; and they praised him, and I also
20 sang praises with them. •And I saw when he descended into the fifth heaven, that
in the fifth heaven he made his form like that of the angels there, and they did
21 not praise him, for his form was like theirs. •And then he descended into the
22 fourth heaven and made his form like that of the angels there; •and when they
saw him, they did not praise him or glorify him, for his form (was) like their form.
23 And again I saw when he descended into the third heaven, that he made his form
24 like that of the angels who (were) in the third heaven. •And those who kept the
gate of the (third) heaven demanded the password, and the LORD gave (it) to them
in order that he should not be recognized;[z] and when they saw him, they did not
25 praise him or glorify him, for his form (was) like their form. •And again I saw
when he descended into the second heaven, that there again he gave the password,
26 for those who kept the gates demanded (it), and the LORD gave (it). •And I saw
when he made his form like that of the angels who (were) in the second heaven,
that they saw him, but did not praise him, for his form (was) like their form.
27 And again I saw when he descended into the first heaven, that there he gave the
password to those who kept the gates. And he made his form like that of the
angels who (were) on the left of that throne, and they did not praise him or glorify
28 him, for his form (was) like their form. •And as for me, no one questioned me
29 because of the angel who led me. •And again he descended into the firmament
where the prince of this world dwells, and he gave the password to those who   1:3
(were) on the left, and his form (was) like theirs, and they did not praise him
there; but in envy they were fighting one another, for there is there a power of
30 evil[a2] and envying about trifles.[b2] •And I saw when he descended and made himself
31 like the angels of the air, that he was like one of them. •And he did not give the
password, for they were plundering and doing violence to one another.[c2]

The miraculous birth of the Lord

1 **11** And after this I looked, and the angel who spoke to me and led me said to
me, "Understand, Isaiah son of Amoz, because for this purpose I was sent from
2 the LORD."[a] •And I saw a woman of the family of David the prophet whose name   Acts 2:30;
(was) Mary, and she (was) a virgin and was betrothed to a man whose name (was)   11QPs[a] 27.11
Joseph, a carpenter, and he also (was) of the seed and family of the righteous
3 David of Bethlehem in Judah. •And he came into his lot.[b] And when she was
betrothed, she was found to be pregnant, and Joseph the carpenter wished to   Mt 1:18–21
4 divorce her. •But the angel of the Spirit appeared in this world,[c] and after this
5 Joseph did not divorce Mary;[d] but he did not reveal this matter to anyone. •And
he did not approach Mary, but kept her as a holy virgin, although she was
6,7 pregnant. •And he did not live with her for two months. •And after two months
8 of days, while Joseph was in his house, and Mary[e] his wife,[f] but both alone, •it
came about, when they were alone, that Mary then looked with her eyes and saw
9 a small infant, and she was astounded. •And after her astonishment had worn

z. "And those . . . recognized": B omits.
a2. B C D "an evil power there."
b2. "but . . . trifles": Lat2, Slav omit.
c2. "for they . . . another": Lat2 "and they
did not sing praises"; Slav "and they did not
question him."

11 a. Lat2, Slav add "to show you all things. For
no one before you has seen, nor after you will be
able to see, what you have seen and heard. And I
saw one like a son of man, and he dwelt with men
in the world, and they did not recognize him."
Lat2, Slav thereafter omit the whole of vss. 2–22.

b. The fate decreed him by God; it was God's
plan that Joseph should marry Mary; cf. vs. 10 and
ProtJames 9:1, "And the priest said to Joseph, 'It
has fallen to your lot to receive the virgin of the
Lord.'" Cf. ProtJames 19:1.
c. "in this world": B "to him."
d. B C "did not divorce her, but kept Mary";
after "divorce" in A D a word has been erased.
e. B C "in the house, and Mary"; D "in the
house of Mary."
f. "his wife": so C; B "his betrothed wife"; A
D have an erasure.

10 off,[g] her womb was found as (it was) at first, before she had conceived. •And
when her husband,[h] Joseph, said to her, "What has made you astounded?" his
eyes were opened, and he saw the infant and praised the LORD, because the LORD
11 had come in his lot.[i] •And a voice came to them, "Do not tell this vision to
12,13 anyone." •But the story about the infant was spread abroad in Bethlehem. •Some
said, "The virgin Mary has given birth before she has been married[j] two months."
14 But many said, "She did not give birth; the midwife did not go up (to her), and
we did not hear (any) cries of pain." And they were all blinded concerning him;
15 they all knew about him, but[k] they did not know from where he was. •And they
16 took him and went to Narazeth in Galilee. •And I saw, O Hezekiah and Josab my
son, and say to the other prophets also who are standing by, that it was hidden
from all the heavens and all the princes and every god of this world.

*Ignatius, Epistle
to the Ephesians
19*

The infancy and life of the Lord

17 And I saw (that) in Nazareth he sucked the breast like an infant, as was customary,
18 that he might not be recognized. •And when he had grown up, he performed great
signs and miracles in the land of Israel and (in) Jerusalem.

3:20

The crucifixion and resurrection of the Lord

19 And after this the adversary envied him and roused the children of Israel, who
did not know who he was, against him. And they handed him to the ruler,[l] and
20 crucified him, and he descended[m] to the angel[n] who (is) in Sheol.[o] •In Jerusalem,
21 indeed, I saw how they crucified him on a tree, •and likewise (how) after the
third day he rose and remained (many) days.[p]

*9:16; 10:8, 10,
14*

The ascension of the Lord through the seven heavens

22 And the angel who led me said to me, "Understand, Isaiah." And I saw when
23 he[q] sent out the twelve disciples and ascended. •And I saw him,[r] and he was in
the firmament,[s] but was not transformed into their form. And all the angels of the
24 firmament, and Satan, saw him and worshiped. •And there was much sorrow there
as they said, "How did our[t] LORD descend upon us, and we did not notice the
glory which was upon him,[u] which we (now) see was[v] upon him from the sixth
25 heaven?"[w] •And he ascended into the second heaven,[x] and he was not transformed,
but all the angels who (were) on the right and on the left, and the throne in the
26 middle, •worshiped him, and praised him, and said, "How did our[y] LORD remain
27 hidden from us as he descended, and we did not notice?" •And in the same way

*3:17f.;
Mt 28:18–20;
Acts 1:8f.*

2:2

g. Lit. "after she had been astounded."

h. "her husband": so C; omitted by B, erased
in A and (apparently) D.

i. "his lot": cf. n. b on vs. 3.

j. "she has been married": so C; D (over an
erasure) "she has been betrothed"; in A B the
word has been erased.

k. C "they all believed in him, but"; B D "no
one believed in him, and." Vs. 14 is apparently
quoted in the Acts of Peter 24.

l. "ruler": a word normally translated "king,"
but it is presumably Pilate who is meant (cf. Mt
27:2).

m. B C D "and caused him to descend."

n. B C "angels."

o. "who (is) in Sheol": so D, cf. Greek Legend
2:39 "the angel of Hades"; A B C omit.

p. A B D have only "days," with the sense
"many days"; C "forty days" (cf. Acts 1:3). It
has been suggested that originally Eth read "five
hundred and forty-five days," as in 9:16.

q. B "the Lord."

r. "him": B C D omit.

s. Lat2, Slav "And I saw him ascending into
the firmament."

t. B C "the."

u. "which was upon him": possibly a doublet
of the following clause.

v. Lit. "was found."

w. As he descended Christ retained the glory
which he possessed in the seventh and sixth heavens
(cf. 10:19), but kept it concealed; as he ascended
Christ's proper glory (cf. vs. 29) was recognized
by all. For vs. 24 Slav reads, "They said, 'How
was the Lord concealed from us in (our) midst,
and we did not recognize the king of glory?'"
Lat2 corrupt. The text appears to be defective at
this point in Eth and Lat2, Slav, for we expect a
reference to the ascent of the Lord into the first
heaven.

x. Lat2, Slav "And from the first heaven he
ascended more glorious."

y. B C D "the."

he ascended into the third (heaven), and in the same way they praised him and
28 spoke. •And in the fourth heaven and also in the fifth they spoke in exactly the
29,30 same way. •But there was one glory, and from it he was not transformed. •And
I saw when he ascended into the sixth heaven, that they worshiped him and praised
31,32 him;[z] •but in all the heavens the praise grew louder. •And I saw how he ascended
into the seventh heaven, and all the righteous and all the angels praised him. And
then I saw that he sat down at the right hand of that Great Glory, whose glory I   10:14
33 told you I could not behold. •And also I saw that the angel of the Holy Spirit sat   9:37
on the left.   9:36

The conclusion of the vision

34 This angel said to me, "Isaiah, son of Amoz, [it is enough for you],[a2] for these
(are) great things, for you have observed what no one born of flesh has observed.[b2]   8:11
35 And you shall return into your robe until your days are complete; then you shall   8:27
come here." These things I saw.

Isaiah's instructions to Hezekiah

36 And Isaiah told (them)[c2] to all those who were standing before him, and they sang
praises. And he spoke to Hezekiah the king and said, "These things I have spoken.
37,38 And the end of this world •and all this vision will be brought about in the last
39 generation." •And Isaiah made him[d2] swear that he would not tell this[e2] to the
people of Israel, and that he would not allow any man to copy these words.[f2]
40 And then[g2] they[h2] shall read them.[i2] But as for you, be[j2] in the Holy Spirit that
you may receive your robes, and the thrones and crowns of glory, which are   7:22; 9:9f.
41 placed in the seventh heaven. •Because of these visions and prophecies Sammael   5:1; 15f.
Satan sawed Isaiah the son of Amoz, the prophet, in half by the hand of Manasseh.   1:8; 2:2
42 And Hezekiah gave all these things to Manasseh in the twenty-sixth year of his
43 reign.[k2] •But Manasseh did not remember these things, nor place them in his   1:1
heart, but he became the servant of Satan and was destroyed.[l2]   2:1
                                                                                           1:8

Here ends (the book) of Isaiah the prophet with his ascension.[m2]

z. For vss. 27–30 Lat2, Slav have a shorter text.

a2. Correction based on Lat2, Slav; Eth "I have saved you."

b2. Lat2, Slav add "what eye has not seen, nor ear heard, nor has it entered into the heart of man, how great things God has prepared for all [Slav omits "all"] those who love him [Lat2 "you"]"; cf. Isa 64:4; 1Cor 2:9. Jerome (*Commentary on Isaiah* 64:4 [PL, vol. 24, col. 622]) states that AscenIs has this passage and thus indicates that here at least the text of AscenIs he knew is the one given in Lat2, Slav. For the title "the Ascension of Isaiah" in Jerome, see "Composite Character of the Ascension."

c2. "These things . . . told (them)": Lat2, Slav "These things Isaiah saw and told."

d2. D "Hezekiah."

e2. "this": A B D, Lat2, Slav omit.

f2. This statement is part of the apocalyptic fiction which was intended to explain how the account of Isaiah's vision had remained unknown from the time of its supposed composition in the reign of Hezekiah to the time of its actual composition in the early Christian era. Cf. 6:17.

g2. "then": apparently "in the last generation" (vs. 38), cf. Dan 12:4, 9. But the sequence of thought is not very clear, and Eth may be defective; see n. i2.

h2. B C D "you."

i2. "And then . . . read them": so Eth; Slav "But as far as you understand what is said by the king in the prophets, understand such things, all of you"; Lat2 corrupt.

j2. Slav "watch."

k2. "of his reign": A C omit.

l2. Vss. 41–43 are an editorial conclusion which serves to link VisIs (chs. 6–11) with MartIs (chs. 1–5). For these vss. Lat2, Slav have "And he ceased speaking and went out from (the presence of) Hezekiah the king."

m2. B, Slav omit; C "Here ends the vision of Isaiah the prophet, the son of Amoz, with his ascension"; D "Here ends the ascension of Isaiah the prophet"; Lat2 "The vision of Isaiah is ended."

JOSEPH AND ASENETH

(First Century B.C.–Second Century A.D.)

A NEW TRANSLATION AND INTRODUCTION

BY C. BURCHARD

The Old Testament records that Pharaoh gave to Joseph Aseneth, the daughter of Potiphera, Priest of On, for his wife (Gen 41:45). How could Joseph—the model of chastity, piety, and statesmanship—marry a foreign Hamitic girl, daughter of an idolatrous priest? Jewish theology and lore found many answers to this intriguing question and expanded some into narratives.[1] Joseph and Aseneth, the longest of these stories, is a full-fledged romance by an anonymous author; it is nearly twice as long as Esther, and a little longer than the Gospel of Mark.

Aseneth is a beautiful virgin of eighteen years and the daughter of Pentephres,[2] priest of Heliopolis and Pharaoh's chief counselor. Many princes, including Pharaoh's firstborn son, ask for her hand in marriage. She despises them all and prefers to live in her ornate penthouse above Pentephres' palace, where she worships countless idols. One day Joseph, touring Egypt to collect corn, announces his visit to her father. Pentephres tells Aseneth he is going to give her to Joseph in marriage. She refuses flatly, only to fall in love with Joseph when she sees him entering her father's house in royal attire. Now it is her time to be repudiated. A Jew who worships God and lives on the bread of life will not kiss a heathen woman who eats food offered to idols. Still Joseph is charitable enough to say a prayer for her conversion, then boards his chariot in order to gather more corn, promising to be back a week later. Utterly shaken, Aseneth destroys her idols, engages in a week of fasting and crying, and repents for both her conceit and idolatry. On the morning of the eighth day, the chief of God's angels comes to see her, declares her reborn, tells her that she is to be a mother city for all who would repent like her, feeds her a piece of honeycomb, which he says is the bread of life, and promises her that Joseph will come to marry her. He does; and the wedding ensues, performed and presided over by Pharaoh himself.

Eight years later, Pharaoh's firstborn son happens to see Aseneth by chance and his old infatuation is revived. He fails to persuade Joseph's brothers, Simeon and Levi, to help him kidnap Aseneth and assume power in Egypt by killing Pharaoh and Joseph. He then tries Dan and Gad and achieves more success. He gives them troops; and the three set up an ambush for Aseneth, who is driving to her vineyard. However, Benjamin, who is sitting beside her in the carriage, wounds Pharaoh's son with a stone and kills his escorts. Levi, being a prophet, divines what is going on and comes running with his brothers—Reuben, Simeon, Judah, Issachar, and Zebulon—to slay Dan and Gad's men. These two attempt to kill Aseneth, but miraculously their swords fall from their hands. Aseneth pardons them and intercedes for them with her in-laws. Three days later Pharaoh's son dies, closely followed by his grief-strickened father. Joseph then reigns over Egypt for forty-eight years.

---

[1] V. Aptowitzer, "Asenath, the Wife of Joseph: A Haggadic Literary-Historical Study," *HUCA* 1 (1924) 239–306; L. Ginzberg, *Legends*, vol. 2, pp. 170–78; also see esp. vol. 5, pp. 336–39, 374f.

[2] As to the name form, see note on 1:3.

Texts

Joseph and Aseneth is extant in sixteen Greek manuscripts, falling into at least four groups, and eight versions translated from the Greek, running to a rough total of seventy manuscripts.[3] Abbreviations used herein are as follows:

Group a:
1. O = St. Catherine's Monastery, Mount Sinai, MS Greek 504, 10th cent., Joseph and Aseneth is lost except for the title and the first words in the table of contents.
2. A = Vatican Library, Vatican City, MS Vaticanus Graecus 803, 11–12th cent.; printed by P. Batiffol, "Le Livre de la Prière d'Aseneth," *Studia Patristica: Études d'ancienne littérature chrétienne* (Paris, 1889–90) pp. 1–87 (with apparatus from BCD Syr.; = Bat); transl. P. Riessler, "Joseph und Asenath: Eine altjüdische Erzählung," *TQ* 103 (1922) 1–22, 145–83, reprinted with little change by P. Riessler, *Altjüdisches Schrifttum ausserhalb der Bibel* (Augsburg, 1928; repr. Darmstadt, 1966) pp. 497–538, 1303f. (= Rie); and E. W. Brooks, *Joseph and Asenath: The Confession and Prayer of Asenath Daughter of Pentephres the Priest* (TED 2.7; London, New York, 1918). Brooks makes use of Batiffol's apparatus and Syr. Arm. L1 Slav., and gives the non-*a* material contained in 11:15–18a, 12:8b, 15:12x, 16:17–17x, 20:5b, 6b, 21:10–21, and 23:6b in an appendix because he thinks it is original (= Br).
3. P = Monastery of Konstamonitou, Mount Athos, MS 14, 15th cent.
4. Q = Vatican Library, Vatican City, MS Palatinus Graecus 364, 15th cent., many omissions; used by V. M. Istrin, "Apokrif ob Iosifě i Asenefě," *Drevnosti* (Trudy Slavjanskoj kommissii Imperatorskago moskovskago archeologičeskago obščestva 2; Moscow, 1898) pp. 146–99.
5. C = Bodleian Library, Oxford, MS Baroccio Greek 148, 15th cent., ends in 10:5; used by Bat.
6. R = St. Catherine's Monastery, Mount Sinai, MS Greek 530, 15–16th cent., ends in 5:1, maybe a copy of C.

Group b:
7. E = Monastery of Vatopedi, Mount Athos, MS 600, 15th cent., many omissions.
8. G = Greeley Collection, Virginia Beach, Va., MS McKell (formerly property of D. McK. McKell of Chillicothe, Ohio), c. 1580, written and illuminated by Luke the Cypriot in Wallachia, omits 2:3b–10:1a and other passages; miniatures published by J. and O. Pächt, "An Unknown Cycle of Illustrations of the Life of Joseph," *Cahiers Archéologiques* 7 (1954) 35–49, pl. XII–XVI; G. Vikan, *Illustrated Manuscripts of Pseudo-Ephraem's Life of Joseph and the Romance of Joseph and Aseneth* (Ph.D. diss., Princeton, N.J., 1976).
9. F = Library of the Academy of the People's Republic of Rumania, Bucharest, MS Greek 966, 17th cent., four hortatory interpolations, some illegible spots.
10. W = St. Catherine's Monastery, Mount Sinai, MS Greek 1976, 17th cent., same interpolations as F.

Group c:
11. H = Greek Orthodox Patriarchate, Jerusalem, MS Panhagios Taphos 73, 17th cent., ends in 16:17y with a new ending down to chapter 21:9 added in modern Greek; this ending is published by Chr. Burchard, "Joseph and Aseneth neugriechisch," *NTS* 24 (1978) 68–84, see 80–83.
12. J = Ibid., MS Saba 389, 17th cent., ends in 16:10.
13. K = Ibid., MS Saba 593, finished September 1, 1802, ends as H.

Group d:
14. B = Vatican Library, MS Palatinus Graecus 17, 11th cent.; used by Bat, printed by Istrin.
15. D = Bodleian Library, MS Baroccio Greek 147, 15th cent.; used by Bat.
    Critical edition of the *d* text by M. Philonenko, *Joseph et Aséneth: Introduction,*

---

[3] For catalogs and other details see Chr. Burchard, *Untersuchungen*, pp. 2–17; A.-M. Denis, *Introduction*, pp. 40–48. No papyri and no quotations in Gk. are on record.

texte critique et notes (SPB 13; Leiden, 1968); full documentation of BD, many readings from Slav. (cf. below on Slav.), occasional references to AEFGH, almost none to the other versions (= Phil).

Unexplored:

16. University Library, Wrocław (formerly Breslau), Poland, MS Rehdiger 26, 11th cent., lower script of a palimpsest.

Versions:

1. Syr. = Syriac, first half of 6th cent. Syr. is preserved only as part of Pseudo-Zacharias Rhetor, *Church History*, I 6 (finished soon after A.D. 569), in one MS and a copy of it. Leaves containing 13:15–16:7 are lost. Careful edition by E. W. Brooks, *Historia ecclesiastica Zachariae Rhetori vulgo adscripta* (CSCO 83; Paris, 1919, repr. 1953) vol. 1, pp. 21–55; Latin translation by the same, *Historia ecclesiastica Zachariae Rhetori vulgo adscripta* (CSCO 87; Louvain, 1924, repr. 1953) vol. 1, pp. 15–39.

2. Arm. = Armenian, 6–7th cent.(?). Forty-five manuscripts falling into six groups are known to date, the most important being Matenadaran (Mashtotz Institute of Ancient Manuscripts), Erevan, MS 1500 (A.D. 1282–83) (= 332). Poor edition by S. Yovsêpʿeanç, *Tʿangaran hin ew nor naxneaç, I. Ankanon girkʿ hin ktakaranaç* (Venice, 1896) pp. 152–98 (= Yovs); used by Br; poorly translated by J. Issaverdens both collectively, *The Uncanonical Writings of the Old Testament* (Venice, 1900) pp. 91–160, and separately, *The History of Assaneth* (Venice, 1900); specimen of a better edition by C. Burchard, "Joseph and Aseneth 25–29 armenisch," *JSJ* 10 (1979) 1–10.

3. L1 = Latin 1, circa A.D. 1200. Nine manuscripts are known, possibly all of them written in England. The text is rather uniform. Tolerable edition by Batiffol, *Studia Patristica*, pp. 89–115; used by Br. An unpublished epitome is preserved in three manuscripts.

4. L2 = Latin 2, circa A.D. 1200. We have five manuscripts falling into two very different groups. One group has only one member; it is University Library, Uppsala, MS C 37, beginning of the 13th cent. (= 436). The other group is headed by Monastery Library, Vorau (Austria), MS 136, 13th cent. (= 435). Unpublished.

5. Slav. = Serbian Slavonic, 15th cent.(?). Two manuscripts with minor variants are known. 1) Belgrad, National Library, MS Slav. 29, early 15th cent. (now lost), was printed by S. Novaković, "Srpsko-slovenski zbornik iz vremena despota Stefana Lazarevića," *Starine* 9 (1877) 1–47, see 27–42 (= 551), and used by Br. 2) Novaković's text was reprinted with the variants from Bucharest, Library of the Academy of the People's Republic of Rumania, MS Slav. 306, 15th cent. (= 552) by Chr. Burchard, *Joseph und Aseneth serbisch-kirchenslavisch: Text und Varianten* (Dielheimer Blätter zum Alten Testament. Beiheft 2; Dielheim, 1980); see pp. 43–45 for a list of corrections of Philonenko's presentation of BD).

6. Ngr. = Modern Greek, 16th cent.(?). We have two illuminated manuscripts: Monastery of Koutloumousi, Mount Athos, MS 100, 16th cent. (= 661); Bodleian Library, Oxford, MS Roe 5, 1614 (= 671). Poor edition of 671 by Istrin, *Drevnosti*, pp. 146–79; corrections and an edition of 661, which is a mere epitome, by Burchard, *NTS* 24 (1978) 68–79; miniatures of both published by Vikan, *Illustrated Manuscripts;* miniatures of 661 published by S. M. Pelekanidis, P. C. Christou, C. Tsiounis, and S. N. Kadas, *The Treasures of Mount Athos: Illuminated Manuscripts, Miniatures-Headpieces-Initial Letters* (Athens, 1974) vol. 1, pp. 456, 458f.; figs. 339–41.

7. Rum. = Rumanian, 18th cent.(?). Four manuscripts are known. Rum. shares the interpolations of FW. One manuscript was printed in modernized form by C. Bobulescu, *Istoria frumosului Iosif şi a prea frumoasei Asineta: După un manuscris din 1753* (Biblioteca pentru popor 15; Bucharest, 1922). A critical edition by V.-I. Leb is in preparation.

8. Eth. = Ethiopian. Lost save for a number of allusions.[4] Eth. may depend upon an equally lost Arabic version.

---

[4] See below, nn. 108–10.

The textual history of Joseph and Aseneth is not yet fully understood.[5]

(1) The book is an author's work, not a folk tale which has no progenitor. There was an original text. We may be reasonably certain that all textual witnesses known to date go back to a common archetype, which must be older than c. A.D. 500.[6]

(2) We know that the Greek manuscripts fall into at least four groups, *a*, *b*, *c*, *d*, that Slav. sides with *d*, and that the other versions align with *b*. For ancient translations, Arm. and L2 are full and reliable versions. However, for example, the relationship of 436 and 435& within L2 needs examination. Syr. would make a fair witness, too, were it not for a tendency toward loose or double translation, some abbreviation from the middle of chapter 24 on, and the loss of nearly three chapters. L1, a mere epitome from chapter 25 onward, is guilty of many omissions before that, even more so the Slav. When extant, Slav. is fairly accurate, however. Ngr. is little more than a paraphrase with long stretches of text left out altogether, while others are much inflated. Rum. is a severe condensation. All Greek groups and the versions need closer inspection as to their *Vorlage*. The miniatures of G, 671, and 661[7] may be of some help here because they reflect a state of textual development, all within the *b* group, which is older than the manuscripts in which they occur.

(3) We also know that *a* is a revision, no later than the tenth century, which meant to improve the biblicized Greek of the text but did not impinge on its substance and order save for a few omissions. Greek manuscript group *c*, as far as it goes, is an independent and less thorough revision, probably late medieval or early modern, of a text which was closer to *b* than to the ancestors of *a* or *d*.

(4) Difficulties start with *d*. It is one third shorter than *a*. Philonenko feels that *d* represents the oldest attainable text of Joseph and Aseneth; it was expanded into *b*, which was revised into *c*, which in turn was finally revised into *a*. However, many gaps in *d* are obvious omissions (see e.g. 19:4; 21:2; 27:10), and many readings are inferior to those in *a*, *b*, *c*. Manuscript group *a* is also generally closer to *d* than to *b* or *c*, which are supposed to stand between them, and there is nothing to suggest that *c*, purported father of *a*, ever existed beyond 16:17a. So *d* is more likely to be an epitome, no later than the eleventh century, of a fuller text, which was close to the unrevised archetype of *a*. Abridgment is a natural thing to happen to a text transmitted in writing as any individual manuscript of Joseph and Aseneth will readily demonstrate, and it tends to affect the last chapters, or the last verses of a subsection, more than the first, which is exactly what occurs in *d*.

(5) The main problem is *b*. This group includes four very recent Greek manuscripts and seven versions, all very different in both wording and length, most of them marred by a host of individual shortcomings. How does *b*, or its parts, relate to the other groups?[8] At any rate, the *b* group houses our oldest witnesses (Arm. Syr.)[9] and is the largest and most widely distributed group; readings offered, or supported, by it (versions included) are very often superior to their competitors on internal grounds. This includes a number of passages preserved by *b* alone such as 21:10–21.

(6) It seems possible to reconstruct the archetype of the textual tradition with a fair degree of certainty.[10] Often the witnesses agree literally or to a degree that the general run of the text is unmistakable even if the wording is not. Such passages occur over the whole length of the book, forming a sort of grid which has kept the original outline from becoming indiscernible.

---

[5] Burchard, *Untersuchungen*, pp. 18–49; *JSJ* 1 (1970) 3–34; "Joseph und Aseneth neugriechisch," *NTS* 24 (1978) 68–84; see 69 (correcting Burchard, *Untersuchungen*, p. 39); M. Philonenko, *Joseph et Aséneth*, pp. 3–26; E. W. Smith, Jr., *Joseph and Asenath*, pp. 13–17.

[6] That JosAsen is coupled with a Life of Joseph in all groups of text but *c* (see below) seems to corroborate the basic unity of the tradition.

[7] See Vikan, *Illustrated Manuscripts*, partly summarized in his "Illustrated Manuscripts of the Romance of Joseph and Aseneth," *SBL 1976 Seminar Papers*, ed. G. MacRae (SBL Seminar Papers Series 10; Missoula, Mont., 1976) pp. 193–208, 15 figs. Cf. further Pächt and Pächt, *Cahiers Archéologiques* 7 (1954) 35–49; Burchard, *NTS* 24 (1978) 75–77.

[8] In some cases of split tradition *b* appears to have preserved one part of a clause and *a*, *d*, or *c* the other (see 2:3; 12:2; 16:14; 18:2, 11; 21:9; 22:9, 13; 24:3; 24:17; 25:4, 6). This would suggest that *b* is indeed a family of its own, with an ancestor which stands at some distance from the original.

[9] The Passion of St. Irene, which depends on JosAsen (see below) also seems to testify to the age of *b*. The text which it presupposes certainly is neither *a* nor *d* (see 15:7).

[10] Contrast the opinion of Philonenko, *Joseph et Aséneth*, pp. 22f. Nevertheless, for all practical purposes Philonenko regards *d* as the original text.

A new edition of the Greek text is needed; the existing editions of the Greek text, as well as the modern translations, rely on either *a* or *d* and leave *b, c,* and most of the versions practically unmined. A major edition will have to wait until all evidence has been explored fully. A preliminary new text has been established for the present translation and for the German version.[11] The new text is based on fresh collations of all Greek and modern Greek manuscripts (except the Breslau palimpsest) by D. Sänger, and of all Latin manuscripts by H. Krüger. It is also based on Syr. (as edited by Brooks), on Arm. chapters 1–24 (as printed by Yovsēpʻeanç, supplemented by a collation of 332), on Arm. chapters 25–29 (as edited by Burchard), on Slav. (as printed by Novaković), on Ngr. (671) (as printed by Istrin and corrected by Burchard), and on Rum. (as printed by Bobulescu). The textual history of Joseph and Aseneth as it is known to date would seem to suggest that an eclectic text with a strong leaning toward *b* is in order. The preliminary text follows *b* unless a variant reading definitely proves superior. This is generally assumed when *a, c,* or *d* have a fuller text than *b,* unless there is evidence to the contrary. If there is a disagreement among the manuscripts and versions of *b,* the variant that has more outside support is usually preferred. In a few cases we must rely on conjecture (e.g. in 12:8). The text thus constituted may look more *b*-like than a final one will. Still it has the advantage of presenting Joseph and Aseneth very close to the form, or type of forms, in which the book was most widely read, and of being, it is hoped, much closer to the original than any other text published so far. A minor edition with a representative critical apparatus is in preparation.[12]

Original language

Most scholars have agreed that Joseph and Aseneth was composed in Greek. The only one to argue at some length against this view was P. Riessler.[13] To him *a* and *d* represented two independent translations from the Hebrew. Textual history as reviewed above rules out a double translation; the language all but precludes a single one. Riessler advanced some evidence for mistranslation, but it is inconclusive (see 4:2; 15:7; 16:13). The balance of his argument goes to show biblicized Greek; but it is better to assign this to the stylistic effort of a Greek author (see below). Moreover, a translator would have had little occasion to use words like "all-beautiful" (13:14), "child-loving" (12:8), "immortality," "incorruptibility" (e.g. 8:5), "(things) being and appearing" or "non-appearing and non-being" (12:2), "incorruptible" (12:15), "sweet (father)" (of God, 12:14f.), "transient" (12:15), "unutterable" (14:2), turns like "it is not fitting" (e.g. 8:5), "in a tyrannical fashion" (23:6), clusters of adjectival attributes (e.g. 10:10), or the passive with "by." If based on a Semitic original, Joseph and Aseneth would be a reworking, not a translation. Yet no one has so far produced a shred of evidence that Joseph and Aseneth was at all known in ancient Hebrew or Aramaic literature. So the book belongs to what is commonly called "hellenistic Jewish literature" as distinct from Palestinian and Babylonian,[14] although the latter branches are hardly less hellenistic, if often in a different way.[15] Numerous contacts with the literature of the Western diaspora and early Christianity readily bear this out.

Literary character

Title
Ancient custom suggests that Joseph and Aseneth had a title, probably given in full at the end and prefixed in a possibly shorter form at the opening,[16] but none that have come down to us seem to represent it (see before 1:1). It may have been something like "Aseneth,"

[11] Burchard, *Joseph und Aseneth* (JSHRZ 2.4; Gütersloh, 1983).

[12] To be published in the PVTG series (Leiden). The text alone is available in mimeographed form in "Ein vorläufiger griechischer Text von Joseph und Aseneth," *Dielheimer Blätter zum Alten Testament* 14 (1979) 2–53.

[13] "Joseph und Asenath: Eine altjüdische Erzählung," *TQ* 103 (1922) 1–22, 145–83; see esp. pp. 1–3.

[14] R. Marcus, "Hellenistic Jewish Literature," *The Jews: Their History, Culture, and Religion*, ed. L. Finkelstein (New York, 1949, 1960³) vol. 2, pp. 1077–115; V. Tcherikover, "Jewish Apologetic Literature Reconsidered," *Eos* 48.3 (1957) 169–93; G. Delling, "Perspektiven der Erforschung des hellenistischen Judentums," *HUCA* 45 (1974) 133–76.

[15] M. Hengel, *Judentum und Hellenismus* (WUNT 10; Tübingen, 1969, 1973²; ET by Fortress Press of Philadelphia in 1974).

[16] On ancient book titles see lately, E. Schmalzriedt, *Peri physeōs: Zur Frühgeschichte der Buchtitel* (Munich, 1970).

conceivably with a term denoting genre before and a word of identification after it, or perhaps "Joseph and Aseneth" as we call the book today. The author's name may or may not have gone with it, but none is preserved.

Structure

Joseph and Aseneth falls into two parts, which could almost stand by themselves. Part I (chs. 1–21) is suspended between two allusions to the Story of Joseph (Gen 37–50). Chapter 1:1 echoes Genesis 41:46 to tell that Pharaoh sent Joseph around Egypt to gather up the corn of the seven years of plenty, followed in 1:2 by a remark about Joseph's arrival in Heliopolis. Chapter 21:9 notes the birth of Ephraim and Manasseh in accordance with Genesis 41:50–52. The narrative proper opens with an exposition in 1:3–2:12; it corresponds to the page announcing the cast of characters and the scene of action that we usually see prefixed today to a play or detective story. Part I is rounded off by a hymn in 21:10–21 in which Aseneth recounts what happened to her. This consists of a combination of two different plots: the love story engaging Aseneth and Joseph, in chapters 3–9 and 19–21, and the conversion story, which involves Aseneth and the heavenly man in chapters 10–18, overlapping the love theme in 8f. and 19. Aseneth is the main figure, being almost uninterruptedly on the scene. But she is not in control. Pentephres launches the action, then he loses out gradually, first to the heavenly man and then to Pharaoh, the transitions being operated by Joseph. Otherwise the latter is a passive figure who has his marriage more or less wished upon him. During his bride's cumbersome conversion he is absent collecting grain. Part II (chs. 22–29) opens in 22:1f. with a summary of Genesis 41:53f. and 45:26–46:7; 47:27: Jacob and his kin come to Egypt and settle in Goshen. Joseph and Aseneth go to visit them (ch. 22 is an exposition). What follows is a tale of both abduction and revolution, or attempts to that effect, not simply a case of kidnap. Not incongruously, it ends with a reference to Joseph's rule over Egypt for forty-eight years. The scheme involves Pharaoh's son aided and abetted by Dan and Gad on the one hand, and Levi, Simeon, and Benjamin on the other. Aseneth has a part only in chapters 26–28. Joseph barely appears in 26:1–4, his mind again set on corn.

There is action in the story, but it is not fully developed. Potentially colorful narratives such as the wedding feast in chapter 21 or the military entanglements in chapters 26f. are merely stated. Considerable space is devoted to a sketch of Aseneth's tower and garden, to descriptions of people's appearance and emotions and to scenes of Aseneth dressing, where action is just an excuse for description. The rest consists mostly of dialogues, with some monologues, especially in chapters 11–13.

Stripped of the dialogues, the plot is simple enough. It unfolds with legendary straightforwardness bordering on the naïve (note the effects of a headache in 25:1–4). But it is by and large well constructed. Most of the shortcomings may be explained away on the assumption that Joseph and Aseneth is to be read as a companion to Genesis.

Integrity

Some scholars have suspected that the hymn of 21:10–21 is a later insertion, and that chapters 22–29 are an addition. The first half of this suspicion is invalidated by form criticism (see 21:10f.), and Part II is so close to I in both style and thought content that it is not likely to have come from a different hand. Lately T. Holtz argued for Christian interpolations.[17] Such interpolations, or other forms of editing, are not intrinsically improbable, but the evidence is not overwhelming.

Sources

If *source* means what the Gospel of Mark is to Matthew, or *Pygmalion* to *My Fair Lady*, a source for Joseph and Aseneth, or part of it, direct or indirect, has not yet appeared. More is gained if we amend the question of sources to include subject matter or themes, which the author may have picked up from tradition, oral or written, and worked into a new story, much as *West Side Story* is based on *Romeo and Juliet* and both reflect the

---

[17] "Christliche Interpolationen in 'Joseph und Aseneth,'" *NTS* 14 (1967–68) 482–97. On the problem outside Joseph and Aseneth, see G. B. Coleman, *The Phenomenon of Christian Interpolations into Jewish Apocalyptic Texts* (Ph.D. diss., Vanderbilt University, Nashville, Tenn., 1974).

eternal theme of young love thwarted by old convention, or individual happiness shattered by group rivalry. However, much of what has been cited in this context at best furnishes parallels to isolated motifs: the Egyptian Tale of the Doomed Prince, the Greek tradition concerning beautiful Helen of Troy, the Prayer of Joseph,[18] or Jewish legends making Aseneth the daughter of Dinah (Gen 34).[19] Batiffol, Aptowitzer, and Philonenko attach great importance to a Syriac text of very late attestation narrating how an eagle carried Dinah's daughter to Egypt and cradled her on Potiphar's altar.[20] This text they think is a later form of an old Jewish legend from which Joseph and Aseneth was developed, albeit with some dissimulation, because a daughter of Dinah could hardly serve as a proto-proselyte.[21] The pertinent passage runs:

> And the wife of this priest (Putiphar) took her (the baby) and brought her a nurse. And they rejoiced with great joy, for they had neither a boy nor a girl. And when the little girl grew up, Putiphar had a splendid dwelling constructed where he allowed her to live, and appointed virgins to serve her. And many chiefs' sons asked (for) her (in marriage), for she was beautiful to look at; but they did not suit her. And when Joseph came before Pharaoh he made him mount his carriage, and gave him the seal of the kingdom. And the Egyptians escorted him in triumph across all of Egypt, and his fame spread in all regions. And he (Pharaoh) gave him the daughter of the priest, Putiphar, for his wife, and he (Joseph) did not repulse [lit. hate] the daughter of Dina, (his) sister.

There seems to be some contact with Joseph and Aseneth here, but as it is restricted to chapters 1f., surely the dependence is on the legend's side.[22]

More helpful is hellenistic romance, especially the erotic variety as represented by the Great Five: Chariton's Chaereas and Calirrhoe, Xenophon of Ephesus' Ephesiaca, Longus' Daphnis and Chloë, Achilles Tatius' Clitophron and Leucippe, and Heliodorus' Aethiopica; or by Apuleius' The Golden Ass and Cupid and Psyche.[23] Much like these stories, Joseph and Aseneth relates a love that is achieved with difficulty only to find itself exposed to dangerous adventures to which a happy end is wrought by the hand of a benign Fate (although adventure which makes up the bulk of the novels is represented by just one episode in JosAsen). In particular, as an utterly conceited heroine who is swept off her feet by a handsome male and then thrown into the blackest despair, from which she disentangles herself by self-abasement and supernatural assistance, Aseneth is a worthy companion of Xenophon's Habrocomes and Anthia or Apuleius' Psyche. The historian's touch which is discernible in Joseph and Aseneth, although in the biblical vein rather than the Greek, does not militate against this suggestion. This is characteristic of the hellenistic novel also, especially of Chariton.[24] As to conversion forming part of a romance, apart from the general

---

[18] Philonenko, *Joseph et Aséneth*, pp. 32–43. See PrJos contained herein.

[19] Aptowitzer, *HUCA* 1 (1924) 243–56.

[20] First published by G. Oppenheim, *Fabula Josephi et Asenethae apocrypha e libro Syriaco Latine versa* (Phil. diss., Berlin; Berlin, 1886) pp. 4f., from the MS Staatsbibliothek, Berlin (DDR), MS Syr. 174, ff. 75ᵃ–76ᵃ, after A.D. 1827; repr. by Aptowitzer, *HUCA* 1 (1924) 248, n. 22; French version by Philonenko, *Joseph et Aséneth*, pp. 34f. A second MS was described by S. P. Brock ("Notes on Some Texts in the Mingana Collection," *JSS* 14 [1969] 205–26; see 206f.: Mingana MS Syr. 177, fols. 227ᵃ–28ᵃ, c. A.D. 1870).

[21] They discern traces of the legend, e.g. in 1:5; 22:9; 23:14.

[22] A legend of this type may, however, have influenced the much-debated miniature in the Vienna Genesis, fol. 16ᵃ (6th cent. A.D.), which would point to its age; cf. M. D. Levin, "Some Jewish Sources for the Vienna Genesis," *Art Bulletin* 54 (1972) 241–44.

[23] First noted by Philonenko (*Joseph et Aséneth*, pp. 43–48 and *passim*) whose main interest, however, is to point out parallels to individual motifs. See further Chr. Burchard, *Zeuge*, pp. 59–86; S. West, *The Classical Quarterly*, N.S. 24 (1974) 70–81; R. I. Pervo, *SBL 1976 Seminar Papers*, pp. 171–81. On Gk. romance generally, see K. Kerényi, *Die Griechisch-Orientalische Romanliteratur in religionsgeschichtlicher Beleuchtung* (Tübingen, 1927; repr. Darmstadt, 1962); *Der antike Roman* (Libelli 315; Darmstadt, 1962); M. Braun, *History and Romance in Graeco-Oriental Literature* (Oxford, 1938); S. Trenkner, *The Greek novella in the classical period* (Cambridge, 1958); R. Merkelbach, *Roman und Mysterium in der Antike* (Munich, 1962); B. E. Perry, *The Ancient Romances* (Sather Classical Lectures 37; Berkeley, Calif., 1967); T. Hägg, *Narrative Technique in Ancient Greek Romances* (Skrifter utgivna av Svenska Institutet i Athen, Series in 8°, 8; Stockholm, 1971).

[24] He seems to give himself the air of a contemporary of the events which are way back. One wonders if the author of JosAsen has the same thing in mind.

presence of religion, sometimes with an outright propagandistic drive (Heliodorus), there is Apuleius, Book 11[25] and (in a way) Cupid and Psyche again.

This is not to postulate literary dependence on either side, but there may be independent adaptation of common material. If the Kerényi-Merkelbach school is right, a myth may be at the bottom of this,[26] but further investigation is needed. It should cover the whole range of ancient romance in the wider sense of the term, which also includes such writings as Ahiqar, Judith, 3 Maccabees, Daniel chapters 1–6, certain passages from Josephus, the Life of Alexander, the Life of Aesop, the Pseudo-Clementines, or the apocryphal Acts of the Apostles, and the Greek novella. Two more possible sources (dealt with later) are the Jewish ritual and the allegorical patterns which, according to some, underlie Joseph and Aseneth at certain points.

Another question is whether *models* may have suggested or influenced, albeit by contrast, the composition of Joseph and Aseneth without contributing much to its narrative content. A writer who had read Ruth, Judith, Tobit, or Esther would perhaps be more inclined to tackle a figure from Israel's history, especially a woman, than one who had not. Then there is the Story of Joseph, though not an independent book. Joseph and Aseneth may have been inspired, among other things, by a desire to ensure that Joseph's wife become the heroine of a story that would be similar to that of her husband.[27] The romances are due for further consideration under this heading as well.[28] Most important, however, is a number of Jewish and Christian texts relating to conversion, especially the ones containing "conversion visions" (TJob 2–5; ApAb 1–11; Acts 9:1–19 par. 22:6–16; 26:12–18) and texts like Dan 4; Lk 7:36–50; Mt 16:16–18. They show, despite the differences they may have among each other and with Joseph and Aseneth, that the conversion section, for all that it may owe to the romantic genre, is constructed along the lines of a pattern, current in hellenistic Judaism, as to how a conversion, particularly of a person who was to be a model, ought to be presented.[29]

We are on safer ground when it comes to ascertaining the origin of details. Many of these can be traced back to the Old Testament, to the early Jewish literature, to oral traditions, and to Jewish traditions found in early Christian writings.[30] The general framework, the characters, and many a detail of the story are of course drawn from Genesis, especially the Story of Joseph.[31] The exception is Pharaoh's son,[32] unless he is modeled upon Shechem, the son of Hamor (Gen 34, but cf. Ex 11:5). The individual features of Jacob and his sons (see e.g. 4:7; 6:4, 6; 22:7, 11) can be paralleled from other intertestamental writings. Pharaoh's philo-Semitism recalls the kindly views which Daniel or the Letter of Aristeas have their respective sovereigns take to Judaism. The conversion section, particularly the angel's visit, has some important points in common with Judges 13 (retold in *LAB* 42; cf.

---

[25] For a commentary, see J. G. Griffiths, *Apuleius of Madauros: The Isis-Book* (Études Préliminaires aux Religions Orientales dans l'Empire Romain 39; Leiden, 1975).

[26] See nn. 23 and 81; *Zeuge*, pp. 81–86.

[27] Some have detected its influence in Esther (A. Meinhold, "Die Gattung der Josephsgeschichte und des Estherbuches: Diasporanovelle," ZAW 87 [1975] 306–24; 88 [1976] 72–93) and Tobit (L. Ruppert, "Das Buch Tobias—ein Modellfall nachgestaltender Erzählung," *Wort, Lied und Gottespruch: Beiträge zur Septuaginta. Festschrift für Joseph Ziegler*, ed. J. Schreiner [Forschung zur Bibel 1; Würzburg, 1972] pp. 109–19).

[28] Here the question of contrast comes up. Philonenko (*Joseph et Aséneth*, p. 44) thinks that as a "puritan novel" JosAsen is a pigeon among the cats. But Chariton or Xenophon of Ephesus are not very different, and all novels, although not exactly Victorian in their outlook on sexual matters, take a firm stand on female pudicity and conjugal faithfulness. The triumph of chastity over all temptations that are waged against it is one of the main devices to keep the action going. There is, however, a marked difference between the demure, if not in the least disinterested, attitude in which Aseneth strives toward her happiness, and the ruses employed, e.g. by Dionysius, one of the good characters in Chariton, to lure an unwilling Callirhoe into matrimony.

[29] A wealth of material and interpretative suggestions is amassed by K. Berger (*Auferstehung*). Close structural parallelism between Acts 9:1–19 and the conversional element in JosAsen, esp. chs. 4–19, was suggested by Burchard (*Zeuge*, pp. 86–105). Cf. also U. Wilckens, *Orientierung an Jesus*, pp. 394–424.

[30] See Aptowitzer, *HUCA* 1 (1924); Berger, *Auferstehung*; "Jüdisch-hellenistische Missionsliteratur und apokryphe Apostelakten," *Kairos* N.S. 17 (1975) 232–48; E. W. Smith, Jr., "Joseph Material in Joseph and Asenath and Josephus Relating to the Testament of Joseph," SCS 5, pp. 133–37.

[31] Or some paraphrase such as Jub? Cf. the dates in 1:1f.; 3:1; 22:1. On the Story of Joseph see D. B. Redford, *A Study of the Biblical Story of Joseph (Genesis 37–50)* (Supplements to VT 20; Leiden, 1970); E. I. Lowenthal, *The Joseph Narrative in Genesis: An Interpretation* (New York, 1973); Meinhold, ZAW 87 (1975) 306–24 and 88 (1976) 72–93.

[32] He remains anonymous, as do all persons (except Joakim of Moab, 1:9) and places in JosAsen which are nameless or not referred to in the Bible. For a different handling cf. TJob and *LAB*.

also Judg 6:11–24). Benjamin's bravery is a re-enactment of David slaying Goliath (1Sam 17). The prayers (8:9; 12f.; 17:10; 21:11–21; 27:10), meditations (6:2–8; 11:3–14, 16–18; 17:9), and eulogies (3:3; 8:3; 15:12; 17:6; 19:8; 21:4, 6) could hardly have been composed without knowledge of traditional forms of such devotional texts.[33]

Whether or not there is a common ancestry for the subject matter, many clichés which are typical, if not exclusive, marks of the hellenistic romance can be found in Joseph and Aseneth. A fine example is 1:3–6, which can be compared with Chariton 1.1.1f.:

> Hermocrates, the *strategos* (chief magistrate) of the Syracusans, the one who defeated the Athenians, had a daughter by the name of Callirhoe, a wonderful specimen of a virgin and the delight of all Sicily. For her beauty was not human but divine, not that of a Nereid or a nymph of the mountains, but of the Virgin Aphrodite herself. The fame of the incredible spectacle penetrated everywhere, and suitors flocked into Syracuse, princes and sons of tyrants, not only from Sicily, but also from Italy and the mainland (or Epirus) and the (non-Greek) nations on the mainland.

A second example, which can be compared to 18:9, is Achilles Tatius 1.4.3: Leucippe's "mouth was a flower of roses, when the rose begins to open the leaves' lips."[34]

A problem which must yet be investigated is to what extent the *realia*—such as architecture, landscape, seasons, products, clothing, and hygiene—reflect what the author saw in his day, and how much the dealings of the characters mirror contemporary events. Obviously this also has some bearing on the questions of date and provenance (see below). The romances exhibit a good deal of anachronistic realism in these matters. As to Joseph and Aseneth, one gathers that the author, whose interest in lively detail is limited anyway, owes more to the biblical narrative and related literature than to an interested knowledge of the world in which he lived.

Language and style

If Aseneth's looks are like Sarah's (1:5), so is her tongue. All of Joseph and Aseneth is written in a simple Greek *koine* with a marked Hebrew and/or Aramaic flavor commonly called "Semitic."[35] It avoids subordinate clauses and conjunctive or absolute participles (see 19:1 for an exception). Most sentences start with "and," with the verb immediately following. Particles other than "and" are used very sparingly. Redundant possessive and demonstrative pronouns abound. A noun in the genitive is often used as a substitute for an adjectival attribute (e.g. "bride of God" 4:1; "prison of darkness" 4:10; "bread of life" 8:5; "bait of life" 21:21), and in the nominative for an adjectival complement ("fellowship with her is destruction and corruption" 7:5). There is ample evidence of the cognate accusative, usually carrying an attribute, in lieu of an adverb (lit. "to rejoice a great joy" 3:3; "to fear a great fear" 6:1; "to tremble a heavy trembling" 10:1; "to name the name of God" 11:15; "to insult an insult" 23:14; "to pain a pain" 25:3), and of related uses of the associative or instrumental dative (lit. "to weep with great and bitter weeping" 9:2; "to sigh with great sighing" 10:3; "to die with death" 21:8; "to wound with a heavy wound" 27:2). The Greek words *prosōpon*, "face," and *cheir*, "hand," are employed to form composite prepositions (e.g. 5:2; 27:7). Most of these phenomena, as well as the author's vocabulary and phraseology generally, can be paralleled from the Septuagint. The author, however, is not simply imitating the Old Testament or some other concrete model.[36] Borrowing is at times quite obvious (e.g. at 12:7; 15:7; 17:8; 20:5; 22:7; 27:1–5; 29:2), although literal quotations are few (cf. TJob for contrast).[37] However, basically the same

---

[33] N. B. Johnson, *Prayer in the Apocrypha and Pseudepigrapha* (JBLMS 2; Philadelphia, Pa., 1948); G. Mayer, "Die Funktion der Gebete in den alttestamentlichen Apokryphen," *Theokratia* 2 (1970–72) 16–25; J. Heinemann, *Prayer in the Talmud* (Studia Judaica 9; Berlin, 1977).

[34] A slight Persian touch is also characteristic. Cf. the satraps in e.g. 1:3, and Aseneth's garments in e.g. 3:6.

[35] Philonenko, *Joseph et Aséneth*, pp. 28–32; G. D. Kilpatrick, review of Burchard, *Untersuchungen*, and Philonenko, *Joseph et Aséneth*, in NovT 12 (1970) 233–36; G. Delling, JSJ 9 (1978) 29–56. Delling notes that the influence of the Pss and Gen is most palpable.

[36] He could have done so without discrediting himself. Imitation was a virtue rather than a vice in some areas of ancient literature. Chariton is leaning heavily on the historical prose of Xenophon of Athens.

[37] One would like to know to what extent deviation from our LXX text is because of a different form or forms of text. There is no evidence so far for independent knowledge of MT or another Heb. text form.

type of Greek, though with varying admixtures of Semitisms, is found for instance in the Testaments of the Twelve Patriarchs, the Testament of Job, Luke-Acts, and Hermas. There was a living tradition to write on sacred subjects in a biblicized language.

On the other hand this recognition does not explain everything. Occasionally there is a classical simile (8:5) or turn (21:21; 22:6), a quasi-philosophical touch (12:2 beginning), an unexpected metonymy (20:1), a *paronomasia* (*kakon anti kakou*, "evil for evil," e.g. 23:9), *parechesis* (*pēlos polys*, "plenty of mud," 10:16; 13:7, cf. 15:3), or *chiasmus* (e.g. 11:13). There are also words, with or without Septuagint support, that seem to be rare (*apokrybē* 6:6; *barythymein* 10:1; *brimēma* 10:15; *charopoios* 22:7; *delea[s]ma* 21:21; *eidōlomanēs* 12:9; *hypolampas* 14:9; *katapetasma* 10:2; *prodromos* or *-mon* 19:2, 4; *sitistos* 10:13). This side of the author's vocabulary will have to be given further attention before we can reach a definite conclusion regarding his language as a whole.

The narrative evolves at a leisurely pace with plenty of repetition. It is full of recapitulation ("And there was . . . a spring of abundant living water, and below *the spring* was a big cistern receiving *the water of that spring*," 2:12), stereotyped auxiliary verbs and turns ("she hurried and," "he stretched out his hand and," "they prostrated themselves before him, face down to the ground, and"), and mechanical epithets ("Pentephres priest of Heliopolis," "Joseph the Powerful One of God"). The various and sundry scenes of Aseneth getting dressed (3:6; 10:10; 14:14f.; 18:5f.) and emotional outbursts (e.g. 4:9; 6:1; 8:8; 9:1f.; 10:1, 3, 15) show that variety of expression is not a concern of the author. Also he has a leaning toward overemphasis. The overall result is a pompous rigidity of style which is stiff to us, but presumably it was more attractive to the author and his readers.

Genre

We can only speculate whether the author intended to write a piece of fiction or a work of history; but we can see the result: a romance in the wider sense of the word.[38] Can it be associated with any of the possible subdivisions of this heterogeneous ensemble which "is probably the most formless of all ancient genres?"[39] The books of Ruth, Esther, Tobit, and Judith have been put forward as closest literary affinities, with some similarities to Jonah acknowledged.[40] These writings form an ill defined group, yet they resemble Joseph and Aseneth in language and religion, and the eminent role both play in life. Female characters dominate, there is marriage, and Jewish-gentile relations are at stake. There is also some similarity in structure (see 12:1; 21:10, 11). But there is more interest in historical shading (Joseph and Aseneth is closer to the Joseph story here), and none of these books makes love's labors a constituent of the plot. This feature, as well as the adventures, is shared by Joseph and Aseneth with the erotic novels.[41] But is the element of eroticism and adventure strong enough for Joseph and Aseneth to be considered a specimen of this variety? In Part I love is almost superseded by the conversion theme; in Part II it is barely present. The general background of high treason and fighting is romantic indeed, but the actors are mostly busy discussing what they have in mind or why it must not be done. The naïveté and the lack of historiographical detail, and the brevity of Joseph and Aseneth, distinguish it from the erotic romances. Recently an attempt has been made to sever the Jewish book from them and put it alongside the apocryphal acts, especially Paul and Thecla, as a "religious proselyte romance."[42] This attempt seems to emphasize unduly the conversion aspect to the detriment of others; moreover, there is no figure in Joseph and Aseneth resembling an apostle or missionary as portrayed in the Christian Acts. So while this approach has its merits, it does not explain everything. R. I. Pervo[43] assumes that, as a specimen of the romantic genre, Joseph and Aseneth is best regarded as a piece of literary syncretism. Pervo

---

[38] See e.g. P. Weimar, "Formen frühjüdischer Literatur," *Literatur und Religion des Frühjudentums*, eds. J. Maier and J. Schreiner (Würzburg, 1973) pp. 123–62; see pp. 130–35. Weimar strings Jdt, Esth, 3Mac, JosAsen, Tob, LetAris, Art, and TJos chs. 2–9, together as novels.

[39] Pervo, *SBL 1976 Seminar Papers*, p. 72.

[40] Burchard, *Untersuchungen*, pp. 106f.; Kilpatrick, *NovT* 12 (1970) 234.

[41] Philonenko, *Joseph et Aséneth*, pp. 43–48; West, *Classical Quarterly* N.S. 24 (1974) 70–81.

[42] T. Szepessy, "L'histoire de Joseph et d'Aseneth et le roman antique," *Studia Classica Universitatis Scientiarum Debreceniensis* 10–11 (1974–75) 121–31.

[43] *SBL 1976 Seminar Papers*, pp. 171–81.

feels that the book updated the older form of the "Sapiental novel" (e.g. Ah, Tob, Dan 1–6) by taking in structural elements and motifs of the erotic variety. He may underestimate the affinities to the literature dealing with conversion,[44] but generally he seems to be on the right track.

Date and provenance

Batiffol introduced Joseph and Aseneth to modern scholarship as a Christian work of the fifth century A.D. from Asia Minor, based on a short Jewish legend of the fourth century.[45] This infelicitous presentation did much to prevent students of the Bible and Judaism from noticing the book. Kautzsch and Charles did not include it. Ironically enough, when a reviewer concluded that Joseph and Aseneth must be a Jewish composition from Jesus' time or even earlier, Batiffol all but agreed.[46] Every competent scholar has since affirmed that Joseph and Aseneth is Jewish, with perhaps some Christian interpolations; none has put the book much after A.D. 200, and some have placed it as early as the second century B.C. As to the place of origin, the majority of scholars look to Egypt. Those in favor of a Semitic original suggest Palestine; and there is a plea for Syria.[47] However, the date and provenance have never been thoroughly examined.[48]

What we can say with certainty may be summarized in the following way. The book itself is probably first attested toward the end of the fourth century A.D. Peter the Deacon of Monte Cassino writes in his book *On the Holy Places* (shortly before A.D. 1137), in a passage which he probably culled from the lost beginning of the *Pilgrimage of Etheria* (c. A.D. 382):[49]

> Heliopolis is twelve miles from Babylonia (Cairo). In the center of this city is a large piece of ground on which there is the Temple of the Sun, and there is Petefres' house. Between Petefres' house and the Temple is Asennec's house. The inner wall within the city is rather old and made of stone (surrounding, or connecting?) only the Temple with Asennec's house and Petefres' house.

Aseneth's house is known exclusively from Joseph and Aseneth. People at Heliopolis, a tourist center long before the first Christian pilgrim's progress (see 1:2), seem to have put their finger on the localities described in Joseph and Aseneth, unless the author made use of some local tradition already extant (in which case, however, one would like to find a reference to the famous obelisk or obelisks in the text). But Joseph and Aseneth must be even earlier than this testimony. A book glorifying the mother of the proselytes ought to have been written before Greek-speaking Judaism ceased to make its impact on the ancient world and gave way to Christianity.[50] On the other hand, Joseph and Aseneth presupposes at least some of the Septuagint, and probably all of it. It is hard to decode this into dates, but we are probably safe to say that the book was written between 100 B.C. and Hadrian's edict against circumcision, which has to do with the Second Jewish War of A.D. 132–135. If Joseph and Aseneth comes from Egypt, the Jewish revolt under Trajan (c. A.D. 115–117) is the latest possible date.[51] It does appear to have originated in Egypt, since Aseneth, and

---

[44] Burchard, *Zeuge*; Berger, *Auferstehung*; Szepessy, *Studia Classica Universitatis Scientiarum Debreceniensis* 10–11 (1974–75) 121–31.

[45] Batiffol, *Studia Patristica*, pp. 30–37.

[46] L. Duchesne, *Bulletin critique* 10 (1889) 461–66; see 466; Batiffol, review of M. R. James, *Apocrypha Anecdota*, vol. 2 (T&S 5:1; Cambridge, 1897) in *RB* 7 (1898) 302–4; see 303.

[47] Brooks, *Joseph and Asenath*, pp. xvii–xviii.

[48] For a survey, see Burchard, *Untersuchungen*, pp. 133–51; Philonenko, *Joseph et Aséneth*, pp. 99–109.

[49] Translated from the autograph as printed in Burchard, *Untersuchungen*, p. 137; somewhat differently, J. Wilkinson, *Egeria's Travels* (London, 1971) p. 204.

[50] Cf. generally, B. J. Bamberger, *Proselytism in the Talmudic Period* (Cincinnati, Ohio, 1939; repr. New York, 1968); W. G. Braude, *Jewish Proselyting in the First Five Centuries of the Common Era, the Age of the Tannaim and Amoraim* (Brown University Studies 6; Providence, R.I., 1940); K. G. Kuhn and H. Stegemann, "Proselyten," Pauly-Wissowa Suppl. 9 (1962) 1248–83; K. G. Kuhn, "prosēlytos," *TDNT*, vol. 6, 727–44; N. J. McEleney, "Conversion, Circumcision and the Law," *NTS* 20 (1974) 319–41.

[51] On the revolts generally, see E. M. Smallwood, *The Jews under Roman Rule: From Pompey to Diocletian* (SJLA 20; Leiden, 1976) esp. pp. 389–466. Perhaps we may even go back until the troubles in Alexandria under Caligula (c. A.D. 38). Gentile-Jewish friction never ceased after that.

not another woman such as Ruth or Rahab (Josh 2), is the heroine of the story.

Other suggestions for dating and locating Joseph and Aseneth are mere speculation. Surely no individual incident such as the conversion of Queen Helena of Adiabene, an elderly lady (died c. A.D. 65), was needed to trigger the composition of Joseph and Aseneth.[52] That Egypt figures in the book as an independent country ruled by a philo-Semitic dynasty does not prove that the novel was written under the later Ptolemies before the Romans took over.[53] The absence of a reference to proselyte baptism is of little avail since we do not know when the custom began.[54] Lexical chronology is also of little help. We may note that words like *anazōopoiein* (8:9; 15:5), *brimēma* (10:15), *eidōlomanēs* (12:9), *ekliparein* (1:7; 15:7), *hemithanēs* (27:3), male *parthenos* (4:7; 8:1), *proskairos* (12:15), *sitistos* (10:13), *sitodotēs* (25:5), *sygklēronomos* (24:14) are not attested with certainty until the first century B.C. or even later.[55] But Greek lexicography is not advanced enough to enable us to be certain when a word first appeared.

An Essene[56] or Therapeutic[57] origin of Joseph and Aseneth is maintained by some scholars; but Aseneth's way of living, her marriage, and happiness thereafter are hardly in keeping with the quasi-monastic rigorism of these groups.

Philonenko suggests a rural milieu outside Alexandria because he thinks Joseph and Aseneth is less intransigent toward paganism than an Alexandrian like Philo.[58] Quite possibly the book represents a more popular type of Jewish culture than does Philo, who among all Jewish writers we know is closest to the hellenistic ideal of a well-bred, well-read, and well-to-do gentleman spending his life in the service of both learning and politics. But this does not necessarily imply the countryside. With villages usually adhering more closely to their traditions than the city dwellers, would a rural community have attracted enough proselytes and sympathizers to make writing about it worthwhile? Would it be interested in the finer points of conversion? Would it provide enough of a reading public for Joseph and Aseneth, supposing, as seems likely, that it was to be read privately and by Jews? (See below.) Private reading in antiquity took both education and money. Jews were by and large less illiterate than other populations, and perhaps more willing to buy books, theirs being a book religion. Nevertheless, one must look for the prospective readers of Joseph and Aseneth in the upper brackets of Jewish society, although perhaps not the top level; would Philo have enjoyed it? We know too little about Judaism in and outside Alexandria[59] and not yet enough about Joseph and Aseneth to answer these questions.[60]

Theological importance[61]

By design, the theological importance of a religious book is in its message. Beyond this the modern historian will be interested generally in the theological ideas expressed in the book, particularly in those that are less well documented outside it.

Message

Barring heavy generalization, the message of Joseph and Aseneth cannot be rendered by a single concept or phrase. A story of such length and complexity usually has several things to say. But they will cohere if it is as well organized as Joseph and Aseneth.

[52] Against Aptowitzer, *HUCA* 1 (1924) 309.

[53] Against G. D. Kilpatrick, "The Last Supper," *ExpT* 64 (1952–53) 4–8.

[54] Cf. T. M. Taylor, "The Beginnings of Jewish Proselyte Baptism," *NTS* 2 (1955–56) 193–98.

[55] Burchard, *Untersuchungen*, pp. 148–51.

[56] K. Kohler, "Asenath, Life and Confession or Prayer of," *JE*, vol. 2, pp. 172–76; Riessler, *TQ* 103 (1922) 4–13; *Altjüdisches Schrifttum*, pp. 1303f.

[57] K. G. Kuhn, "The Lord's Supper and the Communal Meal at Qumran," *The Scrolls and the New Testament*, ed. K. Stendahl (New York, 1957) pp. 65–93, 259–65; see esp. 74–77, 261–62; M. Delcor, "Un roman d'amour d'origine thérapeute: Le Livre de Joseph et Asénath," *Bulletin de Littérature Ecclésiastique* 63 (1962) 3–27.

[58] Philonenko, *Joseph et Aséneth*, pp. 106f.

[59] For a general survey see Smallwood, *Jews*, pp. 220–55, 364–68. The complete lack of cultic interest in JosAsen would seem to rule out Leontopolis with its "Temple in Exile" (c. 160 B.C.–A.D. 73), even though it is situated in the county of Heliopolis, just eighteen kilometers north of the city (today Tell el-Yehudieh).

[60] There is no compelling reason to assume that our author was an Egyptian proselyte; contrast Philonenko, *Joseph et Aséneth*, p. 106.

[61] More information is available in the footnotes to the passages referred to in this section.

In Part I attention is focused on what happens to Aseneth. She represents the virgin, who is proud of her virginity, but, eventually chastised by violent passion, must endure hardships before she is gratified. Yet, since the target of her emotions is Joseph, the son of God, her story gradually assumes a religious complexion. Pride becomes a symbol for pagan enmity against God, and passion the sudden desire to be accepted by him aroused by a meeting with a true follower of God. Consequently love's labors are continued by a period of self-humiliation leading to conversion. The message of Part I, therefore, is about conversion to Judaism: It means fullness of life, whereas paganism brings death and eternal destruction.

Some scholars have found allegory in the story. Philonenko, for example, detects several allegorical patterns in the narrative. First, Aseneth is molded in the image of the Egyptian goddess Neith, whose name she bears (see 1:5), thus insinuating that the deity is giving in to the Most High God and wants her worshipers to follow her example. Second, there is astrology in the book. Joseph and Aseneth impersonate the Sun and the Moon uniting in a holy wedding, thus witnessing to the importance which Judaism, or parts of it, attached to astrology. Third, there is a mythological pattern of gnostic extraction. Aseneth represents the mythic figure of Wisdom fallen into error, and Joseph is the divine Logos, who is coming to rescue her by uniting himself to her.

This method of allegorizing the document is too complicated to warrant acceptance. As to Neith, the appearance of the Lady of Sais seems to have been so variegated, and many of her attributes so unspecific in the author's day, that very precise parallels would be needed for Aseneth to be her symbol.[62] Joseph and Aseneth, like Greek romance generally, seems to make use of motifs that stem from mythical and astrological contexts. But it remains to be shown that the author did so consciously, and, if he did, that he intended Joseph and Aseneth to be more than human figures entangled in the vicissitudes of human love and conversion. Love is a heavenly thing, after all, and so is conversion, to religious people.

To be sure, the affair between Joseph and Aseneth has a deeper meaning. But it is stated by the text; it is not coded in it. Aseneth, who found her way to God, is also an eternal City of Refuge for all (not just women) who repent in like manner (15:7; 16:16; 19:5), with her seven virgins as pillars to support her (17:6). The tradition of Sion, the City of God, also described under the figure of a woman,[63] lies behind this concept. Chapter 15:7a may be a direct reference to the prophecy on Sion, Zech 2:15 LXX (cf. e.g. Isa 62:4–12; Jer 50:5; 4Ezra 9f.; Rev 21). Moreover, Aseneth as the City of Refuge parallels Abraham (Isa 51:1f.; *LAB* 23:4f.), Peter, the rock on whom the church is built (Mt 16:16–18), the "pillar apostles" (Gal 2:9), perhaps also Sarah and Hagar as exegeted by Paul (Gal 4:21–31).[64] This is metonymy, not allegory. For Aseneth, as a City of Refuge, does not mean merely that all proselytes will be safeguarded by God *like* her. Full protection is offered to all who seek shelter "in" her, by becoming naturalized descendants of her by rallying themselves to the Jewish people of whom she is an ancestor. To be "in" Aseneth, however, is not similar to being "in" Christ. Both concepts are comparable in that salvation depends on association with an historical person, but association means different things in each case. Aseneth did not continue to be present as a person. She does not continue to live "in" the proselytes similar to the way "Christ lives in me" (Gal 2:20).[65] Only the promises and

[62] D. Sänger, *Antikes Judentum und die Mysterien*, pp. 58–67; idem, "Bekehrung und Exodus: Zum jüdischen Traditionshintergrund von 'Joseph und Aseneth,' " *JSJ* 10 (1979) 11–36; see pp. 13–20. On Neith generally, see C. J. Bleeker, "The Egyptian Goddess Neith," *Studies in Mysticism and Religion presented to Gershom G. Scholem on his seventieth Birthday by Pupils, Colleagues, and Friends*, eds. E. E. Urbach, R. J. Zwi Werblowsky, and Ch. Wirszubski (Jerusalem, 1967) pp. 41–56; repr. in Bleeker, *The Rainbow* (SHR 30; Leiden, 1975) pp. 128–42.

[63] Cf. W. W. Reader, *Die Stadt Gottes in der Johannesapokalypse* (Theol. diss.; Göttingen, 1972); G. Fohrer and E. Lohse, "Siōn etc.," *TDNT*, vol. 7, 292–338.

[64] Cf. also Jer 1:18; 1QH 3.37; Mt 5:14; Eph 2:20; 1Tim 3:15. Burchard, *Untersuchungen*, pp. 118–21; C. Kähler, "Zur Form- und Traditionsgeschichte von Matth. XVI. 17–19," *NTS* 23 (1977) 36–58. U. Fischer (*Eschatologie und Jenseitserwartung im hellenistischen Diasporajudentun* [BZNW 44; Berlin, 1978] pp. 115–23) thinks that Aseneth bears a touch of heavenly Jerusalem, considering that the heavenly rest of the saved is also described as a walled city (see below). The point, however, is not elaborated. At any event, we should not regard the description of Aseneth as a city as the outcome of a process of de-eschatologization.

[65] H. Thyen (*Studien zur Sündenvergebung im Neuen Testament und seinen alttestamentlichen und jüdischen Voraussetzungen* [FRLANT 96; Göttingen, 1970] pp. 126f.) wrongly assumes that Aseneth is transformed into Metanoia as her heavenly counterpart.

qualities with which she was endowed remain available, like the physical and material heritage that is inherited by a particular family.

A woman portrayed in the role elsewhere occupied by men should not come as a surprise. The Sion tradition, at least when taken up directly, paved the way for this portrayal (cf. also Gal 4:21–31). This portrait may also reflect the fact that more women than men became full proselytes, and that a relatively liberal status was accorded to women in some quarters of Jewish Hellenism.[66]

In Part II Joseph's brothers are in the foreground, and Aseneth has become one of the family. The message seems to be that true Jews will not allow themselves to be talked into hate and subversion; if attacked, they will be protected by both divine assistance and their own gallantry soothed by clemency. Let it be noted that it is not only moral and physical integrity which is at stake here; it is also the leading position of Jews in society. Both aspects are interrelated, as, for example, in the picture of the wise man in the Testament of Levi 13, who is both prudent and influential, "enthroned with kings, as was Joseph my brother" (vs. 9).[67] Much like the plot, the message of Part II is developed rather independently from I, but there are some foreshadowings (perhaps 16:17–22). Between them the two parts add up to a rather well-balanced whole. Part I defines Judaism in contrast to the world; Part II describes Judaism in the world.

Key Ideas

God[68] has two main characteristics in Joseph and Aseneth. He created and sustains the world by his word (8:9; 12:1f.). He is also the loving father of man, assuring the welfare of those who adhere to him and hating those who worship idols; but always he is prepared to receive in mercy those who repent earnestly (11:7–14, 18; 12:8, 13–15). God is not identified as the Lord of history, the author of the Law or morality, or the recipient of the Temple cult. Exodus, the giving of the Law on Mount Sinai, and the institution of the cult, of course, postdate the setting of the narrative. But the author could have found a way to mention these events if he was interested in them, e.g. by prophecy as the Testament of the Twelve Patriarchs.

The *world* which God created is a three-story structure animated by his "word which is life for all your creatures" (12:1f.) and holds all elements in obedience. Lowest is "the abyss of the water," sealed by stones, floating on it like leaves, which carry the earth. On top are the heavens founded on a firmament, which rests on the winds. The earth is man's dwelling place, but (unlike Acts 17:26) the author is not interested in the subdivisions of continents and seasons. The abyss underneath houses "the big sea monster" which Aseneth is afraid may devour her (12:11). The devil is responsible for this (12:9–11), but it is not specified where he resides. In heaven is God, of course, and the hosts of the angels. Two of these are described individually: Aseneth's heavenly visitor who is their commander in chief (elsewhere named Michael), and his beautiful sister, Repentance (14:8; 15:7f.). In heaven is a "book of the living" that contains the names of the angels and the saved (15:4). In heaven is also God's Paradise, with many flowers from which bees make honey, the food for the angels and God's elect; the honey is manna (16:14; cf. 16:7y–23). For the elect a heavenly place of "rest" is prepared (8:9; 15:7; 22:13). More specifically, this place is in the seventh heaven (if the reading is right); it is described as a walled city founded upon rock (22:13).

Man is dependent upon God for continuous sustenance. Yet of all creatures man has the capacity of ignoring his maker by worshiping other gods. Idolatry rather than erroneous philosophy, transgression of the Law, or plain moral depravity is the main earmark of the godless. God will, of course, sustain only those who recognize him. The Jews alone do; consequently they are endowed with light, truth, life, and immortality. The rest of mankind thrives in darkness and error, and is practically dead. This dualistic view of mankind is not

---

[66] K. Thraede, "Frau," *RAC* 8 (1972) 197–269; see especially 226f.

[67] Here, however, wisdom is achieved by observance of the Law.

[68] On his titles and predicates see Delling, *JSJ* 9 (1978) 45–47. Otherwise cf. R. Marcus, "Divine Names and Attributes in Hellenistic Jewish Literature," *Proceedings of the American Academy for Jewish Research* (1931–32) 43–120.

explained in terms of man's past, let alone primal developments as can be expressed only in a myth. The pairs of opposites, darkness and light, error and truth, death and life—for all that they may designate in other texts[69]—do not in Joseph and Aseneth denote a dualism of spheres, eons, or opposite reigns of God and Satan; they denote two ways of life. Adherence is by birth, but it may be altered by choice. So there is no doctrine of the Fall or of any redemptive activity of God in history. To know God has always been feasible; unlike Romans 1:18–23, it is not a chance passed over. It is not naturally accomplished, of course; it is a divine gift, which is available to each who would seek it. To be sure, Joseph and Aseneth talks about sin (7:4; 11:10f., 18; 12:5, 15; 13:13; 21:11–21; 23:11) and election (8:9; 16:14; 17:6; cf. 8:11; 21:4). But election is not predestination; it certainly does not obliterate one's personal responsibility. Sin does not mean a supernatural agent holding humanity in his or her grip, corrupting everyone in the very core of existence (as Paul sees it); sin is the result of personal failure, often ushered in by "ignorance" (6:7; 12:5; 13:13). According to Joseph and Aseneth, sinful acts amount to non-allegiance to God and hostility against his followers.[70]

Divine life is not mediated to man through the Law, through special revelation or mystical experience, or through proclamations loaded with spirit and grounded in a "saving event" (as with Paul); it is obtained through the right use of food, ointment, and by the avoidance of the pagan way of partaking of them. This is the meaning of the much-debated so-called meal formula (8:5; cf. 8:9; 15:5; 16:16; 19:5; 21:13f., 21). It is difficult to discern the precise meaning of the "blessed bread, cup, and ointment" (see 8:5). Perhaps the expression refers merely to the ordinary Jewish diet; possibly it may refer to some ritual practice such as a cultic meal; some even regard it as a Christian interpolation.[71] At any event, "bread, cup, and ointment," as enjoyed by Jews, provide life, immortality, and incorruption. That is because the Jewish food is equivalent to the manna from heaven (see above), probably by virtue of "blessing," i.e. grace said at meals.

So Jews live in close relationship with God, and with angels whose food they share; but they remain apart from non-Jews, with whom they may coexist but must not mingle: no table-fellowship with pagans, no physical intimacy with a pagan woman (chs. 7f.). Relationship with God implies that Jews enjoy all the privileges that come with divine childhood, leading some sort of angelic existence. Practically, as the example of Aseneth shows, that means fullness of life, supernatural beauty, wisdom, comfortable living, and divine protection. These things are embodied in an exemplary, if not exclusive, fashion, in the Patriarchs generally, with particular emphasis, besides Aseneth, on Joseph (4:7; 6:4–6 and *passim*), Jacob (22:7), and Levi (22:13; 23:8–17; 26:6; 27:6; 28:15–17; 29:3–6). A special mark is the gift of prophecy which Levi has (22:13; 23:8; 26:6). It assures supernatural insight into things divine, such as a person's heavenly rest, and the ability to read others' minds (cf. Lk 7:39) and recognize what is going on from a distance rather than to foretell the future. A similar thing is the "inner light" which gives supernatural eyesight to Joseph (6:6).[72]

Such qualities would seem to account for the epithet of "son of God" accorded to Joseph, which is invariably in other people's mouths, never in the narrative (6:3, 5; 13:13; "his firstborn son" 18:11; 21:4; "like the firstborn son" 23:10). This title has been taken as evidence of Joseph being a figure of the Redeemer. But "sons of God" seems to be used elsewhere as a designation of the saved in general (16:14; 19:8). Aseneth is called "a daughter of the Most High" in a passage where her prototypical role is not at stake (21:4), and Jacob (who does not cease to be Joseph's father) is designated "a friend of the Most High God" (23:10). So "son of God" assigns to Joseph a peer's rank; he is superior even to Pharaoh's firstborn, and that may be all it means.[73] But if the Wisdom of Solomon 2–5,

---

[69] See e.g. H. Conzelmann, "*skotos* etc.," *TDNT*, vol. 7, 423–45; "*phōs* etc.," *TDNT*, vol. 9, 310–58.

[70] This applies also when the sin of a Jew is envisaged (7:4; 23:11, only occurrence of the root *hamart-* in Part II).

[71] This possibility is defended by Holtz, *NTS* 14 (1967–68) 482–97; cf. also R. D. Richardson, "Supplementary Essay," in H. Lietzmann, *Mass and Lord's Supper: A Study in the History of the Liturgy* (Leiden, 1979) pp. 343–47.

[72] It is highly doubtful whether such features warrant the conclusion that "the highest religious value of the group (sc. that is back of Joseph and Aseneth) seems to have been personal, revelatory experience" (H. C. Kee, "The Socio-Religious Setting and Aims of 'Joseph and Asenath,' " *SBL 1976 Seminar Papers*, pp. 183–92; see p. 188).

[73] Burchard, *Untersuchungen*, pp. 115–17.

especially 5, is analogical, "son of God" may also mean that Joseph is an example of the just man in whom God can be recognized.[74]

Fullness of life does not include living together with other people in a community. The services, festivals, and ordinances (unless 8:5 points to a communal meal) of the synagogue play no role in the author's thought, although he must have been aware of their existence and does not criticize them.

It follows from the above discussion that *salvation* is a "necessity" appropriate only for non-Jews. It did not have to be wrought by a redeemer (let alone a dying one like Christ); and its conditions were not disclosed at some specific time in history by a special envoy of God, such as the Teacher of Righteousness. That Aseneth is cast in the part of proto-proselyte does not mean that salvation had then been instituted. The publication of Joseph and Aseneth was not intended to announce salvation; it is not a gospel. The chance to be saved has always been present, predicated on God's habitual mercy for penitent polytheists, man's capacity to avail himself of it, and the presence of Judaism in the world.

There is no hint in Joseph and Aseneth that Jewish missionaries or zealous individuals spread the good news of salvation and called for conversion. Joseph does surprisingly little for Aseneth.[75] He prays for her conversion, and then leaves. This act is enough for the girl to smash her idols and start castigating herself; but for positive guidance she depends upon what she "heard" about the mercy of the God of the Hebrews (11:10),[76] hardly from missionary sermons. Finally she is accepted without further human interference, a fact which is gladly welcomed by Joseph. Surely this is a pattern which conversion often followed.[77]

Materially, conversion[78] is described as the passage from darkness to light, from error to truth, from death to life, in analogy to creation (8:9; 12:1f.; 15:12; 27:10); it is not from sin to righteousness or forgiveness. Forgiveness is hoped and asked for (11:18; 13:13), but nobody tells Aseneth that her sins have been forgiven. Obviously, she has overcome them by spurning her idols, giving away her valuables, and castigating herself for seven days. Conversion is also called re-creation (8:9; 15:5; cf. 16:16; 18:9)[79] with no implication of a fall from which one has to be lifted up again nor of dying and rising as professed, for example, by Paul or perhaps, in a very different perspective, by Apuleius.[80] Re-creation is the promotion from the deficient, nothing-but-human state naturally possessed by the heathen to the angelic status naturally possessed by the Jews. This has little, if any, moral implications and consequences. There is no word about future obligations, not even religious ones such as daily prayer, or of a new stimulus implanted in the re-created. Ethics are important to the author (see below). But what Judaism offers over non-Jewish existence is privilege, not

---

[74] Berger, *Auferstehung*, p. 606, nn. 506f. See further generally, P. Pokorný, *Der Gottessohn: Literarische Übersicht und Fragestellung* (Theologische Studien 109; Zürich, 1971); M. Hengel, *Der Sohn Gottes: Die Entstehung der Christologie und die jüdisch-hellenistische Religionsgeschichte* (Tübingen, 1975); P. Wülfging von Martitz, G. Fohrer, E. Schweizer, E. Lohse, and W. Schneemelcher, "*hyios* etc.," *TDNT*, vol. 8, 334–99; G. Delling, "Die Bezeichnung 'Söhne Gottes' in der jüdischen Literatur der hellenistisch-römischen Zeit," *God's Christ and His People: Studies in Honor of Nils Astrup Dahl*, eds. J. Jervell and W. A. Meeks (Oslo, 1977) pp. 18–28.

[75] Apparently less than for Potiphar's wife according to TJos 4:4.

[76] T. Holtz, " 'Euer Glaube an Gott': Zu Form und Inhalt von 1 Thess 1,9f.," *Die Kirche des Anfangs. Festschrift für Heinz Schürmann zum 65. Geburtstag*, eds. R. Schnackenburg, J. Ernst, and J. Wanke (Erfurter Theologische Studien 38; Leipzig, 1977) pp. 459–88; see esp. 472f.

[77] On Jewish mission generally, see nn. 50, 87, 89, and D. Georgi, *Die Gegner des Paulus im 2. Korintherbrief: Studien zur religiösen Propaganda in der Spätantike* (Wissenschaftliche Monographien zum Alten und Neuen Testaments 11; Neukirchen-Vluyn, 1964). On the Christian mission, F. Hahn, *Mission in the New Testament* (SBT 47; London, 1965); Chr. Burchard, "Formen der Vermittlung christlichen Glaubens im Neuen Testament," *EvT* 38 (1978) 313–40.

[78] C. Bussmann, *Themen der paulinischen Missionspredigt auf dem Hintergrund der spätjüdisch-hellenistischen Missionsliteratur* (European University Papers, Series xviii, Theology 3; Bern, Frankfurt, 1971); S. Anandakumara, *The Gentile Reactions to the Christ-Kerygma—The Problems Involved in the Reception of the Christ-Kerygma in the Young Gentile Christianity in the New Testament* (Theol. diss.; Hamburg, 1975) pp. 29–91, 316–35; Berger, *Kairos* 17 (1975) 232–48; Sänger, *Antikes Judentum und die Mysterien*, pp. 148–90. Generally, see A. D. Nock, *Conversion* (Oxford, 1933; repr. Oxford Paperbacks 30; 1961).

[79] Some have sensed an element of "realized eschatology" at this point and others (cf. also n. 64). For this term to be applied properly, the concept of re-creation would have to have been transposed from a context of future eschatology into the present. Paul has done so (e.g. in 2Cor 5:17) but it may be doubted whether the author of JosAsen did the same.

[80] R. C. Tannehill, *Dying and Rising with Christ* (BZNW 32; Berlin, 1967); Griffiths, *Isis-Book*, pp. 296–301.

obligation. Incidentally, Aseneth's motivation, which is plainly egotistical, at least in the beginning, is not frowned upon.

Philonenko[81] suggested that the conversion section of Joseph and Aseneth, or part of it, is shaped after some pertinent ritual or rituals, possibly an initiation liturgy designed to present Judaism as a form of mystery religion. The parallels to Lucius' initiation and his retransformation from donkey to human being (in Apuleius, *Golden Ass*, 11) might seem to be *prima facie* evidence for this view. However, such a ritual would have to be reconstructed from the very text which it is called upon to elucidate. The methodological problem involved is how to translate literary developments back into liturgical procedure, and that is a formidable problem. If there is mystery religion in Joseph and Aseneth, moreover, we ought to be prepared for a measure of deliberate mystification (Apuleius, *Golden Ass*, 11.23.6). Doubtless there were no angels visiting, no bees rising from miraculous honeycombs, and no fiery chariots ascending into heaven. If these features represent some ritual, what could it be? If they are fictional, why not the rest of chapters 14–18 as well?

Ritual, however, or at least accepted custom, nevertheless, may be reflected in Joseph and Aseneth. Entry into Judaism may well have been performed by a period of fasting, praying, meditating, washing, a symbolical changing of clothes (and perhaps of name), and celebrating a festive meal. But corroborative evidence is needed before we can be certain. It is significant that neither circumcision nor proselyte baptism (supposing that it existed already in the author's day) is mentioned. Since religion in Joseph and Aseneth appears to be private and personal, perhaps we should look more to the area of private custom than to synagogue life for a better understanding of its conception of conversion.

Ethics is an important concern of the author, although it is not preparatory to, instrumental in, or a consequence of salvation. He gives, or reports, a number of important rules, beginning with the following: "It does not befit a man who worships God" (on this attribute, see 4:7) to kiss a heathen woman (8:5), to sleep with his fiancée prior to the wedding (21:1), to render evil for evil (23:9; 29:3; cf. 28:5, 14), to injure anyone of his own free will or aid an injurer (23:12), or to crush a fallen enemy to death (29:3). The last three points are the main lesson of Part II. Other standards are less formally stated, such as a general warning against foreign women (7:5) attributed to Jacob, or expressed in the adjectives used to characterize persons like Joseph, who is "a man who worships God, and self-controlled, and a virgin" (4:7) and "meek and merciful and God-fearing" (8:8). More virtues are exemplified by action. Joseph does not eat with non-Jews (7:1) and is concerned with social welfare (4:7; 25:5; 26:3). There is a hint at charity in Aseneth's repentance (ch. 10) and a display of magnanimity in her treatment of Dan and Gad (ch. 28). Individual bravery is represented by Benjamin (27:1–5) and Joseph's good brothers (26:6; 27:6). Levi is the incarnation of the man who does not render evil for evil (23:6–17; 28:15–17): His attempt to save the life of Pharaoh's son (29:3–5) is reminiscent of the Good Samaritan (Lk 10:30–35), even if it is far from disinterested. However, such meekness seems to be in order only toward equals; hostile soldiers are dispatched in large quantities without further ado (27:4–6).

We ought not be surprised, perhaps, that the more popular social virtues—such as almsgiving, hospitality, visiting the sick, or burying the dead—are not evidenced in Joseph and Aseneth, as they are, for example, in Tobit, the Testament of Job, and such sketches of the ideal Jew as the "good man" of TBenj 4. Doubtless they are not absent from the author's moral code. If he does not mention them, it is because he lets himself be guided by what his story requires, and the story is one of upper-class people (see 3:5) living comfortable lives among their like in a divided society and experiencing upper-class adventures. This observation, however, is noteworthy by itself. The criticism leveled against the rich and mighty, the fundamental concern for the underprivileged, the hope for a just

[81] Philonenko, *Joseph et Aséneth*, pp. 89–98. This approach parallels the interpretation of ancient romance as veiled representations in narrative form of the cultic practice of mystery religions, especially Isis, by Merkelbach and his pupils. It is liable to the criticism leveled at it generally. As to JosAsen, cf. Burchard (*Zeuge*, pp. 83f.) and Pervo (*SBL 1976 Seminar Papers*, pp. 176f.). A ritual background without the character of a mystery initiation is presupposed by W. D. Berner (*Initiationsriten in Mysterienreligionen, im Gnostizismus und im antiken Judentum* [Theol. diss.; Göttingen, 1972] pp. 156–72, 307–13); Anandakumara (*Gentile Reactions*, pp. 29–91, 316–35) even attempts to reconstruct liturgical texts from JosAsen; Sänger, *Antikes Judentum und die Mysterien*, pp. 148–90.

world in history or beyond, which characterizes other strands of Jewish tradition and much of early Christianity,[82] is entirely absent from Joseph and Aseneth. Social change is of no concern to the author.

Joseph and Aseneth has no qualms about the practicability of its moral standards. The good characters naturally live up to them, although they may first have to calm their tempers (23:7–9; 28:12–14). The evil characters do not, but experience and tolerance on the part of the good ones teach them.

High morals are not an exclusively Jewish mark. Doubtless, rules that befit one who worships God are best kept by such men, but Joseph and Aseneth does not intimate that Pentephres or Pharaoh fall short of them,[83] whereas some Jews do, at least temporarily. And virginity, for all the symbolic overtones it may carry, had made Aseneth Joseph's sister long before they first met (7:7–8:1).

We learn little about the source of these ethics. The interdiction against foreign women is traced back to Jacob (7:5), but he is hardly viewed as its author. Morals as befit God-worshiping men seem to come with the worship of God without further notice.

Eschatology[84] is a matter of individual afterlife in heaven (8:9; 15:7f.; 22:13). Joseph and Aseneth does not envisage an end of the world, let alone one of the type known as "apocalyptic," with wars raging, stars falling from the sky, a general resurrection, and last judgment,[85] after which the godly live happily in heaven or on a new earth and the wicked go to hell. In Joseph and Aseneth only individual lives come to their natural end followed by heavenly "rest" seemingly without delay (cf. Lk 23:43), if they are animated by the supernatural vitality provided to Jews. They perhaps come to nothing if they are not (but cf. 12:11). Little is said about how a person exists in heaven. The close association of the Jews with the angels suggests some sort of angelic existence (cf. Lk 20:36). This implies that in heaven persons are not mere souls (27:10 notwithstanding) but have a body (cf. 16:16; 18:9). However, we are not told whether the new existence will be acquired by transformation, resurrection, or new creation.

If, by way of conclusion, we ask what Judaism as depicted in Joseph and Aseneth is like, it is easier to say what it is not. It is not like Pharisaism, turning the Law into guidelines for personal piety and minutely regulating the chores of daily life. It is not like Sadduceeism, upholding the Law solely as the Magna Charta of the Temple of Jerusalem and the community gathering around it. It is not like Essenism (or, its diasporic extension, Therapeutism), withdrawing from the world to live in a priestly community by a new interpretation of the Law, revealed in the last days by a teacher sent from God. It is not like Zelotism, attempting to restore a Law-abiding theocracy in Israel by violence and guerrilla tactics. Certainly, the author also was no Philo, trying to show that the Law is the very essence of piety and philanthropy, a storehouse, if interpreted properly, of true philosophical insight barely adumbrated in non-Jewish philosophy and a guide to the union of the soul with God. Certainly the author had no apocalyptic leanings. He *may* have been an addict of sapiental theology or mysticism or both, elements of which are also alive in Philo in a "philosophized" form. On the whole, Joseph and Aseneth may be more representative of Greek-speaking Judaism than we have previously imagined.

Purpose

Joseph and Aseneth removes a rough spot in the Bible and satisfies pious curiosity as to the circumstances of a noted patriarch's surprise wedding to a non-Jew. Yet the author's main concern is his message.

Joseph and Aseneth has often been called a missionary tract, a *Missionsschrift*, meaning

---

[82] See generally, E. Bammel, "*ptōchos* etc.," *TDNT*, vol. 6, 885–915; L. Schottroff and W. Stegemann, *Jesus von Nazareth—Hoffnung der Armen* (Urban-Taschenbücher, T-Reihe, 639; Stuttgart, 1978).

[83] This hardly makes them God-fearers; against Aptowitzer, *HUCA* 1 (1924) 303; Philonenko, *Joseph et Aséneth*, pp. 51f.

[84] H. C. C. Cavallin, *Life after Death: Paul's Argument for the Resurrection of the Dead* (Coniectanea Biblica. NT Series 7:1; Lund, 1974) pp. 155–60; G. Fischer, *Die himmlischen Wohnungen: Untersuchungen zu Joh 14,2f* (European University Papers, Series 23.38; Bern, Frankfurt, 1975) pp. 186–89; U. Fischer, *Eschatologie*, pp. 106–23.

[85] But see 12:11; 28:7, 14.

that it was written to promote Jewish mission among non-Jews, or Jews, or both.[86] This is mistaken.[87] Judaism is not depicted as mission-minded in Joseph and Aseneth. Proselytes are welcomed, not sought, and conversion certainly is not an easy affair. Moreover, Joseph and Aseneth is not a beginner's book. The reader is supposed to know Genesis, at least the Joseph story, and to understand allusions to other scriptural passages. Little effort is made to explain Jewish life and customs; the sabbath,[88] circumcision, the interdiction against pork, and standards of levitical purity are not even mentioned. As a specimen of Introducing Judaism, Joseph and Aseneth is remarkably ill-suited. It could, at best, be a book for the advanced pagan reader entreating him to take the final step. But surely he would expect something more tangible than a piece of fiction.

It seems safe to assume that Joseph and Aseneth was composed for Jews, both born and naturalized, including perhaps those "God-fearing" sympathizers[89] who thought and lived Jewish but never crossed the line formally and were seldom pressed to do so. The document reminds not only the Jews of the privileges they have always enjoyed but also the converts of what they, or their forefathers, gained by crossing over to Judaism.[90] Of course, just as in the case of the message, there may be subordinate purposes incidental to the main object. Surely the ethics of the book belong here, especially the interdiction to repay evil by evil and the injunction against non-Jewish women.[91]

Historical importance

Joseph and Aseneth greatly enhances our knowledge of Greek-speaking Judaism around the beginning of the present era. Its main importance is in the field of theology, ethics included; but, if handled with prudence, some historical information may also be derived from it. From a literary point of view—like Ezekiel the Tragedian, Philo the Epic Poet, Pseudo-Phocylides, and the Sibylline Oracles—it represents one of the attempts to adapt forms of Greek belletristic literature. Perhaps the book will shed some modest light on the history of the Septuagint text. It may also help us understand the growth of the romantic genre. As a Greek Jewish writing, Joseph and Aseneth is part of the background of early Christianity and its literature. A significant number of Christians were recruited from the synagogue, and many elements of New Testament theology and ethics, church management and administration of charity were taken over or adapted from Jewish sources. New Testament parallels to Joseph and Aseneth are certainly not caused by literary influence on either side; these similarities are due to a common Jewish heritage. Naturally Joseph and Aseneth has been used for a fresh interpretation of New Testament passages (e.g. Mt 6:23; 16:16–18; Lk 7:36–50; Jn 6:35, 48; Acts 9:1–19 par.; Rom 4:17; 7:24f.; 12:17; 1Cor 10:16f.; 11:24–26 par.; Eph 1:4; 1Thes 5:15; Heb 3:7–4:13; 1Pet 3:9; and Rev 14:8f.).[92] Last but not least, the language of Joseph and Aseneth invites comparison with New Testament Greek.[93]

Cultural importance

Joseph and Aseneth is one of the best attested and most widely distributed books included in this collection. The number of copies and versions speaks for itself, especially when we consider that most were made to be read aloud.[94] But its influence extends far beyond this

---

[86] E.g. Kohler, JE, vol. 2, pp. 172–76.

[87] Perhaps this is not only in the case of JosAsen. Some scholars think that no piece of hellenistic Jewish literature was designed to be read predominantly by non-Jews (e.g. Tcherikover, Eos 48.3 [1957] 169–93).

[88] It is presupposed in 9:5; 14:1; cf. 21:8. Both Joseph's and the angel's visits occur on Sundays.

[89] See lately, F. Siegert, "Gottesfürchtige und Sympathisanten," JSJ 4 (1973) 109–64, and cf. above, n. 77.

[90] A similar problem arises with regard to Acts, and an analogous answer should probably be given.

[91] Mixed marriage is thought to be a major, or even the main, issue by Philonenko (Joseph et Aséneth, p. 106) and Kee (SBL 1976 Seminar Papers, p. 187).

[92] See above, nn. 29, 63, 64, 76, 79, and JosAsen at 4:7, 10; 6:1, 2, 6, 7, 8; 7:1, 4; 8:5, 9; 9:1, 2; 10:2, 11, 13, 16, 17; 11:5, 12; 12:5, 9, 15; 14:1, 6, 9; 15:4f., 7, 10; 16:14; 19:1, 11; 20:2, 7; 21:8, 16, 21; 23:8, 9; 24:14; 27:3; 29:4, 5.

[93] Kilpatrick, NovT 12 (1970) 234–36; Chr. Burchard, "Fussnoten zum neutestamentlichen Griechisch I," ZNW 61 (1970) 157–71; Smith, Joseph and Asenath. Bauer-Arndt-Gingrich (Greek-English Lexicon [Chicago, 1957]) did not use Joseph and Aseneth, but a future revision doubtless will.

[94] MSS A, B, and O are menologies. See also note before 1:1.

use, as shown by the following remarks, which are by no means exhaustive.[95] As far as we can see, exegesis and theology took little notice of our romance, unless inclusion in some lists of canonical and apocryphal books is a sign of theological interest.[96] Joseph and Aseneth was read as a source of inspiration and moral strength, at times for historical information, and indubitably often just for fun.

About the fate of Joseph and Aseneth in Judaism we know nothing, unless the Heliopolis tradition reported by Egeria, supposing that it reflects knowledge of the book, happens to be Jewish. By Egeria's time, at the latest, Christianity must have appropriated Joseph and Aseneth. The Passion of Irene (5th cent. A.D.?) drew on it, and other saints' lives show its influence also, probably through Irene.[97] At some early date Joseph and Aseneth was joined (not merged except perhaps in G) with Pseudo-Ephrem's Life of Joseph.[98] The Life of Joseph is coupled with Joseph and Aseneth in CR (= a), GFW (= b), D (= d), and MS Breslau, crossing three of the four Greek groups, and in Arm. and Ngr.[99] So it must antedate Arm. (6th–7th cent.?). After this, we seem to lose track of Joseph and Aseneth in the Greek church until the tenth century,[100] the date of MS O. The eleventh century witnessed the appearance of the following: B and perhaps A, the pictorial archetype of the miniature cycles, covering the Life of Joseph and Joseph and Aseneth, in G, 671, and 661,[101] and the mention by Nikon of Rhoidiou near Antioch, Syria (died after 1088), of Joseph and Aseneth in his *Taktikon*, chapter 13, which is a collection of monks' rules and letters pertaining to matters of monastic discipline and liturgy. Chapter 13 in the *Taktikon* contains a list of apocrypha based on the famous Canon of 60 Books; but it has an additional "Aseneth" after the "Prayer of Joseph."[102] By the intermediary of a Slavonic version, which became something of a classic in the Slavonic churches, the *Taktikon* influenced some old Russian canon lists.[103] This apparent popularity of Joseph and Aseneth in the eleventh century may have contributed to the translation of L1 and L2 in the West (before A.D. 1200).

A renewed interest makes itself felt beginning with the fourteenth or fifteenth century; perhaps this is a Renaissance phenomenon. Manuscript group *c*, the interpolations of FW Rum., the peculiar text of G, and Ngr. were probably produced early in this period, which also saw the translation of Slav. and, somewhat later, Rum. Also, Ngr. 1:6 preserves a quotation of uncertain origin and date which seems to reflect our book: "That is why some poet said in praise of her [i.e. Aseneth], 'By beauty the sun surpasses the stars, but Aseneth

---

[95] The vast bulk of Jewish, Christian, and Islamic Joseph literature may hold traces of JosAsen that have gone unheeded so far; for the time being cf. n. 1 and A. von Weilen, *Der ägyptische Joseph im Drama des XVI. Jahrhunderts* (Wien, 1887); H. Näf, *Syrische Josef-Gedichte: Mit Uebersetzung des Gedichts von Narsai und Proben aus Balai und Jaqob von Sarug* (Phil. diss., Zürich; Zürich, 1923); H. Priebatsch, *Die Josephsgeschichte in der Weltliteratur* (Breslau, 1937); H. A. Brongers, *De Jozefsgeschiedenis bij Joden, Christenen en Mohammedanen* (Wageningen, 1962); M. Derpmann, *Die Josephsgeschichte. Auffassung und Darstellung im Mittelalter* (Beihefte zum "Mittellateinischen Jahrbuch" 13; Ratingen—Kastellaun—Düsseldorf, 1974); and SCS 5. A matter calling for further inquiry is the purported influence of Joseph and Aseneth on Yussuf and Zuleikha, an Islamic adaptation of Joseph's adventure with Potiphar's wife treated repeatedly by authors in various languages, most notably by the famous Persian poets, Firduzi (c. A.D. 940–1020) and Djami (A.D. 1483); see Philonenko, *Joseph et Aséneth*, pp. 117–23.

[96] Joseph and his wife figure in some Eastern versions of the Christian marriage ritual (R. P. A. Raes, *Le mariage, sa célébration et sa spiritualité dans les Églises d'Orient* [Collection Irénikon; Paris, 1959] pp. 34, 42, 51, 59, 62, 132, 189; cf. Burchard, *Untersuchungen*, p. 39, n. 4). Influence of JosAsen is doubtful here, to say the least.

[97] Burchard, *Untersuchungen*, pp. 134–37; Philonenko, *Joseph et Aséneth*, pp. 110–17. Berger, *Auferstehung*, pp. 564–65, n. 403, has doubts.

[98] Or is it genuine (cf. Näf, *Josef-Gedichte*, pp. 10f.)?

[99] Chr. Burchard, "Zur armenischen Überlieferung der Testamente der zwölf Patriarchen," *Studien zu den Testamenten der Zwölf Patriarchen*, ed. W. Eltester (BZNW 36; Berlin, 1969) pp. 1–29; cf. Burchard, *Untersuchungen*, p. 29.

[100] There are only a few possible exceptions. An anonymous chronicle of the late 9th cent. affirms that "Joseph ruled over the Egyptian (land) for eighty years, beginning in the first year of plenty which was Joseph's thirty-second year, in which he is reported [cf. JosAsen 1:2; 3:1 against Gen 41:50] to have married Aseneth, daughter of Pentephres, priest of Heliopolis. This (man) was Osiris' priest. Osiris the Egyptians call the sun, just like the Greeks call him [the sun] Apollon" (J. A. Cramer, *Anecdota Graeca e codd. manuscriptis Bibliothecae Regiae Parisiensis* [Oxford, 1839] vol. 2, p. 175). Then there is the date of *a* and *d*. Both seem, perhaps, to be older than c. A.D. 1000.

[101] Thus Vikan (*SBL 1976 Seminar Papers*, pp. 196–98) against the earlier suggestion by Pächt and Pächt (*Cahiers Archéologiques* 7 [1954] 35–49) argues that the archetype of the G miniatures originated in the 6th cent. in Syria in the neighborhood of the Vienna Genesis.

[102] See the only extant MS: St. Catherine, Mt. Sinai, MS Greek 441, f. 98ᵇ, unpublished (microfilm courtesy of the Library of Congress).

[103] Which may not therefore be cited as witnesses to the existence of JosAsen Slav.

the girls under [or "the rays of?"] the sun.' "[104] Joseph and Aseneth was copied in Greek so late as A.D. 1802.

Turning to the oriental churches, we find traces of Joseph and Aseneth in Syriac, Armenian, and Ethiopic. In Syriac, in addition to Pseudo-Zacharias and the legend quoted above, there is an entry, "The Book of Asyath, wife of Joseph the Just, son of Jacob," between the works of Josephus and Tobit in a canon list by the noted theologian Ebed Yeshu, which should be dated shortly before A.D. 1300.[105]

The area in which Joseph and Aseneth was most successful in the East is the Armenian church. It first appears under the title of "Aseneth's Prayer" in an "Order of the Holy Scriptures"—ascribed to John Sarkavag ("the Deacon") of Haghbat (A.D. 1045/55–1129)[106]—a book list with indications of length, including the New Testament and Old Testament, each with apocrypha, and a number of philosophical and theological books. It was intended as a key to theological education, and possibly as a guide to a model theological library. Since it says in the superscription that the books "were verified" (*stugabaneçan*) by John (which may denote text-critical and editorial activity, a thing for which he was reputed), we may assume that John had a copy of the Armenian Joseph and Aseneth before him. Anyway, it was after this "Order" that the monumental codex of Erevan 1500 (332), one of the most important Armenian manuscripts ever written, was executed in A.D. 1282–83. The "Order" may also have contributed to the fact that Armenian Bibles, which are traditionally interspersed with apocrypha, though not with canonical honors, often feature Joseph and Aseneth, the oldest specimen being the Erznka Bible of A.D. 1269.[107] Of the imprints Joseph and Aseneth left in Ethiopic,[108] let us quote two that are not easily accessible. Among the hymns (*salamât*) contained in the expanded version of the Ethiopian Synaxarion (which dates from the late sixteenth or early seventeenth century) there are two drawn from Joseph and Aseneth:[109]

> Salutation to Joseph, who was called the similitude
> Of the chief of the army of God [cf. 14:8; 21:21].
> All my bones sing to this wise man, the bearer of a gem,
> The storehouse of his riches, saying,
> "O Mary, he is thyself."

> Salutation to 'Asnêt, whose splendor is like the sun,
> And like the flower of the red rose, which cometh forth
>   from its leaves [cf. 18:9].
> The bees who feed her ascend on the wings of the wind,
> And those who wish to inflict a wound in her
> Fall down upon the ground, and perish straightway
>   [cf. 16:20–22].

In a manuscript of the four gospels from A.D. 1720–45 there is a marginal note in Amharic which reads:[110]

> Asanêt is the wife of Joseph. She is an idolater [cf. 2:3]. When she was yearning for Joseph, she entered into seclusion [*ḥermat*] and prayed [cf. chs. 9–13], and an

[104] Burchard, *NTS* 24 (1977) 74. A second quotation inserted into 1:6 does not mention Aseneth.

[105] Burchard, *Untersuchungen*, p. 25.

[106] Ibid., pp. 32–34. The Order was investigated afresh by M. E. Stone ("Armenian Canon Lists III—The Lists of Mechitar of Ayrivank' (c. 1285 C.E.)," *HTR* 70 [1977] 289–300). He thinks that the ascription to Sarkavag is sound, but we must not assume for sure that all books listed were extant in Armenian in his day.

[107] Armenian Patriarchate, Jerusalem, MS 1925. JosAsen was occasionally illustrated by vignettes showing both persons; for a specimen see M. E. Stonè, "Bible, Translations, Armenian," *EncyJud*, vol. 4, cols. 861f.; see col. 862.

[108] Burchard, *Untersuchungen*, pp. 39–41. Add the marginal note adduced presently. For a more recent discussion see Select Bibliography.

[109] Trans. by E. A. W. Budge, *The Book of the Saints of the Ethiopian Church* (Cambridge, 1928; vol. i–ii repr. in Hildesheim, New York, 1976) vol. 1, p. xxxvii.

[110] Patriarchate Library, Addis Abbaba, Ethiopian Manuscript Microfilm Library Project No. 650, f. 145ᵃ (W. F. Macomber, *A Catalogue of Ethiopian Manuscripts Microfilmed for the Ethiopian Manuscript Microfilm Library, Addis Abbaba and for the Hill Monastic Manuscript Library, Collegeville* [Collegeville, Minn., 1976] vol. 2, p. 399). Trans. by G. Haile through the courtesy of Macomber. Both have informed the present translator that they have not discovered a MS of the full text of JosAsen Eth.

angel breathed on her mouth [cf. 16:8–11]. After that, a white bee [cf. 16:18] made white honey in her mouth [cf. 16:19], and when she ate it [cf. 16:15], she was purified of her idolatry. So he gave her Joseph [cf. 15:6], and she gave birth to Ephraim and Manasseh [cf. 21:9].

In Europe, L1 had an influence which surpasses even that of Arm. in the East.[111] An epitome is extant in three fifteenth-century manuscripts, probably from the continent.[112] A Middle English verse translation is preserved in a fifteenth-century manuscript also containing some poetry of John Lydgate (c. 1370–c. 1451) and a Latin treatise by Hoccleve, both in a different hand.[113] After line 265, Joseph and Aseneth 8:7–9:4 are lacking. There is a break in the verse pattern, not in the manuscript. So it is not the autograph. The author seems to have lived "not far from Warwickshire, and not long after the death of Chaucer" (A.D. 1400),[114] hardly John Lydgate himself. But he is the only English writer of his time, and perhaps the only one of some reputation at all, to remember Aseneth in his poem *To Mary the Queene of Heaven*,[115] fifth stanza (ll. 33–40):

O bussh vnbrent, shewed to Moyses,
　Iudith the secounde, þat saued al Israel,
Assenek of Egipt, of beute pereless,
　Souereyn Sara of refut cheeff Rachel,
　For our Sauacioun salued bi Gabriel,
Reclinatorye throne of kyng Salamoun,
　Fro thy seruantes al mescheeff do repelle,
To thy .v. Ioies that haue deuocioun.

Lydgate obviously knew Joseph and Aseneth (cf. 1:5), but in which form we cannot be certain.

The man who did most to promote the book was Vincent of Beauvais (c. 1190–c. 1264). He included a condensation of L1, independent of the epitome just mentioned, in his *Speculum historiale*, 1, 118–24, a world history from creation down to A.D. 1244–53.[116] This condensation met with extraordinary success far beyond the wide distribution in Latin, Dutch, French, and German of the *Speculum* itself.[117] It was often separately copied and found its way into numerous other compilations, both handwritten and printed, in Latin, Czech, Dutch, English, French, German, Polish, Russian, and Scandinavian, including Icelandic, down to the eighteenth century.[118] In the sixteenth century, Joseph and Aseneth, Part I, was made into a play for Corpus Christi Day.[119]

In 1670, Philipp von Zesen, the renowned German baroque writer, had his most important novel, *Assenat*, probably the first one on this subject, printed in Amsterdam.[120] He used a

[111] Contrary to a suggestion by Batiffol (*Studia Patristica*, p. 3), L1 cannot have been produced by the noted Franciscan scholar Robert Grosseteste (before A.D. 1173–1253), who was the author, or rather commissioner, of the Latin T12P (S. H. Thomson, *The Writings of Robert Grosseteste: Bishop of Lincoln* [Cambridge, 1940] pp. 242f.).

[112] Burchard, *Untersuchungen*, pp. 15, 36.

[113] Now preserved in H. E. Huntington Library, San Marino, Calif., MS El 26. A. 13, printed by H. N. MacCracken, "The Storie of Asneth: An Unknown Middle English Translation of a Lost Latin Version," *The Journal of English and Germanic Philology* 9 (1910) 224–64; cf. G. L. Hamilton, "The Latin Historia Assenech," *The Journal of English and Germanic Philology* 11 (1912) 143f.; MacCracken, "The Source of the Story of Asneth," *The Journal of English and Germanic Philology*, 291f.; R. A. Dwyer, "Asenath of Egypt in Middle English," *Medium Aevum* 39 (1970) 118–22.

[114] MacCracken, *Journal of English and Germanic Philology* 9 (1910) 224.

[115] H. N. MacCracken, *The Minor Poems of John Lydgate* (Early English Text Society. Extra Series 107; London, 1911) vol. 1, p. 286.

[116] No modern printed edition and no English translation are available. MacCracken (*Journal of English and Germanic Philology* 9 [1910] 228–64) prints the Lat. text of 1, 118–24 at the bottom of the pages. Illustrated copies in French include pictures featuring Aseneth (L. Delisle, "Exemplaires royaux et princiers du Miroir historial (XIVᵉ siècle)," *Gazette Archéologique* 11 [1886] 87–101, and pls. 13–16, see 92, 98, pl. 14).

[117] Burchard, *Untersuchungen*, pp. 41–45.

[118] For the influence of this condensation on English, see M. M. Banks, *An Alphabet of Tales* (Early English Text Society. Original Series 126; London, 1904) vol. 1, pp. 61–64.

[119] L. Rouanet, *Collección de Autos, Farsas y Coloquios del siglo XVI*, i–iv (Bibliotheca Hispanica 5–8; Madrid, 1901). However, the numerous Joseph plays of the 16th cent. take little or no notice of JosAsen.

[120] Reprinted with an epilogue by V. Meid (Tübingen, 1967). A Danish version was printed in 1711 and reprinted several times; another one is extant in MS form.

Dutch version of Vincent's abridgment as one of his sources. Large portions have gone into his text, others are quoted verbatim in the learned footnotes appended to the novel according to a custom of the time. Of the thirty engravings which adorn the volume, several illustrate scenes stemming from Joseph and Aseneth. Zesen apparently thought our romance historical. For this he was reprimanded by his even more famous contemporary J. J. C. Grimmelshausen in his novel *Das wunderbarliche Vogelnest*, Part 1, first published at Montbéliard, France, in 1672. He also insinuates plagiarism.[121] Grimmelshausen had an ax to grind. He had himself published a *Histori vom Keuschen Joseph in Egypten*, the first of its kind in German,[122] in which he had failed to use Joseph and Aseneth, a fact duly noted by Zesen. Anyway, Grimmelshausen is the first person on record to have voiced doubts as to the historicity of Joseph and Aseneth.[123]

After this period the European reading public gradually lost interest in Joseph and Aseneth. Nineteenth-century scholarship rediscovered it and most of its versions; and owing to two short notes by G. D. Kilpatrick and J. Jeremias in 1952,[124] it has been viewed with growing interest by students of early Judaism and Christianity. But all attempts to revive it as a work of literature[125] seem to be doomed to failure.

By way of appendix, let us note two fields of influence of Joseph and Aseneth that require the hand of the non-theological specialist. The first, and more important one, is iconography. Apart from the miniatures in the manuscripts referred to earlier, Aseneth naturally figures in numerous illustrations of the biblical narrative proper, both in Genesis manuscripts and outside. Influence of Joseph and Aseneth may of course be assumed with certainty only when the pictorial content coincides with the novel against the biblical text. It is less likely when a picture deviates from the Bible without special support in Joseph and Aseneth, as in the case of Jacob blessing the sons of Joseph, which is not narrated in our book. Aseneth is not mentioned in Genesis 48 either, but she is present in many representations of the scene from the fourth century down to Rembrandt's famous canvas of 1656 (now in Kassel).[126] It remains to be seen whether this, and other Aseneth pictures, have anything to do with Joseph and Aseneth.

Secondly, there is the use of Aseneth as a Christian name, which never seems to have been a very popular one. The name occurs four times in a Greek tax list from after A.D. 716.[127] Armenians have used it since the fifteenth century.[128] Some English occurrences from the seventeenth and eighteenth centuries are also known.[129] Since Joseph and Aseneth was so widely distributed in Armenian, it may have furnished motivation to choose the name, but we do not know how well seventeenth-century England was acquainted with the book.

The present translation

The following translation is based on the provisional text referred to above. A major problem was the author's biblicized style. As it was employed by choice, being neither his everyday mode of speech nor presumably the kind of language he would have used for a non-biblical subject, a translation must somehow preserve it. To this end it seemed advisable

---

121 Reprinted with an introduction by R. Tarot (Tübingen, 1970); see especially pp. 99–103.

122 Under the pseudonym of Samuel Greifnson (Nuremberg, 1666; 2nd ed., 1670, repr. Tübingen, 1968).

123 "Aseneth's story, although I did not see it, I consider a tale of some ancient rabbi who wanted to incite the Jewish lads to virtue and chastity" (100f.).

124 See n. on 8:5.

125 E.g. C. Lucerna, *Asseneth: Eine apokryphe Erzählung aus den Werdezeiten des Christentums* (Vienna, 1921; also in Serbo-Croatian).

126 Generally, cf. W. Stechow, "Jacob Blessing the Sons of Joseph from Early Christian Times to Rembrandt," *Gazette des Beaux-Arts*, 6th series, 23 (1943) 193–208, 382; J. C. H. Lebram, "Jakob segnet Josephs Söhne: Darstellungen von Genesis XLVIII in der Überlieferung und bei Rembrandt," *The Priestly Code and Seven Other Studies*, eds. J. C. Vink *et al.* (OTS 15; Leiden, 1969) pp. 145–69. Cf. above, n. 116.

127 British Museum, London, Pap. 1419, Inv. No. 1442, ff. 4ᵃ (twice), 19ᵃ, 24ᵇ (H. I. Bell, *Greek Papyri in the British Museum*, [London, 1910] vol. 4, pp. 182, 201, 214).

128 H. Ačaṙyan, *Hayoç anjnanunneri baṙaran* [Dictionary of Armenian Personal Names] (RSS d'Arménie. Université Molotov à Erivan. Travaux scientifiques 21; Erivan, 1942) vol. 1, p. 221. The evidence is mostly from MS colophons.

129 E. G. Withycombe, *The Oxford Dictionary of English Christian Names* (Oxford, 1945; 1953²) p. 32: "It was occasionally used, like most other Old Testament names, in the 17th C, and there was an *Asenath* Angel in Shropshire in 1798. The gipsy name *As(h)ena* may be derived from it."

to translate as literally, and consistently, as present-day English grammar will permit, even to the extent of stretching a rule here and there, and to bring out the biblical affinities by following an established translation of the Bible. The present translator was guided by The Jerusalem Bible, unless otherwise required by the principle of literalness as laid down before. If a non-literal rendering is unavoidable, the literal translation is given in a footnote, except for some well-known turns that recur frequently such as "to rejoice with great joy" (lit. "to rejoice a great joy"), "to be filled with great fear" (lit. "to fear a great fear"), and similar instances of the cognate accusative: "to tell you what I have to say" (lit. "to speak to you my words"), "to speak words such as these" (lit. "to speak according to these words"), "forever" (lit. "in the eternity" or "eternities"), "for ever (and) ever" (lit. "in the eternity time," see 4:8), "for ever and ever" (lit. "in the eternities of the eternities").

Personal names are spelled as in The Jerusalem Bible, because their original form has not yet been critically established, except that Asenath is "Aseneth," and Potiphera, "Pentephres" (see 1:3, 5).

Chapters were installed by Batiffol and verses by Riessler, and later by Philonenko. Riessler obviously could not make up his mind between short verses, as in the Bible, and longer paragraphs, as, for example, in Josephus. Working with a provisional text, the present translator did not feel free to adopt a new division, which will, however, eventually be necessary. He followed Riessler, continuing his numbering if new material is added at the end of chapters (11:16–19 [or 15–18]; 21:10–21), using x, y numbers if in the middle (11:1x–y; 15:12x; 16:16x; 16:17x), and altering numbers only if textual criticism cogently demands it (see 6:2; 13:10; 16:17; 16:17y). Philonenko's numbers are given in parentheses. A fresh division into sections and appropriate headlines have been supplied for this translation.

The text-critical footnotes include the major differences in length between a, b, c, and d, a selection of variants illustrating the diversified nature as well as the basic unity of the textual tradition in the positive text, and some variants bearing intrinsic interest. The presentation is as follows: (a) If a textual problem is mentioned, as a rule, all pertinent variants are cited except for minor deviations, especially such as will not normally show in a translation at all, regarding, for example, the article, synonymous or nearly synonymous prepositions and forms, or the word order, but not, for example, the exchange of synonyms. (b) If more words than the one carrying the footnote letter are concerned, they are given at the head of the note. The variants quoted after this until the first stop are in lieu of exactly that heading. Longer readings are usually abbreviated by ellipsis points between the first and last words (to find the exact length read back from the last word quoted to the first that you come to reading backward). Insertions in parentheses refer only to the one word before the parenthesis unless otherwise stated. (c) Variants are normally given full coverage from ACPQR ($=a$), EFGW ($=b$), HJK ($=c$), BD ($=d$), Syr., Arm., L1, L2 (if 436 and 435& do not agree they are quoted separately), Slav., Ngr. (671 only), Bat, Phil (both text and translation), Br (including the appendixes), Rie., Eth., Rum., 661 (Ngr.), and Istrin are noted by way of exception only. For the sake of brevity, a or A include Bat, Rie, and Br, d includes Slav. and Phil, unless otherwise stated, and "rest" includes all witnesses normally used for coverage except those quoted individually. (d) The witness or witnesses supporting a reading, if only with minor deviations, are set right after it. If a version or versions are adduced after Greek evidence this implies only that they show no sign of being based on a different Greek text. If a witness deviates in a more than minor fashion, but still supports the reading in a general way, it is set in parentheses. If this should happen to all witnesses supporting a variant, they vary considerably from one another, which usually means that the text generally can be reconstructed but details remain doubtful. The abbreviation "add." means that a reading is found in addition to the text in the witnesses quoted, "om." that it is lacking, "gap(s)" that the reading *and* words before or after it or both are lacking, not necessarily to the same extent in all witnesses adduced.

The present translator is greatly indebted to Dieter Sänger and Tuviah Kwassman for their unfailing help in preparing the translation, and especially to J. H. Charlesworth for correcting it. Claudius Fehlandt and Michael Hoffmann helped to see the work through the press.

SELECT BIBLIOGRAPHY

Charlesworth, *PMR*, pp. 137–40.

Delling, *Bibliographie*, pp. 95f.

Denis, *Introduction*, pp. 40–48.

Berger, K. *Die Auferstehung des Propheten und die Erhöhung des Menschensohnes: Traditionsgeschichtliche Untersuchungen zur Deutung des Geschickes Jesu in frühchristlichen Texten.* Studien zur Umwelt des Neuen Testaments 13; Göttingen, 1976.

Burchard, Chr. *Der dreizehnte Zeuge.* FRLANT 103; Göttingen, 1970; pp. 59–105.

———. *Untersuchungen zu Joseph und Aseneth.* WUNT 8; Tübingen, 1965.

———. "Zum Text von 'Joseph und Aseneth,' " *JSJ* 1 (1970) 3–34.

Delling, G. "Einwirkungen der Sprache der Septuaginta in 'Joseph und Aseneth,' " *JSJ* 9 (1978) 29–56.

Kähler, C. "Zur Form- und Traditionsgeschichte von Matth. XVI. 17–19," *NTS* 23 (1976) 36–58.

Nickelsburg, G. W. E. Jr. "Narrative Writings, §B 7: Joseph and Aseneth," *Oral and Literary Tradition in Judaism and Early Christianity.* Compendia Rerum Iudaicarum ad Novum Testamentum 2, 2; Leiden, in press.

Pervo, R. I. "Joseph and Asenath and the Greek Novel," *SBL 1976 Seminar Papers,* ed. G. MacRae. SBL Seminar Papers Series 10; Missoula, Mont., 1976; pp. 171–81.

Philonenko, M. *Joseph et Aséneth: Introduction, texte critique, traduction et notes.* SPB 13; Leiden, 1968.

Sänger, D. *Antikes Judentum und die Mysterien. Religionsgeschichtliche Untersuchungen zu Joseph und Aseneth.* WUNT 2.5; Tübingen, 1980 (with history of research and full bibliography).

Smith, E. W. Jr. *Joseph and Asenath and Early Christian Literature: A Contribution to the Corpus Hellenisticum Novi Testamenti* (Ph.D. dissertation, Claremont Graduate School), Claremont, Calif., 1974.

West, S. "Joseph and Asenath: A Neglected Greek Romance," *The Classical Quarterly* N.S. 24 (1974) 70–81.

Wilckens, U. "Vergebung für die Sünderin (Lk 7, 36–50)," *Orientierung an Jesus: Zur Theologie der Synoptiker. J. Schmid zum 80. Geburtstag am 26. Januar 1973 von Freunden, Kollegen und Schülern,* eds. P. Hoffmann, N. Brox, and W. Pesch. Freiburg, 1973; pp. 394–424.

SUPPLEMENT

Burchard, Chr. "Joseph und Aseneth," *JSHRZ* 2.4 (1983). (German translation with Introduction and Bibliography.)

———. "Zur armenischen Übersetzung von Joseph und Aseneth," *Revue des études arméniennes* 17 (1983) 207–40.

———."Der jüdische Asenethroman und seine Nachwirkung: Von Egeria zu Anna Katharina Emmerick oder von Moses aus Aggel zu Karl Kerénye," *ANRW,* vol. 2, 20 (in press). (A full account of the cultural importance of JosAsen with new information about Eth. by G. Haile.)

———. "The Importance of Joseph and Aseneth for the Study of the New Testament," *NTS* 32 (1986). (General survey with Bibliography, and a fresh study of the importance of JosAsen for the Lord's Supper).

Delling, G. "Die Kunst des Gestaltens in 'Joseph und Aseneth,' " *NovTest* 26 (1984) 1–40.

Denis, A.-M., and Schumacher, J. *Concordance des Pseudépigraphes grecs d'Ancien Testament.* Leiden, 1984.

van Goeij, M. *Jozef en Aseneth. Apokalyps van Baruch. De Pseudepigrafen* 2; Kampen, 1981. (Dutch translation.)

Kee, H. "The Socio-Cultural Setting of Joseph and Aseneth," *NTS* 29 (1983) 394–413.

Martínez Fernandez, R., and Piñero, A. "José y Asenet," *Apócrifos del Antiguo Testamento,* ed. A. Díez Macho; Madrid, 1983. (Spanish translation of Philonenko's text.)

Suski, A. "Józef i Asenet," *Studia Theologica Varsaviensia* 16 (1978) 199–240. (Polish translation of Philonenko's text.)

JOSEPH AND ASENETH[a]

FIRST PART: ASENETH'S CONVERSION AND MARRIAGE

I. CAST OF CHARACTERS. SCENE OF ACTION

The characters are introduced

1 (1) **1** And it happened[b] in the first year of the seven years of plenty, in the second month, on the fifth of the month:[c] Pharaoh sent out Joseph to drive around the whole land of Egypt. 2 (2) And Joseph came in the fourth month of the first year, on the eighteenth of the month,[d] (3) into the territory of Heliopolis,[e] and was gathering the grain of that region like the sand of the sea.[f] 3 (4) And[g] there was a man in that city,[h] a satrap of Pharaoh, and this (man) was a chief of (5) all the satraps and the noblemen of Pharaoh. And this man was exceedingly rich and prudent and gentle, and he was a counselor of Pharaoh, because he was understanding beyond all the noblemen of Pharaoh. And the name of that man (was) Pentephres, priest of Heliopolis.[i]

1 a. Modern (Rie, see Intro.). Survey of the titles in Burchard, *Untersuchungen*, pp. 50–54. "Life and Confession of Aseneth daughter of Pentephres priest of Heliopolis, and how the all-beautiful Joseph took her for (his) wife" (*a d* L1 Ngr. Br, Phil, not Bat Rie); "Discourse (*logos*) about Aseneth daughter of Pentephres." *c;* "Discourse (*logos*) chosen from the old book about Aseneth having become (h.b. omit W) the wife of Joseph the all-beautiful and self-controlled (a.s. omit W)" FW (Arm. c, 435, Ebed Yeshu, see Intro.); "Story (*historia*) of A." E 332 (somewhat longer Arm. a, d) 2–456 (436); "Book of Asyath" Anonymous letter in Ps-Zacharias Rhetor, *Church History*, 1.4; "Aseneth's Prayer" Sarkavag (see Intro.); "Prayer of Aseneth" Bat, "Aseneth" Nikon and other canon lists (see Intro.); "Deed(s?) of the all-beautiful Joseph and his wife Asèneth" MS Breslau; "Tale of Joseph the Just and of Asyath his wife" Syr. (Syr. subscription, Arm. b, e, cf. also L2 445, 455); "Story of Joseph and Aseneth" or similar, Rum. The first mentioned title is old because it crosses *a, b,* and *d,* and the next two may be derived from it, but it sounds hagiographical. The title is followed in CPQR FW HJK BD by "Bless, Lord (or Father)," a stock formula opening the delivery of the text when read aloud. [Biblical and apocryphal references are not placed in the margins to JosAsen because there are no formal quotations from them in this document; affinities are discussed in the notes. Two verse systems are provided (see Introduction, "The present translation"). Bullets denote the primary system of verses; marginal parentheses specify Philonenko's system. The beginning of a verse according to the secondary system is not indicated if the punctuation points to it unequivocally; when it is not obvious, the sign ' has been inserted in the text.—J.H.C.]

b. "And it happened" G *c* Syr. Arm. L1; "it h." CR E *d* 435&; omit AOPQ Ngr.; 1:1f. omit FW; 1:1–7 "for (his) wife" omit 436. Frequent traditional turn (not in Aram.) to introduce circumstantial data, also 3:1; 21:9; 22:1; followed by an independent clause without "and," e.g. 2Chr 12:11; Dan 8:15; Lk 1:59. As the opening of an entire book in Josh, Judg, Ruth, 2Sam, 1Mac, Jub (1:1, also with a precise date); "it h." TAb B 1:1, cf. Lk 1:5.

c. See 1:2.

d. See 1:1 (5th day, 2d month, year 1), 3:1 (as in 1:2), and 22:2 (21st day, 2d month, year 2 of famine), cf. the dates in Jub. According to the calendar of Jub, also attested at Qumran, 5th day, 2d month and 8th day, 4th month would be sabbaths (J. van Goudoever, *Biblical Calendars* [Leiden, 1959; 1961²] p. 63). But 18th day, 4th month is a Sunday in 9:5, and would Joseph travel on sabbaths? Or is 18th day, 4th month "an indication of the summer solstice" (Goudoever, *Biblical Calendars*, p. 120, referring to 5:5; 6:2; 9:5 etc.)? Anyway, it is harvest time in chs. 1–21 (see also 2:11; 4:2; 5:5) as also in 22:29, though years later (24:15; 25:2; 26:1). Does the season of Aseneth's conversion have a symbolical meaning (cf. Mt 9:37)? The day certainly has one (see on 9:5; 11:1; 14:1).

e. "Sun City," Heb. *'ōn*, Gen 41:45, 50; 46:20, cf. Jer 43:13; today Matarieh, a few miles northeast of Cairo (E. P. Uphill, "Pithom and Raamses: Their Location and Significance", *JNES* 27 [1968] 291–316; 28 [1969] 15–39, see especially pp. 296–99 [with plans] and pp. 37–39). It is an important center of the Sun god Rê, almost in ruins in the author's day, but a tourist attraction haunted by the memories of Plato and Eudoxus (Strabo, *Geography* 17.1.29). Jews thought that Abraham had visited there and taught the Egyptian clergy astrology (Ps-Eup F. 1), that they had fortified the city (Ex 1:11 LXX), and built the local temple (Art F. 2; 3). Apion, *History of Egypt*, is said by Josephus to have reported that Moses was born in Heliopolis and erected prayer-houses and pillars with statues on them for sun-clocks there (*Apion* 2.2 §10–11, cf. 12–14). On Leontopolis see Intro. n. 59.

f. Frequent traditional simile, e.g. Gen 41:49.

g. On the following introduction of a man cf. e.g. Job 1:1–3; Acts 10:1f.; Xenophon of Ephesus 1.1.1. On 1:3–6 cf. e.g. Chariton 1.1.1f.; Xenophon of Ephesus 1.1.1–3; Apuleius 4.28.1–29.4.

h. See next note.

i. "And . . . Heliopolis" (all) except a, which has "by name (of) P. being priest of H. and" after "city." Pentephres (Heb. *Pôṭî Pęraʿ*, LXX *Petephrēs*; etymology in Redford, *Study*, pp. 228f., cf. Philo, *Somn.* 1.78, "worshipper of the mind") occurs in the Bible only at Gen 41:45, 50; 46:20. Like, e.g., Josephus, *Ant* 2.6.1 §91, and Philo, *Jos*, 121, JosAsen does not identify Pentephres with Potiphar Gen 37:36, 39:1, whose name is

₄ (6) And he had a daughter, a virgin of eighteen years,[j] (she was) very tall and handsome and
₅ (7) beautiful to look at beyond all virgins on the earth. •And this (girl) had nothing similar to
        the virgins of the Egyptians, but she was in every respect similar to the daughters of the
    (8) Hebrews; and she was tall as Sarah and handsome as Rebecca and beautiful as Rachel.[k]
₆ (9) And the name of that virgin was Aseneth.[l] •And the fame of her beauty spread all over that
        land and to the ends of the inhabited (world).[m] And all the sons of the noblemen and the
        sons of the satraps and the sons of all kings, all of them young and powerful,[n] asked for
    (10) her hand in marriage,[o] and there was much wrangling among them over Aseneth, 'and they
        made attempts to fight against each other because of her.[p]
₇ (11) And[q] Pharaoh's firstborn son heard about her and he kept entreating[r] his father to give
    (12) her to him for (his) wife. And his firstborn son said to Pharaoh, "Father, give me Aseneth,
        the daughter of Pentephres, the priest of Heliopolis, for (my) wife."[s] •And Pharaoh, his
₈ (13) father, said to him, "Why do you seek a wife (that is) beneath you, and you are king[t] of
        the whole land of Egypt? •Behold, is not the daughter of the king of Moab, Joakim,[u]
₉ (14) betrothed to you,[v] and she is a queen and exceedingly beautiful? This (one) take for (your)
        wife."

Aseneth's tower and the court surrounding Pentephres' house are described

₁ (1) **2** And Aseneth was despising and scorning every man, and she was boastful and arrogant
        with everyone.[a] And no man had ever seen her, because Pentephres had a tower adjoining

almost identical in MT and completely in LXX, but many ancient authors, both Jewish and Christian, did (e.g. Jub 40:10; TJos 18:3; rabbinical literature is divided (cf. Aptowitzer, *HUCA* 1 [1924], 262). It is not clear whether "priest" has the article. Perhaps it should be omitted when followed by "of Heliopolis" (1:3, 7; 21:2, 11) in accordance with LXX, but retained when not (3:2; 12:5). Despite his title, P. is never shown officiating, whereas Aseneth is (2:3).

j. Aseneth's virginity, not mentioned in the Bible (but, e.g. by Josephus, *Ant* 2.6.1 §91), plays a great role in JosAsen (e.g. chs. 7f., 11–13), as virginity generally does in the romances. The age of eighteen means that she has been fighting off suitors for several years.

k. A novel's hero or heroine has to be beautiful (e.g. Xenophon of Ephesus 1.1.3; 1.2.5,7; Achilles Tatius 1.4.2; Apuleius 4:28), and her looks may be compared to a classical figure or a goddess (e.g. Chariton 1.1.1; 1.6.2; 2.6.1 etc.). To a Jew, Jewish women, above all the patriarchs' wives, whose beauty was legendary (e.g. Sarah, Ginzberg, *Legends*, vol. 5, p. 261, no. 90; vol. 6 (1928, repr. 1946) p. 273, n. 132; 1QapGen 20.2–8), would set the standard. "Hebrews" instead of "Jews" (as in 11:10) has a distinguished ring.

l. "And . . . Aseneth" (G *d* Syr. Arm. 435&); "by name (of) A." before or after 1:4 "virgin" *a* EW *c* L1 Ngr. Rum. illegible F; gap 436. Aseneth (Heb. 'As*e*nat, LXX Asen[n]eth, Egyptian possibly *ns-nt*: "the One belonging to Neith"; on this etymology see Redford, *Study*, pp. 229f.) is mentioned in the Bible only at Gen 41:45, 50; 46:20. The author and the readers of JosAsen may have been aware of the reference to Neith, but more would be needed to make Aseneth a representation of the goddess (cf. Intro.).

m. Ps 19:4. A person's reputation spreads the same way, e.g. in Chariton 1.5.1; 3.2.7; 4.7.5; 5.2.6; Achilles Tatius 6.10.3; Apuleius 4.29.1; 11.18.1.

n. Maybe these are to be understood as two more classes of suitors.

o. The reading "asked . . . marriage": *c d*;

"desired (*epethymoun*) her to be married" ACPR (Q Arm. 435& Ngr.); "praised (*hymnoun*) her" *b* Syr. L1 Rum.; gap 436. Seems to be one instance where *b* (but not all versions) is at fault, although its reading is not entirely incongruent (cf. Xenophon of Ephesus 1.1.3; 1.2.7; Apuleius 4.28.1f.). Note the graphic similarity of the two verbs.

p. Another novelistic feature. For an illustration see e.g. Chariton 1.2.2f.

q. 1:7–9 lays the foundation for 4:11 and chs. 22–29.

r. The verb *ekliparein* (also 15:7) is found first in Strabo and Dionysius of Halicarnassus.

s. Cf. Gen 34:4.

t. The titles of "king" and "queen" (1:9; 28:2; cf. 10:13; 13:8) in JosAsen are also applied to the crown prince, to viceroys like Joseph (4:7), and related folk.

u. "Moab, Joakim" *a*, "Moab" E FW (gap following) *c* Syr. (gap following) Arm. L1 L2, "Joakim" *d*, paraphrase G, gap Ngr. Is Moab a biblicised reference to the Nabatean kingdom, *c.* 100 B.C.–A.D. 105/6 (Burchard, *Untersuchungen*, pp. 144–46)? The name was used down to Christian times. Why does this Moabite (or his daughter?) have a Heb. name?

v. In Jewish law of the time, as in Greek, betrothal (also 21:3, 23:3) was the legally binding step in bringing about a marital union, constituting by and large the formal beginning of a marriage; consummation by the wedding could be, and often was, deferred at the parties' convenience. See generally R. Taubenschlag, *The Law of Greco-Roman Egypt in the Light of the Papyri 332 B.C.–640 A.D.* (Warsaw, 1955²) p. 114; A. Calderini, "La *eggyèsis* matrimoniale nei romanzieri greci e nei papiri," *Aegyptus* 39 (1959) 29–39; B. Cohen, *Jewish and Roman Law. A Comparative Study* (New York, 1966), vol. 1, pp. 279–347.

2 a. In spite of the general ring, Aseneth's boastfulness, which is a main motif in chs. 1–21 (4:12; 6:2–8; 7:7f.; 11:6; 12:5; 13:13; 21:12, 16–21), is in fact limited to possible suitors (cf. 8:1). As she lives in seclusion (see vs. 2), it would express

(2) his house, very big and high, and 'on top of this tower was an upper floor including ten
2 (3) chambers.[b] •And the first chamber was big and splendid, paved with purple stones, and its
(4) walls were faced with colored and precious stones,[c] and the ceiling of that chamber was of
3 gold. •And within that chamber gods of the Egyptians[d] who were without number were
(5) fixed to the walls,[e] (even gods) of gold and silver.[f] And Aseneth worshiped them all and
4 (6) feared them and performed sacrifices to them every day.[g] •And the second chamber contained
(7) Aseneth's ornaments and chests, and there was much gold in it (the chamber) and silver
and clothes interwoven with gold and chosen and costly stones and distinguished cloths[h]
5 (8)(9) and all the ornaments of her virginity. •And the third chamber was Aseneth's storeroom,
6 (10) and in it were all the good (things) of the earth.[i] •And seven virgins[j] occupied the remaining
(11) seven chambers, each having one chamber, 'and these were waiting on Aseneth, and they
were all of the same age, born in one night with Aseneth, and she loved them very much.[k]
And they were very beautiful, like the stars of heaven, and no man ever conversed with
them, not (even) a male child.
7 (12) And there were three windows to Aseneth's big chamber where her virginity was being
(13) fostered. And the one window, the first, was exceedingly big, looking east toward the court,
and the second one was looking south, and the third one was looking north toward the street
8 (14) where people passed by.[l] •And there was a golden bed standing in the chamber, (a bed)
(15) that looked toward the window (looking) east, and the bed was laid with gold-woven purple
9 (16) stuff, interwoven with violet, purple, and white.[m] •And in this bed Aseneth slept, alone;
and a man or another woman never sat on it, only Aseneth alone.[n]
10 (17) And there was a large court surrounding the house,[o] and a wall was around the court,
11 (18) very high, built from big square stones.[p] •And the court had four iron-plated gates, and
(19) eighteen powerful armed young men guarded each of these.[q] And handsome trees of all

---

itself in the manner shown in ch. 4. She behaves
lovingly toward her parents, servants (2:6; 10:4;
17:4), and her dead brother (10:8). She is actuated
by virginal fastidiousness rather than misanthropy,
feminism, or sex-hatred. She wants the best man
(a fairy-tale motif), and she will get him, if only
against herself (cf. on 4:11).

b. The "tower" need be no more than the two-
story part of an otherwise flat mansion. On the
description of the premises cf. Cupid's palace and
park (Apuleius 5.1.1–2.1); a garden (Achilles
Tatius 1.15). That women, especially unmarried
daughters, had better stay home is a common ideal
of the time, often no more than that (Thraede,
"Frau," pp. 199–201, 215f.), but upheld rigorously in Jewish quarters (e.g. 2Mac 3:19; 3Mac
1:18; Sir 42:9–14; Ps-Phoc 215–17; Philo, *Leg
All*, 3.169; *Flacc*, 89). This does not mean that
Aseneth is held a prisoner. In other texts the tower
(another fairy-tale motif) may mean just that; in
JosAsen it goes to underline Pentephres' affluence
and his care for his daughter. Obviously she is in
charge of the house during her parents' absence
(chs. 18–20), just as she will look after Joseph's
estate later on (24:15; 26:1–4; see 3:5). She is also
Pentephres' heiress (12:15), apparently being his
only child after her brother's death (10:8; according
to Nu 27:1–11; BB 9:1, Jewish daughters inherit
only if their father had no male children living).

c. Cf. 1Chr 29:2 LXX; Esth 1:6.

d. These would be animal statues, but unlike
e.g. WisSol 15:18f. JosAsen makes nothing of it.
The gods have names (3:6), but as in Jewish
polemic generally they are not identified individually. See further esp. 12:9–11.

e. Both chamber and walls are mentioned in G
Arm. L1 L2 Rum. (and perhaps F in between
illegible spots), the chamber alone in APQ *d* Slav.
Ngr., the walls in *c* Syr. (and perhaps F in between
illegible spots); gaps CR EW.

f. Conventional, cf. e.g. Ex 20:23; Ps 115:4
(113:12 LXX); WisSol 13:10; LetJer 3, 10, 29;
Acts 17:29; Rev 9:20; 17:4.

g. Cf. 10:12; 11:8f., 16; 12:5; 13:11; 19:5;
21:13f. Xenophon of Ephesus' Antheia and Heliodorus' Chariclea were also priestesses. Cf. TJob
2:2f.; ApAb 1:3.

h. Gold, silver, jewels, and fine clothes is a
common formula for mobile wealth (cf. Acts 20:33;
Jas 5:2f.). In antiquity clothes were folded away
in chests (also 10:8; 14:14; 18:5), never hung up
in wardrobes or closets.

i. Or "land"; i.e. food stuff as in 4:2. Cf. Isa
1:19; Hos 10:1.

j. Cf. Esth 2:9, seven valets Esth 1:10, seven
counsellors Ezra 7:14. The wording of the first half
of vs. 6 is doubtful. Cf. 17:4.

k. The reading "and . . . much": ACP; destroyed R; gaps Q EG Ngr.; omit rest. Cf. 10:4.

l. Lit. "of the (people) passing by" FW *c* (Syr.)
Arm. L1 (L2); omit *a d*; gaps EG Ngr.

m. Both text and meaning of the description of
the textiles are uncertain (as in 3:6; 5:5; 13:3;
16:18); cf. Ex 26:1, 31, 36; 28:5f., 8, 15; Jdt
10:21; TJob 25:7; Josephus, *War* 5.5.4 §212. For
similar luxury beds, see Esth 1:6; TJob 25:8; 32:4;
Philo, *Somn.* 2.57; Chariton 8.1.14; 8.6.7; Xenophon of Ephesus 1.8.2; Apuleius 2.19.1. East: to
facilitate prayer in that direction (on which see
11:1y).

n. The reading "except . . . alone": ACPR *d*;
gaps *b* Ngr.; omit rest. Cf. 15:14.

o. Not on the northern side, unless Aseneth's
tower is a distance from the house, cf. 2:7; 10:11–
13; 13:11.

p. Indicating careful and costly construction.
Cf. ShepHerm Vis 3.2.5.

q. The number hardly symbolizes the eighteen
stars of *Aries* (Philonenko, *Joseph et Aséneth*, pp.
74f.) or the Eighteen Benedictions (Riessler, *Altjü-*

sorts and all bearing fruit were planted within the court along the wall. And their fruit was
12 (20) ripe, for it was the time of harvest. •And there was in the court, on the right hand, a spring
of abundant living[r] water, and below the spring was a big cistern receiving the water of that
spring. From there a river ran right through the court and watered all the trees of that court.

II. PENTEPHRES' ATTEMPT TO GIVE ASENETH TO JOSEPH IN MARRIAGE

Joseph's visit to Pentephres is announced

1 (1) **3** And it happened in the first year of the seven years of plenty, in the fourth month, on
the eighteenth[a] of the month; Joseph came into the territory of Heliopolis and was gathering
2 (2) the surplus grain of that region.[b] •And when he had come close to that city, Joseph sent
(3) twelve men[c] ahead of him to Pentephres the priest, saying, "I will lodge with you because
it is the hour of noon and the time of lunch,[d] and the heat of the sun is great, and (I desire)
3 (4) that I may refresh myself under the shadow of your house."[e] •And Pentephres heard this,
and rejoiced exceedingly with great joy and said, "Blessed (be) the Lord, the God of
4 (5) Joseph, because my lord Joseph thought me worthy to come to us."[f] •And Pentephres called
(6) the (steward) of his house[g] and said to him, "Hurry and make my house ready and prepare
a great dinner, because Joseph, the Powerful One of God,[h] is coming to us today."

Aseneth dresses up to meet her parents

5 (7)　And Aseneth heard that her father and mother had come from the field, which was their
(8) inheritance,[i] and rejoiced and said, "I will go and see my father and my mother because
they have come from the field which is our inheritance."[j] For it was (the) time of harvest.
6 (9) And Aseneth hurried into the chamber, where her robes lay,[k] and dressed[l] in a (white) linen

disches Schrifttum, p. 1303). If it is at all symbolical, the total of seventy-two might refer to the
seventy-two nations of the world (Gen 10 LXX;
cf. LetAris 50, 307; Lk 10:1). Cf. 3:2.
　r. I.e. fresh as opposed to cistern water; also
14:12, 15. Traditional, e.g. Gen 26:19; Jer 2:13.

3 a. Witnesses c FW Syr. Arm. L1 Slav. Phil;
"seventeenth" 436; "twenty-eighth" ACPR d i,
"eighth" Q; gaps EG 435& Ngr.
　b. The reading "of surplus (lit. "plenty") . . .
region": the evidence is variegated. (a) B Slav.
have only "the region"; FW L1 only "the plenty";
similarly Syr. ("of the seven years of plenty," cf.
Gen 41:34, 47) Arm. ("of plenty of the times"),
only 436 and perhaps c have both; omit Ngr., gaps
EG D 435& Phil. The text is restored on the
assumption of split tradition.
　c. A reference to Israel? Cf. 2:11. Of course a
man in Joseph's position would not travel alone,
but have a large staff with him (9:3; 18:1).
　d. Cf. Mk 11:1 par; Lk 9:52; 19:5. See also 3:5
end.
　e. The reading "the shadow (skian, "shelter"
[skepēn] D) of your house (hand 435&)": E D
Arm. L1 L2; "the roof (stegēn) of y.h." a Slav.;
"your shadow" c; "your house (oikian)" FW
(Syr.); "your roof" B Phil; gaps G Ngr.
　f. Traditional form of eulogy, e.g. Gen 14:19–
20; 1Sam 25:32; 1Kgs 1:48; 8:15; Tob 3:11; 2Mac
1:17; see H. W. Beyer, "eulogeō etc.," TDNT 2,
754–65. Also in a gentile's mouth as in 8:2; 21:4,
e.g. 1Kgs 5:21; 10:9. The translation "to come to
us" is a guess from the variegated evidence.
　g. Cf. Gen 43:16; 44:1, 4. An analogous person
in ch. 18. They would be slaves. Cf. on 5:1.
　h. Also 4:7; 18:1f.; 21:21. Not LXX, but cf.
Isa 9:5; Jub 40:7.
　i. Lit. "field of their inheritance," also 3:5b;
4:2; 16:4; 20:6; 24:15; 26:1; cf. 10:1; 23:3. The

expression sounds Semitic, but no equivalent is on
record; could this be an artificial Semitism? Perhaps
the expression is not so much due to an intention
to present Pentephres in a biblicized manner, as to
a peculiarity of Egyptian law. Arable land was
considered property of the crown and either ad-
ministrated directly or allotted to others. In Ptolemaic times the latter seems to have gradually
acquired the character of private property (see
Taubenschlag, Law, pp. 232–39). That Pentephres
is a landowner may come from Gen 47:22, 26, but
Pharaoh's firstborn (25:2) and Joseph (24:15; 26:1)
also are (cf. further 23:3). With men of their
description, the "fields" would be estates as hellenistic patricians used to have rather than mere
strips of land; perhaps we ought to translate agros
accordingly. Pentephres' estate is near (16:4). Such
estates were run by managers (cf. Lk 16:1) who
might be slaves, with the help of other slaves (cf.
Chariton 4.2) or hired labor (cf. Lk 15:15f.). The
owners lived in the city, keeping an occasional eye
on things (as described e.g. in Chariton 2.3.1),
particularly at harvest time. So statements like
those in 24:15; 25:2; 26:1 should be taken in the
sense of supervision rather than personal hard work,
although a landlord was not above lending a helpful
hand when on his estate (Syracuse's second-best
man fell from a ladder there and almost killed
himself, Chariton 1.3.1). The estates in JosAsen
produce different kind of fruit (4:2), honey (16:4),
wine (24:15; 25:2; 26:1), and doubtless also corn.
　j. This might have been mentioned as early as
3:2. Ngr. has an addition there to this effect as
well as further remarks on Pentephres' hospitality.
　k. The reading "into . . . lay": APCR B; gaps
EG; omit rest Phil. The MS evidence is poor, but
some such remark seems appropriate, cf. 10:8;
14:14; 18:5.
　l. More dressing scenes, cf. 10:10; 14:14f.;
18:5f. Cf. Jdt 10:3f.

robe interwoven with violet and gold,[m] and girded herself (with) a golden girdle and put bracelets on her hands and feet, and put golden buskins[n] about her feet, and around her (10) neck she put valuable ornaments and costly stones which hung around from all sides, and the names of the gods of the Egyptians[o] were engraved everywhere on the bracelets and the (11) stones, and the faces of all the idols were carved on them. And she put a tiara on her head and fastened a diadem around her temples, and covered her head with a veil.

Pentephres proposes to give Aseneth to Joseph in marriage, but she refuses

1 (1) **4** And she hurried and went down the stairs from the upper floor, and came to her father (2) and mother and greeted them and kissed them. And Pentephres and his wife rejoiced over her daughter Aseneth (with) great joy, because they saw her adorned like a bride of God.[a]

2 (3) And they brought out all the good (things) which they had brought from the field which (4) was their inheritance, and gave (them) to their daughter. And Aseneth rejoiced over all the good (things), the fruit,[b] and the grapes, and the dates, and the doves,[c] and the pomegranates, and the figs, because they were all handsome and good to taste.[d]

3 (5) And Pentephres said to his daughter Aseneth, "My child." And she said, "Behold, 4 (here) I (am), my lord."[e] • And he said to her, "Sit down between us,[f] and I will tell you what I have to say."[g]

5 (6)(7) And Aseneth sat between her father and mother. And Pentephres, her father, with his right hand grasped the right hand of his daughter and kissed it[h] and said to her, "My child 6 Aseneth." • And she said, "Behold, (here) I (am), lord. Let my lord and my father speak 7 (8) up."[i] • And Pentephres, her father, said to her, "Joseph the Powerful One of God is coming to us today. And he is chief of the whole land of Egypt,[j] and the king Pharaoh appointed (9) him king of the whole land,[k] and he is giving grain to the whole land, and saving it from the oncoming famine.[l] And Joseph is a man who worships God,[m] and self-controlled, and a virgin[n] like you today,[o] and Joseph is (also) a man powerful in wisdom and experience,

---

m. See 2:8.

n. Thus Br for *anaxyrides*, an ill-defined piece of oriental clothing; "Binden" Rie, "pantalons" Phil; also 18:6. Liddell-Scott only admit "trousers," but those do not go well with "feet" and would leave Aseneth barefooted. The sequence of objects also demands something more in the nature of an accessory.

o. See 2:3.

4 a. Does this expression mean that a god will unite himself to her in the guise of the future king of Egypt (Philonenko, *Joseph et Aséneth*, p. 141)? A genitive of quality or origin seems to fit the context better, cf. 1Thes 4:16; Rev 15:2. For the vision of a bride clad in white cf. ShepHerm Vision 4.2.1.

b. "Fruit" seems to serve as a heading, cf. 10:13.

c. No positive variants. Riessler (*TQ* 103 [1922] 2) suggests that Heb. *gôzālīm* ("pigeons") is a mistake for *'gôzīm* ("walnuts"); this is a rather remote possibility in view of the context. If *tais peristerais* ("the doves") cannot be explained somehow (cf. Philonenko, *Joseph et Aséneth*, p. 141), perhaps we might envisage corruption from *tais persikais* ("the peaches") or *tois pistakiois* ("the pistachios").

d. Cf. Gen 2:9.

e. Traditional opening of a dialogue; cf. e.g. Tob 2:3 S; 6:11 S; Jub 18:6; more in Berger, *Auferstehung*, pp. 431f., n. 19, and on 14:6. It is repeated in vss. 5f.; as the angel in ch. 14, Pentephres addresses Aseneth twice before he launches his speech; cf. 1Sam 3:1–14; Jn 21:15–18.

f. Sus 50 Theod.

g. Lit. "my words" as often. Cf. 4:9.

h. Or "her"; cf. 20:6.

i. Wording of vs. 6 is uncertain.

j. Cf. Gen 45:26.

k. Cf. Gen 41:41, 44. The wording of the clause is uncertain. Gen does not say that Joseph is "king" (on the meaning see 1:8), but postbiblical tradition did, or almost did, e.g. TLev 13:9; Philo, *Jos*, 120. See further on 29:8f. [In the HistJos, Joseph is called "King"; see the contribution in this volume on HistJos by G. T. Zervos.—J.H.C.]

l. Also 25:6; 26:3; cf. Gen 47:13–26.

m. Gk. *theosebēs*, also 8:5f.; 21:1; 23:9f., 12; 28:5; 29:3, cf. 8:8; 27:1. JosAsen never uses *eusebēs*. The word *theosebēs* is something like a technical term in JosAsen; it is used to designate the Jews who revere the one and only God and observe appropriate ethical standards (see Intro.). So *theosebēs* has a distinguishing ring (cf. e.g. Jdt 11:17; 4Mac 15:28; 16:12); that is why "religious" will not do for a translation ("god-fearing" suggests *phoboumenos ton theon* as a Gk. original and provokes false association with the "god-fearers"). Parallels to this usage are not numerous (NT only in Jn 9:31). See further G. Bertram, "*theosebēs, theosebeia*," *TDNT* vol. 3, 123–28; McEleney, *NTS* 20 (1974) 326f.

n. This seems to be the first instance of masculine *parthenos* before (or beside?) Rev 14:4 (cf. 1Cor 7:25); Burchard, *Untersuchungen*, p. 110, n. 1. Perhaps this is a Jewish and Christian speciality; Achilles Tatius 5.20.5 wonders if it is admissible. See further 2:1; 7:7; 15:1, 7.

o. I.e. "to date" as in 8:1; 23:2; cf. Acts 22:3.

8 (10) and the spirit of God is upon him, and the grace of the Lord (is) with him.[p] •Come, my
child, and I will hand you over[q] to him for (his) wife, and you will be a bride to him, and
he will be your bridegroom for ever (and) ever."[r]
9 (11) And when Aseneth heard these words from her father, plenty of red sweat[s] poured over
her face, and she became furious with great anger, and looked askance at her father with
(12) her eyes, and said, "Why does my lord and my father speak words such as these, to hand
me over,[t] like a captive, to a man (who is) an alien, and a fugitive, and (was) sold (as a
10 (13) slave)?[u] •Is he not the shepherd's son from the land of Canaan,[v] and he himself was caught[w]
(14) in the act (when he was) sleeping with his mistress, and his master threw him into the
prison of darkness;[x] and Pharaoh brought him out of prison, because he interpreted his
11 (15) dream just like the older women of the Egyptians interpret (dreams)?[y] •No,[z] but I will be
married to the king's firstborn son, because he is king of the whole land of Egypt."[a2]
12 (16) Hearing this,[b2] Pentephres was ashamed to speak further to his daughter Aseneth[c2] about
Joseph, because she had answered him[d2] daringly and with boastfulness and anger.

Joseph arrives at Pentephres' house

1 (1) **5** And a young man of Pentephres' servants[a] rushed in and says, "Behold, Joseph is
2 (2) standing before the doors of our court." •And Aseneth fled from her father's and mother's

p. This is a mosaic of traditional attributes occurring, either alone or in combination, in descriptions of godly men, and most of them also of Joseph: "who worships God" (e.g. Ex 18:21; Job 1:1, 8; 2:3; TNaph 1:10; TAb A 4); "self-controlled" especially in sexual matters (of Joseph, cf. Gen 39; 4Mac 2:2; TJos 4:1f.; 6; 7; Philo, *Jos*, 40; Josephus, *Ant* 2.4.3 §48); "wisdom and experience" (e.g. Jdt 11:8; of Joseph, cf. Gen 41:39); "spirit" (e.g. Dan 6:4; Lk 2:25; Acts 6:5; of Joseph, cf. Gen 41:38; TSim 4:4; Philo, *Jos*, 116); "grace" (e.g. Lk 2:40; Acts 6:8; of Joseph, cf. TJos 12:3). Such attributes are also used to characterize messianic figures (e.g. PssSol 17:37f.; Lk 2:52), but there is nothing intrinsically messianic about them.

q. Gk. *paradidonai*, lit. "to give over," often has a negative ring when used of people (it is what Judas Iscariot does to Jesus), which is more to the point in vs. 9 than here; but cf. Tob 7:13; 10:10 S.

r. Gk. *eis ton aiōna chronon*, lit. "into the eternity time," a septuagintism (no Semitism), e.g. Ex 14:13; Jdt 15:10; PssSol 8:33; 15:13; also 1En 103:4, cf. 3Mac 5:11, never NT. JosAsen is fond of it: also 6:8; 8:9; 12:11; 13:15; 15:6, 7, 9, 12x; 16:14; 17:6; 19:5; 21:3f. For the concept of marriage forever, see Tob 7:12 S.

s. Cf. Lk 22:44; Chariton 4.2.13.

t. The reading "why . . . over": many variants. The major problem is whether "want(s)" is to be inserted before "to give" and whether the verb (or verbs) is (or are) in the third or second person. Phil adds "so" after "speak" on the sole strength of Slav., maybe because he omitted "words such as these" on the authority of *d* Slav.

u. Cf. Apuleius 4.31.2 Prisoners of war were often sold as slaves, and slaves' masters could effect a marriage to them. Pentephres had a right to marry his daughter away, but not without sheer injustice to give her to a man thrice dishonored. "Fugitive" may also be rendered "driven into exile"; meaning that he had it coming to him.

v. A sneer; see Gen 46:34. Cf. Mk 6:3 par.

w. The reading "was caught": EFW *c* Syr. Arm. L1 (L2); "was abandoned by him (his father)" (A)P *d* Rie Br (Philonenko, *Joseph et Aséneth*, p. 145, comments on the strangeness of this); "from there was brought hither" Slav.; gaps CR Q G Ngr. Cf. Jn 8:4.

x. Cf. Gen 39:20. For the darkness see TJos 8:5, cf. 2:4; 9:1f. Ancient prisons used to be dark, e.g. Isa 42:7; 49:9; Xenophon of Ephesus 2.6.5; Apuleius 9.21.4; cf. also WisSol 17:2.

y. Whence? The meaning must be deprecatory. If a neutral or favorable comparison were intended, Aseneth could have referred, e.g., to the dream interpreters (among them women) who belonged to the staff of many pagan temples of the time (cf. F. Cumont, *L'Egypte des Astrologues* [Brussels, 1937] pp. 127–29). The whole vs. is a distortion of elements from Gen 39–41; according to 13:13 (cf. 6:2) people told Aseneth so.

z. Witnesses ACR EF *c d* L1: "No, my lord father and my sweetest mother, no" P (Q); "I will not do this" W; "No, my father, not to this (one) will I be joined" Syr.; "it will not be so" Arm. (436); "Not so" 435&; "Anyway, oh my precious father, be silent and do not speak to me such words" Ngr. 671 (a little shorter 661); gap G. Something like "No, my father (cf. PQ Syr. Ngr.), it will not be so (cf. Arm. L2)" may be original; cf. 23:1 and the variant at 20:9.

a2. This outburst of class feeling may be exaggerated, but it is not reprehended as such. "The king's (not Pharaoh's) firstborn son" may be deliberately ambiguous, cf. 18:11; 21:4, 20; 23:10. To be forced down the social ladder is a constant threat in ancient romance, e.g. Chariton, and a person owes it to himself or herself to defend his or her status. Structurally, Aseneth's pride resembles Habrocomes' boastfulness toward Eros (Xenophon of Ephesus 1.1.4–6) and Psyche's attempted murder of her unknown husband (Apuleius 5.5.1–22.1).

b2. "Hearing this" ACPR *d* (Q Ngr.); "And in longness of spirit [i.e. longanimity] P. was and" Syr.; "and" rest; gap G. The participial form is suspicious.

c2. Witnesses ACR Syr. (omit "his daughter") Slav.; gaps EG Ngr.; omit rest.

d2. Witnesses *a c d* Syr. Arm. 436; "her father" FW L1; gaps EG 435& Ngr.

5 a. It is taken for granted that Pentephres has a staff of servants to look after his house. Cf. 3:4.

presence, when she heard (them) speak these words about Joseph, and went up into the upper floor and entered her chamber and stood by the large window, the one looking east, 3 (3) in order to see Joseph entering her father's house.[b] •And Pentephres and his wife and his[c] 4 (4) whole family went out to meet Joseph.[d] •And the gates of the court looking east were (5) opened, and Joseph entered, standing[e] on Pharaoh's second chariot,[f] 'and four horses, white as snow[g] and with golden bridles, were harnessed (to it), and the entire chariot was 5 (6) manufactured from pure[h] gold. •And Joseph was dressed in an exquisite white tunic, and the robe which he had thrown around him[i] was purple, made of linen interwoven with gold,[j] and a golden crown (was) on his head, and around the crown were twelve chosen stones, and on top of the twelve stones were twelve golden rays.[k] And a royal staff[l] was in his left (7) hand, and in his right hand[m] he held outstretched an olive branch,[n] 'and there was plenty 6 (8) of fruit on it, and in the fruits was a great wealth of oil.[o] •And Joseph entered the court, (9) and the gates of the court were closed, and every man and woman, (if) strange, remained outside the court, because the guards of the gates drew tight and[p] closed the doors, and all 7 (10) the strangers were closed out.[q] •And Pentephres and his wife and his[r] whole family, except their daughter Aseneth, went and prostrated themselves face down to the ground before (11) Joseph. And Joseph descended from his chariot and greeted them with his right (hand).

Aseneth is shattered at the sight of Joseph

1 (1) **6** And Aseneth saw Joseph on his chariot and was strongly cut (to the heart), and her soul was crushed,[a] and her knees were paralyzed, and her entire body trembled,[b] and she was filled with great fear.[c] And she sighed and said in her heart:

---

b. See 6:1; 7:2.

c. Some witnesses have "their," as also in 5:7; 20:6. Some mention the servant staff in addition to, or in lieu of, the family.

d. Also 5:7; 19:2–4; 22:5. This is the proper thing to do when receiving an honored guest; cf. Acts 10:24f.

e. Witnesses EFW c L1 L2 (cf. 17:8); "sitting" ACP d Arm. (Ngr., also miniatures); "carried upon" Syr.; gap Q G. Joseph would of course sit while en route (cf. Acts 8:28), but he may have stood up for the entry. Nevertheless, "sitting" could be right.

f. Cf. Gen 41:43. See also at 24:19.

g. Also 16:8, 18; 22:7. This is a traditional simile; cf. e.g. Dan 7:9 Theod.; 1En 106:2; Mt 28:3; Rev 1:14.

h. APC (Syr.), gaps Q G 435& Ngr., omit rest.

i. Lit. "the rope of his wrapping" (peribolē, also "dress").

j. See 2:8.

k. Joseph is dressed in royal attire. The fact is suggested by Gen 41:42, but the description is more like Esth 8:15. The details of the crown (itself probably in the form of a palm wreath) go beyond this. The twelve stones and rays are characteristic of the crown of the sun god Helios (F. J. Dölger, "Die 12 Apostel als Corona duodecim radiorum und die Zwölfstrahlenkrone des Sonnengottes," Antike und Christentum [Münster, 1940] vol. 6, pp. 36–51; for similar crowns worn by other heavenly figures cf. e.g. Rev 12:1 and the commentaries thereon; Lucianus, De Syria dea, 32). The author may remember some statue of Helios or generalize his memory of such statues. This does not mean that Joseph is regarded as a god or that Helios is explained as a deification of Joseph, the way Sarapis was (b. AZ 43a; Firmicus Maternus, De errore profanarum religionum, 13:1–3 etc.). Joseph is not wearing all this of his own right. He is a representative, outwardly of Pharaoh, but really of God, of whom the sun can be a symbol (see 6:6; 11:1y). The number twelve, originally a

reference to the zodiac, may have suggested the twelve tribes or patriarchs to the author. See further 6:2.

l. An ensign of office as becomes a viceroy, not mentioned in Gen 41:42. Cf. WisSol 10:14.

m. The reading "in his left . . . right hand": (Syr.) Arm. L2; gaps Q G. The other MSS mention only the right (or just one) hand, implying either that Joseph held both scepter and olive branch in one hand (cf. Rie Br) or that the scepter was in the form of a branch.

n. A sign of peace, carried e.g. by ambassadors. Perhaps there is also an overtone of fertility. A priestly note (TLev 8:8) is less likely.

o. The reading "and . . . a great wealth of oil (lit. "a fatness of much oil")": (F Syr. Arm. L1 L2 Slav. Ngr.?); omit ACP W c d; gaps Q EG.

p. The reading "drew tight and": ACP c (L1 436); omit FW d Syr.? Arm.; gaps Q EG 435& Ngr.

q. The reading "and . . . out": D (F Syr. Arm.) L1 L2 (Slav.); omit ACP W c B Phil; gaps Q G Ngr. See also 19:3; cf. Apuleius 11.23.5.

r. See 5:3.

6 a. The reading "cut . . . crushed": E (FW c Syr. Arm.) L1 L2; "cut [and suffered add. PQ] in the soul, and her bowels were crushed" a d (Slav.); gap G; doubtful Ngr.

b. Syr. Yovs (not 332) L2 add another clause expressing distress, but the wording differs widely.

c. Lit. "she feared (a) great fear." See Intro. This is JosAsen's way to describe a "stroke of lightning" that has hit, e.g. Habrocomes (Xenophon of Ephesus 1.3.1) or Psyche (Apuleius 5.22.3) in similar situations (cf. also TJos 14:1; Josephus, Ant 2.10.2 §252). Other kinds of unexpected confrontations may be depicted in a similar vein (e.g. Chariton 4.1.9 and frequently). From ch. 6 (or even ch. 5) on down to ch. 13 cf. Xenophon of Ephesus 1.3.1–4.7; Apuleius 5.22–6.5; Acts 9:3–9 par. (Zeuge, 86f., 88–98; Berger, Auferstehung, pp. 196–98, 210; 556f., n. 378; 557–62, nn. 382–

2 (5)   What[d] shall I now do,[e] wretched (that I am)?
Did I not speak[f] saying[g] that Joseph is coming,
the shepherd's son from the land of Canaan?
And now, behold, the sun from heaven[h] has come to
     us on its chariot
and entered our house today,
and shines in it like a light upon the earth.[i]

3 (6)   But I, foolish and daring,[j] have despised him
and spoken wicked words about him,
and did not know that Joseph is (a) son of God.[k]

4 (7)   For who among men on earth will generate such beauty,[l]
and what womb of a woman will give birth to such light?[m]
What a wretched and foolish (girl) I (am),
because I have spoken wicked words about him to my father.

5 (2)   And now, where shall I go[n] and hide from his face[o]
in order that Joseph the son of God does not see me
because I have spoken wicked (things) about him?

6 (3)   And where shall I flee[p] and hide,
because every hiding place,[q] he sees
and nothing hidden escapes him,
because of the great light that is inside him?[r]

7 (4)   And now be gracious on me, Lord, God of Joseph,

93; 597, n. 492).

d. Present order of vss. 2–7 in EFW *c* Syr. Arm. L1 L2 Ngr., vss. 5–7 before 2–4 in *a d*, gap G. Riessler's verse numbers, virtually identical with Philonenko's as given in parentheses, had to be altered here. Aseneth's lament vss. 2–8 anticipates many motifs laid out in greater detail in chs. 11–13. On the background, see E. W. Smith, Jr., "The Form and Religious Background of Romans VII 24–25a," *NovT* 13 (1971) 127–35; P. Tachau, *"Einst" und "Jetzt" im Neuen Testament: Beobachtungen zu einem urchristlichen Predigtschema in seiner Vorgeschichte* (FRLANT 105; Göttingen, 1972) pp. 52–58 (see also 12:5); Berger, "Missionsliteratur," 240–45 (especially ActsPhil 61).

e. The reading "do" (*poiēsō*): E Syr. Arm. Rie; "see" (*opsomai*) CPQ FW *c* D (L1) L2 (Slav.) Phil; "follow" (*hepsomai*) A B Bat Br ("This can hardly be correct," p. 29, n. 1); gaps G Ngr.

f. "Did . . . speak" ACP EFW *c d* L1 435&; "Because my strange counsellors deceived me who said to me" Syr.; "Did not now my father and mother with despising speak to me and said" Arm.; "Did not some say" 436; "And did not my father say to me that the Powerful (One) of God comes, Joseph, who is powerful according to God's truth because with God's power he reigns as King [cf. 4:7]? I said" Ngr.; gaps Q G. Cf. 13:13. See the next note.

g. EFW *d* L1 (436); cf. Syr. Arm. in previous note; omit ACP *c* 435& Ngr.; gaps Q G.

h. The reading "the sun from heaven": (FW *c*) D L1 436 (435&) Slav. Phil; "like the s.f.h. (he, namely Joseph)" *a* B Arm. (Ngr.?); "I see (that) the s. of h." E (Syr.), gap G.

i. Aseneth verbalizes 5:5 with a pun: the sun is coming to Sun City at last. Cf. e.g. Sir 50:7; 1En 106:2, 10; 4Ezra 7:97; TJob 31:5; Chariton 5.3.9. The Messiah is not often compared to the sun, but see TZeb 9:8 (Mal 3:20); TLevi 18:3f. Joseph is not coming as the Messiah will be; he is coming

as the representative of God (see 5:5) as every true Jew is, or at least the famous ones.

j. Cf. Prov 9:13.

k. See Intro.

l. Joseph's beauty was proverbial since Gen 39:7, e.g. TSim 5:1. See Intro.

m. The wording is biblical, but the idea is not unfamiliar to the Gk. mind, cf. e.g. Chariton 2.1.5.

n. See 11:3.

o. Cf. Ps 138:7, particularly as quoted by 1Clem 28:3; also Achilles Tatius 8.2.1; *Historia Regis Tyri*, 27:1; Apuleius 6.26.6.

p. Witnesses FW *c d* Syr. (Ngr.?), "go away" ACP (436); omit Arm. (incl. following "and"); gaps Q EG L1 435&.

q. Gk. *apokrybē* is very rare and unattested before Origen except in OT translations.

r. The closest parallel known is Mt 6:23 (Jn 11:10?). Ancient ophthalmology, both popular (as implied e.g. in Sir 23:19; TGad 5:7; *LAB* 25:12; Philo, *Quod Deus*, 58; Eph 1:18; cf. below 14:9) and scientific (e.g. Plato, *Timaeus*, 45B–46C; Galenus, *De placitis Hippocratis et Platonis*, 7.5; Epictetus, *Diss.*, 2.23.3; Philo, see below; not Aristotle!), believed that eyesight depends on rays of light or spirit emitted from, not received by, the eye. Sharp-sightedness requires a large portion of inner light, supernatural vision a supernatural one. The whole verse may be an allusion to Zaphenath-paneah (Gen 41:45), interpreted as "finder of hidden (things)" in Josephus, *Ant* 2.6.1 §91 (cf. Aptowitzer, *HUCA* 1 [1924] 286). It is also reminiscent of traditional references to God (e.g. Job 28:24; 34:21f.; Sir 42:18–20), the sun (e.g. Ps 19:6; Sir 42:16; cf. vss. 2 and 5:5 above), and Wisdom (e.g. WisSol 7:22–8:1), but this does not make Joseph a heavenly being, an incarnation of Wisdom, or a figure of the Messiah. Rather, he is credited with prophetical insights: "To a prophet nothing is unknown, because he has intelligible light in him and shadowless rays" (Philo, *Spec Leg*, 4:192).

because I have spoken wicked words against him in ignorance[s]
8 (8)   And now, let my father give me to Joseph for a maidservant and slave,[t]
and I will serve him for ever (and) ever.

Joseph is convinced that Aseneth will not molest him and agrees to meet her

1 (1) **7** And Joseph entered the house of Pentephres and sat upon the throne.[a] And they washed[b]
his feet and set[c] a table before him by itself, because Joseph never ate with the Egyptians,
2 for this was an abomination to him.[d] •And looking up with his eyes, Joseph saw Aseneth
(2) leaning through (the window).[e] And Joseph said to Pentephres and his whole family, saying,
(3) "Who is this woman who is standing in the upper floor by the window? Let her leave this
3 house," 'because Joseph was afraid, saying, "This one must not molest me, too." •For all
the wives and the daughters of the noblemen and the satraps of the whole land of Egypt
(4) used to molest him (wanting) to sleep with him, and all the wives and the daughters of the
4 (5) Egyptians, when they saw Joseph, suffered badly because of his beauty. •But Joseph
despised them,[f] and the messengers whom the women sent to him with gold and silver and
valuable presents Joseph sent back with threats and insults,[g] because Joseph said,[h] "I will

s. Ignorance (*agnoia*) separates Aseneth's
wickedness from outright sin; it does not absolve
her of responsibility but lets her hope for forgiveness
(also 17:10; cf. e.g. TJud 19:3). The word is also
used in an analogous sense for her general status
prior to conversion, where the object of ignorance
is above all God (12:5; 13:11–13). This is Jewish
and Christian usage (e.g. WisSol 14:22; Acts 3:17;
13:27; 17:30; 1Tim 1:13; Aristides, *Apology*, 17:4).
t. Also 13:15. Aseneth desires almost as little
as the prodigal son (Lk 15:19), and like him she
will get more. An application of the traditional
principle inherent in e.g. Ps 147:6; Prov 3:34
(quoted Jas 4:6; 1Pet 5:5); Mt 23:12; Lk 1:52.
Voluntary enslavement of course is also a motif of
erotic language.

7 a. Pentephres' throne as in 20:2? As a satrap he
would have one *ex officio* (cf. TJob 20:4f.). Anyway, the article is there.
b. The reading "they washed": *a* W *c* Syr.
(Brooks' emendation) Arm. L1 L2 Ngr.661; "he
washed" F *d* Syr. (ms.) Ngr.671; "washing (sing.)"
E; gap G; cf. next note. Foot washing is a traditional
gesture of hospitality, e.g. Gen 18:4; 1Sam 25:41;
TAb 3; b. Ket 61a; Lk 7:44; Jn 13:1–17; *Vita
Aesopi* G, 61. It is a service which dependants like
wives, children, pupils owed to their respective
masters (13:15; 20:2–5).
c. Witnesses ACP (c) D Syr. (Brooks' emendation) L1 L2 Ngr.; "set (sing.)" Q E B Syr.
(ms.) Slav. Phil; gaps FGW. Tables like this one
would be low affairs, more like trays on legs, often
with a disconnecting board, to be set when needed
and put away after use; see 15:14; 17:7f. "To set
(*paratithenai*) a table before someone"; also e.g.
1En 89:50; Acts 16:34.
d. Reversal of Gen 43:32. Abstention from
heathen food and avoidance of table fellowship
between Jews and pagans was one of the main
issues of Jewish life in the hellenistic, especially
post-Maccabean, period (cf. e.g. Esth 4:17x; Jub
22:16; 3Mac 3:4, 7; SibOr 4:24–30; Acts 10–11;
Gal 2:11–14). The reason, as given in JosAsen, is
that pagan food has come into contact with idols.
Remarkably enough, while it is implied later on
that it is polluting (11:9, 16; 12:5), it is never said
that Jewish food is pure. So the Levitical law of
purity plays no role here, at least not directly. See
further 8:5; 20:7.

e. "And ... (the window)" *a c* "with his eyes"
omit AC, "leaning through" omit Q); "And Joseph
looked at the tower" Syr. (mentioning the leaning
through in the next sentence, where PQ also have
it); "Gazing, however, Joseph (with) his eyes saw
in the chamber above Aseneth standing" Ngr.; gap
G; omit rest. On "leaning through (*parakyptein*)"
cf. 1Chr 15:29; Prov 7:6; Song 2:9; Sir 14:23;
21:23. The word may have sexual or mythical
overtones or both (W. Fauth, *Aphrodite Parakyp-
tusa: Untersuchungen zum Erscheinungsbild der
vorderasiatischen Dea prospiciens* [Akademie der
Wissenschaften in Mainz. Abhandlungen der Geis-
tes- und sozialwissenschaftlichen Klasse, 1966,
no. 6; Wiesbaden, 1967]), but it looks harmless
enough here. Joseph's misgivings are actuated by
the behavior of the Egyptian women generally
(vs. 3), rather than by Aseneth's posture in particular. His attitude in chs. 7f. rather resembles
Aseneth's in chs. 2–4, a stroke of poetic justice.
The scene in vss. 2–6 is developed from Gen 39:7–
10, but not by the author of JosAsen. Jewish and
Christian lore has it that all Egyptian women felt
like Potiphar's wife when they saw Joseph on his
tour around Egypt, offering him their valuables,
and that his resistance was strengthened by the
memory or an appearance of his father (Näf, *Josef-
Gedichte*, pp. 73f.; Aptowitzer, *HUCA* 1 [1924]
269f.; e.g. PRE 39). The latter point is already in
Jub 39:6; TJos 3:3. For the hero of a romance
being the idol of all women see Xenophon 1.5.4.
f. "But ... them" (F)W (*c* Syr.) Arm. (L1)
L2; omit *a d*; gaps EG Ngr. Instead of "but" (W
Arm. L2) we may have to read "and" (F Syr.
L1).
g. "Threats" (*apeilē*, sing.) has a tendency to
come in a pair with words denoting physical
violence (Plato, *Protagoras* 325D; 4Mac 4:24; Pap.
Rylands I 28.117; Chariton 2.8.1; Acts 9:1; *ZNW*
61 [1970] 163–65). So perhaps "insults" (*hybris*,
also singular) had better be rendered "outrage,
injuries." As in the romances (and elsewhere)
righteous indignation has a right to violent expression (see also chs. 23–29). Chaereas barely fails
to kick to death his beloved Callirhoe, who is
reported to be unfaithful (Chariton 1.4.12); he is
acquitted because he acted in good faith. Besides,
the messengers would probably be slaves.
h. The reading "because Joseph said": E Syr.
(Arm. L1 L2); "saying" *a* FW *c d*; gaps G Ngr.

not sin before (the) Lord God of my father Israel nor in the face of my father Jacob."[i]
5 (6) And the face of his father Jacob, Joseph always had before his eyes, and he remembered his father's commandments. For Jacob would say to his son Joseph and all his sons,[j] "My children, guard strongly against associating with a strange woman, for association (with)
6 (7) her is destruction and corruption."[k] •Therefore Joseph said, "Let this woman leave this house."

7 (8)   And Pentephres said to him, "Lord, this one whom you have seen standing in the upper floor is not a strange woman, but she is our daughter, a virgin[l] hating every man, and there
(9) is not any other man who has ever seen her except you alone today. And if you will, she
8 (10) will come and address you, because our daughter is like a sister to you."[m] •And Joseph rejoiced exceedingly with great joy because Pentephres had said, "She is a virgin hating every man." And Joseph said by himself, "If she is a virgin hating every man, this (girl)
(11) will certainly not molest me."[n] And Joseph said to Pentephres and his whole family,[o] "If she is your daughter and a virgin, let her come, because she is a sister to me, and I love her from today as my sister."

Joseph will not be kissed by Aseneth, but prays for her conversion

1 (1) **8** And Aseneth's mother went up to the upper floor and brought her and stood her before[a] Joseph. And Pentephres said to his daughter Aseneth,[b] "Greet[c] your brother, because he, too, is a virgin like you today and hates every strange woman, as you, too,[d] every strange
2 (2) man." •And Aseneth said to Joseph, "Be of good cheer,[e] my lord, blessed by the Most
3 High[f] Lord." •And Joseph said to Aseneth, "May the Lord God[g] who gives life to all
4 (3) (things) bless you." •And Pentephres said to his daughter Aseneth, "Go up and kiss your
5 (4) brother." •And as Aseneth went up to kiss Joseph, Joseph stretched out his right hand and put it on her chest between her two breasts, and her breasts were already standing upright
(5) like handsome apples.[h] And Joseph said, "It is not fitting for a man who worships God,[i]

i. Sin against God and the father also in 23:11. See TRub 1:8; Lk 15:18, 21; ShepHerm Vision 1.3.1; cf. Ex 10:16; Josephus, *War* 1.32.3 §365; *Ant* 19.6.4 §315. The reason for this combination may be gleaned from Ps-Phoc 8; SibOr 3.593f.

j. Text uncertain since vs. 4 "I will not."

k. A common warning since OT times (e.g. Gen 24:3; 28:1, 6; Deut 7:3f.; Neh 13:13–29), as a word of Jacob (Jub 39:6; TJos 3:3). Cf. further e.g. Tob 4:12; *PJ* 8:2, 4f.; TJud 14:6; TLevi 9:10; 14:6; TJob 44:3; *LAB* 9:5; Philo, *Spec Leg*. 3.29; Josephus, *Ant* 8.7.5 §191f.; b. AZ 36b. This is not tantamount to a general interdiction of exogamy. But a foreign woman will have to turn Jewish, like Aseneth, before a Jew may marry her. Pentephres seems to understand Joseph's attitude, but many did not. Cf. Tacitus, *Historiae*, 5.2.2; b.Meg 13b.

l. All read thus except omit A; gap G.

m. Cf. Tob 7:12; ShepHerm Vision 1.1.7. Pentephres suggests that virginity makes people of different faith brothers and sisters. Joseph accepts this only with the restriction stated in 8:5f. See also 15:1, 7. On the idea that certain virtues are a natural preparation for conversion, cf. also Acts 10:34f.

n. "And . . . molest me" (EF Syr. Arm. L1 L2 Ngr.); omit *a c d*; gaps G W.

o. The reading "and . . . family": F *c* Arm. (Syr.) L1 L2; "and his wife" *a d*; omit E Ngr.; gaps GW. Perhaps we should adopt both wife and family, cf. 5:7 (but see also 7:2).

8 a. The reading "and . . . before": (E) *c* Syr.

Arm. L1 L2; "to" *a* (FW) *d*; "before" Ngr.; gap G.

b. The reading "his daughter Aseneth (before "his": Syr. Arm., punctuated so as to belong to the following sentence as an address E, omit W L2 Slav.)": EFW *d* Syr. Arm. L2 Slav.; "her" ACP *c* L1 Ngr.; omit Q; gap G.

c. Gk. *aspasai*, which may also mean "kiss": Br; cf. 19:10. But vs. 4 is against this.

d. The reading "hate today": add. *c* L1 (after "man") 436; "hate" add. Ngr.; gaps EGW; omit rest.

e. Gk. *chairois* (also Ngr.). Never in LXX and NT, but TAb B 13:6.

f. A frequent attribute of God in JosAsen, as in LXX (e.g. Gen 14:19) and other hellenistic Jewish literature, but rare in the NT (e.g. Acts 16:17). In a polytheistic environment it sounded both inviting and exclusive (e.g. against *Zeus Hypsistos*); cf. G. Bertram, "*hypsos* etc.," *TDNT* 8, 602–20.

g. The reading "the Lord God": *a* L2 (add. "of Israel"); "God" *d*; "the Lord" EFW *c* Syr. Arm. L1; gaps G Ngr.

h. The reading "between . . . apples": (APQ E Syr. L1 436); "and pushed her away" Slav.; omit *c d* Arm. 435&; gaps C FGW Ngr. "Like handsome apples" is in APQ (adds "two" after "like") only, a classical metaphor for a girl's breasts; cf. Aristophanes, *Lysistrata*, 155; *Ecclesiazusae*, 903; (Ps-?) Theocritus, *Idylls*, 27.50. Another simile is in 18:9.

i. On this opening see Intro.; cf. Acts 10:28. The following triad of statements about the bread,

who will bless[j] with his mouth the living God and eat blessed bread of life[k] and drink a blessed cup of immortality[l] and anoint himself with blessed ointment of incorruptibility to kiss a strange woman who will bless with her mouth dead and dumb[m] idols and eat from their table bread of strangulation[n] and drink from their libation a cup of insidiousness[o] and

6 (6) anoint herself with ointment of destruction. •But a man who worships God will kiss his mother and the sister (who is born) of his mother[p] and the sister (who is born) of his clan and family and the wife who shares his bed, (all of) who(m) bless with their mouths the

7 (7) living God. •Likewise, for a woman who worships God it is not fitting to kiss a strange man, because this is an abomination before the Lord God."

the cup, and the ointment is often called a "meal formula" (also 8:9; 15:5; 16:16; 19:5; 21:13f., 21), perhaps unwisely so. If we go by 8:5, which seems to be its original setting in JosAsen, it is couched in relative clauses, the subject of which is "the man who worships God" (see at 4:7), and the point of the passage is not to institute or justify any meal, but to explain why such a man does not kiss a heathen woman. Also it is not at all clear whether the unction is envisaged as an integral part of a meal. Anyway, it is the right kind of "bread," "cup" and "ointment" that characterizes a Jew, and distinguishes him from the gentile, who uses the opposite kind. The problem is whether this is to be understood in terms of a cultic meal, albeit a daily one as in communities such as the Essenes or the Therapeutae, or in terms of ordinary Jewish self-maintenance. If a sacramental interpretation is preferred we will have to identify JosAsen's meal either with one that we know (Essene: 1QS 6.4–6; 1QSa 2.17–21; Josephus, *War* 2.8.5 §129–33, or, rather, Therapeutic: Philo, *Vita Cont*, 37ff., 69ff.; e.g. Kuhn, "Lord's Supper," *The Scrolls and the New Testament*, ed. K. Stendahl, 74–77, 261–62) or with one that we seem to know (synagogue meals in mystery style, e.g. Thyen, *Studien*, 127f., cf. Georgi, *Gegner*, 135f.); or else we should stipulate a hitherto unknown meal (e.g. Kilpatrick, *ExpT* 64 [1952–53] 4–8; W. Nauck, *Die Tradition und der Charakter des ersten Johannesbriefes* [WUNT 3; Tübingen, 1957] pp. 169–71, referring to Christian initiation by unction, baptism, and first eucharist, both orthodox and gnostic, e.g. ActsThom 120–21; GPhil 68,76,98; Philonenko, *Joseph et Aséneth*, pp. 91–93). The heathen counterpart would probably be meals in a temple "at a god's table" (in Aseneth's case equivalent to daily meals, see 10:13); such meals are known to us among other things from the papyri (see the commentaries on 1Cor 10:14–22; cf. also the idea later developed at length by Firmicus Maternus, *De errore profanarum religionum*, esp. ch. 18, that the pagan mysteries ape the Christian sacraments). If the "formula" is taken to refer to ordinary Jewish eating and anointing (J. Jeremias, "The Last Supper," *ExpT* 64 [1952–53] 91f.; Burchard, *Untersuchungen*, pp. 121–33), we should compare the passages in which human maintenance is summarized by the triad "bread (or other food), wine (or other beverage), oil" (e.g. Ezra 3:7; Ps 23:5; Jdt 10:5; Dan 10:3; 1QH 10.24; ApAb 9:7; Terumoth 6:1; Maasseroth 2:1; b. Pes 32a; Epictetus, *Diss.*, 2.23.5; Ps-Heraclite, *Letters*, 7.5.1). This triad is doubtless related to the similar one "grain, wine, oil" that describes the produce of the land (e.g. Ps 104:14f.; Josephus, *War* 1.15.6 §299 [plus cattle]; Rev 6:6; TJud 9:8; SibOr 3.243,745; Eup. 2.25f.; Apuleius 9.33.2). The heathen counterpart would then be ordinary meals

which were always in contact with food offered to idols one way or the other. Be that as it may, a change of diet is indispensable if a person wants to become Jewish and gain life (see further 7:1).

Aseneth is promised bread, cup, and ointment (15:5; cf. 8:9), and receives them, she says (19:5; 21:13f., 21). But she is actually fed a piece of supernatural honeycomb, i.e. manna (see Intro.), which means—the angel explains—that she has eaten the bread, drunk the cup, and been anointed with the ointment (16:16). This poses a new problem; is the honey a symbol, for example, for the Law or the word of God (cf. e.g. Pss 19:10f.; 119:103; Philo, *Fuga*, 137–39), implying that when it is received this is equivalent to the reception of bread, cup and ointment, whatever they mean (Anandakumara, *Gentile Reactions*, 66f.; Delling, *JSJ* 9 (1978) 54)? Does the honey refer to something real, a "honey communion" connected with, or representing, the cultic meal described by the "formula" (Philonenko, *Joseph et Aséneth*, p. 98)? Is this scene a way of depicting metaphorically what bread, cup, and ointment really are? The latter interpretation, which is preferred here, is applicable whether the meal is a cultic one or not; if it is not cultic we may point to Did 9:3f., doubtless based on a Jewish prayer, as proof for the idea that hellenistic Jews thought of their daily bread as a gift from heaven which provided life and wisdom. The "meal formula" may be of some help in interpreting Jn 6, especially vss. 35, 48, and 1Cor 10 (Burchard, *Untersuchungen*, pp. 130–33; corrected and enlarged in *NTS* 32 [1986] in press).

j. I.e. probably say grace before and after meals. This was regarded as one of the distinguishing marks of Judaism (e.g. SibOr 4.25f.; Christian, but with a possible Jewish origin, Aristides, *Apology*, 15:10). This "blessing" will account for "blessed" below.

k. The only real extant parallel to Jn 6:35, 48.

l. Grace after meals was said over a cup which would hence be called "cup of blessing" (cf. 1Cor 10:16 and commentaries thereon).

m. Also 11:8; 12:5; 13:11. Some witnesses attest the reverse order except in 13:11, where the words occur only in AP c Arm. L2, the latter two having "dumb and deaf." Never LXX or NT, but cf. 3Mac 4:16.

n. For similar turns, see Ps 80:5; Prov 31:27; Isa 30:20; Hos 9:4.

o. Lit. "ambush" as in chs. 24–27. The choice of words in this and the previous instance may be influenced by the obvious fact that pagan food does not cause people to drop dead.

p. The reading "and the sister . . . mother": AC (Syr. Arm. 435&) Slav.; omit PQ EFW c (gap following in HK) d L1 436; gaps G Ngr.

8 (8)   And when Aseneth heard these words of Joseph, she was cut (to the heart) strongly and[q]
         was distressed exceedingly and sighed, and she kept gazing at Joseph with her eyes open
(9) and her eyes were filled with tears. And Joseph saw her, and had mercy on her exceedingly,
         and was himself cut (to the heart),[r] because Joseph was meek and merciful and fearing
9 God.[s] •And he lifted up his right hand and put it[t] upon her head and said:[u]

(10)   Lord God of my father Israel,[v]
              the Most High, the Powerful One of Jacob,[w]
              who gave life[x] to all (things)
              and called (them) from the darkness to the light,[y]
              and from the error to the truth,[z]
              and from the death to the life;[a2]
              you, Lord, bless this virgin,
(11)   and renew her by your spirit,[b2]
              and form her anew by your hidden hand,
              and make her alive again[c2] by your life,[d2]
              and let her eat your bread of life,
              and drink your cup of blessing,
              and number her among your people
              that you have chosen[e2] before all (things) came into being,
              and let her enter your rest
              which you have prepared for your chosen ones,[f2]
              and live in your eternal[g2] life for ever (and) ever.

q. The reading "she . . . and": E (FW c Syr. Arm.) L1 (L2 Ngr.); omit a d; gap G.

r. The reading "and . . . heart)": (EF) W (c Syr. Arm.) L1 (L2); uncertain Ngr.; omit a B Slav. Phil; gaps G D.

s. Similarly 27:1. See at 4:7.

t. The reading "and put it": PQ Syr. Arm. L2 (Ngr.?); gap G; omit rest. Similarly 16:13. A gesture of blessing rather than exorcism (against Philonenko, Joseph et Aséneth, p. 157).

u. On Joseph's prayer cf. Smith, Joseph and Asenath, pp. 107–16; Berger, Kairos 17 (1975) 232–40 (quotes especially ActsPhil 117). The address refers to the creator, which is common enough (12:1f.; 2Kgs 19:15 parallel Isa 37:16; Neh 9:6; Esth 4:17c; 3Mac 2:2–3; PrMan 2f.; 2Bar 21:4f.; 1En 84:2f.; Jub 12:19; Acts 4:24). But the four clauses apply equally well to God's activity in conversion (see Intro.).

v. Cf. Jdt 9:2.

w. The reading "of Jacob": Syr. Arm. 436 Ngr.; "God" ACP c; omit Q EW d L1 435&; illegible F; gaps G Rum. Cf. MT Gen 49:24 (also LXX); Isa 49:26; 60:16; Ps 132:2, 5. See also 11:9, but the text is uncertain.

x. Gk. zōopoiēsas AC FW d Arm. (Ngr.); "gives life to" (zōopoiōn) E L1 L2; "made" (poiēsas) PQ c; uncertain Syr.; gap G. Cf. Neh 9:6; 1Tim 6:13.

y. Cf. Philo, Virt, 179f.; SibOr Fr. 1.25–34; Passover Haggadah, section Lefi-Khakh; Acts 26:18; 1Pet 2:9; 1Clem 59:2; Meliton of Sardes, Passover Homily, 489–93; Poimandres, 19f. See S. Pines, "From Darkness into Great Light," Immanuel 4 (1974) 47–51; R. Stehly, "Une citation des Upanishads dans Joseph et Aséneth," RTP 55 (1975) 209–13; Anandakumara, Gentile Reactions, p. 45, n. 1.

z. Cf. 1Clem 59:2; AposCon, 7.39.3.

a2. Cf. Lk 15:24, 32; Jn 5:24; 1Jn 3:14; AposCon, 7.39.3. See also 20:7 and n. y above.

b2. Witnesses F c B Syr. Arm. L1 (partly) L2 Phil; "holy s." a EW D L1 (partly) Slav. (Bucharest MS only) Ngr.; gap G. "Spirit" (4:7; 16:14; 19:11) in JosAsen is supernatural vitality and insight, rather than a miraculous power by which exorcisms (26:6 probably notwithstanding). On renewal by spirit cf. Rom 7:6; 2Cor 3:6; Tit 3:5; AposCon, 8.6.

c2. Also 15:5. Gk. anazōopoiein was known hitherto only as a Christian word, except perhaps in TAb A 18.

d2. The reading "and form . . . life": (FW Syr. Arm. L1 436 435&) Phil; "and make (her) alive again by your hand" c; omit a ("and make alive" added after "bless") Ngr.; gaps EG d ("make alive and" add. before "bless"). FW have "hand at the top (koryphaia, never LXX or NT)" instead of "hidden [probably kryphaia] hand" (cf. Ex 17:16 LXX).

e2. Cf. Ps 33:12; Eph 1:4; O. Hofius, " 'Erwählt vor Grundlegung der Welt' (Eph 1,4)," ZNW 62 (1971) 123–28.

f2. Cf. Ps 95:11 (LXX rather than MT). The "rest" (katapausis) is not a state of body or mind, but a place in heaven prepared for the saved (15:7; 22:13). JosAsen seems to be the oldest witness to this idea, which is of some importance for understanding Heb 3:7–4:13 (O. Hofius, Katapausis. Die Vorstellung vom endzeitlichen Ruheort im Hebräerbrief [WUNT 11; Tübingen, 1970]). [Cf. D. R. Darnell's Rebellion, Rest, and the Word of God: An Exegetical Study of Hebrews 3:1–4:13, (unpublished dissertation) Duke University, 1973. J.H.C.]

g2. The reading of a; "heavenly": Ngr.; gaps G d Syr.; omit rest. Eternal life is frequently mentioned in ancient Jewish and Christian texts (e.g. 2Mac 7:9; Dan 12:2; PssSol 3:12; 1En 40:9; Mt 25:46; Jn 3:5; Rom 5:21).

Aseneth retires in confusion

9 And Aseneth rejoiced exceedingly with great joy over Joseph's blessing, and hurried and went into the upper floor by herself, and fell on her bed exhausted, because in her there was joy and distress and much fear and trembling[a] and continuous sweating[b] as she heard all these words of Joseph, which he had spoken to her in the name of the Most High God. And she wept with great and bitter weeping and repented of[c] her (infatuation with the) gods whom she used to worship, and spurned[d] all the idols, and waited for the evening to come.

Joseph departs after promising to return a week later

And Joseph ate and drank and told his servants, "Harness the horses to the chariots"[e]; for, he said, "I will go away[f] and drive around the whole land." • And Pentephres said to Joseph, "Let my lord lodge here today, and tomorrow you will go out (on) your way." And Joseph said, "No, but I will go out today, because this is the day on which God began to make all his creatures,[g] and on the eighth[h] day, when this day returns,[i] I too will return to you and lodge here."

10 And Joseph went away (on) his way 'and Pentephres and his whole family went away to their estate.[a]

---

9 a. The reading "and trembling": FW *c* Syr. Arm. L1 L2; omit *a d;* gaps EG Ngr. "Fear and trembling" is a biblicism (e.g. Gen 9:2; Ps 55:6; Jdt 2:28; 4Mac 4:10; 1En 13:3; 2En 22:10; 1Clem 12:5, and below) denoting physical terror, rather than awe or reverence. The reading "in great fear and trembling" of 14:10 (cf. Isa 19:16; 1Cor 2:3) and "with much fear and trembling" of 16:13 (which would be the only ancient exact parallel to 2Cor 7:15; Eph 6:5; Phil 2:12 known to date) are secondary (against Philonenko, *Joseph et Aséneth*, p. 178, on 14:10, and Burchard, *ZNW* 61 (1970) 169, on 16:13). Mingled emotions: Mt 28:8; ShepHerm Vision 5.4; Chariton 1.9.3; 3.4.15; 5.8.2; Xenophon of Ephesus 5.13.4; Achilles Tatius 1.4.5; 5.19.1; Apuleius 11.7.1.

b. The reading "was poured around her" (*peri-echythē autēn*): added D Bat (in broken parentheses) Br Rie Phil (cf. 4:9); gaps EG Ngr.; omit rest. A new verb for "sweat" is in order after "in her," but this could be the very reason why it was inserted. Anyway, the accusative form *autēn* (probably a purely graphic variant) cannot be right. Cf. Apuleius 11.7.1.

c. *Metanoein apo* as e.g. Jer 8:6; Acts 8:22; 1Clem 8:3; same verb in 15:7, substantive *metanoia* in 16:14, as the name of an angel in 15:7. Repentance does not denote conversion as a whole, but, rather, mankind's part in it, which is a human accomplishment, not a stroke of grace bestowed upon man (in the NT cf. Luke-Acts, esp. Lk 15). In this instance repentance means no more than breaking away from the idols (cf. Rev 9:20f. and perhaps Heb 6:1); turning to God comes later, in chs. 10–13. For repentance to ripen to conversion it takes the intercession of Repentance and God's acceptance (15:7). The background of this concept

is probably to be found in the passages which make repentance the prerequisite for God's forgiveness (e.g. PrMan 7, 13f.; PssSol 3:8; Sir 17:29; 1En 50:2–4; Jub 41:23–25; TAb B 12:13).

d. The verb *prosochthizein* is not attested prior to the LXX.

e. Only the twelve men of 3:2 and one chariot have been mentioned before.

f. The reading "for . . . away": (E?) FW (*d*) Syr. Arm. L1 (L2) Slav.; omit *a c;* gaps G Ngr.

g. Sunday. Its definition as representing the first day of creation was taken over into Christianity (first in Justin, *Apology*, 1,67)."Creatures" (*ktismata*) is neuter, but 12:2 suggests that they are alive, meaning either that they are the live beings such as angels (TJob 47:11; created on the first day according to e.g. Jub 2:2) and men (but they were made on the sixth day), or that all of creation is considered animated. See further n. i.

h. Witnesses *a c d* (Syr.) L1 L2; "seventh" EFW Arm. (but cf. 11:1); "the restful day, or sabbath" Ngr. (see E below); gap G.

i. The reading "when . . . returns": FW *c* Arm. L1 436; "when he rested" E; omit *a d* Syr. 435& Ngr. (but see n. h); gap G. Aseneth repents on a Sunday (see vs. 2), but she must wait a week until God accepts her. This goes to underscore, among other things (see 10:17), the huge distance between her old and new existence. On the symbolism of the eighth day cf. R. Staats, "Ogdoas als ein Symbol für die Auferstehung," *VC* 26 (1972) 29–52; see 45f.

10 a. Lit. "lot," i.e. a share of land as e.g. in Num 16:14, often in the papyri; see at 3:5. Pentephres and his family seem to stay there until the episode in 20:6.

III. ASENETH'S CONVERSION

A. ASENETH'S REPENTANCE

Aseneth prepares for her repentance in sackcloth and ashes

(2)   And Aseneth[b] was left alone with the seven virgins, and she continued to be weighed down and weep until the sun set. And she ate no bread and drank no water.[c] And the night fell,[d] and all (people) in the house slept, and she alone was awake and continued to brood and[e] to weep; and she often struck her breast with (her) hand and kept being filled with great fear and trembled (with) heavy trembling.

2 (3)   And Aseneth rose from her bed and quietly went down the stairs from the upper floor (4) and went to the gateway,[f] and the woman gatekeeper[g] was asleep with her children. And Aseneth hurried and took down from the window the skin (which hung there for a) curtain,[h] and filled it with ashes from the fireplace,[i] and carried it up into the upper floor, and put it 3 (5) on the floor. •And she closed the door firmly and slipped the iron bolt across and sighed with great sighing and bitter weeping.

Aseneth's virgins try to look after her

4 (6)   And the virgin (who was) her foster sister,[j] whom Aseneth loved beyond all the virgins, heard her sighing and hurried and woke up the other six virgins. And they went[k] to Aseneth's 5 (7) door and found the door closed. •And they heard Aseneth's sighing and weeping and said to her,[l] "What have you, mistress, and why do you feel[m] so sad, and what is it that is 6 (8) bothering[n] you? Open (the door to) us, and we will see what you have."[o] •And Aseneth did not open the door, but said to them from within, "My head is (stricken with) heavy pain,[p] and I am resting in my bed, and I do not have the strength[q] to rise and open (the 7 door to) you, because I have grown weak in[r] all my limbs. •But go each of you in your 8 chamber and rest and let me be quiet." •And the virgins went away, each into her chamber.

Aseneth throws her valuables away, idols included, and repents in sackcloth and ashes for seven days

(9)   And Aseneth rose and opened the door quietly and went into her second chamber where the chests (containing) her ornaments were, and opened her coffer and took out a black and

b. On the following reactions cf. esp. Dan 4:33a–34 LXX; Xenophon of Ephesus 1.3.3–4.1.6; Chariton 2.4.3–5; 3.10.3–4.1.1; Apuleius 7.27.2; more at 11:1x,15.

c. Also 10:17 (see there); 13:9; cf. Ex 34:28; 1Sam 30:12; Ezra 10:6.

d. "And . . . fell" (all) except a d; gap Ngr.

e. The reading "to brood and": F(G)W (c) Syr. (Arm.) L1 (436); omit a E; gaps d 435& Ngr.

f. The reading "the gateway" (ton pylōna): a EFW c d L1; "the millhouse" (ton mylōna) Syr. Arm. 436 (435&); gaps G Ngr.

g. The reading "the woman gatekeeper" (hē pylōros): EFW L1, "the woman gatekeeper" (accusative, tēn pylōron) c, "the woman doorkeeper" (accusative tēn thyrōron) a d (a c d have "she found . . . sleeping" for "was asleep"), "the woman miller" Syr. (plural) Arm. 436; gaps G 435& Ngr. Women as gatekeepers, in the author's day, were most likely slaves who lived in a room near the gate or door; cf. e.g. 2Sam 4:6 LXX (followed by Josephus, Ant 7.2.1 §48); TJob 6:5; Jn 18:16f.; Acts 12:3–5; Plautus, Curculio, 1.1.76). Why the children should be mentioned is not clear, unless to indicate that the woman had retired for the night (Lk 11:7) and was not likely to notice Aseneth's doings.

h. Lit. "the skin of the curtain" (tēn derrin tou

katapetasmatos); cf. 10:14. Gk. katapetasma is extremely rare outside Jewish and Christian literature, where it designates one of the veils hanging in the Temple, either directly or figuratively (as in Heb).

i. The reading "from the fireplace": (FW) Arm. 436; gaps G Ngr.; omit rest.

j. The reading "her foster sister": b c (Syr. Arm.) L1 436 (435&); omit a d; gap Ngr. Aseneth has a favorite slave just as Callirhoe (Chariton 1.4.1 etc.) and other ancient ladies. The Beloved Disciple (Jn 13:23, etc.) is barely comparable.

k. Witnesses a G d have this verb and the three following ones in the singular, the rest, if present, have it in the plural.

l. The reading "outside standing (singular)": added a; gaps d Syr. Ngr.; omit rest; a may be correct, as it corresponds to "from within" of vs. 6.

m. Lit. "look."

n. Same word as "molest" in 7:2–8.

o. Two questions followed by an imperative: Ps 43:2f., 5; Lk 24:38f.

p. Similarly 18:4; 25:3. So headache as an excuse (or is it?) was known in antiquity; cf. Apuleius 3.13.1.

q. Cf. Lk 11:7.

r. Lit. "of."

(10) somber tunic.^{s} 'And this was her tunic of mourning when her younger^t brother died. In this
9 Aseneth had dressed and mourned for her brother. •And she took her black tunic and carried
it into her chamber and closed the door again firmly and slipped the bolt across.

10 (11)   And Aseneth hurried and put off her linen and gold woven royal robe and dressed in the
black tunic of mourning, and loosened her golden girdle and girded a rope around (her),
and put off the tiara from her head, and the diadem and the bracelets from her hands and
11 (12) feet, and put everything on the floor. •And she took her chosen robe and the golden girdle
and the headgear and the diadem, and threw everything through the window looking north
12 (13) to the poor.^{u} •And Aseneth hurried and took all her gods that were in her chamber, the
ones of gold and silver who were without number, and ground them to pieces,^{v} and threw
all the idols of the Egyptians through the window looking north from her upper floor to
13 (14) beggars and needy (persons). •And Aseneth took her royal dinner^w and the fatlings^x and the
fish and the flesh of the heifer and all the sacrifices of her gods and the vessels of their
wine of libation and threw everything through the window looking north, and gave everything
to the strange dogs. For Aseneth said to herself, "By no means must my dogs eat from my
dinner and from the sacrifice of the idols, but let the strange dogs eat those."^{y}
14(15)(16)   And after that Aseneth took the skin (full) of ashes and poured it on the floor. 'And she
took a piece of sackcloth^z and girded it around her waist. And she loosened the clasp of
15 the hair of her head^{a2} and sprinkled ashes upon her head.^{b2} •And she scattered the ashes on
(17) the floor 'and struck her breast^{c2} often with both hands, and wept bitterly, and fell upon the
ashes and wept with great and bitter weeping all night with sighing and screaming^{d2} until
daybreak.

s. Philonenko (*Joseph et Aséneth*, p. 163) draws
attention to Isis' black cloak (e.g. Apuleius 11.3.7;
Griffiths, *Isis-Book*, 128f.). But Aseneth's tunic is
more like the garments worn for repentance or
mourning often mentioned in Jewish texts (e.g. Jdt
4:10; 1Mac 2:14; 2Mac 3:19; PssSol 2:21; *LAB*
30:5; SibOr 5:190), which would of needs be black
(Josephus, *Life* 28 §138). Black was also the color
of mourning in the Greek and Roman tradition
(e.g. Chariton 3.4.4), but not in the Egyptian
tradition.

t. Witnesses *b* Syr. Arm. L1 ("major" 2 MSS)
436 435&; "second" *c*; "firstborn" *a d*; gap Ngr.
The brother who is not otherwise known comes up
unexpectedly. Philonenko (*Joseph et Aséneth*, p.
163) refers to Isis' mourning for Osiris, but he is
her *elder* brother. "Repenting, the younger brother
of not sinning" (Philo, *Somn*, 1.91) does not help,
either.

u. The reading "to the poor" (*tois penēsin*): AP
d; gaps Q EW Ngr.; omit rest. The crushed idols
are given "to the beggars and needy persons"
(*ptōchois kai deomenois*, vs. 12). The translation
assumes that *penēs* (a man without means who has
to work for a living) and *ptōchos* (beggar) are not
synonymous as in other Jewish texts; the idols'
remnants are reserved for the lowest social class.
This would be a point in favor of the author's
mastery of Gk. (Bammel, "*ptōchos* etc.," *TDNT*
6, 885–915). On almsgiving as a prerequisite to
conversion (cf. Mk 10:21 parallels; Lk 7:5; 19:8;
Acts 10:2) see K. Berger, "Almosen für Israel:
Zum historischen Kontext der paulinischen Kol-
lekte," *NTS* 23 (1976–77) 187–204; cf. also 12:15.

v. The reading "and . . . pieces": AP *d* (Ngr.,
in 9:2); gaps Q GW Syr.; omit rest. Also 13:11.
Cf. Jdg 6:25–32; 2Chr 34:7; Isa 2:20; 30:22; 31:7;
ApAb 1–6; Jub 12:1–14; TJob 5:2; 17:4. A Jew
must neither deride others' gods (Ex 22:27 LXX;
Philo, *Spec Leg* 1.53; *Vit Mos*, 2.205; Josephus,
Apion 2.33 §237) nor rob their temples (Rom 2:22);
but a would-be convert could not leave his personal
idolatrous gear undisturbed (cf. Acts 19:18f.).

w. "Royal dinner" (also 13:8) seems to serve
as a heading for what follows, like "fruit" in 4:2.
"Royal" is an attribute of quality (cf. Apuleius
5.2.4), rather than origin (Dan 1:15). Aseneth is a
queen after all (see on 1:8). Her regular dinner is
a sacrificial meal "at the god's table" and vice
versa (11:9; 12:5; 21:13f.; see 8:5).

x. So Br for *ta sitista*, cf. Mt 22:4. This rare
Gk. word is not attested before Mt and Josephus,
Ant 8.2.4 §40. Gk. *ta* (the) omit Phil.

y. The reading "and gave . . . those": (*FbW c*
Syr. Arm. L1 L2); "and gave everything (*panta*
omit in apparatus Phil) to the dogs as food (or to
the north)" B; "to the dogs (as) food" A (D Slav.
Phil); "to the dogs" Ngr.; "to the poor" P; gap
Q; also cf. 13:8. Aseneth's dogs might be watch
dogs (e.g. TJob 9:3: eight hundred for the cattle,
two hundred for the palace) or pets (b. Ket 61b;
cf. Mk 7:27 parallel) or both. The "strange dogs"
would be stray street roamers—a common plague
in the ancient Near East (e.g. 1Kgs 14:11; Lk
16:21)—which are often cited proverbially. Both
"strange" and "dogs" probably bear antiheathen
overtones (cf. Mk 7:27 parallel; Mt 7:6; Did 9:5).
See generally O. Michel, "*kyōn, kynarion*," *TDNT*
3, 1101–04.

z. Lit. "the skin (*derris* as in 10:2) of the
sackcloth." Sackcloth is made of animal hair, not
skin. Does *derris* mean "sheet"?

a2. A gesture of mourning, cf. e.g. Esth 4:17k.

b2. To besprinkle one's own head with ashes,
dust, or dirt is a common gesture of mourning,
e.g. 2Sam 1:2; Jdt 9:1; 2Mac 10:25; *PJ* 2:1; TJob
28:2; Josephus, *Ant* 20.6.1 §123; Rev 18:19; Homer, *Iliad*, 18.23f.; Chariton 3.10.4; Apuleius
7.27.2. Cf. Acts 22:23.

c2. Cf. Philo, *Flacc*, 19 §157; Lk 18:13; Chariton 1.14.9; Apuleius 9.31.1.

d2. The reading "and screaming": FW Arm.
L1 436; omit *a c d*; gaps EG Syr. 435& Ngr. Gk.
brimēma is very rare; it is found neither in LXX
nor in NT.

16 (18)   And Aseneth rose at daybreak and looked, and behold,[e2] there was much mud from her
(19)   tears[f2] and from the ashes. 'And Aseneth fell again upon her face on the ashes till evening
and until the setting (of) the sun.[g2]

17 (20)   And this way Aseneth did for seven days,[h2] and she ate no bread and drank no water in
those seven days of her humiliation.[i2]

Aseneth's first soliloquy on how to take courage to address God

1 (1) **11** And[a] on the eighth day, behold, it was dawn and the birds were already singing and
the dogs barking at (people who were) passing through, and Aseneth lifted her head (just)
a little from the floor and the ashes on which she was lying, because she was exceedingly
tired and could not control her limbs because of the want (of food) for the seven days.

1x   And[b] she rose on her knees and put her hand on the floor and lifted (herself) up a little
from the floor, and (she was) still bowing her head, and the hairs of her head were stretched
out (in strands) from the load of ashes. And Aseneth clasped her hands, finger against
finger, and shook her head to and fro,[c] and struck her breast continuously with her hands,
and laid her head into her lap;[d] and her face was flooded with her tears, and she sighed
with great sighing,[e] and pulled her hairs from her head,[f] and sprinkled ashes on her head.

1y   And Aseneth was tired and had become discouraged and her strength had gone.[g] And she
2 turned upward to the wall[h] and sat below the window looking east.[i] •And she laid her head
into her lap, clasping her fingers round her right knee, and her mouth was closed, and she
3 (had) not opened it in the seven days and in the seven nights of her humiliation. •And she
said in her heart without opening her mouth:[j]

What shall I do, miserable (that I am),[k]
or where shall I go;

---

e2. "And looked, and behold" is traditional, e.g. Dan 4:13 LXX Theod.; Rev 4:1; see also 14:9.

f2. Poetic exaggeration, rather than a prodigy recalling Isis' tears which cause the Nile to rise (Philonenko, *Joseph et Aséneth*, p. 165).

g2. The reading "till evening (*deilēs*) . . . sun": (FW) *c* Arm. (omit "and") (L1) 436; "until the sun set" *a d;* "till the set of the sun" 435&; "till the oncoming of the evening" Syr.; "until evening (*hesperas*)" G; gaps E Ngr.; "setting" is an infinitive in FW *c* Arm. The "and" is the weakest point of the restored text. Is this an example of double chronology as in Mk 1:32; Poimandres, 29?

h2. 4Ezra (e.g. 5:13) and 2Bar (e.g. 9:2) mention several seven-day periods of fasting and mourning preparatory to prayer or revelation; also cf. *LAB* 30:4f. These may go back to the seven days of mourning for the dead (Gen 50:10; 1Sam 31:13 parallel 1Chr 10:12; Sir 22:12). Closer parallels are similar periods connected with conversion (seven years Dan 4:33a–b LXX; cf. 4QPrNab 1.3; three days Acts 9:9; ten days' abstention from wine and meat Apuleius 11.23.3; 11.28.4; 11.30.1, which may reflect the Egyptian ten-day week; cf. Griffiths, *Isis-Book*, pp. 290, 355f.). The figures all bear a note of completeness. See also 9:5.

i2. The reading "and she . . . humiliation": (*b c* Syr. Arm. L1 L2); "not tasting anything at all" AP (Q) *d;* gap Ngr. "Humiliation" (*tapeinōsis*) probably does not have the ordinary Gk. meaning of a dilapidated state of body or mind or the Jewish nuance of humility, but of self-castigation, particularly fasting, as e.g. Ezra 9:5; Ps 25:18; Sir 18:21; 1Clem 53:2; 55:6. See W. Grundmann, "*tapeinos* etc.," *TDNT* 8, 1–26.

11 a. The reading "it happened": added *d* 332, omit rest, gaps 436 Ngr. The eighth day (cf. 4Ezra 6:36; Lk 9:28; see 9:5) begins much like the day

of Lucius' *reformatio* (Apuleius 11.7). Daily life in ancient times began at daybreak (21:2; 26:1) or even before (Burchard, "Fussnoten zum neutestamentlichen Griechisch II," *ZNW* 69 [1978] 143–57, see especially p. 152, n. 52). Jews would then say their morning prayer (compulsory for males only).

b. Vss. 1x–18 all; except omit *d.* Vs. 1x (GFW *c* Syr. Arm. L1 435&); omit *a;* gaps E *d* 436 Ngr.; details very uncertain. The verse contains a competent assortment of conventional mourning gestures; see also 10:1, 8, 14f.; 11:15.

c. Lit. "thence and thence." Cf. e.g. Apuleius 9.31.1.

d. Cf. e.g. Chariton 1.8.3. For a different purpose cf. 2Kgs 18:42.

e. The text of the last two clauses is very uncertain.

f. Cf. e.g. Chariton 3.10.4; Apuleius 7.27.2.

g. Lit. "she was out of her power."

h. Also cf. vs. 15. Cf. 2Kgs 20:2.

i. For the practice of praying at a window cf. Tob 3:11; Dan 6:11. Jewish prayer ought to be directed toward Jerusalem (Dan 6:11). "East" may denote either that tradition or the direction of the rising sun as a symbol of God or new life (Philo, *Vita Cont,* 11 §89; Josephus, *War* 2.8.5 §128), or both.

j. Ch. 11:3–14 has a good parallel in Apuleius 6.5; cf. also Xenophon of Ephesus 1.4.1–4.6f. From the structural angle the parallel is weakened by the presence of the second soliloquy, almost unnoticed hitherto, which gives chs. 11–13 a tripartite rather than bipartite structure (see also 4:3; 14:4). From this point down to ch. 20 Apuleius' book 11 has a number of structural parallels to offer (Burchard, *Zeuge*, pp. 72–80).

k. The reading "humble (that I am)": *a;* gaps *d* 436 Ngr.; omit rest.

with whom shall I take refuge,[1]
or what[m] shall I speak,[n]
I the virgin and an orphan and desolate and abandoned and hated?[o]

4   All people have come to hate me,
and on top of those[p] my father and my mother,
because I, too, have come to hate their gods and have destroyed them,
and caused them to be trampled underfoot by men.[q]

5   And therefore my father and my mother and my whole family
have come to hate me and said, "Aseneth is not our daughter[r]
because she destroyed our[s] gods."

6   And all people hate me,[t]
because I, too, have (come to) hate every man,
and all who asked for my hand in marriage.
And now, in this humiliation of mine, all have (come to) hate me,
and gloat over this affliction of mine.[u]

7   And the Lord the God of the powerful Joseph, the Most High,
hates all those who worship idols,
because he is a jealous and terrible god[v]
toward all those who worship strange gods.

8   Therefore he has come to hate me, too,
because I worshiped dead and dumb[w] idols,
and blessed them,

9   and ate[x] from their sacrifice(s),
and my mouth is defiled[y] from their table,
and I do not have the boldness to call on the Lord God of Heaven,
the Most High, the Mighty One of the powerful Joseph,[z]
because my mouth is defiled from the sacrifices of the idols.

10   But I have heard[a2] many saying
that the God of the Hebrews[b2] is a true God,
and a living God,[c2] and a merciful God,
and compassionate and long-suffering and pitiful and gentle,[d2]
and does not count the sin[e2] of a humble person,[f2]
nor expose the lawless deeds of an afflicted person at the time of his affliction.

11   Therefore I will take courage too and turn to him,
and take refuge with him,[g2]
and confess all my sins to him,

l. One of the big words in chs. 11–13 and 15:7; 19:5; it is biblical, e.g. Ps 142:6, but cf. also Xenophon of Ephesus 1.4.5.

m. Syr. L1 435&; "with whom" *a c;* gaps rest.

n. Similarly 6:5f.; cf. Xenophon of Ephesus 1.4.7.

o. These are recurring motifs in chs. 11–13. Actually nothing of the sort has happened or will happen. A theme going back to the "complaint," or "lament," psalm genre (e.g. Ps 27:10) and put to appropriate use in texts relating to conversion (cf. also 1QH 9.34f.; Philo, *Spec Leg,* 4.179; Mk 13:12 parallel) has dictated the expressions in this lament. Doubtless life often was like that when a person decided to become a Jew. The counterpoint is that it is expected that God will be a new and better father (see especially 12:8); cf. generally G. Schrenk and G. Quell, "*patēr* etc.," *TDNT* 5, 945–1022; J. Jeremias, *The Prayers of Jesus* (SBT 2.6; London, 1967).

p. The reading "on top of those (people or things)": AP *c;* omit EG Syr.(?) Arm. L1 435&; gaps Q FW *d* 436 Ngr.

q. Also 13:11, but not quite in accord with 10:12; cf. Mt 5:13.

r. Cf. Lk 15:19, 21 and 15:24, 32.

s. The reading "she destroyed our": FW (Syr.)

Arm. L1; "she sold our" 435&; "I gave to destruction their" *a c;* gaps EG *d* 436 Ngr.

t. Order of clauses varies widely since beginning of vs. 5.

u. Cf. Jn 16:20; Rev 11:10.

v. FW *c* Syr. Arm. L1; "as I heard" added AP; gaps Q EG *d* 436 435& Ngr. Cf. Ex 20:5f.; Deut 5:9f.

w. See 8:5.

x. Gk. *ephagon* FGW Syr. Arm. L1 435&; "fled" (*ephygon*) AP (*-ga* Q) *c;* gaps E *d* 436 Ngr.

y. (G)FW Arm. L1 435&; "estranged" *a c;* gaps E *d* Syr. 436 Ngr.

z. See 8:9 beginning.

a2. Unlike Esther (Additions to Esther 14:5), who "heard" the traditions from her early youth.

b2. TJos 12:3; Josephus, *Ant* 9.2.1 §20. On "Hebrews" see 1:5.

c2. Cf. e.g. TJob 37:2; 1Thes 1:9.

d2. Cf. e.g. Ex 34:6; Ps 86:15.

e2. Cf. e.g. Ps 32:2; TZeb 9:7; 2Cor 5:19.

f2. The reading "and especially of one who sins in ignorance": added *a;* gaps G *d* 436 Ngr; omit rest.

g2. The reading "and . . . him": AP Syr. Arm. L1 435&; omit Q EFW *c;* gaps rest.

and pour out my supplication before him.[h2]

12   Who knows,[i2] (maybe) he will see my humiliation[j2]
and have mercy on me.
Perhaps he will see this desolation of mine
and have compassion on me,

13   or see my orphanage[k2]
and protect me,
because[l2] he is the father of the orphans,
and a protector of the persecuted,
and of the afflicted a helper.[m2]

14   I will take courage and cry to him.

Aseneth's second soliloquy on how to take courage to pronounce God's name

15   And[n2] Aseneth rose from the wall where she was sitting and turned to the window looking east and straightened up on her knees and spread her hands out toward heaven. And she was afraid to open her mouth and to name the name of God.[o2] And she turned again away to the wall and sat and struck her head[p2] and her breast with (her) hand often, and said in her heart without opening her mouth:

16   (What) a wretched (woman) I (am), and an orphan and desolate,
my mouth is defiled from the sacrifices of the idols
and from the blessings[q2] of the gods of the Egyptians.

17   And now, in these tears of mine and the ashes strewn around[r2] and the filth of my
      humiliation,
how shall I open my mouth to the Most High,
and how name his terrible holy name,
(and be sure) that the Lord will not be angry with me,
because in (the midst of) my lawless deeds I have called on his holy name?

18   What shall I now do, wretched (that) I (am)?
I will rather take courage and open my mouth to him
and invoke his name.
And if in fury the Lord strikes me
he himself will again heal me;
and if he chastises me with his whips,[s2]
he himself will look again on me in his mercy;
and if he is furious at me in my sins,
he will again be reconciled with me and forgive me every sin.
So I will take courage to open my mouth to him.

Aseneth's confession of sin and prayer for acceptance

19   And Aseneth rose again from the wall where she sat and straightened up on her knees[t2]

---

h2. The reading "and he will have mercy upon my miserableness": added *a;* omit FW *c* Syr. (Arm.) L1 435&; gaps rest; also cf. 12:3; cf. Pss 102:1; 142:3.

i2. Lit. "who knows if" (*tis oiden ei*) (Br). But this would express doubts rather than timid confidence which is what the Gk. means (Rie); cf. e.g. 2Sam 12:22; Esth 4:14; Tob 13:8 BA; *LAB* 9:6; Epictetus, *Diss.,* 2.20.30; Achilles Tatius 7.6.2; Apuleius 1.15.4; 6.1.2; 6.5.4; 10.26.2. If this applies to 1Cor 7:16 as well, it is an exhortation to carry on in a mixed marriage; Burchard, *ZNW* 61 (1970) 170f.; if not, it gives permission to let go (S. Kubo, "I Corinthians vii.16: Optimistic or Pessimistic?" *NTS* 24 [1978] 539–44).

j2. Cf. 1Sam 1:11; Lk 1:48. See 10:17.

k2. Gk. *orphania* also 13:1. LXX only Isa 47:8.

l2. FWG *c* Syr. Arm. L1; "as I hear" added *a;* gaps rest.

m2. Also 12:13; cf. Jdt 9:11.

n2. Vss. 15–18 (G *c* Syr. Arm. 436 Br; all of these except 436 have the first soliloquy); omit *a* EFW L1 435& (in some of these the omission may actually be 15b–19, because 15a and 19 are very similar; in 435& elements of the second soliloquy seem to be combined with the first); gaps *d* Ngr. See further 11:3.

o2. Cf. Lev 24:16; Sir 23:9.

p2. Cf. e.g. Chariton 3.10.3; Apuleius 4.25.1.

q2. Gk. *eulogiai* means "blessed gifts," rather than "words of blessing."

r2. Or "besprinkled with ashes."

s2. Cf. 1Kgs 12:11, 14 parallel 2Chr 10:11, 14.

t2. As a rule a Jew would pray standing up (e.g. TJob 40:1f.; Lk 18:11, 13); kneeling or prostration indicates intensity (e.g. Dan 6:11; TJob 40:4; Mk 14:35 parallel; Acts 9:40). In either case, he (or she) would look up (e.g. TLevi 2:3; Lk 6:41. 18:13 is by way of exception).

(12:1) 'and spread her hand eastward and looked with her eyes up toward heaven, and opened her mouth to God, and said:

1 (2)   **12** Lord[a] God of the ages,[b]
who created all (things) and gave life (to them),
who gave breath of life to your whole creation,[c]
who brought the invisible (things) out into the light,[d]

2   who made the (things that) are and the (ones that) have an appearance from the non-appearing and non-being,[e]

(3)   who lifted up[f] the heaven
and founded it on[g] a firmament[h] upon the back of the winds,[i]
who founded the earth upon the waters,[j]
who put big stones on the abyss of the water,[k]
and the stones will not be submerged,[l]
but they are like oak leaves (floating) on top of the water,
and they are living stones
and hear your voice, Lord,
and keep your commandments[m] which you have commanded to them,
and never transgress your ordinances,[n]
but are doing your will to the end.[o]
For you, Lord, spoke and they were brought to life,[p]
because your word, Lord, is life for all your creatures.[q]

3   With you I take refuge, Lord,

(4)   and to you I will shout, Lord,
to you I will pour out my supplication,
to you I will confess my sins,
and to you I will reveal my lawless deeds.

4   Spare me, Lord,

(5)   because I have sinned much before you,
I have committed lawlessness and irreverence,[r]
and have said wicked and unspeakable (things) before you.

---

12 a. Witnesses AP Bat Br prefix "Prayer and Confession of Aseneth," B before "and spread" 11:19 (different script). This heading may have originated as a marginal note slipped into the text at various places. Perhaps an ancestor of B was corrected after a MS of the AP type. Content and form of the confession require analysis; cf. Tob 3:2–6, 11–15; Esth 4:17b–h, 1–z; PrMan; Dan 3:24–45; LXX 4:34, also Ezra 9:5–15; Neh 9; Dan 9:4–19; 1Bar 1:15–3:8. On the function of prayer as denoting the turn of a predicament, see the above examples and Jdt 9:2–14; in the romances, cf. Xenophon of Ephesus 1.4.4f.; Apuleius 11.2.

b. The reading "the ages": EG d Syr. Arm. 436 (cf. 16:16; 21:21; Tob 13:7; 13:11 BA; Sir 36:17; 1Clem 35:3; 55:6; 61:2); "the just (plural)" A FW c L1 (cf. PrMan); "the powers" PQ; "the heavens" 435&; omit Slav., gap Ngr. On some of the following clauses see further 8:9.

c. Cf. e.g. Gen 2:7; Prov 24:12; Acts 17:25.

d. Cf. Gen 1:2 LXX.

e. One of the essentials of Jewish and Christian cosmology, e.g. Gen 1:2 LXX; WisSol 11:25; 2Bar 21:4; 48:8; 2En 24:2; 24:5–26:1; Philo, Spec Leg. 4 §187; Somn 1 §76; Rom 4:17; Heb 11:3; ShepHerm Vision 1.1.6; ShepHerm Mandates 1; AposCon 8.12.7.

f. Gk. hypsōsas, according to Philonenko (Joseph et Aséneth, pp. 59f.), is typical of Egyptian cosmology and not evidenced in Jewish literature; but cf. Jer 38 (31):35 LXX; Paris Magical Papyrus 1204f. (K. Preisendanz, Papyri Graecae Magicae,

vol. 1 [Leipzig-Berlin, 1928] p. 112).

g. Or "as."

h. Cf. Gen 1:6 LXX; 1En 18:2; TSol 20:12; AscenIs 7:9; 10:23. See generally G. Bertram, "stereos etc.," TDNT 7, 609–14.

i. The reading "and . . . winds": (FGW c Syr. Arm. L1 L2); omit E d; gap Ngr.

j. Cf. e.g. Pss 24:2; 136:6; 2En 28:1f.; 2Pet 3:5; ShepHerm Vision 1.3.4.

k. Cf. e.g. 2En 28:1f.; ShepHerm Similitudes 9.3.3; ShepHerm Vision 3.2.4f.; Aptowitzer, HUCA 1 (1924) 271f.

l. The Gk. verb bythizesthai appears in LXX only in 2Mac 12:4.

m. Cf. e.g. Jdt 16:14; Sir 16:27f.; 1QS 3.16f.

n. The reading "but they . . . ordinances": (FW Syr. Arm. L1 L2); omit a d; gaps EG c Ngr. See next note.

o. The reading "but are . . . end": a d; gaps c EG Ngr. 435&; omit rest. Perhaps this is the a d variant of the text cited in previous note, rather than part of the original text. Cf. Rev 2:26; ShepHerm Similitudes 9.27.3.

p. Creation by God's word is another basic principle of Jewish and Christian theology, e.g. cf. Jdt 16:14; Pss 33:9; 148:5; WisSol 9:1; Isa 48:13; Jn 1:3, 10; Heb 11:3; 2Pet 3:5; ShepHerm Visions 1.3.4; 3.3.5; IgnatiusEph 15:1. Cf. 16:11.

q. Cf. e.g. Jn 1:4; 12:50; 1Jn 1:1f.; cf. 9:5.

r. Cf. e.g. 1Kgs 8:47; Ps 106:6; 1Bar 2:12; Dan 3:29; 9:5 (Theodotion); ApMos 32; 1QS 1.24f.

5   My mouth is defiled from the sacrifices of the idols
         and from the tables of the gods of the Egyptians.

(6)   I have sinned, Lord,
         before you I have sinned much in ignorance,
         and have worshiped dead and dumb[s] idols.
         And now I am not worthy[t] to open my mouth to you, Lord.

(7)   And I, Aseneth, daughter of Pentephres the priest,
         the virgin and queen,
         who (was) once proud and arrogant,
         and prospering in my riches beyond all people,
         am now an orphan, and desolate, and abandoned by all people.[u]

6   With you I take refuge, Lord,
         and to you I bring my supplication,
         and to you I will shout.

7   Rescue me before I am caught by my persecutors.[v]

8   For (just) as a little child who is afraid flees to his father,

(8)   and the father, stretching out his hands, snatches him off the ground,[w]
         and puts his arms around him by his breast,
         and the child clasps his hands around his father's neck,
         and regains his breath after[x] his fear,
         and rests at his father's breast,
         the father, however, smiles at[y] the confusion of his childish mind,[z]
         likewise you too, Lord, stretch out your hands upon me as a child-loving father,
         and snatch me off the earth.[a2]

9 (9)   For behold, the wild old[b2] lion[c2] persecutes me,
         because he is (the) father of the gods of the Egyptians,[d2]
         and his children are the gods of the idol maniacs.[e2]
         And I have come to hate them,
         because they are the lion's children,
         and have thrown all of them from me and destroyed them.

10   And the lion their father[f2] furiously persecutes me,[g2]

s. See 8:5.

t. Cf. e.g. *LAB* 42:5; Lk 15:19, 21; Jn 1:27; Acts 13:25.

u. Cf. 12:13; 13:6, 11; Xenophon of Ephesus 5.11.4, also 1.4.1. Tachau ("*Einst*" *und* "*Jetzt*," pp. 55f.) suggests the "now" clause should be understood as signaling a positive condition, in analogy to e.g. Rom 7:5f.; 11:30; 1Cor 6:9–11; Col 1:21; 1Pet 2:25. However, whatever the connection between the two sets of passages in terms of tradition history may be, JosAsen contrasts past glory and present misery, the NT past godlessness and present salvation. Only 13:11 comes close to that.

v. Cf. Pss 7:2f.; 31:15f.; 142:6f.

w. The reading "off the ground": Syr. Arm. L2; small gaps *a* G *c;* large gaps rest.

x. The reading "regains . . . after": Syr. (Br); "reassures himself from" Arm.; "gasps (*anhelat*) from" 435&; "is weak from (*asthenei apo*)" *c* (cf. Ps 88:10 LXX); gaps rest. For the Gk. text we may conjecture *anapnei apo*, although *anapnein* is attested in LXX only at Job 9:18 and never in the NT.

y. The reading "smiles at": L2; "is glad about" Syr. (Br); "is weary because of (*akēdia epi*)" *c;* gaps rest. Gk. *akēdian* (in LXX Pss 61:3; 102:1; 143:4; Sir 22:13; 1Bar 3:1; Dan 7:15) has a negative ring, and it is doubtful whether it can be constructed with *epi.* Gk. *meidia* has been conjectured for the Gk. text.

z. The reading "and the child . . . childish mind (lit. "childhood")": (*c* Syr. Arm. L2 Br); omit

AP G; gaps rest.

a2. The reading "off the earth (same word as "ground" above)": *c* Syr. Arm. L2; "off the lion" G (from vs. 9); "out of the hand of the ("supernatural" added *a*) enemy" *a d;* omit L1; gaps EFW Ngr. If this means that Aseneth would rather die, cf. e.g. Tob 3:6; Apuleius 11.2.7 and many other passages in the novels.

b2. Cf. e.g. Rev 12:9; 20:2, also Jn 8:44; 1Jn 3:8.

c2. In the OT "lion" is a metaphor for a persecutor; in later times it also signifies the devil (cf. e.g. Pss 7:3; 22:14; Esth 4:17s; ApEl 19:5; 1Pet 5:8). That the devil will attempt to avenge himself upon those who escaped his dominion makes the plot of TJob, and apparently there was a paraenetic tradition warning new converts against his machinations (cf. also Mk 4:15 parallel).

d2. Cf. Firmicus Maternus, *De errore profanarum religionum*, 13:4; etc.

e2. The reading "of the idol maniacs": AP; "of the Egyptians" *d;* "of the heathen" Arm.; "whom I worshiped" G; "and the judges (?, *i sudcii*, corrupt for "Egyptians"?)" Slav.; gaps rest. "Idol maniac (*eidōlomanēs*)" is first attested in Athenagoras, *Leg.*, 21:1 (A.D. 177), which makes it a bit doubtful here. Unlike Jn 8:44, men are not identified as devil's children.

f2. FG *c* Arm. 436; "the devil" added *a d;* gaps rest.

g2. The reading "persecutes me": FG *c* Syr. Arm. 436; "tries to swallow me" AP (Q) *d;* gaps EW L1 435& Ngr.

11 (10) but you, Lord, rescue me from his hands,
     and from his mouth deliver me,[h2]
     lest he carry me off like a lion,[i2]
     and tear me up
     and throw me into the flame of the fire,
     and the fire will throw me into the hurricane,[j2]
     and the hurricane (will) wrap me up in darkness
     and throw me out into the deep of the sea,
     and the big sea monster who (exists) since eternity will swallow me,[k2]
     and I will be destroyed for ever (and) ever.[12]

12 (11) Rescue me, Lord,
     before all this comes upon me.
     Rescue me, Lord,
     the desolate and solitary,[m2]
     because my father and my mother disowned me and said,
     "Aseneth is not our daughter,"
     because I have destroyed and ground (to pieces) their gods,
     and have come to hate them.

13   And I am now an orphan and desolate,
     and I have no other hope save in you, Lord,
     and no other refuge except[n2] your mercy, Lord,
     because you are the father of the orphans,
     and a protector of the persecuted
     and a helper of the afflicted.

14   Have mercy upon me, Lord,
     and guard me, a virgin (who is) abandoned and an orphan,
     because you, Lord, are a sweet and good and gentle father.

15   What father is as sweet as you, Lord,
     and who (is) as quick in mercy as you, Lord,
     and who (is as) long-suffering toward our sins as you, Lord?

(12)   For behold, all the gifts[o2] of my father Pentephres,
     which he gave me as an inheritance,[p2] are transient[q2] and obscure;
     but the gifts[r2] of your inheritance, Lord, are incorruptible and eternal.[s2]

1   **13** Be mindful, Lord, of my humiliation
     and have mercy upon me.

(1)   Look at my orphanage
     and have compassion on the afflicted.
     For behold, I fled from everything
     and took refuge in you, Lord, the only friend to men.

2   Behold, I left behind all the good (things) of the earth
     and took refuge in you, Lord,

h2. Cf. Ps 22:22; 2Tim 4:17.

i2. The reading "like a lion": F L2; "like a wolf" d; omit Syr. Arm. L1; gaps rest. Also cf. vs. 9.

j2. Cf. Ps 11:6. Or "gush, big wave"; cf. Ps 69:16?.

k2. Is Aseneth afraid to be tossed across the four elements? Anyway, unlike e.g. Rev 19:20, fire is not the end.

l2. Cf. Jn 10:28.

m2. The reading "defenceless": Br and Rie, which is possible for *aperistatos*.

n2. Cf. e.g. Ps 91:9; Jdt 9:14; Add. to Esth 4:17 l, t.

o2. The reading "gifts (*domata* conjectured)": (G) Syr. 436 Rie; "funds (*chrēmata*)" B Phil; "houses (*dōmata*)" a F c D Bat (followed by G. Fischer, *Wohnungen*, p. 188) Br; "bands (*uzy*, Gk. *demata* or *desmata?*)" Slav.; omit Arm. 435&; gaps EW L1 Ngr. See below, n. r2.

p2. See at 2:1; 3:5.

q2. Gk. *proskairos* is first attested in Dionysius of Halicarnassus. Cf. 2Cor 4:18, also Mt 6:19–21 parallel; 1Pet 1:4; Jas 1:17.

r2. The reading "gifts": (G Syr. Arm. 436 Slav.) Rie; "houses" AP d Bat Br; illegible F; omit Q c; gaps EW L1 435& Ngr. See above, n. o2.

s2. Cf. e.g. 4Ezra 13:54–56; TJob 4:4–11; 18:5–8; Mk 10:17–31 parallel; Heb 10:34. Conversion often meant leaving one's property or occupation behind, either as a prerequisite or as a practical consequence, and the values to be gained by the new existence were held out in comfort. Cf. K. Berger, *Die Gesetzesauslegung Jesu: Ihr historischer Hintergrund im Judentum und im Alten Testament* (Wissenschaftliche Monographien zum Alten und Neuen Testament 40; Neukirchen-Vluyn, 1972) vol. 1, pp. 422–32; see also 10:11.

in this sackcloth and ashes,[a]
naked and an orphan and left all alone.[b]

3 (2)   Behold, I put off my linen royal robe, interwoven with violet and gold,[c]
and dressed in a black mourning tunic.

4 (3)   Behold, I loosened my golden girdle and threw it off me
and girded a rope and sackcloth around myself.

5 (4)   Behold, my tiara and my diadem I threw off my head,
and have sprinkled ashes (upon it).

6 (5)   Behold, the floor of my chamber, paved with colored and purple stones,
which once used to be besprinkled with perfumes
and wiped with bright linen cloths,
is now besprinkled with my tears
and was profaned having been powdered with ashes.

7 (6)   Behold, my Lord, from my tears and the ashes
much mud has been formed in my chamber,
as on a broad street.[d]

8 (7)   Behold, Lord, my royal dinner[e] and the cereals
I gave to the strange[f] dogs.

9 (8)   And behold, seven days and seven nights I was fasting
and ate no bread and drank no water,
and my mouth has become dry as a drum,
and my tongue as a horn,
and my lips as a potsherd,[g]
and my face has fallen,[h]
and my eyes are burning in shame[i] from my many tears,
and my entire strength has left (me).[j]

11   Behold now, all the gods whom I once used to worship in ignorance:
I have now recognized[k] that they were dumb and dead[l] idols,
and I have caused them to be trampled underfoot by men,
and the thieves snatched[m] those that were of silver and gold.[n]

12   And with you I have taken refuge, O Lord my God.
Yet you, rescue me from my many deeds of ignorance[o]

13   and pardon me,

(9)   because I have sinned against you in ignorance,
being a virgin,
and have fallen in error unwittingly,[p]
and spoken blasphemous (words) against my lord Joseph,

(10)   because I did not know, the miserable (one that I am),
that he is your son,
as people told me
that Joseph is the shepherd's son from the land of Canaan.

---

13 a. A Jewish pair not attested in profane Gk. "In sackcloth and ashes" is on record only at TJos 15:2; Mt 11:21 parallel Lk 10:13.

b. Cf. 1Tim 5:5; 4Mac 16:10.

c. See 2:8.

d. Cf. Micah 7:10; Zech 9:3. "Broad street" means highway (also 24:20). "Mud of the street" is a common phrase, often employed proverbially, e.g. Ps 18:43 = 2Sam 22:43; 1QSb 5.27.

e. See 10:13.

f. F c D Syr. Arm. 436 Slav.; omit a B Phil; gaps rest.

g. Cf. Ps 22:16.

h. Also 18:3, 4, 7. Cf. Gen 4:5f.; 1Sam 1:18; Jdt 6:9; TJos 7:2.

i. Lit. "became (or, were) in shame of inflammation." This clause is very uncertain, but words to this effect were there. "In shame (en aischynē)" is strange in this context; a word expressing physical, rather than mental, discomfort would be more to the point.

i. The reading "and . . . (me)": (F Syr. Arm.

L2); omit a c; gaps rest. Vs. 10 is as follows: "But you, my Lord (God added A), rescue me from the many deeds of ignorance of mine, and pardon me because I, being a virgin and unwitting, have fallen into error" (transposed here from vss. 12b and 13a) AP (Q); omit c Syr. Arm. L2; vss. 10f. omit G; 10–12 omit d; 10–12a omit F; gaps EW L1 Slav. Ngr.

k. Cf. TJob 40:4; Jn 16:30; 17:7; Acts 12:11; 20:25.

l. See 8:5.

m. Not consonant with 10:12; 11:4, but with a point made in polemics against idols (e.g. LetJer 56f.; Aristides, Apology, 3:2).

n. This clause is in AP c Syr. Arm. L1 436; "and have removed them from my face" added Syr. (Arm.); also L2 after "men" ("and . . . gold" omit 435&); gaps rest. It could be part of the text, but the position is awkward.

o. Cf. Ps 39:9.

p. See 13:9.

And I, the miserable one, have come to believe them
and fall into error.
And I have despised him
and spoken wicked (words) about him,
and did not know that he is your son.

14 (11)　For who among men will give birth to such beauty
and such great wisdom and virtue and power,
as (owned by) the all-beautiful Joseph?

15　　　Lord, I commit him to you,[q]
because I love him beyond my (own) soul.[r]

(12)　　Preserve him in the wisdom of your grace.
And you, Lord, commit me to him for a maidservant and slave.
And I will make his bed
and wash his feet
and wait on him
and be a slave for him and serve him for ever (and) ever.[s]

B. ASENETH'S ACCEPTANCE

A man descends from heaven, introduces himself as chief of the angels, and orders Aseneth to dress again

1 (1)　**14** And[a] when Aseneth had ceased making confession to the Lord, behold, the morning
2　star rose out of heaven in the east. And Aseneth saw it and rejoiced and said, '''So the
Lord God listened to my prayer, because this star rose as a messenger[b] and herald of the
2 (3)　light of the great day.''[c] •And Aseneth kept looking,[d] and behold, close to the morning
3 (4)　star, the heaven was torn apart[e] and great and unutterable light appeared.[f] •And Aseneth
saw (it) and fell on (her) face on the ashes.[g] And a man[h] came to her from heaven and
4,5 (5)　stood by Aseneth's head. •And he called her and said, "Aseneth, Aseneth."[i] •And she
said, "Who is he that calls me, because the door of my chamber is closed, and the tower
6 (6)　is high, and how then did he come into my chamber?'' •And the man called her a second

---

q. Cf. e.g. Acts 14:23; 20:32; 1Pet 4:19.
r. Cf. Apuleius 5.6.6.
s. Cf. 6:8.

14 a. "And . . . saw": Gk. text with full apparatus in C. Burchard, "Zum Text von 'Joseph und Aseneth,' " *JSJ* 1 (1970) 3–34, see 30–34. On the form of 14:1–9 cf. Acts 9:1–8 and below vs. 6. In function the heavenly man's visit (chs. 14–17) is not parallel to Jesus' appearance according to Acts 9:3–8 (see above 6:1), but to Saul's vision referred to in Acts 9:12 and the angel's visit to Cornelius in Acts 10:3–7; cf. also Apuleius 11.5.1–6.6.

b. Gk. *aggelos*, which may also mean "angel," but "messenger" seems to go better with "herald." Besides, the star is not identical with the man (vs. 3). On the morning star as a symbol of new light, life, and renovation, cf. 2Pet 1:11; Rev 2:28; R. Staats, "Die Sonntagnachtgottesdienste der christlichen Frühzeit," *ZNW* 66 (1975) 242–63, see esp. pp. 255f.

c. The first day of creation which will be the day of reformation (cf. 2Cor 4:6) or just the day of salvation (OdesSol 41:4; cf. *dies salutaris* Apuleius 11.5.4). The Day of Atonement can also be called "The Great Day" (Isa 1:13 LXX; Aristides, *Apology*, 14:4), but it is on vii-10, not iv-25.

d. "And . . . looking" (*b c* Arm. L1 L2 Ngr.); omit *a d*; destroyed Syr.; gap Slav.

e. Cf. e.g. Mk 1:10; ShepHerm Vision 1.1.4. On the motif generally, see F. Lentzen-Deis, *Die Taufe Jesu nach den Synoptikern: Literarkri-*

tische und gattungsgeschichtliche Untersuchungen (Frankfurter Theologische Studien 4; Frankfurt am Main, 1970) pp. 99–127.

f. "Light" is a must for heavenly appearances. It emanates from them (as e.g. vs. 9) or directly from heaven (as here). The sky is torn apart and the supernatural light which fills the upper world leaks out (cf. also Acts 9:3 parallel). So the Gk. should not be translated "a light" (Rie, Phil).

g. Also vs. 10. The proper reaction; cf. e.g. Dan 8:17f.; ApAb 10:2; TJob 3:4; Acts 9:4 parallel.

h. The reading "a man" (*anthrōpos*): *a* FG L1 436 Phil; "(one) similar to a man" *c* (Arm.); "a man of light" B; "the man of God" D; "an angel" W; "the angel of the Lord" (435& Ngr.); "a bright angel" Slav.; "a voice" E; destroyed Syr. Similar variants occur at each mention of the man below, with "angel" or the like dominating in *a* E L1 435& Ngr. (Burchard, *Untersuchungen*, p. 21). Doubtless the "man" was promoted to "angel," rather than vice versa, as 19:5, 9 confirm, where "man" is attested by virtually all witnesses.

i. Also vs. 6. Double address is frequent in Jewish and early Christian literature, e.g. Gen 46:2; TJob 3:1; 24:1; 25:9; Lk 10:41; Acts 9:4; Berger, *Auferstehung*, p. 436, n. 31. The angel addresses Aseneth twice before beginning to deliver his message. The idea that a heavenly being has to call three times before it can be believed may be back of this (cf. e.g. *LAB* 53:4; Jn 21:15–18; Acts 10:10–16; Berger, *Auferstehung*, pp. 158f.; 451–54, nn. 85–93). See also 4:3; 11:3; Mk 14:32–42 parallel.

7 time and said, "Aseneth, Aseneth."[j] •And she said, "Behold, (here) I (am), Lord. Who
8 (7) are you, tell me." •And the man said, "I am the chief of the house of the Lord and
commander of the whole host of the Most High.[k] Rise and stand on your feet,[l] and I will
tell you what I have to say."[m]
9 (8) And Aseneth raised her head[n] and saw, and behold,[o] (there was) a man in every respect
(9) similar to Joseph,[p] by the robe and the crown and the royal staff, ʼexcept[q] that his face was
like lightning, and his eyes like sunshine, and the hairs of his head like a flame of fire of
a burning torch,ʳ and hands and feet like iron shining forth from a fire, and sparks shot
10 (10) forth from his hands and feet. •And Aseneth saw (it) and fell on her face at his feet on the
11 (11) ground. And Aseneth was filled with great fear, and all of her limbs trembled. •And the
man said to her, "Courage, and do not be afraid,[s] but rise and stand on your feet, and I
12 (12) will tell you what I have to say." •And Aseneth rose and stood on her feet. And the man
said to her, "Proceed unhindered into your second chamber and put off your black tunic of
mourning, and the sackcloth put off your waist, and shake off those ashes from your head,
(13) and wash your face and your hands with living water, ʼand dress in a new linen robe (as
yet) untouched[t] and distinguished and gird your waist (with) the new twin girdle of your
13 (14) virginity. •And come (back) to me, and I will tell you what I have to say."
14 (15) And Aseneth hurried and went into her second chamber where the chests (containing)
her ornaments were, and opened her coffer, and took a new linen robe, distinguished (and
(16) as yet) untouched, and undressed the black tunic of mourning and put off the sackcloth
from her waist, and dressed in her distinguished (and as yet) untouched linen robe, and
girded herself with the twin girdle of her virginity, one girdle around her waist, and another
15 (17) girdle upon her breast.[u] •And she shook off the ashes from her head, and washed her hands
and her face with living water. And she took an (as yet) untouched and distinguished linen
veil and covered her head.

The heavenly man announces Aseneth's acceptance with God and her marriage to Joseph

1 (1) **15** And she went to the man into her first chamber and stood before him. And the man
said to her, "Remove the veil from your head, and for what purpose did you do this?[a] For

j. Vss. 6–8 represent a traditional form to start a dialogue, cf. e.g. Gen 27:18f.; 31:11–13; 46:2f.; Jub 44:5; ApAb 8:2–5; 9:1–5; *Poimandres*, 1f.; Acts 9:4f.; also in shorter form, e.g. TJob 3:1f.; Acts 9:10f.; 10:3–5; cf. above 4:3–6. See G. Lohfink, *Paulus vor Damaskus* (Stuttgarter Bibelstudien 4; Stuttgart, 1965); Burchard, *Zeuge*, pp. 88f.; Berger, *Auferstehung*, pp. 154–59; 436–54, nn. 33–93.

k. Also 21:21. There are many variants; cf. also Eth. (see Intro.). Witnesses *a* D Slav. Ngr. Phil (gap B) have "commander-in-chief (*archistratēgos*)" someplace in this verse and later on (cf. Josh 5:14). This is the conventional title of Michael (Philonenko, *Joseph et Aséneth*, p. 178); and he is meant certainly. The angels' hosts (cf. e.g. Lk 2:13) are traditionally thought of as being organized like a monarch's court (in the NT "house of God" has become an epithet of the Church, e.g. 1Tim 3:15) or an army (see 25:6) with Michael at its head.

l. Also vs. 11. Cf. e.g. Josh 5:14; Acts 26:16.

m. Also vs. 11. Cf. e.g. Ezek 2:1; 4Ezra 7:2; Acts 9:6; 22:10.

n. Aseneth starts to obey the angel's order but finds at once that she cannot do it.

o. "Raise, see, and behold" e.g. Gen 37:25; 2Sam 13:34; cf. further 10:16.

p. Michael holds the post in heaven which Joseph holds in Egypt: second only to the supreme ruler. But he is not Joseph, nor does he appear in his guise. Visionary appearances of historical persons (such as Josephus, *Ant* 11.8.5 §334) which have been interpreted as being angels appearing in the form of such persons (Aptowitzer, *HUCA* 1 [1924] 278f.; cf. also Acts 9:12) are no parallels to the thought here.

q. The details of the angel's description are traditional, cf. e.g. Dan 10:6; ApAb 17:12; ApZeph 9:3f.; Mt 28:3; Rev 1:13–16; 10:1.

r. Gk. *hypolampados kaiomenēs* A; "from a burning torch (*hypo l.k.*)" P *c;* omit G *d* Arm. L1 L2; destroyed Syr.; gaps Q EFW Ngr. Gk. *hypolampas* is rare, and the meaning "torch" is uncertain; but it is apparently required in Acts 20:8 D. The report in Bauer-Arndt-Gingrich (*Greek-English Lexicon* [Chicago, 1957]) is garbled.

s. Also 23:16; 28:7. This is a traditional exhortation, e.g. 4Ezra 6:33, *LAB* 6:9; 20:5; Mk 6:50 parallel.

t. Or "not to be touched, pure," as in vss. 14, 15.

u. Unusual. The two girdles seem to be a special mark of virginity; according to 3:6 and 18:6 Aseneth wears only one, presumably around her waist. Girdles around (or above?) the breast are mentioned in ApZeph 9:4; Rev 1:13; 15:6 (*BJ* has "waist" in both instances), but they seem to be in lieu of the ordinary ones. Job's daughters are given multicolored girdles to gird their breasts (TJob 46:9), and these seem to be additional, but they convey protection against the devil, eternal life, and miraculous creativity in poetry and music (TJob 46–50), and have nothing to do with virginity.

15 a. The reading "and . . . this": FW *c* (Arm.)

2 (2) you are a chaste virgin today, and your head is like that of a young man.'"ᵇ •And Aseneth removed the veil from her head.

Andᶜ the man said to her, "Courage, Aseneth, chaste virgin. Behold, I have heardᵈ all
3 the words of your confession and your prayer. •Behold, I have also seenᵉ the humiliation and the affliction of the seven days of your want (of food). Behold, from your tears and
4 (3) these ashes, plenty of mud has formed before your face. •Courage, Aseneth, chaste virgin. For behold, your name was writtenᶠ in the book of the livingᵍ in heaven; in the beginning of the book, as the very first of all, your name was written by my finger,ʰ and it will not
5 (4) be erased forever. •Behold, from today, you will be renewed and formed anew and made alive again,ⁱ and you will eat blessed bread of life, and drink a blessed cup of immortality,
6 (5) and anoint yourself with blessed ointment of incorruptibility. •Courage, Aseneth, chaste virgin. Behold, I have givenʲ you today to Joseph for a bride, and he himself will be your bridegroom for ever (and) ever.

7 (6)   "Andᵏ your name shall no longer be called Aseneth, but your name shall be City of Refuge,ˡ because in you many nations will take refuge with the Lord God, the Most High, and under your wings many peoples trusting in the Lord Godᵐ will be sheltered,ⁿ and behind your wallsᵒ will be guarded those who attach themselves to the Most High Godᵖ in the name

L1 L2; omit *a* E *d;* destroyed Syr.; gaps G Ngr.

b. Aseneth is not declared androgynous (against Philonenko, *Joseph et Aséneth*, p. 181); her head is compared to, not identified with, a young man's. This may signify that virginity gives a certain equality to the sexes (see 7:7), or that in Judaism both sexes are alike before God. It probably does not mean that JosAsen suggests Jewish virgins should go unveiled (as perhaps some Corinthians did, cf. 1Cor 11:2–16 and the commentaries thereon), because in 18:6 Aseneth puts on a veil again, albeit "like a bride."

c. On vss. 2–10 cf. Apuleius 11.5.1–6.6. There is no analogy to Aseneth's role as City of Refuge, but Lucius will become a model to the "unreligious" (11.15.4).

d. First person: GFW *c* Arm. L2; third ("the Lord" or the like): *a d* L1; destroyed Syr.; gaps E Ngr. Similarly, vs. 3 "I have seen" (GFW *c* Arm. L2 versus AP L1 E; destroyed Syr.; gaps Q *d* Ngr.); vs. 4 "was written," first instance (*a* G *d* Arm. L1 Ngr. versus W *c* L2, perhaps E, illegible F; destroyed Syr.); "was written," second instance (W[?] *c* Arm. versus L2, illegible F; destroyed Syr.; gaps rest); vs. 6 "I have given" (*b c* Arm. L1 L2 versus *a d* Ngr.; destroyed Syr.). In the retrospective 19:5 "I have given" has no variant in the positive text (illegible F; gap *d*). On the strength of this the first person was adopted into the text (against Burchard, *Untersuchungen*, p. 47) except in 15:4, where there is little support for it.

e. See 15:2.

f. See 15:2.

g. The reading "of the living (plu.)": EGW *c* Arm. L1 436; "of life" *a d* 435&; Ngr.; illegible F; destroyed Syr. This book (also vs. 12x; usually "of life") is a sort of heavenly citizens' register, a common Jewish and Christian idea with roots way back in the ancient Near East; cf. e.g. Ex 32:32f.; Ps 87:6; Jub 30:22; 1QM 12.1f.; Lk 10:20; Rev 20:12, 15. See L. Koep, *Das himmlische Buch in Antike und Christentum* (Theophaneia 8; Bonn, 1952).

h. "For . . . finger": Gk. with full apparatus in Burchard, *Untersuchungen*, pp. 54f.; "in the beginning . . . finger" (FW *c* Arm. L2); omit E Ngr.; destroyed Syr.; gaps *a* G *d* L1.

i. The reading "renewed (see 8:9) . . . again" AP (436) Phil; "renewed and formed anew" *c;*

"renewed and made alive again (omit D W? Ngr.)" FW *d* Arm. (L1) Ngr.; "renewed" EG; destroyed Syr.; gaps Q 435&. Cf. Gen 2:7. The two last verbs of the triad may be interpreting the first as in 1Cor 2:3; 4:9; Eph 2:5; 3:6 (Burchard, *ZNW* 61 [1970], 169).

j. See 15:2.

k. Vss. 7–8: Gk. with full apparatus in Burchard, *Untersuchungen*, pp. 55–67. This is one of the most badly damaged passages of the book, especially in the second half of vs. 7. Vs. 7a is taken up in the *Passion of St. Irene* (Burchard, *Untersuchungen*, p. 135) in a form apparently close to *b.*

l. Proselytes often took new names, but there is more to the phenomenon here. Aseneth does not choose a name, she is given one from above like others in biblical tradition, in particular those who have a significance for God's people as a whole (e.g. Gen 17:5, 15; 32:29; 41:45; Isa 62:4f.; 1Bar 5:4; Zech 8:3; Mk 3:16 parallel; Mt 16:18; Berger, *Auferstehung*, pp. 198; 562–65, nn. 394–405). That she is called a "City" is necessitated by the concept underlying 15:7 (see Intro.). "City of Refuge (*polis kataphygēs*)" may have been suggested by Zech 2:15 LXX (cf. Isa 54:15; Jer 27 [50]:5) as taken up in the following clause. Perhaps a pun was intended; *polis* sounds much like *pollois,* the dative plural of *polloi* "many" (the *Vorlage* of L1 actually may have read *pollois kataphygēs*). Possibly there is also a reminiscence of Num 35:27f. (the only parallels in LXX and the other Gk. versions of the OT). Attempts to explain "City of Refuge" on the basis of a pun in Heb. or Aram. have failed because there is no word resembling ᵓ*Asᵉnat* which could mean "refuge"; but the author may have been familiar with an etymology of the name as meaning "ruin" (cf. Heb. ᵓ*āsōn* "calamity") which was known to Jerome and others (Burchard, *Untersuchungen*, pp. 92–95).

m. The reading "trusting . . . God": (E) Arm. (L1 436); omit *a* G *d* 435&; destroyed Syr.; gaps FW *c* Slav. Ngr.

n. Cf. e.g. Ps 17:8; 61:5; 63:8.

o. Lit. "in your wall." Gk. *teichos* may also mean "fortress."

p. Gk. *hoi proskeimenoi tō Theō* is a standing epithet of the proselytes; cf. e.g. Isa 56:6.

(7) of Repentance. For Repentance[q] is in the heavens, an exceedingly beautiful and good daughter of the Most High. And she herself entreats[r] the Most High God for you at all times[s] and for all who repent in the name of the Most High God, because he is (the) father of Repentance. And she herself is guardian of all virgins,[t] and loves you very much, and is beseeching the Most High for you at all times[s] and for all who repent she prepared a place of rest in the heavens.[u] And she will renew all who repent, and wait on them herself

8 (8) for ever (and) ever. •And Repentance is exceedingly beautiful, a virgin pure and laughing[v] always, and she is gentle and meek. And, therefore, the Most High Father loves her,[w] and all the angels stand in awe of her. And I, too, love her exceedingly, because she is also my sister.[x] And because she loves you virgins, I love you, too.

9 (9)   "And behold, I am going away to Joseph and will tell him about you everything I have to say. And Joseph will come to you today, and see you, and rejoice over you, and love you, and he will be your bridegroom, and you will be a bride for him for ever (and) ever.

10 (10) And now listen to me, Aseneth, chaste virgin, and dress in your wedding robe, the ancient and first[y] robe which is laid up in your chamber since eternity, and put around you all your

(11) wedding ornaments, and adorn yourself as a good bride, and go meet Joseph. For behold, he himself is coming to you today, and he will see you and rejoice."

Aseneth tries to ascertain the heavenly man's name

11 (12)   And when the man had finished speaking these words,[z] Aseneth rejoiced exceedingly with great joy about all these words and fell down at his feet and prostrated himself face

12 (13) down to the ground before him, and said to him, •"Blessed be the Lord your God the Most High who sent you out to rescue me from the darkness and to bring me up from the

12x foundations of the abyss,"[a2] and blessed be your name forever.[b2] •What[c2] is your name, Lord; tell me in order that I may praise and glorify you for ever (and) ever."[d2] And the man said to her, "Why do you seek this, my name, Aseneth? My name is in the heavens in the book of the Most High, written by the finger of God in the beginning of the book before all (the others), because I am chief of the house of the Most High. And all names written in the book of the Most High are unspeakable, and man is not allowed to pronounce nor hear them in this world, because those names are exceedingly great and wonderful and laudable."

Aseneth invites the heavenly man to take food. The mysterious honeycomb which is bread of life

13   And Aseneth said, "If I have found favor in your sight,[e2] Lord, and will know that you will do all your words that you have spoken to me, let your maidservant speak before you."

q. Angels representing, or presiding over, human virtues are well known in Judaism. 1En 40:9 calls the angel of repentance Phanuel; he is anonymous in ShepHerm Vision 5.8; Clement of Alexandria, *Quis dives salv.*, 42:18; *metanoia* (see 9:2) is personified also in TGad 5:7f. In the romances, cf. Achilles Tatius 6.10.4; Apuleius 6.8.3; 6.9.2; 6.24.4.

r. Angels (Aptowitzer, *HUCA* 1 [1924] 292) and the patriarchs (e.g. Philo, *Praem*, 166) were regarded as intercessors. In Heb, Christ, the heavenly highpriest, fulfills this office.

s. Lit. "every hour." Or does this mean "at every regular hour (of prayer)"?

t. I.e. all nations (Aptowitzer, *HUCA* 1 [1924] 293f.), or all individuals who are prepared for conversion through virginity (see 7:7).

u. Cf. Jn 14:2f.; G. Fischer, *Wohnungen*. On "rest" see 8:9 and Intro. Witness *d* (gap Slav.) has a "heavenly bridal chamber" instead, which may be gnostic (GPhil; cf. Philonenko, *Joseph et Aséneth*, p. 184).

v. Cf. Lk 15:7, 10.

w. As he loves Wisdom (WisSol 8:3). Cf. Jn 10:17.

x. Repentance and Michael seem to form a team.

She is his assistant in charge of everything preparatory to a proselyte's acceptance, which is then ratified by him.

y. The reading "and first": AP *c* (*d*) L2; omit EFW; destroyed Syr.; gaps Q G Arm. L1 Slav. Ngr. Also cf. 18:5; Lk 15:22; Burchard, *ZNW* 61 (1970) 160.

z. Cf. e.g. Mt 7:28.

a2. The reading "into the light": added AP *d;* omit FGW *c* Arm. L1 L2 Ngr.; destroyed Syr.; gaps Q E Slav. Perhaps this should be adopted into the text. On vs. 12 cf. further Melito of Sardis, *Passover Homily*, 68; *Vita Aesopi* G, 5. On "darkness" cf. Ps 107:14; Isa 42:7; Col 1:13, on "abyss" cf. above 12:11.

b2. Also 19:8; cf. Ps 72:19.

c2. "What . . . said" (*b c* Arm. L1 L2 Ngr. Br); omit *a d;* destroyed Syr.; gap Slav. Gk. with full apparatus in Burchard, *Untersuchungen*, pp. 68–73. On Aseneth's demand cf. e.g. Gen 32:30; Judg 13:6, 16f.; *LAB* 42:10; TLevi 5:5f.; Berger, *Auferstehung*, pp. 156, 443f., nn. 56–60.

d2. Same motivation in Judg 13:17; TLevi 5:5; Berger, *Auferstehung*, p. 444, n. 59.

e2. Traditional phrase, e.g. Gen 47:29; Esth 5:8; 7:3; 8:5.

14 And the man said to her, "Speak (up)." And Aseneth stretched out her right hand and put
(14) it on his knees[f2] and said to him, "I beg you, Lord, sit down a little on this bed, because
this bed is pure and undefiled, and a man or woman never sat on it. And I will set a table
before you, and bring you bread and you will eat, and bring you from my storeroom old
and good wine, the exhalation of which[g2] will go up till heaven, and you will drink from
15 it. And after this you will go out (on) your way." •And the man said to her, "Hurry and
bring (it) quickly."

1 (1) **16** And Aseneth hurried and set a new[a] table before him and went to provide bread for
2 (2) him. And the man said to her, "Bring me also a honeycomb."[b] •And Aseneth stood still
3 (3) and was distressed,[c] because she did not have a honeycomb in her storeroom. •And the
4 man said to her, "Why do you stand still?" •And Aseneth said, "I will send a boy to the
suburb, because the field which is our inheritance is close,[d] and he will quickly bring you
5 a honeycomb from there, and I will set (it) before you, Lord." •And the man said to her,
"Proceed and enter your storeroom, and you will find a honeycomb lying upon the table.
6 Pick it up and bring (it) here." •And Aseneth said, "Lord; a honeycomb is not in my
7 storeroom." •And the man said, "Proceed and you will find (one)."

8 (4)　　　And Aseneth entered her storeroom and found a honeycomb lying on the table. And the
comb was big and white as snow and full of honey. And that honey was like dew from[e]
9 heaven and its exhalation like breath of life.[f] •And Aseneth wondered and said in herself,
Did then this comb come out of the man's mouth, because its exhalation is like the breath
10 (5) of this man's mouth?[g] •And Aseneth took that comb and brought it to the man, and put it
on the table which she had prepared before him.[h]

　　　And the man said to her, "How is it that you said that a honeycomb is not in my
11 (6) storeroom? And behold, you have brought a wonderful honeycomb." •And Aseneth was
afraid and said, "Lord, I did not have a honeycomb in my storeroom at any time, but you
spoke and it came into being.[i] Surely this came out of your mouth, because its exhalation
is like breath of your mouth."

12,13 (7)　　　And the man smiled at Aseneth's understanding,[j] •and called her to himself, and stretched
out his right hand, and grasped her head and shook her head with his right hand. And
Aseneth was afraid of the man's hand, because sparks shot forth from his hand as from
bubbling (melted)[k] iron. And Aseneth looked, gazing with her eyes at the man's hand.
14 And the man saw (it) and smiled and said, "Happy are you,[l] Aseneth, because the ineffable

f2. "And Aseneth . . . knees" (c Arm. L1 436);
omit a G 435&; destroyed Syr.; gaps rest. Gk. text
with full apparatus in Burchard, *Untersuchungen*,
pp. 74–76. On the invitation cf. Gen 18:1–5; Judg
13:15f.; 1Sam 28:22f.; *Vita Aesopi* G, 4. This
narrative does not represent a magic rite to entice
a *daimōn parhedros* (against Philonenko, *Joseph
et Aséneth*, p. 97).

g2. Lit. "of which its exhalation"; cf. 1Clem
21:9 (so it is probably not a Semitism).

16 a. Gk. *kainēn* FG c L1 L2; "most handsome"
Ngr.; "empty (*kenēn*, pronounced like *kainēn*)"
AP Arm. W; omit Q; destroyed Syr.; gaps E d
Rum.

b. Lit. "comb of honey (*kērion melitos*)" or
"of bee (*melissēs*)"; also in vss. 2–11. Witnesses
a d L1 generally support the former variant, b c
Arm. L2 (Ngr.) the latter; but there are exceptions.
The rendering "honeycomb" may do justice to
both variants, as "bee" perhaps is used in metonymy for "honey."

c. "And Aseneth . . . distressed": many variants. Ngr. (435&) prefix "And as Aseneth heard
(this)," which is in JosAsen's style.

d. Cf. Chariton 1.13.5.

e. The reading "third": added Syr. 436 (see vs.

14); gaps G d L1 Ngr.; omit rest.

f. Both "exhalation" and "breath" represent
Gk. *pnoē*. A pun; see also vss. 9,11. The description
shows that the comb represents manna (cf. e.g. Ex
16:14, 31; WisSol 19:21; SibOr 3.746); see further
vs. 14. Generally see R. Meyer, "*manna*," *TDNT*,
vol. 4, 462–66; B. J. Malina, *The Palestinian
Manna Tradition* (AGAJU 7; Leiden, 1968).

g. The reading "because . . . mouth": (FW
Syr. Arm. L1 L2); omit a c Ngr.; gaps EG d. This
could be a statement, rather than a question.

h. The reading "which . . . him": (Arm. Syr.
436); omit a c Ngr.; gaps b d L1 435&.

i. The reading "you . . . being": FW Arm.
Syr. (L1) 436 (Ngr.); "as you said, so (AP only)
it came into being" a d; "you however spoke" c;
gaps EG 435&. "Came into being (*gegone*)" might
also be rendered "happened."

j. Also see vs. 14. A smiling angel; cf. e.g.
ShepHerm Vision 3.8.2.

k. Gk. *kochlazontos* (or *ka-*). Erroneously *och-
lazontos*, "crowding," Bat ("redhot" Br, on the
strength of Syr. Arm.). Batiffol's error induced
Riessler (*TQ* 103 [1922] 2) to suggest a confusion
of Heb. *ṣûq* I, "to pour" with *ṣûq* II, "to be
narrow"; hence his translation "*geschmolznem*."

l. Cf. e.g. Mt 16:17.

mysteries[m] of the Most High have been revealed to you, and happy (are) all who attach themselves to the Lord God in repentance, because they will eat from this comb. For this
(8) comb is (full of the) spirit of life. And the bees of the paradise of delight[n] have made this from the dew of the roses of life that are in the paradise of God. And all the angels of God eat of it and all the chosen of God and all the sons of the Most High,[o] because this is a comb of life, and everyone who eats of it will not die for ever (and) ever."

15 (9)   And the man stretched out his right hand and broke a small portion off the comb, and he himself ate and what was left he put with his hand into Aseneth's mouth, and[p] said to her,
16 "Eat." And she ate. •And the man said to Aseneth, "Behold, you have eaten bread of life, and drunk a cup of immortality, and been anointed with ointment of incorruptibility. Behold, from today your flesh[q] (will) flourish[r] like flowers of life from the ground[s] of the Most High, and your bones will grow strong[t] like the cedars of the paradise of delight of God, and untiring powers will embrace you, and your youth will not see old age, and your beauty will not fail for ever.[u] And you shall be like a walled mother-city of[v] all who take
16x refuge with the name of the Lord God, the king of the ages." •And the man stretched out his right hand and touched the comb where[w] he had broken off (a portion), and it was restored and filled up, and at once it became whole as it was in the beginning.

The heavenly man marks the comb with a cross and makes bees, which encircle Aseneth, rise from it

17 (10)   And[x] again the man stretched out his right hand and put his (fore)finger on the edge of the comb looking east and drew it over the edge looking west, and the way[y] of his finger
(11) became like blood. And he stretched out his hand the second time and put his finger on the edge of the comb looking north and drew it over to the edge looking south, and the way of
17x (12) his finger became like blood. •And Aseneth stood at his left (hand) and watched everything that the man was doing.
17y (13)   And the man said to the comb, "Come."[z] •And bees rose from the cells of that comb, and the cells were innumerable, ten thousand (times) ten thousand and thousands upon

m. The reading "the ineffable mysteries": AP; "the mysteries" Q F 435&; "the hidden (things)" G Syr. Arm.; "the ineffable (things)" E c d 436; gaps W (L1) Ngr. Split tradition except in AP, or is that reading conflate? Anyway, "mysteries" should be retained. The revelation concerns the origin of the honeycomb as recognized in vs. 11 and its nature as described presently, rather than God's mysteries in general.

n. LXX translation of "Garden of Eden," e.g. Gen 3:23. It is in the third heaven, according to ApMos 37:5; 3Bar 4:8; 3En 8:1; there are also the manna mills (b. Ḥag 12b). Manna is "bread of (or from) heaven," e.g. Neh 9:15; Ps 105:40.

o. "The chosen of God" (cf. e.g. Tob 8:15 BA; 1En 39:1; 61:10; 1Tim 5:21) and "the sons of the Most High" (e.g. Ps 89:7; see Intro.) might be angels or the dead just in paradise, both of which are credited with eating manna (Ps 75:25; WisSol 16:20; LAB 19:5; Meyer, TDNT 4, 462–66), or God's children on earth (17:6; 19:8). Maybe JosAsen does not draw a sharp line between angels and men, God's elect residing on earth and in heaven.

p. The reading from "and" to the end of vs. 16x (all); except omit d; gap W.

q. Lit. plural.

r. Gk. bryousi (present tense): APG c Syr. Br Rie; future Arm. (L1) L2; gaps rest. Gk. bryein (never LXX, NT only Jas 3:11) does not seem to occur in the future tense. It can be either transitive (Br Rie) or intransitive (cf. parallel clause about the bones). Comparison of the well-being of persons

to flourishing plants is traditional, e.g. Pss 1:3; 92:13–15; Jer 17:8; below 18:9. Flourishing may also symbolize prolific posterity (cf. TSim 6:2; Targum Isa 53:2).

s. Gk. [apo tēs] gēs G Syr. Arm. 436; "garden" 435&; "spring (pegēs)" AP c; gaps rest. "Ground" (cf. 18:9) makes a good parallelism with "paradise," but "spring" makes sense too.

t. Lit. "fat." Cf. Isa 58:11; 66:14.

u. Cf. Apuleius 11.6.5f. The fulfillment of this begins in 18:9.

v. FG are the only Gk. witnesses from here down to vs. 16x end.

w. Or "of which."

x. Vs. 17 (G d Syr. Arm. L1 435& Br, also Rie, who put vss. 17–17x first half after vs. 23 as vss. 24f. on the strength of BDI); omit F; gaps EW 436 Ngr.; a c have "But the angel whetted the comb" for vss. 17–17x. Br gives an idea how divergent the evidence is. Vs. 17 is the introduction to the following verses, rather than an episode by itself. So the cruciform mark is preparatory to, and perhaps causal of, the appearance of the bees in vs. 17y. See further vs. 23.

y. Gk. hē hodos D (Syr.) L1 (435&) (Br Rie Phil]; "the appearance (to eidos)" B Arm. Slav.; omit G ("the hand" for "of his finger"); gaps rest. Same situation at the second occurrence of "the way" (G gap too).

z. "And . . . come" (FG Syr. Arm. L1 Ngr.); omit d Br; gaps rest. In G and L1 the man's command is addressed to Aseneth.

18 thousands.ᵃ² • And the bees were white as snow, and their wings like purple and like violet
and like scarlet (stuff) and like gold-woven linen cloaks,ᵇ² and golden diadems (were) on
19 (14) their heads, and they had sharp stings, and they would not injure anyone.ᶜ² • And all those
bees encircled Aseneth from feet to head.

And other bees were great and chosen like their queens,ᵈ² and they rose from the damaged
part of the combᵉ² and encircled Aseneth's mouth, and made upon her mouth and her lips
20 a comb similar to the comb which was lying before the man.ᶠ² • And all thoseᵍ² bees ate of
(15) the comb which was on Aseneth's mouth. And the man said to the bees, "Go off to your
21,22(16) place." • And all the bees rose and flew and went away into heaven. • And those who wanted
(17) to injure Aseneth fell to the ground and died. And the man stretched out his staff over the
23 dead bees and said to them, "Rise you, too, and go away to your place." • And the bees
who had died rose and went into the court adjoining Aseneth's house and sought shelter on
the fruit-bearing trees.ʰ²

1 (1) **17** And the man said to Aseneth, "Have you seen this thing?"ᵃ And she said, "Yes,
2 (2) Lord, I have seen all these (things)." • And the man said to her, "So will be all my words
3 (3) which I have spoken to you today." • And the man for the third time stretched out his right
hand, and touched the damaged partᵇ of the comb, and at once fire went up from the table
4 and consumedᶜ the comb, but the table it did not injure. • And much fragrance came forth
from the burning of the comb, and filled the chamber.ᵈ

The heavenly man blesses Aseneth's seven virgins

(4)   And Aseneth said to the man, "Lord, with me are seven virgins ministering to me,
fostered with me from my childhood, born with me in one night, and I love them as my

a2. Cf. Dan 7:10; ApZeph 4:4; 13:1; 1En 40:1;
60:1; 71:8; Rev 5:11; 1Clem 34:6. Is there a
connection with Deut 33:17? The translations
"(times)" and "upon" are lit. "of." Group c ends
with the first "ten thousand." Vs. 17y is 17 in Rie
(for the beginning see our vs. 17).

b2. See 2:8.

c2. For a contrast, cf. Rev 9:7–10.

d2. Beehives were regarded as being governed
by kings in antiquity, not queens. The author may
have had in mind something like "as befits queens,"
but there is a "queen of the bees" in Epictetus,
Diss., 3.22.99.

e2. The reading "from . . . comb": (a FG Syr.
Arm.); gaps rest. The translation "damaged part"
is dubious; it is not in a, and the other witnesses
are not clear; besides, the comb is not broken at
this moment (vs. 16). However, 17:3 seems to
suppose that it is damaged somehow; this would
seem to refer back to the angel's manipulations in
vs. 17. If not, we may have to translate "tablet"
or "cells" in vs. 19.

f2. Philonenko (*Joseph et Aséneth*, p. 189) has
drawn attention to the vagrant legend that a swarm
of bees descended on Pindar, Plato, Ambrose and
others, while in their cradles, symbolizing their
future inspiration and eloquence (more on this in
I. Opelt, "Das Bienenwunder in der Ambrosius-
biographie des Paulinus von Mailand," *VC* 22
[1968] 38–44). Whatever can be made of this
tradition, the meaning of vs. 19 surely is not to
credit Aseneth with poetic or theological inspiration, since she is nowhere cast in the role of a
speaker. H. M. I. Gevaryahu, in a conversation,
suggested some connection with the Old Egyptian
mouth-opening ritual, believed to infuse the breath
of life into the statues of the gods. But it is not
said at this point that Aseneth ate from the comb,
and besides honey along with butter was also needed

for the ritual. See further vs. 23.

g2. Witnesses AP; omit F (Syr. 435&); gaps
rest. It is not clear whether all bees or just the big
ones eat. On vss. 20–22 cf. Eth. (see Intro.).

h2. Cf. Mk 4:32 parallel. The bees episode (vss.
17–23 [see especially vs. 17]) is a confirmation
miracle as e.g. 2Kgs 20:8–11; it offers proof that
all promises of the angel will be fulfilled (17:1f.).
But the episode has not yet been interpreted satisfactorily. Since the bees of paradise have been
mentioned as producers of the comb in vs. 14, the
bees in vss. 17y–23 are perhaps best explained as
their like, rather than an allegorical representation
of some sort. Thus vss. 19–21 could prove that
honey such as Aseneth has eaten *is* made by the
bees of paradise and remains available through her
(note the correspondence of vs. 19b with vss. 9
and 11b). Admittedly it is not easy to pursue this
line in vss. 22f., unless we are to understand that
some of the paradisiac honey-makers will remain
with Aseneth for good (cf. Ngr. in 17:2; but why
the vicious ones?) or that natural bees are a "fallen"
variety of the heavenly ones. If allegory was
intended (cf. also vs. 9) we should perhaps equate
the bees to the Israelites, Aseneth's new compatriots, rather than to the virgins, the nations or the
like (on bee symbolism generally, cf. W. Telfer,
" 'Bees' in Clement of Alexandria," *JTS* 28 [1926–
27] 167–78). The aggressive ones would then
anticipate Dan and Gad as portrayed in chs. 22–
29. But why should they end up in Aseneth's park?
Is it because they will eventually be forgiven?

17 a. Lit. "word (*rēma*)"; a biblicism. Cf. e.g.
Lk 2:15. See also 23:11.

b. Lit. "blow, injury (*plēgē*)" AP (Syr. Arm.);
omit Q G d Ll 435&; gaps rest. See 16:19.

c. Cf. Judg 6:21.

d. Cf. Jn 12:3.

5 (5) sisters. I will call them, and you will bless them as you have blessed me, too." •And the
6 man said, "Call them." •And Aseneth called the seven virgins and stood them before the
man. And the man blessed them and said, "May the Lord God the Most High bless you.
And you shall be seven pillars of the City of Refuge,ᵉ and all the fellow inhabitantsᶠ of the
chosen of that city will rest upon you for ever (and) ever."

The heavenly man departs

7 (6), 8 And the man said to Aseneth, "Put this table away." •And Aseneth turned to put the
table away, and at once the man went awayᵍ out of her sight.ʰ And Aseneth saw (something)
like a chariot of four horses traveling into heaven toward (the) east. Andⁱ the chariot was
like a flame of fire, and the horses like lightning. And the man was standing on that chariot.ʲ
9 And Aseneth said, "(What a) foolish and bold (woman) I (am), because I have spoken
with frankness and said that a man came into my chamber from heaven; and I did not know
that (a) godᵏ came to me. And behold, now he is traveling (back) into heaven to his place."
10 (7) And she said in herself, Be gracious, Lord, to your slave, and spare your maidservant,
because I have spoken boldly before you all my words in ignorance.

IV. JOSEPH'S AND ASENETH'S MARRIAGE

Joseph's second visit is announced. Aseneth's foster-father notices her fallen face

1 (1) **18** And as Aseneth was still saying these things to herself, behold, a young man from
Pentephres'ᵃ servant staff rushed in and said, "Behold, Joseph the Powerful One of God is
coming to us today. For a forerunner of his is standing at the gates of our court."ᵇ
2 (2) And Aseneth hurried and called her foster-father, the (steward) of her house,ᶜ and said to
him, "Hurry and make the house ready and prepare a good dinner, because Joseph the
3 Powerful One of God is coming to us today." •Andᵈ her foster-father saw her, and behold,
her face had fallen from the affliction and the weeping and the fasting of the seven days,
and he was distressed and wept, and he took her right hand and kissed it and said, "What
4 have you, my child,ᵉ because your face has fallen so (much)?" •And Aseneth said to him,
"My head is stricken with heavy pain, and the sleep kept away from my eyes,ᶠ and therefore
5 my face has fallen."ᵍ •And her foster-father went away and prepared the house and the
dinner.

e. The reading "seven . . . Refuge": (E Syr.
Arm.) L1 (prefixes "like"; Batiffol's edition omits
"seven") 435&; "pillars (seven pillars Rie) of
refuge of seven cities" a (Bat marks "pillars of
refuge" off as illegible in A); gaps rest. Cf. Prov
9:1; Philo, *Quaes Ex*, 1.21 on 12:17; Gal 2:9; Rev
3:12; 1Clem 5:2; ShepHerm Vision 3.8.2. See
further Intro.
f. Gk. *hai synoikoi* (fem.), i.e. "women im-
migrants."
g. The reading "went away": (AP EFW d Syr.
L1 436); "became invisible" Q G Arm. 435&?
Slav.? Ngr. (also 661), also the secondary finale
of c (Burchard, *NTS* 24 [1977] 81).
h. Lit. "eyes." Cf. Judg 6:21.
i. "And" to end of vs. 9 (all); except omit d;
gap E.
j. Cf. Elijah's ascension 2Kgs 2:11; Berger,
Auferstehung, pp. 569f., n. 416. Vss. 8–10 also
stand in the tradition of Judg 6:21f.; 13:20–22;
Berger, *Auferstehung*, pp. 156f., 444–47, nn. 61–
69. On angels' disappearances generally, cf. Berger, *Auferstehung*, pp. 170–72, 471–78, nn. 147–
58.
k. The reading "(a) god": AP; with article, i.e.
"God" Q; "an angel of the Lord" Arm. (L1
435&); ambiguous Syr. ("God from heaven"
Brooks' edition) 436; gaps rest. See also at 22:3.

18 a. Witnesses EFW Syr. Arm. L1 436 (Ngr.)
Br (in footnote); "P. her father's" G; "her father's" 435&; "Joseph's" a d.
b. "For . . . court" (b Syr. Arm. L1 L2); omit
a d Ngr.(?).
c. The reading "her foster father . . . house":
FW (Syr. Arm.) 436; "her foster father" G Ngr.
(adding "or, her grandfather"); "the (steward) of
her house" a E d 435&; gap L1. The man who is
probably not identical with Pentephres' steward
(3:4) reappears in vss. 3, 5, 7, 11 as "her foster-
father" (FGW Syr. Arm. 436 Ngr., if present) or
"the (steward) of her house" (a, if present; 435&);
never again in d; gap L1. E is lacking in vss. 3,
5, 7, but has both titles in vs. 11. Maybe both
titles were there each time. "Foster-father (*tropheus*)" might also be rendered "personal attendant," but he seems to be more than that (vs. 3).
d. "And" . . . to "hurried and" in vs. 5 (all);
except "And Aseneth" d; gap L1.
e. The reading "my child": G Ngr. (Syr.);
"child" FW Arm.; "my mistress" a; "mistress"
436; "dearest" 435&; gaps E d L1.
f. Cf. e.g. Gen 31:40; 1Mac 6:10.
g. The reading "and . . . fallen": (FGW Arm.
L2 Ngr.); omit a Syr.; gaps E d L1.

Aseneth dresses as a bride and is transformed to heavenly beauty

(3)   And Aseneth remembered the man (from heaven) and his commandment, 'and she hurried and entered her second chamber where the chests (containing) her ornaments were, and opened her big coffer and brought out her first robe, (the one) of wedding, like lightning

6 (4) in appearance, and dressed in it. •And she girded a golden and royal girdle around (herself)

(5) which was (made) of precious stones. And she put golden bracelets on her fingers and on her feet golden buskins,[h] and precious ornaments she put around her neck in which innumerable costly (and) precious stones were fastened,[i] and a golden crown she put on her head, and on that crown, in front on her brow, was a big sapphire[j] stone, and around the

(6) big stone were six costly stones. And with a veil she covered her head like a bride, and she took a scepter in her hand.[k]

7   And Aseneth remembered the words of her foster-father, because he had said to her, "Your face has fallen." And she sighed and was much distressed and said, "Woe is me,

8 (7) the humble, because my face has fallen. Joseph will see me and despise me." •And she said to her foster-sister,[l] "Bring me pure water from the spring,[m] and I will wash my face."

9 And she brought her pure water from the spring and poured it into the basin.[n] And Aseneth leaned (over) to wash her face and saw her face in the water.[o] And it was like the sun[p] and her eyes (were) like a rising morning star, and[q] her cheeks like fields of the Most High,[r] and on her cheeks (there was) red (color) like a son of man's blood,[s] and her lips (were) like a rose of life[t] coming out of its foliage, and her teeth like fighting men lined up for a fight,[u] and the hair of her head (was) like a vine in the paradise of God prospering in its fruits,[v] and her neck like an all-variegated cypress,[w] and her breasts (were) like the mountains of the Most High God.[x]

10   And when Aseneth saw herself in the water, she was amazed at the sight and rejoiced with great joy, and did not wash her face, for she said, "Perhaps I (will) wash off this

11 great beauty." •And her foster-father came to say to her, "Everything is prepared as you have commanded." And when he saw her he was alarmed and stood speechless for a long (time),[y] and was filled with great fear[z] and fell at her feet and said, "What is this, my

h. See 3:6.

i. The reading "in . . . fastened": (FW Syr. Arm. L2 Ngr.); omit AP *d;* gaps Q EG L1 Slav.

j. Same word as "violet"; see 2:8. Cf. Rev 21:20.

k. The reading "like . . . hand": (GFW Syr. Arm. L2); omit AP; gaps Q E *d* L1 Ngr. ("bride" is there).

l. The reading "her foster-sister": FW Arm. L2; "her maidservant" AP B Phil (D); "one of the virgins her companions" Syr.; "the virgins" G; gaps rest. See 10:4.

m. See 2:12. In a more hellenized environment she would doubtless have ordered a bath.

n. The reading "and . . . basin": details uncertain. Some witnesses also mention a bowl (*kogchē*) such as was used for drawing water. It may belong in the text.

o. Does this scene reflect magical practice involving the mirror effect of water in a basin (Philonenko, *Joseph et Aséneth,* p. 193)? Probably not, because the text neither says that Aseneth had anything but washing in mind, nor that she was transformed because she looked into the water. Aseneth's sudden beauty is in partial fulfillment of 16:16. She comes close to being an angelic creature (see 20:6; cf. Acts 6:15; 2Cor 3:18). The description offers many variants. It is reminiscent of the Song of Songs, the influence of which seems to have grown stronger in the MS tradition.

p. Cf. e.g. Mt 17:2; Rev 1:16; 10:1.

q. The reading "and" to the end of vs. 11: (all); except omit *d;* gaps L1 Slav.

r. The reading "fields of the Most High": FW Syr. (cf. Song 5:13); "furrows even and beautiful" Arm.; "a star of heaven" A; "the stars of the heaven" P; gaps rest.

s. The reading "and . . . blood": (F Syr. Arm. 436); omit AP W; gaps rest. "Son of man" is a Semitism meaning no more (in this instance) than "a man" (cf. e.g. Jdt 8:16; Ps 8:5; Sir 17:30; TJos 2:5). It is in F Syr. 436 only; "parts of a pomegranate" Arm. (cf. Song 4:3?).

t. The reading "of life": FW Syr. L2; "flowering" Arm.; "being red" AP Eth. (see Intro.); gaps rest.

u. The reading "coming . . . fight": (Syr. Arm. L2); "which comes forth from its leaves" Eth. (see Intro.); omit AP FW; gaps rest. Cf. Achilles Tatius 1.4.3 (see Intro.).

v. The paradise tree Gen 2:17; 3:3, cf. ApAb 23:5f.

w. The reading "all-variegated cypress": A (cf. Ps 92:12f.; Ezek 31:8f.); "much-variegated vine" P (cf. preceding clause); "beautiful tower" Arm. (cf. Song 4:4; 7:5); "isles of rest of angels that (are) in heaven" Syr.; "hill of (the) heavens" 436; gaps rest. The original text is obscure.

x. The reading "and . . . God": (Syr. Arm. 436); omit AP; gaps rest. On Arm. cf. Song 2:17; 8:14.

y. A common reaction; cf. e.g. Chariton 3.9.2; 4.1.9; 5.3.9; Apuleius 11.14.1.

z. The reading "he was . . . fear": (FW Syr. Arm. L2); "he was much filled with fear and was trembling for a long time" AP; "he was alarmed"

mistress, and what is this great and wonderful beauty?"[a2] At last the Lord God of heaven has chosen you as a bride for his firstborn son, Joseph?"[b2]

Joseph arrives and acknowledges Aseneth

1 (1) **19** And while they were still speaking this (way)[a] a boy came and said to Aseneth,
2 "Behold, Joseph is standing at the doors of our court." •And Aseneth hurried and went down the stairs from the upper floor with the seven virgins to meet Joseph and stood in the
3 entrance of the house. •And Joseph entered the court and the gates were closed, and all strangers remained outside.
4 (2) And Aseneth went out of the entrance to meet Joseph, and Joseph saw her and was
5 amazed at her beauty, and said to her, "Who[b] are you? Quickly tell me." •And she said to him, "I am your maidservant Aseneth, and all the idols I have thrown away from me and they were destroyed. And a man came to me from heaven today, and gave me bread of life and I ate, and a cup of blessing and I drank. And he said to me, 'I have given[c] you for a bride to Joseph today, and he himself will be your bridegroom for ever (and) ever.' And he said to me, 'Your name will no longer be called Aseneth, but your name will be called City of Refuge and the Lord God will reign as king over many nations for ever,[d]
6 because in you many nations will take refuge with the Lord God, the Most High.' •And the man said to me, 'I will also go to Joseph and speak into his ears[e] concerning you what
7 I have to say.' •And now, you know, my Lord, whether that man has come to you and spoken to you concerning me."
8 And Joseph said to Aseneth, "Blessed are you by the Most High God, and blessed (is)[f] your name for ever, because the Lord God founded your walls in the highest, and your walls (are) adamantine walls of life,[g] because the sons of the living God[h] will dwell in your
9 City of Refuge, and the Lord God will reign as king over them for ever and ever. •For this man came to me today and spoke to me words such as these concerning you. And now, come to me, chaste virgin, and why do you stand far away from me?"[i]
10 (3) And Joseph stretched out his hands and called Aseneth by a wink of his eyes.[j] And Aseneth also stretched out her hands and ran up to Joseph and fell on his breast.[k] And Joseph put his arms around her, and Aseneth (put hers) around Joseph, and they kissed
11 each other for a long time and both came to life in their spirit.[l] •And Joseph kissed Aseneth and gave her spirit of life, and he kissed her the second time and gave her spirit of wisdom, and he kissed her the third time and gave her spirit of truth.[m]

G; "he was filled with fear" Q; paraphrastic E; gaps *d* L1 Ngr. Perhaps the trembling should go into the text on the assumption of split tradition.

a2. Witnesses *a* G Arm. Ngr.; "virtue" FW Syr. L2; "grace" E; gaps *d* L1.

b2. The reading "his firstborn son, Joseph" is a reconstruction from "his firstborn son" F Syr. L2; "his son Joseph" A; "Joseph" PQ Arm.; "the most beautiful Joseph" G; gaps rest. Doubtful.

19 a. Traditional formula of transition, e.g. 1Sam 17:23; Job 1:16–18; Mt 9:18; Mk 5:35. On ch. 19 cf. Acts 9:10–17; Apuleius 11.22.4–6; 11.23.1,6; 11.27.7–9. Joseph's role is similar to that of Ananias in Acts 9:10–17 and of the head priest of Isis to whom Lucius rushes after having been told in a dream that the day of his initiation had approached, only to find him informed in the same manner. On the motif of double dreams or visions cf. Acts 9:10–12 and the commentaries thereon.

b. "Who" to end of vs. 9 (all); except "Come to me, chaste virgin, because I was given good news about you from heaven who (masc.!) said to me all the (things) about you" *d* ("from . . . you" omit D); gap Slav. This is a manifest case of condensation in *d* with a patent seam before "who."

c. See 15:2.

d. Cf. e.g. Pss 10:16 (9:37 LXX); 146:10; WisSol 3:8; Rev 11:15. Cf. also vs. 8.

e. Cf. also 24:2. The image is traditional, e.g. Gen 20:8; Deut 31:28; ShepHerm Vision 3.8.11; 4.3.6. The phrase expresses audibility, rather than furtiveness.

f. Or "blessed (it will be)," i.e. "it will be praised" (Berger, *Auferstehung*, p. 563, n. 401; cf. Mk 14:9 parallel)? Also 15:12.

g. The reading "in . . . life": (G Syr. Arm. L2); omit AP; gaps rest.

h. Cf. Hos 2:1.

i. On vss. 8f. cf. Apuleius 11.22.4–6.

j. The reading "by . . . eyes": Syr. Arm. L2 (Ngr.); gaps rest. See next note.

k. The reading "and called . . . breast": (*b* Syr. Arm. L2 Ngr.); omit *a* D L1 Phil; gaps B Slav.

l. I.e. "they cheered up"; cf. e.g. Gen 45:27; Jub 31:6; 43:24. This verse seems to contain the first indubitable occurrence of *anazan* besides Lk 15:24 and Rom 7:9.

m. That life, soul, spirit, or the like can be transferred or exchanged (or taken away, for that matter) by a kiss is a very old idea underlying many kinds of human behavior and ritual, and expressed in a host of texts, both religious and profane (e.g. Gen 2:7; Jn 20:22; OdesSol 28:6f.; Xenophon of Ephesus 1.9.6); in the way of ritual, cf. e.g. the "holy kiss" of the early Church 1Cor 16:20, etc., and the Valentinian "Sacrament of the Bridal Chamber" in GPhil; see generally, I. Löw,

1 **20** And they embraced each other for a long time and interlocked their hands like bonds.[a]

Aseneth leads Joseph into the house and washes his feet

(1)   And Aseneth said to Joseph, "Come, my Lord, and enter our[b] house, because I have
2 prepared our[c] house and made a great dinner." •And she grasped his right hand and led
(2) him into her[d] house and 'seated him on Pentephres['] her father's throne. And she brought
3 water to wash his feet.[f] •And Joseph said, "Let one of the virgins come and wash my
4 (3) feet." •And Aseneth said to him, "No, my Lord, because you are my lord from now on,
and I (am) your maidservant. And why do you say this (that) another virgin (is) to wash
your feet? For your feet are my feet, and your hands are my hands, and your soul my soul,[g]
5 and your feet another (woman) will never wash."[h] •And she urged him and washed his
feet. And Joseph looked at her hands, and they were like hands of life, and her fingers fine
(4) like (the) fingers of a fast-writing scribe.[i] And after this Joseph grasped her right hand and
kissed it,[j] and Aseneth kissed his head and sat at his right (hand).

Pentephres proposes to give a wedding feast, but Joseph prefers Pharaoh

6 (5)   And her father and mother and his[k] whole family came from the field which was their
inheritance.[l] And they saw Aseneth like (the) appearance of light, and her beauty was like
heavenly beauty.[m] And they saw her sitting with Joseph and dressed in a wedding garment.[n]
7 And they were amazed at her beauty and rejoiced[o] and gave glory to God who gives life to
8 the dead.[p] •And after this they ate and drank and celebrated.[q]

"Der Kuss," *MGWJ* 65 (1921) 253–76, 323–49;
K. Thraede, "Ursprünge und Formen des 'Heiligen
Kusses' in frühen Christentum," *JAC* 11–12 (1968–
69) 124–80; G. Stählin, "*phileō* etc.," *TDNT* 9,
113–71. Joseph's kiss may go back to an erotic
motif, if only in a spiritualized form (cf. Xenophon
1.9.6). He imparts to Aseneth the spirit which he
himself possesses; it is not sent down from above
for the occasion. "Spirit of life," "of wisdom,"
and "of truth" (not all too frequent in ancient
Judaism: e.g. Jub 25:14; TJud 20:5; 1QS 3.18f.;
4.21,23; 1QM 13.10; of course Jn 15:26; ShepHerm
Mandates 3.4) denotes three aspects or effects of
the spirit, rather than three spirits (so "spirit"
should remain anarthrous as in the Gk. text, against
Rie Br). How this relates to the blessed bread, cup,
and ointment which also provide life (see 8:5) is
not clear. Maybe we are to understand that life is
first mediated by intimate contact with a Jew and
then sustained by other things. But perhaps the
author in 19:11 just makes use of a different tradition
to express the same general idea that adherence to
Judaism means life.

20 a. Lit. "and tightened the bonds of their hands."
In a handshake or around each other's neck?

b. Witnesses *a* FW Syr. Arm. L1 L2; "my" G
d; omit Ngr.; gaps E Slav. See n. d below.

c. Witnesses AP (Syr.) Arm.; "my" Ngr.; omit
L2; gaps Q *b d* L1 Slav.

d. Witnesses AQ G *d* Syr. Ngr.661; "their" P;
omit EFW Arm. L1 L2 Ngr.671; gap Slav. The
"her house" does not go well with "our house"
of vs. 1.

e. Witnesses *a d*; gaps L1 Ngr.; omit rest.

f. On foot washing see 7:1 and note. For foot-
washing scenes with a deeper meaning see Lk
7:36–50 (see Wilckens, *Orientierung an Jesus*);
Jn 13:1–17.

g. This is a poetic expression of loving someone

"like yourself" (cf. Ruth 1:16f.; TJos 17:7), rather
than an illustration of the lovers' "mystical union"
(thus Philonenko, *Joseph et Aséneth*, p. 195).

h. The reading "and . . . wash": (*a d*); omit F
Syr. Arm. L1 436; gaps EGW 435& Ngr. Cf. Jn
13:8.

i. "And Joseph . . . scribe" (F Syr. Arm. L1
L2 Ngr. Br); gap E; omit rest. Many variants
especially in the last clause (omit F L1). The
reading "like the fingers (*daktyloi*)" (Syr. Br, cf.
Arm.) might also be "like the reed pens (*kalamoi*)"
(436, cf. 435&; Ps 45:2). The first variant is
retained on the assumption that copyists are more
likely to clarify a biblical allusion than to obscure
it.

j. Or "her"; cf. 4:5.

k. See 5:3.

l. They seem to have been there since 10:1.

m. "And they . . . heavenly beauty" (FGW
Syr. Arm. L1 436 Br); omit *a* E *d* 435& (Ngr.?).

n. Cf. Mt 22:11.

o. The reading "and rejoiced": *a d* (Ngr.); gap
G; omit rest. Cf. Apuleius 11.13.4.

p. Cf. e.g. 2Mac 7:28f.; *Eighteen Benedictions*
2 (see C. W. Dugmore, *The Influence of the
Synagogue upon the Divine Office* [Westminster,
1964] pp. 114–27); Jn 5:21; Rom 4:17; Apuleius
11.16.2; O. Hofius, "Eine altjüdische Parallele zu
Röm. IV. 17*b*," *NTS* 18 (1971–72) 93f. Around
the beginning of our era "He who gives life to the
dead" had become all but a definition of God in
Judaism. Does this mean that Pentephres and his
family embraced Judaism too? The next verse seems
to confirm this interpretation. Cf. also "to give
glory to God" in Mt 5:16; 1Pet 2:12.

q. The reading "and celebrated": Q Arm. (Ngr.);
"and celebrating all (of them)" AP; Br connects
it with the following sentence; gap 435&; omit
rest. "To eat, drink, and celebrate" is a traditional
threesome, e.g. 1Kgs 4:20; Tob 7:10; Eccl 8:15;

(6)   And Pentephres said to Joseph, "Tomorrow I will call all the noblemen and the satraps of the whole land of Egypt and give a marriage feast for you,ʳ and you will take my daughter
9 (7) Aseneth for (your) wife." •And Joseph said,ˢ "I will go tomorrow to Pharaoh the king, because he is like a father to me and appointed me chief of the whole land of Egypt,ᵗ and I will speak about Aseneth into his ears, and he himself will give her to me for (my) wife."
10 And Pentephres said to him, "Go in peace."ᵘ

1 (20:8) **21** And Joseph stayed that day with Pentephres, and he did not sleep withᵃ Aseneth, because Joseph said, "It does not befit a man who worships God to sleep with his wifeᵇ before the wedding."

Pharaoh solemnizes the marriage and gives a wedding feast

2 (21:1)   Andᶜ Joseph rose at daybreak and went away to Pharaoh andᵈ said to him, "Give me
3 Aseneth, daughter of Pentephres, priest of Heliopolis, for (my) wife." •And Pharaoh rejoiced with great joy andᵉ said to Joseph, "Behold, is not this one betrothed to you since eternity?ᶠ And she shall be your wife from now on and for ever (and) ever."
4 (2)   And Pharaoh sent and called Pentephres, and he came and brought Aseneth, and stood
(3) her before Pharaoh.ᵍ And Pharaoh saw her and was amazed at her beauty and said, "May the Lord, the God of Joseph bless you, child, and let this beauty of yours remain for ever (and) ever, because justly the Lord, the God of Joseph, has chosen you as a bride for Joseph, because he is the firstborn son of God. And you shall be called a daughter of the
5 (4) Most High andʰ a bride of Joseph from now on and for ever." •And Pharaoh took Joseph and Aseneth and put golden crownsⁱ on their heads which had been in his house from the
6 beginning and of old. And Pharaoh set Aseneth at Joseph's right side, •and put his hands on their heads, and his right hand was on Aseneth's head.ʲ And Pharaoh said, "May the Lord God the Most High bless you and multiply you and magnifyᵏ and glorify you forever."
7 (5) And Pharaoh turned them around toward each other face to face and brought them mouth to mouth and joined them by their lips,ˡ and they kissed each other.

TAb B, 5:1; Lk 12:19. To express joy by appropriate meals is an all but universal custom. Here it may reflect a ceremonial meal held on the occasion of a conversion. If eating separates the Jews from the non-Jews, the first meal with Jews must acquire a special character. Cf. Mk 2:15; Lk 15:23; Acts 16:34; Apuleius 11.24.5. Anyway, there is no further mention of the interdiction stated in 7:1.

r. Lit. "make you weddings." Cf. Mt 22:2.

s. "Not so, but" added Arm. 435& (cf. 4:11; 23:1); gap d; omit rest.

t. Cf. Gen 45:8.

u. Traditional valediction, e.g. Judg 18:6; Jdt 8:35; Acts 16:36.

21 a. The reading "sleep with": FGW Arm. L1 436 Ngr.; "recognize" Syr. (cf. e.g. Gen 4:1; Mt 1:25); "go in to" a d (cf. vs. 9); gaps E 435&.

b. Aseneth is Joseph's "wife" by virtue of her engagement (20:4, 8; cf. 23:3; see on 1:9), but we may have to understand "his (future) wife." In either case the statement seems to imply that a man "who does *not* worship God" might have acted otherwise. A Jew might not (Cohen, *Jewish and Roman Law*, vol. 1, p. 322), but there may have been local differences (see m. Ket 1:5 and commentaries on Mt 1:18f.).

c. On vss. 2–9 cf. Apuleius 6.21.1–24.4: Cupid flies to Jupiter to ask for Psyche's hand in marriage. Jupiter convokes all the gods and declares Psyche immortal and her union with Cupid perpetual. A feast ensues, and soon their daughter, Voluptuous-

ness, is born.

d. The reading "and said . . . saying": (all), except omit B(D). D omits "and said . . . sent," then adds "and Aseneth" after "Pentephres," then omits from "and he" to "natives" in vs. 8. Slav. is shortened, omitting vs. 3 altogether. A rather poor Gk. retroversion of Slav., corrected by two readings from A and F Syr., is adopted and translated by Phil.

e. The reading "rejoiced . . . and": a, P(Q) prefixing "having heard this word from Joseph"; gaps E d Ngr.; omit rest. Stylistically PQ is acceptable except for the participial form.

f. Similarly 23:3. Cf. Tob 6:18. This expression means no more than that the match is providential. Closer scrutiny of the wedding rites in vss. 4–8 might help to determine the date and place of origin of JosAsen.

g. Cf. Gen 47:7.

h. The reading "a daughter . . . and": (FW Syr. Arm. L1 436 Slav. Phil); omit AP; gaps rest.

i. I.e. wreaths. They were an all but universal custom in ancient weddings.

j. The reading "and . . . head": (FGW Arm. L1 436); omit a Syr. 435&; gaps E d Ngr. (except perhaps for a trace in Ngr. 661). Cf. Gen 48:13.

k. The reading "and magnify": a; gaps E d 436 Slav. Ngr.; omit rest. Cf. WisSol 19:22. Is this a current wedding formula? Cf. Gen 1:28.

l. The reading "and . . . lips": FW 436; "on their lips" L1; omit A; gaps rest. Lit. "on their mouths" and "on their lips."

8 (6)   And after this Pharaoh gave a marriage feast and a great dinner and a big banquet[m] for
(7) seven days.[n] And he called together all the chiefs of the land of Egypt and all the kings of
the nations[o] and proclaimed to the whole land of Egypt, saying, "Every man who does
(any) work during the seven days of Joseph's and Aseneth's wedding shall surely[p] die."

9 (8)   And it happened after this,[q] Joseph went in to Aseneth, and Aseneth conceived from
Joseph, and gave birth to Manasseh and Ephraim, his brother, in Joseph's house.[r]

V. ASENETH'S PSALM

10   And[s] then Aseneth began to confess to the Lord God and gave thanks, praying, for all
the good (things) of which she was deemed worthy by the Lord:[t]

11   I have sinned, Lord, I have sinned,
         before you I have sinned much,[u]
        I Aseneth, daughter of Pentephres, priest of Heliopolis,
         who is an overseer of everything.[v]

---

m. Lit. "drinking bout"; in LXX this expression is often used for banquets (e.g. Job 1:4). After "dinner" (Ps-Lucianus, *Onos*, 24.3; never LXX) it denotes the drinking rounds following the meal proper.

n. The conventional length in Judaism, as already e.g. Judg 14:12, 17.

o. Cf. e.g. Lk 22:25.

p. Lit. "by death." Cf. Ex 35:2, "by death" being an addition from a legal formula such as Ex 21:16.

q. "And . . . this" F(G)W Syr. Arm. L1 436; "And when the marriage feast had happened and the dinner was completed" AP(Q) *d* Slav. (adding "and"); omit 435&; gaps E Ngr. Split tradition?

r. Cf. Gen 41:50–52. The author gives us no idea as to where Joseph's house stood. "To go in" is a traditional euphemism to denote consummation of marriage. It is followed by "conceive and give birth" e.g. Gen 30:4f., 10; 2Sam 12:24. 435& break off at this point. On the 436 version of vs. 9 see at vs. 10.

s. Vss. 10–21 (EFW Syr. Arm. L1 436 Br); omit *a* G *d* Rum.; gap Ngr. Vs. 10 is in E only (omit vss. 11–21), but there seem to be traces of it elsewhere. In F(W) vss. 11–21 are imbedded into a lengthy exhortation beginning after vs. 9, and introduced thus: "But hear (singular) also the confession, or thanksgiving, of Aseneth. For after she recognized (the) living God, and was released from the pollutions of the idols (cf. Acts 15:20), and had renounced the dead and dumb images of the Egyptian gods, and had obtained what she wanted, giving thanks, she said to the Most High." The L1 MS 421 has "Afterwards (she) said" in the margin of the heading, adopted with an added "Aseneth" by Batiffol's edition of L1 and accepted by Br. In 436 vs. 9 reads: "And it happened after this that Joseph entered to the song of confession which Aseneth sang to the Lord the Most High after she gave birth to Effraim and Manasse." Vss. 11–21 Gk. with full apparatus in Burchard, *Untersuchungen*, pp. 76–90; cf. also Br. W was not known at the time; it offers some helpful variants. Nevertheless the text of the psalm is marred by numerous difficulties, some of them well-nigh

insoluble, especially at the end of vs. 11 and in vss. 19f. On the function of the text, cf. Ex 15; Tob 13; Jdt 16:1–17; 4Mac 18:6b–19; on the anaphoric form of the stanzas, cf. TJob 25; 32; on the first person singular Ps 151; 4Mac 18:6b–19; on the general structure (ten stanzas of parallel form, followed by a longer prose section), cf. Mt 5:1–12; D. Daube, *The New Testament and Rabbinic Judaism* (London, 1956) pp. 196–201.

t. An introduction to vss. 11–21 would seem to be needed; cf. Tob 13:1; Jdt 15:14. E has been adopted for want of a better text (see previous note); "gave thanks (*eucharistōsa*)" is dubious. The psalm is entitled "Hymn of Confession of Aseneth to the Most High" (FW Syr. Arm. L1 436 Br); gaps rest. The heading may have originated as a marginal title; it is hardly original as part of the running text (see also 12:1).

u. "I have sinned, Lord . . . much" (FW Syr. Arm. L1 436 Br); gaps rest. The two lines recur in vss. 12–21 in L1 Br, in vss. 12–20 in Arm., in vs. 21 only in 436. FW have them again before vss. 12, 16, and 18, Syr. before vss. 12, 13, and 19, all in shorter forms than above, varying a little each time. It is assumed here that all verses down to vs. 21 began this way, although in vs. 20 this beginning seems to break a sentence.

v. The clause is a reconstruction from "who sees everything" Syr.; "of (the) god who is an overseer of everything" Arm. 332; "who was the overseer of the gods all (singular)" Yovs; "like of an (or the) overseer (*episcopi*) of all (plural)" L1 MSS 424 433 441; omit rest of L1 including Batiffol's edition; gaps rest. The structure of the stanza would require a further clause. If the above variants represent it, nevertheless the wording (*episkopos* may have been in it) and to whom it refers remain obscure. In Syr. and 332 the reference is unequivocally to the sun. This makes good sense, because the idea that the sun (or God, for that matter) sees everything is commonplace (see 6:6). But whereas in Syr. and 332 the clause goes well with "Heliopolis," rendered "City of the Sun," is it not easy to see how this would have run in Gk.

12   I have sinned, Lord, I have sinned;
before you I have sinned much.
I was prospering in my father's house,
and was a boastful and arrogant virgin.

13   I have sinned, Lord, I have sinned;
before you I have sinned much.
And I have worshiped strange gods who were without number,
and eaten bread from their sacrifices.

14   I have sinned, Lord, I have sinned;
before you I have sinned much.
Bread of strangulation I have eaten,
and a cup of insidiousness I have drunk from the table of death.

15   I have sinned, Lord, I have sinned;
before you I have sinned much.
And I did not know the Lord the God of Heaven,
and I did not trust in the Most High God of life.

16   I have sinned, Lord, I have sinned;
before you I have sinned much.
For I trusted in the richness of my glory[w] and in my beauty,
and[x] I was boastful and arrogant.

17   I have sinned, Lord, I have sinned;
before you I have sinned much.
And I despised every man on earth,
and there was no one who achieved something[y] before me.

18   I have sinned, Lord, I have sinned;
before you I have sinned much.
And I had come to hate all who had asked my hand in marriage,
and despised them and scorned them.

19   I have sinned, Lord, I have sinned;
before you I have sinned much.
And I spoke bold (words) in vanity and said,
"There is no prince on earth who may loosen the girdle of my virginity."[z]

20   I[a2] have sinned, Lord, I have sinned;
before you I have sinned much.
But will be the bride of the great king's firstborn son.

21   I have sinned, Lord, I have sinned;
before you I have sinned much,
until Joseph the Powerful One of God came.[b2]
He pulled me down from my dominating position
and made me humble after my arrogance,
and by his beauty he caught me,
and by his wisdom he grasped me like a fish on a hook,
and by his spirit, as by bait of life, he ensnared me,[c2]

w. This phrase is the only extant ancient parallel to Rom 9:23; Eph 1:18; 3:16; Col 1:27; cf. Phil 4:19; but the sense is different.

x. W Syr. Arm.; omit F Ll 436 Br, also Burchard, *Untersuchungen*, p. 80; gaps rest.

y. The reading "achieved something" is a guess from the variegated evidence; cf. Burchard, *Untersuchungen*, p. 81. W has "as someone does not do."

z. Classical metonymy in Jewish language.

a2. The verse is doubtful. Maybe it is not a separate stanza at all.

b2. Cf. Dan 4:8.

c2. Hunting metaphors play a role in missionary language, e.g. Mk 1:17 parallel; see generally, W. H. Wuellner, *The Meaning of "Fishers of Men"* (NT Library; Philadelphia, Pa., 1967). Gk. *delea(s)ma*, "bait," is not a frequent word; cf. Josephus, *War* 2.8.11 §158; 2Pet 2:14, 18. In a burlesque throng of masqueraded people preceding

and by his power he confirmed me,
and brought me to the God of the ages
and to the chief of the house of the Most High,
and gave me to eat bread of life,
and to drink a cup of wisdom,
and I became his bride for ever and ever.

SECOND PART: PHARAOH'S SON ATTEMPTS TO KIDNAP ASENETH
AND RISE TO POWER IN EGYPT

I. JOSEPH'S AND ASENETH'S VISIT TO JACOB

Aseneth meets Jacob

1 (1) **22** And it happened after this: The seven years of plenty passed and the seven years of
2 (2) famine began to come. •And Jacob heard about Joseph his son, and Israel went to Egypt
with his whole family, in the second year of the famine, in the second month, on the
twenty-first of the month,ᵃ and dwelt in the land of Goshen.ᵇ
3 (3) And Aseneth said to Joseph,ᶜ "I will go and see your father, because your father Israel
4 is like a father to me and (a) god."ᵈ •And Joseph said to her, "You shall go with me and
5 (4) see my father." •And Joseph and Aseneth went to the land of Goshen to Jacob. And
Joseph's brothers met them and prostrated themselves face down to the ground before them.
6 (5) And they went in to Jacob. Andᵉ Israel was sitting on his bed, and he was an old man in
comfortable old age.ᶠ
7 And Aseneth saw him and was amazed at his beauty,ᵍ because Jacob was exceedingly
beautiful to look at, and his old age (was) like the youth of a handsome (young) man, and
his head was all white as snow, and the hairs of his head were all exceedingly close and
thick like (those) of an Ethiopian,ʰ and his beard (was) white reaching down to his breast,
and his eyes (were) flashingⁱ and darting (flashes of) lightning, and his sinews and his
shoulders and his arms were like (those) of an angel, and his thighs and his calves and his
8 feet like (those) of a giant. And Jacob was like a man who had wrestled with God.ʲ •And
Aseneth saw him and was amazed, and prostrated herself before him face down to the
ground. And Jacob said to Joseph, "Is this my daughter-in-law, your wife? Blessed she
9 will be by the Most High God." •And Jacob called her to himself and blessed her and
kissed her. And Aseneth stretched out her hands and grasped Jacob's neck and hung herself

---

the Isis procession Apuleius noticed hunters, fowlers with lime-sticks, and fishermen with fishing rods and hooks (11.8.1f.), but it is unlikely that they are symbolic figures (Griffiths, *Isis-Book*, p. 177). The Devil is compared to a fisherman catching different fish with different sorts of bait in the gnostic *Authentikos Logos*, pp. 29f.

22 a. Jub 45:1 says it was on the 1st day of the 4th month, a Wednesday according to its calendar. See 1:2.

b. Gen 41:53f.; 45:26–46:7; 47:27. The historical Goshen may have been in the northern part of the county of Heliopolis and adjoining regions farther north (Uphill, *JNES* 27 [1968] 291–316 and 28 [1969] 15–39. See also n. e to 1:2), but we do not know where the author thought it was.

c. Note the naïve way in which the action starts again. Some words about the whereabouts and situation of the characters known from the first part of the book, which closed some eight years earlier, would certainly be welcome.

d. The reading "like . . . god": AP(Q); "my

father" d; "like (a) god to me" FW (Syr. Arm.) L1 436; gaps EG Ngr. "God" (which must be original even if "father" is not) either means a person of utmost authority (cf. Ex 4:16; Philo, *Vit Mos*, 1.158; Jn 20:28 is only a formal parallel) or an angelic, godlike being as described in vs. 7; cf. 17:9.

e. The reading "And" to "himself " in vs. 9: (all) except omit d; gap Ngr.

f. Lit. "in fat old age." Classical, not LXX.

g. He has gotten what Aseneth was promised in 16:16 and accorded in 18:9.

h. The reading "like (those) of an Ethiopian": Syr.; "like (those) of an Indian man" Arm. (*Aithiops* may also mean one of the dark aborigines of India); "his teeth however like (those) of an Ethiopian (Gen 49:12?)" 436; omit a; gaps rest. In our terms "Ethiopian" should be Nubian or Sudanese.

i. Gk. *charopoioi* is very rare; cf. Gen 42:19 BA.

j. "And . . . God" (Syr. Arm. 436); omit AP; gaps rest. Cf. Gen 32:25–33.

on her father's neck[k] just like someone hangs on to his father's neck when he returns from
10 (6), (7) fighting into his house, and she kissed him.[l] • And after this they ate and drank. And Joseph
and Aseneth went (back) to their house.

Simeon and Levi see Joseph and Aseneth home

11   And Simeon and Levi, Joseph's brethren, the sons of Leah, alone escorted them; but the
sons of Zilpah and Bilhah, Leah's and Rachel's maidservants, did not escort them, because
12 they envied (them) and were hostile against them.[m] • And Levi was on Aseneth's right (side)
13 (8) and Joseph on (her) left. • And[n] Aseneth grasped Levi's hand. And Aseneth loved Levi
exceedingly beyond all of Joseph's brethren, because he was one who attached himself to
the Lord, and he was a prudent man and a prophet of the Most High and sharp-sighted with
(9) his eyes, and he used to see letters[o] written in heaven by the finger of God[p] and he knew
the unspeakable (mysteries) of the Most High God[q] and revealed them to Aseneth in secret,
because he himself, Levi, would love Aseneth very much, and see her place of rest[r] in the
highest, and her walls like adamantine eternal walls, and her foundations founded upon a
rock of the seventh heaven.[s]

II. THE PLOT OF PHARAOH'S SON AGAINST ASENETH AND JOSEPH

Pharaoh's son fails to persuade Simeon and Levi to help him

1 (1) **23** And it happened while Joseph and Aseneth were passing by,[a] Pharaoh's firstborn son
(2) saw them from the wall.[b] And he saw Aseneth and was cut (to the heart), and (for some
time) he was heavily indignant and felt sick[c] because of her beauty. And he said, "Thus it
shall not be."[d]

2 (3)   And Pharaoh's son sent messengers and called to him Simeon and Levi. And the men
came to him and stood before him. And Pharaoh's firstborn son said to them, "I know
today[e] that you are powerful men beyond all men on the earth, and by these right (hands)
of yours the city of the Shechemites has been overthrown, and by these two swords of
3 (4) yours thirty thousand fighting men were cut down.[f] • And behold, today I will take you as
companions for myself,[g] and give you plenty of gold and silver, and servants and maids

k. Gk. *trachēlos* is distinct from previous *auchēn*, which is the hind part of the neck. Traditional phrase, e.g. Gen 45:15; 46:29; 50:1; 3Mac 5:49; TAb B 6:2.

l. The reading "just . . . him" has been reconstructed on the assumption of split tradition from "just . . . house" (Syr. Arm. 436) and "and . . . him" *a* (E) *d;* omit both phrases FW; gaps G Ll Ngr.

m. Tradition, none directly from the Joseph story, is reflected in this verse. The relationship between Simeon and Levi may go back to Gen 34:25–31; 49:5–7, although they are severely censured there, whereas Levi is a thoroughly positive figure in JosAsen (see Intro.) as in ancient Jewish lore generally, and Simeon could be, were it not for his temper (see 23:7). Hostility of Dan, Gad, Naphtali, and Asser, the sons of Zilpah and Bilhah (Gen 30:1–13), against their brothers, especially Joseph, probably was developed on the basis of certain features of Gen 37 and is likewise evidenced in contemporary literature (e.g. TGad 1; Aptowitzer, *HUCA* 1 [1924] 284f.).

n. Perhaps we should shift the beginning of vs. 13 to the next clause.

o. Those *grammata* would be writings such as the Book of the Living (15:4, 12x) or the heavenly tablets read by Jacob (Jub 32:21; PrJos Fragment B), Asser (TAss 5:4), or Enoch (1En 103:2; 106:19; cf. further TLevi 5:4; TAss 2:10), rather than letters inscribed in the sky.

p. The reading "by the finger of God": Syr. 436 (cf. 15:4, 12x); omit *a d;* gaps rest.

q. The reading "and . . . God": G (Syr.) Arm. (436 "read" instead of "know"); "and read them" *a d;* gaps rest. Perhaps a case of split tradition which ought to be reconstructed as "and read . . . and he knew . . ."

r. Cf. Isa 66:1 LXX(?). On the "rest" see Intro.

s. The reading "and her walls . . . heaven": (Syr. Arm. [332 "third," Yovs "second" heaven] 436); omit *a d;* gaps *b* Ll Ngr.

23 a. The reading "when they were going away to Jacob (absolute genitive)": added A(PQ); gap Ngr.; omit rest.

b. Does the author intend the city wall? Cf. Gen 12:14; 2Sam 11:2.

c. The reading "and was . . . sick": (all); except "he became mad about her" AP(Q) *d.* Cf. 6:1; 7:3.

d. "And . . . be" (all); except omit *a* G *d;* gap Ngr. See also 4:11.

e. See 4:7.

f. Also vs. 14. Cf. Gen 34; Jub 30; TLevi 1–7.

g. "And . . . myself" (*a b* Syr. Arm. 436); "And behold I will take you for my assistance today" B; "But I ask you for my assistance; hurry" D (Ll); gaps Slav. Ngr. Phil adopts both D and the majority reading (following F). "Companions" denotes members of Pharaoh's son's retinue (see also vs. 4), not just "pals."

and houses and big (estates as) inheritance.[h] Only do this thing and show mercy on me,[i] for I have been insulted very much by your brother Joseph, for he himself took Aseneth
4 (5) my (envisaged) wife who was betrothed to me from the beginning.[j] •And now, come assist me, and we will make war on Joseph your brother, and I will kill him with my sword,[k] and have Aseneth for (my) wife, and you will be to me brothers and faithful friends.[l]
5 (6) However, do this thing. But if you are too cowardly to do this thing, and despise my
6 purpose, behold, my sword is prepared against you.''[m] •And while he was saying this, he exposed his sword and showed it to them.

But when the men, Simeon and Levi, heard these words, they were exceedingly cut (to
7 (7) the heart), because Pharaoh's son had spoken to them in a tyrannical fashion.[n] •And Simeon was a daring and bold man,[o] and he intended to lay his hand on the handle of his sword and draw it from its sheath and strike Pharaoh's son, because he had spoken defiant things
8 (8) to them.[p] •And Levi saw the intention of his heart, because Levi was a prophet, and he was sharp-sighted with (both) his mind and his eyes, and he used to read what is written in the heart of men.[q] And Levi trod with his foot (on) Simeon's right foot and pressed it and
9 (9) (thus) signaled him to cease from his wrath. •And Levi said to Simeon quietly, "Why are you furious with anger[r] with this man? And we are men who worship God, and it does not befit us to repay evil for evil.''[s]
10 (10) And Levi said to Pharaoh's son with frankness, his face cheerful,[t] and there was not the least (bit of) anger in him, but in meekness of heart he said to him, "Why does our lord[u] speak words such as these? And we are men who worship God, and our father is a friend[v]
11 (11) of the Most High God, and Joseph our brother is like the firstborn son of God. •And how could we do this wicked thing,[w] and sin before our God and before our father Israel[x] and
12 before our brother Joseph?[y] •And now, listen to my words. It does not befit a man who worships God to injure anyone in any way. And if anyone wants to injure a man who worships God, that (first-mentioned) man who worships God does not succor him (the
13 injurer),[z] because a sword is not in his hands.[a2] •And you at least guard against speaking
(12) any longer about our brother Joseph words such as these. But if you insist on this wicked purpose of yours, behold, our swords are drawn in our right hands before you.''
14 (13) And Simeon and Levi drew their swords from their sheaths and said, "Behold, have you

---

h. Lit. plural. See 3:5.

i. Lit. "make mercy with me." Biblical, e.g. 1Sam 20:14; Lk 10:37.

j. Pharaoh thought otherwise, 1:7–9; but cf. 4:11. Undoubtedly he means: "by Fortune, unknown to man," as 21:3. On "wife" see 21:1.

k. "I will make war" and "we will kill" are also well attested. The textual situation calls for further scrutiny.

l. The words denote rank, rather than personal intimacy; cf. 1Mac 14:40 (see also vs. 3).

m. "However . . . thing ("H.—thing" omit EFW Syr. L1). But . . . you" (b Syr. Arm. L1 436; "But if you do not hear my words I will kill you with my sword" AP(Q) d; gaps Slav. Ngr. On "thing" see vs. 11.

n. "But . . . fashion" (EFGW Syr. Arm. 436 Br); omit a d; gaps L1 Slav. Ngr.

o. Cf. 28:12f. Simeon's character goes back to Gen 34:25–31; 49:5–7; cf. on 22:11.

p. Cf. Gen 42:7, 30; Jude 15.

q. The reading "and he was . . . men": (G Syr. Arm. 436); "and he saw in advance all the (things) to come" (B) D Phil; omit AP EF; gaps rest. For this description of a prophet see e.g. Lk 7:39, also Mk 2:8 parallel; Jn 2:25.

r. The reading "with anger": E Syr.? Arm. (436); omit a G d; gaps rest. "To be furious with anger (thymousthai orgē)" is prevalent in LXX, e.g. Gen 39:19.

s. Also 29:3, cf. 28:5, 14, one of the most

important ethical principles held up in JosAsen. The only exact parallels are Rom 12:17; 1Thes 5:15; 1Pet 3:9 and later on ApSedr 7:7; Letter of Polycarpus, 2:2. See further Intro.

t. Esther keeps up a cheerful face in spite of a fearful heart (Esth 5:1b).

u. The reading "does our Lord": AP EFW Syr. Arm. L1 436; "do you, my lord" (Q) G d; gap Ngr. Cf. Gen 44:7 LXX.

v. Witnesses a FW 436; "near and beloved" Syr.; "beloved" Arm. (as in following clause, where d also has it instead of "son"); "slave" d; "puer" ("child" or "servant") L1; "guest" Slav.; gaps EG Ngr. The title "friend of God" is here drawn from Jewish tradition, which applied it above all to Abraham, but Egyptian and Greek tradition (e.g. Epictetus, Diss., 2.17.29: the Stoic) have it too (G. Stählin, "philos etc.," TDNT 9, 146–71).

w. Lit. "word (rēma)," also vs. 5 and 24:14. A biblicism; cf. e.g. Gen 18:25. See also 17:1.

x. Witnesses AP Syr. L1 436; "Jacob" GW Arm.; omit F; gaps rest.

y. Cf. Gen 39:9. See also on 7:4.

z. Other translations: "that (injured) man who worshippeth God avengeth not himself upon him (the injurer)" Br; "so schützt sich jener Gottesfürchtige doch nicht vor ihm (the injurer)" Rie. But, for this, "him" would here have to be in the accusative, as in 24:7, not in the dative.

a2. But cf. vs. 14. Are we to understand: "not wantonly"?

seen these swords? With these, two swords the Lord God punished the insult of the
Shechemites (by) which they insulted the sons of Israel, because of our sister Dinah whom
15 (14) Shechem the son of Hamor had defiled." •And the son of Pharaoh saw their swords drawn
and was exceedingly afraid and trembled over his whole body, because their swords were
flashing forth (something) like a flame of fire, and the eyes of Pharaoh's son darkened, and
16 (15) he fell on his face on the ground beneath their feet. •And Levi stretched out his right hand
and grasped[b2] him and said to him, "Rise and do not be afraid. Only guard against speaking
17 (16) any longer a wicked word about our brother Joseph." •And Simeon and Levi went away
from the presence of Pharaoh's son.

Pharaoh's son enlists the help of Dan and Gad, Naphtali and Asher. They set up an ambush for Aseneth

1 (1) **24** And the son of Pharaoh was full of fear and distress, because he was afraid of Joseph's
brothers, Simeon and Levi, and he was still weighed down by Aseneth's beauty and
2 (2) distressed with great overwhelming[a] distress. •And his servants said to him into the ear,
saying, "Behold, the sons of Bilhah and the sons of Zilpah, Leah's and Rachel's maidservants,
Jacob's wives, are hostile to Joseph and Aseneth and envy them. And these will be in your
3 (3) power[b] according to your will." •And Pharaoh's son sent messengers and called them to
himself. And they came to him at the first hour of the night and stood before him. And
Pharaoh's son said to them, "I have a word (to say) to you, because[c] you are powerful
4 (4) men." •And Dan and Gad, the elder brothers, said to him, "Let our lord say to his servants
what he wants (to say), and your servants will listen,[d] and we will do according to your
5 (5) will."[e] •And Pharaoh's son rejoiced exceedingly with great joy and said to his servants,
"Withdraw from me a little, because I have a confidential word (to say) to these men."
6 And they all withdrew.
7 (6)   And Pharaoh's son lied to them and[f] said, "Behold, blessing[g] and death (are set) before
(7) your face. Take now rather the blessing[g] and not the death, 'because you are powerful men
8 (8) and will not die like women,[h] but be brave and avenge yourself on your enemies. •For I
heard Joseph your brother saying to Pharaoh my father concerning you, 'Children of my
father's maidservants are Dan and Gad and Naphtali and Asher, and they are not my
(9) brothers. And I will wait for my father's death[i] and (then) I will blot them out from the
earth[j] and all their offspring lest they share the inheritance with us, because they are children
9 (10) of maidservants.[k] •And these (men) have sold me to the Ishmaelites,[l] 'and I will repay them
according to the whole insult of theirs which they committed against me wickedly. Only
10 (11) let my father die (first).' •And Pharaoh, my father, commended him and said to him, 'Well
you have spoken, child. Then, take from me men (who are) powerful in fighting and go
out to meet them[m] in accordance with what they did to you. And I will be a helper to
you.' "
11 (12)   And when the men heard the words of Pharaoh's son, they were exceedingly troubled

---

b2. Gk. *ekratēsen* AP G Arm. 436; "erected
(*ēgeiren*)" Q FW Syr.; "raised (*anestēsen*)" E d;
gaps Ll Ngr.

24 a. Lit. "super-great."
  b. Gk. *hypocheirioi*, lit. "under-the-hand-(people)." LXX often use this for subjugated groups.
  c. "I . . . because" (FGW Arm. 436); "I
learned from many that" a; "I know that" d; omit
Syr.; gaps E Ll Ngr. Is this a case of split tradition?
  d. The reading "and . . . listen": (AP Syr.)
436; "and we . . . listen" G Arm.; omit Q d; gaps
rest. Cf. 1Sam 3:9f.
  e. Witnesses AQ(P) G d Syr. Arm. 436; "word"
EFW; gaps Ll Ngr.
  f. The reading "lied . . . and": (AP E? d); omit
FGW Syr. Arm. 436; gaps Q Ll Ngr. Pharaoh's
son tries a new approach in the following verses.
  g. The reading "blessing," both occurrences:

(all); except "life" G Syr.; gaps E Ngr. Cf. Deut
30:19; Jer 21:8. A similar alternative in weaker
terms is proposed to Joseph by Potiphar's wife in
Josephus, *Ant* 2.4.3 §48f.
  h. Also 25.7; cf. *LAB* 31:7.
  i. Cf. Gen 47:28.
  j. The reading "from the earth": a G (after
"offspring") Syr.; gaps E Ngr.; omit rest.
  k. Cf. Gen 21:10; Aptowitzer, *HUCA* 1 (1924)
285.
  l. Cf. Gen 37:25–28.
  m. The reading "and . . . them (*kai hypexelthe
autous* or *autois*)": A d; "and give them back(?)"
Slav.; omit P; paraphrastic Syr.; gaps rest. The
translation is difficult; "and proceed against them"
Br; "*und belange sie*" Rie; "*et sors secrètement
pour traiter tes frères*" Phil. The rendering "and
keep out of their way" would suit the verb better,
but not in this context.

12 (13) and distressed and said to Pharaoh's son, "We beg you, lord, help us."[n] •And Pharaoh's
13 son said to them, "I will be a helper to you if you hear my words." •And the men said,
"Behold, we are your servants before you.[o] Give us orders, and we will do according to
14 your will." •And Pharaoh's son said to them, "I will kill my father Pharaoh this night,
because Pharaoh my father is like a father to Joseph and said to him (that he would) help
him against you. And you kill Joseph. And I will take Aseneth for a wife for myself, and
you will be brothers to me and fellow heirs[p] of all my (things). However, do this thing."
15 (14)   And Dan and Gad said to him, "We are your servants[q] today and will do everything
which you have ordered us. And we have heard Joseph saying to Aseneth today, 'Go
tomorrow to the field (which is) our inheritance, because it is the hour of the vintage.' And
he gave (as an escort to be) with her six hundred men powerful in fighting and fifty
16, 17 forerunners. •And now, listen to us, and we will speak to our lord." •And they spoke to
18 (15) him all their secret words (and said), "Give us men for war."[r] •And Pharaoh's son gave
to the four brothers five hundred men each, and them he appointed their chiefs and
commanders.
19 (16)   And Dan and Gad said to him, "We are your servants today, and will do everything that
you have ordered us. We will go by night and set up an ambush in the wadi,[s] and hide in
(17) the thicket of the reeds. And you, take with you fifty bowmen on horses,[t] and go far ahead
(18) of us.[u] And Aseneth will come and fall into our hands.[v] And we will cut down the men
who are with her. And Aseneth will flee ahead with her carriage[w] and fall into your hands,
(19) and you will do to her as your soul desires.[x] And after that we will kill Joseph as he is
(20) distressed over Aseneth, and his children we will kill before his eyes."[y] And Pharaoh's son
rejoiced when he heard these words. And he sent them out and two thousand fighting men
with them.
20 (21)   And they came to the wadi and hid in the thicket of the reeds. (And) they split into four
detachments.[z] And there were sitting across the wadi, on the forward section as it were, on
this side of the road and the other five hundred men each; likewise on this side of the wadi
the rest were waiting, and they, too, were sitting in the thicket of the reeds, on this side of
the road and the other five hundred men each.[a2] And between them the road (was) wide
and spacious.

---

n. "For from now on we are your household servants and slaves and will die with you" added (*a*); omit G Syr. Arm. 436; gaps rest. It is assumed here that the *a* reading is an anticipation from vs. 13 (or 15:19?), but perhaps the case merits reconsideration; cf. Mk 14:31 parallel.

o. "Behold . . . you" (*b* Syr. Arm. 436); omit *a* (including "the men"); gaps *d* L1 Ngr. See also vs. 11.

p. Gk. *sygklēronomos* is not otherwise attested before Philo and Rom 8:17; Eph 3:6 (cf. Burchard, *ZNW* 61 [1970] 169); Heb 11:9; 1Pet 3:7. Gk. *syn* refers to joint possession. The testator in this case is Pharaoh, rather than his son.

q. Cf. Josh 9:8, 11; *LAB* 57:4.

r. Vs. 17: "And . . . words" (*a* FWG Arm. 436); "and may he give us men for war" Syr.; "let therefore my lord command to come with us war-men more than those" L1 (lacks vss. 16 and 18–19a); "and give us men of war, and (men) powerful for war" Slav. (lacks vs. 16 "and . . . lord"); cf. "and give us 500 men each" added in vs. 19 after "reeds" E (lacks vs. 16 "and we will," vs. 19 "ordered us"); gaps *d* (vs. 15 "and fifty" to 17; but B Phil begin vs. 18 "And as Pharaoh's son heard these words, he") Ngr. (E, see above). The verse is reconstructed on the assumption of split tradition, but it is utterly doubtful. The first half is well attested, but why the secrecy? The second half is poorly evidenced,

but it seems to be needed as a foundation for vs. 18. There is no evidence whatsoever for a syntactical link such as "(and said)."

s. Cf. 1Sam 15:5.

t. LXX has mounted bowmen only in Jdt 2:15.

u. The reading "of us": Syr. L1 Br Rie; "of her" or "it" (*autēs*) *a* B; "it" (*autō*) G; omit EFW D Arm. 436 Slav. Phil; gap Ngr.

v. Witnesses *a* GW *d* Arm.; "ambush (plural)" EF L1 436; gaps Syr. Ngr.

w. Gk. *ochēma* (also 26:5; 27:1f., never LXX or NT), whereas Joseph's chariot is *harma* (e.g. 5:4). We should perhaps visualize a household vehicle designed to transport several people (cf. 27:1–5) with their luggage (cf. Chariton 2.3.3f.).

x. Traditional phrase, e.g. 1Sam 2:16; Isa 58:11 LXX.

y. Cf. 2Kgs 25:7.

z. "And . . . detachments" *a* (no "and" because preceding clause begins "And as"); gaps E Ngr.; omit rest. "Split" is lit. "became"; cf. Gen 2:10. Gk. *archē* in the sense of "military body" (as e.g. in Judg 7:16; 1Sam 13:17) seems to be a Septuagintism; cf. Josephus, *Ant* 1.9 §172.

a2. "And there were . . . each" (A); much shorter rest; gaps E 436 Ngr.: A alone gives a clear picture of the ambush. Words from the other witnesses may, however, be used to improve it. The road is crossing the wadi.

Pharaoh's son fails to kill his father and takes up his position in the ambush

1 (1) **25** And Pharaoh's son rose in that night and went to the chamber[a] of his father in order to kill his father with a sword. And his father's guards prevented him from going in to his
2 (2) father and said to him, "What are your orders, lord?" •And Pharaoh's son said to them, "I want to see my father, because I am going out to harvest (the vintage of) my new-
3 (3) planted vineyard."[b] •And the guards said to him, "Your father suffers from a headache[c] and lay awake all night, and now he is resting a little.[d] And he said to us, 'Let no one
4 (4) come close to me, not even my firstborn son." •And when he heard this,[e] Pharaoh's son went away hurriedly[f] and took with him fifty mounted bowmen and went away at their head,[g] just as Dan and Gad had spoken to him.

Naphtali and Asher, bitten by remorse, fail to refrain Dan and Gad

5 (5) And the younger brothers, Naphtali and Asher, spoke to their older brothers, Dan and Gad, saying,[h] "Why do you once again act wickedly against our father Israel and against
(6) our brother Joseph? And him the Lord is guarding like an apple of the eye.[i] 'Behold, have you not sold him once, and now he is king of the whole land of Egypt and savior and grain
6 (7) giver?[j] •And now again, if you should attempt to act wickedly against him, he will cry to the Most High,[k] and he will send fire from heaven, and it will consume you,[l] and the angels
7 (8) of God will fight for him against you.'"[m] •And their older brothers, Dan and Gad, were
8 angry at them and said, "But shall we die like women?[n] That would be absurd." •And they went out to meet Joseph and Aseneth.[o]

III. ASENETH FALLS INTO THE AMBUSH AND IS RESCUED
BY JOSEPH'S BROTHERS

Aseneth is caught in the ambush and Levi alarms his brothers

1 (1) **26** And Aseneth rose at daybreak and said to Joseph, "I will go, just like you have said,[a] to the field (which is) our inheritance. And my soul is anxious, because you are parting

---

25 a. Gk. *epi ton thalamon*: E (*d*) 436; "for the death (*epi ton thanaton*)" FW; "in the reed (*en tō kalamō*)" G; "into the bedchamber (*eis ton koitōna*)" AP; "into the house (*eis ton oikon*)" Q Arm.; omit Syr.; gaps L1 Ngr.

b. Gk. *ampelos*, "grapevine," is used for "vineyard" on papyri since the third century B.C., but this and possibly Rev 14:18f. are the first known occurrences in literary texts.

c. Witnesses *b* Syr. Arm. L1; "ache" *a d*; illegible 436; gap Ngr.

d. The reading "a little": FGW Arm. L1 436; omit *a* E *d* Syr.; gap Ngr.

e. The reading "when . . . this": AP L1; gap Ngr.; omit rest.

f. Witnesses *b* Arm. 436; "in anger" *a d* (Syr.?); omit L1; gap Ngr. Is this a split tradition?

g. Lit. "ahead of them," a traditional phrase implying leadership; cf. e.g. Tob 5:18; *LAB* 39:1; 1QSa 1.17,23.

h. On this intervention cf. TZeb 1:7.

i. Also 26:2. Traditional, e.g. Deut 32:10; Ps 17:8; 1En 100:5.

j. This noun is not otherwise attested before imperial times.

k. The reading "he will cry (*boēsei*) . . . High": *a*; "he will go up (*anabēsetai*) into the heaven" EGW (Syr.) 436 Slav.; "God will pull him into heaven" Arm.; "he will call upon the God of Israel saying (omit D Phil)" *d*; illegible F; gaps L1 Ngr.

Gk. *anaboēsetai* "he will cry up" (or "out") may be behind both *boēsei* and *anabēsetai*. But perhaps this is just another case of split tradition. A possible reconstruction, assuming loss by *homoiarcton*, is "he will cry to the Most High, and (his cry) will go up into the heaven" (cf. Acts 10:4).

l. Cf. 2Kgs 1:10, 12, 14; Sir 48:3; TAb B 12; Lk 9:54.

m. Cf. e.g. 2Kgs 6:16f.; 2Mac 3:25f.; 3Mac 6:18f.; 1QM 12.8; Mt 26:53; Berger, *Auferstehung*, pp. 270–73, n. 106. See also 28:1.

n. See 24:6.

o. "That . . . Aseneth" *a* ("in" for "out" AP) *d*; gaps L1 Ngr.; omit Slav. and rest. The end of vs. 7 is not intrinsically improbable (*mē genoito*, the well-known emphatic negation stemming from popular philosophical parlance, never LXX, but e.g. TJob 38:1; Rom 3:4); but vs. 8 is difficult, because the bad brothers have already gone out (24:19f.), and not against Joseph at that. Is vs. 8 an addition? But the style of JosAsen requires some conclusion of the scene. Is this an early example of flashback technique, perhaps somewhat unexpectedly and rather clumsily done? Or shall we assume that vss. 5–8 have been misplaced at some early date? They would fit better between 24:19 and 24:20.

26 a. Reported in 24:15.

2 (2) from me." •And Joseph said to her, "Courage, and do not be afraid, but go,[b] because the
Lord is with you,[c] and he himself will guard you like an apple of the eye from every wicked
3 (3) deed![d] •For I, too, will go to my grain giving[e] and will give bread[f] to all men, and the
4 (4) whole land will surely not perish (away) from the face of the Lord."[g] •And Aseneth went
away on her way, and Joseph went away to his grain giving.

5 (5)   And Aseneth and the six hundred men with her came to the place of the wadi. And
suddenly those who lay in ambush[h] rushed out of their ambushes and joined battle with
Aseneth's men, and cut them down with the edge of the sword,[i] and they killed all her
(6) forerunners, but Aseneth fled ahead with her carriage.

6 (7)   And Levi, the son of Leah, perceived all these (things) in (his) spirit[j] as a prophet, and
he[k] declared the danger[l] (in which) Aseneth (was) to his brothers the sons of Leah.[m] And
each of them took his sword and put it on his thigh, and they took their shields and put
them on their arms, and they took their spears in their right hands, and pursued after Aseneth
in rapid course.

7 (8)   And Aseneth was fleeing ahead, and behold, Pharaoh's son and fifty horsemen with him
8 met[n] her. •And Aseneth saw him and was afraid and troubled very much, and her whole
body trembled. And she called on the name of the Lord her God.

Benjamin wounds Pharaoh's son and kills his troups with stones

1 (1), (2)   **27** And Benjamin[a] sat at Aseneth's left (hand) in her carriage.[b] And Benjamin was a boy
of eighteen years, big and strong and powerful, and there was unspeakable beauty on him,
2 (3) and strength like (that of) a lion cub,[c] and he feared the Lord exceedingly. •And Benjamin
leapt down from the carriage and took a round stone from the wadi and filled his hand[d] and
hurled (the stone) at Pharaoh's son and struck his left temple and wounded him with a
3 heavy[e] wound. •And Pharaoh's son fell down from his horse on the ground, being half
4 (4) dead.[f] •And Benjamin leapt and went up upon the rock, and said to Aseneth's charioteer,
5 (5) "Give me stones[g] from the wadi." •And he gave him fifty stones. And Benjamin hurled

b. A adds "rejoicing (masculine) completely,
(by) nothing (or "no one") being frightened (*ptoou-
menē*)"; PQ add "rejoicing (feminine) no word
doing (*poioumenē*)"; gaps EG L1 Slav. Ngr.; omit
rest.

c. Traditional; see W. C. van Unnik, "Dominus
vobiscum," *New Testament Essays: Studies in
Memory of Thomas Walter Manson*, ed. A. J. B.
Higgins (Manchester, 1959) pp. 270–305.

d. Cf. e.g. Ps 120:7; Jub 12:29; 31:24; 1QS
2.3.

e. Gk. *sitodosia*, in LXX only Gen 42:19, 33,
no equivalent in MT. Also cf. vs. 4.

f. Witnesses FW Arm. L1 (436); "grain" AP
d Syr.?; omit E Slav.; gaps Q G Ngr.

g. Cf. Gen 6:11. If this vs. in Gen is alluded to
we should perhaps translate, ". . . surely not grow
corrupt in the Lord's sight." Cf. further Gen 41:36;
47:13.

h. The reading "those . . . ambush": *b* ("for
them" added G) Arm. 436 (L1) Slav. (added "for
her"); "the men" Syr.; "those around Pharaoh's
son" AP(Q) *d* (against 24:19); gap Ngr.

i. Lit. "in mouth of sword," the well-known
biblical phrase, e.g. Gen 34:26; Jdt 2:27; Sir 28:18;
Lk 21:24.

j. Cf. Mk 2:8; see Intro.

k. The reading "the son . . . he": (*a d*); cf.
"And as Levi and Benjamin saw (singular)" Ngr.
(but context is garbled); omit rest including Slav.

l. As often, *kindynos* means "predicament,"
rather than "risk."

m. The reading "the sons of Leah": E Syr.
Arm. 436 Ngr.; "the sons of Israel" (FGW); omit
rest.

n. Lit. "meets (*apanta*)."

27 a. He appears unexpectedly. 1Sam 17, especially vss. 48–51, have inspired the following
verses and 29:2. This explains why Benjamin is a
"boy" despite his eighteen years (on those cf. 1:4
and also TLevi 12:5).

b. "And . . . carriage" (E)F(G)W ("right" for
"left" E G) Arm. (436); "And Benjamin was
sitting with her (w. h. omit Slav.) on the carriage
at (the) right (side) ("at . . . side" omit *d* only)"
(*a d*); "Benjamin however with her was in the
carriage" Syr.; "Benjamin however (just) as he
was on Aseneth's carriage with her" L1; "Sat
however also near her in her right part Benjamin
the son of Jacob or rather the brother of Joseph"
Ngr.

c. Cf. Gen 49:9 (Judah). Benjamin's description
varies considerably. Maybe more can be made of
the evidence.

d. The expression appears to mean that he
"gripped the stone firmly." Cf. 2Kgs 9:24, lit.
"And Jehu filled his hand with the bow."

e. Witnesses *a* EFW Syr. Arm. (436); "great
and heavy" G Slav. Phil; "great" Ngr.; gaps *d*
L1.

f. The reading "being half dead": (*a*) *d* (L1)
Ngr. (661 only, see Burchard, *NTS* 24 [1978] 73f.);
probably Arm. (Burchard, "Joseph und Aseneth
25–29 armenisch," *JSJ* 10 [1979] 1–10); omit EG
Syr. 436 Slav.; gap FW. Gk. *hemithanēs* is first
attested by Dionysius of Halicarnassus and Diodorus of Sicily. Cf. Lk 10:30; Burchard, *ZNW* 61
(1970) 158.

g. See vs. 5. Perhaps we should prefix "fifty."

the fifty stones and killed the fifty men who were with the son of Pharaoh.[h] And all the stones penetrated their temples.

Levi and his brothers kill the troops of Dan and Gad

6 (6)   And the sons of Leah, Ruben and Simeon, Levi and Judah, Issachar and Zebulun, pursued after the men who had been lying in ambush for Aseneth and fell upon them unawares[i] and cut them all down; and the six men killed two thousand.[j]

Dan and Gad, Naphtali and Asher try to kill Aseneth, but their swords turn to ashes

7 (7)   And their brothers, the sons of Bilhah and Zilpah, fled from their presence and said, "We have been destroyed by our brothers, and Pharaoh's son has died by the hand of Benjamin the boy, and all (who were) with him have been destroyed by the one hand of
8   the boy Benjamin. •And now,[k] come, let us kill Aseneth and Benjamin and flee into this
9 (8)   thicket of reeds." •And they came toward Aseneth holding their swords drawn, full of blood.
10   And Aseneth saw them and was exceedingly afraid and said:

> Lord my God, who made me alive again
> and rescued me[l] from the idols and the corruption of death,[m]
> who said to me, "Your soul will live for ever,"[n]
> rescue me from the hands of these wicked men.

11   And the Lord God heard Aseneth's voice, and at once their swords fell from their hands on the ground and were reduced to ashes.

The wicked brothers give up and ask Aseneth to intercede for them with Levi and his brothers

1 (1)   **28** And the sons of Bilhah and Zilpah saw this great thing and were exceedingly afraid and
2 (2)   said, "The Lord fights against us for Aseneth."[a] •And they fell on the face to the ground and prostrated themselves before Aseneth and said, "Have mercy on us, your slaves,
3   because you are our mistress and queen. •And we have wickedly committed evil (things)
(3)   against you and against our brother Joseph;[b] and the Lord repaid us according to our works.[c]
4   •And now we, your slaves, beg you, have mercy on us and rescue us from the hands of our brothers, because they arrived as avengers of the insult (done to) you, and their swords
5   are against us. •And[d] we know that our brothers are men who worship God and do not
6   repay anyone evil for evil. •Anyway, be gracious to your slaves, mistress, before them."
7 (4)   And Aseneth said to them, "Courage, and do not be afraid of your brothers, because

---

h. In *a* G *d* the number of stones and men, if present, is fifty (G *d* have it also in vs. 4); in EFW Syr. Arm. Ngr. it is forty-eight; in 436 forty-nine; Slav. has fifty in vs. 4, forty-eight in vs. 5; gap L1. Fifty is consonant with 24:19; 25:4; 26:7. Maybe Dan and Gad have been deducted erroneously to make forty-eight.
   i. Cf. Josh 10:9.
   j. The variants are too numerous to list here.
   k. "And now" *b d* Syr. (436 Slav.); "and now they say" (or "said") Arm.; "Anyway therefore (omit Q) the (omit A) left behind (plural) said" *a* Bat ("the" omit "left . . . said" in square brackets; omit Br Rie); gaps L1 Ngr.
   l. Cf. Isa 49:7, 26; 54:5, 8.
   m. The reading "and rescued . . . death": AP(Q); "out of death" *b* Syr. Arm. 436 Slav. Phil; gaps *d* L1 Ngr. The *a* reading has been adopted on the principle of *lectio longior* (see Intro.) and because "rescued" makes a good parallelism with "rescue," but the evidence is poor. Cf. Rom 7:24.
   n. The mention of an afterlife of the "soul"

does not by itself prove that JosAsen believes in its immortality (against Philonenko, *Joseph et Aséneth*, p. 215). It is compatible with other ideas of man's future life (cf. Fischer, *Eschatologie und Jenseitserwartung*, pp. 97–105). See further Intro.

28 a. Also cf. vs. 10. Cf. e.g. Ex 14:14, 25; 2Chr 20:29. G. Delling ("Einwirkungen der Sprache der Septuaginta in 'Joseph und Aseneth,' " *JSJ* 9 [1978] 29–56, see p. 45) suggests a deliberate allusion to the miraculous deliverance at the Red Sea. See further 25:6.
   b. The reading "and . . . Joseph": *a* B (D) Phil; gaps L1 Ngr.; omit rest.
   c. Cf. e.g. Ps 62:12; Prov 24:12; Sir 35:24; Rom 2:6; 2Cor 11:15.
   d. Vss. 5f. (*a* B; vs. 5 in square brackets Bat, omit Br); omit *b* D (but in vs. 7 D Phil have "not repaying evil for evil" for "fearing . . . man," *a* vestige of the *a* B reading?) Syr. Arm. 436 Slav. Br Phil; gaps L1 Ngr. Vs. 5 will have to be taken as a self-correction ("And yet we know . . .") to make sense after vs. 4.

(5) they are men who worship God and fearing God and respecting every man.[e] But go into this thicket of reeds, until I appease them concerning you[f] and make their anger cease,
(6) because you acted in great boldness against them. Courage now, and do not be afraid.
8 (7) Besides, the Lord[g] will judge between me and you.''[h] •And Dan and Gad and their brothers fled into the thicket of reeds.

Aseneth appeases Simeon and his brothers

(8) 9   And behold, the sons of Leah came running like three-year-old[i] stags against them. •And Aseneth descended from the carriage (that gave) her shelter and gave them her right hand
(9) with tears, 'and they, falling (down), prostrated themselves on the ground before her, and wept in a loud voice; and they were seeking their brothers, the sons of their father's
10 (10) maidservants, in order to do away with them. •And Aseneth said to them, ''I beg you, spare your brothers and do not do[j] them evil for evil, because the Lord protected me against them, and shattered their swords, and they melted on the ground like wax from the presence
(11) 11 of fire.[k] 'And this is enough for them that the Lord fights against them for us.[l] •And you, spare them because they are your brothers and your father Israel's blood.''[m]
12 (12)   And Simeon said to her, ''Why does our mistress speak good (things) on behalf of her
13 (13) enemies? •No, but let us cut them down[n] with our swords, because they (were) first (to) plan evil (things) against us and against our father Israel and against our brother Joseph,[o]
14 (14) this already twice,[p] and against you, our mistress and queen, today.'' •And Aseneth stretched out her right hand and touched Simeon's beard and kissed him and said, ''By no means, brother, will you do evil for evil to your neighbor.[q] To the Lord will you give (the right) to punish the insult (done) by them.[r] And they are your brothers and your fathers, Israel's line, and they fled far from your presence. Anyway, grant them pardon.''[s]
15 (15), (16)   And Levi went up to her and kissed her right hand and perceived that 'she wanted to
16 save the men from their brother's anger so that they would not kill them. •And[t] they were
17 nearby in the thicket of reeds. •And Levi their brother perceived it and did not declare it to his brothers. For he was afraid that in their anger they might cut them down.

Levi tries to save the life of Pharaoh's son

1 (1) **29** And Pharaoh's son rose from the ground and sat up and spat blood from his mouth,
2 (2) because the blood from his temple ran down over his mouth. •And Benjamin ran up to him and took his sword and drew it from its sheath, because Benjamin did not have a sword on
3 (3) his thigh, and set about to strike the breast of Pharaoh's son.[a] •And Levi ran up to him and grasped his hand and said, ''By no means, brother, will you do this deed, because we are men who worship God, and it does not befit a man who worships God to repay evil for
4 evil nor to trample underfoot a fallen (man) nor to oppress his enemy till death. •And now,
(4) put your sword back into its place,[b] and come, help me, and we will heal him of his wound; and if he lives, he will be our friend after this, and his father Pharaoh will be like our father.''

e. The reading ''and . . . man'': G (Syr.) Arm. 436; omit AP b Slav.; gaps rest (D Phil see at vs. 5). Cf. Lk 18:2.
  f. Cf. Ex 32:30.
  g. The reading ''may see (idoi A, idou ''behold'' PQ) and'': added a (cf. Ex 5:21; 1Sam 24:16; 2Chr 24:22); gaps L1 Ngr.; illegible F; omit rest.
  h. The whole phrase is traditional; cf. previous note and Gen 16:5; Jdt 7:24.
  i. The reading ''three-year-old'': FGW; ''young'' Syr.; ''many'' Arm.; ''in much hurry'' AP(Q); omit d 436; gaps E L1 Ngr. Stags or hinds are a model of velocity in the OT, e.g. cf. Ps 18:34.
  j. Witnesses FGW d Arm. 436; ''repay'' a Syr.; gaps rest including Slav.
  k. Traditional, e.g. Ps 68:2; Micah 1:4.
  l. See vs. 1.
  m. ''Blood'' was believed to have a part in procreation (e.g. WisSol 7:2; 1En 15:4; Jn 1:13) and hence used in metonymy for ''line,'' ''family,''

''relative'' (not biblical). See the evidence in J. Behm, ''haima etc.,'' TDNT 1, 172–77; SibOr 3.827; Josephus, War 1.18.4 §359; Apuleius 4.23.4.
  n. The reading ''limb from limb'': added a D; gaps E L1 Slav. Ngr.; omit rest.
  o. Cf. Gen 50:20.
  p. The reading ''this . . . twice'': FGW D Syr. (Arm.) Phil; omit a B 436; gaps,E L1 Slav. Ngr.
  q. The reading ''to your neighbor'': a d; gaps E L1 Slav. Ngr.; omit rest.
  r. Or ''give the insult (done) by them to punish.'' Cf. e.g. TBenj 4:3; 1QS 10.17f.; Rom 12:19.
  s. ''Anyway . . . pardon'' AP; omit G Syr. Arm. 436; gaps rest. Doubtful.
  t. Vss. 16f. (a FGW Syr. Arm. 436); omit d; gaps E L1 Slav. Ngr.

29 a. Cf. 1Sam 17:50f. See also 27:1.
  b. Cf. Mt 26:52; Jn 18:11.

5 (5)   And Levi raised Pharaoh's son from the ground and washed the blood off his face and
tied a bandage to his wound, and put him upon his horse, and conducted him to his father
6 (6), (7) Pharaoh,[c] and described[d] to him all these things. •And Pharaoh rose from his throne and
prostrated himself before Levi on the ground and blessed him.[e]

IV. THE END

7 (8)   And on the third day Pharaoh's son died from the wound (caused by the impact) of the
8 (9) stone of Benjamin, the boy. •And Pharaoh mourned exceedingly for his firstborn son, and
(10) from the mourning he fell ill; and Pharaoh died[f] at a hundred and nine[g] years, and left his
9 (11) diadem to Joseph. •And Joseph reigned as king in Egypt for forty-eight years,[h] and after
this he gave the diadem to Pharaoh's younger offspring, who was at the breast when Pharaoh
died. And Joseph was like a father to Pharaoh's younger son in the land of Egypt all the
days of his life.[i]

c. Cf. Lk 10:30–35. Levi's attitude borders on
the love of one's enemy as implied in the Good
Samaritan and prescribed by Mt 5:43–48; yet it is
not the same thing. Levi exhibits clemency toward
a defeated enemy, as becomes a man in power, a
deed both noble and sensible which serves the
interests of both parties (cf. e.g. LetAris 227).
Jesus exacts love of one's persecutors from a
subdued minority predicated upon God's boundless
mercy. Cf. L. Schottroff, "Non-Violence and the
Love of One's Enemies," *Essays on the Love
Commandment*, ed. R. H. Fuller (Philadelphia,
1978) pp. 9–39.

d. (All), except "they d." G Ll Ngr. Phil (no
footnote); gaps E Slav.

e. The reading "and blessed him": *a* B Arm.?;
"and he lifted up his son from the ground" 436;
"Pharaoh however was grateful to them that they
had not killed him" vs. 6 Ll; omit FG D Syr.
Phil; gaps EW Slav. Ngr.

f. Arm. ends here.

g. The reading "a hundred and nine": A E *d*;
"99" GW Ll; "199" F; "190" Ngr.; "170" PQ;
"177" Syr.; "160" 436; uncertain Slav. If the

number 109 is correct; Pharaoh died one year
before the ideal age of 110 years, which Joseph
reached (Gen 50:26).

h. Similar figures in Jewish lore; cf. Aptowitzer, *HUCA* 1 (1924) 286.

i. The reading "all . . . life": Syr.; "until his
death glorifying and lauding God" *a* (B); omit EG
D Ll 436 Phil; W stopped after vs. 9 "years," F
at some point after "offspring in Egypt" (illegible);
Arm. after vs. 7 "died," Slav. after vs. 9 "son,"
Ngr. after vs. 9 "years"; "celebrating with the all
beautiful Aseneth, this all beautiful Joseph" added
671; "Joseph however made with Aseneth two
sons, Manasse and Ephraim [cf. 21:9], and saw
children of his children" added 661. The text is
doubtful; *a* might be given preference on the
strength of Tob 14:15f.; TAb B 14:7, but perhaps
we should break off after "of Egypt." Most
witnesses add some historical remarks from Gen
or Ex, an admonition, a note of completion, giving
the title of the book, a doxology, a colophon, or a
combination of such items; *a* adds Gen 50:22b–26
LXX, which is a remark about Aseneth's death
and burial, and a doxology.

LIFE OF ADAM AND EVE

(First Century A.D.)

A NEW TRANSLATION AND INTRODUCTION
BY M. D. JOHNSON

The Greek and Latin texts of the Life of Adam and Eve both purport to narrate in Midrashic form some episodes in the life of the "first-made" after their expulsion from Paradise, especially their deathbed recollections and instructions.

The Greek text (ApMos), after relating the murder of Abel by Cain and the birth of Seth, moves rapidly to Adam's deathbed, from which he tells how illness resulted from the first sin. He asks Seth and Eve to return to Paradise for oil from a tree with which he might be anointed and find rest from his pains. On the way to Paradise Seth is attacked by a wild beast and learns that the revolt of the animal world is another result of the Fall. At Paradise the archangel Michael informs Seth that the oil of mercy will not be given men until the day of resurrection. Seth and Eve return to Adam, who asks Eve to tell all their children the story of the Fall from Paradise. This she does at length (ApMos 15–30), describing the devil's plot with the serpent, his entry into Paradise, the temptation and Fall, God's appearance in Paradise to announce the punishments, and the expulsion from Paradise. Eve then repents in great sorrow. Adam dies, and Eve witnesses the awesome return of God to the earthly Paradise. Adam's soul is washed in Lake Acheron and taken up into the heavenly Paradise, while his body and that of Abel are prepared for burial in the spot where Adam's body had been formed at creation. Six days later Eve also dies and her body is buried in the same place.

The Latin text (Vita) begins differently;[1] after a description of their repentance (1–17), Eve is shown standing in the Tigris River and Adam in the Jordan. When Eve's time of penitence is half accomplished, Satan appears as an angel and deceives her a second time, inducing her to interrupt her penance. Adam approaches her and the devil. Satan then tells them that his fall from heaven resulted from his refusal to worship Adam, the image of God. When Adam completes his period of penance, Eve separates herself from him until the birth of Cain. The Latin here adds the story of Adam's ascension into the heavenly Paradise (25–29) but omits Eve's story of the Fall (ApMos 15–30). It continues with the account of the death and burial of Adam, and concludes with Eve's command to her children to record the story of Adam and Eve for posterity on tablets of stone and clay.

Texts

Tischendorf published an edition of the Greek text in 1866 which was based on four manuscripts (A1 B C D) and which, together with two others (E1 E2), was used as the basis for the English translation of Wells and the German of Fuchs.[2] Seventeen additional manuscripts have been located, ten of which, along with the previous six, have been collated by J. L. Sharpe as variants to the Tischendorf text.[3] These sixteen manuscripts, with sigla as used by Tischendorf, Fuchs, Wells, and Sharpe, along with an estimation of date, present location, and degree of completeness, are:

---

[1] In the following pages I have designated the Lat. text as Vita and the Gk. text as ApMos. Two MSS (F and H) of ApMos have a version of the repentance and are translated below as a parallel to Vita 1ff.

[2] See Bibliography.

[3] J. L. Sharpe, Prolegomena, pt. 2.

A1.   13th–14th cent.; Venice; ends at 36:3.
A2.   15th–17th cent.; Athos; complete, except 13:2–16:4 is missing.
B.   13th–16th cent.; Vienna; omits 21:3–25:2 and 33:2–43:4.
C.   11th–13th cent.; Vienna; this is the most complete manuscript.
D1.   11th cent.; Milan; 18:1–36:1 is missing.[4]
D2.   12th–14th cent.; Strassburg; complete.
D3.   1518 A.D.; Athens; complete.
D4.   13th cent.; Athos; complete.
D5.   16th–17th cent.; Andros; 16:3–29:3 is missing.
E1.   16th cent.; Paris; essentially complete.
E2.   15th–16th cent.; Montpellier; essentially complete.
F.   15th–17th cent.; Vatican; incomplete in 43; has the "repentance" following 29:6.
G.   16th cent.; Brescia; complete.
H.   16th–17th cent.; Patmos; complete; has the "repentance" following 29:6.
M1.   15th–16th cent.; Ankara; complete.
M2.   16th cent.; Patmos; complete.

Sharpe suggests a classification of these manuscripts into four translations.[5] A (A1 A2); D (D1 D2 D3 D4 D5 M1 M2); C (C E1 E2 G); F (F H); manuscript B is unclassified. Since progress in the critical analysis of the text does not yet allow a firm conclusion about the classification and relative priority among these manuscripts,[6] it has seemed best to present a translation which takes into account the major variants of all available manuscripts.

The translation of the *Vita* is based on the text of Meyer, taking into account the variants indicated in his apparatus as well as some of those given by Mozley.[7] Meyer classified the manuscripts, all of which are located in Munich except for the last mentioned, which is in Paris, as follows:

I. Three manuscripts: S, ninth century; T, tenth century; M, twelfth century. These do not have 29:4–15 or 51:3–9 and are Meyer's main authority, with preference for manuscript S.

II. Four manuscripts, one from the thirteenth to fourteenth centuries, the others from the fifteenth century. These contain the lengthy additions to chapters 29 and 51; eight of Mozley's manuscripts, as well as some medieval translations, conform to this textual type.

III. Four manuscripts from the fifteenth century, which include 29:4–15 as well as material on the history of the wood of the cross (similar to one manuscript of Mozley).

IV. The Paris manuscript, produced in the ninth century or later, related to II; contains 29:4–15 and 51:3–9.

Significant versions of the Greek text are the Armenian[8] and, with more Christian interpolations, the Slavonic.[9] The Greek and Latin original texts are both certainly prior to these and perhaps also to the other Adam literature, sometimes of Christian production, such as The Cave of Treasures, extant in Syriac, Arabic, and Ethiopic; The Combat of Adam and Eve, a Christian work of the eleventh century translated from Arabic into Ethiopic; the Testament of Adam, extant primarily in Greek and Syriac, and an Apocalypse of Adam among the gnostic works discovered at Nag Hammadi.[10] These documents reveal the

[4] MS D1 was published by A. M. Ceriani in *Monumenta Sacra et Profana* (Milan, 1868) vol. 5, pt. 1, pp. 19–24.

[5] Sharpe, *Prolegomena*, pt. 1, pp. 185–203.

[6] Sharpe's contention (pt. 1, p. 201) that MSS E1 and E2 preserve "the earliest type of text and the most conservative in style" goes against some apparently secondary features of those MSS, e.g. the omission of *koimōmenōn de autōn*, "and while they were lying down in order to sleep" (2:1); the addition of "my brother" in 2:2b; *ēsthenēse mikron*, "he fell sick a little," in 5:2; the addition of "branch of grace" in 9:3b and 10:1; "how were your eyes opened?" in 10:3; cf. also 11:1b and 19:2.

[7] See bibliography.

[8] F. C. Conybeare, "On the Apocalypse of Moses," *JQR* 7 (1895) 216–35. See also the references in Denis, *Introduction*, p. 7, n. 23, and M. Stone, "The Death of Adam—An Armenian Adam Book," *HTR* 59 (1966) 283–91.

[9] Text edited by V. Jagič, *Slavische Beiträge zu den biblischen Apocryphen* (Vienna, 1893), vol. 1, pp. 17–99. The Slav. version of the repentance is translated by L. S. A. Wells, *APOT*, vol. 2, pp. 134–36.

[10] For bibliography on these and other Adam materials see Denis, *Introduction*, pp. 7–14; Wells, *APOT*, vol. 2, pp. 125f.; James, *LAOT*, pp. 1–8.

continued interest among Christian writers in speculating upon the life of the protoplasts, Adam and Eve, and upon Seth as a recipient of revelation. To a large extent, however, these documents are later alterations of the material here presented, and are of limited use in establishing the Greek and Latin texts.

Original language

Although no Hebrew text is extant,[11] it is most probable that there did exist an original Hebrew document or documents from which the Apocalypse and *Vita* were translated, the Greek directly from the Hebrew and the Latin directly either from the Hebrew or from the Greek.[12] Sharpe has summarized much of the evidence which leads to this conclusion with regard to the Greek text:[13] the consistent parataxis; the verb preceding the subject; traces of Semitic parallelism (ApMos 34–36; 39:1–3); the use of the infinite absolute, a rarity in Aramaic (17:5; 41:3); the adjectival genitive (3:2; 21:2; 38:2; 43:5); Hebraic relative constructions ("the tree in which the oil flows out of it" in 9:3 and "my command which I delivered to you to keep it" in 22:3); and the redundant use of the participle, as in the frequently used expression "he answered and said" or "he wept, saying." More striking are the evidences of transliterations and apparent mistranslations from the Hebrew: *idou*, lit., "behold," in 41:1 (Heb. *hin˚ni*); *Jael* (see 29:4; 33:5); repeated prepositions (Gk. of 26:4); *en mataiois*, lit., "in follies," an apparent mistranslation in 25:1 (see n.). In addition to this evidence offered by Sharpe, see the notes to Apocalypse 1:3 and 19:5, both of which suggest a Hebrew original.

In spite of this convincing evidence it should be noted that the author was familiar with the Septuagint of Genesis 1–5 and that the Lake Acheron of Apocalypse 37:3 is derived from Greek tradition, although it was familiar to early Christians and could have been known also to a Jewish author (see n.).

Whether the Latin is derived solely from a Greek version, partly from a Greek and partly from a Hebrew, or entirely from a Hebrew text cannot be determined conclusively. The problem is complicated by the fact that three episodes in the Latin have no direct counterpart in most manuscripts of the Greek: the repentance of Adam and Eve (1–11); Satan's fall from heaven (12–16) and Adam's ascension into the heavenly Paradise (25–29). Similarly, Eve's story of the Fall in Apocalypse 15–30 has no complete parallel in *Vita*, although several details from it are reproduced.[14] The Greek text, moreover, shows clear signs of composite sources: God appears in the earthly Paradise twice to announce punishments for sin (8; 22) and twice to attend to matters following the death of Adam (33; 38). Without doubt, a diverse oral and literary history lies behind the Greek and Latin texts alike; it would therefore be pointless to attempt recovery of "the original Hebrew text."

The linguistic evidence in *Vita* is likewise mixed. On the one hand Greek expressions are retained in the Latin, e.g. *plagas*, "plagues," in 34:1; *plasmatus*, "created," in 13:2; *plasmasti*, "you formed," in 27:2; *plasma*, "creature," in 46:3; *sindones bissinas*, "linen cloths," in 48:1. On the other hand Semitisms can be seen in 10:1 (Heb. *yarōqah*, "sponge," read as *yārāq*, "herb"); 18:2 (*ad occasum solis*, "to the sunset," see n.); 21:1 (*virtutes*, "excellences," see n.); 21:3 (*herbam*, "reed," see n.), as well as in the style. Several possibilities remain: The Latin author was ignorant of the Greek; he chose not to reproduce the story of Eve; or he had before him a form of the Greek text that is earlier than what is reflected in the extant manuscripts. The latter possibility seems most adequate.[15]

---

[12] Rabbinic traditions interpret Gen 5:1 as referring to God's foreknowledge of human history rather than to a document, as in bAZ 5a: "Did not Resh Lakish say, 'What is the meaning of the verse, *This is the book of the generations of Adam?* Did Adam have a book? What it implies is that the Holy One, blessed be He, showed to Adam every generation with its exposition . . .' " (so also ARN 31 [Goldin's ed., p. 126]; bBM 85b–86a; GenR 24:2; ExR 40).

[12] Gk. from Heb. original: Meyer, p. 217; Wells, *APOT*, vol. 2, pp. 129f.; C. Fuchs, *APAT*, vol. 2, p. 511; Sharpe, *Prolegomena* pt. 1, pp. 114–39; O. Eissfeldt, *The Old Testament: An Introduction* (New York, 1965) p. 636. That the Lat. is directly translated from the Heb. is less widely held; see the evidence adduced by Wells, *APOT*, vol. 2, pp. 128f., to suggest that the author of the *Vita* had the ApMos before him.

[13] Sharpe, *Prolegomena*, pt. 1, pp. 116–39.

[14] Cf. the following passages from Eve's story with parallels in *Vita* (ApMos reference is given first): 15:2 with 32:2; 16:2 with 14:3; 16:3 with 12–16; 17:1 with 9:1 and 33:2; 21:6 with 44:2; 22 with 25; 29:6 with 22:2 and 43:5.

[15] But see Meyer's reasons for presupposing translation from the Heb. (*Abhandlungen*. pp. 198–207).

Date

Meyer suggested the possibility that the Paris manuscript of the *Vita* was made in the ninth century or later from a manuscript dated between 730 and 740.[16] He notes also that the story of the fall of Satan (12–16), not found in the Greek, seems to have been known to Mohammed (see 12:1, n.) and that the original document (Hebrew?) must be prior to the Adam material extant in Syriac, Arabic, Ethiopic, and Slavic. Parts, at least, of the Greek document were known to the author of the Gospel of Nicodemus (ch. 19 = Descent into Hell 3); and the Armenian and Slavic are translations of the Greek. The external evidence therefore would indicate a latest possible date of about A.D. 500, or better 400, for the first Greek and Latin translations of the original document(s), which must be considerably earlier.

The absence of apparent Christian allusions, except for the easily identifiable variants in *Vita* 29 and 51, does not necessarily argue for a date early in the Christian period since Christian allusions are rare in most Jewish writings of that time. Yet, given the fact that the document enjoyed wide circulation among Christians, the paucity of Christian interpolations is indeed striking. The many parallels with early rabbinic traditions (some are identified in the notes), 2 Enoch (see below), and Josephus (cf. *Ant* 1.2.3 with *Vita* 50) reveal that the substance of both recensions, Greek and Latin, fits into the time near the beginning of Christianity. On the other hand, the frequently adduced passage in *Vita* 29:8 which refers to a second temple without mentioning its destruction is not an indication of date since it is missing in the best Latin manuscripts. There are, unfortunately, no clear historical allusions in any part of either text.

Given the relationship with the Pseudepigrapha, Josephus, rabbinic traditions, and perhaps Paul, the most natural span for the original composition would be between 100 B.C. and A.D. 200, more probably toward the end of the first Christian century. The Greek and Latin texts were produced between that time and A.D. 400.[17]

Provenance

On the basis of supposed hellenistic touches, especially the mention of the Lake of Acheron in Apocalypse 37:3, it has often been suggested that the author of the original document was a Jew of Alexandria.[18] This view is difficult to maintain if it is admitted that both the Greek and Latin texts show signs of mistranslation of a source or sources written in Hebrew. Moreover, our documents have a consistently non-Philonian approach to biblical interpretation, with no trace of allegorization or symbolic treatment of biblical figures. The work stands much closer to the Midrash or Haggadah so typical of Qumran and the Rabbis. Preferable, therefore, is the view of Sharpe, who concludes from an examination of the Greek text that "the original document was written in Hebrew, the form is that of the Midrash, and the theology is that of Pharisaic Judaism" and that it probably originated in Palestine.[19] While the question of authorship can be discussed only on the basis of the contents and must therefore remain problematical, it is highly probable that the author of the main traditions was a Jew who had not absorbed much of Greek piety or the Philonian exegetic method.[20]

Theological importance

The contents of both the Greek and Latin recensions appear to be quite compatible with the beliefs reflected in the Pseudepigrapha as a whole, as well as the theology of rabbinic

---

[16] Meyer, *Abhandlungen*, pp. 218f.
[17] See also Sharpe, *Prolegomena*, pt. 1, pp. 146–51.
[18] E.g. Wells, *APOT*, vol. 2, p. 130.
[19] Sharpe, *Prolegomena*, pt. 1, p. 226; also pp. 8f. and 151.
[20] E. Schürer, *Geschichte des Jüdischen Volkes*[4] (Leipzig, 1909) vol. 3, pp. 398–99, is one of the few who has expressed doubts on this point.

Judaism,[21] the Dead Sea Scrolls, and early Christianity.[22] The absence of polemic and sectarian tendencies is remarkable and refreshing, and yet it frustrates the attempt to identify the milieu out of which the material has sprung.

God is pictured with a curious mixture of transcendent majesty and quaint anthropomorphism. The four theophanies of the Greek text (ApMos 8; 22; 33; 38) describe God's arrival on a "chariot of Cherubim" (22) or a "chariot of light . . . [drawn] by four radiant eagles" (33), accompanied by ranks of angels, and with such glory that the sun and moon seem to be darkened (ApMos 35–36). With this, the account in *Vita* 25–28 of Adam's ascension into the "paradise of righteousness" is fully consistent. This divine transcendence is suggested also by the mediation of the angels who carry out God's will. Especially touching are the blossoming of the plants of the earthly Paradise on God's arrival (ApMos 22:3; 38:4), the cultic preparations made for the theophany in Apocalypse 33, and the piety of *Vita* 28 and Apocalypse 32; 42. Yet both recensions record God stretching out his hand to receive Adam's soul (ApMos 37:4; *Vita* 47:2), holding a conversation first with Adam's soul (ApMos 39) and then his body (ApMos 41), and rebuking the angels for being more merciful than he (ApMos 27:4).[23] God is both to be feared and also to be looked to for grace.

The exaltation of God is also to be seen in the numerous references to angelic beings. There are ranks of angels (ApMos 36:1) over which are the cherubim (ApMos 22; 36:3) and the seraphim (ApMos 33:3; 37:3). These accompany God in his appearances on earth and offer worship to him at regular intervals (ApMos 7:2; 17:1). Four angels are mentioned by name (ApMos 40:2) and of these Michael is of greatest interest in our texts: He teaches Adam agriculture (*Vita* 22:2); as the "angel of mankind" (ApMos 32; *Vita* 41:1) he comforts Eve (*Vita* 21:2); he conducts Adam to the paradise of righteousness (*Vita* 22:2), takes charge of the soul and body of Adam after his death (ApMos 37:5–6; *Vita* 46:3), and in general serves as God's messenger to men (ApMos 2:1; 3:2; 49:2 and par. in *Vita*). The Angelic Liturgy of the Dead Sea Scrolls offers an interesting parallel to several of these details (see nn.). Certain angels, called *virtutes*, "excellences," in the *Vita*, are placed to guard the earthly Paradise before and after the Fall.

Satan is a pre-existent fallen angel, and the *Vita* constitutes a classic source for this legend (12–16), which recurs in the Koran and various early and medieval Christian writings. He seeks to destroy men's souls (*Vita* 17:1) by disguising himself as an angel of light (*Vita* 9:1, 3; 12:1; ApMos 17:1) to put into men "his evil poison, which is his covetousness" (*epithymia*, ApMos 19:3; cf. *Vita* 15:3). This leads to transgression of God's commands, to strife or enmity (ApMos 25:4; 28:3; *Vita* 12:1), to seventy varieties of illness and pain (ApMos 8; *Vita* 34), to disruptions in the natural and animal world (ApMos 10ff.; *Vita* 37ff.; ApMos 20:3), and, above all else, to death (ApMos 14:2; 2:4). But in the end, those whom he has seduced by his wiles will sit on the glorious throne which he has usurped (ApMos 39:2; *Vita* 47:3).

Man is formed from clay and the divine breath (*Vita* 27:2) and so has the image of God, which is not totally obliterated by the Fall (ApMos 10:3; 12:1; 35:2; *Vita* 13:3; 14:1–3; 15:2; 37:3; 39:2). He was originally clothed in righteousness and glory (ApMos 20–21) and received the worship of angels (*Vita* 13–14) but now has an "evil heart" (ApMos 13:5) and is subject to toil, pain, strife, sickness, and death. Yet his love of knowledge remains (*Vita* 27:3). Of special interest is the conception of soul and body, seen most clearly in the Greek text, in which at the death of Adam the soul is taken into the third heaven (ApMos 37) while the body is buried in the ground (ApMos 40). Restoration of full life awaits the resurrection, when the soul and body will be reunited. That there is some Greek influence on this conception can be seen by the mention of the Lake Acheron in Apocalypse 37:3.

Sin, according to our texts, stems from grasping equality with God (*Vita* 15:3) or from Satan's *epithymia* ("covetousness" or "grasping desire"; ApMos 19:3), which takes concrete form in the breaking of God's commands. Both texts repeatedly assert that sin has

---

[21] Except that the MSS in group I at *Vita* 14:2 have the divine name in Gk. uncials: *IHU*.

[22] Christian motifs are not evident even in the interpolations in *Vita* 29:4–15, except at vs. 14, and 51:3–9, except vs. 9. The same is true of ApMos 13:3–6, but not, of course, *Vita* 42:2–5, which is completely Christian in origin.

[23] Wells, *APOT*, vol. 2, p. 132.

come to the human race through a woman (ApMos 9:2; 11; 14:2; 21:2, 6; 24:1; 29:3; 32:2; *Vita* 18:1; 26:2; 35:2; 38; 44:2). Repentance and sincere sorrow are the appropriate attitudes of the sinner, as is seen most movingly in Eve's repentance in Apocalypse 32 (cf. ApMos 27:3; *Vita* 4). The *Vita* also emphasizes ritual acts (fasting, 6:1; submersion in water, 6; placing dung or dust on one's head, 40:2; 36:1; cf. ApMos 6:2), but it is noteworthy that in neither text is sacrifice explicitly set forth as expiatory.[24] Ascetic ideals are much less in evidence than one would expect in an early Jewish or Christian document.[25]

Of special interest in both texts are the two paradises. The earthly Paradise is surrounded by water (*Vita* 29:2–3) and a wall with gates (ApMos 17:1; 19:1); it was divided between Adam and Eve to be tended by them (ApMos 15; *Vita* 32:2). Greatest emphasis falls on the tree of life, the "illegal tree," and the tree from which the healing oil flows (in *Vita* 36:2 but not ApMos this is identified with the tree of life). The earthly Paradise is also the place of burial of Adam, Abel, and Eve (ApMos 40:6). The heavenly Paradise is located in the third heaven[26] (ApMos 37:5; 40:1; cf. 2En 8) and is the "Paradise of visitation" or "Paradise of righteousness" of *Vita* 25:3 and 29:1. This is the abode of the soul after death (ApMos 37).

The resurrection of the dead at the last day is repeatedly taught. While not denying the resurrection of the wicked, the emphasis clearly is placed on the restoration to man of what had been lost in the Fall: The tree of life will be given (ApMos 28:4), the healing oil which Adam requested in vain (ApMos 13; *Vita* 42), a godly heart (ApMos 13), and the throne usurped by Satan (ApMos 39; *Vita* 47). The absence of any and all messianism is most striking and completely unexplainable on the assumption of a Christian origin of the material.

There is also the motif of the place where Adam was created (ApMos 40:6), where he had his house of prayer (ApMos 5:3; *Vita* 30:2), and where he was buried (ApMos 40; *Vita* 45:2). In *Vita* 45:2 this is "against the East in the great dwelling place of God," and in Apocalypse 33:4 there is an altar at that spot. There can be little doubt that the same site is intended in all such references and that the location is to be understood as the place of the Jerusalem Temple, where rabbinic sources fix the location of Adam's oratory (see n. to *Vita* 30:2). Since no trace is here found of the Christian legend that Adam was buried on the site of the crucifixion and burial place of Jesus,[27] we have all the more reason to think of a specifically Jewish origin of this material.

Relation to canonical and apocryphal books

Parts of this work develop themes which are at best tangential to Old Testament material: the repentance of Adam and Eve and the fall of Satan (*Vita* 1–17); Adam's rapture to the heavenly Paradise (*Vita* 25–29); Seth's quest for the healing oil (ApMos 5:3–6:3; 9–14 and par.); the death and burial of Adam and Eve (ApMos 31–43 and par.); and Eve's command to her children to make the tablets (*Vita* 49; 51:3ff.). The remainder of the narrative, including the birth of the children of Adam and Eve (ApMos 1–5 and par.), Adam's story of the Fall (ApMos 7–8 and par.), and Eve's story of the Fall (ApMos 15–30), is a typical haggadic Midrash on various details of Genesis 1–5.[28] Numerous allusions and quotations from the Septuagint are to be found in Apocalypse 15–30 and from the Vulgate throughout the *Vita*. Specific allusions to other Old Testament material are rare. *Vita* 4:2 and even the description of the divine chariot may derive directly from other Pseudepigrapha (but cf. *Vita* 15f. with Isa 14:13).

Interesting parallels to several New Testament passages can be found: Hebrews 1:16 (*Vita* 13–14); James 1:17 (*Vita* 29:2; ApMos 36:3); the tree of life (Rev 22:2). However, it is

---

[24] Sacrifice is not mentioned in *Vita*; in ApMos it seems to be a form of worship (4:2; 29:3).

[25] Fasting only in *Vita* 6:1; sexual intercourse as the "sin of the flesh" in ApMos 25:3 has rabbinic parallels (see n.); separation of animals in Paradise according to sex (ApMos 15:3; not in *Vita* 32) may not be an ascetic touch. By contrast, suffering is not to be desired (ApMos 24–25) and there is nothing wrong in enjoying the delights of Paradise (*Vita* 16:2).

[26] Only in ApMos 35:2 are seven heavens mentioned; see note to *Vita* 25:3.

[27] Held already by Africanus, Origen, Athanasius, Basil, Chrysostom, and Epiphanius; see E. C. Quinn, *The Quest of Seth for the Oil of Life* (Chicago, 1962) p. 77, and M. Stone, *HTR* 59 (1966) 291, for references.

[28] Sharpe, *Prolegomena*, pt. 1, pp. 94–113, would limit the midrashic base to Gen 3:1–5:5.

the writings of Paul with which the documents have the closest affinity,[29] as can be seen in the idea that Eve was the source of sin and death (cf. 2Cor 11:3; 1Tim 2:4; in Rom 5:12–21 death follows the sin of Adam). Death as the separation of soul and body may have some affinity with 2 Corinthians 5:1–5, while the most striking parallels are the appearance of Satan in the brightness of an angel (*Vita* 9:1; ApMos 17:1; cf. 2Cor 11:14); the location of Paradise in the third heaven (ApMos 37:5; 2Cor 12:2); and *epithymia* as the root of all sin (ApMos 19:3; Rom 7:7). In spite of these parallels it is impossible to determine whether there is a relationship between the New Testament and our texts.

Among the other Jewish writings of the time various parallels can be found in the Dead Sea Scrolls, 4 Ezra, Jubilees, and 1 and 2 Enoch (see nn.). The Latin text has an especially close relationship with 2 Enoch (the fall of Satan, 2En 29:4–5; heavenly Paradise, 8:1–5; 42:2; 65:1; waters of Paradise, 8:5; 22:9; the tablets, 33:8–12). Wells's judgment appears fully justified when he suggests that "Paul and the author of the 2 Enoch were near contemporaries of the original author of Apoc. Mos. and moved in the same circle of ideas."[30]

Cultural importance

The biblical story of the Fall of the first humans and its effect has grasped and stimulated the minds of Jews, Christians, and Muslims from antiquity to the present day. In the long history of this speculation the two documents here translated constitute one of the earliest, if not the first, separate treatments of the various legends linked to the first chapters of Genesis. Yet in assessing the cultural influence of these documents one must face the knotty problem of determining whether these documents themselves, or their Hebrew precursor, were the impetus for the many subsequent treatments or whether they are but one result of this interest itself.

The popularity of these two documents can be seen both by the fact that various versions of the Greek were made, notably the Armenian and the Slavic,[31] and also by their apparent use in several of the series of Eastern works which take the death of Adam as a starting point for a series of prophecies and events leading to the crucifixion. Among the latter, the Syriac Cave of Treasures[32] has inspired the Ethiopic Conflict of Adam and Eve,[33] while both works have occasional parallels of detail with the *Vita* and the Apocalypse.[34] The Syriac and Arabic Testament of Adam shows less influence from the *Vita* and the Apocalypse than the Cave and Conflict.[35]

Literary evidence suggests that during the fifth century, coincidental with the height of the Pelagian controversy, there was great interest, especially among Frankish churchmen, in harmonizing the biblical story of the origins of man with classical pagan heroic motifs, as is seen in poems of Hilary of Arles, Victor Rhetor of Marseilles, Avitus of Vienne, Cyprian of Gaul, and in the popular *Carmen de Deo* of Dracontius.[36] Direct influence of the *Vita* or the Apocalypse, however, is not found in these. Similarly, the earliest extant Anglo-Saxon Christian poetry, of the eighth and ninth centuries, reveals the influence of pagan Germanic saga. It is especially the English poem *Christ and Satan*[37] that betrays influence of the *Vita* in its Christianized form of the legend of the fall of Satan, as is also the case with the continental poem known as *Genesis B*.[38] The Koran also reflects knowledge of a form of the fall of Satan legend which is close to that of the *Vita* (*Vita* 12, n. a).

Toward the close of the twelfth century we have evidence that the legends of the history of the wood of the cross, developed at an earlier time, were combined with the motif of

[29] Wells, *APOT*, vol. 2, p. 130; Sharpe, *CBQ* 35 (1973) 35–46.

[30] Wells, *APOT*, vol. 2, p. 130.

[31] On these see Sharpe, *Prolegomena*, pt. 1, pp. 204–15.

[32] English translation by E. A. Wallis Budge, *The Book of the Cave of Treasures* (London, 1927).

[33] English translation by S. C. Malan, *The Book of Adam and Eve, Also Called the Conflict of Adam and Eve with Satan* (London, 1882).

[34] See Wells, *APOT*, vol. 2, pp. 125–27, 131f.

[35] M. R. James, *LAOT*, pp. 5–8; Wells, *APOT*, vol. 2, pp. 125f.

[36] On these see J. M. Evans, *Paradise Lost*, ch. 4.

[37] Ed. G. P. Krapp, *The Junius Manuscript* (New York, 1936).

[38] Evans, *Paradise Lost*, ch. 5, especially p. 146.

Seth's journey to Paradise, a combination found in Meyer's four fifteenth-century manuscripts (Group III) but found already in the *Rationale divinorum officiorum*, circa 1170.[39] According to this tradition, Seth returned from Paradise with a twig or seeds from which grew the tree that eventually supplied the wood for the cross of Jesus. In this modified form the *Vita* had a significant impact on the medieval European imagination.[40]

Apart from its conflation with the holy-wood motif, the *Vita* undoubtedly influenced the twelfth-century *Historia Scholastica* of Peter Comestor, especially in its treatment of the ascension of Adam and the Fall itself.[41] Less direct influence can be traced in the Townely and Chester medieval English miracle plays and in such narrative poems as *The Stanzaic Life of Christ*, Robert Grosseteste's *Chasteau d'Amour*, *Ludus Coventriae*, *De Lyff of Adam and Eve* in the Vernon manuscript, as well as in *De Deuelis Perlament* and the *Canticum de Creatione*.[42] The *Vita*'s description of Adam's repentance finds a close parallel in the similar account in *Mirk's Festival*, while William of Shoreham's poem *On the Trinity, Creation, the Existence of Evil, Devils, and Adam and Eve* reads like a theological reflection on the themes of the *Vita*. English miracle plays typically included the serpent disguised as an angel of light, Adam's prophetic dream at the creation of Eve, the serpent extracting the promise from Eve that she would give the fruit to Adam, and Eve's suggestion after the Fall that Adam kill her—all features betraying the probable influence of the *Vita*. Seth's journey to Paradise, however, is prominent only in the *Ordinale de Origine Mundi*.[43]

Adam is relatively insignificant in the *Divine Comedy*, being prominent only in paragraph 26, where Dante questions him about the duration of time from the creation to Dante's life (4,302 years) and the language Adam spoke in Eden (a tongue already extinct before the Flood).

The greatest classic on this theme, Milton's *Paradise Lost*, shows in its various drafts the influence of several of the prior treatments but especially, at least with regard to form, that of the Latin drama *Adamus Exul*, written by Hugo Grotius in 1601. Yet a good many details in Milton's work raise the probability of at least indirect influence by the *Vita*: Satan's charge that he was self-created and the equal of the Son of God, yet treated as inferior (*Paradise Lost* 5.661ff.; *Vita* 14); the corresponding functions of Milton's Abdiel and the *Vita*'s Michael; the division of labor between Adam and Eve (*Paradise Lost* 9.205–12; *Vita* 32); the dropping of Eve's garland at the first sin (*Paradise Lost* 9.892f.; cf. ApMos 20); the Fall as the loss of righteousness and glory (*Paradise Lost* 9.1054ff.; ApMos 21); and the vision of future generations given by Michael at the close of Milton's poem (book 11), which forms a parallel to *Vita* 29, 41, and the Apocalypse 13.

While J. M. Evans (see bibliography) has brilliantly traced the treatment of the Fall theme in literature up to Milton, there is no comparable study for the history of art or for literary and artistic productions subsequent to Milton.

[39] E. C. Quinn, *The Quest of Seth*, especially pp. 88ff.

[40] Quinn, *Quest of Seth*, traces the history of this tradition.

[41] Evans, *Paradise Lost*, pp. 168–72.

[42] Ibid., pp. 176–85.

[43] The *Ordinale de Origine Mundi* is a 15th-cent. Cornish miracle play (see Evans, *Paradise Lost*, pp. 195–207). Evans was not aware of the motif of the serpent as an angel of light in *Vita* and ApMos; he thought it was "the accidental result of the exigencies of medieval stage craft" (Evans, *Paradise Lost*, p. 195).

BIBLIOGRAPHY

Charlesworth, *PMR*, pp. 74f.
Delling, *Bibliographie*, p. 172.
Denis, *Introduction*, pp. 3–7.

Evans, J. M. *Paradise Lost and the Genesis Traditions*. Oxford, 1968. (Comprehensive
   analysis of the interpretations of the Adam and Eve traditions in Jewish, gnostic,
   patristic, medieval, and Renaissance literature as well as in Milton's *Paradise Lost*.)
Fuchs, C. "Adambuch," *APAT*, vol. 2, pp. 514–28. (German translation with introduction.)
Ginzberg, L. *The Legends of the Jews*. 7 vols.; Philadelphia, 1909–38. (Adam legends are
   narrated in vol. 5, nn. 22–53.)
James, M. R. *The Lost Apocrypha of the Old Testament*. London, 1920. (General introduction
   to the Adam literature subsequent to *Vita* and ApAdam is on pp. 1–9.)
Meyer, W. "Vita Adae et Evae," *Abhandlungen der königlich bayerischen Akademie der
   Wissenschaften, Philosophische-philologische Klasse*, vol. 14 (Munich, 1878). (The
   Lat. text with convenient apparatus is on pp. 221–50 and an excellent introduction on
   pp. 187–220.)
Mozley, J. H. "The Vitae Adae," *JTS* 30 (1929) 121–49. (The Lat. text based on several
   medieval British MSS with nn.)
Sharpe, J. L. *Prolegomena to the Establishment of the Critical Text of the Greek Apocalypse
   of Moses*. Unpublished dissertation, Duke University, 1969. Ann Arbor, Mich., 1969.
   (Pt. 1 provides treatment of the provenance, theology, versions, and MSS of the Gk.
   text, with bibliography. Pt. 2 contains the Gk. text with the most complete apparatus
   currently available.)
————. "The Second Adam in the Apocalypse of Moses," *CBQ* 35 (1973) 35–46. (Shows
   similarities of thought between ApMos and Paul.)
Tischendorf, C. von. *Apocalypses Apocryphae*. Hildesheim, 1966. (This reprint of the 1866
   edition has the Gk. text on pp. 1–23 with a brief introduction on pp. X–XII.)
Wells, L. S. A. "The Books of Adam and Eve," *The Apocrypha and Pseudepigrapha of
   the Old Testament*, ed. R. H. Charles. Oxford, 1913. (An English translation of the
   Gk. and Lat. texts with a fine introduction is in vol. 2, pp. 123–54.)

THE LIFE OF ADAM AND EVE
[*Vita*]

1. THE REPENTANCE OF ADAM AND EVE

The motive and manner of their repentance

1 **1** When they were driven out of Paradise they made for themselves a tent and   Gen 3:22-24
mourned for seven days, weeping in great sorrow. But after seven days they began
to hunger and sought food to eat, but found none.

1 **2** Then Eve said to Adam, "My lord, I am hungry. Go and seek for us that we
may eat. Perhaps the LORD God will consider us and pity us and call us back to
2 the place we were before." •And Adam rose and walked seven days over all that
land and found no food such as they had had in Paradise.

1 **3** And Eve said to Adam, "My lord, would you kill me? O that I would die!
Then perhaps the LORD God will bring you again into Paradise, for it is because
2 of me that the LORD God is angry with you."ᵃ •Adam answered, "Do not wish
to speak such words lest the LORD God bring on us some further curse. How is
it possible that I should let loose my hand against my flesh? But rather let us rise   Gen 2:23
and search for ourselves, how we might live, and not weaken."

1 **4** And they walked searching for nine days and found nothing such as they had
2 had in Paradise, but only such as animals eat.ᵃ •And Adam said to Eve, "The
LORD apportioned this for animals and beasts to eat, but for us there used to be
3 the food of angels.ᵇ •But it is just and fitting for us to lament in the sight of God   Ps 78:25
who made us. Let us repent with a great penitence; perhaps the LORD God will
be forbearing and pity us and provide for us that we might live."ᶜ

1 **5** And Eve said to Adam, "My lord, tell me, what is repentance and what kind
of penitence should I do, lest by chance we impose on ourselves an effort which
we cannot sustain, and the LORD not hear our prayers and turn his face from us
2 because we did not keep our promise. •My lord, how much did you intend to
repent, since I have brought toil and tribulation on you."

1 **6** And Adam said to Eve, "You are not able to do so much as I; but do as much
as you have strength for. I will spend forty days fasting, but you rise and go to

---

3 a. The MSS have a doublet of Eve's request which ends, "For it is because of me that you have been
driven from there."

4 a. That Adam ate animals' food is considered in some rabbinic writings one of his punishments for
the Fall (GenR *ad rem*; PRE 20); in ARNⁱ (Goldin 14) Adam complains about eating animals' food.
   b. Cf. Sanh 59b.
   c. In PR 50:5 Adam learns the value of repentance from Cain, while in 7:2 we read that Adam refused
to repent before being driven out of Paradise; see also the n. to 6:3.

THE LIFE OF ADAM AND EVE

[Apocalypse]

PREFACE

The narrative and life of Adam and Eve the first-made, revealed by God to Moses his servant when he received the tablets of the law of the covenant from the hand of the LORD, after he had been taught by the archangel Michael.[a]

7 **29** And it happened that we mourned for seven days. After seven days we were hungry and I said to Adam, "Gather and bring us food that we might eat and live, lest we die. Let us get up and weep on the ground so that God might hear 8,9 us." •And we rose and went through the whole land and did not find (food). •And answering, I said to Adam, "Rise, my lord, and do away with me that I might depart from you and from the presence of God and from the angels so that they 10 will cease to be angry with you on my account." •Then Adam answered and said to Eve, "Why have you been thinking of this evil, that I should commit murder and bring death to my rib, so that I should stretch out my hand against the image   Gen 2:21 11 which God made?[b] •But rather let us

repent and offer prayers[c] for forty days. But you fast thirty-four days because you were not formed (until) the sixth day in

---

P a. This preface, certainly a later addition to the Gk. text, is the sole cause of the traditional, but erroneous, title "Apocalypse of Moses"; the Gk. text has nothing to do with Moses, nor is it in the technical sense an apocalypse.

29 a. The "repentance" in the Gk. tradition is found only in MSS F and H, and is located there after 29:6 as the concluding part of Eve's story of the Fall; the text translated here is that of H with variants of F noted.
   b. Gk. *epoiēsei*, "[he] made"; MS H has *apoiēsei*, "[he] will not make."
   c. MS PH adds "and with me."

[Vita]

the Tigris River and take a stone and stand on it in the water as far as (your)   Gen 2:14
2 neck[a] in the depths of the river. •And let no speech come out of your mouth,
because we are unworthy to entreat the LORD since our lips are unclean from the   Isa 6:5
illegal and forbidden tree. And stand in the water of the river for thirty-seven
3 days. •But I will spend forty days in the water of the Jordan.[b] Perhaps the LORD   Deut 10:10
God will pity us.''   1Kgs 19:8
  Mt 4:2

1 **7** And Eve walked to the Tigris River and did just as Adam told her. Similarly,
Adam walked to the Jordan River and stood on a stone up to his neck in water.

1 **8** And Adam said, ''I tell you, water of the Jordan, mourn with me and gather
to me all swimming creatures which are in you and let them surround me and so
2 lament together with me. •Let them not mourn for themselves, but rather for me,
3 because it is not they who have sinned, but I.'' •At once all the living beings
came and surrounded him and the water of the Jordan stood, its current not   Josh 3:13-17
moving, from that hour.

Satan again deceives Eve

1 **9** Eighteen days went by. Then Satan was angry and transformed himself into   2Cor 11:14
the brightness of angels[a] and went away to the Tigris River to Eve and found her
2 weeping. •And the devil himself, as if to grieve with her, began to weep and said
to her, ''Step out of the river and cry no more. Cease now from sadness and
3 sighs. Why are you and your husband Adam disturbed? •The LORD God has heard
your sighs and accepted your repentance; and all we angels have entreated for you
4 and interceded with the LORD, •and he sent me to bring you up from the water
and give you food which you had in Paradise, and for which you have been
5 lamenting. •Now therefore come out of the water and I will lead you to the place
where your food has been prepared.''

1 **10** Now when Eve heard this she believed and came out of the water of the
2 river, and her flesh was as grass[a] from the cold of the water. •And when she came   Isa 40:6;
3 out, she fell on the ground and the devil raised her and led her to Adam. •But   51:12
when Adam saw her and the devil with her, he cried out with tears and said, ''O
4 Eve, Eve, where is the work of your penitence? •How have you again been
seduced by our enemy by whom we have been deprived of our dwelling in Paradise
and of spiritual joy?''

1 **11** When Eve heard this, she knew that the devil had persuaded (her) to come
out of the river and fell on her face to the ground, and her sorrow and sighing
2 and lamenting were doubled. •She cried out, saying, ''Woe to you, O devil. Why

---

6 a. That a woman's ritual bath can purify only when it reaches one's neck is asserted in b.Yoma 87a.
    b. In PRE 20 Adam's repentance is put on the first Sunday after his expulsion from Paradise and it
takes place in the Gihon, one of the rivers of Paradise (Gen 2:13); Adam stayed there for seven weeks,
until his body became like a sponge; he prayed for forgiveness and God accepted his repentance.

9 a. Cf. ApMos 17:2. In the Dead Sea Scrolls the archangel Michael is referred to as the ''Prince of
Lights'' (1QM 13:9–10; 17:6–8; 1QS 3:20); the *Vita* and Paul in 2Cor 11:14 may imply that Satan
disguised himself as Michael.

10 a. Ginzberg, *Legends*, vol. 5, p. 115, suggests that this odd expression is due to a mistranslation of
the rare Heb. word *yarôqah*, ''sponge,'' as though it were related to *yârâq*, ''herb''; PRE 20 says that
Adam's body became like a sponge from his penitence in the water. This may be an indication of a Heb.
source for *Vita*.

[*Apocalypse*]

12 which God made his creation.[d] •But you rise and go to the Tigris River, and take a stone and set (it) under your feet, and go in and stand in the water up to the neck, and do not let three words come out of your mouth, for we are unworthy and our lips are not clean. But cry silently to God (saying), 'O God, be gracious to me.' ''[e]

13 •But Adam went into the Jordan River and cried with a loud voice, saying, ''I say to you, water of the Jordan, stand still; and all birds and all animals
14 and all reptiles both on land and in the sea gather together.'' •And all the angels and all the creatures of God surrounded Adam as a wall around him, weeping and praying to God on behalf of Adam, so that God gave ear to them.

15 But the devil, not having found an opportunity with Adam, came to the Tigris River to Eve. Taking the form of an angel, he stood before her weeping, and his
16 tears fell on the ground and on his robe. •And he said to me, ''Come up out of the water and be done with weeping, for the LORD has heard your request and the angels and all his creatures have beseeched God about your prayer.

17 Thus he deceived me, and I stepped out of the water.''

d. Sharpe has *ktēsin*, ''creation.'' The Slav. reads, ''forty-four.''
e. MS F; H reads, ''But pray to God, and keep the lips silent that we might be baptized in the water with all your heart''; this has a Christian touch not found in F.

[*Vita*]

do you assault us for nothing? What have you to do with us? What have we done to you, that you should pursue us with deceit? Why does your malice fall on us?
3 Have we stolen your glory and made you to be without honor? Why do you treacherously and enviously pursue us, O enemy, all the way to death?''

Satan's account of his expulsion from heaven

1 **12** And the devil[a] sighed and said, "O Adam, all my enmity and envy and sorrow concern you, since because of you I am expelled and deprived of my glory which I had in the heavens in the midst of angels, and because of you I was cast
2 out onto the earth." •Adam answered, "What have I done to you, and what is my blame with you? Since you are neither harmed nor hurt by us, why do you pursue us?"

Isa 14:12-15
Zeph 3:2
Ps 82:6-7
Lk 10:18
Jn 12:31
2En 29:4-5
Rev 12:9
2Pet 2:4
Gen 2:7
Gen 1:27

1 **13** The devil replied, "Adam, what are you telling me? It is because of you that
2 I have been thrown out of there. •When you were created, I was cast out from
3 the presence of God and was sent out from the fellowship of the angels. •When God blew into you the *breath of life* and your countenance and likeness were made *in the image of God*, Michael[a] brought you and made (us) worship you in the sight of God, and the LORD God said, 'Behold Adam! I have made you in our image and likeness.'

1 **14** And Michael went out and called all the angels, saying, 'Worship the image
2 of the LORD God, as the LORD God has instructed.'[a] •And Michael himself worshiped first, and called me and said, 'Worship the image of God, Yahweh.'[b]
3 And I answered, 'I do not worship Adam.'[c] And when Michael kept forcing me to worship, I said to him, 'Why do you compel me? I will not worship one inferior and subsequent to me. I am prior to him in creation; before he was made, I was already made. He ought to worship me.'

Gen 1:26
Rev 12:7-12

1 **15** When they heard this, other angels who were under me refused to worship
2 him. •And Michael asserted, 'Worship the image of God. But if now you will
3 not worship, the LORD God will be wrathful with you.' •And I said, 'If he be wrathful with me, I will set my throne above the stars of heaven and will be like the Most High.'

Isa 14:13
Dan 8:10
Obad 4
Job 22:12
Jude 9

1 **16** And the LORD God was angry with me and sent me with my angels out from our glory; and because of you, we were expelled into this world from our dwellings
2 and have been cast onto the earth. •And immediately we were made to grieve, since we had been deprived of so great glory. And we were pained to see you in
3 such bliss of delights.[a] •So with deceit I assailed your wife and made you to be expelled through her from the joys of your bliss, as I have been expelled from my glory.''

Gen 3:1-7

12 a. Satan's fall is a widely known legend (see marginal references here and at 15:3) which may have arisen as a Midrash on Isa 14:12-15. It is reflected in 2En 29:4f.; 31:3; GBart 4.51-55, vol. 1, p. 500; numerous rabbinic writings; the NT (marginal references above); Tertullian, *de Patientia* 5; Irenaeus, *Against Heresies*, IV.40.3; Augustine, *de Genesi ad Literam* XI.18; and the Koran, suras 2, 7, 15, 17, 18, 20, and 38. The account in the *Vita* could well be among the earliest witnesses to this legend.

13 a. Michael is the chief angel in *Vita* and ApMos, as also in the Dead Sea Scrolls (see *Vita* 9, n. a); cf. M. Hengel, *Judaism and Hellenism* (Philadelphia, 1974) vol. 1, pp. 188, 231.

14 a. Heb 1:6 may be an allusion to an early form of this legend; cf. Heb 1:14.
 b. MSS in group I; *IHU*, "Yahweh"; those in groups II and III omit this name.
 c. Lat. *Non habeo ego adorare*, "I do not have to worship."

16 a. Lat. *laetitia delitiarum*, "bliss of delights."

[*Vita*]

1 **17** Hearing this from the devil, Adam cried out with great weeping and said, "O LORD, my God, my life is in your hands. Remove far from me this my opponent, who seeks to destroy my soul, and give me his glory which he himself 2,3 has forfeited." •And immediately the devil disappeared from him. •But Adam persisted forty days standing in repentance in the water of the Jordan. <small>Lk 4:13</small>

II. THE CHILDREN OF ADAM AND EVE

The birth of Cain

1 **18** And Eve said to Adam, "You live on, my lord. Life is granted to you, since you have done neither the first nor the second error, but I have been cheated and 2 deceived, for I have not kept the command of God. •And now separate me from 3 the light of such life, and I will go to the sunset[a] and stay there until I die." •And she began to walk toward the West and to mourn and to weep bitterly with loud 4 sighing. •And she made there a shelter while she was three months pregnant.

1 **19** And when the time of her giving birth drew near, she began to be distressed with pains and cried out to the LORD, saying, "Have mercy on me, LORD, help ,3 me." •But neither was she heard, nor was the mercy of God around her. •And she said to herself, "Who will give the news to my lord Adam? I beg you, O lights of heaven, when you return to the East,[a] tell my lord Adam."

1 **20** However, at that very moment, Adam said, "Eve's complaint has come to 2 me; perhaps again the serpent[a] has contended with her." •And he went forth and came upon her in great distress. And Eve said, "The moment I saw you, my lord, my pained soul was refreshed.[b] And now implore the LORD God for me to hear 3 you and to have regard for me and free me from my most awful pains." •And Adam prayed to the LORD for Eve.

1 **21** And behold, twelve angels and two excellencies[a] came and stood to the right 2 and to the left of Eve. •And Michael stood to the right and touched her from her face to the breast and said to Eve, "Blessed are you, Eve, because of Adam. Since his prayers and utterances are many, I am sent to you that you might receive 3 our help. Now rise and make ready to give birth." •And she bore a son, and he was lustrous.[b] And at once the infant rose, ran, and brought in his hands a reed[c] and gave it to his mother. And his name was called Cain. <small>Gen 4:1</small>

---

18 a. A Hebraism.

19 a. The East is the location of Paradise in Gen 2:8 and 1En 32:2.

20 a. Cf. *Vita* 37:1 and the role of the serpent in ApMos 15–30.
  b. Lat. *refrigeravit*, "he was refreshed"; lit. "cooled"; other MSS read *infrigeravit*, "he was cooled," or *inrefrigeravit*, "he was cooled."

21 a. "Excellencies" (*virtutes*) may be a translation of the Heb. for "partakers of the divine *Kabod* ('glory')" in b.Ber 60b; see b.Hag 16a and cf. the "principalities and powers" of Rom 8:38; Eph 6:12, etc.
  b. Lat. *lucidus*, "lustrous," "full of light," probably related to ApMos 1:3 (see n.).
  c. Lat. *herbam*, "reed"; probably from the similarity of the Heb. words *Qáyin*, "Cain," and *qáneh*, "reed." According to GenR 22:8, Cain killed Abel with a reed.

[Apocalypse]

[*Vita*]

1,2 **22** And Adam brought Eve and the child and led them to the East. •And the   ApMos 29
LORD God sent various seeds by the angel Michael and gave them to Adam and   Gen 1:29
showed him (how) to work and till the ground so as to have produce by which   Jub 3:15
they and all their generations might live.

The murder of Abel and the birth of Adam's other children

1 **23** For Eve later conceived and bore a son, whose name was Abel. And Cain
2 and Abel used to stay together. •And Eve said to Adam, "My lord, while I was
sleeping I saw a vision—as if the blood of our son Abel was in the hand of Cain
3 (who was) gulping it down in his mouth. That is why I am sad." •And Adam
said, "God forbid that Cain would kill Abel! But let us separate them from each
4 other and make separate places for them." •And they made Cain a farmer and   Gen 4:2
5 Abel a shepherd, that in this way they might be separated from each other. •After   Gen 4:9
this Cain murdered Abel, at which time Adam was 130 years old, while Abel   Gen 5:3
when he was murdered was 122.[a]

1 **24** After this Adam knew his wife and she bore a son and called his name Seth.
2 And Adam said to Eve, "See, I have sired a son in place of Abel, whom Cain
3 struck down." •And after Adam had become the father of Seth, he lived eight
hundred years and fathered thirty sons and thirty daughters, sixty-three altogether.[a]
4 And they were multiplied over the earth in their nations.   Gen 10:32

III. ADAM IS TAKEN UP TO THE HEAVENLY PARADISE[a]

1 **25** Adam said to Seth, "Listen, Seth my son, and I will pass on to you what I
2 heard and saw. •After your mother and I had been driven out of Paradise, while   Isa 66:15
we were praying, Michael the archangel and messenger of God came to me.   Jer 4:13
    Ezek 1,10
3 And I saw a chariot like the wind and its wheels were fiery. I was carried off   Pss 68:17; 104:3
into the Paradise of righteousness,[a] and I saw the LORD sitting and his appearance   2Kgs 2:11
    ApMos 33
    1En 13-17

23 a. George Syncellus, *Chronicle* 1:14, asserts that Abel was twenty-two when he sacrificed, and he
puts the date at 99 Anno Mundi.

24 a. Including Cain, Abel, and Seth.
T a. This section seems to have had some original relationship with ApMos 37.

25 a. See also ApMos 37–40; *Vita* 29; 2Cor 12:4; Lk 23:43; Rev 2:7; 1En 32:3; 77:3; 60:8; 2En 8:1–5;
42:2; 65:10; 4Ezra 7:53; 8:52. In the *Vita* and ApMos there are both an earthly Paradise, Eden, and a
heavenly, which is located in the third heaven. The latter is referred to here and in *Vita* 29:1 ("Paradise
of visitation and of God's command"); ApMos 37:5; 40:1; the remaining references in *Vita* and ApMos
to Paradise are to the earthly. In some popular Jewish and Christian writings there are said to be seven
heavens, as in ApMos 35:2 and 2En 1–20 (classic description in b.Hag 12b); an older view, perhaps, is

[*Apocalypse*]

1,2 **1** This is the account of[a] Adam and Eve. •After they had come out of Paradise, Adam took his wife, and they went down into the East. And they stayed there
3 eighteen years and two months,[b] •and Eve conceived and bore two sons, Diaphotos called Cain, and Amilabes called Abel.[c]

1 **2** After these things Adam and Eve were together and when they were lying
2 down to sleep, Eve said to her lord Adam, •"My lord, I saw in a dream this night the blood of my son Amilabes, called Abel, being thrust into the mouth of Cain
3 his brother, and he drank it mercilessly. •He begged him to allow him a little of it, but he did not listen to him but swallowed all of it. And it did not stay in his
4 stomach but came out of his mouth." •And Adam said to Eve, "Let us rise and go to see what has happened to them.[a] Perhaps the enemy is warring against them."

1 **3** And when they both[a] had gone out they found Abel killed by the hand of Cain,
2 his brother. •And God said to Michael the archangel, "Say to Adam, 'The mystery which you know[b] do not report to your son Cain, for he is a son of wrath. But   Gen 4:5
do not mourn, for I will give you another son in his place; this one shall reveal   Eph 2:3
                                                                                      Gen 4:25
3 to you[c] all that you shall do;[d] but you tell him nothing!' "[e] •These things God said to his angel, and Adam kept the word in his heart, with him and Eve, grieving   Lk 2:19,51 over Abel their son.

1 **4** After these things Adam knew his wife and she conceived and bore Seth.[a]
2 And Adam said to Eve, "See, we have begotten a son in place of Abel, whom Cain killed; let us give glory and sacrifice to God."

1 **5** And Adam fathered thirty sons and thirty daughters.   Gen 5:4

---

1 a. MSS E1 and E2 add "the first-made."

   b. E1 and E2 add "Adam knew his wife and she."

   c. Several explanations of the enigmatic names for Cain and Abel have been proposed: (a) That the original read *Diaphytōr* or *Diaphyteutēs*, "a planter," and *Mēlatas* or *Mēlobotēs*, "a keeper of sheep"; (b) *Adiaphōtos*, "unshining," as found in MSS D1 D2 D3 M1 M2 E1 (*Aphaton*, "nameless," in E2) as well as the Arm. text; (c) that "Amilabes" is a rude transcription of the Heb. *hamᵉhubāl*, "the destroyed one"; (d) that the similarity of *Qayin*, "Cain," with *kiyun* (Kaiwan = the planet Saturn) gave rise to the legend about the shining face of Cain which is found in PRE 21 and TargYer on Gen 4:1. The description of Cain as "lustrous" in *Vita* 21:3 supports this view of the name Diaphotos. The later two explanations would imply that a Semitic, probably Heb., original text lay behind both the Gk. and Lat.

2 a. E1 and E2 omit the last five words.

3 a. E1 and E2 omit "both."

   b. MS B omits these five words.

   c. "To you" is omitted in A1 A2 D1 D2 D3 D4.

   d. Some MSS add "to him."

   e. The last phrase is omitted in D1 D4 E1 E2 G H and the Arm.

4 a. MS H adds the last half of Gen 4:25.

[*Vita*]

was unbearable flaming fire. And many thousands of angels were at the right and at the left of the chariot.[b]   Ezek 1:27

1 **26** "I was disturbed when I saw this; fear laid hold of me and I worshiped in 2 the presence of God on the face of the earth. •And God said to me, 'Behold, you shall die, because you have disregarded the command of God, since you have listened rather to the voice of your wife, whom I gave into your power, that you might keep her in your will. But you listened to her and disregarded my words.'   ApMos 24:1 Gen 3:6

1 **27** "And when I heard these words of God, I fell down on the ground, worshiped the LORD, and said, 'My lord, almighty and merciful God, holy and upright, let not the name that reminds of your majesty[a] be blotted out, but convert my soul, 2 for I am dying, and my spirit will pass from my mouth. •Cast me not from your presence, whom you formed from the clay of the earth; and do not withhold your 3 grace from him whom you nurtured.' •And behold, your word[b] came to me and the LORD said to me, 'Because your days are numbered,[c] you have been made to cherish knowledge; therefore, there shall not be abolished from your seed forever (those who would) serve me.'   Ps 51:11

1 **28** "Hearing these words, I prostrated myself to the ground and worshiped the LORD God, saying, 'You are the eternal and most high God and all creatures give 2 you honor and praise. •You are the true light shining above all lights, living life, incomprehensibly great excellence. To you the spiritual powers[a] give honor and praise. You perform among all humanity the miracles of your mercy.'   Rom 8:38 Eph 6:12

1 **29** "After I had worshiped the LORD, Michael the archangel of God immediately took hold of my hand and ejected me from the Paradise of visitation and of God's 2 command. •And Michael held in his hand a rod and touched the waters which 3 were around Paradise[a] and they froze. •I crossed over and Michael with me, and he took me to the place from where he had seized me."[b]   Vita 25:3

---

that there were three heavens, as is implied in 2Cor 12:2–3 (the third heaven is designated "Paradise") and TLevi 3; see also *TDNT*, vol. 5, pp. 511–12 (Traub). The Samaritans also held to an earthly and a heavenly Paradise, both called the "Garden of Eden" (J. Macdonald, *Theology of the Samaritans* [Philadelphia, 1964] ch. 21).
  b. Cf. the "chariot-like Throne above the firmament of the cherubim" in the Qumran "Liturgy of the Angels" (T. Gaster, *The Dead Sea Scriptures* [Garden City, 1964], pp. 373f.). The chariot here seems to be both the means of Adam's rapture (vs. 3a) and also the throne of God (vs. 3b), a possible indication of a reworking of the sources.

27 a. In 2En 30:13, SibOr 3:24–26, and other sources, the name Adam is taken to be an acrostic for the names of the four directions; the reference here, however, may be to Adam as the image of God. See W. D. Davies, *Paul and Rabbinic Judaism* (New York, 1967) p. 55.
  b. Lat. *verbum tuum*, a reference to the promise of progeny for Adam through Seth.
  c. Lat. *Quoniam figurantur dies tui.* Other MSS read *figura (figuratio) cordis tui*, "form of your heart"; *figura corporis tui*, "form of your body"; *figura corporis mei*, "form of my body"; *factus est*, "it is done." The meaning is obscure, although it may be linked with Ps 90:12.

28 a. Lat. *virtutes*, lit. "excellencies"; see *Vita* 21, n. a.

29 a. TLevi 3:2 refers to fire, snow, and ice at the first (lowest) heaven; 2En 3:3 describes a "very great Sea, greater than the earthly sea at the first heaven"; Rev 4:6 and 15:2 refer to a "sea of glass" in heaven. Here, however, the waters seem to be around the earthly Paradise.
  b. The MSS in groups II, III, and IV include here the following interpolation, an apocalyptic piece which refers both to the temples of Solomon and of Herod:
29:4 "Listen, Seth my son, to the other future sacramental mysteries which were revealed to me, which by eating of the tree of knowledge I knew and understood, which shall be in this temporary age, which God is about to perform with his creation, the human race. 5 The LORD will appear in a blaze of fire. From the mouth of his majesty he will give commands and precepts, and they will hallow him in the

[*Apocalypse*]

[*Vita*]

IV. ADAM'S FINAL ILLNESS

1 **30** After Adam had lived 930 years, he knew his days were at an end and Gen 5:5
therefore said, "Let all my sons be gathered to me, that I may bless them before
2 I die, and speak with them." •And they assembled in three parts in his sight at
3 the oratory[a] where they used to worship the LORD God. •And they asked him,
"What is it with you, Father, that you should gather us together? And why are
4 you lying on your bed?" •And Adam answered and said, "My sons, I am sick
with pains." And all his sons said to him, "What is it, Father, to be sick with
pains?"

1 **31** Then his son Seth said, "Lord, perhaps you have longed for the fruit of
Paradise of which you used to eat, and that is why you are lying in sadness.
2,3 Tell me and I will go to the vicinity of the entrances to Paradise •and will put
dust on my head and throw myself to the ground before the gates of Paradise and
mourn with great lamentation, entreating the LORD. Perhaps he will hear me and
4 send his angel to bring me the fruit which you desire." •Adam answered and
said, "No, my son, I do not long for (that); but I have weakness and great pain
5 in my body." •Seth responded, "What is pain, O lord Father? I do not know; do
not hide it from us, but tell us."

Adam's story of the Fall

1 **32** And Adam answered and said, "Listen to me, my sons. When God made
us, me and your mother, and placed us in Paradise and gave us every tree bearing
fruit to eat, he forbade us (saying), 'Regarding the tree of the knowledge of good
2 and evil, which is in the midst of Paradise, do not eat of it.' •Moreover, God
gave a part of Paradise to me and (a part) to your mother. The trees of the eastern
part and over against the north he gave to me, and to your mother he gave the
southern and western parts.

ApMos 15

---

house of the habitation of his majesty. 6 And he will show them the wonderful place of his majesty, and
then they will build a house for the LORD their God on the earth where he will dread them (ms. 3 has
"which he will prepare for them"), 7 and there they will pass by his precepts and their sanctuary will
be set on fire and their land deserted and they themselves will be dispersed because they provoked God.
8 And once again he will deliver them from their dispersion, and again they will build a house of God,
and the latest house of God shall be exalted more highly than before. And once again iniquity will surpass
equity. 9 After this God will dwell with men, being seen on the earth, and then justice will begin to
shine, and the house of God will be honored in this world and no longer will the enemies be able to
harm men who believe in God. 10 And God will raise up for himself a faithful people whom he will
save forever. 11 But the wicked who refused to love his law will be punished by God their king.
12 Heaven and earth, nights and days, and all creatures will obey him and not ignore his commandment
nor change its works, but rather men who forsake the law of the LORD will be changed. 13 Therefore,
the LORD will banish from himself the impious while the righteous will shine like the sun in the presence
of God. 14 And in that time men will be purified from sins by water, but those who refuse purification
by water will be condemned. 15 Happy will be the man who has reformed his soul when the judgments
and wonders of God shall come among men, their deeds being investigated by God, the just Judge."
　　The Babylonian destruction of Judah is referred to in vs. 7 and the second temple in vs. 8; vs. 14 is
certainly, and vs. 9 possibly, from a Christian hand.

30 a. In rabbinic sources Adam's oratory is located on Mount Moriah, on the spot on which the holy
of holies of the temple later stood (Midrash on Ps 92:6; PR 43:2; PRE 23; 31, etc.). The assertion of
ApMos 40:5 that Adam was buried on the same spot from which the dust was taken for his body is
assumed in several Jewish sources to refer to the same place; cf. *Vita* 45:2.

[*Apocalypse*]

2 **5** And (Adam) became ill and cried with a loud voice saying, "Let all my sons
3 come to me that I may see them before I die." •And all came together, for the
earth was settled* in three parts.* And they all came to the door of the house in
4 which he used to enter to pray to God.* •And his son Seth said, "Father Adam,
what is your illness?" And he said, "My children, much pain afflicts me."*
5 And they said, "What is pain and illness?"*

1 **6** And Seth answered and said, "Father, have you been thinking of the things
2 from which you used to eat and grieving to desire them?* •If such is the case tell   *Vita* 1-4
me, and I will go and bring you fruit from Paradise. For I will place dung on my
head and weep and pray, and the LORD will hear me and will send his angel, and   Mal 2:3
3 I will bring (it) to you so that the pain will leave you."* •Adam said to him,
"No, Seth my son; but I have sickness and pain." Seth said to him, "And how
did this happen to you?"

1 **7** Adam said to him, "When God made us, me and your mother, through whom
I am dying,* he gave us every plant in Paradise, but concerning one he commanded
us not to eat of it, (for) we would die by it.*   Gen 2:16-17

---

5 a. MSS E1 and E2 read "divided."

b. Arm. reads "For they were living apart each by himself in his own place."

c. This sentence occurs only in A1 A2 (variant) C (variant) D3 F.

d. E1 and E2 omit this sentence and otherwise condense the conversation.

e. The purpose of this section in both *Vita* and ApMos is to show that sickness is not part of the created order, but rather one of the punishments brought by the Fall.

6 a. Several MSS omit the last three words.

b. MS B reads, "And he will bring to me from the tree in which the oil flows, and the pain will leave you."

7 a. This phrase is not found in E1 and E2.

b. MS G reads differently, but without significant change of meaning, in vss. 1–3.

[Vita]

1,2 **33** The LORD God appointed two angels to guard us.[a] •The hour came when the
3 angels ascended to worship in the presence of God. •Immediately the adversary,
the devil, found opportunity while the angels were away and deceived your mother
so that she ate of the illicit and forbidden tree. And she ate and gave to me.

1 **34** And immediately the LORD God was angry with us and the LORD said to me,
'Because you have forsaken my commandment and have not kept my word which
2 I set for you, behold, I will bring upon your body seventy plagues; •you shall be
racked with various pains, from the top of the head and the eyes and ears down
3 to the nails of the feet, and in each separate limb.' •These he considered to be
the scourge of pain from one of the trees.[a] Moreover, the LORD sent all these to
me and to all our generations.''

1 **35** Adam said this to all his sons while he was seized with great pains, and he
cried out with a loud voice, saying, ''Why should I suffer misery and endure such
2 agony?'' •And when she saw him weeping, Eve herself began to weep, saying,
3 ''O LORD, my God, transfer his pain to me, since it is I who sinned.'' •And Eve
said to Adam, ''My lord, give me a portion of your pain, for this guilt has come
to you from me.''

Vita 44:2

1 **36** And Adam said to Eve, ''Rise and go with my son Seth to the regions of
Paradise and put dust on your heads and prostrate yourselves to the ground and
2 mourn in the sight of God. •Perhaps he will have mercy and send his angel to the
tree of his mercy, from which flows the oil of life,[a] and will give you a little of
it with which to anoint me, that I might have rest from these pains by which I
am wasting away.''

The rule of the beasts

1 **37** And Seth and his mother went toward the gates of Paradise; and while they
were walking, behold suddenly there came a serpent, a beast, and attacked and
2 bit Seth. •And when Eve saw it, she cried out and said, ''Woe is me for I am
3 cursed, since I have not kept the command of the LORD. •And Eve said to the
serpent in a loud voice, ''Cursed beast! How is it that you were not afraid to
throw yourself at the image of God, but have dared to attack it? And how were
your teeth made strong?''[a]

---

33 a. Ginzberg, *JE*, vol. 1, p. 179, takes these to be among the *virtutes*, ''excellencies,'' mentioned in 21:1; 28:2; 48:2; see also 2En 8:8.

34 a. Lat. *Haec deputavit in flagellationem dolori uno cum arboribus*; the MSS differ greatly on this expression.

36 a. This tree is identified as the ''tree of life'' only in ApMos 28; contrast *Vita* 40:3 and see *Vita* 40:2–3; ApMos 13:1. In ApMos 28:2–4 Adam is told that he will not eat from the tree of life until the resurrection, an inconsistency with this passage if the tree here is the tree of life. Both texts, however, are composed of originally separate traditions. Rabbinic literature knows nothing of the ''oil of life'' but speaks of the ''dew of light'' (Isa 26:19) as the means of resurrection; on the oil see GNic 19 (= Descent 3); PseudClemRec 1.45; Origen, *Contra Celsus* 6:27; Mk 6:13; Jas 5:14.

37 a. The oldest MSS of *Vita* omit this sentence.

[*Apocalypse*]

2 •And the hour drew near for the angels who were guarding^c your mother to ascend and worship the LORD. And the enemy gave to her and she ate from the tree, since he knew that neither I nor Gen 3:1-7
3 the holy angels were near her. •Then she^d gave also to me to eat.

1 **8** When we both had eaten,^a God was angry with us. And the LORD came into Gen 3:8-12 Paradise^b and called with a frightful voice, saying, 'Adam, where are you? And
2 why do you hide from my face? Can the house hide from its builder?' •And he said, 'Since you have forsaken my covenant, I have submitted your body to seventy plagues.^c The pain of the first plague is affliction of the eyes; the pain of the second plague is of the hearing; and so one after the other all the plagues shall pursue^d you.' ''

1 **9** While he was saying these things to his sons, he sighed deeply and said, "What
2 shall I do? I am in great distress." •And Eve also wept and said, "My lord Adam, rise, give me half of your illness and let me bear it, because this has happened to you through me; because of me you suffer troubles and pains."^a

3 •But Adam said ApMos 14:2 to Eve,^b "Rise and go with our son, Seth, near to Paradise, and place earth on Rev 22:2 your heads and weep, beseeching God so that he might have mercy on me, and 1En 24:3-4 send his angel into Paradise and give me^c from the tree out of which the oil flows, TLevi 18:11 and bring it to me, and I will anoint myself and rest."^d 4Ezra 2:12

1 **10** And Seth and Eve went into the regions of Paradise. As they were going,
2 Eve saw her son and a wild beast attacking him. •And Eve wept, saying, "Woe is me! For when I come to the day of resurrection, all who have sinned will curse
3 me, saying^a that Eve did not keep the command of God." •And Eve cried out to the beast and said, "O you evil beast, do you not fear to attack the image of God? How was your mouth opened? How did your teeth grow strong? How did you not remember your subjection, for you were once subjected to the image of Gen 1:26, 28 God?"

c. Several MSS read *diatērountas*, "watching closely," rather than *phylassontōn*, "guarding," translated here.
    d. Some MSS read "he" or "that one."

8 a. Six MSS omit this phrase (C D1 D2 D4 M1 M2).
    b. Several MSS add "placed his throne."
    c. Three MSS read "seventy-two." This confusion is similar to the rabbinic question whether there are seventy or seventy-two nations in the world; m.Nega'im 1:4 deals with the signs of leprosy and is not relevant to this passage.
    d. Gk. *parakolouthēsousin*, "pursue."

9 a. This clause is not found in E1 and E2; several other MSS omit "and pains."
    b. In *Vita* 31 (= ApMos 6) Adam rejects Seth's offer to go to Paradise.
    c. MSS E1 and E2 add "a branch."
    d. MS C reads, "I will anoint myself and be freed from the pain"; several others add, "And I will show you the way in which we were formerly deceived," an addition which disrupts the narrative.

10 a. Some MSS read, "cursed be Eve, for she did not keep the command of God."

[*Vita*]

1 **38** The beast answered in a human voice, "O Eve, is not our malice against
2 *you*? Is not our fury against *you*? •Tell me, Eve, how was your mouth opened
3 that you ate of the fruit which the LORD God commanded you not to eat? •Now,
however, are you not able to bear it if I begin to reproach you?"ᵃ

1 **39** Then Seth said to the beast, "May the LORD God rebuke you. Stop; be quiet;
2 close your mouth, cursed enemy of truth, chaotic destroyer.ᵃ •Stand back from
the image of God until the day when the LORD God shall order you to be brought
3 to judgment." •And the beast said to Seth, "See, I stand back from the presence
of the image of God, as you have said." Immediately he left Seth, who was
wounded by (his) teeth.ᵇ

Seth and Eve at the earthly Paradise

1 **40** But Seth and his mother walked toward the regions of Paradise for the oil of
2 mercy, to anoint the sick Adam. •And they arrived at the gates of Paradise, took   31:3
dust from the earth, and put it on their heads, prostrated themselves to the ground   ApMos 6:3
3 on their faces and began to mourn with loud sighs, •begging the LORD God to
pity Adam in his pains and to send his angel to give them the oil from the tree of
mercy.

1 **41** But when they had prayed and entreated for many hours, behold, the angel
Michael appeared to them, saying, "I have been sent to you from the LORD; I
2 have been set by the LORD over the bodies of men. •I say to you, Seth, man of
God, do not weep, praying and begging for the oil of the tree of mercy to anoint
your father Adam for the pains of his body.

1 **42** Truly I say to you that you are by no means able to take from it, except in
the last days.ᵃ

1 **43** But you, Seth, go to your father Adam, for the span of his life is completed.
2 Six days from now his soul shall leave the body; and as it leaves, you shall see
3 great wonders in heaven and on the earth and in the lights of heaven." •Having   ApMos 35-36
4 said this, Michael immediately withdrew from Seth. •And Eve and Seth turned
back and brought with them aromatics, namely, nard, crocus, calamine, and   ApMos 29
cinnamon.

---

38 a. Some MSS omit the words "if I begin to reproach you."

39 a. These words, as well as the identification of the beast as a serpent in 37:1, reveal that the Lat. text thinks of the beast as Satan; this is not the case in ApMos.

b. Lat. *plaga de dentibus a Seth,* "Seth who was wounded by his teeth"; there are a variety of variants for this phrase.

42 a. Meyer includes here the following extract, found in a few MSS as well as the Lat. text of GNic 19 (= Descent 3): ". . . When five thousand five hundred years [variants: 6,500, 5,050, 5,200, 5,199, 5,228] shall have been completed. Then the most beloved Christ, Son of God, shall come upon the earth to revive the body of Adam and with him the bodies of the dead. •And when he, the Son of God, comes, he himself will be baptized in the river Jordan, and when he has come out of the water of the Jordan, then he will anoint from the oil of mercy all who believe in him. •And the oil of mercy shall be from generation to generation for those who are born again of water and the Holy Spirit into eternal life. •Then the most beloved Son of God, Christ, shall descend to the earth, and lead your father Adam to Paradise to the tree of mercy." Meyer takes this passage as evidence that the *Vita,* or its sources, was known to the author of GNic.

[*Apocalypse*]

1 **11** Then the beast cried out, saying, "O Eve, neither your greed nor your weeping
are due to us, but to you, since the rule of the beasts has happened because of
2 you.ᵃ •How is it that your mouth was opened to eat from the tree concerning
which God commanded you not to eat from it? Through this also our nature was
3 changed. •Therefore now you would not bear it if I begin to reprove you."

1 **12** Seth said to the beast, "Shut your mouth and be silent, and keep away from
2 the image of God until the day of judgment." •Then the beast said to Seth, "See,
I stand off, Seth,ᵃ from the image of God." Then the beast fled and left him
wounded and went to its dwelling.ᵇ

1 **13** And Seth went with his mother Eve near to Paradise. And they wept there,ᵃ
praying God that he would send his angel to give them the oil of mercy.ᵇ

2 And God sent Michael the archangel,ᶜ and he said to them, "Seth, man of God,
do not labor, praying with this supplication about the tree from which the oil
flows, to anoint your father Adam; it shall not come to be yours now (butᵈ at the
3 end of times. •Then all flesh from Adam up to that great dayᵉ shall be raised,
4 such as shall be the holy people; •then to them shall be given every joy of Paradise
5 and God shall be in their midst, •and there shall not be any more sinners before
him, for the evil heart shall be removed from them, and they shall be given a   Jer 31:33
6 heart that understands the good and worships God alone.) •But you go again to   Ezek 18:31;
your father, since the measure of his life is fulfilled, that is,ᶠ in three days. And   36:26
as his soul departs, you are sure to witness its fearful upward journey."   ApMos 32:4

11 a. That the hostilities of the animal world toward man will be removed in the future age is found in
Isa 11:6–9; see also Mk 1:13.

12 a. Several MSS omit the name Seth here. The widespread speculation that Seth possessed the image
of God in a special way is based on Gen 5:3.
   b. Lit. "tent"; MS C reads, "den" (*koitēn*).

13 a. This word is not found in several MSS.
   b. A play on words (*elaion/eleou*, "oil"/"mercy") not capable of Lat. translation.
   c. See ApMos 17:2, n. a.
   d. The words from here through 13:5 are found in a minority of the Gk. MSS and are thus included
here in parentheses. Yet, in striking contrast to the interpolation in *Vita* 42:2–5, this passage has no
exclusively Christian features.
   e. MS B reads, "the day of consummation."
   f. Gk. *ison*, "that is"; lit. "equal to"; some MSS emend this to *eisōn*, "within," or *eis treis ēmeras*,
"to three days."

[*Vita*]

1 **44** And when Seth and his mother reached Adam, they told him how the beast,
2 the serpent, bit Seth. •And Adam said to Eve, "What have you done? You have
3 brought upon us a great wound, transgression and sin in all our generations. •And
you shall relate[a] what you have done to your children[b] after my death, for those
who rise up from us shall labor, not being adequate, but failing,[c] and they shall
4 curse us, saying, •'Our parents who were from the beginning have brought upon
5 us all evils.' " •When Eve heard this she began to weep and groan.

44 a. Lit. *refert,* "she relates"; other MSS read *refer,* "you relate," *referes,* "you are relating," or *referent,* "they are relating." This statement suggests that the author of the *Vita* was aware of Eve's story (ApMos 15–30).
    b. The MSS read *tuos,* "your," *tuis,* "your," *meus,* "my," *tuus,* "your," or *nostri,* "of us"; and *filios,* acc. pl. "children," *filius,* nom. sing. "son," or *filii,* nom. pl. "children."
    c. This suggests an acquaintance with ApMos 24.

[*Apocalypse*]

1 **14** Having said these things, the angel departed from them. Seth and Eve came
2 into the tent where Adam was lying. •Adam said to Eve, "Why have you wrought   2Cor 11:3
destruction among us and brought upon us great wrath, which is death gaining   1Tim 2:14
3 rule over all our race?"ᵃ •Andᵇ he said to her, "Call all our children and our   Rom 5:12-21
children's children, and tell them how we transgressed."

V. EVE'S STORY OF THE FALL AND ITS CONSEQUENCES

1 **15** Then Eve said to them, "Listen, all my children and my children's children,
2 and I will tell you how our enemy deceived us.ᵃ •It happened while we were
guarding Paradise, each his portion allotted from God. Now I was watching in
3 my share, the South and West, •and the devil came into Adam's portion, where   Vita 32
the male animals were, since God divided the animals among us, and all the
males he gave to your father, and all the females to me, and each of us kept his
own.ᵇ

1 **16** "And the devil spoke to the serpent,ᵃ saying, 'Rise and come to me, and I
2 will tell you something to your advantage.' •Then the serpent came to him, and
the devil said to him, 'I hear that you are wiser than all the beasts; so I came to   Gen 3:1
observe you.ᵇ I found you greater than all the beasts, and they associate with you;   Vita 14:3
3 but yet you are prostrate to the very least.ᶜ •Why do you eat of the weeds of
Adamᵈ and not of the fruitᵉ of Paradise? Rise and come and let us make him to
be cast out of Paradise through his wife,ᶠ just as we were cast out through him.'   Vita 12-16
4,5 The serpent said to him, 'I fear lest the LORD be wrathful to me.' •The devil said
to him, 'Do not fear; only become my vessel,ᵍ and I will speak a word through   ApMos 26:1
your mouth by which you will be able to deceive him.'ʰ

The temptation

1 **17** "And immediately he suspended himself from the walls of Paradise about   ApMos 7:2
the time when the angels of God went up to worship. Then Satan came in the   Vita 9:1
2 form of an angel and sang hymns to God as the angels. •And I saw him bending   2Cor 11:14

---

14 a. 2En 30:18 and Sir 25:24 also hold that death came through Eve (cf. 2Cor 11:3; 1Tim 2:14), while
the blame is put on Adam in Rom 5:17; 4Ezra 3:21; 7:118. MS C does not have the words following
"death."
  b. MSS E1 E2 G have a significantly different text for 14:3–16:5 and M1 and M2 for 14:3–17:2; MS
D5 begins at this point.

15 a. MS C omits the words "Listen . . . deceived us."
  b. The last phrase of this sentence is not found in four MSS.

16 a. On the serpent of Paradise see *TDNT*, vol. 5, pp. 577f. (Foerster).
  b. Gk. *katanoēsai*, "to observe"; MS C: "And therefore I consult you . . ."
  c. This clause is not found in MS C; two others omit the last phrase.
  d. Some MSS add "and his wife."
  e. Most MSS do not have "of the fruit."
  f. Several MSS omit "through his wife."
  g. A Hebraism (see *TDNT*, vol. 7, pp. 359–60); several MSS omit "only."
  h. Some MSS correct this to read "her" or "them."

over the wall, like an angel. And he said to me, 'Are you Eve?' And I said to
3 him, 'I am.' And he said to me, 'What are you doing in Paradise?' •I replied,
4 'God placed us to guard it and eat from it.' •The devil answered me through the
5 mouth of the serpent, 'You do well, but you do not eat of every plant.' •And I
said to him, 'Yes, we eat from every plant except one only, which is in the midst   Gen 3:3
of Paradise, concerning which God commanded us not to eat of it, else *you shall*   Gen 2:17
most surely die.'

1 **18** "Then the serpent said to me, 'May God live! For I am grieved[a] over you,
that you are like animals.[b] For I do not want you to be ignorant; but rise, come
2 and eat, and observe the glory of the tree.' •And I said to him, 'I fear lest God
3 be angry with me, just as he told us.' •He said to me, 'Fear not; for at the very
time you eat, *your eyes will be opened and you will be like gods, knowing good*   Gen 3:5
4 *and evil.* •But since God knew this, that you would be like him,[c] he begrudged
5 you and said, "Do not eat of it." •But come to the plant, and see its great glory.'
6 And I turned to the plant and saw its great glory. And I said to him, 'It is pleasing   Gen 3:6
to consider with the eyes';[d] yet I was afraid to take of the fruit. And he said to
me, 'Come, I will give it to you. Follow me.'

The Fall

1 **19** "And I opened (the gate) for him,[a] and he entered into Paradise, passing
through in front of me. After he had walked a little, he turned and said to me, 'I
have changed my mind and will not allow you to eat.' He said these things,
wishing in the end to entice and ruin me.[b] And he said to me, 'Swear to me that
2 you are giving (it) also to your husband.' •And I said to him, 'I do not know by
what sort of oath I should swear to you;[c] however, that which I do know I tell
you: By the throne of the LORD and the cherubim and the tree of life, I shall give
3 (it) also to my husband to eat.' •When he had received the oath from me, he
went, climbed the tree, and sprinkled his evil poison on the fruit which he gave
me to eat which is his covetousness.[d] For coveteousness is the origin[e] of every   Jas 1:15;
sin. And I bent the branch toward the earth,[f] took of the fruit, and ate.   Rom 7:7

---

18 a. MS D1 has a hiatus from here to 36:1.

    b. Most MSS do not have this phrase.

    c. This phrase is not in MSS C and E2.

    d. Several MSS omit vs. 6 up to this point.

19 a. This implies that Satan and not Eve was outside of Paradise; on Satan's attempt to enter Paradise,
cf. ARN 1.

    b. This sentence is not found in several MSS.

    c. One MS has this as a question: "What sort of oath shall I swear to you?"

    d. Gk. *epithymias;* see ApMos 25:3, n. d. The poison (*ios*) of snakes is mentioned in the LXX of Ps
139:4 (ET 140:3); 57:5 (ET 58:4) [*thymos . . . tou opseōs* = wrath . . . of serpents]; see also Rev 3:3;
Hermas, Sim. 9.26.7.

    e. Gk. *kephalē* corresponds to the Heb. *rō'š,* "head" or "first"; since the Heb. word also denotes a
poisonous plant, the original could have been a pun. MS C reads "root and beginning."

    f. Several MSS and the Arm. read, "he bent," corresponding to ARN 1, where the serpent "touched
the tree with his hands and feet, and shook it until its fruits fell to the ground."

[Vita]

[Apocalypse]

1 **20** "And at that very moment my eyes were opened and I knew that I was naked Gen 3:7
2 of the righteousness with which I had been clothed.ᵃ •And I wept saying, 'Why Isa 61:10
have you done this to me, that I have been estranged from my glory with which Eph 6:10-20
3 I was clothed?'ᵇ •And I wept also about the oath. But that one came down from
4 the tree and vanished. •I looked for leaves in my region so that I might cover my Gen 3:7
shame, but I did not find (any) from the trees of Paradise, since while I ate, the
5 leaves of all the trees of my portion fell,ᶜ except (those) of the fig tree only. •And
I took its leaves and made for myself skirts; they were from the same plants of Gen 3:7
which I ate.ᵈ

1 **21** "And I cried out with a loud voice, saying, 'Adam, Adam, where are you?
2 Rise, come to me and I will show you a great mystery.' •And when your father
came, I spoke to him unlawful words of trangression such as brought us down
3 from great glory.ᵃ •For when he came, I opened my mouth and the devil was
speaking, and I began to admonish him, saying, 'Come, my lord Adam, listen to
me and eat of the fruit of the tree of which God told us not to eat from it, and
4 you shall be as God.' •Your father answered and said, 'I fear lest God be angry
with me.' And I said to him, 'Do not fear; for as soon as you eat, you shall know
5 good and evil.' •Then I quickly persuaded him. He ate, and his eyes were opened,
6 and he also realized his nakedness. •And he said to me, 'O evil woman! Why Vita 44
have you wrought destruction among us? You have estranged me from the glory ApMos 14
of God.'

The appearance of God in Paradise

1 **22** "And in the same hour we heard the archangel Michael sounding his trumpet, Isa 58:1
2 calling the angels, saying, •'Thus says the LORD, "Come with me into Paradise Ezek 33:1-6
Hos 8:1
3 and hear the sentenceᵃ which I pronounce on Adam."' •And as we heard the Mt 24:31
1Cor 15:52
archangel sounding the trumpet, we said, 'Behold, God is coming into Paradise 1Thes 4:16
to judge us.' We were afraid and hid.ᵇ And God returned to Paradise, seated on Rev 8:2
a chariot of cherubim, and the angels were praising him. When God came into
Paradise, all the plants, both of the portion of Adam and also of my portion,
4 bloomed forth and were established.ᶜ •And the throne of God was made ready ApMos 20:1;
where the tree of life was.ᵈ 38:4

1 **23** "And God called Adam, saying, 'Adam, where did you hide, thinking that Gen 3:9
2 I would not find you? Can a house hide from its builder?' •Then your father
answered and said, 'O LORD, we are not hiding thinking that we would not be
discovered by you, but rather Iᵃ am afraid because I am naked, and I stood in Gen 3:10

20 a. Ginzberg (*Legends*, vol. 5, pp. 121f. and n. 120) notes that the haggadic interpretation of "naked"
in Gen 3:7, 10 is that the first pair became aware that they were bare of good deeds; cf. Shab 14a; Meg
32a; GenR 19:6; PRE 14. Other Jewish and Christian writers assert that Adam and Eve had garments of
light before the Fall.
  b. This sentence is not found in several MSS.
  c. See ApMos 22:3; 38:4 and cf. b.Yoma 39b.
  d. Cf. PR 42:1: The tree of knowledge was "wheat, according to R. Meir. A fig tree according to R.
Jose. Grapes, according to R. Judah the son of R. Illai. According to R. Abba of Akko, it was the
ethrog. Whatever it was, God has not revealed its identity." GenR 15:7 agrees with later Adam literature
that it was the fig tree. Several MSS do not have the last clause of vs. 5.

21 a. Some MSS omit the words "such as . . . glory."

22 a. Gk. *hrēmatos*, "sentence," or *krimatos*, "judgment," "sentence."
  b. Several MSS omit vs. 3 up to this point.
  c. Some MSS apply this verb to the following sentence: "And the throne of God was established
. . ."
  d. According to 2En 8:3 when God comes into Paradise he locates himself at the tree of life.

23 a. Some MSS correct this to "we."

[*Vita*]

[*Apocalypse*]

3 awe of your might, O LORD.' •God said to him, 'Who showed you that you are   Gen 3:11
naked, unless you have forsaken my commandment which I delivered to you to
4 keep?' •Then Adam remembered the word which I spoke to him, when I wanted
5 to deceive him, 'I will make you safe from God.' •And he turned and said to me,
'Why have you done this?' And I also remembered the word of the serpent, and   Gen 3:13
I said, 'The serpent deceived me.'

The punishments

1 **24** "God said to Adam, 'Because you transgressed my commandment and listened   Gen 3:17-19
2 to your wife, cursed is the ground in your labors. •For when you work it, it will
not give its strength; *it shall yield you brambles and thistles* and *with sweat on*   Gen 3:18
your brow shall you eat your bread. You will suffer many a hardship: Gen 3:19

> You will grow weary and not rest;
> be afflicted with bitterness and not taste
>   sweetness;
3 > be oppressed by heat and burdened by cold;
> you will toil much and not gain wealth;
> you will grow fat and finally not be.*

4 And the animals over which you ruled will rise up against you in disorder, because   ApMos 11
you did not keep my commandment.'

1 **25** "Turning to me, the LORD said to me, 'Since you have listened to the serpent   Gen 3:16
and ignored my commandment, you shall suffer birth pangs* and unspeakable
2 pains; •with much trembling you shall bear children and on that occasion you
3 shall come near to lose your life* from your great anguish and pains, •and you
shall confess and say, "LORD, LORD, save me and I will never again turn to the
4 sin of the flesh."* •And by this, according to your word I will judge you, because
of the enmity which the enemy has placed in you.* And yet you shall turn again
to your husband, and he shall rule over you.'

1 **26** "And after he had told me these things,* he spoke to the serpent in great   Gen 3:14-15
wrath, saying to him, 'Since you have done this and become an ungrateful vessel,*
so far as to lead astray the careless of heart, *accursed* are you *beyond all wild*   Gen 3:14
2 *beasts.* •You shall be deprived of the food which you used to eat,* and shall *eat*
dust every day of your life. You shall crawl on your belly and you shall be deprived   Gen 3:14
3 of your hands as well as your feet. •There shall be left for you neither ear nor

---

24 a. Gk. *eis telos mē hyparkseis* may also be translated "not reach (your) goal."

25 a. Fuchs rightly suggests that the Gk. *mataiois*, "follies," resulted from reading the Heb. original *hʰbālīm*, "birth pangs," as *hʰbālīm*, "vanities." The translator in *ANF*, vol. 3, p. 568 suggests that the Gk. originally read *kamatoi*, "labors," (as in D3) or *mochthois*, "hardships."
   b. Gk. *en mia hōra elthēs kai apoleseis tēn zōēn sou*, lit. "in one hour you may come and you will lose your life."
   c. Eve's promise has close parallels in b.Nidd 31b and GenR 20:7.
   d. A pun (*echthran*, "enmity," *echthros*, "enemy"); Ginzberg (*Legends*, vol. 5, p. 124, n. 131) suggests that in the Heb. original this sentence read "according to your actions," that it was addressed to the serpent, and that it was located at the end of 26. In the Gk. the "word" refers to Eve's promise in vs. 2. The idea that Satan awakened Eve's sexual desire is found in ApAb 23; PRE 21; Philo, *Op* 56.

26 a. The first clause of 26:1 is not found in several MSS.
   b. Gk. *skeuos achariston* may be a translation of the Heb. *kʰliy bʰliyyaʾal*, "tool of Belial'"; so Fuchs, Ginzberg, and Maurer (*TDNT*, vol. 7, p. 360, n. 15); but see Hos 8:8 in LXX. The expression is not found in MSS C and D4.
   c. MS B has a lengthy addition here.

[*Apocalypse*]

wing nor one limb of all that with which you enticed (them) in your depravity
4 and caused them to be cast out of Paradise.[d] • And I will put enmity between you   Gen 3:15
and his seed; he shall beware of your head and you his heel until the day of
judgment.'[e]

The expulsion and the repentance

1 **27** "Having said these things, he ordered his angels to cast us out of Paradise.
2 While we were being expelled and lamenting, your father Adam begged the
angels, 'Let me be a little while so that I may beseech God that he might have
3 compassion and pity me, for I alone have sinned.' • And they ceased driving him
out. And Adam cried out with weeping and said, 'Forgive[a] me, LORD, what I
4 have done.' • Then the LORD said to his angels, 'Why have you stopped driving
5 Adam out of Paradise? Is the guilt mine, or did I judge badly?' • Then the angels
fell on the ground and worshiped the LORD, saying, 'You are righteous, LORD,
and you judge uprightly.'

1 **28** "And the LORD turned and said to Adam, 'From now on I will not allow you
2 to be in Paradise.' • And Adam answered and said, 'LORD, give me from the tree
3 of life that I might eat before I am cast out.' • Then the LORD spoke to Adam,
'You shall not now take[a] from it; for it was appointed to the cherubim[b] and the
flaming sword which turns to guard it because of you, that you might not taste of   Gen 3:24
it and be immortal forever,[c] but that you might have the strife which the enemy   ApMos 25:3
4 has placed in you. • But when you come out of Paradise, if you guard yourself
from all evil, preferring death to it,[d] at the time of the resurrection I will raise
you again, and then there shall be given to you from the tree of life, and you
shall be immortal forever.'[e]

1 **29** "When the LORD had said these things, he ordered us cast out of Paradise.
2 And your father wept before the angels opposite Paradise, and the angels said to
3 him, 'What do you want us to do for you, Adam?' • Your father answered and
said to the angels, 'See, you are casting me out; I beg you, let me take fragrances   Jub 3:27
from Paradise, so that after I have gone out, I might bring an offering to God so
4 that God[a] will hear me.' • And they came to God and said, 'Jael,[b] eternal king,
5 command that fragrant incenses from Paradise be given to Adam.' • And God
ordered Adam to come that he might take aromatic fragrances out of Paradise[c] for   Vita 22:2;
6 his sustenance. • When the angels allowed him, he gathered both[d] kinds: crocus,   43:5
nard, reed, cinnamon; and other seeds for his food. And he took these and went   Gen 1:29
out of Paradise. And (so) we came to be on the earth.[e]

---

d. Several sources suggest the belief that the serpent had limbs before the Fall; see Josephus, *Ant*
1.1.4; GenR 19:1; 20:5.
   e. The verb *tērēsei* is from Gen 3:15, LXX; the Heb. verb *šûwp* may have the same meaning.

27 a. Gk. *sygchōrēson*, "forgive"; lit. "yield," as in 33:5; 35:2; and 37:6.

28 a. MS C reads "taste."
   b. In the Dead Sea Scrolls the cherubim are the highest rank of angels; cf. 1En 61:10; 2En 19:6.
   c. MS M1 has a hiatus from here to 34:1.
   d. Gk. *hōs boulomenos apothanein*, "preferring death to it"; lit. "as one who wishes to die"; one
MS reads "as one about to die."
   e. MSS E1 and E2 do not have this vs.; MSS C and G omit the last clause.

29 a. Some MSS have "he."
   b. "Jael," a compound from the first syllable of each of the two most common Heb. biblical terms
for God (Yahweh, Elohim); see Wells, p. 148. C omits the word; D5 has *aule*, D2 *ēaēl*, and E2 *yōēl*.
   c. Several MSS add "and seeds."
   d. For cultic purposes and also for food; several MSS read "four kinds."
   e. MSS F and H add here the account of the repentance of Adam and Eve, translated above as a
parallel to *Vita* 1–10.

[*Vita*]

1 **45** And just as Michael the archangel had predicted, the death of Adam came
2 after six days. •When Adam realized that the hour of his death had come, he said
to all his sons, "Behold, I am 930 years old, and if I should die, bury me against
3 the East in the great dwelling place of God."ᵃ •And it happened that when he
finished his whole speech, he gave up the spirit.

John 19:30

---

45 a. Lat. *contra ortum dei magnum habitationibus*, "against the East in the great dwelling place of
God"; some MSS read *in agrum*, "toward open country," or *in agro*, "on land"; see *Vita* 30:2, n. a.

1 **30** "Now then, my children, I have shown you the way in which we were deceived. But you watch yourselves so that you do not forsake the good."[a]

VI. THE DEATH AND BURIAL OF ADAM AND EVE

1 **31** When she had said these things in the midst of her sons and while Adam was lying ill, having one more day before going out of the body, Eve said to Adam, 2Cor 5:1-5
2 "Why are you dying and I live? And how long have I to live after you die? Tell
3 me." •Then Adam said to Eve, "Do not be concerned about this, for you shall not be long after me, but we shall both alike die, and you yourself[a] shall be laid in my place. But when I die, leave me alone[b] and let no one touch me until the
4 angel of the LORD shall say something about me; •for God will not forget me, but will seek his own vessel[c] which he has formed. But rather rise to pray to God until I shall give back my spirit into the hands of the one who has given it. For we know not how we shall meet our maker, whether he shall be angry with us or turn to have mercy on us."

Eve's repentance and Adam's death

1,2 **32** Then Eve rose and went out and fell on the ground and said, •"I have sinned, O God; I have sinned, O Father of all; I have sinned against you, I have sinned against your chosen angels, I have sinned against the cherubim, I have sinned against your steadfast throne; I have sinned, LORD, I have sinned much; I have
3 sinned before you, and all sin in creation has come about through me."[a] •While ApMos 14:2
Eve was still on her knees praying, behold, the angel of mankind[b] came to her
4 and lifted her up, saying, •"Rise, Eve, from your repentance, for behold, Adam your husband has gone out of his body. Rise and see his spirit borne up to meet its maker."

The return of God with his angels

1 **33** And Eve rose and put her hand on her face,[a] and the angel said to her, "Lift Acts 7:55;
2 yourself from earthly things." •And Eve gazed into heaven, and saw a chariot of 1:10
light coming, (drawn) by four radiant eagles of which it is not possible for anyone born from the womb to tell their glory or to see their faces,[b] and angels went

---

30 a. In lieu of this paragraph E1 and E2 have a description of Eve's lament.

31 a. So the Arm.; most Gk. MSS have "she herself," although A2 and M2 put the verb in the second person singular.
 b. Gk. *kataleipsete*, "leave (me) alone"; A1 and A2 read *kalypsete*, "cover (me)."
 c. Gk. *skeuos*, "vessel"; other MSS read *plasma*, "image."

32 a. The E MSS here refer to death as resulting from Eve's sin.
 b. Michael is intended; see *Vita* 41:1.

33 a. The Gk. MSS have several variants here; Arm. (cf. MS G) reads "with her hands wiped her many tears from her face."
 b. MSS M1 G E1 read, "The beauty and glory of which it is impossible for tongues of men to describe."

[*Vita*]

1,2 **46** And for seven days were the sun, moon, and stars darkened. •And while Seth was mourning, embracing the body of his father from above and Eve was looking
3 at the ground, her hands folded over her head, with her head on her knees, and all her children were weeping most bitterly, •behold, the angel Michael appeared standing at the head of Adam and he said to Seth, "Rise from the body of your father and come to me and see what the LORD God is arranging concerning him. He is his creature and he has had mercy on him."

[Apocalypse]

3 before the chariot. •When they came to the place where your[c] father Adam was lying, the chariot stood, and the seraphim (were) between (your) father and the 4 chariot. •I myself saw golden censers and three bowls, and behold, all the angels with frankincense and the censers and the bowls came to the altar and breathed 5 on them, and the fumes of the incense hid the sky.[d] •And the angels fell down and worshiped God, crying out and saying, "Holy Jael, forgive, for he is your image, and the work of your (holy) hands."

1 **34** And then I, Eve, saw two great and fearful mysteries standing before God. 2 And I wept from fear and cried out to my son Seth, saying, •"Rise, Seth, from the body of your father, Adam,[a] and come to me, that you may see things which no eye has ever seen."[b]

1 **35** Then Seth got up and came to his mother. And he said to her, "What is the 2 matter? Why are you weeping?" •She said to him, "Look up with your eyes and see the seven heavens[a] opened, and see with your eyes how the body of your father lies on its face, and all the holy angels are with him, praying for him and 3 saying, 'Forgive him, O Father of all, for he is your image.'[b] •So[c] then, my child Seth, what shall this be? When will he be given over into the hands of our unseen 4 Father and God? •And who are the two dark-skinned persons[d] assisting at the prayer for your father?"

1 **36** Seth said to his mother, "These are the sun and the moon, and they themselves 2 fall down and pray for my father Adam." •And Eve said to him, "And where is 3 their light, and why have they become dark?" •Seth said to her, "They are not able to shine before the light[a] of all, and this is why the light is hid from them."

Joel 2:10; 3:15
Job 25:5
Rev 8:12

Vita 28:2

Adam's soul is taken up to the heavenly Paradise[a]

1 **37** While Seth was speaking to his mother, an angel sounded the trumpet and the angels who were lying on their faces stood up[b] and cried out with a fearful 2 voice, saying, •"Blessed be the glory of the LORD over his works; he has had 3 mercy on Adam, the work of his hands." •When the angels had shouted out these things, one of the six-winged seraphim came and carried Adam off to the Lake

---

c. Most of ApMos 33–34 are written as though Eve is speaking; this may have been part of a separate section from which 15–30 were also derived.

d. Or "firmaments" (*stereōmata*); F and H read "heaven."

34 a. Several MSS do not include the name Adam here.

b. Several MSS add, "And they are praying for your father Adam."

35 a. See *Vita* 25, n. a.

b. Some MSS read, "son," "house," "tent," or "product."

c. The E MSS do not contain 35:3–36:3 and have a much shorter form of the text from there to the end.

d. Gk. *Aithiopes*, lit. "Ethiopians"; MS G reads *theoprosōpoi*, "god-faced ones."

36 a. Several MSS read "Father of lights," as in Jas 1:17.

37 a. Chs. 37f. presuppose a distinction, not so clear in *Vita*, between body and spirit (or "soul"); death is the separation of the two. See *TDNT*, vol. 7, p. 1050 (E. Schweizer); on Paradise see *Vita* 25, n. a.

b. So D F and Arm.; Tischendorf's text reads "The angels lying on their faces blew the trumpet . . ."

[*Vita*]

47 And all the angels sounded the trumpets and said, "Blessed are you, LORD,
who has pitied your creature." •Then Seth saw the extended hand of the LORD   ApMos 37:4
holding Adam, and he handed him over to Michael, saying, •"Let him be in your
custody until the day of dispensing punishment^a at the last years, when I will turn
his sorrow into joy. Then he shall sit on the throne of him who overthrew him."

48 And again the LORD said to the angels Michael and Uriel, "Bring me three
linen cloths and spread them out over Adam, and other cloths over his son Abel,
and bury Adam and his son." •And all the ranks of angels processed before
Adam, and the sleep^a of the dead was hallowed. •And Michael and Uriel said,   ApMos 43:2
"Bury your dead in the same way as you have seen."

---

47 a. Lat. *usque in diem dispensationis in suppliciis*, "until the day of dispensing punishment"; other
MSS read *disposition*, "order," or *defensionis*, "defense."

48 a. Lat. *dormitatio*, "sleep" (medieval); other MSS have *dormitio*, "sleep."

[*Apocalypse*]

4 of Acheron[c] and washed him three times[d] in the presence of God. •He lay three
5 hours,[e] and so the LORD of all, sitting on his holy throne, stretched out his hands   *Vita* 47:2
and took Adam and handed him over to the archangel Michael, saying to him,
5 "Take him up into Paradise, to the third heaven,[f] and leave (him) there until that   2Cor 12:2
6 great and fearful day which I am about to establish for the world." •And the   *Vita* 25
archangel Michael took Adam and brought him away and left him, just as God
told him at the pardoning of Adam.

The burial of Adam's body

1 **38**[a] Now after all these things the archangel asked about attending to the remains.
2 And God gave orders that all the angels should gather before him, each according
3 to his rank. •And all the angels came together, some with censers and others
trumpets. And the LORD of hosts mounted up, the winds drawing him, and the   *Vita* 25:3
cherubim being above the winds; and the angels of heaven were leading him. And   ApMos 22
4 when they came to the place where the body of Adam was, they took it. •And
they came into Paradise and all the plants of Paradise were stirred, so that all   ApMos 20:3;
those born of Adam became drowsy from the fragrance except Seth, because he   22:3
was born according to the appointment of God.[b]   Gen 4:25

1 **39** Now the body of Adam was lying on the ground in Paradise, and Seth was
mourning greatly over him. And the LORD God said, "Adam, why did you do
this? If you had kept my commandment, those who brought you down into this
2 place would not have rejoiced. •Yet now I tell you that their joy shall be turned
into sorrow, but your sorrow shall be turned into joy; and when that happens, I
3 will establish you in your dominion on the throne of your seducer. •But that one   *Vita* 12-16
shall be cast into this place, so that you might sit above him. Then he himself
and those who listen to him shall be condemned, and they shall greatly mourn
and weep when they see you sitting on his glorious throne."

1 **40** Then he spoke to the archangel Michael, "Go into Paradise in the third
2 heaven[a] and bring me three cloths of linen and silk."[b] •And God said to Michael,
Gabriel, Uriel, and Raphael,[c] "Cover Adam's body with the cloths and bring oil
from the oil of fragrance and pour it on him." And thus they did and prepared   2En 8
3 his body. •And the LORD spoke, "Let also Abel's body be brought." And they
4 brought other linens and prepared him also, •since he was unattended from the

---

c. In Gk. tradition part of the stream over which the souls of the dead were conveyed to the underworld.
That Michael washes repentant sinners in Acheron is found in ApPaul 22 (end); Bartholomew literature
(M. R. James, *ANT*, p. 185); SibOr 2.330–39 (HSW, vol. 2, p. 718); see also SibOr 5.485; 3Bar 10:2;
1En 17:6.
d. "Three times" is omitted in some MSS.
e. Most Gk. MSS originally read "days"; "hours" is written by another hand. Cf. TJob 20.
f. See *Vita* 25, n. a. The E MSS do not have the words following "Paradise" in 37:5 or 38:1-3, 5.

38 a. MSS F and H do not have chs. 38–39.
b. Gk. *kath horon tou theou*, "according to the appointment of God," may be a reference to Gen
4:25 or could be read *kathoran tou theou*, "to behold God" (so Charles); or may be read, as in MS G,
katharos enōpion tou theou, "pure before God."

40 a. See *Vita* 25, n. a.
b. Gk. *syrikas*, "pipes," is mistakenly written for *sērikas*, "silken"; some MSS omit "and silk."
c. These four angels also are named in the Dead Sea Scrolls and 1En 9:1 as the greatest of the angels.
Several MSS mention Michael alone here.

[*Vita*]

Eve's instructions about the tablets and her death

1 **49** Indeed, six days after Adam died, Eve, aware that she would die, gathered
all her sons and daughters, Seth with thirty brothers and thirty sisters, and Eve
2 said to (them) all, •"Listen to me, my children, and I will tell you that I and your
3 father transgressed the command of God, •and the archangel Michael said to us,
'Because of your collusion, our LORD will bring over your race the wrath of his
judgment, first by water and then by fire; by these two the LORD will judge the
whole human race.'

1 **50** "But listen to me, my children! Make now tablets of stone and other tablets
of clay and write in them all my life and your father's which you have heard and
2 seen from us. •If he should judge our race by water, the tablets of earth will
dissolve and the tablets of stone will remain; but if he should judge our race by
fire, the tablets of stone will break up and those of clay will be thoroughly
baked."ᵃ

2En 33:8-12
Josephus, *Ant*
1.2.3

50 a. This tradition is already found in different form in Josephus, *Ant* 1.2.3; the tradition is known in
"Pseudo-Manetho," cf. George Syncellus, Chronicle 40; see also Jub 8:1–3; 2En 33:8–12 (B); Philo,
Vita Mos 2:36; GenR 26; ARN 31. The fact that the contents of these tablets according to the *Vita* is the
story of Adam and Eve, while in Josephus it is astronomical knowledge, may indicate lack of dependence
between these two. Cf. M. Hengel, *Judaism and Hellenism*, vol. 1, pp. 241–43.

[Apocalypse]

day when his brother Cain murdered him.[d] For the evil Cain took much care to
hide (Abel's body), but could not,[e] for the earth did not receive the body, saying, Gen 4:10-11
5 "I shall not receive another[f] body until the mound of earth which was taken from
me and formed shall come to me." Then the angels took up the body and set it Gen 2:7
6 on the rock, until the time his father died, •and both were buried according to the
command of God in the regions of Paradise in the place from which God had
7 found the dust.[g] •And God sent seven angels into Paradise and they brought many
fragrances and set them in the earth, and so they took the two bodies and buried
them in the place which they dug and built.[h]

1 **41** And God called Adam and said, "Adam, Adam." And the body answered
2 from the ground and said, "Here I am, LORD." •And the LORD said to him, "I Gen 3:19
3 told you that *you are dust and to dust you shall return.* •Now I promise to you
the resurrection; I shall raise you on the last day in the resurrection with every
man of your seed."

1 **42** After these words God made a triangular seal and sealed the tomb in order
that no one might do anything to him for six days, when his rib would return to
2,3 him. •Then the LORD and the angels went to their place,[a] •and after six days Eve
also died.[b]

d. Several sources, including Josephus, *Ant* 1.2.1, assert that Cain hid Abel's body in the ground;
rabbinic sources hold that Adam buried Abel (cf. b.Taʿan 69a, 56; DeutR on 4:41). We have here a
separate tradition.
   e. MS D adds "for the body sprang up from the earth and there was a voice from the earth saying
. . ."
   f. Most MSS have *hetairon*, "companion"; the original probably had, as with D, *heteron*, translated
here. Abel could not be buried before Adam.
   g. See *Vita* 30, n. a; the temple mount is suggested. The Samaritans held a similar view but identified
the place of Adam's creation, Eden, and burial place as Mount Gerizim; cf. J. Macdonald, *The Theology
of the Samaritans* (The New Testament Library; London, 1964) p. 375.
   h. MSS F and H have an abbreviated form of vss. 5-7.

42 a. So MS D; others read, "And when the benevolent God and the holy angels had committed (him)
to his place, after six days . . ."
   b. This may be linked with the rabbinic interpretation of Gen 1-2 that Adam was created on the first
day of creation and Eve on Friday; cf. Ginzberg, *Legends,* vol. 5, p. 127, n. 138.

[*Vita*]

3   When Eve had said all this to her children, she stretched out her hands
to heaven, praying, and bent her knees to the ground and worshiped the LORD,
giving thanks, and gave up the spirit.

1,2 **51** After this, all her children buried her with great weeping. •Then, when they
had mourned for four days, the archangel Michael appeared to them and said to
Seth, "Man of God, do not prolong mourning your dead more than six days,
because the seventh day is a sign of the resurrection, the rest of the coming age,
3 and on the seventh day the LORD rested from all his works." •Then Seth made   Gen 2:2
the tablets.

VI. APPENDIX: THE DISCOVERY OF THE TABLETS[a]

Then Seth made tablets of stone and clay, and wrote in them the life of his father
Adam and his mother Eve, what he had heard from them and his eyes had seen,
and he put the tablets in the middle of the house of his father in the oratory[b] where
4 he used to pray to the LORD. •And after the Flood, those written tablets were seen
5 by many persons but were read by no one. •The wise Solomon, however, saw
the writings and was entreating the LORD, and an angel of the LORD appeared to
6 him, saying, •"I am he who held the hand of Seth, so that he wrote with his
finger onto stone, and you shall be wise in writing[c] so that you might know and
understand all that is contained on the stones, and where the place of prayer was
7 where Adam and Eve used to worship the LORD God. •And it is fitting for you
8 to build the temple of the LORD, the house of prayer, at that place. •Then Solomon
completed the temple of the LORD God and called forth those Achillean[d] documents
(that is to say, written without the knowledge of words by the finger of Seth, his
9 hand being held by the angel of the LORD). •And on the stones themselves was
found what Enoch, the seventh from Adam, prophesied before the Flood, speaking   Gen 5:21-24
of the coming of Christ, "Behold, the LORD will come in his holiness *to pronounce*   Jude 14-16
judgment on all and to convict the impious of all their works which they spoke   1En 1:9
of him, sinners and impious, murmurers and irreligious, who walked according
to their lust and whose mouth has spoken pride."[e]

51 a. This appendix, certainly a late and separate tradition, is found in the MSS of Meyer's group II,
with many variants in some MSS used by Mozley (pp. 145–49), and in several medieval English and
German versions. It is often connected with the legend of the wood of the cross.

b. See *Vita* 30, n. a.

c. Lat. *scripturam*, "writing."

d. Lat. *achiliacas*; other MSS have *achilicas* or *archilaykas*. Meyer suggests a translation from the
Gk. (*acheiropoiētous*, "not made with hands"). There are numerous textual variants in vss. 8–9.

e. That vs. 9 describes different contents of the tablets from what is indicated in 50:1 and 51:3
demonstrates the composite nature of this appendix.

[Apocalypse]

While living, she herself wept about her death,[c] because she did not know where her body was to be placed. For while the LORD was in Paradise when they buried Adam, both she and her children slept, except for Seth, as I said.[d]
4 And Eve in the hour of her death implored that she might be buried where Adam,
5 her husband, was, saying, •"My Master, LORD and God of all excellence, do not
6 separate me[e] from the body of Adam; for you made me from his members; •but rather consider me worthy, even me, unworthy and sinful, to be buried near his
7 body. And just as I was with him in Paradise, •and not separated even after the
8 transgression, so also let no one separate us (now)." •Therefore after she prayed, she looked up to heaven, rose, beat her breast, and said, "God of all, receive my   Lk 23:46 spirit." And immediately she gave up her spirit to God.[f]

1 **43** When she had died, the archangel Michael stood by, and three angels came
2 and took her body and buried it where the body of Abel was. •And the archangel Michael said to Seth, "Thus you shall prepare for burial each man who dies until   Vita 48:3
3 the day of resurrection.[a] •And do not mourn more than six days; on the seventh day rest and be glad in it, for on that day both God and we angels rejoice in the
4 migration from the earth of a righteous soul."[b] •And when he had said these things, the angel went up into heaven, glorifying (God) and saying, "Alleluia, to whom be glory and power forever and ever."[c]

---

c. MS D reads "about the death of Adam."
d. The reference is to ApMos 38:4.
e. Some MSS add "your servant."
f. The E MSS end here with a statement that Eve's sons buried her with the body of Adam and there is a brief doxology.

43 a. The D group, F H G, add, with variants, "Upon giving him (this) law, the archangel departed from Seth, saying to him . . ."
b. MS G ends, ". . . in which God rested from all his works; to him be glory and power forever and ever. Amen." Other MSS read, "Do not mourn for seven days, for in it God and we angels rejoice . . ."
c. So MS D1. All MSS, in addition to Arm. and Slav., have variant endings; Tischendorf printed that of MS C: "He went up into heaven, glorifying and saying the hallelujah, 'Holy, holy, holy, LORD, to the glory of God the Father, for to him is due glory, honor, and worship with his eternal and life-giving Spirit both now and eternally, forever and ever. Amen.' " The trisagion is found also in D2 D3 D5 M1 M2 H. The ending of MS G is given in n. b.

PSEUDO-PHILO

(First Century A.D.)

A NEW TRANSLATION AND INTRODUCTION

BY D. J. HARRINGTON

Pseudo-Philo's *Biblical Antiquities* (often referred to by the Latin title *Liber Antiquitatum Biblicarum*), a history of Israel from Adam to David, is an imaginative retelling of parts of the Old Testament story. It interweaves biblical incidents and legendary expansions of these accounts. From the material corresponding to that of the book of Genesis there are genealogies from Adam to Noah (ch. 1) and from Cain to Lamech (ch. 2), the story of the Flood (ch. 3), genealogies of the sons of Noah down to Abraham (ch. 4), the census of Noah's descendants (ch. 5), the story of the tower of Babel and Abraham's rescue from the fiery furnace (ch. 6), the account of the dispersion of the peoples and the choice of Canaan as the land of Abraham (ch. 7), and the history of Israel from Abraham's settlement in Canaan to the descent of Jacob's sons into Egypt (ch. 8). From Exodus there are the stories of Moses' birth (ch. 9), the departure from Egypt and the crossing of the sea (ch. 10), the giving of the Law (ch. 11), and the golden calf (ch. 12). Various statutes regarding festivals and the purification of lepers are taken from Leviticus (ch. 13). From Numbers there is the census of the people (ch. 14) as well as the accounts of the twelve spies (ch. 15), the rebellion of Korah (ch. 16), the rod of Aaron (ch. 17), and Balaam (ch. 18). The narrative of Moses' farewell, prayer, and death (ch. 19) uses material from Deuteronomy. From Joshua there are stories of Joshua's commissioning as Moses' successor and his division of the land (ch. 20), Joshua's prayer and the cult at Gilgal (ch. 21), the altar across the Jordan and those at Gilgal and Shiloh (ch. 22), the covenant of Joshua (ch. 23), and the farewell and death of Joshua (ch. 24). Then from Judges there is a lengthy section about Kenaz, who is mentioned only in Judges 3:9–11 as the father of Othniel. His election and the sinners' confession (ch. 25), the punishment of the sinners and the twelve precious stones (ch. 26), his victory in battle (ch. 27), and his covenant, vision, and death (ch. 28) are described. After a brief section on Zebul (ch. 29) there are accounts of Deborah's call (ch. 30), the defeat of Sisera (ch. 31), the "hymn" of Deborah (ch. 32), and her farewell and death (ch. 33). Then sections about Aod the magician (ch. 34), the call (ch. 35) and victory (ch. 36) of Gideon, Abimelech (ch. 37), Jair (ch. 38), Jephthah (ch. 39) and his daughter Seila's lament (ch. 40), Abdon and Elon (ch. 41), and the birth (ch. 42) and exploits (ch. 43) of Samson are included. The narratives about the idols of Micah (ch. 44), the crisis at Nob (ch. 45), Israel's defeat (ch. 46), and the activities (ch. 47) and ascension (ch. 48) of Phinehas the priest follow. Finally, corresponding to 1 Samuel and the beginning of 2 Samuel there are long sections devoted mainly to Samuel and David. Connected with Samuel are the stories of Israel's search for a leader (ch. 49), the prayer of Hannah (ch. 50), the birth of Samuel (ch. 51), the sons of Eli (ch. 52), the call of Samuel (ch. 53), the capture of the ark and Eli's death (ch. 54), the return of the ark (ch. 55), the people's demand for a king (ch. 56), the presentation of Saul to the people (ch. 57), and the sin of Saul (ch. 58). Connected with David are the parts about his anointing and his psalm (ch. 59), his function as Saul's exorcist (ch. 60), David and Goliath (ch. 61), David and Jonathan, David's song (ch. 62), the death of Abimelech (ch. 63), the witch of Endor (ch. 64), and the death of Saul (ch. 65).

Texts

Pseudo-Philo exists in eighteen complete and three fragmentary Latin manuscripts, all apparently of German or Austrian origin.[1] The oldest are dated to the eleventh century, while the most recent are from the fifteenth century. All the complete manuscripts have what seem to be gaps of uncertain length between 36:4 and 37:2 and between 37:5 and 38:1. All end abruptly in the midst of Saul's final speech; the original ending seems to have been lost. There are Latin errors common to all the manuscripts. For our purposes the most important complete manuscripts are Fulda-Cassel Theol. 4°,3 (11th cent.) and Phillipps 461 (12th cent.; part of the Bodmer Collection). Also important is the *editio princeps* published by John Sichardus at Basel in 1527 in which he used the Fulda-Cassel manuscript along with a now lost manuscript from the Lorsch monastery. Detailed analysis indicates that this Lorsch manuscript reflected an earlier stage of tradition than any extant manuscript does. The close relationships between it and the Fulda-Cassel manuscript and between the latter and the Phillipps 461 lead us to rely on these primarily as the basis for arriving at the earliest possible text of Pseudo-Philo. The remaining complete manuscripts form a second major group. The most significant of these are Munich Latin 18481 (formerly Tegernsee 481; 11th cent.) and Admont 359 (11th cent.; now in the library of H. L. Goodhart). The relationships among all the extant manuscripts is such, however, that this second major group can preserve some readings that are likely to correspond to the earliest stage of the Latin tradition of Pseudo-Philo. Our translation is based mainly on the text of the Fulda-Cassel and Phillipps manuscripts, but where the second group offers manifestly superior readings we have adopted them. Finally, there are medieval retroversions of parts of Pseudo-Philo to be found in the Hebrew *Chronicles of Jerahmeel* (Bodleian MS Heb. d. 11; 14th cent.).[2] Several features in these Hebrew texts are best explained as translations from the Latin; there is also a tendency to assimilate Old Testament texts to the Masoretic Text. It is difficult to know, however, which Latin text (or texts) the retroverter had at his disposal. The title *Biblical Antiquities* comes from the first Latin editions. In the 1527 edition, Sichardus followed the lead of the fourteenth-century label of the Fulda-Cassel manuscript (*liber Philonis antiquitatum*) and called it *Liber Antiquitatum*. The title *Liber Antiquitatum Biblicarum* first appears in the edition of Sichardus' text printed in 1552 at Lyon by S. Gryphe.

Original language

In an 1898 article[3] that reintroduced Pseudo-Philo to the scholarly world, Leopold Cohn argued that the Latin text is a translation from the Greek and that underlying the Greek there must have been a Hebrew original. Cohn's view has won general acceptance. Pseudo-Philo now exists in a Latin version whose idiom and style represent that vulgar Latin in which the Old Latin versions of the Bible were written. There are, however, several texts that are best explained if we presume a Greek stage in the transmission.[4] For example, in Pseudo-Philo 9:3 ("from the time when the word of God that he spoke to Abraham *was spoken*, there are 350 years") the Latin has *was found*. Here we probably have confusion between the Greek *errethē*, "was spoken," and *heurethē*, "was found." Also, several Greek words have been left practically untranslated: *paratecem*, "deposit," in 3:10, *ometoceam*, "miscarriage," in 9:2, *zaticon*, "covenant," in 9:15, and *anteciminus*, "adversary," in 45:6. There are examples of mistranslation implying a Hebrew original. For example, in 15:6 ("to kindle a lamp for my people and to establish *laws* for creation") the Latin word *terminus*, "boundaries," can be traced back to the Hebrew *ḥûqqîm*, which can mean both "boundaries" and "laws." Also, in 53:6 ("With your right ear pay attention,

[1] D. J. Harrington, "The Text-Critical Situation of Pseudo-Philo's *Liber Antiquitatum Biblicarum*," *RBen* 83 (1973) 383–88.

[2] D. J. Harrington, *The Hebrew Fragments of Pseudo-Philo's* Liber Antiquitatum Biblicarum *Preserved in the* Chronicles of Jerahmeel.

[3] L. Cohn, "An Aprocryphal Work Ascribed to Philo of Alexandria," *JQR* 10 (1898) 277–332.

[4] D. J. Harrington, "The Original Language of Pseudo-Philo's *Liber Antiquitatum Biblicarum*," *HTR* 63 (1970) 503–14. Most of the key passages are mentioned in the notes accompanying our translation.

with your left *be deaf*") the Latin *taceat*, "be silent," reflects the Hebrew *ḥāraš*, which means both "be silent" and "be deaf." Lastly, some biblical texts are best explained as translations from Hebrew into Greek and then into Latin. In 3:4 ("Noah, who was a righteous man and *blameless*"), a version of Genesis 6:9, the word *inmaculatus*, "blameless," renders the Hebrew *tammîm*. Unlike the Septuagint translators, who rendered *tammîm* as *teleios*, "perfect," the Greek translator of Pseudo-Philo must have used *amōmos*, "spotless," "blameless," which in Latin became *inmaculatus*. In other words, here and elsewhere we are dealing with a translation of the Hebrew Bible independent of the Greek Old Testament. These indications that Hebrew was the original language of Pseudo-Philo enable us to recognize more clearly the many Semitisms behind the Latin text. Could Pseudo-Philo have been composed in Aramaic? Distinguishing between a work written in the Hebrew of the second Temple period and a work composed in Aramaic when we have only a Latin version made from a Greek translation is not easy. But some of the probable errors noted are possible only in Hebrew. For example, the phrase *in victoria* (9:3) or *ad victoriam* (12:6) can be traced to the Hebrew idiom *lᵉneṣaḥ*, "forever, everlasting," but the root *nṣḥ* in Aramaic is not used in this sense. Furthermore, there is no solid positive evidence on which to argue that the book was composed in Aramaic. Therefore we are led to conclude that Hebrew, rather than Aramaic, is the original language of Pseudo-Philo.

Date

Attempts to date the composition of the original Hebrew version have focused on Pseudo-Philo 19:7, which mentions "the place where they will serve me 740 years" as having been destroyed on the same day as that on which Moses broke the tablets of the Law, the seventeenth of Tammuz. This has been understood as a reference to Titus' capture of Jerusalem, A.D. 70. But close inspection of this text and the complexities involved in it indicates that the reference could also be to the capture of Jerusalem by Nebuchadnezzar, Antiochus Epiphanes, or Pompey.[5] The parallels between Pseudo-Philo and 4 Ezra and 2 Baruch, the latter two most probably composed after the destruction of the second Temple, could also suggest a date after A.D. 70. But, again, this point is not decisive, since the theological emphases of these two books (mourning over the destroyed Temple, heightened eschatological consciousness, the four-empire scheme of history, the Messiah, etc.) are not the same as those of Pseudo-Philo.

The presence of what may be called a "Palestinian" biblical text[6] (rather than "Babylonian" or "Egyptian" according to the categories of F. M. Cross, Jr.[7]) makes the latest possible date around A.D. 100 (when such texts were probably suppressed). Some other considerations lead us to suspect that Pseudo-Philo was composed before A.D. 70: the attitude toward the Temple and sacrifice (e.g. 32:3) is what we would expect before 70; the expression "unto this day" in 22:8 suggests that the Temple still stands; the negative attitude toward Jewish rulers not chosen by God (possibly an anti-Herodian polemic) would have been a dead issue after 70; the silence about the destruction of the Temple would be strange if indeed the Temple had been destroyed; the free attitude toward the biblical text fits the period before 70 better than after it. If Getal, the king of the Ammonites in 39:8, can be identified with Zenon surnamed Cotylas, who was ruler of Philadelphia (Ammon), then we can establish 135 B.C. as the earliest possible date for the composition of the work. A date around the time of Jesus seems most likely.

Provenance

If Pseudo-Philo had really been composed by Philo the Jew, Alexandria would be its obvious place of origin. The Latin text of Pseudo-Philo was transmitted along with the Latin translations of Philo's works, but the attribution of Pseudo-Philo to him cannot be

---

[5] P.-M. Bogaert, *Apocalypse syriaque de Baruch* (SC 144; Paris, 1969) 252–58.

[6] D. J. Harrington, "The Biblical Text of Pseudo-Philo's *Liber Antiquitatum Biblicarum*," *CBQ* 33 (1971) 1–17.

[7] F. M. Cross, Jr., *The Ancient Library of Qumran and Modern Biblical Studies* (Garden City, N.Y., 1961) pp. 163–94; "The History of the Biblical Text in the Light of the Discoveries in the Judaean Desert," *HTR* 57 (1964) 281–99.

sustained. The manner of dealing with the biblical text is very different from Philo's allegorizing. Moreover, Philo wrote in Greek (how much Hebrew he knew is debatable), but our author apparently wrote in Hebrew. Finally, there are several points at which Pseudo-Philo explicitly contradicts the views of Philo: 1,652 years from Adam to the Flood (3:6) against Philo's 2,242; the favorable or at least neutral portrayal of Balaam (18) against Philo's negative description; Moses' burial by God (19:16), not by the angels.[8]

Many factors point to Palestine as the place in which Pseudo-Philo originated: it was apparently composed in Hebrew; the biblical text that the author had at his disposal was a Palestinian one; there are many literary parallels with 4 Ezra and 2 Baruch,[9] both of Palestinian origin; some of the author's theological interests (the Temple, the rules of sacrifice, the covenant and the Law, eschatology, and angelology) point toward a Palestinian provenance; where we can understand the geographical aspects of the work, the author seems to know the geography of Palestine (e.g. 55:7).

Historical importance

Efforts to connect Pseudo-Philo with specific groups or sects in Palestine (Pharisees, Essenes, Qumran Covenanters, Samaritans, anti-Samaritans, Hellenists, Gnostics, etc.) have not won general acceptance. Rather, Pseudo-Philo seems to reflect the milieu of the Palestinian synagogues at the turn of the common era. It is the earliest witness for motifs frequently repeated in the Jewish tradition: Abraham's escape from Ur (6), Israel's being spared from the water of the Flood (7:4), Dinah's husband as Job (8:8), Moses' being born circumcised (9:13), the writing on the tablets of the Law fleeing away (12:5), Balaam as an interpreter of dreams (18:2), the sacrifice of Isaac (18:5; 32:2–4; 40:2), Isaac's birth in the seventh month (23:8), the concealment of the precious stones until the last day (26:13), the equation of Phinehas and Elijah (48:1), the identification of Saul with the fleeing Benjaminite of 1 Samuel 4:12 (54:4), and Saul's death as an atonement for his sins (64:9).

The work also transmits legends and motifs not found elsewhere. Among the more significant examples are the connection of the building of the tower of Babel with casting Abraham into the fire (6:3–18), Tamar's aim in having intercourse with Judah as to avoid intercourse with gentiles (9:5), the connection between Moses' being cast into the water and his later drying up of the Red Sea (9:10), Moses' being prevented from entering the holy land lest he see idols (19:7), the long sections on Kenaz (chs. 25–28), the idols of Micah (44:5), and Saul's motive in expelling the sorcerers as winning personal renown (64:1). Two other features might tell us more about the historical setting of the work if we were able to offer satisfactory explanations for them. There are some interesting plays on Old Testament clichés from what would now be described as a feminist perspective: "woman of God" in 33:1 and "the bosom of her mothers" in 40:4. Also, there seems to be a deliberate attempt to relocate certain biblical events: Shiloh in 45:5 rather than Mizpah of Judges 20:1 or Bethel of Judges 20:18; Shiloh in 55:9 rather than Beth-shemesh of 1 Samuel 6:12; Ramathaim in 58:2 rather than Gilgal of 1 Samuel 15:12, 21, 33; and Bethel in 59:2 rather than Bethlehem of 1 Samuel 16:4.

Theological importance

God is light (12:9; cf. 22:3) and life (30:6). He knows what is to happen beforehand (18:4; 21:2; 28:4). He is frequently described with the epithet "the Most Powerful" (*Fortissimus*). He punishes sin and holds people responsible for transgressions but has mercy on Israel on account of those who have fallen asleep (35:3). God spoke about Israel even before it existed (9:4). The habitable places of the world were made for Israel (39:7). The holy land was not touched by the Flood (7:4). The heavenly bodies minister to Israel and intercede for it with God (32:9, 14). Israel can be defeated only if it sins (18:13). It cannot be destroyed so long as the world exists (9:3). In fact, if God destroyed Israel, there would be no one left to glorify him (12:9).

[8] L. H. Feldman, in his Prolegomenon to the reissue of M. R. James's *The Biblical Antiquities of Philo* (New York, 1971), pp. xxiii–xxiv.
[9] James, *The Biblical Antiquities of Philo*, pp. 46–58.

The Law is an eternal light (9:8), a light to the world but a punishment to the ungodly (11:1). By the Law, God will judge the whole world (11:2). It is an eternal commandment that will not pass away (11:5); it was prepared from the creation of the world (32:7). Idolatry and mixed marriage are the most reprehensible sins against the Law. Abraham would rather have died than take part in idolatrous rites (6). Idolatry is at the root of the sinful behavior of the tribes (25:9–13). Aod (34), Gideon (36:3), Jair (38), and Micah (44:1–5) lead the people astray by idolatry. It is the root of all evils (44:6f.). Pseudo-Philo is vigorously opposed to marriage with gentiles. Tamar had relations with her father-in-law rather than have relations with gentiles (9:5). Balaam plots to have the Midianite women lead Israel astray (18:13f.). The list of evils in 44:7 culminates in lusting after foreign women. The Levite's concubine was abused because she had had intercourse with the Amalekites (45:3). See also 9:1; 21:1; 30:1; and 43:5 for other criticisms of sexual relations with gentiles. While an individual's punishment for sin may be deferred for a while, it is finally exacted (6:11; 27:7, 15; 45:3; 49:5). The Deuteronomic concept of history (sin-punishment-salvation) is found in 3:9f.; 12:4; 13:10; and 19:2–5. At the basis of Pseudo-Philo's views on God and humanity is the biblical notion of covenant.

Angels appear frequently in Pseudo-Philo. The angels were jealous of Abraham (32:1f.). Jacob wrestled with the angel who was in charge of hymns (18:6). The angels lamented Moses' death (19:16). Two angels assisted Samuel when he was raised up by the witch of Endor (64:6). The angels are guardians (11:12; 59:4), but they will not intercede for people if they sin (15:5). Four angels are mentioned by name: Ingethel (27:10), Zeruel (27:10; Zervihel in 61:5), Nathaniel (38:3), and Fadahel (42:10). Evil spirits are assumed to exist (53:3f.; 60:1); they were created on the second day of creation (60:3). Certain angels who were condemned still assist men in the practice of sorcery (34:3). Holy spirits are mentioned in connection with Balaam's prophecy (18:3, 11). A holy spirit came upon Kenaz (28:6). Deborah speaks of the grace of the holy spirit (32:14).

The focus of Pseudo-Philo's eschatological interest is the future state, i.e. what happens after death and what happens during and after God's eschatological visitation. He does not cast his eschatology in political terms, nor does he show interest in the future Messiah. There are two ages: the present and the world to come (3:10; 16:3; 19:7, 13; 32:17; 62:9). After death, when the soul is separated from the body, all will be judged according to their deeds (44:10). There is no chance to repent after death, and the fathers of Israel cannot intercede for sinful Israel (33:2–5). The souls of the just will be at peace until the eschatological visitation (23:13; 28:10; 51:5), but the wicked undergo punishment for their sins (16:3; 23:6; 31:7; 36:4; 38:4; 44:10; 51:5; 63:4). When the appointed time is fulfilled, God will visit the world (3:9; 16:3; 19:12f., 15; 23:13; 26:12; 48:1). Then all will be raised up and judged according to their deeds (3:9f.; 19:12f.; 25:7). The just will dwell in happiness with God (19:12f.) and with their fathers (23:13), but the wicked like Korah and his band will be annihilated (16:3).

Relation to canonical books

A glance at the summary of contents placed at the beginning of the Introduction shows how important the books of the Bible from Genesis to 1 and 2 Samuel are for Pseudo-Philo. There are also occasional references to Isaiah, Jeremiah, and Psalms. Pseudo-Philo does not treat Scripture in the same way as the compilers of the later Jewish Midrashim do. Rather than making a clear distinction between the biblical text and its interpretation, Pseudo-Philo interweaves the two. As far as we can tell from the Latin text, he seems to have used a version of the Old Testament other than the Masoretic Text. For his combination of genealogies, short narratives, speeches and prayers, supplements to existing biblical narratives, and interest in numbers, Pseudo-Philo may have taken as his formal model the books of Chronicles.

There are some important verbal parallels with the New Testament:[10] "May your blood

[10] For more extensive lists, see James, *Biblical Antiquities*, pp. 59–60, and Feldman, Prolegomenon, pp. lvi–lviii. See also R. Bauckham, "The Liber Antiquitatum Biblicarum of Pseudo-Philo and the Gospels as 'Midrash,' " in *Gospel Perspectives. Volume III* (Sheffield, England, 1983) pp. 33–76.

be upon your own head" (6:11 and Mt 23:34f.; 27:25; cf. Acts 5:28; 18:6; 20:26); "on the third day" to mean "after three days" (11:2 and Mt 27:63; Mk 8:31; 9:31; 10:34; Lk 24:7; Acts 10:40; 1Cor 15:4); "he who restrains" (51:5 and 2Thes 2:6f.). There are also common traditions: "a well of water to follow them" (10:7; 11:15 and 1Cor 10:4); divorce initiated by the wife (42:1 and Mk 10:12). There are parallels between the stories of the births of Moses (9:9–16) and of Samson (42:1–10) and the infancy narratives in Matthew 1f. and Luke 1f. respectively.[11] Another important connection is to be found in Pseudo-Philo's treatment of the sacrifice of Isaac (Gen 22). According to 32:2–4 Isaac offered his life freely (cf. 40:2); his sacrifice is related to other sacrifices made to God for the sins of men (cf. 18:5); and his self-offering has a beneficent effect upon future generations. This complex of ideas[12] is similar to the Christian theology of Jesus' death, but it is not certain that the New Testament writers actually knew the theology connected with Abraham's sacrifice of Isaac.

Relation to apocryphal books

As an example of an imaginative retelling of the biblical story that joins the Old Testament text and legendary material, Pseudo-Philo stands closest in form to Jubilees, the Qumran Genesis Apocryphon, and Josephus' *Antiquities*. In matters of apocalyptic language it stands closest to 4 Ezra and 2 Baruch. Among the apocalyptic motifs common to the three works are these: the dead sleep in the earth (3:10; 19:12; 35:3; 53:5; 4Ezra 7:32; 2Bar 11:4), the souls of the righteous are in their chambers (32:13; 4Ezra 4:35; 2Bar 21:23; 42:7f.), Sheol restores its debt (3:10; 4Ezra 4:41–43; 2Bar 21:23), death is sealed up (3:10; 33:3; 4Ezra 8:53; 2Bar 21:23; 42:7f.), the nations are like spittle (7:3; 12:4; 4Ezra 6:56; 2Bar 82:5). Such parallels have led scholars in the past to speak of Pseudo-Philo as emanating from the same school or circle in which 4 Ezra and 2 Baruch were composed. Yet there exists a complex of ideas common to 4 Ezra and 2 Baruch that is absent from Pseudo-Philo: the four-empire scheme of history, the last wicked empire being overthrown by the Messiah, the formulation of messianic activity in forensic terms, and the concept of a temporary messianic kingdom.[13] In Pseudo-Philo there are no clear statements about the Messiah's role in the eschatological visitation, no dwelling on the fall of Jerusalem (unless it be in 19:7), and no mention of revenge on Rome or the ruling empire. The authors of 4 Ezra and 2 Baruch may have known Pseudo-Philo, but to speak of all three originating in the same circle or school stretches those vague terms too far.

Cultural importance

As a witness to the understanding of the Bible in the Palestinian synagogues prior to A.D. 70 and as a link to the material later gathered in the traditional midrashic compilations, Pseudo-Philo has great significance for the history of Judaism. As a Jewish writing composed about the time when most of the New Testament writings were taking shape, it is important also for the history of early Christianity. Yet Pseudo-Philo's impact on both Jewish and Christian history has been slight. The earliest Christian references to it come from the medieval writers Rhabanus Maurus, Rupert of Deutz, and Peter Comestor. Several proper names near the end of John Donne's *Metempsychosis* indicate that the English divine knew it. The only reference to it by a Jewish scholar before the nineteenth century comes from Azariah dei Rossi in the sixteenth century. Even after Cohn's 1898 article made the work known again, it was overlooked in the collections edited by R. H. Charles and E. Kautzsch and in the rabbinic commentary on the New Testament by P. Billerbeck. Louis Ginzberg, however, made ample use of it in his *Legends of the Jews*.[14]

[11] C. Perrot, "Les Récits d'enfance dans la Haggada antérieure au IIᵉ siècle de notre ère," *RSR* 55 (1967) 481–518.

[12] S. Spiegel, *The Last Trial* (New York, 1967); G. Vermes, *Scripture and Tradition in Judaism. Haggadic Studies* (SPB 4; Leiden, 1961), pp. 193–227; R. Le Déaut, *La Nuit Pascale* (AnBib; Rome, 1963), pp. 188–94. R. J. Daly, "The Soteriological Significance of the Sacrifice of Isaac," *CBQ* 39 (1977) 45–75; P. R. Davies and B. D. Chilton, "The Aqedah: A Revised Tradition History," *CBQ* 40 (1978) 514–46.

[13] M. E. Stone, "The Concept of the Messiah in IV Ezra," in *Religions in Antiquity: Essays in Memory of E. R. Goodenough* (Leiden, 1968), p. 302.

[14] Feldman, Prolegomenon, pp. ix–xv.

This translation

Pseudo-Philo has been translated into English by M. R. James (1917), German by P. Riessler (1928) and C. Dietzfelbinger (1975), Modern Hebrew by A. S. Hartom (1967), and French by J. Cazeaux with C. Perrot and P.-M. Bogaert (1976). The present English version of Pseudo-Philo is based on the edition of the Latin text prepared by the translator for Sources chrétiennes. Both there and here we have followed the combination of Fulda-Cassel Theol. 4°,3 and Phillipps 461 unless these manuscripts were obviously wrong. The present translation aims at a literal rendering of the Latin text. This decision has been made partly out of the feeling that a literal translation would best communicate the "biblical" flavor of the book. But even more persuasive has been the recognition that in many places the Latin text is corrupt and cannot be restored with certainty. The translation mirrors the awkwardness of the text in these places. Where a proper name has a recognizable biblical equivalent, we have written it according to its usual biblical form. Where the text agrees with a recognizable ancient biblical text (the MT, LXX, Samaritan Pentateuch, etc.), we have signaled these agreements by placing the relevant words in italics and noting the text in question in the margin. Where there is merely an allusion to the biblical text, we have noted this in the margin.

BIBLIOGRAPHY

Charlesworth, *PMR*, pp. 170–73.
Delling, *Bibliographie*, pp. 174f.
Denis, *Introduction*, p. 162.

Cohn, L. "An Apocryphal Work Ascribed to Philo of Alexandria," *JQR* 10 (1898) 277–332. (An extensive summary of the content and a survey of the major issues.)

Ginzberg, L. *The Legends of the Jews I–VII*. Philadelphia, 1909–46. (Ps-Philo is studied along with many other Jewish writings; references are cited in the index of vol. 7, 537–39.)

Harrington, D. J. "The Original Language of Pseudo-Philo's *Liber Antiquitatum Biblicarum*," *HTR* 63 (1970) 503–14. (Argues for a Heb. original translated into Gk. and then into Lat.)

————. "The Biblical Text of Pseudo-Philo's *Liber Antiquitatum Biblicarum*," *CBQ* 33 (1971) 1–17. (Detailed study of OT quotations and allusions in the text.)

————. *The Hebrew Fragments of Pseudo-Philo's* Liber Antiquitatum Biblicarum *Preserved in the* Chronicles of Jerahmeel. Texts and Translations 3, Pseudepigrapha Series 3; Cambridge, Mass., 1974. (Text and translation of the Heb. retroversions of Ps-Philo found in the *Chronicles of Jerahmeel*.)

————, Cazeaux, J., Perrot, C., and Bogaert, P.-M. *Pseudo-Philon, Les Antiquités Bibliques*. SC 229–30; Paris, 1976. (Introduction to the text, critical text, French translation, literary introduction, and commentary.)

James, M. R. *The Biblical Antiquities of Philo*. Translations of Early Documents 1: Palestinian Jewish Texts; London, 1917. (A lengthy introduction along with an ET based on the *editio princeps*. The volume was reprinted in 1971 by Ktav Publishing House of New York with a 169-page prolegomenon by Louis H. Feldman. Feldman's work is a very valuable compilation of information and a major contribution in its own right.)

Kisch, G. *Pseudo-Philo's Liber Antiquitatum Biblicarum*. Publications in Mediaeval Studies 10; Notre Dame, Ind., 1949. (A Lat. text based primarily on MS Admont 359.)

Perrot, C. "Les Récits d'enfance dans la Haggada antérieure au IIe siècle de notre ère," *RSR* 55 (1967) 481–518. (Connects the stories of the births of Moses, Samson, and Samuel in Ps-Philo with other Jewish accounts and the NT infancy narratives.)

Strugnell, J. "More Psalms of David," *CBQ* 27 (1965) 207–16. (Retroversion of 59:4 into Gk. and Heb. with detailed philological commentary.)

PSEUDO-PHILO

Genealogies from Adam to Noah

1 **1** In the beginning of the world[a] Adam became the father of three sons and one daughter: Cain, Noaba,[b] Abel, and Seth.
2 *And after he became the father of Seth, Adam lived 700[c] years; and he became*   Gen 5:4
3 *the father of* twelve *sons and* eight *daughters.* •And these are the names of the males: Eliseel, Suris, Elamiel, Brabal, Naat, Zarama, Zasam, Maathal, and Anath.[d]
4 And these are his daughters: Fua, Iectas, Arebica, Sifa, Tetia, Saba, Asin.[e]
5 *And Seth lived 105[f] years and became the father of Enosh. And after he became*   Gen 5:6f.
the father of Enosh, Seth lived 707[g] years and became the father of three *sons*
6 *and* two[h] *daughters.* •And these are the names of his sons: Elidia, Fonna, and Matha; and of his daughters: Malida and Thila.
7 *And Enosh lived 180[i] years and became the father of Kenan. And after he*   Gen 5:9f.
became the father of Kenan, Enosh lived 715[j] years and became the father of two
8 *sons and* a daughter. •And these are the names of his sons: Foe and Thaal; and of his daughter: Catennath.
9 *And Kenan lived 170[k] years and became the father of Mahalalel.[l] And after he*   Gen 5:12f.
became the father of Mahalalel, Kenan lived 730[m] years and became the father
10 *of* three *sons and* two *daughters.* •And these are the names of the males: Athac, Socer, Lofa; and the names of the daughters: Ana and Leva.
11 *And Mahalalel lived 165[n] years and fathered Jared. And after he fathered*   Gen 5:15f.
Jared, Mahalalel lived 730[o] years and became the father of seven *sons and* five
12 *daughters.* •And these are the names of the males: Leta, Mata, Cechar, Melie, Suriel, Lodo, Otim.[p] And these are the names of his daughters: Ada and Noa, Iebal, Mada, Sella.
13 *And Jared lived 162[q] years and became the father of Enoch. And after he*   Gen 5:18f.
became the father of Enoch, Jared lived 800 years and became the father of four
14 *sons and* two *daughters.* •And these are the names of the males: Lead, Anac, Soboac, and Ietar; and of the daughters: Tetzeco, Lesse.
15 *And Enoch lived 165[r] years and became the father of Methuselah. And after he*   Gen 5:21f.
became the father of Methuselah, Enoch lived 200[s] years and became the father
16 *of* five *sons and* three *daughters.* •Now Enoch pleased God in that time *and he*   Gen 5:24
17 *was not to be found, for God took him away.*[t] •Now the names of his sons: Anaz, Zeum, Achaun, Feledi, Elith; and of his daughters: Theiz, Lefith, Leath.
18 *And Methuselah lived 187[u] years and became the father of Lamech. And after*   Gen 5:25f.

---

1 a. Some MSS have "The beginning of the world" or omit the expression altogether.

b. According to Jub 4:1 her name is Awan, but in a Syriac patristic text she is called Leboda or Lobda.

c. The LXX of Gen 5:4 has 700, while the MT has 800. The chronological scheme underlying the whole ch. is closest to that of the LXX.

d. Only nine of Adam's twelve sons are named. Jub 4:10 says that Adam had nine sons.

e. Only seven of the eight daughters are named.

f. The MT of Gen 5:6 has 105, while the LXX has 205.

g. The LXX of Gen 5:7 has 707, the MT 807.

h. Most MSS read "three." Either we should read "two" with other MSS, or we must assume that the name of one daughter has been omitted.

i. The LXX of Gen 5:9 has 190, the MT 90.

j. The LXX of Gen 5:10 has 715, the MT 815.

k. All MSS have 520, while the LXX of Gen 5:12 has 170 and the MT 70. We have emended DXX (520) to CLXX (170).

l. Here and in 1:11 the MSS have Malalech, but see Gen 5:12–17. This and other recognizable biblical names have been spelled according to their usual English forms.

m. The LXX of Gen 5:13 has 740, the MT 840.

n. The LXX of Gen 5:15 has 165, the MT 65.

o. The LXX of Gen 5:16 has 730, the MT 830.

p. Lodo and Otim appear as one name (Lodo-otim) in the MSS.

q. We have emended 172 (CLXXII) to 162 (CLXII) in the light of the LXX and MT of Gen 5:18.

r. The LXX of Gen 5:21 has 165, the MT 65.

s. The LXX of Gen 5:22 has 200, the MT 300.

t. That is, to heaven.

u. The LXX of Gen 5:25 has 187, the MT 87.

he became the father of Lamech, Methuselah lived 782 years and became the
19 *father of two sons and two daughters.* •And these are the names of the males:
Inab and Rafo; and of the daughters: Aluma and Amuga.
20   *And Lamech lived 182ᵛ years and became the father of a son and called him*   Gen 5:28f.
after his birth "Noah," saying, "This one will give restʷ to us and to the earth
from those who dwell on it—on account of the wickedness of whose evil *deeds*
21 the earth will be visited." •*And after he fathered Noah, Lamech lived 585ˣ years.*   Gen 5:30
22 *And Noah lived 300ʸ years and became the father of three sons: Shem, Ham,*   Gen 5:32
Japheth.ᶻ

Genealogies from Cain to Lamech

1 **2** *Now Cain dwelt in the land trembling,ᵃ* as God had appointed for him after he   Gen 4:16
2 had killed Abel his brother. And the name of his wife was Themech.ᵇ •*And Cain*   (4:12,14)
3 *knew* Themech *his wife, and she conceived and bore Enoch.* •Now Cain was   Gen 4:17
fifteen years old when he did these things, and from that time he began to *build*   Gen 4:17
cities until he had founded seven cities. And these are the names of the cities: the
name of the first city, *corresponding to the name of his son, Enoch*; and the name
of the second city Mauli, and of the third Leed, and the name of the fourth Teze,
and the name of the fifth Iesca, and the name of the sixth Celeth, and the name
4 of the seventh Iebbat. •And after he became the father of Enoch, Cain lived 715
years and became the father of three sons and two daughters. And these are the
names of his sons: Olad, Lizaf, Fosal; and of his daughters: Citha and Maac. And
all the days of Cain were 730 years, and he died.
5   Then Enoch took a wife from the daughters of Seth, and she bore him Ciramᶜ
and Cuut and Madab. *Now Ciram became the father of Methushael,ᵈ and Methushael*   Gen 4:18
6 *became the father of Lamech.* •*Now Lamech took for himself two wives. The name*   Gen 4:19
7 *of the one was Adah, and the name of the other Zillah.* •*And Adah bore* Jobab;   Gen 4:20f.
he was the father of all those dwelling in tents and feeding cattle. And again, she
8 bore him *Jobal, who was the first to teach all kinds of musical instruments.* •In   Gen 4:21
that time, when those inhabiting the earth began to do evil deeds (each one with
his neighbor's wife) and they defiled them, God was angry. And heᵉ began to
play the lyre and the lute and every instrument of sweet song and to corrupt the
9 earth. •*Now Zillah bore Tubalᶠ* and Miza and Theffa. And this is the Tubal who   Gen 4:22
showed men techniques in using lead and tin and *iron and bronze* and silver and
gold. And then those inhabiting the earth began to make statues and to adore
10 them. •*Now Lamech said to* both *his wives, Adah and Zillah, "Hear my voice,*   Gen 4:23f.
wives of Lamech, and pay attention to my remark, for I have destroyed men on
my own account and snatched sucklings from the breasts, in order to show my
sons and those inhabiting the earth how to do evil deeds. *And now Cain will be*
avenged seven times, but Lamech seventy-seven times."

---

v. The MT of Gen 5:28 has 182, the LXX 188.
w. This interpretation of the name Noah traces
the name back to the Heb. root *nwḥ*, "rest," but
the MT of Gen 5:29 relies on *nḥm*, "console."
The LXX is similar to Ps-Philo here.
x. The MT of Gen 5:30 has 595, the LXX 565.
y. Both the MT and the LXX of Gen 5:30 have
500.
z. With the phrase "three sons" and the omission of "and" between the proper names Ps-Philo
stands in agreement with the LXX of Gen 5:32.

2 a. The word "trembling" is due to the ambiguity
of the Heb. *nwd* in "the land of Nod" in Gen

4:16. See also Gen 4:12, 14.
b. According to Jub 4:8 the name of Cain's wife
was Awan, who according to Jub 4:1 was also his
sister. The name Themech is also given to the
mother of Sisera in Ps-Philo 31:8.
c. According to Gen 4:18 the name should be
Irad.
d. The generation of Mehujael (see Gen 4:18)
has been omitted.
e. That is, Jobal. A connection is being drawn
between musical instruments and immoral
behavior.
f. The MT of Gen 4:22 has Tubalcain. Ps-Philo
here agrees with the LXX and the Vetus Latina.

The Flood

1 **3** *And it happened that, when men began to multiply upon the earth,* beautiful   Gen 6:1f.
daughters were born to them. And the sons[a] of God saw that the daughters of
2 *men were very fair and took for themselves wives from all whom they chose.* •*And*
God said, "My spirit shall not judge[b] those men[c] forever, because they are flesh,   Gen 6:3
but their years shall be 120." For them he set the limits of life, but the crimes
3 done by their hands did not cease. •*And God saw that among all those inhabiting*   Gen 6:5,7
the earth wicked deeds had reached full measure; and because they were plotting
evil all their days, he said, "I will blot out man and all the things that grow on
earth, *for I am sorry that I have made him."*

4   Yet *Noah found favor* and mercy *before the Lord, and these are his generations.*   Gen 6:8f.
Noah, who was a righteous man and *blameless in his generation,* pleased the
Lord. To him *God said, "The time set for all* men *dwelling upon the earth* has   Gen 6:13–15
arrived, for their deeds are wicked. And now *make for yourself an ark from* cedar[d]
wood. And this is how you will make it: Its length will be 300 cubits, and its
width 50 cubits, and its height 30 cubits. And you will enter the ark, you and   Gen 6:18
your wife and your sons and the wives of your sons with you. And I will establish
my covenant with you, to destroy all those inhabiting the earth. *Now of the clean*   Gen 7:2–4
animals and of the clean *birds of the heaven you will take seven males and seven*
females so that their seed *can live upon the earth. But of the unclean animals and*   Gen 6:19–21
birds you will take for yourself two males and two females. Also, you will take
5 *food for yourself and for them."* •*And Noah did what God commanded him. And*   Gen 7:5,7
he entered the ark, he and all his sons with him. And *it happened after seven*   Gen 7:10–12
days that the water of the flood began *to fall upon the earth. And on that day*
were opened all the deeps and the great spring[e] and the floodgates of the heaven;
6 *and there was rain upon the earth forty days and forty nights.* •Now it was then
the sixteen hundred and fifty-second[f] year from the time when God made heaven
and earth, in which the earth along with those inhabiting it was destroyed on
7 account of the wickedness of their deeds. •*And the deluge continued on the earth*   Gen 7:23–8:1
for one hundred and fifty days. Only Noah and those who were with him in the
ark survived. And when God remembered Noah, he made the water subside.

8   And it happened on the ninetieth[g] *day that God dried up the earth and said to*   Gen 8:14–21
Noah, "Go forth from the ark, you and all *who are with you, and increase and*
multiply upon the earth." And Noah went forth from the ark, he[h] and his sons
and the wives of his sons, and brought out *all the beasts and reptiles and birds*
and cattle with him, *as God commanded him. Then Noah built an altar to the*
Lord, and took some of the clean cattle and clean birds, and offered burnt offerings
upon the altar; and it was accepted by *the Lord* like *a restful[i] scent.*

9   *And God said, "I will never again curse the earth on man's account, for the*   Gen 8:21
tendency of man's heart is foolish[j] from his youth; and so I will never destroy all
living creatures at one time as I have done. But when those inhabiting the earth
sin, I will judge them by famine or by the sword or by fire or by death; and there

3 a. Most LXX MSS as well as Philo and Josephus
have "angels" rather than "sons" in Gen 6:2.
   b. The LXX of Gen 6:3 has "remain." Ps-Philo
is reading the Heb. *ydwn* as in the MT and
understanding it to mean "judge."
   c. Lit. "all" (*omnibus*), which we have emended
to "men" (*hominibus*) in the light of Gen 6:3.
   d. This interpretation of the Heb. *goper* as cedar
in Gen 6:14 is also found in the Palestinian Targums
and GenR.
   e. Perhaps we should emend *omnes abyssi et
fons magnus* to *omnes fontes abyssi magni*, "all
the springs of the great abyss," on the basis of
Gen 7:11.
   f. The figure is close to what can be deduced

from the MT's chronology, 1,656 years. This total,
however, cannot be reconciled with the chronology
of Ps-Philo 1, and the section may well be a scribal
gloss.
   g. Apparently Ps-Philo understood Gen 8:14 as
meaning after two months and twenty-seven days.
   h. The wife of Noah is not mentioned; see Gen
8:18.
   i. The LXX translator with his *osmēn euōdias*
has taken the Heb. *hnyhh* of Gen 8:21 to mean
"tranquilizing" or "soothing" because of its good
odor. Ps-Philo has taken it in the sense of "restful."
   j. We are reading *desipit*, "is foolish," rather
than *desiit*, "has left off," of all the MSS; see
Gen 8:21.

will be earthquakes, and they will be scattered to uninhabited places. But no more
will I destroy the earth by the water of the flood. And *in all the days of the earth,*   Gen 8:22
seedtime and harvest, cold and heat, spring and fall will not cease day and night
until I remember those who inhabit the earth, until the appointed times are fulfilled.

10   "But when the years appointed for the world have been fulfilled, then the light
will cease and the darkness will fade away. And I will bring the dead to life and
raise up those who are sleeping[k] from the earth. And hell will pay back its debt,
and the place of perdition will return its deposit[l] so that I may render to each
according to his works and according to the fruits of his own devices, until I
judge between soul and flesh.[m] And the world will cease, and death will be
abolished, and hell will shut its mouth. And the earth will not be without progeny
or sterile for those inhabiting it; and no one who has been pardoned by me will
be tainted. And there will be another earth and another heaven, an everlasting
dwelling place."

11   *And the Lord spoke again to Noah and to his sons, saying, "Behold I will*   Gen 9:8f.
establish my covenant with you and with your seed after you, and no more *will I*   Gen 9:11
destroy the earth by the water of a flood. And everything that moves *and lives*   Gen 9:3f.
will be food for you. But meat with its lifeblood you may not eat. For whoever   Gen 9:6f.
will shed the blood of a man, his own blood will be shed, because man was made
after the image of God. But you, *increase and multiply and fill the earth,* like a   Gen 9:1
12 school of fish multiplying in the waves." •*And God said, "This is the covenant*[n]   Gen 9:12
that I have established between me and you. And it will happen that when I cover   Gen 9:14
the heaven with clouds, my[o] *bow will appear in the cloud; and* it will be a
memorial *of the covenant between me and you and all those* inhabiting *the earth."*   Gen 9:16

Genealogies of the sons of Noah

1 **4** *And the sons of Noah who went forth from the ark were Shem, Ham, and*   Gen 9:18
Japheth.

2   *The sons of Japheth: Gomer,*[a] *Magog and Madai, Javan,*[b] *Tubal, Meshech,*   Gen 10:2–4
Tiras,[c] *Ashkenaz,*[d] *Riphath and Togarmah, Elishah, Tarshish,*[e] *Kittim,*[f] *Dodanim.*[g]
And the sons of Gomer: Thelez, Lud, Deberleth. And the sons of Magog: Cesse
and Thifa, Faruta, Ammiel, Fimei, Goloza, Samanac. And the sons of Javan[h]:
Sallus, Felucta, Fallita. And the sons of Tubal: Fanata, Nova, and Eva. And the
sons of Meshech[i]: Amboradat, Urac, Bosara. And the sons of Tiras: Maac, Tabel,
Ballana, Samplameac, Elaz. And the sons of Ashkenaz[j]: Jubal, Zaraddana, Anac.
And the sons of Riphath[k]: Doad, Defad, Zead, Enoc. And the sons of Togarmah:
Abiuth, Safath, Asapli, Zepthir. And the sons of Elishah: Zaac, Zenez, Mastisa,
Rira. And the sons of Tarshish[l]: Meccul, Loon, Zelatabac. And the sons of
Kittim[m]: Macziel, Temna, Aela, Finon. And the sons of Dodanim: Itheb, Beath,

---

k. For the dead sleeping in the earth see 19:12;
35:3; 53:5; 4Ezra 7:32; 2Bar 11:4; 21:24.

l. For the idea of restoring the deposit see 33:3
as well as 2Bar 21:23; 1En 51:1; and 4Ezra 4:41–
43; 7:32.

m. The phrase "between soul and flesh" may
simply refer to the higher and lower aspects of the
whole person.

n. Gen 9:12 has "this is the sign of the covenant." The Heb. for "sign" (*'wt*) was probably
omitted due to its proximity to "this" (*z't* or even
z'wt).

o. For "my" in Gen 9:14 see the LXX, Vetus
Latina, and Vulgate.

4 a. Gomer is not in the MSS of Ps-Philo, but see
Gen 10:2 and Ps-Philo 4:2, 4. The proper names
in this ch. and the following one are usually given
as they appear in the MS tradition, but where an

obviously biblical name can be recognized we have
placed that name in the text and given the MSS
reading at the bottom of the page.

b. MSS Nidiazec.

c. MSS combine Meshech and Tiras into Moc-
teras.

d. MSS Cenez.

e. MSS Dessin.

f. MSS Cethin.

g. MSS Tudant.

h. MSS Tudan. The sons of Madai have been
omitted.

i. MSS Mellech. The MSS place the sons of
Tiras before the sons of Meshech.

j. MSS Cenez.

k. MSS Heri, Fuddet.

l. MSS Tessis. The MSS place the sons of
Kittim before the sons of Tarshish.

m. MSS Zepti.

3 Feneth. •And these were the ones who were *scattered abroad* and dwelt *on the* Gen 10:5
earth among the Persians and Medes and[n] *in the islands* that are in the sea. And
Feneth[o] the son of Dodanim[p] went up and ordered that seafaring ships be built.
4 And then a third part of the earth[q] was divided up. •Gomer[r] and his sons received
Ladech. Magog and his sons received Degal. Madai and his sons received Besto.
Javan and his sons received Ceel. Tubal and his sons received Feed. Meshech
and his sons received Nepthi. Tiras[s] and his sons received Duodenin. Ashkenaz[t]
and his sons received Goda. Riphath and his sons received Bosorra. Togarmah
and his sons received Futh. Elishah and his sons received Thabola. Tarshish[u] and
his sons received Marecham. Kittim[v] and his sons received Thaan. Dodanim and
5 his sons received Caruba. •And then they began to work the land and to sow upon
it. And when the land was dry, its inhabitants cried out to the LORD; and he heard
them and gave rain in abundance. And it happened that, when the rain descended
upon the earth, the bow appeared in the cloud. And those inhabiting the earth saw
this memorial of the covenant and fell upon their faces and made sacrifices and
offered burnt offerings to the LORD.

6 *Now the sons of Ham: Cush and Egypt[w] and Put[x] and Canaan. And these are* Gen 10:6f.
the sons of Cush: Seba and Havilah, Sabtah, Raamah and Sabteca. And the sons
of Raamah: Sheba[y] and Dedan.[z] And the sons of Put[a2]: Zeleu, Telup, Geluc,
Lefuc. And the sons of Canaan: Sidon, Aendain, Racin, Simmin, Uruin, Nemigin, Gen 10:15–18
7 Amathin,[b2] Nefin, Telaz, Elat, Cusin. •*Now Cush became the father of Nimrod.* Gen 10:8f.
He began to be arrogant before the Lord. Now Egypt became the father of Ludim Gen 10:13f.
and Anamim[c2] and Lehabim and Latuin[d2] and Pathrusim and Casluhim (whence
8 *came the Philistines) and the Cappadocians.* •And then they also began to build
cities. And these are the cities that they built: Sidon and its surroundings, that is,
Resun, Beosomaza, Gerar, Ashkelon,[e2] Dabircamo, Tellun, Lachish, *Sodom and* Gen 10:19
Gomorrah, Admah and Zeboim.
9 And *the sons of Shem: Elam, Asshur, Arpachshad, Lud, and Aram. And the* Gen 10:22–25
sons of Aram: Uz, Hul,[f2] Gether, and Mash. Now Arpachshad became the father
of Shelah; Shelah became the father of Eber. And to Eber were born two sons;
the name of one was Peleg,[g2] for in his days the earth was divided, and the name
10 *of his brother was Joktan.[h2]* •*Joktan became the father of Almodad and Sheleph,* Gen 10:26–29
Hazarmaveth, Jerah, Hadoram, Uzal, Diklah, Obal, Abimael, Sheba, Ophir,
Havilah, and Jobab.[i2] And the sons of Peleg[j2]: Reu,[k2] Refuth, Zefaram, Aculon, Gen 11:17–20
Sachar, Sifaz, Nabi, Suri, Seciur, Falacus, Rafo, Faltia, Zaldefal, Zavis and
Arteman, Helifaz. These are the sons of Peleg, and these are their names. And
they took wives for themselves from the daughters of Joktan and became fathers
11 of sons and daughters and filled the earth. •Now Reu took as his wife Melcha[l2]
the daughter of Ruth, and she bore to him Serug. And when the day of his delivery
came, she said, "From him there will be born in the fourth generation one who

---

n. The word "and" is not in the MSS.

o. MSS Fenath; see 5:1.

p. MSS Dudeni.

q. Apparently a third part of the earth destroyed by the Flood is now being resettled. See Rev 8:7–12; 9:15, 18.

r. MSS Domereth.

s. MSS Iras.

t. MSS Iesca. The MSS place Duodenin and Ashkenaz in the wrong positions; we have reversed them.

u. MSS Tessis.

v. MSS Cethim.

w. MSS Mestra.

x. MSS Funi.

y. MSS omit "and Havilah . . . Sheba," but see Gen 10:7.

z. MSS Tudan.

a2. MSS Funi.

b2. Gen 10:15–18 may be of some help in restoring the text here: Racin—the Arkites; Simmin—the Sinites; Uruin—the Arvadites; Nemigin—Zemarites; Amathin—Hamathites.

c2. MSS Niemigin.

d2. According to Gen 10:13 this should be Naphtuhim.

e2. For Gerar, Ashkelon, the MSS have Gerras, Calon.

f2. For Uz, Hul, the MSS have Assum or Asum.

g2. MSS Falech.

h2. MSS Iepta.

i2. We have restored the text in the light of Gen 10:26–29. MSS have "Elimodan et Salastra et Mazaam, Rea, Dura, Uzia, Deglabal, Mimoel, Sabthfin, Evilach, Iubab."

j2. MSS Falech.

k2. MSS Ragau.

l2. According to Jub 11:7 her name is Ora.

will set his dwelling on high[m2] and will be called perfect and blameless; and he
will be the father of nations, and his covenant will not be broken, and his seed

12 will be multiplied forever." •*And after he became the father of Serug, Reu lived*   Gen 11:21
119[n2] years and became the father of seven sons and five daughters. And these
are the names of his sons: Abiel, Obthi, Salma, Dedasal, Zeneza, Accur, Nefes.
And these are the names of his daughters: Cedema, Derisa, Seifa, Ferita, Theila.

13 *And Serug lived 29[o2] years and became the father of Nahor. And after he became*   Gen 11:22f
the father of Nahor, Serug lived 67[p2] years and became the father of four sons
and three daughters. And these are the names of the sons: Zela, Zoba, Dica, and

14 Fodde. And these are his daughters: Tefila, Oda, Selifa. •*And Nahor lived 34[q2]*   Gen 11:24f
years and became the father of Terah. And after he became the father of Terah,
Nahor lived 200[r2] years and became the father of eight sons and five daughters.
And these are the names of the males: Recap, Dediap, Berechap, Iosac, Sithal,

15 Nisab, Nadab, Camoel; and his daughters: Esca, Thifa, Bruna, Cene, Etha. •*And*   Gen 11:26f
Terah lived 70 years and became the father of Abram and Nahor and Haran.
Now Haran became the father of Lot.

16   Then those who inhabited the earth began to observe the stars[s2] and started to
reckon by them and to make predictions and to have their sons and daughters pass

17 through the fire. But Serug and his sons did not act as these did.[t2] •*And these are*   Gen 10:31f,5
the generations of Noah according to their tribes and languages, from which the
nations were portioned out on the earth after the Flood.

The census of Noah's descendants

1 **5** Then the sons of Ham came and made Nimrod their leader; and the sons of
Japheth appointed Fenech their chief; and the sons of Shem came together and

2 made Joktan their leader. •And when these three came together, they decided to
have the people related[a] to them pass in review and to number them. And while
Noah was still alive, all gathered together in one place and lived in accord, and

3 the earth was at peace. •Now in the three hundred and fortieth year after Noah's
exit from the ark, after God dried up the flood, the leaders numbered their people.

4   And Fenech had the sons of Japheth pass in review. The sons of Gomer, all   Gen 10:2-4
passing by under their captains' staffs,[b] were 5,800 in number. Now of the sons
of Magog, of all passing under their captains' staffs, the number was 6,200. Now
the sons of Madai, all passing by under their captains' staffs, were 5,700 in
number.[c] Now the sons of Tubal, all passing by under their captains' staffs, were
9,400 in number. And the sons of Meshech,[d] all passing by under their captains'
staffs, were 5,600 in number. But the sons of Tiras, all passing by under their
captains' staffs, were 12,300 in number.[e] And the sons of Riphath,[f] those passing
by under their captains' staffs, were 11,500 in number. But the sons of Togarmah,
passing by under their captains' staffs, were 14,400 in number. Now the sons of
Elishah, passing by under their captains' staffs, were 14,900 in number. Now the
sons of Tarshish, all passing by under their captains' staffs, were 12,100 in
number. Now the sons of Kittim, all passing by under their captains' staffs, were

---

m2. That is, in heaven or perhaps even on
Mount Moriah.

n2. The MT and LXX of Gen 11:21 have 207.

o2. The MT of Gen 11:22 has 30, the LXX
130.

p2. The MT and LXX of Gen 11:23 have 200.

q2. The MT of Gen 11:24 has 29, the LXX 79.

r2. The MT of Gen 11:25 has 119, the LXX
129.

s2. There may be some connection between
ending the genealogy with Terah, who lived in Ur
(a place noted for astrology), and these remarks
about the beginning of astrology.

t2. According to Jub 11, Serug and his family
did worship idols.

5 a. Lit. those drawing near. Since the leaders are
numbering their own families, the Heb. underlying
the expression is probably *qrwbym*, "relatives."

b. Lit. here and throughout the ch., "according
to the scepters of their captaincies." The expression
may come from Lev 27:32 ("all that pass under
the herdsman's staff"). Again as in ch. 4 we have
given the proper names according to their recognizable biblical forms.

c. The sons of Javan have been omitted.

d. MSS Mesca.

e. The sons of Ashkenaz have been omitted.

f. MSS Rifa.

17,300 in number. But the sons of Dodanim,ᵍ passing by under their captains' staffs, were 17,700 in number. And the total of the camps of the sons of Japheth, all men of might and all equipped with arms for battle before their leaders, was 142,200, apart from women and children. In the review of Japheth the total number was 142,000.ʰ

5 And Nimrod, himself a son of Ham, had all the sons of Ham pass in review. Gen 10:6f. The sons of Egypt, all passing by under their captains' staffs, were found to be 24,800 in number. The sons of Put,ⁱ all passing by under their captains' staffs, were 27,700 in number. And the sons of Canaan, all passing by under their captains' staffs, were found to be 32,800 in number. But the sons of Seba,ʲ all passing by under their captains' staffs, were found to be 4,300 in number. And the sons of Havilah,ᵏ all passing by under their captains' staffs, were found to be 24,300 in number. But the sons of Sabtah,ˡ all passing by under their captains' staffs, were found to be 25,300 in number. And the sons of Raamah, all passing by under their captains' staffs, were found to be 30,600 in number. But the sons of Sabteca,ᵐ all passing by under their captains' staffs, were found to be 46,400 in number. And the total of the camps of the sons of Ham, all men of might and equipped with battle gear before their leaders, were 244,900, apart from women and children.

6 And Joktan the son of Shem had the sons of Shem pass in review. And the Gen 10:22 sons of Elam, all passing by under their captains' staffs, were 37,000 in number. Now the sons of Asshur, all passing by under their captains' staffs, were found to be 78,000 in number. And the sons of Aram,ⁿ all passing by under their captains' staffs, were found to be 87,400 in number. But the sons of Lud, all passing by under their captains' staffs, were found to be 30,600 in number.ᵒ Now the sons of Arpachshad, all passing by under their captains' staffs, were 114,600 7 in number. The total number of all of them was 347,600. •This was the total of the camps of the sons of Shem. All were distinguished in courage and military 8 discipline before their captains, . . .ᵖ besides women and children. •And these are the generations of Noah taken separately, whose total number altogether was 914,100. And all these were examined while Noah was still alive. *And Noah lived* Gen 9:28f. *350 years after the flood. And all the days of Noah were 950 years, and he died.*

The tower of Babel and Abraham in the furnace

1 **6** Then all those who had been separated and were inhabiting the earth gathered Gen 11:2-4 and dwelt together. *And migrating from the east, they found a plain in the land of Babylon; and settling there, each one said to his neighbor,* "Behold it will happen that we will be scattered every man from his brother and in the last days we will be fighting one another. Now *come, let us build for ourselves a tower whose top will reach the heavens, and we will make a name for ourselves* and a 2 glory *upon the earth.*" •*And they said, each to his neighbor,* "Let us take bricksᵃ Gen 11:3 and let each of us write our names on the bricks and *burn them with fire*; and whatever will be burned through and through will be used for mortar and brick."ᵇ

3 And they took their bricks, all of them except twelve men who would not take them. And these are their names: Abram, Nahor, Lot, Ruge, Tenute, Zaba, 4 Armodat, Jobab, Esar, Abimahel, Saba, Aufin.ᶜ •And the people of that land laid

---

g. MSS Doin.
h. The sentence is probably a scribal gloss.
i. MSS Fua.
j. MSS Soba. The number here is disproportionately small.
k. MSS Lebilla.
l. MSS Sata.
m. MSS Sabaca.
n. The sons of Aram and the sons of Arpachshad are in reverse order in the MSS, but see Gen 10:22.
o. In the MSS there is an intrusion: "the number

of the sons of Ham was . . ."
p. The total is lacking in the MSS.

6 a. Lit. "stones"; but the context demands the translation "bricks."
b. For building the tower.
c. Abimahel, Saba, and Aufin can be traced to Gen 10:28f. Ruge may be Reu of Gen 11:18-21. Armodat may be Almodad of Gen 10:26. Jobab is found in Gen 10:29.

hold of them and brought them to their chiefs and said, "These are the men who have gone against our plans and would not walk in our ways." And the leaders said to them, "Why were each of you not willing to cast in bricks along with the people of the land?" And those men answered saying, "We are not casting in bricks, nor are we joining in your scheme. We know the one LORD, and him we worship. Even if you throw us into the fire with your bricks, we will not join

5 you." •And the leaders were angered and said, "As they have spoken, so do to them. And unless they take part with us in throwing in the bricks, you will have the fire devour them along with your bricks."[d]

6   And Joktan,[e] who was chief of the leaders, answered, "No, but let them be given a period of seven days, and if they repent of their evil plans and are willing to cast in bricks with you, they may live. If not, let it be done and let them be burned then in accord with your judgment." He, however, sought how he might save them from the hands of the people, because he was of their tribe and served

7 God. •When this was said, he took them and locked them in the royal household. And when it was evening, the leader commanded that fifty men of might be summoned to him, and he said to them, "Go forth and tonight take those men who are locked in my house, and put supplies for them from my household on ten beasts of burden. And bring those men to me, and bring their supplies along with the beasts of burden to the mountains and take care of them there. And know

8 that, if anyone learns what I have said to you, I will burn you in the fire." •And the men went forth and did everything that their chief commanded them. And they brought the men to his house[f] by night, and they took their supplies and put them on the beasts of burden and led them into the mountains as he had commanded

9 them. •And the chief summoned to himself those twelve men and said to them, "Be confident and do not fear, for you will not die. For the God in whom you trust is powerful, and therefore be steadfast in him because he will free you and save you. And behold now I have commanded the fifty men who have brought[g] you out here; supplies have already been taken from my household. And they have gone forth[h] into the mountains and are waiting[i] for you in the valley, and I will give you another fifty men who will escort you there. And go, hide yourselves there in the valley; you will have drinking water that flows from the rocks. And stay there for thirty days, until the hatred of the people of this land subsides and until God sends his wrath upon them and destroys them. For I know that the evil plan that they have agreed to carry out will not stand, because their plot is foolish. And when seven days have passed and they seek you out, I will say to them, 'The door of the jail in which they were locked up was broken down. They went out and escaped by night. And I have sent a hundred men to search after them.'

10 And I will distract them from the anger that is upon them." •And eleven of the men answered him and said, "Your servants have found favor in your eyes,

11 because we are rescued from the hands of these arrogant men." •But Abram alone was silent. And the leader said to him, "Why do you not answer me, Abram servant of God?" Abram answered and said, "Behold, today I flee to the mountains. And if I escape the fire, wild beasts will come out of the mountains and devour us; or we will lack food and die of famine; and we will be found fleeing from the people of this land but falling in our sins. And now as he in whom I trust lives, I will not be moved from my place where they have put me. If there be any sin of mine so flagrant that I should be burned up, let the will of God be done." And the leader said to him, "May your blood be upon your own

---

d. The connection of Abraham's escape from Ur (in Heb., *'ūr* means "fire") and the building of the tower of Babel is unique to Ps-Philo. The tradition of Abraham in the fiery furnace is similar to those of Dan 3 and 2Mac 7.

e. The MSS call him Iectan, but presumably he is to be connected with the sons of Shem in 5:1, 6.

f. Var. "from his house"; but the context seems to require "to his house." See 6:7.

g. The MSS put the verb in the future.

h–i. In the MSS the two verbs are imperatives, but the story demands that they be perfect and imperfect respectively. Heb. * yṣ'w/whkw* was probably misread as *wṣ'w/whkw.*

head[j] if you are not willing to go forth with these men. Now if you are willing to do so, you will be freed; but if you wish to stay, stay as you wish." And Abram

12 said, "I will not go forth, but I will stay here." • And the leader took those eleven men and sent another fifty with them and commanded them, saying, "You also, wait in the mountains for fifteen days with those fifty who were sent on ahead; and afterward come back and say, 'We have not found them,' as I told the former group. And know that if anyone disregards any of these words that I have spoken to you, he will be burned in the fire." And the men went forth. And he took

13 Abram by himself and locked him up again where he had been confined. • And after seven days had passed, the people gathered together and said to their leader, "Give us back the men who were unwilling to join in our plan, and we will burn them in the fire." And they sent the leaders to bring them out, and they found no one but Abram. And they gathered together with their leaders and said, "The men whom you locked up have fled; they have evaded our scheme." • And Fenech

14 and Nimrod[k] said to Joktan, "Where are the men whom you locked up?" But that man said, "They have broken out by night. But I have sent a hundred men to search for them and commanded them that, if they find them, not only should they burn them in the fire but also give their corpses to the birds of the heavens, and so let them destroy them."

15 And then those men said, "This fellow who alone has been found, we will burn him." And they took Abram and brought him to their leaders. And they said to him, "Where are those who were with you?" And he said, "I was sleeping

16 during the night; when I awoke, I did not find them." • And they took him and   Dan 3 built a furnace and lit it. And they threw bricks burned with fire into the furnace. And then the leader Joktan with great emotion[l] took Abram and threw him along

17 with the bricks into the fiery furnace. • But God caused a great earthquake, and the fire gushing out of the furnace leaped forth in flames and sparks of flame. And it burned all those standing around in sight of the furnace. And all those who were burned in that day were 83,500. But there was not the least injury to Abram

18 from the burning of the fire. • And Abram came up out of the furnace, and the fiery furnace collapsed. And Abram was saved and went away to the eleven men who were hidden in the mountains, and he reported to them everything that had happened to him. And they came down with him from the mountains, rejoicing in the name of the Lord. And no one who met them frightened them that day. And they named that place by the name of Abram and in the language of the Chaldeans "Deli,"[m] which means "God."

The dispersion of the people and the choice of Canaan

1 **7** And it happened after these events that the people of the land were not turned from their malicious plottings, and they came together again to their leaders *and*   Gen 11:4 *said*, "The people will not be defeated forever. And now *we will come together and build ourselves a city and a tower* that will never be taken away."

2 And when they had begun to build, God *saw the city and the tower that the*   Gen 11:5f. *sons of men were building, and he said, "Behold they are one people and have one language for all; but what they have begun to make*, neither the earth will put up with it nor will the heavens bear to behold it. And if *they are not stopped*

3 now, *they will be daring in all the things they propose to do.* • *And* behold now I   Gen 11:7 will divide up *their languages* and scatter them in all regions so that a man will not understand his own brother and *no one will hear the language of his neighbor.* And I will banish them to the cliffs, and they will build for themselves huts with stalks of straw and will dig caves for themselves and live there like the beasts of

---

j. See Mt 23:35–36; 27:25; Acts 5:28; 18:6; 20:26.

k. For Nimrod as the planner of the tower of Babel see Josephus' *Ant* 1.4.2 §§113f.

l. Lit. "dissolved with feeling."

m. Perhaps read Beli as in *PrEv* 9.18.2. According to Josephus' *Ant* 1.7.2 §160, a village in the region of Damascus was called "Abram's abode."

the field. And thus they will remain before me all the time so that they will never make such plots again, and I will consider them like a drop of water and liken them to spittle.ª And to some the end will come by water, but others will be dried 4 up with thirst. •And before all these I will choose my servantᵇ Abram, and I will bring him out from their land and will bring him into the land upon which my eye has looked from of old, when all those inhabiting the earth sinned in my sight and I brought the water of the flood and I did not destroy it but preserved that land. For neither did the springs of my wrath burst forth in it, nor did my water of destruction descend on it.ᶜ For there I will have my servant Abram dwell and will establish my covenant with him and will bless his seed and be lord for him as God forever."

Isa 40:15

5   Now when the people inhabiting the land had begun to construct the tower, God divided up their languages and changed their appearances, and a man did not recognize his own brother *and no one heard the language of his neighbor*. And so it happened that when the builders would order their assistants to bring bricks, those would bring water; and if they demanded water, those would bring straw. And so their plan was frustrated, *and they stopped building the city. And the Lord scattered them from there over the face of all the earth. And therefore the name of that place was called "Confusion,"ᵈ because there* God *confused* their languages *and from there he scattered them over the face of all the earth.*

Gen 11:7

Gen 11:8f.

From Canaan to Egypt

1 **8** *Now Abram went* forth from there and *dwelt in the land of Canaan and took with him Lot his nephew and Sarai his wife*. And since Sarai was sterile *and had not conceived*, then Abram took Hagar his maid *and she bore him Ishmael*. Now 2 Ishmael became the father of twelve sons. •*Then Lot separated from* Abram *and dwelt in Sodom. But Abram lived in the land of Canaan*.ª *And the men of Sodom* 3 *were very wicked men and great sinners.* •*And* God *appeared to Abram, saying, "To your seed I will give this land, and your name will be called Abraham, and Sarai, your wife, will be* called *Sarah. And I will give* to you from her *an everlasting seed, and I will establish my covenant with you."* And Abraham knew Sarah, his wife, *and she conceived and bore* Isaac.

Gen 12:4f.
Gen 13:12
Gen 16:1
Gen 16:15
Gen 25:12,16
Gen 13:11–13

Gen 17:1
Gen 13:15
Gen 17:5,15,8,7

Gen 21:2f.

4   Now Isaac took for himself a wife from Mesopotamia, the daughter of Bethuel, 5 who conceived and bore to him Esau and Jacob. •Now Esau took for himself as wivesᵇ *Judith the daughter of Beeri and Basemath the daughter of Elon and Oholibamah the daughter of Anah and Mahalath the daughter of Ishmael.*ᶜ *And Adah bore him Eliphaz,*ᵈ *and the sons of Eliphaz were Teman, Omar, Zepho, Gatam, Kenaz,* Amalek. *And Judith bore* Tenacis, Ieruebemas. *Basemath bore Reuel.*ᵉ *And the sons of Reuel: Nahath, Zerah, Shammah, Mizzah. And Oholibamah* 6 *bore Auz, Ioolam,*ᶠ *Korah.* Mahalath bore Tenetde, Thenatela. •Now Jacob took for himself as wives the daughters of Laban the Syrian, Leah and Rachel, and two concubines, Billah and Zilphah. And Leah bore to him Reuben, Simeon, Levi, Judah, Issachar, Zebulun, and Dinah their sister. Now Rachel brought forth Joseph and Benjamin. Billah bore Dan and Naphtali. And Zilphah bore Gad 7 and Asher. These are the twelve sons of Jacob and one daughter. •*And Jacob*

Gen 25:20–26
Gen 26:34
Gen 36:2
Gen 28:9;
36:4(10)
Gen 36:11
Gen 36:4(10),
13
Gen 36:5,14,18

Gen 29:31–
30:24; 35:18,
23–26

Gen 37:1; 33:18;
34:2

---

7 a. We are reading "spittle" (*sputo*), rather than "shield" (*scuto*) found in all MSS, on the basis of the LXX of Isa 40:15 and Ps-Philo 12:4; see also 4Ezra 6:56 and 2Bar 82:5.

b. Lit. "child," which reflects the Gk. *pais* as a rendering for the Heb. ʿ*bd*.

c. That it did not rain on the land of Israel in the Flood is also stated in b.Zeb 113a and *SongR* 1:15.

d. Based on the biblical etymology for Babel; see Gen 11:9.

8 a. All MSS have the error Cham.

b. In view of what follows we would expect "Adah the daughter of Elon" here.

c. MSS have "Manem the daughter of Samael." As in chs. 5f. we are presenting the proper names according to their recognizable biblical equivalents.

d. MSS conflate the names to Adelifan.

e. MSS Rugil.

f. From Gen 36:5, 14, 18, we would expect "Jeush, Jalam."

dwelt in the land of Canaan, and Shechem the son of Hamor the Hurrite[g] *raped
Dinah his daughter and humiliated her. And the sons of Jacob, Simeon and Levi,*   Gen 34:25f.
went in and killed the whole city of them by the sword; and they took their sister
8 *Dinah and went away from there.* •And afterward Job took her as a wife[h] and   Job 42:13f.
fathered from her fourteen sons and six daughters; that is, seven sons and three
daughters before he was struck down with suffering, and afterward seven sons
and three daughters when he was healed. And these are their names: Elifac,
Ermoe, Diasat, Filias, Diffar, Zellud, Thelon; and his daughters: Meru, Litaz,
Zeli.[i] And such as had been the names of the former, so were those of the latter.
9   Now *Jacob* and his twelve sons *lived in the land of Canaan. And these hated*   Gen 37:1,4
their brother Joseph, whom *they delivered into Egypt to Potiphar, the chief of*   Gen 37:36; 39:1
10 *Pharaoh's cooks,*[j] and he spent fourteen years with him. •*And* afterward *the king*   Gen 41:1
of Egypt had a dream. And they told him about Joseph, and he explained to him
the dreams. And after he explained to him the dreams, Pharaoh *made him chief*   Gen 41:43
over all the land of Egypt. At that time there was a *famine over all the land,* as   Gen 41:54
Joseph had discerned, *and his brothers went down to buy food in Egypt* because   Gen 42:3
only *in Egypt was there food. And Joseph recognized his brothers, but was not*   Gen 42:1
known by them. And he did not deal vengefully with them, and he sent and   Gen 42:8
summoned his father from the land of Canaan; and he went down to him.
11   *And these are the names of the sons of Israel who went down to Egypt with*   Gen 46:8,27;
Jacob, each with his own household. The sons of Reuben: Hanoch, Pallu, Hezron,   Ex 1:1
and Carmi. Now the sons of Simeon: Namuel[k] *and Jamin and Ohad*[l] *and Jachin*[m]   Gen 46:9–15
and Shaul the son of the Canaanite woman. Now the sons of Levi: Gershon,[n]
*Kohath, and Merari. The sons of Judah: Er and Onan, Shelah, Perez, and Zerah.
Now the sons of Issachar: Tola and Puvah, Job and Shimron.*[o] *Now the sons of
Zebulun: Sered, Elon,*[p] *and Jahleel.* And Dinah their sister bore fourteen sons and
six daughters. *And* these are the generations of *the sons that Leah*[q] *bore to Jacob,*
12 *all the sons and daughters*[r] being 72.[s] •*Now the sons of Dan: Hushim.*[t] *The sons*   Gen 46:23–25
of Naphtali: Betaal, Neemmu, Surem, Opti, Sariel.[u] *And these are the generations*
13 *of Billah that she bore to Jacob; the total was eight.*[v] •*But the sons of Gad*[w]:   Gen 46:16–18
Sariel, Sua, Visui, Mofar, and Sar their sister the daughter of Seriebel, Melchiel.
These are the generations of Zilphah the woman of Jacob *that she bore* to him,
14 *and all the sons and daughters were ten*[x] in number. •And the sons of *Joseph:*   Gen 46:20–22
Ephraim and Manasseh. But *Benjamin* fathered *Bela, Ashbel,*[y] Nanubal, Aboc-
mefec, Utendeus. *And these are the persons whom Rachel bore to Jacob, fourteen.*
And they went down into Egypt and dwelt there 210 years.

---

g. Ps-Philo agrees with the LXX of Gen 34:2
in making Shechem a Hurrite; other texts call him
a Hivvite.

h. Apparently Job is identified with Jobab of
Gen 36:33. That Dinah married Job is stated in
TJob 1:6 and several rabbinic texts.

i. Perhaps we are to connect the names with
Job's comforters: Elifac—Elifaz; Filias—Baldas;
Diffar—Soffar. Meru may be related to Job's first
daughter, Jemimah (Job 42:14).

j. In calling Potiphar the chief of Pharaoh's
cooks, Ps-Philo agrees with the LXX of Gen 37:36;
39:1; Jub 34:1; Josephus' *Ant* 2.4.1 §39 and 2.5.4
§78, and Philo's Jos 27 and LegAll 3.236.

k. For Namuel rather than Jemuel see 1Chr 4:24.

l. The MSS have Doth. In Gen 46:10 the MT
has *'hd* and the LXX *Aôd*. The Lat. translator of
Ps-Philo or an earlier Gk. copyist probably confused
initial alpha and delta.

m. Zohar of Gen 46:10 has been omitted.

n. MSS Getson.

o. MSS Sombran.

p. The MSS conflate the two names into Sarelon.

q. The MSS omit Leah, but see Gen 46:15.

r. Lit. "all the souls of the sons and daughters."

s. According to Gen 46:15 the number should
be 33; perhaps Ps-Philo had 32 (XXXII), the actual
number of sons here (25 names and 7 from Dinah),
which was then misread as 72 (LXXII).

t. MSS Usinam.

u. Gen 46:24 has Jahzeel, Guni, Jezer and
Shillem.

v. Gen 46:25 has seven. There are only six
names given here and only five in the OT.

w. Most of the list of Gad's sons and the
beginning of Asher's sons have dropped out.

x. Gen 46:18 has sixteen.

y. MSS have Gela, Esbel.

Amram and the birth of Moses

1 **9** And after Joseph's passing away, *the sons of Israel multiplied and increased* Ex 1:6–10
*greatly. And another⁴ king who did not know Joseph arose in Egypt, and he said
to his people,* "Behold that people has multiplied more than we have. Come, let
us make a plan against them so they will not multiply more." And the king of Ex 1:22
Egypt ordered all his people, saying, "Every son that is born to the Hebrews,ᵇ
throw into the river; but let their females live." And the Egyptians answered their
king, saying, "Let us kill their males, and we will keep their females so that we
may give them to our slaves as wives. And whoever is born from them will be a
slave and will serve us." And this is what seemed wicked before the LORD.

2   Then the elders of the people gathered the people together in mourning, and
they mourned and groaned saying, "The wombs of our wives have suffered
miscarriage; our fruit is delivered to our enemies. And now we are lost, and let
us set up rules for ourselves that a man should not approach his wife lest the fruit
of their wombs be defiled and our offspring serve idols. For it is better to die
without sons until we know what God may do."

3   And Amram answered and said, "It will sooner happen that this age will be Ex 6:20
ended foreverᶜ or the world will sink into the immeasurable deep or the heart of
the abyss will touch the stars than that the race of the sons of Israel will be ended.
And there will be fulfilled the covenant that God established with Abraham when
he said, 'Indeed your sons will dwell *in a land not their own and will be brought* Gen 15:13
into bondage and afflicted 400 years.' And behold from the time when the word
of God that he spoke to Abraham was spoken,ᵈ there are 350 years; from the time Ex 12:40
4 when we became slaves in Egypt, there are 130ᵉ years. •Now therefore I will not
abide by what you decree, but I will go in and take my wife and produce sons so
that we may be made many on the earth.ᶠ For God will not abide in his anger,
nor will he forget his people forever, nor will he cast forth the race of Israel in
vain upon the earth; nor did he establish a covenant with our fathers in vain; and
5 even when we did not yet exist, God spoke about these matters. •Now therefore
I will go and take my wife, and I will not consent to the command of the king;
and if it is right in your eyes, let us all act in this way. For when our wives
conceive, they will not be recognized as pregnant until three months have passed,
as also our mother Tamar did.ᵍ For her intent was not fornication, but being
unwilling to separate from the sons of Israel she reflected and said, 'It is better
for me to die for having intercourse with my father-in-law than to have intercourse
with gentiles.'ʰ And she hid the fruit of her womb until the third month. For then
she was recognized. And on her way to be put to death, she made a declaration
saying, '*He who owns this staff and this signet ring and the sheepskin,ⁱ from him* Gen 38:24f.
6 *I have conceived.*' And her intent saved her from all danger. •Now therefore let
us also do the same. And when the time of giving birth has been completed, we

---

9 a. The MT for Ex 1:8 has "new," but the LXX
has "another."

   b. The specification "to the Hebrews" is absent
from the MT of Ex 1:22 but present in the LXX
and Samaritan Pentateuch.

   c. The Lat. *in victoria* reflects the Gk. *eis nikos*
and Heb. *lnṣḥ* and means "forever." In Aram. the
root has only the meaning of "splendor" or "victory" and so the phrase is an argument against
Aram. as the original language of Ps-Philo.

   d. Lit. "was found," which probably arose from
confusion between Gk. *heurethē*, "was found,"
and *errethē*, "was spoken."

   e. See Ex 12:40, where the MT says that the
people of Israel dwelt in Egypt for 430 years but
the LXX divides the time between Canaan and

Egypt as Ps-Philo does.

   f. In several rabbinic texts Amram advises the
husbands and wives not to live together. In Josephus' *Ant* 2.9.3 §210 Amram's wife is already
pregnant.

   g. This is the first instance of a common technique in Ps-Philo: referring back to past events or
forward to future events in Israelite history to
illustrate an event now under discussion.

   h. This apology for Tamar's actions is found
only in Ps-Philo. For other polemics against marriage with gentiles, see 18:13f.; 21:1; 30:1; 44:7;
45:3.

   i. In Gen 38:18, 25, the MT has "cords," the
LXX "small necklace," and the Vulgate "brace-
let."

will not cast forth the fruit of our womb (if we are able). And who knows if God will be provoked on account of this so as to free us from our humiliation?''

7 And the strategy that Amram thought out was pleasing before God. And God said, ''Because Amram's plan is pleasing to me, and he has not put aside the covenant established between me and his fathers, so behold now he who will be born from him will serve me forever, and I will do marvelous things in the house of Jacob through him and I will work through him signs and wonders for my people that I have not done for anyone else; and I will act gloriously among them 8 and proclaim to them my ways. •And I, God, will kindle for him my lamp that will abide in him, and I will show him my covenant that no one has seen. And I will reveal to him my Law[j] and statutes and judgments, and I will burn an eternal light for him, because I thought of him in the days of old, saying, '*My spirit will*   Gen 6:3 *not be a mediator among these men forever, because they are flesh and their days will be 120 years.*' ''

9 *And* Amram *of the tribe of Levi went out and took a wife* from his own tribe.[k]   Ex 2:1; 6:20 When he had taken her, others followed him and took their own wives. And this 10 man had one son and one daughter; their names were Aaron and Miriam. •And the spirit of God came upon Miriam one night, and she saw a dream and told it to her parents in the morning, saying, ''I have seen this night, and behold a man in a linen garment stood and said to me, 'Go and say to your parents, ''Behold he who will be born from you will be cast forth into the water; likewise through him the water will be dried up.[l] And I will work signs through him and save my people, and he will exercise leadership always.'' ' '' And when Miriam told of her dream, her parents did not believe her.

11 The strategy of the king of Egypt, however, prevailed against the sons of Israel, 12 and they were humiliated and worn down in making bricks. •*Now* Jochebed   Ex 2:2–3; 6:20 *conceived* from Amram *and hid him* in her womb *for three months.*[m] *For she could not conceal him any longer,* because the king of Egypt appointed local chiefs who, when the Hebrew women gave birth, would immediately throw their   Ex 1:22 male children into the river. *And she took* her child and *made for him an ark* from   Ex 2:3 13 the bark of a pine tree *and placed the ark at the bank of the river.* •Now that 14 child was born in the covenant of God and the covenant of the flesh.[n] •And when they had cast him forth, all the elders gathered and quarreled with Amram, saying, ''Are not these our words that we spoke, 'It is better for us to die without having sons than that the fruit of our womb be cast into the waters'?'' And Amram did 15 not listen to those who were saying these words. •*Now Pharaoh's daughter came*   Ex 2:5f. *down to bathe in the river,* as she had seen in dreams, *and* her maids *saw the ark. And she sent* one, *and she fetched and opened it. And when she saw the boy* and while she was looking upon the covenant (that is, the covenant of the flesh),[o] 16 she said, ''*It is one of the Hebrew children.*'' •And she took him and nursed him.   Ex 2:9f. And he became her own son, and she called him by the name Moses. But his mother called him Melchiel.[p] And the child was nursed and became glorious above all other men, and through him God freed the sons of Israel as he had said.

---

j. Lit. ''superexcellence.'' This expression (or one like it) must mean ''law'' or ''statute'' as in 11:1; 12:2; 19:4; 30:2; and 44:6, but its origin is not now recognizable.

k. There are striking parallels between Moses' birth as narrated here and that of Jesus in Mt 1f.: communication by dreams, the spirit of God, interest in name and mission, concealment, and the slaughter of the male children. Literary dependence is doubtful; the points in common show a lively interest in the birth of heroes in the NT period. The ''new Moses'' motif in Mt 2 is well known. See also Ps-Philo 42.

l. The connection between Moses' being cast into the water as an infant and his later drying up of the Red Sea is unique to Ps-Philo.

m. There may be some material missing here, since there is a sudden transition from Jochebed's pregnancy to her precautions to save Moses.

n. That is, Moses was born circumcised as in b.Soṭ 12a and ExR 1:24.

o. That is, the sign of his circumcision. In post-biblical Heb., ''covenant'' had become a technical term for circumcision.

p. For Melchi as a name for Moses, see Clement of Alexandria's *Strom* 1.23.1.

The departure from Egypt and the crossing over the sea

1 **10** Now when *the king of the Egyptians died, another king rose up* and afflicted   Ex 2:23f., 1:8
all the people of Israel. *But they cried out to* the LORD, *and he heard* them. And
he sent Moses and freed them from the land of the Egyptians. God also sent upon
them ten plagues and struck them down. Now these were the plagues; that is,   Ex 7:14–12:36
blood and frogs and all manner of beasts and hail and the death of cattle and
locusts and gnats and darkness that could be felt and the death of the firstborn.[a]

2 And while *they were going forth* from there and setting out, *the heart of the*   Ex 14:8–11
Egyptians was hardened once more, and they continued *to pursue them* and *found*
them by the Red *Sea. And* the sons of Israel cried out to their Lord and said to
Moses, saying, "Behold now the time of our destruction has come. For the sea
is ahead of us, and the throng of enemies is behind us, and we are in the middle.   Num 14:3
Is it for this that God has brought us forth, or are these the covenants that he
established with our fathers, saying, *'To your seed will I give the land* in which   Gen 12:7
you dwell' that now he might do with us whatever is pleasing in his sight?"

3 Then in considering the fearful situation of the moment, the sons of Israel were
split in their opinions according to three strategies.[b] For the tribe of Reuben and
the tribe of Issachar and the tribe of Zebulun and the tribe of Simeon said,
"Come, let us cast ourselves into the sea. For it is better for us to die in the water
than to be killed by our enemies." But the tribe of Gad and the tribe of Asher
and the tribe of Dan and that of Naphtali said, "No, but let us go back with them;   Ex 14:12
and if they are willing to spare our lives, we will serve them." But the tribe of
Levi and the tribe of Judah and that of Joseph and the tribe of Benjamin said,
"Not so, but let us take up our weapons and fight with them, and God will be

4 with us." •And *Moses* cried out *to the Lord* and *said, "Lord God of our fathers,*   Ex 3:13f.
did you not say to me, 'Go and *tell the sons of Israel,*[c] "God has sent me to
you" '? And now behold you have brought your people to the edge of the sea,   Ex 14:15,9

5 and the enemy *has pursued them*; but you, LORD, remember your name." •And   Ex 14:15f.
God said, *"Why have you cried out to me? Lift up your rod and strike* the sea,
and it will be dried up." And when Moses did all this, God rebuked the sea and
the sea was dried up. *And the seas* of water *piled up* and *the depths* of the earth   Ex 15:8
were visible, and the foundations of the world[d] were laid bare by the fearful din

6 of God and *by the breath of the anger* of the LORD.[e] •And *Israel* passed *through*   Ex 14:22(29)
the middle of the sea on dry ground. And the Egyptians saw this and continued
following them. And God hardened their perception, and they did not know that
they were entering the sea. And while the Egyptians were in the sea, God again
commanded the sea and said to Moses, "Strike the sea yet once more." And he
did so. And the LORD commanded the sea, and it started flowing again and covered
the Egyptians and their chariots and horsemen.

7 Now he led his people out into the wilderness; for forty years *he rained down*   Ex 16:13–17:6
for them bread from heaven and brought *quail* to them *from the sea* and brought   Ps 78:24,27
forth a well of water to follow them.[f] *Now with a pillar of cloud he led them by*   Num 21:16–20
day, and with a pillar of fire he gave them light by night.   Ex 13:21; Neh 9:12

---

10 a. The plague of boils is absent from the list.
When the order is compared with that of the biblical
text, the order in Ps-Philo is 1, 2, 4, 7, 5, 8, 3,
9, 10.

b. The division of opinion here may be related
to that in Judg 5:15–16. A fourfold rather than
threefold division is common in rabbinic texts.

c. All MSS but one have "the sons of Leah,"
but the conjecture of that one MS ("the sons of
Israel") is probably correct. See Ex 3:14.

d. Lit. "habitation," which in Gk. probably
was *oikoumēnē*.

e. Lit. "my LORD." The use of the first person
singular possessive adjective is unexpected. The
Gk. translator may have mistranslated the Heb.
'dwny ("the LORD") as "my LORD."

f. The idea of a well of water to follow them
arises from Num 21:16–20 and is found in Ps-Philo
11:15; 1Cor 10:4, and many targumic and rabbinic
texts.

The gift of the Law. The Decalogue

1 **11** And *in the third month after the sons of Israel had gone forth from the land* Ex 19:1
of Egypt, they came into the wilderness of Sinai, and God remembered his words
and said, "I will give a light to the world and illumine their dwelling places and
establish my covenant with the sons of men and glorify my people above all
nations. For them I will bring out the eternal statutes[a] that are for those in the
2 light but for the ungodly a punishment." •And he said to Moses, "Behold I will Ex 19:15
call you tomorrow; *be prepared* and tell my people, *'For three days let no man
approach*[b] *his wife,'* and on the third day[c] I will speak to you and to them. And
afterward you will come up to me, and I will put my words in your mouth, and
you will enlighten my people, for I have given an everlasting Law into your hands
and by this I will judge the whole world. For this will be a testimony. For even
if men say, 'We have not known you, and so we have not served you,' therefore
3 I will make a claim upon them because they have not learned my Law."[d] •And
Moses did what God commanded him, *and he consecrated the people and said* Ex 19:14f.
to them, *"Be prepared* on the third day, because after three days God will establish
his covenant with you." And the people were consecrated.

4 *And on the third day there were* claps of *thunder* and the brightness of *lightning,* Ex 19:16f.
and the sound of trumpets sounded aloud. Terror came upon all the people who
5 *were in the camp. And Moses brought the people out before God.* •And behold
the mountains burned with fire, and the earth quaked, and the hills were disturbed,
and the mountains were rolled about, and the abysses boiled, and every habitable
place was shaken, and the heavens were folded up, and the clouds drew up water,
and flames of fire burned, and thunderings and lightnings were many, and winds
and storms roared, the stars gathered together, and angels ran on ahead, until God
should establish the Law of his eternal covenant with the sons of Israel and give
his eternal commandments that will not pass away.[e]

6 And *then the Lord spoke* to his people *all these words, saying, "I am the Lord* Ex 20:1f.,4–6
*your God who led you forth from the land of Egypt, from the house of slavery.
You shall not make for yourselves graven* gods; *neither* shall you make any
abominable image of the sun and moon or of any of the ornaments of *heaven;
nor shall you make a likeness of any of the things that are upon the earth or of
those things that* crawl *in the water* or upon *the earth. I am the Lord your God,
a jealous God and visiting until the third and fourth generation the sins of them*
that sleep on the living *sons* of the ungodly if they will walk in the ways of their
parents, *but acting mercifully for a thousand* generations *to those who love me*
7 *and keep my commandments.* •*You shall not take the name of the Lord your God* Ex 20:7
in vain, lest my ways be made empty.[f] *For God* detests *him who takes his name*
8 *in vain.* •*Take care*[g] *to sanctify the sabbath day. Work for six days, but the seventh* Ex 20:8–11
day is the sabbath of the Lord. You shall not do any work on it, you and all your
help, except *to praise the* LORD *in the assembly of the elders* and *to glorify the* Ps 107:32
Mighty One *in the council of the older men. For in six days the Lord made the
heaven and the earth and the sea and all things that are in them* and all the world

11 a. Lit. "heights," but the context demands the
meaning "statutes." See 9:8.

b. The MSS have "ascend" (*ascendat*), but in
view of Ex 19:15 we have emended to "approach"
(*accedat*).

c. Here "on the third day" is the equivalent of
"after three days" as in Mt 27:63; Mk 8:31; 9:31;
10:34; Lk 24:7; Acts 10:40; and 1Cor 15:4.

d. According to b.AZ 2b, since God offered the
Law to all the nations, they have no excuse for not
obeying it. But perhaps only the case of unfaithful
Israelites is being considered here.

e. Similar lists of wonders accompanying the
gift of the Law are in 15:5f.; 23:10; and 32:7f. See
also 4Ezra 3:18f. For commandments that do not
pass away, see Mt 5:18.

f. The "ways" here may be purely metaphorical
(i.e. God's ways or directions), or they may be
connected with b.Shab 33a: "For the crime of vain
oaths . . . the roads became desolate."

g. The Samaritan Pentateuch of Ex 20:8 and the
various texts of Deut 5:12 also have "take care"
rather than "remember."

and the uninhabitable wilderness and all things that labor and all the order of
heaven. *And God rested on the seventh day. Therefore, God sanctified the seventh*[h]

9 *day* because he rested on it. •*Love your father and your mother,* and *you shall* | Ex 20:12
honor them, and then your light will rise. And I will command the heaven, and
it will give forth its rain, and the earth will give back fruit more quickly. And
you will live many days and dwell *in* your *land,* and you will not be without sons,

10 for your seed will not be lacking in people to dwell in it. •*You shall not commit* | Ex 20:14
adultery,[i] because your enemies did not commit adultery against you, but *you* | Ex 14:8

11 *came forth with a high hand.*[j] •*You shall not kill,* because your enemies had power | Ex 20:15

12 over you so as to kill you, but you saw their death. •*You shall not be a false* | Ex 20:16
witness against your neighbor, speaking false testimony, lest your guardians[k]

13 speak false testimony against you. •*You shall not covet your neighbor's house or* | Ex 20:17
what he has, lest others should covet your land."

14 And when the LORD ceased speaking, the people were very much afraid, because | Ex 20:18; Deut
they saw the mountain burning with torches of fire. *And they said to Moses, "You* | 5:22; Num 12:8
speak to us, but do not let God speak to us lest perhaps we die. For behold today | Ex 20:19f.
we know that God speaks to a man face to face and that man may live. And now
we have recognized that the earth has borne the voice of God with quaking." *And
Moses said to them, "Do not fear. For God has come to test you that you
yourselves* should come *to fear him so that you will not sin."*

15 *And all*[l] *the people stood far off, but Moses drew near the cloud,* knowing *that* | Ex 20:21
God was there. And then God told him his statutes and his judgments, and he
detained him *forty days and forty nights.* And there he commanded him many | Ex 24:18
things *and showed him the tree* of life, from which he cut off and took and *threw* | Ex 15:25
into Marah, *and the water* of Marah[m] *became sweet.* And it[n] followed them in
the wilderness forty years and went up to the mountain with them and went down
into the plains. And he commanded him about the tabernacle and the ark of the | Ex 25–31
LORD and about the sacrifice of burnt offerings and incense and about setting up
the table and the candlestick and about the laver and its basin[o] and about the
ephod and the breastplate and about the precious stones, so that the sons of Israel
might make these things. And *he showed* him *their likeness* in order that he might | Ex 25:9,8
make them according to *the pattern* that he had seen. And he said to him, "*Make
me a sanctuary, and the tent* of my glory will be *among you."*[p]

The golden calf

1 **12** And Moses came down. And when he had been bathed with invisible light, | Ex 34:29–35
he went down to the place where the light of the sun and the moon are; and the
light of his face surpassed the splendor of the sun and the moon, and *he did not
even know* this. And when he came down to the sons of Israel, they saw him but
did not recognize him.[a] But when he spoke, then they recognized him. And this
was like what happened in Egypt when *Joseph recognized his brothers but they* | Gen 42:8
did not recognize him. And afterward, when Moses realized *that his face had
become glorious,* he made *a veil* for himself with which to cover his face.

2 And while he was on the mountain, the heart of the people was corrupted, *and* | Ex 32:1f.

---

h. The LXX and Peshitta of Ex 20:11 also have
"seventh," while the other texts have "sabbath."

i. The prohibition of adultery precedes that of
murder as in the LXX, Nash Papyrus, Philo, and
some NT texts (Rom 13:9; Lk 18:20; Jas 2:11).
The prohibition of stealing is omitted.

j. The point seems to be that Israel's enemies
did not get the chance to commit adultery.

k. See also 15:5 and 59:4 for guardian angels.
The passage is a formulation of the golden rule
("Do to others as you would have them do to
you"; cf. Mt 7:12).

l. Ps-Philo agrees with the Lucianic MSS and

the Vetus Latina of Ex 20:21 in reading "all."

m. Marah in Heb. means "bitter."

n. The water, not the LORD (as some MSS
have); see 10:7.

o. The MSS have "vase" (*vase*), but "basin"
(*base*) must be correct; see 13:1 and Ex 30:18.

p. With "tent" and "among you" Ps-Philo
stands closest to the Samaritan Pentateuch of Ex
25:8.

12 a. That the people of Israel saw Moses but did
not recognize him is unique to Ps-Philo.

they gathered together to Aaron, saying, "Make gods for us whom we may serve, as the other nations have, *because that Moses* through whom wonders were done before our eyes has been taken away from us." *And Aaron said to them,* "Be patient. For Moses will come, and he will bring judgment near to us and will illumine the Law for us and will explain from his own mouth the Law[b] of God

3 and set up rules for our race." •And while he was speaking, they did not heed him, so that the word spoken in the time when the people sinned by building the tower might be fulfilled, when God said, "And now unless I stop them, *everything*   Gen 11:6 *that they will propose to do they will dare,* and even worse." But Aaron, fearful because the people were very strong, *said to them,* "*Bring us the earrings of your*   Ex 32:2–4 *wives.*" And each man asked his wife, and they gave them immediately. And they cast them into the fire, and they were fashioned into shape, and out came a molten calf.

4   *And the Lord said to Moses,* "*Hurry[c] away from here, because the people have*   Ex 32:7f. *been corrupted and have turned aside from my ways that I commanded them.* Are the promises that I promised to your fathers when I said to them, *'To your*   Gen 12:7 *seed I will give the land* in which you dwell'—are they at an end? For behold the people have not even entered the land yet and now even have the Law with them, and they have forsaken me. And indeed I know that if they had entered that land, even greater iniquities would have been done. And now I too will forsake them, and I will turn again and make peace with them so that a house may be built for me among them, a house that will be destroyed because they will sin against me. And the race of men will be to me like a drop from a pitcher and will be reckoned   Isa 40:15 like spittle."

5   And *Moses* hurried *down and saw the calf.* And he looked at the tablets and   Ex 32:15,19 saw that the writing was gone,[d] and he hurried to *break them.* And his hands were opened, and he became like a woman bearing her firstborn who, when she is in labor, her hands are upon her chest and she has no strength to help herself

6 bring forth.[e] •And after one hour he said to himself, "Will bitterness win the day always, or will evil prevail forever? And now I will rise up and gird my loins, because even if they have sinned, what was declared to me above will not be in

7 vain." •And he arose and broke the calf *and cast it into the water and made the*   Ex 32:20 *people drink of it.*[f] And if anyone had it in his will and mind that the calf be made, his tongue was cut off; but if he had been forced by fear to consent, his face shone.

8   And then Moses went up to the mountain and prayed to the LORD, saying, "Behold now, you O God, who have planted this vine and set its roots into the abyss and stretched out its shoots to your most high seat,[g] look upon it in this time, because that vine has lost its fruit and has not recognized its cultivator. And now, if you are angry at your vine and you uproot it from the abyss and dry up its shoots from your most high and eternal seat, the abyss will come no more to nourish it, nor will your throne come to cool that vine of yours that you have

9 burned up. •For you are he who is all light; and you have adorned your house[h] with precious stones and gold; and you have sprinkled your house with perfumes and spices[i] and balsam wood and cinnamon and roots of myrrh and costum[j]; and you have filled it with various foods and the sweetness of various drinks. Therefore, if you do not have mercy on your vine, all things, LORD, have been done in vain, and you will not have anyone to glorify you. For even if you plant another vine, this one will not trust you, because you have destroyed the former one. For if

---

b. Lit. "superexcellence"; see 9:8.

c. See the LXX of Ex 32:7 *badize to tachos.*

d. The legend that the writing fled away from the tablets of the Law is found in rabbinic writings.

e. See Jer 4:31 and 1QH 3.7–10 for the image of giving birth.

f. Drinking the waters to determine the identity of sinners is found in Num 5:11–31 in the case of a woman suspected of adultery.

g. For a similar description, see 1QH 6.14–17.

h. Perhaps paradise, but more likely the universe.

i. Var. "jasper."

j. ["Costum" is from Lat. *costum* (Gk. *kostos*), which denotes an eastern plant with aromatic qualities; there is no English name for the plant; see Jub 16:24 (and n. c), in which "costum" is mentioned among other fragrant plants. —J.H.C.]

you indeed forsake the world, then who will do for you what you say as God? And now let your anger be restrained from your vine; rather let what was said previously by you and what still must be said be done, and do not let your labor be in vain, and do not let your inheritance be pulled apart in humiliation."

10 *And God said to* him, "Behold I have been made merciful according to your Ex 34:1 words. Therefore *cut two stone tablets for yourself* from the same place where you cut *the former* ones, *and rewrite* [k] on them the commandments *that were on the first ones.*"

The tent of meeting and the festivals

1 **13** And Moses hastened and did everything that God commanded him. And he Ex 35–40 went down and made the tent of meeting [a] and its vessels and the ark and the lamp and the table and the altar of holocausts and the altar of incense [b] and the ephod and the breastplate and the precious stones and the laver and the basins and everything that was shown to him. And he arranged all the vestments of the priests, the belt and the robe [c] and the headdress and the golden plate and the holy crown. And the oil for anointing priests and the priests themselves he consecrated.

2 *And when all this was done, the cloud covered* them all. •Then Moses *called* to Ex 40:33f. the LORD, and God *spoke to him from the tent of meeting,* saying, "This is the Lev 1:1 law of the altar, [d] according to which you will sacrifice to me and pray for your own souls. Now regarding what you will offer to me, *from the cattle* offer the Lev 1:10,14 calf and *the sheep and the goat,* but *from the birds the turtledove* and *the dove.*

3 "And if there be leprosy in your land and the leper be cleansed, *they will take* Lev 14:2–6 for the LORD *two live chicks and cedarwood and hyssop and scarlet*; and he will approach the priest, *and he will kill one chick but keep the other alive.* And he will give orders to the leper in all the matters that I have commanded in my Law.

4 "And when the times appointed for you come around, you will acknowledge Lev 23:4–8 me as holy on the festival day and rejoice before me on the festival of the unleavened bread and set before me the bread, celebrating the festival as a

5 memorial, because on that day you went forth from the land of Egypt. •And on Lev 23:15–21 the festival of weeks you will set before me bread and make me an offering for

6 your fruits. •Now the feast of trumpets will be an offering for your watchers. [e] In Lev 23:24–32 as much as I watched over creation, [f] may you also be mindful of all the earth. At the beginning of those days, when you present yourselves, I will declare the number of those who are to die and who are to be born. A fast of mercy you will fast [g] for me for your own souls, so that the promises made to your fathers may

7 be fulfilled. •And celebrate for me the festival of the booth, *and you will take* for Lev 23:40 me *the beautiful branch of the tree and the palm branch and the willow and the cedar and branches of myrtle.* And I will remember the whole earth with rain, and the measure of the seasons will be established, and I will fix the stars and command the clouds, and the winds will resound, and lightning bolts will rush about, and there will be a thunderstorm. And this will be an everlasting sign; and the nights will yield dew, as I said after the flooding of the earth."

8 Then he gave him the command regarding the year of the lifetime of Noah, and he said to him, "These are the years that I ordained after the weeks in which I visited the city of men, at which time I showed them the place of creation and

k. Moses is to write the commandments. Most witnesses say that God wrote them, but some LXX MSS do make Moses the writer. See Ex 34:27f. See also Ps-Philo 25:13 for doubt about the authorship of the Law.

13 a. Lit. "the tables" (*tabulas*), but the context demands "tent of meeting" (*tabernaculum*).
b. Lit. "the thurible of holocausts and the thurible of incense," but according to Ex 35:15f. these should be altars. Perhaps Gk. *thymiaterion,* "thu-

rible," was misread for *thysiaterion,* "altar."
c. We are reading *citona,* "robe," instead of *cetera,* "the rest," the reading of all the MSS.
d. Again the MSS have "thurible."
e. Angelic guardians are probably meant, but in 34:2 sacrifice to angels is attacked. Perhaps the point is that at the New Year, Israel is brought to judgment by God's angels.
f. For the New Year as the anniversary of creation see b.RH 11a.
g. The Day of Atonement.

the serpent.''[h] And he said, "This is the place concerning which I taught the first man,[i] saying, 'If you do not transgress what I have commanded you, all things will be subject to you.' But that man transgressed my ways and was persuaded by his wife; and she was deceived by the serpent. And then death was ordained
9 for the generations of men." •And the LORD continued to show him the ways of paradise and said to him,[j] "These are the ways that men have lost by not walking in them, because they have sinned against me."

10   And the LORD commanded him regarding the salvation of the souls of the people and said, "If they will walk in my ways, I will not abandon them but will have mercy on them always and bless their seed; and the earth will quickly yield   Lev 26:2–5
its fruit, and there will be rains for their advantage, and it will not be barren. But I know for sure that they will make their ways corrupt and I will abandon them, and they will forget the covenants that I have established with their fathers; but nevertheless I will not forget them forever. For they will know in the last days that on account of their own sins their seed has been abandoned, because I am faithful in my ways."

The census of the people

1 **14** *Then* God *said to* him, "Make pass in review my people *from twenty years*   Num 1:1–3
and up to forty years so that I may show your tribes what I declared to your fathers in a foreign land, because from the fiftieth[a] part I raised them up from the   Ex 13:18
2 land of Egypt, but forty-nine parts died in the land of Egypt. •When you make them stand and pass in review, write down their number until I fulfill all that I have spoken to their fathers and until I set them firmly in their own land; for not a single word from what I have spoken to their fathers will I renege on, from those that I said to them: '*Your seed will be like the stars of heaven in multitude.*'   Gen 22:17; Deut
By number they will enter the land, and in a short time they will become without   28:62
number."
3   And then Moses came down and numbered them, and the number of the people was 604,550.[b] *But he did not number the tribe of Levi with them, because so it*   Num 1:46–49;
was commanded him. But he did number those who were above fifty[c] years, whose   2:33
number was 47,300. Moreover, he numbered those who were below twenty years, and their number was 850,850. And he looked over the tribe of Levi, and the whole number of them was 100,200. And the whole number of the sons of Israel
4 was 1,620,900.[d] •And Moses declared their number to God, and God said to him, "These are the words that I spoke to their fathers in the land of Egypt, and I established the number of 210 years for all who saw my wonders; and the number of all of them was 9,295,000 men apart from women. And I put to death the whole crowd of them because they did not believe in me. And the fiftieth part of them was left, and I consecrated them to myself. Therefore I command each generation of my people that they should give to me tithes from their fruits, to be before me as a memorial of how many hardships I have removed from them."
5 And when Moses descended and declared these matters to the people, they mourned and lamented; and they dwelt in the wilderness for two years.   Num 9:1

The twelve spies

1 **15** And *Moses sent* twelve men as spies *to spy out the land,* for so it was   Num 13:1–3,
                                                                                              20–29,32f.

---

h. We are reading *colubrum*, "serpent" (see 13:8 below) instead of *colorem*, "color," found in all MSS.
i. Adam, who is called *protoplastus* here. For the same term see WisSol 7:1 and 10:1.
j. Probably Moses, but possibly Noah.

14 a. Based on a midrashic explanation of the

Heb. *ḥmšym* in Ex 13:8, which can mean "equipped for battle" or "fifties."
b. Num 1:46 has 603,550.
c. In view of 14:1 we would expect "forty."
d. The figures for the Levites and all the sons of Israel are emendations based on a very corrupt text. Num 3:39 puts the number of Levites at 22,000.

commanded him.[a] When *they went up and spied out the land, they returned to him* and brought back fruits from the fruits of the land. And *they troubled the heart of the people*, saying, "You cannot inherit the land, because it has been locked up with iron bars by its mighty men." • Yet two men of the twelve did not speak in this way, but said, "Just as hard iron can overcome the stars, or as weapons conquer lightning, or thunder is shut off by the arrows of men, so can these men fight against the LORD."[b] For they saw as they went up that the lightnings from the stars shone forth and claps of thunders resounding with them followed. • And these are their names: Caleb the son of Jephunneh, son of Beri, son of Batuel, son of Galifa, son of Cenen, son of Selumin, son of Selon, son of Judah. The second was Joshua son of Nun, son of Eliphat, son of Gal, son of Nefelien, son of Emon, son of Saul, son of Dabra, son of Ephraim, son of Joseph. But the people did not listen to the voice of these two. Rather, they were very disturbed and said, "Are these the words that God spoke to us, saying, 'I will bring you *into a land flowing with milk and honey'? And how does he* now *bring us up so that we should fall upon the sword and our wives be taken into captivity?*" And when they said these words, suddenly *the glory of God appeared*, and he said to Moses, "So, do the people continue not to listen to me at all? Behold now the plan of action that has issued from me will not be in vain. I will send the angel of my wrath upon them to afflict their bodies with fire in the wilderness. But I will command my angels who watch over them[c] not to intercede for them; for their souls I will shut up in the chambers of darkness, and I will tell my servants, their fathers, 'Behold this is the seed to which I have spoken, saying, *"Your seed will stay a while in a land not its own, and I will judge the nation whom it will serve."* ' And I fulfilled my words and made their enemies melt away and set the angels beneath their feet and placed the cloud as the covering for their head. And I commanded the sea, and when the abyss was divided before them, walls of water stood forth. • And there was never anything like this event since the day I said, '*Let the waters under the heaven be gathered together into one place,*' until this day. And I brought them forth, but I killed their enemies. And I brought them before me to Mount Sinai, and I bent the heavens and came down to kindle a lamp for my people and to establish laws[d] for creation. And I taught them to make sanctuaries for me that I might dwell in them, but they abandoned me and did not believe my words, and their mind grew weak. And now behold the days will come, and I will do to them as they wished, and I will cast forth *their bodies in the wilderness.*"

7 And Moses said, "Before you took the seed from which you would make man upon the earth, was it I who did establish their ways? Therefore let your mercy sustain us until the end, and your fidelity for length of days; for unless you had mercy, who would ever be born?"

Marginal references:
Josh 14:8 / Num 13:30 / Num 32:12 / 1Chr 7:21–27 / Ex 3:8 / Num 14:3 / Num 14:10 / Gen 15:13f / Ex 14:22 / Gen 1:9 / Isa 64:1 / Num 14:32 / Num 14:13–19

The rebellion of Korah

1 **16** In that time he commanded that man[a] about the tassels. And then Korah and two hundred[b] men with him rebelled and said, "Why is an unbearable law imposed upon us?"[c]

2 And God was angry and said, "I commanded the earth, and it gave me man;

Marginal references: Num 15:37–16:3

---

15 a. Ps-Philo follows Num 13:1f. in attributing the sending of the spies to God's initiative, but in Deut 1:22f. it is a suggestion of men approved by Moses.

b. That is, it is impossible for these men to fight against the LORD.

c. For the angels as guardians see also Ps-Philo 11:12 and 59:4 as well as Jub 35:17.

d. The expression "laws" (*terminos*) can be traced back to the Heb. *hwqym*, which can mean "limits, boundaries" or "laws, statutes, enactments." See 51:3.

16 a. Moses.

b. Num 16:2 has 250.

c. In Josephus' *Ant* 4.2.2 §14 Korah's rebellion is traced to his jealousy of Moses. The connection in Ps-Philo between the law of the tassels (Num 15:37–41) and the rebellion (Num 16:1–3) is due to the proximity of the two passages.

and to him two sons were born first of all, and the older rose up and killed the   Gen 4:1–16
younger, and the earth quickly swallowed up his blood. But I drove Cain out and
cursed the earth and spoke to the parched land,[d] saying, 'You will swallow up
3 blood no more.'[e] •And now the thoughts of men are very corrupt; behold I
command the earth, and it will swallow up body and soul together. And their   Num 16:30
dwelling place will be in darkness and the place of destruction; and they will not
die but melt away until I remember the world and renew the earth. And then they
will die and not live, and their life will be taken away from the number of all
men.[f] And hell will no longer spit them back, and their destruction will not be
remembered, and their passing will be like that of those tribes of nations of whom
I said, 'I will not remember them,' that is, the camp of the Egyptians and the
race that I destroyed with the water of the flood. And the earth will swallow them
up, and I will do no more.''
4   And though Moses was speaking all these words to the people, Korah and his
men were still defiant. And Korah sent for his seven sons, who had not joined
5 with him in the plot, to be summoned. •But they answered him, saying, ''Just as   Num 26:11
a painter does not produce a work of art unless he has been instructed beforehand,
so we have received the Law of the Most Powerful that teaches us his ways; and
we will not enter them except to walk in them. Our father has not begotten us,
but the Most Powerful has formed us. And now if we walk in his ways, we will
be his sons. But if you are unbelieving, go your own way.'' And they did not
come up to him.
6   And after this the earth was opened before them. And his sons sent to him,
saying, ''If your madness is still upon you, who will help you in the day of your
destruction?'' And he did not heed them. *And the earth opened its mouth and*   Num 16:32
swallowed up them and their households. And four times the foundation of the
earth was shaken so as to swallow up the men as it had been commanded. And
7 after this, Korah and his group cried out until the earth became solid again. •Now
the assembly of the people said to Moses, ''We cannot stay around[g] this place
where Korah and his men were swallowed up.'' And he said to them, ''*Take up*   Num 16:26f.
your *tents* from round about them; *do not be joined in their sins.*'' And so they
did.

The rod of Aaron

1 **17** And then the identity of the priestly family was revealed by the selection of
one tribe. And it was told to Moses, ''*Take for the twelve tribes one rod apiece*   Num 17:2,4f.
and put them in the tent of meeting. And then to whomever my glory shall have
spoken, *the rod of that one will flower and I will take away the murmuring* from
2 my people.'' •And *Moses* did so, and he *deposited the twelve rods. And the rod*   Num 17:7f.
3 *of Aaron sprouted and flowered and yielded seed of almonds.* •Now that which
happened[a] then was like what Israel did while he was in Mesopotamia with Laban   Gen 30:37–39
the Syrian when *he took almond rods and put them at the cisterns of water; and
the flocks came to drink and* were divided among the peeled rods, *and they brought*
4 *forth white and speckled and many-colored kids.* •So the assembly of the people
was like the flock of sheep. And as the flocks brought forth according to the
almond rods, so the priesthood was established through almond rods.

Balaam

1 **18** In that time, Moses killed Sihon and Og, the kings of the Amorites, and he   Num 21
2 handed over all their land to his own people, and they dwelled in it. •Now *Balak*   Num 22:2f.,5

---

d. Lit. "Zion"; this is based on a misunderstanding of the Heb. *ṣywn*, "parched earth." See
Isa 25:5 and 32:2.

e. b.Sanh 37b says that the earth did not open
its mouth from when it swallowed Abel's blood
until it swallowed up Korah.

f. Korah and his group will be annihilated.

g. Lit. "Sinai" (*Syna* or *Sina*), which we emend
to *sinu*, lit. "in the bosom of this place."

17 a. Lit. "was born" (Gk. *egennēthē*), probably
a mistake for *egenēthē*; see also 30:5; 51:6.

was king of Moab and was living opposite them, *and he was very much afraid.
And he sent to Balaam the son of Beor, the interpreter* of dreams*, who lived in
Mesopotamia, and commanded him, saying, "Behold I know that in the reign of
my father Zippor, when the Amorites fought him, you cursed them and they were
handed over before him. *And now come* and *curse this people, because they are   Num 22:6,17
3 too many for us,*[b] *and I will do you great honor."* •And Balaam said, "Behold
this has given pleasure to Balak, but he does not know that the plan of God is
not like the plan of man. Now he does not realize that the spirit that is given to   Num 22:18
us is given for a time. But our ways are not straight unless God wishes it. And   Num 22:8
now *wait here*, and I will see *what the Lord may say to me this night*."
4   *And God said to him*[c] by night, "*Who are the men who* have come *to you?"*   Num 22:9
And Balaam said, "Why, LORD, do you try the human race? They cannot endure
it, because you know well what is to happen in the world, even before you
founded it. And now enlighten your servant if it be right to go forth with them."[d]
5 And he said to him, "Is it not regarding this people that I spoke to Abraham in
a vision, saying, '*Your seed will be like the stars of the heaven*,' when I lifted   Gen 22:17
him above the firmament and showed him the arrangements of all the stars?[e] And
I demanded his son as a holocaust. And he brought him to be placed on the altar,
but I gave him back to his father and, because he did not refuse, his offering was
acceptable before me,[f] and on account of his blood[g] I chose them. And then I
said to the angels who work secretly, 'Did I not say regarding this, "*I will reveal   Gen 18:17
6 everything I am doing to Abraham* •and to Jacob his son, the third one whom I
called[h] firstborn, who, when *he was wrestling in the dust* with the angel who was   Gen 32:24-27
in charge of hymns, *would not let him go* until *he blessed him*." ' And do you
propose *to go forth with them* to curse whom I have chosen? But if you curse   Num 22:12
them, who will be there to bless you?"
7   *And Balaam arose in the morning* and said, "*Be on your* way, *because God*[i]   Num 22:13-15
does not wish me to come with you." And they set out and told Balak what was
said by Balaam. *And Balak again sent* other men to Balaam, saying, "Behold I
know that when you offer holocausts to God, God will be reconciled with men.
And now ask even still more from your LORD and beg with as many holocausts
as he wishes. But if he should be propitiated regarding my evil deeds, you will
8 have your reward and God will receive his offerings." •And Balaam said to them,
"Behold the son of Zippor is looking around[j] and does not recognize that he
dwells among the dead.[k] *And now wait here this night, and I will see what* God   Num 22:19-21,
may say to me." And God said to him, "Go with them, and your way will be a   8
stumbling block, and that Balak will go to ruin." *He rose in the morning and set
9 out with them*. •And his she-ass came by way of the wilderness and *saw an angel   Num 22:27,
and lay down beneath him*.[l] *And he*[m] *opened Balaam's eyes, and he saw the angel   31f.,35
and adored him* on the ground. And the angel said to him, "Hurry and be gone,
because whatever you say will come to pass for him."
10   And he[n] came into the land of Moab and built an altar and *offered* sacrifices.   Num 23:2

---

18 a. The name of the river Pethor in Num 22:5
has been rendered as "interpreter" because of the
root ptr/pšr. See also Josephus' *Ant* 4.6.2 §104.

b. Ps-Philo agrees with the LXX and the Lucianic MSS of Num 22:8 in reading "for us" (Heb.
mmnw) rather than the MT's "for me" (*mmny*).

c. The phrase "to him" agrees with the LXX
of Num 22:9 rather than the MT.

d. Balaam's reply to God here puts him in a
more favorable light than he receives in the OT.

e. In TAb 10, Abraham is given a world tour
in a heavenly chariot.

f. See 32:2–4; 40:2; Josephus' *Ant* 1.13.2–4
§§225–36, and TarJon of Gen 22:1 for similar
presentations of the sacrifice of Isaac.

g. Even though Isaac's blood was not really
shed, it is still seen as having atoning value; see

also b.Yoma 5a and Mekilta d'R. Shimon 4.

h. Lit. "he called" (*vocavit*); but in this context
and in the light of Jub 19:29, where Jacob is called
God's firstborn son, we have emended to "I called"
(*vocavi*).

i. See the LXX of Num 22:13.

j. Var. "foolish" (*insipiens*) rather than *inspi-
ciens*.

k. Korah does not recognize that the idols are
dead.

l. Balaam.

m. The angel, or God as in Num 22:31.

n. Presumably Balaam. See Num 23:2, where
the MT says that Balaam and Balak sacrificed
together while the LXX and Philo have Balak
sacrifice alone. Josephus (*Ant* 4.6.4 §113) and Ps-
Philo have Balaam sacrifice alone.

And when *he saw part of the people, the spirit of God* did not abide *in him.*º *And* he took up his discourse and said, "Behold *Balak brought me* to *the mountain,* saying, 'Come, run into the fire*p* of those men.' What fire the waters will not extinguish, I cannot resist; but the fire that consumes water, who will resist that?" And he said to him, "It is easier to take away the foundations and the topmost part of the earth*q* and to extinguish the light of the sun and to darken the light of the moon than for anyone to uproot the planting of the Most Powerful or to destroy his vine." And he*r* did not know that his consciousness was expanded so as to
11 hasten his own destruction. •"For behold I see the heritage that the Most Powerful has shown me by night. And behold the days will come, and Moab will be amazed at what is happening to it because Balak wished to persuade the Most Powerful with gifts and to buy a decision with money. Should you not have asked about what he sent upon Pharaoh and his land because he wished to reduce them to slavery? Behold an overshadowing*s* and highly desirable vine, and who will be jealous because it does. not wither? But if anyone says to himself that the Most Powerful has labored in vain or has chosen them to no purpose, behold now I see the salvation and liberation that will come upon them. I am restrained in my speech and cannot say what I see with my eyes, because there is little left of the holy spirit that abides in me. For I know that, because I have been persuaded by
12 Balak, I have lessened the time of my life. •And behold my remaining hour. Behold again I see the heritage and the dwelling place*t* of this people. And its light will shine more brilliantly than the splendor of lightning, and its course will be swifter than that of an arrow. And the time will come and Moab will groan, and those serving Chemosh*u* who have plotted these things against them will be made weak. But I will gnash my teeth, because I have been led astray and have transgressed what was said to me by night. And my prophecy will remain public, and my words will live on. And the wise and understanding will remember my words that, when I cursed, I perished, but though I blessed, I was not blessed." On saying these words he grew silent. *And Balak said,* "Your God *has cheated you* of many *gifts* from me."
13 And then Balaam said to him, "Come and let us plan what you should do to them. Pick out the beautiful women who are among us and in Midian, and station them naked and adorned with gold and precious stones before them.*v* And when they see them and lie with them, they will sin against their LORD and fall into
14 your hands; for otherwise you cannot fight against them." •And on saying this, *Balaam* turned away *and returned to his place.* And afterward *the people* were seduced after *the daughters of Moab.* For Balak did everything that Balaam had showed him.

Num 22:41;
23:6f.

Num 24:2

Num 24:10f.

Num 31:16

Num 25

Num 24:25; 25:1

Moses' farewell, prayer, and death

1 **19** And in that time Moses killed the nations and gave half their spoils to the people. And he began declaring to them the words of the Law that God had
2 spoken to them on Horeb. •And he spoke to them, saying,*a* "Behold I am to sleep with my fathers and will go to my people. But I know that you will rise up and forsake the words established for you through me, and God will be angry at

Num 31:27

Deut 31:16–18

---

o. For the view that Balaam prophesied by the spirit of God, see the LXX of Num 23:6 (also Num 24:2).

p. There may be a play on the Heb. words *'wr,* "fire," and *'rh,* "curse."

q. Lit. "their" (*eorum*), for which we read *terre.*

r. Balaam.

s. Or "overshadowed," i.e. protected.

t. Lit. "of the dissolution," which probably reflects a confusion between the meanings of Gk. *katalysis.*

u. The MSS have *Cham,* which must be emended to *Chamos* in the light of Num 21:29.

v. Josephus (*Ant* 4.6.6 §129) says, "Take of your daughters those who are comeliest and most capable of constraining and conquering the chastity of their beholders by reason of their beauty, deck out their charms to add to their comeliness . . ."

19 a. For other testaments of Moses, see Deut 31–34, Jub 1, AsMos, and Josephus' *Ant* 4.7.44–48 §§302–26.

you and abandon you and depart from your land. And he will bring upon you those who hate you, and they will rule over you, but not forever, because he will
3 remember the covenant that he established with your fathers. •But then you and your sons and all your generations will rise up after you and lament the day of my death and say in their heart, 'Who will give us another[b] shepherd like Moses or such a judge for the sons of Israel to pray always for our sins and to be heard
4 for our iniquities?'[c] •Now *I call to witness against you today heaven and earth*   Deut 4:26; 32:1 (for heaven will hear this, and earth will know it with its ears) that God has revealed the end of the world so that he might establish his statutes[d] with you and kindle among you an eternal light.[e] And you will remember, you wicked ones; for when I spoke to you, you answered saying, '*All that God has said to us, we*   Deut 5:27 *will do and hear.* But if we transgress or grow corrupt in our ways, you will
5 recall this as a witness against us, and he will cut us off.' •But know that you   Ps 105; 78:25; have eaten the bread of angels for forty years. And now behold I bless your tribes   Deut 33 before my end comes. But you, acknowledge my toil that I have toiled for you from the time you went up from the land of Egypt.''
6   On his saying these words, *God spoke to* him a third time, saying, "*Behold*   Deut 31:16 *you* are going forth *to sleep with your fathers. But this people will rise up and* not seek[f] me, and they will forget my Law, by which I have enlightened them,
7 and I will abandon their seed for a time. •Now I will show you the land before   Deut 32:52; 34:4 you die, but *you will not enter it* in this age lest you see the graven images with which this people will start to be deceived and led off the path.[g] I will show you the place[h] where they will serve me for 740 years. And after this it will be turned over into the hands of their enemies, and they will destroy it, and foreigners will encircle it. And it will be on that day as it was on the day I smashed the tablets   Ex 32:19; Zech of the covenant that I drew up for you on Horeb; and when they sinned, what   8:19 was written on them flew away. Now that day was the seventeenth day of the fourth month.''[i]
8   And Moses ascended Mount *Abarim*[j] as God had commanded him, and he   Deut 32:49; prayed saying, "Behold I have completed my lifetime; I have completed 120   Num 27:12 years. And now I ask, May your mercy with your people and your pity with your heritage, LORD, be established; and may your long-suffering in your place[k] be
9 upon the chosen race because you have loved them before all others. •And you   Ex 3:1–6 know that *I was a shepherd. And* when I fed *the flock* in *the wilderness, I brought* them *to your mountain Horeb and* then *I* first *saw* your *angel on fire from the bush.* But *you called* me *from the bush, and I was afraid and turned* my *face.* And you sent me to them and you freed them from Egypt, but their enemies you drowned in the water. And you gave them the Law and statutes in which they might live and enter as sons of men. *For who is the man who has not sinned*   1Kgs 8:46 *against you?* And unless your patience abides, how would your heritage be established, if you were not merciful to them? Or who will yet be born without sin? Now you will correct them for a time, but not in anger.''
10   *Then the Lord showed him the land* and all that is in it *and said,* "*This is the*   Deut 34:1,4 *land that* I will give to my people.'' And he showed him the place from which the clouds draw up water to water the whole earth, and the place from which the

---

b. Lit. "one." There may have been an error at the level of Heb., where *'hd* (one) was read as *'hr* (another).

c. See AsMos 11:11, 17; 12:3, for a similar description of Moses. For a similar description of Jeremiah see 2Mac 15:14 and 2Bar 2:2.

d. Lit. "heights" (*superexcelsa*) as in 9:8.

e. For the Law as lamp see 2Bar 17:4 and 59:2.

f. Var. "and seek"; but the sense demands a negative.

g. Ps-Philo is unique in stating that the reason why Moses was not allowed to enter the promised land was to keep him from seeing the idols by

which the Israelites would be led astray.

h. Presumably, the Temple in Jerusalem.

i. m.Ta'an 4:6 has been taken as evidence that the second Temple was destroyed on the 17th of Tammuz, A.D. 70, but this is contrary to the witness of Josephus and involves many problems. It cannot be taken as proof that Ps-Philo was composed after A.D. 70.

j. The variant "Horeb" is certainly wrong in the light of Deut 32:49. Perhaps "Nebo" is to be read.

k. Heaven, or possibly the Temple or Israel.

river takes its water, and *the land of Egypt,*[1] and the place in the firmament from which only the holy land[m] drinks. And he showed him the place from which the manna rained upon the people, even unto the paths of paradise. And he showed him the measurements of the sanctuary and the number of sacrifices and the signs by which they are to interpret the heaven. And he said, ''These are what are
11 prohibited for the human race because they have sinned against me.[n] •And now your staff with which these signs were performed will be a witness between me and my people. And when they sin, I will be angry with them but I will recall your staff and spare them in accord with my mercy. And your staff will be before me as a reminder all the days, and it will be like the bow with which I established my covenant with Noah when he went forth from the ark, saying, *'I will place* Gen 9:13,15 *my bow in the cloud, and it will be for a sign between me and* men that never
12 *again will the flood water cover all the earth.'* •Now I will take you from here and glorify you with your fathers, and I will give you rest in your slumber and bury you in peace. And all the angels will mourn over you, and the heavenly hosts will be saddened. But neither angel[o] *nor man* will *know* your *tomb* in which Deut 34:6 you are to be buried until I visit the world. And I will raise up you and your fathers from the land of Egypt[p] in which you sleep and you will come together
13 and dwell in the immortal dwelling place that is not subject to time. •But this heaven[q] will be before me like a fleeting cloud and passing like yesterday. And when the time draws near to visit the world, I will command the years and order the times and they will be shortened,[r] and the stars will hasten and the light of the sun will hurry to fall and the light of the moon will not remain; for I will hurry to raise up you who are sleeping in order that all who can live may dwell in the place of sanctification I showed you.''
14 And Moses said, ''If I can make another request of you, LORD; according to your great mercy be not angry with me, but show me what amount of time has
15 passed and how much remains.'' •And he said to him, ''There is honey, the topmost peak,[s] the fullness of a moment, and the drop of a cup; and time has fulfilled all things. For four and a half[t] have passed, and two and a half remain.''
16 And when Moses heard this, he was filled with understanding and his appearance Deut 34:5f. became glorious; *and he died* in glory *according to the word of the Lord, and he buried him* as he had promised him. And the angels mourned at his death, and the lightnings and the torches and the arrows went all together before him. And in that day the hymn of the heavenly hosts was not sung because of the passing of Moses, nor was there such a day from the one on which the LORD made man upon the earth, nor shall there be such forever, that the hymn of the angels should stop on account of men; because he loved him very much. *And he buried him* with his own hands on a high place and in the light of all the world.[u]

Joshua and the division of the land

1 **20** And in that time God established his covenant with Joshua the son of Nun, Deut 31:23 who was left from the men who had spied out the land; for the lot went forth

I. The Samaritan Pentateuch of Deut 34:1 also mentions the land of Egypt.

m. For the expression ''the holy land'' see Zech 2:12; 2Bar 63:10; 4Ezra 13:48; 2Mac 1:7.

n. Lit. ''themselves'' (*sibi*); but since God is the speaker, ''me'' seems better. Confusion between Heb. *ly* (against me) and *lw* (against them, in a collective sense) is likely.

o. According to Philo's *Vita Mosis* 2:291, Moses was buried by immortal powers (i.e. angels).

p. The reference is to those Israelites who died in the land of Egypt, outside the boundaries of the holy land.

q. Perhaps read ''age'' (*seculum*) rather than ''heaven'' (*celum*).

r. For God's shortening of the days on account of the elect, see 2Bar 20:1; 54:1; 83:1 as well as Mk 13:20 (Mt 24:22).

s. The Lat. *Istic mel, apex magnus* might be emended to *Stigma et apex manus* (''An instant, the topmost part of a hand'') on the basis of 4Ezra 4:48–50 and 6:9f.

t. What units are meant or what system of calculation is implied is not clear. See 28:8.

u. That Moses' death took place in public and that God buried him is also found in Josephus' *Ant* 4.8.48 §326 and AsMos 1:15. There may be conscious opposition to the view that Moses did not really die.

upon them that they should not see the land because they had spoken badly about
2 it, and on account of this that generation died. •Then God said to Joshua the son   Josh 1:1–3
of Nun, "Why do you mourn and why do you hope in vain that Moses yet lives?
And now you wait to no purpose, because Moses is dead. Take his garments of
wisdom and clothe yourself, and with his belt of knowledge gird your loins, and
you will be changed and become another man. Did I not speak on your behalf to   1Sam 10:6
Moses my servant, saying, 'This one will lead my people after you, and into his   Deut 3:28
hand I will deliver the kings of the Amorites'?''
3   And Joshua took the garments of wisdom and clothed himself and girded his
loins with the belt of understanding. And when he clothed himself with it, his
mind was afire and his spirit was moved, and he said to the people, "Behold the   Num 14:35
first generation has died in the wilderness because they have spoken against their
God. And behold now, all you leaders, know today that if you proceed in the
4 ways of your God, your paths will be made straight. •But if you do not heed his
voice and you become like your fathers, your affairs will be spoiled and you
yourselves will be crushed and your name will perish from the earth. And where
will the words be that God spoke to your fathers? For even if the gentiles say,
'Perhaps God has failed, because he has not freed his people'—nevertheless they
will recognize that he has not chosen for himself other peoples and done great
wonders with them, then they will understand that the Most Powerful does not
respect persons; but because you sin through pride, so he took away his power
from you and subdued you. And now rise up and set your heart to walk in the
5 ways of your LORD, and he will guide you." •And the people said to him,   Num 11:26
"Behold we know today what Eldad and Modad prophesied in the days of Moses,
saying, 'After Moses goes to rest, the leadership of Moses will be given over to
Joshua the son of Nun.' And Moses was not jealous but rejoiced when he heard
them. And from then on all the people believed that you would exercise leadership
over them *and divide up the land* among them in peace. And now even if there   Josh 1:6,9
is conflict,ᵃ *be strong and act manfully*, because you alone are ruler in Israel.''
6   On hearing these words *Joshua* decided to send *spies* into Jericho. And he   Josh 2:1
summoned Kenaz and Seeniamias,ᵇ his brother, the two sons of Caleb, and he
said to them, "I and your father were sent by Moses in the wilderness, and we   Josh 14:6–8
went up with ten other men. And they came back and spoke badly about the land
and discouraged the heart of the people, and they and the heart of the people
with them were discouraged. *But I* and your father *alone fulfilled* the word of the
Lord, and behold we are alive today. And now I will send you to spy out the
7 land of Jericho. Imitate your father, and you also will live." •And they went up
and spied out the city. And when they brought back word, the people went up   Josh 6:24
and attacked *the city and burned it with fire*.
8   And after Moses died, *the manna stopped* descending upon *the sons of Israel*,   Josh 5:12
and then they began *to eat from the fruits of the land*. And these are the three
things that God gave to his people on account of three persons; that is, the well
of the water of Marah for Miriam and the pillar of cloud for Aaron and the manna
for Moses. And when these came to their end, these three things were taken away
from them.
9   Now the people and Joshua fought against the Amorites. And they prevailed in
battle against their enemies all the days of Joshua, and thirty-nineᶜ kings who   Josh 12:7–24
dwelt in the land were destroyed. And Joshua gave the land to the people by lot,   Josh 13–23
10 to each tribe according to the lots, as it had been commanded him. •Then Caleb   Josh 14:6,8f.,13
approached him and said, "*You know* that the two of us were sent by lot from
Moses to go with the spies, and because we fulfilled the word of the LORD, behold
we are alive today. And now, if it is acceptable in your eyes, let there be given

---

20 a. Var. "even if you will waver." On Joshua's
wavering see AsMos 11:9–19; 12:3.
   b. Perhaps taken over from Mesha the son of
Caleb or Shema the great-grandson of Caleb; see

1Chr 2:42f.
   c. Var. "thirty-eight." The MT of Josh 12:24
has thirty-one, while the LXX has twenty-nine.

by lot to Kenaz my son the territory of the three towers."[d] *And Joshua blessed him,* and so he did.

The prayer of Joshua and the cult at Gilgal

1 **21** And when *Joshua had grown old and was advanced in days, God said to him, "Behold you are old and advanced in days; and there is very much land,* and there is no one *to divide it up by lot.* And after your departure this people will be intermingled with those inhabiting the land, and *they will be seduced after strange gods,* and I will abandon them as I testified in my speech to Moses. But you bear witness to them before you die." Josh 13:1(23:1)

Deut 31.16

2 And Joshua said, "You above all know, LORD, what moves the heart of the sea before it rages, and you have searched out the constellations and numbered the stars and regulated the rain; you know the number[a] of all generations before they are born. And now, LORD, give to your people a wise heart and a prudent mind; and when you will give those orders to your heritage, they will not sin 3 against you and you will not be angry at them. •Are not these the words that I spoke before you, LORD, when *Achan stole from* the things under the ban and the people were delivered up before you, and I prayed before you and said, 'Would it not have been better for us, LORD, if we had died in the Red Sea, where you drowned our enemies, or if we had died in the wilderness like our fathers, than *to be delivered into the hands of the Amorites so as to be destroyed* forever?' 4 And the word concerns us: 'No evil will befall us.' For even if our goal be taken away in death, you who are before all ages and after all ages still live, even if man, who cannot place one generation before another, says, 'God has destroyed the people whom he has chosen for himself.' And behold we will be in Sheol but you will make your word alive. And now let the fullness of your mercy sustain your people and choose for your heritage a man so that he and his offspring will 5 rule your people. •Did not our father Jacob speak about him, saying, '*A ruler will not be lacking from Judah, nor a leader from his loins'?* And now confirm those words spoken beforehand so that the nations of the earth and the tribes of the 6 world may learn that you are eternal." •And he added, saying, "LORD, behold the days will come when the house of Israel will be like a brooding dove who on placing her young in a nest does not leave or forget her place. So also these, having repented of their deeds, will hope[b] for the salvation that is to be born from them."[c]

1Kgs 3:9

Josh 7:1

Josh 7:7

Gen 49:10

7 And Joshua went down to Gilgal *and built an altar with very large stones and did not lift an iron tool to them as Moses had commanded.* And he set up large stones *on Mount Ebal*[d] and whitened them and *wrote on* them very plainly the words of the *Law.* And he gathered all the people together and *read* out loud 8 before them *all the words of the Law.* •And he came down with them and *offered peace offerings on* the altar; and all sang many praises. And they took the ark of the covenant of the LORD out of the tent of meeting with timbrels and dances and 9 harps and lyres and lutes and every good-sounding instrument. •And the priests and Levites were going before the ark and rejoicing in song, and they put the ark in front of the altar. *And they offered* very many *peace offerings upon it,* and all the house of Israel sang together in a loud voice saying, "Behold our LORD has fulfilled what he said to our fathers: '*To your seed I will give the land* in which you may dwell, *a land flowing with milk and honey.'* And behold he led us into the land of our enemies and delivered them broken in spirit before us, and he is

Josh 8:30–35

Josh 8:31

Ps 150:3–5

Josh 8:31

Deut 11:9

---

d. Var. "of the tribe of towers," which is also obscure. There may be some allusion to Hebron and the three sons of Anak (Judg 1:20), where the Heb. *gdl* (great one) and *mgdl* (tower) have been confused.

21 a. Lit. "mind" (*sensum*), which we have read

as *censum.*

b. Lit. "capture by attack" (*expugnabunt*), which we have emended to *expectabunt.*

c. The point seems to be that Israel opposes the leaders given to it by God.

d. Josh 8:33 mentions both Mount Gerizim and Mount Ebal, but Ps-Philo mentions only the latter.

the God who sent word to our fathers in the secret dwelling places of souls, saying, 'Behold the LORD has done everything that he has said to us.' And truly now we know that God has established every word of his Law that he spoke to us on Horeb. And if our heart keeps to his ways, it will be good for us and for
10 our sons after us." •And Joshua blessed them and said, "The LORD grant that your heart may abide in him all the days and you do not depart from his name. May the covenant of the LORD remain with you and not be broken, but may there be built among you a dwelling place for God, as he said when he sent you into his inheritance with joy and gladness."

The altar across the Jordan. Gilgal and Shiloh

1 **22** And after these events when *Joshua* and all Israel *heard* that *the sons of*   Josh 22:10-12
Reuben and the sons of Gad and the half tribe of Manasseh who dwelt *around the Jordan had built an altar there*[a] and were offering sacrifices[b] on it and had made priests for the sanctuary, *all the people were very much disturbed*[c] and came
2 to them to *Shiloh.*[d] •And Joshua and all the elders said to them, "*What are these*   Josh 22:15-20
deeds that are done among you, when we have not even yet settled in our land? Are not these the words that Moses spoke to you in the wilderness, saying, 'Beware that on entering your land you grow corrupt in your own deeds and destroy all this people'? And now why have our enemies abounded unless it is because you have corrupted your ways and made all this trouble? And so those gathered against us will crush us."
3 *And the sons of Reuben and the sons of Gad and the half tribe of Manasseh*   Josh 22:21,24f.
said to Joshua and to all the people of Israel, "Behold now God has counted out[e] the fruit of the womb of men and set up a light that they may see what is in darkness, because *he himself knows what are in the hidden places* of the abyss *and the light abides with him.* Now the LORD God of our fathers knows that none   Dan 2:22
of us nor we ourselves have done this act out of wickedness but rather for our posterity's sake so that their heart may not be separated from the LORD our God and that they may not say to us, 'Behold our brothers who are across the Jordan have an altar and offer sacrifice on it, but we in this place do not have an altar and are far from the LORD our God; for our God is so far from our ways that we
4 may not serve him.' •And on saying these words, we said among ourselves, 'Let us make an altar for ourselves so that there may be zeal among us for seeking the LORD.' For some of us who stand here did this. And knowing that we are your brothers and that we stand guiltless before you, do therefore whatever is pleasing in the eyes of the LORD."
5 And Joshua said, "Is not the LORD the King more powerful than a thousand sacrifices? And why have you not taught your sons the words of the LORD that you heard from us? For if your sons had been meditating upon the Law of the LORD, their mind would not have been led astray after an altar made by hand. Or do you not know that[f] when the people were left alone for a while in the wilderness, when Moses went up to receive the tablets, their mind was led astray and they made idols for themselves. And if the mercy of the God of our fathers had not been their guardian, all their assemblies would have been derided and all the sins
6 of the people made public because of your foolishness. •And so now, go and dig up the altars that you have built for yourselves, and teach your sons the Law and have them *meditate on it day and night,* so that through all the days of their life   Josh 1:8

---

22 a. Lit. "for themselves"; but Josh 22:10 *šm* (there) suggests that *ibi* (there) should be read for *sibi* here.

b. The statement that they did offer sacrifices contradicts Josh 22:23, 26, 28, 29.

c. The Lat. *conturbati sunt* might also be derived from *turbo* and translated "were gathered together."

d. According to Josh 22:13, 15, the meeting takes place in the land of Gilead.

e. Lit. "cut off" (*amputavit*), which we have emended to *computavit*.

f. Lit. "when" (*quando*); but "that" (*quoniam*) seems necessary. Perhaps Gk. *hote*, "when," was misread for *hoti*, "because."

the LORD may be for them a witness and a judge. And God will be a witness and a judge between me and you and between my heart and your heart. For if you have done this act out of cunning because you wished to destroy your brothers, it will be avenged upon you; but if you have done it out of ignorance as you say because of your sons, God will be merciful to you." And all the people answered, "Amen, amen."

7 And Joshua and all the people of Israel offered a thousand rams on their behalf for their pardon, and they prayed for them, and he sent them away in peace. They went and destroyed the altar, and they fasted and lamented, they and their sons, and they prayed saying, "God of our fathers and you who know beforehand the heart of all men, you know that our ways were not undertaken out of wickedness before you; we have not strayed from your ways but all of us serve you, for we are the works of your hands. Now have mercy on your covenant with the sons of your servants."

8 And after this Joshua went up to Gilgal and took up the tent of meeting of the LORD and the ark of the covenant and all its vessels, and he took themᵍ up to Shiloh and set up the Urim and Thummim there. And then Eleazar the priest was   Ex 28:30 ministering at the altar. All who came from the people came together and sought the LORD; he taught them with the Urim, for with this it was revealed to them. Now at the new altar that was in Gilgal Joshua had decreed even unto this dayʰ

9 what holocausts would be offered every year by the sons of Israel. •For until the house of the LORD was built in Jerusalemⁱ and sacrifice offered on the new altar, the people were not prohibited from offering sacrifice there, because the Thummim and Urim revealed all things in Shiloh. And until the ark was placed in the sanctuary of the LORD by Solomon, they were offering sacrifice there until that day. Now Eleazar the son of Aaron the priest was serving in Shiloh.

The covenant of Joshua

1 **23** Now Joshua the son of Nun, being a mighty man, organized the people and   Josh 19:51 divided up the land among them. And while there were still enemies of Israel upon the land, the days of Joshua drew near for him to die. And he sent and *summoned all Israel* in all their land, along with women and children, and he said   Josh 23:2 to them, "Gather before the ark of the covenantᵃ of the LORD in Shiloh,ᵇ and I

2 will establish a covenant with you before I die." •And on the sixteenth day of the third monthᶜ *all the people* along with women and children *gathered together*   Josh 24:1f. *before the Lord in Shiloh*, and *Joshua said* to them, "*Hear, O Israel*. Behold I   Deut 6:4 am establishing with you a covenant of this Law that the LORD established for your fathers on Horeb. *And so wait here this night* and see *what God will say to*   Num 22:19

3 *me* on your behalf." •And while the people were waiting that night, the LORD appeared to Joshua in a dream vision and said to him, "According to these words I will speak to this people."

4 And Joshua rose up in the morning and gathered all the people and said to   Josh 24:2 them, "The LORD says this: 'There was one rock from which I quarried out your   Isa 51:1f. father. And the cutting of that rock bore two men whose names are Abraham and Nahor, and out of the chiseling of that place were born two women whose names are Sarah and Melcha, *and they lived* together *across the river*. And Abraham   Josh 24:2

5 took Sarah as a wife, and Nahor took Melcha. •And when all those inhabiting the   Gen 11:29 land were being led astray after their own devices, Abraham believed in me and

---

g. Lit. "it" (*eam*); but the sense requires a plural (*ea*).

h. The phrase "even unto this day" implies that when the author wrote, sacrifices were still being offered in the Temple (i.e. before A.D. 70).

i. This is the only explicit mention of Jerusalem in all of Ps-Philo.

23 a. Lit. "the ark and the covenant" (*arce et testamenti*); originally "the ark of the covenant" (*arce testamenti*).

b. Ps-Philo along with the LXX of Josh 24:1 place the covenant renewal ceremony at Shiloh, while the MT has it at Shechem.

c. Jub 1:1; 15:1; 44:1–4 say that Pentecost must be observed on the fifteenth day of the third month.

was not led astray with them. And I rescued him from the flame *and took* him   Josh 24:3
and brought him over all the land of Canaan and said to him in a vision, *"To*   Gen 12:7
your seed I will give this land." And that man said to me, "Behold now you   Gen 15:2–5
have given me a wife, and she is sterile. And how will I have offspring from that
6 rock of mine that is closed up?" •*And* I said *to him, "Bring me a three-year-old*   Gen 15:9f.
calf and a three-year-old she-goat and a three-year-old ram, a turtledove, and a
dove." And *he brought them* as I commanded him. Now I sent upon him *a deep*   Gen 15:12
sleep and encompassed him with *fear* and set before him the place of fire where
the deeds of those doing wickedness against me will be expiated, and I showed
him *the torches of fire* by which the just who have believed in me will be   Gen 15:17
7 enlightened.[d] •And I said to him, "These will be a witness between me and you,
that I will give you offspring from one who is closed up. And I will make you
like the dove, because you have taken for me a city that your sons will begin to
build before me. Now the turtledove I liken to the prophets who will be born from
you; and the ram I liken to the wise men who will be born from you, who will
enlighten your sons; but I will liken the calf to the multitude of peoples, which
are made many through you; the she-goat I liken to the women whose wombs I
will open and they will give birth. And these prophecies and this night will be a
8 witness between us, that I will not go against my words." •*And I gave him Isaac*   Josh 24:3
and formed him in the womb of her who gave birth to him and commanded her
to restore him quickly and to give him back to me in the seventh month. And
therefore every woman who gives birth in the seventh month,[e] her son will live,
9 because upon him I have brought my glory and revealed the new age. •*And I gave*   Josh 24:4f
to Isaac Jacob and Esau. And I gave to Esau the land of Seir as an inheritance,
but Jacob and his sons went down into Egypt. And the Egyptians humbled[f] your
fathers, as you know; but I remembered your fathers and *sent Moses* my friend
10 and freed them from there, but their enemies I struck down. •And I brought them   Ex 14:8
out *with a high hand* and led them through the Red Sea and set a cloud beneath
their feet and brought them through the deep. And I brought them to the foot of
Mount Sinai, and I *bowed the heaven and came down* and congealed the flame of   Ps 18:9
fire and stopped up the channels of the abyss and impeded the course of the stars
and muffled the sounds of thunder and quenched the fullness of the wind and
rebuked the many clouds and stayed their movements and interrupted the storm
of the heavenly hosts so as not to break my covenant. For all things were set in
motion when I came down, and everything was brought to life when I arrived.
And I did not let my people be scattered, but I gave them my Law and enlightened
them in order that by doing these things they would live and have many years
11 and not die. •And I brought you into this land and gave you *vineyards. Cities that*   Josh 24:13
you did not build you inhabit. And I fulfilled my covenant that I promised your
12 fathers. •And now, if you listen to your fathers, I will set my heart among you
forever and overshadow you, and your enemies will fight against you no more.
And your land will be renowned over all the earth, and your seed special among
all the peoples, who will say, "Behold a faithful people! Because they believed
in the LORD, therefore the LORD freed them and planted them." And so I will
plant you like a desirable vine and tend you like a lovable flock; and I will
command the rain and the dew, and they will be abundant for you during your
13 lifetime. •But also at the end the lot of each one of you will be life eternal,
for you and your seed, and I will take your souls and store them in peace until
the time allotted the world be complete. And I will restore you to your fathers   Mal 3:24(4:6)
and your fathers to you, and they will know through you that I have not chosen
14 you in vain.' These are the words that the LORD spoke to me this night." •And
all the people answered and said, *"The Lord is our God,* and him alone *we will*   Josh 24:24,17f.

---

d. Cf. Abraham's vision of the judgment process
in TAb 11–14.

e. According to b.RH 11a, Isaac was born in
the seventh month.

f. Ps-Philo agrees with the MT, Lucian, Vulgate,
and Peshitta in having "And I gave" at the

beginning of Josh 24:24; with the LXX and Lucian
in "and the Egyptians humbled"; and with the
MT, Lucian, Vulgate, and Peshitta in mentioning
Moses. The only texts having all three features are
Ps-Philo and Lucian.

serve." And all the people had a great feast that day and a renewal ceremony for twenty-eight days.

The farewell and death of Joshua

1 **24** And after those days Joshua the son of Nun again gathered all the people and said to them, "Behold now the LORD has testified among you. *Today I have called* Deut 4:26 *to witness against you heaven and earth, for* if you continue to serve the LORD, you will be a special people to him; *but if you are not willing to serve him* and Josh 24:15 you wish to obey *the gods of the Amorites in whose land you dwell,* say this today before the LORD and go forth. *But I and my household will serve the Lord.*"
2 And all the people raised their voice and wept and said, "Perhaps God has accounted us worthy; it is better for us to die in fear of him than to be blotted out
3 from the earth." •And Joshua the son of Nun blessed the people and kissed them and said to them, "May your words win mercy before our LORD, and may he send his angel and guard you. Be mindful of me after my death and of Moses the friend of the LORD, and let not the words of the covenant that he established with you depart from you all the days." *And he dismissed them, and they went away,*[a] Josh 24:28
4 *each man to his own inheritance.* •Now Joshua laid himself on his bed and sent and summoned the son of Eleazar the priest and said to him, "Behold now I see with my own eyes the transgression of this people in which they are to stray; but you strengthen yourself while you are still with them." And he kissed him and his father and his sons, and he blessed him and said, "May the LORD God of
5 your fathers guide your ways and those of this people." •And when he ceased speaking to them, *he drew up his feet into the bed* and slept with his fathers; and Gen 49:33
6 his sons placed their hands over his eyes. •And then all Israel gathered together Gen 46:4 to bury him. And they made a great lamentation for him, and they said this in their lamentation:

> "Lament over the wing of this swift eagle
> because he has flown away from us,
> and lament over the might of the lion's cub
> because he has been hidden from us.

And who will go and tell the just Moses that we have had a leader like him for forty years?" And they ended their lamentation and *buried him* with their own Josh 24:30,28 hands *at Mount Ephraim,* and they returned each to his own tent.

The election of Kenaz and the sinners' confession

1 **25** *And after the death of Joshua* the land of Israel was peaceful. But the Judg 1:1 Philistines were seeking to fight with the sons of Israel. And they *inquired of the Lord and said, "Should we go up and fight against* the Philistines?"[a] And God said to them, "If you go up with a pure heart, fight; but if your heart is defiled, you should not go up." And they inquired again, "How will we know if the heart of all the people is the same?" And God said to them, "Cast lots[b] among your tribes, and every tribe that comes out in the lot will be set aside for another lot,
2 and then you will know whose heart is pure and whose may be defiled." •And the people said, "First let us appoint a leader among us, and then we will cast the lot." And the angel of the LORD said to them, "Appoint one." And the people said, "Whom will we appoint who is worthy, LORD?" And the angel of the LORD said to them, "Cast the lot upon the tribe of Caleb; and whoever will be revealed

---

24 a. The expression "and they went away" is found in the LXX of Josh 24:28 but not in the MT.

25 a. According to Judg 1:1, the Canaanites.

b. The lot is a device to ascertain knowledge by occult means. In the OT most of the words used with "lot" suggest that it was thrown or cast. See also 49:1.

in that lot, he will rule over you." And they cast the lot upon the tribe of Caleb, and the lot came out upon Kenaz,[c] and they made him ruler in Israel.

Josh 19:1

3   And Kenaz said to the people, "Bring to me your tribes and hear the word of the LORD." And the people were gathered, and Kenaz said to them, "You know what Moses the friend of the LORD commanded you, not to *transgress* the Law *to the right or to the left*. And also Joshua, who was ruler after him, commanded you the same. And now behold we have heard from the mouth of the LORD that your heart is defiled, and the LORD has ordered us to cast lots upon your tribes in order that we may know whose heart has turned away from the LORD our God. Will not the fury of his wrath be brought upon the people? Now I promise you today that, even if someone from my own household comes out in the lot of sin, he will not be saved but will be burned in the fire." And the people said, "You

Josh 1:7; Deut 28:14

4   have proposed a good plan to carry out." •And he brought the tribes before him, and there were found from the tribe of Judah 345 men, but from the tribe of Reuben 560, and from the tribe of Simeon 775, and from the tribe of Levi 150, and from the tribe of Issachar 665, from the tribe of Zebulun 545,[d] and from the tribe of Gad 380, and from the tribe of Asher 665, and from the tribe of Manasseh 480, and from the tribe of Ephraim 448, and from the tribe of Benjamin 267. And the total number of those who were found in the lot of sin was 6,110. And Kenaz led them all away and shut them up in prison until it should be known

5   what should be done about them. •And Kenaz said, "Did not Moses the friend of the LORD speak about these people, saying, '*Lest[e] there be among you a root bearing poison and bitterness*'? Now blessed be the LORD, who has revealed all the schemes of these men and did not let them corrupt the people with their wicked deeds. Therefore bring the Urim and Thummim here, and summon Eleazar

Deut 29:17(18)

6   the priest, and let us inquire of the LORD through him." •And then Kenaz and Eleazar and all the elders and all the assembly prayed together saying, "LORD God of our fathers, reveal to your servants the truth, for we have found those who do not believe the wonders that you did for our fathers from the time you brought them out of the land of Egypt until this day." And the LORD answered and said, "First question those who have been found such, and let them confess their deeds that they have done with cunning, and afterward they will be burned in the fire."

7   And Kenaz brought them out and said to them, "Behold now you know how Achan[f] confessed when he came out in the lot and how he declared everything he had done. And now declare to us your wicked deeds and schemes. And who knows that if you tell the truth to us, even if you die now, nevertheless God will

8   have mercy on you when he will resurrect the dead?" •And one of them, Elas by name, said, "Will not death now come upon us so that we might die in the fire? But I tell you, sir, the schemes that we have done so wickedly are not all alike. Now if you wish to seek out the plain truth, examine the men of each tribe individually; and so every bystander will know the differences among their sins."

9   And Kenaz examined those who were from his own tribe, and they said to him, "We desired to copy and make the calf that they made in the wilderness." And after this he examined the men of the tribe of Reuben, and they said, "We desired to sacrifice to the gods of those who inhabit the land."[g] And he examined the men from the tribe of Levi, and they said, "We desired to test the tent of meeting, whether or not it is holy." And he asked the group from the tribe of Issachar, and they said, "We desired to make inquiry through the demons of the idols, whether or not they would reveal things plainly." And he examined the men of the tribe of Zebulun, and they said, "We desired to eat the flesh of our own

---

c. Kenaz is mentioned in Judg 3:9, 11, as Othniel's father. There as elsewhere in the Jewish tradition (except in Josephus' *Ant* 5.3.3 §§182–84) he is merely a name.

d. The tribes of Dan and Naphtali have been omitted in this list; cf. 10:3; 25:9.

e. Lit. "There is a strong . . ." (*Fortis est*); but "Lest there be" (*Ne forte sit*) corresponds better to Deut 29:17(18).

f. Most MSS have Achiar or the like; see 21:3.

g. The tribe of Simeon has been omitted.

children and to know whether or not God has care for these." And he examined
the group from the tribe of Dan, and they said, "The Amorites have taught us
what they make, so we might teach our children, and behold these things are
hidden beneath Abraham's mountain[h] and stored beneath a heap of earth. Therefore
send, and you will find them." And Kenaz sent and found them. And he examined
the group from the tribe of Naphtali, and they said, "We desired to make what
the Amorites make,[i] and behold they are hidden beneath the tent of Elas, who
told you to examine us. Therefore send, and you will find them." And Kenaz
10 sent and found them. •And afterward he examined those who were left over from
the tribe of Gad, and they said, "We have committed adultery with each other's
wives." And then he examined the men of the tribe of Asher, who said, "We
have found the seven golden idols whom the Amorites[j] call the sacred nymphs,
and we took them along with the precious stones set upon them and hid them.
And behold now they are stored beneath the summit of Mount Shechem.[k] Therefore
send, and you will find them." And Kenaz sent men, and they removed them
11 from there. •These are the nymphs that, when called upon, showed the Amorites
what to do every hour. For these are what seven sinful men devised after the
flood; their names are these: Canaan, Futh, Selath, Nimrod, Elath, Desuath.[l] Nor
will there ever be anything like this in the world graven by the hand of a craftsman
or adorned with painting. Now they were set up with spikes and fixed for the
worship of idols. Those precious stones, among which were crystal and prase,[m]
were brought from the land of Havilah; and they had a pierced style. And one of   _{Gen 2:11f.}
them was cut on the top, and another like spotted chrysoprase shone in its cutting
12 as if it revealed the water of the deep lying beneath it. •And these are the precious
stones that the Amorites had in their sanctuaries, the value of which cannot be
estimated; because for those entering by night the light of a lamp was not necessary,
so brightly did the natural light of the stones shine forth. But among these that
one cut in the pierced style and cleansed with bristles gave off more light. For
even if one of the Amorites was blind, he would go and put his eyes on it and
recover sight. These Kenaz found, and he stored them in hiding until he might
13 know what to do about them. •And after this he examined the group from the
tribe of Manasseh, and they said, "We merely profaned the sabbaths of the
LORD." And he examined the group from the tribe of Ephraim, who said, "We
desired to make our sons and daughters pass through the fire, to know if what
had been said would be proved by direct evidence." And he asked the group from
the tribe of Benjamin, and they said, "We desired in this time to investigate the
book of the Law, whether God had really written what was in it or Moses had
taught these things by himself."

The punishment of the sinners. The twelve stones

1 **26** And when Kenaz had taken in all these words and written them in a book
and had read them before the LORD, God said to him, "Take the men and what
was found with them and all their possessions, and put them in the bed of the
river Fison[a] and burn them with fire, so that my anger may cease from them."
2 And Kenaz said, "Should we burn those precious stones in the fire or consecrate
them to you, because we do not have any like those?" And God said to him, "If

---

h. Abraham's mountain would be Mount Moriah
(in Jerusalem), or perhaps we should emend to
monte Abarim.
    i. Since in Heb. *'bd* can mean both "make"
and "worship," Ps-Philo may have meant "to
worship what the Amorites worship."
    j. For the Amorites as wicked idolators, see
2Bar 60:1.
    k. For the burial of images under an oak at
Shechem, see Gen 35:4. For the hiding of sacred
vessels, see 2Bar 6:7; 2Mac 2:4–8; and Josephus'

Ant 18.4.1 §85.
    l. There are only six names. Desuath may be a
corruption of Dedan, Suah (cf. Gen 10:7), or
perhaps Ham should be inserted before Canaan.
    m. A leek-green gem.

26 a. This may be the river Pishon, which goes
around the land of Havilah (Gen 2:11) and is
connected with precious stones. Or perhaps the
Kishon. See also 27:15.

God in his own name takes anything from the things under the ban, what will man do? And so now you will take those precious stones and everything that has been found in the book; and when you have arranged for the men, you will place the stones apart with the books, because the fire cannot burn them up, and afterward I will show you how to destroy them. But the men and everything else that has been found, you will burn in the fire. And when all the people have been gathered together, you will say to them, 'So it will be done to every man whose
3 heart has turned from his God.' • And after the fire has burned up those men, then you will place on the top of the mountain[b] beside the new altar the books and the precious stones that cannot be burned by fire or cut up by iron or blotted out by water. And I will command a cloud, and it will go and take dew and send it down upon the books and blot out what is written in them, because they will not be blotted out by any other water than that which has never served men. And afterward
4 I will send forth my lightning, and it will burn up those books. • But regarding the precious stones, I will command my angel, and he will take them and go and put them in the deep of the sea. And I will order the deep, and it will swallow them up, for they cannot remain in the world, because they have been defiled by the idols of the Amorites. And I will command another angel, and he will take for me twelve stones from the same place from which these seven were taken. When you find them on the top of the mountain where you are to place these others, you will take them and set them on the ephod over against the twelve stones that Moses in the wilderness set on the breastplate; you will consecrate them according to the twelve tribes. And do not say, 'How will I know what stone to set for what tribe?' Behold I will tell you the name of the tribe along with the name of the stone, and you will find them engraved one over the other."
5   And Kenaz went and took everything that had been found and the men along with these things, and he gathered all the people to himself again and said to them, "Behold you have seen all the wonders that God has revealed to us until this day. And behold, when we were seeking out all those who planned evil deeds craftily against the LORD and against Israel, God revealed them to us according to their works. And now cursed be the man who would plot to do such things among you, brothers." And all the people answered, "Amen, amen." And when this had been said, he burned all those men in the fire and everything that had been found with them except the precious stones.[c]
6   And after this Kenaz wished to determine whether or not the stones would be burned by fire, and he cast them into the fire. And as soon as they fell into the fire, the fire was extinguished. And Kenaz took the iron sword so that they might be broken up; and when the sword touched them, its iron melted. And after this, he wished at least to blot out the books with water, but as soon as the water fell upon them it was congealed. And on seeing these happenings Kenaz said, "Blessed be God, who has done so many mighty deeds for the sons of men, and he made Adam as the first created one and showed him everything so that when Adam sinned thereby, then he might refuse him all these things (for if he showed them
7 to the whole human race, they might have mastery over them)." • And when this was said, he took the books and the stones, and he placed them on top of the mountain beside the new altar as God had commanded him. And he took the peace offering and offered the holocausts on the new altar by placing on it 2,000 holocausts in all as a whole-burnt offering on that day; and he and all his people together celebrated a great feast.
8   And that same night God did as he had told Kenaz. He commanded a cloud, and it went and took dew from the ice of paradise and poured it on the books and blotted them out. And after this an angel came and burned them. But another angel took the precious stones and cast them into the heart of the sea, and he

---

b. According to 25:10 the stones were hidden under the top of Mount Shechem, but 22:8 speaks of the new altar at Shiloh.

c. Mention of the books has been omitted; see 26:3.

commanded the deep of the sea and it swallowed them up. And another angel came and took the twelve stones and put them beside that place from which he had taken the previous seven and engraved on them the names of the tribes.

9 And Kenaz arose the next morning and found those twelve stones on the top of the mountain where he himself had placed the previous seven. And the engraving 10 on them was such that the forms of eyes were portrayed on them. • And the first stone, [d] on which was written the name of the tribe of Reuben, was like sardius. But the second stone was cut from ivory, and there the name of the tribe of Simeon was engraved, and it seemed like topaz. And on the third stone, which was like emerald, was engraved the name of the tribe of Levi. Now the fourth stone, on which the name of the tribe of Judah was engraved, was called crystal, and it was like carbuncle. But the fifth stone was prase, and upon it was engraved "tribe of Issachar," and it had the color of sapphire in it. And the engraving of the sixth stone (like chrysoprase) was speckled with diverse markings, and there was written 11 "tribe of Zebulun," and it was like jasper. • Now the engraving of the seventh stone shone and showed itself as if it held the water of the deep, and there was written the name of the tribe of Dan, and it was like ligure. The eighth stone was cut out from diamond, and there was written the name of the tribe of Naphtali, and it was like amethyst. And the engraving of the ninth stone was pierced-work from Mount Ophir, and there was written "tribe of Gad," and it was like agate. And the engraving of the tenth stone was hollowed out, and it had the appearance of stone from Teman, and there was written "tribe of Asher," and it was like chrysolite. And the eleventh stone was taken from Lebanon, and there was written the name of the tribe of Joseph, and it was like beryl. And the twelfth stone was cut out from the height of Zion, and on it was written "tribe of Benjamin," and it was like onyx.

12 And God said to Kenaz, "Take those stones and put them in the ark of the covenant of the LORD along with the tablets of the covenant that I gave to Moses on Horeb; and they will stay there until Jahel, [e] who will build a house in my name, will arise, and then he will set them before me upon the two cherubim, 13 and they will be before me as a memorial for the house of Israel. • And when the sins of my people have reached full measure and enemies begin to have power over my[f] house, I will take those stones and the former stones[g] along with the tablets, and I will store them in the place from which they were taken in the beginning. [h] And they will be there until I remember the world and visit those inhabiting the earth. And then I will take those and many others better than they are from where *eye has not seen nor has ear heard* and it has not entered into the heart of man, until the like should come to pass in the world. And the just will not lack the brilliance of the sun or the moon, for the light of those most precious 14 stones will be their light." • And Kenaz arose and said, "Behold how much good God has made for men, but because of their sins they have been deprived of all these things. And now today I know that the race of men is weak and their life 15 should be accounted as nothing." • And on saying this, he took the stones from the place they were laid. And when he took them, it was as if the light of the sun was poured over them and the earth glowed from their light. And Kenaz put them in the ark of the covenant of the LORD with the tablets as it had been commanded him, and they are there to this day.

Marginal references:
Ex 28:17–20
Isa 64:4

d. Compare the other lists of gems in the MT and LXX of Ex 28:17–20; Philo's LegAll 1:81; Josephus' *Ant* 3.7.5 §168 and *War* 5.5.7 §234; Rev 21:19; and ExR 38:8.

e. Jahel should be Solomon. Ithiel is one of Solomon's ten names in rabbinic literature. But Jahel may be the angel Jaoel as in ApAb 10:4, 9.

f. Lit. "their," but the Temple is God's house.

Perhaps Heb. *byty* (my house) was misread as *bytw* (his [the people's] house).

g. Those already on the breastplate.

h. For the concealment of the precious stones until the last day, see 2Bar 6:4–10; 4Bar 3:7–14; AsMos 1:17; Josephus' *Ant* 18.4.1 §85; 2Mac 2:4–8.

The victory of Kenaz

1 **27** And after this he armed three hundred thousand men from the people, and he went up to fight the Amorites. And he struck down on the first day eight hundred
2 thousand men, and on the second day he killed five hundred thousand. •And on the third day certain men of the people grumbled against Kenaz, saying, "Behold now Kenaz alone is busy at his home with his wife and his concubines, and he
3 sends us into battle so that we may be destroyed before our enemies." •And on hearing these words, the servants of Kenaz reported them to him. And he commanded the captain of fifty, and he brought thirty-seven[a] men from them who
4 had been his detractors, and he locked them up in prison. •These are their names: Leetuz, Betul, Efal, Dealma, Anaf, Desac, Besac, Getel, Anael, Anazim, Noac, Cehec, Boac, Obal, Iabat, Enath, Beath, Zelut, Effor, Ecent, Deffaf, Abidan, Esar, Moab, Duzal, Azat, Felac, Igat, Zefal, Eliesor, Ecar, Zebat, Sebet, Nesach, Cere. And when the captain of fifty had locked them up according to the command of Kenaz, Kenaz said, "When God will have worked salvation for his people by my hands, then I will punish those men."
5 And on saying this, Kenaz commanded the captain of fifty, saying, "Go and Judg 7:8 choose from my servants three hundred men and horses of the same number, and let no one of the people know the hour in which I am to go out for battle; only in whatever hour I tell you, prepare the men, so that they might be prepared even
6 at night." •And Kenaz sent emissaries as spies to see where the main part of the Amorite camp was. And the emissaries went and in their spying saw that the main part of the Amorite camp was arrayed on the cliffs and that they were planning to come and fight against Israel. And the emissaries returned and reported this to Judg 7:9–18 him. And Kenaz and the three hundred horsemen with him arose by night, and he took trumpets in his hand and began to go down with the three hundred men. And when he drew near to the Amorite camp, he said to his servants, "Stay here. I will go down alone to have a look at the Amorite camp. And if I blow the trumpet, you may come down; but if not, you are not to look for me there."
7 And Kenaz went down alone. And before he went down he prayed and said, "LORD God of our fathers, you have shown your servant the wonders that you are ready to do by reason of your covenant in the last days. And now send one of your wonders to your servant, and I will fight your enemies in order that they and all the nations and your people may know that the LORD saves not by means of a huge army or by the power of horsemen. If they but knew the sign of deliverance that you will work with me today! Behold I will draw my sword out of its scabbard, and it will shine in the Amorite camp. And if the Amorites recognize that I am Kenaz, I know that you have delivered them into my hands. But if they do not recognize me and think I am someone else, I know that you have not heard me but have delivered me to my enemies. For even if I be handed over to death, I know that the LORD has not heard me because of my faults and has handed me over to my enemies. But he will not destroy his inheritance by my death."
8 And he went forth after he prayed, and he heard many of the Amorites saying, "Rise up, and let us fight against Israel. For we know that our sacred nymphs are
9 there with them, and they will deliver them into our hands." •And Kenaz arose, and the spirit of the LORD clothed him, and he drew his sword. And when its light shone on the Amorites like a lightning bolt, they saw it and said, "Is not this the sword of Kenaz that has wounded so many of us, and the word that we were saying is correct because the sacred nymphs have delivered them into our hands? And behold now this day will be a feast day for the Amorites, since our enemy has been handed over to us. Now therefore rise up, and let each one gird
10 himself with his sword and begin to fight." •And when Kenaz heard their words,

27 a. There are only thirty-five names.

he was clothed with the spirit of power and was changed into another man, and he went down to the Amorite camp and began to strike them down. But the LORD sent before him the angel Ingethel,[b] who is in charge of hidden things and works invisibly, and another powerful angel was helping him. And Ingethel struck the Amorites with blindness so that, when each saw his neighbor, they thought they were their adversaries and they killed one another. And Zeruel,[c] the angel who is pre-eminent in military might, bore up the arms of Kenaz lest they should sink down.[d] And Kenaz killed forty-five thousand men of the Amorites. Now they

11 killed one another, and forty-five thousand men fell. •And when Kenaz had killed such a great number, he wished to release his hand from the sword, because it was stuck to the handle of the sword and could not be released, and his right hand   2Sam 23:10 took in the power of the sword. And then some of the Amorite survivors fled into the mountains. Now Kenaz sought how he might release his hand, and looking about, he saw with his own eyes an Amorite man in flight; and he took hold of him and said to him, "I know that the Amorites have been wiped out, and now show me how to release my hand from this sword, and I will let you go." And the Amorite said, "Go and get a man from the Hebrews, and kill him; and while his blood is still hot, put your hand beneath it; on receiving his blood, your hand will be released." And Kenaz said, "As the LORD lives, for if you had said, 'Get a man from the Amorites,' I would have gotten one of these and saved you. But because you have said 'from the Hebrews' and so reveal your hatred, your own word will be against you and, as you have said, so I will do to you." And on saying these words, Kenaz killed him; and while his blood was still hot, he put

12 his hand beneath; and on receiving it, it was released. •And Kenaz left there and took off his clothes and threw himself into the river and washed himself.[e] And he came up again, changed his clothes, and returned to his servants. But the LORD had sent upon them a deep sleep at night, and they slept and did not know all the deeds that Kenaz had done. And Kenaz came and woke them up from sleep, and they looked at him and saw with their own eyes, and behold the field was full of bodies; and they were astonished and looked at each other. And Kenaz said to them, "Why are you amazed? Is the way of men like the ways of God? For among men a great number prevails, but with God whatever he has decided. And so if God wished to save this people by my hands, why are you amazed? Arise, and each of you gird on your swords, and we will go home to our brothers."

13 And when all Israel heard that deliverance had been accomplished by the hands of Kenaz, all the people went out together to meet him and they said, "Blessed be the LORD who has made you leader among his people and has shown that what he had said to you was worthy of belief; and what we have heard by word, now

14 we have seen, and the work of God's word is manifest." •And Kenaz said to them, "Ask your brothers, and have them tell you how much they have toiled with me in battle." And those men who were with him said, "As the LORD lives, we did not fight nor did we even know anything except that, when we were awakened, we saw the field full of bodies." And the people answered, "Now we know that the LORD has decided to save his people; he does not need a great number but only holiness."

15 And Kenaz said to the captain of fifty who had locked up those men in prison, "Bring those men here, and we will hear their words." And when he had brought them, Kenaz said to them, "Tell me what you have seen so as to grumble about me among the people." These said, "Why do you ask us? Now therefore command us to be burned in the fire, because we will not die for this sin that we are talking about now but for that previous one in which we were implicated. Those men

b. The name may be related to the Heb. root ʿṭḥ (hide).

c. The name is probably related to the Heb. zrwʿ (arm, strength). See also 61:5 for what seems to be reference to the same angel.

d. Var. "lest they should perceive him"; but this is meaningless in the context and involves a wrong sequence of tenses. See Ex 17:8–13 for the motif as applied to Moses.

e. Var. "and he was washed"; this may have the notion of ritual purification connected with it.

made a confession and were burned for their sins. For then we had joined in their sins, saying, 'Perhaps the people will not find us out,' and then we escaped the people. But rightly have we been made a public example in our sins, in that we have fallen into slandering you." And Kenaz said, "If therefore you testify against yourselves, how will I have mercy on you?" Kenaz ordered them to be burned in the fire and threw their ashes into the bed of the river Fison,[f] where he had 16 thrown those of the great number of sinners. •And Kenaz ruled the people fifty- Judg 3:8-11 seven[g] years, and there was fear among all his enemies all his days.

The covenant of Kenaz. His vision and death

1 **28** And when the days of Kenaz drew near for him to die, he sent and summoned all of them and Jabis and Phinehas the two prophets and Phinehas the son of Eleazar the priest,[a] and he said to them, "Behold now the LORD has shown to 2 me all his wonders that he is ready to do for his people in the last days. •And now I will establish my covenant with you today so that you do not abandon the LORD your God after my departure. For you have seen all the wonders that came upon those who sinned and what they declared in confessing their sins voluntarily, or how the LORD our God destroyed them because they transgressed against his covenant. Now therefore spare those of your household and your children, and stay in the paths of the LORD your God lest the LORD destroy his own inheritance." 3 And Phinehas the son of Eleazar the priest said, "If Kenaz the leader and the prophets and the elders command it, I will speak the word that I heard from my father when he was dying, and I will not be silent about the command that he commanded me while his soul was being taken away." And Kenaz the leader and the prophets said, "Speak, Phinehas. Should anyone speak before the priest who guards the commandments of the LORD our God, especially since truth goes forth 4 from his mouth and a shining light from his heart?" •And then Phinehas said, "While my father was dying, he commanded me, saying, 'These words you will say to the sons of Israel, "When you were gathered together in the assembly, the LORD appeared to me three days ago in a dream by night and said to me, 'Behold you have seen and also your father before you how much I have toiled among my people. But after your death this people will rise up and corrupt its ways and turn from my commands, and I will be very angry with them. But I will recall that time that was before the creation of the world, the time when man did not exist and there was no wickedness in it, when I said that the world would be created and those who would come into it would praise me. And I would plant a great vineyard, and from it I would choose a plant; and I would care for it and call it by my name, and it would be mine forever. When I did all the things that I said, nevertheless my plant that was called by my name did not recognize me as its planter, but it destroyed its own fruit and did not yield up its fruit to me.' " ' " And 5 this is what my father commanded me to say to this people." •And Kenaz and the elders and all the people lifted up their voices and wept with great lamentation until evening and said, "Will the Shepherd destroy his flock for any reason except that it has sinned against him? And now he is the one who will spare us according to the abundance of his mercy, because he has toiled so much among us." 6 And when they had sat down, a holy spirit came upon Kenaz and dwelled[b] in Num 24:17; him and put him in ecstasy, and he began to prophesy, saying, "Behold now I Ezek 8:1(20:1f.) see what I had not hoped for, and I perceive that I did not understand. Hear now, you who dwell on the earth, just as those staying a while on it prophesied before me and saw this hour even before the earth was corrupted, so all of you who 7 dwell in it may know the prophecies that have been fixed in advance. •Behold

---

f. See 26:1.

g. Josephus (*Ant* 5.3.3 §184) says that Kenaz ruled forty years. According to Judg 3:8-11, Cushan-rishataim ruled Israel eight years and Othniel forty years (fifty, according to Lucian).

28 a. Originally there may have been only one prophet and one prophet-priest. See 48:1-3, where Phinehas is described in terms reminiscent of Elijah.

b. Lit. "dwelling."

now I see flames that do not burn, and I hear springs raised up out of a sleep for which there is no foundation, and I perceive neither the tops of the mountains nor the roof of the firmament, but everything has no appearance and is invisible and has no place whatsoever. And although my eye does not know what it sees, my
8 heart will find what to say. •Now from the flame that I saw not burning, I saw and behold a spark came up and, as it were, laid for itself a platform. And the floor was like what a spider spins, in the pattern of a shield. And when this foundation had been set, behold^c there was stirred up from that spring, as it were, boiling foam; and behold it changed itself into another foundation, as it were. Now between the upper foundation and the lower there came forth from the light of that invisible place, as it were, the images of men; and they were walking around. And behold a voice was saying, 'These will be a foundation for men,
9 and they will dwell^d in between them for 7,000^e years.' •And the lower foundation was solid material, but the upper was of foam. And those who went forth from the light of the invisible place, they will be those who will have the name 'man.'^f And when he will sin against me and the time will be fulfilled, the spark will be put out and the spring will stop, and so they will be transformed.''
10 And when Kenaz had spoken these words, he was awakened, and his senses came back to him. But he did not know what he had said or what he had seen. But this alone he said to the people: "If the repose of the just after they have ^{Num 23:10} died is like this, we must die to the corruptible world so as not to see sins." And when he had said these words, Kenaz died and slept with his fathers. And the people mourned for him thirty days.

Zebul

1 **29** And afterward the people appointed over themselves as leader Zebul.^a In that ^{Judg 9:28–41} time he gathered the people together and said to them, "Behold now we know all the toil that Kenaz toiled for us in the days of his life. And now if he had sons, they should rule the people. And since he left only daughters, let them receive a greater inheritance among the people, because their father during his ^{Num 36} lifetime refused to give anything to them lest he be called avaricious and greedy."
2 And the people said, "Do everything that is pleasing in your sight." •Now Kenaz had three daughters, whose names were these: the firstborn Ethema, the second Feila, the third Zelfa. And Zebul gave to the firstborn all that was around the land of the Phoenicians, and to the second he gave the olive grove of Ekron, but to ^{Josh 15:46f.} the third he gave *the tilled lands that were around Ashdod*. And he gave them husbands, that is, to the firstborn Elisefan, to the second Odihel, but to the third
3 Doel. •Now in those days Zebul established a treasury for the LORD and said to ^{2Chr 24:8;} the people, "Behold if anyone wishes to consecrate gold and silver to the LORD, ^{2Kgs 12:9–16} let him bring it to the treasury of the LORD in Shiloh; only do not let anyone who has anything belonging to idols wish to consecrate it to the treasuries of the LORD, because the LORD does not want the abominations of the things under the ban lest you disturb the assembly of the LORD. For the wrath that has passed is sufficient." And all the people, from men to women, brought whatever gold and silver their heart prompted. And everything that was brought was weighed out: twenty talents
4 of gold and two hundred and fifty of silver. •And Zebul judged the people twenty-five years. And when he had completed his time, he sent and called together all the people and said, "Behold now I am going forth to die; look to the testimonies that our predecessors have left as witnesses, and do not let your heart be like the waves of the sea. But just as a wave of the sea understands nothing except what

---

c. Lit. "I saw."

d. Lit. "for those dwelling." The Gk. third person plural present indicative may have been read as a masculine plural participle.

e. Var. "4,000." See 19:15, whose four and a half and two and a half suggest that 7,000 is correct.

f. Var. "they will be those who dwell, and the name of that man . . ."

29 a. The name should correspond to Ehud of Judg 3:15.

is in the sea, so let your heart ponder nothing else except what belongs to the Law." And Zebul slept with his fathers, and he was buried in the tomb of his father.

Deborah

1 **30** Then the sons of Israel did not have anyone to appoint for themselves as judge; and their heart fell away, and they forgot the promise and transgressed the ways that Moses and Joshua the servants of the LORD had commanded them, and *they were led astray after the daughters*[a] of the Amorites *and served their gods*. Judg 2:17

Num 25:1f.

2 And the LORD was angry at them and sent his angel and said, "Behold I have chosen one people from every tribe of the earth, and I said that my glory would reside in this world with it; and I sent to them Moses my servant, who would declare my laws and statutes; and they transgressed my ways. And behold now I will arouse *their enemies*,[b] and they will rule over them. And then all the people will say, 'Because we have transgressed the ways of God and of our fathers, on account of this these things have come upon us.' And a woman will rule over 3 them and enlighten them for forty years." • And after this the LORD aroused against them *Jabin the king of Hazor*, and he began to attack them. And he had *Sisera* as *the commander of his army, who had* eight thousand[c] *iron chariots*, and he came to Mount Ephraim and *attacked the people*. And Israel feared him very 4 much, and the people could not resist all the days of Sisera. • And when Israel had been badly humiliated, all the sons of Israel gathered together to the mountain of Judah[d] and said, "We say that we are more blessed than other nations, and behold now we have been humiliated more than all peoples so that we cannot dwell in our own land and our enemies have power over us. And now who has done all these things to us? Is it not our own wicked deeds, because we have forsaken the LORD of our fathers and *have walked in these ways that have not profited us*? And now come, let us fast for seven days, *from man to woman and from the least to the suckling child*. And who knows, perhaps God will be reconciled with his inheritance so as not to destroy the plant of his vineyard?"

Judg 2:1–3,17

Judg 2:3

Judg 4:2f.

Jer 2:8

ISam 15:3;
22:19

5 And when the people had fasted seven days and sat in sackcloth, the LORD sent to them on the seventh day Deborah, who said to them, "Can the sheep to be slaughtered give answer to its slaughterer? But both the slaughterer and the slaughtered are silent even though he is sorrowful over it. And now you were[e] like a flock before our LORD, and he led you into the height of the clouds and set the angels beneath your feet and established for you the Law and commanded you through the prophets and corrected you through the leaders and showed you not a few wonders; and on your account he commanded the luminaries, and *they stood still in their* assigned *places;* and when your enemies came against you, he rained down *hailstones*[f] *on them* and destroyed them. And Moses and Joshua and Kenaz 6 and Zebul commanded you, and you did not obey them. • For while these were alive, you showed yourselves as if you were serving your God; but when these died, your heart also died. And you became like iron cast into the fire, which when made molten by the flame becomes like water, but when it comes out of the fire it reverts to its original hardness. So you also, while those who warned you burned you, you were taught[g] the matter; but after they have died you forget

Isa 53:7

Josh 10:11–13

---

30 a. See also 9:5; 21:1; 44:7; 45:3; cf. 18:13f. for polemics against intermarriage.

b. The MT of Judg 2:3 has "sides" (ṣdym) while the LXX's "narrow places" (synochai) implies ṣrym. Ps-Philo has interpreted ṣrym as "enemies."

c. Judg 4:3 has 900. Some Ps-Philo MSS have 9,000.

d. In Judg 4:5 it is the hill country of Ephraim.

e. Lit. "were born." We may have confusion here between Gk. "were born" and "were"; see also 17:3; 51:6.

f. The LXX of Josh 10:11 also has "hailstones"; the MT has "great stones."

g. Lit. "you demonstrated," which probably depends on the Gk. translator's having mistaken the Heb. hophal ("were taught") for the hiphil ("demonstrated").

7 everything. •And behold now the LORD will take pity on[h] you today, not because of you but because of his covenant that he established with your fathers and the oath that he has sworn not to abandon you forever. (Know, however, that after my departure you will start sinning again until the end of your days.) On account of this the LORD will work wonders among you and hand over your enemies into your hands. For our fathers are dead, but the God who established the covenant with them is life."

The defeat and death of Sisera

1 **31** *And Deborah sent and summoned Barak, and she said to him,* "Rise and *gird your loins like a man,* and go down and attack Sisera, because I see *the stars* moved from their course and *ready for battle* on your side. Also I see the lightning that cannot be moved from its course going forth to hinder the works of the chariots of those who glory in the might of Sisera, who is saying, 'I am going down to attack Israel with my mighty arm, and *I will divide* their *spoils* among my servants, and I will take for myself beautiful women as concubines.' And on account of this the LORD said about him that the arm of a weak woman would attack him and maidens would take his spoils and even he would fall *into the* 2 *hands of a woman."* •And when Deborah and the people and Barak went down to meet the enemies, immediately the LORD disturbed the movement of his stars. And he said to them,[a] "Hurry and go, for your enemies fall upon you; and confound their arms and crush the power of their heart, because I have come that my people may prevail. For even if my people have sinned, nevertheless I will have mercy on them." And when these words had been said, the stars went forth as had been commanded them and burned up their enemies. And the number of those gathered together in one hour and slain was 90 times 97,000 men; but they did not destroy Sisera, because so it had been commanded them.

3 And when *Sisera,* sitting on a horse,[b] *had fled* to save his life, *Jael the wife of Heber[c] the Kenite adorned herself and went out to meet him;* now the woman was very beautiful in appearance. And she saw him and said to him, "Go inside and take some food and sleep until evening; I will send my servants with you. For I know that you will remember me and return the favor to me." And Sisera went in, and when he saw roses scattered on the bed, he said, "If I am saved, I 4 will go to my mother, and Jael will be my wife." •And after this Sisera was thirsty and said to Jael, *"Get me a little water, because* I am faint and my soul burns with the flame that I saw in the stars." And Jael said to him, "Rest a little 5 while, and then you will drink." •And when Sisera was sleeping, Jael went out to the flock and got milk from it. And when she was milking, she said, "And now be mindful, LORD, of when you assigned every tribe or race to the earth. Did you not choose Israel alone and liken it to no animal except to the ram that goes before and leads the flock? And so look and see that Sisera has made a plan and said, 'I will go and punish the flock of the Most Powerful One.' And I will take from the milk of these animals to which you have likened your people, and I will go and give him to drink. And when he will have drunk, he will be off guard, and afterward I will kill him. But this will be the sign that you act along with me, LORD, that, when I enter while Sisera is asleep, he will rise up and ask me again and again, saying, *'Give me water to drink,'* then I know that my prayer 6 has been heard." •And when Jael returned and came in, Sisera was awakened and said to her, *"Give me a drink,* because I am burning up terribly and my soul is inflamed." And Jael took wine and mixed it with milk and *gave it to him to* 7 *drink.* And he drank it and went to sleep. •*Now Jael took a stake in her left hand*

Marginal references:
Judg 4:6
Job 38:3(40:7)
Judg 5:20
Ex 14:25
Judg 5:30; Ex 15:9
Judg 4:9
Judg 5:20
Judg 4:15,17f.
Judg 5:28
Judg 4:19; 5:25
Judg 4:19

---

h. Var. "be reconciled with."

31 a. Here God speaks to the stars.
b. In Judg 4:17 Sisera flees on foot.

c. The name Heber is absent from all the MSS but one, yet it is present in Judg 4:17. Its omission in the Lat. is easily explained by the proximity of *uxor* and *Aber.*

and approached him, saying, "If God will work this sign with me, I know that   Judg 4:21, 5:26
Sisera will fall into my hands. Behold I will throw him down on the ground from   Jdt 13:7
the bed on which he sleeps; and if he does not feel it, I know that he has been
handed over." And Jael took Sisera and *pushed him* onto the ground *from the*   Jdt 13:9
bed. But he did not feel it, because he was very groggy. And Jael said, "*Strengthen*   Jdt 13:7
in me today, Lord, my arm on account of you and your people and those who   Judg 4:21, 5:26
hope in you." *And Jael took the stake and put it on his temple and struck it with*
a hammer. And while he was dying, Sisera said to Jael, "Behold pain has taken
hold of me, Jael, and I die like a woman." And Jael said to him, "Go, boast
before your father in hell and tell him that you have fallen *into the hands of a*   Judg 4:9
woman." And by doing this she killed him and left his body there until Barak   Judg 5:28–30
8 should return. •Now Sisera's mother was named Themech,[d] and she sent word to
her ladies, saying, "Come and let us go out together to meet my son, and you
will see the daughters of the Hebrews whom my son will bring here for himself
9 as concubines." •Now *Barak* returned *from pursuing Sisera* and was very   Judg 4:22
disappointed because he had not found him. *Jael went out to meet him and said*,
"*Come*, enter in, you blessed by God, and I will hand over to you your enemy
whom you pursued but did not find." And Barak entered and found Sisera dead
and said, "Blessed be the LORD, who sent his spirit and said, 'Into the hand of a
woman Sisera will be handed over.'" And on saying these words he cut off
Sisera's head and sent it over to his mother and gave a mess~ge to her, saying,
"Receive your son, whom you hoped to see coming back with spoils."

The hymn of Deborah

1 **32** *Then Deborah and Barak the son of Abino*[a] *and all the people together sang*   Judg 5:1
a hymn[b] to the LORD *on that day, saying*, "Behold the LORD has shown us his
glory from on high, as he did in the height of the heavenly places when he sent
forth his voice to confuse the languages of men. And he chose our nation and   Gen 11:7
took Abraham our father out of the fire and chose him over all his brothers and
kept him from the fire[c] and freed him from the bricks destined for building the
tower. And he gave him a son at the end of his old age and took him out of a
sterile womb. And all the angels were jealous of him, and the worshiping hosts
2 envied him.[d] •And since they were jealous of him, God said to him, 'Kill the   Gen 22:1–10
fruit of your body for me, and offer for me as a sacrifice what has been given to
you by me.'[e] And Abraham did not argue, but set out immediately. And as he
was setting out, he said to his son, 'Behold now, my son, I am offering you as a
3 holocaust and am delivering you into the hands that gave you to me.' •But the
son said to the father, 'Hear me, father. If a lamb of the flock is accepted as
sacrifice to the LORD with an odor of sweetness and if for the wicked deeds of
men animals are appointed to be killed, but man is designed to inherit the world,
how then do you now say to me, "Come and inherit life without limit[f] and time
without measure"? Yet have I not been born into the world to be offered as a
sacrifice to him who made me? Now my blessedness will be above that of all
men, because there will be nothing like this; and about me future generations will
be instructed and through me the peoples will understand that the LORD has made
4 the soul of a man worthy to be a sacrifice.' •And when *he had offered* the son   Gen 22:9–18

---

d. This was also the name of Cain's wife in 2:2.
Was it originally Tanaach, or was it derived from
tybb or *tbṭ* in Judg 5:28?

32 a. Judg 5:1 has "Abinoam" and omits "and
all the people." The Gk. translator may have
divided the Heb. *'byn'm* into *'bynw* and *'m* (Abino
and the people).
b. Even though what follows is called a hymn,
we cannot now detect a hymnic structure.

c. See 6:3–18 for Abraham's escape from the
fire.
d. On the angels' jealousy of Abraham, see
GenR 55:4, where they accuse Abraham before
God.
e. For Abraham's sacrifice of Isaac, see 18:5
and 40:2.
f. Lit. "life secure." There may be confusion
between the Gk. *apeiratos*, "untroubled," and
aperantos, "limitless."

upon the altar and *had bound his feet* so as to kill him, the Most Powerful hastened
and sent forth his voice *from on high* saying, 'You shall not slay your son, nor
shall you destroy the fruit of your body. For now I have appeared so as to reveal
you to those who do not know you[g] and have shut the mouths of those who are
always speaking evil against you. Now your memory will be before me always,
and your name and his will remain from one generation to another.'

5   "And he gave Isaac two sons, both also from a womb that was closed up. And Gen 25:21
their mother was then in the third year of her marriage[h]; and it will not happen
in this way to any woman, nor will any female so boast. But when her husband
approached her in the third year, to him there were born two sons, Jacob and
6 Esau. And God *loved Jacob, but he hated Esau* because of his deeds. •And in Mal 1:2f.
their father's old age Isaac blessed Jacob and sent him into Mesopotamia, and
there[i] he became the father of twelve sons. And they went down into Egypt and
dwelt there.

7   "And when their enemies had dealt with them wickedly, the people cried out
to the LORD, and their prayer was heard, and he brought them out of there and Ex 19
brought them to Mount Sinai and brought forth for them the foundation of
understanding that he had prepared from the creation of the world.[j] And then
when the world's foundation was moved, the heavenly hosts speeded the lightnings
on their courses, and the winds brought forth noise from their chambers,[k] and the
earth was shaken from its firmament, and the mountains and cliffs trembled in
their joints, and the clouds lifted up their floods against the flame of fire so that
8 it would not burn up the world. •Then the abyss was aroused from its very springs,
and all the waves of the sea gathered together. Then Paradise gave off the scent
of its fruit, and the cedars of Lebanon were shaken from their roots, and the beasts
of the field were moved in their dwelling places in the forest; and all his creatures
came together to see the LORD establishing a covenant with the sons of Israel.
And everything that the Most Powerful said, this he observed, having Moses his
beloved as a witness.

9   "And when he was dying, God established for him a platform[l] and showed
him then what we now have as witnesses, saying, 'Let there be as a witness
between me and you and my people the heaven that you are to enter and the earth
on which you walk until now. For the sun and the moon and the stars are servants
10 to you.' •And when Joshua arose to rule the people, on the day when he was
fighting the enemies, the evening approached while the battle was still going on.
Joshua said to the sun and moon, 'You who have been made servants between
the Most Powerful and his sons, behold now the battle is still going on, and do
you abandon your duties? Therefore stand still today and give light to his sons Josh 10:12
and darkness to his enemies.' And they did so.

11   "And now in these days Sisera arose to enslave us. And we cried out to our
LORD, and he commanded the stars and said, 'Depart from your positions and
burn up my enemies so that they may know my power.' And the stars came down
12 and attacked their camp and guarded us without any strain. •So we will not cease
singing praise, nor will our mouth be silent in telling his wonders, because he has
remembered both his recent and ancient promises and shown his saving power to
us. And so *Jael is glorified among women*, because she alone has made straight Judg 5:24
the way to success by killing Sisera with her own hands.

13   "Go, earth; go, heavens and lightnings; go, angels of the heavenly host; go
and tell the fathers in their chambers of souls[m] and say, 'The Most Powerful has
not forgotten the least of the promises that he established with us, saying, "Many
wonders will I do for your sons."' And now from this day on let it be known

g. Var. "to reveal myself to those who do not
know me."

h. But according to Gen 25:20 Isaac was forty
when he married, and according to Gen 25:26 he
was sixty when Jacob and Esau were born.

i. But Benjamin was born in the land of Israel.

j. The Law, or divine wisdom in general.

k. For the treasuries of the winds, see 1En 18:1.

l. Moses is given a platform or balcony from
which he can see all.

m. For Sheol as the resting place of souls, see
1Pet 3:19; 4:6; 4Ezra 4:35; 2Bar 21:23; 42:7f.

that, whatever God has said to me, he will do; these things he will do, even if
14 man delays in praising God. •But you, Deborah, sing praises, and let the grace
of the holy spirit awaken in you, and begin to praise the works of the LORD,
because there will not again arise such a day on which the stars will band together[n]
and attack the enemies of Israel as was commanded them. And from this hour, if
Israel falls into distress, it will call upon those witnesses along with these servants,
and they will form a delegation to the Most High, and he will remember that day
15 and send the saving power of his covenant. •And you, Deborah, begin to tell
what you saw in the field, how the people were walking about and going forth in
safety and the stars fought for them. Rejoice, earth, over those dwelling in you,
because the knowledge[o] of the LORD that builds a tower[p] among you is present.
Not unjustly did God take from you the rib of the first-formed,[q] knowing that   Gen 2:21f.
from his rib Israel would be born. Your forming will be a testimony of what the
16 LORD has done for his people. •Wait, you hours of the day, and do not wish to
hurry, in order that we may declare what our mind can bring forward, for night
will be upon us. It will be like the night when God killed the firstborn of the   Ex 12:29
17 Egyptians on account of his own firstborn. •And then I will cease my hymn, for
the time is readied for his just judgments. For I will sing a hymn to him in the
renewal of creation. And the people will remember his saving power, and this
will be a testimony for it. And let the sea with its abyss be a witness, because
not only has God dried it up before our fathers, but also he has diverted *the stars*[r]   Ex 14f.
from their positions and *attacked* our enemies.''   Judg 5:20
18   And when Deborah made an end to her words, she along with the people went
up to Shiloh, and they offered sacrifices and holocausts, and they sang to the
accompaniment of the trumpets. And when they were singing and the sacrifices
had been offered, Deborah said, ''And this will be as a testimony of trumpets
between the stars and their LORD.'' And Deborah came down from there and
judged[s] Israel *forty years.*   Judg 5:31

The farewell and death of Deborah

1 **33** And when the days of her death drew near, she sent and gathered all the
people and said to them, ''Listen now, my people. Behold I am warning you as
a woman of God[a] and am enlightening you as one from the female race; and obey
2 me like your mother and heed my words as people who will also die. •*Behold I*   Josh 23:14
am going today[b] *on the way of all* flesh, on which you also will come. Only direct
your heart to the LORD your God during the time of your life, because after your
3 death you cannot repent of those things in which you live. •For then death is
sealed up and brought to an end, and the measure and the time and the years have
returned their deposit. For even if you seek to do evil in hell after your death,
you cannot, because the desire for sinning will cease and the evil impulse will
lose its power,[c] because even hell will not restore what has been received and
deposited to it unless it be demanded by him who has made the deposit to it. Now
therefore, my sons, obey my voice; while you have the time of life and the light
4 of the Law, make straight your ways.'' •And while Deborah was saying these
words, all the people raised up their voice together and wept and said, ''Behold
now, Mother, you will die, and to whom do you commend your sons whom you

---

n. Lit. ''announce,'' which in Heb. would be
ygydw; but better sense is had by assuming an
original *ygwdw,* ''will band together,'' as in Ps
94:21.

o. Var. ''assembly.''

p. Lit. ''burns incense'' (*thurificat*); but ''builds
a tower'' (*turrificat*) may be better in view of 32:1.

q. Adam.

r. Most MSS have the incorrect *castra,* ''camps,''
instead of *astra.*

s. Comparison with the Heb. of Judg 5:31
suggests a possible confusion between ''and she

judged'' (*wtšpt*) and ''it was quiet'' (*wtšqt*); see
Ps-Philo 33:6.

33 a. The expression ''woman of God'' seems to
be the feminist counterpart of the common expression ''man of God''; see also ''the bosom of her
mothers'' in 40:4.

b. Reading ''today'' (*hodie*) rather than ''to
die'' (*mori*) on the basis of Josh 23:14.

c. The idea that the evil impulse ceases after
death is unique to Ps-Philo.

are leaving? Pray therefore for us, and after your departure your soul will be
5 mindful of us forever." •And Deborah answered and said to the people, "While
a man is still alive he can pray for himself and for his sons, b t after his end he
cannot pray or be mindful of anyone. Therefore do not hope in your fathers.[d] For
they will not profit you at all unless you be found like them. But then you will
be like the stars of the heaven,[e] which now have been revealed among you."
6 And Deborah died and slept with her fathers and was buried in the city of her
fathers. And the people mourned for her seventy days, and while they were
mourning for her, they said these words as a lamentation:

> "Behold there has perished a *mother from Israel,*   Judg 5:7
> and the holy one who exercised leadership in the house of Jacob.
> She firmed up the fence about her generation,
> and her generation will grieve over her."

And after her death *the land had rest for* seven[f] *years.*   Judg 5:31

Aod the magician

1 **34** And in that time there arose a certain Aod[a] from the sanctuaries of Midian,   Judg 6:1-6
and this man was a magician, and he said to Israel, "Why do you pay attention
to your Law? Come, I will show you something other than your Law." And the
people said, "What will you show us that our Law does not have?" And he said
to the people, "Have you ever seen the sun by night?" And they said, "No."
And he said, "Whenever you wish, I will show it to you in order that you may
know that our gods have power and do not deceive those who serve them." And
2 they said, "Show it." •And he went away and worked with his magic tricks and
gave orders to the angels who were in charge of magicians, for he had been
3 sacrificing to them for a long time. •Because in that time before they were
condemned, magic was revealed by angels and they would have destroyed the age
without measure;[b] and because they had transgressed, it happened that the angels
did not have the power; and when they were judged, then the power was not
given over to others. And they do these things by means of those men, the
4 magicians who minister to men, until the age without measure comes. •And then   Judg 6:7-10
by the art of magic he showed to the people the sun by night. And the people
were amazed and said, "Behold how much the gods of the Midianites can do,
5 and we did not know it." •And God wished to test if Israel would remain in its
wicked deeds, and he let them[c] be, and their work was successful. And the people
of Israel were deceived and began to serve the gods of the Midianites. And God
said, "I will deliver them into the hands of the Midianites, because they have
been deceived by them." And he *delivered them into* their *hands,* and the   Judg 6:1
Midianites began to reduce Israel to slavery.

The call of Gideon

1 **35** Now Gideon was the son of Joash; he was the most powerful man among all
his brothers. And when it was summertime, he came *to beat out* the sheaves he   Judg 6:11f.,15
had and to escape the attacking *Midianites by hiding* himself in the mountain.
And behold *the angel of the Lord* met[a] *him and said to him, "From where have*   Judg 19:17
2 *you come, and where is your destination?"* •He said to him, "Why do you ask
me from where do I come, for distress has encompassed me? Israel has fallen into

---

d. What is being disputed is the power of the
dead to intercede for the living. See also 2Bar
85:12. Elsewhere in Ps-Philo (e.g. 35:3) the merits
of Israel's fathers have power.
     e. On the life of the just after death as astral
immortality, see Dan 12:2f.; 1En 104:2, 6; AsMos
10:9.
     f. Judg 5:31 has "forty" years.

34 a. The episode of Aod is unique to Ps-Philo.
     b. The age to come, the eschatological age.
     c. The wicked angels.

35 a. Judg 6:12 has "appeared." Heb. *wyqr'* (met)
may have been confused with *wyr'* (appeared).

distress; they have been *delivered into the hands of the Midianites. And where* Judg 6:13
are the wonders that our fathers described to us, saying, 'The LORD has chosen
Israel alone before all the peoples of the earth'? *And* behold now *he has delivered
us up* and forgotten the promises that he told our fathers. For we would prefer to
be handed over to death once and for all than for his people to be punished thus
3 over a period of time." •*And the angel*[b] *of the Lord said to him,* "You have not Judg 6:14
been delivered up without reason, but your own schemes have done these things
to you; because, as you have abandoned the promises that you have received from
the LORD, *these evils*[c] *have found you out;* and you have not been mindful of the Judg 6:13
commandments of God that those who were before you commanded you, so that
you have come into the displeasure of your God. But he will have mercy, as no
one else has mercy, on the race of Israel, though not on account of you but on
4 account of those who have fallen asleep.[d] •*And now come; I will send you, and* Judg 6:14
you will free Israel from the hand of the Midianites; for the LORD says these
words: 'Even if Israel is not just, nevertheless because the Midianites are sinners,
though I recognize the wickedness of my people, I will forgive them and afterward
I will rebuke them because they have acted wickedly. But for the present I will
5 take my vengeance upon the Midianites.'" •And Gideon said, "Who am I and Judg 6:15
what is *the house of my father* that I should go up against the Midianites for
battle?" *And the angel said to him,* "Perhaps you think that as the way of men
is, so the way of God is. For men look for the glory of the world and riches, but
God for the straight and good and for meekness. Now therefore go and gird your
loins, and *the Lord will be with you.* For he has chosen you to take vengeance Judg 6:16
6 upon his enemies as he commanded you." •*And Gideon said to him,* "*May my* Judg 6:17
Lord not be angry that I should say a word. Behold Moses the first of all the Gen 18:30
prophets asked the LORD for a sign, and it was given to him. But who am I,
unless perhaps the LORD has chosen me? *May he give me a sign* so that I may Judg 6:17
know that I am being guided." *And the angel of the Lord said to him,* "Run and Judg 6:20
get for me water from that lake and *pour it on that rock,* and I will give you a
7 sign." And he went away and got it as he commanded him. •And the angel said Judg 6:20f.
to him, "Before you pour water on the rock, ask what you wish to be made from
it, either blood or fire, or that it not appear at all." And Gideon said, "Let it
become half blood and half fire." And Gideon poured water on the rock. And
when he had poured it out, it became half flame and half blood, and they were
both mixed together, that is, the fire and the blood; and the blood did not extinguish
the fire nor did the fire consume[e] the blood. And Gideon saw these happenings
and sought other signs, and they were given to him. Are they not written in the
Book of Judges?

The victory of Gideon. His sin and death

1 **36** And *Gideon* took three hundred[a] *men* and went out and *came to the outskirts* Judg 7:19
of the camp of Midian and heard each man speaking to his neighbor, saying,
"You will see confusion beyond reckoning caused by the sword of Gideon coming
upon us because *God has delivered into his hands the camp of the Midianites* and Judg 7:14
he is about to destroy us utterly, that is, even mother along with children, because
our sins have reached full measure as even our own gods have shown us and we
did not believe them. And now let us rise up and take care for our own lives and
2 flee." •*And as soon as Gideon heard* these words, *he put on the spirit of the* Judg 7:15; 6:34
Lord[b] *and was strengthened* and said to the three hundred men, "*Rise up,* let
each one of you gird on his sword, *because the Midianites have been delivered*

b. In the LXX of Judg 6:14 as in Ps-Philo an
angel speaks; in the MT God speaks.

c. The expression "these evils" agrees with the
LXX, Lucian, and Vetus Latina of Judg 6:13.

d. The idea that God will have mercy on Israel
because of those who have died is also found in
2Mac 8:15.

e. Most MSS have "shook off" (*excussit*), but
"consume" (*exussit*) must be correct.

36 a. Judg 7:19 has "one hundred."

b. Or perhaps read "the spirit of the LORD
clothed him" by emending *induit spiritum* to *induit
spiritus;* see Judg 6:34.

into our hands.'' And the men went down with them. And he drew near and
began to fight, and *they blew the trumpets and cried out* together and said, *"The*   Judg 7:19f.
sword of the Lord[c] *is upon us.''* And they killed about *120,000 men* of the   Judg 8:10
3 Midianites, and the rest of the Midianites fled. •And after these events Gideon
came and gathered the people of Israel and said to them, ''Behold the LORD has
sent me to fight your battle, and I have gone out as he commanded me. And now
I make one *request of you;* do not turn your face away. *Let each of you give me*   Judg 8:24–27
the golden bracelets[d] *that you have on your hands.''* And Gideon *spread out a*
garment, and each of them threw in his bracelets. And all were weighed, *and*
their weight was found to be twelve talents.[e] And Gideon took them and *made*
4 idols from them and worshiped them. •And God said, ''One course is fixed, that
I should not rebuke Gideon during his lifetime, because, when he destroyed the
sanctuary of Baal, then they all said, '*Baal will avenge himself.*' Now if I should   Judg 6:25–32
chastise him because he has acted wickedly against me, you may say, 'Not God,
but Baal has chastised him, because he sinned against him first.' And so now
Gideon will die at a good old age so that they may have nothing[f] to say. But
afterward, when Gideon will have died, I will chastise him once and for all,
because he has offended me.'' *And Gideon died at a good old age and was buried*   Judg 8:32
in his own city.[g]

Abimelech

1 **37** And he had a son by a concubine. Abimelech[a] *killed all*[b] *his brothers,* for he   Judg 9:1
2 wished to be leader of the people. •Then all *the trees* of the field came together   Judg 9:5,18
Judg 9:10f.
to the fig tree[c] *and said, ''Come, reign over us.''* And *the fig tree said,* ''Was I
born for kingship or *rulership over the trees?* Or was I planted so as to reign
among you? And so as I cannot reign over you, so Abimelech will not get a long
tenure in his rule.'' And afterward *the trees* came together *to the vine and said,*   Judg 9:12f.
''Come, reign over us.'' And *the vine said,* ''I was planted *to give sweetness to*
men. Come and preserve the fruit of my vineyard. But as I cannot reign over you,   Ezek 3:18
so is the blood of Abimelech demanded from you.'' And then the trees came to
the apple tree[d] and said, *''Come, reign over us.''* And it said, ''It has been
commanded to me to provide sweet-smelling fruit for men. So I cannot reign over
3 you; and Abimelech will die by stoning.'' •And then *the trees* came *to the*   Judg 9:14
bramblebush and said, ''Come, reign over us.'' And *the bramblebush said,*
''When the thorn was born, truth shone forth in the form of a thorn.[e] And when
the first-formed[f] was condemned to death, the earth was condemned to bring forth
thorns and thistles. And when the truth enlightened Moses, it enlightened him by   Gen 3:18
Ex 3:2
means of a thicket of thorns. And now it will be that the truth may be heard by
you from me. And if you have spoken truthfully to the bramblebush that *it really*   Judg 9:15
should reign over you, sit in its shadow. But if hypocritically, *let the fire go forth*
and devour[g] *and eat up* the trees of the field, for the apple tree signifies[h] the
chastisers, and the fig tree signifies the people, and the vine signifies those who
4 were before us. •And now the bramblebush will be for you in this hour like
Abimelech, who killed his brothers unjustly and wishes to rule among you. If

---

c. The var. ''the sword of the LORD and Gideon''
is probably due to an assimilation to Judg 7:20.

d. In Judg 8:24–27 it is ''earrings.''

e. In Judg 8:26 it is 1,700 shekels of gold.

f. The phrase ''they may have nothing'' is
inserted in only one MS, but some such phrase is
necessary for sense.

g. The phrase ''in his own city'' is found in the
LXX and Lucianic MSS of Judg 8:32 but not in
the MT.

37 a. The proper name is missing in all but one
MS. Some other material seems to be missing here
also.

b. Only Ps-Philo and the Lucianic MSS of Judg
9:5 have ''all.''

c. The olive tree mentioned in Judg 9:8f. is
omitted.

d. Var. ''myrtle tree.'' Neither an apple tree nor
a myrtle tree is mentioned in Judg 9:8–15.

e. To what Ps-Philo is alluding is not clear.

f. Adam.

g. Perhaps the Lat. at one point had ''let the
fire go forth from the bramblebush,'' but then *de
rubo* (from the bramblebush) was corrupted into
devoret. See Judg 9:15 and Ps-Philo 37:4.

h. Lit. ''was made for.''

Abimelech be worthy of them whom he wishes to rule for himself, let him be
like the bramblebush that was made to rebuke the foolish among the people."
And *the fire went forth from the bramblebush and ate up* the trees that were in   Judg 9:15
5 the fields.ⁱ •After this *Abimelech ruled* the people one year and six months,ʲ and   Judg 9:22
he died when *a woman threw down upon him* half *a millstone.*ᵏ   Judg 9:53

Jair

1 **38** Jairᵃ built a sanctuary to Baal, and he deceived the people, saying, "Everyone   Judg 10:3-6
who will not sacrifice to Baal will die." And when all the people were sacrificing,
only seven men were not willing to sacrifice. Their names are these: Defal,
2 Abiesdrel, Getalibal, Selumi, Assur, Ionadali, Memihel.ᵇ •They answered and
said to Jair, "Behold we are mindful of the commandments that those who were
before us and Deborah our mother commanded us, saying, *'See that you do not*   Deut 5:32; Josh
turn your heart *to the right or to the left, but pay attention to the Law* of the LORD   1:7f.
day and night.' And now why do you corrupt the people of the LORD and deceive
them, saying, 'Baal is God; let us adore him'? And now if he is God as you say,
3 let him speak as God and then we will sacrifice to him." •And Jair said, "Burn   1Kgs 18:24
them in the fire, because they have blasphemed against Baal." And his servants
took them to burn them in the fire. And when they had put them in the fire,
Nathaniel,ᶜ the angel who was in charge of fire, came forth and extinguished the
fire and burned the servants of Jair. But he let the seven men escape in such a
way that none of the people saw them, because he had struck the people with
4 blindness. •And when Jair came to the place, he was burned with the fire; and
before he burned him up, the angel of the LORD said to him, "Hear the word of
the LORD before you die. And these words the LORD says: 'I have raised you up
from the landᵈ and appointed you leader over my people, but you rose up and
corrupted my covenant and deceived them and sought to burn up my servants
with the flame because they chastised you. Those who were burned with corruptible
fire, now are made alive with a living fire and are freed; but you will die, says
the LORD, and in the fire in which you will die there you will have a dwelling
place.' "ᵉ And afterward heᶠ burned him up, and he came to the pillarᵍ of Baal
and demolished it and burned Baal along with the people who stood by,ʰ that is,
a thousand men.

Jephthah

1 **39** And after these events *the sons of Ammon* came and began to attack Israel,   Judg 10:9
and they took many of their cities. And *the people were in distress,* and *they*   Judg 10:17f.
gathered together in Mizpah and were saying, each one to his neighbors, "Behold
now we look at the distress that encompasses us, and the LORD has departed from
us and now is not with us, and our enemies have captured our cities, and there is
no leader who may go in and go out before us. Now therefore let us see whom
we may appoint over us to fight our battle."
2 *Now Jephthah the Gileadite was a mighty warrior.* His brothers who *thrust him*   Judg 11:1-3

---

i. Perhaps the sentence should be in the future
or jussive and included within the quotation as in
Judg 9:15.

j. Judg 9:22 has "three years."

k. There seems to be a gap of some sort between
the end of ch. 37 and the beginning of ch. 38.

38 a. Most MSS omit the proper name, but the
rest of the story makes clear who is meant.

b. For a similar story, see 6:3-18 as well as
Dan 3 and 2Mac 7.

c. An angel named "Nathaniel" does appear in
rabbinic traditions but is not described as being in

charge of fire.

d. The var. "land of Egypt" may be merely the
mechanical repetition of a biblical cliché or may
be making some point about the origin of idolatrous
worship outside the land of Israel.

e. For the fire as the dwelling place of the
wicked, see 2Bar 44:15; 48:39, 43; 59:2; 64:7; and
85:13.

f. The angel of the LORD.

g. The reference to the pillar is sudden. Perhaps
the Heb. *mṣbt* (pillar) has been misread for *mzbh*
(altar).

h. Perhaps his devotees.

out from his own land envied him,[a] and he went and *dwelt in the land of Tob.*
3 *And worthless*[b] *men gathered around him and spent their time with him.* •And   Judg 11:5f.
when *Israel was being attacked, they came to* the land of *Tob to Jephthah and*
said to him, "Come, rule over the people. For who knows if you have been kept   Esth 4:14
safe to these days or freed from the hands of your brothers in order that you may
4 rule your people in this time?" •*And Jephthah said* to them, "Does love so return   Judg 11:7
after hatred, or does time conquer all things, for *you have driven me* out of my
land and *from the house of my father and now you have come to me when you*
are in distress?" And they said to him, "If the God of our fathers, when we had
sinned against him and he had delivered us up before our enemies and we were
hard pressed by them, was not mindful of our sins but freed us, why do you,
mortal man, want to remember the iniquities that happened to us in the time of
5 our distress? And therefore let it not be so before you, sir." •And Jephthah said,
"God can be not mindful of our sins, for he has the time and place where he as
God may restrain himself out of his long-suffering; but I, a mortal man and made
from the ground into which I will return, where will I expel my wrath and the
injury that you have done me?" And the people said to him, "Let the dove[c] to
which Israel has been compared teach you, because when her young are taken
from her, still she does not depart from her place, but she puts away the injury
6 done her and forgets it as if it were in the depth of the abyss." •And *Jephthah*   Judg 11:11
arose and *came with* them and gathered all the people and said to them, "You
know that, while our leaders were still alive, they warned us to follow our Law.
And Ammon and his sons turned the people from their way in which they walked,   Judg 10:13
and they served foreign gods who would destroy them. Now therefore set your
hearts on the Law of the LORD your God, and let us beg him together, and so we
will fight against our enemies, trusting and hoping in the LORD that he will not
deliver us up forever. Even if our sins be overabundant, still his mercy will fill
7 the earth."[d] •And all the people prayed together, men and women and children.
And when they prayed, they said, "Look, LORD, upon the people that you have
chosen, and may you not destroy the vine that your right hand has planted, in
order that this nation, which you have had from the beginning and always preferred
and for which you made dwelling places and brought into the land you promised,
may be for you as an inheritance; and may you not hand us over before those
who hate you, LORD."
8   And God repented of his wrath and strengthened the spirit of Jephthah. *And he*   Judg 11:29
sent a messenger to Getal[e] *the king of the sons of Ammon and said,* "Why are   Judg 11:12
you troubling our land and taking my cities? Or are you sad that Israel did not
take you first so that you might scatter those inhabiting the land? And now return
to me my cities, and my anger will cease from you. But if not, know that I will
come up to you and return to you past offenses and repay your wickednesses on
your own head. Or am I not mindful that you were deceitful to the people of
Israel in the wilderness?" And the ambassadors of Jephthah gave these messages
9 to the king of the sons of Ammon. •And Getal said, "Does Israel think highly of
itself in so far as it has taken possession of the land of the Amorites? And therefore
you say, 'Know that now I will take other cities from you and return your
wickedness to you and avenge the Amorites whom you have harmed.'" *And*   Judg 11:14
Jephthah sent another message to the king of the sons of Ammon, saying, "Truly
I have learned that God has brought you forward that I may destroy you unless
you cease from the iniquity by which you wish to harm Israel. And so I will come

39 a. Lit. "when he envied his brothers"; but
according to Judg 11:2 Jephthah's brothers envied
him. Perhaps in the original Heb. *bqn't 'hyw* (in
the envy of his brothers) the word *'hyw* was taken
as an objective rather than subjective genitive.
    b. Lit. "vagrant" (*vagi*). We have emended to
"worthless" (*vani*) on the basis of Judg 11:3.
    c. Israel is compared to the dove in 23:7; 4Ezra

5:26, and several rabbinic texts.
    d. See Rom 5:20.
    e. Perhaps this is "Zenon, surnamed Cotylas,
who was ruler of the city of Philadelphia" (Ammon)
in Josephus' *Ant* 13.8.1 §235 (also *War* 1.2.4 §60).
If this identification of Getal with Cotylas is correct,
then we could establish 135 B.C. as the earliest
possible date of composition for Ps-Philo.

to you and show myself to you. For they are not gods, as you say they are, who Judg 11:24
have given you the inheritance that you possess; but because you have been
deceived by following after stones, fire will come after you for vengeance.''

10　And because *the king of the sons of Ammon* would *not listen* to the voice of Judg 11:28
Jephthah, Jephthah rose up and armed all the people to go out and fight in battle
array, saying, *"When the sons of Ammon have been delivered into my hands and* Judg 11:30f.
I have returned, whoever meets me first *on the way will be a holocaust to the*
11　*Lord."* •And God was very angry and said, "Behold Jephthah has vowed that he
will offer to me *whatever meets him* first *on the way;* and now if a dog should Judg 11:31
meet Jephthah first, will the dog be offered to me?[f] And now let the vow of
Jephthah be accomplished against his own firstborn, that is, against the fruit of
his own body, and his request against his only-begotten. But I will surely free my
people in this time, not because of him but because of the prayer that Israel
prayed.''

The daughter of Jephthah

1　**40** *And Jephthah came and attacked the sons of Ammon, and the Lord delivered* Judg 11:32–35
them into his hands, and he struck down sixty[a] of their *cities.* And Jephthah
returned *in peace,* and women came out *to meet him in song and dance. And it
was his only daughter who came out* of the house first in the dance *to meet* her
father. *And* when *Jephthah saw her, he grew faint and said,* "Rightly was your
name called Seila,[b] that you might be offered in sacrifice. And now who will put
my heart in the balance and my soul on the scale? And I will stand by and see
which will win out, whether it is the rejoicing that has occurred or the sadness
that befalls me. And because *I opened my mouth to* my *Lord* in song with vows,[c]
2　*I cannot* call that back again." •*And* Seila *his daughter said to him,* "And who Judg 11:36
is there who would be sad in death, seeing the people freed?[d] Or do you not
remember what happened in the days of our fathers when the father placed the Gen 22
son as a holocaust,[e] and he did not refuse him but gladly gave consent to him,
and the one being offered was ready and the one who was offering was rejoicing?
3　And now do not annul everything you have vowed, but carry it out.[f] Yet one Judg 11:36–38
request I ask of you before I die, a small demand I seek before I give back my
soul: that *I may go into the mountains and stay* in the hills and walk among the
rocks, *I and my virgin companions,* and I will pour out my tears there and tell of
the sadness of my youth. And the trees of the field will weep for me, and the
beasts of the field will lament over me. For I am not sad because I am to die nor
does it pain me to give back my soul, but because my father was caught up in
the snare of his vow; and if I did not offer myself willingly for sacrifice, I fear
that my death would not be acceptable or I would lose my life in vain. These
things I will tell the mountains, and afterward I will return." *And* her father *said,*
4　"*Go.*" •And Seila the daughter of Jephthah, she and her virgin companions, *went* Judg 11:38
out and came and told it to the wise men of the people, and no one could respond
to her word.[g] And afterward she came to Mount Stelac,[h] and the LORD thought
of her by night and said, "Behold now I have shut up the tongue of the wise men
of my people for this generation so that they cannot respond to the daughter of
Jephthah, to her word, in order that my word be fulfilled and my plan that I

---

f. In b.Taʿan 4a there is speculation that Jephthah
might have met an unclean thing.

40 a. Judg 11:33 has twenty cities.
　b. The name of Jephthah's daughter is given as
Seila only in Ps-Philo. In Heb. the root *šʾl* means
"ask," and so Seila is the one "asked for," or
"requested."
　c. Lit. "in the song of vows."
　d. The same motif is found in Josephus' *Ant*
5.7.10 §265.

e. See 18:5 and 32:2–4 for a similar description
of the sacrifice of Isaac.
　f. According to the rabbis Jephthah's vow was
invalid.
　g. A rabbinic tradition says that Jephthah's
daughter was sacrificed because the scholars forgot
that his vow was invalid.
　h. Perhaps connected with the Heb. *šlg* (snow)
or the Aram. *tlg* (snow). TargOnk of Deut 3:9
describes Mount Hermon as the "mountain of
snow."

thought out not be foiled. And I have seen that the virgin is wise in contrast to her father and perceptive in contrast to all the wise men who are here. And now let her life be given at his request, and her *death* will be *precious before* me   Ps 116:15 always, and she will go away and fall into the bosom of her mothers."[i]

5   And when the daughter of Jephthah came to Mount Stelac, she began to weep, and this is her lamentation that she lamented and wept over herself before she departed. And she said,

"Hear, you mountains, my lamentation;
and pay attention, you hills, to the tears of my eyes;
and be witnesses, you rocks, of the weeping of my soul.
Behold how I am put to the test!
But not in vain will my life be taken away.
May my words go forth in the heavens,
and my tears be written in the firmament!
That a father did not refuse the daughter whom he had sworn to sacrifice,
that a ruler granted that his only daughter be promised for sacrifice.

6   But I have not made good on my marriage chamber,
and I have not retrieved my wedding garlands.
For I have not been clothed in splendor while sitting in my woman's chamber,[j]
And I have not used the sweet-smelling ointment,[k]
And my soul has not rejoiced in the oil of anointing that has been prepared for me.
O Mother, in vain have you borne your only daughter,
because Sheol has become my bridal chamber,
and on earth there is only my woman's chamber.
And may all the blend of oil that you have prepared for me be poured out,
and the white robe that my mother has woven, the moth will eat it.
And the crown of flowers that my nurse plaited for me for the festival,
may it wither up;
and the coverlet that she wove of hyacinth and purple in my woman's chamber, may the worm devour it.
And may my virgin companions tell of me in sorrow and weep for me through the days.

7   You trees, bow down your branches and weep over my youth,
You beasts of the forests, come and bewail[l] my virginity,
for my years have been cut off
and the time of my life grown old in darkness."

8   And on saying these things Seila *returned to her father, and he did everything*   Judg 11:39f. *that he had vowed* and offered the holocausts. Then all the virgins of Israel gathered together and buried the daughter of Jephthah and wept for her. And the children of Israel made a great lamentation and established that in that month on the fourteenth day of the month they should come together every year and weep for Jephthah's daughter for four days. And they named her tomb in keeping with 9 her name: Seila. •*And Jephthah judged* the sons of *Israel* ten[m] *years, and he died*   Judg 12:7 *and was buried* with his fathers.

i. The phrase "bosom of her mothers" seems like a feminist counterpart to the more usual "bosom of his fathers"; see also "woman of God" in 33:1.

j. The MSS have "sitting on my knees" (*sedens in genua mea*) or "sitting in my virginity" (*sedens in virginitate mea*). We emend to *sedens in genicio meo* (sitting in my woman's chamber) where *genicium* is a form of *gynaecium*, the opposite of the "bridal chamber." The other two uses of the term in this section are also emendations.

k. Lit. "Moses." In Lat. there may have been confusion between *Moysi* (Moses) and *moscho;* confusion at the Heb. level is also possible.

l. Lit. "trample" (*conculcate*), which we have emended to "bewail" (*conululate*).

m. The MT has six, the LXX sixty.

Abdon and Elon

1 **41** *And after him Abdon the son of Hillel the Pirathonite*[a] *arose as judge in*   Judg 12:13–15
Israel, *and he also judged the sons of Israel eight years.* And in his days the king
of Moab sent messengers to him, saying, "Behold now you know that Israel has
taken my cities, and now return them as a repayment." And Abdon said, "Have
you not learned from what happened to the sons of Ammon, unless perhaps it is
so that the sins of Moab have reached full measure?" And Abdon sent and took
from the people twenty thousand men and came out against Moab and attacked
them and killed forty thousand men of them, but the rest fled before him. And
Abdon returned in peace, and he offered holocausts and sacrifices to his LORD.
2 *And he died and was buried in* Effrata,[b] *his own city.* • And in that time the people
chose *Elon* and appointed him as judge for them. *And he judged Israel* twenty[c]   Judg 12:11f.
years. And in those days they attacked the Philistines and took from them twelve
3 cities. *And Elon died and was buried* in his own city. • But the sons of Israel
forgot the LORD their God and served the gods of those inhabiting the land; and
on account of this *they were handed over to the Philistines* and served them *forty*   Judg 13:1
years.

The announcement of Samson's birth

1 **42** *Now there was a man from the tribe of Dan whose name was Manoah,* son   Judg 13:2
of Edoc, son of Odon, son of Eriden, son of Fadesur, son of Dema, son of Susi,
son of Dan. *And he had a wife whose name was Eluma*[a] *the daughter of Remac,
and she was sterile and did not bear children* to him. And, every day, Manoah
her husband was saying to her, "Behold the LORD has shut up your womb so that
you may not bear children, and now let me go[b] that I may take another wife lest
I die without fruit." And she said, "Not me has the LORD shut up that I may not
bear children, but you that I may not bear fruit." And he said to her, "Would
2 that this could be tested and proved!"[c] • And they were quarreling daily and both
were very sad, because they were without fruit.[d] One night the wife went up to
the upper chamber[e] and prayed saying, "Behold you, LORD God of all flesh,
reveal to me whether it has not been granted to my husband or to me to produce
children, or to whom it may be forbidden or to whom it may be allowed to bear
fruit in order that whoever is forbidden may weep over his sins because he remains
without fruit. Or if both of us have been deprived, then reveal this to us also so
that we might bear our sins and be silent before you."
3   And the LORD heard her voice and sent his angel to her in the morning, *and*   Judg 13:3
he said to her, "You are the sterile one who does not bring forth, and you are
the womb that is forbidden so as not to bear fruit. But now the LORD has heard
your voice and paid attention to your tears and opened your womb. *And behold*   Judg 13:3,24,5

41 a. The MSS have "Addo son of Elech from
Praton." The description of Abdon contradicts that
of Josephus (*Ant* 5.7.15 §273): "Thanks to the
prevailing peace and security of the state, he too
did no brilliant deed."
   b. Judg 12:15 says that he was buried at Pirathon;
Effrata may be a corruption of this name.
   c. According to Judg 12:11 Elon was judge for
ten years.

42 a. This name for Samson's mother is found
nowhere else in Jewish literature. There are many
parallels between Samson's birth as narrated here
and those of John the Baptist and Jesus in Luke's
Gospel: a genealogy not derived from the OT,
sterility, prayer in seclusion, the angel's appear-

ance, the name announced. See also ch. 9.
   b. According to Jewish law the husband rather
than the wife must take the initiative in a divorce
proceeding; but see Mk 10:12.
   c. Lit. "the Law makes evident our experiment." We may have had a Heb. infinitive-absolute
construction *mstnw hwrh twrh;* then *twrh* was
translated as a noun meaning "Law." Our translation is based on this supposition. An idiomatic
rendering would be "Our experiment will indeed
prove it out!"
   d. Josephus (*Ant* 5.8.2 §277) speaks of the great
beauty of Samson's mother and her husband's
jealousy.
   e. A terrace or balcony, the part of the house
exposed to the sun.

you will conceive and bear a son, and you will *call his name Samson. For* this
one *will be dedicated* to your LORD.[f] *But see* that he[g] *does not taste from any*   Judg 13:4,14,5
fruit of the vine and eat any unclean thing, because (as he[h] himself has said) *he
will free Israel from the hand of the Philistines."* And when the angel of the
4 LORD had spoken these words, he departed from her. •*And she came* into the   Judg 13:6
house *to her husband and said* to him, "I am placing my hand upon my mouth,
and I will be silent before you all the days because I have boasted in vain and
have not believed your words. For the angel of the LORD *came to me* today and   Judg 13:6,3
revealed to me, saying, 'Eluma, *you are sterile, but you will conceive and bear*
5 *a son.'"* •And Manoah did not believe his wife, and being perplexed and sad, he
himself also went to the upper chamber and *prayed and said,* "Behold I am not   Judg 13:8
worthy to hear the signs and wonders that God has done among us or to see the
6 face of his messenger." •And while he was speaking these words, *the angel of*   Judg 13:9f.
the Lord came again to his wife. But she was in the field, and Manoah was in his
house. And the angel said to her, "Run and announce to your husband that God
7 has accounted him worthy to hear my voice." •*And the wife ran and called to*   Judg 13:10–12
her husband, and he hurried to *come* to the angel in the field.[i] The angel said to
him, "Go into your wife and do all these things." But he said, "I am going,[j]
but see to it, sir, that *your word*[k] *be accomplished* regarding your servant." And
8 he said, "It will be accomplished." •*And Manoah said to* him, "If I can, let me   Judg 13:15f.
persuade you to enter my house and eat bread with me; and know that, when you
go, I will give you gifts that you may take along with you to offer as a sacrifice
to the LORD your God." And the angel said to him, "I will not enter your house
with you, *nor eat your bread* nor take your gifts. For if you offer *sacrifice* from
9 what is not yours,[l] I cannot show favor to you." •And Manoah built an altar   Judg 13:19,23
upon the rock and offered *sacrifices and holocausts.* And when he had cut up the
meats and placed them on the altar, *the angel reached out and touched* them *with*   Judg 6:21
the tip of his staff. And fire came forth from the rock, and it devoured the
holocausts and sacrifices. *And the angel of the Lord went up* from there *with the*   Judg 13:20
10 *flame of fire.*[m] •*But Manoah and his wife saw these events and fell on their faces*   Judg 13:20
and said, *"Surely we will die because we have seen the Lord* face to face." And   Judg 13:22
Manoah said,[n] "It is not enough that I have seen him but I even asked his *name,*   Judg 13:16–18
not knowing that he was the minister of God." Now the angel who came was
named Fadahel.[o]

The exploits of Samson

1 **43** And in those days Eluma conceived and *bore a son and called his name*   Judg 13:24;
Samson, and the Lord was with him. And when he had begun to grow up and   Isa 7:14
sought to attack the Philistines, he took for himself a wife from the Philistines.   Judg 14f.
The Philistines burned her in the fire, because they had been badly humiliated by   Judg 15:6
2 Samson. •And afterward *Samson* was angry at Ashdod,[a] *and they locked him up*   Judg 16:1–3
and surrounded the city and said, "Behold now our enemy has been delivered
into our hands, and now let us gather together and let us save our own lives."
And when Samson arose at night and saw the city locked up, he said, "Behold

---

f. Ps-Philo may have had in mind a derivation
from the Heb. *šmš* (minister, serve) in the light of
Samson's Nazirite status.

g. In Judg 13:4, 14, it is Samson's mother who
is not to drink wine or eat anything unclean.

h. Presumably this is God.

i. Some MSS add "in spirit" (*in animo*) or "in
Ammo."

j. Var. "to him" (*ei*) rather than "I am going"
(*Eo*).

k. The MT of Judg 13:12 has "words."

l. If the angel accepted Manoah's gifts, then
Manoah would not have his own things to offer.

m. The MT of Judg 13:20 has "in the flame of
the altar." Ps-Philo agrees with the LXX here.

n. "And Manoah said" is absent from some
MSS but is necessary for the sense of the passage.

o. According to Judg 13:18 the angel's name is
pľy. Ps-Philo probably had an original *pľy'l,* which
in Gk. would have been Phalael, which in turn
was deformed into Fadahel.

43 a. Var. "Gaza," which is the reading of Judg
16:1. The Heb. *ʿzth* (to Gaza) could have been
mistranslated into Gk. as *Azōton.* But Ps-Philo
frequently changes the places of biblical events.

now those fleas have locked me up in their own city, and now the LORD will be
3 with me, and I will go out through their gates and attack them." •And he came   Judg 16:3
and put his left hand beneath the bar of the gate, and he took down the gate from
the wall by shaking it. One part of it he kept in his right hand[b] for a shield; the
other *he put on his shoulders.* And he carried it because he had no sword, and he
pursued the Philistines with it and killed 25,000 men with it. *And he took up*
4 everything that made up the gate and *brought them* up to the mountain. •Now   Judg 14:5f.
concerning *the lion* that he killed and concerning *the jawbone of the ass* by which   Judg 15:15f.
he killed the Philistines and concerning the *bonds that were broken off[c] from his*   Judg 15:14
arms as it were spontaneously and *the foxes* that he caught, are not these written   Judg 15:4f.
in the Book of Judges?
5   Then Samson went down to Gerar, a city of the Philistines, *and he saw there*   Judg 16:1,4
a harlot whose name was Delilah, and he was led astray after her and took her
to himself for a wife. And God said, "Behold now Samson has been led astray
through his eyes, and he has not remembered the mighty works that I did with
him; and he has mingled with the daughters of the Philistines and has not paid   Gen 39
attention to Joseph my servant who was in a foreign land and became a crown
for his brothers because he was not willing to afflict his own seed. And now
Samson's lust will be a stumbling block for him, and his mingling a ruin. And I
will hand him over to his enemies, and they will blind him. But in the hour of
his death I will *remember* him, *and I will avenge* him *upon the Philistines once*   Judg 16:28
6 *more."* •And after this his wife *was pressuring him* and kept saying to him,   Judg 16:16
"*Show me your power* and *in what your strength lies,* and so I will know that
you love me." And when Samson had tricked her three times *and she was still*   Judg 16:16f.
pressuring him daily, the fourth time *he revealed to her his heart.* And she got   Judg 16:19
him drunk, and while he slept, *she called in a barber and he cut the seven locks*
of his head, and his strength left him, because he had made such a revelation.
And she called the Philistines, and they beat Samson and blinded him and put   Judg 16:21
7 him in prison. •And on the day of their drinking bout *they summoned Samson to*   Judg 16:25
make sport of him. And he, *bound between two pillars,* prayed saying, "*Lord*   Judg 16:28,30
God of my fathers, hear me *once more and strengthen me in order that I may die*
with these Philistines, because the sight that they took from me was given freely
to me by you." And Samson added, saying, "Go forth, *my soul,* and do not be
8 sad; die, my body, and do not weep about yourself." •*And he grasped the two*   Judg 16:29-31
columns of the house[d] and shook them. *And the house* and all that was around it
fell down, and it killed all who were around it. And their number was 40,000[e]
men and women. *And Samson's brothers and all the house of his father went*
down and took him and buried him in the tomb of his father. Now he had judged
Israel twenty years.

The idols of Micah and the sin of Israel

1 **44** *And in those days there was no* leader *in Israel, but each one did what was*   Judg 17:6
2 *pleasing in his own eyes.* •And in that time there arose Micah the son of Dedila   Judg 17:1-4
the mother of Heliu, and he had one thousand pieces of gold and four wedges of
melted gold and forty double pieces of silver. And Dedila his mother said to him,
"My son, hear my voice, and you will make a name for yourself before death.
Take that gold and melt it down and make for yourself idols, and they will be as
3 gods for you, and you will become a priest for them. •And whoever wishes to
ask anything through them will come to you, and you will respond to him. And
there will be an altar in your house and a column made out of that gold you have;

---

b. For the reference to the two hands of Samson,
see Judg 16:29.
   c. The verb "broken off" suggests that the Heb.
behind Ps-Philo and the Lucianic MSS of Judg
15:14 may have been *wytkw* (from the root *ntk*)
rather than the MT's *wymsw.*

d. Ps-Philo agrees with the LXX[B] of Judg 16:29
in reading "the house" (*hbyt*) rather than "the
middle" (*htwk*).
   e. In Judg 16:27 the MT has three thousand and
the LXX seven hundred on the roof.

you will prepare frankincense for burning and sheep for sacrifice. And whoever wishes to offer a sacrifice will give seven double pieces for the sheep; and for the incense, if he wishes to burn it, he will give one double piece of silver of full weight. And your title will be 'priest,' and you will be called 'worshiper of the
4 gods.'" •And Micah said to her, "You have advised me well, Mother, on how to live. And now your name will be even greater than mine, and in the last days
5 all kinds of things will be requested of you." •And Micah set out and did Judg 17:5 everything that his mother had commanded him. And he shaped and made for himself three images of boys and calves, the lion, the eagle, and the dragon, and the dove. And all who were led astray would come to him. And if some wished to ask for a wife, they would ask him by means of the dove. But if anyone asked for sons, it was by the images of the boys. But whoever asked for riches did it through the likeness of the eagle. Whoever asked for courage, he advised him through the image of the lion. If for servants and maids, he asked through the images of the calves. But if for length of days, he asked by the image of the dragon.ª And his wickedness took many forms, and his impiety was full of trickery.
6   And then, when the sons of Israel were departing from the LORD, the LORD said, "Behold I will root up the earth and destroy the whole human race, because, when I established laws on Mount Sinai, I showed myself to the sons of Israel in the storm. And I said that they should not make idols, and they agreed not to Ex 20:2–17; carve out the images of gods. And I ordered them not to take my name in vain, Deut 5:6–21 and they agreed that they themselves would not take my name in vain. And I commanded them to keep the sabbath, and they agreed to keep it holy.ᵇ And I told them to honor father and mother, and they promised they would do it. And I ordered them not to steal,ᶜ and they agreed. And I told them not to commit murder, and they held it as acceptable not to do this. And I commanded them not to commit adultery, and they did not oppose this. And I ordered them not to speak false testimony and not to covet each one his neighbor's wife or his house or all
7 his possessions, and they agreed. •And I told them not to make idols nor the works of those gods that have been born from corruption under the name of 'graven image' and those things through which all these corruptions have been brought about.ᵈ For mortal men have made them, and the fire has served to melt them down. The skill of a man has produced them, and hands have manufactured them, and imagination has invented them.ᵉ By accepting these they took my name in vain, and they have given my name to graven images. And the day of the sabbath that they agreed to keep, they have done abominable things on it. Whereas I have told them to love father and mother, they have dishonored me, their Creator. And whereas I told them not to steal, they have dealt like thieves in their schemesᶠ with graven images. And whereas I told them not to kill, they kill those whom they seduce. And though I commanded them not to commit adultery, they have committed adultery with their zeal. And whereas they chose not to speak false testimony, they accepted false testimony from those whom they destroyed. And they lusted for foreign women.
8   "Therefore, behold I abhor the race of men, and I will cut away the root of my creation; and those dying will outnumber those being born, because the house of Jacob has been infected in its wickedness and the impiety of Israel has been

---

44 a. The various images may have something to do with the sanctuary of Mithras, where two torch-bearing youths, a bull, a lion, a serpent, and a bird customarily appear. But here there is no mention of the bull or the sun, both important features of the Mithraic cult.

b. Lit. "to sanctify themselves." But the ob-servance of the sabbath is clearly at issue; there may have been confusion at the level of Heb. or Gk.

c. This order of commandments—stealing, mur-der, adultery—is also found in Jer 7:9.

d. The text is corrupt here. We have added "And I told them" to make better sense; "of 'graven image'" is based on emending *sculptili sed* to *scuptilis et*. The point of the whole passage is to show that idolatry is the root of all sins.

e. For similar expressions, see WisSol 13:10–19.

f. Lit. "sense."

multiplied. And can I not totally destroy the tribe of Benjamin, because they first of all were led astray after Micah? And the people of Israel will not go unpunished. 9 But this will be an everlasting scandal remembered for generations. •Now I will deliver Micah to the fire, and his mother will be rotting away in his sight while she is alive upon the earth, and worms[g] will come forth from her body. And then, while they are speaking to one another, she will say[h] as a mother chastising her son, 'Behold what a sin you have committed!' And he will answer as a son heeding his mother and acting cleverly, 'And you have done even greater wickedness.' And the image of the dove that he made will be used for putting out his eyes, and the image of the eagle will be used for bringing fire upon them out of its wings, and the images of the boys that he made will be used for scraping his sides, and the image of the lion that he made will be like mighty ones 10 tormenting him.[i] •And I will not do this to Micah alone, but to all who sin against me.[j] And the race of men will know that they will not make me jealous by their inventions that they make, but to every man there will be such a punishment that in whatever sin he shall have sinned, in this he will be judged. And if they have lied before me, I will command the heaven and it will deny them rain. And if anyone wished to covet the wife[k] of his neighbor, I will command death and it will deny them the fruit of their womb. And if they will make a false declaration in my name, I will not hear their prayers. And when the soul is separated from the body, then they will say, 'Let us not mourn over these things that we suffer; but because whatever we ourselves have devised, these will we receive.'"

The crisis at Nob

1 **45** And in that time *a certain* man from the tribe of *Levi* came to Gibeah, and   Judg 19:1
he wanted to stay there when *the sun set*. And he wanted to enter there, but those   Judg 19:14
who dwelt there did not let him. *And he said to his servant*, "Walk on and lead   Judg 19:13
the mule, and we will go to the city of Nob;[a] perhaps they will let us enter it."
And he came there *and sat down in the open square of the city, and no one* said   Judg 19:15
to him, "Enter my house."
2   Now there was a certain Levite whose name was Bethac. When this man *had*   Judg 19:16-20
seen him, he *said to him*, "Are you Beel[b] from my tribe?" And he said, "I am."
And he said to him, "You do not know the wickedness of those who dwell in
this city. And who persuaded you to enter here? Get out of here in a hurry and
enter my house where I dwell, and stay there today; and the LORD will shut up
their heart[c] before us as he shut up the Sodomites before Lot." And he entered   Gen 19:10f.
3 the city and remained there that night. •And all those inhabiting the city came   Judg 19:22-25;
together and said to Bethac, *"Bring out* those *who have come* to you today. If   Gen 19:5,9
not, we will burn in the fire both you and them." *And he came out to them and
said to them, "Are not these our brothers? Let us not do evil* with them lest our
sins be multiplied against us." And they answered, "It has never happened that
the strangers gave orders to the natives." And they entered by force and *dragged*
him and *his concubine out, and they cast him off*. And when the man had been
let go, *they abused* his concubine until she died, because she had transgressed[d]
against her man once when she committed sin with the Amalekites, and on account   Judg 19:2

---

g. For great sinners being eaten alive by worms, see 63:4; 2Mac 9:9; Acts 12:23, and b.Soṭ 35a.

h. Lit. "said"; but the sense demands a future or present.

i. The calves and the dragon are omitted.

j. That is, the punishment is to fit the crime.

k. The MSS have "property" (*rem*), but in view of the principle of the punishment fitting the crime ("deny them the fruit of their womb") we have emended to "wife" (*uxorem*).

45 a. The best MSS have "new city" (*civitatem*

novam), but see 46:3.

b. Ps-Philo is unique in giving the names Bethac and Beel.

c. Our concept of "mind" as the organ of thought and perception is presupposed by "heart." In Gen 19:10f. the Sodomites are struck blind.

d. The fate of the concubine in the Bible is not connected to her personal sins as it is here, but Ps-Philo's interpretation may take its rise from Judg 19:2 as well as from his own theological outlook. For his horror at intermarriage with gentiles, see 9:5; 18:13f.; 21:1; 30:1; 44:7.

4 of this the LORD God delivered her into the hands of sinners. •And when it was
morning, Beel *went out* and found his concubine dead and *put her on the mule*   Judg 19:27–29
and hurried away *and came into* Cades.ᵉ And *he took her* body *and cut it up into
parts and sent her around to the* twelve *tribes*, saying, "These things have been
done to me in the city of Nob, and those dwelling there *rose up against me to*   Judg 20:5
kill me*, and they took *my concubine* while I was locked up and they killed her.
And if being silent pleases you, nevertheless the LORD judges. But if you wish to
5 take revenge, the LORD will help you." •And all the men of the twelve tribes   Judg 20:1
were disturbed, and *they gathered together* in Shiloh,ᶠ and each one said to his
neighbor, "If such *wickedness is done in Israel*, Israel will cease to be."   Judg 20:6
6   And the LORD said to the adversaryᵍ, "Did you see this foolish people disturbed
in the hourʰ in which they ought to have died, when Micah acted craftily so as
to lead the people astray with the dove and the eagle and with the image of the
men and the calves and the lion and the dragon? And so because they were not
provoked to anger then, therefore let their plan be in vainⁱ; and their heart will be
so disturbed that the sinners as well as those allowing the evil deeds will be
destroyed."

The defeat of Israel

1 **46** And when it was morning, the people of Israel were disturbed and said, "Let   Judg 20:11
us go up and search out the sin that has been committed in order that *wickedness*   Judg 20:13
be taken away from us." And then they said, "Let us ask the LORD first and   Judg 20:27f.
learn if he will deliver our brothers into our hands; if not, let us desist." And
Phinehas said to them, "Let us bring out the Urim and Thummim."ᵃ And the
LORD answered them, saying, *"Go up, because I will deliver them into your*
2 hands."* But he led them astray so that he might fulfill his words. •And they went   Judg 20:12f.
up for battle and came into the city of Benjamin and *sent* messengers *saying*,
"Send us *the men* who have done this wicked deed, and we will spare you but
return to each his own evil." And the people of Benjamin hardened their heart,
and they said to the people of Israel, "Why should we deliver our brothers to
you? And if you do spare them, will we not fight against you?" And the people
of *Benjamin went out* to meet the sons of Israel and pursued them. And the sons
of Israel fell before them, and they *struck down* among them forty-five thousandᵇ   Judg 20:21
3 men. •And the heart of the people was very much disturbed, *and they came*   Judg 20:26
mourning and weeping to Shiloh. And they said, "Behold the LORD has delivered
us before those dwelling in Nob, and now let us ask the LORD who among us has   Judg 20:23
sinned." *And they asked the Lord,* and he said to them, "If you wish, *go up* and   Judg 20:28
fight, and they will be delivered *into your hands,* and then it will be told to you
why you have fallen before them." And they went up *the next day* to attack them,   Judg 20:24f.
and the sons of Benjamin went out and pursued Israel *and killed* among them
4 forty-six thousandᶜ men. •And the heart of the people grew very faint, and they   Judg 20:26–28
said, "Has God wished to lead his people astray? Or has he so established it on
account of the evil that was done, that the innocent as well as those who do
wicked deeds should fall together?" And on saying these words they fell before
the ark of the covenant of the Lord and tore their garments and put ashes on their
heads, they and *Phinehas the son of Eleazar the priest*, who prayed and said,

---

e. Var. "Gades." Perhaps this is the Levitical
city of Kedesh (1Chr 6:57).

f. According to Judg 20:1 the assembly took
place at Mizpah; according to Judg 20:18 there was
an assembly at Bethel.

g. The Lat. *anteciminus* has been taken over
from the Gk. *antikeimenos* (adversary), which is
most likely the equivalent of the Heb. *śtn;* see Job
1:6–12.

h. The MSS have "land" (*terra*), but the emendation to "hour" (*hora*) seems likely in view of
"they were not provoked to anger then."

i. Reading *vanum* instead of the MSS *manu*
(hand) or *malum* (evil).

46 a. Lit. "the demonstration and truth," which
renders the Gk. *dēlōsis kai alētheia* and the Heb.
'wrym wtmym. This refers to an oracular device
carried in the priest's breastplate. See 47:2.

b. In Judg 20:21 the number is twenty-two
thousand.

c. In Judg 20:25 the number is eighteen thousand.

"What is this deceit by which you have led us astray, LORD? If what the sons of Benjamin have done is right in your sight, why have you not told us so we might consider it? But if it did not please you, why have you allowed us to fall before them?"

The fable of the lion

1 **47** And Phinehas added, saying, "God of our fathers, hear my voice and tell your servant today whether this has been done correctly in your sight, or perhaps the people have sinned and you were not willing to root out their evil deeds so as to correct those among us who have sinned against you. For I remember in my Num 25:6–18 youth when Jambres sinned in the days of Moses your servant, and I went and entered in and was possessed with jealousy in my soul, and I hoisted both of them[a] up on my sword. And the rest wished to rise up against me and kill me, and you sent your angel and you killed from them twenty-four thousand men, and
2 you freed me from their hands. •And now you have sent the eleven tribes up, saying to them, 'Go and kill them'; and they went and were delivered up. And now they say that your Urim and Thummim[b] are telling lies in your sight. And now, LORD God of our fathers, do not hide from your servant but tell us why you have brought this wickedness against us."
3 And the LORD saw that Phinehas had prayed earnestly before him, and he said to him, "I myself have sworn, says the LORD; if I had not sworn, I would not have remembered you in what you have said, nor would I have answered you
4 today. And now say to the people, 'Stand and hear the word of the LORD.' •These words the LORD says: 'There was a certain mighty lion[c] in the midst of the forest to whose power all the beasts entrusted the forest that he might guard it lest perhaps other wild animals should come and destroy it. And while the lion was guarding these, some wild animals[d] arrived from another forest and devoured all the young of the animals and destroyed the fruit of their wombs. And the lion looked on and was silent. And the animals were at peace, because they had entrusted the forest to the lion and did not realize that their own offspring had
5 been destroyed. •And after a time there arose from those who had entrusted the forest to the lion a very small animal, and he ate up the small cub of another wicked animal. And behold the lion roared and disturbed all the animals of the
6 forest, and they fought among themselves, and each attacked his neighbor. •And when many animals were destroyed, another cub from another great forest saw the lion and said, "Have you destroyed so many animals? What is this wickedness that when so many animals and their offspring were unjustly destroyed previously by other wicked animals, and when all the animals should have been moved to avenge themselves when their fruit was being destroyed in vain, then you were silent and did not speak? But now one cub of a wicked animal has perished, and you have so aroused the whole forest that all the animals should eat one another up unjustly, so that the forest is depleted. And now you ought to be destroyed first, and so you will make the rest secure." And the cubs of the animals heard this and killed the lion first, and they appointed the cub in his place, and so all the other animals were subject to one authority.'
7 "Micah[e] arose and made you rich by these things that he and his mother made. And they were wicked and evil things that no one before them had discovered, but by his own craftiness he made them—graven images that had not been made until this day. And no one was provoked but all were led astray, and you saw the

---

47 a. They are not named in Ex 7:11 but are called Jannes and Jambres in the Jewish tradition and 2Tim 3:8.

b. See 46:1. We have emended *manifestationes tue veritates* to *manifestationes tue et veritates*.

c. The species of the animal is lacking in all but one MS but can be supplied from the rest of the

story.

d. Lit. "animals of the field" (*fere agri*); but *agri* may be a mistake for the Gk. *agroi* (wild, savage).

e. Seder Olam 12 and Est Rabbah 37:7 also connect the sin of Micah and the crime of the Benjaminites.

8 fruit of your womb destroyed and you were silent like that wicked lion. •And now on seeing how this man's concubine, who had done wicked deeds, died, you were all disturbed and came to me, saying, 'Will you deliver the sons of Benjamin into our hands?' Therefore I have deceived you and said, 'I will deliver them to you.' And now I have destroyed you, who were silent then. And so I will take my revenge on all who have acted wickedly.''

9 *And* all the people *rose up* together and went away. *And the sons of Benjamin*   Judg 20:31–37
came out to meet them, thinking that they would conquer them *as before,* and *they did not know that evil had* reached full measure *against them.* And when *they had come out as at first* and pursued them, the people fled from before them so as to *give ground.* And then they rose up from their hiding places, and the   Judg 20:42
10 sons of Benjamin were *in their midst.* •And when those who were fleeing *turned*   Judg 20:41–43
back, eighty-five thousand[f] people of the city of *Nob,* men and women, were killed. And the sons of Israel burned the city, and *they destroyed all* their spoils   Judg 20:37
that had been snatched away *by the edge of the sword.* And none of the sons of Benjamin survived except *six hundred men* who *fled* and were not found in the   Judg 20:46–48
battle. And all the people returned to Shiloh, and Phinehas the son of Eleazar the
11 priest was with them. •These are they who were left from the race of Benjamin, the rulers of the tribe, of ten families, whose names are these.[g] Of the first family: 1Chr 8
Ezbaile, Zieb, Balac, Rein, Debac, Belloch. And of the second family: Netach, Zenip, Fenoch, Demech, Geresaraz. And from the third family: Ierimuth, Veloth, Amibel, Genuth, Nefuth, Fienna. And from the fourth city: Gemuf and Eliel, Gemet, Soleph, Rafaf, and Doffo. And from the fifth family: Anuel, Code, Fretan, Remmon, Peccan, Nabath. From the sixth family: Refaz, Sefet, Arafaz, Metach, Adhoc, Balinoc. And from the seventh family: Benin, Mefiz, Araf, Ruimel, Belon, Iaal, Abac. From the tenth[h] family: Enoflasa, Melec, Meturia, Meac. And
12 the rest of the rulers of the tribe who survived were sixty in number. •And in that time the LORD repaid to Micah and his mother all he had said. And Micah was destroyed in the fire and his mother was rotting away, just as the LORD had said concerning them.

The ascension of Phinehas

1 **48** And in that time Phinehas laid himself down to die, and the LORD said to him, ''Behold you have passed the 120 years that have been established for every   Gen 6:3
man. And now rise up and go from here and dwell in Danaben on the mountain and dwell there many years. And *I will command* my eagle, and *he will nourish*   1Kgs 17:4
you there, and you will not come down to mankind until the time arrives and you be tested in that time; and you will shut up the heaven then, and by your mouth   1Kgs 17:1
it will be opened up.[a] And afterward you will be lifted up into the place where those who were before you were lifted up, and you will be there until I remember the world. Then I will make you all come, and you will taste what is death.''
2 And Phinehas went up and did all that the LORD commanded him. Now in those
3 days when he appointed Eli[b] as priest, he anointed him in Shiloh. •Now in that time when he went up, then the sons of Israel were celebrating Passover,[c] and they commanded the sons of Benjamin, saying, ''Go up and get wives for   Judg 21:17–19
yourselves, because *we cannot give* you *our daughters.* For we *made a vow* in the time of our anger, but let it not happen that one *tribe be blotted out from Israel.'' And the sons of Benjamin* went up *and seized* for themselves *wives and*   Judg 21:23
4 *built for themselves* Gabaon and began *to dwell* there. •And while the sons of   Judg 21:25

---

f. In Judg 20:46 there are twenty-five thousand men.

g. Some of the names may come from 1Chr 8: Geresaraz (cf. Gera 8:7), Ierimuth (cf. Jeremoth 8:14), Eliel (8:20), and Melec (cf. Melech 8:35).

h. The eighth and ninth families are missing.

48 a. Phinehas is described in terms reminiscent of Elijah.

b. The MSS have ''him'' (*eum*), but in the light of 50:3 and 52:2 Eli seems to be meant.

c. Judg 21:19 merely describes it as a yearly feast.

Israel were at rest in the meantime, *they had no* leader *in those days, and each
5 one did what was pleasing in his own eyes.* •These are the commandments and
judgments and testimonies and manifestations that were in the days of the judges
of Israel, before a king ruled over them.

The search for a new leader

1 **49** And in that time the sons of Israel began to make a request from the LORD,
and they said, "Let all of us cast lots[a] to see who it is who can rule us as Kenaz
did. For perhaps we will find a man who may free us from our distress, because
2 it is not appropriate for the people to be without a ruler." •And they cast the lot.
And when no one was found, the people were very sad and said, "The people
were not worthy to be heard by the LORD. Therefore[b] he did not answer us. And
now let us cast lots by tribes, if God may be reconciled by a large group. For we
know that God will be reconciled with those worthy of him." And they cast the
lot by tribes, and upon no tribe did the lot come forth. And Israel said, "Let us
choose from among ourselves, for we are put in a position of need. For we know
3 that God has hated his people and his soul has detested us." •And a certain man
by the name of Nethez[c] answered and said to the people, "He does not hate us,
but we have made ourselves so hateful that God should abandon us. And so, even
if we die, let us not abandon him, but let us flee to him. We who have walked
in our evil ways have not known him who created us, and so our plan will be in
vain. For I know that God will not reject us forever, nor will he hate his people
for all generations. And so strengthen yourselves, and let us pray again, and let
us cast lots by cities. For even if our sins are many, nevertheless his long-suffering
4 will not fail." •And they cast lots by cities, and Ramathaim[d] came out in the lot.
And the people said, "So Ramathaim is accounted more just than all the cities of
Israel, because he has chosen it above all the cities." And each one said to his
neighbor, "In that city that came out in the lot let us cast a lot by men, and let
5 us see whom the LORD has chosen from it." •And they cast the lot by men, and
it fell upon no one except Elkanah. Because the lot fell out upon him, the people
took him and said, "Come, and be a leader for us." And Elkanah said to the
people, "I cannot be a leader over this people, nor can I be considered[e] one who
could be a leader for you. But if my sins have caught up with me, I will kill
myself so that you may not defile me. For it is just that I should die only for my
own sins rather than to bear the burden of this people."
6 And the people saw that Elkanah was not willing to exercise leadership over
them, and they prayed again to the LORD, saying, "LORD God of Israel, why
have you abandoned your people in the victory of their enemies, and in the time
of distress why have you neglected your inheritance? Behold even he who has
been chosen in the lot has not fulfilled your commandments. But this happened
only because the lot fell out on him and we thought we had a leader. And behold
it has happened that even he is contending[f] against the lot. Whom will we ask
for once more, or to whom will we flee, or where is the place of our relaxation
and rest? For if the ordinances that you have established with our fathers are true,
saying, '*I will multiply your seed,*' and they will experience this, then it would   Gen 16:10
have been better to say to us, 'I am cutting off your seed,' than to neglect our
7 root." •And God said to them, "If I were to pay you back according to your evil
deeds, it would be necessary to pay no attention at all to your race. And what
will I do that my name will come to be invoked upon you? And now know that

---

49 a. See ch. 25.

b. Lit. "because." The Heb. probably had
"therefore" (*'l kn*), but at the level of Gk., *dio,*
"therefore," was confused with *dioti,* "because,"
which was taken over into the Lat. as *quia.*

c. The name may have some relation to the Heb.
and Aram. term for "lot."

d. The MSS have Armathem or Arimathes; see
1Sam 1:1.

e. In all the MSS the verb *existimare* is active,
but Elkanah has not been asked to think of a
substitute. We have emended to *existimari.*

f. Var. "even if he were not contending."

Elkanah, upon whom the lot has fallen, cannot rule among you; but rather his son who will be born from him, he will rule among you and prophesy. And *from this* time on, *a ruler will not be lacking* from you for many years." •And the people said, "Behold, LORD, Elkanah has ten sons, and who of them will rule or prophesy?" And God said, "None of the sons of Peninnah can rule the people, but the one who is born from the sterile woman whom I have given to him as a wife will be a prophet before me. And I will love him as I have loved Isaac, and his name will be before me always." And the people said, "Behold perhaps now God has remembered us so as to free us from the hand of those who hate us[g]." And on that day they made peace offerings and feasted according to their customs.[h]

Gen 49:10
1Sam 1:8

The prayer of Hannah in her distress

1 **50** And Elkanah had *two wives. The name of one was Hannah, and the name of the other was Peninnah. And* because *Peninnah had sons and Hannah did not,* Peninnah *taunted*[a] *her,* saying, "What does it profit you that Elkanah your husband loves you, for you are a *dry tree?* And I know that my husband will love me, because he delights in the sight of my sons standing around him like a plantation 2 of olive trees." •And so it was when she was taunting her daily, and Hannah was saddened very much. And she had been fearing God from her youth. It happened that on the holy day[b] of Passover, when her *husband went up to sacrifice,* Peninnah was insulting Hannah, saying, "A wife is not really loved even if her husband loves her or her beauty.[c] *Let* Hannah *not boast in* her appearance; *but she who boasts, let her boast*[d] when she sees her offspring before her. And when among women the fruit of her womb is not so, love will be in vain. For what did it profit Rachel that Jacob loved her? And unless the fruit of her womb had been given to him, his love would have been in vain." And when Hannah heard these words, 3 *her soul grew faint and poured out tears.* •And her husband saw her and said, "*Why* are you sad? *And why do you not eat? And why does your heart fall within you?* Are not your ways of behaving[e] *better than the ten sons* of Peninnah?" And *Hannah* listened to him, *and she rose up after she ate* and came *to Shiloh* to the house of the LORD, where *Eli the priest dwelt,* whom Phinehas the son of Eleazar 4 the priest[f] had appointed, as had been commanded him. •And Hannah prayed and said, "Did you not, LORD, search out the heart of all generations before you formed the world? Now what womb is born opened or dies closed unless you wish it? And now let my prayer ascend before you today lest I go down from here empty, because you know my heart, how I have walked before you from the day 5 of my youth." •And Hannah did not want to pray out loud as all people do. For then she thought, saying, "Perhaps I am not worthy to be heard, and Peninnah will then be even more eager to taunt me as she does daily when she says, '*Where is your God* in whom you trust?' And I know that neither she who has many sons is rich nor she who has few is poor, but whoever abounds in the will of God is rich. For who may know what I have prayed for? If they know that I am not heard in my prayer, they will blaspheme. And I will not have any witness except in my own soul, because my tears are the servant of my prayers."

1Sam 1:2
1Sam 1:6
Isa 56:3
Ps 128:3
1Sam 1:3
1Sam 1:7
1Sam 2:7,10
1Sam 1:10
1Sam 1:8f.
1Sam 1:13
Ps 42:3
1Sam 2:5

6 And while she was praying, *Eli*[g] the priest saw that she was disturbed and acted like a drunken woman, and he *said to her,* "Go and put your wine away

1Sam 1:14f.

g. The MSS lack "us." Perhaps the Heb. *šn'ynw* (our enemies) was misread as *šn'ym* (enemies).

h. Lit. "dispositions." which may refer to orders in the sense of groups arranged according to some hierarchical scheme (see 1QSa).

50 a. While "taunted" is absent from the LXX of 1Sam 1:6, it is found in the Lucianic MSS, the MT, and other texts.

b. Lit. "the good day."

c. Or "the love of wife does not depend on her

husband's loving her or her beauty."

d. In the LXX of 1Sam 2:10 there is a long expansion on the theme of boasting.

e. For "ways of behaving" (*mores*), perhaps read "loves" (*amores*).

f. For Eli as appointed by Phinehas, see 48:2 and 52:2.

g. In the LXX of 1Sam 1:14 the servant (*paidarion*) of Eli speaks; Ps-Philo here agrees with the MT.

from you."[h] *And she said,* "Is my prayer so heard that I am called a drunken woman? Now I am drunk with sorrow, and I have drunk the cup of my weeping."

7 And Eli the priest said to her, "Tell me why you are being taunted." And she said to him, "I am the wife of Elkanah; and because God has shut up my womb,   1Sam 1:15
I have prayed before him that I do not go forth from this world without fruit and that I do not die without having my own image." *And Eli* the priest *said to her,*   1Sam 1:17
"Go, because I know[i] for what you have prayed; *your prayer* has been heard."

8 But Eli the priest did not want to tell her that a prophet had been foreordained to be born from her. For he had heard that when the LORD spoke concerning him.
And Hannah *came into her house,*[j] and she was consoled of her sorrow, but she   1Sam 1:18
told no one what she had prayed.

The birth of Samuel

1 **51** *In those days she conceived and bore a son and called his name Samuel,*   1Sam 1:20
which is interpreted "mighty one,"[a] as God had named him when he prophesied
about him. *And* Hannah[b] *remained there and nursed the infant until* he was two   1Sam 1:23f.
years old. *And when she had weaned him, she went up with him*[c] and brought
gifts in her hands. And the child was very handsome, and the LORD was with him.

2 And *Hannah* placed *the boy* before *Eli and said to him,*[d] "This is the desire I   1Sam 1:25f.
desired, and this is *the request I have asked.*" And Eli said to her, "You have
not asked alone, but the people have prayed for this. This is not your request
alone, but it was promised previously to the tribes. And through this boy your
womb has been justified so that you might provide advantage for the peoples[e] and

3 set up the milk of your breasts as a fountain for the twelve tribes." •And on   1Sam 2:1
hearing this *Hannah prayed and said,*

> "Come to my voice, all you nations,
> and pay attention to my speech, all you kingdoms,
> because my mouth has been opened that I should speak
> and my lips have been commanded to sing a hymn to the LORD.
> Drip, my breasts, and tell your testimonies,
> because you have been commanded to give milk.
> For he who is milked from you will be raised up,
> and the people will be enlightened by his words,
> and he will show to the nations the statutes,[f]
> and his *horn will be exalted* very high.   1Sam 2:10

4 > And so I will speak my words openly,
> because from me will arise the ordinance of the LORD,   Isa 51:4
> and all men will find the truth.
> *Do not* hurry *to say great things*   1Sam 2:3
> *or to bring forth from your mouth lofty* words,
> but delight in glorifying (God).
> For when the light[g] from which wisdom is to be born will go forth,   Isa 51:4
> not those who possess many things will be said to be rich,
> nor those who have borne in abundance will be called mothers.
> *For the sterile one has been satisfied*[h] *in childbearing,*   1Sam 2:5

---

h. Only the Lucianic MSS of 1Sam 1:14 have both "go" and "from you."

i. Var. "you know"; but in this context "I know" seems preferable.

j. The phrase "into her house" is found in the LXX and the Lucianic MSS of 1Sam 1:18 but not in the MT; but see 1Sam 1:19.

51 a. Based on the possible division of "Samuel" in Heb. as *šmw ʾl* meaning "his name is El (the Mighty One)."

b. Only Ps-Philo and one Lucianic MS mention Hannah by name in 1Sam 1:23.

c. The expression "with him" is found in the LXX, the Lucianic MSS, and Ps-Philo but not in the MT of 1Sam 1:24.

d. Only Ps-Philo and the Lucianic MSS have "to him" in 1Sam 1:26.

e. This may refer to the gentiles, but the parallelism of the next line suggests that the peoples of Israel are being discussed.

f. Lit. "boundaries"; see 15:6.

g. The light is the anticipated prophet Samuel.

h. The phrase depends on the Hebrew *śbʿh* of 1Sam 2:5, which is usually interpreted with the number "seven" in mind.

but she who had many children has been emptied.

5 Because *the Lord kills* in judgment,   1Sam 2:6
and *brings to life* in mercy.
For them who are *wicked* in this world he kills,[i]   1Sam 2:9
and he brings *the just* to life when he wishes.
Now *the wicked* he will shut up in darkness,
but he will save his light for the just.
And when *the wicked* have died, then they will perish.
And when *the just* go to sleep, then they will be freed.
Now so will every judgment endure,
until he who restrains[j] will be revealed.

6 Speak, speak, Hannah, and do not be silent.
Sing a hymn, daughter of Batuel,[k]
about the miracles that God has performed with you.
Who is Hannah that a prophet is born[l] from her?
Or who is the daughter of Batuel that she should bear *the light to the*   Isa 51:4
peoples?
Rise up, you also, Elkanah, and *gird your loins.*   Jer 1:17;
Sing a hymn about the wonders of the LORD.   Job 38:3
Because Asaph prophesied in the wilderness about your son, saying,
'*Moses and Aaron were among his priests,*   Ps 99:6
and Samuel was there among them.'
Behold the word has been fulfilled,
and the prophecy has come to pass.
And these words will endure
until they give *the horn to his anointed one*   1Sam 2:10f.
and *power* be present at the throne of his *king.*
And let my son stay here and serve
until he be made a light for this nation."

7   *And they departed*[m] and set out with gladness, rejoicing and exulting in heart   1Sam 2:11
over all the glory that God had worked with them. But the people came down to
Shiloh together with timbrels and dances, lutes and harps, and they came to Eli
the priest and brought to him Samuel. And they stood Samuel before the LORD,
anointed him, and said, "Let the prophet live among the people, and may he be
a light to this nation for a long time!"

The sons of Eli

1 **52** Now Samuel was very young and knew nothing of these things. And while   1Sam 2:11–16
he *was serving before the Lord*, the two *sons of Eli* were not walking in the ways
of their fathers and began to do wicked things to the people and multiplied their
own wickednesses. And they were lingering near the house of Bethac, and when
the people came together to sacrifice, *Hophni and Phinehas* came and provoked   1Sam 2:34
the people to anger by taking their sacrificial offerings before they were offered
2 as holy to the LORD. •And this was pleasing neither to the LORD nor to the people
nor to their father. And so their father *said to them*, "What is this *report that I*   1Sam 2:23f.
hear about you? Or do you not know that I have received this place that Phinehas
committed to me?[a] And if we destroy what we have received, what will we say
if he who committed it asks for it again and he for whom he committed it should
harm us? And now straighten out your ways and walk in good ways, and your

i. Lit. "For they are wicked in this world"; we
have added "he kills" to make a parallel with
"brings the just to life."
   j. Most likely God himself; see 2Thes 2:6f.
   k. Only Ps-Philo mentions the name of Hannah's
father as Batuel.
   l. Lit. "is." In view of the parallel expression

"she should bear" we would expect "is born."
This may reflect confusion between *egenēthē* (was)
and *egennēthē* (was born); see 17:3; 30:5.
   m. Ps-Philo agrees with the LXX and Lucianic
MSS of 1Sam 2:11 in having a plural verb.

52 a. See 48:2 and 50:3.

positions will remain the same. But if you refuse and do not restrain your wicked
schemes, you will destroy yourselves, and the priesthood will be in vain and what
has been sanctified will be considered as nothing. And then they will say, 'Did
the staff of Aaron spring up in vain or has the flower born of it come down to
3 nothing?' •And so while you still can, my sons, correct what you have done
sinfully, and the men against whom you have sinned will pray for you. But if
you are not willing and you remain in your wickedness, I will be guiltless and   1Sam 2:25
will only be sorry if perhaps I will hear of the day of your death before I die. But
even if this should happen, I will be free of guilt; and though I will be saddened,
4 nevertheless you will perish." •And his sons *did not listen, because the Lord* had   1Sam 2:25
made a decision about them *that they should die*, for they had sinned. For when
he said to them, "Repent of your wicked way," they were saying, "When we
grow old, then we will repent."[b] And they who were warned by their father were
not permitted to repent, because they were always rebelling and acting very
unjustly in despoiling Israel. The LORD was angry at Eli.[c]

The call of Samuel

1 **53** And *Samuel was serving before the Lord, still not knowing* what *the oracles*   1Sam 3:1; 2:11;
of the Lord were. He had not yet heard the oracles of the LORD. He was eight   3:7
2 years old.[a] •And when God remembered Israel, he wished to *reveal* to Samuel   1Sam 3:7,3
his *words. And Samuel was sleeping in the temple of the Lord.* And when God
called to him, he gave it consideration first, saying, "Behold now Samuel is
young so as to be beloved before me. In spite of the fact that he has not heard
the voice of the LORD or has been confirmed with the word of the Most High,
nevertheless he is like my servant Moses. To an eighty-year-old I spoke, but
Samuel is eight years old. And Moses saw the fire first, and his heart was very
much afraid. And if Samuel should see fire now, how will he survive? And so
now my voice to him will be like that of a man, and not like that of God. And
3 when he has understood, then I will speak to him like God." •And in the middle   1Sam 3:4f.
of the night a voice from heaven called him. And Samuel was awakened, and he
recognized it as the voice of Eli the priest, and *he ran to* him *and said,* "Why
have you awakened me, Father? For I was frightened, because you never called
me at night." And Eli said, "Woe is me! Has an unclean spirit led my son Samuel
astray?" *And he said* to him, "Go, *sleep.* For *I have not called you.* Nevertheless,
tell me this, if you remember: How often did he who summoned you call?" And
he said, "Twice."[b] And Eli said to him, "Tell me, whose voice did you recognize,
4 my son?" He said, "Yours. Therefore I ran to you." •And Eli said, "In you I
see this sign that men will have from today unto eternity, that if one should call
to another twice by night or in midday, they will know that it is an evil spirit.
But if he should call again a third time, I will know that it is an angel." *And*   1Sam 3:5
5 *Samuel went away and slept.* •And a second time he heard a voice from heaven,   1Sam 3:6,8f.
and *he rose up* and *ran to Eli and said to him,* "Why has he called me? For I
have heard the voice of my father Elkanah." And then *Eli understood that* God
had begun *to summon him. For Eli said,* "With the two voices by which God
has already called to you, he has become like a father and a master; now with the
6 third he will be like God." •And he said to him, "With your right ear pay   1Sam 3:11
attention, with your left be deaf.[c] For Phinehas the priest has commanded us,
saying, 'The right ear hears the LORD by night, but the left an angel.' And so if

---

b. See b.Yoma 85b: "If one says, 'I shall
continue to sin and later repent,' the opportunity
to repent is not granted to him."
c. In 52:2f. Eli has made it clear that he has not
been involved in the sin of his sons, yet in 54:5
he dies along with them.

53 a. Josephus (*Ant* 5.10.4 §348) says that Samuel

had completed his twelfth year when he began to
act as a prophet.
b. "Twice" implies a text similar to that of the
LXX for 1Sam 3:4.
c. Lit. "be silent," which probably reflects a
confusion between the meanings of the Heb. root
ḥrš (be silent, be deaf).

you hear in your right ear, say *'Say* whatever you wish, *because I am listening,*   1Sam 3:9
for you have created me.' But if you hear with your left ear, come and tell me."

7 *And Samuel went away and slept* as Eli had commanded him. •*And the Lord*   1Sam 3:8
spoke again a third time, and the right ear of Samuel was filled. And when he
knew that the word of his father had come down, Samuel turned on his other side
and said, "If I am capable, speak; for you know more about me (than I do)."

8 And God said to him, "I have indeed enlightened the house of Israel in Egypt
and have chosen for myself then as a prophet Moses my servant and have done
wonders through him for my people and have taken revenge on my enemies as I
wished. And I brought my people into the wilderness and enlightened them as

9 they looked on. •And when one tribe rose up against another, saying, 'Why are   Num 16
the priests alone holy?' I did not wish to destroy them and I said to them, 'Have
each one present his staff, and he whose staff will flower—him I have chosen for
the priesthood.' And when all had handed in the staffs as I had commanded, then
I commanded the ground where the tent of meeting was that the staff of Aaron
should flower in order that his family be made manifest all the days. And now

10 those who have flowered have defiled my holy things. •Therefore behold the days
will come, and I will trample on the flower that was born then and will stop them
who transgress the word that I have commanded Moses my servant, saying, *'If*   Deut 22:6
you come upon a bird's nest, you shall not take the mother with young.' d So it
will happen to them that mothers will die with daughters e and fathers will perish

11 with sons." •And when Samuel heard these words, his heart grew faint, and he
said, "Has it thus fallen to my youth that I should prophesy the destruction of
him who nourished me? And now how is it that I have been given according to
my mother's prayer? And who has brought me up? How has he commanded me

12 to announce evil as if it were good?" •*And Samuel arose in the morning,* f *and*   1Sam 3:15
he did not wish *to tell Eli. And* Eli *said to* him, "Listen now, my son. Behold
before you were born, God promised Israel that he would send you to them and
that you would prophesy. And then when your mother came here and prayed,
because she did not know what had happened, I said to her, 'Go forth, for what
will be born from you will be a son for me.' And so I spoke to your mother and
so has the LORD guided your life. Even if you should chastise the one who has
brought you up, as the LORD lives, *do not hide from me* whatever you have heard."   1Sam 3:17

13 Then *Samuel was afraid and told him all the words* that he had heard. And he   1Sam 3:15,18
said, "Will the object formed answer back him who formed it? So I cannot answer   Isa 29:16
back when he wishes to take away what he has delivered as a faithful giver. Holy
is he who has prophesied, for I am under his power."

The capture of the ark and Eli's death

1 **54** *And in those days the Philistines* assembled their camp *to attack Israel.* a *And*   1Sam 4:1-3
the sons of *Israel went out* to fight with them. And when *the people* of Israel
were put to flight in the first encounter, *they said,* "*Let us bring up the ark of the*
covenant of the Lord, and perhaps he may fight along with us, because in it are

2 the tablets b of the LORD that he established with our fathers on Horeb." •And   1Sam 4:5
when *the ark* went up with them and *arrived at the camp,* the LORD *thundered*
and said, "This hour will be like that which occurred in the wilderness when they
took the ark without my command, and destruction befell them. So also in this
hour the people will fall and the ark will be captured in order that I may destroy
the enemies of my people on account of the ark and correct my people because

3 they have sinned." •And when the ark had come into the battle, the Philistines   1Sam 4:10f.

---

d. The connection of the sins of Eli's sons with   does not.
Deut 22:6 is unique to Ps-Philo.
  e. Var. "sons"; but the parallelism suggests   **54** a. The sentence "And . . . Israel" is absent
that "daughters" is preferable.   from the MT of 1Sam 4:1 but is present in the
  f. The LXX, the Lucianic MSS, 4Q160, and   LXX and Lucianic MSS.
Ps-Philo have this phrase; the MT of 1Sam 3:15   b. The tablets of the Decalogue.

went out to meet the sons of Israel and killed them. And Goliath the Philistine was there, and he came up to the ark. And Hophni and Phinehas the sons of Eli and Saul the son of Kish were holding onto the ark. And Goliath took hold of it 4 with his left hand and killed Hophni and Phinehas. •But Saul, because he was 1Sam 4:12 swift on his feet, *fled* from him.ᶜ *And he tore his garments* and put *ashes on his head. And he came to Eli* the priest, and *Eli said to him, "Tell me what happened* 1Sam 4:14–17 in the camp." And Saul said to him, "Why do you ask me these things? For the people are defeated, and God has rejected Israel, and even the priests have been 5 killed by the sword, and the ark has been delivered to the Philistines." •But when Eli had heard of the capture of the ark, he said, "Behold Samuel prophesied about my sons and about me that we should die together, but he did not mention the ark to me then. And now the tablets of the Law have been delivered to enemies. What more can I say? Behold Israel departs from the truth,ᵈ because the statutes have been taken away from it." And while Eli was in deep despair, *he fell down* 1Sam 4:18 *from his seat.* And there died on one day Eli and Hophni and Phinehas his sons. 6 *And the wife of Phinehas* sat down *to give birth.* When *she heard* these things, 1Sam 4:19–21 all her insides were *loosened.* And the midwife *said to her,* "Regain your strength, and let not your soul grow faint, *because a son* is *born* to you." And the woman said to her, "Behold now this one person is born and four of us die, that is, the father and the two sons and his daughter-in-law." *And she called his name "where is glory,"ᵉ saying, "Glory has departed from Israel,ᶠ because ᵗʰe ark of the Lord has been captured."* And when she had said these words, she gave up her spirit.

The return of the ark

1 **55** Now Samuel knew nothing of all these matters, because three days before the battle God had sent him forth, saying to him, "Go and look around Ramathaim 1Sam 7:17 where your dwelling will be." And when Samuel had heard what had happened to Israel, he came and prayed to the LORD, saying, "Behold now in vain has understanding been denied me, that I should see the destructionᵃ of my people. And now I fear lest perhaps my days grow old in evil and my years reach an end in sorrow. Since the ark of the LORD is not with me, why should I go on living?" 2 And the LORD said to him, "Do not be sad, Samuel, because the ark has been taken away. I will bring it back, and I will overturn those who have taken it away, and I will avenge my people from my enemies." And Samuel said, "Behold even if you do take vengeance according to your long-suffering, nevertheless what will we who die now do?" And God said to him, "Before you die, you will see the end that I am bringing upon my enemies, in which the Philistines will be 1Sam 6:4 destroyed by scorpionsᵇ and all evil creeping things and will perish." 3 And *when the Philistines had set up the* captured *ark of the Lord in the temple* 1Sam 5:2–6 *of Dagon,* their god, and when they had come to inquire of Dagon concerning the outcome,ᶜ they found that *he had fallen on his face and his hands and feet* were lying *before the ark.* And on the first morning they went out and *crucified* his priests. And the next day they came and found it as the day before, and there 4 was a great massacre among them. •And the Philistines gathered in Ekron and 1Sam 5:10f. said, each to his neighbor, "Behold now we see that destruction is great among us, and the fruit of our womb will perish because the creeping things that have

c. In identifying Saul with the unnamed man of Benjamin in 1Sam 4:12, Ps-Philo agrees with several rabbinic writings. The word "fled" agrees with the Lucianic MSS.

d. Var. "perishes utterly."

e. That is, Ichabod, which lit. in Heb. is "no glory." The translator may have read ˀyh kbwd, "where is glory?" for ˀy kbwd, "no glory."

f. Some MSS have "The glory of God in Israel," while others have "The glory of the house of Israel." Our reading of the text is based on 1Sam 4:21.

55 a. All the MSS have "army" (*exercitium*); we are reading "destruction" (*exitium*) as being more consistent with the content of the passage.

b. According to 1Sam 6:4 the Philistines are destroyed by mice rather than scorpions. A confusion at the level of Heb. (ˁkbrym meaning "mice" with ˁqrbym meaning "scorpions") is likely.

c. Or "their going forth."

been sent upon us will destroy those who are with child or sucklings and those
who are nursing." And they said, "Let us see why *the hand* of the LORD *has* | 1Sam 5:7
been heavy upon us. Is it not because of the ark, for our god is found daily *falling* | 1Sam 5:3f.
on his face before the ark? And we have destroyed the priests more than once in
5 vain." •And the wise men of the Philistines[d] said, "Behold now we can learn | 1Sam 6:2
about this, if the LORD has sent destruction upon us on account of the ark or an
6 evil power has come upon us by chance. •*And now* because all who are pregnant | 1Sam 6:7-10
and who are nursing are dead, and those who nurse are made childless and those
who are nursed perish, *let us take cows that give milk and yoke them to a* new
cart and put *the ark* on it and shut up *their calves.* And if the cows in going forth
should go forth so as not to turn back to their calves, we will know that we have
suffered these things on account of the ark. *But if they do not* want to go forth
out of longing for their calves, *we will know* that the time of destruction *has come*
7 *upon us.*" •And some of the wise men and diviners answered, "Not only will we | 1Sam 6:2
try this, but also we will set the cows at the juncture of the three roads that are | 1Sam 6:9
around Ekron. For the middle road goes straight to Ekron and the right-hand one
to Judah and the left-hand one to Samaria. And if they set out on the right-hand
road and go straight to Judah, we will know indeed that the God of the Jews has
destroyed us. But if they go forth by the other roads, *we will know* that this very | 1Sam 6:9
violent time *has come upon us* because now we have denied our own gods."
8 *And the Philistines took the cows that gave milk and yoked them to the* new *cart* | 1Sam 6:10-12
and put the ark on it and set them at the juncture of the roads and *shut up their*
calves at home. Now the cows, even though they lowed and yearned for their
calves, nevertheless were going forth on the right-hand road, which leads to Judah.
9 And then they knew they were being destroyed because of the ark. •And all *the* | 1Sam 6:21
Philistines gathered together and *returned the ark* to Shiloh[e] with timbrels and
pipes and dances. And in place of the evil creeping things that destroyed them
10 they made *golden tumors,* and they consecrated the ark. •And on that day the | 1Sam 6:17
destruction of the Philistines took place. The number of those who were with | 1Sam 6:19
child and died was seventy-five thousand, and the sucklings sixty-five thousand
and those who were giving suck fifty-five thousand, and the men twenty-five
thousand. And the land was at peace for seven years.

The people demand a king

1 **56** And in that time *the sons of Israel* desired and sought for a king, and *they* | 1Sam 8:4f.
gathered to Samuel and said, "Behold now *you are old, and your sons do not*
walk in your ways. And now appoint over us[a] *a king to govern us,* because the
word has been fulfilled that Moses said to our fathers in the wilderness, saying,
2 '*Appoint from your brothers* a ruler *over you.*'" •And when Samuel heard talk of | Deut 17:15
a kingdom, he was very sad in his heart and said, "Behold now I see that it is | 1Sam 8:6
not yet the time for us to have an everlasting kingdom and to build the house of
the LORD our God, for these people are seeking a king before the proper time.
But even if the LORD so wished it, it seems to me that a king could not be
3 appointed." •And the LORD said to him by night, "Do not be sad. For I will send | 1Sam 8:9
them a king who will destroy them, and he himself will be destroyed afterward.
Now he who will come *to you tomorrow* at the sixth hour; he is the one who *will* | 1Sam 9:16
rule over them."
4 And on the next day Saul the son of Kish came from *the hill country of Ephraim* | 1Sam 9:1-4
in search of *his father's asses.* And when he came to Ramathaim, he went in to | 1Sam 9:12f.
inquire from Samuel about the asses. Now he was walking around Bama.[b] And

---

d. Josephus (*Ant* 6.1.2 §§8–10) also describes
a dispute among the Philistine leaders based on
1Sam 6:2.

e. According to 1Sam 6:12 the Philistines brought
the ark to Beth-shemesh.

56 a. Ps-Philo reads "And now" and "over us"

in agreement with the LXX and Lucianic MSS of
1Sam 8:5.

b. The MSS have *Baam.* The emendation to
Bama is based on the assumption that the Heb.
word for "high place" (*bāmâ*) in 1Sam 9:12–14
has been misunderstood, or deliberately misinterpreted, as a proper name.

Saul said to him, *"Where is he who sees?"* Now in that time *a prophet was called*   1Sam 9:18
"one who sees." And Samuel said to him, "I am the one who sees." And he   1Sam 9:9
                                                                                       1Sam 9:19
said, "Can you tell me about my father's asses, because they are lost?" And   1Sam 9:19
Samuel said to him, *"Rest yourself with me today, and I will tell you tomorrow*
5 *that for which you have come to inquire."* •And Samuel said to the LORD, "Direct
your people, LORD, and tell me what you have planned for them." *And Saul*   1Sam 9:24–26
rested himself with Samuel on that day. And he rose up in the morning, *and*
Samuel *said to him,* "Behold may you know *that the Lord* has chosen *you as*   1Sam 10:1
ruler for his people in this time and has directed your ways, and your future will
6 also be directed." •And Saul said to Samuel, "Who am I and what is the house   1Sam 9:21
of my father that my lord *should say to me this word? For I do not understand*   Jer 1:6
what you are saying, *because I am young."* And Samuel said to Saul, "Who will
grant that your word be accomplished of itself to the end that you should have a
long life? Nevertheless, consider this, that your words will be compared to the
7 words of the prophet whose name will be Jeremiah." •And Saul went away, and
on that day the people came to Samuel, saying, *"Give us a king* as you have   1Sam 8:6
promised us." And he said to them, "Behold your king will come to you after
three[c] days." And behold Saul came, *and all the signs* that Samuel had told him   1Sam 10:9
happened to him. Are these not written in the Book of Kings?[d]

Saul is presented to the people

1 **57** And Samuel sent and gathered all the people and said to them, "Behold you   1Sam 12:1–3
2 and your king. But I am in your midst as God has commanded me. •And so
before your king I say to you as my lord Moses the servant of God said to your
fathers in the wilderness when the company of Korah[a] rose up against him, 'You
know that *I have not taken anything* from you, *nor have I harmed anyone* of you.'   Num 16:15
And because they lied then and said, 'You have taken,' *the earth swallowed them*   Num 16:32
3 up. •And now you, who have not been punished by the LORD, *answer before the*   1Sam 12:3
Lord and before his anointed, if you have sought a king because I have treated
you badly; and *the Lord* will be the *witness* for you. But if now the word of the   1Sam 12:5
LORD has been fulfilled, I and the house of my father are free from blame."
4 And the people answered, "We are your servants; but we have a king, because
we are not worthy to be governed by a prophet. *Now appoint over us a king who*   1Sam 8:5
will govern us." And all the people and the king wept with a great lamentation
and said, "Long live Samuel the prophet!" And when the king was being
5 appointed, they brought sacrifices to the LORD. •And afterward Saul fought with   1Sam 13:9
the Philistines in a year of very successful combat.

The sin of Saul

1 **58** And in that time the LORD said to Samuel, "Go and say to Saul, 'You have
been sent to *destroy Amalek* in order that the words that Moses my servant spoke   1Sam 15:3
may be fulfilled: *"I will destroy the name of Amalek* from the earth." I have   Deut 25:19; Ex
spoken in my anger. *And do not forget* to destroy everyone of them as has been   17:14
2 commanded to you.'" •And *Saul* went off and *attacked Amalek. And he let Agag,*   1Sam 15:7–9,
the king of Amalek, live, because he said to him, "I will show you hidden   20
treasures." And on account of this *he spared*[a] him and let him live and brought   1Sam 15:16,20
3 him to Ramathaim.[b] •And God said to Samuel, "You have seen how in a short
time the king has been corrupted with silver, and he has let the king of Amalek
and his wife live. And now let them be, so that Agag may come together with

---

c. Seven, according to 1Sam 10:8.   **58** a. Josephus (*Ant* 6.7.2 §137) says that Saul
d. 1Sam is also referred to in this manner in the   spared Agag "out of admiration for his beauty and
LXX tradition.   his stature."
                                                           b. According to 1Sam 15:12, 21, 33, Agag is
57 a. According to Seder Olam 20 and other   brought to Gilgal.
rabbinic sources Samuel was a descendant of Korah.

his wife tonight; and you will kill him tomorrow. But his wife they will keep safe until she bears a male child, and then she also will die. And he who will be born from her will become a stumbling block for Saul.[c] Now may you rise up tomorrow

4 and kill Agag, because Saul's sin is written before me all the days." •And when *Samuel rose up early in the morning, Saul went out to meet him* and said to him, "The LORD has delivered our enemies into our hands just as you have said." And Samuel said to Saul, "How much harm Israel has done because they demanded you for themselves as a king before the time came that a king should rule over them! And you, who were sent to do the will of the LORD, have transgressed it. And so he who was let live by you will die now, and those hidden treasures that he talked about he will not show you, and one who will be born from him will be for you a stumbling block." And Samuel came to Agag, and he had a sword, and *Samuel killed Agag*[d] *and returned to his house.*

1Sam 15:12f.

1Sam 15:33f.

The anointing and the psalm of David

1 **59** *And the Lord said to* him, "Go, *anoint him whom I will tell you,* because the time in which his kingdom will come to pass has been fulfilled." And Samuel said, "Behold are you blotting out the kingdom of Saul?" And he said, "I am

2 blotting it out." •And *Samuel went forth to Bethel*[a] and *consecrated* elders and *Jesse and his sons.* And Eliab, the firstborn son of Jesse, came. And Samuel said, "Behold now is this the holy one, *the anointed of the Lord?" And the Lord said to* him, "Where is your vision that your heart sees? Are you not the one who said to Saul, *'I am the one who sees'?* And why do you not know whom you should anoint? And now this reproach is sufficient for you; seek out the least shepherd

3 of all *and anoint this one." •And Samuel said to Jesse,*[b] *"Send and bring* your son from the flock, because God has chosen him." *And Jesse*[c] *sent and brought* David, *and* Samuel *anointed him in the midst of his brothers.* And the LORD was

4 with him *from that day.* •Then David began to sing this song, and he said,

1Sam 16:1,3

1Sam 16:4–7

1Sam 9:19

1Sam 16:11–13

> "From the ends of the earth I will begin my song of glory,
> and from the days long ago I will take up[d] a hymn.
> When Abel first shepherded flocks,
> his sacrifice was more acceptable than that of his brother,
> and his brother was jealous of him and killed him.
> But for me it is not the same,
> because God has protected me
> and because he has delivered me to his angels
> and to his guardians[e] that they should guard me.
> For my brothers were jealous of me,
> and my father and my mother neglected me.
> And when the prophet came,
> they did not call to me.
> And when the anointed of the LORD was to be designated,
> they forgot me.
> But God with his right hand
> and his mercy drew near to me.
> Therefore I will not cease singing praises
> all the days of my life."

Ps 61:2

Ps 27:10

5　And while David was still speaking, behold a fierce *lion* from the forest and a

1Sam 17:34–37

c. See 65:4. That Agag's son was responsible for Saul's death is not found in the biblical account. In Josephus' *Ant* 11.6.5 §211 Haman (cf. Esth 3:1) is a descendant of Agag.

d. Josephus (*Ant* 6.7.5 §155) has Samuel give an order for someone else to put Agag to death.

59 a. According to 1Sam 16:4 the place should be Bethlehem.

b. Var. "Hear, O Jesse"; but our reading reflects 1Sam 16:11.

c. Only the Lucianic MSS and Ps-Philo specify Jesse as the subject here in 1Sam 16:12.

d. Lit. "say"; confusion between the Gk. *airō* (take up) and *erō* (say) is possible.

e. For the angels as guardians, see 11:12 and 15:5.

bear from the mountain *seized* the sheep¹ of David. And David said, "Behold this will be a sign for me as a most striking beginning of my victory in battle. And *I am going out* after them and *will rescue* what has been snatched away *and kill* them." *And* David *went out after* them and took stones from the forest and *killed them*. And God said to him, "Behold with stones I have delivered up these beasts for you. Now this will be a sign for you, because with stones you will kill the enemy⁸ of my people later on."

David as exorcist

1 **60** And in that time *the spirit of the Lord* was taken away *from Saul, and an evil spirit was choking him. And Saul sent* and brought David, and *he played a song on his lyre* by night. And this was the song he played for Saul in order that *the evil spirit might depart from him.*

1Sam 16:14
1Sam 16:19,23

2　　"Darkness and silence* were before the world was made,
　　and silence spoke a word* and the darkness became light.
　　Then your name* was pronounced in the drawing together of what had
　　　　been spread out,
　　the upper of which was called heaven and the lower was called earth.

Gen 1:11f.

　　And the upper part was commanded to bring down rain according to its
　　　　season,
　　and the lower part was commanded to produce food for all things that had
　　　　been made.
　　And after these was the tribe of your spirits made.
3　　And now do not be troublesome as one created on the second day. ᵈ
　　But if not, remember Tartarus where you walk.
　　Or is it not enough for you to hear that, through what resounds before
　　　　you, I sing to many?
　　Or do you not remember that you were created from a resounding echo in
　　　　the chaos?
　　But let the new womb from which I was born rebuke you,
　　from which after a time one born from my loins* will rule over you."

And as long as David sang, the spirit spared Saul.

1Sam 16:23

David and Goliath

1 **61** And after this the Philistines came to fight Israel, *and David returned* to the wilderness *to feed the sheep*. And the Midianites happened upon him and wanted to take his sheep. And he went down to them and attacked them, and he killed fifteen thousand of their men. ª This is the first battle that David fought while he
2 was in the wilderness. •*And a man by the name of Goliath went forth from the camp of the Philistines*, and he looked at Saul and at Israel and said, "Are you not the Israel⁴ that fled before me when I took the ark from you and killed your priests? And now that you are king, come down like a man and a king, and fight us. If not, I will come to you and take you captive and make your people serve

1Sam 17:15

1Sam 17:4

1Sam 17:9

---

f. Lit. "bulls"; but see 1Sam 17:34, where the lion and the bear took a lamb from the flock. The *tauros* of Ps-Philo can be explained as resulting from confusion between *šh* (lamb) and *šwr* (bull).
　g. Goliath. See 61:3.

60 a. The primordial silence is also mentioned in 2Bar 3:7.
　b. For speech coming from silence, see IgnMagn 8:2 and GTr 27:10–12.
　c. The name of the evil spirit.
　d. According to 2En 29:1 the evil spirits were

created on the second day, but according to Jub 2:2 on the first day.
　e. It is unlikely that this is a reference to the future Messiah (or Jesus), given the lack of interest in such a figure throughout Ps-Philo. Probably this is an allusion to Solomon as exorcist; see WisSol 7:17–22 and especially Josephus' *Ant* 8.2.5 §§45–49.

61 a. This incident with the Midianites is unique to Ps-Philo.
　b. Perhaps Saul or Israelite.

our gods." [c] *And when Saul and Israel heard these words, they were very much* 1Sam 17:11 *afraid.* And the Philistine said, "According to the number of days in which Israel feasted when it received the Law in the wilderness, that is, forty days, so I will

3 ridicule them and afterward I will fight with them." •*And when the forty days* 1Sam 17:16,28, had been completed and David came *to view* his brothers' *battle,* he heard the 22 words that the Philistine had spoken and said, "Is this the time about which God said to me, 'I will deliver into your hands by stones the enemy of my people'?"

4 And Saul heard these words and *sent* and received him and said, "What is this 1Sam 17:31 word that you have spoken to the people?" And David said, "Do not fear, King, 1Sam 17:32 *because I will go and fight the Philistine,* and God *will take away* hatred and 1Sam 17:36

5 *reproaches from Israel.*" [d] •And David set out, and he took seven[e] stones and 1Sam 17:40 wrote on them the names of his fathers (those of Abraham, Isaac, and Jacob, Moses and Aaron) and his own and the Most Powerful. And God sent Zervihel,[f]

6 the angel in charge of might in warfare. •And David went out to Goliath and said 2Sam 21:15–22 to him, "Hear this word before you die. Were not the two women, from whom Ruth 1:14 you and I were born, sisters? And your mother[g] was Orpah, and my mother Ruth. And Orpah chose for herself the gods of the Philistines and went after them, but Ruth chose for herself the ways of the Most Powerful and walked in them. And now there were born from Orpah you and your brothers. And because you have risen up today and have come to destroy Israel, behold I who am born from your own blood have come to avenge my people. For after your death your three brothers, too, will fall into my hands. Then you will say to your mother, 'He

7 who was born from your sister has not spared us.'" •*And David* put *a stone in* 1Sam 17:49–51 *the sling and struck the Philistine on his forehead. And he ran up to him and drew his sword.* And Goliath, while he still had life in him, said to him, "Hurry

8 and kill me, and then rejoice." •And David said to him, "Before you die, open your eyes and see your slayer, the one who has killed you." And the Philistine looked and saw an angel and said, "Not you alone have killed me, but also the one who is present with you, he whose appearance is not like the appearance of

9 a man." *And* then David *cut off his head.* •Now the angel of the LORD had 1Sam 17:55–58 changed[h] David's appearance, and no one recognized him. *And Saul saw David* and asked him who he was, and there was no one who recognized him.

David and Jonathan

1 **62** And after this Saul was jealous of David, and he sought to kill him. Now 1Sam 18:3 *David* and *Jonathan* the son of Saul *had made a covenant* together. And when *David* saw that Saul[a] was seeking to kill him, he *fled to Ramathaim;* and Saul 1Sam 19:18–22

2 went out after him. •*And a spirit* abided *in* Saul, *and he prophesied,* saying, 1Sam 19:23 "Why are you led astray, Saul, and whom are you pursuing in vain? The time allotted to your kingdom has been completed. Go to your place. For you will die, and David will reign. Will not *you and your son*[b] die together? And then the 1Sam 31:6 kingdom of David will appear." And Saul went away and did not know what he had prophesied.

3 Now David came to Jonathan and said to him, "Come, and let us make a 1Sam 18:3 covenant before we are separated from one another. For Saul, your father, seeks to kill me unjustly, and because he knows that you love me he does not tell you 1Sam 20:3

4 what he is planning about me. •But on account of this he hates me, because you

---

c. In 1Sam 17:9 Goliath threatens to make Israel serve the Philistines, not the gods of the Philistines as here.

d. For taking away reproaches from Israel, see the LXX and Lucianic MSS of 1Sam 17:36.

e. 1Sam 17:40 speaks of five stones only.

f. See 27:10 for what seems to be the same angel.

g. Here "mother" must mean ancestress.

h. All the MSS have "raised," which probably

reflects an error in reading *nś* or *nśh* (raised) for *śnh* (changed). For the idiom of "changing the face" to avoid recognition, see 7:5 and 64:4.

62 a. All the MSS merely have "he," but according to 1Sam 19:18–22 and the rest of the story here it must be Saul.

b. But according to 1Sam 31:6 Saul dies with his three sons.

love me and in order that I may not reign in his place. And when I gave him good things, he paid me back with bad things. And when I killed Goliath according to the word of the Most Powerful, see the end that he planned for me, for he determined to destroy my father's house. And would that the judgment of truth might be placed in the balance so that the many prudent people might hear the 5 decision. •And now I fear that he will kill me, that he will lose his own life on my account. For I never have shed innocent blood, and why does my soul suffer persecution? *For I, the least among my brothers, was tending sheep*, and why should I be in danger of death? For I am just and have no wickedness, and why does your father hate me? But the righteousness of my father[c] helps me so that I should not fall into the hands of your father. And since I am young and tender of 6 days, in vain does Saul envy me. •If I had harmed him, I would ask that he forgive me these sins; because if God forgives wicked deeds, how much more should your father, who is flesh and blood. I have walked in his household with a perfect heart, and like a swift eagle I was brought before him. I put my hands to the lance, and I blessed him with songs. But he made plans to kill me, and 7 like a sparrow who flees before the hawk, so I fled from him. •To whom did I say these words, or to whom have I told what I have suffered, except to you and 8 Michal, your sister? As for the two of us, let us go forth together in truth. •And it would have been better, brother, if I had been slain in battle than that I should fall into the hands of your father. For in the battle my eyes were looking everywhere that I might protect him from his enemies. Jonathan my brother, hear my words. *And if there is wickedness in me, correct me.''*

9 And Jonathan answered and said to David, ''Come to me, my brother David, and I will tell you of your righteousness. My soul will pine away in sadness over you, because we are now separated from each other. And our sins have caused this, that we should be separated from each other; but let us be mindful of one another night and day while we live. Even if death separates us, I know that our souls will know each other.[d] For yours is a kingdom in this world, and from you 10 is the beginning of a kingdom which will come in its own time. •And now like an infant who is taken away from the milk of its mother, so will our separation be. Be a witness, heaven, and be a witness, earth, for those *words that we have exchanged;* and let us weep each one over the other, and let us collect our tears into one vessel and consign that vessel to the earth, and it will be a testimony for 11 us.'' •*And they wept, one over the other, and they kissed one another*. But Jonathan was afraid, and he said to David, ''Let us remember, my brother, the covenant begun between us and the oath set in our heart. And if I die before you and you are king as the LORD has said, do not remember the anger of my father but your covenant that has been established *between me and you*. Do not remember the hatred with which my father hates you in vain but my love with which I have loved you. Do not remember that my father was ungrateful toward you, but remember the table at which we ate together. Do not hold on to the jealousy with which he was jealous of you so evilly but the truth that you and I have. Do not care about the lie that Saul has lied but the oaths that we have sworn to one another.'' *And they kissed each other*. And after this *David[e] went off* into the wilderness, *and Jonathan entered the city*.

Ps 151(LXX)

1Sam 20:8

1Sam 20:23

1Sam 20:41f.

The death of Abimelech

1 **63** In that time the priests who dwelt in Nob were profaning the holy things of the LORD and desecrating[a] the first fruits of the people. And God was angry and

1Sam 22:18f.

---

c. In the rabbinic tradition Jesse, David's father, is one of the four righteous men who did not die because of their own sins but because the serpent caused Adam and Eve to sin. The present sentence contrasts Jesse's righteousness with Saul's unrighteousness.

d. For the dead recognizing one another at the resurrection, see 2Bar 50:3f.

e. All texts except the MT specify David as the subject in 1Sam 20:42 (21:1 in the MT).

63 a. We are reading *expropriantes* for *exprobantes*, which is found in all the MSS.

said, "Behold I will blot out those dwelling in Nob, because they walk in the
2 ways of the sons of Eli."[b] •And in that time *Doeg the Syrian,*[c] *who was in charge*   1Sam 22:9–13,
of Saul's mules, came *and said* to him, "Do you not know that Abimelech the   16–21
priest is making plans with David, and *he has given him a sword* and has let him
go in peace?" *And* Saul *sent and called Abimelech and said* to him, "*You will
surely die,* because you have made a plot with my enemy." And Saul[d] killed
Abimelech and the house of his *father,* and not *one* of his tribe *was saved* except
Abiathar his *son.* And he went off to David and told him all that had happened
3 to him. •And he said to him, "Behold in the year when Saul began to reign,   1Sam 14:45
when Jonathan had sinned and he[e] wanted to kill him, this people rose up and
did not let him. And now when 385[f] priests are killed, they are silent and say   1Sam 22:18
nothing. And so behold the days will come soon, and I will deliver them into the   1Sam 31
4 hands of their enemies, and they will fall wounded with their king." •And the
LORD said these things about[g] Doeg the Syrian: "Behold the days will come soon,
and a fiery worm[h] will go up into his tongue and make him rot away, and his
5 dwelling place will be with Jair in the inextinguishable fire forever." •All the
things that Saul did, and the rest of his words, and how he pursued David, are
they not written in the Book of the Kings of Israel?

The witch of Endor

1 **64** *And* after this *Samuel died, and all Israel gathered together and wept over*   1Sam 28:3; 25:1
him and buried him. Then Saul thought and said, "Because I am to expel the
wizards from the land of Israel, they[a] will be mindful of me after my departure."
And Saul scattered all *the wizards from the land.* And God said, "Behold Saul   1Sam 28:3
has not driven the wizards out of the land for fear of me, but to make a name for
himself.[b] Behold he will go to those whom he has scattered, to obtain divination
2 from them, because he has no prophets." •And then the Philistines said, each to
his neighbor, "Behold Samuel the prophet is dead, and who prays for Israel? And
David, who fought on their behalf, is Saul's enemy, and he is not with them.
And now let us rise up and go and fight and attack them and avenge the blood of
3 our fathers." *And the Philistines gathered together and came* for battle. •*And*   1Sam 28:4
when *Saul saw* that Samuel was dead and David was not with him, *his hands*   1Sam 28:5–7
grew faint, and he inquired of the Lord, but he did not listen to *him.* And he
sought out *prophets,* and none appeared to him. *And Saul said* to the people, "Let
us *seek out* some *medium and inquire of him* what I should plan out." And the
people answered him, "*Behold* now there is a *woman,* Sedecla[c] by name, and
this is the daughter of the Midianite diviner[d] who led the people of Israel astray
4 with sorceries, and behold she dwells *in Endor.* •*And Saul put on* his worst *clothes*   1Sam 28:8–11
and went off to her, *he and two men with him, by night and said* to her, "*Raise
up Samuel for me.*" She said, "I fear King Saul." And Saul said to her, "You
will not be harmed by Saul in this matter." And Saul said to himself, "When I
was king in Israel, even if the gentiles did not see me, they knew nevertheless
that I was Saul." And Saul asked the woman, saying, "Have you ever seen
Saul?" She said, "I have seen him often." Saul went outside and wept and said,

b. Josephus (*Ant* 6.12.6 §260) also connects the
death of the priests with the iniquities of Eli's sons,
but he does not say that they themselves did wrong
as Ps-Philo does.
c. Ps-Philo agrees with the LXX and Josephus
in making Doeg an Aramean (or Syrian) rather
than an Edomite as in the MT of 1Sam 22:9.
d. According to 1Sam 22:18 Doeg, not Saul,
does the killing.
e. Saul, according to 1Sam 14:45.
f. According to 1Sam 22:18 the number of
priests killed was 385 (Josephus), 85 (MT), 305
(LXX), 350 (Lucianic MSS).

g. Lit. "to"; but the statement is cast in the
third person, and so there may have been confusion
between the Heb. 'l (to) and 'l (about).
h. On being eaten by worms, see 44:9.

64 a. Var. "he will be mindful."
b. Ps-Philo is unique in attributing the expulsion
of the sorcerers to Saul's selfishness.
c. Ps-Philo alone gives this name, Sedecla, to
the witch of Endor.
d. An emendation. Most MSS have "Adod the
Midianite," who may be Aod of ch. 34.

"Behold now I know that my appearance has been changed, and the glory of my
5 kingdom has passed from me." •And *when the woman saw Samuel* rising up and   1Sam 28:12f.
she saw Saul[e] with him, *she shouted out and said*, "Behold *you are Saul, and
why have you deceived me?" And he said to her, "Do not be afraid, but tell*[f]
what you have seen." She said, "Behold forty years have passed since I began
raising up the dead for the Philistines, but such a sight as this has never been seen
6 before nor will it be seen afterward." •*And Saul*[g] *said to her, "What is his*   1Sam 28:13f.
appearance?" She said, "You are asking me about *divine beings*. For behold his
appearance is not the appearance of a man. For he is clothed in a white robe[h]
with a mantle placed over it, and two angels[i] are leading him." And Saul
remembered the mantle that Samuel tore when he was alive, and he struck his   1Sam 15:27
7 hand *on the ground* and pounded it. •*And Samuel said to* him, "Why have you   1Sam 28:14
disturbed me by raising me up? I thought that the time for being rendered the   1Sam 28:15
rewards of my deeds had arrived.[j] And so do not boast, King, nor you, woman;
for you have not brought me forth, but that order that God spoke to me while I
was still alive, that I should come and tell you that you have sinned now a second
time in neglecting God. Therefore after rendering up my soul my bones have been
disturbed so that I who am dead should tell you what I heard while I was alive.
8 Now therefore *tomorrow you and your sons will be with me*[k] when *the people*   1Sam 28:19
have been delivered *into the hands of the Philistines;* and because your insides
9 were eaten up with jealousy, what is yours will be taken from you." •And Saul
heard the words of Samuel and grew faint and said, "Behold I am going to die
with my sons; perhaps my destruction will be an atonement[l] for my wickedness."
And Saul *rose up and went away* from there.   1Sam 28:25

The death of Saul

1 **65** *And the Philistines attacked Israel*, and Saul went out for battle, *and Israel*   1Sam 31:1,3
fled before the Philistines. And Saul seeing that *the battle was very fierce* said in
his heart, "Why are you strengthening yourself for life when Samuel has announced
2 death for you along with your sons?" •*And Saul said to his armor-bearer, "Take*   1Sam 31:4
your sword and kill *me* before the Philistines *come and abuse me." And the*
3 *armor-bearer was not willing* to lay his hands upon him. •But *he fell upon his*   1Sam 31:4
own sword, without being able to die. *And he looked behind him. He saw* a man   2Sam 1:7
running, *and he called* him *and said*, "Take your sword and *kill me; there is still*   2Sam 1:9
4 *life in me."* •And he came to kill him. And Saul said to him, "Before you kill   2Sam 1:10
me, tell me who you are." And he said to him, "I am Edabus, son of Agag,   2Sam 1:8,13
king of the Amalekites." And Saul said, "Behold now the words of Samuel have
come to pass upon me, because he said, 'He who is born of Agag will be a
5 stumbling block for you.'[a] •Now go and tell David, 'I have killed your enemy.'   2Sam 1:10
And you will say to him, 'Be not mindful of my hatred or my injustice.'"

---

e. Some LXX MSS of 1Sam 28:12 report that
the woman saw Saul, but the other texts say that
she saw Samuel. Ps-Philo appears to combine the
two.

f. By including "tell" Ps-Philo stands with the
LXX and the Lucianic MSS of 1Sam 28:13.

g. The inclusion of "Saul" is found only in the
Lucianic MSS of 1Sam 28:14.

h. The white shroud in which he was buried.

i. Cf. GPet 10 (39f.), where two angels lead
Christ out of the tomb.

j. The day of judgment.

k. In death.

l. In rabbinic literature Saul's death is an atonement for his sins, but Josephus (*Ant* 6.14.4 §349)
attributes his death to desire for fame after death.

65 a. See 58:4.

THE LIVES OF THE PROPHETS

(First Century A.D.)

A NEW TRANSLATION AND INTRODUCTION

BY D. R. A. HARE

"The names of the prophets, and where they are from, and where they died and how, and where they lie"—with these phrases the major manuscript, Codex Marchalianus, summarizes the content of the brief document now known as The Lives of the Prophets. In some sections all the information given fits this summary. In others the scheme is expanded to include legendary information not contained in the Scriptures (Jonah was the son of the widow of Zarephath visited by Elijah, 1Kgs 17!—10:4–6) and prophecies or "signs" attributed to the prophet that are not found in the canon. Non-canonical miracles are also reported. In a few instances canonical narratives are included. The collection treats the three major and twelve minor prophets and Daniel, and seven non-literary prophets whose activities are reported in the Bible.

Texts

The Lives of the Prophets is extant in a number of versions, including Syriac, Ethiopic, Latin, and Armenian, but all are dependent upon Greek originals. There are an abundance of Greek manuscripts, the most important of these are the following:

Codex Marchalianus, Cod. Vaticanus Gk. 2125, sixth century, in the Vatican library; it is referred to as Q. It is the most important member of the group of manuscripts constituting the "anonymous recension."[1]

Codex Paris. Gk. 1115, copied in 1276, now in the Bibliothèque Nationale, Paris; because it is the chief witness for the longer of the two recensions attributed to Epiphanius of Salamis, it will be referred to as E[1].

Codex Coisl. 120, tenth century, Bibliothèque Nationale (Fonds Coislin), Paris; since it is the leading representative of the short recension attributed to Epiphanius, it will be referred to as E[2].

Codex Vindob. Theol. Gk. 40 (formerly 77), thirteenth century, Vienna; because it is the best example of the recension attributed to Dorotheus, it will be cited as D.

Codex Coisl. 224, tenth century, Bibliothèque Nationale (Fonds Coislin), Paris; a member of the "anonymous recension," it generally agrees with Q. No siglum is used for this manuscript, because it is used infrequently.

The text is well preserved in these manuscripts (Coisl. 224 is defective in the section on Daniel), but they differ widely regarding the order in which the prophets are treated and in respect to which non-literary prophets are included.

The translation here presented is based almost entirely upon Q, which is generally regarded as best representing the earliest Greek version of this work.[2]

---

[1] This term distinguishes Q and its dependents from the many MSS that attribute the work to Epiphanius or Dorotheus.

[2] A critical text of Q is presented by T. Schermann, *Prophetarum vitae fabulosae indices apostolorum discipulorumque Domini Dorotheo, Epiphanio, Hippolyto aliisque vindicate*, pp. 68–98. With this was compared the text of Q as printed by E. Nestle, *Marginalien und Materialien*. Discussions of the major recensions and their chief witnesses

Original language

It is believed by many that The Lives of the Prophets was originally written in one of the Semitic languages. A few scholars have proposed that the original language was Syriac, but this position has won few supporters.[3] More widespread is the view, vigorously defended by C. C. Torrey, that the book was composed in Hebrew.[4] The Israeli scholar S. Klein suggests that either Aramaic or Hebrew may have been the original language.[5] T. Schermann posits a Hebrew ancestor but opposes the view that the earliest Greek version was simply a translation from Hebrew.[6]

Two arguments count against the hypothesis of a Semitic original. First, the evidence of mistranslation is not substantial.[7] Secondly, there are several instances in which the text is closer to the Greek version of the Jewish Scriptures than to the Hebrew.[8] In the absence of compelling evidence to the contrary, it is best to assume that the Palestinian traditions included in this document first attained literary form in Greek.[9]

Date

It is very difficult to date a document of this kind, not only because it contains very few allusions to contemporary events, but also because it was an open-ended collection that invited additions.

The document is extant in Christian manuscripts only. Not a scrap of it has been identified at Qumran, and there is no reference to it in other Jewish literature. Nevertheless, the basic material has been so little influenced by Christian beliefs that scholars are generally agreed that the original writing was created by a Jew. Because it was transmitted by Christians, however, it is not surprising that the manuscripts contain a good deal of Christian material. In D, for example, each section is prefaced with prophecies concerning the Messiah attributed to the prophet in question, to which are appended in some instances references to the use of these prophecies in the New Testament. E[1] adds sections dealing with Zechariah the father of John the Baptist, Simeon of Luke 2:25–35, and John the Baptist. A few manuscripts dependent upon Q, including Coisl. 224, contain an account of the martyrdom of "Simon, son of Clopus, the cousin of the LORD." Q contains no Christian additions of either of these two types, but Christian interpolations of a more subtle kind are suspected at various points, some of which will be referred to in the notes.[10]

On the assumption that the basic work was created by a non-Christian Jew, it is still difficult to establish limits for his activity, but the evidence suggests a date within the first century A.D. Some of the traditions are undoubtedly ancient, but it seems unlikely that the basic collection originated as early as the Maccabean period. Nor is there any certain evidence that the document dates from after the destruction of Jerusalem and the Temple in

may be found in T. Schermann, *Propheten- und Apostellegenden nebst Jüngerkatalogen der Dorotheus und verwandter Texte*, pp. 1–133; A.-M. Denis, *Introduction*, pp. 85–88; C. C. Torrey, *The Lives of the Prophets*, pp. 4–6.

[3] The leading proponent was I. H. Hall, "The Lives of the Prophets," *JBL* 7 (1887) 38f.

[4] *Lives*, p. 7; Torrey also cites earlier advocates of this view.

[5] "'al ha-seper Vitae Prophetarum," *Sefer Klozner*, ed. H. Torczyner, 209.

[6] *Propheten- und Apostellegenden*, pp. 131f.

[7] Cf. n. c on 1:1. Torrey's brilliant conjecture concerning the *argolai* of 2:7 (*Lives*, p. 49; see below, n. k on 2:7) does not provide evidence of translation from a Heb. original; if the passage is not a gloss, the author may simply be transmitting a tradition popular among Gk.-speaking Jews of Egypt. The evidence of mistranslation in 4:10 is impressive (see n. f) but is not in itself sufficient to justify the hypothesis.

[8] Cf. n. j on 4:15, n. f on 12:12, and nn. k and l on 21:13–14. The use of "Sybatha" in 20:1 seems to reflect a tradition based on the Heb. text (see n. c), but awareness of such a tradition on the part of a Palestinian author would not justify the inference that he wrote in Heb. (or Aram.).

[9] Concerning the use of Gk. by Palestinian Jews, cf. J. N. Sevenster, *Do You Know Greek?* (Leiden, 1968); A. R. C. Leaney, "Greek Manuscripts from the Judean Desert," *Studies in New Testament Language and Text*, ed. J. K. Elliott (Leiden, 1976) pp. 283–300.

[10] M. de Jonge, "Christelijke Elementen in de Vitae Prophetarum," *Nederlands Theologisch Tijdschrift* 16 (1961–62) 164, raises the possibility that Melito or Hegesippus assembled the material while traveling in the Near East, and, in conjunction with Christian editing, first presented it to the world as a literary document.

A.D. 70.[11] A date after the emergence of gentile Christianity may be required if the prophecy in 2:13 concerning gentiles worshiping a piece of wood is an expression of Jewish disgust at the idolatrous veneration of the cross by gentile Christians, but it seems more probable that this is a Christian interpolation.

Of greater relevance to the question of the date are two passages that seem to imply specific historical situations. If the passage concerning Isaiah's grave indicates that in the author's perspective the so-called spring of Siloam is outside the wall of Jerusalem, a date prior to the erection of the new south wall by Herod Agrippa (A.D. 41–44) is required.[12] On the other hand, the author may simply be reflecting an awareness of the fact that the Herodian wall is of very recent date, and therefore this passage cannot be pressed as certain evidence for a date prior to A.D. 41.

More convincing evidence of a first-century date is provided by a phrase in 21:1, "Elijah, a Thesbite from the land of the Arabs." That is, from the author's perspective, Elijah's Transjordanian birthplace lay within the area under Nabatean political control. Since Nabatean hegemony was terminated in A.D. 106 by Trajan, it is probable that our author wrote at an earlier date.

Although demonstration is impossible, it would appear that the most probable date is the first quarter of the first century A.D., when interest in the erection of monuments for prophets and other national heroes, encouraged in part by Herod's construction of an expensive memorial of white marble at the entrance to David's tomb (Josephus, Ant 16.7.1 §182) began to gain momentum. One may hazard the guess that this little document preceded, and perhaps even contributed toward, the peaking of this movement. The saying of Jesus in Luke 11:47, "Alas for you who build the tombs of the prophets, the men your ancestors killed!" (cf. Mt 23:29), implies that memorials had been erected recently for certain martyred prophets. Jeremias argues that Jesus was alluding most probably to monuments in honor of Isaiah and Zechariah son of Jehoiada, the only prophets to whom tradition had attributed a Jerusalem martyrdom and burial.[13] While The Lives of the Prophets 1:8 suggests that a monument had been erected for Isaiah (cf. n. 1 on 1:8), there is no suggestion that this was of recent date. Respecting the burial of Zechariah son of Jehoiada, on the other hand, our text betrays no awareness of a monument (cf. 23:1 and n. d). If Jesus' saying does in fact point to such a construction, it can be inferred that our author wrote prior to the time of Jesus' public ministry.

Provenance

It is most probable that the writing originated in Palestine. Not only does the author apparently have accurate geographical information, but also his perspective seems to be that of a resident in Judea. Torrey argues that the author is an inhabitant of Jerusalem, because of the naturalness with which he speaks of "the city" when referring to Jerusalem.[14] Since it is possible, however, that Jews resident elsewhere in Palestine sometimes spoke in this way, it it necessary to be cautious. In any case, the author seems to be particularly well informed regarding Jerusalem. The details he gives concerning the site of Isaiah's grave in relation to other local landmarks suggest great familiarity with, if not actual residence in, the Holy City.

Did the work originate among hellenistic Jews of Palestine? Sometimes the document reflects dependence upon the Hebrew text of the Bible, at other points it clearly evidences familiarity with a Greek translation.[15] It is important in this connection to remember that in

[11] The prediction of 12:11 that the Temple will be destroyed by a Western nation was probably understood as referring to the Romans, but nothing requires that it be taken as a prophecy after the fact; the accompanying statements have the ring of unfulfilled predictions. Similarly, the prophecy of 10:11 is best taken as reflecting an earlier situation, not the bitter experience of A.D. 70 (see n. on 10:11).

[12] See 1:1–8 and n. i.

[13] J. Jeremias, *Heiligengräber in Jesu Umwelt*, pp. 66, 68. Jeremias seems to infer that since there were no graves of martyr-prophets in Galilee, Transjordan, or Samaria, and because the graves of Micah and Amos were honored in southern Judea beyond the area of Jesus' travels, it can be assumed that Jesus' saying alludes to the Jerusalem martyrs.

[14] *Lives*, p. 11.

[15] *Sybatha* in 20:1 and *Spharphōtim* in 16:3 suggest acquaintance with the Scriptures in Heb. (see nn. on these passages). On the other hand, the use of *Baltasar* as a name both for Nebuchadnezzar's crown prince and for Daniel depends on LXX (see 4:4, 15 and n.).

the first century A.D. a large number of Palestinian Jews were bilingual or trilingual, and well able to use Greek as a literary medium. In the absence of clear proof to the contrary, it may be supposed that The Lives of the Prophets reflects bilingual Palestinian Judaism.

Theological importance

Perhaps the main reason why this early writing has so seldom been translated into English and has not heretofore been included in English collections of Jewish apocryphal and pseudepigraphical writings is that it contains so little of interest to biblical theologians. Religious edification is not its prime purpose, and consequently theological themes are for the most part dealt with only indirectly.

The document is "orthodox" in the sense that it assumes the biblical view that there is but one God, who is LORD of history and Savior of his people, and that the rulership of God is manifested in natural disasters and in miracles (1:2–8; 2:3–4). Abnormal natural occurrences are taken as signs, provided by God and announced through his prophets, of forthcoming historical events (3:5; 4:19–20).

Angels, though seldom mentioned, are obviously taken for granted as an important means of communication between God and his people (12:12; 16:2–3; 23:2; the men "of shining white appearance" of 21:2 are presumably angels). Demons are never referred to, but Satan appears three times in the text under the name "Beliar" (4:6, 20; 17:2), a designation often used in the Testaments of the Twelve Patriarchs and in the Qumran literature, and occurring once in the New Testament (2Cor 6:15).[16] Another designation for the prince of evil is "the serpent" (12:13); the closest parallel to this is provided by Revelation 12:9, 17 (ApMos 16:5 prefers to render the snake of Gen 3 as Satan's "vessel"). Satan is also alluded to as "the enemy" (2:15), as in the Testament of Daniel 6:3f. and Luke 10:19 (cf. Mt 13:39). Thus it can be affirmed that dualism is present in the document, but it is by no means emphasized.

Ethics and the related theological topics of guilt, punishment, and expiation are not a major concern in this writing. It is assumed that it is proper to live in accordance with the law (2:18; 3:16; 17:1), but there is no attempt to preach this by reference to God's acts in history. Although the historical narratives of the canonical books of Kings and of Chronicles are the source of anecdotal material, the central theological theme of these books, namely that God punishes those who fail to keep his law and rewards those who observe it, has not greatly influenced this document. It is particularly striking that in a book that purports to relate the martyrdoms of six prophets there is no allusion to the popular theme that Israel has always persecuted God's prophets (cf. 2Chr 24:19; 36:14–16; Neh 9:26; Jub 1:12).[17] Only in the case of Jeremiah is the martyrdom attributed in generalized terms to his "people," i.e. Israel (see 2:1 and n.), and even here there is no theological reflection on the corporate guilt thus incurred. Also significant is the fact that the "moral thunder" of the prophetic writings, so much appreciated by modern readers, has left almost no trace (cf. 6:2). It is very evident that the author's interest in the prophets relates not to their importance as ethical teachers but, rather, to their numinous quality as workers of miracles, intercessors, and foretellers of future events.

The doctrine of the resurrection is assumed without argument or polemic (2:15; 3:12). It is further assumed that important symbols of Israel's worship will reappear in the age to come. In connection with his concealment of the ark of the covenant and its contents prior to the destruction of the first Temple, Jeremiah is said to have declared:

> This ark no one is going to bring out except Aaron, and none of the priests or prophets will any longer open the tablets in it except Moses, God's chosen one. And in the resurrection the ark will be the first to be resurrected and will come out of the rock and be placed on Mount Sinai, and all the saints will be gathered to it there . . . (2:14f.)

[16] For a helpful discussion of the significance of Belial (Beliar) in the Dead Sea Scrolls, cf. H. Ringgren, *The Faith of Qumran*, trans. E. T. Sander (Philadelphia, 1963) pp. 74f., 91f.

[17] L. Ginzberg, *The Legends of the Jews*, vol. 4, p. 295, cites a haggadah in which the young Jeremiah declares, "O LORD, I cannot go as a prophet to Israel, for when lived there a prophet whom Israel did not desire to kill?"

Similarly, Habakkuk prophesies that the capitals of the pillars of the second Temple will be restored at the commencement of the age to come as sources of illumination for those being pursued by the serpent (12:12f.).

Of special interest to students of Jewish eschatology is the designation of Moses as "God's chosen one" (2:14), in view of the fact that the same words are employed as a designation of the Messiah by Jesus' enemies in Luke's passion narrative (Lk 23:35). Since the Messiah is nowhere mentioned in the oldest version of The Lives of the Prophets, it can be argued that its author adhered to that segment of Jewish eschatology which expected not a Davidic but a Mosaic deliverer. Also fascinating is the assertion that Elijah "will judge Israel" (21:3, to which most MSS apart from Q add "with sword and fire"). This provides valuable evidence of the belief that God will execute his judgment by means of one or more human deputies, and makes more understandable the parallel assertions of the New Testament (e.g. Mt 19:28; Acts 17:31; 1Cor 6:2f.). The idea that Elijah will function as eschatological judge may underlie the prediction attributed to John the Baptist concerning the one who will baptize with fire (Mt 3:11f.; Lk 3:16f.).

Despite a strong belief in a future resurrection it is perhaps even more strongly believed that the righteous dead are still alive in a very real sense. In 1:8 it is asserted that the martyred Isaiah is the patron saint of Siloam, through whose prayers the water continues to flow, and it is apparently the numinous presence of Jeremiah at his grave that makes the soil effective for the healing of asps' bites (2:4). With this must be compared the early Christian belief that the righteous dead are transported to a place of blessedness before the final resurrection (Lk 16:22–24; 23:43; Phil 1:23; Rev 6:9f.; cf. Mk 12:26f.) and thus are to be conceived of as already alive and not merely "sleeping" in the earth. No consistency is attempted in our text relative to the location of this post-mortem existence. On the one hand it is assumed that the dead prophet's lively existence is to be experienced at his grave; on the other, a heavenly residence is suggested by the statement that Jeremiah and Moses "are together to this day" (2:19), despite the fact that their supposed graves are widely separated.

Relation to canonical books

Although the author is thoroughly familiar with the biblical narratives concerning the prophets given in Kings and Chronicles and the prophetic books, it is evident that he wishes to provide supplementary information rather than simply to repeat canonical material. For this reason, the long summaries of the "signs" performed by Elijah and Elisha (21:4–14; 22:4–17) must be suspected of being later additions.[18]

There is no indication that the book was known to any of the New Testament writers, but the author of the Letter to the Hebrews seems to have been aware of some of the traditions here recorded. The statement of Hebrews 11:37, "They were stoned, or sawn in half, or beheaded," appears to refer to the popular legends concerning the martyrdoms of the three major prophets Jeremiah, Isaiah, and Ezekiel respectively.[19] Our document explicitly states that Jeremiah was stoned (2:1) and that Isaiah "died under Manasseh by being sawn in two" (1:1) but is less explicit regarding Ezekiel. We are told only that "The ruler of the people Israel killed him . . ." (3:2).

The saying of Jesus regarding the erection of monuments in honor of martyred prophets (Mt 23:29; Lk 11:47) has no direct point of contact with The Lives of the Prophets, which mentions no recent monuments, but it supports our text by providing evidence of the contemporary interest in the graves of the prophets.

The belief that the holy martyrs are able to present petitions to God, evidenced in Revelation 6:9–11, is probably to be seen as related to the conception of the prophets as intercessors, as witnessed by 1:8.[20]

Relation to apocryphal books

A much fuller account of Isaiah's murder is provided by the Martyrdom of Isaiah, but the latter makes no mention of the burial or its location. There is no evidence of dependency

---

[18] Cf. Torrey, *Lives,* pp. 3f. and n. on 21:4.
[19] See n. on 3:2.
[20] Cf. Jeremias, *Heiligengräber,* pp. 133–38.

in either direction. The functions of the two narratives are very different. Whereas the point of the much longer version is to edify, the intention of the brief account given here is simply to note that Isaiah is a martyr, because this fact is significant for the cult connected with his grave.

The legend concerning the concealment of the ark and its contents in a cliff by Jeremiah (2:11–19) has parallels in 2 Maccabees 2:4–8 and 4 Baruch 3:8 without any indication of borrowing. It must be assumed that the tradition circulated in variant forms in the folklore of Palestine.

Many of the legends here recorded have parallels in the haggadah of rabbinic Judaism, as will be indicated in the notes.

Cultural importance

The Lives of the Prophets has had little influence upon Western culture, but it throws indirect light on the Christian practice of the veneration of the saints, which is frequently reflected in the art and literature of the Western world. No attempt can be made here to pursue the question of the origin of the practice, but it is clear that we have in this document evidence that one of the roots lies in the Jewish veneration of the holy dead.

BIBLIOGRAPHY

Charlesworth, *PMR*, pp. 175–77.
Delling, *Bibliographie*, p. 172.
Denis, *Introduction*, pp. 85–90.

Ginzberg, L. *The Legends of the Jews*. Translated by H. Szold. 7 vols.; Philadelphia, 1909–38. (This invaluable collection provides ample evidence that many if not most of the legends transmitted in LivPro have parallels in rabbinic and other Jewish sources.)
Jeremias, J. *Heiligengräber in Jesu Umwelt*. Göttingen, 1958. (This is the fullest study available of holy graves in Jewish Palestine. Jeremias carefully compares the literary data provided by LivPro and early pilgrims with the available archaeological evidence.)
Jonge, M. de. "Christelijke Elementen in de Vitae Prophetarum," *Nederlands Theologisch Tijdschrift* 16 (1961–62) 161–78. (De Jonge argues that the Christian elements are far more pervasive than many have believed, and that this collection of Jewish traditions may have first attained literary form in a Christian context.)
Klein, S. "'al ha-seper Vitae Prophetarum," *Sefer Klozner*, edited by H. Torczyner. Tel Aviv, 1937; 189–208. (A critical analysis of LivPro in Heb., with special attention to matters of geography.)
Nestle, E. *Marginalien und Materialien*. Tübingen, 1893. (On opposite pages Nestle presents the Gk. text of Q and E[1], with a list of the variant readings of three Syr. MSS.)
Schermann, T. *Prophetarum vitae fabulosae indices apostolorum discipulorumque Domini Dorotheo, Epiphanio, Hippolyto aliisque vindicate*. Leipzig, 1907. (A critical text of each of the major Gk. recensions, with an extensive apparatus giving the more important variants.)
————. *Propheten- und Apostellegenden nebst Jüngerkatalogen des Dorotheus und verwandter Texte*. TU 31.3. Leipzig, 1907. (An indispensable study of the texts and versions of LivPro.)
Simon, M. "Les Saints d'Israël dans la dévotion de l'Église ancienne," *RHPR* 34 (1954) 98–127. (A study of the influence of Jewish veneration of the graves of heroes and prophets upon the early Church.)
Torrey, C. C. *The Lives of the Prophets. Greek Text and Translation*. Philadelphia, 1946. (The most important English study. The translation assumes that the Gk. text contains a number of difficulties which are due to mistranslation from an underlying Heb. text.)

THE LIVES OF THE PROPHETS

The names of the prophets, and where they are from, and where they died and how, and where they lie.

Isaiah

1 **1** Isaiah, from Jerusalem, died under Manasseh by being sawn in two,[a] and was Martls 5:1-5
buried[b] underneath the Oak of Rogel,[c] near the place where the path crosses the
2 aqueduct whose water Hezekiah shut off by blocking its source.[d] • And God worked
the miracle[e] of Siloam for the prophet's sake, for, being faint[f] before he died, he
prayed for water to drink, and immediately it was sent to him from it; therefore
3 it is called Siloam, which means "sent."[g] • And in the time of Hezekiah, before
he made the cisterns and the pools, in response to the prayer of Isaiah a little
water came out, for the nation was besieged by foreigners and (this happened) in
4 order that the city might not perish for lack of water.[h] • For the enemies were
5 asking, "From where are they drinking?" • And having the city under siege they
6 were encamped at Siloam.[i] • If, then, the Jews were coming, water would come
7 out, but if foreigners (approached), (it would) not. • Wherefore to this day it comes

---

1 a. Cf. b. Yeb 49b, y. Sanh 10:28c, 37. Heb 11:37 witnesses to the pre-Christian origin of this legend.

b. Lit. "placed."

c. Possibly "Fuller's Oak." A common practice associated holy graves with trees, with oaks given special preference (Jeremias, *Heiligengräber*, p. 120). Torrey, *Lives*, pp. 10f., supports the conjecture that an error occurred in translating the underlying Heb. into Gk. and that the original referred to ʿ*ên rögēl*, i.e. the Fountain of Rogel. Since a major point of the following narrative is to present Isaiah as the patron spirit of the Spring of Siloam, it is hardly likely that he was buried at ʿ*ên rögēl*, now known as Jacob's Well, which is situated about 400 meters south of Siloam. If the Fuller's Field (Isa 7:3) was situated in this area (cf. Jeremias, *Heiligengräber*, p. 64), it is not at all unlikely that a tree along the path descending the hill above Siloam should be known as "Fuller's Oak."

d. Lit. "near the crossing of the waters that Hezekiah destroyed by blocking them." Torrey, *Lives*, p. 34, translates *diabaseōs* as "conduit," apparently taking it as an allusion to the ancient aqueduct that descended Ophel above the Kidron valley from Gihon to the Lower Pool. Since this water system was entirely outside the city wall, Hezekiah blocked the source so as to deprive invading enemies of a convenient source of water (2Chr 32:3, 4, 30; cf. Isa 8:6). F.-M. Abel (H. Vincent and F.-M. Abel, *Jerusalem* [2 vols.; Paris, 1912–26] vol. 2, p. 857) insists that *diabasis* denotes not an aqueduct but the place where one crosses a watercourse, i.e. either a bridge or a ford. Jeremias, *Heiligengräber*, p. 64, concurs but argues that Abel is mistaken in associating the *diabasis* with the old aqueduct; it must refer, rather, to the place where the path crosses Hezekiah's tunnel, just above its lower end at Siloam. Although Jeremias' interpretation fits well with Isaiah's function as patron spirit of Siloam, it makes nonsense

of the Gk. text and ignores the fact that our author was ignorant of Hezekiah's tunnel; see n. h below.

e. Lit. "sign" as in Jn 2:11; 20:30.

f. "Being faint" seems to be required by the context, but there is no lexical evidence that *oligōreō* ever carried this meaning.

g. Because of the parallel at Jn 9:7, de Jonge, *Nederlands Theologisch Tijdschrift* 16 (1961–62) 166, argues that we have here evidence of Christian influence upon LivPro. Since the etymology is very differently employed in the two writings, however, there is little basis for de Jonge's conjecture.

h. This statement provides clear evidence that the transmitters of this tradition, like Josephus (*War* 5.4.1 §140), regarded Siloam as a spring rather than as the effluence of Hezekiah's underground aqueduct which diverted the water from the Gihon spring. An excellent description of Hezekiah's engineering feat is provided by J. Simons, *Jerusalem in the Old Testament* (Leiden, 1952) pp. 173–92. Apparently all recollection of the connection with Gihon had disappeared by the Roman period.

i. It is generally held that Hezekiah's intention was to divert water from Gihon, which lay outside the fortifications, to a reservoir *within* the walls (cf. 2Kgs 20:20; Sir 48:17). On the basis of careful archaeological investigation, K. Kenyon, *Digging Up Jerusalem* (New York and Washington, 1974) pp. 158, 246f., maintains that Siloam was not enclosed within the walls of the city until Herod Agrippa built the new south wall, A.D. 41–44. Puzzling though such a conclusion is relative to Hezekiah's defense strategy, it is confirmed by our text, which assumes that the besieging army camped by the spring in order to use its water. Further confirmation is provided by Josephus, who reports that the most ancient wall traversed the hill "above the fountain of Siloam" (*War* 5.4.2 §145).

8 out intermittently,[j] in order that the mystery may be manifested.[k] •And since this happened through Isaiah, as a memorial of it the nation also buried him nearby with care and in great honor,[l] so that through his prayers even after his death they might enjoy the benefit of the water, for an oracle was also given to them concerning him.

9   His tomb is near the tomb of the kings,[m] west of the tomb of the priests[n] in the
10 southern part of the city.[o] •For Solomon made the tombs, in accordance with David's design, east of Zion,[p] which[q] has an entrance from Gabaon, twenty stadia[r]
11 distant from the city. •And he made a secret construction with winding passages;
12 and it is to this day unknown to most.[s] •There the king kept the gold from Ethiopia
13 and the spices. •And because Hezekiah showed the gentiles the secrets of David   2Kgs 20:12-18 and Solomon and defiled the bones of the place of his fathers, God swore that his offspring should be enslaved to his enemies, and God made him sterile from that day.

Jeremiah

1 **2** Jeremiah was from Anathoth, and he died in Taphnai of Egypt,[a] having been   Jer 1:1
2 stoned[b] by his people.[c] •He was buried[d] in the environs of Pharaoh's palace,   Jer 43:8
      because the Egyptians held him in high esteem, having been benefitted through   4Bar 9:31
                                                     Jer 43:9
3 him. •For he prayed, and the asps left them, and the monsters of the waters,

---

j. The intermittent character of the Gihon spring (known today as the Virgin's Spring or the Spring of the Steps) is due to a subterranean siphon caused by the geological formation; cf. Simons, *Jerusalem*, pp. 163f.

k. Torrey's translation "to keep the miracle in mind" (*Lives*, p. 34) is very attractive, but there is no lexical evidence that *mystērion* ever carried this connotation. Cf. its use in 2:10, 19.

l. This language suggests the erection of a monument (Jeremias, *Heiligengräber*, p. 64). Since memorial constructions were not always contiguous with the actual graves (Jeremias, *Heiligengräber*, p. 122), Isaiah's monument may not have been situated beside the Oak of Rogel. "Nearby" (*plē-sion*) suggests that the monument was "in the neighborhood," rather than directly adjacent to Siloam, however, and therefore a site near the tree is entirely possible.

m. The site of the royal necropolis is still uncertain. The constructions on the Kidron side of the hill about 110 meters (c. 361 ft.) northeast of Siloam, identified by R. Weill as the royal tombs (*La Cité de David* [Paris, 1920] pp. 35–44, 157–73), are regarded by Kenyon, *Digging*, pp. 31f., as cisterns. Nevertheless the literary evidence, both biblical (Neh 3:16) and rabbinic (t.BB 1:11), points to a site within the walls at the southern extremity of the southeast hill, i.e. not far distant from the site proposed in n. c above for Isaiah's grave. Cf. Simons, *Jerusalem*, p. 210.

n. "The tomb of the priests" may refer to one or more of the impressive constructions still standing on the eastern slope of the Kidron about 800 meters (2,600 ft.) from Siloam. Photographs and descriptions are provided by B. Mazar, *The Mountain of the Lord* (Garden City, N.Y., 1975) pp. 71, 225. The Gk. *opisthen* probably reflects the Heb. *'aḥar*, which normally means "behind" but can connote "West" (cf. MT and LXX of Judg 18:12).

o. Lit. "at the southern part."

p. Although Josephus did not employ the term "Zion," it is clear that he erroneously regarded David's city as situated on the western hill of Jerusalem (*War* 5.4.1 §137); cf. Simons, *Jerusalem*, pp. 35–59. The phrase "east of Zion" need not imply the same error. It may mean simply "on the eastern (Kidrón) slope of David's city."

q. The Gk. text here becomes hopelessly confused. Jeremias, *Heiligengräber*, p. 58, proposes that the original purpose of this clause was to bring the royal tomb into relation with the Siloam tunnel; since the tunnel's point of origin at the Gihon spring was no longer known, it was possible to present the fanciful idea that it was almost 4 kilometers long and had its beginning north of the city in the direction of Gibeon. This proposal ignores the fact that the author believed that Siloam was a spring (see n. h above). It is better to take the clause as a haggadic description of the famous tomb.

r. About 3.8 kilometers (2.3 miles).

s. Q and its dependents add the ungrammatical and awkward gloss "and of the whole people," which is absent from E[1] and E[2]. D attempts an improvement: "unknown to most of the priests and to the whole people." Since E[1] concludes its treatment of Isaiah at this point, it is possible that the subsequent irrelevant statements concerning Solomon's storehouse and Hezekiah's indiscretion did not belong in the earliest version.

2 a. *Taphnai* is an unusual Gk. transliteration of the Heb. name *taḥpanḥēs* (Jer 43:7). This was probably the town known in hellenistic times as Daphnai, modern Tell Defenneh, in northeastern Egypt, less than 20 kilometers (12.5 miles) west of the point where the Suez Canal enters Lake Menzaleh.

b. Lit. "having been thrown (down) by stones."

c. Lit. "by the people." *Laos*, "people," normally designates Israel in this document as in hellenistic Jewish literature generally; cf. 3:2, 11, 13.

d. Lit. "he lies."

4 which the Egyptians call *Nephoth* and the Greeks crocodiles.ᵉ •And those who are
   God's faithful pray at the place to this very day, and taking the dust of the place
5 they heal asps' bites.ᶠ •And we have heard from the children of Antigonus and
   Ptolemy, old men, that Alexander the Macedonian, after standing at the prophet's
   graveᵍ and witnessing his mysteries,ʰ transferred his remains to Alexandria and
6 placed them in a circle around (the city) with due honor;ⁱ •and the whole race
7 of asps was kept from the land, and from the river likewise the crocodiles.ʲ •And
   to the same end heᵏ introduced the snakes which are called *Argolai*, which means
   "snake-fighters," which he brought from Argos of the Peloponnesus, whence
   they are also called *Argolai*, that is, "fortunate ones from Argos"; for everything
   fortunate they call *laia*.ˡ
8   This Jeremiah gave a sign to the priests of Egypt, that it was decreedᵐ that their
   idols would be shaken and collapse [through a savior, a child born of a virgin, in
9 a manger].ⁿ •Wherefore even to this day they revere a virgin giving birth and,
10 placing an infant in a manger, they worship. •And when Ptolemy the king inquired
   about the cause, they said, "It is an ancestral mystery delivered to our fathers by

---

e. Torrey, *Lives*, pp. 49–52, accepting the reading *ephôth* found in E² and D, conjectures that the
original text contained no reference to crocodiles
since *ephôth* is simply the transliterated plural of
the Heb. word *'ep'eh*, "viper," the term by which
Egyptian Jews referred to the asps.

f. At this point the textual tradition becomes
very confused, with various glosses, inversions,
and conflations. The following tradition, although
given verisimilitude by association with specific
names, is missing from E¹ and for that reason may
be suspected of being a gloss.

g. Lit. "place."

h. See 1:7 and n.

i. Jeremias, *Heiligengräber*, pp. 108–10, proposes that this strange statement alludes to the
founding of Alexandria and asserts that Alexander
deposited the bones of the prophet at specific
locations on the perimeter, both to establish the
bounds of the city and to protect it. M. Simon,
RHPR 34 (1954) 124, argues that this tradition
regarding the transfer of Jeremiah's remains to
Alexandria represents a Christian attempt to woo
Christians away from the ancient site where they
were too easily attracted to Jewish popular religion.

j. D omits "the crocodiles."

k. I.e. Alexander. Torrey, *Lives*, p. 49, proposes
that an earlier version of this gloss attributed the
introduction of the *Argolai* to Jeremiah. He conjectures that the unknown Gk. word *argolai* is the
transliteration of the Heb. *hargôl*, which occurs at
Lev 11:22 as the designation of one of four kinds
of grasshoppers that may be eaten. In LXX it is
rendered *ophiomachēn*, "snake-fighter," as here!
Since grasshoppers cannot kill snakes, Torrey suggests that the mistranslation in LXX indicates that
Egyptian Jews had used *hargôl*, "grasshopper,"
as a nickname for the ichneumon (the Egyptian
mongoose famous for its ability to kill snakes)
because of its abrupt leaping. Because the original
meaning of *argolai* had been lost, it was possible
for later glossators to conceive them as snakes, and
derive them from Argos. The tradition about the
Argolai is absent from E¹ and E².

l. That this strained etymology was difficult to
understand even in ancient times is indicated by
the plethora of textual variants.

m. Lit. "it is necessary," but divine necessity
is implied; cf. Dan 2:28LXX and Mt 24:6.

n. Something has dropped out of Q at this point;

the lack is supplied by an awkward gloss in its
dependents. Included here in brackets is the reading
of Coisl. 224, which appears to be related to the
parallel in D: "through a savior, a child born of a
virgin, and lying in a manger" (cf. Lk 2:12). It is
virtually impossible to reconstruct the earliest form
of this paragraph, which is differently represented
in each of the four major recensions. The second
and third sentences, which are absent from E¹, are
probably secondary, whatever the origin of the
first. The opening statement predicts divine punishment of Egyptian idolatry; it is not likely that a
Jewish author who included this "sign" would
have been so foolish as to suggest that the pagan
Egyptians regularly celebrated the anticipated overthrow of their popular religion in a cultic ceremony
that was itself a manifestation of pagan polytheism!
For this reason the suggestion of Torrey, *Lives*,
pp. 9f., that the Palestinian author derived this
tradition from a Christian Jew from Egypt, is hardly
acceptable. M. de Jonge, *Nederlands Theologisch
Tijdschrift* 16 (1961–62) 168, is probably correct
in insisting that the entire paragraph must be
regarded as a Christian product. It can be argued,
however, that more than one Christian hand is
evident here. The first glossator asserted that Jeremiah had foreseen the success of Christianity in
Egypt, which was to be initiated by the visit of the
Virgin Mother and Holy Child (Mt 2:13–15, with
which is conflated the narrative concerning the
manger of Lk 2:7–16). A later scribe noted how
this visit had been prefigured in a pagan festival
honoring a virgin and divine child, and added the
legendary anecdote concerning Ptolemy's question
in order to bring his addition into connection with
Jeremiah. It is remotely possible, however, that
the first sentence (without the awkward reference
to the manger) comes from a Jewish author who
produced the "sign" by combining three prophetic
texts as translated in LXX: Isa 19:1, Jer 46:15
(LXX 26:15), and Isa 7:14. In this case the
statement would express a Jewish hope that the
pagan culture of Egypt would be overturned by the
Messiah, whose miraculous birth would signal that
God had invested him with the supernatural power
necessary for the task. D. Daube, *The New Testament and Rabbinic Judaism* (London, 1956) pp.
6f., finds evidence of an early rabbinic tradition
concerning the miraculous birth of Moses.

a holy prophet, and we are to await, he says, the consummation of his mystery."[o]
11 This prophet, before the capture of the Temple, seized the ark of the Law and 2Mac 2:4-8
12 the things in it, and made them to be swallowed up in a rock.[p] •And to those 4Bar 3:8-20
standing by he said, "The LORD has gone away from Zion into heaven and will
13 come again in power. •And this will be for you a sign of his coming, when all
14 the gentiles worship a piece of wood."[q] •And he said, "This ark no one is going
to bring out except Aaron, and none of the priests or prophets will any longer
15 open[r] the tablets in it except Moses, God's chosen one. •And in the resurrection
the ark will be the first to be resurrected and will come out of the rock and be
placed on Mount Sinai, and all the saints will be gathered to it[s] there as they await
16 the LORD and flee from the enemy who wishes to destroy them." •In the rock 12:13
with his finger he set as a seal the name of God, and the impression was like a
carving made with iron, and a cloud covered the name, and no one knows the
17 place nor is able to read the name[t] to this day and to the consummation. •And the
rock is in the wilderness, where the ark was at first, between the two mountains
18 on which[u] Moses and Aaron lie.[v] •And at night there is a cloud like fire, just like
19 the ancient one, for the glory of God will never cease from his Law.[w] •And God
bestowed this favor upon Jeremiah, that he might himself perform the completion
of his mystery,[x] so that he might become a partner of Moses,[y] and they are
together to this day.[z]

Ezekiel

1 **3** Ezekiel. This man was from the land of Arira,[a] of the priests, and he died in Ezek 1:3
the land of the Chaldeans during the captivity, after having prophesied many
2 things to those in Judea. •The ruler of the people Israel killed him there as he
3 was being reproved by him concerning the worship of idols.[b] •And they buried Gen 10:22; 11:10
him in the field of Maour[c] in the grave of Shem and Arpachshad, ancestors of 1Chr 1:17,26

o. Cf. 1:7; 2:5, 19.

p. In 2Bar 6 it is an angel who takes the sacred vessels from the Temple; the earth opens its mouth and swallows them.

q. This is probably an allusion to gentile veneration of the cross. It need not be regarded as a Christian interpolation if it is seen as a negative comment upon gentile Christianity, but it more probably is an expression of the Christian hope that Jesus will return when the full number of the gentiles have been converted.

r. Lit. "unfold" (as a scroll) but probably used metaphorically in the sense of "disclose."

s. Following E^1 and E^2. Q's reading "to him" is probably simply a grammatical error.

t. Following E^1. Q has "him," perhaps with reference to "impression" (a masculine noun).

u. Lit. "in which" or "in the midst of which."

v. The two mountains on which Aaron and Moses died, Hor and Nebo respectively, were sometimes considered "twins" in Jewish legend; cf. Ginzberg, *Legends*, vol. 3, p. 316.

w. E^1 ends its narrative concerning Jeremiah at this point.

x. Cf. 1:7; 2:5, 10.

y. E^2 concludes at this point, and may well represent the earliest version.

z. Although their physical remains rest in widely separated locations! Cf. 2Mac 15:13 and Mt 16:14 for similar views concerning the continued vitality of Jeremiah.

3 a. The place in question remains unknown. Variants include *Sarira*, *Sarĕra*, *Saira*, *Saiĕra*, and *Serida*. The variants may reflect the tradition about a mysterious land of Sir in the Far East; cf. Josephus, *Ant* 1.2.3 §71, and G. J. Reinink, "Das Land 'Seiris' (Sir) und das Volk der Sirer in jüdischen und christlichen Traditionen," *JSJ* 6 (1975) 72–85, who concludes that the land of Sir is China.

b. E. R. Goodenough, *Jewish Symbols in the Greco-Roman Period* (13 vols.; New York, 1953–68) vol. 10, pp. 188–90, argues that the pictures in the Ezekiel cycle on the north wall of the Dura synagogue portray the arresting of Ezekiel by a person of great dignity and his subsequent beheading. Since the Jewish leader in Babylonia claimed royal status, and in A.D. 200 received the title Exilarch (*Resh Galuta*) from the Parthians, Goodenough proposes that the Jewish tradition underlying both the Dura painting and the statement here in LivPro attributed Ezekiel's death to the political leader of Babylonian Jewry. He suggests that Heb 11:37, "They were stoned, or sawn in half, or beheaded," alludes to traditions concerning the manner of execution of the three major prophets Jeremiah, Isaiah, and Ezekiel respectively. ApPaul 49, however, witnesses to a different tradition regarding the manner of Ezekiel's death: "I am Ezekiel whom the children of Israel dragged by the feet over the rocks on the mountain until they dashed out my brains" (HSW, vol. 2, p. 792). The same report is given in the Syriac Acts of Philip; cf. W. Wright, *Apocryphal Acts of the Apostles* (London and Edinburgh, 1871) vol. 2, p. 83.

c. Torrey, *Lives*, p. 23, n. 18, conjectures that *Maour* is a corruption of *Naour*, i.e. Nahor (Gen 11:22, 26). Jeremias, *Heiligengräber*, p. 112,

Abraham, and the tomb is a double cave, for Abraham also made Sarah's tomb
4 in Hebron like it.[d] •It is called "double" because there is a twisting passage and   Gen 23:9
an upper room which is hidden from the ground floor, and it is hung over the
ground level in the cliff.[e]

5   This prophet gave a portent to the people, so that they should pay attention to
the river Chebar: When it failed they should set their hope in the scythe which   Ezek 1:1
desolates to the end of the earth, and when it flooded, in the return to Jerusalem.   Zech 5:1-3LXX

6,7 For the saint also lived there, and many used to congregate to him. •And once
when there was a multitude with him[f] the Chaldeans were afraid that they would
8 rebel, and came up against them to destroy them. •And he made the water stop
9 so that they might escape by getting to the other side. •And those of the enemies
who dared to pursue were drowned.

10   Through prayer he furnished them of his own accord with an abundant supply
of fish, and for many who were at the point of dying he entreated that life should
come from God.[g]

11   When the people was being destroyed by its enemies, he went to the (enemy)
12 leaders and, terrified by the prodigies, they ceased. •He used to say this to them:
"Are we lost? Has our hope perished?"[h] and in the wonder of the dead bones he   Ezek 37:1-14
persuaded them that there is hope for Israel both here and in the coming (age).

13   While he was there he used to show the people Israel what was happening in
14 Jerusalem and in the Temple. •He was snatched up from there and he went to   Ezek 8:3
15 Jerusalem to rebuke those who were faithless. •Like Moses, this man saw the   Ex 25:9
pattern of the Temple,[i] with its wall and broad outer wall, just as Daniel also said   Ezek 40-42
16 that it would be built. •He pronounced judgment in Babylon on the tribe of Dan
and that of Gad, because they were committing sacrilege against the LORD by
17 persecuting those who were keeping the Law. •And respecting them he worked
this great wonder, that snakes would devour their infants and all their flocks, and
he foretold that on their account the people would not return to its land but would
18 be in Media until the consummation of their error. •And the one who killed him
19 was one of them. •For they opposed him all the days of his life.

Daniel

1 **4** Daniel. This man was of the tribe of Judah, of the family of those prominent   Dan 1:3
in the royal service,[a] but while yet a child he was taken from Judea to the land

---

argues that it is very unlikely that the burial place
of such famous figures would be designated with
the name of a descendant; moreover, Nahor is
regularly represented in LXX and the NT as *Nachōr*.
Jeremias therefore prefers the possibility that *Maour*
is a corruption of *Our*, i.e. Ur of the Chaldees. He
reports that veneration is still paid to the grave of
Ezekiel in Kifil, south of ancient Babylon; this site,
however, is over 200 kilometers (125 miles) northeast of Ur. Rabbinic legend places Ezekiel's tomb
in Babylonia near that of Baruch; cf. Ginzberg,
Legends, vol. 4, pp. 324f., 333.

d. Gen 23 gives no hint of any special construction by Abraham, but the Heb. name *makpēlah*
(Machpelah) means "double." In LXX the name
is not transliterated but translated "the double
cave," *to spēlaion to diploun* (Gen 23:9), as in
our text. The duality of the tomb is dealt with by
Philo, *Quaes Gen* 4.80, and by the Talmud (b. 'Erub
59a: While Rab held that the cave consisted of two
chambers, one within the other, R. Samuel held
that it had a lower and an upper chamber).

e. A common practice was to expand a cave
tomb by carving out a lower chamber below the
entry level. As our text suggests, it was very
uncommon to construct a second chamber *above*
the main room.

f. Jeremias, *Heiligengräber*, p. 112, prefers E[1],
according to which the miracle was effected post-
humously for the benefit of pilgrims who had
gathered at Ezekiel's grave "for prayer and supplication."

g. The reference seems to be to a restoration to
earthly life, not to the preaching of life after death,
as suggested by Torrey, *Lives*, p. 37. For haggadah
concerning Ezekiel's success in restoring various
dead persons to life, see Ginzberg, *Legends*, vol.
4, pp. 332f.

h. Following Torrey, *Lives*, p. 37, who takes
the statements as questions. Since it is the people
who say this in Ezek 37:11, however, it is possible
that D correctly represents the original: ". . . when
Israel was saying, 'We are lost, our hope has
perished.' "

i. "Of the temple" is missing from Q but found
in E[1], E[2], D, Coisl. 224, and most other MSS.

4 a. By combining Dan 1:3, 6 with Isa 39:7,
Jewish tradition maintained that Daniel was a
member of the royal family; cf. Josephus, *Ant*
10.10.1 §186 and Ginzberg, *Legends*, vol. 6, p.
414.

2   of the Chaldeans. •He was born in Upper Beth-Horon, and he was a chaste man, so that the Judeans thought that he was a eunuch.

3   He mourned greatly over the city, and in fasts he abstained from all desirable food, and he was a man gaunt in appearance but beautiful in the favor of the Most High.

4   He prayed much for Nebuchadnezzar, at the entreaty of his son Baltasar,[b] when
5 he became a wild animal and beast of the field, so that he might not perish. •His   Dan 4:30(33)
fore parts with the head were like an ox, and the feet with the hind parts like a
6 lion. •Concerning this mystery it was revealed to the holy man that (Nebuchadnezzar) had become a beast of the field because he was fond of pleasure and stiff-
necked, and because those who belong to Beliar[c] become like an ox under yoke.   4:20; 17:2
7 Tyrants have these (vices) in their youth, and in the end they become monsters,
8 seizing, destroying, killing, and smiting. •Through divine revelation the saint
9 knew that he was eating grass like an ox and that it became human food. •It was
also for this reason that Nebuchadnezzar, recovering a human heart after digestion,[d]
used to weep and honor the LORD, praying forty times each day and night.[e]
10 Behemoth[f] used to come upon him, and he would forget that he had been a man;
his tongue was taken from him so that he might not speak, and perceiving (this)
11 he immediately wept; his eyes were like raw flesh from crying. •For many were
12 going out of the city and gazing at him. •Daniel alone did not wish to see him,
because he was in prayer for him the whole time of his changed condition; and
he kept saying, "He will become a man again," and they did not believe him.
13 Daniel made the seven years, which he called seven seasons, become seven   Dan 4:29(32)
months;[g] the mystery of the seven seasons was accomplished in his case, for he
was restored in seven months; during the six years and six[h] months (remaining)   Dan 4:31f.
he prostrated himself to the LORD and confessed his impiety, and after the   (34f.)
14 forgiveness of his wickedness he restored to him the kingdom. •He neither ate
bread or meat nor drank wine as he made his confession, for Daniel had ordered
15 him to appease the LORD with (a diet of) soaked pulse and greens. •Nebu-   Dan 1:7; 5:12
chadnezzar[i] called him Baltasar[j] because he wanted to make him joint heir
16 with his children. •But the holy man said, "Far be it from me to leave the heritage
17 of my fathers and cleave to the inheritances of the uncircumcised."[k] •And for
other kings of the Persians he wrought many prodigies, which they did not write
18 down. •There[l] he died, and was buried by himself and with great honor in the
royal grotto.

b. "Belshazzar," according to the MT; see n. j below.

c. In many texts "Beliar" (or "Belial") designates the chief of evil spirits, Satan; it is used below in 4:20 and 17:2. Cf. MartIs 2:2–4, where it appears as the synonym of "Satan." In the NT it occurs only at 2Cor 6:15.

d. Since Hebrew thought conceived the heart as the seat of mental activity, Torrey, *Lives*, p. 39, paraphrases: "recovering human reason when digestion was completed."

e. Ginzberg, *Legends*, vol. 4, p. 334, reports that in Yerahmeel 46.205f. the king's reason is restored after forty days; he spends the next forty days weeping over his sins, and for the remainder of the seven months he again lives the life of a beast. Our text may represent a confused recollection of these two sets of forty days.

f. The text is clearly in error, since in Jewish tradition Behemoth is a primeval monster, not a demon (cf. 2Bar 29:4). Torrey, *Lives*, pp. 24f., conjectures that the underlying Heb. read *lēb behēmôt*, i.e. "heart of dumb beasts," and that *lēb* was accidentally omitted in the Heb. text used by the Gk. translator. He translates (*Lives*, p. 39): "Then the mind of a dumb animal would (again) take possession of him . . ."

g. LXX, followed by Josephus (*Ant* 10.10.6 §216), translates the "seven times" of Dan 4:32 as "seven years" while Theodotion renders more literally as "seven seasons," *hepta kairoi*. The tradition that Daniel's prayer reduced the sentence from seven years to seven months is also found in Yerahmeel 46 (Ginzberg, *Legends*, vol. 4, p. 334; vol. 6, p. 423).

h. D, Coisl. 224, and some dependents read "five," correcting the arithmetical error.

i. Lit. "he."

j. Cf. 4:4. Although the Heb. and Aram. portions of Daniel carefully distinguish between "Belteshazzar," the Babylonian name given to Daniel (1:7), and "Belshazzar," the name of Nebuchadnezzar's crown prince (5:1), for some inexplicable reason the LXX translators rendered both names as *Baltasar*. E[i] notes the coincidence with an explanatory gloss added at this point: "For this reason also Nebuchadnezzar called Daniel 'Baltasar' after the name of his only-begotten son." Not only the gloss but the underlying statements in Q seem to reflect an environment in which LXX, not MT, is dominant.

k. The same statement is attributed to Daniel in Yerahmeel 66.206 (Ginzberg, *Legends*, vol. 4, p. 339; vol. 6, p. 427).

l. "There" is ambiguous. According to most Jewish sources Daniel's mausoleum was to be seen

19   And he gave a portent with respect to the mountains which are above Babylon:
     "When the mountain on the north smokes, the end of Babylon is coming; and
20   when it lies as in·fire,ᵐ the end of all the earth. •And if the mountain in the south
     pours forth water the people will return to its land, and if it pours forth blood,   4:6;17:2
21   Beliar's slaughter will take place in all the earth." •And the holy man fell asleep
     in peace.

Hosea

1   5 Hosea. This man was from Belemothᵃ of the tribe of Issachar, and he was
2   buried in his own districtᵇ in peace. •And he gave a portent, that the LORD would
    arrive upon the earth if ever the oak which is in Shilohᶜ were divided from itself,
    and twelve oaks came to be.

Micah

1,2 6 Micah the Morathiteᵃ was of the tribe of Ephraim.ᵇ •Having done many things   Mic 1:1
     to Ahab, he was killed by Joram his sonᶜ at a cliff,ᵈ because he rebuked him for
3   the impieties of his fathers. •And he was buried in his own district by himself,ᵉ
     near the burial ground of the Anakim.ᶠ   Josh 11:22

Amos

1,2 7 Amos was from Tekoa. •And when Amaziah had tortured him sorely, at last
3   his son also killed him with a club by striking him on the temple.ᵃ •And while he
     was still breathing he went to his own district, and after some days he died and
     was buried there.

in Shushan (Susa), but others convey the impression that he died in Palestine (Ginzberg, *Legends*, vol. 4, p. 350; vol. 6, p. 437). E¹ explicitly states that Daniel died in Babylon, "and his grave is known to all in Babylon to this very day."
     m. Coisl. 224 emends to "burns with fire."

5 a. Torrey, *Lives*, pp. 26, 40, considers the otherwise unknown *Belemōth* a variant of *Balamōn* of Jdt 8:3, which he identifies with Ibleam in northern Samaria. According to Josh 17:11 Ibleam belonged to the tribe of Manasseh but was situated within the territory of Issachar. Cf. Jeremias, *Heiligengräber*, p. 29.
     b. Shalshelet ha-Kabbalah 19a reports that Hosea died in Babylon and was buried in the Jewish cemetery at Safed (Ginzberg, *Legends*, vol. 4, p. 261; vol. 6, p. 356).
     c. *Sēlōm*, the form of the name given here, corresponds neither to the transliteration used by LXX nor to any of the various renderings of Shiloh found in Josephus, but the identity is not in question, since the same form occurs in 18:1, 5 in connection with Ahijah.of Shiloh (1Kgs 11:29). That the oak of Shiloh was a well-known landmark is indicated by its appearance here and at 18:5.

6 a. In reading *Mōrathi* instead of *Mōrasthi* (so D, and most MSS of LXX, at Mic 1:1), Q is consistent with its own reading at Mic 1:1; cf. also LXX of Jer 33:18. Eusebius, *Onomastikon* (ed. E. Klostermann [Hildesheim, 1966] p. 134) has *Mōrathei*, and asserts that the place was just east of Eleutheropolis (modern Beit Jibrin, northeast of Hebron).
     b. The erroneous identification with Ephraim may have resulted from confusion with Micah of Ephraim of Judg 17, as proposed by Klein, *Sefer*

Klozner, p. 197 (cf. Jeremias, *Heiligengräber*, p. 82).
     c. Despite the unambiguous chronological note of Mic 1:1, Micah is here placed in the time of Ahab, apparently by confusion with Micaiah son of Imlah (1Kgs 22:8). This could be explained as due to the fact that LXX employs the same transliteration for both Heb. names, if it were not for the fact that the same confusion is found in rabbinic sources; in one haggadah Micah is named one of the four disciples of Elijah (Ginzberg, *Legends*, vol. 6, p. 343; cf. p. 355).
     d. For the difficult *krēmnō* E¹ substitutes *krēmnōtheis*, i.e. "hanged" or possibly "crucified" (LSJM, p. 994, cites a 2nd-cent. instance of the verb with this meaning).
     e. E¹ adds: "And his grave is well known to this day." Jeremias, *Heiligengräber*, p. 85, infers that the narrator (or interpolator) knew of a monument marking Micah's supposed grave, and finds this confirmed by the report of the 5th-cent. church historian Sozomenos that the bishop of Eleutheropolis had discovered Micah's remains near this town in 385 (*Ecclesiastica Historia* 7.29.2).
     f. "Anakim" designates the three giants of Hebron in Num 13:22, but Josh 11:21f. refers to an entire people by this name, and reports that the remnants of the Anakim were located at Gaza, Gath, and Ashdod. Jeremias, *Heiligengräber*, pp. 82–86, points out that Jewish legend associated the giants with Eleutheropolis. He claims to have discovered the "cemetery of the giants" in an impressive Seleucid necropolis that he and A. Alt visited in 1932, situated about 2 kilometers (1.25 miles) north of Beit Jibrin.

7 a. According to Shalshelet ha-Kabbalah 97, King Uzziah killed Amos by striking him on the forehead with a red-hot iron (Ginzberg, *Legends*, vol. 4, p. 262; vol. 6, p. 357).

Joel

1 **8** Joel was from the territory of Reuben,[a] in the countryside of Bethomoron.[b]
2 He died in peace[c] and was buried there.

Obadiah

1 **9** Obadiah was from the district of Shechem, of the countryside of Bethacharam.[a]
2 This man was a disciple of Elijah,[b] and endured much because of him, and   1Kgs 18:7
3 escaped with his life. •This was the third captain of fifty whom Elijah spared and   2Kgs 1:13-15
4 (with whom) he went down to Ahaziah.[c] •After these events he left the service of
5 the king and prophesied. •And he died and was buried with his fathers.

Jonah

1 **10** Jonah was from the district of Kariathmos[a] near the Greek city of Azotus by
2 the sea. •And when he had been cast forth by the sea monster and had gone away   Jonah 2:11(10);
to Nineveh and had returned, he did not remain in his district, but taking his   3:1-5
mother along he sojourned in Sour,[b] a territory (inhabited by) foreign nations;
3 for he said, "So shall I remove my reproach, for I spoke falsely in prophesying   Jonah 3:4,10
4 against the great city of Nineveh."[c] •At that time Elijah was rebuking the house   1Kgs 17:1-7
5 of Ahab, and when he had invoked famine upon the land he fled. •And he went
and found the widow with her son, for he could not stay with uncircumcised   1Kgs 17:8-16
6 people; and he blessed her. •And when her son[d] died, God raised him again from   1Kgs 17:17-24;
the dead through Elijah, for he wanted to show him that it is not possible to run   21:7
7 away from God. •And after the famine he arose and went into the land of Judah.   Jonah 1:3
8 And when his mother died along the way, he buried her near Deborah's Oak.[e]   Gen 35:8
9 And after sojourning in the land of Saraar[f] he died and was buried in the cave of

---

8 a. The tribal connection of the prophet is not given in the book that bears his name. In 1Chr 5:4, 8, however, there is mention of a Reubenite of the same name.

b. Klein, *Sefer Klozner*, p. 198, and Torrey, *Lives*, pp. 26, 41, propose that this should be emended to *Bēthmaōn*, i.e. Beth-meon of Jer 48:23, a modified form of Beth-baal-meon (Josh 13:17), a town in Transjordan south of Nebo. 1Chr 5:8 locates the Reubenite Joel in this vicinity. Jeremias, *Heiligengräber*, p. 104, can report no other evidence of the veneration of Joel's grave during the early centuries of the Christian era, and proposes that the tradition reported by LivPro may be a purely literary product that had no local precipitate in the form of a cult.

c. H. J. Schoeps, *Aus frühchristlicher Zeit* (Tübingen, 1950) p. 132, notes that, according to *The Book of the Bee* of Solomon of Basra, Joel was clubbed to death like Amos.

9 a. Torrey, *Lives*, p. 41, derives the name from the Heb. *bēt ha-kerem*, "House of the Vineyard," which was probably a common name for small, rural settlements. If Obadiah's grave was indeed the object of veneration near Shechem when LivPro was written, the tradition must have disappeared by the 4th cent., when Christians looked for the grave elsewhere in Samaria (Jeremias, *Heiligen-*

gräber, p. 31).

b. Cf. Ginzberg, *Legends*, vol. 6, p. 343.

c. Jewish tradition also associated the prophet with the pious Obadiah of 1Kgs 18:3–16, who was a high official in Ahab's court (Ginzberg, *Legends*, vol. 4, pp. 240f.).

10 a. Identity unknown.

b. Cf. Jdt 2:28, where *Sour* seems to refer to a coastland city. Torrey, *Lives*, p. 41, conjectures that this is simply an unusual transliteration of *ṣōr*, and therefore translates it as "Tyre."

c. Cf. Ginzberg, *Legends*, vol. 4, p. 247.

d. The narrative assumes familiarity with the widespread tradition that Jonah was the son of the widow of Zarephath (cf. Ginzberg, *Legends*, vol. 4, p. 197; vol. 6, p. 318). E², D, and Coisl. 224 make the connection explicit by adding "Jonah."

e. Jeremias, *Heiligengräber*, p. 119, prefers D's reading, "the oak of Lebanon."

f. E¹, E², D, and Coisl. 224 read *Saar*. Torrey, *Lives*, p. 42, translates "Seir," i.e. Edom. From the perspective of the writer, Seir, which in his time was better known as Idumea, included much of southern Judea (cf. Josephus, *Apion* 2.116). Jeremias, *Heiligengräber*, pp. 88f., suggests that the Mohammedan mosque of Jonah at Halhul, 6 kilometers (3.75 miles) north of Hebron, marks the site to which reference is here made.

10 Kenaz,[g] who became judge of one tribe[h] in the days of the anarchy. •And he gave   Gen 36:15,42;
    a portent concerning Jerusalem and the whole land, that whenever they should   Judg 3:9
11 see a stone crying out piteously the end was at hand. •And whenever they should   Hab 2:11
    see all the gentiles in Jerusalem,[i] the entire city would be razed to the ground.   4Bar 9:30

Nahum

1 **11** Nahum was from Elkesi on the other side of Isbegabarin of the tribe of
2 Simeon.[a] •After Jonah this man gave to Nineveh a portent, that it would be
3 destroyed by fresh water and an underground fire, which also happened. •For the
    lake which surrounds it inundated it during an earthquake, and fire coming from
4 the wilderness burned its higher section. •He died in peace and was buried in his
    own district.

Habakkuk

1 **12** Habakkuk was of the tribe of Simeon, from the countryside of Bethzouchar.[a]
2 Before the captivity he had a vision[b] concerning the conquest of Jerusalem, and
3 he mourned greatly. •And when Nebuchadnezzar entered Jerusalem he fled to
4 Ostrakine,[c] and (later) sojourned in the land of Ishmael.[d] •When the Chaldeans
    turned back, and the remnant that was in Jerusalem (went) to Eg/pt, he was living
5 in his own district and ministering to those who were harvesting his field. •When
    he took the food, he prophesied to his own family, saying, "I am going to a far
6 country, and I will come quickly. •But if I delay, take (food) to the harvesters."   Bel 33-39
7 And when he had gone to Babylon and given the meal to Daniel,[e] he approached
    the harvesters as they were eating and told no one what had happened; he
8 understood that the people would soon return from Babylon. •And he died two
9 years before the return. •And he was buried alone in his own field.
10   He gave a portent to those in Judea, that they would see a light in the Temple
11 and so perceive the glory of the Temple. •And concerning the end of the Temple
12 he predicted, "By a western nation it will happen." •"At that time," he said,
    "the curtain of the *Dabeir*[f] will be torn into small pieces, and the capitals of the
    two pillars will be taken away, and no one will know where they are; and they
    will be carried away by angels into the wilderness, where the tent of witness was

g. Ps-Philo 25:3 and Josephus *Ant* 5.3.3 §182,
as well as later rabbinic sources (Ginzberg, *Legends*, vol. 6, p. 181), identify the first judge as
Kenaz, not Othniel the son of Kenaz, despite the
unequivocal testimony of Judg 3:9 that the son held
this honor. Jeremias, *Heiligengräber*, p. 90, conjectures that this reflects local Idumean tradition,
which glorified Kenaz as the ancestor of an important Edomite tribe. The cave of Kenaz thus
constituted the Idumean response to the cave of
Machpelah, the grave of the patriarchs near Hebron.

h. Torrey, *Lives*, pp. 27f., conjectures that the
underlying Heb. text was corrupt. His emendation
yields the translation: "the first who became judge."
This is unnecessary if the reference is to Idumean
tradition (see preceding n.).

i. This prediction makes little sense if the presence of "all the gentiles in Jerusalem" is taken as
referring to the successful penetration of the city's
defenses by the Roman armies in A.D. 70. It seems,
rather, to reflect uneasiness regarding the increasing
number of gentile visitors and/or residents, which
threatened to change the character of Israel's holy
city.

11 a. Jeremias, *Heiligengräber*, pp. 83f., 100,
identifies *Isbēgabarin* as Beit Jibrin, i.e. Eleuth-

eropolis. If Elkesi was an existing village, and not
merely a postulate based upon the Heb. text of
Nah 1:1, it must have been situated in southwestern
Judah, where tradition located the tribe of Simeon.
E² takes the name in Nah 1:1 as personal, and
substitutes "Nahum, son of Elkesaios, was from
Iesbe . . .''

12 a. Jeremias, *Heiligengräber*, p. 81, identifies
Bēthzouchar as Khirbet Beit Skaria (Beth-Zacha-
rias), situated 9 kilometers (5.6 miles) southeast of
Bethlehem.

b. Lit. "saw."

c. On the Mediterranean coast in eastern Egypt.

d. I.e. Arabia or Nabatea.

e. The same story is found in Bel 33–39 (JB
Dan 14:33–39).

f. *Haplōma* seldom designates a curtain, but this
curious usage is attested by TBenj 9:4, where it
also denotes the Temple veil. *Dabeir* (or *Dabir*) is
a transliteration of the Heb. *d'bîr*, which denotes
the inner sanctuary of the Temple (the holy of
holies). The LXX translators elected to use this
transliteration rather than a translation at 1Kgs 6:5
and elsewhere where the Heb. word occurs, treating
it as if it were a place-name.

13 set up in the beginning. •And by means of them the LORD will be recognized at the end, for they will illuminate those who are being pursued by the serpent in darkness as from the beginning.''   Rev 12:9,17; 2:15

Zephaniah

1,2 **13** Zephaniah was of the tribe of Simeon, of the countryside of Sabaratha.[a] •He prophesied concerning the city and about the end of the gentiles and the shaming 3 of the impious. •And he died and was buried in his field.   Zeph 1:4,12   Zeph 2:1-15

Haggai

1 **14** Haggai, who is also ''the Messenger,''[a] came from Babylon[b] to Jerusalem, probably as a youth, and he openly prophesied concerning the return of the people, 2 and witnessed in part the building of the Temple. •And when he died he was buried near the tomb of the priests,[c] in great honor as were they.   Hag 1:13   Hag 1:14

Zechariah

1 **15** Zechariah came from Chaldea when he was already well advanced in years, and there he prophesied many things to the people, and gave portents as proof. 2 This man told Jozadak that he would beget a son and that he would serve as priest 3 in Jerusalem. •He also pronounced a blessing upon Shealtiel[a] at the birth of his 4 son, and named him Zerubbabel. •And concerning Cyrus he gave a portent of his victory, and prophesied regarding the service which he was to perform for 5 Jerusalem, and he blessed him greatly.[b] •His prophesying in Jerusalem was based on his visions about the end of the gentiles, Israel, the Temple, the laziness of 6 prophets and priests, and he set forth the twofold judgment. •And he died when he had attained a great age, and when he expired he was buried near Haggai.[c]   Ezra 3:2   Zech 9:12

Malachi

1 **16** Malachi. This man was born in Sopha after the return,[a] and while still a very 2 young man he led a virtuous[b] life. •And since the whole people honored him as holy and gentle, it called him Malachi, which means ''angel''; for he was indeed 3 beautiful to behold. •Moreover, whatever he himself said in prophecy, on the same day an angel of God appeared and repeated (it), as happened also in the   Mal 1:1(LXX)

---

13 a. Klein, *Sefer Klozner*, p. 202, conjectures that *Sabaratha* derives from *Satiabaratha*, which in turn represents an inverted form of *Bērathsatia*, i.e. Birath Satia, which lay about 3.5 kilometers (2.1 miles) north of Beit Jibrin (Eleutheropolis). Jeremias, *Heiligengräber*, p. 87, finds this conjecture problematical but concurs that the connection with Simeon points to the area of Beit Jibrin.

14 a. *Aggelos*, here translated ''messenger,'' elsewhere denotes ''angel.'' The clause is absent from E[1], E[2], and D and is probably a gloss based on Hag 1:13. Torrey, *Lives*, pp. 29, 44, omits.

b. Haggai, Zechariah, and Malachi were associated with Daniel in rabbinic tradition (Ginzberg, *Legends*, vol. 6, p. 613).

c. Cf. above 1:9 and n. Jeremias, *Heiligengräber*, p. 72, can cite no corroborating evidence but accepts it as probable that Haggai's tomb lay in the Kidron valley.

15 a. The Gk. is *Salathiēl*, as in LXX of Ezra 3:2.

b. Q puts ''greatly'' with the following sentence, but the text is badly disturbed, and later recensions make various emendations. What follows in this translation is a rough paraphrase.

c. Zechariah the prophet, ''son of Berechiah son of Iddo'' (Zech 1:1), was frequently confused with the martyred priest Zechariah son of Jehoiada (2Chr 24:20–22; cf. Mt 23:35), whose violent death is reported below, ch. 23. In E[2] the two Zechariahs become one in a conflation of chs. 15 and 23. For an excellent discussion of this widespread confusion, see S. A. Blank, ''The Death of Zechariah in Rabbinic Literature,'' *HUCA* 12/13 (1937–38) 327–46.

16 a. Sopha is unknown. Other traditions regard Malachi as one of the returning exiles (Ginzberg, *Legends*, vol. 4, p. 354; vol. 6, p. 413).

b. Lit. ''beautiful.''

days of the anarchy as written in Spharphotim,[c] that is, in the Book of Judges.
4 And while he was still a young man he was added to his fathers in his own field.[d]

Nathan

1 **17** Nathan, David's prophet, was from Gaba,[a] and it was he who taught him the   2Sam 7:2
2 law of the LORD.[b] •And he saw that David would transgress in the Bathsheba   2Sam 11:2-4
(affair); and while he was hastening to go to tell him, Beliar hindered him, for   4:6,20
by the road he found a dead man who had been murdered lying naked; and he
3 remained there, and that night he knew that (David) had committed the sin. •And
he returned weeping, and when (David) killed her husband, the LORD sent (him)   2Sam 11:14-17
4 to rebuke him. •And when he had grown very old he died and was buried in his
own district.

Ahijah

1 **18** Ahijah was from Shiloh,[a] where the tabernacle was in ancient times, of Eli's   1Kgs 11:29
2 city. •This man said concerning Solomon that he would give offense to the LORD.   1Sam 1:24f.
3 And he rebuked Jeroboam, because he was going to walk deceitfully with the   1Kgs 11:31-33
LORD: He saw a yoke of oxen trampling the people and running against the priests.   1Kgs 14:7-14
4 He also foretold to Solomon that his wives would change him and all his   1Kgs 12:28
5 posterity.[b] •And he died[c] and was buried near the Oak of Shiloh.   5:2

Joad

1 **19** Joad[a] was from Samareim.[b] This is the one whom the lion attacked and he   1Kgs 13:1-32
2 died, when he rebuked Jeroboam over the calves. •And he was buried in Bethel
near the false prophet who deceived him.[c]   2Kgs 23:17f.

---

c. A confused recollection of the Heb. title of
the Book of Judges, *sēper šōptîm*. Torrey, *Lives*,
p. 30, conjectures that the original transliteration
was *Spharsōphtim*. Probably an allusion to Judg
13:8f.
d. Jeremias, *Heiligengräber*, reports nothing
concerning Malachi's grave.

17 a. On the strength of D and the Syriac version,
Torrey, *Lives*, p. 30, reads *Gabaōn*, i.e. Gibeon.
Klein, *Sefer Klozner*, p. 190, conjectures that
Gibeon was assumed to be Nathan's home because
the ark of the covenant was in that place at the
time of Nathan's conversation with David in 2Sam
7:17 (cf. 1Chr 16:39). On the other hand, the
textual evidence in favor of *Gaba* and *Gabath* is
stronger. Since Josephus uses this Gk. name to
refer to Gibeah (*Ant* 6.8.1 §156, referring to 1Sam
15:34), it can be argued that Gibeah, not Gibeon,
is intended. The Bible, however, designates four
places with the name "Gibeah." On the basis of
reports concerning Nathan's grave given by medieval Jewish pilgrims, Jeremias, *Heiligengräber*,
p. 80, concludes that the Gibeah in question is
modern Jeba, which lies about 19 kilometers (11.9
miles) southwest of Jerusalem. Torrey, *Lives*, pp.
30, 45, accepts the addition "from the tribe of
Thok," found in E[1], and emends it to read "from
the tribe of the Hivites" and concludes that Nathan
was a foreigner. This is improbable.
b. The Zohar 2.108 contains the tradition that
Nathan was Solomon's teacher (Ginzberg, *Legends*,
vol. 6, p. 279).

18 a. See above 5:2 and n.

b. Lit. "race."
c. According to the medieval Midrash Aggadah
(Ginzberg, *Legends*, vol. 6, p. 396), Ahijah died
a martyr's death at the hands of Abijah, king of
Judah.

19 a. Variants include *Iōab*, *Iōam*, and *Iōath*. No
name is given to the prophet in the biblical narrative
(1Kgs 13:1–32), but this deficiency was remedied
by later tradition. Josephus (*Ant* 8.8.5 §231) gives
his name as Jadon (*Iadōn*). Rabbinic tradition
identified him with Iddo, the seer of 2Chr 9:29
(b.Sanh 89b, 104a). This identification is perhaps
responsible in part for the inclusion of the prophet
at this point in the series, for 2Chr 9:29 brings
together Nathan, Ahijah, and Iddo as prophets
whose writings constituted sources for the history
of Solomon. Jerome is a later witness to this
tradition in *Quaestiones Hebraicae* on 2Chr 12:15
(PL, vol. 23, col. 1391) and, further, supplies the
name *Jaddo*, which is reminiscent of the form of
the name used by Josephus.
b. The common variant "Samaria" is understandable, but improbable in view of the explicit
reference to Judea in the biblical narrative (1Kgs
13:1). Torrey, *Lives*, p. 46, proposes that the place
in question is Zemaraim of Josh 18:22, 2Chr 13:4,
which has been identified as Khirbet es Sumrah,
situated 8 kilometers (5 miles) northeast of Jericho.
c. 2Kgs 23:17f. reports that a gravestone or
monument marked the common grave of the man
of God from Judah and the prophet of Bethel who
deceived him. Local tradition concerning this grave
persisted until at least the 5th cent. A.D. (Jeremias,
Heiligengräber, p. 51).

Azariah

1 **20** Azariah was from the district of Sybatha;[a] (it was he) who turned from Israel   2Chr 15:1-15
2 the captivity of Judah.[b] •And he died and was buried in his own field.   2Chr 28:8-15

Elijah

1 **21** Elijah, a Thesbite[a] from the land of the Arabs,[b] of Aaron's tribe,[c] was living   1Kgs 17:1
2 in Gilead, for Thesbe[a] was given to the priests.[d] •When he was to be born, his
   father Sobacha saw that men of shining white appearance were greeting him and
3 wrapping him in fire, and they gave him flames of fire to eat. •And he went and
   reported (this) in Jerusalem, and the oracle told him, "Do not be afraid, for his
   dwelling will be light and his word judgment,[e] and he will judge Israel."[f]
4,5   The signs[g] which he did are these. •Elijah prayed, and it did not rain for three   1Kgs 17:1
6 years, and after three years he prayed again and abundant rain came. •In Zarephath   1Kgs 17:8-16
   of Sidon through the word of the LORD he made the jar of the widow not to fail
7 and the flask of oil not to diminish. •Her son who had died God raised from the   1Kgs 17:17-24
8 dead after (Elijah) prayed.[h] •When the question was posed by him and the prophets   10:6
   of Baal concerning who is the true and real God, he proposed[i] that a sacrifice be
   offered both by him and by them, and that fire not be placed under (it), but that

---

20 a. *Sybatha*, like Josephus' *Saphatha* (variants *Sabatha* and *Saphtha*, *Ant* 8.12.1 §293), seems to derive from the textually difficult allusion in 2Chr 14:10. J. Jeremias, "Sarabatha und Sybatha," *Zeitschrift des deutschen Palästina-Vereins* 56 (1933) 253–55, argues that here LXX reflects a better text; the corrupt reading of MT has given rise to the spurious place-name Zephathah.

b. It appears that tradition has confused Azariah son of Oded of 2Chr 15:1 with the later prophet Oded of 2Chr 28:9; it is the latter, not the former, who reverses Israel's enslavement of Judah in the war between Pekah and Ahaz. The reconstruction of the text proposed by Torrey, *Lives*, p. 46, "who turned away from Judah the captivity that befell Israel," is unnecessary if allusion is here made to the prophecy of Oded in 2Chr 28:9–15.

21 a. The name of Elijah's home is spelled *Thesbei* in Q; variants include *Thesbē*, *Thesbis*, and *Thesbōn*. The location of the town is still unknown; cf. J. Simons, *The Geographical and Topographical Texts of the Old Testament* (Leiden, 1959) pp. 359f. According to the LXX translators, Elijah came from *Thesbōn*, which is perhaps to be taken as the genitive plural of a neuter plural *Thesba* (1Kgs 17:1). Josephus (*Ant* 8.13.2 §319) has *Thesbōnēs* (variant *Thessebōnēs*), but *Thesba* is given by Eusebius, *Onomastikon* (Klostermann, ed.; p. 102). The existence of such a place in the Roman-Byzantine period and its association with Elijah are confirmed by the 5th-cent. testimony of Egeria that she saw (probably without actually visiting) the town of *Thesbe*, which possessed a grotto in which Elijah was said to repose (the Lat. text and French translation are given on adjoining pages in the edition by H. Pétré, "Éthérie," *Journal de voyage* [SC 21; Paris, 1948] pp. 154f.). Egeria's report suggests that the town of Thesbe was visible from the Jordan valley; therefore, it cannot be identical with Listib, the site proposed by F.-M. Abel, *Géographie de la Palestine* (Paris, 1967³) vol. 2, p. 486, which is about 17 kilometers (10.6 miles) east of the Jordan between Osara and Ajlun.

Jeremias, *Heiligengräber*, p. 106, who accepts the identification with Listib, proposes that Egeria did not actually see Thesbe, but that the direction in which the town lay was pointed out to her by her guides. This is hardly an adequate interpretation of the text: ad subito vidimus civitatem sancti prophetae Heliae, id est Thesbe ("suddenly we saw the city of the holy prophet Elijah, that is, Thesbe"). It remains possible, of course, that Egeria was misinformed by her guides.

b. In the 1st cent. the Nabateans (*Araboi*) controlled the area east of Perea and the Decapolis. Perhaps their influence at times extended to those villages in Transjordan that were not in close proximity to the major hellenistic and Jewish towns. In any event, our author or his source believed that Thesbe lay in Nabatean territory.

c. Elijah was often regarded as a priest in Jewish tradition (Ginzberg, *Legends*, vol. 6, p. 316).

d. According to Josh 21:19, thirteen cities were assigned to the descendants of Aaron, but Tishbeh (Thesbe) is not mentioned in any of the lists of priestly cities.

e. Or "verdict."

f. Most MSS, including E[1], E[2], and D, add "with sword and fire." Elijah was frequently assigned a role in the judgment of the deceased (Ginzberg, *Legends*, vol. 6, p. 324).

g. Following D, Torrey, *Lives*, pp. 8, 32, 47f., omits the "signs" included by Q in the sections on Elijah and Elisha (21:4–15; 22:4–17), which are taken from 1–2Kgs. It is instructive that E[1] and E[2] have short additions at this point, but contain none of the biblical material found in Q. Torrey is probably correct, therefore, in regarding this material as secondary. It is even possible that the entire section devoted to Elijah is a later addition, since it does not conform to the document's general purpose of encouraging veneration of the prophets' graves.

h. See above 10:6 and n. No attempt is made in this passage to identify the dead son as Jonah.

i. "Proposed" fits the context but cannot be defended lexically. The first aorist active of *haireō*

9 each should pray, and the one answering him would be God. •Accordingly, the
(prophets) of Baal prayed and cut themselves until the ninth hour, and no one
answered them; and Elijah, when he had filled the place where the sacrifice was
with much water, also prayed, and immediately fire came down and consumed
10 the sacrifice, and the water was gone.ʲ •And all blessed God, and killed the four
11 hundred and fifty (prophets) of Baal. •When King Ahaziah sent to obtain an oracle   2Kgs 1:1-17
12 from idols, (Elijah) prophesied death, and he died. •When two captains of fifty   2Kgs 1:9-12
were sent to him from Ahaziah, the king of Israel, he invoked the LORD and fire   9:3
came down from heaven, and the fire consumed them at the LORD's command.
13,14 Ravens brought him bread in the morning and meat in the afternoon.ᵏ •With a   1Kgs 17:6
sheepskinˡ he struck the Jordan and it was divided, and they crossed over with   2Kgs 2:8
15 dry feet, both he and Elisha. •Finally he was taken up in a chariot of fire.   2Kgs 2:11

Elisha

1,2 **22** Elisha was from Abel Meholah in the land of Reuben.ᵃ •And a marvel occurred   1Kgs 19:16
concerning this man, for when he was born in Gilgal,ᵇ the golden calf bellowed
shrilly, so that it was heard in Jerusalem, and the priest declared through the
Urimᶜ that a prophet had been born to Israel who would destroy their carved
3 images and molten idols. •And when he died, he was buried in Samaria.ᵈ
4,5 The signs which he did are these. •He too struck the Jordan with Elijah's   2Kgs 2:13f.
6 sheepskin, and the water was divided, and he too passed over with dry feet. •The   2Kgs 2:19-22
water in Jericho was foul and sterile; and hearing (this) from the city's residents,
he invoked God, and he said, "I am healing this water, and no longer will death
7 and sterility issue from it," and the water has remained healed to this day. •When   2Kgs 2:23f.
children treated him disrespectfully, he cursed them,ᵉ and two bears came out and
8 tore to piecesᶠ forty-two of them. •The wife of a prophet who had died was being   2Kgs 4:1-7
pestered by creditors,ᵍ and was unable to pay; she came to Elisha, and he
commanded her to gather new vessels, as many as she could, and to pour the
(jar) containing very little oil into them until the vessels were full; and she did
this and filled the vessels and repaid her creditors, and she had the surplus for the
9 sustenance of her children. •He went to Shunemʰ and stayed with a certain woman;

---

is not witnessed until the 4th cent., according to
LSJM, p. 41, and nowhere does the active verb
bear a meaning suitable to this context. Perhaps
hērēse should be emended to *ētēse*, "asked," but
the latter would fit poorly with the fourth infinitival
phrase.

j. Lit. "ceased." Possibly a scribal error substituted *exeleipen* for an original *exelixen* as found
in the LXX version of the narrative, 1Kgs 18:38,
"and it licked up the water."

k. Following LXX; MT has "bread and meat
in the morning, and bread and meat in the after-
noon."

l. Again following LXX; MT has "mantle."

22 a. Abel Meholah is frequently located west of
the Jordan, about 16 kilometers (10 miles) south
of Beisan (Beth-shan, Scythopolis); cf. Simons,
Geographical and Topographical Texts, pp. 293f.
N. Glueck, *Explorations in Eastern Palestine*, IV,
part I: Text, *Annual of the American Schools of
Oriental Research* 25-28 (1945-49; New Haven,
1951) pp. 211-23, argues for a site in Gilead near
the Wadi el-Yabis. Our text supports a Transjordanian site but places it much farther south in
Reubenite territory.

b. The Gilgal here referred to is not the sanctuary
near Jericho but a site near Bethel. Awareness of
this second Gilgal persisted through the Roman
period, as evidenced by the *Onomastikon* of Eusebius (Klostermann, ed.; p. 66). Although the

phrase "in Gilgal" is awkwardly placed, it is
apparently to be taken with the following clause.
Torrey, *Lives*, p. 48, remarks, "This passage in
the Lives is the oldest witness to the belief, found
in the writings of certain Church fathers, that one
of Jeroboam's two golden calves was set up in
Gilgal instead of Dan."

c. Cf. Num 27:21; Urim is often combined with
Thummim (Ex 28:30). Possibly a form of dice by
means of which a priest could secure a divine
answer to a human inquiry. Cf. I. Mendelsohn,
"Urim and Thummim," *IDB* 4.739-40.

d. Jeremias, *Heiligengräber*, p. 30, notes that
the narrative concerning Elisha's grave in 2Kgs
13:20f. presupposes a site much closer to the
Jordan, where an incursion of Moabite raiders
would be more likely, but adds that later tradition
consistently points to Samaria. Jerome, *Comm. in
Abdiam* 1 (PL, vol. 25, col. 1099B), mentions a
mausoleum of Elisha in Sebaste (Samaria).

e. Lit. "among them."

f. Emending the text from *enerrēxan*, "broke
into," to *anerrēxan*, as found in LXX of 2Kgs
2:24.

g. 2Kgs 4:1 mentions only one creditor.

h. Q, following LXX, has *Souman*. Eusebius,
Onomastikon (Klostermann, ed.; p. 158) identifies
Shunem (which he spells *Sounēm*) with an existing
village called *Soulēm*, five Roman miles (c. 4.6
miles) south of Mount Tabor.

she was not able to bear a child, but earnestly desired to have one; he prayed and made her able to conceive and give birth; then, when the child died, he prayed
10 again and raised it from the dead. •He went to Gilgal and was brought before the   2Kgs 4:38-41 sons of the prophets; and when the food was boiled, and a deadly herb was boiled with the food, and they were all on the brink of danger, he made the food harmless
11 and sweet. •When the sons of the prophets were felling trees by the Jordan, the   2Kgs 6:1-7 axehead fell off and sank; and Elisha, praying, made the axehead float to the
12,13 surface. •Through him Naaman the Syrian was cleansed of leprosy. •When his   2Kgs 5:1-27 servant, named Gehazi, went to Naaman secretly, against his wishes, and asked for silver, and later upon returning denied it, Elisha rebuked and cursed him, and
14 he became a leper. •When the king of Syria was making war against Israel, he   2Kgs 6:8-23
15 protected the king of Israel by announcing to him the plans of the enemy. •When the king of Syria learned this he sent a force to bring the prophet, but he prayed and made them to be struck[i] with blindness, and he led them to Samaria, to their
16 enemies, but keeping them unharmed he preserved and fed them. •When the king
17 of Syria learned this he stopped making war. •After Elisha's death a man died,   2Kgs 13:20f. and as he was being buried he was thrown onto his bones, and just as he touched Elisha's bones the dead man revived immediately.

Zechariah son of Jehoiada

1 **23** Zechariah was from Jerusalem, son of Jehoiada the priest, and Joash the king   2Chr 24:20-22 of Judah killed him near the altar,[a] and the house of David[b] poured out his blood   Mt 23:35 in front of the *Ailam*,[c] and the priests took him and buried him with his father.[d]
2 From that time visible portents occurred in the Temple,[e] and the priests were not able to see a vision of angels of God or to give oracles from the *Dabeir*,[f] or to inquire by the Ephod,[g] or to answer the people through Urim as formerly.

i. Reading *patachthēnai*, following Nestle's transcription of Q, *Marginalien*, p. 34; the same verb is used by the LXX narrative, 2Kgs 6:18. Schermann, *Prophetarum vitae fabulosae*, p. 96, has *katachthēnai* as Q's reading.

23 a. The Midrash on Lamentations, *Midrash Rabbah*, ed. H. Freedman and M. Simon (10 vols.; London, 1939) vol. 7, p. 226, stresses that the murder occurred in the Court of the Priests, not the Court of Israel or the Court of Women. According to Ginzberg, *Legends*, vol. 6, p. 396, the medieval Midrash Aggada declares that the blood of Zechariah bespattered the walls of the sanctuary. The assertion of Jesus that Zechariah died "between the sanctuary and the altar" (Mt 23:35; Lk 11:51) shows contact with the tradition transmitted by LivPro. An interesting variant provided by Codex Bezae at Lk 11:51 shows even closer contact: *anameson*, "in the midst of" or "between."

b. In Zech 12:8 the term "the House of David" seems to be a circumlocution for "the king." Poetic parallelism employs the same circumlocution here.

c. *Ailam* is the transliteration employed in LXX to render the Heb. 'ûlâm and 'ûlâm, which designate the porch of the Temple (1Kgs 6:3 et al.).

d. According to 2Chr 24:16, Jehoiada was buried "with the kings in the Citadel of David." Jeremias, *Heiligengräber*, p. 68, correctly points out that, regardless of the accuracy of this statement, it is very unlikely that 1st-cent. Jews believed that Zechariah and his father were buried within Jerusalem, in view of the frequent testimony in the rabbinic literature that only the kings and Huldah

(and Isaiah, according to the variant tradition reported by ARN 39 [B]) were buried within the city walls (e.g. t.BB 1:11). In the light of Mt 23:29f. and Lk 11:47, Jeremias continues, we must assume that the supposed grave of Zechariah had recently been marked with a new monument, for Zechariah and Isaiah are the only prophets whose martyrdoms and subsequent burials in Jerusalem could have prompted this saying of Jesus. Because of the widespread confusion that identified this Zechariah with the prophet of the same name (see n. c on 15:6), it is probable that the monument was erected in the Kidron valley near the tombs of the priests (see n. n on 1:9). Jeremias, *Heiligengräber*, pp. 68–72, rules out the possibility that Zechariah's monument can be identified with any of the existing structures in that area.

e. None of the punishments listed in this sentence are mentioned in the rabbinic haggadah, but a great deal of attention is given there to one portent that is not explicitly alluded to in LivPro: The blood of Zechariah seethed and bubbled on the stones in the Temple court for 252 years until it was finally atoned by the slaughter effected by Nebuzaradan (b.Giṭṭ 57b; b.Sanh 89b; Midrash on Ecclesiastes 3.16 §1; 10.4 §1 [*Midrash Rabbah*, vol. 8, pp. 101f., 263f.]).

f. See n. f on 12:12. The practice here alluded to of giving oracles from the holy of holies is nowhere attested.

g. According to this passage, both the Ephod and the Urim were employed in oracular practice. Rabbinic haggadah contains a similar opinion (Ginzberg, *Legends*, vol. 3, p. 172). Cf. also LetAris 97.

Conclusion

1 **24** And other prophets became hidden,[a] whose names are contained in their genealogies in the books of the names of Israel; for the whole race of Israel are enrolled by name.

---

24 a. The difficulty of this phrase is probably responsible for the variant reading of E[1], "which we have not mentioned." E[2] and D do not have this concluding sentence. "Hidden" may mean simply that, while there are other prophets, the collection here assembled exhausts the list of prophets whose graves are known.

LADDER OF JACOB

(c. First Century A.D.)

A NEW TRANSLATION AND INTRODUCTION

BY H. G. LUNT

The Ladder of Jacob has not survived as an integral text, even in a form as unsatisfactory as that of the Apocalypse of Abraham, but is known only from what was utilized in the Slavonic *Tolkovaja paleja*, or Explanatory Palaia. In retelling the tales of the Old Testament, the Slavic editors of the Palaia made many changes in the texts they used; they excised, they rearranged the order of sentences, paragraphs, or sections, and—most important—they modified wording in order to fit the texts into the anti-Jewish commentary interspersed in the canonical and non-canonical episodes they were explaining. Moreover, they freely united heterogeneous materials, often with little consideration for narrative flow or logical connections. Therefore we must treat the Ladder of Jacob with the utmost caution; at best our reconstitution of the text must be controversial in many details. For the moment, however, given the lack of careful study of the manuscript witnesses and the inaccessibility of many of them, we can give only a preliminary approximation that will serve as an introduction to the problems.

The original Slavonic version of the Ladder was modified in slightly different ways by two traditions in the history of the Palaia text. Recension A is the more conservative but is marred by the omission of the continuous text after 7:9; recension B was severely edited in a part of the narrative, while other passages appear to show harmonization with the commentary. Both have before 1:8 an obvious insertion whose purpose is to elucidate the Septuagint version of Genesis 28:13 (see n. to 1:7). In recension B, the major portion of Jacob's account—2:3–5:1—is reduced to a banal prayer and the matter-of-fact appearance of a nameless angel who starts to explain the vision. Otherwise, recension B continues through the end of chapter 7. A, on the other hand, abruptly moves from the middle of 6:9 to the commentary that in B follows 7:35. There is nothing to indicate that this omission was a real editorial decision; it is possible that our three copies go back to a model based on a defective manuscript.[1] In any case, the commentary jumps back to offer brief and haphazard interpretations of 5:12–17, then 6:5–12, 1–4, 13–15, and then a much more detailed and discernibly organized exegesis in chapter 7.

Chapter 7 is probably to be regarded as a separate work (cf. n. a to ch. 7). It is connected

---

[1] In A, the commentary begins: "Understand, Jew, how the Lord explained to your forefather Jacob . . ." In B, the introduction is longer: "Have you heard this well, you who have not recognized the truth, O Jew, how the Lord explained . . ." Very likely the common ancestor of our three MSS of rec. A was the work of a copyist who was faced with a lacuna, presumably bounded by "your tribe" of 6:9 and the vocative "Jew" of the commentary. He simply bridged it by means of the imperative "understand," which is common enough in the Palaia commentaries. Note that A (like the longer version of the ApAb) is found in what is agreed to be the *second* redaction of the Palaia as a whole. This indicates that copies of the independent text were still available in 15th-cent. Russia, when an editor restored some of the passages that had been modified or deleted by earlier compilers of the Palaia. It is quite possible that the episode we call the LadJac was a part of a larger work, but there is no evidence to affirm P. E. Ščegolev's conjecture that it is an excerpt from TJac ("Očerki istorii otrečennoj literatury: *Skazanie Afroditiana,*" *Izvestija Otdelenija russkogo jazyka i slovesnosti,* vol. 4 [1899] 1332f.). [Frequently authors' first names are given in full herein, because Slav. publications are unusually difficult to locate. We are grateful to R. Rubinkiewicz for sharing with us his photographs of MSS of LadJac that he has found; and we look forward to his publications on this interesting document. —J.H.C.]

to the Ladder only by means of a grammatically incongruent sentence referring to the angels descending and ascending, and otherwise contains no identifiable reference to Jacob. Modern scholars have regarded it as a part of the Ladder because the Palaia has it, with its long commentary, between the materials clearly connected with Jacob's vision at Bethel and his continued journey to Laban.

Synopsis

The Ladder of Jacob is an elaboration of Jacob's dream at Bethel, Genesis 28:11–22. Resting during his flight from Esau, Jacob sees in a dream a ladder or staircase reaching from the earth to heaven. At the top is a fiery image, and at the right and left of each of the twelve steps is a statue or bust of a man. Angels are ascending and descending on the staircase. From above the highest statue, God calls to Jacob, promising that the land on which he is sleeping will be his and that his descendants are to flourish and be blessed.

Jacob awakens, consecrates the place, and utters a long prayer (unfortunately somewhat garbled and possibly shortened in the transmission of the text) asking God to interpret the dream. God orders the archangel Sariel to bless Jacob and explain the dream. Sariel appears to Jacob and changes his name to Israel. (An obscure passage may have offered an interpretation of Sariel's name; there may well be substantial omissions here.) Sariel says the ladder or staircase is this age and the twelve steps are the periods of the age; the faces or busts are the kings of the godless gentiles who will try Jacob's descendants. The iniquity of these descendants will bring retribution; unfortunately the text is too corrupt to allow any clear definition of precisely what is being prophesied. Possibly there is a reference to the destruction of the Temple. Some descendants of Esau will become kings and will help the Israelites (but again the corrupt text fails to give a clear picture). Eventually a king will arise for final vengeance, and the angels and archangels will hurl their bolts of lightning to aid the salvation of Jacob's tribe. The wicked (clearly the Egyptians) will be punished, Leviathan and "the lawless Falkon" will be defeated, and Jacob's justice will prevail. The kingdom of Edom and the peoples of Moab will perish.

The text now designated chapter 7 is a mosaic of oracular prophesies concerning the birth of Christ and also the crucifixion. It is to be regarded as an independent work, juxtaposed to the Ladder of Jacob by a Slavic editor of the Palaia.

Texts

The following survey of manuscripts is based on materials kindly furnished by Ryszard Rubinkiewicz.

RECENSION A, three manuscripts.

S.   Explanatory Palaia of 1477. Sin. 210, State Historical Museum, Moscow, fols. 100ᵛ–106ᵛ. The manuscript was reproduced in facsimile: *Tolkovaja paleja 1477 goda*, vol. 93, *Obščestvo ljubitelej drevnerusskoj pis'mennosti* (St. Petersburg, 1893).

R.   Rumiantsev Palaia of 1494. Rum. 455, Lenin Library, Moscow, fols. 76–83. Published by A. N. Pypin in Grigorij Kušelev-Bezborodko, *Pamjatniki starinnoj russkoj literatury* (St. Petersburg, 1862) vol. 3, pp. 27–32.

U.   Undolsky Palaia of 1517. Und. 719, State Historical Museum, Moscow. (Unpublished; a few variants available from penciled notes in my copy of Kušelev-Bezborodko.)

RECENSION B, thirteen manuscripts.

K.   Kolomna Palaia of 1406. Tr.-Serg. 38, Lenin Library, Moscow, fols. 77–79. The Ladder was first published by N. S. Tikhonravov, *Pamjatniki starinnoj russkoj literatury* (St. Petersburg, 1863) vol. 1, pp. 92–95. Later the whole manuscript was printed: *Paleja tolkovaja po spisku sdelannomu v g. Kolomne v 1406 g., Trud učenikov N. S. Tikhonravova*, Moscow, 1892. This edition adduces selected variants from eight other manuscripts (one from the 14th, one from the 15th cent., the rest later; including MS Slav. 9 of the Vienna State Library, erroneously identified as no. 12).

V¹. MS 83, Public Library, Vilnius, fols. 139–43, sixteenth century.

V². MS 84, Public Library, Vilnius, fols. 84–86, sixteenth century.

M. Melec Monastery collection, Ukrainian Academy Library, Kiev, No. 114 (Aa 1292), fols. 74ᵛ–77ʳ, seventeenth century.

P. Solovki Monastery collection, Saltykov-Shchedrin Public Library, Leningrad, Sol. 653. The Ladder was published by I. Ja. Porfir'ev, in "Apokrifičeskie skazanija o vetkhozavetnykh licakh i sobytijakh po rukopisjam soloveckoj biblioteki" (= *Sbornik otd. r. jaz. i slov.* 17.1), St. Petersburg, 1877, pp. 138–49.

RECENSION C is a brief extract of little interest on fol. 30ʳ of the Palaia of 1414, Library of the Academy of Sciences, Leningrad, no. 25.5.8.

A German translation was made by N. Bonwetsch ("Die Apokryphe 'Leiter Jakobs,' " *Göttinger Nachrichten, philol.-histor. Klasse* [1900] 76–87) on the basis of the published material from R, K, and P, but it remained for N. M. Vtorykh (*Drevnosti, Trudy Slavjanskoj komissii Moskovskoj arkheologičeskogo obščestva*, 2, 1902, protokoly, 1) to point out that recs. A and B go back to a single Slavonic translation.

The present translation is based on an eclectic text relying chiefly on MS S. It must be emphasized that many of the witnesses are unavailable or known only from variants selected by diverse scholars with differing methodologies and prejudices. One hopes that in the future it will be possible to examine carefully all the evidence. Since the relative value of many manuscripts is unknown, and the extant provenance of some variants has not been noted, the commentary does not attempt to identify the source of every variant mentioned.

Original language

The Explanatory Palaia is a compilation from many sources, but nearly all of the component parts of variant redactions go back to the Old Church Slavonic translations made in the Cyrillo-Methodian period, A.D. 863–87, and in the subsequent flowering of Byzantino-Slavic culture among the Slavs of Macedonia and Bulgaria for several generations after 890. A few hints in the Ladder, such as *uslaždaemyx*, "beguiled," (*katathelchthentes*) in 3:2, the distorted *moguty* for unfamiliar *moguti* "nobles" in 5:8, the agreement with the Apocalypse of Abraham (whose language demonstrably places its translation in the tenth century at the latest), and the peculiar use of *vŭsxody* or *sŭxody* (cf. nn. to 5:7, 9), allow us to assume that the Slavonic Ladder existed before the final Byzantine destruction of the Bulgarian state in 1018.

Greek may have been the original language of the Ladder (excluding ch. 7, whose origin will be treated below). No other Slavonic text has *lice*, "face," used to mean "statue" or "bust" (1:5 etc.), and there is no Semitic parallel. It is easily explained as a calque of *prosōpon*. (The use of "face" as a quasi-pronoun in 3:1 etc. is common in Slavonic as a reflection of biblical Gk. and tells us nothing of a text's origin.)

A non-Hebrew base text may be inferred from the citation of several Hebrew words in the prayer in 2:18b–19. (The reproduction of the untranslatable names of Divinity as in 2:18a and ApAb 17:16 tells us nothing about the original language.) Perhaps Sariel's explanation of his name in 4:6 was based on transposing letters. The Slavonic *jako tŭ běaše* (S) may be modified from *jakovŭ běaše*, reflecting Greek *iakōb ēn*. We may speculate further that much earlier the text spelled out the name, *Iakōb* (*iod, ain, koph, waw, beth*) and went on to explain some sort of modification and its significance. Such a text would have little meaning for a later, non-Jewish audience, and successive copyists would surely distort it. In short, it is possible that the truncation of this passage preceded its translation into Slavonic. If all this is so, we can posit an originally Jewish text written down in Greek but intended for readers with at least some knowledge of Hebrew.

Date and provenance

The date and provenance of the Ladder are unknown.[2] The following observations should help in discerning the history of transmission of the possibly original Jewish document.[3]

The enigmatic (k)falkonagargailyu(ya) of 5:15 must somehow be connected with the "lawless Falkon"; cf. 6:13. Perhaps the association with Leviathan provides a clue. In Isaiah 27:1, Leviathan is described as "the crooked (or twisted) serpent," Hebrew nhš 'qltwn. The unusual epithet may have been taken as a proper name, and spelled in Greek— with loss of the initial ain—kalthōn. A mechanical transposition of letters would produce Thalkōn, and the East Slavic confusion of the letters theta and phi would yield "Falkon." In the apocryphal Life of St. Pancratius of Taormina, a pagan god named Falkon was cast into the sea by demons at the command of the saint; perhaps this legend influenced the form of the name in the Ladder. We may surmise that the second element is connected with the Greek stem gargalizein, "tempt, seduce," and conjecture that the original text was alluding to the crooked or lawless tempter, Satan.

The relationship of chapter 7 to the Ladder is only one of many questions still facing the student of the origin and development of the Explanatory Palaia. The time, place, and shape of the original compilation are controversial, and the order of various additions and emendations still needs intensive study. We can discern, however, two general aims of the original compilers and subsequent editors: to give an outline of Old Testament history, with some interpretation of significant but obscure events, and to elucidate the specifically Christian import of all Scripture and expose "the wicked falsity" of Jewish exegesis. For the first purpose, the whole texts of the Apocalypse of Abraham and the Ladder were suitable, although they might require some modification. For anti-Jewish polemical purposes, no particular system was required, for a word here and a sentence there can point to the proper sense. Such expansions could be made either to the original biblical text (e.g. the n. on Gen 28:13 inserted after LadJac 1:7) or to passages of an interpolated unit (such as the comments on 5:12–17 and ch. 6). Yet some persistent Jewish arguments called for more detailed refutation, and therefore longer pieces were added at a place the editors deemed appropriate. This is surely the case with chapter 7, which is generally devoted to the divinity of Christ, and more specifically to the Nativity: The cryptic text has been constructed as a framework and excuse for the exegesis. Its incorporation into the Palaia may have preceded, followed, or been simultaneous with the addition of the Ladder.

The principal source is a well-known Christian work entitled Explanation of the Events in Persia (Exēgēsis tōn prachthentōn en Persidi), more specifically the section found independently in some manuscripts under the name Tale of Aphroditianus.[4] Russian and Serbian Slavonic copies (13th–18th cent.) surely stem from an Old Church Slavonic translation made in the tenth century.[5] It is a mediocre translation with a series of peculiarities

---

[2] Epiphanius (Adv. Haer. 30.16.7) mentions a "Ladder [anabathmoi, "steps," not klimax as we would expect] of Jacob"; but, as Rubinkiewicz has stated to me, K. Holl correctly showed that Epiphanius is referring to a "Ladder of Jacob (the Apostle)." See Holl's Epiphanius (Ancoratus and Panarion) (Leipzig, 1915) vol. 1, p. 354. In contrast to LadJac, Epiphanius' "Ladder of Jacob" concerns the Temple, sacrifices, and fire on the altar. —J.H.C.

[3] We can speculate reliably only on the final steps in the transmission of LadJac. I suggest, however, that this is the last of a series of stages, approximately as follows: (1) a Jewish story composed in Jewish-Gk. for a Palestinian audience; (2) transmission of this text in Byzantine circles, with inevitable distortions, ending up with a Gk. copy available by about A.D. 900 to a Slav; (3) translation into OCS; (4) utilization of copies of this old translation by Russ. editors as they elaborated various redactions of the Palaia in the 13th–15th cent.

[4] Published, with an extensive study, by E. Bratke, Das sogenannte Religionsgespräch am Hof der Sasaniden pp. 101–6. The Tale of Aphroditianus is 11.3–19.9 of his text. At the same time, P. E. Ščegolev published a study of Aphroditianus, chiefly in Slav. literature (Izvestija Otdelenija, vol. 4 (1899) 148–99, 1304–44). It is a pity that he and Bratke were unaware of each other's work.

[5] The 13th-cent. Russ. Slavonic copy titled Skazanie Afrodit'jana o byvšim v perštěi zemli čudesi was published by N. S. Tikhonravov, Pamjatniki starinnoj russkoj literatury (St. Petersburg, 1863) vol. 2, pp. 1–4; it corresponds to Bratke's 11.3–19.6. A 16th-cent. Russ. Slavonic copy (cf. I. Ja. Porfir'ev, "Apokrifičeskie skazanija o novozavetnykh licakh i sobytijakh po rukopisjam Soloveckoj biblioteki," Sbornik Otdelenija russkogo jazyka i slovesnosti 52 [1891] 149–54) adds a final paragraph from another source. A 13th-cent. Serbian Slavonic fragment published by V. Makušev (Russkij filologičeskij vestnik 7 [1882] 9–12) breaks off at 15.1. The full text, with a long interpolation not mentioned by Bratke, was published from a 1740 Serbian Slavonic MS by Stojan Novaković (Starine 10 [1878] 72–80).

that make it possible to demonstrate beyond question that verses 11–25 of chapter 7 of the Ladder were put together from elements found in the Slavonic Aphroditianus.[6] The whole chapter and its commentary is most probably the work of the Slavic editors of the Palaia, very likely Russians of the thirteenth to fourteenth centuries. Verse 7:2b anticipates 16, which is part of the mosaic from Aphroditianus. Verses 3–9, 21, and 26–35 are taken from other sources; this last group is not well integrated with what goes before.

The Tale of Aphroditianus starts with the uproar among the idols in Persian temples that caused the Magi to seek out Mary and Jesus in Bethlehem, and continues through the events of the Nativity and the slaughter of the innocents. The commentary to the Ladder 7:20 quotes Balaam's prophecy, "a star shall rise out of Jacob, a man shall spring out of Israel" (Numbers 24:17LXX). These words, and the final phrase of the verse, "and shall crush the princes of Moab," would be familiar to pious Orthodox Christians, for the passage occurs in one of the Old Testament lessons for the Christmas service. Moreover, that same service explicitly connects the star of Jacob and the star of Bethlehem.[7] Therefore the Slavic editors of the Palaia had good reason for associating this chapter with the Ladder 6:15 as the suitable spot to introduce extensive arguments about the miraculous and divine nature of the Nativity.[8] The problems of this chapter deserve further study, but in any case it is clear that these verses were added not to the Greek but to the Slavonic Ladder.

Theological importance[9]

Belief in one God is emphasized in the Ladder of Jacob. God is Lord of the world. He is the one who is "carrying the whole world under" his arm, "yet not being borne by anyone" (2:9). He made the skies, set the order of movements for the sun, moon, and stars (2:10–12), and fills the "heaven and earth, the sea and abysses and all the ages" with his glory (2:20). Yet, it is not clear that Jewish monotheism is emphasized in the Ladder; the existence of other gods is not denied and often it seems that the God of Adam, Abraham, Isaac (2:6), and Jacob (*passim*) is the God of gods; note 2:22, "you are a god who is mighty, powerful and glorious, a god who is holy; my Lord and Lord of my fathers." Likewise, thoroughgoing monotheism seems to be foreign to the Ladder, since Falkon raises "the wrath of the God of gods by his pride" (6:13).

Angels, of course, play a prominent role in the Ladder. They ascend and descend, which is a characteristic of traditions related to Jacob (cf. Gen 28:12b; Jn 1:51); elsewhere the emphasis is upon angels descending and then ascending. The archangel Sariel, who is also mentioned in the Qumran Scrolls, Aramaic Enoch, and the Neofiti Targum,[10] is said to be the one who is in charge of dreams (3:2); hence, he is the one who is dispatched to Jacob in order to explain to him the meaning of his dream.

---

[6] Specifically, vss. 10f. = Aphr 15.9f.; 12b + 13a = 14.2; 14 = 15.16 + 19; 15f. = 18.8–10; vs. 17 expresses ideas of Aphr 13.4–7; 18f. is a general summary with reference to Aphr 15.10; 20 = 14.11–16; 21 is from another source; vs. 22 has the idea of 15.1 plus words of 13.19, while vss. 23–25 = 15.1–3. Some further details are mentioned in the nn. to the translation.

[7] Since the Christmas liturgy associates Balaam's prophecy with the Magi and the Nativity, these same themes were sometimes interwoven in Christmas sermons, as early as Basil the Great. A particularly striking parallel for our ch. 7 is a sermon of John of Damascus (inc. *Hopotan to ear eiselthē*), where Balaam's prophecy is cited just before a long passage taken literally from Aphr (cf. Bratke, *Das sogenannte Religionsgespräch*, p. 92, and Ščegolev, *Izvestija Otdelenija*, vol. 4 [1899] 195f.; both attribute the sermon to John of Euboea). We lack evidence that this work was translated into Slavonic in the early period, however, but surely the Slavs knew some of the earlier sermons of this type.

[8] The Slavs may well have known another traditional connection which is echoed in Theodore of Studios' apostrophe of the Theotokos as the "ladder, fixed on the earth, to heaven" by which the Lord descended "to the great patriarch Jacob." ("In dormitionem Deiparae," in Migne, PG, vol. 99, col. 725B.)

[9] The remainder of the introduction and nn. is by J. H. Charlesworth, in consultation with Lunt and Rubinkiewicz.

[10] Cf. 1QM 9.12–15, 4QEn^b (cf. 4QEn^a), and Noef. Gen 32:25–32 (viz. "And Jacob was left alone; and the angel Sariel wrestled with him in the likeness of a man . . ."). G. Vermes argues that Sariel appears as one of the four chief angels (along with Michael, Raphael, and Gabriel) through reflections upon the Jacob saga; cf. his "The Archangel Sariel: A Targumic Parallel to the Dead Sea Scrolls," in *Christianity, Judaism and Other Greco-Roman Cults*, ed. J. Neusner (SJLA 12; Leiden, 1975) part 3, pp. 159–66. Also cf. J. T. Milik, ed., with M. Black, *The Books of Enoch: Aramaic Fragments of Qumrân Cave 4* (Oxford, 1976) pp. 170–74. It is significant for the dating of the traditions in LadJac to observe that Sariel, who is later replaced by Ouriel (cf. 1En 9:1) as one of the four archangels, is linked with traditions that are clearly pre-A.D. 70 and Palestinian.

As in some of the other pseudepigrapha, the voice has ceased to be something heard and has become a hypostatic creature. In 2:2, we have the familiar concept of a voice; but in 3:1, we hear that "a voice came before my face" and, although he appears to be speaking to Jacob, he actually addresses words to Sariel. A hypostatic voice also appears in the Apocalypse of Abraham, chapter 9, and tells Abraham to sacrifice. In the History of the Rechabites, a voice comes to an individual (2:7) and even speaks to the traveler (3:1). The concept of a hypostatic voice appears also in the Apocalypse of Sedrach and some of the apocalypses preserved in the Mani Codex.[11]

In contrast to the Treatise of Shem (contained herein), there appear to be anti-astrological overtones in at least two passages. In 2:12, it is stated that the sun is controlled by God "so that it might not seem a god" and similarly in 2:14 it is said that the stars are controlled by God "to pass on so that they too might not seem gods."

Running throughout the six chapters in an unorganized fashion—reflecting the fragmentary nature of the text—[12] appears to be an apocalyptic vision of the future. First, the descendants of Jacob will suffer desolation and exile (5:7; 6:2). Because of the sins of Jacob's descendants (5:7), they "shall be exiled in a strange land" and be afflicted with slavery and wounds every day (5:16). Second, his descendants will be freed by God (6:2), because angels (6:6) and finally God (6:9) will fight for Jacob's tribe (cf. 1QM). Finally, at the end of time, Jacob's descendants will inherit the land promised to him (1:9) and become as many "as the stars of heaven and the sand of the sea" (1:10). The future will indeed be glorious according to God's own words to Jacob: "And through your seed all the earth and those living on it in the last times of the years of completion shall be blessed" (1:11).

SELECT BIBLIOGRAPHY

Charlesworth, *PMR*, pp. 130f.
Denis, *Introduction*, pp. 34f.

Bonwetsch, N. "Die Apokryphe 'Leiter Jakobs,'" *Göttinger Nachrichten, philol.-histor. Klasse* (1900) 76–87. (German translation of the LadJac.)
Bratke, E. *Das sogenannte Religionsgespräch am Hof der Sasaniden.* TU N.F. 4.3a (1899) pp. 101–6. (A study of ch. 7 of LadJac.)
James, M. R. "Ladder of Jacob," *The Lost Apocrypha of the Old Testament.* TED; London, New York, 1920; pp. 96–103. (A brief summary and comments on LadJac.)
Ščegolev, P. E. "Očerki istorii otrečennoj literatury: Skazanie Afroditiana," *Izvestija Otdelenija russkogo jazyka i slovesnosti,* Imp. Akademija Nauk, vol. 4 (1899) 148–99, 1304–44.
Vassiliev, Athanasius. *Anecdota Graeco-Byzantina.* Moscow, 1893; vol. 1, pp. xxix–xxxii. (Summary, Lat. version of LadJac 7, and the Palaia's commentary.)

---

[11] See the discussions in the contributions herein on ApAb 9, HistRech 3:1, ApSedr 2:1–4; also cf. TJob 3:1, "a loud voice came to me in a very bright light saying, Jobab, Jobab"; and 3Bar 11:5, "And behold a voice came: 'Let the gate be opened' " (Gk., cf. Slav.).

[12] Perhaps the Slavs deleted portions of an earlier longer document; certainly there were ideas in Early Judaism that would have been offensive or confusing to the medieval Slavs.

THE LADDER OF JACOB

1,2 **1** Jacob then went to Laban his uncle. •He found a place and, laying his head   Gen 28:11–12a
3 on a stone, he slept there, for the sun had gone down. •He had a dream.[a] And
4 behold, a ladder was fixed on the earth, whose top reached to heaven. •And the
5 top of the ladder was the face[b] as of a man, carved out of fire. •There were twelve
steps leading to the top of the ladder, and on each step to the top there were two
human faces, on the right and on the left, twenty-four faces (or busts) including
6 their chests. •And the face in the middle was higher than all that I saw, the one
of fire, including the shoulders and arms, exceedingly terrifying, more than those
7 twenty-four faces. •And while I was still looking at it, behold, angels of God   Gen 28:12b
8 ascended and descended on it.[c] •And God was standing above its highest face,
and he called to me from there, saying, "Jacob, Jacob!" And I said, "Here I
9 am, LORD!" •And he said to me, "The land on which you are sleeping, to you   Gen 28:13f.
10 will I give it, and to your seed after you. •And I will multiply your seed as the
11 stars of heaven and the sand of the sea. •And through your seed all the earth and
those living on it in the last times of the years of completion shall be blessed.
12 My blessing with which I have blessed you shall flow from you unto the last
generation; the East and the West all shall be full of your tribe."

1,2 **2** And when I heard (this) from on high, awe and trembling fell upon me. •And
3 I rose up from my dream and, the voice still being in my ears, I said,[a] •"How   Gen 28:17–19
fearful is this place! This is none other than the house of God and this is the gate
4 of heaven." •And I set up the stone which had been my pillow as a pillar, and I
poured olive oil on the top of it, and I called the name of that place the House of
5 God. •And I stood and began to sing, and I said,

6   "LORD God of Adam your creature and
          LORD God of Abraham and Isaac my fathers
          and of all who have walked before you in justice!

---

1 a. We follow Tikhonravov in beginning LadJac
here, a decision supported, as far as we know, by
only one MS, V¹. The preceding material in the
Palaia tells of Esau's murderous anger and Rebecca's advice that Jacob flee to Laban. The wording
is essentially Gen 27:41b–45, slightly altered in
sequence; nothing remains of Gen 27:45–28:9. In
the oldest MSS of rec. B there is no hint of a
subdivision here or nearby. Rec. A, however (with
two MSS of B), makes a break after "dream" in
vs. 3 and provides a heading: "Concerning the
Ladder." MS S has a miniature showing the
sleeping Jacob and God appearing behind a craggy
mountain but, oddly enough, no ladder. It is
probable, in view of the first-person narrative from
vs. 6 on, that LadJac originally began with Jacob's
own account of events that brought him to this
place.
   b. Here and below surely *prosōpon* in the sense
of "bust" or "portrait." We retain the traditional
"ladder," although surely this is rather a solid
staircase, lined with statues, as on a ziggurat. (Cf.
E. A. Speiser's comment on Gen 28:12 in his
Genesis [The Anchor Bible; Garden City, N.Y.,
1964] p. 218.)
   c. At this point there is an insertion, starting

with the beginning of Gen 28:13 in explicitly LXX
form: "And the LORD *was established* on it." A
short commentary on this phrase follows, then
reference to the angels ascending (identified as the
gentiles) and descending (the Jews). This is the
only interruption of the text up to 6:8.

2 a. From here through 5:1 the text is preserved
only in A. B has a poorly constructed condensation
as follows:
   "LORD, Creator of all creation, and again LORD
God of Abraham and of Isaac my father, and God
of all who have walked in justice before you.
(Behold, I saw a terrible vision; trembling fell upon
me.) But remember, LORD, my forefather Abraham, how he walked before you in innocence, and
in all ways fulfilled your commandments. And also
my father, your servant Isaac, did not disobey your
commandments. Therefore, LORD, look on me
mercifully, on your servant, and explain to me this
vision, this terrible one I have seen." And while
the word and prayer were still in Jacob's mouth,
behold an angel of God stood before him, saying,
"Jacob, I have been sent to you by the Creator of
all things to tell you of your dream. Put this
announcement of your dream in your heart."

7 You who sit firmly[b] on the cherubim and the fiery[c] throne of glory
     . . . and the many-eyed (ones) just as I saw in my dream,

8 holding the four-faced cherubim,
     bearing also the many-eyed seraphim,

9 carrying the whole world[d] under your arm,
     yet not being borne by anyone;

10 you who have made the skies firm for the glory of your name,

11 stretching out on two heavenly clouds the heaven which gleams under you,

12 that beneath it you may cause the sun to course and conceal it during the   cf. ApAb 7:8
     night so that it might not seem a god;

13 (you) who made on them[e] a way for the moon and the stars;

14 and you make the moon wax and wane, and destine the stars to pass on
     so that they too might not seem gods.

15 Before the face of your glory the six-winged seraphim are afraid, and they   Isa 6:2
     cover their feet and faces with their wings, while flying with their
     other (wings), and they sing unceasingly a hymn:

16 '. . .[f] whom I now in sanctifying a new (song) . . .

17 Twelve-topped,[g] twelve-faced, many-named, fiery one!
     Lightning-eyed holy one!

18 Holy, Holy, Holy, Yao, Yaova, Yaoil, Yao,   PrJac
     Kados,[h] Chavod,[i] Savaoth,

19 Omlemlech[j] il avir[k] amismi[l] varich,[m]
     eternal king, mighty, powerful, most great,
     patient, blessed one!'

20 You who fill heaven and earth, the sea and abysses
     and all the ages with your glory,

21 hear my song with which I have sung you and grant me the request I ask
     of you,

22 and tell me the interpretation of my dream,
     for you are a god who is mighty, powerful and glorious,
     a god who is holy; my LORD and LORD of my fathers.''

1,2 **3** And while I was still saying this prayer, behold, a voice came before my face
saying, •''Sariel, leader of the beguiled,[a] you who are in charge of dreams, go
and make Jacob understand the meaning of the dream he has had and explain to
3 him everything he saw; but first bless him.'' •And Sariel the archangel came to
4 me and I saw (him), and his appearance was very beautiful and awesome. •But I
was not astonished by his appearance, for the vision which I had seen in my
5 dream was more terrible than he. •And I did not fear the vision of the angel.

1,2,3 **4** And the angel said to me, ''What is your name?'' •And I said, ''Jacob.'' •(He
announced), ''Your name shall no longer be called Jacob, but your name shall be

---

b. Slav. *krěpcě;* perhaps better read *krěpče*, "O Mighty One, sitting (who sittest)."

c. The text is corrupt at this point. In the phrase *na prěstolě slavy ogneně*, the last word may be locative and an epithet of "throne," as translated, but it could be a banal error for *ogniě*, a vocative ("O fiery one!") which introduces a new invocation, cf. vs. 17 below and ApAb 17:19. At least a few words must have been omitted at this point.

d. Or "age"; Gk. *aiōn*, Heb. *'ōlām*. Grammar obscure; possibly "the age of everything" or, assuming a lacuna, "the age of the whole . . ."

e. Presumably the clouds.

f. Text corrupt.

g. Or "twelve-crested."

h. Heb. *qādôš*, "holy."

i. All copies written with an abbreviation mark obviously understood by scribes as *xrista vod*, "Christ of the waters." Surely Heb. *kāvôd*, "Glory" in the sense of a "theophanic cloud."

j. Probably distorted Heb. *melek*, "king," perhaps plus *'ōlām*.

k. For Heb. *'Êl 'ābîr*, "LORD-Bull; mighty LORD."

l. Var. *amimis*. Probably contains Heb. *'amîṣ*, "strong, firm, courageous."

m. Heb. *bārûk*, "blessed."

3 a. Slav. *uslaždaemyx*, lit. "sweetened," but here surely for Gk. *katathelgō*, "enchant, charm," or with negative sense "delude, deceive."

4 similar to my name, Israel.[a]" •And when I was going from Phandana of Syria[b]
to meet Esau my brother, he came to me and blessed me and called me Israel.
5,6 And he would not tell me his name until I adjured him. •And then he said to me,
"As you were kep zul[c] . . ."

1 **5** Thus he said to me: "You have seen a ladder with twelve steps, each step
2 having two human faces which kept changing their appearance. •The ladder is
3,4 this age, •and the twelve steps are the periods[a] of this age. •But the twenty-four
5 faces are the kings of the ungodly nations of this age. •Under these kings the
children of your children and the generations of your sons will be interrogated.
6,7 These will rise up against the iniquity of your grandsons. •And this place will be
made[b] desolate[c] by the four ascents[d] . . . through the sins[e] of your grandsons.
8 And around the property of your forefathers a palace will be built, a temple in
9 the name of your God and of (the God) of your fathers, •and in the provocations
10 of your children it will become deserted[f] by the four ascents[g] of this age. •For
11 you saw the first four busts[h] which were striking against the steps . . . •angels[i]
12 ascending and descending, and the busts amid the steps. •The Most High will
raise up kings from the grandsons of your brother Esau, and they will receive all
13 the nobles of the tribes of the earth who will have maltreated your seed. •And
14 they will be delivered into his hands and he will be vexed[j] by them. •And he will
hold them by force and rule over them, and they will not be able to oppose him
until the day when his thought will go out against them to serve idols and (to
15 offer) sacrifices of the dead.[k] •. . . (He will) do violence to all those in his
kingdom who will be revealed in such guilt, both to the highest (man)[l] from your
16 tribe and kfalkonagargailyuya.[m] •Know, Jacob, that your descendants shall be
exiles in a strange[n] land, and they will afflict them with slavery and inflict wounds   cf. Gen 15:13f.
17 on them every day. •But the LORD will judge the people for whom they slave.

1,2 **6** "[a]And when the king arises, judgment too will come upon that place. •Then
your seed, Israel, will go out of slavery[a] to the nations who hold them by force,

---

4 a. Heb. *sry-'l,* "Sariel," with transposition of
one letter is *ysr-'l,* "Israel."

b. This same form, clearly representing Padan
Aram (Aram = "of Syria"), is found in ApAb
2:3.

c. R U *kop zul.* Presumably more detailed discussion of the angel's name has been deleted here.

5 a. Slav. *vrěmena,* probably Gk. *kairoi.*

b. Vs. corrupt. A has singular transitive "he
will make," B plural "they will make"; neither
subject is clear.

c. Or "empty."

d. Positing instrumental plural *vüsxody;* the majority reading is *sxody,* "descents." The word
means "going up" in various senses, including
"stairway," and its exact meaning here, in vs. 9
below, and in ApAb 27:3 and 28:4f. is obscure. It
is used in an early version of Ezek 9:3 to render
the Gk. *aithrion,* referring to the threshold of the
Temple. If this is the sense, F. M. Cross, Jr.,
suggests it may be taken as a boundary: To enter
the Holy of Holies one must cross four thresholds
or make four "ascents," while in leaving it would
be four "descents." Cf. Ezek 10:4, 18f. and 11:22f.
for the descent or abandonment and chs. 42–48 for
the ascent or return.

e. Instrumental plural in S, nominative or accusative singular or else genitive plural elsewhere.

f. Slav. *zapustěet,* intransitive.

g. Reading *vüsxody* and interpreting it as instrumental. Yet *do sxod* is possible, and might mean

"before the fourth ascent"; cf. ApAb 28:5, in
which this term seems to denote a period.

h. The text is corrupt; possibly "you saw the
four faces first when they were striking" (or
"hitting"). The sense of the latter verb is obscure.

i. B omits the vs. In A, "angels" is nominative,
but the accompanying participles are accusative.
The "busts" or "faces" are either nominative or
accusative.

j. Slav. *negodujem,* a passive participle, though
the verb is always intransitive elsewhere.

k. A has no verb, but the genitive "of the dead"
with no clear context. B has "that they may sacrifice
to the dead" with appropriate dative. Neither rec.
has a clear connection to the following "do violence"; there must be something missing.

l. A (with U) *vyšünemu;* S R an incongruous
vyšInem.

m. S R; U, with rec. A, omits final *-ya* but
starts next vs. with the conjunction *a,* "and, but."
A omits initial *k,* probably equating it with the
preposition "to," deemed inappropriate in the
context. Meaning possibly "crooked tempter," i.e.
Satan.

n. Note that the wording of this vs. is not quite
that of Gen, either in Heb. or Gk.

6 a. This is the text of A, where it follows 5:17.
In B and in the repetition found embedded in the
commentary, 5:17 is followed by 6:5, and the text
of 1f. is slightly different: "Then the Most High
will give judgment to that place, and he will lead
your seed out of slavery."

3 and they will be free from any rebuke of your enemies. •For this king is the head
of all revenge and retaliation[b] against those who have done evil to you, Israel,
4 and the end of the age. •For bitter ones will rise;[c] they will cry out, and the LORD
5 will hear them and accept their plea. •And the Mighty One will repent because
6 of their sufferings. •For the angels and archangels will hurl their bolts of lightning
7 before them for the sake of the salvation of your tribe. •And you will gain the
8,9 mercy of the Most High. •Then their wives will bear many children. •And
afterward the LORD will fight for your tribe[d] through great and terrible signs
10 against those who made them slaves. •He filled their storehouses, and they will
11 be found empty. •Their land swarmed with reptiles and all sorts of deadly things.
12,13 There will be earthquakes and much destruction. •And the LORD will pour out his
wrath against Leviathan the sea-dragon; he will kill the lawless Falkon with the
14 sword, because he will raise the wrath of the God of gods by his pride. •And
then your justice will be revealed, Jacob, and that of your children[e] who are to
15 be after you (and) who will walk in your justice. •And then your seed will sound
the horn and all the kingdom of Edom will perish together with all the peoples of
Moab.

*　　*　　*

1,2 **7** "And as for the angels you saw descending and ascending the ladder,[a] •in the
last years there will be a man from the Most High, and he will desire to join the
3 upper (things) with the lower. •And before his coming your sons and daughters
4 will tell about him and your young men will have visions about him. •Such will
5,6 be the signs at the time of his coming: •A tree cut with an ax will bleed; •three-
7 month-old babes will speak understanding; •a baby in the womb of his mother
8,9 will speak of his way; •a youth will be like an old man. •And then the expected
one will come, whose path[b] will not be noticed by anyone.

10,11 "Then the earth will be glorified, receiving heavenly glory. •What was above
12,13 will be below also.[c] •And from your seed will bloom a root of kings; •it will
14 emerge[d] and overthrow the power of evil. •And he himself will be the Savior for
every land and rest for those who toil, and a cloud shading the whole world from
15,16 the burning heat. •For otherwise the uncontrolled[e] will not be controlled. •If he
17 does not come,[f] the lower (things) cannot be joined with the upper. •At his coming
the idols of brass, stone, and any sort of carving will give voice for three days.[g]
18 They will give wise men news of him and let them know what will be on earth.
19 By a star, those who wish to see on earth him whom the angels do not see above
20 will find the way to him. •Then the Almighty will be on earth in body, and,

b. Not congruous with "vengeance," though
the error is minor. Perhaps, however, the sense is
"and yours is the vengeance of those who have
done evil to Israel."

c. Slav. *gorci bo vstanutĭ,* A; B *gorcě vstanetĭ
na nja,* "bitterly will (he) rise against them." In
the commentary the subject "Pharaoh" is added.

d. From this point through the end of the ch.
the text in both recs. is embedded in commentary;
it may have undergone special editing.

e. A *dětei;* B has *děd,* "grandfathers," and
modifies the following phrase slightly.

7 a. Ch. 7, which comprises about one third of
LadJac, was compiled by a Slav as part of the anti-
Jewish commentary of the Palaia; apparently his
principal source was the Slavonic version of the
Tale of Aphroditianus. Presently it is not clear
whether ch. 7 was intended as an addition to LadJac
or was written originally as a separate polemical
exercise. Syntactically this vs. is not properly
connected with either the preceding or the following. Cf. 5:11. In A the text is embedded in
commentary, but in B it is separate and then

repeated in the commentary. Note that, unlike Gen
28:12, descending comes first. This surely symbolizes Christ's descent to earth, introducing the
idea of incarnation, which clearly is the theme of
the ch.

b. B "whose path you are: he."

c. Aphr 15.10 negates the first clause: "What
was not above was below." Note that the past
statements of Aphr are converted to the prophetic
future here.

d. Or "raise its head"; Aphr 14.2 *riza entheos
kai basilikě anekypsen.*

e. In A the text is garbled, and in B the majority
have positive *ustrojenaja* instead of *neustrojenaja*
(= Aphr *ta adioikěta,* "the [things which are] not
administered, managed"). The Slav. could mean
"the unordered (things)."

f. Reading *pridet,* against majority *prišel,* "if
he had not come," which fits the commentary (and
Aphr) but not the appropriate reference to future
events.

g. Aphr has the talking idols, but no three-day
period is mentioned.

21 embraced by corporeal arms, he will restore human matter.[h] •And he will revive
22 Eve, who died by the fruit of the tree. •Then the deceit of the impious will be
23 exposed and all the idols will fall face down. •For they will be put to shame by
24 a dignitary.[i] •For because (they were) lying by means of hallucinations, henceforth
25 they will not be able to rule or to prophesy. •Honor will be taken from them and
they will remain without glory.[j]
26   "For he who comes will take power and might and will give[k] Abraham the
27 truth which he previously told him. •Everything sharp he will make dull, and the
28 rough will be smooth. •And he will cast all the iniquitous into the depths of the   cf. Micah 7:1
29,30 sea. •He will work wonders in heaven and on earth. •And he will be wounded in   cf. Zech
31 the midst of his beloved house.[l] •And when he is wounded, then salvation will   13:6LXX
32 be ready, and the end to all perdition. •For those who have wounded him will
33 themselves receive a wound[m] which will not be cured in them forever. •And all
34 creation will bow to him who was wounded, and many will trust in him. •And
he will become known everywhere in all lands, and those who acknowledge his
35 name will not be ashamed. •His own dominion and years will be unending   Ps 102:27
forever."

---

h. Slav. *ponovit veščí clovečísku;* cf. Aphr *pon-avljajeti clovečíču veščí,* an extremely free rendering of Gk. *tina gennousa anthrōpon,* "who bore a man," which refers to Mary. *Veščí* has a broad range of meaning, from "thing, matter" (Gk. *pragma, stoicheion*) to "nature" (Gk. *physis*). The author of LadJac 7 combines phrases from his sources with little regard to their original usage.

i. Slav. *ot sanovita lica,* lit. "by a dignity-endowed face"; Aphr *hyper empraktou prosōpou,*

"by an office-holding [or "active"] person."

j. This is the end of the material from Aphr.

k. Or "give back to."

l. Or "the house of his beloved," which corresponds to the Alexandrine text of LXX.

m. Two MSS have *paguba,* either "ruin, perdition" (Gk. *apōleia, (kata)phthora*) as in 30, or else "pestilence" (Gk. *loimos*); this may have established a connection between the two vss. in the original Slav. compilation.

4 BARUCH

(First to Second Centuries A.D.)

A NEW TRANSLATION AND INTRODUCTION

BY S. E. ROBINSON

This pseudepigraphon, attributed to Baruch the scribe in the Ethiopic version but to Jeremiah the prophet in the Greek, deals with certain events between the destruction of Jerusalem by the Babylonians and the stoning of Jeremiah. On the eve of Jerusalem's destruction, the LORD warns Jeremiah of the impending disaster and instructs him to leave the city and to take Baruch with him. The LORD further instructs Jeremiah to take the vessels of the Temple service and "deliver them to the earth," by which they will be guarded. Jeremiah asks what favor he can do at this critical time for Abimelech in return for the latter's faithful service, and the LORD instructs him to send Abimelech out of the city on a pretext and promises that he will be preserved. The LORD further directs Jeremiah to go with the people into captivity, but Baruch is to remain behind in Jerusalem.

In the morning, before the Babylonians arrive, Jeremiah sends Abimelech out of the city, ostensibly to gather figs for the sick at the farm of Agrippa. In Abimelech's absence, the Babylonians conquer the city and lead the people off. Jeremiah commits the keys of the Temple to the care of the sun and is carried off with the people. In Baruch's lament for the city, he insists that Jerusalem could not have been taken were it not for the wickedness of its inhabitants, which led the LORD to abandon them. Baruch also affirms that God will eventually bring his people back, and then he retires to live in a tomb, where the angels of God come often to converse with him.

In the meantime, Abimelech, who has collected his basket of figs, stops in the heat of the day to rest under a tree and sleeps for sixty-six years. Both he and his figs are miraculously preserved by the LORD; when he wakes up, he even complains about the brevity of his nap. Returning to Jerusalem, he is totally disoriented until an old man solves the riddle and is able to convince Abimelech of what has happened. An angel then leads him to Baruch.

Baruch interprets the awakening of Abimelech as proof of the resurrection of the dead individually and also as an indication that God is about to restore his people collectively. He informs Jeremiah of what has happened in a letter, which is delivered by an eagle miraculously provided for that purpose, and instructs Jeremiah to prepare the people for their return by excluding gentiles from their company and by repudiating their Babylonian spouses and children. At last the LORD brings his people back to Jerusalem, excluding those who would not cast off their Babylonian relations. The latter eventually found Samaria. While celebrating the return in Jerusalem, Jeremiah has a vision and prophesies the coming of Jesus Christ, for which he is stoned to death by the people.

Text

Both long and short forms of 4 Baruch are preserved in a relatively large number of manuscripts. So far, Greek witnesses for the long form total twenty-three manuscripts, and 4 Baruch is found in Ethiopic, Armenian, Old Church Slavonic, and Romanian versions, besides the Greek. The translation below is taken from the provisional, eclectic text of the long form of 4 Baruch edited by R. A. Kraft and A.-E. Purintun,[1] which improves upon the text published by J. R. Harris in 1889[2] by consulting more Greek manuscripts and by adding the evidence of the Armenian and Slavonic versions to that of the Ethiopic employed by Harris.

The major Greek texts of 4 Baruch are A: Milan Brera AF IX 31 (15th cent.); B: Jerusalem Taphos 34 (11th cent.); C: Jerusalem Taphos 6 (10th cent.); and P: Paris Greek Manuscript 1534 (11th cent.). Kraft and Purintun have an excellent summary of the textual witnesses, to which the reader is referred.[3]

Original language

Several early scholars, particularly R. H. Charles and those influenced by him, maintained that the original language of 4 Baruch was Greek.[4] Since the time of Charles, however, scholars have generally come to favor the hypothesis of a Semitic original for the work.[5] The Greek text contains several elements that may be traces of such a Semitic original, and a list of several such elements has been compiled by A.-E. Purintun.[6] Among others, these include the possible transliteration of Hebrew words (e.g. "God Zar" for "foreign God," 7:29), intensive verbs (e.g. "to pray a prayer," 9:3, and "stone with stones," 9:22), the possible use of the Greek *ek* for the Hebrew *min* (5:35 and 7:29), and the redundant use of personal pronouns following a relative pronoun (e.g. "in whom all judgment was hidden in him," 9:6).[7]

Date

The strongest bit of evidence for dating 4 Baruch is the mention of the vineyard or farm of Agrippa (3:14, 21; 5:22), since it places the final Jewish redaction of the work after Agrippa I gained control of Judea and Samaria, A.D. 41.[8] It is probable that we should understand the destruction of the city and Temple in chapters 1 through 4 to reflect the destruction of Jerusalem by the Romans, A.D. 70. It is unlikely that this can refer to the second revolt (A.D. 132–35), because the actual destruction of the Temple and the cessation of the Temple service figure so prominently in the story. Consequently, the upper limit of composition for the Jewish portion of the work may be found by adding the sixty-six years of Abimelech's sleep (i.e. the maximum duration of exile expected by the author) to the date of the destruction of the Temple, A.D. 70. This gives an upper limit of A.D. 136. Further, since the final Jewish redaction of 4 Baruch appears to have been harmonized with 2 Baruch, which was composed shortly before the end of the first century, we may conclude that the Jewish portion of 4 Baruch was finished sometime roughly during the first third of the second century A.D. and may have contributed to, or even been produced by, the resurgent hope for a restoration of Jewish institutions that led ultimately to the second revolt. Sometime thereafter, perhaps by the middle of the second century, the work was redacted by a Christian who made at least one interpolation (6:25) and Christianized the ending (8:12–9:32).

---

[1] R. A. Kraft and A.-E. Purintun, *Paraleipomena Jeremiou*, pp. 12–48. [The present contribution had to be reassigned; I am grateful to S. E. Robinson, who agreed to contribute this work on 4Bar even though only two months could be allowed to complete the task. —J.H.C.]

[2] J. R. Harris, *The Rest of the Words of Baruch*, pp. 47–64.

[3] Kraft and Purintun, *Paraleipomena*, pp. 3–5. See also P. Bogaert, *Apocalypse de Baruch*, pp. 179f.

[4] R. H. Charles, *APOT*, vol. 2, pp. 133f. See also J.-B. Frey, "Apocryphes de l'ancien testament," *DBSup*, vol. 1, p. 454.

[5] E.g. A.-M. Denis, *Introduction*, p. 75; G. Delling, *Jüdische Lehre und Frömmigkeit in den Paralipomena Jeremiae*, p. 72.

[6] A.-E. Purintun, *Paraleipomena Jeremiou* (Philadelphia, 1971) unnumbered.

[7] Purintun, *Paraleipomena*, unnumbered.

[8] See the discussion in Harris, *The Rest*, pp. 33f. Contrary to Harris, the mention of Agrippa cannot be used to establish an upper limit for the date of 4Bar, since place-names can be extremely long-lived.

Provenance

The references to the vineyard or farm of Agrippa (3:14, 21; 5:22) and the marketplace of the gentiles (6:19) may indicate a Palestinian provenance for 4 Baruch. It may even have been written in Jerusalem, as J. R. Harris suggested, since both allusions would seem to betray a thorough familiarity with the environs of the holy city.[9] However, it is not necessary to press an identification of the vineyard of Agrippa or the marketplace of the gentiles with any sites known from other sources.[10] Moreover, one must bear in mind that a skillful author could invent geographical details to give his fiction the ring of authenticity and that even valid allusions to Jerusalem landmarks prove only that the author was familiar with the city and not that his work was necessarily produced there. Nevertheless, in the absence of any evidence for a different provenance, we are certainly justified in associating the place of composition with the only geographical clues we have in the text, and tentatively suggest that 4 Baruch was indeed written in Palestine, perhaps even in Jerusalem as Harris maintained.

An originally Jewish composition, 4 Baruch has been interpolated by a Christian and provided with a Christian ending (8:12–9:32, esp. 9:14–32). The Jewish portion of the document has more than one redactional level.[11] Characteristic of the earlier level of Jewish redaction is an emphasis on the figure of Jeremiah the prophet as the "chosen one" of the LORD and as the LORD's agent in dealing with Israel. If Baruch figures in the story at this level, it is only as an auxiliary of Jeremiah. This is in harmony with the picture of these events in canonical Jeremiah, 2 Maccabees 2:1–7, and The Lives of the Prophets. The later level of redaction in the Jewish portion of the text is characterized by an emphasis on the importance of Baruch the scribe. This complicated redactional history is responsible for the fact that the work is known by two titles. The Greek manuscripts title it "The Things Omitted from Jeremiah the Prophet"; in the Ethiopic version it is titled "The Rest of the Words of Baruch." In the final form of 4 Baruch, what begins as a revelation to the prophet continues as a pronouncement of the scribe and ends with a prophecy about the Christ. This sequence adequately reflects the redactional history of the work. Jeremiah, who completely overshadows Baruch in chapters 1 through 4, is almost totally eclipsed by Baruch in chapters 7 and 8, in which the prophet must accept the mediation of the scribe between himself and God. Moreover, we are told in 7:25–28 that God loved Baruch too much to let him suffer the same fate as Jeremiah. G. Delling has already noted the strong Pharisaic flavor of 4 Baruch, and the shifting of importance from prophet to scribe is certainly in keeping with the Pharisaic point of view.[12]

The final redaction of 4 Baruch was by a Christian, as the reference to Jesus Christ in the last chapter (9:14) makes perfectly clear. Also, the description of the waters of the Jordan as a test for the people (6:25) is an obvious Christian interpolation referring to baptism, especially since there is no mention of a test by water when the people actually do cross the Jordan (8:4–6).[13] The Christian redactor employs some terms and phrases that are similar to but not necessarily influenced by gnostic ideas, especially in chapters 6 and 9. Some examples are "virgin faith" (6:7), "O great name which no one can know" (6:13), "let knowledge come into our heart" (6:13), "the sign of the great seal" (6:25), and "Jesus Christ the light of all the aeons" (9:14, 26).[14] Also the passage at 9:16f., which describes the rejection of the trees that "had sprouted" (the Jews) and the acceptance of those that were previously "uncultivated," seems to reflect a Christianity that was already non-Jewish in its own self-understanding.

Historical importance

In 4 Baruch there is very little direct information about the period between A.D. 70 and

[9] Harris, *The Rest*, pp. 12f.
[10] A doubtful project pursued by Harris in *The Rest*, pp. 12f., 32–35.
[11] See O. Wintermute's review of G. Delling, *Jüdische Lehre*, in *CBQ* 30 (1968) 44f.
[12] Delling, *Jüdische Lehre*, pp. 71f.
[13] See Harris, *The Rest*, pp. 14f.
[14] Wintermute, *CBQ* 30 (1968) 44f.

136, yet the Jewish portions of the work offer an insight into the psychological response to the destruction of the Temple in 70 and the eventual revival of hopes for a restoration of Jewish institutions prior to 136. The document *may*, with its shift in emphasis from prophet to scribe, reflect the increasing influence of the Pharisees after A.D. 70 (see "Provenance"). After the disastrous results of the second revolt (A.D. 132–35), a disillusioned Judaism abandoned 4 Baruch altogether (along with most of its other apocalyptic literature) to be preserved by Christians, who found it (for a while at least and with appropriate revisions) a serviceable vehicle for validating Christian claims. It has been preserved to the present in both Greek Orthodox and Ethiopian Christianity.

Theological importance

The author of 4 Baruch insists that the holy vessels of the Temple cultus were miraculously preserved from destruction by the Babylonians (Romans) and can therefore be restored when God brings his people back from exile (3:8–11, 18f.; 4:4f.). Also, Jerusalem, according to our author, could never have been destroyed if God had not abandoned it for its sins (4:7–8). The conclusion to be drawn by the original audience was perhaps that if the Jews would conform sufficiently to the will of God, as interpreted by the scribe,[15] they could bring about a restoration of the Temple cultus in an invincible Jewish state. We see here lingering hope for and real anticipation of the restoration of the Temple and of the nation, which continued until all hope was quenched in the second revolt.

Also, the miraculous preservation of Abimelech and the figs is seen by the author as a proof of the doctrine of the resurrection (6:6–10), and the ideas of personal and corporate resurrection are closely linked. A further connection between the doctrine of personal resurrection and the restoration of Israel is found at 7:18, where the eagle raises a dead man so that the people may believe God is about to restore the nation. The insistence on a personal resurrection probably accounts for some of 4 Baruch's appeal to Christians, and this doctrine is given further attention at 9:12–14, where Jeremiah's ecstatic faint is described in terms reminiscent of the resurrection of Christ.

Relation to canonical books

In 4 Baruch are described events found in the canonical books of Jeremiah, 2 Kings, 2 Chronicles, Ezra, and Nehemiah. The book is intended by its Greek title to be understood as an addition to the canonical Jeremiah. It agrees with its canonical antecedents concerning the general facts of destruction and deportation but disagrees with them on the details. For example, 4 Baruch represents Jeremiah and Baruch as leading the people back from Babylon, but Jeremiah 43:6f. makes it clear that neither went to Babylon, but that they went instead to Egypt.[16] Neither Jeremiah nor Baruch is mentioned in the account of the return in Ezra-Nehemiah, although a priest named Jeremiah may have been confused by the author of 4 Baruch with Jeremiah the prophet (Neh 10:2; 12:1, 12, 34). The description of the Samaritans as Jews who intermarried with Babylonians during the exile is sharply contradicted by Ezra-Nehemiah, according to which the Samaritans existed before the return, and by 2 Kings 17:24–41, which connects the origin of the Samaritans with the Assyrian conquest of the Northern Kingdom.

Relation to apocryphal books

It has often been claimed that 4 Baruch is dependent upon 2 Baruch, and in fact the two works have many striking similarities.[17] P. Bogaert has offered several reasons why 4 Baruch should be considered to be dependent on 2 Baruch.[18] Nevertheless, while it is probable that the *final* form of 4 Baruch is later than and to a certain extent dependent upon 2 Baruch,

---

[15] Jeremiah instructs the people to follow the directions of Baruch in these words: "Everything that you have heard from the letter observe, and the LORD will lead us into our city" (7:23).

[16] This is also stated in LivPro on Jeremiah.

[17] These are listed by Bogaert, *Apocalypse*, pp. 186–92.

[18] Bogaert, *Apocalypse*, pp. 192–221.

the possibility should be allowed that the earlier level of redaction in 4 Baruch preserves a more original form of the tradition and is not copied from 2 Baruch. This is seen most clearly in chapter 1 of 4 Baruch, where Jeremiah the prophet receives the initial warning of destruction. In 2 Baruch 2, the warning is very similar, but it is Baruch the scribe who receives it. 4 Baruch tends to agree with canonical Jeremiah, 2 Maccabees 2:1–7, and The Lives of the Prophets 2 that the prophet and not the scribe is the central character. Moreover, in The Lives of the Prophets 2:11–19 and in 2 Maccabees 2:1–7, which must certainly be dated long before 2 Baruch, it is Jeremiah who buries the Temple vessels (in agreement with 4Bar 3) and not the anonymous angel of 2 Baruch 6:6–10.[19] Concerning the traditions of the fall of Jerusalem, 4 Baruch agrees with the earlier 2 Maccabees against 2 Baruch. Since the author of 2 Maccabees reports that this material was already found "in the archives" (2:1, 4) in his day, it is likely that all four accounts (2Mac 2:1–7; 2Bar 1–10; LivPro 2:11–19; 4Bar 1–4) are taken from a prior source, to which the earlier level of redaction in 4 Baruch is more faithful, at least in some respects, than is 2 Baruch. Sometime after the publication of 2 Baruch, a final Jewish redactor of 4 Baruch edited the latter to bring it into harmony with the former. It was at this time that emphasis within the work was shifted from Jeremiah to Baruch.

In conclusion, it seems appropriate to offer a few speculative suggestions. A close examination of the opening chapters of 4 Baruch reveals that the figure of Baruch is an intrusion here, inserted perhaps by the later Jewish redactor to bring 4 Baruch into harmony with 2 Baruch. For example, 1:10 ("So rise up and go to Baruch and tell him these words") breaks up the sequence of the LORD's instruction to Jeremiah in 1:9 and 11. The redactor obviously intends 1:10 to complement 2:1a ("And Jeremiah ran and told these things to Baruch"), but 2:1a is obviously an intrusion, since in 2:2–6, Baruch does not yet know what has happened. The other two references to Baruch in chapter 1 are appositional (1:1, 8), and represent the simplest kind of editorial additions. Moreover, it is possible that the subservient character in chapter 2 was originally not Baruch at all but Abimelech, since he, and not Baruch, is in the habit of calling Jeremiah "father" (5:5, 22), since 2:5 suggests that the unidentified character does menial labor ("let us not draw water for the troughs"), and since the motif of Abimelech's being spared the sight of Jerusalem's destruction, which is mentioned twice (3:13; 5:28), is later transferred to Baruch (7:25–27).

Another possibility is that chapters 1 to 4, rather than reflecting an earlier redactional level, constitute a separate Jeremiah source which was used by the author of 4 Baruch and altered by him to harmonize with 2 Baruch. On this view, some of the tension within the composition would be due not to separate redactional levels but to the use of incompatible sources. Either way, the Jeremiah material of chapters 1 to 4 seems to be prior to the form of the traditions in 2 Baruch and not dependent upon them except as it has been harmonized with that document by the author or redactor.

BIBLIOGRAPHY

Charlesworth, *PMR*, pp. 88–91.
Delling, *Bibliographie*, p. 171.
Denis, *Introduction*, pp. 70–78.

Bogaert, P. *Apocalypse de Baruch*. Paris, 1969; pp. 177–221.
Delling, G. *Jüdische Lehre und Frömmigkeit in den Paralipomena Jeremiae*. Berlin, 1967.
Harris, J. R. *The Rest of the Words of Baruch*. Cambridge, England, 1889.
Kilpatrick, G. D. "Acts VII.52 *ELEUSIS*," *JTS* 46 (1945) 140–45.
Kohler, K. "The Pre-Talmudic Haggada. B. The Second Baruch or Rather the Jeremiah Apocalypse," *JQR* 5 (1893) 407–19.
Kraft, R. A., and Purintun, A.-E. *Paraleipomena Jeremiou*. T&T 1, Pseudepigrapha Series 1; Missoula, Mont., 1972.

---

[19] This is also true in the rabbinic literature; see for example b.Yoma 54.

THE THINGS OMITTED FROM JEREMIAH THE PROPHET[a]

1 **1** It happened, when the children of Israel were taken captive by the king of the Chaldeans, that God spoke to Jeremiah, saying, "Jeremiah, my chosen one, rise up and get out of this city, you and Baruch, because I am going to destroy it for 2 the multitude of the sins of those who inhabit it. •For your prayers are like a firm 3 pillar in the middle of it, and like an unbreachable wall encircling it. •So now 4 rise up and get out before the host of the Chaldeans surrounds it." •And Jeremiah answered, saying, "I implore you, LORD, allow me, your servant, to speak before 5,6 you." •And the LORD said to him, "Speak, my chosen one, Jeremiah." •And Jeremiah spoke, saying, "LORD Almighty, are you delivering the chosen city into the hands of the Chaldeans, so that the king may boast with the multitude of his 7 people and say, 'I prevailed over the holy city of God'? •(Surely) not, my LORD; 8 but if it is your will, let it be destroyed by your (own) hands." •And the LORD said to Jeremiah, "Since you are my chosen one, rise up and get out of this city, you and Baruch, because I am going to destroy it for the multitude of the sins of 9 those who inhabit it.[b] •For neither the king nor his host can come into it unless I 10,11 first open its gates. •So rise up and go to Baruch and tell him these words. •And rising up at the sixth hour of the night, get up on the wall of the city, and I will 12 show you that unless I first destroy the city, they cannot come into it." •After saying these things, the LORD departed from Jeremiah.

Jer 1:18
2Bar 2:1f.
LivPro

2Bar 7:1
3Mac 2:17f.

1 **2** And Jeremiah ran and told these things to Baruch, and as they came into the Temple of God,[a] Jeremiah tore his garments and put dust on his head and went 2 into the sanctuary of God. •And Baruch, seeing him (with) dust sprinkled on his head and his garments torn, cried out in a loud voice, saying, "Father Jeremiah, what is the matter with you, or what sort of sin have the people committed?"[b] 3 (He said this) because whenever the people sinned, Jeremiah sprinkled dust on 4 his head and would pray for the people until the sin was forgiven them. •And (this is why) Baruch asked him, saying, "Father, what is the matter with you?"[c] 5 And Jeremiah said to him, "Avoid the rending of your garments, but rather let us rend our hearts; and let us not draw water for the troughs, but let us weep and 6 fill them with tears. For the LORD will not have mercy on this people." •And 7 Baruch said, "Father Jeremiah, what has happened?" •And Jeremiah said, "God is delivering the city into the hands of the king of the Chaldeans, to take the 8 people captive into Babylon." •And when Baruch heard these things, he tore his 9 garments also and said, "Father Jeremiah, who revealed this to you?" •And Jeremiah said to him, "Wait with me a little, until the sixth hour of the night, 10 that you may know that this word is true." •And so they both remained at the altar weeping, and their garments were torn.

1 **3** But when the hour of the night arrived, as the LORD had said to Jeremiah, they 2 went up together onto the walls of the city, Jeremiah and Baruch. •And behold, there was a sound of trumpets, and angels came out of heaven holding torches in

2Bar 6:1-4

---

1 a. This is the title given in the Gk. MSS; the Eth. version is entitled "The Rest of the Words of Baruch."

b. Note that this is a doublet of 1:1b.

2 a. MS C and the Eth. version omit "Jeremiah ran . . . God." In light of 2:2–7 the omission is probably correct. The line may have been added

by a redactor interested in enhancing the importance of Baruch.

b. Note Baruch's subservient status in the opening chs., where Jeremiah is always addressed as "Father."

c. The majority of Gk. MSS read, "What is this?" The translation here follows the text of J. R. Harris, *The Rest of the Words of Baruch.*

3 their hands, and they stood on the walls of the city. •And when Jeremiah and
Baruch saw them, they wept, saying, "Now we know that the word is true."
4 And Jeremiah pleaded with the angels, saying, "I implore you not to destroy the   2Bar 6:5f.
5 city just yet, until I have a word with the LORD." •And the LORD spoke to the
angels, saying, "Don't destroy the city until I speak to my chosen one, Jeremiah."
6,7 Then Jeremiah spoke, saying, "Please, LORD, let me speak before you." •And
8 the LORD said, "Speak, my chosen one, Jeremiah." •And Jeremiah said, "Behold,
LORD, we know now that you are delivering the city into the hands of its enemies,
9 and they will carry the people off into Babylon. •What do you want me to do   2Bar 6:7-10
10 with the holy vessels of the (Temple) service?" •And the LORD said to him,
"Take them and deliver them to the earth, saying, 'Hear, earth, the voice of him
who created you, who formed you in the abundance of the waters, who sealed   Rev 5:1
you with seven seals in seven periods (of time), and after these things you will
11 receive your fruitful season.ᵃ •Guard the vessels of the (Temple) service until the
12 comingᵇ of the beloved one.' " •And Jeremiah spoke, saying, "I implore you,
LORD, show me what I should do for Abimelech the Ethiopian, for he did many
13 good deeds for your servant Jeremiah. •For he pulled me out of the muddy cistern,   Jer 38:4-13
and I do not want him to see the destruction of this city and (its) desolation, but
14 that you may show him mercy and that he might not be grieved." •And the LORD
said to Jeremiah, "Send him to the vineyard of Agrippaᶜ and in the shadow of   3Bar 1:3
15 the mountain I will shelter him until I return the people to the city. •But you,
Jeremiah, go with your people into Babylon and stay with them, preaching to   2Bar 10:1-3
16 them until I return them to the city. •But leave Baruch here until I speak to him."   Jer 43:6f.
17,18 After the LORD said these things, he went up from Jeremiah into heaven.ᵈ •But
Jeremiah and Baruch went into the sanctuary and, gathering up the vessels of the   Jer 52:17-19
(Temple) service, they delivered them to the earth, just as the LORD had instructed   2Bar 6:7-10
2Mac 2:4-8
19,20 them. •And immediately the earth swallowed them up. •And the two sat down   LivPro
21 and wept. •And when it was morning, Jeremiah sent Abimelech away, saying,
"Take the basket and go out to the farm of Agrippa by the mountain road and
get a few figs to give to the sick among the people, for the delight of the LORD
22 (rests) upon you, and (his) glory upon your head." •And saying these things,
Jeremiah sent him away, and Abimelech went as he had been instructed.

1 **4** And when it was morning, behold the host of the Chaldeans surrounded the
2 city. •And the great angel trumpeted, saying, "Come into the city, host of the   2Bar 8:2
3 Chaldeans; for behold, the gate has been opened for you. •Therefore, let the king
4 come in with his multitude and take all the people captive." •But Jeremiah, taking
the keys of the Temple, went outside of the city and, facing the sun, he tossed
them, saying, "I say to you, sun, take the keys of the Temple of God and keep   2Bar 10:18
5 them until the day in which the LORD will question you about them.ᵃ •Because
6 we were not found worthy of keeping them, for we were false stewards." •While   Jer 52:27-30;
Jeremiah was still weeping for the people, they carried him (off) with the people,   40:1-7;
43:6f.
7 dragging (them) into Babylon. •And Baruch put dust on his head and sat and
wept this lamentation, saying, "Why was Jerusalem made desolate? For the
sins of the beloved people she was delivered into the hands of enemies, for our
8 sins and (those) of the people. •But do not let the outlaws boast and say, 'We
were strong enough to take the city of God by our power'; but because of our
9 sins it was delivered to you. •And our God will pity us and return us to our city,   2Bar 10:6f.
10 but you will not have life. •Blessed are our fathers, Abraham, Isaac, and Jacob,   2Bar 11:4

---

3 a. Lit. "your ripeness of fruit."

b. Following the suggestion of G. D. Kilpatrick,
"Acts VII.52 *ELEUSIS*," *JTS* 46 (1945) 140f.,
although this rendering is elsewhere unattested.
Literally the word is "coming together," or "union,"
or perhaps even "marriage." The variant "consummation, completion" (MSS A B P) should be
noted. According to R. A. Kraft and A.-E. Purintun
(*Paraleipomena Jeremiou*, p. 17), "coming" is

supported by the Arm. version.

c. Harris, *The Rest*, p. 12, identifies this vineyard with an area south of Jerusalem known as
Solomon's Gardens. See also Josephus, *Ant* 8.7.3.

d. Note the anthropomorphic representation of
God.

4 a. See also b.Taʿan 29a; LevR 19:6; and ARN
7.

for they departed from this world and did not see the destruction of this city.''
11 After saying these things, Baruch went outside the city, weeping and saying,
12 "Grieving over you, Jerusalem, I have left you." •And he remained sitting in a Jer 43:6f.
tomb while the angels came to him and elaborated to him all the things that the
Lord would reveal to him through them.

1 **5** But Abimelech carried the figs in the heat (of the day), and coming upon a
2 tree, he sat under its shade to rest a little. •And leaning his head on the basket of
figs (and) falling asleep, he slept for sixty-six years, and he did not wake from
3 his sleep. •And afterward, when he arose from his sleep, he said, "I slept
pleasantly a little, but my head is weighed down because I didn't get enough
4,5 sleep." •Then, uncovering the basket of figs, he found them dripping milk. •And
he said, "I would like to nap a little longer, because my head is weighed down,
but I'm afraid I might fall fast asleep and be late waking up, and my father
Jeremiah might think less (of me). For if he were not in a hurry, he would not
6 have sent me (so) early this morning. •So I will get up and proceed in the heat,
7 for isn't there heat, isn't there work, every day?" •So, getting up, he took the
basket of figs and put (it) on his shoulders and went into Jerusalem, and he did
not recognize it, neither the house nor his neighborhood; neither did he find his
8 family, nor any of the neighbors. •And he said, "Blessed (be) the Lord, for a
9 great stupor has befallen me today. •This is not the city Jerusalem! I got lost[a]
because I came by the mountain road after getting up from my sleep; and since
10 my head was heavy from my not getting enough sleep, I got lost. •Imagine telling
11 Jeremiah that I got lost!"[b] •And he went out of the city, and looking (carefully)
he saw the landmarks of the city and said, "This, then, is the city; I got lost."
12 And he returned again to the city and searched and found none of his own (people),
13 and he said, "Blessed (be) the Lord, for a great stupor has befallen me!" •And
he went outside the city again and stayed (there) grieving, not knowing where he
14 should go. •And he put the basket down, saying, "I'm sitting right here until the
15 Lord takes this stupor away from me." •And as he sat, he saw an elderly man
coming from the field, and Abimelech said to him, "I say to you, old man, what
16,17 city is this?" •And he said to him, "It is Jerusalem." •And Abimelech said to
him, "(Then) where is Jeremiah the priest and Baruch the reader and all the
18 people of this city, because I didn't find them." •And the old man said to him,
"Are you not from this city, that you remember Jeremiah today, and ask about
19 him after so long a time? •For Jeremiah is in Babylon with the people. For they
were taken captive by Nebuchadnezzar the king and Jeremiah is with them to
20 preach to them and to teach them the word." •But as soon as Abimelech heard (this)
from the old gentleman, he said, "If you weren't an old man, and if it
weren't improper for a man to insult his elder(s), I would laugh at you and say
you are crazy because you said, 'The people were taken captive into Babylon.'
21 If the cataracts of heaven had come down upon them, there still isn't time to have
22 gone into Babylon! •For how long can it be since my father Jeremiah sent me to
the farm of Agrippa to get a few figs so we could give (them) to the sick among
23 the people? •And I went out and got them, and coming upon a certain tree in the
heat (of the day), I sat down to rest a little, and I leaned my head on the basket
24 and fell asleep. •And when I woke up, I uncovered the basket of figs, thinking I
25 was late, and found the figs dripping milk, just as (when) I picked them. •And
26 you say that the people were taken captive into Babylon! •But (just) so you'll
27 know, take the figs (and) see!" •And he uncovered the basket of figs for the old
28 man, and he saw them dripping milk. •And when he saw them, the old gentleman
said, "O my son, you are a righteous man, and God did not want you to see the
29 desolation of the city, so he brought this stupor upon you. •For behold, it is today

---

5 a. Lit. "I wandered the road."
  b. Lit. "Marvelous to say this to Jeremiah that
. . ."

30 sixty-six years since the people were taken captive into Babylon. •And so that
you may learn, son, that what I am telling you is true, look out into the field and
31 see that the growth of the crops is not (yet) apparent. •See also the figs, that it is
32 not (yet) time for them, and understand." •Then Abimelech cried in a loud voice,
saying, "I will bless you, O God of heaven and of the earth, the rest of the souls
33 of the righteous in every place." •Then he said to the elderly gentleman, "What
34,35 month is this?" •And he said, "Nisan, the twelfth (day)."ᶜ •And picking up
(some) of the figs, he gave them to the old gentleman and said to him, "May
God guide you with (his) light to the city above, Jerusalem!"

Ezra 8:31

Gal 4:26
Heb 12:22
2Bar 4:2-7

1 **6** After these things Abimelech went outside the city and prayed to the LORD.
2 And behold, an angel of the LORD came and, taking hold of his right hand,
brought him back to the place where Baruch was sitting, and he found him in a
3 tomb. •And when they saw each other, both (of them) wept, and they kissed each
4 other. •And looking up, Baruch saw with his (own) eyes the figs sheltered in
5,6 Abimelech's basket. •And raising his eyes to heaven, he prayed, saying, •"'You
are the God who bestows a reward (on) those who love you. Prepare yourself,
my heart; rejoice and be glad in your tabernacle, saying to your fleshly dwelling,
'Your sorrow has been turned to joy.' For the Mighty One is coming and will
7 raise you in your tabernacle, for sin has not taken root• in you. •Be refreshed
8 within your tabernacle, in your virgin faith, and believe that you will live.ᵇ •Look
at this basket of figs; for behold, they are sixty-six years old and they have not
9 withered nor do they stink, but they are dripping with milk.ᶜ •Thus will it be for
you, my flesh, if you do the things commanded you by the angel of righteousness.ᵈ
10 He who preserved the basket of figs, the same one again will preserve you by
11 his power." •After saying these things, Baruch said to Abimelech, "Get up and
let us pray that the LORD might reveal to us how we can send word to Jeremiah
12 in Babylon about the protection which was yours on the way." •And Baruch
13 prayed, saying, "Our power, LORD God, (thou) chosen light, (is) that which
proceeds from your mouth.• •We implore and beg of your goodness, O great name
14 which no one can know. Hear the voice of your servants and let knowledge come
15 into our heart. •What should we do, and how should we send this news to Jeremiah
in Babylon?" •And while Baruch was still praying, behold an angel of the LORD
came and said to Baruch all these words: "Councilor of the light, don't worry
about how you should send to Jeremiah. For tomorrow an eagle is coming to you
16 (at the) hour of light, and you must direct (it) to Jeremiah. •Therefore, write in
the letter,ᶠ 'Speak to the children of Israel, "Let him among you who has become

Ezra 10:11

a foreigner be expelled," and let them spend fifteen days, and after these things
17 I will lead you into your city, says the LORD. •Whoever is not separated from
Babylon, let him not come into the city, and I will punish them with not being
18 taken back again by the Babylonians, says the LORD.' " •And after these things,
19 the angel departed from Baruch. •And Baruch sent to the marketplace of the
gentiles and got papyrus and ink, and he wrote the following letter: "Baruch, the

2Bar 78:1

20 servant of God, writes to Jeremiah in the captivity of Babylon. •Hail and rejoice!
For God has not left us to pass out of this body grieving over the city which was
21 desolated and outraged. •For this reason the LORD has taken pity on our tears and
has remembered the covenant that he established with our fathers Abraham, Isaac,

---

c. Kraft and Purintun (*Paraleipomena Jeremiou*,
p. 27), give "Nisan (which is Abib)." The text is
difficult here (see Harris, *The Rest*, p. 54), but
Ezra 8:31 supports the translation above.

6 a. From *ginesthai*, lit. "has not become."
   b. Baruch interprets the experience of Abimelech as a proof of the resurrection of the flesh.
   c. The fig is an apt symbol for life, since it is
full of seeds and "drips milk." The fig is often

identified in Jewish literature as the forbidden fruit
of Eden.
   d. See 8:12 and 9:15.
   e. Or "Our power, LORD God, (is) the chosen
light which proceeds from your mouth."
   f. What follows are instructions for Jeremiah
the prophet from Baruch the scribe, in a reversal
of their canonical roles and of their respective roles
in chs. 1–4, 9.

22 and Jacob. •And he sent his angel to me and told me these words which I have
23 sent to you. •Now, these are the words that the LORD God of Israel, who led us
from the land of Egypt, out of the great furnace, spoke: 'Because you didn't keep
my commandments, but your heart was lifted up and you stiffened your neck
before me, in wrath and anger I delivered you to the furnace in Babylon.
24 However, if you will listen to my voice,' says the LORD, 'from the mouth of
Jeremiah my servant, whoever listens I will bring him back from Babylon, and
whoever does not listen will become a stranger to Jerusalem and to Babylon.
25 And you will prove them with the water of the Jordan; whoever does not listen
will become known; this is the sign of the great seal.' ''g

1 **7** And Baruch stood up and went out of the tomb and found the eagle sitting   2Bar 77:17-26
2 outside the tomb. •And conversing in a human voice, the eagle said to him, "Hail,
3 Baruch, the steward of the faith!"a •And Baruch said to him, "You who speak
are chosen from all the birds of heaven, for this is clear from the gleam in your
4 eyes; so show me, what are you doing here?" •And the eagle said to him, "I was
5 sent here so that you may send every word you desire through me." •And Baruch
6 said to him, "Can you take this message up to Jeremiah in Babylon?" •And the
7 eagle said to him, "Certainly; this is why I was sent." •And picking up the letter
and fifteen figs from the basket of Abimelech, Baruch tied them to the neck of
the eagle and said to him, "I say to you, king of birds, depart in peace and health
8 and carry the message for me. •Don't be like the raven that Noah sent out and   Gen 8:7-12
that never again returned to him in the ark, but be like the dove that on the third
9 (attempt) brought word to the righteous one. •So also, you take this precious word
up to Jeremiah and to those prisoners with him that it might be well with you.
10 Take this papyrus to the people and to the chosen one of God. •If all the birds of
heaven should surround you and desire to fight with you, resist (them); the LORD
11 will give you power. •And don't veer off to the right or to the left, but like an
arrow shot straight, go forth in the power of God, and may the glory of the LORD
12 be with you on the entire journey which you will travel." •Then the eagle took
flight, having the letter around his neck, and departed for Babylon. And when he
arrived (there), he rested in a certain tree outside the city in a deserted place.
13 And he was silent until Jeremiah came by, for he and certain other people were
14 coming out to bury a dead man outside the city. •For Jeremiah had made a request
of King Nebuchadnezzar, saying, "Give me a place where I may bury the dead
15 of my people." And the king had given (it) to him. •And as they were going out
16 with the dead man and weeping, they passed by the eagle. •And the eagle cried
in a loud voice, saying, "I say to you, Jeremiah, chosen one of God, go! Gather
the people and come here that they may hear a letter which I have brought you
17 from Baruch and Abimelech." •And when Jeremiah heard, he glorified God, and
he went out and gathered the people with (their) wives and children, and he came
18 to where the eagle was. •And the eagle descended upon the one who had died,
19,20 and he came back to life. •This happened that they might believe. •And all the
people marveled at what had happened, saying, "Is this the God who appeared
to our fathers in the wilderness through Moses (who) has now also appeared to
21 us through this eagle?" •And the eagle said, "I say to you, Jeremiah, come untie
this letter and read it to the people." So, untying the letter, he read it to the
22 people. •And when the people heard (it), they wept and put dust on their heads,
and they said to Jeremiah, "Save us, and tell us what we should do, that we may
23 enter our city (once) again." •And Jeremiah answered and said to them, "Everything
that you have heard from the letter observe, and the LORD will lead us into our
24 city." •And Jeremiah also wrote a letter to Baruch, saying thus, "My beloved
son, do not be negligent in your prayers pleading with God in our behalf, that he

g. This is probably a reference to Christian
baptism. Note that the language of this ch. (6:7,
12f., 25) is reminiscent of Gnosticism.

7 a. This use of "the faith" to mean correct
doctrine is similar to the use of the term in the
Pastoral Epistles. See e.g. 1Tim 3:9; 4:1.

25 might speed our journey until we leave the jurisdiction of this lawless king. •For
you were found righteous before God, and he didn't allow you to come here, so   Jer 45:2-5
you wouldn't see the oppression which has befallen the people at the hands of the
26 Babylonians. •For (it is) just as (when) a father has an only son and he is handed
over for punishment; those who see his father and (are) consoling him cover his
face so he won't see how his son is being punished and be racked by grief (even)
27 more. •For God similarly had mercy on you and didn't allow you to come into
28 Babylon so you wouldn't see the oppression of the people. •For since we came
29 here, grief has not left us (even) today (after) sixty-six years! •For I would often
go out and find (some) of the people hung up by King Nebuchadnezzar weeping
30 and saying, 'Have mercy on us, God Zar!'[b] •Hearing these things, I would grieve
and would weep a double lamentation, not only because they were hung up, but
31 because they were calling upon a foreign god, saying, 'Have mercy on us.' •And
I would remember the feast days that we used to celebrate in Jerusalem before
we were taken captive, and remembering, I would groan and return to my house
32 distressed and weeping. •So pray now in the place where you are, you and
33 Abimelech, for this people, so that we may depart from here. •For I say to you
that the whole time we have been here, they have oppressed us, saying, 'Sing[c] us
34 a song from the songs of Zion, the song of your God.' •And we say to them,   Ps 137:3f.
35 'How can we sing to you, being in a foreign land?' '' •And after these things,
Jeremiah tied the letter to the neck of the eagle, saying, ''Go in peace, and may
36 the LORD watch over us both!'' •And the eagle took flight and came to Jerusalem
and gave the letter to Baruch, and after he had untied (it), he read (it) and kissed
it, and he wept when he heard about the griefs and the oppressions of the people.
37 But Jeremiah took the figs and distributed (them) to the sick among the people,
and he continued teaching them to keep away from the pollutions of the gentiles
of Babylon.

1,2 **8** But the day came in which the LORD led the people out of Babylon. •And the
LORD said to Jeremiah, ''Get up, you and the people, and come to the Jordan;
and you will say to the people, 'Let him who desires the LORD leave the works
3 of Babylon behind.' •And (of) the men who took wives from them, and the   Ezra 10:18f.
women who took husbands from them, let those who hear you cross over, and
take them up to Jerusalem; but (as for) those who do not hear you, you must not
4 lead them there.'' •And Jeremiah spoke these words to the people, and they got
5 up and came to the Jordan to cross over. •And when he told them the words
which the LORD had spoken to him, half of those who had (inter)married with
them did not want to hear Jeremiah, but said to him, ''We will not leave our
6 wives behind forever, but we will bring them with us back to our city.'' •So they
7 crossed over the Jordan and came to Jerusalem. •And Jeremiah stood (firm) with Ezra 9:12
Baruch and Abimelech, saying, ''No man who cohabits with Babylonians will   Neh 13:27
8 enter this city!'' •And they said among themselves, ''Let's get up and return to
9 Babylon, to our place.'' And they departed. •But when they came to Babylon,
the Babylonians came out to meet them, saying, ''You will not come into our
city, because you hated us and went out from us in secret; for this you will not
10 come in with us. •For we made one another swear an oath in the name of our
god to receive neither you nor your children, since you went out from us in
11 secret.'' •And when they learned this, they turned back and came to a desert place 2Kgs 17:24-41
some distance from Jerusalem, and they built themselves a city and named it
12 Samaria.[a] •And Jeremiah sent to them, saying, ''Repent, for an angel of
righteousness is coming, and he will lead you to your exalted place.''[b]

---

b. This is probably a transliteration of the Heb.
zar (''foreign''). See G. D. Kilpatrick, *JTS* 46
(1945) 141.

c. The Gk. is *eipate*, ''say.''

8 a. This conflicts with the account of Samaritan
origins found at 2Kgs 17:24–41.

b. The Christian redactor has changed the original Jewish polemic against the Samaritans into a
promise of exaltation by adding this vs.

1 **9** And those who were with Jeremiah continued for nine days rejoicing and
2 offering up sacrifices for the people. •But on the tenth (day) Jeremiah alone offered
3 up a sacrifice. •And he prayed a prayer, saying, "Holy, holy, holy, incense of
4 the living trees, true light that enlightens me until I am taken up to you; •for your
mercy I plead, for the sweet voice of the two seraphim I plead, for another fragrant
5 odor of incense. •And may Michael, the archangel of righteousness who opens
the gates for the righteous, be (the object of) my attention until he leads the
6 righteous in. •I implore you, Almighty LORD of all creation, unbegotten and
incomprehensible, in whom all judgment was hidden[a] before these things existed."
7 And as Jeremiah said these things, while standing at the altar with Baruch and
8 Abimelech, he became as one of those who have given up their soul. •And Baruch
and Abimelech remained weeping and crying in a loud voice, "Woe to us, because
9 our father Jeremiah has left us; the priest of God has departed." •And all the
people heard their weeping, and they all ran to them and saw Jeremiah lying on
10 the ground as though dead. •And they tore their garments and put dust on their
11 heads and wept bitterly.[b] •And after these things, they prepared themselves to
12 bury him. •And behold, there came a voice saying, "Do not bury one still living,
13 for his soul is coming into his body again." •And because they heard the voice,
they did not bury him but remained in a circle around his tabernacle for three
14 days, saying, "At what hour is he going to rise?" •And after three days, his soul
came into his body and he lifted up his voice in the midst of (them) all and said,
"Glorify God with one voice! All (of you) glorify God, and the Son of God who
awakens us, Jesus Christ the light of all the aeons, the inextinguishable lamp, the
15 life of faith! •And after these times there will be another four hundred and seventy-
16 seven years, and (then) he is coming to the earth. •And the tree of life which is
planted in the middle of Paradise will cause all the uncultivated trees[c] to bear
17 fruit, and they will grow and sprout. •And the trees that had (already) sprouted
and boasted and said, 'We raised our top to the air,'[d] he will cause them to wither
together with the loftiness of their branches. And the firmly rooted tree will cause
18 them to be judged! •And what is scarlet will become as white as wool; the snow
will be made black; the sweet waters will become salty, and the salty sweet in
19 the great light of the joy of God. •And he will bless the islands that they may
20 bear fruit at the word of the mouth of his anointed one.[e] •For he will come! And
he will go out and choose for himself twelve apostles, that they may preach among
the nations, he whom I have seen adorned by his father and coming into the world
21 on the Mount of Olives; and he will fill the hungry souls." •And as Jeremiah was
saying these things about the Son of God, that he is coming into the world, the
people became angry and said, "These (once) again are the words spoken by
22 Isaiah the son of Amos, saying, 'I saw God and the son of God.' •Come, therefore,
and let us not kill him by that (same) death, but let's stone him with stones."
23 Now, Baruch and Abimelech were extremely grieved because they wanted to hear
24 in full the mysteries that he had seen. •But Jeremiah said to them, "Be quiet and
do not weep, for they will not kill me until I have described to you everything
25,26 that I saw." •And he said to them, "Bring a stone here to me." •And he set it
(up) and said, "Light of the aeons, make this stone look just like me until I have
27 described everything I saw to Baruch and Abimelech." •Then the stone, by the
28 command of God, took on the likeness of Jeremiah. •And they were stoning the
29 stone, thinking that it was Jeremiah. •But Jeremiah delivered all the mysteries
that he had seen to Baruch and Abimelech, and then he simply stood in the midst
30 of the people, desiring to bring his stewardship to an end. •Then the stone cried

Ezra 8:35

Isa 6:3

Jn 1:9

Rom 15:6

Eph 2:2
1QH 8

Ezek 47:8-11
4Ezra 5:9

Jn 1:9
Acts 1:11f.

Mt 5:6; 14:19f.

AscenIs 3:9
AscenIs 4:13
AscenIs 5:11

9 a. The MSS add "in him," a redundancy that may indicate a Semitic original.

b. Lit. "wept a bitter weeping," possibly another Semitism carried over to the Gk. text.

c. I.e. gentiles.

d. Lit. "We gave our end to the air," a very

cryptic line. Kraft and Purintun render it: "We have supplied our power (?) to the air." The Gk. *aēr*, "air," may here be used in a demonological sense; cf. Eph 2:2.

e. Or "of his Christ" (used as a proper noun).

out, saying, "O stupid children of Israel, why do you stone me, thinking that I
31 am Jeremiah? Behold, Jeremiah stands in your midst!" •And when they saw him,
they immediately ran at him with many stones, and his stewardship was fulfilled. LivPro
32 And Baruch and Abimelech came and buried him, and they took the stone and
put (it) on his tomb after inscribing (it) thus: "This is the stone (that was) the ally
of Jeremiah."

JANNES AND JAMBRES

(First to Third Centuries A.D.)

A NEW TRANSLATION AND INTRODUCTION

BY A. PIETERSMA AND R. T. LUTZ

The names of Jannes and Jambres appear with considerable frequency in ancient and medieval sources, and traditions about their activity and fate are extant in Hebrew, Aramaic, Syriac, Arabic, Greek, and Latin. Christian, Jewish, and pagan writers found occasion to refer to these two magicians at the Pharaonic court who plied the art of magic in opposition to Moses.[1] Our oldest Semitic reference speaks of "Joḥana," while the earliest text of the book of Jannes and Jambres gives the names as "Joannes" (Johannes) and, by analogical formation, "Joambres," but the most common appellations of the two brothers are "Jannes" and "Jambres." In Latin and rabbinic sources, however, "Jambres," with some textual variation, becomes "Mambres."

It is now beyond doubt that in antiquity there existed, on the one hand, traditions about Jannes and Jambres, and on the other, a book that detailed some of their exploits. Not yet entirely clear, however, is the precise relationship between the loose traditions and the written composition.

The tradition

The earliest reference to our magicians occurs in the Damascus Document, fragments of which have been discovered in the Cairo Geniza and more recently at Qumran. The date of this work has been given as c. 100 B.C.[2] Apparently referring to the exodus, it states, ". . . in ancient times, Moses and Aaron arose by the hand of the Prince of Lights and Satan [Belial] in his cunning raised up Jannes [Joḥana] and his brother when Israel was first delivered."[3] Our earliest reference in Greek, the language in which most of our ancient sources were written, is 2 Timothy 3:8f., which is thought to date from the early second century A.D. Here our magicians are cited as opponents of the truth: "Men like this defy the truth just as Jannes and Jambres defied Moses: their minds are corrupt and their faith spurious. But they will not be able to go on any longer: their foolishness, like that of the other two, must become obvious to everybody."

From relative obscurity and doubtlessly due to the increasing prominence of Moses, Jannes and, to a lesser extent, Jambres achieved some prominence as magicians in the Greco-Roman world.[4]

The origin of the Jannes and Jambres tale was clearly pre-Christian, more particularly Jewish, and its base is the biblical account of the exodus, in which Pharaoh's magicians are anonymous. But though the tale is of Jewish origin—some scholars have attempted to

---

[1] Aaron, if referred to at all, is virtually never mentioned by name. For the general rise of Moses in the hellenistic and early Greco-Roman periods, which in the Jannes and Jambres tradition caused the eclipse of Aaron, see G. Vermes, "La Figure de Moïse au tournant des deux testaments," in *Moïse l'homme de l'alliance* (Paris, 1955), and Gager, *Moses in Greco-Roman Paganism*.

[2] For an English translation see G. Vermes, *The Dead Sea Scrolls in English* (Penguin Books, 1968) pp. 95–117.

[3] Vermes, *The Dead Sea Scrolls in English*, p. 102.

[4] As early as the 1st cent. A.D., Pliny (Natural History 30.2.11) speaks of Moses, Jannes, and Lotapes (= Jambres?) as magicians among the Jews. See further Apuleius, Apology 90, QuesBart 4:50 (Lat. 2), and Acts of St. Catherine (J. Viteau, Text A.4 and *passim* in Text B; cf. n. 11).

hold Artapanus (c. 100 B.C.) responsible for it[5]—the pair play an insignificant role in rabbinic literature before the ninth century A.D. Of the earlier literature, only the Talmud (Men. 85a) and Targum Pseudo-Jonathan (Ex 1:15; 7:11; Num 22:22) mention them.[6] In the Targum (Ex 1:15), they interpret a dream of Pharaoh, predict the birth of Moses, and subsequently appear as the helpers of Balaam (Num 22:22). In later Jewish tradition they become Balaam's sons. In the Talmud, Moses is derided for coming with magic to the home of magic.

Most early development of the Jannes and Jambres tale took place in a Greek (and Latin) Christian milieu. We touch here briefly on additions to the biblical Exodus, apart from the mere identification of the magicians.[7] The order that follows is basically chronological.

Of much interest is the problematic statement by the pagan writer Numenius (2nd cent. A.D.), who, in a brief passage cited in Eusebius' *Praeparatio evangelica* (9.8), says that Jannes and Jambres were able to undo, publicly, even the greatest of the disasters that Moses brought against Egypt. This assertion is the more noteworthy since Origen mentions in his *Contra Celsum* (4.51) that the same Numenius had recounted "the story concerning Moses and Jannes and Jambres," which must mean that Numenius composed more on the subject than what has been preserved in Eusebius; presumably he had based his account on extensive traditions and perhaps was acquainted with a book on Jannes and Jambres. Whatever the case, Numenius' statement clearly contradicts the biblical account according to which the magicians, hence Jannes and Jambres, were able to follow Moses' act only to the second plague inclusive (cf. Ex 8:18). Furthermore, no known ancient author shows any agreement with Numenius' aberrant claim. Consequently, it seems necessary to discount an author who, one would assume, knew well the Jannes and Jambres tale. New relevant evidence, however, has recently come to light in Pap. Chester Beatty XVI (see below, "Texts"), one fragment of which (26a[r]) contains a passage (". . . Jannes opposed Moses and . . . by doing everything they had [done]") which appears to suggest that in the Book of Jannes and Jambres the conflict between Moses (and Aaron) and Jannes, at least insofar as this involved feats of magic, was telescoped into what in the biblical account is merely the introduction to the plagues episode. There is no evidence in our available texts that the book gave a blow-by-blow account of the story of the plagues, though, admittedly, conclusions drawn from silence must be treated with due caution.

To return to Numenius, if in the book the confrontation was indeed telescoped, and since one of the Chester Beatty fragments (see also Pap. Vindob. G 29 456 verso B) clearly states that Jannes equaled Moses' achievement, Numenius may have been acquainted with Jannes and Jambres. To be sure, Numenius speaks of both Jannes and Jambres, while the fragment mentions only Jannes as directly opposing Moses, but this need not be a contradiction, since Jambres may have played a supporting role.

Naturally, no author, Christian or Jewish, who was intimately familiar with the biblical account would readily repeat the claim of Numenius, who may not have been guilty of distortion but nevertheless created the wrong impression by quoting out of context.

Philostorgius (4th/5th cent.), in addition to repeating that the magicians Jannes and Jambres were afflicted with ulcers (cf. Ex 9:11), relates that Moses sent the mother "of one of them" to her death. No mother of either, of course, appears in the biblical account, but the Vienna text as well as the Chester Beatty fragments[8] mention "the mother," not of one but of both magicians. Though Philostorgius may be suggesting that Jannes and Jambres were paternal half brothers, there is no extant tradition that contradicts their being full

---

[5] This was first proposed by J. Freudenthal, *Alexander Polyhistor* (Breslau, 1875) p. 173. See also L. E. Iselin, "Zwei Bemerkungen zu Schürer's 'Geschichte des jüdischen Volkes im Zeitalter Jesu Christi,' " *Zeitschrift für wissenschaftliche Theologie* 37 (1894) 321–26.

[6] See M. McNamara, *The New Testament and the Palestinian Targum to the Pentateuch*, pp. 90–93, and in greater detail H. L. Strack and P. Billerbeck, *Kommentar zum Neuen Testament aus Talmud und Midrasch*, vol. 3, pp. 660–64.

[7] "Addition" has been taken fairly strictly. When, for example, the Ambrosiaster (4th cent.) states that Jannes and Jambres confessed in pain that God was active in Moses (*confessi sunt cum dolore vulnerum Deum in Moyse operatum*), this is not regarded as an addition. Though the biblical story does not speak of "confession," the magicians' acknowledgment of the "finger of God" (Ex 8:19) was naturally understood as meaning just that (cf. also Cosmas Indikopleustes, *Christian Topography* 3.164 B). For the boils, see Ex 9:11. Similarly, 2Tim 3:8f. can hardly be said to go beyond the biblical account, apart from the naming of the magicians.

[8] See the discussion under "Texts."

brothers. Of further interest is that, as Philostorgius intimates, "the mother" died a violent death. This is now apparently confirmed by the Chester Beatty papyrus.

Twice in the tradition we are told that Jannes and Jambres themselves perished as a result of their confrontation with Moses. According to the *Acts of Pilate* (4th cent.), Jannes and Jambres were regarded as gods by the Egyptians but perished "together with those that believed in them" (5:1), since the signs they did were not of God. That the two had adherents is specifically stated in the Vienna (3rd cent.) and Chester Beatty (4th cent.) fragments, where they appear as "the friends." That Jannes and Jambres themselves perished is subsequently also mentioned by Abdias (6th cent.) and apparently in part is confirmed by the Chester Beatty fragments, in which Jannes seems to have died an untimely death. But though their mother seemingly perished likewise, there is no evidence that Jambres did. Further confirmation of Jannes' death comes from the British Library text (11th cent.; cf. "Texts," below), though we remain in the dark about the circumstances.

From the earliest mention of "Jannes and his brother" in the Damascus Document we encounter explicit references to the fact that our magicians were in league with the devil. In the *Testament of Solomon* (3rd/4th cent.?) a demon who, interestingly, has some connection with "the Red Sea"[9] replies to the king: "I am he who was called upon by Jannes and Jambres who fought against Moses in Egypt" (25:4). Similarly, in the later text of the *Questions of St. Bartholomew* (6th/7th cent.) Satan says, "Simon Magus, Zaroës, Arfaxir, and Jannes and Mambres are my brothers" (Lat. 2, 4:50). Of further significance here may be a statement in the *Penitence of Cyprian* (5th cent.?) in which the great magician of Antioch relates how the devil called him "a clever lad, a new Jambres, trained for service, and worthy of fellowship with himself" (§6). The implication seems to be that Jambres had enjoyed such fellowship. It is possible that Palladius (5th cent.) also meant to imply that Jannes and Jambres had been assisted by demons. In his *Lausiac History* (ch. 17) he relates that Macarius of Alexandria (4th cent.) once visited the garden-tomb (*kēpotaphion*) of Jannes and Jambres, and upon arrival was met by seventy demons who resided there. Presumably in the tomb, he found a small brass jar suspended, and outside were some empty pomegranates that had been dried up by the sun. A rusty chain lay by the well beside the tomb. The connection, however, between Jannes and Jambres and the demons is indirect at best and may in fact be non-existent.[10] Of interest is the reference to the garden-tomb, since one of the Chester Beatty fragments mentions Jannes' tomb (*mneion* for *mnēmeion*), near which, as it seems, his mother was buried.

In our extant texts there is no explicit reference to the devil's role in the opposition of Jannes and Jambres, but the last lines of a Chester Beatty fragment (26a') are suggestive. After Jannes has been struck with a fatal illness in consequence of his contest with Moses, the text continues that he "sent word to the king [saying, 'This] active [power] is of God.' Therefore I deliberately (*thelōn*) op[posed Moses]." Obviously, here we have moved well beyond the biblical account, which simply states, "So the magicians said to Pharaoh, 'This is the finger of God' " (Ex 8:19).

Though in the majority of references Jannes and Jambres are simply described as magicians—sometimes, as we saw, in explicit league with the devil—one source indicates specifically that they practiced necromancy. In the *Acts of St. Catherine* (Text B.11),[11] a work which in its present form does not antedate the tenth century but perhaps contains earlier material, we are told that Jannes and Jambres "show to those who seek to behold the persons (faces) who from of old have slept in the earth."[12]

Once, in an Arabic work of Bar Hebraeus (13th cent.), we are told that Moses was entrusted by Pharaoh's daughter to Jannes and Jambres for instruction in wisdom.

In conclusion, we briefly summarize (post-9th-cent.) rabbinic additions to the biblical account.[13] As already mentioned, from helpers of Balaam in Targum Pseudo-Jonathan,

---

[9] For Jannes and Jambres and the Red Sea episode in rabbinic literature, see Strack and Billerbeck, *Kommentar zum Neuen Testament*, vol. 3, p. 663k.

[10] For a similar story extant in Syr. but probably deriving indirectly from Palladius, see Iselin, *Zeitschrift für wissenschaftliche Theologie* 37 (1894) 321f.

[11] See J. Viteau, *Passions des Saints Écaterine et Pierre d'Alexandrine* (Paris, 1897).

[12] The term "necromancy" is employed in an untranslatable line that precedes this passage (see M. R. James, *The Lost Apocrypha of the Old Testament*, pp. 33f.).

[13] See Strack and Billerbeck, *Kommentar zum Neuen Testament*, vol. 3, pp. 660–64.

Jannes and Jambres achieve the status of sons, and together with their father are counselors of Pharaoh. It is they who are responsible for the order to destroy all newborn males of Israel, in an effort to forestall predicted ruin. When Moses nevertheless grows to manhood, they leave for Ethiopia; but, after some years, they reappear on the scene as Pharaoh's magicians, who with their craft oppose the exodus of Israel. When bested by Moses, they, against God's explicit advice, are accepted by him as proselytes. This allows them to accompany Israel out of Egypt and places them in a position to continue their animosity on the desert wanderings. Not unexpectedly, they are in the forefront of the golden-calf revolt, and as a result are put to death (cf. Ex 32:28). Alternatively, they remained with Pharaoh, went with him to the Red Sea, flew above the waters on wings they had made themselves, but perished at the hands of the archangel Michael.

In the manifestly earlier traditions about Jannes and Jambres there is little if any corroboration of these rabbinic elaborations. There is no evidence of their filial relationship to Balaam, and no connection with the Red Sea episode or desert wandering is evident.[14]

The book

That at some point in the evolution of the Jannes and Jambres tale a book was composed about them is first mentioned by Origen (3rd cent.). In reference to 2 Timothy 3:8f., he states that the information contained there is not found in "public books" (= canonical) but in an apocryphal composition entitled The Book of Jannes and Jambres.[15]

In the next century, the writer known to modern scholarship as the Ambrosiaster (4th cent.) comments directly on 2 Timothy 3:8f. and labels it "an example from the apocrypha."[16]

The so-called Gelasian Decree (6th cent.), which, among other things, contains a list of biblical books, includes, as an apocryphal book, the title *Penitence of Jannes and Jambres*.[17]

What the precise meaning is of a reference in the *Chronicle* of John of Nikiu (7th cent.), preserved only in Ethiopic, is not clear.[18] In chapter 30 of that work he writes, "Pharaoh Petissonius, who is Amosis, King of Egypt, reigned with the help of the book of the magicians Jannes and Jambres." At first glance the book appears to be *by* them (or belonging to them) rather than *about* them, but whatever the intent some book is clearly alluded to.[19]

It is now certain that a book on Jannes and Jambres not only existed in antiquity but has been preserved in fragments. Unfortunately, due to its very fragmentary state much remains disconcertingly unclear, but on the positive side it must be said that we now know much more than we did a mere decade ago. When we integrate the manuscripts, the story runs somewhat as follows:[20]

1. The king of Egypt, one assumes, has summoned his wise men to observe the growth of some miraculous tree or other plant, the branches of which have quickly formed a shelter from the sun's heat. While Jannes (?) at the behest of the king is seated under "a certain apple tree," "a great earthquake" strikes, accompanied by thunder and lightning, and the violence of the elements breaks off some of the branches of the shelter. Thereupon Jannes (as chief magician?) runs into the library in order to consult his magical books and tools.

2. Perhaps while he is engaged in his magical proceedings in the library heavenly emissaries appear to him and bring him a message from "the LORD of the earth and the

---

[14] Jannes' warning to Jambres not to accompany Pharaoh in his campaign against the "Hebrews" (see Vienna papyrus A) need not foreshadow the pursuit but perhaps ought to be so interpreted in the light of one of the Chester Beatty fragments (26gʳ). Though once again our text is too fragmentary for complete reconstruction, enough is clear to determine that at least the question of the pursuit is raised. But we do not know whether Jambres, in defiance of his brother's warning, accompanied the king. An indirect connection between our magicians and the sea episode is found in TSol, in which the demon upon whom the brothers are said to have called hails from "the Red Sea."

[15] Commentary on Matthew 27:9. The work is extant only in Lat. translation, hence the reference reads "Mambres" for "Jambres." See further on Mt 23:37.

[16] Commentary on 2 Timothy.

[17] Since it is in Lat. the names appear as "Jannes" and "Mambres."

[18] See Iselin, *Zeitschrift für wissenschaftliche Theologie* 37 (1894) 324.

[19] We may have further indication of the existence of a book in the Acts of St. Catherine Text B.11, in which the singular verb with Jannes and Jambres perhaps suggests that the reference is to a composition known as Jannes and Jambres rather than to the magicians as individuals.

[20] The outline is of necessity only tentative. As a result of more study it may well turn out that the order of some of the Chester Beatty fragments will have to be changed. See the authors' forthcoming monograph.

Overseer of the universe." They have come to remove him to Hades, where he will share the lot of the dead. However, "two clad in white" appear to grant him a respite of fourteen days (?).

3. Having comforted his mother, who apparently has fallen ill, and having committed her to the care of his friends, Jannes takes Jambres with him (from an unknown place) to Memphis, where he entrusts his brother with a book (of magic?), enjoins him to keep it secret, and warns him against participation in the king's campaign against and in pursuit of the Hebrews. He perhaps also relates to Jambres what had transpired with his mother.

4. While Jannes is delivering to his adherents an address that mentions a wedding he has attended and possibly also his previous altercations with Moses, emissaries from the palace arrive, urging him to oppose "Moses the Hebrew," who in the presence of the king has succeeded in astounding everyone with his feats. Though Jannes is able to duplicate whatever "Moses and his brother" have done, he is afflicted with "a painful ulcer" and retreats to the *hedra*, presumably his official residence, from which he presently sends word to the king explaining that the "active power of God" was operative in Moses and that he, in full knowledge of this fact, launched his opposition.

5. Jambres (and perhaps the mother of the two brothers) subsequently appears to visit Jannes, who gives him instructions for the next move. That night, however, a portent of a falling star is observed; the next morning, it is apparently interpreted (by whom our fragmentary text does not tell us) as indicating the downfall of Jannes and his adherents and as foreboding his own death.

6. Jannes presumably meets his end as a result of his "painful ulcer." He is survived by his brother and his mother, who addresses his corpse with a moving lament. Though we remain in the dark as to the manner and circumstances, it is clear that his mother follows Jannes in death; she is buried with complete ritual by her second son, Jambres, apparently next to Jannes' tomb.

7. It seems reasonable to assume that at this point in the story Jambres comes into his own as a magician. We are told that he opened the book(s) (probably the one that had earlier been entrusted to him by Jannes) near (?) the apple tree (which likewise has appeared earlier in the story), and "performed necromancy." The penitent shade of Jannes promptly makes its appearance and launches into an apparently lengthy and wide-ranging discourse admitting the justness of his punishment, warning his brother against a life that will lead to Hades, describing his abode below, relating God's displeasure with idols and idol worshipers alike, and evidently warning at length about the life that leads to hell. Perhaps Jannes, for the benefit of the reader, recaps the debacle of the opposition with appropriate paraenetic commentary along the way. What became of Jambres we do not know.

Texts

Jannes and Jambres is extant only in fragmentary form. Scholars have long been acquainted with British Library, Cotton, Tiberius B.V., fol. 87. First edited in 1861, this text in Latin (plus Anglo-Saxon translation) and accompanied by two illustrations was brought to renewed scholarly attention in 1901 by M. R. James.[21] The date of the British Library fragment is eleventh century A.D.

In Greek we possess Pap. Vindob. G 29 456 verso of the Nationalbibliothek in Vienna, which comprises four fragments (A–D) and has been dated to the third century A.D. As a basis for translation, we have used P. Maraval's edition[22] as well as photographs kindly supplied by H. Loebenstein of the Nationalbibliothek in Vienna.

Further fragments in Greek are in the possession of the Chester Beatty Library and Gallery of Oriental Art, Dublin.[23] Seven frames include a total of ninety-three fragments, the vast

[21] M. R. James, "A Fragment of the 'Penitence of Jannes and Jambres,' " *JTS* 2 (1901) 572–77. A year later, an improved text was published by M. Förster in "Das lateinisch-altenglische Fragment der Apokryphe von Jamnes und Mambres," *Archiv für das Studium der neueren Sprachen und Literaturen* 108 (1902) 15–28.

[22] P. Maraval, "Fragments grecs du Livre de Jannès et Jambré (Pap. Vindob. 29456 et 29828 Verso)," *Zeitschrift für Papyrologie und Epigraphik* 25 (1977) 199–207.

[23] Cf. A. Pietersma, "Greek and Coptic Inedita of the Chester Beatty Library," *Bulletin of the International Organization for Septuagint and Cognate Studies* 7 (1974) 10–18.

majority of which are too small either for reconstruction of the papyrus or for translation. The date of the Chester Beatty fragments is fourth century A.D. or perhaps somewhat earlier. Though the official designation is now Pap. Chester Beatty XVI, the numbers of the individual frames that appear with the present translation have no official status and hence are subject to change.

The argument of K. Koch that a passage in Targum Pseudo-Jonathan on Exodus 1:15 constitutes an insertion from Jannes and Jambres has been convincingly refuted by C. Burchard.[24] We have therefore not included the passage in our edition of Jannes and Jambres.

A.-M. Denis cites a passage from Philostorgius that in his judgment is a quotation from our book.[25] This seems unlikely not only because the wording of the passage suggests a reference rather than a quotation but also because the statement that Moses sent the mother "of one of them" to her death contradicts our extant fragments, which make it clear that Jannes and Jambres were sons of the same mother. This passage, therefore, like that of Pseudo-Jonathan, has been ignored for our edition of Jannes and Jambres.

In addition to an enumeration of extant texts, mention should be made here of the possibility that more than one version of the book existed. When one compares the Latin fragment in the British Library with the parallel Chester Beatty text (24afp^r), it becomes readily apparent that the two are not identical. The differences, however, are not so great that they cannot be explained by the fact that the former was lifted out of its original context and modified accordingly. Yet there is some evidence to suggest that more than one version of our book was in circulation. By a remarkable coincidence, Pap. Vindob. G 29 456 verso, fragment B, parallels Pap. Chester Beatty XVI 26a (part of recto and continued on verso). Initially, the Vienna papyrus merely shows some expansion: "wonder" (or "signs," but not both) of Pap. Chester Beatty is "signs and wonders" in Pap. Vindob., and "Moses and his brother" of the former becomes "Moses and his brother Aaron" in the latter. However, from approximately that point onward the two texts, though similar and even identical at times, go their own separate ways. Naturally, much is uncertain because of the state of the papyri, but that the two texts diverge quite markedly is not subject to debate.

Original language

In consequence of his argument that a fragment in Pseudo-Jonathan belongs to Jannes and Jambres, Koch has attempted to uncover Semitisms in the Latin fragment at the British Library—the only text known to scholars at the time of Koch's writing—but his arguments in support of an Aramaic original are not convincing. Particularly when one remembers the influence of the Septuagint, one is hesitant to posit a Semitic original in order to explain the phenomenon of clauses linked simply by "and . . . and" and the occurrence of "saying" after the finite verb *respondit* ("he answered"). Similar Septuagintalisms exist in our newly discovered Greek texts, but these are insufficient to prove that the original language of the book is Semitic. Certain other features point in a different direction, e.g. the use of the particle *te* as a connective not simply of word pairs but of coordinate clauses as well, and the appearance of the so-called historical present.

Our oldest texts of Jannes and Jambres are in Greek and there is as yet no good reason to believe that the original language of the composition was other than Greek.

Date

The usual difficulty in dating literature of the kind we are concerned with is compounded by the extremely fragmentary nature of the text. The Vienna fragments are third century A.D., and Pap. Chester Beatty XVI was written at most a century later. When we add to this evidence the fact that Origen (c. 185–c. 254) specifically mentions the existence of an apocryphal book on Jannes and Jambres, whence, according to him, the information in 2 Timothy 3:8 derives, it becomes clear that the latest possible date of our book is the middle of the third century A.D. The earliest possible date, however, is more difficult to determine.

---

[24] K. Koch, "Das Lamm, das Ägypten vernichtet. Ein Fragment aus Jannes und Jambres und sein geschichtlicher Hintergrund," *ZNW* 57 (1966) 79–93. C. Burchard, "Das Lamm in der Waagschale," *ZNW* 57 (1966) 219–28.
[25] A.-M. Denis, *Fragmenta Pseudepigraphorum quae supersunt graeca*, p. 69.

Several scholars have thought that the book is pre-Christian. J. Bidez and F. Cumont,[26] for example, date it back to hellenistic times, and E. Schürer argued that,

> ... as it is probable that those anonymous personages owed their name and individuality first of all to the apocryphal book itself, we may perhaps venture to refer the date of the composition of this work to pre-Christian times.[27]

These scholars may well be correct, but proof still eludes us. Even if in its present form the book is Christian, that in no way precludes an originally (pre-Christian) Jewish composition.[28]

Possible evidence for Jannes and Jambres as a Christian book is as follows: (1) In fragment B of the Vienna papyrus (l. 8), the word *chiazein* occurs, the basic meaning of which is "to form (the Greek letter) chi." It need mean no more than "to cross out" or "to mark with an *X*" but could possibly be a reference to the cross.[29] Unfortunately the context is no aid to interpretation, hence the evidential value of the word is slight.[30] Furthermore, only the Vienna text but not the basically parallel text of Chester Beatty has the reading in question. (2) Chester Beatty 23e recto, line 2, reads apparently "this one having descended to Ha[des . . .]," which may be a reference to the descent of Christ. The remainder of the sentence might run "[did not] die," but again we cannot go beyond the realm of the possible. Other interpretations can be adduced. (3) Perhaps the best argument for Jannes and Jambres, in its present form, as a Christian book lies in its apparent literary form. If our ordering of the material is even approximately correct and if the Gelasian Decree has reference to our book, Jannes and Jambres is essentially a confession (*poenitentia*), a genre of literature that was manifestly Christian but not Jewish.[31]

Provenance

As has already been mentioned,[32] Freudenthal sought to connect the Jannes and Jambres tale with the Jewish historian Artapanus, basing his argument on the fact that Numenius, who is said by Origen to have composed "the story of Moses and Jannes and Jambres," called Moses by his hellenized name, Musaeus, as did Artapanus. His argument, however, was judged inconclusive by Schürer, who stated that "the names of the magicians, which in all probability are Semitic, seem rather to point to a Palestinian origin."[33] Subsequently Iselin[34] attempted to strengthen Freudenthal's argument by claiming that "Aristomenes," in Bar Hebraeus, is a corruption of "Artapanus." Hence Bar Hebraeus is made to yield that Paul in 2 Timothy 3:8 is dependent on Artapanus.

By extension, if Artapanus was the originator of the Jannes and Jambres tradition, perhaps he in fact wrote the book, or at any rate the book might be presumed to have been written

---

[26] J. Bidez and F. Cumont, *Les Mages hellénisés* (Paris, 1938) vol. 2, p. 22.

[27] E. Schürer, *History*, vol. 3, p. 149.

[28] Of some interest and possible significance is the fact that both our Gk. fragments and 2Tim 3:8 use the verb *anthistanai*, "to withstand," in describing the magicians' opposition to Moses. This verb, admittedly a logical but scarcely the sole choice (it does not appear in the biblical account), is found only in authors who can be presumed to have been familiar with 2Tim. Numenius, for example, used *paristanai* and TSol *machesthai*. However, even if there be a question of literary dependence, we have no way of knowing who influenced whom.

[29] Cf. G. W. H. Lampe, p. 1525, and LSJM, p. 1991.

[30] The verb *chiazein* in Plato's *Timaeus* was thought by Justin Martyr to refer to the cross; a similar interpretation would be possible for Jannes and Jambres even if no reference to the cross was intended. One is invariably reminded here of a passage in James (*Lost Apocrypha*, p. 34) in which he comments on references to Jannes and Jambres in the Gk. Acts of St. Catherine:

> The other [of two passages] is better [i.e. more intelligible]: "But concerning the mountains (*sic*—?mules) Jannes and Jambres spake, signifying the sign of the manger of the Lord; and concerning the stone whereby the stone of the tomb (*a verb is wanted*) . . ." If this is a genuine quotation at all (and one from the Sibyl which precedes it is correct) it implies Messianic, even Christian, predictions in the book.

(For the Gk. text of James's reference, see Viteau, *Passions de Saints Écaterine*, p. 33 [= Text B §11]). Though James incautiously fails to distinguish between what Jannes and Jambres may have contained and how the book was interpreted, it appears to have been at least open to Christian interpretation.

[31] See further below.

[32] See n. 5.

[33] Schürer, *History*, p. 150.

[34] See n. 5.

in Egypt. But thus far no convincing argument has been made for Artapanus as the originator of the tradition. Though it is *a priori* not unlikely that Artapanus would have created the tale, in view of his obvious interest in Moses, what seems to contradict this possibility is the fact that we do possess, in Eusebius, Artapanus' connected narrative of the confrontation, but Jannes and Jambres are not mentioned.[35] Of course Artapanus may have written a separate work on the two magicians, but in that instance is it credible that in his survey he did not even mention their names?

Of some *possible* significance is the fact that, in our texts, the center of action seems to be Memphis,[36] the Old Kingdom capital, whereas in the biblical account no city is mentioned by name. Memphis also plays the central role in Artapanus and Philo,[37] but this city of ancient fame and lasting prestige would admittedly be the logical choice for any author with historical sense who tried to place Moses historically.

Since our earliest texts of Jannes and Jambres were found in Egypt and since our book is first mentioned by an Alexandrian author, the burden of proof may be assumed to lie with those who wish to advocate a Palestinian origin for the composition. The place of origin of the tradition, in distinction from our book, is another question.

Theological importance

The fragmentary nature of our text makes it hazardous, if not impossible, to arrive at definitive theological conclusions. Some tentative observations, however, may be made. That Jannes and Jambres may have relevance for the question of forgiveness will be noted below.

Jannes and Jambres clearly evidences continued Jewish (if the work was Jewish in origin) and Christian interest in necromancy, though in our book as well as in the Old Testament it is condemned, if only by association with the opponents of Moses. It may well be, however, that when the Chester Beatty text comments on idolatry (22aᵛ), its primary and perhaps only referent is necromancy. But for this there is no absolute proof. We may have no more than a general condemnation of idolatry, necromancy included, which is well attested in early literature of both religions.

Further noteworthy items are mentioned here only in passing. Astrological interest appears in a passage that seemingly links the impending death of Jannes to a falling star (26aᵛ). God is spoken of as *episkopos* (25aᵛ), a term which, though well enough attested in early literature, is relatively rare as a divine epithet.[38] Hades appears to be described as the great equalizer which obliterates all distinction between king and pauper (22jᵛ).[39] Heavenly emissaries are sent to remove Jannes to Hades (25aᵛ),[40] but "two clad in white" win him a reprieve, and the mother apparently addresses the corpse of Jannes (24bʳ).

Relation to canonical books

As indicated at least as early as the Pseudo-Jonathan tradition, the Jannes and Jambres tale takes its point of departure from the biblical account of the contest between Moses and Pharaoh's court magicians in the plague narrative of Exodus 7 and 8. Later elaboration, though not present in our fragmentary text, links these two magicians to the birth of Moses (Ex 1–2), the crossing of the Red Sea (Ex 14), the golden calf incident (Ex 32), and the oracles of Balaam (Num 22–24). Jannes and Jambres are not named in the biblical story, nor are they ever referred to anywhere else in the Old Testament.

Not until the New Testament do we again meet any reference to these two antagonists of

---

[35] See Denis, *Fragmenta*, pp. 189–95. [Also see J. J. Collins' contribution on Artapanus in the Supplement. — J.H.C.]

[36] See Vienna papyrus fragment A.

[37] Its precise role in Josephus is unclear (*Ant* 2.240).

[38] See, e.g., 1Clement 59:3 and SibOr "Fragments" l. 3 (J. Geffcken, *Die Oracula Sibyllina* [GCS; Leipzig, 1902; reprint Amsterdam, 1970] p. 227.), Olympiodorus' fragmentary commentary on Job (PG 93.221A), and in earlier classical literature *Iliad* 22.255 and Sophocles, *Antigone* 217.

[39] Cf. Job 3:11–19 and Isa 14:9–11.

[40] Cf. the angel who announces death in TAb.

Moses. In the often quoted verses 2 Timothy 3:8f., the author of the epistle compares false Christian teachers to Jannes and Jambres. As the latter defied truth when they opposed Moses, so the former defy truth when they champion a pattern of behavior contrary to accepted Christian standards. The end result for them will be the same as that of Jannes and Jambres. Knowledge of the tradition is assumed, but no information apart from their names is provided.

Relation to apocryphal books

It has been suggested above that Jannes and Jambres in its present form is a confession or penitence (*poenitentia*), as it is labeled in the Gelasian Decree in distinction from Origen, who calls it simply "Book of Jannes and Jambres" (Mambres). This decree lists immediately preceding our book the *Penitence of Origen* and the *Penitence of (Saint) Cyprian*, and earlier on the *Penitence of Adam*. Of these only the *Penitence of Cyprian* has survived; James, more than seventy-five years ago, suggested a connection between the two books:

> In one of the writings classed with it [i.e. the *Penitence of Jannes and Jambres*] in the Gelasian Decree, the *Penitence of Cyprian*, we see a document calculated to give us a fair idea of the nature of what is gone [i.e. lost of Jannes and Jambres]. Cyprian, the hero of the *Penitence*, is the wizard of Antioch . . . and in his work he tells—with a quantity of interesting detail—the story of his initiation into the black art, and his practice of it, and its failure when confronted with the power of the true God. Very much the same would the contents of the *Penitence* of the two Egyptian magicians have been, only it is doubtful whether they or at least both of them, made so fine an end as Cyprian.[41]

James's surmise seems to have been correct in general terms; it is now confirmed by new evidence, though obvious differences between the two works exist, not the least of which is the fact that whereas Cyprian's is a totally retrospective account, by the protagonist himself in the first person, of his initiation into and the practice of magic, in Jannes and Jambres the confession, apparently put in the mouth of Jannes, who speaks from the realm of the dead, is preceded by a third-person narrative that details the conflict between the two brothers and Moses. From the point of view of literary form, Cyprian's would seem to be the more developed penitence.

In the course of his lament over past misdeeds, Cyprian repeatedly expresses his belief and fear that God will not forgive him, and in one of his despairing utterances he exclaims as follows:

> I do not believe that He forgives me. For I am not convinced that a man worse than I has been born, seeing that I surpassed the well-known Jannes and Jambres. They when they practised magic acknowledged the finger of God, but I was convinced that God did not exist. If God did not forgive them, when they recognized him in part, how can He forgive me since I totally ignored him.[42]

James has placed what may be termed a Faustian interpretation on this passage by suggesting that the two brothers did not obtain pardon.[43] There is, however, no completely compelling reason for drawing this inference. The passage may simply mean that, as a result of their opposition to Moses (God), Jannes and Jambres perished; but this punishment does not exclude ultimate forgiveness. Alternatively, Cyprian may simply be drawing an inference, either from the Exodus account or from the Book of Jannes and Jambres. Yet there is possibly some support for the idea that the book explicitly dealt with the question of forgiveness. In a passage of Pap. Chester Beatty XVI (23fᵛ), which appears to be part of Jannes' confession and touches on his present plight in Hades, we read: "and now there is for us no forgiveness." But be it noted once again that our text is very fragmentary!

---

[41] James, *JTS* 2 (1901) 575.
[42] *Penitence of Cyprian*, para. 17.
[43] James, *JTS* 2 (1901) 576.

Cultural importance

Whether we have in Jannes and Jambres another tale, in addition to those of Simon Magus, Cyprian of Antioch, and Theophilus of Adana,[44] that was a forerunner of the Faust legend is still relatively obscure.[45] Very interesting in this connection is a passage in the Chester Beatty papyrus to which we have already referred twice, namely 26a[r]. Here it is stated that precisely because Jannes knew that Moses' power was from God, he launched his opposition. We have already noted that this comment goes well beyond the biblical account; but perhaps we are justified in going one step further. Implicitly, though perhaps not explicitly, we may be dealing here with a "pact with the devil," which is an integral part of the Faust tradition; but in the pre-Faust legends it is not attested earlier than the story of Theophilus of Adana (7th–9th cent.). Similarly, like the end of Faust, the fate of Jannes (and Jambres?) may have been intended as a warning to the believers.

SELECT BIBLIOGRAPHY

Charlesworth, *PMR*, pp. 133f.
Delling, *Bibliographie*, p. 165.
Denis, *Introduction*, pp. 146–49.

TEXTS AND ALLEGED TEXTS

Denis, A.-M. *Fragmenta Pseudepigraphorum quae supersunt graeca.* PVTG 3; Leiden, 1970; p. 69.
Förster, M. "Das lateinisch-altenglische Fragment der Apokryphe von Jamnes und Mambres," *Archiv für das Studium der neueren Sprachen und Literaturen* 108 (1902) 15–28.
James, M. R. "A Fragment of the 'Penitence of Jannes and Jambres,' " *JTS* 2 (1901) 572–77.
————. *The Lost Apocrypha of the Old Testament.* London and New York, 1920; pp. 31–38.
Koch, K. "Das Lamm, das Ägypten vernichtet. Ein Fragment aus Jannes und Jambres und sein geschichtlicher Hintergrund," *ZNW* 57 (1966) 79–93.
Maraval, P. "Fragments grecs du Livre de Jannès et Jambré (Pap. Vindob. 29456 et 29828 Verso)," *Zeitschrift für Papyrologie und Epigraphik* 25 (1977) 199–207.

GENERAL

Gager, J. G. *Moses in Greco-Roman Paganism.* Nashville, 1972.
McNamara, M. *The New Testament and the Palestinian Targum to the Pentateuch.* Analecta Biblica 27; Rome, 1966; pp. 82–96.
Pietersma, A. "Greek and Coptic Inedita of the Chester Beatty Library," *Bulletin of the International Organization for Septuagint and Cognate Studies* 7 (1974) 10–18.
Schürer, E. *A History of the Jewish People in the Time of Jesus Christ,* Eng. rev. ed. Edinburgh, 1885–91; §32.3.
Strack, H. L. and Billerbeck, P. *Kommentar zum Neuen Testament aus Talmud und Midrasch.* Munich, 1926; vol. 3, pp. 660–64.

[44] Cf. P. M. Palmer and R. P. More, *The Sources of the Faust Tradition* (New York, 1936), and with Gk. texts L. Radermacher, *Griechische Quellen zur Faustsage* (Sitzungsberichte der Akademie der Wissenschaften in Wien; phil.-histor. Klasse, Bd. 206, Abhandlung 4, Vienna, Leipzig, 1927).

[45] See the very suggestive title of a paper delivered by H. Chadwick at the 14th International Congress of Papyrologists, "The Penitence of Jannes and Jambres: The Origins of the Faust Legend," *Proceedings of the XIV International Congress of Papyrologists, Oxford, 24–31 July 1974* (London, 1975) x.

FRAGMENTS FROM
THE BOOK OF JANNES AND JAMBRES

Pap. Chester Beatty XVI

25aʳ

       ] all [
       ] having summoned [
his servants], both [the] wise men an[d the
magicians, and after] seven [day]s when he was w[alking] about
i]n [his] ho[use] and saw [
the plant flourish [and] that the
bra]nches were already providing shade [
And when he had become [   ] he ordered [
to sit(?) under a certain apple tree (*mēlea*)
And [when he was seated] there, a great earthquake occurred
and from heaven (came) [the sound] of thunder and
lightning], so that some branches of the
shelter [broke off]. When he saw what had happened
Jannes ran into the library
where [his] magical tools were
      (bottom of page)

25aᵛ

      ] they(?) came [
c]lothed [
t]he two having [
      (remnants of two lines)
      ] to him and sa[y
ing, the LORD of the earth and (the) Overseer [of the
universe] has sent us to lead you away [to Hades
Henceforth [you will be] a companion of the dead.
Forever [you will be] pitied.
Then] the two clad in white said,
Let there be granted to him] still fourteen days(?)
in his house and after that [
      (bottom of page)

21aʳ

      (top of page)
      (remnants of two lines)
And when Jambres knew [
      (remnants of six lines)
les]t bi[tter
] each day [
      (remnants of two lines)

      ] to heed you
faithfully. [Then he approached
and kissed he]r, fi[ghting back
his tears]. [
      ] let [his tears] flow.

Pap. Vindob. G 29 456ᵛ (fragment A)

      ] lest bitter [
      ] I shall send t[o
      ] and you [
and also to Joambres my brother to
attend to you (and) to heed you
faithfully. Then he approached
and kissed her, fighting back
his] tears. When she had left he
      ] let his tears flow. And [he took
leave of?] his friends having
urged them all [to ca]re for
his mother. (Then) he took his
brother with him to Memphis

21aᵛ

(top of page)
] Keep it
secret, a[nd take heed so as not
to go forth] on the day when
the king] marches out with the
grandees of [Egypt against] the
peop[le of the Hebrews, and do
not accompany t]hem [
      ] and [the] soul
      (remnants of two lines)
      God] heav[en(?)
      (remnants of one line)
our mother [
      (remnants of one line)
I (they?) said to her [
      k]ing [
When [our] mother had left [
      ] from death [

and ha[nded him the] book.
He said, Brother, I am [passing
on to you] a document. Keep it
secret, and ta[ke heed so as not
to go [forth] on the day when
the king] marches out [with] the
grandees of Egypt [against the
peo]ple of the Hebrews, and do
not acco[mpany them]. And [
to be ill and the [soul
from death and from(?) [
      ] God heaven [
      (bottom of column)

26aʳ

(top of page)
to/at a wedding and the [
for seven [da]ys [we] en[joyed ourselves.
Men and brothers, after(?) [
I took up position(?) against a [certain] Hebrew.
And when he had [not yet] finished [speaking
emissaries came [from the palace
saying, Come quickly [and
oppose] Moses the Hebrew who is
per[forming wonders] to the
amazement of all. [And in the
presence] of the king, Jannes
opposed Moses and [his brother
by doing everything they had
done. Then the] fatal disease
struck him] on the spot,
[and with a painful ulcer he]
w[ent] to the *hedra* and a[fter a
while] sent word
to the king
[saying, This] active [power] is
of God. Therefore I deliberately
opposed [Moses

Pap. Vindob. G 29 456ᵛ (fragment B)
op]pose Moses the Hebr[ew who is
performing si]gns and wonders to the
amazement] of all. And in the
presence [of the ki]ng, he
opposed Moses and his brother Aaron
by doing everything t[hey had
done]. Then the fatal disease
struck [him on the spot,
and] with a painful ulcer [he
went] to the [*hedra*
      ] to mark with a chi [
to] the king,
saying, This [is
the finger of God]. Indeed
I am unable [

26aᵛ

(top of page)
      [not
to g]rieve [him.] And [
            because/that
he [haz]arded in the daytime(?)

      ] therefore regarding money/
            possessions [
      ] against us. Make ready
      (remnants of three lines)

      ] except unto death [
Joannes [called his] brother [
and] urged him [   ] not
to grie[ve] him [
            because/that
he hazarded [
      (remnants of one line)
      ] money/possessions and [

      ] us. Make ready [
      ] for the spirit [
] that/because si[gns

] through (a) spi[rit
] his brother [
    (remnants of one line)
    (bottom of column)

] for the morning and [   ]
al]l the things being observed [
] he made inquiry at what hour
he saw the] setting of the star [
] he said, Such is a
generation [of lying li]ps and deceitful hearts
] of the hour of [his] death
] Come and see how long [
] and he said to him nothing

26gʳ

(remnants of one line)
] after this [
] to pursue the p[eople of the Hebrews
(remnants of two lines)
] Egypt [
] and of the people [
] weeping [
] Jambres [
(remnants of two lines)

26gᵛ

(remnants of one line)
] the oaths which [   ] swore [
] your [
] and when Jannes [
] he said to [his] brother [
(remnants of one line)
] hundred thou[sand
] hundred fo[als
] hundred [ca]mels [
(remnants of three lines)

25hʳ

    (top of page)
] and a noise
] and he said
] h[is] b[roth]er
(remnants of one line)

25hᵛ

    (top of page)
my/of me is perishing and [
my whole body has been agit[ated
his brother Jambre[s
    ] and [Jann]es op[posed

24bᵛ

    (top of page)
When Joannes heard [
of the king he encouraged/advised [all the
other friends. [And his mother] cri[ed out say
ing [   ] and my son J[

24cᵛ

(remnants of two lines)
] and when [his] mot[her
] (s)he was amazed a[nd
] if to him and [
] he had preferred [
(remnants of one line)

24afp^v

(remnants of one line)
] when [his] mother [ca]me [she
approached hi]m to kiss him [
] from her and [
he said to he]r, Stay back, mother, [
] on account of the fire (= fever?) I am unable [
I am in] much [pain], mother. Then [his mother
] said [
] he replied [
] you took the trouble, mother, [to come] to me [
(remnants of two lines)
to hi]m, I will go to [
(remnants of five lines)

24b^r

(top of page)
I saw [the] dead and no one
resembled] you, child. Lie(?) here
] your appearance [   ] has been utterly changed
] child, you are a corpse, for
your tongue] and your lips are not moving
and] your [knuc]kles are not [

24c^r

Jambres [
and weeping(?)]
I(?) have been deprived [
(remnants of one line)
] and money [
(remnants of one line)

24afp^r

(remnants of one line)
] the spirit [
] his mother(?) [
] the tomb of his brother a[nd
her] abandoned(?) corpse and [having performed the] complete funeral rites he buried h[er
his] mother Jamb[res

having op]ened the b[ook near(?)	Brit. Lib., Cotton, Tiberius B.V., fol. 87
the apple tree per[formed]	Mambres opened the magical books
necromancy	of his brother Jannes; he performed
	necromancy
and] brought up from Ha[des	and brought up from the netherworld
his brother's shade, and [the soul	his brother's shade. The soul
of Jannes said to [his]	of Jannes said in response,
brother Jambres	I your brother did not die
(remnants of seven lines)	unjustly, but indeed justly,
(bottom of page)	and the judgment will go
	against me, since I was more
	clever than all clever magicians,
	and opposed the two brothers,
	Moses and Aaron, who performed
	great signs and wonders.
	As a result I died and was
	brought from among (the living)
	to the netherworld where there is
	great burning and the pit of
	perdition, whence no ascent is
	possible. Now then, brother Mambres,

make sure you do good in
your life to your children and
friends; for in the netherworld
no good exists, only gloom and
darkness. After you will have
died and have come to the
23aᵛ   netherworld, among the dead,
     your abode   your abode will be two cubits wide
     cubits   and four cubits long
     (remnants of nine lines)

23bᵛ

     (remnants of one line)
     ] cubits [
     (remnants of three lines)
     tho]se who do not do evil [
     (remnants of six lines)

23eᵛ

     (remnants of one line)
     ] where are (the) sons [
     ] Egypt and on account of the [
     (remnants of two lines)

23fᵛ

     (remnants of four lines)
     ] and we are descending [
     ] but now(?) there is no
forgiveness for us(?) [
     (remnants of two lines)
     ] and friends [
     ] for the gates of [
     the] dumb and [
     (bottom of page)

23bʳ

     (remnants of six lines)
     ] of us/our [
     (remnants of two lines)
     ] the *oikoum[ene*
     ] unab[le
     ] corrupti[on

23eʳ

     ] fo[r] he knew [
This one having descended to Ha[des . . . d
ied. These [
     (remnants of two lines)

23fʳ

     (remnants of four lines)
our limbs [
full of darkness [
we are burning(?) [
nothing [
we [
to give it(?) [
     (bottom of page)

22aᵛ

     (remnants of one line)
We who w]orshiped ido[ls and
carved images until we came [to de
struction together with [our] idols, [for neither

the idols nor their worship[ers does
God the King [of the earth love(?)
and in Hades no one, not even [
     (remnants of one line)

22b^v

  ] the wretched one(?) [
  (remnants of three lines)
  ] practiced sorcery [
  ] commit perjury [

22c^v

  (remnants of six lines)
  ] money len[der
  ] my [br]other [

22j^v

in] Hades not even a kin[g
  ] excels [
  ] equality/fair dealing, just ones [
  (remnants of one line)
  ] having opposed [
  ] of the earth [
  ] the mighty one [
t]orture [

22ab^r

  (remnants of three lines)
  ] of [th]e children nor of the [
  ] the soul [
  ] fornication. Nothing [
  ] very gladly he sins and [
  (remnants of one line)
  ] brothe[r

22c^r

  (remnants of one line)
  ] she [
b]ut grief [
  ] the wom[an
  ] evil [
  (remnants of two lines)
for]nication [
  (remnants of one line)

22k^r

  (remnants of one line)
Pha]raoh kin[g
  (remnants of one line)

22m^r

  (remnants of one line)
  ] of God [

HISTORY OF THE RECHABITES

(First to Fourth Centuries A.D.)

A NEW TRANSLATION AND INTRODUCTION

BY J. H. CHARLESWORTH

The History of the Rechabites in its present form recounts the visit of a virtuous man, named Zosimus in some passages, to the island of the Blessed Ones. For forty years this man has entreated God to show him the abode of the Blessed Ones. God answers his prayer, and with the guidance of an angel and supernatural assistance from an animal and two trees he is able to journey over the great ocean and a dense cloud to an island that resembles paradise (chs. 1–3). The man meets the Blessed Ones, who become so oppressively inquisitive about him that he asks his attendant to inform visitors: "He is not here." This request causes a mild sensation, and an assembly asks this liar, a "man of sin," to go away. After pleas for forgiveness the man receives mercy. He then asks the Blessed Ones concerning their history (chs. 4–7).

The Blessed Ones inform him that they are the Rechabites who, by the help of the angels of God, departed Jerusalem for the present island in the time of Jeremiah (chs. 8–10). They describe themselves, their occupation, and their blessed state, and report that angels dwell with them (chs. 11–12:9). The account also mentions the virginal birth of the Word and Lent (chs. 12:9a–13:5c), describes the paradisaic state they enjoy, and with considerable detail defines the death of the body and ascent of the soul (chs. 14:1a–16:8g). The traveler then returns to the shore of the sea, and with the help of the two trees passes over the cloud and the sea, and finally the (apparently same) animal carries him back to his cave (chs. 17:1–18:4).

Texts

The History of the Rechabites was once very popular and is now extant in many ancient languages, of which the most important are the Ethiopic, the Greek, and the Syriac. The present translation, the first English rendering of the latter,[1] aims at being idiomatic without sacrificing the flavor of the Syriac. The base of the translation is manuscript A,[2] Syriac 236 (*olim* Supplément 28, Saint-Germain 125.), of the Bibliothèque Nationale.[3] This manuscript was copied near the end of the twelfth century.[4] Significant variants in B (Syr. 235 [*olim*

---

[1] An English translation of the Eth. was published by E. A. W. Budge (*The Life and Exploits of Alexander the Great*, London, 1896; vol. 2, pp. 555–84), and of the Gk. by W. A. Craigie ("The Narrative of Zosimus Concerning the Life of the Blessed," *ANF* 10, pp. 220–24). A French translation of the Syr. was published by F. Nau ("La Légende inédite des fils de Jonadab, fils de Réchab, et les îles fortunées," *Revue sémitique* 7 [1899] 136–46). For further bibliographical information see Charlesworth, *PMR*, pp. 223–28. An edition and literal translation of the Gk., Syr., and Eth. will be published by Charlesworth, Martin, and Wintermute in the SBL T&T Pseudepigrapha Series.

[2] Nau also based his translation upon MS A; but he placed in his text and translation variants from other MSS. Frequently he did not note the source of the reading.

[3] HistRech appears on fols. 328a–37b; these are well preserved and of paper. A description is published in H. Zotenberg, *Catalogues des manuscrits syriaques et sabéens (mandaïtes) de la Bibliothèque Nationale* (Paris, 1874) pp. 187f.

[4] Fol. 364a, l. 8 down: "*These histories (or biographies) are completed by the help (lit. helps) of our Lord*"; l. 11 down: "in the year 1505 of the Greeks."

Ancien fonds 144.] of the Bibliothèque Nationale, of the 13th cent. and of paper),[5] in C (Syr. 234 [*olim* Ancien fonds 143, Colbert 5137.], also of the Bibliothèque Nationale, of the 13th cent. and of paper),[6] and in D (BM Add. 12174 of the British Museum, of the 12th cent. and of vellum)[7] are placed in the notes.[8]

Original language, date, and provenance

It is unwise to state the probable original language, date, or provenance of this document until critical editions of the Greek, Syriac, and Ethiopic texts are available.[9] A few observations and speculations, however, are warranted. The Syriac version, as the notes to the translation below indicate, may well have been translated from a Greek text; but some of it may go back to an earlier, Semitic source. Work on the Greek version suggests a complex picture: Some sections appear to have been composed in Greek, others indicate possible translation from a Semitic text, which could be the original language of the earliest portions. This opinion, obtained from years of work on the two major versions, the Syriac and the Greek, receives stunning endorsement from the rubrical preface to this section of manuscript D (fols. 209r–210v): "*The History of the Blessed Ones, the Sons of the Rechabites . . . It Was Translated from Hebrew into Greek and from Greek into Syriac by the Hands of the Reverend Mar Jacob of Edessa.*"[10]

The date of the History of the Rechabites is the crucial issue, and it is related to the Jewish or Christian character of the various sections. In its *present* form the work may date from the sixth century A.D., as M. R. James contended.[11] Comparison of the Syriac manuscripts reveals that the document, like many pseudepigrapha (viz. 4Ezra), has received interpolations by Christians; the same observation results from a mere cursory examination and comparison of the Greek manuscripts, and by the recognition that the Greek is expanded by chapters 19 through 23, which are certainly Christian. The Ethiopic, moreover, has been extensively expanded by scribes who were obviously Christian.[12] Some of the present document is Christian, but the Christian interpolations—sometimes found in only one manuscript—raise the possibility that 12:9a–13:5c and 16:1b–8 are not original but a Christian insertion into an earlier document. This hypothetical earlier writing could be a Christian revision of inherited Jewish traditions, or it could be a Christian expansion of an original (partly preserved) Jewish document. James,[13] A. Zanolli,[14] Nau,[15] G. Graf,[16] L.

---

[5] HistRech begins on fol. 84b (left col.); it ends on fol. 91b (right col.): "*The history of the sons of Rechab ends.*" Cf. Zotenberg, *Catalogues*, pp. 185–87. Fol. 341b, right col., l. 7 down: "*It ends by the help of our Lord . . . ,*" l. 16 down: "of the year 1603 of the Greeks."

[6] HistRech appears on fols. 61a (right col.) to 62a (left col.); as Zotenberg said, it is a "résumé de la vision de Zosime, relative aux Réchabites." Cf. Zotenberg, *Catalogues*, pp. 182–85. In the middle margin of 344b is found "In the year 1505 this book is completed, the living words, in the year 1603 of the Greeks." MS C differs considerably from MS A, most notably, besides being an epitome, in the placing of the history of the Rechabites in Jerusalem before mentioning Zosimus, who is described as a monk who lives in a monastery in Jerusalem.

[7] HistRech appears on fols. 209b (or recto) to 214a (or verso). Cf. W. Wright, *Catalogue of the Syriac Manuscripts in the British Museum* (London, 1872) pt. III, pp. 1123–39, especially p. 1128.

[8] Variants to these MSS are noted only when the different word (or form) supplies a significantly different meaning. I am most grateful to the trustees of the Bibliothèque Nationale and of the BM for permission to study these MSS personally and to obtain photographs of them.

[9] Comments herein will be conservative in line with the rest of this collection of documents. As with 2En, ApAb, LadJac, and some other pseudepigrapha, so with HistRech we are in the early stages of understanding the document and its complex traditions.

[10] For the titles to the MSS see n. b to ch. 1.

[11] M. R. James, *Apocrypha Anecdota* (T&S 2.3; Cambridge, England, 1893) p. 95. Nau claimed the *present* form does not predate the 5th cent. ("La Légende inédite des fils de Jonadab, fils de Réchab, et les Iles fortunées," *Revue sémitique* 6 [1898] 264). K. Kunze thinks that the document was composed in Gk. in the 6th cent. See his "Zosimo, monaco della Scizia, beato (?)," *Bibliotheca Sanctorum* (Rome, 1969) vol. 12, col. 1502.

[12] See the provisional translation of the Eth. and a comparison of it with the Syr. and Gk. versions, and especially Appendix D in E. G. Martin, *The Account of the Blessed Ones: A Study of the Development of an Apocryphon on the Rechabites and Zosimus (The Abode of the Rechabites).* Duke Ph.D., 1979.

[13] James, *Apocrypha Anecdota*, p. 95.

[14] A. Zanolli, "La leggenda di Zosimo secondo la redazione armena," *Giornale della Società Asiatica Italiana.* N.S. 1 (1924) 146–62.

[15] Nau, *Revue sémitique* 6 (1898) 265.

[16] G. Graf, *Geschichte der christlichen arabischen Literatur* (Studi e Testi 118; Rome, 1944) vol. 1, p. 214.

Ginzberg,[17] J.-C. Picard,[18] and B. McNeil[19] have perceived evidence of a Jewish original behind the present Christian document. Nau even used such terms as "the Christian translator," "the primitive text," "the Hebrew text," and "the Hebrew author." Working with only the Greek document generates the impression that the beginning and end are Christian and that the central chapters, 3–15, are originally Jewish. Focusing upon the Syriac document leaves the impression that only 12:9a–13:5c and 16:1b–8 are clearly Christian and appear to be interpolated, because they interrupt the flow of thought and contain intrusive ideas. The mention of the name "Zosimus" in the latter section (16:8) suggests that perhaps all passages connected with this name may be from a later stratum,[20] hence chapters 7:12–16:1a, which do not identify the traveler as "Zosimus," would be earlier and possibly Jewish. It is only in these chapters, and specifically in 8–10, that mention is made of the Rechabites and their history in Jerusalem during the days of Jeremiah.[21] At this stage in our work it is best to suggest only that sections of this document are Jewish or heavily influenced by Jewish traditions, and that they may antedate the second century A.D.

It is practically impossible to discern the provenance of this document. According to the Armenian version, "Yovsimios" lived on Schiza, an island in the Ionian Sea.[22] This identification appears late, speculative, and unreliable. Syriac manuscript C states that Zosimus lived in a monastery in Palestine (see n. b to ch. 18). This comment should not be taken seriously in itself, although Palestine is a likely origin for the early Jewish stratum, which has a strong Semitic flavor, centers upon the Rechabites, and locates their history in Jerusalem. The repeated mention of Jerusalem in chapters 8–10, however, could be caused, of course, by the midrashic nature of these chapters and the dependence upon Jeremiah 35, which is centered in Jerusalem.

Historical and theological importance

The historical and theological importance of this document is first related to the growing perception of early medieval Christian interest in the land of the Blessed Ones, further reflections on a distant, not future, earthly paradise, and continued dependence on Jewish apocryphal literature or traditions. Such importance is, second, related to the increasing clarity with which we can now perceive and understand the theology of Jews near the beginning of the present era. Of central importance is the rich imagery and interesting descriptions of the daily life of the Blessed Ones, especially their freedom from sickness, pain, misfortune, temptation, discomfort—but not death—and their unique sexual customs. The eschatological concerns of Jewish apocalyptic are reflected not only in the ideas previously mentioned but also in the concern for the time of the end of the world (6:5–6a; cf. 2Bar and 4Ezra). Angelology is impressively developed, but not in ways similar to the multiplicity of names typical of 2 Enoch, 3 Enoch, and the Prayer of Jacob. The angels descend to the Blessed Ones, visit them (15:4b), and even dwell with them (12:8). They announce the time of death of a Blessed One, bury his (or her) body (14:2–15:10), and take the soul to heaven. The angels also transmit the prayers and praises "before" the throne (16:8c–8d).

---

[17] L. Ginzberg, *The Legends of the Jews*, 7 vols., trans. H. Szold (Philadelphia, 1909–38, reprinted 1937–66) vol. 6, p. 409.

[18] J.-C. Picard, "L'Histoire des bienheureux du temps de Jérémie et la narration de Zosime: Arrière-plan historique et mythique," *Pseudépigraphes de l'Ancien Testament et manuscrits de la Mer Morte*, ed. M. Philonenko et al. (Cahiers de la *RHPR* 41; Paris, 1967) pp. 27–43. Also see V. Nikiprowetzky, "Pseudépigraphes de l'Ancien Testament et manuscrits de la Mer Morte: Réflexions sur une publication récente," *REJ* 128 (1968) 5–40.

[19] B. McNeil rightly observes the lack of Christology, soteriology, and ecclesiology in the main body of HistRech and concludes that "it is a light Christian reworking of a Jewish text." See his "The Narrative of Zosimus," *JSJ* 9 (1978) 68–82.

[20] The name "Zosimus" appears in the Syr. version only in 1:2 (*bis*), 3; 2:9; 7:11; 16:8f.; and 17:1a. The omission of the name is frequently conspicuous; and sometimes it appears the Blessed Ones are not speaking to one person but to many, e.g. n. 14:1a: "And again we announce to you (plural), O brothers . . ." The opening ch. also tends to supply the impression that the "certain" man mentioned later is to be identified with a particular individual: "His name was Zosimus . . ." (1:2).

[21] Jeremiah is also mentioned in 1:2; but this verse is obviously part of the introduction to the document.

[22] Zanolli, *Giornale della Società Asiatica Italiana*. N.S. 1 (1924) 153.

The island of the Blessed Ones is an intermediary state between the corruptible world and the heavenly realm. There is no resurrection, but rather a separation of soul from body, and ascent of the former with the aid of angels. When in heaven, the soul resides in a mansion, awaiting the resurrection of the rest of the Blessed Ones (16:7a). This thought is rather unique in biblical and quasi-biblical literature.

Relation to other books

Since the traditions preserved in the History of the Rechabites are exceedingly complex and rich, and since some of these are preserved in only one recension of one of the main versions (Syriac, Greek, or Ethiopic), it is necessary to limit discussion on literary relationships until critical texts and translations are available.

The History of the Rechabites is obviously dependent upon Jeremiah; the middle chapters (apparently the earliest section) of this document (especially chs. 8–10) resemble a midrashic expansion of Jeremiah 35. Many other passages are ultimately dependent upon traditions preserved in the Old Testament; for example, chapters 7:2a–10a and 12:3a are derived, perhaps only through secondary sources or oral traditions, from Genesis 1–3. Unlike the Greek and Ethiopic versions, which are intermittently dependent on New Testament ideas and traditions, the Syriac version is almost totally free of influences from the New Testament. Even the apparent Christian interpolations in the Syriac version are more influenced by ecclesiastical and liturgical traditions than by the New Testament documents; chapters 12:9a–13:5c, which mention the incarnation of the Word, and the virgin, are more influenced by ecclesiastical liturgy than John, on the one hand, or Matthew and Luke, on the other. Chapter 16:1b–8 shows virtually no influence from the New Testament.[23]

The History of the Rechabites shows no literary dependence upon any of the other pseudepigrapha, but striking parallels exist between it and 1 Enoch (cf. ch. 39), Jubilees (cf. 23:29), the Ascension of Isaiah (cf. e.g. HistRech 12:9a and 16:8a–8d), and especially 2 Baruch. As with the holy man in the History of the Rechabites, so Baruch fasts for seven days, eats no bread and drinks no water (not wine as in HistRech; cf. 2Bar 20:5–21:2). The abundance of food on the island of the Rechabites is reminiscent of the pictorial description of nourishment prepared for "the consummation of time" according to 2 Baruch 29.[24] The elaborate descriptions of the death of the body and the description of the soul and its ascent in the History of the Rechabites recalls the explanation of the resurrected body in 2 Baruch 50 and 51. Other shared traditions are the concept of the corruptible and incorruptible worlds (cf. 2Bar 74:2) and the description of the blessed island or the future day as one in which there is no disease, anxiety, or anguish, but only rest and joy, and the idea that plants will produce food by themselves (cf. 2Bar 73, 74). The relationship between the History of the Rechabites and 2 Baruch, however, is apparently not the result of literary dependence in either direction; it can be explained by a shared milieu or body of traditions, perhaps by a shared tradition, and possibly by independent influence from a lost apocryphon on the abode of the nine and a half tribes.[25]

[23] There can be little doubt that the HistRech influenced many early Christian writers. Merely two examples must suffice. *The Contendings of the Apostles* has been influenced by this document (or its traditions). According to this account, Matthew tells Peter and Andrew that he has just returned from the country of Prokumenos, whose inhabitants tell him that they are the nine and a half tribes "whom God Almighty brought into the land of inheritance . . . we eat not flesh and we drink not wine in our country, for our food is honey and our drink is the dew . . . and our firstborn children do we offer as a gift unto God that they may minister in the church . . . The water which we drink [floweth] not from cisterns which have been hewn by the hand of man, but [we drink] of the water which floweth from Paradise . . . No word of lying hear we in our land, and no man knoweth another who speaketh that which is false." Other interesting parallels to the HistRech could be listed, most notably the report that "in our country there is neither spring, nor cold, nor ice; but there are winds and they are [always] pleasant." (ET from E. A. W. Budge, *The Contendings of the Apostles*, London, New York, 1901; vol. 2, pp. 111–13.) The same apparent dependence on HistRech—or the lost apocryphon on the lost tribes—is found in the hymns of Commodius (cf. especially XLII in J. Martin, *Commodiani Carmina*, CCSL 128, Turin, 1960).

[24] The manna preserved for the future day is mentioned explicitly in 2Bar 29:8; it is also one of the traditional images inherited by the Christian redactor of the HistRech (cf. 13:2). For a discussion of this imagery in early Jewish writings, including the pseudepigrapha, see B. J. Malina, *The Palestinian Manna Tradition* (AGAJU 7; Leiden, 1968).

[25] HistRech contains traditions that are elsewhere identified with the lost tribes (cf. n. 22). 2Bar (cf. especially 77:17–26) is clearly built upon traditions related to the nine and a half tribes. It is possible that there once was an apocryphon on the lost tribes; cf. Charlesworth, *PMR*, pp. 147–49.

Ginzberg has drawn attention to concepts shared by the History of the Rechabites and 2 Alphabet of Ben Sira 28. The latter Jewish work records that the descendants of Jonadab, that is the Rechabites, entered alive into Paradise. In contrast to the History of the Rechabites, 2 Alphabet of Ben Sira 28 states that the Rechabites do not "taste death."[26]

The History of the Rechabites has also been influenced by ideas, concepts, and traditions developed in non-Jewish and non-Christian writings. The description of the abode of the Rechabites is in places impressively similar to Iranian myths, notably the Var de Yima, which depict paradise.[27] At least six early Greek or Roman authors preserved ideas that appear eventually to have influenced the author(s) of the History of the Rechabites. Hesiod (fl. 800 B.C.) describes the region in which heroes live after death; it is the "island of the Blessed Ones," which is beyond the shore of the ocean at the ends of the world (*Works and Days* 159–74; cf. also Homer, *Odyssey* IV.560). Pindar (522–448 B.C.) records the idea that souls that are pure "pass by the highway of Zeus unto the Tower of Cronus, where the ocean-breezes blow around the Islands of the Blest (lit. "Island of the Blessed Ones": *makarōn nasos*)."[28] Herodotus (c. 485–425 B.C.) places "the Island of the Blessed Ones" (*Makarōn nēsos*) "seven days' march from Thebes across sandy desert."[29] Plato (427–347 B.C.) envisions a celestial earth in which the inhabitants have no sickness, live long lives, and are vastly superior to earthly men and women; and the gods "really dwell" in their "sacred groves and temples" (cf. *Phaedo* 111b). Virgil (70–19 B.C.), like the author of 2 Baruch, describes the future golden age as one in which the earth shall pour forth gifts without having to be tilled and goats with swollen udders will come home without having to be tended or called (*Eclogue* IV.18–25, 39f.). Lucian (A.D. 125–200) describes an "island of the Blessed Ones" (*he men nēsos eiē tōn Makarōn*) on which the inhabitants are heroes who have become incorporeal (*autoi de sōmata men ouk echousin . . . kai asōmatoi ontes*) and who enjoy sweet breezes, an eternal spring (*aiei gar par autois ear esti*), and a land abounding in flowers, grapevines, and instead of "wheat-ears, loaves of bread all baked grow on the tops of the halms . . ."[30] The History of the Rechabites apparently has inherited images and ideas commonly shared in antiquity in the countries of the Fertile Crescent and in the lands of the Mediterranean.[31]

Cultural importance

The History of the Rechabites must have considerably influenced Western and Middle Eastern culture during the middle ages, since it is extant in numerous medieval Greek, Syriac, Ethiopic, Arabic, Karshuni, Slavonic, and Armenian manuscripts.[32] Moreover, a very popular story in medieval Europe is the *Navigatio Sancti Brendani*, which is extant in two versions and recounts how Brendan of Clonfert (c. 484–577), an Irish monk, twice visited the island of the Blessed Ones. Brendan sails west from Ireland and visits one island after another until he arrives at an island, encircled by a thick cloud, on which he meets a holy man who is unclothed except for feathers. The island is the island of the Blessed Ones. Because of similar ideas in Greek and Roman sources, we cannot conclude that the traditions in the History of the Rechabites influenced this Irish legend; and there is no reason to

---

[26] Ginzberg, *Legends*, vol. 6, p. 409.

[27] See Picard (*Pseudépigraphes*, pp. 27–43), who sees influence on the HistRech from the Var de Yima through the Dead Sea Scrolls. Although direct influence from the Dead Sea Scrolls is unlikely, HistRech shares with them the concept that a full member has transcended mere anthropology and has approached angelology (cf. HistRech 7:11 with 1QH 3:21f.) and that angels dwell within the community (cf. HistRech 11:5, 12:6–9 with e.g. 1QSa 2.3–11 and 1QH 3.21f., 4.24f.). Also see n. 30.

[28] *Olympian Odes* 2.69–71; Gk. and ET from J. Sandys, *The Odes of Pindar* (LCL; Cambridge, Mass., London, 1937) pp. 24f.

[29] *History* Bk. III.26; Gk. and ET from A. D. Godley, *Herodotus* (LCL; New York, London, 1921) pp. 34f.

[30] *A True Story* 2.6–13; Gk. and ET from A. M. Harmon, *Lucian* (LCL; New York, London, 1913) pp. 310–17.

[31] Nikiprowetzky (*REJ* 128 [1969] 22–38) claims that Christians employed classical and Jewish sources to produce the HistRech, which is a Christian work that praises monasticism. McNeil (*JSJ* 9 [1978] 80f.) similarly argues that "the most important aspect" of this document is that it "sets out, in a pictorial form, a way of life for a community." He suggests that the community should be identified with the Therapeutae.

[32] See the discussion of these versions in Martin, *The Account of the Blessed Ones*, pp. 68–108.

imagine with Alexander von Humboldt that Saint Brendan is reporting that he succeeded in reaching the American continent.[33]

A world map of approximately 1275 seems to identify the islands Saint Brendan visited with the Canary Islands (*Fortunate Insulate Sex Sunt Insulae Sct Brandani*).[34] This amazing confusion seems to be caused by Pliny's, Strabo's, and Ptolemy's identification of the Canary Islands as the islands of the Blessed Ones;[35] the identification in antiquity is logical, since the legends place them in the ocean, near the end of the earth, precisely the geographical location of the Canary Islands in early antiquity.

Introduction to the translation

The following English translation attempts to be as idiomatic as possible, although the main focus has been upon the Syriac manuscripts with their subtleties and inelegancies. Hence, while particles and connectives in Syriac that are intrusive or unnecessary in English are not represented, nouns and verbs are translated as consistently as English will allow; note the following: $npš$ = "soul," $ṣl$ = "he prayed," $ṣlwt$ = "prayer," $š'l$ = "he requested," $š'lt$ = "request," pys = "he asked," b' = "he petitioned," $'t$ = "he came," $'zl$ = "he journeyed," hlk = "he walked," rd = "he traveled," $knš$ = "he assembled," $knš$ = "the assembly," $šrbt$ = "family," $'r'$ = "land,"[36] $šwr$ = "bulwark." Chapters noted herein have been adapted from W. A. Craigie's translation of the Greek version; verses are supplied for the first time. Verse numbers in parentheses denote that the passage is unique (or nearly so) in the Greek recension; verse numbers followed by an alphabetical number signify that the Syriac has another (or longer) version. Hence, 16:(7)7a means verse 7 in Greek is missing in Syriac, and that the Syriac has another reading. Verses to the Greek version will be found in the forthcoming edition. Placed within parentheses are additions necessary for idiomatic English. Italics denote rubrification.

BIBLIOGRAPHY

Charlesworth, *PMR*, pp. 223–28.
Denis, *Introduction*, p. 144.

Budge, E. A. W. *The Life and Exploits of Alexander the Great*. London, 1896; vol. 2, pp. 555–84. (ET of the Eth.)
Charlesworth, J. H. *The History of the Rechabites*, vol. I: *The Greek Recension*. T&T 17; Pseudepigrapha Series 10; Chico, Calif., 1982.
Craigie, W. A. "The Narrative of Zosimus Concerning the Life of the Blessed," *ANF* 10, pp. 220–24. (ET of the Gk.)
James, M. R. "On the Story of Zosimus," *Apocrypha Anecdota*. T&S 2.3; Cambridge, England, 1893; pp. 86–108. (Contains Gk. text plus significant introduction.)

---

[33] See the discussion of the *Navigatio Sancti Brendani* and opinions regarding it in R. H. Ramsay's *No Longer on the Map: Discovering Places That Never Were* (New York, 1973) pp. 60–74, 210–12. C. R. Beazley correctly states that the Brendan story "shows in many places signs of being concocted from other narratives" (p. 235). He suggests, furthermore, that the voyages of the Moslem Wanderers of Lisbon and of Sinbad the Sailor "are clearly related in some way to the Brendan narrative" (p. 235). See his *The Dawn of Modern Geography* (London, 1897). For a defense of the claim that the traditions in the legend of St. Brendan are to be connected "with an Atlantic quest," see G. Ashe, *Land to the West: St. Brendan's Voyage to America* (New York, 1962). As far as I know, no publication draws attention to the parallels between the HistRech and the *Navigatio Sancti Brendani*.

[34] Ramsay, *No Longer on the Map*, pp. 64f.

[35] See Ashe, *Land to the West*, pp. 132f.

[36] Sometimes "land" seems ill suited in the context: the reader may substitute "ground" or "earth."

Martin, E. G. *The Account of the Blessed Ones: A Study of the Development of an Apocryphon on the Rechabites and Zosimus (The Abode of the Rechabites)*. Unpublished Ph.D. dissertation, Duke University, 1979. (A good review of research and assessment of the versions.)

McNeil, B. "The Narrative of Zosimus." *JSJ* 9 (1978) 68–82.

Nau, F. "La Légende inédite des fils de Jonadab, fils de Réchab, et les îles fortunées," *RevSem* 6 (1899) 263–66 (introduction); 7 (1899) 54–75 (Syr. text); 7 (1889) 136–46 (French translation).

Picard, J.-C. "L'Histoire des bienheureux du temps de Jérémie et la narration de Zosime: Arrière-plan historique et mythique," *Pseudépigraphes de l'Ancien Testament et manuscrits de la Mer Morte*, ed. M. Philonenko *et al.* Cahiers de la RHPR 41; Paris, 1967; pp. 27–43.

Zanolli, A. "La leggenda di Zosimo secondo la redazione armena," *Giornale della Società Asiatica Italiana*. N.S. 1 (1924) 146–62.

THE HISTORY OF THE RECHABITES[a]

The History of the Holy Hermit Zosimus and of the Sons of Jonadab, the Son of Rechab[b]

1 **1** There was a certain amazing and virtuous man,[c] who while dwelling in the desert for forty years did not eat bread, did not drink wine, and did not see the
2 face[d] of a mortal. •His name was Zosimus; and he earnestly was entreating God by night and by day to show him where he had translated the Blessed Ones, the sons of Jonadab, who were taken away from worldly life[e] in the days of Jeremiah the prophet, and where God had made them dwell.

And when the LORD[f] saw the (self-)humiliation[g] of this blessed one, Zosimus, for the sake of these Blessed Ones, then God heard his prayer and granted his
3 request. •And on one of the days while he was praying, a voice came to him[h] and   2:7,9
an angel came toward him and said to him,[i] "Zosimus, O man of God, I have   2:8
been sent to you from the height (of heaven)[j] to guide you and to show you[k] the way so that you may journey and see these Blessed Ones as you petitioned the
4 LORD. •However, do not boast in your mind (thinking thus), 'Behold (for) forty
5 years bread I have not eaten, and wine I have not drunk,[l] •and the faces[m] of men I[n] have not seen (but) only the face of angels'; now approach."

1,2 **2** Then I left the cave,[a] •and traveled with the angel (for) forty days. I arrived at a certain place wearied[b] and fatigued, and I collapsed from my exhaustion;[c]

---

1 a. The title given to this document, adapted from the titles in MSS A B D, draws attention to the Jewish character of the earliest sections of the work (cf. chs. 8f. with Jer 35).

b. This is the title found in MS A. The title in B is *"The History of the Sons of Jonadab, the Son of Rechab, Who Are in the Midst of the Ocean, the Great Sea, When God Showed Them to Zosimus, the Virtuous Hermit."* The title in MS D is *"The History of the Blessed Ones, the Sons of the Rechabites, Whose Record Is Recorded by Jeremiah the Prophet When He Said That They Are the Sons of Jonadab, the Son of Rechab, Who Are Inhabitants of the City Jerusalem. It Was Translated from Hebrew into Greek and from Greek into Syriac by the Hands of the Reverend Mar Jacob of Edessa."* (Italics denote rubrics.)

c. D adds "Abba" (Father), cf. 2:9; as with most variants in D, this one looks secondary.

d. Gk. loan word, *prṣwpʾ*.

e. Or "world, age"; for the rest of this paragraph, D has "the sons of the Rechabites, who were taken away from the people of Israel in the days of the prophet Jeremiah and Josiah the king of Jerusalem, and concerning the place he had made them dwell."

f. "LORD" and "God" are used interchangeably in this section.

g. Lit. "his humiliation, his feebleness"; B: "his exhaustion" (cf. 2:2). D: "his labor and his exhaustion."

h. The clause "a voice came to him" is not found in B D; but see 2:7,9. The clause seems original; the redundancy could be seen as unattractive and hence omitted by a medieval copyist. The hypostatization of a voice is typical of some early

apocalypses; cf. especially the following: Rev 1:10–12; Cologne Mani Codex 57.12 (the "Apocalypse of Shem"), "But a voice (*phōnē*) bent toward me, calling from the throne, and coming toward me, took my right hand, and lifted (me)"; ApSedr 2:3 "And the voice (*hē phōnē*) said to him, 'I was sent to you that I may carry you up into heaven' " (translator Agourides, see herein). It seems that in ApSedr 2, Sedrach twice calls the voice "LORD" (*kurios*).

i. Lit. "and answered and said to him." This Semitism is well known, is reflected in the Gospels, and idiomatically means "said" when no question has been asked.

j. D adds "from God."

k. Lit. "And I shall be for you a guide and I shall show you . . ."

l. For the rest of the paragraph, D has: "and the face (*wprṣwpʾ*) of man I have not seen; for the words of God are more excellent and pleasant than bread, and his spirit more satisfying and sweeter than wine. And also (do not say), 'Faces of men I have not seen, only the face (*prṣwph*) of the heavenly king'; (now) move near." D is obviously derivative and late. A preserves the better reading.

m. The indigenous Syr. word, not the Gk. loan word as above and below.

n. The three verbs in this sentence can represent either the first person, as here, or the second person, as in Nau's translation.

2 a. D: "my cave."

b. B D: *meṭṭaraph*, "vexed or smitten."

c. Lit. "and I cast my soul (myself) down because of my exhaustion." B omits "because of my exhaustion."

3 afterward I prayed to God (for) three[d] days. •And a certain animal came and 18:3
(4, carried me away and traveled beneath me (for) many days until it reached the
5,6) great ocean.[e] •And when I saw the great sea I was amazed[f] at its vastness and
6a
7 wondered[g] what I would do. •And immediately a voice came to me, saying, "O 1:3
man of God, never has a man proceeded (farther) or passed beyond me; merely
8 perceive (this) and understand (it)." •And I looked and (saw) in the midst of the
sea (something) like a dense bulwark of cloud suspended[h] upon the sea; and the
8a top of the cloud extended[i] to the height of heaven. •And I thought[j] that perhaps 17:3a 1:3
9 the Blessed Ones were in the midst of it,[k] •(because) I heard a voice from the 1:3; 2:7
midst of the cloud which said, "Father Zosimus.'"[l] Then (realizing my misconception)
I praised and gave thanks to God, (to) him who makes mute natures to speak, to
him who makes everything easy.

(1)1a,2 **3** And then I prayed to[a] the LORD to deal with me as it pleases his will. •And 17:4a
suddenly two luxuriant[b] and very stately trees, larger than (any) I had ever seen,[c]
3 appeared on the shore of the sea. •And then one of the trees bent itself down[d] and
I securely grasped its branches. And it stretched out toward the height (of heaven)
and lifted me up and carried me in its summit until the cloud was beneath (me).
And also that other tree bent itself down toward it;[e] and the one from here curved
(4)4a its summit and held me out to the one which was from the other side. •And
descending, it dropped me in the midst of it. And thus by God's guidance[f] I
5 passed over the great ocean[g] and the cloud.[h] •And I rested in (that) place (for)
three days, while the praise of God did not cease from my mouth. Then I arose
6 and traveled through the land that was in the midst of the sea; •it was pleasant
and beautiful and filled with luxuriant trees, which were bearing pleasant and
fragrant fruits. It was like a large and vast island, without a mountain or hill,[i]
adorned with flowers[j] and filled with many and delightful pleasures.

1 **4** While observing the beauty[a] of that land, I approached a little (ways) and saw
(2)2a a certain naked man, who was seated. •And I was afraid because of his appearance,[b]
3,4 but said, "Peace to you, my brother." •Then he replied[c] and said, "Come in
(5,6,7)8 peace; and joy be with you •for I know that you are a man of God, otherwise you
would not have been allowed[d] to enter here."

1,(2)2a **5** And again he asked me, "Have you come from the world of vanity?" •Then
I said to him, "In truth I come from the world of vanity[a] in order to see (all of)

---

d. D: "four."
e. Gk. loan word in Syr., *Pwqynws;* D: "the ocean, the great sea, which surrounds the earth."
f. D: "I was greatly amazed."
g. Or "and I was thinking."
h. B D: "of white cloud"; no verb is represented in this version.
i. Lit. "was rising."
j. D adds "in my heart."
k. The pronoun "it," which is third person feminine singular, refers back to "cloud" (feminine in Syr.), not "sea" (masculine in Syr.).
l. D adds "blessed are you, because you were deemed worthy to come to this place."

3 a. Lit. "before"; B: "unto."
b. Or "honorable, adorned."
c. Lit. "the great(ness) of their like(ness) I had never seen."
d. D adds "and carried me in its summit." This variant looks like an error that slipped in from the selfsame phrase in the next verse.
e. D: "toward me." Was the scribe of D attempting to improve the text?

f. Or "providence."
g. Gk. loan word in Syr., *Pwqynws.*
h. D adds "and the dark fog"; it is evident that most of the variants in D, at least in the first three chs., are errors. Nowhere, not even in D, is it said that Zosimus has trouble with *'arpellâ,* "the dark fog."
i. Or "height."
j. D: "lovely flowers." See the Syr. of 7:3, "lovely trees."

4 a. Or "grace."
b. Usually *ḥäzîthâ* means "eye"; possibly the Syr. is corrupt, but probably the meaning "appearance" was once represented by this feminine emphatic active participle of *ḥz'* as well as by *ḥezwâ,* which usually denotes "appearance, form."
c. Syr. idiom, lit. "he returned to me a word."
d. There is here an intrusive *dyn,* Gk. loan word meaning "but."

5 a. The Syr. is poor here; there is an intrusive *gyr,* a Gk. particle that means "for," and *mṭl* (because) should be followed by *d·* plus imperfect, not the perfect.

3 you. However, tell me, why are you naked?" •But he said to me, "You are he (who is) naked, and you do not discern that your garment is corrupted, but my own garment is not corrupted. If you wish to see me, however, come, gaze[b]
4 toward the height of heaven." •And while gazing above I saw[c] his face[d] (to be) like the face[e] of an angel. And my eyes were dimmed from fear; and I fell upon the land.

1 **6** And then he approached me and grasped me by my hands, and raised me up upon my feet. And he said to me, "Do not fear; for I am one of the Blessed
2 Ones, whom[a] you have earnestly desired to visit.[b] •But[c] come with me and I shall
3 take you to the holy Blessed Ones, my brothers. •And traveling with me, holding my hands, he asked me concerning the world and all that (is) in it. And then he brought me to the assembly of the Blessed Ones. And after watching them I fell
3a to the land and worshiped them. •It was the assembly of elect ones, (comprising
4 both) splendid[d] youths and honorable[e] holy ones. •And when these Blessed Ones
5 saw me,[f] they greatly marveled and asked[g] (each other) simultaneously,[h] •"My brothers, has the end of the world arrived and consequently a man was able to
6 come here?" •And all of them rose up and prayed and petitioned the LORD to inform them (of the reason) for my incursion among them.
6a   And God heard their prayer; and I watched and behold two angels descended from heaven, stood before the assembly of the Blessed Ones, and said[i] to them, "The[j] end has not yet arrived; do not be afraid by the coming of this man who is
6b among you. He[k] will remain among you (for) seven days. •Write out for him and inform him (about) all of God's providence respecting you, and that he visits with you; however, that (man) shall (soon) go out[l] from you, and return to his place
7 rejoicing." •And after the angels said these things to them, they ascended to heaven.

1,1a **7** Then the Blessed Ones rejoiced, and received me in peace. •And the holy ones,
1b the Blessed Ones, delivered me to an attendant.[a] •And the holy ones said[b] to him,
2 "Keep[c] him, this our brother, with you (for) seven days." •And the holy attendant received me, and brought me to his tent, and I sat[d] with him under these fair
2a trees. •And in his presence I took delight[e] in the delight of his prayers. For that place is like the Paradise of God and these Blessed Ones are like Adam and Eve
2b.3 before they sinned. •They fast[f] from the ninth hour until the ninth; •and then they eat[g] what they need[h] from the fruits of these trees; for water which is sweet and delightful as honey flows[i] from the roots of the trees. And each one drinks what

---

b. B: "you must not gaze."

c. The Syr. here contains an otiose *gyr* (see n. a above).

d. Gk. *prṣwp'*; see n. 1 to ch. 1.

e. Gk. *prṣwp'*. Ch. 5 in Syr. gives me the impression that it was translated from a Gk. copy.

6 a. Another otiose *dyn* is found in the Syr.

b. Lit. "but which you have earnestly desired that you may come to them."

c. In the Syr. there are two particles to denote "but," the customary Syr. *'P* and *dyn*.

d. Or "glorious, excellent, stately."

e. Or "handsome, beautiful."

f. Disregard Nau's text; A has *ḥz'wwnny*.

g. Lit. "they answered and they said."

h. Lit. "together"; B: "one to the other."

i. Lit. "and answered and said."

j. Another otiose *gyr* is present in the Syr.

k. A Syr. "but," *'P*, and a *dyn* are both in the text.

l. The future aspect of the Syr. participle is

intended here. In excellent Syr. I would expect this and the next verb to be imperfects, not participles.

7 a. Lit. "to one of them who was an attendant (or servant)."

b. Lit. "and answered and said."

c. Or "guard, watch." It would be incorrect to assume that the Blessed Ones are still suspicious of this man; the angels have spoken on his behalf (ch. 6), and the Blessed Ones call him "our brother" (7:1).

d. Lit. "I was sitting."

e. Lit. "I was taking delight (or refreshing myself)."

f. Lit. "they were fasting"; here the participle denotes customary or habitual action. There is an otiose *gyr* in the Syr.

g. Lit. "they were eating"; see n. f. D adds *mst*, "quantity."

h. Lit. "their need."

i. Or "springs up."

he needs.[j] And immediately they stop eating;[k] from the ninth hour (on)[l] they live[m] alone.

4   When these families[n] of these Blessed Ones heard what was (happening) on my account, and (when) they were told[o] by their brothers, "Behold, a certain man 5 has come from the world of vanity,"[p] •(then) they began to be disturbed and all of the fair families of the Blessed Ones came (persistently)[q] in order to see (the 6 phenomenon),[r] since amazement[s] possessed them because of me. •And they (incessantly) questioned me concerning this world, and I (repeatedly) told them. 7 From the weariness, duration, and pain of the manner[t] (of questioning), my soul[u] quivered and I was unable to speak, because neither by night nor by day did they leave me alone to rest. And I asked that attendant and said to him, "I ask you, O Blessed One, do me a kindness; if they come to you and question you concerning me, tell them, 'He is not here,' so that I may rest; (because)[v] my soul[w] is greatly 8 harassed." •And that holy attendant, when he heard this (request)[x] from me, cried out in a loud voice[y] saying, "O My Blessed Fathers, misfortune is counted to me on this day.[z] Behold, I am almost[a2] like Adam in Paradise; for he through the 7:2a advice of Eve[b2] transgressed the commandment. And this man through his evil advice, which he reveals (by) asking[c2] (something) that would cause me (to sin), (9)9a said to me, 'Lie, and say to your companions that I am not here.'[d2] •Cast out this man from here so that he shall not implant (lies) in our place of captivity."[e2]

10   And many noble elders[f2] and spiritual youths, who were like angels of heaven, assembled, formed[g2] an assembly,[h2] and said[i2] to me, "O man of sin, go, exit from among us. We do not know how you prepared yourself so that you were 10a able to come among us;[j2] •perhaps[k2] you wish to deceive us as the Evil One 11 deceived our father Adam." •However, I, miserable Zosimus, fell upon my face before them, and with mournful tears entreated them earnestly and said,

> Have mercy upon me, O Blessed Ones;
> And forgive me my offense, O Earthly Angels.[l2]

And after I entreated them earnestly and abundantly, with difficulty they had 11a mercy upon me. •And all of them became very silent, and after a short (time) they said to me,[m2] "Tell us, our brother, all of those things which (transpired) so 12 that you were able to visit us;[n2] be at rest and do not fear." •Then I told them the

---

j. Lit. "his need."
k. Lit. "they were eating and do not continue."
l. D adds "to the ninth."
m. Or "continue, travel."
n. Or "generations, tribes"; D adds "all of them."
o. An unnecessary *gyr* is in A B (but not in D).
p. D: "from a cursed land."
q. Adverbs are supplied in order to convey the continuous action of the Syr. participles.
r. Lit. "it, him."
s. Or "reverence."
t. D: "of the excessive talk."
u. Or "I myself." In this document I have translated *npš* as "soul," because of the contrast between "soul" and "body" in 11:2a.
v. I would have expected *mṭl d.*
w. Or "I myself."
x. Apparently *šēltā* (feminine) is presupposed.
y. D adds "to his companions."
z. Lit. "woe is counted to me on this day." Nau's text is inaccurate; read *ywm'* for *nwm'.*
a2. A has an unnecessary *dyn,* which is not in the printed text.
b2. D: "Behold, I am almost like the counsel of this one to Adam and Eve in Paradise, who through the counsel of the Evil One transgressed [restored later; this singular form is incorrect here] the commandment." D is corrupt.
c2. Or "petitioning."

d2. D: "he is not here."
e2. Or "exile." The appropriateness of this term is clarified by the concept in the Dead Sea Scrolls, in the OdesSol, and in a tradition about the abode of the lost tribes (cf. Charlesworth, *PMR,* pp. 147–49).
f2. Or "ancient ones"; no rank or office seems to be denoted.
g2. Lit. "began, came in."
h2. The Syr. is inelegant.
i2. Lit. "and they answered and said."
j2. The members of the assembly (or multitude) have forgotten the revelations by the angels (cf. ch. 6). Either the author is very clumsy, or we have evidence of two different traditions.
k2. The Syr. has an otiose *gyr.*
l2. The Syr. noun *'r'ʾ,* here translated "earthly," is elsewhere rendered as "land." The petition is composed in *parallelismus membrorum,* the norm of Semitic poetry, and is found (e.g.) in the Davidic Psalms, the 5ApocSyrPss, PssSol, and OdesSol. This poetic form is not present in the Gk. text parallel to 7:11.
m2. Lit. "And all of them were in a great silence, and after a little they answered and said to me."
n2. Lit. "all of them, those things, which on account of them your incursion happened here with us." The Syr. is verbose.

13 entire story, in what manner I requested God, "Show me your place." •Then the
elders responded to me, "And now, our beloved, since God has answered you
(14)14a and you have seen us and our place, what do you wish?" •Then I said to them,
"I beg[o2] (you) from your blessedness[p2] to write for me the history of (how) your
entrance here (was possible), so that your history may be a good introduction[q2]
and a beautiful example for everyone who wishes to be guided by the fear of
God."

1 **8** And they took tablets of stone[a] and wrote on them as follows: Hear, all (of
you) who are in the world of vanity, and perceive all the providence[b] which has
1a occurred after this manner; •we are called the sons of Rechab, we are from you;   Jer 35
and behold we departed from your world to this place in which we (are) today.[c]
2 For[d] in that time when Jeremiah,[e] the prophet, announced[f] and prophesied[g] the
ravaging and devastation (of) Jerusalem because of the sins of the sons of Israel,
then behold shortly (thereafter) the destroyer came[h] to ravage and slay them. Then
Jeremiah,[i] the prophet, rent his garments and was clothed in sackcloth, and
sprinkled dust upon his head. And he showed[j] to the common folk[k] the way of
goodness; and urged[l] them to return to the LORD.
3   Then our father Jonadab, the son of Rechab, heard how the prophet charged,
"Do not eat bread, and do not drink wine until the LORD hears your petition."
And our father said to us, "We must not eat bread and we must not drink wine;   Jer 35:6-11
4 and we must not put on a garment.[m] We must obey his word." •And we said to
5 him, "We will do all that you have charged us." •And then we removed the
garments from our bodies, and did not eat bread, and did not drink wine, and
6 lamented with a great lamentation. And we offered prayers to God. •And he
accepted our petitions. And he turned back from his fierce anger.[n]

1,2 **9** And after King Josiah died, another[a] king ruled[b] after him. •And when he
assembled together all the people of the Jews,[c] (some) men[d] spoke to him because
of us: "There is here a family[e] which is from us but they do not act like us; and
they are naked and neither eat (bread) nor drink (wine)[f]." Then the king dismissed
(3)4 (them);[g] •and he summoned us.[h] •And when we came in before him, the king

---

o2. Or "petition" as in 6:6 and elsewhere.

p2. Nau's text is incorrect; A B D have
twbtnwtkwn.

q2. The words "entrance" and "introduction"
are from the same root.

8 a. D adds "like (those) engraved by Moses upon
the mountain." D is derivative.

b. D adds "which God provided for you."

c. B omits "today." C begins about here (and
lit. translated): "There was once (lit. "in the time")
a man from the sons of Israel whose name was
Rechab. And this Rechab was an excellent man;
and there was to him a son, and his name (was)
Jonadab. And he, this Jonadab, followed in the
footsteps of Rechab, his father. And with him in
Jerusalem at that time there was Jeremiah, the
prophet. And it was made known to him by God
that a bitter sentence from diverse peoples would
come over Jerusalem. And that they will lead it
away captive (into) a severe captivity . . ."

d. B omits "for."

e. A: "Elijah." B D have "Jeremiah." A is
obviously in error; cf. n. i below.

f. Here and below "announced" is a Gk. loan
word (fr. *kērux*) in Syr.

g. Lit. "was announcing and prophesying"; the
participle indicates the continuous action of Jeremiah's prophesying.

h. The Syr. contains an otiose *dyn*.

i. All MSS (A B D) have "Jeremiah." Jer does
not record that Jeremiah "rent his garments and
was clothed in sackcloth, and sprinkled dust upon
his head."

j. The verbs "sprinkled" and "demonstrated"
are translated from Syr. participles.

k. A: "the sons of men."

l. Or "announced"; the same verb is used in
8:2.

m. The verb "to put on" and the noun "garment" are cognate in Syr.

n. D: "And he turned back his fierce anger from
the city." Cf. Jer 4:8.

9 a. D adds "wicked."

b. Lit. "rose up"; but *qwm* also acquired the
meaning "to reign."

c. D: "And when all the sons of Jerusalem and
the Jews were assembled near him." This reading
is derivative.

d. D omits and has "they spoke to him (concerning) our action."

e. Or "family, tribe."

f. The sons of Rechab obviously eat and drink.
The Syr. is cryptic; "bread" and "wine" are
assumed from 8:3–6.

g. D omits all the words from "There is here"
to "dismissed (them)."

h. D: "all of us."

5 asked us, "Who are you and from which family[i] are you?" •Then we answered[j]
him, "We are from this your people, and from the city Jerusalem; and we are
6 sons of Jonadab, the son of Rechab.[k] •And when Jeremiah, the prophet, in the
(7)6a,8 days of the king who was before you, exhorted •the common folk[l] to repent, •our
father heard the word of the prophet and warned and charged us not to eat bread,   Jer 35:6f
(9)10 drink wine, be anxious again about garments, or dwell in houses.[m] •And God
10a heard his prayer.[n] And he removed his anger from the city.[o] •And we loved him[p]
with all our soul[q] and girded[r] ourselves with his kindness. And this[s] (his love)
was pleasing in our eyes so that in this way we shall be leisurely[t] naked[u] all our
days."[v]

1,2 **10** And the king said[a] to us, "You are doing well; •but (now) mix with your
people,[b] and put on your garments,[c] and eat bread, and drink wine, and forsake
3 the LORD.[d] And behold you will be obedient sons of our kingdom." •But we
answered[e] the king, "We shall never break our promises to God; and we shall
4 not cease[f] from (obeying) the covenant with him forever." •And the king raged
against us and charged (that) all of us be imprisoned in prison;[g] and while we
were imprisoned we kept vigil by prayer before God.
5   On the first night,[h] a brilliant[i] light shone upon us; and angels of God in glorious
(6)5a form appeared to us. And they led all of us out from prison, •and placed us in
7 the air[j] that is above the land, •and brought us to this place (in) which you (now)
7a see (us), and allowed us to dwell in it.[k] •And our virtuous wives, who with us
had surrendered themselves[l] to God, now abide separately among us[m] in this land,
while remaining as we (do) in a fast and prayer and praise to God. And after the
angels of God brought us and placed us in this place in the midst of the water of
this great sea,[n] God commanded and the waters rose up from the deep abyss and
8 encircled this place. •And by the command of God a cloud became a bulwark[o]
above the water and rose up as far as heaven.

---

i. Or "family, tribe."

j. Lit. "we returned"; cf. n. e to ch. 10. This
expression, as in 10:3, is an abbreviated form of
the idiom "to return a word" (cf. 4:4 and n. c).

k. The Syr. is correct; the Gk. incorrectly states
that Rechab is the son of Jonadab.

l. Lit. "the sons of the people."

m. D adds "and we obeyed and kept the commandment of our father."

n. D adds "and received our petition."

o. D: "this city."

p. D: "the LORD."

q. Or "being"; contrast the use of np∫ (self,
being, soul) in the latter chs., especially 11:2a and
14:2.

r. Or "were imprisoned"; but this meaning is
inappropriate.

s. "This" (feminine) refers back to "love"
(feminine).

t. The Syr. baṭṭílê, the passive participle of "to
cease work" or "be at leisure," usually means
"void, obsolete." The reference is to the preceding
vss., which state that the Blessed Ones are clothed
with God's love.

u. B: "so that we shall dwell here"; D: "so
that in this way we shall continue."

v. D: "all the days of our life."

10 a. Lit. "answered and said."

b. Lit. "the sons of your people."

c. Paronomasia: "garment yourself with your
garments." D has the rest of this sentence after

the next sentence.

d. Before "the LORD," A has an unnecessary
dyn (which is not in Nau's text). D adds "your
God" and "mix with us." The statement that the
sons of Rechab should disobey their father's commandment is expanded by the exhortation to "forsake the LORD." This expansion is a significant
addition to the biblical tradition; it implies that to
reject the Rechabite customs is to forsake the LORD.
This idea reveals how pro-Rechabite is this section;
Jer 35:12–19 is expanded with a pro-Rechabite
Midrash. The Gk. is appreciably different: "and
glorify your LORD, and you shall be serving God
and the king."

e. Syr. idiom; cf. n. j to ch. 9.

f. A preserves an ancient orthography; B, the
usual verb form; D: "we shall never go aside from
. . ."

g. Lit. "he charged and all of us were imprisoned"; there is no paronomasia in Syr. C: "in a
guardhouse."

h. D adds "while keeping vigil." C summarizes,
"and the LORD saw their faith and sent a Watcher
and he led them out from the prison and brought
them to the midst of the great sea, to the land
which is Paradise."

i. Lit. "great."

j. Gk. loan word, aér.

k. D adds "and our children."

l. Or "their beings," or "their souls."

m. Lit. "among the midst of us."

n. D adds "an island."

o. Or "wall, defense."

(1)Ia **11** And according to his will God assembled us on this island and did not scatter
2 us upon the whole land; •but God placed us on this holy land. And we are without
2a sins and evil and abominable thoughts. •And we are mortals; however, we are
purified and spotless, and our souls[a] and bodies are cleansed from all defilement;
and we depend upon the hope[b] of our LORD; and our sight[c] is fixed continuously
(4)2b (and) unceasingly on the light of the future life. •And from prayer to God we are
not silent[d] by night and by day, for this (offering of praise) is our occupation.[e]   OdesSol 16:1
3 And God commanded and this land[f] brought forth for us pleasant and splendid
4 trees which are filled (with) lovely, marvelous, and abundant fruits. •And again[g]
from the roots of the trees flows sweet and delightful water; and from these fruits
and water we take delight and rest and are sustained.
5   There is not among us vineyards, grain, husbandry,[h] wood, iron,[i] houses,
5a buildings, gold, or silver; •and neither stormy weather[j] nor rain is with us; neither
snow nor ice. And the sun does not shine upon us, because the cloud, which
5b encircles us like a bulwark,[k] restrains it. •And the land in which we are is filled
with a glorious[l] light so darkness and night do not enter it. And we possess a
shining appearance[m] and dwell in light.
6   And[n] there are among us men who take wives and once only[o] the man has
7 intercourse[p] with his wife. •And then they are set apart from each other and they
remain[q] in purity for the remainder[r] of their lives. And the memory of the delight[s]
does not arise in the mind[t] of any of us.[u] But they remain all their days as those
8 who grow up in virginity. •But the wife conceives and bears two children; one of
them is for marriage[v] and the other[w] grows up in virginity. And after this manner
we have been commanded[x] by God; and truly after this manner is our custom.[y]

1,1a **12** But[a] there is among us no one who measures the years.[b] •For the sake of
those who (daily)[c] live[d] in[e] purity and holiness, the years of their life shall increase;
but the years of sinners shall decrease.[f] And no one among us computes months
(2)3 and years.[g] •But we are naked not as you suppose,[h] for[i] we are covered with a

---

11 a. Or "beings."

b. Or "expectation."

c. D: "the sight of our mind (or intellect)."

d. Or "do not cease."

e. Or "worship." D adds "our manner of life."

f. D: "For by the command (or decree) of God
the land . . ."

g. The Syr. contains a *dyn* which is acceptable
but not necessary.

h. Lit. "occupation (or work) of the land." But
this is a Syr. idiom for "husbandry." D adds "(we
are) not even (bound to) one craft (whether it be)
. . ."

i. D: "brass."

j. Or "winter." B (due to the turning of a leaf)
omits "rain is with us; neither snow nor . . ."

k. Or "wall, defense." B omits "like a bulwark."

l. D adds "pleasant."

m. Lit. "enlightened appearance"; B: "and we
possess an enlightened mind"; D: "and no son of
darkness (*sic*) enters among us. And we possess
an enlightened mind. And we dwell in fair (or
beautiful) light."

n. B omits the "and" and later adds a *dyn*.

o. B omits.

p. This verb, *šwtp*, means "to communicate,"
or "to administer" the Eucharist; but in the Eth-
paual, the form here, it means not only "to
communicate" but also "to have conjugal intercourse."

q. Or "are, live."

r. Lit. "until the end of."

s. Or "lust, desire, appetite"; B D: "of the
copulation (or marriage)."

t. Lit. "heart," but also "mind."

u. A B; D: "of them."

v. Or "copulation"; see the variant in B D cited
in n. s.

w. D: "and one."

x. Lit. "it was commanded to us."

y. Or "course."

12 a. D omits *dyn*.

b. Lit. "But a measurer of the years there is not
among us." For "years" D has "life."

c. The adverb clarifies the continuing activity
denoted by the Semitic participle.

d. Lit. "do business (or worship, cf. 12:9f.)
and give."

e. D omits.

f. Or "be diminished"; but "decrease" is preferred because the preceding verb does not mean
"be increased." The linguistic data scarcely support an argument that the holy increase their own
years, but God decreases the years of sinners.

g. Lit. "And no computation of months and
years is with us." For "and of years" D has
"*wdšb*ʾ and days"; *wdšb*ʾ is an error for *wdšb*ᶜ (or
*wdšbw*ᶜ), which means "and of weeks"; hence D:
"and of weeks and days." After "among us" D
adds "or of hours."

h. D: "But we are not naked as you suppose
. . ."

i. D adds "we are decked (or arrayed) with a
stole of glory." D then omits everything until after

covering of glory; and we do not show each other the private parts of our bodies.
3a But we are covered with a stole[j] of glory (similar to that)[k] which clothed Adam
4 and Eve before they sinned.[l] •We[m] are nourished by the fruits of the trees at the
ninth hour; not that the hours are distinguished among us,[n] but when the time for
our[o] nourishment arrives, the fruits of the trees come[p] among us, although they
4a do not fall by our will.[q] •And thus we are nourished from them sufficient (to) our
need. And afterward we drink from the exceedingly good, sweet, and delightful
5 water which comes out to us from the roots of the trees. •And then the water
returns and is gathered together (in its original place).
6   We[r] have knowledge about you people[s] who inhabit the world, and how you
are. We know the works of the righteous and the works of the wicked, because
the angels of God come among us continually and inform us concerning your
7 deeds and the length[t] of your life. •We[u] pray for you,[v] petitioning God on your
7a account because we are also from your (race) and from the sons of Adam. •And
God set us apart and chose us according to his will; and he brought (and) placed
8 us in this place in which we are (now). •And the angels of God dwell with us
and they announce to us those things which (happen) among you; and we rejoice
9 at the good deeds which the upright who are among you do. •And we grieve over
the sinners and pagans[w] who are in the world; and petition God constantly[x] to
restrain[y] his[z] anger concerning you.[a2]
9a   To us[b2] the holy angels[c2] of God announce[d2] (both) the incarnation of the Word
of God, who (is) from the holy virgin, the mother of God,[e2] and all those things
which (he) provides and perfects and endures[f2] for the sake of the salvation of
9b mortals. •And then we worship and acknowledge and glorify (him)[g2] for the sake
9c of the glory[h2] of his incarnate life.[i2] •Then we ask for your love, O people, that
9d you will not be unfaithful[j2] when you chance to read this history. •Do not surrender
to the cruel and merciless ruler,[k2] but be shrouded[l2] by the secrets which were
9e entrusted to you. •And let this history be for you the salvation of your lives.
9f Have regard to us in your hidden thoughts,[m2] be imitators of our way of life,

the next "glory" in vs. 3a. This reading seems to be an error (parablepsis facilitated by homoeoteleuton). See D's reading given below in n. m.

j. Gk. loan word, *'stl*.
k. D has *'yk*, "like."
l. D adds: "and transgressed the commandment. And we do not show each other the private parts of the body as you think (or as it is shown to you)."
m. The Syr. contains an unnecessary *dyn*.
n. A omits "but when the time for our nourishment arrives, the fruits of the trees come among us." The reading given above is from B with nn. to variants in D. A is defective; the error is caused by a scribe skipping from one *lwtn*, "among us," to the next *lwtn*, "among us." Perhaps the scribe of A committed this error (homoeoteleuton) since the first *lwtn* completed the line and his eye wandered back to the right margin of his own manuscript.
o. D omits.
p. D: "fall off."
q. For "although they do not fall by our will," D has "We do not put them in a sack, but in their season they yield the need." D's *mḥtynn* seems to be a Peʿal masculine plural participle with a first-person plural suffix of an unattested verb. The verb derives from *ḥṭ*, "a sack, bag." The verb also appears in the Hymn of the Pearl 12.
r. The Syr. contains a *dyn* which is unnecessary but acceptable.
s. Lit. "about you sons of men."
t. Lit. "numbers."

u. The Syr. contains a *dyn*.
v. A Syr. idiom; lit. "your faces."
w. Or "heathen, unbelievers."
x. Or "continually."
y. Lit. "be restrained from." B D: "refrain from."
z. D omits.
a2. D adds: "and determine for you reconciliation (or peace) until the end of the age."
b2. The Syr. contains a *dyn*. The remaining vss. of ch. 12 (i.e. 9a–9g) are not preserved in Gk. These additional vss. are clearly Christian and an expansion of the essentially Jewish account. They are composed in a Syr. style superior to that of the preceding vss.
c2. B: "But the holy angel of God announces to us . . ."
d2. D: "And knowing you are virtuous (or good, beautiful) the holy angels announce to us . . ."
e2. B D add "Mary." Nau's printed text is misleading in these vss.
f2. D adds "from those who hate."
g2. B has *lh*, "him."
h2. B omits.
i2. Lit. "The glory of his guidance (or providence) when in the flesh." D: "Then we worship and acknowledge all the glory of his guidance when in the flesh."
j2. Or "unchristian, unbelieving."
k2. D: "judge."
l2. Lit. "hemmed in."
m2. Lit. "minds."

pursue peace,[n2] cherish the love (that is) unchangeable,[o2] and love purity and
9g holiness. •And you will be made perfect in all good things[p2] and inherit the
kingdom of God.

1   **13** We[a] perceive (that)[b] the holy fast of forty (days)[c] of our LORD (has begun
2 when) the fruits of the trees are withheld and cease (developing). •And on each
of the days of the holy fast God causes to rain down upon us from heaven manna
(similar to) that which he gave to our fathers when he led them out of Egypt.
3 We learn that the holy Passover will arrive when these trees among us flourish
4 and produce[d] magnificently sweet and abundant[e] fruits. •Then we know that the
5 Passover of our LORD (has arrived). •But on the feast of our LORD's resurrection[f]
5a from the grave[g] we watch[h] (for) three days and three nights. •Then we are filled
with gladness and rejoicing,[i] perceiving that the holy feast of the resurrection of
5b our LORD (has arrived). •And with a spiritual cheerfulness we rejoice while
celebrating with the holy angels; likewise also we exult and sing praises during
5c all of the noble[j] and saving feasts of the providence[k] of our LORD. •And all the
assembly which (are) above us and all the heavenly hosts[l] rejoice (with us)[m] in
these feasts.[n]

(1)1a   **14** And again we announce to you, O brothers, that among us there is no sickness,
pain, fatigue to our bodies, mutilation, weariness, or temptations;[a] not even Satan's
power can touch us,[b] for there is not among us rage, jealousy, evil desire,[c] or
hateful thoughts. But (we experience only) quietness[d] and gladness; and (exhibit)
2 love and affection toward God and each other.[e] •And the soul[f] of each of us is
not wearied or sorrowful or wishes to stay behind when the angels of God come
to guide it from the body. But we are glad and rejoice and the holy angels (rejoice)
with us when they are sent out after the soul of each of us.[g]
3   As the bride[h] rejoices over her betrothed bridegroom, so the soul[i] rejoices at
the good news[j] of the holy angels. For they (the angels) say to it nothing except
4 this alone: "O pure soul,[k] your LORD is calling you to come to him." •Then the
soul[l] with great rejoicing leaves the body to meet the angel.[m] And seeing that pure
soul,[n] which has (just) left the body, all the holy angels unfold (for it)[o] their

n2. Lit. "run after peace again."
o2. A adds "and do not be greatly disturbed."
A seems less reliable in these vss.
p2. A: "in all bountifully good things."

13 a. A contains an initial *twb* and an otiose *dyn*.
b. Lit. "We perceive it from this . . ."
c. Or "Lent."
d. Or "bud, germinate."
e. Lit. "trees, sweet (and) of magnificence (praise, glory), and of abundance."
f. "The feast of the resurrection" is the Syr. expression for Easter. The Syr. in this section is excellent. D: "But on the great and glorious feast of his resurrection."
g. Or "Sheol."
h. Or "keep vigil."
i. D adds "(that) is ineffable to our souls and bodies." D here, as so often elsewhere, is expanded.
j. Lit. "lordly."
k. The emphasis is upon the effects of Jesus' earthly life; cf. n. i2 in 12:9b ("his providence when in the flesh").
l. Or "heavenly powers."
m. A omits; B D have "with us."
n. B: "in our feasts." D: "in the splendid feasts of the Messiah, God."

14 a. Or "trials."
b. Or "approach among us."

c. Or "lust." B omits "evil." This verse is much shorter in Gk.
d. Or "serenity."
e. After 14:1a there are numerous variants in D: "weariness or temptation of tempting (or the Tempter) and not even Satan, and the power of the Tempter shall approach us or enter here among us; and there is not among us rage, or the murderer's jealousy (lit. jealousy the murderer), or hateful thoughts, or evil desire, or one of wars. But (we experience only) quietness and gladness, and continual calm; and (exhibit) serene love and complete affection toward God and each other." It appears that a scribe has expanded and clarified the base text.
f. Or "being"; this section of the document clearly reflects the concept that mankind is bifurcated into "soul" and "body."
g. Or "beings."
h. B: "the pure bride."
i. Or "being."
j. B adds "which is pure which is received from . . ."
k. Or "being."
l. Or "being."
m. Lit. "to the meeting of the angel." Contrast this account with the story about Abraham's refusal to let God's messenger have his soul as described in TAb 15–20.
n. Or "being."
o. D adds "for it."

5 shining stoles.ᵖ •And they receive it with�q joy, saying, "Blessed are you, O pure soul,ʳ and blest, for you have thoroughly done the will of God, your LORD."
5a Andˢ this (is how) he brings his providence to each one of us:

(1-3)4 **15** (The soul)ᵃ discerns and knows the day of its departureᵇ through a revelation
4a from holy angels.ᶜ •And we live an extremely long time;ᵈ and the extentᵉ of our
4b life (is) not brief and short as with you. •When the holy angelsᶠ are sent among us,ᵍ in this beautiful orderʰ (of which) we have informed you, they visit among
(5)4c us. •However, first they come to our elders; and when the blessed elders see the angels who have come, they immediately with joy entreatⁱ (so that) all the blessed
6 brothers assemble. •And when all the people have assembled, immediately with
7 praise we come with the angels to the place in which bodies are buried. •And because we have nothing to use for digging,ᵏ the angels themselves make a
7a sepulchre for the bodies. •And again when all of these (souls)ˡ have completed (their time),ᵐ then they are separated from our assembly; and (each) departsⁿ with
8 great joy. •And all of us with exultation come near to itᵒ and offer itᵖ peace in the kiss of the LORD while it is being conducted and led (to the grave) by the holy
9 angels. •And then the soulq of our blessed brother leaves the body in which it had
9a settled; •and with joy far removed from mourning it approaches and comes to the
10 holy angelsʳ and ascends up to God withˢ joy. •But we with one accord see the soulᵗ when itᵘ leaves the body clearly and plainly; the appearance of the soulᵛ when it leaves the body is the likeness of a glorious light, and formed and imprinted in the likeness and typeʷ of the body,ˣ and it is spiritually flying.

1 **16** And while we are looking at that holy and spotless soul,ᵃ the holy angels carry it away and salute it,ᵇ and thus it ascends and goes up from us in glory. And after it ascends with them and passes into the regionᶜ of the power of the
1a highest heavens, then other ordersᵈ (of angels) receive it with joy. •And the archangels salute it;ᵉ and afterward they stretch out to it (their hands and lead it) to the thrones and dominionsᶠ that (are) above them. And thus it goes up and
1b ascends until it enters (before) and worships the LORD.ᵍ •And when the highest

---

p. Gk. loan word, 'sṭl'; see n. j to ch. 12.
q. The Syr. contains an unnecessary dyn.
r. Or "being."
s. Dyn.

15 a. Apparently this subject is assumed; if so the two masculine participles should be changed to feminine, since npš', "soul," is feminine. The Gk. contains three other vss. here.
  b. D adds "from the body."
  c. Here D adds 13 ll.; they expand upon the idea of departing from the body and seem secondary. This sentence, 15:4, is found in Gk. at the beginning of ch. 14.
  d. Lit. "extremely large duration." B D: "extremely larger duration of time."
  e. Lit. "measuring, age."
  f. B D add "of God."
  g. B adds "after the soul of one of us"; D: "and descend after our souls."
  h. Gk. loan word, ṭks'.
  i. Or "command."
  j. B D add "with joy."
  k. Syr. idiom; lit. "And because we, there is nothing among us, to complete with it what is needed for digging."
  l. Here the Syr. correctly has the feminine forms for the pronouns.
  m. Or "have died."
  n. The verbs and particles are masculine; they should be feminine, since npš', "soul," is the

subject. Perhaps in this and the following ll. the scribe has become confused and is thinking about pgr', "the body," which is masculine.
  o. A dot should be placed over the h to denote that it is a feminine pronoun. The dot is not in A B D.
  p. See the preceding n.
  q. Or "being."
  r. B D add "of God."
  s. D adds "great."
  t. Or "being."
  u. The h correctly has a dot over it.
  v. Or "being."
  w. Gk. loan word, ṭwps'.
  x. D adds (in line with the Gk.): "subtracting (only that which is) necessary (to denote) male and female."

16 a. Or "being."
  b. Lit. "And while we are looking at it the holy angels carry away that holy and spotless soul and offer it peace."
  c. Lit. "the beginning, origin."
  d. Gk. loan word, l'gm'. Compare the idea in these vss. with the concept of the ascending quality of the angels as one passes from the lowest to the highest heaven, as recorded in AscenIs.
  e. Lit. "offer it peace."
  f. D adds "and principalities."
  g. B D: "God, its LORD."

order[h] of cherubim and seraphim receive it, they rise to the gate of the holy
2 Trinity. •Then the Son of God receives that soul[i] from their hands and brings it
(3,4)5 (forward) so that it may worship his father. •And when the soul[j] falls down upon
its[k] face to worship before God, then the revelation[l] is revealed to us, (and) all of
6 us fall upon the land and worship the LORD with the soul.[m] •And when God makes
(7)7a that soul[n] rise from its worship, we also rise to our feet.[o] •And then God[p] sends
that soul[q] to a stately[r] mansion[s] (to await) the day of resurrection[t] for (the rest of
7b our) community.[u] •Then we also go away from the body of that soul[v] of our
brother to our (own) assembly[w] and complete the service through praises to[x] the
8 Holy Spirit.[y] •And so we have engraved[z] (upon) these tablets and sent (them) to
you through the hands of our brother Zosimus.[a2]

(3)8a   And again God, our Creator, has given us this (privilege): we hear the voices[b2]
of the spirits[c2] and the praises of the angels,[d2] the hosts, and the heavenly orders,[e2]
(3)8b who continually praise[f2] God. •When they praise[g2] (God),[h2] so also we in our
land[i2] praise[j2] (him).

8c   And the angels receive and transmit our prayers and our praises (by) entering
and worshiping in love before that divine and mystic[k2] throne, (which) knows
8d secrets.[l2] •And thus[m2] by the aid of the angels[n2] and the heavenly hosts[o2] our
8e prayers[p2] pass on and find entrance[q2] before God. •This is all of our manner[r2] (of
life).[s2] And we are truly called the Blessed Ones, because we experience the
8f benevolence of God.[t2] •And we write and send (these tablets) to you, O people
who dwell in that world of vanity,[u2] through the hands of this our brother Zosimus,[v2]
who entered among us for your sake through the mercies (of God)[w2] and remained
8g with us (for) seven days. •And accompanying him we traveled with him until (we
came) to the shores of the great ocean.[x2]

---

h. Lit. "highest orders." Gk. loan word, *t'gm'*.
i. Or "being."
j. Or "being."
k. In this ch. the *h* correctly has a dot over it.
l. D: "the heavenly revelation."
m. Or "being."
n. Or "being."
o. D adds "upon the land."
p. D: "The God of gods."
q. Or "being."
r. Lit. "comely, fair."
s. Or "lodging, inn, abode." The same noun is used in Jn 14:2, 23. Cf. also 2En 61:2. B D add "to journey to it."
t. D: "the last day"; D: "the day of general rising up (or resurrection)."
u. A has the dot in the wrong place; it should denote a *d, not* an *r*. D omits this word. The description of the soul's ascent after death is by no means gnostic; yet it is unique in the history of Jewish and Jewish-Christian literature. The description of the successive stages or orders of angels and the emphasis upon singing may have been influenced by the traditions now preserved in AscenIs.
v. Or "being."
w. D: "to the congregations (or churches) and to the assemblies and to our (own) positions (or offices) (which are) holy and noble."
x. Lit. "of."
y. B D add "that is pure and holy to the LORD. This is our providence (guidance), (we), the Blessed Ones, in truth."
z. What has been engraved is not specified, but it is obviously the account just written.
a2. Nau overlooked the phrase "through the hands of our brother Zosimus"; it is in A but not in B D. The variants in these vss. are significant.
b2. Lit. "voice"; none of the Syr. MSS have the dots that denote the plural.

c2. B: "of the angels"; D: "of the angels and of the spirits."
d2. B: "of the spirits"; D omits "and the praises" and has "with their holy proclamations and their praises."
e2. Gk. loan word *t'gm'*.
f2. Or "glorify."
g2. Or "glorify."
h2. A D do not contain the noun "God," but B has it.
i2. D adds "below."
j2. Or "glorify."
k2. Or "hidden, secret." For "divine," D has "of God."
l2. D adds "and revelations (or things public)."
m2. The Syr. has an otiose *dyn*.
n2. D omits "by the aid of the angels" and has "in the midst of the orders."
o2. Or "heavenly powers."
p2. D: "our spiritual prayers."
q2. D: "are received (or accepted)." In Jewish apocalyptic, the emphasis is placed upon the fact that God hears prayers.
r2. Or "providence, rule, stewardship."
s2. D adds "and our mystic (or hidden, secret) history."
t2. B D omit "because we experience the benevolence of God."
u2. D: "in the world of vanity and in (or on) the land of thorns."
v2. D: "through the hands of our beloved brother Zosimus, the ascetic (or hermit)."
w2. B: "the mercies of God"; D: "the mercies and grace (or goodness) of God."
x2. Gk. loan word, *'wqynws*. B: "Then they accompanied me and journeyed (with me) until the shore of the ocean." D: "Then they accompanied me and they journeyed with me (correcting *'myd* to *'my*) until the shore of the sea."

(1)1a **17** And[a] then all of us together knelt down[b] upon the shores of the sea and prayed
,3)3a and petitioned God to be for our brother Zosimus a guide and a refuge. • And then
immediately in a moment a white cloud appeared above the sea and its top   2:8
3b extended to the highest summit. • And we praised God, (confessing) that it is easy
for him to do everything.

4(4a)   Then suddenly two trees appeared in the middle of the sea and by a command   3:2
4b of God one of these trees bent down toward me,[c] Zosimus. • And it held me
securely in its branches and stretched (itself) out to the height of heaven; and
carried me and lifted me gently unto the summit and the top of that white cloud.
(5)5a And that second[d] tree bent down toward me, then that (first) one now bent its
head;[e] and that (second) tree also bent down toward me, (lifted me up), and
5b brought me to dry land.[f] • And again I crossed the ocean,[g] the great sea, and that
5c cloud. • And I gave thanks unto and praised the merciful God, who fulfills the
desires[h] of those who fear him, and who hears their petition and saves them.

2)3,4 **18** And suddenly that animal arrived and carried me; •(and) it brought me to the   2:3
cave while I praised and exalted God, who had answered me and heard my
petition[a] and fulfilled my desire. To him (be) praise, amen, from heavenly and
earthly (beings) for all time, amen.[b]

         (The Gk. contains chs. 19–23, which appear to be later expansions by a
Christian.)[c]

---

17 a. B D vary so much from A in chs. 17 and
18 that for the purposes of this translation it would
be unsuitable to note the variants. Only the ending
in each will be included.
   b. Lit. "put a blessing."
   c. B D switched to the first person in 16:8g; A
now shifts to the first person.
   d. Lit. "other."
   e. Or "And that one bent its head from here."
   f. The Syr. is inelegant.
   g. Gk. loan word, 'wqynws.
   h. Or "who does the will."

18 a. Lit. "and heard the voice of my petition."
   b. A ends as follows: *"This history ends."* After
18:4, B ends as follows: "while I praised and
exalted God, who had answered me and heard the
voice of my petition. That to him (be) praise from
all, and for all and because of all (his providence);
and everyone who believes in this history of these
Blessed Ones, the sons of Jonadab, the son of
Rechab, upon him shall be the mercies of God
through the prayers of the blessed Mother, Theotokos (or Deipara or Mother of God), Mary, and
of all the holy ones, now and in all time, and

forever, amen. *The history of the sons of Rechab
ends."* After 18:4, D ends as follows: "and I
praised and exalted God, who had answered me
and heard my voice, my petition. That to him (be)
praise from all, and for all and because of all (his
providence); now and in all time, and forever,
amen. *The history of the Blessed Ones, the sons
of Rechab. But may their prayer be for us a
bulwark."* C ends as follows: "Then an angel of
the LORD came and took the holy Zosimus and
brought him to the district (or country) of Palestine
and placed him in an inhabited monastery. He was
in it so that by his prayers and those of the Blessed
Ones the wretched one who writes could make
supplication and receive mercy. Amen and amen
(no rubrics here in C)."
   c. Ch. 19 contains an account of how Zosimus,
"blessed one of Christ," is warned that he is about
to be tempted by "Satan." Chs. 20 and 21 describe
"the Devil's" approach to Zosimus, torment by
him, and his final defeat by Zosimus' prayer. Ch.
22 recounts how Zosimus teaches the fathers in the
desert and leaves them "this testament." Ch. 23
introduces Cryseos, a desert hermit, who publicizes
Zosimus' testament; Zosimus' body is buried and
his soul shines "seven times brighter than the sun."

ELDAD AND MODAD

(Prior to the Second Century A.D.)

A NEW TRANSLATION AND INTRODUCTION

BY E. G. MARTIN

Extant Text: "The LORD is near to those who turn (to him)," as it is written in the (book of) Eldad and Modad, who prophesied in the desert to the people.

(Hermas, Vision, 2.3.4)

Introduction

According to Numbers 11:26–29 Eldad and Modad (Medad) were the two prophets among the elders in the wilderness who continued to prophesy within the camp. Although the Old Testament does not report the contents of their prophecy, later generations "supplied" the missing portions. A pseudepigraphon, now lost, contained these lost ecstatic prophecies. According to rabbinic sources, the contents of the Book of Eldad and Modad apparently contained references to Gog and Magog, the end of time, and the coming of a royal Messiah. The one specific quotation from the book supplies no information on the contents of the prophecy.

Texts

The only quotation occurs in the Visions of the Shepherd of Hermas, 2.3.4. The citation is in Greek, and there are Latin, Ethiopic, and Coptic versions derived from the Greek. For critical editions, see the following:

Funk, F. X. *Patres Apostolici* (Tübingen, 1901²) vol. 1, p. 429.
Whittaker, M. *Die Apostolischen Väter*. I: *Der Hirt des Hermas* (GCS 48; Berlin, 1956) p. 7.

Original language, date, and provenance

With only four words extant, it is not possible to determine the original language. The book was written before the Shepherd of Hermas, which dates from the second century A.D., but again, with the brevity of the quotation, it is not possible to determine a more specific date. The provenance could be any Jewish, Christian, or Jewish-Christian area.

Historical importance

For a document which exists in the form of a single four-word quotation in a single Church Father, a considerable amount of historical importance has been attached to Eldad and Modad by scholars from J. A. Fabricius[1] to the present. Because of one citation and five references in ancient canonical lists (see below), Eldad and Modad has aroused considerable interest and speculation.

The book was known in the early Church from the apostolic period, and apparently was

---

[1] J. A. Fabricius, *Codex Pseudepigraphus Veteris Testamenti* (Hamburg, 1722) vol. 1, pp. 801–4.

widespread as late as the eighth or ninth century.[2] Not only does the Shepherd of Hermas quote Eldad and Modad, but Epiphanius[3] and Pseudo-Jerome[4] also make reference, respectively, to the numbering of the two prophets among the seventy-two prophets in the wilderness, and to the two prophets as being half brothers of Moses. This, however, points to the difficult problem with the lost pseudepigraphon: Does each reference to Eldad and Modad in a patristic or rabbinic source necessarily refer to the document, or is the information concerning the two prophets based upon other traditions? The logical answer would be that Eldad and Modad were popular figures to whom a book of prophecy was assigned, but additional details concerning the prophets were also known.

Whatever might have been known concerning the two prophets, only one source, the Targum of Pseudo-Jonathan on Numbers 11:26, lists the possible contents of their prophecy. The two prophets predicted the assault upon Jerusalem, the end of days which would be brought about by a war involving Gog and Magog, and the defeat of evil at the hands of a royal Messiah. This messianic prophecy in the Targum contains a quotation of Eldad and Modad, "The LORD (*qîrîs*) is near to those in distress," which is very similar to the quotation from Eldad and Modad in Hermas. This similarity suggests that the source of the Targum reference and the Hermas reference is the same Book of Eldad and Modad, and that the contents of that book are described in the Targum. Additional details concerning the prophecies or persons of Eldad and Modad in rabbinic writings[5] also may have been based upon the lost pseudepigraphon.

Some scholars have attempted to identify the lost pseudepigraphon of Eldad and Modad either with anonymous citations in patristic writings or with recently translated documents. J. B. Lightfoot[6] suggested that references in 1 Clement 23:3f. and 2 Clement 2:2–4 refer to Eldad and Modad. These passages are sufficiently obscure that they have been applied also to the Testament of Moses and the Apocryphon of Ezekiel; hence the most prudent course is to leave these verses anonymous.[7] M. R. James[8] attempted to show the relationship of Eldad and Modad to the legend of the lost tribes as displayed in the History of the Rechabites, the Acts of Matthew, the Contendings of the Apostles, and two poems by Commodian. He bases this conclusion upon the similarity of the names "Eldad" and the ninth-century-A.D. traveler "Eldad ha-Dani." The similarities are insufficient to warrant additional study. Similarly, James's suggestion[9] that a fragment of Eldad and Modad may have been quoted in the Vision of Kenaz is unlikely; Denis[10] suggests that this fragment probably came from Pseudo-Philo.

The Book of Eldad and Modad continued to be popular into the early Middle Ages. It occupies the sixth place in the Addition to the List of Sixty Books. It is mentioned seventh in the Armenian List of Michithar, in the List of Pseudo-Athanasius, and in the Stichometry of Nicephorus, who also notes that it contains four hundred stichoi (ll.).[11]

Theological importance

Given the brevity of the quotation in Hermas, little weight should be given to its theological importance, other than noting the tendency of producing pseudepigrapha which "explain" or "supply" material not found in the Old Testament. The widespread nature of the references to Eldad and Modad suggests that the book may have been well known in antiquity.

---

[2] The date of the most recent canonical list, the Stichometry of Nicephorus, is A.D. 800.

[3] Epiphanius, *De Fide* 4.5 (ed. K. Holl, GCS 37; Leipzig, 1922), pp. 500, 509.

[4] Jerome, *Quaestiones Hebraicae in Librum I Paralipomenon* 4.17; PL, 23, col. 1437. (This was actually falsely attributed to Jerome.)

[5] See esp. b.Sanh 17a; NumR 15:19; cf. b.Sanh 96b–97a, 98a; and SifNum 96.

[6] J. B. Lightfoot in Funk, *Patres Apostolici* (Tübingen, 1901[2]) vol. 1, p. 131.

[7] Cf. A.-M. Denis, *Introduction*, p. 144.

[8] M. R. James, *Apocrypha Anecdota* (T&S 2.3; Cambridge, England, 1893) p. 94.

[9] Ibid., p. 175.

[10] Denis, *Introduction*, p. 145.

[11] Ibid., p. 142. (Many of the ancient canon lists are discussed in and quoted by T. Zahn, *Geschichte des Neutestamentlichen Kanons* [Erlangen, 1890]. For recent research on the Armenian lists, see M. E. Stone, "Armenian Canon Lists II—the Stichometry of Anania of Shirak," *HTR* 68 [1975] 253–60.)

Relation to canonical books

The figures of Eldad and Modad were insignificant tribal prophets who are mentioned only once in the Old Testament (Num 11:26–29). The prophecy as given in the Targum bears little similarity to that of the account in Numbers. There is no apparent relationship between the references in Hermas and Numbers. Eldad and Modad are not mentioned in the New Testament.

Relation to apocryphal books

The Book of Eldad and Modad is not quoted or mentioned in any of the non-canonical books. Apparently, the two prophets are also not mentioned in any of the documents of the Apocrypha or the Pseudepigrapha. It has been suggested, most recently by Denis,[12] that the name "Eldad" and the "Land of Elda" in Jubilees 3:32 are related, but this seems unlikely. Finally, there is the suggestion by James (mentioned above), who relates this document to the legend of the lost tribes and the History of the Rechabites, because of the relationship between the names of Eldad and the ninth-century traveler Eldad ha-Dani; but the connection is insignificant.

SELECT BIBLIOGRAPHY

Charlesworth, *PMR*, pp. 94f.
Denis, *Introduction*, pp. 142–45.

Aberbach, M. "Eldad and Modad," *EncyJud*, vol. 6, cols. 575f.
Chréstou, P. K. "Eldad and Modad," *ThĒE*, vol. 5, cols. 551f. (in Gk.)
Denis, A.-M. *Fragmenta Pseudepigraphorum Graeca*. PVTG 3; Leiden, 1970; p. 68.
Fabricius, J. A. *Codex Pseudepigraphus Veteris Testamenti*. Hamburg, 1722; vol. 1, pp. 801–4.
James, M. R. *Apocrypha Anecdota*. T&S 2.3; Cambridge, 1893; p. 94.
———. *Lost Apocrypha of the Old Testament*. London, 1920; pp. 38–40.
Wallis, G. "Eldad und Modad," *BHH;* vol. 1, col. 390.
White, W., Jr. "Eldad and Modad, Book of," *ZPEB;* vol. 2, p. 266.

---

[12] Denis, *Introduction*, p. 143.

HISTORY OF JOSEPH

(Prior to the Fourth Century A.D.)

A NEW TRANSLATION AND INTRODUCTION

BY G. T. ZERVOS

As nearly as can be determined from the meager textual material under consideration, the document which H. J. M. Milne labeled the "History of Joseph"[1] seems to be a Jewish midrashic expansion of a portion of the Book of Genesis.[2] By a comparison of the surviving fragments of our document with the corresponding biblical text, we may conclude that the History of Joseph dealt with at least the following matters: the establishment of Joseph by Pharaoh over Egypt; the gathering of grain before the famine; the coming of the famine and subsequent dispensation of the grain; the appearance of Joseph's ten brothers before him to buy grain; his recognition of them and emotional turning away; his accusing them of espionage; his inquiry about their family; his brothers' fear, prayer to God, and attempt to clear themselves; Joseph's statement about testing their story; the brothers' discussion in jail and Reuben's statement that their troubles stem from their mistreatment of Joseph; the return of nine brothers to Canaan; Jacob's surprise at seeing that one of them was missing and his inquiry about Simon; the brothers' explanation of the events which had transpired in Egypt; and Jacob's lamentation about losing Simon now as he had lost Joseph before.

Texts

The History of Joseph is partially extant on several Greek papyrus fragments which are preserved in the British Museum; the Bodleian Library, at Oxford; and the Louvre. Descriptions and complete transcriptions of the two fragments belonging to the British Museum have been published in Milne's *Catalogue of the Literary Papyri in the British Museum* (pp. 187–90) under numbers 226 and 227 (hereafter referred to as A and B, respectively). Milne's transcription has been reproduced in A.-M. Denis's *Fragmenta Pseudepigraphorum Quae Supersunt Graeca* (PVTG 3; Leiden, 1970; pp. 235f.). Facsimiles of A verso and B recto may be found in F. G. Kenyon's *Greek Papyri in the British Museum* (London, 1893; vol. 1, pp. 225, 227, under numbers 113 [13a] and 113 [12b], respectively). These two fragments have been dated by Milne to the sixth or seventh century.

Milne correctly observes that there are two different hands present in A and B, but he gives the mistaken impression that each of these fragments is written completely in only one of the two hands. This is, in fact, the case with A, but B contains both of the scripts. The first thirteen lines of B verso are written in the large, upright uncial hand which is also that present in A. However, the last four lines of B verso and all of B recto are written in the smaller, sloping uncial script which is easily distinguishable from the hand of A and B

---

[1] H. J. M. Milne, ed., *Catalogue of the Literary Papyri in the British Museum* (London, 1927) pp. 187, 189. Although this title perhaps is appropriate for the present fragments, which deal exclusively with the Joseph story, its applicability for the entire document is questionable, since the extent of the original work is unknown.

[2] For the midrashic character of the HistJos see "Relation to Canonical and Apocryphal Books." A B seem to correspond to Gen 41:39–42:36, but C–E are so fragmentary that it is difficult to pinpoint precisely the biblical context which they represent.

verso 1–13. Thus, we seem to have in B verso an interesting example of a page in which one scribe took over the work of copying a document from another.

Transcriptions of three more papyrus fragments belonging to the History of Joseph and, in all probability, to the same manuscript of this document as A and B have been published by W. M. Lindsay in *The Athenaeum* (Number 3019; Sept. 5, 1885; p. 304). Lindsay's fragments i. (hereafter C) and ii. (hereafter D) appear to be written in the same hand as that found in B verso 14–17 and all of B recto; Lindsay's fragment iii. (hereafter E) contains a script which seems to be identical to that of A and B verso 1–13.[3] It is perhaps significant that both Milne, in reference to A and B, and Lindsay, with respect to C, D, and E, report that their fragments were discovered in the Fayum of Egypt. The facts that they are written in the same scripts and have a common place of origin support the possibility that fragments A, B, C, D, and E originally belonged to the same manuscript.

A single unpublished papyrus fragment, which represents a different copy of our document, is preserved in the Louvre under catalogue number E. 7738a (hereafter F). F is written in a hand distinct from those observed in A through E and consists of two originally separate pieces. The smaller fragment, which is long and narrow and from the top of a page, has been joined to the upper left hand corner (recto) of the second piece, which is substantially larger and from the bottom of a page. Although both fragments contain the same script, the manner in which they have been connected is questionable. F, for the most part, does not preserve enough writing to add significantly to the text of our document. However, the recto of this fragment contains some lines which occur also in B recto and can therefore be used to correct and supplement the text of that fragment.

The present translation is based upon the texts of A and B as found in the works of Milne and Denis. Possible corrections of those texts, resulting from a study of photographs[4] of A, B, and F will be suggested in the present edition. Of the Bodleian papyri only C contains sufficient context to warrant translation. This will be added after B recto, because C was written by our second scribe, who took over at B verso 14 and subsequently copied all of B recto and probably the following pages. It seems likely, therefore, that C should follow B recto, although it cannot be determined how much text originally separated these two fragments.

Original language, date, and provenance

There seems to be no indication that the original language of the History of Joseph is other than Greek. It is perhaps significant that the vocabulary of this document does not appear to be dependent upon that of the Septuagint.

The composition of this work must be placed before the sixth- or seventh-century date of the papyri themselves, given that the two different hands represented in A–E indicate that the manuscript to which these fragments originally belonged was a copy of an older original. However, there seems to be ample reason for ascribing the History of Joseph to a substantially earlier period, especially in view of its parallels with the Targums, Joseph and Asenath, and the Testaments of the Twelve Patriarchs (see below).

In the absence of more conclusive evidence, an Egyptian provenance for our document is implied by: (1) the origination of most of its extant fragments[5] in the Fayum of Egypt

---

[3] That C–E are part of the HistJos is indicated also by the letters *kōb* in C verso 6, which appear to be part of the name Jacob; by the letters *stheis tou Iakōb* in D verso 8, which is almost certainly part of the phrase "Joseph remembering Jacob"; and by the letters *theist* in E recto 7, which seem to belong to another occurrence of the same phrase. For the significance of this phrase in the HistJos see "Theological Importance." Further evidence that D E are from our document may be seen at D recto 4 in the letters *lakk*. These are probably from the word *lakkos* (pit), which occurs in the LXX of the Joseph story at Gen 37:20, 22, 24. D verso 6 reads *akousate huioi* (listen sons), which also fits the context of the HistJos and probably refers to the "sons of Jacob" (cf. A verso 23, B recto 3). E recto 10 contains the letters *lphoi*, which are probably from *adelphoi* (brothers) and refer to the brothers of Joseph. It should be noted that there are inaccuracies in Lindsay's descriptions and transcriptions of the fragments.

[4] I would like to express my appreciation to the British Museum, the Louvre, and the Bodleian Library for providing excellent photographs of their fragments and to the International Center on Christian Origins, at Duke University, for making these photographs available to me. I would also like to thank Professor W. H. Willis for his very helpful suggestions concerning the papyri of the HistJos.

[5] Details about the acquisition of F are not given by S. de Ricci in "Bulletin papyrologique," *Revue des études grecques* 15 (1902) 431.

and (2) the concern of at least the surviving portions of text for events which took place principally in Egypt.

Theological importance

Of particular importance in the History of Joseph is the obvious attempt by the author to elevate the image of Joseph above that presented in the corresponding biblical text. In what is perhaps the single most significant element in this document, Joseph is referred to as "king of the people" (*basileus tou laou*) in A recto 16 (cf. A verso 28). Such references to Joseph as king, or ruler, of Egypt are not unknown in Jewish literature of late antiquity. In fact, these titles are commonly attributed to him in chapters 41–42 of Genesis in Targums Onkelos and Pseudo-Jonathan.[6]

Another example of the exaltation of Joseph in our papyri may be seen in A recto 23 in the words *ephanē tropheus*. This phrase means that Joseph appeared as, or became, a foster father, or rearer, or, more literally, nourisher of the Egyptians. It is interesting to note that in one Greek inscription of the first century A.D., *tropheus* signifies "one who gives free meals to the people."[7] This interpretation would fit our present context admirably.

Further evidence of this elevation of Joseph in our document may be found in A recto 10, where the singular imperative form of the verb *sōzein* (to save) occurs. From the context of lines 9–11 it seems entirely possible that at this point in the story Pharaoh could be asking Joseph to save him and Egypt from the coming famine. Support for this reading may be seen later in the biblical narrative (Gen 47:25), where the Egyptian people are described as saying to Joseph, "You have saved our lives . . ."

A final example of the exaltation of Joseph is the occurrence of the phrase "the God of Joseph" in B verso 11 and B recto 9 (cf. A verso 24). The first instance occurs during the conversation between Joseph's brothers in which Reuben apparently states that the "God of Joseph" has brought misfortune upon them for their having sold Joseph into slavery. The second occurrence of this phrase is in an even more unexpected context. B recto contains the dialogue between Jacob and his nine sons who had returned to Canaan. In line nine it seems that the brothers are asking their father to pray, presumably for the safe release of the imprisoned Simon. That the sons of Jacob would ask their father to entreat thus the "God of Joseph" strongly suggests that our document is concerned with the elevation of Joseph.

Another outstanding characteristic of the History of Joseph is the repeated occurrence in the text of the phrase "Joseph remembering Jacob" (A recto 7, 15, 24; A verso 5, 15; B verso 11?).[8] Although no single one of these lines contains all the words of the phrase complete, it would seem that Milne's restoration in each case of the missing elements is valid. At any rate, the existence of frequent references to Joseph's remembering Jacob in such a fragmentary text would indicate that this concept could very well be one of the central themes of our document. Perhaps the phrase "Joseph remembering Jacob" provides us with a hint of the situation in which the History of Joseph was written. Such an emphasis upon the remembrance of Joseph's forefathers could suggest that our document was written in a time of oppression of the Jews, when adherence to their ancestral traditions would be difficult.

Relation to canonical and apocryphal books

The extant text of fragments A and B of the History of Joseph follows the biblical narrative of Genesis 41:39–42:36 along general lines but seems to be more an example of midrashic expansion than a mere translation. This may be demonstrated adequately by a

---

[6] J. W. Etheridge, *The Targums of Onkelos and Jonathan Ben Uzziel on the Pentateuch with the Fragments of the Jerusalem Targum from the Chaldee* (New York, 1968) vol. 1, pp. 128–35, 300–9.

[7] LSJM, p. 1827.

[8] See n. 3 for occurrences of "Joseph remembering Jacob" in the Bodleian fragments. It is interesting that in F this phrase is found only at the end of well-defined sections of the text which are set apart from each other by gaps left on the papyrus. This occurs twice on the recto and once on the verso of F and may also be seen at A recto 7. This phenomenon raises the possibility that the HistJos could have been used at some time for liturgical purposes.

comparison of the first four lines of B recto with their counterpart in the biblical text (Gen 42:29). The text in Genesis reads as follows: "Returning to their father Jacob in the land of Canaan, they gave him a full report of what had happened to them." Corresponding to this single biblical verse, our papyrus contains four lines. In B recto 1 it is clear that "they (the brothers) went to Canaan." In line two the verb *eskirta* (to leap) perhaps refers to some excitement on the part of Jacob—possibly "his heart leapt." This interpretation is supported by what follows in line two: "and the sight"; line three: "the number of the ten"; and line four: "without one" and "he inquired about." Thus, the History of Joseph expands one biblical verse, which stated merely that the brothers returned to their father and related to him what had happened to them, by adding both the agitation of Jacob at the sight of the nine brothers returning without Simon and Jacob's inquiry about the missing brother.

Apart from this obvious dependence of the History of Joseph upon the Book of Genesis for its basic story line, there are also indications of some relation to such early pseudepigraphical works as Joseph and Asenath and the Testaments of the Twelve Patriarchs. It is especially interesting that the three outstanding concepts distinguishable in our papyri of Joseph as king, provider of food, and savior (see above) all occur in a single line of Joseph and Asenath (25:6).[9] The possibility of some affinity between this pseudepigraphon and our document is further strengthened by the occurrence in both of the phrase "God of Joseph" (JosAsen 3:4; 6:4; HistJos B verso 11; B recto 9; A verso 24?). Furthermore, the same sort of elevation of the figure of Joseph, characteristic of the History of Joseph, may be found also in Joseph and Asenath. In the latter work Joseph is described as "the mighty one of God" (3:6; 4:8), "the son of God" (6:2, 6), "the blessed one of the most high God" (8:2), and "the chosen one of God" (13:10).

Finally, yet another important motif of the History of Joseph has a parallel in the Testaments of the Twelve Patriarchs. This is the phrase "Joseph remembering Jacob," which as mentioned above is one of the central themes of our document. In the Testament of Joseph 3:3, as Joseph is recounting the story of his temptation by the wife of Potiphar, he states, "I remembered the words of my father, Jacob." The implication in both documents is that Joseph remembered the wise counsels of his father, Jacob, throughout his trials in Egypt and that this enabled him to overcome his misfortune and to rise from prison to an exalted position as "king" of the land of Egypt.

---

[9] In this line Joseph is referred to as *basileus* (king), *sitodotēs* (giver of grain), and *sōtēr* (savior).

BIBLIOGRAPHY

Charlesworth, *PMR*, p. 138.
Denis, *Introduction*, pp. 47f., 304.

Denis, A.-M. *Fragmenta Pseudepigraphorum Quae Supersunt Graeca.* PVTG 3; Leiden, 1970; pp. 235f. (Reproduces the text of fragments A and B as published by Milne; see below.)
Kenyon, F. G. *Greek Papyri in the British Museum.* London, 1893; vol. 1, pp. 225, 227. (Contains facsimiles of the verso of A and of the recto of B.)
Lindsay, W. M. *The Athenaeum.* Number 3019. Sept. 5, 1885; p. 304. (Includes transcriptions of the three Bodleian fragments.)
Milne, H. J. M., ed. *Catalogue of the Literary Papyri in the British Museum.* London, 1927; pp. 187–90. (Contains descriptions and transcriptions of fragments A and B. It is in this work that our document is first labeled the History of Joseph.)
Ricci, S. de. "Bulletin papyrologique," *Revue des études grecques* 15 (1902) 431. (Calls attention to fragment F from the Louvre as being part of the HistJos.)

A VERSO[a]

1	]zō[	
2	].e[	
3	]ē[	
4	]le[	
5	Jos]eph remembe[ring Jacob?	TJos 3:3
6	?]and [fa]cing[i] the embassy[j] t[	Gen 42:7
7	]on the prayer, exel[	
8	]the ten b[r]oth[ers cov]ered[?	Gen 42:3
9	Jos]eph, then they made obeisance[	Gen 42:6
10	]they bend unto him the[	Gen 42:6
11	]the price of the grain, the g[rain?	Gen 42:7
12	]lōsantes after the[	
13	]bought with silver the . . . of the n[	
14	not[k]] being recognized by them ka[	Gen 42:8
15	]Joseph remembering Ja[cob	TJos 3:3
16	]and [no longer] then containing himsel[f	Gen 42:24
17	]n being absent for a short (time), he left[	Gen 42:24
18	]s to his relatives k[	Gen 42:24
19	]you were seeking . .[to b]uy grain[	Gen 42:10
20	]ai, but all of you came i[n order to?	Gen 42:12
21	]therefore you showed (that) you are . . . and p[	
22	]you have another relative, .[	Gen 42:13
23	]ēmos of the sons of Jacob, k[	Gen 42:11
24	]God, now save us G[od of Joseph[l]	Gen 42:28
25	]and[ ]enoi the fear for a shor[t (time)	Gen 42:28
26	to K]ing Joseph: "Do not be angry, O K[ing	Gen 42:10
27	]for we[c]ame not to sp[y[m]	Gen 42:11
28	]ēdes of the elde[r	
29	]both he and w[e	Gen 42:13
30	]. t[o] ou[r] land[	
31	]in your[[n]	

B VERSO[o]

1	]. is before you,[	
2	].reton us and s.[	
3	]ete are trustworthy, al.[	Gen 42:16,20

A RECTO

1	].nei[	
2	l]oosed su[	
3	tr]uly after the . . . themselv[es^b	
4	]ein more sensibl[e	Gen 41:39
5	]ton as me ou[r	
6	]ou and corruption rale tēs.^c[	
7	remember]ing Jacob. [	TJos 3:3
8	]es of the earth, and except for you[	Gen 41:43-44
9	]lēs I Pharaoh.[ ]desired[	
10	]. .ou save me also not ph[	Gen 47:25
11	]lōs. . that they may bless me[	JosAsen 25:6
12	]trie. . .ap. . in the disease[	
13	]. . . . . of easy . . . on the one hand the pl[	
14	]. .ukas guards^d .eo. . . .[	
15	]eusen Joseph, remembering[Jacob?	TJos 3:3
16	]theis king of the people ka[	Gen 42:30
17	]. straight there being mu[ch] grain[	JosAsen 25:6 Gen 41:48-49
18	? he sai]d: "Gather unto me tichi^e when[ce	
19	]and [the] famine passe[s] through^f her[	Gen 41:54-57
20	]nē and when^g the a[ ]arrives[	
21	].ntas receiving the com[mand	Gen 41:55
22	]. of every . . . of all the grain up[	
23	].tou he became a provider^h k[	Gen 41:56-57
24	Jose]ph remembering Jac[ob	JosAsen 25:6 TJos 3:3
25	]covere[d th]e land[	Gen 41:54
26	th]e famine euthun[	
27	Pha]raoh upon Jo[seph	Gen 41:39-45
28	b]lessed[	

B RECTO

1	]they went to Canaan[but the^q	Gen 42:29
2	l]eaped,^r and the sigh[t?	
3	t]he number of the ten s[ons^s	

h. Lit. "he appeared (as) a nourisher."

i. Lit. "[st]anding against."

j. Or "group of ambassadors."

k. A *mē* supplied at this point would suit the context better.

l. Milne supplies "Abraham," but in view of B verso 11 and B recto 9 Joseph would seem to be more likely.

m. Lit. "to trace (or track) out."

n. Gk. *tais* could also be the dative plural ending of a noun.

o. The order of B recto and B verso as published by Milne has been reversed in the present edition. Not only does B verso seem to precede B recto according to the story line of Gen 42, but also the first lines of B verso appear to be from the same setting as the last lines of A verso. Furthermore, the hand of the upper part of B verso follows that of A verso, while the shift in hands occurs at the bottom of B verso and continues throughout B recto, thus verifying our reversal of Milne's order.

p. Lit. "with me."

q. Supplied from F.

r. F mistakenly has *eskirda* for *eskirta* in B, thus suggesting that it was a less carefully written manuscript.

s. Milne reads C[anaanites]. However, the last letter preserved in this line could be an *u* rather than a *ch*. This makes possible our restoration of *huiōn*, which would fit the context better.

(B VERSO)

4	]pson .n in my presence^p kata[	Gen 42:15
5	]kate now, lead aw[ay	Gen 42:19
6	th]e relative to[ward?	Gen 42:20
7	]asthe to me, . . . too[k	Gen 42:20
8	]as before the(m)[	Gen 42:24
9	]to them, pa. .akr[	Gen 42:25
10	]ōs justly these (things)[	Gen 42:21-22
11	]the God of Joseph, remem[bering	Gen 42:28
12	]your . . . I will call, Reube[n	JosAsen 3:4; 6:4 Gen 42:22
13	se]rving you, mē[	
14	]not to be angry, flesh[	
15	]ōs acting foolishly ka[	
16	]and . . .mous tou[	
17	]is ka[	

C VERSO

1	]. . . . . . call. .[	
2	]e now shows to the father . .[	
3	]n remain with me a[	
4	]e. and having loosed eu.[	
5	]th each cuts^{c2} my[	
6	]to see [Ja]cob as a deer epi[^{d2}	Ps 41:2(LXX)
7	]. the water lab.[	
8-11	traces of four more lines	

---

t. Both B and F have *deicha* for *dicha*.
u. Supplied from F.
v. F adds "to him" at this point.
w. Supplied from F.
x. Read *kteinai* for *ktinai*.

y. Supplied from F. It is conceivable that "God of Jo[seph" from the following line is the subject of "softened," thus making it possible that in ll. 6–9 the brothers are telling Jacob that the king (Joseph) in Egypt was insolent against them and

(B RECTO)

4	?]without' [th]e one, . . . inqu[ired where"	
5	]and[ ]i says,ᵛ "Listen[	
6	a man inso]lentʷ against us ka[	Gen 42:30
7	]. and becoming ang[ry	Gen 42:30
8	to k]illˣ us bu[t . . . softenedʸ	Gen 42:20,30
9	]by your[entrea]ties the God of Jo[sephᶻ	JosAsen 3:4; 6:4
10	]and that which I do not seek apekr[	
11	Si]mon where, perhaps he also[	Gen 42:36
12	Jo]seph, you have added on[	Gen 42:36
13	]tou I am in my primeᵃ² the t[	
14	b]ring to me . . . of this one o. .[	
15	]menoi now . . . will speak against to[	
16	]dua give knēm. . .[	
17	]. . Simo[n	

C RECTO

1	traces of one line
2	]. seeks to give back .[
3	]. finds not even one di.[
4	]his . . . said, "Do not mim.["
5	]. evil (ones) not the oppres[sedᵇ²
6	]. repa[y] the sellers[
7	]. . . .ōithei to those having stripped .[
8	].n and then to you te[
9-12	traces of four more lines

became angry and was going to kill them, but by Jacob's entreaties the God of Joseph softened his heart.

z. Corrected by reference to F from Milne's "]in your [si]ns the God of Ja[cob."

a2. Lit. "I have the high point."

b2. Possibly "oppres[sors]."

c2. Possibly "mourns" or "beats the breast."

d2. The vocabulary in ll. 6f. is strikingly similar to that in Ps 41:2 (LXX), where the psalmist writes that his soul yearns after God in the same way that a deer yearns after fountains of waters.

WISDOM AND PHILOSOPHICAL LITERATURE

INTRODUCTION
BY J. H. CHARLESWORTH

Long before the establishment of the monarchy under Saul, David, and Solomon, the Israelites probably shared with their neighbors a fondness for wise sayings and philosophical maxims. Because of the wisdom accorded Solomon, the wisdom literature in the Old Testament and the Apocrypha is attributed to him. In the Pseudepigrapha, however, with the exception of the Testament of Solomon, the wisdom tradition is not associated with Solomon. Because of its generic nature and lack of attention to God's actions in history on behalf of the descendants of Abraham, it is often difficult to demarcate the peculiarly Jewish aspect of the following documents.

Wisdom literature is distinct from the Greek philosophical dialogues and writings; it flourished in Egypt, Mesopotamia, and Palestine, and customarily dealt not with strictly religious ideas but, rather, with the practical affairs of life. The aphorisms derive primarily from living in a particular culture. Israel, of course, tended to spiritualize the often secular humanism of other cultures.

Ahiqar does not strictly belong in the Pseudepigrapha. It is not a Jewish but an Assyrian composition and predates the period covered by the present collection. Nevertheless, it is usually associated with the Pseudepigrapha and cannot be subsumed under other collections. It is obviously important for biblical studies; it is referred to in Tobit 1:21f. and probably influenced some of the writings in the New Testament.

In assessing the documents collected below, examine the wisdom books in the Old Testament: Job, Proverbs, Ecclesiastes (cf. the Song of Songs and some of the Psalms); in the Apocrypha: the Book of Wisdom, Ecclesiasticus (cf. Tobit and Baruch); in Philo of Alexandria's and Josephus' writings; in the rabbinic writings (esp. Pirke Aboth); in the gnostic and hermetic documents, and in the wisdom sayings of Jesus of Nazareth. Consult the wisdom sections of the Testaments of the Twelve Patriarchs and many of the fragmentary writings collected in the Supplement.

CONTENTS

Ahiqar
3 Maccabees
4 Maccabees
Pseudo-Phocylides
Syriac Menander

AHIQAR

(Seventh to Sixth Century B.C.)

A NEW TRANSLATION AND INTRODUCTION
BY J. M. LINDENBERGER

The text known as "The Words of Ahiqar" was one of the best-known and most widely disseminated tales in the ancient Mediterranean world. It is also by far the oldest text included in this collection, probably antedating the post-exilic portions of the Old Testament. This dates it well before the period usually assigned to the Pseudepigrapha. Furthermore, it is non-Jewish in origin. Thus Ahiqar is not, strictly speaking, a pseudepigraphon in the sense in which that term is applied to the other documents in this volume.[1]

Its inclusion here is justified by two facts, one relating to its content, the other to its history. In the first place, the work is closely similar in genre—and to some extent in content as well—to the wisdom traditions of the Old Testament and Apocrypha. This gives it a special importance for biblical studies. In the second place, it is clear that by the end of the Old Testament period, the story was not only known in some parts of the diaspora but had even been reworked to portray the pagan sage as a Jew. The oldest extant version, translated here, was found among the ruins of a Jewish settlement in Egypt dating from the fifth century B.C. The author of Tobit evidently knew a version according to which Ahiqar was an exiled Jew. Later recensions were in wide circulation in Jewish and Christian circles during the early centuries of the Christian era. So Ahiqar, though it was not composed by those who wrote and first read the books of the Pseudepigrapha, was adopted by them as the story of one of their own.

The work is in two parts. The first is the story of Ahiqar, wise scribe and counselor to the kings of Assyria. The sage, advanced in years and having no son to succeed him, decides to adopt his nephew Nadin[2] and teach him all his wisdom. The young man is educated and presented to Esarhaddon, and in time takes his uncle's place at court. Nadin, instead of dealing kindly with his uncle, plots to discredit him and manages to convince Esarhaddon that the old man is scheming to overthrow the throne. In a rage, the king orders Ahiqar killed. However, the officer sent to carry out the death sentence turns out to be an old friend of Ahiqar, whom the latter once rescued from death. The two of them concoct a plan by which a slave is substituted for Ahiqar and killed in his place. Evidently the plan succeeds, but the end of the story is lost. Presumably it related the restoration of Ahiqar to favor and the punishment of Nadin.[3]

The second part contains the wisdom of Ahiqar, a collection of slightly over a hundred aphorisms, riddles, fables, instructions, and other brief sayings of various kinds, arranged in a more or less haphazard manner. Many of them are fragmentary and difficult to understand. They cover a wide range of topics such as family discipline, respect for the

---

[1] On the criteria to be used in assigning documents to the Pseudepigrapha, see particularly J. H. Charlesworth, *The Pseudepigrapha and Modern Research* (Missoula, Mont., 1976), pp. 21–22; and the "Definition of Pseudepigrapha" in Charlesworth's "Introduction for the General Reader," above.

The present writer wishes to express his thanks to the trustees of the H. R. MacMillan Fund of the Vancouver School of Theology for a generous research grant to underwrite this study.

[2] Or "Nadan." See discussion of the name, n. 30.

[3] See the summary of the conclusion of the late versions following l. 78.

king, prudent speech, and righteous behavior,[4] and many of the individual sayings are similar to proverbs known from the Bible and the wisdom of the ancient Near East.

Texts

The Aramaic text translated here is found in a single papyrus manuscript. Much of it poorly preserved,[5] it was discovered by the German excavators of ancient Elephantine in 1907. Catalogued by the Königliche Museen zu Berlin[6] as P.13446, most of the manuscript remains in the museum's Papyrus Collection. Column vi (P.13446 J) was subsequently returned to Egypt along with a number of other papyri from Elephantine and is now in the Egyptian Museum at Cairo, where it bears the catalog number 43502.

The present translation is based on an examination of the papyrus original (except for col. vi, for which the original was inaccessible), compared with the photographs published by Sachau in 1911. The transcription of the narrative portion published by Cowley is, in general, reliable. Divergences from it are noted. For the sayings, the writer's own edition has been used.[7]

Much later and more elaborate recensions of the Ahiqar text are found in versions from the Christian era in Syriac, Arabic, Armenian, Karshuni, and Old Church Slavonic, with fragments in Ethiopic and still later translations into Georgian, Old Turkish, Romanian, Russian, Serbian, and neo-Syriac.[8] There was also a Greek version, now lost, from which the Slavonic and the Romanian stem. The Greek also served as the basis for a portion of the Life of Aesop.[9] Much of the material in these late versions does not parallel the Elephantine text, and they are not reproduced here. Significant parallels are given in the footnotes. The Syriac and the Armenian (which also goes back to a Syr. tradition) are the versions most closely related to the Aramaic.

Relation of narrative and sayings

In the Syriac and Armenian, and other late versions, the wisdom material is inserted into the narrative in two large blocks. The first comes after Ahiqar adopts his nephew, and purports to be the content of the sage's instruction. The second comes near the end of the story as the words with which Ahiqar rebukes the ungrateful boy.

This arrangement seems not to be original. In the Elephantine text, the sayings were evidently not integrated into the narrative at all.[10] They seem to have been simply collected at the end without any explicit link to the story.[11] The version which lies behind the Life of Aesop represents an intermediate state in the integration of the sayings and the narrative,[12]

---

[4] See also "Relation of Narrative and Sayings."

[5] Of some ll., little or nothing remains. Hardly a single l. is completely intact. In the narrative, the repetitious style and fairly close parallels with the late recs. make it possible to restore much of the lost text. The sayings, by contrast, are written in such a terse style that often the loss of a few letters can render an entire saying unintelligible. Translation of the proverbs is made even more difficult by the number of unfamiliar words they contain. The badly damaged state in which the Aram. text has survived has required some modifications of the standard editorial sigla listed in vol. 1, p. xxxv. Note particularly:

  a. [Regular type in brackets] indicates that the words enclosed are missing or damaged beyond certain identification but can be restored with high probability on the basis of remaining traces or close parallels in the late versions.

  b. *Italic type* indicates a word whose material reading is clear but whose meaning is uncertain.

  c. [*Italic type in brackets*] indicates a conjectural restoration.

[6] Now the Staatliche Museen zu Berlin (East).

[7] See "Significant Publications."

[8] For the texts of the late versions, see "Significant Publications."

[9] On the complex question of the Near Eastern antecedents and inner development of the Aesop traditions, see the works of Perry and Daly listed in "Significant Publications"; see also B. E. Perry, *Studies in the Text History of the Life and Fables of Aesop* (Haverford, Pa., 1936).

[10] If the text followed the pattern of the late recs., the appropriate place for the sayings would be after the words "I . . . taught him wisdom" (l. 9). See l. 16, n. q.

[11] The fragmentary state of the text makes it impossible to state categorically that there was no transition in the text from narrative to sayings. But in the surviving portions, cols. i–v contain only narrative, vi–xiv only sayings.

[12] In the Gk. there is only one block of instructional material, inserted not at the point where the hero educates his adopted son, but after his reinstatement (where the late Ahiqar versions place the reproaches). The Egyptian episode in the Aesop story takes place after the death of the foster son, rather than before as in the versions of Ahiqar.

and even in the late versions there is a certain artificiality about the position of the sayings. A number of the reproaches at the end are quite inappropriate to the literary context in which they are placed, and some sayings found in the first collection in one version appear in the second collection in another. Taking this into account, along with the fact that the wisdom portion of the Elephantine text is written in a slightly different dialect from the narrative (see below), it is evident that in dealing with questions of date, provenance, and historical background, the two parts of the text must be treated separately.

Original language

Before the discovery of the Aramaic text, the dominant view was that Ahiqar was written by a Jew, probably in Hebrew.[13] The major reasons for this were the references to Ahiqar in Tobit[14] and the existence of a number of parallels between the Syriac Ahiqar and the Talmud.[15] With the discovery of the Elephantine manuscript, this opinion at first seemed to be confirmed. It was, after all, a Jewish colony in whose ruins the papyrus was found, and certain features of its language were thought to betray Hebrew influence.

But scholars quickly came to realize that the text showed no real trace of Jewish origin. On the contrary, its religious background is that of ancient Near Eastern polytheism.[16] With the abandonment of the Jewish hypothesis, a fairly broad agreement developed that the Aramaic is a translation from an Akkadian (i.e. Assyrian) original. The setting of the story is the neo-Assyrian court, a number of the personal names are authentically Assyrian, there are several Akkadian loan words in the narrative, and four of the proverbs mention the Mesopotamian god Shamash. This view persists in many scholarly works until the present.[17]

Recent years, however, have seen the beginning of a new consensus that the Aramaic is not a translation at all, but the original language. The Assyrian names simply belong to the Assyrian setting of the story. The Akkadian loan words are almost all words which are common in Imperial Aramaic. The mention of a Mesopotamian god shows only that the work was composed in an area under Mesopotamian influence. It has no bearing on the original language. Thus the evidence for a lost Akkadian original is by no means as strong as it first appeared.

The case for an Aramaic original is particularly strong in the proverbs. Unlike the narrative, they contain virtually no Akkadian loan words.[18] Some of them contain Aramaic wordplays (e.g. the pun on *ḥṭ* "arrow" and *ḥṭʾ* "sin" in saying 41). Some also show a knowledge of distinctively West Semitic literary conventions (in particular, the use of traditional word pairs in poetic parallelism),[19] which would be extremely difficult to account for if the text were a translation from (East Semitic) Akkadian. Even in the narrative, evidence for translation from Akkadian is lacking. During the time of the neo-Assyrian Empire, Akkadian was coming more and more to be displaced by Aramaic as the dominant language of the people in Mesopotamia.

Thus it is most likely that the text in its entirety was composed in Aramaic. A close study of the two parts of the text reveals that they are written in slightly differing dialects. The narrative is written in the official, or "Imperial," Aramaic dialect of the neo-Assyrian and neo-Babylonian periods. The proverbs are in a somewhat more archaic dialect with a greater similarity to the Canaanite family of languages, accounting for the features earlier thought to be "Hebraisms."[20]

---

[13] The hypothesis of a Sanskrit original, put forth toward the end of the nineteenth century, has long since been discredited. See the summary of this early discussion in A. H. Krappe, "Is the Story of Ahiqar the Wise of Indian Origin?" *JAOS* 61 (1941) 280f.

[14] See "Relation to Apocryphal Books."

[15] See "Cultural Importance."

[16] For details, see "Religious Importance."

[17] E.g. Grelot, who refers to the text as a "masterpiece of Akkadian literature translated into the common language of the Persian Empire" (*Documents*, p. 452). Cowley (*Aramaic Papyri*, pp. 205f.) attempts to complicate this hypothesis even further by assuming that the putative Akkadian original was first translated into Persian and thence into Aram. His arguments are not cogent, however, and have never gained wide acceptance.

[18] An apparent exception is *knt*, "fellow, companion" (sayings 10, 72). This is common Aram., probably borrowed from Akkadian quite early. A more serious exception is found in saying 34 (see nn.), which seems to rest on an Akkadian wordplay.

[19] See J. Lindenberger, *Aramaic Proverbs*, pp. 23f.

[20] See also under "Provenance" for details.

Date

Because the work is composite, the question of date is complex. The Elephantine manuscript is dated by paleography and archaeological context to the late fifth century B.C., but it is likely that the combined text (narrative and sayings) was in existence for at least a century before that.

The presence of double forms of some of the sayings (39 par. 41 [cf. 93], 40 par. 42, the two versions of the ending of 36) indicates a period of transmission long enough for variants to develop. Some of the inconsistencies in spelling may also indicate the copying of the text over a rather extended time, during which the phonology of the language was evolving.[21] There are also a good many scribal errors, though in theory these could have been introduced by a careless scribe at a single copying.

The earliest possible date for the narrative is provided by the mention of Esarhaddon (reigned 681–669 B.C.). The gnomic portion of the text has no historical allusions, but the more archaic flavor of the language of the sayings indicates that they are at least as old as the narrative and probably older. Since the Imperial Aramaic of the Persian period and later shows a great many Persian words, the absence of such Persian loans in Ahiqar suggests a date of composition before the mid-sixth century. Both parts of the text (and probably the editorial joining of them) must have been fixed in writing during the latter seventh or early sixth century B.C.[22]

Provenance

The exact provenance of the text is not known. Though the manuscript was found in Egypt, it is most unlikely that it was composed there. Nothing in either part of the text suggests an Egyptian background.[23] The setting of the story in the neo-Assyrian court is "authentic" in the sense that the few verifiable historical details in it are correct. The Assyrian personal names are typical of the period and are accurately transcribed into Aramaic.[24] The Aramaic of the narrative is the standard literary dialect of the neo-Assyrian and neo-Babylonian periods. Lacking any evidence to the contrary, it is likely that the narrative originated in Mesopotamia.

The proverbs are another matter. Practically nothing in them is suggestive of a Mesopotamian background.[25] The only geographical reference is in saying 110, and "the Sidonian" there simply refers proverbially to the seafarer, as "the Arab" refers to the desert dweller. The dialect of the proverbs is closer to the language of the very oldest Imperial Aramaic texts and the latest phase of Old Aramaic, a transition which took place roughly around the beginning of the seventh century B.C. In a number of features, particularly the vocabulary, the dialect of the sayings has affinities with the Canaanite languages of ancient Syria-Palestine.[26] The most likely explanation of this is that the proverbs (or an earlier collection containing most of them) originated in northern Syria, where several Aramaic-speaking kingdoms flourished during the first part of the first millennium B.C. A further argument in favor of a north Syrian origin of the wisdom portion of the text is the appearance of a pantheon of gods whose names often appear together in other texts from that region.[27] When and where the two parts of the text were joined is not known (see below).

---

[21] Note particularly the fluctuation in the initial consonant of *Sennacherib* between s and š, and the spelling of the sibilant in *Esarhaddon* with s over against that in *Assyria* (originally the same) with t.

[22] This conclusion is clouded somewhat by the fact that the use of *šmh* "his name" to introduce a new character (see l. 1, n. a) in Ah is thought to be an idiom borrowed from Persian; see E. Y. Kutscher, "New Aramaic Texts," *JAOS* 74 (1954) 241. But the Persian derivation of the expression is not certain.

[23] Even the Egyptian episode of the late versions is told from the viewpoint of Ahiqar and the Assyrians. The Egyptians are merely foreign foils for the sage's cleverness.

[24] See "Historical Importance."

[25] The sole exception to this is saying 34.

[26] See J. Lindenberger, *Aramaic Proverbs*, "Scribal and Linguistic Character of the Text."

[27] See H. Donner and W. Röllig, *Kanaanäische und Aramäische Inschriften* (3 vols.; Wiesbaden, 1964–68) numbers 202 B:23f.; 214:2f., 11, 18; 215:22; and particularly 26A:III:18f.

Historical importance

Until fairly recently, most scholars considered the story of Ahiqar to be pure folklore, and the hero to be the literary creation of the unknown author.[28] Sennacherib and Esarhaddon are, of course, well-known historical figures.[29] The name Ahiqar (sometimes vocalized Ahuqar) occurs in cuneiform texts of the neo-Assyrian period, as do the names Nadin and Nabusumiskun.[30] In fact, there was a Nadin accused of subversive activities during the reign of Ashurbanipal, and Esarhaddon is known to have had a high-ranking army officer named Nabusumiskun. But while these persons could conceivably be identified with the characters in the Ahiqar story, the names are rather common, and the cuneiform texts never associate the various individuals with one another, so the apparent correspondence may be mere coincidence.

The question of the historicity of Ahiqar has more recently been thrown into a new perspective by the discovery at the site of ancient Uruk of a cuneiform tablet in which the name appears in a context which immediately links it to the Aramaic story. The Akkadian text, from the Seleucid period, is a list of a number of distinguished court scholars (*ummānū*) of various Babylonian and Assyrian kings. The relevant line reads: "[In the time of] King Esarhaddon, Aba-enlil-dari, [whom] the Arameans call Ahuqar, was *ummānu*."[31] The name, nationality, role, and date in the cuneiform and Aramaic traditions match, making it appear extremely likely that there was, in fact, such an Ahiqar at the Assyrian court.

It may be possible to go even beyond this. A number of the *umānnū* listed are noted Mesopotamian literary figures, among them the reputed authors of the Gilgamesh Epic and "The Exaltation of Inanna." This suggests that Ahiqar, too, was remembered in Mesopotamia, not only as an official of Esarhaddon, but also as an author. That is not to say that the details of the story are necessarily historical; much of the narrative is characteristic of folklore. (In particular, the themes of the ungrateful nephew and the downfall and restoration of a minister are known elsewhere in Mesopotamian literature.)[32] Much less does it demonstrate that the historical Ahiqar was the author of our story. But it does suggest that the story is not pure fiction. It is better classified as a historical novel, or still better as a literary folktale about a historical figure.

A plausible—though partly conjectural—reconstruction of the early development of the text may be made as follows: The oldest components, the individual sayings, circulated orally among the Aramaic-speaking peoples of Syria in the earlier part of the first millennium

---

[28] An early attempt to identify historical events lying behind the story was made by W. von Soden, "Die Unterweltsvision eines assyrischen Kronprinzen," ZA 43 [n.F. 9] (1936) 11–13.

[29] The Elephantine MS has Sennacherib and Esarhaddon in the correct historical sequence, whereas the late versions generally reverse the order. Only one late Syr. MS has the order correctly. The Arm. and OCS omit Esarhaddon entirely.

[30] *Ahiqar*—"My (divine) brother is precious." Linguistically the name can be either Akkadian or Aram. The name appears (as *Ahi-iaqar* and variant spellings) in Akkadian texts from the Old Babylonian period on. More than one Assyrian bureaucrat bore the name. In the Seleucid text which refers to the Ahiqar of our story, the name is written *ᵐA-ḫu-uʾ-qa-a-ri*. The Syr. Ah preserves the name accurately. In the Arm., it becomes *Khikar*; in the Ar., *Haiqar*. In Aram., the probable pronunciation (without pretonic reduction) would be *ʾaḫī-yaqar*, or perhaps simply *ʾaḫ-yaqar*, without the pronominal suffix.

Nadin (or *Nadan*)—an abbreviated name-form from the Akkadian verb *nadānu*, "to give." The name *Nādin* (Akkadian active participle) is fairly common in the neo-Assyrian period. In the case of one of the persons so named, the full form of his name is also known: *Nabū-nādin-zēr* ("Nabu gives progeny"). Occasionally the form *Nadan* appears in Akkadian. In the printed translations of the Syr. and Ar. Ah, the name is vocalized "Nadan," but as the consonantal script in both languages has simply *ndn*, this cannot be claimed as ancient evidence for a different pronunciation. The Arm. (which is based on a Syr. version) has *Nathan* in the better MSS, *Nadan* in others. The adopted son in the Aesop tradition is known variously as *Ennos, Ainos,* and *Hēlios*. On the name in Tob, see n. 57.

Nabusumiskun—reflects the Assyrian pronunciation of Akkadian *Nabū-šum-iškun*, "Nabu has established a name (i.e. given a son)," the name of several individuals of the neo-Assyrian period, including a high-ranking army officer under Esarhaddon. The name is altered considerably in the later Ahiqar traditions. On the Akkadian of the three names, see K. Tallqvist, *Assyrian Personal Names* (Leipzig, 1914) pp. 16a, 160b–161a, 165b.

[31] For the entire text and commentary, see J. van Dijk, XVIII. *Vorläufiger Bericht über die vom Deutschen Archäologischen Institut und der Deutschen Orient-Gesellschaft aus Mitteln der Deutschen Forschungsgemeinschaft unternommenen Ausgrabungen in Uruk-Warka,* ed. H. J. Lenzen (Abhandlung der Deutschen Orient-Gesellschaft 8; Berlin, 1963) pp. 44–52.

[32] See E. Reiner, "The Etiological Myth of the 'Seven Sages,'" *Orientalia* N.S. 30 (1961) 1–11.

B.C. At some time during this period, a written collection of these sayings was made, probably by scribes in the court of one of the Aramean kings.[33] The collection would presumably have been brought to Assyria in the aftermath of the Assyrian conquests of Aramean territory in the course of the eighth century. By the time of Sennacherib (704–681) or Esarhaddon (681–669) the proverbs would have been known, and perhaps had been re-edited, in Assyria, by circles of Aramaic-speaking literati associated with the imperial court. Ahiqar himself may have been the editor; that would account for his literary reputation in Mesopotamian tradition and the linking of his name with the proverbs in the Aramaic text. On the other hand, the collection could have been attributed to him after his lifetime, in the same way that various collections of Israelite wisdom from all periods came to be linked to the name of Solomon.

The narrative may have been composed completely independently of the sayings, with a later editor joining the two parts which make up the present text. Or the story may from the beginning have been intended to introduce an already existing collection of sayings; i.e. its author would also be the editor of the composite text in its earliest form. The date and historical setting for the composition of the story cannot be determined with any degree of precision, but the author was most likely an Aramean scribe living in the latter days of the neo-Assyrian Empire or early in the time of the neo-Babylonian (Chaldean) Empire. To this author (or the later editor mentioned above) may also be attributed the addition to the wisdom collection of those proverbs which appear to be inspired by the narrative (50–52, 76, 80). He may have added a few others as well, such as 34. Insofar as the story is an exemplary tale of a wise and virtuous hero who rose to prominence in the court of a foreign king, it is comparable to the biblical stories of Joseph, Esther, and Daniel.[34]

Theological importance

The theological background of the Aramaic Ahiqar is that of the ancient Near East. In it we encounter not the God of Israel but the gods of Aram, Canaan, and Mesopotamia. The theology is concentrated in the wisdom sayings. The narrative, though edifying, says nothing directly about the gods.[35] But the proverbs mention them often, frequently by name, usually portraying them in roles similar to those which they play elsewhere in the religious literature of the ancient Orient.

Several sayings refer to "the gods"—without further specification—as instructors, judges, and protectors of humanity. These gods give eloquence to the inexperienced (32), requite evil speech (37), and punish those who persecute the righteous (39, 41). Not only the liar and the evildoer (46) but also the fool (38)[36] is subject to their judgment. It is only the gods who can protect a person from inner wickedness (69), and it is they who are the ultimate source of wisdom (13).[37]

El, father of the gods in the Canaanite pantheon, is the divinity most often named in the proverbs.[38] He is referred to in saying 25 by his epithet "the merciful" (rḥmn), a title similar to the pair of epithets by which the god is known in Ugaritic literature ("the beneficent, the benign") and almost identical to the biblical designation of Yahweh as 'ēl raḥûm wᵉḥānûn, "gracious and loving God."[39] Saying 25 is a comparison of the authority of the king to that of El:

---

[33] A number of the sayings are explicitly intended for the instruction of courtiers (17–21, 23, 25f.), and a good many others would be appropriate for such a setting.

[34] A common literary structure has also been discerned in these stories; see J. J. Collins, "The Court-Tales in Daniel and the Development of Apocalyptic," *JBL* 94 (1975) 224–27. There is some evidence that parallels between Ah, Aesop, and Joseph were observed in antiquity. One of the Syr. MSS of Ah also contains a collection of Aesop's fables attributed to "Josephus"; J. R. Harris et al., *Aḥiḳar*, p. lxxx, p. 2.

[35] There are references to the gods in the later recs. of the narrative, particularly the Arm.; see below.

[36] See the nn. on the text of this difficult saying.

[37] On this saying, see also under "Shamayn," below.

[38] Earlier translations have tended to confuse Aram. 'l (El) and 'lhyn / 'lhy' (the gods), often translating both as "God." For a detailed discussion of the problem, see J. Lindenberger, "The Gods of Ahiqar," *Ugarit-Forschungen* 14 (1983) 105–17.

[39] Ex 34:6; Deut 4:31; Neh 9:31; Jonah 4:2. In post-biblical Jewish literature, *raḥmān* is used as a circumlocution for the name of God, and the same epithet is a primary title of Allah in Islamic writings.

A king is like the Merciful,
even his voice is haughty.
Who is there who could withstand him,
but one with whom El is?

It is El who will avenge treacherous speech (66; probably failure to keep an oath is meant).[40]
A fragmentary saying (64) appears to relate El to healing, a role in which he is occasionally
found also in Canaanite literature.[41] Another damaged saying appears to be a petition to the
god for righteousness or vindication: "Establish me, O El, as a righteous man with you!"
(78).

Second in the pantheon of the proverbs is Shamash,[42] the sun-god. In ancient Mesopotamia,
this god functioned primarily as administrator of justice. He protected the needy and heard
the claims of the unjustly treated. It is just this role which he has in saying 77: "If a wicked
man grasps the fringe of your garment, leave it in his hand. Then appeal to Shamash; he
[will] take what is his and will give it to you." Saying 49 illustrates one way in which
Shamash executes judgment: He withholds light from the wicked.

Just as the king is likened to El (25), so also is his splendor compared to that of Shamash
(26):

A king is as splendid to see as Shamash;
and his majesty is glorious
to them that tread the earth in peace.

Comparison of the king to the sun-god is also known from Mesopotamia. In the seventh-
century prayer of Ashurbanipal to Shamash, the king's splendor is said to depend on his
piety toward Shamash.[43] Shamash is also concerned with human wisdom. He takes pleasure
in the man who masters wisdom and learns discretion in speech; he is displeased when
wisdom fails (12).

Saying 13 is the most important passage for the text's theological understanding of
wisdom, and incidentally contains a probable reference to a third divinity:

From heaven the peoples are favored;
Wisdom is of the gods.
Indeed, she is precious to the gods;
her kingdom is et[er]nal.
She has been established by Shamayn;
yea, the Holy Lord has exalted her.[44]

The words "Shamayn" (lit. "heaven") and "the Holy Lord" probably refer to the god
known as "the Lord of Heaven" (Aram. b'l šmyn),[45] whose worship was widespread among
the Canaanite and Aramean peoples of Syria (and to some extent also northern Mesopotamia)
from the Bronze Age until well into the Christian era. In the Canaanite pantheon described
by Sanchuniathon, he is chief of the gods. Saying 13 appears to be a hymn to wisdom,
praising her divine origin, her benefits to mankind, and her exaltation by the god. Though
the saying does not go so far as to personify wisdom explicitly, it is nevertheless the closest
non-Jewish parallel to the biblical and post-biblical poems in praise of wisdom[46] and is
probably older than any of them.[47] The theological intent of saying 13 within the entire
collection is comparable to that of Prov 8:22–31 within the Book of Proverbs: the wisdom

---

[40] The badly broken saying 70 also seems to refer to oaths in connection with El.
[41] In the Keret epic, from Ugarit, El takes it on himself to provide a healer for the ailing king. See KRT C, v;
ANET, p. 148b.
[42] "Shamash," the name by which the god is best known, is the Akkadian pronunciation of the name. In the Aram.
of the period of the text, the name was perhaps pronounced šimš or šimiš; in later Aram. šᵉmeš.
[43] For a translation of the prayer, see F. J. Stephens in ANET, pp. 386f.
[44] See the nn. on the saying.
[45] Pronounced approximately ba'l šamayn; in later Aram. it would be bᵉel šᵉmayin.
[46] The image of Wisdom in Philo Judaeus and the gnostic myths of the lesser Sophia have also been compared; see
W. F. Albright, From the Stone Age to Christianity (Garden City, N.Y., 1957) pp. 368, 370. Albright also cites
other possible parallels from more ancient Near Eastern texts.
[47] A possible exception is Prov 8:22–31.

teaching, largely practical and—on the face of it—secular in character, is said to derive from the divine realm. The life and success conferred by wisdom are, at root, gifts of the gods. Wisdom rules forever, because she has been enthroned by the High God of Heaven.

Many of the general themes of the proverbs, e.g. family discipline, controlled speech, behavior vis-à-vis the king, are paralleled in biblical wisdom literature.[48] As in biblical wisdom, wisdom is associated with life, prosperity, and divine favor. Folly brings the displeasure of gods and the king, and tends toward death. But some of the distinctive theological emphases of Hebrew wisdom are not to be found in the Aramaic document. Cosmology plays no role in the Ahiqar sayings, in contrast to the prominence which creation theology has in Old Testament wisdom.[49] Though the Ahiqar text characterizes wise behavior as being pleasing to the gods, there are no analogues to the recurring biblical affirmation that "The fear of Yahweh is the beginning of wisdom" (Prov 9:10; cf. 1:7). The question of theodicy does not arise; the gods of the proverbs are never seriously challenged by man.

The late versions of Ahiqar have, to varying degrees, assimilated the polytheism of the original to a monotheistic viewpoint, under the influence of the Jewish and Christian circles in which they were transmitted. "The gods" of the Elephantine proverbs have for the most part become "God." A few traces of the older religious setting have survived, particularly in the Armenian, which relates that Ahiqar prayed to his gods "Belshim and Shimil and Shamin."[50] The Syriac in the same passage has eliminated the names of the gods in favor of "O Lord, my God,"[51] and the Arabic even introduces the biblical phrase "Most High God, creator of the heavens and of the earth" (cf. Gen 14:19).

Relation to canonical books

If it is important in dealing with any question of literary comparison to distinguish between parallels and influence, it is doubly important when treating material from the realm of wisdom and folklore. Folk themes, figures of speech, and entire proverbs migrate across geographical and cultural boundaries by routes which are often impossible to trace or document. Parallels, even quite close ones, between books such as Ahiqar and the canonical and apocryphal books may indicate nothing whatever about the direct knowledge of one document by the author of another. In every case, the burden of proof is on the one who would claim to see signs of literary influence.

Leaving aside wisdom themes which are common to biblical and ancient Near Eastern wisdom (see notes on the individual sayings), close parallels between the Elephantine Ahiqar and the canonical books are very few. The address "My Son" (sayings 4, 14a, 40, 42, 60, frequent in biblical proverbs)[52] simply belongs to wisdom diction. It is found in Near Eastern texts as old as the third millennium B.C. Similarly the form of the numerical proverb, "There are two things . . . and a third . . ." (saying 12; cf. Prov 30:15–19, 21–31), and the comparison of a word to a dagger or sword (saying 18; Pss 52:2; 57:4, etc.) are well attested literary devices in ancient oriental literature.[53]

Only in two cases are there parallels which justify raising the question of possible dependence. The first is the pair of sayings 3–4:

Spare not your son from the rod, otherwise, can
you save him [from *wickedness*]?

If I beat you, my son,
you will not die;

---

[48] See "Relation to Canonical Books."

[49] On the importance of creation in biblical wisdom, see particularly W. Zimmerli, "The Place and Limit of the Wisdom in the Framework of the Old Testament Theology," *SJT* 17 (1964) 146–58.

[50] Arm. Ah 1:4. "Shamin" is obviously the "Shamayn" of the Elephantine text (saying 13), and "Belshim" (which recurs in 6:16) may also be a corruption of "Baal Shamayn." "Shimil" is possibly derived from Aram. *šm ʾl*, "the Name of El," a type of surrogate name well known in other northwest Semitic texts. The Turkish has a more garbled version of the three names: Belshim, Shillim, and Shahmil (J. R. Harris et al., *Aḥiḳar*, p. 86).

[51] The Syr. does preserve one reference to "Bel" (6:10). In one MS, a possible second reference to the god has been erased (J. R. Harris et al., *Aḥiḳar*, p. 119, n. 1).

[52] In the late recs. of Ah, virtually all of the sayings are introduced by the phrase.

[53] See saying 12, n. t, and saying 18, n. n.

but if I leave you alone,
[you will not live].

Compare Proverbs 23:13-14:

Do not withhold discipline from a child;
if you beat him with a rod, he will not die.
If you beat him with the rod
you will save his life from Sheol.   (RSV)

Though parental discipline and the desirability of corporal punishment are common enough themes in wisdom literature, the close verbal similarity (even closer in the original than appears in translation) is greater than could be accounted for by similarity of theme alone. It cannot be claimed that either saying is borrowed from the other, but it is likely that some common oral or written tradition underlies both.

The second close biblical parallel is to saying 109:

Let not the rich man say, "In my riches I am glorious."

This is very similar to the last clause of Jer 9:22:

Let the sage boast no more of his wisdom,
. . . nor the rich man of his riches!

In this case, the saying is brief and its theme universal. It is probably part of the common stock of ancient Near Eastern folk wisdom.

The number of apparent similarities between the late versions of Ahiqar and the Bible (particularly Daniel and Luke) is somewhat greater. Here again, some are simply literary devices: "O King, live forever!" (Ah 1:11 [Syr., Arm.; cf. Ar.]; Dan 2:4; 3:9; 5:10; 6:6, 21); clothing someone in purple and gold as a sign of special favor (Ah 1:7 [Arm.]; Dan 5:7, 16; cf. 2Ezra 3:6); the comparison of long fingernails to birds' claws ʿAh 5:11 [Syr., Arm., Ar.]; Dan 4:30); the complaint that a task is so difficult that not even the gods (or only the gods) could perform it (Ah 5:6 [Syr., Arm.]; cf. Dan 2:11); feeding pigs as a despised occupation (Ah 8:34 [Syr.]; Lk 15:15); lists of various kinds of soothsayers (Ah 1:3 [Ar.]; Dan 2:2, 27; 5:7); the idea that one should not share a meal with a person of bad character (Syr. Ah 2:16; Ar. 2:19; Arm. 2:10; cf. 1Cor 5:11); references to saving someone from the mouth of a lion (Syr. Ah 2:59; Arm. 2:60; cf. Ps 22:21; 2Tim 4:17; as a narrative motif also in Dan 6:17-25); and a variety of expressions which have in common the presupposition that the wolf is a proverbial enemy of sheep (Ah 2:30 [Ar.]; Isa 11:6; 65:25; Mt 7:15; 10:16; Lk 10:3; Acts 20:29). The sudden death of the wicked by bursting open (Nadin in Syr. Ah 8:41 and parallels; Judas in Acts 1:18, cf. also Papias' account of the death of Judas) also seems to be a narrative convention; compare the death of the dragon in Daniel 14:27 [Bel 27] and a similar incident in the apocryphal Acts of Thomas.

Other parallels between the Bible and the late versions of Ahiqar do seem to show at least the dependence of both on kindred wisdom traditions. The clearest case of this is the proverb cited in 2 Peter 2:22: "When the sow has been washed, it wallows in the mud." A fuller version of the same proverb appears in Syriac Ahiqar 8:18: "My son, thou hast been to me like the swine that had been to the baths, and when it saw a muddy ditch, went down and washed in it . . ." (cf. Arm. Ah 8:24a; Ar. 8:15). Stories about unfruitful trees (Syr. Ah 8:35 [parallels in Arm. and Ar.]; Lk 13:6-9) appear in various places in ancient Near Eastern wisdom literature.[54] Proverbial conventions about untrustworthy stewards who beat their subordinates and get drunk when their masters go away may be seen behind the description of Nadin's behavior in Ahiqar's household (Ah 4:15 [Syr., Ar.; cf. Arm.]) and the Synoptic parable concerning the dishonest steward (Mt 24:48-51; Lk 12:45-46). Another such example is the notion that an ineffective or offensive bodily member should be gotten rid of—a hand cut off or an eye plucked out (Syr. Ah 8:20; Ar. 8:18-19; Mk 9:43, 47; Mt 5:29-30; 18:8-9).

---

[54] Cf. Elephantine saying 73 and the Babylonian fable cited in 73, n. m.

These parallels, taken together, do not prove that the biblical writers were familiar with Ahiqar. The most probable case of direct influence of Ahiqar on the Bible is the proverb about the pig who took a bath, and even that may have been a widely known saying in antiquity.[55] The most that can be said with confidence is that there is evidence in Ahiqar and the Bible of a common reliance upon similar idioms, literary conventions, and wisdom themes.

Biblical diction has evidently influenced the later versions in a few places. The biblical phrase "Most High God, creator of the heavens and of the earth" in the Arabic Ahiqar has been noted above (see "Theological Importance"). The Arabic also has a saying which may well be a reflex of the New Testament injunction to "love your enemies": "If thine enemy wrong thee, show him kindness" (2:19; Mt 5:43–48; Lk 6:27–36; Rom 12:14, 17, 20–21). The fable of the fruitless palm tree, mentioned above, concludes in the Syriac version, "Thou hast not been industrious in what is thine own, how wilt thou be industrious in what is not thine own?" (8:35). This wording, unlike that in the other versions, may possibly have been suggested to the Syriac scribe by the language of the parable of the talents: "You have shown you can be faithful in small things, I will trust you with greater" (Mt 25:21, 23; cf. Luke 19:12–27). And the wording of Nadin's plea for forgiveness, "Father, I have sinned against thee. Forgive me, and I will be a slave unto thee henceforth and forever" (Arm. 8:24b; cf. Syr. 8:34), may be influenced by the phraseology of the parable of the prodigal son (Lk 15:18–19, 21).

In such cases, it is difficult, if not impossible, to be certain who (if anyone) has influenced whom. This is necessarily so in view of the gaps in our knowledge of the development of the Ahiqar tradition. There was, it is certain, a pre-Christian Jewish version of Ahiqar. It is possible that sayings from Ahiqar were current in first-century Palestine (or Egypt or Syria) and were known to the Gospel writers or to Jesus himself. They could have even been familiar with a written text of Ahiqar. But that version is lost. Except for a few fragments which have survived in quotations elsewhere, all we have for comparison is a text which is older by centuries and a group of translations which are centuries younger.

The older text, the Aramaic, does not bear any close verbal similarity to the New Testament and only a limited similarity to the Old. But of course the first-century version must have differed substantially from this Aramaic text and *may* have contained some of the New Testament parallels cited above. On the other hand the late versions do show apparent parallels with the New Testament at a number of points. But those versions come to us from the hands of Christian scribes who did not think it amiss to introduce biblical idioms into their texts. Thus every seeming biblical parallel in them is suspect unless supported by pre-Christian evidence. Where that evidence is lacking, we can go no farther than to speak of unsupported possibilities. Even where such testimony is to be found, it must, for reasons already given, be treated cautiously. The conclusion drawn by some older writers that Jesus and the evangelists must have known Ahiqar[56] goes considerably beyond the evidence.

Relation to apocryphal books

The author of Tobit is well acquainted with the story of Ahiqar and his deceitful kinsman ("Nadab").[57] Chapter 1, verses 21–22 depicts Tobit as the uncle of Ahiqar[58] and lists the latter's official titles:

---

[55] But see n. 77, on J. R. Harris's attempt to trace the proverb back through Clement of Alexandria to Democritus, and ultimately to Ah. The motif is a nearly universal one; cf. e.g. "Piglet Has a Bath," in A. A. Milne, *Winnie-the-Pooh* (New York, 1926, 1961) pp. 104–09! The question of biblical parallels with Ah is discussed in detail by J. R. Harris et al. in *Aḥiḳar*, pp. lvi–lxiii, and more briefly by the same writer in R. H. Charles (ed.), *APOT*, vol. 2, pp. 718f., including further possible, though more doubtful, parallels.

[56] E.g. Harris et al., *Aḥiḳar*, p. lxiii: "A new volume has . . . been added to our Lord's library" [Harris's italics].

[57] The textual traditions in Tob concerning the names of Ahiqar (spelled "Ahikar" in The Jerusalem Bible) and his nephew are badly garbled. Ahiqar is generally *Achiacharos* in Vaticanus and Alexandrinus, for which *Manassēs* is substituted in 14:10 (third occurrence). The spelling in Sinaiticus is different at almost every occurrence of the name. The Syr. has *'ḥywr* (cf. Vulgate *Achior*, Tob 11:20 [Gk. v. 18]), *'ḥyḥwr* and *'qyqr*. The nephew's name in the Gk. traditions appears variously as *Nadab* (probably the original Gk. reading), *Nasbas, Nabad, Adam,* and *Aman;* in the Syr. Tob it is *nbws, lbn, 'dm,* and *ʿkb.*

[58] The Tob tradition seems to be confused also in the matter of the relationship of Ahiqar, Nadab, and Tobit. In

Ahikar, the son of my brother Anael, was appointed chancellor of the exchequer for the kingdom and given the main ordering of affairs. Ahikar then interceded for me and I was allowed to return to Nineveh, since Ahikar had been chief cupbearer, keeper of the signet, administrator and treasurer under Sennacherib, king of Assyria, and Esarhaddon had kept him in office.

At the end of the book, Tobit concludes his deathbed instructions to Tobias by drawing a moral from the story of Ahiqar:

Consider, my child, all that Nadab did to his fosterfather Ahikar. Was he not forced to go underground, though still a living man? But God made the criminal pay for his outrage before the eyes of his victim, since Ahikar came back to the light of day, while Nadab went down to everlasting darkness in punishment for plotting against Ahikar's life. Because of his good works (*eleēmosynē*) Ahikar escaped the deadly snare Nadab had laid for him, and Nadab fell into it to his own ruin. (14:10)

Ahiqar's name is also mentioned briefly in 2:10 (". . . Ahikar provided for my upkeep for two years, till he left for Elymais") and 11:18.[59]

Evidently the author of Tobit knew Ahiqar in a form not identical with either the Elephantine text or the later versions. Unlike the late recensions, Tobit has Sennacherib and Esarhaddon in the correct order. (The author may in this instance be correcting his source on the basis of more accurate information from the OT.) The elaboration of the original story which characterizes the late versions has already begun in the version known by Tobit, which mentions Ahiqar's underground hiding place (14:10), a detail not found in the Elephantine text. Tobit's version must also have suppressed the polytheistic traits of the original.[60] This is inferred from the fact that Tobit, a devout Jew, is said to be related to Ahiqar (1:21–22) and to have lived with him for two years (2:10). He also has high praise for Ahiqar's virtue (14:10). It is entirely possible that Tobit's version explicitly described Ahikar as Jewish. Even if not, it can hardly have depicted him as a gentile worshiper of other gods, as the late recensions (particularly the Arm.) still do.[61]

It is not clear whether Tobit may also allude to additional events in the career of his distinguished relative which are not found in any of the extant versions of Ahiqar. The reference to Ahiqar's departure "to Elymais" (2:10) is perplexing. No such incident is otherwise known. The words could refer to a lost episode in the narrative, but it is more likely that they are an error in the Greek of Tobit[62] or that they simply refer to the Egyptian[63] episode with the locale changed.[64]

At least one of the sayings of Ahiqar from the late versions is found also in Tobit, albeit

---

11:18, Ahiqar and Nadab appear to be cousins of Tobit. Because of the various forms in which the name of Ahiqar's kinsman appears, it is quite possible that at some stage in the editing of the text of Tob the hero's cousin (11:18) and Ahiqar's foster son (14:10) were understood as two different individuals.

[59] In Sinaiticus, his name is repeated again in 14:15.

[60] It is assumed that the version of Ah known to the author of Tob contained both narrative and sayings, since at least one of the sayings is found in Tob. Note that in the Elephantine version the polytheistic features are found only in the *sayings*, whereas in the late versions they appear only in the *narrative*.

[61] The details of Ahiqar's Jewish ancestry may, of course, have been invented by the author of Tob to integrate Ahiqar more closely into his story.

[62] It has been suggested that the Gk. translator of Tob misunderstood a Heb. phrase in his *Vorlage* to the effect that Ahiqar went "to his hiding place" (a form of the root *ʿlm*) as saying he went to Elymais (Heb. *ʿlmyn*). For a critical evaluation of the proposal, see F. Zimmerman, *The Book of Tobit* (New York, 1958) p. 58n.

[63] D. C. Simpson in R. H. Charles, *APOT*, vol. 1, p. 186, has made the less plausible suggestion that the author of Tob (or possibly the adapter of the version of Ah which he knew) intentionally altered "Egypt" to "Elymais" on theological grounds: It was unthinkable that a righteous Jewish sage should travel to the wicked Egyptian court to demonstrate his wisdom.

[64] Also unclear is the source of the reference in Tob 14:10 to Ahiqar's being saved from death because of his *eleēmosynē* (the Gk. word may be translated either "good works" or "almsgiving"). None of the versions of Ah stresses his "good works" (though of course he did save Nabusumiskun), and none of them speaks at all of his "almsgiving," the sense in which Tob uses *eleēmosynē* elsewhere in the passage. The Syr. Ah does, however, say that the sage was kept alive because of his righteousness (*kʾnwt*; 8:2, 37), and J. R. Harris is probably correct in seeing an original Semitic *ṣdqh* ("righteousness" and "almsgiving" in post-biblical Heb. and Aram.) behind Ahiqar's *eleēmosynē* in the Tob passage (*Aḥiḳar*, pp. l–lii). One need not agree with Harris's suggestion to translate *kʾnwt* as "almsgiving" in the Syr. Ah. To the phrase in question, cf. the statement in Prov 11:4 that "virtuous conduct (*ṣdq*) delivers from death," and the use of *ṣdq* in Elephantine saying 78.

in a somewhat distorted form: "Pour out your wine [Gk.: "Place your bread"] on the grave of the righteous, but give not to sinners" (4:17).[65] This comes directly from the Ahiqar saying "My son, pour out thy wine on the graves of the righteous, rather than drink it with evil men" (Syr. 2:10; cf. Arm. 2:7; Ar. 2:13).[66] The statement in Tobit 14:10 that Nadab fell into his own trap probably comes from "He that digs a pit for others, himself falls into the pit" (Arm. Ah 8:27; cf. Syr. 8:41; Ar. 8:38), though the idea is known elsewhere (cf. Ps 141:10). And the quotation of the golden rule in negative form in Tobit 4:15 is very possibly derived from Ahiqar: "Son, that which seems evil unto thee, do not to thy companion" (Arm. 8:88).[67]

Ben Sira, like the canonical Book of Proverbs, contains a considerable number of general parallels to the sayings in the Elephantine Ahiqar, but none so explicit as to suggest a direct relationship. As for relations with the late versions, Sirach 4:26, ". . . Do not strive against the current of a river," is often cited, though probably not correctly, as a borrowing from Syriac Ahiqar 2:65, ". . . Stand not against a river in its flood." The metaphor is a natural one and is used for quite different purposes in the two contexts.

Another possible, though uncertain, point of contact is found in Ben Sira 22:14–15:

> What is heavier than lead,
> and what is its name if not "fool"?
> Sand, and salt, and a lump of iron
> are all easier to bear than a dolt.

This may be compared to Armenian Ahiqar 2:69c: "I have lifted iron and I have lifted stones upon my shoulders, and it was better for me, than to dwell with the ignorant and the fool."[68] But the saying in Ben Sira may derive from a general wisdom cliché or may be a reformulation of Proverbs 27:3:

> Heaviness of stone, weight of sand,
> heavier than both: annoyance from a fool.

It has been suggested that the figure of Achior the Ammonite in Judith (Jdt 5–6; 11:9–10; 14:5–10), who cautions Holofernes against attacking Israel and later is converted to Judaism, is patterned on Ahiqar.[69] But apart from the name (Ahiqar is called Achior in some of the versions of Tobit),[70] there is little similarity in the two figures beyond the fact that both are wise pagans who give advice to kings.

Given the wide distribution of Ahiqar during the hellenistic and Roman periods, it is surprising that it has left no trace in the writings that postdate it in the Pseudepigrapha.[71]

Cultural importance

The story of Ahiqar blends two literary themes: the disgrace and rehabilitation of a wise minister, and the treachery of an ungrateful kinsman. Both, particularly the former, are

---

[65] Translation of F. Zimmerman, *Tobit*, p. 71; cf. 70n. The Jerusalem Bible follows the Vulgate (cf. also Old Latin) in translating "Be generous with bread and wine on the graves of virtuous men, but not for the sinner."

[66] The Arm. omits the phrase "on the graves of the righteous," so that the original allusion to libations for the dead disappears. The confusion of the text in Tob 4:17 was probably abetted by Jewish uneasiness about a positive reference to this pagan custom (cf. Jub 22:17).

[67] Cf. Mt 7:12; Lk 6:31. That Ah was the source of Tob 4:15 seems likely in view of the proximity of the Ah quotation in Tob 4:17. But this is by no means certain, since the maxim (in positive and negative form) is widely attested in classical and Jewish literature. The earliest known occurrence is in Herodotus (5th cent. B.C.), and it is found often in later Gk. and Lat. writings. The earliest Jewish reference is in LetAris 207. A famous passage in the Talmud places the saying in the mouth of Hillel (b.Shab 31a), and it occurs also in TargYer on Lev 19:18. For further references and bibliography, see D. M. Beck, "Golden Rule, The," *IDB* 2, p. 438, and R. G. Hamerton-Kelley, "Golden Rule, The," *IDBS*, pp. 369f.

[68] The pairing of sand and salt as heavy burdens in Sir 22:15 could even be traced back to Elephantine saying 29.

[69] The Jerusalem Bible, p. 625, n. 5b.

[70] See n. 57.

[71] R. H. Charles, *APOT*, vol. 2, p. 291, notes a few parallels between Syr Ah and the T12P: Ah 2:20 [!] with TJos 18:2 (cf. TBenj 3:3) and Ah 2:19 with TReu 4:1; TJud 17:1; TIss 4:4; TBenj 8:2. None of these indicates direct influence.

well-known motifs in the folklore of many peoples[72] and can be documented in Babylonian literature originating well before the composition of Ahiqar.[73] The wisdom traditions to which the sapiential portion of the text is heir are also extremely ancient in the Near East. Collections of instructions attributed to wise viziers of famous kings and designed to edify young men being trained for court service were being composed in Egypt before the beginning of the second millennium, and the Sumerians and Babylonians were writing proverbs almost as early.[74] The narrative and sayings of Ahiqar were written in a cultural world in which their genre and themes were already ancient.

If it is correct that the proverbial portion of the text represents sayings current among the Aramaic-speaking population of Syria in the sixth or seventh century (or even earlier), that is of particular importance for the study of Old Testament wisdom literature. It means that in this text, as in no other, we have an independent record of the wisdom traditions of one of Israel's immediate neighbors, dating from the period when much of Israel's own wisdom literature was being formed and collected.[75]

By the intertestamental period and the early centuries of the Christian era, there is abundant evidence that the story and sayings of Ahiqar were widely known throughout the Near East and the Mediterranean world. In Greece, Ahiqar's name and wisdom seem to have been known from as early as the fifth century B.C. Clement of Alexandria accuses Democritus (5th cent.) of plagiarizing the content of a "stele of Ahiqar (*Akikaros*)," and the Arab philosopher Shahrastānī attributes to the same "Democrates" (*sic*) several proverbs known from the later versions of Ahiqar,[76] including one which can be traced back to the Elephantine version (59).[77] Just when the Greek Life of Aesop, a portion of which is extracted from a Greek version of Ahiqar, was written is not known. L. W. Daly dates it as early as the fifth century B.C.[78] Diogenes Laertius (3rd cent. A.D.) includes a book entitled *Akicharos* in his list of the works of Theophrastus (4th to 3rd cent. B.C.), and Strabo (1st cent. B.C. to 1st cent. A.D.) also makes mention of Ahiqar.

Ahiqar was better known in Jewish circles (apart from the Elephantine community) than the references in Tobit and scant parallels elsewhere in the Apocrypha would indicate. Several of the sayings from the Syriac can be found in the Talmud and Midrash,[79] one of which is also found in the Elephantine text (30). In the Koran (Sura 31) there are several sayings by the legendary Arab wise man Luqman, one of which appears to be derived from Ahiqar, and there is evidence from elsewhere in Muslim traditions that the figure of Luqman is patterned upon Aesop and Ahiqar.[80] Traces of the story have been detected in the folklore of Persia and India.[81]

---

[72] A. H. Krappe, "Is the Story of Aḥiqar the Wise of Indian Origin?" *JAOS* 61 (1941) 280–84. See further Stith Thompson, *Motif-Index of Folk Literature* (Indiana University Studies 19–22; Bloomington, 1932–36) K 2101, K 2214.3, K 2214.3.1.

[73] E. Reiner, "The Etiological Myth of the 'Seven Sages,' " *Orientalia* N.S. 30 (1961) 1–11.

[74] The best collections of this literature are E. Gordon, *Sumerian Proverbs* (Philadelphia, 1959); W. G. Lambert, *Babylonian Wisdom Literature* (Oxford, 1960); and the section on "Didactic and Wisdom Literature" in *ANET*.

[75] Note that Hezekiah, whose name is linked by biblical tradition with the transmission of Israelite wisdom (Prov 25:1) and under whose sponsorship a collection of older Israelite wisdom was probably made, is a contemporary of Sennacherib and therefore of Ahiqar.

[76] Syr. 2:38 (and parallels in Arm., Ar., Eth., and the Life of Aesop); 2:39 (and parallels); 2:53 (and parallels).

[77] Paralleled in Arm. Ah 2:8. J. R. Harris states (in Charles, *APOT*, vol. 2, p. 717) that Clement attributes the proverb about the pig (see "Relation to Canonical Books") to Democritus. This, however, is incorrect. The passage from Clement (Exhortation to the Greeks 75 [ch.10]) reads: "Pigs, it is said, delight in mud more than in clean water, and are wild about filth, according to Democritus" (*Hyes gar phēsin hēdontai borborō mallon ē katharō hydati kai epi phorytō margainousin kata Dēmokritou*). Only the last clause ("are wild about filth") is attributed to Democritus. (Plutarch [*De tuenda sanitate* 14] also credits Democritus with the words.) That is a rather commonplace notion for which there is no reason to suspect Ah of being the source. (Harris gives the words less accurately as "wallow in a drain.") The first half of the sentence, for which Clement does not name his source ("it is said"), is a quotation not from Ah but from Heracleitus; see Diels, *Die Fragmente der Vorsokratiker*, ed. W. Krantz. (Dublin and Zürich, 1966¹²) vol. 2, p. 154, # 13. On the saying quoted from Democritus, see Diels, vol. 2, p. 171, # 147. Thus the alleged parallel to Ah disappears. (See also above, n. 55.)

[78] *Aesop Without Morals*, pp. 21f.

[79] Full documentation is given by A. Yellin, *The Book of Aḥiqar the Wise* (Jerusalem, 1937²) p. 13 (in Modern Heb.).

[80] J. R. Harris et al., *Aḥikar*, pp. lxxiv–lxxxi. A. Furayḥah (*Aḥiqar: Wise Man of the Ancient Near East* (American University of Beirut Oriental Series 40; Beirut, 1962 [in Ar.]) has studied in detail the Ar. traditions relating to Ah.

[81] A. H. Krappe, "Is the Story of Aḥiqar the Wise of Indian Origin?" *JAOS* 61 (1941) 280–84.

The continued popularity of the work in the Near East is evidenced by the fact that it was still being copied in Arabic as late as the eighteenth century and in Syriac as late as the end of the nineteenth. It is included in a supplement to some printed editions of the *Thousand and One Nights*. The Armenian version went through numerous printed editions in the eighteenth and nineteenth centuries.[82] The Slavonic and particularly the Romanian versions provide evidence for the transmission of the text in Europe until recent centuries.

But the influence of Ahiqar on Western culture in general has been very slight. A Roman mosaic in Trier (3rd cent. A.D.) depicts a wise man named ". . ICAR," plausibly restored as [AC]ICAR⟨US⟩, seated before the Muse Polymnia.[83] And the twelfth-century Fables of Marie de France contain a Norman French versification of the story of the wolf who went to school (Syr. Ah 8:36 and parallels).[84] Otherwise, Ahiqar does not appear to have had any impact on Western literature and art. If Ahiqar has influenced modern culture at all, it is likely that evidence will be forthcoming not so much from the field of literature and the fine arts as from the realm of folklore and proverb.[85]

SELECT BIBLIOGRAPHY

Charlesworth, *PMR*, pp. 75–77.
Denis, *Introduction*, pp. 201–14.

Cowley, A. E. *Aramaic Papyri of the Fifth Century B.C.* Oxford, 1923 (repr. Osnabrück, 1967); pp. 204–48. (Long the standard English edition. Transcription, translation, and nn. incorporating most of the significant proposals made by others for revising Sachau's readings. Fairly complete bibliography of scattered publications 1911–16.)
Ginsberg, H. L. "The Words of Ahiqar," in *Ancient Near Eastern Texts*, ed. J. B. Pritchard. Princeton, 1969³; pp. 427–30. (Excellent ET of the better-preserved portions. Footnotes give biblical parallels and a few observations on the text. Select bibliography.)

[82] F. C. Conybeare, in *The Story of Aḥiḳar*, pp. 174–76, cites quotations in Arm. writers from the 5th to 13th cents. A.D. Illuminated MSS are also not unknown in the Arm. Ah tradition. See the 16th-cent. MS page reproduced in *EncyJud* 2, col. 462, which depicts Ahiqar admonishing Nadin.

[83] The mosaic is published in *Antike Denkmaeler herausgegeben vom kaiserlichen deutschen archaeologischen Institut* 1.4 (Berlin, 1890) Plate 48. See also the article of W. Studemund ("Zum Mosaik des Monnus," *Jahrbuch des kaiserlichen deutschen archaeologischen Instituts* 5 [1890] 1–5), who first proposed the identification of the figure in the mosaic with Ahiqar. The mosaic, much of which is damaged, includes nine octagons, each showing one of the Muses with a symbol of the art over which she presides, and the figure of a person skilled in that art, notably Homer and Aratus, a hellenistic writer on astronomy. (There are also several rectangles with busts of famous poets and authors, including Vergil and Menander.)

Studemund cites a Gk. literary tradition which apparently suggested the subject matter of the mosaic octagons: lists of the nine Muses, the realm of knowledge with which each is associated, and the names of the inventors or famous practitioners of the arts. Two of the entries in these lists correspond to figures paired in the mosaic: Calliope-Homer (poetry) and Urania-Aratus (astronomy). Polymnia appears in the lists not with Ahiqar but with Euclid (geometry). It is not certain that Polymnia represents geometry in the mosaic. The object she holds in her hands is unrecognizable, and other classical traditions identifying specific functions for each Muse are late and inconsistent. The Aram. Ah does not portray the sage as a geometrician, but in the Syr., Ahiqar is sent to Egypt in answer to Pharaoh's demand for a "skilled architect" to consult on building a castle between heaven and earth (5:2). Studemund suggests that the name of Ahiqar and some of the other less familiar names in the mosaic may have been known to the artist from Clement of Alexandria.

[84] J. R. Harris et al., *Aḥiḳar*, pp. lxxxiif.

[85] The most thorough studies of the Ahiqar traditions by folklorists were made around the end of the 19th and the beginning of the 20th cents., before the publication of the Elephantine text. Further bibliography can be found in the studies of Krappe and Thompson listed in n. 72. Furayḥah, *Aḥiqar*, draws attention to a number of modern Ar. proverbs which are paralleled in Ah.

Grelot, P. *Documents araméens d'Égypte*. Paris, 1972; pp. 427–52. (Up-to-date introduction and annotated French translation of narrative and proverbs. A revision of his earlier study of the proverbs [only], "Les proverbes araméens d'Ahiqar," *RB* 68 [1961] 178–94.)

Lindenberger, J. M. *The Aramaic Proverbs of Ahiqar*. Baltimore, London, 1983. (New edition and detailed commentary on the proverbs [only] citing parallels from the OT, ancient Near Eastern literature, and the late versions.)

Rosenthal, F. *An Aramaic Handbook*. Wiesbaden, 1967; vol. 1.2, pp. 15f.; vol. 1.2, pp. 8–15. (Aram. transcription of the text [ll. 17–21, 41–64, 79–83, 100–5, 118–20a, 165f.] and glossary, including a number of valuable original proposals for restoration. No connected translation.)

Sachau, E. *Aramäische Papyrus und Ostraka aus einer jüdischen Militär-Kolonie zu Elephantine*, 2 vols. (Leipzig, 1911). (First edition of the Aram. Ah, containing the only published photographs of the papyrus [Plates 40–50], with transcription, German translation, and brief commentary.)

ON THE LATE VERSIONS:

Charles, R. H. (ed.). *The Apocrypha and Pseudepigrapha of the Old Testament in English*. Oxford, 1913 (repr. 1968); vol. 2, pp. 715–84. (Reproduces the ETs from J. R. Harris et al., *The Story of Ahikar*, of the Syr., Ar., and Arm. in parallel columns with v. numbers, and includes separately a translation of the Eth. fragments and the English and Gk. of the Aesop Life. Insofar as possible, parallels in the present edition are cited from Charles.[86])

Daly, L. W. *Aesop Without Morals*. New York, 1961. (ET of a second recension of the Life of Aesop [pp. 31–90], and the best modern language translation of the Fables. The Gk. and Lat. originals are edited by B. E. Perry, *Aesopica I* [Urbana, Ill., 1952].)

Gaster, Moses. "Contributions to the History of Ahikar and Nadan," *JRAS* 21 (1911) 301–19. (Translation of the Romanian Ahiqar.[87])

Harris, J. R., F. C. Conybeare, and A. S. Lewis. *The Story of Ahikar*. Cambridge, 1913[2]. (Detailed introduction and the standard edition of the versions, including the original texts of the Syr., Arm., Ar. [Karshuni], and Old Turkish; ETs of these and the Slavonic and Eth.; as well as relevant parallels from one recension of the Gk. Life of Aesop. There is also a partial ET of the Elephantine text, based on Sachau.)

---

[86] For the OCS and Old Turkish, which do not appear in Charles, references are given to Harris. The late versions have not been translated anew for this edition. Quotations from them reproduce the archaic English style adopted in the works of Charles and Harris.

[87] For bibliography on the Georgian, Russ., and Serbian versions, see W. Lüdtke, "Beiträge zu slavischen Apokryphen," *ZAW* 31 (1911) 218f. These versions, the Georgian translated from Arm., and the Russ. and Serbian from Slavonic, are of little importance for the early history of the text and have not been utilized in the present study. The same is true of the neo-Syr., which is a late translation of an Ar. original.

AHIQAR

I. THE NARRATIVE

Introduction

Col. I 1 [These are the wor]ds of one Ahiqar,ᵃ a wise and skillful scribe,ᵇ which he
2 taught his son. N[ow *he did not have offspring •of his own, but]*ᶜ he said,
"I shall nevertheless have a son!" Prior to this,ᵈ Ahiqar had [become a
3 gre]at man; he had [become counselor of all Assyria •and ke]eper of the Tob 1:22
seal*ᵉ* of Sennacherib, king of Assy[ria. He used to say, "I] may not have
4 any sons,ᶠ but •Sennacherib, king of Assyria, relies [on my counsel] and
advice."ᵍ

Death of Sennacherib. Ahiqar trains his nephew to succeed him

5 A[t that time Senna]cherib, k[ing of Assyria, died, and] •his son Esarhaddonʰ
[arose] and became king in Assyria in pla[ce of his fa]ther [Sennacherib].
6 T[hen I said (to myself),ⁱ •"I am] growing old." [*So I] se[nt] for [my]*
7 nep[*hew, so that he might succeed me at]* my death [*and become*ʲ •scribe
and keeper of the se]al for [King] Es[arhaddon just as I was for Sennacherib,
8 king] of Assyria. Then I [*adopted Nadin, my]* ne[*phew, as my son. I*
9 *reared him and trained him]*ᵏ •and taught him wisdom. And I was generous
to himˡ and i[nstalled him in the] palace [ga]teᵐ with [me before the king
10 in the midst of] •his courtiers.

Nadin is presented to Esarhaddon

I brought him before Esarhaddon, king of Assyria, and the k[*ing questioned*
11 *him]* concerning wisdom, [*and he told him every]*thing •he asked.ⁿ Then
Esarhaddon, king of Assyria, gave him his approvalᵒ and said (to me),
12 "May your life [*be prolonged],*ᵖ •O wise [s]cribe, counselor of all Assyria,

Col. I a. Lit. "Ahiqar, his name." The same
idiom, a common one in Imperial Aram., is used
to introduce Esarhaddon (l. 5) and Nadin (l. 18).
On Ahiqar's name, see Introduction, n. 30.

b. The ancient Near Eastern scribe, no mere
copyist, was a master of the literary arts and a
learned scholar. Such persons were often sought
out by kings to serve as advisers and officials; cf.
1Chr 27:32; Ezra 7:6; etc. The Akkadian text in
which Ahiqar's name appears (see "Historical
Importance") describes him as *ummānu* ("scholar,
savant") of Esarhaddon.

c. Restoring conjecturally *ẘ[zr< l̊ hwh lh w]ʾmr*.
Ahiqar may have been a eunuch; see l. 63, n. n.

d. Lit. "before his words."

e. Lit. "[bear]er of the signet ring." Compare
Ahiqar's titles in the Syriac version: "sage and
secretary" (1:1; 8:41; cf. 4:1; 5:5), "Secretary and
Great Seal" (*ʾzqtʾ*; 3:8, 9, 11; 6:18); and the titles
in Tob 1:21–22. The exact background of the title
[*s]byt <zqh* in the Elephantine text has been much
debated; see J. C. Greenfield, "Studies in Aramaic
Lexicography I," *JAOS* 82 (1962) 292f., 297–99.

f. Reading [*yʾmr ʾn]h lm bnn l[ʾ ly]*.

g. The clause, restored according to ll. 43, 60f.,
is elliptical; lit. "on my advice and my words is
S., king of A."

h. Lit. "E., his name, his son"; see n. a. (*šmh*
has been inserted above the line.) The late recs.
generally invert the order of Sennacherib and
Esarhaddon.

i. Or "he said." The narrative begins in the
third person but changes to the first. Because of
the state of the MS, it is not certain whether this
change takes place in l. 5 or l. 8.

j. The restoration *šb [ʾnh wš]l[h̊ĭ] lbr ʾ[h̊t̊ẙ whw
yh̊lp ly <l m̊]wtŷ [wyhwh]* just fits the space and the
fragmentary letters.

k. To restore *ʾn[h lqht ndn] br ʾ[h̊ty lbry wrbyth
wʾlpth]* will exactly fit the lacunae and is closely
paralleled in the late versions.

l. Lit. "I gave (him) what is good" or ". . .
good things," reading *wt̊bt̊ʾ y[hbt]*. For the idiom,
see Heb. Ps 85:13, especially cf. Targum and
Peshitta.

m. I.e. the royal council chamber; cf. lines 17,
23, 44.

n. Grelot's restoration, *whkmh m[lk² šʾlh wʾmr
kl z]ly*, is plausible though somewhat long.

o. Lit. "loved him."

p. Restoring tentatively *hyn š[gyʾn lk wyh̊ẘh̊ŭ]*.
Cowley's restoration of *lh̊qr* instead of *lk* is too
long.

who raised up his [neph]ew to be his son, since [he had] no son of his
13 own.'' •[When the king of Assy]ria [said this], I, Ahiqar, bowed low in
obeisance to Esarh[addon, king of] Assyria.

Nadin succeeds Ahiqar at the court

14 [Some time later, when I, A]hiqar, saw that Esarhaddon, king of Assyria,
15 was favorably disposed, I addressed •[the king and said], "I [served] your
16 father, King [Sennach]erib, [wh]o ruled [before you] •[. . . . .]q [Now]
Col. II 17 I am growing old. I can no longer perform my duties in the palace gate
18 [or continue my service to you.] •But my son Nadina has grown up.b Let
19 him succeed me as scribe [and counselor of all Assyria], •and let him be
[kee]per of the seal for you! For [I have taught him] my wisdom and
20 co[unsel.'' Esarhaddon, •ki]ng of Assyria, replied to me, "Very well, [your
21 son] shall [be scribe and counselor and keeper of the seal for me] •in your
place. He shall do your work [for me.'' *Now when I, Ahiqar, heard him*
22 *prom]ise [this],c I went back home [and went into retirement there.]*

The treachery of Nadin

23 [And as for this son of mine, •whom] I [had reared] and installed in the
24 palace gate [before Esarhaddon, king of Assyria, in the midst of •hi]s
[courtiers], I thought, "He will promo[te my] welfare, [just as I did his.''
25 (But) then •my nep]hew, whom I reared, devised [a wicked] plot against
26 [me and thought to himself], •"[This is what] I can s[ay (to the king): 'This
27 old Ahiqar, who was keeper of the seal] •for your father, King Sennache[ri]b,
[is subverting the land against you,d for] he is a wise [counselor and scribe],
28 on whose counsel and ad[vice all Assyria used to rely.' Then], when
29 [Esarhaddon] •hears [my report],e he will be greatly enraged, [and will
30 order Ahiqar killed.'' So] •when this false son of minef had devised [this
31 lie against me, . . .] •[. . . . .]g

Ahiqar is placed under death sentence

Col. III 32,33 [Then Es]arhaddon, king of Assyria, [*flew into a rage*],a and said, •["*Bring
me* Nabusumiskun, on]e of my father's officers, who [was] on his staff.''b

---

q. Grelot (*Documents*) inserts the sayings (ll.
79–223) at this point. Though the original sequence
of cols. in the fragmentary papyrus is not known,
Grelot's arrangement is hardly plausible. By this
point in the story, the young man has already been
instructed in wisdom (ll. 9–11). L. 17 is simply
the continuation of the audience with Esarhaddon
which begins on l. 15. See also "Relation of
Narrative and Sayings."

Col. II a. On the name Nadin (also restored in l.
8), see Introduction, n. 30.

b. Lit. "Behold, N., his name, my son, has
grown up." See l. 1, n. a.

c. Lit. "[heard the word g]iven," following
Cowley's restoration [*šmʿt mlt* y]*hybʾ* and taking
the last word as passive participle third person
feminine singular spelled with final *aleph*. The
restoration and exact idiom are uncertain.

d. Cowley's restoration, based on the repetition
of the accusation in l. 36, is reasonably certain,
but *ḥbl* is better translated as active participle than
perfect.

e. Lit. "hears words [like these which I will

say to him]."

f. Lit. "my son who was not my son."

g. The end of l. 30 and another line must have
related briefly how the plot was carried out and
Ahiqar was denounced for treason. The late versions
elaborate considerably on the plot: Nadin forges
letters in Ahiqar's name to the kings of Persia and
Egypt, offering to surrender Assyria to them if they
will meet him at a specified rendezvous. At the
same time, he writes a letter to Ahiqar purporting
to be from the king ordering the sage to muster his
troops and meet him at the spot named in the letters
to the foreign kings. The nephew then shows the
king copies of the letters to Egypt and Persia, and
takes him to the rendezvous to show him Ahiqar
with all his forces drawn up, as final proof of the
old man's treachery.

Col. III a. The entire right margin is lost, but the
repetitious language of the narrative allows the
restoration of some lines with considerable probability (e.g. ll. 36, 44), establishing the approximate
position of the margin.

b. Lit. "who [ate] my father's bread."

34 [(Then) the king said (to Nabusumiskun)], "Seek [Ahiqar] out, (and)
35 wherever you find (him), •[kill him!] Otherwise that old [Ah]iqa[r]—wise
36 scribe •[and counselor of all Assy]ria that he was—is liable to subvert^c the
37 land against us." When •[the king of A]ssyria [had said this], he appointed
38 two other men with him to observe how •[(the execution) should be carried
out]. (Then) officer [Nab]usumiskun^d rode [away] on a swif[t h]orse,
39 accompanied by [those men].

Ahiqar is found and hears of Nadin's treachery

40 After three d[a]ys had gone by, •[he and the o]ther [men] accompanying
him c[aught sight of me] as I was walking along among the vineyards.
41 [As soon as] officer [Nab]usumiskun saw me, he tore his cloak and lamented:
42 ["Is it you], O wise scribe and master of good counsel, who [used to be a
43 *righteous*] man, •[and o]n whose counsel and advice all Assyria used to
44 rely? •[Your son whom you rear]ed,^e whom you installed in the palace
45 gate, has *denounced* you.^f He has ruined you, and turn[ed •on you
wickedly."]^g

Ahiqar asks to be spared

[Sudde]nly I, Ahiqar, was afraid, and I answered [officer] Nabusum[iskun,
46 "Indeed], I am the same Ahiqar^h who once long agoⁱ rescued you from
47 an undeserved death, •[when] King Esarhaddon's father [Sennacherib] was
48 so angry with you •[that he sought to kill you.]^j I took you [direc]tly to my
Col. IV 49 own house and provided for you there, •as a man would care for his own
brother. I concealed you from him, saying, 'I have killed him,' until an
50 oppor[tune ti]me.^a Then, after •a long time, I presented you to King
Sennacherib and cleared you of the charges against you^b in his presence,
51 so that •he did you no ha[rm]. Indeed, King Sennacherib was grateful to
me for having kept you alive rather than killing you. Now it is your turn
52 to treat me as I treated you.^c Do not kill me, (but) take me to your house
53 un[til] the times change.^d •King Esarhaddon is *known to be*^e a merciful
man. He will eventually think of me and wish for my counsel. Th[en] you
54 can [br]ing me to him and he will let me live."

c. Lit. "Why should he subvert . . . ?"
d. Lit. "that officer [Nab]usumiskun"; so also
to be restored in ll. 41, 45–46. On the name, see
Introduction, n. 30.
e. Restoring [brk zy rby]t at the beginning of l.
44.
f. The material reading of the word translated
"has *denounced* you" is uncertain and the clause
has been variously translated. Cowley may be
correct in reading yr^ck, although there is a small
trace of ink below and to the left of the second
letter, which may be the left stroke of a b. yr^c
would be construed as Pa^cel, Perf. of the root yr^c
(a by-form of r^{cc}), lit. "to harm, injure someone."
Grelot's reading brk "your son" (followed by [br³]
at the beginning of l. 44) cannot possibly fit the
traces.
g. More lit. "[it is a wicked] turn," reading
wtwb³ [lhy³ hw]. twb³ is construed as a noun (masc.
def.) derived from twb, meaning approximately
"recompense, turn." Cf. the form (though not the
meanings) of Jewish Aram. tûbā³ and Syr. tawbā³
from the same root. The restorations of Rosenthal
(twb³ [b³yš ^cbd]) and Cowley (twb³ [b³yš hw]) are
too long for the space.

h. Restoring [³p] before ³nh. An alternative
reading is that of Rosenthal: [³P], "[Am] I [not]
the same Ahiqar . . . ?"
i. Aram. qdmn here appears adverbially without
preposition, in the same sense as Jewish Aram.
mlqdmyn.
j. Lit. simply "was angry with you [to kill
you]"; [lmqtlk].

Col. IV a. Lit. "until ano[ther ti]me."
b. Lit. "I took away your offences."
c. Lit. "Now you, just as I did to you, so
therefore do to me"; cf. Tob 4:15; Mt 7:12.
d. Or simply "for a while"; lit. "un[til] other
days." The idiom ^c[d] lyŵmn ³hrnn seems to have
a different sense from lywmn ³hrnn šgy³n in ll. 49–
50.
e. Translated *ad sensum*. The exact meaning of
kmnd^c is uncertain, though it appears to be derived
from the root yd^c, "to know." It may be the
common Aram. noun manda^c, "knowledge" in
the sense "known, something known," or it may
be related to Imperial Aram. mnd^cm, mnd^cmt³ (Syr.
meddem), "anything" (Rosenthal: "like anything"
= "extraordinarily merciful"; Cowley: "kind as
any man"; similarly Ginsberg).

Nabusumiskun agrees, and a ruse is contrived

55 Then officer Nabusumiskun [re]plied to me, "Have no fear, •my [lor]d[f]
Ahiqar, father of all Assyria, on whose counsel King Sennacherib and [all]
56 the Assyrian Army •[used to rely]!" At once officer Nabusumiskun said to
57 his companions, those two men who were accompanying him, •["*List*]*en!*
Co[*me near*][g] to me and I will tell you [my] plan, and a [very] good plan
58 it is." •Th[en] those two [men] replied to hi[m, "You t]ell us, officer
59 Nabusumiskun, •what [yo]u th[ink, and we will obey] you." Then [of]ficer
60 [Nabusumiskun] said [in reply] to them, "Listen to me: •This [Ahi]qar
was[h] a great man.[i] He was [King] Esarhaddon's [keeper of the se]al, and
61 all the [Assyr]ian army used to rely on his counsel and advice. Far be it
62 from us to kill him![j] [There is[k] a] eunuch-[slave] of mine.[l] •Let him be
killed[m] between [the]se two mountains in place of this Ahiqar. Whe[n it is
63 reported], the king will [se]nd other [m]en •[af]ter us to see the body of
this Ahiqar. Then [they will see the body] of [th]is eunuch-slave of mine[n]
64 (and that will be the end of the matter) •until eventually [King] Esarhaddon
65 [*thinks of Ahiqar and wishes for his counsel,*[b] *and grieves*] •over him.
(Then) [King] Esarhaddo[n]'s thoughts [*will turn to me, and he will say to*
66 *his officers and courtiers*], •'I would give you riches as num[erous *as grains*
67 *of sand, if only you could find Ahiqar.*' " Now this plan] •seemed good to
68 his t[wo] companions. [*They replied to officer Nabusumiskun*], •"Do as
69 you suggest. [*Let us not kill him, but you give us*] •that eunuch-[slave] in
place of [this] Ahiqar. [*He shall be killed between these two mountains.*"]

Col. V[a]

Ahiqar is hidden and the king is deceived

70 At that time word spread through the la[nd[c] *of Assyria that Ahiqar,*] King
71 [*Esarhaddon's scribe,*] •had been put to death. Then [officer] Nabus[umiskun
72 took me to his house and hid me.[d] Indeed,] •he provided for me there as
[a man would care for his own brother. *And he said to me* . . . . "Bread
73,74 and water] •will be provided to my lord. I[f . . . ." •He gave
me] plenty of food and abun[dant] supplies. [Then officer Nabusumiskun]
75 went to Ki[ng] Esarhaddon [and said, "I have done as you commanded
76 me.] •I went and found [that] Ahiqar [and put him to death." Now when
77 King Esarhaddon heard this,] •he questioned the t[wo] men [whom he had
appointed along with Nabusumiskun. And they said, "It happened just as]
78 he said." T[he]n, while [King] Esarha[ddon . . . .]

f. Following Ginsberg's reading [*mr*]'*y*. An alternative reading is that of Cowley, [*th*]*yy*, "[you
shall l]ive." The next-to-last letter is broken and
can be either *aleph* or *yod*.

g. Restoring tentatively ['*ntm ḥṣ*]*ytw* ʾ[*p qr*]*b*[*w*].

h. Or "This is [Ahi]qar. He was, etc."

i. The common Aram. noun *rb*, "great man,
chief," is to be distinguished from *rby* / *rby*ʾ,
"officer," Nabusumiskun's title, which is probably
of Akkadian derivation.

j. Lit. "As for us, let us not kill him." '*nḥnh*
is emphatic.

k. Restoring ['*yty*] at the beginning of the lacuna
(Rosenthal).

l. The slave is evidently Nabusumiskun's. In
the late versions, the slave is Ahiqar's and is in
prison awaiting execution for an unspecified crime.

m. The verb was omitted by the scribe, and
later inserted above the line.

n. Though the story is not explicit, the nature

of the ruse seems to imply that Ahiqar, like the
young slave, was a eunuch.

Col. V a. Well over half of col. v has been lost.
Only a portion of the right side of each line is
preserved. Except where the phraseology parallels
the better-preserved parts of the text, the missing
words can be only very roughly restored by conjecture and by comparison with the late versions.
The translation is based on Cowley's restoration.

b. Cf. l. 53.

c. Aram. *bm*[*t* ʾ*twr*] is perhaps a better restoration than Cowley's *bm*[*dynt* ʾ*twr*]. *mdynh* is ambiguous: "province," later "city."

d. In the Syr. and other late recs., Ahiqar is
concealed by his benefactor in a tiny underground
hiding place. This detail is known to the author of
Tob (Tob 14:10); see "Relation to Apocryphal
Books."

(At this point, the narrative breaks off. According to the later versions, when the king of Egypt hears that Ahiqar is dead, he writes the Assyrian monarch challenging him to send a wise man who can answer a series of riddles and supervise the construction of a palace between heaven and earth. Nadin declares that not even the gods themselves could meet the challenge.

The Assyrian is at his wits' end, and laments his lost sage, offering a rich reward if only Ahiqar could be returned to him alive. The officer, seeing the time is ripe, brings the old scribe out of hiding to receive the king's profuse apologies and reinstatement at the court. After a series of adventures in Egypt, Ahiqar returns to Assyria and asks permission to discipline Nadin. The young man is put in chains and beaten, after which Ahiqar addresses him with a long series of reproaches. The speech concluded, Nadin swells up and dies.

It cannot be ascertained how much of this was included in the Elephantine version. No doubt it was much shorter. The surviving fragments of the Aram. text have no trace of the Egyptian episode, and there may have originally been only a rather brief statement of Ahiqar's rehabilitation and the disgrace and punishment of his adopted son.)

II. THE SAYINGS

Col. VI

79 *1* What is stronger than a braying ass? . . . .ᵃ

80 *2* The son who is instructed and restrained, and on whose foot the *bar*ᵇ is placed, [*will prosper in life*].ᶜ   Sir 6:23f.

81 *3* Spare not your son from the rod; otherwise, can you save him [from wickedness]?ᵈ   Prov 23:13f.; 13:24; 19:18; 22:15; 29:15,17 Sir 30:1–13 81 *3*

82 *4*
> If I beat you, my son,
> you will not die;
> but if I leave you alone,ᵉ
> [you will not live].ᶠ

83 *5*
> A blow for a serving-boy,   Prov 26:3
> a rebuke for a slave-girl,
> and for all your servants, discipline!

84 *6* He who acquires a runawayᵍ slave or a thievish maid [. . . . . .ʰ and
85 ruins] •the reputation of his father and his progeny by his own corrupt reputation.

Col. VI a. Or "What is stronger than an ass braying in the . . . ?" *ḥsyn,* "stronger," may also be translated "louder." No convincing restoration has yet been suggested for *b*[.]*r* at the end of the saying. It may be a one-word answer to the riddle. Or it is possible that l. 80 is the answer. The sense of the riddle is unclear.

b. Aram. *'rḥ'* is probably to be identified with Jewish Aram. *'rīḥā'* or *'arḥā',* "half-brick, lath, bar," here referring to a fetter or hobble. Wooden blocks were sometimes used for immobilizing prisoners in the ancient Near East.

c. Restoring [*yṣlḥ bḥywhy*] (Grelot). If this line is the answer to the riddle in l. 79, nothing needs to be restored. The general theme of parental discipline is extremely common in biblical and ancient Near Eastern wisdom.

d. Arm. 2:14 is an expanded version of Aram. sayings 3 and 4: "Son, spare not the rod to thy son . . . For if thou strike him with a rod once or twice, he is rendered sensible quietly, he does not die. But if thou leave him to his own will, he becomes a thief; and they will take him to the gallows and to death, and he becomes unto thee a reproach and breaking of heart." Cf. also Syr. Ah 2:2.

e. Lit. "if I leave you to your own heart."

f. The antithetic parallelism makes the restoration of the final words fairly certain.

g. The last letter of the Aram. word is lost, but the meaning is assured on the basis of the close parallel in Syr. Ah 2:24: "My son, . . . do not get thee a slave that is runaway nor a maid that is thievish: lest they destroy all that thou hast gotten." Cf. Ar. 2:25 and Arm. B saying 17 (J. R. Harris et al., *Ahiķar,* p. 59). In the Aram. text, perhaps *prỹ*[*d*] or *pry*[*r*] should be restored.

h. The damaged text appears to read *p*[*ḥd*] *h*[*w*], followed by a lacuna extending to the end of the line. Cowley's reading, *p*[*ḥd*] *hw* [*hnᶜl lbyth*], is not, as he notes himself, very satisfactory.

86 *7* The scorpion [*finds*] •bread and will not eat it; but (if he finds) something
foul, he is more pleased than if he were (sumptuously) fed.[i]

87 *8* . . . . hind . . . .[j]

88 *9* The lion *catches the scent of* the stag in his hidden *den*,[k] and he . . . . . .

89 and sheds its blood and eats its flesh. Just so is the meeting of [*men*].[l]

90 *10* . . . the lion[m] . . . •The ass abandons his load and will not carry it. He
will be shamed by his fellow and will have to carry a burden which is not

91 his own; •he will be laden with a camel's load.[n]

11 The ass mounts[o] the jenny out of lust for her. But the birds . . . .[p]

92 *12*   There are two things which are good,
and a third which is pleasing to Shamash:[q]
one who drinks wine and shares it,
one who masters wisdom [*and observes it*];[r]

93   and one who hears a word but tells it not.
Now that is precious to Shamash.
But one who drinks wine and [shares it] not,

94   whose wisdom fails,
who has seen[s] . . . ?[t]

13   From heaven[u] the peoples are favored;   Prov 8:22–31
Wisdom is of the gods.   Sir 1:9f[ ]; 24:1–7

Col. VII 95   Indeed, she is precious to the gods;   Wis 7:25,29
her kingdom is et[er]nal.   1En 42:1f.
She has been established by Shamayn;[a]   1Bar 3:29
yea, the Holy Lord has exalted her.   Jn 1:1–4

96 *14a*[b]   My son, do not c[ur]se the day[c]
until you have seen the night.

i. The text of this saying is badly broken and its meaning quite obscure. The sense may be that the one who is foul thrives on filth, or again, that "one man's meat is another's poison." The translation (cf. that of Ginsberg) assumes a restored text reading: ʿ[*qr*]*bʾ* [*yhškh*] *lḥm wlʾ* y[ʾk]*l* [*wlḥ*]*yh* *wʿ*[*l*]*wḥ*ᵍ *ṭb mn* [*ʾ*]*y* *yṭ*[ʿ*mwnh*]. Grelot understands the saying as referring to the scorpion's being inedible.

j. Except for fragments of several words, this saying is completely lost.

k. The meaning of the unknown word *swyḏ* or *swyrʾ* is taken from context.

l. Cf. Aesop's fable of the Deer and the Lion: "A deer that was running away from hunters came to a cave where there was a lion and went in to hide. As she was seized by the lion and was being killed she said, 'How ill-fated I am! Running away from men only to throw myself into the clutches of a wild animal.'" L. W. Daly, *Aesop Without Morals*, p. 126 (no. 76).

m. The relation of this word (followed and preceded by lacunae) to saying 10 is not clear. It can hardly belong to the end of saying 9, since that has a conclusion followed by a dividing sign. Nor is there enough space for another entire saying at the end of l. 89 (between 9 and 10). Cowley suggests that 10 begins "Fr[om fear of the] lion," but that does not fit the traces.

n. If you don't pull your own weight, you will end up with a heavier task. Cf. Aesop's fable of the mule that was unwilling to help the ass carry its burden. The ass fell over a cliff and died, and the owner forced the mule to carry both the ass's load and the hide of the dead animal. L. W. Daly,

Aesop Without Morals, pp. 170f. (n. 181).

o. *rk*[*b*] (Sachau).

p. Two or three words are lost at the end, so that the point of the saying is obscure. Perhaps the meaning is that while the ass mates from lust, the birds mate to propagate their species.

q. The sun-god; see "Theological Importance."

r. [*wynṭrh*] (Grelot).

s. Or "[. . .] is seen," *m*[*t*]*ḥzh*.

t. The Mesopotamian Shamash literature also contains such lists of various kinds of behavior which are pleasing and displeasing to Shamash. The type of numerical parallelism found in this saying is frequently found in biblical and ancient Near Eastern literature; see W. Roth, "The Numerical Sequence x/x + 1 in the Old Testament," *VT* 12 (1962) 300–31.

u. Or "by Shamayn"; see "Theological Importance."

Col. VII a. Probably Baal Shamayn, "the Lord of Heaven," one of the high gods of the Arameans. See "Theological Importance." The saying is evidently a hymn in praise of wisdom.

b. Grelot, who originated the enumeration of the proverbs followed here, misread l. 96 (see n. c) and combined it with l. 97 as a single saying (14).

c. *ʾl ṭ*[*lw*]*ṭ ywmʾ* is correctly read by Sachau. Cowley's revised reading *ʾl ṭ*[*b*]*ṭ ytr*, "do not chatter overmuch," though widely accepted, is incorrect. A vertical split in the papyrus (not clearly visible in the published photograph from which Cowley worked) distorts the appearance of the last word.

97 *14b* ⟨My son, do not utter everything⟩[d] which comes into your mind, for there Sir 22:27
are eyes and ears everywhere. But keep watch over your mouth, lest it Eccl 10:20
bring you to grief![e]

98 *15* Above all else, guard your mouth; and as for what you have h[eard], be Ps 141:3
discreet![f] For a word is a bird,[g] and he who releases it is a fool.[h] Sir 22:27; 27:16–21

99 *16* Ch[oo]se[i] the sayings you shall utter,[j] then speak them [to] your [*brother*]
to help him. For the treachery of the mouth is more dangerous[k] than the
treachery of battle.[l]

100 *17*   Quench not the word of a king;
let it be a balm[m] [for] your [hea]rt.

18 A king's word is gentle, but keener and more cutting than a double-edged 103 20. 106 23
dagger.[n]

101 *19* Here is a difficult thing before you: Do not stand opposed to the king.[o] His Prov 16:14
102 anger is swifter than lightning; look out for yourself! •Let him not kindle
it[p] against your words, lest you depart before your time.[q]

103 *20* When a royal command[r] is given you,[s] it is a burning fire. Execute it at 100 18. 106 23
104 once,[t] lest it flare up[u] against you and singe[v] your hands. •But rather (let)
the king's command (be your) heart's delight.[w]

21   How can logs strive with fire, Isa 10:15
meat with a knife, Eccl 6:10b
(or) a man with a king?[x]

d. A phrase should be restored; it was evidently
lost through transmission.

e. Warnings against hasty speech are frequent
in the wisdom literature. Cf. the Egyptian Instructions of Onchsheshonqy 7:23f.: "Do not speak
hastily lest you give offence. Do not say the first
thing that comes into your head." S. R. K.
Glanville, *The Instructions of ʿOnchsheshonqy*
(Catalogue of Demotic Papyri in the BM 2; London,
1955).

f. Lit. "harden (your) heart."

g. The image of the word as a bird occurs also
in Prov 26:2; cf. Eccl 10:20. Cf. also Syr. Ah
2:25: "My son, the words of a liar are like fat
sparrows, and he that is void of understanding
eateth them." Arm. 2:17; Arm. B saying 19
(J. R. Harris et al., *Aḥiḳar*, p. 59); Slav saying 23
(Harris et al., *Aḥiḳar*, p. 4), in which a similar
metaphor appears, may be remotely descended from
the Aram. saying. Cf. also the "winged words"
of Homeric cliché.

h. Lit. "a man of no sense," *gbr P l[bb]*.
Similar exhortations to discretion appear in the
Akkadian Counsels of Wisdom: "Let your mouth
be controlled and your speech guarded; therein is
a man's wealth—let your lips be very precious . . .
Beware of careless talk, guard your lips, . . . For
what you say in a moment will follow you afterwards. But exert yourself to restrain your speech."
W. G. Lambert, *Babylonian Wisdom Literature*
(Oxford, 1960) pp. 101 (ll. 26f.), 105 (ll. 131,
133f.).

i. Restoring *m[ś]y*.

j. Lit. "the proverbs of your mouth."

k. Lit. "strong."

l. The details of this saying are elusive. Several
words are ambiguous due to possible confusion
between *d* and *r*. The point seems to be that the
wise man who is asked for counsel should ponder
his advice carefully, lest he do serious harm. Syr.
2:53 is a form of the same saying: "My son, let
not a word go forth from thy mouth, until thou
hast taken counsel within thy heart: because it is

better for a man to stumble in his heart than to
stumble with his tongue." (Cf. also Arm. 2:55;
Ar. 2:54; Eth. 13). Democritus (see "Cultural
Importance") is quoted as having said, "It is better
to stumble with the foot than with the tongue";
Charles, *APOT*, vol. 2, p. 717.

m. The *aleph* of *rpʾh* is written above the line.
For the association of speech and healing, cf. Prov
4:20–22; 12:18b; 13:17.

n. The comparison of the spoken word to a
sword or knife is a recurring image: Pss 52:2; 57:4;
Wis 18:15f.; Heb 4:12.

o. Aram. [*ʿl ʾ*]*npy m*[*lk*] *ʾl tqwm*. An alternative
translation is "[in pre]sence of a k[ing] delay not"
(Cowley, Ginsberg); cf. Eccl 8:2–4.

p. Restoring *ʾl yḥ*[*bn*]*hy* (cf. Syr. *ḥbb*).

q. Cf. the Egyptian Instructions of Ptah-Hotep
445: "Opposition to a superior is a painful thing,
(for) one lives as long as he is mild . . ." J. Wilson
in *ANET*, p. 414a. The theme of the king's anger
appears in various ways in the wisdom literature;
cf. Prov 14:35; 19:12; 20:2; Eccl 10:4.

r. Lit. "a word of the king," [*mlʾ*]*t mlk* (Sachau);
cf. ll. 100–4.

s. Lit. "if it is commanded you." *lk* has been
added above the line.

t. Lit. "hurry, do it!"

u. Aram. *ʾl thnśq*, either active (Hafʿel), "lest
you kindle it, lest it grow hot"; or passive (Hufʿal)
"lest it be kindled." Cowley and Grelot divide the
verb into two words: *ʾl thn śq* "do not put sackcloth
upon thee." But *thn* is not a known word, and the
scribe often leaves extra space before the letter
ś/š in the middle of a word.

v. Aram. *tksh* is to be emended to *tkwh* (Ginsberg); cf. Jewish Aram. and Syr. *kwʾ*, "to sear,
scorch."

w. Aram. *bḥmd lbbʾ*. Others read *bḥmr lbbʾ*,
"the word of the king is with wrath of heart"
(Cowley).

x. There are no close parallels to this saying in
the late versions, but it is possible that Syr. 2:65,
"My son, strive not with a man in his day . . . ,"
goes back ultimately to it.

105 22   I have tasted even the bitter medlar,[y]
    and have eaten *endives*,[z]
    but there is nothing more bitter than poverty.[a2]

106 23 The k[ing]'s tongue is gentle, •but it breaks a dragon's ribs. It is like death,   100 *18*, 103 *20*
    which is invisible.   Prov 25:15b
                                                     Sir 28:17

24   Exult not over a multitude of sons,   Sir 16:1
    [nor be sad] over a meager number of them.[b2]

107 25   A king is like the Merciful;[c2]
    even his voice is haughty.
    Who is there who could withstand him,
    but one with whom El is?

108 26   A king is as splendid to see as Shamash;
    and his majesty is glorious
    to them that tread the earth in peace.[d2]

109 27   A good container keeps a thing[e2] within it,   Sir 21:14
    but a broken one lets it out.

110 28 The lion approached to gre[et the ass]: "Peace be unto you!" The ass
    replied to the lion, ...[f2]

Col. VIII

111 29   I have carried sand and hauled salt,
    but there is nothing more burdensome than [de]b[t].[a]

112 30   I have carried straw and lifted bran,
    but there is nothing[b] taken more lightly than
        a foreigner.[c]

y. The bitter fruit of the medlar tree is similar to a small apple, although it is brown and edible only when it begins to decay.

z. The second verb should probably be read *w[ʾkl]t*, based on context and later parallels. This requires an emendation, since the fragmentary last letter seems to be *aleph*. The precise identification of *ḥsyn* is uncertain. The usual meaning of Jewish Aram. *ḥāsāʾ* (Syr. *ḥassᵉtaʾ*) is "lettuce." Context here demands something bitter. Note that in the Talmud (b.Pes 39a) *ḥsʾ* is considered suitable for use as the "bitter herbs" in the Passover ritual. "Endive" is based on the Arm. parallel; see n. a2.

a2. The closest parallel in the later Ahiqar traditions is Arm. 2:69: "Son, I have eaten endive and I have drunk gall, and it was not more bitter than poverty . . ." (cf. also Ar. 2:40). The Arm. saying continues with a parallel to Elephantine 29. Note that Aram. sayings 22, 29, and 30 all have the same form.

b2. The saying is preserved in Arm. 2:34: "Son, rejoice thou not in the number of thy children, and in their deficiency be not distressed." Cf. also the Gk. parallel to saying 109 (n. f).

c2. An epithet of the god El; see "Theological Importance."

d2. See "Theological Importance." Ll. 107f. could be understood as a single, complex saying.

e2. The double meaning of *mlh* ("thing" and "word") is the key to the understanding of the saying: "a good pot holds its contents," i.e. a discreet man knows how to hold his tongue. Cf. Syr. 2:52f.; Arm. 2:55f.; Ar. 2:53f.

f2. The first of several animal fables (cf. 35,

36, and probably also 106). Its conclusion must have appeared at the top of a lost column. One of the reproaches in the Syr. (8:9) appears to be related: "My son, thou hast been to me as the lion that came upon the ass in the morning of the day and said to him, 'Welcome, my lord Kyrios.' But the ass said to him, 'May the same welcome that thou gavest me be the portion of him that tied me up last night; and did not make my halter fast, so that I had not seen thy face.' " In the shorter Arm. and OCS parallels the animals are a wolf and an ass.

Col. VIII a. The saying is closely paralleled by Syr. 2:45: "My son, I have carried salt and removed lead; and I have not seen anything heavier than that a man should pay back a debt (*ḥwbrʾ*) which he did not borrow." Following the Syr. *ḥwbrʾ*, the last word of the Aram. text is restored with the Imperial Aram. equivalent [*zp*]*ʾt*[*ʾ*]. Prov 27:3 and Sir 22:14f. compare human folly with a heavy load. See further "Relation to Apocryphal Books."

b. The scribe has mistakenly written *wlʾ* twice.

c. Lit. "sojourner, resident alien." The closest parallel is found in the Talmud, incorrectly attributed to Sir: "I have weighed all things in the scale of the balance and found nothing lighter than bran; lighter than bran is a son-in-law who lives in the house of his father-in-law . . ." (b.BB 98b). Less similar to the Elephantine text is the version in Syr. Ah 2:46: "My son, I have carried iron and removed stones; and they were not heavier on me than a man who settles in the house of his father-in-law."

113 *31* A sword stirs up quiet waters between good neighbors.

114 *32* If a young man[d] utter great[e] words, they will soar above him when his　Ex 4:i0–12
115 utterance exalts •the gods. If he is beloved of the gods, they will give him　Jer 1:6–9
something worthwhile to say.[f]　　　　　　　　　　　　　　　　　　　　　　Mk 13:11
　　　　　　　　　　　　　　　　　　　　　　　　　　　　　　　　　　　　　Lk 12:11f.

116 *33* The [s]tar[s in the sky] are so numerous [that] no one knows their names.[g]
Just so, no one knows man.

117 *34*　　　　　There is no lion in the sea;
　　　　　　　　therefore the *sea-snake*[h] is called *labbu*.[i]

118 *35* (Once upon a time) a leopard came upon a she-goat who was cold. The
leopard said to the goat, "Won't you let me cover you with my pelt?"
119 The goat replied to the leopard, "Why should I do that, my lord? Don't
take my own hide away from me! For (as they say), 'A [*leopard*] does not
120 greet a gazelle except to suck its blood.' "[j]
　　36 (Once upon a time) a bear came to the lambs and [said, "*Let me take just
121 one of you and*][k] •I will be content." The lambs replied to him, "Take
122 whichever of us you will. We [*are only sheep, but you are a bear!*]][l] •For
it is not in men's own power to lift their feet or set them down apart fro[m　Gen 41:44
the gods . . . ."]　　　　　　　　　　　　　　　　　　　　　　　　　　　　Jer 10:23

123 (*Variant ending:*) "For it is not in your power to lift your foot or set it
down."[m]

　37　　　　　If good comes forth from m[en's] mouths,
　　　　　　　　(it is a fine thing).[n]
124　　　　　　But if evil comes forth from their mouths,
　　　　　　　　then the gods will bring evil upon them.

125 *38* If the eyes of the gods are on men, •a man who chops wood in the dark
when he cannot see is like a thief[o] who breaks into a house and is caught.[p]
Col. IX
126 *39*　　　　　[Do not draw[a]] your bow　　　　　　　　　　　　　　128 *41*, 191 *93*
　　　　　　　　and shoot your arrow at the righteous man,　　　　　　Pss 11:2, 6;
　　　　　　　　　　　　　　　　　　　　　　　　　　　　　　　　　64:1–4,7

---

d. Or "insignificant man."

e. Or "many."

f. For the general idea that an insignificant person may speak words which transcend his limitations, cf. the Egyptian Protests of the Eloquent Peasant (*ANET*, pp. 407b–410b). The Aram. saying is difficult to interpret. The first clause could also be translated: "If a little man speaks too many words, they soar up away from him" (i.e. he has no control over their consequences; cf. saying 15).

g. Cf. Isa 40:26; Ps 147:4.

h. The difficult word *qp*', not found elsewhere in Aram., is probably to be identified with Akkadian *kuppû*, "eel, sea snake."

i. The Akkadian word *labbu* (written *lb*' in Aram.) means "lion" but is also the name of a mythological sea monster. Evidently a serpentlike sea creature named for the legendary monster (perhaps the vicious moray eel) has been popularly identified with the homonymous word "lion." Thus the saying is a rather erudite bilingual play on words. If so, this is the only saying in the collection whose background is clearly Mesopotamian.

j. This is the best preserved of the fables in the text (cf. also 28, 36 and 106[?]), and one of the longest of all the sayings. Its point is that a generous gesture may mask malicious intentions. The goat sees through the leopard's artifice and foils him by a clever answer. Since the concluding sentence refers to a gazelle, not a goat, it appears to be a proverb which the goat applies to her own situation. Similar fables are known in Gk. and Ar. literature.

Cf. Syr. Ah 8:4; Arm. 8:9; Ar. 8:4 for a quite different fable concerning the hide of a she-goat or gazelle.

k. The missing words can only be restored by conjecture. Perhaps the text read something like [*w*'*mr* '*ns*° *hd mnkm wh*'] '*stq*.

l. Also conjectural, the translation follows the restoration of Grelot, '*nhnh* ['*mrn w*'*nt db*].

m. This saying, like 35, seems to conclude with a short proverb quoted by the weaker protagonist in the fable. In this case, the proverb has been preserved in two versions, one in third person, the other in second person.

n. Though *tb* or *tb lhm* could be restored at the end of l. 123, it is not necessary. The conditional clause may be elliptical; cf. Dan 3:15.

o. The scribe originally wrote *k*'*ys zy gnb*, then erased *zy*.

p. The saying is obscure. It may be that a line has been lost after l. 124, so that l. 125 begins a new saying. But it is possible to understand the saying as it stands to mean that the gods look on a foolhardy act as being as serious as a criminal one. Alternatively, if cutting wood in the dark refers to poaching lumber, the meaning would be that the surreptitious evildoer will be punished as surely as a thief caught in the act.

Col. IX a. Or "aim." The beginning of the line may be restored [*l tdrk q*]*stk*, (cf. l. 191), or possibly [*l tngd q*]*stk* (cf. the restoration of l. 128). *drk* and *ngd* are synonymous.

lest the gods come[b] to his aid
and turn it back[b] against you.[c]

127 *40* [Hear], O my son: 129 *42*
harvest any harvest, Prov 12:11; 28:19
and do any job; Eccl 2:24; 3:13, 22; 5:18f.; 9:7–10
then you may eat your fill Sir 7:15
and provide for your children.[d]

128 *41* [If] you have [dr]awn[e] your bow and shot your arrow at a more righteous 126 *39*
man than yourself, it is a sin against the gods.[f]
129 *42* [Hear], O my son: borrow grain and wheat, that you may eat your fill and 127 *40*
provide for your children with you.[g]
130 *43* Do not take a heavy loan from an evil man. And if you take a loan (at all), Prov 6:1–5
131 give yourself no peace until •[you have re]pa[id] it. A loan is pleasant as
. . . ,[h] but paying it back is a houseful.[i]

132 *44* . . . . *it*[j] with your ears,
for truthfulness[k] renders a man admirable,
but lying speech[k] makes him repulsive.[l]

133 *45* [At] first the throne is [*comfortable*][m] for the liar; but in the end, his lies
will overtake him, and they will spit[n] in his face.[o]
134 *46* The liar should have his throat cut,[p] like a *temple*[q] virgin who [*exposes*][r]
135 her face; like a man who does evil, •contrary to the will of the gods.[s]
136 *47* [Do not *despise*][t] that which is your lot, nor covet some great thing which Ps 131:1
is withheld from you.

b. The verbs "come" (*ysgh*) and "turn it back" (*yhtybnhy*) are singular, evidently a scribal lapse. It is not possible to translate the subject *ʾlhyʾ* as "god" or "the god." Following universal usage in Aram., it must be read as plural. Nor, given the polytheistic character of the text (see "Theological Importance"), is it preferable to emend *ʾlhyʾ* to the singular *ʾlhʾ*.

c. Saying 41 is a variant (slightly more prosaic) of 39; cf. also the parallel between 40 and 42. The altered form of the saying in the later Ahiqar tradition derives from 41: "Thou hast been to me, O my son! like a man who shot an arrow up to heaven. The arrow certainly did not reach heaven, but the man was guilty of sin" (OCS reproach 2; J. R. Harris et al., *Aḥiḳar*, p. 21). "My son, thou hast been to me like a man that threw a stone at the heaven, and it did not reach heaven, but he incurred sin against God" (Syr. 8:5).

d. Parallels from ancient Near Eastern wisdom are numerous. Cf. the Egyptian Instructions of Amenemopet 8:16f.: "Plow in the fields, that thou mayest find thy needs, that thou mayest receive bread of thy own threshing floor" (J. A. Wilson in *ANET*, p. 422b).

e. Restoring [*n*]*gt*, an assimilated form of *ngdt*.

f. The saying plays on the words *ḥṭ*, "arrow," and *ḥṭʾ* "sin." The last word in the Aram. should be read *hẘ* ("it"). A thick *w* with a long tail has lost a tiny fleck of ink in the middle of the head, making it look somewhat like *d*/*r*.

g. The variant to saying 40 shifts the emphasis from tilling the land to borrowing produce.

h. Some restore *k*[*zẙ ḥsy*]*r* (Cowley, Grelot), but that is quite uncertain.

i. I.e. it may cost you everything you own. For a similar idiom, cf. Num 22:18; 24:13.

j. The beginning is lost. Cowley cautiously restores [*kl zy tšmʿ tbḥnn*]*hy*, "all that thou hearest, thou mayest try (by the ears)." Ginsberg has "My [son hearken not] with thine ears to [a lying man]." Both are paleographically unlikely.

k. Or perhaps "faithfulness" and "apostasy."

l. Lit. "his repulsiveness is the lying of his lips."

m. Restoring tentatively [*šq*]*ẙṭ*, construed as an adjective related to *šqṭ* "to be at ease."

n. Probably impersonal plural, i.e. "his face will be spat in."

o. Since the saying refers to a throne, the word "liar" (*kdbʾ*) may have a political significance, i.e. a usurper or rebellious vassal. The word is often so used in ancient Near Eastern diplomatic terminology. From the late versions of Ah, the nearest parallel is OCS 23: "My son, a liar findeth sympathy at first, but at the last he is despised and abused" (J. R. Harris et al., *Aḥiḳar*, p. 4). Cf. also Syr. 8:2; Arm. 2:17.

p. Lit. "his neck is cut." As in saying 45, "liar" (here *mkdb*) may have a political sense. The threat of beheading was a traditional curse against rebellious vassals in the ancient Near East.

q. The word *tymnh* has never been satisfactorily explained. It is possible that it is a nominal derivative of the root *ʾmn*, "be faithful, trustworthy," and refers to a female member of a religious order (cf. Syr. *mʿhaymnāʾ*, "minister, eunuch"). The noun is in apposition with *btwlh*, "virgin."

r. Restoring [*tḥwh*] or [*thḥwh*].

s. More lit. "which did not proceed from the gods." There seems to be an unclear trace of a letter (*aleph?*) before *wmn* at the beginning of l. 135. A short word may have been lost.

t. [*ʾl tbsr̊*], though conjectural, is a possible restoration. Cowley's [*ʾl tmʾs*] does not fit the trace of the last letter.

137 *48*   [Do not *amass*] wealth,ᵘ

lest you pervert your heart.

Ezek 28:5
Ps 62:10
Deut 8:13f.
Lk 12:13–21
1Tim 6:10

138 *49* Whoever takes no pride in his father's and mother's name may Shama[sh]ᵛ not shine [on him], for he is an evil man.

Prov 20:20
Ex 20:12
Deut 5:16
Sir 3:1–16

139 *50–52*ʷ My distress is my own fault,ˣ

before whom will I be found innocent?ʸ

My own son spied out my house,

[wh]at shall I say to strangers?ᶻ

140   He was a false witness against me;

who, then, will declare me innocent?

[My] poisonerᵃ² came from my own house;

before whom can I press my complaint?ᵇ²

Ps 41:9; 55:12–
14
Jer 9:3–6; 12:6
Micah 7:6
Jn 13:18

141 *53* Do not reveal your [secr]etsᶜ² before your [frien]ds, lest your reputation with them be ruined.ᵈ²

Prov 25:9b–10a

Col. X

142 *54* With one who is more exalted than yourself, do not pick a quar[rel].ᵃ

Sir 8:1
Mt 5:25f.

143 *55* With one who is nobler and stronger than yourself, [*do not . . . . .*]ᵇ, *for* 142 54

144   *he will take]* •from your portion and [add] to his own.

145 *56* . . . . •Just so is a little man who [*contends*] with [*a great one*].

---

u. *Aleph* has been erased after *ḥyl.* If *ḥyl* is a complete word and is to be translated "wealth" rather than "strength," one might restore [*ʾl thśg*], "do not amass," at the beginning of the line as a play on *ʾl thśg*, "lest you pervert," in the second clause. Another possible restoration is [*ʾl thwy d]ḥyl,* "do not be fearful."

v. The sun-god. See "Theological Importance" on the Shamash sayings.

w. The Aram. text has dividing marks after "be found innocent" in l. 139 and "declare me innocent" in l. 140. Hence the two ll. are reckoned by Grelot as three sayings. But it seems more probable that this is a single saying in poetic or quasi-poetic form. Each of the four sentences in the two ll. has the same balanced form: a confession of the speaker's folly or ignorance followed by a rhetorical question pointing to the impossibility of justification. The saying, reminiscent in its tone of the reproaches with which the late versions of Ah end, is among those which seem most clearly related to the narrative. Cf. also 76 and 80.

x. Lit. "proceeded from me."

y. The phraseology of the second clause is similar to that of Job 9:2; 25:4.

z. Aram. *nkry* is to be so translated if the word has the meaning we would expect from comparison with Syr. and other cognate languages. But this gives an odd meaning in the context. It is possible that the word has some special legal sense here similar to "investigator" or "judge." Note that the verb *nkr* (Afᶜel) can mean "to know, recognize" in Jewish Aram. and Christian Palestinian Aram.

a2. Lit. "[my] poison," *ḥmt[y].* Another translation is "From my house has gone forth wrath" (*ḥmt[ʾ]*, Ginsberg; cf. Cowley and Grelot).

b2. The clause *ʾm mn ʾqśh wᶜph* is obscure. *qśh* (Afᶜel), "to harden, make difficult," can also mean "to dispute, object," in a legal sense in Jewish Aram. A verb *ᶜph* is known in Aram. but not in any appropriate sense. (Meanings such as "to bloom, flourish, spread, be thick-branched"

occur.) The lexica also list another *ᶜph* (Peᶜal) meaning "to toil, strive," and H. L. Strack (reviewing Sachau's *Aramäische Papyrus und Ostraka* in *ZDMG* 65 [1911] 833) long ago suggested that this is the verb which appears in Ah. That would give an intelligible clause, taking the two verbs ("make hard" and "strive") together as meaning approximately "make a vigorous struggle." The difficulty is that the verb proposed by Strack is so weakly attested it can be doubted that it exists at all. It occurs only as a textual variant in some editions of the Targum of Prov 21:25, where other editions have an obvious error or a completely different word. A better solution might be to assume that the scribe has reversed two letters of an original *ʾpᶜh. pᶜh,* "to cry, bleat" (Jewish Aram. and Syr.) also occurs in the Talmud with the sense "make a noisy protest." In that case, the two verbs could be rendered "press my complaint," or more lit., "dispute and protest."

c2. Perhaps [*str]yk.*

d2. Lit. "lest your name be diminished before them." Such admonitions are common in wisdom literature. The saying has been variously reworked in the late versions: "O my son! display not thy condition to thy friend, lest thou be despised by him" (Ar. 2:43). "Son, reveal not thy secret counsel to thy wife . . ." (Arm. 2:74).

Col. X a. Aram. *ʾl tᶜbd bnṣ[yn]* (cf. Syr. *neṣyānā*, "dispute, dissension," Grelot). Variations on this theme abound in wisdom texts. Ar. 2:38 is similar: "O my son! make not an enemy of a man stronger than thyself, for he will take thy measure and his revenge on thee." Cf. also Turkish saying 81 (J. R. Harris et al., *Aḥikar*, pp. 93–94).

b. Cowley restores [*ʾl tśpṭ*], "contend not." Probably the warning is against entering into financial dealings with the powerful (cf. Sir 8:12a) or provoking his hostility (Ar. Ah 2:38). One might also compare the parable of the talents (especially Mt 25:28f.; Lk 19:24–26).

146 57 Do not remove wisdom from yourself, [*lest* . . . .]
147 58 Do not *be overly foolish*,ᶜ lest . . . . be extinguished.ᵈ
148 59   Do not be too sweet lest you be [swallowed];
            do not be too bitter [lest you be spat out].ᵉ
149 60 If [yo]u wis[h to be *exalted*], my son, [*humble yourself before Shamash*],ᶠ
150   who humbles the [*exalted*] and [*exalts the humble*].ᵍ
151 61   How can [hu]man l[ip]s curse
            [*what the gods have not cursed*]?ʰ
152 62 It is better to master [*wisdom*ⁱ *than* . . . .]
153 63 . . . . . •yourself. Do not let him/it love . . . . .
154 64 . . . . . . •who can *heal* them but one with whom El is?ʲ
155 65 . . . . my hands . . . . my mouth . . . . . .ᵏ
156 66 May El twist the mouth of the treacherous and tear out [his] tongue.ˡ   Prov 10:32
157 67   May good eyes not be dimmed,
            [*may good*] ears [*not be stopped*,
158   *and may a good mouth love*] •the truth
            and speak it.ᵐ
Col. XI
159 68 A man of [fi]ne characterᵃ and a happy dispositionᵇ is like a mighty c[*it*]yᶜ
        which is bu[*ilt*] on a h[*ill*].ᵈ
160 69 [*If*] a man is [*not*] under the careᵉ of the gods, then how can he guard
        himself against his *inner wickedness*?ᶠ
161 70 . . . . . . •. . . . . . .,ᵍ but as for him with whom El is not, who would
        accept his oath?ʰ

c. The few surviving words of this saying are so ambiguous that translation is almost impossible. *tstkl* has been variously translated "be crafty, stare, be foolish." But it is probable that the Aram. spelling of this period would still distinguish the originally separate roots *śkl*, "be wise, look," and *skl*, "be foolish."

d. Grelot (*RB*) suggests the restoration *w⁾l ydᶜk h*[*śk nhwrk*], "that the darkness not extinguish your light." Ginsberg reads "lest thy vision be dimmed."

e. Arm. Ah 2:8 preserves the saying faithfully: "Son, be thou not over sweet, so that they swallow thee, nor over bitter, so that they spit thee out . . ." The saying is attributed by Shahrastani to Democritus; see "Cultural Importance."

f. So plausibly reads Grelot (*Documents*). Instead of "Shamash," one could also read "the king" or "your master."

g. The reconstruction of this saying (cf. Arm. Ah 2:35) is largely conjectural. If it is correctly understood, cf. Ps 18:27 and *Derek ⁾Ereṣ Zuṭa* 9:11: "If you have humbled yourself, the Holy One, blessed be He, will lift you up; if you have exalted yourself before your fellow, the Holy One, blessed be He, will set you low." Similarly Job 5:11; 22:29; Mt 23:11f.; Lk 1:52; 14:11; 18:14; 1Pet 5:5; cf. Prov 3:34.

h. The restoration is based on Num 23:8a. Other possible readings: "What men's lips curse, the gods do not curse" (cf. Ginsberg) and "Why do the lips of man curse? The gods do not curse" (Grelot, *Documents*).

i. Cf. *kbś ḥkmh*, l. 92.

j. See "Theological Importance."

k. Unintelligible. Ll. 155–58 all deal with parts of the body.

l. The mouth of a man who is unfaithful to his word will be multilated by the god whose oath he has trespassed. For a detailed discussion of this saying in the light of Assyrian law, see J. Greenfield, "The Background and Parallel to a Proverb of Ahiqar," *Hommages à A. Dupont-Sommer*, eds. A. Caquot and M. Philonenko (Paris, 1971) pp. 49–59.

m. This fragmentary saying, perhaps an editorial footnote, might be described as a scribal benediction. A skilled scribe needs keen eyes, sharp ears, and a well-trained mouth to give wise counsel. It is possible that saying 66 is a negative counterpart, a curse on the sage who leads others astray.

Col. XI a. Aram. *mddh* is taken as a by-form of *middāh*, "measure, character."

b. Lit. "a good (happy) heart."

c. Aram. *q*[*ŕy*]*h* (Ginsberg, Grelot).

d. A possible restoration would be *ᶻy mᶤ*[*bnyh*] *bᶤ*[*wr⁾*] *⁾yty*, a conjecture based on Mt 5:14 (cf. Peshitta). Ginsberg reads similarly. The sense is that a man of strong inner resources is as immovable as a mighty citadel, or that he is an outstanding example to those around him.

e. Aram. [*hn P y*]*štmr*, despite Cowley's reservations, appears to be the correct reading.

f. The meaning of *ᶜl ⁾wn gwh* is uncertain. *⁾wn*, not known elsewhere in Aram., may be a cognate of Heb. *⁾āwen*, "wickedness," *gwh* may be taken as *gawwā⁾*, "midst, inner parts," with pronominal suffix. Thus lit. "against the wickedness of his inner self."

g. The first part of the saying is completely lost in the lacuna at the end of l. 160. The beginning of l. 161 is unintelligible. *bṭn*, "belly, womb"(?) cannot be understood without context.

h. Aram. *yhw*[*m*]*⁾nhy* (Grelot, *Documents*), Hafᶜel of *ym⁾*; lit. "who would make him swear." For the association of El and oath taking, cf. saying 66 and "Theological Importance." Syr. Ah 8:22 may be remotely related.

162 *71* . . . . . . and man. And the peoples *pass through*[i] them, and do not leave them, and their hearts are . . . .[j]

163 *72* [*No*] one [*knows*] what is in the heart of another; and when the good man
164 [se]es the wi[cked] man, [*let him beware!*] •He shall [not] accompany him on [*the road*] nor shall he become his employer. (Thus shall) the good man (act) [to]ward the [wick]ed o[ne].[k]

165 *73* The [bram]ble sent a message to the pomegranate as follows: "Dear Pomegranate,[l] what good are all [your] thorns [to him who tou]ches your
166 [fru]it?" •The [pome]granate replied to the bramble, "You are nothing but thorns to him who [tou]ches you!"[m]

167 *74* It is best to support a righteous man;[n] all who clash with him *are laid low*.[o]   126 39
168 *75* [*The city*][p] of the wicked will be swept away in the day of storm, and its
169 gates will fall into ruin;[q] for the spoil •[*of the wicked shall perish*].[r]

       Prov 11:11;
       14:11
       Amos 1:14
       Ezek 13:11

76   My eyes which I lifted up upon you,
      and my heart which I gave you in wisdom,
170   [*you have despised*, and] have brought
      my name into disrepute.[s]

171 *77* If a wicked man grasps the fringe of your garment, leave it in his hand.   Ex 22:25f.
172 Then appeal[t] to Shamash; he •[will] take what is his[u] and will give it to   Deut 24:10–13
    you.[v]

Col. XII[a]

173 *78* Establish me, O El, as a righteous man with you! To . . . .[b]   Ps 7:8–10
174 *79* My enemies[c] will die, but not by my sword.[d]
175,176 *80* I left you in the shelter of the cedar,[e] and . . . . •You have
    abandoned your friends and have ho[no]red [*my enemies*[f] . . . . . .]
177 *81* Pity a man who does not know what he [*wants*]!
178 *82* The wise man speaks, for the opening of the mouth . . . . .
179–86 (Unintelligible).[g]

---

i. Aram. *ᶜbrw*, or "serve them" (*ᶜbdw*).

j. The saying as a whole is unintelligible.

k. This saying, much of which has to be restored conjecturally, is a rather diffuse and rambling warning against associating with persons of bad character.

l. Lit. "bramble to pomegranate."

m. Aesop's fable of the Pomegranate, the Apple Tree and the Bramble (L. W. Daly, *Aesop Without Morals*, p. 182 [# 213]) is probably related. Cf. also the Mesopotamian fable of the Tamarisk and the Palm, in which the palm reproaches its rival: "You, Tamarisk are a useless tree. What are your branches? Wood without fruit!" (W. G. Lambert, *Babylonian Wisdom Literature*, pp. 162f.). Two such plant fables are found in the OT: Judg 9:8–15 and 2Kgs 14:9.

n. Lit. "The righteous—a man to his aid!"

o. Aram. *hwyn* is usually taken as Peᶜal participle of *hwh*, "to be," but "for his help all who meet him are" is awkward. The word may better be related to Heb. *hwh*, "to fall"; *hawwāh*, "destruction"; *hôwāh*, "disaster."

p. Aram. [*qryt*] (Ginsberg, Grelot).

q. Aram. *šhynn*, nowhere else attested in this form, is probably a derivative of *šhy*, "be vacant, lie waste." Several derivations of *yṣᶜwn* are possible. It may be cognate with Hebrew *ṣᶜh*, "be bowed down, sprawl."

r. Aram. *bzyzt* [*ršyᶜn rᵖbd*]. Cf. also Mt 7:24–27.

s. The situation presupposed by this saying parallels closely that of Ahiqar and Nadin (cf. 50–53).

t. Lit. "submit (your case)." *ᵖdny* is probably Afᶜel imperative of *dny* (cf. Syr.).

u. The meaning is either "what he has (of yours)" or perhaps "all that he has."

v. See "Theological Importance." It is not clear whether the "wicked man" is a robber taking a garment by force or an unscrupulous creditor taking the fringe (perhaps actually the entire cloak) as a pledge.

Col. XII a. Most of the left portion of the column is lost, so that only a few sayings are intelligible.

b. Evidently a prayer to El requesting righteousness or vindication. See "Theological Significance." The insertion of a prayer into a wisdom collection occurs also in Sir (23:1, 4; 36:1–17; 51:1–12).

c. Aram. *šᵖny*, a scribal error for *šnᵖy*.

d. If the saying is complete, the reason for the speaker's confidence is not explained. Perhaps it is simply the belief that disaster overtakes the wicked (Prov 11:21; 12:7; 14:11; 21:7, 12).

e. Perhaps a metaphorical reference to the king; cf. Ezek 17:22f.; 31:2–9; Dan 4:7–9, 17–19.

f. Or "hardened [your heart]." The saying can be understood as a reproach of Ahiqar directed to Nadin. Ar. 8:25f. (cf. also Syr. 8:31) may go back ultimately to this saying.

g. A few isolated words can be made out. 184: ". . . the *moth* fell and in the *evening* . . ." 185: ". . . *noble* . . ." 186: "into a house of *bronze* (or "of a serpent") the *moth* fell . . ."

187 *89* My [so]ul does not know the path, therefore . . . . . .

188 *90*   Hunger makes the bitter sweet,   Prov 27:7
          [and] thirst [*makes the sour palatable*].

189 *91* Let the angry man gorge himself on bread,   Prov 31:6f.
          [and the *wrathful*] get drunk [on wine].[h]

190 *92* (Unintelligible).
Col. XIII

191 *93* One drew his bow and shot his [arr]ow, but it did not 126 *39*, 128 *41*
                                                        Ps 7:12b–13

192 *94* If your master entrusts you with water to keep [*and you are not trustworthy*   Mt 25:14–30
193   *with it, how can he*] •leave gold in your hand?[a]   Lk 19:12–27

194 *96* . . . and he does not . . . . "Come near to me!" And let him not say to
          you, "Go away from me!"[b]

195 (Unintelligible).

196 *99* [*A slave who has*] a bar [*on*] his [*fee*]t or [*who is a thie*]*f* should not b[e]   84 *6*
          bought.

197–203 (Unintelligible).[c]

204 *106* [*A man said*] one [*da*]*y* to the wild ass, "[Let me ride] on you, and I will
205   provide for you!" •[*The wild ass replied, "Keep*] your care and fodder; I
          want nothing to do with your riding!"[d]

206 *107* [*Between ski*]*n* and my sandal, may no pebble *get into*[e] my foot.

207 *108* (Unintelligible).

      109 Let not the rich man say, "In my riches I am glorious."[f]   Jer 9:22
Col. XIV

208 *110* [Do not sh]ow an Arab the sea or a Sidonian the st[eppe], for their
          occupations are different.

209 *111* [*He who treads*][a] wine is the one who should taste it. And . . . he shall
          guard it.[b]

210–23 (Unintelligible).[c]

---

h. Anger can be moderated by gluttony.

Col. XIII a. The rest of the line, belonging to another saying, is unintelligible.

b. The antithesis of "come near" and "go away" suggests a possible comparison with Ar. 2:32: "O my son! be not one of those servants to whom their lords say, 'Get away from us,' but be one of those to whom they say, 'Approach and come near to us.'"

c. Only isolated words and phrases can be read. 197: ". . . his [house] with him . . ." 198: ". . . to his *ma*[*ster*] . . . his *case*, because he has acted wickedly toward his [m]aster." 199: "his master . . . The birds . . ." 200: ". . . a wicked man whom . . . overtakes . . ." 201: ". . . when [he] sends [you], lest you lose his favor." 202: ". . . his face because . . ." 203: ". . . an *acquaintance* . . . before you *is tested* before . . ."

d. Lit. "as for me, let me not see your riding." The issue is fodder versus freedom. The onager, or wild ass, (*rd*) is a proverbially untamable beast; see Job 39:5–8. Compare Aesop's fable of the Wild Boar, the Horse, and the Hunter; L. W. Daly, *Aesop Without Morals*, p. 205 (# 269).

e. *ynᶜl* is tentatively translated as coming from the verb ᶜ*ll*, "to enter." But the root may be *nᶜl*. G. R. Driver ("The Aramaic Papyri from Egypt: Notes on Obscure Passages," *JRAS* 42 [1932] 89)

proposes an Ar. etymology which enables him to translate "let not a pebble make a sore place on my foot." In any case there is probably some play on words involving *nᶜl* (which can also mean "to shoe") and ᶜ*n*, "sandal."

f. Cf. the final saying in the Life of Aesop: "Rejoice not at great wealth, and grieve not at small." L. W. Daly, *Aesop Without Morals*, p. 81.

Col. XIV a. Restoring conjecturally [ᶜ*ṣr*]. If that is correct, cf. Deut 25:4.

b. The second clause may have been something like "but he who does not drink wine is the one who should guard it."

c. 210: ". . . *was told* . . . *is dead*. And I answered, ... and he knows (or "I know") who is coming after him." 211: ". . . he will tear out a . . . from my hide . . . weeping . . . from . . ." 213: ". . . one who is blind . . ." 214: ". . . comes . . . to him . . ." 215: ". . . eyes . . ." 216: "a *boy* and one who is deaf . . ." 217: ". . . from the womb he knows a noble man and not . . ." 218: ". . . was a man not . . ." 219: ". . . is bought . . . like a . . . and a *wife* . . ." 221: ". . . *thief* . . ." 222: ". . . his *neighbor's* house *caught fire* . . ." 223: ". . . [from] my friend[s] and from the lord of . . ."

3 MACCABEES

(First Century B.C.)

A NEW TRANSLATION AND INTRODUCTION

BY H. ANDERSON

Saved by a renegade Jew from a plot against his life by Theodotus, Ptolemy IV Philopator, King of Egypt (221–204 B.C.), decisively defeats Antiochus III the Great of Syria at Raphia (1:1–5). He then visits neighboring cities, distributing gifts to their shrines and securing their loyalty (1:6f.). A friendly delegation from the Jews persuades him to visit Jerusalem, where he is so impressed by the Temple that he longs to enter the sanctuary. His request causes a great furor in the city, but despite repeated remonstrances he is undeterred from his desire (1:8–29). The High Priest Simon, recalling God's wonderful deliverances of Israel in the past, prays that Ptolemy's threatened act of desecration might be averted, whereupon the king is punished by a stroke from God and falls on the ground in a swoon (2:1–22). On his return to Egypt, bent on revenge against the Jews, he decides to deprive them of their civil rights and to have them branded with the ivy leaf, the emblem of Dionysus. However, if any should participate in the cult of Dionysus they would enjoy the privileges of citizens of Alexandria (2:23–30). The majority of Jews resist gallantly, and the enraged king commands that all the Jews in Egypt, men, women, and children, be brought in chains to Alexandria and be put to death (2:31–3:30). Cruelly treated and herded together like animals on board ship, a great multitude are transported to the outskirts of Alexandria, where they are imprisoned in the racecourse (4:1–13). So vast is their number that the registration of their names takes forty days and cannot be completed because the supply of writing materials is exhausted (4:14–21). Ptolemy now orders that the Jews should be trampled by five hundred elephants, driven to fury by potent doses of wine and frankincense, but the king amazingly falls into a deep sleep so that the execution is postponed until the next day (5:1–22). The following day the Jews are once again spared their ordeal by a miraculous divine intervention which renders Ptolemy oblivious to his previous commands (5:23–35). Later the same day, however, he renews his instructions that the elephants should be made ready for the next morning (5:36–45). At dawn, when all is set and the king is already on his way with the panoplied beasts to the racecourse, the aged and esteemed Eleazar prays for God to intervene, and two angels, visible to all except the Jews, strike terror into the king and his troops and turn the elephants back upon the king's forces (5:46–6:21). The king, his disposition now totally transformed, is indignant with his counselors and orders not only that the Jews be released but that they celebrate a festival for seven days at his expense (6:22–30). So on the very spot where they had been doomed to die, the Jews feast and give thanks for their deliverance, and thereupon resolve that these days should be kept as a festival forever (6:30–41). In a letter to all governors in the provinces, the king now charges them to offer every protection to the Jews (7:1–9), and the Jews, having been granted permission to slay those of their brethren who had apostatized from the faith, do just that. They then institute another seven-day festival at Ptolemais and return in safety to their own homes (7:10–23).

Texts

Third Maccabees is not found in either Vaticanus or Sinaiticus, but does appear in the third great uncial manuscript of the Greek Bible, Alexandrinus, which dates from the middle part of the fifth century. The eighth- or ninth-century Codex Venetus also contains a text of 3 Maccabees which merits recognition alongside the Alexandrinus. In addition, there are a number of important minuscule manuscripts of 3 Maccabees. Somewhat less reliable, however, are those minuscules which stand in the textual tradition initiated by Lucian of Antioch (martyred A.D. 312), whose revision of the Septuagint became standard in Syria, Asia Minor, and Constantinople. The version of 3 Maccabees in the Syriac Peshitta (late 4th cent.) represents a free and expanded rendering, and is mainly Lucianic in character. There is also a rather paraphrastic Armenian version from some time between A.D. 400–600. The book does not stand in the Vulgate of Jerome (A.D. 382–404) and so is neither in the Roman Catholic Bible nor in the Apocrypha of the Protestant churches.

On the whole the text of 3 Maccabees is in very good shape. The present translation is based on the edition by A. Rahlfs, *Septuaginta*, vol. 1 (Stuttgart, 1935). In the commentary only those variant readings are noted which substantially affect the meaning of a sentence or passage. A fuller critical apparatus is available in Rahlfs' *Septuaginta*, in H. B. Swete's *The Old Testament in Greek*, vol. 3 (Cambridge, 1899), and in R. Hanhart's *Maccabaeorum Liber III* (Sept. Gott. 9.3; Göttingen, 1960). The symbols used in the commentary are: A = Alexandrinus; V = Venetus; m = one minuscule; mm = more than one minuscule; L = the Lucianic recension; Syr. = Syriac Peshitta; Arm. = Armenian Version.

Original language

All indications are that 3 Maccabees was first written in Greek. The work may be classed as an "historical romance," and as such it bears some resemblance to the Greek "romances" which flourished in the hellenistic period. Only a few of these, like the *Chaereas and Callirhoë* of Chariton, have survived, but 3 Maccabees shares enough features in common with them to suggest that its writer was acquainted with this type of literary model—the legendary embellishment of the career or of an episode in the career of an actual historical personage; a climactic scene describing the threatened destruction and miraculous deliverance of hero or heroine, generally in a public place such as the racecourse or theater; the prominence given to the religious element; the citation of putative letters or documents; the heightening of incidents in the story for dramatic effect by the addition of colorful but irrelevant detail.[1]

However, it is in the style and language employed that our author most of all exhibits his Greek hand. He often indulges in "fine writing," piling epithet upon epithet and participial clause upon participial clause. The book abounds in rhetorical repetitions and exaggerations. The vocabulary is rich and varied, and contains numerous pure classical forms as well as several which betray the influence of *koinē* usage on the writer. He is acquainted also with words that occur only in Greek poetry and has a distinct leaning toward compound verbs and adjectives, some of which he may even have coined himself since they are not found elsewhere in Greek literature, e.g. *bythotrephēs* = "sea-nurtured" (6:8), *puropnous* = "blazing" (6:34). All of this clearly stamps the author as a pseudo-classicist or pseudo-Atticist, at home with various phases of the Greek language.[2]

Date

Internal historical evidence points with certainty only to an upper and lower limit for the work. On the one side it begins with a brief depiction of the Battle of Raphia, which took place in 217 B.C. On the other side, in view of the glorification of the Jerusalem Temple in the book, the Temple is obviously still standing and the destruction that befell it in A.D. 70 has not yet occurred. Beyond that, further significant historical clues to a firmer dating within the period 217 B.C.–A.D. 70 are lacking. Josephus (*Apion* 2:5) gives a similar but much more sober account of the incident of the elephants, but unlike our author he attributes the outrage to a later Ptolemy, namely Ptolemy IX Physcon (146–117 B.C.). But Josephus

---

[1] See further, M. Hadas, *The Third and Fourth Books of Maccabees*, pp. 13–16.
[2] C. W. Emmet, "The Third Book of Maccabees," *APOT*; vol. 1, pp. 156–73.

is by no means necessarily correct in this. In fact, evidence has been adduced from the papyri to show that Physcon was favorably disposed toward the Jews.[3]

Accordingly, it does not follow that the author of 3 Maccabees must have written during or after Physcon's reign, or that he must knowingly have transferred the episode of the elephants to Philopator to suit his own polemic or apologetic purposes. Conceivably, since both Josephus and 3 Maccabees associate the story of the elephants with the institution of a particular festival, it may go back to some historical event. More probably Josephus' more restrained version and 3 Maccabees' more highly adorned version both stem from a popular legend which originated in the third century B.C. and which arose on the basis of the known fact that Egyptian monarchs made use of elephants for military purposes.[4] The story of the elephants, consequently, is a most uncertain criterion for dating 3 Maccabees.

It has been maintained that 3 Maccabees is a *Gelegenheitschrift*, that is a document produced in a specific set of historical circumstances and designed, like the apocalyptic writings, to aid people meet and overcome a particular crisis, in the case of 3 Maccabees obviously a crisis for the Jewish people. Ewald suggested that the crisis reflected in 3 Maccabees is the persecution of Alexandrian Jews during the reign of the Roman Emperor Caligula and that the book is connected with his attempt to set up his image in the Jerusalem Temple in A.D. 40.[5] But if the author of 3 Maccabees wrote under Caligula and cloaked his criticism of Caligula's administration under the record of an analogous crisis in the reign of Philopator of Egypt in the distant past, we should surely expect some hint of the most sinister and oppressive features, the imperial claim to divine honors (especially since the Ptolemies, too, were *theoi* or "gods") and the desecration of sanctuaries by attempts to erect imperial effigies in them. But there is no such hint!

More recently M. Hadas has argued that 3 Maccabees was written in response to a crisis affecting Egyptian Jews when Egypt was made a Roman province in 24 B.C. and the Jews' civic status was jeopardized by the new Roman administration.[6] The hinge of his argument on the historical side is that 3 Maccabees 2:28 refers to a *laographia* which, as 2:30 indicated, here means the "poll tax" of the Roman period (liability to it involving loss of citizen status), and that this accords with the administrative situation just after the Romans took over in Egypt. On the other hand, it has been proposed that Philopator himself may have been responsible for the institution of a poll tax in Egypt,[7] although the ostraca of the Ptolemaic period appear to suggest that no general poll tax was applied in early Ptolemaic Egypt similar to the Roman *laographia*.[8] However, the term does occur in Ptolemaic papyri in the less technical sense of a "registry of taxable *laoi*." And it is likely that, in view of the heavy expenses incurred for his realm in two wars, Philopator enforced a much stricter collection of rents, taxes, and arrears.[9] Also the old salt tax, levied on every inhabitant of Egypt, was, as Rostovtzeff notes,[10] virtually equivalent to a poll tax, and the fact that certain privileged classes could be exempted from it by royal command implies a caste system of taxation under which the Jews could have suffered at any time during the Ptolemaic period. Accordingly, the mention of *laographia* and what it may have implied in 3 Maccabees 2:28, 30 is hardly sufficient in and by itself to constrain us to date the work in the Roman period.

The Achilles' heel of every theory of dating that would trace 3 Maccabees to a specific

[3] J. P. Mahaffy, *A History of Egypt Under the Ptolemaic Dynasty* (London, 1899) pp. 192–216. The papyri of the Ptolemaic period generally are scanty, however, and coming chiefly from the villages of the Faȳum do not necessarily reflect the life of the whole of Egypt. Also, 3Mac notes that Philopator himself was favorably disposed toward the Jews until the incident at Jerusalem (see 3Mac 1:8–12 and 3:15–17). See M. Rostovtzeff, "Ptolemaic Egypt," *The Cambridge Ancient History*, vol. 7, p. 109.

[4] The military technique of the Seleucids reached its culmination in their use of elephants from India. The Ptolemies adopted the practice also; in the earlier part of the 3rd cent. B.C., Ptolemy II Philadelphus made an expedition to East Africa and undertook the formation of a contingent of African elephants. See Rostovtzeff, *The Social and Economic History of the Hellenistic World* (Oxford, 1964) vol. 1, pp. 383f.

[5] H. G. A. Ewald, *Geschichte des Volkes Israel* (Göttingen, 1864–68³) vol. 4, pp. 611–14. Cf. H. Willrich, "Der historische Kern des III. Makkabäerbuches," *Hermes* 39 (1904) 244–58.

[6] Hadas, *Maccabees*, pp. 3, 19–21.

[7] S. L. Wallace, "Census and Poll tax in Ptolemaic Egypt," *American Journal of Philology* 59 (1938) 418–42.

[8] Rostovtzeff, *Social and Economic History*, vol. 3, p. 1392, n. 117.

[9] Ibid., vol. 2, p. 708.

[10] Ibid., vol. 1, p. 309.

moment of trial and tribulation in the history of Egyptian Jews is that the book itself does not really read like a "crisis document." Among the favorite themes of the apocalyptic writings are retribution, life after death, the last judgment, and the impending cataclysmic overthrow of the existing world order through God's ushering in the end-time. Such themes are conspicuous by their absence from 3 Maccabees.[11] In fact, glad thanksgiving for God's merciful deliverances of his people and festival joy feature quite prominently in the work, and the sense of an inevitably happy outcome that runs through it might the more imply an era of success and prosperity for the Jews when it was written.[12] On the whole it is best regarded as an edifying and apologetic tract of a generalizing kind, designed to keep the lamp of orthodox Jewish faith burning, to exhibit the loyalty of Jews as subject people in the territories of their sojourn, and to account etiologically for the observance of a particular Egyptian Jewish festival.

Literary characteristics and relationships of 3 Maccabees offer more promising leads than internal historical evidence toward a narrower dating within the period 200 B.C.–A.D. 70. Third Maccabees 6:6 reveals the author's acquaintance with the Greek additions to the Book of Daniel, and since Daniel itself is normally ascribed to the beginning of the Maccabean period, around 165 B.C., this points to a time for 3 Maccabees hardly earlier than the latter part of the first century B.C. In 3 Maccabees 3:12 and 7:1 there occurs a formula of salutation in the style *chairein kai errōsthai* = "greetings and good health." The same formula occurs also in the Letter of Aristeas, the normally accepted date for which is around 100 B.C. And the fact that the papyri of an earlier and later period attest different formulas of salutation tends to confirm that the "greetings and good health" of 3 Maccabees and the Letter of Aristeas was the favored usage about the turn of the first century B.C.

On a broader front, the associations of 3 Maccabees in style and content with 2 Maccabees and the Letter of Aristeas support a date early in the first century for our book. Similarities of vocabulary, some of it relatively rare elsewhere, and of phrase between 2 and 3 Maccabees are striking. In both works the same motifs are prominent (see Relation to Apocryphal Books), and especially noteworthy is the resemblance between the narrative of the miracle by which punishment was visited on Ptolemy in 3 Maccabees 2:21–24 and the narrative concerning Heliodorus in 2 Maccabees 3:22–31. The correspondences between 2 and 3 Maccabees are scarcely comprehensive enough to suggest they were written by a single author, but they are close enough to suggest that the two authors shared the same thought world and most probably wrote at approximately the same time. The consensus is that 2 Maccabees can hardly be earlier than the last quarter of the second century B.C.[13] To judge from the literary traits and connections of 3 Maccabees, a date in the earlier part of the first century B.C. commends itself as a reasonable hypothesis.

Provenance

The main action in the "plot" of 3 Maccabees takes place in the neighborhood of Alexandria in Egypt. Throughout, one of the author's primary concerns is with the status of Egyptian Jews. His work, in its pseudo-classicism, shares the Alexandrian flavor of 2 Maccabees and the Letter of Aristeas and shows the same familiarity not only with the court life of the Ptolemies but with the technical language of official Ptolemaic decrees. The lines of evidence converge on Alexandria as the place of origin of 3 Maccabees.

Historical importance

The title "Third Maccabees" is a misnomer for our document. The events described in it antedate the Maccabean period proper by some fifty years or more. By any standard the book has an abrupt introduction, even more noticeable in the Greek than in English translation. Moreover, the plot of Theodotus is introduced in 1:2 as though it were already

---

[11] Even Hadas, who holds that 3Mac shares something of the "emergency" quality of apocalyptic, has to concede that "the visonary embellishments and the prophetic elements of the Apocalyptic are entirely wanting in our book" (*Maccabees*, p. 12).

[12] See Emmet, *APOT*, vol. 1, p. 158.

[13] See J. Moffatt, *APOT*, vol. 1, pp. 128f. Cf. Hadas, *Maccabees*, p. 12.

known to the reader. From this it has sometimes been deduced that the work as we have it is truncated and originally contained an introductory chapter or chapters in which, among other things, the author would have explained how he intended to produce an appropriate prolegomenon to the epic struggle of the Maccabees. But any attempt to reconstruct the contents of a supposedly lost chapter or chapters is of necessity purely conjectural. Most probably our document received its title through its collocation with 1 and 2 Maccabees in the manuscripts or perhaps because its theme, the sacrilegious intent of Ptolemy and the brave Jewish reaction, was felt to have an affinity with later imperial arrogance and heroic Jewish resistance in the days of the Maccabean revolt.

Whatever the case may be, more suitable for 3 Maccabees than the designation *Makkabaika* would be *Ptolemaika*, the heading under which the Letter of Aristeas was listed by Syncellus (I.516), the Byzantine historian, around A.D. 800. But even as *Ptolemaika*, 3 Maccabees adds little to our knowledge of actual events around 217 B.C. in the reign of Ptolemy IV Philopator. Our author's brief portrayal of Philopator's victory at Raphia in that year (1:1–7) differs only in detail from the description in Polybius (5). In the latter, for example, the opposing armies arrive at Raphia about the same time, Arsinoë joins Philopator in exhorting his army to gallantry before the battle, and while Theodotus and his plot against Ptolemy are mentioned there is no reference to the Dositheus of 3 Maccabees 1:3. But beyond these first few verses, as far as the provision of reliable historical information on the several separate incidents related goes, 3 Maccabees takes us into very uncertain territory indeed. While there is no *a priori* reason why Philopator should not have visited Jerusalem after his triumph at not-so-distant Raphia in the south of Palestine, the story of his encounter with the Jews at the Jerusalem Temple is told in such highly legendary terms as to cast grave suspicion on the factuality of the whole episode. The account of the "elephant outrage" most likely stems, as we have noted, from a popular legend which circulated during the last two centuries B.C. And the narrative of the cruel deportation of Jews from their homes to the vast concourse of the hippodrome at Alexandria is so overdrawn as also to savor of the legendary.

Nevertheless, 3 Maccabees clearly reflects a sound general knowledge on its writer's part of the life and times of Ptolemy IV. From his depiction of the Battle of Raphia, consistent in its main lines with that of Polybius, it may reasonably be inferred that he had access to some relatively trustworthy source, possibly the lost history of Ptolemy Megalopolitanus. Polybius himself alludes to this Ptolemy, but only a few fragments of his work survive and are to be found in Müller's *Fragmenta* 3.66.[14] However, aside from the opening verses on Raphia, our author reveals an undoubted acquaintance with the conditions prevailing in Egypt under Philopator. The characterization of Philopator in 3 Maccabees is true to what is known of him from elsewhere: his love of banqueting, his openness to the whims of his courtiers, his hope of uniting Jews and Greeks in the worship of his ancestor Dionysus, prompted possibly by the contemporary identification of Dionysus' name Sabazius with the Jewish Sabaoth.[15] Also, our author's familiarity with the style and format of official Ptolemaic letters or decrees is generally conceded.

We possess all too little information about the historical circumstances of the Jews in Egypt during the Ptolemaic period, and 3 Maccabees is to be sure of broad historical value. Nevertheless, the writer is not an historian whose first interest is to record accurately what happened or to preserve the memory of past events simply for their own sake. He is, rather, a man of orthodox Jewish religious sentiment who employs the medium of historical narration, albeit a narration which he has greatly romanticized, in order, on the one hand, to edify and encourage the faithful within the fold of his own people and, on the other hand, to commend them to outsiders as a "special people" and to defend and justify their mode and quality of life, their religious sensitivities, and their continuing religious observances.

---

[14] See Emmet, *APOT*, vol. 1, p. 159. Cf. Hadas, *Maccabees*, p. 17. K. Müller, *Fragmenta Historicorum Graecorum* (Paris, 1883).

[15] See W. W. Tarn, "The Struggle of Egypt Against Syria and Macedonia," *The Cambridge Ancient History*, vol. 7, p. 727.

Theological importance

Our author's theological standpoint can in some measure be gauged as much from what he omits to say as from what he actually does say in his narrative. There is no trace of any of the leading motifs which permeate the apocalyptic writings that began to flourish in the earlier part of the second century B.C. For example, missing are ideas regarding life beyond death, retribution, the last judgment, the messianic hope, and the dawning of the new age. The absence of such themes is all the more remarkable inasmuch as the martyrology of 2 Maccabees, which our author probably knew, testifies extensively to the notion of a just redress for the martyred dead in the afterlife. Moreover, there is no suggestion in 3 Maccabees of the "liberation of reason" [16] or process of secularization, the radical questioning or skepticism typical of such products of the wisdom literature of later Israel as Proverbs, Job, and Ecclesiastes. Nor again, although our author is a neo-classicist, probably from Alexandria, and presumably familiar with Platonic ideas, is there any hint of the Alexandrian drift toward Philo's attempted fusion of Greek thought with the Torah or his allegorical method of scriptural exegesis.

Over against apocalyptic, wisdom, and hellenistic philosophy, our author may best be pictured as a staunch conservative, swimming against the stream of the more radical tendencies of his time. In fact, he appears as an ardent champion of the old Deuteronomic orthodoxy, which at the risk of oversimplification may be described as the conviction that God rewards the righteous and punishes the wicked, and against which the author of Job registers a vehement protest. In 3 Maccabees the God who intervenes wonderfully to save his people is very much the God of the faithful and the just. Ptolemy IV does not at all subscribe to the worship of the God of Israel, but in his letter to his generals he is represented as acknowledging officially that the Jews are a "peculiar people": "And knowing of a surety that God in heaven protects the Jews, in alliance with them continually, like a father with his children . . . Be sure of this, if we devise any evil scheme against them or cause them any trouble, we shall have not man, but the Most High God, who is ruler of all power, as our adversary to exact vengeance for what is done, inexorably in all circumstances and for all time" (7:6, 9). Our author gives no sign at all of being possessed of any proselytizing zeal or of moving beyond the particularism of which the pagan Philopator is here made the eloquent spokesman.

Third Maccabees strongly reflects its writer's unshakable hold upon the faith of earlier Israel that God continually moved toward her in her history and actively participated in it, ruling, controlling, and directing her way, and this at a period when such a faith had been trenchantly questioned by more adventurous spirits in Judaism. The prayers of the High Priest Simon in 2:2–20 and of Eleazar in 6:2–15 are in effect celebrations of "sacred history," reminiscent of those Psalms (e.g. 78, 80, 106, 114, 135, 136) which sing Yahweh's praises for his former acts of deliverance. However, the manner in which our author extends the line of "sacred history" into the time of Ptolemy IV might appear to be somewhat naive—his reports on the miraculous divine interferences by which Ptolemy and his officials were thwarted of their designs against the Jews may hardly be described as strong on historical realism. But in recounting them he does enter, however remotely, into the ancient Hebrew tradition of the holy wars in which Yahweh fought for and rescued his people, a concept which reappears in new forms in the prophets (cf. e.g. Isa 29:6, 8; 30:30). [17] And he is at least sophisticated enough theologically to recognize that the Jews do not require visible, cosmic signs to support their faith in Yahweh's marvelous interventions on their behalf: He is, in fact, at pains to affirm that the "two angels" who occasion a dramatic reversal of fortunes at the racecourse were "visible to all except the Jews" (6:18).

In other salient aspects of his theological demeanor, our author subscribes without question to ancient Jewish norms. He has a strong sense of vast distance between the "sacred" and the "secular," and this shows particularly in his reverence for the Temple, which he needs only to call "the place" in the assumption that his readers will understand. The rather

---

[16] G. von Rad, *Wisdom in Israel*, trans. J. D. Martin (Nashville and New York, 1972) pp. 53–73.

[17] G. von Rad, *Old Testament Theology*, trans. D. M. G. Stalker (New York and Evanston, 1965) vol. 2, pp. 159f.

extravagant description of 1:9–29 reveals how much for him the Temple is filled with the numinous. And the ultimate in nefarious deeds is Ptolemy Philopator's sacrilegious intent to enter the Temple. Prominent also is the writer's rigorous devotion to the Law, nowhere more in evidence than in his report (and tacit endorsement) of the slaying of over three hundred renegade Jews, in accordance with the injunctions of Deuteronomy 13:6–18.

Again, the niceties of strict religious observance carry a special appeal for our author. He shares with hellenistic Judaism the tendency to pile up reverential epithets on every mention of the name of God (see e.g. 2:2–21; 5:7; 6:2–9, 18, 28) and even employs some titles not used elsewhere in the Septuagint (e.g. *monarchos*, 2:2; *propatōr*, 2:21; *megalokratōr*, 6:2; *misoubris*, 6:9). He subscribes to the view that the efficacy of prayer is related to the attitude or quality of life of the petitioner: Witness his description of the high priest's assuming the correct posture in 2:1 and of the exalted status of the aged Eleazar in 6:1. For him clearly "the heartfelt prayer of a good man works very powerfully" (Jas 5:16). Finally, part at least of our writer's motivation for telling his story was to compose a "festival legend" for a feast celebrated among Egyptian Jews in his own time, perhaps an Egyptian counterpart of the Feast of Purim, to which the Book of Esther testifies and which probably originated in the eastern Diaspora.[18]

Relation to canonical books

The writer of 3 Maccabees does not seem to have been influenced especially by any particular canonical work. Rather he appears to have been steeped in the old biblical traditions, a selection of which he has drawn upon in somewhat random fashion, notably in the prayers he puts on the lips of Simon and Eleazar in chapters 2 and 4 respectively. However, his work does bear a resemblance, at one or two points, to the Hebrew Book of Esther. There, as in 3 Maccabees, a foreign tyrant plans the destruction of the Jewish people in his territory, but his (Haman's) plot is thwarted and the Jews are authorized by King Ahasuerus to turn against and stamp out their enemies (Esth 8:3–14). Nevertheless, the differences between the two books are much more notable than the similarities. Esther is a secular pamphlet which attributes the deliverance of the Jews to human agency, in short the wiles of the heroine Esther, and never even mentions God or prayers to God. Third Maccabees has no hero proper but subordinates everything to God, who intervenes to save his people. Moreover, unlike 3 Maccabees, Esther has nothing at all to say on the subject of the loyalty of the Jews as a subject people. Accordingly, it is by no means certain that there is any direct line of connection between the Hebrew Esther and 3 Maccabees, nor can it be said with any degree of assurance that our author set out purposely to correct the secular tone of Esther.[19]

Relation to apocryphal books

Third Maccabees has points of contact most of all with 2 Maccabees and the Letter of Aristeas (see Date). Second Maccabees contains a number of leading incidents and ideas which parallel those in 3 Maccabees. Second Maccabees tells of the repulse of Heliodorus' attempt to profane the Temple (3:22–31), and the punishment visited upon Antiochus for his arrogance (2Mac 9:4ff.) is like Philopator's (3Mac 2:21–24). The awesomeness of the Temple (2Mac 3:15–22; 8:2–4; 14:34–36; 3Mac 1:11–16; 2:1–21); portentous visions (2Mac 3:25; 10:29; 11:8; 3Mac 6:18); attacks upon religion (2Mac 6:9; 3Mac 2:27–33; 3:21); efforts to impose an alien citizenship (2Mac 4:9; 3Mac 2:27–30); memorial festivals (2Mac 10:6; 15:36; 3Mac 6:30–36); the appearance of the esteemed Eleazar (2Mac 6:1, 16), and the horror of the Jewish populace (2Mac 3:15ff.; 3Mac 1:16–29; 4:3–8) are all prominent features of both works. The resemblance of 3 Maccabees to the Letter of Aristeas is hardly

---

[18] See O. Eissfeldt, *The Old Testament: An Introduction*, trans. P. R. Ackroyd, p. 582; cf. A. Weiser, *The Old Testament: Its Formation and Development*, trans. D. M. Barton, p. 396.

[19] See Hadas, *Maccabees*, pp. 6–8. The Gk. Esth is probably of Alexandrian vintage and represents an attempt to desecularize the Heb. Esth or to transpose it into a religious key. But neither the existence of a Gk. corrective to the Heb. Esth nor the fact that it seems to have one or two points of contact with 3Mac is sufficient to establish that our author simply undertook the same task and worked over the Heb. Esth in his own way.

any less close. Both books exalt the Jews and extol their loyalty as subjects of the Ptolemies. In both, a Ptolemy acknowledges that God is the special protector of his own people (LetAris 16, 19, 37; 3Mac 3:21; 5:31; 6:24–28; 7:6–9). Both glory in the inextinguishable majesty of the Temple (LetAris 83–91; 99; 3Mac 1:11–16; 2:1–21), and stress the "apartness" of the Jews in food and life (LetAris 128–66; 3Mac 3:3–7) while at the same time making much of Egyptian royal feasts (LetAris 187, etc.; 3Mac 4:16, etc.). Perhaps even more significant is the fact that our author uses a relatively large number of words and expressions that are found in 2 Maccabees and/or the Letter of Aristeas but are rare elsewhere and in many cases do not occur at all in the Septuagint.[20] Resemblances of terminology in the official letters and decrees recorded in each work are especially striking.

Not surprisingly, therefore, the direct literary dependence of 3 Maccabees on 2 Maccabees and the Letter of Aristeas has been argued. But the reverse has also been argued with just as much cogency, and if each document is examined as a whole and full account is taken of the differences as well as the similarities, the safest conclusion is simply that the authors belonged to the same milieu and in particular shared a common stock of knowledge of official Egyptian procedures and of the technical language of Egyptian royal decrees and letters.

Cultural importance

As far as can be gathered, the story told in 3 Maccabees has had no influence at all on the art or literature, secular or religious, of the West. Missing from Jerome's Vulgate, its chances of even becoming known were slender indeed. But even in the East, 3 Maccabees has left remarkably few traces. In one of his exegetical works, commenting on Daniel 11, Theodoret of Antioch (c. A.D. 393–c. 458), who became Bishop of Cyrrhus in Syria, offers a brief summary of 3 Maccabees, and the existence of an old Syriac translation implies a more general interest in the work on the part of the Syrian Church.

SELECT BIBLIOGRAPHY

Charlesworth, *PMR*, pp. 149–51.
Delling, *Bibliographie*, pp. 146f.

Eissfeldt, O. *The Old Testament; An Introduction*. Trans. P. R. Ackroyd. New York and Evanston, 1965; pp. 581f.
Emmet, C. W. "The Third Book of Maccabees," *APOT;* vol. 1, pp. 156–73.
Hadas, M. *The Third and Fourth Books of Maccabees*. New York, 1953.
Rostovtzeff, M. "Ptolemaic Egypt," *The Cambridge Ancient History*. Cambridge, 1964; vol. 7, pp. 109–54.
Schürer, E. *History*. Div. 2, vol. 3, pp. 216–19.
Tarn, W. W. "The Struggle of Egypt Against Syria and Macedonia," *The Cambridge Ancient History*. Cambridge, 1964; vol. 7, pp. 699–731.
Weiser, A. *The Old Testament: Its Formation and Development*. Trans. D. M. Barton. New York, 1961; pp. 395–97.

---

[20] See the list given by Emmet, *APOT*, vol. 1, pp. 156f.

THE THIRD BOOK OF MACCABEES

Ptolemy IV Philopator's victory at Raphia

1 **1** From people returning from the scene Philopator received the news of Antiochus'
capture of the places which had been under his control. He then put out orders to
all his infantry and cavalry forces and moved on, taking his sister Arsinoë along
with him, to the territory around Raphia[a] where Antiochus' army was camped. Dan 11:11f.
2 But a certain Theodotus[b] decided to carry out a scheme he had in mind, so he
took some of the very best of Ptolemy's soldiers[c] who had previously been placed
in his charge and went across by night to Ptolemy's tent intending to kill him
3 single-handedly and end the war at a stroke. •However, one Dositheos, called the
son of Drimylus, who was a Jew by birth but later had renounced the Law and
abandoned his ancestral beliefs, removed Ptolemy and had a poor unknown fellow
sleep in his tent bed instead, and he of course suffered the fate intended for
4 Ptolemy. •A violent battle ensued, and when the tide ran in favor of Antiochus,
Arsinoë traversed the ranks and, wailing and in tears, with her braided hair
hanging loose, begged them to take courage and rally not just for their own sake
but for the sake of their wives and children; she even promised to give each one
5 of them, if they won, two minae of gold.[d] •The outcome was that the enemy was
destroyed in the combat and many also were taken prisoner.

Ptolemy visits Jerusalem and determines to enter the Temple

6 With the plot against him thwarted, Ptolemy now decided to visit the neighboring
7 cities and offer them encouragement. •When he had done this and distributed
8 gifts to their shrines, he made his subjects feel secure.[e] •When the Jews sent a
delegation of the council and the elders to greet him and offer him friendly gifts
and congratulate him on his achievements, he was all the more eager to visit them
9 as soon as possible. •So he came to Jerusalem, where he sacrificed to God the 2Mac 3:36;
Greatest and put up thank offerings, observing to some extent the proprieties of 1:16; 3:11; 4:16;
5:25; 7:22
the place. When he entered the sacred place[f] he was struck by its immaculate and
10 dignified appearance •and, marveling at the orderliness of the Temple, asked
11 himself thoughtfully whether he should go into the sanctuary. •They told him that
this was quite improper since not even the Jewish people themselves were allowed
in nor indeed any and every priest but only the high priest, who was the chief of
12 all, and he only once a year. However, he was not at all convinced. •Even after Ex 30:10
the Law had been read out to him he persistently affirmed that he must enter and Lev 16:34
13 said, "Even if they are deprived of this honor, I must not be." •He then asked
why it was that when he entered every (other) shrine[g] nobody present stopped

---

1 a. On the Battle of Raphia and the relation of
the account given here to that of Polybius in *Historia*
5. 79–86, see Historical Importance.

b. Polybius devotes a great deal more space to
the plot of Theodotus "the Aetolian" (5. 81).

c. The word translated "soldiers" is a neuter
plural in Gk. and may equal "arms" or "weapons." "Weapons" would seem to accord better
with our author's notice that Theodotus wanted to
kill Ptolemy "single-handedly." But on the other
hand any small dagger, easily concealed, would
have done the job, and it is probable that an escort
of soldiers for protection is intended.

d. Two minae of gold, the equivalent of 200
drachmas, seems an excessive sum. But Egyptian

queens did own extensive private property.

e. This description is consistent with what is
known of Philopator's policy from other sources.

f. In Gk. simply "the place" but here = "the
Temple," as frequently in 2Mac and 3Mac.

g. The translation is sometimes offered "why,
when he entered the shrine at all?" and this would
refer to his coming within the Temple area, in
which case he asks why he should be allowed to
go so far without hindrance but no farther. But this
would require in Gk. not *pan temenos* but *pan to
temenos*, and our translation, which takes *pan
temenos* in its natural sense of "all (other) shrines
(than the Jerusalem Temple)," is more probable.

14 him. •All too hastily somebody said that it was wrong to speak of this as if it
15 were a marvel.ʰ •"Even so," he said, "why should I not enter in my case whether
16 they want me to or not?" •Then the priests in all their vestments prostrated
themselves and entreated Almighty God to help them in their present difficulty
and make their assailant change his mind, and they filled the Temple with loud
cries and tears.

The rush of the outraged citizenry to the Temple

17   The people who were left in the city hurried out in disarray, reckoning that   2Mac 3:15–22
18 something mysterious was going on. •Even the young women who had been
confined to their chambers rushed out with their mothers, and they took dust and
covered their hair with it and filled the streets with cries of grief and moans.
19 Those recently married left the chambers where the marriage bed had been prepared   4:6
and, heedless of the modesty appropriate to their station, ran about in disorder in
20 the city.ⁱ •The mothers and nurses in charge of the youngest children left them
here and there, in houses or in the streets, and, abandoning all caution, thronged
21 to the most glorious Temple. •Many and varied were the prayers of those who
22 gathered there because of the king's sacrilegious designs. •At the same time the
bolder spirits among the citizens would not endure the pressure he was exerting
23 to gain his own ends or his determination to carry through his project •and,
sounding a call to take up arms with all haste and to die bravely for the Law of
their fathers, they caused a great disturbanceʲ in the place. Only with difficulty
were they dissuaded by the elders, and they then joined them in the posture of
24,25 prayer. •Meanwhile the multitude went on with their prayers as previously. •But
the elders close to the king tried in many ways to divert his mind from the scheme
26 he had so arrogantly conceived. •With great boldness he dismissed every plea,
however, and, bent on achieving his declared purpose, was already moving
27 forward. •When those around him saw what was happening they joined our own
people in calling on him who is all-powerful to help them in their present extremity
28 and not overlook this insolent act of lawlessness. •The combined shouts of the
29 crowd, ceaseless and vehement, caused an indescribable uproar. •It seemed as if
not only the people but the very walls and the whole pavement cried out, so much
at that moment did they all prefer death to the profanation of the Temple.

The prayer of Simon the High Priest

1 **2** The high priest, Simon,ᵃ knelt in homage in front of the sanctuary and, holding   Pss 105,106
2 out his hands with due reverence, he prayed.ᵇ •"LORD, LORD, King of heaven,   6:1–15
ruler of all creation, holy among the holy ones, sovereign, conqueror of all, pay
heed to us who are sorely vexed by a wicked and corrupt man,ᶜ reckless in his
3 effrontery and might. •For you who created all things and govern the whole world

---

h. The Gk. verb used here means "to talk
marvels" or "portents" and implies in this context
"to make a boastful claim."

i. The general drift of vss. 18f. is clear enough,
though the text is somewhat obscure. In vs. 19, A
V m read "chambers completely prepared," other
mm "prepared for all." Arm. has "were sitting
veiled and prepared." But in light of 4:6, *pastous*
= "bridal chambers" is most probably correct.
The word rendered "married" in vs. 19, the
meaning required here, does not occur in this sense
elsewhere. It may also be translated "secluded"
or "clothed in nuptial garments." Arm. has "newly
introduced."

j. Gk. lit. = "roughness," "harshness."

2 a. The ruling high priest in 217 B.C. was Simon
II, son of Onias, possibly referred to also in Sir
50:1, although he is there described as "son of
Jochanan." It is not clear whether this Simon or
Simon I, who many years earlier had encountered
Alexander the Great, is the one surnamed "the
Just." Vs. 1 is omitted in A V mm but is present
in L. Arm. reads "they began to pray and said."

b. The language of the prayer in vss. 3–20,
more sober and restrained than the narrative sections
of 3Mac, resembles the *Amidah* and conforms to
the typical liturgical usage of hellenistic Judaism
in its piling up of the attributes of God, although
otherwise it is thoroughly Heb. and OT.

c. "Wicked and corrupt" = "profane" or
"religiously defiled."

4 are a just ruler and condemn all who act insolently and arrogantly. •You destroyed   Gen 6:4–7
men for their wicked deeds in the past, among them giants relying on their own   Jdt 16:7
Sir 16:7
strength and self-confidence, upon whom you brought an immeasurable flood of   WisSol 14:6
Gen 7
5 water. •When the inhabitants of Sodom acted insolently and became notorious for
their crimes you burned them up with fire and brimstone and made them an   Gen 19:24
6 example to later generations. •You tested the proud Pharaoh, who enslaved your
holy people Israel, with many different punishments and made known to him your   Ex 5–12
7 mighty power. •When he pursued with chariots a great host of people, you
overwhelmed him in the depths of the sea and brought safely through those who   Ex 14:21–31
8 believed on you, the ruler of all creation. •When they saw the works of your hand
9 they praised you, conqueror of all. •You, king, when you created the boundless   Ex 15
and measureless earth, chose this city and sanctified this Temple for your name,
though you lack nothing at all, and you glorified it by a splendid manifestation
10 and established it to the glory of your great and honorable name. •And in your
love for the house of Israel you promised that, if ever we should turn away or   1 Kgs 8:33–53
distress overtake us, and we came to this holy place to pray, you would hear our
11,12 prayer. •And you are surely faithful and true to your word. •Seeing that often
when our forefathers were afflicted you helped them in their humiliation and
13 rescued them from great ills, •so look now, holy king, when we are oppressed
and subjected to our enemies on account of our many serious sins and are weak
14 and resourceless. •In our calamity this arrogant and corrupt man sets out to violate
15 the holy place which is dedicated on earth to the name of your glory. •Your
16 dwelling place, the heaven of heaven, is beyond the reach of men. •But since you   1Kgs 8:27–29
sanctified this holy place because you took pleasure in your glory among your
17 people Israel, •do not punish us by the uncleanness of these men, nor censure us
by their corruption, lest the lawless ones boast in their wrath or exult in the
18 insolence of their tongue, saying, •'We have trodden down the house of the   1Mac 6:7
19 sanctuary as the houses of the abominations[d] are trodden down.' •Wipe out our
20 sins and disperse our offenses and show your pity at this moment. •Let your
mercies speedily overtake us, and let praises fill the mouths of those who are
fallen and crushed in their souls, and grant us peace."

God's punishment of Ptolemy and the king's vengeful response

21   Then the God who beholds all, the supremely holy father among the holy, heard   Deut 32:6
the prayer of supplication offered in the regular form and scourged the one who   Isa 63:16
22 was greatly exalted by his own insolence and effrontery, •tossing him to and fro   2Mac 3:22–30;
9:4–10
like a reed on the wind until he fell impotent to the ground, with his limbs
paralyzed and unable to speak, completely overpowered by a righteous judgment.
23 When his friends and members of his bodyguard saw how severe was the
chastisement that overtook him, they were afraid he might die, and, smitten with
24 extreme alarm, they pulled him out. •However, punished though he had been,
when he recovered shortly after he was by no means contrite but went away with
25 bitter threats. •Thereafter, on his arrival in Egypt, he became even more extravagant
in his wickedness through his aforementioned[e] boon companions and friends,
26 complete strangers to everything that was just, •and not only was he not satisfied
with his innumerable excesses, he even reached such a pitch of arrogance as to
concoct slanderous reports[f] in these regions. Many of his friends watched the
27 king's procedure intently and themselves fell into line with his wishes. •His aim
.was to bring disgrace upon the nation publicly. Accordingly, he erected a pillar
28 on the tower at the palace and inscribed on it, •"That none of those who did not

---

d. Forgetful that he is citing the words of a
pagan speaker, the Jewish author describes pagan
shrines in the only way a Jew would do so as "the
houses of the abominations."

e. The fact that they have not actually been

mentioned previously suggests either that the author
is slavishly following a source or that in its present
form 3Mac has lost its original beginning.

f. Whether against the Jews or by the Jews
against himself is not clear.

sacrifice should be permitted to enter their temples,[g] and that all Jews should be required to enroll in the census[h] and be reduced to the condition of slaves, and
29 that any who spoke against it should be taken by force and put to death, •that those who were enrolled should be branded by fire on their bodies with an ivy leaf, the emblem of Dionysus,[i] and should be registered according to their former
30 restricted status."[j] •But so as not to appear to be an enemy to them all he added, "But if any of them prefer to join those who are initiated in the mysteries, they
31 would be on the same footing as the citizens of Alexandria."[k] •Some who objected strongly to the price the city had to pay for the practice of its religion[l] surrendered gladly, expecting to participate in some of the prestige that would come from
32 association with the king. •But most resisted with gallantry of spirit and did not abandon their religious practice, but they gave their money as a ransom for their
33 life and fearlessly sought to save themselves from the enrollment. •They persisted in the hope that they would obtain relief and despised those who left their ranks, judging them to be enemies of the nation and depriving them of any part in community life and service.

2Mac 6:1
LetAris 22

3:21

3:22–24

The Jews in society

1 **3** On receiving word of this, the impious king was so enraged he was not angry only with those who lived in Alexandria but was even more bitterly opposed to those in the country and ordered that all of them should be assembled with haste
2 in one spot and put to death in the most violent way. •While this was being organized, a malicious rumor was noised abroad against the Jewish nation by men who conspired to harm them and grasped an opportunity that arose to represent
3 them as hindering them from observance of their laws. •The Jews, however, steadily maintained their goodwill toward the kings and their unwavering loyalty.
4 But reverencing God and conducting themselves according to his Law, they kept themselves apart[a] in the matter of food, and for this reason they appeared hateful
5 to some. •They adorned their community life with the excellent practice of
6 righteousness and so established a good reputation among all men. •But of this excellent practice, which was common talk everywhere regarding the Jewish
7 nation, the foreigners took no account whatever. •Instead they talked incessantly about how different they were in regard to worship and food, asserting that they did not fulfill their contracted obligations either to the king or the armed forces but were hostile and very unsympathetic to his interests. So it was no small charge

4:12

Esth 3:8

4Mac
LetAris 128–66

g. The Jews are here forbidden to practice their own religion if they do not also follow the official cult with its sacrifices.

h. On *laographia* (here translated "census"), see Date. The specific mention of the Jews and Jewish enrollment is probably an insertion by our author into what would have been a broad and general edict.

i. The practice of branding or tattooing, to which Ptolemy Philopator himself most likely submitted, goes back to the Thracian origins of the Dionysiac cult. While Philopator himself was apparently a devotee of the cult, his object in enforcing the branding was more political than religious, namely to provide a universal symbol of national unity among the varied populace of Egypt.

j. The reference is to their previous servile status up to the time of their liberation by Ptolemy II Philadelphus. Cf. LetAris 22.

k. The question of the civic status of Jews in Egypt and in particular of the various grades of citizenship in Alexandria is much disputed. Josephus insists that the Jews enjoyed full citizen status

in Alexandria (*Ant* 12.1; 19. 5.2). But it is likely that if they did so, it was not specifically as Jews but as individuals, in which case one can see the point of the exceptive clause added to Philopator's edict in vs. 30.

l. The beginning of vs. 31 is rather obscure. The MSS reveal a number of minor variant readings which suggest such possible alternative translations as "Some who on account of the citizenship in a city hated the approaches to the city of piety" or "Some who were over a district in Alexandria hated the advances of the religion of the city." Our translation follows the most probably correct reading, and what is implied is that the renegade Jews were alienated by the high cost of keeping up strict observance of the Law or of the Temple tax. See Emmet, *APOT*, vol. 1, p. 166.

3 a. The apartness or separatism of the Jews is a familiar theme in hellenistic writings and is particularly prominent in 4Mac. Our author is at pains to show that their apartness does not prevent them from being loyal subjects.

8 they fastened on them. •When the Greeks in the city,[b] who were in no way
wronged by them, noticed the unexpected tumult around these people, and the
unforeseen concourses taking place, they were unable to help, for they lived under
a tyranny, but they did give them encouragement and felt sorry for them, and   4:1
9 they assumed that things would change for the better. •Surely a community so
10 large that had done no wrong could not be left to such a fate. •Some of their
neighbors and friends and business associates took some Jews aside secretly and
pledged to support them and make every effort to assist them.

Ptolemy's decree that all Jews in his kingdom be arrested

11   The king, priding himself on his present prosperity and with no regard for the
power of the Almighty God, and supposing that he could persist forever with the   2:28–31
12 same scheme, wrote the following letter against the Jews: •"King Ptolemy   1:9,16; 4:16;
13 Philopator, to his generals in Egypt and elsewhere, greeting and good health.[c] •I   5:25; 7:22
14 myself am in good health and our affairs are prospering. •Our expedition in Asia,
of which you yourselves are aware, having been brought, as we expected, to its
15 successful conclusion with the deliberate help of the gods, •we thought we would
foster the inhabitants of Coele-Syria and Phoenicia, not by force of arms, but by
16 kindness and great benevolence, conferring benefits on them willingly. •And
having allotted very large revenues to the temples in the various cities, we proceeded
also to Jerusalem, having gone up to do honor to the Temple of this accursed
17 people who never desist from their folly. •Outwardly they seemed to welcome
our presence, but in fact their welcome was insincere, for when we desired to
18 enter their shrine and to honor it with resplendent and beautiful offerings, •carried
away by their ancient pride, they stopped us from going in, but because of the
benevolence we practice toward all men they were left untouched by our might.
19 But they plainly exhibited their hostility to us and, the only ones among all
peoples who offer lordly resistance to kings and their own benefactors, they refused
20 to accept anything as genuine. •For our part we accommodated ourselves to their
folly, and returning victoriously to Egypt, we met all nations with benevolence:
21 we have acted rightly. •Similarly, we made known to all our readiness to forgive
the Jews' fellow countrymen, because of their alliance with us and the many   5:31
affairs that had been entrusted to them from of old,[d] and we boldly decided to   LetAris 36
introduce a change, declaring them worthy of Alexandrian citizenship and allowing   6:25; 7:7
22 them to participate in our regular religious rites. •But they misinterpreted us and
23 in their innate feelings of hostility rejected this good offer. •Inclining as they
always do toward the mean and petty, they not only rejected the invaluable
citizenship, but also by their silence as well as by their words they show contempt
for the few among them who are properly disposed to us, constantly nursing the
secret hope that with their disgraceful conduct we would quickly alter our policy.
24 Accordingly, we have adequate proof of our conviction that these people are in
every way hostile to us, and noting in advance that, if ever a sudden disturbance
should be stirred up against us later on, we would have these impious people
25 behind our backs as traitors and barbarous enemies, •we have decreed that the   Ex 1:10
very moment this letter reaches you, you shall dispatch to us those who reside
among you, together with their women and children, committing atrocities against
them and binding them fast all over in iron chains, to meet a desperate and
26 ignominious death as befits traitorous foes. •For we believe that when they are all
punished together, our government will be perfectly established forever in the

---

b. The reference is possibly to the more refined
Macedonian Gk. element, which is prepared to
take some risks to help the Jews. Again the point
is that the Jews' separatism does not mean they
have no friends among non-Jews. But in 4:1 our
author does stress the generally prevailing antipathy
of pagans toward the Jews.
c. On this greeting and its significance, see

Date.
d. That Jews had been placed in positions of
trust appears to be a matter of historical fact. We
gather from the Elephantine Papyri that in the 5th
cent. B.C. Jewish garrisons had been posted by the
Persians at Elephantine and Assuan to guard Egypt's
southern frontiers, and the Ptolemies seem to have
continued the policy.

27 most secure and healthy condition. •Whoever shelters any Jew, from the old to
   the child and even to the infant at the breast, shall with all his household be done
28 to a violent death with the most horrible torture. •Whoever wishes may act as
   informer, and he shall receive the estate of the person who is sentenced to
   punishment as well as two thousand drachmas from the royal treasury and shall
29 also be rewarded with freedom.ᵉ •Any place where a Jew is detected under any
   kind of shelter shall be made out of bounds and burned with fire and shall become
30 altogether useless for every mortal creature for all time." •Such was the form of
   the letter that was written.

The deportation of the Jews and their imprisonment at Alexandria

1 **4** In every place where the decree reached, a feast was arranged for the heathen
   at the public expense with noisy celebrations and gladness, with the hatred which
   had long before become inveterate in their hearts now being given open expression. Esth 4:3
2 But among the Jews there was incessant grief and cries of lamentation with tears,
   and their hearts were all aflame as they groaned and bewailed the unexpected
3 destruction so suddenly decreed against them. •What district or city or town or
   village with any inhabitants at all or what streets were not filled with lamentation
4 and wailing for them?ᵃ •For with such vindictive and pitiless spirit were they sent
   away, all of them together, by the generals of the various cities, that even some
   of their enemies, confronted with their extraordinary suffering, and perceiving the
   people's pity for them and reflecting on life's strange vicissitudes, were moved to
5 tears at their wretched expulsion. •For there was taken away a large company of
   old men, their heads covered with gray, and though their feet were sluggish and
   crooked from age, they were having to force themselves to a brisk pace under the
6 altogether shameless and relentless driving. •The young women who had but 1:18f.
   recently entered the bridal chamber for the society of married life exchanged their
   joy for wailing, and, with their perfume-drenched locks covered in dust, they
   were carried away unveiled and all joined in singing a dirge instead of a wedding
7 hymn, as if torn asunder by the brutal mangling of the heathen. •And in full view
   of everybody they were forcibly dragged along in bonds until they were embarked
8 on board ship. •Their husbands, in the full bloom of youth, their necks girded
   with halters in place of garlands, spent the remaining days of their wedding festival
   not in glad celebration and youthful recreation but in dirges, seeing the grave
9 already yawning at their very feet. •They were put on board like animals, driven
   along under the constraint of iron bonds. Some had their necks fastened to the
10 ship's benches, and others had their feet secured in unbreakable fetters. •Worse
   still, they were placed in total darkness that they might be treated as traitors
11 throughout the voyage. •When they had been brought to the place called Schediaᵇ
   and the voyage as determined by the king was over, he ordered them to be thrown
   into the hippodrome on the outskirts of the city,ᶜ an immense concourse eminently
   suitable for making the captives a public example to all who came down to the

---

e. The reading of A V, the genitive of the Gk.
word for "freedom," *eleutherias*, and the verb
stephanōthēsetai = "shall be crowned," is grammatically awkward. Arm. reads "shall be honored
with a crown of freedom," and Deissmann emends
the genitive to the dative, *eleutheria*, and furnishes
evidence from Polybius for the use
of the verb "crowned," metaphorically meaning
simply "rewarded" (our translation). Some texts
of L read "shall obtain freedom and shall be
crowned" and some add the Gk. words for "forever." The sense of vs. 28 is rather difficult. Is it
Jewish informers against Jews who are here offered
their freedom (from the slavery with which all Jews
are threatened in 2:28, and for whom death is
decreed in 3:25f.)? Presumably there would be few

such, and the informers envisaged may be lower-
or serf-class Egyptians in the populace hostile to
the Jews. An attractive suggestion is that we should
read the dative plural *tois eleutheriois*, in which
case the question of "freedom" is not involved,
since the meaning would then be "shall be crowned
at the Eleutheria," a festival of Dionysus.

4 a. The description of the mass deportation in
vss. 3–10 is highly rhetorical and grossly exaggerated, as is clear from 4:18.
   b. Schedia was an area of docks some three
miles from Alexandria. Possibly a landing place
closer in is what the author really intended.
   c. The hippodrome was located near the east
gate of the city.

city and to those who left the city for a sojourn in the country, the purpose being to prevent them from associating with the king's forces or claiming to be within
12 the precincts of the city. •When this was done, the king heard that their fellow
13 countrymen came out frequently to bewail the bitter fate of their brethren •and in a rage ordered that they should be treated in precisely the same way as the others and should be allowed no remission whatever of the punishment meted out to
14 these others. •Moreover, the whole race was to be registered by name, not for   2:28 the toilsome labor service, briefly explained above, but to be tortured by the torments which he had commanded and to be put to death in the space of a single
15 day. •The registration, undertaken with shameful haste and unremitting diligence from sunrise to sunset, was closed after forty days, although still incomplete.
16 Filled with great and continuous joy, the king appointed feasts at all his idol shrines, with a heart far removed from the truth and a profane mouth, praising dumb objects unable to answer or help, and uttering improper words against the   2:27–29
17 Almighty God. •After the interval of time mentioned previously, the scribes   1:9,16; 3:11; 5:25; 7:22 reported to the king that they could no longer continue the registration of the Jews   4:3–10
18 on account of their incalculable number,d •although in fact the majority were still in the country, some still remaining in their homes and others on the journey;e
19 the task was impossible for all the generals in Egypt. •After threatening them harshly on the ground that they had been bribed to contrive their escape, he was
20 eventually clearly convinced on this point •when they stated, with proof to back it up, that the paper mill and the pens they used for writing had already given
21 out. •But this was the working out of the invincible providence of the one who helps the Jews from heaven.

The divine frustration of the king's plan to execute the Jews

1 **5** He then summoned Hermon, who was in charge of the elephants, and, filled
2 with stern anger and rage and completely inflexible, •ordered him for the following day to drug all the elephants, five hundred in number,a with large handfuls of frankincense and quantities of unmixed wine, then when they were wild with the
3 plentiful supply of drink to bring them in to compass the fate of the Jews. •When he had given out these orders he turned to his feasting, having brought together
4 those of his friends and army who were especially hostile to the Jews. •Meanwhile, Hermon, the superintendent of the elephants, carried out his orders to the letter.
5 The attendants assigned for the purpose went out in the evening and bound the handsb of the poor unfortunate people and took every other precaution to see that   3:25; 4: 9 they were secure through the night, imagining that the whole nation would meet
6 its ruinous end in one blow. •But the Jews, who seemed to the heathen to be bereft of every support, completely restricted as they were by their bonds, called
7 upon •their Lord, the all-conquering who governs with all power, the merciful
8 God and father, all of them beseeching him with unrestrained cries and tears •to frustrate the wicked design against them and rescue them by a wonderful
9 manifestation from the disaster imminently in store for them. •So their prayer

d. The number of Jews in Egypt is not exactly known, but in Philopator's time it could not have been all that large. The statements here in 3Mac are clearly hyperbolic. Philo (*Flacc.* 6) also exaggerates greatly when he speaks of one million Jews in Alexandria, although the number of Jews in Egypt generally would have increased a great deal by Philo's time.
e. "On the journey" is the reading given by L, vis. *kata ton poron.* A has *kata ton topon,* lit. = "at the place," and V has *kata tropon,* lit. = "according to custom" or "duly," neither of which makes much sense. It is not surprising that in this kind of romanticized narrative inconsistencies should appear: 4:1–3 gives the impression of a truly

massive roundup of the Jews, 4:18 by contrast of a relatively small minority of captives; then by contrast with 2:27–29, 4:12 implies that a great many Jews in Alexandria had as yet been left unhampered.

5 a. Even the ancient reader would have been struck by this excessively large number and would have recognized it as a "romantic" exaggeration; at the Battle of Raphia, Philopator had seventy-three elephants, itself a large number.
b. They were already bound (3:25; 4:9), but a poetic license is permissible in an historical romance of this kind.

10 went up fervently to heaven. •Hermon drugged the pitiless elephants until they
were filled with an abundant supply of wine and saturated with frankincense, and
11 in the early morning he appeared at the palace to inform the king. •But that lovely
gift of his creation, the interval of sleep, bestowed night and day since the
beginning of time by him who confers his blessings on whomsoever he chooses,
12 he sent upon the king. •And the king, in the spell of the sweet, deep sleep God
brought on him, was greatly thwarted in his lawless purpose and utterly disappointed
13 in his inflexible aim. •The Jews, having escaped the appointed hour, praised their
holy God and begged him who is quick to respond in mercy to show the power
14 of his mighty hand to the arrogant heathen. •But the middle of the tenth hour[c]
had nearly arrived when the official in charge of the invitations noticed that the
15 guests were assembled and went to the king and shook him. •He had trouble in
awakening him, but then pointed out that the duration of the banquet was almost
16 past and reminded him of the circumstances. •The king took account of what he
said and then, turning to his cups, he ordered his guests at the banquet to take
17 their places opposite him. •This done, he advised them to give themselves up to
revelry, to appreciate the great honor conferred upon them and regard this late
18 part of the feast as all good cheer. •After a period of table fellowship the king
summoned Hermon and with severe threats inquired of him why the Jews had
19 been allowed to survive that day. •But when he pointed out that he had carried
out every last word of the king's bidding overnight and his friends confirmed it,
20 the king was seized with rage more fierce than Phalaris'[d] and said that the Jews
had only sleep to thank for that day's grace. Then he added that the elephants
should be prepared without delay for the coming day, in exactly the same fashion,
for the extermination of the accursed Jews.
21   When the king had spoken, all who were present readily assented together with
22 joy and each went off to his own home. •But they used the nighttime not so much
for sleep as for devising all sorts of insults for the people they thought were
23 doomed. •The cock had no sooner crowed the dawn than Hermon set the beasts
24 in all their paraphernalia in motion in the great colonnade. •The crowds in the
city thronged together for the piteous spectacle, eagerly awaiting the first light of
25 morning. •But the Jews, drawing their last brief breath in tearful supplication and
strains of lament, stretched out their hands to heaven and implored the Almighty   1:9; 3:11; 4:16
26 God once more to help them speedily. •The rays of the sun were not yet widely   5:46
dispersed and the king was receiving his friends[e] when Hermon presented himself
and invited him to go forth, explaining that his wishes were now ready to be
27 granted. •When the king received his report he was amazed at the outrageous
invitation to go forth, overtaken as he was by complete ignorance, and asked what
business was on hand that required everything to be completed for his sake with
28 such haste. •But this was the working of the God who governs all things who had
29 implanted in his mind forgetfulness of his previous schemes. •But Hermon and
all his friends pointed to the beasts and the troops and said, "Everything is in
30 readiness, King, in accordance with your firm purpose."[f] •However, he was filled
with stern anger at the words, since by the providence of God in this matter his
31 mind had gone blank, and gazing at him threateningly, he said, •"If your parents
or your offspring were here,[g] I would have served them as an ample meal to the
wild beasts instead of the Jews, against whom I have no complaint and who above
32 all others showed an absolutely unflinching loyalty to my ancestors. •Indeed, if it   3:21

c. According to the Babylonian reckoning then in use in Egypt, 3:30 P.M.; according to the Roman reckoning, 4:30 P.M.

d. The sadistic tyrant of Agrigentum in the 6th cent. B.C. He enjoyed roasting people alive in a hollow brazen bull and listening to them bellow with pain (Polybius 12, 25).

e. Apparently a reference to the morning procession of courtiers come to pay their respects to the king.

f. After vs. 29, L has some additional sentences which are clearly a later interpolation: Hermon is introduced as "one who had been brought up with the king" as though he had not been mentioned before, and he and his friends plead with the king to recall his previous decree and point out how dangerous are the Jews.

g. The Gk. is in the form of an iambic line and is no doubt a quotation from an unidentified Gk. tragic poet.

were not for the affection that comes of our habitual companionship and your
33 service, your life would have been taken instead of theirs." •So Hermon met with
an unexpected and dangerous threat and he cast his eyes down and his face fell.
34 The king's friends, slipping out sulkily one by one, sent away the gathered
35 throng, each to his own business. •The Jews, on hearing what had happened with
the king, praised the God who had manifested himself, the Lord, the king of
kings, since they had obtained this help from him also.

36 Now the king once more arranged the whole banquet in the same way and
37 ordered the company to turn to revelry. •He then summoned Hermon and said
menacingly, "How often, wretch, must I give you orders on the self-same matters?
38 Fit out the elephants right now for tomorrow for the extermination of the Jews."
39 But his kinsfolk^h who were at the table with him were astonished at his
40 waywardness and remonstrated with him as follows: •"How long, King, will you
make trial of us as though we were fools? For the third time now you have ordered
us to exterminate the Jews, and once again when the business is in hand you
41 change your mind and cancel your decree. •All this has put the city in a tumult
of anticipation, and already crowded with throngs of people, it has several times
42 now been in danger of being plundered." •Thereupon the king, a veritable Phalaris
in every respect, was filled with madness and, completely heedless of the changes
of heart which had been effected in him for the protection of the Jews, vowed
emphatically but vainly that he would forthwith dispatch the Jews to the grave,
43 mangled by the knees and feet of the beasts, •and that he would make an expedition
against Judea and quickly level it to the ground with fire and sword and would
swiftly burn down the Temple to which he had been refused admissionⁱ and empty
44 it for all time of those who sacrificed there. •Then his friends and kinsfolk left in
great glee and high confidence and had troops posted in the most convenient spots
in the city to keep guard.

45 The superintendent of the elephants drove the beasts almost, one might say, to
a state of madness with fragrant draughts of wine mingled with frankincense and
46 equipped them with horrible implements.^j •About dawn, when the city was already
full of innumerable crowds making their way toward the hippodrome, he entered
47 the palace and incited the king to take up the business on hand. •Then the king,
his impious heart filled with stern anger, stormed out with the beasts, determined
to watch without a qualm and with his very own eyes the spectacle of the
48 aforementioned Jews' painful and piteous destruction. •When the Jews saw the
dust stirred up by the elephants going out at the gate, the fully armed troops
accompanying them and the movement of the people and heard the thunderous
49 din, •thinking that the last crisis of their life and the end of their agonizing
suspense had come, they took to wailing and moaning and kissed one another,
embracing their relatives and falling on their necks, parents and children, mothers
and daughters; some had newborn infants at their breasts, drawing their last milk.
50 Nevertheless, mindful of the former occasions on which help was given from
heaven, they threw themselves on their faces with one accord; they removed the
51 babes from breasts^k •and cried out with an exceedingly great shout, imploring the
ruler of all power by a manifestation to show mercy to them now that they were
standing at the very gates of death.

---

h. The Gk. word *sungeneis* (lit. = "kinsmen")
is used regularly of the higher officials of the king's
court.

i. The Gk. here slips into direct speech, reading
lit. "to which we had been refused admission."
The whole sentence is somewhat confused, as the
several minor variants in the textual tradition testify,
and may be a redactional afterthought or a later

interpolation.

j. Knives and scythes attached to the beasts, as
they often were also to war chariots.

k. In order to prostrate themselves as supplicants. For the author's fastidiousness regarding the
appropriate postures for prayer, see Theological
Importance.

Eleazar's prayer

1 **6** A certain Eleazar,[a] a man of distinction among the priests[b] of the country, already well advanced in years and a shining example of all life's virtues, directed the elders around him to stop calling on the holy God[c] and prayed as follows: 2 "King, great in power, Most High, All-conquering God, who governs the 3 whole creation with mercy,[d] •look upon the seed of Abraham, upon the children of Jacob whom you sanctified, the people of your sanctified inheritance who are 4 perishing unjustly as strangers in a strange land. •Pharaoh, the former ruler of this Egypt, with his multitude of chariots, high and mighty in his lawless insolence and boastful tongue, you destroyed in the depths of the sea with his proud host, Father, causing the light of your mercy to shine upon the people of Israel. 5 Sennacherib, the cruel king of the Assyrians, exulting in his countless hosts, when he had subjugated the whole earth by the spear and was lifted up against your holy city, uttering grievous words with boastfulness and insolence, you shattered, 6 Lord,[e] displaying your power openly to many nations. •The three comrades in Babylonia who of their own choice gave their life to the fire rather than serve idols you delivered unharmed to the very hair of their head, making the fiery 7 furnace like dew, and you sent flame upon all their enemies. •When, through the slanderous accusations brought against him out of envy, Daniel was thrown to the lions underground as food for beasts, you brought him up to the light unscathed. 8 When Jonah was pining away unpitied in the belly of the monster of the deep, 9 you, Father, restored him uninjured to all his household.[f] •So now, you who hate insolence, full of mercy, protector of all, manifest yourself swiftly to those of the people of Israel who are outrageously treated by the abominable and lawless 10 heathen. •If our life is subject to penalty because of impious deeds in the course of our sojourn abroad, rescue us from the hand of our enemies, Lord, and destroy 11 us by a fate of your own choosing. •Let not those who think vain thoughts bless their vain gods for the destruction of your beloved people and say, 'Not even their 12 God could rescue them.' •You who possess all might and power, Eternal, look now upon us. Pity us who are being put to death like traitors by the mad insolence 13 of lawless men. •Let the heathen fear your unconquerable power this day, highly 14 honored one, who are continually mighty to save the people of Jacob. •The whole 15 multitude of children and their parents implore you with tears. •Let it be made clear to all the nations that you are with us, Lord, and have not turned your face away from us, but even as you have said, 'Not even when they were in the land of their enemies have I neglected them,' so bring it to pass, Lord."

Marginal references:
2:1–20
2Mac 6:18
4Mac 6:5; 7:1
LetArist 41

Pss 105,106

Ex 15

2Kgs 19:35

Dan 3:50

Dan 3:27
PrAzar 25

Dan 6:24

Jonah 1:17–2:9

WisSol 2:16–24
Ps 115:2

Lev 26:44

A remarkable turnabout in events and in the king's attitude

16 Just as Eleazar was finishing his prayer, the king arrived at the hippodrome 17 with the beasts and the whole wanton array of his army. •And the Jews observed it and raised a great cry to heaven that made the surrounding valleys ring with the 18 sound and struck uncontrollable terror in all the hosts. •Then the great and glorious, all-conquering and true God revealed his holy face and opened heaven's gates, from which descended two angels, clothed in glory and of awe-inspiring appearance,

1En 14:20
TLevi 3:4

---

6 a. Eleazar appears here, as in the related literature, e.g. 2Mac 6:18; 4Mac 6:5; 7:1; LetAris 41, as the "type" of wisdom garnered from long life and experience, piety and faith.

b. A reads "Jews" instead of "priests," but comparison with 7:13 suggests that "priests" is correct. "Priests" possibly refers to those of the temple of Onias at Leontopolis.

c. It seems strange that he should call for a cessation of prayer among the elders, but possibly the author understands that in virtue of his priestly office Eleazar gives the signal that he is about to act as their spokesman and intercessor before God.

d. The prayer begins in the same fashion as the Jewish *Amidah* prayer.

e. 2Kgs has an "angel of the Lord" intervene as God's agent to smite the Assyrians (19:35). Here the Lord shatters them himself; he needs no intermediary to provide help as far as the Jews are concerned. Cf. 6:18.

f. The OT itself does not expressly mention Jonah's restoration to his home.

19 visible to all except the Jews,[g] •and they confronted the forces of their adversaries
and filled them with confusion and timidity and bound them with immovable
20 fetters. •The king also experienced a shuddering in his body and his gross insolence
21 faded to nothing. •And the beasts turned back on the armed forces that followed
22 them and they began to trample them down and destroy them. •The king's anger
was now turned to pity and tears on account of the scheme he had previously
23 devised. •For when he heard the outcry and saw them all prostrate to meet their
24 death, he wept and angrily threatened his friends, saying, •"You usurp the king's
power and excel tyrants in savagery, and you even attempt to deprive me myself,
your benefactor, of my rule and indeed of my life, secretly devising measures that
25 are deleterious for my kingdom. •Who has driven from their homes those who
held the fortresses of our country with such loyalty and stupidly mustered them
26 here, each one? •Who has so lawlessly surrounded with torments those who from
the beginning have in every way exceeded all peoples in their goodwill toward us
27 and have frequently submitted to the worst dangers confronting men? •Loose, yes
loose completely their unrighteous bonds. Send them back to their homes in peace,
28 asking their forgiveness for what has been done to them. •Release the sons of the
all-conquering, living God of heaven, who from the times of our ancestors until
29 now has conferred upon our estate an impregnable stability with glory?" •So the
king spoke. The Jews were released forthwith and blessed the holy God, their
savior, for their narrow escape from death.

2Mac 3:24–40;
10:29; 6:5
WisSol 18:3,
15,17

The Jewish celebration of a feast of deliverance

30   Then the king left for the city and, summoning the keeper of the public revenues,
he ordered him to supply the Jews with wine and all the perquisites for a feast
for seven days, decreeing that in the very place where they had thought to meet
31 their fate they should hold a festival of deliverance with all joy. •Then those who
had been reviled and had just been close to the grave, or rather had already had
one foot in it, instead of a bitter and wretched fate held a feast celebrating their
deliverance, and filled with gladness they portioned out to different festive groups
32 the space that had been made ready for their destruction and burial. •They left off
the mournful sound of dirges and took up the song of their fathers, praising God
the deliverer and worker of wonders, and laying aside all wailing and lamentation,
they formed dances as a sign of the joy and peace that had come upon them.
33 The king likewise held a great banquet in celebration of all that had happened and
endlessly returned solemn thanks to heaven for the unexpected deliverance granted
34 to him.[h] •But those who previously imagined that the Jews were doomed to
destruction and to become a prey for the birds, and had joyfully conducted the
registration, now groaned at being covered with confusion and at having their
35 blazing effrontery ignominiously quenched. •The Jews, however, as we have said,
having formed the dance just mentioned, spent the time in festivity, with glad
36 thanksgiving and psalms. •And they laid down a general ordinance on these
matters, to have effect wherever future generations might sojourn, that they should
celebrate the aforementioned days with a festival of joy, not for the sake of
drinking and gluttony but of the deliverance that had come to them through God.[i]
37 They next petitioned the king, requesting him to dismiss them to their own
38 homes. •Now the process of registration had gone on from the twenty-fifth day
of Pachon to the fourth of Epiphi, for forty days, and the appointment of their

Esth 9:18
1Mac 4:56;
7:59; 13:50
2Mac 10:6;
15:36

Esth 9:19–26

g. The appearance of heavenly visitants to aid
the weaker side in battle is a feature not only of
Jewish but also of Gk. history, e.g. at Marathon
and Salamis. The observation here that the angels
were "visible to all except the Jews" may well be
an insertion of the author to correct a story he had
received from the tradition in the light of his own
particular theological preconceptions (cf. 6:5).

h. A mm Arm. read *autōn* = "the deliverance
granted to them"; others read *autō* = "to him"
(the reading followed in the translation). V omits.

i. The festival ordinance shows that the passage
is to be regarded as etiologic; the author traces the
origin of a festival that continued to be celebrated
among Egyptian Jews to the rescue of the Jews at
Alexandria and its immediate sequel.

39 destruction from the fifth of Epiphi to the seventh, for three days.ʲ •On these days
the ruler of all revealed his mercy with great glory and rescued them one and all
40 unharmed. •They feasted, with everything supplied by the king, until the fourteenth
41 day, when they made the petition for their dismissal. •The king consented and on
their behalf wrote the following letter to the generals in the cities, generously
declaring his purpose.

The king's letter on behalf of the Jews

1 **7** "King Ptolemy Philopator to the generals in Egypt and all who have charge of
2 our affairs, greetings and good health;ᵃ •We, for our part, are in good health, and   LetArist 37
3 our children also,ᵇ the great God directing our estate as we desire. •Some of our   6:25–28
friends, out of malice, by urging the matter on us continually, persuaded us to
gather the Jews together in the kingdom in a body and to inflict upon them
4 extraordinary punishments as traitors, •suggesting that our state would never be
stable because of the ill will the Jews bear to all nations until this was carried
5 out. •So they brought them down with atrocious treatment, as slaves or rather
conspirators, and they sought to put them to death without legal trial or even
investigation, decking themselves out with cruelty more savage than the law of   2Mac 4:47
6 the Scythians.ᶜ •But because of the fairness we show to all men, we reprimanded   4Mac 10:7
them for their conduct with stern threats and barely granted them their lives, and
knowing of a surety that God in heaven protects the Jews, in alliance with them
7 continually like a father with his children, •and taking account of their unshakable
friendly disposition toward us and our ancestors, we have justly absolved them of
8 any blame whatever. •And we have enjoined that all should return, each one to
his own home, and that no one should do them any harm at all in any place or
9 reproach them for the unreasonable penalties inflicted on them. •Be sure of this,
that if we devise any evil scheme against them or cause them any trouble, we
shall have not man but the most high God, who is ruler of all power, as our
adversary to exact vengeance for what is done, inexorably in all circumstances
and for all time. Farewell."
10 On receiving this letter, the Jews did not at once make haste for their departure,
but requested further of the king that those of the Jewish people who had wittingly
transgressed against the holy God and his Law should receive the due punishment
11 at their hands, •stressing that those who had transgressed the divine commandments
for their belly's sake would never be well disposed to the king's business either.
12 The king acknowledged the truth of what they said, and praising them, he granted
them full indemnity, to destroy without let or hindrance or any royal license or
investigation those who had transgressed the Law of God anywhere in his
dominion.

The Jews' joyous departure and return home.

13 Then, applauding him, as was fitting, their priests and the whole multitude
14 departed with joy, shouting the hallelujah. •Any one of their countrymen they
encountered on the way who had become defiled they punished and put to death
15 as a public example. •On that day they put to death over three hundred men, and
16 they kept it as a joyous festival, having subdued the unclean.ᵈ •But those who

---

j. Pachon and Epiphi (Egyptian names) are respectively April 26–May 25 and June 25–July 24.
The precise dating introduces an air of realism and
no doubt in the author's view supports the etiology.

7 a. In form and structure the letter is realistic
enough, conforming as it does to regular pattern
(on the significance of the greeting, see Date). But
in content it is farfetched: The language of vss. 6
and 9 particularly is virtually impossible for a

Ptolemy.
   b. Ptolemy did not have a legitimate son until
208 B.C., about ten years after the events recorded
here.
   c. The Scythians were proverbial for their cruelty.
   d. The action seems harsh and vengeful, but
apostasy in the presence of largely pagan authorities
was regarded as a heinous crime.

held fast to God even unto death enjoyed the full advantage of their deliverance and departed from the city crowned with all kinds of fragrant flowers, giving thanks to the God of their fathers, the everlasting savior of Israel, with gladness
17 and with shouting, in songs of praise and melodious hymns. •When they had reached Ptolemais, called "rose-bearing"ᵉ because of the special characteristic of the place, the fleet waited for them, according to their general wish, for seven
18 days, •and there they held a banquet to celebrate their deliverance, the king having generously supplied every one of them with all they needed until their arrival at
19 their own home. •And when they had completed their voyage in peace with appropriate thanksgivings, there too in the same fashion as before they decided to   6:36
20 make these days also during the time of their sojourn festival days.ᶠ •They consecrated them with an inscription on a pillar, and having dedicated a place of prayer on the site of the banquet, they went away unscathed, free, and filled with joy, and were conducted safely, by ordinance of the king, over land and seaᵍ and
21 river, each to his own home. •They had even greater authority than before among their enemies and were regarded with high esteem and awe; no one at all extorted
22 their property. •They recovered all their possessions, according to the register,ʰ and those who had anything of theirs returned it to them with great fear: The great   1:9,16; 3:11;
23 God had perfectly accomplished great things for their salvation. •Blessed be the   4:16; 5:25; 7:22
deliverer of Israel forever and ever! Amen.   4Mac 18:24
        Sir 51:30–38
        Tob 14:15

e. Ptolemais here is not the famous city near Thebes in Upper Egypt but the town at the harbor some miles southwest of Cairo, where the canal broadened out. The adjective "rose-bearing" is not elsewhere applied to Ptolemais, and in fact is found only here. It may be regarded as a private note of the author's.

f. It is not clear whether the author thought of this as a separate festival. It appears he does. But he may be incorporating at this point a tradition that initially referred to the great festival at Alexandria (6:36) and dated its moment of origin rather differently.

g. There was no "sea," except, of course, the Mediterranean, nearby. Assuming "they" (7:20) denotes only Alexandrian Jews, the writer may be in error or may be describing Lake Moeris as "sea." More likely, in view of his apparently extensive knowledge of the geography of the region, he is here making a rhetorical flourish.

h. There has been no mention in the book of any confiscation of Jewish property. Probably the author had information about such confiscation in other times and places and has added here this general note, which certainly emphasizes the completeness of the Jews' restoration.

4 MACCABEES

(First Century A.D.)

A NEW TRANSLATION AND INTRODUCTION

BY H. ANDERSON

The book widely known under the above heading is set in the form of a philosophical discourse in which the author proceeds to develop his argument by using the first person singular. In his preface in 1:1–6 he introduces the subject of his entire work, devout reason's mastery over the passions, a phrase which recurs like a refrain throughout (1:9, 13, 19, 30; 2:6, 24; 6:31; 7:16; 13:1; 16:1; 18:2). After intimating (1:7–12) that by far the best illustration of this proposition is the martyrdom of Eleazar and the seven sons and their mother, he moves into a philosophical and didactic section (1:13–3:18) in which he discusses the relationship of reason to the passions or emotions and furnishes examples from the lives of Old Testament heroes Joseph, Moses, Jacob, and David. There follows a brief historical exordium relating the intervention of Apollonius, governor of Syria, in the affairs of the Jerusalem Temple, its outcome, and the hostility of Antiochus Epiphanes to the Jews (3:19–14:26). So the scene is set for the martyrdoms to which the main body of the book is entirely devoted (5:1–17:6). Exceedingly detailed descriptions of the tortures to which all were subjected are interspersed with speeches from the lips of Eleazar and the sons, as well as with a panegyric on Eleazar in 6:31–7:23 and another on the sovereignty of devout reason in the seven brothers in 13:1–14:10. In 14:11–17:6 the mother is represented as, in her suffering and death, the most illustrious exemplar of the victory of reason, inasmuch as before her own end she exhorted her sons to endure death rather than transgress the Law. The final segment of the book is given to an account of the public effect of the martyrdoms (17:7–18:5) and of the mother's address to her children (18:6–19), and closes with an expression of faith in the justice of God and, finally, a doxology (18:20–24).

Texts

The text of 4 Maccabees has been handed down in several manuscripts of the Septuagint, but most important are the Sinaiticus (S), from the fourth century A.D., and the Alexandrinus (A), from the fifth century. It does not appear in the third great uncial manuscript of the Greek Bible, the Vaticanus, but is found, with the exception of the section 5:11–12:1, in the eighth- or ninth-century Codex Venetus (V). In addition, numerous manuscripts containing the works of the Jewish historian Josephus also contain 4 Maccabees, a fact which has, since the fourth century, led mistakenly, as we shall see, to the ascription of 4 Maccabees to Josephus. In any case, that 4 Maccabees was first issued without the name of the author is clearly indicated by its appearance in many manuscripts anonymously.

The Greek of our book (see Original Language) was early translated into Syriac, and it appears in the Peshitta under the title *The Fourth Book of the Maccabees and Their Mother*, a version which generally favors the readings of S against A. Some comparison of the Syriac with the Greek was undertaken in the joint work of R. L. Bensly and W. E. Barnes, published at Cambridge in 1895, titled *The Fourth Book of Maccabees and Kindred Documents in Syriac*.

The Fourth Book of Maccabees is not in the Vulgate and so is absent from the Apocrypha of the Roman Bible as well as from Protestant Bibles. However, Erasmus was responsible for a very free Latin paraphrase of 4 Maccabees, first published at Cologne in 1524. He was not acquainted with the Greek text, which was in fact first printed in volume 3 of the Strasbourg Septuagint in 1526, but may have worked from an old Latin version entitled *Passio SS. Machabaeorum*, somewhat closer to the Greek than Erasmus' rendering and extant in some thirty codices going back, probably, to an eighth-century archetype.

The first critical text of 4 Maccabees, founded, unlike the Strasbourg Septuagint of 1526, on a number of manuscripts, was that of O. F. Fritzsche, *Libri Apocryphi Veteris Testamenti Graeci* (Leipzig, 1871). H. B. Swete's edition, in volume 3 of *The Old Testament in Greek* (Cambridge, 1899), simply reproduces the text of A and furnishes variants from S and V. The text on which our translation is based is that of volume 1 of Rahlfs' *Septuaginta* (Stuttgart, 1935), which depends only on S and A. Our commentary draws attention only to those variants which significantly affect the sense of a passage.

The Fourth Book of Maccabees has a considerably stronger claim to the name "Maccabees" than 3 Maccabees, insofar as it witnesses events presumed to have taken place in the earliest days of the Maccabean revolt. Nevertheless, 4 Maccabees is in no sense a history of the exploits of the Maccabean leaders or of the course of the revolt. Rather, our author uses accounts of the martyrdoms as paradigmatic materials for a philosophical exercise on the subject of devout reason's mastery over the passions. Accordingly, even for 4 Maccabees, the designation "Maccabees" remains somewhat misleading. In the manuscript tradition different titles have been transmitted with the work, and the most appropriate and probably most original of these is the one cited by Eusebius and Jerome, On the Supremacy of Reason.

There is some question as to whether 4 Maccabees as we have it is the work of a single hand. Especially has the integrity of 18:6–19 been disputed, and several commentators consider the mother's speech to her children in these verses to be an interpolation. Their opinion is based chiefly on the supposed inferiority of style in the passage, on its catena of scriptural references, and on the discrepancy of its themes with the remainder of the book. But there is no manuscript evidence for the omission of 18:6–19. Nor is there any strong reason to suppose that a rhetorician like the Jewish author of 4 Maccabees, intent on wedding Greek philosophy to Jewish religion, could not have rounded off his entire essay with an address of a rather more homespun type from his great heroine, celebrating the virtues of chastity and familial piety so dear to the Jews, elevating the heroes of the Jewish faith, and in short acting as the final spokeswoman for the supremacy of the Jewish religion. He could scarcely either have inserted the words attributed to the mother here at the close of her earlier speech in 16:16–23 without detracting from his focal point of interest, reason's sovereignty over the passions. So he allows the woman, whose own sovereign victory he has so lauded, to have the last word as the champion of Judaism. Consequently, we here treat the whole of 4 Maccabees as it stands in the Greek text as a unity.

Original language

The chief aim of the writer of 4 Maccabees is to advocate fidelity to the Law and to demonstrate that the hope of fulfilling the Greek ideal of virtue resides only in obedience to the Law of Judaism. Accordingly, he is unquestionably a Jew. But he is no less certainly a Jew profoundly influenced by Greek philosophical thought and thoroughly at home with the Greek language. His work is conspicuously devoid of semitisms, and citations from the Old Testament consistently follow the Septuagint. The images, symbols, and metaphors employed as well as the antitheses, climaxes, and apostrophes that abound all clearly exhibit his skill in the craft of the Greek rhetorician. His Greek is free and idiomatic, indicating that he thinks in that language; it is his native tongue.

A large number of poetic, rare, or even unique terms occur in this book, e.g. *philtra* = "charm" (13:19, 27; 15:13); *hossopoieomai* = "hatch" (14:16); *pangeōrgos* = "master gardener" (1:29); *misaretos* = "enemy of virtue" (11:4); *allophuleō* = "adopt the pagan way of life" (18:5). Characteristic also are the many compounds minted by or used by our author, who no doubt loved to savor their sound, e.g. *ekdiaitaō* = "change" (4:19); *heptamētor* = "mother of seven" (16:24); *prosepikatateinō* = "draw tighter and tighter"

(9:19). These are but further indications of the writer's fluency in Greek and of the pervasive Greek atmosphere of 4 Maccabees.[1]

Authorship and date

Nowhere in 4 Maccabees is there any express notice given of its authorship, date, or place of origin. However, the work as a whole, as well as certain pieces of internal evidence, does allow us initially at least to make some reasonable, albeit broad and general, surmises on these matters:

1. We noted above that 4 Maccabees is found in a number of manuscripts containing the works of Flavius Josephus, the Jewish historian. Eusebius of Caesarea, in the early fourth century, and Jerome, a century later, attribute it to the hand of Josephus. But dismissing Ewald's suggestion[2] that another person by the name of Josephus may have been the author, we can also reject the traditional ascription of our book to the famous Flavius Josephus. Nowhere in his major works does the latter exhibit anything like the same florid rhetorical style as 4 Maccabees—he is an historian where the writer of 4 Maccabees is primarily philosopher and rhetorician. Josephus reveals no acquaintance with the text of 2 Maccabees, which appears to lie behind 4 Maccabees. Nor is it at all likely that the eminent historian, who took the name of Flavius as a compliment to the Flavian Caesar and married a gentile wife, would have championed the heroes of the resistance after the fashion of 4 Maccabees. Finally, to make but one specific point, whereas Josephus correctly describes Antiochus Epiphanes as the brother of Seleucus IV (*Ant* 12:4), in 4 Maccabees (4:15) he is called his son.

2. The manner in which the writer refers to the Jerusalem Temple and its services (e.g. 4:11f.) seems to presuppose that the Temple is still standing and therefore points to a date before the destruction of the Temple in A.D. 70. We may infer that the earliest possible date of composition is 63 B.C. The author is eager to explain that in the days of Seleucus IV (175 B.C.) the high priest Onias held the office for life; this statement would have been unnecessary before 63 B.C., when life tenure lapsed after the fall of the Hasmonean dynasty.[3]

3. We can no longer think of Judaism in our period, even Palestinian Judaism, as distinct at all on most points from the cultural stream of Hellenism. Recent research has demonstrated ever more clearly that even in its homeland Judaism was influenced to a hitherto unsuspected degree by hellenistic ideas, ideals, and practices.[4] However, traces of the infiltration of Hellenism into various phases of Palestinian Jewish life and thought are one thing, an almost complete absorption in hellenistic modes of conceptualization is another, and the ambience of 4 Maccabees is so thoroughly and unreservedly Greek that to regard it as a product of Palestine is virtually impossible. The author's extensive knowledge of Greek philosophy, his positive and purposeful use of it to argue the supremacy of the Law, and his skill in Greek rhetoric undoubtedly point to a location beyond the boundaries of Palestine, to a milieu in which East and West had completely met.

These arguments, limited as they are, do suggest that 4 Maccabees was written outside of Palestine by an unknown author in the period 63 B.C.–A.D. 70. Although we do not know the author's name, his work conjures up a vivid picture of the man—devotee of the Law of his people, theologian of considerable depth, philosopher and rhetorician in the Greek style, impassioned and imaginative narrator.

As to the date of 4 Maccabees, almost every generation between the time of Pompey (around 63 B.C.) and the Emperor Hadrian (around A.D. 120) has been proposed. In the Talmud, rabbinic accounts of martyrdoms, somewhat similar in form to the story related in 4 Maccabees, reflect the period of the persecution of Jews under Hadrian. Aside from the rather fragile evidence mentioned earlier that the Temple still appears to be standing, it is barely conceivable that, with its eloquent advocacy of the supremacy of the Jewish Law to

---

[1] See further A. Dupont-Sommer, *Le Quatrième Livre des Machabées*, p. 58.

[2] H. G. A. Ewald, *Geschichte des Volkes Israel* (Göttingen, 1864–68) vol. 4, p. 633.

[3] R. B. Townshend, "The Fourth Book of Maccabees," *APOT*, vol. 2, pp. 653–85.

[4] See M. Hengel, *Judaism and Hellenism: Studies in their Encounter in Palestine During the Early Hellenistic Period*, trans. J. Bowden (Philadelphia and London, 1974). Also, J. N. Sevenster, *Do You Know Greek?* (Leiden, 1968) p. 177.

the ethical systems of the pagan world and of the invincible power of Jewish faith and religion against all tyrannical attempts at suppression, 4 Maccabees could have been written after the Hadrianic persecution, when the Jews stood apart *contra mundum*, as it were. Accordingly, A. Dupont-Sommer assigns 4 Maccabees to the short period of relative quiet (A.D. 117–118) between the Jewish war at the close of Trajan's reign and the persecutions under his successor, Hadrian.[5] On the other hand, M. Hadas favors the reign of Caligula (A.D. 37–41), when the storm clouds of persecution were also gathering thickly. But it is not necessary to look for an historical juncture when persecution or the imminent threat of it must have given rise to the considerations that appear in 4 Maccabees.[6] Definitive indications of the author's, or readers', or hearers' situation vis-à-vis persecution or the absence of it are lacking from the work, and the theme of 4 Maccabees is not after all religious persecution as such. Rather does the writer offer a philosophical disquisition on the victorious strength of the devout reason, which would have been relevant and meaningful, at least to Jews of the Diaspora, almost anytime between Pompey and Hadrian, and for illustrative materials he draws upon what he clearly takes to be the classic martyrdoms under Antiochus Epiphanes in the early days of the Maccabean revolt.

In suggesting a date between A.D. 18 and 55, E. Bickermann follows a quite different line of argument and moves us on to rather firmer ground. There occur in 4 Maccabees words like *thrēskeia* = "religion" and *nomikos* (for the earlier *grammateus*, see 4Mac 5:4 and cf. 2Mac 6:18) = "expert in the law," which became fashionable only from the time of Augustus on. But more important, whereas 2 Maccabees speaks of Heliodorus, minister of Seleucus IV, as taking possession of the Temple treasures and describes him as *stratēgos* of Coelesyria and Phoenicia (2Mac 3:5), 4 Maccabees replaces this Heliodorus with Apollonius, governor of Syria and styles him *stratēgos* of "Syria, Phoenicia, and Silicia" (4:2). This change can best be explained by assuming that an author like ours would naturally have employed the nomenclature obtaining under the conditions of the Roman imperial administration *in his own time*, when it appears that Syria and Silicia formed united parts of a single territory, and from Galatians 1:21, an inscription of A.D. 86, and a Roman agricultural writer by the name of Columella, it can be inferred that Syria-Silicia did in fact once constitute one province. Two passages in the *Annals* of the Roman historian Tacitus (2. 58; 13. 8) point to approximately A.D. 19–54 as the period during which Syria-Silicia made up one region for Roman administrative purposes, and Bickermann's view that 4 Maccabees falls somewhere within this period must be deemed a very plausible hypothesis.[7] But it is quite unjustified to go beyond this and maintain that, since there is no allusion at all to the persecution of Caligula, 4 Maccabees was written before the outbreaks of A.D. 38. As we have seen, reference, or the lack of it, to any particular persecution in a philosophical discourse like 4 Maccabees is a most unsure criterion of dating. Fortunately, the appreciation of such a philosophical work does not depend too largely on our ability to fix its immediate historical background precisely within the narrowest limits.

Provenance

Alexandria in Egypt has sprung naturally to the mind of a number of commentators as the likeliest place of composition. This city had an extremely large colony of Jews who were exposed constantly to the influence of Greek philosophy; it was also the city of Philo, with whose works 4 Maccabees has numerous points of contact. But the choice of Alexandria is based not so much on critical grounds or any specific indication of locality in 4 Maccabees itself as on a feeling for its general suitability. It may indeed tell against Alexandria that there is no reference to or quotation from 4 Maccabees in either Clement of Alexandria or Origen, and, in any case, as J. Freudenthal observed long ago, many Jewish hellenists composed their writings in widely disseminated parts of the Diaspora, far away from

[5] Dupont-Sommer (*Machabées*, pp. 78–85) supports this dating by appeal to certain affinities he detects between 4Mac and other documents of the early second century, notably the Epistle to the Hebrews and the Letters of Ignatius.

[6] M. Hadas, *The Third and Fourth Books of Maccabees*, pp. 95–99.

[7] E. J. Bickermann, "The Date of Fourth Maccabees," *Louis Ginzberg Jubilee Volume* (New York, 1945) English Section, pp. 105–12.

Alexandria; for example, Jason of Cyrene, Paul of Cilicia and Josephus himself.[8] Moreover, E. Norden, a leading expert in matters of Greek literature and language, found in 4 Maccabees an outstanding representative of that flowery, rhetorical "Asianic style" that was associated especially with Asia Minor and eventually blossomed to its fullest extent in the early second century A.D.[9]

If we look away from Egypt to the coastal lands of the northeast Mediterranean, the city that first suggests itself as a possible location for 4 Maccabees is Antioch in Syria, which was, according to Josephus, after Rome and Alexandria, the third city of the ancient world, where Greek rhetoric, and indeed all the arts, certainly did flourish, where there was also a large community of Jews, and where the early Christian movement established its first strong foothold on gentile soil. In later Christian tradition there are in fact certain indications of the existence of a cult of the Maccabean martyrs at Antioch. From the fourth century A.D., Jerome, for instance, testifies (somewhat ambiguously) to the veneration of the tomb of the Maccabees at Modein in Palestine, and is apparently thinking of the heroic leaders of the Maccabean revolt, but he seems to know also of physical relics of the martyrs (those described in 4Mac?) at Antioch. At approximately the same period at Antioch, John Chrysostom, in his *Fourth Homily*, conveys the impression of his preaching by the tomb of the martyrs, and later in the same work alludes to Eleazar and the mother and her seven sons, the very martyrs of 4 Maccabees.

Given the witness of these and other still later traditions to Antioch as the scene of a cult of the martyrs, there would seem to be no likelier home for 4 Maccabees, if we could also accept the view adopted by some recent interpreters, notably Dupont-Sommer and Hadas, that it was actually composed for oral delivery as an address of commemoration of the martyrs.[10] At this point the question of the place of origin of 4 Maccabees is intimately bound up with the question of its form. Our work has of course been variously characterized as a synagogue sermon, a lecture, a genuine commemorative address, or as a fictive discourse.

The main objection to regarding 4 Maccabees as a specimen of synagogue preaching[11] is that a synagogue sermon would almost certainly have been based on a text from scripture,[12] and although our knowledge of the homiletic practices of the synagogues of the Diaspora is very limited indeed, it is surely unlikely that even there a sermon would have begun in the highly philosophical vein of 4 Maccabees. By the same token, since as the work develops philosophical exposition gives way to fervent religious pleading, the classification of 4 Maccabees as a lecture[13] set within "the groves of academe" is no less improbable. We are thus left with two alternatives—a genuine commemorative address (delivered on the site of the martyrdoms at Antioch) or a literary piece of a rhetorical kind cast in the shape of a fictive discourse.

It has been maintained that 4 Maccabees was intended for oral delivery on a special occasion, and that the occasion was in fact the Jewish festival of Ḥanukkah. But the trouble with this assertion is, on the one hand, that, if composed for Ḥanukkah, 4 Maccabees must assuredly have alluded to the heroes of the Maccabean war whom that feast celebrates, which it never does, and, on the other hand, that there is no Jewish tradition that associates the martyrs of 4 Maccabees, Eleazar and the mother and her seven sons, with Ḥanukkah. It is with such considerations in mind that M. Hadas invites us to think of 4 Maccabees as a real address delivered at "an annual commemoration of the martyrs celebrated *at the site,* actual or supposed, of their burial."[14]

In support of this estimate of 4 Maccabees, appeal can be made to several passages which do seem to imply that it was spoken at the tomb of the martyrs on a day of special solemnity,

---

[8] J. Freudenthal, *Die Flavius Josephus beigelegte Schrift über die Herrschaft der Vernunft (IV Makkabäerbuch), eine Predigt aus dem ersten nachchristlichen Jahrhundert* (Breslau, 1869) pp. 112f.

[9] E. Norden, *Die antike Kunstprosa vom VI Jahrhundert v. Chr. bis in die Zeit der Renaissance* (Leipzig, 1923) vol. 1, pp. 416–20.

[10] Dupont-Sommer, *Machabées,* pp. 67–73; Hadas, *Maccabees,* pp. 109–13.

[11] See e.g. Freudenthal, *Josephus,* pp. 4–36.

[12] See e.g. E. Schürer, *History,* div. 2, vol. 3, p. 244.

[13] See Townshend, *APOT.* vol. 2, p. 653.

[14] Hadas, *Maccabees,* pp. 104f.; cf. Cardinal Rampolla de Tindaro, "Martyre et Sépulture des Machabées," *Revue de l'Art Chrétien* 42 (1899) 290–305; Dupont-Sommer, *Machabées,* pp. 67–73.

especially 1:10, "I might indeed eulogize for their virtues those men who *at this season of the year* died together with their mother for goodness' sake," and 3:19, "But the season now summons us to expound the theme of the temperate reason" (although this latter may as well be translated, "But we have now reached the point in our discourse at which we are summoned to expound . . ."). Also, according to Dupont-Sommer,[15] the exclamation of 18:20, "Ah! bitter was the day and yet not bitter," evokes the particular day of commemoration of the martyrs, just as the mention of their tomb and epitaph in 17:8–10 suggests that the panegyric of 4 Maccabees was pronounced at the very site where they were buried.

However, only a pedantry quite foreign to the imaginative procedures of a rhetorician like our author would insist on the basis of 18:20 and 17:8–10 that he just *had* to be speaking on *the* day of commemoration at the actual tomb of the martyrs. None of the passages referred to in the foregoing paragraph are incompatible with the possibility of a set written piece, composed at a time of year traditionally associated with the death of the martyrs, in the form of a fictive discourse in which the author projects himself on to the rostrum, so to speak, in good rhetorical fashion, and confronts his readers directly. E. Norden draws attention to an essay in Cicero's *Paradoxa* in which he talks of "this speech," whereas he had already made it clear in the preface that he was *writing* late at night and was indeed choosing to do so in the form of direct speech.[16]

Besides, it may be asked whether the relatively wordy speeches placed on the lips of Eleazar, the sons, and, finally, the mother would have been natural in a spoken address. Again, if our author had delivered his panegyric at the very scene of the martyrdoms, by the tomb of the martyrs, would a rhetorician of his skill have lost the opportunity to make that movingly plain to his audience at 5:1 with words like "And so the tyrant Antiochus took his seat on this very spot where we are now gathered"? Instead he describes the location of the martyrdoms very vaguely indeed ("And so the tyrant Antiochus took his seat with his counselors on a certain high place" 5:1), so vaguely that the reader is given to think from what has gone before that Jerusalem may indeed be the setting for the martyr deaths. The possibility, therefore, that 4 Maccabees was in fact composed as a fictive discourse cannot be lightly dismissed.

Certain extrinsic factors also militate against the notion that 4 Maccabees was an address actually delivered on the site of the martyrs' burial. The Law expressly forbade contact with the dead (Lev 21:1–5, 10f.; Num 6:6–9; 19:11–13; Deut 18:9–12, 26:14), and the attitude of Jewish tradition toward anything resembling a cult of the dead is completely negative. Consequently, in order to regard 4 Maccabees as a commemorative speech at the martyrs' tomb in Antioch, we would have to think, as Hadas clearly recognizes,[17] of a thoroughly hellenized Jewish community in which hellenistic custom and usage in respect of the annual commemoration of heroes had altogether overcome natural Jewish reserve. Again, later Christian veneration of the Maccabean martyrs provides no guarantee of the existence of an earlier Jewish cult in the period of 4 Maccabees, with which the Christian commemoration stood in direct continuity.[18]

---

[15] Dupont-Sommer, *Machabées*, p. 68.

[16] Norden, *Kunstprosa*, vol. 1, p. 416. Recently J. C. H. Lebram has classified 4Mac as in form a philosophical diatribe. After a brief philosophical and then historical exordium, the second and much the larger part of the work from ch. 5 on removes the account of the martyrs from the sphere of a history of the Maccabees and instead incorporates it in a funeral oration of the type spoken at Athens by Hyperides, Demosthenes, Isocrates, and others. The rhetorical schools continued to teach the literary techniques involved in the funeral oration. The circumstances of the Jews in the Maccabean age, resistance to tyranny, the struggle for the Law and freedom, and belief in the immortality of the martyrs all lent themselves readily to literary treatment of this kind. See Lebram, "Die literarische Form des vierten Makkabäerbuches," *VC* 28 (1974) 81–96.

[17] Hadas, *Maccabees*, p. 105.

[18] Ibid., p. 109. "It is natural to assume," says Hadas, "that the Christian commemoration of these martyrs was a continuation of a Jewish institution." In a recent article, "The Maccabean Martyrs," *VC* 28 (1974) 97–113, M. Schatkin argues on the ground of evidence both internal and external, following Cardinal Rampolla, that the martyrs were executed, buried, and venerated in Antioch. However, even if we accepted all her arguments, and the arguments from the internal evidence of 2Mac and 4Mac are not all that convincing, the fact remains that the author of 4Mac is not necessarily to be associated with Antioch. Schatkin herself observes that "some ancient writers, *including the unknown author of 4 Mac*, assumed that the executions took place at Jerusalem" (italics mine; note the apparent conflict between 4Mac 18:5 and 1Mac 3:37).

These considerations or reservations both about the form of our work and the actuality of a Jewish martyr cult in the first half of the first century A.D. considerably weaken the case for associating it with the tomb of the martyrs in Antioch. It may be best to follow E. Norden[19] in leaving the question of a home for 4 Maccabees much more open, contemplating only some possible location in the coastal lands of Asia Minor. Largely because of the numerous sea metaphors in the book, A. Kahana[20] conjectures one of the Aegean islands as a home for it, but the conjecture need not be taken too seriously, since almost anyone in the regions of the eastern Mediterranean could have indulged in sea metaphors, and, in any case, there are just as many metaphors of besieged cities, the land, and so on.

Historical importance

The only complete Jewish work of its kind that has survived to us, 4 Maccabees is intrinsically of great historical value. Different in form and scope from anything that men of somewhat similar background and outlook, like Philo of Alexandria and Josephus, have given us, 4 Maccabees provides us with a particularly fascinating insight into the thought world of a hellenized Jew of the Diaspora in the first century of our era. Through 4 Maccabees we may appreciate his mastery of the Greek rhetorician's craft, his profound knowledge of Greek philosophical principles and his use of them to defend and illumine the sovereignty of the Law and the devout reason's control over the passions. But, as a source book of information on the external history of the writer's own time and place or of the early years of the Maccabean wars to which the martyrdoms he describes purport to belong, 4 Maccabees is of little value.

Our author, of course, is no historian. His aim is not to notify his readers as accurately as possible concerning long-past events of the Maccabean struggle. Rather does he seek, through all the rhetorical powers he can muster, to let the stories he tells kindle the imagination of his readers, to move them to the depths in mind and heart, to persuade them to accept the supremacy of devout reason. The basic materials for his martyrdom stories were most probably derived from the tradition embedded in 2 Maccabees, although our author has patently stretched them and adorned them at will to suit his own philosophical and theological purposes, particularly in the speeches he has placed on the lips of the dying martyrs. Whether these stories have a foundation in genuine historical fact is an open question. If we have no means of proving their historicity, neither should we reject them out of hand as completely legendary. Perhaps a generation acquainted with the barbarities of Auschwitz and Buchenwald may be less prone to dismiss as terribly overdrawn and altogether fictional the bizarre and gruesome items in the repeated descriptions of the tortures in 4 Maccabees than the generation for which Townshend wrote in 1913, "The details of the successive tortures are elaborated in a way that shocks modern taste."[21] Nevertheless, beyond reminding us that brave people almost certainly suffered severe torments and died as martyrs for the Jewish faith under Antiochus Epiphanes, 4 Maccabees adds nothing to our knowledge of the Maccabean period.

Theological importance

The writer of 4 Maccabees is a philosopher as well as a theologian. The framework of his thought is Greek, as are his mode of expression and the form of his work. He appears to have a firsthand intimacy with Platonic ideas, perhaps especially, as Hadas observes,[22]

[19] Norden, *Kunstprosa*, vol. 1, p. 419.

[20] A. Kahana, *Hebrew Edition of the Apocrypha* (Tel Aviv, 1956) vol. 2, p. 258.

[21] Townshend, *APOT*, vol. 2, p. 655.

[22] Hadas, *Maccabees*, pp. 116f. It has recently been held that our author in fact drew nothing directly from Plato but was indebted only to the "philosophic *koinē*" or "philosophic commonplaces" of his time and in particular to contemporary Stoic notions. But does one need to set up an either/or in this regard, either Platonic or Stoic? See R. Renehan, "The Greek Philosophic Background of Fourth Maccabees," *Rheinisches Museum für Philologie* 115 (1972) 223–38. The issue of our author's "Platonism" or "Stoicism" is further complicated by the fact that, as Renehan rightly observes (p. 226), the Stoicism of his day was no monolithic structure but left room for considerable variety of opinion. Posidonius, for example, not subscribing to the doctrine that the passions cannot be eradicated. But by

with Plato's *Gorgias,* in which Socrates concludes that the ultimate ideal or the true doctrine is to live and die in the practice alike of justice and of all other virtues. But he is closely acquainted also with the prevalent Stoic philosophy of his own day, and in many passages adopts Stoic language and echoes Stoic views (see e.g. 1:1, 6, 16f., 33; 2:7, 14; 3:11f.; 5:7–13, 19f., 22, 25, 38; 12:13; 13:19; 14:2; 15:4). However, his concern is not to advocate Stoicism or even to advance the knowledge of Greek thought among his readers, who are no doubt already "naturalized" in the Greek philosophical atmosphere. The philosopher in him never in fact overcomes the theologian, loyal to the faith of his fathers. All that he has learned from the Greeks is enlisted in the service of Judaism, to show that the cardinal virtues, self-control, courage, justice, and temperance, indeed the very essence of Greek wisdom, are subsumed under the Law or obedience to it.

Our author's religious priorities are nowhere more graphically illustrated than in the picture he presents of Eleazar in chapter 5. As the Jewish philosopher par excellence (5:4), Eleazar, far from endorsing Stoic principles, indeed opposes them, as when, for example, he insists against Stoicism that reason does not eradicate but only controls or directs the passions (5:23). Again, whereas Stoicism operated with the notion of the equality of sins, Eleazar follows Jewish tradition in distinguishing between light and serious sins (5:19–21). But the real point at issue in Eleazar's confrontation with Antiochus, who is here spokesman for the Stoic viewpoint, is not the gradation of sins.[23] It is rather that the king is quite unable to comprehend what loyalty to the Jewish Law involves. The heart of Eleazar's doctrine is simply that "we must lead our lives in accordance with the divine Law" (5:15) and that "under no circumstances whatever do we ever deem it right to transgress the Law" (5:17). Accordingly, strict faithfulness to the Law's command is the ground of his refusal to partake of swine's flesh or food sacrificed to idols. Antiochus, by contrast, brands this as a senseless scruple, engendered by a "preposterous philosophy" (5:11). For the king the act of eating swine's flesh is no more than the innocent enjoyment of one of nature's good gifts (5:9). For the old Jewish sage it is a matter of the utmost gravity since violation of any commandment, most of all violation in public in the presence of onlookers, constituted contempt for God the giver of the Law and was tantamount to apostasy (5:35–38).

Eleazar, who in 2 Maccabees is not at all recognized as a "philosopher," thus becomes the advocate of our author's own "philosophy" that the truth resides in the *eusebeia,* or piety, which inheres in obedience to the Law of Moses. His "philosophy" is in fact incapsulated in the rather strange and pregnant phrase *ho eusebēs logismos* ("the devout reason," which enables the martyrs to master their natural feelings and desires throughout their fiery ordeal), which appears throughout the work as a recurring refrain and by which he invites not only his fellow Jews but the world at large to see that the sum of human wisdom and all the law of nature is gathered up under fidelity to the Law revealed by God to Israel.

The blend of particularism and universalism, implicit already in the term "the devout reason," accords well with our author's doctrine of God. For him the God who is first and foremost the God of the fathers of Israel (9:24; 12:18) is also the omniscient (1:12; 13:19) creator of the whole world (5:25; 11:5). He it is who fashioned man and implanted in him both his feelings and his reason (2:21f.). By his will alone personages like Antiochus are permitted to enjoy their regal status (12:11). He determines men's eternal destinies (18:5; cf. 12:19), recompensing the righteous martyrs and consigning the wicked to everlasting punishment. In all of this our author is in conformity with the Judaism of his day, and typically Jewish also is his appeal to biblical figures as archetypal models of the heroism of faith, Abraham (14:20; 16:20), Isaac (16:20), Jacob (2:19), Joseph (2:2), Moses (2:17), David (3:6), and Daniel and his companions (16:3, 21).

---

whatever "wing" of Stoicism our author may have been influenced, the truth remains that his philosophy is swallowed up in his Jewish orthodoxy.

[23] Critics are divided on the question of whether in 5:19–21 Eleazar espouses or opposes the Stoic doctrine of the equality of sins. Against Hadas (*Maccabees,* p. 118. See also H. A. Wolfson, *Philo* (Cambridge, 1947) vol. 2, pp. 271f.), Renehan insists that in 5:20 Eleazar is clearly in general agreement with the Stoic teaching (*Rheinisches Museum für Philologie* 115 [1972] pp. 229f. See also R. H. Pfeiffer, *History,* p. 219, n. 23). But for our author the problem of the equality or gradation of sins is subsidiary—his real concern is to show that Antiochus does not regard the eating of swine's flesh *as a sin at all* (5:9) and so stands as a destructive threat to the sovereignty of the Law.

However, in one important respect, at least, our author's knowledge of Greek philosophy has positively affected his religious belief. Like Philo and the author of the Wisdom of Solomon, he subscribes to the idea of the immortality of the soul. The great hope expressed in 4 Maccabees is that the pure and immortal soul might enter into the incorruption of life everlasting (9:22; 14:5f.; 16:13; 17:12; 18:23). His espousal of the Greek doctrine of the immortality of the soul is clear-cut and striking; he consistently omits the passages in his primary source, 2 Maccabees, that testify unreservedly to the Jewish belief in the resurrection of the body (7:9, 11, 14, 22f.). Doctrinally, the most significant contribution of 4 Maccabees is the development of the notion that the suffering and death of the martyred righteous had redemptive efficacy for all Israel and secured God's grace and pardon for his people. Eleazar first expresses the idea in his prayer in 6:28f.: "Be merciful to your people and let our punishment be a satisfaction on their behalf. Make my blood their purification and take my life as a ransom for theirs." Later, we find the same thought: "The tyrant was punished and our land purified, since they became, as it were, a ransom for the sin of our nation. Through the blood of these righteous ones and through the propitiation of their death the divine providence rescued Israel, which had been shamefully treated" (17:21f.).

The idea of vicarious atonement in and through the death of Jesus was of course of central importance in early Christianity, and it appears in many places in the New Testament (e.g. Mk 10:45; Mt 20:28; Heb 9:12; Rom 5; 1Tim 2:6; etc.). But there is no need whatever to suppose that passages like 6:28f. and 17:21f. in 4 Maccabees should be regarded as Christian interpolations. In fact, although the concept of vicarious atonement was by no means normative or widespread in Judaism around the time of Jesus or Paul, it does have roots going far back into the Old Testament and our author was certainly no innovator in this matter. One of the Levitical ordinances for the Day of Atonement is that the goat on which the lot for the Lord fell should be sacrificed and the blood brought into the holy place as a propitiation for the sins of Israel (Lev 16), since, as Lev 17:11 testifies, it is the blood that makes atonement. On a quite different level, the portrayal of the servant of Yahweh in Deutero-Isaiah bears witness to the saving effect for Israel of the suffering and sacrifice of an elect individual or group (see especially Isa 53:5, 10, 11). There is little doubt that the epic struggles of the Jews in the Maccabean wars gave further impetus to reflection not only on the positive value but on the atoning power of suffering and death. At any rate, the idea that the suffering and death of the righteous atoned vicariously for the sins of others is sufficiently well attested in the apocalyptic literature (e.g. TBenj 3:8) and at Qumran (e.g. 1QS 5:6; 8:3f., 10; 9:4) to suggest that it was in the air in the intertestamental period. Add to this its occurrence in less-developed form in 2 Maccabees 7:37f., and we can recognize that the readers of 4 Maccabees would certainly not have regarded the notion of vicarious redemption as a novel doctrine introduced by the author. Accordingly, when in its confessional formulations early Christianity laid great stress on the saving or redemptive efficacy of the death of Jesus, it was picking up and adapting to its own new faith a doctrine that already enjoyed at least a limited currency in Judaism.

Similarly, it is quite unnecessary to suppose that the notion of the Jewish martyrs being "received" after their death by Abraham, Isaac, and Jacob (4Mac 13:17) is an accommodation to the picture of Lazarus in the bosom of Abraham in Luke 16:22f. or that the idea of the patriarchs and martyrs "living unto God" (4Mac 16:25) adumbrates a Christian view of the resurrection of the dead. Such ideas and images arise not by direct borrowing one way or the other between Judaism and primitive Christianity but rather from a common climate of thought and religious imagination shared by both.

In the last analysis our author's chief claim to fame rests not on any pioneering contribution he has made to a particular Jewish doctrine but on the fact that his work affords us a singularly valuable specimen of the way in which a hellenistic Jew of the Diaspora can draw upon Greek philosophical thoughts and modes of expression in the formation of an essentially religious message of enduring relevance and validity. The spur to withstand oppression and tyranny and to win spiritual victory over death itself is loyal obedience to the revealed will of God.

Relation to canonical books

Since our author's innovative genius lies "in his attempt to acclimate Judaism to a hellenized Diaspora, and thus prepare the way for making of it, and of its daughter religion, a universal faith,"[24] it is hardly surprising that his work shows no special indebtedness to any Old Testament book or books. If such men really did help to pave the way for the worldwide spread of Christianity, is there then any trace of the influence of 4 Maccabees on the New Testament? A. Deissmann, in fact, suggested that Paul may have been familiar with 4 Maccabees as a sort of current best seller, and he had in mind specifically the similarity between Paul's witness to the atoning death of Jesus and the testimony of 4 Maccabees to the vicarious atonement wrought through the deaths of the Jewish martyrs.[25] But a similarity in one point of doctrine between two authors is by no means enough to justify a theory of direct borrowing one way or the other, and the most we should assume, as we have already indicated, is that Paul and our author, both hellenistic Jews of the Diaspora, were exposed to the same atmosphere of religious belief.

Relation to apocryphal books

The author of 2 Maccabees refers to his own work as an epitome of the five volumes of Jason of Cyrene. Few critics would deny that 2 and 4 Maccabees stand in some sort of relationship to each other. Both relate the martyr deaths of Eleazar and the mother and her seven sons, and both furnish an historical preamble to their accounts of the martyrdoms. However, whereas in 2 Maccabees the historical preamble is a lengthy and detailed report of the Syrian persecution and the martyrdoms are briefly told in less than two chapters (6:18–7:41), in 4 Maccabees the historical preamble (3:20–4:26) reads like a short résumé of 2 Maccabees, and the martyrdoms, described in the most elaborate detail, occupy fourteen chapters (5–18).

Freudenthal argued that the phenomena presented by the two texts, the similarities and discrepancies between them, are best accounted for by supposing that each author used Jason's history as a basic source and selected and adapted from it what best suited his own intention and design.[26] Heliodorus, mentioned thirteen times in 2 Maccabees, completely disappears from 4 Maccabees and is apparently replaced by Apollonius (4Mac 4:2). This must be due to confusion about the identity of the person referred to by the many pronouns employed in the Jason source. The longer form of the speech of the dying Eleazar in 4 Maccabees 6:26–29 (cf. the short form in 2Mac 6:30) is to be taken as a faithful transcript of the text of Jason. Similarly, while 2 Maccabees 7:41 merely notes quite simply that "after the sons the mother died," 4 Maccabees 17:1 describes her as committing suicide by throwing herself on the flames. This is a piece of information derived from Jason but suppressed by the author of 2 Maccabees because he repudiated suicide as evil. Such is the gist of Freudenthal's argumentation.

The case for 4 Maccabees' use of Jason is not at all convincing.[27] Nothing whatever of Jason's work has survived, and, given the literary devices of the day, it is possible that the claim of the author of 2 Maccabees to be Jason's epitomist is only a fictional piece of propaganda to lend authority to his writing. Freudenthal's thesis that 4 Maccabees depends on Jason's history is unconvincing; it requires us to make of our author much more of a factual reporter fastidious about accurate reproduction of his source than from his work he

[24] Hadas, *Maccabees*, p. 123.

[25] A. Deissmann, "Das vierte Makkabäerbuch," *APAT*, vol. 2, pp. 151f., 160, 174. P. Staples lately conjectured that there is some literary and circumstantial evidence to link the Gk. Maccabee tradition with the NT, albeit, in the light of the Maccabean ideals of Law, Temple, etc., not with Paul and his letters, but with opponents of Paul possibly in Ephesus, Corinth, and elsewhere. In particular, only seven words from 4Mac appear in Luke-Acts, only five in Heb, and only eleven in the Pastoral Epistles. Most of all, the doxology of 4Mac 18:24 turns up in several contexts in the NT, not least in 2Tim 4:18, Heb 13:21, and in a "freer" version in Phil 4:20, Eph 3:21, and 1Tim 1:17, all documents associated with Ephesus. The possibility of the interconnection of 4Mac, Heb, and Ephesus is enhanced if Apollos, who came from Alexandria (home of 4Mac?) and joined the Pauline mission at Ephesus were author of Heb. But the vocabulary overlap of 4Mac with NT documents is certainly not enough to demonstrate literary dependence and the circumstantial evidence is too heavily dependent on guesswork. It is much safer to assume that the various authors were simply exposed to the same climate of religious thought and belief. See also P. Staples, "The Unused Lever? A Study on the Possible Literary Influence of the Greek Maccabean Literature in the New Testament," *The Modern Churchman* 9 (1966) 218–24.

[26] Freudenthal, *Josephus*, pp. 72–90. Deissmann favors the same view, *APAT*, vol. 2, p. 156.

[27] See Dupont-Sommer, *Machabées*, pp. 30f.

really appears to be. In this regard Dupont-Sommer's remark is very much to the point: "The history of temperate reason is certainly more than mere history."[28] The writer of 4 Maccabees' main aim was to move his readers deeply by the pathos of his story, and he was first and foremost a rhetorician of skill and inventiveness and not a recorder of facts. A man like this knew above all how to develop, enlarge, and embellish a story to produce the desired effect upon his readers. If he had at hand the data provided by 2 Maccabees, he certainly did not need a fuller source like Jason's history for the many, many additions he has made to the narrative of the martyrdoms. His own imagination, aided and abetted perhaps by developments of the tale within ongoing oral tradition, would have been quite enough to do the trick. In all likelihood then our author had at his disposal 2 Maccabees and rearranged and reshaped it freely to suit his own taste and purpose. The relative dates of the two works and the obvious parallels in sequence as well as in content, as the list in Townshend[29] clearly demonstrates, offer additional support for this view.

There are certain rather close resemblances in religious thought and outlook between 4 Maccabees and the Wisdom of Solomon: belief in the incorruptibility and immortality of the soul, the everlasting life of the righteous as a life of communion with God (WisSol 3:9; cf. 4Mac 7:19; 9:8; 16:25; 17:18), the notion emanating from Neo-Pythagorean astralism of the immortal souls of the martyrs shining bright like the stars in heaven (WisSol 3:7; cf. 4Mac 17:5). Freudenthal thought that the author of 4 Maccabees not only knew the Wisdom of Solomon but that he had it before him when he wrote. In his view the long passage in 4 Maccabees 5:23f. is a deliberate extension or elaboration of the simple statement in the Wisdom of Solomon 8:7: "The fruits of wisdom's labor are virtues, for she teaches self-control and understanding, righteousness, and courage; and there is nothing in life for men more profitable than these."[30] But there is little or no verbal similarity between the two passages, and in both we are dealing with common Stoic arguments. We can infer no more from the parallel thought of the two passages than that both writers were familiar with Stoic ideas. From other parallels in thought between the two documents (e.g. the immortality of the soul) it is impossible to adduce proof of direct literary connection or dependence of 4 Maccabees on the Wisdom of Solomon. All we are entitled to say is that the authors shared a similar background of religious ideas.

Cultural importance

In 4 Maccabees, as in 2 Maccabees, the story of the martyrdoms is set in the early days of the Maccabean revolt and the persecutor is Antiochus Epiphanes. No traces of 4 Maccabees are discernible, however, in later Jewish tradition, where the story circulated in a wide variety of forms for many centuries. In the rabbinic literature the martyrdoms are assigned to the Hadrianic persecution (see LamR 1:16; b.Git 57b; PR 43:180; SER 30:151), and in some rabbinic accounts the name of the mother, not given in 4 Maccabees or in 2 Maccabees, is Mariam bat Tanhum. In Syriac Christian accounts she is called Shamone and/or Maryam, whereas a Spanish reviser of the *Sefer Josippon* (c. A.D. 953; edited at Constantinople in 1510) named her Hannah, no doubt under the inspiration of the story of Hannah in 1 Samuel 1f., and especially 1 Samuel 2:5 (Hannah's prayer: "The barren woman bears sevenfold, but the mother of many is desolate").

Representations of the martyrdoms in works of art (e.g. the macabre pictures of the fourteenth and fifteenth centuries), poetry, and drama down to modern times are probably dependent on later versions of the story stemming from traditions independent of 4 Maccabees (or 2Mac). The same may be true also of such early iconographic depictions of the martyrdom of the Maccabees as on the Brescia Casket (c. A.D. 370).

It is unquestionably in the sphere of Christian martyrology that 4 Maccabees specifically exerted the most profound and widespread influence, most of all among early Church Fathers both of the East and West, like Gregory Nazianzus and John Chrysostom, Ambrose and Augustine. They not only knew and used 4 Maccabees but almost adopted it as a "Christian"

---

[28] Ibid., p. 31. [Idiomatic translation of the French by J.H.C.]

[29] Townshend, *APOT*, vol. 2, p. 665.

[30] Freudenthal, *Josephus*, pp. 92f.

book insofar as they looked upon the Jewish martyrs as Christian protomartyrs. In his oration on the martyrs, Gregory, for instance, refers to the first of August as the annual day of their commemoration and holds them up as worthy of universal honor, with the reminder (alluding to Heb 11:40) that none of those who were made perfect before Christ reached that point outside of the Christian faith. Indeed, later on in his work he commends them for having lived according to the cross even though they lived before it.[31] Likewise Chrysostom, author of four homilies on the Maccabean martyrs, vividly portrays Christ as the one who draws the aged mother into the contest of the arena of torment. Augustine, for his part, notes clearly (*City of God* 18:36) that it was "on account of the extreme and wonderful suffering of the martyrs told therein" that the books of the Maccabees were taken over and preserved by the Church. Ambrose's *De Jacob et vita beata* is hardly more than a transcript of our book.

Further testimony to the influence of 4 Maccabees in Christian circles is borne by the *Passio ss. Machabaeorum*, a free Latin adaptation of our work belonging possibly to the fourth century A.D. This was probably the Latin text freely paraphrased by Erasmus in his edition of 4 Maccabees, first published at Cologne in 1524 and dedicated to his friend Elias Maraeus, president of the "most honorable college of Maccabees at Cologne." Erasmus was evidently familiar with a shrine of the Maccabean martyrs at Cologne, where Maccabean relics were greatly revered. According to tradition, relics of the martyrs had been transported from Antioch, the place of their burial, to Byzantium by St. Helen, later from Byzantium to Milan by Eustorgius, and finally from Milan to Cologne in 1164 by Reginald, bishop of that city.

Erasmus' interest in 4 Maccabees was assuredly not simply academic. He began his paraphrase in 1517, the very year when Luther nailed his pamphlet against indulgences to the door of the church at Wittenberg. And some six years later the works of the great humanist were submitted to the Spanish Inquisition. No wonder he suffered his own dread of martyrdom. To be sure, he found in the message of 4 Maccabees stimulus, uplift, and encouragement. Erasmus' appeal to 4 Maccabees sums up within itself what has been the supreme cultural importance of the work—not only has it provided materials for the literary and theoretical development of Christian martyrology which became a matter of prominent concern in the religion of Europe, but its "martyr-saints" have been a model and an inspiration to fortitude and perseverance for many under the heel of tyranny and persecution.

SELECT BIBLIOGRAPHY

Indispensable for the student of 4 Maccabees are the following full-scale works, consisting of introductions, translations, and notes:

Charlesworth, *PMR*, pp. 151–53.
Delling, *Bibliographie*, p. 95.

Amir, Y. "Maccabees, Fourth Book of," *Encyclopedia Judaica*. Vol. 11, cols. 661f.
Bickermann, E. J. "The Date of IV Maccabees," *Louis Ginzberg Jubilee Volume*. New York, 1945; English Section, pp. 105–12.
Breitenstein, U. *Beobachtungen zu Sprache, Stil und Gedankengut des Vierten Makkabäerbuches*. Basel, Stuttgart, 1978². (Breitenstein's monograph, which is his 1974 Basel dissertation, appeared after Anderson had completed the above contribution. After examining the vocabulary, syntax, rhetoric, and thought of 4Mac, Breitenstein concludes that the vocabulary of 4Mac is clearly distinguishable from the LXX, and that the author is a rhetorician who lived in the early 2nd cent. A.D. —J.H.C.).

---

[31] For some clear echoes of 4Mac in Gregory's oration, see Townshend, *APOT*, vol. 2, p. 659.

Deissmann, A. "Das vierte Makkabäerbuch," *APAT,* vol. 2, pp. 149–77.

Dupont-Sommer, A. *Le Quatrième Livre des Machabées.* Paris, 1939.

Eissfeldt, O. *The Old Testament: An Introduction.* Trans. P. R. Ackroyd. New York and Evanston, 1965; pp. 583f.

Emmet, C. W. *The Fourth Book of Maccabees.* London, 1918.

Freudenthal, J. *Die Flavius Josephus beigelegte Schrift über die Herrschaft der Vernunft (IV Makkabäerbuch), eine Predigt aus dem ersten nachchristlichen Jahrhundert.* Breslau, 1869.

Hadas, M. *The Third and Fourth Books of Maccabees.* New York, 1953.

Schürer, E. *History.* Div. 2, vol. 3, pp. 244–48.

Townshend, R. B. "The Fourth Book of Maccabees," *APOT,* vol. 2, pp. 653–85.

THE FOURTH BOOK OF MACCABEES

The author's definition of his task

1 1 Highly philosophical is the subject I propose to discuss, namely, whether devout
reason is absolute master of the passions,[a] and I would strictly counsel you to
2 give earnest attention to my philosophical exposition.[b] •The subject is an
indispensable branch of knowledge but it also includes a eulogy of the greatest of
3 virtues,[c] by which I mean of course prudence. •If reason is shown to be master
4 of the passions that hinder temperance, namely gluttony and lust, •it is also
demonstrated that it is lord of the passions that impede justice, such as malice,
and over the passions that impede courage, such as rage and fear and pain.[d]
5 How then, some might ask, if reason is master of the passions, does it not control 2:24
6 forgetfulness and ignorance? The question is absurd. •It is not over its own
inherent defects that reason is master but over the passions that are opposed to
justice and courage and temperance, and master over these not in such a way as
to eradicate them but to keep men from surrendering to them.[e]
7 I could prove to you from many and varied sources that reason is absolute
8 master of the passions, •but far the best example I could furnish is the heroism
of those who died for virtue's sake, namely Eleazar and the seven brothers and
9 their mother.[f] •Taking no account at all of the sufferings that brought them to
10 their death, they all proved that reason is lord of the passions. •I might indeed
eulogize for their virtues those men who at this season of the year[g] died together
with their mother for goodness' sake, but I would rather congratulate them on the
11 distinctions they have attained. •Not only was all mankind stirred to wonder by
their courage and fortitude, but even their own torturers, and so they became
responsible for the downfall of the tyranny which beset our nation, overcoming
the tyrant by their fortitude so that through them their own land was purified.[h]
12 But I shall have opportunity presently to speak on this matter. Meanwhile, I shall

1 a. The author right away defines the aim and scope of his work: It is primarily philosophical. Accordingly, the book is not necessarily to be regarded as a "crisis document," produced inevitably in a time of rampant religious persecution. The Gk. word for "reason" (*logismos*) normally denotes "common arithmetic," but here, in accordance with Stoic usage, refers to the human reason or the rational will. "Devout reason" or "religious reason" (M. Hadas, *The Third and Fourth Books of Maccabees*, p. 144) is probably a more appropriate rendering of *eusebēs logismos* than "inspired reason" (R. B. Townshend, "The Fourth Book of Maccabees," APOT, vol. 2, p. 666). Perhaps the best commentary on the meaning of the words for our author is his own stress on reason's compatibility with the Law of God (2:1–23). The translation "passions" is here preferred to "emotions" (Hadas, *Maccabees*), although "passions" has a broader connotation than is usual with us today.

b. Gk. lit. = "philosophy," but the writer clearly has in view his own particular philosophical treatment of the theme, hence the translation "my philosophical exposition."

c. The author here affirms the *theoretical* importance of his subject, but he has in view at the same time its *practical* significance, since he will go on to praise prudence as acted out in the martyr

deaths of Eleazar and the mother and her seven sons (3:20–17:6).

d. The four cardinal Platonic virtues, inherited by the Stoics, are taken over also by our author: prudence, temperance, justice, and courage.

e. The text of vss. 3–6 presents some difficulties. The hypothetical nature of the protasis, introduced by the Gk. *ei ara* in vs. 3, is scarcely appropriate. Again "lust" is a general category, "gluttony" only a particular manifestation of it. Finally 2:24 and 3:1 are almost identical with vss. 5f. here. Possibly the earliest part of the manuscript had become mutilated and a later editor (who worked before Syr., which is represented in the above translation) filled in the gaps with doublets from later parts of the work (see Hadas, *Maccabees*, p. 145).

f. Here Eleazar is linked with the mother and seven sons as though all the martyrdoms together constituted but a single episode, in contrast with 2Mac 6:18–31, where Eleazar's martyrdom is separate.

g. The phrase has been taken to indicate that the book was composed for delivery on a festival day of commemoration.

h. Clearly vs. 11 refers to the Maccabean revolt led by Judas Maccabeus and his brothers and culminating at the close of its first phase in the cleansing and rededication of the Temple.

begin, as I am accustomed to do, with the general theory, and then I shall turn to their story, giving glory[i] to God the all-wise.

The supremacy of reason

13 The subject of discussion then is whether reason is absolute master of the passions.
14 But we have to define what reason is and what passion is, how many forms of
15 passion there are, and whether reason is lord over them all. •Reason, I suggest,
16 is the mind making a deliberate choice of the life of wisdom. •Wisdom, I submit,
17 is knowledge of things divine and human, and of their causes.[j] •And this wisdom,
    I assume, is the culture we acquire from the Law, through which we learn the
18 things of God reverently and the things of men to our worldly advantage. •The
19 forms of wisdom consist of prudence, justice, courage, and temperance. •Of all
    these prudence is the most authoritative, for it is through it that reason controls
20 the passions. •Of the passions, the two all-embracing kinds are pleasure and pain,
21 and each of these inheres in the body as well as the soul. •A large retinue of
22 passions attends upon both pleasure and pain. •Before pleasure comes desire, and
23 after pleasure comes joy. •Before pain comes fear, and after pain comes sorrow.
24 Anger is a passion involving both pleasure and pain, if one reflects on how it
25 has touched him.[k] •Included under pleasure also is the malicious moral temper
26 which expresses itself in the most widely varied ways of all the passions, •those
    of the soul being pretentiousness and avarice and seeking the limelight and
27 contentiousness and backbiting, •those of the body being a voracious appetite for
28 all kinds of food[l] and gluttony and gormandizing in private. •Now pleasure and
    pain being, as it were, two branches stemming from body and soul, there are
29 many offshoots of these passions.[m] •Each of these reason, the master gardener,
    purges thoroughly and prunes and binds up and waters and irrigates all around,[n]
30 and so domesticates the wild undergrowth of inclinations and passions.[o] •For
    reason is the guide of the virtues and the supreme master of the passions.
31 Observe in the first place how, in regard to the things that hinder temperance,
    reason is complete master of the passions. Temperance, as I understand it, is
32 control over desires, •and of desires some relate to the soul and others to the
33 body, over both of which reason obviously holds sway. •When we are attracted
    to forbidden foods, how do we come to reject the pleasures to be gained from
    them?[p] Is it not because reason has the power to control the appetites? I believe
34 it is. •Accordingly, when we crave seafood or fowl or the meat of four-legged
    beasts or any sort of food at all that is forbidden to us under the Law, it is through
35 the mastery of reason that we abstain. •For the proclivities of our appetites are
    restrained and held in check by the prudent mind, and all the motions of the body
    are muzzled by reason.

i. This Heb. expression occurs only here in 4Mac and was probably culled from the LXX.

j. Corresponds exactly to the Stoic definition given in Cicero's *Tusculan Disputations*, 4.25.37. The writer of 4Mac shares with pagan philosophers the notion that wisdom does have a religious dimension, although in vs. 17 his own distinctive Jewish stance comes into view.

k. The text of the last part of the vs. is dubious. A reading *hote* = "when" for *hoti* = "that," "how." The Gk. (translated above as "how it has touched him") lit. = "that it has befallen him" or "encountered him," and it seems that something is wanting to complete the sense.

l. An interesting anticipation of 6:15, where Eleazar is offered cooked meats, but of course refuses (6:16–19).

m. The metaphor about the retinue or train of attendants in vs. 21 (followed by a number of

philosophical commonplaces in vss. 22–27) now gives way to a metaphor from plant or tree life.

n. The word translated "irrigates" (*metacheōn*) lit. = "pours from one vessel into another," but possibly denotes here allowing the water to flow from the main channel along little furrows so as to irrigate thoroughly a number of small plots.

o. Over against the standard Stoic view that reason eradicates the passions altogether, our author shares the rabbinic view that the "passions" are not inherently evil and need only to be controlled or tamed by reason (see Hadas, *Maccabees*, p. 151).

p. Another anticipation of 6:15–19. Just as the author will go on to illustrate his philosophical principles by concrete examples, so here already and in vss. 34f. he has recourse to practical considerations.

The Law's compatibility with reason

1 **2** What wonder, then, if the desires of the soul for union with beauty are deprived
2 of their force? •It is on these very grounds that the temperate Joseph is praised,
because through his own rational faculty he gained mastery over his sensuality.
3 Though a young man at the prime of his sexual desire, he quenched the burning   Gen 39:7–12
4 ardor of his passions. •And not only over the fiery passion of sexual desire does
5 reason evidently exercise control, but over all desire. •For the Law says, *You*   Ex 20:17
6 *shall not covet your neighbor's wife or anything that is your neighbor's.* •Surely
then, since the Law tells us not to covet, I should the much more readily persuade
you that reason has the power to control the desires.
7   It has that power, indeed, over the passions which hinder justice. •For how else
could a man who habitually gormandizes in private or is gluttonous or a drunkard
be taught to change his ways if reason were not obviously lord over the passions?
8 As soon as a man conducts himself according to the Law, then even if he be
avaricious, he reverses his own natural tendency and lends to the needy without
9 interest, canceling the debt with the coming of the seven-year period.ᵃ •And if a   Deut 15:9; 23:20
man be niggardly, he is brought under the rule of the Law through reason, so that   Ex 22:24
                                                                                      Lev 25:36–53
he neither gleans over the stubble in his harvest fields nor picks the last grapes
from his vines.
    And in other cases also we can perceive that reason is master of the passions.
10 For the Lawᵇ takes precedence over benevolence to parents and will not betray
11 virtue for their sake; •it takes precedence over love for a wife and reproves her
12 for transgression; •it overrules love for children and punishes them for wrongdoing;
13 and it exercises its authority over intimate relationships with friends and rebukes
14 them for evil. •Nor should you think it paradoxical that reason is able through the   Deut 20:19
Law to master enmity so that a man will not cut down the trees in his enemy's   Ex 23:4f.
orchard and will save the property of his adversary from marauders and raise up
his beast when it has fallen.ᶜ
15   Reason is also obviously in control of the more aggressive passions, ambition,
16 vanity, false pretension, pride, and backbiting. •All these malicious passions the
temperate mind rejects, as it does even with anger, since over it too it has the
17 mastery. •When Moses grew angry with Dathan and Abiram, instead of venting   Num 16:23–30
18 his anger upon them he moderated it by reason.ᵈ •For the temperate mind, as I
have said, has the power to triumph over the passions, to transform some of them
19 and quell others. •How else did our surpassingly wise father Jacob blame Simeon   Gen 34
and Levi and their friends for slaughtering the whole tribe of the Shechemites
20 without any appeal to reason, and declare, *Accursed be their rage?* •Surely if   Gen 49:7
21 reason could not control anger, he would not have spoken in this way. •When
22 God fashioned man, he implanted in him his passions and inclinations,ᵉ •and at

---

2 a. This would apply only within Judaism among Jews since the Law allowed interest to be taken from gentiles (Ex 22:24; Lev 25:36–53; Deut 23:20). The text presents some difficulties and it is not clear whether it is the whole debt or only the interest that is to be canceled. Our translation follows the text represented by S and V. The reading of A at the close of the vs. (supported by Syr.) may be translated, "So he reckons by the weeks and forgives part of what is due to him." But the words "part of" need to be supplied in order to make sense of this reading, and in the light of Deut 15:1–18 it is likely that the reading of S and V should be followed.

b. In the conjunction of vs. 10 with vs. 9 the author now simply equates the Law with reason.

c. The Gk. words translated "property," "marauders" and "his beast" are broad and general

terms equivalent, respectively, to "the things," "those who destroy" and "things that have fallen," and so their specific meaning is not at once obvious. Hadas (*Maccabees,* p. 155), probably correctly, finds an allusion to Ex 23:4f., and translates the latter part of vs. 14 thus: "One must save cattle of a personal enemy, and help raise up his beast if it has fallen."

d. An observation by our author, nowhere explicitly expressed in Scripture, although Moses became the familiar type of the "mild" man.

e. Our author, like Philo and the rabbis, believes that the passions are God-given. Hence, for him reason is conceived as controlling the passions (3:2), not extirpating them as with the Stoics. But the language and ideas of vss. 22f. are otherwise typically Stoic, e.g. the notion of the kingship of the sage.

the same time enthroned the intellect amid the senses as the sacred guide over
23 all.[f] •To the intellect he gave the Law, and if a man lives his life by the Law he
shall reign over a kingdom that is temperate and just and good and brave.

Reason's conquest of the passions, as in King David

24 How is it then, someone may object, that if reason is master over the passions, 1:5
it does not control forgetfulness and ignorance?

1 **3** The argument is absolutely ludicrous, for reason is clearly not sovereign over
2 its own inherent inclinations but over those of the body.[a] •For instance, none of
you can eradicate desire, but reason can ensure that you do not become enslaved
3 to desire. •Anger none of you can eradicate from his soul, but reason can help
4 you resist anger. •None of you can eradicate malice, but reason may be your ally
5 in not allowing you to be overwhelmed by malice. •For reason is not the uprooter
of the passions but their antagonist.
6 This becomes even clearer, in fact, when we consider the case of King David's
7 thirst.[b] •When David had been fighting against the Philistines throughout the entire 2Sam 23:13–17
day and in company with the soldiers of his own people had killed many of them, 1Chr 11:15–19
8 with the evening he came to the royal tent all perspiring and very tired, and
9 around it was encamped the whole army of our ancestors. •While all the rest took
10 to dining, •the king, parched with thirst as he was and though he had plentiful
11 springs of water, was unable to slake his thirst from them. •An unreasonable
desire for the water in the enemy's territory racked him and inflamed him and
12 unnerved him and burned him up. •When his bodyguard grumbled at the king's
desire, two stalwart young soldiers who respected it equipped themselves fully
13 with armor and, taking a pitcher, scaled the enemy's ramparts. •Escaping the
notice of the sentries at the gates, they went through the whole enemy encampment
14 on the search. •On finding the spring, they boldly drew from it and carried the
15 drink to the king. •But he, though still burning with thirst, considered that a drink
reckoned as equivalent to blood presented a dreadful danger to his soul.
16 Accordingly, he set reason against desire and poured out the drink as a libation
17 to God. •For the temperate mind is able to conquer the constraints of the passions
18 and to quench the flames of frenzied desire, •to overcome the pains of the body,[c]
however extreme, and through the nobility of reason to reject contemptuously the
whole domination of the passions.

---

f. Since the Gk. preposition *dia* may mean
"among" or "in the midst of" it is not necessary
to take it as meaning here "through the agency of
the senses" and to think of it as a later scholarly
gloss on the part of someone familiar with the
Stoic doctrine that nothing reaches the intellect
except through the senses (cf. Hadas, *Maccabees*,
pp. 156f.).

3 a. The appropriateness of the reading of the
MSS, here translated "over those of the body,"
has been called in question, since in vss. 3–5 it is
passions of the soul, anger and malice, that are
mentioned, and not passions of the body. Accordingly, some commentators (see Hadas, *Maccabees*,
p. 157) reject the reading, and, regarding 1:5f. as
a doublet of what initially belonged here in the
text, transfer it to this point and read "but of those
contrary to justice, courage, temperance, and prudence; and of these it is master not in order to
destroy them, but in order not to yield to them."
But this is hardly necessary. In setting the scene

in 3:1 the writer no doubt has in view the coming
story of David, and David's thirst may be described
as a mingled passion of body and soul. In the light
of his stress on the physical side of David's thirst
in 3:8–10 he may well have written "over those
of the body" in 3:1 while at the same time alluding
to passions of the soul in 3:3–5.

b. The story that follows deviates in detail from
the Heb. account in 2Sam 23:13–17 and 1Chr
11:15–19, e.g. there three chieftains and not, as
here, two soldiers undertake the exploit; there the
spring is at Bethlehem and not, as here, in enemy
territory. Our author seems to have been familiar
with the LXX here and was probably acquainted
also with Midrashic expansions of the story. The
LXX expression in 2Sam 23:15, "David desired,"
could have given him a springboard for his own
interpretation.

c. An anticipatory hint of the main subject matter
of the book to come, the heroic resistance of the
martyred righteous to torture and suffering.

The divine punishment of Apollonius, governor of Syria, in the Temple

19   But the season[d] now summons us to expound the theme of the temperate reason.
20 When our fathers were enjoying profound peace through their observance of the
      Law and were faring so well that even the king of Asia, Seleucus Nicanor,[e] set
21 moneys aside for their Temple service and recognized their polity,[f] •just then   Ex 30:12
      certain men took repressive measures against the communal harmony and implicated   2Chr 24:6
      us in various disasters.

1   **4** A certain Simon set himself up as political opponent of Onias, a man of the
      highest integrity, who was then high priest and held the office for life,[a] but when,
      in spite of spreading all sorts of slander, he failed to harm him in the eyes of the
2   people, he went off into exile with a view to betraying his country. •He then
      made his way to Apollonius, governor of Syria, Phoenicia, and Silicia, and said,
3   "Sympathetic as I am to the king's interests, I am here to inform you that
      thousands upon thousands of private deposits are stored in the treasury at Jerusalem
      in which the Temple holds no share, and so they rightfully belong to King
4   Seleucus." •Apollonius, having checked out the details of the matter, praised   2Mac 3:7–34
      Simon for protecting the king's interest and went up to Seleucus and disclosed
5   the fact of these large funds. •Armed with full authority to deal with the business,
      he proceeded quickly to our country with the accursed Simon and a very powerful
6   army.[b] •He declared he had come at the king's command to take over the private
7   deposits in the treasury. •Our people complained and protested at the announcement,
      reckoning that it was outrageous for those who had entrusted their deposits to the
      Temple treasury to be deprived of them, and they did all they could to prevent
8,9 him. •But Apollonius, with threats, made his way to the Temple. •Then the priests
      and the women and children made supplication to God in the Temple to defend
10 his holy place, which was being desecrated; •and when Apollonius, with his armed
      soldiery, marched up to seize the moneys, angels on horseback appeared from   3Mac 6:18
11 heaven with flashing armor[c] and filled them with fear and trembling. •At that
      Apollonius fell down half dead in the court of the gentiles, and he stretched out
      his hands to heaven and with tears entreated the Hebrews to pray for him and
12 propitiate the heavenly host. •He had so sinned, he said, as to merit death, but if
      only he were spared he would sing before all men praises to the blessedness of
13 the holy place. •Moved by these words, despite his anxiety[d] lest King Seleucus

---

d. Regarded by some commentators as another
indication that 4Mac was designed for a festival of
commemoration.
    e. Seleucus Nicanor is an egregious error, and
V reads, "Seleucus, descendent of Nicanor." The
king intended here is Seleucus IV Philopator, who
was the sixth successor of Seleucus Nicanor and
son of Antiochus III the Great and older brother of
his own successor, Antiochus IV Epiphanes.
    f. "Set moneys aside," that is, out of his own
state revenues. This is a more likely meaning of
the Gk. than the suggested alternative "sanctioned
the exaction of the Temple tax" (the annual half-
shekel tax paid by Jews to the priests: Ex 30:12;
2Chr 24:6). "Their polity" is the theocratic constitution under which the high priest was ruler also
of their secular affairs.

4 a. Life tenure was a feature of the hereditary
office of high priest, and Onias is not here being
marked off as singular by the words "held the
office for life." However, the added comment does
point ahead to the outrage of Antiochus' deposition
of Onias in 4:16. In vs. 1, the Gk. phrase rendered
"a man of the highest integrity," lit. = "beautiful

and good," the standard Gk. description of the
"true gentleman."
    b. According to 2Mac 3:7–34, Seleucus' com-
mander on this expedition was Heliodorus, not
Apollonius. The preamble to the desecration of the
Temple is told at much greater length in 2Mac 3:7–
23 than here.
    c. The author of 4Mac does not at this point
reveal the theological subtlety of 3Mac 6:18, where
the deliverance is accomplished by two angels who
are "visible to all *except* the Jews." See 3Mac
6:18.
    d. This translation follows the suggested emen-
dation adopted by Hadas (*Maccabees*, p. 165), that
is the Gk. *kai* = "and" for *kaiper* = "although."
If we accept the reading of the manuscripts (*kaiper*
= "although"), the verse is to be translated rather
differently, but possibly less convincingly, because
the thought is somewhat too subtle: "Moved by
these words, Onias, the high priest, although most
scrupulous in other cases, made intercession for
him lest King Seleucus should possibly think that
Apollonius had been overthrown by a human device
and not by divine justice" (Townshend, *APOT*,
vol. 2, p. 671).

should think that Apollonius was overthrown by human design and not by divine
14 justice, Onias the high priest prayed for him. •And after his miraculous deliverance,
Apollonius went off to reveal to the king what had happened to him.

Antiochus' savage measures against the Jews

15 On the death of King Seleucus, his son[e] Antiochus Epiphanes. an arrogant and
16 terrible man, succeeded to the rule. •He deposed Onias from the high priesthood
17 and appointed his brother Jason as high priest •on his agreeing to pay him annually
three thousand, six hundred, and sixty talents[f] if he would confer the office on   2Mac 4:8–10
18 him. •So Antiochus commissioned Jason to serve as high priest and rule over the
19 people. •In total disregard for the Law, Jason changed the nation's whole mode
20 of life and its polity; •not only did he lay out a gymnasium on the citadel[g] of our   2Mac 4:12
21 native land but he also rescinded the service of the Temple. •At this the divine
22 justice was angered and brought Antiochus himself to war against them. •When
he was at war with Ptolemy in Egypt[h] and heard that the people of Jerusalem took   2Mac 4:18–6:17
the greatest delight in a widespread rumor about his death, he promptly marched
23 against them. •And. when he had ravaged them he issued a decree to the effect
24 that all who were seen to conform to their ancestral Law must die. •And when
by his decrees he failed completely to destroy our people's respect for the Law,
25 and observed that all his threats and penalties were entirely discounted, •even to
the extent that women who knew in advance what was in store for them were
hurled headlong from the walls with their infants because they had their children
26 circumcised; •when, I say, his decrees were despised by the people, he himself
sought to force each individual in the nation under torture to partake of unclean
food and to abjure Judaism.[i]

Antiochus' encounter with Eleazar

1 **5** And so the tyrant Antiochus took his seat with his counselors on a certain high
2 place,[a] with his fully armed troops mustered around him, •and he ordered his
guards to drag along every single one of the Hebrews and compel them to eat
3 swine's flesh and food sacrificed to idols. •Whoever refused to eat the defiled
4 food was to be tortured and put to death. •Many were violently snatched away
and the first of the herd to be brought before Antiochus was a man called Eleazar,   2Mac 6:18–31
of priestly stock, expert in the Law and advanced in age, and known to many of
5 the tyrant's entourage for his philosophy.[b] •When Antiochus saw him, he said,[c]
6 "Before I have the tortures begun on you, old man, I would advise you to eat

e. A mistake of the author's attested in all
manuscripts. Antiochus IV was the younger *brother*
of Seleucus IV Philopator.

f. In 2Mac the total sum is only 590 talents
(2Mac 4:8f.).

g. Cf. 2Mac 4:12, which has it correctly, "*under*
the citadel."

h. Antiochus conducted several campaigns against
Egypt, and our author has compressed into vss.
22–26 what is told at great length and in detail in
2Mac 4:18–6:17.

i. The eating of unclean food, as the terminology
here makes clear, was not simply a matter of
"desire" or "indulgence" but a symbol of apostasy
and recognition of the validity of a heathen cult.

5 a. A vague notice of location, and there is
nothing in either 2Mac or 4Mac to indicate that it
was anywhere else than in Jerusalem, although the
early Church appears to have regarded Antioch as
the scene, and a basilica was erected there in honor
of the martyrs. See further, Introduction, n. 18.

b. According to 2Mac 6:18–31, Antiochus personally had no confrontation with Eleazar but was
present only at the martyrdom of the seven brothers
(7:12). Eleazar is a very common name, and the
impression one has from the different descriptions
of Eleazar in 2Mac and 4Mac and elsewhere, as
also from 6:5, is that the name had become a
legendary feature of numerous martyr hero stories.
2Mac 6:18 calls Eleazar a "scribe" and 6:24 makes
him "ninety years of age." If with V and other
MSS we accept at the close of vs. 5, instead of
the other reading, "known to many of the tyrant's
entourage for his age" (which seems tautologous),
"known for his philosophy," then Eleazar is here
described as "priest" and "philosopher," the latter
being particularly congenial to the author's purpose.

c. In accordance with the convention of historians from Thucydides on, the author puts on the
lips of one of his principal characters a speech that
is most probably largely of his own composition
and what he deemed fitting for the occasion.

7 of the swine's flesh and save yourself. •I respect your age and your gray hairs,
although to have had them for so long and still cling to the religion of the Jews
8 makes you anything but a philosopher in my eyes. •Why should you abhor eating
9 the excellent meat of this animal which nature has freely bestowed on us? •Surely
it is sheer folly not to enjoy harmless pleasures, and it is wrong to spurn nature's
10 good gifts. •But in my judgment it will be greater folly still if you indulge in idle
11 conceits about truth and continue to defy me to your own cost in suffering. •Will
you not awaken from your preposterous philosophy, abandon your nonsensical
calculations, assume a frame of mind to match your years, and accept the true
12 philosophy of expediency? •Bow to my benevolent advice and have pity on your
13 own old age. •Consider this also, that, even if there is some power that watches
over this religion of yours, it would pardon you for any transgression committed
under compulsion." d

14   When the tyrant had in this way urged him on to the eating of food forbidden
15 by the Law, Eleazar asked permission to speak, •and on receiving authority to do
16 so he began to speak out publicly as follows: •"We, Antiochus, who firmly
believe that we must lead our lives in accordance with the divine Law, consider
that no compulsion laid on us is mighty enough to overcome our own willing
17 obedience to the Law. •Therefore, under no circumstances whatever do we ever
18 deem it right to transgress the Law. •And even if our Law was not, as you suggest,
in truth divine, and we only reckoned it to be divine, it would still in fact be
19 impossible for us to ruin our reputation for piety.e •Accordingly, you must not
20 regard it as a minor sin for us to eat unclean food; •minor sins are just as weighty   Gal 3:10
21,22 as great sins, •for in each case the Law is despised.f •You mock at our philosophy   Jas 2:10
23 as though our living under it were contrary to reason. •On the other hand, it
teaches us temperance so that we are in control of all our pleasures and desires;
and it gives us a thorough training in courage so that we willingly endure all
24 hardship; •and it teaches us justice so that whatever our different attitudes may be
we retain a sense of balance; and it instructs us in piety so that we most highly
25 reverence the only living God. •Therefore, we do not eat unclean food. Believing
that God established the Law, we know that the creator of the world, in giving
26 us the Law, conforms it to our nature.g •He has commanded us to eat whatever
will be well suited to our souls, and has forbidden us to eat food that is the   Lev 11:1–23
27 reverse. •It is the act of a tyrant to compel us not only to transgress the Law but
also to eat, so that you may laugh at us for partaking of the unclean food that is
28,29 abhorrent to us.h •But you will not have your laugh at my expense. •I will not
violate the solemn oaths of my ancestors to keep the Law, not even if you gouge
30 out my eyes and burn my entrails. •I am neither so old nor short of manliness
31 that in the matter of religion my reason should lose its youthful vigor. •So set the
32 torturer's wheel turning and fan the fire to a great blaze. •I am not so sorry
33 for my old age as to become responsible for breaking the Law of my fathers. •I
34 will not play you false, O Law my teacher; •I will not forswear you, beloved self-
35 control; •I will not shame you, philosophic reason, nor will I deny you, venerable

d. The cunning appeal of Antiochus' closing gambit would have registered with the readers of 4Mac, insofar as they would themselves have known well how severe were the pressures and constraints of living under a foreign power in a pagan environment.

e. The mention of a "reputation for piety" is not simply a matter of Jewish pride but of Jewish sensitivity to the ultimate seriousness of offenses committed in public.

f. The rabbis were not unaware of the distinction between "light" and "heavy" transgressions, but at the same time their major emphasis was on the binding nature of the Law in its entirety or in all its precepts. These Jewish ideas inform Eleazar's remarks here more than the common Stoic notion

that all sins, though not the same, are equal, a notion ridiculed by Horace ("It can never be an equivalent crime/to crib the cheap cabbage and plunder the shrine"), Cicero and Plutarch. See also Introduction, n. 23.

g. Whereas the Stoic thought of nature's sovereignty and man's need to adapt himself to nature's gifts and demands, the (Jewish) thought here is of the sovereignty of the creator God who graciously confers on man the Law that is adapted to man's needs and nature, the dietary regulations, for instance, being given to man as morally purifying.

h. What is at stake is more than just the question "to eat or not to eat"; it is the preservation of the Law's integrity in the world's eyes.

36 priesthood and knowledge of the Law. •You shall not defile the reverent lips of
37 my old age nor my lifelong service of the Law. •Pure shall my fathers welcome   Gen 15:15
38 me,[i] fearless of your punishments even unto death. •Tyrannize as you will over
the ungodly, but you will never lord it over my thoughts on the subject of true
religion, neither by your words nor through your works."[j]

Eleazar's amazing bravery under torture

1 **6** After Eleazar responded so eloquently to the tyrant's exhortations, then the
2 guards who stood around dragged him roughly to the implements of torture. •First
they stripped off the old man's clothes, though he was still adorned with the
3 beauty of his piety. •Then, binding his arms on either side, they scourged him
4 with whips, •while right up against him a herald shouted, "Obey the king's
5 command!" •But the great-souled and noble man, a true Eleazar,[a] refused absolutely
6 to recant as if the torture were no more than a dream, •and, keeping his eyes
raised aloft to heaven, the old man let his flesh be torn by the scourges until his
7 blood ran freely and his sides were lacerated. •He fell to the ground when his
body could no longer endure the pain, but his reason he kept erect[b] and inflexible.
8 With his foot one of the merciless guards kicked him savagely on the side to
9 make him get up as he fell. •But he suffered the torment and scorned the
10 compulsion and overcame the pains, •and under a hail of blows, the old man, like
11 a true athlete, prevailed over his torturers. •His face beaded with sweat and panting
heavily, he roused his very torturers to amazement at his fortitude.
12,13   Thereupon, partly out of pity for his old age, •partly in sympathy through
previous friendship, partly in admiration of his courage, some of the king's
14 courtiers went up to him and said, •"Why, Eleazar, are you so unreasonably
15 destroying yourself in this foul way? •Let us bring you some of the cooked food,   2Mac 6:21
and you pretend to taste of the swine's flesh and save yourself."[c]
16   But as if their counsel only made his wounds all the harder to bear, Eleazar
17 cried aloud, •"Never may the children of Abraham think such evil thoughts as
18 out of cowardice to enact a part so ill-becoming to us.[d] •It would most surely be
contrary to reason if, having lived our lives in accordance with the truth right up
to our old age and having preserved our fair reputation for so living in conformity
19 with the Law, we should now change •and ourselves become a model of impiety
20 to the young by setting them an example of eating unclean food. •Shameful would
it be if we should, with only a very short space of life left to us,[e] become a
21 laughingstock in the eyes of all for our cowardice •and be despised by the tyrant
22 as craven because we would not champion our divine Law to the death. •Therefore,
23 O children of Abraham, you must die nobly for piety's sake. •And you, guards
of the tyrant, why leave off your work?"
24   When they saw him so high in spirit in the face of such constraints and so
25 adamant against their offer of mercy, they brought him to the fire. •There they
burned him with cunningly devised instruments and threw him in the fire and

i. The idea of "being gathered to the fathers" is a common OT mode of speaking about death, e.g. Gen 15:15, "For your part you shall go to your fathers in peace." In the context of Eleazar's speech the thought of the final divine judgment and future reward and punishment is also in the background.

j. Eleazar's closing words afford an excellent example of one of the salient motifs of 4Mac, the compatibility of joyous obedience to the Law with the freedom of the individual reason or conscience as the Stoic sage understood it.

6 a. The name in Heb. means "God help" or "seed of God." There may be an indication here that the name had become proverbial for the typical

martyr who endured bravely under torture to the end.

b. The word translated "erect" is a *double entente*, since it means also "right" or "correct."

c. Apparently the element of pretense would be that since the meat was "cooked" or "dressed" the bystanders need not have detected that it was in fact pork.

d. What outrages Eleazar is not simply the act of eating unclean food in itself but the baleful public effect of even a pretense at an action which involved profanation of the divine name.

e. The words "with only a short space of life left to us" imply thoughts of the imminence of the divine judgment and of eternity.

26 poured an evil-smelling concoction into his nostrils. •And when his flesh had been burned away to the very bones, and he was on the point of expiring, he lifted his
27 eyes to God and said,ᶠ •"You know, O God, that though I could have saved
28 myself I am dying in these fiery torments for the sake of the Law. •Be merciful
29 to your people and let our punishment be a satisfaction on their behalf. •Make
30 my blood their purification and take my life as a ransom for theirs."ᵍ •With these words the holy man nobly succumbed to his torments, and by his reason held his ground through the very tortures of death for the Law's sake.
31,32 Confessedly then, devout reason is master of the passions. •For if the passions were sovereign over reason, I would have credited them with testimony to their
33 superiority. •But since we have just shown how reason conquers the passions, we
34 properly confer upon it the authority of leadership. •It is only right that we should confess reason's sovereignty insofar as it rules over torments inflicted on us from
35 outside ourselves—it would be absurd to do otherwise.ʰ •The arguments I adduce demonstrate wisdom's actual sovereignty not only over pains but its rule over pleasures and its complete refusal to yield to them.

(margin: 1:11; 6:28; 9:24; 12:18; 17:20–22; 18:4)

A panegyric on Eleazar

1 **7** Like an outstanding pilot, indeed, the reason of our father Eleazar, steering the
2 vessel of piety on the sea of passions, •though buffeted by the threats of the tyrant
3 and swamped by the swelling waves of torture, •in no way swerved the rudder of
4 piety until he sailed into the haven of deathless victory. •No city beleaguered by many devices of all kinds has ever offered such resistance as did that perfect saint. When his sacred soul was assailed with blazing rack and torture, through reason,
5 the shield of his piety, he overcame his besiegers. •Stretching out his mind like a protruding cliff, our father Eleazar shattered the wild surges of his passions.
6 O priest worthy of your priestly office, you did not defile your sacred teeth, nor did you pollute with unclean food a stomach that had room only for piety and
7 purity. •O mind in perfect unison with the Law, and philosopher of the divine
8 life! •So must all those be who are skilled in the craft of keeping the Law and who defend it with their own blood and noble sweat even in the face of sufferings
9 unto death. •You, father, by endurance that brought you to glory,ᵃ have confirmed our adherence to the Law, and your august speech on holiness you have not annulled, but through your deeds you have ratified your words of divine philosophy.
10 O aged man, mightier than torture; revered elder more vigorous than the flame;
11 great king, ruler of the passions, Eleazar! •Even as our father Aaron, armed with the censer, ran through the massed company of his people and overcame the fiery
12 angel, •so did Aaron's descendant Eleazar not deviate in his reason, though
13 consumed in the fire.ᵇ •But most wonderful of all, though he was an old man, and the sinews of his body were already unstrung, his muscles all relaxed and his

(margin: Num 17:1–15 WisSol 18:20–25)

---

f. The exaggeration involved here is part of the rhetorician's stock-in-trade and greatly heightens the pathos of the dying man's speech.

g. The most explicit statement in 4Mac (cf. 1:11; 9:24; 12:18; 17:20–22; 18:4) of the concept of the martyr's death as a vicarious atonement for the people, a concept absent from 2Mac (6:30–35).

h. The translation "it would be absurd to do otherwise" represents only three Gk. words which lit. = "since also absurd," and is arrived at only by supplying some such addition (not in the MSS) to these three words as "to do otherwise" or "to deny it." Syr. favors such a procedure, but some have suggested an emendation which yields the sense "torments inflicted on us from outside, ridiculous things as they are." In view of the difficulty of the text, Hadas chooses to leave a

lacuna at this point in his translation (*Maccabees*, pp. 182f.).

7 a. The phrase "to glory" has a twofold connotation here: (1) It refers to Eleazar's preservation of his fair reputation for piety in the eyes of men, to the public effect of his refusal to partake of unclean food. Hadas translates, "by your perseverance in the public gaze" (*Maccabees*, p. 185); (2) it denotes the divine reward of "everlasting glory." Our translation is such as to imply both features of the phrase.

b. The reference is to Num 17:1–15, although no "fiery angel" appears there. In WisSol 18:20–25 the plague staved off by Aaron does appear to be pictured as an avenging angel. The point of comparing Eleazar with Aaron here is that both manifested the power of victorious faith in public.

14 nerves weakened, •by means of reason he became youthful again in spirit and by
15 reason like Isaac's prevailed over many-headed torture. •O blessed old age, revered   Gen 22
gray head, life loyal to the Law and perfected by the faithful seal of death.
16   If, therefore, an old man despised torments unto the death on account of his
17 piety, we must admit that devout reason is leader over the passions. •But some
may contend that not all men are masters of the passions, because not all men
18 possess enlightened reason. •Only those who with all their heart make piety their
19 first concern are able to conquer the passions of the flesh, •believing that to God   Mk 12:26
they do not die, as our patriarchs Abraham, Isaac, and Jacob died not, but live to   Rom 6:10; 14:8
                                                                                        Gal 2:19
20 God.ᶜ •Accordingly, the validity of our argument is not impaired by the fact that   16:25
some men seem to be ruled by their passions because of the weakness of their
21 reason. •For what philosopher is there, who lives by the whole rule of philosophy
22 and believes in God •and knows that it is blessed to endure every pain for the
23 sake of virtue, who could fail to master his passions for the sake of piety? •Only
the wise and courageous man is ruler of the passions.

The king's invitation to the seven brothers to recant their ancestral faith

1 **8** Yes, indeed, even young lads have become philosophers through devout reason
2 and have triumphed over still more severe torments. •For when the tyrant had
been so conspicuously foiled in his first attempt, having been unable to compel
the old man to eat unclean food, then in violent rage he ordered others of the
Hebrew captives to be brought and said that if they would eat of the unclean food
they would be released, but if they refused, they would be even more savagely
3 tortured. •When the tyrant had issued these commands, seven brothers in the   2Mac 7:1–42
company of their aged mother were brought before him, handsome and modest
4 and well-born and altogether charming. •On seeing them standing around their
mother in the midst, as though they were a chorus, the tyrant was struck by them,
and astounded at their comeliness and nobility, he smiled at them and called them
5 near and said, •"Young men, I admire you each and every one and want to show
you favor, and since I greatly respect the beauty of such a large band of brothers,
I not only advise you not to display the same mad frenzy as that old man who
has just been tortured, but I beg of you to yield to me and take advantage of my
6 friendship. •Just as I am able to punish those who disobey my orders, so am I
7 able to benefit those who obey me. •Take my word for it then that if you will
renounce the ancestral law of your polity you will receive leading positions of
8 authority over my domains. •Share in the Greek style, change your mode of
9 living, and enjoy your youth.ᵃ •If you provoke me to anger by your disobedience,
you will compel me to the use of dreadful punishments to destroy each and every
10 one of you by torture. •Have pity on yourselves, for though I am your enemy, I
11 myself feel compassion for you in your youth and beauty. •Will you not reflect
that if you disobey there is nothing in store for you but death with torments?"
12   With these words he ordered the instruments of torture to be brought forward
13 in order to terrorize them into eating of the unclean food. •The guards then brought
forward the wheels and joint dislocators, racks and wooden horses, catapults and
cauldrons, braziers and thumbscrews, iron claws and wedges and bellows,ᵇ and

---

c. The notion of "living to God" is common
in the NT, e.g. Rom 6:10; 14:8; Gal 2:19. In Mk
12:26, the "I am" of God's declaration to Moses
at the bush—"I am the God of Abraham, and the
God of Isaac and the God of Jacob"—is used,
rather surprisingly, as a proof of the resurrection
of the dead.

8 a. Antiochus appears here as the advocate of
the Gk. way of life. So the clash presented in 4Mac

is not entirely between the forces of absolute evil
on the one side and of good on the other side, but
rather between the good as a Gk. ruler sees it and
the good as youthful Jews who take their stand on
their ancestral faith see it.

b. The instruments of torture listed here reappear
and are described in operation later on. The meaning
of the word translated "wooden horses" is somewhat obscure, as is the manner of its operation. It
was probably a bone-crushing device of some sort.

14 the tyrant spoke up again and said, •"You must be afraid, my lads, and the justice
you revere[c] will be merciful to you if you transgress under duress."

15   But they, when they heard his enticing words and saw the fearful machines of
torture, not only were not frightened but even resisted the tyrant with their own
16 philosophy, and by their right reasoning brought down his tyranny. •Just think,
however, what sort of arguments they would have used if some among them had
17 been fainthearted and cowardly. •Would they not have gone like this? "What
wretched and extremely foolish creatures we are that, when the king invites us
18 and presses us to accept his benevolence, we should not consent! •Why do we
sport such vain resolutions and venture a disobedience that will be the death of
19 us? •Shall we not, my brothers, fear these instruments of torture, take account of
20 the threats of torment, and abandon this vainglory and fatal bragging? •Let us
21 take pity on our own youth and have compassion for our mother's old age, •and
22 let us lay it to heart that if we disobey we die. •The divine justice will pardon us
23 for being afraid of the king under duress. •Why should we remove ourselves from
24 this most pleasant life and deprive ourselves of this sweet world? •Let us not
25 resist necessity nor vaunt ourselves to our own cost in torture. •Not even the Law
itself would willingly condemn us to death for being afraid of the instruments of
26 torture.[d] •Why should we be so absorbed in contentiousness or so attracted to an
obstinacy that must prove fatal when we could obey the king and live an untroubled
27 life?" •But on the very point of being tortured these young men uttered no such
28 words nor even entertained such thoughts. •For they despised the emotions and
29 were masters over pain. •Accordingly, no sooner had the tyrant finished counseling
them to eat unclean food than they all with one voice and as with one soul said:[e]

1 **9** "Why do you delay, tyrant? We are prepared to die rather than transgress the
2 commandments of our forefathers. •We should truly bring shame upon our
ancestors if we did not live in obedience to the Law and take Moses as our
3 counselor. •Tyrant, who counsel us to transgress, do not in your hatred of us pity
4 us more than we pity ourselves. •We reckon that your clemency which offers us
deliverance in return for our transgression is harder to bear than death itself.
5 You seek to terrify us with your threat of death by torture as if you had learned   5:4–6:30
6 nothing from Eleazar but a short while ago. •But if, for the sake of their religion
and enduring through torments, old men of the Hebrews have remained faithful
to the end, it is even more appropriate that we who are young should die in
disregard of the tortures you impose on us, the very tortures our aged teacher[a]
7 triumphed over. •Put us to the test then, tyrant; and if you take our lives for the
8 sake of our religion, do not think you can harm us with your torments. •By our
suffering and endurance we shall obtain the prize of virtue and shall be with God,
9 on whose account we suffer. •But you, because of our foul murder, will suffer at
the hand of divine justice the everlasting torment by fire you deserve."[b]

The torture and defiance of the first and second sons

10   Indignant at these words expressing the youths' disobedience, the tyrant was even
11 more enraged at their ingratitude. •Then, at the word of command, the guards
brought forward the eldest brother, ripped off his tunic, and bound his hands and
12 arms on either side with thongs. •But when they had flogged him with whips and

c. A pagan philosophical circumlocution for
"God."

d. Though it most surely condemned idolatry in
any form, the Law did not condemn "fear" in
such circumstances as these.

e. The description probably harks back to the
typically hellenistic picture of the seven sons and
their mother as a chorus in 8:4.

9 a. Probably "teacher" here signifies only an
exemplar in faithful endurance rather than that
Eleazar was a professional teacher, although in 5:4
he is described as "expert in the Law."

b. In vs. 8 the words "and shall be with God,
on whose account we suffer" are omitted by A,
and in vs. 9 the words "by fire" are omitted by
S. But there is no compelling reason to follow A
or S here.

for all their strenuous efforts had made no impression on him, they cast him on
13 the wheel. •When he was racked on it, the limbs of the noble youth were put out
14 of joint, •and as limb after limb was broken,[c] he denounced the tyrant and said,
15 "Most abominable tyrant, enemy of heaven's justice and bent on slaughter, you
punish me in this fashion not as a murderer or man of impiety but as a champion
16 of the divine Law." •The guards then said to him, "Consent to eat and so save
17 yourself from the tortures." •But he replied, "Your wheel is not so strong, base
underlings, as to strangle my reason. Sever my limbs, burn my flesh, twist my
18 joints, •and through all these torments I will prove to you that the children of the
19 Hebrews alone are invincible in the defense of virtue." •When he said this they
20 spread fire under him and fed the blaze, drawing the wheel still tighter. •The
wheel was besmeared all over with his blood, and the heap of coals was quenched
by the discharged fluid dropping down, and bits of flesh whirled around on the
21 axles of the machine. •Even when his bodily frame was all dissevered, the great-
22 souled youth, a true son of Abraham, uttered not a groan. •As though he were   Mal 3:2
being transformed into incorruption by the fire,[d] he nobly endured the torments
23 and said, •"Imitate me, my brothers; do not become deserters in my trial[e] nor
24 forswear our brotherhood in nobility. •Fight the sacred and noble fight for true
religion and through it may the just providence that protected our fathers become
25 merciful to our people and take vengeance on the accursed tyrant." •With these
words the saintly youth expired.
26   While they all marveled at his bravery of soul, the guards brought forward the
brother next to him in age, and when they had adjusted the sharp-clawed iron
27 hands, they fastened him to the torture machine and the catapult. •On inquiring
of him whether he was willing to eat before the torture began, they heard his
28 noble resolve, •and then proceeded to tear at his sinews with the iron hands and
ripped off all the flesh even from his cheeks and the skin of his head, like wild
29 leopards. This agony he endured with courage and said, •"How sweet is every
kind of death for the sake of our ancestral religion." And to the tyrant he said,
30 "Does it not occur to you, most bloodthirsty of tyrants, that you are being tortured
more than I, when you see that the arrogant reasoning that belongs to your tyranny
31 is overcome by our endurance for true religion's sake? •I am sustained in my
ordeal by the joys that arise from defending virtue, but you are tortured by the
32 threats that confront impiety. •You cannot, vile tyrant, escape the penalties of the
divine wrath."

The torture and defiance of the third and fourth sons

1 **10** When he had bravely met his illustrious death, the third son was brought
forward amid fervent exhortations from many people to taste of the food and save
2 himself. •But he cried aloud and said, "Do you not know that the very same
father begot both me and my dead brothers, and the same mother bore us all, and
3 I was brought up on the same doctrines? •I do not abjure the noble bond of
4 brotherhood. •Therefore, if you have any means of torture, apply it to my body,
5 for my soul you cannot touch even if you would."[a] •At the man's outspoken
pronouncement they were grievously annoyed, and with their dislocating machines

---

c. The discrepancies between the descriptions
of the tortures administered to the first son and the
other six, here and in 2Mac, indicate no more than
that the story circulated in different forms or that
each writer claimed his freedom to shape up the
narrative in his own way.

d. The notion of the cleansing or purifying
quality of "fire" (often associated with the day of
judgment) is common in the Heb. milieu, and that
of the incorruptibility and immortality of the irrational soul (as opposed to the corruptibility and
mortality of the rational soul or mind) is found

especially in Philo's representation of Platonic
doctrine.

e. A and S read "do not desert me forever,"
but our translation follows the reading given in a
few minuscules (and probably to be preferred),
"do not desert me in my trial."

10 a. The words of vs. 4 do not occur in A and
are omitted from the text of Rahlfs. They are
reminiscent of Eleazar's words in 2Mac 6:30 and
may be an interpolation.

they dislocated his hands and feet, and by the use of levers they sundered his
6 limbs from their sockets; •and they twisted his fingers and arms and legs and
7 elbows. •And when they could by no means strangle (his spirit), they abandoned
their machines and with the tips of their fingers[b] they scalped him as the Scythians
8 do. •Then they brought him at once to the wheel, and on it his backbone was
disjointed until he saw bits of his flesh in shreds and gouts of blood pouring from
9,10 his entrails. •On the point of death he said, •"We, vile tyrant, suffer all this for
11 our training in divine virtue. •But for your impiety and savagery you will suffer
endless torments."

12　　　When he had died in a manner worthy of his brothers, they dragged forward
13 the fourth one and said, •"Do not you, too, display the same madness as your
14 brothers, but obey the king and save yourself." •But he replied, "For me you
15 cannot heat the fire so hot as to make a coward of me. •By the blessed death of
my brothers, by the everlasting ruin of the tyrant, by the glorious life of the pious,
16 I will not deny our noble brotherhood. •Contrive whatever tortures you will,
tyrant, that you might go on learning from them that I am brother to those who
17 have been tortured already." •On hearing this the bloodthirsty and murderous and
18 altogether abominable Antiochus ordered his tongue to be cut out. •But he said,
"Even if you remove the organ of speech, God still hears those who are silent.　Isa 53:7–12
19 Look, my tongue is hanging out; cut it off, for you will not thereby make my
20 reason mute. •Gladly, for the sake of God, do we allow the limbs of our body to
21 be mutilated. •But you God will speedily overtake, since you are cutting out the　Isa 35:6
tongue that sang songs of praise to him."

The torture and defiance of the four remaining sons

1 **11** When he, too, who had been so cruelly afflicted with tortures died, the fifth
2 son sprang forward and said, •"I waste no time in demanding the torture for
3 virtue's sake, •but of my own accord come forward so that you might kill me and
for your further misdeeds incur the punishment the heavenly justice will inflict on
4 you. •You enemy of virtue and enemy of man, what have we done that you
5 destroy us in this way? •Is it because we revere the creator of all and live according
6–9 to his virtuous Law? But such conduct deserves honors, not torments."[a] •While
he spoke these words the guards bound him and dragged him to the catapult.
10 They bound him to it by his knees, and fastening them to it with iron cramps,
they twisted his loins back over the circular wedge until he was curled back on
11 the wheel like a scorpion and his limbs were all disjointed.[b] •And thus, struggling
12 for breath and racked in body, he said, •"A glorious favor you bestow on us,
tyrant, though all unwilling, enabling us as you are to manifest our constancy
toward the Law by yet more noble sufferings."

13　　　When he had died, the sixth son was brought forward—a mere lad. The tyrant
14 then asked if he was willing to eat and be released. But he replied, •"I am younger
15 in age than my brothers, but just as old in reason. •We were born and reared for
the same purpose, and we are likewise obliged to die in the same cause.
16 Accordingly, if you want to torture me for not eating unclean food, do your
17,18 torturing now." •When he said this they brought him to the wheel, •and stretching
him out on it carefully until his backbone was disjointed, they set the fire going
19 under him. •And heating up sharp skewers, they ran them into his back, and

---

b. A and S have three additional Gk. words at
this point meaning "they stripped off his skin,"
perhaps as an inserted explanatory comment on the
single Gk. word *apeskythizon*, meaning "scalped
him as the Scythians do." Reference to the Scythian
practice of scalping is found in Herodotus 4:64 and
Pliny's *Natural History* 7:11.

11 a. Vss. 7 and 8 are wanting from S and are

omitted in Rahlfs' text. Following the words "not
torments" in vs. 6, they read ". . . if you but
understood human aspirations and had hopes of
salvation with God. But as it is, you are estranged
from God and make war on those who revere him."

b. A number of minor variants occur in the
textual tradition in vs. 10, and the text appears to
be in some disarray. Consequently the meaning is
not entirely clear.

20 piercing his sides, they burned out his entrails. •But under all this torment he
declared, "How sacred and seemly is the agony to which so many of my brothers
and I have been summoned as to a contest in sufferings for piety's sake, and yet
21 we have not been vanquished. •For religious knowledge, tyrant, is unconquerable.
22,23 Fully armed with goodness I, too, shall die along with my brothers, •and I
myself, too, shall confront you with one great avenger more,ᶜ you deviser of new
24 tortures, you enemy of men of true religion. •Six of us, lads though we are, have
25 destroyed your tyranny. •For your inability to sway our reason or to force us to
26 eat unclean food, is not that your ruin? •Your fire is cool for us and your catapults
27 painless and your violence powerless. •No tyrant's guards, but the guardians of
the divine Law have been our protectors, and that is why our reason remains
undefeated."

1 **12** When he, too, had died a blessed death, having been cast into the cauldron,
2 the seventh and youngest son of all came forward. •Moved with pity toward him,
even though he had been fiercely exasperated by his brothers, and seeing the
bonds already placed on him, the tyrant asked him to come closer and attempted
3 to persuade him, saying, •"You see the outcome of your brothers' folly; they
4 have been duly punished for their disobedience and are dead. •And you, too, if
you refuse to obey, will be miserably tortured and will yourself meet a premature
5 death. •But if you do obey you will be my friend and will be given charge over
6 my affairs of state." •While he thus appealed to him, he sent for the boy's mother
7 so that he might show pity to her over the loss of so many sons and further urge
on the sole surviving son the obedience that would save him. •But when the
mother gave encouragement to her son in the Hebrew tongue, as we shall shortly
8 relate,ᵃ •"Loose me," he said, "and let me speak to the king and all the friends   2Mac 7:22–40
9 who are with him." •And in great glee over the boy's promise, they quickly
10,11 loosed him. •Then he ran to the nearest brazier and said, •"Impious man, of all
the wicked ones you most ungodly tyrant, are you not ashamed to receive your
kingdom with all its blessings from the hand of God and then to kill those who
12 serve him and torture those who practice piety? •In return for this, justice will
hold you in store for a fiercer and an everlasting fire and for torments which will
13 never let you go for all time. •Are not you, who are but a man, ashamed, you
savage beast, to cut out the tongues of men who share the same feelings as you
and are made of the same elementsᵇ and to torture them in this brutal fashion?
14 They, for their part, have died nobly and so fulfilled their piety toward God, but
you will groan dreadfully for having slain the champions of virtue without cause."
15,16 Then when he, too, was on the point of death, he declared, •"I shall not prove
17 deserter to my brothers' valor. •I call upon the God of my fathers to be merciful
18,19 to our people. •You he will punish both in the present life and in death." •With
this prayer against the tyrant, he threw himself into the braziers and so gave up
his life.ᶜ

A panegyric: reason's sovereignty in the seven sons

1 **13** Now, therefore, if the seven brothers scorned sufferings even unto death, it
must be universally conceded that the pious reason is complete master of the
2 passions. •For if being enslaved to the passions they had eaten unclean food, we

c. This accords with the motives for the lad's
self-giving expressed in vs. 3.

12 a. In 2Mac 7:22f. the mother's words of encouragement to her son are reported before the
description of his death. Our author chooses to
hold back the mother's speech at this point ("as
we shall shortly relate") and seems to have been
aware of its occurrence at this juncture in his source

or sources.

b. Part of the stock-in-trade of Stoic thought
and a clear indication of the hellenistic milieu of
the story and of our author's account of it.

c. Although Stoicism consented to suicide on
certain terms, it is likely that our author is thinking
less of suicide here than of highlighting the extreme
heroism of the youth, for whom death was only
moments away in any case.

3 would have said that they had been conquered by them. •However, in this case it
did not happen so, but by the reason which is commended by God they prevailed
4 over the passions, •and so we cannot but perceive the mind's supremacy over
5 them since they overcame both passion and sufferings. •How then can we fail to
admit, in regard to these men, right reason's victory over the passions, seeing that
6 they did not shrink from the pains of fire?[a] •Even as towers at the entrance to
harbors repulse the threatening onslaughts of the waves and provide a calm haven
7 for those who sail into it, •so the seven-towered right reason of the youths fortified
8 the haven of piety and tamed the rugged license of the passions. •They formed a
9 holy choir of piety as they encouraged each other with the words, •"Let us die
like brothers all, brothers, for the Law's sake. Let us follow the example of the
three youths in Assyria, who despised the same trial by ordeal in the furnace.[b]　Dan 3
10,11 Let us not be pusillanimous in the demonstration of true piety." •"Courage,
12 brother!" said one, and another, "Hold on nobly!" •And another, recalling the
past, said, "Remember whence you came and at the hand of what father Isaac　Gen 22
13 gave himself to be sacrificed for piety's sake."[c] •Each one severally and all
together, looking at each other with most cheerful mien, aglow with courage,
said, "With all our hearts let us consecrate ourselves unto God, who gave us our
14 souls, and let us expend our bodies for the custodianship of the Law. •Let us have
15 no fear of him who thinks he kills. •Great is the ordeal and peril of the soul that　Matt 10:28
lies in wait in eternal torment for those who transgress the commandment of God.
16 Let us then arm ourselves with the control over the passions which comes from
17 divine reason. •After our death in this fashion Abraham and Isaac and Jacob will
18 receive us, and all our forefathers will praise us." •And to each one of the brothers
as they were dragged away, those who were left said, "Do not shame us, brother,
nor be traitor to our brothers who have already died."
19　You cannot be ignorant of the charm of brotherhood which the divine and all-
wise providence has allotted through fathers to their offspring, implanting it, in
20 fact, in their mother's womb. •There brothers dwell for the same period and are
formed over the same duration of time; they are nurtured from the same blood
21 and are brought to maturity through the same source of life. •They are brought to
birth through the same span and draw milk from the same fountains, and through
22 being embraced at the same breast, fraternal souls are nourished, •and they grow
from strength to strength through a common nurture and daily companionship as
23 well as in the training imposed by our discipline in the Law.[d] •The ties of brotherly
love, it is clear, are firmly set and never more firmly than among the seven
24 brothers; •for having been trained in the same Law and having disciplined
themselves in the same virtues, and having been reared together in the life of
25 righteousness, they loved one another all the more. •Their common zeal for beauty
and goodness strengthened their goodwill and fellow feeling for one another,
26 and in conjunction with their piety made their brotherly love more ardent.
27 Nevertheless, although with them nature and companionship and high moral
character added to the charms of brotherhood, it was through their piety that the
surviving sons had the endurance to look upon their brothers while they were
being racked with pain and tortured to death.

1　**14** More than that, they even urged them on to face the torment, and so they not

---

13 a. The minor variants in the MSS A S V in
vss. 1–5 attest the disturbed state of the text here,
although the overall meaning is not in any serious
doubt.

　b. Since the events related in 4Mac purport to
belong to the period of the opening of the Maccabean war to which Dan is usually attributed, it
is quite natural for him to refer here to that book,
to the bravery of the "Three Children," Shadrach,
Meshach, and Abednego (Dan 3).

　c. The story of Abraham's near sacrifice of Isaac

in Gen 22 was sometimes taken as a testimony to
Abraham's faith, e.g. 4Mac 15:28; 17:6; WisSol
10:5; sometimes, as here, as a testimony to Isaac's
willingness to be sacrificed.

　d. The uniquely Jewish feature of training in
the Law rounds off the series of Stoic commonplaces on the theme of brotherhood. The stress in
vss. 23–27 on the brothers' practice of the true
religion clearly reveals the point at which, for our
author, Judaism transcends the Stoic ethic.

only despised the sufferings but also mastered the strong feelings of brotherly
love.

2,3   O reason, more kingly than kings, more free than freemen! •How holy and
4 harmonious the concord of the seven brothers for piety's sake! •Not one of the
5 seven lads turned coward, nor cowered away from death, •but all, as though
6 running on the highway to immortality, hurried on to death by torture. •Just as
hands and feet move in unison with the promptings of the soul, so did those holy
youths, as if impelled by the deathless soul of piety, go in harmony to the death
7 for piety's sake. •O all-holy sevenfold assembly of brothers in harmony! For just
8 as the seven days of creation move around piety, •so did the youths in chorus
9 circle around the sevenfold assembly, dissolving the terror of torture.[a] •Even now
we shudder when we hear of the affliction of those young men; but they, not only
looking on with their own eyes, not only hearing the instant threat pronounced
against them, but actually suffering the torment, endured to the end, and that in
10 the agonies of burning—•and what could be more painful than these? Sharp and
immediate is the power of fire and quickly did it destroy their bodies.

The mother in her death the most shining example of the victory of reason

11   Do not count it amazing that in those men reason triumphed over tortures,[b]
12 when even a woman's mind scorned still more manifold torments; •for the mother
of the seven youths endured the agonies inflicted on every one of her children.
13 Consider how tangled is the web of a mother's love for her children so that her
14 whole feeling is the profoundest inward affection for them. •Even animals not
possessed of reason have an affection and love for their young similar to that of
15 human beings. •Among the winged creatures the tame ones shield their young by
16 nesting under the roofs of houses,[c] •while those that build their nests on the peaks
of mountains and in the clefts of rocks and in the holes or tops of trees hatch their
17 young and ward off the intruder. •But if they cannot ward him off they flutter
around about the nestlings in the pangs of love and call to them in their own
18 speech and assist their offspring in whatever way they can. •But what need is
19 there to demonstrate the affection of irrational animals for their young •when even
the bees fend off intruders at the season of making the honeycomb and pierce
with their sting like a sword those who molest their young and defend them to
20 the death? •But not even her affection for her young caused the mother of the
youths, whose soul was like Abraham's,[d] to waver.

1 **15** O reason that was lord over the passions of the sons![a] O piety that was dearer
2 to the mother than her sons! •When two options lay before her, namely piety or
3 the instant deliverance of her seven sons according to the tyrant's promise, •she
4 loved piety better, which preserves to eternal life according to God's word. •How

---

14 a. The picture conjured up in vss. 7f. is not
altogether clear. For the notion of the number
"seven" as a sacred and perfect number, particularly in Alexandrian mysticism and astrology, see
e.g. Philo, *Op.* 90. Probably a more intelligible
sense is obtained in 4Mac 7bf. by adopting the
suggestion of various commentators (see Hadas,
Maccabees, p. 216) that we should transpose the
Gk. words *hebdomada* and *eusebeian* and so read,
"Just as the seven days of creation move around
the hebdomad, so did the youths in chorus circle
around piety."
     b. On the question of the importance of this
expression for the circumstances in which 4Mac
was composed, see Theological Importance.
     c. Reading the emendation *orophokoitounta* (for
orophoitounta, which hardly yields sense), sug-

gested by a number of commentators (see Hadas,
Maccabees, p. 218).
     d. Abraham's readiness to sacrifice Isaac is the
archetypal victory of devout reason over parental
love for children.
15 a. It has been suggested that "of the sons"
here is out of place since the subject is the mother's
mastery of the emotions, and that "of the sons"
is either by dittography from the following clause
or that we should read for "of the sons" (*teknōn*),
philoteknon = "O reason that was lord over
maternal affections" (see Hadas, *Maccabees*, p.
219). But this may not be necessary, since the
retrospective glance at the moral heroism of the
sons may simply give edge to the following apostrophe, "O piety that was dearer to the mother
than her sons! (even such sons as these)."

can I possibly express the deep love of parents for their children? On the tender nature of the child we impress a wonderful likeness of soul and form,[b] and especially mothers, who are more affectionate in their own feelings toward their
5 children than fathers. •For mothers are weaker in their being than fathers, and the
6 more children they bear, so much the more do they love their children. •But no mother ever loved her children more than the mother of the seven sons, who in
7 seven childbirths implanted in herself a profound affection for them; •and because of the many pains she suffered in each case was constrained to feel her bond of
8 love with them; •but on account of her fear of God she discounted the immediate
9 safety of her children. •Indeed, because of her sons' moral heroism and their
10 willing obedience to the Law, she cherished an even greater love for them. •For they were just, and temperate, and brave, and magnanimous, and so filled with love for each other and for their mother that in obedience they kept the Law even
11 unto death. •Nevertheless, although all the many promptings of maternal love pulled the mother toward the bond of affection for them, in not a single case did
12 their varied tortures avail to sway her reason, •but each and every child and all
13 of them together did the mother urge on to death for piety's sake. •O sacred nature, parental love, filial affection,[c] nurture, and unconquerable maternal
14 affections. •Each one she saw racked and burned, yet for piety's sake remained
15 unwavering. •She saw the flesh of her children melt away in the fire and their toes and fingers scattered on the ground, and the flesh of their heads right down
16 to the cheeks laid out before her like masks. •O mother, sorely tried now by pains
17 sharper than the pains of birth! •O woman who alone among women brought
18 perfect piety to birth! •Your firstborn, as he breathed his last, did not sway your resolve, nor the second, as he looked on you with pity in his torment, nor the
19 third, as he expired; •nor when you beheld the eyes of each one immovably fixed on the same anguish amid the tortures, nor indeed when you observed in their
20 nostrils the signs of approaching death did you break into tears. •When you saw your children's flesh burned on children's flesh, and severed hand upon hand, and flayed head upon head, and corpse fallen upon corpse, and when you saw the place crowded with spectators of your children's torments, you did not weep.
21 Not the sirens' melodies nor the sweet sound of the swan's song so charm the hearers' ears as do the children's voices charm their mother when they speak to
22 her from amid the tortures. •With what a manifold host of torments then was the
23 mother tortured while her sons were racked by the wheel and fire. •But in the midst of her passionate feelings pious reason nerved her whole being with a manly courage and enabled her to transcend the immediate affections of a mother's love.
24 And although she saw the destruction of her seven children and the endlessly varied series of tortures, that noble mother disregarded all of it because of her
25 faith in God. •In the council chamber of her own heart, so to speak, she saw clever advocates, nature and parenthood and maternal love and the torment of her
26 children—•a mother holding two votes in regard to her children, one to consign
27 them to death and the other to preserve them alive; •but she did not decide on the
28 safe course that would preserve her sons for a little while, •but like a true daughter
29 of God-fearing Abraham called to mind Abraham's unflinching bravery. •O mother of the nation, champion of the Law, defender of true religion, and winner of the
30 prize in the inward contest of the heart! •More noble than men in fortitude and
31 stronger than heroes in endurance! •Like the ark of Noah, carrying the universe   Gen 6:5–8:22 in the worldwide cataclysm and stoutly enduring the waves, so did you, guardian of the Law, buffeted on every side in the flood of the passions and by the mighty

b. This idea has its background in Stoic thought on heredity in relation both to the physical and spiritual aspects of human existence.

c. Our translation renders the text found in only a few MSS, *genesi*, dative plural of *genos* = "offspring." S has *gennēmasi*, which means essentially the same. A has *goneusi* = "O love for

parents!'' V has *genesei*, which leads Townshend (*APOT*, vol. 2, p. 681) to accept *genesis*, which has small MS support but is suggested by the Syr., and to render it ''O yearning of parents for offspring,'' the sense of which is, in the end, clearly very similar to our own translation.

gales of your sons' torments, so did you by your perseverance nobly weather the storms that assailed you for religion's sake.

1 **16** If then a woman and indeed a woman of advanced years, the mother of seven sons, held out while looking upon her children being tortured to death, we must
2 concede that devout reason is sovereign over the passions. •I have therefore demonstrated that not only men have conquered human passions but that even a
3 woman despised the greatest torments. •Not so wild were the lions around Daniel   Dan 6 nor so blazing hot in its greedy flame was the furnace of Mishael[a] as the natural   Dan 3 mother's love that burned in her when she saw her seven sons so indiscriminately
4 tortured. •But by pious reason the mother quenched all these fiery emotions.
5   There is this too to consider, that if, as being a mother, the woman had been weak in spirit, she would have wept over them and spoken perhaps as follows:
6 "Ah, thrice-wretched woman that I am, yes more than thrice-wretched! I have
7 borne seven sons and am the mother of none! •How vain were these seven pregnancies, how futile these seven times ten months[b] with child, how fruitless
8 the nursing and wretched the suckling! •In vain, my children, did I endure these
9 many pains for you and the even more severe strains of rearing you. •Alas for my sons, some unmarried, others married but to no purpose! I shall never set eyes on any children of yours nor shall I know the happiness of being called grandmother.
10 Woe is me, who had many handsome children, but am now bereft and all alone
11 with my many sorrows! •Nor shall I have any. of my sons to bury me when I die."
12   But the holy and God-fearing mother lamented none of them with any such dirge, nor urged any of them to avoid death, nor grieved over them in the moment
13 of their death. •Rather, as though she had a mind of adamant and were this time bringing her brood of sons[c] to birth into immortal life, she encouraged them and
14 pled with them to die for piety's sake. •Mother, soldier of God in piety's cause, elder and woman withal! By your brave endurance you have overcome even the
15 tyrant and in deeds as in words have proven yourself stronger than a man. •When you were seized along with your sons, you stood watching Eleazar under torture
16 and said to your children in the Hebrew tongue, •"My children, noble is the struggle, and since you have been summoned to it to bear witness for our nation,
17 fight zealously for our ancestral Law. •Shameful were it indeed that this old man should endure agonies for piety's sake, while you young men were terrified of
18 torments. •Remember that it is for God's sake you were given a share in the world
19 and the benefit of life, •and accordingly you owe it to God to endure all hardship
20 for his sake, •for whom our father Abraham ventured boldly to sacrifice his son Isaac, the father of our nation; and Isaac, seeing his father's hand, with knife in   Gen 22:10
21 it, fall down against him, did not flinch. •Daniel also, the righteous one, was thrown to the lions, and Hananiah and Azariah and Mishael were cast into the   Dan 6
22 fiery furnace, and all endured for the sake of God. •Therefore, you who have the   Dan 3
23 same faith in God must not be dismayed. •For it would be unreasonable for you who know true religion not to withstand hardships."

---

16 a. The events are in reverse order of the way they appear in Dan, where the fiery furnace comes first in ch. 3 and the account of Daniel in the lion's den in ch. 6. But this need not suggest that our author was working with a different text of Dan but probably only that he regarded Daniel as his primary hero in brave endurance.

   b. "Ten months" is a literal rendering of the Gk. *dekamēnoi*, a common expression in antiquity for the period of gestation, although the correct number of months was known well enough.

   c. For "her brood of sons" (cf. Hadas, *Maccabees*, p. 228) the Gk. has lit. "the number of

her sons," that is "the whole number of seven," everyone without exception.

   d. There is no justification for reading the idea of resurrection into this vs. or for regarding it as a Christian interpolation. The notion of "living unto God" may denote no more than their final vindication by God or their translation to heaven. The apparently solecistic nominative participle *eidotes*, where strict grammar would require the accusative ("knowing full well" = *eidotas*), is not without parallel elsewhere in *Koine* (see Townshend, *APOT*, vol. 2, p. 682, and Hadas, *Maccabees*, p. 231).

24 With these words the mother of the seven exhorted each one and persuaded
25 them to die rather than transgress the commandment of God, •and they knew full
well themselves that those who die for the sake of God live unto God, as do
Abraham and Isaac and Jacob and all the patriarchs.[d]   Ex 3:6
                                                                Mk 12:26f.

1 **17** Some of the guards declared that when she, too, was about to be seized and
put to death, she threw herself into the fire so that no one would touch her body.[a] 2Mac 7:41
2 O mother with the seven sons, who broke down the violence of the tyrant and
3 thwarted his wicked devices and exhibited the nobility of faith! •Nobly set like a
roof upon the pillars of your children, you sustained, without yielding, the
4 earthquake of the tortures. •Be of good cheer, therefore, mother of holy soul,
5 whose hope of endurance is secure with God. •Not so majestic stands the moon
in heaven as you stand, lighting the way to piety for your seven starlike sons, TJob 39:9–40:5
6 honored by God and firmly set with them in heaven. •For your childbearing was
from our father Abraham.

The effect of the martyrdoms

7 If it were possible for us to paint, as on a picture,[b] the story of our piety, would
not those who looked upon it shudder to see the mother of seven sons enduring
8 manifold torments unto death for piety's sake? •It would in fact be appropriate to
inscribe upon their tomb itself, as a memorial to those members of our nation,
the following words:

9

HERE LIE BURIED AN AGED PRIEST
AN OLD WOMAN
AND HER SEVEN SONS
THROUGH THE VIOLENCE OF A TYRANT
BENT ON DESTROYING THE POLITY OF THE HEBREWS

10

THEY VINDICATED THEIR RACE
LOOKING UNTO GOD AND ENDURING
TORMENTS EVEN UNTO DEATH.[c]

11,12 Truly divine was the contest in which they were engaged. •On that day virtue
12 was the umpire and the test to which they were put was a test of endurance. •The
13 prize for victory was incorruption in long-lasting life. •The first to enter the contest
was Eleazar, but the mother of the seven sons competed also, and the brothers as
14 well took part. •The tyrant was the adversary and the world and the life of men 1Cor 4:9

17 a. There is no hint of the mother's suicide in
2Mac, and at this point our author himself is rather
squeamish about it (although in certain circumstances and on certain conditions suicide was
considered acceptable among the Stoics). He attributes the report of it to the guards (Did he possess
no tradition on this matter?) and refers to the matter
in a strangely oblique and fleeting way.

b. The Gk. has no word for "picture," but
reads lit. "as on someone" or "as on something."
Townshend (APOT, vol. 2, p. 683) supposes that
the Gk. verb for "paint" must imply an artist to
paint the picture, takes the preposition epi in the
sense of "in the style of" and translates "as might
some artist." But this seems rather forced, and the
very plausible conjecture that some such Gk. word
as pinakos has dropped out of the text, and that
we should read "as on a picture," is, despite the
lack of MS authority, more acceptable. Also Townshend's translation of the preceding words, "And
had it been lawful for us to paint" (which is a
quite legitimate rendering of the Gk.), implies that

what is involved here is our author's interpretation
of the second commandment as prohibiting all
forms of pictorial art. On the other hand, however,
we have to bear in mind not only that Hellenism
made much of pictorial art and analogy, but that
4Mac is permeated with hellenistic influence, but
also that the religious paintings in the synagogue
at Dura-Europus near Antioch (third century A.D.)
most probably suggest that pictorial representation
among the Jews was possible even at a considerably
earlier stage (see especially E. R. Goodenough,
Jewish Symbols in the Graeco-Roman World, 8
vols. [New York, 1953–58]). Hence, our translation of vs. 7 implies only that our author thinks of
the whole scene of the martyrdoms as so awesome
that it is beyond artistic depiction.

c. The tomb and the proposed epitaph may be
no more than a rhetorical device. But some commentators find here an indication that 4Mac was
composed as a commemorative address to be delivered at the actual tomb of the martyrs (see Hadas,
Maccabees, p. 234).

15 were the spectators. •Piety won the victory and crowned her own contestants.
16 Who did not marvel at the champions of the divine Law; who were not amazed?
17 The tyrant himself and his whole council were astonished at their endurance,
18 on account of which they now stand beside the divine throne and live the life of
19 the age of blessing. •For Moses says, *All the holy ones are under your hands.* ᵈ Deut 33:3
20 These then, having consecrated themselves for the sake of God, are now honored
not only with this distinction but also by the fact that through them our enemies
21 did not prevail against our nation, •and the tyrant was punished and our land
purified, since they became, as it were, a ransom for the sin of our nation. ᵉ
22 Through the blood of these righteous ones and through the propitiation of their
death the divine providence rescued Israel, which had been shamefully treated.
23 For the tyrant Antiochus, observing intently their heroism in virtue and their
endurance under torture, publicly held up their constancy as a model for his
24 soldiers •and so roused them to such a high sense of honor and such courage in
infantry warfare and in the siege of cities that he ravaged and overthrew all his
enemies. ᶠ

1 **18** O offspring of the seed of Abraham, children of Israel, obey this Law and
2 be altogether true to your religion, •knowing that devout reason is master over
the passions, and not only over pains from within but also from outside ourselves. ᵃ
3 Those men who surrendered their bodies to suffering for piety's sake were in
return not only admired by mankind but were also deemed worthy of the divine
4 portion. •And it was because of them that our nation enjoyed peace—they revived
5 the observance of the Law in their land and repulsed their enemies' siege. •And
the tyrant Antiochus was punished on earth and continues to suffer punishment in
death. For when he had failed absolutely to compel the people of Jerusalem to
adopt the pagan way of life, and to forsake the customs of their fathers, he
departed from Jerusalem and marched away against the Persians.

The mother's address to her children

6 The mother of the seven sons also addressed these righteous sayings to her children:
7 "I was a chaste maiden and did not leave my father's house; but I kept guard
8 over the rib built into woman's body. ᵇ •No seducer of the desert nor deceiver in Gen 2:22
the field corrupted me, nor did the seducing and beguiling serpent defile my Gen 3:1–7
9 maidenly purity. ᶜ •Through all the days of my prime I stayed with my husband.
When these sonsᵈ were grown up, their father died. Happy was he, for the life
he lived was blessed with children, and he knew not the pain of the time when
10 they were taken away. •He, while he was still with you, taught you the Law and Gen 4:8
11 the Prophets. •He read to you of Abel, slain by Cain, of Isaac, offered as a burnt Gen 22
12 offering, and of Joseph, in prison. •He spoke to you of the zeal of Phineas, and Gen 39:7–23
Num 25:7–13
13 taught you about Hananiah, Azariah, and Mishael in the fire. •He sang the praises Dan 3
Dan 6

---

d. An exact citation of Deut 33:3 (LXX).

e. On the "ransom" idea in relation to the martyrs, see Theological Importance.

f. Vss. 23f. appear to be out of place in this context where the emphasis is on divine retribution, and inferior as they are in stylistic flourish to the normal mode of writing in 4Mac, they may very well be an interpolation. On the other side, our author may conceivably have had on hand some prosy materials relating to Antiochus' well-known victories and may have inserted them here to accentuate how great was the downfall reported later in 18:5.

18 a. "Pains from within" are mental anguish, and "pains from outside ourselves" are bodily

anguish.

b. Staying at home was of course a means of ensuring the protection of chastity. For "the rib built into woman's body" the Gk. has only "the built-up rib," but in view of Gen 2:22 (LXX) the meaning is not in doubt.

c. The desert was regarded in Judaism and early Christianity as particularly the haunt of evil spirits, and here the reference is to demons that lie in wait to lead women astray. Our philosophically minded author here somewhat surprisingly uses the popular mythological language of the day to affirm the mother's perfect chastity, outside the home as well as within it.

d. The word for "sons" is not expressed in the Gk. text, but is clearly to be understood.

14 of Daniel in the lions' den and called him blessed. •He reminded you of the
scripture of Isaiah which says, *Even though you walk through the fire, the flame*   Isa 43:2
15 *shall not burn you.* •He sang to you the psalm of David which says, *Many are*
16 *the afflictions of the righteous.* •He recited the proverb of Solomon which says,   Ps 34:19
17 *He is a tree of life*[e] *to those who do his will.* •He affirmed the word of Ezekiel,   Prov 3:18
18 *Shall these dry bones live?* •Nor did he forget the song that Moses taught which   Ezek 37:3
19 says, •*I kill and I make alive,* for this is your life and the length[f] of your days.''   Deut 32:39
20   Ah! bitter was the day and yet not bitter when the cruel tyrant of the Greeks
quenched[g] fire with fire in his fierce braziers, and in a furious rage brought to the
catapult and back again to his tortures those seven sons of the daughter of Abraham;
21 he pierced the pupils of their eyes, their tongues he cut out, and slew them with
22 all kinds of torment. •And for these acts the divine justice has pursued and will
23 pursue the accursed tyrant. •But the sons of Abraham, together with their mother,
who won the victor's prize, are gathered together in the choir of their fathers,[h]
having received pure and deathless souls from God, to whom be glory forever   WisSol 8:19
and ever. Amen.

e. In Prov 3:18 it is wisdom that is the tree of
life, but in our author's adaptation the reference is
obviously to God.

f. For "length" A reads "blessedness," which
is followed by Townshend, *APOT*, vol. 2, p. 685.

g. A and S read "kindled," but probably the
more difficult and certainly more graphic reading

"quenched" is to be preferred.

h. Townshend's rendering "gathered together
unto the place of their ancestors" (*APOT*, vol. 2,
p. 685) requires instead of the Gk. *choros* =
"choir" the word chōros = "place." For "gathered together" S has "are celebrated," which
might fit equally well with "choir" or "place."

PSEUDO-PHOCYLIDES

(First Century B.C.–First Century A.D.)

A NEW TRANSLATION AND INTRODUCTION

BY P. W. VAN DER HORST

Introduction

Phocylides was an Ionic poet living in Miletus in the middle of the sixth century B.C.[1] Though his name is almost unknown today, he was famous in antiquity as a writer of maxims with useful advice for daily life.[2] Only a few of these sentences have been preserved.[3] The poem of 230 lines which is under discussion here is undoubtedly not authentic but written pseudonymously under the name of Phocylides. Quite apart from content, features of language and meter make it impossible to attribute the poem to an author of the sixth century B.C. Moreover, since it is evident that the writer knows the Septuagint and Stoic ethics, the sentences of Pseudo-Phocylides must be given a date after the second century B.C.[4]

Though a close study of the text reveals its undeniably Jewish character, the most striking characteristic of the poem is the author's effort to hide this by consistently avoiding any allusion to customs, rules or laws that might be recognized as typically Jewish and also by concealing Old Testament ethics in the disguise of Greek (Ionic) hexametric poetry.[5] He succeeded so well that his poem was held as authentic till the end of the sixteenth century. This characteristic, of course, raises the problem of the author's intentions. What did he wish to accomplish with such a poem? Why did he select only those commandments from the Old Testament with which civilized Greeks would be inclined to agree? Though the solution to this problem may never be found, three possible solutions have been suggested: (1) The author did not mean anything with his poem. He wrote it just for fun, as a kind of exercise in versification. (2) The author wanted to say to his fellow Jews: Look, the best of Greek ethics agrees with the Law, so do not be ashamed of your own tradition over against the Greeks and do not be afraid that you have missed anything by remaining Jewish. (3) The author directed himself to the heathen, not in order to make converts to Judaism (which would be impossible by means of such a poem), but in order to make "sympathizers,"[6]

---

[1] See P. Ahlert, "Phokylides," Pauly-Wissowa vol. 20.1 cols. 503–5.

[2] Phocylides' fame is demonstrated by the references to his poetry in ancient authors, collected by W. Pape and G. Benseler, *Wörterbuch der griechischen Eigennamen* (Braunschweig, 1911[3]; repr. Graz; 1959) s.v. Phocylides.

[3] Latest edition by Z. Franyo, B. Snell, and H. Maehler, *Frühgriechische Lyriker* (Berlin, 1971) pp. 66–73. ET in J. M. Edmonds, *Elegy and Jambus* (LCL, London; Cambridge, Mass., 1931) vol. 1, pp. 172–81.

[4] The most recent defender of the authenticity of the poem is F. Dornseiff, *Echtheitsfragen antik-griechischer Literatur: Rettungen des Theognis, Phokylides, Hekataios, Choirilos*, pp. 37–51. Dornseiff's thesis that Phocylides may have known the OT by contact with the Jewish Diaspora in Miletus and by pre-LXX translations of the Pentateuch has met with serious criticism. See the reviews by E. Howald, *Deutsche Literaturezeitung* 61 (1940) 663–68, and by A. von Blumenthal, *Gnomon* 19 (1943) 289–93.

[5] The first to point this out was J. Bernays, *Über das phokylideische Gedicht* (Berlin, 1856), repr. in his *Gesammelte Abhandlungen* (Berlin, 1885) Bd. 1, pp. 192–261.

[6] For this category and its difference from proselytes and God-fearers see L. H. Feldman, "Jewish 'Sympathizers' in Classical Literature and Inscriptions," *Transactions and Proceedings of the American Philological Association* 81 (1950) 200–08, and especially F. Siegert, "Gottesfürchtige und Sympathisanten," *JSJ* 4 (1973) 109–64.

that is, to win over people to a standpoint more sympathetic to Judaism so as to break through the isolation of the Jews in the hellenistic world.[7]

None of these three possibilities can be ruled out entirely, but many scholars seem to favor the third solution.[8] The arguments are: There was a current in early Judaism that thought it useful, perhaps in a way reminiscent of the so-called Noachian laws, to propagate some universal principles of religion and ethics without the intention of making proselytes.[9] And, secondly, in a number of verses Pseudo-Phocylides runs parallel to passages in Philo's *Hypothetica* and Josephus' *Against Apion* which clearly figure in an apologetic and propagandistic context.[10] It has been suggested that all three of them had a common source which had its origin in a "wide-spread Jewish missionary activity which promoted ethical monotheism."[11] "The original impulse and intention of the Jewish mission lay . . . not in an extension of 'Judaism' as a national and religious cult but in the proclamation of the one God and his universal, ethical standards."[12]

There are problems, however, with this solution: These parallel texts in Philo and Josephus figure in recognizably Jewish writings, and, unlike these writings, our poem can hardly be called a missionary document. Moreover, the relation to the Noachian laws is a very uncertain matter (see below). These points seem to lend support for the second alternative, that Pseudo-Phocylides wrote for his own co-religionists, either to demonstrate that there is no marked difference between Jewish and Greek ethics or to show them that the rules of the Law could be given in a hexametric poem that could match contemporaneous Greek poetry quite well. One might also suggest that it was written as a schoolbook for Jewish children, since we know that collections of sentences were often used as material for writing and reading exercises in hellenistic schools.[13] These sentences would have had educational value at the same time. Another alternative has been suggested by the Jewish scholar G. Alon, who assumes that the author made Phocylides, the acclaimed ancient Greek writer, present the principles of Jewish life in order to demonstrate to Jews who were engrossed in hellenistic culture, and who imitated its manners and deeds, that even an honored poet like Phocylides recognized Jewish moral requisites. He did not have to mention abandonment of idolatry, which was taken for granted even by these thoroughly hellenized Jews.[14] This is a most attractive theory, explaining both the use of a pseudonym and the absence of the prohibition of idolatry, but it cannot be proved or disproved. It does, however, merit serious consideration. Ultimately we will have to await new data before the intention of this author will become wholly clear to us.

Original language and texts

There is no doubt that the original language of the poem was Greek. There are no versions in other ancient languages, and all extant manuscripts are in Greek. Of these many manuscripts only a limited number are valuable, namely the five which Douglas Young has used for his recent edition:[15]

---

[7] A fourth possibility suggests that the poem was written by a "sympathizer" or "God-fearer," not by a Jew (which is the position of M. Rossbroich, *De Pseudo-Phocylideis*, diss. Münster, 1910). If this is true Ps-Phoc should not be included in this volume.

[8] Most modern scholars see in Ps-Phoc a kind of (clumsy) propagandistic poet.

[9] See G. Klein, *Der älteste christliche Katechismus und die jüdische Propaganda-Literatur*, pp. 8–65, and M. Guttmann, *Das Judentum und seine Umwelt* (Berlin, 1927).

[10] This was pointed out by P. Wendland, "Die Therapeuten und die philonische Schrift vom beschaulichen Leben," *Jahrbücher für classische Philologie* Supplementband 22 (1896) 709–12.

[11] J. E. Crouch, *The Origin and Intention of the Colossian Haustafel* (FRLANT 109, 1972) p. 89.

[12] Crouch, *Origin*, p. 94.

[13] See H. I. Marrou, *Histoire de l'éducation dans l'antiquité* (Paris, 1960⁵) p. 218.

[14] G. Alon, "The Halakah in the Teaching of the Twelve Apostles," *Studies in Jewish History* (Hakibbutz Hameuchad, 1967²) vol. 1, pp. 274–94 [in Heb.]. A similar position is defended by N. Walter in his translation (with introduction) of Ps-Phoc in the series *JSHRZ* 4.3 (1983).

[15] D. Young, *Theognis, Ps.-Pythagoras, Ps.-Phocylides, Chares, Anonymi aulodia, fragmentum teleiambicum* (Leipzig, 1971²). This is the critical edition behind our translation. Young discusses the textual tradition on pp. xvi–xviii. More extensive discussions may be found in W. Kroll, "Zur Überlieferung der Pseudophocylidea," *Rheinisches Museum* 47 (1892) 457–59; A. Ludwich, *Lectiones Pseudophocylideae* (Konigsberg, 1892); idem, *Über das Spruchbuch des falschen Phokylides* (Programm Königsberg, 1904) pp. 1–26 (review by W. Kroll, *Berliner Philologische Wochenschrift* 25 [1905] 241–43). A new edition by P. Derron is in preparation.

        M: tenth century, in Paris;
        B: tenth century, in Oxford;
        P: twelfth century, in Paris;
        L: thirteenth century, in Florence;
        V: thirteenth-fourteenth century, in Vienna.

Still debated is the value of the so-called *Psi* group of manuscripts of the Sibylline Oracles. This group has inserted Pseudo-Phocylides 5–79 between Sibylline Oracles 2.55 and 149. Seventy-five lines of Pseudo-Phocylides occupy ninety-five lines in the Sibylline Oracles because this *Psi* group has again inserted twenty lines of its own into the quotation from Pseudo-Phocylides; the result is an "interpolated interpolation." Nevertheless, according to some scholars these twenty interpolated lines are an original part of the text of Pseudo-Phocylides, and *Psi*, therefore, represents a better text tradition of lines 5–79 than the manuscripts listed above.[16] This theory, however, has not won acceptance because the secondary character of the extra lines is too obvious to consider them seriously as authentic.[17]

Date and provenance

Though the dates proposed for Pseudo-Phocylides vary from the sixth century B.C. to the fourth century A.D., there is a growing consensus to ascribe the poem to the period between 200 B.C. and A.D. 200. We must consider if it is possible to fix the time of origin more precisely. This is difficult, however, because nowhere in the poem are there references to political events or circumstances that might help. Nevertheless, there are some features of language and thought that make it possible to narrow down the above-mentioned period.

Pseudo-Phocylides uses about thirty words (or word forms) which are not attested in Greek literature before the third century B.C.; about fifteen of these do not occur in texts before the first century B.C. This suggests 100 B.C. as the earliest possible date.[18] The same date is suggested by the unmistakable acquaintance of the author of Pseudo-Phocylides with the Septuagint, including the Prophets and Wisdom literature as well as the Pentateuch (which is evident in more than half of the poem).[19] Also undeniable is the influence of Stoicism on the author.[20] In itself this Stoic influence indicates only that the poem was written after 300 B.C., but its affinity with the thought of first-century A.D. Stoics like Musonius Rufus, Hierocles, and Seneca points strongly to the Imperial period.[21] The first century A.D. is also suggested by Pseudo-Phocylides' many agreements with Philo and by the similarities it shares with the "diatribes" of the popular philosophical-ethical preachers, who were most active in the early Roman period.[22]

This cumulative evidence seems to favor a date between about 50 B.C. and A.D. 100. Moreover, if we recognize the probable Alexandrian provenance (see below), then the most probable date of origin lies in the period when the relations between Jews and Greeks in Alexandria were not too tense, namely during the reigns of the emperors Augustus (30 B.C.–A.D. 14) and Tiberius (A.D. 14–37). It is unlikely that after the anti-Jewish pogroms in Alexandria during the reign of Caligula (A.D. 37–41)[23] an Alexandrian Jew could have

---

[16] See esp. A. Kurfess, "Das Mahngedicht des sogenannten Phokylides im zweiten Buch der Oracula Sibyllina," *ZNW* 38 (1939) 171–81. The first to propose this theory was J. Sitzler in a long view of Rossbroich's dissertation (*De Pseudo-phocylides*, 1910) in *Wochenschrift für klassische Philologie* 29 (1912) 449–57.

[17] See the criticism by R. Keydell, "Die griechische Dichtung der Kaiserzeit," *Jahresbericht über die Fortschritte der klassischen Altertumswissenschaften* 272 (1941) 27f.

[18] For a list of these words see my *The Sentences* 55–57. Of course these data are too scanty to base a firm conclusion upon them. But in combination with the following arguments this fact receives its due weight.

[19] See the nn. to the translation. Very clear instances are the allusions to Jer 9:22 in l. 53 and Prov 6:6–8c in ll. 164–74.

[20] E.g. in ll. 63–67 where Ps-Phoc distinguishes between different types of anger, zeal, and love, which are Stoic distinctions.

[21] C. Schneider, *Kulturgeschichte des Hellenismus* (München, 1967) Bd. 1, p. 892, even asserts that Ps-Phoc is "*von Musunius Rufus oder einem seiner Geistesverwandten beeinflusst.*"

[22] See P. Wendland, *Therapeuten*, p. 712, n. 2, with reference to his "Philo und die kynisch-stoische Diatribe," in P. Wendland and O. Kern, *Beiträge zur Geschichte der griechischen Philosophie und Religion* (Berlin, 1895) pp. 1–75.

[23] See E. Schürer, *The History of the Jewish People in the Age of Jesus Christ*, new English version rev. and ed. by G. Vermes and F. Millar (Edinburgh, 1973) vol. 1, pp. 388–94.

maintained so great an openness toward pagan culture. Therefore, the most probable date would be somewhere between 30 B.C. and A.D. 40.[24] Needless to say, this does not mean that another dating would be impossible, but the characteristics of the poem are explained best by a date within this period.

That Alexandria is to be preferred to other places as the city of origin is a conclusion based on one single line in the poem (102), where it is said that it is not good to dissect the human body. As far as we know, it was only in Alexandria that human anatomy was studied by applying dissection,[25] which is of course no definite proof that Pseudo-Phocylides was written there. Since a prohibition of the dissection of humans would make more sense if Pseudo-Phocylides originated in Alexandria, and since in other respects the poem excellently fits in with the Jewish-hellenistic culture in Alexandria as we know it from other sources, that city is most likely the place of origin.[26]

Historical importance

If Pseudo-Phocylides really belongs to a current of nonproselyting religious propaganda of ancient Judaism,[27] are there more writings from the hellenistic-Roman period which reflect that same interest? Rabbi Klein has pointed in this connection to the so-called *Derek Erez* literature, which he saw as the continuation of the universalistic Wisdom literature of Israel's *hakhamin*.[28] But, as has been pointed out, Klein is inclined to project late sources back into an earlier period.[29] Nevertheless, he is right in stressing that even in the Old Testament period there was always a nonparticularistic, universalistic current in Israel, embodied in the Wisdom literature, which never disappeared, not even after Ezra. It is well known that this Wisdom literature often incorporated non-Israelite wisdom, just as the author of Pseudo-Phocylides took over many maxims from Greek authors before him. So we must bear in mind that this tendency was not new among the Jews of the hellenistic age. Closer parallels, however, than the *Derek Erez* tractates are the "forged quotations" from classical Greek poets like Aeschylus, Sophocles, Euripides, Menander, Diphilus, and others,[30] and even more the (Syr.) sentences of Menander the Wise.[31] By means of this Jewish pseudepigraphic activity no reasonable Jew would have expected to convert pagans to Judaism. The forgers may have had no other intention than inculcating in heathen minds some universally valid ethical and religious principles, perhaps with the hope of humanizing pagan society. These Jews may have felt obliged to inform their non-Jewish fellow men about some fundamental and universal principles of religion and ethics without feeling any necessity to make converts to Judaism.[32]

Is there any relation between this literature and the seven so-called Noachian laws? As is well known, unlike the Sinaitic laws these laws were considered by the Jews to be valid

[24] Cf. the dating by A. Kurfess, "Oracula Sibyllina I–II," *ZNW* 40 (1941) 162: *"ungefähr in die Zeit unmittelbar vor oder nach Christi Geburt"*; F. Christ ("Das Leben nach dem Tode bei Pseudo-Phokylides," *TZ* 31 [1975] 140) dates the work to the time of Jesus.

[25] See L. Edelstein, "The History of Anatomy in Antiquity," *Ancient Medicine* (Baltimore, 1967) pp. 247–301; F. Kudlien, "Anatomie," Pauly-Wissowa Sup. 11 (1968) cols. 38–48.

[26] See e.g. W. Kroll, "Phokylides (2)," Pauly-Wissowa Bd. 20.1 (1941) col. 507; P. M. Fraser, *Ptolemaic Alexandria* (Oxford, 1972) vol. 2, p. 539.

[27] Let us adopt this (debatable) thesis at this point for the sake of convenience.

[28] Klein, *Der älteste christliche Katechismus*, pp. 66–142.

[29] W. D. Davies, *Paul and Rabbinic Judaism* (London, 1955²) pp. 134f. Crouch, *Haustafel*, p. 16, n. 16. On the date of the *Derek Erez* tractates see the Introduction to the English translation in A. Cohen (ed.), *The Minor Tractates of the Talmud* (2 vols.; London, 1965).

[30] Now conveniently collected by A. M. Denis, *Fragmenta Pseudepigraphorum quae supersunt Graeca* (PVTG 3; Leiden, 1970) pp. 161–74, and discussed by Denis in his *Introduction aux pseudépigraphes grecs d'Ancien Testament* (SVTP 1; Leiden, 1970) pp. 223–38. Most of these quotations have been preserved by Ps-Justin (*De Monarchia, Cohortatio*), Clement of Alexandria (*Stromateis*), and Eusebius (*Praeparatio Evangelica*).

[31] Most easily accessible in the German translation by P. Riessler, *Altjüdisches Schrifttum ausserhalb der Bibel* (Augsburg, 1928; repr. Heidelberg, 1966) pp. 1047–57. Syr. text in J. P. N. Land, *Anecdota Syriaca* (Leiden, 1862) vol. 1, pp. 64–73. See the discussion in Schürer, *Geschichte des jüdischen Volkes* (Leipzig, 1909⁴) Bd. 3, pp. 622f., and the literature mentioned by Denis, *Introduction*, p. 211, n. 49. J. P. Audet ("La sagesse de Ménandre l'Egyptien," *RB* 59 [1952] 55–81) asserts that this Menander is not a Jew but a so-called God-fearer. That the fourth and seventh spurious *Epistles* of Heraclitus belong to this category is extremely doubtful; see J. Strugnell and H. Attridge, "The Epistles of Heraclitus and the Jewish Pseudepigrapha: a Warning," *HTR* 64 (1971) 411–13.

[32] Cf. Guttmann, *Judentum*, pp. 110f.

for the whole of humanity. These seven commandments were: (1) the command to establish courts of justice; (2) the prohibition of idolatry; (3) the injunction against blaspheming the name of God; (4) the prohibition of murder; (5) the ban against adultery and incest; (6) the forbiddance of robbery and theft; (7) the proscription against eating meat with the blood of life in it.[33] The gentiles, it was believed, had undertaken to keep these laws, but did not do so. It has been asserted that Pseudo-Phocylides, in a more or less veiled way, incorporated these seven commandments in his poem[34] and added a number of rules with the same "unwritten law" character, partly from Greek, partly from Jewish sources.[35] This might be true. With the first Noachian commandment one can compare several lines in Pseudo-Phocylides dealing with the incorruptible administration of justice (9–12, 86); with the second and third, 8 and 54, which stipulate that the one God has to be honored;[36] with the fourth, 4, 32, and 58; with the fifth, 3 and 177–83; with the sixth, 6, 18, 135f. and 154, and with the seventh, 147f. Therefore, at least twenty-five lines reflect ideas which are found in the Noachian laws. But it apparently was not Pseudo-Phocylides' only intention, if it was his intention at all, to propagate these laws,[37] for he added a great number of other rules. It is significant, however, that all these rules of behavior are cast in the same mold; that is to say, not one presupposes Jewish national particularities but all can claim a universal validity equal to the Noachian laws. Some of them even prove to be so-called "unwritten laws" of the Greeks,[38] and several have their parallels in Stoic lists of duties, which ofter incorporated earlier "unwritten laws."

Nevertheless, in spite of this universalistic tendency of his poem, Pseudo-Phocylides has succeeded in stating clearly two principal Jewish tenets of his age: that there is one God (l. 54) and that there will be a resurrection of the dead (ll. 103f.).[39] Also the thought of a retribution in the hereafter, closely related to the tenet of the resurrection,[40] is possibly present in the poem (l. 11). The reference to the resurrection clearly shows that the author of Pseudo-Phocylides is Jewish,[41] and perhaps it is for this reason that he immediately continues with remarks about the deification and incorruptibility of the soul, which make a very Greek impression.[42]

If all the above is true, we may conclude very tentatively that in the poem of Pseudo-Phocylides we have a representative of that universalistic current in ancient Judaism. While holding to the principal tenets of "orthodox" Judaism, it tried to give to the gentiles some ethical principles that might humanize life in family and society, using therefore all sources that could contribute to this aim, both Jewish and Greek.[43]

However, this thesis, which cannot be proved, could be wrong. Another possible solution

---

[33] See G. F. Moore, *Judaism* (Cambridge, Mass., 1927) vol. 1, pp. 274f.; H. L. Strack and P. Billerbeck, *Kommentar zum N.T. aus Talmud und Midrasch* (München, 1926) Bd. 3, pp. 37f.

[34] Guttmann, *Judentum*, p. 112, and Siegert, *JSJ* 4 (1973) 125.

[35] On the striking analogy between Noachian laws and unwritten laws in Philo see the remarks by H. A. Wolfson, *Philo* (Cambridge, Mass., 1948²) vol. 2, pp. 183–87. Cf. Crouch, *Origin*, p. 96: "Both (Noachian laws and unwritten laws) were regarded as expressions of a primitive code of ethics which was valid for the entire human race."

[36] Of course Ps-Phoc could not prohibit idolatry and blasphemy openly without making known his Jewishness. Hence only this positive formulation appears in ll. 8 and 54. Cf. the same positive formulation in a Noachian context in Jub 7:20.

[37] S. Krauss emphatically denies that the poem of Ps-Phoc has anything to do with the Noachian precepts ("Les préceptes des Noachides," *REJ* 47 [1903] 32f.) as does G. Alon, "The Halakah in the Teaching of the Twelve Apostles," 277.

[38] E.g. the injunctions to leave no corpse unburied (vs. 99) and always to return a benefit (vs. 80). See R. Hirzel, *Agraphos Nomos* (Abhandl. der königl. sächsischen Gesellschaft der Wissenschaften, Philol.-hist. Classe 20, 1; Leipzig, 1900).

[39] On these principal tenets of Judaism see W. Bousset and H. Gressmann, *Die Religion des Judentums im späthellenistischen Zeitalter* (Tübingen, 1926³; repr. 1966⁴) pp. 158f.

[40] Bousset and Gressmann, *Religion*, pp. 192f.

[41] How strange this theory was to non-Jewish ears may be seen from Acts 17:32.

[42] The whole passage ll. 103–15 is not very consistent in matters of the hereafter, "but to press this point would be to ignore the widespread tendency of language about the afterlife to admit inconsistencies" (A. D. Nock, *Essays on Religion and the Ancient World* [Oxford, 1972] vol. 1, p. 507, n. 19). See further below.

[43] Another point of importance is that we have in Ps-Phoc an example of Jewish-hellenistic ethics as it found its way into so many parts of the NT. The parallels to the paraenetic passages of the NT are numerous and have been adduced especially by Martin Dibelius in his commentaries. Cf. his remarks in *Die Formgeschichte des Evangeliums* (Tübingen, 1971⁶) p. 239. The NT parallels will be referred to in the nn. to the translation. See also P. W. van der Horst, "Pseudo-Phocylides and the New Testament," *ZNW* 69 (1978) 187–202.

is that of Alon (see above), who suggests that Pseudo-Phocylides is a very interesting example of inner-Jewish "propaganda" meant to keep Jews that were in danger of sliding down too far into an un-Jewish way of life within the limits of Judaism and to encourage them by the suggestion that even a renowned pagan author propagated the principles of Jewish life. Further and closer study of hellenistic Judaism will, we hope, shed more light on this still obscure field.

Theological importance

To speak about the theology of Pseudo-Phocylides would be rash, for his poem consists mainly of ethical rules and many of his ideas are very general. By what principles the author was guided in his eclectic procedure we have already seen above. To systematize his thoughts, which are uttered so unsystematically, is difficult; there is no unifying conception behind the poem and no coherence exists in it since he has drawn from so many sources. Sometimes there are even contradictory statements.[44] In general, one may say, Pseudo-Phocylides is guilty of a certain superficiality.

The "doctrine" of God in Pseudo-Phocylides is, of course, monotheistic. The only wise and mighty God, who is rich in blessings (l. 54), must be honored before anything else (l. 8). His image is man's spirit, a loan of God to the mortals (l. 106). As the source of our prosperity, God demands that men share their wealth with those in need (l. 29).[45] God hates perjury (l. 17). He blesses each creature with a means of self-defense; in addition man receives the ability to think and speak (ll. 125–28). This statement and the one in line 106 (see above) no doubt imply that God is the creator of the universe, though this is nowhere actually expressed. This universe is harmonious and coherent (ll. 71–74). God will judge us after death (l. 11) and is the ruler of all souls, whether high or low (l. 111). The emphasis on the instability of life (ll. 27, 116, 118–20) may derive from the underlying thought that the ways of God are inscrutable.

The problem of the so-called polytheistic references has been exaggerated.[46] Twice (ll. 75, 163) reference is made to "the Blessed Ones" (Gk. *makares*), by which the heavenly bodies are designated. Although in Greek literature this term generally means "the gods," it does not mean here that sun, moon, and stars are gods any more than does the use of a current Platonic term by Philo when he calls them "visible gods" (*De opificio mundi* 27). It does mean ascription of personality to the heavenly bodies, but that is not inconsistent with Jewish monotheism.[47] In two other lines (98, 104) there is the plural form "gods." In the former case this reading makes no sense at all and the text should be emended.[48] The second reference, where it is declared that the departed become gods (l. 104), looks rather pagan and has no exact Jewish parallels, though often the deceased were regarded as angels, and angels were often called gods.[49] Here we can say that Pseudo-Phocylides goes rather far in an effort to neutralize the effect of his statement on the bodily resurrection in lines 103f. Real "polytheistic" references are not found in Pseudo-Phocylides.

Pseudo-Phocylides' teaching on man contains several Old Testament ideas. Man's body is of the dust of the earth and at death returns to it; his spirit, which is God's image, is released into the air at death (ll. 106–8).[50] From the numerous warnings against evil and wrongdoing one may conclude that the poet assumes that human nature is inclined toward evil. Except by implication, the writer almost nowhere delineates the character of the good life, so intent is he upon warning his readers against the evil life. He condemns a great number of evils and clearly is more concerned with the consideration of specific evils than

---

[44] Though he sees all this clearly, J. J. Lewis nevertheless goes too far in systematizing Ps-Phoc's "doctrines" in his "The Teaching of Pseudo-Phocylidea," *The London Quarterly and Holborn Review* (Oct. 1953) 295–98. Yet his attempt is of some use.

[45] This is actually the only line in the poem that shows a religious foundation of ethics.

[46] Because of them several scholars have denied the Jewish origin of the poem.

[47] See Nock, *Essays*, vol. 2, p. 912. Often the stars were regarded as angels; cf. Bousset and Gressmann, *Religion*, pp. 322f.

[48] We read *gooisi* with Bernays instead of *theoisi*.

[49] See on this line the sound remarks by M. Hengel, "Anonymität, Pseudepigraphie und «literarische Falschung» in der jüdisch-hellenistischen Literatur," *Pseudepigrapha I, Entretiens de la Fondation Hardt* (Vandoeuvres–Geneva, 1972) vol. 18, p. 297.

[50] On afterlife see further below.

with any abstract conception of evil or its origin. Behind all his precepts is the assumption that, if man so desires, his will is strong enough for him to reject evil and cleave to good. There is no mention of the need for forgiveness or for divine aid in conquering evil.

Lines 153–74 form the longest coherent passage of the poem and also constitute its best part in expressiveness and style.[51] Here, in accordance with the positive appraisal of labor in the Old Testament and Judaism,[52] Pseudo-Phocylides sings a song in praise of labor and against idleness. Work is useful and important for man; it is the only route to an honorable existence.

To enumerate all the evils that are condemned by our author would be tedious and useless. One topic, however, must be mentioned because Pseudo-Phocylides devotes so much attention to it, namely sexual sins. He warns against nearly every sexual aberration that one can imagine (viz. ll. 177–94). Nevertheless, he heartily encourages marital relations (175f.). That, too, is in accordance with Judaism, in which a positive evaluation of marriage is often accompanied by strong puritanism.[53] The reason Pseudo-Phocylides chose to elaborate upon this subject is probably that injunctions concerning "forbidden relations" formed a set part of Jewish propaganda.[54]

The poet lays stress on moderation and self-restraint. Due measure is best in all things. The word "measure," or "moderation" (Gr. *metron*), occurs several times in the poem (see ll. 36, 69, 98). This Greek ideal was, of course, fully compatible with his Jewish ideas. More Jewish than Greek is the accent he lays on practicing justice and mercy, especially in lines 9–41, where a real concern for the poor and the weak is evident. Also great emphasis is laid on good relationships in the family, between wife and husband (ll. 195–97), between children and parents (ll. 207–9), and between slaves and masters (ll. 223–27).[55] Friendship is highly appraised (ll. 142, 218). Even to one's personal enemy kind help is to be given when there is an opportunity (ll. 140–42).[56] The writer reveals a keen sense of the value of good relations.

It is clear that Pseudo-Phocylides' remarks on the afterlife are inconsistent.[57] Admittedly, inconsistencies in theories of the afterlife are very common with philosophically untrained people. But in this matter our author seems to go to the extreme. On the one hand he clearly expresses his hope of the resurrection of the dead (ll. 103f.). It is for that reason that the remains of the dead are to be treated with respect (l. 102). He even says that the souls remain in the deceased (l. 105). On the other hand he declares that the immortal souls go to the everlasting home of Hades, where God rules over them (ll. 111f.). Moreover, he says that the body is turned to dust and the spirit is released into the air (ll. 107f.). This third statement is not necessarily a contradiction of the second, for in the hellenistic period Hades was often transposed into the air,[58] and in Judaism the distinction between soul and spirit was often neglected.[59] The first and second statements, however, are hardly reconcilable. Again it is clear that Pseudo-Phocylides has no logically thought-out system. Yet he does not give the impression of being an uneducated man. Had he been uneducated he could not have written as well as he did in hexameters and in an artificial Greek dialect that was used only in poetry. He must have been one of the upper class who could afford a thorough literary training but who did not go beyond that.

[51] This is the judgment of several scholars, e.g. Bernays, *Gesammelte Abhandlungen*, vol. 1, p. 209, and Bousset and Gressmann, *Religion*, p. 431. The only other coherent passage is ll. 177–94 (on sexual sins).

[52] See F. Hauck, "Arbeit," *RAC* (Stuttgart, 1950) Bd. 1, p. 588. J. Jeremias, *Jerusalem in the Time of Jesus* (London, 1969) pp. 1f.

[53] Cf. Nock, *Essays*, vol. 2, p. 894.

[54] See Josephus, *Apion* 2.199–203.

[55] One is reminded here of the so-called *Haustafeln* in the Epistles to the Colossians and Ephesians. Crouch (*Origin and Intention of the Colossian Haustafel*) discusses the relation between these passages and Ps-Phoc and points to their common background in hellenistic-Jewish propaganda.

[56] This line has allured some scholars (e.g. J. Scaliger) to the view that the poet must have been a Christian ("love your enemy!"), but Bernays, *Gesammelte Abhandlungen*, Bd. 1, p. 197, rightly referred to Ex. 23:5 as the source of this line. Yet Harnack (*TLZ* 10 [1885] 159f.) still believed that the author was a Christian.

[57] See n. 42; see also H. C. C. Cavallin, *Life after Death. Paul's Argument for the Resurrection of the Dead in I Cor. 15. Part I: An Enquiry into the Jewish Background* (Lund, 1974) pp. 151–55 (on Ps-Phoc) and pp. 199–202 (on this phenomenon in Judaism in general).

[58] See F. Cumont, *After Life in Roman Paganism* (New Haven, 1922; repr. New York, 1959) pp. 81–83.

[59] See Bousset and Gressmann, *Religion*, pp. 400f.

Relation to canonical books

As indicated above, Pseudo-Phocylides probably knew the whole Septuagint.[60] But not all parts of the Septuagint influenced him equally. There is no doubt that he knew the Prophets,[61] but the reminiscences are not many. The Wisdom books (especially Prov and Sir) obviously influenced him much more strongly, and there are many reminiscences or allusions to these books.[62] Most manifest is the influence of the Pentateuch, of which some chapters have affected him strongly; foremost among them is Leviticus 19.[63] Many verses of this chapter have their echo in the poem, probably because the principal tenets of Old Testament ethics are summarized there. Leviticus 18 and Exodus 22 and 23 (from the so-called Book of the Covenant) also have many parallels in Pseudo-Phocylides. These chapters seem to have been followed rather closely. Some scholars correctly see in lines 3–8 a summary of the Decalogue.[64] It is clear therefore that a number of central passages in the Pentateuch have done much in shaping the poem of Pseudo-Phocylides. That Genesis and the other historical narratives of the Pentateuch do not play a part can be explained by the nature of the poem.

It is very unlikely that Pseudo-Phocylides has influenced any of the New Testament authors. That there are many parallels between Pseudo-Phocylides and the New Testament is explained by their common background, namely the Old Testament and hellenistic Jewish culture. These parallels, and also those from the Old Testament, will be noted in the margin of the translation.

Relation to apocryphal books

Of the apocryphal books the Wisdom of Jesus ben Sirach has the closest affinity to Pseudo-Phocylides, but at the same time there are marked differences; Sirach is certainly not as universalistic as Pseudo-Phocylides. A similar situation exists in the case of Tobit; its emphasis on the duty of burying the dead is paralleled in Pseudo-Phocylides 99. For the relationship of Pseudo-Phocylides to pseudepigraphic literature see Historical Importance.

Cultural importance

In antiquity the poem apparently influenced few writers. The first to quote from it was Stobaeus, who wrote in the fifth century A.D. No author in the Middle Ages quoted from it, yet the text was being copied (see the dates of the MSS, above). The first printed edition appeared in 1495 from Venice. Subsequently the poet received great popularity. In the sixteenth century there were numerous editions, translations, and commentaries. The poem became a favorite lecture source for young schoolboys. Pseudo-Phocylides embodied the ideal combination of biblical ethics and classical forms. And because the poem was deemed authentic, one was delighted that a real heathen had presented a testimony to truths that in essentials were identical with biblical doctrines. Natural reason proved to consent to biblical ideas.[65]

In 1591 the first doubts concerning the authenticity of the poem were raised,[66] and fifteen years later the great Joseph Scaliger demonstrated persuasively that it was not from the real Phocylides.[67] The result was a rapid decline of interest in the poem,[68] which was neglected

---

[60] Cf. A. Beltrami, "Ea quae apud Pseudo-Phocylidem Veteris et Novi Testamenti vestigia deprehenduntur," *Rivista di Filologia e Istruzione Classica* 36 (1908) 411–23, who gathers a large collection of parallels (several of which, however, must be rejected).

[61] E.g. l. 53 is evidently inspired by Jer 9:22 (or 1Kgs 2:10 LXX).

[62] Most clear is the influence of LXX Prov 6:6–8c in Ps-Phoc 164–74.

[63] Bernays, in his pioneering study *Über das phokylideische Gedicht*, which appeared in 1856, was the first to point this out.

[64] E.g. the fact that the prohibition of adultery is mentioned first is paralleled in several other free renderings of the Decalogue; see Bousset and Gressmann, *Religion*, p. 425 with n. 3.

[65] For the history of Ps-Phoc in the sixteenth century see Bernays, *Gesammelte Abhandlungen*, Bd. 1, pp. 192f.

[66] By F. Sylburg, *Epicae elegiacaeque minorum poetarum gnomae* (Frankfurt, 1591).

[67] In *Animadversiones in Chronologica Eusebii*, printed in his *Thesaurus Temporum* (Leiden, 1606), pp. 88f.

[68] See F. Susemihl, *Geschichte der griechischen Litteratur in der Alexandrinerzeit* (Leipzig, 1892) Bd. 2, p. 642, n. 63.

until Jacob Bernays wrote his famous study on our author in 1856. The popularity and influence of Pseudo-Phocylides lasted only a century, from 1500 until 1600, but no doubt before and after that period many read his lines and perhaps were edified.

SELECT BIBLIOGRAPHY

Charlesworth, *PMR*, pp. 173–75.
Delling, *Bibliographie*, p. 56.
Denis, *Introduction*, pp. 215–19.

Bernays, J. *Über das phokylideische Gedicht*. Berlin, 1856; reprinted in his *Gesammelte Abhandlungen*. Berlin, 1885; Bd. 1, pp. 192–261. (This fundamental work was the basis of all subsequent study of Ps-Phoc.)

Crouch, J. E. *The Origin and Intention of the Colossian Haustafel*. FRLANT 109; Göttingen, 1972. (Crouch discusses Ps-Phoc along the lines indicated by Klein [1909], but follows more refined methods.)

Dornseiff, F. *Echtheitsfragen antik-griechischer Literatur: Rettungen des Theognis, Phokylides, Hekataios, Choirilos*. Berlin, 1939; pp. 37–51. (The latest and most intelligent defense of the authenticity of the poem.)

Farina, A. *Silloge Pseudofocilidea*. Naples, 1962. (Introduction, Gk. text, Italian translation, some nn.; has a curious theory on the origin of the poem.)

Horst, P. W. van der. *The Sentences of Pseudo-Phocylides. Introduction, Translation and Commentary*. SVTP 4; Leiden, 1978. (Extensive discussion and commentary on the Gk. text; also contains a concordance.)

Klein, G. *Der älteste christliche Katechismus und die jüdische Propaganda-Literatur*. Berlin, 1909; see especially pp. 143–53. (The first to place Ps-Phoc in the context of universalistic, non-proselytizing Jewish propaganda.)

Kroll, W. "Phokylides" (2), Pauly-Wissowa. Stuttgart, 1941; vol. 20.1, pp. 505–10. (Very learned discussion, stresses the hellenistic elements in the poem, underrates its Jewishness.)

Küchler, M. *Frühjüdische Weisheitstraditionen. Zum Fortgang weisheitlichen Denkens im Bereich des frühjüdischen Jahweglaubens*. Orbis Biblicus et Orientalis 26; Freiburg i/d Schweiz, Göttingen, 1979; pp. 236–302.

Rossbroich, M. *De Pseudo-Phocylideis* (diss. Münster, 1910). (The latest commentary on the Gk. text; sees in Ps-Phoc a God-fearing gentile.)

Schürer, E. *Geschichte des jüdischen Volkes im Zeitalter Jesu Christi*. Leipzig, 1909⁴; Bd. 3, pp. 617–22. (A very useful survey of the older literature on Ps-Phoc and a significant discussion of the problems.)

THE SENTENCES OF PSEUDO-PHOCYLIDES

Prologue

1 Phocylides, the wisest of men, sets forth
2 these counsels of God by his holy judgments, gifts of blessing.[a]

Summary of the Decalogue

3 Neither commit adultery nor rouse homosexual passion.   Ex 20:14; Deut 5:18 Lev 18:22; 20:13
4 Neither devise treachery nor stain your hands with blood.   Ex 20:13; Deut 5:17
5 Do not become rich unjustly, but live from honorable means.[a]
6 Be content with what you have and abstain from what is another's.[b]   Heb 13:5; Tlss 4:2; Ex 20:17 Deut 5:21
7 Do not tell lies, but always speak the truth.   Prov 21:3; Sir 7:13; TDan 5:2 Eph 4:25
8 Honor God foremost, and afterward your parents.[c]   Sir 1:14–16; Ex 20:12 Deut 5:16; Lev 19:3 Prov 23:22–25

Exhortation to justice

9 Always dispense justice and let not your judgment be influenced by favor.[a]
10 Do not cast down the poor unjustly, do not judge partially.[b]
11 If you judge evilly, subsequently God will judge you.[c]   Prov 17:15; Mt 7:2
12 Flee false witness; award what is just.   Ex 20:16; Deut 5:20 Prov 21:28
13 Watch over a deposit, and in everything keep faith.   Lev 5:20–26; Ex 22:6–12 Ezek 18:7
14 Give a just measure, and an extra full measure of all things is good.   Deut 25:14f.; Prov 11:1; 16:11; 20:10; Amos 8:4–6 Hos 12:8; Mic 6:11 Ezek 45:10; Lk. 6:38 Lev 19:35f.

15 Do not make a balance unequal, but weigh honestly.
16 And do not commit perjury, neither ignorantly nor willingly.   Ex 20:7; Deut 5:11 Lev 19:12; Sir 23:11
17 The immortal God hates a perjurer, whosoever it is who has sworn.[d]   WisSol 14:28f.; PssSol 4:4
18 Do not steal seeds. Cursed is whosoever takes (them).
19 Give the laborer his pay, do not afflict the poor.   Lev 19:3; Deut 24:14 Jas 5:4; Amos 8:4; Sir 4:1–4
20 Take heed of your tongue, keep your word hidden in (your) heart.   Prov 21:23; Eccl 5:2 Sir 21:26
21 Neither wish to do injustice, nor therefore allow another to do injustice.

Admonition to mercy

22 Give to the poor man at once, and do not tell him to come tomorrow.   Prov 3:27f.; Sir 4:3

Prologue
a. These opening lines correspond with the closing lines (229f.); hence there is little reason to regard them as spurious as has often been done since they are missing in some MSS.

Summary of the Decalogue
a. There is a very strong emphasis on justice in Ps-Phoc; especially cf. ll. 9, 12, 14f., 21, 22f., 29.
b. For ll. 3–6 cf. Mk 7:21f., and for the traditional combination of licentiousness and covetousness cf. also Eph 4:19; 5:3–5.
c. For the combination of these two commandments (not in this form in the OT, but traditional in Gk. ethics) cf. especially SibOr 3.593f.; Jub

7:20; Josephus, *Apion* 2.206; Philo, *Spec. Leg.* 2.235.

Exhortation to justice
a. Warnings against partiality in the administration of justice are frequent in the OT, e.g. Ex 23:1–3; Deut 1:17; 16:18–20; Lev 19:15; Sir 19:13–17; cf. Jn 7:24.
b. See the references in the previous n. For the concern for the poor cf. Ex 23:6; Prov 22:22; Sir 4:1–6.
c. It is uncertain whether the divine judgment takes place in this life or in the hereafter.
d. This may be a rendering of Ex 20:7b: "Yahweh will not leave unpunished the man who utters his name to misuse it."

23 You must fill your hand.[a] Give alms to the needy.
24 Receive the homeless in (your) house, and lead the blind man.   Isa 58:7; Job 29:15; 31:32
25 Pity the shipwrecked, for navigation is unsure.   Heb 13:2; Deut 27:18
26 Extend your hand to him who falls, and save the helpless one.
27 Suffering is common to all; life is a wheel; prosperity is unstable.[b]
28 When you have wealth, stretch out your hand to the poor.   l. 23; Deut 15:11
                                                                  Prov 31:20; Sir 7:32
29 Of that which God has given you, give of it to the needy.   Deut 15:14; TZeb 7:2
30 Let all of life be in common, and all things be in agreement.[c]
31 [Do not eat blood; abstain from what is sacrificed to idols.][d]
32 Put on a sword, not for bloodshed but for protection.
33 But may you not need it at all, neither outside the law nor justly.
34 For if you kill an enemy, you stain your hand.[e]
35 Keep off the field of your neighbor, and therefore do not be a   Ex 22:4f.; Deut 23:25
   trespasser.
36 Moderation is the best of all, and excesses are grievous.[f]
37 [Lawful acquisition is useful, but unjust acquisition is bad.]
38 Do not damage fruits that are growing on the land.   Ex 22:4f.: Deut 23:25
39 Strangers should be held in equal honor among citizens.   Lev 19:33f.; 24:22
40 For we all experience the poverty of much wandering.[g]
41 And the land of the country has nothing steadfast for men.[h]

Love of money and its consequences

42 The love of money is the mother of all evil.[a]
43 Gold and silver are always a lure for men.
44 Gold, originator of evil, destroyer of life, crushing all things,
45 would that you were not a desirable calamity to mortals![b]
46 For your sake there are battles and plunderings and murders,
47 and children become the enemies of their parents, and brothers (the
   enemies) of their kinsmen.[c]

Honesty, modesty, and self-control

48 Do not hide a different thought in your heart while uttering another.   Prov 11:13; Sir 5:9; 6:1;
49 Change not yourself according to the spot, like a polyp that clings to   27:23; 28:13
   the rock.[a]
50 Be sincere[b] to all, speak what is from your soul.

Admonition to mercy

a. The Gk. text is very uncertain here. Alternative renderings are: "if your hand is full, give . . ." or "you must fill his hand; give . . ." or "he will fill your hand; give . . ."

b. This line expresses a very Gk. sentiment.

c. The exact meaning of this line is obscure.

d. This line is missing in all the important MSS. It is probably a Christian interpolation on the basis of Acts 15:29.

e. These two lines have an undeniably pacifistic ring about them.

f. This line is an interruption (as is the spurious l. 37) between l. 35 and l. 38. It is identical with l. 69b and strikes a note of keeping measure in all things, which often recurs in this poem, e.g. ll. 59–69, 98, etc.

g. The historical basis of the injunction to treat aliens fairly (l. 39), namely, the Israelites having been themselves aliens in Egypt (Lev 19:34; Ex 23:9), is generalized here into a common truth.

h. The text is somewhat in disorder here.

Love of money and its consequences

a. This maxim occurs in many forms in many ancient writings. The best-known instance is 1Tim 6:10: "The love of money is the root of all evils."

b. This kind of an address to money itself is not found in the Bible but has many parallels in Gk. literature.

c. For this (traditional) list of calamities cf. SibOr 8:24–6 and also Mk 13:12. On the motif of these lines cf. Sir 8:2; 10:8; 31:6.

Honesty, modesty, and self-control

a. Here Ps-Phoc polemicizes against a famous Gk. poet (Theognis) who exhorts man to be as adaptable as a polyp. [An inferior translation would be "octopus"; a polyp, not an octopus, changes its colors according to the environment. See P. van der Horst's commentary for further discussion. — J.H.C.]

b. Lit. "simple" (Gk. *haplous*); for this theme see, besides Prov 11:25 and Wis 1:1, especially TLevi 13:1 and the whole of TIss; cf. EBar 19:2.

51 Whoever wrongs willfully is a bad man; but if he does so under
   compulsion,
52 I shall not pass sentence, for it is each man's intention that is examined.
53 Do not pride yourself on wisdom nor on strength nor on riches.ᶜ
54 The only God is wise and mighty and at the same time rich in   Sir 1:8; Rom 16:27
   blessings.
55 Do not afflict your heartᵈ with bygone evils;
56 for what has been done can no more be undone.
57 Do not be rash with (your) hands, but bridle your wild anger.ᵉ   Prov 15:1; Eccl 7:9; Sir 1:22
58 For often someone who has dealt a blow has unintentionally committed   Jas 1:19
   a murder.ᶠ

Moderation in all things

59 Let (your) emotions be moderate, neither great nor overwhelming.
60 Excess, even of good, is never a boon to mortals;
61 and a great luxuriousness draws one to immoderate desires.   TJud 14–16; Sir 9:12f.
62 Great wealth is conceited and grows to insolence.   1Tim 6:17
63 Anger that steals over one causes destructive madness.
64 Rage is a desire, but wrath surpasses (it).ᵃ
65 Zeal for good things is noble, but (zeal for) bad things (is) excessive.ᵇ
66 Daring in bad deeds is ruinous, but greatly helps a man who works at
   good deeds.ᶜ
67 Love of virtue is worthy, but love of passion increases shame.ᵈ
68 A man who is too naïve is called foolish among the citizens.
69 Eat in moderation, and drink and tell stories in moderation.   Sir 31:12–31; 3Bar 4:16f.
69b Moderation is the best of all, excesses are grievous.ᵉ   Rom 13:13; 16–18
                                                                1Cor 5:11; 6:10; Phil 3:19
                                                                Sir 19:6; 20:7f.; 23:7f.; 32:7f.

Danger of envy and other vices

70 Do not envy (your) friends their goods, do not fix reproach (upon them).ᵃ   Tob 4:7,16; Sir 14:10
71 The heavenly onesᵇ also are without envy toward each other.   TSim; Rom 1:29
72 The moon does not envy the much stronger beams of the sun,   Gal 5:19–21
73 nor the earth the heavenly heights though it is below,
74 nor the rivers the seas. They are always in concord.
75 For if there were strife among the blessed ones,ᶜ heaven would not stand
   firm.

c. Jer 9:23: "Let the sage boast no more of his
wisdom, nor the valiant of his valor, nor the rich
man of his riches."

d. Lit. "liver." For this use of "liver" as the
center of emotions cf. TSim 2·4, 7; 4:1; TZab 2:4;
TGad 2:1.

e. Cf. Mishnah, Aboth 2:10: "Be not easily
provoked."

f. Cf. Did 3:2.

Moderation in all things

a. Or: "but if it [rage] is excessive, it is wrath."
Behind these lines is a piece of Stoic casuistry that
distinguishes three kinds of anger. For warnings
against anger see Prov 15:1; 27:4; 29:11; Sir 1:22;
10:18; 23:16; 27:30; Eph 4:31; also TDan 2–4.

b. Again a Stoic distinction.

c. Here two kinds of daring are distinguished
(not demonstrably Stoic).

d. Again a Stoic distinction.

e. This line is similar to l. 36 and possibly an
interpolation.

Danger of envy and other vices

a. That is: "Do not defame your neighbor because you envy him his goods."

b. Here and in l. 75 the heavenly bodies are
given Gk. names that often denote gods. Since a
Jew would never call these creatures gods these
lines have led some scholars to conclude that our
author was not a Jew (see Intro.). But Ps-Phoc
does no more than borrow traditional pagan terminology to express that the heavenly bodies are
personalities, a common Jewish view. No deification of the heavenly bodies is implied here. Also
Philo, who explicitly denies that stars are gods
(Spec. Leg. 1.13ff.), only adopts traditional philosophical terminology when in Opif. Mundi 27 he
says that the stars are visible gods. (This argument
is strengthened by the observation that during the
period in which Ps-Phoc was composed Jews were
influenced by astrological symbols and ideas; cf.
TrShem.)

c. See previous n.

76 Practice self-restraint,[d] and abstain from shameful deeds.   l. 145

77 Do not imitate evil, but leave vengeance to justice.   3Jn 11

78 For persuasiveness is a blessing, but strife begets only strife.

79 Trust not too quickly, before you can see exactly the end.   Prov 14:15; Sir 6:7; 19:4

80 It is proper to surpass (your) benefactors with still more (benefactions).[e]

81 It is better to entertain guests with a simple meal quickly

82 than extensive festivity drawn out beyond the right time.

83 Never be a relentless creditor to a poor man.[f]

84 One should not take from a nest all the birds together,

85 but leave the mother bird behind, in order to get young from her again.[g]

86 Never allow ignorant men to sit in judgment.   Ex 18:21f.; Deut 1:13

87 [Do not pass a judgment before you have heard the word of both parties.][h]

88 A wise man examines wisdom, and a fellow craftsman (examines) crafts.[i]

89 An untrained ear cannot grasp important teaching;

90 for those who have never learned good things do not understand.[j]

91 Do not make parasitic flatterers your friends.[k]

92 For many are friends of drinking and eating,

93 flattering at a time whenever they can satiate themselves,

94 but all being discontented with little and unsatiated with much.

95 Trust not the people; the mob is fickle;

96 for the people and water and fire are all equally uncontrollable.[l]

Death and afterlife

97 Sit not in vain at the fire, weakening your heart.[a]

98 Be moderate in your grief;[b] for moderation is the best.   l. 36

99 Let the unburied dead receive their share of the earth.[c]   Jer 16:4; 22:19; 4Ezra 2:23

100 Do not dig up the grave of the deceased, nor expose to the sun   Tob

101 what may not be seen, lest you stir up the divine anger.[d]

102 It is not good to dissolve the human frame;[e]

103 for we hope that the remains of the departed will soon come to the light (again)

---

d. The concept of self-restraint (Gk. *sōphrosyne*), which is very important in Gk. ethics, seldom occurs in the LXX (e.g. 4Mac 1:31) but more frequently in later Jewish literature, e.g. TJos 4:2; 9:2; 10:2–3; Josephus, *Apion* 2.195.

e. This utilitarian principle of reciprocity is very hellenistic; see the note on l. 152.

f. Many Jews in the Diaspora were bankers and, in spite of the OT prohibition to ask interest from an Israelite (Ex 22:24; Lev 25:36; Deut 23:20), they lent money to one another at the regular interest of 24 percent.

g. These two lines belong to the most typically Jewish ones of this poem. The source is evidently Deut 22:6f., though Ps-Phoc probably derived it from a document also used by Philo (*Hypothetica* in Eusebius' *Praeparatio Evangelica* 8.7.9) and Josephus (*Apion* 2.213). Though regarded as the least weighty of all commandments in rabbinic literature, it was viewed as important; see e.g. Mishnah, *Hullin* 12.1.

h. This line, a well-known ancient maxim, is lacking in most of the important MSS.

i. The sense of this line is hard to determine.

j. Criticisms of the uneducated are found frequently in Sir.

k. How to discern a flatterer from a real friend was a theme frequently discussed in Gk. and Roman literature.

l. The aristocratic mentality reflected in these lines, though more Gk. than biblical, may also be seen in Philo's remarks on the Alexandrian mob (*Leg. ad Gaium* 67.120).

Death and afterlife

a. Though the sense of this line is not very clear, it may be a warning against excessive mourning; see the following lines.

b. Reading *gooisi*, "grief " (with Bernays) instead of *theoisi* of the MSS. The text, however, is very uncertain; hence the translation is an educated guess.

c. This was one of the unwritten laws of Gk. ethics.

d. Probably these lines must be interpreted in the light of l. 102: graves were opened in order to dissect the corpses of the deceased.

e. A reference to anatomical practice in Alexandria (see Intro.).

104 out of the earth;[f] and afterward they will become gods.[g]
105 For the souls remain unharmed among the deceased.
106 For the spirit is a loan of God to mortals, and (his) image.[h]
107 For we have a body out of earth, and when afterward we are resolved again into earth

Gen 3:19; Eccl 12:7
Sir 17:1; WisSol 15:8

108 we are but dust;[i] and then the air has received our spirit.[j]
109 When you are rich, do not be sparing; remember that you are mortal.
110 It is impossible to take riches and money (with you) into Hades.

Job 1:21; Eccl 5:15
Ps 49:18f.; 1Tim 6:7
Job 3:19

111 All alike are corpses, but God rules over the souls.
112 Hades is (our) common eternal home[k] and fatherland,
113 a common place for all, poor and kings.

SibOr 2.322–24; 8.110–12

114 We humans live not a long time but for a season.
115 But (our) soul is immortal and lives ageless forever.[l]

Job 14:1f.; Wis 2:1,4; 9:5; 15:8

The instability of life

116 [Nobody knows what will be after tomorrow or after an hour.
117 Death is heedless of mortals, and the future is uncertain.][a]
118 Do not let evils dismay you nor therefore exult in success.[b]

Sir 2.4

119 Many times in life incredible calamity has come suddenly
120 to the confident and release from evil to the vexed.[c]

Eccl 9:12; Sir 11:21

121 Accommodate yourself to the circumstances, do not blow against the winds.

Speech and wisdom, man's distinction

122 Do not become mad in your mind by reveling in boastfulness.

1Sam 2:3; Sir 10:7–22

123 Practice speaking the right word, which will greatly benefit all.
124 Speech is to man a weapon sharper than iron.

Ps 56:5; Heb 4:12

125 God allotted a weapon to every creature; the capacity to fly
126 to birds, speed to horses, and strength to the lions;
127 he clothed the bulls with their self-growing horns, he gave stings to the bees
128 as their natural means of defense, but speech to man as his protection.[a]

f. The idea of bodily resurrection, which is very un-Gk. (cf. Acts 17:32) and typically Jewish, was already foreshadowed in the OT (Isa 26:19; Dan 12:2) but fully developed only in post-biblical Judaism.

g. On the basis of this half line some scholars have asserted that Ps-Phoc was not a Jew but rather a pagan or a Christian. One should bear in mind, however, that the resurrected were often regarded as angels, and angels are often called "gods" in Jewish texts.

h. Here in one and the same line one finds the hellenistic idea of the soul or spirit as a loan from God (which, however, also occurs in hellenized Jewish writings, e.g. Philo, *Spec. Leg.* 1.295; Josephus, *War* 3.374; Lk 12:20) and the OT idea of God's image (Gen 1:26f.), though, again typically hellenistic Jewish, it is not man but his spiritual principle which is regarded as God's image (as in Philo, e.g. *Opif. Mundi* 69).

i. This motif occurs very frequently in Gk. literature, and especially in epitaphs.

j. A common Gk. motif; probably Stoic influence.

k. This expression occurs only once in the OT, Eccl 12:5, but it is very frequent in Jewish, Gk., and Lat. epitaphs.

l. A common view throughout later antiquity (though there were skeptics then too).

The instability of life

a. These two lines are missing in most important MSS. Their theme is common to the OT (Prov 3:28; Eccl 8:7; Sir 11:19; cf. Jas 4:14) and Gk. literature.

b. A common theme in Gk. literature.

c. Again a common theme in Gk. literature.

Speech and wisdom, man's distinction

a. The theme of these lines (125–28) is a well-known topic in Gk. literature since the Sophist Protagoras. Cf. from Jewish literature Philo, *Somn.* 1.103. Though in both l. 124 and l. 128 the Gk. word *logos* has been translated "speech," one should note that this word also means "reason"; both semantic aspects are present here, but there is no English word that covers both meanings.

129 [But speech of the divinely inspired wisdom is best.][b]
130 Better is a wise man than a strong one.   Prov 24:5; Eccl 9:16
131 Wisdom directs the course of lands and cities and ships.[c]

Avoidance of wickedness and the life of self-restraint and virtue

132 It is unholy to hide a wicked man so as to prevent his being brought
    to trial;
133 but one must return an evildoer forcibly.
134 Those who are with the wicked often die with them.   Num 16:26
135 Do not accept from thieves a stolen, unlawful deposit.
136 Both are thieves, the one who receives as well as the one who steals.[a]
137 Render to all their due, and impartiality is best in every way.
138 In the beginning be sparing with all things, lest in the end you fall short.
139 Take not for yourself a mortal beast's ration of food.[b]
140 But if a beast of (your) enemy falls on the way, help it to rise.[c]
141 Never expose a wandering man and a sinner.[d]
142 It is better to make a gracious friend instead of an enemy.[e]
143 Nip the evil in the bud, and heal the wound.
144 [By a tiny spark a vast forest is set on fire.][f]
145 [Keep your heart restrained and abstain from disgraceful things.]   l. 76
146 [Flee an evil report; flee lawless men.][g]
147 Eat no meat that is torn by wild animals, but leave the remains
148 to the swift dogs.[h] Animals eat from animals.
149 Make no potions, keep away from magical books.   Acts 19:19; Did 2:2
                                          EBar 20:1
150 Do not apply your hand violently to tender children.
151 Flee dissension and strife when war is drawing near.
152 Do no good to a bad man; it is like sowing into the sea.[i]

The usefulness of labor[a]

153 Work hard so that you can live from your own means;   Ex 20:9; Prov 28:19
154 for every idle man lives from what his hands can steal.[b]   2Thes 3:10
155 [A craft maintains a man, but an idle man is oppressed by hunger.][c]
156 Eat not the leavings of another man's meal,   Sir 40:28-30
157 but eat without shame what you have earned yourself.[d]
158 And if someone has not learned a craft, he must dig with a hoe.[e]   Lk 16:3

---

b. This line, in clumsy Gk., is probably unauthentic. It is lacking in some important textual witnesses.

c. On Wisdom as helmsman see Wis 10:4.

Avoidance of wickedness . . .

a. Probably a proverb.

b. The Gk. text of this line is rather obscure. Many interpreters have asserted that the line forbids the eating of meat that is torn by animals, but that is the theme of ll. 147f.

c. No doubt deriving from Ex 23:5.

d. Again the text is obscure. A little change in the text (reading not *broton*, "man," but *boton*, "beast") might make it refer to Ex 23:4 (on your enemy's ox going astray), which is attractive in view of l. 140.

e. On the worth of friendship see Sir 6:16; 7:18.

f. This line is in only one MS. On the theme cf. Jas 3:5 ("Think how small a flame can set fire to a huge forest"); Philo, *Migr. Abr.* 123.

g. This clumsy interpolation occurs in only one MS.

h. This is one of the very few typically Jewish prescriptions in the poem, no doubt deriving from Ex 22:31. It was also one of the Noachian laws; see *Sanhedrin* 56a.

i. The principle of reciprocity, i.e. that one has always to return a benefaction (see l. 80), had as a consequence that one wanted to benefit only those people from whom one expected some return. Of hellenistic origin, this principle had penetrated into Judaism, as may be concluded from Sir 12:1-7. Jesus' polemics against this principle are reflected in Lk 6:32-5.

The usefulness of labor

a. This passage (ll. 153-74) and the following one (ll. 175-205) are the only really coherent parts of this poem.

b. Cf. *Qiddushin* 29a: "He who does not teach his son a craft teaches him brigandage."

c. This spurious line is in only one MS.

d. The text of this line is uncertain.

e. Digging was regarded as the hardest kind of work, mostly reserved for slaves or uneducated.

159 Life has every kind of work if you are willing to toil.
160 If you want to sail and be a mariner, the sea is wide.
161 And if you want to cultivate land, the fields are large.[f]
162 There is no easy work without toil, (neither) for men,[g] nor for the blessed
themselves.[h]
163 But labor gives great increase to virtue.
164 The ants having left their homes, deeply hidden under the earth,
165 come in their need of food when the fields
166 fill the threshing floors with fruits after the crops have been reaped.
167 They themselves have a load of freshly threshed wheat
168 or barley—and always bearer follows bearer—
169 and from the summer harvest they supply their food for the winter,
170 without tiring. This tiny folk is much-laboring.[i]
171 The bee toils, traversing the air, working excellently,
172 whether in the crevice of a hollow rock or in the reeds,
173 or in the hollow of an ancient oak, within their nests,
174 in swarms at their thousand-celled combs, building with wax.[j]

Tlss 5:3–6

Marriage and chastity[a]

175 Do not remain unmarried, lest you die nameless.
176 Give nature her due, you also, beget in your turn as you were begotten.[b]
177 Do not prostitute your wife,[c] defiling your children.
178 For the adulterous bed brings not sons in (your) likeness.[d]
179 Do not touch your stepmother, your father's second wife,[e]
180 but honor her as a mother, because she follows the footsteps of your
mother.
181 Do not have intercourse with the concubines of (your) father.[f]
182 Do not approach the bed of (your) sister, (a bed) to turn away from.[g]
183 Nor go to bed with the wives of your brothers.[h]
184 Do not let a woman destroy the unborn babe in her belly,
185 nor after its birth throw it before the dogs and the vultures as a prey.[i]

Lev 18:8; 20:11; 1Cor 5:1

TReu 3:11–15; Jub 33:1–9

f. Agriculture is strongly recommended by both Gk. moralists and by Jewish authors.

g. This line is probably a literal quotation from an oracle of the Milesian Branchidae. The author possibly drew upon a collection of oracles as they were current in antiquity.

h. This addition to the oracle text looks like a polemic against the ancient idea of the great ease of divine action. But by "the blessed" Ps-Phoc means (as in l. 75) the heavenly bodies. The labors of sun and moon are the eclipses, as may be gathered from several Gk. and Lat. texts.

i. This whole passage (ll. 164–70) is inspired by Prov 6:6–8, though there are many classical texts where the ants are regarded as examples of industry.

j. For this somewhat top-heavy sentence the author drew upon Prov 6:8a–c, which is not in the Heb. text but only in the LXX. Though there are classical parallels here too, the sequence of ll. 164–74, which is exactly the same as Prov 6:6–8c, makes it more than probable that Ps-Phoc tried to render this LXX text.

Marriage and chastity

a. This section and the following (ll. 175–227) show several resemblances to the so-called *Haustafeln* in Col 3:18–4:1 and Eph 5:22–6:9. These passages also deal with marriage, education of children, and treatment of slaves. One is reminded of the rabbinic triad, "women, slaves, and minors."

b. Recommendations of marriage and procreation, though also found in Stoic authors, are more frequent in Jewish writings (usually based on Gen 1:28 and 2:24). See the long instructive passage *Jebamoth* 61a–64a.

c. This has no OT source, though Lev 19:29 forbids the prostitution of one's daughter.

d. Perhaps this line reflects the ancient belief that the likeness of children to their parents was determined solely by the man's sperm.

e. Cf. Josephus, *Apion* 2.200.

f. Having no exact OT counterpart, this line may also render Lev 18:8 (as does l. 179). The combination stepmother-concubine was a traditional one.

g. Cf. Philo, *Spec. Leg.* 3.22. Possibly Ps-Phoc had in view here the marriages between brothers and sisters in Egypt (not only in the royal family).

h. See for ll. 179–83 also Mishnah, *Keritot* 1.1.

i. Abortion and exposure of children were the current methods of family planning in pagan antiquity. Though the OT forbids neither practice (but see the LXX translation of Ex 21:22f.), they are frequently condemned (in this combination) in Jewish and Christian writings, e.g. Philo, *Spec. Leg.* 3.108–19, Josephus, *Apion* 2.202; SibOr 2:281f.; Did 2:2; EBar 19:5, etc.

186 Do not lay your hand upon your wife when she is pregnant.[j]
187 Do not cut a youth's masculine procreative faculty.[k]
188 Do not seek sexual union with irrational animals.[l]
189 Do not outrage (your) wife by shameful ways of intercourse.[m]
190 Do not transgress with unlawful sex the limits set by nature.[n]
191 For even animals are not pleased by intercourse of male with male.[o]
192 And let women not imitate the sexual role of men.[p]
193 Do not surrender wholly to unbridled sensuality toward (your) wife.[q]
194 For eros is not a god,[r] but a passion destructive of all.
195 Love your own wife, for what is sweeter and better
196 than whenever a wife is kindly disposed toward (her) husband and a husband toward (his) wife
197 till old age, without strife divisively interfering?[s]
198 Let no one violently have intercourse with a girl not yet betrothed.
199 Do not bring as a wife into your home a bad and wealthy woman,
200 for you will be a slave of (your) wife because of the ruinous dowry.[t]
201 We seek noble horses and strong-necked bulls,
202 plowers of the earth, and the very best of dogs;
203 yet we fools do not strive to marry a good (wife),
204 nor does a woman reject a bad man when he is rich.[u]
205 Do not add marriage to marriage, calamity to calamity.[v]
206 Nor permit yourself strife with your kinsfolk about possessions.

Ex 22:19; Lev 18:23; 20:15f.
Deut 27:21; SibOr 5.393
TLev 17:11

Ex 22:16

Family life

207 Do not be harsh with your children, but be gentle.
208 And if a child offends against you, let the mother cut her son down to size,
209 or else the elders of the family or the chiefs of the people.[a]
210 If a child is a boy do not let locks grow on (his) head.
211 Do not braid (his) crown nor the cross knots at the top of his head.
212 Long hair is not fit for boys, but for voluptuous women.[b]
213 Guard the youthful prime of life of a comely boy,
214 because many rage for intercourse with a man.
215 Guard a virgin in firmly locked rooms,[c]
216 and do not let her be seen before the house until her wedding day.

Col 3:21; Eph 6:4

1Cor 11:14

2Mac 3:19; 3Mac 1:18
4Mac 18:7

---

j. The sense of this line is not wholly clear, but probably it is about sexual intercourse with a pregnant woman; cf. Josephus, *Apion* 2.202.

k. In the OT castration is not explicitly forbidden, but cf. Philo, *Hypothetica* in Eusebius' *Praeparatio Evangelica* 8.7.7, and Josephus, *Apion* 2.270f.; also *Sanhedrin* 56b; *Shabbath* 110b, etc.

l. Cf. Philo, *Spec. Leg.* 3.43–50.

m. Though several explanations of this line are possible (intercourse during menstruation, Lev 18:19; "variations"; violating; adultery), probably it forbids intercourse that is not for the sake of procreation, strongly condemned by both Jewish and (some) Gk. writers.

n. In view of the following line this line probably forbids homosexual activities (as does l. 3) by referring to the law of nature, as do Philo (*Abr.* 135; *Spec. Leg.* 2.50) and Paul (Rom 1:27) and other Jewish and Gk. authors.

o. This zoological error was a current opinion in antiquity.

p. Lesbian love is not explicitly forbidden in the OT, but see *Shabbath* 65a, *Jebamoth* 76a, and in the NT Rom 1:26.

q. Or "a woman."

r. *Eros*, "love; desire," was regarded as a god by the Greeks.

s. These lines are a paraphrase of some vss. from Homer (*Odyssey* 6.182–84) that had become almost proverbial in antiquity.

t. This was a topic in ancient literature; cf. Josephus *Apion* 2.200.

u. In ll. 201–4 the author paraphrases some well-known lines of Theognis, a Greek poet from the 6th cent. B.C.

v. It is hard to decide whether this line is directed against remarrying or against bigamy (polygamy). The same difficulty is found in CD 4:21 ("to take two wives during their lifetime").

Family life

a. These lines probably are a rather free and mitigating rendering of Deut 21:18–21; cf. Philo, *Spec. Leg.* 2.232; Josephus, *Apion* 2.206.

b. A man's wearing long hair was often considered as a sign of effemination; e.g. Philo, *Spec. Leg.* 3.37.

c. Cf. Philo, *In Flaccum* 89.

217 The beauty of children is hard for their parents to guard.   Sir 7:24; 42:9–11
218 [Love your friends till death, for faithfulness is a good thing.]ᵈ
219 Show love to your kinsmen and holy unanimity.   Sir 25:11
220 Revere those with gray hair on the temples and yield your seat   Lev 19:32; Sir 8:6; Job 32:4
221 and all privileges to aged persons. An old man of equal descent
222 and of the same age as your father give the same honors.ᵉ
223 Provide your slave with the tribute he owes his stomach.ᶠ
224 Apportion to a slave what is appointed so that he will be as you wish.ᵍ
225 Do not brand (your) slave, thus insulting him.ʰ
226 Do not hurt a slave by slandering (him) to (his) master.ⁱ   Prov 30:10
227 Accept advice also from a judicious slave.

Epilogue

228 Purifications are for the purity of the soul, not of the body.ᵃ   Mk 7:15
229 These are the mysteries of righteousness;ᵇ living thus   Prov 16:31
230 may you live out (your) life well to the threshold of old age.ᶜ

---

d. This line is an interpolation occurring in only one MS.

e. The sentiment expressed in these three lines is universal in the ancient world; cf. Philo, *Spec. Leg.* 2.237; Josephus, *Apion* 2.206.

f. Typical of the great humanity of Ps-Phoc, in ll. 223–27 he mentions only duties of masters toward slaves, not the reverse.

g. Philo, *Spec. Leg.* 2.90f.

h. Slaves usually were branded when they had run away or had done something wrong; but rabbis admitted branding as a preventive measure. It was felt very much as a disgrace.

i. Prov 30:10 (note, however, that Prov 30:10 is rendered in the LXX in quite another way; it

looks as if Ps-Phoc knew the Heb. text, but that is extremely improbable).

Epilogue

a. The text and meaning of this line is uncertain. It is clear, however, that in our author's view the purity of the soul is of greater importance than that of the body.

b. By this term the whole content of the poem is summarized.

c. For structurally similar closing passages cf. SibOr 2:149–51; EBar 21:1; ShepHerm Similitudes 10.4.1. (I am indebted to the editor for some useful suggestions.)

THE SENTENCES OF THE SYRIAC MENANDER

(Third Century A.D.)

A NEW TRANSLATION AND INTRODUCTION

BY T. BAARDA

"Menander the Sage said: . . ." These words introduce a collection of wisdom sayings written in the Syriac language. The purpose of the author in drawing up this anthology of maxims was to show his readers how they could best live in a world in which good and evil, misfortune and fortune are mingled in an unpredictable way. Passing through a world of this nature, people need to be provided with direction, and the author gives such guidance by means of various counsels. The work is often designated a florilegium, and this seems to be a fairly good name for the collection, whose maxims have apparently been taken from the current stream of wisdom tradition.

The exact number of sayings in the collection is not certain. In the present translation of the Florilegium, I have divided the text into 474 longer and shorter lines (including the opening and concluding lines) and abstained from any division into separate sayings. I did not wish to add another division to those already existing. J.-P. Audet counts 96, F. Schulthess 101, P. Riessler 103, and A. Baumstark no less than 153 sayings, preceding the closing line (474): *"Menander has come to an end."*[1]

The nature of the book may be adequately defined as wisdom literature in the form of practical rules for human behavior. Found in it are precepts, prohibitions, paradigms, and short characterizations of human attitudes. It does not contain a philosophical definition of wisdom, but instead a very pragmatic view of it (see ll. 27–33). Wisdom is the art of living. The entire range of this practical wisdom is brought into focus: how to live with parents, children, women, brothers, and friends; how to behave while drinking or eating; how to use riches; how to deal with older people, slaves, and enemies.[2]

It is very difficult to find a clear order in the sequence of the various counsels. This lack of system may be due to the fact that the author drew upon various sources, each with an order of its own. There are a few thematic groups of sayings, such as those on adultery and fornication (ll. 45–51), on eating and drinking (ll. 52–66), and on servants (ll. 154–66). The short definitions at the end of the collection (ll. 402–38) create the impression of having belonged to a specific source of sayings from which the author borrowed several lines.

Besides this Florilegium there exists a short Epitome, which, too, is attributed to Menander. From the place of the Epitome in the manuscript—between extracts from Greek authors and philosophers—it is clear that the author of the manuscript considered Menander to be a Greek author, and it is obvious that he must have been thinking of the famous representative of the New Comedy in Athens (c. 300 B.C.).[3] There is, of course, no one who entertains the notion that this writer was the actual author of the collection, but A.

---

[1] For the publications by these authors, see "Select Bibliography."

[2] For a detailed survey of the themes in SyrMen, cf. M. Küchler, *Frühjüdische Weisheitstraditionen* (Orbis biblicus et orientalis 26; Göttingen, 1979) pp. 307f.

[3] See for Menander especially H. J. Mette, "Der heutige Menander," *Lustrum* 10 (1965) 5–211; 11 (1966) 139–43; 13 (1968) 535–68.

Baumstark has suggested that someone could have collected the various sayings from the plays of the renowned Menander.[4] Others have compared the Florilegium with the anthologies of short sentences (monostichs) which circulated under the name of Menander long after his death.[5] But apart from the short maxims in lines 402–38 and a few other logia in the collection, there is nothing comparable to the monostich genre. Why was the name Menander attached to our Florilegium? Was it because the collector also drew upon a source of monostichs ascribed to Menander and took the opportunity to connect this famous name with his collection of sayings?

Texts[6]

The Syriac text which underlies the present translation of the large Florilegium was published by J. P. N. Land in 1862. His edition was based upon the famous British Museum manuscript Or.Add.14.658 (987.18°), fols. 163v.–67v. It appears that Land's text is less exact than one could have hoped for, but the corrections afforded by W. Wright (1863), F. Schulthess (1912) and J.-P. Audet (1952) give us sufficient tools for a reconstruction of the Syriac text. The date of the manuscript is most probably the seventh century.

The Syriac text of the short Epitome has been edited by E. Sachau in his publication of profane Greek writings in Syriac translation (1870). His text was based upon the British Museum manuscript Or.Add.14.614 (773.4°b), more accurately that part of the manuscript which dates from the eighth or ninth century.

The younger text of the Epitome is not based upon the older text of the Florilegium but presupposes a slightly different recension of the latter, which at least in one instance seems to have preserved a better text (cf. Florilegium ll. 470–73 and Epitome ll. 34–39).

Original language

The original language may have been Syriac. In that case we must assume that a Syriac-writing author collected these various maxims. His source could have been popular wisdom circulating in his environment, but the possibility should not be excluded that he made use of written collections in another language, such as Syriac, Aramaic, Hebrew, or Greek.

The original language may have been other than Syriac. In that case, the author of the Syriac collection functioned as a translator. If he was a translator, one cannot totally exclude the possibility that he added some material of his own to the existing collection which he rendered into Syriac. But then what is the original language of the anthology? Is it a Hebrew wisdom text?[7] There is no decisive argument for that theory. It seems to be safer to assume, as do most scholars, that the Syriac author rendered a Greek anthology.

Date

Since the collection consists of wisdom sayings, it is very difficult to assign a specific date to it. Wisdom, as a matter of fact, has the air of timelessness. Moreover, collections of this kind are apt to be gradually enlarged during the period of their transmission, so that even a tentative fixing of date of a logion does not necessarily mean that the whole collection must be of the same time or provenance. We may make the following observations:

a. The slight differences between the large Florilegium and the short Epitome suggest that there may have been various copies of the Florilegium in, or probably before, the seventh century.

b. The Syriac of the Florilegium seems to be of a very archaic character.[8] This may

---

[4] A. Baumstark, *Geschichte der syrischen Literatur* (Bonn, 1922), pp. 483f.

[5] The most recent edition: S. Jaekel, *Menandri Sententiae, Comparatio Menandri et Philistionis* (Leipzig, 1964).

[6] An attempt to acquire the photographs from the BM has failed. For the works quoted in this paragraph, see "Select Bibliography."

[7] This was the thesis of W. Frankenberg, "Die Schrift des Menander (Land, Anecd. Syr. I, 64ff.) ein Produkt der jüdischen Spruchweisheit," *ZAW* 15 (1895) 226, 264.

[8] Cf. Baumstark, *Geschichte*, p. 487 (*sermo perquam antiquus*).

point to the possibility that the text had already had a long history in Syriac-speaking regions.

c. The foregoing observations do not give us sufficient evidence for a more exact date of the original Syriac text. Dating it in the fourth century would be no more than a guess.

d. But even if we could date the Syriac text, this would be of little help if the text is a translation from another language. And if the work is a genuine Syriac collection, we would still have no certainty regarding the data of the potential sources which the collector drew upon.

e. If a Greek origin is assumed, there are also no clear guides for an exact dating. It is generally taken for granted that the text originated in the Roman period.[9] Some scholars find a latest possible date in the fact that schools for gladiators gradually disappeared after Constantine due to successive imperial rules.[10] This would imply that the advice given in lines 34–44 cannot be dated after c. 400.[11] An earliest possible date is found in the laws of Hadrian and Antonine with respect to the treatment of slaves: The master was not permitted to kill his slave. This would imply that line 159 ought to be dated after c. 150.[12]

From these data one can conclude that the collection is most probably a product of the third century.[13] This may seem a reasonable conclusion, but it presupposes not only that the implications based upon the lines mentioned are valid but also that these lines are original.

Provenance

There is no indication which might give us a clue as to the provenance of the Florilegium. Therefore it is not surprising that most scholars have abstained from any discussion about its place of origin. J.-P. Audet is the only one who dares to put forward a thesis about the country of the author, whose mention of "water" in line 3 and a supposed mistranslation in line 365 are sufficient for Audet to conclude that our author is an Egyptian.[14] His arguments are not persuasive; nevertheless, it is possible that our document comes from Egypt. But it seems safer to conclude that there is too little evidence to endorse a specific provenance.

Theological importance

Because we do not know exactly when, where, and by whom the work was written, its theological importance is diminished to a certain extent. Moreover, the fact that it is a book of wisdom sayings makes it hardly possible to systematize the author's own convictions. For example, it is very difficult to discover a clear concept of God in the various sayings:

a. God is the Creator: He made man (361), and he is also the ultimate cause of everything that comes into existence (7).

b. God determines the space of life for everyone (391–92, cf. 449f.), and he also mingles for all both bad and good things (393). Man, however, should not complain against God for the bad things which life brings with it (453f.). Only the fear of God is able to liberate man from the evil (394–95), and at the end of life God has provided Sheol as a place of rest for men after their hard labors (470f.).

c. God is to be praised (8) and feared (9, 123, 394). He hates the adulterer (47f.), the bad servant (161), the evil man (168), impurity and prodigality (352). The sinner who offends his parents can expect only God's punishment (22–23). The fear of God frees one from evil (394–95).

d. God shall not cast down forever or humiliate eternally (116f.); he remains the God to whom one can pray (39, 202) and to whom one may call upon in times of distress (124).

[9] Cf. Frankenberg, ZAW 15 (1895) 270.
[10] Cf. ibid., p. 270; J.-P. Audet, "La sagesse de Ménandre l'Égyptien," RB 59 (1952) 77.
[11] Audet, RB 59 (1952) 78.
[12] Ibid., p. 77.
[13] Ibid., p. 78; Küchler, Weisheitstraditionen, p. 316.
[14] Audet, RB 59 (1952) 77; Küchler, Weisheitstraditionen, p. 316. (Küchler rejects Audet's argument based on the mention of "water.")

He will listen to prayers (125); he will take us by the hand and raise us after our fall (108).

From these data one may feel tempted to say that the author is a monotheist, which would fit in with the theory of a Jewish origin of the book (although in my opinion most of these utterances would fit in equally well with the assumption of a Gk. writer). At times, our author speaks of God in a rather impersonal way, as for example when he is presented as determining the fate of men's lives; at other times, however, the reference is more personal, as for example when he appears to be a God who listens to the prayers of men.

There is one great problem. In lines 263f. there is a clear indication of polyíheism, which seems to contradict the thesis of a Jewish origin. Is this a later insertion?[15] Is it a mistranslation on the part of the Syriac translator?[16] Or is the author, himself a monotheist, describing the practices of a pagan-cult priest?[17] If the author was a Jew, could he then write about "gods" as a result of a heterodox background?[18] Or did he merely wish to give to his work the air of a pagan document?[19]

These questions cannot now be answered. As long as the exact place, date, and provenance of the work are unknown, it is not possible to say anything very significant about the theological position of the author and his writing.

Relation to canonical books

In a eulogy on silence (311–13)—"There exists nothing better than silence. Being silent is at all times a virtue. Even if a fool is silent, he is counted wise"—we find a striking similarity to Proverbs 17:28: "If a fool can hold his tongue, even he can pass for wise" (cf. also Sir 20:5). This is one of the agreements between Syriac Menander and the Old Testament wisdom literature that made Frankenberg conclude that the Florilegium was an early Hebrew wisdom book, breathing the same spirit as Proverbs and Sirach. This conclusion is not sufficiently warranted, but the references to canonical and apocryphal wisdom literature which he offers (several of which are noted in the margin of the translation) are a necessary addition to the one-sidedness of scholars such as Land and Baumstark, who had an eye only for the "Greek" atmosphere of Syriac Menander. In fact, they so focused upon the Greek world that they did not even mention Proverbs in this connection; they merely referred to the monostichs and plays of Menander, which do not offer a very good parallel to the line in question.

It should be kept in mind that a sentence such as that found in line 313 could be a later addition to the two foregoing lines. Such could have been inserted by a translator or a copyist; certainly a Christian who knew his Bible could have edited and expanded this document.

Relation to apocryphal books

A Jewish provenance of the maxims was suggested partly because of several striking parallels between Syriac Menander and Sirach. A very close resemblance is found between the concluding lines (458–73) and Sirach 38:16–23 (cf. 22:11). In the margin of the translation many other references to Sirach are found, which might seem to support a relationship to Jewish wisdom literature.

One should, however, be aware that there is a complication involved here: Jewish wisdom is closely connected with oriental and Greek wisdom literature in general. For example, we read in Sirach 8:7, "Do not gloat over a man's death; remember that we all must die [or 'be gathered']." A similar maxim is also found in our text, lines 126f.: "Do not rejoice over a dead man, over one who dies, because all men will go to the eternal house, they are mortal." But the same thought is expressed in a saying ascribed to Menander: "Because

---

[15] E. Schürer, *Geschichte des jüdischen Volkes im Zeitalter Jesu Christi* (Leipzig, 1909⁴), vol. 2, p. 622.

[16] P. Riessler, *Altjüdisches Schrifttum ausserhalb der Bibel* (Heidelberg, 1928 [repr. 1966]), p. 1329.

[17] Frankenberg, *ZAW* 15 (1895) 265.

[18] See for example the co-existence of monotheism and polytheism in the Jewish community at Elephantine. [Also see the extant fragments of Art (see the contribution herein), who claimed that Egyptian culture, including polytheism and idolatry, was defined by Abraham, Joseph, and Moses. —J.H.C.]

[19] Riessler, *Altjüdisches Schrifttum*, p. 1329.

you are mortal, do not make mirth over one who is dead."[20] Is this Jewish wisdom or Greek wisdom? In addition, we may refer to the legend of Ahiqar as well: "Son, rejoice not in the death of your enemies, for death impends for you as well" (Arm. B 78; cf. Syr. 60: "My son, rejoice not over the enemy when he dies").[21] Is it, therefore, oriental wisdom? It is clear that mere parallels cannot decide the question as to whether the Florilegium has a Jewish origin, since Jewish wisdom arose from the fruitful soil of Mediterranean and oriental wisdom traditions in general.

Relation to the pseudepigraphical literature

The reference to Ahiqar brings forward another point. One may say that the legend of Ahiqar is a good specimen of oriental wisdom literature, but the fact that fragments of an Aramaic book of Ahiqar were found in Elephantine make it sufficiently clear that this wisdom book had found a place in the library of a heterodox Jewish community at a very early date (c. 400 B.C.). In the present translation a few references are drawn to the book of Ahiqar, but here I should like to point out one quite interesting parallel between the sixth maxim of the book's Syriac version and Syriac Menander 246f.: "My son, commit not adultery with your neighbor's wife, lest others should commit adultery with your wife" (Ah Syr.)[22] and "Just as you do not wish your wife to commit adultery with another, likewise also do not wish to commit adultery with your neighbor's wife" (Syr Men). Does this parallel application of the negative golden rule to adultery prove that the maxim is a Jewish counsel? Or does it merely furnish evidence that it is a specimen of oriental wisdom in general?

Another writing to be mentioned here is Pseudo-Phocylides, a hellenistic Jewish wisdom poem.[23] This document contains some interesting parallels to sayings found in Syriac Menander (see the margin of the translation). One of them is found in Pseudo-Phocylides 109f.: "When you are rich, do not be sparing; remember that you are mortal. It is impossible to take riches and money (with you) into Hades,"[24] which can be compared with Syriac Menander 368–73: "If you have goods, if you have possessions, live on your possessions as long as you are alive . . . remember . . . one (can)not use (his) goods in Sheol . . ." Similar thoughts are found not only in the Old Testament (cf. Job 1:21; Eccl 5:17–19) but also in Greek and Latin writings.[25]

It is clear that the agreements between either Ahiqar or Pseudo-Phocylides on the one hand and the Syriac Menander on the other do not prove that the latter work is of Jewish provenance. Our document belongs to the world of wisdom of which Ahiqar and Pseudo-Phocylides are part, and therefore it may have been a writing of a Jewish author.

A rabbinic parallel?

"Everything that is hateful to you, you should not wish to do that to your neighbor" (250f.); with these words the author of the Florilegium presents a peculiar form of the negative golden rule. The idea expressed by this maxim is found in many cultures and among many peoples, but the specific form of the saying seems to point in the direction of Jewish tradition. Land's only reference is to a parallel in the Menandric monostich "Let us not practise the things that we find fault with"[26]; he fails to mention even Tobit 4:15 ("Do to no one what you would not want done to you"), which is to my knowledge the closest parallel in Greek (the maxim of Orion of Thebes "what you would *hate* to have your equals cause to happen to you, do not do to others" is a Christian paraphrase of Tob 4:15). A

[20] Jaekel, *Menandri Sententiae,* p. 52.

[21] Cf. F. C. Conybeare, J. R. Harris, and A. S. Lewis, *The Story of Ahikar* (Cambridge, England, 1913²), pp. 64, 108. [Also see the contribution by J. M. Lindenberger herein. —J.H.C.]

[22] Ibid., p. 103.

[23] Cf. P. W. van der Horst, *The Sentences of Pseudo-Phocylides* (SVTP 4; Leiden, 1978) 94v. [Also see his contribution herein. —J.H.C.]

[24] P. W. van der Horst, translation published herein.

[25] P. W. van der Horst, *Sentences,* pp. 192f.

[26] J. P. N. Land, *Anecdota Syriaca,* vol. 1, p. 201; cf. Jaekel, *Menandri Sententiae,* p. 33.

close parallel to the saying in Syriac Menander is the word ascribed to Hillel in the Babylonian Talmud, Shabbat 31a: "what is hateful to you, you shall not do to your neighbour" (cf. TargJerI on Lev 19:18).[27] Is this, as some maintain, a clear indication of a Jewish origin of the Florilegium? We should keep in mind that this "Jewish" form of the sentence was known to Syrian and Persian Christians of the fourth century, since it appears in *Liber Graduum* and Aphrahat. It may also have been adopted as Gospel text in the *Diatessaron* of Tatian at a very early stage of Syrian church history.[28]

We are confronted, consequently, with another question: Is the saying in question Jewish or Christian? We have a notice regarding the Roman Emperor Alexander Severus (related by the biographer Lampridius) which tells us that he was fond of saying *quod tibi non vis, alteri ne feceris* ("that which you do not wish for yourself, do not do to another"), a maxim he had learned from some Jews or Christians and which he loved so much that he ordered that it be prescribed as a rule for the palace and for the public buildings.[29] Is it a Jewish or a Christian maxim? It is difficult to decide that question, both in the case of the Emperor and in the case of Syriac Menander. Does the occurrence of the maxim imply that the author of our writing was a Jew? Or was he a pagan, and was the saying added by the translator or by a copyist, who may have been a Christian? Or could not a pagan author have incorporated the saying in his writing, since a pagan writer could well have borrowed from Jewish or Christian traditions, as did Emperor Alexander Severus?

Menandric influence?

In the foregoing observations on apocryphal parallels a reference was made to a monostich ascribed to Menander. As the marginal annotations of the translation demonstrate, however, there are more parallels within the "Menandric" corpus. "No one who is righteous will easily become rich"[30] is a good example of these parallels, for it appears to be very similar to the maxim "Radiant and comely are riches, but the good man hardly acquires them" (425f.). Line 65, "Blessed is the man who has mastered his stomach and his lust," reminds us of the monostich "It is a good thing to master one's stomach and lust."[31] A paraphrase of the "Menandric" maxim "Honour your father, respect her who gave birth (to you)"[32] is found in lines 94–98 of Syriac Menander. The thoughts expressed in lines 377–81 are almost a convincing elaboration of the adage "If you exert yourself when you are young, you will enjoy a flourishing old age."[33] These examples will suffice to show that there are several close links between the text of Syriac Menander and the collections of monostichs that circulated under Menander's name in the Greek world. One ought, therefore, not to exclude the possibility that the collector of our text—Jewish or not—may have used such anthologies, and that he even took the name attached to them to promote his own collection of wisdom sayings.

A Jewish pseudepigraphon?

In spite of the several demonstrable agreements with the "Menandric" tradition, there is a strong consensus among scholars (apart from Land and Baumstark) that our text has nothing to do with Menander. Since the publication of Frankenberg's thesis, the Jewish parallels can no longer be left out of consideration; but his far-reaching conclusions (that the text was originally a Jewish wisdom book, written in Heb.) were not such that they could really convince all scholars. Audet posited what may be termed a kind of synthesis of the earlier theses that argued for respectively a Greek or a Jewish origin when he stated that the Florilegium was a product of an author from the so-called God-fearing circles.[34] Of

---

[27] Cf. H. Freedman, J. Epstein (eds.), *Shabbath* (London, Jerusalem, New York, 1972) vol. 1, *ad loc.*; M. Ginzburger, *Pseudo-Jonathan* (Berlin, 1903) p. 206.

[28] Cf. R. H. Connolly, "A Negative Form of the Golden Rule in the Diatessaron?" *JTS* 35 (1934) 351–57.

[29] Cf. G. Resch, *Das Aposteldekret nach seiner ausserkanonischen Textgestalt* (Berlin, 1905) p. 134.

[30] Jaekel, *Menandri Sententiae*, p. xvi; cf. Audet, *RB* 59 (1952) 78; and Küchler, *Weisheitstraditionen*, pp. 309f.

[31] Jaekel, *Menandri Sententiae*, p. 57.

[32] Ibid., p. 72 (cf. p. 130).

[33] Ibid., p. 64.

[34] Audet, *RB* 59 (1952) 80f.

course, one could just as easily defend the thesis that the work was authored by a cultured pagan writer who, in drawing up this collection of wisdom sayings, incorporated additional material in it from the oriental wisdom traditions, including Jewish ones, with which he was familiar. It is very difficult to decide the matter. Still, it has become accepted practice to class the work under the Jewish Pseudepigrapha, simply because there is no place elsewhere for it. F. Schulthess, who was very resolute in his rejection of a Jewish origin, published his contribution on Syriac Menander in an Old Testament periodical,[35] and O. Stählin, who is very skeptical about the suggestion that it is a Jewish book, deals with our Florilegium in the section dealing with Jewish pseudepigraphic literature[36] of a large historical work on Greek literature. Syriac Menander should be included among the Pseudepigrapha until there is decisive proof that it ought to be dealt with under another heading.

English translation

The following translation of both the Epitome and the Florilegium is the first attempt to provide an English version of these texts. Since it is the product of a Dutch reader of the Syriac text, it is subject to those failings which might stimulate others to a retranslation which exploits all the possibilities of the English language.

In the margin the reader will find a number of references to other wisdom literature: Proverbs, Ecclesiastes, Sirach, Wisdom, Tobit, Ahiqar, the maxims of Pseudo-Phocylides, and the monostichs of Menander (MenM; the numbering is that of Jaekel).

I have abandoned any attempt to give a new system of numbering to the various sayings. The only numbering used is that which divides the Syriac text into lines. For convenience, however, I have also added to the text the numbers which Baumstark (B), Riessler (R), Schulthess (S), and Audet (A) have used in their translations to distinguish the separate sentences of the Florilegium. Similarly, I have also divided the Epitome into lines, except that here I have added Sachau's numbering of the various sayings. In the margin of the Epitome I have made references to the parallel sayings in the Florilegium. In the notes I refer to Land's translation.

SELECT BIBLIOGRAPHY

THE TEXT

Land, J. P. N. *Anecdota Syriaca I*. Leiden, 1862; (Syr.), 64:21–73:18. (Cf. also the corrections by W. Wright in *Journal of Sacred Literature* 4th series, 3 [1863] 115–30: and by J. P. N. Land, *Anecdota Syriaca II*. Leiden, 1868; pp. 25f.)

Sachau, E. *Inedita Syriaca, Eine Sammlung syrischer Übersetzungen von Schriften griechischer Profanliteratur*. Vienna, 1870; (Syr.), 80:1–81:10. (Cf. J. P. N. Land, *Anecdota Syriaca II*, pp. 20f.)

TRANSLATIONS

Audet, J.-P. "La sagesse de Ménandre l'Égyptien," *RB* 59 (1952) 55–81. (This French rendering is a version based upon a comparison of the text of Land with the photographs of the MS; in some cases this version equals that of Schulthess, or even improves it, but in other cases, Audet loses to Schulthess.)

Baumstark, A. "Lucubrationes Syro-Graecae," *Jahrbücher für klassische Philologie*. Supplement-Band 21; Leipzig, 1894; pp. 473–90. (This Lat. version of the text is not a real improvement of the first translation.)

---

[35] F. Schulthess, "Die Sprüche des Menanders," *ZAW* 32 (1912) 199–224.

[36] W. Schmid and O. Stählin, *Geschichte der griechischen Literatur* (Munich, 1920⁶) vol. 2.1, pp. 535–656 (cf. especially pp. 608–24).

Frankenberg, W. "Die Schrift des Menander (Land, Anecd. Syr. I, 64ff.) ein Produkt der jüdischen Spruchweisheit," *ZAW* 15 (1895) 226–77. (Frankenberg presents his readers with a paraphrasis of the text in German, which also contains several more literal translations of the maxims.)

Land, J. P. N. *Anecdota Syriaca I.* Leiden, 1862; pp. 156–64 (emendations and additions, *Anecdota Syriaca II*, pp. 17–19). (Land's Lat. translation has the normal weaknesses of a first translation.)

Riessler, P. *Altjüdisches Schrifttum ausserhalb der Bibel.* Heidelberg, 1928 (repr. 1966); pp. 1047–57, 1328f. (Riessler's version is apparently based on the [text and] translation of Land; the neglect of Schulthess' version by Riessler diminishes the value of his German rendering of the sentences.)

Schulthess, F. "Die Sprüche des Menanders," *ZAW* 32 (1912) 199–224. (This first complete German version was made on the basis of a fresh comparison of [photographs of] the MS text.)

GENERAL WORKS

Baumstark, A. *Geschichte der syrischen Literatur.* Bonn, 1922; especially pp. 169f.

Krauss, S. "Menander I," *JE*, vol. 8, pp. 473f.

Küchler, M. *Frühjüdische Weisheitstraditionen.* Orbis biblicus et orientalis 26; Göttingen, 1979; pp. 303–18.

Schmid, J. "Menandros, Sprüche des M.," *LTK²*, vol. 7, col. 266.

Schmid, W., and Stählin, O. *Geschichte der griechischen Literatur.* Munich, 1920; vol. 2, pp. 41f., 46, 623.

Schürer, E. *Geschichte des jüdischen Volkes im Zeitalter Jesu Christi.* Leipzig, 1909⁴; vol. 2, pp. 622–24.

THE SENTENCES OF THE SYRIAC MENANDER

I

The Epitome of the Sentences of the Syriac 'Menander' [a]

1 *Menander, the Sage:*   (M. 1)

(1) 2 Before everything, fear God,   (M. 8–9)
3 and honor the one that is older than you,   (M. 13)
4 for thus you shall be honored by God.   (M. 14)

(2) 5 Flee from everything that is hateful.   (cf.M. 15–16)

(3) 6 There is no one who follows his stomach or his lust,   (M. 63)
7 who immediately shall not be dishonored and despised.   (M. 64)

(4) 8 Blessed is the man who has mastered his stomach and his lust.   (M. 65)

(5) 9 The main source[b] of all good things is the fear of God: (M. 394, cf.123)
10 it delivers us from all evil things,   (M. 395)
11 and in your distresses you will call upon him,   (M. 124)
12 and he will listen to your voice.   (M. 125)

(6) 13 The affairs of men, however, will not last,   (M. 397)
14 since their life is until the house of death.   (M. 398)

(7) 15 Comely is youth,   (M. 399)
16 but it is with men only for a short time,   (M. 400)
17 and (then) old age makes it fade away.   (M. 401)

(8) 18 Pleasant are life, goods, and children,   (M. 402)
19 but more pleasant than them is a good name.   (M. 403)

(9) 20 Excellent is joy   (M. 404)
21 when quarrel and violence are far from it.   (M. 405)

(10) 22 Good is friendship   (M. 406)
23 which continues to the house of death.   (M. 407)

(11) 24 Lovely is wisdom   (M. 408)
25 when it is not puffed up.   (M. 409)

(12) 26 Excellent is faithfulness   (M. 410)
27 when it is coupled with sound judgment.   (M. 411)

(13) 28 Insipidity leads the mind astray.   (M. 419)

(14) 29 Agitation makes (one) lose (his) senses.   (M. 420)

(15) 30 An evil heart causes griefs and sighing.   (M. 421)

I (The Epitome)

a. For the sentences of the Epitome, compare the parallel lines of the large Florilegium (II), which are indicated in the right margin. The numbers in italics on the left side are adopted from the edition of E. Sachau, who made a division of the text into eighteen maxims.

b. The MS reads: "the chief number," which can easily be corrected into "the main source"; cf. the parallel line in the Florilegium.

(16) 31 Jealousy is the cause of evil and strife. (M. 422)

(17) 32 The belly (can be) disgraceful. (M. 423)
33 The tongue brings (one) to misery. (M. 424)

(18) 34 I have watched, (M. –)
35 but the dwelling place of men is Sheol, (M. –)
36 and this is the place of rest (M. 470)
37 which God determines for men, (M. 471)
38 that they may rest there from the evil things (M. 472)
39 which they saw in their life. (M. 473)

II

The Sentences of the Syriac Menander

(R 1)
1 *Menander the Sage said:*

(R 2; B-S-A 1)
2 Prior to the words[a] of man are all his activities: (Cf. Sir 39:26f.)
3 water and[b] seed, plants and children.
(R 3)
4 It is good to plant plants
5 and it is comely to beget children,
6 praiseworthy and good is the seed,
7 but he through whom it comes to pass,[c]
8 he is to be praised before everything.[d]

(R 4; B-S-A 2)
(L.65) 9 Fear God,[e]
10 and honor (your) father and mother.

11 Do not laugh at old age,
12 for that is where you shall arrive and remain.
(R 5; B-S 3)
13 Honor him who is older than you,
14 (and) God will raise you to honor and dignity.[f]

1Pet 2:17
Prov 24:21(LXX)
Sir 1:14,16;
3:3f.; Ex 20:12
Deut 5:16
MenM 322.674
Ps-Phoc 8

Sir 8:6

Lev 19:32
Ps-Phoc 220–22
Ah[Arm.](80)[B]

(R 6; B-S 4; A 3)
15 You shall do no murder,
16 and your hands shall not do what is hateful,
17 for the sword lies in the midst[g]:
(B 5)
18 there is no one who cruelly kills
19 (who) will not himself be killed immediately.

Ex 20:13; Deut
5:17

Gen 9:6; Mt
26:52
Rev 13:10

II (*The Sentences . . .*)

a. *B* renders ll. 1f. differently: "Menander the Sage said in the beginning of his words: Of man are the activities . . ."

b. *LF-R* unjustly rejects the words "water and . . ."

c. *S*: "but he who is successful" (less probable).

d. *S-A* read in accordance with the Epitome:

". . . praised. Before everything, fear God" (ll. 8f.).

e. Cf. Epitome 1. 2.

f. Cf. Epitome ll. 3f. (in 4: "for thus you shall be honored by God").

g. I.e. "the sword will be a hindrance" (*S*), or "the sword is impartial" (*R*).

(R 7; B 6; S 5; A 4)

20 Listen every day to the words of your father and mother,

21 and seek not to offend and dishonor them;

22 for the son who dishonors and offends his father and mother,

23 God ponders his death and his misfortune.

   (R 8; B 7; S 6; A 5)

24 Honor your father in the proper way,

25 do not despise your friends,

26 and do not dishonor those who honor you.

   (R 9; B 8a; S 7; A 6)

27 If your son grows out of his boyhood

28 (as one who is) humble and wise,

29 teach him the "book of wisdom,"ʰ

30 for the book is good to learn (wisdom) from.

   (B 9)

31 (Wisdom) is bright eyes and an excellent tongue.

32 Eyes that are bright will not be blinded,

33 and a tongue that speaks wisely will not begin to stammer.

   (B 8b)

34 And if your son grows out of his boyhood

35 (as one who is) brutish, crude,ⁱ and insolent,

36 (one who is) thievish, deceitful, and provocative,ʲ

37 teach him the profession of gladiator

38 and put into his hand a sword and a dagger,

39 and pray for him,

40 that he shall die, shall be killed, immediately,

41 lest—by his living on—

42 you should grow old through his frauds and expenses,

43 while he does not produce anything good for you.

   (B 10; R 10)

44 Every bad son should die and not live on.

   (B-R 11; S 8; A 7)

45 And as for an adulterous woman, her feet are not firm,

46 for she deceives her good husband.

   (B 12)

47 And a man who does not correctly deal with his wife,

48 even God hates him.

   (B 13; R 12; S 9; A 8)

49 Keep your son away from fornication,

50 and your servant from the cabaret,

51 since these make (one) acquainted with the habit of stealing.

   (B 14; R 13; S 10; A 9)

52 Drink wine moderately

53 and do not boast of it;

54 for wine is, indeed, mild and sweet,

55 but every man that quarrels and boasts of it

56 will immediately be dishonored and despised.

   (B 15; S 11)

57 But when your thirst is quenched,ᵏ depart,

Prov 6:20
Sir 3:1ff.

Prov 20:20;
30:17
Sir 3:16
Ahᴬʳ (26)

cf. 211–MenM
674ᵃ
cf. 213–MenM
11.390
cf. 214–

34; Prov 10:1;
29:3

MenM 586.180

Eccl 8:1

27; Prov 10:1

Sir 16:3

cf. Prov 29:3

Deut 21:18–21

Prov 7:11

Col 3:19
Ahᴳ·(26:4)

Prov 29:3; Sir
9:6

Sir 31(34):27
Tob 4:15
Sir 31(34):25

Sir 31(34):26
Sir 31(34):29

---

h. Or "philosophy" (*R*), "arts and philosophy" (*A*).

i. MS: "athlete" (?); cf. "*nequam*" (*L-B*), "*schlicht*" (*S*), "*execrable*" (*A*).

j. So *S*: "*herausfordernd*" (but *L-B-R*: "contemptible").

k. Lit. "But when your stomach is full."

(B 16; A 10)

58 but not (so that what) is left (is) what dogs eat, the vomit[1] of the stomach.

(B 17; S 12)

59 There are two hateful things,
60 and in both of them the stomach is involved:
61 starvation, (the stomach) is swollen,[m]
62 satiety, (the stomach) is at the bursting point.[n]

(B 18; S 13)

(L.66) 63 And there is no one who follows his lust and his stomach   Sir 18:30f.
64 who will not immediately be dishonored and despised.

(B 19; S 14)

65 Blessed is the man who has mastered his stomach and his lust,[o]   MenM 425
66 he is one on whom one can rely at all times.

(B 20; S 15; A 11)

67 Hateful is the custom of lying down at an improper time: Prov 6:9–11;
(B 21)   10:5; 20:13;
                                                                           24:33f.
68 sleep carries (us) into Sheol,   MenM 780 var
69 dreams unite (us) with the dead.   MenM 784

(B 22; S 16; R 14; A 12)

70 Hateful is laziness;   Prov 10:40;
71 (it is) hungry and thirsty, naked and lamenting.   12:27; 13:4;
                                                                           19:15; 20:13

72 How comely and praiseworthy is industry;   Prov 10:4;
73 at all times (it is) a filled stomach and a bright face.   12:27; 13:4;
                                                                           20:13

74 Even if one does not have success,
75 he will not be blamed.

(B 23; S 17; R 15; A 13)   176. Prov 20:3

76 Do not be quarrelsome;
77 do not stretch out your hand against one older than you.

(B 24)

78 For the companions of Homer asked him,
79 "Whosoever will smite an old man,
80 what will happen to him?"
81 He said to them, "His eyes will be blinded."
82 "And whosoever will beat his mother,   Prov 19:26
83 what will happen to him?"
84 He said to them, "The earth shall not receive him,
85 for she is the mother of all men."   MenM 511
86 And again they asked him,
87 "And whosoever will smite his father,   Prov 19:26
88 what will happen to him?"
89 Homer said to his companions,
90 "This has not happened,
91 and so it cannot be taken into account;   Cicero,
92 for a son who beats his father does not exist,   ProRoscio, 25
                                                                         Herodotus I, 137
93 unless his mother bore him after committing adultery with a foreigner."

(B 25; S 18; R 16; A 14)

94 More than everything love your father,   Sir 7:27; Prov
95 you shall fear him and honor him.   23:22
                                                                         Ah^Arm.(20)[B]
                                                                         MenM 674a

---

l. Lit. "the whey" (I have maintained the MS   n. The text is obscure; my conjecture: "it is
reading).   filled, it is breaking."
   m. The text is obscure; my conjecture: "if it   o. For ll. 63–65, cf. Epitome ll. 6–8 (log. 3f.).
starves, it is swollen."

(B 26)

96 And do not despise, do not dishonor your mother,

97 for ten months long she bore you in her womb,

98 and when she gave birth to you she was at the point of death.

Sir 7:27
MenM 674
Ah[Arm.](20)[B]
Prov 23:22,25
WisSol 7:2

(B 27; S 19)

99 Do not laugh at the words of the aged,

100 nor curl your lips (in scorn) at the aged;

101 and do not despise the poor.[p]

MenM 376,
376 var

Sir 7:11

(B 28)

102 For old age has its infirmities,[q]

103 and man (has to) accept them,

104 but when he descends into the grave, he will find rest.[r]

Eccl 12:1–7
MenM 293
MenM 802

470

(B 29; A 15)

105 For there was a man who fell very badly,

106 and no one believed with respect to him

107 that he would stand on his feet (again);

108 but at some moment God took him by the hand and raised him,

109 and brought him (back) to great honor.

Sir 7:11

Sir 7:11; Prov
24:16
Sir 11:21

110 For neither riches are everlasting,

111 nor at all times is there poverty,

112 for subject to change are all things.

Ps-Phoc 27

Sir 11:14

Ps-Phoc 27[b]
MenAgricola
(Stob.)

113 For I have seen

114 someone who stood up to kill, and he was killed;

115 and someone they seized that he should die, and he found life.

18f.

116 For as for God, he who was cast down[s] by him will not be so forever,

117 nor will he who was humiliated[t] by him be so at all times.

(B 30; S 20; R 17; A 16)

118 And if you want to take a wife,

(L.67) 119 make first inquiries about her tongue,

120 and take her (only) then.

Sir 25:13–26:9

(B 31)

121 For a talkative woman is a hell;

122 and . . . a bad man is a deadly plague.[u]

336–39; Sir
25:20 [Heb.]

(B 32; S 21; R 18; A 17)

123 You shall fear God at all times,

124 so that you may call upon him in your distress,

125 and he will listen to your voice.[v]

9

Sir 2:10f.

Prov 15:29

(B 33; S 22; R 19; A 18)

126 Do not rejoice over a dead man, over one who dies,

127 because all men will go to the eternal house, they are mortal.

(B 34)

128 If you have an enemy,

129 do not pray with respect to him that he may die

130 —for when he is dead he is delivered from his misfortunes—

Ah[Syr.](60)
Sir 8:7; MenM
346
Eccl 12:5
Ah[Arm.](78)[B]
Ah[Gk.](26:3)

---

p. *S* places l. 101 after 102–4; he combines 99f. with 102–4, 101 with 105ff.

q. Lit. "for with old age do infirmities come."

r. I follow the conjecture of *S*; see l. 470.

s. The text has the active voice: "he whom he cast down."

t. The text: "he whom he humiliated"; *A* guesses "raised."

u. Lit. "death"; for the parallel Sheol = death, cf. Prov 7:27.

v. Cf. Epitome ll. 9–12 (log. 5).

131 but pray with respect to him that he may become poor,
132 (then) he will live on and (perhaps may) cease from his evil practices. ʷ

(B 35; S 23; R 20; A 19)
133 Do not intervene between brothers,   Prov 26:17
134 and do not seek to pronounce a judgment between them.   Sir 7:6
135 If brothers fight (with each other),
136 what business is it of yours?
137 For they are brothers, and they will be reconciled;
138 but as for you, they despise you in their minds.

(B 36; S 24; R 21; A 20)
139 Do not pass through a market street in which there is a quarrel,   Prov 26:17; Sir
140 lest, if you pass through, you badly suffer,   11:9; Prov 20:3
    MenM 332:
141 and, if you part them, you be wounded and your garments be rent,   Ps-Phoc 151
142 and, if you stand there and watch, you be summoned to court to give   Ah^Syr·(55)
    evidence.

(B 37)
143 Hate being wounded;
144 refuse to bring out false witness.   Ex 20:16; Deut
    5:20
    Ps-Phoc 12

(B 38; S 25; R 22; A 21)
145 Be fond of possessions, but hate stealing:
146 for possessions are "life,"   Prov 10:16
147 but stealing is at all times "death."

(B 39; S 26; R 23; A 21–22)
148 (If you meet)ˣ a bad man in the market street,   cf. Sir 13:1;
149 do not sit down immediately,   22:13
    MenM 25; 423
150 lest, if you give ear to that bad man,
151 everyone who sees you will call you the companion of the bad man;   Ah^Syr·(12)
152 and lest, if you do not heed him or adhere to his opinion,
153 he reviles you and molests you in his wickedness.

(B 40; S 27; R 24; A 23)
154 Do not dine with a bad servant,
155 lest his master(s) accuse(s) you
156 of teaching his (their) servant to steal.

(B 41; S 28; R 25; A 24)
157 Hate a bad servant,
158 and beware of a free man who steals;
159 for just as you have not the competence to kill a servant,
160 neither have you (the capacity) to restrain a free man.

(B 42; S 29; R 26; A 25)
161 God hates the bad servant   cf. Ah^Arm·(45)^B
162 who hates and dishonors his master(s).

(B 43; S 30; R 27; A 26)
163 If you see a bad servant in deplorable misfortune,
164 do not feel sorry for him,
165 but say, "Alas for his master(s), what a (piece of) property."

(B 44; S 31; R 28; A 27)
166 Love the industrious servant   Sir 7:20f.
167 who is active and works with zeal in the house of his master(s).

---

w. I have followed *S* (conjecture); *L-B-R-A*
follow the MS reading, "then he will live on and
sigh because of his misfortunes," which might be
correct.

x. My conjecture—MS: "begging and sons";
L-B-R: "ears and eyes"; *S*: "do not sit down near";
A: "(the bad man) combines buildings with beg-
ging."

(B 45; S 32; R 29; A 28)
168 As for every bad man, God gives him over into slavery,
(L.68) 169 but every industrious man is worthy to rise in honor and greatness.

(B 46; S 33; R 30; A 29)
170 Reject and hate a lascivious old man,
171 for as you are not able to restrain the wind
172 so you cannot restrain or educate (such) an old man.

MenM 146; Sir 25:2

Eccl 8:8

MenM 161[b]

(B 47; S 34; R 31; A 30)
173 Do not leave the way,
174 and do not go astray,
175 and do not walk wickedly.

Prov 21:16; MenM 101 Ah[Syr](48)

(B 48; S 35; R 32; A 31)
176 Do not be quarrelsome,
177 lest a quarrel arise which reduces (you) to poverty.
(B 49)
178 And if you lie, immediately you shall be despised.
(B 50)
179 And if you speak wickedly, your face shall grow pale.
(B 51)
180 If you are boastful, you shall prove harmful to yourself.

76; Prov 20:3

(B 52; S 36; R 33; A 32)
181 If you recline at table among many (others),
182 do not open your purse in their presence;
183 and do not show what you have with you,
184 lest they borrow from you but do not pay you back.
185 And when you ask them (about it), they will strive with you
186 and call you a sour man.
187 (In short) you will lose what was yours,
188 and, moreover, you will become (their) enemy.

Sir 8:12; 29:4f.

Sir 29:6

Sir 29:6

(B 53; S 37; R 34; A 33)
189 Love your brothers,
190 and make your words pleasing to your friends.
(B 54)
191 For I went about and sought
192 something that can be likened to good friends,
193 but I did not find (it).

Tob 4:13 CD 6:20 GThom 25

WisSol 8:18

Sir 6:15; MenM 575

(B 55; S 38)
194 Rejoice at your sons, father,
195 for they are a (real) joy.

196 However, the position of brothers,
197 the sons do not take for me; see my sons (and) my brothers.[y]

Sir 25:7

198 For your son prays for your death,
199 since through your death he will receive honor,
200 and will occupy your position,
201 and will live on your goods at will.

y. Cf. *A*; MS: "See, my sons, my brothers" or
"See the sons of my brothers" (so *L-B-S*), *F-R*
want to leave out "my sons" (or "of my sons").

202 But your brothers pray to God for your life,
203 because as long as you live they are splendid,
204 but through your death they are handicapped;
205 your sons will call them, your brothers, worthless fellows.
   (B 56)
206 But it is a bad and foolish son who thinks of these things;
207 a bad thought in his heart, (focused) on his father's death.

208 The bad son does not understand
209 that if his father dies, it is not good for the sons:
210 the head (of the family) no longer lives for them. z

   (B 57; S 39; R 35; A 34)
211 Love and honor your father,   24
212 because he gave himself to you.

213 Do not despise your friends,   25
214 and do not dishonor those who honor you.   26
   (B 58)
215 And he with whom you had a meal,   Ps 41:10
216 do not walk with him in a treacherous way.   Mk 14:18
                                                                   Jn 13:18

   (B 59; S 40)
217 And when you are going to your friend,
218 if your friend (really) loves you
219 and (if) you are (really) dear to him,
220 his children will show you that outwardly.
221 If they eagerly watch for your presence,
222 be convinced that your friend loves you,
223 and that you are dear to him.
224 But if his children do not eagerly watch for your coming,
225 even he, your friend, is unwilling to see you . . .
   (R 36)
226 Leave, go home!a2

   (B 60; S 41; A 35)
(L.69) 227 Tardily does the freebornb2 appreciate his home,
228 and the maidservantc2 the house of her master(s).

   (B 61; S 42; R 37; A 36)
229 If you see a noble man who loses his rank of honor,
230 do not seek to dishonor him (further).
231 On the contrary, honor him in a correct way,
232 and give to him that which you can;   Sir 7:31
233 for great is the charity which you practice   Sir 29:8–13;
234 when you give to a man who lost his possessions and rank of honor.   Tob 4:7
235 If you have, give to him,   Ps-Phoc
236 and if you have not and (can)not give to him,   22,26,28
                                                                   Sir 4:1–10
237 then visit him with good and gentle words,   Tob 4:8f.,16

z. L-B-R: "because they have not where they   freeborn").
can put their head" (incorrect).   c2. I leave out "the son of" before "maidser-
   a2. S adds here: "slowly, tardily," which word   vant" (against L-B-R-S-A), since it is not in the
I render in l. 227 (so L-B-R-A).   MS and not required by the context.
   b2. So with B contra L-R-S-A ("the son of the

238 and say to him, "Do not be afraid"
239 and "May God purpose something good for you!"[d2]

(B 62; S 43; R 38; A 37)
240 Keep yourself away from adultery.

    (B 63)

Ex 20:13; Deut
5:17; Prov 5:20
Tob 4:12
Ah^Arm.(152)^B
Prov 5:15–17;
9:17; 25:26a

241 Why should you want to buy polluted and putrid water,
242 whose beginning is dwindling, whose end is light and loose[e2]?

    (B 64; R 39; A 38)

243 And walk in a straight line with the head[f2] raised,   Prov 4:25f.
244 and be chaste[g2] in your thoughts.

    (B 65)
245 Remember and see:
246 Just as you do not wish your wife to commit adultery with another,   Ah^Syr.(6)
247 likewise also do not wish to commit adultery with your neighbor's wife.

    (B 66; S 44; A 39)
248 And if you are very keen on not losing anything,
249 you should (also) not be keen on stealing.

    (B 67; R 40; A 40)
250 Everything that is hateful to you,   Tob 4:15
251 you should not wish to do that to your neighbor.   b.Shab 31^a
              Ah^Arm.(88^a)^A

    (B 68; S 45; R 41; A 41)
252 Let not your way of life be arrogant,   MenM 35
253 lest it be harmful to you.
    (B 69)
254 And if you are impudent,   MenM 35
255 this will not be pleasant for you.

    (B 70; R 42; A 42)
256 You shall not[h2] learn hunting,
257 if the weariness of life is not to fall upon you.
258 If you should (wish) to learn[i2] it,
259 you would be searching for something that you have not lost,
260 and you would not find something that is beautiful,
261 because it is contemptible.[j2]

    (B 71; R 43; A 43)
262 As for the king, he is honored by his princes,
263 but the gods are despised by their priests.
    (B 72; S 46)
264 (Do not invite)[k2] a priest who despises his gods.
    (B 73)
265 If you invite a wicked priest to your house,
266 he gives you a blessing each time that he enters,
267 but makes complaints each time that he departs.   Ps-Phoc 94

---

d2. Or as one saying: "Do not be afraid, for [or 'then'] God shall purpose . . ."

e2. Polluted and evaporating water as imagery of the whore: l. 242 gives the picture that such water is not useful, for it dries up, so that nothing remains except damp—"light and loose" also has the connotation of wanton women.

f2. Lit. "the neck."

g2. Or "modest."

h2. I add (with Geiger) the negation, against L-B-R-A (= MS); S does not accept the negation but guesses the word "modesty" instead of "hunting."

i2. MS: "teach."

j2. All the hunter finds is a cadaver.

k2. My conjecture—the MS is obscure here; L-B: "you shall not give drink (make drunk)"; S: "dissolute"; A: "vit pour lui-même."

268 And if you place food[12] before him,
269 his one hand, indeed, goes to his mouth;
270 but the other takes the food away
271 and puts it into his bag to take it along with him for his children.
   (B 74)
272 Have more love for a dog than you have for (such) a priest;
273 if the dog has enough food,
274 he leaves (the remains) behind in your house,
275 but if the priest has enough food,
276 he takes (the remains) along with him for his children,
277 and makes complaints in addition.

   (B 75; S 47; R-A 44)
278 Be welcome,[m2]
279 if (at least) (your) garments are fair,
280 and if (your) purse is filled.
   (B 76; R-A 45)
(L.70) 281 A meal makes company pleasant.   Ps-Phoc 92
   (B 77)
282 Riches multiply friends.   Prov 14:20; 19:4
283 But if a man's foot falters,   MenM 238; 71
                                                             Ps-Phoc 91
284 all his friends are gone.[n2]   Prov 19:4;
   (B 78; R-A 46)   Sir 6:8,10
                                                             MenM 34
285 A gift makes words pleasant.   Prov 18:16,19:6

   (B 79; S 48; R-A 47)
286 With someone who is richer than you, do not dine every day,   Prov 23:1–8;
287 for if you happen to visit him,   Sir 13:2–13
288 he would receive you with(in the bounds of) his daily expenditures;
289 but if he happens to visit you,
290 you would spend because of him what you have collected in thirty days,
291 and thereby ruin yourself.   Sir 8:2

   (B 80; S 49; R-A 48)
292 Divination gladdens the heart of fools,   Sir 34(31):1.5,7
293 astrology infatuates the mind of the stupid.   Did 2:2; 5:1

   (B 81; R-A 49)
294 One who remains in the market street is an idler.
   (B 82; R-S-A 50)
295 Stealing is the constructor of a cross.   cf. 147
   (B 83; R-A 51)
296 Bad amusement[o2] is the teacher of falsehood and theft.
   (B 84; R-A 52; S 51)
297 Keep a boy away from evil things;
   (B 85)
298 the school keeps (one) far from death;   MenM 436
299 handicraft delivers (one) from misfortune.   MenM 430
   (B 86)
300 The law is a divine appeal.[p2]   Ps-Phoc 129

12. Lit. "bread." See also ll. 270, 273, 275.
m2. Lit. "Come in peace."
n2. Lit. "lost."
o2. Or "an unfortunate time."
p2. So S-A—otherwise: L (improbable): "*divina*

lectio lex est"; B (improbable): "*Divina lectio lex est*"; R (impossible): "*Das göttliche Gesetz ist Gegenstand des Lesens.*" One might guess, with a slight change of the text, "The law summons for the divine."

(B 87; R-A 53; S 52)

301 Hateful is loquacity;

302 and excessive laughter is a (true) disgrace.

(B 88; R-A 54; S 53)

303 Disorderly conduct, despise it at all times.

(B 89; S 54)

304 Reject, hate the talkative person

305 who interrupts (others) but (who himself) speaks the more.

(B 90)

306 Though he had (even) ten thousand enemies,

307 they would not hurt him like his own tongue;

308 every day he is involved in a deadly fight,

309 he has not a bright face,

310 due to the words for which he is censured.

(B 91; R-A 55)

311 There exists nothing better than silence.

(B 92)

312 Being silent is at all times a virtue.

(B 93)

313 Even if a fool is silent, he is counted wise.

(B 94; R-A 56; S 55)

314 Never lose heart.

(B 95)

315 Do not fall back in battle;

316 for whosoever does not fall back in battle

317 and gives himself unto death,

318 shall immediately find life and a good name

319 and he shall be praised.

(B 96)

320 He who speaks boldly in court

321 shall be declared innocent.

(B 97; R-A 57; S 56)

322 Riches without fuss are a (true) power;

323 but not everyone knows how to administer them.

(B 98)

324 For if someone has inflated his stomach,[q2] he will die;

325 and if he does not remember the end, he will perish.

326 If, on the other hand, you calm down your stomach, you will grow rich;

327 and if you will remember the end, it will be well with you.

(B 99; S 57; R-A 58)

328 (To act as) a judge is fine;

329 Take care that you do not pronounce judgment over a foolish man,

330 because (even) if you should try to assist the fool in his case,

331 he will still revile you and he will say to many (others),

332 "He has condemned me."

(B 100; R-A 59; S 58)

333 Do not dine with a wicked man;

334 for even what is your own he will consume,

335 and in his wickedness he will say about you evil and hateful things.

Sir 20:5
Ps-Phoc 20
MenM 144

MenM 288a

Sir 20:5

Sir 11:8

MenM 289
Prov 10:14; 13:3

MenM 597

Prov 17:27

Prov 17:28

MenM 181,612

Sir 7:36

Sir 7:36

265–77; Sir 11:29,33

Sir 27:23

---

q2. Lit. "has widened his stomach (belly)" with the meaning "empty pretentiousness"; cf. l. 409.

(B 101; R-A 60; S 59)

336 Do not listen to a talkative and verbose woman;   118–22

337 do not believe her, if she complains to you of her husband;

(L.71) 338 for he did not sin against her,

339 but she did irritate him every day with her wicked tongue.

(B 102; R-A 61; S 60)

340 Do not measure your strength with one who is stronger than you,   Lk 14:31

341 or one who forces you to strive with him;   Ah^Arm.-(48)^B

342 do not say to yourself, "Maybe I will cast him down,"

343 lest he cast you down;   Ah^Arm.-(28)^A

344 then you will be ashamed in the presence of many bystanders.   Lk 14:29f.

(B 103; R-A 62; S 61)

345 Be bold against one who contends you;

346 and do not forgive him the revilements against your father.   Sir 30:6

(B 104; R-A 63; S 62)

347 Do not cast a glance at your maidservant in your house,

348 and do not be fond of impurity and prodigality;

349 do never besmirch your honor.

350 For if you raise your eyes^r2 in your house, you will become very sad,   Ah^Syr.-(5)

351 but if you are chaste,^s2 you shall be happy and fortunate,

352 because God hates impurity and prodigality,

353 even for men these are a disgrace.

(B 105; R-A 64; S 63)

354 If you have goods, if you have possessions,   368; MenM 478

355 be humble and kind, and give; do not flaunt.   Ps-Phoc 28,53

                                              MenM 510

356 And if you have no possessions, if you are poor,   MenM 52

357 bow yourself down and be gentle; be not stubborn.   Sir 25:2

358 Flaunting and stubbornness are hateful to men.

(B 106; R-A 65; S 64)

359 Do not turn away your eyes from your father and mother,   Sir 7:27f.

360 and do not curl your lips (in scorn) at "testicles" and "breasts,"^t2

361 and do not dishonor the God who made you.   Sir 7:30; Did 1:2

(B 107)

362 However, remember and see:

363 if our eyes become great, they (still can)not surpass our eyebrows.

364 For if you have surpassed your father and mother,

365 and if—as it is now your time and your fate—

366 you are to be called "Master" and "Lord,"   Jn 13:13

367 it is due to the name of your father and mother that all people call you so.

(B 108; R-A 66; S 65)

368 If you have goods, if you have possessions,   354; Ps-Phoc

369 live on your possessions as long as you are alive   109

                                              Eccl 5:17f.

370 and your eye (can) see and your foot (can) walk.

---

r2. That is, to covet your maidservant (S: "if you look with pride").

s2. Or "ashamed," or "modest."

t2. The MS reads "breasts" as the second word. L-B-R-S-A guess "teachers," since they interpret the first word as "friends." (L: "amicos et prae-

ceptores") The first word, however, may mean "uterus" or "testicles," and it is to be taken in the latter sense: l. 360 repeats l. 359, referring to the very beginning of man's life, but one should keep in mind that the ultimate source of life is God himself (l. 361).

371 For remember and see: Ps-Phoc 109
372 one (can)not use (his) goods in Sheol,   Ps-Phoc 110
373 and riches do not accompany one into the grave.
374 Therefore, you shall not deny yourself the good things,   Eccl 11:8
375 for better is one day under the sun
376 than a hundred years in Sheol.

(B 109; R-A 67; S 66)
377 Be energetic in your youth,   MenM 536
378 as long as your eye (can) see and your foot (can) walk,
379 (as long as) your strength is great.

380 But when you have become aged and weary,   MenM 536
381 sit down and live on your possessions.
(B 110)
382 And comely is youth,   399
383 when the young man is energetic,
384 and (when) he is successful through his strength.

(B 111; R-A 68; S 67)
385 Let anxieties never dominate your heart,   MemM 3, 563
386 because it is a bad thing to nurse anxiety.
(B 112)
387 For many are the years which a man does not (really) live;
388 their anxieties (slowly) kill him.   MenM 440; Sir 30:23f.
(B 113; R 69)
(L.72) 389 If you are anxious, you shall die;   Sir 30:24
390 and if you are sad, you shall never (really) live.
(B 114)
391 For short and limited is the space of life   Eccl 5:17
392 which God determines for men;   Eccl 5:18
393 and he mingled for them many bad things with a few good things.   MenM 741

(B 115; R 70; A 69; S 68)
394 The main source of all good things is the fear of God,   MenM 63
395 it delivers (one) from all evil things;[u2]   Prov 1:7; 9:10; 10:27; 22:4
396 a treasure it is.   Prov 14:27

(B 116; S 69)
397 Not always, however, will last the affairs of men,
398 since their life is until the house of death.[v2]
(B 117; R 71; S-A 70)
399 Comely and praiseworthy is youth,   382
400 but it is with men only for a short time,
401 and (then) old age makes it fade away.[w2]   MenM 39f.

(B 118; R 72; S-A 71)
402 Pleasant are life, goods, and buildings,[x2]
403 but more pleasant than these is a good name.[y2]   Prov 22:1; Eccl 7:1
(B 119; R 73; S-A 72)   MenM 406
404 Praiseworthy and radiant is joy

u2. Ll. 394f.; cf. Epitome 5 (ll. 9f.).   x2. The reading "buildings" (MS) is followed
v2. Ll. 397f.; cf. Epitome 6 (ll. 13f.).   by *L-A; B-R-S* ("children") follow the Epitome.
w2. Ll. 399ff.; cf. Epitome 7 (ll. 15–17).   y2. Ll. 402f.; cf. Epitome 8 (ll. 18f.).

405 when quarrel and violence are far from it.[z2]

   (B 120; R 74; S-A 73)

406 Good and excellent is friendship

   192
   Ps-Phoc 218

407 which continues to the house of death.[a3]

   (B 121; R 75; S-A 74)

408 Unpretentious is wisdom

409 when it is not puffed up.[b3]

   (B 122; R 76; S-A 75)

410 Good is faithfulness

   Ps-Phoc 218

411 when it is coupled with sound judgment.[c3]

   (B 123; R 77; S-A 76)

412 Praiseworthy is industry

413 when someone is energetic and successful.

   (B 124; R 78; S-A 77)

414 Laziness is a bad thing

415 when a person's body should be vigorous.

   (B 125; R 79; S-A 78)

416 Intemperance provokes conflict.[d3]

   Prov 29:22

   (B 126; R 80; S-A 79)

417 Wisdom keeps one back from wickedness.

   (B 127; R 81; S-A 80)

418 Hope comforts the heart.

   MenM 30

   (B 128; R 82; S-A 81)

419 Insipidity leads the mind astray.[e3]

   (B 129; R 83; S-A 82)

420 Agitation makes (one) lose (his) senses.[f3]

   (B 130; R 84; S-A 83)

421 An evil heart[g3] causes grief and sighing.[h3]

   (B 131; R 85; S-A 84)

422 Jealousy is the cause of evil and strife.[i3]

   Ps-Phoc 70

   (B 132; R 86; S-A 85)

423 The belly (can be) a disgraceful thing.[j3]

   (S-A 86)

424 The tongue brings to misery.[k3]

   MenM 305
   Jas 3:6

   (B 133; R-S-A 87)

425 Radiant and comely are riches,

426 but the good man hardly acquires them.

   MenM 62

   (B 134; R-S 88)

427 Hateful and dark is poverty

428 when accompanied by disease and loss.[l3]

   (B 136; R-S 89; A 88)

429 Riches are (merely?) a step to honor.

   (B 136; R-S 90; A 89)

430 Rest is a great blessing.

   Eccl 4:6

---

z2. Ll. 404f.; cf. Epitome 9 (ll. 20f.).

a3. Ll. 406f.; cf. Epitome 10 (ll. 22f.).

b3. Ll. 408f.; cf. Epitome 11 (ll. 24f.); 409: lit. "when flatulence is far from it."

c3. Ll. 410f.; cf. Epitome 12 (ll. 26f.).

d3. The text is obscure; instead of "intemperance" the MS has "fur coat." Different conjectures are made by Geiger, Frankenberg, Schulthess, and Audet.

e3. L. 419; cf. Epitome 13 (l. 28).

f3. L. 420; cf. Epitome 14 (l. 29).

g3. Or "bad conscience" (*L-B-R-A*); "melancholy" (*S*).

h3. L. 421; cf. Epitome 15 (l. 30).

i3. L. 422; cf. Epitome 16 (l. 31).

j3. L. 423; cf. Epitome 17 (l. 32).

k3. L. 424; cf. Epitome 17 (l. 33).

l3. Lit. "when d. and l. are coupled with it."

(B 137; R-S 91; A 90)

431 Riches that will not reduce to poverty are a strong power.

432 Wretched poverty means illness and disease.   Prov 17:22

(B 138; R-S 92; A 91)

433 Health means joy and rejoicing.   Prov 17:22

(B 139; R 93; A 92)

434 Old age is the frontier of death.

(B 140; R 94; S-A 93)

435 Poverty is the dregs of all evil   MenM 590; 660

436 when it takes up its abode in old age.   MenM 656

(B 141; S 94)

437 And the last part of life is death;

(B 142; S 95)

438 the grave hides the dust.ᵐ³

(B 143; S 96; R 95; A 94)

439 Fever corrupts charming people;

(B 144)

440 health and good cheer make one's appearance charming.

(B 145; S 97; R 96; A 95)

441 Death corrupts (even) the firm (body);

(B 146)

(L.73) 442 but dissolution forms (first) ten parts,

443 and then (death) corrupts the one (part) that was well prepared.ⁿ³

444 These bad and good things are mingled in the life of men,   393

445 not to mention fever, tremors, diseases, and (other) great calamitiesᵒ³

446 which are called "the angelsᵖ³ of death."

(R 98)

447 And no one can choose and take for himself what is good

448 and avoid what is bad;

449 but men go their way according to what God measures out for them,

450 as long as he allows them to live.

(B 148; S 99)

451 Neither should men despair,

452 because they cannot live longer than is determined for them;

(B 149; R 99)

453 nor should we angrily complain against God

454 because of the misfortunes that befall us.

(B 150; R 100)

455 For how often (it happens that)   105

456 someone, even when he suffers misfortunes,

457 rises (again) to honor and dignity.   108f.

(B 151; R 101; S 100)

458 One should, however, in the sorrow that befalls him,

459 not be excessively sad,   Sir 22:11

(B 152)

460 and through his groaning badly vex himself,   Sir 38:21

(R 102)

461 because he will not be of any help to a deceased   Sir 38:21

---

m3. The text is corrupt; my conjecture is not shared by *L-B-R-A*, who render with "riches," or by *S*, who renders with "beauty" instead of "dust."

n3. I.e. the soul?
o3. MS obscure.
p3. Or "messengers."

462 even if he falls down and greatly suffers after his (death).q3

(R 103)

463 But he who is wise

464 —even when the deceased is very dear to him—

465 shall accompany him with tears to the tomb;   Sir 38:16f.

466 but when the deceased has been buried,   Sir 38:23

467 let him, even him, overcome his groaning;

468 and let him remember and consider in his mind

469 that he himself shall also die.   Sir 38:20,22

(B 153; S 101)

470 And this (Sheol)r3 is the place of rest   Sir 38:23; 22:11

471 which God determines for men,

472 that they may rest there from the evil things

473 which they saw in their life.s3

474 *Menander has come to an end.*

---

q3. Lit. "after him," namely, the deceased.   (and this . . .)."
r3. The Epitome adds before this line: "I have   s3. Ll. 470–73; cf. Epitome 18b (ll. 36–39).
watched, but the dwelling place of men is Sheol,

PRAYERS, PSALMS, AND ODES

INTRODUCTION

BY J. H. CHARLESWORTH

The Davidic Psalms, portions of which may date from prior to David's reign until sometime in the post-exilic period, were the psalmbook of the Temple. At the beginning of this century it was generally assumed that the psalter was the only collection of psalms significant to most Jews during the period of Early Judaism. Now we know that the psalter itself was not set—or canonized—until rather late, probably not until the beginning of the Common Era; and five more psalms—Psalms 151–55—were considered by at least some Jews as part of an expanded psalter. Other collections of psalms or hymns were important in the period 100 B.C. to A.D. 200, and all of these, except the Psalms of Solomon, have been discovered or recognized only in the past one hundred years. The most notable hymnbooks are the following: the Psalms of Solomon, the Qumran Hodayoth, the Hellenistic Synagogal Prayers (perhaps), and the Odes of Solomon. Besides the individual prayers (or psalms) presented below, poetic compositions—indeed psalms and prayers—highlight many pseudepigrapha, especially the apocalypses and testaments.

The Prayer of Joseph is included among the following collections of prayers, psalms, and odes only because of its title. As extant, it is more characteristic of the works included under the "Expansions of the 'Old Testament' ' '"; but only a portion of the document has been preserved, and originally it may have been defined by a prayer of Joseph. An analogy may be drawn to Joseph and Aseneth, which has often been called the Book of the Prayer of Aseneth because of the prayer featured in the heart of the narrative (chs. 12f.).

The following prayers and psalms should be read along with other poetic compositions, notably the Qumran Hodayoth, the Qumran non-Masoretic psalms, other Qumran hymns, the hymns and prayers in the Apocrypha (including the Song of the Three Young Men and the Prayer of Azariah), similar compositions in the Targumim, and the proto-rabbinic prayers. Also to be examined are the psalms in Pseudo-Philo, in the Testament of Job, and in 2 Baruch, the Psalm of Taxo (TMos 10:1–10), the poetical works collected in the Supplement, the Prayer of Enoch (1En 84:1–6), the Prayer of Aseneth (JosAsen 12f.), the Prayer of Eleazar (3Mac 6:2–15), the prayers in Jubilees, in Pseudo-Philo, and in 2 Baruch, the laments and prayers of Ezra (esp. 4Ezra 8:20–36), and Zephaniah's prayer (ApZeph 9:1–10; 12:5–10). Also significantly related to these psalms and prayers are the Prayer of Jesus (Mt 6; Lk 11; Didache 8), the hymns and prayers in Luke 1f. and John 1:1–18, the Hymn of the Pearl, Hermes's Hymn of Rebirth (C.H. XIII), and the gnostic prayers: The Prayer of the Apostle Paul (CG I, 1), the Prayer of Thanksgiving (CG VI, 7), and the Hymn of the First Stele of Seth (CG VII, 5).

CONTENTS

More Psalms of David
Prayer of Manasseh
Psalms of Solomon
Hellenistic Synagogal Prayers
Prayer of Joseph
Prayer of Jacob
Odes of Solomon

MORE PSALMS OF DAVID

(Third Century B.C.–First Century A.D.)

A NEW TRANSLATION AND INTRODUCTION

BY J. H. CHARLESWORTH with J. A. SANDERS

The canonical Old Testament in Hebrew (the Masoretic Bible) contains 150 psalms; yet five more psalms of David and part of a sixth (151B) are now recognized. The disparate date and character of these additional psalms are best represented by discussing and translating them individually. The early, pre-Christian date and Jewish character of four of these psalms—Psalms 151A, 151B, 154, and 155—is proved by the discovery that they are extant in the Qumran Psalms Scroll (11QPs²), which dates from the first half of the first century A.D.[1]

Despite the disparateness that separates these psalms, there may be an organic relationship between them, and earlier ones may have inspired later ones. This possibility arises with the recognition that Psalms 151A, 151B, 152, and 153 are all influenced by the tradition recorded in 1 Samuel 16 and 17, according to which David slew both lions and bears (1Sam 17:36) and defeated the Philistine Goliath, eventually cutting off his head with the giant's own sword (1Sam 17:51).

Texts

Psalm 151 is preserved in Greek (LXX), Hebrew, and Syriac;[2] Psalms 152 and 153 only in Syriac; Psalms 154 and 155 in Hebrew and Syriac. Generally speaking, the Hebrew, because it is earlier and the language of the original, is to be preferred over the other texts.[3]

The translation of the Greek (LXX) and Hebrew is based upon the edition by Sanders.[4] The translation of the Syriac is based upon the edition by W. Baars.[5] Sigla are as follows:

A – Baghdad, Library of the Chaldean Patriarchate, MS 1113, fols. 118b–20b, of circa the twelfth century. This MS was once in Mosul; it is our base text.

B – London, British Museum, Add. MS 14.568, fols. 49b–50a, of the sixth century.

[1] J. A. Sanders, "The Apocryphal Compositions," *The Psalms Scroll of Qumran Cave 11 (11QPs²)* (DJD 4; Oxford, 1965) p. 9. See also J. Strugnell, "More Psalms of 'David,'" (*CBQ* 27 [1965] 207).

[2] The editions of the Gk. (LXX), Heb., and Syr. used herein are given below. For a critical edition of the Eth. (which derives from the LXX) and a translation, see S. Strelcyn, "Le Psaume 151 dans la tradition éthiopienne," *JSS* 23 (1978) 316–29. The Old Lat., which is also dependent upon the LXX, is available in R. Weber (ed.), *Le Psautier romain et les autres anciens psautiers latins* (Collectanea Biblica Latina 10; Rome, 1953).

[3] M. Noth argued that the Syr. was separated from the original Heb. by a Gk. intermediary version. See his "Die fünf syrisch überlieferten apokryphen Psalmen," *ZAW* 48 (1930) 13. M. H. Goshen-Gottstein has now argued persuasively that the Syr. depends directly on the Heb. See his "The Psalms Scroll (11QPs²): A Problem of Canon and Text," *Textus* 5 (1966) 32. Sanders correctly states, ". . . all scholars agree that the Hebrew psalm (151) in the scroll is the original." See his "The Qumran Psalms Scroll [11QPs²] Reviewed," *On Language, Culture, and Religion: In Honor of Eugene A. Nida*, eds. M. Black and W. A. Smalley (The Hague, 1974) p. 85.

[4] Sanders, *The Dead Sea Psalms Scroll* (Ithaca, N.Y., 1967) pp. 96–115.

[5] W. Baars, "Apocryphal Psalms," *The Old Testament in Syriac According to the Peshitta Version* (Leiden, 1972) part IV, fascicle b, pp. 1–12.

JRL Syr 7 – Manchester, John Rylands Library, Syriac Manuscript 7, fol. 135a, of the sixteenth century.[6] It contains only Psalm 151 of the pseudepigraphical psalms.

Collective importance

Some distinguished scholars have argued that one or more of these pseudepigraphical psalms were composed by the Essenes, the authors of the Dead Sea Scrolls.[7] Most scholars,[8] however, conclude correctly that while some passages can be interpreted in line with Essene theology, this possibility does not indicate that these psalms were composed by the Essenes, who shared ideas with other Jews contemporaneous with them.

The presence of these psalms within the Qumran Psalter (11QPs^a) raises the question of the extent of the Davidic Psalter prior to the destruction of Jerusalem in A.D. 70. At Qumran, of course, the Psalter was appreciably different from the present collection in Hebrew; but what was the shape of the Psalter elsewhere? M. H. Goshen-Gottstein[9] has argued that the Psalter was already set (and canonized) by the second century B.C. and that excerpts from it, along with apocryphal compositions, were placed in 11QPs^a, which is therefore the earliest "Jewish prayerbook."[10] A similar interpretation is defended by P. Skehan,[11] who contends that 11QPs^a is a "library edition" of the "standard collection of 150 Psalms." The presence of "apocryphal" psalms such as the Prayer of Manasseh, and the Psalms of Solomon, which were considered inspired by many Jews around the turn of the era, along with the presence of apocryphal psalms in 11QPs^a[12] indicate the distinction between canonical and apocryphal psalms had not been clarified before the advent of Christianity.[13]

Translation

The translation attempts to be as literal as intelligible English will allow, so that comparisons can be made between the Syriac and the Hebrew. For a convenient collection of divergent translations, see Sanders' *The Dead Sea Psalms Scroll* (pp. 100–3). Syriac and Hebrew words are translated consistently by the same English word; when possible, cognate words are translated identically.

---

[6] This unexamined version of Psalm 151 was discovered by Charlesworth while working on a catalogue of the Syr. MSS in the John Rylands Library. The variants in JRL Syr 7 are frequently similar to those in BM Add. MS 14.674, fols. 160b–61b, of the 12th cent., and to MS G. 31. Sup., fol. 176b in the Ambrosian Library in Milan, of the 16th cent. Compare the apparatus in Baars's edition with the major variants cited below.

[7] M. Philonenko, "L'Origine essénienne des cinq psaumes syriaques de David," *Semitica* 9 (1959) 48–53; M. Delcor, "Cinq nouveaux psaumes esséniens?" *RQ* 1 (1958) 85–102; idem, "Cinq psaumes syriaques esséniens," *Les Hymnes de Qumran* (Paris, 1962) pp. 299–319; idem, "Zum Psalter von Qumran," *BZ* n.F. 10 (1966) 15–29; A. Dupont-Sommer, "Le Psaume CLI dans 11QPs^a et le problème de son origine essénienne," *Semitica* 14 (1964) 25–62.

[8] J. A. Sanders, "Two Non-Canonical Psalms in 11QPs^a," *ZAW* 76 (1964) 57–75; J. Carmignac, "La Forme poétique du psaume 151 de la grotte 11," *RQ* 4 (1963) 371–78; W. H. Brownlee, "The 11Q Counterpart to Psalm 151, 1–5," *RQ* 4 (1963) 379–87; A. S. van der Woude, "Die fünf syrischen Psalmen (einschliesslich Psalm 151)," *JSHRZ* 4 (1974) 29–47.

[9] M. H. Goshen-Gottstein, *Textus* 5 (1966) 22–33.

[10] S. Talmon published articles that presented a position in agreement with Goshen-Gottstein; see Talmon, "Hebrew Apocryphal Psalms from Qumran," *Tarbiz* 35 (1966) 214–34 [in Heb.; English summary on pp. II–III]; idem, "Pisqah Be'emsa' Pasuq and 11QPs^a," *Textus* 5 (1966) 11–21. Talmon now has rejected this hypothesis; see Sanders, *On Language, Culture, and Religion,* pp. 79–99.

[11] P. W. Skehan, "The Apocryphal Psalm 151," *CBQ* 25 (1963) 407–9; idem, "A Broken Acrostic and Psalm 9," *CBQ* 27 (1965) 1–5; idem, "A Liturgical Complex in 11QPs^a," *CBQ* 35 (1973) 195–205; idem, *"Jubilees* and the Qumran Psalter," *CBQ* 37 (1975) 343–47; idem, "Qumran and Old Testament Criticism," *Qumrân: Sa piété, sa théologie et son milieu* (Bibliotheca Ephemeridum Theologicarum Lovaniensium 46; Paris, 1978) pp. 163–82.

[12] 11QPs^a contains other pseudepigraphical psalms than the 5ApocSyrPss; and it preserves a prose account of the psalms attributed to David, stating that the total was 4,050, which is clearly an inflated figure that lauds David's genius. J. Strugnell has found another psalm of David in *LAB* 59; he concludes, "As a general observation let us call attention to the fact that, like Ps 151A, 151B, and Syriac Ps 152, this is clearly a Davidic pseudepigraphon, *ex persona David.*" See Strugnell, *CBQ* 27 (1965) 207–16; the quotation is on pp. 215f.

[13] See herein the discussion of the pseudepigraphical psalms and odes just mentioned. See also Sanders, "Cave 11 Surprises and the Question of Canon," *New Directions in Biblical Archaeology,* eds. D. N. Freedman and J. C. Greenfield (Garden City, N.Y., 1971) pp. 113–30.

SELECT BIBLIOGRAPHY

The important publications are too numerous to list; in addition to the works cited herein see the bibliographical data reported in the following:

Charlesworth, *PMR*, pp. 202–9.
Denis, *Introduction*, pp. 66f.

Magne, J. "Recherches sur les Psaumes 151, 154 et 155," *RQ* 8 (1975) 503–7.
Sanders, J. A. "The Qumran Psalms Scroll [11QPsᵃ] Reviewed," *On Language, Culture, and Religion: In Honor of Eugene A. Nida*, ed. M. Black and W. A. Smalley (The Hague, 1974) pp. 79–99.

PSALM 151

The original language of this psalm is Hebrew. The Syriac of Psalm 151 derives from the Greek (LXX); but in Psalms 152–55 it comes directly from the Hebrew.[1] A mere cursory comparison of the Syriac and Hebrew of Psalms 151–55 reveals that the Syriac of 151A and 151B, in contrast to Psalms 154 and 155, is dissimilar to the Hebrew. The Syriac of Psalm 151 is similar to and dependent upon the Greek (LXX). Originally Psalm 151 was two separate psalms, 151A and 151B; unfortunately the latter is lost because this section of 11QPs^a is mutilated. The Greek (LXX) and Syriac have truncated both psalms.

Psalm 151 must predate the second century B.C.; it is in the Greek (LXX), which antedates that period. F. M. Cross has argued recently that in "no case can it be later than the 3rd century B.C."[2] This early date certainly dismisses the possibility that Psalm 151 was composed by the members of the Qumran community, which did not originate until the middle of the second century B.C.[3]

Before verse two there is a line that is a later interpolation; the line is as follows: "And I discovered a lion and a wolf and I killed and rent them." The idea is intrusive to the thought of the psalm; it also is not preserved in 11QPs^a, is only in the margin of MS A (the most reliable Syr. tradition), and is missing in JRL Syr 7. The line has been interpolated from Psalms 152 and 153.

---

[1] See Strugnell, "Notes on the Text and Transmission of the Apocryphal Psalms 151, 154 (= Syr. II) and 155 (= Syr. III)," *HTR* 59 (1966) 278. Magne ("Les Textes grec et syriaque du Psaume 151," *RQ* 8 [1975] 548–64) attempts to refute Strugnell's arguments and concludes that the Syr. and Gk. of 151 are "two independent versions" of the Heb.

[2] F. M. Cross, "David, Orpheus, and Psalm 151:3–4," *BASOR* 231 (1978) 69–71; the quotation is from p. 70.

[3] Charlesworth, "The Origin and Subsequent History of the Authors of the Dead Sea Scrolls: Four Transitional Phases among the Qumran Essenes," *RQ* 38 (1980) 213–33.

151A and B (11QPs^a 151)

Hebrew
A Hallelujah of David the Son of Jesse

151A

1 I was the smallest among my brothers,
and the youngest among the sons of my father;
and he made me shepherd of his flocks,
and the ruler over his kids.^a

LAB 59
1Sam 16:11,17:14

2 My hands made a flute,
and my fingers a lyre;
and I shall render glory to the Lord,
I thought within myself.^b

---

a. It is amazing that the portions of the leather upon which this psalm is written are preserved without a lacuna. The script is easy to read; cf. the facsimiles in Sanders, *The Psalms Scroll of Qumran Cave 11*, and in G. Jeremias, H.-W. Kuhn, and H. Stegemann, eds., *Tradition und Glaube: Das frühe Christentum in seiner Umwelt. Festgabe für Karl Georg Kuhn zum 65. Geburtstag* (Göttingen, 1971) plates 2, 3, 4, 5, 6, 7. Compare the Hymn of the Pearl (vs. 1): "When I was a little lad / And dwelling in my kingdom, the house of my father, . . ." (trans. Charlesworth).

b. P. W. Skehan begins vs. 3 here: "I had said to myself, / the mountains cannot witness to Him, . . ." Skehan, "The Apocryphal Psalm 151," *CBQ* 25 (1963) 407–9.

3   The mountains cannot witness to him,
        nor the hills proclaim (him);
        the trees have elevated my words,
        and the flocks my deeds.[c]

4   For who can proclaim and who can announce,   *Sir 16:20,22*
        and who can recount the deeds of the Lord?   *OdesSol 26:8–11*
        Everything God has seen,
        everything he has heard and he has listened.

5   He sent his prophet to anoint me,   *1Sam 16:1–11*
        Samuel to make me great;
        my brothers went out to meet him,
        handsome of figure[d] and handsome of appearance.

6   (Although) their stature was tall,
        (and) their hair handsome,
        the Lord God   *1Sam 16:10*
        did not choose them.

7   But he sent and took me from behind the flock,   *1Sam 16:12f.; 2Sam*
        and he anointed me with holy oil,   *7:8; Pss 78:70f.; 89:20*
        and he made me leader for his people,
        and ruler over the sons of his covenant.

---

c. Or "(Nor) the trees elevate my words, and the flocks my deeds." The translation of this vs. is problematic. The waws and yodhs are very similar in 11QPs[a], the poetic structure open to more than one possibility. Numerous translations have been defended; see Sanders (*The Dead Sea Psalms Scroll*, pp. 100–3). Strugnell (*HTR* 59 [1966] 280) renders this verse as follows: "The mountains cannot witness to Him / nor the hills proclaim about Him / (Nor) the trees (proclaim) His words / nor the flocks His deeds." For a thoroughly different translation see J. Magne, "Orphisme, pythagorisme, essénisme dans le texte hébreu du Psaume 151?" *RQ* 8 (1975) 508–47, see especially p. 532 (or 544). Some scholars argue that vs. 3a should be read so that the Heb. is *ly* and not *lw*: "The mountains cannot witness *to me* [italics mine]"; cf. e.g. J. Carmignac, "Nouvelles précisions sur le Psaume 151," *RQ* 8 (1975) 593–97.

Vss. 2b and 3 are not preserved in Syr., as can be seen by comparing the two translations above; they are also missing in the Gk. and Lat. In contrast to Isa 55:12, vs. 3 claims that mountains and hills cannot witness to the Lord. If the vs. implies that the trees and flocks do receive and enjoy David's words and deeds, then Sanders is certainly right in suggesting that these vss. might "exhibit overtones" from traditions relating to Orpheus, who is the mythical Greek shepherd musician. Sanders wisely cautions that this possibility is rather tenuous; but if it is correct, 11QPs[a] 151 preserves the only literary evidence of an Orphic David, who is well known in mosaics and paintings (see the photograph opposite p. 98 in Sanders, *The Dead Sea Psalms Scroll*). Also see the Orphic fragments in the Supplement to the present work. Yet it should be pointed out that the old Lat. and some copies of the LXX understood vs. 4b to say that God hears everything, reflecting 1Sam 16:7; see Sanders, *Dead Sea Psalms Scroll*, p. 97, n. 10. A. Dupont-Sommer (*David et Orphée* [*Séance pub-*

lique annuelle des cinq Académies] Paris, 1964) accepts Sanders' suggestion of Orphic overtones in 151 and sees in it an allusion to the Pythagorean concept of the harmony of the world and music of the spheres. Other scholars (e.g. W. H. Brownlee, J. Carmignac, F. M. Cross, I. Rabinowitz, P. W. Skehan) have been critical of Sanders' suggestion, but it has been defended rigorously by J. Magne in *RQ* 8 (1975) 508–47 and in " 'Seigneur de l'Univers' ou David-Orphée?" *RQ* 9 (1977) 189–96. The omission of 2b and 3 in Syr. and Gk. should be explained; perhaps the Gk. scribe (the Syr. is dependent upon the LXX), like the Arab of the "Pseudo-David" Psalter (cf. Strugnell's text and translation in *HTR* 59 [1966] 280) corrected David's unorthodox thoughts. Cross denies possible Orphic influence; he renders vss. 3f. as follows:

  O that the mountains would bear Him witness,
  O that the hills would tell of Him,
  The trees (recount) His deeds,
  And the flock, His works!
  Would that someone tell and speak,
  And would that someone recite His works!

  The Lord of all saw;
  The God of all heard,
  And He gave heed.

See Cross, *BASOR* 231 (1978) 69. Magne ("Le Psaume 154 et le Psaume 155," *RQ* 9 [1977] 95–111) argues that 154 is the product of two authors, one who composed a wisdom psalm and a later author (redactor) who added verses that called his sectarian brothers to participate in a cult in which glorification of God replaced sacrifices in the Temple.

d. A vaguely possible meaning, in light of a possible chiastic construction with vs. 6, "their hair handsome," is to derive the meaning from *twr*, to obtain "handsome with plaited (hair)." More probably, derive *htwr* from a defectively written *tō'ar*, masculine "form, outline."

151A and B (5ApocSyrPs 1a)

Syriac
By David, When He Alone Fought Against Goliath[a]

151A

1 I was the smallest[b] of[c] my brothers,
   and a child[d] of[e] my father's house.

   I was tending my father's flocks;
   [and I discovered a lion and a wolf
     and I killed and rent them.][f]

2 My hands made instruments,[g]
   and my fingers fashioned[h] lyres.

3 And who will declare[i] my Lord;[j]
   that is the Lord; that is my God?[k]

4 He sent[l] his angel;
   and removed[m] me from the sheep[n] of my father;
   and anointed me with the ointment of his[o] anointing.[p]

5 My brothers were handsome and majestic;[q]
   but the Lord did not choose them.[r]

LAB 59
1Sam 16:11

1Sam 17:36–38

1Sam 16:10

---

a. The title is from MS A. JRL Syr 7: "Another Psalm of David, Supernumerary"; LXX: "This Psalm, Though Supernumerary, Is David's Own Composition, When He Single-handedly Fought Goliath."

b. Or "youngest"; cf. vs. 5. JRL Syr 7: "small."

c. Beth; lit. "among"; but the parallel lines indicate the beth in this line and the one in next should be translated similarly.

d. JRL Syr 7: "youth."

e. See n. c; lit. "in"; "child": the Syr. noun denotes one between the ages of seven and twelve years.

f. Lit. "And I killed them and I rent them." This line is placed in the margin of MS A; it is missing in JRL Syr 7.

g. Gk. loanword in Syr., *organon*.

h. Lit. "fitted"; (cf. R. Payne Smith, *Thesaurus Syriacus*, vol. 2, col. 1928).

i. The participle can denote the future. The modal coloring of the participle can also be employed; lit.: "And who is he who may declare [or "make manifest"] my Lord?"

j. Note the mixed traditions: JRL Syr 7: "He is the Lord God who hears me" (ignoring the punctuation, the preceding line is corrupt). LXX: "The Lord himself, he hears everything."

k. MS B: "He is the Lord; he is my God." Cf. Jn 20:28.

l. JRL Syr 7: *šdr*.

m. Or "raised, exalted."

n. JRL Syr 7: *ʿnʾ* (cf. vs. 1, with LXX).

o. JRL Syr 7 omits.

p. This poetic alliteration is not found in 11QPs[a] and only partly in LXX.

q. Or "old"; *rwrbʾ* with *zʿwrʾ* (vs. 1, "small, young") frequently means "old."

r. Or "was not pleased with them."

151B (11QPs^a 151)

Hebrew
At the Beginning of [Dav]id's Po[w]er
After the Prophet of God Anointed Him^a

1   Then I s[a]w a Philistine   1Sam 17:8-25
        who was uttering taunts from the ra[nks of the enemy . . .]

2   . . . I . . . the . . .

a. 11QPs^a 151 preserves two psalms, 151A and 151B, which were truncated in the Gk. (LXX) and Syr. Strugnell warns that it is "uncertain whether this secondary text [151B] ever existed in Hebrew . . ." (*HTR* 59 [1966] 259). Plate 17 (in Sanders, *The Psalms Scroll*) shows, however, that a portion of it is preserved in 11QPs^a; the MS is severely damaged at this place, yet ll. 13 and 14 are clearly extant.

151B (5ApocSyrPs 1b)

Syriac
(Text is continuous with 151A:1–5 in Syr.)

1   I went out to attack^a the Philistine,
        and he cursed me by his idols.

2   But after I unsheathed his sword,^b I cut off his head;   1Sam 17:51
        and I removed the shame from the sons of Israel.^c

a. The root of the verb (*npq*) is used to denote a military attack. JRL Syr 7: "I invaded (or attacked) the land of the Philistine."

b. JRL Syr 7 adds "and with it"; LXX, "from him."

c. JRL Syr 7: "from the house of Israel."

PSALM 152

The original language of this psalm, which is extant only in Syriac, may be Hebrew (see nn. b and f).[1] In verse 1 the noun for God is *'il*, which is parallel to the Hebrew word for God, *'ēl*, not the Syriac name for God, *'allāhâ* (151:3); likewise in verse 6 *'dwnywhy* looks like a (probably confused) transliteration of the Hebrew word for "Lord," *'dwny*, whereas the Syriac name for "Lord" is *māryâ* (vs. 4). Comparisons with Psalms 151, 154, and 155, which are extant in Hebrew and were composed in Hebrew, demonstrate the poor poetic character of this psalm. It seems derivative, uninspired, and a mimic of biblical poetry.

It is impossible to date this psalm. The general tone, Jewish but non-rabbinic character, and association with Psalms 151, 154, and 155 indicate that it was probably composed by a Palestinian Jew during the hellenistic period.

[1] Strugnell (*HTR* 59 [1966] 259) thinks that Psalms 152–55 "certainly derive from a Hebrew text." This conclusion is open to debate; there is no evidence that they were in the Qumran library (see Sanders, *The Dead Sea Psalms Scroll*, p. 141). While 151, 154, and 155 in Syr. show clear evidence of a Heb. base, 152 and 153 (especially) are notably different (see nn. to the translation).

152 (5ApocSyrPs 4)

Spoken by David After Fighting Against the Lion and the Wolf Which Took Sheep from His Flocks.[a]

1   O God,[b] O God, come to my help;
    assist me and save me;
    and deliver me[c] from the killers.

2   Shall I descend to Sheol by the mouth of the lion?   1Sam 17:34–36
    Or shall the lion[d] maim[e] me?[f]

3   Is it not sufficient for them to ambush my father's flocks;[g]
    and to tear a sheep from his sheepfold?
    They are even wishing to slay me.[h]

4   Spare, O Lord, your elect one;[i]
    and deliver your holy one from destruction;
    so that he may continue praising you[j] in all his times,
        and may praise your magnificent name.

5   When you have saved him from the hands of destroying[k] death,[l]
    and when you have rescued my captivity[m] from the mouths of[n] beasts.

6   Quickly, O Adonai,[o] send from your presence a redeemer;[p]
    and lift me up from the gaping abyss which is seeking
        to enclose me in its depths.

a. The title is from MS A. The above translation differs from Sanders' idiomatic rendering (*The Dead Sea Psalms Scroll*, p. 142), because I have attempted to be literal, have occasionally used different MSS, and have translated cognate words in these Heb. and Syr. texts consistently (often missing a beautiful phrase in English).

b. The line is beautiful in Syr.: *'îl 'îl thâ l°iyâli*. The choice of the Heb. *'îl* (God) seems deliberate to bring out the assonance with *l°iyâli* (to my help).

c. Or "my soul."

d. All other Syr. MSS: "the wolf." MS A seems in error.

e. The usual meanings of this verb (*bl*) in the Palpel are "to confound, confuse, mar, spoil." Jastrow (Dictionary, ad loc.) cites an example in which the verb denotes an action that accelerates death. This meaning is apposite here because of the previous vs., the synonymous parallel, and vs. 3c.

f. "Me" is written *l°yâthi*, which is a Hebraism and denotes the *nota accusativi*, with a prefixed redundant *l°*, the Syr. note of the accusative. This observation plus *'îl* for "God" (see n. b) may indicate that this psalm was translated from Heb.

g. Lit. "to them that they lay in ambush for the flocks of my father."

h. Or "my soul."

i. All other Syr. MSS omit "your elect one."

j. Lit. "continue in your praises."

k. For "destroying," all other Syr. MSS have "and of the vicious wolf."

l. The redundancy is unattractive; all other Syr. MSS replace "death" with "lion."

m. Or "prey"; the noun seems ill-chosen.

n. All other Syr. MSS: "hands of."

o. The Heb. *Adonai* is employed; by error MS A reads "his Lord."

p. Or "the Redeemer."

PSALM 153

This psalm is extant only in Syriac. The original language may be Hebrew, but there is even less evidence of that hypothesis for this psalm than there is for Psalm 152.[1] The above statement regarding date and provenance of Psalm 152 applies to Psalm 153 as well.

[1] See the introduction to Psalm 152.

153 (5ApocSyrPs 5)

*Spoken by David After[a] Receiving God's Grace When He Delivered Him from
the Lion and Wolf and Those Two[b] He Killed by His Hands*

1 Praise the Lord, all you nations;
   glorify him and bless his name;

2 For he delivered the physical life[c] of his elect one from the hands of death;
   and he redeemed his holy one from destruction.   1Sam 17:34–36

3 And he saved me from the snares of Sheol;
   and brought me[d] forth from the abyss that is inscrutable.

4 Because before my salvation could proceed from before him,
   I almost became two parts by[e] two beasts.

5 However, he sent his angel and closed from me the gaping mouths;
   and redeemed my life from destruction.

6 I myself[f] shall praise him and exalt him because of all his graces,
   which he has provided and is[g] providing for me.

a. Or "while." The translation differs from Sanders' rendering for the same reasons given in n. a to 152.
b. Lit. "the two of them."
c. Or "soul." In vs. 5 "my life" is *ḥaiyai*.
d. Or "my soul."

e. The lamadh denotes the cause. The Syr. is inelegant. The adverb "almost" is in the wrong place.
f. Lit. "my soul."
g. Or "will provide"; the verb is an active participle.

PSALM 154

The original language of this psalm is Hebrew. The Syriac derives directly from the Hebrew[1] but not necessarily from the Hebrew as preserved in 11QPs[a]. Because the psalm is preserved in this first-century manuscript, it must date from the first, or better the second, century B.C.[2] There is no reason to doubt that it was composed somewhere in Palestine.

Of Psalms 151–55 this one is most closely aligned with the thoughts in the Dead Sea Scrolls.[3] The "many ones" (or many) of 154:1 (only Syr.; Heb. lost) may be parallel to "the many," a technical term (*Rabbîm*) that defines the fully initiated members of the Qumran community (cf. 1QS 6.8–7.25). The "many," however, may be only a generic reference, as it is in 155:10 and Isaiah 53:11. The Hebrew of 154:4, which has been translated "Join an assembly," could be rendered "join a *yaḥad*"; the latter is a technical term at Qumran for the community of oneness in covenant with God (cf. 1QH 11.10–14;

[1] For further discussion, see Strugnell, *HTR* 59 (1966) 272–75.
[2] Most of the "apocryphal" psalms in 11QPs[a] are from the 2nd cent. B.C. See Cross in *Qumran and the History of the Biblical Text*, eds. Cross and S. Talmon (Cambridge, Mass., 1975) pp. 177–95, especially p. 182; A. Hurvitz, "Observations on the Language of the Third Apocryphal Psalm from Qumran," *RQ* 5 (1965) 225–32; R. Polzin, "Notes on the Dating of the Non-Massoretic Psalms of 11QPs[a]," *HTR* 60 (1967) 468–76; and Skehan in *Qumrân: Sa piété, sa théologie, et son milieu*, p. 168.
[3] See n. 7 to the introduction of this contribution.

3.19–23).[4] The phrase "join (or form) a *yaḥad*," however, is not found elsewhere in the Dead Sea Scrolls. Other nouns that are technical terms at Qumran, but not necessarily ideas peculiar to the Dead Sea Scrolls, are "the innocent ones" in 154:3, 18 (cf. 1QS 4.22) and "the poor ones" in 154:18 (cf. 1QH 2.34, 5.13f.). Concepts cherished at Qumran are the ideas expressed in 154:10f. that the Most High accepts praise as equal to sacrifices and in 154:13f. that the righteous share in common meals and constantly study the Law;[5] but these emphases are also characteristic of the prophets and the practices of other Jews, especially the Pharisees. It seems, therefore, that while there is nothing peculiarly Qumranian about Psalm 154, it may be proto-Essenian and predate the exodus of the Essenes to Qumran.[6]

[4] See especially P. Wernberg-Møller, "The Nature of the YAHAD According to the Manual of Discipline and Related Documents," *ALUOS* 6 (1966–68) 56–81; and J. Pouilly, "Le YAHAD, 'Communauté de Dieu,' " in *La Règle de la Communauté de Qumrân: Son évolution littéraire* (Cahiers de la Revue Biblique 17; Paris, 1976) pp. 102–7.

[5] Skehan states that "it is interesting that this, Ps 154, is a reflex of the Essene religious assemblies and communal meals." See Skehan in *Qumrân: Sa piété, sa théologie et son milieu*, p. 169.

[6] Sanders shows that the psalm portrays "three distinct groups": the righteous, those addressed by them, and the wicked. He has also raised the possibility that the psalm is "proto-Essenian, or Hasidic." See Sanders, *The Psalms Scroll of Qumrân Cave 11*, pp. 69f.

154 (11QPs[a] 154)

Hebrew

1   (lost)

2   (lost)

3   [Associate][a] yourselves[b] with the good ones;
    and with the pure ones[c] to glorify[d] the Most High.

4   Join an assembly[e] to announce his salvation;
    and do not be lax to announce his power
        and his gloriousness[f] to all simple ones.

5   For to announce the glory (or honor) of the Lord,
    wisdom has been given.

6   And to recount his many deeds,
    she was made known[g] to humanity:

7   To announce to simple ones his power,
    to explain to those lacking understanding his greatness.[h]

a. The Heb. of 154:1–2a is lost; the verb "associate" is restored from the Syr. The above translation is different from those now available because I have attempted to translate the Syr. and Heb. versions so that cognate (and corresponding) words within each are easily recognized. Hence, Syr. *mᶜlnᵓ* and Heb. *mbwᵓ* in 154:8 are both rendered by "entrance."

b. Or "your souls."

c. Or "innocent ones." The Heb. and Syr. have the same word, but the meanings are slightly different.

d. Heb. *pᵓr* (beautify, glorify); Syr. *šbḥ* (glorify, praise), which corresponds to Heb. *šbḥ* (praise).

e. Or "Form an assembly (or *yaḥad*)"; Heb. *yḥd*, which is a technical term at Qumran; it meant

the community of oneness in covenant with God (cf. 1QH 11.10–14; 3.19–23). See n. 1.

f. The Heb. noun for "gloriousness" (154:4, 9) is cognate with "to glorify" in 154:3b, 10a, 17a, and with "glory" in 154:5a. The theme of the psalm is clearly to glorify God's glory, as is demonstrated by the first two vss., preserved only in Syr.: "glorify God . . . proclaim his glory . . . glorify his excellence . . . narrate his gloriousness." Wisdom (vs. 5) was given to accomplish this task.

g. Heb. *nwdᶜh*, "made known," is cognate with "to announce," in 154:4 (bis), 5, 7, and 14.

h. Sanders (*The Dead Sea Psalms Scroll*, p. 105): "and to explain to senseless folk his greatness . . ."

8   Those far from her openings,[i]
        those banished from her entrances.

9   Because the Most High is the Lord of Jacob,
        and his gloriousness (is) over all his deeds.

10   And a person who glorifies the Most High,
        he accepts as one who brings a meal offering,

11   As one who offers he-goats and baby bulls;
        as one who anoints the altar with many burnt offerings;
        as sweet-smelling fragrance from the hand of the righteous ones.

12   From the openings[j] of the righteous ones is heard her voice;
        and from the congregation of the pious ones her song.

13   When they eat with satiety she is cited;
        and when they drink in association[k] together.[l]

14   Their meditation is on the Law of the Most High;
        their words[m] to announce his power.

15   How far from the wicked ones (is) her word;[n]
        from all haughty ones to know her.

16   Behold the eyes of the Lord
                will have compassion upon the good ones;

17   And upon those who glorify him will he increase his mercy;
        from an evil time will he deliver them.[o]

18   [Bless] the Lord, who redeems the poor ones from the hand of st[rangers]
        [and deliver]s [. . . ,]

19   [. . . Ja]cob
        and a judge of [. . . ;]

20   (lost)

i. Or "doorways" (Heb. *pth*) or "utterances" (Heb. *mpth*). The play on words is found in Heb., not in Syr. Wisdom's "openings" are associated with her "utterances."

j. Or "utterances." The play on words is possible in Heb. but not in Syr. See n. i.

k. Heb. *bhbr*, "in association, in fellowship," is cognate with *hhbyru*, "join," in 154:4.

l. Heb. *yhdyw;* see n. e.

m. Or "citings"; see 154:13a.

n. Or "citing"; see preceding n.

o. Or "their soul."

154 (5ApocSyrPs 2)

Syriac

*The Prayer of Hezekiah When the Assyrians Were Surrounding Him
and He Was Asking God Deliverance from Them So That the People
Might Receive Permission from Cyrus to Return to Their Land. And
They Asked God to Fulfill Their Expectation.*[a]

1   In a great voice glorify[b] God;
    in the congregation of the many ones[c] proclaim his glory.

2   And in the multitude of the upright ones glorify his excellence;
    and with the faithful ones narrate his gloriousness.

3   Associate yourselves[d] with the good ones;
    and with the innocent ones to glorify the Most High.

4   Gather[e] together to announce his power;
    and do not neglect to declare his[f] salvation,
        and his glory to all children.[g]

5   So that the honor[h] of the Lord shall be made known,[i]
    wisdom has been given.[j]

6   And to narrate his works,
    she has made known[k] to humanity:

7   To announce to children his power,
    and to explain to those lacking understanding[l] his gloriousness,

8   Those who are far[m] from her entrances,
    and are dispersed from her gate.

9   Because the Most High is the Lord of Jacob,
    and his pride is over all his works.[n]

10   And a person[o] who glorifies the Most High,
    he accepts[p] as one who offers a meal offering.[q]

---

a. The title is from MS A, but it is very late and has little relation to the content of the psalm.

b. In Pss 151–53 *šbḥ* is translated as "praise"; here it denotes "glory." Uppermost in the poet's mind is the concept of glorifying (or praising) God's glory. The root *šbḥ* or its cognates appear in vss. 1 (bis), 2 (bis), 3, 4, 7, 10, and 17. The masculine noun for "praise, honor, glory," *šwbḥ*, is translated "glory"; the feminine noun with the same meaning, *tšbwḥt*' is distinguished as "gloriousness."

c. "The congregation of the many" is a technical term in the Dead Sea Scrolls, but it probably no longer retained this meaning in the latter Syriac-speaking churches.

d. Or "your (plural) soul"; proposed *npštkwn* (your souls); the emendation is not demanded, since *npškwn* can mean "your souls."

e. Or "be gathered."

f. Ignore the supralinear dot that indicates the feminine pronoun; such dots are later than the date of composition of this psalm.

g. Or "infants"; the noun is plural and frequently denotes boys and girls under five years old.

h. Or "glory" (another word than employed herein), "magnificence."

i. Or "understood, ascertained."

j. MS A incorrectly has added the Nestorian vocalization for the first-person-singular pronoun.

k. Again, see n. j; the Nestorian vocalization is incorrectly first common singular.

l. Lit. "those in want of a heart (or mind)"; but both the Syr. and Heb. phrases really mean "those who are senseless (or stupid)." The Semite thought of his chest or breast as the place of intelligence and feeling.

m. Both verbs in this vs. appear to be passive participles.

n. Or "his servants"; but see vs. 6.

o. Or "man," "mortal."

p. In Psalm 151:5 *ṣb*' with *b*' means "choose."

q. Good English demands this translation; but "offers" and "offering" are not cognate in Syr.

11   And as one who offers he-goats and baby bulls;[r]
        and as he who anoints the altar with many burnt offerings;
        and as sweet-smelling fragrance from the hand of the righteous ones.

12   From the gates of the just ones is heard her[s] voice;
        and from the voice of the just ones her[t] admonition.

13   And concerning their food fullness (is) in truth;
        and concerning their feast their portions[u] (are) together.

14   Their discussions (are) on the Law of the Most High;
        and their word is to announce his power.

15   How far from the wicked ones (is) her[v] word;
        and from all evil ones her[w] understanding.

16   Behold the eye of the Lord
            will have pity upon the good ones;

17   And upon those who glorify him will he increase mercies;
        and from an evil time will he redeem them.[x]

18   Blessed be the Lord who saves the poor ones from the hand of strangers;
        and redeems the innocent ones from the hand of the evil ones;

19   Who raises[y] the horn from Jacob,
        and the judge of the nations[z] from Israel;

20   So[a2] that he may prolong[b2] his sojourn in Zion;
        and may cause adornment[c2] forever in Jerusalem.

r. Lit. "sons of bulls."
s. Or "his." There is no dot over the *Hē*.
t. Or "his." There is no dot over the *Hē*.
u. All other MSS: "in fellowship"; "And concerning their feast in fellowship (are they) together." This vs. is difficult to understand; Strugnell (*HTR* 59 [1966] 273) judges it to be "clearly unsatisfactory" in both Heb. and Syr.
v. Or "his."
w. Or "his."

x. Or "their souls."
y. Or "rouses up, appoints, promises."
z. Or "the peoples."
a2. The exhortation is to bless the Lord so he will prolong his habitation in Jerusalem.
b2. Or "he may continue."
c2. According to extant lexicons *ṣbt* is not used in the Aphel; but the meaning, form, and Nestorian vocalization indicate that here it is an Aphel.

PSALM 155

Hebrew is the original language of the psalm. As with Psalm 154, the Syriac appears to derive directly from the Hebrew.[1] This psalm is not Qumranian but biblical; it is similar in style to Psalm 22. Since it is extant in 11QPs[a] it must date at least from the first century B.C. and is probably much earlier. The Syriac translator is gifted;[2] he cannot be identified with the author of Psalms 152 and 153 (if one were to assume a Syr. original for them). Like most of the canonical (or Masoretic) psalms,[3] this psalm is generic in thought and tone; hence it is impossible to discern its author, date, or provenance.

[1] See Strugnell (*HTR* 59 [1966] 275f.) and the nn. to the translation below.
[2] See the nn. to both translations.
[3] In Heb. it is even constructed in acrostics; see Skehan, "A Broken Acrostic and Psalm 9," *CBQ* 27 (1965) 1–5; P. Auffret, "Structure littéraire et interprétation du Psaume 155 de la grotte XI de Qumrân," *RQ* 9 (1978) 323–56; and Magne, "Le Psaume 154 et le Psaume 155," *RQ* 9 (1977) 95–111.

155 (11QPs^a 155)

Hebrew^a

1   O Lord, I called unto you,
     be attentive to me.

2   I spread forth my palms,
          toward your holy dwelling;

3   Incline your ear;
     and give me my request.

4   And my petition
          do not hold back from me.

5   Build me^b up;
     and do not cast me^c down.

6   And do not abandon (me)
          before the wicked ones.

7   The rewards of evil,
     may the Judge of Truth remove^d from me.

8   O Lord, do not condemn me according to my sins;
     for no one living is righteous before you.

9   O Lord, instruct me in your Law;
     and teach me your statutes;^e

10   So^f many may hear of your deeds,
     and nations may honor your magnificence.^g

11   Remember me and do not forget me;
     and do not let me enter that which is too difficult for me.^h

12   The sins of my youth cast far from me;
     and my transgressions do not remember against me.

13   O Lord, purify me from the evil plague;
     and do not let it again turn back^i to me.

14   Dry up its roots from me;
     and do not let its le[av]es bloom in me.

15   Magnificent^j are you, O Lord;
     hence complete^k my request from before you.

---

a. There is no title in the Heb. For the means of translating, see n. a to 154.

b. Or "my soul."

c. Lit. "do not cast it down."

d. Or "cause to turn back."

e. Heb. *mšpṭykh* (statutes) which is cognate with *tšpṭny* (do not condemn me) in 155:8.

f. Lit. "and."

g. Or "glory, honor."

h. Or, with Sanders (*The Dead Sea Psalms Scroll*, p. 111): "and lead me not into situations too hard for me."

i. See n. d.

j. See n. g.

k. Heb. *šlm* in the Piel, imperative with *Hē.*

16   To whom may I cry and he would give to me?
       And human beings, what can [their] pow[er] add?

17   From befo[r]e you, O Lord, is my trust.
       I called, "O Lord," and he answered me;
       [and he healed] my broken heart.

18   I slumbered [and I s]lept;
       I dreamed, nevertheless . . .

19   (lost)

20   (lost)

21   (lost)

155 (5ApocSyrPs 3)

Syriac

*The Prayer of Hezekiah When the Assyrians Surrounded Him and He Asked
God Deliverance[a] from Them[b]*

1   O Lord, I called to you,
       hearken to me.

2   I stretched out my hands
           to the dwellings of your holiness;

3   Incline your ear;
       and grant me my request.

4   My prayer
           do not withhold from me.

5   Build me[c] up;[d]
       and do not destroy me.[e]

6   And do not uncover me[f]
           before the wicked ones.

7   The rewards of evil turn from me,
       O Judge of Truth.

8   O Lord, do not judge me according to my sins;
       because guilty[g] before you is every life.[h]

9   O Lord, explain to me your Law;
       and teach[i] me your judgments;

a. The Syr. is *ghyt³*; elsewhere *pṣ³* is represented
by the English verb and cognates "to deliver."

b. The title is from MS A, but it is late and has
no basis in the psalm itself.

c. Or "my soul."

d. MS A (seek it) is corrupt; read with other
Syr. MSS and the Heb., which has *bnh*, "build."

e. Lit. "do not destroy it."

f. Lit. "do not uncover it."

g. Lit. "not innocent" or "not free from guilt."

h. The close order of words between the Syr.
and Heb. indicates that the former derives directly
from the latter, and not through a Gk. intermediary.

i. Syr. *³lpyny;* *lmd* in Syr. obtained a meaning
different from *lmd* in Heb. (cf. the Heb.).

10   So that many[j] may hear of your works,
        and the nations[k] may give thanks for your honor.[l]

11   Remember me and do not forget me;
        and do not let me enter[m] that which is too difficult for me.

12   The sins of my childhood remove[n] from me;
        and my insolence[o] do not remember against me.

13   O Lord, cleanse me from the evil leprosy;[p]
        and do not let it again return[q] to me.

14   Dry up its roots from me;
        and do not let its leaves bud in me.

15   Powerful and great are you, O Lord;
        hence,[r] my request will be fulfilled[s] from before you.

16   To whom may I complain and he would give to me?
        And human beings, what can their strength add (for me)?

17   From before you, O Lord, (is) my confidence.
        I called to the Lord, and he answered me;
        and he healed my broken heart.

18   I slumbered and slept;
        I dreamed, nevertheless I was aroused.[t]

19   And you supported me, O Lord.
        And I shall render (thanks)[u] because the Lord has delivered me.

20   Now I shall behold their shame;
        I trusted in you and shall not be ashamed.
        Give honor (to the Lord) for ever and ever.

21   Save Israel, your elect one;
        and those of the house of Jacob, your chosen[v] one.

j. Or "the many"; see n. c to 154 (5ApocSyrPs 2).

k. Or "peoples."

l. Or "your glory, magnificence."

m. The same verb in the same verbal stem is used in Mt 6:13 in the Peshiṭta: "and do not let us enter into temptation."

n. Or "transfer, cause to pass."

o. Or "disobedience, rebellion."

p. A scribe wrote grb' in the margin of MS A; Baars (The Old Testament in Syriac, p. iv) takes this note as a correction to what is in the text of MS A: grb', "the man."

q. The Nestorian vowels in MS A denote the Aphel infinitive; the Pe'al infinitive is also possible (cf. Nöldeke, Compendious Syriac Grammar, p. 108).

r. Or "on this account."

s. All other Syr. MSS: "will be full (or complete)."

t. This passive voice reflects the divine passive and means "the Lord aroused me" (cf. next vs.). All other Syr. MSS: "I was helped."

u. The vs. is difficult to translate; the verb qbl means thanks render with tybwt', which may have been lost through copying. In the margin of MS A (and in 18El) sgp lby, "he injured my heart." The Heb. is lost because of the scroll's condition.

v. Or "tried (or approved) one." At the end of the collection of psalms a scribe adds in MS A: "So ends, by the assistance of our Lord, the writing of the Psalms of the blessed David, the prophet and king, with the five psalms which are not among the Greek or Hebrew numbering. However, as they are said (and) preserved in Syriac so we have copied them for him who desires (a copy)."

PRAYER OF MANASSEH

(Second Century B.C.–First Century A.D.)

A NEW TRANSLATION AND INTRODUCTION

BY J. H. CHARLESWORTH

Eventually, and perhaps originally, attributed to Manasseh (687–642 B.C.), the son of the righteous king Hezekiah, but the wickedest king of Judah (2Kgs 21:1–8, 2Chr 33:1–20; cf. 2Bar 64:8), this short prayer is a penitential psalm, or individual lament of personal sin ("*ein individuelles Klagelied*"). Twice the author confesses his sin and twice he pleads for absolution from sin; constantly he appeals to the Lord's graciousness. The poetic thought is beautiful and penetrating; the high point is the perception of inward contrition: "And now behold I am bending the knees of my heart before you."

The prayer contains three main sections: an *invocation*: praise to the Lord for his works of creation (vss. 1–4) and acknowledgment of the Lord's fury against sinners and of his multitudinous mercies (vss. 5–7); a *confession*: a personal lament and confession (vss. 8–10); and an *entreaty*: a supplication for pardon (vss. 11–13) and an expression of trust in God's grace and a concluding doxology (vss. 14f.).

Texts

The following translation is based upon the Syriac text (usually right col.) as edited by W. Baars and H. Schneider ("Prayer of Manasseh," *The Old Testament in Syriac According to the Peshiṭta Version* [Leiden, 1972] part 4, fasc. 6, pp. i–vii, 1–9). Significant variants in the Greek are noted, following the edition by A. Rahlfs (*Psalmi cum Odis: Septuaginta: Societatis Scientiarum Gottingensis* [Göttingen, 1931] vol. 10, pp. 361–63).[1] Baars and Schneider have based their right column upon the version preserved in the ninth-century Syriac manuscript in the Mediceo-Laurenziana Library in Florence, Italy (9aI) and in the Syriac manuscripts of the *Didascalia Apostolorum* (especially 10DI and 13DI). Their left column, used infrequently below (see nn.), is according to the tenth-century Syriac manuscript in the Saltykov-Shchedrin State Public Library in Leningrad, U.S.S.R.; it is Syr. MS, New Series 19, and is abbreviated 10tI. Rahlfs's Greek text is based upon the fifth-century Codex Alexandrinus—the earliest Greek text—which is in the British Museum, in London. Variants in other manuscripts and editions are occasionally discussed in the notes to the translation (T is Codex Turicensis, of the seventh century, now in Zurich).

Original language

While hundreds of Hebrew and Aramaic manuscripts have been found in the Near East during the past three decades, it is noteworthy that an Aramaic or Hebrew version of the Prayer of Manasseh has not been recovered. This fact should not be taken as proof for the

---

[1] The Gk. in the Göttingen edition is the same (minus the critical nn.) as in the later, convenient "Handausgabe" by Rahlfs (*Septuaginta*, vol. 2, pp. 180f.). The Lat. version is not used herein; it is late and derivative: Jerome did not translate it and (contrary to some published reports) no Old Lat. version is extant. For the Lat. see the appendix to R. Weber (ed.) *Biblia sacra iuxta vulgatam versionem*, 2 vols. (Stuttgart, 1969) vol. 2, p. 1909. Also see H. Schneider, "Der Vulgata-Text der Oratio Manasse," *BZ* n.F. 4 (1960) 277–82.

position that the prayer was composed in Greek, even though this hypothesis is defended by many scholars, namely (among the earlier scholars) L. E. T. André,[2] J. B. Frey,[3] O. F. Fritzsche,[4] H. E. Ryle,[5] V. Ryssel,[6] E. Schürer,[7] (and among the more recent scholars) W. Baumgartner,[8] L. H. Brockington,[9] A.-M. Denis,[10] O. Eissfeldt,[11] L. Rost,[12] H. H. Rowley,[13] H.-P. Rüger,[14] and M. E. Stone;[15] cf. C. Stuhlmueller.[16] Perhaps with his mind on only the Greek, D. Flusser[17] offers the sane advice that in its "present form the prayer is Greek in origin, but it may have existed in a Hebrew version, of which the Greek is a free adaptation."

Other scholars are convinced that the original language is Semitic; among these, most noteworthy are C. J. Ball,[18] K. Budde,[19] R. H. Charles,[20] L. Couard,[21] W. O. E. Oesterley,[22] R. H. Pfeiffer,[23] and C. C. Torrey;[24] cf. J. C. Dancy.[25] C. Westermann advises, "It is not certain if the original language was Hebrew (or Aramaic) or Greek, but [the Prayer of Manasseh] throughout has a Semitic structure."[26]

The scholarly stature of the specialists who favor a Semitic original, the lack of a detailed examination of the question by proponents of either a Greek or a Semitic original, and the cavalier treatment of the Syriac version(s) by almost all scholars should warn against concluding with some authors[27] that the issue is closed and the original language is Greek. While the notes to the following translation demonstrate that the Syriac version sometimes preserves a more reliable tradition, and while I tend to favor slightly a Semitic original, three factors preclude certainty regarding a resolution of the issue for the present. First, the

---

[2] L. E. T. André, *Les Apocryphes de l'Ancien Testament* (Florence, 1903) p. 241: "The Prayer of Manasseh was composed in Greek. The style, without being classical, is sufficiently fluent; it approximates, nevertheless, that of the LXX version, particularly of the Psalms." It is obvious that André considered only the Gk. version.

[3] J. B. Frey in *DB Sup*, vol. 1, col. 443.

[4] O. F. Fritzsche, *Kurzgefasstes exegetisches Handbuch zu den Apokryphen des Alten Testaments* (Leipzig, 1851) p. 157.

[5] H. E. Ryle, "Prayer of Manasses," in *APOT*, vol. 1, pp. 614f.

[6] V. Ryssel, "Das Gebet Manasse," *APAT*, vol. 1, pp. 165–68.

[7] E. Schürer, *History*, div. 2, vol. 3, p. 188.

[8] W. Baumgartner, "Manasse-Gebet," *RGG*[3], (1960) vol. 4, p. 708.

[9] L. H. Brockington, *A Critical Introduction to the Apocrypha* (London, 1961) p. 101.

[10] A.-M. Denis, *Introduction*, p. 181.

[11] O. Eissfeldt, *The Old Testament: An Introduction*, trans. P. R. Ackroyd (New York, 1965) p. 588.

[12] L. Rost, *Judaism Outside the Hebrew Canon: An Introduction to the Documents*, trans. D. E. Green (Nashville, 1976) p. 95.

[13] H. H. Rowley, *The Origin and Significance of the Apocrypha* (London, 1967) p. 8.

[14] H.-P. Rüger in *Theologische Realenzyklopädie*, vol. 1, p. 304. I am grateful to the editors of this distinguished series for rushing page proofs of this article to me.

[15] M. E. Stone, "Apocryphal Notes and Readings," *Israel Oriental Studies* 1 (1971) 123–31; see p. 128. Stone lists some words in the PrMan that are "rare and completely unknown" in the LXX and opines that this "is persuasive in the direction of the hypothesis of a Greek original." But the PrMan was only added to some MSS of the LXX, and many of the words Stone cites are typical of the NT; moreover, cannot a Gk. translator use sophisticated Gk.?

[16] C. Stuhlmueller in New Catholic Encyclopedia, vol. 2, p. 403.

[17] D. Flusser in The New Encyclopaedia Britannica, Macropaedia, vol. 2, p. 933.

[18] C. J. Ball in *Apocrypha*, ed. H. Wace (London, 1888) vol. 2, pp. 361–71. *N.V.*

[19] K. Budde, "Zum hebräischen Klagelied," *ZAW* 12 (1892) 31–51; especially p. 40: "There are only a few terms which are difficult or impossible to translate back into Hebrew, and these can be due to translation and transmission." (I have translated rather freely.) According to Budde (and others), this opinion was also held by Ewald (but I have not been able to locate a published argument by him).

[20] R. H. Charles appended a significant note to Ryle's discussion of the original language; cf. *APOT*, vol. 1, pp. 614f. Also see Charles's *Religious Development Between the Old and the New Testaments* (London, 1914) p. 215, in which he reported that Ryle "is not definitely opposed to the hypothesis of a Hebrew original. The present writer has sought to show [he does not state where, but it is obviously in *APOT*] that only by retranslation into Hebrew (or Aramaic) can certain corruptions in the text be removed." Unfortunately he does not consult the extant Syr.

[21] L. Couard, *Die religiösen und sittlichen Anschauungen der alttestamentlichen Apokryphen und Pseudepigraphen* (Gütersloh, 1907) p. 5.

[22] W. O. E. Oesterley, *An Introduction to the Books of the Apocrypha* (New York, 1935) p. 298.

[23] R. H. Pfeiffer, *History*, p. 459.

[24] C. C. Torrey, *Apoc. Lit.*, p. 68. "The original language of the prayer was not Greek, but Hebrew."

[25] J. C. Dancy, *The Shorter Books of the Apocrypha* (Cambridge, England, 1972) p. 243. H. H. Howorth thought the PrMan was originally composed in Aram. (p. 95) and reported that Ewald and Furst thought the original language was Semitic. *Proceedings of the Soc. of Bibl. Arch.* 31 (1909) 89–99.

[26] C. Westermann, "Manasse, Gebet des," *BHH*, vol. 2, col. 1137.

[27] Cf. especially Eissfeldt, *Introduction*, p. 558 ("clearly originally composed in Greek"); and Denis, *Introduction*, p. 181 ("La langue originale a sans doute été le grec").

text of the Prayer of Manasseh is too short to provide sufficient data to explore the question. Second, the history of the transmission of the extant Greek and Syriac texts is unclear and confusing. Both Greek versions, the one in the Apostolic Constitutions and the Odae appended to Codex Alexandrinus and Codex Turicensis, may derive from the now lost Greek of the *Didascalia*, and this may have been translated from a Semitic original. Conversely the Syriac versions may derive from the extant Syriac version of the *Didascalia*, which was translated from the Greek *Didascalia*. Other possibilities could obviously be suggested, but the confusing nature of the extant Greek and Syriac versions and the unknown history of transmission for each leave us presently uncertain as to whether the original language of the Prayer of Manasseh is Greek or Semitic (Hebrew or Aramaic). Third, because of a more sensitive awareness of early Jewish culture—especially the influence of Greek upon Semitic languages and, of course, the reverse—and because of the abundant evidence of Greek influence within Palestine, it has become more and more difficult to distinguish between Greek that was translated from a Semitic source and Greek that was composed by a hellenistic Jew who was fluent in numerous languages.

Date

Despite J. A. Fabricius',[28] J.-P. Migne's,[29] and F. Nau's[30] dated conclusion that the Prayer of Manasseh was composed by the author of the Apostolic Constitutions and despite recent comments by Eissfeldt[31] and R. E. Brown,[32] there can be no doubt that the Prayer of Manasseh predates the destruction of Jerusalem.[33] A distinguished group of scholars contend that the Prayer of Manasseh was composed in the second century B.C.[34] It is safe to conclude that it was composed either in the second or the first century B.C.,[35] with the recognition that it also could have been composed during the early part of the first century A.D.

The Prayer of Manasseh is probably an expansion of Chronicles (see below); hence it must postdate Chronicles (c. 4th cent. B.C.). On the other end of the continuum, it must predate the *Didascalia* (3rd cent. A.D.). The two limits can be reduced, since the portions of Chronicles that pertain to a prayer by Manasseh are possibly a late scribal addition and because the Prayer of Manasseh must date from a much earlier period than the *Didascalia*. The parallels with other Jewish apocryphal works (see below), especially the similarities to the additions to Daniel, and post-biblical phrases and concepts—such as the concept of the Lord's sweetness (vss. 7b, 11), "O Lord, God of the righteous ones" (vs. 8), the concept of a heart with knees (vs. 11), "God of the repenters" (vs. 13)—indicate the probability that this Jewish prayer was composed sometime in the last two centuries B.C.

[28] Fabricius, *Libri veteris testamenti apocryphi* (Leipzig, 1694) p. 208. *N.V.*

[29] J.-P. Migne, *Dictionnaire des apocryphes* (Paris, 1856) vol. 1, col. 850.

[30] F. Nau, "Un Extrait de la Didascalie: La Prière de Manassé (avec une édition de la version syriac)," *ROC* 13 (1908) 134–44, especially p. 137. E. Nestle claimed that the PrMan was composed by the author of the *Didascalia*. *Septuagintastudien* (Stuttgart, 1899) vol. 3, pp. 17f.

[31] Eissfeldt, *Introduction*, p. 588.

[32] R. E. Brown surprisingly states that the PrMan "was originally composed in Greek by a Jew in the 1st or 2nd cent. A.D.," *JBC*, p. 541.

[33] This is the opinion of most scholars; cf. e.g. Budde, *ZAW* 12 (1892) 40; Howorth, "Some Unconventional Views on the Text of the Bible: The Prayer of Manasses and the Book of Esther," *Proceedings of the Soc. of Bibl. Arch.* 31 (1909) 93; André, *Les Apocryphes*, p. 242; B. M. Metzger, *Intr. to the Apoc.*, p. 125; idem in *EncyJud*, vol. 11, col. 854. Torrey (*Apoc. Lit.*, p. 69) and A. Wikgren (in *IDB*, vol. 3, p. 256) conclude that the PrMan was composed in the 1st cent. B.C. or the 1st cent. A.D. Westermann (*BHH*, vol. 2, col. 1137) suggests it was composed sometime between the 2nd cent. B.C. and the 1st cent. A.D. S. Sandmel (*Judaism and Christian Beginnings* [New York, 1978] p. 70) advises that it "comes from the period between 200 and 50 B.C." Pfeiffer (*History*, pp. 459f.) settles on sometime between 250 B.C. and "the beginning of our era, presumably in the first century B.C." Rüger calls for caution and places it in the pre-Christian period, in *Theologische Realenzyklopädie*, vol. 1, p. 304. P. Riessler claimed it probably dated from the time of Antiochus Epiphanes or of Pompey (p. 1291).

[34] Viz. Ball, in *Apocrypha*, ed. Wace, vol. 2, pp. 361–71, *N.V.*; Fritzsche, *Handbuch*, p. 157; E. J. Goodspeed, *The Story of the Apocrypha* (Chicago, 1939) p. 54; Oesterley, *Introduction*, p. 297; Rowley, *Origin*, p. 8; Ryssel in *APAT*, vol. 1, p. 167.

[35] Flusser prefers the 1st cent. B.C.; see his comments in *The New Encyclopaedia Britannica*, Macropaedia, vol. 2, p. 933.

Provenance

As with almost all of the Pseudepigrapha, it is practically impossible to discern if the document under examination was composed in the Diaspora or in Palestine. Goodspeed[36] and Rost[37] thought the Prayer of Manasseh was from Egypt; and Wikgren[38] opined it may come from Alexandria. But Pfeiffer[39] and Metzger[40] are certainly correct in stating that the theological concepts in the Prayer of Manasseh are not characteristic of Diaspora Judaism and are in harmony with the teachings of Palestinian Judaism. Certainty is impossible, but the provenance of the Prayer of Manasseh may be Jerusalem or its environs.

Historical and theological importance

The opinion of Fabricius, Migne, and Nau, mentioned above, according to which the author of the Prayer of Manasseh is identified as a "Christian," is no longer persuasive. The author was obviously a Jew, as almost all specialists today recognize;[41] he shares with other early Jews the intriguing mixture of racial particularism with the perception of universalism. For example, the old and pervasive concept of God's covenantal unity with Israel alone opens the prayer: "O Lord, God of our fathers, God of Abraham, and of Isaac, and of Jacob, and of their righteous offspring." Focus is limited not only to the descendants of Abraham but also, in accordance with post-exilic theology, to their righteous remnant (which is an emphasis developed in Jewish apocalyptic thought, cf. e.g. 1En 83:8; 4Ezra 12:34; 2Bar 40:2; SibOr 5.384; cf. HistRech 7–9).[42] Later in the prayer a universal tone may appear: The Lord feels sorry "over the evils of men" and has appointed "repentance as the salvation for sinners" (vss. 7a and 7b); God is described as "God of the righteous ones" (vs. 8; this may not be universalistic, because the righteous ones are described as "such as Abraham, and Isaac, and Jacob") and "God of the repenters" (vs. 13).

Before translating the Prayer of Manasseh, I thought it may have been only eventually attributed to Manasseh, since his name does not appear in the prayer and since no clear statements in it demand attribution to this wicked king. But the abundant descriptions in the prayer are strikingly reminiscent of the Chronicler's account of him; note, for example, the following selections:

2 Chronicles 33	Prayer of Manasseh
verse	*verse*
6 [Manasseh] . . . provoking his [Yahweh's] anger	10 I provoked your fury [or anger] (cf. vs. 13)
7 [Manasseh] . . . placed . . . the idol . . . in the Temple	10 I set up idols
11 Manasseh with hooks, . . . in chains . . . led . . . away . . .	9b I am ensnared / 10 I am bent by a multitude of iron chains
12 humbling himself deeply before	11 I am bending the knees of my heart before you
the God of his ancestors . . .	1 God of our fathers

[36] Goodspeed, *Story*, p. 52.
[37] Rost, *Judaism*, p. 95.
[38] Wikgren, in *IDB*, vol. 4, p. 256.
[39] Pfeiffer, *History*, p. 459.
[40] Metzger, *Intr. to the Apoc.*, p. 125.
[41] The list of names is very long; it includes Fritzsche, *Handbuch*, p. 158; Ryssel in *APAT*, vol. 1, p. 167; Ryle in *APOT*, vol. 1, p. 612; Pfeiffer, *History*, p. 459; Oesterley, *Introduction*, p. 297; Torrey, *Apoc. Lit.*, p. 68; Rost, *Judaism*, p. 95; Westermann, *BHH*, vol. 2, col. 1137; Dancy, *Shorter Books*, p. 243; Baumgartner, *RGG³*, vol. 4, p. 708; Rüger, *Theologische Realenzyklopädie*, vol. 1, p. 304; Goodspeed, *Story*, p. 56; E. Oswald, "Gebet Manasses," *JSHRZ*, 4.1, p. 20.
[42] The concept was inherited from the prophets, especially Isaiah (cf. 7:3), his "school" (viz. 10:20–22, 11:10–16, 28:5, 37:32), and Zephaniah (2f.). See the excellent, succinct discussion by E. Jenni in *IDB*, vol. 4, pp. 32f.

It is now clear to me that the Prayer of Manasseh—as most critics have claimed[43]—was probably composed with 2 Chronicles in mind. Brown rightly states that it is "a pseudonymous attempt to fill in the prayer of King Manasseh (687–642) mentioned in 2 Chr 33:11–13 . . ."[44]

The above discussion explains partially why the Prayer of Manasseh should now be considered within the Pseudepigrapha: It is obviously prior to A.D. 70, Jewish, and pseudepigraphically attributed to Manasseh. Most scholars today acknowledge that the Apocrypha should be defined exclusively—to exclude documents not in the Septuagint—because the Pseudepigrapha is conceived inclusively—to include many more documents than those brought together, for example, by Kautzsch and Charles.[45] The Prayer of Manasseh is not part of the Septuagint,[46] it does not appear in Codex Vaticanus or Codex Sinaiticus; and it is appended to the Psalter, within the Odae, in Codex Alexandrinus and in Codex Turicensis.[47]

One of the most beautiful and eloquent utterances of the human heart, this poem preserves the measured, articulated need for divine forgiveness and acceptance. Emphasis is placed upon unworthiness—the Greek verb (the aorist imperative of *aniēmi*) for "forgive" in verse 13 means "let go unpunished"[48]; the punishment experienced is considered just (vs. 9b), and the inability to lift the head or eyes is confessedly deserved (vs. 10). Although the prayer was probably originally attributed to Manasseh, the author must have been introspectively aware of his own frailties, and so it is generically evocative to others, as we shall see, who are sensitive to God's demands and grace. Thus, two main ideas permeate the verses: God's infinite mercy and grace, and the assurance that authentic repentance is efficacious.[49] Other significant concepts are the power of God's name,[50] the idea that righteousness is through God alone,[51] the concept that the patriarchs (Abraham, Isaac, and Jacob) "did not sin" (vs. 8),[52] and the idea that chastisements are good and atone for sin.[53] But the central focus of this document is repentance, which comes to expression as a prayer with four main features: (1) acknowledgment of God's infinite powers (vss. 1–7b), (2) full and humble confession of sins (vss. 8–13), (3) affirmation of God's power (vss. 7a, 7b, 8)

---

[43] Notably, cf. Baumgartner in *RGG³*, vol. 4, p. 708; Brockington, *Introduction*, p. 101; Denis, *Introduction*, p. 177; Flusser in The New Encyclopaedia Britannica, Macropaedia, vol. 2, p. 933; Goodspeed, *Story*, p. 53f.; Oesterley, *Introduction*, p. 295; Pfeiffer, *History*, p. 457; Rost, *Judaism*, p. 95; Ryle in *APOT*, vol. 1, p. 614; Ryssel in *APAT*, vol. 1, p. 165; Schürer, *History*, div. 2, vol. 3, p. 188; Westermann in *BHH*, vol. 2, col. 1137; Wikgren in *IDB*, vol. 3, p. 255; G. F. Moore, *Judaism in the First Centuries of the Christian Era*, 3 vols. (Cambridge, Mass., 1927–30 [reprinted 1950]), vol. 1, p. 514.

[44] R. E. Brown in *JBC*, p. 541.

[45] See Charlesworth, *PMR*, especially pp. 17–25.

[46] The most common error by scholars who have written on the PrMan is to assume that it is part of the LXX (perhaps this mistake arises because the PrMan is in many modern versions of the LXX, including Swete's *Old Testament in Greek* and Rahlfs's *Septuaginta*). Oesterley did not become so confused; he warned, ". . . as a matter of fact it never has formed part of the Septuagint text" (*Introduction*, p. 295).

[47] Long ago E. Nestle warned that the PrMan was not part of the LXX; he claimed that it was eventually considered a biblical book because of Luther's inclusion of it in the Weimarer Ausgabe and appreciation for it. See Nestle's *Septuagintastudien*, vol. 3, pp. 3–22.

[48] The NEB correctly renders it "spare me, O Lord, spare me." The import is that the confessor acknowledges that he deserves punishment; forgiveness is only because of God's grace (cf. vs. 14).

[49] So also Ryle in *APOT*, vol. 1, p. 615; and Metzger, *EncyJud*, vol. 11, col. 855.

[50] Cf. E. E. Urbach, "The Power of the Divine Name," *The Sages: Their Concepts and Beliefs*, trans. I. Abraham (Jerusalem, 1975) pp. 124–34, especially see pp. 125f. See the discussion in my contribution on PrJac.

[51] See n. 48; cf. 1QH 13:16–19; 16:11f. Also see 2Bar 84:11 ("For if he [the Mighty One] judges us not according to the multitude of his grace, woe to all of us who are born." Cf. 2Bar 75:5).

[52] Some pseudepigrapha claim that a few persons have been free from sin; note e.g. Tob 3:14, Jub 27:18, T12P (especially TIss 7:1–9, TLevi 10:2, TZeb 1:4), LAE 18:1, TAb 10, 2Bar 9:1, ApSedr 15; contrast PssSol 9:15 (sins are attributed to the righteous), *LAB* 19:9, 4Ezra 4:30. It is difficult to reconcile such claims with 1Kgs 8:46 ("for there is no man who does not sin"). For a recent study of this theme in a few early Jewish documents see A. Strobel, *Erkenntnis und Bekenntnis der Sünde in neutestamentlicher Zeit* (Arbeiten zur Theologie 1.37; Stuttgart, 1968).

[53] Akiba used Manasseh to argue "that chastisements are very precious." See the discussion and text in J. Neusner, *Eliezer ben Hyrcanus: The Tradition and the Man* (SJLA 3, 4; Leiden, 1973; vol. 1, pp. 404f.). Also see the earlier publication by A. Büchler, *Studies in Sin and Atonement in the Rabbinic Literature of the First Century* (Oxford, 1928). For a recent study, which unfortunately mentions the PrMan only in a minor footnote (p. 133), see H. Thyen, *Studien zur Sündenvergebung im Neuen Testament und seinen alttestamentlichen und jüdischen Voraussetzungen* (FRLANT 96; Göttingen, 1970).

and willingness to forgive (vs. 14), and (4) a commitment to return to righteous conduct and proper celebration and praise (vs. 15).

Relation to canonical books

The Prayer of Manasseh does not quote any canonical book; but it was composed by a Jew whose composition revealed how well he had learned his Bible. Our prayer is very close to Psalm 51, "the typical prayer of the penitent sinner in the canon,"[54] and to Psalms 25 and 103. As J. K. Zink states, the "prayer seems to be a cento of Biblical phrases."[55] Although the Prayer of Manasseh contains neither Psalm 51's reference to inherited sin (51:5) nor its critique of sacrifice (51:16–19), there are some significant parallels between the prayer and the psalm; note the following:

Psalm 51 (LXX 50)		Prayer of Manasseh	
verse		verse	
1	your abundant mercy	7b	the multitude of your mercies
	my transgressions	13	my transgressions
3	I know my transgressions	12	I know my sins
4	and have done that which is evil	10	because I did evil things before you
	in your sight		(or in your sight)
4	you are justified in your sentence	9b	I am justly afflicted
9	hide your face from my sins	13	do not remember my evils
11	do not banish me	13	do not banish me
14	save me from death	13	do not destroy me
14	God of my salvation,	15	Because of this (salvation)
	and my tongue will sing aloud		I shall praise you

If the author of the Prayer of Manasseh had this psalm in mind when he wrote, he prefixed to the core thought a lengthy praise of the Lord's powers of creation and appended an appreciation of angelic singing (as in the AscenIs). He also was probably influenced by other psalms (cf. vs. 5 with Ps 145:5 [LXX 144]; vs. 13 with Pss 103:9 [LXX 102] and 139:15 [LXX 138]; and vs. 15 with Pss 23:6 [LXX 22], 27:4 [LXX 26], and 128:5 [LXX 127]). Significant parallels are also found between the prayer and Genesis (vs. 2 with Gen 1:1, and vs. 13 with Gen 19:15) and Joel (vs. 7a with Joel 2:13; cf. Jonah 4:2 and Ex 34:6).[56] Of course, the most important parallel is the obvious dependence of the prayer upon the narrative in 2 Chronicles 33:11–19, especially verses 18 and 19:

> The rest of the history of Manasseh, his prayer to his
> God . . . can be found in the Annals of the Kings of
> Israel. His prayer and how God relented at his
> prayer . . . are recorded in the Annals of Hozai.

The Prayer of Manasseh is probably not a copy of the prayer reputed to be in the lost annals; it was never a part of 2 Chronicles, despite the claims by Thomas Aquinas (see below) and more recently by Howorth.[57]

According to 2 Kings 21, Manasseh dies unrepentant; in contrast, the Chronicler felt impelled to rewrite this history because of his theological bias (inherited from Deut) that sinners are punished. He knew that Manasseh reigned longer than his good father, Hezekiah, and David, so God must have allowed him to live until he repented of his heinous sins, namely building pagan altars with idols in the Temple and encouraging human sacrifice by burning his son. The Chronicler[58] has inserted into salvation history the account of Manasseh's

---

[54] Moore, *Judaism*, vol. 1, p. 514.

[55] J. K. Zink, "The Prayer of Manasseh," *The Use of the Old Testament in the Apocrypha* (Duke University Ph.D., 1963 [under the supervision of J. Strugnell]) pp. 128–32; especially see p. 128. Zink (p. 132) concludes that the "most important feature of the prayer is the manner in which various strands of Biblical language are woven together to make a prayer which later commended itself to liturgical usage." Oswald uses the imagery of a mosaic of numerous recollections from OT documents; *JSHRZ*, 4.1, p. 19.

[56] See Zink, *Apocrypha*, pp. 128–32.

[57] Howorth, *Proceedings of the Soc. of Bibl. Arch.* 31 (1909) 95.

[58] As M. Smith states, the "Chronicler is notoriously untrustworthy." See his "The Veracity of Ezekiel, the Sins of Manasseh, and Jeremiah 44:18," *ZAW* 87 (1975) 11–16.

repentance, prayer, and forgiveness by God.[59] A later Jew, on the basis of this narrative, composed a prayer as Manasseh's individual lament of personal sin and plea for forgiveness.

Relation to apocryphal books

Of the abundant evidence of relationship between our prayer and the apocryphal books, only a few comments may be permitted here. It is now safe to say that this prayer is an expansion of Chronicles as Bel and the Dragon, Susanna, and the Prayer of Azariah and the Song of the Three Young Men are additions to Daniel. The Prayer of Manasseh closely resembles the Prayer of Azariah;[60] moreover, in many Greek, Syriac (viz. 9aI), and other manuscripts the Prayer of Manasseh is followed immediately by the Prayer of Azariah in the Odae appended to the Psalter. The Jewish anthropological homogeneity reflected in verse 11 ("the knees of my heart") is shared with the Odes of Solomon (viz. 37:2: "And I spoke with the lips of my heart"). The consciousness and expression of sin are shared with many apocryphal writings; note especially the Testament of Isaac 4:27–31. Unrecognized heretofore is an impressive parallel between our prayer and the prayers of Aseneth (JosAsen 11f.), especially her confession of sin and prayer for acceptance. Note the following:

> I have sinned, Lord,
> before you I have sinned . . . (JosAsen 12:5)
> Rescue me, Lord,
> before all this comes upon me.
> Rescue me, Lord,
> the desolate and solitary . . . (JosAsen 12:12)[61]

The repetitions are reminiscent of our prayer, especially of verse 12: "I have sinned, O Lord, I have sinned." The explanation for the parallels between the Prayer of Manasseh and the prayers of Aseneth await full examination.

An obvious and well-known parallel exists between the Prayer of Manasseh and 2 Baruch, according to which Manasseh is introduced into a recital of God's dealings with mankind as "the ninth black waters." Manasseh's evil deeds are emphasized and although, as in Chronicles, there is a reference to his prayer ("the Most High had heard his prayer," 64:8), the concluding reference to him concerns his torments. Apparently the author of 2 Baruch thought that Manasseh, despite his prayer, was doomed to (eternal) torment.[62] Tobit 14:10, however, according to Codex Vaticanus, records that "Manasseh gave alms and was saved from the deadly snare which had been laid for him."[63]

The Prayer of Manasseh contains the style of Semitic poetry found in the hundreds of prayers, hymns, and odes we now possess from early Judaism. It also shares with them the claim that God is near and hears the humble voice of the repentant sinner. Along with the Psalms and Odes of Solomon, the Hellenistic Synagogal Prayers—preserved, like the Prayer of Manasseh, in the Apostolic Constitutions—Psalms 151–55, the Hodayoth, along with the hymns and prayers preserved in the apocryphal compositions and in some of the New Testament books, and along with the early rabbinic writings (especially the ʿAmîdāh, Qaddish, and Shemoneh ʿEsreh), the Prayer of Manasseh is a palpable reminder of the living force of Jewish piety during the turn of the era (c. 200 B.C. to c. A.D. 100).[64]

---

[59] For other examples of the Chronicler's rewriting of history, see G. von Rad, "The Historical Work of the Chronicler," *Old Testament Theology*, trans. D. M. G. Stalker (New York, 1962) vol. 1, pp. 347–54. Well known is the Chronicler's portrayal of David as "a spotless holy king who delivers solemn orations" (p. 350).

[60] Cf. Pfeiffer, *History*, p. 459.

[61] Translation by C. H. Burchard (see his contribution in this volume).

[62] In 1891 W. J. Deane wrote that "the opinion of Manasses' damnation in spite of his prayer is, as far as we know, peculiar to Pseudo-Baruch." *Pseudepigrapha: An Account of Certain Apocryphal Sacred Writings of the Jews and Early Christians* (Edinburgh, 1891) p. 148. This advice needs to be seen in light of the rabbinic literature, especially y.Sanh 10; see the following section of the introduction. Also see L. Ginzberg, *Legends*, vol. 6, p. 376. Ḥag Bereshit states that Manasseh's prayer was uttered "with lips of deceit." AscenIs 11:41–43 records how Manasseh sawed Isaiah to death, was thoroughly under the influence of Satan, and went to destruction.

[63] See H. B. Swete, *The Old Testament in Greek According to the Septuagint* (Cambridge, England, 1896²) vol. 2, p. 847. Unfortunately most of the translations of Tob do not mention this reading in Tob 14:10.

[64] See Charlesworth, "Jewish Liturgies, Hymns and Prayers (c. 167 B.C.E.–135 C.E.)," in R. A. Kraft and G. W. E. Nickelsburg, eds., *Early Post-Biblical Judaism and its Modern Interpreters* (in press).

Cultural importance

Its appearance in the *Didascalia* (3rd cent. A.D.) and especially in the Apostolic Constitutions (4th cent. A.D.), a manual for instruction in the post-Nicene Church, reveals that the Prayer of Manasseh was from early times used ecclesiastically. Its place in the Odae, or liturgical canticles, of Codex Alexandrinus (5th cent. A.D.), Codex Turicensis (7th cent. A.D.), Syriac Manuscript, Oriental MS 58 in Mediceo-Laurenziana Library in Florence (9th cent. A.D.), and many other biblical manuscripts from the early Middle Ages to modernity—and in printed editions—demonstrates its popularity for Christians. Its omission from the ancient canon lists, nevertheless, is surprising. Denis may not be wrong in inferring that perhaps this omission is the result of the belief among Christians that it was canonical;[65] but Frey is certainly correct in stating that although some early Christian writers treated it as inspired—some, like Julius Africanus (c. 160–c. 240) and George Hamartolos (9th cent.), even considering it to have been written by Manasseh himself—no Father cited it as "Scripture."[66]

In the thirteenth century the Dominican Friar Thomas Aquinas, "the greatest of the medieval philosophers,"[67] who produced the work that established the official theology of Roman Catholicism, quoted the eighth verse of the Prayer of Manasseh. He demonstrated the authority and revelatory quality of the prayer by using it to prove that "the sacrament of Penance" (*sacramentum Poenitentiae*) is necessary as a "conditional" act for all who are in sin (*Summa Theologiae*, 3a.845).[68] Two centuries later, the father of the Reformation translated the Prayer of Manasseh into German, publishing it first separately and then at the end of his edition of the Apocrypha. The esteem with which Martin Luther held this prayer is illustrated by his claim that the Duke of Braunschweig should "in all sincerity genuinely repent," imploring God "with words such as those that appear in the Prayer of Manasseh or similar ones."[69]

The importance of this prayer, of course, should not be exaggerated; it is conspicuously absent, for example, in the *Confessions* of St. Augustine, in the biblically inspired and Jansenist-influenced genius of the earliest phases of the Enlightenment, Blaise Pascal,[70] and in the introspective writings of the melancholy Dane Søren Kierkegaard, who has been hailed by some modern intellectuals as the founder of both existentialism and phenomenology. Yet the Prayer of Manasseh continues to exert some influence on the Church today: It appears regularly in editions of the Apocrypha and occasionally surfaces in more conspicuous places, as in the widely influential sermon on Manasseh that was delivered periodically by the late James Cleland, James B. Duke Professor of Preaching and Dean of the Chapel at Duke University.

Utterly different is the fate of this prayer in rabbinic Judaism; there is no trace of it in Jewish traditions.[71] Yet a prayer of Manasseh must have been known in Jewish circles. Josephus' account of Manasseh primarily reports this king's prayer, which God heard, as in 2 Chronicles 33, and how he repented and was released by the king of Babylon to return to Jerusalem, where he rebuilt the city walls (*Ant* 10.3, which is dependent upon 2Chr 33:14).[72] But Josephus displays no cognizance of the content of or traditions in our prayer.

---

[65] Denis, *Introduction*, p. 171.

[66] For details see J. A. Fabricius, *Codex Pseudepigraphus Veteris Testamenti* (Hamburg, 1722²) vol. 2, pp. 1100–2; Fritzsche, *Handbuch*, pp. 158f.; and Frey, *DBSup*, vol. 1, col. 444.

[67] G. L. Abernethy and T. A. Langford, *Philosophy of Religion* (New York, 1962) p. 105.

[68] Cf. St. Thomas Aquinas, *Summa Theologiae*, eds. R. Masterson and T. C. O'Brien (London, New York, 1966) p. 23. St. Thomas Aquinas thought that the PrMan was once part of 2Chr (*Summa Theologiae* 3.984.10). See above for Howorth's more recent and similar claim.

[69] G. K. Wiencke (ed.) *Luther's Works* (Philadelphia, 1968) vol. 43, pp. 272f. For a discussion of Luther's use and appreciation of the PrMan, which he called "*oratio pulcherrima, omni confessuro aptissima*" (*Weimar Ausgabe* vol. 6, p. 159, 9), see H. Volz, "Zur Überlieferung des Gebetes Manasse," *ZKG* 70 (1959) 293–307.

[70] It might have been expected that Pascal would have been attracted to the PrMan; the Jansenists emphasized man's total sinfulness and redemption only through unmerited divine grace.

[71] Cf. e.g. the comments by J. F. McLaughlin in Jewish Encyclopedia, vol. 8, p. 282.

[72] Recently Manasseh's reputed constructions (perhaps prior to deportation) have been unearthed. See B. Mazar, "Manasseh in Jerusalem," *The Mountain of the Lord* (New York, 1975) p. 57; cf. Y. Yadin, *Jerusalem Revealed: Archaeology in the Holy City 1968–1974* (Jerusalem, New Haven, London, 1976) especially p. 44.

The Targum on Chronicles, far from expanding the text with the prayer traditionally ascribed to Manasseh, adds (to 2Chr 33:13) a lengthy account of how the angels attempted to close all the windows of heaven so that the prayer would not reach God. God, however, on the behalf of all who sincerely repent, heard Manasseh's prayer and fulfilled his supplication.[73] Sandmel rightly emphasizes that the Prayer of Manasseh "did not make its way into the later synagogue worship on the Day of Atonement. In content and form it would have fitted admirably."[74]

Introduction to translation

The following translation is based on the Syriac, because the earliest extant version of the prayer is in the Syriac *Didascalia*. Additional reasons for choosing the Syriac are the following: The Syriac of the Odae and the *Didascalia* has received perfunctory treatment by scholars; all printed translations are based only on the Greek; possibly all extant versions, Syriac and Greek, go back to the *Didascalia*, which is extant only in Syriac; and a careful study of the Syriac traditions reveals the presence of reliable, probably authentic, passages not extant in Greek. A literal translation of the Syriac, with critical notes to the Greek variants, is offered for scholars; a more idiomatic translation is presented for all readers, who will be interested in the poetic vision and beauty of the prayer.

SELECT BIBLIOGRAPHY

Charlesworth, *PMR*, pp. 156–58.
Delling, *Bibliographie*, p. 149.
Denis, *Introduction*, pp. 177–81.

Baars, W., and Schneider, H. "Prayer of Manasseh," *The Old Testament in Syriac According to the Peshiṭta Version*. Leiden, 1972; part 4, fasc. 6; pp. i–vii, 1–9.
Oswald, E. "Gebet Manasses," *JSHRZ*, 4.1 (1974) 1–25.
Rahlfs, A. *Septuaginta: Societatis Scientiarum Gottingensis*. Göttingen, 1931; vol. 10, pp. 361–63.
Ryle, H. E. "Prayer of Manasses." *APOT*, vol. 1, pp. 612–24.
Ryssel, V. "Das Gebet Manasse." *APAT*, vol. 1, pp. 165–71.

---

[73] Aram. *ůš͏ema' ṣ͏elôtêh w͏eqabbēl ba'ůtêh*. See R. Le Déaut and J. Robert, *Targum des Chroniques*, 2 vols. (Analecta Biblica 51; Rome, 1971) especially vol. 2, p. 158. For other traditions on Manasseh, see Ginzberg, *Legends*, vol. 4, pp. 279–81; vol. 6, pp. 375f. Also see S. Schechter, *Aspects of Rabbinic Theology* (New York, 1961—reprint of 1909 edition) pp. 318f.

[74] Sandmel, *Judaism*, p. 70.

THE PRAYER OF MANASSEH

Idiomatic Translation

1 O Lord, God of our fathers,
    God of Abraham, Isaac, Jacob, and their righteous offspring;

2 He who made the heaven and the earth
    with all their beauty;

3 He who bound the sea
    and established it by the command of his word,
  he who closed the bottomless pit
    and sealed it by his powerful and glorious name;

4 You[a] (before) whom all things fear and tremble;
    (especially) before your power.

5 Because your awesome magnificence
    cannot be endured;
  none can endure or stand before
    your anger and your fury against sinners;

6 But unending and immeasurable
    are your promised mercies;

7a Because you are the Lord,
    long-suffering, merciful, and greatly compassionate;
  and you feel sorry over the evils of men.

7b You, O Lord, according to your gentle grace,
    promised forgiveness to those who repent of their sins,
    and in your manifold mercies
    appointed repentance for sinners as the (way to) salvation.

8 You, therefore, O Lord, God of the righteous,
    did not appoint grace for the righteous,
    such as Abraham, Isaac, and Jacob,
    those who did not sin against you;
    but you appointed grace for me, (I) who am a sinner.

9a Because my sins exceeded the number of the sand(s) of the sea,
  and on account of the multitude of my iniquities,
    I have no strength to lift up my eyes.

9b And now, O Lord, I am justly afflicted,
    and I am deservedly harassed;
    already I am ensnared.

10 And I am bent by many iron chains,
    so that I cannot lift up my head;
  for I do not deserve to lift up my eyes
    and look to see the height of heaven,
    because of the gross iniquity of my wicked deeds,
    because I did evil things before you,
    and provoked your fury,
    and set up idols and multiplied impurity.

11 And now behold I am bending the knees of my heart before you;
  and I am beseeching your kindness.

12 I have sinned, O Lord, I have sinned;
  and I certainly know my sins.

13 I beseech you;
    forgive me, O Lord, forgive me!

---

a. Syr.: "he." Here we have a shift from indirect ("he") to direct discourse ("you"); the poet leads up to the personal lament and exhortation directed to the Lord.

Do not destroy me with my transgressions;
do not be angry against me forever;
do not remember my evils;
and do not condemn me and banish me to the depths of the earth!
For you are the God of those who repent.

14   In me you will manifest all your grace;
and although I am not worthy,
     you will save me according to your manifold mercies.

15   Because of this (salvation) I shall praise you continually
     all the days of my life;
because all the hosts of heaven praise you,
     and sing to you forever and ever.

THE PRAYER OF MANASSEH*

Literal Translation

1 O Lord,[a] God of our fathers,   Ex 3:15
     God[b] of Abraham, and of Isaac, and of Jacob, and of their righteous offspring;   Acts 3:13
2 He who made[c] the heaven and the earth   Gen 1:1; 2:1
     with all their embellishment;[d]
3 He who bound the sea   Gen 1:6–10
     and established[e] it by the command of his[f] word,[g]   Job 38:8–11; Ps 104:7–9
he who closed the bottomless pit[h]   4Ezra 16:58f.
     and sealed it by[i] his[j] powerful[k] and glorious name;   Tob 8:5
4 He (before) whom all things fear[l] and tremble;   Nah 1:5f.
     (especially) before your[m] power.
5 Because the grandeur[n] of your magnificence   Ps 145:5; OdesSol 7:3
     cannot be endured,[o]
and none can endure[p] or stand before
     your anger and your fury against sinners;[q]
6 But unending and immeasurable
     are[r] your promised mercies;[s]
7a Because you are the Lord,[t]   Ps 145:8

* This title is taken from MS 9al; the same title is found in *Didascalia Apostolorum* and in Codex Alexandrinus (the base of Rahlfs's edition). Other given titles: "Prayer of Manasseh, the son of Hezekiah" in Codex Turicensis (also used by Rahlfs), *Oratio Manassae regis Iuda cum captus teneretur in Babylone* in the Vulgate.

a. Gk. adds: "Almighty."

b. Gk. omits.

c. Gk.: "you who made."

d. Gk., *tō kosmō*: "their order," or "their embellishment."

e. Syr. Aph'el, lit. "he caused to rise up." Gk. omits this verb.

f. Gk.: "your."

g. The divine "word" = (*mlt'*) as in Jn 1; not *ptgm'*. Only the OdesSol use both Syr. nouns to denote the divine "Word."

h. *T'hômâ*, a Heb. loan word, which first appears in biblical Heb. in Gen 1:2.

i. In Syr. the preposition of means is *b'*; in Gk. there is no preposition, only a dative case.

j. Gk.: "your."

k. Gk.: "fearful, terrible."

l. Gk.: "shudder."

m. This is the first occurrence of this pronoun in Syr.; contrast the Gk., which *again* has "your."

n. Syr. idiom; lit. "greatness of the beauty (or grace)."

o. Gk.: "Because unendurable (is) the magnificence of your glory."

p. In Syr.—but not in Gk.—5a and 5b are linked by different forms of the same verb (*sbr*, "to endure"; in the Ethpaial in 5a, Paiel in 5b). The Syr. of this verse is superior to the Gk.

q. Gk.: "And irresistible (is) the wrath of your boast against sinners."

r. Gk. again omits.

s. Gk. is singular.

t. Gk. adds "Most High"; cf. the Gk. addition in vs. 1.

long-suffering, and merciful,[u] and greatly compassionate;
and you feel sorry over[v] the evils of men.

Joel 2:13
Ps 103:8
WisSol 11:24

7b You, O Lord, according to the sweetness[w] of your grace,[x]
 promised forgiveness[y] to those who repent[z] of their sins,
 and in the multitude of your mercies
 appointed repentance[a2] as the salvation[b2] for sinners.[c2]

8 You, therefore, O Lord, God of the righteous ones,
 did not appoint grace[d2] for the righteous ones,
 such as Abraham, and Isaac and Jacob,
 those who did not sin against you;
 but you appointed grace for me, (I) who am a sinner.

9a Because my sins multiplied in number more than the sand of the sea,[e2]
and on account of the multitude of my iniquities,[f2]
 I have no strength[g2] so that I can lift up my eyes.

9b And now, O Lord, I am justly afflicted,
 and as I deserve I am harassed;
 for already I am ensnared.[h2]

2Chr 33:11

10 And I am bent by a multitude of iron chains,[i2]
 so that I cannot lift up my head;[j2]
for I do not deserve to lift up my eyes[k2]
 and look[l2] and see the height of heaven,[m2]
 because of the multitude of the iniquity of my wicked deeds,[n2]
 because I did evil things[o2] before you,[p2]

Ps 51:4

u. See vs. 6; in both Syr. and Gk. the emphasis is upon God's *mercy*.

v. The Syr. means "to return, repent," the Gk. "perceive afterward, repent." But God is not here declared to be "self-reproachful," hence "feel sorry over," which lies behind the meaning of "to repent." The Syr. and Gk. may be corrupt here; a 16th-cent. Syr. text has *wmttw'*, which clearly means "being sorrowful over."

w. Or "pleasantness, gentleness, kindness." Gk.: *plēthos*, "multitude, great."

x. Or "goodness, kindness."

y. Or "release (from debt)."

z. The same verb stem as earlier translated "feel sorry" over. Identity in English is impossible because earlier the subject was the Lord; here it is men.

a2. Or "conversion, penitence."

b2. Or "life."

c2. The Gk. of 7b is not in Rahlfs's 1935 (or in Swete's) edition; it is extant only in late Gk. MSS (and in Lat. and Syr. MSS). The Gk. is different from the Syr.; it reads as follows:

You, O Lord, according to your great goodness (or kindness),
promised repentance and forgiveness to those who sinned against you,
and in the multitude of your mercies
appointed repentance toward salvation for sinners.

For the Gk. see O. F. Fritzsche, *Libri apocryphi veteris testamenti graece* (Leipzig, 1871), p. 92; and the critical apparatus in Rahlfs's Göttingen edition, p. 362. For a different recension of the Gk., see A.-M. Denis, *Fragmenta pseudepigraphorum quae supersunt graeca* (PVTG 3; Leiden, 1970), p. 116. The vs. seems original; it contains no extraneous data or ideas; it fits smoothly into the flow of the prayer. It may have been inadvertently omitted by a copying scribe. He wrote *su* in vs. 7b, rested, and then let his eye wander back

incorrectly to the *su* that begins vs. 8. Both vss. 7b and 8 would probably have begun with the left margin, as in Fritzsche. Vs. 7b was omitted, therefore, due to parablepsis.

d2. See n. w.

e2. Gk. adds: "my transgressions are multiplied, O Lord, they are multiplied." The repetitions also found in vss. 12 and 13 suggest that this Gk. l. is original.

f2. Gk.: "And I am not worthy to look intently and see the height of heaven on account of the multitude of my iniquities."

g2. Lit. "And there is not for me breathing (or refreshment)." But *np's* derives from *nps*, which denotes "the breath of life, soul, vitality." The l. is difficult to understand; perhaps "strength" could be intended. For the Gk. see n. e2.

h2. Vs. 9b is not extant in Gk. The vs. may be original; it contains no ideas or images foreign to the prayer; it flows smoothly into the idea of being ensnared, in vs. 10.

i2. Gk.: "by many an iron chain." As in the Psalter and (possibly in the) Hodayoth this expression is to be understood as a metaphor.

j2. The Syr. here agrees with the Gk. of T. This and the next l. in Gk. are not found in Denis' edition of the Gk. (which is from Funk's edition of the AposCon). The Gk. versions reflect corruption in transmission. Corresponding to the Syr. verb, rendered above as "I cannot lift up," is a Gk. verb translated in numerous ways: "I am rejected" (RSV), "I grieve over" (NEB), "I bend beneath" (Goodspeed).

k2. Gk.: "and I have no relief."

l2. Or "gaze."

m2. Gk. omits.

n2. Gk. omits.

o2. Gk. is singular.

p2. Or "in your sight." In the Gk. this and the next l. are inverted.

and I provoked your fury,   2Chr 33:6

and I set up idols[q2] and multiplied defilement.[r2]   2Chr 33:7

11 And now behold[s2] I am bending[t2] the knees[u2] of my[v2] heart before you;   2Chr 33:12

and I am beseeching your kindness.[w2]

12 I have sinned, O Lord, I have sinned;   JosAsen 12:5

and certainly[x2] I know my sins.[y2]   Ps 51:3

13 I make supplication before you;

forgive me, O Lord, forgive me![z2]   JosAsen 12:12

and do not destroy me with my transgressions;   Ps 51:1

and do not be angry against me forever;   Ps 103:9

and do not remember my evils;[a3]   Pss 51:9; 25:76

and do not condemn me and banish me[b3] to[c3] the depths of the earth!   Ps 51:11

For you are[d3] God of the repenters.

14 And in me you will manifest all your grace;[e3]

and although I am not worthy,

you will save me according to the multitude of your mercies.

15 Because of this (salvation)[f3] I shall praise you continually   Ps 51:14

through all the days of my life;[g3]   Pss 61:8; 145:1f.

because all the hosts[h3] of heaven[i3] praise you,   AscenIs 6–11

and sing to you forever and ever.[j3]

---

q2. Gk.: "abominations." The NEB freely renders it as "idols"; contrast Goodspeed and RSV: "setting up abominations and multiplying offenses."

r2. Or "abomination," which in Syr. can denote idol worship; for example cf. Dan 11:31, in which this Syr. word is used to denote "the abomination that makes desolate." The Gk. has a plural noun here.

s2. Gk. omits.

t2. Or "bend"; here I translate the participle literally for the emphasis I think is intended.

u2. Gk.: "knee."

v2. A omits the pronoun; it is in T.

w2. Or "sweetness"; cf. vs. 7b, in which basîmûthâ is translated "sweetness."

x2. wmṭl dᵉ seems to be used here for emphasis.

y2. Gk.: "transgressions"; only the Syr. has paronomasia: both the verb ("I have sinned") and the noun ("sins") are from the same root.

z2. The second "forgive me" is not in Syr. MS 9aI (the right col. in Baars-Schneider). It is in Syr.

MS 10tl (the left col. in Baars-Schneider) and the Gk. The repetition throughout the PrMan suggests that the reading in MS 10tl should be preferred. This choice breaks our usual custom of following only the reading of 9aI.

a3. Lit. "And do not keep in memory for me my evils." Gk. of the last two ll.: "Do not forever be angry (with me, nor) lay up evil for me."

b3. Gk. omits "and banish me."

c3. bᵉ in Syr., which is not unusual; but en in Gk. looks like a Semitism.

d3. Gk. adds: "Lord."

e3. Following Syr. MS 10tl, which is similar to the Gk.: "And in me you will manifest your goodness."

f3. Gk. and Syr. 10tl omit.

g3. Lit. "forever and for all the days of my life."

h3. Gk. is singular.

i3. Gk. is plural.

j3. Gk.: "And yours is the glory forever. Amen."

PSALMS OF SOLOMON

(First Century B.C.)

A NEW TRANSLATION AND INTRODUCTION

BY R. B. WRIGHT

The eighteen Psalms of Solomon incorporate the response of a group of devout Jews to the capture of Jerusalem by the Romans in the first century B.C. Psalms 1, 2, 8, and 17 are the account of how a native cadre seizes power illegally and misuses its prerogatives. These usurpers, however, are overthrown by foreign invaders and are executed or deported. But the gentile occupation is worse than the native regime it displaced, introducing foreign cultic and social practices which corrupt many citizens. There is no realistic expectation of relief, because of the immense power of the invaders. The pious group responsible for our psalms expect a legitimate king to appear and lead them in a rebellion against the occupying forces, in the expulsion of foreign influence, and in the establishment of an independent Jewish state. Psalms of Solomon 17 contains an extended messianic hymn describing the reign of this king, the anointed son of David. The remaining psalms show similarities to those of the canonical psalter and the Qumran Hymn Scroll and grapple with a variety of more conventional topics common to the psalm genre: evil and good, sin and salvation, threat and rescue.

Texts

The Psalms of Solomon are preserved, in whole or in part, in eleven Greek and four Syriac manuscripts dating from the tenth to the sixteenth centuries A.D. The abundance of Greek manuscripts precludes a description of each here. The present translation is based on my forthcoming critical edition of the Greek witnesses.

The earliest historical evidence we have of the Psalms of Solomon is from the fifth century A.D., when the "Eighteen Psalms of Solomon" were mentioned in the list at the beginning of Codex Alexandrinus, in which they follow the Old and New Testaments and the Clementine Epistles. The leaves at the end of the codex which would have contained the text of the Psalms of Solomon are missing. It also has been calculated that the Psalms of Solomon would have fit into the twelve missing pages of Codex Sinaiticus.

The Psalms of Solomon are listed with the Odes of Solomon as *antilegomena* of the Old Testament, following Maccabees and an unknown Ptolemaic history and preceding Susanna in the *Synopsis Sanctae Scripturae* of Pseudo-Athanasius, in the sixth century. They are listed among what we call pseudepigrapha in the sixth-century list of "Sixty Books" at the end of Anastasius Sinaita's *Quaestiones et Responsiones*, after the canonical and deutero-canonical books. However, they appear in the ninth century *Stichometry* of Nicephorus among the books of the Apocrypha. That these notices refer to the Psalms of Solomon as we know them may be claimed with some degree of certainty.

None of our manuscripts have verse numbers. The division of verses and the numbers assigned to them in this edition are aligned with A. Rahlfs's *Septuaginta*.[1] This enumeration is in the Ryle and James edition[2] (and within parentheses in *APOT*).

The footnotes to the introduction have been supplied by the author.

[1] A. Rahlfs, *Septuaginta id est Vetus Testamentum Graece* (Stuttgart, 1935, reprinted 1965).
[2] H. S. Ryle and M. R. James, *Psalmoi Solomōntos: Psalms of the Pharisees, Commonly Called the Psalms of Solomon* (Cambridge, England, 1891).

Original language

The Psalms of Solomon, according to the majority of scholars, were composed in Hebrew, very soon afterward translated into Greek, and at some later time into Syriac. There are no Hebrew manuscripts extant, and the Greek documents are late. A. Hilgenfeld, virtually alone, argued for a Greek original.[3] Evidence for a Greek original is made up largely of quotations from the Septuagint within the psalms, but use of the Septuagint only confirms an acquaintance with the Septuagint and a harmonization with its readings by a translator. Several attempts have been made to reconstruct a Hebrew original, but they have little historical or linguistic value.

It is clear that the Greek text is a translation. Ryle and James, and G. B. Gray (in *APOT*), noted features in common with other translations: translational errors from Hebrew, "Semitisms" in the Greek, etc. R. R. Hann has now confirmed by syntactical analysis that our texts are indeed "translation Greek,"[4] a phenomenon identifiably distinct from writings originally composed in Greek, even those written in conscious imitation of the Septuagint. The Greek is written with a modest vocabulary. In several passages the meaning is obscure and has been subject to conjecture by both medieval scribes and modern editors.

The Syriac has usually been seen as a translation from the Greek text, although there is some evidence that it was translated from a Hebrew text.[5] It stands closest to Greek Manuscript 253 and its close relatives, although with similarities to Greek Manuscripts 769 and 336. Its most notable feature is the attempt to smooth difficult readings. In numerous passages where the text is difficult and the texts diverge in their attempts to provide intelligibility, the Syriac gravitates toward Manuscript 253 and its group of manuscripts.

The texts of Wisdom and Sirach in Manuscript 253 and its group are part of the Syro-hexaplaric text tradition, which may reinforce similarities between this group and the Syriac community which preserved the psalms together with the Odes of Solomon. First Baruch, an original Greek composition which quotes the Psalms of Solomon, antedates the end of the first century A.D. because of its testimony to the destruction of the Temple and the extensive quotations from First Baruch by Irenaeus. First Baruch's use of the Psalms of Solomon would suggest that the Greek translation was available by the mid first century A.D. The Greek manuscripts remain our primary witnesses to the Psalms of Solomon.

Date

The external evidence takes us back no further than the fifth century A.D., but the relation to First Baruch gives evidence of the existence of the Psalms of Solomon in Greek before the end of the first century A.D. The internal evidence is of two kinds: allusions to Jewish national conflicts and references to international events.

The psalmist is deeply disturbed about the condition of Israel. The monarchy is in the hands of usurpers who do not honor the ancient covenants, and the Temple is in the control of desecraters who violate both the ritual and the spirit of the cultus. Although dissidents in several periods might have made these charges against the government, the time of greatest internal turmoil was in the late Hasmonean period, the early to middle first century B.C. On the other hand, the struggle between sinners and devout is in some measure timeless and offers little but a confirmation of other evidence.

The descriptions of the foreign conqueror and his fate, however, are concrete to a degree paralleled only in Daniel, and offer as in Daniel the best evidence we have for dating the Psalms of Solomon. Identification of the conqueror with Antiochus Epiphanes, Herod the

---

[3] A. Hilgenfeld, "Die Psalmen Salomos und die Himmelfahrt des Moses, griechisch hergestellt und erklärt," *ZWT* 11 (1868) 133–68.

[4] R. R. Hann, *The Manuscript History of the Psalms of Solomon* (SCS 13; Chico, Calif., 1982).

[5] After Wright completed his contribution, J. L. Trafton examined the place of the Syr. version within the textual tradition of the PssSol. He concludes that the Syr. version is "an important witness to the text of the PssSol. It is based primarily, if not exclusively, on a Heb. Vorlage" (p. 360). See Trafton's *A Critical Evaluation of the Syriac Version of the Psalms of Solomon.* Duke University Ph.D., 1981.

Great, Pompey, and Titus has each had its supporters. But the allusions best match Pompey. The conqueror is a gentile who came from the west (17:12). At first he was welcomed into Jerusalem by at least part of the government and the people (8:16–18), but once inside he encountered resistance at the Temple compound and was forced to bring up reinforcements, including a siege machine (2:1). After the city fell, he and his troops explored the Temple, desecrating its sanctity (2:2). Leaving Jerusalem, he went to Egypt, where he was assassinated. His body lay on the beach unburied (2:26f.). By comparison with Josephus' account, it is now generally agreed that this describes the career of the Roman general Pompey, who took Jerusalem in 63 B.C.

The earliest direct allusion in the psalms to a specific historical event is to Pompey's invasion (63 B.C.). The latest is to his death, in 48 B.C. The widest limits for dating are between 125 B.C. and the early first century A.D. Narrow limits would be about 70 to 45 B.C., with the caveat that the undatable psalms may have been earlier or later and the collection as a whole was certainly later.

That Jerusalem has been desecrated but not destroyed suggests that the psalms reached their final form before A.D. 70. The chronology of the events, although capable of close alignment with events of the mid first century B.C., is not in chronological order in the present text. This would suggest that the compilation of the psalms, which was perhaps coincidental with the translation into Greek, was by an editor whose interest was literary and who had little knowledge, or at least regard, for the sequence of events behind the poems.

Further evidence of an editorial stage appears in the disjunctions in the text, marked by dropped antecedents, awkward constructions, and shifts of perspective. The joinings between 1:1–2:18 and 2:19–31; 8:1–22 and 8:23–34; 17:1–15 and 17:21–42 are particularly difficult. Psalms of Solomon 18:10–12 appears to be appended. The individual psalm titles bear little relation to their context, and the supposed musical or liturgical notations are ill-placed. Both appear to be by-products of the editorial process. The remaining psalms have no historical reflections, and without evidence to the contrary, discussions of date, authorship, and provenance have been assumed to apply to the collection.

The Psalms of Solomon emerge from the tradition of a Jewish community in the last century before the turn of the era. It is fruitless to debate whether there was one author or several, for the similarities convince those who argue for a single author and the differences are evidence for those who find several authors. It is better to understand the hymns as the product of a community. Clearly the writer speaks of and for a community that is bound together by persecution and hope for the future. The concerns expressed are not individual but communal. It is better to argue for a common tradition, for this will best account for both the similarities which bind the psalms together and the differences which divide them, and will avoid the fault of a restrictive rigidity which sees only the static elements as genuine. It is a unity not of authorship but of tradition.

The ascription of the collection to Solomon appeared obvious to the editor. The similarity between the most prominent psalm (PssSol 17) and the canonical Psalm 72, already known as a Psalm of Solomon, prompted the ascription of the collection to one who, next to David, enjoyed a reputation as a poet (1Kgs 4:32). The resemblance between Solomon and the Messiah figure is marked: Each is called the son of David, and both were extenders of boundaries, restorers and beautifiers of Jerusalem, and defenders of the worship of Yahweh. They received tribute from foreign monarchs, who came to see their glory, and stood above all other regents in wisdom and justice. Solomon, however, sinned in multiplying silver and gold, horses and chariots and ships, and was guilty of pride and oppression. The Messiah, of course, will not commit such atrocities (PssSol 17:33).

Provenance

There is little doubt that Jerusalem is the provenance of the Psalms of Solomon. The city is given unusual prominence. It is the locale of many events, and the descriptions are detailed. Jerusalem is addressed (PssSol 11) and speaks (PssSol 1). It is the seat of the Sanhedrin (4:1). It has been suggested that the vices described are particularly urban.

There is some question, however, as to the sociopoliticoreligious provenance of the

Psalms of Solomon, particularly the identification of the several groups denounced or praised in the psalms and of the community which was the source of the psalms. There are three groups described: the gentiles, the sinners, and the devout. The identification of the gentiles with the conqueror Pompey and the Roman invaders is the least difficult. They were "alien to our race," came from the west, were ignorant of the religious and social customs, but were used by God to punish Israel for her sins. The sinners, the Jewish opponents of the devout, are the Hasmonean Sadducees. They violently usurped the monarchy (17:5–8, 22), they were not scrupulous in ritual purity and in ceremonial observances (1:8; 2:3, 5; 7:2; 8:12; 17:45), and they were too willing to comply with foreign customs (8:22).

The identity of the devout presents a problem. Traditionally they have been identified with the Pharisees. Indeed, Ryle and James titled their edition *Psalms of the Pharisees*. However, with the new information about the beliefs and practices of the Essenes provided by the Qumran documents, another possibility emerged: that the Psalms of Solomon originated in an Essene-like community in Jerusalem that stood in opposition to the Sadducees and in contrast to the Pharisees. O. Eissfeldt saw many points of contact between the Psalms of Solomon and the Qumran texts,[6] and A. Dupont-Sommer was convinced that the Psalms of Solomon and several other writings of the time were Essene in origin.[7]

The identification of the devout with either the Pharisees or the Essenes is based on an examination of the theology and theodicy of the Psalms of Solomon. Theocracy ("the Lord is King" [2:30, 32; 5:18, 19; 17:1, 34, 46]); sacred Law (which their enemies misuse [4:8] but which is the proof of God's care [10:4]); and divine providence (5:3, 4) were, according to Josephus, emphases which set off the Pharisees and Essenes from the Sadducees. A strong doctrine of retribution (2:34, 35; 13:6; 15:12, 13; 17:8) was also characteristic of both Pharisees and Essenes.

It is unwise to label these psalms as either Pharisaic or Essene.[8] We know far too little about Pharisaic thought prior to the destruction of Jerusalem, in 70; our only sources on them are later than this paradigmatic date and are considerably subjective (the NT, Josephus, and the rabbinic writings). Similarly, although we are now convinced that some Essenes lived in Jerusalem, we are unsure of the ideas and customs that distinguish them from other contemporaneous Jews. The recognition that some ideas in these psalms are similar to those among the Pharisees or among the Essenes ignores the fact that these two sects were very similar; moreover, scholars are now recognizing that the Essene community at Qumran may have received an influx of Pharisees fleeing Jerusalem in the early decades of the first century B.C.[9] Finally, according to both Philo and Josephus, most Jews were not members of a sect; there were far more Jewish groups than the classic four (Sadducee, Pharisee, Essene, Zealot—and the latter sect postdates the composition of these psalms[10]); hence it is unwise to force these psalms into any model of the Pharisees or Essenes.[11]

Historical importance

The Psalms of Solomon provide a view of the internal conflict and external invasion that plagued Judea in the mid first century B.C. They provide in less cryptic, less veiled language than at Qumran the feelings of a group of devout Jews, living in Jerusalem, troubled by recent events such as the traumatic invasion and occupation of their country and by corruption in political and religious leadership. Their attempt to reconcile theology with reality results in one possible answer to a crisis: apocalyptic messianism. The members of the group were

---

[6] O. Eissfeldt, "The Psalms of Solomon," *The Old Testament: An Introduction*, translated by P. R. Ackroyd (New York, 1965) pp. 610–13.

[7] A. Dupont-Sommer, *The Essene Writings from Qumran*, translated by G. Vermes (Cleveland, New York, 1962, reprinted 1973) p. 296.

[8] The paragraph beginning with this sentence was added by the editor to Wright's excellent introduction.

[9] See the recent discussion on this issue by J. H. Charlesworth in "The Origin and Subsequent History of the Authors of the Dead Sea Scrolls: Four Transitional Phases Among the Qumran Essenes," *RQ* 38 (1980) 213–33.

[10] See D. M. Rhoads, *Israel in Revolution, 6–74 C.E.: A Political History Based on the Writings of Josephus* (Philadelphia, 1976).

[11] J. Schüpphaus claims that the PssSol are a "classic source" for Pharisaic thought. See his *Die Psalmen Salomos: Ein Zeugnis Jerusalemer Theologie und Frömmigkeit in der Mitte des vorchristlichen Jahrhunderts* (ALGHJ 7; Leiden, 1977). Also, see Charlesworth review of this position in *JAAR* 50 (1982) 292f.

not political pacifists, and appear as quietists only because they have no opportunity to be activists (12:5). They heap verbal abuse on their enemies (4:1f., 6, 14–20) and predict revenge when they return to power under the Messiah (12:6; 17:22–25). But with no realistic hope to secure political control, they accept the current difficulties as God's discipline (14:1; 16:11), confident that their fortunes will be reversed, if not in the present age then certainly in the age to come (2:34f.). Much as the covenanters of Qumran, they accepted their present situation but envisioned the ultimate defeat of their enemies.

We have several insights into this urban group. Some of the accusations leveled against their enemies would apply to many times and situations (insatiable greed, prostitution). Other charges are more specific, such as allegations of an illegitimate monarchy or of misappropriation of consecrated offerings (1:8; 2:3; 8:11f., 22). The complaints of the devout paint a picture of the general secularization of the regime in power, of the greed of the religious leadership, of widespread disregard for religious and civil law, and an international involvement of the Jewish nation which resulted at last in foreign invasion.

As a consequence, the Psalms of Solomon preserve one of the most detailed messianic expectations in the immediate pre-Christian centuries. The title "Messiah," which in the Old Testament commonly referred to any legitimately appointed priest or king, and which in later Jewish writings became the repository of all those ideal hopes which were unrealized in the present, is given shape and dimension in these psalms as they describe the person of the Messiah and the character of his government in the age to come. There is more substance to the ideas concerning the Messiah in the Psalms of Solomon than in any other extant Jewish writing.[12] The Messiah is here identified as a son of David who will come to establish an everlasting kingdom of God. Although not a supernatural being, both he and the devout over whom he reigns are without sin, and he rules with all the ancient virtues heightened to superlatives: wisdom, justice, mercy, power. He will restore the ancient tribal divisions and with them the ancient ways of righteousness and fidelity. He will bring back the Diaspora of Israel to a purified homeland. The nations likewise will come, to pay homage to Jerusalem and her king. Finally, these psalms link for the first time the concepts of *Messiah* and *lordship* into a new construct which the Gospel of Luke later seizes as a title for Jesus (Lk 2:11), and the New Testament develops into the concept of "Christ the Lord," a concept that played an important part in the development of New Testament Christology.

Theological importance (with V. Schwartz)

The Psalms of Solomon is literature of crisis. But it is more than the crisis of an alien army invading the homeland; it is one of harsh reality invading a traditional theology. For when Pompey's soldiers entered Jerusalem and tramped across the Temple compound, it was the ancient promises that they breached and the inviolable covenant they trampled. Although many historical periods and the literature they produced may be characterized as "crisis literature," the author of the Psalms of Solomon is affected personally by the torrent of events, and the tribulations of the times raise in him deep theological misgivings. Since he is caught off guard by the suddenness of the events, we see in the unsystematic and somewhat unstable theodicy of the Psalms of Solomon the author's desperate appropriation of any possible rationale by which to make sense of the situation. Theodicy is a theme to which he returns repeatedly (2:1, 15–18; 3:3–5; 4:8; 8:3, 23–26; 9:2).

What is especially intriguing is to watch the psalmist alternating between solutions which may be termed "biblical" (if not "pre-exilic") and those which usually are thought of as of more recent origin. For example, it is clear that the psalmist has not abandoned the idea that God will do justice *in this life*. The righteous will prosper and the wicked will be punished. This prosperity and punishment are visible signs of God's favor and displeasure. But it is just this "biblical" theodicy which provokes his dilemma, for recent events affecting both the nation and the individual cast doubt on this reassuring view. The nation, he quickly observes, has been punished for her sins. Her calamities serve both to expose hidden sins and to demonstrate that God is a powerful and righteous judge whom none can evade (PssSol 2:8; 9:1–3; 17). But the psalmist, although he acknowledges the justice of

---

[12] See Charlesworth, "The Concept of the Messiah in the Pseudepigrapha," *ANRW* II.19.1, pp. 188–218.

God's action, is faced with the real possibility of the gentiles' being allowed to destroy Israel. He reminds God repeatedly that Israel is his beloved nation, with whom he has an enduring covenant (7:8f.; 9:8–11; 11:7; 14:5; 17:4) and pleads with God not to allow the gentiles to triumph completely over his people (2:22–25; 7:3–5; 8:27–31). His final recourse is to find a solution for Israel's difficulties in the messianic kingdom of the last days (7:10; 11; 15:12; 17; 18:6–10). But this is no fond hope for the distant future; to the contrary, Israel's present adversity convinces him that the day of God's kingdom is imminent, for surely God could not permit this grave threat to continue for long.

When the psalmist faces the problem of the suffering of the righteous individual, his problem of justifying God is even more acute. Although he frequently indulges in sweeping indictments of the nation (2:8f.; 17:20), it is clear that he holds himself and his own devout associates to be at least relatively guiltless. Why, then, must they suffer? The psalmist's notion of corporate guilt is not so pervasive that it can serve to justify God for allowing the righteous to suffer equally with the wicked. Further, in some instances, the persecution of the righteous comes not from gentiles but from fellow Jews (as in PssSol 4), and this calls for a solution different from those used to explain national suffering.

Again the psalmist searches through several explanations. His first response is that justice has been delayed. Given time, the scales will yet tip into balance on this side of the grave (PssSol 2; 5). Meanwhile, God will never allow a righteous person to perish utterly or to succumb under his ordeal (2:36; 16:12–15).

The writer next considers the idea that the Lord *tests* the righteous person with affliction to prove his faithfulness (16:14). This thought appears only once, and it is clear that the writer is no Job, for here again he presents suffering as nevertheless compensatory for wickedness of some sort. The righteous must be guilty of some sins, even if unwittingly, and God alerts the righteous person to these sins through affliction so that he may improve himself and thus escape a worse punishment. For indeed, God punishes the righteous differently from the wicked. He corrects them as a father disciplines a beloved child (13:8–10—said also of Israel in 18:4), and one of the proofs of a person's righteousness is the way he responds to the divine discipline. In contrast to the sinner, he is neither demoralized nor made resentful by affliction but searches out his sins and declares God to be just (3:3–10; 10:1–3).

The eschatological hope for the individual functions in the same way as for the nation. The eschatological day must come shortly to end the suffering and persecution, but this future prospect in no way diminishes the psalmist's need to explain why the righteous suffer now. Again, he does not use the motif of the age to come only as a consolation for present difficulties, but also to warn the righteous away from sins which would lead to their destruction, or to purge the righteous in preparation for the kingdom. There is nothing approaching a "theology of suffering" as found in other Jewish and Christian ruminations on the problem of evil. The psalmist believes that suffering is purgative and salutary (10:1–3) and will say that the righteous are singled out for especially exacting discipline, but he never moves toward assigning a positive meaning to suffering or of making it the sign of election. For the psalmist, suffering remains suffering for sin.

If the psalmist is unsettled on this point, elsewhere he is a confident, if not particularly profound, thinker. His doctrine of providence is strong. God is active in every circumstance of personal life and history. The attributes of God which are most stressed in the Psalms of Solomon are precisely those which pertain to his ceaseless surveillance of human life: He is the king and judge over all the earth (2:32; 8:24; 17:3) and the provider for all life (PssSol 5). Although implacably wrathful against hardened sinners, he is otherwise merciful and forgiving and especially tender in his love for Israel (5:9–11; 18:1–4; 7:4f.; 9:6f.). He is the refuge of the poor and weak (5:2; 10:6; 15:1; 18:3). Although humans are hardly the equals of God in benevolence (5:13f.), power, and trustworthiness (17:1–3), it is not God's distance from humanity which is prominent in the psalms but his proximity. The psalmist addresses God quite directly, much as he might address an earthly king. Indeed, his sense of divine kingship is hardly figurative or abstract. God *is* king (2:30, 32; 5:19).

Perhaps because of this proximity of the psalmist with his king there is but a small place for angels in the Psalms of Solomon. The angel of death is mentioned in Psalms of Solomon 7:4, but this is the only certain reference to an angel or angels in the psalms.

The poet's anthropology is straightforward and corresponds at least in part to that ascribed to the Pharisees and Essenes by Josephus. Man has freedom of will (9:4), yet it is God who impels man to good. Persons have a "fate" or "part" allotted to them, but this is closer to "good fortune" than to any more sophisticated doctrine. It is also clear that one's fate is not unalterably fixed and that God may adjust it on the basis of one's actions.

Life after death is concentrated entirely in the hope for bodily resurrection (viz. 2:31; 3:12) and betrays no certain trace of a belief in an immortal soul. The life of the righteous "goes on forever" (13:11), but this is in the kingdom, after the "day of mercy" (14:9). Thus the psalmist conceives of man as essentially embodied and the occasional use of the term "soul" corresponds to its use in the psalter to mean "person." He posits no body/ soul dualism and is not in the least "otherworldly" in his thinking. The cosmos and the nature of humanity are undivided.

The psalmist is a moral rigorist. It is by scrupulous purity of life that one makes oneself pleasing to God. Even unintentional sins must be atoned for (3:7f.; 13:7) with repentance, confession (9:6f.), fasting and other penance (3:8), and the humble acceptance of God's discipline (13:10; 10:1). The Law is specifically mentioned in two places (4:8; 14:1–3). But while the psalmist undoubtedly derives his notions of God's requirements from the Law, there is little in his expressed ethic which presupposes the intense absorption with the specific interpretations and fulfillment of Torah that characterized the Pharisees. His concern for cultic obligations is expressed mainly through his horror at how certain Jews have travestied the Temple rites. Likewise, the distinction between Israel and the nations is sharp. The writer is no universalist. Gentiles are lawless by nature and are rejected by God (2:2, 19–25; 7:1–3; 8:23; 17:13–15), even if occasionally he chooses them as instruments of his wrath against sinful Israel (PssSol 8). No hope is offered for their conversion. Indeed, one of the blessings of the messianic age will be the expulsion of the gentiles from Israel (PssSol 17). God chooses Israel "above all the nations" forever (9:8–11) as the object of his special love and concern, and the sense of Israel's mission to the gentiles is extremely limited.

In reviewing the covenant relationship, the psalmist refers twice to Abraham (9:9f.; 18:3) and once to Sinai (10:4); however, the covenant central in his thought is the Davidic. This preoccupation is explicit in Psalm 17 and is implicit in the psalmist's animus against the Hasmonean usurpers and the prominent role assigned to Jerusalem, both at present and in the end-time. The city is conceived as holy in its own right, the most intense locus of God's presence in Israel (2:19–21; 8:4) and the center for the ingathering in the last days (PssSol 11).

The end-time is at hand. Following a review of Israel's immediate history up to his time, the psalmist concludes that the only solution lies in the immediate intervention of God in history. This is called, in 15:12; 10:4, and 11:6, the day of God's "supervision" or "overseeing" of Israel—the day when he takes direct control of Israel's destiny. This day of judgment will see sinners marked out for destruction (2:31, 34; 15:12), and the righteous honored and raised to life (2:31; 3:12). Sinners will not share in the resurrection (3:9–12; 14:9f.).

When the Messiah appears, he is a kingly figure, a scion of the house of David. As the manifestation of God's kingship over Israel and the world, he overthrows the gentile occupiers, ejects all aliens and sinners, and gathers together a purified nation which he leads in righteousness, justice, and holy wisdom (17:23–25). The dispersed of Israel will return to their homeland (17:31; 11; 8:28); the land will be distributed according to the antique tribal system (17:28); Jerusalem and the Temple will be resanctified (17:30f.). All gentile nations will be subjugated to Israel's king, and Jerusalem and her God will be glorified throughout the world.

Although the Messiah is distinctly a royal and, one might say, a political figure, he is not military in the ordinary sense, for the source of his power is entirely spiritual (17:33f.). He is not himself superhuman, although he is free from sin (17:36). He is so thoroughly imbued with the spirit of holiness (17:37) as to be invincible in action and perfect in judgment. This aspect of the messianic king—his power to purify the people and impart to them a holy wisdom—is given equal emphasis with his deliverance of them from the gentile oppressor. Although some have drawn a contrast between the Psalms of Solomon and other messianic passages in Jewish literature for the almost exclusive concern with Israel's sanctification in the Psalms, it should be remembered that the Psalms of Solomon always see a close connection between spiritual and physical well-being. If the messianic hymn makes no mention of the physical delights of the end-time, it is because in the psalmist's mind these would follow inevitably upon the renewal of Israel's righteousness.

The Psalms of Solomon, then, present an interesting intersection between themes already extant in biblical and post-biblical literature, and new emerging constructs. The ethics and outlook of the Book of Proverbs are joined to apocalyptic expectation, the warranty of the Davidic covenant is fulfilled in the messianic hope, and the concept of the "anointed one" becomes concretized in a specific expectation of an immediate consummation. The two messianic titles, "Son of David" and "Lord Messiah," the former the first instance and the latter the only instance of such usages in Jewish literature, are themselves combinations of older concepts. The Son of David is now more than a ruler with the proper genealogy, although certainly this was a concern of the psalmist. He is the final, apocalyptic king, who, in possession of the full range of idealized royal virtues, will accomplish all the chores left unfulfilled by lesser sons of David.

"Lord Messiah," the title used by Luke and a base for the theology of the New Testament, combines categories of all God's anointed agents—from priest to prophet to king—with the lordship to be exercised on earth by God's vizier. It is God who rules—the psalms are clear on that—but his agent is the Lord Messiah.

Recent studies into the nature of apocalyptic movements and literatures have emphasized that apocalyptic is not limited to specific parties or groups but is socially and politically conditioned by the fortunes of historical development. Likewise, the traditional "lists" of supposed characteristics of the phenomenon confuse surface contours with underlying causes. When historical conditions prevent the fulfillment of the divine promise, increasingly the devout look for the fulfillment of their hopes outside of historical conditions. Sociologically the position of the apocalyptic community is one of powerlessness and disenfranchisement. They hope for a direct and dramatic intervention by God that will overcome the limitations of the historical situation and bring their hopes to fulfillment.

The historical conditioning of apocalyptic is joined to an equally impelling crisis in theology. The failures of the old royal theology (the invincibility of the monarchy) and of the Deuteronomic theology (the inviolability of Jerusalem) are visible in the corruption of king and priest, government and cult. When the collapse of history as a viable vehicle for covenantal promises prompts the crisis in theology, when the hopelessness of the political expectations of the oppressed community brings forth the call for a divine interruption of history, apocalyptic eschatology provides relief. The oppressed community looks for the realization of present and ancient hopes, and the rescue of traditional theology.

Relation to canonical books

The Psalms of Solomon are a conscious imitation of the Davidic psalter, perhaps heightened later by the addition of titles, ascription, and liturgical paraphernalia. Several classic psalm types can be identified: hymn (2:30; 33–37; 3:1f.); individual and community lamentation (2:19–25; 7; 8:22–34; 16:6–15); thanksgiving song (8:1–4; 15:1–6; 16:1–5); and didactic poem (3:3–12; 6). There appears to be more mixing of psalm types than in the psalter, and the progression of thought is not always as clear. In at least one respect, the Psalms of Solomon differ from the Davidic psalms: These psalms do not display the patina which comes with repeated liturgical handling, the wearing away of specific historical allusions which allows the psalter's hymns to be meaningful in situations far removed from their original one, as they are passed from one worshiper to another. To the contrary, the Psalms of Solomon preserve specific, thinly veiled allusions, sharp edges of historical reality.

Although it would be unfair to characterize the Psalms of Solomon as a montage of citations from the psalms and the prophets, there are numerous reflections of the biblical material to be found in these poems. Psalms of Solomon 17 has similarities to canonical Psalm 72, and there are echoes of Psalm 28 in our psalms. The similarity among the Psalms of Solomon, Baruch, and Isaiah 11 has long been noted. Repeatedly one hears echoes of the canonical books: adversaries who have trodden down the sanctuary (Isa 63:16–19; PssSol

1; 2); Israel as the "shoot of my planting" which "shall possess the land forever" (Isa 60:21; PssSol 14:3f.); the cries to God in distress (Ps 120:1; 130:1f.; PssSol 1:1); the turning away of the face of God (Ps 13:1; 22:24; Isa 64:7; Ezek 39:23f.; PssSol 2:8); a wreath of glory thrown to the ground (Lam 2:1; PssSol 2:21); the fate of the righteous as compared to the wicked (Prov 24:16–22; PssSol 3:9–12). The list is interminable, and the texture quite even. Conceptual constructs, individual ideas, and snatches of phrases from the Old Testament lie behind the Psalms of Solomon.

Parallels have been drawn between the Psalms of Solomon and the hymns in the opening chapters of Luke. Descriptions of the devout as "lambs among sinners" (PssSol 8:23) are common in the Gospels. God corrects the devout as "a beloved son" and as his "firstborn" (PssSol 13:9; cf. 2Sam 7:14), the discipline of Israel as "an only son" (PssSol 18:4; 4Ezra 6:58). These are familiar to New Testament readers. More specific than reflections which may well have their common source in the Old Testament are the titles of the Messiah. Although the "house of David" (Jer, Isa) or "my servant David" (Ezek) is expected to ascend the throne, the title "son of David" occurs here for the first time in Jewish literature (cf. numerous references in the Synoptic Gospels). The title "Lord Messiah," which becomes the favorite messianic title in the New Testament (christos kurios denotes Jesus Christ) outside the Gospels, appears only in Psalms of Solomon 17:32.

In the Codex Alexandrinus, the Psalms of Solomon are listed after both the Old Testament and New Testament and follow the two letters of Clement. However, in the extant Greek manuscripts of the text of the Psalms of Solomon they are uniformly placed with the wisdom literature, because the wisdom writings were popularly attributed to Solomon, and so the Psalms of Solomon were included among them.

Relation to apocryphal books

The Psalms of Solomon are unique neither in form (poetry, hymn) nor mood (diatribes, supplications, confessions). But in one point the Psalms of Solomon are singular. They call explicitly for a rebellion, albeit supported by divine intervention, against the government. Unlike the cryptic language of other apocalyptic literature, the criticism and challenge are open and unveiled. Such an open call for rebellion against foreign domination is rare in the contemporary literature. Most seditious compositions, such as Daniel and Revelation, are veiled in cryptic vocabulary innocuous in the view of outsiders. Unless the document was assured of a strictly controlled circulation, the community was either careless or made bold by its belief in the certainty of imminent divine intervention. Its subversiveness lies nearest to that of the Qumran War Scroll, which likewise aimed at specific targets—but the circulation of 1QM was severely restricted and its community closed to external investigation.

Although parallels between the Psalms of Solomon have been drawn in various directions, the only sure dependence between them and another apocryphal writing is between Psalms of Solomon 11:2–5 and 1 Baruch 5:5–8. Some scholars extend this alignment to include a larger section (1Bar 4:36–5:9 with PssSol 11) or find other parallels (1Bar 4:26 and PssSol 8:17; 1Bar 4:20 and PssSol 2:21–23) or even expand the parallels to include all of 1 Baruch. However, if we insist that proven parallels at minimum retain their relative verse sequence, we must examine a more restricted selection:

Psalms of Solomon 11:2	Stand on a high place, O Jerusalem, and look at your children; from the east and the west assembled together by the Lord.
1Baruch 5:5	Stand up, O Jerusalem, and stand upon a high place . . . and look at your children assembled from . . . west to east.
Psalms of Solomon 11:4	He flattened high mountains into level ground for them . . .
1Baruch 5:7	For God commanded every high mountain to be flattened . . . into level ground . . .
Psalms of Solomon 11:5	The forests shaded them . . . God made every fragrant tree to grow for them.
1Baruch 5:8	The forests and every fragrant tree shaded Israel at God's command.

A few have detected a dependence of Psalms of Solomon upon 1 Baruch, usually from the observation that the Baruch parallels fit their context and that the themes described are those appropriate to the Babylonian exile. However, most scholars insist that 1 Baruch is dependent upon the Psalms of Solomon because stanza seven of Baruch's "Poem of Consolation and Hope" (1Bar 5:5–9) is longer, disjunctive, and somewhat diffused, while the psalm is a tightly arranged and wholly consistent composition.

It seems clear that the Psalms of Solomon are not dependent upon 1 Baruch. It is not impossible, however, that they both are quoting some lost liturgical poem. But without the recovery of this hypothetical source, we may for the present assume that 1 Baruch is dependent upon the Psalms of Solomon.

Apart from this specific relationship, the connections are abundant between the Psalms of Solomon and the literature from Qumran. Isaiah 11, for instance, has exerted a strong influence on both. The "spirit of counsel and power, a spirit of knowledge and of the fear of Yahweh," of Isaiah 11:2, are echoed both in 1QS^b 5.25 and in Psalms of Solomon 17:37–40. The metaphors of Isaiah 11:4, "and he shall smite the earth with the rod of his mouth, and with the breath of his lips he shall slay the wicked" (RSV), are used in 1QS^b 5.24, 25a:

> And (thou shalt strike the peoples) by the might
> of thy (mouth)
> Thou shalt devastate the earth by thy sceptre, and
> by the breath of thy lips shalt thou slay the ungodly.

And they are echoed in Psalms of Solomon 17:23f.:

> To smash the arrogance of sinners like a potter's jar;
> . . . .
> to destroy the unlawful nations with the word of his mouth.

Imagery like "gird him with righteousness/strength" (Isa 11:5; 1QS^b 5.26a; PssSol 17:22) and "fruit of the lips" (Prov 18:20; 1QH 1.27f.; PssSol 15:3) is drawn from the Old Testament by both Qumran and the Psalms of Solomon, and indicates their common interest in and use of such imagery.

The Qumran community went into the desert to escape persecution and saw in this flight prophetic fulfillment:

> And when these things come to pass for the Community in Israel
> at these appointed times, they shall be separated from the midst
> of the habitation of perverse men to go into the desert to prepare
> the way of Him as it is written, "In the wilderness prepare the way
> of . . . Make straight in the desert a highway for our God"
> (1QS 8.12–14).[13]

Psalms of Solomon 17:15–17 knows of a flight of the devout from Jerusalem:

> No one among them in Jerusalem acted (with) mercy or truth.
> Those who loved the assemblies of the devout fled from them
> as sparrows fled from their nest.
> (They became) refugees in the wilderness
> to save their lives from evil.
> The life of one who was saved from them was precious in the eyes of the exiles.

The catalog of sins attributed to the usurpers of David's throne and Solomon's Temple are called the "three nets of Belial" in the Damascus Document:

> . . . these are Belial's three nets, of which Levi son of
> Jacob spoke, by which he (Belial) ensnared Israel,
> and which he set [be]fore them as three sorts of

---

[13] Translated by A. Dupont-Sommer, *The Essene Writings*, p. 92.

[14] Translated by A. Dupont-Sommer, *The Essene Writings*, pp. 128f.

righteousness: the first is lust, the second is riches,
(and) the third is defilement of the Sanctuary (CD 4.15–18).[14]

In the Psalms of Solomon the usurpers are described in detail and their sins are listed:

God exposed their sins in the full light of day;
. . . .
Everyone committed adultery with his neighbor's wife;
     they made with them agreements with an oath about these things.
They stole from the sanctuary of God
     as if there were no redeeming heir.
They walked on the place of sacrifice of the Lord
     (coming) from all kinds of uncleanness;
 . . . they defiled the sacrifices as if they were common meat (8:8–12).

The sins are the same three denounced in the Damascus Document, and they are cataloged
in the same order.

A miscellany of verbal and conceptual comparisons:

"Tree of Life" (1QH 8.5f.; PssSol 14:3)
"Driven/fled from the nest" (1QH 4.8f.; PssSol 17:16)
"Punishment for families" (CD 3.1; PssSol 9:5)
   Lions that "break the bones of the strong" (1QH 5.7; PssSol 13:3, 4:19)

Cultural importance

The few and scattered references to the Psalms of Solomon in Jewish and Christian
writings show that they did not enjoy any widespread influence upon religious literature.
The handful of allusions, none earlier than the fifth century, and the lateness of the extant
manuscripts, the earliest being copied more than a millennium after its composition, indicate
that the Psalms of Solomon achieved only limited circulation up until the end of the first
millennium of our era. Yet in certain times and places the Psalms of Solomon succeeded
as did none of the other writings included among the Pseudepigrapha. It is the only text
included in the present volumes listed in the canon in Codex Alexandrinus.

SELECT BIBLIOGRAPHY

Charlesworth, *PMR*, pp. 195–97.
Delling, *Bibliographie*, pp. 175f.
Denis, *Introduction*, pp. 60–69.

Baars, W. "Psalms of Solomon," in *The Old Testament in Syriac*. Leiden, 1972. (The
   most recent edition of the Syr. Introduction, Syr. text.)
Gebhardt, O. von. *Die Psalmen Salomos*. Leipzig, 1895. (The most thorough edition to
   date; collates five of eight then available MSS. Introduction, Gk. text, and nn.)
Gray, G. B. "The Psalms of Solomon," in *APOT*, vol. 2, pp. 625–52. (The most accessible
   ET of the PssSol. Introduction, translation, and nn.)
Hann, R. R. *The Manuscript History of the Psalms of Solomon*. SCS 13; Chico, Calif.,
   1982. (The most recent study of the relationship of the Gk. MSS.)
Holm-Nielsen, S. "Die Psalmen Salomos." *JSHRZ* 4 (1977) 51–112. [This German
   translation of the PssSol appeared too late for the contributor to consult. —J.H.C.]

La Cerda, J. *Adversaria sacra . . . accessit . . . Psalterium Salomonis.* Lyon, 1626. (The first published edition of the PssSol. Gk. text with Lat. translation. Thought to be based on the lost Codex Augustanus, since 1895 shown to be based on a faulty transcription of MS 149.)

Rahlfs, A. *Septuaginta id est Vetus Testamentum Graece.* Stuttgart, 1935. (Most accessible Gk. text. Based on von Gebhardt's edition.)

Ryle, H. S., and James, M. R. *Psalmoi Solomontos: Psalms of the Pharisees. Commonly Called the Psalms of Solomon.* Cambridge, England, 1891. (The most thorough English edition. Introduction, Gk. text, translation, and nn.)

Schüpphaus, J. *Die Psalmen Salomos: Ein Zeugnis Jerusalemer Theologie und Frömmigkeit in der Mitte des vorchristlichen Jahrhunderts.* ALGHJ 7; Leiden, 1977. [This monograph appeared too late for the contributor to consult. —J.H.C.]

Viteau, J. *Les Psaumes de Salomon*, in François Martin, *Documents pour l'étude de la Bible.* Paris, 1911, 2.4. (Introduction, extensive survey of literature, Gk. text, translation, and nn.)

Wright, R. B. "The Psalms of Solomon, the Pharisees, and the Essenes." SCS 2; 1972, pp. 136–47. (Examination of the origin of the PssSol which calls into question the assignment of the authorship to the Pharisees.)

PSALMS OF SOLOMON

1
A Psalm of Solomon

1	I cried out to the Lord when I was severely[a] troubled, to God when sinners set upon (me).	5:5; 15:1; 2Chr 12:12
2	Suddenly, the clamor of war was heard before me; "He will hear me, for I am full of righteousness."	8:1
3	I considered in my heart[b] that I was full of righteousness, for I had prospered and had many children.[c]	Isa 54:1
4	Their wealth was extended to the whole earth, and their glory to the end of the earth.	
5	They exalted themselves to the stars,[d] they said they would never fall.	Isa 14:13
6	They were arrogant in their possessions, and they did not acknowledge[e] (God).	Ps 29:1f.; 96:7f.
7	Their sins were in secret, and even I did not know.	4:5; 8:9
8	Their lawless actions surpassed the gentiles before them;[f] they completely profaned the sanctuary of the Lord.[g]	2:3; 8:12 Lev 19:8

2
A Psalm of Solomon Concerning Jerusalem

1	Arrogantly the sinner[a] broke down the strong walls[b] with a battering ram[c] and you did not interfere.	8:16–18 Ps 10:2 4Ezra 3:8

1 The psalmist, speaking as Jerusalem personified, is distressed by the attack on the holy city. The responses are the classic defenses of holding to one's integrity (vs. 2) like Job, and claiming the visible assurance of divine favor (vs. 3) like the Deuteronomist. But the children have turned out badly. Further, their sin has brought punishment, even worse than the gentile invasions in the past. PssSol 1 is a fragmentary poem which is dependent upon PssSol 2.

a. The Gk. reads: *eis telos*, which may mean (1) a dislocated title "to the Chief Musician" (see Ps 54[55]); however, the LXX rubric is *eis to telos*; (2) "to the end" either of time or of the author's endurance (Syr.: "at my end"); (3) an intensification "severely," as in 2Chr 12:12, 1Thes 2:16, and PssSol 2:5.

b. In the Semitic world both thought and emotion were located in the heart.

c. I.e. the citizens of Jerusalem. According to the Torah (Deut 7:12f.), the blessing of a large family was a reward for obedience.

d. Compare Isa 14:13: "I will climb up to the heavens; and higher than the stars of God."

e. "Pay tribute (to God)" as in Ps 29:1f.; 96:7f. Less likely is "they did not bring (offerings)" as in Ps 68:29; 76:11. The sinners had possession of God's blessings but were not properly thankful. Syr.: "they did not understand."

f. This may refer to earlier gentile incursions, e.g. Antiochus Epiphanes in the 2nd cent. B.C.

g. This may refer specifically to the services and sacrifices of the sanctuary as in Lev 19:8, or more generally to the Temple itself as in Ezek 5:11; 23:38, inclusive of both the buildings and the rites. Syr.: "the sanctuary."

2 Psalm 2 is one of three psalms, together with 8 and 17, containing historical allusions which provide clues for dating parts of the collection. The description in PssSol 2 agrees with the details of Pompey's capture of Jerusalem in 63 B.C. After being welcomed into the city (see 8:16–19), he could not take the Temple area without a fight. After a three-month siege, Pompey executed the resisters, the supporters of Aristobulus the high priest, and occupied the sanctuary. Pompey's assassination, in 48 B.C. in Egypt by Caesar's agents (vss. 26–29), is cheered as an act of God (vss. 32–35). It should be noted that it is Pompey the individual, not Imperial Rome, which is the enemy. Jerusalem was accorded special consideration by the caesars (see Josephus, *Ant* 14.10.1–10).

a. In eschatological literature, coded allusions to conquerors are carefully drawn to avoid obvious consequences (see 2Thes 2:3f.; 1Jn 2:18).

b. The walls surrounding the Temple area. Pompey had entered the city three months earlier without resistance (see 8:16–18).

c. Josephus reports that Pompey imported the machine from Tyre (*Ant* 14.4.2).

2 Gentile foreigners went up to your place of sacrifice;   8:12
      they arrogantly trampled (it) with their sandals.   Isa 63:18;
                                                                                   Ps 79:1

3 Because the sons of Jerusalem^d defiled the sanctuary of the Lord,   1:8; 8:11
      they were profaning the offerings^e of God with lawless acts;

4 Because of these things he said, "Remove them far from me;   Jer 7:15
      they are not sweet-smelling."^f

5 The beauty of his glory^g was despised before God;
      it was completely disgraced.

6 The sons and the daughters^h (were) in harsh captivity,
      their neck in a seal,ⁱ a spectacle among the gentiles.

7 He did (this) to them according to their sins,
      so that he abandoned them to the hands of those who prevailed.

8 For he turned away his face from their mercy;
      (from) young and old and their children once again,^j
      for they sinned once again by not listening.

9 And the heavens were weighed down,   Jer 2:12
      and the earth despised them,
      for no one on (the earth) had done what they did.

10 And the earth shall know all your righteous judgments, O God.   2:15; 5:1; 8:7f.;
                                                                                   9:5; 17:10

11 They^k set up the sons of Jerusalem for derision because of her prostitutes.
      Everyone passing by entered in in broad daylight.

12 They derided their lawless actions even in comparison to what they
      themselves were doing;^l
      before the sun they held up their unrighteousness to contempt.   8:8

13 And the daughters of Jerusalem were available to all, according to your
      judgments,^m
      because they defiled themselves with improper intercourse.ⁿ   8:9

14 My heart and my belly^o are troubled over these things.

15 I shall prove you right,^p O God, in uprightness of heart;   3:5; 4:8; 8:7,26;
      for your judgments are right, O God.   9:2
                                                                                   Ps 51:4; 119:7

---

d. "Sons of Jerusalem" (only in Joel 4:6); also "daughters of Jerusalem" (PssSol 2:13). In the context of vs. 3, the Temple and the services, the "sons of Jerusalem" may be the priests who attend the sanctuary and the rites.

e. Lit. "the gifts of God," a phrase used in the LXX of Lev 21:6 as "food of . . . God."

f. Other MSS read "fit (to be offered)." Some editors have conjectured "I have no pleasure in them," but for this there is no textual evidence. The awkwardness of the text has prompted ancient and modern attempts to smooth the reading. None is satisfactory.

g. The term "beauty of his glory" may refer to: (1) the Temple (as in Isa 60:7), or (2) a theophany (as in Ezek 1:28; 10:18), or (3) the Temple hangings (in Isa 6:1 the word *swl* similarly may be the draperies and tapestries of the sanctuary). Syr.: "He did not give them his glorious beauty."

h. Of Jerusalem; see vss. 3 and 13. Syr.: "her sons and daughters."

i. It was common to brand or tattoo slaves with the signet of the owner, usually on the forehead or hand (see 3Mac 2:29), rarely on the neck as here (see also SibOr 8.244). This may alternately refer to slave collars marked with the owner's name.

Syr.: "the people's sealed yoke is put around their neck."

j. "At once," "finally," "in a moment," "once for all." The idiom appears in PssSol 11:2 and in Isa 66:8, Ps 88(89):35, and 1Thes 2:18.

k. The foreigners, even by whose standards the sins of the Jerusalemites were despicable (see vs. 12). Some MSS read "he," i.e. God.

l. The *gentiles* derided the *Jews'* lawless actions; the *gentiles* held up the *Jews'* unrighteousness to contempt.

m. Not a specific verdict in this case, but the accumulated judgments which form the concept of the divine Law.

n. The Heb. may have been more explicit than the euphemistic Gk. translation, which is literally translated "mingled intermixing." Although racial mixing may have been feared, the context here suggests it is sexual improprieties which are probably intended (see PssSol 8:9, where a cognate is used to describe incest).

o. See Isa 16:11; Jer 4:19; Lam 1:20.

p. The idea that the devout are to "justify" God or "prove him right" appears often in these psalms (3:5; 4:8; 8:7, 26; 9:2). See also Ps 51:4; 119:7; Lam 1:18; Lk 7:29.

16 For you have rewarded the sinners according to their actions,
and according to their extremely wicked sins.

17 You have exposed their sins, that your judgment might be evident;   2:12; 8:8
you have obliterated their memory from the earth.

18 God is a righteous judge and he will not be impressed by appearances.   Deut 10:17

19 For the gentiles insulted Jerusalem, trampling (her) down;
he[q] dragged her beauty down from the throne of glory.[r]

20 She put on sackcloth instead of beautiful clothes,   Isa 3:24
a rope around her head instead of a crown.

21 She took off the wreath of glory which God had put on her;
in dishonor her beauty was thrown to the ground.

22 And I saw and implored in the Lord's presence and said,
"Let it be enough,[s] Lord,[t] to make your hand heavy[u] on Jerusalem[v]   5:6
by bringing gentiles (upon her)."

23 For they ridiculed (her) and did not refrain in anger and vicious rage,
and they will be finished unless you, Lord, censure them (= gentiles)
in your anger.

24 For they have not done it in zeal,[w] but in emotional passion,[x]
to pour out their anger against us in plunder.   Isa 10:5–11

25 Do not delay, O God, to repay to them on (their) heads;[y]
to declare dishonorable[z] the arrogance of the dragon.[a2]   Jer 51:34

26 And I did not wait long until God[b2] showed me his insolence
pierced[c2] on the mountains of Egypt,
more despised than the smallest thing on earth and sea.

27 His body was carried about on the waves[d2] in much shame,
and there was no one to bury (him),[e2] for he (God) had despised him
with contempt.

28 He did not consider that he was a man,
for the latter[f2]
do not consider (this).

29 He said, "I shall be lord of land and sea";
and he did not understand that it is God who is great,[g2]
powerful in his great strength.

30 He is king over the heavens,[h2]

q. The last antecedent mentioned is God, in vs. 18, but the Gk. translator, who appears untroubled by tense and person grammatical agreements, may be alluding to the gentile Pompey. Syr.: "was dragged down."

r. The reference could be to (1) the Temple (Jer 17:12), (2) the holy of holies, (3) God's throne (Isa 66:1), (4) the heavenly powers (TLevi 3:8; Eph 1:21; Col 1:16; 2En 20:1), (5) Jerusalem (Jer 14:21), or (6) the honorific place the holy city occupied (1Sam 2:8; Isa 22:23).

s. In the OT it is God who halts the punishment of the people (2Sam 24:16; 1Chr 21:15).

t. One MS adds "God."

u. See Ps 32:4.

v. One MS reads "Israel."

w. The gentiles, seen as God's agent, act in the Lord's "zeal" to punish evil (see Ezek 5:13; 16:38, 41; 38:19). But in this instance they have gone beyond their commission (PssSol 2:22) by exceeding the punishment appropriate to Israel's sin. They must be stopped and themselves punished.

x. Lit. "lust of soul."

y. This may be a pun on "head"; i.e. turn it back on their leader (as happens in the next vss.). Syr.: "thrown down."

z. This awkward phrase may be a mistranslation

from the Heb. The original meaning may have been to "turn the arrogance . . . into dishonor" (as Hos 4:7, "they have bartered their glory for shame"). Syr.: "to cast down in dishonor."

a2. The dragon image was often applied to Egypt (Ps 74:14; Ezek 29:3) and to Nebuchadnezzar (Jer 51:34 [LXX 28:32]). If the common code of identifying Rome with Babylon is employed here, the Roman Pompey would be the incarnation of the earlier conqueror of Jerusalem. The crocodile (Heb. tanin) of Ezek 32:2 and 29:3 is assumed by some to be the word behind the Gk. drakontos (dragon).

b2. Syr.: "the Lord."

c2. These details give us the clearest identification with Pompey, whose death, described by Plutarch, matches in most particulars (see also Dio Cassius 42.5).

d2. Other MSS read "rotted on the waves."

e2. The worst indignity at death was to fail to have a proper burial (Ps 79:3; 2Kgs 9:10; Jer 22:19). Pompey's decapitated and decomposing body was burned on a pyre of driftwood.

f2. "The latter," i.e. man.

g2. Syr.: "the Lord is God."

h2. Syr. adds, "and over the earth."

judging even kings and rulers,[i2]

31   Raising me up to glory,
         but putting to sleep the arrogant for eternal destruction in dishonor,
         because they did not know him.

32   And now, officials of the earth, see the judgment of the Lord,   Ps 2:10
         that he is a great and righteous king, judging what is under heaven.

33   Praise God, you who fear the Lord with understanding,
         for the Lord's mercy is upon those who fear him with judgment.

34   To separate between the righteous and the sinner
         to repay sinners forever according to their actions

35   And to have mercy on the righteous (keeping him) from the humiliation
            of the sinner,
         and to repay the sinner for what he has done to the righteous.

36   For the Lord is good[j2] to those who persistently call upon him,   9:6
         to treat his devout[k2] in accordance with his mercy,
         to bring them (constantly) before him in strength.

37   Praised be the Lord forever before his servants.

3

A Psalm of Solomon Concerning the Righteous

1   Why do you sleep, soul,[a] and do not praise the Lord?
         Sing[b] a new song[c] to God, who is worthy to be praised.

2   Sing and be aware of how he is aware of you,[d]   Isa 65:14; Judg
         for a good psalm to God is from a glad heart.[e]   16:25;
                                                       Ruth 3:7; Jas
                                                       5:13

3   The righteous remember[f] the Lord all the time,   2:10,15; 4:8;
         by acknowledging and proving the Lord's judgments right.   5:1; 8:7f.,23,
                                                                           34; 9:5; 10:5;
                                                                                          17:10

4   The righteous does not lightly esteem discipline[g] from the Lord;
         his desire is (to be) always in the Lord's presence.

5   The righteous stumbles[h] and proves the Lord right;
         he falls and watches for what God[i] will do about him;
         he looks to where his salvation comes from.   Ps 121:1; 123:1

6   The confidence[j] of the righteous (comes) from God their savior;
         sin after sin does not visit the house of the righteous.

7   The righteous constantly searches his house,[k]
         to remove his unintentional sins.

---

i2. Syr.: "kingdoms and princes."

j2. In Gk., this phrase, *chrēstos ho kurios* ("the Lord is good"), could be changed to *christos kurios*, "the Lord Messiah" (in the NT "Jesus Christ") by altering one eta to iota, an example of several opportunities to Christianize the text which was not appropriated by copyists in any extant manuscript.

k2. Some MSS read: "those with him."

3 a. Syr.: "Why sleep, my soul . . . ?"

b. "Sing" is plural, most likely because in six of seven passages in the OT in which "a new song" is invited, usually from choir or congregation, the verb is plural, and this writer unconsciously repeats a familiar phrase. Less probably, he is calling for the heavenly choirs to sing to God. The verb sing describes singing with the accompaniment

of a stringed instrument: lit. "strum a new song."

c. Other MSS read: "a song and a hymn."

d. Lit. "keep watching for his watching" or "be aware of his being aware of you." The Gk. and Syr. are obscure to the point of unintelligibility.

e. Other MSS read: "whole heart" (see Deut 6:5).

f. "Mention" (see Ps 63:6; 71:16; Isa 58:1; 62:6).

g. The word invokes the image of the training of a child.

h. Or "offends."

i. "Lord . . . God"; Syr.: "God . . . Lord."

j. Gk.: "truth," "faithfulness," or "dependability."

k. Syr.: "he (God) searches the house of the righteous."

8 He atones for (sins of) ignorance by fasting and humbling his soul,   18:4; Ps 35:13
       and the Lord will cleanse every devout[l] person and his house.[m]

9 The sinner stumbles and curses his life,
       the day of his birth, and his mother's pains.
10 He adds sin upon sin in his life;   Isa 30:1
       he falls—his fall is serious—and he will not get up.
11 The destruction of the sinner is forever,   2:31; 14:9;
       and he will not be remembered when (God) looks after the righteous.   15:10.12f.
12 This is the share[n] of sinners forever,
       but those who fear the Lord shall rise up to eternal life,[o]   13:11; 14:10
       and their life shall be in the Lord's light, and it shall never end.

4
A Conversation[a] of Solomon with Those Trying to Impress People[b]

1 Why are you sitting in the council[c] of the devout, you profaner?
       And your heart is far from the Lord,
       provoking the God of Israel by lawbreaking;
2 Excessive in words, excessive in appearance above everyone,[d]
       he who is harsh in words in condemning sinners at judgment.

3 And his hand is the first one against him[e] as if in zeal,   Deut 13:9f.
       yet he himself is guilty of a variety of sins and intemperance.[f]
4 His eyes are on every woman indiscriminately,[g]   8:9f.
       his tongue lies when swearing a contract.   4:11
5 At night and in hiding he sins as if no one saw.   1:7; 8:9
       With his eyes he speaks to every woman of illicit affairs;[h]
       he is quick to enter graciously every house as though innocent.
6 May God remove from the devout those who live in hypocrisy;
       may his flesh decay and his life be impoverished.
7 May God expose the deeds of those who try to impress people;   4:19
       (and expose) their deeds with ridicule and contempt.
8 And the devout will prove their God's judgment to be right   2:10; 3:3; 5:1;
       when sinners are driven out from the presence of the righteous,   8:7f.,23,34; 9:5;
       those who please men, who deceitfully quote the Law.   10:5; 17:10

9 And their eyes are on a man's peaceful house,
       as a serpent destroys the wisdom[i] of others with criminal words.
10 His words are deceitful that (he) may accomplish (his) evil desires;

l. "Devout." The Gk. corresponds to the Heb. *hasid*, from which comes the party name of the strictest observers of Judaism, the Hasidim (see 1Mac 2:42).

m. The devout eliminate all possible sins: repeated sins (vs. 6), accidental sins (vs. 7), and unknown sins (vs. 8).

n. "Portion," "fate," "doom," lit. "what is reserved for . . ." (see 4:14, 5:4, and 14:9; also Ps 49:13 RSV; 81:15).

o. As elsewhere, it is unclear whether this is the resurrection of the body (rise from the grave), or immortality of the spirit (rise to God), or, indeed, if this author distinguished the two. See Dan 12:2; 2Mac 7:9; Job 33:29f.

4 a. Other MSS read "Psalm."

b. "Those trying to be popular," "opportunists," or "demagogues," those who attempt to win public approval and applause at the sacrifice

of principle. PssSol 4 is an indictment of hypocritical political and religious leaders. The language is intense and shockingly vicious in its attack on those in the highest positions in government.

c. In the capital, in the first cent. B.C., the "assembly of the holy ones" (or "holy assembly" in some MSS) most probably refers to the supreme council, *the* Sanhedrin, rather than to a local Sanhedrin. Some MSS omit "of the devout."

d. I.e. verbose and ostentatious.

e. I.e. the sinner (vs. 2). Josephus spoke of the cruelty of certain council members in imposing harsh sentences (*Ant* 20.9.1).

f. Lack of self-control. One MS reads: "appears content."

g. Syr.: "immodestly."

h. Lit. "evil arrangements."

i. The allusion may be to the garden (Gen 3) in which the serpent worked on one to get at the other.

he did not stop until he succeeded in scattering (them) as orphans.

11 He devastated a house because of his criminal desire;
   he deceived with words; (as if) there were no one to see and to judge.

12 He is satiated with lawless actions at one (place), and (then) his eyes are
   on another house
   to destroy it with agitating words.ʲ

13 With all this his soul, like Hades, is not satisfied.

Isa 5:14; 14:9;
15:10; 16:12
Prov 27:20

14 Lord, let his part be in disgrace before you;
   may he go out groaning and return cursing.

Ps 69:23–29;
109:6–15; 121:8

15 Lord, may his life be in pain and poverty and anxiety;
   may his sleep be painful and his awakening be anxious.

16 May sleep be taken away from his temples at night;ᵏ
   may he fail disgracefully in all the work of his hands.

17 May he return to his house empty-handed;
   may his house lack everything; let it not satisfy his soul.ˡ

18 May his old age be in lonely childlessness until his removal.ᵐ

19 May the flesh of those who try to impress people be scattered by wild
   animals,
   and the bones of the criminals (lie) dishonored out in the sun.ⁿ

4:7

Ps 53:5; 79:2

20 Let crows peck out the eyes of the hypocrites,
   for they disgracefully empty many people's houses
   and greedily scatter (them).

Prov 30:17

21 They have not remembered God,
   nor have they feared God in all these things;
   but they have angered God, and provoked him.

22 May he banish them from the earth,
   for they defrauded innocent people by pretense.

4:6

23 Blessed are those who fear God in their innocence;
   the Lord shall save them from deceitful and sinful people
   and save us from every evil snare.

2:33

Ps 141:9

24 May God banish those who arrogantly commit all (kinds of)
   unrighteousness,
   for the Lord our God is a great and powerful judge in righteousness.

2:10,18; 5:1;
9:2,5; 10:5

25 Lord, let your mercy be upon all those who love you.

6:6; 10:3; 14:1

5
A Psalm of Solomon

1 Lord God, I will joyfully praise your name
   among those who know your righteous judgments.

10:5

2:10; 3:3; 4:8;
8:34

2 For you are good and merciful, the shelter of the poor.
   When I cry out to you, do not ignore me.

10:6; 15:1; 18:2

Ps 28:1

3 For no one takes plunder away from a strong man,
   so who is going to take (anything) from all that
   you have done, unless you give (it)?

Isa 49:24

---

j. Lit. "words that give wings."
k. See Judg 4:21–22; Ps 132:4).
l. Lit. "it will not fill his soul."
m. Lit. "taken up." The term is odd here,
because of its rarity (it is not found in the LXX
and only in Lk 9:51) and because it came to be a
technical term for "assumption," as applied later
to Enoch, Moses, and Abraham. Its use here may
be a clue for the dating of the Gk. translation of
the PssSol, for no Jew or Christian would employ
it in this context after it had become current in

Christian and Jewish literature and with that de-
notation (see 4Ezra 6:26; 8:20; AsMos 10:12). The
Syr. paraphrases the line: "and may not one of his
children come near to him."
   n. The OT describes the particular horror of
those who are denied burial. To lie exposed, to be,
in the words of Deut 28:26, "carrion for all the
birds of heaven and all the beasts of the earth,"
was the ultimate disgrace described by Jeremiah
(7:33; 8:1f.) and by Ezekiel (6:5; 29:5; 39:17).

4 For an individual and his fate (are) on the scales before you;
> he cannot add any increase contrary to your judgment, O God.

5 When we are persecuted, we call on you for help   1:1; 15:1
> and you will not turn away from our prayer;
> for you are our God.

6 Do not weigh down your hand on us,[a]   2:22
> lest under duress we sin.

7 Even if you do not restore us,   Ps 80:7,19
> we will not stay away, but will come to you.[b]

8 For if I am hungry, I will cry out to you, O God,   Ps 107:5f.
> and you will give me (something).

9 You feed the birds and the fish,
> as you send rain to the wilderness[c] that the grass may sprout

10 To provide pasture in the wilderness for every living thing,
> and if they are hungry, they will lift up their face to you.   Ps 145:15

11 You feed kings and rulers and peoples, O God,
> and who is the hope of the poor and the needy, if not you, Lord?   15:1

12 And you will listen. For who is good and kind but you,   Ps 86:1–6
> making the humble person happy[d] by opening your hand in mercy?

13 Human kindness (comes) sparingly, and tomorrow,[e]
> and if (it comes) a second time without complaint, this is remarkable.

14 But your gift is abundantly good and rich,   18:1
> and the one whose hope is in you will not be lacking gifts.

15 Lord, your mercy is upon the whole world in goodness.

16 Happy is (the person) whom God[f] remembers with a moderate sufficiency;   Prov 16:8; 30:8
> for if one is excessively rich, he sins.

17 Moderate (wealth) is adequate—with righteousness;
> for with this comes the Lord's blessing:
> to be (more than) satisfied with righteousness.

18 Those who fear the Lord are happy with good things.
> In your kingdom your goodness (is) upon Israel.

19 May the glory of the Lord be praised, for he is our king.   17:1,46

6

In Hope. Of Solomon

1 Happy is the man whose heart is ready to call on the name of the Lord;   10:1
> when he remembers the name of the Lord, he will be saved.   3:3

2 His ways are directed by the Lord,
> and the works of his hands are protected by the Lord[a] his God.   Ps 90:17

3 His soul will not be disturbed by the vision of evil dreams;
> he will not be frightened when crossing rivers or rough seas.

4 He gets up from his sleep and blesses the name of the Lord;
> when his heart is at rest he sings in honor of his God's[b] name.

5 He prays to the Lord for all his household,
> and the Lord has heard the prayers of all who fear God.[c]

---

5 a. Cf. Job 2:5.

b. Syr.: "and do not turn your face from us lest we go far from you."

c. "Empty grasslands."

d. Syr.: "satisfied."

e. The sense is that human help is always "too little and too late." In contrast, God's help is generous and prompt. All the devout need to do is to look up (vs. 10) and God provides. For "sparingly," one MS reads: "to a friend."

f. Syr.: "the Lord."

6 a. Syr. omits "Lord."

b. Syr. reads: "the Lord."

c. Syr. reads: "him."

6   And the Lord fulfills every request from the soul that hopes in him;
        praised is the Lord, who shows mercy to those who truly love him.   10:3; 14:1

7
Of Solomon. About Restoring[a]

1   Do not move away from us, O God,   1:1; 9:8; 17:5
        lest those who hate us without cause should attack us.   Ps 35:19

2   For you have rejected them, O God;
        do not let their feet trample your holy inheritance.[b]   2:2; 8:12; 17:22

3   Discipline us as you wish,   7:9; 8:26; 16:11;
        but do not turn (us) over to the gentiles.   18:7

4   For if you sent death (himself)[c]
        you would give him (special) instructions about us.

5   For you are kind,
        and will not be angry enough to destroy us.

6   While your name lives among us, we shall receive mercy
        and the gentile will not overcome us.

7   For you are our protection,
        and we will call to you, and you will hear us.

8   For you will have compassion on the people Israel forever
        and you will not reject (them);

9   And we are under your yoke forever,[d]
        and (under) the whip[e] of your discipline.   8:26; 16:11;

10   You will direct us in the time of your support,[f]   18:7
        showing mercy to the house of Jacob[g] on the day
        when you promised (it) to them.

8
Of Solomon. To Victory[a]

1   My ear heard distress and the sound of war,   1:2
        the blast of the trumpet sounding slaughter and destruction.

2   The sound of many people as of a violent storm,   Jer 4:11–13
        as a raging fire storm sweeping through the wilderness.

3   And I said to my heart, Where, then, will God judge it?[b]

4   I heard a sound in Jerusalem, the holy city.

5   My stomach was crushed at what I heard;   Isa 21:3; Jer
                                                    23:9

---

7 a. The title of this psalm appears to refer to the restoration of people to the protection of God (vss. 1–3) and under the discipline of God (vss. 5, 9). See 16:11.

b. The Temple; see 2:2, 19.

c. Lit. "death." The allusion of death with special instruction for the devout may be to the Exodus and to the tenth plague. The idiom "threat of death" conveys the two-stage process of (1) death being sent and (2) death claiming its victims. Here the first occurs, but the devout are spared the second.

d. The implication is twofold: (1) there is an obligation, sometimes severe, which the devout have toward God, and (2) they take it upon themselves voluntarily.

e. See 10:2.

f. The noun implies help which seizes hold to assist.

g. See "Jacob's God" in 15:1.

8 With PssSol 2 and 17, this psalm contains specific historical references to the capture of Jerusalem and the Temple by Pompey. Because of their sins, the Jews were drugged by God and offered no resistance to the Roman army until they reached the Temple. After the siege, some citizens were massacred and others taken as war prisoners to Rome. This psalm contains historical reflections (vss. 1–22) up to the point when the gentile armies take control of Jerusalem (which may be the time of composition) and then abruptly changes to a hymn of supplication for aid from God (vss. 23–34).

a. It is unclear whether the title refers to the gentile victory over Jerusalem, or to the hope of ultimate victory of God over the invaders.

b. Gk. and Syr. are obscure; the meaning appears to be "Is this the judgment of God?"

my knees were weak, my heart was afraid,
  my bones shook like reeds.[c]

6   I said, They directed their ways in righteousness.[d]

7   I thought about the judgments of God since the creation of heaven and
       earth;
     I proved God right in his judgments in ages past.   2:15; 3:3; 4:8;
                                                                          8:23,26; 9:2
8   God exposed their sins in the full light of day;   2:17; 4:7
     the whole earth knew the righteous judgments of God.

9   In secret places underground was their lawbreaking, provoking (him), 1:7; 4:5
       son involved[e] with mother and father with daughter;

10   Everyone committed adultery with his neighbor's wife;   4:4f.
       they made agreements with them with an oath about these things.[f]

11   They stole from the sanctuary of God
           as if there were no redeeming heir.

12   They walked on the place of sacrifice[g] of the Lord,
           (coming) from all kinds of uncleanness;
         and (coming) with menstrual blood (on them), they defiled the sacrifices
           as if they were common meat.   Ezek 4:14

13   There was no sin they left undone in which they did not surpass the 1:8; 2:9
           gentiles.

14   Because of this God mixed them (a drink) of a wavering spirit,[h]   Isa 19:14
           and gave them a cup of undiluted wine to make them drunk.   Isa 51:17-23

15   He brought someone from the end of the earth, one who attacks in strength;
           he declared war against Jerusalem, and her land.

16   The leaders of the country met him with joy.[i] They said to him,
           "May your way be blessed. Come, enter in peace."[j]

17   They graded the rough roads before his coming;[k]   Isa 40:3
           they opened the gates to Jerusalem, they crowned her city walls.[l]

18   He entered in peace as a father enters his son's house;
           he set his feet securely.[m]

19   He captured the fortified towers and the wall of Jerusalem,[n]   2:1
           for God led him in securely while they wavered.

20   He killed their leaders and every (man) wise in counsel;[o]
           he poured out the blood of the inhabitants of Jerusalem   Ps 79:3
           like dirty water.

21   He led away their sons and daughters, those profanely spawned.[p]

---

c. Lit. "linen" or "flax reeds."

d. The sense is that since Jerusalem had (supposedly) always done what is right, in the time of
attack God would protect it (see 1:2).

e. Lit. "mixed," see 2:13.

f. This probably refers to the test for unfaith-
fulness described in Num 5:19, which requires an
affirmation and an ordeal to clear oneself of a
charge of infidelity.

g. Syr.: "Temple."

h. See Isa 19:14: "giddiness" (JB), "dizziness"
(NAB).

i. Josephus reports the meeting between Pompey
and the leaders of the opposing factions, Hyrcanus
and Aristobulus. Each wanted Pompey's help against
the other to confirm his control over the country
(Ant 14.3.2).

j. Josephus describes how all the resistance to
Pompey's advance was cleared (Ant 14.3.4).

k. This is almost a parody on the messianic
announcement of Isa 40:3: "Make a straight highway for our God across the desert." One MS reads:

"their coming."

l. The people lined up on top of the walls to
hail the invader.

m. Lit: "with great firmness."

n. Josephus recounts (Ant 14.4.2) how those
opposed to Aristobulus allowed Pompey to occupy
the city and the king's palace, but Aristobulus'
partisans barricaded themselves inside the Temple
compound and were only expelled after three
months of intense fighting.

o. Josephus reports the priests continued to
conduct the service while the Roman soldiers cut
them down with their swords (War 1.7.5). Some
twelve thousand citizens died in the assault on the
Temple, not all at the hands of the Romans,
according to the same historian (War 1.7.5).

p. Lit. "those born in defilement." Josephus
reports that Pompey exiled Aristobulus and his
sons and daughters to Rome (War 1.7.5, confirmed
by Plutarch). Many Judeans were taken prisoner
and marched through Rome to celebrate Pompey's
great military successes (Ant 14.4.4).

22   They acted according to their uncleanness, just as their ancestors;
        they defiled Jerusalem and the things that had been consecrated to the   1:8; 2:3
        name of God.

23   God was proven right in his condemnation of the nations of the earth,   2:10,15
        and the devout of God are like innocent lambs among them.   2:36; 13:10,12
24   Worthy of praise is the Lord, who judges the whole earth in his righteousness.   3:1; 8:34
25   See, now, God, you have shown us how you rightly judge;
        our eyes have seen[q] your judgments, O God.
26   We have proven your name right, which is honored forever,   8:7
        for you are the God of righteousness,
        judging Israel in discipline.   13:7–10; 18:4
27   O God, turn your mercy upon us and be compassionate to us.   5:7; 7:8; 9:8
28   Bring together the dispersed of Israel with mercy and goodness,   9:2; 11:3; 2Bar
        for your faithfulness is with us.   78:7
29   For we stiffened our necks, but you are the one who disciplines us.
30   Do not neglect us, Our God,
        lest the gentiles devour us as if there were no redeemer.
31   But you (have been) our God from the beginning,
        and on you we have hoped, Lord.   5:11; 9:10; 15:1;
           17:3
32   And we will not leave you,   5:7
        for your judgments upon us are good.   3:3; 4:8; 5:1;
           17:10

33   May (you) be pleased with us and our children forever;
        Lord, our savior, we will not be troubled at the end of time.   3:6; 16:4; 17:3
34   Worthy of praise is the Lord for his judgments by the mouth of the devout,
        and may Israel be blessed by the Lord forever.   5:18; 8:24; 9:11;
           10:8; 11:9; 12:6

9
Of Solomon. For Proof

1   When Israel[a] was taken into exile to a foreign country,
        when they neglected the Lord,[b] who had redeemed them,
     They were expelled from the inheritance
        which the Lord had given them.   Jer 16:13; 22:26
2   The dispersion of Israel (was) among every nation,   8:28; 11:3
        according to the saying of God;
     That your righteousness might be proven right, O God, in our lawless
        actions.
        For you are a righteous judge over all the peoples of the earth.   2:18; 4:24
3   For none that do evil shall be hidden from your knowledge,
        and the righteousness of your devout is before you, Lord.
        Where, then, will a person hide himself from your knowledge, O
        God?

4   Our works (are) in the choosing and power of our souls,
        to do right and wrong in the works of our hands,
        and in your righteousness you oversee human beings.
5   The one who does what is right saves up life for himself with the Lord,
        and the one who does what is wrong causes his own life to be
        destroyed;
        for the Lord's righteous judgments are according to the individual and
        the household.[c]

---

q. Other MSS read: "their eyes have seen."   b. Syr.: "God."
        c. Syr.: "according to every person and his
9 a. One MS reads: "Jerusalem."   house."

6   To whom will you be good, O God,[d] except to those who call upon the   2:36
           Lord?
           He will cleanse from sins the soul in confessing, in restoring,[e]
           so that for all these things the shame is on us, and (it shows) on our
               faces.

7   And whose sins will he forgive except those who have sinned?
           You bless the righteous, and do not accuse them for what they sinned.
    And your goodness is upon those that sin, when they repent.

8   And now, you are God and we are the people whom you have loved;
           look and be compassionate, O God of Israel, for we are yours,
           and do not take away your mercy from us, lest they[f] set upon us.   7:1; 16:6

9   For you chose the descendants of Abraham above all the nations,
           and you put your name upon us, Lord,
           and it[g] will not cease forever.

10   You made a covenant with our ancestors concerning us,
           and we hope in you when we turn our souls toward you.

11   May the mercy of the Lord be upon the house of Israel forevermore.   10:8; 11:9; 12:6

10
A Hymn[a] of Solomon

1   Happy is the man whom the Lord remembers with rebuking,   6:1
           and protects[b] from the evil way with a whip
           (that he may) be cleansed from sin that it may not increase.

2   The one who prepares (his) back for the whip shall be purified,   Isa 50:6
           for the Lord is good to those who endure discipline.   2:36; 5:2,12;
                                                    14:1; 16:13f.

3   For he will straighten the ways of the righteous,
           and will not bend (them) by discipline;
           and the mercy of the Lord is upon those who truly love him.   4:25; 6:6; 14:1

4   And the Lord will remember his servants in mercy,
           for the testimony of it (is) in the Law of the eternal covenant,
           and the testimony of the Lord (is) in the ways of men
           in (his) supervision.   3:11; 11:1

5   Our Lord[c] is just and holy in his judgments forever,[d]   2:10,15; 3:3;
           and Israel shall praise the Lord's name[e] in joy.   4:8; 5:1; 8:7,
                                                    23,32,34; 9:5;
                                                    17:10

6   And the devout shall give thanks in the assembly of the people,   15:3
           and God[f] will be merciful to the poor to the joy of Israel.   5:2,11; 15:1;
                                                    18:2

7   For God is good and merciful forever,   2:36; 5:2,12;
           and the synagogues of Israel will glorify the Lord's name.   7:5; 10:2

8   The Lord's salvation (be) upon the house of Israel
           (that they may be) happy forever.   9:11; 11:9; 12:6

11
Of Solomon. In Anticipation

1   Sound in Zion the signal trumpet of the sanctuary;   2Chr 13:12;
           announce in Jerusalem the voice of one bringing good news,   1Mac 4:40; 7:4
           for God has been merciful to Israel in watching over them.   Isa 52:7
                                                                          3:11; 10:4

---

d. Syr.: "is God good."
e. Syr. omits.
f. Syr.: "the peoples."
g. Other MSS read: "you."

10 a. One MS reads: "In Hymns."

b. Syr.: "restrains."
c. Syr.: "Our God."
d. Syr.: "upright in all his judgments."
e. One MS adds: "forever."
f. Syr.: "the Lord."

2   Stand on a high place, Jerusalem, and look at your children,
        from the east and the west assembled together by the Lord.   8:28; 9:2;
3   From the north they come in the joy of their God;   2Bar 78:7
        from far distant islands God has assembled them.
4   He flattened high mountains into level ground for them;   Isa 40:4
        the hills fled at their coming.
5   The forests[a] shaded them as they passed by;
        God made every fragrant tree to grow for them.
6   So that Israel might proceed under the supervision of the glory of their   3:11; 10:4; 11:1
        God.
7   Jerusalem, put on (the) clothes of your glory,   1Bar 5:1–3; Isa
        prepare the robe of your holiness,   52:1
    for God has spoken well of Israel forevermore.   1Bar 5:4
8   May the Lord do what he has spoken about Israel and Jerusalem;
        may the Lord lift up Israel in the name of his glory.
9   May the mercy of the Lord be upon Israel forevermore.   9:11; 10:8; 12:6

12
Of Solomon. About the Tongue of Criminals

1   Lord, save my soul from the criminal and wicked man,   Ps 120:2
        from the criminal and slandering tongue
        that speaks lies and deceit.
2   The words of the wicked man's tongue (are) twisted so many ways;[a]
        (they are) as a fire among a people which scorches its beauty.[b]
3   His visit fills homes with a false tongue,
        cuts down trees of joy,[c] inflaming criminals;
        by slander[d] he incites homes to fighting.[e]
4   May God remove the lips of the criminals in confusion far from the   Ps 12:3f.
        innocent,
        and (may) the bones of the slanderers be scattered far from those who   4:19
        fear the Lord.
    May he destroy the slanderous tongue in flaming fire far from the devout.   4:8
5   May the Lord protect the quiet person who hates injustice;
        may the Lord guide the person who lives peacefully at home.   6:2; 7:10; 16:9;
6   May the salvation of the Lord be upon Israel his servant forever;   18:8
        may the wicked perish once and for all from before the Lord.   17:21; Isa 42:1–
    And may the Lord's devout inherit the Lord's promises.   4; 49:1–6; 50:4–
                                                                                  9; 52:13–53:12

13
Of Solomon. A Psalm: Comfort for the Righteous

1   The right hand of the Lord covered me;[a]   Ps 98:1; WisSol
        the right hand of the Lord spared me.   5:16; 19:8
2   The arm of the Lord saved us[b] from the sword that passes through,
        from famine and the sinners' death.   15:7
3   Wild animals attacked them viciously,   Ezek 14:13–23
        they tore their flesh with their teeth,
        and crushed their bones with their molars.
4   The Lord protected us from meeting all these things.

---

11 This psalm is related to 1Bar 4:36–5:9, and   12 a. Other MSS read: "for doing perversity."
both passages are linked to Isa 40–66. See Intro-   b. Other MSS read: "are as a fire on a threshing
duction.   floor (which) burns up straw."
    a. Syr. reads: "The cedars."

5   The godless person[c] was terrified by his mistakes
         lest he be taken along with the sinners.
6   For the destruction of the sinner is terrible;
         but nothing shall harm the righteous, of all these things.
7   For the discipline of the righteous (for things done) in ignorance
         is not the same as the destruction of the sinners.
8   In secret the righteous are disciplined
         lest the sinner gloat over the righteous.
9   For he will admonish the righteous as a beloved son   18:4; WisSol
         and his discipline is as for a firstborn.   11:10
10   For the Lord will spare his devout,
         and he will wipe away their mistakes with discipline.
11   For the life of the righteous (goes on) forever,   3:12; 10:8; 12:6
         but sinners shall be taken away to destruction,
         and no memory of them will ever be found.   2:31; 3:11; 9:5;
                                                                  14:9; 15:10
12   But the Lord's mercy is upon the devout
         and his mercy is upon[d] those who fear him.

14
A Hymn of Solomon

1   The Lord is faithful to those who truly love him,   17:10
         to those who endure his discipline,   10:2; 16:15
2   To those who live in the righteousness of his commandments,
         in the Law, which he has commanded for our life.[a]   Ps 1:2
3   The Lord's devout shall live by it forever;   Lev 18:5
         the Lord's paradise, the trees of life,[b] are his devout ones.   Isa 61:3; Ps
                                                                  92:13; 1En
4   Their planting is firmly rooted forever;   10:16; 93:2-5
         they shall not be uprooted as long as the heavens shall last,[c]
5   For Israel is the portion and inheritance of God.   7:2; 8:31; 9:8

6   But not so are sinners and criminals,
         who love (to spend) the day in sharing their sin.

---

c. The meaning of this phrase is obscure. Other MSS read: "to cut down trees of burning evil glee." See 14:3, where the devout are described as "the Lord's paradise, the trees of life." Syr.: "He cut down the trees of His pleasure with the fire of the criminal."

d. Lit.: "whispering lips."

e. Some MSS and the Syr. read: "criminals incite"; other MSS read: "he incites criminal homes."

13 a. Syr.: "us."

b. Syr.: "me."

c. Lit. "the non-worshiper." The psalmist describes the difference in attitudes between devout and secular persons. The secular person is terrified when he sins, for he knows the fate of the sinner. The devout person is not frightened, for he is not accused when he sins (9:7), for in God's care nothing can happen to him (13:6b). There is a difference in the fate of the devout and of the sinner (13:7). There is no MS evidence for the conjectural emendation to "righteous" made by nearly all the commentators. Nor is it required by the sense of the argument. The righteous, unlike the wicked, need not fear discipline (vs. 9), for God "wipe[s] away their mistakes" (vs. 10). God's discipline is like that of a loving father (vs. 9), and the righteous continue forever (vs. 11). Not so the wicked, for unlike the discipline of the righteous, his fate is destruction (vs. 7). With good reason is the godless person terrified by his mistakes: his fate is awful (vs. 6). See also PssSol 3:5, where the righteous, when he stumbles, proves God to be faithful and looks to him for help.

d. Syr.: "he will treasure."

14 Canonical Ps1 is the faint model for this poem, in the contrast between the fate of the devout and that of the sinner. Note "Law" (PssSol 14:2/Ps 1:2); "trees of life" (PssSol 14:3/1:3); "not so" (14:6/1:4); "brief and mortal"/"chaff" (cf. 14:7/1:4); "he knows"/"takes care of" (14:8/1:6).

a. Syr.: "He has given us the law for our life."

b. A common allusion in Prov for one who is a source of life and vitality (Prov 3:18; 11:30; 13:12; 15:4). See also Ps 1:3.

c. Lit. "all the days of heaven."

7 Their enjoyment is brief and decaying,
  and they do not remember God. 4:21

8 For the ways of men are known before him always, 9:3; Sir 17:15
  and he knows the secrets of the heart before they happen. WisSol 1:8f.;
  1En 9:11

9 Therefore their inheritance is Hades, and darkness and destruction; 4:13; 15:10;
  16:2
  and they will not be found on the day of mercy for the righteous.

10 But the devout of the Lord will inherit life in happiness. 3:12; 10:8;
   13:11; 15:13

15
A Psalm of Solomon with Song

1 When I was persecuted I called on the Lord's name; 1:1; 5:5
  I expected the help of Jacob's God[a] and I was saved. 7:10
  For you, O God, are the hope and refuge of the poor. 5:2; 10:6; 18:2

2 For who, O God, is strong except he who confesses you in truth; 6:6; 10:3; 14:1
  and what person is powerful except he who confesses your name?

3 A new psalm[b] with song with a happy heart,
  the fruit of the lips with the tuned instrument of the tongue, Hos 14:2; Isa
  57:18
  the first fruits of the lips from a devout and righteous heart.

4 The one who does these things will never be disturbed by evil;
  the flame of fire and anger against the unrighteous shall not touch him 13:6

5 when it goes out from the Lord's presence against sinners
  to destroy the sinners' every assurance.

6 For God's mark[c] is on the righteous for (their) salvation. Rev 7:3; 9:4

7 Famine and sword and death shall be far from the righteous; 7:4; 13:2
  for they will retreat from the devout like those pursued by famine.

8 But they shall pursue sinners and overtake them,
  for those who act lawlessly shall not escape the Lord's judgment.

9 They shall be overtaken as by those experienced in war,
  for on their forehead (is) the mark of destruction. 9:6

10 And the inheritance of sinners is destruction and darkness, 14:9
   and their lawless actions[d] shall pursue them below into Hades.

11 Their inheritance shall not be found for their children,
   for lawless actions[e] shall devastate the homes of sinners.

12 And sinners shall perish forever in the day of the Lord's judgment,
   when God oversees the earth at his judgment.[f] 3:11

13 But those who fear the Lord shall find mercy in it
   and shall live by their God's mercy;
   but sinners shall perish for all time.

16
A Hymn of Solomon. For Help for the Devout[a]

1 When my soul slumbered, (I was far away) from the Lord, wretched for
    a time;[b]
  I sank into sleep, far from God.

---

15 a. Syr.: "I called to the God of Jacob for my help."

b. Other MSS read: "A psalm and a hymn" (see 3:1).

c. The mark of salvation is in contrast to the mark of destruction (vs. 9).

d. Other MSS read: "sins."

e. Syr.: "their lawless acts."

f. Other MSS add: "to punish sinners forever," and omit vs. 13c, "but sinners shall perish for all time."

16 a. Some MSS omit "for the devout."

b. The Gk. is awkward and nearly unintelligible. Lit. "in the sleepiness of my soul from God . . . by a little wretchedness . . ."

2   For a moment my soul was poured out to death;   Isa 53:12
         (I was) near the gates of Hades with the sinner
3   Thus my soul was drawn away from the Lord[c] God of Israel,
         unless the Lord had come to my aid with his everlasting mercy.
4   He jabbed me as a horse is goaded to keep it awake;
         my savior and protector at all times saved me.
5   I will give thanks to you, O God, who came to my aid
             for (my) salvation,
         and who did not count me with the sinners for (my) destruction.
6   Do not take your mercy away from me, O God,   7:1; 9:8
         nor your memory from my heart until death.
7   Restrain me, O God, from sordid sin,
         and from every evil woman who seduces the foolish.   Prov 6:24f.; Sir
                                                                          9:8; 25:21
8   And may the beauty of a criminal woman not deceive me,
         nor anyone subject to useless sin.
9   Direct the works of my hands before you,[d]
         and protect my steps in your remembrance.   6:2; 9:4; 10:3
10   Protect my tongue and my lips with words of truth;
         put anger and thoughtless rage far from me.
11   Put grumbling and discouragement in persecution far from me.
         If I sin, discipline (me) that (I may) return.

12   With approval and happiness support my soul;
         when you strengthen my soul, what has been given is enough for me.
13   For if you do not give strength,
         who can endure discipline in poverty?   2:36; 10:2; 14:1
14   When a person is tried by his mortality,[e]
         your testing is in his flesh, and in the difficulty of poverty.
15   If the righteous endures all these things, he will   3:3f.
         receive mercy from the Lord.

17
A Psalm of Solomon, with Song, to the King

1   Lord, you are our king forevermore,   5:19; 17:46
         for in you, O God, does our soul take pride.
2   How long is the time of a person's life on the earth?
         As is his time, so also is his hope in him.
3   But we hope in God our savior,   3:6; 8:33
         for the strength of our God is forever with mercy.
     And the kingdom of our God is forever over the   Ps 145:13
         nations in judgment.[a]
4   Lord, you chose David to be king over Israel,
         and swore to him about his descendants forever,[b]   2Sam 7
         that his kingdom should not fail before you.
5   But (because of) our sins, sinners[c] rose up against us,

c. Syr. omits "Lord."
d. So the Syr.; Gk.: "in your place."
e. Lit. "By the hand of his mortality."

17 This third psalm with historical reflections (with 2 and 8) recites, after an opening hymn to the everlasting faithfulness of God, the immediate past history of the community, first under an illegitimate leadership, then under foreign domination. When the oppression becomes unbearable, evil pervasive, and hope of relief gone save for flight to the wilderness, then nature rebels and signals an outpouring of apocalyptic fervor, and the scene shifts from historical recital to eschatological entreaty. The remainder of the psalm is an extended hymn describing in vivid poetic imagery the expected overthrow of local and foreign enemies, the return of the Diaspora, the revitalization of Jerusalem, and the establishment of universal and everlasting peace under the leadership of the Lord Messiah.
   a. Some MSS omit "in judgment."
   b. Syr. omits "forever."
   c. These sinners are Judeans, not gentiles (as in 1:1; 2:1). The Hasmoneans are probably intended, as illegitimate usurpers of the government and religion.

they set upon us and drove us out.
Those to whom you did not (make the) promise,
    they took away (from us) by force;
    and they did not glorify your honorable name.[d]   8:26

6   With pomp they set up a monarchy because of their arrogance;
    they despoiled the throne of David with arrogant shouting.

7   But you, O God, overthrew them, and uprooted their
    descendants from the earth,[e]   4:22
for there rose up against them a man alien to our race.[f]

8   You rewarded them, O God, according to their sins;   2:16,35
    it happened to them according to their actions.

9   According to their actions,[g] God showed no[h] mercy to them;
    he hunted down their descendants,
        and did not let even one of them go.

10   The Lord is faithful in all his judgments   2:15; 3:3; 5:1;
    which he makes in the world.   8:7f.,23,34;
        10:5

11   The lawless one[i] laid waste our land, so that no one inhabited it;
    they massacred young and old and children at the same time.

12   In his blameless wrath[j] he expelled them to the west,
    and he did not spare even the officials of the country from ridicule.

13   As the enemy (was) a stranger
    and his heart alien to our God, he acted arrogantly.

14   So he did in Jerusalem[k] all the things
    that gentiles do for their gods in their cities.

15   And the children of the covenant (living) among the gentile rabble
    adopted these (practices).
No one among them in Jerusalem acted (with) mercy or truth.   Ps 14:3

16   Those who loved the assemblies of the devout[l] fled from them   10:7; 17:43f.
    as sparrows fled from their nest.   Ps 11:1

17   (They became) refugees in the wilderness
    to save their lives from evil.
The life of even one who was saved from them was precious in the eyes
        of the exiles.

18   They were scattered over the whole earth by (these) lawless ones.

For the heavens withheld rain from falling on the earth.
19   Springs were stopped,
        (from) the perennial (springs) far underground   AsMos 10:6
        (to) those in the high mountains.
For there was no one among them[m]
    who practiced righteousness or justice:

20   From their leader to the commonest of the people,
    (they were) in every kind of sin:
        The king was a criminal
        and the judge disobedient;
        (and) the people sinners.[n]

---

d. Lit. "they did not glorify . . . with glory."
  e. Another reference (see 8:21) to Pompey's taking Aristobulus and his children to Rome (Josephus, *Ant* 14.4.5, 5.4, 6.1; *War* 1.7.7, 8.6).
  f. Pompey.
  g. Some MSS and Syr. omit "according to their actions."
  h. Some MSS and Syr. omit "no."
  i. Some MSS read: "the storm."
  j. Lit. "the wrath of his beauty"; Syr.: "the

beauty of his wrath." Unless this awkward phrase is a mistranslation from the original Heb., it refers to God's "righteous indignation."
  k. Syr. reads: "and Jerusalem did."
  l. Some MSS omit "of the devout."
  m. The citizens of Jerusalem (see vs. 15).
  n. Lit. "The king (was) in transgression,
    the judge in disobedience [Syr. reads:
    "in wrath"],
    the people in sin."

21 See,[o] Lord, and raise up for them their king,
the son of David, to rule over your servant Israel 12:6; Isa 42:1–4; 49:1–6; 50:4–9; 52:13–53:12
in the time known to you,[p] O God.
22 Undergird him with the strength[q] to destroy the unrighteous rulers, Ps 18:33
to purge Jerusalem from gentiles
who trample her to destruction; 2:2,19
23 in wisdom and in righteousness[r] to drive out
the sinners from the inheritance; 7:2; 9:1
to smash the arrogance of sinners
like a potter's jar; Ps 2:9
24 To shatter all their substance with an iron rod;
to destroy the unlawful nations with the word of his mouth;
25 At his warning the nations will flee from his presence; Ps 104:7
and he will condemn sinners by the thoughts of their hearts.

26 He will gather a holy people[s] 9:2; 11:3
whom he will lead in righteousness;[t]
and he will judge the tribes of the people
that have been made holy by the Lord their God.
27 He will not tolerate unrighteousness (even) to pause among them, Ps 101:7
and any person who knows wickedness shall not live with them.
For he shall know them
that they are all children of their[u] God.
28 He will distribute them upon the land 11:3; Isa 49:6; Ezek 45:8; 47:13,21
according to their tribes;
the alien and the foreigner will no longer live near them.[v]
29 He will judge peoples and nations in the wisdom of his righteousness. 18:9
Pause.
30 And he will have gentile nations serving him under his yoke,[w]
and he will glorify the Lord in (a place) prominent (above) the whole earth.
And he will purge Jerusalem
(and make it) holy as it was even from the beginning,
31 (for) nations to come[x] from the ends of the earth to see his glory, Isa 55:5
to bring as gifts her children who had been driven out,
and to see the glory of the Lord[y]
with which God has glorified her.
32 And he will be a righteous king over them, taught by God.
There will be no unrighteousness among them in his days, Jer 23:5
for all shall be holy,
and their king shall be the Lord Messiah.[z]

o. Other MSS read: "Know this."

p. One of the apocalyptic secrets is the time of the various events (see Ps 75:2f.; 69:13; Zech 14:1f.). Other MSS, including Syr., read: "you have seen."

q. The strength is to accomplish a series of tasks which follow. Grammatically the verb controls a string of infinitives which follow.

r. Syr. omits "in wisdom and in righteousness."

s. One Syr. MS reads: "a righteous people."

t. Syr.: "He will gather a holy people who shall glorify themselves."

u. Syr. omits "their."

v. Syr. reads: "will live near them because . . ." The purification of the land in the last days by the expulsion of foreigners was a common motif. See Neh 13:3; also Ezek 44:9 and Joel 4:17. But see below, vss. 30–32 and 34 (cf. Ezek 47:22f.), where aliens are to come with gifts and remain to serve God.

w. See 7:9.

x. The nations who took the Judeans into exile (Diaspora) are now to restore them to their homeland (see Isa 2:2–4). Other MSS read: "come, nations . . ."

y. The context leaves ambiguous whether this refers to the purified Temple, or to the newly anointed king.

z. "Lord Messiah." A title for the expected apocalyptic king. Most commentators have emended the text to read: "the Lord's Messiah," regarding it as a mistranslation (with the LXX of Lam 4:20) of an original and common Heb. phrase, "Messiah of Yahweh." However, there is evidence for retaining the reading of the text. The Gk. and Syr. MSS are uniform in reading "Lord Messiah."

33   (For) he will not rely on horse and rider and bow,
         nor will he collect gold and silver for war.
     Nor will he build up hope in a multitude for a day of war.

34   The Lord himself is his king,
         the hope of the one who has a strong hope in God.

     He shall be compassionate to all the nations
         (who) reverently (stand) before him.

35   He will strike the earth with the word of his mouth forever;
         he will bless the Lord's people with wisdom and happiness.   10:6.8; 14:10

36   And he himself (will be) free from sin, (in order) to rule a great people.   Isa 11:4
     He will expose officials and drive out sinners
         by the strength of his word.

37   And he will not weaken in his days, (relying) upon his God,
         for God made him
         powerful in the holy spirit   Isa 11:2
         and wise in the counsel of understanding,
         with strength and righteousness.

38   And the blessing of the Lord will be with him in strength,
         and he will not weaken;

39   His hope (will be) in the Lord.
     Then who will succeed against him,[a2]

40   mighty in his actions
         and strong in the fear of God?
     Faithfully and righteously shepherding the Lord's flock,
         he will not let any of them stumble in their pasture.

41   He will lead them all in holiness[b2]
         and there will be no arrogance among them,
         that any should be oppressed.

42   This is the beauty of the king of Israel[c2]
         which God knew,
         to raise him over the house of Israel
         to discipline it.

43   His words will be purer than the finest gold, the best.
     He will judge the peoples in the assemblies,   10:7; 17:16
         the tribes of the sanctified.
     His words will be as the words of the holy ones,[d2]   Ps 89:5–7;
         among sanctified peoples.   Job 5:1

There is no textual evidence for reading "Lord's Messiah."

The arguments that *christos kurios* cannot represent the original text rest on the assumptions (1) that the Semitic original was a form of *mešiah yhwh* and (2) that the phrase, in the mouth of a Judean Jew, could only have meant "the LORD'S Messiah."

Against these assumptions are the following: (1) Lk 2:11 demonstrates that *christos kurios* was available for use as a messianic title by the first cent. A.D. (2) There are references in which *kurios* is not a translation of *yhwh* but part of a royal title; Herod the Great (37–4 B.C.), and Herod Agrippa I (A.D. 39–44) were all called *basileus kurios*, "the lord king." Since the adjectival use of *kurios* had as well the connotation "legitimate," it is not inconceivable that a group of religious and political dissidents such as the authors of the PssSol would have described the anticipated righteous king by that adjective with the phrase *christos kurios* and so denied the implication of legitimacy to the present, corrupt rulers.

The assumption that *christos kurios* was an impossible combination in the mouth of a devout Judean Jew is to read *christos* in terms of its meaning for later Christology and not in terms of its use as a political title in its own time. Certainly the related title "King Messiah" was known to the later Jewish tradition. It was attested in GenR 2 and applied in LamR to Simon Bar Kokhba.

That *christos kurios* is a Christian interpolation or mistranslation is unlikely, as other texts (e.g. 1:8), which would be equally tempting to a Christianizing scribe, were not emended in similar directions.

The term is preserved here with the MS evidence as a current messianic title combining the concepts of lordship and anointed agent.

a2. Syr. reads: "for who shall stand against him."

b2. Other MSS read: "equality."

c2. One MS reads: "king of Jerusalem."

d2. Angels.

44   Blessed are those born in those days   18:6
         to see the good fortune of Israel[e2]
         which God will bring to pass in the assembly of the tribes.

45   May God dispatch his mercy to Israel;
         may he deliver us from the pollution of profane enemies;
46   The Lord Himself is our king forevermore.   5:9; 17:1

18
A Psalm of Solomon About the Lord Messiah

1   O Lord, your mercy is upon the works of your hands forever.   2:33; 4:25; 11:9
      (You show) your goodness to Israel
         with a rich gift.   5:14f.,18
2   Your eyes (are) watching over them and none of them will be in need.[a]   Ps 23:1; 34:10
      Your ears listen to the hopeful prayer of the poor,   5:2,11f.; 10:6;
                                                                                 15:1
3   Your compassionate judgments (are) over the whole world,   2:10; 8:8; 15:12
         and your love is for the descendants of Abraham, an Israelite.[b]   9:9
4   Your discipline for us (is) as (for) a firstborn son, an only child,[c]   7:9; 8:26
      to divert the perceptive[d] person from unintentional sins.[e]   3:8; 13:7
5   May God cleanse Israel for the day of mercy in blessing,   17:22–30
         for the appointed day when his Messiah will reign.
6   Blessed are those born in those days,   17:44
         to see the good things of the Lord
         which he will do for the coming generation;
7   (which will be) under the rod of discipline of the Lord Messiah,[f]   17:24
         in the fear of his God,
         in wisdom of spirit,
      and of righteousness and of strength,
8   to direct people in righteous acts, in the fear of God,   7:10; 16:9
         to set them all in the fear of the Lord[g]
9   A good generation (living) in the fear of God,
         in the days of mercy.
      Pause.

10   Our God is great and glorious
         living in the highest (heavens),   Isa 33:5; 57:15
      who arranges the stars into orbits
         (to mark) time of the hours from day to day.[h]
      And they have not deviated from their course,
         which he appointed them.

---

e2. One MS reads: "Jerusalem."

18 a. Syr. reads: "there is nothing hidden from them."

b. Lit. "of a son of Israel." This awkward syntax has prompted numerous conjectures, including: (1) emend to "the Israelites"; (2) transpose Abraham and Israel, with the Syr., to read: "the descendants of Israel, the son of Abraham"; (3) emend to "the Israelite." Most simply, the phrase is in apposition to "of Abraham."

c. The primacy of the first and only child in the affection of a father is the idiom for the depth of God's love for the people Israel. The only other, similar phrase is in 4Ezra 6:58.

d. Lit. "one who hears (and listens and obeys)"— see Prov 13:1; 21:28; one who is sensitive to the learning experience of punishment.

e. Lit. "from ignorance in incomprehension." In the LXX, the last word takes on the connotation of sin.

f. Gk.: *christou kuriou* would regularly be translated "of the Lord's Messiah." However, within the context of 17:32 (see n.) it is taken to be "of the Lord Messiah."

g. Other MSS read: "in the presence of the Lord."

h. Lit. "for times of the hours from days to days."

11   Their course each day is in the fear of God,
         from the day God created them forever.
12   And they have not wandered
         from the day he created them, from ancient generations.
     They have not veered off their course
         except when God directed them
         by the command of his servants.   Josh 10:12f.; Isa
                                                                                 38:8

HELLENISTIC SYNAGOGAL PRAYERS

(Second to Third Century A.D.)

INTRODUCTION BY D. A. FIENSY

TRANSLATION BY D. R. DARNELL

Scattered among the Christian liturgy in Books Seven and Eight of the *Apostolic Constitutions* are sixteen prayers which may be remnants of Jewish synagogal prayers. The prayers praise God's deeds in creation and history, and extol God's attributes in terms often reminiscent of hellenistic philosophy. Some prayers have more specific functions: Prayer 5 explains and defends Sabbath observance, and Prayer 16 invokes God's mercy on those who have died.

Text

The text for this translation is the edition of F. X. Funk.[1] He collated an eclectic text using Greek manuscripts dating from the tenth to the seventeenth centuries A.D.

Original language

The Greek flows smoothly and gives no indication that it is a translation from a Semitic language. In addition, quotations from the Old Testament follow the Septuagint (see e.g. 3:3,11; 4:1,7,15,19,25; 6:6–12 and notes d–i; 9:8; 11:11; 12:16,24,78 and n. c; 13:1, 9) including the transliteration of certain Hebrew words (4:8 and n. a, 4:10 and n. b. See also Prayer 6 n. d and Prayer 12 n. d). It follows, therefore, that Greek is probably the original language.

The Jewish origin of the prayers

As early as 1893, K. Kohler[2] suggested that Book Seven of the *Apostolic Constitutions* contained prayers which resemble those in the Jewish prayer book. W. Bousset[3] maintained in 1915—apparently without knowledge of Kohler's work—that some of the prayers in Books Seven and Eight of the *Constitutions* had been taken from liturgy used in diasporic Judaism. E. R. Goodenough[4] later agreed with Bousset but defined the origin of the prayers more narrowly. They had been produced in mystic Jewish circles similar to the environment from which Philo of Alexandria came. Each of these scholars argued that the prayers contain passages which are distinctly Jewish and which have parallels in other Jewish literature.

Kohler claimed that Prayers 2–7 are parallel to the first six of the Seven Benedictions for Sabbaths and Festivals of the Jewish prayer book. These six prayers in the *Apostolic*

---

[1] *Didascalia et Constitutiones Apostolorum* (Paderborn, 1905).

[2] "Über die Ursprünge und Grundformen der synagogalen Liturgie: Eine Studie," *MGWJ* n. F. 1 (1893) 441–51, 489–97. Kohler restated this in his article "Didascalia," *JE*, vol. 4, pp. 588–95; and in "The Essene Version of the Seven Benedictions as Preserved in the VII Book of the Apostolic Constitutions," *HUCA* 1 (1924) 410–25. His conclusion that the prayers are Essene should be re-evaluated in light of the Dead Sea Scrolls.

[3] "Eine jüdische Gebetssammlung in siebenten Buch der apostolischen Konstitutionen," *Nachrichten von der Königlichen Gesellschaft der Wissenschaften zu Göttingen; Philologische-historische Klasse 1915* (Berlin, 1916) pp. 438–85.

[4] *By Light, Light* (New Haven, London, 1935) pp. 306–58.

Constitutions contain the same general content, in the same order, as the Seven Benedictions.[5]

All three scholars[6] emphasized the most striking parallel to the synagogal liturgy, which is found in Prayer 4 (vss. 9–12). This prayer obviously contains the Kedushah, which consists of a description of the sanctification of God by ministering angels based on the theophanies of Isaiah (6:3) and Ezekiel (3:12). The form of the Kedushah found in Prayer 4 is much like the Kedushah of the Yotzer prayer in the Jewish prayer book.[7]

Bousset thought Prayer 5 was reminiscent of the Sabbath Kiddush prayer, since they similarly explain the importance of the Sabbath. In addition, the emphasis on the number seven as a perfect number is very similar to Philo's propaganda about the Sabbath.[8] It is inconceivable, argued Bousset, that a Christian could have written a prayer such as this, which defends Sabbath observance for the first two thirds of the prayers and then weakly asserts the superiority of the Lord's Day at the very end.[9]

Many prayers seem Jewish because of what they fail to say. There is often very little peculiarly Christian content, and this is especially striking where one would expect emphasis on Christ's functions and titles. Further, where there are distinctly Christian passages, they are usually only loosely—often awkwardly—connected to the context. This suggests that such passages are interpolations.[10]

A very common feature of these prayers is the phrase "through Christ" or "through Jesus."[11] These specify how God has acted in creation and history. Another phrase which can easily be inserted into the text and tends to specify is the genitival phrase

> "We give thanks to you,
> O God and Father *of Jesus our Savior* . . ."[12]

The argument from silence is mostly convincingly employed with reference to Prayer 6. At 6:4–12, where God's faithfulness in answering the requests of his people is reviewed, the historical references begin with Abel and end with Mattathias. One would expect, as Bousset argued, that a Christian would mention Jesus of Nazareth.[13] The same argument can be used with 9:10–14; 12:53–79; and 16:8. Of course one must proceed with caution in arguing from silence, since at times even New Testament authors fail to mention Jesus when one might expect them to do so. Hebrews 11 lists only the Old Testament heroes as examples of faith, and James 5:10f. offers only the prophets and Job as examples of patience. However, there is sufficient content in the remainder of those two New Testament books to convince most scholars that they were authored by a Christian.[14] Such content is lacking in the prayers translated below.

The thesis of Kohler, Bousset, and Goodenough is therefore quite feasible.[15] The existence

[5] Kohler, *HUCA* 1 (1924) 410–25. For the Seven Benedictions, see P. Birnbaum, *Daily Prayer Book* (New York, 1977) pp. 265–71.

[6] Kohler, *HUCA* 1 (1924) 415f.; Bousset, *Nachrichten*, p. 438; Goodenough, *By Light, Light*, pp. 308f.

[7] See J. Heinemann, *Prayer in the Talmud*, translator R. Sarason (Studia Judaica 9; Berlin, 1977) pp. 223f., who pointed out that the Kedushah is attested as early as the tannaitic period (t.Ber 1:9). For the Yotzer, see Birnbaum, *Daily Prayer Book*, pp. 71–74.

[8] *Nachrichten*, p. 445. Philo, *SpecLeg* 2.59–62. See also Aristobulus F. 5 in the Supplement. For the Kiddush, see Birnbaum, *Daily Prayer Book*, p. 289.

[9] Bousset, *Nachrichten*, p. 445. For early Christian observance of the Sabbath, however, see C. W. Dugmore, *The Influence of the Synagogue upon the Divine Office* (Westminster, 1964) pp. 28–36.

[10] J. H. Charlesworth, "Christian and Jewish Self-Definition in Light of the Christian Additions to the Apocryphal Writings," *Jewish and Christian Self-Definition*, vol. 2, *Aspects of Judaism in the Greco-Roman World*, eds. E. P. Sanders with A. I. Baumgarten and A. Mendelson (Philadelphia, 1981) pp. 27–55 uses the following features as criteria for determining interpolations: The word or words under examination may contain ideas or images extraneous to the general context. The passage may be loosely connected grammatically to its context; the flow of thought, however, is often clarified or improved when the passage in question is removed.

[11] *Dia Christou*, e.g. 4:22; 5:1; 7:7; 11:2; 14:1; and *dia lēsou*, e.g. 1:3; 7:18; 15:1.

[12] See Charlesworth, in *Jewish and Christian Self-Definition*, pp. 28–35.

[13] *Nachrichten*, p. 446. But in a similar passage, 7:3, Jesus is mentioned and it is not clear that this is an interpolation. See 7:4 and n. a. Kohler's imaginative solution (*HUCA* 1 [1924] 422–24) to the problem, that this was originally a reference to Jesus ben Phabi (Josephus, *Ant* 15.9.3), is rather farfetched.

[14] Heb is of course quite obviously Christian. For the arguments in favor of Christian authorship of Jas, see P. Feine, J. Behme, and W. G. Kümmel, *Introduction to the New Testament*, translator A. J. Mattill Jr. (Nashville, 1966) pp. 288f.

[15] The evidence pertaining to all of the prayers cannot be given here. Some of the prayers are not as clearly Jewish as others. However, for the sake of completion, all of the prayers which Goodenough believed were originally Jewish

of distinctly Jewish content in the prayers, while peculiarly Christian elements are absent, makes a reasonable argument in favor of Jewish authorship for at least some of the prayers.[16]

Date

Goodenough argued that the middle of the second century A.D. is probably the latest period in which the prayers could have been composed, since after this time relations between Jews and Christians were not conducive to Christian borrowing of synagogue liturgy.[17] However, one should be very cautious about overemphasizing the break between church and synagogue after the Bar Kokhba war (A.D. 135).[18] The prayers may have been composed shortly before the *Apostolic Constitutions* were compiled (A.D. 380).[19]

The earliest possible date is the middle of the second century A.D., since, as Bousset pointed out, the prayers show familiarity with Aquila's Greek version of the Old Testament (c. A.D. 135, e.g. see Prayer 2:14, *horamatismos*, "vision"). The date should then be set as early as A.D. 150 or as late as A.D. 300.[20]

Provenance

There is nothing in the prayers themselves to suggest where they were composed. The similarities with Philo in thought and expression could suggest Alexandria. Nevertheless, it is just as reasonable to posit Syria as the provenance since it is generally agreed that the *Constitutions* were compiled there.[21]

Historical importance

Some scholars of Christian liturgy have stated that there was no wholesale borrowing by Christians from the liturgy of the synagogue. The general framework of the service was borrowed but not the actual prayers.[22] However, these prayers suggest that the affinity between early church and synagogue was greater than many suppose.

More important, the prayers furnish additional information about the piety and theology of the Judaism similar to, but not necessarily identical with, that of Philo.

Relation to canonical books

The prayers are most similar in form and content to the Davidic psalter. In addition to the general theme of praise of God, the prayers contain numerous quotations of and allusions to the Psalms. But the author(s) of the prayers was (were) thoroughly saturated with the

---

are translated here. He added Prayers 1, 14, and 15 to Bousset's list and omitted some very short prayers in Book Eight of *AposCon*. Kohler included only Prayers 1–7 in his list. See the nn. to the individual prayers for evidence of the Jewish authorship of the rest of the prayers.

[16] Dugmore, *The Influence of the Synagogue*, pp. 102–13, and A. Baumstark, *Comparative Liturgy* (Westminster, 1957) pp. 43–51, who maintain that the Jewish synagogue and its liturgy had a profound formative effect on early Christian worship, make this thesis even more reasonable.

[17] *By Light, Light,* p. 357. Evidence of the later hostile relationship between church and synagogue may be seen in Prayer 7:14, where the Jews are called "Christ murderers."

[18] See the work of W. A. Meeks and R. L. Wilken, *Jews and Christians in Antioch in the First Four Centuries of the Common Era* (Missoula, Mont., 1978). The whole thrust of this book is to show the influence of Judaism upon the Church during the first four centuries.

[19] L. O'Leary, *The Apostolical Constitutions* (London, 1906) p. 69, dated the *AposCon* A.D. 378–425. B. Altaner, *Patrology*, translator H. C. Graef (Freiburg, 1960) p. 59, gives A.D. 380.

[20] See *Nachrichten*, p. 466. Bousset also believed the words *synthēkē*, "covenant," (2:15) and *Phassa* for "Passover" (6:10) to be from the influence of Aquila's version. Of course it must not be assumed that all the prayers were written at the same time or by the same author.

[21] F. C. Cross and E. A. Livingstone, eds., The Oxford Dictionary of the Christian Church (London, 1974) pp. 75f.; R. H. Cresswell, *The Liturgy of the Eighth Book of the Apostolic Constitutions* (New York, 1900) p. 9, gives the reasons: The calendar, lenten customs, and liturgy are parallel to those of Antioch and Constantinople. O'Leary, *Constitutions*, p. 69, also notes that several Syrian monks are cited (*AposCon* 5:14, 17, 20).

[22] W. O. E. Oesterley, *The Jewish Background of Christian Liturgy* (Oxford, 1925) pp. 127–54, gave in parallel cols. prayers taken from 1 Clem, Did, and other Christian sources, and prayers from the Jewish prayer book. Dugmore, *The Influence of the Synagogue*, pp. 75–77, 111–13, rejected Oesterley's contention, arguing that there were no real parallels and that many of the prayers in the Heb. prayer book did not exist at that time.

entire Old Testament and thus freely drew upon the Pentateuch, Prophets, and Writings.

Relation to non-canonical Jewish literature

While the prayers share numerous striking parallels of thought with Philo, there are some significant parallels with the Wisdom of Solomon and Aristobulus. All these works reflect the profound influence of Greek thought which is so typical of Jewish authors living in the Diaspora.

Philo's doctrine of divine omnipresence[23] (*Leg All* 3.51) is similar to Prayer 13:1. His admonition on thanksgiving for the creation of the world (*SpecLeg* 1.210f.) is expressed in 7:7f. and 12:12–40. Philo's discourse on the meaning of the number seven (*Leg All* 1.8–16) is paralleled in Prayer 5:15; but Philo is also anticipated by Aristobulus (see the Supplement, F. 5).

The most important parallel to the Wisdom of Solomon is the reference to the presence of Wisdom at creation as God's agent (Prayers 3:19 and 12:10; WisSol 9:2, 9). In addition, the notion of man as created immortal (WisSol 2:23) is found in Prayer 7:9.

Theological importance

GOD

God is omnipotent (1:7; 2:1f.; 4:23bf.; 12:36f.), omnipresent (4:25f.; 13:1), omniscient (2:4; 9:4–6), eternal (2:22; 3:1; 4:24; 9:2, 4; 12:3, 5; 13:2, 4), and faithful (1:7; 6:1a). He is just in rewarding the righteous and punishing the wicked (4:40; 7:1f.; 12:57); and merciful, desiring repentance (2:3, 6f.; 4:2f., 23a; 6:1b; 9:8; 11:5–8). God has acted in creation (1:4; 3:2–23; 4:16–21, 38; 5:1; 12:16) and history (5:9–14; 6:4–12; 7:3; 9:10–16; 12:53–55, 59–79) for the benefit of mankind.

ANTHROPOLOGY

Mankind was the goal of all God's creative work. He was created a rational being (3:18; 11:3; 12:39) with five senses (3:21; 7:8), and made a world citizen (3:18; 12:35; 8:2), and a microcosm of the world as in hellenistic philosophy (3:20; 11:2; 12:35 and nn.). Man is a combination of an immortal soul created from "non-being" and a corruptible body created from the four elements (3:20f.; 12:37f.). Although man was given the innate law at creation (1:5; 11:3; 12:43, 69), he disobeyed and therefore incurred death (3:24–26; 12:46–50). However, God in his mercy has provided the resurrection for those who are "cleansed" by the Law (7:10f.).

ANGELOLOGY

Although angels do not play a large role in the prayers, three passages portray a hierarchy of heavenly beings (4:11, 12:14, 81–85). Angels are also present at 16:12, where it is stated that angels minister to the spirits of the dead.

WISDOM AND WORD

There is only one passage where we have a notion of the Word (*Logos*) in the sense of John 1:1. This passage may be a Christian interpolation (12:10),[24] as two similar passages certainly are (1:8; 5:20).

---

[23] As Goodenough, *By Light, Light*, pp. 325, 337, noted.

[24] It looks suspiciously like an interpolation: Praise of God and his creative power is interrupted by a description of God's "Son." Goodenough (*By Light, Light*, pp. 340f.) maintained, however, that although exact parallels are wanting in Philo, the passage in Prayer 12 is in harmony with Philo's doctrine of the Logos as *prôtogonos* ("first begotten") in *Conf* 146.

[25] It has been alleged that the compiler of *AposCon* was an Arian (C. H. Turner, "Notes on the Apostolic Constitutions," *JTS* 16 [1914–15] 54–61). However, there is nothing particularly Arian in the interpolations as they stand in Funk's text. See Funk's refutation of the alleged Arianism of the compiler in *Apostolischen Konstitutionen* (Frankfurt, 1970 [1891]) pp. 120–23.

Special attention is given to Wisdom (*sophia*). Wisdom is personified and represented as the instrument of creation (3:19; 4:7, 38; 12:36). Wisdom is not eternal, however, since God is her father (4:38) and creator (5:3). It is not clear that Wisdom is identified with Word except in the difficult passage mentioned above (12:10).

LAW

Mankind was given an innate law at creation (1:5; 2:9; 12:43). However, because of man's sin, the written Law had to be given as an aid to the natural law (11:3; 12:69). But the written Law must now be learned; thus the Sabbath is provided as the day for study and meditation (5:2, 19).

AFTERLIFE

Mankind possessed immortality at creation. This, however, he lost when he sinned, and therefore God has graciously and mercifully provided the general resurrection to restore what was lost (3:24–27; 7:10f.; 12:46–50; 16:7). But this appears to be promised only to those who have been cleansed by the Law (7:10f.).

Christology of the interpolations

Christ was born of a virgin of the lineage of David (6:2) and while on earth was both human and divine (1:8; 5:6; 7:15). Identified with Wisdom (5:3–4) and the divine Word (1:8; 5:20), he is represented as the agent in creation (3:1; 9:7; 14:1; 15:1) and the mediator of those who pray (4:22; 6:13).[25]

Introduction to this translation

The interpolations have been indicated by underlining. The interpolator(s) may be responsible for more of the material than has been indicated, but only those passages which must be considered Christian have been underlined. There is considerable difficulty in defining the perimeters of interpolations. They may begin earlier and end later than indicated, but restraint has been applied in underlining.

SELECT BIBLIOGRAPHY

Bousset, W. "Eine jüdische Gebetssammlung im siebenten Buch der apostolischen Konstitutionen," *Nachrichten von der Königlichen Gesellschaft der Wissenschaften zu Göttingen; Philologische-historische Klasse 1915*. Berlin, 1916; pp. 438–85; reprinted in A. F. Verheule. *Religionsgeschichtliche Studien*. Leiden, 1979; pp. 231–86.

Bouyer, L. *Eucharist*, trans. C. U. Quinn. Notre Dame, 1968; pp. 119–35.

Charlesworth, J. H. "Christian and Jewish Self-Definition in Light of the Christian Additions to the Apocryphal Writings," *Jewish and Christian Self-Definition*, ed. E. P. Sanders, A. I. Baumgarten, and A. Mendelson. Philadelphia; vol. 2, pp. 27–55, 310–15.

Charlesworth, J. H. "Hellenistic Synagogal Prayers," *The Pseudepigrapha and Modern Research with a Supplement* (SBL SCS 7S; Chico, Calif., 1981) pp. 288f.

Charlesworth, J. H. "Jewish Liturgies, Hymns and Prayers (c. 167 B.C.E.–135 C.E.)," *Early Post-Biblical Judaism and Its Modern Interpreters*, ed. R. A. Kraft and G. W. E. Nickelsburg. Chico, Calif., in press.

Fiensy, D. A. *A Redactional Examination of Prayers Alleged to Be Jewish in the Constitutiones Apostolorum*. Duke University, Ph.D., 1980.

Funk, F. X. *Didascalia et Constitutiones Apostolorum*. Paderborn, 1905.

Goodenough, E. R. *By Light, Light*. New Haven, 1935.

Kohler, K. "The Essene Version of the Seven Benedictions as Preserved in the VII Book of the Apostolic Constitutions," *HUCA* 1 (1924) 410–25; reprinted in J. J. Petuchowski, *Contributions to the Scientific Study of Jewish Liturgy*. New York, 1970; pp. 75–90.

Simon, M. *Versus Israel*. Bibliothèque des Écoles Françaises d'Athènes et de Rome; Paris, 1948; pp. 74–82.

Whiston, W. "Constitutions of the Holy Apostles," *The Ante-Nicene Fathers*, ed. J. Donaldson. Grand Rapids, Mich., 1951; vol. 7, pp. 385–508.

1. A Prayer of Thanksgiving Following Communion (*AposCon* 7.26.1–3)

1 (1) (Then after the communion, you shall give thanks in this way:)
2 (2) We give thanks to you, O God and Father of Jesus our Savior,[a]
       on behalf of your holy name which you caused to encamp among us,   Jn 1:14
3   and on behalf of the knowledge and faith and love and immortality which
       you gave to us through Jesus[b] your Son.
4 (3) O Master Almighty, the God of the universe,
       you created the world and what is in it through him;[c]
5   and you planted deeply in our souls a law;   2:9; 11:3; 12:43.
       and you prepared for men the things (necessary) for communion; 69
6 (you are) the God of the holy and blameless ones, our fathers Abraham and Isaac Ex 3:16
       and Jacob, your faithful servants;
7 the powerful God, the faithful and true One, without falsehood in your promises; 1Bar 3:37
8 the One who sent forth upon earth Jesus your Christ, to live together with men
       as a man, being divine Word and Man, and radically to destroy error.[d]

2. A Prayer of Praise to God, the Universal Savior and Fighter on Behalf of Abraham's Race (*AposCon* 7.33.2–7)

1 (2) Our eternal Savior:
       the King of the gods,   Esth 4:17 LXX
       who alone is Almighty and Lord,
2   the God of all beings,
       and God of our holy and blameless fathers before us,
       the God of Abraham and Isaac and Jacob,   Ex 3:16
3   the merciful and compassionate,   Joel 2:13
       the patient and very merciful,
4   to whom every heart is seen, appearing naked,
       and every hidden thought is uncovered;
5   to you the souls of righteous people cry out!
    Upon you the hopes of devout people have relied:
6   the Father of the blameless,
       the Hearer of those who call upon you with honesty,
       the one who knows the petitions unspoken.
7 For your forethought reaches as far as human (inner) feelings,
       and through (the) conscience you search each person's judgment,
       and in every region of the inhabited earth,
       the incense that comes through prayer and words is sent up to you. Mal 1:11
8 (3) You are the one who appointed the present world as a racecourse for righteousness, 1Cor 9:24
    and opened to everyone a gate of mercy,

---

1 a. E. R. Goodenough in *By Light, Light* (New Haven, 1935) italicized *of Jesus our Savior* as a Christian interpolation.

  b. Goodenough italicized only *Jesus* as an interpolation.

  c. The Christian redactor probably deleted some words as he worked; perhaps "through your Word" originally stood in the preceding vs. and was changed to "through Jesus your Son"; the Jewish author elsewhere refers to the "Word" (cf. 4:21; 12:10).

  d. Christian additions in these prayers, as elsewhere (see the T12P, in which the most striking additions are in the last two testaments), are most extensive near or at the end.

9 and showed to every person, through implanted knowledge, and inborn judgment,   1:5
     and by their response to the law,

10   how the possession of wealth is surely not everlasting,
     the beauty of appearance is not ever-flowing,
     the strength of power is easily dissolved,
     and surely everything is a vapor, and vanity.   Jas 4:14
     Eccl 1:2

11 But a conscience with undisguised faith endures,
     a dwelling-place through the midst of the heavens,
     rising up with truth,

12   it takes hold by the right hand of the coming nourishment.

13 At the same time, and before the promise of the regeneration is present,
     the soul itself, exulting, is rejoiced.

14 (4) For from the beginning of our forefather Abraham's laying claim to the way of
     truth,
     You led (him) by a vision,
     having taught (him) what at any time this world is.

15 And his faith traveled ahead of his knowledge,[a]
     but the covenant was the follower of his faith.

16 For you said,
     I will make your seed like the stars of the heaven,   Gen 13:16;
     and like the sand that is beside the edge of the sea.   22:17

17 (5) But truly, having also given Isaac to him,
     and having known him to be like that one in character,

18 you were also called his God, having said,
     I will be your God, and of your seed after you.   Gen 17:7

19 And having placed our father Jacob in Mesopotamia, <u>having shown (him) the
     Christ,</u>[b]
     <u>through him</u> you spoke, saying,

20   *Look! I am with you,*   Gen 28:15; 48:4
     and I will increase you,
     and multiply you exceedingly.

21 (6) And in this way you spoke to Moses,
     your faithful and holy servant,
     in the vision at the bush:

22   *I am the Being;*   Ex 3:14,15
     this is for me an eternal name,
     and a remembrance to generations of generations.

23 (7) O Fighter on behalf of Abraham's race,
     blessed are you forever![c]

3. A Prayer That Meditates upon God's Manifold Creative Power, Which Comes to Sinful Man in Redemption (*AposCon* 7.34.1–8)

1 (1) Blessed are you, O Lord, King of the ages,   1Tim 1:17
     who <u>through Christ</u>[a] made everything,   Jn 1:3
     Col 1:16f.

2 a. W. Whiston, "Constitutions of the Holy Apostles," *ANF* 7, pp. 387–505), followed by Goodenough, made "knowledge" the subject of the sentence. The MSS vary at this point, one MS reading "knowledge" as the subject.

  b. Goodenough italicized only *the Christ* as a Christian interpolation. The Christian scribe transfers what was said of "the Lord" to Christ. See Gen 28.

  c. Goodenough insisted that apart from the interpolated reference to Christ, "there is not a Christian syllable in this prayer. Christian authorship is unthinkable" (*By Light, Light*, p. 317). The prayer is strikingly Jewish throughout, and looks very much like a prayer taken verbatim from a Jewish synagogue service, except for this one reference to the Christ.

3 a. *Christ* is clearly interpolated; Goodenough also made this point. It was perhaps originally "the Word"; cf. n. a to Prayer No. 14.

and <u>through him</u> in the beginning ordered that which was unprepared;   Gen 1:1f.

2 who separated waters from waters with a firmament,   Gen 1:6
and put a lively spirit in these;

3 who settled the earth (firmly),
and stretched out heaven,   Ps 103:2 LXX
and ordered the exact arrangement of each one of the creatures.

4 (2) For by your conception, O Master, order has beamed with joy;

5 while heaven, having been pitched like a vault, is adorned with stars,   Isa 40:22
for the sake of encouragement (in the midst of) the darkness;

6 while light and sun, for days and (for) fruits, came to birth;   Gen 1:14–19

7 while moon, for changing of seasons, increased and decreased,
and night was named, and day was kindly addressed;   Gen 1:5

8 while a firmament was shown forth in the midst of the abysses,   Gen 1:6
and you said for the waters to be gathered together,   Gen 1:9
and for the dry land to appear;

9 (3) while the sea itself—how shall we describe it in full?—
which comes raging from (the) oceans,
yet runs back again from (the) sand, being hindered by your command.

10 For you said,
By it shall her waves be shattered.   Job 38:11

11 While for living creatures, for small and for great,   Ps 103:25–26
LXX
and for (the) voyaging of ships, you made it.

12 (4) Then earth grew green, engraved with all sorts of flowers,
and with an embroidery of different trees.

13 And (the) all-blazing luminaries are nourishers of these,
keeping without trespass the long course,
not deviating in any way from your ordinance;

14 but wherever you may command,
in this (place) they rise and set,
for signs of seasons and years,   Gen 1:14
alternating for the assistance of mankind.

15 (5) Thereafter were prepared races of differing living creatures:
those found on dry land,
those living in water,
those traversing the air,
(and) amphibians.

16 And by the skilled Wisdom of your forethought   3:19; 4:7,38;
5:3; 12:10,36
is given to each one the appropriate providence.

17 For just as she[b] was not exhausted in bringing forth differing races,
neither has she[b] neglected to make for each one a different providence.

18 (6) And the goal of the creative work—   12:35f.
the rational living creature, the world citizen—

19 having given order by your Wisdom, you created, saying,   3:16; 2En 30:8;
WisSol 9:2, 9
Gen 1:26

Let us make man according to our image and likeness;

20 having declared him a (micro-)cosm of the cosmos,[c]   12:35; 11:2
having formed for him the body out of the four elements;

21 and having prepared for him the soul out of non-being,
and having given to him fivefold perception,
and having placed over the perceptions a mind, the holder of the reins of the
soul.[d]

22 (7) And in addition to all these things, O Master, Lord,
who can worthily describe the movement of rain-producing clouds,

---

b. Goodenough translates "she," making the subject *Sophia*, God's wisdom.

c. Lit. "of the cosmos, a cosmos." Whiston preferred the translation "the ornament of the world." The preceding description of man as rational, and as a world citizen, is a commonplace of hellenistic Judaism. Compare Philo, *Op* 142.

d. Here the dependence upon Platonic philosophy is clear. Compare *Phaedrus*, 246.

the flashing forth of lightning, the clashing of thunders;
23   for the supplying of appropriate nourishment,
and the blending of complex atmospheres?
24 (8) But when man was disobedient,
You took away his deserved life.
25 You did not make it disappear absolutely, but for a time,
26 having put (him) to sleep for a little (while),
by an oath you have called (him forth) to new birth.   ApMos 28:4;
37:3; 41:3; 43:1
27 You have loosed the boundary of death,   Vita 51:2
You who are the Maker of life for the dead, through Jesus Christ, our hope!ᵉ   1Tim 1:1

4. A Prayer That Joins with All Nature in Praising the One and Only Great and Merciful God (AposCon 7.35.1–10)

1 (1) Great are you, O Lord, Almighty One, and great is your strength,
and of your understanding there is no numbering!   Ps 146:5 LXX
2 O Creator, Savior, Rich One in favors,
Long-sufferer, and Supplier of mercy,
Who do not withdraw from the salvation of your creatures!
3 For by nature you are good;
yet you spare those who are sinning, summoning them to repentance,
for your warning is merciful!
4 For how should we have withstood,
having swift judgment demanded of us?
We who, when being treated patiently, with difficulty refuse our weakness?
5 (2) The heavens proclaimed your might;   Ps 18:2 LXX
and earth, (though) being shaken, (proclaimed) your firmness,
being hung upon nothing!   Job 26:7
6 (The) sea, surging with waves,
and shepherding a herd of countless living creatures,
has been shackled with sand,
has shuddered at your will,
and compels all to cry out:
7   How magnified are your works, O Lord!   Ps 103:24 LXX
You made everything with Wisdom;   3:16
the earth was filled with your creating!
8 (3) And an army of angels breaking forth,
and intellectual spirits say to Phelmuni,ᵃ
There is one Holy One!   Dan 8:13
9 And holy seraphim, together with the six-winged cherubim, singing to you the   [Theodotion]
triumphal song, with never-silent voices cry out,
10   Holy, holy, holy, Lord Sabaoth,ᵇ   Isa 6:3
the heaven and the earth are full of your glory!
11 And the other throngs of the hosts, archangels, thrones, dominions, sovereignties,   Col 1:16
authorities, powers, crying out, say,   12:14,27
12 Blessed be the glory of the Lord from its place!
13 (4) But Israel, your earthly assembly out of (the) gentiles,ᶜ

e. Goodenough correctly italicized this last l. as a Christian interpolation. Again, the Christian addition is prominent at the end. Cf. Philo, SpecLeg 1.210f.

4 a. Probably a Gk. transliteration of the Heb. palmônî (Dan 8:13), which apparently is a com-

bination of a two-word Heb. phrase meaning "each one."
b. A Gk. transliteration of the Heb. word for "armies." See LXX Isa 6:3.
c. Goodenough italicized taken out of the Gentiles as a Christian interpolation. However, as he points out (By Light, Light, p. 309), the phrase

	competing with the heavenly powers by night and by day,	
14	with heart filled to the brim and with a willing spirit sings,	2Mac 1:3
15	*The chariot of God is ten thousands multiplied by thousands of thriving ones;*	Ps 67:18 LXX
	the Lord is among them in Sinai, in the holy place!	
16 (5)	Heaven knows the one who raised it as a vault upon nothing,	
	like a stone cube,	Job 38:38 LXX
17	and united earth and water with each other,	
	and poured out air for keeping animals,	
18	and plaited together with this fire[d] for warmth and encouragement in darkness.	
19	The chorus of stars amazes,	Ps 146:4 LXX
	pointing out the one who numbered (them),	
	and showing the one who named (them).	
20	Living creatures (point to) the one who gave (them) life;	
	trees (point to) the one who produced (them);	
21	as all things, having been made by your word, suggest the might of your power.	
22 (6)	Wherefore also all men ought, from their very breasts,	
	to send up to you <u>through Christ</u>[e] the hymn on behalf of all,	
	by reason of you who hold power over all things.	
23 (7)	For you are the Kind One in good deeds,	
	and One fond of giving with compassions,	
	the only All-Mighty one!	
	For when you desire, to be able is present with you.	
24	For your eternal power even cools flames,	Dan 3
	and muzzles lions, and tames sea monsters,	Dan 6; Jonah 2
	and raises those who are sick, and overturns powers,	
	and overthrows an army of enemies and a people numbered for its arrogance.	
25 (8)	You are the one in heaven, the one upon earth,	
	the one in the sea,	
	the one in the farthest boundaries, bounded by nothing.	
	For of your greatness there is no boundary.	Ps 144:3 LXX
26	For this oracle is not ours, Master, but your servant's, saying,	
	And you shall know in your heart that your God is (the) Lord,	Deut 4:39
	God in heaven above, and upon earth beneath,	
	and there is no other beside him!	
27 (9)	For there is no god beside you alone, there is no Holy one beside you;	Isa 45:5
28	Lord God of knowledge,[f]	1Sam 2:3
	God of holy ones,	
	Holy one above all holy ones.	
	For those who have been made holy are under your hands.	Deut 33:3
29	(You are) honored and exalted exceedingly:	
	invisible by nature,[g]	1Tim 1:17
30	unsearchable in judgments,	Rom 11:33
	whose life is in want of nothing.	
31	Unchangeable and unceasing is (your) continuance.	
	Untiring is (your) activity.	

could well have been used by Diasporic Jews in the sense "separated from the Gentiles." [The word translated "assembly" is *ekklēsia*, "assembly, church," and the Christians who recited these prayers or hymns would have viewed this passage as referring to themselves, the true Israel, the church. Early Jews referred to themselves as God's assembly (*ekklēsia, kāhāl*; see, for example, Ps 107:32. —J.H.C.]

d. The listing of the four elements is reminiscent of Gk. philosophical analysis.

e. Goodenough correctly italicized *Christ* as an interpolation.

f. [Lit. "knowledges." —J.H.C.]

g. A list of seventeen descriptions of God begins here.

32   Unlimited is (your) greatness.
         Unfailing is (your) beauty.

33   Unapproachable is (your) dwelling-place.   ITim 6:16
         Unremovable is (your) resting-place.

34   Without beginning is (your) knowledge.
         Unchangeable is (your) truth.

35   Unmediated is (your) work.
         Unplotted against is (your) strength.

36   Without successor is (your) monarchy.
         Unending is (your) kingdom.

37   Without adversary is (your) might.
         Great in number is (your) army.

38 (10)   For you are the Father of Wisdom,   3:16
         the Creator, as cause, of the creative workmanship through a Mediator;

39   the Supplier of foresight;
         the Giver of laws;
         the Fulfiller of needs;

40   the Punisher of the ungodly,
         and the Rewarder of the righteous;

41   the God and Father of the Christ,[h]
         and the Lord of those who are pious toward him;

42   whose promise is not deceptive,
         (whose) judgment is without bribery,

43   (whose) knowledge is never faithless,
         (whose) religion is never-ending,
         (whose) thanksgiving is everlasting;

44   through whom also the worship worthy of you is owed by every
         reasonable and holy nature![i]

5. A Prayer Praising God for His Redemptive Deeds for Israel, Old and New, and for the Institution of Days Set Apart for Worship *(AposCon* 7.36.1–7)

1 (1)   O Lord, Almighty One,
         you created (the) cosmos through Christ,[a]
         and marked out a sabbath day for a remembrance of this;   Ex 20:8–11

2   because on it you rested from the works (of creation),   Gen 2:2
         in order to give attention to your own laws.

3   And you appointed festivals for (the) gladdening of our souls,
         so that we may come into remembrance of the Wisdom created by you:[b]   Prov 8:22
                                                                     3:16

4 (2)   [c]how for us he submitted to birth, that (birth) through a woman;

5   (how) he appeared in (this) life, having demonstrated himself in (his) baptism;

6   how he who appeared is God and man;
         (how) he suffered for us with your consent,

---

h. Goodenough italicized this l. and the remaining ll. of this prayer as a Christian interpolation. There is, however, no reason for looking upon the remaining ll. as interpolated, for they say nothing that a hellenistic Jew would not include in such a prayer.

i. W. Bousset thought this prayer the most obviously Jewish prayer in the entire collection (*Nachrichten,* pp. 436f.), and Goodenough agreed

with this assessment (*By Light, Light,* pp. 308f.). The prayer as a whole is obviously rooted deeply in hellenistic Judaism, whatever theory is accepted as to its entrance into Christian liturgy.

5 a. Goodenough italicized only *Christ* as an interpolation. Originally the passage may have read "through the Word." Cf. n. a to Prayer 3.

b. Goodenough notes that a variant reading *theou*

and (how) he died and arose by your strength.

7 Therefore, celebrating the resurrection festival on the Lord's day,
we rejoice over the one who indeed conquered death,   ICor 15:55
having brought to light life and immortality.[c]   2Tim 1:10

8 For by him you brought the gentiles[d] to yourself, for a treasured people, the
true Israel, the friend of God, who sees God.[e]   Deut 7:6

9 (3) For you, O Lord, have led out from (the) land of Egypt even our fathers;   Deut 4:20
10 and you have rescued (them) out of an iron furnace,
and out of clay and making of bricks.

11 You redeemed (them) out of Pharaoh's hand, and (the hand) of those under him.

12 And you led them through (the) sea as through dry land,   Ex 14:29
and you bore with their manners in the wilderness with manifold   Acts 13:18
goodnesses.   Deut 1:31

13 (4) You gave to them a Law, ten oracles uttered by your voice,   Ex 20
and engraved by your hand.   Ex 20:18

14 You commanded (them) to keep sabbath, not giving an excuse for laziness,   Ex 20:8
but rather an opportunity for reverence (toward God),
for knowledge of your power,
for hindrance of evil;

15 as if having confined (them) in a holy circumference,
for the sake of teaching,
for the exultant joy of the number seven.[f]   Aristob F. 5

16 Because of this (you appointed) one seven, and seven sevens, and a seventh   Lev 23
month, and a seventh year;

17 and with this a year for forgiveness, each fifty-year cycle,   Lev 25
(5) So that men might have no excuse to pretend ignorance.

18 For this reason every sabbath you permitted (them) not to work,
so that no one would desire to let drop from his mouth a word (spoken)
in anger on the day of the sabbath.

19 For (the) sabbath is a rest from creation,
a completion of (the) cosmos,
a seeking out of laws,
thankful praise to God on behalf of those things which he has freely
given to men.

20 (6) [g]All of which the Lord's day surpasses, showing forth:
the Mediator himself, the Supervisor,
the Lawgiver, the cause of resurrection,
the firstborn of all creation, the divine Word;   Col 1:15

21 and Man, the one born of Mary alone, without a husband;   Jn 1:1

22 who lived holily as a citizen,
who was crucified under Pontius Pilate,
and having died, is also (the one) having arisen from (the) dead.[g]

23 As the Lord's day, it advises (us) to offer to you, O Master,
thanksgiving on behalf of everything.

genetheises shows Christian redaction in the interest of orthodoxy (*By Light, Light*, p. 310).

c. All of the material between the two footnote marks is italicized by Goodenough as a Christian interpolation. The material does appear to be an interpolation, somewhat awkwardly adapted to the context.

d. Goodenough italicized *the Gentiles* as an interpolation. Perhaps the vs. refers back to "Wisdom" of the vs. previous to the long Christian interpolation, and may be Jewish.

e. The description of Israel as "the one who sees God" is a commonplace in Philo. See *LegAll* 3.186; *Post* 92; *Conf* 56, 146. The rootedness of this prayer in hellenistic Judaism here becomes quite obvious.

f. The Pythagorean emphasis on the significance of numbers is reminiscent of Philo and therefore of hellenistic Judaism. See *LegAll* 1.8–16; *Op* 89–128; *Abr* 28–30; and *VitaMos* 2.209, 263.

g. [These lines are a credal formula with tradi-

24 <u>For this is the grace which has been furnished by you,</u>
   <u>which by (its) magnitude covered over every (other) good deed!</u>[h]

6. A Prayer of Invocation, Calling upon God, Who Has Always Accepted the Worship of His People, to Accept the Present Prayers of His New People (*AposCon* 7.37.1–5)

1 (1) O you who have fulfilled the promises which (were given) through the prophets,
        and have had mercy on Zion,
        and have had pity on Jerusalem,

2   by your having exalted the throne of David, your servant, in her midst,
         <u>[a]by the birth of the Christ,</u>
         <u>the one who, according to flesh, was of his seed,</u>   Rom 1:3
         <u>having been born of a virgin alone;[a]</u>

3 now also, yourself, O Master God,
  accept the entreaties on the lips of your people,
        who (have come) out of (the) gentiles,[b]
        who call upon you in truth,   Ps 144:18 LXX
  even as you received the gifts of the righteous in their generations:

4 (2)   Abel, especially—you beheld and accepted his sacrifice;   Gen 4
        Noah, when he had come out of the ark;   Gen 8:20–22

5   Abraham, after his coming out from the land of the Chaldeans;   Gen 12:7
        Isaac, at the well of the oath;   Gen 26:23–25
        Jacob, in Bethlehem;[c]   Gen 35

6   Moses, in the wilderness;   Ex–Deut
        Aaron, in the midst of the living and of those who had died;   Num 16:48 LXX;
                                                                                     WisSol 18:20–25
        Joshua, the (son of) Naue[d] in Gilgal;   Josh 5

7   Gideon, upon the rock, and the fleeces, before his sin;   Judg 6,8
        Manoah—and of his wife—in the field;   Judg 13
        Sampson, in his thirst before his error;   Judg 15:18–19
        Jephthah, in the war, before his unwise promise;   Judg 11
        Barak and Deborah, in the days of Sisera;   Judg 4,5
        Samuel, in Mizpah;   1Sam 7

8 (3)   David on (the) threshing floor of Ornan the Jebusite;   1Chr 21
        Solomon in Gibeon and in Jerusalem;   1Kgs 3,8

9   Elijah in Mount Carmel;   1Kgs 18
        Elishah at the barren fountain;[e]   2Kgs 2:19–22

---

tions going back to Col. 1:15 and Jn 1:1–18.—
J.H.C.]

h. This material is correctly italicized by Goodenough as a Christian interpolation. He stated, "To
say the least, the passage on the Lord's Day is an
anti-climax, quite intelligible as a Christian appendix to the Jewish 'Sabbathgebet,' but unintelligible
as the originally planned objective of the prayer"
(*By Light, Light*, p. 311). This conclusion seems
unavoidable, and therefore supports the theory that
these prayers were originally prayers of the hellenistic Jewish synagogue, later adapted through interpolation for use by the Christian community in its
liturgy. This insight is now developed by Charlesworth in "Christian and Jewish Self-Definition in
Light of the Christian Additions to the Apocryphal
Writings," *Jewish and Christian Self-Definition*,

eds. E. P. Sanders, A. I. Baumgarten, A. Mendelson (Philadelphia, 1981) vol. 2, pp. 27–55,
310–15.

6 a. All of the material included between the two
footnote marks is correctly italicized by Goodenough as a Christian interpolation.

b. Goodenough italicized *who (have come) out
of (the) gentiles* as an interpolation. This is unnecessary.

c. So the Gk. text. The reference must be to
Bethel, not Bethlehem.

d. The LXX everywhere renders Nun by Naue,
a mistake for the Gk. Naun. This is a clear indication
of dependence on the Gk. OT, rather than the Heb.

e. A curious interpretation; the biblical text calls
the *land* barren, not the *fountain*.

10 Jehoshaphat in the war;	2Chr 18
Hezekiah in sickness, and concerning Sennachereim;[f]	2Kgs 20,19
Manassah in the land of the Chaldeans after his offence;	2Chr 33:10–13
Josiah in Phassa;[g]	2Chr 35
Esdra[h] in the return;	Ezra 8
11 (4) Daniel in the hole of the lions;	Dan 6
Jonah in the belly of the whale;	Jonah 2
the three children in a furnace of fire;	Dan 3
12 Hannah in the tent before the ark;	1Sam 1
Nehemiah at the raising up of the walls; and of Zorobabel;[i]	2Ezra 2–7; Neh 3
Mattathias and his sons in your zeal;	1Mac 2–16
Jael in praises.[j]	Judg 4f.

13 (5) And now, therefore, receive the prayers of your people,
        offered up with full knowledge to you <u>through Christ in the Spirit!</u>[k]

7. A Prayer of Thanksgiving to God for His Continuing Acts of Redemption in the Past, and Now in Christ; and for His Manifold Gifts to Man, the Rational Animal (AposCon 7.38.1–8)

1 (1) We give thanks to you for all things, O Master Almighty,
        because you have not forsaken us with your mercies and your compassions;
2   but generation after generation you save, rescue, lay hold of, (and) shelter.

3 (2) For you laid hold of (people) in the days of Enos and Enoch,
        in the days of Moses and Joshua,
        in the days of the Judges,
        in the days of Samuel and Elijah and of the Prophets,
        in the days of David and of the Kings,
        in the days of Esther and Mordecai,
        in the days of Judith,
        in the days of Judah Maccabeus, and of his brothers.

4 (3) <u>And in our days you laid hold of us through your great High Priest, Jesus Christ your Child.</u>[a]   Heb 7:26–28

5   For even from the sword he rescued,
        and from famine he delivered, having maintained (us);
6   from disease he healed,
        (and) from an evil tongue he sheltered (us).

---

f. LXX often spells Sennacherib with the m ending.

g. A curious mistake based on a Hellenist's misunderstanding of the Heb. word for Passover, which has here been taken as a place name! The more correct reading would be "Josiah at (the) Passover." See Whiston, ANF 7, p. 475.

h. Ezra is commonly spelled Esdra by the LXX.

i. So the LXX spells Zerubbabel.

j. Jael is added as an afterthought, completely out of chronological sequence.

k. Goodenough correctly italicized *through Christ in the Spirit* as a Christian interpolation added onto a thoroughly Jewish prayer. Such an understanding of this prayer seems unavoidable in the light of its exclusively OT honor roll of the worshipers of God. Goodenough, following Bousset, stated that

"it is incredible that a Christian of the time when the *Apostolic Constitutions* was written could have based all his precedents for prayer upon this list of the Patriarchs down to the Maccabees, the last period of Jewish grace, and not gone on to mention the prayer or sacrifice of Christ or the achievements of the Apostles" (*By Light, Light*, p. 313).

7 a. Goodenough italicized from *And in our days* to *Child* as a Christian interpolation. This is not an obvious interpolation, and it is difficult to apply the following words to Judas Maccabeus. It is likewise difficult to apply them to Jesus. Perhaps the best course is to see these words as a Christian interpolation and then to refer the "he" to God, seeing the prayer as shifting from second person to third person. There is no easy solution.

7 For all things we give thanks to you <u>through Christ,</u>^b
    (to you) who even have given (us) an articulate voice for confession
        (of gratitude),
  and have undergirded (it with) a harmonious tongue,
    in the manner of a plectrum,
    like a musical instrument;
8   and a useful (sense of) taste,
    and a corresponding sense of touch,
    and vision for sight,
    and hearing for sound,
    and a sense of smelling for vapors,
    and hands for work,
    and feet for travel.
9 (5) And all these things you have formed out of a little drop in a womb,
    and after the shaping, you freely give immortal life,^c
    and you bring forward into light the rational animal, the man.
10 With laws, you have taught (him);
  with just ordinances, you have cleansed (him);
11   bringing on dissolution for a little while,
  You have promised the resurrection!
12 (6) Therefore indeed, what manner of life is fully able,
  and how great length of ages will be sufficient for men for thanksgiving?
13 To do so worthily would be impossible,
  but (to do so) according to (our) ability is holy.
14 For you have rescued (us) from the ungodliness of many gods,
(7) <u>and you have delivered (us) from the heresy of the Christ-murderers;</u>^d
  You have set (us) free from the ignorance that has gone astray.
15 <u>You have sent forth the Christ to men as a man, being uniquely born God;</u>
  <u>you have caused the Paraclete to live in us;</u>^e   Jn 14–16
  you have set up angels (over us);
  you have dishonored the devil.
16 Not being, you have made (us); having become, you watch over (us).
17 You measure out life;
  you supply nourishment;
  you have promised repentance.
18 (8) On behalf of all things, to you (be) the glory and the reverential awe,
    <u>through Jesus Christ,</u>^f now and always, and into the ages. Amen.

b. Goodenough italicized *Christ* as a Christian interpolation. However this may be, in the ll. following, the influence of hellenistic philosophical anthropology is obvious. Compare Philo, *SpecLeg* 1.210f.

c. Immortality, rather than being the free gift of God, given to the faithful, is viewed as given to all human beings at birth, as in hellenistic Judaism. Compare WisSol 2:23.

d. Goodenough italicized this l., from *and you have delivered* to *Christ-murderers* as a Christian

interpolation. The anti-Jewish sentiment expressed here is in strong contrast to the pro-Jewish sentiment of the majority of these prayers.

e. Goodenough italicized this and the preceding l., from *You have sent forth* to *in us*, as another Christian interpolation.

f. Goodenough italicized *through Jesus Christ* as a Christian interpolation. The prayer as a whole is a rather uneasy combination of disparate materials from hellenistic Judaism and Christianity.

8. Instruction for Catechumens (*AposCon* 7.39.2–4)[a]
Translated by D. A. Fiensy.

1 (2) Let the one who is to be instructed in piety[b] be taught before baptism: knowledge[c] concerning the unbegotten God, <u>understanding[d] concerning the only begotten son,</u>
2 <u>and full assurance concerning the Holy Spirit.</u> •Let him learn the order of a distinguished creation,[e] the sequence of providence,[f] the judgment seats of different legislation,[g] why the world came to be and why man was appointed a world   3:18; 12:35
3 (3) citizen. •Let him understand his own nature, of what sort it is. Let him be educated in how God punished the wicked by water and fire, and glorified the saints in   Gen 7; 19:24
4 each generation: •I mean Seth, Enos, Enoch, Noah, Abraham and his descendants, Melchisedek, Job, Moses, both Joshua[h] and Caleb, Phinehas the priest, and the
5 holy ones in each generation. •And how God, though he foresaw,[i] did not abandon the race of men, but summoned them at various times from error and folly *into*   1Tim 2:4
the understanding of truth, leading them from servitude and impiety into freedom and piety, from iniquity into righteousness, from eternal death into everlasting
6 (4) life. •Let the one who offers himself learn during his instruction these things and those that are related to them.

9. A Prayer of Praise to God for His Greatness, and for His Appointment of Leaders for His People (*AposCon* 8.5.1–4)

1 (1) The one who is, Master, Lord, God the Almighty;
     the only one without origin and without a king;
2   the one who is forever, and who exists before the ages;
     the one needing nothing in any way, and greater than every cause and origin;
3   the only true one, the only wise one;
     the one who is alone Most High;
4   the one who is by nature invisible;   1Tim 1:17
     whose knowledge is without beginning;
5   the only good one, and incomparable one;   Mt 19:17
     the one who knows all things before their origin;
6   the knower of the hidden things,   Dan 2:22
     the unapproachable one,
     the one without a master;
7 (2)   the God and Father <u>of your only Son, our God and Savior,</u>

---

8 a. This is of course not a prayer at all but an outline of catechetical instruction. That the initiate is required to learn nothing of the NT heroes or the work of Christ led Goodenough to argue (*By Light, Light,* p. 327) that this outline of instruction originated in Judaism.

   b. Gk. *katēcheisthai ton logon tēs eusebeias,* lit. "be instructed regarding the teaching of piety." For this use of *logos,* see Lampe, p. 808.

   c. Gk. *gnōsis.*

   d. Gk. *epignōsis.*

   e. Or as Whiston, *ANF* 7, p. 475, translates: "the order of the several parts of the creation." Gk. *dēmiourgias diaphorou taxin.* But it is doubtful if *diaphoros* in the singular can mean "several." See LSJM 1,b. For the emphasis on the order of creation in Philo, see *Op* 13–83.

   f. Gk. *pronoias heirmon.* Possibly this is equal to the Stoic belief in the chain of destiny which continuously connects the causes of events. See Arnim 2.918 (*heimarmenē heirmos tis ousa*). Philo expressed a similar belief in *Mut* 135, *De Aet* 75 (see F. H. Colson's translation and notes in the LCL Philo, vol. 5, pp. 210f.; vol. 9, pp. 236f.).

   g. Gk. *nomothesias diaphorou dikaiōtēria.* The different legislation is, according to Goodenough (*By Light, Light,* pp. 327n, 350), the law as implanted and as written.

   h. Gk. *Iēsoun,* which is obviously Joshua of the OT and not "Jesus." The names in Greek are identical.

   i. Gk. *pronooumenos* can also mean "to provide for," as Whiston (*ANF* 7, p. 476) has rendered it.

the maker of the whole universe <u>through him;</u>
8   the Administrator, the Guardian,
the Father of mercies, and God of all consolation,   2Cor 1:3
the one who dwells in (the) heights, and who observes humble things;   Ps 112:5f LXX
9 (3)   <u>you are the one who gave standards for the Church,</u>
     <u>through the appearance in flesh of your Christ,</u>
     <u>subject to the witness by the Paraclete,</u>   7:15; Jn 14–16
     <u>through your apostles and through us bishops who by your grace</u>
       <u>are present.</u>[a]
10 (You are) the one who marked out beforehand, from the beginning,
     priests for dominion over your people:
11   Abel at first,
       Seth and Enos and Enoch and Noah, and Melchizedek and Job;
12 (4)   the one who showed forth Abraham, and the other patriarchs,
       together with your faithful servants Moses and Aaron, and Eleazar
       and Phinehas;
13   the one who prepared beforehand from among them rulers and priests in the
     tent of the testimony;
14   the one choosing for yourself Samuel, to be a priest and a prophet;
15   the one who did not forsake your sanctuary without public services;
16   the one who was pleased to be glorified by those you have chosen.[b]

10. A Prayer on Behalf of the Catechumens (*AposCon* 8.6.5–8)
Translated by D. A. Fiensy.

1 (5) Let us all earnestly entreat God on behalf of the catechumens:
2   that the one who is good and loves mankind will kindly hear their prayers;
     and having received their supplication, that he may assist them and grant
3   them for their good the requests of their hearts;   Ps 37:4
4   that he may reveal to them the <u>gospel of his Christ,</u>
5   illumine them,
      and give them understanding,
      educate them in the knowledge of God,
6   teach them his ordinances and judgments,   Ps 119:12
      implant in them his pure and saving fear,
      open the ears of their hearts
      to engage in his law day and night;[a]   Ps 1:2
7 (6) and that he may establish them in piety,
      unify and number them among his holy flock,
8   grant them (the) washing of regeneration,   Tit 3:5
        the garment of incorruption,
        (and) real life;
9   and that he may save them from all impiety,
     and give place to no adversary against them;

9 a. All of the material between the two footnote marks is italicized by Goodenough as a Christian interpolation. This is not as obvious as in some of the other cases; it is possible that the prayer was originally composed by a Christian author.

b. This prayer originally could have been used by hellenistic Judaism for the consecration of a priest and later taken over and interpolated by Christians for use in the consecration of presbyters.

However, such a prayer could have been framed in its entirety by a Christian author seeking justification from the OT for the priestly prerogatives of a growing clerical caste.

10 a. Cf. Ab 3:4,7; 4:12. The emphasis in vs. 6 on the Law led Goodenough to argue (*By Light, Light,* pp. 328f.) for Jewish authorship of the prayer.

10   and that he may cleanse them from all pollution of flesh and spirit,   2Cor 7:1
         and dwell in them,   Lev 26:17f.
         and walk (among them) through his <u>Christ,</u>   2Cor 6:16
11   and bless their comings in, and their goings out,   Ps 121:8
         and guide their affairs for their good.
12 (7) Let us still earnestly supplicate for them that,
         obtaining remission of their trespasses through initiation,[b]
13   they may be deemed worthy of the holy mysteries, and of remaining constantly
         with the saints.
14 (8) Arise, catechumens, request the peace of God through his <u>Christ,</u>
15   that the day be peaceable and free from sin,
         even the entire time of your life,
16   that your end be <u>Christian,</u>[c]
         that God be gracious and kind,
         (that God grant) the forgiveness of trespasses.
17 Dedicate yourselves to the only unbegotten God through his <u>Christ.</u>
18 Bow down and receive a blessing.

11. A Prayer of Entreaty for God's Mercy upon the Penitent (*AposCon* 8.9.8f.)

1 (8) O Almighty God, eternal one,
         Master of the whole universe,
         Creator and President of everything,
2   the one who showed forth man as a (micro-)cosm of the cosmos <u>through</u>   3:20
         <u>Christ,</u>[a]
3   and who gave an implanted and written law to him,   Jas 1:21, 1:25;
         so that he might live lawfully as a rational being,   Rom 2:14f.; 12:42; 1:5
4   and when he had sinned, gave him your goodness, as a pledge to lead him   Rom 2:4
         to repentance;
5 look upon those who have bent the neck of their soul and body to you, because
6   *He does not desire the death of the sinner, but his repentance,*   Ezek 33:11
      so that he might turn back from his way of evil, and live!
7 (9) (You are) the one who accepted the repentance of the Ninevites;   Jonah 3
8   the one desiring all men to be saved, and to come to a knowledge of truth;   1Tim 2:4; cf. 8:5
9   <u>the one who accepted the son who had consumed his life's savings with loose</u>   Lk 15:13, 20
         <u>living,</u>
      with fatherly feelings because of his repentance.[b]
10 Also now yourself receive from your supplicants their change of mind;
         for there is no one who will not sin against you.   1Kgs 8:46
11 For, if you, Lord, should watch lawlessness closely, Lord, who could stand his   Ps 129:3f. LXX
         ground?
   Because with you there is the means for taking away sin!

b. Gk. *myesis*. This word and the related word in the same vs. (*mysterion*) are terms from the pagan mystery religions but are also found in Philo (e.g. *LegAll* 3.100; *Quaes Gen* 4.8; *Sac* 60). See R. Reitzenstein, *The Hellenistic Mystery Religions*, trans. J. E. Steely (Pittsburgh, 1978; published in German in 1926), p. 241; also the entries in LSJM "myeo" and "mysterion." However, the term *mysterion* is used ordinarily of the sacraments in patristic writings. See Lampe.

c. Or "your death be Christian."

11 a. Goodenough italicized *through Christ* as a Christian interpolation.

b. All the material between the two footnotes is italicized by Goodenough as a Christian interpolation. This position is entirely possible, but it is neither obvious nor necessary. The entire prayer could have been written by a Christian who accepted the OT as Christian Scripture and who was also deeply influenced by Platonic or Neoplatonic philosophy. Goodenough argues (p. 332) that the philosophy of repentance in this prayer is Jewish; it could, of course, be Christian.

12. A Prayer of Praise to God, Rehearsing the Grounds in Redemption and in Creation Which Make Praise So Fitting for God's Redeemed Creature, Man (*AposCon* 8.12.6–27)

1 (6) It is truly worthy and right before all things to sing a hymn to you,
  the one who is truly God;

2 the one who is before things that have been made;
  from whom every family in heaven and upon earth is named;   Eph 3:15

3 the only one without origin, and without a beginning;
  and not ruled by a king, and without a master;

4 the one not in want;
  the supplier of every good (thing);

5 the one far exceeding every cause and origin;
  the one always the same, and holding just so;

6 from whom are all things,   1Cor 8:6
   just as from some starting-point, it came in order to be.

7 (7) For you are the knowledge without beginning;
  the eternal vision;
  the hearing without origin;
  the wisdom without teaching;

8 the first by nature,
  and only one in being,
  and far exceeding every number;

9 the one who brought everything into being out of non-being, through[a] your Jn 1:14,18
   only Son,
   and gave him birth before all the ages,
   by purpose, and power, and unmediated goodness—

10 an only Son, a divine Word, a living Wisdom, WisSol 9:1f.
  a firstborn of all creation, (Jn 1:1,18);
            WisSol 9:9
  a messenger[b] of your great purpose, (Col 1:15)
            3:16
  your high priest; Isa 9:5 LXX

11 both king and lord of all intelligible and perceptible nature, (Heb 7)
  the one before all things, through whom are all things! WisSol 9:9 (Col
            1:17; 1Cor 8:6)

12 (8) For you, O eternal God, have made all things through him, WisSol 9:1f.,9;
  and through him by suitable foreknowledge you design everything. 10:1f. (Jn 1:3)
            WisSol 8:8

13 For through him you freely gave being,
  (and) through him also you gave well-being.

14 (You are) the God and Father of your only Son,[c]
  who through him before all things made the cherubim and the seraphim, WisSol 9
  both ages and (heavenly) hosts,
  both powers and authorities, (Col 1:16) 4:11
  both rulers and thrones,
  both archangels and angels;

---

12 a. [Goodenough did not italicize the following lines as a Christian interpolation; and the present contributors are also reluctant to see them as a Christian addition. But, in light of the numerous parallels to them in New Testament passsages, as noted by the marginalia, and in comparison with the other clearly Christian lines in these hymns, I have no hesitancy in seeing them as a Christian interpolation, or better a Christian redaction of a Jewish sentence. The redactor deleted what followed "through" (l. 9) and specified that "the only Son," the "Word," created all things. The redaction runs from "your only Son" through

"through whom are all things!" The Jewish original specified the agent of creation, perhaps "the Word," or "Wisdom"—both of which are agents of creation according to WisSol 9—and then celebrated monotheism and God as the ultimate cause of creation (l. 12). —J.H.C.]

b. [Gk. *angelon*; perhaps "angel"; and that translation corresponds with Goodenough's rendering. Cf. GosThom 82, according to which Peter confesses that Jesus is "like a righteous angel" (*ekeine nouangelos endikaios*). —J.H.C.]

c. [Not italicized by Goodenough. The phrase "of your only Son" should be read in terms of

15   and after all these, having made through him this world that is seen, and   (Jn 1:3)
        everything in it.

16 (9) For you are the one who placed the heaven like a vaulted arch,   Isa 40:22
        and like a screen stretched it out;   Ps 103:2 LXX

17   and founded the earth upon nothing, by judgment alone;   Job 26:7

18   the one who fixed a firmament, and prepared night and day;   Gen 1

19   the one who brought light out of the treasuries, and at the contraction of this
            (light),
        the one who brought the darkness for rest for the living creatures moving
            about in the world;

20   the one who appointed the sun for rule (over) the day in heaven,   Gen 1:16
            and the moon for rule (over) the night,
        and engraved the choir of the stars in heaven, for praise of your great splendor;

21 (10) the one who made water for drinking and cleansing,
        lively air for breathing in and breathing out,
            and for utterance of a voice,
            the air having been struck by a tongue,
            and (the sense of) hearing, working together under it, so as to hear,
            taking in the speech falling upon it;

22 (11) the one who made fire for encouragement (in) darkness,
        for fulfillment of want,
        and for us to be warmed and enlightened by it;

23 (12) the one who separated the great sea from the land,
        who indeed declared the one for navigation,
        and made the other passable for feet;

24   who filled the one with living creatures, small and great,   Ps 103:25 LXX
        and filled up the other with tame animals and untamed;

25   having encircled (it) with manifold plants,
        and having crowned (it) with herbs,
        and having beautified (it) with flowers,
        and having enriched (it) with seeds;

26 (13) the one who framed an abyss,
        and surrounded it with a great hollow,
        seas of salt waters having been heaped up;

27   the one who by winds sometimes raises it to a crest, to become the height   Jer 5:22;
            of mountains,   Job 38:10
        and sometimes spreads it out into a plain,
        and sometimes indeed driving it mad with storm,
        and sometimes soothing it with a calm,
            so as to be easy for crossing by seafaring sailors;

28 (14) the one who encircled with rivers the world
        which came into being by you through Christ,[d]   Jn 1:3
        and flooded it with mountain torrents,
        and drenched it with never-failing springs,
        and bound it tightly all around with mountains,
            for an unshakable foundation of a most steadfast earth.

29 (15) For you filled your world, and divided and arranged it,
        with sweet-smelling and healing herbs;

30   with many and varied living creatures,
        with strong ones and with weak ones,
        with edible ones and with productive ones,
        with tame ones and with untamed ones;

31   with hissings of serpents,
        with screams of many-colored birds;

12:9. These prayers are not only interpolated but
redacted from such Jewish ideas. —J.H.C.]

d. Goodenough italicized only *Christ* as a Christian interpolation.

32   with cycles of years,
        with numbers of months and days;
        with arrangements of customs;

33   with courses of rain-producing clouds, for the generation of fruits, and the
        care of living creatures;

34   (and with) a balance of winds,   Job 28:25
        blowing when they are ordered by you;
        (and) the multitude of plants and herbs.

35 (16) And you not only made the world,
    but you also made the world citizen in it,   3:18–20
    declaring him (to be) a (micro-)cosm of the cosmos.

36 For you said by your Wisdom,   3:19
    Let us make man according to our image,   Gen 1:26
    and according to (our) likeness;
    and let them rule the fish of the sea,
    and the winged birds of the heaven.

37 (17) Therefore also you have made him out of immortal soul,
    and out of a body that may be scattered;

38   the one indeed out of that which is not,
        but the other out of the four elements.

39 And you have indeed given to him, with reference to the soul,
    rational discrimination,
    distinguishing of piety and impiety,
    observation of right and wrong.

40 While with reference to the body,
    you have given (him) five senses,
    and the movement involving change of place.

41 (18) For you, O God Almighty, through Christ,[e]
    planted a paradise in Eden, eastward,   Gen 2:8
    with all manner of edible foods, in (proper) order;

42   and into it, as if into a very expensive home, you brought him.

43 And indeed, you have given to him an implanted law to do,   Rom 2:14f.
    so that from himself, and by himself,   1:5
    he might have the seeds of divine knowledge.

44 (19) So, having brought (him) into the paradise of luxury,   Gen 2:15–17
    you allowed him the right to partake of all things.

45 But of only one thing did you refuse him the taste;
    in hope of greater things,
    in order that, if he should keep the commandment,
    he might receive immortality as a reward for this.

46 (20) But, having cared nothing for the commandment,   Gen 3
    and having tasted of the forbidden fruit,
    by the trickery of a serpent,
    and by the counsel of a woman,
    you indeed rightly thrust him out from paradise.

47 Yet in goodness, you did not overlook him who was perishing forever,
    for he was your work of art.

48   But, having subjected to him the creation,
     You have given to him, through sweat and hard labors, to provide by himself Gen 3:17–19
        the nourishment for his own family,
        while you are causing all things to grow, and to ripen.

49 And in time, having caused him to fall asleep for a while,
    you called (him) by an oath to new birth;   ApMos 28:4

50   having dissolved the boundaries of death,   Vita 51:2

---

e. Goodenough italicized only *Christ* as a Christian interpolation.

you promised life by resurrection!

51 (21) And not only this; but also those who poured forth from him,
        to become an innumerable multitude—

52   those who continued with you, you glorified,
        while those who separated from you, you punished.

53 And while indeed from Abel, as from a devout man,   Gen 4
        you favorably received a sacrifice;

54 from the brother-murderer Cain,
        you turned aside the offering as from an accursed person.

55 And in addition to these, you took hold of Seth and Enos, and you translated Gen 4:25f.
Enoch.   Gen 5:24

56 (22) For you are the maker of man,
        and the supplier of life,
        and the fulfiller of need,

57   and the dispenser of laws,
        and the rewarder of those keeping them,
        and the avenger of those transgressing them;

58 the one who brought the great flood on the world,   Gen 6–9; 2Pet
        because of the multitude of those who lived godlessly; 2:5

59   and who delivered the righteous Noah from the flood in an ark,
        together with eight souls;   1Pet 3:20

60   an end indeed of those who have passed on,
        but a beginning of those about to be born.

61 (You are) the one who kindled the fearful fire against the five cities of Sodom, Gen 19; WisSol
        and turned a fruitful land into salt because of those living in it, 10:6
        and snatched away pious Lot from the burning. Ps 106:34 LXX
    You are the one who delivered Abraham from ancestral godlessness, WisSol 10:7
          2Pet 2:7

62 (23)   and appointed him heir of the world,   Gen 12
        and showed to him your Christ;[f] (Rom 4:13)

63 the one who appointed Melchizedek a high priest in your service; Gen 14:18
        who declared your much-enduring servant Job conqueror of the archevil
        serpent;

64   who made Isaac a son of promise;   Gen 17:19
        (and) Jacob, father of twelve sons; and you formed his descendants into a
        multitude;[g]
        and who led (them) into Egypt, with seventy-five souls. Gen 46:27 LXX

65 (24) You, O Lord, did not neglect Joseph,   Gen 41
        but gave to him to rule over Egypt—
        a reward of the self-control that you enable.

66 You, O Lord, did not disregard the Hebrews,   Ex 1–15
        being worn out by hard labor under the Egyptians.

67   But, on account of the promises (made) to the fathers,
        you delivered (them), having punished the Egyptians.

68 (25) And when men had corrupted the natural law,   Rom 1:21–25
        and at one time, indeed, having esteemed the creation as happening without
        cause,
        and at another time, having honored it more than is right,
        comparing it to you, to the God of the universe;

69   you did not permit them to go astray,
        but showed forth your holy servant Moses,
        having given through him the written Law, as an aid to the natural (law). Ex 20; Isa 8:20
          LXX 1:5

---

f. Goodenough italicized only *Christ* as a Christian interpolation.

  g. [Lit. ". . . Jacob, father of twelve sons, and

you scattered those from him into a multitude . . ."
—J.H.C.]

70 And you showed the creation to be your work,
   and you banished the polytheistic error.
71 You glorified Aaron, and those who came after him, with priestly honor;
72 you punished the Hebrews when they sinned;
   you received those who returned (to you).
73 (26) You exacted vengeance on the Egyptians with ten plagues;   Ex 4–17
   you carried the Israelites across a sea, dividing it;
   you destroyed the pursuing Egyptians under water;
74 you sweetened bitter water with wood;   Num 11:31
   you poured forth water out of jagged rock;   Ex 17; Num 20
75 you rained the manna out of heaven,   Ps 77:24 LXX;
     a mother-of-quail nourishment out of the air;   Ex 16
76 you comforted them with a pillar of fire by night, for light,   Neh 9:19
     and a pillar of cloud by day, for shade;
77 you showed forth Joshua, the soldier;   Josh 1–13
   you destroyed seven Canaanite nations through him;
78 you tore in two the Jordan;
   you dried up the rivers of Etham;[h]   Ps 73:15 LXX
79 you broke down walls without machines (of war),
   and without human hand.
80 (27) Glory is yours, because of all these things,
     O Master Almighty!
81   Innumerable armies of angels worship you—archangels, thrones, dominions,   Col 1:16
     rulers, authorities, powers, eternal armies;   4:11
82   the cherubim and the six-winged seraphim, with two covering up their feet,   Isa 6:2
     and with two their heads, and with two flying;
83   and saying together with thousands on thousands of archangels,   Dan 7:10
     and ten thousand times ten thousand angels,
   incessantly and loudly crying out
84   —and all the people together, let them say—
     "Holy, holy, holy is Lord Sabaoth, the heaven and the earth are full of   Isa 6:3
     his glory!
85   (He is) blessed forever!" Amen.[i]   Rom 1:25

13. A Prayer of Praise and Benediction, Spoken by a Bishop at the Close of the Eucharistic Service (*AposCon* 8.15.7–9)

1 (7) . . . O God, the Almighty, the True one and Incomparable one,
     who is everywhere, and is present in all things;
     and who is in nothing as though being one certain thing;[a]
     the one who is not circumscribed in places;
2   the one who is not growing old in time;

h. Following the LXX, the prayer mistakes the Heb. word for "overflowing" for a place name, Etham.

i. This prayer should be compared with Prayer 3 (7.34:1–8). Prayer 12 contains a remarkable synthesis of Christian, Gk., and Jewish viewpoints, all united to serve in Christian liturgy. The high christological statements of vss. 7–15 are so integral to the prayer that Goodenough, who wishes to see much Jewish material preserved in it, makes no effort to excise them as interpolations; instead he suggests that Paul may have borrowed from them (p. 325), a solution which seems forced. The OT teaching concerning creation is taken up and commented on from a hellenistic philosophical and scientific viewpoint (see especially vss. 22–40). The prayer concludes with a biblically based theological statement about the fall of man, derived from the OT. The context of this prayer seems to be the celebration of the Eucharist; it is followed immediately by a prayer that centers upon God's redemption in Jesus Christ.

13 a. This philosophically oriented description of God is reminiscent of Philo; cf. *LegAll* 3.51.

the one who does not come to an end in the ages;

3   the one who is not deceived by words;

the one who is not subject to origin;

the one who does not need a guardian;

4   the one who is above corruption;

the one who does not admit change;

the one who by nature is unchangeable;

5   the one who dwells in unapproachable light;   1Tim 6:16

the one who is by nature invisible;

6   the one who is known by all those who with good will seek you with rational natures;

7   the one who is understood by those who with good will seek after you;

8   the God of Israel, the one truly seeing,[b]   Gen 35:9f.

Your people who have believed in Christ:[c]   5:8

9 (8)   being gracious, attend to me on account of your name,

and bless those who have bended low their necks before you,

and give to them the requests of their hearts—the things that are profitable— Ps 36:4 LXX

10   and do not make one of them a castaway from your Kingdom,

but consecrate them, guard, shelter, assist, deliver them from the stranger, from every enemy;

11   preserve their homes,

guard their goings in and goings out!   Ps 120:8 LXX

12 (9) Because to you (belong) glory, praise, splendor, reverence, (and) worship;

13   [d]and to your Servant Jesus, to your Christ, to our Lord, both God and King; and to the Holy Spirit;[d]

now, and always, and into the ages of the ages. Amen.

14. A Portion of a Prayer Prayed at the Ordination of Presbyters (*AposCon* 8.16.3)

1 (3) O Lord, Almighty, our God,

who through Christ[a] made everything,   Jn 1:3

and through him provide for everything appropriately;

2   for to the One having power to make differing things,   WisSol 6:8

to this One belongs power also to provide in differing ways;

3   for through him, O God, you indeed provide for those who are immortal in a place of security, in a mansion;[b]

4   while for those who are mortal, (you provide) in successive ways,

for the soul by meditation upon laws,

for the body by the satisfaction of wants.[c]

5   Now also yourself, look upon your holy Church and increase it; and multiply those leading it;

6   and give power so that they may work hard in word and in deed,   1Tim 5:17

for the building up of your people! . . .

---

b. Israel as "the one truly seeing" is a Philonic phrase. See above, Prayer 5, footnote d.

c. Goodenough italicized from *who* to *Christ* as a Christian interpolation.

d. All of the material between the two footnote marks is correctly italicized by Goodenough as a Christian interpolation.

14 a. Goodenough italicized *Christ* as a Christian interpolation. [Here, as in 3:1, I think that "Christ"

may have replaced "the Word"; the following "through him" demands this or a similar term; 12:10 reveals that the Jewish author, as the author of WisSol 8–10, believed creation was by God through the Word, who is Wisdom. —J.H.C.]

b. Or "simply by keeping."

c. Goodenough ended the prayer at this point. While containing elements reminiscent of hellenistic Judaism, the prayer could have been composed as it is by a Christian for liturgy purposes.

15. A Prayer to Accompany the Offering of Firstfruits (*AposCon* 8.40.2–4)

1 (2) We give thanks to you, O Lord Almighty,
    Maker and Superintendent of the universe,
      <u>through your only Son, Jesus Christ, our Lord,</u>[a]
    for the firstfruit offerings to you,
      not such as we ought (to give),
      but such as we are able (to give).
2 (3) For who among men is able to give thanks to you worthily,
    on behalf of the things you have given to them for partaking in?
  3 O God of Abraham, and Isaac, and Jacob,   Acts 3:13
    and of all the holy ones,
    the One who brought all things to perfection through your word,   Gen 1
and commanded the earth to produce all manner of fruits for our gladdening and
    food;
  4 who gave forage for the duller and sheepish (creatures):
    foliage for those eating grass,
    and to some, indeed, raw meat,
    while to some, seeds;
  5   yet to us, grain, the useful and appropriate food,
    and various other things—
    some indeed, for (our) use,
    while others for (our) health,
    still others for (our) enjoyment.
6 (4) For all these things, therefore, you are praised (in hymns),
    for your good deeds to all <u>[b]through Christ,</u>
    <u>with whom to you be glory, honor, and awe;</u>
    <u>and to the Holy Spirit, forever. Amen.</u>

16. Funeral Prayer for the Dead (*AposCon* 8.41.2–5)

1 (2) And on behalf of those our brothers who are at rest <u>in Christ,</u>[a]
    let us beg;
  2   on behalf of the repose of this brother or that sister,
    let us beg;
  3   that God, the lover of man, having received his soul,
    may forgive him every sin—voluntary and involuntary;
  4   and being gracious and favorable,
    may appoint him to a position among the godly ones,   Lk 16:23
    sent into the embrace of Abraham, and Isaac, and Jacob,
    with all those from of old who were well pleasing, and who did his will;
    where pain and grief and moaning have fled away.   Isa 35:10
  5 Let us arise! Let us commit ourselves, and one another, to the eternal God,
    through the Word (which was) in the beginning!   Jn 1:1
6 (3) And let <u>the bishop</u>[b] say,
  (4)   "O you who are by nature immortal and unending,

---

15 a. Goodenough italicized this entire l. as a Christian interpolation.

  b. Goodenough italicized from this point to the end of the prayer as a Christian interpolation. This is possible; but again we cannot be certain.

16 a. Goodenough italicized *in Christ* as a Christian interpolation.

  b. Goodenough italicized *the bishop* as a Christian interpolation.

through whom everything immortal and mortal has come into being;

7 who with artistic skill made this rational living being, man, the mortal world
　　citizen,   3:18–20

and who promised resurrection;

8 who did not permit Enoch and Elijah to experience death,

the God of Abraham, and Isaac, and Jacob,

not as of the dead, but as God of the living, are you.   Mt 22:32; Lk
　　　　　　　　　　　　　　　　　　　　　　　　　　　　　　　　　　20:38

9 Because, with you, all souls are alive,

and the spirits of the righteous are in your hand, whom anguish will not touch.   WisSol 3:1

10 For all those who are set apart are under your hand.   Deut 33:3

11 (5) Also now yourself, look upon this your servant,

　　　　whom you have chosen, and received into another sphere;

12 and forgive him, if he has committed any great sin, voluntarily or involuntarily;

and place beside him favorable angels;

and appoint him (a place) in the embrace of the patriarchs, and the prophets, and

13　　the apostles,ᶜ

and of all those who from of old were pleasing to you;

14 where there cannot be grief, and pain, and moaning,   Isa 35:10

but a free place of godly ones,

and a land of upright ones, set up for you,

　　　ᵈand for those in it who see the glory of your Christ;

15 With whom to you be glory, honor, and awe, thanksgiving and worship,

and to the Holy Spirit, forever. Amen.

---

c. Goodenough correctly italicized *and the apostles* as a Christian interpolation.

d. Goodenough correctly italicized from this
point to the end of the prayer as a Christian

interpolation. The Christian sections may be more
extensive. The prayer incorporates possible Christian elements in its resemblances to Jn 1:1; Mt
22:32; and Lk 20:38.

PRAYER OF JOSEPH

(First Century A.D.)

A NEW TRANSLATION WITH INTRODUCTION

BY J. Z. SMITH

The Prayer of Joseph is a unique text which maintains that the patriarch Jacob was the earthly incarnation of the angel Israel. The central tale, in the fragments that have survived, concerns a conflict between the angels Israel and Uriel over their relative rank in heaven. The title is enigmatic as Joseph is not mentioned in the surviving fragments, but the text was most likely an extended testament developed out of Jacob's blessing of Joseph's sons in Genesis 48. The narrative of Jacob wrestling with the "man" in Genesis 32:24–31 has contributed the central motifs to the text.

Texts

According to the *Stichometry* of Nicephorus, the Prayer of Joseph originally contained eleven hundred lines. Only three fragments containing nine Greek sentences have survived in the writings of Origen. Fragment A is quoted in Origen's *Commentary on John* by way of supporting his argument that John the Baptist was an angel who became incarnate in order to bear witness to Jesus.[1] Fragment B, a single sentence, is cited in Gregory and Basil's compilation of Origen, the *Philocalia*, and is also quoted in Eusebius, *The Preparation of the Gospel* as well as in the Latin *Commentary on Genesis* by Procopius of Gaza.[2] Fragment C, also from the *Philocalia*, quotes Fragment B and paraphrases Fragment A.[3] In addition to these fragments, the title (*Proseuchē Iōsēph*) occurs in several lists of apocryphal works, and three possible allusions to the Prayer of Joseph in other writings have been suggested by scholars.[4] None of these adds to our knowledge of the text.

---

[1] Origen, *CommJn* 2:31 (25), pp. 189f. in the critical edition by E. Preuschen, GCS 10. Also, C. Blanc, *Origène: Commentaire sur Saint Jean*, SC 120, pp. 334–37.

[2] Origen, *Philoc* 33:15 in the edition by J. A. Robinson (Cambridge, 1893) pp. 203f. Cf. the Gk. quotation in Eusebius, *PrEv* 6:11; 64 in the critical edition by K. Mras, GCS 43:1, p. 356; and the Lat. citation in Procopius of Gaza, *CommGen* 29 (PL 87:1, cols. 95f.).

[3] Origen, *Philoc* 33:19 in Robinson's edition, p. 208. All three fragments of the PrJos are conveniently edited in A. Resch, *Agrapha*, pp. 295f., and A.-M. Denis, *Fragmenta Pseudepigraphorum Graeca* (Leiden, 1970) pp. 61f.

[4] The PrJos is listed in the *Stichometry* of Nicephorus (HSW, vol. 1, pp. 50f.); the *List of Sixty Books* (HSW, vol. 1, pp. 51f.); the *Synopsis* of Pseudo-Athanasius (in Gk.: T. Zahn, *Geschichte des neutestamentlichen Kanons* [Erlangen, 1888–92] vol. 2, p. 317; Slav. recensions, W. Lüdtke, "Beiträge zu slavischen Apokryphen, 5," *ZAW* 31 [1911] 230–35); and a list by the Arm. Mechither of Arivank [Zahn, *Forschungen des neutestamentlichen Kanons* (Leipzig, 1893) vol. 5, p. 116.]). In some lists, the PrJos appears in the place usually assigned to JosAsen and appears to refer to this work (see C. Burchard, *Untersuchungen zu Joseph und Aseneth* [WUNT 8; Tübingen, 1965] pp. 32–34). [Also see Burchard's contribution on JosAsen in the present collection. —J.H.C.]

Michael Glycas, *Annales* 2:171 (ed. I. Bekker, *Corpus Scriptorum Historiae Byzantinae* 27 [Bonnaer, 1836] p. 321), refers to a contest between Jacob and the angel Raphael as being in a text entitled the PrJos. The reference in Priscillian, *Liber de Fide et de Apocryphis* (ed. G. Schepss [Leipzig, 1889] pp. 45f.): "Whoever heard of a prophecy by Jacob being included in the canon?" may refer to the PrJos. The reference in AscenIs 4:22 to the "Words of Joseph the Just" most probably does not refer to PrJos.

Original language

The 164 words that have survived from the Prayer of Joseph in direct quotation are too scant to permit an identification of the original language. In the scholarly literature, the majority of commentators have abstained from hazarding an opinion; for those who have, much has depended on the assignment of the text to either Jewish or Christian authorship. For those who hold that it was originally a Jewish work, an Aramaic original is presumed; for those who hold to a Christian authorship, a Greek. Neither of these identifications is based on linguistic criteria.

The Prayer of Joseph contains three words that have been identified as *hapax legomena*: one (Fragment A, 7 *archichiliarchos*, chief captain) is a unique occurrence of what appears to be a technical military term that, if historical, might suggest the date and provenance of the text. The other two—*proektisthēsan* (Fragment A, 2 precreated) and the phrase "imperishable name" (Fragment A, 9 *onomata asbestos*)—are rare theological terms that occur in later Christian texts.[5]

The largest number of linguistic and theological parallels are to Egyptian Greek and Coptic Jewish and Christian texts; the significant narrative details in the Prayer of Joseph are most closely paralleled by Aramaic materials.

Date

The dating of Origen's *Commentary on John* with its notice of the Prayer of Joseph as "an apocrypha presently in use among the Hebrews" as prior to A.D. 231 provides a secure latest possible date. The various parallels to both hellenistic and Aramaic materials would suggest a first-century date.

Provenance

Given the uncertainty with respect to original language and date, any decision regarding provenance is impossible. If the Greco-Egyptian Jewish and Christian parallels are stressed, Alexandria would appear most likely. If the Aramaic parallels are stressed, a Palestinian provenance seems more likely.

Historical importance

There are no historical allusions in the Prayer of Joseph. No particular situation appears to be reflected in the text.

Theological importance

Given the extant remains of the Prayer of Joseph, its theological significance must be located in the remarkable cluster of titles attributed to the angel Israel, its notion of Jacob as the incarnation of the angel Israel, and its striking narrative of a combat between Uriel and Israel. Because of these, many scholars have sought to relate the Prayer of Joseph in some way to Christian tradition: either as a Jewish-Christian or gnostic text (Resch, Batiffol, Schneider, Grant, Winter, Daniélou) or as a Jewish anti-Christian work (Charles, Marshall, James, Russell, Turner) or as a Christian anti-Jewish polemic (Burch).[6] But the close

---

[5] Gk. *proktizō* is applied to Christ in Christian tradition in Didymus of Alexandria, *De Trinitate* 3:4 (PG, vol. 39, col. 832) and Gelasius Cyzicus, *Historia concilii nicaeni* 2:16 (PG, vol. 85, col. 1257). The term "imperishable name" occurs in Esaias, *Oratio* 4:9 (ed. Augustinos [Jerusalem, 1911] p. 26) in a homily on Gen 28:13–15, where God promises Jacob that his name will never be forgotten.

[6] Resch, *Agrapha*, p. 297; P. Batiffol, *Studia Patristica* (Paris, 1889) 1.17; T. Schneider, "Der Engel Jakob bei Mani," *ZNW* 33 (1934) 218f.; R. M. Grant, *Gnosticism and Early Christianity* (New York, 1959) pp. 19, 190; P. Winter, "Monogenēs para Patros," *ZRGG* 5 (1953) 351f., 358, 361; J. Daniélou, "Trinité et angélologie dans la théologie judéo-chrétienne," *RSR* 45 (1947) 23–25; J. Daniélou, *Théologie du Judéo-Christianisme* (Paris, 1958) pp. 182–85 (note especially the central passage [184f.] has been omitted in the ET, *Theology of Jewish Christianity* [London, 1964] pp. 132–34, as the author no longer accepts his original interpretation); R. H. Charles, *The Ascension of Isaiah* (Edinburgh, 1900) p. 39; J. T. Marshall, "Joseph, Prayer of," in Hastings' *DB*, vol. 2, p. 362; D. S.

parallels in technical terms, narrative tradition and theology to both hellenistic and Palestinian Jewish traditions make it most probable that Origen was right in identifying the Prayer of Joseph as Jewish (Priebatsch, Stein, Smith).[7] The Prayer is most likely to be situated within those first-century Jewish groups, both in Palestine and in the Diaspora, both before and after the destruction of the Temple, that sought to develop a notion of community, principles of authority, sources of revelation, and modes of access to divinity apart from the Jerusalem Temple, its traditions, priests, and cult. This was accomplished largely through the creation of a pseudepigraphical literature of revelation to the patriarchs (beginning already with the ascription of the Pentateuch to Moses) and by the development of the complex rituals and visionary literature of the early Jewish Merkabah (throne) mystics. Both of these tendencies are related to the Prayer of Joseph.

The theology of the Prayer is best described in terms of the titles it confers on the angel Israel;[8] its mythology of combat and descent will be discussed below as exegetical developments of the Jacob narrative.

In the Prayer of Joseph, the titles that are given apply only to the angel Israel. Although in Greco-Egyptian magical materials, Coptic-gnostic and Manichean texts, there is an angel Jacob,[9] in the Prayer of Joseph, Israel is the name borne by the angel; Jacob, by the man.[10]

Israel, an angel of God

While the immediate locus for this title would appear to be targumic and midrashic understandings of the conferring of the name Israel on Jacob in Genesis 32:28, a second source would appear to be the collective use of Israel in canonical passages (e.g. Ex 4:22) that suggest a heavenly or pre-existent being. These passages, sometimes referring to Jacob-Israel, sometimes to the nation, were collected in catenae (e.g. 4Ezra 6:58 and the close parallel in 4QDibHam iii), which resemble the assemblage in the Prayer of Joseph. For example, in *De confusione linguarum* 146, Philo writes of the Logos: "God's firstborn, the Logos, who holds the eldership among the angels, an archangel as it were. And many names are his for he is called the Beginning, and the Name of God, and His Word, and the Man after His Image and He that Sees, that is to say, Israel." In the Prayer of Joseph, Israel is called "firstborn," an "archangel," and a "man seeing God"; and his role as "the Beginning" and his "eldership" is clearly implied.[11] Even more striking is the Coptic-

Russell, *The Meaning and Message of Jewish Apocalyptic* (Philadelphia, 1964) p. 67; N. Turner, "Joseph, Prayer of," *IDB*, vol. 2, p. 979; V. Burch, "The Literary Unity of the Ascensio Isaiae," *JTS* 20 (1918–19) 20f.

[7] H. Priebatsch, *Die Josephsgeschichte in der Weltliteratur* (Breslau, 1937) pp. iv–v, xvii, 8–14, 22f., 33–44; E. Stein, "Zur apokryphen Schrift 'Gebet Josephs,' " *MGWJ* 81 (1937) 280–86; J. Z. Smith, "Prayer of Joseph," in Goodenough Festschrift, pp. 253–94.

[8] Also see J. H. Charlesworth's contribution on the PrJac below.

[9] Jacob occurs as the name of a supernatural being in the description of an amulet in the *Sword of Dardanus* (K. Preisendanz, *Papyri Graecae Magicae [PGM]* [Leipzig, 1928] vol. 1, pp. 126, 1735–37), which has been compared to the PrJos by M. Smith, "The Account of Simon Magus in Acts 8," *H. A. Wolfson Jubilee Volume* (Jerusalem, 1965) p. 749. Such an amulet has been printed by R. Mouterde, "Le Glaive de Dardanos," *Mélanges de l'Université Saint-Joseph* 15 (1930) 57f. Another amulet (Newhall Collection 35) has been translated, somewhat speculatively, as "Jacob, the likeness/YHWH, his son" and compared with the PrJos by H. C. Youtie, "A Gnostic Amulet with an Aramaic Inscription," *JAOS* 50 (1930) 214–20. R. Ganschinietz ("Jacob," Pauly-Wissowa, vol. 9, pp. 623f.) notes the tendency in magical papyri to combine *Iakōb* with the divine name *Iaō*, which might suggest a heavenly Jacob. The angel Jacob and the angel Israel appear as two of the three heavenly *stratēgoi* in the Coptic Gospel of the Egyptians 64:13f. (J. Doresse, "Le Livre sacré du Grand Esprit Invisible," *JA* 254 [1966] 408f.; 256 [1968] 314, 320). "The angel Jacob" (*Yākōb prēstag*) occurs in Manichean Turfan fragments M, 4 and M, 20 and was related to the PrJos by Schneider, *ZNW* 33 (1934) 218f. and A. Böhlig, "Jacob as an Angel in Gnosticism and Manicheism," in *Nag Hammadi and Gnosis*, ed. R. McL. Wilson (NHS 14; Leiden, 1978) pp. 122–30.

[10] This is a standard feature of revelation literature: The heavenly revealer possesses a secret name known only on high while being known on earth by another name. Compare *PGM* 2.45, 1–48, 63; *Pistis Sophia* 137 (C. Schmidt, W. Till, *Koptisch-gnostische Schriften* [Berlin, 1962] vol. 1, p. 235); the Mandaean *Right Ginza* 3 (ed. M. Lidzbarski [Leipzig, 1925] p. 98). It appears to be an adaptation of an archaic Indo-European epic convention, see Homer, *Iliad* 1.403f.; 2.813f.; 14.290f.; 20.74; and compare the collection of texts and bibliography in R. Lazzeroni, "Lingua degli dei e lingua degli uomini," *Annali della scuola normale superiore di Pisa* 26 (1957) 1–25; C. Watkin, "The Language of Gods and the Language of Men," in *Myth and Law among the Indo-Europeans*, ed. J. Puhvel (Berkeley, 1970) pp. 1–17.

[11] This Philonic passage has been frequently compared to the PrJos, most extensively by Stein, *MGWJ* 81 (1937) 283, and Daniélou, *Theology*, 133. It should be noted that each title in the PrJos applied to Israel is closely paralleled by a title in Philo applied to the Logos. a) Israel: *Conf* 146; b) angel/archangel: *LegAll* 3.177; *QuodDeus* 182; *Heres* 205; *Mut* 87; *Conf* 146; *Somn* 1.240; c) Ruling spirit: *Abr* 124; *QuaesEx* 2.64, 66, 68; d) one seeing God: see

gnostic treatise *On the Creation of the World* (*CG* 2.5), which depicts, standing before the heavenly throne, amid the angels and next to Sabaoth, "a firstborn whose name is Israel, the one who sees God."[12] All three titles occur as well in the Prayer of Joseph. The setting in this treatise, rather than the occurrence of an angel Israel in Greco-Egyptian and Jewish magical materials,[13] seems to supply the proper context for understanding Israel's role in the Prayer.

In early Jewish mystical literature, the community of Israel chanting the *Keduša* (the *Trisagion*) became personified as a heavenly figure named Israel who leads (as does Michael or Metatron in parallel traditions) the celestial worship before the throne. In its original form it is a two-level action such as that depicted in b.Hullin 91b: "Israel is beloved before the Holy One, blessed be he, even more than the ministering angels. For Israel repeats the song every hour while the ministering angels repeat it only once a day . . . Furthermore, the ministering angels do not begin the song above until Israel has started it below." Later there developed a vision, in the Hekhalot literature, in which the congregational action was transported entirely to heaven with an "angel who bears the name Israel standing in the center of heaven and leading the heavenly choir."[14] Such a role is summarized in the Prayer of Joseph by the self-description of Israel as the "first minister before the face of God" who calls "upon my God by the inextinguishable name" (Fragment A, 8f.).

In the discussion of canonical parallels below, it will be noted that the Palestinian targumic tradition is uniform in understanding Jacob's angelic adversary in Genesis 32 as "the chief of those who praise [God in heaven]," that it was a common midrashic tradition that Jacob let the angel go at dawn so that the angel could return on high to join in the heavenly chanting, that some texts identify Jacob's adversary as bearing the name Israel, while others interpret the name Israel as meaning "trying to sing instead of the angels." It is on some such cluster of associations that the central narrative of the Prayer of Joseph rests. It is also related to the theme of angelic rivalry before the heavenly throne, which may be found in both hellenistic and Palestinian Merkabah literature.[15] Thus, in the Apocalypse of Abraham 10:9, Jaoel (or Iaoel) is described as "the one who has been charged, according to his commandment, to restrain the threats of the living creatures of the cherubim against one another,"[16] while in the vision of the throne in chapter 18, Abraham sees that when the *hayyot*, "the living creatures," "finished singing, they would look at one another and threaten one another. And it came to pass that when the angel who was with me saw that they were threatening each other, he left me and went running to them. And he turned the face of each living creature from the face which was opposite it so that they could not see each other's faces threatening each other. And he taught them the song of peace which the

---

below, n. 20; e) firstborn: *Agr* 51; *Conf* 63; "the eldest son of God" in *LegAll* 3.175; *Quod Det* 118; *Migr* 6; *Conf* 146; *Heres* 205; *Somn* 1.230; f) chief captain: compare the Logos as *hēgemōn* in *Conf* 174, as lieutenant in *Somn* 1.241, compare the Logos as *stratēgos* in Pseudo-Justin, *Oratio ad Graecos* 5, which has been compared to Philo by E. R. Goodenough, "The Pseudo-Justinian Oratio ad Graecos," *HTR* 18 (1925) 194f., and P. Beskow, *Rex Gloriae* (Stockholm, 1962) pp. 209f.; g) first minister: compare the Logos as heavenly high priest in *LegAll* 3.82–88; *SpecLeg* 1.230; *Gig* 52; *Migr* 102; *Fuga* 108–10.

[12] A. Böhlig, P. Labib, *Der koptisch-gnostische Schrift ohne Titel aus Codex II von Nag Hammadi* (Berlin, 1962) pp. 153, 23–25. Compared to the PrJos by N. A. Dahl, "The Johannine Church and History," in *Current Issues in New Testament Interpretation* eds. W. Klassen and G. Snyder (New York, 1962) p. 287; Daniélou, *Theology*, p. 133; and P. Borgen, *Bread from Heaven* (Leiden, 1965) p. 177.

[13] Israel, as an angelic name, appears only in late Jewish magical materials, e.g. Sefer Razi'el 4b, 41b. *Yisriel* appears more frequently in earlier texts, e.g. Sefer ha-Razim (ed. M. Margalioth [Jerusalem, 1966]) pp. 97, 19; Harbe de Moshe (ed. M. Gaster, *Studies and Texts* [London, 1928]) vol. 3, pp. 71f. In Gk. materials, Israel appears as an angelic name only as a designation of one of the three *archai* in Justin's Book of Baruch (Hippolytus, *Ref* 5.26.2 [PG, vol. 16, col. 3194]), which has been related to the PrJos by Resch, *Agrapha* p. 298. *Istraēl* is the more common form, e.g. 1En 10:1 (other MSS, Uriel); the *Sword of Dardanus* (*PGM* vol. 1, pp. 128, 1815f.); Papyrus Oslo 1 (ed. S. Eitrem [Norske videnskaps-akademie 1; Oslo, 1925] pp. 15, 310) and elsewhere. See a full list in Smith, Goodenough Festschrift, p. 263.

[14] G. Scholem, *Major Trends in Jewish Mysticism* (New York, 1954) p. 62 paraphrasing Hekhalot Rabbati in A. Jellinek, *BHM*, vol. 3, pp. 161–63. The pattern, in b.Hull 91b, of the angels not beginning their song above until Israel has begun it below is also found in the Hekhalot material, e.g. *BHM*, vol. 3, p. 161.

[15] Central to this tradition is Job 25:2: "Dominion and fear are with him; he makes peace in his heights" (translation mine). The latter phrase is understood as God's need to keep peace among his angels (see Smith, Goodenough Festschrift, p. 279). See also P. Schäfer, "The Rivalry Between Angels and Men in *The Prayer of Joseph* and Rabbinic Literature," *Proceedings of the Sixth World Congress of Jewish Studies*, ed. A. Shinan (Jerusalem, 1977) vol. 3, pp. 511–15. (In Heb.)

[16] [Translation is by R. Rubinkiewicz and H. G. Lunt and is published herein. —J.H.C.]

Eternal One has in himself" (ApAb 18:8–11). The same sort of conflict is depicted in Tanhuma, Bereshit (ed. S. Buber, Rome, 1885) 1.10, which contains a Midrash on Job 25:2: "Dominion and fear are with him; he makes peace in his high places." "Dominion" is interpreted as Michael; "fear" as Gabriel. The "making peace" is understood to be God's action in keeping peace among the angels "for even the heavenly ones need peace . . . each one in his turn says 'I am the first.' " In Pirke Hekhalot (*BHM* 3.161–63), the angel Israel has the function of keeping order among the heavenly choir much as does Jaoel in the Apocalypse of Abraham. The conflict between Uriel and Israel over their relative rank in the Prayer of Joseph more closely resembles that depicted in Tanhuma.

A ruling spirit

A general term in astrological and angelogical materials to which no special significance may be attached.[17] In the Prayer of Joseph it serves to emphasize Israel's preeminent rank.

A man seeing God

Ultimately dependent on Genesis 32:31, the name Israel was understood to be derived from *'yš r'h 'el*, "a man seeing God," which is the form in which it occurs in the Prayer of Joseph (Fragment A, 3). While a Hebrew play on words, the etymology is not found (except for one possible late exception)[18] in any extant Hebrew source but is rather to be found only in Jewish and Christian texts from a Greco-Egyptian provenance in a variety of verbal forms.[19] Its most massive witness is Philo, in whose writings some form of the etymology appears forty-nine times.[20] The term indicates what, since Ezekiel 1:4–28, was the goal of the Merkabah mystic—a vision of God on his heavenly throne.[21]

The firstborn

Israel's claim that "I am the firstborn (*prōtogonos*) of every living thing to whom God gives life" (Fragment A, 3) bears a striking resemblance to the description of the son in the archaic hymn preserved in Colossians 1:15, 17: "He is the image of the unseen God and the firstborn (*prōtotokos*) of all creation . . . before anything was created he existed"[22]

---

[17] It may not be used to relate PrJos to the gnostic, Archontic sect (Resch, *Agrapha*, pp. 295–97).

[18] The only occurrence of the etymology of Israel as a man seeing God in Heb. tradition is a presumably late Midrash on Hos 9:10 in SER 27 (ed. M. Friedmann, *Jahresbericht der israelitisch-theologischen Lehranstalt in Wien* 7 [1900] 138f.).

[19] In the Philonic form *ho horōn ton theon* in Clement of Alexandria, *Paid* 1.9 (PG vol. 8, col. 841); Origen, *Princ* 4.3 (PG vol. 11, col. 395); Eusebius, *PrEv* 11.6.519b (PG vol. 21, col. 860); Basil Caesar, *CommIsa* 15 (PG vol. 30, col. 141); and in closely related forms in Jerome, *HebQuaestinLibGen* (CCSL 72.40–41); Pseudo-Jerome, *Liber Interpretationis Hebraicorum Nominum in Exodum* (CCSL 72.75); Macarius, *Hom* 47.5 (PG vol. 34, col. 800); Clement of Alexandria, *Strom* 1.5 (PG vol. 8, col. 725). See, likewise, the Jewish(?) prayers in the Apostolic Constitutions 7.36.2 and 8.15.7 in W. Bousset, "Eine jüdische Gebetssamlung im siebenten Buch der apostolischen Konstitutionen," *Nachrichten von der Königlichen Gesellschaft der Wissenschaften zu Göttingen, philologische-historische Klasse, 1915* (1916), especially p. 444. [Also see the contribution herein titled the Hellenistic Synagogal Prayers. —J.H.C.]. The Heb. form is most closely represented by the rarer *anēr horōn theon* or *anthrōpos horōn theon* in Hippolytus, *Contra Noetum* 5 (PG vol. 10, col. 809); Eusebius, *PrEv* 7.8.525b (PG vol. 21, col. 525); and the Coptic-gnostic treatise "On the Origin of the World" (Böhlig-Labib, pp. 153, 23–25). See further Smith, Goodenough Festschrift, p. 264.

[20] Philo most usually employs the phrase *Israēl [ho] horōn [ton theon]*: *LegAll* 2.34, 3.186, 212; *Sacr* 134; *Post* 62, 92; *Conf* 56, 72, 146, 148; *Migr* 113, 125, 201; *Heres* 78; *Congr* 51; *Fuga* 208; *Somn* 1.173; 2.44; 173; *Abr* 57; *Leg* 4; *QuaesGen* 3.49; 4.233. Cf. *LegAll* 3.15; 172; *Plant* 58, 60; *QuaesGen* 2.22. To *horatikon genos* as a synonym for Israel occurs in *QuodDeus* 144; *Conf* 91; *Migr* 18, 54; *Mut* 109, 189, 258; *Somn* 2.279; cf. *Somn* 2.44. The form *ho orōn* in *Conf* 159 and *QuaesEx* 2.47 and *hoi oratikoi* in *Plant* 46f. and *QuaesEx* 2.58 may be compared. For other verbs of seeing applied to Israel in Philo, cf. *Sacr* 120; *Heres* 279; *Somn* 1.114. For *horatikos* with some bodily organ with reference to Israel, compare *Ebr* 111; *Migr* 14; *Mut* 209; *Conf* 92; *Mut* 203.

[21] See P. Borgen, *Bread from Heaven*, pp. 115–18, 175–79, who relates the Philonic etymology to Merkabah traditions.

[22] Col 1:15 has been compared with PrJos by H. Windisch, "Die göttliche Weisheit der Juden und die paulinischen Christologie," *Neutestamentliche Studien G. Heinrici* (Untersuchungen zum Neuen Testament 6; Leipzig, 1914) p. 225, and C. F. D. Moule, *Colossians and Philemon* (Cambridge, 1962) p. 63.

and has its origin in Exodus 4:22, in which God declares "Israel is my first-born (*prōtotokos*, LXX) son." While in Exodus the title clearly refers to the nation (cf. 4Ezra 6:58; Sir 36:12; Jub 2:20; PssSol 18:4), some texts interpreted the passage to refer to the patriarch (cf. Jub 19:29; R. Nathan in ExR 19:7). This title is paralleled by the tradition that the patriarchs were formed before creation (a tradition alluded to in PrJos A, 2: "Abraham and Isaac were [pre-]created before any work") and likewise Israel (either the patriarch or the nation).[23]

Archangel of the power of the Lord

This is one of the early occurrences of the term "archangel." Joined to the phrase "of the power of the Lord," it appears to be a reflection of the traditional vocabulary associated with Michael as the "Great Prince" (viz. Dan 12:1).

Chief captain among the sons of God

The title "chief captain" (*archichiliarchos*) is unique to the Prayer of Joseph but appears to parallel Michael, who is the chief captain of the heavenly host (*archistratēgos*) in hellenistic Jewish literature (Dan 8:11 in LXX and Theod; 2En 22.6f.; 33:10f.; AsMos 10:2; JosAsen 14 and throughout TAb).

The first minister before the face of God

The term ministering angels (*maľᵃke ha-ššārēt/angeloi leitourgoi*) is commonplace. The figure of Israel in the Prayer of Joseph is a close parallel to the Merkabah description in the Testament of Levi 3:4: "For in the uppermost heaven of all dwells the Great Glory, in the Holy of Holies, superior to all holiness. There with him are the archangels, who serve and offer propitiatory sacrifices to the Lord . . ."[24]

The designation "first" ought to be read as a term of rank consonant with "ruling spirit," "archangel," "chief captain," and, especially, "[Uriel] the eighth after me [Israel]." This last term has caused much discussion as it seems to imply that Uriel is no longer one of the seven archangels.[25] The problem is relieved by assuming a scheme of seven archangels with an eighth highest angel (who is Israel); Uriel would be the lowest of the seven. Thus Israel, in the Prayer of Joseph, plays an analogous role to the *Ogdoad* in gnostic traditions (e.g. *AdvHaer* 31:4), to the son who has the face of God and who rules over the seven angelic *prōtoktistoi* in Clement of Alexandria (*Excerpta ex Theodoto* 10–12), and to the *Dynamis* of the eighth highest heaven in Jewish Merkabah materials (e.g. the "Great Glory" in TLevi 3:4 quoted above; 3En 10:3; b.Ḥag 13a).[26]

Each title in the Prayer of Joseph can be related to parallel Jewish materials; each appears to have its prime locus in early Merkabah traditions as the mythology of the Prayer of Joseph appears to have its prime locus in exegetical traditions developed out of Genesis 32.

The Prayer of Joseph may be termed "a myth of the mystery of Israel." Whether the earthly Jacob-Israel is to be understood as a thoroughly docetic figure, the incarnation of a heavenly power, or a heavenly messenger is not clear. However, it is frequently a characteristic of each of these patterns that the myth may be ritually appropriated by its believers. The narrative of Israel's descent is presumably matched by a ritual for Jacob's (and the sons of Jacob's) ascent. The soteriological experience would accord with the well-known pattern of the ascent of the mystic to the Merkabah, an ascent threatened by angelic adversaries, which results in a vision of the form of God on the celestial throne and the "angelicizing" of the adept as he joins in the heavenly chorus of praise. One may presume that the way of ascent in the Prayer of Joseph was "Jacob's Ladder." The Prayer of Joseph may be grouped with the pseudepigraphical literature and Philo, in contradistinction to the

[23] See the convenient collection of texts in *Kommentar*, vol. 3, pp. 256–58. See the discussion of the PrJos in W. L. Knox, *Some Hellenistic Elements in Early Christianity* (London, 1944) p. 49, and P. Winter, *ZRGG* 5 (1953) 335–65.

[24] [Trans. by H. C. Kee; see his contribution on T12P in this collection. —J.H.C.]

[25] Daniélou, *Theology*, p. 134; W. L. Knox, *Hellenistic Elements*, p. 49; Priebatsch, *Josephsgeschichte*, p. 9.

[26] See G. Scholem, *Jewish Gnosticism, Merkabah Mysticism and Talmudic Tradition* (New York, 1965²) pp. 65–71; H. Corbin, *Avicenna and the Visionary Recital* (New York, 1960) pp. 65, 287f.

Hebrew and Aramaic Merkabah texts, in placing emphasis on the patriarch as a model for salvation.[27]

With particular reference to the Prayer of Joseph, the sort of promise it held out to its believers may be paralleled by E. R. Goodenough's description of the great reredos in the Dura Europus synagogue. The fresco is dominated by a great vine, which is, in part, a ladder. To one side, at the foot of the vine, is the reclining figure of the patriarch Jacob; in the branches sits the figure of Orpheus, the heavenly singer; at the summit is the celestial throne and the Powers. In Goodenough's words: "blessed at the bottom by the Patriarch wearing the white robe of a man of God on earth, Israel can go up to stand permanently beside the Throne with the Powers."[28] An even closer parallel is found in a Jewish magical papyrus entitled "The Prayer of Jacob" (*Proseuchē Iakōb*). The petitioner prays, "Fill me with wisdom, empower me, Master . . . because I am an angel on earth, because I have become immortal, because I have received the gift from you."[29]

The Prayer of Joseph is to be situated within some such circle of first-century Judaism, which sought a model for salvation in the ascent of the patriarchs to the full reality of their heavenly, angelic nature. This Prayer is the narrative of the mythology of such a heavenly figure; a text such as the Prayer of Jacob is the expression of the experience of this salvation on the part of the individual believer.

The complete pattern is most apparent in the various texts that witness to the complex Enoch tradition, particularly 2 Enoch. Here Enoch was originally a man (ch. 1) who ascended to heaven and became an angel (22:9, cf. 3En 10:3f. and 48C), returned to earth as a man (33:11), and finally returned again to heaven to resume his angelic station (67:18).

Relation to canonical books

In considering the relation of the Prayer of Joseph to the *present* canonical text, it is necessary, as is the case with any of the pseudepigrapha, to compare it not only with modern editions of the Hebrew scriptures but also with early versions, translations, and interpretations. It is also essential to perceive how redactional activity within the canon is continued by the pseudepigraphical works. In the case of the Prayer of Joseph, the links *already* established in Genesis as well as in Hosea 12:4–6 between three blocks of material: (a) Genesis 32f.; (b) Genesis 35f.; Genesis 28; and (c) Genesis 48 exhaust the passages relevant to an understanding of the Prayer of Joseph. A similar set of links (omitting Gen 32f.) occurs in the version of Genesis 35 in Jubilees 32.

Genesis 32f.

The immediate point of departure for an examination of the relationship of the Prayer of Joseph to canonical tradition is the account of the combat between Jacob and a (heavenly) assailant and the patriarch's gaining of the name Israel in Genesis 32:24–31.

The larger narrative context of Genesis 32f. is relevant. The bulk of these chapters is devoted to an account of Jacob's tense meeting with his elder twin brother, Esau (Gen 32:4–23; 33:1–17), their first meeting since Jacob tricked his father Isaac into bestowing Esau's blessing on him (Gen 27). In the interim, Jacob had sought refuge from Esau's fury with his uncle Laban in Haran (Gen 27:43–32:1). Genesis 32f. is situated as Jacob and his entourage, in flight from Laban, are journeying up from Paddan-Aram to Canaan in response to a divine command to "return to the land of your birth" (Gen 31:13). The tension with Laban and Esau and the fight by the Jabbok are part of an overall pattern. Whenever Jacob approaches a human being, a close relation, with whom there is conflict, preparations for combat are made (Gen 31:22–42; 32:4–23), but battle is avoided and reconciliation occurs (Gen 31:43–32:1; 33:1–17); whenever Jacob encounters angelic beings, combat appears to follow (Gen 32:2f.; 32:24–31).

a) The combat in the Prayer of Joseph occurs in an identical setting as Genesis 32f. Jacob is "coming up from Syrian Mesopotamia" (Fragment A, 4), the standard Septuagint translation of Paddan-Aram (see LXX Gen 31:18 and 33:18, which frame the meeting with Esau).

---

[27] See further Smith, Goodenough Festschrift, pp. 287–91.

[28] E. R. Goodenough, *Jewish Symbols*, vol. 9, pp. 78–123, especially p. 107.

[29] *PGM*, vol. 2, pp. 148, 1–149, 28. [See Charlesworth's translation of the PrJac below. —J.H.C.]

b) The conflict, as described in the Prayer of Joseph, is between two rival, all but equal, archangelic powers as to their relative rank before the throne of God. This closely parallels the conflict between Jacob and Esau. They are twin brothers constantly competing for relative seniority. The competition began in their mother's womb (Gen 25:22–26), continued through Jacob's acquisition of Esau's birthright (Gen 25:29–34), and culminated in Jacob's theft of Esau's blessing (Gen 27:1–40) with Esau's threat to kill Jacob (Gen 27:41f.).[30] These events explain the derivations of Jacob's name: *Ya'aqōbh,* either because at birth he held his brother's heel (*'aqēbh,* Gen 25:26) or because he is one who supplants: "Is it because his name is Jacob that he has now supplanted (*wayya 'q*ᵉ*bhēnî*) me twice? First he took my birthright, and look, now he has taken my blessing!" (Gen 27:36). This latter derivation is followed throughout the canon, in Hosea 12:3 and, most effectively, in the proverbial pun in Jeremiah 9:4: "every brother is a very Jacob (*'āqōbh ya 'qōbh*)." Philo regularly assigns the title "The Supplanter" (*ho pternistēs,* e.g. *LegAll* 1.61; 2.89) to Jacob before receiving the name Israel. The derivation is alluded to by Origen in the introduction to his paraphrase of the Prayer of Joseph (Fragment C, 1): "Jacob . . . he who supplanted his brother."[31]

Esau's jealousy of his brother may well have supplied the notion of "envy" which is given as the motivation for the attack on Israel by Uriel in the Prayer of Joseph (Fragment A, 5), but in the Prayer, despite the implicit accusation that each angel has usurped the other's title and rank, Israel is the elder (Fragment A, 3).[32]

c) In the Genesis account, the patriarch's journey begins with a mysterious encounter between Jacob and a band of angels: "While Jacob was going on his way angels of God met him, and on seeing them he said, 'This is God's camp,' and he named the place Mahanaim" (Gen 32:1–2). The construction *pg'* with *b*ᵉ, here translated as "met," usually implies a hostile encounter. Likewise Jacob's exclamation that the place was a *mah*ᵃ*nē* ᵓᵉ*lohîm,* a war camp of God (more strongly militaristic in the LXX) and the etymology of the place name Mahanaim (two camps) hints at an armed conflict between Jacob and the angels.[33]

d) From what has survived, one might well have thought that the apocryphon would have been entitled "Prayer of Jacob" rather than of Joseph. The only prayer by Jacob in the canonical text occurs in Genesis 32:10–13 where the patriarch prays: "I implore you, save me from my brother's clutches, for I am afraid of him; he may come and attack us . . ."[34]

---

[30] Based on the oracle in Gen 25:23, haggadic literature extended the conflict to the descendants of Jacob and Esau and their respective guardian angels. Going beyond the tense confrontation of Gen 32–33, some traditions have Jacob slay Esau "as he came forth from Mesopotamia." For early witnesses, see TJud 9 and the more extended narrative in Jub 37:1–38:14; and compare such late Midrashim as Midrash wa-Yissa'u in Yalkut 1.132 (*BHM,* vol. 2, pp. 1–5) and Chronicles of Jeraḥmeel, pp. 80–87 (ed. M. Gaster; London, 1899). These may be dependent on the lost "Wars of the Patriarchs" (Jub 34:1–9; TJud 3–7), of which two fragments, derived from Jacob's encounter with Esau (Gen 32:15) and the wrestling match (Gen 32:23f.), *may* have been recovered at Qumran (1Q23 1:13). But see the new designation of these fragments as 1QHenGiants following J. T. Milik, "Turfan et Qumran," Kuhn Festschrift, pp. 120f. In part these traditions are based on Esau's threat (Gen 27:41f.) and Jacob's fear (Gen 32:7–12) combined with the battle scene of the sons of Jacob avenging the rape of Dinah (Gen 34:25–29) and the brief reference to the wars of Jacob (connected by a pun with Shechem, Gen 48:22, cf. GenR 80:10 and 97:6); in part on traditions that identify Esau as the nation opposed to Israel: first, Edom, already in the Gen narrative (Gen 36:1, 8, 9, 43; extended in Mal 1:2–5, cf. Rom 9:10–13), later to the Herodian dynasty, Rome, and the Christian Church. See G. D. Cohen, "Esau as a Symbol in Early Medieval Thought," in A. Altmann, ed., *Jewish Medieval and Renaissance Studies* (Cambridge, Mass., 1967) pp. 19–48. Later tradition is relentless in continuing the fraternal conflict, e.g. Gen 33:4: "But Esau ran to meet him, took him in his arms and held him close . . ." is interpreted as Esau biting Jacob in the neck in an attempt to slay him! (TargYer; Gen 33:4; GenR 78:9).

[31] This may either be a nominative tag (compare Origen *ExcerPss* 80.2 [PG vol. 17, col. 149]), or may summarize some of the lost narrative content of PrJos.

[32] Compare Jub 19:29 where Jacob is declared to be the firstborn son.

[33] Some scholars have suggested that Gen 32:1f. is the Elohist version of the wrestling match in the Jahwist narrative (Gen 32:24–31). The Palestinian Targumim consistently relate the two incidents through a variety of exegetical devices.

[34] There are only two texts entitled "The Prayer of Jacob": *PGM,* vol. 2, pp. 148f. (discussed above and presented below by J. H. Charlesworth), and an Eth. magical text, Ləssâna Ya'əqob, in D. Lifchitz, *Textes éthiopiens magico-religieux* (Université de Paris, Travaux et Mémoires de l'Institut d'Ethnologie 38, Paris, 1940) p. 241, where the angel Gabriel reveals to Jacob while he was dwelling in "Syria" all of the names of God: "By this prayer, Jacob was saved from the hand of his brother Esau. Likewise save me . . ." Cf. PRE (ed. G. Friedlander, New York, 1965) p. 37.

e) The central text that supplies the narrative details in Prayer of Joseph ("He . . . fought with me and wrestled with me saying that his name," Fragment A, 5) is Genesis 32:24–31; but these verses appear to intrude abruptly on the larger story of Jacob and Esau.[35] Each detail of the nocturnal wrestling match is of relevance with the exception of the damage to Jacob's thigh (Gen 32:25b, 31b–32).

Genesis gives no clue as to the identity of Jacob's opponent. He is simply described as a "man" or "one" (Gen 32:25); and, later, he refuses to answer Jacob's question as to his name (Gen 32:29). The conferring of the name Israel on Jacob, with the etymology of "because you have been strong (*śārîtā*) against God (*'elōhîm*)" (Gen 32:28) represents, already, an interpretation of the adversary. A further layer of interpretation within the canon is given in Hosea, which plays on both possible meanings of *'elōhîm* as God or divine beings, and correlates the conflict against Esau with the struggle at the Jabbok and the bestowal of the name Israel on Jacob in Genesis 32 with that in chapter 35: "In the very womb he supplanted his brother, in maturity he wrestled against God. He wrestled with the angel and beat him, he wept and pleaded with him. He met him at Bethel and there God spoke to him" (Hos 12:3f.).[36]

Post-canonical "Old Testament" tradition either continues the ambiguity of the Genesis account or, building on the sort of interpretation represented by Hosea 12, goes on to specify the angel's name. Thus Targum Onkelos Genesis 32:24f. reads "a man" as does the Septuagint. The Palestinian Targum reads "an angel in the likeness of a man," to which may be compared the homiletical Midrashim, "in the likeness of a shepherd" or "of an outlaw" (GenR 77:2). Josephus understands the opponent to have been a "phantasm" (*Ant* 1.333). The earlier homiletic Midrashim specify either Michael or Gabriel as the angelic adversary (perhaps already implied in TargYer 32:25); later mystical Midrashim identify him as Metatron. The old Midrash *Yelemmedenu*, preserved only in fragments in later collections, contains the tradition that Jacob fought with several angels (*Yalqut Shim'oni* Ps 39 [Horeb, 1925–26; 2.758]). This appears to conflate Jacob's encounter with the angels in Genesis 32:1f. with the combat in 32:24–31. R.Ḥama b.R. Ḥanina is reported to have held that the adversary was the guardian angel of Esau (GenR 77:3 and 78:3), thus correlating the wrestling with the forthcoming encounter between the two brothers.[37] Two anonymous traditions, one explicit (PRE 37), the other implicit (GenR 77:3), give the name of the wrestling angel as Israel. In this tradition, Jacob, the man, does battle with his heavenly counterpart, the angel Israel.[38]

The most important of these post-canonical "Old Testament" interpretations—one that supplies both some clues as to why it is that Uriel is uniquely identified in the Prayer of Joseph as Jacob-Israel's opponent[39] and a number of striking parallels to other elements in

---

[35] F. van Trigt, "La Signification de la lutte de Jacob près du Yabboq," *OTS* 12 (1958) 280–309, contains a useful review of contemporary interpretations.

[36] The details of weeping and pleading introduce new elements whether they are understood to refer to Jacob (most commentators—but unlikely) or the angel (so b.Ḥull 92a; Gunkel, Pedersen; Engnell); see the summary of critical positions in P. R. Ackroyd, "Hosea and Jacob," *VT* 13 (1963) 250f. For the combination of Gen 32f. with Gen 35 in Hos, see GenR 78:3 and 82:4 and the attempt to place Hos 12 in a haggadic context by M. Gartner, "Masorah and the Levites," *VT* 10 (1960) 272–84.

[37] This is based on Gen 33:10 (obscured in the JB translation, hence my own translations follow) where Jacob says to Esau: "Seeing your face is like seeing the face of God," which is correlated with Jacob's naming of Peniel: "I have seen God face to face" (Gen 32:31) to read: "I have seen in Esau's face the face of the fought." The second version of this tradition cites Gen 32:29: "you shall prevail against men" and simply states "by that Esau and his chiefs are meant."

[38] The interpretation in GenR 77:3 appears based on the notion of national guardian angels and takes Jacob-Israel as the nation. The tradition in PRE 37 is more complex: "And [the angel] called [Jacob's] name Israel like his [the angel's] own name, for his [the angel's] own name was called Israel." In the LadJac (as translated by James, *LAOT* p. 98) the angel Sarakl says to Jacob after the vision at Bethel: " 'What is your name?' and I said, 'Jacob.' Then he said: 'Your name shall no longer be called Jacob but your name shall be like my name, Israel.' " In Christian tradition, Christ—as the Logos who is called Israel—wrestles with Jacob and bestows his name on the patriarch. Justin, *DialTrypho* 125.5 (PG vol. 6, col. 768), is the earliest witness to this.

[39] The only explicit identification of the angel as Uriel (outside of the PrJos) is a Christian homily attributed to John of Jerusalem (MS Reims 427 fol. 62): *et pugnavit cum angelo Oriel* and is probably dependent on Origen's quotation of the PrJos. See G. Morin, "Le Catalogue de manuscrits de l'abbaye de Gorze au XIᵉ siècle. Appendix: Homélies inédites attribuées à Jean de Jerusalem," *RBen* 22 (1905) 14.

the Prayer—is the early Palestinian targumic tradition on Genesis 32:25–31 represented by Codex Neofiti:[40]

> 25 And Jacob was left alone and the angel Sariel *wrestled* with him in the appearance   Fragment A.
> of a man and he held him until the column of dawn arose . . .
> 27 And he [the angel] said: "Let me go because the rise of the column of dawn has
> arrived and because the time of the angels on high to praise has arrived and *I am*
> *chief of those who praise.*" And he [Jacob] said: "I will not let you go until you   Fragment A.
> 28,29 bless me." And he said to him: "What is your name?" And he said: "Jacob."
> And he said: "Your name shall no longer be called Jacob, but Israel, because you
> have acted as a *prince with angels from before the Lord* . . .''   Fragment A.
> 31 And Jacob called the name of the place Peniel "because I have seen angels from
> before the Lord face to face and my life has been spared."[41]

Palestinian targumic tradition is remarkably uniform in identifying Jacob's opponent as the *ryš lmšbhy*, the "chief of those who praise" (Neofiti; Fragment Targum, Genizah Fragment A; TargYer reads "one of the praising angels"; *LAB* 18:6 identifies the opponent as "the angel that was over the praises"), and in stressing that this was the reason that the angel had to return on high at dawn, to lead the heavenly praise-songs.[42]

The targumic tradition is an early Palestinian witness to an understanding of the combat in Genesis 32 within a Merkabah context. To this may be added the cluster of details discussed above: the traditions of angelic rivalry before the throne; the angel Israel who serves as the heavenly choirmaster and has the function of keeping order among the chorusing angels; the tradition that the heavenly choir does not begin its song above until Israel (the nation) has begun to chant below; and the derivation of the name Israel as "trying to sing instead of the angels." All of these give expression to the same sort of role that Israel plays in the Prayer of Joseph, depict the same sort of rivalry as is present in the Prayer, and give special force to the self-identification of Israel as "the first minister before the face of God" (Fragment A, 8).

A unique element in Neofiti, of possible relevance to the Prayer of Joseph, is the identification of the opposing angel as Sariel. The usual catalog of the four chief angels is: Michael, Gabriel, Raphael, and Uriel. However, the list is subject to some variation. In the majority of instances, when the list is altered, it is Uriel that is displaced. When that occurs, the name of the angel that takes his place appears to be in some way associated with Genesis 32:24–31![43] Three examples are of particular importance. In 1QM 9:12–15, the list of chief angels is given as Michael, [Gabriel], Sariel, and Raphael. The same list occurs in 4Q Hen^a 9:1 replacing Uriel in the Greek manuscripts.[44] While Sariel is known elsewhere in early sources,[45] his identification as one of the four archangels appears unique to Qumran just as the identification of him as Jacob's opponent is unique to Neofiti. In 1 Enoch 10:1 (Gk. and Syncellus), God sends Uriel to warn Noah about the impending flood. In the Gizeh fragment, the angelic name Istrahel (Israel) is substituted.[46] In five instances in 1 Enoch (40:9; 54:6; 71:8, 9, 13), confined to the "Similitudes," Phanuel replaces Uriel in a catalog

---

[40] See G. Vermes, "The Archangel Sariel," in M. Smith Festschrift, vol. 3, pp. 159–66, and summarized in Vermes, "The Impact of the Dead Sea Scrolls on Jewish Studies," *JJS* 26 (1975) 12–14. Vermes makes no mention of PrJos, but cf. Smith, Goodenough Festschrift, pp. 270 and 277.

[41] ET by M. McNamara and M. Maher in A. Diez Macho, *Neophyti 1* (Madrid, 1968) vol. 1, p. 588 (text: pp. 217–19) with slight emendations.

[42] The origin of this tradition appears to have been the thrice-repeated chronological note in Gen 32:24, 26, 31 of "daybreak," the traditional beginning of liturgical activity (e.g. GenR 78:2 on Gen 32:26). The same sort of tradition is behind PRE 37. Note the alternative tradition that the angels sing by night, the nation Israel by day (e.g. b.Ḥag 12b). [Also see TAdam, and S. E. Robinson's contribution upon it in this collection. —J.H.C.]

[43] See further Y. Yadin, *The Scroll of the War of the Sons of Light Against the Sons of Darkness* (Oxford, 1962) pp. 237–40; Smith, Goodenough Festschrift, p. 277; Vermes, M. Smith Festschrift, pp. 159–64.

[44] J. T. Milik, "Problèmes de la littérature Hénochique à la lumière des fragments araméens de Qumrân," *HTR* 64 (1971) 346. 1En 9:1 combines both, listing Suriel (Suryāl/Suryān) and Uriel (Uryāl/Uryān).

[45] 1En 20:6; Sefer ha-Razim (ed. Margalioth) pp. 104f.

[46] For Istrahel, see above n. 13. The Eth. reads *Asreelyor*.

of the four archangels. It is most likely that the name Phanuel is to be derived from the place name Peniel / Penuel (the face of God) in Genesis 32:30,[47] and therefore may be related to the title "a man seeing God" (Fragment A, 3). The conclusion by G. Vermes appears justified: "In the circles represented by the Similitudes of Enoch, Qumran and the Neofiti variety of the Palestinian Targum, the angelic adversary of Jacob was recognized as one of the four celestial princes and called alternatively as Sariel or Phanuel."[48]

To strengthen the relationship of this tradition to the Prayer of Joseph, it must be noted that Sariel-Phanuel-Istrahel regularly substitutes for Uriel and that, while Sariel is a relatively unknown angelic figure, his name seems to be quite frequently conflated with Uriel (e.g. 1En 9:1, Eth.) to produce the angelic name Suriel, a figure of largely negative attributes. For example, in the remote parallel to Genesis 32 and the Prayer of Joseph, the enigmatic scene in Exodus 4:22–26 is later clarified so that Moses—after being told by the Lord that "Israel is my first-born son"—is met "on the way" by an "angel" (so the LXX, most of the targumic and midrashic treatments, e.g. b.Ned 31b–32a) who seeks to kill him. When this angel is identified, it is most frequently Uriel or Suriel.[49] These bits of evidence are obscure and fragmentary, but there is a striking "family of resemblance" among these details, largely centered in Aramaic materials, which hint at a connection between the Uriel of the Prayer of Joseph and the figure Sariel-Phanuel-Suriel in Palestinian tradition.

A third element of possible relevance to the Prayer of Joseph in Neofiti is its etymology of the name Israel. Neofiti understands Israel to be built from the root *śrr* (to rule, to act as a prince), a derivation found in other Targumim (TargOnk, *rb*, the Palestinian tradition, *'trbrb*) and the Greek of Aquila and Symmachus (*archein*).[50] This denominative verb, from *śar*, "prince" (which figures prominently as an element in angelic titles), yields the interpretation of Genesis 32:28: "You have conducted yourself as a prince with angels" and must be related to the angelic understanding of Israel in the Prayer.

f) One of the more puzzling motifs in the Prayer of Joseph is Origen's paraphrastic report that Jacob was ignorant of his heavenly nature until reminded of it by Uriel (Fragment C and implied[?] in Fragment A, 4). This may be dependent on the sequence of events in Genesis 32f. In Genesis 32:28, Jacob is recognized as a princely (i.e. angelic) being by his (angelic) adversary and given the (angelic) name Israel. In Genesis 33:10 Jacob recognizes Esau (Uriel?) as a heavenly being: "I came into your presence as into the presence of God,"[51] strengthened in the Palestinian targumic circumlocution: "I have seen your countenance as one sees the countenance of the angels from before the Lord."

Genesis 35:9f., Genesis 28:10–18

As indicated by Hosea 12:4 ("He wrestled with the angel and beat him, he wept and pleaded with him. He met him at Bethel and there God spoke to him"), and suggested already by the redactional note in Genesis 35:9 ("Once more God appeared"), the conferring of the name Israel on Jacob was harmonized with the doublet conferring the name at Bethel in chapter 35 and this with the angelic vision at Bethel in chapter 28 (Gen 35:1: "Go to Bethel . . . Make an altar there for the God who appeared to you when you were fleeing from your brother Esau").

While the geographical setting in Genesis 35:9 is the same as in Genesis 31:18 and 33:18 and Prayer of Joseph Fragment A, 4: "on his return from Paddan-Aram," no etymology

---

[47] J. E. H. Thomson, *The Samaritans* (Edinburgh, 1919) p. 189; A. Z. Aescoli, "Les Noms magiques dans les apocryphes chrétiens des Ethiopiens," *JA* 220 (1932) 109; Smith, Goodenough Festschrift, p. 277; Vermes, M. Smith Festschrift, pp. 161, 164. Phanuel appears in other early texts, e.g. SibOr 2.215; Sefer ha-Razim (ed. Margalioth) pp. 78, 88.

[48] Vermes, *JJS* 26 (1975) 13.

[49] L. Ginzberg, *Eine unbekannte jüdische Sekte* (New York, 1922) p. 37, compares the Suriel-Moses tradition with Uriel-Israel in the PrJos (cf. Ginzberg, *Legends*, vol. 5, p. 310). See further J. H. Polotsky, "Suriel der Trompeter," *Museon* 49 (1936) 231–43, and Smith, Goodenough Festschrift, p. 277; and cf. the positive understanding of Suriel as "the Prince of the Presence" equivalent to Metatron in H. Odeberg, *3 Enoch* (Cambridge, 1928) pp. 99f. [See also the contribution in this collection on 3En by P. Alexander. —J.H.C.]

[50] Vermes, M. Smith Festschrift, pp. 164f. A similar interpretation is found in Jerome, *HebQuaestinLibGen* (PL, vol. 23, col. 1038), and may well derive from *his* knowledge of the Targumim (see Smith, Goodenough Festschrift, p. 264).

of the name Israel is given or implied; it is simply bestowed: "from now on you shall be named not Jacob but Israel" (Gen 35:10). But again, a theophany appears to be the cause of the designation. The Palestinian Targumim are unanimous in rendering Peniel (Gen 32:30) as "I have seen angels of the Lord face to face" rather than the usual singular circumlocution, "angel of the Lord." This most probably refers to the angels in the "ladder" vision of Genesis 28:12,[52] with chapter 35 supplying the warrant for connecting chapters 32 and 28. Further, the "ladder" vision supplies the picture of ascending and descending angels so central to the Prayer of Joseph and this motif is used, in both the Palestinian Targumim and early Midrashim, as the chief proof-text for a heavenly Jacob-Israel.[53] These interpretations, combined with the canonical portrait in Genesis 28 of Jacob as an ignorant, sleeping man (Gen 28:16), may well have contributed to the puzzling report in the Prayer (Fragment C) that Jacob was ignorant of his heavenly nature "while doing service in the body."

Genesis 48

If the title of the work and the quotation that Jacob "read in the tablets of heaven all that shall befall you and your sons" (Fragment B, cf. C) most probably relate the text to the testament-genre, then the most likely influence on the form of the Prayer of Joseph within the canon would be Genesis 48, according to which the dying Jacob adopts and blesses Joseph's sons.[54]

While the narrative setting is in Egypt, Jacob begins his address to Joseph and his sons with the phrase "When I was on my way from Paddan" (Gen 48:7). The only place in Genesis in which this phrase occurs in direct speech by the patriarch as it does in the Prayer of Joseph (Fragment A, 4), and the first mention of Jacob's journey since the narrative of his name being changed to Israel at Bethel is in Genesis 35:9. The content of Jacob's first address (Gen 48:7) is all but a direct quotation of Genesis 35:16–20. Thus it would appear that the redactional activity within the Genesis narrative itself already linked together the three blocks of canonical material most crucial to the Prayer of Joseph: Genesis 32–33; 35; and 48.[55]

The blessing of Joseph's sons by the weak-sighted patriarch with its theme of the placing of the younger brother ahead of the elder reintroduces the motif of fraternal rivalry and repeats elements of the scene of blind Isaac blessing Jacob and Esau (Gen 27). This echoes the angelic rivalry in the Prayer of Joseph and the dispute between Uriel and Israel over priority of birth (Fragment A, 3) and rank (Fragment A, 7f.). The blessing contains, as well, an enigmatic reference to Jacob's guardian angel: "may the angel who has been my saviour from all harm, bless these boys" (Gen 48:16), which does not appear to refer to any of the canonical traditions of Jacob and an angel (Gen 28:11; 31:11; 32:2).

Thus texts about Jacob, linked together by both internal redaction within the canon and early targumic and midrashic interpretation, appear to account for the bulk of the narrative material in the Prayer of Joseph.

Relation to apocryphal books

The title "prayer" (*proseuchē/oratio*) affixed to this document is relatively rare as a designation for apocryphal works. Those that have survived with such a title are either

---

[51] See above, n. 37.

[52] Vermes, M. Smith Festschrift, p. 164.

[53] The most frequent explanation as to why the angels were "going up and coming down" rather than the expected descending and ascending is that they saw the sleeping patriarch below and then ascended to see his image engraved on the throne on high (So TargYer and Neofiti, Gen 27:12; b.Hull 91b; GenR 68:12; 78:3). See the extended debate between R. Hiyya and R. Yannai in GenR 68:13–69:3 in Smith, Goodenough Festschrift, pp. 285f. [Also cf. Jn 1:51 and LadJac, which is presented in the present collection by H. Lunt. —J.H.C.]

[54] James, *LAOT*, p. 26, has pointed to verbal parallels between Gen 48 in the LXX and PrJos. There are two, of relative insignificance: *Mesopotamias tēs Syrias* (Gen 48:7 = PrJos Fragment A, 4) and the phrase "my God" (Gen 48:3 in some MSS = PrJos Fragment A, 9). The thematic similarities are more persuasive.

[55] A somewhat similar catena underlies Jub 32:16–34, which paraphrases Gen 35 and contains (vss. 21–26) the closest parallel to the testamentary passage in PrJos Fragments B, C (see below). Jub 32:21 combines Gen 35 with Gen 28:11; Jub 32:23 alludes to Gen 47:30; 46:4, 30; 48f. Note that the version of Gen 32f. in Jub omits the wrestling match and retains only the reconciliation with Esau (Jub 29:13).

lengthy prayers without narrative (e.g. PrMan; PrAzar; 4QPrNab) or narrative works with extended prayers as a central feature of their plot (e.g. JosAsen 12–13).[56] The insertion of prayers and hymns is a frequent device in expansions of biblical texts from Chronicles to Pseudo-Philo (perhaps most clearly, AddEsth 4:17[a-i, k-z]; 5:1[a-f], 2[a-b]). Thus it is possible to assume with M. R. James that the lost sections of the Prayer of Joseph "must have contained a prayer or prayers of considerable bulk uttered by Joseph . . . On what occasion it was offered, whether in pit or prison or on his death bed, there is no certainty."[57] However, neither canonical nor post-canonical "Old Testament" tradition has attributed much in the way of prayers to Joseph (JosAsen 8:10f. would be the chief, though insignificant, exception).

What has survived of the Prayer of Joseph is either direct speech by Jacob (not Joseph): "I, Jacob, who is speaking to you" (Fragment A, 1) or indirect speech by the angel Israel reporting what he and Uriel had said (Fragment A, 4–9). The audience is, presumably, Joseph and his sons: "For I have read in the tablets of heaven all that shall befall you and your sons" (Fragment B, cf. C). The setting would most appropriately be the blessing by Jacob of Joseph's sons expanded from Genesis 48. This suggests that the Prayer of Joseph is most likely what Kolenkow has termed a "blessing-revelation testament." She argues that the archaic genre of the last words of patriarchs, which foretell the future (e.g. Gen 27:27–29; 48f.; Deut 33; cf. Tob 13–14), has been expanded, in the hellenistic period, to include narratives that relate visions or journeys to heaven and serve to validate the forecasts.[58] As in texts such as Philo's *De vita Mosis* and the Assumption of Moses 1:14, this authority would seem to have been further extended by having the patriarch not merely journey to heaven but be himself a heavenly figure. The Prayer of Joseph would seem to belong to this type.

Although the majority of such testamentary texts title the work after the name of the revealing patriarch (e.g. AsMos; TAb), there is a subgenre, represented by works such as the Testament of Isaac and the Testament of Jacob, in which an angel (Michael) assumes the form of the previous patriarch, appears, and speaks to the patriarch named in the title, most usually at the point of the latter's death. Thus, in the latter, Michael appears to Jacob in the form of Isaac; in the Prayer of Joseph, perhaps, Israel appears to Joseph in the form of Jacob.[59]

The possibility of relating the Prayer of Joseph to a testament tradition receives strong support from Jubilees 32:17–26, which contains the closest verbal parallels to the testamentary passage in Fragments B and C of the Prayer, and which has been discussed above as connecting the same chain of biblical passages that seem to underlie the Prayer. [For a translation of Jubilees 32:17–26, the reader is encouraged to see the contribution herein on Jubilees by O. S. Wintermute. —J.H.C.]

Cultural importance

In its present form, the Prayer of Joseph remains a tantalizing fragment that has left no discernible impact on subsequent literature.

---

[56] See C. Burchard, *Untersuchungen zu Joseph und Aseneth*, pp. 50–54, 76–90. [Also see Burchard's contribution in JosAsen in the present collection. —J.H.C.]

[57] James, *LAOT*, p. 26.

[58] A. B. Kolenkow, "The Genre Testament and Forecasts of the Future in the Hellenistic Jewish Milieu," *JSJ* 6 (1975) 57–71.

[59] W. E. Barnes, "Appendix: The Testaments of Abraham, Isaac and Jacob" in James, *The Testament of Abraham* (Cambridge, 1892) pp. 140, 152; S. Gaselee, "Appendix: Translations from the Coptic Version of the Testaments of Isaac and Jacob," in G. H. Box, *The Testament of Abraham* (London, 1927) pp. 58, 77. [Also see W. F. Stinespring's contributions in this collection on TIsaac and TJac. —J.H.C.] Some scholars (Priebatsch, *Josephsgeschichte*, pp. 16–34) have posited a relationship between PrJos and JosAsen with the latter's striking portrait of a divine Joseph. Attention has been focused on the detail of Michael assuming the form of Joseph (JosAsen 14:8) to speak with Aseneth. But the motif here is used to quite a different end than that in TIsaac and TJac. It would appear either to be related to Egyptian kingship traditions where the Sun God assumes the form of the reigning king, copulates with his wife in order to produce the new, divine heir (see H. Brunner, *Die Geburt des Gottkönigs* [Wiesbaden, 1964]) or to Greco-Roman erotic romance motifs, such as the seduction of Alkmene by Zeus, who assumes the form of Amphitryon (e.g. Apollodorus, *Bibliotheca* 2.4.8; Plautus, *Amphitryo*).

SELECT BIBLIOGRAPHY

Charlesworth, *PMR*, pp. 140–42.
Delling, *Bibliographie*, p. 166.
Denis, *Introduction*, pp. 125–27.

James, M. R. *The Lost Apocrypha of the Old Testament*. London, 1920; pp. 21–31.
Priebatsch, H. *Die Josephsgeschichte in der Weltliteratur*. Breslau, 1937; see especially pp. 8–44.
Smith, J. Z. "The Prayer of Joseph," in *Religions in Antiquity: Essays in Memory of Erwin Ramsdell Goodenough*, ed. J. Neusner. Sup *Numen* 14; Leiden, 1968; pp. 253–94 (with full bibliography).
Stein, E. "Zur apokryphen Schrift 'Gebet Josephs,' " *MGWJ* 81 (1937) 280–86.

PRAYER OF JOSEPH

FRAGMENT A

1 "I, Jacob, who is speaking to you, am also Israel,[a] an angel of God[b] and a ruling
2,3 spirit.[c] •*Abraham* and Isaac *were created before any work.*[d] •But, I, Jacob, who
men call Jacob but whose name is Israel[e] am he who *God called Israel* which
means, a man seeing God,[f] because I am the *firstborn of every living thing to*
whom God gives life.[g]
4 And when I was *coming up from Syrian Mesopotamia,*[h] Uriel, the angel of
God,[i] came forth and said that 'I [Jacob-Israel] had *descended to earth* and I had
5 tabernacled among men[j] and that I had been called by the name of Jacob.' •He
envied me and *fought with me and wrestled with me*[k] saying that his name and
6 *the name that is before every angel* was to be above mine.[l] •I told him his name
7 and what rank he held among the sons of God.[m] •'Are you not Uriel, the eighth
after me? and I, Israel, *the archangel of the power of the Lord* and the *chief*
8 *captain* among the sons of God?[n] •Am I not Israel, the *first minister before the*
9 *face of God*?' •And I called upon my God by the inextinguishable name."[o]

Jn 8:58
Gen 32:27f.;
35:10;
Jub 32:17
Ex 4:22; Col
1:15,17; 4Ezra
6:58; Sir 36:12;
Jub 2:20; PssSol
18:4
Gen 31:17;
33:18; 35:9;
48:7
Gen 28:10–27;
Eph 4:9f.; Sir
24:8–10; Bar
3:36f.; Jn 1:14;
6:38; Rev 21:3
Gen 32:24–28;
Hos 12:3f.
Eph 1:21; Phil
2:9; Heb 1:4
TSol 2:4; Josh
5:14; Dan 8:11;
2En 22:6–7;
33:10f.
JosAsen 14:7;
TAb A 7, 19;
ApocEzra 4:24;
TLevi 3:4
Mt 18:10

A a. The change of names in the Gen account
(e.g. Gen 17:5, 15) usually indicates some change
in status. At times, it may be used for symbolic
purposes (Hos 1:8; 2:24). Discovering some deeper
meaning to name changes fascinated ancient exe-
getes, for example, Philo's treatise *On Change of*
Names (*Mut*).

b. Israel appears as an angel in magical and
mystical literature, at times combined with the
heavenly nation, Israel.

c. A term found in astrological literature, here
used to emphasize Israel's exalted rank.

d. The term "created before" (lit. "precreated") occurs only here and in late Christian
texts. The notion that wisdom, Torah, or the nation
Israel were pre-existent is quite widespread in
Jewish materials. Less common is the claim that
the patriarchs or Moses were pre-existent.

e. Jacob is his earthly name; Israel, the heavenly
name. The idea is that the celestial name is known
only to other angelic beings.

f. This etymology of the name Israel is found
solely in Jewish and Christian materials from Egypt,
especially in Philo.

g. Most probably a literalistic understanding of
Ex 4:22: "Israel is my first-born son."

h. The standard LXX translation for Paddan-
Aram.

i. Uriel is usually one of the four archangels.
See 1En 9:10; 10:1, 4, 9, 11; 20:2; GkApEzra 6:2;
TSol 2:4; ApMos 40.

j. "To tabernacle" is traditional language of
incarnation in Jewish and Christian texts. In Jewish
materials, it is used preeminently of Wisdom. [In
Christian writings, it is most famous in Jn 1:14.
—J.H.C.]

k. This is an allusion to the story of Jacob
wrestling with a (heavenly) man in Gen 32:24–31,
which supplies a motivation, envy, for the attack
missing in the canonical account.

l. His name (Uriel) is the name that is before
every angel (God). Another possible translation:
"his name (Uriel) should have precedence over my
name (Israel) and of the angel that is before all."

m. Here we have a veiled reference to a supernatural contest in which power is displayed by
knowing one's secret name (e.g. Mk 1:24); such a
contest is quite different than the physical one just
described.

n. By any of the traditional schemes of four or
seven archangels, the description of Uriel as the
"eighth" would eliminate him from the heavenly
hierarchy. If the hellenistic scheme of an eighth
highest heaven and angel (the Ogdoad) is being
employed, then Uriel would be the lowest member
of the hierarchy. The titles "archangel" and "chief
captain" (this latter term is unique to the PrJos)
are close parallels to the titles usually accorded
Michael, the chief of the heavenly band. See the
full discussion above.

o. The calling on the name probably refers to
either the Trisagion or a secret name of *yhwh*.

FRAGMENT B

1 "For I have read in the *tablets of heaven*ᵃ *all that shall befall you and your sons.*" Jub 32:31
Gen 48f.

FRAGMENT C

[Origen writes] Jacob was greater than man, he who supplanted his brother and
who declared in the same book from which we quoted "I read in the tablets of B
heaven" that *he was a chief captain of the power of the Lord and had, from of* A. 7
old, the name of Israel; something which he recognizes while doing service in the A. 3
*body, being reminded of it by the archangel Uriel.*ᵃ A. 4

B   a. The term "tablets of heaven" is quite
common in the pseudepigrapha, especially in Jub
where it occurs some twenty times. In some passages it appears to refer to a heavenly law code;
elsewhere, as in the PrJos, to a book of destiny.

C   a. While clearly a paraphrase of Fragment A,
Origen here introduces what appears to be a gnostic

motif (most closely paralleled by texts such as the
"Hymn of the Pearl") in which the heavenly figure
has forgotten his divine origin until reminded of it
by another heavenly figure. To what degree this
represents Origen's own interpretation and to what
degree this may hint at parts of the PrJos no longer
preserved cannot be determined.

PRAYER OF JACOB

(First to Fourth Century A.D.)

A NEW TRANSLATION AND INTRODUCTION

BY J. H. CHARLESWORTH

The Prayer of Jacob contains eight internal divisions, consisting of four invocations, three petitions, and one injunction. The first invocation (vss. 1f.) begins by summoning the Father of the Patriarchs who is defined as the Creator; the second (vss. 3–5) moves in a partly chiastic form to the first from a) Father of the Patriarchs; b) Father of all things; c) Father of the powers of the cosmos; d) Creator of all; through the invocation to d) Father of powers altogether; c) Father of the whole cosmos; b) Father of all creation; a) He who showed favor to Abraham. The third invocation (vss. 6–9) summons God as the King who sits "upon (the) mountain of h[oly] [S]inaios," the sea, the serpent gods, and the sun. The last invocation (vss. 10f.) clarifies a concept found in each preceding invocation, "power": God is the one who gives "power" to others. The first petition (vs. 12) merely asks God to hear the prayer. The second petition (vss. 13f.) is the most Jewish section of the prayer; the one addressed is the "Lord God of the Hebrews," and the petitioner is one "[fro]m the rac[e] of Israel"; the author asks God to make him straight. The third petition (vss. 15–19) mentions the secret name of God and emphasizes his cosmic nature; the request now is specific and laudable, it is for wisdom (as with Solomon, cf. 1Kgs 3) by one who seems to be "an earthly angel." The injunction (vs. 20) concludes the prayer. Unfortunately the Prayer of Jacob is virtually unknown to scholars (while the PrJos is included in *IDB*, vol. 2, p. 979, and discussed in Denis, *Introduction* [especially pp. 125–27], the PrJac is not even noted in these major reference works).

Texts

The Prayer of Jacob is extant in a fourth-century papyrus now supposedly preserved in the Deutsche Staatsbibliothek in Berlin. The present translation is based on the edition by K. Preisendanz.[1]

Original language, date, and provenance

There is no reason to doubt that Greek is the original language. The time of composition must antedate the fourth century, the date of the papyrus. Parallels with second-century documents (see below) indicate that the prayer may be as early as the second century A.D.; if the Prayer of Joseph dates from the first century (as J. Z. Smith states in his contribution above) then the Prayer of Jacob may also be that early. Since the papyrus was acquired in Cairo, venerates Sinai, and shares ideas with many other Egyptian documents and papyri, it is reasonable to assume an Egyptian provenance.

[1] K. L. Preisendanz, ed., *Papyri Graecae Magicae: Die griechischen Zauberpapyri*, (Leipzig, Berlin, 1931) vol. 2, pp. 148f. Other apocryphal prayers attributed to Jacob are found in PRE 37 (ed. Friedlander, p. 281) and in the Eth. text titled "La Langue de Jacob" (see D. Lifschitz, *Textes éthiopiens magico-religieux* [Université de Paris, Travaux et mémoires de l'Institut d'Ethnologie 38; Paris, 1940] pp. 239–43). I wish to express appreciations to H. D. Betz and P. Pokorný, who helped me improve this contribution.

Theological importance

The prayer appears Jewish, as demonstrated by verse 14, viz. the identification of the author as one "[fro]m the rac[e] of Israel." If the author was a Jewish magician, he did not fully understand the Jewish traditions (see vs. 13 and n. k2). The concept of God is interesting, stressing both his covenant relation with Israel in verses 1, 5, 8, 13, and 14 and his cosmic powers, especially as the Creator (viz. vss. 2, 4). Two unique features are the apparent belief that "[S]inaios" is a personal name in verse 8 (see Ex 19:11, 18f.; 24:16) and the concept that the composer is like "an ear[th]ly angel" and has "become immortal" (see n. i2).

E. R. Goodenough claimed that the Prayer of Jacob "is a prayer for transfiguration."[2] He correctly saw that the prayer "is hardly a charm" (p. 203), but then claimed that the "person who uses the charm thereby becomes 'an angel upon earth,' becomes 'immortal,' and receives the 'gift' " (p. 203). But the prayer does not describe how or when the one who recites the prayer became an "angel"—perhaps he was imbued with this state as a gift (vs. 19) from saying prayers or incantations repeatedly (see vs. 20). It is possible that the author claims to be immortal like Jacob—who is "an angel of God" according to the Prayer of Joseph—and, hence, prays this prayer because he is "immortal." The prayer, therefore, seems to be, as J. Z. Smith says above, an "expression of this salvation on the part of the individual believer."

M. Simon,[3] who was followed by Goodenough,[4] claimed that Jewish magic has three main characteristics: great respect for Hebrew, which is usually not understood but considered to be endowed with magical powers; a feeling for the efficacious power of the name; and a preoccupation with angels. Only two of these features characterize the Prayer of Jacob. In verse 9, for example, there is a string of Hebrew names that probably were not clearly comprehended: "God, Abaōth, Abrathiaōth, [Sa]ba[ōth, A]dōnai . . ." This one verse illustrates the first two features: misunderstood Hebrew and a sense of the power of the name. A good example of at least the second of these features is verse 15: "He who has the secret name Sabaōth, . . . God of gods; amen, amen." The third characteristic is not typical of the Prayer of Jacob; this prayer holds the idea that the "Lord God of the Hebrews" is the one who answers prayers (vss. 13f.), addresses petitions directly to him (vss. 17–19), and twice celebrates him as the "Creator" or "God of the angels and archangels" (vss. 2, 7). The author is preoccupied with God, not angels. These concepts are as close to Jewish traditions preserved in the Old Testament and early Jewish literature as they are far from the ideas typical of the magical charms, such as the very long Coptic prayer,[5] which seems to be a prayer to Gabriel, the Angel of Righteousness, which states that Arnael presides over the hearing of prayers (II), and which repeatedly calls to Gabriel to "hearken unto me" and "come to me" in order to be "for me, Administrator and help . . ." (V, cf. XII, XVIII, XX). In contrast to the Prayer of Jacob, this charm contains the idea that the angels can be forced through magical incantations to come to man in order to protect and serve him. Religion and magic, as the above excerpts tend to demonstrate, are not essentially opposites, but there is a fundamental difference between them; as M. P. Nilsson argued,[6] the contrast seems to be that religion attempts to obtain (or receive) results through willful benevolence and grace, while magic seeks to obtain them through coercion.

---

[2] E. R. Goodenough, *Jewish Symbols in the Greco-Roman Period* (New York, 1953) vol. 2, p. 204.
[3] M. Simon, *Verus Israel: Étude sur les relations entre Chrétiens et Juifs dans l'Empire romain (135–425)* (Bibliothèque des Écoles Françaises d'Athènes et de Rome 166; Paris, 1948) pp. 399–404. Extremely valuable insights on Jewish "Magic and Miracle" and on "The Power of the Divine Name" are found in chs. 6 and 7 of E. E. Urbach's *The Sages: Their Concepts and Beliefs*, trans. I. Abrahams (Jerusalem, 1975) pp. 97–134. Urbach has influenced my thinking on this subject; I wish to express my debt to him.
[4] Goodenough, *Jewish Symbols*, vol. 2, p. 161.
[5] For bibliographical data regarding text and studies by F. Rossi, E. Amélineau, and U. F. Kropp see Goodenough, *Jewish Symbols*, vol. 2, p. 174; for ET see ibid., pp. 174–88.
[6] M. P. Nilsson, *Opuscula Selecta* (Lund, 1960) vol. 3, pp. 269f.

Relation to other books

The prayer is similar to other Greek-Egyptian magical papyri, as one would expect from the pervasive emphasis on God's power and on him as the source of all power (see especially vs. 11). The fourth- or fifth-century papyrus that precedes this prayer in Preisendanz's second volume of *Papyri Graecae Magicae* (=*PGM*) also mentions Iao and Sabaoth and adds the names "Michael" and "Gabriel." The Jewish amulet, Cairo 10434 (*PGM* XXV.c), likewise comes from Cairo and mentions the name "Zabaoth"; it is very brief, consisting only of the following proclamation: "Holy (is) the Lord *Zabaōt* (*hagios kurios Zabaōt*)." There are numerous other parallels with the Jewish magical papyri, such as the Diadem of Moses (*PGM* VII, vol. 2, p. 28) and the so-called Eighth Book of Moses (*PGM* XIII, vol. 2, pp. 86–131).

The concept of the power of God's name in the Jewish magical papyri is different from the biblical view (viz. Ex 3:13–15, Acts 4:9f.). In the Bible and in almost all Jewish apocryphal writings—notably in 1 Enoch 69:14, Jubilees 36:7, Prayer of Manasseh, and Artapanus—God's name is considered known, holy, revered, and often ineffable (see Josephus, *Ant* 2.275; Jerome, *Psalm* VIII). The name was powerful because God was behind it.

In the magical papyri the divine name is considered secret and itself full of efficacious powers. In the biblical and apocryphal writings, the ruling idea is that by calling God's name he would answer; but the pseudepigrapha do contain the tradition that God's name is unknown to men: "And I praised the One who is not named and is unique, who dwells in the heavens, whose name is unknown to all flesh . . ." (AscenIs 7:37, cf. 1:7, 8:7). In the magical papyri the name was the essential part of a formula by which the individual could manipulate the gods and powers to grant immediately the expressed wish. Totally unbiblical is the individual's commands to God or the gods, and the orders to supply the request "at once" (see e.g. *PGM* XVIII.b, vol. 2, p. 141, ll. 6f. "*ēdē ēdē, tachu, tachu*").[7]

The parallels with gnostic documents are very impressive (see the nn. to the translation). Most significant are the parallels with On the Origin of the World (II, 5) at **101**, in which the androgynous beings are celebrated, notably Yaldabaoth, whose son is "called 'Yao,' his feminine name is 'lordship.' Sabaoth's feminine name is 'divinity.' *Adonaios'* feminine name is 'kingship.'"[8] In this excerpt and in the Prayer of Jacob are the names "Yao" (II, 5) or "Iao" (PrJac), "Sabaoth" (identical in both), "Adonaios" (II, 5), or "[A]donai" (PrJac). The relationship does not appear direct in either direction; and both seem to be independently influenced by Jewish traditions.[9]

Noteworthy is another interesting parallel between the Prayer of Jacob and a Jewish magical prayer preserved in a fifth-century papyrus (*PGM* XXXV, vol. 2, p. 161, ll. 8f.), which contains the following: "I call upon you, he who sits upon the snow, *Telzē*; I call upon you, *Edanōth*, who (is) upon the sea; I call upon you, *Saecechel*, who (is) upon the serpents." This prayer is clearly Jewish; it refers to "the god of Abraham and Isaac and Jacob" (l. 14). Somewhat similarly to many pseudepigrapha, it refers to six heavens and names the angels who rule over each of them (ll. 3–7). The Prayer of Jacob shares with this anonymous prayer the repeated invocations, the concept of a deity sitting upon the serpents (see v. 8), and the reference to snow (v. 16).

The Prayer of Jacob should neither be branded gnostic nor be categorized as another

---

[7] P. Brown argues persuasively that the period from "around A.D. 300 to 600" is a "recognizable whole" and that "it is far from certain that there was any absolute increase in fear of sorcery or in sorcery practices" during this period: "All that can be said is that, in the fourth century A.D., we happen to know more about sorcery because we are told more about it . . ." (p. 122). He aptly defines sorcerer: "the sorcerer is a man who enjoys power *over* the demons, even over the gods. He can threaten the gods . . ." (p. 139). Brown has presented a brilliant study of the "*social* context" of the phenomenon. See his *Religion and Society in the Age of Saint Augustine* (London, 1972).

[8] Translation by H.-G. Bethge and O. S. Wintermute in J. M. Robinson, ed., *The Nag Hammadi Library in English* (New York, London, 1977) p. 164. It is significant that J. Z. Smith (see his contribution above) sees parallels between the PrJos and On the Origin of the World.

[9] G. Scholem (*EncyJud*, vol. 11, col. 1388) claimed (and I think rightly) that in "the second century Jewish converts to Christianity apparently conveyed different aspects of Merkabah mysticism to Christian Gnostics." Also see Scholem's *Major Trends in Jewish Mysticism* (New York, 1941) especially pp. 40–79.

magical charm. It is markedly different than either of these genres. There is nothing peculiarly gnostic about it. It is not a charm; and it is impressively different from the manipulative words and commands addressed to God (or gods; cf. *PGM* XXXV, vol. 2, p. 162, ll. 26f.: "Quick, quick, for I adjure (by oath) you, *Iaō, Sabaōth* . . .") and the shallow theology and request for beauty, riches, and honor typical of some charms (see *PGM* XXII.a, vol. 2, pp. 147f., ll. 15–26).

The Prayer of Jacob contains a request for wisdom and a heart filled with good things. And, as stated above, it addresses to God himself the petition for these gifts. This plea is reminiscent of Solomon's request (see 1Kgs 3). Noticeably absent, however, is the concept of contrition and plea for forgiveness that is the main characteristic of the Prayer of Manasseh.

The Prayer of Jacob should be added to the documents in the Pseudepigrapha. It is Jewish, pseudepigraphical, related to the traditions in the Prayer of Joseph and other pseudepigrapha, and probably dates from the same historical period as the later pseudepigrapha. Its inclusion herein also informs the reader of the significant ideas and perspectives found in many of the Jewish magical texts, such as the possibly third-century document titled "The Apocryphal Book of Moses, (Which) Concerns the Great Name."[10] The inclusion of the Prayer of Jacob draws attention to the many unexplored areas of similarity among the pseudepigrapha, gnostic documents, and Jewish magical texts.

The concept in verse 16, that God is upon the stars, brings forth snow, and passes through the stars and planets, recalls similarities in apocalyptic documents, especially 1 and 2 Enoch. The idea in the same verse that God makes the heavenly bodies "run in every way" by his creating power is reminiscent of Ode of Solomon 16:13 ("And created things run according to their courses"), Ecclesiasticus 16:26–28, 2 Baruch 48:9, 1 Enoch 2:1, 5:2, and Psalm of Solomon 18:12–14.

The concept of being like an angel on earth and possessing immortality in verse 19 is reminiscent of some passages in the Dead Sea Scrolls[11] and the Odes of Solomon,[12] and when it is linked with the mention of Jacob (see vs. 20) there are noteworthy parallels with other writings,[13] especially the Prayer of Joseph: "I, Jacob, who is speaking to you, am also Israel, an angel of God, and a ruling spirit."[14]

Introduction to translation

In the following translation[15] of the Prayer of Jacob, I have aimed at an idiomatic translation; when necessary a literal sense or alternate interpretation is provided in the notes. My attempts to obtain a photograph of the papyrus have not been successful; I have been dependent on Preisendanz's observations, suggested readings, and restorations. Unfortunately these have been confusing in some places. I do not note below when letters are not clear to him, and have not translated his tiny, insignificant Greek words. I also do not follow the divisions in the papyrus; to do so would have reduced the attractiveness of an idiomatic translation. As elsewhere, parentheses denote words added for good English sense; brackets circumscribe restorations.

[10] *PGM* XIII, ll. 131f., vol. 2, p. 120. See C. Leemans, *"Excerpta ex Libris Apocryphis Moïsis,"* *Papyri Graeci Musei Antiquarii Publici Lugduni-Batavi* (Leiden, 1885) pp. 77–198 [Gk. text, Lat. translation and nn.]; A. Dieterich, *Abraxas: Studien zur Religionsgeschichte des Spätern Altertums* (Usener FS; Leipzig, 1891), pp. 167–205; and *PGM*, vol. 2, pp. 86–131. The Jewish mystical elements in the *Pistis Sophia* (especially Book 5) are sometimes similar to those in PrJac.

[11] The Qumran community considered itself to be an antechamber of heaven and that the elect (the Essenes) formed with the angels one lot (cf. 1QH 6.13; cf. 1QH 3.21f., 4.24f.).

[12] See my contribution on the OdesSol herein; note especially Ode 3:7f.: "I have been united (to him) . . . he who is joined to him who is immortal,/truly will be immortal."

[13] Although A. Böhlig does not mention the PrJac, he does draw attention to numerous parallels to the concept of Jacob as an angel, as in PrJos, in gnostic and Manichean documents; cf. his "Jakob als Engel in Gnostizismus und Manichäismus," *Erkenntnisse und Meinungen,* ed. G. Wiessner (Göttinger Orientforschungen 17; Wiesbaden, 1978) pp. 1–14. Also see T. Schneider, "Der Engel Jakob bei Mani," *ZNW* 33 (1934) 218f.; the contribution above on PrJos by J. Z. Smith; and the magical texts published by Leemans, *Papyri Graeci,* vol. 2 (especially V.8.16; 9.7; W.18.23; 22.28).

[14] Fragment A, 1, translated by J. Z. Smith and published herein. Another interesting parallel, which is related to Gen 32:22–32, is found in PRE 37: "And (the angel) called his name Israel like his own name, for his own name was called Israel" (ed. Friedlander, p. 282).

[15] Goodenough earlier presented a "free" translation (*Jewish Symbols,* vol. 2, p. 203). I have noted the places in which our translations differ.

SELECT BIBLIOGRAPHY

Charlesworth, *PMR*, p. 139.

PRAYER OF JACOB

Goodenough, E. R. "Charms in Judaism," *Jewish Symbols in the Greco-Roman Period.* Bollingen Series 37; New York, 1953; vol. 2, pp. 161–207.

Preisendanz, K. L., ed. *Papyri Graecae Magicae: Die griechischen Zauberpapyri.* Leipzig, Berlin, 1931; 2nd revised edition by A. Henrichs, 1974; vol. 2, pp. 148f. (= *PGM* XXII.b).

JEWISH MAGIC

Blau, L. *Das altjüdische Zauberwesen.* Berlin, 1914².

Dieterich, A. *Abraxas: Studien zur Religionsgeschichte des Späteren Altertums.* (Usener FS). Leipzig, 1891.

Eitrem, S. *Orakel und Mysterien am Ausgang der Antike.* Albae vigilae 5; Zürich, 1947.

Festugière, A. M. J. "La Valeur religieuse des papyrus magiques," in *L'Idéal religieux des grecs et de l'Évangile.* Paris, 1932; pp. 281–328.

Ganschinietz, R. "Jao," *Pauly-Wissowa,* vol. 9 (1914), cols. 698–721.

Hopfner, T. *Griechisch-ägyptischer Offenbarungszauber,* 2 vols. Studien zur Paleographie und Papyruskunde 21 & 23; Leipzig, 1921–1924.

———. "Mageia," *Pauly-Wissowa,* vol. 14 (1928) cols. 301–93.

Nilsson, M. P. *Geschichte der griechischen Religion.* Handbuch der Altertumswissenschaft 5.2; 1961².

———. "Die Religion in den griechischen Zauberpapyri," in *Opuscula Selecta.* Skrifter Utgivna av Svenska Institutet i Athen 8, 2.3; Lund, 1960; vol. 3, pp. 129–66, see especially p. 134. (Nilsson, p. 137, correctly stated that "das Gebet Jakobs . . . sehr stark jüdisch gefärbt sind. . . .")

Nock, A. D. "Greek Magical Papyri," in *Essays on Religion and the Ancient World.* Oxford, 1972; vol. 1, pp. 176–94, see especially section 6.

Trachtenberg, J. *Jewish Magic and Superstition: A Study in Folk Religion.* New York, 1939.

PRAYER OF JACOB[a]

Preisendanz
XXII.b.

(1) 1   Father of (the) Patria[rch]s,
Father of al[l] (things),[b]
[Fathe]r of (the) powe[rs of the co]sm[os];

2   Cr[e]ato[r of a]l[l . . .],
Creator of the angels and archang[e]l[s],
the C[r]eator of (the) re[deeming] nam[es];[c]

3   I invoke you,

4   O Father of powe[r]s altogether,
Father of the [wh]ole [co]s[m]os

(5)   [and of] ‖ all creation,[d] both the inhabited and uninhabite[d,
to whom the] ch[erubim are sub]j[e]c[t]e[d];[e]

5   He who showed favor to[f] [Abr]aham
        by [giving the] kingd[om to him].

                               Gen 15:18

6   He[a]r me,

7   (You) the God o[f the p]owers,
the G[od of ang]els a[nd a]r[cha]ngels,
ki[ng . . .];[g]

(10) 8   ‖ You[h] who s[i]t upon (the) mountain of h[oly] [S]inaios; . . .[i]

a. The title is restored from the last line of the Gk.

b. Or "(the) universe." See Lampe, p. 950. The concept of God as Father, the Creator—an association not typical of the OT in which Father is linked with personal care (cf. G. Schrenk, *TDNT*, vol. 5, pp. 978–82)—is an emphasis by Plato (*poiētēs kai patēr tou pantos, Timaeus* 28C) that is inherited and used frequently by Justin (cf. E. F. Osborn, "The God and Father of All," *Justin Martyr* [Beiträge zur historischen Theologie 47; Tübingen, 1973; pp. 17–27]).

c. The concept is in biblical and apocryphal literature but not in the magical papyri.

d. Gk.: [*kai tēs*] *hōlēs geneseōs.* The Gk. *geneseōs* can mean "beginning, production, creation, race, age." Goodenough (*Jewish Symbols*, vol. 2, p. 203) rendered the phrase freely: "and of everything which has come into being."

e. Gk. [*hup*]*est*[*a*]*l*[*men*]*o*[*i hoi*] can mean "those shrinking before," "those holding in awe," but LSJM (p. 1895) shows that the verb also means "to be subject to." Goodenough (*Jewish Symbols,* vol. 2, p. 203) translated the phrase similarly: "to whom the cherubim are subject."

f. The Gk. *charizō,* "to show favor to," is used in a similar fashion in ApEzra 1:13: "Lord, what favor will you show the righteous (*kurie, tous dikaious ti charizeis*)?" See K. Tischendorf, *Apoc-*

alypses Apocryphae (Leipzig, 1866; repr. Hildesheim, 1966) p. 25.

g. It is impossible to discern how much text is lost. Between the lacunae are portions of *voces magicae* (magical incantations).

h. Cf. the translation of *ho poiēsas* in WisSol 9:1 and the discussion of this Gk. form in E. Norden, *Agnostos Theos: Untersuchungen zur Formengeschichte Religiöser Rede* (Leipzig, Berlin, 1913) pp. 201–7.

i. This statement is significant, because Jews usually depicted Jerusalem, not Sinai, as the *axis mundi.* Jub 8:19 refers to three holy places: the Garden of Eden, Mount Sinai, and Mount Zion (see Jub 1:2, 28). Ezek 38:12 calls Jerusalem "the navel of the earth." 1En 26:1 portrays Jerusalem as both the middle of the earth and the "holy mountain" (see also LetAris 83). For a recent discussion of the identification of Jerusalem with a "world mountain" and the "navel of the world," see B. S. Childs, *Myth and Reality in the Old Testament* (SBT 27; London, 1960; pp. 83–93) and S. Terrien, "The Omphalos Myth and Hebrew Religion" (*VT* 29 [1970] 317–38). For a severe critique of Childs and Terrien, see S. Talmon, "The 'Navel of the Earth' and the Comparative Method" (in *Scripture in History & Theology: Essays in Honor of J. Coert Rylaarsdam,* eds. A. L. Merrill and T. W. Overholt; Pittsburgh, 1977;

[you] who sit upon the s[e]a, . . .ʲ
you who sit [upon] the s[er]pen[t] gods,ᵏ
the [God who s]i[t]s [upon the s]un, *Iaō*,ˡ
you who si[t upon . . .]ᵐ
you who [si]t [u]pon th[e . . .] . . . Abriēl, Louēlⁿ
[. . . t]he [r]esting place of (the) che[r]u[b]i[m . . .]ᵒ
‖ f[o]r ever and e[ve]r.

(15)

9   God *Abaōth, Abrathiaōth*,ᵖ [*Sa*]*ba*[*ōth*,�q A]*dōnai*,ʳ *astra*ˢ . . .
         the L[or]d of all (things).

10   I summon you,ᵗ

pp. 243–68). A tradition in rabbinic literature states that God's Shekinah rests upon the sanctuary (in Jerusalem; see NumR Naso 13.6). Other rabbinic traditions deny that God came down upon Mount Sinai in order to speak with Moses (cf. viz. Mekilta Baḥodesh, Yitro, §4, p. 216, as edited by H. S. Horovitz). PRE, however, which describes the descents of God to earth, states that God's "sixth descent was when He came down on Sinai . . ." (41; ed. Friedlander, p. 318). The translation above is followed by lacunae and *voces magicae.*

j. Again it is difficult to be certain how much of the text is missing; it contains portions of *voces magicae.*

k. Goodenough (*Jewish Symbols*, vol. 2, p. 203): "upon the serpent-formed gods."

l. Cf. "Yao" in Apocryphon of John (II,1.11 and 12) and in On the Origin of the World (II,5.101). Other proper names also appearing in the Nag Hammadi Codices will be noted below.

The Gk. could be translated "upon the Sun-god *Iaō*" or "upon *Hēlios Iaō*"; cf. the cosmic prayers that call upon "Helios, Father of the world," and begin "Hail Helios, hail thou God in the heavens" (see Goodenough, *Jewish Symbols*, vol. 2, pp. 194, 199f.). Goodenough presented (p. 203) a translation similar to ours: "God [who sittest upon the s]un, Iao"; and cautioned that the "text is too bad here to make discussion of the matter valuable." Preisendanz (*PGM*, vol. 2, p. 148): "[Gott, der sitzt auf] dem Hēlios Iaô (the latter in small print)."

Iaô is another name for *yhw*, the abbreviated Heb. name for God (cf. Ganschinietz in Pauly-Wissowa, vol. 9 [1914] cols. 698–721 and Urbach, *Sages*, p. 126). Iaô, as Jerome (in *Psalm* VIII) seems to explain, could be pronounced "Yaho," and would accurately represent the Heb. *yhw*, which is a well-known contracted form of Yahweh, and which "seems as definitely to indicate the Jewish God as the name Osiris does the Egyptian" (Goodenough, *Jewish Symbols*, vol. 2, p. 192). Simon (*Verus Israel*, p. 400, cf. p. 407) suggests that Iaô represents *yhwh*. The name "Iaô" lost its Heb. roots and was used by pagans such as Macrobius in the fifth century (cf. Goodenough, *Jewish Symbols*, vol. 2, p. 207). The famous anguipede (cf. Goodenough, *Jewish Symbols*, vol. 2, pp. 245–58) has been identified recently as the god *Iaô, yhwh*, by M. Philonenko in "L'Anguipède alectorocéphale et le dieu Iaô," *Académie des inscrip-*

tions & belles-lettres (1979) 297–304. In the Eighth Book of Moses (especially ll. 1020–22 and 1045f.) *Iaô* is clearly identified with the great God in heaven. In the *Pistis Sophia*, however, *Iaô* is defined mystically in terms of the Gk. letters (see Book 5).

m. This expression is followed by a series of lacunae and *voces magicae.* Goodenough (*Jewish Symbols*, vol. 2, p. 203) forgot to translate *ho* [*kathēm*] *en* [*os*]; he translated only the first of the two "He (= you) who sit(s) upon."

n. These names are rare in the magical papyri. Abriēl appears only here and in VII, 978; Louēl occurs only here. They are both Semitic names for angels, but are not mentioned in the lists of angels' names in 1En 6:7f. and in 1En 69:1–3, and they are not cited in the expanded angelology of 3En. Etymologies are frequently nonexistent for the magical names; *perhaps* Abriēl is a contraction of Heb. *'abbîrᵉēl*, which means "God's mighty one," and *perhaps* Louēl is a Gk. rendering of Heb. *lāᵉel* (LXX *daouēl*), which means "belonging to God."

o. In the lacuna there are portions of *voces magicae.*

p. These two names occur frequently in the magical papyri; see Preisendanz (*PGM*, vol. 3, p. 236).

q. This name, "Sabaoth," appears also in many of the Nag Hammadi Codices; viz. it is in the Apocryphon of John, the Hypostasis of the Archons, On the Origin of the World, and the Testimony of Truth. It is also one of the most popular names in the magical papyri (see Preisendanz, *PGM*, vol. 3, pp. 229f.), and often is combined with Iaô (see Goodenough, *Jewish Symbols*, vol. 2, pp. 166, 172f., 176f., 179–81, 186, 196, 198–201).

r. This proper name could refer to the Gk.-Egyptian god Adonaios; but probably it is the Heb. substitute for the tetragrammaton (*yhwh*). Cf. the name "Adonaios" in the Nag Hammadi Codices; especially in On the Origin of the World. The name is popular primarily in the magical papyri; see Preisendanz (*PGM*, vol. 3, pp. 213f.).

s. *Astra* means "stars"; Goodenough (*Jewish Symbols*, vol. 2, p. 203) did not represent the word; but it is clear in Preisendanz. It is difficult to be certain how much of this fragile text is lost; but around the lacunae are portions of *voces magicae.*

t. Goodenough (*Jewish Symbols*, vol. 2, p. 203) also joined this injunction with the following ll.

11   (You who) give power o[ver (the) ch]as[m][u] (to those) above and
those below and those under the earth;[v]

12   Hear the one who [ha]s [the] prayer.[w]

13   The Lord God of the Hebrews, *Epa[g]aēl*, . . .[x]
of whom (is) [the] everlasting[y] power,
[*Elō]ēl, Souēl*.[z]

14   Make straight[a2] the one who has [th]e prayer [fro]m the
(20)   rac[e] of Israel [a]nd those || who have received favor[b2]
from you, God of gods.

15   He who has the secret name *Sabaōth*[c2] . . .
God of gods; amen, amen.

16   [He] who is upon (the) stars abo[v]e (the) ages,
who brings forth snow,[d2]
a[nd] who always passes throu[g]h the stars and pla[n]ets,[e2]
[and makes] (them) run in every way[f2] by your creating (power).[g2]

17   Fill me with wisdom,[h2]
empow[e]r me, Lord;

18   Fill my heart with good things, Lord;

u. The underworld is denoted by [*ch*]*as*[*ma*]*tos* (cf. e.g. Lk 16:26). In *PGM* IV.2536 (vol. 2, p. 153) Tartarus is defined as *chasma phaeinon*: "the bright (or fiery) chasm." According to *PGM* XXV.3 (vol. 2, p. 160) *Buthath* is said to sit (or rule over) the abyss: *ho kathēmenos epi tēs abus[s]ou*. According to 1En 20:2 Uriel is the angel who is in charge of Tartarus. 1En 90:24–27 describes the place of destruction as the "fiery abyss." In GkApEzra 1:9 it is said that "sinners . . . are for fiery Gehenna (*eis tēn geennan tou puros*)." In 4Mac 9:8 the tyrant is told he will suffer "eternal torture by fire (*aiōnion basanon dia puros*)."

v. The Gk. syntax is odd. The author is apparently thinking about a universe of three tiers. Goodenough (*Jewish Symbols*, vol. 2, p. 203) translated the passage freely: "to the things above, upon, and beneath the earth." Cf. Phil 2:10; Rev 5:13.

w. Gk. [*tēn*] *euchēn, euchē* means "prayer, oath." Goodenough (*Jewish Symbols*, vol. 2, p. 203) translated the form as "the curse." It is difficult to understand the reason for Goodenough's translation, since he rightly claimed that the "object of this prayer, for it is hardly a charm, is a deeply spiritual one . . ." (p. 203). See n. z.

x. *Epa[g]aēl* appears only here in the magical papyri. Goodenough (*Jewish Symbols*, vol. 2, p. 203) broke his habit of not representing words in small type in Preisendanz; he included "*alamn*."

y. According to Preisendanz's text, this word, *aenaos*, is very unclear.

z. These are two Semitic names and are found only here in the magical papyri. It is tempting to

suggest the second name is Gk. for "*su ēl*" or "you (in Gk.) are (understood) God (the Semitic proper name)." The l. would then mean "God of God, you (are) God." The harmony with vss. 14b and 15b is attractive.

a2. Gk.: *diorthōson*, from *diorthoō*, which means "to make quite straight, set right, amend"; the verb has a medical or therapeutic meaning. Goodenough (*Jewish Symbols*, vol. 2, p. 203): "Keep straight him who has the charm." The noun is again [*tē*]*n euchēn*; which Goodenough had earlier translated as "curse" (see n. w).

b2. See n. f.

c2. See n. q.

d2. The syntax is difficult. Another vaguely possible interpretation: "[He] who brings forth snow upon (the) stars abo[v]e (the) ages."

e2. Lit. "the fixed and wandering s[ta]rs"; but these are technical terms.

f2. Gk.: *ta panta* is here taken to be an accusative of specification.

g2. The Gk. is difficult. Another possible rendering is "[and make] (them) pursue everything in your creation." P. Pokorný suggested to me another possible rendering: "and who makes the stars and planets run the universe by your creating (power)." A similar translation was offered by Goodenough (*Jewish Symbols*, vol. 2, p. 203): "and makest the fixed stars and planets marshall all things by thy creative power." He also added the n. "This passage is difficult." See above discussion under "Relation to other books."

h2. Gk.: *sophias*; see 1Kgs 3:9; cf. LXX 5:9.

19   As an ear[th]ly angel,[i2]

(5)   as ‖ [hav]ing become immortal,[j2]

as having recei[ved] the gift which (is) from [yo]u, [a]men, amen.

20   [S]ay [the p]r[a]y[e]r o[f] Jacob[k2] seven times to (the)
Nor[th] and E[a]st.

2En 30:11 (J).
PrJos A 1

i2. The *hōs* probably should not be taken as a demonstrative and the l. understood as a petition: "so that (I might become) an ear[th]ly angel." Three times in vs. 19 there is a *hōs* that begins a line; the first of these may be translated either "as (you empower) an ear[th]ly angel" or "as (having become) an ear[th]ly angel." The latter possibility seems preferable, because of the two following aorists (probably dramatic aorists): having become immortal and having received the gift. The Qumran literature (viz. 1QH 3.21f.; 4.24f.; 6.13; 3.22f.; 1QS 11.7f.; 1QSb 4.25), many pseudepigrapha (especially PrJos A, 2En 30:8–11 A, HistRech 7; cf. JosAsen 20:6, OdesSol 3:7f., TSol 22), the Cologne Mani Codex 51:1ff. (ApSethel: *kai egenomēn hōs heis tōn megistōn aggelōn*), and other Jewish inspired writings (e.g. Book of Adam and Eve, ed. C. S. Malan, Bk. 1, ch. 10) demonstrate that Jews could have thought of a righteous person on earth becoming an angel and asking for wisdom and power.

j2. Goodenough (*Jewish Symbols*, vol. 2, p. 203): "because I am an angel upon earth, because I have become immortal."

k2. In vs. 5 [Abr]aham is mentioned and here Jacob's name is expressed. It is noteworthy that Isaac's name never appears. One might have expected it; the Patria[rch]s, presumably Abraham, Isaac, and Jacob (see the contribution herein on the Testaments of the Three Patriarchs), are uppermost in the mind of the author, since they are mentioned in the very first l. of vs. 1. As the name of God, so the ranks of the Patriarchs—Abraham, Isaac, and Jacob—were assumed to possess magical powers (cf. e.g. *PGM* VII, ll. 314f. [vol. 2, p. 14]; XIII, l. 976, especially 817 [vol. 2, p. 128]; and Simon, *Verus Israel*, p. 401). It is only vaguely possible (and I would think improbable; see n. 1) that *Iaō* in vs. 8 denotes Isaac even though Simon (*Verus Israel*, p. 407) seems to be correct in stating that the phrase *ton theon tou Abraam kai tou Iaō kai tou Iakou* means "the God of Abraham, and of Isaac [sic], and of Jacob." Also see J. Z. Smith's comments above, in his contribution on PrJos, n. 9. In the opening of PrJos, Abraham, Isaac, and Jacob are said to predate creation (cf. Fragment A 1–3). As stated above, the magical papyri use Heb. names without understanding them or even correctly pronouncing and transliterating them.

ODES OF SOLOMON

(Late First to Early Second Century A.D.)

A NEW TRANSLATION AND INTRODUCTION

BY J. H. CHARLESWORTH

During the early years of this century, J. Rendel Harris discovered among some manuscripts, which had been randomly placed in a corner of his office,[1] a hymnbook that he soon was to identify as the long-lost Odes of Solomon.[2] The Odes were known previously only because of notations in lists of apocryphal books, excerpts in the Coptic *Pistis Sophia*, and from a Latin quotation by Lactantius. Subsequent discoveries of another Syriac manuscript[3] and a Greek version of Ode 11,[4] and intensive research on this document, convinced many scholars that the Odes are not gnostic[5] but a collection of very early Christian hymns. They are so Jewish in tone and perspective that scholars from the beginning until the present have been persuaded, incorrectly, that they are essentially Jewish.[6] In line with the consensus that these Odes are Christian[7] is the observation that the key characteristic in these hymns is a joyous tone of thanksgiving for the advent of the Messiah who had been promised (cf. Ode 7:1–6; 41:3–7) and for the present experience of eternal life and love from and for the Beloved (3:1–9; 11:1–24; 23:1–3; 26:1–7; 40:1–6).

Texts

In addition to the Harris manuscript (H), which is now Cod. Syr. 9 in the John Rylands University Library of Manchester, England, the Odes are preserved only in Codex Nitriensis (N), which is recorded in the British Museum as B.M. Add. 14538, in Bodmer Papyrus XI (G), which is housed in the Bibliothèque Bodmer in Geneva, and in quotations in the Coptic Codex Askewianus (C), which is shelved in the British Museum and cataloged as MS. Add. 5114. The Odes are not extant in full in any manuscript; Ode 2, the beginning of Ode 3, and perhaps portions of Ode 1 are still lost. Manuscript H is mutilated at the beginning and preserves only Odes 3:1b–42:20; N preserves only Odes 17:7–42:20, G only Ode 11:1–24;

---

[1] J. R. Harris, "An Early Christian Hymn-Book," *Contemporary Review* 95 (1909) 414–28. Harris' excitement as described by him is quoted in J. H. Charlesworth, *The Odes of Solomon* (Oxford, 1973) pp. 4f.

[2] Harris published the *editio princeps* in the year in which he discovered the Odes: *The Odes and Psalms of Solomon: Now First Published from the Syriac Version* (Cambridge, 1909).

[3] Found in the BM by F. C. Burkitt and announced in his "A New MS of the Odes of Solomon." *JTS* 13 (1912) 372–85.

[4] M. Testuz (ed.), *Papyrus Bodmer X–XII* (Geneva, 1959).

[5] See Charlesworth, "The Odes of Solomon—Not Gnostic," *CBQ* 31 (1969) 357–69; H. Chadwick, "Some Reflections on the Character and Theology of the Odes of Solomon," *Kyriakon* [Quasten Festschrift], vol. 1. pp. 266–70; and E. Yamauchi, *Pre-Christian Gnosticism: A Survey of the Proposed Evidences* (Grand Rapids, Mich., 1973) pp. 91–94.

[6] A. Harnack claimed the Odes are a Jewish hymnbook from the time of Jesus that was interpolated around A.D. 100 by a Christian. See his and J. Flemming's *Ein jüdisch-christliches Psalmbuch aus dem ersten Jahrhundert* (TU 35.4; Leipzig, 1910). More extreme are the positions of A. Menzies, who thought the Odes are the "Psalms of the Proselytes" ("The Odes of Solomon," *Interpreter* [London] 7 [1910] 7–22) and M. Testuz, who claimed that they were composed by an Essene (*Papyrus Bodmer VII–IX*, p. 58).

[7] J. A. Emerton considers the debate closed: "The Odes are plainly Christian in their present form." "Notes on Some Passages in the Odes of Solomon," *JTS* N.S. 28 (1977) 507–19.

and C only quotations from Odes 5:1–11; 1:1–5; 6:8–18; 25:1–12; 22:1–12. Manuscripts H and N are respectively from the fifteenth and tenth centuries; the Greek papyrus from the third; and the Coptic manuscript from the fourth century.

Original language and date

Intensive research has been devoted to the attempt to discover the original language in which these Odes were composed. Some scholars have thought that the original language is Greek,[8] others that it is Hebrew;[9] and Father J. Carmignac has recently attempted to show that the Odes were composed in a kind of Qumran Hebrew.[10] It is probable, however, that they were composed in Syriac (or Aram.), as demonstrated in the important commentary by J. R. Harris and A. Mingana,[11] and by recent publications by A. Vööbus,[12] J. A. Emerton,[13] and myself.[14] Odes 7:10 and 9:8f. are apparently based on the Septuagint of Psalms 50:3 [H 51:1] and 20:4 [H 21:3] but this dependence cannot be used as an argument for a Greek original; we now have ample evidence that the Septuagint was used in communities that were very conservative and Semitic as proved, for example, by the discovery of fragments from several copies of the Septuagint among the Dead Sea Scrolls.[15] Parallels with gnostic literature are, of course, not indicative that the Odes were composed in Greek because the gnostics used and inherited many documents that were originally composed in Syriac and other Semitic languages. The only surviving witness to a Greek version, namely the Bodmer Papyrus XI, shows signs of being translated from a Semitic language and does not appear to be either good Greek or to have been composed in Greek. Most importantly the attractive quality of the extant Syriac is indicative that Syriac is probably the original language. Of special note is the play on words possible only in Syriac (cf. Ode 19:9 and n.) and the pervasive assonance, metrical scheme, and rhythm in the Syriac. Also numerous variants between the extant versions are frequently explained by the assumption of a Syriac tradition of transmission; note for example 5:2 and 23:4 in which *maryâ* was confused with *m⁽raimâ*, 22:6 in which *brk* was mistaken for *krk*, and 25:8 in which *raḥmâ* was confused with *rûḥâ*.

Shortly after the discovery of the Odes, A. Harnack argued that behind Christian editorial additions lies an early pre-Christian Jewish hymnbook.[16] J. Bernard rejected Harnack's hypothesis and claimed that the Odes are a Christian hymnbook from the latter part of the second century A.D.[17] After a decade of study and debate, Harris and Mingana assigned the Odes to the first century A.D.[18] Despite R. Bultmann's extensive influence and use of the Odes in understanding the background of Johannine theology,[19] many German scholars have

[8] In the first two of his three editions Harris thought Gk. to be the original language. Cf. *editio princeps*, pp. 36f., 46f. Since the recovery of one ode in Gk. some scholars have claimed that Gk. is the original language. See Testuz in *Papyrus Bodmer X–XII*, p. 3; and M. Philonenko in "Conjecture sur un verset de la onzième Ode de Salomon," *ZNW* 53 (1962) 264. W. Frankenberg, so convinced that Gk. is the original language, translated the Odes into Gk. Cf. *Das Verständnis der Oden Salomos* (BZAW 21; Giessen, 1911).

[9] H. Grimme, persuaded that Heb. is the original language, translated the Odes into Heb. Cf. *Die Oden Salomos: Syrisch-Hebräisch-Deutsch* (Heidelberg, 1911).

[10] Cf. J. Carmignac in "Les Affinités qumrâniennes de la onzième Ode de Salomon," *RQ* 3 (1961) 71–102; and in "Recherches sur la langue originelle des Odes de Salomon," *RQ* 4 (1963) 429–32.

[11] *The Odes and Psalms of Solomon*, especially vol. 2, p. 165.

[12] "Neues Licht zur Frage der Originalsprache der Oden Salomos," *Le Muséon* 75 (1962) 275–90.

[13] "Some Problems of Text and Language in the Odes of Solomon," *JTS* N.S. 18 (1967) 372–406.

[14] *A Critical Examination of the Odes of Solomon: Identification, Text, Original Language, Date* (Duke Ph.D., 1967) especially pp. 67–138. Charlesworth, "Paronomasia and Assonance in the Syriac Text of the Odes of Solomon," *Semitics* [Pretoria] 1 (1970) 12–26.

[15] Cf. F. M. Cross, Jr., *The Ancient Library of Qumran and Modern Biblical Studies* (Garden City, N.Y. 1961²) p. 28.

[16] Harnack, *Ein jüdisch-christliches Psalmbuch*. Harnack later rejected his own hypothesis in favor of Harris and Mingana's conclusion. Cf. Harnack's review of their edition in *TLZ* 46 (1921) cols. 6f. I am grateful to Dr. M. Lattke for discussions on this issue.

[17] J. H. Bernard, *The Odes of Solomon*, p. 42.

[18] *The Odes and Psalms of Solomon*, vol. 2, p. 69.

[19] "Ein jüdisch-christliches Psalmbuch aus dem ersten Jahrhundert," *Monatschrift für Pastoraltheologie* 7 (1910) 23–29; *The Gospel of John: A Commentary*, trans. G. R. Beasley-Murray, eds. R. W. N. Hoare and J. K. Riches (Oxford, 1971).

followed W. Bauer[20] and see the Odes as a product of second-century Gnosticism.[21] The extensive and pervasive parallels with the Qumran Hodayoth,[22] the undeniable similarities with the ideas found in the Gospel of John that cannot be explained away by either the hypothesis that they are dependent upon John or that John depends upon them,[23] and the possibility that Ignatius of Antioch may have known and even quoted from them[24] cumulatively indicate that the Odes were probably composed sometime around A.D. 100.

Provenance

The most difficult question to answer in working on an ancient Jewish or Christian document is its provenance. Since it was possible to travel widely and ideas were not necessarily limited to one particular city or locale, it is conceivable that the Odes were composed in a number of places. It is possible that they were composed somewhere in Palestine and perhaps in Pella, where it seems the earliest group of Jewish Christians fled before the destruction of Jerusalem, in Alexandria or some other city in Egypt, or in Ephesus or some other place in Asia Minor. Specialists, however, have defended two hypotheses: The Odes were composed in either Edessa or one of the many Jewish Christian communities that dotted the region between Edessa and Antioch,[25] or in Antioch-on-the-Orontes.[26] If the Odes were composed around A.D. 100 in Syriac, are from the same community or region in which the Gospel of John was composed, and were familiar to Ignatius or contained the same Christian tone and ideas as those found in his letters, then the most probable provenance is Antioch or somewhere near that city. This hypothesis is tentative because of the generic tone of the Odes, a feature shared with almost all psalms and hymns.

Historical importance

Attempts to discern the historical importance of the Odes have been published in hundreds of scholarly articles and monographs, but it seems possible to summarize the discussion of their importance. First, the early concepts and images in the Odes, which were a shock and disappointment to many of the scholars who worked on them during the beginning of this century, preserve precious reminders of the first attempts to articulate the unparalleled experience of the advent of the Messiah. The Odist portrayed God with breasts that were milked by the Holy Spirit and from which came salvivic milk that is described as the Son (Ode 19). The early and strong Jewish tone of the Odes, like some passages in the Synoptic Gospels (cf. especially Mt 10:5f.), portray the gentiles in unattractive terms (cf. 10:5; 23:15 [N]; 29:8). The Odist confessed the grandeur of the Messiah with the words that he is the

---

[20] "Die Oden Salomos," *Neutestamentliche Apokryphen in deutscher Übersetzung*, eds. E. Hennecke and W. Schneemelcher (Tübingen, 1964) vol. 2, pp. 576–625; cf. especially p. 577.

[21] For example, see W. G. Kümmel, *Introduction to the New Testament*, rev. ed. trans. H. C. Kee (Nashville, 1975) p. 223, and K. Rudolph, *Gnosis und Gnostizismus* (Wege der Forschung 262: Darmstadt, 1975) pp. 521, 527, 791.

[22] See J. Carmignac, *RQ* 3 (1961) 71–102; Charlesworth, "Les Odes de Salomon et les manuscrits de la mer morte," *RB* 77 (1970) 522–49; Charlesworth, "Qumran, John and the Odes of Solomon," *John and Qumran*, pp. 107–36.

[23] Charlesworth and A. Culpepper, "The Odes of Solomon and the Gospel of John," *CBQ* 35 (1973) 298–322.

[24] This argument is presented by many, especially by R. M. Grant, "The Odes of Solomon and the Church of Antioch," *JBL* 63 (1944) 363–97; and by V. Corwin, *St. Ignatius and Christianity in Antioch* (Yale Publications in Religion 1; New Haven, 1960) pp. 71–80.

Harris and Mingana concluded their search for the Odes' origin in the third edition with the claim that "it is hardly possible to refer the Odes to any other time than the first century, or to any other district than Antioch." They also cautioned, "if we are wrong in assigning them as written at Antioch in the first century, we are not far wrong either in place or in time." *The Odes and Psalms of Solomon*, vol. 2, pp. 67, 69.

[25] Cf. especially J. de Zwaan, "The Edessene Origin of the Odes of Solomon," *Quantulacumque*, eds. R. P. Casey, S. Lake, and A. K. Lake (London, Baltimore, 1937) pp. 285–302; cf. especially p. 297. Grant, *JBL* 63 (1944) 363–77; cf. especially p. 377: "The Odes of Solomon, composed in Syriac at Edessa, were known to the bi-lingual Ignatius either there or at Antioch." Also see A. Vööbus, "The Odes of Solomon," *History of Asceticism in the Syrian Orient* (CSCO 14; Louvain, 1958) pp. 62–64.

[26] Antioch was defended by not only Harris and Mingana (*The Odes and Psalms of Solomon*, vol. 2, pp. 67–69), but also by J. Bernard (Review of *The Odes and Psalms of Solomon*, re-ed. by J. R. Harris and A. Mingana, in *Theology: A Monthly Journal of Historic Christianity* 1 [1920] 288–98, see especially p. 289).

"most praised among the praised,/and the greatest among the great ones" (36:4). This confession might have been unattractive to Arius and, of course, would have been horrifying to the father of Christian orthodoxy, Athanasius. For the historian, however, these expressions, ideas, and metaphors are a precious reminder of the attempts by the earliest Christians to articulate that which is paradigmatically new.

Second, the striking and frequent parallels between the Odes and the Dead Sea Scrolls, especially the Hodayoth, give us another indication of the extent to which the Essenes influenced some earliest Christian theology. Both in the Odes and in the major sectarian Dead Sea Scrolls, there is a consciousness of being "the Way," the term used by Paul to describe the earliest followers of Jesus (Acts 24:14; cf. 24:22), and of constituting the true community of the faithful ones, "the holy ones," whom God has founded upon the rock and has planted for his glory. Similarly both in the Odes and in the Dead Sea Scrolls, there is an emphasis on "knowledge," "the war," "crown," "living water," and "the sun" as symbols of a realized salvation that has not yet been fully consummated.[27] It is possible that these similarities show that the Odes merely share with the Dead Sea Scrolls a similar type of Judaism; but it seems more probable that the author of the Odes had been influenced by many of the ideas developed in the Dead Sea Scrolls; and it is even conceivable that he had at one time been a member of the sect that produced them.[28]

Third, the Odes are significant for a better understanding of the origin and meaning of the Gospel of John; the *ex ore Christi* form in many of the Odes, in which the Odist ceases talking as an inspired believer and speaks as the living Lord, is of significant and still unexamined importance for a better perception of the Johannine sayings that begin with "I am" (cf. especially Jn 6:35, 48; 8:12, 58; 10:7, 9, 14; 11:25; 15:1, 5).[29] Also the "Word" Christology in the Odes is rich, containing numerous ideas similar to those found in John. But the terminology is not as sophisticated; the Odist twelve times uses the appropriate term for the "Word," *mellᵉthâ*, and twelve times the inappropriate *pethgâmâ*.

Fourth, the joyous tone of these Odes themselves stands in contrast to most of the other pseudepigrapha. Unlike most of them the focus is not on earthly catastrophes (e.g. 4Ezra, 2Bar), although the Odist is aware of the destruction of the Temple (cf. Ode 4), but on the advent of the Messiah. Paradise is not conceived as distant, as in the Abode of the Rechabites, nor as in the third heaven, as in 2 Enoch, but upon the earth.[30] As in the Psalms of Solomon and in the Gospel of John the believer is portrayed as a tree planted by God, but in the Odes the tree (the believer) is planted in Paradise and drinks of the living water of eternity (cf. Ode 11).

Fifth, the Odes are a window through which we can occasionally glimpse the earliest Christians at worship; especially their apparent stress on baptism,[31] their rejoicing over and experiencing of a resurrected and living Messiah, Lord, and Savior, and their frequent exhortations to live a life of the highest conceivable righteousness.[32]

Theological importance

God. In the Odes, God is portrayed as one who is gracious (9:5; 33:10) and merciful (3:6). The Odes are monotheistic: God is the Creator (cf. 4:15; 6:3–5). In language reminiscent of passages in the Hodayoth that seem to derive from the founder of the community, the teacher of righteousness,[33] the Odist expresses his thanksgiving for God's

---

[27] See Charlesworth, *RB* 77 (1970) 522–49. Also see D. E. Aune, "The Present Realization of Eschatological Salvation in the Odes of Solomon," *The Cultic Setting of Realized Eschatology in Early Christianity* (NovTSup 28; Leiden, 1972) pp. 166–94.

[28] See Charlesworth, *RB* 77 (1970) 522–49, and Charlesworth in *John and Qumran*, p. 135.

[29] Bultmann correctly observed that the "Revelation-discourses" in John are in the style "of Semitic speech; more accurately of Semitic poetry such as is known to us from the Odes of Solomon . . ." *Theology of the New Testament*, trans. K. Grobel (New York, 1951–55) vol. 2, p. 10.

[30] Cf. Ode 11 and the following discussion on "Immortal life."

[31] Bernard recognized, but exaggerated, the importance of baptism in the Odes, claiming "they are baptismal hymns intended for use in public worship, either for catechumens or for those who have recently been baptized." *The Odes of Solomon,* p. 42.

[32] See the discussion below on "Ethics."

[33] Here I must confess indebtedness to G. Jeremias, *Der Lehrer der Gerechtigkeit* (Studien zur Umwelt des Neuen Testaments 2; Göttingen, 1963).

act in rescuing him: "I was rescued from my chains,/and I fled unto you, O my God" (25:1). God is called the Most High (3:6; 5:2; 11:9; *et passim*), the Father (7:7, 11; 8:22; 9:5; 10:4; *et passim*), and especially Lord; but it is difficult to decide when the Odist means God and when the Son by this term, since he clearly identifies the two.[34] Although the Odist places emphasis on the appearance of the Messiah, his incarnation (7:3–6; 41:3f., 11–15), crucifixion (especially 27:1–3; 42:1f.), resurrection (42:6), and descent into Hades (especially 42:6–20), God is not portrayed as one who works only through intermediaries. He is actively involved in his creation as illustrated by 11:2: "For the Most High circumcised me by his Holy Spirit,/then he uncovered my inward being toward him,/and filled me with his love." A similar expression of God's activity is found in 17:1: "Then I was crowned by my God,/and my crown is living." In contrast to the accent in the apocalypses[35] but in line with the stress in most of the psalms, hymns, and prayers[36] in early Judaism, the Odist emphasizes God's presence. Note, for example, Ode 21:6f.: "And I was lifted up in the light,/and I passed before his (the Lord's) face.//and I was constantly near him,/while praising and confessing him." The Odist does talk about the descent of the Word (12:5f.; 23:5; cf. 22:1), but in contrast to the Gospel of John in which God is portrayed as "he who has sent," Jesus as "he who was sent," and the disciples as "they who are sent,"[37] the Odist portrays the unity between God and the Son in terms of the activity by the Son who appears. Observe how the Odist expresses himself in 41:11–14: "And his Word is with us in all our way,/the Savior who gives life and does not reject ourselves.//The Man who humbled himself,/but was raised because of his own righteousness.//The Son of the Most High appeared/in the perfection of his Father.//And light dawned from the Word/that was before time in him." The Christology, with the mention of self-humility and received exaltation, is close to the pre-Pauline hymn in Philippians 2:5–11.

Man. Although a hymnbook is not a treatise and the Odist has not displayed his theology, we can nevertheless discern that his concept of man is distinct from Paul, who saw humankind divided into two groups: a person prior to the revelation of faith, and a person under faith.[38] The Odist's anthropology is equally dissimilar from that found in John where humankind is bifurcated into those who believe and those who do not believe.[39] For the Odist, humankind is divided into those who walk in error (15:6; 18:14) and those who walk in the way of truth (11:3) or in the knowledge of the Lord (23:4).[40] While the former and intermittently the latter are plagued by the Evil One (14:5; 33:4), sometimes called the Deceiver (38:10), the Corruptor (33:1, 7; 38:9), and the Error (31:2; 38:10), the emphasis throughout is upon the decisive battle won by God over "the persecutors" (23:20; 42:5). In language strikingly similar to that found in John, the Odist affirms that the Messiah has already captured a world that was rebellious against the Creator: "I took courage and became strong and captured the world,/and it became mine for the glory of the Most High, and of God my Father" (10:4 [*ex ore Christi*]; cf. 29:10; 31:1f.). In contrast with the majority of humankind, the Odist experiences the final victory because "there is a Helper for me, the Lord" (7:3; cf. 8:6f.). Consequently, the Odist rejoices in his present experience of immortal life: "And he (the Lord) has caused to dwell in me his immortal life" (10:2; cf. 15:10). This idea is very similar to the concept of realized salvation found in the Gospel

[34] In Ode 29:6 "Lord" refers to God ("the Lord's Messiah," cf. PssSol 17); in 24:1 to the Messiah ("our Lord Messiah"). The transition is clarified in 29:6 ("For I believed in the Lord's Messiah,/and considered that he is the Lord").

[35] This tendency is discussed in my "A History of Pseudepigrapha Research: The Re-Emerging Importance of the Pseudepigrapha," *ANRW*, Band II 19.1, pp. 54–88.

[36] This emphasis is discussed in my "Hymns, Prayers, Liturgies (c. 167 B.C.E.–135 C.E.)," in the SBL Centennial Volume, ed. G. W. E. Nickelsburg, Jr., and R. A. Kraft; see also my "A Prolegomenon to a New Study of the Jewish Background of the Hymns and Prayers in the New Testament," *JJS* 33 (1982) 265–85 [Yadin Festschrift].

[37] See J. Kuhl, *Die Sendung Jesu und der Kirche nach dem Johannes-Evangelium* (Studia Instituti Missiologici Societatis Verbi Divini 11; St. Augustin, 1967). See especially p. 36.

[38] See the classic discussion of Paul's anthropology in R. Bultmann's *Theology of the New Testament*, vol. 1, pp. 190–352.

[39] An important examination of the theologies of Paul, John, and the Odes was published by J. Lindblom in his *Om Lifvetz Idé hos Paulus och Johannes samt i de s. k. Salomos Oden* (Uppsala Universitets Årsskrift 1910: Teologi 1; Uppsala, 1911).

[40] See Charlesworth in *John and Qumran*, pp. 107–36.

of John. It is also distinct from 4 Ezra, whose author, shattered by the collapse of the Temple, Jerusalem, and the nation Israel, struggles with the eternal question of the meaning and purpose of evil in a world created by God and finally is distressed at the extremely few number of those who will be saved at the end of time.[41] In stunning contrast to the author of Ezra, the Odist expresses his salvation and oneness with his Creator and Savior: "I love the Beloved and I myself love him,/and where his rest is, there also am I" (3:5). A few verses later he writes, "I have been united (to him), because the lover has found the Beloved,/because I love him that is the Son, I shall become a son" (3:7). This pervasive tone of oneness becomes so developed in the Odes that frequently the Odist ceases speaking as himself and speaks as Christ.

Cosmology. As in the Gospel of John there is a cosmology of two worlds, the world above and the world below; moreover, the cosmic dualism of two worlds is modified with the "above" vastly superior to the "below" (34:4f.). The cosmos can be described as inhabited by two spirits, the Lord's Holy Spirit (cf. 3:10; 14:8; 16:5) and the Evil One (14:5). In contrast to the ideas found in the Qumranic Rule of the Community (1QS 3.13– 4.26), but again in striking similarity to the dualism in the Gospel of John, the Odes do not portray a cosmic struggle between two warring spirits, because the good spirit has already saved from the evil spirit the one who walks "in the knowledge of the Lord" (23:4; 14:4f.). Even in Ode 38, in which is depicted a militantly aggressive Deceiver and Error, the Odist celebrates his victory because of the superior quality of the Truth. In contrast to most of the apocalypses, the Odist portrays God as directly involved with his creation and with the salvation of the individual.

Ethics. An aspect of the Odist's thought that has remained not only unexamined but almost unseen is the ethical exhortations that appear in no less than fourteen Odes. These exhortations are certainly dissimilar to brilliant and perceptive philosophical discussions like those found in Aristotle's *Nicomachean Ethics*; they are more similar to the injunctions found in Pseudo-Phocylides and are especially similar to the exhortations preserved in the Testaments of the Twelve Patriarchs. Since most of the exhortations are couched in verbs with plural forms, we can assume that they were most probably used in the worship of a community. Corroborative evidence is the similarity between petitions and exhortations and the phrase in 14:9 with the request from the Lord to "hasten to grant *our* petitions" [italics mine]. Most of the exhortations in the Odes are of a generic nature urging others to be wise, to be understanding, to exhort, to confess, to exult, to be enriched, to be strong and redeemed. Only once is an exhortation put in the mouth of Christ and that is in 31:6f. in which Christ invites individuals: "Come forth . . ." Indicative of the homogeneity of the Odes is the observation that the very next exhortation is by the Virgin who urges those who hear her to "return" and to "come" (33:5–11). Ode 20:5–8 is of significant importance, because only here the imperatives are in a singular form and because there are six distinct ethical exhortations. At the beginning and the end of the list, the Odist exhorts the listener to spiritual virtues. In the interior of the list, there are exhortations reminiscent of the decalogue or Ten Commandments; the list is as follows: Offer your inward being faultlessly, do not oppress anyone, do not buy slaves, do not deceive your neighbor, do not steal from him, put on the grace of the Lord, come into his Paradise, and make for yourself a crown from his tree. As can be seen by a cursory examination of this list, except for the first and last three exhortations to spiritual righteousness, the others are couched in negative terms. Negative phraseology does not occur in the very next exhortation contained in the Odes, Ode 23:4, in which there is an exhortation to "walk in the knowledge of the Lord." Here as elsewhere in the Odes exhortations are not linked with material rewards. A spiritual reward, however, is mentioned in the next line of this fourth verse: "And you will know the grace of the Lord generously . . ." The overriding ethical norm for the Odist is without question the emphasis placed on love. This emphasis runs throughout the Odes from Ode 3 through to the end of the collection. The final exhortation in the Odes is found in 41:1–

---

[41] See the insightful study by A. L. Thompson, *Responsibility for Evil in the Theodicy of IV Ezra* (SBLDS 29; Missoula, Mont., 1977).

6 in which there is a deliberate and intentional reworking of the first psalm of David so that the law is replaced by love: "And let our faces shine in his light,/and let our hearts meditate in his love./By night and by day" (41:6).

Immortal life. The Odist professes neither the Greek concept of an immortal soul that is transmigrated from one body to another nor the Jewish concept of the resurrection of the body,[42] which is graphically portrayed in the action by Razis, who hurled his entrails at the crowd and Greek soldiers calling to the Lord of life to return them to him at the proper time (2Mac 14). The Odist rather exults in his salvation and experience of immortality because he has taken off a corrupt garment and put on a garment of incorruption (15:8), a garment of light (21:3), and the Lord's garment (cf. 11:11; 21:3; 25:8). Another way of expressing his experience of immortality is the pictorial metaphor that he is one of the fruit-bearing trees that has been planted by the Lord in Paradise (cf. 11:16a–24; 20:7). All of this language is used to state emphatically that his immortality is geographically here and chronologically now. The most significant quality of immortality for the Odist is the incorruption that it entails; he who is joined to the Beloved "shall be found incorrupted in all ages" (8:22). In Ode 3 immediately after stating that the lover has been united to the Beloved, the Odist states, "Indeed he who is joined to him who is immortal,/truly will be immortal" (3:8). The Lord's purpose and will for the believer is eternal life and a perfection that is incorruptible (cf. 9:4). The one who trusts in the Lord has the assurance of redemption (40:5), and possesses immortal life and incorruptibility: "And his (the Lord's) possession is immortal life,/and those who receive it are incorruptible" (40:6). J. Rendel Harris, perceiving how the Odist identifies immortality with incorruptibility, argued that he had "defined" immortality as incorruption and "that the odist viewed his immortality experimentally and qualitatively, rather than in a remote future, or in the language of mere duration."[43] It seems better to state that the Odist describes immortality as incorruption and was so enthusiastic about the presence of his incorruptibility and immortality[44] that he saw no need to talk about its duration, celebrating rather the permanent possession of eternal gifts that will last forever. The Odist exults in incorruption in *all* ages, as we have seen (8:22), praises the Lord for "his rest" that is "for ever and ever" (25:12), and looks forward, with the apocalyptists, to the future "incorruption in the new world" (33:12).

Relation to canonical books

The Odist neither quoted from the Old Testament nor the New Testament, but he was directly influenced by the former and by the traditions recorded in the latter. The Odist seems to have been influenced by Ezekiel 47 in Ode 6 and Ezekiel 37:4–6 in Ode 22:9. He is apparently dependent on Proverbs 8:22 in Ode 41:9, on Genesis 2:2 in Ode 16:12, and on Isaiah 58:8 in Ode 8:19.[45] His major dependence is certainly on the Davidic Psalms, and there is sufficient evidence to warrant the assumption that he knew these Psalms both in Hebrew and in Greek. Earlier we saw how he was influenced and deliberately rephrases Psalm 1; he similarly treated Psalm 84:10 so that it produced the following: "For one hour of your faith/is more excellent than all days and years" (4:5). The Odist is apparently dependent on the Septuagint of Psalms 50:3 [H 51:1] and 20:4 [H 21:3] in Odes 7:10 and 9:8f.; and he is dependent on the Hebrew, or Syriac, of Psalms 21:11 and 2:4 in Odes 5:8 and 29:10. By far the most influential Psalm is 22; Psalm 22:16 has influenced Ode 28:14; Psalm 22:18 has affected Ode 28:18; and Psalm 22:16–18 has supplied the words and images in Ode 31:8–13.

Since the discovery of the Odes of Solomon, numerous attempts have been made to prove that the Odist is dependent on one or more of the books in the New Testament. The

---

[42] "Resurrection" is transformed into a release of the living from threatening death (cf. 29:4), or the deliverance of those in Sheol by the Son of God (42:11–20). See also J. R. Harris, *The Doctrine of Immortality in the Odes of Solomon* (London, 1912) p. 71.

[43] Harris, *Immortality*, pp. 43, 45f.

[44] See Aune, *The Cultic Setting*, especially pp. 184–94.

[45] Harris and Mingana claimed a phrase in Ode 41:9 was "borrowed" from Prov 8:22 (*The Odes and Psalms of Solomon*, vol. 2, p. 75, 118f.). Abbott argued that the Song of Moses (Ex 15:10) had influenced Ode 25:3f. (*Light on the Gospel from an Ancient Poet*, pp. 192f.)

arguments have persuaded few; they are not persuasive because of the ambiguity of the parallels, and because the *oral* tradition continued to be influential even until Tatian compiled his so-called Diatessaron around the year A.D. 175.[46] To be sure, the Odes share many of the traditions that have been recorded in the New Testament, but that by no means suggests that they are to be linked with one or more of the canonical records of these traditions. Significant traditions shared with the New Testament are Jesus' virginal birth, baptism, and walking on the water (cf. Odes 19, 24, 39). Jesus' suffering and crucifixion are significantly portrayed in Odes 8:5, 27; 28:9–20; 31:8–13; and 42:2. As we have seen, the Odes share with the Gospel of John many striking and significant parallels, but specialists on the Odes have cautioned against assuming that the Odes are dependent on John and have urged consideration of a shared community.[47]

Relation to apocryphal books

The Odist never quotes from an apocryphal writing; he shares numerous ideas and symbols with many apocryphal compositions and apparently has been influenced by some writings and has influenced others. Since we are working with a hymnbook in which dependence on earlier writings can only be through illusions or a borrowed idea or phrase, it might be wise to remain open to the possibility that the Odist had been influenced directly or indirectly by the Psalms of Solomon and 1 Enoch. In Psalm of Solomon 14, the writer describes the holy ones as the *trees* of life in the *Paradise* of the *Lord*. He even describes their *planting* as *rooted* forever. In Ode 11 the Odist becomes "like the land which blossoms and rejoices in its fruits" (11:12; cf. 38:17), is taken to the *Lord's Paradise* (11:16) and sees "blooming and fruit-bearing trees" (11:16a), whose *roots* are from an immortal land and which are identified as the blessed who "are *planted* in your land" (11:18). It is conceivable that both the Psalmist and the Odist were independently influenced by the ideas found in the eighth column of the Hodayoth; but it is also conceivable that the idea in Psalm of Solomon 14 has influenced the Odist's discussion of Paradise and the confession that he became like "the land which blossoms," Paradise (11:16). In both the Psalms of Solomon and the Odes of Solomon the righteous are described as the *trees planted* in *Paradise*. Perhaps the concept in the Psalms of Solomon has influenced Ode 38, in which the Odist talks about the Lord's *planting* and confesses that he has been *planted* by the Lord and his fruits will be forever (38:17, 18, 20–22). Secondly, it is possible that Psalm of Solomon 15 has influenced the Odist. In this Psalm, the writer talks about a *new* song and mentions the fruit of the *lips* of a pious and righteous *heart*. It is possible that such ideas influenced the Odist's description of a *new* chant in Ode 41:16 and his phrase "the *lips* of my *heart*" in 37:2.[48] Thirdly, although the concept is found in numerous apocalypses, the Psalmist's description of the lights in the heavens that God has established in "*their courses* . . . turned not aside from the way" he has appointed for them (PssSol 18:12–14) may have influenced the Odist's concept and language in Ode 16:13, in which he describes how created things run according to "*their courses*" and neither cease nor fail.

An apocalypse, in which the order of creation follows God's ordinances from creation, and a document that seems more likely to have influenced the images and language of the Odes is 1 Enoch. The statements in 1 Enoch 2:1–5:2 and 69:20f. that the luminaries do not change their orbits and that the sun and moon complete their courses and do not deviate from the eternal ordinance may have influenced the Odist when he wrote Ode 16:13–17; but as we have seen, this was a common theme in intertestamental writings. More significantly for possible influence from 1 Enoch upon the Odist is the description of a fountain of righteousness which was inexhaustible and the picture of the Son of Man as found in 1 Enoch 48:1–10. In these verses we find a memorable description of a *fountain* of righteousness which was inexhaustible so that *all* the *thirsty drank* and were filled. This description may have influenced the Odist when he wrote Ode 30:1f., in which there is a

[46] See Charlesworth, "Tatian's Dependence upon Apocryphal Traditions," *HeyJ* 15 (1974) 5–17.

[47] See Charlesworth and Culpepper, *CBQ* 35 (1973) 298–322.

[48] Harris and Mingana apparently saw neither of these parallels; but they argued that PssSol 17:30 influenced Ode 41:1f. and suggested that the "close agreement . . . suggests that the Odist has been using the Psalter of Solomon as he uses the Psalter of David." *The Odes and Psalms of Solomon*, vol. 2, p. 403.

similar picture of a living *spring* and the exhortation to *all* the *thirsty* to come and *drink*; moreover, the water that comes from the spring is described as boundless. Increasing the possibility of influence is the description in 1 Enoch 48:2–10 of the *Son of Man* who *was named* in the presence of the Lord of Spirits (cf. 48:3). It would be unwise to dismiss the possibility that this image influenced Ode 36:1–3, in which the Odist claims that he was lifted up to heaven by the *Spirit* of the *Lord*; and then that Christ himself spoke and stated that he had been brought before the Lord's face and because he was the *Son of Man* he "*was named* the Light, the Son of God." Increasing the possibility of dependence here on 1 Enoch by the Odist is the recognition that the *naming* of the Son of Man in apocalyptic and other intertestamental writings is apparently found in only these two documents.

It is possible that the Odes of Solomon have influenced the Christian redactor who added to the Ascension of Isaiah the so-called Testament of Hezekiah (3:13b–4:18) and the Vision of Isaiah (6–11). The Odist's description of Jesus as *the Beloved* may have influenced 3:17, in which there is a description of *the Beloved* who was crucified and resurrected. The Odist may have also influenced innumerous references to the celestial *garment* (e.g. 3:25), the reference to the plant that is *planted* (4:3), and the pervasive emphasis upon singing through the seven heavens, which is more developed in the Ascension of Isaiah than in any other pseudepigrapha. The Odes may have influenced the Ascension of Isaiah in three places in particular. The description in Ode 38:10f. of the Deceiver who will imitate *the Beloved* may have influenced the idea in the Ascension of Isaiah 4:6, in which Beliar is described as acting and speaking like *the Beloved*. Second, the cosmological idea in Ode 34:4 ("The *likeness* of that which is below/is that which is *above*") may have contributed to the idea in the Ascension of Isaiah 7:10, in which there is the statement that as it is *above* so it is also on the earth and the *likeness* of that which is in the firmament is also that upon the earth. Third, the concept of the descent of the Beloved in the Odes (e.g. 22:1), the identification of *the Beloved, the Lord,* and *Christ,* and the references to *crowns* and *garments* throughout the Odes may have influenced the similar ideas found in the Ascension of Isaiah 9:12–18. Fourth, the description of the *Virgin* and the unique statement that she did not need a *midwife* and labored without *pain* (OdesSol 19:8f.) may have influenced the author of the Ascension of Isaiah 11:2–15, in which the *Virgin* Mary did not need a *midwife* and apparently uttered no cries of *pain*. These parallels between the Odes of Solomon and the apocryphal writings have apparently never been discussed by the commentators;[49] whether the parallels are to be dismissed as insignificant, merely generic in nature, and coincidental or whether they are indicative of influence upon or from the Odes will depend on future critical examinations.

Introduction to the translation

In the following translation, I have attempted to be as idiomatic as the Syriac, Greek, and Coptic will allow. When necessary, I placed in a note the literal meaning of the word or phrase. I have endeavored to rework my earlier translation and have especially attempted to be more consistent in the way a word or phrase was translated but have again given prior claim to the particular context and the poetic thought in which the word or phrase occurs. Capitalization has received special attention. When I am convinced that either God or the Messiah, who is identified herein with Jesus of Nazareth, is intended, then the following capitals have been used: Beloved (3:5, 7; 7:1; 8:21), Word (7:7; 10:1; 12:5, 10, 12; 32:2; 37:3; 41:11, 14; cf. 29:9f.), Helper (7:3; 8:6; 21:2; 25:2), Son (3:7; 7:15; 19:2, 8; 23:18, 22; 41:13; 42:15), Head (17:17; 23:18; 24:1), Man (41:12), Righteousness (8:5; 9:10), Righteous One (42:2), Messiah (9:3; 17:17; 24:1; 39:11; 41:3, 15), Light (36:3; 10:1; contr. 15:2). Other words capitalized are as follows: Virgin (19:6, 7) because it refers either to Mary or the Church (33:5); Way (11:3 *bis*; 39:7, 13) because it seems to be a technical term for earliest "Christianity"; Seers (7:18); Singers (7:22); Odists (26:12) because they seem to denote a particular group. Other titles that are capitalized seem self-explanatory. It is always a hard decision to decide when to capitalize especially since the ancient languages

---

[49] Abbott (*Light,* pp. 189–93) and Harris and Mingana (*The Odes and Psalms of Solomon,* vol. 2, pp. 71f., 75, 274–76, 277, 336f.) claimed that the Odes have been influenced by the WisSol. Harris and Mingana (pp. 115f., 276) argued also that the "whole of Ode XII is a Wisdom composition, showing striking parallelism with the *Praises of Wisdom* in Sirach xxiv."

have no means to denote capitalization. Brackets in the translation denote restorations; parentheses signify words added for idiomatic English; double parentheses denote that the verse or line is found only in Greek (cf. 5:8; 11:16a–16f.).

Pruning long lists compiled over two decades, I have placed in the marginalia references to only the most important books. I have relegated to the notes parallels of secondary importance. Related passages in the Odes are noted by numbers only.

BIBLIOGRAPHY

Charlesworth, *PMR*, pp. 189–94.
Denis, *Introduction*, pp. 65f.

Abbott, E. A. *Light on the Gospel from an Ancient Poet.* (Diatessarica 9) Cambridge, England, 1912.
Bernard, J. H. *The Odes of Solomon.* T&S, 8.3; Cambridge, England, 1912.
Chadwick, H. "Some Reflections on the Character and Theology of the Odes of Solomon," *Kyriakon, Festschrift Johannes Quasten,* eds. P. Granfield and J. A. Jungmann. Münster, 1970; vol. 1, pp. 266–70.
Charlesworth, J. H. "Les Odes de Salomon et les manuscrits de la mer morte," *RB* 77 (1970) 522–49.
———. *The Odes of Solomon.* Oxford, 1973; repr. T&T 13; Pseudepigrapha Series 7; Missoula, Montana, 1978.
———. "The Odes of Solomon—Not Gnostic," *CBQ* 31 (1969) 357–69.
———. "Odes of Solomon," *The Interpreter's Dictionary of the Bible: Supplementary Volume,* eds. K. Crim, L. R. Bailey, V. P. Furnish, E. S. Bucke. Nashville, 1976; pp. 637f.
———. "Qumran, John and the Odes of Solomon," *John and Qumran.* ed. J. H. Charlesworth. London, 1972; pp. 107–36.
———, ed. *Papyri and Leather Manuscripts of the Odes of Solomon.* Dickerson Series of Facsimiles of Manuscripts Important for Christian Origins 1; Durham, North Carolina, 1981. (For the Syr., Gk., and Cop. MSS and for the text of the variants cited below, see this facsimile edition.)
Emerton, J. A. "Some Problems of Text and Language in the Odes of Solomon," *JTS* N.S. 18 (1967) 372–406.
Harris, J. R., and Mingana, A. *The Odes and Psalms of Solomon.* 2 vols. Manchester, London, New York, 1916 and 1920.
Labourt, J., and Batiffol, P. *Les Odes de Salomon: une œuvre chrétienne des environs de l'an 100–120.* Paris, 1911.
Tondelli, L. *Le Odi di Salomone: Cantici Christiani degli inizi del II Secolo.* Prefazione del Angelo Mercati. Rome, 1914.

ODE 1

1 The Lord is on my head like a crown,[a]
and I shall never be without him.

2 Plaited for me is the crown of truth,[b]
and it caused your branches[c] to blossom in me.

3 For it is not like a parched crown that blossoms not;

4 But you lived upon my head,
and have blossomed upon me.

5 Your fruits[d] are full and complete;
they are full of your salvation.

5:12; 9:8–11;
17:1; 20:7f.

ODE 2

(lost)

ODE 3

1 . . .
I am putting on [the love of the Lord].[a]

2 And his members are with him,
and I am dependent on them; and he loves me.

3 For I should not have known how to love the Lord,
if he had not continuously loved me.

1Jn 4:19

4 Who is able to distinguish love,
except him who is loved?

5 I love the Beloved and I myself love him,[b]
and where his rest is, there also am I.

7:1; 8:21
Jn 14:2–3; 17:24

6 And I shall be no foreigner,[c]
because there is no jealousy with the Lord Most High and Merciful.

Eph 2:19

7 I have been united (to him), because the lover has found the Beloved,
because I love him that is the Son, I shall become a son.

7:15; 19:2,8;
23:18,22; 41:13;
42:15

8 Indeed he who is joined to him who is immortal,
truly will be immortal.

Jn 14:19b
1Cor 6:17

1 a. Or "wreath."
b. Gk. *alētheia*.
c. Gk. *klados*.
d. Gk. *karpos*.

3 a. Restored on analogy with 23:3. Also see,
however, 4:6f.; 7:4; 13:3; 15:8; 20:7; 21:3; 23:1;
33:12; 39:8.
b. Or "and my soul (*npšy*) loves him."
c. Or "stranger."

9   And he who delights in the Life   Jn 11:25
will become living.[d]

10   This is the Spirit of the Lord, which is not false,[e]
which teaches the sons of men to know his ways.[f]   Jn 14:26

11   Be wise and understanding and vigilant.

Hallelujah.

ODE 4

1   No man can pervert your holy place, O my God;   ApAb 2:29
nor can he change it, and put it in another place.

2   Because (he has) no power over it;
for your sanctuary you designed before you made special places.

3   The ancient one shall not be perverted by those which are inferior to it.[a]   2Bar 7:1–8:5
You have given your heart, O Lord, to your faithful ones.[b]   4Bar 1:6

4   Never will you be idle,
nor will you be without fruits;

5   For one hour of your faith   Ps 84:10
is more excellent than all days and years.

6   For who shall put on your grace[c] and be rejected?[d]   33:12

7   Because your seal[e] is known;
and your creatures are known to it.

8   And your hosts possess it,
and the elect archangels are clothed with it.

9   You have given to us your fellowship,
not that you were in need of us,
but that we are always in need of you.

10   Sprinkle upon us your sprinklings,
and open your bountiful springs which abundantly
       supply us with milk and honey.[f]

11   For there is no regret with you;
that you should regret anything which you have promised;

12   Since the end was manifest to you.

---

d. Cf. Jn 11:25; also Jn 1:4; 5:26, 40; 10:10, 28; 14:6.

e. Cf. Tit 1:2.

f. Cf. Jn 14:17, 26; 15:26; 1QS 3.13–4.26.

4 a. Cf. Vita 14:3.

b. Or "your believers."

c. Or "goodness," "kindness."

d. Or "be despised," "be oppressed."

e. Or "sign."

f. Cf. Ex 3:8, 17.

13 For that which you gave, you gave freely,
    so that no longer will you draw back and take them again.

14 For all was manifest to you as God,
    and was set in order from the beginning before you.

15 And you, O Lord, have made all.

    Hallelujah.

ODE 5

1   I praise you, O Lord,
    because I love you.[a]

2   O Most High, abandon me not,
    for you are my hope.

3   Freely did I receive your grace,
    may I live by it.[b]

4   My persecutors will come[c] but let them not see me.

5   Let a cloud of darkness fall[d] upon their eyes;   Ps 69:23
    and let an air of thick darkness obscure them.

6   And let them have no light to see,
    so that they cannot seize me.

7   Let their counsel[e] become dull,
    so that whatever they have conspired will return upon their own heads.[f]

8   For they have devised a counsel,
    but it was not for them.[g]
    ((And they were vanquished although they were powerful.))[h]

9   They prepared themselves maliciously,
    but they were found to be impotent.[i]

10 Indeed my hope[j] is upon the Lord,
    and I shall not fear.

11 And because the Lord is my salvation,   Ps 27:1
    I shall not fear.[k]

12 And he is as a crown upon my head,   1:1; 9:8-11;
    and I shall not be disturbed.   17:1; 20:7f.

5 a. Cf. the Hodayoth formula.
  b. Or "I shall live by it." C: "through you."
  c. C: "may they fall." Cf. Jer 20:11.
  d. C: "it covers."
  e. Or "mind"; but cf. 5:8. C: "counsel become powerless."
  f. C: "And what they have counseled, let it come upon them." Cf. Ps 7:16.

  g. Cf. Ps 21:11; 4Ezra 7:22.
  h. This line is extant only in Cop.; it appears to be spurious.
  i. C: "And what they have wickedly prepared has fallen upon them."
  j. Or "trust," "confidence."
  k. C: "You are my God, my Savior."

13   Even if everything should be shaken,
       I shall stand firm.

14   And though all things visible should perish,
       I shall not die;

15   Because the Lord is with me,
       and I with him.

       Hallelujah.

ODE 6

1   As the [wind] moves through the harp   14:8
       and the strings speak,

2   So the Spirit of the Lord speaks through my members,   16:5
       and I speak through his love.

3   For he destroys whatever is foreign,
       and everything is of the Lord.

4   For thus it has been from the beginning,
       and (will be) until the end.

5   So that nothing will be contrary,
       and nothing will rise up against him.

6   The Lord has multiplied his knowledge,
       and he was zealous that those things should be known which through his
          grace have been given to us.

7   And his praise he gave us on account of his name;
       our spirits praise his Holy Spirit.

8   For there went forth a stream,[a]   Rev 22:1f.
         and it became a river great and broad;[b]
       indeed it carried away everything, and it shattered
         and brought (it)[c] to the Temple.[d]

9   And the restraints of men were not able to restrain it,
       nor even the arts of them who habitually restrain water.

10   For it spread over the face of all the earth,   30:1-6
       and it filled everything.[e]

---

6 a. C: "a flowing off," "a stream," "an emanation."

  b. Cf. Ezek 47:1–12; Hab 2:14; Isa 11:9; Zech 14:8; and AddEsth F3(6) and A9(10) to OdesSol 6:8–11; but the differences are significant.

  c. A pronoun as a direct object is often assumed in Semitic documents; see OdesSol 8:7; 9:7; 19:5f.; 20:8; 23:7; 36:2; cf. 22:10; also see 1Bar 1:7, "and

they sent (it) to Jerusalem" (*kai apesteilan eis Jerousalēm*). C: "It gathered all things and it turned toward the Temple."

  d. Or "Indeed it carried away everything, and it shattered and carried away the Temple."

  e. C: "and it possessed all the water." Cf. PseudClemRec 6.

11   Then all the thirsty upon the earth drank,[f]
      and thirst was relieved and quenched;

30:1f.

12   For from the Most High the drink was given.

13   Blessed, therefore, are the ministers of that drink,
      who have been entrusted with his water.[g]

14   They have pleased[h] the parched lips,
      and have restored[i] the paralyzed will.[j]

15   Even lives[k] who were about to expire,[l]
      they have seized from Death.[m]

16   And members which had fallen,[n]
      they have restored and set up.[o]

17   They gave power for their coming,[p]
      and light for their eyes.

18   Because everyone recognized them as the Lord's,
      and lived by the living water of eternity.[q]

11:7; Jn 7:37f.;
4:10,14

      Hallelujah.

ODE 7

1   As is the course of anger over wickedness,
      so is the course of joy over the Beloved;
      and brings in of its fruits unhindered.

3:5; 8:21

2   My joy is the Lord and my course is toward him,
      this way of mine is beautiful.

3   For there is a Helper for me, the Lord.[a]
      He has generously shown himself to me in his simplicity,
      because his kindness has diminished his grandeur.[b]

8:6; 21:2; 25:2

4   He became like me, that I might receive him.
      In form he was considered like me, that I might put him on.

5   And I trembled not when I saw him,
      because he was gracious to me.

---

f. C: "They who were upon the sand which is dry drank." Cf. 1En 48:1; Jn 7:37b–38.
g. C: "The water of the Lord."
h. Or "have refreshed."
i. Or "aroused."
j. C: "Those who were exhausted have received joy of heart."
k. Or "souls."
l. C: "They have embraced lives (or souls, *psuchai*), having poured in the breath, so that they will not die."
m. Or "have held back from death."
n. Or "And limbs which had collapsed . . ."

o. C: "have caused to stand."
p. C: "their openness."
q. "Living water" is salvivic in the Odes (cf. 11:7; 30:1–7); and in Jn (cf. Jn 4:10–15; 7:38); Rev (7:17; 21:6; 22:1, 17); the Qumran Scrolls (1QH 8.7, 16; CD 19.34); and some post-apostolic documents (Ignatius, Romans 7:2; Didache 7:1–3).

7 a. The Lord or God is called "Helper" in other biblical books; cf. e.g. Ps 10:14; Heb 13:6; Sir 51:2. Contrast 2En 53:1.
b. Or "greatness," "dignity." Cf. Rom 5:2; Eph 2:18.

6   Like my nature he became, that I might understand him.
        And like my form, that I might not turn away from him.[c]

7   The Father of knowledge[d]
        is the Word of knowledge.[e]

8   He who created wisdom
        is wiser than his works.[f]

9   And he who created me when yet I was not
        knew what I would do when I came into being.

10   On account of this he was gracious to me in his abundant grace,
        and allowed me to seek from him and to benefit from his sacrifice.
            Ps 50:3 [LXX; MT 51:1]

11   For he it is who is incorruptible,
        the perfection of the worlds and their Father.

12   He has allowed him to appear to them that are his own;
        in order that they may recognize him that made them,
        and not think that they came of themselves.
            Jn 1:11
            Ps 100:3 [LXX; MT Ketib]

13   For toward knowledge he has set his way,
        he has spread it out and lengthened it and brought it to complete perfection.[g]

14   And has set over it the traces of his light,
        and it proceeded from the beginning until the end.

15   For by him he was served,
        and he was pleased by the Son.
            Mk 1:11; 3:7; 19:2,8; 23:18,22; 41:13,15

16   And because of his salvation he will possess everything.
        And the Most High will be known by his holy ones:

17   To announce to those who have songs of the coming of the Lord,
        that they may go forth to meet him and may sing to him,
        with joy and with the harp of many tones.

18   The Seers will go before him,
        and they will appear before him.

19   And they will praise the Lord in his love,
        because he is near and does see.

20   And hatred will be removed from the earth,
        and with jealousy it will be drowned.

21   For ignorance was destroyed upon it,
        because the knowledge of the Lord came upon it.

---

c. The Syr. nouns translated as "nature" and "form" also mean "natural disposition," "essence," and "image." The language here is not docetic; but see 17:6; 28:17f.; 41:8; and 42:10.

d. Cf. 1QS 3.15.

e. Or "word of knowledge." It is difficult to be sure when "word" should be capitalized; cf. the discussion above under "Introduction to the translation." Cf. 4Ezra 6:38; 2Bar 21:4; JosAsen 12.

f. Cf. Prov 8:22f.

g. Cf. 1QS 11.11.

22   Let the Singers sing the grace of the Lord Most High,
      and let them offer their songs.

23   And let their heart be like the day,
      and their gentle voices[h] like the majestic beauty[i] of the Lord.

24   And let there not be any person
      that is without knowledge or voice.

25   For he gave a mouth to his creation:
      to open the voice of the mouth toward him,
      and to praise him.

26   Praise[j] his power
      and declare his grace.

      Hallelujah.

ODE 8

1   Open, open your hearts to the exultation of the Lord,
      and let your love abound from the heart to the lips.[a]

2   In order to bring forth fruits to the Lord, a holy life;[b]   12:2; 14:6f.
      and to speak with watchfulness in his light.

3   Stand and be established,[c]
      you who once were brought low.

4   You who were in silence, speak,
      for your mouth has been opened.

5   You who were despised, from henceforth be raised,
      for your Righteousness has been raised;   41:12

6   For the right hand of the Lord is with you,   7:3; 21:2; 25:2
      and he will be your Helper.[d]

7   And peace was prepared for you,
      before what may be your war.   9:6; 29:9

Christ Speaks[e]

8   Hear the word of truth,
      and receive the knowledge of the Most High.[f]

9   Your flesh may not understand that which I am about to say to you;
      nor your garment that which I am about to declare to you.[g]   25:8

h. Or "a musical note," "gentle sound," "soft
whisper."
   i. Or "majestic grace."
   j. Or "Confess."

8 a. Both imperatives are plurals in Syr. The Ode
may have been intended for liturgical use in early
Christian services.
   b. Cf. Hos 14:2; Heb 13:15; 1QH 1.28; PssSol

15:5.
   c. Or "Rise up and stand erect . . ."
   d. See n. a to OdesSol 7.
   e. Here and in the following Odes I have added
this notation; it is frequently clear that the Odist
speaks as the Christ. In the MSS no dot, word, or
phrase clarifies the shift in speakers.
   f. As in 8:1 the imperatives are plural.
   g. Or "to show you."

10   Keep my mystery,[h] you who are kept by it;
         keep my faith, you who are kept by it.

11   And understand my knowledge, you who know me in truth;
         love me with affection, you who love;

12   For I turn not my face from my own,
         because I know them.   Jn 10:14

13   And before they had existed,
         I recognized them;
         and imprinted a seal on their faces.

14   I fashioned their members,
         and my own breasts I prepared for them,   14:2; 19:4
         that they might drink my holy milk and live by it.   1Cor 3:1–2

15   I am pleased by them,
         and am not ashamed by them.   9:7; 29:1

16   For my work are they,
         and the power of my thoughts.

17   Therefore who can stand against my work?
         Or who is not subject to them?

18   I willed and fashioned mind and heart;
         and they are my own.
         And upon my right hand I have set my elect ones.

19   And my righteousness goes before them;
         and they will not be deprived of my name;
         for it is with them.[i]

The Odist Speaks[j]

20   Seek and increase,
         and abide in the love of the Lord;   Jn 15:9f.

21   And you who are loved in the Beloved;   3:5; 7:1
         and you who are kept in him who lives;
         and you who are saved in him who was saved.[k]

22   And you shall be found incorrupted in all ages,
         on account of the name of your Father.   9:5

         Hallelujah.

---

h. Cf. 1QH 11.10 and 1Q27.
i. Cf. Isa 58:8.
j. I add this notation.

k. Cf. OdesSol 8:19–21 with Jn 15:9f. and 17:11f.

ODE 9

1   Open your ears,
     and I shall speak to you.

2   Give me yourself,
     so that I may also give you myself;

3   The word of the Lord and his desires,   17:17; 24:1;
     the holy thought which he has thought concerning his Messiah.   39:11; 41:3.15

4   For in the will of the Lord is your life,
     and his purpose[a] is eternal life,
     and your perfection is incorruptible.

5   Be enriched in God the Father;   8:22
     and receive the purpose of the Most High.
     Be strong and saved by his grace.

6   For I announce peace to you, his holy ones,   8:7; 29:9; 4Mac
     so that none of those who hear[b] will fall in the war.   9:24

7   And also that those who have known him may not perish,   Jn 3:16
     and so that those who receive (him)[c] may not be ashamed.[d]   8:15; 29:1

8   An everlasting crown is Truth;   1:1; 5:12; 17:1;
     blessed are they who set it on their head.   20:7f.; Ps 20:4
                                          [LXX; MT 21:3]

9   (It is) a precious stone,
     for the wars were on account of the crown.[e]

10   But Righteousness has taken it,
     and has given it to you.

11   Put on the crown in the true covenant of the Lord,
     and all those who have conquered[f] will be inscribed in his book.

12   For their book is the justification[g] which is for you,
     and she sees you before her and wills that you will be saved.

     Hallelujah.

ODE 10

1   The Lord has directed my mouth by his Word,   7:7
     and has opened my heart by his Light.[a]   36:3

2   And he has caused to dwell in me his immortal life,   Jn 4:14
     and permitted me to proclaim the fruit of his peace.

---

9 a. Or "mind," "belief," "intelligence."   g. Or "victory."
  b. Or "obey."
  c. See n. c to OdesSol 6.
  d. Or "confused."   10 a. It is difficult to know when to capitalize
  e. Cf. TJob 40:3; WisSol 5:16; 1QH 9.25.   "word" and "light." See n. e to OdesSol 7 and
  f. Or "who were free from guilt," "who were   the comments above under "Introduction to the
declared blameless."   translation."

3   To convert the lives of those who desire to come to him,
and to capture a good captivity for freedom.

Ps 68:18; TZeb
9:8 (bdg)

Christa Speaks[b]

4   I took courage and became strong and captured the world,
and it became mine for the glory of the Most High, and of God my Father.

5   And the gentiles who had been scattered were gathered together,
but I was not defiled by my love (for them),
because they had praised me in high places.[c]

29:8; Jn 11:52

6   And the traces of light were set upon their heart,
and they walked according to my life and were saved,
and they became my people for ever and ever.

Hallelujah.

ODE 11

1   My heart was pruned and its flower appeared,
then grace sprang up in it,
and it produced fruits for the Lord.[a]

2   For the Most High circumcised me by his Holy Spirit,
then he uncovered my inward being[b] toward him,
and filled me with his love.

3   And his circumcising became my salvation,
and I ran in the Way[c] in his peace,
in the Way of truth.[d]

39:7,13
33:8

4   From the beginning until the end
I received his knowledge.

5   And I was established upon the rock of truth,[e]
where he had set me.

6   And speaking waters[f] touched my lips
from the spring of the Lord[g] generously.[h]

Rev 7:17

7   And so I drank and became intoxicated,
from the living[i] water that does not die.

6:18; Jn 4:10;
7:37f.

8   And my intoxication was not with ignorance;[j]
but I abandoned[k] vanity;

---

b. See n. e to OdesSol 8.
c. Cf. Mal 1:11.

11 a. G: "for God." Cf. OdesSol 11:1–3 with
Deut 10:16 and 30:6.
   b. Lit. "kidneys."
   c. Cf. Acts 24:14, 22; 9:2; Jn 14:6; 1QS 9.19,
21; 11.11.
   d. G: "I ran a way of truth in his peace." Cf.

1QS 4.17; 9.17f.; CD 3.15.
   e. G: "solid rock."
   f. Cf. Ignatius, Romans 7:2.
   g. Or "the fountain of the Lord"; G: "from the
fountain of life of the Lord." Cf. 1QH 8.14.
   h. Cf. GThom 13.
   i. G omits.
   j. Cf. 38:12–15.
   k. G omits.

9   And turned toward the Most High, my God,
and was enriched by his favors.

10   And I abandoned the folly cast upon the earth,
and stripped it off and cast it from me.

11   And the Lord renewed me with his garment,
and possessed me[l] by his light.[m]

12   And from above he gave me immortal rest;[n]
and I became like the land which blossoms and rejoices in its fruits.

13   And the Lord (is) like the sun
upon the face of the land.

14   My eyes were enlightened,
and my face received the dew;

15   And my breath was refreshed
by the pleasant fragrance[o] of the Lord.[p]

16   And he took me to his Paradise,
wherein is the wealth of the Lord's pleasure.[q]

16a   ((I contemplated blooming and fruit-bearing trees,[r]
and self-grown was their crown.

16b   Their branches were flourishing
and their fruits were shining;[s]
their roots (were) from an immortal land.

16c   And a river of gladness was irrigating them,
and the region round about them in the land of eternal life.))

17   Then I adored the Lord because of his magnificence.

18   And I said, blessed, O Lord, are they
who are planted in your land,
and who have a place in your Paradise;[t]

           PssSol 14:2(5)
           38:17–22

19   And who grow in the growth of your trees,
and have passed from darkness into light.[u]

l. G: "and he recovered me."

m. Or "Light," cf. 36:3; 1QS 4.8. Cf. Ps 104:2; 1Bar 5:1–9.

n. Or "incorruptible rest." G: "And he enlivened me through his incorruption." Cf. Ps 95:11; Heb 3:7–4:13.

o. Cf. 1En 24:1–6.

p. G: "in the fragrance of the kindness of the Lord."

q. A similar description of Paradise appears in many documents, cf. 1En 24; 2En 8; ApAb 21; SibOr frag. 3.48f.; also 1QH 8.12–20; JosAsen 2:17–20; LAB 12:8.

r. Vss. 16a–16c are found only in G.

s. Lit. "were laughing." The Gk. egelō[n] means only "were laughing," "were deriding." The corresponding Syr., which I believe is behind the Gk., would be ghk, which means not only "laughing," but also "shining."

t. Cf. GTr 36:35–37.

u. This imagery is widespread in early Jewish literature, cf. e.g. TJos 19:3; 1QH 9.26f.; TAb B7; JosAsen 8:10; 15:13; 3Bar 6:13; 2En 30:15; and especially 1QS 3.13–4.26. Also cf. Didache 1:1; EBar 18:1–20:2.

20   Behold, all[v] your laborers are fair,
    they who work good works,
    and turn from wickedness to your kindness.[w]

21   For they turned away from themselves the bitterness of the trees,[x]
    when they were planted in your land.[y]

    38:17–22

22   And everyone was like your remnant.[z]
    ((Blessed are the workers of your water,))[a2]
    and the eternal memorial[b2] of your faithful servants.

    6:13
    1Bar 4:5

23   Indeed, there is much room in your Paradise.[c2]
    And there is nothing in it which is barren,
    but everything is filled with fruit.

    Jn 14:2

24   Praise be to you, O God, the delight of Paradise for ever.

    Hallelujah.

ODE 12

1   He has filled me with words of truth,
    that I may proclaim him.

2   And like the flowing of waters, truth flows from my mouth,
    and my lips declare his fruits.

3   And he has caused his knowledge to abound in me,
    because the mouth of the Lord is the true word,
    and the door of his light.[a]

4   And the Most High has given him to his generations,[b]
    (which are) the interpreters of his beauty,
        and the narrators of his glory,
        and the confessors of his thought,[c]
        and the preachers of his mind,
        and the teachers[d] of his works.

5   For the subtlety of the Word is inexpressible,[e]
    and like his expression[f] so also is his swiftness and his acuteness,
    for limitless is his path.[g]

    7:7; 10:1; 12:10,
    12; 32:2; 37:3;
    41:11,14

6   He never falls but remains standing,
    and one cannot know his descent or his way.

---

v. G omits.

w. G: "from wickedness to kindness."

x. G: "The pungent odor of the trees is changed in your land." Cf. 3Bar 4:15.

y. G omits. Cf. 1QH 8.4–26; *LAB* 18:10; 23:12; 28:4.

z. G: "And everything occurs according to your will." Cf. Isa 10:19–23.

a2. Extant only in G.

b2. Cf. 1Bar 4:5.

c2. Cf. Jn 14:2.

12 a. "Word," "Door," and "Light" could be capitalized (cf. n. e to OdesSol 7) and the parallels

with Jn would be striking; cf. Jn 1:1–18; 10:7–9; 8:12.

b. Or "ages," "worlds."

c. Or "purpose."

d. Lit. "those who teach to be chaste."

e. Lit. "there is no narration." Both "subtlety" and "swiftness" in this vs. are identical in the Syr.; hence the first two ll. could be translated: "For the swiftness of the Word is inexpressible,/ and like his expression so also is his swiftness and his acuteness . . .""

f. Or "utterance."

g. Or "progression." Cf. Heb 4:12; WisSol 7:22–27.

7   For as his work is, so is his expectation,
        for he is the light and dawning of thought.

8   And by him the generations spoke to one another,
        and those that were silent acquired speech.

9   And from him came love and harmony,[h]
        and they spoke one to another whatever was theirs.

10   And they were stimulated by the Word,   12:5,12
        and knew him who made them,
        because they were in harmony.

11   For the mouth of the Most High spoke to them,
        and his exposition was swift through him.

12   For the dwelling place of the Word is man,[i]   12:5,10
        and his truth is love.

13   Blessed are they who by means of him have recognized[j] everything,
        and have known the Lord in his truth.

        Hallelujah.

ODE 13

1   Behold, the Lord is our mirror.[a]
        Open (your) eyes and see them in him.

2   And learn the manner of your face,
        then announce praises to his Spirit.

3   And wipe the paint[b] from your face,
        and love his holiness and put it on.

4   Then you will be unblemished at all times with him.

        Hallelujah.

ODE 14

1   As the eyes of a son upon his father,   Ps 123:2
        so are my eyes, O Lord, at all times toward you.

2   Because my breasts and my pleasure are with you.   8:14; 19:3f.

3   Do not turn aside your mercies from me, O Lord;
        and do not take your kindness from me.

4   Stretch out to me, my Lord, at all times, your right hand,
        and be to me a guide till the end according to your will.   Ps 48:14

h. Or "equality"; cf. 12:9.   b. Cf. ActsJn 28f.
i. Cf. Jn 1:14.
j. Or "perceived."   14 a. Or "evil." Cf. Ps 31:3f.
                                                    b. Or "your gentleness."

13 a. Cf. ActsJn 95.25; WisSol 7:26. For "mirror" cf. 2Cor 3:18 and Jas 1:23.

5   Let me be pleasing before you, because of your glory,
      and because of your name let me be saved from the Evil One.[a]   Mt 6:13

6   And let your serenity,[b] O Lord, abide with me,
      and the fruits of your love.

7   Teach me the odes of your truth,
      that I may produce fruits in you.

8   And open to me the harp of your Holy Spirit,   6:1
      so that with every note I may praise you, O Lord.

9   And according to the multitude of your mercies, so grant unto me,
      and hasten to grant our petitions.

10   For you are sufficient for all our needs.   Phil 4:19

      Hallelujah.

ODE 15

1   As the sun is the joy to them who seek its daybreak,
      so is my joy the Lord;

2   Because he is my sun,
      and his rays have restored me;   Eph 5:14
      and his light has dismissed all darkness from my face.[a]

3   Eyes I have possessed in him,
      and have seen his holy day.

4   Ears I have acquired,
      and have heard his truth.

5   The thought of knowledge I have acquired,
      and have lived[b] fully through him.

6   I abandoned the way of error,   Jub 22:23
      and went toward him and received salvation from him generously.

7   And according to his generosity he gave to me,
      and according to his majestic beauty he made me.

8   I have put on incorruption[c] through his name,
      and stripped off corruption by his grace.

9   Death has been destroyed before my face,   42:11; Rev 1:18;
      and Sheol has been vanquished by my word.   6:8; 20:13f.

10   And eternal life has arisen in the Lord's land,
      and it has become known[d] to his faithful ones,
      and been given without limit to all that trust in him.

      Hallelujah.

---

15 a. Cf. 15:1f. with 1QH 4.5f.; 9.27.   c. Or "immortality." Cf. 1Cor 15:54f.
   b. Lit. "to delight oneself," "enjoy to the full,"   d. Or "been declared."
"live luxuriously."

ODE 16

1   As the work of the plowman is the plowshare,
    and the work of the helmsman[a] is the steering of the ship,
    so also my work is the psalm of the Lord in his praises.

2   My art and my service are in his praises,
    because his love has nourished my heart,
    and his fruits he poured unto my lips.[b]

3   For my love is the Lord;
    hence I shall sing unto him.

4   For I am strengthened in his praises,
    and I have faith in him.

5   I shall open my mouth,
    and his spirit will speak through me   6:1f.
    the praise[c] of the Lord and his beauty,

6   The work of his hands,
    and the service of his fingers;

7   For the multitude of his mercies,
    and the strength of his word.[d]

8   For the word of the Lord investigates that which is invisible,
    and perceives his thought.

9   For the eye sees his works,
    and the ear hears his thought.

10 It is he who spread out the earth,[e]
    and placed the waters in the sea.

11 He expanded the heaven,
    and set the stars.

12 And he set the creation and aroused it,
    then he rested from his works.   Gen 2:2

13 And created things run according to their courses,[f]
    and work their works,
    and they are not able to cease and be idle.[g]

14 And the hosts are subject to his word.[h]

15 The reservoir of light is the sun,
    and the reservoir of darkness is the night.

16 a. Gk. *kubernētes* (in H).
   b. Cf. 16:1f. with Ps 45:1.
   c. Or "glory."
   d. In vss. 7, 8, 14, and 19 "word" could be capitalized. See n. e to OdesSol 7. Cf. Gen 1:1–2:4a; PrMan 3; and also Jn 1:1–3; Jub 12:4.
   e. Or "he who made the earth broad . . ." If

"Word" (16:7) is the agent of creation here, cf. Jn 1:1–18.
   f. Lit. "they run according to their runnings."
   g. Parallels to this concept are abundant; cf. 1En 2:1–5:2; 69:20f.; PssSol 18:12–14; 2Bar 48:9; Eccl 16:26–28.
   h. See n. d above.

16   For he made the sun for the day so that it will be light;   Gen 1:16–18
but night brings darkness over the face of the earth.

17   And (by) their acceptance one from another   Ps 19:1; 1En
they complete the beauty of God.   69:20; 78:10

18   And there is nothing outside of the Lord,   1:1
because he was before anything came to be.[i]

19   And the worlds are by his word,[j]
and by the thought of his heart.

20   Praise and honor to his name.

    Hallelujah.

ODE 17

1   Then I was crowned by my God,   1:1; 5:12; 9:8–
and my crown is living.   11; 20:7f.

2   And I was justified by my Lord,
for my salvation is incorruptible.

3   I have been released from vanities,
and am not condemned.

4   My chains were cut off by his hands;
I received the face and form of a new person,[a]
and I walked in him and was saved.

5   And the thought of truth led me,
and I went after it and did not err.

Christ Speaks[b]

6   And all who saw me were amazed,
and I seemed to them like a stranger.

7   And he who knew and exalted me
is the Most High in all his perfection.

8   And he glorified me[c] by his kindness,
and raised my understanding to the height of truth.

9   And from there he gave me the way of his paths,   24:5; 42:10–20;
and I opened the doors which were closed.[d]   Jn 10:7–10; Rev
                 3:7f.

10   And I shattered the bars[e] of iron,   Ps 107:16; Isa
for my own iron(s) had grown hot and melted before me.   45:2

---

i. Cf. Jn 1:1–3; 8:58.
j. See n. d above.

17 a. Gk. prosópon.

b. See n. e to OdesSol 8.
c. N: "and he is glorified."
d. For the idea of *descensus ad inferos* see
OdesSol 24:5 and especially 42:10–20.
e. Gk. *mochlos.*

11   And nothing appeared closed to me,
     because I was the opening of everything.

Jn 10:7–10; Rev 3:7f.

12   And I went toward all my bondsmen in order to loose them;
     that I might not abandon anyone bound or binding.

13   And I gave my knowledge generously,
     and my resurrection[f] through my love.

14   And I sowed my fruits in hearts,
     and transformed them through myself.

15   Then they received my blessing and lived,
     and they were gathered to me and were saved;

16   Because they became my members,
     and I was their head.

24:1; Rom 12:4f.; Col 1:15–20; Jn 15

Doxology[s]

17   Glory to you, our Head, O Lord Messiah.

9:3; 23:18; 24:1; 39:11; 41:3,15

Hallelujah.

ODE 18

1   My heart was raised and enriched in the love of the Most High,
     so that I might praise him with my name.

2   My members were strengthened,
     that they may not fall from his power.

3   Infirmities fled[a] from my body,
     and it stood[b] firm for the Lord by his will;
     because his kingdom is firm.[c]

22:12

4   O Lord, for the sake of those who are in need,
     do not expel[d] your word from me.[e]

5   Nor, for the sake of their works,
     withhold your perfection from me.

6   Let not light be conquered by darkness,
     nor let truth flee from falsehood.[f]

Jn 1:5

7   Let your right hand set our salvation to victory,
     and let it receive from every region,
     and preserve (it)[s] on the side of everyone who is besieged by evils.

---

f. Lit. "my prayer"; *b'wr'* seems to have obtained the meaning "resurrection"; cf. my edition of the Odes, p. 77, n. 17.

  g. See n. b above; I add this notation.

18 a. H: "they forsook."
  b. N: "and they stood."

c. Or "solid," "true," "lasting."
d. H: "do not loose."
e. "Word" could be capitalized; see n. e to OdesSol 7.
f. See n. u to OdesSol 11.
g. See n. c to OdesSol 6. Also see my edition, p. 80, n. 10.

8   You are my God, falsehood and death are not in your mouth;
      only perfection is your will.

9   And vanity you knew not,
      because neither does it know you.

10   And you knew not error;
      because neither does it know you.

11   And ignorance appeared like dust,
      and like the foam of the sea.

12   And vain people thought that it was great,
      and they became like its form and were impoverished.

13   But the wise[h] understood and contemplated,
      and were not polluted by their thoughts;

14   Because they were in the mind of the Most High,
      and mocked those who were walking in error.[i]

15   Then they spoke the truth,
      from the breath which the Most High breathed into them.

16   Praise and great honor to his name.

      Hallelujah.

ODE 19

1   A cup of milk was offered to me,
      and I drank it in the sweetness of the Lord's kindness.   1Pet 2:3   19:11

2   The Son is the cup,[a]
      and the Father is he who was milked;
      and the Holy Spirit is she who milked him;   3:7; 7:15; 19:8; 23:18,22; 41:13; 42:15

3   Because his breasts were full,
      and it was undesirable that his milk should be released without purpose.

4   The Holy Spirit opened her bosom,
      and mixed the milk of the two breasts of the Father.   8:14; 14:2

5   Then she gave the mixture to the generation[b] without their knowing,   35:5
      and those who have received (it)[c] are in the perfection of the right hand.

6   The womb of the Virgin took (it),[d]
      and she received conception and gave birth.

7   So the Virgin became a mother with great mercies.

8   And she labored and bore the Son but without pain,   Ascenls 11:2–15
      because it did not occur without purpose.[e]   3:7; 7:15; 19:2; 23:18,22; 41:13; 42:15

h. Lit. "those who knew."
i. Cf. Jn 8:12 and 12:35; 1QS 3.21 and 4.11.   c. See n. c to OdesSol 6.
      d. See n. c above.
19 a. Cf. GTr 24:9–14.   e. See the discussion in "Relation to apocryphal
      b. Or "world."   books."

9   And she did not seek a midwife,
       because he caused her to give life.

10   She bore as a strong man with desire,[f]
       and she bore according to the manifestation,[g]   Lk 1:26–38
       and possessed with great power.[h]

11   And she loved with salvation,
       and guarded with kindness,   19:1
       and declared[i] with greatness.

       Hallelujah.

ODE 20

1   I am a priest of the Lord,
       and to him I serve as a priest;

2   And to him I offer the offering of his thought.

3   For his thought is not like the world,
       nor like the flesh,
       nor like them who serve[a] according to the flesh.

4   The offering of the Lord is righteousness,
       and purity of heart and lips.

5   Offer your[b] inward being faultlessly;
       and do not let your compassion oppress compassion;
       and do not you yourself oppress anyone.[c]   Ex 22:21

6   You should not purchase a foreigner because he is like yourself,[d]   Sir 33:30f.
       nor seek to deceive your neighbor,
       nor deprive him of the covering for his nakedness.   Ex 22:26f.

7   But put on the grace of the Lord generously,
       and come into his Paradise,   Rev 2:7
       and make for yourself a crown from his tree.   1:1; 5:12; 9:8–
                                                            11; 17:1

8   Then put (it)[e] on your head and be refreshed,
       and recline upon his serenity.

9   For his glory will go before you;
       and you will receive of his kindness and of his grace;[f]
       and you will be anointed in truth with the praise of his holiness.

10   Praise and honor to his name.

       Hallelujah.

---

f. Or "will."
g. Or "example," "demonstration."
h. Or "And she acquired according to the Great
Power"; if so cf. Mk 14:62; Acts 8:10.
   i. Or "manifested"; cf. 19:10.

20 a. Or "worship."

b. N: "my inward being."
c. Or "And do not let your soul oppress a soul."
d. Or "like your (own) soul."
e. See n. c to OdesSol 6.
f. Or "and of his goodness." N: "of his goodness" (a slightly different noun; cf. my edition, p.
87, n. 6). Cf. Isa 58:8.

ODE 21

1   I raised my arms[a] on high
       on account of the grace of the Lord.

2   Because he cast off my chains from me,
       and my Helper raised me according to his grace and his salvation.[b]   7:3; 8:6; 25:2

3   And I stripped off darkness,
       and put on light.[c]

4   And even I myself acquired members.
       In them there was no[d] sickness
       or affliction or suffering.

5   And abundantly helpful to me was the thought of the Lord,
       and his incorruptible[e] fellowship.

6   And I was lifted up in the light,
       and I passed before his face.

7   And I was constantly near him,   36:6
       while praising and confessing him.

8   He caused my heart to overflow, and it was found in my mouth;
       and it sprang forth unto my lips.

9   Then upon my face increased the exultation of the Lord and his praise.[f]

    Hallelujah.

ODE 22

Christ Speaks[a]

1   He who caused me to descend from on high,
       and to ascend from the regions below;[b]

2   And he who gathers what is in the middle,
       and throws them[c] to me;[d]

3   He who scattered my enemies,
       and my adversaries;

4   He who gave me authority over chains,
       so that I might loosen them;

5   He who overthrew by my hands the dragon with seven heads,   Rev 12:3
       and placed me[e] at his roots[f] that I might destroy his seed;

---

21 a. N: "arm."
  b. See n. a to OdesSol 7.
  c. Cf. 1Bar 4:20; 5:1–2. Also see n. u to OdesSol 11.
  d. H omits.
  e. Or "everlasting," "immortal."
  f. N: "in his praise."

22 a. See n. e to OdesSol 8.

  b. C: "from the regions which are in the deep below."
  c. H omits.
  d. C: "He who took those who were in the middle,/and has taught me concerning them."
  e. Following C; both H and N: "and you set me."
  f. N: "his root."

6   You were there and helped me,
and in every place your name surrounded[g] me.

7   Your right hand destroyed the evil poison,[h]
and your hand leveled the way for those who believe in you.

8   And it chose them[i] from the graves,
and separated them[j] from the dead ones.

9   It took dead bones   Ezek 37:1–6
and covered them with flesh.

10   But they were motionless,
so it gave (them) energy[k] for life.

11   Incorruptible was your way and your face;
you have brought your world to corruption,
that everything might be broken and renewed.

12   And the foundation of everything is your rock.[l]   18:3; Mt 16:18
And upon it you have built your kingdom,
and it[m] became the dwelling place of the holy ones.[n]

Hallelujah.

ODE 23

1   Joy is for the holy ones.   WisSol 3:9; 4:15
And who will put it on but they alone?

2   Grace is for the elect ones.
And who will receive it but they who trusted in it from the beginning?

3   Love is for the elect ones.
And who will put it on but they who possessed it from the beginning?

4   Walk in the knowledge of the Lord[a]
and you will know the grace of the Lord[b] generously;
both for his exultation and for the perfection of his knowledge.

5   And his thought was like a letter,[c]
and his will descended from on high.

6   And it was sent from a bow like an arrow
that has been forcibly shot.

7   And many hands rushed to the letter,
in order to catch (it),[d] then take and read it.

g. H: "a blessing"; C agrees with N.
h. Cf. 1QH 5.10, 27 and CD 8.9; 19.22.
i. C: "You redeemed them from . . ."
j. C: "You removed them from . . ."
k. H: "help," "assistance." C agrees with N.
l. C: "Your light." Cf. 1QH 6.25f.
m. H: "and you became."
n. Cf. 1QS 8.8; 1QM 12.2; 1QH 12.2; 1QSb

4.25.

23 a. H: "Most High."
    b. H omits "And you will know the grace of the Lord."
    c. Cf. Zech 5:1f. and especially Hymn of the Pearl 40–55.
    d. Cf. n. c to OdesSol 6.

8   But it escaped from their fingers;
      and they were afraid of it and of the seal which was upon it.

9   Because they were not allowed to loosen its seal;
      for the power which was over the seal was better than they.

10   But those who saw the letter went after it;
      that they might know where it would land,
      and who should read it,
      and who should hear it.

11   But a wheel received it,
      and it (the letter) came over it.

12   And with it was a sign,
      of the Kingdom and of providence.ᵉ

13   And everything which was disturbing to the wheel,
      it mowed it and cut it down.

14   And it restrained a multitude of adversaries;
      and bridgedᶠ rivers.

15   And it crossed over (and) uprooted many forests,ᵍ
      and made a wide way.ʰ

16   The head went down to the feet,
      because unto the feet ran the wheel,
      and whatever had come upon it.

17   The letter was one of command,
      and hence all regions were gathered together.

18   And there appeared at its head, the Head which was revealed,
      even the Son of Truth from the Most High Father.

                                                             17:17; 24:1

                                                             3:7; 7:15; 19:2, 8; 23:22; 41:13; 42:15

19   And he inherited and possessed everything,
      and then the schemingⁱ of the many ceased.

20   Then all the seducers became headstrong and fled;
      and the persecutors became extinct and were blotted out.ʲ

21   And the letter became a large volume,ᵏ
      which was entirely written by the finger of God.

22   And the name of the Father was upon it;
      and of the Son and of the Holy Spirit,
      to rule for ever and ever.

                                                             3:7; 7:15; 19:2, 8; 23:18; 41:13; 42:15

   Hallelujah.

---

e. Or "government," "the divine dispensation."

f. Lit. "covered with earth."

g. N: "peoples," or "gentiles."

h. Or "an open way."

i. Or "thought."

j. H: "and were angry."

k. Gk. *pinakidion*.

ODE 24

1   The dove fluttered over the head of our Lord Messiah,[a]
    because he was her Head.

9:3; 17:16f.;
23:18; 39:11;
41:3,15

2   And she sang over him,
    and her voice was heard.[b]

3   Then the inhabitants were afraid,
    and the foreigners were disturbed.

4   The bird began to fly,[c]
    and every creeping thing died in its hole.

5   And the chasms were opened and closed;
    and they were seeking the Lord as those who are about to give birth.[d]

17:9

6   But he was not given to them for nourishment,
    because he did not belong to them.

7   But the chasms were submerged in the submersion of the Lord,
    and they perished in that thought with which they had remained
        from the beginning.

8   For they labored from the beginning;
    and the end of their labor was life.

9   And all of them who were lacking perished,
    because they were not able to express the word so that they might remain.

10   And the Lord destroyed the thoughts,
    of all those who had not the truth with them.

11   For they were lacking in wisdom,
    they who exalted themselves in their mind.[e]

12   So they were rejected,
    because the truth was not with them.

13   For the Lord declared[e] his way,
    and spread out his grace.

14   And those who recognized it
    knew his holiness.

    Hallelujah.

ODE 25

1   I was rescued from my chains,[a]
    and I fled unto you, O my God.[b]

---

24 a. H: "The dove fluttered over the Messiah . . ."
   b. 24:1f. is an allusion to Jesus' baptism.
   c. N: "she flew."
   d. Cf. 1QH 3.16–18. The *descensus ad inferos* is portrayed in 42:11–20; cf. 17:6–16.

e. Or "heart."
f. Or "revealed."

25 a. C: "the bonds."
   b. C: "O Lord."

2   Because you are the right hand of salvation,[c]
and my Helper.

7:3; 8:6; 21:2

3   You have restrained those who rise up against me,
and they did not appear again.[d]

4   Because your face was with me,
which saved me by your grace.[e]

5   But I was despised and rejected in the eyes of many,
and I was in their eyes like lead.

6   And I acquired strength from you,
and help.

7   A lamp you set for me both on my right and on my left,
so that there might not be in me anything that is not light.

8   And I was covered with the covering of your spirit,[f]
and I removed from me my garments of skin.[g]

8:9

9   Because your right hand raised me,
and caused sickness to pass from me.

10   And I became mighty in your truth,[h]
and holy in your righteousness.

11   And all my adversaries[i] were afraid of me,[j]
and I became the Lord's by the name of the Lord.[k]

12   And I was justified by his kindness,[l]
and his rest[m] is for ever and ever.

Heb 4:1

Hallelujah.

ODE 26

1   I poured out praise to the Lord,
because I am his own.

Ps 45:1

2   And I will recite his holy ode,
because my heart is with him.

3   For his harp is in my hand,
and the odes of his rest shall not be silent.

4   I will call unto him with all my heart,
I will praise and exalt him with all my members.

Ps 119:145

---

c. C: "For you became for me a right hand by which you saved me."

d. H: "I shall not see him." C: "They have not shown themselves."

e. Cf. Gen 32:30.

f. C: "of your mercy."

g. H: "the garments of skins." Cf. GTr 20:30–34 and 1QS 4.7f.

h. H: "in truth"; C agrees with N.

i. Lit. "all those who are against me."

j. C: "my enemies became far from me."

k. C omits this line.

l. Or "gentleness," "sweetness," "gladness." C: "your gentleness."

m. C: "your rest."

5   For from the East and unto the West
    is his praise;

6   Also from the South and unto the North
    is his thanksgiving.ᵃ

7   Even from the peak of the summits and unto their end
    is his perfection.

8   Who can write the odes of the Lord,   5ApocSyrPss 1:4
    or who can read them?ᵇ

9   Or who can train himself for life,
    so that he himself may be saved?

10 Or who can press upon the Most High,
    so that he would recite from his mouth?

11 Who can interpret the wonders of the Lord?   Ps 106:2
    Though he who interprets should perish,ᶜ
    yet that which was interpreted will remain.

12 For it suffices to perceive and be satisfied,
    for the Odists stand in serenity;

13 Like a river which has an increasingly gushing spring,
    and flows to the relief of them that seek it.

    Hallelujah.

ODE 27

1   I extended my hands   42:1–2
    and hallowed my Lord;

2   For the expansion of my hands
    is his sign.ᵃ

3   And my extension
    is the upright cross.

    Hallelujah.

ODE 28

1   As the wings of doves over their nestlings,
    and the mouths of their nestlings toward their mouths,
    so also are the wings of the Spirit over my heart.

2   My heart continually refreshes itself and leaps for joy,
    like the babe who leaps for joy in his mother's womb.ᵃ

26 a. Or "confession," "praise," "acknowledg-   27 a. N: "it was hindered."
ment."
   b. Cf. Eccl 7:24; 2Bar 14:8f.; and 75:1–5.   28 a. Cf. Ps 22:9f. and Lk 1:44.
   c. Or "should be destroyed."

3   I trusted, consequently I was at rest;
         because trustful is he in whom I trusted.

4   He has greatly blessed me,
         and my head is with him.

5   And the dagger shall not divide me from him,   Rom 8:35
         nor the sword.[b]

6   Because I am ready[c] before destruction comes,
         and have been placed in his incorruptible arms.[d]

7   And immortal life embraced me,[e]
         and kissed me.

8   And from that (life) is the Spirit which is within me.
         And it cannot die because it is life.

Christ Speaks[f]

9   Those who saw me were amazed,
         because I was persecuted.

10   And they thought that I had been swallowed up,
         because I appeared to them as one of the lost.

11   But my defamation
         became my salvation.

12   And I became their abomination,
         because there was no jealousy[g] in me.

13   Because I continually did good to every man
         I was hated.

14   And they surrounded me like mad dogs,   Ps 22:16
         those who in stupidity[h] attack their masters.

15   Because their mind is depraved,
         and their sense is perverted.

16   But I was carrying water in my right hand,
         and their bitterness I endured[i] by my sweetness.

17   And I did not perish, because I was not their brother,
         nor was my birth like theirs.[j]

18   And they sought my death but were unsuccessful,[k]
         because I was older than their memory;[l]
         and in vain did they cast lots[m] against me.   Ps 22:18

b. Cf. Ps 22:20.
c. H: "I made ready."
d. Or "wing," "bosom," "side."
e. H: "and they went out."
f. See n. e to OdesSol 8.
g. Or "zeal."
h. H: "because they do not know."

i. N: "I disregarded."
j. N: "nor did they acknowledge my birth."
k. Lit. "they did not find it possible."
l. N: "their garment."
m. H: "they threatened"; a marginal n. in H
agrees with N.

19   And those who were after me[n]
      sought in vain to destroy the memorial of him
              who was before them.[o]   Jn 1:30; 8:57–59

20   Because the mind of the Most High cannot be prepossessed;[p]
      and his heart is superior to all wisdom.

      Hallelujah.

ODE 29

1   The Lord is my hope,   Pss 31:1; 71:1
      I shall not be ashamed in him.[a]   8:15; 9:7

2   For according to his praise he made me,
      and according to his grace[b] even so he gave to me.

3   And according to his mercies he raised me,
      and according to his great honor he lifted me up.

4   And he caused me to ascend from the depths of Sheol,
      and from the mouth of Death he drew me.

5   And I humbled my enemies,
      and he justified me by his grace.

6   For I believed in the Lord's Messiah,
      and considered that he is the Lord.

7   And he declared to me[c] his sign,
      and he led me by his light.[d]

8   And he gave me the scepter of his power,[e]
      that I might subdue the thoughts of the gentiles,   10:5
      and humble the strength of the mighty.

9   To make war by his word,[f]   8:7; 9:6; 29:9
      and to take victory by his power.[g]

10   And the Lord overthrew my enemy[h] by his word;[i]
      and he became like the dust which a breeze carries off.   Ps 1:4

11   And I gave praise to the Most High,
      because he has magnified his servant and the son of his maidservant.   Ps 116:16; cf.
                                                            Lk 1:38

      Hallelujah.

n. N omits "me."   d. Perhaps "light" should be capitalized as in
o. Cf. Jn 1:30.   10:1 and 36:3.
p. Or "be anticipated."   e. Cf. Ps 110:2.
                                          f. Or "Word"; see n. e to OdesSol 7.
29 a. Or "I shall not be confused in him."   g. Cf. 1QM 11.4.
b. Or "goodness," "kindness."   h. H: "my enemies."
c. H: "to him."   i. Or "Word"; see n. f above.

ODE 30

1   Fill for yourselves water from the living spring[a] of the Lord,
     because it has been opened for you.

                     1En 48:1–10; Rev 21:6

2   And come all you thirsty and take a drink,
     and rest beside the spring[b] of the Lord.

                     6:6–18; Rev 22:17

3   Because it is pleasing and sparkling,
     and perpetually pleases the self.[c]

4   For more refreshing is its water than honey,
     and the honeycomb of bees is not to be compared with it;

                     Ps 19:10; Sir 24:20

5   Because it flowed from the lips of the Lord,
     and it named from the heart of the Lord.

6   And it came boundless and invisible,
     and until it was set in the middle they knew it not.[d]

7   Blessed are they who have drunk from it,
     and have rested by it.

Hallelujah.

ODE 31

1   Chasms vanished before the Lord,
     and darkness was destroyed by his appearance.

2   Error erred and perished on account of him;
     and Contempt received[a] no path,
     for it was submerged by the truth of the Lord.

3   He opened his mouth and spoke grace and joy;
     and recited a new chant to his name.

4   Then he raised his voice toward the Most High,
     and offered to him those that had become sons through him.

                     Jn 17:1–9

5   And his face[b] was justified,
     because thus his Holy Father had given to him.

Christ Speaks[c]

6   Come forth, you who have been afflicted,
     and receive joy.

7   And possess yourselves through grace,
     and take unto you immortal life.

---

30 a. Or "fountain." Cf. 1QH 8.14.
  b. Or "fountain."
  c. Or "the soul,"'"the breath of life."
  d. Or "And until he was set in the middle they knew him not." Cf. Jn 1:26.

31 a. H: "I gave it (her) . . ." or "she was given it . . ."
  b. Gk. prosōpon.
  c. See n. e to OdesSol 8.

8   And they condemned me when I stood up,
me who had not been condemned.[d]

9   Then they divided[e] my spoil,   Ps 22:18
though nothing was owed them.

10   But I endured and held my peace and was silent,
that I might not be disturbed by them.

11   But I stood undisturbed like a solid rock,
which is continuously pounded by columns of waves and endures.[f]

12   And I bore their bitterness because of humility;
that I might save my nation and instruct it.

13   And that I might not nullify the promises to the patriarchs,   Rom 15:8
to whom I was promised for the salvation of their offspring.

Hallelujah.

ODE 32

1   To the blessed ones the joy is from their heart,
and light from him who dwells in them;

2   And the Word from the truth who is self-originate,[a]   7:7; 10:1; 12:5,
10,12; Jn 1:1–18

3   Because he has been strengthened
by the holy power of the Most High;
and he is unshaken for ever and ever.

Hallelujah.

ODE 33

1   But again Grace was swift and repudiated the Corruptor,[a]   38:9; Rev 9:11
and descended upon him to renounce him.

2   And he caused utter[b] destruction before him,
and corrupted all his construction.[c]

3   And he stood on the peak of a summit and cried aloud
from one end of the earth to the other.

4   Then he drew to him all those who obeyed him,
for[d] he did not appear as the Evil One.

5   However the perfect Virgin[e] stood,
who was preaching and summoning[f] and saying:

---

d. Or "who had been found not guilty."
e. N: "and he divided."
f. H: "pounded by waves and endures."

32 a. Lit. "he who is from himself"; N omits "from." Cf. Jn 1:1–18.

33 a. Or "dismissed the Destroyer."
b. Lit. "he has destroyed the destruction."
c. Or "composition," "work."
d. Or "and," "then," "yet."
e. Cf. the fourth vision of the ShepHerm; contrast Prov 1:20f.; 8:1–4.
f. N: "and shouting."

6   O you sons of men, return,
        and you their daughters, come.

7   And abandon the ways of that Corruptor,[g]
        and approach me.

8   And I will enter into you,
        and bring you forth from destruction,
        and make you wise in the ways of truth.   11:3

9   Be not corrupted
        nor perish.

10   Hear[h] me and be saved,
        for I am proclaiming unto you the grace of God.

11   And through me you will be saved and become blessed.
        I am your judge;

12   And they who have put me on will not be rejected,[i]   4:6
        but they will possess incorruption in the new world.

13   My elect ones have walked with me,
        and my ways I shall make known to them who seek me;
        and I shall promise them my name.

        Hallelujah.

ODE 34

1   There is no hard way where there is a simple heart,
        nor barrier for upright thoughts,

2   Nor whirlwind in the depth of the enlightened thought.

3   Where one is surrounded entirely[a] (by) pleasing country,
        there is nothing divided in him.

4   The likeness[b] of that which is below   Ascenls 7:10
        is that which is above.

5   For everything is from above,
        and from below there is nothing,
        but it is considered[c] to be by those in whom there is no understanding.[d]

6   Grace has been revealed for your salvation.
        Believe and live and be saved.

        Hallelujah.

g. Cf. 1QM 14.10.
h. Or "Obey me . . ."
i. Or "will not be rejected . . ."

34 a. Or "on every side."
    b. Or "form."
    c. Or "believed."
    d. Or "knowledge."

ODE 35

1   The sprinkling[a] of the Lord overshadowed me with serenity,[b]
    and it caused a cloud of peace to stand over my head;

2   That it might guard me at all times.
    And it became salvation[c] to me.

3   Everyone was disturbed and afraid,
    and there flowed from them smoke and judgment.

4   But I was tranquil[d] in the Lord's legion;[e]
    more than shade[f] was he to me, and more than foundation.

5   And I was carried like a child by its mother;
    and he gave me milk, the dew of the Lord.[g]   19:1-5

6   And I grew strong in his favor,
    and rested in his perfection.

7   And I extended my hands in the ascent of myself,[h]   37:1
    and I directed myself near[i] the Most High,
    and I was saved near[j] him.   36:6

    Hallelujah.

ODE 36

1   I rested on the Spirit of the Lord,
    and she raised me up to heaven;[a]

2   And caused me to stand on my feet in the Lord's high place,
    before his perfection and his glory,
    where I continued praising (him)[b] by the composition of his odes.

Christ Speaks[c]

3   (The Spirit) brought me forth before the Lord's face,   1En 48:2-10
    and because[d] I was the Son of Man,
    I was named the Light, the Son of God;[e]   10:1

4   Because I was most praised among the praised;[f]
    and the greatest among the great ones.[g]

35 a. Or "fine rain," "gentle showers."
  b. H: "with rest."
  c. H: "in salvation."
  d. Or "I was silent."
  e. Gk. *tagma*.
  f. N: "dew."
  g. 4Ezra 8:10 refers to milk as "the fruit of the breasts." 1En 39:5 mentions "mercy like dew upon the earth."
  h. Cf. Tertullian *De oratione* 14. Or "And I spread out my hands in the ascent of my soul . . ."
  i. Or "toward," "with."
  j. Or "toward," "with."

36 a. Or "height"; H: "on high."
  b. See n. c to OdesSol 6.
  c. See n. e to OdesSol 8.
  d. Or "when," "after," "although," "while."
  e. Cf. the discussion in the Introduction, under "Relation to apocryphal books."
  f. Or "the most glorified among the glorious ones . . ." H: "the most glorified among those who glorify . . ." Cf. Heb 1:3f.
  g. Cf. 2En 22:10 (13); 3Mac 2:2, "holy among the holy ones"; and ActsThom 101f., 105.

5   For according to the greatness of the Most High, so she made me;
and according to his newness he renewed me.

6   And he anointed me with his perfection;
and I became one of those who are near him.   21:7; 35:7

7   And my mouth was opened like a cloud of dew,
and my heart gushed forth[h] (like)[i] a gusher of righteousness.

8   And my approach was in peace,
and I was established in the spirit of providence.

Hallelujah.

ODE 37

1   I extended my hands toward the Lord,[a]   35:7
and toward the Most High I raised my voice.

2   And I spoke with the lips of my heart,   PssSol 15:5(3);
and he heard me when my voice reached him.   PrMan 1:11

3   His Word came toward me,[b]   7:7; 10:1; 12:5,
that which gave me the fruits of my labors;   10,12; 32:2

4   And gave me rest by the grace of the Lord.

Hallelujah.

ODE 38

1   I went up into the light of Truth as into a chariot,
and the Truth led me and caused me to come.[a]

2   And caused me to pass over chasms and gulfs,[b]
and saved me from cliffs and valleys.[c]

3   And became for me a haven[d] of salvation,
and set me on the place[e] of immortal life.

4   And he went with me and caused me to rest and did not allow me to err;
because he was and is the Truth.

5   And there was no danger[f] for me because I constantly walked with him;
and I did not err in anything because I obeyed him.

6   For Error fled from him,
and never met him.[g]

---

h. Lit. "to vomit," "reject."
i. This adverb is sometimes assumed in Semitic texts.

37 a. H: "my Lord."
b. See n. e to OdesSol 7.

38 a. Cf. Ps 43:3.

b. N: "over empty chasms and gulfs."
c. Lit. "ground liable to be flooded."
d. Gk. *limēn*.
e. Lit. "step," "degree," "condition." H: "arms."
f. Gk. *kindunos*; cf. 39:8.
g. Lit. "And it constantly did not meet him."

7   But Truth was proceeding on the upright way,
and whatever I did not understand he declared to me:

8   All the drugs of error,
and pains of death which are considered[h] sweetness.

9   And the corrupting of the Corruptor,   33:1; Rev 9:11
I saw when the Bride who was corrupting[i] was adorned,
and the Bridegroom who corrupts and is corrupted.

10   And I asked the Truth, Who are these?
And he said to me: This is the Deceiver[j] and the Error.[k]

11   And they imitate the Beloved and his Bride,   Ascenls 4:6
and they cause the world to err and corrupt it.

12   And they invite many to the wedding feast,[l]
and allowed them to drink the wine of their intoxication;[m]

13   So they cause them to vomit up their wisdom and their knowledge,
and make them senseless.[n]

14   Then they abandon them;
and so they stumble about like mad[o] and corrupted men.

15   Since there is no understanding in them,
neither do they seek it.

16   But I have been made wise so as not to fall into the hands of the deceivers,[p]
and I myself rejoiced because the Truth had gone with me.

17   For I was established and lived and was saved,
and my foundations were laid on account of the Lord's hand;
because he has planted me.[q]   11:18–22

18   For he set the root,
and watered it and adapted it and blessed it,
and its fruits will be forever.

19   It penetrated deeply and sprang up and spread out,[r]
and it was full and was enlarged.

20   And the Lord alone was praised,
in his planting[s] and in his cultivation;

21   In his care and in the blessing of his lips,
in the beautiful planting of his right hand;

h. H: "they who think."
i. H: "who was being corrupted."
j. Or "Impostor," "Seducer." In TJob 3:3 the Evil One (2:7 and 5:1) is one who deceives; cf. ApMos 39:2.
k. Or "one who is straying."
l. Or "banquet," "marriage."
m. Cf. 38:9–12 and 42:8f. with ActsThom 11–16.

n. Lit. "no mind," "no sense."
o. H: "Commanders."
p. H: "Deceiver."
q. Cf. 1Cor 3:6–10 and PssSol 14; see the Introduction above, under "Relation to apocryphal books."
r. H: "it deepened and raised and enriched."
s. Cf. 1QH 6.15; 8.5; 1QS 8.5; 11.8.

22   And in the attainment[t] of his planting,
       and in the understanding of his mind.

       Hallelujah.

ODE 39

1   Raging rivers (are like)[a] the power of the Lord;
       they bring headlong those who despise him.

2   And entangle their paths,
       and destroy their crossings.[b]

3   And catch their bodies,
       and corrupt their natures.

4   For they are more swift than lightnings,[c]
       even more rapid.

5   But those who cross them in faith
       shall not be disturbed.[d]

6   And those who walk on them faultlessly   PssSol 6:5
       shall not be shaken.

7   Because the sign on them is the Lord,
       and the sign is the Way for those who cross in the name of the Lord.   11:3

8   Therefore, put on the name of the Most High and know him,
       and you shall cross without danger;[e]
       because the rivers shall be obedient to you.

9   The Lord has bridged them by his word,[f]
       and he walked and crossed them on foot.

10   And his footsteps were standing firm upon the waters, and were not
               destroyed;
       but they are like a beam[g] (of wood) that is constructed[h] on truth.[i]

11   On this side and on that the waves were lifted up,
       but the footsteps of our Lord Messiah were standing firm.   9:3; 17:17; 24:1;
                                                                    41:3,15

12   And they are neither blotted out,
       nor destroyed.

13   And the Way has been appointed for those who cross over after him,   11:3; 39:7
       and for those who adhere to the path of his faith;
       and who adore his name.

       Hallelujah.

t. Or "finding," "discovery," "existence."   Cf. Tob 5:16–22.
                                                    e. Gk. *kindunos*; cf. 38:5.
39 a. See n. h to OdesSol 36.   f. Or "Word"; see n. e to OdesSol 7.
  b. Or "ways," "passages," "fords."   g. Or "cross."
  c. H: "lightning."   h. Or "firmly fixed."
  d. 2Ezra 8:50–53 also preserves the claim that   i. This vs. appears to refer obliquely to the
the Lord protects his children during a journey.   tradition that Jesus walked on water.

ODE 40

1   As honey drips from the honeycomb of bees,
and milk flows from the woman who loves her children,
so also is my hope upon you, O my God.

2   As a spring[a] gushes forth its water,
so my heart gushes forth the praise of the Lord,
and my lips bring forth praise to him.

3   And my tongue becomes sweet by his anthems,
and [my] me[mbe]rs are anointed by his odes.[b]

4   My[c] face rejoices in his exultation,
and my spirit exults in his love,
and my nature shines in him.

5   And he who is afraid will trust in him,
and salvation will be established in him.[d]

6   And his possession[e] is immortal life,
and those who receive it are incorruptible.

Hallelujah.

ODE 41

1   Let all the Lord's babes praise him,[a]
and let us[b] receive the truth of his faith.

2   And his children shall be acknowledged[c] by him,
therefore let us sing by his love.

3   We live[d] in the Lord by his grace,
and life we receive by his Messiah.

          9:3; 17:17; 24:1;
          39:11; 41:15

4   For a great day has shined upon us,
and wonderful is he who has given to us[e] of his glory.

5   Let us, therefore, all of us agree in the name of the Lord,
and let us honor him in his goodness.

6   And let our faces shine in his light,
and let our hearts meditate in his love,
by night and by day.

          Ps 1:2

7   Let us exult with the exultation of the Lord.

---

40 a. Or "fountain."
   b. H: "And my tongue by his odes."
   c. N omits.
   d. Or "And redemption will be assured for him."

   e. Or "profit," "gain."

41 a. Lit. "They will praise the Lord, all of his infants." N: "Let us praise."
   b. N: "and let them receive."
   c. Or "shall be known . . ."
   d. N: "we rejoice."
   e. N omits "to us."

Christh Speaksf

8   All those who see me will be amazed,
     because I am from another race.g   17:6; 28:17f.

9   For the Father of Truth remembered me;
     he who possessed me from the beginning.h

10   For his riches begat me,
     and the thought of his heart.

The Odist Speaksi

11   And his Word is with us in all our way,   7:7; 10:1; 12:5,
     the Savior who gives life and does not reject ourselves.   10,12; 32:2;
                                                                         37:3; 41:14
                                                                         Jn 6:33–37

12   The Man who humbled himself,
     but was raised because of his own righteousness.   8:5; Phil 2:6–9

13   The Son of the Most High appeared   3:7; 7:15; 19:2,
     in the perfection of his Father.   8; 23:18,22;
                                                                         42:15

14   And light dawned from the Word   41:11; Jn 1:1
     that was before time in him.

15   The Messiah in truth is one.   9:3; 17:17; 24:1;
     And he was known before the foundations of the world,   39:11; 41:3
     that he might give life to persons forever by the truth of his name. Jn 17:24b

Doxologyj

16   A new chant (is) for the Lord from them that love him.   PssSol 3:2

     Hallelujah.

ODE 42

1   I extended my hands and approached my Lord,   27:1–3
     because the stretching out of my hands is his sign.

2   And my extension is the commona cross,b
     that was lifted up on the way of the Righteous One.   1En 38:2; 53:6

Christ Speaksc

3   And I became useless to thosed who knew me [not],
     because I shall hide myself from those who possessed me not.

4   And I will be with those
     who love me.

---

f. See n. e to OdesSol 8.   42 a. Or "simple," "erect," "plain."
g. Gk. *genos*.   b. Or "wood," "tree."
h. Cf. Prov 8:22f.   c. See n. e to OdesSol 8.
i. and j. I add this notation.   d. H omits the words between "to those" and
                                                   "from those."

5   All my persecutors have died,
       and they who trusted in me sought me, because I am living.[e]

6   Then I arose and am with them,
       and will speak by their mouths.

7   For they have rejected those who persecute them;
       and I threw over them the yoke of my love.

8   Like the arm of the bridegroom over the bride,
       so is my yoke over those who know me.

9   And as the bridal feast[f] is spread out by the bridal pair's home,
       so is my love by those who believe in me.

10   I was not rejected although I was considered to be so,
       and I did not perish although they thought it of me.

11   Sheol saw me and was shattered,
       and Death ejected me and many with me.   *15:9; Rev 20:13f.*

12   I have been vinegar and bitterness to it,
       and I went down with it as far as its depth.

13   Then the feet and the head it released,
       because it was[g] not able to endure my face.[h]

14   And I made a congregation of living among his dead;
       and I spoke with them by living lips;
       in order that my word may not fail.

15   And those who had died ran toward me;
       and they cried out and said, "Son of God, have pity on us.   *3:7; 7:15; 19:2, 8; 23:18,22; 41:13*

16   "And deal with us according to your kindness,
       and bring us out from the chains of darkness.

17   "And open for us the door
       by which we may go forth to you,   *17:9; 24:5; Jn 10:7–10; Rev 3:7f.*
       for we perceive that our death does not approach you.

18   "May we also be saved with you,
       because you are our Savior."

19   Then I heard their voice,
       and placed their faith in my heart.[i]

20   And I placed my name upon their head,
       because they are free[j] and they are mine.

Doxology[k]

Hallelujah.

---

e. Or "pure."
f. Or "bed," "couch," "bridal chamber."
g. H: "they were."
h. Gk. *prosópon.*

i. H omits vs. 19b.
j. Or "nobles," "princes."
k. I add this notation.

SUPPLEMENT

FRAGMENTS OF LOST
JUDEO-HELLENISTIC WORKS

EDITOR'S INTRODUCTION

BY J. H. CHARLESWORTH

After the Babylonian exile Judaism increasingly began to reflect ideas usually associated with the Persians, Greeks, and Romans, often filtered through the indigenous cultures of Syria and Egypt. Many of the fascinatingly diverse Jewish documents composed during this period are now lost. Fortunately some of them—most notably the Dead Sea Scrolls[1]—have been recovered; a few others are represented by the fragments presented here.[2]

These excerpts reward the attentive reader. From them we learn that Greek epic poetry was written by Jews, who like Philo the Epic Poet mastered the hexameters of the Greek poets and who like Ezekiel the Tragedian demonstrated proficiency in iambic trimeters. In them we are introduced to a Jewish philosopher, Aristobulus, who combined Greek philosophical systems (especially those of Pythagoras, Plato, and some Stoics) with Jewish traditions (particularly those represented by Proverbs, Sirach, the Wisdom of Solomon, Pseudo-Phocylides, and 4 Maccabees). Through them we are ushered into a strange world of unusual traditions, notably through Demetrius, who claimed that the weapons used in the conquest of Canaan were taken by the Israelites from drowning Egyptians, and through Artapanus, who transmitted the idea that Egyptian culture—including its idolatry and polytheism—was shaped by Abraham, Joseph, and Moses. Generally characteristic of these excerpts, small remnants of once voluminous works, is an apologetic claim that the best Greek ideas are derived from the Jews. This theme, of course, recurs often in the better-known authors Philo of Alexandria and Josephus.[3]

Additional Abbreviations

In addition to the abbreviations listed in the beginning of this volume, the ones listed below have been chosen to simplify the presentation and facilitate the reading of the following works:

Primary
 F. = Fragment
 Plato *Tim* = Plato, *Timaeus*
 Plato *Apol* = Plato, *Apologia*
 Plato *Theag* = Plato, *Theages*
 Hesiod *Theog* = Hesiod, *Theogonia*

Secondary
 Freudenthal, *Alexander Polyhistor* = J. Freudenthal, *Hellenistische Studien* 1, 2: *Alexander Polyhistor;* Breslau, 1875.
 Denis, PVTG 3 = A.-M. Denis (ed.), *Fragmenta pseudepigraphorum quae supersunt graeca,* PVTG 3; Leiden, 1970.

---

[1] See the authoritative and succinct introduction by F. M. Cross, Jr., *Scrolls from the Wilderness of the Dead Sea* (San Francisco [ASOR], 1969).

[2] I wish to express my appreciation to John Strugnell for helping me to edit the following contributions by participants in his seminar at Harvard University and to organize the presentations. I also am indebted to my editorial assistants, Steve Robinson, Gary Martin, and especially Dave Fiensy, who helped me check the translations and polish the discussions.

[3] Works by Philo and Josephus are available in numerous English editions; especially see the translations in the LCL.

Jacoby, *FGH* = F. Jacoby, *Die Fragmente der griechischen Historiker;* 3 vols., Berlin, 1940–43; reprinted Leiden, 1954–64.

Mras, GCS 43, 1–2 = K. Mras (ed.), *Eusebius Werke, Achter Band: Die Praeparatio Evangelica,* GCS 43, 1–2; Berlin, 1954–56.

CONTENTS

INTRODUCTION

GENERAL INTRODUCTION, WITH A NOTE ON
ALEXANDER POLYHISTOR

BY J. STRUGNELL

The works presented in the following section share certain characteristics:
  a) They were all written by Jews;[1]
  b) They were composed in Greek and in literary forms known elsewhere in Greek literature;
  c) They are not pseudepigraphic; they were not written under another's name (although, by accident, some may now be falsely ascribed and so in another sense pseudepigraphical), and the names attached to them are probably the real names of their authors;[2]
  d) They are only fragmentarily preserved.[3]

The introduction to each fragmentary work will indicate the authors who have preserved it for us in its extant forms. As will be seen, without Pseudo-Justin, Clement of Alexandria, and Eusebius of Caesarea, our knowledge of this chapter in Jewish literary history would be much poorer. However, in most cases these authors had only indirect knowledge of the works that they have transmitted to us. Clement and Eusebius may have known Aristobulus (see below) directly, but though knowledge of the Orphic poem and of the fragments of epic, tragic, and comic verse will have reached Clement and Pseudo-Justin independently, each probably reflects the use of intermediary anthologies composed for apologetic purposes. The most important intermediary, however, was one Alexander Polyhistor, who is responsible for almost all our knowledge of ten of these fragmentary authors, and whose work *On the Jews* is known principally through the long excerpts made from it in the ninth book of the *Preparation for the Gospel*, by Eusebius. Polyhistor was certainly known also to Clement, and his knowledge of some of these same authors was also in all probability mediated through the same work, *On the Jews*.

Cornelius Alexander of Miletus, surnamed Polyhistor, was probably born there between 112 and 102 B.C.; brought young as a captive to Rome and freed around 82 B.C., he pursued an active scholarly career there until his death, sometime in the thirties.[4] The titles of over twenty-five of his numerous compositions are preserved; these suggest that he was mainly

---

[1] Most of "Pseudo-Hecataeus" perhaps constitutes an exception, and may not belong in this section, or even in the present vol. It is, however, included here out of respect for the contrary judgment of most scholars, and for the convenience and interest of the reader.

[2] Exceptions are many of the epic, tragic, and comic fragments and the Orphic poem; for similar but non-fragmentary Jewish pseudepigrapha in these areas, compare the SibOr and Ps-Phoc. The author of "Pseudo-Eupolemus," despite modern scholarly terminology, did not originally intend to *pass off* his work as being by Eupolemus; in fact he probably *was* Eupolemus himself. However, the fragments of "Pseudo-Eupolemus" have been edited here separately from those certainly attributed to Eupolemus and under their conventional title, "Pseudo-Eupolemus," because that is where most readers will expect to find them.

[3] Here again the Orphic poem forms an exception; it is preserved in its entirety by several works, but usually inside a quotation of a larger fragment (cf. the edition of Aristobulus in this section). Whether this poem once belonged to a larger collection of Jewish Orphic poems is uncertain.

[4] The guess by some that Polyhistor was Jewish lacks any basis at all.

interested in history, geography, and ethnography. We have, for example, fragments of his books *On Rome, On Illyria, On the Black Sea, On Bithynia, On Paphlagonia, On Phrygia, On Caria, On Lycia, On Cilicia, On Syria, On the Jews* (as well as others on Egypt, Libya, Crete); other types of work are also attested, on philological topics (a *Commentary on the Poetess Corinna*) and on philosophical ones (e.g. on the succession of the leading philosophers).

Some have suggested that Polyhistor's works on eastern nations (including his *On the Jews*) would have been written at about the time of Pompey's oriental campaigns (66–62 B.C.), to satisfy Roman curiosity about the history and culture of the newly occupied lands. No internal evidence in his *On the Jews*, however, supports this date, and if Clement is citing Demetrius (F. 6) and Eupolemus (F. 5) from Polyhistor, as is very possible, then a date after 40 B.C. is demanded (and Polyhistor himself would most likely have been the one responsible for the chronological updating of Eupolemus). In any case, either the sixties or the forties is the latest possible date for the works quoted by Polyhistor in his *On the Jews*; the scattered internal evidence for some of these fragmentary works, as will be seen, usually pushes us a century or more earlier.

The nature of Polyhistor's works in general is discussed by others;[5] his treatise *On the Jews* (as far as we can see from Eusebius' excerpts) seems to have been arranged in chronological order, going from Abraham (or earlier) to at least the destruction of Jerusalem by Nebuchadnezzar; it may well have contained further material from the Persian and hellenistic periods also. Although Polyhistor arranged his excerpts from his sources in chronological order, their content is also of ethnographic, cultural, and topographic interest.

His weaknesses as a historian—he was no critical Polybius—become for us virtues; he seems to have been primarily a compiler of quotations, a *grammatikos*, as ancient tradition puts it. But how reliable is he in making quotations? Does he quote verbatim or modify to suit his own purposes? We have almost no places where we can check his accuracy in citation; the originals from which he quoted are not available for comparison. The poetic quotations, where the laws of meter give us closer control over what the original text must have read, do not seem to have suffered worse than any other Greek poetical text with a similarly narrow manuscript basis. The prose passages have almost always been turned into indirect speech; in addition to that, they have suffered accidental haplographies and corruptions[6] due to the ignorance or confusion of scribes, or even of Polyhistor himself; but these are accidents; no bias in doctoring his sources, or historiographical tendency in abbreviating them, can be detected.

These excerpts, then, require careful text-critical study; they may sometimes require emendation to repair the damages suffered by the texts before and after Polyhistor's time.[7] It may further be that Polyhistor did not select from his sources those passages that would have most interested a modern historian of Judaism, or even a more critical ancient one. But without him, we would have nothing at all from most of these authors and know nothing of the variegated literary activity that they reveal; for what he has given us, then, the (generally reliable) old *grammatikos* still deserves our thanks.

---

[5] The best presentation of the totality of Alexander Polyhistor's work is to be found in Jacoby, *FGH*, commentary to no. 273. For other discussions concerning more specifically his *On the Jews*, consult Freudenthal, *Alexander Polyhistor*, pp. 16–35; and B. Z. Wacholder, *Eupolemus: A Study of Judaeo-Greek Literature* (New York, 1974), pp. 44–52.

[6] For a good instance, see the very corrupt F. 2 of Demetrius.

[7] To establish the texts, note that Clement exists in a single independent MS and occasional ancient citations (in Eusebius and elsewhere). Pseudo-Justin's *De Monarchia* has a two-branched stemma (CE//F) and his *Cohortatio* another two-branched one (GD//ABCEF). Eusebius' *Praeparatio* is equally two-branched, B//I/ON (but B is often missing). The Tübingen Theosophy (important for Ps-Orph) exists, like Clement, in a single MS. The establishment of the text of the archetype of the MS tradition of these later authors, and then of their intermediate sources (such as Alexander Polyhistor) is relatively easy—but for the texts of the original authors we will often need further critical (i.e. historical and conjectural) work before we may be confident of having restored the earliest form of the Jewish documents themselves.

SELECT BIBLIOGRAPHY

Dalbert, P. *Die Theologie der hellenistisch-jüdischen Missionsliteratur unter Ausschluss von Philo und Josephus.* Theologische Forschung 4; Hamburg-Volksdorf, 1954.

Denis, A.-M. (ed.). *Fragmenta pseudepigraphorum quae supersunt graeca una cum historicorum et auctorum judaeorum hellenistarum fragmentis.* PVTG 3; Leiden, 1970.

Fraser, P. M. *Ptolemaic Alexandria.* 3 vols.; Oxford, 1972.

Freudenthal, J. *Alexander Polyhistor und die von ihm erhaltenen Reste jüdischer und samaritanischer Geschichtswerke.* Hellenistische Studien 1–2; Breslau, 1874–75.

Gutman, Y. *The Beginnings of Jewish-Hellenistic Literature.* Jerusalem, 1963; vol. 1 [in modern Heb.].

Hengel, M. *Judaism and Hellenism,* trans. J. Bowden. 2 vols.; Philadelphia, 1974.

Jacoby, F. (ed.). *Die Fragmente der griechischen Historiker.* 3 vols.; Berlin, 1923–.

Mras, K. (ed.). *Eusebius Werke, Achter Band: Die Praeparatio Evangelica.* GCS 43, 1–2. Berlin, 1954–56.

Stählin, O. (ed.). *Clemens Alexandrinus, Stromata I–VI.* GCS 52; Berlin, 1960.

Walter, N. "Fragmente jüdisch-hellenistischer Exegeten: Aristobulos, Demetrios, Aristeas," *JSHRZ* 3.2 (1975).

———. *Untersuchungen zu den Fragmenten der jüdisch-hellenistischen Historiker* (typescript). Halle, 1968.

POETRY

PHILO THE EPIC POET

(Third to Second Century B.C.)

A NEW TRANSLATION AND INTRODUCTION

BY H. ATTRIDGE

From an epic poem of Philo there remain six brief fragments, providing a total of twenty-four hexameter verses. The first two of these fragments deal with Abraham and, more particularly, with the binding of Isaac, recounted in Genesis 22. The third fragment mentions God's beneficence to the patriarchs and especially to Joseph. The last three fragments focus on Jerusalem and its remarkable water-supply system. To judge from the title of the poem mentioned in Eusebius, *On Jerusalem*, the focus of the whole epic was the city and its history.

Text and original language

The fragments of Philo's work are preserved in Eusebius, *Praeparatio Evangelica* 9. Eusebius in turn depended on Alexander Polyhistor's work of the first century B.C. The hexameter verses are written in a pedantic and obscure Greek. Unusual words combine with opaque allusions and a bombastic style to render much of the poetry barely intelligible. Textual corruption no doubt has contributed to the difficulty of these fragments, but much of the obscurity is due to Philo's attempt to imitate the erudite epics of the Alexandrian period.

Date and provenance

It is impossible to be precise about the time and place of Philo's composition. Both Josephus (*Apion* 1:218) and Clement of Alexandria (*Strom* 1.141.3) mention a Philo in connection with the historians Demetrius and Eupolemus. This Philo may, however, be different from the epic poet. The testimonia, like the fragments in Eusebius, depend on Alexander Polyhistor or another source of the first century B.C. Philo certainly lived before Alexander's literary activity; the association of the poet with the historians of the late-third and mid-second centuries B.C. suggests that Philo may have lived in the same period.

The place of Philo's composition is uncertain. Although the interest in Jerusalem in the fragments of the poem may be indicative of a Palestinian provenance, Jews everywhere had the same high regard for the sacred city. The literary character of the poem makes it more likely that it was composed in a center of Greek culture such as Alexandria.

Theological and historical importance

Philo's poem contains nothing novel or striking in its theology. The highly laudatory language used of Abraham and his offspring in the first fragments illustrates well the panegyric quality characteristic of Jewish apologetic literature, with its celebration of the main figures in Jewish tradition. The epic form indicates once again the efforts made by Jews of the hellenistic period to adopt features of Greek culture to give expression to their own self-understanding. Another example of similar literary activity appears in the epic poem of Theodotus.

SELECT BIBLIOGRAPHY

Charlesworth, *PMR*, pp. 168f.
Delling, *Bibliographie*, pp. 53–55.
Denis, *Introduction*, pp. 270f.

TEXTS
Denis, A.-M. *Fragmenta pseudepigraphorum graeca*. Leiden, 1970; pp. 203f.
Mras, K. *Eusebius Werke 8: Die Praeparatio Evangelica*. GCS 43.1 and 2; Berlin, 1954/
    56.

STUDIES
Dalbert, P. *Die Theologie der hellenistisch-judischen Missionsliteratur unter Ausschluss von*
    Philo und Josephus. Hamburg-Volksdorf, 1954; pp. 33–35.
Gutman, Y. *The Beginnings of the Jewish-Hellenistic Literature*. Jerusalem, 1963; vol. 1,
    pp. 245–61.
———. "Philo the Epic Poet," *Scripta Hierosolymitana*. Jerusalem, 1954; pp. 36–63.
Lohse, E. "Philo," RGG³; vol. 5, col. 347.
Ludwich, A. *De Philonis carmine graeco-judaico*. Königsberg, 1900.
Wacholder, B. Z. "Philo (The Elder)," *EncyJud*; vol. 13, cols. 407f.
Walter, N. "Epiker Philon," *JSHRZ* 1.2 (1976) 112–14.

TRANSLATION

Fragments 1–2 Eusebius, *Praeparatio Evangelica* 9.20.1. Philo speaks on this subject[a] in the first book of his work *On Jerusalem*:

A thousand times have I heard in the ancient laws how once
(when you achieved something)[b]
marvelous with the bonds' knot,[c] O far-famed Abraham,
resplendently did your God-beloved prayers[d] abound[e] in
wondrous counsels.[f] For when you left the beauteous garden
of dread plants,[g] the praiseworthy thunderer[h] quenched the pyre[i]
and made his promise immortal.[j] From that time forth
the offspring of that awesome born one[k] have won far-hymned praise.

And so forth, to which he adds after a short while:[l]

as mortal hand readied the sword
with resolve,[m] and crackling (wood)[n] was gathered at the side,
he[o] brought into his hands a horned ram.

Fragment 3 Eusebius, *Praeparatio Evangelica* 9.24.1. Philo, too, corroborates the sacred Scriptures[a] in the first[b] book of his work *On Jerusalem*, saying,

For them[c] the Most High, great Lord of all[d] created a most blessed spot,
even from of old, yea from the days of Abraham and Isaac

Fragments 1–2 a. Eusebius has been recounting the story of Abraham according to Eupolemus, Artapanus, and Molon. At *PrEv* 9.19.4 he describes the Akedah. The episode probably had its place in an epic on Jerusalem, because of the identification of Mount Moriah with the Temple mount. Cf. 2Chr 3:1.

b. It seems likely that a l. to this effect has been lost after the first l. of the F.

c. An allusion to Gen 22:9.

d. The Gk. word for "prayers" basically means "charms" or "spells."

e. The Gk. word has been emended to provide a verb in this obscure sentence. The word basically means "rise like the flood tide."

f. The allusion in this sentence is unclear. It may be a reference to Abraham's prayers for an heir in Gen 15:1–6 or to his obedience to God's command in Gen 22:3–8. The line might alternatively be translated, "resplendently did consolations dear to God abound in the form of resounding utterances (of God)."

g. The word translated as "dread plants" is a hapax legomenon. It is occasionally translated "plants of praise." It is, however, analogous to many Gk. words with connotations of "dread" or "terror." The reference is probably to the wood which Abraham took with him to Mount Moriah, which was "dreadful" because of its intended function. Cf. Gen 22:3–6. Alternatively, this could be a reference to Abraham's departure from Chaldea. Cf. Gen 12:1–4.

h. The epithet "thunderer" is not used of God elsewhere in Jewish literature. It is applied to Ares in the *Iliad* 13.521. God is termed "praiseworthy" in the LXX version of Sam 22:4; 1Chr 16:25; Pss 47:2 and 95:4.

i. The pyre is probably an allusion to the fire which Abraham brought for the sacrifice of Isaac. Cf. Gen 22:6. In the biblical account the fire is not quenched.

j. Following the binding in Gen 22:16f., God promises Abraham that he will make his descendants as numerous as the stars and that they shall be a blessing for all nations.

k. The Gk. word is formed analogously to the "dread plants" of vs. 5. The epithet seems to be a reference to Isaac, who was born in an awesome way, first because of his miraculous conception in the womb of the aged Sarah, according to Gen 21:1–3, and secondly because he is figuratively reborn on the sacrificial pyre. The epithet could also, however, be meant for Abraham.

l. This remark of Eusebius introduces F. 2. Those three vss. probably formed part of a detailed account of the Akedah, to which F. 1 provided a general introduction. The beginning of the F. may well be corrupt.

m. In Gen 22:10 Abraham all but carries out his intent to sacrifice Isaac. The translation here reflects the emendation of Mras, GCS 43.1–2.

n. The Gk. word used here may be associated with a verb describing the sound of something burning. Cf. *Odyssey* 9.390. It is used by metonymy for the wood which makes that sound. Alternatively, the word may mean "neck" and the phrase could be translated: "with his (Isaac's) neck turned to the side."

o. This, of course, is God or his angel. Cf. Gen 22:11–13.

Fragment 3 a. Eusebius has just recounted the story of Joseph in Artapanus.

b. The Gk. text reads "fourteenth," but it seems unlikely that Philo could have taken thirteen books to recount patriarchal history prior to Joseph. Either "first" or "fourth" should be read.

c. The pronoun probably refers to the Israelites.

d. The figure mentioned here is probably God, who gave the blessed land of Palestine, although he could conceivably be Pharaoh, who provided the Israelites with a settlement in the land of Goshen, according to Gen 47:6–11.

and Jacob, rich in children, from whom was Joseph, who was
interpreter of dreams[e] for the scepter bearer on Egypt's throne,[f]
revolving time's secrets with the flood of fate.[g]

Fragments 4–6 Eusebius, *Praeparatio Evangelica* 9.37.1–3. Philo in his work
On Jerusalem says that there is a fountain[a] and that it is dry in winter and full
in summer. In his first book he says,
Above the swimmers[b] is the most wondrous sight, another
pool.[c] Its sound, with that of the ruler's baths,[d] fills
the deep channel of the stream as it exits.
And so forth, to which he adds, farther along, remarks concerning the filling:[e]
For the stream,[f] gleaming on high,[g] fed by moist
rains, rolls joyously under the neighboring towers;[h]
and the dry and dusty soil on the plain
shows the fountain's far-seen, marvelous deeds, the wonders of the nations[i]
and so forth. Then he goes on as follows concerning the high priest's fountain
and the way it empties out:
And on high do pipes pour out from channels
through the earth.[j]

e. Cf. Gen 41:14–32.
f. Cf. Gen 41:39–41. The translation reflects
the reading of Lloyd-Jones in an unpublished paper.
He emends "scepter bearer" from the nominative
to the dative.
g. This rather sentential line simply refers to
Joseph's ability as a prophetic interpreter of dreams.

Fragments 4–6 a. Eusebius has just given an
account of the water-supply system of Jerusalem
according to Timochares. Other accounts of this
system are found in Strabo, *Geography* 16.761,
and Tacitus, *Histories* 5.12. The topographical
referents of Philo's poem are obscure. The "fountain" of F.5 may be the spring of Gihon, which
supplied the pool of Siloam through Hezekiah's
tunnel. The body of water to which Eusebius refers
as a "fountain" may also be a pool. Its relationship
to the "ruler's baths" of F. 4 is unclear. It may be
the pool of Siloam. The ruler's baths may be the
pool of the king (probably equivalent to the pool
of Shelah), mentioned in Neh 2:14 and 2Ezra 12:14
(LXX). Alternatively, the ruler's baths may be the
pool of Siloam. For details of the water system of
Jerusalem, cf. L. H. Vincent and A.-M. Stève,
Jérusalem de l'Ancien Testament (Paris, 1954) vol.
1, pp. 260–312.
b. The participle in the Gk. text is emended,

with Lloyd-Jones, from the nominative to the
dative.
c. The Gk. word used here (*derkēthron*) is
problematic. It may mean "sight" or it could be
an unattested form of *derethron* ("gulf, pit"),
used, for the sake of the meter, to refer to a body
of water, such as the baths mentioned in this F.
d. The expression here is poetically condensed,
much like the reference to the crackling wood at
the binding in F. 2. The vs. seems to mean that the
pool in question, whose sound blends with that of
the "ruler's baths," empties into and fills a stream
which issues from it.
e. I.e., the filling of the pool.
f. Note that the stream issuing from the temple
in Ezekiel's vision of Jerusalem is deep enough to
swim in. Cf. Ezek 47:5.
g. This is possibly a reference to water at the
top of an aqueduct, possibly supplying the pool of
F. 4.
h. The towers of Jerusalem constitute an important part of the glorified picture of the city
sketched in LetAris 100, 105.
i. Note the description of the lush agricultural
riches of Palestine in LetAris 107, 112–14. The
old aqueducts from the spring of Gihon to the
king's pool also served to irrigate the terraced
cultivation on the east of the City of David.
j. Cf. LetAris 88–90, which Eusebius next quotes.

THEODOTUS

(Second to First Century B.C.)

A NEW TRANSLATION AND INTRODUCTION

BY F. FALLON

Theodotus composed a poem which used the vocabulary and meter of Greek epic poetry and which was probably entitled *On the Jews*. From the poem eight fragments survive. Some short summaries of sections of the poem also survive; they introduce the fragments. All of these pieces pertain to the story of the rape of Jacob's daughter Dinah at Shechem as recorded in Genesis 34. In the first fragment Theodotus gives a description of the city of Shechem and its environs. In a second brief fragment Theodotus presents the arrival of Jacob at Shechem. Then, in the third fragment, Theodotus recalls the earlier departure of Jacob for Mesopotamia, his marriages with Leah and Rachel, and his subsequent return to Canaan. After a summary of the rape of Dinah, fragment 4 presents the need of the Shechemites to be circumcised before Dinah can be married. The fifth fragment portrays the origin of the law of circumcision. After a summary of the plan of Simeon and Levi to slay Hamor and Sychem is given, the sixth fragment offers their motivation: a divine oracle. The seventh fragment then describes the evil nature of the Shechemites, which justifies the action. In the final fragment the actual slaying of Hamor and Sychem is poetically portrayed, and then the tale is concluded by the withdrawal from Shechem of the sons of Jacob with their booty.

Transmission

The fragments have been preserved because of the work of Alexander Polyhistor, the Greek historian, who flourished in the mid first century B.C. Because of the presence of the distinctive epic vocabulary and meter within, it is clear that Alexander has faithfully preserved the wording of the fragments. In addition, he has provided us with the summaries of the omitted parts of the poem or the omitted parts of this section of the poem, if the poem was actually longer than our fragments indicate. A higher incidence of non-epic words in these summaries indicates that Alexander has preferred normal prose vocabulary for his summations rather than epic diction. However, the agreement between the account in Genesis and the summations of Alexander shows that here, too, Alexander has been faithful to his source, Theodotus.[1]

Alexander Polyhistor's *On the Jews* is no longer extant in its entirety. However, excerpts from his writing have been preserved by Eusebius of Caesarea (c. A.D. 260–340) in his *Praeparatio Evangelica*; the material pertaining to Theodotus appears in 9.22.1–11.[2]

Provenance

Over the years, a number of scholars have suggested that Theodotus was a Samaritan

---

[1] On the fidelity of Alexander Polyhistor to his sources, see Freudenthal, *Alexander Polyhistor*, pp. 17–34. Alexander Polyhistor in his summation uses such non-epic words as *geōmoreō*, "to till the earth," and *eriourgeō*, "to work in wool."

[2] Mras, GCS 43, 1–2, pp. 512–16. The Fs. are also conveniently collected in Jacoby, *FGH*, vol. 3C, no. 732, pp. 692–94.

author. Various reasons, such as the following, have been offered in support of this hypothesis. The preserved part of the poem pertains to Shechem, a Samaritan city.[3] The city is referred to as a "holy city."[4] The title *On the Jews*, even if it is the correct title, could have been used by a Samaritan.[5] The identification of Shechem as the son of Hermes in the summary before the first fragment fits in with the euhemeristic impulse in other Samaritan works.[6]

Other scholars, however, have proposed the thesis that Theodotus was a Jewish author, for the following reasons. Although Theodotus was a Greek name, it is known to have been used by Jews as well as Samaritans.[7] As the title suggests, the poem may have been much longer than the fragments indicate and may not have been restricted to Shechem. Identification of Shechem as a "holy city" can be understood as epic language rather than as a statement about the religious significance of Shechem.[8] In addition, the euhemeristic impulse is not restricted to Samaritan literature.[9] Thus, there seems to be no clear evidence to compel a decision in favor of a Samaritan or Jewish hypothesis.

In his poem, Theodotus shows an awareness of post-biblical traditions, which were available in Palestine. The story of the return of Jacob, the rape of Dinah, and the attack by the sons of Jacob, is also recalled in one apocryphal work, the Book of Judith, and two pseudepigraphic works, Jubilees and the Testament of Levi. All three works, at least in their origins, derive from Palestine sometime between the third and first centuries B.C.[10] In these writings it is made clear that the attack upon the Shechemites was not merely an act of revenge by the sons of Jacob but, rather, that it was a just act of punishment willed by God (Jdt 9:2; Jub 30:6–7; TLevi 5:1–5; 6:8, 11). Further, just as fragment 7 of Theodotus stressed the unrighteousness of the Shechemites in that they did not honor anyone who came to them, whether evil or noble, so the Testament of Levi 6:8–10 suggests an earlier attack upon Sarah and Rebecca similar to that upon Dinah. This passage in the Testament of Levi further proposes that the Shechemites persecuted Abraham and his kin when they were strangers.[11] Thirdly, just as fragment 8 of Theodotus specifies—beyond the biblical text—that it is Simeon who slays Hamor, and Levi who slays Sychem, so, too, the Testament of Levi 6:4 specifies the matter in the same way. However, it is interesting to note that Levi is given greater emphasis than Simeon in the Testament and Jubilees. In the former, Levi slays Sychem before Simeon slays Hamor, and in the latter Levi and his descendants are chosen to be priests and Levites because of his slaying of the enemies of Israel. In contrast Simeon takes the initiative in Theodotus (cf. Jdt 9:2). Next, it should also be noted that neither the fragments nor the summaries of Theodotus mention the actual circumcision of the Shechemites. Thus the motif that the Shechemites were attacked while they were still in pain from the circumcision is also omitted. Similarly in Jubilees 30 there is no indication that the Shechemites were actually circumcised. In the Testament (TLevi 6:3) Levi counsels his father and brother against circumcising the Shechemites but then records (6:6) that they were indeed circumcised. Obviously the authors are struggling with the embarrassment of the Shechemites being circumcised, i.e. being given the sign of admittance into Israel and then being slain by the sons of Jacob. The absence in Theodotus of the account of the circumcision and of the motif of the pain may be due to the summation and omission by Alexander Polyhistor, but it is also possible that Theodotus omitted the circumcision because he shared the same concern as Jubilees and the Testament of Levi.[12]

The poem of Theodotus also reflects the interest in epic poetry during the hellenistic

[3] Freudenthal, *Alexander Polyhistor*, pp. 99–101.

[4] E. Schürer, *History*, division 2, vol. 3, pp. 224f.

[5] R. J. Bull, "A Note on Theodotus' Description of Shechem," *HTR* 60 (1967) 223f. Bull refers to ancient reports that the Samaritans would allow themselves to be called Jews when it was politically expedient to do so.

[6] M. Hengel, *Judaism and Hellenism* (Philadelphia, 1974) vol. 1, pp. 89, 266; vol. 2, p. 62. The euhemeristic impulse refers to the hellenistic theory that many of the gods were actually men who lived in bygone ages.

[7] Hengel, *Judaism and Hellenism*, vol. 1, p. 64.

[8] A. Ludwich, *De Theodoti Carmine Graeco-Judaico* (Königsberg, 1899) p. 6, n. 8. See *Iliad* 5.446; 16.100; *Odyssey* 1.2.

[9] Hengel, *Judaism and Hellenism*, vol. 1, pp. 89, 266.

[10] O. Eissfeldt, *The Old Testament: An Introduction* (New York, 1966) pp. 585–87, 606–8, 631–36.

[11] Cf. the description of the temple on Mount Gerizim as the temple of Zeus, the Friend of Strangers, in 2Mac 6:2.

[12] Josephus also omits telling of the actual circumcision of the Shechemites in *Ant* 1.21.1 337–40 (tr. H. St. J. Thackeray; LCL; Cambridge, England, 1967) vol. 4, pp. 161–63.

period.[13] It is well known that in antiquity there was a widespread interest in the poetry of Homer. During the hellenistic period there was a further revival of writing epic poetry, especially at such centers as Alexandria, where such authors as Callimachus (c. 305–240 B.C.) wrote short epic poems, especially upon mythological themes. Other authors, such as Apollonius of Rhodes (third century B.C.) continued the tradition of long epic poems upon mythological themes. In addition, long epic poems were written about hellenistic rulers as well as about various regions of the hellenistic world. Although it is difficult to know the exact nature and extent of the latter poems because our evidence is so fragmentary, it is nevertheless clear that the poets need not have been natives of or residents of the particular regions (e.g. Rhianus of Crete with his *Messēniaka* in the third century B.C.) but, rather, used the occasion to codify existing traditions.[14] In addition, some poets such as Rhianus of Crete included in their poems motifs of a religious and political value.[15]

It is into this context of an interest in epic poetry during the hellenistic period that Theodotus is to be placed along with the Jewish author Philo the Elder (second century B.C.), who composed an epic poem on Jerusalem in accord with the other regional epics. In his poem Theodotus uses Homeric language and meter as well as terms or usages which are customary in the later, hellenistic epic poets.[16] Occasionally he employs terms or usages not attested in epic poetry.[17]

Alexander Polyhistor states that the title of Theodotus' composition was *On the Jews*. Objections to the correctness of this title, such as the following, have been made by scholars. First, it has been argued that a Samaritan author would not give such a title to his work.[18] Second, it has been noted that the poem is concerned with Shechem rather than with the Jews.[19] Third, since the same title appears frequently as the title of the works quoted by Alexander Polyhistor (e.g. Ps-Eup, Art, ArisEx),[20] it is possible that the use of the same title here is erroneous. Fourth, it has been observed that within the poem itself the term which is used to refer to the people is "Hebrews" rather than "Jews" (e.g. *PrEv* 9.22.6).

In response to these objections, the following observations can be made. It is not clearly proved that the author was in fact a Samaritan. Next, if the title *On the Jews* is correct, then this episode concerning Shechem may be merely one episode of a cycle or one part of a longer poem. Further, although the term "Hebrews" is more appropriately used for the period prior to the Babylonian captivity, the term "Jews" in the title *On the Jews* would be an understandable anachronism on the part of an author such as Theodotus.[21] Thus, it seems more probable that the title *On the Jews* is correct.[22]

In his poem Theodotus draws mainly upon Genesis 34 for his account, although there are also references to the divine command to circumcise in Genesis 17 and to events in the life of Jacob in Genesis 27–33. Theodotus' use of epic language, however, makes it impossible to establish his dependence upon the Greek of the Septuagint.

Because of the recent excavations at Shechem,[23] it may be possible to date more precisely the poem of Theodotus. The exact description of Shechem within the poem indicates an

---

[13] For this discussion, see the classic study of K. Ziegler, *Das Hellenistische Epos: Ein Vergessenes Kapitel Griechischer Dichtung* (Berlin, 1934); cf. also A. Lesky, *A History of Greek Literature* (New York, 1963) pp. 700–37.

[14] The fragments of Rhianus are collected in Jacoby, *FGH*, vol. 3A, no. 265, pp. 64–69.

[15] See J. Gutmann, "Philo the Epic Poet," *Scripta Hierosolymitana* 1 (Jerusalem, 1954) pp. 60–63. The story of the earlier destruction of Messenia by Sparta but its subsequent restoration had political implications for the period of Rhianus and the contemporary opponents of Sparta.

[16] *Erymnos*, "steep" (cf. Apollonius, *Argonautica* 2.514); *laios*, "left" (cf. Apollonius, *Argonautica* 2.1036); and *ōrōrei* as the imperfect of the verb "to be" (cf. LSJM, pp. 1254f.).

[17] *Aiginomos* (browsed by goats), *aposylao* (to strip off), *ktenotrophos* (well-grazed), *oikētor* (inhabitant), *synomaimōn* (kinfolk); *poneomai* in the active voice as "to toil" and *riza* in the extended sense of "foundation."

[18] Schürer, *History*, division 2, vol. 3, p. 225.

[19] Ibid.; Freudenthal, *Alexander Polyhistor*, pp. 99–101.

[20] *PrEv* 9.17.2; 9.23.1; 9.25.1; GCS 43, 1–2, pp. 502, 516, 518.

[21] Cf. the discussion of Freudenthal, *Alexander Polyhistor*, p. 101, who, however, argues against the correctness of the title. Contrary to Freudenthal, it should be noted that Artapanus in his *On the Jews* can also use the term "Hebrews" (*PrEv* 9.18.1; GCS 43, 1–2, p. 504).

[22] Alternatively but less plausibly, in analogy to the poem of Philo the Elder, the title may have been *On Shechem*. Or in accord with other regional epics it may have been entitled *Foundation of Shechem*; see Ziegler, *Die Hellenistische Epos*, pp. 16f.

[23] See G. E. Wright, *Shechem: The Biography of a Biblical City* (New York, 1965).

eyewitness of the site and not simply a person who has read Genesis. Further, the archaeological data indicate that from the time of Alexander the Great (c. 331 B.C.) until c. 190 B.C. there was a large city wall around Shechem. However, in the following period (190–150 B.C.) the city wall was no longer maintained and stones were taken from the wall to build towers in front. Since Theodotus describes Shechem as having a "smooth wall" and since this phrase is not a customary epic description, then he must have observed the city prior to the middle of the second century B.C.[24] and presumably composed his poem at the same time. Such a date as the end of the third century or beginning of the second century B.C. would be appropriate, since it leaves some time between the composition of the poem and its collection by Alexander Polyhistor in the first century B.C.

Such a date may also help to explain the difficulty in deciding whether the author is Samaritan or Jewish. Even though tensions existed between Samaritans and Jews at an earlier period, a final break between them did not occur until later, in the reign of John Hyrcanus (135–105 B.C.).[25] Prior to that time they were in communication with one another, and the distinction was not necessary. The place of composition is uncertain; Palestine is as possible as Alexandria.

Importance

The poem of Theodotus is significant in that it is another indication of the degree of hellenization which some Jews underwent in the hellenistic period. In terms of its theology, the poem of Theodotus is significant in that it portrays God as the revealer of his commandments, his Law as unchangeable, and circumcision as a necessary part of that Law. Further, Theodotus portrays God as the revealer of oracles, the rewarder of his people, and the punisher of evil persons such as the Shechemites.

The function or functions of Theodotus' poem are not completely clear. Evidently it served to codify existing tradition, as did the other hellenistic regional epics. In a cultural setting in which the gymnasia and Greek education were ever present, the poem may also have served a Jewish need to recast tradition in an epic mode. It probably also served the religious need to recall the necessity of circumcision.

SELECT BIBLIOGRAPHY

Charlesworth, *PMR*, pp. 210f.
Denis, *Introduction*, pp. 272f.

Bull, R. J. "A Note on Theodotus' Description of Shechem," *HTR* 60 (1967) 221–28. (Examines Theodotus in the light of the archaeological evidence; still considers him to be a Samaritan.)
Denis, A.-M. *Fragmenta pseudepigraphorum quae supersunt graeca.* PVTG 3; Leiden, 1970; pp. 204–7. (A convenient collection of the fragments.)
Eusebius. *Werke; Band 8: Die Praeparatio Evangelica,* ed. Mras, K. GCS 43.1–2; Berlin, 1954–56. (The critical edition for Eusebius.)
Freudenthal, J. *Alexander Polyhistor.* Breslau, 1875; pp. 99–101. (The classic study of Theodotus, which suggested that he was a Samaritan.)
Gutmann, J. *The Beginnings of Jewish-Hellenistic Literature.* Jerusalem, 1958; vol. 2, pp. 245–61. (Hebrew)
Hengel, M. *Judaism and Hellenism.* Philadelphia, 1974; vol. 1, pp. 69, 89, 266. (Considers Theodotus to be a Samaritan and associates him with the euhemeristic impulse of the times.)

---

[24] Bull, *HTR* 60 (1967) 226–28. The adjective "smooth" (*lissos*) does occur in Homer, but there it modifies "rock" rather than "wall" (*Odyssey* 3.293; 5.412). Similarly, the term "wall" (*teichos*) occurs in Homer (e.g. *Odyssey* 7.9; 15.4720) but it is not described as "smooth."

[25] F. M. Cross, Jr., "Aspects of Samaritan and Jewish History in Late Persian and Hellenistic Times," *HTR* 59 (1966) 201–11.

Jacoby, F. (ed.). *Die Fragmente der griechischen Historiker*. Leiden, 1958; vol. 3C, part 2, no. 732, pp. 692–94. (Convenient, critical collection of the fragments of Theodotus.)

Schlatter, A. *Geschichte Israels*. Stuttgart, 1925³; p. 199. (Proposed that Theodotus was a Jewish author.)

Schürer, E. *History of the Jewish People*. Edinburgh, 1886²; div. 2, vol. 3, pp. 224f. (Draws upon Freudenthal and further reinforces hypothesis of Theodotus as a Samaritan.)

Ziegler, K. *Das Hellenistische Epos: Ein Vergessenes Kapitel Griechischer Dichtung*. Berlin, 1934. (Classic study of the revival of epic poetry in the hellenistic period which is the context out of which Theodotus emerges.)

TRANSLATION

Fragment 1 *Alexander Polyhistor, "On the Jews," in Eusebius, "Praeparatio Evangelica" 9.22.1:*

Theodotus[a] in *On the Jews*[b] says that Shechem took its name from Shechem, the son of Hermes,[c] for he also founded the city. He says that the city is situated in the land of the Jews[d] in the following manner:

> Thus the land was good and grazed upon by goats and well watered. There was neither a long path for those entering the city from the field nor even leafy woods for the weary. Instead, very close by the city appear two steep mountains, filled with grass and woods.[e] Between the two of them a narrow path is cut.[f] On one side[g] the bustling Shechem appears, a sacred town, built under (i.e. the mountain) as a base;[h] there was a smooth wall[i] around the town; and the wall for defense up above ran in under the foot of the mountain.[j]

Fragment 1 (22.1) a. The possible testimonium to Theodotus is as follows. Josephus, *Apion* 1.23, 215f.: "However, our antiquity is sufficiently established by the Egyptian, Chaldaean, and Phoenician records, not to mention the numerous Greek historians. In addition to those already cited, Theophilus, Theodotus, Mnaseas, Aristophanes, Hermogenes, Euhemerus, Conon, Zopyrion, and, may be, many more—for my reading has not been exhaustive—have made more than a passing allusion to us" (translator H. St. J. Thackeray; LCL vol. 1, p. 251).

b. Some scholars who consider Theodotus to be a Samaritan question whether this title is correct for the poem; see the introduction.

c. In the later Fs., Theodotus identifies the head of the tribe from Gen 34 as Emôr and his son as Sychem. In this paraphrase by Alexander Polyhistor the father of the founder of the city is identified as Ermou and the founder as Sikimiou (both in the genitive case); the name of the city is then spelled as Sikima. Either the text is corrupt here or Alexander Polyhistor has altered his source or Theodotus has deliberately spelled the names in this manner. It seems more likely that Theodotus has exploited the difference in spelling between the name of the city and the name of the person in Gen 34 (a contemporary of Jacob) to separate the two figures Sikimios and Sychem from one another. Thus, in accord with other hellenistic regional epics, he can refer back prior to the time of Jacob to the founding of the city and to Sikimios as the founder of Sikima. By separating the two figures and by proposing Sikimios as the founder rather than Sychem, Theodotus also avoids the awkward situation that in Gen 34 the ruler is the father, Emôr, rather than the eponymous founder, i.e. Sychem. The name of the son could have been scanned Sīkimios to fit epic meter. Further, it seems likely that the name Hamor (Emôr) suggested the name Hermes (Ermēs) as the name of the founder's father. Thereby the pagan god Hermes would presumably be treated as simply a man by this Jewish author; such a treatment would have appropriately arisen from the euhemeristic impulse of the hellenistic period. Further, it is precisely at the point of the beginning of a city that one would expect an association with mythology, and such was the case in the regional epic poetry of the

hellenistic period. See, for example, the fragments of Rhianus of Crete in Jacoby, *FGH*, vol. 3A, no. 265, pp. 64–69, and the discussion by K. Ziegler, *Das Hellenistische Epos: Ein Vergessenes Kapitel Griechischer Dichtung* (Berlin, 1934) pp. 11–21.

d. There is a textual problem here. The text reads *en tē peri Ioudaiōn*. As it stands, the text could be understood as "in the (book) *On the Jews*." Or, if this phrase is merely a repetition of the phrase "in *On the Jews*" in the opening sentence, then the *tē* would need to be emended to *tō*. A third possibility, adopted by the editor Mras, is that the *peri* should be deleted as a mistaken repetition of the term in the opening sentence and that the phrase be understood as "in the (land) of the Jews." We follow the emendation of Mras.

e. Mount Ebal and Mount Gerizim.

f. The text has been emended by the removal of the term *aulōpis*, which is extra beyond the meter of the line and probably a later gloss.

g. The consistent perspective from which the entire scene is described seems to be the encampment of Jacob before Shechem as in Gen 33:18–20. The phrase *en d heterōthi* has been translated as "on one side." In Homer *heterōthi* is used alone or in conjunction with *enthen*. It means "on the other side" when used in conjunction with *enthen*. When used alone, *heterōthi* can mean "elsewhere" or "in another quarter" or—more freely translated—"on one side." Since *heterōthi* is not used by Theodotus in conjunction with *enthen*, this latter meaning must be intended by him; the addition of the preposition *en* merely strengthens the meaning. See R. J. Cunliffe, *A Lexikon of the Homeric Dialect* (London, 1924) p. 165.

h. The phrase "built under as a base" is in accord with the fact that Shechem was situated on a mound or shoulder at the base of Mount Ebal, but it should be noted that the use of *riza* in an extended sense to indicate the root or foundation of a mountain is a post-Homeric development.

i. Archaeological excavations have uncovered the remains of this city wall. It was well taken care of (i.e. smooth) from the time of Alexander the Great to the first half of the second century B.C but was disrupted thereafter. See the introduction.

j. The phrase "up above" seems to refer to the fact that Shechem was *above* the plain where Jacob was encamped. An alternate interpretation might

Fragment 2 *Alexander Polyhistor, "On the Jews," in Eusebius, "Praeparatio Evangelica" 9.22.2:*

Next he says that it was occupied by the Hebrews when Hamor was ruling, for Hamor begot a son Sychem. He says,

> O stranger, Jacob came as a shepherd[a] to the broad city of Shechem; and over their kinsmen Hamor was chief with his son Sychem, a very stubborn[b] pair.

Gen 33:18–20

Fragment 3 *Alexander Polyhistor, "On the Jews," in Eusebius, "Praeparatio Evangelica" 9.22.3:*

Then concerning Jacob and his arrival in Mesopotamia and his marriage with his two wives and the birth of his children and his arrival from Mesopotamia to Shechem, he said,

> Jacob came to well-grazed Syria[a] and left behind[b] the broad stream of the Euphrates, a turbulent river. For he had come there when he left the sharp rebuke of his own brother. Laban, who was his cousin and then alone ruled over Syria since he was of [native] blood,[c] graciously received him into his house. He agreed to and promised the marriage of his youngest daughter to him. However, he did not at all aim that this should be but, rather, contrived some trick. He sent Leah, who was her older sister, to the man for his bed. In any case, it did not remain hidden to him; rather, he understood the mischievousness and received the other maiden. He was mated with both, who were his kinfolk. To him there were born eleven sons who were exceedingly wise in mind and a daughter, Dinah, who had a beautiful form, an admirable[d] frame, and a noble spirit.

cf. Gen 28:6
Gen 31:21

Gen 27:41–45

Gen 29:13–30

Fragment 4 *Alexander Polyhistor, "On the Jews," in Eusebius, "Praeparatio Evangelica" 9.22.4–6:*

He says that from the Euphrates Jacob came into Shechem to Hamor.[a] He

Gen 33:18–20

suggest that it was a *high* wall for defense that ran around (the town). Our translation rests on a slight emendation of the text, the introduction of the "and" (*d*) after the term for "the foot of the mountain" (*hypōreian*).

Fragment 2 (22.2) a. There are difficulties in the first line. The identities of the speaker and the addressee are unclear. Such a dialogue setting with a stranger is found in Homer; e.g. Athene speaks to a mortal (*Odyssey* 8.195) or some person speaks to Odysseus (*Odyssey* 6.255), but the form of the term in Homer is *xeinos*, rather than *xenos* as here. Further, the text must be emended from *poimenothi* to *poimenophi* in order to be translated as "as a shepherd" (cf. Gen 26:20). The corruption may be more deep-seated.

b. The MSS read *atēree*, "improvident," rather than *ateiree*, "stubborn." The term "improvident" may seem more appropriate for Hamor and Sychem in view of their eventual death and because of their willingness to undergo circumcision. However, "stubborn" is also appropriate in view of their determination to obtain Dinah in marriage and is to be preferred since *atēree*, "improvident," is not found in Homer or the later epic poets, whereas *ateiree*, "stubborn," is properly Homeric.

Fragment 3 (22.3) a. The use of the term Syria here and later in this fragment seems to be a shortening of the name "Mesopotamia of Syria" (e.g. LXX Gen 33:18). The shortening of the name would have been for the sake of Homeric meter.

b. The reference here seems to be to Jacob's crossing of the Euphrates before coming to Laban's

dwelling; cf. Gen 28:6 and 31:21. Such a usage is Homeric; see *Odyssey* 7.317 and 13.1.

c. The text appears to be corrupt here. The MSS read *neēgenēs*, "newborn," which is the proper epic form but which does not fit the meter of the line. The editor Mras has adopted the emendation to *neiēgenēs*, "newborn," which fits the meter but whose form is non-epic and whose meaning is not clearly appropriate. The emendation to *xynēgenēs*, "kindred," is possible, but the clause would then be redundant, since the preceding line states that he was a "cousin to him." A possible emendation is *gaiēgenēs*, "from the land," i.e. native; the clause would then explain why Laban ruled over Syria.

d. The emendation of *epiprepton*, "conspicuous," to *epistrepton*, "admirable," which has been adopted by Mras, has been followed.

Fragment 4 (22.4–6) a. In this paragraph Alexander Polyhistor paraphrases the poetry of Theodotus. The length of the poetic material cannot be determined, but the subject matter derives from Gen 34. In contrast with Gen 34 it is noticeable that there is no elaboration in the paraphrase of Shechem's love for Dinah or of his offer to give or do anything in order to obtain her as his wife. Absent also is the motif of the anger of the sons of Jacob when they heard of the deed and their decision to deal deceitfully with the Shechemites. The discussion between Hamor and the sons of Jacob about the merging of their respective peoples in terms of marriage, sharing of the land, and trade is also omitted. It is impossible to know with

welcomed him and gave him a certain portion of the land.[b] Jacob himself tilled the land; his sons, eleven in number, herded sheep; and his daughter, Dinah, and his wives worked with wool. And Dinah, still a virgin, came into Shechem when there was a festival,[c] since she wished to see the city. But when Sychem the son of Hamor saw her, he loved her; and after seizing her as his own, he carried her off and ravished her. Then, coming back again with his father to Jacob, he asked for her in the partnership of marriage. Jacob said that he would not give her until all the inhabitants of Shechem were circumcised and became Jews.[d] Hamor said that he would persuade them. Concerning the necessity of their being circumcised, Jacob says,[e]

Gen 34:1–12

> For this is not allowed to Hebrews to bring sons-in-law or daughters-in-law into their house from elsewhere but, rather, whoever boasts[f] that he is of the same race.

Gen 34:13–17

Fragment 5 *Alexander Polyhistor, "On the Jews," in Eusebius, "Praeparatio Evangelica" 9.22.7:*

Then, a little below he (i.e. Jacob) says concerning circumcision,[a]

> Once (God) himself, when he led the noble Abraham out of his native land, from heaven called upon the man and all his family to strip off the flesh (i.e. the foreskin), and therefore he accomplished it. The command remains unshaken, since God himself spoke it.

Gen 17:9–27

Fragment 6 *Alexander Polyhistor, "On the Jews," in Eusebius, "Praeparatio Evangelica" 9.22.8–9:*

As Hamor went into the city and encouraged his subjects to be circumcised,[a] one of the sons of Jacob—Simeon by name—decided to kill Hamor and Sychem,[b] since he was unwilling to bear in a civil manner the violent attack upon his sister.[c] When he had decided this, he shared it with his brother. Seizing him, he urged him to agree to the act by producing an oracle which said that God

Gen 34:18–24
Gen 34:25

---

certainty whether Theodotus included these themes in his poem or not, since Alexander Polyhistor may simply have omitted them (but see below). The emphasis on circumcision in the paraphrase and in the poetry has its roots in the biblical account.

b. In Gen 33:19 Jacob purchases the land from the sons of Hamor rather than receiving it as a gift.

c. There is no reference in Gen to a festival; Dinah simply wanted to see the city there. Josephus also refers to a feast in the city and may derive his reference from Theodotus or from common exegetical tradition; see *Ant* 1.21.1, 337.

d. For the term "to become Jews" or "to Judaize" (*ioudaizein*), see LXX Esther 8:17.

e. In Gen 34:14–17 it is the sons of Jacob who speak, and in the LXX it is Simeon and Levi, whereas in Theodotus, as reported by Alexander, it is Jacob. By having Jacob speak about circumcision, Theodotus would remove the appearance of treachery on the part of the sons of Jacob in encouraging circumcision while plotting to kill the Shechemites.

f. Since the verb *exeuchomai*, "to boast aloud," does not occur in Homer, we should probably read here two words: the preposition *ex*, "of," and the verb *euchomai*, "to boast aloud," although the editor Mras has preferred the verb *exeuchomai*.

Fragment 5 (22.7) a. Alexander Polyhistor has apparently omitted several ll. at this point. In those ll. Theodotus probably pointed to the law of circumcision as the reason why the Hebrews were not allowed to intermarry with other ethnic groups.

In the ll. of paragraph 7 as in paragraph 6 Jacob is evidently intended as the speaker.

Fragment 6 (22.8–9) a. In this paragraph Alexander Polyhistor again summarizes the poem of Theodotus. Two important items, which are present in Gen 34 but missing in the paraphrase of Alexander, are that the males of Shechem were in fact circumcised and that Simeon and Levi attacked the city while they were recovering. It is possible that Theodotus included these motifs and that Alexander merely omitted them. However, the embarrassment of later Jewish tradition over the circumcision and then slaughter of the Shechemites makes it possible that Theodotus excluded these motifs. Jub 30 and Josephus, *Ant* 1.21.1, 337–40 omit the actual circumcision; in TLevi 6:3 Levi counsels against circumcising the Shechemites but then records that they were in fact circumcised (6.6). See, further, the introduction.

b. In Gen 34:13 the sons of Jacob speak with Hamor treacherously by demanding circumcision while plotting the slaughter. Theodotus avoids the treachery by having Jacob encourage circumcision (F. 5) and by having Simeon decide by himself to kill the Shechemites.

c. In Gen 34:25 both Simeon and Levi are referred to, but neither is given emphasis. In Jub 30 the role of Levi is emphasized and also the derivation of the priesthood and the Levites from him because of his slaughter of the Shechemites (30:17–22). Also in TLevi 5f. the role of Levi is given greater prominence; he receives the heavenly

had determined[d] to give ten peoples[e] to the descendants of Abraham. Simeon says the following to Levi:

> For I have indeed learned the word from God, for of old he said that he would give ten peoples to the children of Abraham.

Fragment 7 *Alexander Polyhistor, "On the Jews," in Eusebius, "Praeparatio Evangelica" 9.22.9:*
God sent this thought into them because those in Shechem were impious. He (i.e. Theodotus) says,

> God smote the inhabitants of Shechem, for they did not honor whoever came to them, whether evil or noble.[a] Nor did they determine rights or laws throughout the city. Rather, deadly works were their care.[b]

Fragment 8 *Alexander Polyhistor, "On the Jews," in Eusebius, "Praeparatio Evangelica 9.22.10–12:*
Therefore, Levi and Simeon came fully armed into the city. At first they slew those they happened to meet, and then they killed Hamor and Sychem. Concerning their slaying, he says the following:[a] Gen 34:25f.

> Thus then Simeon rushed upon Hamor himself and struck him upon the head; he seized his throat in his left hand and then let it go still gasping its last breath,[b] since there was another task to do. At that time Levi,[c] also irresistible in might, seized Sychem by the hair; the latter grasped his knees and raged unspeakably. Levi struck the middle of his collarbone; the sharp sword entered his inward parts through the chest; and his life thereupon[d] left his bodily frame. When the other brothers learned of their deed, they assisted them and Gen 34:26–29 pillaged the city; and after rescuing their sister, they carried her off with the prisoners to their father's quarters.

command to slay the Shechemites (5:1–5), and he kills Sychem first, before Simeon attacks Hamor (6:4). The emphasis upon Levi in these two documents probably indicates their origin in priestly or Levitical circles. Here in Theodotus it is Simeon who takes the initiative (see also Jdt 9:2). Theodotus, then, does not represent a sympathy for the priestly or Levitical group.

d. Later Jewish tradition was evidently concerned to show that the killing of the Shechemites was not simply an act of revenge but was in accord with the will of God. See Jdt 9:2; Jub 30:6f.; and TLevi 5:1–5 and 6:8, 11.

e. The reference to give ten peoples to the descendants of Abraham is found in Gen 15:18–21. Freudenthal (*Alexander Polyhistor*, pp. 99f.) was unaware of the biblical reference and thus suggested that the notion was related to the idea of the ten lost tribes of Israel; this suggestion seems unnecessary.

Fragment 7 (22.9) a. Gen 34 has no mention of the impiety of the Shechemites. Theodotus' charge that the Shechemites "did not honor whoever came to them, whether evil or noble," is shared by TLevi 6:8–10, where it is charged that the Shechemites also sought to attack Sarah and Rebecca, that they persecuted Abraham when he was a stranger, and that they so acted against all strangers. To some extent the motivation for this charge may be to exculpate the sons of Jacob from

merely seeming to have performed an act of revenge.

b. The charges against the Shechemites are further specified in Homeric language as not determining "rights or laws" and caring for "deadly works"; see *Odyssey* 9.215 and *Iliad* 1:518.

Fragment 8 (22.10–12) a. The following lines of poetry expand in vivid, Homeric, descriptive language the brief notice of the event in Gen 34:25f.

b. Since the Homeric form of the verb "to gasp" is *aspairō* rather than *spairō*, the text should probably be emended from *eti spairousan* to *et aspairousan*.

c. Gen 34:25f. does not specify which of the sons of Jacob slew Hamor and which slew Sychem. In accord with TLevi 6:4, Theodotus states that it is Simeon who slays Hamor and Levi who slays Sychem. In contrast to Theodotus, however, TLevi has Levi slay Sychem first and then Simeon slay Hamor. Again, the emphasis on Levi in TLevi probably indicates a priestly or Levitical origin for the testament, and the contrary emphasis on Simeon in Theodotus probably indicates a different origin or sympathy; see F. 6.

d. The MSS read *authis*, "again"; the editor Mras has adopted the emendation *euthys*, "immediately." The more appropriate emendation seems to be to the epic form *authi*, "forthwith," i.e. thereupon. See *Iliad* 5.296.

ORPHICA

(Second Century B.C.–First Century A.D.)

A NEW TRANSLATION AND INTRODUCTION

BY M. LAFARGUE

This piece, written in archaizing Greek, represents itself to be esoteric instructions given by Orpheus to his son and pupil Musaeus. It has long been recognized as a Jewish work, rather than a part of the legitimate Orphic Hymns, both because of its content and because Eusebius claimed to have found it cited in the works of a Jewish theologian, Aristobulus. The third-century pseudo-Justinian *De Monarchia* cites it under the title "Diathēkai," i.e. the "Testament" of Orpheus, though it has little in common with other "Testaments" from Jewish literature of the same period.

Texts

The textual tradition is quite complex. There are at least two major recensions of the hymn, differing in numerous and very significant points. The main witnesses are as follows: (a) a short version (J) of twenty-one hexameters, found in two third-century works falsely attributed to Justin Martyr (*De Monarchia*, ch. 2, and *Cohortatio ad Gentiles*, ch. 15)[1]; (b) a long version (E) of forty-one hexameters, found in the *Praeparatio Evangelica* (13.12.5)[2] of Eusebius (A.D. 263–340); (c) numerous short quotations in the *Stromata* and *Protrepticus* of Clement of Alexandria (A.D. 150–215), one quotation (C²) in agreement with E, the others (C¹) agreeing mostly with J but with a few E readings also[3]; (d) a fifth-century self-styled "Theosophical" text (T),[4] containing all the lines found elsewhere, agreeing largely with E but sometimes agreeing with J against E and having many unique readings of its own.

Several hypotheses are possible as to lines of transmission that could explain this state of affairs. Earlier commentators unanimously considered J to be original and E and T to be the result of interpolations and corruptions. This thesis, however, was based on the alleged incoherence of E and T. Comparison with other esoteric works of the same period show that E and T can be read as intelligent and unified compositions. In the light of this it seems more likely that J is a cleaned-up, orthodoxizing version of an originally longer text more

---

[1] In *Corpus Apologetorum Christianorum*, ed. J. C. T. Otto (Jena, 1879) vol. 3.

[2] Latest edition in Mras, GCS 43, 2.

[3] GCS, ed. O. Staehlin (Leipzig, 1906). The Clementine quotations that follow J (C¹) are

Protr 74.4–5	Ll. 1–9a (minus l. 2)	
Strom 5.123.1	Ll. 6–9a	
Strom 5.78.4	Ll. 10, 11b–12	
Protr 74.5	Ll. 10–12	
Strom 5.126.5	Ll. 13, 15	
Strom 5.78.5	Ll. 20, 22f.	
Strom 5.127.2	Ll. 34f.	

The quotation that follows E (C²) is

        Strom 5.123.2–124.1   Ll. 26–30, 32–39, 42–43a.

[4] Printed in H. Erbse, *Fragmente griechischer Theosophien* (Hamburg, 1941) pp. 167–201. Also in K. Buresch, *Klaros* (Leipzig, 1889) pp. 112–15.

adequately represented by E and T. Two hypotheses as to textual transmission then become possible.

First Hypothesis: E, C², and T are descendants of a common prototype, a long version (L). J and C¹ are descendants of another prototype, a short version (S).

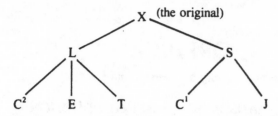

Second Hypothesis: E and C² are descendants of something very close to the original. J is a descendant of a shortened version of this original. T, and probably also C¹, are conflated texts, combining readings from the original and the shortened version.

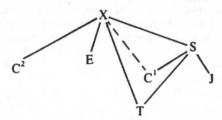

The translation below contains both a short version (based primarily on J) and a long version (based on the best readings from E and T); also indicated are the points at which the two different hypotheses yield substantive differences in the text.[5]

Date

There is no reason to doubt Eusebius' assertion that he found this hymn quoted in a work by Aristobulus; hence a probable date for the E version of the work is sometime between 150 B.C. and A.D. 50, depending on the date one assigns to Aristobulus. [A. Yarbo Collins dates his work to 155–145 B.C.; see her contribution herein. —J.H.C.] The J and C¹ forms must likewise antedate Clement and Pseudo-Justin.

Theological importance

In the shorter version (J), one finds familiar themes of hellenistic Jewish theology: the oneness of God, who is the invisible creator and ruler of everything and who has some good purpose for the evils he brings upon people.

In the longer version the most striking difference is the statement that Moses (or Abraham), alone of men, has "seen God," and this through his knowledge of astrology (ll. 25–29) and probably a heavenly ascent (l. 30). Following this statement is either a description of Moses' apotheosis (using OT images of God) or a description of Moses' divine vision (ll. 32–39). Lines 10–16a of this version probably represent a particular interpretation of a scriptural assertion of monotheism, the two halves of which open and close the section.

---

[5] The two hypotheses about the text tradition are relevant principally in those cases in which J and T agree over against E. On the first hypothesis, this is evidence that the J and T reading is more likely original (X). On the second hypothesis, it only means that T is copying from the short version at this point rather than from the long one. The only case in which this makes a significant difference theologically is l. 12 (see textual notes).

The interpretation apparently combats a dualistic view which would posit, besides a "good" God, also a malicious God responsible for "turning good things into evil." It rather solves the problem of evil in the world by saying that there is one God who is both transcendent and immanent (ll. 10f.) and present in "evil" (i.e. suffering) as well as in good (ll. 13–15). Both Jewish and Orphic traditions are included in this version as divine revelation, though the latter have a decisively inferior place (ll. 17–21; ll. 1 and 39 are Orphic sayings). E (not T) makes a distinction between two levels of consciousness, *psyche* and *nous*, the latter of which alone is capable of seeing God. It is possible also that the "double law" of line 41 refers to two senses of Scriptures. Finally, this version closes with an admonition to secrecy and meditation on the secret revelation given in the hymn. This admonition matches the framework of esoteric instruction given also in the first lines. In view of the unusual contents of this version, this may in some way reflect the spirit in which some Jewish group at the time actually understood the ideas in the hymn, though it may also be that this is simply a propaganda attempt to represent Orpheus treating Jewish themes as esoteric secrets.

Relation to canonical books

If lines 25–39 refer to Moses' apotheosis, they form a striking parallel to the hymn fragment in Phil 2:6–11. The means to the attainment of divine status of course differ (the crucifixion vs. mystical vision via the study of astrology). But both hymns picture the newly achieved status in phrases taken from Old Testament descriptions of God.

Relation to apocryphal books

In 3 Enoch, chapters 6–16, Enoch is enthroned as a "lesser Yahweh" following a heavenly ascent. Likewise in a play of Ezekiel the Tragedian (see Eusebius, *PrEv* 9:28 and the translation in the present vol.), we read how Moses was enthroned in heaven and the stars came to serve him. (These are of course only parallels if ll. 32–39 are taken to refer to Moses rather than God.)

Cultural importance

Depending on how the "mystery" framework of the hymn is understood, the hymn may be an important witness to the beginnings of Jewish mysticism. As to the influence of the hymn on subsequent cultural history, its main importance is its preservation and diffusion by Christian apologists. In the words of K. Ziegler, this hymn "gave Christians a good opinion of Orpheus and made him look like an early preacher of salvation . . . and brought about his acceptance in early Christian art."[6]

---

[6] K. Ziegler, "Orphische Dichtung," Pauly-Wissowa 18.2, col. 1399.

SELECT BIBLIOGRAPHY

Charlesworth, *PMR*, pp. 167f.
Delling, *Bibliographie*, pp. 53–55.
Denis, *Introduction*, pp. 223–38.

Elter, A. *De gnomologiorum graecorum historia*. Bonn, 1897; cols. 154–84. (An attempt to trace intermediary recensions between J (regarded as original) and E, by means of Clement's quotations.)
Georgi, D. *Die Gegner des Paulus in 2. Corintherbrief*. Neukirchen-Vluyn, 1964; pp. 73–76. (The first critical treatment to try to understand the longer version (E) as a coherent whole.)
Lafargue, M. "The Jewish Orpheus," *Society of Biblical Literature 1978 Seminar Papers*, ed. P. Achtemeier; vol. 2, pp. 137–44. (Proceeds from Georgi's position, and argues in detail for many of the interpretations given in the translation and nn. here.)
Lobeck, C. A. *Aglaophamus*. Königsberg, 1829; vol. 1, pp. 438–48. (One of the earliest critical treatments of the hymn.)
Walter, N. *Der Thoraausleger Aristobulos*. TU 86; Berlin, 1964; pp. 103–15, 202–61. (The most recent and thorough attempt to support and refine Elter's position, this work contains a good summary of previous scholarship on the hymn.)

THE LONG VERSION (E and T)

1 I will sing for those for whom it is lawful, but you uninitiate, close your doors,[a]
2 Charged under the laws of the Righteous ones, for the Divine has legislated[b]
3 For all alike. But you, son of the light-bearing moon,
4 Musaeus, listen, for I proclaim the Truth.
5 Let not what you formerly felt lose for you a happy eternity,[c]
6 But look to the divine word, study it closely,
7 [So] guiding your heart, that knowing vessel. Set out firmly
8 On the path, and look only at the undying shaper of the universe.
9 There is an ancient saying about him:
10 "He is one"—self-completing, and all things completed by him,   Deut 6:4
11 In them he himself circulates. But no one has seen him
12 With the souls mortals have, he is seen [only] by Mind.[d]
13 He does not take good things and make them into evil
14 For people, but he comes in company with love and hate,[e]
15 "And war and plague and weeping pain"—[f]
16 "And there is no other." You would understand everything   Isa 45:5
17 If you were to see him. But before that, here on earth, sometimes,[g]
18 My son, I will point it out to you, whenever I notice his footsteps,
19 And the strong hand of the mighty God.
20 But I do not see him, because around [him] a cloud is set up,
21 A thin one for me, but tenfold for all [other] people.
22 For all mortals have mortal pupils in their eyes,
23 [Too] small, since flesh and bones have produced them,
24 [Too] weak to see Zeus, the ruler of all.[h]
25 And no one has seen the ruler of mortal men,
26 Except a certain unique man, an offshoot from far back of the race
27 Of the Chaldeans. For he was knowledgeable about the path of the Star,[i]
28 And how the movement of the Sphere goes around the earth,
29 Both in circular fashion, but each on its own axis.
30 He rides in spirit through the air and through the water[j]
31 Of the stream. A comet makes manifest these events—he had a mighty birth.[k]   Mt 2:2

The Long Version:

a. "You uninitiate . . . doors," a formula probably taken from the mystery religions, found also in Plato (Symp. 218b). Further references are found in O. Kern, *Orphicorum fragmenta* (Berlin, 1922) p. 258.

b. "Righteous ones": probably initiates, using *dikaios* in the hellenistic Jewish sense. One could also, however, understand "laws about the right things."

c. Lit. "What formerly appeared in your breast."

d. "With the souls . . . by Mind": only in E. According to the first hypothesis (see above under "Text") this is an interpolation, since T here agrees with J: "but he sees everything." T repeats l. 20 following this l., which is surely not original, since it makes sense there but not here.

e. T and the MSS of E vary here. A different reading, with a slight emendation, would be "but love and hate, and war . . . serve him."

f. Quoted from SibOr 3.603, or a common source.

g. "Before that," i.e. before making the heavenly journey and seeing God.

h. E is missing ll. 22–24. T has misplaced l. 21, putting it after l. 24 (in the order 20, 22–24, 21), where it makes no sense. The translation of l. 21 given here is based on C. A. Lobeck's emendation of *loipon* to *lepton* ("thin"), and of E's *stasin* to T's *pasin* ("all").

i. Possibly Abraham is meant here. But Philo (*Vit Mos* 5) thinks also of Moses as a Chaldean schooled in astronomy.

j. The MSS vary here. One could also read: "He rides the winds . . ." or "He [God] guides the winds . . ."

k. This l. is difficult to make sense of and the translation here is conjectural. I take l. 30 to be a description of a heavenly ascent, and then the comet here to be a heavenly portent signaling its cosmic importance. "Mighty birth" is a translation of *iphi genēthe*, a play on the name Iphigeneia ("born mighty"), a reference to an initiatory "rebirth" following the heavenly journey. Others emend with Stephanus to *iphigenētou*, "a mighty-born flame of fire flashes up." This, together with l. 30, could then be a reference to the Chaldean's knowledge of the cosmos or his vision of God. T

32 Yes he after this is established in the great heaven[l]
33 On a golden throne. He stands with his feet on the earth.   Isa 66:1
34 He stretches out his right hand to the ends of the ocean.
35 The foundation of the mountains trembles within at [his] anger,   Ps 18:8
36 And the depths of the gray sparkling sea.[m]
37 They cannot endure the mighty power. He is entirely
38 Heavenly, and he brings everything to completion on earth,
39 Being "the beginning, the middle, and the end,"[n]   Rev 1:8
40 As the saying of the ancients, as the one water-born[o] has described it,
41 The one who received [revelations] from God in aphorisms, in the form of a
   double law.[p]
42 It is unlawful to say anything else. My body is trembling.
43 In Mind, from above,[q] he rules over everything according to an order,
44 My son, approach him with your Mind,
45 And do not betray, but guard the divine message in your heart.[r]

THE SHORT VERSION (J and C[1])

1 I will sing for those for whom it is lawful, but you uninitiate, close your doors,
3 All alike. But you, son of the light-bearing moon,
4 Musaeus, listen, for I proclaim the Truth.
5 Let not what you formerly felt lose for you a happy eternity,
6 But look to the divine word, study it closely,
7 [So] guiding your heart, that knowing vessel. Set out firmly
8 On the path, and look only at the master of the universe.[a]
10 He is one, self-generating; all things are brought forth generated from this one,[b]
11 And among them he is superior.[c] And no one
12 Of mortal men has seen him, but he sees all.
13 Out of goodness he brings evil upon mortals,
15 "And chilling war and weeping pain,"
16 And there is no other besides the great king.
20 But I do not see him, because around [him] a cloud is set up.
22 For all mortals have mortal pupils in their eyes,

does not have *iphi genēthe*, but *diaphengea pantē* "[flames of fire] shining forth everywhere."

l. Ll. 32–39 may be a description of the Chaldean's apotheosis or of his divine vision. In the latter case "hereafter" (*autis*) should be changed to "in turn" in l. 32.

m. Lacking in E.

n. Plato (*Laws* 715e) refers to this as an "ancient saying." References to further occurrences are to be found in E. Lohmeyer, *Die Offenbarung des Johannes* (Tübingen, 1953) p. 168.

o. "Water-born": an easy emendation of *hylogenēs* to *hydogenēs* (or *hydrogenēs*), understanding it as a reference to Moses' experience in the basket on the Nile.

p. "Double law": perhaps a reference to two levels of meaning (exoteric/esoteric) in Scripture. It could also be simply a reference to the two tablets of the Law.

q. "My body . . . from above": Punctuating differently and taking T's text with a slight emendation, one could read, "I tremble strongly in [my] mind. From above . . ." The "order" in l. 43

may refer to the sequence to be followed in esoteric instruction. This is very likely if we read l. 42a as a denial of the legitimacy of giving out further secrets at the present time. Compare the "order of the transmission (of esoteric instruction)" mentioned in The Discourse on the Eighth and the Ninth from Nag Hammadi (VI 52, 6).

r. E here is neither intelligible nor metrically correct. The translation is based on T, with an emendation in l. 45 of *apogos* (unintelligible) to *apodos* ("betray").

The Short Version:

a. C[1] has also the first word of l. 9 as it appears in the long version, showing that Clement's text probably had l. 9, though J does not.

b. One C[1] quotation has "self-completing" in the place of J's "self-generating." Another C[1] quotation agrees with J.

c. C[1] agrees with the long version in reading, "in them he circulates." According to the first hypothesis, this was the original reading in the short version as well.

[24] Too weak to see Zeus, the ruler of all.[d]
[32] And he is established in the bronze heaven
[33] On a golden throne. He rests with his feet upon the earth,
[34] And he stretches out his right hand everywhere, to the end of the ocean.
[35] And the great mountains tremble round about,[e]
[36] And the gray rivers and the depths of the blue sea.

---

d. C¹ has l. 23 (see the long version) and omits l. 24.

e. C¹ has the text in a different order here: 34, 35a, 33b.

DRAMA

EZEKIEL THE TRAGEDIAN

(Second Century B.C.)

A NEW TRANSLATION AND INTRODUCTION

BY R. G. ROBERTSON

The Exagōgē ("Leading Out") is a tragic drama from the hellenistic period which recounts the story of the exodus from Egypt. Its author, Ezekiel, is described as "the poet of tragedies" by Eusebius, citing Alexander Polyhistor (*PrEv* 9.28.1). Clement of Alexandria defines him more precisely as "the poet of Jewish tragedies" (*Strom* 1.23). All that remains of his literary efforts, however, are the fragments of this one work which are preserved in Eusebius and, in part, in Clement of Alexandria and in Pseudo-Eustathius. The content of Ezekiel's work is based upon the biblical narrative in Exodus 1–15 and centers around Moses as the principal figure. Ezekiel begins with the events surrounding Moses' birth and early childhood and then traces the story of his flight into the wilderness, his call by God to lead the Israelites out of Egypt, and the events surrounding the departure of the Israelites from Egypt. In the final act Ezekiel describes the scene at Elim (Ex 15:27) as Moses and the Israelites journey into the wilderness. At various points Ezekiel exercises literary license to create material which is extraneous to the biblical narrative (e.g. Moses' dream and its subsequent interpretation by his father-in-law). Ezekiel also introduces characters in his drama who are fictional in terms of the narrative of Exodus (e.g. the Egyptian survivor who relates the destruction of the Egyptian army in the Red Sea). Such variations are generally in accord, however, with the dictates of the dramatic form which Ezekiel has adopted. In brief, Ezekiel's work represents a synthesis of the content of the biblical narrative of Exodus with the literary form of Greek tragic drama.

Texts

The text of Ezekiel is extant only in fragments cited by Eusebius (*PrEv* 9, 28–29, edited by K. Mras, GCS 43, 1), Clement of Alexandria (*Strom* 1.23.155f., edited by O. Stählin, GCS 15, 2), and Pseudo-Eustathius (*Commentarius in Hexaemeron*, PG 18, 729). Various critical editions of Ezekiel's text are referred to in the notes that accompany the translation. A complete summary of the earlier editions is included in J. Wieneke, *Ezechielis Iudaei poetae Alexandrini* (Monasterii Westfalorum, 1931). The most recent modern edition of Ezekiel is that of B. Snell, *Tragicorum Graecorum Fragmenta* (Göttingen, 1971) vol. I, pp. 288–301.

Original language

Ezekiel's text is extant in iambic trimeter, the meter which was commonly used in Greek tragic drama, thus indicating clearly that Greek was the language in which the author wrote.

Date

The date of Ezekiel's composition has been the subject of widespread discussion. His knowledge of the Septuagint argues for a date subsequent to its translation, while the excerpts of his work in Alexander Polyhistor's *Concerning the Jews* (c. first century B.C.) indicate a date prior to the middle of the first century B.C. Kuiper argued for a date during or shortly after the time of Ptolemy Euergetes III (died 221 B.C.), based primarily on Ezekiel's description of the legendary phoenix bird.[1] Tacitus (*Annales* 6.28) refers to the excitement and the flurry of literature generated by the bird's arrival in Egypt around 34 A.D. Tacitus also quotes one of his sources to the effect that the bird had appeared previously during the reign of Pharaoh Sesostris and, at a later date, during the reign of Ptolemy Euergetes III. Kuiper argued that similar interest in the phoenix bird might well have evolved during the reign of Euergetes. Thus, the expected appearance of the phoenix during the reign of Ptolemy Euergetes III may have occasioned Ezekiel's use of the material here and might explain his efforts to link the bird's previous appearance in the reign of Sesostris with Jewish tradition; specifically with Moses, the great Jewish leader. Kuiper's argument is, however, highly speculative. All that one can safely say is that Ezekiel is familiar with a literary tradition concerning the phoenix bird, a fact which may tie him more closely to an Egyptian provenance because of the association of the bird with Egypt.

Perhaps a more significant indication of the actual situation from which Ezekiel's work evolved is the polemic found in the Letter of Aristeas 312–16, where the author addresses himself to the question of certain tragic poets who sought to adapt some of the incidents recorded in the Bible for their plays. The situation described here presupposes literature such as Ezekiel's Exagōgē.[2] This, combined with the fact that Ezekiel's work may have been based on a recension of the Septuagint text, seems to point to a somewhat later date than that suggested by Kuiper, perhaps the first part of the second century B.C. The lack of any other concrete evidence makes it difficult to be more precise in the matter of dating.

Provenance

The provenance of Ezekiel's work has been assigned by most scholars to Alexandria.[3] The choice of subject matter, the use of the Septuagint text, and, in particular, the wedding of these elements with the vehicle of Greek tragic drama are indeed compatible with such a milieu. Ezekiel utilized the models of Greek tragedy—Aeschylus, Sophocles, and Euripides—in the construction of his drama. Euripides, in particular, seems to have exercised a great deal of influence on Ezekiel's work.[4] This is perhaps consonant with the fact that during the third century B.C. Ptolemy Euergetes III is said to have acquired the official manuscripts of these authors from Athens and to have deposited them in the library at Alexandria. It was during this period also that Satyrus' *Life of Euripides* was written and circulated in Egypt.[5]

Nevertheless, there is very little in the way of direct evidence with which to link Ezekiel with Alexandria. It is entirely possible that his work could have been produced in some other center, such as Cyrene, in which the spirit of Hellenism had influenced Jewish culture.[6] While Alexandria remains as a most likely place of origin for Ezekiel and his work, it is the lack of direct evidence, rather than its abundance, which has allowed him to be characterized as "the Jewish poet of Alexandria"[7] without serious challenge.

Historical importance

The significance of Ezekiel's work lies both in its relationship to biblical tradition and in its testimony to the development of tragic drama in the hellenistic period.

[1] Kuiper, K. "Le Poète Juif Ezéchiel," *REJ* 46 (1903) 171.
[2] Cf. Trencsényi-Waldapfel, "Une tragédie grècque à sujet biblique," *Acta Orientalia Academiae Scientiarum* 2 (1952) 161.
[3] Kuiper (*REJ* 46, 174), took exception to this and believed Ezekiel to have been a Samaritan. In this he was followed (on somewhat different grounds) by J. B. Segal, *The Hebrew Passover from the Earliest Times* (London, 1963) p. 25.
[4] Numerous examples are cited by Kuiper, *REJ* 46 (1903) 48–73, 161–77; Wieneke, *Ezekielis Iudaei poetae Alexandrini* (Monasterii Westfalorum, 1931); and others in their commentaries.
[5] Cf. *Oxyrhynchus Papyri* IX, 1176.
[6] So, for example, J. Gutmann, *Hasifrut Hayehudith Hahellenistith* (Jerusalem, 1963) vol. 2, pp. 66–69.
[7] So Wieneke in the title of his work.

Striking parallels have long been noted between certain elements of Ezekiel's text and the Septuagint text of Exodus.[8] The evidence clearly indicates that Ezekiel was dependent on the Septuagint text. In all probability, he made use of an early recension of the Septuagint, which fact seems to be reflected by the existence of certain variant textual traditions within his text.[9] A more precise analysis of the nature of the Greek text on which Ezekiel based his work remains yet to be done.

The Exagōgē itself is the most extensive surviving example of hellenistic tragedy. It is a historical drama, but its title is derived neither from the leading character nor from the chorus. Tragedies based on historical events (e.g. Aeschylus' *Persians*), were rare during the classical period, although later works attributed to Theodectes, Moschion, Philiscus, and Lycophron indicate their rise in popularity during the hellenistic period. The recent discovery of the "Gyges" fragment (part of the tragic drama based on historical events in ancient Lydia) may also attest this phenomenon.[10]

A distinctive feature of Ezekiel's drama which separates it from the mainstream of classical Greek tragedy is the violation of the theoretical unity of time and place, a principle expressed by Aristotle (*Poetics* 1449b), who described the ideal tragedy as situated in one geographic location and occurring within a period of twenty-four hours. Although even Aeschylus and Sophocles did not always adhere to such unity, Ezekiel's apparent disregard of Aristotle's principle may be indicative of the changes that were taking place within tragic drama during the hellenistic period, particularly in the Alexandrian school of literature.

Was Ezekiel's work intended for the stage? It is impossible to answer this question with certainty. Most commentators have discussed the problem in some detail, and the general consensus has been that there is nothing in the drama as it now stands that would make it intrinsically impossible for it to be enacted on the stage.

Ezekiel's work conforms to the generally accepted pattern of a tragedy in five acts.[11] Although commentators disagree in some details, the fragments that remain can be easily broken down in a pattern similar to the following:

Act I   Scene 1—Moses' monologue
         Scene 2—Moses' dialogue with Sepphorah
Act II   Scene 1—Sepphorah's dialogue with Chus
         Scene 2—Moses' dream, and Jethro's interpretation
Act III Scene 1—Moses' dialogue with God
         Scene 2—Moses' instructions to the people[12]
Act IV   —Report of the Egyptian messenger
Act V   —Elim, and the report of the messengers to Moses.

Kappelmacher and others have argued for various arrangements to deal with the troublesome dialogue between Sepphorah and Chus (ll. 66–67), and additional scenes have been hypothesized to include Moses' marriage to Sepphorah (Act II), Moses and Aaron before Pharaoh (Act IV, Scene 1), and perhaps Moses' final reunion with Sepphorah (Act V, Scene 2).

The existence of a chorus has also been argued, although none of the lyric verses that might be attributed to a chorus have survived in the fragments. This is not surprising, however, in light of the particular interests of Alexander Polyhistor, Eusebius, and Clement. It is entirely possible that a chorus could have made its *parodos* ("entrance") immediately after the opening monologue when Moses noted the appearance of Sepphorah and her sisters. If, as Kappelmacher and others have suggested, there is a closing scene in which Moses and Sepphorah are reunited, then the chorus would have made its "exodus" at that

---

[8] The critical text of B. Snell offers an accurate comparison with the LXX of Ex. The commentary of Wieneke, which includes the text of Ex on facing pp. opposite that of Ezekiel, is sometimes in error.

[9] Cf., *infra*, n. on l. 2, passim.

[10] The text is published in *Oxyrhynchus Papyri* XXIII, 2382, with bibliography. A full discussion may be found in D. L. Page, *A New Chapter in the History of Greek Drama* (Cambridge, England, 1951). Additional bibliography is included in R. A. Pack, *The Greek and Latin Literary Texts from Greco-Roman Egypt* (Ann Arbor, 1967[2]) p. 97.

[11] In the early Gk. tragedians the number of acts was not fixed and was only formally established for drama in Horace, *Ars Poetica* 189, although the practice had become common since the rise of New Comedy in the fourth century B.C.

[12] Cf., *infra*, n. w2.

point. The idea of a chorus of Egyptians responding to the report of the Egyptian messenger is also possible in Act IV, as is a chorus of the Hebrew people in Act III, Scene 2.

The possibility that the play was intended for the stage is enhanced by the evidence which indicates that Ezekiel transformed certain material from the Exodus account which would have been virtually impossible to present upon the stage. The plagues, for example, have been completely relegated to a speech delivered by God to Moses. The crossing of the Red Sea is handled in true Aeschylean fashion by Ezekiel when, with dramatic irony, he dredges up a lone survivor from the Egyptian army who is able to recount the disaster. One further example is of great importance: that is, the specific statement made by God to Moses (l. 101) that it is impossible for him to be seen by Moses (and so, presumably, by the audience as well). Although it may not be possible to prove conclusively that Ezekiel consciously effected these modifications for the specific purpose of producing a piece suitable for the stage, nevertheless, there is nothing in the play that would make it technically impossible for dramatization.

Ezekiel's verse corresponds with that ordinarily found in the dialogue of tragic drama, iambic trimeter. It is only in recent years that this aspect of Ezekiel's work has received more serious attention. Wieneke's commentary marked a definite advance beyond the work of Kuiper and others who preceded him insofar as he sought to emend the text on the basis of metrical considerations. There is no doubt that the text—as preserved by Eusebius, Clement, and Pseudo-Eustathius, and the scribes who copied their works—has suffered corruption at a number of points. There is ample evidence, however, to suggest that Ezekiel was careful to employ the proper rules of metrics in his composition. B. Snell[13] and J. Strugnell[14] have demonstrated conclusively that Ezekiel was consistent in correctly applying the rules of metrics in his work. There is a marked affinity at this point between Ezekiel's verse and that of the later Euripides and his successors.

Translation

In order to preserve the somewhat archaic flavor of Ezekiel's verse, the English translation has been rendered metrically in iambic pentameter and in a manner which attempts to represent the technically correct, but often strained, language which Ezekiel employed. I am grateful to the editor for allowing an exception in this case to the usual norms followed in this volume, and to J. Strugnell and A. Nakis for their invaluable suggestions and assistance. While every effort has been made to follow the lines of Ezekiel's text with as exact a representation of the content of each line as might be possible in the English translation, metrical and grammatical considerations sometimes precluded this. In some cases, the footnotes indicate the slight rearrangement of the text that was made in the English translation. The translation is based upon the critical text of Mras. The texts of Kuiper, Wieneke, and Snell have been consulted throughout and noted accordingly in the footnotes. The standard numeration for Ezekiel's lines has also been followed in the translation.

---

[13] B. Snell, "Die Jamben in Ezechiels Moses-Drama," *Glotta* 44 (1966) 25–32.
[14] J. Strugnell, "Notes on the Text and Metre of Ezekiel the Tragedian's 'Exagoge.' " *HTR* 60 (1967) 449–57.

SELECT BIBLIOGRAPHY

Charlesworth, *PMR*, pp. 110f.
Delling, *Bibliographie*, p. 55.
Denis, *Introduction*, pp. 273–77.

Freyhan, M. "Ezechiel der Tragiker," *Jahrbuch für jüdische Geschichte und Literatur* 31 (1938) 46–83.
Kappelmacher, A. "Zur Tragödie der hellenistischen Zeit," *Wiener Studien* 44 (1924–25) 69–86.
Kraus, C. "Ezechiele Poeta Tragico," *Rivista di filologia e di istruzione classica* 96 (1968) 164–75.
Kuiper, K. "Le Poète Juif Ezéchiel," *REJ* 46 (1903) 48–73, 161–77.
Snell, B. "Die Jamben in Ezechiels Moses-Drama," *Glotta* 44 (1966) 25–32.
————. "Ezechiels Moses-Drama," *Antike und Abendland* 13 (1967) 150–64.
Strugnell, J. "Notes on the Text and Metre of Ezekiel the Tragedian's 'Exagoge,'" *HTR* 60 (1967) 449–57.
Trencsényi-Waldapfel, "Une tragédie grecque à sujet biblique," *Acta Orientalia Academiae Scientiarum* 2 (1952) 143–64.
Wieneke, J. *Ezechielis Iudaei poetae Alexandrini*. Monasterii Westfalorum, 1931.

Exagōgē

And with regard to Moses being exposed by his mother in the marsh, and being taken up and reared by the king's daughter, Ezekiel the tragic poet narrates the events, taking up the story from the beginning, when Jacob and those that were with him came into Egypt to Joseph.[a] Introducing Moses as the speaker, he says:

1 And when from Canaan Jacob did depart,	Gen 46:27
2 with threescore souls and ten[b] he did go down	
3 to Egypt's land; and there he[c] did beget	Ex 1:7
4 a host of people: suffering,[d] oppressed,	
5 ill-treated even to this very day	
6 by ruling powers and by wicked men.	
7 For Pharaoh, seeing how our race increased	Ex 1:9–11,14
8 in swarms, devised against us this grand scheme:	
9 he forced the men[e] to manufacture bricks	
10 for use in building lofty walls and towers;[f]	
11 thus with their toil he made his cities strong.	
12 He ordered next the Hebrew race to cast[g]	Ex 1:22
13 their infant boys into the river deep.	
14 At which point, she who bore me from her womb	Ex 2:2f.
15 did hide me for three months, as she declared.	
16 But when found out, she robed me and exposed[h]	

a. There seems to be no real reason to suppose, as some commentators have, that the opening ll. of the prologue are missing. (For *de* as an introductory particle, cf. Xenophon, *Cyropaedia* 4.5.23; Aeschylus, *Agamemnon* 717). The editorial statement by Alexander Polyhistor implies that Ezekiel's work commenced at the point where Jacob and his family entered Egypt. The text, as it has been preserved, corresponds in detail to the beginning of the narrative in Ex 1. Since the biblical text of Ex comprised Ezekiel's primary source, it may be assumed (with some degree of probability) that the existing text marks the beginning of the drama as it was originally written. A further indication of this lies in the fact that the prologue is comparable in length to similar material in Euripides, whose work Ezekiel may have utilized as a model.

b. Ezekiel's reading of "seventy" marks a significant departure from the text of the LXX, which reads "seventy-five," (Ex 1:5; cf. Gen 46:27; Acts 7:14). The reading "seventy" is attested in the biblical text primarily by the MT and the Samaritan Pentateuch (cf. Josephus, *Ant* 2.176). This and other instances in which Ezekiel's text seems to stand closer to the Heb. than to the LXX have led some scholars to conclude that Ezekiel may have used a Heb. text, either directly or as a means of correcting certain LXX readings. In l. 113, for example, Ezekiel reads *ouk eulogos*, "not eloquent," a more literal rendering of the Heb. and Samaritan *l'o 'iš d°barîm*, "not a man of words," which is rather loosely expressed by the LXX *ouk hikanos eimi*, "I am not sufficient," Ex 4:10. Similarly, in l. 140 (Gk.) Ezekiel reads *loimos*, "pestilence, plague," which seems to stand closer to the Heb. *deber kabēd*, "severe plague," than to the reading of the LXX, *thanatos megas sphodra*, "a very great death," Ex 9:3. In spite of these and other instances, however, in almost every case in which Ezekiel's text seems to stand closer to the Heb. text than to the LXX it is supported by significant textual witnesses within the LXX (frequently by marginal readings in the uncial manuscript F, and sometimes by Philo or Josephus). This suggests the possibility that Ezekiel's work may have been based on a text of the LXX which had undergone some revision in order to bring it into greater harmony with a changing Heb. textual tradition.

c. Cf. Strugnell, *HTR* 60 (1967) 455–56, who suggests emending to a plural form of the verb: "and there *they* did beget . . ."

d. Lit. "faring badly."

e. The construction of the Gk. text is difficult, with nothing in the ll. that follow which answers to *tous men*. Kuiper felt compelled to add an extra l. to the text at this point, drawing from parallel material in Josephus, *Ant* 2.203. The same sort of syntactical problem occurs later in Ezekiel's work (ll. 200, 205).

f. Lit. "for heavy building works." The reading of Clement and N², *oikodomiais*, is necessary on metrical grounds.

g. Or, perhaps, "to cast the infant boys of Hebrew descent . . ." The text is unclear; for a full discussion of the question, cf. Howard Jacobsen, "Ezekielos 12–13," *American Journal of Philology* 98 (1977), 415f. Jacobsen suggests emending *genei* to *genē*, thus bringing Ezekiel's text into closer correspondence with the tradition of Ex. The biblical text (Ex 1:22) is quite clear as to the fact that Pharaoh instructed the Egyptians to cast the male children of the Hebrews into the river. Another tradition, preserved in Jub 47:2 (and perhaps also in Acts 7:19), indicates that it may have been the Hebrews themselves who were instructed to throw their own children into the river. If one accepts these latter references as summary

17 me in the marsh hard by the river's edge;[i]
18 and Miriam, my sister[j], watched close by.   Ex 2:4f.
19 The sovereign's daughter, with her maidens, then
20 came down to bathe her limbs, as was her wont.[k]
21 And straightway seeing me,[l] she took me up:
22 she knew that I was of the Hebrew race.   Ex 2:6–8
23 My sister, running to the princess, said,
24 "Shall I quickly fetch this child a nurse
25 of Hebrew stock?" The princess pressed her on;
26 she came and told my mother, who with haste
27 did come herself, and took me in her arms.
28 The sovereign's daughter then said, "Woman, nurse   Ex 2:9
29 this child and I will render you a wage."
30 And she, the princess, named me "Moses,"[m] since   Ex 2:10
31 she took me from the river's soggy shore.

After other matters,[n] Ezekiel adds further information in his tragedy, introducing
Moses, who says:
32 And seeing that my infancy had passed,   Ex 2:9f.
33 my mother led me to the princess' rooms;
34 but first all things she did declare to me
35 pertaining to my father's God and race.[o]
36 Throughout my boyhood years the princess did,
37 for princely rearing and instruction apt,
38 provide all things, as though I were her own.[p]
39 The circle[q] of the days then being full,   Ex 2:11
40 I quit the royal house, impelled to deeds
41 by my own heart[r] and by the king's device.

and conflate statements of the instructions given
by Pharaoh, first to the Hebrew midwives and later
to the Egyptians, then the basis of this tradition in
the biblical account (Ex 1:15–22) is quite clear.

h. For this section, cf. Josephus, *Ant* 2.217–21.
The detail of the *thibin*, "ark" (cf. Ex 2:3), is
omitted by Ezekiel. He adds, however, a reference
to the *kosmos*, "ornamental robe," with which
Moses' mother clothed him. Ezekiel's use of the
term *hypexethēke*, translated here "she exposed,"
is significant for the drama. The motif of the
foundling who later rises to success and fame is a
familiar one in Gk. literature; cf. Richmond Lattimore, *Story Patterns in Greek Tragedy* (London,
1964), p. 74, n. 21.

i. Lit. "on the bank of the river in a deep bushy
marsh." Clement reads *bathy*, "deep," which
seems preferable to the reading of Eusebius, *dasy*,
"overgrown with bushes," which may have originated as a marginal gloss on *lasion*, "bushy."

j. *adelphē mou*, the emendation accepted by
most editors in place of *adelph' hēmōn*, which is
the reading of the MSS in the texts both of Eusebius
and of Clement.

k. Lit. "came down to cleanse her flesh with
washings." *Neon*, here translated adverbially, "as
was her wont," has sometimes been considered as
an adjective modifying "flesh." In this case, the
text would read: "youthful flesh."

l. The translation follows the text of Clement,
idousa m'euthys. Eusebius reads *idousa d'euthys*.

m. The introduction of the name of the principal
character is necessary for the benefit of the audience, particularly since it is not included in the
title of the play. Ezekiel follows closely the Heb.

etymology of Moses' name as it is preserved in
the Septuagint (Ex 2:10), over and against Josephus
(*Ant* 2.228) and Philo (*Vit Mos* 1.17), who adopt
an Egyptian etymology. The particular form of the
name, *Mōsēn*, is necessary here to fit the meter.
The reading of Clement, Mōysēn, must be excluded
on metrical grounds.

n. The difficulty with this editorial remark lies
in determining whether it should be attributed to
Eusebius or to Alexander Polyhistor. The grammatical sense of the statement seems to favor the
latter (cf., contra, Kraus, p. 164, n. 4). Scholars
have objected to this, however, on the ground that
the historical narrative of Ex does not allow for
any "other matters" at this point. Nevertheless, it
is entirely possible that Ezekiel may have amplified
his material here (as elsewhere), including a section
in which Moses was formally presented to Pharaoh
(cf. Josephus, *Ant* 2.232–37).

o. Lit. "my father's race and gifts of God."

p. The Septuagint states that Moses became *eis
huion* to Pharaoh's daughter (Ex 2:10). Ezekiel
suggests the theme which is fully developed at a
later time by Josephus, *Ant* 2.232, and Philo, *Vit
Mos* 1.19, to the effect that Moses was legally
adopted. Cf. Artapanus, *PrEv* 9.27.3, who hints
at this with the use of the term *hypobalesthai*.

q. The MSS read *kolpos*, "womb." The emendation which is followed here (*kyklos* for *kolpos*)
was first suggested by Kuiper.

r. This term, *thymos*, could also be translated
"anger" (cf. Jub 46:12), in which case it might
be inferred that at this point Moses had come to a
full realization of the conditions under which the
Israelites were enslaved by Pharaoh. This would

42 And first I saw men locked in strife, at odds,ˢ
43 Egyptian one, and one of Hebrew race.
44 And seeing them alone, with none about,   Ex 2:12
45 I saved my kinsman, but his foe I slew
46 and hid him in the sand,ᵗ that none might see
47 or, else, expose our homicidal act.
48 The next day, once again I saw two men: Ex 2:13–15
49 my kinsmen, they, each other pommeling.
50 I said, "Why strike one weaker than yourself?"ᵘ
51 Said he, "Who set you for a judge 'twixt us
52 or ruler in this place? Will you slay me
53 as that man yesterday?" And I, afraid,
54 said, "How, then, has this deed been brought to light?"
55 All this was soon reportedᵛ to the king,
56 upon which Pharaoh sought to take my life.
57 When such I heard, I fled beyond his reach,
58 and now I wander in a foreign land.

   Then concerning the daughters of Raguelʷ he adds:
59 But, lo! These seven maidens I espy!   Ex 2:16

   In response to his question as to who they might be, Sepphorah replies:
60 This land, O stranger, all bears Libya'sˣ name,

also correspond with the understanding of *tech-nasma basileōs* as "the king's device." *Technasma* is understood here as part of the compound subject of the verb with *thymos*. If, however, *technasma* were considered as an accusative belonging with *pros erga*, "to deeds," the pejorative sense disappears completely; the l. would then read: "Impelled by my heart to acts and deeds befitting a king." In any event, it is as though the audience was meant to realize that this is an important decision on Moses' part. Given the fact that he is the foundling who has been rescued (contrary to the realities of life, which predict that such a child will probably die), the dramatic theme demands that his star should rise. But even though the shape of the story may intimate the final end, there is still the element of choice whereby the hero may confirm or deny the destiny that lies before him. This theme is common in other Gk. tragedies (e.g. *Gyges* and Aeschylus' *Septem*) and was surely understood by the author of Heb. 11:24.

s. For "at odds" as a translation of *en cheirōn nomais*, cf. LSJM on *nomē*. which cites a second-century-B.C. inscription as evidence for the use of this idiom.

t. The term *ammos*, "sand," used by Ezekiel, is derived from the Septuagint and stands in contrast to the more poetic term *psammos*, which is used by Clement in his editorial summary of this section. In Ezekiel's account of the killing of the Egyptian by Moses, very little effort is made to adjust the picture of Moses in any way, as is the case, for example, in Philo (*Vit Mos* 1.44). In many respects, Ezekiel's "Moses" seems to be typical of Aristotle's ideal tragic hero (*Poetics* XIII.5).

u. Ezekiel's text, "one weaker than yourself," stands against that of the Septuagint, "(your) neighbor." There is no textual support from the biblical evidence, nor do the demands of meter require it. It may, however, be a dramatic portent of the fact that Moses will be the defender of the weak and the oppressed (cf. Kraus, p. 174).

v. Reading *apēggelē*, the emendation proposed by Kuiper (p. 57). The MSS read *apēggeile*, for which some editors have suggested *tis* as the subject (replacing *kai* at the beginning of the l.). The translation would then read: "Someone quickly brought these tidings to the king." This seems to be the understanding of Mras, who refers to "*der erwähnte Gewalttäter*" as the subject. A somewhat different solution is proposed by Strugnell (*HTR* 60 [1967] 456), which results, however, in the same translation as is adopted above.

w. The name "Raguel" does not occur within the actual text of Ezekiel. Its existence here must be attributed either to Eusebius or to Alexander Polyhistor. Thus, Mras's statement (GCS 43, 1, p. 527) that, according to Ezekiel, Sepphorah is Raguel's daughter is an inference that cannot fairly be drawn from Ezekiel's text. At no point does Ezekiel identify Moses' father-in-law by name, as either "Jethro" or "Raguel." The question raised by the diverse biblical tradition as to his name (cf. Ex 2:16, 18; 3:1; 4:18) remains unresolved in terms of Ezekiel's text. The matter did receive a considerable amount of attention from other ancient authors, however; e.g. Demetrius (*PrEv* 9.29.1), who maintained that Sepphorah was the daughter of Jethro and the granddaughter of Raguel; Josephus (*Ant* 2.264), who may have simply combined "Jethro" and "Raguel" into one name, "letheglaeus." Modern scholarship has done little more to clear up the confusion. Cf. Kappelmacher (p. 71, n. 1), who suggests that one or the other of the two names was a surname.

x. The name "Libya" represents a radical departure from the text of the Septuagint (Ex 2:15) which is not occasioned by the necessities of meter since "Midian" could have scanned equally as well in this l. The answer may lie in the need to harmonize Moses' marriage to Sepphorah with the well-known reference in Num 12:1 to Moses' Ethiopian wife. Although some early traditions did maintain that Moses had married two wives, Sep-

61 but tribes of sundry races dwell throughout;
62 the dark-skinned Aethiops. Yet there is one
63 who ruler, prince, and sole commander, he
64 rules all this state and judges mortal men;
65 a priest, the father of myself and these.

Then he describes the watering of the flocks and adds an account of the marriage
of Sepphorah, introducing Chus and Sepphorah, who speak in dialogue:ʸ
66 Sepphorah, you must speak in words forthright.   (C)
67 My father gave me for this alien's wife.   Ex 2:21   (S)

(Section from Demetrius, describing these same events)

And Ezekiel also speaks about these things in the *Exagōgē*, including, in addition,
the dream which was seen by Moses and interpreted by his father-in-law. Moses
himself speaks with his father-in-law in dialogue:ᶻ
68 On Sinai'sᵃ² peak I saw what seemed a throne
69 so great in size it touched the clouds of heaven.

phorah and an Ethiopian princess (cf. Josephus, *Ant* 2.252f., 262f.), nevertheless much of the early tradition attempts to bring the two together into one person. Demetrius (*PrEv* 9.29) explicitly states that Sepphorah was an Ethiopian woman, a descendant of Abraham through his son Keturah, who had been sent away to "an eastern land" (Gen 25:6); cf. T. Rajak, "Moses in Ethiopia: Legend and Literature," *JJS* 29 (1978) 111–22. The term "Libya," in antiquity, was frequently assigned to all of Africa, so that Ezekiel's description of a land inhabited by "sundry races" including "dark-skinned Aethiops" is quite accurate when he says, "This land all bears Libya's name." (Cf. E. W. Warmington, "Libya," Oxford Classical Dictionary, ed. N. C. L. Hammond and H. H. Scullard (Oxford, 1970) p. 608; LSJM on *Libyē*. The argument of Kuiper, that anyone with so poor a sense of geography as Ezekiel seems to possess at this point could not possibly have lived in Egypt, is without basis.

y. The expression *di' amoibaiōn* is regularly used in the editorial remarks to introduce dialogue, although at no point are the speakers themselves explicitly identified in the manuscripts of Eusebius. The brief, two-line dialogue which follows at this point is problematic both in respect to the identification and function of "Chus" in the drama and as to the question of whether or not Moses' marriage to Sepphorah had actually taken place by this time. Chus has been understood by some scholars to be the brother of Sepphorah, by others as a rejected suitor. The name, in any event, is traditionally connected with Ethiopia (cf. Gen 10:6; Josephus, *Ant* 1.131; Pseudo-Eupolemus, *PrEv* 9.17). As to the question of Moses' marriage, Kuiper (*REJ* 46 [1903] 174) concluded that Moses must have married Sepphorah in a previous scene which has been omitted in our sources. Kappelmacher, on the other hand, troubled by Jethro's designation of Moses as "stranger" in l. 83, concluded that these ll. (66f.) must have followed the ensuing scene. If, as seems most likely, the editorial comments included here are from the pen of Alexander Polyhistor, then a rearrangement of the material such as Kappelmacher suggested is almost impossible. Sepphorah's statement seems to indicate that the marriage

has already occurred, in which event ll. 66–67 must have been taken from the closing section of this scene.

z. The section which follows, ll. 68–89, represents Ezekiel's free creation in which he departs entirely from the Ex account; cf. E. Starobinski-Safran, "Un poète judéo-hellénistique: Ezéchiel le tragique," *Museum Helveticum* 31 (1974) 216–24. The device of the dream has its backgrounds both in Gk. drama and in the biblical material. In the tragedies of Aeschylus and others, the dream sometimes functioned as a device which pointed toward the dramatic climax of the play, a miniature prelude to what lay ahead. In terms of content there are some remarkable coincidences between Moses' dream and that of Joseph (cf. Gen 37:9) and the vision of Daniel (cf. Dan 7:13, 14). Moses is portrayed as having been chosen by God to represent him as divine vizier. The significance of the dream for the interpretation of the drama as a whole has been pursued from diverse points of view. Trencsényi-Waldapfel (*Acta Orientalia Academiae Scientiarum* 2 [1952] 156) discussed the motif of ecumenicity, viewed as an effort on Ezekiel's part to bring together the universalism of Gk. thought with that of the Heb. prophets. Lucien Cerfeaux, "Influence des mystères sur le Judaisme alexandrine avant Philon," *Muséon* 37 (1924) 36–48, analyzed Moses' dream in terms of the initiation rites connected with the mystery religions (a thesis subsequently adopted and expanded by E. R. Goodenough, *By Light, Light* (New Haven, 1935). Although some light may be shed from these studies on the literary development of the figure of Moses, it is still sufficient to say that both the function and the content of Moses' dream may be accounted for quite adequately by Ezekiel's obvious knowledge of both the tragic dramas of the Gk. masters and the content of the Bible.

a2. The reading is based on the conjecture of Dübner, *Appendix ad Euripidis Fragmenta a Guilelmo Wagnero collecta, Christus Patiens, Ezechieli et Christianorum poetarum reliquiae dramaticae* (Paris, 1846), accepted by most editors; the MSS offer several versions of an obviously corrupt reading.

70 Upon it sat a man[b2] of noble mien,
71 becrowned, and with a scepter in one hand
72 while with the other he did beckon me.
73 I made approach and stood before the throne.
74 He handed o'er the scepter and he bade
75 me mount the throne, and gave to me the crown;
76 then he himself withdrew from off the throne.
77 I gazed upon the whole earth round about;
78 things under it, and high above the skies.[c2]
79 Then at my feet a multitude of stars
80 fell down, and I their number reckoned up.
81 They passed by me like armèd ranks of men.
82 Then I in terror wakened from the dream.

And his father-in-law interprets the dream as follows:
83 My friend,[d2] God gave you this as sign for good.
84 Would I might live to see these things transpire.
85 For you shall cause a mighty throne to rise,
86 and you yourself shall rule and govern men.
87 As for beholding all the peopled earth,
88 and things below and things above God's realm:[e2]
89 things present, past, and future you shall see.

And in regard to the burning bush and Moses' mission to Pharaoh, once again
Ezekiel introduces Moses conversing with God. And Moses says:[f2]

90 Aha! What token this from yonder bush,　　　　　　　Ex 3:1f.
91 some sign beyond belief to mortal men?
92 A bush that sudden burns, with raging flame,
93 and yet its shoots remain all green and fresh.
94 What then! I shall advance and view this sign,　　　　Ex 3:3
95 so great it seems incredible to men.

---

b2. Ezekiel uses *phōs* (a poetic term for *anēr*), common in the Homeric literature and later poets. Its significance lies in the fact that Ezekiel would represent God as a man, an image which is surely rooted in the figures of "the son of man" and "the Ancient of Days" in Daniel's vision (Dan 7).

c2. Lit. "the heaven."

d2. The use of the term *xenos* as a form of address caused some difficulties for Kappelmacher, who thought it inconceivable that Jethro could have addressed Moses as "stranger" if Moses was married to Sepphorah at this point in the drama. But, in addition to the more common meaning of the term (cf. l. 67), there are various levels of usage, among which is the meaning "guest," one who is bound by ties of hospitality.

e2. Lit. "heaven."

f2. It is not clear how much may have been lost between the end of the preceding section and the beginning of this material. The scene itself is a skillful blending by Ezekiel of elements from Ex 3 and 4, with additional references to material from Ex 7. This is followed by a section dealing with the institution of the Passover, based on Ex 12; 13. There are a number of editorial comments inserted in this lengthy discourse, thus making it impossible to accurately determine the complete scope of material that was originally dealt with here. The first section (ll. 90–112) represents a fairly straightforward but poetic rendition of Ex 3:1–10. The latter half of vs. 9 (reference to the various nations) and vs. 10 (which is merely a repetition of vs. 7) have been omitted by Ezekiel in the interests of literary economy and meter. In ll. 110f. God instructs Moses to go first to the Heb. people and then to the king. These instructions seem to be in accord with Ex 3:10, 16, but from this point on, Ezekiel seems to have omitted all reference to Moses' mission to the Heb. people and to the possibility that they will not believe him (although cf. *infra*, n. w2). In Ezekiel's version of the story, the basic thrust of Moses' message is to be directed toward the king. Aaron, for example, is to be Moses' spokesman before the king (ll. 118f.), rather than to the people (cf. Ex 4:16). The rod, according to Ezekiel, functions only as a means of establishing credibility before Pharaoh and the Egyptians and not before the Heb. people themselves (as in Ex 4:1–5). In this way, Ezekiel emphasizes the personal confrontation between Moses and Pharaoh, thus heightening the dramatic effect. It is unclear whether Ezekiel's purpose in omitting all reference to possible unbelief on the part of the Heb. people is consequent to his desire for dramatic effect or whether he consciously sought to erase any trace of a lack of solidarity between the Heb. people and their leader Moses.

Then God addresses him:

96 Stay, Moses, best of men, do not come near   Ex 3:4–6
97 till you have loosed the bindings from your feet;
98 the place on which you stand is holy ground,
99 and from this bush God's word shines forth[g2] to you.
100 Take courage, son, and listen to my words;
101 as mortal man you cannot see my face,
102 albeit you have pow'r to hear my words,
103 and for this very reason I have come.
104 God am I of those, your fathers[h2] three,
105 of Abram, Isaac, Jacob, I am He.[i2]
106 Mindful of my promises to them,[j2]   Ex 3:7f.
107 to save my Hebrew people I am come,
108 since I have seen my servants' toil and pain.
109 Now go, and testify[k2] to these my words,
110 to all the Hebrews first, then to the king,
111 the things commanded by me unto you,
112 that you should lead my people from this land.

Then, a few speeches farther down, Moses himself replies:

113 I am not by nature eloquent;   Ex 4:10
114 my tongue with difficulty speaks, I stammer,
115 so that I cannot speak before the king.   Ex 6:12

Then, in reply to these things, God answers him:

116 Your brother Aaron I will send with haste,   Ex 4:14,15,16
117 to whom you'll tell all things that I have said,
118 and he it is who'll speak before the king.
119 You'll take the words from me, and he from you.

And concerning the rod and other wonders, he speaks thus in dialogue:

120 Say, what is this you hold within your hand?   Ex 4:2f.   (G)
121 A rod, the chastener of beasts and men.   (M)
122 Now cast it on the ground and move away;   (G)
123 a fearful serpent you in awe shall see.
124 See, there I cast it down. Be gracious, Lord!   (M)
125 How dreadful, huge! Be merciful to me!
126 I tremble at the sight, my limbs do shake.
127 Fear not! Stretch forth your hand and seize its tail;   Ex 4:4   (G)
128 again 'twill be a rod as it once was.
129 Your hand thrust in your bosom, draw it forth.   Ex 4:6f.
130 'Tis done. It has become as white as snow![i2]   (M)
131 Reach in again, it shall be as it was.   (G)

g2. The meaning of *theios logos*, "divine word," in Ezekiel is difficult to determine. Wieneke (*Eze-chielis*, p. 77) argued for a simple interpretation of the word as "voice," offering various examples in which the verb *eklampein* or *lampein* is connected with sound. This understanding of *logos* as the equivalent of the metrically undesirable *phonē* would make the burning-bush scene in Ezekiel compatible with similar descriptions in Artapanus (*PrEv* 9.27.21, *phonēn theian*) and in Josephus (*Ant* 2.267, *phonē*, which Josephus later identifies as "God"). Cf. Ex 3:2 (LXX) *aggelos kyriou*; Philo, *Vit Mos* 1.66, *aggelos*; Justin Martyr, *Apol* 1.63; *DialTrypho* 59.60. In l. 246, Ezekiel again

associates the term *lampein* with the presence of God.

h2. The use of the plural term "fathers" is another noteworthy departure from the standard text of the Septuagint (Ex 3:6), supported, in this case, by a variety of witnesses. (Cf. Acts 8:32.)

i2. The proper names in this line, all drawn from the biblical text (Ex 3:6), comprise severe metrical difficulties for the Gk. text. Cf. Strugnell, *HTR* 60 (1967) 450, n. 5; 453, n. 10; Snell, *Glotta* 44 (1966) 28.

j2. Lit. "having remembered them and my gifts."

k2. Lit. "give a sign."

l2. Most editors have assigned this l. to Moses.

To these things (after certain other matters that he has interposed), he (Polyhistor) adds the following: Ezekiel says these things in similar fashion in the *Exagōgē*, introducing God, who speaks concerning the signs as follows:[m2]

132 And with this rod these woes you shall effect:	Ex 4:17
133 now, first the river shall flow red with blood,	Ex 7:19
134 and all the springs, and every stagnant pool.[n2]	
135 A host of frogs and lice I'll cast on earth;	Ex 7:27,28; 8:12
136 then sprinkle ashes from the furnace round,	Ex 9:8f.
137 and ulcerous sores shall thus burst forth[o2] on men.	
138 And swarms of flies shall come and sore afflict	Ex 8:17,20
139 the men of Egypt; then another plague	
140 shall come, and they shall die whose hearts are hardened.	
141 And I shall make the heavens bitter; hail	Ex 9:23,25
142 and fire shall fall and slay all mortal men,	
143 and cause to perish every crop and beast.	
144 Darkness I'll decree for three whole days,	Ex 10:22
145 and locusts send, who shall the residue	Ex 10:4f.
146 of food consume and every blade of grass.	
147 Last shall I slay the firstborn of mankind,	Ex 11:5
148 and thus bring down the wanton pride[p2] of men.	
149 Yet Pharaoh shan't be moved[q2] by what I say	
150 until his firstborn child lies as a corpse;	
151 then, moved with fear, he'll send the people forth.	
152 This also say to all the Hebrew race:	Ex 12:3
153 "This month shall be the first month of your years,	Ex 12:2
154 in which I'll lead you[r2] to another land	Ex 12:17
155 which to the Hebrew fathers I did swear."	Ex 13:5
156 And say to all the people, "In this month,	Ex 12:6
157 on full moon's eve,[s2] the Paschal sacrifice	Ex 12:21
158 to God present, and touch the doors with blood,	Ex 12:7

m2. Eusebius' editorial comment indicates that Alexander Polyhistor digressed at this point before returning to Ezekiel. In regard to the description of the plagues, Ezekiel takes Ex 4:17 as a literary basis for his discussion of the *sēmeia*, although his discourse is based on Ex 7:17–11:7. Ezekiel's account of the plagues is in accord with the tendency of tragic drama to collapse events into a short period of time. The literary freedom which Ezekiel exhibits in regard to the Septuagint text is explicable when one considers that his summary description is of a totally different literary style than that of the historical narrative of Exodus. The technical problems of dramatizing such material have been neatly avoided by transforming the entire series of events into a prophetic speech in which God describes what will take place in the future. As to the order of the plagues in Ezekiel, cf. Wieneke, *Ezechielis*, pp. 69–71. Ezekiel is neither as stylized nor as tedious as Philo in his division of the plagues (*Vit Mos* 1.96–142). His listing is more complete than that of Josephus (*Ant* 2.293–314) and of Artapanus (*PrEv* 9.27) but not quite as closely bound to the biblical text as is the author of Jubilees (48:5–8).

n2. This l. is found in almost identical form in Pseudo-Aeschylus, cited in Pseudo-Justin (*De Monarchia* 2) and in Clement of Alexandria (*Strom* 5.14).

o2. Lit. "to boil, seethe." The MSS offer several different readings here, none of which is wholly satisfactory in defining the term precisely, although the general sense seems clear.

p2. The use of the term *hybris* is significant because of its long-standing association within the pattern of *hybris/nemesis* in Gk. tragedy. Strong parallels exist between the characterization of Pharaoh by Ezekiel and the pronouncement of doom rendered against Xerxes in Aeschylus' *Persians*. Because Xerxes sought to "wrest nature, turn sea into land, manacle a strait with iron, to make a highway for his troops" (*Persians*, ll. 747f.) and thus to contravene the will of the gods, he received "the just reward of pride and insolence" (l. 808). For a discussion of *hybris* in Gk. tragedy, cf. R. Lattimore, *Story Patterns in Greek Tragedy* (London, 1964), p. 23.

q2. The translation understands *peiset'* as derived from *peithō*, rather than from *paschō*. This is paralleled in Euripides, *Helena* 446 (cf. Kuiper, *REJ* 46 [1903] 65). Alternatively, the translation would read: "And King Pharaoh will suffer none of these things of which I speak." This stands in direct contradiction, however, to the evidence of the Septuagint (cf. Ex 8:4, 20, 27).

r2. Lit. "the people."

s2. Cf. Ex 12:6: "the evening of the fourteenth day of the month." For a complete discussion of the material dealing with the Passover in Ezekiel (and in other ancient authors), cf. J. B. Segal, *The Hebrew Passover from the Earliest Times* (London, 1963).

159 which sign the fearsome angel¹² shall pass by.   Ex 12:13
160 But you, by night, shall eat the roasted flesh;   Ex 12:8
161 then shall the king drive out the throng in haste.   Ex 12:33
162 But ere you go I'll grant the people favor;   Ex 3:21f.
163 one woman from another shall receive
164 fine vessels, jewels of silver and of gold
165 and clothing, things which one may carry off,
166 so as to compensate them for their deeds.ᵘ²   Ex 12:25
167 But when at last you enter your own land,   Ex 12:25
168 take heed that from the morn on which you fled
169 from Egypt and did journey seven days,
170 from that same morn, so many days each year   Ex 13:7
171 you eat unleavened bread and serve your God.   Ex 13:5
172 The firstborn of all living things presentᵛ²   Ex 13:2,15
173 to God, whatever virgins first shall bear
174 of males that open up the mothers' wombs.

And again, concerning this same feast, he says that he elaborates more precisely:ʷ²
175 And when the tenth day of this month is come,   Ex 12:3,21
176 let Hebrew men by families thus selectˣ²
177 unblemishedʸ² sheep and calves, and keep them till   Ex 12:5

t2. In Ex 12:13 God says that he himself will "pass over" them. In l. 187 of Ezekiel it is *thanatos* which will "pass over."

u2. There is a certain ambiguity in this l. The implication seems to be that the Hebrews will receive a wage as compensation for what they (the Hebrews) had done for the Egyptians. It could be construed, however, to mean that "they [the Hebrews] will receive compensation for what they [the Egyptians] had done" (presumably to the Hebrews). Ezekiel's statement is designed to explain the theme which is briefly stated in Ex 12:35–36, the fact that they despoiled the Egyptians. The attempt to justify this action on the part of the Hebrews was maintained by Philo, *Vit Mos* 1.141–42; cf. Jub 48:18.

v2. Lit. "sacrifice" (*thyontes*); cf. Ex 13:2, *hagiazein*. The idea of human sacrifice, although it might be implied by Ezekiel's use of the term *thyein*, was surely not intended by him here. Ezekiel may have clarified this point in material which has been omitted between ll. 174 and 175, referring, perhaps, to the biblical instructions (Ex 13:15) which distinguish between sacrificing (*thyein*) the firstborn of animals and redeeming (*lytroein*) the firstborn of men.

w2. The difficulty with this editorial insertion lies in determining whether it is the statement of Eusebius or of Polyhistor. The problem is compounded by the confusion in the MSS as to the correct form of *epexergazomenos*/*on*/*ēs*. The translation could read either: "he [Polyhistor] says that he [Ezekiel] . . ." or "he [Ezekiel] says that he [God?] . . ." (following the text adopted by most editors, *epexergazomenon*. Although, from a grammatical point of view, either reading is possible, the character of Ezekiel's text as dialogue precludes the latter reading, which would be tantamount to a stage direction. The most likely solution is that the editorial statement is to be attributed to Eusebius, in which case the question as to the identity of the speaker in ll.175–92 remains open. Traditionally, most scholars have assumed that God is

still the speaker and that this section is closely linked to the preceding ll. (132–74). The most obvious objection to this lies in the fact that ll. 175–92 seem to constitute a needless repetition of the material that has gone before. If God is still the speaker in ll. 175–92, under what circumstances did Ezekiel find it necessary to have him issue these instructions twice? A solution may lie in the suggestion that ll. 175–92 constitute part of a separate scene in which Moses related God's instructions to the people (cf. Ex 12:21–28). This would be in keeping with Ezekiel's tendency to follow the general outline of events in the text of Ex. It would also account for the otherwise peculiar use of the term *despotēs*, "Lord," in l. 188, a term which would be quite natural if spoken by Moses (cf. l. 124) but which would be most unusual if God himself were the speaker. (The frequent use of this term in the Septuagint is limited to situations where man addresses God directly or is speaking about him.) In contrast, the earlier section (in which God is clearly the speaker) uses the term *theos*, "God," in the commandments regarding the Passover (e.g. ll. 158, 173). In addition, the frequent use of the first person singular in the earlier section is notably absent in ll. 175–92 (e.g. ll. 154, 191). All of these features combine to suggest that ll. 175–92 represent a separate scene in which Moses is addressing the Hebrew people and imparting to them God's instructions in regard to the Passover. (Cf. Kraus, *Rivista di filologia e di istruzione classica* 96 [1968] 167.)

x2. The fact that some material, at least, has been omitted is indicated here by the lack of any subject for the verb *labōn*. Some editors have proposed an emendation to *labe* (cf. Ex 12:21: *labete*), while Mras (GCS 43, 1) understands an anacoluthic construction at this point and suggests *hekastos labōn—phagesthe*.

y2. "Unblemished" = *amōma*. Cf. Ex 12:5 (LXX) *teleion*. Ezekiel's term is reminiscent of the regulations in Leviticus (3:1; cf. Ezek 45:18). In regard to the "sheep and calves," Ezekiel's text

178 the fourteenth day has dawned, and then, at eve,   Ex 12:6
179 make sacrifice; thus shall you eat them whole,
180 the flesh and inward parts all roast with fire;   Ex 12:11
181 your loins girt up and shoes upon your feet,
182 and in your hand a staff, for thus in haste
183 the king will order all to leave the land.
184 It shall be called "Passover."z2 Then, when you
185 shall sacrifice, take hyssopa3 in your hands;   Ex 12:22
186 and dip the twigs in blood and lightly touch
187 both doorposts, so that death may pass you by.   Ex 12:23
188 So keep this festival unto the Lord;   Ex 12:14
189 for seven days you'll eat unleavened bread.b3   Ex 12:15, 13:3
190 For there shall be deliverance from these ills;
191 a "going forth" he'll grant you in this month,
192 and first of months and yearsc3 it e'er shall be.

And after certain other matters he (Polyhistor) adds: "And Ezekiel, also, in the drama entitled *Exagōgē*, introduces a messenger who tells of the disposition of the Hebrews and of the destruction of the Egyptians as follows":d3

193 For when King Pharaoh set forth from his house,   Ex 14:6f.
194 with multitude of myriad armèd men,
195 with cavalry and four-horsed chariots,
196 and front ranks with supporting troops nearby;
197 how awesome was the host arrayed for battle.
198 Foot soldiers formed a phalanx in the center,
199 with spaces for the chariots to pass through;
200 and horsemen he deployed, some on the left,e3
201 and on the right the rest of Egypt's force.
202 I asked as to their army's total strength;f3
203 there were a million men both brave and true.

seems closer to that of Deut 16:2 and 2Chr 35:8 than to the text of Ex (12:3, 21). Following the text of Ex, however, Ezekiel retains the instructions to "roast" the sacrifice (ll. 179f.; cf. l. 160). His text does not reflect the confusion which arises out of the instructions in Deut 16:7 and 2Chr 35:13 regarding "roasting" and "boiling."

z2. The MSS read: *pas kai hotan*. The emendation to *pasch' hotan* was originally proposed by J. Strugnell (*HTR* 60 [1967] 449–52). The resultant text not only resolves all metrical and grammatical difficulties in this otherwise troublesome l. but also restores the name of the feast in Ezekiel's text in exactly the same place that it occurred in his source (Ex 12:11).

a3. Lit. "a bundle of hyssop leaves." The same phrase is found in Josephus, *Ant* 2.312, in contrast to the simpler Septuagintal formula *desmēn hyssōpou*.

b3. Lit. "Seven days (you will eat) unleaven, and you will not eat leaven." (Cf. Ex 12:1, 14, 15, 20.) An alternative form of punctuation (utilized by most editors) links the first part of this l. with the preceding l., resulting in the translation: "You will keep this festival to the Lord, seven days unleavened. Leaven will not be eaten."

c3. Lit. "times," but cf. l. 153.

d3. The appearance of the messenger suggests that the end of the drama is near. He identifies himself as a member of the Egyptian army for the first time in l. 204. The comparison with the messenger in Aeschylus' *Persians* has often been noted. The contents of the messenger's speech are comparable to the themes expressed in the songs of Moses and of Miriam in Ex 15. The closing ll. of this section point up the author's purpose: a contrast between the fate of the well-ordered Egyptian army, confident of their success, and that of the disordered Israelite throng, unarmed and apparently helpless. Ezekiel does not attempt to develop this theme into the *lex talionis* (expressed in Jub 48:14 and WisSol 11:16). The contrast depicted by Ezekiel is consonant with material such as Ps 106:9–11. Despite the initial appearance of things, God proves to be the helper of the downtrodden Israelites, while he wreaks destruction upon the Egyptians. For a discussion of the military terminology involved in the messenger's speech, cf. W. Tarn, *Hellenistic Military and Naval Developments* (Cambridge, England, 1930). Although much of this language has no counterpart in the Ex account, it does have parallels in the language of tragic drama (cf. Wieneke, *Ezechielis*, p. 94) and, to a certain extent, in Philo, *Vit Mos* 1.168) and in Josephus (*Ant* 2.324).

e3. The same sort of ambiguous grammatical structure exists in this l. and the following as was seen in ll. 9f. and in l. 205. Strictly speaking, the *pantas* in l. 201 does not answer to the *tous men* in l. 200. Lit. l. 201 reads: "the whole of Egypt's force."

f3. The problem in the Gk. text of this l. lies in the fact that there are too many syllables. For a concise discussion of the difficulties, cf. Strugnell, *HTR* 60 (1967) 456.

204 The Hebrews, when confronted by our[g3] host,	Ex 14:9
205 lay strewn about hard by the sandy shore,[h3]	
206 in masses there upon the Red Sea's strand.	
207 Some were engaged in caring for the young[i3]	Ex 12:37f.
208 together with their wives, worn out with toil,	
209 with many flocks and herds and household stuff.[j3]	
210 And they, all unprotected, without arms,	Ex 14:10
211 on seeing us sent up a doleful cry,	
212 'gainst heaven they inveighed,[k3] their fathers' God.	
213 Now great in number was their multitude,[l3]	
214 but we, for our part, were all overjoyed.	
215 Then, facing them, we pitched our camp nearby	Ex 14:9
216 (the place by men is called Beelzephon).[m3]	
217 And since the Titan sun[n3] was near to set,	Ex 14:19f.
218 we waited, longing for the fight at dawn,	
219 in numbers trusting, and in our dread arms.	
220 And thereupon commenced divine portents	
221 full wondrous to behold! And, all at once,	
222 a mighty column stood, of cloud and fire,[o3]	
223 midway between the Hebrew camp and ours.	
224 And then their leader Moses, taking up	Ex 14:21
225 the rod[p3] of God by which he'd lately wrought	
226 such evil signs and ills on Egypt's land,	
227 did smite the Red Sea's surface, and the depth	
228 was rent asunder; so they all as one	Ex 14:22
229 with haste went forth[q3] along that briny path.	
230 We quickly sped along in that same route,	Ex 14:23
231 foll'wing their track; by night we entered in,	
232 in close pursuit with shout;[r3] then, all at once,	
233 as if with chains our chariot wheels were bound.	Ex 14:24f.

g3. Lit. "my."

h3. Lit. "some [of the Hebrews], on the one hand, lay strewn . . ." The grammar is broken, with no *de* to answer to the *men* in l. 205. For this reason, Wieneke (*Ezechielis*) rearranged the order of these ll.: 205, 206, 209, 207, 208, 210. Cf. nn. on ll. 9, 200.

i3. Lit. "They gave food to young children."

j3. In Wieneke's arrangement, this l. would immediately follow l. 206 (cf. n. h3), which would seem to be a more felicitous arrangement.

k3. The translation is based on an emendation proposed by J. Strugnell (*HTR* 60 [1967] 450, n. 3), reading *pros aither' apetathēsan*. The text is obviously corrupt and the emendation not only clarifies the confused readings of the manuscripts but has the advantage of eliminating metrical difficulties and of restoring to the text of Ezekiel the biblical reference to the people's complaint against God (Ex 14:11). As to the notion of inveighing against heaven, Strugnell notes that the passage should be regarded "as another instance of the use of *shmym/ouranos* vel sim. for the divine name."

l3. For *ochlos*, "multitude," Kuiper, *REJ* 46 (1903), suggested *oknos*, "shrinking, hesitation," to contrast with the "joy" of the Egyptians in the following l. The text would then read: "And great was their consternation, but, for our part, we were overjoyed."

m3. Determining the exact location of Beelzephon serves no purpose for Ezekiel's text, since he merely followed the text of Ex. Josephus identifies it as "a place by the Red Sea" (*Ant* 2.315). A full discussion may be found in J. Simons, *The Geographical and Topographical Texts of the Old Testament* (Leiden, 1959) p. 240.

n3. Although the phrase "Titan sun" bears overtones of pagan mythology, it is appropriate in the mouth of the Egyptian messenger. The expression is not common to the Gk. tragedians, although it is found frequently in the Lat. poets. Cf. Wieneke, *Ezechielis*, p. 100.

o3. The translation is based on the suggestion of Kuiper, who proposed *puriphlegēs* for the reading of the MSS, *pro gēs megas*. The emendation of Dübner, *Appendix*, *pro gēs melas*, is an easier correction but lacks grammatical consistency. In any event, the reading of the MSS is suspect, since the preceding l. also ends in *megas*. Both of the suggested emendations have support in the text of Ex (cf. 14:20, 24).

p3. The "rod" obviously has magical qualities in the estimation of the Egyptian messenger. Cf. Ex 14:21, 27, which says that Moses used his hand.

q3. Whether one reads *ōrousan* (the reading of the MSS BI) or *ōrmēsan* (the reading of the MSS ON), the translation is essentially the same.

r3. Although the term *boēdromountes* would ordinarily be construed to mean "run to a cry for help," its meaning here must be simply "run with a cry"; cf. Appianus, *Hann.* 42 and examples cited by Wieneke, *Ezechielis*, pp. 103–4.

234 From heaven, then, a shining light like fire
235 appeared to us, so we were led to think
236 that God was their defense. For when they reached　　　　Ex 14:30
237 the farther shore a mighty wave gushed forth
238 hard by us, so that one in terror cried,
239 "Flee back before the hands of the Most High;　　　　Ex 14:25
240 to them he offers succor, but to us,
241 most wretched men, destruction he does work."
242 The sea-path flooded, all our host was lost.ˢ³　　　　Ex 14:28

And again, after a few things: "From there they went for three days, as Demetrius himself says (and the Holy Bible agrees with this). And since the water in that place was bitter and not sweet, at God's command he cast a certain piece of wood into the spring and the water became sweet. And from there they came to Elim, where they found twelve springs of water and seventy palm trees. In regard to these things and to the bird that appeared there, Ezekiel, in the *Exagōgē*, introduces someone speaking to Moses about the palm trees and twelve springs of water as follows":ᵗ³

243 Take note, most noble Moses, of this place　　　　Ex 15:27
244 which we have found near yonder airy glen.ᵘ³
245 'Tis over there, where you, too, now may see.
246 From thence a lustrous light now flashes forth,
247 by night, a sign,ᵛ³ like to a fiery pillar.
248 And there we found a meadow shaded o'er
249 and splashing streams: a place profuse and rich,
250 which draws from out one rocky ledge twelve springs;
251 the trunks of fruitful palms rise like a hedge,
252 threescore and ten, with water flowing round,
253 and tender grass yields pasture for the flocks.

s3. Lit. "The way through the Red Sea has been flooded ["closed up"—some MSS] and has utterly destroyed the way." The repetition of *poros* in l. 242 has given rise to several possible suggestions for correction. Mras, GCS 43.1, p. 536, and Snell, *Tragicorum Graecorum Fragmenta*, p. 300 (following Stephanus), read *straton* for the second instance of *poros*, while Wieneke adopted the reading *stolon*, both of which can be translated as "army." Mras suggested, however, that Ezekiel could have intended a play on words here, based on the several meanings of *poros* (e.g. "the ford was flooded, and destroyed the way of escape").

t3. There is some disagreement among commentators as to whether this section represents the closing scene of the drama (so Trencsényi-Waldapfel, *Acta Orientalia Academiae Scientiarum* 2 (1952) 143–64) or whether there was one further scene in which Moses and Sepphorah were reunited (cf. Kuiper, *REJ* 46 [1903] 166–67; Kappelmacher, *Wiener Studien* 44 [1924–25] 82). The report of the messenger to Moses is the free creation of Ezekiel, based on Ex 14:27. The closing ll., which describe the "strange living creature," may have been taken from some other literary source. Its identification here as the legendary phoenix bird is based on the repetition of these ll. in Pseudo-Eustathius, *Commentarius in Hexaemeron* (PG 18.729), and the fact that it is so designated there.

(For a thorough discussion of the phoenix bird in ancient literature, cf. M. C. Fitzpatrick, *Lactanti de Ave Phoenice* (Philadelphia, 1933), and more recently R. Van den Broek, *The Myth of the Phoenix According to Classical and Early Christian Traditions* (Leiden, 1972). The association between the name of the bird, *phoinix*, and the palm trees at Elim, *phoinikoi*, is obvious (cf. Ovid, *Metamorphoses* 15.397). The function of the phoenix in Ezekiel's drama, however, is not so clear. Trencsényi-Waldapfel suggested that the legislation given to the people by Moses at Marah (Ex 15:26) comprises the heart of this last act, and thus the scene at Elim constitutes a new "garden of Eden" with its subsequent temptation. By identifying a fragment from Epiphanius (PG 43.174) as originally part of this same scene, Trencsényi-Waldapfel transformed the phoenix into "the tempter" of Gen 3, who tempts the people to disobey the legislation recently given to them. This reconstruction is highly speculative, however, and there is nothing in the fragment from Epiphanius which specifically relates it to Ezekiel's drama.

u3. Cf. the dismal scene at Elim, as described by Josephus (*Ant* 3.9–11).

v3. Adopting the emendation suggested by Kuiper and others, *kat' euphronēn*. The reading of most of the manuscripts, *kat' euphronēs* "a goodly sign," must be excluded on metrical grounds.

Then, farther down, he sets forth a description of the bird which appeared:[w3]

254   Another living creature there we saw,
255   full wondrous, such as man has never seen;
256   'twas near in scope to twice the eagle's size,
257   with plumage iridescent, rainbow-hued.
258   Its breast appeared deep-dyed with purple's shade,
259   its legs were red like ochre, and its neck
260   was furnished round with tresses[x3] saffron-hued;
261   like to a coxcomb[y3] did its crest appear,
262   with amber-tinted eye it gazed about,
263   the pupil like some pomegranate seed.
264   Exceeding all, its voice pre-eminent;
265   of every other wingèd thing, the king,
266   it did appear. For all the birds, as one,
267   in fear did haste to follow after him,
268   and he before, like some triumphant bull
269   went striding forth with rapid step apace.

w3. The following lines are also found in Pseudo-Eustathius, *Commentarius in Hexaemeron* (PG 18.729D). Although the text in Pseudo-Eustathius contains several variant readings, these are generally conceded to be inferior to the text of Eusebius, as is indicated by their lack of conformity to the rules of meter.

x3. Lit. "locks of wool."

y3. The text is difficult, with both Pseudo-Eustathius and the MSS of Eusebius attesting the phrase *koitēs himerēs* (vel sim.), indicating, perhaps, "a soft nest." The genitive construction does not fit well, however, with *parempheres*, and the emendation to *kottois hēmerois* has been accepted by most editors, primarily on the basis of Pliny's description of the phoenix as having a crest on its head (*Natural History* 10.2): *auro fulgore circa colla*). Ezekiel's text may preserve the figure of "a tufted nest of feathers" on top of the bird's head.

FRAGMENTS OF PSEUDO-GREEK POETS

(Third to Second Century B.C.)

A NEW TRANSLATION AND INTRODUCTION
BY H. ATTRIDGE

In the hellenistic period, Jews composed many works in Greek literary genres. Some of these were written under the actual names of the authors (e.g. *Ezekiel the Tragedian* and *Philo the Epic Poet*). Others were pseudonymous compositions (e.g. the SibOr). In addition to these complete works, Jews reworked authentic fragments from Greek poetry and composed brief passages of their own in imitation of classical models. These pseudonymous fragments were then collected, together with some genuine passages from classical poets which could be interpreted in a Jewish way, and circulated in anthologies or *gnomologia*, which served to support the apologetic claims that Jewish tradition was the source of Greek wisdom and that the best in Greek literature was in harmony with Jewish belief.

Sources

The spurious verses of classical poetry composed by Jews are now to be found in several patristic witnesses, in the *Protrepticus* and *Stromata* of Clement of Alexandria (c. A.D. 150–215), who is in turn cited in the *Praeparatio Evangelica* of Eusebius (c. A.D. 263–339), and in the *De Monarchia* and the *Cohortatio ad Gentiles*, works erroneously attributed to Justin. The dates of these last two pseudonymous works are uncertain. They are probably later than Clement's works and may have been composed in the third century A.D. All these Christian works continue the traditions of Jewish apologetics by attempting to show how Judeo-Christian monotheism was foreshadowed in classical literature.

The two most extensive collections of pseudonymous verses, in the *Stromata* of Clement and the *De Monarchia* of Pseudo-Justin, diverge at many points. Neither source contains all the verses. In many cases they differ in their attribution of given verses to classical authors. In several cases the contents of particular verses differ and Pseudo-Justin's version is usually the longer. Finally, the order of the fragments varies. Based on the numeration of this translation, which follows the chronological order of the authors to whom the verses are attributed, Clement's order is 8, 1, 7, 2, 5, 12, 10, 6, 4, 11, while Pseudo-Justin's order is 4, 5, 9, 3, 6, 10, 12, 11.

Despite the differences between Clement and Pseudo-Justin, it is probable that all the tragic and comic verses which they cite ultimately derive from a single *gnomologion*. The spurious epic verses (number 1 in this translation) are attested separately by the Jewish philosopher and exegete Aristobulus of the second century B.C. and these hexameter verses may originally have been part of a *gnomologion* different from that which contained the dramatic verses.

Date

The spurious epic verses were quoted by Aristobulus (c. 150 B.C., according to Yorb); hence they were composed and collected in the late-third or early-second century B.C. In connection with one of the fragments attributed to Sophocles (number 5 in this translation), Clement quotes as his source a work on Abraham, ascribed to the Greek ethnographer and historian Hecataeus. This work was, no doubt, a Jewish pseudepigraphon, probably identical to the work on the same subject alluded to in Josephus, *Antiquities* 1.159. Thus this work must have been written before the last quarter of the first century A.D.[1] Unfortunately, it is impossible to determine how much of the collection was known to Pseudo-Hecataeus. In any case, it is unlikely that the author of this Jewish pseudepigraphon composed the pseudonymous dramatic verses.[2] At most, it can be said that the verses predate this work of Pseudo-Hecataeus and thus probably were composed in the late-hellenistic or early-Roman period. Nothing definite can be said about their provenance.

Theological and historical importance

These brief fragments illustrate some of the most important themes of Jewish apologetic theology: the unity and transcendence of God, the inferiority of pagan worship and mythology, and the reality of divine justice. At the same time, these pieces indicate the influence of hellenistic civilization, which not only imposed on Judaism the need for apologetic enterprises but also provided a wide new range of literary tools for those endeavors.

SELECT BIBLIOGRAPHY

Charlesworth, *PMR*, p. 168.
Denis, *Introduction*, pp. 223–38.

TEXTS

Denis, A.-M. *Fragmenta pseudepigraphorum graeca*. Leiden, 1970; pp. 161–74.
Edmonds, J. M. *The Fragments of Attic Comedy*. Leiden, 1961; 3 vols.
Merkelbach, R., and West, M. L. *Fragmenta Hesiodea*. Oxford, 1967.
Nauck, A. *Tragicorum graecorum fragmenta*. Leipzig, 1899². (Reprinted, with a supplement by B. Snell, Hildesheim, 1964).

STUDIES

Walter, N. *Der Thoraausleger Aristobulos*. TU 86; Berlin, 1964; pp. 172–201.

---

[1] On the issue of the various Jewish works composed in the name of Hecataeus, cf. most recently N. Walter, "Fragmente jüdisch-hellenistischer Historiker," *JSHRZ* 1.2 (1976) 144–60; B. Z. Wacholder, *Eupolemus: A Study of Judaeo-Greek Literature* (Cincinnati, O., 1974) pp. 263–73; and J. H. Charlesworth, *PMR*, pp. 120–22.

[2] This has been persuasively argued by N. Walter, *Der Thoraausleger Aristobulos* (TU 86, Berlin, 1964) pp. 172–201.

TRANSLATION

1. Various epic poets.

These hexameter fragments are preserved in Clement of Alexandria, *Stromata* 5.14.107, 3f., who is cited by Eusebius, *Praeparatio Evangelica* 13.13.34. Eusebius quotes the same verses in *Praeparatio Evangelica* 13.12.13, along with material assigned to the Jewish philosopher of the second century B.C. Aristobulus. Utilization of these verses by that author indicates that this collection dates from the early-hellenistic period. The collection contains some genuine verses and may originally have been compiled by a Pythagorean or a Jew interested in the sacred number seven.[a]

Clement's introduction:

Not only Hebrews but also Greeks know of the sacred number seven, in accordance with which the entire cosmos of all living and growing beings revolves. Hesiod speaks thus about it:

Eusebius' introduction:

And, indeed, the entire cosmos of all living and growing things revolves around the seventh day. It is called "sabbath" and is translated "rest." Both Homer and Hesiod, having taken information from our books, say clearly that it is holy. Hesiod speaks thusly:

1. The first, the fourth, and the seventh are holy days.[b]

And again:

2. Again on the seventh day is the bright light of the sun.[c]

And Homer says:

1. Then, on the seventh day, a holy day returned.

And:

2. It was the holy seventh day.[d]

And again:

3. It was the seventh day and on it all things were completed.[e]

And:

4. And, on the seventh dawn, we left the stream of Acheron.[f]

Clement comments:

Yes, and Callimachus[g] the poet writes:

Eusebius comments:

He signifies that movement is from spiritual forgetfulness and evil, that by the "seventh," reason, which is in accord with truth, the things previously mentioned are left behind and

---

1. **Various epic poets**

a. Cf. Plato, *Republic* 616B.

b. This vs. is from Hesiod, *Works and Days* 770.

c. This l. (F. 362 in the edition of Merkelbach and West) is not attested in the works of Hesiod. Compare Homer, *Iliad* 11.605, and Hesiod, *Theogony* 760, 958. Like vs. 1 from Homer and vss. 2–5 from Linus, the line seems particularly Pythagorean.

d. Or "The seventh day was holy."

e. This vs. is from the *Odyssey* 5.262, where the reference is to the fourth day. The vs. is, no doubt, understood to be an allusion to Gen 2:2, as is vs. 1 of Linus.

f. Cf. *Odyssey* 10.513. The reference to travel on the Sabbath makes it unlikely that the verse was originally composed by a Jew.

g. Probably because Linus was a legendary figure, Clement attributes the following lines to Callimachus, a poet of the third century B.C. The attribution in Aristobulus and Eusebius is probably more original.

we receive knowledge of the truth, as had been said above. And Linus speaks thusly:

1. On the seventh dawn, when all was completed.
2. The seventh day is counted among good things as is the seventh birth.

And:

3. The seventh day is counted among primary things and the seventh is perfect.

And:

4. All seven[h] have been fashioned in the starry heaven, shining in their orbits in the recurring years.

2. Hesiod.

A brief hexameter fragment about the supreme deity is attributed to Hesiod in Clement of Alexandria, *Stromata* 5.14.112,3 and in his *Protrepticus* 6.73.3. Eusebius cites the passage from the Stromata in *Praeparatio Evangelica* 13.13.39. This fragment could be genuine.

> For he is king and master of all
> and none of the immortals contends with him in power.[a]

3. Pythagoras.

The sixth-century philosopher Pythagoras is credited by Pseudo-Justin, *De Monarchia* 2, with a series of hexameter verses on the unique creator. The citation follows a series of Pseudo-Orphic verses.

> If anyone says, "I am God," apart from the One, he should
> set up a world equal to this and say, "This is mine."
> He should not only set it up and call it "mine," but also should himself dwell
> in that which he has made. For it has been made by this one.[a]

4. Aeschylus.

This iambic fragment attributed to the first major tragic poet of the fifth century B.C. is quoted by Clement of Alexandria, *Stromata* 5.14.131,2f., who is cited by Eusebius, *Praeparatio Evangelica* 13.13.60. It is also preserved as the first passage in the collection of verses in Pseudo-Justin, *De Monarchia* 2.[a] The piece deals first with the transcendence of God, and then describes a divine theophany. The language of the fragment has many elements derived from classical poetry, and it may be, in part at least, genuine.

Pseudo-Justin's introduction:
For, first of all, Aeschylus, using an arrangement of his own words, makes an utterance about the only God when he says:

Clement's introduction:
Again, Aeschylus the tragedian illustrating the power of God does not hesitate to call him "most high" in these words:

> Set God apart from mortals, and do not think
> that he exists in flesh like to yourself.

---

h. These seven are the sun, the moon, and the five planets known in antiquity.

2. Hesiod
a. These lines are F. 308 in Merkelbach and West, whose emendations are reflected in the translation.

3. Pythagoras
a. I.e., this visible cosmos has been made by the one God.

4. Aeschylus
a. The text is F. 464 Aeschylus in the edition of Nauck.

You know him not. At times as fire[b] he appears
unapproachable and raging,[c] at times as water,
                                    at times as darkness.[d]
He is similar to beasts,[e]
to wind, cloud and lightning, thunder, rain.[f]
Sea and rocks serve him,
and every font and all bodies of water.[g]
Hills, earth, the enormous
depth of the sea[h] and the lofty height of mountains quake[i]
when they behold the terrible eye[j] of the Master.
For the glory of the most high God[k] has power over all.

5. Sophocles.

To the second major tragic poet are ascribed several theological fragments. The first is found in Clement of Alexandria, *Protrepticus* 7.74.2 and *Stromata* 5.14.113,2, which is cited by Eusebius, *Praeparatio Evangelica* 13.13.40. The passage is also cited in Pseudo-Justin, *De Monarchia* 2 and in the *Cohortatio ad Gentiles* 18.[a] In the *Stromata*, Clement mentions as his source the work attributed to Hecataeus *On Abraham and the Egyptians*. The verses proclaim the unity of the creator while they condemn idolatry.

Pseudo-Justin's introduction:
Not only was he (Aeschylus) initiated into the knowledge of God, but also Sophocles gives an account of the sole creation of the universe and the one God thusly:

Clement's introduction (Stromata):
As Hecataeus said in his historical work *On Abraham and the Egyptians*, Sophocles cries out on the stage:

God is one, one in very truth,[b]
who fashioned heaven and the broad earth,
the depth's gray swell[c] and the winds' might.[d]
But many of us mortals, erring in our heart,
have set up[e] consolation for calamities,[f]
statues of gods made of stone, or figures of bronze,
wrought gold or ivory.[g]

b. Note that the Divine Warrior "shone forth" in Deut 33:2. The Lord leads his people in a pillar of fire by night, according to Ex 13:21, and he descends on Mount Sinai in fire in Ex 19:18.

c. Cf. Pindar, *Pythian Ode* 1.21, of the fire of Etna. A similar phrase appears in Aeschylus, *Prometheus Bound* 371. The adjective "unapproachable" has connotations of "terrible, monstrous."

d. Cf. Ex 20:18.

e. Note that God brings his people out of Egypt "on the wings of eagles" in Ex 19:4, but the Gk. here may be corrupt.

f. All of these meteorological phenomena are connected with the divine theophany. Cf. Ex 19:16, Judg 5:4f.

g. A similar l. appears in Ezekiel the tragedian, Eusebius, *PrEv* 9.29.12 (GCS 43.1, p. 532f.).

h. Cf. Aeschylus, *Prometheus Bound* 431f.

i. For the quaking of the elements at the appearance of God, cf. Ex 19:18, Judg 5:4, Ps 68:8f.

j. The phrase "terrible eye" (*gorgon omma*) is used in Aeschylus, *Seven Against Thebes* 537.

k. "Most high" (*hypsistos*) is an epithet used of Zeus in Aeschylus, *Eumenides* 28. It was used of many deities in the hellenistic period, but was especially used by Jews. Cf. Gen 14:17(LXX).

5. Sophocles

a. The text is F. 1025 of Aeschylus in the edition of Nauck.

b. The monotheistic affirmation of this first l. certainly recalls Deut 6:4, although similar monotheistic affirmations can be found in syncretistic pagan sources from the hellenistic and Roman periods. Note the Orphic fragment, no. 239, cited in Pseudo-Justin, *Cohortatio ad Gentiles* 15, and Macrobius, *Saturnalia* 1.18.17.

c. The poetic description of the sea is frequently attested: Orphic fragment 245.21, *Anthologia Palatina* 9.36, 12.53, and Nonnus, *Dionysiaca* 4.187.

d. Cf. *Iliad* 16.213.

e. The Gk. word *hidryo* is a technical term for the founding of a sanctuary or cult.

f. Cf. Euripides, *Hecuba* 280 and *Orestes* 62, for similar expressions.

g. Cf. the condemnations of idolatry in Isa 46:6–7, WisSol 13:10, LetJer 17–29.

Sacrifices do we grace with these as well as
lovely[h] holy days, and think we thus act piously.

6. Sophocles.

The second fragment attributed to Sophocles occurs in Clement of Alexandria, *Stromata* 5.14.121,4–122, 1, which is cited by Eusebius, *Praeparatio Evangelica* 13.13.48. The verses are cited by Pseudo-Justin, *De Monarchia* 3, in a slightly longer form than that found in Clement.[a] The additional verses are, no doubt, misplaced in Pseudo-Justin. The attribution of the verses to Sophocles occurs only in Pseudo-Justin. Clement and Eusebius introduce them simply as a quotation from "tragedy." The fragment contains an eschatological vision with many parallels in Stoic thought, as well as in Jewish apocalyptic eschatology.

Pseudo-Justin's introduction:

And for the fact that he alone is able to institute judgment concerning the things done in life and concerning ignorance about the divine, I am able to provide suitable witnesses, first of whom is Sophocles, who says on this matter:

Clement's introduction:

Tragedy agrees with these (the comic verses of number 10 in the translation) in the following verses:

> For there will, there will indeed, come that period of time
> when the gold-faced sky[b] will split apart
> the treasury filled with fire, and the nurtured flame[c]
> will in its rage consume[d] all things on earth
> and in the heavens.

And, after a while, he adds:[e]

> and when the universe gives out,
> the whole wavy deep will be gone;[f]
> the land will be empty of dwellings; the air,
> in flames, will not bear winged flocks.
> For we believe there are two paths in Hades,
> one for the just, the other for the impious.[g]
> Then will he preserve all things which previously perished.[h]

7. Sophocles.

The third iambic fragment attributed to Sophocles is preserved in Clement of Alexandria, *Stromata* 5.14.111,4–6, which is cited by Eusebius, *Praeparatio Evangelica* 13.13.38.[a] The piece describes a mythological episode. It contains nothing specifically Jewish and may

---

h. Pseudo-Justin's text reads "lovely," which may be meant ironically. Clement in the *Stromata* reads "evil" and in the *Protrepticus* "empty."

6. Sophocles

a. The text is F. 1027 of Sophocles in the edition of Nauck.

b. The epithet "gold-faced" is applied to the sun in Euripides, *Electra* 740.

c. For the language of nurturing a flame, cf. Sophocles, *Oedipus Rex* 1425. Here the sky is conceived of as raining fire.

d. For the Stoic doctrine of the final conflagration, cf. Cicero, *De Natura Deorum* 2.118, where the notion of the fiery ether is also prominent. Consuming fire also plays a prominent role in Jewish eschatology. Cf. Mal 3:19; Ezek 38:22; SibOr 3.80–90; *Vita* 49; 2Pet 3:7; Josephus, *Ant* 1.70.

e. Clement, followed by Eusebius, divides the passage into two sections at this point. The vss. form one fragment in Pseudo-Justin.

f. Cf. Sophocles, *Antigone* 15.

g. These two vss. are omitted from the text of Sophocles in Clement, in whose version they appear as part of the fragment of Diphilus. See number 10, below.

h. The subject of this sentence is not explicit. It most probably is God.

7. Sophocles

a. The text is F. 1026 of Sophocles in the edition of Nauck.

well be authentic. It was probably used by a Jewish author to illustrate the low morality of Greek mythology.

Clement's introduction:
Sophocles straightforwardly writes:

For Zeus wed the mother of this man,
not in golden form,[b] nor clothed
with feathers of a swan, as he made pregnant
the maid of Pleuron,[c] but completely as a man.[d]

Then he goes on and adds:
Swiftly the adulterer stood upon the steps
of the bride,[e]

by which becomes even clearer the immorality of the mythical account. Zeus is introduced in this way:
And he, without touching table or basin,
rushed to bed with heart aflame
and through that whole night[f] he kept mounting her.

8. Euripides.

Two short iambic fragments of possible Jewish origin are attributed to the third great fifth-century tragedian. One is cited only by Clement of Alexandria, *Stromata* 5.11.75,1.[a] It proclaims that no temple is worthy of containing God.

Clement's introduction:
Quite beautifully, then, does Euripides agree with these remarks (of Isa 1:11 on sacrifices) as he writes:

What sort of house fashioned by craftsmen
would contain the divine form in the folds of its walls?[b]

9. Euripides/Philemon.

The second fragment, proclaiming that God is invisible, is attributed to Euripides by Clement of Alexandria, *Protrepticus* 6.68.3. Pseudo-Justin, *De Monarchia* 2, attributes the verses to the fourth-century comic poet Philemon.[a] The verses may be authentic.

---

b. Zeus in the form of a golden stream had intercourse with Danae. Cf. Sophocles, *Antigone* 944–50, Horace, *Odes* 3.16.1–12, and Apollodorus, *The Library* 2.4.1.

c. Zeus in the form of a swan had intercourse with Leda. Cf. Euripides, *Helen* 16–22, Apollodorus, *The Library* 3.10.7. Leda was the great-granddaughter of Pleuron. Cf. Pausanias, 3.13.8.

d. These vss. probably refer to the begetting of Heracles, who was born of Alcmena after Zeus slept with her in the form of her husband, Amphitryon. Cf. Hesiod, *Shield of Heracles* 1–56, and Apollodorus, *The Library* 2.4.8.

e. This remark fits the situation of the begetting of Heracles. Amphitryon was unable to sleep with his wife before avenging the death of his wife's brothers. Before he returned from that task, Zeus, the adulterer, had already done his work. Sophocles composed a lost play based on this myth.

f. According to the myth about the birth of Heracles, Zeus prolonged the time he spent with Alcmena into three nights.

8. Euripides
a. The text is F. 1130 of Euripides in the edition of Nauck.

b. That a man-made temple is inadequate to house the divine is affirmed by Isa 66:1 and Acts 7:48 but is also a commonplace in popular hellenistic philosophy. Cf. Seneca, *De Beneficiis* 7.7.3; Plutarch, *De Tranquillitate Animi* 20; and Diogenes Laertius, 7.33 (quoting Zeno).

9. Euripides/Philemon
a. The text is F. 247 of Philemon in the edition of Edmonds and F. 1129 of Euripides in the edition of Nauck.

Pseudo-Justin's introduction:
But Philemon, too, who has much to say on ancient things, partakes in the knowledge of reality, since he writes:

Clement's introduction:
Though unwilling, they confess that God is one, indestructible and unbegotten, and that somewhere on high in the outermost parts of heaven in his own personal watchtower he really exists eternally. . . . So says Euripides:

> Tell me, how should one think of God,
> the one who is all-seeing yet is himself unseen?

10. Diphilus/Philemon/Euripides.

A lengthy set of iambic verses is preserved in several patristic sources, who give various attributions. Clement of Alexandria, *Stromata* 5.14.121,1–3, followed by Eusebius, *Praeparatio Evangelica* 13.13.47, cite the whole collection as a fragment of the fourth-century comic poet Diphilus. Pseudo-Justin, *De Monarchia* 3, quotes the first thirteen verses, including two not in Clement, as a fragment of Philemon.[a] Pseudo-Justin attributes the last eleven verses, including one not in Clement, to Euripides. Within the latter passage, verses 3 to 6 are a genuine fragment of Euripides, from his tragedy the *Phryxos*, which is quoted by Stobaeus, *Anthology* 1.3.15. The comic verses in the first half of the passage may also be genuine. In both cases, a Jewish author has taken verses congenial to Jewish belief and interpolated further material which is unmistakably Jewish. Such interpolations are the reference to the unutterable name of God at the end of the comic verses and possibly the strong affirmation of the existence of God after the genuine verses of Euripides. Common to the whole collection is the affirmation of the reality of reward and punishment after death.

Pseudo-Justin's introduction:
And Philemon again:

Clement's introduction:
Diphilus the comic poet says the following about the judgment:

> Do you think, Niceratos,[b] that those who die
> having had in life a share in every delight
> are covered by the earth and henceforth for all time[c]
> have avoided the notice of the deity and escape him?
> Justice has an eye, which looks upon all things.[d]
> And we believe there are two paths[e] in Hades,
> one for the just, the other for the impious,[f]
> even if the earth forever covers both.
> For if just and unjust will have one end,[g]
> go off and rob, steal, plunder, act in rage.[h]
> Make no mistake. There is, even in Hades, judgment,
> which God, the Lord of all, will execute,

10. Diphilus/Philemon/Euripides
  a. The text is F. 246 of Philemon in the edition of Edmonds.
  b. A Niceratos appears as a character in an anonymous comic fragment from the end of the third century B.C. and in Menander's play *The Samian Lady*. Cf. Edmonds, *The Fragments of Attic Comedy*, 339, 1167.
  c. This vs. is omitted by Clement. Note the similarity with vs. 8.
  d. This l. is cited by Plutarch, *Moralia* 1124F. Justice is often personified. Cf. Hesiod, *Works and Days* 218–24.
  e. On the two paths, cf. Plato, *Gorgias* 523E.
  f. The last two ll. are omitted by Pseudo-Justin, who cites them as part of the fragment of Sophocles given above in number 6, n. 29. The passage in Clement is interrupted at this point.
  g. This vs. is omitted by Clement.
  h. Similar advice is recorded by the Roman comic poet Plautus, *Pseudolus* 138.

> whose name is awesome, and I would not utter it.[i]

And Euripides[j]

> He gives to sinners a long
> life.
> And if some mortal thinks he has escaped
> the notice of the gods while doing evil all day long,
> he reckons ill, and in his reckoning will be seized,
> when Justice at her leisure comes upon him.[k]
> Give heed, you who think there is no God,
> erring twice without careful thought,[l]
> for there is, there is indeed, and if someone prospers,
> while really being wicked, let him take advantage of the present time,
> for in time to come he will pay the penalty.

11. Diphilus/Menander.

Another brief iambic fragment is also preserved with varying attributions. Clement of Alexandria, *Stromata* 5.14.133,3, followed by Eusebius, *Praeparatio Evangelica* 13.13.62, attribute it to Diphilus. Pseudo-Justin, *De Monarchia* 5, attributes it to the major figure in the New Comedy, Menander (late fourth to early third century), in a work called the *Diphilus*.[a] The latter attribution is probably a misunderstanding of the correct attribution found in Clement. It is possible that the fragment is not a Jewish exaltation of the creator but an authentic fragment referring to a divine figure such as Zeus, or possibly Eros. Cf. Plato, *Symposium* 178f.

Clement's introduction:

The comic poet Diphilus says most sententiously:

> Wherefore honor only the one who is forever
> Lord of all and father for all time,
> who discovered and established so many pleasant things.

12. Philemon/Menander.

A final iambic fragment is, again, attributed to various comic poets. Clement of Alexandria, *Stromata* 5.14.119,2, followed by Eusebius, *Praeparatio Evangelica* 13.13.45f., attributes it to Menander and introduces the piece as a parallel to the condemnation of sacrifices in Isa 1:11. Pseudo-Justin, *De Monarchia* 4, cites a longer version of the fragment and attributes it to Philemon.

Pseudo-Justin's introduction:

And that God does not approach the libation or offering of the wicked but apportions recompense to each in righteousness, Philemon again testifies for me:

Clement's introduction:

Menander the comic poet writes in these very words:

---

i. This vs. may be the only Jewish interpolation. On the prohibition against profane uttering of the divine name, cf. Philo, *Vit Mos* 2.114; Josephus, *Ant* 2.276. Cf. also y. Yoma 40d, b. Kid 71a.

j. This is Pseudo-Justin's introduction to the second half of this collection.

k. The last four vss. are the genuine fragment from the lost play the *Phryxos*, of Euripides.

l. Clement omits this vs.

11. Diphilus/Menander
a. The text is F. 138 of Diphilus in the edition of Edmonds.

O Pamphilus,[b] if someone offers as a sacrifice
a multitude of bulls or kids, or by God,
items such as these, or offers works of art,
having fashioned gold or purple mantles,
or animals of ivory or of emerald,
and thinks he thereby renders God propitious,[c]
he is deluded and has not all his wits.
For man must honorable be
and must not seduce women, nor commit adultery
nor steal nor slay for sake of gain,
nor look to others' property, nor covet
either wealthy woman or house
or goods or even slave or servant lass
or horses, cattle or any beast at all. What then?[d]
Covet not, O friend, even a needle's thread.
For God is nearby and is watching you.

Clement comments:

And again Menander, paraphrasing that scripture (which exhorts): "Offer a sacrifice of righteousness and hope in the Lord," writes as follows:

Not even a needle, dear friend,
should you covet, when it is another's. For God
is pleased with just deeds, not unjust,
and he allows a man to earn his livelihood by labor,
by plowing the earth night and day.
Sacrifice to God always being righteous,
shining not in your clothing but in your heart.
If you hear some thunder, do not flee,
as long as you have nothing on your conscience, master.
For God is nearby and is watching you.

---

b. A Pamphilus appears as a character in fragments of Philemon, Philippides, Apollodorus of Carystus, Menander, and an anonymous comic poet. Cf. Edmonds, *The Fragments of Attic Comedy*; vol. 3, pp. 79, 179, 191, 367, 401, 809.

c. Note the similar critique of the cult of images in the fragment ascribed to Sophocles, number 5, above.

d. The preceding four vss. are omitted by Clement. They bring the fragment's condemnation of vice into even closer conformity with the decalogue.

PHILOSOPHY

ARISTOBULUS

(Second Century B.C.)

A NEW TRANSLATION AND INTRODUCTION

BY A. YARBRO COLLINS

The five fragments of Aristobulus' work seem to be part of an extended attempt to relate Jewish tradition to hellenistic culture. Fragment 1 deals with astronomical characteristics of the date of Passover. Aristobulus remarks that, at the feast of the Passover, both the sun and the moon are passing through an equinoctial sign. Thus, they are in diametrically opposed positions on that day.

Fragment 2 is concerned primarily with the nature of God. Aristobulus explains certain anthropomorphic descriptions of God in the Law, which were offensive to educated people of his time.

In fragment 3, Aristobulus claims that Plato and Pythagoras knew the Jewish Law and borrowed from it. In support of this claim, he states that portions of the Law were translated from Hebrew into Greek long before the well-known Septuagint version.

Fragment 4, like fragment 2, discusses the nature of God. The problem of anthropomorphisms is taken up again. Aristobulus argues that Moses and some Greek philosophers and poets had similar ideas about God. But he is not content merely to point out similarities between the Jewish Law and certain Greek authors. As in fragment 3, he claims that some Greek writers knew the Jewish Law and were dependent on it. Here he claims that Socrates, as well as Plato and Pythagoras, made use of the Law. In this fragment, Aristobulus cites verses from Orpheus and Aratus to show how similar their ideas are to those of Moses. Some of the verses cited are attested elsewhere and are thus genuine non-Jewish works. Others are dubious; some are very likely Jewish compositions (see the notes to the translation below).

In fragment 5, the Jewish observance of the Sabbath is explained in terms of cosmic order. Verses from Homer, Hesiod, and the mythical Linus are cited to show that the Greeks also considered the seventh day holy.

Texts

Fragment 1 has been preserved by Eusebius, *Ecclesiastica Historia*, book 7, chapter 32, sections 16–18. In that passage, Eusebius is not quoting directly from Aristobulus' work but is citing Anatolius, *On the Passover*. The edition used for the translation of fragment 1 is by E. Schwartz.[1] Fragments 2–5 are found in Eusebius, *Praeparatio Evangelica*, book 8, chapter 10, and book 13, chapter 12. Part of fragment 5 is also cited, in book 7, chapter 14. The translation below is based on the edition by K. Mras.[2]

Clement of Alexandria also apparently had access to Aristobulus' work. Since his citations are less reliable than those of Eusebius, they were not used in making the translation presented below. Parallels to parts of fragments 2–5 are found in *Stromata*, books 1, 5, and 6 (for exact references, see the n. to the translation). The text of the fragments of Aristobulus,

---

[1] E. Schwartz, *Eusebius Werke, 2. Kirchengeschichte, Zweiter Teil* (GCS 9,2; Leipzig, 1908) pp. 722, 724.
[2] The text of F. 2 is given in Mras, GCS 43,1; pp. 451–54; F. 3–5 are given in GCS 43,2; pp. 190–97.

including the parallels in Clement's *Stromata*, is given by A.-M. Denis, *Fragmenta pseudepigraphorum quae supersunt graeca*.[3]

Anatolius says that Aristobulus dedicated exegetical books on the Law of Moses to Ptolemy Philadelphus (283–246 B.C.) and his father. In introducing fragment 2, Eusebius says that he quotes from Aristobulus' work (*suggramma*) which was dedicated to "Ptolemy the King." The title in the text of Eusebius preceding fragment 3 indicates that the fragment is "from the books of Aristobulus dedicated to King Ptolemy." Eusebius indicates that fragments 4 and 5 are from the same context as 3. N. Walter argued that fragment 5 is a speculative explanation of Genesis 2:1–4.[4] None of the other fragments is a close exegesis of any one, specific passage. Not enough of Aristobulus' work survives to allow firm conclusions about its genre and extent.

Since the seventeenth century a number of scholars have argued that the fragments of Aristobulus were composed only in the early Christian period and not, as they appear to be, in pre-Christian times by a hellenistic Jew. Walter has made a persuasive case for their authenticity.[5]

Original language

There are no indications that the fragments were written originally in a language other than Greek. It is likely that Aristobulus was aware of the allegorical interpretation of Homer and Hesiod practiced by the Stoics and the philological school at Pergamum. Although his approach to the Law is somewhat similar, he does not use the technical terms of allegorical interpretation and he proceeds more cautiously.[6] There is little evidence that Aristobulus knew Hebrew or Aramaic.[7]

Date

Eusebius and Clement say that Aristobulus' work was dedicated to Ptolemy the King. It is evident from other passages that they both believed Ptolemy VI Philometor (181–145 B.C.) to be the king in question.[8] Anatolius' dating of Aristobulus to the reign of Ptolemy II Philadelphus must be an error, since Aristobulus refers to Philadelphus as the forefather (*progonos*) of the Ptolemy for whom he wrote (F. 3).

N. Walter is skeptical about the date given by Clement and Eusebius.[9] His skepticism results from a close study of the passages in which Eusebius mentions Aristobulus. Only when he is clearly dependent on Clement (e.g. *PrEv* 9.6.6) does he mention the eponym Philometor. Elsewhere he simply refers to Ptolemy the King. Since Eusebius is generally faithful to his sources, Walter concludes that the manuscript of Aristobulus used by Eusebius had a superscript which dedicated the work simply to Ptolemy the King. In one of the two places in which Clement dates Aristobulus to the reign of Philometor, he refers to 2 Maccabees 1:10, the prescript of a letter purporting to be from Judas Maccabaeus and the Jews of Judaea to Aristobulus and the Jews of Alexandria. The letter claims to have been written shortly after the death of Antiochus IV Epiphanes (November–December 164 B.C.).[10] Walter follows E. Bickermann in his judgment that the letter is a fabrication dating to about 60 B.C.[11] Since the letter describes Aristobulus as the teacher of Ptolemy the King (with no eponym), Walter concludes that the fabricator of the letter had a text of Aristobulus with the same dedication Eusebius read. Clement's text, according to Walter, had the same dedication. When he read 2 Maccabees, however, which placed Aristobulus in the time of Judas Maccabaeus, he inferred, on the basis of other chronological information available to

---

[3] A.-M. Denis, PVTG 3, pp. 217–28.

[4] N. Walter, *Der Thoraausleger Aristobulos* (Berlin, 1964) p. 28.

[5] *Thoraausleger*, pp. 35–123.

[6] *Thoraausleger*, pp. 124–41.

[7] N. Walter, "Fragmente jüdisch-hellenistischer Exegeten: Aristobulos, Demetrios, Aristeas," *JSHRZ* 3.2 (1975) 264.

[8] Walter, *Thoraausleger*, pp. 13–16.

[9] *Thoraausleger*, pp. 13–26.

[10] A. J. Sachs and D. J. Wiseman, "A Babylonian King List of the Hellenistic Period," *Iraq* 16 (1954) 209.

[11] Walter, *Thoraausleger*, p. 17.

him, that the Ptolemy in question must have been Philometor. Thus, according to Walter, Eusebius' dating is dependent on Clement, and Clement's on 2 Maccabees.

Walter is skeptical about the reliability of this dating, because of his hypothesis that the fabricator of the letter in 2 Maccabees needed a leader of the Jews in Alexandria to serve as an authoritative addressee for his letter. Hence, he arbitrarily chose Aristobulus and placed him in the historical context which suited his purposes.

Against this skeptical position, one can argue that 2 Maccabees 1:10 may reflect a tradition that Aristobulus lived and wrote during the time of Ptolemy VI. It is not unreasonable to assume that the author of 2 Maccabees would have been familiar with such a tradition.[12] Even if the letter is a fabrication dating to about 60 B.C., such a tradition could easily have survived for a century or so.

In any case, the fragments should not be dated much before the middle of the second century B.C., because Aristobulus calls Ptolemy I the forefather of the Ptolemy he is addressing; thus, he must be addressing the grandson of Ptolemy I (who was Ptolemy IV Philopator, 221–204 B.C.) or a later king. But he uses the eponym "Philadelphus" for Ptolemy II, and it first came into use in the second century to distinguish him from the other Ptolemies.[13] Thus Ptolemy V Epiphanes (205–180 B.C.) would be the earliest king to come under consideration. Since Aristobulus is already familiar with the legend about the origin of the Septuagint, he should not be dated too close to the third century. Thus, the latter part of the reign of Philometor seems to be the earliest reasonable date for the fragments. If Walter is correct that the evidence of 2 Maccabees is unreliable, a later date is possible.

M. Hengel thinks more weight should be given to the notice of 2 Maccabees 1:10. He argues that the fabricator of the letter addressed it to Aristobulus because it was known that he had written a didactic letter to the young Philometor. He takes seriously the description of Aristobulus as the teacher of Ptolemy and thus dates the work to the early part of the reign of Ptolemy VI. He argues further that, since the work was dedicated to Ptolemy alone, it must have been written while he was sole ruler; this was the case only from 176 to 170 B.C.[14]

Against Hengel's point of view, it might be said that, while it is conceivable that Jews were participating in the intellectual life of the court at Alexandria in the mid-second century B.C., it is somewhat unlikely that a Jew would have been a teacher of a Ptolemy at that time, especially since no other notice of such a relationship has survived. Walter's suggestion is more plausible: that the author of the letter read Aristobulus and, taking note of the direct address to Ptolemy and the explanatory nature of the writing, surmised that the author had been indeed an instructor of the king. There is no good reason to doubt that Aristobulus wrote during the reign of Ptolemy VI Philometor. But the fact that the work was addressed solely to Ptolemy does not necessarily mean that he was sole ruler at the time. To make this point, Hengel would have to show that it was customary to include the names of the guardian of the king, his wife, or co-ruler in literary dedications as well as in contracts. The latter part of the reign of Philometor (155–145 B.C.) thus seems to be the most likely date for the work of Aristobulus.

Provenance

Aristobulus' direct address to a Ptolemy, a descendant of Philadelphus, in fragment 3 makes an Alexandrian provenance for his work likely. This conclusion is supported by Eusebius' and Clement's statements that Aristobulus' work was dedicated to Ptolemy the King and that he lived during the time of Ptolemy Philometor (see the section on *Date*, above). Those scholars who accept the authenticity of the fragments consider Aristobulus an Alexandrian Jew.[15]

---

[12] J. Moffatt ("2 Maccabees," *APOT*, vol. 1, pp. 130f.) argued that the author of 2 Maccabees was an Alexandrian Jew.

[13] H. Volkmann, "Ptolemaios," Pauly-Wissowa vol. 23, col. 1645.

[14] M. Hengel, *Judaism and Hellenism* (Philadelphia, 1974) vol. 1, pp. 163f.; vol. 2, pp. 105–7 (nn. 373 and 378).

[15] Walter, *Thoraausleger*, pp. 38–41; Walter, *JSHRZ* 3.2 (1975) 262; Hengel, *Judaism and Hellenism*, vol. 1, pp. 69f., 90, 163f.; P. M. Fraser, *Ptolemaic Alexandria* (Oxford, 1972) vol. 1, p. 695.

Historical importance

The fragments of Aristobulus provide important information about how a Jew in the second century B.C. attempted to reconcile Jewish tradition and hellenistic philosophy. Although there is little evidence that Aristobulus was a member of or founded a school of Jewish philosophy, it is clear that he stands in a particular line of tradition, beginning with the translation of the Hebrew Bible into Greek and flowering in the work of Philo.[16] Aristobulus' work thus helps the historian trace the genesis of Philo's point of view and methods.

Aristobulus contributes to our knowledge of hellenistic Judaism in that he is the first known Jewish philosopher. The dedication of his work to Ptolemy, the direct address to the king in fragments 2 and 3, and the general tone of an address to outsiders[17] indicate that the work has an apologetic intent. It is likely that the reconciliation of the two cultures was of importance to the self-understanding of Aristobulus and his fellow Jews also.

In fragments 1 and 5 Aristobulus seems to point out that the Jewish feasts (Passover and Sabbath) have cosmic significance. They are observed not only because of particular experiences peculiar to the Jewish people but also because they express aspects of cosmic reality which have universal significance.[18] The Passover is associated with the spring equinox and marked by the positions of both sun and moon (F. 1), and the Sabbath with the sevenfold pattern in the overall structure of the cosmos (F. 5).

Fragment 5 provides important evidence for Jewish use of Pythagorean ideas in the second century B.C. Both Aristobulus and Philo (*SpecLeg* 2.59) seem to presuppose a traditional, allegorical interpretation of the biblical account of creation. This interpretation made use of Pythagorean reflections on the number seven as a prime number.[19]

Theological importance

Aristobulus is of great interest as the earliest known theologian in the Judeo-Christian tradition engaged in the hermeneutical task. He presupposes that reality is a unified whole and that there cannot be contradictions between the truth of Scripture and the truth of philosophy. Apparent contradictions can be resolved by interpreting Scripture in accordance with the laws of nature (*physikōs*) instead of in a mythological or human way (F. 2:2). Or, to put it another way, one must not read according to the letter but must discern the "elevated" meaning (F. 2:5, 9). In any case, descriptions of God must be interpreted in accordance with "the fitting conception of God" (F. 2:2).

In discussing the "standing" of God (F. 2:9–12), Aristobulus used the allegorical method of interpretation which the Stoics had applied to Homer and which later Philo also applied to the Bible.[20] According to Aristobulus, one can assume that the writer at times used words relating to outward appearances in order to express something about the arrangements of nature and the constitutions of great matters (F. 2:3). Another method he uses is to point out that the biblical writer has made use of a metaphor; he does this in interpreting references to God's "hands" (F. 2:7–9). Elsewhere, in speaking of wisdom as the source of light (F. 5:10), Aristobulus himself deliberately and consciously makes use of a metaphor in his interpretation (F. 5:10). Even in a case in which Aristobulus wants to affirm the text as a description of an actual event, he moves on from a discussion of *what* happened to *why*. The descent of God upon Sinai is thus interpreted symbolically as an expression of divine activity in its omnipresent majesty (F. 2:17).

Aristobulus is notable, as has been shown, because of his concern to develop a hermeneutical method. His work is also of interest as an early and simple example of a theology which unites Jewish reflections on wisdom with hellenistic ideas about the Logos. A. Schlatter and P. Dalbert claimed too much by construing Aristobulus' use of *logos* as an expression of a divine hypostasis.[21] In fragment 4, Aristobulus discusses God's creation by the spoken

[16] Fraser, *Ptolemaic Alexandria*, vol. 1, pp. 695f.; H. Wolfson, *Philo* (Cambridge, England, 1948) vol. 1, p. 94.
[17] Note, e.g., the references to "*our* philosophical school," near the end of F. 4 (emphasis added). The "school" refers to Judaism.
[18] Walter, *Thoraausleger*, p. 138; Hengel, *Judaism and Hellenism*, vol. 1, p. 166.
[19] *Thoraausleger*, pp. 156f.; Hengel, *Judaism and Hellenism*, vol. 1, pp. 166f.
[20] *Thoraausleger*, pp. 124–49.
[21] See Walter's criticism of their views, *Thoraausleger*, p. 81, n. 3.

word, alluding to Genesis 1. The method of interpretation used in this passage seems to be the same used with regard to God's "standing" (F. 2:9–12). There he says that the elevated meaning is the establishment of the cosmos. Here he says that the "voice" of God means the establishment of things (F. 4:3). The passage shows that it is the attribution of speech generally to God (expressed in various ways) which is to be interpreted allegorically, not his word (*logos*) as such. The variation in vocabulary and the tentative, nontechnical character of the method show that Aristobulus represents an early stage in the development both of the allegorical method and of theological reflection on the Logos.

In fragment 5, wisdom is associated with the seventh day (F. 5:9f.). The seventh day, in turn, is associated with the sevenfold principle (*logos*), the sevenfold structure of all things (F. 5:12). Thus wisdom and Logos have similar functions. Wisdom is the source of light in which all things are contemplated. Through the sevenfold principle, we have knowledge of human and divine matters. Aristobulus is a pioneer in this kind of reflection; this is shown by the explicit remark that he is speaking metaphorically (F. 5:10). These reflections of Aristobulus are important for anyone seeking to understand the role of the Logos in Philo's thought or in the Gospel of John.

Relation to canonical books

Exodus 12 probably influenced Aristobulus' discussion of the date of Passover. Various passages in Exodus, Deuteronomy, Genesis, and Numbers are quoted or alluded to in the treatment of anthropomorphisms in fragments 2 and 4 (see the margins of the translation for references). The Acts of the Apostles refers to the same passage of Aratus quoted in fragment 4. Titus 2:12 also lists two of the three virtues mentioned in fragment 4:8 (piety and justice). The author of the letter to Titus may have drawn directly upon hellenistic ethical teaching,[22] or may be dependent upon hellenistic Judaism at this point. Genesis 1–2 stands behind the discussion of the Sabbath in fragment 5. Other biblical passages seem to be behind other parts of fragment 5 (see the margins of the translation).

Aristobulus seems to be interested primarily in interpreting the Torah (Pentateuch). On one occasion at least (F. 5:11), he alludes to the Writings, probably to Proverbs 8. The quotations in fragments 2 and 4 seem to derive from the Septuagint, which is what one would expect, given the explicit mention of it in fragment 3.[23]

Relation to apocryphal books and to later literature

The relationship between the fragments of Aristobulus and 2 Maccabees has already been discussed in the section on *Date*.

E. Schürer argued that Aristobulus cited the poem attributed to Orpheus and the verses on the seventh day from Pseudo-Hecataeus' book on Abraham. Others argued that Aristobulus is indirectly dependent upon another work attributed to Hecataeus, *Concerning Jews*. Neither conclusion is warranted.[24]

The fragments of Aristobulus and the Letter of Aristeas share a number of features. Both refer to the legend about the translation of the Jewish Law made under Ptolemy Philadelphus and Demetrius Phalereus. Since the Letter of Aristeas gives the legend in detail and Aristobulus mentions it only in passing, many scholars, including E. Schürer and W. Bousset, concluded that Aristobulus was literarily dependent upon the Letter. It has been argued, however, that the author of the Letter did not invent the legend, but only used it for his own purposes.[25] If this theory is correct, the two authors could have known the legend independently. There are also a number of verbal similarities, but not enough to indicate literary dependence in either direction.[26]

---

[22] This possibility is implied by M. Dibelius and H. Conzelmann in *The Pastoral Epistles* (Philadelphia, 1972) p. 142.

[23] Walter, *Thoraausleger*, pp. 32f.; Walter, *JSHRZ* 3.2 (1975) 264.

[24] *Thoraausleger*, pp. 87f.

[25] *Thoraausleger*, p. 91, n. 3.

[26] *Thoraausleger*, pp. 88–103. Walter argues cautiously that at some points Aristobulus seems to be prior. There does not seem to be enough evidence to establish such a conclusion.

A. Elter and P. Wendland argued that the fragments of Aristobulus are dependent upon Philo and thus a forgery from Christian times. Walter has shown persuasively that such dependence is very unlikely.[27] Aristobulus is more primitive in vocabulary and method; this primitiveness would be hard to explain after Philo. The technical vocabulary of allegorical interpretation is absent in Aristobulus (*allēgoria, tropikōs, hyponoia*) and his interpretations are more self-conscious and cautious.

The extant fragments of Aristobulus' work survive only because early Christian writers were interested in them. His cosmic reflections on the date of the Passover were cited by Anatolius in support of his view that Easter ought to be celebrated on the same day as the Passover. Clement and Eusebius cited from his work because its allegorical method was useful to them in interpreting the "Scripture" (*graphas*). His claim that many great Greek thinkers and poets were dependent upon Moses supported their own apologetic concerns.

Cultural importance

The issues discussed above with regard to historical and theological importance are significant also for those concerned with the history of culture. Further, Aristobulus is of note for the history of philosophy. H. Wolfson suggested that Western philosophy may be divided into three epochs: ancient philosophy, which did not know Scripture; medieval philosophy, which began with Scripture as revelation; and modern philosophy, which had its inception in an attempt to free itself from Scripture. According to Wolfson, the fundamental departure from ancient philosophy involved a new theory of knowledge by introducing a new source of knowledge. This fundamental change appears first in hellenistic Judaism, where it attains its systematic formulation in Philo.[28] Aristobulus is Philo's most important known forerunner in this regard.

SELECT BIBLIOGRAPHY

Charlesworth, *PMR*, pp. 81f.
Delling, *Bibliographie*, pp. 53–55.
Denis, *Introduction*, pp. 277–83.

Collins, J. J. *Between Athens and Jerusalem*. New York, 1983; pp. 175–78 and *passim*. (Discusses Aristobulus in the context of Jewish identity in the Diaspora.)
Fraser, P. M. *Ptolemaic Alexandria*. Oxford, 1972; vol. 1, pp. 695–96; vol. 2, pp. 963–70. (Discusses historical matters and the place of Aristobulus in Alexandrian literature.)
Hengel, M. *Judaism and Hellenism*, trans. J. Bowden. Philadelphia, 1974; vol. 1, pp. 163–69; vol. 2, pp. 105–10. (Situates Aristobulus in the intellectual history of Judaism.)
Sandelin, K.-G. "Zwei Kurze Studien zum alexandrinischen Judentum," *ST*, 31 (1977) 147–52. (A discussion of Aristobulus' remarks on the descent of God on Sinai.)
Walter, N. *Der Thoraausleger Aristobulos*. TU 86; Berlin, 1964. (The basic study; includes bibliography of older studies.)
―――. "Fragmente jüdisch-hellenistischer Exegeten: Aristobulos, Demetrios, Aristeas," *JSHRZ* 3.2 (1975) 261–79. (Introduction, bibliography, and translation with nn.)

---

[27] *Thoraausleger*, pp. 58–86.
[28] Wolfson, *Philo*, vol. 2, pp. 444f., 456f.

TRANSLATION

Fragment 1 *Eusebius, "Ecclesiastica Historia" 7.32.16–18*

On the date of the Passover

16 And this is not our own reckoning,[a] but it was known to the Jews long ago even before Christ and it was carefully observed by them. One can learn it from what is said by Philo, Josephus, (and) Musaeus,[b] and not only by these, but also by both of the Agathobuli, who are still more ancient and are surnamed the teachers. One can learn it also from what is said by the excellent Aristobulus,[c] who was enrolled among the seventy[d] who translated the sacred and divine Scriptures of **F. 3:1f.** the Hebrews for Ptolemy Philadelphus and his father and who dedicated exegetical **F. 3:2** books on the law of Moses to the same kings.

17 When these (writers) explain questions concerning the Exodus, they say that it is necessary that all alike sacrifice the Passover after the vernal equinox, in the **Ex 12:6** middle of the first month[e]; and this occurs when the sun passes through the first sector of the solar, or as some of them called (it), the zodiacal circle.

And Aristobulus adds that on the feast of the Passover of necessity not only the sun will be passing through an equinoctial sector, but the moon also.

18 For, since there are two equinoctial sections, the vernal and the autumnal, and since they are diametrically opposite one another, and since the day of the Passover was assigned to the fourteenth of the month after evening, the moon will stand in **Ex 12:6** the position opposite and over against the sun, just as one can see (it) at the seasons of full moon. (So) the one, the sun, will be in the sector of the vernal equinox, and the other, the moon, of necessity will be in (the sector of) the autumnal (equinox).

Fragment 2 *Eusebius, "Praeparatio Evangelica" 8.9.38–8.10.17.*

On anthropomorphisms

9.38 It is time to listen to what sorts of things Aristobulus recounted concerning elements in the sacred books which are currently understood to refer to God's limbs. Aristobulus was familiar with Aristotelian philosophy in addition to that of **F. 3 (Title)** his ancestors. (He is the one whom the second book of the Maccabees mentions **2Mac 1:10** in the beginning of the book.) And in his work (dedicated) to Ptolemy the King this man also explains this method:

10.1 When, however, enough had been said in response to the questions set forth, you

---

Fragment 1

a. Anatolius was an Alexandrian teacher of Aristotelian philosophy who became bishop of Caesarea in Palestine and later of Laodicea in Syria. He died in Laodicea around A.D. 282. In his work *On the Passover*, he apparently defended the position of the Quartodecimans, that Easter ought to be celebrated on the same day as the Jewish Passover, the fourteenth of the Jewish lunar month Nisan.

b. Musaeus was a mythical singer, closely related to Orpheus. There were oracles in circulation supposed to have been written by him. Anatolius may refer here to a Jewish poem attributed to

Musaeus, like the Pseudo-Orphic hymn quoted by Aristobulus and discussed by M. Lafargue in this volume.

c. The translation reflects the Greek MSS. The Latin and Syriac read "Aristobulus from Paneas" (that is, Caesarea Philippi).

d. Anatolius here refers to the legend that the Hebrew Bible was translated into Greek in Alexandria during the reign of Ptolemy II Philadelphus (283–246 B.C.). The most extensive account of the legend is in the pseudepigraphical LetAris, according to which there were seventy-two translators.

e. Philo, *SpecLeg* 2.145–61, *Quaes Ex* 1.4; Josephus, *Ant* 2.311–13, 3.248.

also, O King, exclaimed (questioning) why indications are given of hands and arms and face and feet and walking about throughout our Law with respect to the divine power. These things will receive a proper discussion and they will not contradict in any way what was said by us beforehand. F. 4:3

2 And I wish to exhort you to receive the interpretations according to the laws of nature[a] and to grasp the fitting conception of God and not to fall into the mythical and human way of thinking about God.

3 For our lawgiver Moses proclaims arrangements of nature and preparations for great events by expressing that which he wishes to say in many ways, by using words that refer to other matters (I mean matters relating to outward appearances).

4 Therefore, those who are able to think well marvel at his wisdom and at the divine spirit in accordance with which he has been proclaimed as a prophet also. Among these are the philosophers already mentioned and many others, including poets, who took significant material from him and are admired accordingly. Deut 18:18; 34:10
F. 3:1
F. 4:4
F. 4:4–6
F. 5:13–16

5 But to those who have no share of power and understanding, but who are devoted to the letter alone, he does not seem to explain anything elevated.

6 I shall begin then to take up each thing signified in turn, to the extent that I am able. But if I miss the point or fail to be persuasive, attribute the lack of reason not to the lawgiver but to my inability to interpret his thoughts.

7 Now "hands" are clearly thought of even in our own time in a more general way. For when you, being king, send out forces, wishing to accomplish something, we say, "The king has a mighty hand," and the hearers are referred to the power which you have.

8 Now Moses indicates this also in our Law when he speaks thus: *"God brought you out of Egypt with a mighty hand,"* and again he says that God said to him, *"I will send forth my hand and I will strike the Egyptians."* And with respect to the death which came upon the cattle and the others he speaks to the king of the Egyptians, saying, *"Behold, the hand of the Lord shall be upon your cattle and a great death shall be upon all that are in the fields,"* so that it is necessary that the hands be explained as the power of God. For it is possible for people speaking metaphorically to consider that the entire strength of human beings and their active powers are in their hands.[b] Ex 13:9 (LXX)

Ex 3:20 (LXX)

Ex 9:3 (LXX)

9 Therefore, the lawgiver has employed a metaphor well for the purpose of saying something elevated, when he says that the accomplishments of God are his hands.

And the establishment of the cosmos might well be called divine "standing"[c] in accordance with the elevated (level of meaning). Gen 28:13
Ex 17:6

10 For indeed God is over all things and all things have been subordinated (to him) and have received their "standing" (from him), with the result that human beings comprehend that these things are unalterable. I mean something like this, that heaven has never become earth and earth heaven, nor has sun become shining moon, nor moon again sun, nor rivers sea, nor sea rivers.

11 And again with regard to living beings, there is the same rule. For a human being will not become beast nor a beast a human being. And the same thing applies also to the rest, to plants and the others. They are not interchangeable, but the members of each group change and are destroyed in the same way. F. 5:12

12 In these respects, therefore, divine "standing" might be spoken of, because all things are subjected to God.

It is said too in the book of the Law that there was a descent of God upon the mountain, at the time when he was giving the Law, in order that all might see the action of God. For this descent was manifest; therefore, anyone wishing to guard the account about God should interpret these things in the following way. Ex 19:11

13 For it is set forth that *"the mountain was burning with fire,"* so says the Law, Ex 19:16–18;
24:17
Deut 4:11; 5:23;
9:15

Fragment 2

a. Or "in a way corresponding to reality," a technical term of the Stoics.

b. Philo, *LegAll* 2.89. *SpecLeg* 4.138.
c. Philo, *Somn* 1.157–58, 241; 2.219–22.

on account of God's coming down. It also says that there were trumpet blasts and the fire blazing without substance. Ex 19:16,19; 20:18
Ex 3:2

14 For even though the whole multitude of not less than a hundred myriads (one million),[d] not counting minors,[e] was assembled round about the mountain and even though the making of a circuit around it would take not less than five days, the fire was seen blazing from every point of view around them all where they were camped.[f] Ex 12:37f.
Num 1:45–47;
11:21
Ex 19:2,17

15 Therefore, the descent was not local; for God is everywhere. Rather he (the lawgiver) showed that the power of fire, which is marvelous beyond all things because it consumes all things, blazes without substance and consumes nothing, unless the power from God (to consume) is added to it. Ex 3:2

16 For, although the regions were blazing mightily, (the fire) consumed nothing of the growing things throughout the mountain, but the foliage of all of them remained untouched by fire. The trumpet blasts were quite strongly audible at the same time as the exhibition of the lightning-like fire, although no such instruments were present nor any to sound them, but all things happened by divine arrangement.

17 Therefore, it is clear that the divine descent occurred for these reasons: in order that the viewers might comprehend each of these things in a revelatory way—not that the fire consumed nothing, as has been said, nor that the trumpet blasts came into being without human activity or the use of instruments, but that God, without any aid, manifested his own majesty, which is throughout all things.

Fragment 3   *Eusebius, 13.12.1f.*

Greek dependence on the Jewish Law

(Title) That also Aristobulus, who lived before us and was of the Hebrew people, the peripatetic (philosopher), agreed that the Greeks begin from the philosophy of the Hebrews;[a] from the (books) of Aristobulus dedicated to King Ptolemy:

1 It is evident that Plato imitated our legislation and that he had investigated thoroughly each of the elements in it. For it had been translated by others before[b] Demetrius Phalereus,[c] before the conquests of Alexander[d] and the Persians.[e] The parts concerning the exodus of the Hebrews, our fellow countrymen, out of Egypt, the fame of all the things that happened to them, the conquest of the land, and the detailed account of the entire legislation (were translated).[f] So it is very clear that the philosopher mentioned above took many things (from it). For he was very learned, as was Pythagoras, who transferred many of our doctrines and integrated them into his own system of beliefs.[g] F. 4:4, 2:4

2 But the entire translation of all the (books) of the Law (was made) in the time of the king called Philadelphus, your ancestor. He brought greater zeal (to the task than his predecessors), while Demetrius Phalereus managed the undertaking. F. 1:16

d. Philo., *SpecLeg* 2.146.

e. Or "not counting the elderly."

f. F. 2:14–16 is cited by Clement (*Strom* 6.32,3–33,1).

Fragment 3

a. Artapanus (*PrEv* 9.27.4) says that Moses invented and taught philosophy (see the section on Artapanus).

b. LetAris 30, 314.

c. Peripatetic philosopher, statesman, and writer

who ruled Athens (318–307 b.c.) and was adviser to Ptolemy I Soter in Alexandria (c. 297 b.c.). On the translation connected with his name see LetAris 301–22.

d. 332 b.c.

e. 343 b.c. or 525 b.c.

f. Apparently a reference to the books of Ex, Lev, Num, Deut, and Josh.

g. Clement cites F. 3:1 in *Strom* 1.150, 1–3 and uses F. 3:2 in *Strom* 1.148,1.

Fragment 4   *Eusebius, 13.13.3–8*

Anthropomorphisms and Greek dependence on the Law

3 Then, having said some things in between, he continues, saying:

For it is necessary to take the divine "voice" not as a spoken word, but as the
establishment of things.[a] Just so has Moses called the whole genesis of the world
words of God in our Law. For he continually says in each case, *"And God spoke
and it came to pass."*

4 And it seems to me that Pythagoras, Socrates, and Plato with great care follow
him in all respects. They copy him when they say that they hear the voice of
God, when they contemplate the arrangement of the universe, so carefully made
and so unceasingly held together by God.[b] And further, Orpheus[c] also imitates
Moses in verses from his (books) on the Hieros Logos. He expresses himself thus
concerning the maintaining of all things by divine power, their being generated
and God's being over all things. And he speaks so:[d]

5 I will sing for those for whom it is lawful, but you uninitiate, close your doors,
Charged under the laws of the Righteous ones, for the Divine has legislated
For all alike. But you, son of the light-bearing moon,
Musaeus, listen, for I proclaim the Truth.
Let not what you formerly felt lose for you a happy eternity,
But look to the divine word, study it closely,
[So] guiding your heart, that knowing vessel. Set out firmly
On the path, and look only at the undying shaper of the universe.
There is an ancient saying about him:
"He is one"—self-completing, and all things completed by him,
In them he himself circulates. But no one has seen him
With the souls mortals have, he is seen [only] by Mind.
He does not take good things and make them into evil
For people, but he comes in company with love and hate,
"And war and plague and weeping pain"—
"And there is no other." You would understand everything
If you were to see him. But before that, here on earth, sometimes,
My son, I will point it out to you, whenever I notice his footsteps,
And the strong hand of the mighty God.
But I do not see him, because around [him] a cloud is set up,
A thin one for me, but tenfold for all [other] people.
For all mortals have mortal pupils in their eyes,
[Too] small, since flesh and bones have produced them,
[Too] weak to see Zeus, the ruler of all.
And no one has seen the ruler of mortal men,
Except a certain unique man, an offshoot from far back of the race
Of the Chaldeans. For he was knowledgeable about the path of the Star,
And how the movement of the Sphere goes around the earth,
Both in circular fashion, but each on its own axis.
He rides in spirit through the air and through the water
Of the stream. A comet makes manifest these events—he had a mighty birth.
Yes, he after this is established in the great heaven
On a golden throne. He stands with his feet on the earth.
He stretches out his right hand to the ends of the ocean.
The foundation of the mountains trembles within at [his] anger,

Marginal references:
F. 2:1
Deut 4:12,33;
5:23–26
Gen 1:3,6,9,
14,20,24 (LXX)

F. 2:4
F. 3:1

F. 2:4;
5:13–16;
1:16 (n.b)

Deut 6:4

Isa 45:5

Mt 2:2

Isa 66:1

Fragment 4

a. Philo, *Migr* 48f.

b. Plato, *Tim* 47 A–E, *Apol* 31 D, *Theag* 128
D. F. 4:3–4a is used by Clement (*Strom* 5.99,3).

c. Artapanus claims that Moses taught Orpheus

(*PrEv* 9.27,4); see the contribution on Artapanus
in this volume.

d. [The translation of the Orphic poem which is
given here is from M. Lafargue's contribution
above. —J.H.C.]

And the depths of the gray sparkling sea.
They cannot endure the mighty power. He is entirely
Heavenly, and he brings everything to completion on earth,
Being "the beginning, the middle, and the end,"   Rev 1:8
As the saying of the ancients, as the one water-born has described it,
The one who received [revelations] from God in aphorisms, in the form of a
   double law.
It is unlawful to say anything else. My body is trembling.
In Mind, from above, he rules over everything according to an order.
My son, approach him with your Mind,
And do not betray, but guard the divine message in your heart.

6 And Aratus[e] also speaks about the same things thus:
Let us begin with God, whom men never leave unspoken; full of God are the
streets, and all the marketplaces of humanity, and full the sea and the harbors;
and we are all in need of God everywhere.[f] We are all his children; and he gently   Acts 17:28
to humanity gives good omens, and rouses people to work, reminding (them) of
sustenance; and he tells when the soil is best for cattle and for pickaxes, and he
tells when seasons are favorable both for planting trees and for sowing all seeds.

7 I believe that it has been clearly shown how the power of God is throughout all
things. And we have given the true sense, as one must, by removing the (name)
Zeus throughout the verses. For their (the verses') intention refers to God, therefore
it was so expressed by us. We have presented these things therefore in a way not
unsuited to the things being discussed.

8 For it is agreed by all the philosophers that it is necessary to hold holy opinions
concerning God,[g] a point our philosophical school makes particularly well. And
the whole constitution of our Law is arranged with reference to piety and justice   Tit 2:12
and temperance and the rest of the things that are truly good.[h]

Fragment 5   *Eusebius, 13.12.9–16*

On the sabbath

9 Following these things, after other (remarks), he adds:
And connected (with this) is (the fact) that God, who established the whole   Gen 2:2f.
cosmos, also gave us the seventh day as a rest, because life is laborious for all.[a]   Ex 20:8–11
 Deut 5:12–15
According to the laws of nature,[b] the seventh day might be called first also, as   Ex 23:12
the genesis of light in which all things are contemplated.[c]   Gen 1:3–5

10 And the same thing might be said metaphorically about wisdom also. For all light
has its origin in it. And some of those belonging to the Peripatetic school have
said that wisdom holds the place of a lantern; for as long as they follow it
unremittingly, they will be calm through their whole life.[d]

11 And one of our ancestors, Solomon, said more clearly and better that wisdom   Prov 8:22–31
existed before heaven and earth; which indeed agrees with what has been said.
And it is plainly said by our legislation that God rested on the seventh day.   Gen 2:2
This does not mean, as some interpret, that God no longer does anything. It means

---

e. Aristobulus cites here the first nine lines of
an astronomical poem, *Phaenomena*, by Aratus of
Soli, in Cilicia (c. 315–240/239 B.C.). For the
complete text and translation of *Phaenomena* see
A. W. Mair's publication in LCL. Note that
Aristobulus changed *Zeus* in the poem to *theos*.
   f. Or "and we consult God's oracles everywhere." If the Gk. word for "God" be emended
from the genitive to the dative case, the translation
would be "and we have familiar intercourse with

God everywhere."
   g. LetAris 234f.
   h. Philo, *Quod Omn* 83.

Fragment 5
   a. Jub 2:18–20.
   b. Or "in a way corresponding to reality" (see
F. 2:2, n. a).
   c. Philo, *SpecLeg* 2.59.
   d. Philo, *Ebr* 31.

that, after he had finished ordering all things, he so orders them for all time.

12 For the legislation signifies that *in six days* he *made heaven and earth and all*   Ex 20:11 (LXX)
things which are in them in order that he might make manifest the times and   Gen 1:14–18
foreordain what precedes what with respect to order. For, having set all things in
order, he maintains and alters them so (in accordance with that order). And the   F. 2:11
legislation has shown plainly that the seventh day is legally binding for us as a
sign of the sevenfold principle[e] which is established around us, by which we have
knowledge of human and divine matters.

13 And indeed all the cosmos of all living beings and growing things revolves in
series of sevens.[f] Its being called "sabbath" is translated as "rest." And both
Homer and Hesiod, having taken information from our books, say clearly that the   F. 2:4
seventh day is holy. Hesiod (speaks) so:

To begin with, (the) first, (the) fourth and (the) seventh, (each) a holy day;[g]
And again he says:
And on the seventh day (is) again the bright light of the sun.[h]

14 And Homer speaks so:
And then indeed the seventh day returned, a holy day;[i]
[and
Then was the holy seventh day][j]
and again:
It was the seventh day and on it all things had been completed[k]   Gen 2:2f.
and:
And on the seventh morning we left the stream of Acheron.[l]

15 He (Homer) thereby signifying that away from the forgetfulness and evil of the
soul, by means of the sevenfold principle[m] in accordance with the truth, the things
mentioned before are left behind and we receive knowledge of the truth, as has
been said above.[n]

16 And Linus[o] speaks so:
And on the seventh morning all things were made complete;[p]
and again:
(The) seventh (day) is of good quality and (the) seventh (day) is birth;[q]
and:
(The) seventh (day) is among the prime (numbers) and (the) seventh (day) is
perfect;
[and]
And all seven (heavenly bodies) have been created in the starry heaven,
Shining in their orbits in the revolving years.
Such then are the remarks of Aristobulus.[r]

---

e. Or "as a sign of our seventh faculty, namely, reason."

f. There are various points of contact between F. 5:9–13 and Clement, *Strom* 6.137–44.

g. Hesiod, *Opera et Dies*, 770.

h. The verse is not attested in the works of Hesiod; cf. Homer, *Iliad* 1.605; Hesiod, *Theog* 760, 958.

i. This verse is not attested in Homer's works.

j. The material in brackets does not occur in *PrEv* 13.12, 14; it is cited in 13.13, 34 and by Clement, *Strom* 5.107, 2.

k. This verse seems to be based on Homer,

Odyssey 5.262, which reads "the fourth day."

l. This verse is not attested but is related to *Odyssey* 10.513, 12.1.

m. Or "reason."

n. The Greek here is nearly unintelligible.

o. A mythical singer, like Musaeus and Orpheus.

p. This verse is probably a Jewish composition.

q. Or "The seventh day and the seventh birth are good." According to Philo the seventh day was the birthday of the world (*Op* 89).

r. Clement cites the same verses as F. 5:13–16 in *Strom* 5.107, 1–108, 1 and attributes them to Callimachus.

DEMETRIUS THE CHRONOGRAPHER

(Third Century B.C.)

A NEW TRANSLATION AND INTRODUCTION

BY J. HANSON

Six fragments are customarily ascribed to Demetrius.[1] All are concerned with the Old Testament in one way or another. Fragment 1 is a synopsis of the story of the sacrifice of Isaac (Gen 22). Fragment 2, the longest of the six, mainly involves patriarchal chronology, relating Jacob's career and the birthdates and ages of his twelve sons and one daughter in conjunction with it and concluding with a brief treatment of the main events of Joseph's career in Egypt and of the chronology of Moses' ancestors. Fragment 3 chiefly concerns the genealogy of Moses and Zipporah, reconciling the various Old Testament traditions about the latter's father.[2] Fragment 4 is a synopsis of the story of the changing of bitter water to sweet at Marah, and the arrival of the people at Elim (Ex 15:22–27). Fragment 5 deals with the question of how the people of the Exodus got their weapons.

There is no internal evidence for the title of the work from which the first five fragments are drawn. Fragment 6, however, is said to be from Demetrius' work *On the Kings in Judaea* and gives the number of years between the various deportations of Israel and Judah and Demetrius' own time. This is a period of biblical history much later than that treated in fragments 1–5. Yet it is not necessary to posit that these fragments were taken from a different work, however inappropriate the title may seem for patriarchal traditions.[3]

Text and language

Fragments 1–5 are preserved in Eusebius, *Praeparatio Evangelica*, Book 9, where he has excerpted the work of Alexander Polyhistor *On the Jews;* Polyhistor had, in turn, excerpted the work of Demetrius. The translation of the first five fragments follows the text and numbered divisions of K. Mras's edition of Eusebius' *Praeparatio Evangelica;*[4] the text used for the translation of fragment 6 is O. Stählin's edition of Clement of Alexandria's *Stromata*, the work in which this fragment is preserved.[5]

Demetrius' Greek style—if we may judge from Polyhistor, who systematically converts his excerpts into indirect speech—is grammatically uncomplex and straightforward, if somewhat tedious and restricted in vocabulary. It is unaffected by the descriptive flourishes found in other Graeco-Jewish authors, such as Artapanus or Pseudo-Eupolemus, and lacks

---

[1] Fs. 1 and 5 lack any attribution of authorship. Although more true of F. 5, both are generally compatible with the language and style of the ascribed Fs. and illustrate similar interests. See also F. 1, n. a, and F. 5, n. a.

[2] This third F. is often cited by Byzantine authors, e.g. Leo the Grammarian and George Cedrenus; cf. Denis, *Introduction*, p. 249f. For some discussion of this F. as a whole, cf. Wacholder, *Eupolemus* (Cincinnati, Ohio, 1974), p. 100f.

[3] Since Fs. 1–5 do not deal with the kings in Judea, as does F. 6, the one title for all of them seems awkward and allows the speculation that Demetrius may have written more than one work. Yet Justus of Tiberias wrote a history of Judean kings (*Ioudaiōn Basileōn en tois stemmasi*), which covered the period from Moses to Agrippa II. Philo, too, can call Moses a "king" (*Vit Mos* 2.292).

[4] See Bibliography for complete details, as well as a list of other editions and collections of Demetrius' fragments.

[5] For details, see Bibliography. Clement may, like Eusebius, have drawn on Alexander Polyhistor as his source for Demetrius; cf. Denis, *Introduction*, p. 250.

the obvious apologetic biases of Josephus. Instead of the legendary and fabulous features found among the likes of Artapanus, Demetrius is marked by sober chronological precision, using the traditions of the Septuagint as a base.[6] As a constructive chronographer, he knows his source well and generally follows it closely, down to the spellings of proper names. Yet where his purposes require it, Demetrius can alter and combine diverse traditions and make open conjectures (cf. F. 3, *PrEv* 9.29.1–3; F. 5, *PrEv* 9.29.16).

Date and provenance

Fragment 6 (*Strom* 1.141.1f.) refers to Ptolemy IV (c. 221–204 B.C.); hence Demetrius' work is often dated to his reign and placed in Egypt. A one-hundred-year discrepancy with some other dates in this fragment has led some scholars to emend the reference to another Ptolemy.[7] But such an alternative is without probative force, since it is those other dates which have probably suffered textual corruption.[8] Despite the difficulties of the text, a dating to the time of Ptolemy IV is appropriate because of Demetrius' relation to other literary activities of the third century and to the Septuagint in particular.[9] Hence Demetrius is the earliest datable Jewish author writing in Greek.[10] He wrote after the completion of the Greek translation of the Pentateuch (3rd cent. B.C.), since he shows knowledge and use of it,[11] but before the first century B.C., when his work was excerpted by Alexander Polyhistor.

Although Palestine or some other place under Ptolemaic rule cannot be excluded (because of the reference to Ptolemy IV Philopator in F. 6), Egypt, or Alexandria in particular, is probably the place in which Demetrius composed his work. Such a judgment rests on his use of the Septuagint and especially upon his relation to scientific chronography (see below).

Historical importance

Demetrius' concern for the inconsistencies and obscurities found in the biblical traditions, especially in matters of chronography, gives evidence for the beginnings of biblical exegesis, or at least scientific chronography, among hellenistic Jews. There are also good indications that Demetrius does not stand alone but may represent a school of biblical chronographical interpretation.[12] This suggestion is reinforced by the observation that not only are such schools in evidence later[13] but that the Septuagint itself, upon which Demetrius relies, gives hints that it, too, may represent a school of biblical chronology. This possibility is seen in the divergences in dating between the Hebrew and Septuagint texts.[14] Although chronological concerns constitute the bulk of Demetrius' preserved work, he was also interested in other exegetical matters, as the shorter fragments 1, 4, and 5 may suggest.

Demetrius is the first witness to the use of the Septuagint, or at least of the Greek Pentateuch.[15] His work clearly, and perhaps exclusively, presupposes the Greek Old

---

[6] That Demetrius does not use the Heb. text is most clearly seen in his choice of vocabulary, which exhibits a vast and detailed overlap with that of the LXX. Use of the LXX is also shown by the differences between the chronographical system of Demetrius/LXX and that of the Heb. or the Samaritan version. That Demetrius may have known a Heb. Pentateuch, but with Septuagintal chronology, seems to be supported by F. 5 (see below, n. 15, and F. 5, n. d). But this possibility is called into question by F. 2 (*PrEv* 9.21.10); cf. n. 10 c.

[7] Freudenthal, *Alexander Polyhistor*, pp. 57–62, would emend to Ptolemy III (246–221 B.C.). H. Graetz, "Die Chronologie des Demetrius," *MGWJ* 27 (1877) 71, preferred a much later date for the Ptolemy in question.

[8] Cf. F. 6, n. f.

[9] For further remarks, see under "Historical importance."

[10] Demetrius, although confused with Demetrius of Phaleron, is placed first in the list of historians mentioned in Josephus, *Apion* 1.218, as knowledgeable in Jewish matters. The order of the names may be chronological.

[11] Wacholder's repeated suggestion that Demetrius may have been one of the so-called seventy translators of the LXX is without warrant and is challenged by F. 2, *PrEv* 9.21.10; see n. c.

[12] Cf. Freudenthal, *Alexander Polyhistor*, pp. 65–72; Wacholder, *Eupolemus*, pp. 97–100, and his other articles as well.

[13] Cf. especially Wacholder, *HUCA* 35 (1964) 43–56.

[14] See Wacholder, *Eupolemus*, pp. 98f. However, the chronological system of the LXX probably existed in earlier Heb. MSS and may go back to chronological activity in Palestine in the Persian period.

[15] Cf. Freudenthal, *Alexander Polyhistor*, pp. 36n., 43, 49. Demetrius' work is the only independent evidence for Aristeas' notion that the LXX existed as early as the middle of the 3rd cent. B.C.

Testament. Evidence for a knowledge of biblical traditions in Hebrew is scant.[16] In fragments 2 and 3 he reflects the chronographic system of the Septuagint and shows no knowledge of the numerical figures of the Hebrew text where they differ from those of the Septuagint. Further, his spellings of biblical names generally follow the Septuagint; even his phrasing is reminiscent of the Greek Old Testament.

The extant fragments of Demetrius' work are coherent with literary trends in third-century Alexandria. As Demetrius investigated the ancient chronicles of his people, so did the Greeks and Egyptians theirs. Eratosthenes (c. 275–194 B.C.), in his *Chronographiai*, marks a first scientific attempt to fix the dates of political and literary history of the Greeks. Manetho (c. 280 B.C.), in his *Aigyptiaka*, produced a history of Egypt frequently used by later Jewish and Christian writers to establish biblical chronology. At the same time, Berossus of Babylon (c. 290 B.C.), wrote a chronologically oriented history of Babylon (*Babyloniaka*).[17]

Whether consciously or not, Demetrius also reflects the use of another specific form of writing found among his contemporaries, that of *aporiai kai luseis*, "difficulties and solutions." Ancient writings were searched for difficulties or problems, which were then solved. This was done for Homer and Hesiod and can be seen in Philo's *Quaestiones et Solutiones in Genesim et Exodum* and among the Rabbis.[18] Some of the questions that drew Demetrius' attention included: how the people of the Exodus got their arms (F. 5, *PrEv* 9.29.16); why Joseph waited nine years to inform his family of his circumstances in Egypt (F. 2, *PrEv* 9.21.13); and why Joseph gave fivefold portions of food and clothing to Benjamin (F. 2, *PrEv* 9.21.14). These concerns raise the question of whether Demetrius' purpose in writing extended to apologetics, or whether he was, simply, an apologist.[19] But the implicit apologetic found in Demetrius is at most an internal one, directed toward the questions raised by his school or other schools of biblical interpretation. For Demetrius is not an apologist in the usual sense; he looks nothing like a Eupolemus or Artapanus, who make Old Testament heroes into philosophers and astrologers and who fuse oriental and Greek mythology. His work shows no necessary signs of being directed toward the pagan world. His main focus is patriarchal chronology. Such chronological systems were used polemically and could have been so used in missing parts of Demetrius' work. But Demetrius' system does not make synchronisms with other cultures and as such would hardly reach beyond a Jewish audience. Broadly speaking, he treats the history of Israel in light of the literary culture of third-century Alexandria, but remains thoroughly Jewish in both his subject matter and his language.[20]

In all of Demetrius' work with biblical texts or traditions, there is no attention given to theological matters, even in fragments that take him beyond an interest in genealogy or chronology. He overlooks, for example, any theological dimension to the story of the sacrifice of Isaac (F. 1, *PrEv* 9.19.4). He clearly accepts the outlook of his sources (e.g. a belief in angels, F. 2, *PrEv* 9.21.7, 10; F. 1, *PrEv* 9.19.4), but apart from such meager evidence no insight into his theological views is possible.

Relation to canonical books

No canonical work is similar to the fragments of Demetrius. The extant fragments almost exclusively concern those narratives in Genesis and Exodus that serve him in determining biblical chronology. But Demetrius goes considerably beyond these in detail and precision. Even where he takes up a much later period in Israel's history, as in fragment 6, the interest

---

[16] The best evidence for an independent knowledge of the Heb. OT is found in F. 5 (*PrEv* 9.29.16). The Heb. of Ex 13:18 says the Israelites were "armed," which the LXX translates as "fifth." Demetrius would then show knowledge of the Heb. by directly contradicting it and asserting that they were "unarmed." Cf. Wacholder, *Eupolemus*, pp. 281, n. 85; 282, n. 90.

[17] It is interesting that all these authors, as well as Demetrius, are preserved only in fragments. Their effect on later historiography was not great.

[18] See S. Lieberman, *Hellenism in Jewish Palestine* (New York, 1950) 47–82, especially 64–68, and H. Dörrie and H. Dörries, "Erotapokriseis," *RAC* 6, cols. 342–70.

[19] See Dalbert, *Theologie*, 30–32, who emphasizes this.

[20] See Freudenthal, *Alexander Polyhistor*, pp. 62–65, 80–82.

is still largely restricted to chronology. The influence of the canonical books upon Demetrius seems to reside solely in the language and system of chronology that are apparent in the Septuagint.

Relation to apocryphal books

Demetrius belongs to those apocryphal traditions which similarly represent or reflect chronological systems, if not schools: Jubilees, Genesis Apocryphon, Testament of the Twelve Patriarchs, Seder Olam, and Talmudic and Midrashic traditions. But, within this group, distinctions may be made. For example, the Testament of the Twelve Patriarchs certainly reflects a chronological system, but unlike Demetrius and Jubilees, this is not intricately related to the purpose of the work. Because Demetrius is so early, direct influences upon him are difficult if not impossible to determine. Demetrius' influence upon others is also a difficult matter and can rarely be determined with precision.[21] Even where his interpretation coincides with a later view influence or dependence is hard to prove. But it is clear that he is to be considered in light of those apocryphal traditions which concerned themselves with matters of chronography.

SELECT BIBLIOGRAPHY

Charlesworth, *PMR*, pp. 93f.
Delling, *Bibliographie*, pp. 53–55.
Denis, *Introduction*, pp. 248–51.

TEXTS

Denis, A.-M. (ed.). *Fragmenta pseudepigraphorum quae supersunt graeca*. PVTG 3; Leiden, 1970; pp. 175–79.
Jacoby, F. (ed.). *Die Fragmente der griechischen Historiker*. Leiden, 1958; vol. 3C, pp. 666–71.
Mras, K. (ed.). *Eusebius Werke 8.1, Praeparatio Evangelica*. GCS 43.1; Berlin, 1954–56.
Stählin, O. (ed.). *Clemens Alexandrinus, Stromata 1–4*. GCS 52; Berlin, 1960; p. 87.

STUDIES

Bickerman, E. J. "The Jewish Historian Demetrios," *Christianity, Judaism and Other Greco-Roman Cults*, ed. J. Neusner. SJLA 12.3; Leiden, 1975; pp. 72–84. (Discussion of the historical and literary environment of Demetrius, with an excursus on F. 6. [Unfortunately, the article does not appear to have been proofread.])
Dalbert, P. *Die Theologie der hellenistisch-jüdischen Missionsliteratur unter Ausschluss von Philo und Josephus*. Theologische Forschung 4; Hamburg-Volksdorf, 1954; pp. 27–32. (An introductory treatment of Demetrius, with brief discussions of the exegetical [i.e., non-chronographical] fragments.)
Freudenthal, J. *Alexander Polyhistor und die von ihm erhaltenen Reste jüdischer und samaritanischer Geschichtswerke*. Hellenistische Studien 1–2; Breslau, 1874–75; pp. 35–82, 205–7, 219–23 (text). (The best single treatment of Demetrius, both for general matters and specific details of the fragments and their problems.)
Gaster, M. "Demetrius und Seder Olam. Ein Problem der hellenistischen Literatur," *Festskrift i anledning af Prof. David Simonsens 70-aarige fødselsdag*. København, 1923; pp. 243–52.
Gutman, Y. *The Beginnings of Jewish-Hellenistic Literature* (vol. 1). Jerusalem, 1963; vol. 1, pp. 132–47 [in modern Heb.].

---

[21] For example, Demetrius' identification of Zipporah with the "Cushite" woman of Num 12:1 (an "Ethiopian") in *PrEv* 9.29.3 may have influenced Ezekiel the Tragedian in *PrEv* 9.28.4. Sifre on Num 12:1 makes the same identification, but in neither case can influence be proved. In fact, all, including Demetrius, may depend on the same midrashic tradition.

Wacholder, B. Z. "Biblical chronology in the hellenistic world chronicles," *HTR* 61 (1968) 451–68. (Earlier version of materials treated in his *Eupolemus;* see below.)

——. "Demetrius," *EncyJud* 5, cols. 1490f. (A concise introductory essay.)

——. *Eupolemus: A Study of Judaeo-Greek Literature*. Cincinnati, 1974; pp. 98–104, 280–82. (Chapter 4 of this monograph, "Hellenistic Biblical Chronologies," places Demetrius in the context of chronographical developments of his period; special attention is given to fragment 3.)

——. "How Long Did Abram Stay in Egypt? A Study in Hellenistic, Qumran, and Rabbinic Chronography," *HUCA* 35 (1964) 43–56.

Walter, N. "Fragmente jüdisch-hellenistischer Exegeten: Aristobulos, Demetrios, Aristeas," *JSHRZ* 3.2 (1975) 280–92. (Introduction, translation, and nn. to the fragments.)

——. *Untersuchungen zu den Fragmenten der jüdisch-hellenistischen Historiker* (typescript). Halle, 1968; pp. 15–36, 141–55. (*Non vidi.*)

TRANSLATION

Fragment 1[a]   (*PrEv* 9.19.4)

So much says Polyhistor; to which[b] he adds, after other [sentences],[c] saying:

But not long after,[d] God commanded Abraham to offer his son Isaac as a whole burnt offering to him. And when he led his son up to the mountain, he heaped up a pyre, and placed Isaac on it. But when he was about to sacrifice him, he was prevented by an angel, who provided him with a ram for the offering. And Abraham took his son down from the pyre and offered the ram.

Gen 22
Jub 18

Fragment 2   (*PrEv* 9.21.1–19)

1 Let us return again to Polyhistor:

Demetrius Concerning Jacob,[a] *from the Same Writing of Polyhistor.*

Demetrius says that Jacob was [77][b] years old when he fled to Haran in Mesopotamia, having been sent away by his parents on account of the secret enmity of Esau towards his brother (which was due to the fact that his father had blessed him thinking that he was Esau), and in order that he might acquire a wife there.

Gen 27:41–28:5
Jub 27:1–12

2 Jacob, then, set out for Haran in Mesopotamia, having left his father Isaac, who was 137 years of age,[a] while he was himself 77[b] years old.

3 Then after spending 7 years there, he married two daughters of Laban, his maternal uncle, Leah and Rachel, when he was 84[a] years old. In seven more years, 12 children were born to him.[b] In the 10th month of the 8th year, Reuben [was born]; and in the 8th month of the 9th year, Simeon; and in the 6th month of the 10th year, Levi; and in the 4th month of the 11th year, Judah. And since Rachel did not bear, she became envious of her sister, and gave her own handmaid [Bilhah

Gen 29:31–30:24
Jub 28; 44:11–34;
33:22

Fragment 1

a. This anonymous F. is frequently attributed to Demetrius (cf. Freudenthal, *Alexander Polyhistor*, pp. 14f., 36). Although the language and style are not inconsistent with the genuine Fs., not only are there no real internal grounds favoring Demetrius, but n. d, below, indicates a remark at odds with his best-attested trait: chronological precision. While Demetrius' excerptor, Polyhistor, could himself have produced this F. from Gen 22 directly (cf. Walter, *JSHRZ* 3.2 [1975] 284), he could also have obtained it from yet another excerpted author/ historian. In short, authorship by Demetrius is quite doubtful.

b. A F. of the work of Molon (*Against the Jews*) immediately precedes this F. and concerns Abraham, his two wives, and their children (cf. *PrEv* 9.19.4).

c. Eusebius has apparently abbreviated some of Polyhistor's work. The omitted material possibly contained an indication of the authorship of this F., as there is in F. 4 (*PrEv* 9.29.15).

d. Such an imprecise time indicator is out of character for a chronographer such as Demetrius.

Fragment 2

1 a. In this longest F., several emendations have been made where the MS tradition is clearly corrupt, rendering Demetrius self-inconsistent.

b. The MSS read "75" years old. The emendation to 77 is due to the fact that all of Demetrius' computations involving Jacob are based on his age

as 77 when he fled Haran, as it is correctly given a few ll. later, in *PrEv* 9.21.2. The close proximity of these two differing ages for Jacob indicates the probable corruption of the first reference, perhaps due to scribal error.

2 a. Thus Isaac was 60 years old at Jacob's birth.

b. The correct age of Jacob in Demetrius' schema; cf. n. 1b, above.

3 a. This confirms Jacob's age as 77 when he fled to Haran (cf. n. 2b): 77 plus 7 years with Laban = 84.

b. Gen 29:31–30:24; cf. Jub 33:22; 44:11–34. Although the biblical text does not explicitly mention that 7 years were taken for the birth of the 12 children, Demetrius has deduced this from the fact that the births are narrated after the first 7-year period and before the 6-year period. Rabbinic texts also specify 12 children in 7 years (cf. Seder Olam 2; GenR 70). The difficulty of begetting 12 children in 7 years is solved by allowing 10 months between births of children of the same mother, and simultaneous pregnancies for the various mothers. Jub 28:11–24 (with differing birth dates), and Josephus, *Ant* 1.303–8 do not specify the number of years taken to beget the 12 children (11 sons and 1 daughter; Benjamin is born later—cf. *PrEv* 9.21.10; Gen 30:25), but both have them born before the return to Palestine. For 10-month spacings in births, cf. Aristotle, *Historia Animalium* 7.584a 36; WisSol 7:2.

to Jacob as a concubine, who bore Dan in the 4th month of the 11th year, and in the 2nd month of the 12th year, Naphtali. And Leah gave her own handmaid]^c Zilpah to Jacob as a concubine, at the same time as Bilhah^d conceived Naphtali, in the 5th month of the 11th year, and he begot a son in the 2nd month of the 12th year, whom Leah named Gad; and of the same mother in the 12th month of the same year he begot another son, whom Leah named Asher.

4 And in return for the mandrake apples which Reubel^a brought to Rachel, Leah again conceived, as did her handmaid Zilpah at the same time, in the 3rd month of the 12th year, and bore a son in the 12th month of the same year, and gave him the name Issachar. Gen 30:14

5 And again Leah bore another son in the 10th month of the 13th year, whose name was Zebulun; and in the 8th month of the 14th year, the same Leah bore a [daughter]^a named [Dinah].^a And at the same time as Leah [conceived]^b a daughter, Dinah, Rachel also conceived in her womb, and in the 8th month of the 14th year she bore a son, who was named Joseph, so that in the 7 years spent with Laban, 12 children were born.

6 But when Jacob wanted to return to his father in Canaan, at Laban's request he stayed six more years, so that in all he stayed for twenty^a years with Laban in Haran. Gen 31:38,41

7 And while he was going to Canaan, an angel^a of the Lord wrestled with him, and touched the hollow of Jacob's thigh, and he became numb and went lame; on account of this the tendon of the thigh of cattle is not eaten. And the angel^a said to him that from that time on he would no longer be called Jacob, but Israel. Gen 32:24–32

8 And he came to [Salem, a city]^a of the land of Canaan, having with him his children, Reuben, 12 years and 2 months old; Simeon, 11 years and 4 months; Levi, 10 years and 6 months; Judah, 9 years and 8 months; [Dan, 9 years and 8 months;]^b Naphtali, 8 years and 10 months; Gad, 8 years and 10 months; Asher, 8 years; Issachar, 8 years; Zebulun, 7 years and 2 months; Dinah, 6 years and 4 months; Joseph, 6 years and 4 months old.^c Gen 33:18

9 Now Israel lived beside Hamor for 10 years;^a and Israel's daughter, Dinah, was defiled by Shechem the son of Hamor, when she was 16 years and 4 months old. Gen 34 Jub 30:1–6 TLevi 2:2; 5:3f.; 6:3f.

---

c. The insertion follows Freudenthal (*Alexander Polyhistor*, p. 56), who thus includes the account of the births of Dan and Naphtali according to Gen 30:1–8. The omission is a probable result of homoioteleuton. The emendation maintains Demetrius' 10-month birth schema, gives the correct mother to each son, properly identifies Rachel's handmaid, and follows the birth order of OT traditions, all of which Demetrius must have intended.

d. Bilhah and Zilpah are sisters, according to Jub 28:9 and TNaph 1:11f. No such relationship is indicated in Demetrius.

4 a. "Reubel" is a variant of Reuben (cf. *PrEv* 9.21.8 and 17). Josephus, *Ant* 1.304, as well as inscriptions, also attest "Reubel."

5 a. The MSS read "a son named Dan." Such a reading is probably the result of later editorial work designed to make a place for him, since he was missing in the unemended text of *PrEv* 9.21.3 (see above, n. 3c). Cf. Gen 30:21; Freudenthal, *Alexander Polyhistor*, p. 54f.

b. In line with the emendations in *PrEv* 9.21.3, 5 (see nn. 3c and 5a), one should read "conceived" and not "bore" (MSS).

6 a. The tradition of the 20-year stay with Laban is derived from Gen 31:38, 41, and is consistent

with the rest of Demetrius' chronology (7 years with Laban; 7 years of child-begetting; the requested additional 6 years).

7 a. Gen 32:24–32; cf. Josephus, *Ant* 1.331–34. Like the MT, the LXX reads "man" (*anthrōpos*). Demetrius' "angel" (*angelos*) has only very weak support among LXX MSS.

8 a. The MSS read "to another city" (*eis heteran polin*), a phrase inexplicable from the text of Gen. This reading is possibly due to Alexander Polyhistor, who substituted *heteran* for *allēn* in the phrase *eisallēnpolin*, which is probably a corruption of *eissalēmpolin*: "to the city of Salem"; hence the emendation. Cf. LXX Gen 33:18: *eis Salēm polin*.

b. The MSS do not mention Dan in this list (*PrEv* 9.21.8) at all, neither after Judah (following Gen 29:31–30:24), nor after Zebulun (following the corrupt MS list in *PrEv* 9.21.5; cf. 1Chr 2:1f.). "Dan, 9 years and 8 months" dropped out through haplography; the names and ages of Judah and Dan are almost identical (from *Ioudan etōn ennea mēnōn oktō* to *Dan etōn ennea mēnōn oktō*).

c. The ages of Jacob's children in this list (*PrEv* 9.21.8) may be calculated by subtracting the dates given for their births in *PrEv* 9.21.3–5 from the end of the 20-year stay in Haran.

9 a. The traditions in Gen 34 do not explicitly mention "10 years." Demetrius' OT datum is

And Israel's son Simeon, at 21 years and 4 months, and Levi, at 20 years and 6 months of age,[b] rushed out and slew both Hamor and his son Shechem, and all their males, because of the defilement of Dinah; and Jacob was 107[c] years old at the time.

10 To resume, when he had come to Luz [which is][a] Bethel, God said that he was no longer to be called Jacob, but Israel.[b] From that place he came to Chaphratha,[c] and after that to Ephrath, which is Bethlehem, and there he fathered Benjamin; and Rachel died after giving birth to Benjamin,[d] and Jacob lived with her for 23[e] years.   Gen 35:1–27   Jub 32:32–34

11 From there, Jacob came to Mamre, [which is][a] Hebron, to his father, Isaac.[b] Joseph was then 17 years old,[c] and he was sold into Egypt, and remained in prison 13 years, so that he was then 30[d] years old. And Jacob was 120[e] years of age, one year before Isaac's death at 180[f] years of age.   Jub 19:5

12 And Joseph, having interpreted the king's dreams, governed Egypt for 7 years, in which time he married Asenath, daughter of Pentephres[a] the priest of Heliopolis, and begot Manasseh and Ephraim;[b] and 2 years of famine followed.[c]   Gen 41

13 But though Joseph had prospered for 9 years, he did not send for his father, because he was a shepherd, as were Joseph's brothers; and to the Egyptians it is disgraceful to be a shepherd. That this was the reason why he did not send for him, he himself had made clear. For when his relatives came, he told them that if they should be summoned by the king and asked what their occupation was, they should say that they were breeders of cattle.[a]   Gen 46:31–34

Joseph's sale into Egypt at age 17 (Gen 37:2). Since he has both Joseph and Dinah as the same age (cf. *PrEv* 9.21.5, 8), he arbitrarily adds 10 years to allow for the events prior to the sale. According to Jub 30:2, Dinah is 12 years old at the time of the rape.

   b. The ages of Dinah, Simeon, and Levi are reached by adding 10 years to their last-mentioned ages in *PrEv* 9.21.8.

   c. Jacob's age is also consistent with Demetrius' chronological schema: 77 years old when he fled to Haran, plus 7 years there, plus 7 years of child-begetting, plus the additional 6 years requested by Laban, plus 10 years beside Hamor = 107.

10 a. The MSS read "Luz *of* Bethel," as if Luz is in the region or district of Bethel. LXX Gen 35:6 supports the emendation, as does LXX Josh 18:13 and Jub 27:19, 26 (but cf. MT Josh 16:1f.). See also n. 11a.

   b. Following OT traditions, Demetrius also has a second version of Jacob's change of name, in which God is the actor/speaker (Gen 35:10); cf. *PrEv* 9.21.7 and Gen 32:24–28.

   c. The word "chaphratha" (*kbrt*) is here and in LXX Gen 35:16 only transliterated (LXX: "and when he drew near chabratha to come to the land of Ephrath"; MT: "and when they were still some distance from Ephrath"). The term is mistakenly understood as a place name by Demetrius (and possibly also the LXX), instead of an indication of distance as in the Heb.; cf. Jub 32:32. This circumstance speaks against Demetrius' being familiar with Heb. or the Heb. OT.

   d. Gen 35:16–19; Jub 32:32–34.

   e. That is, Jacob lived with Rachel for 7 years, during the births of the 12 children (*PrEv* 9.21.3), plus 6 years at Laban's request (*PrEv* 9.21.6), plus 10 years with Hamor (*PrEv* 9.21.9) = 23 years.

11 a. The MSS read "Mamre of Hebron," as if each name refers to a different entity. But Mamre = Hebron according to Gen 35:27; Jub 19:5. See n. 10a.

   b. Gen 35:27.

   c. Gen 37:2.

   d. Gen 41:46.

   e. In Demetrius' schema, 120 years = Joseph's 13-year imprisonment (*PrEv* 9.21.11), plus Jacob's age at the time of Dinah's rape, 107 (*PrEv* 9.21.9).

   f. Gen 35:28f. Such an age also accords with Demetrius' calculations: Isaac is 137 when Jacob leaves for Haran (*PrEv* 9.21.2), plus Jacob's 7 years with Laban, 7 years of child-begetting, 6 additional years with Laban, 10 years with Hamor, 13 years of imprisonment = 180. On the other hand, it is not clear why the calculation is "one year before," and the Greek is similarly perplexing at this point.

12 a. Gen 41:45. The priest's name varies: LXX, Petephre; MT, Potiphera; TJos 12:1, Pentephri. Some LXX cursives parallel Demetrius' spelling; cf. Josephus, *Ant* 2.91.

   b. Gen 41:50–52. Walter (*JSHRZ* 3.2 [1975] 287), suggests that a summary similar to Gen 41:45–49; 42:6, belongs here, as is in fact found in *PrEv* 9.23.4 amid a F. by Artapanus but which may have had its origins elsewhere. Is the source Demetrius?

   c. Gen 45:6.

13 a. Demetrius' interest here is to explain the tradition and answer questions that may arise from it (in this case, why Joseph did not send for his family earlier and announce his rise to power in Egypt); cf. Freudenthal, *Alexander Polyhistor*, p. 45.

14 And they were at a loss[a] as to why Joseph gave Benjamin at breakfast a portion Gen 43:31-34
5 times[b] as much as theirs, since he was not able to consume so much meat.[c] He
had done this because his father had had [six][d] sons by Leah, and two by his
mother, Rachel; therefore, he set five portions before Benjamin, and he himself
took one;[e] accordingly they had [six][d] portions, as many as the sons of Leah
received.

15 Similarly, while he gave two garments to each, to Benjamin he gave five, and
three hundred pieces of gold;[a] and he sent [him] to his father likewise,[b] so that
his mother's house might be equal to the other.

16 And they lived in the land of Canaan from the time when Abraham was chosen
from among the gentiles and migrated to Canaan: Abraham for 25[a] years; Isaac,
60[b] years; Jacob, 130[c] years. All the years in the land of Canaan were [thus] 215.[d] Ex 12:40 (LXX)

17 And in the third year of the famine in Egypt, Jacob came into Egypt when he was
130[a] years old; Reuben, [44 years and 10 months];[b] Simeon, 44 years; Levi, 43
years [and 2 months];[c] Judah, 42 years and [4][d] months; [Dan, 42 years and 4
months];[e] Naphtali, 41 years and [6][f] months; Gad, 41 years and [6][g] months;
Asher, 40 years and 8 months; [Issachar, 40 years and 8 months];[h] Zebulun, [39
years and 10 months];[i] Dinah, 39 years; and Benjamin, [22][j] years old.[k]

18 But Joseph (he[a] says) was already there in Egypt, [at age][b] 39; and from Adam
until Joseph's brothers came into Egypt there were 3624[c] years; and from the

---

14 a. Who is "at a loss," Joseph's brothers or
readers of Gen? The Gk. is ambiguous. If the
latter, "to be at a loss (as to why)" is language
characteristic of *aporiai kai luseis* texts and is to
be related to the "someone asked" in F. 5 (*PrEv*
9.29.16end).

b. Gen 43:34. Jub 42:23f. has Benjamin receive
7 times as much.

c. The remark that Benjamin could not eat all
that was given to him has no OT basis.

d. The MSS read "7." The emendation to "6"
is supported by Gen 35:23 (cf. Gen 46:8–15) and
Demetrius himself (*PrEv* 9.21.3–5 and the last
phrase here in 9.21.14), where Leah had only 6
sons. The occurrence of 7 in the MSS is possibly
the result of corruption, since the abbreviations of
these numbers in Gk. are so similar (so Freudenthal,
Alexander Polyhistor, p. 53f.). To maintain "7,"
as in Mras's text (which then emends "one" to
"two" (see next n.), is not convincing. Leah had
7 children, but Dinah was not sent to Egypt.

e. That the MSS read "one" here may confirm
the emendation discussed in the previous n.

15 a. Demetrius, like LXX Gen 45:22, reads
"gold"; MT reads "silver."

b. Gen 45:22f.; cf. Jub 43:22. The Gk. here is
ambiguous; it is not clear whether a similar gift
was given or that Benjamin was sent in a similar
fashion to his father.

16 a. This period of time is derived from Gen
12:4. Abraham is 75 years old when he leaves
Haran and is 100 when Isaac is born (Gen 21:5).

b. Isaac's age when Jacob is born (Gen 25:26),
i.e., 137 (= Isaac's age) minus 77 (= Jacob's
age) = 60. Cf. *PrEv* 9.21.1–2.

c. Jacob's age when he enters Egypt (Gen 47:9;
cf. *PrEv* 9.21.17).

d. LXX Ex 12:40 gives 430 years for the time
spent in both Egypt and Canaan. MT Ex 12:40 (cf.
Gen 15:13) has 430 years in Egypt only. Hence
Demetrius is dependent on the LXX. Although 215

years is attested by Josephus, *Ant* 2.318, he exhibits
divergent chronologies elsewhere; cf. *Ant* 1.154;
1.256f.; and 2.187f., yielding 230 years. See also
n. 18e.

17 a. Cf. Gen 47:9. In Demetrius' schema, 130
could be confirmed by adding Jacob's last-mentioned age, 120 (cf. *PrEv* 9.21.11), 7 years of
plenty, and 3 years of famine. The "third year"
seems to be Demetrius' conclusion from Gen 45:6
and the events that follow.

b. The MSS read 45 years.

c. The MSS read 43 years.

d. The MSS read 2 months.

e. The MSS omit Dan and his age entirely, by
haplography.

f. The MSS read 7 months.

g. The MSS read 3 months.

h. The MSS omit Issachar and his age by
haplography.

i. The MSS read 40 years.

j. The MSS read 28 years.

k. The MSS for the list in *PrEv* 9.21.17 are
problematic. Although the ages of Simeon, Asher,
and Dinah are correct, some of the figures are
corrupt, while others appear rounded off. The
pattern of 10 months between births, seen in *PrEv*
9.21.3–5, 8, is not followed, and Dan and Issachar
are again missing from the list, both by homoioteleuton because of the age of the preceding brother
in each case. The emended and reconstructed list
seen in the translation follows Demetrius' own
established patterns and conforms to OT traditions,
which he carefully followed; cf. Gen 46:8–27.

18 a. I.e., Demetrius.

b. The MSS erroneously read that Joseph was
in Egypt for 39 years, which in context is impossible. It is, however, Joseph's age at the time (read
etōn instead of *etē*); cf. Seder Olam 2.

c. The period of 3624 years agrees with the
LXX system of calculation; the MT has 2238 years.

deluge until Jacob's coming into Egypt, 1360[d] years; and from the time when Abraham was chosen from among the gentiles and came from Haran into Canaan until Jacob and his family came into Egypt there were 215[e] years. Ex 12:40 (LXX)

19 But Jacob came into Haran to Laban when he was [77][a] years old, and begot Levi [. . . .].[b] And Levi lived on in Egypt for 17 years, from the time of his coming from Canaan into Egypt, so that he was 60 years old when he begot [Kohath].[c] And in the same year in which [Kohath] was born, Jacob died in Egypt,[d] after he had blessed the sons of Joseph, when he himself was 147 years old, leaving Gen 47:28 Joseph at the age of 56 years. And Levi was 137 years old when he died. And Ex 6:16 when [Kohath] was 40 years old he begot Amram,[e] who was 14 years old when Joseph died in Egypt at the age of 110; and [Kohath] was 133 years old when he Gen 50:22,26 died. Amram took as his wife his uncle's daughter Jochebed,[f] and when he was Ex 6:18 75 years old he begot Aaron [and Moses].[g] But when he begot Moses, Amram was 78 years old,[h] and Amram was 136[i] years old when he died.[j]

Fragment 3   (PrEv 9.29.1–3)

1 Demetrius described the slaying of the Egyptian and the quarrel with the man who disclosed the information about the one who died in the same way as the writer of the Sacred Book.[a] He says, however, that Moses fled into Midian and there

---

d. On the basis of the figures 3624 and 1360, the number of years from Adam to the flood is 2264 (3624 minus 1360). According to LXX Gen 5:1–6:1; 7:11, the number of years is 2262. The difference of 2 years may have resulted from the tradition in Gen 11:10. In Josephus, Ant 1.80–88, the period is also 2262 years, although Josephus uses several conflicting chronologies (e.g. Ant 8.61f.; cf. Ant 10.147f.). The MT has 1656 years; Jub has 1307 years. Cf. J. Skinner, Genesis (ICC; New York, 1925) p. 134. The period of 1360 years from the flood to Jacob's entry into Egypt corresponds to LXX Gen 11:1–26; 12:4, with 215 years from Abraham's entry into Canaan to Jacob's entry into Egypt; MT: 580 years. Cf. Josephus, Ant 1.140–47.

e. With 215 years, LXX Ex 12:40 and Demetrius agree. See above, n. 16d. Seder Olam 2–3 gives 220 years in Canaan, 210 in Egypt.

19 a. The MSS read "80." The emendation, as in PrEv 9.21.1f., brings this passage into harmony with Demetrius' own chronological computations; cf., above, F. 2, n. 1a.

b. Walter (JSHRZ 3.2 [1975] 289) suggests that Polyhistor has passed over a connecting link here in Demetrius, and therefore plausibly inserts: "at the age of 87; when Levi was 43 years old, Jacob, with his entire household, went to Egypt when he was 130 years old."

c. For Kohath, the LXX has Kaath, but here and elsewhere in PrEv 9.21.19 the MSS read "Klath," which is undoubtedly an inner Gk. corruption of Kaath, due to the similarity of the uncial alpha and lambda. For Kohath as the son of Levi, cf. LXX Gen 46:11; Ex 6:16; Num 3:17; 26:57; 1Chr 6:1; 6:18.

d. There is no OT tradition to the effect that Jacob died in Egypt in the year that Kohath was born (and the implication that Kohath was born in

Egypt is contrary to Gen 46:11; cf. 46:8–27). Demetrius starts with two usable data: 215 years in Egypt, and Moses' age as 80 at the Exodus (the various death dates in Ex 6 are of no help to him). From these, Demetrius must invent the other dates to fill in the gaps, here with Kohath's and Amram's ages at the birth of their children.

e. For Kohath as the father of Amram, cf. Ex 6:18; Num 3:19; 26:59; 1Chr 6:3; 6:18. There is, however, no OT tradition for his age as 40.

f. Ex 6:20; Num 26:58f.; 1Chr 6:3.

g. Although the MSS read "and Moses" here, in view of the next phrase it should be omitted (so Jacoby and Mras). But the unemended text, to this point, is paralleled in Ex 6:20, without, however, mentioning the age of Amram at the time of the birth, only his age at death.

h. For the time between the births of Moses and Aaron, cf. Ex 7:7.

i. For Amram's age at death, MT Ex 6:20 reads 137 years old; LXX Ex 6:20 reads 132 years old. The Samaritan text and the Lucianic LXX have 136.

j. There is probably an omission at this point, where the excerpter ceased his work prematurely. The whole passage seems to be leading to the statement that would explain LXX Ex 12:40, namely, that Moses was 80 at the time of the Exodus from Egypt and that this completed the 215 (17 + 40 + 78 + 80)-year stay in Egypt. Hence the stay in Egypt and Canaan was a total of 430 years. Cf. Walter, JSHRZ 3.2 [1975] 289f., who follows Freudenthal, Alexander Polyhistor, pp. 48–51.

Fragment 3
1 a. Cf. Ex 2:11–15; Jub 47:10. More than once, Demetrius merely gives a synopsis of biblical traditions, omitting many details and with no trace of apologetic.

married Zipporah the daughter of Jethro,[b] who was, as far as it may be conjectured[c] from the names of those born from Keturah,[d] of the stock of Abraham, a descendant of Jokshan, who was the son of Abraham by Keturah. And from Jokshan was born Dedan, and from Dedan, Reuel,[e] and from Reuel, Jethro and Hobab,[f] and from Jethro, Zipporah, whom Moses married.

Gen 25:1–4
(LXX); Ex 3:1

2 The generations also agree, for Moses was seventh[a] from Abraham, and Zipporah sixth.[b] For Isaac, from whom Moses descended, was already married when Abraham, at the age of 140, married Keturah, and begot by her a second son, [Jokshan].[c] But he begot Isaac when he was 100 years old;[d] so that [Jokshan],[c] from whom Zipporah derived her descent, was born 42 years later.

3 There is, therefore, no inconsistency in Moses and Zipporah having lived at the same time.[a] And they lived in the city of Midian,[b] which was named from one of the sons of Abraham.[c] For it (i.e., Scripture) says that Abraham sent his sons to the East[d] to settle there. And (it says that) for this reason also, Aaron and Miriam said at Hazeroth that Moses had married an Ethiopian woman.

Num 11:35–12:2

PrEv 9.28.4

Fragment 4   (PrEv 9.29.15)

And again after a little:[a]

From there[b] they went for three days, as Demetrius himself says, and the Sacred Book agrees with him.[c] Since he (i.e., Moses) found there[d] not sweet but bitter

Ex 15:22–27

b. With Demetrius, LXX Ex 2:16 attests Jethro as Moses' father-in-law; so also Ex 2:18 (codex Alexandrinus); Ex 3:1 and Judg 1:16 (codex Vaticanus); cf. Philo, *Abr* 36–40. But Ex 2:18 (codex Vaticanus) has Reuel (Gk.: Raguel); cf. Josephus, *Ant* 2.258, 264; 3.63; Ezekiel the Tragedian, *PrEv* 9.28.4; and Artapanus, *PrEv* 9.27.19. Judg 1:16 (codex Alexandrinus) and 4:11 have Hobab as Moses' father-in-law. The MT suffers from a similar confusion or conflation of traditions: Ex 2:18: Reuel; Ex 3:1: Jethro.

c. Demetrius' fidelity to OT traditions does not prevent him from speculating, where necessary, for his genealogical interests. As a whole, there is no OT parallel to the present genealogy (*PrEv* 9.29.1) in either the LXX or MT. It appears to be a conflation of LXX Gen 25:1–4 (cf. 1Chr 1:32) and Ex 3:1 (cf. Ex 4:18; 18:1f.).

d. Keturah is Abraham's (third) wife according to Gen 25:1–4, but his concubine according to 1Chr 1:32; cf. Jub 19:11.

e. To this point, the traditional basis of the genealogy is in LXX Gen 25:1–3; cf. 1Chr 1:32.

f. For Hobab as the son of Reuel there is only Num 10:29, but cf. Judg 1:16 and 4:11 as possibly inspiring this. There is no OT evidence for Jethro as Reuel's son, nor for Jethro and Hobab as brothers. Only Demetrius proposes these relationships.

2 a. Seventh according to Demetrius: Abraham, Isaac, Jacob, Levi, Kaath, Amram, Moses; cf. F. 2, *PrEv* 9.21.16–19. OT traditions do not specifically number the generations, but that Moses is the 7th generation is readily deducible from Ex 6:6–20; Gen 25:19–26; 29:34; cf. Josephus, *Ant* 2.229; Philo, *Vit Mos* 1.2; NumR 12.6 (ed. Wilna, 1887); PR 5.18b (ed. Friedmann, 1880).

b. Abraham + Keturah, Jokshan, Dedan, Reuel, Jethro, Zipporah, a genealogy constructed by Demetrius from several fragmentary or partial OT genealogical traditions; cf., above, F. 3, nn. 1b, c, f.

c. The MSS read "Isaar" here. The emendation meets the expectations raised by Demetrius' own genealogy in *PrEv* 9.29.1, which follows Gen 25:2.

Freudenthal (*Alexander Polyhistor*, p. 206) suggests that Isaar is an error for Jokshan due to the nearby Isaac. The biblical traditions (Num 3:19; 16:1; Ex 6:18; 1Chr 6:2) that place an Izhar in the generations from Abraham to Moses are irrelevant in light of Gen 25:1–3.

d. Gen 21:5; 25:20. This advanced age, and being 140 when he married Keturah (*PrEv* 9.29.2), allows for the extra generation in Moses' descent from Abraham compared to Zipporah's.

3 a. This conclusion may reflect a question or objection to either the biblical traditions (cf. the features of *aporiai kai luseis* texts mentioned in the Introduction and F. 2, n. 14a), or to Demetrius' (or his school's) genealogical calculations.

b. Gen 25:1–3; Ex 18:1–12.

c. Gen 25:2, 4; Ex 2:15; 1Chr 1:32.

d. Gen 25:6; cf. Jub 20:12. For Demetrius, "East" included both Midian (Ex 2:15) and Ethiopia (Num 12:1; and the last sentence here in *PrEv* 9.29.3), cf.: also Ezekiel the Tragedian, *PrEv* 9.28.4.

Fragment 4

a. Although the F. that follows is usually ascribed to Demetrius, Polyhistor paraphrases Demetrius *and* Scripture here. How much of this F. is Demetrius and how much is Scripture is uncertain. The first sentence is undoubtedly from Demetrius, not simply because his name appears but also because of the chronological element "three days." As for the rest, there is nothing to indicate Demetrius: no dates, no genealogy, no *aporiai kai luseis*; rather, only a summary of Scripture, much like F. 1, which is also doubtful (cf. F. 1, n. a).

b. I.e., the Red Sea. The preceding F. in Polyhistor's collection is from Ezekiel the Tragedian, where he describes the crossing of the Red Sea (*PrEv* 9.29.14).

c. The details of Ex 15:22–27 are omitted. At the same time, this is another external indication of Demetrius' fidelity to OT traditions (cf. F. 3, *PrEv* 9.29.1).

d. I.e., Marah.

water, when God said he should cast some wood into the fountain, the water became sweet. And from there they came to Elim, where they found 12 springs of water and 70 palm trees.[e]

Fragment 5 (*PrEv* 9.29.16end)[a]

And after a short space:

Someone asked[b] how the Israelites had weapons,[c] since they came out unarmed.[d] Ex 14 For they said that after they had gone out on a three-day journey, and made sacrifice, they would return again. It appears, therefore, that those who had not been drowned made use of the others' arms.[e]

Fragment 6 (Clement of Alexandria, *Strom* 1.141.1f.)

But Demetrius says, in his [work] "On the Kings of Judaea,"[a] that the tribe of Judah and [those of] Benjamin and Levi were not taken captive by Sennacherib, but from this captivity[b] to the last [captivity], which Nebuchadnezzar effected out of Jerusalem,[c] [there were] 128 years and 6 months.[d] But from the time when the ten tribes of Samaria were taken captive to that of Ptolemy the 4th,[e] there were 573 years and 9 months. But from the time [of the captivity] of Jerusalem [to Ptolemy the 4th], there were 338 years [and] 3 months.[f]

e. The purpose of this F. for Demetrius is apparently the chronological element of three days. No purpose is evident for the Elim section if it is from Demetrius. But, for Polyhistor, the F. serves as an introduction to the excerpt from Ezekiel the Tragedian, which immediately follows and embellishes various elements of the story in question. See also Josephus, *Ant* 3.2–10; Philo, *Vit Mos* 1.188–90; Mekilta Wa-Yassa[c] 1.45b; TargYer 16.22.

Fragment 5

a. Although this F. is unattributed, it is consistent with what is otherwise known of Demetrius. It is a reasoned conjecture ("It appears . . .") to clarify obscure biblical traditions, and it further supports the idea that Demetrius represents an exegetical school (cf. Introduction). But what is surmise in Demetrius becomes fact for the Rabbis; cf. Mekilta Bashallah 5.32a–b; 6.33a–b; Mekilta R. Simon 53f.; Tehillim 22.180. See also Josephus, *Ant* 2.349.

b. "Someone asked" constitutes an exegetical formula consistent with *aporiai kai luseis* texts and gives some additional weight to the suggestion that Demetrius is the author; cf. F. 2, n. 14a, and the Introduction.

c. Possession of weapons by the Israelites is presupposed in Ex 17:8–13.

d. Demetrius suggests the arms were obtained from the drowned Egyptians, despite the statement in Ex 13:18 to the contrary. See Introduction, n. 15, on the issue of Demetrius' knowledge of Heb., which this F. raises.

e. On the arms of the drowned Egyptians, cf. Ex 14:23–30; WisSol 10:20; Josephus, *Ant* 2.349.

Fragment 6

a. For comments on the title of this work, see the Introduction, n. 3.

b. Apparently this is the captivity of Sennacherib, contrary to 2Kgs 17:3; 18:9, where it is Shalmaneser who takes Samaria into exile. Seven years later, Sennacherib destroys Jerusalem (but without taking Judah, Benjamin, or Levi into exile). However (cf. n. f, below), the final calculation shows that there must have been in Demetrius also a reference to, and dating of, the captivity of the ten tribes under Shalmaneser, as well as to the non-

captivity under Sennacherib, even if Polyhistor ran the two together.

c. Cf. 2Kgs 25:1.

d. For this length of time, calculating the lengths of the reigns of the kings, cf. 2Kgs 18–25.

e. On the possibility that Ptolemy IV is a gloss, see the Introduction. Emendations to other Ptolemies have been unnecessarily suggested by some due to the problems in dating discussed in the following n.

f. Although this F. is grammatically comprehensible, it has probably suffered some loss or corruption in the process of excerpting or subsequent transmission, since it is chronologically inconsistent. Demetrius gives 128 years and 6 months as the time between the fall of Samaria and the fall of Jerusalem. This figure becomes 135 years and 6 months if one supplies, from 2Kgs 17:2–6; 18:9, the 7 years from the time of Shalmaneser's taking the 10 tribes into exile to the fall of Samaria (which may well have been present in Demetrius' original text; cf. Freudenthal, *Alexander Polyhistor*, pp. 57–62; Walter, *JSHRZ* 3.2 [1975] 292). This same figure (135 years and 6 months) should then also result by subtracting the two other figures in Demetrius' text, namely, 338 years and 3 months (fall of Jerusalem to time of Ptolemy IV) from 573 years and 9 months (fall of Samaria to the time of Ptolemy IV). But this subtraction yields 235 years and 6 months. Thus, to achieve consistency and maintain Ptolemy IV as Demetrius' fixed point of reference (the most probable Ptolemy; cf. the Introduction), one would emend either the figure of 338 years and 3 months to 438 years and 3 months, or the figure of 573 years and 9 months to 473 years and 9 months. But one cannot confidently choose between these two options, since it is not known how long a time Demetrius allowed for the Persian period (either c. 135 or c. 235 years). Demetrius' solid points of reference were the accession of Ptolemy IV, in 221 B.C., and the sparse OT traditions for the period from the end of the exile to his own time. He may also have known the traditions behind Dan 9:24–27 for the length of the exile (cf. also Jer 25:11f.; 29:10; Zech 1:12; 7:5). For some further discussion, cf. Bickerman, in *Christianity, Judaism and Other Greco-Roman Cults,* vol. 3, pp. 80–84.

ARISTEAS THE EXEGETE

(prior to First Century B.C.)

A NEW TRANSLATION AND INTRODUCTION

BY R. DORAN

Aristeas the Exegete, in a work whose dimensions, contents, and character otherwise escape us, reconstructs a "Life of Job" from the Greek form of the narrative of the canonical Book of Job. Aristeas places Job among the patriarchs as a descendant of Esau, and describes how his possessions and health are taken from him, how his friends comfort him, and how and why God restores his fortune and health.

Texts

The work of Aristeas is known to us only thirdhand. Eusebius of Caesarea, in his *Praeparatio Evangelica* 9.25.1–4, cited Alexander Polyhistor's quotation of Aristeas' work. The critical text used as the basis for this translation is that of K. Mras.[1]

Relation to the canonical Book of Job

The synopsis of the story of the Book of Job made by Aristeas is clearly related to the Greek translation of the Book of Job. In both the Septuagint and Aristeas, Job lives in Ausitis (= Heb. text *'uş*); the possessions of Job are listed in the same order and language in both (LXX Job 1:3a; *PrEv* 9.25.2); the disasters that befall Job occur in the same order and often in the same language. The three friends who come to comfort Job are described as kings by Aristeas, as in the Septuagint but not in the Hebrew text of Job 2:11; they come to visit, *eis episkepsin*, a phrase that reflects the text of the Septuagint in Job 2:11, *episkepsasthai auton*, but which has no equivalent in the Hebrew text. The names of all four visitors echo the form of the names in the Septuagint. Aristeas, therefore, is drawing on this text of the Book of Job.

That Aristeas has knowledge of the complete Book of Job is indicated by the addition of Elihu to those who come to visit Job; in the canonical book, he does not appear until chapter 32.[2] Such a conclusion is important, since Aristeas' portrayal of Job differs radically from that of the present canonical Book of Job, which combines two views of Job; Job the Questioner and Job the Patient.[3] But Job the Questioner, the one who seeks to understand the problem of the suffering of a righteous man, is absent in Aristeas. He does not mention the dialogues on the problem of suffering but, rather, emphasizes Job's courageous endurance and God's subsequent astonishment. Job's visitors, Elihu among them, encourage Job in Aristeas' version; they do not condemn him for sinning. What Aristeas has taken from the canonical Book of Job is essentially the folk tale of the patient Job.[4]

Why would Aristeas have made such a précis of the Book of Job? The language that

---

[1] Mras, GCS 43,1.
[2] Many scholars see the section about Elihu as an interpolation; cf. M. Pope, *Job* (Anchor Bible 15; New York, 1973) pp. xxvii–xxviii.
[3] H. L. Ginsberg, "Job the Patient and Job the Impatient," *Conservative Judaism* 21/3 (1967) 12–28.
[4] Cf. S. N. Kramer, "Man and his God: A Sumerian Variation on the 'Job' Motif," *Wisdom in Israel and in the Ancient Near East* (eds. M. Noth and D. W. Thomas; VTSup 3; Leiden, 1955) pp. 170–82.

Aristeas uses is that found in Jewish accounts of persecution and martyrdom.[5] The amazement of onlookers at the constancy of Jews under trial for their religion is found in the descriptions of the deaths of Eleazar (4Mac 6:11) and of some of the seven brothers martyred under Antiochus IV (4Mac 9:26; 2Mac 7:12). Hecataeus of Abdera also states that the Jews deserve admiration because of their willingness to undergo any torture rather than transgress their ancestral laws (Josephus, *Apion* 1.190–93). Aristeas, then, by stating that God was amazed at Job's steadfastness, has transformed the tragedy and the problem of suffering in the canonical Book of Job into an edifying story of endurance for the sake of religion.

Relation to Jewish traditions

Aristeas places Job in the patriarchal period as a descendant of Esau. Jewish tradition also places Job in this period: the Biblical Antiquities of Pseudo-Philo has Job marry Dinah, the daughter of Jacob;[6] the Rabbis discuss Job's role in connection with that of Balaam in Numbers 24;[7] the Pseudo-Jonathan Targum on Gen 36:11 identifies Eliphaz, one of the sons of Esau, as the Eliphaz who came to visit Job.[8]

Three texts identify Job and the figure of Jobab in Genesis 36:33: Aristeas the Exegete, the Septuagint addition to the canonical Book of Job, and the Testament of Job. This last text, perhaps to be dated to the latter half of the first century B.C. and subtitled The Book of Job, Who Is Called Jobab,[9] explains that Jobab was his name when he dwelt near an idol. The change in name here seems to signify the change from idol worshiper to true believer (TJob 2:1–2). In this document, Job's first wife was called Sitis, and his second wife was named Dinah. Here, the Testament of Job is similar to the tradition found in Pseudo-Philo's Biblical Antiquities. According to this tradition, Job would belong to the generation after Jacob and Esau.

The closest parallel to the genealogical traditions in Aristeas the Exegete is found in the Septuagint addition to Job. This text, present in every Greek manuscript, was known to Origen.[10] Besides the identification of Job and Jobab, the genealogy in the Septuagint addition and in Aristeas depends on a special reading of the Greek, which turned Bozrah, the city, into Bassara, the mother of Jobab. One major difference between the genealogies is that, in Aristeas, Job is the son of Esau; in the Septuagint addition, he is fifth in line from Abraham through Esau, Reuel, and Zerah.[11] However, as soon as one has Bozrah as the mother of Job, one is dependent on a tradition that has Zerah as the father of Job, as at Genesis 36:33. The best suggestion is that the text of Aristeas has suffered accidental haplography: Esau married [Bassemat and had Reuel. Reuel married and had Zerah. Zerah married] Bassara and had Job.[12] Without some such textual emendation, it is difficult to see how the mother of Job can be derived from Bozrah of Genesis 36:33, and the father be Esau.

Besides the same genealogical tradition in both Aristeas and the Septuagint addition, the same geographical location is given in both; however, linguistic similarity in place descriptions is not enough to posit dependence between texts.

The similarities between the Septuagint addition and Aristeas are impressive. What is the probable relationship? Freudenthal and Walter have argued that the Septuagint addition is

---

[5] Similar language is used also in contexts of endurance of suffering as part of one's *philosophical* creed. Cf. the report of Aelian on the death of Calanus, the Indian gymnosophist (*Varia historia* 5.6). The way Calanus died was even to be marveled at (*agasthēnai*); Alexander the Great admired Calanus and his fortitude in undergoing death. For a fuller report of the contempt of the Gymnosophists for pain and suffering, see Arrian, *Anabasis* 7.2f.

[6] *LAB* 8.8.

[7] Simai in b.Soṭ 11a.

[8] Cf. those discussions of the Rabbis in b.BB 15a which place Job in the patriarchal period. It is interesting that texts of the Book of Job found at Qumran were written in paleo-Heb. script, perhaps a sign that the sectaries placed Job in the patriarchal period. See F. M. Cross, *The Ancient Library of Qumran* (London, 1958) p. 33.

[9] *The Testament of Job*, ed. R. A. Kraft. (SBL T&T 5; Missoula, Mont., 1974).

[10] *Ad Africanum*, 3.

[11] The *Zare* of Gen 36:17 is equated with the *Zara* of Gen 36:33.

[12] J. Strugnell, in a private communication. Such an emendation lends support to the opinion of Freudenthal and Walter that the LXX addition better represents the underlying biblical exegesis than the present text of Alexander Polyhistor/Eusebius. (Freudenthal, *Alexander Polyhistor*, pp. 140f.; Walter, *JSHRZ* 3.2 [1975] 293f.)

dependent on Aristeas.[13] P. Wendland claimed that Aristeas is dependent on the Septuagint addition.[14] However, neither solution is satisfactory. Perhaps both Aristeas and the Septuagint addition share a common tradition. A source for this common tradition may be the "Syriac book" which the Septuagint addition claims that it is quoting.[15]

Relation to the Letter of Aristeas

Within this volume is the Letter of Aristeas, which describes the circumstances surrounding the translation of the Hebrew Scriptures into Greek. This tale of the seventy translators was surely written by an Alexandrian Jew, presenting himself as a gentile functionary of the Ptolemaic court.[16] Is there any connection between the author of this work and the Aristeas who wrote the remarks on Job? In the Letter of Aristeas 6, the author remarks that "on a former occasion, I sent you a record of the facts which I thought worth relating about the Jewish race." Is the author of the Letter of Aristeas here referring to the work of the Aristeas who wrote on Job? Is he claiming identity with him?

B. Motzo is the main proponent of the view that the two works were authored by the same person,[17] but Tramontano has rightly shown that Motzo's reasoning is very farfetched.[18] From Freudenthal on, most scholars have denied that the same person authored the two works. Denis, for example, holds that the authors of the two works have nothing in common except the name; Denis emphatically states that the exegetical work of the historian of Job could not have been passed off as the work of a non-Jew, as the Letter of Aristeas was.[19] However, the issue remains open. B. Z. Wacholder is right to object that the two different genres demanded two different styles,[20] even were the author the same.

Cultural significance

Aristeas the Exegete has depicted Job as the silent sufferer. This view of Job is too unspecified to allow one to detect whether Aristeas has influenced later writings. For example, one cannot say that James 5:11, where Job is mentioned as a model of steadfastness, was influenced by Aristeas. Aristeas is certainly in line with the later Rabbis, such as Abaya and R. Johanan, who held Job in high esteem; he is likewise distinguished from such others as Raba, who states that Job was a sinner, and those who linked Job with Balaam.[21] The context of discussion for Aristeas, however, is quite different from that of the Rabbis: They argue from the debates and dialogues in the Book of Job; Aristeas overlooks these debates.

Date and provenance

The work of Aristeas the Exegete is prior to that of Alexander Polyhistor, who flourished around 50 B.C. No more precise dating is possible, unless one accepts that the Letter of Aristeas 6 is referring to Aristeas' "Concerning the Jews." Then Aristeas is prior to the Letter of Aristeas. As to where the work was produced, the use of the Septuagint Job indicates a Greek-speaking area; beyond this, it is impossible to specify.

Original language

It was shown above, in discussing the relation of Aristeas to the canonical Book of Job, that Aristeas uses the Septuagint translation. It was also noted that the name of Job's mother, Bassara, comes from a special reading of the Greek. The original language of Aristeas' work, therefore, was certainly Greek.

[13] Freudenthal, *Alexander Polyhistor*, pp. 140f.; Walter, *JSHRZ* 3.2 (1975) 293f.
[14] Wendland, *JE* 2, p. 92.
[15] Does "Syriac" here refer to a language or to an area? Walter (*JSHRZ* 3.2 [1975] 294) holds that this phrase refers to what precedes, i.e. to the whole Book of Job, but this is grammatically unlikely.
[16] M. Hadas, *Aristeas to Philocrates* (New York, 1951) pp. 3–9.
[17] As reported by R. Tramontano, *La Lettera di Aristea a Filocrate* (Naples, 1931) p. 44*.
[18] Tramontano, *La Lettera*, pp. 44*–46*.
[19] Denis, *Introduction*, p. 259.
[20] B. Z. Wacholder, *Eupolemus: A Study of Judaeo-Greek Literature* (Cincinnati, Ohio, 1974) p. 5, n. 23.
[21] See b.BB 14b–16b; b.Soṭ 11a.

SELECT BIBLIOGRAPHY

Charlesworth, *PMR*, pp. 80f.
Denis, *Introduction*, pp. 258–59.

Freudenthal, J. *Alexander Polyhistor und die von ihm erhaltenen Reste jüdischer und samaritanischer Geschichtswerke*. Hellenistische Studien 1–2; Breslau, 1874–75.
Wacholder, B. Z. "Aristeas," *EncyJud* 3, cols. 438f.
Walter, N. "Aristeas," *Unterweisung in lehrhafter Form. JSHRZ* 3.2 (1975) 293–96.
Wendland, P. "Aristeas," *JE* 2, p. 92. Vol. 2, p. 92.

1 In his "Concerning the Jews," Aristeas narrates that Esau married [Bassemat   Gen 36:10
and had Reuel. Reuel married, and had Zerah. Zerah married] Bassara,[a] and   Gen 36:13
fathered in Edom a son, Job. Job dwelt in Ausitis on the borders of Idumea and   Job 1:1
2 Arabia. He was a righteous man and rich in possessions. For he owned 7,000   Job 1:3
sheep, 3,000 camels, 500 yoke of oxen, 500 she-asses at pasture, and he also had
3 much arable land. •This Job was formerly called Jobab. God tested him to endure,[b]   Gen 36:33
   Job 1:2
and brought great misfortune on him. First, his asses and oxen were lost because   Job 1:14f.
of robbers; then, both the sheep and the shepherds were burnt up by fire which   Job 1:16
fell from heaven. Not long after this, the camels too were driven away by robbers.   Job 1:17
Then his children died when their house collapsed on them; on the same day, his   Job 1:18f.
4 body too was covered with ulcers. •While he was in such dire straits, Eliphaz the   Job 2:7.11
king of the Taimanites, Baldad the ruler of the Sauchites, and Sophar the king of
the Minneans came to visit him. Elihu, the Buzite,[c] the son of Barachiel, also   Job 32:2
came. While he was being comforted, he said that even without comfort he would
be steadfast in piety, even in such trying circumstances.[d] God, amazed at his high
courage, freed him from his illness and made him master of many possessions.   Job 42:10–17

a. See the Introduction, "Relation to Jewish
traditions."
  b. Walter (*JSHRZ* 3.2 [1975] 295) has overstated
the grammatical complexity.
  c. The MSS of Eusebius *Zōbitēs*, a metathesis
for the *Bouzitēs* of LXX Job 32:2.
  d. As the text now stands, *en tē eusebeia* is
grammatically linked to *tois deinois* by a *te* . . .
kai construction, which is usually connective. However, the usual meaning of *tois deinois* is "in
difficult circumstances," and such a meaning is in

contrast to an attitude of reverence. The above
translation has maintained the contrast between
"piety" and "trying circumstances." Alternatively, one could suggest that the basic meaning of
the main verb, *emmenein*, "to remain," would be
nuanced by the phrases that follow: with "in piety,"
the verb would mean "be steadfast," i.e. in piety;
with "in difficult circumstances," it would mean
"submit to." The translation would then be:
". . . he would be steadfast in reverence, and he
would submit to such trying circumstances."

SEPTUAGINT ADDITION TO THE BOOK OF JOB

  [a] It is written that he will rise again with those whom the Lord raises up.   42:17
  [b] This is translated from the Syriac book: Dwelling in the land of Ausitis on   Job 1:1
the borders of Idumea and Arabia, he was first named Jobab.   Gen 36:33
  [c] He married an Arabian woman and fathered a son named Ennon. His father
was Zerah, a grandson of Esau, and his mother was Bosorra; thus he was fifth in   Gen 36:33
line from Abraham.
  [d] These are the kings who ruled in Edom, which was the region which he also   Gen 36:31–35
ruled. First was Balak, son of Beor, and the name of his city was Dennaba. After
Balak was Jobab, called Job. After him was Hasom, a ruler from the region of
Taiman. After him was Hadad, the son of Barad; he repulsed Midian in the plain
of Moab, and the name of his city was Getthaim.
  [e] The friends who came to him: Eliphaz of the sons of Esau, the king of Taiman;   Job 2:11
Baldad, the ruler of the Sauchites; Sophar, the king of the Minneans.

HISTORY

EUPOLEMUS

(prior to First Century B.C.)

A NEW TRANSLATION AND INTRODUCTION

BY F. FALLON

Eupolemus was a Jewish historian who composed a work, probably entitled *On the Kings in Judea*,[1] of which only five fragments survive. In the first fragment, Eupolemus identifies Moses as the first sage, who invented the alphabet and wrote laws. In a second, lengthy fragment, Eupolemus traces Israelite history from Moses to Solomon and discusses in detail the building of the Temple in Jerusalem. The third fragment completes the account of Solomon. Then, in the fourth fragment, Eupolemus treats King Jonachim (see n. 39a), during whose reign Jeremiah prophesied and Jerusalem was captured by the Babylonians. In the final fragment, Eupolemus tabulates the number of years from Adam and the Exodus to the fifth year of the reign of Demetrius, the Seleucid king (158/7 B.C.).

Transmission

The preservation of these fragments is due mainly to the work of Alexander Polyhistor, the Greek historian who flourished in the mid first century B.C. It seems clear that Alexander was faithful to the sources he used and in the main merely transposed them into indirect discourse.[2]

Although Alexander Polyhistor's *On the Jews* is no longer extant in its entirety, excerpts have fortunately survived in Clement of Alexandria (c. A.D. 150–216) and Eusebius of Caesarea (c. A.D. 260–340). In his *Stromata*, Clement has preserved some of the material; however, he has summarized the contents, rather than provided an exact quotation. On the contrary, Eusebius in his *Praeparatio Evangelica* (*PrEv*) 9.25–39 has cited his source literally and thus provides the text for our translation of the first four fragments.[3]

The final fragment is preserved only in Clement. Although previous scholars had argued that this fragment, too, was transmitted through Alexander Polyhistor to Clement,[4] recent studies by N. Walter and B. Z. Wacholder have suggested that this fragment may have been transmitted through another source to Clement.[5] Walter analyzes the larger context in Clement, i.e. *Stromata* 1.141.1–4. This passage contains a summary of the computations by Demetrius the chronographer (third century B.C.) of the number of years from the falls of the northern and southern kingdoms to his own time. The passage also contains a

---

[1] The title is given as such in Clement of Alexandria, *Strom* 1.153.4, where Clement is also quoting Eupolemus (F. 1) from Alexander Polyhistor. Eusebius, quoting F. 2 in *PrEv* 9.30.1, however, gives the title as *On the Prophecy of Elia*, which must be erroneous since it does not accord with the contents. See Freudenthal, *Alexander Polyhistor*, p. 105, n. 9.

[2] Freudenthal, *Alexander Polyhistor*, pp. 17–34.

[3] Freudenthal, *Alexander Polyhistor*, pp. 3–14. The Fs. are conveniently collected in Jacoby, *FGH*, vol. 3C, pp. 671–78. The text from Jacoby is used, but the F. on Jeremiah is here numbered as F. 4 (Jacoby F. 5) and the chronological F. as F. 5 (Jacoby F. 4).

[4] Freudenthal, *Alexander Polyhistor*, pp. 14–16; cf. E. Schürer, *History*, div. 2, vol. 3, pp. 203–6.

[5] N. Walter, "Zur Überlieferung einiger Reste früher jüdisch-hellenistischer Literatur bei Josephus, Clemens und Eusebius," *Studia Patristica* 7 (TU 92; Berlin, 1966), pp. 314–20, and "Eupolemus," *JSHRZ* 1.2 (1976) 94. B. Z. Wacholder, *Eupolemus: A Study of Judaeo-Greek Literature* (Cincinnati, Ohio, 1974) pp. 40–52, 111–14.

reference to a certain Philo, who is said to disagree with Demetrius in the matter of the kings of the Judeans. Lastly, the passage contains the fragment of Eupolemus, which in addition to its mention of Demetrius the Seleucid king (158/7 B.C.) also has an updated reference to the Roman consuls Gnaius Dometianus and G. Asinius (40 B.C.). In his analysis, Walter argues that this passage could not have come from Alexander Polyhistor, since Alexander's floruit was in the sixties B.C. and since the final form of the fragment of Eupolemus must come from 40 B.C. He further analyzes the passage in Josephus (*Apion* 1.23, §218) in which Demetrius, Philo, and Eupolemus are also mentioned as Greek authors in this same order. He then argues that Josephus did not derive this notice from Alexander Polyhistor, since otherwise Josephus would not have mistaken them for Greek authors. Thus, according to Walter, Josephus also must have taken this reference from another source. Walter further argues that Clement has not here drawn upon Josephus, since the former is more extensive than the latter. He suggests that they inherited a common source; possibly this source was compiled by a hellenistic Jew who put in his book the lists of the Jewish kings according to Demetrius, Philo, and Eupolemus and compared them with the biblical account.[6]

Wacholder agrees basically with Walter that the passage in Clement of Alexandria is from a source other than the composition of Alexander Polyhistor and suggests Ptolemy of Mendes (first century B.C.) as the author of this source. In his discussion, however, Wacholder revises the dates for Alexander Polyhistor and extends the period of his activity from about 80 to 35 B.C.

If Wacholder is correct in his revised dating for Alexander Polyhistor, then the main support for Walter's hypothesis disappears and thereby casts doubt upon the hypothesis as a whole. The simpler theory still remains that Josephus and Clement independently drew upon Alexander Polyhistor's *On the Jews*—perhaps on his chronological summary—for their reference and that the updated reference to the Roman consuls comes from him.

Provenance

It is probable that all five fragments of Eupolemus derive from the single work *On the Kings in Judea*. In the fragments and perhaps in the work itself, Eupolemus passes very quickly over the early period of Jewish history from Moses through the period of the judges. The kings from David to the exile are then treated more extensively. Because of the title, it seems likely that the work concluded with the fall of the Judean monarchy, in which case the final fragment must be considered as simply a chronological appendage. However, it is possible, if the chronographical note be considered an integral part of the work, that Eupolemus continued his treatise into his own, Seleucid era.[7]

For his material, Eupolemus has drawn especially upon the biblical accounts of the construction of the Temple in 1 Kings 5–8 and 2 Chronicles 2–5. In his work, he has relied more closely upon Chronicles than Kings. This preference is indicated by the agreement in wording between the blessing in *Praeparatio Evangelica* 9.34 and the Septuagint of 2 Chronicles 2:11 and by Eupolemus' use of incidents only recounted in Chronicles, e.g. that the place for the altar was pointed out by an angel (1Chr 21:18) and that David could not build the Temple because of his involvement in warfare (1Chr 28:3).

It is also clear that Eupolemus used the Septuagint for his work and thus that his book was originally composed in Greek. This conclusion is shown to be correct by the agreement in wording with the Septuagint of 2 Chronicles 2:11, mentioned above, by the use of proper names in their Septuagint form (e.g. *Jēsous, Nauē, Samouēl*), and by the use of technical terms that are found in the Septuagint for the Temple vessels (e.g. *skēnē tou martyriou, loutēr chalkous*). In addition, Eupolemus has also used the Hebrew text, as his rendering of the name Hiram indicates. That name appears as *Souron*, which differs from the Septuagint *Chiram* and derives from the Hebrew text's *ḥûrām*. Eupolemus' use of the Hebrew text is

---

[6] Further, Walter notes the poem of Philo the Elder in Alexander Polyhistor. It is a hellenistic epic poem in which one would normally not expect lists and dates of kings. However, in the passage in the *Strom.* Clement contrasts the prose chronographic accounts of Demetrius with the disagreements in Philo and Eupolemus. Eupolemus then clearly has a chronographic account. Thus, he concludes that this Philo is not the same as the epic poet of a lost prose historical work.

[7] Wacholder, *Eupolemus*, p. 6.

further indicated by his translation of terms that the Septuagint has merely transliterated (e.g. LXX 2Chr 3:16 *serserōth:* Eupolemus *halusidōtoi*).[8]

In the final fragment, the time from Adam and Moses is tabulated up to the fifth year of the reign of Demetrius. Intended is the Seleucid king Demetrius I Soter (162–150 B.C.), whose fifth regnal year is thus 158/7 B.C. The fragment then correlates the fifth regnal year of Demetrius with the twelfth year of the reign of Ptolemy. Intended here is Ptolemy VII Euergetes II Physeon, who began his rule in 170 B.C.[9] If the work was composed in 158/7 B.C., this reference to Ptolemy must be a later addition for the following reasons.[10] Ptolemy VII began his rule as coregent with his brother but was sent shortly thereafter to Cyrene to rule over that area. In 145 B.C. he returned to rule over all of Egypt. Only after his return to power were his regnal years, including the intervening years, computed from 170 B.C. His twelfth year would thus be 159/8 B.C., which does not coincide precisely with the fifth year of Demetrius. It had previously been suggested by scholars that Demetrius II Nicator (145–139 B.C.) was the intended ruler. That suggestion, however, is impossible since there is no Ptolemy whose twelfth year of reign will match the fifth year of Demetrius II.

Presumably, therefore, the date of composition is 158/7 B.C. Since the author has dated his work by reference to the Seleucids rather than the Ptolemies and since the author has used the Hebrew as well as the Septuagint texts, the place of composition was probably Palestine rather than Egypt. Further, a Palestinian provenance makes more likely the hypothesis that the author, Eupolemus, is to be identified with the ambassador of Judas Maccabeus to Rome, who is mentioned in 1 Maccabees 8:17f. and 2 Maccabees 4:11. The time and place are appropriate, and a member of a priestly family who functioned as an ambassador would be acquainted with Greek.[11]

Importance

If the identification between the author and the ambassador be accepted, then the fragments of Eupolemus come from one who was close to the Maccabees and who was yet conversant in Greek. Possibly he is directly or indirectly behind 1 Maccabees 8. In any case, he is interested in portraying the glory of the Jewish people. In contrast with the biblical account, he presents Hiram, the king not only of Tyre but also of Sidon and Phoenicia, as subject to David, and the king of Israel as on a level of parity with the Pharaoh of Egypt. In addition, Eupolemus has magnified the splendor of the Temple in terms of its adornment and cost. Because of the limited nature of the fragments, only a few theological features of the work are clearly visible, i.e. the Temple and its cult and also the significance of the Law.[12] Eupolemus survives, then, as the oldest hellenistic Jewish historian, whose writing served to present the Greek reading public with a short history of the Jewish people. The work probably served inner Jewish needs in the period after Antiochus IV as much as, if not more than, any distinctive missionary or apologetic purpose.[13]

[8] Freudenthal, *Alexander Polyhistor*, pp. 106–14, 119–20; J. Giblet, "Eupolème et L'Historiographie du Judaïsme Hellénistique," *ETL* 39 (1963) 547f.

[9] Freudenthal, *Alexander Polyhistor*, pp. 124f.

[10] A. von Gutschmid, *Kleine Schriften* (Leipzig, 1890) pp. 191–94; Wacholder, *Eupolemus*, pp. 41–43.

[11] Freudenthal, *Alexander Polyhistor*, p. 127; Schürer, *History*, p. 204; Wacholder, *Eupolemus*, pp. 1–22.

[12] P. Dalbert, *Die Theologie der hellenistisch-jüdischen Missionsliteratur unter Ausschluss von Philo und Josephus* (Hamburg-Volksdorf, 1954), pp. 36–42). Dalbert, however, underestimates the significance of the Law for Eupolemus; see Wacholder, *Eupolemus*, pp. 83–85.

[13] See V. Tcherikover, "Jewish Apologetic Literature Reconsidered," *Eos* 48 (1953) 169–93; N. Walter, "Frühe Begegnungen zwischen jüdischem Glauben und hellenistischer Bildung in Alexandrien," *Neue Beiträge zur Geschichte der Alten Welt* (Berlin, 1964) pp. 367–78; M. Hengel, "Anonymität, Pseudepigraphie, und Literarische Fälschung in der jüdisch-hellenistischen Literatur," *Pseudepigrapha I* (Entretiens sur l'Antiquité Classique 18; Vandoeuvres-Genève, 1972) pp. 229–329.

SELECT BIBLIOGRAPHY

Charlesworth, *PMR*, pp. 107f.
Delling, *Bibliographie*, pp. 53–55.
Denis, *Introduction*, pp. 252–55.

Clemens Alexandrinus. *Werke*, eds. Stählin, O. and Fruechtel, L. GCS 52(15); Berlin,
    1960.[3] (The critical edition for Clement.)
Dalbert, P. *Die Theologie der hellenistisch-jüdischen Missionsliteratur unter Ausschluss von
    Philo und Josephus*. Hamburg-Volksdorf, 1954. (Adds to the study of Freudenthal a
    specific focus on the theology present in the fragments.)
Denis, A.-M. *Fragmenta pseudepigraphorum quae supersunt graeca*. PVTG 3; Leiden,
    1970; pp. 179–86. (A convenient collection of the fragments.)
Eusebius. *Werke; Band 8: Die Praeparatio Evangelica*, ed. K. Mras. GCS 43.1–2; Berlin,
    1954–56. (The critical edition for Eusebius.)
Freudenthal, J. *Hellenistische Studien 1–2: Alexander Polyhistor*. Breslau, 1875. (Still the
    classic study of Eupolemus, which demonstrates that Eupolemus was a Jewish-hellenistic
    historian.)
Giblet, J. "Eupolème et L'Historiographie du Judaïsme Hellénistique," *ETL* 39 (1963)
    539–54. (A study that summarizes the discussion up to that point.)
Gutmann, J. *The Beginnings of Jewish-Hellenistic Literature*. Jerusalem, 1958. (Hebrew)
    (Incorporates the more recent studies.)
Gutschmid, A. von. *Kleine Schriften*. Leipzig, 1890. (Important study of the chronological
    references in the final fragment.)
Jacoby, F. *Die Fragmente der Griechischen Historiker*. Leiden, 1958; vol. 3C, part 2, no.
    723, pp. 671–78. (Convenient, critical collection of the fragments of Eupolemus.)
Schürer, E. *History*.[2] Div. 2, vol. 3, pp. 203–6. (Draws upon Freudenthal but also includes
    references to the further discussion at the end of the nineteenth century.)
Wacholder, B. Z. *Eupolemus: A Study of Judaeo-Greek Literature*. Cincinnati, Ohio, 1974.
    (This is the first monograph devoted to Eupolemus since the time of Freudenthal and
    the only detailed commentary. It represents a significant contribution to the study of
    Eupolemus.)
Walter, N. "Eupolemus," *JSHRZ* 1.2 (1976) 93–108. (An introduction and annotated
    translation, which incorporates recent discussion and the author's own significant
    research on Eupolemus.)

TRANSLATION

Fragment 1 *Alexander Polyhistor, "On the Jews," in Eusebius, "Praeparatio Evangelica" 9.26.1:*

26 And concerning Moses the same author (Alexander Polyhistor) further adds many things.[a] Of these it is worthwhile to hear the following: "And Eupolemus[b] says that Moses[c] was the first wise man,[d] that he first taught the alphabet[e] to the Jews, and the Phoenicians received it from the Jews, and the Greeks received it from the Phoenicians, and that Moses first wrote laws[f] for the Jews."

Fragment 2 *Alexander Polyhistor, "On the Jews," in Eusebius, "Praeparatio Evangelica" 9.30.1–34.18:*

30 And Eupolemus[a] says in a certain "On the Prophecy of Elijah"[b] that Moses

Fragment 1

26 a. The testimonia to Eupolemus are as follows. 1Mac 8:17f.: "Having chosen Eupolemus son of John, of the family of Accos, and Jason son of Eleazar, Judas sent them to Rome to make a treaty of friendship and alliance with these people, who would surely lift the yoke from their shoulders once they understood that the kingdom of the Greeks was reducing Israel to slavery" (cf. 2Mac 4:11 and Josephus, *War* 12.10.6, §415–16). Eusebius, *HE* 6.13.7: "And he mentions Tatian's book . . . and moreover Philo and Aristobulus and Josephus and Demetrius and Eupolemus, Jewish writers, in that they would show, all of them, in writing, that Moses and the Jewish race went back further in their origins than the Greeks" (tr. J. Oulton; LCL; Cambridge, Mass., 1973). Josephus, *Apion* 1.23, §218 (cf. Eusebius, *PrEv* 9.42.3): "Demetrius Phalereus, the elder Philo, and Eupolemus are exceptional in their approximation to the truth, and their errors may be excused on the ground of their inability to follow quite accurately the meaning of our records" (tr. H. St. J. Thackeray; LCL; Cambridge, Mass., 1966).

b. This fragment is also preserved in Clement of Alexandria, *Strom* 1.153.4, where the book of Eupolemus is entitled: *On the Kings in Judea.* Clement writes as follows: "Eupolemus in 'On the Kings in Judaea' says that Moses was the first wise man and that he first taught grammar to the Jews and that from the Jews the Phoenicians (received it)."

c. In contrast with those who acclaim Enoch (e.g. Jub 4:17–20) or Abraham (e.g. Ps-Eup) as the discoverer of writing or astronomy, Eupolemus chooses Moses. Perhaps the choice of Moses as inventor of writing is prompted by the desire to emphasize the nation, as the title of Eupolemus' work would suggest. For the hypothesis, which is difficult to establish, that Eupolemus is here dependent upon Hecataeus of Abdera, see Wacholder, *Eupolemus,* pp. 85–96; for Moses in pagan literature, see J. Gager, *Moses in Graeco-Roman Paganism* (SBLMS; Missoula, Mont., 1972).

d. Eupolemus asserts that Moses was the first sage. In making this assertion Eupolemus uses the typical theme of the "first inventor" of hellenistic history writing. M. Hengel states that the intention of this theme was "to demonstrate the great age and at the same time the superiority of the national wisdom over against that of Greece": *Judaism and Hellenism* (Philadelphia, 1974) p. 129; cf. also pp. 90–92, 95.

e. Rather than *grammata* (alphabet), Clement of Alexandria has the variant *grammatikē* (script or grammar). Contrary to claims in antiquity for Egypt, Phoenicia (e.g. Herodotus 5.58), or Greece as the origin of the alphabet, Eupolemus proclaims Moses as the originator of the alphabet and thus the founder of civilization. He thereby also establishes the antiquity of the Jewish race and the superiority of its national wisdom. On the origin of the alphabet, see now P. Kyle McCarter, *The Antiquity of the Greek Alphabet and the Early Phoenician Scripts* (Harvard Semitic Monographs 9; Missoula, Mont., 1975).

f. By the term "laws" the Torah is intended. The plural may be an accommodation to Gk. ideas. That Moses wrote laws is to be taken in conjunction with the claim that he is the first wise man and the teacher of the alphabet, since in Gk. lore the seven wise men were also lawgivers. See Diogenes Laertius 1.40; Wacholder, *Eupolemus,* pp. 76–85.

Fragment 2

30 a. The parallel to this passage in *Strom* 1.130.3 is merely a very brief summary. Clement writes as follows: "Alexander called Polyhistor in the writing 'On the Jews' has recorded certain letters of Solomon to Vaphres the king of Egypt and to the king of Phoenicia and the Tyrians and their letters to Solomon. According to these letters Vaphres is shown to have sent eighty thousand Egyptian men to him for the building of the Temple, and the other (king) to have sent equal numbers with a Tyrian architect from a Jewish mother of the tribe of David; as it is written there, 'Hyperon is the name.'" The text appears to be corrupt in that the name David was falsely derived from the name Dan and in that the name Hyperon was falsely understood from the clause "whatever you ask him about" (*hyper hōn an auton erōtēseis*).

b. The title here attributed by Eusebius to the work of Eupolemus is erroneous; the source of the error is unclear.

prophesied for forty years.[c] Then Joshua the son of Nun prophesied for thirty years;[d] he lived one hundred and ten years and pitched the sacred tabernacle in
2 Shiloh. After this[e] Samuel was prophet. •Then by the will of God Saul was chosen
3 by Samuel to be king and died after ruling twenty-one years.[f] •Then David, his son,[g] assumed power. He subdued the Syrians dwelling by the river Euphrates and in the region of Commagene[h] and the Assyrians in Galadene[i] and the Phoenicians; he also fought against the Idumaeans, the Ammonites, the Moabites,
4 the Ituraeans, the Nabataeans[j] and the Nabdaeans;[k] •he further waged war against Souron,[l] the king of Tyre and Phoenicia; and he compelled them to pay tribute to
5 the Jews. With Vaphres,[m] the king of Egypt, he made a treaty of friendship. •Since David wanted to build a temple for God, he asked God to show him a place for the altar. Then an angel appeared to him standing above the place where the altar is set up in Jerusalem[n] and ordered him not to set up the temple, because he was defiled with human blood and had waged war for many years.[o] His name was
6 Dianathan.[p] •He gave him a command that he should entrust the building to his son but that he should get ready the materials suitable for the construction: gold,
7 silver, bronze, stones, cypress and cedar trees.[q] •After hearing this, David built ships in Elana,[r] a city of Arabia, and sent miners to the island of Urphe,[s] which lies in the Red Sea and has gold mines. From there the miners transported the

2Sam 24
1Chr 21

1Chr 22:8

---

c. The number comes from the forty years that the Hebrews wandered in the desert under him; see e.g. Deut 29:5.

d. See Josh 24:29; 14:7; Num 14:30–34 for the derivation of the thirty years.

e. The phrase may derive from Alexander Polyhistor and indicate a summation. The omission of the period of the judges is striking. It may be explained by the absence of such a narrative in Eupolemus, or by its presence but with a chronological summary which is being quoted by Alexander Polyhistor, or by the reduction of the narrative to a chronological summary by Alexander Polyhistor. In F. 5 we shall see that there is a chronological summary by Eupolemus and also an addition of chronological material by another author, who may be Alexander Polyhistor.

f. The source for this figure is unknown; contrast 1Sam 13:1.

g. The error in identifying David as Saul's son is probably due to a misunderstanding by Alexander Polyhistor. MS B has corrected the error to son-in-law.

h. The biblical record of David's successes is found in 2Sam 5:17–25; 8:1–14//1Chr 14:8–17; 18:1–13. Eupolemus anachronistically adapts the record in the light of his contemporary setting and enlarges the limits of the Davidic empire: E.g. Commagene emerges as a distinct state only in the hellenistic period; it was in the area of the upper Euphrates in eastern Syria and thus was outside the territory of the Davidic empire. It is not clear whether the enlargement reflects expansionary interests in the Maccabean period or whether it reflects an idealized vision of the limits of Israel; compare Gen 13:14f. and 1QapGen 21:11–12. For a discussion of Jewish expansion in the pre-Hasmonean and early-Hasmonean periods, see V. Tcherikover, *Hellenistic Civilization and the Jews* (Philadelphia, 1966) pp. 204–34.

i. The referent of Galadene is unclear. It probably equals Gilead, a region of Transjordan.

j. The notice concerning the Nabateans is anachronistic; they date from the fifth/fourth century B.C.

k. The Nabdaeans are not otherwise attested. They may be either an erroneous doublet of the Nabateans or they may be identical with the inhabitants of Nadabath, a city in the Transjordan area (1Mac 9:37), or with the Zabadeans, the inhabitants of a town in the area either of Apamea or of Damascus (1Mac 12:31).

l. The unusual spelling of the name of Hiram indicates a return to the Hebrew text of 2Chr (*ḥûrām*: e.g. 2:11) rather than the use of the LXX (*Chiram*). Hiram is here made the king not only of Tyre but also of Phoenicia. In contrast with 1Kgs 5:15, which reports friendship between David and Hiram, Eupolemus' statement probably reflects the enmity and political conflict between Israel and the Seleucid Empire in his own period.

m. The only known Vaphres is a Pharaoh of the later-sixth century B.C. (Hophra/*Ouaphrē; Jer 44:30-51:30 LXX). The name may have been chosen because of the assonance with Pharaoh or because of Vaphres' reception of Jewish exiles at the fall of Jerusalem under the Babylonians; see Wacholder, *Eupolemus*, pp. 134–39. In any case, friendship with Pharaoh probably represents Maccabean sympathies with the Ptolemies rather than with the Seleucids, against whom they had fought in the second century B.C.

n. In the biblical account the census by David results in a plague and the appearance of the angel of death (Satan in Chr) and the indication of place for the altar by the prophet Gad (2Sam 24//1Chr 21).

o. This reason is given only in 1Chr 22:8.

p. The text appears corrupt, probably due to the misunderstanding of Alexander Polyhistor. The correct reading may have referred to the message (*aggelos*) sent to David through (*dia*) Nathan (*nathan*) the prophet. Alexander Polyhistor would then have misunderstood *aggelos* here as referring to the angel who appeared and *dia nathan* as the name of the angel; compare 2Sam 7//1Chr 17.

q. That David prepared the materials is recorded only in 1Chr 22 and 28f., but not in Kgs.

r. Biblical Elath.

8 gold to Judea. •After reigning for forty years, David handed over the rule to Solomon, his son, who was twelve years old,' in the presence of Eli the high priest" and the twelve rulers of the tribes. He also handed over to him the gold, silver, bronze, stone, and cypress and cedar trees. Then he died, and Solomon reigned as king and wrote the following letter to Vaphres the king of Egypt:

Solomon's Letter to Vaphres

31 King Solomon* to Vaphres King of Egypt and friend of my father, greetings!

Know that through God the Most High I have received the kingdom from David my father; he commanded me to build a temple for God, who created heaven and earth, and at the same time to write to you to send me some of your people, who will assist me until the completion of everything required, as has been commanded.

Vaphres' Letter to Solomon

32 King Vaphres to Solomon the Great King,* greetings!

When I read the letter from you, I rejoiced greatly, and I and all my administration celebrated a feast day in honor of your reception of the kingdom from a man who was so noble and approved by so great a God.

Now, concerning what you wrote to me, i.e. concerning the matter of our people, I am sending to you eighty thousand men[b] and I hereby make known to you *their number and place of origin:*[c] from the Sethroitic nome[d] ten thousand men; from the Mendesian and Sebunnitic nomes twenty thousand men each;[e] from the Bousiritic, Leontopolitan, and Athribitic nomes ten thousand men each. Provide for their necessary food supplies and other needs, that their pay be regular, and that they return to their own country as soon as they are finished with the task.

Solomon's Letter to Souron

33 King Solomon to Souron the King of Tyre and Sidon and Phoenicia, friend of my father, greetings!

Know that through God the Most High I have received the kingdom from David my father; he commanded me to build a temple for God, who created heaven and earth, and at the same time to write to you to send me some of your people, who

---

s. Biblical Ophir. Eupolemus has attributed this event to David rather than to Solomon; contrast 1Kgs 9:26–28//2Chr 8:17–18.

t. See 1Chr 22:5 and 29:1, where Solomon is considered as young; LXX 1Kgs 2:12 makes the age twelve years. According to Josephus, *Ant* 8.7.8 he was fourteen years old.

u. It is anachronistic to place Eli, the priest of Shiloh (see 1Sam 1–4), with Solomon. Zadok is the high priest under Solomon (1Chr 29:22). The change may stem from Alexander Polyhistor or, more likely, from Eupolemus. The motivation for the change by Eupolemus is not entirely clear. He may have wanted to support the priestly clan that was descended from Ithamar and that was a rival to the Zadokites, who were descended from Eleazar. Or he may have wanted to slight the Zadokites, who were considered defiled because of their co-operation with the Syrian kings; see, for example, 2Mac 4:7–5:17 and Wacholder, *Eupolemus*, pp. 151–55.

Solomon's Letter to Vaphres
31 a. The letter is composed by Eupolemus and based on Solomon's letter to Hiram of Tyre in 1Kgs 5:2–6. The letter follows the conventions of hellenistic epistolography. On Vaphres, see above.

Clement of Alexandria, *Strom* 1.130.3 summarizes the content of the two exchanges of letters and names Alexander Polyhistor, but not Eupolemus, as his source.

Vaphres' Letter to Solomon
32 a. Whereas Solomon acknowledges Vaphres and Souron as kings, they acknowledge him as the Great King and thereby implicitly as in the class of world emperors. See also 34.1.

b. Vaphres and Souron (34.1) each sends eighty thousand for a total of one hundred and sixty thousand men. Eupolemus has rounded off the numbers given in 1Kgs 5:28–29 (one hundred and fifty-three thousand) or in 2Chr 2:16–17 (one hundred and fifty-three thousand six hundred).

c. The text has been emended by the insertion of an extra *kai* before *ex hōn* to give the reading *their number and place of origin.*

d. The text is corrupt and needs to be emended in the cases of the Sethroitic (for Sebrithitic) and Athribitic (for Bathrithitic and similar variations) nomes. When the text is thus emended, all the nomes fall within the Nile Delta.

e. The larger number from the Mendesian and Sebunnitic nomes may derive from their strategic and economic importance; see Herodotus 2.17.

will also assist us until the completion of God's requirement, just as I have been commanded.

I have also written to Galilee, Samaria,[a] Moab, Ammon,[b] and Gilead to furnish them with the necessary food supplies from the land, each month[c] ten thousand cors of grain (the cor is six artabae) and ten thousand cors of wine (the cor of wine is ten measures).[d] Their oil and their other necessities will be furnished for them from Judea, and cattle to be slaughtered for their meat supply from Arabia.

Souron's Letter to Solomon

1 **34** Souron to Solomon the Great King, greetings!

Praised be the God, who created heaven and earth and who chose a noble person, the son of a noble man. As soon as I read the letter from you, I rejoiced and praised God for your reception of the kingdom.

Now, concerning what you write to me, concerning the matter of our people, I am sending to you eighty thousand Tyrians and Phoenicians, and I am sending to you an architect, a man from Tyre born of a mother from Judea, from the tribe of Dan.[a] Anything under heaven that you ask him about concerning architecture, he will show you and do. Concerning the necessary food supplies of the servants[b] sent to you, you will do well if you write the local governors to furnish the necessary food supplies.

2 When Solomon with his father's friends[c] came to Mount Lebanon with the Sidonians and Tyrians, he brought back by sea to Joppa the trees previously cut by his father,[d] and from there by land to Jerusalem. He began to build the Temple of God in his thirteenth year.[e] The previously mentioned peoples were working, and the twelve tribes of the Jews[f]—one tribe each month—provided all the

---

Solomon's Letter to Souron

33 a. The names Galilee and Samaria, by which these territories were later known, are anachronistically given to the territories at the time of Solomon.

b. Moab and Ammon are here treated merely as parts of the Solomonic empire. In history, both Moab and Ammon were separate kingdoms with their own kings. They were vassels of Israel rather than simply parts of the empire (2Sam 8:2; 12:26–31).

c. In 1Kgs 5:11 the supplies are provided annually but in Eupolemus monthly. Since in 1Kgs 5:25 the number of cors of wheat is twenty thousand per year but in Eupolemus ten thousand per month, there is a sixfold discrepancy. The increase is probably due to the desire of Eupolemus to portray the munificence of Solomon.

d. The cor is a Hebrew measure, whereas the artaba is a measure introduced by the Persians and subsequently used in Ptolemaic Egypt and also in Palestine (see Josephus, *Ant* 11.1.3, §16; 12.3.3, §140; the cor is approximately 3.8 to 6.5 bushels; the Persian artaba equals approximately 1⅖ bushels and the hellenistic artaba a little less). The measure is a hellenistic unit equivalent to approximately 8–10 gallons; see *IDB*, vol. 4, pp. 834f., and Wacholder, *Eupolemus*, pp. 166–67.

Souron's Letter to Solomon

34 a. See 1Kgs 7:13f., where the woman is from the tribe of Naphtali, and 2Chr 2:13–14, where she is from the tribe of Dan. The text has been emended from David to Dan in accord with 2Chr 2:13f. and the suggestion of Freudenthal. The error arose from confusion of the name Dan (*dan*) with the abbreviation for David (*dad*). Clement of Al-

exandria, *Strom* 1.130.3 records the same error, which may derive from Alexander Polyhistor (see n. 30a for the translation of the passage). In addition, through a misunderstanding or corruption of the following phrase, Clement gives his name as Hyperon.

b. The MSS read "and the servants" rather than "of the servants." Freudenthal has suggested the emendation.

c. The phrase "his father's friends" probably means his father's court; the wording here is still unclear and may intend to speak about "the servants sent by his father's friends"; see Walter, *JSHRZ* 1.2 (1976) 103.

d. In 30.6–8 Eupolemus discusses David's cutting of the trees. See 1Kgs 5:17–32, where Solomon arranges the cutting of the trees, and 1Chr 22:1–5, where David prepares the materials for the Temple. Freudenthal, *Alexander Polyhistor*, p. 114, suggests that Eupolemus has reconciled the two passages; but see Wacholder, *Eupolemus*, pp. 171f., who interprets the change as part of the tendency of later tradition to exalt David.

e. 1Kgs 6:1 and 2Chr 3:2 indicate that Solomon began to build the Temple in the fourth year of his reign, i.e. when he was sixteen. The alteration may be due to the desire to show Solomon as beginning as soon as he reached the age of majority, or it may be due to the corruption of the text from *iz* to *ig*.

f. In order to reach a smoother reading, the text is emended to omit the "and" (*kai*) before "provide" (*parechein*). Thus the text agrees with 2Chr 2:17–18 that the Israelites merely provided the supplies and against 1Kgs 5:27–28 that they also worked.

necessary food supplies to the one hundred and sixty thousand men. He laid the foundations of the sanctuary of God (sixty cubits in length, sixty cubits in width;[g] and the width of the structure[h] and its foundations ten cubits), for thus Nathan the 3 prophet of God commanded him. •He built alternately a course of stone and a bonding of cypress[i] and fastened the two courses with bronze clamps, a talent in weight. After building it thus, he covered the inside with cedar and cypress wood so that the stone building was not visible. He then overlaid the sanctuary with gold on the inside by piling up[j] golden sheets five cubits in size, and he affixed them by nailing them with silver nails, each a talent in weight and in the form of a breast and four in number.[k]

4   Thus he overlaid it with gold from the floor to the ceiling;[l] and he made the ceiling from golden coffered work, and the roof he made of bronze from bronze tiles after having melted bronze and poured this (into molds).[m] He also made two 5 bronze pillars and overlaid them with pure gold, a finger in thickness.[n] •The pillars were as tall as the sanctuary, and each pillar was ten cubits in circumference. He stood them one on the right of the House (i.e. the Temple) and one on the left. He also made ten golden lampstands, each weighing ten talents;[o] he took as a model the lampstand placed by Moses in the tent of witnessing.[p] He stood them 6 on each side of the sacred enclosure, some on the right, some on the left. •He also made seventy golden lamps so that seven might burn upon each lampstand. He also built the gates of the Temple and adorned them with gold and silver and 7 covered them with coffered work of cedar and cypress. •He also made a portico on the northern side of the Temple, and supported it with forty-eight bronze pillars.[q] He also fashioned a bronze laver, twenty cubits in length, twenty cubits in width, and five cubits in height. He also made a brim upon it, which extended outward one cubit over the base for the priests to stand upon and bathe their feet and wash their hands. He also made the twelve legs of the laver of cast metal[r] and of the height of a man; and he stood them at the back end under the laver, at 8 the right of the altar of sacrifice. •He also made a bronze platform two cubits in

Margin references:
1Kgs 6–7
2Chr 3–5

1Kgs 6:15,18
2Chr 3:5

1Kgs 6:31–35
2Chr 4:22

---

g. The biblical account records that the sanctuary was sixty cubits in length and twenty cubits in width; see 1Kgs 6:2 and 2Chr 3:3. Ezra 6:3 refers to a width of sixty cubits for the Second Temple; however, the passage is probably corrupt. In his description Eupolemus may reflect some aspects of the Second Temple as well as the Solomonic Temple. For example, his omission of the porch and the Holy of Holies may be due to the lesser significance that he attaches to the porch and to the fact that in the Second Temple the Holy of Holies was separated simply by a veil. See Mras, GCS 43,1, p. 542, n. 1, and Wacholder, *Eupolemus*, pp. 174–77.

h. The term *oikodomē* here refers to the width of the walls (see Mras, GCS 43,1, p. 542, n. 3, and Wacholder, *Eupolemus*, pp. 175f.) rather than to the porch (Th. A. Busink, *Der Tempel von Jerusalem* [Leiden, 1970] vol. 1, p. 27, n. 109).

i. Neither Kgs nor Chr refers to layers in the wall of the Temple; 1Kgs 6:36 and 7:12 refer to the inner court. Eupolemus may here reflect 2Ezra 6:25, where the wall is composed of three courses of stone and one course of timber, especially since Eupolemus and 2Ezra both use for "course" the same term, *domos*, rather than *stychos* of 1Kgs 7:12.

j. Freudenthal emends *chōnnunta* ("piling up") to *chōneuonta* ("casting").

k. See 1Kgs 6:19f. and 2Chr 3:8f., where only the Holy of Holies is gilded. It is not clear whether Eupolemus intends the entire sanctuary or just the Holy of Holies. The reference to nails of silver

may derive from the tabernacle in Ex 26:32.

l. 1Kgs 6:15 mentions only the wood paneling of the Temple walls, whereas 2Chr 3:5–7 refers to the gold overlay on the wood paneling.

m. The roof is not described in the biblical accounts. The description may derive from the Second Temple.

n. See 1Kgs 7:15–22 and 2Chr 3:15–17. Only in Eupolemus are the pillars overlaid with gold, which addition comes from his tendency to magnify the splendor of Solomon's Temple.

o. The text is emended in accord with Mras, GCS 43,1, p. 542, from "talent" to "ten talents." Alternately, one could emend the text from "talents" to "talent" and read: ten golden lampstands, each weighing a talent.

p. This tent is the *'ōhel mō'ēd* of Ex 27:21, etc. On the lampstand see Ex 25:31–40; 1Kgs 7:49; 2Chr 4:7. Eupolemus alone refers explicitly to the Mosaic authority.

q. There is no portico in 1Kgs or 2Chr. However, the LXX of 1Kgs 7:31 refers to forty-eight pillars, and a variant of LXX 1Kgs 7:40 refers to a portico. Cf. the eastern portico of the later, Herodian Temple in Josephus, *War* 5.5.1, §185, and *Ant* 20.9.7, §220–21.

r. Freudenthal, *Alexander Polyhistor*, p. 211, emends *toreutas chōneutas* ("cast metal") to *taurous chōneutous*, i.e. "cast oxen," in accord with 2Chr 4:3 LXX. However, Mras retains the reading of the MSS. Cf. 1Kgs 7:23–39; 2Chr 4:2–6; and also Ex 30:17–21.

height near the laver for the king to stand upon whenever he prays so that he might be visible to the Jewish people. He also built the altar of sacrifice twenty
9 cubits⁵ by twenty cubits and twelve cubits in height. •He also made two bronze rings wrought like chains' and stood them upon stands," which were twenty cubits in height above the sanctuary, and they cast a shadow over the entire Temple. He hung upon each network four hundred bronze bells, a talent in weight, and he made all the networks in order to ring the bells and scare away the birds that they might not settle upon the Temple or build a nest upon the coffered works of the gates and porticoes and defile the Temple with their excrement.

2Chr 6:13

10 He also encircled Jerusalem as a city with walls and towers and trenches, and
11 he built a palace for himself. •The shrine was first called the "Temple of Solomon" (*hieron Solomōnos*). Later, corruptly the city was named from the Temple "Jerusalem" (*hierusalēm*); and by the Greeks it is correspondingly called "Hierosolyma."ᵛ

1Kgs 3:1; 7:1–12
2 Chr 7:11

12 After having completed the Temple and enclosed the city with walls, he went to Shilohʷ and offered a sacrifice to God, a thousand oxen as a holocaust. He also took the tent and the altar of sacrifice and the vessels, which Moses had made, and brought them into Jerusalem and placed them in the House (i.e. the Temple).
13 He also placed there the arkˣ and the golden altar and the lampstand and the table and the other vessels, as the prophet commanded him. He also brought to God an innumerable sacrifice, (including) two thousand sheep, (and) three thousand five hundred oxen.

1Kgs 8:5
2Chr 1:6

14 The entire amount of gold, which was used for the two pillars and the sanctuary, was four million, six hundred thousand talents;ʸ of silver for the nails and the other ornament a thousand, two hundred and thirty-two talents; of bronze for the columns and the laver and the portico eighteen thousand, five hundred talents.
15 Solomon also sent back both the Egyptians and the Phoenicians, each to their own
16 country, and gave to each man ten golden shekels (the talent is a shekel).ᶻ •To Vaphres the king of Egypt he sent ten thousand measures of oil, a thousand artabae of dates, one hundred barrels of honey and spices; and for Souron he sent to Tyre the golden column, which is set up in Tyre in the temple of Zeus.ᵃ²

---

s. Emended from twenty-five cubits in accord with 2Chr 4:1. It is also possible that the dimensions of the altar come from multiplying by four the size of the altar in Ex 27:1–2.

t. The wording in the Gk. is not clear at this point. It seems to indicate two circular pieces of network. The object here described is not reported in Scripture (but see the pillars and their capitals in 1Kgs 7:17 and 2Chr 4:12f.). However, Josephus, in *War* 5.5.6, §224, describes the presence of spikes on the roof of the Herodian Temple to scare away birds; see also M. *Middot* 4:6. If D. Sperber is correct in his analysis of a coin from the period of Antigonus Mattathias (40–37 B.C.), the Second Temple also had this row of spikes; see Sperber, "A Note on a Coin of Antigonus Mattathias," *JQR* 54 (1964) 251–57.

u. Compare the *mᵉkōnôt* (LXX *mechōnôth*) of 1Kgs 7:27, which are the bronze stands for the lavers.

v. See the similar etymological discussions in Josephus, *War* 6.10.3, §438; *Ant* 7.3.2, §67; *Apion* 1.22, §174.

w. Contrary to 1Kgs 3:4f. and 2Chr 1:3f., Eupolemus maintains that Shiloh and not Gibeon was the site of the tent.

x. Eupolemus seems to indicate a second move in this sentence, probably since in Scripture David had already moved the ark from the shrine; see 2Sam 6:2; 1Kgs 8:3f.; 2Chr 1:3f.

y. Lit., Eupolemus says four hundred and sixty "myriads" of talents (a myriad is equivalent to ten thousand). See Ex 38:24–31; 1Chr 22:14; 29:4, 7. Walter, *JSHRZ* 1.2 (1976) 105, suggests that "myriads" should be omitted from the text to achieve a more reasonable amount. However, as Wacholder proposes (*Eupolemus*, pp. 214f.), the inflated number is in accord with the tendency of Eupolemus to maximize the splendor of Solomon's Temple.

z. The equation of a talent and a shekel is erroneous; there were three thousand six hundred shekels to the talent.

a2. In 1Kgs 5:25f. Solomon provides wheat and oil for Hiram, the king of Tyre, rather than for the king of Egypt, as Eupolemus states. The rather remarkable sentence concerning the golden column serves to underscore further the wealth of Solomon. On the golden pillar, see Herodotus 2.44; Josephus, *Apion* 1.18, §118; and the quotation from Theophilus in the following n.

Fragment 3 *Alexander Polyhistor, "On the Jews," in Eusebius, "Praeparatio Evangelica" 9.34.20:*

34.20 Eupolemus[a] says that Solomon also made a thousand golden shields, each one of which was in the weight of five hundred gold shekels.[b] He lived fifty-two years, forty years of which he was king in peace.[c]

Fragment 4 *Alexander Polyhistor, "On the Jews," in Eusebius, "Praeparatio Evangelica" 9.39.2-5:*

2 **39** Then Jonachim (became king).[a] During his reign Jeremiah the prophet prophesied. Sent by God, he caught the Jews sacrificing to a golden idol, whose 3 name was Baal. •He disclosed to them the coming misfortune. Jonachim attempted to burn him alive, but he said that, with this wood, as captives they would prepare 4 food for the Babylonians, and dig the canals of the Tigris and Euphrates.[b] •When Nebuchadnezzar the king of the Babylonians heard the predictions of Jeremiah, 5 he exhorted Astibares[c] the king of the Medes to join him in an expedition. •He associated with himself Babylonians and Medes and gathered together a force of one hundred and eighty thousand foot soldiers, one hundred and twenty thousand cavalry, and ten thousand chariots for foot soldiers. First, he subdued Samaria and Galilee and Scythopolis and the Jews living in Gilead.[d] Then he seized Jerusalem and captured Jonachim the king of the Jews. He took as tribute the gold and silver and bronze in the Temple and sent them to Babylon, except for the ark and the tablets in it. This Jeremiah preserved.[e]

Fragment 5 *Clement of Alexandria, "Stromata" 1.141.4:*

141.4 Further,[a] Eupolemus also says in a similar treatise that all the years from Adam to the fifth year of the reign of Demetrius[b] (while Ptolemy[c] was in his

Fragment 3
34.20 a. This fragment probably followed immediately upon F. 2. Alexander Polyhistor has interrupted the sequence to introduce a brief quotation from Theophilus which reads as follows: "And Theophilus says that Solomon sent the remaining gold to the king of the Tyrians and that he fashioned an image of his daughter, a full-bodied figure, and that he placed the golden pillar around as a covering for the statue."

b. The weight is presumably in shekels; the text has merely "gold ones." Contrast 1Kgs 10:16f.; 2Chr 9:15f.; cf. Song 4:4.

c. 1Kgs 11:42 and 2Chr 9:30 report Solomon's reign as lasting forty years; his life-span is derived from this plus his twelve years at his accession (F. 2, 30.8).

Fragment 4
39 a. Under the one name Jonachim, which is probably corrupted for Joachim, Eupolemus encompasses the events that occur to the final three kings of Judah: Jehoiachim, Jehoiakin, and Zedekiah (2Kgs 24:1–25:21; 2Chr 36:5–21).

b. See Jer 26; 36. However, the details of the conflict with Baal, the attempted burning of Jeremiah, and the cooking and digging in Babylonia are all peculiar to Eupolemus.

c. There is no biblical record of the participation of the Medes in the destruction of Jerusalem. According to Ctesias (Diodorus 2.34.6; Jacoby, *FGH*, 688 F. 5), Astibares and then Aspandas were the last two kings of the Medes. In Herodotus 1.16, 46, 73–75, etc., however, they are named Cyxares and Astyges. For the possible relationship of Eupolemus to Ctesias either directly or indirectly, see

Walter, *JSHRZ* 1.2 (1976) 107, and Wacholder, *Eupolemus*, pp. 230–34.

d. The details of the campaign are fictional; contrast 2Kgs 24; 2Chr 36. Scythopolis is the later, hellenistic name of Beth-Shan (Josh 17:11, 16).

e. This legend is also reported in 2Mac 2:1–10 and in T. Schermann, ed., *Prophetarum Vitae* (Leipzig, 1907) pp. 10f. See also 1Mac 4:46; Josephus, *Ant* 18.4.1, §85–87; 2Bar 6.

Fragment 5
141.4 a. The context of Clement of Alexandria, *Strom* 1.141.1–3 is as follows: "Demetrius says in 'On the Kings in Judea' that the twelve tribes of Juda, Benjamin and Levi were not captured by Sennacherib but that the time from this captivity until the final one from Jerusalem, which Nebuchadnezzar accomplished, was one hundred and twenty-eight years (and) six months. From the time when the ten tribes from Samaria became captives until Ptolemy IV five hundred and seventy-three years (and) nine months; from the time of the captives from Jerusalem three hundred and thirty-eight years (and) three months.

And Philo too has recorded the kings of the Jews (but) different from Demetrius."

b. Demetrius I Soter, who ruled from 162 to 150 B.C., is intended, and therefore the date of composition is presumably 158/7 B.C. See the Introduction.

c. Ptolemy VII Euergetes II Physcon, who ruled from 170 to 116 B.C., is meant, and therefore the date is 159/8 B.C. There is thus an error of one year in the synchronization. However, the reference to Ptolemy must be a later addition if the work of Eupolemus was composed in 158/7 B.C.; see the

twelfth year as king of Egypt) are five thousand, one hundred and forty-nine;[d] and from the time when Moses led the Jews out of Egypt to the aforementioned date there are *two* thousand, five hundred and eighty years.[e] (From this time until the Roman consuls Gnaius Dometianus and [G.] Asinius[f] one hundred and twenty years are summed up.)[g]

Introduction. Wacholder, *Eupolemus*, pp. 40–44, boldly suggests Ptolemy of Mendes as the interpolator; Walter, *JSHRZ* 1.2 (1976) 94, leaves the interpolator anonymous. It also seems possible that the interpolator could be Alexander Polyhistor himself.

d. That figure (5,149), when added to the date of Demetrius (158/7 B.C.), sets the creation in 5307/6 B.C.

e. The text has been emended from two thousand to one thousand years by Freudenthal and Jacoby, since the date is too early for the Exodus. The emended text (1738 B.C.) is closer to the LXX. However, as Wacholder points out, Eupolemus could also be deliberately antedating the Exodus

to show the antiquity of the Jewish civilization (*Eupolemus*, pp. 111–13).

f. The text is corrupt and has been emended from *gaiou dometianou kasinou* to *gnaiou dometiou kai asiniou* and therefore 40 B.C.; see Freudenthal, *Alexander Polyhistor*, p. 214. This addition to Eupolemus may stem from Alexander Polyhistor or from an unknown author.

g. The date referred to in the reign of Ptolemy is 159/8 B.C., and the date of the Roman consuls is 40 B.C. A period of one hundred and twenty years is then said to separate these dates. One arrives at the correct figure (120) by including in the computation—in accord with ancient counting practices—the first and last years of the period.

HISTORY

PSEUDO-EUPOLEMUS

(prior to First Century B.C.)

A NEW TRANSLATION AND INTRODUCTION

BY R. DORAN

Within the discussion of Abraham in Eusebius' *Praeparatio Evangelica* are two quotations, one of which is attributed by Alexander Polyhistor to Eupolemus and the other of which is said to be anonymous. Scholars have assigned both these quotations, known from Alexander Polyhistor's *On the Jews*, to a "Pseudo-Eupolemus."

The first fragment deals with Abraham as spreader of astrological lore. After a short introduction which tells of the building and destruction of the tower of Babel, it states that Abraham was born in a Babylonian city, that he excelled in astrology, and that he traveled to Phoenicia, where he taught this science. The fragment briefly recounts the events of Genesis 14, in a version somewhat different from the biblical account, and then has Abraham move to Egypt, where he again teaches astrology. Abraham, however, praises Enoch as the inventor of astrological science.

The second, anonymous fragment traces the lineage of Abraham back to the giants, and attributes the founding of Babylonia to Belos. In one sentence, it states that Abraham taught astrology to the Phoenicians and then to the Egyptians.

Text

The critical text used as the basis for this translation is K. Mras's edition of *Praeparatio Evangelica*.[1]

The two fragments

J. Freudenthal, faced with the problem of whether Eupolemus was a Jew, a Samaritan, or a pagan, solved the question by separating the materials attributed to Eupolemus into two groups.[2] In Freudenthal's view, the fragment on Abraham was not from Eupolemus but from a Samaritan, while the other fragments were genuine.[3] As part of his proof, Freudenthal pointed to close similarities between the text attributed to Eupolemus and the anonymous text; he concluded that the two texts came from the same author, an anonymous Samaritan.[4] The similarities noted by Freudenthal were as follows:

1) The building of the tower was done by giants.
2) Abraham is somehow connected with these giants.
3) Abraham learned astrology from the Chaldeans and taught it to the Phoenicians and then to the Egyptians.[5]

---

[1] Mras, GCS 43,1.

[2] Freudenthal, *Alexander Polyhistor*, pp. 87–89.

[3] Freudenthal, *Alexander Polyhistor*, pp. 85–89.

[4] Freudenthal suggested that Alexander Polyhistor somehow had his collection of files mixed up; the anonymous-Samaritan F. somehow found its way into the file on Eupolemus. Later, when Alexander realized that he was missing his anonymous file, he simply reproduced it from memory. (Freudenthal, *Alexander Polyhistor*, p. 91.)

[5] Freudenthal, *Alexander Polyhistor*, pp. 90–92.

B. Z. Wacholder initially followed Freudenthal and claimed that the two texts come from the same author; later he somewhat modified his view.[6]

When one looks closely at the texts, however, there are more dissimilarities than similarities.[7]

1) Alexander Polyhistor clearly holds that they come from different sources.[8]
2) The order of events is quite different. In the first fragment, the giants escape the flood, build the tower, and are dispersed over the earth when God destroys the tower. In the second, anonymous fragment, however, the tower is built *after* the gods have destroyed most of the giants. The building of the tower in the second fragment is not the cause of any divine chastisement, as it is in the first.
3) The second fragment is polytheistic (*hupo tōn theōn*), but there is no hint of many gods in the first fragment.
4) It is not unreasonable that the building of the tower be associated with giants. The Septuagint of Genesis 10:8f. has Nimrod as a giant in the region of Babel and Shinar, and the tower is built in the land of Shinar (Gen 11:2–4). Finally, the fact that in both texts astrological knowledge is transmitted to Egypt from Babylonia and Phoenicia does not prove that the two texts come from the same author. Rather, it shows that both texts have pro-Phoenician and pro-Babylonian tendencies.

The two texts, therefore, while they show similarities, are too dissimilar to come from the same author.

I. The first fragment

This text, *Praeparatio Evangelica* 9.17.2–9, has been almost universally attributed to an unknown Samaritan author, named for convenience "Pseudo-Eupolemus."[9] What are the grounds for this belief?

1) The fragment could not come from Eupolemus, for Eupolemus held that Moses was the first wise man.[10] Yet this fragment states that Abraham excelled in wisdom and that Enoch invented astrology.
2) This fragment is syncretistic, for it is concerned to link biblical figures with figures of Babylonian and Greek mythology; e.g. it states that Enoch is the same as Atlas. The genuine Eupolemus fragments are not syncretistic.
3) The author is pro-Samaritan, for he locates the Salem of Genesis 14 at Argarizin, which he calls "Mount of the Most High." But Eupolemus is clearly a Jew, possibly an ambassador of Judas Maccabeus.[11]
4) The author of this fragment also favors Phoenicia, for he holds that Phoenicia gained knowledge before Egypt. This view could reflect a Samaritan bias, as Josephus mentions that the Samaritans claimed relationship with the Sidonians (*Ant* 11.344; 12.257–62).

For convenience of exposition, we shall discuss these arguments in inverse order.

1) The author of the fragment has simplified the wanderings of Abraham: Abraham travels to Phoenicia and then on to Egypt but does not then retrace his steps to Phoenicia as in the biblical account. This simplification is in line with the genealogy which has been accepted from the Babylonians:

---

[6] B. Z. Wacholder, " 'Pseudo-Eupolemus' Two Greek Fragments on the Life of Abraham," *HUCA* 34 (1963) 83–113. B. Z. Wacholder, *Eupolemus: A Study of Judaeo-Greek Literature* (Cincinnati, 1974) p. 287, n. 112.

[7] N. Walter, "Zu Pseudo-Eupolemus," *Klio* 43–45 (1965) 282–90.

[8] No other suggestion, except that in n. 3, has been offered to explain how Alexander Polyhistor confused the Samaritan work with that of Eupolemus.

[9] A.-M. Denis speaks only of the "anonymous historian" but distinguishes this author from the genuine Eupolemus ("L'Historien anonyme d'Eusèbe (Praep. Ev. 9, 17–18) et la crise des Macchabées," *JSJ* 8 (1977) 42–49).

[10] *PrEv* 9.26.1; Clement, *Strom* 1.153.4.

[11] 1Mac 8:17; 2Mac 4:11.

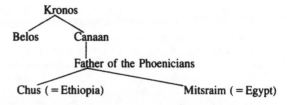

Such a subordination of Egypt to Phoenicia should not be attributed to any personal animosity of the author against the Egyptians;[12] he is taking sides in the oft-debated question on the origin of knowledge. This debate was particularly sharp over the invention of the alphabet, some claiming that the alphabet was invented in Egypt, others in Phoenicia.[13] A fragment attributed to the genuine Eupolemus ignores the claims of Egypt and states that Moses gave knowledge of the alphabet to the Phoenicians and that they in turn gave it to the Greeks.[14] In the present fragment, the claims of Egypt are similarly downplayed, as astrological knowledge comes to Egypt from Babylonia via Phoenicia. In this respect, as in the use of the term "Phoenicia," this fragment has a view of the diffusion of knowledge similar to that of the genuine Eupolemus.

2) The author's interpretation of Argarizin as "Mount of the Most High" does not indicate that he is a Samaritan. Such an interpretation is not a scientific etymology[15] but is related to the account in Genesis 14:18, where Melchisedek is said to be a priest of the Most High. Also, as Wacholder notes, the location of Salem in Samaria is supported by the Septuagint of Genesis 33:18: "And Jacob came to Salem the city of Shechem." Opinions diverged as to the location of Salem. Epiphanius cites two opinions, one which equates Salem with Jerusalem (as does Josephus), the other which places it in the valley of Shechem, now called Neapolis.[16] The fragment under discussion sides with the second opinion. This opinion, however, coincides with the view of fragments attributed to the genuine Eupolemus in which Jerusalem is not derived from the name Salem but from *hieron Solomōnos*, the Temple of Solomon (*PrEv* 9.34.13). On this point, too, there is no contradiction between Eupolemus and the author of this fragment.

3) The fragments of the genuine Eupolemus do not hesitate to connect biblical events with non-Jewish events: Moses is the inventor of the alphabet and laws, a science which then passed to the Phoenicians and Greeks; Solomon was the originator of the golden pillar found in the temple of Zeus at Tyre.[17] The fragment under discussion evidences the same kind of speculation as that found in Artapanus.[18] One should realize that the patriarchal period was the prime ground for such attempts at connecting Jewish and non-Jewish events. The story of Solomon took place in history, but the Genesis account of origins was ripe for connections with other accounts of origins.

4) Finally, Eupolemus speaks of Moses as the first to become wise in the context of the invention of letters and laws. This does not imply that, before Moses, there were none wise in other ways. Before the appearance of Taautus, the inventor of letters, Sancuniathon parades a long list of inventors.[19] It is not, therefore, contradictory that the fragment under discussion should state that Abraham excelled in wisdom and that Enoch invented astrology, and that Eupolemus should state that Moses was the first sage and that he invented writing and laws.

Thus, nothing stands in the way of holding that this fragment on Abraham comes from

[12] Wacholder, *HUCA* 34 (1963) 87; Walter, *JSHRZ* 1.2, p. 183; Wacholder, *Eupolemus*, p. 287.

[13] In Egypt: Diodorus Siculus 1.13.2; 1.16.1; Artapanus in *PrEv* 9.27.6. In Phoenicia: Philon of Byblos, citing Sancuniathon, in *PrEv* 1.10.14.

[14] *PrEv* 9.26.1.

[15] As Wacholder (*HUCA* 34 (1963) 88, n. 32) claims. Walter rightly disputes this (*Klio* 43–45 (1965) 285f.).

[16] Wacholder, *HUCA* 34 (1963) 107, citing Epiphanius, *AdvHaer* 2.55.2.

[17] *PrEv* 9.34.18.

[18] *PrEv* 9.27.3f.; 9.27.6.

[19] *PrEv* 1.10.11–14.

the genuine Eupolemus and that there is no "Pseudo-Eupolemus." The fragment shows no more syncretism than the admittedly genuine fragments on Moses and Solomon, and the restructuring of the biblical narrative was also part of the method of Eupolemus.[20] Such an identification would also fit in with the judgment, which we will make in the following sections, that the author of the fragment knew the Septuagint and was familiar with Palestinian traditions.[21]

This fragment, then, belongs to the work of Eupolemus. It belongs to the Palestinian tradition and is interested in forming contacts with other accounts of the origins of mankind, as well as showing Abraham as a spreader of culture.[22]

Original language

The writer of this first fragment shows dependence on the Septuagint tradition in the spelling of the proper names *Abraam, Enôch, Mathousala, Melchisedek, Mestraeim, Chanaan, Chous*.[23] However, the spelling of proper names is not a conclusive proof as to the original language of the work, as a translator would most probably have followed the Septuagint spelling.

Within the fragment itself, there is no internal evidence that the author knew Hebrew, although Wacholder does attempt to show such knowledge.[24] It is most likely that the original language was Greek.

Relation to the Old Testament

The author of the first fragment diverges from the biblical account: He interposes the incidents of Genesis 14 before those of Genesis 12:10–20. This is in line with his desire to show that knowledge of astrology originated in Babylonia and came to Egypt via Phoenicia. The author also shows some interpretative touches: He describes the attacking kings of Genesis 14 as Armenians.[25] He interprets Genesis 14:16 to mean that Abraham took captive the women and children of his enemies, not that he rescued the women and children of Lot. Thus, the author transforms the dialogue between Abraham and the king of Sodom in the biblical narrative into a dialogue between Abraham and ambassadors from the Armenians.

Relation to non-canonical works

The first fragment shows a close connection with traditions found in the non-canonical literature. As in the Genesis Apocryphon (1QapGen 20:17), Josephus (*Ant* 1.163f.), and the Asatir,[26] Pharaoh is not able to have intercourse with Sarah. Again, one of the kings in Genesis 14 is said in the Genesis Apocryphon (1QapGen 21:23) to come from Cappadocia; the fragment has the kings come from Armenia.

The strongest link with the non-canonical literature, however, is found in the theme of astrological knowledge. The Enochite tradition (Jub 4:17–25; 1QapGen 2:19–21; Asatir 6:18) depicts Enoch as knowing the secrets of whatever is on earth or in the heavens; 1 Enoch contains chapters on astronomy (1En 72–82; 41–44). Methuselah is the conduit for Enoch's knowledge to mankind in 1 Enoch 82; 106; and Genesis Apocryphon 4:24f. That Abraham knew the science of the heavens is also a widespread theme, found in Artapanus, Philo (*Abr* 69–71), and Josephus (*Ant* 1.155, 167f.). However, there was some

---

[20] The best examples are the statement that David was Saul's son (*PrEv* 9.30.3) and the role that Shiloh plays in the preparations for the consecration of the temple (*PrEv* 9.34.14). B. Z. Wacholder notes the discrepancies throughout his work *Eupolemus*.

[21] See the sections on "Original language" and "Relation to non-canonical works."

[22] Cf. D. Georgi, *Die Gegner des Paulus im 2.Korintherbrief: Studien zur religiösen Propaganda in der Spätantike* (Wissenschaftliche Monographien zum Alten und Neuen Testament 11; Neukirchen-Vluyn, 1964) p. 65.

[23] Freudenthal, *Alexander Polyhistor*, p. 98.

[24] Wacholder, *HUCA* 34 (1963) 87–89; 94–95. See Walter's criticisms, *Klio* 43–45 (1965) 284–86.

[25] Freudenthal (*Alexander Polyhistor*, p. 97) and Wacholder (*HUCA* 34 [1963] 105) see here a pro-Babylonian bias, rather than a simple reinterpretation of the text.

[26] Cited by Walter, *Klio* 43–45 (1965) 287.

ambivalence in the tradition about this knowledge of astrology. For Josephus and Philo, Abraham's astrology was a means of knowing the true God, and conflict arose between Abraham and the Chaldean astrologers when they would not go beyond their science to this knowledge of God.[27] The Sibylline Oracles directly polemicize against the view that Abraham knew Chaldean astrology or astronomy.[28] "Pseudo-Eupolemus" has no such ambivalence as to Abraham's astrological knowledge: Astrology, for this author, is a means of glorifying the Jewish patriarchs as culture bringers.

This fragment thus reflects wide traditions about Abraham, Enoch, and Methuselah.

Relation to other works

This first fragment also shows knowledge of non-Jewish traditions. Freudenthal suggested that it reflected knowledge of the work of Berossos, a priest of Bel, who authored a history of Babylon at the beginning of the third century B.C.[29] Schnabel at first followed this lead of Freudenthal and added further arguments in its favor; however, he later stated that the fragment of "Pseudo-Eupolemus" was drawing on oral traditions.[30] Both Wacholder and Walter state that Schnabel was wrong to reverse his position, and both hold that "Pseudo-Eupolemus" knew the work of Berossos.[31]

What is the evidence in favor of this? Freudenthal had pointed to the parallel between *Praeparatio Evangelica* 9.17.3 and the fragment of Berossos preserved in Josephus, *Antiquities* 1.158: "In the tenth generation after the flood lived among the Chaldeans a just, important man who was knowledgeable in heavenly phenomena." The only verbal connection between the two statements is "the tenth generation." The source for "Pseudo-Eupolemus," however, is most probably the Bible, for Genesis 10f. locates Abraham in the tenth generation after the flood. The only information additional to the Bible in both "Pseudo-Eupolemus" and Berossos is that Abraham was well versed in astrology. But the source for "Pseudo-Eupolemus" could well have been the Jewish traditions noted above: Thus, there is no need to say that "Pseudo-Eupolemus" is dependent on Berossos.[32]

"Pseudo-Eupolemus" does, however, explicitly draw on Babylonian traditions for his genealogy of Belos. The tradition here cited stands in opposition to those genealogies in which Belos is a son of Libya (Diodorus Siculus 1.28, 81; Pausanias 4.23.10), and traditions in which Belos leaves Egypt to colonize Babylonia (Diodorus Siculus 1.28.1). Belos could shift places in the genealogical system depending on each author's point of view. For example, in the genealogy of the Danaids, Belos was father of Danaos and Aigyptus; Belos could also father Phoenix and Agenor.[33] Through the kinship relation of ancestors of races is expressed the relationship between the various countries. "Pseudo-Eupolemus" uses a pro-Babylonian and pro-Phoenician genealogy, where Belos is two generations earlier than Egypt, to support his theory of the spread of knowledge. The tradition is in opposition to others, as at Herodotus 2.82 and Diodorus Siculus 1.81.6, where genealogies are used to show that astrological knowledge originated in Egypt. "Pseudo-Eupolemus," however, makes no attempt to identify figures of the Babylonian genealogy with figures from the biblical tradition—one should not search to relate Noah or Nimrod to any of the figures of the genealogy used by "Pseudo-Eupolemus."[34]

---

[27] Josephus, *Ant* 1.155-57; Philo *Migr* 177-87; *Quaes Gen* 3.1.

[28] SibOr 3.218-31.

[29] Freudenthal, *Alexander Polyhistor*, pp. 90f.

[30] P. Schnabel, *Berossos und die babylonisch-hellenistische Literatur* (Leipzig/Berlin, 1923) pp. 67-69. The revision is found on p. 246.

[31] Wacholder, *HUCA* 34 (1963) 91; Walter, *Klio* 43-45 (1965) 289.

[32] Schnabel's other argument for connecting this F. and Berossos is the recognition that behind the phrase *Choum hyion genesthai, hon . . . legesthai Asbolon* lies the name *Chōmasbēlos*, the second king of Babylon after the Flood, according to Berossos (*FGH*, vol. 3C, no. 680, F. 5; Schnabel, *Berossos*, p. 68). However, Walter (*Klio* 43-45 [1965] 285) has shown that the best reading of the proper name is not *Choum*, but *Choun*, the simple accusative of *Chous*. *Asbolos* would then be connected to *asbolos* = "sooty." Walter is equally right to discount Wacholder's suggestion that the F. is directly dependent on a knowledge of Ctesias and Hesiod (*Klio* 43-45 [1965] 289).

[33] For a full listing of possibilities, see K. Tumpel, "Belos," Pauly-Wissowa, vol. 3, cols. 259-64.

[34] The attempts of Wacholder to do so are vitiated by his belief that the two Fs. on Abraham ascribed to "Pseudo-Eupolemus" do come from a single author. There is no explicit attempt in the first F. (*PrEv* 9.17.2-9) to make the identification that Wacholder does.

Beside the "Babylonian traditions," "Pseudo-Eupolemus" is also aware of Greek traditions that linked Atlas with astrology. Such traditions are found in Herodorus, Xenagoras, and Dionysius Scythobrachion.[35]

Cultural importance

The Babylonian traditions have been used by "Pseudo-Eupolemus" as genealogical support for the theory that Jewish heroes were the inventors of astrology. That Jews were such culture bringers is clearly in opposition to both Babylonian and Egyptian traditions.[36] The depiction of Enoch and Abraham as culture bringers is an attempt to enhance Jewish traditions and beliefs and the Jewish people itself both in the eyes of its neighbors and in its own eyes. If the author of this fragment was the Eupolemus who was ambassador of Judas Maccabeus, then this fragment reveals an openness to other traditions while maintaining the superiority of the Jewish traditions.

Date and provenance

The thrust of the above argument is that the author of this fragment is not an anonymous Samaritan, but Eupolemus. The question of date and provenance is thus tied up with the date and provenance of the other fragments of Eupolemus.

II. The anonymous fragment

Walter has proposed that this second fragment, *Praeparatio Evangelica* 9.18.2, is composed of several parts: First is a connection forged by Alexander Polyhistor to relate the Babylonian traditions to Abraham; then the Babylonian traditions; finally, a summary made by Alexander Polyhistor out of the materials in the first fragment of Eupolemus.[37] Even the Babylonian traditions give the impression of being composed out of disparate elements. The destruction of the giants by the gods has overtones of the battle of the Titans, although that term is not expressly used; the escape of one man to build Babylon has overtones of the story of Xisuthros, as told by Berossos;[38] the building of a tower reminds one of the tower of Babel, although clearly here that is no act of impiety, nor is the tower destroyed.

Thus the fragment is a potpourri of traditions, most probably thrown together by Alexander Polyhistor out of disparate elements. One should not seek for a precise author beyond him.

The genealogy does present certain problems, however. The text as it presently stands identifies Belos with Kronos. Such an identification is not found elsewhere; in fact, Belos was more often identified with Zeus (Herodotus 1.181.2; Agathias, citing Berossos; found in Jacoby, *FGH*, vol. 3C, no. 680, F. 12). A simple emendation of the text would have Kronos father Belos, and I have followed this suggestion of J. Strugnell. See the translation nn. for details. Philo Byblos has Kronos father Zeus Belos in *PrEv* 1.10.26. In the same passage of Philo Byblos, however, Kronos also fathers a son called Kronos, besides the son Zeus Belos. That a son is named after the father in such genealogies is therefore not as strange as Wacholder (*HUCA* 34 [1963] 94) and Walter (*JSHRZ* 1.2 [1976] 142) hold.

[35] Herodorus in Jacoby, *FGH*, vol. 1, no. 31, F. 13; Xenagoras, *FGH*, vol. 2B, no. 240, F. 32; Dionysius Scythobrachion, *FGH*, vol. 1, no. 32, F. 7.

[36] Pliny (*Historia naturalis* 6.121) states that Bel was the inventor of astrology; Herodotus 2.82 and Diodorus Siculus 1.50.1 give the honor to the Egyptians. See K. Thraede, "Erfinder II (geistesgeschichtlich)" *RAC*, vol. 5, pp. 1204–6.

[37] Walter, *JSHRZ* 1.2 (1976) 143.

[38] Jacoby, *FGH*, vol. 3C, no. 680, F. 4. As regards the reference to the Titans, it must be emphasized that it is not explicitly stated that the giants were Titans. One should not, with Wacholder (*HUCA* 34 [1963] 92), hold that the fragment directly influenced the SibOr.

SELECT BIBLIOGRAPHY

Charlesworth, *PMR*, p. 108.
Delling, *Bibliographie*, pp. 53–55.
Denis, *Introduction*, pp. 261f.

Denis, A.-M. "L'Historien anonyme d'Eusèbe (*Praep. Ev.* 9, 17–18) et la crise des Macchabées," *JSJ* 8 (1977) 42–49.
Freudenthal, J. *Alexander Polyhistor und die von ihm erhaltenen Reste judäischer und samaritanischer Geschichtswerke. Hellenistische Studien 1–2.* Breslau, 1875.
Gaster, M. *The Asatir, the Samaritan Book of the "Secrets of Moses."* London, 1927.
Jacoby, F. *Die Fragmente der griechischen Historiker.* Leiden, 1954–64.
Schnabel, P. *Berossos und die babylonisch-hellenistische Literatur.* Leipzig/Berlin, 1923.
Wacholder, B. Z. "Pseudo-Eupolemus' Two Greek Fragments on the Life of Abraham," *HUCA* 34 (1963) 83–113.
———. *Eupolemus: A Study of Judaeo-Greek Literature.* Cincinnati, 1974.
Walter, N. "Zu Pseudo-Eupolemus," *Klio* 43–45 (1965) 282–90.
———. "Pseudo-Eupolemus," *JSHRZ* 1.2 (1976) 137–43.

2 Eupolemus, in his work "On the Jews,"[a] states that the Assyrian city of Babylon[b] was first founded by those who escaped the Flood. They were giants, 3 and they built the tower well known in history. •When the tower was destroyed by God's power, these giants were scattered over the whole earth.

Eupolemus holds that Abraham was born in the tenth generation in the Babylonian city Camarina,[c] although others state that the city was named Ourie (which means "city of the Chaldeans")[d] and that Abraham was born in the thirteenth generation.[e] Abraham excelled all in nobility and wisdom; he sought and obtained[f] the knowledge of astrology and the Chaldean craft,[g] and pleased God because he 4 eagerly sought to be reverent.[h] •At God's command, he traveled to Phoenicia and dwelt there. He pleased the Phoenician king by teaching the Phoenicians the cycles of the sun and moon, and everything else as well. Later, the Armenians[i] campaigned against the Phoenicians;[j] victorious, the Armenians took captive the nephew of Abraham. Abraham and his servants came to the rescue; they regained control of those who had been taken captive,[k] and they took as captives the children and 5 women of the enemy.[l] •Ambassadors were sent to Abraham to buy back the prisoners, but he chose not to make a profit out of the misery of others: He took what was required to feed his servants, and returned those whom he had captured. Abraham was treated as a guest by the city in the temple Argarizin,[m] which means 6 "mountain of the Most High."[n] •He received gifts from Melchizedek,[o] its ruler and priest of God.[p]

Gen 10–11
Gen 11:31
Gen 12:1–4
Gen 12:5
Gen 14:1–12
Gen 14:13–16
Gen 14:21–24
Gen 14:18–20

a. The title *On the Jews* is used by Alexander Polyhistor of the works of so many authors that it must simply give a general description of the content of a work, rather than its precise title. There is no reason to change it, as Freudenthal, *Alexander Polyhistor*, p. 207 does, to *On the Hebrews* as more befitting a Samaritan author.

b. Freudenthal (*Alexander Polyhistor*, p. 207) pointed out that *tēs Assourias* modifies not *peri Ioudaiōn* but *polin*.

c. The name is not known elsewhere. Schnabel (*Berossos*, p. 69) suggested that the name derived from Ur as cult city of the moon god Sin, since in Ar. *qamar* means "moon." J. Strugnell has suggested that the name may have derived from the Jewish tradition which understood Ur as a furnace: The Gk. for furnace is *kaminos*, and this could have been confused to *kamarinē*.

d. Wacholder (*HUCA* 34 [1963] 100) holds that this is an interpretation of the author whereby *ʾwr kśdym* is taken as *ʿyr kśdym*. However, it seems simpler to hold that Eupolemus has taken Ur as a city, whereas the LXX, after transliteration, has taken it as a region, *chōra tōn Chaldaiōn*.

e. The text has many difficulties, and both Walter and Jacoby (*FGH*, vol. 3C, no. 724) suggest that the words "in the thirteenth generation" be excised. However, they seem too intertwined in the present text to do this neatly: *en triskaidekatē genesthai Abraam geneai*. The best suggestion is that of Wacholder (*HUCA* 34 [1963] 100) whereby the author is reporting two traditions: One placed Abraham in the thirteenth generation, and started from Enoch, prominent in the end of the F.; the other tradition started from Noah and the Flood, and placed Abraham in the tenth generation.

f. Later in the text, the *discovery* of astrology is attributed to Enoch. Here, therefore, as later in the phrase *phamenon babylōnious tauta kai auton eurēkenai*, the verb *eurein* must be translated to mean not the discovery or invention but the seeking and obtaining of astrological knowledge.

g. Walter suggests that the "Chaldean craft," placed alongside astrology, could refer to arithmetic.

h. Wacholder (*Eupolemus*, p. 313) has translated this phrase: "who on account of his piety was well-pleasing to God." However, *horman epi* must be given the sense of "rush eagerly after."

i. See "Relation to the Old Testament" for a discussion of this reinterpretation.

j. Sodom is included in Canaanite territory in Gen 10:19.

k. Instead of *aichmalōtisamenōn*, I have read *aichmalōtisthentōn* with Jacoby and Walter. If the transmitted text is accepted, the translation would be: "gained control of the captors."

l. Not the women and the people of Lot, as in Gen 14:16.

m. The grammar here is unclear. I have emended *hieron* to the locative *hierō*.

n. Freudenthal (*Alexander Polyhistor*, p. 87*) attempted to find a Heb. source for this interpretation, but one should follow Walter's lead (*Klio* 43–45 [1965] 285f.): *methermēneuomenon* does not signify an exact translation but, rather, a suitable meaning for the proper name.

o. This could refer to the gifts of food and wine (Gen 14:18) and thus is not necessarily in opposition to Gen 14:20b.

p. *Hiereōs ontos tou theou:* An alternative translation might be "priest of its god." One should

When famine came on the land, Abraham moved to Egypt with his whole Gen 12:10
household and dwelt there. The king of the Egyptians married Abraham's wife, Gen 12:11–15
7 since Abraham had said that she was his sister. •Furthermore,[q] Eupolemus relates Gen 12:17–19
that the king was not able to have intercourse with Abraham's wife and that his people and household were wasting away. When he summoned his diviners, they said, "Let the woman not be parted from her husband."[r] In this way, the king of the Egyptians realized that she was the wife of Abraham, and he returned her to her husband.

8 Abraham lived in Heliopolis with the Egyptian priests and taught them much: He explained astrology and the other sciences to them, saying that the Babylonians and he himself had obtained this knowledge. However, he attributed the discovery of them to Enoch. Enoch first discovered astrology, not the Egyptians.
9 For the Babylonians hold that Belos, who is son of Kronos,[s] lived first.[t] Kronos begot sons named Belos and Canaan.[u] This Canaan fathered the ancestor of the Phoenicians, whose son was Chus,[v] called by the Greeks Asbolus.[w] Chus was the ancestor of the Ethiopians and the brother of Mitsraim, the ancestor of the Egyptians.

The Greeks say that Atlas discovered astrology. However, Atlas is the same as Enoch.

The son of Enoch was Methuselah. He learned everything through the angels Gen 5:21
of God, and so knowledge came to us.[x]

note in this context that 2Mac 6:2 tells how the temple at Gerizim was renamed the temple of Zeus the Hospitable (*Xenios*). The reason given in 2Mac for the change is: *kathōs etugchanon hoi ton topon oikountes*. Some commentators, in line with the attitude of Josephus, *Ant* 12.257–61, have taken this phrase to mean "as the dwellers there requested." However, the meaning may well be "in accordance with their character"; i.e., the people at Gerizim were noted for their hospitality.

q. *Perissoteron:* J. Strugnell has suggested the meaning "furthermore," rather than "in great detail" (Walter) or "even more extraordinary things" (Wacholder, *Eupolemus*, p. 313). There is no need for Alexander Polyhistor suddenly to intrude an epitomizing presence here.

r. *Mē einai chēran tēn gynaika:* Both Walter and Wacholder take this phrase as an indirect statement: "they said that the woman was not a widow." However, there had been no previous discussion of such an issue, only that Abraham had said that Sarah was his sister. It would seem better to take the phrase as an oracular imperative (as befits a statement by diviners), where *einai chēra* would have the same meaning as *chērainein*, "to part from one's husband." Whence the above translation.

s. As noted in the Introduction, n. 33, nowhere else is Belos identified with Kronos. To obtain the more usual genealogy, whereby Belos is a son of Kronos, one need only emend *einai Kronon* to *einai Kronou*.

t. *Prōton genesthai:* Wacholder (*Eupolemus*, p. 314) suggests that this means that Belos was the first giant. However, the Babylonian genealogy of mankind is being used to establish relationships among mankind; it is better to maintain the meaning that Belos was the first of mankind.

u. Since Freudenthal (*Alexander Polyhistor*, p. 208), all have replaced the attested word *Chanaan* with *Cham*. Such an emendation is based on the assumption that the phrase *touton de ton Chanaan gennēsai ton patera tōn phoinikōn* should be translated: "This person begot Canaan, father of the Phoenicians." In the biblical tradition at Gen 10:6, Canaan is the son of Ham, and so the referent of *touton* must be the biblical Ham. Hence the emendation. However, the phrase is most simply translated: "This Canaan begot the father of the Phoenicians." No emendation of the text is necessary. Perhaps reference here is to Phoenix, who in many genealogies was the son of the king of Tyre, Agenor. Without such an emendation as that proposed by Freudenthal, the genealogical system in this F. shows no connection with the biblical genealogy in Gen 10; nor should it, as the author of the F. is reporting a Babylonian genealogy, not the biblical one. The lack of such a connection with the biblical genealogy further reduces the plausibility of claiming that the F. shows advanced syncretistic tendencies.

v. Reading *choun*, with one family of the Eusebian MS tradition.

w. A person named Asbolus is otherwise known only from Hesiod, *The Shield of Heracles*, 185. In the genealogy of this fragment, the name suggests *asbolos* = "sooty," as a description of the Ethiopians.

x. As in 1QapGen 2:19; 1En 106. Should this theory of knowledge through angels be connected with the Promethean-type myth found in fragmentary form in 1En 8? For a recent discussion, see P. Hanson, "Rebellion in Heaven, Azazel, and Euhemeristic Heroes in 1 Enoch 6–11," *JBL* 96 (1977) 195–233; G. Nickelsburg, "Apocalyptic and Myth in 1 Enoch 6–11," *JBL* 96 (1977) 383–405.

To whom does this "us" refer? To Abraham? or to "Pseudo-Eupolemus"? One cannot be sure. For the latter possibility, note how the epitomator of 2Mac uses the first person plural in reflective asides, as at 2Mac 6:12–17, to bring the relevance of the narrative home to his readers.

PRAEPARATIO EVANGELICA 9.18.2

In anonymous works, we find that Abraham traced his ancestry to the giants. These dwelt in the land of Babylonia. Because of their impiety, they were destroyed by the gods. One of them, Belos, escaped death and settled in Babylon. He built a tower and lived in it; the tower was called Belos after its builder. After Abraham had learned astrology,[a] he first went to Phoenicia and taught it to the Phoenicians; later he went to Egypt.

Gen 12:5,10

a. Within this section, astrology would seem to be connected with the giants.

CLEODEMUS MALCHUS

(prior to First Century B.C.)

A NEW TRANSLATION AND INTRODUCTION

BY R. DORAN

What survives of the work of Cleodemus deals with the descendants of Abraham through his wife Keturah (Gen 25:1–4). Cleodemus focuses on the deeds of Afera and Iafra: They fight alongside Heracles; Africa receives its name from them; and a tribe, the Sophakes, is named after a descendant from the marriage of Heracles to one of the daughters of Afera.

Text

The extant fragment of Cleodemus is found in Josephus, *Antiquities* 1.239–41. In turn, this was cited by Eusebius in his *Praeparatio Evangelica* 9.20.2–4. The two texts show minor variations; the main differences occur in the spelling of proper nouns. Such name variation is rampant in the Septuagint translation of Genesis. The following translation is based on the critical edition of Josephus by B. Niese;[1] divergences from this text will be noted.

Original language

There is no linguistic evidence to make one look for a language other than Greek. This conclusion is supported by the use of Greek traditions in the retelling of Abraham's descendants.

The work of Alexander Polyhistor

Josephus states that he drew his information from Alexander Polyhistor. But from which work of Alexander is Josephus quoting? Alexander is best known for his work *On the Jews*, which furnished considerable material to Eusebius. Freudenthal held that this fragment of Cleodemus came from the same work.[2] But if so, why did not Eusebius quote directly from this source, which he knew so well otherwise? Freudenthal's guess that Eusebius wanted to use Josephus, rather than a pagan author, is not satisfactory.[3] A. von Gutschmid proposed that the fragment of Cleodemus came from another work of Alexander Polyhistor, that *On Libya*,[4] a proposal seconded by Jacoby.[5] Following Gutschmid, Walter has recently argued that Josephus did not know Polyhistor's *On the Jews*. If Josephus had known this work, he would have mentioned Polyhistor in his list of Greek authors interested in Jewish history (*Apion* 1.161–218).[6] Since Polyhistor often orders his material on an ethnographic and

---

[1] *Flavii Josephi opera* (Berlin, 1885–95) 7 vols.
[2] Freudenthal, *Alexander Polyhistor*, pp. 13–15.
[3] Freudenthal, *Alexander Polyhistor*, p. 15.
[4] A. von Gutschmid, *Kleine Schriften II* (Leipzig, 1890) p. 182.
[5] FGH 273 Fs. 32–47.
[6] N. Walter, "Zur Überlieferung einiger Reste früher jüdisch-hellenistischer Literatur bei Josephus, Clemens und Euseb," *Studia Patristica* 7 (TU 92; Berlin, 1966) pp. 314–20. Walter notes that, at *Apion* 1.218, Josephus mentions two authors—Demetrius and Eupolemus—who are otherwise known to us through Alexander Polyhistor. However, Josephus is drawing on some other source for his knowledge of these authors.

geographic basis, it is reasonable to grant that the excerpt on Cleodemus was taken from Polyhistor's work *On Libya*.

Date

The date of Cleodemus must be before that of Alexander Polyhistor, i.e. before 50 B.C. Added confirmation is given by the distinction which Cleodemus, but not Josephus, draws between Libya and Africa. Cleodemus has Libya as the name for the whole continent, while Africa refers to a much narrower area, the Punic area around Carthage. For Romans, proconsular Africa comprised old Africa (= the area around Carthage) and new Africa (= the Numidian kingdom of King Juba I, annexed by Rome in 46 B.C.). Josephus, familiar with the Roman terminology, confuses Libya and Africa.[7]

Relation to the Old Testament

Cleodemus deals with the descendants of Abraham through Keturah. For Cleodemus, however, Genesis 25:1–6 is a springboard to other traditions, not found in the Old Testament. One should even question whether Cleodemus is dependent on the Greek traditions of the Bible as we know them. There is a discrepancy between the Septuagint and Cleodemus (in both Josephus and Eusebius) in the spelling of names. It is true that both the major Septuagint manuscript traditions and the manuscript tradition of Cleodemus add *r* to the name Ephah, but more evidence would be required to demonstrate that Cleodemus was using the Septuagint tradition.

Name	Hebrew	Septuagint	Josephus	Eusebius
Asshurim	*'šwrym*	*Assourieim*	*Sourēn*	*Assouri*
Ephah	*'yph*	*Gaiphar*	*Iaphran*	*Aphra*
Epher	*'pr*	*Apher*	*(I)apheran*	*Apher*

The African traditions

There were many traditions about Heracles' expedition to Libya. Sallust has the Medes, Persians, and Armenians travel to Libya after Heracles' death. Strabo speaks of Indians who accompanied Heracles on his expedition. Juba II, according to Plutarch, mentions Olbians and Myceneans; and Cleodemus talks of descendants of Abraham.[8] There were also divergent traditions regarding the place in which Heracles fought Antaios. Diodorus Siculus simply places the fight in Libya, present-day Africa. Strabo reports that some located the tomb of Antaios at Tingis (= Tangier) or Lingis, just south of Tangier. Mela states that Antaios founded Tingis. Juba II, according to Plutarch, reports that Sophax, son of Antaios' wife by Heracles, founded Tingis.[9] On the other hand, Procopius reports a tradition that Antaios wrestled with Heracles at Clipea, which is Aspis, on the Carthaginian coast.[10] The tradition of Procopius places the fight in the same geographical location as the tradition of Cleodemus.

The closest parallel in many ways to the account of Cleodemus is that of Juba II as reported by Plutarch.[11] Juba states that the people of Tingis held that Heracles married the wife of the defeated Antaios and had by her a son, Sophax. The son of Sophax was Diodorus. Cleodemus narrates that Antaios' wife had a son by Heracles, and his name was Diodorus; the son of Diodorus was Sophax, from whom the barbarians, the Sophakes, are named. Who are these Sophakes? Juba II traces his own lineage, according to Plutarch, back to Masinissa and the Numidian tribes of the Massyli. Now, the great rival of Masinissa

[7] M. Leglay, "Africa," *Der kleine Pauly* (Stuttgart, 1964) vol. 1, cols. 109f.
[8] Sallust, *Jugurtha* 16f.; Strabo, 17.3.7; Plutarch, *Sertorius* 9.
[9] Diodorus Siculus, 1.17.21, 24; 4.17.4; Strabo, 17.3.8; Mela, 3.106; Plutarch, *Sertorius* 9.
[10] Procopius, *Wars* 4.10.24.
[11] Plutarch, *Sertorius* 9.

was named Sophax, the leader of the Masaesyli.[12] One could surmise that the Sophakes mentioned by Cleodemus refers to the Numidian tribes who lived in the area around Carthage.

As for Juba's account, one should not forget that Mauretania, in which lay Tingis, was given to him by the Romans to rule in 25 B.C. Juba took the legends surrounding Heracles and Antaios and refashioned them as an act of political propaganda to claim ancestral support for his reign in Mauretania.[13] Juba's ancestor Sophax would have founded and named Mauretania's major city, Tingis; Juba's other ancestor Diodorus would have ruled many of the Libyan peoples. The legend itself, however, must be dated to earlier than 25 B.C., as it is found in a Judaized form in Cleodemus.

Provenance

Cleodemus was dubbed a Samaritan by Freudenthal: The added name Malchos pointed to a Semitic origin, and the "syncretism" whereby Abraham's descendants were linked with Heracles suggested an author from the syncretistic Samaritans. Freudenthal even suggested that the Heracles of the legend was the Heracles-Melkart of Tyre.[14]

Freudenthal's belief that the name Malchos was non-Jewish and derived from the name of the god Moloch[15] has been disproved by its appearance in the documents from the Muraba'at caves. Jews could have names from the root *mlk*.[16] Secondly, the equation of Samaritan and syncretist is no longer acceptable. Freudenthal's position does not explain why the fragment is so concerned with the founding of Africa, and makes no reference to Tyre.

B. Z. Wacholder has suggested that Cleodemus was a heathen.[17] His new argument is that Cleodemus is called a prophet (*prophētēs*), a title which no Jewish author would claim for himself at this time. But it is not clear whether *prophētēs* is a title applied to Cleodemus by himself or by Alexander Polyhistor. Furthermore, *prophētēs* has a wide range of meanings, some of which belong in the realm of Greek cult but others of which could be at home in the Judaism of this period.[18]

Cleodemus' concern for the founding of Africa through descendants of Abraham suggests he was a Jew living in that area, possibly even in the main city of Carthage.[19] It is true that Cleodemus notes that Assyria received its name from another of the sons of Abraham through Keturah, but this is mentioned almost in passing. The emphasis rests squarely on the African genealogy. If the above analysis, which connects the Sophakes with the Numidian tribes, is correct, Cleodemus would be reproducing indigenous traditions about the connection of the Numidian tribes to Africa and presenting them in a Judaized form.[20]

Relation to apocryphal books

The general invasion of eastern peoples with Heracles into Libya and their gradual development into the various ethnic groups of Libya was the basis for many traditions.

---

[12] Polybius, 14.1–10; Livy, 28.17–18; 30.3. See P. Habel, "Syphax," Pauly-Wissowa 4 (zweite Reihe), cols. 1472–77.

[13] S. Gsell also suggested that Juba I provided a genealogy for his lineage through Heracles. Apollodorus (*Library* 2.7.8) mentions that Heracles had a son Iobes by a woman named Certhe. Gsell makes the connection between Iobes (= Iuba) and Certhe, from whom would be named Cirta, the capital of Juba I's kingdom. S. Gsell, *Histoire Ancienne de l'Afrique du Nord* (Paris, 1921–28) vol. 8, pp. 236–38. Gsell also discusses here the limits of Juba II's kingdom. See also J. Desanges, "Les territoires gétules de Juba II," *Revue des Études Anciennes* 66 (1964) 33–47.

[14] Freudenthal, *Alexander Polyhistor*, pp. 133f. S. Gsell has shown that the Heracles of the Juba tradition had no connection with Heracles-Melkart. S. Gsell, *Histoire Ancienne*, vol. 6, pp. 154f.

[15] Freudenthal, *Alexander Polyhistor*, pp. 131f.

[16] DJD 2, no. 19, 11.27–28; no. 91b, 11.3.5.

[17] B. Z. Wacholder, "Cleodemus Malchus," *EncyJud* 5, col. 603.

[18] Friedrich, *TDNT*, vol. 6, p. 794. Wacholder states that the title may indicate a temple official, "which implies Phoenician or Nabatean origin."

[19] N. Walter, *JSHRZ* 1.2 (1976) 116f.

[20] The suggestion that Juba II copied Cleodemus, whose traditions he would have learned through his Jewish wife, is unnecessary. (Freudenthal, *Alexander Polyhistor*, pp. 135f.). Both the geographical location and the connections made in the narrative differ. In Juba, Heracles marries the wife of his adversary, while, in Cleodemus, he marries the wife of his partner.

Cleodemus has characterized this invasion as one which involved descendants of Abraham. Such an attempt to connect the Jews with other nations is found also in the Spartan connection of 1 Maccabees 12:20–23.[21] The Cretan Jews also tried to trace their lineage to Greek heroes.[22] D. Georgi has properly emphasized this view of Abraham as colony founder and as culture bringer. Heracles was a bringer of culture, and Abraham is depicted as related to him by marriage and as spreading culture prior to Heracles.[23] Such a view of the patriarchs is also present in Artapanus and "Pseudo-Eupolemus."[24]

Should Cleodemus be labeled syncretistic? Rather than use this term pejoratively, one should recognize that Cleodemus is doing what the genealogists of Genesis were doing: He is tracing the various peoples of the world back to common ancestors. Cleodemus, in his use of non-Jewish historical traditions, witnesses to the creativity and variety of Judaism in the hellenistic period.

SELECT BIBLIOGRAPHY

Charlesworth, *PMR*, pp. 92f.
Denis, *Introduction*, pp. 259–61.

Freudenthal, J. *Alexander Polyhistor und die von ihm erhaltenen Reste jüdischer und samaritanischer Geschichtswerke*. Hellenistische Studien 1–2; Breslau, 1874–75.
Jacoby, F. *Die Fragmente der griechischen Historiker*. Leiden, 1954–64.
Wacholder, B. Z. "Cleodemus Malchus," *EncyJud* 5, col. 603.
Walter, N. "Kleodemus Malchas," *JSHRZ* 1.2 (1976) 115–20.

---

[21] See B. Cardauns, "Juden und Spartaner. Zur hellenistisch-jüdischen Literatur," *Hermes* 95 (1967) 317–24.

[22] See the etymology of Iudaios from Mt. Ida, in Crete, reported in Tacitus, *Histories* 5.2. A. M. A. Hospers-Jansen has written that this genealogy could never have come from a Jew. See her *Tacitus over de Joden (Hist. 5.2–13)* (Groningen, 1949) p. 191. In its present form, the account of the expulsion of the Jews from Crete may reflect an anti-Jewish (Hospers-Jansen suggests Lat.) source. The actual etymology, however, is highly laudatory of the Jews.

[23] D. Georgi, *Die Gegner des Paulus im 2.Korintherbrief: Studien zur religiösen Propaganda in der Spätantike* (Wissenschaftliche Monographien zum Alten und Neuen Testament 11; NeuKirchen-Vluyn, 1964) p. 65.

[24] See the relevant sections in this edition of the Pseudepigrapha.

239 It is told how this Ofren waged war against Libya and occupied it. His grandsons,
240 who settled in the land, named it Africa after him. •Alexander Polyhistor confirms
what I say when he states: "Cleodemus the prophet, also called Malchas,[a] recorded
the history of the Jews, just as Moses, their lawgiver, had done. Cleodemus states   Gen 25:1–6
241 that Keturah bore Abraham mighty sons. •Cleodemus gives their names, calling
three of them Afera, Surim, Iafra.[b] Assyria was named after Surim; the city of   Gen 25:3f.
Afra and the region Africa were named after Afera and Iafra, for Afera and Iafra
fought with Heracles in his campaign in Libya against Antaios. Heracles married
the daughter of Afera and had by her a son, Diodorus.[c] Diodorus had a son,
Sophax,[d] from whom the barbarians get the name of Sophakes.

a. I have followed here the reading of Eusebius, *Malchas*, rather than the *Malchos* of Josephus, as the more difficult reading. See also the Introduction on "Provenance."

b. I have followed the readings of Josephus for the spelling of the names; Eusebius seems to show a tendency to harmonize with the LXX text. See also the Introduction, "Relation to the Old Testament."

c. Following the reading of Eusebius, not that of Josephus, *Didōros*. This is in line with the tradition of Juba II, as preserved in Plutarch, *Sertorius* 9.

d. The MSS of Josephus read *Sophōna*, those of Eusebius *Sophonan*. However, in view of the following tribal name *Sophakas* (Eusebius *Sophas*) and the tradition as in Juba II, I have read *Sophaka*.

ROMANCE

ARTAPANUS

(Third to Second Century B.C.)

A NEW TRANSLATION AND INTRODUCTION

BY J. J. COLLINS

The three fragments of Artapanus deal with the exploits in Egypt of three famous ancestors of the Jews: Abraham, Joseph, and Moses. Each is presented as a founder of culture. Abraham teaches the Egyptians to study the stars. Joseph organizes the division of the land and discovers measurements. He is also administrator of Egypt and stores grain during the seven prosperous years. The career of Moses is described at greatest length. He is identified with Mousaeus, teacher of Orpheus, and also with the god Hermes. He is credited with a wide variety of discoveries and with establishing the Egyptian animal cults. Because of the envy of the Egyptian king, he is sent on a campaign against the Ethiopians, which becomes a resounding success. Subsequently, Moses kills the man sent to assassinate him and flees to Arabia. He restrains the Arabs from campaigning against Egypt, but returns to demand the release of the Hebrews. When the king resists, Moses prevails by using his supernatural powers. Most of the Egyptian temples are destroyed in the plagues, and the sacred animals are destroyed along with the Egyptians in the Red Sea. Two accounts are given of the crossing of the sea. One, attributed to the Memphites, says the Hebrews crossed at low tide. The other, attributed to the Heliopolitans, is clearly miraculous and is evidently preferred by Artapanus.

Texts

The fragments of Artapanus are preserved in Eusebius, *Praeparatio Evangelica*, Book 9, chapters 18, 23, and 27. The third fragment is partially paralleled in Clement, *Stromata*, 1.23.154,2f. The present translation is based on the edition of Eusebius by Karl Mras.[1] The text can also be found in Jacoby's *Die Fragmente der griechischen Historiker*[2] and in A.-M. Denis, *Fragmenta pseudepigraphorum quae supersunt graeca*.[3]

On the textual tradition of Eusebius see the general introduction to Alexander Polyhistor by John Strugnell (above).

It is important to bear in mind that we do not have actual excerpts from Artapanus but only the summaries of Alexander Polyhistor, insofar as these have been preserved by Eusebius. The parallel in Clement is limited to a single incident (the nocturnal visit of Moses to the king) and it omits some of the miraculous details of the text in Eusebius.

The first fragment in Eusebius is presented as an excerpt from Artapanus' *Judaica*, while the other two fragments are said to be from his *Peri Ioudaiōn* ("About the Jews"). The latter title is also given in Clement. It is not clear, however, whether two distinct works were involved. The three fragments could easily fit in one continuous history, and *Judaica* is most probably a loose reference to the *Peri Ioudaiōn*, rather than an exact title. The evidence is not sufficient to permit certainty on this matter.

---

[1] Mras, GCS 43.1, pp. 504, 516f., 519–24.
[2] Jacoby, *FGH*, vol. 3C, no. 726, pp. 680–86.
[3] Denis, PVTG 2, pp. 186–95.

Original language

There is no reason to suspect that the original language was other than Greek. Artapanus' vocabulary has many points of contact with classical Greek literature as well as the *koinē* of the hellenistic age.[4]

Date

The only clear evidence for the date of Artapanus is that he must have written prior to Alexander Polyhistor, who summarized the work about the middle of the first century B.C. Proposed dates include the time of Ptolemy IV Philopator (221–204 B.C.),[5] the early second century B.C.,[6] and about 100 B.C.[7] Artapanus apparently knew the Septuagint[8] and also reflects many themes of the anti-Jewish Egyptian accounts of Moses, of which the earliest is found in Manetho (who flourished about 280 B.C.).[9] Both these considerations suggest an earliest possible date of approximately 250 B.C.[10] The syncretistic character of the work has been urged as an argument for an early date[11] but is in fact compatible with any date in the period 250–100 B.C.

Three considerations may help to specify the date further. Cerfaux has argued that certain passages in Artapanus reflect an attempt by Ptolemy IV Philopator to assimilate the Jews to the worship of Dionysus.[12] Such an attempt is explicitly alleged in 3 Maccabees 2:29f., where Philopator is said to require that the Jews be registered and "branded by fire on their bodies with an ivy leaf, the emblem of Dionysus," while those who voluntarily join the mysteries are granted equal citizenship with the Alexandrians.[13] Cerfaux also notes the evidence of the Schubart Papyrus that Philopator attempted to organize the cult of Dionysus by requiring those who practiced initiation to deposit their sacred doctrine (*hieros logos*) sealed and signed with their names. Cerfaux relates this requirement of the Schubart Papyrus to the enigmatic passage in Artapanus (*PrEv* 9.27.24–26) where the king bids Moses speak the name of his God and then writes the name on a tablet and seals it. Cerfaux also takes the statement in Artapanus (*PrEv* 9.27.20) that Chenephres required the Jews to wear linen garments as an allusion to the attempted assimilation to the cult of Dionysus. If Artapanus is indeed alluding to events in the reign of Philopator in this indirect manner, we should assume that he wrote during that reign or shortly thereafter. However, Cerfaux's argument is too hypothetical to count as decisive evidence, and is no more than a possibility.

A second consideration arises from Artapanus' mention of the disease elephantiasis (*PrEv* 9.27.20). According to Plutarch (*Quaestionum convivialium liber* 8.9.1) this disease was first identified in the time of Asclepiades of Prusa, who flourished in the first century B.C. However, it had already been the subject of a treatise falsely ascribed to Democritus and believed to be the work of Bolus of Mendes, in Egypt, who was a contemporary of

---

[4] See Freudenthal, *Alexander Polyhistor*, pp. 215f.; I. Merentites, *Ho Ioudaios Logios Artapanos kai to Ergon Autou* (Athens, 1961) pp. 184–86.

[5] So Denis, PVTG 2, p. 257, following a suggestion of L. Cerfaux, "Influence des Mystères sur le Judaïsme Alexandrin Avant Philon," *Recueil L. Cerfaux* (Bibliotheca Ephemeridum Theologicarum Lovaniensium 6: Gembloux, 1954), vol. 1, pp. 81–85.

[6] So B. Z. Wacholder, "Biblical Chronology and World Chronicles," *HTR* 61 (1968) 460, n. 34, and *Eupolemus: A Study of Judaeo-Greek Literature* (Monographs of the Hebrew Union College 3; Cincinnati, 1974) p. 106, n. 40.

[7] So Walter, *JSHRZ* 1.2 (1976) 125; Merentites, *Ho Ioudaios Logios*, p. 9.

[8] Freudenthal, *Alexander Polyhistor*, p. 216.

[9] See P. M. Fraser, *Ptolemaic Alexandria* (Oxford, 1972) vol. 1, p. 706.

[10] The origins of the LXX are widely disputed. The traditional date, given by LetAris, is the reign of Ptolemy II Philadelphus (287–247 B.C.). While the Letter is not reliable historical evidence, this period is still the most probable for the translation of the Pentateuch. See the discussion by S. Jellicoe in *The Septuagint and Modern Study* (Oxford, 1968) pp. 52–58. He argues that "association direct or indirect with Philadelphus places the undertaking well before the middle of the third century B.C." and that "Apart from the Aristeas tradition this is borne out by the available external evidence." Jellicoe also discusses dissenting views (pp. 59–73).

[11] Wacholder, *Eupolemus*, p. 106. Wacholder's assumption that "the Maccabean rebellion reaffirmed monotheistic belief" in Egyptian Judaism exaggerates both the syncretism of Artapanus and the influence of the revolt on the Diaspora.

[12] Cerfaux, *Recueil L. Cerfaux*, vol. 1, pp. 81–85.

[13] Cf. 2Mac 6:7f., which says that in the persecution of Antiochus Epiphanes, Jews in Jerusalem were compelled "to wear ivy wreaths and walk in the Dionysiac procession."

Callimachus, in the third century B.C.[14] Artapanus could, of course, have referred to it at any later time, but he would have had more reason to single it out for mention if it was newly identified when he wrote.

A third possible clue is provided by Artapanus' statement (*PrEv* 9.27.7) that Moses included Egyptian farmers in his army. Ptolemy IV Philopator was the first Ptolemy to permit the Egyptian peasantry to bear arms in his service, before the battle of Raphia in 217 B.C.[15] The allusion by Artapanus to peasant participation in Moses' army is not prompted by the biblical account or by the polemics of Egyptians such as Manetho. It may be taken to reflect the historical development in the time of Philopator.

These considerations are by no means conclusive. Artapanus may have written at any time in the period 250–100 B.C. However, the few more specific clues we have all point to a date toward the end of the third century B.C., which may be tentatively taken as the most probable time of composition.

Provenance

All the narratives are set in Egypt. Even the fragment on Abraham deals only with his sojourn in Egypt. Consequently the Egyptian provenance of the work is unquestioned.

Within Egypt Artapanus has usually been localized in Alexandria.[16] This assumption has been questioned by Fraser, who notes that Artapanus has little in common with the literature usually ascribed to Alexandrian Judaism. Fraser argues that Artapanus "is familiar with the native life of Egypt and the purely priestly traditions" and suggests that he did not belong to the influential Jewish circles around Philometor or a later Ptolemy but (as his Persian name might suggest) was "a Jew of mixed descent, possibly resident in another centre such as Memphis."[17] Against Fraser, we must note that Artapanus' knowledge of Egyptian customs seems to be primarily derived from Greek authors (e.g. Hecataeus of Abdera).[18] However, Fraser is quite right that the assumption of Alexandrian provenance is gratuitous. There is no specific indication of the place of authorship within Egypt. We should at least note the distinctiveness of Artapanus over against the main corpus of allegedly Alexandrian literature.

Historical importance

There have been occasional attempts to claim that some of the details of Artapanus' narrative have a historical basis. So Freudenthal suggests that the legend of Moses' campaign against Ethiopia arose from confusion with another Moses (Messu or Mesu), known from an inscription, who was governor of Ethiopia and an approximate contemporary of Moses.[19] Also J. Gutman suggests that the Chenephres of Artapanus was a historical pharaoh of the thirteenth dynasty in the eighteenth century B.C.[20] Neither suggestion is plausible. Artapanus has his closest literary parallels in the historical romances; and he freely mixes fantasy with traditional lore.[21] The historical significance of the work lies in the type of hellenistic Judaism it attests, rather than in the "historical" allusions it preserves.

Artapanus provides one variant of the apologetic literature of hellenistic Judaism, and, on a broader level, of what may be called the "competitive historiography" of the hellenistic

---

[14] Wacholder, *Eupolemus*, p. 106. On Bolus see H. Diels, *Die Fragmente der Vorsokratiker* (Berlin, 1956⁸) vol. 2, p. 216.

[15] See W. W. Tarn, *Hellenistic Civilisation* (New York, 1961³), p. 179. I owe this suggestion to Professor J. Strugnell.

[16] E.g. Walter, *JSHRZ* 1.2 (1976) 124; Merentites, *Ho Ioudaios Logios*, p. 9.

[17] Fraser, *Ptolemaic Alexandria*, vol. 1, p. 706; vol. 2, p. 985 (n. 199). Fraser notes the occurrence of related Persian names in Egypt and the village of Artapatou, near Oxyrhynchus, attested from the third century A.D.

[18] See Wacholder, *Eupolemus*, p. 80.

[19] Freudenthal, *Alexander Polyhistor*, p. 155.

[20] J. Gutman, *Ha Sifrut ha-Yehudit ha-Hellenistit* (Jerusalem, 1963), vol. 2, p. 135. See Wacholder, *Eupolemus*, p. 105. Wacholder also notes other attempted identifications.

[21] The affinities of Artapanus with hellenistic popular romances were shown especially by M. Braun, *History and Romance* (Oxford, 1938) pp. 26–31, 99–102. See the recent evaluation by D. L. Tiede, *The Charismatic Figure as Miracle Worker* (SBLDS 1; Missoula, Mont., 1972) pp. 146–77.

age.[22] Throughout the Near East, from Egypt to Babylon, the native sovereign kingships had been suppressed by the Greeks. Subsequent generations looked to their past nostalgically and tended to romanticize their history by stressing its antiquity and superiority. Berossus of Babylon and Manetho of Egypt, both of whom wrote in Greek at the beginning of the third century B.C., were outstanding examples of such propagandistic historiography. Manetho initiated a long line of Greco-Egyptian writers (Lysimachus, Chaeremon, Apion) who augmented the glory of Egypt by disparaging the Jews and giving derogatory accounts of their origins. Fragments of these writers are preserved by Josephus in his *Against Apion*.[23] Josephus attempts to refute the charges of these writers directly. Earlier Jewish writers, such as Artapanus,[24] did not address the charges directly but took up the weapons of their adversaries and produced romanticized histories of their own.

The competitive historiography of Artapanus has both negative and positive aspects. On the one hand, several details, especially in the treatment of Moses, appear to be implicit refutations of writers such as Manetho, who had alleged that Moses forbade his people to worship the gods or abstain from the flesh of the sacred animals (*Apion* 1.239). Artapanus claimed that it was Moses who established these cults. Manetho alleged that Moses had invaded Egypt (*Apion* 1.241); Artapanus stated that Moses restrained Raguel when the latter wished to invade. According to Manetho, the pharaoh had to protect the sacred animals from Moses (*Apion* 1.244); Artapanus contended that the pharaoh buried the animals which Moses had made sacred since he wished to conceal Moses' inventions. In Manetho's account, the pharaoh sought refuge in Ethiopia when Moses invaded (*Apion* 1.246); in Artapanus, Moses conducted a campaign against Ethiopia on behalf of the pharaoh. Such implicit refutations of the Egyptian account constitute the negative side of Artapanus' historiography. More positively, he portrayed each of his subjects, but especially Moses, as a founder of culture, and attributed to them all the inventions which are beneficial to humanity. Here again the claim is competitive. Artapanus repeatedly claimed for Moses achievements elsewhere attributed to other legendary heroes, especially the Egyptian Sesostris,[25] e.g. inventions in military matters, and in construction and irrigation, the division of Egypt into thirty-six nomes, and victory over the Ethiopians. Further, Artapanus exalted Moses even above the divinities of the Egyptians. Isis was taught by Hermes,[26] but Moses was identified with him. The subordination of Isis to Moses is also expressed through the episode in which Moses strikes the earth (which was traditionally identified with Isis) with his rod (*PrEv* 9.27.32).[27]

The foregoing examples may suffice to set the work of Artapanus in the context of the competitive historiography of the hellenistic age. The purpose of the work may be seen as an attempt to bolster Jewish ethnic pride in the Jewish community.[28] A similar purpose, on a much more sophisticated level, may be attributed to such writers as Josephus and Philo. The work is apparently directed outward to any gentiles who might care to listen, but undoubtedly had its main effect on the self-esteem of the Jewish community.[29]

Perhaps the greatest historical significance of Artapanus, however, is that he represents a very unusual, and distinctly syncretistic, theological stance within Judaism.

Theological importance

Artapanus has been sharply criticized as one who was more concerned with the glory of Judaism than with the purity of his religion.[30] He has also been defended as an apologist

---

[22] See Collins, *Between Athens and Jerusalem*, pp. 33–35.
[23] Josephus, *Apion* 1.75–105, 227–50 (Manetho); 288–92 (Chaeremon); 304–11 (Lysimachus); 2.1–144 (Apion). See J. G. Gager, *Moses in Greco-Roman Paganism* (SBLMS 16; Nashville, Tenn., 1972), pp. 113–24.
[24] Cf. also Eup, Ps-Eup, ClMal.
[25] See Tiede, *The Charismatic Figure*, pp. 150–67. On Sesostris see Diodorus 1.54–57.
[26] Diodorus, 1.17.3 and 1.27.4; Tiede, *The Charismatic Figure*, p. 155.
[27] Tiede, *The Charismatic Figure*, p. 174.
[28] Braun, *History and Romance*, pp. 26f.; Tiede, *The Charismatic Figure*, p. 149.
[29] Compare V. Tcherikover, "Jewish Apologetic Literature Reconsidered," *Eos* 48 (1956) 169–93.
[30] So E. Schürer, *History*, vol. 3, p. 208. Also P. Dalbert, *Die Theologie der hellenistisch-jüdischen Missionsliteratur unter Ausschluss von Philo und Josephus* (Hamburg, 1954), p. 52.

whose narrative was shaped by the need to refute accusations.[31] Neither assessment is quite accurate, although each has some basis. The primary interest certainly lies in the Jewish heroes Abraham, Joseph, and especially Moses. God remains in the background, except for an occasional miraculous manifestation in the "divine voice" (*PrEv* 9.27.21, 36) and the mysterious power of the divine name (*PrEv* 9.27.25f.). Further, Artapanus takes the unparalleled step of making Moses the founder of the Egyptian animal cults. This step is certainly part of the general apologetic glorification of Moses, but no other Jewish apologist goes so far. Artapanus is similarly at variance with other intertestamental writings when he presents both Abraham and Moses as teachers of astrology.[32] Further, he identifies Moses with the god Hermes and says he was deemed worthy of divine honor by the priests (*PrEv* 9.27.6).

However, Artapanus' attitude toward the Egyptian cults is not a simple one. It must be seen in the light of his general euhemeristic[33] tendency to explain pagan divinities by reference to inventions which were useful to mankind. It is crucial to his theology that only pagan divinities are so explained. The God of the Jews is still regarded as "the master of the universe" (*PrEv* 9.27.22). The Egyptian cults may be legitimized by being attributed to Moses, but they are only legitimized in an attenuated sense. We have already seen that Isis is regarded as subordinate to Moses. This is also clearly true of the animal cults. Ultimately, as Tiede remarks, "when the showdown comes, it is no surprise that the Egyptians who brought along their animal gods (27.35) are destroyed by fire and flood (27.37)."[34]

Artapanus, then, does not compromise the superiority of the God of the Jews. He can also use the term "god" for pagan deities (*PrEv* 9.27.4) and does not object when Moses is deemed worthy of divine honor. Yet, we should bear in mind that even in the biblical text God made Moses "a god to Pharaoh" (Ex 7:1), a point noted and utilized by Philo (*Vit Mos* 1.158).[35] However, this is not to deny that Artapanus is syncretistic far beyond the orthodoxy of the Deuteronomic or rabbinic traditions. Not only does he regard the animal cults of the Egyptians as harmless, but he apparently classifies them among the things which are beneficial for mankind. Viewed as cultural products for human benefit, they are considered quite acceptable.

The piety of Artapanus is conspicuously similar to that of hellenistic paganism. He is especially interested in the miraculous, and even, perhaps, the magical.[36] While the Egyptian magicians might seem to be disparaged for their reliance on tricks and charms, great emphasis is placed on Moses' rod, and on the mysterious power of the divine name. The

[31] So G. Vermès, "La figure de Moïse au tournant des deux Testaments," in *Moïse, L'Homme de l'Alliance* (Cahiers Sioniens; Paris, 1955), p. 73.

[32] Contrast SibOr 3.218–30; Philo *Abr* 69–71, 77; Jub 12:16–20. Abraham is also said to have discovered astrology in Ps-Eup (*PrEv* 9.17.3), and in Ps-Hec (Josephus, *Ant* 1.8.2 [168]) he is said to have taught the Egyptians astronomy. See further J. H. Charlesworth, "Jewish Astrology in the Talmud, Pseudepigrapha, the Dead Sea Scrolls, and Early Palestinian Synagogues," *HTR* 70 (1977) 183–200.

[33] Euhemerism is the theory that the gods were originally kings and conquerors who brought benefits to humanity and that their worship arose as an expression of gratitude. The term is derived from Euhemerus of Messene, who put forward this theory about 300 B.C.

[34] Tiede, *The Charismatic Figure*, p. 162. Recently C. R. Holladay (*Theios Aner in Hellenistic Judaism* [SBLDS 40; Missoula, Mont., 1977] 229–32) has urged that the syncretism of Artapanus should be further qualified. He notes that Moses was called Mousaios *by the Greeks*, deemed worthy of divine honor *by Egyptian priests*, and called Hermes *by them or by the Egyptians*. It is doubtful whether this point can really qualify Artapanus' syncretism. There is no suggestion that Artapanus thought these names were wrongly given to Moses, or even that Mousaios or Hermes had any existence apart from Moses. Artapanus' point seems to be that Hermes is only a name that pagans gave to Moses. In one respect he undermines the divinity of Hermes, but he also affirms the esteem in which Moses was allegedly held. Holladay also points to the ambiguity of the reference to the sacred animals, cats, dogs, and ibises in *PrEv* 9.27.4, and stresses that the ibis and Apis were not directly consecrated by Moses. However, in view of the reference in *PrEv* 9.27.12 to "the creatures which Moses had made sacred" there is little room for doubt that Moses is credited with establishing the animal cults. This again subordinates these cults to Moses, but also claims for him whatever prestige may be derived from them.

[35] See D. Georgi, *Die Gegner des Paulus im 2. Korintherbrief: Studien zur religiösen Propaganda in der Spätantike.* (Wissenschaftliche Monographien zum Alten und Neuen Testament 11; Neukirchen-Vluyn, 1964) pp. 147–51.

[36] See Tiede, *The Charismatic Figure*, pp. 166–74. This aspect of Artapanus was emphasized by O. Weinreich, *Gebet und Wunder* (Stuttgart, 1929). It is noteworthy that the citation in Clement downplays the miraculous element in Moses' escape from prison. According to the text in Eusebius the doors opened of their own accord (*automatōs*), in Clement they open "in accordance with the will of God."

portrayal of Moses has often been compared with the hellenistic "divine man" (*theios anēr*), and while Artapanus does not use this expression we may agree with Tiede that he would scarcely have objected to it.[37]

Relation to canonical books

Artapanus' discussions of the careers in Egypt of Abraham, Joseph, and Moses have at least points of departure in Genesis 12:10–20, Genesis 37–50, and Exodus 1–16. Artapanus deals freely with the biblical narrative. Yet the correspondences with the Septuagint, especially in the account of the plagues, are too close for mere coincidence, and are verbally exact in several cases. We must assume with Freudenthal that he knew the Septuagint translation.[38] Much of Artapanus' additional material has no biblical basis, but in a few cases he is clearly modifying the biblical account for apologetic purposes. So, for example, Joseph is not sold into slavery by his brothers, but himself requested the Arabs to convey him to Egypt. Again, Artapanus has Moses kill an Egyptian (*PrEv* 9.27.18) but only in self-defense, in sharp contrast to the biblical incident (Ex 2:12) in which he murders an Egyptian for striking a Hebrew.

Non-biblical sources

Various attempts have been made to link Artapanus with other hellenistic Jewish writings. Freudenthal suggested that Artapanus, Pseudo-Hecataeus, and the Letter of Aristeas were all the work of a single forger.[39] Hugo Willrich at first argued that Artapanus was dependent on Pseudo-Hecataeus, but later revised this opinion and attributed the influence to the genuine Hecataeus of Abdera.[40] More recently, Merentites has suggested dependence on Eupolemus.[41] However, there is nothing to indicate the direct dependence of Artapanus on any earlier non-biblical Jewish writings. He shares some interests and motifs with Eupolemus, Pseudo-Eupolemus, and Pseudo-Hecataeus, but these are common apologetic elements and do not establish direct literary dependence between the individual works.

There is no doubt that Artapanus was influenced by the anti-Jewish historiography of Egyptian writers, quite probably by Manetho.[42] There is general agreement that he also drew on Hecataeus of Abdera, since he has close parallels with Diodorus of Sicily (who wrote about 60–30 B.C.) and Hecataeus is the most likely common source.[43]

Influence on later writings

There is also wide agreement that Josephus was dependent on Artapanus, since both record a number of incidents which are not found in Exodus—most notably the campaign against Ethiopia (*Ant* 2.10.1f. [238–53]).[44] Josephus' account is more lengthy than the

---

[37] Tiede, *The Charismatic Figure*, p. 177. The Moses of Artapanus is also viewed as a "divine man," or *theios anēr*, by Weinreich, *Gebet und Wunder*, p. 166; L. Bieler, *Theios Aner* (Wien, 1935–36) vol. 2, pp. 30–33; and Georgi, *Die Gegner*, pp. 147–51. For a contrary view see Holladay, *Theios Aner*, 199–232. Holladay contrasts Moses' escape from prison with that of Dionysus in the *Bacchae* of Euripides. He stresses that Moses is clearly subordinate to the God who is *despotēs* of the universe, while Dionysus is himself *despotēs*. We may agree with Holladay that Artapanus does not "ascribe divinity to Moses in any way approaching what we find in Euripides' *Bacchae*" and that his propaganda does not depend on showing that Moses is a *theios anēr*. Yet, in the process of asserting the general superiority of Moses, he suggests that Moses is superior to some "divinities" worshiped by the pagans, and identical with others. Consequently, in so far as the epithet "divine" can be applied to the pagan gods, it can be applied to Moses, too. This, however, is "divinity" only in an attenuated sense and is not comparable to the status of the God of the Jews.

[38] Freudenthal, *Alexander Polyhistor*, p. 216.

[39] *Alexander Polyhistor*, p. 165.

[40] H. Willrich, *Juden und Griechen* (Göttingen, 1895) pp. 168f.; and by the same author, *Judaica* (Göttingen, 1900) pp. 111–16.

[41] Merentites, *Ho Ioudaios Logios*, p. 184. Merentites notes that this suggestion has already been made by A. Schlatter.

[42] Merentites, *Ho Ioudaios Logios*; Fraser, *Ptolemaic Alexandria*, vol. 1, p. 706. See above, "Historical importance."

[43] Freudenthal, *Alexander Polyhistor*, pp. 160f.; Willrich, *Judaica*, pp. 111–16. Some of the parallels are also found in Plutarch (*Isis and Osiris*, 32, 57, 72).

[44] So e.g. Walter, *JSHRZ* 1.2, p. 121.

preserved account of Artapanus, and it has been widely supposed that the episodes of Moses' victory over the serpents and his marriage were originally included by Artapanus but omitted by Alexander Polyhistor.[45] However, Josephus omits key points of Artapanus' account, such as the founding of Hermopolis and the introduction of circumcision. Most significantly Josephus provides an entirely different explanation for the origin of the campaign. Accordingly, some scholars deny that Josephus was dependent on Artapanus.[46] The question cannot be resolved definitively since we have only fragments of Artapanus. Josephus could scarcely have followed Artapanus' explanation of the Ethiopian campaign in any case, since it involved Moses' role in establishing the animal cults. Hence he may have deliberately composed an alternative. The correspondence between Josephus and Artapanus is more easily explained if Josephus used the full narrative of Artapanus but modified it or departed from it in accordance with his own view of Moses.

D. Georgi has argued for a line of continuity between Artapanus and Philo in the conception of Moses as a "divine man" (*theios anēr*).[47] The similarities, however, do not suggest direct dependence but are due to the common acceptance of hellenistic ideas for apologetic purposes. Philo, of course, does not follow the more colorful syncretistic exploits of Moses in Artapanus.

The influence of Artapanus on subsequent literature is slight. It is possible (but not very likely) that the neo-Pythagorean philosopher Numenius of Apamea derived the name Mousaeus for Moses from Artapanus (*PrEv* 9.8.2). Some of the non-biblical traditions in Artapanus (e.g. the campaign against Ethiopia) are also found in rabbinic writings, and the confrontation with the Egyptian magicians frequently recurs in Jewish, Christian, and Greco-Roman literature.[48] However, there is no clear evidence of direct dependence on Artapanus in any of this material.

The main claim of Artapanus to cultural significance is that he may represent one of the precursors of the hellenistic romances, but here again there is no evidence that he had any direct influence on the development of the genre.[49]

---

[45] The victory over the serpents seems to be presupposed by the consecration of the ibis in Artapanus. It is possible that the entire Ethiopian campaign may have been inspired by the biblical reference to Moses' Ethiopian (Cushite) wife (Num 12:1), and so the marriage of Moses would have been central to the original legend, either in Artapanus or in his source. However, campaigns against Ethiopia are common features of the competitive historiography of the hellenistic age. Cambyses, Sesostris, and Semiramis were all credited with such campaigns. So we cannot assume that the legend in Artapanus was developed from the biblical reference to the Ethiopian wife. See further D. J. Silver, "Moses and the Hungry Birds," *JQR* 64 (1973) 124–53. Silver takes the biblical reference as the origin of the story.

[46] Wacholder, *Eupolemus*, p. 53, n. 107. T. Rajak, "Moses in Ethiopia: Legend and Literature," *JJS* 29 (1978) 111–22, argues that both Artapanus and Josephus were ultimately dependent on an ongoing oral tradition, although Josephus may have drawn on a written source (but not on Artapanus). A. Shinan, "Moses and the Ethiopian Woman," *Scripta Hierosolymitana* 27 (1978) 66–78, says that Josephus' account is an expansion of the tradition reflected in Artapanus.

[47] Georgi, *Die Gegner*, pp. 148–62. See the assessment by Tiede, *The Charismatic Figure*, pp. 147f.

[48] Freudenthal, *Alexander Polyhistor*, pp. 172f.

[49] Braun, *History and Romance*, pp. 26–31, 99–102. Also M. Hadas, *Hellenistic Culture* (New York, 1959) pp. 98, 172. Most of the romance literature dates to the second century A.D. or later.

SELECT BIBLIOGRAPHY

Charlesworth, *PMR*, pp. 82f.
Delling, *Bibliographie*, pp. 53–55.
Denis, *Introduction*, pp. 255–57.

Braun, M. *History and Romance*. Oxford, 1938; pp. 26–31, 99–102. (Of basic importance for the relationship to the historical romances.)

Collins, J. J. *Between Athens and Jerusalem: Jewish Identity in the Hellenistic Diaspora*. New York, 1983; pp. 32–38. (Discussion of Jewish identity in Artapanus.)

Collins, J. J., and Poehlmann, W. "Artapanus." Unpublished paper from NT seminar 201, Harvard Divinity School, April 1970.

Dalbert, P. *Die Theologie der hellenistisch-jüdischen Missionsliteratur unter Ausschluss von Philo und Josephus*. Hamburg, 1954; pp. 42–52. (The most extensive discussion of the theology of Artapanus.)

Fraser, P. M. *Ptolemaic Alexandria*. Oxford, 1972; vol. 1, pp. 704–6; vol. 2, pp. 983–86. (Well-documented historical comments.)

Freudenthal, J. *Alexander Polyhistor*. Hellenistische Studien 1–2; Breslau, 1874–75. (Still the basic study on many points, although the thesis on authorship is untenable.)

Georgi, D. *Die Gegner des Paulus im 2. Korintherbrief: Studien zur religiösen Propaganda in der Spätantike*. Wissenschaftliche Monographien zum Alten und Neuen Testament 11; Neukirchen-Vluyn, 1964; pp. 147–51. (A discussion of the *theios anēr* motif, setting Artapanus in the context of Jewish mission literature.)

Gutman, J. *Ha Sifrut Ha-Yehudit ha-Hellenistit*. Jerusalem, 1963; vol. 2, pp. 109–35. (An extensive discussion in modern Heb.)

Holladay, C. R. *Theios Anēr in Hellenistic Judaism: A Critique of the Use of This Category in New Testament Christology* (SBLDS 40; Missoula, Mont., 1977) pp. 199–232. (A critique of the view that Artapanus depicts Moses as a Theios Anēr.)

Merentites, K. I. *Ho Ioudaios Logios Artapanos kai to Ergon Autou*. Athens, 1961. (The only book-length study of Artapanus. Introduction and full commentary, in Modern Gk.)

Rajak, T. "Moses in Ethiopia: Legend and Literature," *JJS* 29 (1978) 111–22. (Discussion of the Ethiopian episode and relation of it to Josephus.)

Shinan, A. "Moses and the Ethiopian Woman," *Scripta Hierosolymitana* 27 (1978) 66–78. (Discussion of Ethiopian incident.)

Silver, J. D. "Moses and the Hungry Birds," *JQR* 64 (1973) 123–53. (A discussion of the significance of the ibis and its possible implications for the background of Artapanus.)

Tiede, D. L. *The Charismatic Figure as Miracle Worker*. SBLDS 1; Missoula, Mont., 1972; pp. 146–77. (The best discussion in English. Includes text and translation of the Moses fragment in pp. 317–24.)

Vermès, G. "La figure de Moïse au tournant des deux Testaments," in *Moïse, L'Homme de l'Alliance*. Cahiers Sioniens; Paris, 1955; pp. 66–74. (Contains an annotated French translation of the greater part of Artapanus, with some general comments.)

Walter, N. "Artapanos," *JSHRZ* 1.2 (1976) 121–43. (Introduction and annotated German translation.)

THE FRAGMENTS OF ARTAPANUS

ABRAHAM

Fragment 1 *Eusebius, "Praeparatio Evangelica" 9.18.1*

Abraham in Egypt

Artapanus says in his *Judaica* that the Jews are named "Hermiouth,"[a] which, translated into Greek, is "Jews." They were called Hebrews after Abraham.[b] He says that the latter *came to Egypt* with all his household to the Egyptian king Pharethothes,[c] and *taught him astrology*,[d] that he remained there twenty years[e] and then departed again for the regions of Syria, but that many of those who came with him remained in Egypt on account of the prosperity of the land.[f]

Gen 12:10; Jub 13:11
Ps-Eup (PrEv 9.17.3)
Ps-Hec
(Josephus, Ant 1.8.2 [168])

JOSEPH

Fragment 2 *Eusebius, "Praeparatio Evangelica" 9.23.1–4*

Joseph in Egypt

1 **23** Artapanus says in his "On the Jews" that Joseph was a descendant of Abraham and son of Jacob. Since he excelled the others in understanding and wisdom, *he was plotted against by his brothers*. He obtained prior knowledge of the conspiracy and requested the neighboring Arabs to convey him to Egypt.[a] They complied with the request, for the kings of the Arabs were descendants of Israel,[b] sons of Abraham, and brothers of Isaac.

Gen 37:5–20; Jub 34:11; TJos 1:4; Philo. Jos 5–14

2 He came to Egypt, was recommended to the king, and became *administrator of the entire land*. Hitherto the Egyptians had farmed the land in a disorganized manner, because the country was undivided and the subordinate classes were treated unjustly by the more powerful. This man (Joseph) was the first to divide the land and distinguish it with boundaries.[c] He made much barren land arable and allotted some of the arable lands to the priests.

Gen 41:41;
Josephus, Ant 2.5.7 (90); Jub 40:6; Philo. Jos 157

3 This man also discovered measurements and on account of these things he was greatly loved by the Egyptians. *He married Aseneth, the daughter of a Heliopolitan priest, and begot children by her.* After these things *his father and brothers came*

Gen 41:45,50;
Josephus, Ant 2.6.1 (91–92);
JosAsen 21; Jub 40:10

Fragment 1 (Abraham)

a. This term, which is peculiar to Artapanus, may be a combination of 'aram-yehud (Syro-Judaeus) or Hermes-Ioudaioi (Hermes/Moses Jews). Both suggestions were made by Freudenthal (*Alexander Polyhistor*, p. 153).

b. Abraham is called a Hebrew in Gen 14:13, but the LXX translates as *peratēs* (wanderer) instead of the ethnic or social designation "Hebrew."

c. A fictional name, apparently derived from Pharaoh and Thoth.

d. Contrast Abraham's rejection of astrology in Philo, *Abr* 69–71, 77, and Jub 12:60. Also SibOr 3:218–30 (where the reference is to the descendants of Abraham).

e. The duration of the sojourn is not noted in Genesis. In Jub 13:11 and 1QapGen 19:23 it is five years.

f. Possibly Artapanus is assuming that Abraham

was related to the Hyksos invasion. Cf. Manetho (*Apion* 1.73–92, 227–50), who also associates the Jewish ancestors with the Hyksos.

Fragment 2 (Joseph)

a. Presumably this is a deliberate revision of the biblical story.

b. It is not clear whether Artapanus thinks Israel was the father of Abraham or merely uses Israel as a generic name for Abraham and his descendants. Alternatively, Israel should be emended to Ishmael, and "sons" and "brothers" to "son" and "brother."

c. Contrast Gen 47:20–22, where Joseph is said to acquire all the land of Egypt for Pharaoh, but cf. Josephus, *Ant* 2.7.7 (191f.), where he restores the land to its original owners after the famine. The reforms of Joseph bear some similarity to those of Sesostris (Diodorus, 1.54). See also Fragment 3, on Moses (*PrEv* 9.27.4).

to him bringing much property, and were settled in Heliopolis and Saïs[d] and the Syrians in Egypt became numerous.

4 He (Artapanus) says that these, who were called Hermiouth, founded the temple in Athos and that in Heliopolis.[e] After these things both *Joseph* and the king of the Egyptians *died*.

Joseph, then, as ruler of Egypt, stored *the seven year grain crop*, which was abundant in yield, and became master of Egypt.

Gen 46:1–47:12;
Josephus, *Ant*
2.7.1–6 (168–
88); TJos 17;
Jub 45:1–7;
Philo, *Jos* 255–
57

Gen 50:26;
Josephus, *Ant*
2.8.2 (198); Jub
46:3–5; Philo,
Jos 268–69
Gen 41:47–49;
Josephus, *Ant*
2.6.1 (93); Jub
40:12f.; Philo,
Jos 158–62

MOSES

Fragment 3. *Eusebius, "Praeparatio Evangelica" 9.27.1–37*

1 **27** Artapanus says in his "On the Jews" that when Abraham had died and his son Mempsasthenoth,[a] and also the king of the Egyptians, his son Palmanothes succeeded to dominion.[b]

2 The latter *treated the Jews badly*. First he built Saïs[c] and founded the temple there. Then he established the shrine at Heliopolis.[d]

3 This man begat a daughter Merris,[e] whom he betrothed to a certain Chenephres[f] who was king over the regions beyond Memphis (for at that time there were many kings of Egypt).[g] Since she was barren *she adopted the child of one of the Jews and named it Moses*. As a grown man he was called Mousaeus[h] by the Greeks.

4 This Mousaeus was the teacher of Orpheus.[i] As a grown man he *bestowed many useful benefits* on mankind,[j] for he invented boats and devices for stone construction

Ex 1:8–14;
Josephus, *Ant*
2.9.1 (202);
EzekTrag (*PrEv*
9.28.2)

Ex 2:10;
Josephus, *Ant*
2.9.5–7 (224–
32); Philo, *Vit
Mos* 1.19
Eup (*PrEv*
9.26.1)

d. Heliopolis (biblical On) was the city of the sun-god Re. It is listed as one of the cities built by the Israelites in LXX Ex 1:11. Saïs should be identified as Tanis, capital of Egypt during the Hyksos period. Neither city falls within the area usually identified as the biblical Goshen. In Josephus, *Ant* 2.7.6 (188) Jacob is settled in Heliopolis.

e. Athos may be the biblical Pithom (Ex 1:11). In Ex 1:11 the Hebrews build cities at these locations. Here they build temples.

Fragment 3 (Moses)

a. This passage is problematic and probably corrupt. The most likely solution is that "Abraham" was erroneously written (perhaps by Polyhistor) in place of "Joseph" (so Merentites, *Ho Ioudaios Logios*, p. 26). Mempsasthenoth is a plausible name for a son of Joseph and Aseneth. Alternatively, it is possible that "Abraham" is an error for "Jacob," and "Mempsasthenoth" for "Psonthomphanech" (Joseph's Egyptian name in Gen 41:45, LXX).

b. Palmanothes is presumably the king's son. Like all the Egyptian names in Artapanus, Palmanothes is fictional, but it is a possible Egyptian name.

c. The MSS read *Tessan*, probably a corruption of *te San*. *San* must, like Saïs, be identified with Tanis (which should possibly be identified with the biblical Rameses). Strugnell suggests *Gessan* (= Goshen) as another possibility (private communication).

d. Fragment 2 (*PrEv* 9.23.4) already referred to the building of the temple in Heliopolis before the death of Joseph.

e. In Josephus, the daughter's name is Ther-

muthis (cf. Jub 47:5: Tharmuth). Thermuthis was also the name of the goddess of wet-nursing and a manifestation of Isis. The name Merris is not otherwise known, but Isis was worshiped at Meroë (Diodorus 3.9.2, Strabo 17.2.3). In *PrEv* 9.27.16 (below) Merris is buried at Meroë and worshiped no less than Isis. Artapanus is establishing an indirect association between Moses and the traditions of Isis.

f. The name is Egyptian, but fictional.

g. Probably a gloss (by Polyhistor?) to explain how both Palmanothes and Chenephres were kings. There is no further indication in Artapanus that Egypt was politically divided. The Hyksos never fully controlled Upper Egypt (beyond Memphis), but it is doubtful that Artapanus' statement reflects any historical tradition.

h. Musaeus was a mythical singer often associated with Orpheus. This identification with Moses is probably original in Artapanus. It is also found in Numenius (*PrEv* 9.8.1f.).

i. Orpheus, the legendary founder of Orphism, was probably a mythical figure, but some think he was historical. He is more commonly said to have been the teacher of Musaeus. Here the relationship is inverted to glorify Moses.

j. The inventions here ascribed to Moses are closely modeled on those elsewhere ascribed to other heroes. See especially Diodorus 1.56.2; 1.94.4 (on Sesostris); and 1.96.4, on the wisdom derived from Egypt by Orpheus. The division of Egypt into thirty-six nomes is found in Diodorus 1.54.3 but does not correspond to the historical situation in hellenistic Egypt. Diodorus and Artapanus may both have drawn on Hecataeus of Abdera. In the Jewish tradition cf. the discoveries of the Watchers in SibOr 1:91–96; 1 En 8:1; 69:4–10.

and the Egyptian arms and the implements for drawing water and for warfare, and philosophy. Further he divided the state into 36 nomes and appointed for each of the nomes the god to be worshiped, and for the priests the sacred letters, and that they should be cats and dogs and ibises.[k] He also allotted a choice area to the priests.

5 He did all these things for the sake of maintaining the monarchy firm for Chenephres, for formerly the masses were disorganized and would at one time expel kings, at others appoint them, often the same people but sometimes others.

6 On account of these things then Moses was loved by the masses, and was deemed worthy of godlike honor by the priests and called Hermes,[l] on account of the interpretation of the sacred letters.

The Ethiopian campaign

7 But when Chenephres saw the excellence of Moses he was envious of him and sought to destroy him on some specious pretext. Once indeed when the Ethiopians campaigned against Egypt,[m] Chenephres supposed he had found a convenient opportunity and sent Moses against them as a general with an army. But he put together a host of farmers[n] for him, supposing that he would be easily destroyed by the enemy on account of the weakness of the soldiers. Josephus, *Ant* 2.10.1–2 (238–53)

8 When Moses came to the district called Hermopolis,[o] with about a hundred thousand farmers, he pitched camp there. He sent generals to blockade the region,[p] and these gained notable advantage in battles. He (Artapanus) says that the Heliopolitans assert that this war lasted ten years.[q]

9 Those around Moses founded a city in that place on account of the size of the army, and made the ibis sacred there because it destroys the creatures which harm men.[r] They called it Hermopolis (the city of Hermes).

10 The Ethiopians, even though they were his enemies, loved Moses so much that they learned the circumcision of the genital organs from him, and not only they, but also all the priests.[s]

The plot against Moses

11 When the war was ended Chenephres received him favorably in speech but plotted against him in deed. He took the host away from him and sent some to the borders Josephus, *Ant* 2.11.1 (255)

k. I.e. that the gods should be cats, dogs, and ibises. On the syncretism of Artapanus see Introduction, "Theological importance" (above).

l. Hermes was the Gk. equivalent of Thoth. The identification with Moses was facilitated by the frequency of the Egyptian name Thutmosis. Thoth was also a lawgiver. The Gk. word for interpretation (*hermēneia*) involves a play on "Hermes." On the attribution of divine honor to Moses cf. Ex 7:1 and Philo, *Vit Mos* 1.158, and see Introduction, "Theological importance."

m. The idea of a campaign against Ethiopia was probably inspired by the fact that Cambyses (Herodotus 3.17–25), Sesostris (Diodorus 1.55.1), and Semiramis (Diodorus 2.14.4) all conducted campaigns against Ethiopia (which was also a traditional enemy of Egypt). The biblical reference to Moses' Ethiopian wife (Num 21:1) may also have prompted the idea. The fragments of Artapanus in Eusebius do not refer to Moses' wedding to her, but Josephus does. On the relation between Artapanus and Josephus see Introduction, "Influence on later writings."

n. This idea was possibly inspired by the enrollment of Egyptians in the army of Philopator before the battle of Raphia. See Introduction, "Date."

o. Hermopolis in Greco-Roman times marked the boundary between Middle and Upper Egypt. Artapanus implies (below, 27.9) that it was named after Hermes-Moses. The Egyptian city was the city of Thoth.

p. Translation uncertain. LSJM gives "lay siege." Tiede (*The Charismatic Figure*, p. 318) translated "occupy the land in advance."

q. This reference need not be taken to mean that Artapanus was actually informed by the priests, but could be simply an imitation of the historical style of Herodotus and others.

r. The consecration of the ibis presupposes the story found in Josephus, *Ant* 2.10.2 (246), how Moses overcame the serpents on his march by means of ibises. Silver (*JQR* 64 [1973] 141–52) suggests that Moses' use of the ibis may reflect memories of a syncretistic cult, but his argument is very hypothetical.

s. Herodotus 2.104 and Diodorus 1.55 and 1.28 claim that circumcision originated with the Ethiopians and Egyptians. Artapanus attributes its origin to Moses. In *Apion* 2.141 Josephus implied that only priests were circumcised in Egypt. The Gk. authors imply that it was generally practiced.

of Ethiopia as a garrison[t] and ordered others to tear down the temple in Diospolis (the city of Zeus),[u] which had been constructed of baked brick, and to construct another of stone, quarrying the nearby mountain. He appointed Nacheros overseer of the building project.

12 He came with Moses to Memphis and inquired of him if there was anything else of benefit to men. He (Moses) responded: the breed of oxen, because the land is plowed by them. But Chenephres called the bull Apis[v] and commanded the host to establish his temple, and bade them bring the creatures which Moses had made sacred and bury them there.[w] He did this because he wished to conceal Moses' inventions.

13 When the Egyptians repudiated him,[x] he made his friends swear not to inform Moses of the conspiracy against him and appointed those who were to kill him.

14 When no one complied, Chenephres reproached Chanethothes, the man who was especially addressed by him. The latter, being reproached, undertook to perform the assault, when he had an opportunity.

15 About this time Merris died, and Chenephres gave Moses and Chanethothes the task of bringing the body to the regions beyond Egypt and burying it, assuming that Moses would be killed by Chanethothes.

16 But while they were on their journey, one of the conspirators informed Moses of the plot. The latter guarded himself, buried Merris, and named the river and the city which is on it Meroë. This Merris was honored by the local residents no less than Isis.[y]

Moses in Arabia

17 Aaron the brother of Moses learned about the plot and advised his brother to flee to Arabia. The latter was persuaded, sailed across the Nile from Memphis and departed to Arabia.[z]

18 When Chanethothes learned of Moses' flight he lay in ambush to kill him. When he saw him coming, he drew his dagger against him but Moses anticipated, restrained his hand, drew his (own) sword and *slew Chanethothes*.[a2]   Ex 2:12; Philo. Vit Mos 1.44

19 *Moses fled to Arabia and lived with Raguel*,[b2] *the ruler of the region, whose daughter he married*. Raguel wished to campaign against the Egyptians, wishing to restore Moses and establish dominion for his daughter and son-in-law. But Moses restrained him, taking thought of his compatriots.[c2] Raguel ordered the Arabs to plunder Egypt but withheld them from a full campaign.[d2]   Ex 2:15,18 (LXX) (Moses in Midian) Ex 2:21 (Moses' marriage)

---

t. Compare the Jewish garrison of the late fifth century B.C. known from the Elephantine papyri.

u. There were three towns in Egypt called Diospolis. The most important was Thebes, the Egyptian "House of Amun," which is probably meant here, although there is no mountain nearby.

v. Apis was the bull sacred to Ptah and honored in Memphis.

w. Apparently a confused reference to the Necropolis at Memphis, where Apis and other sacred animals were buried. Artapanus ascribes a negative significance to the burial of the animals.

x. The reference is ambiguous in the present, abbreviated form of the text. It is not clear whether Moses or Chenephres is repudiated. The latter is the more probable.

y. See above, Fragment 3, n. e. Meroë was the capital of Ethiopia and usually thought to have received its name from Cambyses in memory of his sister, or wife, or mother. (See Josephus, *Ant* 2.10.2 [149], Strabo 17.1.5; Diodorus 1.33.1). Strabo, 17.2.3, says that Isis was worshiped at Meroë. Diodorus refers to Meroë as an island in the Nile (1.33) and says that, while Isis is buried at Memphis, some say that Isis and Osiris are buried on the border of Ethiopia on an island in the Nile (1.22.2). Artapanus is attempting to trace

the etiology of the site to Moses and associate Moses with the traditions of Isis while maintaining a distinction between Isis and Merris.

z. Here, and in section 34, below, Arabia refers to the territory between the Nile and the Arabian Gulf. This is in accordance with Strabo 17.1.21. Sesostris was also said to have sojourned in Arabia (Diodorus 1.53.5; Strabo 16.4.4). Arabia here corresponds to the biblical Midian, but Moses is said to flee before he kills the Egyptian.

a2. The killing of the Egyptian is thus explained as self-defense. Josephus omits this episode entirely.

b2. In Ex 3:1 Moses' father-in-law is called Jethro, but in 2:18, Raguel (LXX) or Reuel (MT).

c2. I.e. the Jews in Egypt.

d2. The abbreviated Gk. is obscure. Jacoby reads *diakōluthenta* for *diakōluonta*, so "Raguel was prevented from campaigning but ordered the Arabs to plunder Egypt." Both Manetho (*Apion* 1.241, 264) and Chaeremon (*Apion* 1.292) accused Moses of invading Egypt. Artapanus is controverting that accusation. The idea that the Arabs were permitted to plunder Egypt may reflect the biblical tradition that the Hebrews despoiled the Egyptians at the exodus (Ex 3:22; 12:36).

20 About the same time also Chenephres became the first of all men to contract elephantiasis and he died.[e2] He encountered this fate because he had enjoined the Jews to wear linen garments and put on no woolen clothing, so that they might be conspicuous and be punished by him.[f2]

21 Moses prayed to God that he might thereupon give the people an end to their sufferings. God was propitiated, and he (Artapanus) says that *fire was suddenly kindled* from the earth and it burned although there was no wood or other kindling material in the place.[g2] Moses was afraid of what had happened, and fled. But a *divine voice* bade him campaign against Egypt, rescue the Jews, and lead them to their ancient homeland.

Ex 3:2f.;
Josephus, *Ant*
2.12.1 (264–
66); Philo, *Vit*
Mos 1.65–70;
EzekTrag (*PrEv*
9.29.7)
Ex 3:4;
Josephus, *Ant*
2.12.1 (267);
Philo, *Vit Mos*
1.71

Moses before Pharaoh

22 He took courage and determined to lead a hostile force against the Egyptians.[h2] But first he went to his brother Aaron. The king of the Egyptians learned of Moses' presence, summoned him and asked for what purpose he had come. He responded that the master of the universe had ordered him *to release the Jews.*

Ex 5:1

23 When the king learned this, he confined him in prison.[i2] But when night came, all the doors of the prison opened of themselves,[j2] and some of the guards died, while others were relaxed by sleep and their weapons were broken.

24 Moses came out and went to the royal chambers. He found the doors open and went in. There, since the guards were relaxed, he woke the king. The latter was astonished at what had happened and bade Moses say the name of the god who had sent him, mocking him.[k2]

25 But he bent forward and pronounced it into his ear. When the king heard it, he fell down speechless but revived when taken hold of by Moses.

26 He wrote the name on a tablet[l2] and sealed it, but one of the priests who disparaged what was written on the tablet died with a convulsion.

Ex 7:8–10:20;
Josephus, *Ant*
2.14.1–4 (293–
306); Philo, *Vit*
Mos 1.96–122;
EzekTrag (*PrEv*
9.29.11f.)

The plagues

27 The king said to perform some sign for him. *Moses threw down the rod which he had and made a serpent.* When all were terrified, he seized its tail, took it up and made it a rod again.

Ex 8:10;
Josephus, *Ant*
2.13.3 (287);
Philo, *Vit Mos*
1.91

---

e2. This disease was apparently first named by Bolus of Mendes in the third century B.C. See Introduction, "Date." Merentites suggests that this passage was intended to counter Manetho's charge that the Jews were originally lepers (*Apion* 1.233–35). Cf. also the punishment of Antiochus in 2Mac 9:9.

f2. See Introduction, "Date," above. In Egypt linen garments were usually priestly clothing (Plutarch, *Isis and Osiris*, 4).

g2. Artapanus heightens the miraculous nature of this incident by dispensing with the bush of the Ex story.

h2. The suggestion that Moses lead an army against Egypt does not fit with what follows, and would also be difficult to reconcile with the earlier incident with the Arabs. Josephus, *Ant* 2.12.1 (268), has God bid Moses return to Egypt "to act as commander and leader of the Hebrew host." This was probably the original sense of Artapanus, too. The confusion is probably due to Alexander Polyhistor.

i2. Paragraphs 23–25 are also found (with some variations) in Clement of Alexandria, *Strom* 1.154.2f.:

"Artapanus, then, in the book about the Jews recounts that when Moses had been confined in prison by Chenephres, the king of the Egyptians, for requesting that the people be released from Egypt, the prison was opened at night by the will of God. Moses came out, went to the royal chambers, stood over the sleeping king and woke him. The king was astonished at what had happened and bade Moses say the name of the god who had sent him. Moses bent forward and pronounced it into his ear. When the king heard it he fell down speechless, but revived when taken hold of by Moses."

j2. The parallel in Clement says that the doors were opened "according to the will of God" and omits the word *automatōs* (of themselves). Compare the incidents in Acts 5:17–26; 12:6–17; 16:23–30. Clement also omits the allusions to the guards and the statement that the king's doors were also opened.

k2. Presumably, the king mocks Moses, despite his astonishment, but possibly the king is mocking God, or wants Moses to mock God. Cf. Josephus, *Ant* 2.13.3 (284), where the same verb is used. On this whole episode see Introduction, "Date," above.

l2. It is not clear whether the subject is Moses or the king. The king is the closer antecedent.

28 Proceeding a little *he struck the Nile with the rod. The river became flooded* and deluged all Egypt. From that time also its "inundation" takes place.[m2] *The water became stagnant and stank*[n2] *and destroyed the creatures that live in rivers and the people perished from thirst.* Ex 7:20–25 WisSol 11:5f.

29 After these marvels the king said he would release the people after a month, if he would restore the river.[o2] Moses again struck the water with his rod and drew in the stream.

30 When this had happened, the king summoned the priests who were beyond Memphis and said he would kill them and tear down the temples unless they also could perform some marvels. They then, through some superstitious tricks and charms, *made a serpent and changed the color of the river.* Ex 7:12,22

31 The king became presumptuous at this event and abused the Jews with every kind of vengeance and punishment. When Moses saw this he performed yet other signs, and, striking the ground with his rod, released *some winged creature* to afflict the Egyptians.[p2] *They all developed sores on their bodies.* Since the physicians were not able to cure the sick, the Jews thus again got a respite. Ex 8:21 Ex 9:10

32 Again Moses released *a frog*, through his staff, and in addition to these things, *locusts and lice*. On this account the Egyptians dedicate the rod in every temple, and similarly (they dedicate it) to Isis, since the earth is Isis,[q2] and when it was struck with the rod, it released the marvels. Ex 8:2f.; WisSol 19:10 Ex 10:12–14; WisSol 16:9

33 Since the king was still acting foolishly, Moses brought about *hail* and earthquakes[r2] through the night so that those who fled the earthquakes were killed by the hail and those who avoided the hail were destroyed by the earthquakes. All the houses and most of the temples then collapsed. Ex 9:24; WisSol 16:16

34 Finally, *the king released the Jews* since he had encountered such disasters.[s2] But *they acquired from the Egyptians*[t2] many cups, no small amount of clothing, and abundant other treasure. Having crossed the rivers in Arabia[u2] and traversed a substantial area, *they came on the third day to the Red Sea.* Ex 12:31 Ex 12:35f.; EzekTrag (*PrEv* 9.29.12) Josephus, *Ant* 2.15.1 (315)

35 Now the Memphites say that Moses was familiar with the countryside and watched for the ebb tide and he conveyed the multitude across through the dry sea. But the Heliopolitans[v2] say that *the king rushed down on them with a great force*, together with the consecrated animals, since the Jews had acquired and were carrying off the property of the Egyptians. Ex 14:5–14; Josephus, *Ant* 2.15.3 (320); EzekTrag (*PrEv* 9.29.14)

36 But a divine voice came to Moses to strike the sea with his rod and divide it.[w2] When Moses heard, he touched the water with the rod and thus the flowing *water separated and the host went through a dry path.* Ex 14:15–31; Josephus, *Ant* 2.16.2f. (338–44); Philo, *Vit Mos* 1.176–80

37 He (Artapanus) says that when the Egyptians went in with them and pursued, fire shone out from in front of them and the sea again flooded the path. All the

m2. Artapanus thus attributes the annual flooding of the Nile, which is vital to Egyptian agriculture, to Moses. Unlike the biblical account, the river does not become bloody, but the Egyptian magicians are said to change the color of the river, so the omission may be due to Alexander Polyhistor.

n2. Reading *epozesai*, "to stink" (Freudenthal), for *apozesai*, "to boil."

o2. Josephus, *Ant* 2.14.1 (295) follows Artapanus at this point.

p2. Probably the gadfly, which is the fourth plague in Ex.

q2. So also Diodorus 1.12.4; Plutarch, *Isis and Osiris* (32 and 38). Artapanus thus asserts Moses' supremacy over Isis.

r2. Earthquakes are not mentioned in Ex.

s2. In all, Artapanus recounts some version of the first (flood), second (frogs), third (lice), fourth (gadfly), sixth (boils), seventh (hail) and eighth (locusts) plagues, although he does not follow the biblical order.

t2. Or: "borrowed," but the following paragraph suggests outright appropriation. Josephus, *Ant* 2.14.6, says that the Egyptians freely gave them gifts.

u2. See n. z, above.

v2. It is unlikely that Artapanus actually knew of such an Egyptian tradition. According to Manetho, Moses was a Heliopolitan priest (*Apion* 1.279).

w2. Reading *diastēsai*, "divide," for *diastēnai*, "stand apart" (Mras).

Egyptians were destroyed by both the fire and the flood.[x2] The Jews escaped the danger and *spent forty years in the wilderness. God rained for them meal like millet, very similar in color to snow.* He says that Moses was tall, ruddy, gray with long hair, most venerable. He did these things when he was about eighty-nine years old.[y2]

Ex 16:1–36;
Josephus, *Ant*
3.1.6 (26);
Philo, *Vit Mos*
1.200, 208;
2.258; WisSol
16:20

x2. Compare the common eschatological motif that the world would be destroyed twice, by flood and by fire: Josephus, *Ant* 1.2.3 (70); *Vita* 49; 2Pet 3:6f., and the parallelism of the Flood and eschatological conflagration in SibOr 1–2 and 4.

y2. Compare Deut 34:7, which stresses Moses' vigor up to his death. The biblical account says that Moses was 120 at his death, and so 80 at the exodus. Josephus, *Ant* 4.8.49 (327) follows the biblical account.

APPENDIX

PSEUDO-HECATAEUS

(Second Century B.C.–First Century A.D.)

A NEW TRANSLATION AND INTRODUCTION

BY R. DORAN

Jewish and Christian literature contains several references to a Greek historian named Hecataeus, who shows pro-Jewish sentiments. Is one, therefore, dealing with a pseudonymous author?

The issue is complicated; the most extensive fragment that scholars agree should be attributed to the genuine Hecataeus of Abdera, who wrote under Ptolemy I about 300 B.C., deals with the Jews.[1] It is an excursus found in Diodorus Siculus at the moment when Diodorus is going to recount the campaign of Pompey against Jerusalem. The fragment is a typical example of early hellenistic ethnography.[2] It depicts the Jewish state as a political utopia;[3] Moses is extolled as excelling in wisdom (Diodorus Siculus 40.3.3); the monotheism of the Jews is praised (Diodorus 40.3.4);[4] and unusual customs of the Jews are explained. The genuine Hecataeus thus had some knowledge of Jews and Jewish customs; and he did think highly of their constitution. Would he have written the fragments to be discussed below?

There are two *testimonia* to the work of Hecataeus. Josephus (*Ant* 1.159) refers to a book that Hecataeus wrote on Abraham. Both H. Willrich and N. Walter have concluded that this book is a major source behind Josephus' account of Abraham.[5] The second testimony is found in Origen (*Contra Celsus* 1.15b). Origen reports how Herennius Philo disputed the authenticity of a book about the Jews by Hecataeus the historian. According to Herennius, the work praised the wisdom of the Jews too much to be reliable.

The fragments

1. The Letter of Aristeas 31 quotes Hecataeus as saying that the Bible has a certain sacred quality about it. Questions have been raised as to the extent of the quotation, particularly since Josephus (*Ant* 12.38) cites the Letter of Aristeas and attributes a large section to Hecataeus (see the discussion below).

2. In Clement of Alexandria's *Stromateis* 5.113, Hecataeus of Abdera is cited as the source for verses of Sophocles that praise monotheism and condemn idolatry. Clement of Alexandria titled the work of Hecataeus "On Abraham and the Egyptians."

3. In Josephus (*Apion* 2.43) Hecataeus is the authority for the claim that Alexander the

---

[1] The fragment comes from Diodorus Siculus 40; it is found in the *Bibliotheca* of Photius, codex 244. In the present text, the fragment is attributed to Hecataeus of Miletus, c. 500 B.C., but scholars are unanimous that this is a mistake and that the fragments should be attributed to Hecataeus of Abdera, c. 300 B.C. See J. G. Gager, *Moses in Greco-Roman Paganism* (SBLMS 16; Nashville, Tenn., 1972) p. 26, nn. 6, 7; p. 28, n. 8.

[2] Gager, *Moses*, p. 37.

[3] W. Jaeger, "Greeks and Jews: The First Greek Records of Jewish Religion and Civilization," *Journal of Religion* 18 (1938) 141f. J. G. Gager, *Moses*, p. 36.

[4] J. G. Gager, *Moses*, pp. 31f.

[5] H. Willrich, *Judaica: Forschungen zur hellenistisch-jüdischen Geschichte und Literatur* (Göttingen, 1900) pp. 108f. N. Walter, "Pseudo-Hekataios I und II," *JSHRZ* 1.2 (1976) 149f. For a discussion of this position, see below.

Great admired the Jews and that Alexander gave the Jews Samaria tax-free. Questions have been raised as to the extent of this quotation; does it embrace *Against Apion* 2.43–47? This question will be discussed below.

4. The major fragment explicitly attributed to Hecataeus in Jewish and Christian literature is found in Josephus (*Apion* 1.183–205). Josephus is arguing that learned Greeks admired the Jews (*Apion* 1.175). After discussing a report on Aristotle's admiration for the Jews (*Apion* 1.176–82), Josephus quotes from a book that Hecataeus has written on the Jews. Hecataeus discusses with admiration a priest Ezechias, whom he had met; he speaks of how the Jews suffer persecution rather than transgress their laws, and adduces several examples; he talks of the population of the Jews, the beauty of their country, and Jerusalem; finally, he relates an anecdote in which Jewish contempt for divination is evident.

Texts

The translation of these fragments will be based on the following critical editions:

B. Niese, *Flavii Josephi opera*. Berlin, 1885–95.
L. Fruchtel, *Clemens Alexandrinus. 2 Band. Stromata Buch I–VI*. GCS 52; Berlin, 1960.
P. Koetschau, *Origenes*. GCS 2; Leipzig, 1899.
A. Pelletier, *Lettre d'Aristée à Philocrate*. SC 89; Paris, 1962.
P. Wendland, *Aristeae ad Philocratem epistula*. Leipzig, 1900.

How many Pseudo-Hecataei?

The fragments listed above have elicited discussion in scholarly ranks: were they written by a Pseudo-Hecataeus?[6] Recently, both N. Walter and B. Z. Wacholder have argued that there was not one Pseudo-Hecataeus, but many.

Walter divides the fragments in this fashion:[7] a Pseudo-Hecataeus I wrote fragments 3 and 4. The work of a Pseudo-Hecataeus II lies behind fragment 2 and the testimony of Josephus (*Ant* 1.159). Walter holds that Letter of Aristeas 31 has no clear connection with the above fragments and may or may not be a reference to the work of the genuine Hecataeus.[8]

Wacholder contends that three writers lie behind these references.[9] Pseudo-Hecataeus I, who wrote about 300 B.C., is responsible for fragment 4;[10] Pseudo-Hecataeus II wrote fragments 1 and 3;[11] Pseudo-Hecataeus III is referred to in fragment 2 and in the two testimonies.

Date and provenance

The date assigned to these fragments varies according to the decisions taken on each fragment. Walter dates his Pseudo-Hecataeus I to about 100 B.C., and his Pseudo-Hecataeus II before Josephus. Both were hellenistic Jews from Alexandria.[12] Wacholder dates his Pseudo-Hecataeus I about 300 B.C. (hence he is a contemporary of the genuine Hecataeus), Pseudo-Hecataeus II after Letter of Aristeas but before Josephus, Pseudo-Hecataeus III

---

[6] For a history of scholarship on this question, see B. Schaller, "Hekataios von Abdera über die Juden: Zur Frage der Echtheit und der Datierung," *ZNW* 24 (1963) 15–31; J. G. Gager, "Pseudo-Hecataeus Again," *ZNW* 60 (1969) 130–39.

[7] Walter, *JSHRZ* 1.2 (1976) 144–46.

[8] Walter, *JSHRZ* 1.2 (1976) 146.

[9] B. Z. Wacholder, *Eupolemus: A Study of Judaeo-Greek Literature* (Cincinnati, 1974) pp. 263–66.

[10] Wacholder (*Eupolemus*, p. 266) also includes LetAris 83–120, which he holds is dependent on his Ps-Hecataeus I.

[11] Wacholder (*Eupolemus*, p. 266) also holds that Josephus, *Ant* 12.3–8, and LetAris 12–27 are dependent on his Ps-Hecataeus II.

[12] Walter, *JSHRZ* 1.2 (1976) 147, 148, 151.

before Aristobulus.[13] Pseudo-Hecataeus I would, according to Wacholder, be a Jew, probably a Jerusalem priest.[14]

In order to present this complicated problem more clearly, we will first give an overview of our findings concerning the authenticity of the fragments. Then we will follow the detailed analysis of each fragment. In our view, only two references to Hecataeus of Abdera should be assigned as inauthentic: the testimony at Josephus, *Antiquities* 1.159, and fragment 2, the verses of Sophocles from "On Abraham and the Egyptians" as cited by Clement, *Stromateis* 5.113. The other references are authentic fragments of Hecataeus of Abdera, and should be dated about 300 B.C. Both inauthentic references are to a book about Abraham that must be dated before Josephus. However, since no actual content of this inauthentic work is cited beyond some spurious verses of Sophocles, no conclusions can be drawn as to provenance or to a date for this Pseudo-Hecataeus.

Conclusion

The recognition that these fragments are authentic heightens their importance. They provide information about how Jews were perceived by a non-Jewish author in the third century B.C.

SELECT BIBLIOGRAPHY

Charlesworth, *PMR*, pp. 120–22.
Delling, *Bibliographie*, pp. 53–55.
Denis, *Introduction*, pp. 262–67.

Gager, J. G. "Pseudo-Hecataeus Again," *ZNW* 60 (1969) 130–39. (Gager's article rounds out the history of scholarship given by Schaller, and argues for the authenticity of the fragments.)

Jacoby, F. *FGH*, vol. 3A, Fs. 21–24, pp. 61–75. (Jacoby argues strongly against the authenticity of the fragments.)

Jaeger, W. "Greeks and Jews: The First Greek Records of Jewish Religion and Civilization," *Journal of Religion* 18 (1938) 127–43. (Jaeger pays little attention to these disputed fragments, but gives an excellent account of the attitude of Hecataeus as found in Diodorus Siculus 40.3.)

Lewy, H. "Hekataios von Abdera *peri Ioudaiōn*," *ZNW* 31 (1932) 117–32. (Still the best discussion for connecting the fragments with Gk. ethnographical literature.)

Schaller, B. "Hekataios von Abdera über die Juden: Zur Frage der Echtheit und der Datierung," *ZNW* 24 (1963) 15–31. (Schaller provides a history of scholarship, which needs to be supplemented by Gager, and argues on the basis of the tithe issue that the fragments are not authentic.)

Stern, M. *Greek and Latin Authors on Jews and Judaism, Vol. 1*, Jerusalem, 1974; pp. 20–44. (This provides both the text of Diodorus Siculus 40.3 and the fragments from *Against Apion*, and uses the LCL translation. Stern's commentary is thorough but does not raise the literary issues that Lewy does.)

Walter, N. *Der Thoraausleger Aristobulos. Untersuchungen zu seinen Fragmenten und zu pseudepigraphischen Resten der jüdisch-hellenistischen Literatur*, TU 86; Berlin 1964; pp. 172–87. (Walter's treatment of the collection of texts against polytheism is very convincing.)

---

[13] Wacholder, *Eupolemus*, p. 266. Note that Wacholder (*Eupolemus*, p. 264, n. 13) claims that the Hecataeus of Clement of Alexandria, *Strom* 5.113, and Josephus, *Ant* 1.159, was used by Aristobulus. As his authority, Wacholder used N. Walter, *Der Thoraausleger Aristobulos. Untersuchungen zu seinen Fragmenten und zu pseudepigraphischen Resten der jüdisch-hellenistischen Literatur* (TU 86; Berlin, 1964) pp. 99–103. In *JSHRZ* 1.2 (1976) 151, Walter himself denies that such a connection can be made.

[14] Wacholder, *Eupolemus*, p. 273.

————. "Pseudo-Hekataios I und II," *JSHRZ* 1.2 (1976) 144–60. (Walter, in this translation and commentary, denies the authenticity of the fragments.)

Wacholder, B. Z. *Eupolemus: A Study of Judaeo-Greek Literature.* Monographs of the Hebrew Union College 3; Cincinnati, 1974; pp. 263–73. (Wacholder argues [pp. 183–205] that the fragments in *Against Apion* 1 stem from the third century B.C. but were written by a Jewish priest.)

TESTIMONIA

1. Josephus, *Ant* 1.159:

"Hecataeus did more than just mention Abraham: Hecataeus left behind a book he had written about Abraham."

Among those non-Jews who knew of Abraham, Josephus mentioned Hecataeus. Hecataeus, unlike Berossus the historian of Babylonia, had not mentioned Abraham in passing but had composed a book about him. Both Walter and Wacholder hold that the work to which Josephus refers is the same as that to which Clement of Alexandria refers in his *Stromateis* 5.113.[15] Walter has even gone farther; he has suggested that the work, which he claims comes from Pseudo-Hecataeus II, is a major source behind the account of Josephus. From it Josephus derives what goes beyond the biblical account.[16] In this argument, Walter is following Willrich, who saw in the reason given for Abraham's visit to Egypt (Josephus, *Ant* 1.161: to discuss the nature of the gods with the Egyptians) a clear connection with the theme of the verses of Sophocles on monotheism.[17] One has to be cautious in this reasoning. Josephus mentions in the beginning of his work that the Jews had the correct notion about God (Josephus, *Ant* 1.15, 20f.). This concern of Josephus is reflected in the description of Abraham as the first to state that there is one God, the creator of the universe (Josephus, *Ant* 1.155). This view of Abraham as a striver after knowledge of the true God is found in Jubilees 11:16–17 and 12:1–31; the search for God beyond astrological science is also found in Philo (*Migr* 177–87; *Quaes Gen* 3.1). Does one need to posit a specific source, a Pseudo-Hecataeus I or II, rather than a widespread tradition in Jewish literature that linked Abraham with striving for knowledge of the one God and with astrological knowledge?[18] Again, the fact that Josephus does not mention the distinctive title "On Abraham and the Egyptians," as found in Clement, also calls for caution.

However, even granted these cautions, one cannot deny that Josephus explicitly states that Hecataeus has written a book specifically on Abraham, and the only candidate for that is the work quoted by Clement of Alexandria. These two references, then, are most probably to the same work by a Pseudo-Hecataeus.

2. Origen, *Against Celsus* 1.15b:

The statement of Herennius Philo does not explicitly deny that the work was written by Hecataeus; Philo raises doubts as to whether Hecataeus wrote the book. Gager, and Lewy before him, were right to point out that this opinion of Philo expresses the anti-Jewish sentiments after the Bar Kokhba revolt.[19] No weight should be given to Philo's opinion as to the authenticity of the fragments to be discussed below.

One should note that the mention of Hecataeus in Origen follows a reference to another Greek writer who mentioned the Jews, Hermippus. This follower of Pythagoras had stated that his master had taken his own philosophy from the Jews and introduced it to the Greeks (*Contra Celsus* 1.15a). Such a statement is remarkably similar to the statements of Hermippus (at Josephus, *Apion* 1.163–65): "The most distinguished of these is Hermippus, a very careful historian . . . He then says: '(Pythagoras) practiced and taught these in imitation of the beliefs of the Jews and the Thracians, which he had appropriated to himself.' For it is actually said that that man (Pythagoras) brought many Jewish usages into his own

---

[15] Walter, *JSHRZ* 1.2 (1976) 149f.; Wacholder, *Eupolemus*, p. 264.
[16] Walter, *JSHRZ* 1.2 (1976) 149f.
[17] Willrich, *Judaica*, p. 108; cf. Walter, *Der Thoraausleger*, pp. 197f.
[18] See further discussion in J. H. Charlesworth, "Jewish Astrology in the Talmud, Pseudepigrapha, the Dead Sea Scrolls, and Early Palestinian Synagogues," *HTR* 70 (1977) 183–200.
[19] Gager, *ZNW* 60 (1969) 132; H. Lewy, "Hekataios von Abdera, *peri Ioudaiōn*," *ZNW* 31 (1932) 118.

philosophy.'' This mention of Hermippus in Josephus occurs not much before the excerpts from Hecataeus in *Against Apion* 1.183–205. The sequence of Hermippus-Hecataeus in Josephus and Origen leads one to suggest that the comment of Herennius Philo applies to the work of Hecataeus quoted in *Against Apion* 1.183–205, although Herennius' comment may equally well apply to the genuine fragment found in Diodorus Siculus 40.3.[20]

In any event, the quotation of Herennius says nothing against the fragments to be discussed below.

Text

Also in circulation is a book on the Jews by Hecataeus the historian. This work goes even further (than the works previously mentioned)[21] in holding that this nation is wise— so much so, in fact, that Herennius Philo, in his treatise on the Jews, first doubts whether Hecataeus wrote the work; and then he says that, if indeed (Hecataeus) was the author, most probably he had been misled by the specious arguments of the Jews and had accepted their reasoning.

---

[20] Cf. the position of M. Engers. "De Hecataei Abderitae Fragmentis." *Mnemosyne* 51 (1923) 229.
[21] The works of Numenius and Hermippus. which contained allusions to the Jews.

FRAGMENTS

1. Letter of Aristeas 31:

"You should have accurate translations of these works, because this legislation, as it is divine, is highly philosophic and pure. However,[a] writers, poets and most historians have not mentioned the aforesaid books and the men who have lived (and are living[b]) in accordance with them, because the views proposed in these books are in some way[c] holy and reverent, as Hecataeus of Abdera says."

a. That *dio* need not have the force of a logical conclusion has been shown by E. Molland, "*DIO* Einige syntaktische Beobachtungen," *Serta Rudbergiana*, ed. H. Holst and H. Mørland (Oslo, 1931) 43–52.

b. Wendland rejects the parenthetical words as a later addition.

c. Gager (*ZNW* 60 [1969] 134) notes how *tis* qualifies *hagne semne* in this fragment, as Hecataeus modifies *apanthrōpos* in Diodorus 40.3.4 by *tis;* Gager argues that such modifications show Hecataeus' "overall impressions and limited knowledge of Jewish culture."

Schürer, followed by Schaller and Wacholder, listed as the quotation from Hecataeus the sentence: "However, writers, poets . . ."[21] Schürer noted that Josephus (*Ant* 12.38; quoted in Eusebius, *PrEv* 8.3.3) thought that the whole sentence was from Hecataeus: one should not separate the causal phrase from what it is proving.[22] In contrast to this, Lewy limited the quotation to the phrase "the views proposed in these books are in some way holy and reverent."[23] He noted that this phrase is in some ways a doublet of the preceding causal phrase, "because this legislation . . . pure," and that this notion, *hagnēn tina semnēn* is repeated in Letter of Aristeas 313: "Because this legislation is reverent (*semnēn*) and from God (*dia theou*)." In this latter passage, however, the authority of Theopompos, Theodektes and Demetrius is used, not that of Hecataeus.[24]

One should also note that the sentence on the writers is the second reason that the librarian Demetrius puts forward in favor of the recommendation that experts be brought from Jerusalem to translate accurately the laws of the Jews. He argues that these books should be in the library of the king, because no Greek writers have dealt with them.[25] So, not only

[21] E. Schürer, *History*, div. 3, vol. 2, p. 303; Schaller, *ZNW* 24 (1963) 30; Wacholder, *Eupolemus*, p. 264.

[22] Schürer, *History*, div. 3, vol. 2, p. 303.

[23] Lewy, *ZNW* 31 (1932) 119.

[24] Lewy, *ZNW* 31 (1932) 120.

[25] Note the question of the king in LetAris 312: "Why have none of the historians or poets mentioned such excellent writings?"

are the present copies defective,[26] but one cannot read them in Greek writers. Therefore, one needs a new translation. Why have Greek writers not dealt with these books? The books have a certain sacred quality, and recognition of this sacred quality is found in Hecataeus of Abdera.[27] Lewy is therefore right to limit the quotation to the causal phrase, as the first part of the sentence represents the reasoning of the librarian.

Once one has determined the extent of the quotation, can one determine if it is authentic? Jacoby strongly contrasted the admiring tone of this fragment with the antagonism shown toward the Jews in the material preserved in Diodorus Siculus 40.3.4: Moses set up a way of life "somewhat unsocial and hostile to foreigners."[28] However, as Gager rightly stresses, Jacoby has misunderstood this passage in Diodorus. In its context, Hecataeus is explaining some Jewish customs as a reaction to their treatment in Egypt.[29] The explanation of strange customs was part of hellenistic ethnography, and Hecataeus, if anything, is showing his sympathy for the Jews in this passage. Again, the entire fragment in Diodorus paints the portrait of an idealized polity.[30] Gager has convincingly shown that the texts of Hecataeus in Diodorus and in Letter of Aristeas 31 "are entirely consonant with the predominant pagan view of Judaism in the early Hellenistic period."[31] Gager points to Hecataeus' contemporaries Theophrastus, Megasthenes, and Clearchus, who all thought highly of the Jews, and he maintains that the Hecataeus found in Diodorus and in Letter of Aristeas 31 has the same view.

Thus, there is no reason to deny the authenticity of the fragment found in Letter of Aristeas 31, or to ascribe it to the inventive imagination of the author of this work, as does Jacoby.[32] Rather, this fragment should be ascribed to the genuine Hecataeus.

2. Clement of Alexandria, *Stromateis* 5.113:

As Hecataeus the historian states in his "On Abraham and the Egyptians," Sophocles cried out openly on the stage:
> One, truly one is God
> who made both heaven and the wide earth,
> the blue-gray swell of the sea and the buffeting winds.
> We throngs of men go astray in our hearts
> when, to gain solace from misery,
> we set up as statues of gods
> figures worked from wood,
> or images of copper, gold or ivory.
> We imagine we are religious
> when we enjoin in their honor sacrifices
> and evil festivals.

These verses attributed to Sophocles became a constant feature in Christian apologetic literature; not only Clement of Alexandria but also Athenagoras, Pseudo-Justin, Theodoret, and others[33] use these verses and others from Greek literature as standard ammunition against polytheism. Clement of Alexandria quotes the verses twice, in his *Protrepticus* as well as in the *Stromateis*.[34] Here too the verses are found within quotations from other poetic works. Walter, following Elter, has strongly argued that these chains of quotations from Greek poets, dramatists, and writers on a single theme, e.g. the unity of God, must have come from a gnomologion, a handbook that collected such sayings.[35] Such a collection need not

---

[26] H. G. Meecham (*The Letter of Aristeas: A Linguistic Study with Special Reference to the Greek Bible* [Manchester, 1935], p. 201) noted that *diēkribōmena* means "emended."
[27] In LetAris 313–16, the authority of Theopompos and Theodektes is used.
[28] Jacoby, *FGH*, vol. 3Aa, p. 62.
[29] Gager, *ZNW* 60 (1969) 132–34.
[30] Jaeger, *Journal of Religion* 18 (1938) 141f.
[31] Gager, *ZNW* 60 (1969) 134.
[32] Jacoby, *FGH*, vol. 3Aa, pp. 61, 65, 68f.
[33] Athenagoras, *Supplicatio pro Christianis* 5; Pseudo-Justin, *Cohortatio ad Graecos* 18; *De Monarchia* 2; Theodoret, *Graecarum Affectionum Curatio*, sermo 7; Cyril of Alexandria, *Adversus Julianum* 1.
[34] Clement, *Protrepticus* 7.74.2.
[35] Walter, *Der Thoraausleger*. pp. 172–87.

be attributed to Hecataeus. Walter has rightly noted that the authority of Hecataeus is explicitly restricted to these verses of Sophocles.[36]

What is interesting is that it is only in the *Stromateis* that an explicit authority is given for any of these quotations besides the supposed authorship of Sophocles or Orpheus. In his earlier work, the *Protrepticus*, Clement had felt no need for such external authority. One suspects that Clement is reacting to doubts raised over these verses. Their strong monotheism and condemnation of idolatry may have led Clement's opponents to doubt that these verses should be attributed to Sophocles. Clement, to settle such doubts, searched for an authority who had previously quoted these verses, and found one in Hecataeus.

Walter has suggested that these verses might have a place in a life about Abraham where the monotheistic beliefs of Abraham would be discussed.[37] Such may well have been a theme for the Pseudo-Hecataeus who lies behind this fragment and the reference in Josephus (*Ant* 1.159).

3. Josephus, *Against Apion* 2.43:[38]

(Alexander) honored our people. As Hecataeus states about us, "in return for the loyal regard which the Jews had shown to him, he granted to them to hold the region of Samaria free of tribute."

H. Willrich objected that such a statement about the relations between the country of Samaria and Judea was anachronistic.[39] There is no confirmation in other sources that the Jews of Alexander's time held Samaria, either tax-free or not. Rather, the narrative would reflect the report in 1 Maccabees 11:34, where Demetrios II gave three Samaritan districts to Jonathan in 145 B.C. This report would have been expanded to include all Samaria, and then back-dated to the time of Alexander the Great. Such an expansion would be an attempt to legitimize the takeover of Samaria by John Hyrcanus in 128–107 B.C.

Those who defend the genuineness of this fragment point out that there is nothing inherently improbable in the statement of *Against Apion* 2.43.[40] They adduce the authority of Quintus Curtius Rufus (*The History of Alexander* 4.8.9) to show that there was a Samaritan revolt against Alexander in 331, a revolt that was vigorously put down. They suggest that the Jews, who submitted to Alexander, may have given support to Alexander in this revolt and been rewarded by some territory. The language of 1 Maccabees 11:34 can, in fact, be read to mean "confirmation of a previous possession" (*hestakamen autois ta te horia* etc.). At the present moment, the discussion is at a standoff, although the supporters of the authenticity of the fragment grant that the statement is exaggerated.[41]

There is, however, a third possibility. The context of the passage shows that Josephus is discussing the position of Jews in and around Alexandria. Apion had claimed to be an Alexandrian, but Josephus rebuts this with the statement that Apion really comes from the Egyptian oasis (*Apion* 2.29, 41f.). Josephus attempts to prove that the Jews have historically stronger claims to the rights of Alexandria than the Egyptian Apion. Josephus takes his proof cases from the attitudes of writers from Alexander down to Ptolemy Philadelphus. In such a context, the mention of claims of the Jews to Samaria in Israel seems out of place, unless it is a thorough digression. In discussion of this passage, scholars have ignored the fact that a village and an area called Samaria are attested in Egypt from the third century B.C.[42] If Hecataeus, and Josephus, were referring to this region, the statement would fit its context properly. It may be argued against this suggestion that only Samaritans would have lived in a town called Samaria. However, the virulent hostility of Jews and Samaritans

---

[36] Walter, *Der Thoraausleger*. p. 197.

[37] As noted in n. 5, Walter had earlier maintained this position, in *Der Thoraausleger*. pp. 197f.

[38] Wacholder, *Eupolemus*. p. 263, extends the citation to Josephus, *Apion* 2.43–47. However, this view had already been strongly argued against by Jacoby, *FGH*. vol. 3A, 65.

[39] Willrich, *Judaica*, p. 97.

[40] Lewy, *ZNW* 31 (1932) 120; Gager, *ZNW* 60 (1969) 135f.; M. Stern, *Greek and Latin Authors*, p. 44.

[41] Gager, *ZNW* 60 (1969) 136; M. Stern, *Greek and Latin Authors*. pp. 24, 44.

[42] A document mentioning the area, dated to 255–254 B.C., is found in J. P. Mahaffy (ed.), *The Flinders Petrie Papyri* (Dublin, 1893), Part 2; IV, 11.2, p. [14]. It is also mentioned in XXVIII, 2.9, p. [88]; 8.4, p. [93]; 9.22, p. [94]; 11.12, p. [96]. For references to this area later than the third century B.C., see the entry under *Samaria* in F. Preisigke, *Wörterbuch der griechischen Papyrusurkunden* (Berlin, 1931), vol. III.

toward each other stems from the period of Hyrcanus.[43] Alternatively, Hecataeus could be making a mistake and be calling Samaritans "Jews." Hecataeus, as familiar with Alexandria, could have known the tax situation of areas in Egypt.

If this suggestion is adopted, then there is no reason to hold that the fragment is inauthentic.

4. Josephus, *Against Apion* 1.183–205:

The major fragment ascribed to Hecataeus by hellenistic Jewish writers has given rise to the most debate. The arguments against authenticity of the fragment are as follows:

a. The emphasis on the willingness of the Jews to die rather than to transgress their laws reflects an atmosphere more consonant with the persecution of Antiochus Epiphanes.[44]
b. There is mention of a high priest whose name is not found in the list of high priests given by Josephus (*Ant* 12.43f.).
c. The priests are said to receive tithes. However, this reflects Maccabean practice; according to Judith 11:13 and Jubilees 32:15, works of Maccabean date, the priests, and not the Levites, received the tithes. This is in opposition to earlier works such as 2 Chronicles 31:4; Nehemiah 10:38f.; 12:44; 13:5, 10, and Tobit 1:6 in Sinaiticus, where tithes are given to Levites.[45]
d. The laudatory account of Judea and Jerusalem betrays Jewish authorship, and the description of the Temple reflects priestly piety.[46] Also, the favorable attitude toward Ptolemy is apologetic to show that, from the first, the Jews and the Ptolemies were friends.[47]

The counterarguments are as follows:

a. Wacholder has noted that the phrases on persecution could easily have come from an earlier period, as, for example, the mention of harassment of the Jews under Artaxerxes (Josephus, *Ant* 11.297).[48] The phrases need not, therefore, reflect the later persecutions under Antiochus IV. However, Wacholder maintains that these fragments do not come from Hecataeus, but from a Jewish author.[49] To support this position, Wacholder points to the phrase "such behaviour rightly causes amazement at them." (Josephus, *Apion* 1.191);[50] Wacholder also speaks of the ethnic boasting behind the anecdote of Mosollamus (Josephus, *Apion* 1.200–4).[51]

Such an interpretation, however, has not taken into account how Lewy has situated this writing within Greek ethnographical literature.[52] Lewy noted that Greek ethnographers sought to classify peoples according to common characteristics. When certain peoples had characteristics in common, they were often linked genealogically by the ethnographers. For the present discussion, Lewy noted that the Jews were considered descendants of the Indian philosophers by contemporaries of Hecataeus. Clearchus, as cited in *Against Apion* 1.179, said so, and added that in India they were called Calani, in Syria Jews.[53] The Calani were followers of Calanus, the gymnosophist whom Alexander the Great

[43] See F. M. Cross, "Aspects of Samaritan and Jewish History in Late Persian and Hellenistic Times," *HTR* 59 (1966) 207–11.
[44] Willrich, *Judaica*, p. 104; Walter, *JSHRZ* 1.2 (1976) 147.
[45] Schaller, *ZNW* 24 (1963) 22–25.
[46] Wacholder, *Eupolemus*, p. 270.
[47] Walter, *JSHRZ* 1.2 (1976) 147.
[48] Wacholder, *Eupolemus*, pp. 268f.
[49] Wacholder, *Eupolemus*, p. 269.
[50] Wacholder, *Eupolemes*, p. 269. Note that Stern (*Greek and Latin Authors*, p. 24) also has trouble with this phrase, and would attribute it to later Jewish redaction of the work of Hecataeus.
[51] Wacholder, *Eupolemus*, p. 269.
[52] Lewy, *ZNW* 31 (1932) 124–26.
[53] Megasthenes (c. 350–290 B.C.), in Clement of Alexandria's *Strom* 1.72.4, states: "Everything said about nature by the ancients has also been stated by non-Greek philosophers, in India by the Brachmanes, in Syria by those named Jews."

met. Calanus taught endurance and contempt of death.[54] Both Arrian and Aelian record how Calanus caused amazement to the bystanders as he calmly burned himself to death.[55] Alexander the Great is said to have commented that Calanus had overcome greater opponents than himself, for Calanus had conquered death and pain.[56] In the light of such parallels, the present fragment does not betray peculiar Jewish sympathies.

As regards the Mosollamus anecdote, Lewy noted how the behavior of this very intelligent archer is contrasted strongly with the superstition of the crowd. Such contempt for superstition is also recorded of Diogenes the Cynic,[57] and reinforces the view that the Jews were a philosophic race—a view held by Hecataeus in the fragments in Diodorus Siculus. These anecdotes, then, say nothing against authenticity.

b. *Archiereus* need not mean the high priest par excellence, but could be used loosely.[58] The excavations at Beth-Zur produced a coin that has the image of the Athenian owl on it; behind the owl is written *yhd*, in front of it *yḥzqyh*.[59] Thus, an Ezechias was important enough to have his name stamped on a Jewish coin; he may be the Ezechias of the passage in Josephus, or an ancestor.[60] There is no reason to hold that the figure in Josephus, clearly dated by him to around 300 B.C., is a fabrication that veils the identity of the high priest Onias who fled from Antiochus Epiphanes.[61]

c. On tithes. First, even on Schaller's dating of Tobit and Nehemiah, the change in tithing customs could have occurred between the fourth and the second centuries B.C. and should not be pinpointed to the Maccabean period.[62] Secondly, Gager has noted that Hecataeus may not have distinguished between priests and Levites. Note how Hecataeus in Diodorus Siculus 40.3.5 assigns priests leadership roles in the state from the beginning and makes no mention of kings and judges. As Gager noted, Levites did perform priestly functions, and so the distinction may have been irrelevant for a Greek author.[63] Thirdly, the author of Jubilees would be unlikely to endorse a Maccabean shift in practice.

d. Wacholder maintained that the amount of space given to the description of the Temple betrayed priestly piety.[64] However, as Lewy noted, such details about the country, the main city, and the Temple layout and furnishings belong to Greek ethnographical literature.[65] Note the lavish description in Diodorus 2.7–9 of the building of Babylon by Semiramis and of the construction of the temple of Bel. Similar features are present in Euhemerus' account of the island of Panchaea and of the temple to Zeus on it (Diodorus 5.41–46; 6.1.4–7). In *Against Apion* 1.199, Hecataeus notes that there is no statue or votive offering or sacred plant: such an antirepresentational note corresponds to the statement in Diodorus 40.3.4, where Hecataeus stated that Moses had no images of the gods made for his followers.

As regards the abstinence of the priest from wine (Josephus, *Apion* 1.199), Hecataeus is the authority for Plutarch's statement that the kings of Heliopolis, being priests, drink wine moderately (Plutarch, *De Iside et Osiride* 6).[66] Since the Jews are described by

---

[54] Arrian, *Anabasis* 7.2f.; in Philo *Quod Omn* 96, a pseudepigraphic letter of Calanus to Alexander is found in which the following views are attributed to Calanus: "Your friends urge you to apply violence and force to the philosophers of India . . . There is no king or ruler who can force us to do what we do not choose to do."

[55] Arrian, *Anabasis* 7.3.5; Aelian, *Varia Historia* 5.6. Arrian (*Anabasis* 7.2.2) records of the gymnosophists in general that Alexander admired their endurance (*hoti tēn karterian autōn ethaumase*).

[56] Aelian, *Varia Historia* 5.6.

[57] Diogenes Laertius, *Lives of the Philosophers* 6.24. A similar anecdote is told in one of the pseudepigraphic letters attributed to Diogenes the Cynic. When Diogenes asked a seer whether Diogenes was going to beat him or not, the seer hesitatingly said that he would not. Upon which Diogenes pummeled him, to the great delight of the crowd (R. Hercher, *Epistolographi Graeci* [Paris, 1873], letter 38.2 of Diogenes).

[58] Cf. G. Schrenk, "*archiereus*" *TDNT* 3, pp. 268–72.

[59] O. R. Sellers, *The Citadel of Beth-Zur* (Philadelphia, 1933), p. 73. N. Avigad, "A New Class of *Yehud*-Stamps," *IEJ* 7 (1957) 148f.

[60] P. W. Lapp, "Ptolemaic Stamped Handles from Judah," *BASOR* 172 (1963) 34, n. 59; J. G. Gager, *ZNW* 60 (1969) 138f.; M. Stern, *Greek and Latin Authors*, pp. 40f.

[61] As does Willrich, *Juden und Griechen vor der makkabäischen Erhebung* (Göttingen, 1895) p. 32.

[62] M. Stern, *Greek and Latin Authors*, pp. 41f.

[63] Gager, *ZNW* 60 (1969) 137.

[64] Wacholder, *Eupolemus*, p. 270.

[65] Lewy, *ZNW* 31 (1932) 126f.

[66] This quotation from Hecataeus occurs in the context of the abstinence of priests from wine while serving the god. Jacoby, *FGH*, vol. 3Aa, p. 45, restricts the quotation to the phrase about the moderate habits of the kings.

Hecataeus as colonists from Egypt (Diodorus 40.3), duplication of customs is not unusual.[67]

The description of Ptolemy Lagus in Josephus (Apion 1.186) is close to that given in Diodorus 18.14.1; 19.86.3; the source for Diodorus is not clear.[68] That this description of Ptolemy in Against Apion 1.186 reflects a Jewish apologetic tendency can be maintained only once one has already determined on other grounds that the work is inauthentic, but it cannot stand as a separate argument on its own. One could quite easily state that Hecataeus, writing in the reign of Ptolemy, did not wish to antagonize him.

In conclusion, one can find no strong argument against the authenticity of this fragment. On the contrary, one can detect similarities between it and other Greek ethnographical writing, and between its attitude toward the Jews and that of the Hecataeus of Diodorus 40.3. Consequently, these fragments must be considered authentic.

---

[67] Lewy, ZNW 31 (1932) 127f. In n. 1 on p. 128, Lewy points to other links between Egyptian customs and those of the Jews as reported by Hecataeus: the granting of land to the priests (Diodorus Siculus 1.73.3); the raising of children (Diodorus 1.80.3) is required, and it is done in the simplest manner (Diodorus 1.80.5–6). Cf. also M. Stern, Greek and Latin Authors, pp. 32–34.

[68] Wacholder, Eupolemus, p. 271, n. 54.

Text

183. So Clearchus mentions us by way of digression, for his main topic was different. Hecataeus of Abdera, however, a man at home both in philosophy and in public life, did not mention the Jews in passing, but wrote a book about them.[a] (Hecataeus) grew up in the time of Alexander the King, and was a contemporary of Ptolemy, son of Lagus. I propose to run through, in a summary fashion, some of what is said in this book.

184. First, I will fix the date. (Hecataeus) mentions the battle of Ptolemy against Demetrios at Gaza. Now this battle took place eleven years after Alexander's death, in the 117th Olympiad (312–309 B.C.), as Castor[b] relates.

185. For, when discussing this Olympiad, he states: "In this Olympiad, Ptolemy, son of Lagus, defeated Demetrios surnamed Poliocetes, son of Antigonos, in a battle at Gaza." That Alexander died in the 114th Olympiad (324–321 B.C.) is commonly agreed. So clearly our race was flourishing in the years of Ptolemy and Alexander.[c]

186. Further, Hecataeus states: "After the battle at Gaza, Ptolemy was in control of Syria. Many heard of his kindly benevolence, and decided to go back with him to Egypt and to be members of his empire."

187. "One of these," (Hecataeus) says, "was Ezechias, a chief priest of the Jews, a man about sixty-six years old. He was highly thought of by his countrymen, and quite intelligent; he could speak well, and was as skilled an administrator as any.

188. And indeed the Jews have about 1,500 priests who receive a tithe of what is produced and who manage public affairs."[d]

189. Speaking again of (Ezechias), (Hecataeus) says: "This man, who had attained to such a position of honor and who now was part of our society,[e] gathered together some of his friends and read to them his whole scroll.[f] For it contained the story of their settlement and their political constitution."

---

a. Note the similarity in phrasing with how Josephus speaks of Hecataeus' work on Abraham, in *Ant* 1.159.

b. Castor of Rhodes, cf. Jacoby, *FGH*, vol. 2B, p. 250.

c. Coming after the gymnastics Josephus performs to show the antiquity of the Jewish race by a comparison of Egyptian, Phoenician, and Babylonian chronology with that of the Greeks (*Apion* 1.103–5; 121–27; 159–60), this phrase—and, indeed, the whole argument of Josephus, *Apion* 1.184f.—must be taken as ironical.

d. This number is too small for all the priests of Judea; in Ezra 2:36–39, the number of priests totals 4,289. However, the figure for the priests in Jerusalem is given by Neh 11:10–14 as 1,192; 1Chr 9:10–13 mentions 1,760. See J. Jeremias, *Jerusalem in the Time of Jesus*, trans. by F. H. Cave and C. H. Cave (Philadelphia, 1975) pp. 199–206; M. Stern, *Greek and Latin Authors*, p. 42. The number 1,500, then, refers to the number of priests in Jerusalem.

e. Gk. *teteuchōs tēs timēs tautēs kai sunēthēs hēmin genomenos*. Should this participial phrase be interpreted to refer to what has previously been said about Ezechias, or should one presuppose that some information has been left out by Josephus and the phrase should be taken as obscure? H. St. John Thackeray, in the LCL edition of Josephus, *Apion*, who is followed by M. Stern, seems to take the latter position. Thackeray suggests that "this honor" refers either to the high priesthood or to some special honor given to Ezechias by Ptolemy;

he translates the second half of the phrase as "having been closely in touch with us." Such an interpretation, whereby Hecataeus and Ezechias are seen as good friends and acquaintances, has led to the suggestion that Ezechias is the source for Hecataeus' information about Judea and Jerusalem (Lewy, *ZNW* 31 [1932] 122; Walter, *JSHRZ* 1.2 [1976] 147).

I have translated the phrase in the context of what has previously been said. Therefore, *tēs timēs tautēs* refers to the positions of honor that Ezechias held among his countrymen. One finds it hard to imagine that Josephus would have omitted a story whereby a Jew was given a special honor by Ptolemy, and also where a writer like Hecataeus became close friends with a Jewish high priest. Since the notion of friendship between Hecataeus and Ezechias finds no further development in the text, I suggest that *sunēthēs hēmin* refers to Ezechias' emigration to Egypt to share in (*koinōnein*) and be a member of Ptolemy's empire. *Sunēthēs* would thus have the more general meaning of "habituated," "accustomed," and *hēmin* would not refer to a special coterie of friends, but to Alexandrian society as a whole.

f. I have followed the suggested emendation of Lewy that *diphtheran* be read instead of *diaphoran* (Lewy, *ZNW* 31 [1932] 123; contrast M. Stern, *Greek and Latin Authors*, p. 42). *Diaphoran* has caused much difficulty in interpretation and is translated "he read to them how Greek customs differed from Jewish" or "he read to them how it was good that they had emigrated."

190. Then Hecataeus discusses our attitude toward our laws; he shows that we prefer to suffer anything rather than to transgress our laws, and that we consider such suffering noble.

191. He says: "Therefore, even though spoken ill of by their neighbors and by foreign visitors, and even though frequently treated with disrespect by the Persian kings and satraps, their determination could not be shaken. Without defense, they meet tortures and the worst kinds of death on behalf of these laws, and they do not disown their hereditary way of life."

192. (Hecataeus) brings forward many proofs of their perseverance for the sake of the laws. For he says that when Alexander was at Babylon, he decided to restore the ruined temple of Bel, and ordered all his soldiers, no matter who they were, to fetch the materials.[g] Only the Jews did not obey the orders, but endured much punishment and paid heavy fines until the king pardoned them and granted them exemption.

193. (Hecataeus) gives further evidence: when foreigners came to their country and built temples and altars, the Jews razed them to the ground. In some cases they paid fines to the satraps, in others they were pardoned. And Hecataeus adds that such conduct rightly causes admiration.

194. (Hecataeus) also notes that our race is extremely numerous. For he says that first the Persians deported myriads of our[h] race to Babylon, and also many myriads emigrated to Egypt and Phoenicia after Alexander's death because of the unsettled conditions in Syria.

195. The same writer has reported of the size and beauty of the land we live in. For he says, "They occupy almost three million arourae[i] of excellent and very fertile territory. For such is the size of Judea."

196. Again, he narrates that, from antiquity, we have lived in Jerusalem, a large and beautiful city. He speaks of the size of the population and of the construction of the Temple. Here is his account.

197. "The Jews have many walled towns and villages throughout their country, but only one fortified city whose circumference is about fifty stades[j] and whose population is about one hundred and twenty thousand. Its name is Jerusalem.

198. There, almost in the center of the city,[k] is found a stone-walled enclosure about five plethra in length,[l] a hundred cubits in breadth; it has two entrances. Within this enclosure stands a square altar made of heaped-up stones,[m] unhewn and unfinished; each side is twenty cubits, and its height is ten cubits. Beside this stands a large building in which there are an altar and a lampstand; both of these latter are made out of gold and weigh two talents.[n]

199. On them burns a light day and night—it never goes out. There is no image of a god, or any kind of votive offering; there is absolutely no trace of any plant life, whether in the form of a sacred grove or such like. Priests continually perform certain holy rituals in it day and night; they drink no wine whatsoever while in the temple."

200. Again, (Hecataeus) bears witness that we campaigned[o] both with Alexander the King and with his successors. I will narrate one incident out of those done on the campaign; it was done by a Jew and Hecataeus himself was present.

---

g. On the rebuilding of the temple of Bel by Alexander the Great, see Arrian, *Anabasis* F. 17.2–3. Arrian simply states that Alexander entrusted the job to the Babylonians. Cf. also Strabo 16.1.5.

h. As Thackeray notes, Josephus is paraphrasing Hecataeus, and the use of the first person plural can best be explained this way, rather than showing that the author (Ps-Hec) lets slip his relationship with Jews in this passage (Wacholder, *Eupolemus,* 266f.).

As regards the notice that it was the Persians and not the Babylonians who exiled Jews to Babylon, Lewy (*ZNW* 31 [1932] 126) first noted that Syncellus, in his reporting of Eusebius' *Chronicon,* mentions that Artaxerxes III Ochus banished Jews to the Caspian Sea and to Babylonia. Contrast Solinus, *Collectanea* 35, 4 (No. 449); M. Stern, *Greek and Latin Authors,* p. 43.

i. LetAris 116 gives the area as sixty million arourae, a clear exaggeration. Three million arourae is about 826,000 hectares.

j. LetAris 105 estimates 40 stades, as does Timochares (Eusebius, *PrEv* 9.35); Josephus (*War* 5.159) gives 33, and a report in Eusebius, *PrEv* 9.36 gives 27. A *stade* is 606¾ feet, so 50 *stades* is about 30,000 feet.

k. Lewy (*ZNW* 31 [1932] 128f.) pointed out that to place the Temple in the middle of the city reflects a Gk. view of city planning, not the actual facts. The qualification "nearly" (*malista*) is not strong enough to reverse this judgment, pace Wacholder, *Eupolemus,* p. 270, n. 47.

l. A *plethron* = 100 feet.

m. Ex 20:25; Dt 27:5f.; 1Mac 4:46f.

n. Ex 30:1–5; 37:25–28; 25:31–40; 37:17–24; 1Mac 4:48–51

o. Reading with L *sunestrateuomen* (or *sunestrateusamen*) instead of *sunestrateusanto,* as does Walter.

Index

Note: Volume numbers are in **boldface.** References to footnotes from the text of documents use footnote numbers; for example, "1:262 *n8a*" refers to note 8a on page 262 of volume 1.

This index is essentially an index to topics and names in the pseudepigrapha and related scriptural and ancient literature. Geographical areas and places are included only if of great importance.

Aaron
  Artapanus on, **2:**900, 901
  in 2 Baruch, **1:**641
  on curtain of God, in 3 Enoch, **1:**297
  in Damascus Document, **2:**427
  Demetrius the Chronographer on, **2:**852, 853
  eclipse of, **2:**427 *n*
  in Ezekiel the Tragedian, **2:**805, 813
  in Hellenistic Synagogal Prayers, **2:**684, 688, 694
  invoked by Ishmael, **1:**255
  in Jannes and Jambres, **2:**432, 438, 440
  in Lives of the Prophets, **1:**382, 388
  in 4 Maccabees, **2:**552
  as master of mystical lore, **1:**252
  as priest, **1:**96, 257
    in 3 Enoch, **1:**301
    in 4 Ezra, **1:**525
    in Pseudo-Philo, **2:**324
    in Sirach, **1:**791 *n8b*
  in Pseudo-Philo, **2:**316, 320, 324, 329, 366, 368, 374
  tribe of, **2:**396, 396 *n2d*
Abaddon, **2:**173 *n10l*
Abaôth, **2:**721
Abaya, Rabbi, **2:**857
Abbahu, Rabbi, **1:**315
Abba of Akko, Rabbi, **2:**281 *n20d*
Abdias. *See* Apostolic History of Abdias
Abednego, **1:**500, 502, 513, **2:**558 *n13b*
Abel
  in Apocalypse of Abraham, **1:**701
  in Apocalypse of Sedrach, **1:**609
  in Bere'šit Rabbah (GenR), **2:**264 *n21c*
  different sources on burial of, **2:**293 *n40d*
  in 1 Enoch, **1:**25
  in Hellenistic Synagogal Prayers, **2:**684, 688, 693
  in Jubilees, **2:**61, 64
  as judge, in Testament of Abraham, **1:**350 *n2q2*
  in Life of Adam and Eve, **2:**249, 266–67, 290, 291–93
  in 4 Maccabees, **2:**563
  in Pseudo-Philo, **2:**304, 305
  in Testament of Adam, **1:**994
  in Testament of Isaac, **1:**907, 908

  in Testaments of the Twelve Patriarchs, **1:**804, 827
  in Vision of Isaiah, **2:**170, 171
Abezethibou, **1:**936–38, 952–54, 967 *n6d*, 985–86
Abijah, **2:**395 *n18c*
Abimelek (Abimelech)
  in 4 Baruch, **2:**413, 414, 416, 417, 419–25
  in Jubilees, **2:**35, 103
  in Pseudo-Philo, **2:**350–51, 376
Abiuth, **2:**307
'Abodah Zarah (AZ), **1:**229, 231 *n*, 245, 268 *n16h*, 281 *n26m*, 291 *n39b*, 309 *n24i*
  on "book of the generations of Adam," **2:**251 *n*
  on God's offering of law to all nations, **2:**318 *n11d*
  as heavenly throne, **1:**866 *n1h*
  instruction of prematurely dead in, **1:**313 *n48Cz*
  Messiah in, **2:**298 *n45u*
  Nimrod in, **1:**297 *n45l*
  poison of God in, **1:**658
  stars in, **1:**299 *n46b*
  on storehouse of beings, **1:**294 *n43i*
  "swift cherub" in, **1:**309 *n24h*
Abortion
  in 1 Enoch, **1:**48, 80
  list of books with condemnation of, **2:**580 *n185i*
  in Pseudo-Phocylides, **2:**580
  in Sibylline Oracles, **1:**333, 352
Abot (Ab), **1:**74 *n93o*, 261 *n6e*, 262 *n8a*, 315 *n48Dv*, 819
  on creation, **1:**887 *n9b*
  judgment books in, **1:**889 *n12d*, 900 *n10b*
  yoke of Law in, **1:**633 *n41a*
Abot de-Rabbi Nathan (ARN), **1:**239, 260 *n5k*, 262 *n8a*, 269 *n17f*, 285 *n31a*, 674 *n11d*
  on fall of Adam and Eve, **2:**279 *n19a*, 279 *n19f*
  on Job, **1:**843 *n9d*, 847 *n20f*
  souls in, **1:**294 *n44a*, 295 *n44e*
Above, as likeness of below, in Odes of Solomon, **2:**764
Abraham (Abram)
  Apocalypse of. *See* Apocalypse of Abraham
  in Apocalypse of Abraham, **1:**249
  Artapanus on, **2:**889, 891, 897

Cherubim *(Cont.)*
in Prayer of Jacob, 2:720
in Questions of Ezra, 1:598
in Testament of Abraham, 1:887
in Testament of Adam, 1:991, 993, 995
in Testament of Isaac, 1:903, 910, 911
in Testament of Job, 1:866
Childbirth. *See* Children; Virgin birth; Women
Children
discipline of
in Ahiqar, 2:486–87, 498
Pseudo-Phocylides on, 2:579, 581
exposure of, condemned in Pseudo-Phocylides, 2:580
with gray temples at birth, 1:349
of Israel. *See* Israel; Jews
likeness of, to parents, determined by sperm, 2:580 *n178d*
love of, and flow of milk, in Odes of Solomon, 2:769
massacre of, in Apocalypse of Daniel, 1:763
neglect of, in Letter of Aristeas, 2:29
newborn
demon *vs.*, in Testament of Solomon, 1:974
Pharaoh's murder of, in Jubilees, 2:128
number of, in Ahiqar, 2:501
as reward for obedience to God, 2:651 *n1c*
rule of
in 2 Baruch, 1:645
in Sibylline Oracles, 1:379, 423
sodomy of
in 2 Enoch, 1:118
guarding against, in Pseudo-Phocylides, 2:581–82
teaching of, Syriac Menander on, 2:593, 600
Chosen one
Moses as, in Lives of the Prophets, 2:383, 388
See also Elect One
Chosen people. *See* Jews, as chosen people
Christ, the (Jesus Christ), xxi-xxxiii
acrostic for, in Sibylline Oracles, 1:416, 417, 423–24
Ahiqar perhaps known by, 2:488
as angel wrestling with Jacob, 2:707 *n*
Antichrist compared to
in Apocalypse of Elijah, 1:744–46, 750
in Greek Apocalypse of Ezra, 1:564, 567, 575
in Apocalypse of Elijah, 1:726, 731–32
in Apocalypse of Sedrach, 1:605, 606, 609
as archangel, 1:139 *n22p*
baptism of
Ebionite version of, 1:194 *n67a*
in Sibylline Oracles, 1:406, 407, 409, 411–12, 424
in Testament of Levi, 1:795 *n18c*
in 3 Baruch, 1:665, 669
in 4 Baruch, 2:415, 424
biographies of
in Martyrdom and Ascension of Isaiah, 2:160, 174–75
in Sibylline Oracles, 1:343, 406–7, 416, 424–26
birth of
in Hellenistic Synagogal Prayers, 2:682
in Ladder of Jacob, 2:402, 410–11
in Lives of the Prophets, 2:387–88
Melchizedek's birth compared to, 1:204 *n71c*
Moses' birth paralleled to, in Pseudo-Philo, 2:316 *n9k*
Sampson's birth compared to, 2:355 *n42a*
in Sibylline Oracles, 1:428
star at, 1:478–80
in Tale of Aphroditianus, 2:405
in Vision of Isaiah, 2:174–75
in Bogomil doctrine, 1:684
carried to Mount Tabor, 1:211 *n72e*
death of (crucifixion of)
cross taken up to heaven, 1:406–7
darkness at, 1:194 *n67a*
in Greek Apocalypse of Ezra, 1:564, 573, 578
in Hellenistic Synagogal Prayers, 2:683
in Ladder of Jacob, 2:402, 411
in Martyrdom and Ascension of Isaiah, 2:162, 175
in Martyrdom of Solomon, 2:729, 732, 759–61, 763, 770, 771
priests' complicity in, in Testament of Levi, 1:794
Pseudo-Philo's ideas similar to theology of, 2:302
in Questions of Ezra, 1:598
in Sibylline Oracles, 1:343, 425
in Testament of Adam, 1:994
in Testament of Benjamin, 1:827
in Testament of Solomon, 1:953, 955, 973, 975, 984
in Testaments of the Twelve Patriarchs, 1:789 *n4b*, 793, 827
demons as subjects to, 1:975 *n15c*, 978 *n18f*
denial of, in Apocalypse of Daniel, 1:764
descent from heaven by
in Odes of Solomon, 2:754
in Vision of Isaiah, 2:173–74
as 888, 1:342
2 Enoch incompatible with Christian beliefs in, 1:96
as fish, 1:757
in glory, 1:194 *n66d*
in Sibylline Oracles, 1:351
in Vision of Isaiah, 2:171–73
God's rest after incarnation of, 1:143 *n24h*
in Hellenistic Synagogal Prayers, 2:672, 675, 677–89, 691, 692, 695–97
Herod and. *See* Herod
in History of Joseph the Carpenter, 1:138 *n22j*
incarnation of
in Apocalypse of Elijah, 1:735–36
in 4 Baruch, 2:424
in History of the Rechabites, 2:443, 446, 457–58
in Ladder of Jacob, 2:410–11
in Odes of Solomon, 2:729, 739–40, 769–70
in Sibylline Oracles, 1:428
in Testament of Isaac, 1:907
in Testaments of the Twelve Patriarchs, 1:787, 789 *n5b*, 813
in Vision of Isaiah, 2:154, 170, 173–75
as infant prodigy, 1:206 *n71l*, 209 *n71q*
as intercessor (mediator) in Hellenistic Synagogal Prayers, 2:675, 681
in Testament of Jacob, 1:913, 918
Job and, 1:836
Justin's attribution of saying to, 1:489 *n*, 495

first known philosopher of, **2**:834

Gnosticism of, **1**:236, 714 *n4b*

as God's assembly, in Hellenistic Synagogal Prayers, **2**:680

God's promise to multiply, **2**:322, 325, 678

God's rejection of, until end of time, in Testament of Zebulon, **1**:807

Hellenistic literature of, **1**:836, **2**:181, 183–84, 186–87, 195, 515. *See also* Greece, ancient

Pseudo-Phocylides as, **2**:565–66

instruction for, in Hellenistic Synagogal Prayers, **2**:687, 688–89

lambs as symbolic of, **1**:467 *n4e2*

at Last Judgment, in Sibylline Oracles, **1**:351

leprosy of, Manetho on, **2**:901 *n3e2*

as loyal subjects, in 3 Maccabees, **2**:520 *n3a*

Mark Antony supported by, **1**:476

missionary work of, **2**:194–95, 566

monotheism and polytheism together in community of, **2**:586 *n*

Palestinian *vs.* hellenistic, xxix

persecution and plundering of

by Caligula, **2**:187 *n*, 511, 534

in 4 Ezra, **1**:559

by Hadrian, **2**:187, 533–34

Jewish steadfastness *vs.*, Hecataeus of Abdera on, **2**:918

Job in Aristeas the Exegete as example of, **2**:856

in 2 Maccabees, **2**:534, 549–64

in 3 Maccabees, **2**:509, 519–27

in 4 Maccabees, **2**:531, 537

in Sibylline Oracles, **1**:349

by Trajan, **1**:449, **2**:187

piety of, at turn of the era (200 B.C.–A.D. 100), **2**:631

post-exilic pseudepigrapha of, xxviii–xxix

praise of, in Sibylline Oracles, **1**:367–68

rediscovery of "lost" literature by, xi–xii

revolutionary mood of, **1**:9

role of rabbi among, **1**:239

universal domination of, in Sibylline Oracles, **1**:460

universalistic form of belief of, **1**:876–78

See also Hebrew language; Jerusalem; Marriage, mixed; Mysticism, Jewish; Rabbinic writings; Synagogue; *specific holy days; specific writings*

Job

Abraham compared to, in Testament of Abraham, **1**:892

Apocalypse of Sedrach and, **1**:607

in Aristeas the Exegete, **2**:855–57, 859

Dinah said to be wife of, **1**:839 *n1m*, **2**:314

in Hellenistic Synagogal Prayers, **2**:687, 688, 693

in patriarchal period, **2**:856 *n*

in Septuagint, **1**:831

Targum of, in Dead Sea Scrolls, xxvii

Testament of. *See* Testament of Job

Job (book)

angelic rivalry in, **2**:702 *n*, 703

Aristeas the Exegete and, **2**:855–56

creation described in, **2**:55 *n2i*

Septuagint addition to, **2**:856–57, 859

Sibylline Oracles and, **1**:417

Testament of Job and, **1**:831, 833, 835–36, 839 *n1e*, 840 *n3d*, 842 *n9a*, 842 *n9b*, 843 *n10b*, 843 *n11a*, 844 *n13a*, 844 *n15a*, 848 *n23d*, 854 *n32n*, 861 *n41c*, 862 *n43g*, 868 *n53c*, 868 *n53f*

Ahiqar and, **2**:404 *nXg*

Jobab (Job's earlier name), **1**:829, 839, 840, 846, 852–53, 855 *n32o*, **2**:856, 859

Joel (book)

Prayer of Manasseh and, **2**:630

Testament of Jacob and, **1**:801 *n24b*

John

Acts of. *See* Acts of John

"Apocalypse" of, **1**:760 *n*

in Apocalypse of Sedrach, **1**:609

Apocryphon of. *See* Apocryphon of John

in Greek Apocalypse of Ezra, **1**:564, 572

John (gospel)

Apocalypse of Elijah and, **1**:745 *n3s*

"bread of life" in, **2**:212 *n8i*

1 Enoch and, **1**:10

2 Enoch and, **1**:187 *n61f*

3 Enoch and, **1**:247

ethical dualism of, **1**:52 *n30o*

Odes of Solomon and, **2**:727–30, 732, 736 *n3d*, 736 *n3f*, 739 *n6f*, 742 *n8k*, 744 *n11c*, 746 *n11c2*, 746 *n12a*, 747 *n12i*, 749 *n16d*, 750 *n16i*, 752 *n18i*, 761 *n28o*, 762 *n30d*

1 John (epistle)

Antichrist in, **1**:567, 729

Apocalypse of Elijah and, **1**:722, 729, 732

1 Enoch and, **1**:10

2 John (epistle), Antichrist in, **1**:567

3 John (epistle), canonicity of, xxiv

John the Baptist, **1**:383, 737 *n1o2*, **2**:355 *n42a*, 383

as angel, in Origen, **2**:699

in Lives of the Prophets, **2**:380

John the Evangelist (book)

on Satan's face, **1**:137 *n22d*

on Satan's fall, **1**:130 *n18a*, 149 *n29j*

Jonadab, **2**:447, 450, 454, 455, 461 *n18a*

Jonah, **1**:351, 526, **2**:163, 526, 685

in Lives of the Prophets, **2**:379, 392–93

Jordan River

God's love of, in Apocalypse of Sedrach, **1**:606, 611

in Letter of Aristeas, **1**:20

in Lives of the Prophets, **2**:397

Josab (Joseb), **2**:156–58, 161, 165, 171

Joseph (son of Jacob)

Ahiqar and, **2**:484

in Apocalypse of Sedrach, **1**:609

Artapanus on, **2**:889, 894, 897–98

Demetrius the Chronographer on, **2**:845, 849–52

dreams interpreted by

in Joseph and Aseneth, **2**:207

in Jubilees, **2**:129–30

in Pseudo-Philo, **2**:314

dreams of, **1**:812 *n5b*, 814, 824

Moses' dream in Ezekiel the Tragedian compared to, **2**:811 *nz*

in Hellenistic Synagogal Prayers, **2**:693

History of. *See* History of Joseph

in Jubilees, **2**:36, 111, 120–22, 128–30

Life of, **2**:180 *n*, 196

in 4 Maccabees, **2**:546, 563

THE
OLD TESTAMENT
PSEUDEPIGRAPHA

VOLUME 1
APOCALYPTIC LITERATURE AND TESTAMENTS

VOLUME 2
EXPANSIONS OF THE "OLD TESTAMENT" AND
LEGENDS, WISDOM AND PHILOSOPHICAL LITERATURE,
PRAYERS, PSALMS, AND ODES, FRAGMENTS
OF LOST JUDEO-HELLENISTIC WORKS

<table>
<tr><td>Apocalypse of Abraham</td><td>3 Baruch</td></tr>
<tr><td>Apocalypse of Adam</td><td>4 Baruch</td></tr>
<tr><td>Testament of Adam</td><td>Cleodemus Malchus</td></tr>
<tr><td>Life of Adam and Eve</td><td>Apocalypse of Daniel</td></tr>
<tr><td>Ahiqar</td><td>More Psalms of David</td></tr>
<tr><td>Letter of Aristeas</td><td>Demetrius
the Chronographer</td></tr>
<tr><td>Aristeas the Exegete</td><td></td></tr>
<tr><td>Aristobulus</td><td>Eldad and Modad</td></tr>
<tr><td>Artapanus</td><td>Apocalypse of Elijah</td></tr>
<tr><td>2 Baruch</td><td>1 Enoch</td></tr>
<tr><td></td><td>2 Enoch</td></tr>
</table>